Ray Rankins,
Paul Bertucci,
Chris Gallelli,
Alex T. Silverstein,
et al.

Microsoft®
SQL Server 2005

UNLEASHED

SAMS | 800 East 96th Street, Indianapolis, Indiana 46240 USA

Microsoft® SQL Server 2005 Unleashed

International Standard Book Number: 0-672-32824-0

Library of Congress Cataloging-in-Publication Data

Microsoft SQL server 2005 unleashed / Ray Rankins, et al.
    p. cm.
  ISBN 0-672-32824-0
  1. SQL server. 2. Database management. I. Rankins, Ray.
QA76.9.D3M57365 2007
005.75'85—dc22

                            2007005947

Printed in the United States of America

First Printing: April 2007

10   09   08   4

Trademarks

All terms mentioned in this book that are known to be trademarks or service marks have been appropriately capitalized. Sams Publishing cannot attest to the accuracy of this information. Use of a term in this book should not be regarded as affecting the validity of any trademark or service mark.

Warning and Disclaimer

Every effort has been made to make this book as complete and as accurate as possible, but no warranty or fitness is implied. The information provided is on an "as is" basis. The authors and the publisher shall have neither liability nor responsibility to any person or entity with respect to any loss or damages arising from the information contained in this book or from the use of the CD or programs accompanying it.

Bulk Sales

Sams Publishing offers excellent discounts on this book when ordered in quantity for bulk purchases or special sales. For more information, please contact

> **U.S. Corporate and Government Sales**
> **1-800-382-3419**
> **corpsales@pearsontechgroup.com**

For sales outside of the U.S., please contact

> **International Sales**
> **international@pearsoned.com**

 This Book Is Safari Enabled

The Safari® Enabled icon on the cover of your favorite technology book means the book is available through Safari Bookshelf. When you buy this book, you get free access to the online edition for 45 days.

Safari Bookshelf is an electronic reference library that lets you easily search thousands of technical books, find code samples, download chapters, and access technical information whenever and wherever you need it.

To gain 45-day Safari Enabled access to this book:

- Go to http://www.samspublishing.com/safarienabled
- Complete the brief registration form
- Enter the coupon code EYDB-XJWD-TEH7-QFE6-CG8Q

If you have difficulty registering on Safari Bookshelf or accessing the online edition, please e-mail customer-service@safaribooksonline.com.

Acquisitions Editor
Neil Rowe

Development Editor
Mark Renfrow

Managing Editor
Gina Kanouse

Project Editor
Andy Beaster

Copy Editor
Kitty Jarrett

Indexer
Lisa Stumpf

Proofreader
Paula Lowell

Technical Editor
Ross Mistry

Multimedia Developer
Dan Scherf

Book Designer
Gary Adair

Compositors
Bronkella Publishing
Nonie Ratcliff

Contents at a Glance

Introduction 1

Part I   Welcome to Microsoft SQL Server
1   SQL Server 2005 Overview 11
2   What's New in SQL Server 2005 35

Part II   SQL Server Tools and Utilities
3   SQL Server Management Studio 57
4   SQL Server Command-Line Utilities 89
5   SQL Server Profiler 111

Part III   SQL Server Administration
6   SQL Server System and Database Administration 155
7   Installing SQL Server 2005 173
8   Upgrading to SQL Server 2005 197
9   Client Installation and Configuration 221
10   Security and User Administration 247
11   Database Backup and Restore 291
12   Database Mail 339
13   SQL Server Scheduling and Notification 361
14   SQL Server High Availability 393
15   Replication 415
16   Database Mirroring 481
17   SQL Server Clustering 515

Part IV   Database Administration
18   Creating and Managing Databases 547
19   Creating and Managing Tables 579
20   Creating and Managing Indexes 623
21   Implementing Data Integrity 641
22   Creating and Managing Views in SQL Server 667
23   Creating and Managing Stored Procedures 699

24   Creating and Managing User-Defined Functions 799

25   Creating and Managing Triggers 833

26   Transaction Management and the Transaction Log 873

27   Database Snapshots 919

28   Database Maintenance 945

Part V   **SQL Server Performance and Optimization**

29   Indexes and Performance 969

30   Understanding Query Optimization 1027

31   Query Analysis 1115

32   Locking and Performance 1151

33   Database Design and Performance 1213

34   Monitoring SQL Server Performance 1233

Part VI   **SQL Server Application Development**

35   What's New for Transact-SQL in SQL Server 2005 1273

36   SQL Server and the .NET Framework 1319

37   Using XML in SQL Server 2005 1377

38   SQL Server Web Services 1439

Part VII   **SQL Server Business Intelligence Features**

39   SQL Server 2005 Analysis Services 1473

40   SQL Server Integration Services 1539

41   SQL Server 2005 Reporting Services 1607

Bonus Chapters on the CD

42   Managing Linked and Remote Servers 1663

43   Configuring, Tuning, and Optimizing SQL Server Options 1693

44   Administering Very Large SQL Server Databases 1743

45   SQL Server Disaster Recovery Planning 1771

46   Transact-SQL Programming Guidelines, Tips, and Tricks 1793

47   SQL Server Notification Services 1841

48   SQL Server Service Broker 1875

49   SQL Server Full-Text Search 1913

   Index 1941

Table of Contents

Introduction   **1**

Who This Book Is For 2

What This Book Covers 3

Conventions Used in This Book 5

Good Luck! 7

Part I   Welcome to Microsoft SQL Server

1   SQL Server 2005 Overview   **11**

SQL Server Components and Features 11

     The SQL Server Database Engine 11

     SQL Server 2005 Administration and Management Tools 14

     Replication 18

     Database Mirroring 19

     Full-Text Search 20

     SQL Server Integration Services (SSIS) 21

     SQL Server Analysis Services (SSAS) 22

     SQL Server 2005 Reporting Services 23

     SQL Server Notification Services 23

     SQL Server Service Broker 24

SQL Server 2005 Editions 25

     SQL Server 2005 Standard Edition 25

     SQL Server 2005 Enterprise Edition 26

     Differences Between the Enterprise and Standard Editions of SQL
       Server 26

     Other SQL Server 2005 Editions 27

SQL Server Licensing Models 29

     Developer Edition Licensing 31

     Express Edition Licensing 31

     Mobile Edition Licensing 31

     Choosing a Licensing Model 31

     Mixing Licensing Models 32

     Passive Server/Failover Licensing 32

     Virtual Server Licensing 33

Summary 33

2   What's New in SQL Server 2005   35

New SQL Server 2005 Features 35

SQL Server Management Studio 36

SQL Server Configuration Manager 37

CLR/.NET Framework Integration 37

Dynamic Management Views 38

System Catalog Views 38

SQL Server Management Objects 39

Dedicated Administrator Connection 39

SQLCMD 39

Database Mail 40

Online Index and Restore Operations 40

Native Encryption 40

Database Mirroring 41

Database Snapshots 41

Service Broker 41

SQL Server Integration Services 42

Table and Index Partitioning 42

Snapshot Isolation 43

Business Intelligence Development Studio 44

Query Notification 44

Multiple Active Result Sets 44

New SQL Server Data Types 44

SQL Server 2005 Enhancements 45

Database Engine Enhancements 46

Index Enhancements 46

T-SQL Enhancements 47

Security Enhancements 47

Backup and Restore Enhancements 48

SQL Server Agent Enhancements 49

Recovery Enhancements 49

Replication Enhancements 50

Failover Clustering Enhancements 51

Notification Services Enhancements 51

Full-Text Search Enhancements 52

Web Services Enhancements 52

Analysis Services Enhancements 52

Reporting Services Enhancements 53

Summary 54

Part II   SQL Server Tools and Utilities

3   SQL Server Management Studio   57

What's New in SSMS 57
The Integrated Environment 58
  Window Management 59
  Integrated Help 62
Administration Tools 64
  Using Registered Servers 65
  Using Object Explorer 66
  Using Activity Monitor 68
  Using Log File Viewer 70
Development Tools 71
  The Query Editor 71
  Managing Projects in SSMS 79
  Integrating SSMS with Source Control 81
  Using SSMS Templates 83
Summary 87

4   SQL Server Command-Line Utilities   89

What's New in SQL Server Command-Line Utilities 90
The sqlcmd Command-Line Utility 91
  Executing the sqlcmd utility 92
  Using scripting variables with sqlcmd 94
The dta Command-Line Utility 95
The tablediff Command-Line Utility 98
The sac Command-Line Utility 101
The bcp Command-Line Utility 104
The sqldiag Command-Line Utility 105
The sqlservr Command-Line Utility 107
Removed or Deprecated Utilities in SQL Server 2005 108
Summary 109

5   SQL Server Profiler   111

What's New with SQL Server Profiler 111
SQL Server Profiler Architecture 112
Creating Traces 113
  Events 116
  Data Columns 118
  Filters 121
Executing Traces and Working with Trace Output 123
Saving and Exporting Traces 123

Saving Trace Output to a File 124

Saving Trace Output to a Table 124

Saving the Profiler GUI Output 125

Importing Trace Files 125

Importing a Trace File into a Trace Table 126

Analyzing Trace Output with the Database Engine
  Tuning Advisor 128

Replaying Trace Data 129

Defining Server-Side Traces 131

Monitoring Running Traces 141

Stopping Server-Side Traces 143

Profiler Usage Scenarios 144

Analyzing Slow Stored Procedures or Queries 145

Deadlocks 145

Identifying Ad Hoc Queries 147

Identifying Performance Bottlenecks 148

Monitoring Auto-Update Statistics 150

Monitoring Application Progress 150

Summary 152

Part III   SQL Server Administration

6   SQL Server System and Database Administration   155

What's New in SQL Server System and Database Administration 155

System Administrator Responsibilities 156

System Databases 157

The master Database 158

The resource Database 158

The model Database 158

The msdb Database 158

The distribution Database 159

The tempdb Database 159

Maintaining System Databases 159

System Tables 160

System Views 161

Compatibility Views 161

Catalog Views 164

Information Schema Views 166

Dynamic Management Views 167

System Stored Procedures 170

          Useful System Stored Procedures 170
    Summary 172

7   **Installing SQL Server 2005**   **173**

    What's New in Installing SQL Server 2005 173
    Installation Requirements 173
          Hardware Requirements 174
          Software Requirements 175
    Installation Walkthrough 179
          Install Screens, Step-by-Step 180
    Unattended Installation 191
          Remote Installation 193
    Installing SP1 193
          Unattended SP1 Installation 195
    Summary 195

8   **Upgrading to SQL Server 2005**   **197**

    What's New in Upgrading SQL Server 197
    Using the SQL Server Upgrade Advisor (UA) 198
          Getting Started with the UA 198
          The Analysis Wizard 199
          The Report Viewer 202
    Destination: SQL Server 2005 203
          Side-by-Side Migration 204
          Upgrading In-Place 214
    Unattended Upgrades 219
    Summary 220

9   **Client Installation and Configuration**   **221**

    What's New in Client Installation and Configuration 221
    Client/Server Networking Considerations 222
          Server Network Protocols 222
          The Server Endpoint Layer 224
          The Role of SQL Browser 227
    Client Installation 228
          Installation Requirements 228
          Installing the Client Tools 229
          Installing SNAC 230
    Client Configuration 231
          Client Configuration Using SSCM 232

Connection Encryption 235
Client Data Access Technologies 237
Provider Choices 237
Driver Choices 238
Connecting Using the Various Providers and Drivers 238
General Networking Considerations and Troubleshooting 244
Summary 246

10 Security and User Administration   247
What's New in Security and User Administration 247
An Overview of SQL Server Security 248
Authentication Methods 249
Windows Authentication Mode 250
Mixed Authentication Mode 250
Setting the Authentication Mode 250
Managing Principals 251
Logins 251
SQL Server Security: Users 254
User/Schema Separation 257
Roles 258
Managing Securables 265
Managing Permissions 266
Managing SQL Server Logins 268
Using SSMS to Manage Logins 268
Using T-SQL to Manage Logins 272
Managing SQL Server Users 273
Using SSMS to Manage Users 273
Using T-SQL to Manage Users 275
Managing Database Roles 276
Using SSMS to Manage Database Roles 276
Using T-SQL to Manage Database Roles 277
Managing SQL Server Permissions 277
Using SSMS to Manage Permissions 277
Using T-SQL to Manage Permissions 285
The Execution Context 286
Explicit Context Switching 287
Implicit Context Switching 288
Summary 289

11 Database Backup and Restore   291

What's New in Database Backup and Restore 291

Developing a Backup and Restore Plan 292

Types of Backups 294

    Full Database Backups 294

    Differential Database Backups 295

    Partial Backups 295

    Differential Partial Backups 295

    File and Filegroup Backups 295

    Copy-Only Backups 296

    Transaction Log Backups 296

Recovery Models 296

    Full Recovery 297

    Bulk-Logged Recovery 298

    Simple Recovery 299

Backup Devices 300

    Disk Devices 300

    Tape Devices 300

    Network Shares 301

    Media Sets and Families 301

    Creating Backup Devices 301

Backing Up a Database 302

    Creating Database Backups with SSMS 302

    Creating Database Backups with T-SQL 305

Backing Up the Transaction Log 307

    Creating Transaction Log Backups with SSMS 308

    Creating Transaction Log Backups with T-SQL 309

Backup Scenarios 310

    Full Database Backups Only 311

    Full Database Backups with Transaction Log Backups 311

    Differential Backups 312

    Partial Backups 313

    File/Filegroup Backups 315

    Mirrored Backups 316

    Copy-Only Backups 316

    System Database Backups 317

Restoring Databases and Transaction Logs 317

    Restores with T-SQL 318

    Restoring by Using SSMS 322

    Restore Information 324

Restore Scenarios 326

    Restoring to a Different Database 327

Restoring a Transaction Log 328

Restoring to the Point of Failure 328

Restoring to a Point in Time 331

Online Restores 332

Restoring the System Databases 333

Additional Backup Considerations 335

Frequency of Backups 335

Using a Standby Server 336

Snapshot Backups 337

Considerations for Very Large Databases 337

Maintenance Plans 338

Summary 338

12   Database Mail   339

What's New in Database Mail 339

Setting Up Database Mail 339

Creating Mail Profiles and Accounts 342

Using T-SQL to Update and Delete Mail Objects 345

Setting Systemwide Mail Settings 345

Testing Your Setup 346

Sending and Receiving with Database Mail 347

The Service Broker Architecture 347

Sending Email 347

Receiving Email 354

Using SQL Server Agent Mail 354

Job Mail Notifications 354

Alert Mail Notifications 356

Related Views and Procedures 357

Viewing the Mail Configuration Objects 357

Viewing Mail Message Data 359

Summary 360

13   SQL Server Scheduling and Notification   361

What's New in Scheduling and Notification 361

Configuring the SQL Server Agent 362

Configuring SQL Server Agent Properties 362

Configuring the SQL Server Agent Startup Account 363

Configuring Email Notification 365

SQL Server Agent Proxy Account 367

Viewing the SQL Server Agent Error Log 368

SQL Server Agent Security 370

Managing Operators 370

Managing Jobs 373
    Defining Job Properties 373
    Defining Job Steps 374
    Defining Job Schedules 377
    Defining Job Notifications 379
    Viewing Job History 380
Managing Alerts 381
    Defining Alert Properties 382
    Defining Alert Responses 384
Scripting Jobs and Alerts 387
Multiserver Job Management 388
    Creating a Master Server 388
    Enlisting Target Servers 389
    Creating Multiserver Jobs 390
Event Forwarding 390
Summary 391

14   SQL Server High Availability   393

What's New in High Availability 394
What Is High Availability? 395
The Fundamentals of HA 396
    Hardware 397
    Backup 397
    Operating System 397
    Vendor Agreements 398
    Training 398
    Quality Assurance 398
    Standards/Procedures 398
    Server Instance Isolation 398
Building Solutions with One or More HA Options 400
    Microsoft Cluster Services (MSCS) 401
    SQL Clustering 402
    Data Replication 404
    Log Shipping 406
    Database Mirroring 407
    Combining Failover with Scale-Out Options 408
Other HA Techniques That Yield Great Results 408
High Availability from the Windows Server Family Side 410
    Microsoft Virtual Server 2005 411
    Virtual Server 2005 and Disaster Recovery 412
Summary 412

15   Replication   **415**

What's New in Data Replication 416

What Is Replication? 417

The Publisher, Distributor, and Subscriber Metaphor 418

    Publications and Articles 421

    Filtering Articles 421

Replication Scenarios 425

    The Central Publisher Replication Model 426

    The Central Publisher with Remote Distributor

      Replication Model 427

    The Publishing Subscriber Replication Model 427

    The Central Subscriber Replication Model 428

    The Multiple Publishers or Multiple Subscribers

      Replication Model 429

    The Updating Subscribers Replication Model 430

    The Peer-to-Peer Replication Model 431

Subscriptions 433

    Anonymous Subscriptions (Pull Subscriptions) 434

    The Distribution Database 435

Replication Agents 436

    The Snapshot Agent 437

    The Log Reader Agent 439

    The Distribution Agent 441

    The Merge Agent 442

    Other Specialized Agents 442

Planning for SQL Server Data Replication 443

    Autonomy, Timing, and Latency of Data 443

    Methods of Data Distribution 444

SQL Server Replication Types 444

    Snapshot Replication 444

    Transactional Replication 445

    Merge Replication 446

Basing the Replication Design on User Requirements 447

    Data Characteristics 448

Setting Up Replication 450

    Creating a Distributor and Enabling Publishing 451

    Creating a Publication 456

    Horizontal and Vertical Filtering 463

    Creating Subscriptions 465

Scripting Replication 470

Monitoring Replication 471
    Replication Monitoring SQL Statements 472
    Monitoring Replication within SQL Server Management
        Studio 474
    Troubleshooting Replication Failures 476
    The Performance Monitor 477
    Replication in Heterogeneous Environments 477
    Backup and Recovery in a Replication Configuration 478
    Some Thoughts on Performance 479
    Log Shipping 480
    Data Replication and Database Mirroring for Fault
        Tolerance and High Availability 480
Summary 480

16 Database Mirroring   **481**

What's New in Database Mirroring 481
What Is Database Mirroring? 482
    Copy-on-Write Technology 484
    When to Use Database Mirroring 484
Roles of the Database Mirroring Configuration 485
    Playing Roles and Switching Roles 485
    Database Mirroring Operating Modes 485
Setting Up and Configuring Database Mirroring 486
    Getting Ready to Mirror a Database 487
    Creating the Endpoints 490
    Granting Permissions 492
    Identifying the Other Endpoints for Database Mirroring ... 492
    Creating the Database on the Mirror Server 493
    Configuring Database Mirroring by Using the Wizard 495
    Monitoring a Mirrored Database Environment 501
    Removing Mirroring 505
Testing Failover from the Principal to the Mirror 507
Client Setup and Configuration for Database Mirroring 509
Using Replication and Database Mirroring Together 511
Using Database Snapshots from a Mirror for Reporting 512
Summary 514

17 SQL Server Clustering   **515**

What's New in SQL Server Clustering 516
How Microsoft SQL Server Clustering Works 516
    Understanding MSCS 518
    Extending MSCS with NLB 522

How MSCS Sets the Stage for SQL Server Clustering 523

Installing SQL Server Clustering 524

Configuring SQL Server Database Disks 525

Installing Network Interfaces 527

Installing MSCS 527

Installing SQL Server 528

Failure of a Node 537

The Connection Test Program for a SQL Server Cluster 539

Potential Problems to Watch Out for with SQL

Server Clustering 543

Summary 543

Part IV   Database Administration

18   Creating and Managing Databases   547

What's New in Creating and Managing Databases 548

Data Storage in SQL Server 548

Database Files 549

Primary Files 550

Secondary Files 550

Using Filegroups 551

Using Partitions 554

Transaction Log Files 554

Creating Databases 555

Using SSMS to Create a Database 556

Using T-SQL to Create Databases 559

Setting Database Options 560

The Database Options 561

Using T-SQL to Set Database Options 563

Retrieving Option Information 564

Managing Databases 566

Managing File Growth 566

Expanding Databases 567

Shrinking Databases 568

Moving Databases 572

Restoring a Database Backup to a New Location 573

Using ALTER DATABASE 573

Detaching and Attaching Databases 574

Summary 577

19 Creating and Managing Tables   **579**

What's New in SQL Server 2005 579
Creating Tables 580
    Using Object Explorer to Create Tables 580
    Using Database Diagrams to Create Tables 580
    Using T-SQL to Create Tables 582
Defining Columns 584
    Data Types 585
    Column Properties 590
Defining Table Location 594
Defining Table Constraints 596
Modifying Tables 598
    Using T-SQL to Modify Tables 598
    Using Object Explorer and the Table Designer
      to Modify Tables 601
    Using Database Diagrams to Modify Tables 604
Dropping Tables 605
Partitioned Tables 607
    Creating a Partition Function 608
    Creating a Partition Scheme 610
    Creating a Partitioned Table 612
    Adding and Dropping Table Partitions 614
    Switching Table Partitions 618
Creating Temporary Tables 622
Summary 622

20 Creating and Managing Indexes   **623**

What's New in Creating and Managing Indexes 623
Types of Indexes 624
    Clustered Indexes 624
    Nonclustered Indexes 626
Creating Indexes 627
    Creating Indexes with T-SQL 627
    Creating Indexes with SSMS 631
Managing Indexes 633
    Managing Indexes with T-SQL 633
    Managing Indexes with SSMS 636
Dropping Indexes 637
Online Indexing Operations 637
Indexes on Views 639
Summary 640

21   Implementing Data Integrity   **641**

    What's New in Data Integrity 641

    Types of Data Integrity 642

        Domain Integrity 642

        Entity Integrity 642

        Referential Integrity 642

    Enforcing Data Integrity 642

        Implementing Declarative Data Integrity 643

        Implementing Procedural Data Integrity 643

    Using Constraints 643

        The PRIMARY KEY Constraint 643

        The UNIQUE Constraint 645

        The FOREIGN KEY Referential Integrity Constraint 646

        The CHECK Constraint 650

        Creating Constraints 651

        Managing Constraints 656

    Rules 659

    Defaults 661

        Declarative Defaults 661

        Bound Defaults 662

        When a Default Is Applied 663

        Restrictions on Defaults 664

    Summary 665

22   Creating and Managing Views in SQL Server   **667**

    What's New in Creating and Managing Views 667

    Definition of Views 667

    Using Views 669

        Simplifying Data Manipulation 669

        Focusing on Specific Data 670

        Data Abstraction 670

        Controlling Access to Data 671

    Creating Views 674

        Creating Views Using T-SQL 675

        Creating Views Using the View Designer 679

    Managing Views 681

        Altering Views with T-SQL 681

        Dropping Views with T-SQL 682

        Managing Views with SSMS 682

    Data Modifications and Views 683

Partitioned Views 684
    Modifying Data Through a Partitioned View 688
    Distributed Partitioned Views 688
Indexed Views 690
    Creating Indexed Views 690
    Indexed Views and Performance 693
    To Expand or Not to Expand 696
Summary 697

23 Creating and Managing Stored Procedures   699

What's New in Creating and Managing Stored Procedures 699
Advantages of Stored Procedures 700
Creating Stored Procedures 701
    Creating Procedures in SSMS 702
    Temporary Stored Procedures 709
Executing Stored Procedures 710
    Executing Procedures in SSMS 711
    Execution Context and the EXECUTE AS Clause 713
Deferred Name Resolution 715
    Identifying Objects Referenced in Stored Procedures .. 717
Viewing Stored Procedures 719
Modifying Stored Procedures 722
    Modifying Stored Procedures with SSMS 723
Using Input Parameters 724
    Setting Default Values for Parameters 725
    Passing Object Names As Parameters 728
    Using Wildcards in Parameters 729
Using Output Parameters 731
Returning Procedure Status 732
Using Cursors in Stored Procedures 733
    Using CURSOR Variables in Stored Procedures 738
Nested Stored Procedures 743
    Recursive Stored Procedures 745
Using Temporary Tables in Stored Procedures 749
    Temporary Table Performance Tips 750
    Using the table Data Type 752
Using Remote Stored Procedures 755
Debugging Stored Procedures Using Microsoft Visual Studio .NET .. 756
Using System Stored Procedures 760
Stored Procedure Performance 762
    Query Plan Caching 763

The SQL Server Procedure Cache 763

Shared Query Plans 764

Automatic Query Plan Recompilation 765

Forcing Recompilation of Query Plans 768

Using Dynamic SQL in Stored Procedures 772

Using sp_executesql 774

Startup Procedures 778

T-SQL Stored Procedure Coding Guidelines 781

Calling Stored Procedures from Transactions 783

Handling Errors in Stored Procedures 786

Using Source Code Control with Stored Procedures 789

Creating and Using CLR Stored Procedures 791

Adding CLR Stored Procedures to a Database 792

T-SQL or CLR Stored Procedures? 793

Using Extended Stored Procedures 793

Adding Extended Stored Procedures to SQL Server 794

Obtaining Information on Extended Stored Procedures 795

Extended Stored Procedures Provided with SQL Server 795

Using xp_cmdshell 796

Summary 798

24 Creating and Managing User-Defined Functions   799

What's New in SQL Server 2005 799

Why Use User-Defined Functions? 800

Types of User-Defined Functions 802

Scalar Functions 803

Table-Valued Functions 805

Creating and Managing User-Defined Functions 807

Creating User-Defined Functions 807

Viewing and Modifying User-Defined Functions 818

Managing User-Defined Function Permissions 824

Systemwide Table-Valued Functions 825

Rewriting Stored Procedures as Functions 826

Creating and Using CLR Functions 827

Adding CLR Functions to a Database 828

Deciding Between Using T-SQL or CLR Functions 830

Summary 831

25 Creating and Managing Triggers   833

What's New in Creating and Managing Triggers 834

Using DML Triggers 834

Creating DML Triggers 835

Using AFTER Triggers 837

Using inserted and deleted Tables 841

Enforcing Referential Integrity by Using DML Triggers 845

Cascading Deletes 847

Cascading Updates 849

INSTEAD OF Triggers 851

Using DDL Triggers 859

Creating DDL Triggers 861

Managing DDL Triggers 864

Using CLR Triggers 866

Using Nested Triggers 869

Using Recursive Triggers 870

Summary 871

26 Transaction Management and the Transaction Log   873

What's New in Transaction Management 873

What Is a Transaction? 874

How SQL Server Manages Transactions 874

Defining Transactions 875

AutoCommit Transactions 876

Explicit User-Defined Transactions 876

Implicit Transactions 882

Implicit Transactions Versus Explicit Transactions 884

Transaction Logging and the Recovery Process 885

The Checkpoint Process 886

The Recovery Process 889

Managing the Transaction Log 892

Transactions and Batches 897

Transactions and Stored Procedures 899

Transactions and Triggers 904

Triggers and Transaction Nesting 905

Triggers and Multistatement Transactions 907

Using Savepoints in Triggers 909

Transactions and Locking 911

READ_COMMITTED_SNAPSHOT Isolation 912

Coding Effective Transactions 912

Long-Running Transactions 913

Bound Connections 915

Creating Bound Connections 916

Binding Multiple Applications 917

Distributed Transactions 918

Summary 918

27   Database Snapshots   **919**

What's New with Database Snapshots 920
What Are Database Snapshots? 920
Limitations and Restrictions of Database Snapshots 925
Copy-on-Write Technology 926
When to Use Database Snapshots 927
    Reverting to a Snapshot for Recovery Purposes 927
    Safeguarding a Database Prior to Making Mass Changes 928
    Providing a Point-in-Time Reporting Database 930
    Providing a Highly Available and Offloaded Reporting
      Database from a Database Mirror 930
Setup and Breakdown of a Database Snapshot 932
    Creating a Database Snapshot 932
    Breaking Down a Database Snapshot 938
Reverting to a Database Snapshot for Recovery 938
    Reverting a Source Database from a Database Snapshot 938
    Using Database Snapshots with Testing and QA 939
Setting Up Snapshots Against a Database Mirror 940
    Reciprocal Principal/Mirror Reporting Configuration 941
Database Snapshots Maintenance and Security Considerations 942
    Security for Database Snapshots 942
    Snapshot Sparse File Size Management 943
    Number of Database Snapshots per Source Database 943
Summary 943

28   Database Maintenance   **945**

What's New in Database Maintenance 945
The Maintenance Plan Wizard 946
    Backing Up Databases 948
    Checking Database Integrity 951
    Shrinking Databases 952
    Maintaining Indexes and Statistics 953
    Scheduling a Maintenance Plan 956
Managing Maintenance Plans Without the Wizard 959
Executing a Maintenance Plan 964
Maintenance Without a Maintenance Plan 965
Summary 965

Part V   SQL Server Performance and Optimization

29   Indexes and Performance   **969**

What's New for Indexes and Performance 970
Understanding Index Structures 970

Clustered Indexes 971
Nonclustered Indexes 973
Index Utilization 975
Index Selection 978
Evaluating Index Usefulness 979
Index Statistics 982
The Statistics Histogram 984
How the Statistics Histogram Is Used 986
Index Densities 987
Estimating Rows Using Index Statistics 988
Generating and Maintaining Index and Column Statistics 990
SQL Server Index Maintenance 998
Setting the Fill Factor 1008
Reapplying the Fill Factor 1010
Disabling Indexes 1011
Managing Indexes with SSMS 1012
Index Design Guidelines 1013
Clustered Index Indications 1014
Nonclustered Index Indications 1016
Index Covering 1018
Included Columns 1020
Wide Indexes Versus Multiple Indexes 1020
Indexed Views 1021
Indexes on Computed Columns 1022
Choosing Indexes: Query Versus Update Performance 1024
Summary 1026

30 Understanding Query Optimization   1027

What's New in Query Optimization 1028
What Is the Query Optimizer? 1030
Query Compilation and Optimization 1030
Compiling DML Statements 1031
Optimization Steps 1032
Query Analysis 1032
Identifying Search Arguments 1032
Identifying OR Clauses 1033
Identifying Join Clauses 1034
Row Estimation and Index Selection 1034
Evaluating SARG and Join Selectivity 1035
Estimating Access Path Cost 1040
Using Multiple Indexes 1048
Optimizing with Indexed Views 1056

Join Selection 1059
    Join Processing Strategies 1060
    Determining the Optimal Join Order 1065
    Subquery Processing 1066
Execution Plan Selection 1070
Query Plan Caching 1072
    Query Plan Reuse 1073
    Query Plan Aging 1075
    Recompiling Query Plans 1076
    Monitoring the Plan Cache 1077
Other Query Processing Strategies 1083
    Predicate Transitivity 1083
    Group by Optimization 1083
    Queries with DISTINCT 1084
    Queries with UNION 1084
Parallel Query Processing 1086
    Parallel Query Configuration Options 1088
    Identifying Parallel Queries 1089
Common Query Optimization Problems 1090
    Out-of-Date or Unavailable Statistics 1090
    Poor Index Design 1092
    Search Argument Problems 1092
    Large Complex Queries 1094
    Triggers 1094
Managing the Optimizer 1094
    Optimizer Hints 1096
    Using the USE PLAN Query Hint 1101
    Using Plan Guides 1103
    Forced Parameterizaion 1109
    Limiting Query Plan Execution with the Query Governor 1111
Summary 1113

31 Query Analysis   1115
What's New in Query Analysis 1116
Query Analysis in SSMS 1117
    Execution Plan ToolTips 1118
    Logical and Physical Operator Icons 1121
    Analyzing Stored Procedures 1129
    Saving and Viewing Graphical Execution Plans 1130
SSMS Client Statistics 1132

Using the SET SHOWPLAN Options 1133

    SHOWPLAN_TEXT 1134

    SHOWPLAN_ALL 1136

    SHOWPLAN_XML 1137

Using sys.dm_exec_query_plan 1137

Query Statistics 1139

    statistics io 1139

    statistics time 1142

    Using datediff() to Measure Runtime 1145

    statistics profile 1146

    statistics XML 1146

Query Analysis with SQL Server Profiler 1147

Summary 1149

32 Locking and Performance   **1151**

What's New in Locking and Performance 1151

The Need for Locking 1152

Transaction Isolation Levels in SQL Server 1153

    Read Uncommitted Isolation 1154

    Read Committed Isolation 1155

    Read Committed Snapshot Isolation 1155

    Repeatable Read Isolation 1156

    Serializable Read Isolation 1157

    Snapshot Isolation 1158

The Lock Manager 1160

Monitoring Lock Activity in SQL Server 1160

    Querying the sys.dm_tran_locks View 1161

    Viewing Locking Activity with SSMS 1164

    Viewing Locking Activity with SQL Server Profiler 1167

    Monitoring Locks with Performance Monitor 1169

SQL Server Lock Types 1171

    Shared Locks 1172

    Update Locks 1173

    Exclusive Locks 1174

    Intent Locks 1174

    Schema Locks 1175

    Bulk Update Locks 1176

SQL Server Lock Granularity 1176

    Serialization and Key-Range Locking 1178

    Using Application Locks 1181

Index Locking 1184

Row-Level Versus Page-Level Locking 1185

Lock Escalation 1186

The `locks` Configuration Setting 1186

Lock Compatibility 1187

Locking Contention and Deadlocks 1188

Identifying Locking Contention 1189

Setting the Lock Timeout Interval 1191

Minimizing Locking Contention 1192

Deadlocks 1193

Table Hints for Locking 1203

Transaction Isolation–Level Hints 1204

Lock Granularity Hints 1206

Lock Type Hints 1206

Optimistic Locking 1207

Optimistic Locking Using the `timestamp` Data Type 1207

Optimistic Locking with Snapshot Isolation 1209

Summary 1212

33 Database Design and Performance   1213

What's New in Database Design and Performance 1213

Basic Tenets of Designing for Performance 1214

Logical Database Design Issues 1215

Normalization Conditions 1215

Normalization Forms 1215

Benefits of Normalization 1217

Drawbacks of Normalization 1217

Denormalizing a Database 1218

Denormalization Guidelines 1218

Essential Denormalization Techniques 1219

Database Filegroups and Performance 1225

RAID Technology 1227

RAID Level 0 1227

RAID Level 1 1228

RAID Level 10 1229

RAID Level 5 1230

Summary 1232

34 Monitoring SQL Server Performance   1233

What's New in Monitoring SQL Server Performance 1234

A Performance Monitoring Approach 1235

Performance Monitor 1236
    Performance Monitor Views 1236
    Monitoring Values 1237
Windows Performance Counters 1239
    Monitoring the Network Interface 1239
    Monitoring the Processors 1244
    Monitoring Memory 1250
    Monitoring the Disk System 1254
SQL Server Performance Counters 1257
    MSSQL$:Plan Cache Object 1258
    Monitoring SQL Server's Disk Activity 1259
    Locks 1259
    Users 1259
    The Procedure Cache 1260
    User-Defined Counters 1260
Using DBCC to Examine Performance 1261
    SQLPERF 1262
    PERFMON 1263
    SHOWCONTIG 1263
    PROCCACHE 1264
    INPUTBUFFER and OUTPUTBUFFER 1265
The Top 100 Worst-Performing Queries 1265
Other SQL Server Performance Considerations 1269
Summary 1270

Part VI   SQL Server Application Development

35   What's New for Transact-SQL in SQL Server 2005   1273
The xml Data Type 1274
The max Specifier 1274
TOP Enhancements 1276
The OUTPUT Clause 1280
Common Table Expressions 1284
    Recursive Queries with CTEs 1286
Ranking Functions 1295
    The ROW_NUMBER Function 1295
    The RANK and DENSE_RANK Functions 1298
    The NTILE Function 1299
    Using Row Numbers for Paging Results 1301
PIVOT and UNPIVOT 1305

The APPLY Operator 1309
    CROSS APPLY 1309
    OUTER APPLY 1311
TRY...CATCH Logic for Error Handling 1312
The TABLESAMPLE Clause 1314
Summary 1318

36 **SQL Server and the .NET Framework**   **1319**
What's New in SQL Server 2005 and the .NET Framework 1319
Working with ADO.NET 2.0 and SQL Server 1319
    ADO.NET: Advanced Basics 1320
    What's New in ADO.NET for SQL Server 2005 1324
Developing Custom Managed Database Objects 1331
    An Introduction to Custom Managed Database Objects 1331
    Managed Object Permissions 1332
    Developing Managed Objects with Visual Studio 2005 1334
    Using Managed Stored Procedures 1335
    Using Managed User-Defined Functions (UDFs) 1344
    Using Managed User-Defined Types (UDTs) 1354
    Using Managed User-Defined Aggregates (UDAs) 1363
    Using Managed Triggers 1366
    Using Transactions 1372
    Using the Related System Catalogs 1374
Summary 1375

37 **Using XML in SQL Server 2005**   **1377**
What's New in Using XML in SQL Server 2005 1377
Understanding XML 1377
Relational Data as XML: The FOR XML Modes 1378
    RAW Mode 1379
    AUTO Mode 1385
    EXPLICIT Mode 1389
    PATH Mode 1393
    FOR XML and the New xml Data Type 1396
XML as Relational Data: Using OPENXML 1399
Using the New xml Data Type 1402
    Defining and Using xml Columns 1404
    Using XML Schema Collections 1407
    The Built-in xml Data Type Methods 1411
Indexing and Full-Text Indexing of xml Columns 1430
    Indexing xml Columns 1430
    Full-Text Indexing 1436
Summary 1437

38   SQL Server Web Services   **1439**

What's New in SQL Server Web Services 1439

Web Services History and Overview 1439

The Web Services Pattern 1440

Building Web Services 1442

The AS HTTP Keyword Group 1445

The FOR SOAP Keyword Group 1449

Examples: A C# Client Application 1453

Example 1: Running a Web Method Bound to a
Stored Procedure from C# 1453

Example 2: Running Ad Hoc T-SQL Batches from a
SQL Server Web Service 1458

Example 3: Calling a Web Method–Bound Stored
Procedure That Returns XML 1462

Using Catalog Views and System Stored Procedures 1466

Controlling Access Permissions 1468

Summary 1469

Part VII   SQL Server Business Intelligence Features

39   SQL Server 2005 Analysis Services   **1473**

What's New in SSAS 1473

Understanding SSAS and OLAP 1474

Understanding the SSAS Environment Wizards 1476

OLAP Versus OLTP 1480

An Analytics Design Methodology 1482

An Analytics Mini-Methodology 1483

An OLAP Requirements Example: CompSales International 1485

CompSales International Requirements 1485

OLAP Cube Creation 1486

Using SQL Server BIDS 1487

Creating an OLAP Database 1488

Generating a Relational Database 1523

Cube Perspectives 1524

KPIs 1525

Data Mining 1526

Security and Roles 1536

Summary 1537

40   SQL Server Integration Services   **1539**

What's New with SSIS 1540

SSIS Basics 1540

SSIS Architecture and Concepts 1545

SSIS Tools and Utilities 1549

A Data Transformation Requirement 1555

Running the SSIS Wizard 1556

The SSIS Designer 1566

The Package Execution Utility 1574

    The dtexec Utility 1576

    Running Packages 1577

    Running Package Examples 1580

    The dtutil Utility 1582

    dtutil examples 1585

Using bcp 1586

    Fundamentals of Exporting and Importing Data 1589

    File Data Types 1591

    Format Files 1591

    Using Views 1601

Logged and Non-Logged Operations 1601

    Batches 1602

    Parallel Loading 1602

    Supplying Hints to bcp 1603

Summary 1605

41   SQL Server 2005 Reporting Services   1607

What's New in Reporting Services 2005 1610

    Report Builder 1610

    The Report Viewer Controls 1610

Installing and Configuring Reporting Services 1611

    The Reporting Services System Architecture 1611

    Installing Reporting Services 1613

    Reporting Services Configuration Options and Tools 1615

Designing Reports 1618

    Designing Reports by Using the BIDS Report Designer 1619

    Designing Reports Using Report Builder 1627

    Models and the Model Designer 1629

    A Model Design Example 1631

    Model Security 1643

    Enabling Ad Hoc Reporting 1645

Management and Security 1645

    Deploying Reports 1646

    Scripting Support in Reporting Services 1646

Securing Reports 1647
Subscriptions 1648
Report Execution Options 1650
Performance and Monitoring Tools 1652
The Server Trace Log 1652
The Execution Log 1653
Event Log Entries 1653
Performance Counters 1653
Building Applications for SQL Server Reporting Services
2005 Using the Report Viewer Controls 1653
Using the ASP.NET Report Controls in a Website 1654
Summary 1659

Part VIII   Bonus Chapters on the CD

42   Managing Linked and Remote Servers   1663
What's New in Managing Linked and Remote Servers 1664
Managing Remote Servers 1664
Remote Server Setup 1666
Linked Servers 1671
Distributed Queries 1672
Distributed Transactions 1672
Adding, Dropping, and Configuring Linked Servers 1673
sp_addlinkedserver 1673
sp_linkedservers 1680
sp_dropserver 1681
sp_serveroption 1682
Mapping Local Logins to Logins on Linked Servers 1683
sp_addlinkedsrvlogin 1684
sp_droplinkedsrvlogin 1685
sp_helplinkedsrvlogin 1686
Obtaining General Information About Linked Servers 1687
Executing a Stored Procedure via a Linked Server 1689
Setting Up Linked Servers Through SQL Server Management Studio .. 1689
Summary 1692

43   Configuring, Tuning, and Optimizing SQL Server Options   1693
What's New in Configuring, Tuning, and Optimizing
SQL Server Options 1694
SQL Server Instance Architecture 1694
Configuration Options 1695

Fixing an Incorrect Option Setting 1702

Setting Configuration Options with SSMS 1702

Obsolete Configuration Options 1703

Configuration Options and Performance 1703

    Ad Hoc Distributed Queries 1704

    affinity I/O mask 1704

    affinity mask 1706

    AWE Enabled 1707

    CLR Enabled 1709

    Cost Threshold for Parallelism 1709

    Cursor Threshold 1710

    Default Full-Text Language 1711

    Default Language 1712

    Fill Factor 1714

    Index Create Memory (KB) 1715

    Lightweight Pooling 1715

    Locks 1716

    Max Degree of Parallelism 1716

    Max Server Memory and Min Server Memory 1717

    Max Text Repl Size 1719

    Max Worker Threads 1719

    Min Memory Per Query 1720

    Nested Triggers 1721

    Network Packet Size 1721

    Priority Boost 1722

    Query Governor Cost Limit 1722

    Query Wait 1723

    Recovery Interval 1724

    Remote Admin connections 1724

    Remote Login timeout 1725

    Remote Proc Trans 1725

    Remote Query timeout 1726

    Scan for Startup Procs 1726

    Show Advanced Options 1727

    User Connections 1727

    User Options 1728

    XP-Relate d Configuration Options 1729

    Miscellaneous Options 1730

Database Engine Tuning Advisor 1731

    The Database Engine Tuning Advisor GUI 1731

    The Database Engine Tuning Advisor Command Line 1737

Summary 1742

44 Administering Very Large SQL Server Databases   1743

What's New for Administering Very Large SQL Server Databases 1743

Do I Have a VLDB? 1744

VLDB Maintenance Issues 1745

    Backing Up and Restoring VLDBs 1745

    Checking VLDB Consistency 1749

    Data Maintenance 1751

VLDB Database Design Considerations 1761

    Database Partitioning Options and Issues 1762

Summary 1770

45 SQL Server Disaster Recovery Planning   1771

What's New in SQL Server Disaster Recovery Planning 1772

How to Approach Disaster Recovery 1772

    Disaster Recovery Patterns 1773

    Recovery Objectives 1778

    A Data-Centric Approach to Disaster Recovery 1779

Microsoft SQL Server Options for Disaster Recovery 1780

    Data Replication 1780

    Log Shipping 1782

    Database Mirroring and Snapshots 1782

The Overall Disaster Recovery Process 1784

    The Focus of Disaster Recovery 1784

    SQLDIAG.EXE 1788

    Planning and Executing a Disaster Recovery 1790

Have You Detached a Database Recently? 1791

Third-Party Disaster Recovery Alternatives 1791

Summary 1792

46 Transact-SQL Programming Guidelines, Tips, and Tricks   1793

General T-SQL Coding Recommendations 1794

    Provide Explicit Column Lists 1794

    Qualify Object Names with Schema Name 1796

    Avoiding SQL Injection Attacks When Using Dynamic SQL 1799

    Comment Your T-SQL Code 1806

General T-SQL Performance Recommendations 1807

    UNION Versus UNION ALL Performance 1807

    Use IF EXISTS Instead of SELECT COUNT(*) 1807

    Avoid Unnecessary ORDER BY or DISTINCT Clauses 1808

    Using Temp Tables Versus Table Variables Versus
        Common Table Expressions 1808

        Avoid Unnecessary Function Executions 1809
        Cursors and Performance 1810
        Variable Assignment in UPDATE Statements 1813
    T-SQL Tips and Tricks 1817
        Date Calculations 1817
        Sorting Results with the GROUPING Function 1822
        Using CONTEXT_INFO 1824
        Working with Outer Joins 1826
        Generating T-SQL Statements with T-SQL 1835
        Working with @@error and @@rowcount 1836
        De-Duping Data with Ranking Functions 1837
    Summary 1840

47 **SQL Server Notification Services**   **1841**
    What's New in SQL Server Notification Services 1841
    Requirements and Editions of SSNS 1842
    Making the Business Case for Using SSNS 1843
    Understanding the SSNS Platform Architecture 1844
        Understanding Events 1844
        Understanding Event Providers 1844
        Understanding Subscribers and Subscriptions 1844
        Understanding Event Rules 1845
        Understanding the Notification Cycle 1845
        Understanding Instances 1846
    Building an Effective SSNS Application 1847
        Choosing a Programming Method 1847
        Working with XML Using Management Studio 1848
        Learning the Essentials of ADFs 1850
        Learning the Essentials of ICFs 1863
    Compiling and Running the Sample Application 1866
        Creating the Instance and Application via SSMS 1866
        Creating Subscriptions 1869
        Providing Events to the Application 1871
    Summary 1874

48 **SQL Server Service Broker**   **1875**
    What's New in Service Broker 1875
    Understanding Distributed Messaging 1875
        The Basics of Service Broker 1876
    Designing an Example System 1880

Understanding Service Broker Constructs 1881

    Defining Messages and Choosing a Message Type 1882

    Setting Up Contracts for Communication 1886

    Creating Queues for Message Storage 1887

    Defining Services to Send and Receive Messages 1889

    Planning Conversations Between Services 1890

Service Broker Routing and Security 1901

    Using Certificates for Conversation Encryption 1901

    A Final Note on the Example System 1909

Related System Catalogs 1909

Summary 1911

49   SQL Server Full-Text Search   **1913**

What's New in SQL Server 2005 Full-Text Search 1914

How SQL Server FTS Works 1914

Setting Up a Full-Text Index 1916

    Using T-SQL Commands to Build Full-Text Indexes
        and Catalogs 1916

    Using the Full-Text Indexing Wizard to Build Full-Text
        Indexes and Catalogs 1930

Full-Text Searches 1933

    Contains and ContainsTable 1933

    FreeText and FreeTextTable 1937

    Noise Words 1937

Full-Text Search Maintenance 1938

    Backup and Restore of Full-Text Catalogs 1938

    Attachment and Detachment of Full-Text Catalogs 1938

Full-Text Search Performance 1938

Summary 1939

Index   **1941**

About the Lead Authors

Ray Rankins is owner and president of Gotham Consulting Services, Inc. (www. gothamconsulting.com), near Saratoga Springs, New York. Ray has been working with Sybase and Microsoft SQL Server for more than 20 years and has experience in database administration, database design, project management, application development, consulting, courseware development, and training. He has worked in a variety of industries, including financial, manufacturing, health care, retail, insurance, communications, public utilities, and state and federal government. His expertise is in database performance and tuning, query analysis, advanced SQL programming and stored procedure development, database design, data architecture, and database application design and development. Ray's presentations on these topics at user group conferences have been very well received. Ray is coauthor of *Microsoft SQL Server 2000 Unleashed* (first and second editions), *Microsoft SQL Server 6.5 Unleashed* (all editions), *Sybase SQL Server 11 Unleashed*, and *Sybase SQL Server 11 DBA Survival Guide,* second edition, all published by Sams Publishing. He has also authored a number of articles, white papers, and database-related courses. As an instructor, Ray regularly teaches classes on SQL, advanced SQL programming and optimization, database design, database administration, and database performance and tuning. Ray's ability to bring his real-world experience into the classroom consistently rates very high marks from students in his classes for both his instructional skills and courseware. Ray can be reached at rrankins@gothamconsulting.com.

Paul Bertucci is the founder of Database Architechs (www.dbarchitechs.com), a database consulting firm with offices in the United States and Paris, France. He has more than 26 years of experience with database design, data architecture, data replication, performance and tuning, distributed data systems, data integration, high-availability assessments, and systems integration for numerous Fortune 500 companies, including Intel, 3COM, Coca-Cola, Apple, Toshiba, Lockheed, Wells Fargo, Safeway, Texaco, Charles Schwab, Cisco Systems, Sybase, Symantec, Veritas, and Honda, to name a few. He has authored numerous articles, standards, and high-profile courses, such as Sybase's "Performance and Tuning" and "Physical Database Design" courses. Other Sams Publishing books that he has authored include the highly popular *Microsoft SQL Server 2000 Unleashed*, *ADO.NET in 24 Hours*, and *Microsoft SQL Server High Availability.* He has deployed numerous systems with Microsoft SQL Server, Sybase, DB2, and Oracle database engines, and he has designed/architected several commercially available tools in the database, data modeling, performance and tuning, data integration, and multidimensional planning spaces. Paul's current working arrangement is as Symantec Corporations Chief Data Architect, and he also serves part time as chief technical advisor for a data integration server software company. Paul received his formal education in computer science and electrical engineering from UC Berkeley (Go Bears!). He lives in the great Pacific northwest (Oregon) with his wife, Vilay, and five children, Donny, Juliana, Paul Jr., Marissa, and Nina. Paul can be reached at pbertucci@DBArchitechs.com or Bertucci@Alum.CalBerkeley.Org.

Chris Gallelli is president of CGAL Consulting Services, Inc. His company focuses on consulting services in the areas of database administration, database tuning, and database programming using Visual Basic .NET. Chris has more than 10 years of experience with SQL Server and more than 20 years in the field of Information Technology. He has a Bachelor's degree in Electrical Engineering and a Masters in Business Administration from Union College. Chris was also one of the authors of *Microsoft SQL Server 2000 Unleashed* published by Sams Publishing. Chris currently lives near Albany, New York, with his lovely wife, Laura, and two daughters, Rachael and Kayla. You can contact Chris at CGallelli@gmail.com.

Alex T. Silverstein is managing principal and chief architect of the Unified Digital Group, LLC, a consulting and custom software development firm headquartered near Saratoga Springs, New York. He specializes in designing SQL Server and Microsoft .NET-powered solutions using the principles of Agile development and the Rational Unified Process. Alex has more than a decade of experience providing application development, database administration, and training services worldwide to a variety of industries. He was also a contributing author for *Microsoft SQL Server 2000 Unleashed* published by Sams Publishing. You can reach Alex anytime at alex@unifieddigital.com.

About the Contributing Authors

Tudor Trufinescu joined Microsoft in January 1999, and has since worked on a number of projects and technologies, including Microsoft Metadata services, HTTP-DAV, and SQL Server Reporting Services. He was one of the founding members of the SQL Server reporting services team. His team designed and built the server components of Reporting Services and the report controls included in Visual Studio 2005. Before joining Microsoft, Tudor helped build a number of software solutions, including a workflow and document management application and a real-time production monitoring system. Tudor received his degree in Electronic Engineering and Information Technology from the University of Bucharest, Romania, in 1992. Tudor and his family currently live in Redmond, Washington.

Dedication

I would like to dedicate this book to my beautiful wife of 20 years, Elizabeth, and my son, Jason, for their continued love, support, and understanding during the long hours and lost weekends spent working on this book.

—Ray Rankins

Dedicated to my wife, Vilay, for whom I say "koin hug chow" ("I love you" in Thai/Laotian).

—Paul Bertucci

This book is dedicated to my wife, Laura, and my two daughters, Rachael and Kayla. Keeping an active house quiet while I was working on this book was no small feat but they made it happen. They showed a great deal of patience and understanding during the entire process. Thank you!!!

—Chris Gallelli

I dedicate this work to my girlfriend, Ellen, who patiently endured my absence during the scores of hours devoted to it.

—Alex T. Silverstein

Acknowledgments

I would first like to thank my coauthors for their tireless efforts in helping to turn out a quality publication and their willingness to take on more work when needed to help keep things on track. I would also like to thank Neil Rowe at Sams Publishing for providing us the opportunity to write this book and for his patience in regard to our deadlines.

Most of all, I wish to thank my family, Elizabeth and Jason, for their patience and understanding during the long days and late nights spent working on this book when I should have been spending quality family time with them.

—Ray Rankins

With any writing effort, there is always a huge sacrifice of time that must be made to properly research, demonstrate, and describe leading-edge subject matter. The brunt of the burden usually falls on those many people who are near and very dear to me. With this in mind, I desperately need to thank my family for allowing me to encroach on many months of what should have been my family's "quality time."

However, with sacrifice also comes reward in the form of technical excellence and solid business relationships. Many individuals were involved in this effort, both directly and indirectly, starting with Jeff Brzycki, Jack McElreath, Emily Breuner-Jaquette, Jay Jones, Mark Johnson, Scott Smith, and Walter Kuketz. And special thanks this time must go to my colleagues in France, Yves Moison and Thierry Gerardin. Their expertise in and knowledge of SQL, performance and tuning, and high availability are unmatched. *Merci beaucoup!*

—Paul Bertucci

Writing a book of this size and scope requires a tremendous amount of time and dedication. The time and dedication applies not only to the authors who are writing the book but also to their family members as well. My wife and daughters were very understanding while I was holed up working on this book and that understanding helped make the book happen. My love and thanks to them.

I would also like to thank many of my clients who embraced SQL Server 2005 and adopted the product shortly after it was released. In particular, I would like to thank Ray McQuade and his company Spruce Computer Systems. Spruce has had tremendous success with SQL Server 2005 and they gave me some of the "real-world" experience that was invaluable in creating this book.

—Chris Gallelli

I am most grateful to those whom I am gifted with the opportunity to serve: You are my teachers on this path. To my fellow authors, clients, friends, and mentors: Without you, I would not be the person I am today. Particularly, I'd like to express my appreciation to the men and women at Thomson Learning and at HANYS for making the consulting life a pleasure (and for using the latest technology!); to the staff of Sams Publishing for putting this book together; to my co-authors for trusting in me and providing such an awesome opportunity; to my family, both original and chosen, for their unconditional love; and, finally, to that unknown power that continually drives me on to a better life. Thanks to all who gave me a chance to grow throughout this process.

—Alex T. Silverstein

We Want to Hear from You!

As the reader of this book, *you* are our most important critic and commentator. We value your opinion and want to know what we're doing right, what we could do better, what areas you'd like to see us publish in, and any other words of wisdom you're willing to pass our way.

As a Senior Acquisitions Editor for Sams Publishing, I welcome your comments. You can email or write me directly to let me know what you did or didn't like about this book—as well as what we can do to make our books better.

Please note that I cannot help you with technical problems related to the topic of this book. We do have a User Services group, however, where I will forward specific technical questions related to the book.

When you write, please be sure to include this book's title and author as well as your name, email address, and phone number. I will carefully review your comments and share them with the author and editors who worked on the book.

Email: feedback@samspublishing.com

Fax: 317-428-3310

Mail: Neil Rowe
Senior Acquisitions Editor
Sams Publishing
800 East 96th Street
Indianapolis, IN 46240 USA

Reader Services

Visit our website and register this book at www.samspublishing.com/register for convenient access to any updates, downloads, or errata that might be available for this book.

Introduction

It has been just over six years since SQL Server 2000 was released and just over five years since we published the first edition of *SQL Server 2000 Unleashed*. In that time, SQL Server has established itself as a robust and reliable database platform whose performance and scalability meet the implementation needs of businesses and corporations from simple desktop applications on up to enterprise-wide systems. A number of significant changes and enhancements in SQL Server 2005 further solidify its position in the marketplace as a robust enterprise-wide database system that can compete on the same level as the other major enterprise-wide database products, shifting firmly to providing a database engine foundation that can be highly available 7 days a week, 365 days a year.

One of the biggest challenges we faced when we wrote *SQL Server 2000 Unleashed* six years ago was providing comprehensive, in-depth, all-inclusive coverage of all the features of SQL Server 2000 within a single book. Doing the same for SQL Server 2005 was even more of a challenge. SQL Server 2005 was in development at Microsoft for more than 5 years and represents a major upgrade to SQL Server 2000. Many features of SQL Server 2000 have been replaced completely in SQL Server 2005 (for example, SQL Enterprise Manager and SQL Query Analyzer have been replaced by SQL Server Management Studio), while some have been completely re-architected (for example, Analysis Services), and most others have undergone significant improvements and enhancements. In addition, the number of SQL Server features and components has increased, and many of these features and components (for example, SQL Server Integration Services, Reporting Services, and .NET Framework integration) provide enough material to warrant their own separate titles. After nearly all of the chapters for this book had been completed, we realized we had significantly more information than could reasonably fit into a single book and we had to make some hard decisions as to what to include in print.

We decided that the main focus for the book is for it to provide detailed coverage of the core database server product and the day-to-day administrative and management aspects and tools of SQL Server 2005. We also wanted to be sure to provide extensive coverage of the new features of the SQL Server 2005 database engine, while also providing sufficient coverage of the new components of SQL Server, such as SQL Server Integration Services, Reporting Services, Web Services, and integration with the .NET Framework. We wanted to be sure to provide enough of the necessary information, tips, and guidelines to get you started in making use of these features. However, at the same time, there was a wealth of useful information on various SQL Server 2005 topics and features that had already been written that we didn't want to just simply discard, so we decided that we would include a bonus CD with this book that would contain these additional "bonus" chapters. The chapters included on the bonus CD are described later in this Introduction. Also, as in the past, all of our example scripts, databases, and other material are provided on the bonus CD as well. These, by themselves, offer much value and provide practical guidance on exactly how to create and manage complex SQL Server 2005 solutions.

Our other main goal when writing this book was for it to be more than just a syntax reference. SQL Server Books Online is a fine resource as a syntax reference. This book attempts to pick up where Books Online leaves off, by providing, in addition to syntax where necessary, valuable insight, tips, guidelines, and useful examples derived from our many years of experience working with SQL Server. Although we do provide the core, and sometimes advanced, syntax elements for the SQL commands discussed, SQL Server Books Online provides a much more extensive syntax reference than would make sense to try to duplicate here. As a matter of fact, at times, we may even direct you to Books Online for more detail on some of the more esoteric syntax options available for certain commands.

We hope that we have succeeded in meeting the goals we set out for this book and that it becomes an essential reference and source of expert information for you as you work with SQL Server 2005.

Who This Book Is For

This *Unleashed* book is intended for intermediate- to advanced-level users: for SQL Server administrators who want to understand SQL Server more completely to be able to effectively manage and administer their SQL Server environments, and for developers who want a more thorough understanding of SQL Server to help them write better Transact-SQL (T-SQL) code and develop more robust SQL Server applications. If you are responsible for analysis, design, implementation, support, administration, or troubleshooting of SQL Server 2005, this book provides an excellent source of experiential information for you. You can think of this as a book of applied technology. The emphasis is on the more complex aspects of the product, including using the new tools and features, server administration, query analysis and optimization, data warehousing, management of very large databases, ensuring high availability, and performance tuning.

This book is for both developers and SQL Server administrators who are new to SQL Server 2005 as well as those who are already familiar with SQL Server 2000. At the beginning of each chapter is a brief summary of the major changes or new features or capabilities of SQL Server 2005 related to that topic. If you are already familiar with SQL Server 2000, you can use this information to focus on the information in the chapters that covers the new features and capabilities in more detail.

This book is intended to provide a behind-the-scenes look into SQL Server, showing you what goes on behind the various wizards and GUI-based tools so you can learn what the underlying SQL commands are. Although the GUI tools can make your average day-to-day operations much simpler, every database administrator should learn the underlying commands to the tools and wizards to fully unlock the power and capabilities of SQL Server. Besides, you never know when you may have to manage a server through a telnet session with only a command-line query tool available.

What This Book Covers

The book is divided into the following sections:

- ▶ **Part I, "Welcome to Microsoft SQL Server"**—This section introduces you to the Microsoft SQL Server 2005 environment, the various editions of SQL Server that are available, and the capabilities of each edition in the various Windows environments. In addition, it provides an overview of and introduction to the new features found in SQL Server 2005, which are covered in more detail throughout rest of the book.

- ▶ **Part II, "SQL Server Tools and Utilities"**—This section covers the tools and utility programs that SQL Server 2005 provides for you to administer and manage your SQL Server environments. You'll find information on the various management tools you use on a daily basis, such as SQL Server Management Studio and the new SQLCMD command-line query tool, along with information on SQL Server Profiler. If you are not familiar with these tools, you should read this part of the book early on because these tools are often used and referenced throughout many of the other chapters in the book.

- ▶ **Part III, "SQL Server Administration"**—This section discusses topics related to the administration of SQL Server at the server level. It begins with an overview of what is involved in administering a SQL Server environment and then goes on to cover the tasks related to setting up and managing the overall SQL Server environment, including installing and upgrading to SQL Server 2005 as well as installing SQL Server 2005 clients. This section also includes coverage of security and user administration, database backup and restore, replication, and using the new Database Mail facility. Chapters on SQL Server clustering and SQL Server high availability provide some expert advice in these areas. Database mirroring and task scheduling and notification using SQL Server Agent are also discussed in this section.

► **Part IV, "SQL Server Database Administration"**—This section dives into the administrative tasks associated with creating and managing a SQL Server 2005 database, including the creation and management of database objects, such as tables, indexes, views, stored procedures, functions, and triggers. It also provides coverage of the new Database Snapshot feature of SQL Server 2005 as well as an overview of database maintenance.

► **Part V, "SQL Server Performance and Optimization"**—This section provides information to help you get the best performance out of SQL Server. It begins with a discussion on indexes and performance, one of the key items to understand to help ensure good database performance. It then builds on that information with chapters on query optimization and analysis, locking, database design and performance, and monitoring and optimization of SQL Server performance.

► **Part VI, "SQL Server Application Development"**—This section includes a comprehensive overview of what's new in T-SQL in SQL Server 2005. In addition, chapters in this section provide an overview for developing SQL Server applications within the .NET Framework, working with XML in SQL Server 2005, and SQL Server 2005's built-in Web Services capabilities.

► **Part VII, "SQL Server Business Intelligence Features"**—This section includes a comprehensive overview of SQL Server 2005's built-in business intelligence features: Analysis Services, Integration Services, and Reporting Services.

► **Bonus Chapters on the CD**—In order to be able to provide comprehensive coverage of the new features of SQL Server 2005 and still fit everything in a single book that doesn't require a wheelbarrow to transport, some information had to be omitted from the printed product. However, we have included this information as bonus chapters on the enclosed CD. Most of these bonus chapters cover additional SQL Server components that are not part of the core database engine such as Notification Services, Service Broker, and Full-Text Search. There are also chapters for which there just wasn't room enough to include in the book itself. These chapters provide expert advice and information on remote and linked server management, SQL Server configuration, tuning and optimization, administering very large SQL Server databases, SQL Server Disaster Recovery Planning, and T-SQL programming guidelines, tips, and tricks. In addition, please visit the web page for this book on www.samspublishing.com periodically for any updated or additional bonus material as it becomes available.

► **Book Materials on the CD**—Also included on the CD are many of the code samples, scripts, databases, and other materials that supplement various chapters. This has always been one of the most valuable reasons to buy the *Unleashed* series books. It is our goal to not just discuss a SQL technique or solution, but to also provide working samples and examples that actually do it. Learning by seeing is essential for understanding.

Conventions Used in This Book

Names of commands and stored procedures are presented in a special monospaced computer typeface. We have tried to be consistent in our use of uppercase and lowercase for keywords and object names. However, because the default installation of SQL Server doesn't make a distinction between upper- and lowercase for SQL keywords or object names and data, you might find some of the examples presented in either upper- or lowercase.

Code and output examples are presented separately from regular paragraphs and are also in a monospaced computer typeface. The following is an example:

```
select object_id, name, type_desc
from sys.objects
where type = 'SQ'

object_id    name                            type_desc
----------   -----------------------------   ------------
1977058079   QueryNotificationErrorsQueue    SERVICE_QUEUE
2009058193   EventNotificationErrorsQueue    SERVICE_QUEUE
2041058307   ServiceBrokerQueue              SERVICE_QUEUE
```

When syntax is provided for a command, we have followed these conventions:

Syntax Element	Definition
command	These are command names, options, and other keywords.
placeholder	Monospaced italic indicates values you provide.
{}	You must choose at least one of the enclosed options.
[]	The enclosed value/keyword is optional.
()	Parentheses are part of the command.
¦	You can select only one of the options listed.
,	You can select any of the options listed.
[...]	The previous option can be repeated.

Consider the following syntax example:

```
grant {all ¦ permission_list} on object [(column_list)]
      to {public ¦ user_or_group_name [, [...]]}
```

In this case, *object* is required, but *column_list* is optional. Note also that items shown in plain computer type, such as grant, public, and all, should be entered literally, as shown. Placeholders are presented in *italic*, such as *permission_list* and *user_or_group_name*. A *placeholder* is a generic term for which you must supply a specific value or values. The ellipsis ([...]) in the square brackets following *user_or_group_name* indicates that multiple user or group names can be specified, separated by commas. You can specify either the keyword public or one or more user or group names, but not both.

Some of the examples presented in this book make use of the AdventureWorks database, which is included with SQL Server 2005 (our old friends the pubs and Northwinds databases are no longer provided with SQL Server). However, for many of the examples presented in Part V, larger tables than what are available in the Adventureworks database were needed to demonstrate many of the concepts with more meaningful examples. For many of the chapters in this section, the examples come from the bigpubs2005 database. This database has the same structure as the old pubs database, but it contains significantly more data. A copy of the database, along with an Entity-Relationship (ER) diagram and table descriptions, is also on the CD.

To install the bigpubs2005 database on your system so you can try out the various examples, do the following:

1. Copy the bigpubs2005.mdf file into the SQL Server data folder where you want it to reside.

2. After the file has been copied to the destination folder, ensure that the Read-Only property of the bigpubs2005.mdf file is not enabled (this can happen when the file is copied from the CD). Right-click the file in Windows Explorer and select Properties to bring up the Properties dialog. Click the Read-Only check box to remove the check mark. Click OK to save the changes to the file attributes.

3. Attach the bigpubs2005 database by using a command similar to the following:

```
sp_attach_single_file_db 'bigpubs2005',
    N'D:\MSSQL\DATA\MSSQL.1\MSSQL\Data\bigpubs2005.mdf
```

Note that you might need to edit the path to match the location where you copied the bigpubs2005.mdf file.

Alternatively, you can attach the database by using SQL Server Management Studio. You right-click the Databases node in the Object Explorer and select Attach. When the Attach Databases dialog appears, click the Add button, locate the bigpubs2005.mdf file, and click OK. In the bottom window pane, click the transaction log file entry (it should say Not Found in the message column) and click the Remove button. Next, click the OK button to attach the database. A new transaction log file is automatically created in the same folder as the bigpubs2005.mdf file. For more information on attaching database files, see Chapters 11, "Database Backup and Restore," and 18, "Creating and Managing Databases."

NOTE

In addition to the `bigpubs2005` database, the mdf file for the database that is used for examples in Chapter 39, "SQL Server Analysis Services," (CompSales) is also provided. To install the `CompSales` database, do the following:

1. Copy the `CompSales.mdf` file into the SQL Server data folder where you want it to reside.

2. Ensure that the `Read-Only` property of the `CompSales.mdf` file is not enabled.

3. Attach the `CompSales` database by using a command similar to the following (edit the path to match the location of the `CompSales.mdf` file on your system):

```
sp_attach_single_file_db 'CompSales',
     N'D:\MSSQL\DATA\MSSQL.1\MSSQL\Data\CompSales.mdf
```

Good Luck!

If you have purchased this book, you are on your way to getting the most from SQL Server 2005. You have already chosen a fine platform for building database applications, one that can provide outstanding performance and rock-solid reliability and availability at a reasonable cost. With this book, you now have the information you need to make the best of it.

Many of us who worked on this book have been using SQL Server for more than a decade. Writing about this new version challenged us to reassess many of our preconceived notions about SQL Server and the way it works. It was an interesting and enjoyable process, and we learned a lot. We hope you get as much enjoyment and knowledge from reading this book as we have from writing it.

PART I

Welcome to Microsoft SQL Server

IN THIS PART

CHAPTER 1   SQL Server 2005 Overview   11

CHAPTER 2   What's New in SQL Server 2005   35

SQL Server 2005 Overview

IN THIS CHAPTER

▸ SQL Server Components and Features

▸ SQL Server 2005 Editions

▸ SQL Server Licensing Models

Exactly what is SQL Server 2005? When you first install the product, what are all the pieces you get, what do they do, and which of them do you need?

At its core, SQL Server 2005 is an enterprise-class database management system (DBMS) that is capable of running anything from a personal database only a few megabytes in size on a handheld Windows Mobile device up to a multi-server database system managing terabytes of information. However, SQL Server 2005 is much more than just a database engine.

The SQL Server product is made up of a number of different components. This chapter describes each of the pieces that make up the SQL Server product and what role each plays. Each of these topics is dealt with in more detail later in the book. In addition, this chapter looks at the environments that support SQL Server 2005 and the features available in each of the various SQL Server editions.

SQL Server Components and Features

The main component of SQL Server 2005 is the Database Engine. Before you can use the other components and features of SQL Server 2005, which are discussed in this section, you need to have an instance of the Database Engine installed.

The SQL Server Database Engine

The Database Engine is the core application service in the SQL Server package for storing, processing, and securing data with SQL Server 2005. The SQL Server 2005 Database

Engine is a Windows service that can be used to store and process data in either a relational format or as XML documents. The following are the main responsibilities of the Database Engine:

▶ Provide reliable storage for data

▶ Provide a means to rapidly retrieve this data

▶ Provide consistent access to the data

▶ Control access to the data through security

▶ Enforce data integrity rules to ensure that the data actually means something

Each of these responsibilities is examined in greater detail in later chapters in this book. For now, this chapter provides just a brief overview on each of these points to show how Microsoft SQL Server fulfills these core responsibilities.

Reliable Storage

Reliable storage starts at the hardware level. This isn't the responsibility of the Database Engine, but it's a necessary part of a well-built database. Although you can put an entire SQL database on a single IDE or SATA drive (or even burn a read-only copy on a CD), it is preferable to maintain the data on RAID arrays. The most common RAID arrays allow hardware failures at the disk level without loss of data.

NOTE

For more information on the reliability characteristics and performance implications of the various RAID configurations and guidelines for implementing RAID configurations with SQL Server, see Chapter 33, "Database Design and Performance."

Using whatever hardware you have decided to make available, the Database Engine manages all the data structures necessary to ensure reliable storage of your data. Rows of data are stored in *pages*, and each page is 8KB in size. Eight pages make up an *extent,* and the Database Engine keeps track of which extents are allocated to which tables and indexes.

NOTE

A *page* is an 8KB chunk of a data file, the smallest unit of storage available in the database. An *extent* is a collection of eight 8KB pages.

Another key feature the Database Engine provides to ensure reliable storage is the transaction log. The transaction log makes a record of every change that is made to the database. For more information on the transaction log and how it's managed, see Chapter 26, "Transaction Management and the Transaction Log."

NOTE

It is not strictly true that the transaction log records *all* changes to the database; some exceptions exist. Operations on binary large objects—data of type `image` and `text`—can be excepted from logging, and bulk copy loads into tables can be minimally logged to get the fastest possible performance.

Rapid Data Access

SQL Server allows the creation of indexes, enabling fast access to data. See Chapter 29, "Indexes and Performance," for an in-depth discussion of indexes.

Another way to provide rapid access to data is to keep frequently accessed data in memory. Excess memory for a SQL Server instance is used as a data cache. When pages are requested from the database, the SQL Server Database Engine checks to see if the requested pages are already in the cache. If they are not, it reads them off the disk and stores them in the data cache. If there is no space available in the data cache, the least recently accessed pages (that is, those that haven't been accessed in a while, since they were read into memory) are flushed out of the data cache to make room for the newly requested pages. If the pages being flushed contain changes that haven't been written out yet, they are written to disk before being flushed from memory. Otherwise, they are simply discarded.

NOTE

With sufficient memory, an entire database can fit completely into memory, providing the best possible I/O performance for the database.

Consistent Data Access

Getting to your data quickly doesn't mean much if the information you receive is inaccurate. SQL Server follows a set of rules to ensure that the data you receive from queries is consistent.

The general idea with consistent data access is to allow only one client at a time to change the data and to prevent others from reading data from the database while it is undergoing changes. Data and transactional consistency are maintained in SQL Server by using transactional locking.

Transactional consistency has several levels of conformance, each of which provides a trade-off between accuracy of the data and concurrency. These levels of concurrency are examined in more detail in Chapter 32, "Locking and Performance."

Access Control

SQL Server controls access by providing security at multiple levels. Security is enforced at the server level, at the database level, and at the object level. In SQL Server 2005, security can now also be enforced at the schema level.

Sever-level access is enforced either by using a local user name and password or through integrated network security, which uses the client's network login credentials to establish identity.

SQL Server security is examined in greater detail in Chapter 10, "Security and User Administration."

Data Integrity

Some databases have to serve the needs of more than a single application. A corporate database that contains valuable information might have a dozen different departments wanting to access portions of the database for different needs.

In this kind of environment, it is impractical to expect the developers of each application to agree on an identical set of standards for maintaining data integrity. For example, one department might allow phone numbers to have extensions, whereas another department may not need that capability. One department might find it critical to maintain a relationship between a customer record and a salesperson record, whereas another might care only about the customer information.

The best way to keep everybody sane in this environment—and to ensure that the data stays consistent and usable by everyone—is to enforce a set of data integrity rules within the database itself. This is accomplished through data integrity constraints and other data integrity mechanisms, such as rules, defaults, and triggers. See Chapter 21, "Implementing Data Integrity," for details.

SQL Server 2005 Administration and Management Tools

SQL Server 2005 provides a suite of tools for managing and administering the SQL Server Database Engine and other components. This section provides an overview of the primary tools for day-to-day administration, management, and monitoring of your SQL Server environments.

SQL Server Management Studio (SSMS)

SSMS is the central console from which most database management tasks can be coordinated. SSMS provides a single interface from which all servers in a company can be managed. SSMS is examined in more detail in Chapter 3, "SQL Server Management Studio."

Figure 1.1 shows SSMS being used for some everyday administration tasks.

Figure 1.1 shows a list of registered servers in the upper-left pane. Below that is the Object Explorer, which lets you browse the contents of the databases within a SQL Server instance. The bigpubs2005 database has been expanded, and the right pane shows the columns for the authors table.

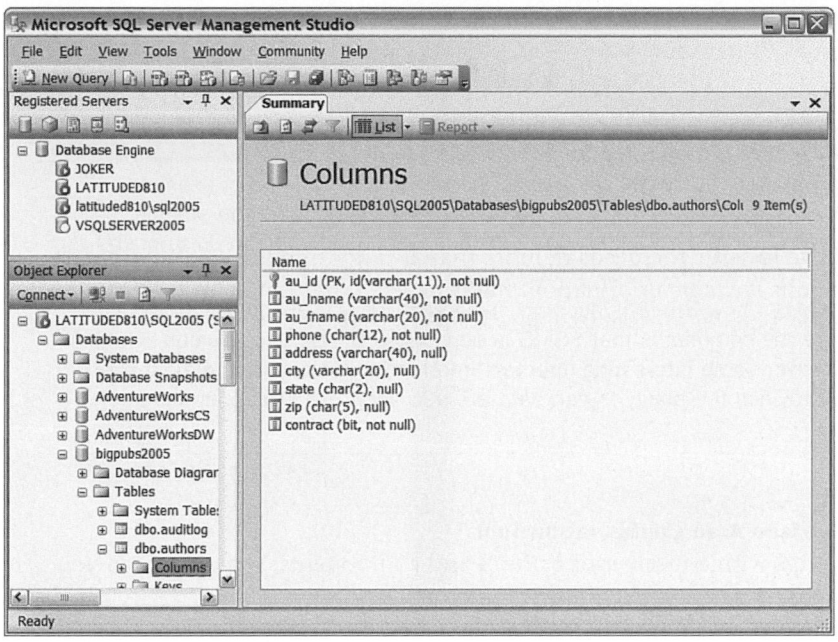

FIGURE 1.1   SSMS, showing a list of columns for the `authors` table in the `bigpubs2005` database.

The following are some of the tasks you can perform with SSMS. Most of these are discussed in detail later in the book:

- ▶ Completely manage many servers in a convenient interface
- ▶ Set server options and configuration values, such as the amount of memory and number of processors to use, the default language, and the default location of the data and log files
- ▶ Manage logins, database users, and database roles
- ▶ Create, edit, and schedule automated jobs through the SQL Server Agent
- ▶ Back up and restore databases and define maintenance plans
- ▶ Create new databases
- ▶ Browse table contents
- ▶ Manage database objects, such as tables, indexes, and stored procedures
- ▶ Generate DDL scripts for databases and database objects
- ▶ Configure and manage replication
- ▶ Create, edit, and analyze Transact-SQL (T-SQL) scripts

▶ Manage and organize scripts into projects and save versions in source control systems such as Visual SourceSafe

---

NOTE

SSMS interacts with SQL Server by using plain old T-SQL commands. For example, when you create a new database through the SSMS interface, behind the scenes, SSMS generates a `CREATE DATABASE` SQL command. Whatever you can do through the SSMS GUI, you can do with T-SQL statements.

If you're curious about how SSMS is accomplishing something, you can run SQL Profiler to capture the commands that SSMS is sending to the server. You can use this technique to discover some interesting internals information. In addition, almost every dialog in SSMS provides the ability to generate a T-SQL script for any actions it performs.

The SQL Server Surface Area Configuration Tool

SQL Server 2005 ships with a number of features and components, some if which you might not need. Stopping or disabling unused components helps to improve security by providing fewer avenues for potential attacks on a system as well as reducing requirements for CPU and memory resources.

You can use the SQL Server Surface Area Configuration tool to verify which SQL Server features and services are enabled and running and to verify which types of connections SQL Server 2005 accepts. You can use this tool to verify or change the state of features, services, and connections.

SQL Server Configuration Manager

SQL Server Configuration Manager is a new tool provided with SQL Server 2005 for managing the services associated with SQL Server and for configuring the network protocols used by SQL Server. SQL Server Configuration Manager provides the same functionality as the multiple tools provided with SQL Server 2000: Server Network Utility, Client Network Utility, and Service Manager. Primarily, SQL Server Configuration Manager is used to start, pause, resume, and stop SQL Server services and to view or change service properties.

SQL Server Agent

SQL Server Agent is a scheduling tool integrated into SSMS that allows convenient definition and execution of scheduled scripts and maintenance jobs. SQL Server Agent also handles automated alerts—for example, if the database runs out of space.

SQL Server Agent is a Windows service that runs on the same machine as the SQL Server Database Engine. The SQL Server Agent service can be started and stopped through either SSMS, the SQL Server Configuration Manager, or the ordinary Windows Services Manager.

In enterprise situations in which many SQL Server machines need to be managed together, the SQL Server Agent can be configured to distribute common jobs to multiple servers through the use of Multiserver Administration. This is most helpful in a wide architecture scenario, in which many SQL Server instances are performing the same tasks with the databases. Jobs are managed from a single SQL Server machine, which is responsible for maintaining the jobs and distributing the job scripts to each target server. The results of each job are maintained on the target servers but can be observed through a single interface.

If you had 20 servers that all needed to run the same job, you could check the completion status of that job in moments instead of logging in to each machine and checking the status 20 times.

The SQL Server Agent also handles event forwarding. Any system events that are recorded in the Windows system event log can be forwarded to a single machine. This gives a busy administrator a single place to look for errors.

More information about how to accomplish these tasks, as well as other information on the SQL Server Agent, is available in Chapter 13, "SQL Server Scheduling and Notification."

SQL Server Profiler

The SQL Server Profiler is a GUI interface to the SQL Trace feature of SQL Server that captures the queries and results flowing to and from the database engine. It is analogous to a network sniffer, although it does not operate on quite that low a level. The Profiler has the ability to capture and save a complete record of all the T-SQL statements passed to the server and the occurrence of SQL Server events such as deadlocks, logins, and errors. You can use a series of filters to pare down the results when you want to drill down to a single connection or even a single query.

You can use the SQL Profiler to perform these helpful tasks:

- ▶ You can capture the exact SQL statements sent to the server from an application for which source code is not available (for example, third-party applications).

- ▶ You can capture all the queries sent to SQL Server for later playback on a test server. This is extremely useful for performance testing with live query traffic.

- ▶ If your server is encountering recurring access violations (AVs), you can use Profiler to reconstruct what happened leading up to an AV.

- ▶ The Profiler shows basic performance data about each query. When your users start hammering your server with queries that cause hundreds of table scans, the Profiler can easily identify the culprits.

- ▶ For complex stored procedures, the Profiler can identify which portion of the procedure is causing the performance problem.

- ▶ You can audit server activity in real-time.

More information on SQL Server Profiler is available in Chapter 5, "SQL Server Profiler."

Replication

Replication is a server-based tool that you can use to synchronize data between two or more databases. Replication can send data from one SQL Server instance to another, or it can include Oracle, Access, or any other database that is accessible via ODBC or OLE DB.

SQL Server supports three kinds of replication:

▶ Snapshot replication

▶ Transactional replication

▶ Merge replication

The availability and functionality of replication might be restricted, depending on the version of SQL Server 2005 you are running.

NOTE

Replication copies the data from your tables and indexed views and even replicates changes to multiple tables caused by a stored procedure, but it does not normally re-create indexes or triggers at the target. It is common to have different indexes on replication targets rather than on the source to support different requirements.

Snapshot Replication

With snapshot replication, the server takes a picture, or snapshot, of the data in a table at a single point in time. Usually, if this operation is scheduled, the target data is simply replaced at each update. This form of replication is appropriate for small data sets, infrequent update periods (or for a one-time replication operation), or management simplicity.

Transactional Replication

Initially set up with a snapshot, the server maintains downstream replication targets by reading the transaction log at the source and applying each change at the targets. For every insert, update, and delete operation, the server sends a copy of the operation to every downstream database. This is appropriate if low-latency replicas are needed. Transactional replication can typically keep databases in sync within about five seconds of latency, depending on the underlying network infrastructure. Keep in mind that transactional replication does not guarantee identical databases at any given point in time. Rather, it guarantees that each change at the source will eventually be propagated to the targets. If you need to guarantee that two databases are transactionally identical, you should look into Distributed Transactions or Database Mirroring.

Transactional replication might be used for a website that supports a huge number of concurrent browsers but only a few updaters, such as a large and popular messaging board. All updates would be done against the replication source database and would be replicated in near-real-time to all the downstream targets. Each downstream target could support several web servers, and each incoming web request would be balanced among the web farm. If the system needed to be scaled to support more read requests, you could simply add more web servers and databases and add the database to the replication scheme.

Merge Replication

With snapshot and transactional replication, a single source of data exists from which all the replication targets are replenished. In some situations, it might be necessary or desirable to allow the replication targets to accept changes to the replicated tables and merge these changes together at some later date.

Merge replication allows data to be modified by the subscribers and synchronized at a later time. This could be as soon as a few seconds, or it could be a day later.

Merge replication would be helpful for a sales database that is replicated from a central SQL Server database out to several dozen sales laptops. As the sales personnel make sales calls, they can add new data to the customer database or change errors in the existing data. When the salespeople return to the office, they can synchronize their laptops with the central database. Their changes are submitted, and the laptops get refreshed with whatever new data was entered since the last synchronization.

Immediate Updating

Immediate updating allows a replication target to immediately modify data at the source. This is accomplished by using a trigger to run a distributed transaction. Immediate updating is performance intensive, but it allows for updates to be initiated from anywhere in the replication architecture.

More details on replication are available in Chapter 15, "Replication."

Database Mirroring

Database mirroring is a new feature available in SQL Server 2005. Database mirroring is primarily a software solution for increasing database availability. Essentially, database mirroring maintains two copies of a single database that reside on different instances of SQL Server, typically on server instances that reside on computers in different locations. In a typical database mirroring scenario, one server instance serves as the primary database to which the client applications connect, and the other server instance acts as a hot or warm standby server.

Database mirroring involves redoing every modification operation that occurs on the primary database onto the mirror database as quickly as possible. This is accomplished by sending every active transaction log record generated on the primary server to the mirror server. The log records are applied to the mirror database, in sequence, as quickly as possible. Unlike replication, which works at the logical level, database mirroring works at the level of the physical log record. The mirror database is an exact copy of the primary database.

For more information on setting up and using database mirroring, see Chapter 16, "Database Mirroring."

Full-Text Search

SQL Server 2005 provides the ability to issue full-text queries against plain character-based data in your SQL Server tables. This is useful for searching large text fields, such as movie reviews, book descriptions, or case notes. Full-text queries can include words and phrases, or multiple forms of a word or phrase.

Full-Text Search capabilities in Microsoft SQL Server 2005 are provided by the Microsoft Full-Text Engine for SQL Server (MSFTESQL). The MSFTESQL service works together with the SQL Server Database Engine. You specify tables or entire databases that you want to index. The full-text indexes are built and maintained outside the SQL Server database files in special full-text indexes stored in the Windows file system. You can specify how often the full-text indexes are updated to balance performance issues with timeliness of the data.

> **NOTE**
>
> The MSFTESQL service is a separate service from the SQL Server Database Engine service. You can enable or disable the MSFTESQL service by using the SQL Server 2005 Surface Area Configuration tool.

The SQL Server Database Engine supports basic text searches against specific columns. For example, to find all the rows where a text column contained the word *guru*, you might write the following SQL statement:

```
select *
   from resume
   where description like '%guru%'
```

This finds all the rows in the resume table where the description contains the word *guru*. This method has a couple problems, however. First, the search is slow. Because the Database Engine can't index text columns, a full table scan has to be done to satisfy the query. Even if the data were stored in a varchar column instead of a text column, an index may not help because you're looking for *guru* anywhere in the column, not just at the beginning. (More information on avoiding situations like this are discussed in Chapter 29, "Indexes and Performance.")

What if you wanted to search for the word *guru* anywhere in the table, not just in the description column? What if you were looking for a particular set of skills, such as "SQL" and "ability to work independently"? Full-text indexing addresses these problems. To perform the same search as before with full-text indexing, you might use a query like this:

```
select *
   from resume
   where contains(description, 'guru')
```

To perform a search that looks for a set of skills, you might use a query like this:

```
select *
  from resume
  where contains(*, 'SQL and "ability to work independently"')
```

For more information on setting up and searching Full-Text Search indexes, see Chapter 49, "SQL Server Full-Text Search" (on the CD-ROM).

SQL Server Integration Services (SSIS)

SSIS is a platform for building high-performance data integration solutions and workflow solutions. You can build extract, transform, and load (ETL) packages to update data warehouses, interact with external processes, clean and mine data, process analytical objects, and perform administrative tasks. In SQL Server 2000, these tasks were performed by Data Transformation Services (DTS). In SQL Server 2005, Microsoft has completely redeployed and rebuilt DTS into SSIS and integrated it into the Business Intelligence (BI) Development Studio/Visual Studio development environments and SSMS.

The following are some of the features of SSIS:

- Graphical tools and wizards for building, debugging, and deploying SSIS packages
- Workflow functions, such as File Transfer Protocol (FTP), SQL statement execution, and more
- SSIS application programming interfaces (APIs)
- Complex data transformation for data cleansing, aggregation, merging, and copying
- An email messaging interface
- A service-based implementation
- Support for both native and managed code (C++ or any common language runtime [CLR]–compliant language, such as C# or J#)
- An SSIS object model

SSIS is a tool that helps address the needs of getting data—which is often stored in many different formats, contexts, file systems, and locations—from one place to another. In addition, the data often requires significant transformation and conversion processing as it is being moved around. Common uses of SSIS might include the following:

- Exporting data out of SQL Server tables to other applications and environments (for example, ODBC or OLE DB data sources, flat files)
- Importing data into SQL Server tables from other applications and environments (for example, ODBC or OLE DB data sources, flat files)
- Initializing data in some data replication situations, such as initial snapshots

 ▶ Aggregating data (that is, data transformation) for distribution to/from data marts or data warehouses

 ▶ Changing the data's context or format before importing or exporting it (that is, data conversion)

For more information on creating and using SSIS packages, see Chapter 40, "SQL Server Integration Services."

SQL Server Analysis Services (SSAS)

SSAS provides online analytical processing (OLAP) and data mining functionality for BI solutions. SSAS provides a rich set of data mining algorithms to enable business users to mine data, looking for specific patterns and trends. These data mining algorithms can be used to analyze data through a Unified Dimensional Model (UDM) or directly from a physical data store.

SSAS uses both server and client components to supply OLAP and data mining functionality for BI applications. SSAS consists of the analysis server, processing services, integration services, and a number of data providers. SSAS has both server-based and client-/local-based analysis services capabilities. This essentially provides a complete platform for SSAS. The basic components within SSAS are all focused on building and managing data cubes.

SSAS allows you to build dimensions and cubes from heterogeneous data sources. It can access relational OLTP databases, multidimensional data databases, text data, and any other source that has an OLE DB provider available. You don't have to move all your data into a SQL Server 2005 database first; you just connect to its source. In addition, SSAS allows a designer to implement OLAP cubes, using a variety of physical storage techniques that are directly tied to data aggregation requirements and other performance considerations.

You can easily access any OLAP cube built with SSAS via the Pivot Table Service, you can write custom client applications by using Multidimensional Expressions (MDX) with OLE DB for OLAP or ActiveX Data Objects Multidimensional (ADO MD), and you can use a number of third-party OLAP-compliant tools. MDX enables you to formulate complex multidimensional queries.

SSAS is commonly used to perform the following tasks:

 ▶ Perform trend analysis to predict the future. For example, based on how many widgets you sold last year, how many will you sell next year?

 ▶ Combine otherwise disconnected variables to gain insight into past performance. For example, was there any connection between widget sales and rainfall patterns? Searching for unusual connections between your data points is a typical data mining exercise.

▶ Perform offline summaries of commonly used data points for instant access via a web interface or a custom interface. For example, a relational table might contain one row for every click on a website. OLAP can be used to summarize these clicks by hour, day, week, and month and then to further categorize these by business line.

SSAS is a complex topic. For more information on MDX, data cubes, and how to use data warehousing analysis services, see Chapter 39, "SQL Server 2005 Analysis Services."

SQL Server 2005 Reporting Services

SQL Server 2005 Reporting Services is a server-based reporting platform that delivers enterprise, web-enabled reporting functionality so you can create reports that draw content from a variety of data sources, publish reports in various formats, and centrally manage security and subscriptions.

Reporting Services includes the following core components:

▶ A complete set of tools you can use to create, manage, and view reports

▶ A report server component that hosts and processes reports in a variety of formats, including HTML, PDF, TIFF, Excel, CSV, and more

▶ An API that allows developers to integrate or extend data and report processing into custom applications or to create custom tools to build and manage reports

There are two design tools for building reports: BI Development Studio, a powerful development tool integrated with Visual Studio .NET 2005, and Report Builder, which is a simpler point-and-click tool that you use to design ad hoc reports. Both report design tools provide a WYSIWYG experience.

Reports are described by Report Definition Language (RDL). RDL contains the description of the report layout, formatting information, and instructions on how to fetch the data. It can optionally contain custom code written in VB .NET that is executed as part of the report.

After a report is defined, it can be deployed on the report server, where it can be managed, secured, and delivered to a variety of formats, including HTML, Excel, PDF, TIFF, and XML. Various delivery, caching, and execution options are also available, as are scheduling and historical archiving.

For more information on designing and deploying reports using Reporting Services, see Chapter 41, "SQL Server 2005 Reporting Services."

SQL Server Notification Services

SQL Server Notification Services is an environment for developing and deploying applications that generate and send notifications. You can use Notification Services to generate and send timely, personalized messages to thousands or millions of subscribers, and you can deliver the messages to a variety of devices, including mobile phones, personal digital assistants (PDAs), Microsoft Windows Messenger, or email accounts.

Notification Services consists of the following:

▶ A Notification Services programming framework that enables you to quickly create and deploy notification applications by using XML or Notification Services Management Objects (NMO)

▶ A reliable, high-performance, scalable Notification Services engine that runs notification applications

In order to receive notifications, subscribers create subscriptions to notification applications. A *subscription* is an expressed interest in a specific type of event, such as when a stock price reaches a specified price or a when a document has been updated. Notifications are generated and sent to the subscriber when a triggering event occurs or notifications can be generated and sent on a predetermined schedule specified by the subscriber.

For more information on building and deploying notification applications using Notification Services, see Chapter 47, "SQL Server Notification Services" (on the CD-ROM).

SQL Server Service Broker

SQL Server Service Broker is a new feature in SQL Server 2005. Service Broker provides a native SQL Server infrastructure that supports asynchronous, distributed messaging between database-driven services. Service Broker handles all the hard work of managing coordination among the constructs required for distributed messaging, including transactional delivery and storage, message typing and validation, multithreaded activation and control, event notification, routing, and security.

Service Broker is designed around the basic functions of sending and receiving messages. An application sends messages to a *service*, which is a name for a set of related tasks. An application receives messages from a *queue*, which is a view of an internal table. Service Broker guarantees that an application receives each message exactly once, in the order in which the messages were sent.

Service Broker can be useful for any application that needs to perform processing asynchronously or that needs to distribute processing across a number of computers. An example would be a bicycle manufacturer and seller who must provide new and updated parts data to a company that implements a catalog management system. The manufacturer must keep the catalog information up-to-date with its product model data, or it could lose market share or end up receiving orders from distributors based on out-of-date catalog information. When the parts data is updated in the manufacturer's database, a trigger could be invoked to send a message to Service Broker with information about the updated data. Service Broker would then asynchronously deliver the message to the catalog service. The catalog service program would then perform the work in a separate transaction. By performing this work in a separate transaction, the original transaction in the manufacturer's database can commit immediately. The application avoids system slowdowns that result from keeping the original transaction open while performing the update to the catalog database.

For more information on using Service Broker, see Chapter 48, "SQL Server Service Broker" (on the CD-ROM).

SQL Server 2005 Editions

You can choose from several editions of SQL Server 2005. The edition you choose depends on your database and data processing needs, as well as the Windows platform on which you want to install it.

For actual deployment of SQL Server in a production environment, you can choose from any edition of SQL Server 2005 except Developer Edition and Evaluation Edition. Which edition you choose to deploy depends on your system requirements and need for SQL Server components.

This chapter examines the different editions of SQL Server and discusses their features and capabilities. Using this information, you can better choose which edition provides the appropriate solution for you.

SQL Server 2005 Standard Edition

The Standard Edition of SQL Server 2005 is the version intended for the masses—those running small- to medium-sized systems who don't require the performance, scalability, and availability provided by Enterprise Edition. Standard Edition runs on any of the Windows 2000 or Windows 2003 Server platforms, and its scalability is limited to up to four processors. There is no built-in memory limitation in SQL Server 2005 Standard Edition as there was in SQL Server 2000; it can utilize as much memory as provided by the operating system.

SQL Server 2005 Standard Edition includes the following features:

- ▶ CLR procedures, functions, and data types
- ▶ SQL Server Analysis Services
- ▶ Service Broker
- ▶ Reporting Services
- ▶ Notification Services
- ▶ SQL Server Integration Services
- ▶ Full-Text Search
- ▶ Built-in XML support
- ▶ SQL Server Profiler and performance analysis tools
- ▶ SQL Server Management Studio

▶ Replication

▶ Two-node failover clustering

▶ Database mirroring (safety full mode only)

▶ Log shipping

The Standard Edition can be installed on any of the Windows 2000 and Windows 2003 Server platforms, as well as Windows XP.

The Standard Edition should meet the needs of most departmental and small- to midsized applications. However, if you need more scalability, availability, advanced performance features, or comprehensive analysis features, you should implement the Enterprise Edition of SQL Server 2005.

SQL Server 2005 Enterprise Edition

The Enterprise Edition of SQL Server 2005 is the most comprehensive and complete edition available. It provides the most scalability and availability of all editions and is intended for systems that require high performance and availability, such as large-volume websites, data warehouses, and high-throughput online transaction processing (OLTP) systems.

SQL Server 2005 Enterprise Edition supports as much memory and as many CPUs as supported by the operating system it is installed on. It can be installed on any of the Windows 2000 and Windows 2003 server platforms.

In addition, SQL Server 2005 Enterprise Edition provides performance enhancements, such as parallel queries, indexed views, and enhanced read-ahead scanning.

Which version is right for you? The next section explores the feature sets of Enterprise and Standard Editions so you can decide which one provides the features you need.

Differences Between the Enterprise and Standard Editions of SQL Server

For deploying SQL Server 2005 in a server environment, either the Standard Edition or the Enterprise Edition of SQL Server is a logical choice. To help decide between the two editions, Table 1.1 compares the major features that each edition supports.

TABLE 1.1   SQL Server 2005 Feature Comparison: Enterprise and Standard Editions

Feature	Enterprise Edition	Standard Edition
Max number of CPUs	Unlimited	4
64 bit support	Yes	Yes
CLR runtime integration	Yes	Yes
Full-Text Search	Yes	Yes
SQL Server Integration Services	Yes	Yes
Integration Services with Basic Transforms	Yes	Yes

TABLE 1.1   Continued

Feature	Enterprise Edition	Standard Edition
Integration Services with Advanced data mining and cleansing transforms	Yes	No
Service Broker	Yes	Yes
Notification Services	Yes	Yes
Reporting Services	Yes	Yes
Replication	Yes	Yes
Log shipping	Yes	Yes
Database Mirroring	Yes	Yes (Single REDO thread with Safety FULL only)
Database snapshot	Yes	No
Indexed views	Yes	Yes (Can be created but automatic matching by Query Optimizer not supported)
Updatable distributed partitioned views	Yes	No
Table and index partitioning	Yes	No
Online index operations	Yes	No
Parallel index operations	Yes	No
Parallel DBCC	Yes	No
Online page and file restoration	Yes	No
Fast Recovery	Yes	No
Failover clustering	Yes	Yes (2-node only)
Multiple-instance support	Yes (50 instances max.)	Yes (16 instances max.)

Other SQL Server 2005 Editions

The Standard and Enterprise Editions of SQL Server 2005 are intended for server-based deployment of applications. In addition, the following editions are available for other specialized uses:

- ▶ Workgroup Edition

- ▶ Developer Edition

- ▶ Express Edition

- ▶ Mobile Edition

Workgroup Edition

SQL Server 2005 Workgroup Edition is intended for small organizations that need a database with no limits on database size or number of users but may not need the full capabilities of the Standard Edition. SQL Server 2005 Workgroup Edition can be used as a front-end web server or for departmental or branch office applications.

Workgroup Edition includes most of the core database features and capabilities of the SQL Server Standard Edition except for the following:

▶ It is limited to two CPUs and a maximum of 3GB of memory.

▶ It does not support failover clustering or database mirroring.

▶ Does not include Analysis Services or Notification Services.

▶ It provides limited support for Reporting Services features.

Developer Edition

The Developer Edition of SQL Server 2005 is a full-featured version intended for development and end-user testing only. It includes all the features and functionality of Enterprise Edition, at a much lower cost, but the licensing agreement prohibits production deployment of databases using Developer Edition.

To provide greater flexibility during development, Developer Edition can be installed in any of the following environments:

▶ Windows 2000 Professional

▶ Any Windows 2000 Server editions

▶ Any Windows 2003 Server editions

▶ Windows XP

Express Edition

The Express Edition of SQL Server 2005 is intended for users who are running applications that require a locally installed database, often on mobile systems, and who spend at least some time disconnected from the network. It replaces the Desktop Edition that was available with SQL Server 2000. Express Edition is a free, lightweight, embeddable and redistributable version of SQL Server 2005. SQL Server Express Edition includes a stripped-down version of SQL Server Management Studio, called SQL Server Management Studio Express, for easily managing a SQL Server Express instance and its databases. Best of all, as your needs grow, your applications seamlessly work with the rest of the SQL Server product family.

The Express Edition can be installed in any of the following environments:

▶ Windows 2000 Professional

▶ Any Windows 2000 Server edition

▶ Any Windows 2003 Server edition

▶ Windows XP

Express Edition supports most of the same features as the Workgroup Edition, with the following exceptions:

- ▶ It is limited to using a maximum of one CPU and 1GB of memory.

- ▶ It limits the maximum database size to 4GB.

- ▶ It does not include Full-Text Search, Notification Services, Reporting Services, or Analysis Services.

- ▶ It does not include SQL Server Integration Services.

- ▶ It supports Service Broker as a client only.

- ▶ It does not include SSMS.

- ▶ It can participate in replication only as a subscriber.

If you need a bit more than the Express Edition offers, but not as much as the Workgroup Edition, Microsoft also provides the Express Edition with Advanced Services. The Express Edition with Advanced Services includes support for Full-Text Search and limited support of Reporting Services for web reporting.

Mobile Edition

The Mobile Edition of SQL Server 2005 is a compact version of SQL Server 2005 that provides T-SQL compatibility and a cost-based Query Optimizer that runs on Windows Mobile devices, including devices running Microsoft Windows CE 5.0, Microsoft Windows XP Tablet PC Edition, Windows Mobile 2003 Software for Pocket PC, and Windows Mobile 5.0. Developers who are familiar with SQL Server 2005 should feel comfortable developing for Mobile Edition.

SQL Server Mobile Edition has a small footprint, requiring only about 2MB. SQL Server Mobile Edition can connect directly with a SQL Server 2005 database through remote execution of T-SQL statements and also supports replication with SQL Server 2005 databases as a merge replication subscriber so that data can be accessed and manipulated offline and synchronized later with server-based version of SQL Server 2005.

SQL Server Licensing Models

In addition to feature sets, one of the determining factors in choosing a SQL Server edition is cost. With SQL Server 2005, Microsoft provides two types of licensing models: processor-based licensing and server-based licensing.

Processor-based licensing requires a single license for each physical CPU in the machine that is running a Microsoft Server product. This type of license includes unlimited client device access. Additional server licenses, seat licenses, and Internet connector licenses are not required. You must purchase a processor license for each installed processor on the server on which SQL Server 2005 will be installed, even if some processors will not be used for running SQL Server. The only exception is for systems with 16 or more processors that allow partitioning of the processors into groups so the SQL Server software can be delegated to a subset of the processors.

NOTE

For licensing purposes, Microsoft bases the number of CPUs in a machine on the number of CPU sockets on the motherboard, not the number of cores on the CPU chip itself. Thus, although a dual-core or quad-core processor chip may appear to the operating system as two or four CPUs, at the time of this writing, each these types of chips is still considered a single CPU for licensing purposes if it occupies only a single CPU socket on the motherboard.

For those who prefer the more familiar server/client access license (CAL), or for environments in which the number of client devices connecting to SQL Server is small and known, two server/CAL-based licensing models are also available:

▶ **Device CALs** —A device CAL is required in order for a device (for example, PC, workstation, terminal, PDA, mobile phone) to access or use the services or functionality of Microsoft SQL Server. The server plus device CAL model is likely to be the more cost-effective choice if there are multiple users per device (for example, in a call center).

▶ **User CALs**—A SQL server user CAL is required in order for a user (for example, an employee, a customer, a partner) to access or use the services or functionality of Microsoft SQL Server. The server plus user CAL model is likely to be more cost-effective if there are multiple devices per user (for example, a user who has a desktop PC, laptop, PDA, and so forth).

The server/CAL licensing model requires purchasing a license for the computer running SQL Server 2005 as well as a license for each client device or user that accesses any SQL Server 2005 installation. A fixed number of CALs are included with a server license and the server software. Additional CALs can be purchased as needed.

Server/per-seat CAL licensing is intended for environments in which the number of clients per server is relatively low, and access from outside the firewall is not required. Be aware that using a middle-tier or transaction server that pools or multiplexes database connections does not reduce the number of CALs required. A CAL is still required for each distinct client workstation that connects through the middle tier. (Processor licensing might be preferable in these environments due to its simplicity and affordability when the number of clients is unknown and potentially large.)

The pricing listed in Table 1.2 is provided for illustrative purposes only and is based on pricing available at the time of publication. These are estimated retail prices that are subject to change and might vary from reseller pricing.

TABLE 1.2   SQL Server 2005 Estimated Retail Pricing

Licensing Option	Enterprise Edition	Standard Edition	Workgroup Edition
Processor Licensing	$24,999 per processor	$5,999 per processor	$3,899 per processor
Server/per-seat CAL license with 5 workgroup CALs	N/A	N/A	$739
Server/per-seat CAL license with 5 CALs	N/A	$1,849	N/A
Server/per-seat CAL license with 25 CALs	$13,969	N/A	N/A

Developer Edition Licensing

The Developer Edition of SQL Server 2005 is available for a fixed price of $49.95. The Developer Edition is licensed per developer and must be used for designing, developing, and testing purposes only.

Express Edition Licensing

The Express Edition of SQL Server 2005 is available via free download from www.microsoft.com/sql. Developers can redistribute it with their applications at no cost by simply registering for redistribution rights with Microsoft. The Express Edition does not require a CAL when it is used on a standalone basis. If it connects to a SQL Server instance running Enterprise Edition, Standard Edition, or Workgroup Edition, a separate user or device CAL is required unless the SQL Server instance it connects to is licensed under the per-processor model.

Mobile Edition Licensing

SQL Server 2005 Mobile Edition is available as a downloadable development product for mobile applications. You can deploy SQL Server Mobile to an unlimited number of mobile devices if they operate in standalone mode (that is, the device does not connect to or use the resources of any SQL Server system not present on the device). If the device connects to a SQL Server instance that is not on the device, a separate user or device CAL is required unless the SQL Server instance is licensed under the per-processor model.

Choosing a Licensing Model

Which licensing model should you choose? Per-processor licensing is generally recommended for instances in which the server will be accessed from the outside. This includes servers used in Internet situations or servers that will be accessed from both inside and outside an organization's firewall. Per-processor licensing might also be appropriate and cost-effective for internal environments in which there are a very large number of users in relation to the number of SQL Server machines. An additional advantage to the per-processor model is that it eliminates the need to count the number of devices connecting to SQL Server, which can be difficult to manage on an ongoing basis for a large organization.

Using the server/per-seat CAL model is usually the most cost-effective choice in internal environments in which client-to-server ratios are low.

Mixing Licensing Models

You can mix both per-processor and server/CAL licensing models in your organization. If the Internet servers for your organization are segregated from the servers used to support internal applications, you can choose to use processor licensing for the Internet servers and server/CAL licensing for internal SQL Server instances and user devices.

Keep in mind that you do not need to purchase CALs to allow internal users to access a server already licensed via a processor license: The processor licenses allow access to that server for all users.

Passive Server/Failover Licensing

In SQL Server 2005, two or more servers can be configured in a failover mode, with one server running as a passive server so that the passive server picks up the processing of the active server only in the event of a server failure. SQL Server 2005 offers three types of failover support:

▶ Database mirroring

▶ Failover clustering

▶ Log shipping

If your environment uses an active/passive configuration in which at least one server in the failover configuration does not regularly process information but simply waits to pick up the workload when an active server fails, no additional licenses are required for the passive server. The exception is if the failover cluster is licensed using the per-processor licensing model and the number of processors on the passive server exceeds the number of processors on the active server. In this case, additional processor licenses must be acquired for the number of additional processors on the passive computer.

In an active/active failover configuration, all servers in the failover configuration regularly process information independently unless a server fails, at which point one server or more takes on the additional workload of the failed server. In this environment, all servers must be fully licensed using either per-processor licensing or server/CAL licensing. Keep in mind that in some log shipping and database mirroring configurations, the standby (passive) server can be used as a read-only reporting server installation. Under this usage, the standby server is no longer "passive" and must be licensed accordingly.

Virtual Server Licensing

Virtualization is defined broadly as the running of software on a "virtual environment." A virtual environment exists when an operating system is somehow emulated (that is, does not run directly on the physical hardware). When you're running virtualization software on a system, one or several applications and their associated operating systems can run on one physical server inside their respective virtual environments.

Running SQL Server 2005 inside a virtual operating environment requires at least one license per virtual operating environment. Within each virtual operating environment, the license allows you to run one or more instances of SQL Server 2005. The license for a virtual operating environment can be a server/CAL license or a processor-based license. If using a processor based license, you must purchase a processor license for each processor that the virtual machine accesses.

Summary

This chapter examines the various platforms that support SQL Server 2005 and reviews and compares the various editions of SQL Server 2005 that are available. Which platform and edition are appropriate to your needs depends on scalability, availability, performance, licensing costs, and limitations. The information provided in this chapter should help you make the appropriate choice.

Chapter 2, "What's New in SQL Server 2005," takes a closer look at the new features and capabilities provided with the various SQL Server 2005 editions.

What's New in SQL Server 2005

IN THIS CHAPTER

▶ New SQL Server 2005 Features

▶ SQL Server 2005 Enhancements

The upgrade from SQL Server 6.5 to 7.0 was pretty significant. In addition to many new features, the underlying SQL Server architecture changed considerably. In comparison, the upgrade from SQL Server 7.0 to 2000 was more of a series of enhancements, additions, and improvements.

Microsoft SQL Server 2005 further extends the performance, reliability, availability, programmability, and ease of use of SQL Server 2000. SQL Server 2005 includes several new features that make it an excellent database platform for large-scale online transaction processing (OLTP), data warehousing, and e-commerce applications.

This chapter explores the new features provided in SQL Server 2005 as well as many of the enhancements to previously available features.

New SQL Server 2005 Features

What does SQL Server 2005 have to offer over SQL Server 2000? The following is a list of the new features provided in SQL Server 2005:

▶ SQL Server Management Studio (SSMS)

▶ SQL Server Configuration Manager

▶ Common language runtime (CLR)/.NET Framework integration

▶ Dynamic management views (DMVs)

▶ System catalog views

▶ SQL Server Management Objects (SMO)

▶ Dedicated administrator connection (DAC)

▶ SQLCMD

▶ Database Mail

▶ Online index and restore operations

▶ Native encryption

▶ Database mirroring

▶ Database snapshots

▶ Service Broker

▶ SQL Server Integration Services (SSIS)

▶ Table and index partitioning

▶ Snapshot isolation

▶ Business Intelligence (BI) Development Studio

▶ Query Notification

▶ Multiple active result sets

▶ New SQL Server data types

The rest of this section takes a closer look at each of these new features and, where appropriate, provides references to subsequent chapters where you can find more information about the new features.

SQL Server Management Studio

One of the biggest changes in SQL Server 2005 that you will notice right away if you have experience with SQL Server 2000 is that SQL Enterprise Manager and Query Analyzer are no longer provided with SQL Server 2005. They have been replaced by a single integrated management console called SQL Server Management Studio (SSMS). SSMS is the tool to use to monitor and manage your SQL Server database engines and databases, as well as Integration Services, Analysis Services, Reporting Services, and Notification Services across your entire SQL Server enterprise. Improvements to the SSMS interface over SQL Enterprise Manager allows database administrators to perform several tasks at the same time, such as authoring and executing a query, viewing server objects, managing objects, monitoring system activity, and viewing online help.

SSMS also provides a Visual Studio–like development environment for authoring, editing, and managing scripts and stored procedures, using Transact-SQL (T-SQL), Multidimensional Expressions (MDX), XML for Analysis, and SQL Server Mobile Edition. SSMS can also integrate with source control software such as Visual SourceSafe to allow you to define and manage your scripts under projects.

SSMS also hosts tools for scheduling SQL Server Agent jobs and managing maintenance plans to automate daily maintenance and operation tasks. The integration of management and authoring in a single tool, coupled with the ability to manage all types of servers, provides enhanced productivity for database administrators.

For an introduction to the capabilities and how to make the most of SSMS, see Chapter 3, "SQL Server Management Studio." In addition, additional features of SSMS are shown in more detail throughout this entire book.

SQL Server Configuration Manager

SQL Server 2005 introduces SQL Server Configuration Manager, a management tool that allows administrators to manage SQL Server services and configure basic service and network protocol options. SQL Server Configuration Manager combines the functionality of the following SQL Server 2000 tools:

- ► Server Network Utility
- ► Client Network Utility
- ► Services Manager

SQL Server Configuration Manager also includes the ability to start and stop and set service properties for the following services:

- ► SQL Server
- ► SQL Server Agent
- ► SQL Server Analysis Services (SSAS)
- ► Report server
- ► Microsoft Distributed Transaction Coordinator (MS DTC)
- ► Full-Text Search

The use of SQL Server Configuration Manager is discussed in various chapters of this book where its use is appropriate.

CLR/.NET Framework Integration

In SQL Server 2005, database programmers can now take full advantage of the Microsoft .NET Framework class library and modern programming languages to implement within SQL Server itself stored procedures, triggers, and user-defined functions written in the .NET Framework language of their choice. Many tasks that were awkward or difficult to perform in T-SQL can be better accomplished by using managed code.

By using languages such as Visual Basic .NET and C#, you can capitalize on CLR integration to write code that has more complex logic and is more suited for computational tasks, such as string manipulation or complex mathematical calculation. Managed code is more efficient than T-SQL at processing numbers and managing complicated execution logic, and it provides extensive support for string handling, regular expressions, and so on.

In addition, two new types of database objects—aggregates and user-defined types—can be defined using the .NET Framework. With user-defined types, you can define your own type that can be used for column definitions (for example, custom date/time data types, currency data types), or you can define other complex types that may contain multiple elements and can have behaviors, differentiating them from the traditional SQL Server system data types.

In addition, you may at times need to perform aggregations over data, such as statistical calculations. If the desired aggregation function is not directly supported as a built-in aggregate function, you have the option to define a custom user-defined aggregate, using the .NET Framework to perform a custom aggregation in SQL Server 2005.

For more information on CLR/.NET Framework integration in SQL Server 2005, see Chapter 36, "SQL Server and the .NET Framework."

Dynamic Management Views

Dynamic Management Views (DMVs) are new to SQL Server 2005 and provide a lightweight means for accessing information about internal database performance and resource usage without the heavy burden associated with tools used in SQL Server 2000. DMVs provide information on internal database performance and resource usage, ranging from memory, locking, and scheduling to transactions and network and disk I/O. DMVs can be used to monitor the health of a server instance, diagnose problems, and tune performance.

An extensive number of DMVs are available in SQL Server 2005. Some DMVs are scoped at the server level, and others are scoped at the database level. They are all found in the sys schema and have names that start with dm_. See Chapter 6, "SQL Server System and Database Administration," for more information on the DMVs available in SQL Server 2005 and how to use them. In addition, other more detailed examples of using DMVs are provided in the chapters in the SQL Server Performance and Optimization section of this book.

System Catalog Views

In SQL Server 2005, the familiar system catalog tables have been replaced with system catalog views. Using catalog views is the preferred method for viewing information that is used by the Microsoft SQL Server database engine. There is a catalog view to return information about almost every aspect of SQL Server. Some of the catalog views return information that is new to SQL Server 2005 or information that was not provided in prior versions. Examples of these include the CLR assembly catalog views and the database mirroring catalog views. Other catalog views provide information that may have been available in prior versions via system tables, system procedures, and so on, but the new catalog views expand on the information that is returned and include elements that are new to SQL Server 2005.

SQL Server 2005 stores the system catalogs in a new hidden system database called the *resource database*. Microsoft chose to make the resource database inaccessible to ensure quick, clean upgrades and to allow rollbacks of intermediate updates or bug fix releases. By implementing the system catalog as a set of views rather than as a directly accessible base table gives Microsoft the flexibility to adjust the catalog schema in the future without affecting existing applications.

For more detailed information on the system catalog views available in SQL Server 2005, see Chapter 6.

SQL Server Management Objects

SQL Server 2005 provides a new programmatic access layer called SQL Server Management Objects (SMO), which is a new set of programming objects that exposes all the management functionality of the SQL Server database. SMO replaces Distributed Management Objects (DMO), which was included with earlier versions of SQL Server. SMO provides improved scalability and performance over DMO.

Dedicated Administrator Connection

In previous releases of SQL Server, under certain circumstances, the system could become inaccessible due to running out of available user connections or other resources that could prevent normal access of the server, even by a system administrator. To help solve this problem, SQL Server 2005 introduces the Dedicated Administrator Connection (DAC), which allows an administrator to access a running server even if the server is not responding or is otherwise unavailable. Through the DAC, the administrator can execute diagnostic functions or T-SQL statements to troubleshoot problems on a server.

SQL Server listens for the DAC on a dedicated TCP/IP port dynamically assigned upon database engine startup. The error log contains the port number the DAC is listening on. By default, the DAC listener accepts connection on only the local port via SSMS or the sqlcmd command-prompt tool. Only members of the SQL Server sysadmin role can connect using the DAC.

To connect to the DAC using the sqlcmd command-prompt utility, you specify the special administrator switch (-A). To connect to the DAC via SSMS, you prefix admin: to the instance name in the connection dialog.

SQLCMD

SQLCMD is the next evolution of the isql and osql command-line utilities that you may have used in prior versions of SQL Server. It provides the same type of functionality as isql or osql, including the ability to connect to SQL Server from the command prompt and execute T-SQL commands. It also offers a number of new script execution options that go beyond what was available before. You can run queries interactively in SQLCMD (as you can with `isql` and `osql`), but the real power of SQLCMD comes into play when you use it to automate T-SQL scripts that are invoked by batch files.

SQLCMD includes a number of new internal and external commands and scripting variables that enhance the execution of T-SQL. With scripting variables, you can store values in variables and have the values span batches.

For more information on using SQLCMD, see Chapter 4, "SQL Server Command-Line Utilities."

Database Mail

SQL Server 2005 introduces Database Mail as a replacement for SQLMail. Database Mail includes a number of new features and enhancements over SQLMail, including support for multiple email profiles and accounts, asynchronous (queued) message delivery via a dedicated process in conjunction with Service Broker, cluster-awareness, 64-bit compatibility, greater security options (such as controlling the size of mail attachments and prohibiting specified file extensions), and simpler mail auditing. Database Mail also utilizes industry-standard Simple Mail Transfer Protocol (SMTP), so you no longer have to have an Extended MAPI mail client installed on the SQL Server machine.

For more information on configuring and using Database Mail, see Chapter 12, "Database Mail."

Online Index and Restore Operations

A new feature of SQL Server 2005 Enterprise Edition is the ability to create, rebuild, or drop an index online. The online index option allows concurrent modifications (updates, deletes, and inserts) to the underlying table or clustered index data and any associated indexes while the index operations are ongoing. This feature allows you to add indexes without interfering with access to tables or other existing indexes.

SQL Server 2005 Enterprise Edition also introduces the ability to perform a restore operation while the database is online. During this operation, only the data that is being restored is unavailable. The rest of the database remains online and available. Earlier versions of SQL Server required that the entire database be offline during the restore process.

For more information on online index operations, see Chapter 20, "Creating and Managing Indexes." For information on online restore, see Chapter 11, "Database Backup and Restore."

Native Encryption

While some encryption functionality existed in previous versions of SQL Server (for example, involving column encryption APIs within user-defined functions or the `PWDENCRYPT` password one-way hash function), it was relatively limited and rarely used. SQL Server 2005 provides significant improvements in this area. SQL Server 2005 introduces built-in native encryption capabilities, which includes added encryption tools, certificate creation, and key management functionality that can be invoked within T-SQL.

T-SQL now includes support for symmetric encryption and asymmetric encryption using keys, certificates, and passwords. SQL Server 2005 includes several new functions to securely create, manage, and use encryption keys and certificates to secure sensitive data. Taking advantage of this new functionality can greatly enhance your database and application security.

Database Mirroring

In SQL Server 2000, there were only two viable methods for maintaining a warm-standby copy of a database: replication and log shipping. SQL Server 2005 introduces another method of maintaining a hot- or warm-standby database: database mirroring. Database mirroring provides the continuous streaming of the transaction log from a source server to a single destination server. In the event of a failure of the primary system, applications can immediately reconnect to the database on the secondary server. The secondary instance detects failure of the primary server within seconds and accepts database connections immediately. Database mirroring works on standard server hardware and requires no special storage devices or controllers.

For more information on configuring and using database mirroring, see Chapter 16, "Database Mirroring."

> **NOTE**
>
> Database mirroring was not available in the GA release of SQL Server 2005 but is included with Service Pack 1.

Database Snapshots

SQL Server 2005 enables database administrators to create database snapshots, which are instant, read-only views of a database that capture the state of the database at a specific point in time. A database snapshot can be used to provide a stable view of data without incurring the time or storage overhead of creating a complete copy of the database. As data in the primary database is modified after the snapshot has been taken, the snapshot facility makes a copy of the data page(s) being modified so it has a pre-modified copy of the page(s), which provide a point-in-time view of the data. In addition to providing a point-in-time snapshot of a database for reporting purposes (for example, an end-of-month snapshot of a database), a snapshot can also be used to quickly recover from an accidental change to a database. The original pages from the snapshot can be quickly copied back to the primary database.

For more information on creating and using database snapshots, see Chapter 27, "Database Snapshots."

Service Broker

The Service Broker feature of SQL Server 2005 provides a scalable architecture for building asynchronous message routing. The Service Broker technology allows internal or external processes to send and receive streams of reliable, asynchronous messages by using extensions to normal T-SQL. Messages can be sent to a queue in the same database as the sender, to another database in the same instance of SQL Server, or to another instance of SQL Server, either on the same server or on a remote server. Service Broker handles all the hard work of managing coordination among the constructs required for distributed messaging, including transactional delivery and storage, message typing and validation, multithreaded activation and control, event notification, routing, and security.

With Service Broker, SQL Server 2005 provides the ability to build loosely coupled, asynchronous database applications. For example, in an order entry system, the system needs to process some parts of an order, such as product availability and pricing, before the order is considered complete. However, other parts of the order, such as billing and shipping, don't have to happen before the system commits the order. If a system can process the parts of the order that can be delayed in a guaranteed but asynchronous manner, an organization can process the core part of the order faster. Service Broker provides this capability.

For more information on Service Broker, see Chapter 48, "SQL Server Service Broker" (on the CD-ROM).

SQL Server Integration Services

SQL Server 2005 replaces Data Transformation Services (DTS) with a completely redesigned enterprise data extraction, transformation, and loading (ETL) platform called SQL Server Integration Services (SSIS). SSIS provides a number of enhancements over what was available in DTS, including the following:

- ▶ A revamped GUI interface hosted in a Visual Studio shell for building, debugging, and deploying SSIS packages

- ▶ SSIS application programming interfaces (APIs) for developing custom SSIS components

- ▶ New control flow components, such as `ForEach Loop`, `For Loop`, and `Sequence`

- ▶ A service-based implementation (the Integration Services service)

For more information on designing and using SSIS, see Chapter 40, "SQL Server Integration Services."

Table and Index Partitioning

In SQL Server 2005 tables and indexes are stored in one or more partitions. Partitions are organizational units that allow you to divide your data into logical groups. Table and index partitioning eases the management of large databases by facilitating the management of a database in smaller, more manageable chunks. For example, a date/time column can be used to divide each month's data into a separate partition. You can assign partitions to different filegroups for added flexibility and ease of maintenance.

Tables with multiple partitions (that is, partitioned tables) are accessed the same way as single-partition tables. DML operations such as INSERT and SELECT statements reference the table the same way, regardless of partitioning.

Generally, partitioning is most useful for large tables. *Large* is a relative term, but these tables typically contain millions of rows and take up gigabytes of space. Oftentimes, the tables that are targeted for partitioning are large tables that are experiencing performance problems because of their size.

Partitioning provides advantages for many different scenarios, including the following:

▶ **Archival and purging**—Table partitions can be quickly switched from a production table to another archive table with the same structure, allowing you to keep a limited amount of recent data in the production table while keeping the bulk of the older data in the archive table. Alternatively, the data in a partition can be switched out to a staging table that can then either be archived or truncated to purge the data.

▶ **Maintenance**—Table partitions that have been assigned to different filegroups can be backed up and maintained independently of each other.

▶ **Query performance**—Partitioned tables that are joined on partitioned columns can experience improved performance because the Query Optimizer can join to the tables based on the partitioned column. Queries can also be parallelized along the partitions.

For more information on table partitioning, see Chapter 19, "Creating and Managing Tables."

Snapshot Isolation

One of the key new features of SQL Server 2005 related to locking and performance is snapshot isolation. Snapshot isolation provides the benefit of repeatable reads without the need to acquire and hold shared locks on the data that is read. The snapshot isolation level allows users to access the last row that was committed by using a transactionally consistent view of the data.

This new isolation level provides the following benefits:

▶ Increased data availability for read-only applications

▶ Minimized locking and blocking problems between read operations and update operations in an OLTP environment

▶ Automatic mandatory conflict detection for write transactions

For more information on snapshot isolation, see Chapter 32, "Locking and Performance."

Business Intelligence Development Studio

SQL Server 2005 introduces the Business Intelligence Development Studio, which is a Visual Studio–based development environment for building business intelligence (BI) solutions that includes templates and project types that are specific to SQL Server 2005 business intelligence. It provides a solutions-based approach for developing BI solutions that includes Analysis Services, Integration Services, and Reporting Services projects.

For more information and a tutorial on designing Analysis Services solutions using Business Intelligence Development Studio, see Chapter 39, "SQL Server 2005 Analysis Services."

Query Notification

With the availability of the Service Broker, SQL Server 2005 also introduces notification support for SQL Server queries. Query Notification is useful for applications that cache database query results in their own private cache area, such as database-driven websites. Rather than having the application repeatedly poll the database to determine whether the data has changed and the cache needs to be refreshed, commands that are sent to the server through any of the client APIs, such as ADO.NET, OLE DB, open database connectivity (ODBC), Microsoft ActiveX Data Objects (ADO), or Simple Object Access Protocol (SOAP), may include a tag that requires a notification. For each query included in the request, SQL Server creates a notification subscription. When the data changes, a notification is delivered through a SQL Service Broker queue to notify the application that data has changed, at which point the application can refresh its data cache.

For more information on using Query Notification, see Chapter 36.

Multiple Active Result Sets

In previous versions of SQL Server, a user connection could have only one pending request per user connection. When using SQL Server default result sets, the application had to process or cancel all result sets from one batch before it could execute any other batch on that connection. SQL Server 2005 provides multiple active result sets (MARS), which allows you to have more than one default result set open per connection simultaneously. In other words, applications can have multiple default result sets open and can interleave reading from them or applications can execute other statements (for example, INSERT, UPDATE, DELETE, and stored procedure calls) while default result sets are open. The existing result set does not need to be cancelled or fully processed first.

For more information on using MARS and configuring client connections to enable MARS, see Chapter 36 and Chapter 9, "Client Installation and Configuration."

New SQL Server Data Types

SQL Server 2005 introduces a brand-new data type, xml, and a new size specification, max, for varchar and varbinary data types.

The xml Data Type

One of the biggest limitations of XML in SQL Server 2000 was the inability to save the results of a FOR XML query to a variable or store it in a column directly without using some middleware code to first save the XML as a string and then insert it into an ntext or nvarchar column and then select it out again. SQL Server 2005 now natively supports column storage of XML, using the new xml data type.

The new xml data type allows relational columns and XML data to be stored side-by-side in the same table. Some of the benefits of storing XML in the database include the traditional DBMS benefits of backup and restore, replication and failover, query optimization, granular locking, indexing, and content validation. In SQL Server 2005, an XML index can be created on both untyped and typed XML columns, and it indexes all paths and values within the entire XML column for faster searching and retrieval of XML data.

The xml data type can also be used with local variable declarations, as the output of user-defined functions, as an input parameter to stored procedures and functions, and much more. XML columns can also be used to store code files, such as XSLT, XSD, XHTML, and any other well-formed content. These files can then be retrieved by user-defined functions written in managed code hosted by SQL Server.

For more information on using the xml data type in SQL Server 2005, see Chapter 37, "Using XML in SQL Server 2005."

varchar(max) and varbinary(max)

In SQL Server 2000, the largest value that could be stored in a varchar or varbinary column was 8000 bytes. If you needed to store a larger value in a single column, you had to use the text or image data type. The main disadvantage of using the text and image data types was that they could not be used in many places where varchar or varbinary data types could be used (for example, as arguments to SQL Server's string manipulation functions, such as SUBSTRING, CHARINDEX, and REPLACE).

SQL Server 2005 introduces the new max specifier for varchar and varbinary data types. This specifier expands the storage capabilities of the varchar and varbinary data types to store up to $2^{31}-1$ bytes of data, the same maximum size as text and image data types. The main difference is that the new max data types can be used just like regular varchar and varbinary data types in functions, for comparisons, as T-SQL variables, and for concatenation. They can also be used in the DISTINCT, ORDER BY, and GROUP BY clauses of a SELECT statement, as well as in aggregates, joins, and subqueries.

For more information on using the max data types, see Chapter 35, "What's New for Transact-SQL in SQL Server 2005."

SQL Server 2005 Enhancements

In addition to the new features in SQL Server 2005, there are a number of enhancements to existing features. This section provides an overview of the major enhancements provided in SQL Server 2005.

Database Engine Enhancements

Several new database-specific enhancements have been added to SQL Server 2005. These changes are focused primarily on the database storage engine. The following are some of the most important enhancements:

- ▶ **Instant file initialization**—New or expanded database files are made available much faster now because the initialization of the file with binary zeros is deferred until data is written to the files.

- ▶ **Partial availability**—In the event of database file corruption, the database can still be brought online if the primary filegroup is available.

- ▶ **Database file movement**—You can now use the ALTER DATABASE command to move a database file. The physical file must be moved manually. This feature was available in SQL Server 2000, but it only worked on tempdb.

In addition, many new table-oriented enhancements are available with SQL Server 2005. This includes features that define how the data in the tables will be stored in the database. The following are two of the key enhancements:

- ▶ **Large rows**—SQL Server 2005 now allows for the storage of rows that are greater than 8060 bytes. The 8060-byte limitation that existed with SQL Server 2000 has been relaxed by allowing the storage of certain data types (such as varchar and nvarchar) on a row overflow data page.

- ▶ **Stored computed columns**—Computed columns that were calculated on-the-fly in prior versions can now be stored in the table structure. You accomplish this by specifying the PERSISTED keyword as part of the computed column definition.

Index Enhancements

The following are some of the most important enhancements available for indexes with SQL Server 2005:

- ▶ **Included columns**—Non-key columns can now be added to an index for improved performance. The performance gains are achieved with covering indexes that allow the Query Optimizer to locate all the column values referenced in the query.

- ▶ **ALTER INDEX**—As with other database objects, such as tables and databases, you can now modify indexes by using the ALTER statement. Index operations that were previously performed with DBCC commands or system stored procedures can now be accomplished with the ALTER INDEX command.

- ▶ **Parallel index operations**—Scan and sort activities associated with index operations can now be done in parallel.

For more information on making use of the enhanced index features, see Chapter 20 and Chapter 29, "Indexes and Performance."

T-SQL Enhancements

SQL Server 2005 provides many enhancements to the T-SQL language that allow you to improve the performance of your code and extend your error-management capabilities. These enhancements include improved error handling, new recursive query capabilities, and support for new SQL Server database engine capabilities. Some of the T-SQL enhancements are as follows:

▶ **Ranking functions**—SQL Server 2005 introduces four new ranking functions: ROW_NUMBER, RANK, DENSE_RANK, and NTILE. These new functions allow you to efficiently analyze data and provide ranking values to result rows of a query.

▶ **Common table expressions**—A common table expression (CTE) is a temporary named result set that can be referred to within a query, similarly to a temporary table. CTEs can be thought of as an improved version of derived tables that more closely resemble a non-persistent type of view. You can also use CTEs to develop recursive queries that you can use to expand a hierarchy.

▶ **PIVOT/UNPIVOT operator**—The PIVOT operator allows you to generate crosstab reports for open-schema and other scenarios in which you rotate rows into columns, possibly calculating aggregations along the way and presenting the data in a useful form. The UNPIVOT operator allows you to normalize pre-pivoted data.

▶ **APPLY**—The APPLY relational operator allows you to invoke a specified table-valued function once per each row of an outer table expression.

▶ **TOP enhancements**—In SQL Server 2005, the TOP operator has been enhanced, and it now allows you to specify a numeric expression to return the number or percentage of rows to be affected by your query; you can optionally use variables and subqueries. You can also now use the TOP option in DELETE, UPDATE, and INSERT queries.

▶ **DML with results**—SQL Server 2005 introduces a new OUTPUT clause that allows you to return data from a modification statement (INSERT, UPDATE, or DELETE) to the processing application or into a table or table variable.

▶ **Exception handling for transactions**—Earlier versions of SQL Server required you to include error-handling code after every statement that you suspected could potentially generate an error. SQL Server 2005 addresses this by introducing a simple but powerful exception-handling mechanism in the form of a TRY...CATCH T-SQL construct.

For more information on the new and enhanced features of T-SQL, see Chapter 35.

Security Enhancements

SQL Server 2005 includes significant enhancements to the security model of the database platform, with the intention of providing more precise and flexible control to enable tighter security of data. Some of the new features and enhancements to improve the level of security for your enterprise data include the following:

- **SQL login password policies**—SQL Server logins can now be governed by a more rigid password policy. This is implemented with new CHECK_POLICY and CHECK_EXPIRATION options that can be selected for a SQL Server login. These options facilitate stronger passwords and cause passwords to expire. The password policy is enforced only on Windows 2003 Server and above.

- **User/schema separation**—In prior versions of SQL Server, the fully qualified name for every object was directly tied to the object owner. With SQL Server 2005, schema names are used in the object namespace instead. This user/schema separation provides more flexibility in the object model and allows for object owners to be changed without affecting the code that references the objects.

- **Module execution context**—The EXECUTE AS option can be used to set the execution context for SQL statements. This allows a user to impersonate another user and is particularly useful for testing permissions.

- **Permission granularity**—The security model in SQL Server 2005 provides a much more granular level of control than earlier versions of SQL Server. This granular control provides some new types of security and allows you to apply security to a new set of database objects.

- **Data Definition Language (DDL) triggers**—Database administrators can now write server- or database-level triggers that fire on events such as creating or dropping a table, adding a server login, or altering a database. These triggers provide an invaluable auditing mechanism to automatically capture these events as they occur.

For more information on the security features in SQL Server 2005, see Chapter 10, "Security and User Administration." For more information on DDL triggers, see Chapter 25, "Creating and Managing Triggers."

Backup and Restore Enhancements

SQL Server builds on the basic set of backup and restore features that exist in SQL Server 2000 with enhancements such as the following:

- **Copy-only backups**—These backups can be made without disrupting the sequencing of other backups (for example, differential or log backups). Because copy-only backups do not affect the restoration chain, they are useful in situations such as when you simply want to get a copy of the database for testing purposes.

- **Mirrored backups**—SQL Server 2005 adds the capability to create additional copies of database backups via mirrored backups. Mirrored backups provide redundancy so that you can overcome the failure of a single backup device or medium by utilizing the mirrored copy of the backup.

▶ **Partial backups**—A partial backup contains all the data in the primary filegroup, any filegroup that is not read-only, and any filegroup that has been explicitly identified for backup. The elimination of read-only filegroups from partial backups saves space, saves time, and reduces the server overhead that is required while performing the backup.

▶ **Online restore**—Online restore allows a filegroup, file, or a specific page within a file to be restored while the rest of the database remains online and available.

See Chapter 11 for more information on the backup and restore capabilities of SQL Server 2005.

SQL Server Agent Enhancements

Microsoft has continued to improve the capabilities of the SQL Server Agent. It has maintained a consistent basis for automation while enriching the feature set. The following are some of the key new features:

▶ **Job Activity Monitor**—A new auto-refreshing tool named Job Activity Monitor has been added to help monitor the execution of scheduled jobs. You can adjust the refresh rate of the screen and specify filtering criteria in order to isolate a job or set of jobs.

▶ **Shared job schedules**—A job schedule can now be shared among jobs that have the same job owner.

▶ **Enhanced SQL Agent security**—Several new roles have been added that provide enhanced security management for the SQL Server Agent. In addition, a separate proxy account can now be defined for each type of subsystem that the SQL Server Agent can interact with.

▶ **Performance improvements**—New thread pooling and reduced job execution delays have improved the performance of SQL Server Agent.

See Chapter 13, "SQL Server Scheduling and Notification," for additional information on SQL Server Agent.

Recovery Enhancements

SQL Server 2005 reduces the amount of time it takes for a database to become available with a new and faster recovery option. In SQL Server 2005, users can access a recovering database after the transaction log has been rolled forward. Earlier versions of SQL Server required users to wait until incomplete transactions had rolled back, even if the users did not need to access the affected parts of the database.

Replication Enhancements

SQL Server 2005 offers a significant number of new features and improvements to replication. Much of what's new for SQL Server data replication revolves around simplifying setup, administration, and monitoring of a data replication topology, including the addition of a new Replication Monitor for ease of use in managing complex data replication operations. Replication Monitor has an intuitive user interface and a wealth of data metrics.

The following are some of the key replication enhancements:

▶ **Replication security enhancements**—The replication security model has changed, allowing more control over the accounts under which replication agents run.

▶ **Simplification of the user interface**—Replication wizards and dialog boxes have been redesigned for SQL Server 2005 to simplify the setup of a replication topology. There are 40% fewer wizard dialogs, and scripting is now integrated into the wizards, providing improved capabilities to script replication setup during or after wizard execution.

▶ **Replication of schema changes**—A much broader range of schema changes can be replicated without the use of special stored procedures. DDL statements are issued at the publisher and are automatically propagated to all subscribers.

▶ **Peer-to-peer transactional replication**—The new peer-to-peer model allows replication between identical participants in the topology (a master/master or symmetric publisher concept).

▶ **Initialization of a transactional subscription from a backup**—Setting up replication between databases that initially contain large volumes of data can be time-consuming and require large amounts of storage. SQL Server 2005 provides a new publication option that allows any backup taken after the creation of a transactional publication to be restored at the subscriber, rather than using a snapshot to initialize the subscription.

▶ **Heterogeneous replication**—Enhancements have been made for publishing data from an Oracle database with transactional and snapshot replication. In addition, there is improved support for many non-SQL Server subscribers.

▶ **Replication mobility**—Merge replication provides the ability to replicate data over HTTPS, with the web synchronization option, which is useful for synchronizing data from mobile users over the Internet or synchronizing data between Microsoft SQL Server databases across a corporate firewall.

▶ **Replication scalability and performance enhancements**—Scalability and performance enhancements include significant improvements to the performance of filtered merge publications and the ability of the Distribution Agent in transaction replication to apply batches of changes, in parallel, to a subscriber.

For more information on using and managing replication with SQL Server 2005, see Chapter 15, "Replication."

Failover Clustering Enhancements

In SQL Server 2005, support for failover clustering has been extended to SQL Server Analysis Services, Notification Services, and SQL Server replication. In addition, the maximum number of cluster nodes has been increased to eight. Other key enhancements to clustering include the following:

▶ **Simpler Microsoft Cluster Service (MSCS) setup**—Installing MSCS has become very easy (with Windows 2003 and above). MSCS is a prerequisite for SQL Server Clustering.

▶ **Cleaner SQL Server Clustering installation wizard**—The much-improved wizard detects and handles most prerequisites and provides for a single point of installation for multiple SQL Server node configurations.

▶ **Increased instances per cluster**—Up to 50 SQL Server instances per cluster are now supported with SQL Server 2005 Enterprise Edition and up to 16 SQL Server instances per cluster for SQL Server Standard Edition.

▶ **Number of nodes in a cluster**—With Windows 2003 Enterprise Edition, you can now create up to eight nodes in a single cluster.

SQL Server 2005 also provides the ability to set up a two-node failover cluster, using SQL Server 2005 Standard Edition. In previous releases, clustering was available only for the Enterprise Edition.

For more information on clustering, see Chapter 17, "SQL Server Clustering."

Notification Services Enhancements

Notification Services was provided as a feature for SQL Server 2000 before SQL Server 2005 was released. SQL Server 2005 provides a number of enhancements to Notification Services, including the following:

▶ **Integration into SSMS**—Notification Services is now integrated into SSMS Object Explorer. Using Object Explorer, you can perform most `nscontrol` command prompt utility tasks, and you can start and stop instances of Notification Services.

▶ **Support for subscriber-defined conditions**—In SQL Server 2005, Notification Services supports a new type of actions, called condition actions, which allow subscribers to define their own query clauses over a predefined data set. Using condition actions allows subscribers to fully define their own subscriptions over the data set.

▶ **Database independence**—SQL Server Notification Services supports using existing databases for instance and application data.

▶ **New management API**—SQL Server Notification Services has a new management API, `Microsoft.SqlServer.Management.Nmo`, that can be used to develop Notification Services instances and applications and to manage those instances and applications.

For more information on the Notification Server architecture and configuring and using SQL Server 2005 Notification Services, see Chapter 47, "SQL Server Notification Services" (on the CD-ROM).

Full-Text Search Enhancements

SQL Server 2005 provides a number of enhancements to the Full-Text Search service to improve the manageability and performance of Full-Text Search. The following are some of the major enhancements:

▶ **Integrated backup and restoration for full-text catalogs**—In SQL Server 2005, full-text catalogs can be backed up and restored along with, or separate from, database data.

▶ **Full-text catalogs included in database attach and detach operations**—SQL Server 2005 preserves full-text catalogs when administrators perform database detach and attach operations.

▶ **Full-text indexing performance improvements**—SQL Server 2005 Full-Text Search includes a major upgrade of the Microsoft Search service to version 3.0, which provides massively improved full-text index population performance and provides one instance of the Microsoft Search service per instance of SQL Server.

For more information on using Full-Text Search for SQL Server 2005, see Chapter 49, "SQL Server Full-Text Search" (on the CD-ROM).

Web Services Enhancements

The main enhancement to Web services in SQL Server 2005 is that you can use HTTP to access SQL Server directly, without using a middle-tier listener such as Microsoft Internet Information Services (IIS). SQL Server 2005 exposes a Web service interface to allow the execution of SQL statements and invocation of functions and procedures directly. Query results are returned in XML format and can take advantage of the Visual Studio Web services infrastructure.

For more information on using SQL Server Web Services in SQL Server 2005, see Chapter 38, "SQL Server Web Services."

Analysis Services Enhancements

SQL Server Analysis Services introduces a number of enhancements, including new management tools, an integrated development environment, and integration with the

.NET Framework. So many things have been changed that it's difficult to list them all. Here are some of the highlights of what has changed for Analysis Services:

▶ Analysis Services is now fully integrated with the SSMS. Many of the same wizards and management aspects of Business Intelligence Development Studio are also available in SSMS.

▶ SQL Server 2005 allows up to 50 separate instances of Analysis Services on one machine with Enterprise Edition and up to 16 separate instances with the Developer and Standard Editions.

▶ Analysis Services is now a cluster-aware application, and failover clustering is completely supported.

▶ SQL Server 2005 supports the XML for Analysis Services 1.1 specification and Analysis Services Scripting Language (ASSL) for XML-based administration.

▶ Proactive caching has been enabled at the partition level, to push data that has changed into cache for immediate access in Analysis Services. This is a big architectural change that directly addresses high-performance query execution of data within online analytical processing (OLAP) cubes that change frequently.

▶ The Unified Dimensional Model (UDM) paradigm provides a powerful metadata abstraction layer to use for all Analysis Services reference needs. It leverages concepts such as dimensions, measures, hierarchies, and so on and provides these simplified reference points to all interfaces and environments.

▶ Perspectives are now available to simplify and control the end user's view into complex cubes.

▶ Several new data mining algorithms have appeared, such as Naïve Bayes, Association, Sequence Clustering, Time Series/Linear Regression, and Neural Network algorithms.

▶ Analysis Services includes more robust usage and integration with SSIS for complex data transformations and filtering of data mining.

For more information on the new features and capabilities of SQL Server Analysis Services (SSAS), see Chapter 39.

Reporting Services Enhancements

The first version of SQL Server Reporting Services shipped in January 2004 for use with SQL Server 2000. However, Reporting Services is now an integrated component of SQL Server 2005, and the new version included in SQL Server 2005 contains a great deal of new features geared toward ease of use, performance, and the improvement of a rich development platform.

Reporting Services is a SQL Server service, similar to the relational database engine or Analysis Services. It allows you to design reports, deploy them on a server, and make them available to users in a secured environment in a variety of online and offline formats.

For more information on the capabilities of Reporting Services and how to use it, see Chapter 41, "SQL Server 2005 Reporting Services."

Summary

SQL Server 2005 provides a number of new and long-awaited features and enhancements. This chapter provides an overview of the new features and enhancements that ship with SQL Server 2005 and Service Pack 1 and Service Pack 2. To learn more, please refer to the other chapters referenced here.

PART II

SQL Server Tools and Utilities

IN THIS PART

CHAPTER 3   SQL Server Management Studio   57

CHAPTER 4   SQL Server Command-Line Utilities   89

CHAPTER 5   SQL Server Profiler   111

SQL Server Management Studio

IN THIS CHAPTER

▶ What's New in SSMS
▶ The Integrated Environment
▶ Administration Tools
▶ Development Tools

SQL Server Management Studio (SSMS) is a new integrated application that provides access to most of the graphical tools you can use to perform administrative and development tasks on SQL Server 2005. SSMS is a replacement for the Enterprise Manager, Query Analyzer, and Analysis Manager that were available in SQL Server 2000. Microsoft has consolidated all those tools into one, with a focus on providing a tool that suits the needs of both developers and database administrators (DBAs).

SSMS is a complicated tool that provides an entry point to almost all of SQL Server's functionality. The functionality that is accessible from SSMS is entirely too much to cover in one chapter. The aim of this chapter is to give a basic overview of SSMS, with a concentration on features that are new to SQL Server 2005. Others chapters in this book focus on the components of SSMS and provide more detailed coverage.

What's New in SSMS

SSMS is an entirely new environment for SQL Server 2005. It encapsulates many of the features previously available in other tools and also offers many new features. The bulk of these new features can be grouped into four major categories: environmental changes, integrated management, enhanced query authoring, and enhanced project management.

The environmental changes are changes that have occurred to the graphical application. SSMS has a new look and feel, and it offers some significant change to the way that windows are managed within the application. The application was rewritten in .NET and has features that are more like the development environment found in Visual Studio. Many windows in SSMS are dockable, can be pinned, and can be set to Auto Hide. In addition, many of the management dialog boxes are now modal, which means they can stay open while you open other windows within the application.

The new integrated management features stem from a consolidation of management tools. SSMS now contains management functionality that was contained in SQL Server 2000's Enterprise Manager, Analysis Manager, SQL Server Service Manager, Query Analyzer, and other tools. The functionality from these tools has been integrated into one environment that shares common Help, a summary window that displays useful information, an Object Explorer tree for easy navigation, and a myriad of other tools that can be accessed from one central location.

The changes related to query authoring are also based on a consolidation of functionality that was contained in several different tools in previous versions of SQL Server. Scripts that were previously created with Query Analyzer or Analysis Services can now be authored in SSMS. A new SSMS window named the Query Editor is an editing tool for the creation of SQL Server scripts. It brings with it many of the great features from the prior tools, such as color coding, syntax checks, and performance analysis, along with some new features, such as Dynamic Help, an XML editor, enhanced templates, and the ability to write scripts without being connected to the database.

The last category of changes in SSMS relates to managing the files or scripts you create when working with SQL Server 2005. SSMS provides a tool to organize scripts, connections, and other, related files into projects. These projects can also be grouped to form a solution. Once again, this functionality is based on the Visual Studio application development environment and the way it organizes development files into projects and solutions. As with Visual Studio, these files can also be managed with source control in SSMS. SSMS provides links to Visual SourceSafe, which allows you to secure the files and manage version control.

This chapter further explores the new features in SSMS. It first examines the features at the environmental level, focusing on how SSMS behaves and how to best utilize the environment. Next, it looks at the administrative tools and what changes have been made to help you better manage your SQL Server environment. Finally, this chapter looks at the development tools that are available with SSMS and the changes that have been made to improve your SQL Server development experience.

The Integrated Environment

Those who have been working with SQL Server for a long time may remember the SQL Enterprise Manager that came with SQL Server 6.5. In some respects, with SSMS, Microsoft has moved back to the paradigm that existed then. Like the SQL Server 6.5 Enterprise Manager, SSMS provides an integrated environment where developers and DBAs alike can perform the database tasks they need. Say goodbye to Query Analyzer, Analysis Manager, and a number of other desperate tools and say hello to SSMS, which provides "one-stop shopping" for most of your database needs.

Window Management

Figure 3.1 shows a sample configuration for the SSMS main display. The environment and the windows that are displayed are completely customizable, with the exception of the document window area. Figure 3.1 shows the document window area displaying the Summary page. The Summary page is the default, but other pages, such as a Query Editor window, can take the focus in this tab-oriented section of the SSMS display.

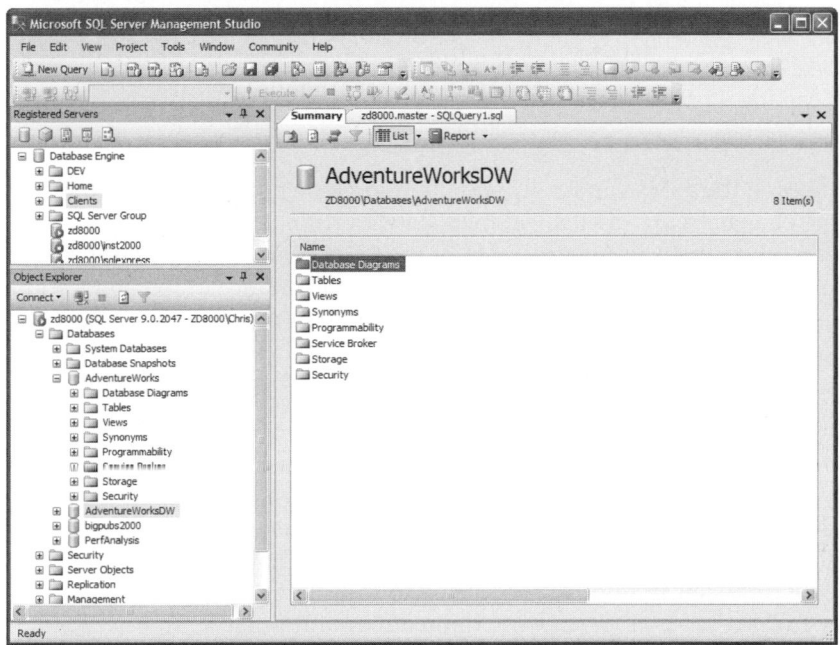

FIGURE 3.1   The SSMS main display.

The dialogs that form the rest of the SSMS display are referred to as *components* and include the Registered Servers and Object Explorer windows that are shown in Figure 3.1, as well as a number of other components that can be displayed via the View menu found at the top of the SSMS display. You can configure each of the component windows in a number of ways; for example, you can have them float, or you can hide, dock, Auto Hide, or display them as tabbed documents in the document window area.

The configuration that you choose for your SSMS display depends on the type of work you do with SQL Server as well as the type of person you are. The Auto Hide feature causes the component window to shrink to a tab along the left or right side of the display. When you mouse over the tab, the window automatically expands and stays expanded as long as the mouse cursor remains in the component window area. Auto Hide helps maximize the working real estate that is available in the document window for query development and the like. Docking many windows can clutter the screen, but it allows you to view many different types of information all at once. This is a matter of personal preference, and SSMS has made it very easy to change.

> **TIP**
>
> You can reposition the component windows by dragging and dropping them to the desired locations. When you are in the middle of a drag and drop, rectangular icons with arrows are displayed at different locations on the SSMS window surface. If you mouse over one of these arrowed icons to select the window location, you see the window destination highlighted. If you release your mouse button while the destination is highlighted, the window docks in that position.
>
> Some users at first ignore the arrow icons and keep hovering the window over the location where you want the window to go. Hovering the window over the desired location does not allow you to effectively dock it. You should save yourself some time and aggravation and use the arrow icons for drag-and-drop positioning.

The other big changes to the SSMS window environment include non-modal windows that are sizable. The change to non-modal windows allows you to perform multiple tasks at once without needing to open another instance of the SSMS application. Enterprise Manager users of SQL Server 2000 were forced to open another instance of the application during many administrative tasks in order to continue with other work. With SSMS, you can launch a backup with the Back Up Database dialog box and then continue working with the Object Explorer or other components in SSMS while the backup is running. This is a great timesaver and helps improve overall productivity.

The ability to size the dialog boxes is another user-friendly change that may seem minor but is quite handy on certain windows. For example, the SQL Server 2000 Enterprise Manager Restore dialog had a fixed size. Viewing the backup set information in this relatively small (nonsizable) dialog box was a challenge. The Restore dialog in SQL Server 2005's SSMS can contain a slew of information related to the backup sets available for restore. The ability to size the windows allows for much more information to be displayed.

The tabbed document window area provides some usability improvements as well. This area, as described earlier, is fixed and is always displayed in SSMS. Component windows can be displayed in this area, along with windows for the Query Editor, diagrams, and other design windows. If desired, you can change the environment from a tabbed display to multiple-document interface (MDI) mode. In this mode, each document is opened in its own window within the document window. The MDI mode manages windows like the SQL Server 2000 Query Analyzer and may be more user-friendly for some people. You can change to MDI mode by selecting Tools, Options and then selecting MDI Environment from the General page.

One particularly useful window that can be displayed in the document window is the Summary page. This new window displays information relative to the node that is selected in the Object Explorer and includes options to produce detailed reports and graphs. The Summary page is displayed in the document window by default when SSMS is launched, but you can also display it by pressing F7 or choosing Summary from the View menu.

TIP

In SQL Server 2000, you could select multiple objects for scripting by selecting the items from the Object Explorer tree in Enterprise Manager. You cannot use the Object Explorer tree to do this with SQL Server 2005, and this has generated some confusion. The solution is the Summary page, which provides a means for doing multiple selections of the objects it displays. You can hold down the Ctrl key and click only those items that you want to script. After you have selected the items you want, you simply right-click one of the selected items and choose the preferred scripting method. This also works with scheduled jobs that are displayed in the Summary page. SQL Server 2000 did not offer this capability.

The reports that are available on the Summary page are often overlooked. Part of the reason for this may be that the reports are not available for every node in the Object Explorer tree. Top-level nodes in the tree are where most of the reports are found. For example, if you select a database in the Object Explorer tree and view the Summary page, you see a Report icon that is enabled on the toolbar at the top of the Summary page. If you click the drop-down arrow next to that icon, you find a list of reports that are available for creation. These reports include Disk Usage, Backup and Restore Events, Top Transactions by Age, and a host of others. Graphs are included with some reports, and you can export or print all these reports. Figure 3.2 shows an example of the Disk Usage report for the AdventureWorks database.

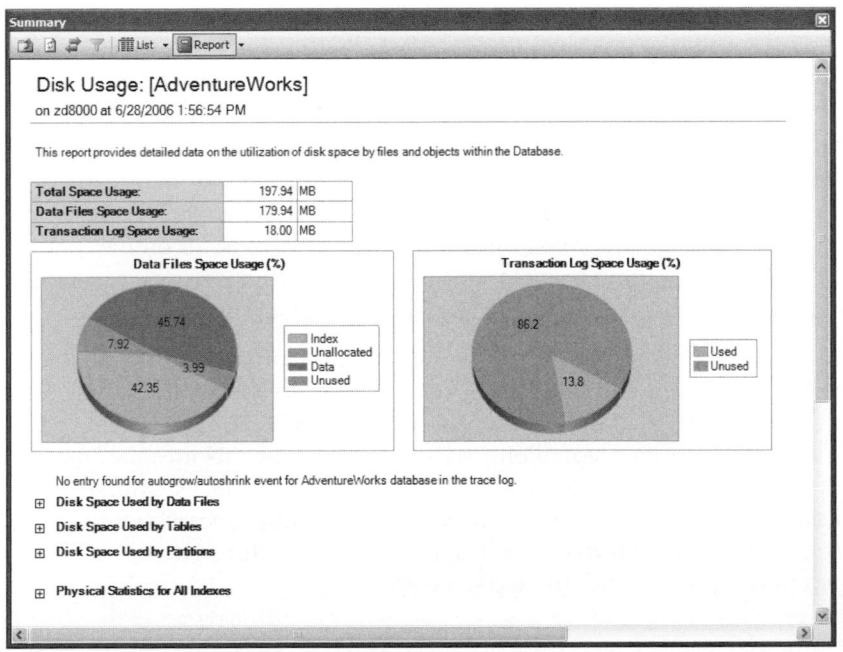

FIGURE 3.2   A Disk Usage summary report.

The graphs are easy to read, and some sections of the report can be expanded to provide more detail. Bullets at the bottom of a report are nodes that can be expanded. For example, the bullets Disk Space Used by Data Files and Disk Space Used by Table at the bottom of Figure 3.2 can be expanded.

Integrated Help

SSMS offers an expanded set of help facilities as well as improved integration into the application environment. The Help sources have been expanded to include both local and online resources. Local help is similar to the Help resources available in past versions and references files that are installed on your machine during the installation process. Local help includes the local SQL Server Books Online resources. Local help files are static and get updated only if another documentation installation is run on the local machine.

Online help is new to SQL Server 2005 and provides access to content that is not static and can be updated with the very latest changes. Three default online resources are provided by default:

- ▶ **MSDN Online**—MSDN Online contains the latest version of the MSDN documentation, including the latest quarterly releases.

- ▶ **Codezone Community**—Codezone Community includes a set of third-party websites that have partnered with Microsoft and provide a wealth of information from sources outside Microsoft.

- ▶ **Questions**—The Questions option allows you to search the forum archives for answers to questions that others have already asked. It also allows you to post your own questions.

The help resources you use on your machine are configurable. You can choose to search online resources first, followed by local help, or you can choose an option that searches local help resources first, followed by online resources. You can also choose specific Codezone online resources to search, or you can eliminate the search of all online resources. Figure 3.3 shows the online help Options window, which allows you to configure your Help options. You access this dialog by selecting Tools, Options.

The Help resources you select are used when you search for content within the Help facility. When you use both local and online resources options, you see results from multiple locations in your search results. Figure 3.4 shows a sample Books Online Document Explorer window with results from a search on "Management Studio." Notice that the panel on the right side of the window lists entries under Local Help, MSDN Online, Codezone Community, and Questions. Each of these sections contains search results that you can access by simply clicking on that area. The number of search results for each section is displayed in parentheses after the section name.

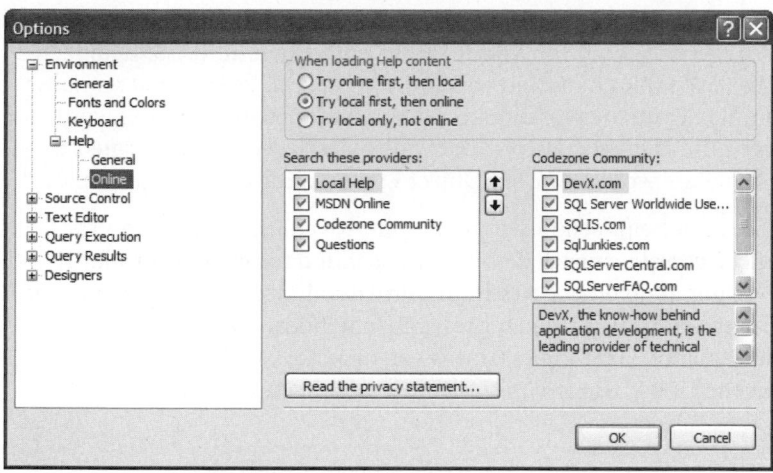

FIGURE 3.3   Setting Help options.

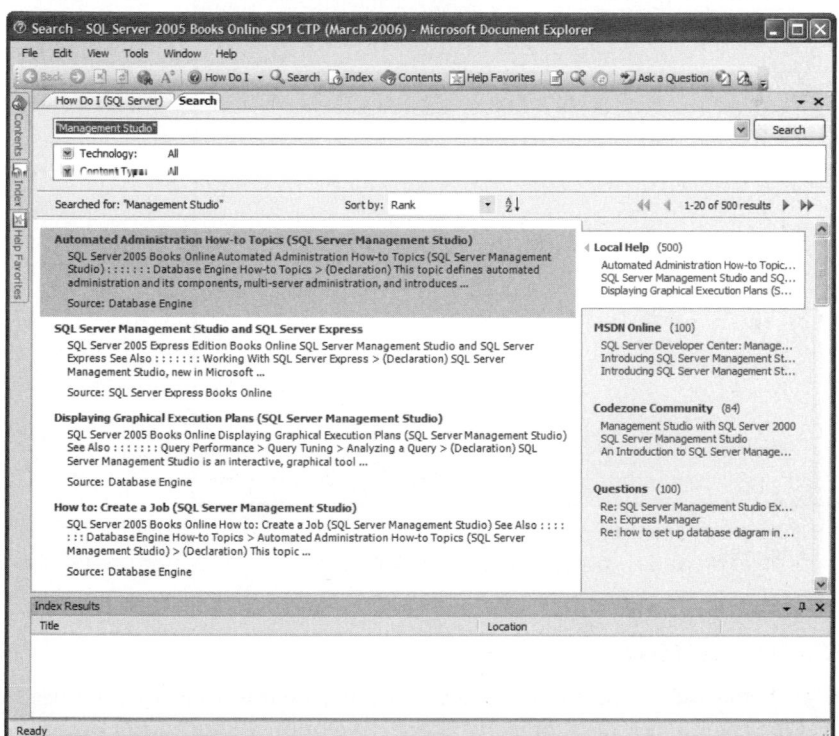

FIGURE 3.4   A Books Online search.

3

One other significant change to the help facilities in SSMS is the addition of Dynamic Help. Dynamic Help is a carryover from the Visual Studio environment. It is a help facility that automatically displays topics in a Help window that are related to what you are doing in SSMS. For example, if you are working in a query window and type the word SELECT to start your query, the Dynamic Help window displays several topics related to the SELECT statement. If you are working in the Object Explorer, it displays Help topics related to the Object Explorer.

Dynamic Help is one of the component windows that you can dock or position on the SSMS surface. To use Dynamic Help, you select Help, Dynamic Help. Figure 3.5 shows an example of the SSMS environment with the Dynamic Help window docked on the right side of the window. The Dynamic Help topics in this example are relative to the SELECT keyword that is typed in the Query Editor window in the middle of the screen.

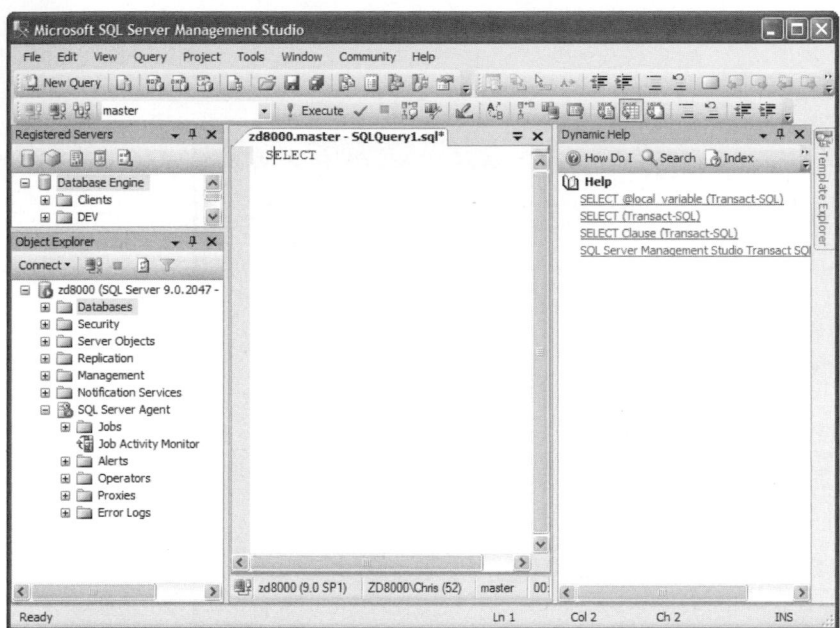

FIGURE 3.5   Dynamic Help.

Administration Tools

The tools that are available with SSMS can be broadly categorized into tools that are used for administering SQL Server and tools that are used for developing or authoring new SQL Server objects. As a matter of practice, developers use some of the administrative tools, and administrators use some of the development tools.

SSMS comes with an expanded set of tools to help with SQL Server administrative tasks. It builds on the functionality that was available in the SQL Server 2000 Enterprise Manager and adds some new tools and functionality to help ease the administrative burden.

Using Registered Servers

Registered servers is a new concept in SQL Server 2005 and represents a new division between managing servers and registering servers. With the SQL Server 2000 Enterprise Manager, the Microsoft Management Console (MMC) tree was displayed on the left side of the Enterprise Manager screen, and it contained servers that had been registered via that tree. Any registered servers or groups were listed in the tree, along with any of the associated objects.

With SQL Server 2005, registered servers are managed and displayed in the Registered Servers component window. The objects associated with these registered servers are displayed in the Object Explorer rather than in the Registered Servers window.

Figure 3.6 shows an example of the Registered Servers window, with several server groups and their associated registered servers. You can add new groups any time; this window offers a handy way of organizing the servers you work with.

FIGURE 3.6   The Registered Servers window.

The servers listed in Figure 3.6 are all database engine servers. These server types are the conventional SQL Server instances, like those you could register in the SQL Server 2000 Enterprise Manager. You can also register several other types of servers. The icons across the top of the Registered Servers window indicate the types of servers that can be registered. In addition to database engine servers, you can also register servers for Analysis Services, Reporting Services, SQL Server Mobile, and Integration Services. The Registered Servers window gives you one consolidated location to register all the different types of servers that are available in SQL Server 2005. You simply click the icon associated with the appropriate server type, and the registered servers of that type are displayed in the Registered Servers tree.

NOTE

The SQL Server 2005 Registered Servers window enables you to register servers that are running SQL Server 2000 and SQL Server 7.0 as well. You can manage all the features of SQL Server 2000 with SQL Server 2005 tools. You can also have both sets of tools on one machine. The SQL Server 2000 and SQL Server 2005 tools are compatible and function normally together.

The SQL Server 2000 Enterprise Manager and Query Analyzer cannot be used to manage SQL Server 2005. You can connect the Query Analyzer to a SQL Server 2005 instance and run queries, but the Object Explorer and other tools are not compatible with SQL Server 2005.

When a server is registered, you have several options available for managing the server. You can right-click the server in the Registered Servers window to start or stop the related server, open a new Object Explorer window for the server, connect to a new query window, or export the registered servers to an XML file so that they can be imported on another machine.

TIP

The import/export feature can be a real timesaver, especially in environments where many SQL servers are managed. You can export all the servers and groups that are registered on one machine and save the time of registering them all on another machine. For example, you can right-click the `Database Engine` node, select Export, and then choose a location to store the XML output file. Then, all you need to do to register all the servers and groups on another machine is move the file to that machine and import the file.

Using Object Explorer

The Object Explorer window that existed in the SQL Server 2000 Query Analyzer has been integrated into SSMS. It has the same tree-like structure that was present in SQL Server 2000 but contains some significant improvements over its predecessor. The most significant feature for those folks managing a large number of database objects is the ability to populate the Object Explorer tree asynchronously. This may not hit home for folks who deal with smaller databases, but those who waited on the synchronous population of Object Explorer in SQL Server 2000 will be excited. The Object Explorer tree in SSMS displays immediately and allows navigation in the tree and elsewhere in SSMS while the population of the tree is taking place.

The Object Explorer is adaptive to the type of server that it is connected to. For a database engine server, the databases and objects such as tables, stored procedures, and so on are displayed in the tree. If you connect to an Integration Services server, the tree displays information about the packages that have been defined on that type of server. Figure 3.7 shows an example of the Object Explorer with several different types of SQL Server servers displayed in the tree. Each server node has a unique icon that precedes the server name, and the type of server is also displayed in parentheses following the server name.

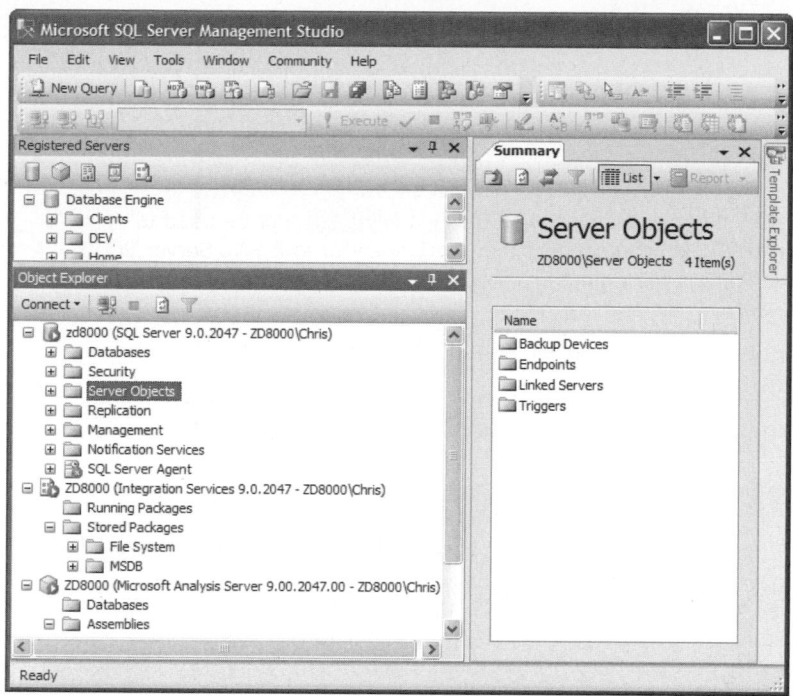

FIGURE 3.7   Multiple server types in Object Explorer.

The objects displayed in the Object Explorer tree can be filtered in SQL Server 2005. The number of filters is limited, but those that are available can be helpful. For example, you can filter the tables that are displayed in Object Explorer based on the name of the table, the schema that it belongs to, or the date on which it was created. Again, for those who deal with large databases and thousands of database objects, this feature is very helpful.

Administrators also find the enhanced scripting capabilities in the Object Explorer very useful. The scripting enhancements are centered mostly on the administrative dialog boxes. These dialogs now include a script button that allows you to see what SSMS is doing behind the scenes to effect your changes. In the past, the Profiler could be used to gather this information, but it was more time-consuming and less integrated than what is available now.

Figure 3.8 shows an example of an administrative dialog, with the scripting options selected at the top. You can script the commands to a new query window, a file, the Windows Clipboard, or a job that can be schedule to run at a later time.

Aside from these features, many of the features and much of the functionality associated with the Object Explorer is similar to what was found in SQL Server 2000. Keep in mind that there are some additional nodes in the Object Explorer tree and that some of the objects are located in different places. There is now a separate node for the SQL Server Agent that contains scheduled jobs and related objects. Linked servers are now located under the Server Objects node, and several new additions are available in the Management node that were found elsewhere in the prior version.

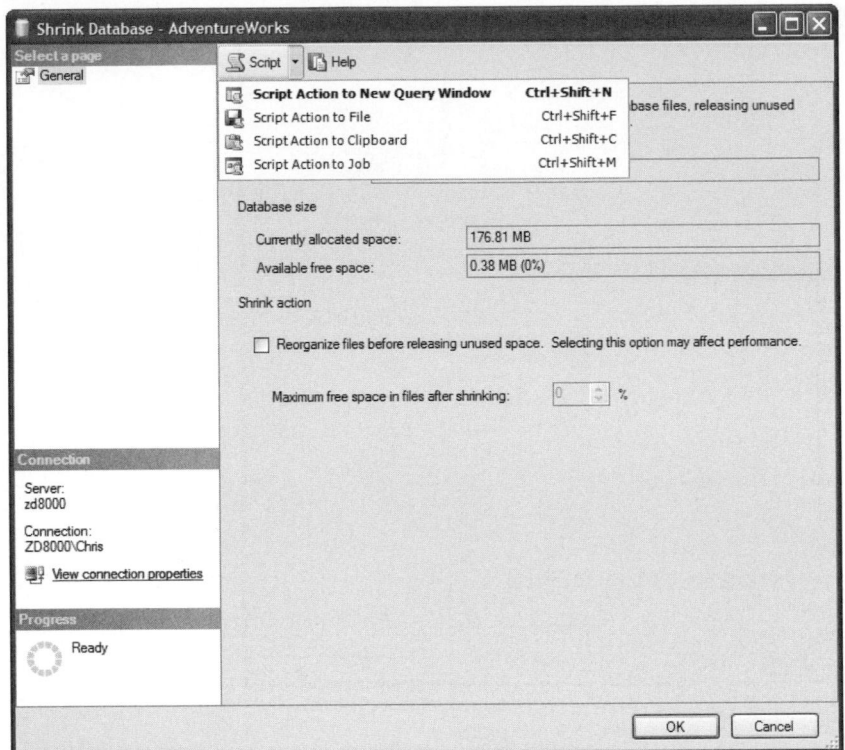

FIGURE 3.8   Scripting from administrative dialogs.

Using Activity Monitor

The functionality that was previously available in the Current Activity node of Enterprise Manager has been ported to a new tool named the Activity Monitor. The Activity Monitor is a non-modal window that is launched from the Object Explorer tree. To access it, you open the Management node of the tree and double-click the Activity Monitor node. Figure 3.9 shows an example of the Activity Monitor window.

The default Process Info page lists current processes on the database server. By default, the system processes are not listed, but you can add them to the display by using the filtering capabilities in the application. If you click the Filter button, a Filter Settings window like the one shown in Figure 3.10 is displayed. You can set the Show System Processes value to True to display all the processes, and you can adjust any of the other filter values to display the desired set of processes.

The other two pages in the Activity Monitor display information about locks on the server. You can display locks by server process ID (SPID) or select locks based on a specific database object. This information is similar to what is retrieved when you run the sp_lock system stored procedure or the sys.dm_tran_locks dynamic management view.

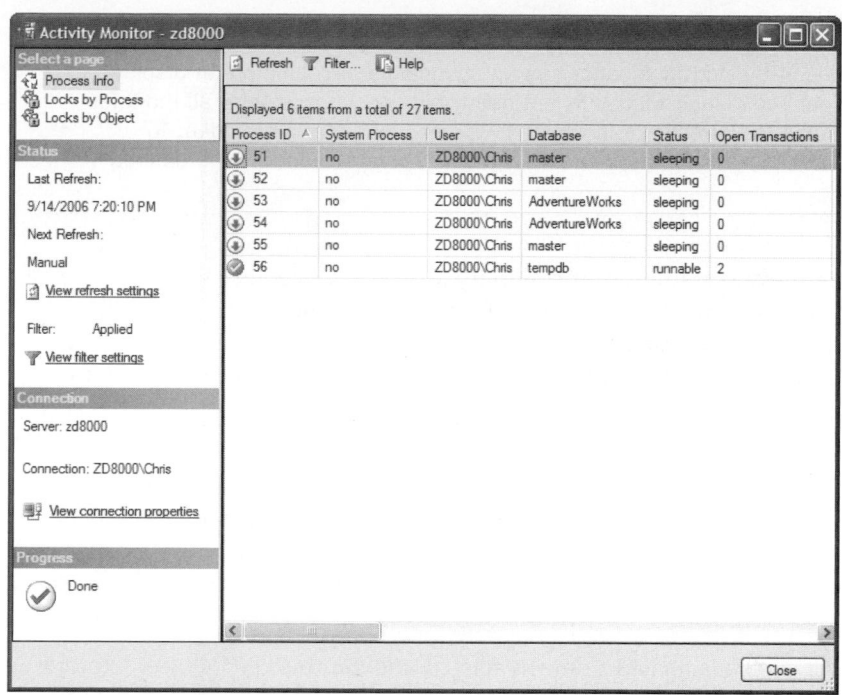

FIGURE 3.9   Process info in the Activity Monitor.

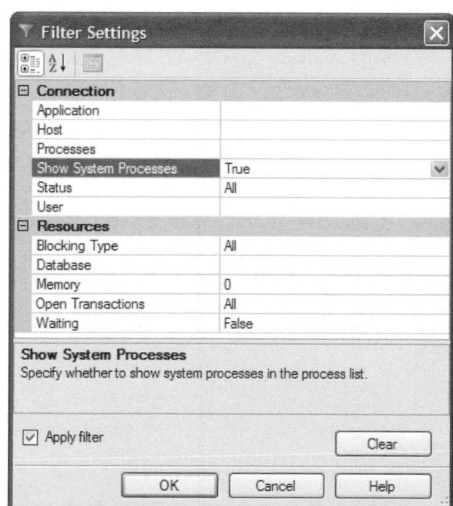

FIGURE 3.10   Filter settings in the Activity Monitor.

> **NOTE**
>
> Each of the pages in the Activity Monitor has an abundance of columns that display useful information. The default window is not nearly big enough to display all the information. You can use the scrollbar to navigate to the columns that are hidden. To rearrange the order of the columns, you simply drag a column header to the desired location.

One of the most impressive features of the Activity Monitor is its ability to refresh the display automatically. You can click the View Refresh settings option on the left side of the screen to adjust the refresh rate. You can select the Auto Refresh Every option and select the number of seconds between refreshes to have the screen automatically refresh.

Using Log File Viewer

The Log File Viewer is another non-modal window that is new to SQL Server 2005. Like the Activity Monitor, it houses information that was previously displayed in the document window in the SQL Server 2000 Enterprise Manager. It can display log files that are generated from several different sources, including Database Mail, SQL Server Agent, SQL Server, and Windows NT.

The Log File Viewer can be launched from the related node in the SSMS Object Explorer. For example, you can select the Management node and expand SQL Server Error Logs. If you double-click one of the error logs listed, a new Log File Viewer window is launched, displaying the SQL Server log file entries for the log type selected (see Figure 3.11).

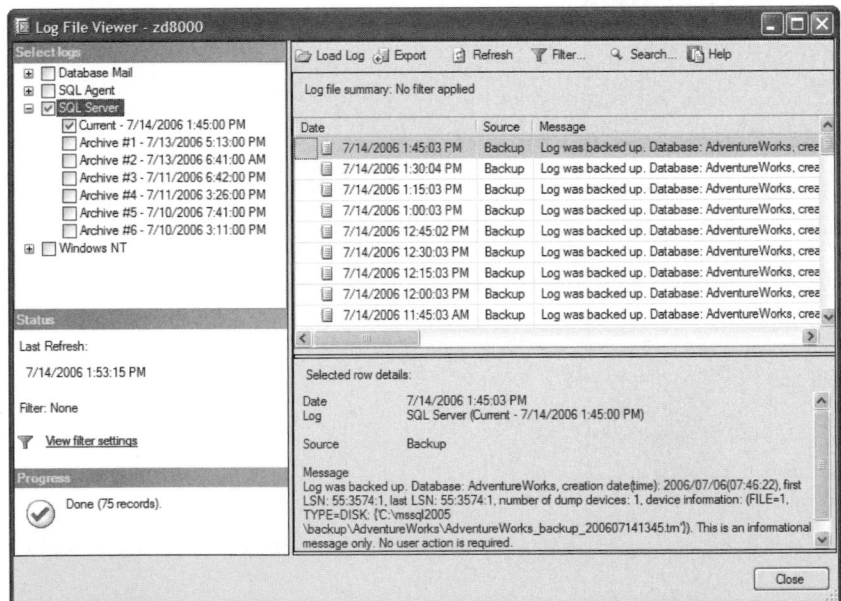

FIGURE 3.11   SQL Server logs displayed in the Log File Viewer.

> **NOTE**
>
> By default, entries are shown in the SQL Server Log File Viewer from newest to oldest. This is different from the default order in the SQL Server 2000 Enterprise Manager, which displayed the log file entries from oldest to newest.

One of the first things you notice when you launch the Log File Viewer is that there is a tree structure at the top-left corner of the screen that shows the log files you are viewing. You can see that there are four different log types available: Database Mail, SQL Agent, SQL Server, and Windows NT. You can choose to display multiple log files within a given log type (for example, the current SQL Server log and Archive #1) or you can select logs from different sources. For example, you can display all the current log entries for SQL Server and the current log entry for the SQL Server Agent.

When multiple logs are selected, you can differentiate between the rows shown on the right side of the Log File Viewer by looking at the Log Source column and the Log Type column. The Log Source values match up with the names that are shown in the tree structure where the log was selected. The Log Type column shows the type of log, such as SQL Agent or SQL Server. Rows from the different log types are displayed together and sorted according to the date on which the row was created. The sort order cannot be changed.

> **TIP**
>
> You can rearrange the order of the columns shown in the Log File Viewer. You simply click the column header and drag the column to the desired location. When viewing rows for more than one log type or multiple logs, it is best to drag the Log Type and Log Source columns to a location that is easily viewed so that you can distinguish between the entries.

Other noteworthy features in the Log File Viewer include the ability to filter and load a log from an external source. You can filter on dates, users, computers, the message text, and the source of the message. You can import log files from other machines into the view by using the Load Log facility. This works hand-in-hand with the Export option, which allows you to export the log to a file. These files can be easily shared so that others can review the files in their own Log File Viewer.

Development Tools

SSMS delivers an equally impressive number of enhancements for database developers. These new tools are based on tools such as Query Analyzer that were available in prior versions of SQL Server. They deliver the same functional value available in prior releases and offer enhancements that address some of the shortcomings.

The Query Editor

The Query Editor sits at the top of the list for new development tools in SSMS. The Query Editor, as its name indicates, is the editing tool for writing queries in SSMS. It contains much of the functionality that was contained in SQL Server 2000's Query Analyzer. The ability to write Transact-SQL (T-SQL) queries, execute them, return results, generate execution plans, and many of the other features you may be familiar with in Query Analyzer are also available with the Query Editor.

One main difference with the Query Editor is that is has been integrated into the SSMS environment. In SQL Server 2000, the Query Analyzer was a separate application with its own independent interface. In SQL Server 2005, SSMS houses the query-editing capabilities along with all the administrative capabilities.

> **NOTE**
>
> The biggest upside to the integration of the query-editing tool into the SSMS environment is that you can find almost anything you need to administer or develop on your SQL Server database in one spot. There is no need to jump back and forth between applications. One possible downside, however, is that SSMS may be much more than some database developers need.

Clicking the New Query button, opening a file, and selecting the Script to File option from a list of database objects in the Object Explorer are just a few of the ways to launch the Query Editor. Figure 3.12 shows the Query Editor window with a sample SELECT statement from the AdventureWorks database. The figure shows the Query Editor window displayed on the right side of the screen and the Object Explorer on the left side.

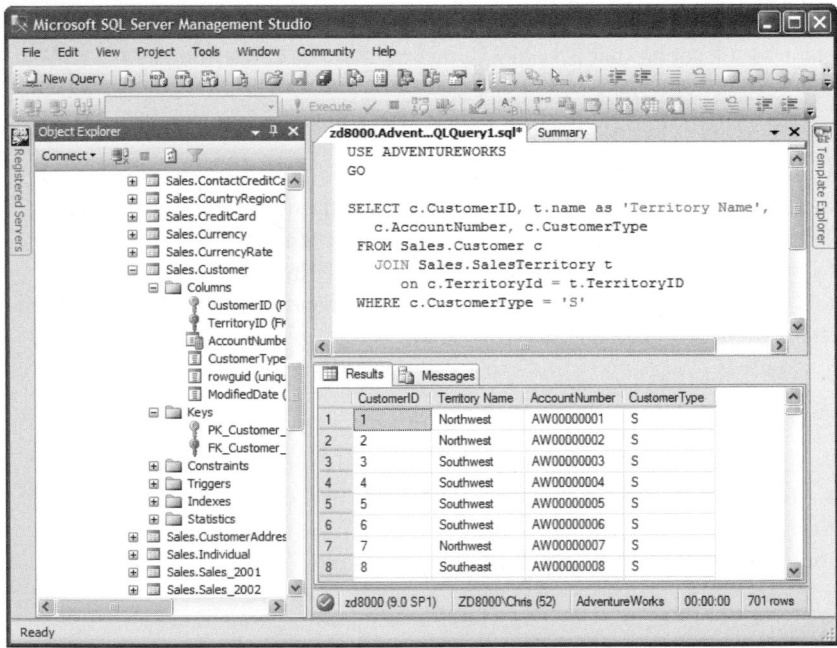

FIGURE 3.12   The Query Editor window in SSMS.

The basic editing environment within the Query Editor is similar to Query Analyzer. The top portion of the Query Editor window contains the query. The bottom portion contains the results of an executed query. The results can be displayed as text, displayed in a grid format, or output as XML. However, in the Query Editor, windows are by default managed differently than with Query Analyzer. Multiple Query Editor windows are displayed in a tabbed format; in comparison, Query Analyzer displayed a separate window for each query.

TIP

The tabbed document display has some advantages, but you can set an option in SSMS that causes the Query Editor to behave much like the Query Analyzer. To do this, you select Tools, Options to launch the Options dialog. The default page has a section named Environmental Layout. If you choose the MDI Environment option, you set SSMS in MDI mode instead of the tabbed layout.

Query Editor Types

The Query Editor in SQL Server 2005 enables you to develop different types of queries. You are no longer limited to database queries based on SQL. You can use the Query Editor to develop all types of SQL Server Scripts, including those for SQL Server Analysis Services (SSAS) and SQL Server Mobile Edition. The SSAS queries come in three different flavors: multidimensional expressions (MDX), data mining expressions (DMX), and XML for analysis (XMLA). Only one selection exists for creating SQL Server Mobile Edition scripts.

You see these new query options when you create a new query. When you select New from the SSMS menu, you can choose what type of query to create. You use the Database Engine Query choice to create a T-SQL query against the database engine. The other new query options correspond to SSAS and SQL Server Mobile Edition. The toolbar on SSMS also has icons that correspond to each type of query that can be created.

Each query type has a code pane that works much the same way across all the different types of queries. The code pane, which is the topmost window, color-codes the syntax that is entered, and it has sophisticated search capabilities and other advanced editing features that make it easy to use. The features that are new to SQL Server 2005 and apply to all the editor types include line numbering, bookmarks, hyperlinks in the comments, and a color-coded indicator that is shown in front of each line that has changed since the script was opened.

Other code pane features are available only for certain types of queries. IntelliSense, which automatically completes syntax and arguments, is available for all queries except database engine queries. Squiggles, which are wavy lines that appear below a word in the editor to indicate possible syntax errors, are available with MDX, DMX, and XML queries. The MDX, DMX, and XML editors also offer code outlining, which enables you to expand and collapse code segments to make it easier to review code.

Disconnected Editing

New to SQL Server 2005 is the ability to use the code editor without a database connection. When creating a new query, you can choose to connect to a database or select Cancel to leave the code pane disconnected. To connect to the database at a later time, you can right-click in the code pane window and select the Connect option. You can also disconnect the Query Editor at any time or choose the Change Connection option to disconnect and connect to another database all at once.

Along with disconnected editing are some changes to the Windows behavior that are worth noting. The biggest changes relate to the behavior of query windows that are currently open at the time that a file is opened for editing. With SQL Server 2000 Query Analyzer, the currently selected window would be populated with the contents of the file that you were opening. Prior to this replacement, a prompt would be displayed that asked whether you wanted to save your results. If the query window was empty, the contents would be replaced without the prompt for saving.

With SQL Server 2005, a new query window is opened every time a new file is opened. The new window approach is faster but can lead to many more open windows in the document window. You need to be careful about the number of windows/connections you have open. Also, you need to be aware that the tabbed display shows only a limited number of windows. Additional connections can exist even if their tabs are not in the active portion of the document window.

Editing SQLCMD Scripts in SSMS

SQLCMD is a command-line utility that is new to SQL Server 2005. You can use it for ad hoc interactive execution of T-SQL statements and scripts. It is basically a replacement for the ISQL and OSQL commands that were used in prior versions of SQL Server. (OSQL still works with SQL Server 2005, but ISQL has been discontinued.)

What's new to SSMS is the ability to write, edit, and execute SQLCMD scripts within the Query Editor environment. The Query Editor in SSMS treats SQLCMD scripts in much the same way as other scripts. The script is color-coded and can be parsed or executed. This is possible only if you place the Query Editor in SQLCMD mode, which you do by selecting Query, SQLCMD Mode or selecting the SQLCMD mode icon from the SSMS toolbar.

Figure 3.13 shows a sample SQLCMD script in SSMS that can be used to back up a database. This example illustrates the power and diversity of a SQLCMD script that utilizes both T-SQL and SQLCMD statements. It uses environment variables that are set within the script. The script variables DBNAME and BACKUPPATH are defined at the top of the script with the SETVAR command. The BACKUP statement at the bottom of the script references these variables, using the convention $(*variablename*), which substitutes the value in the command.

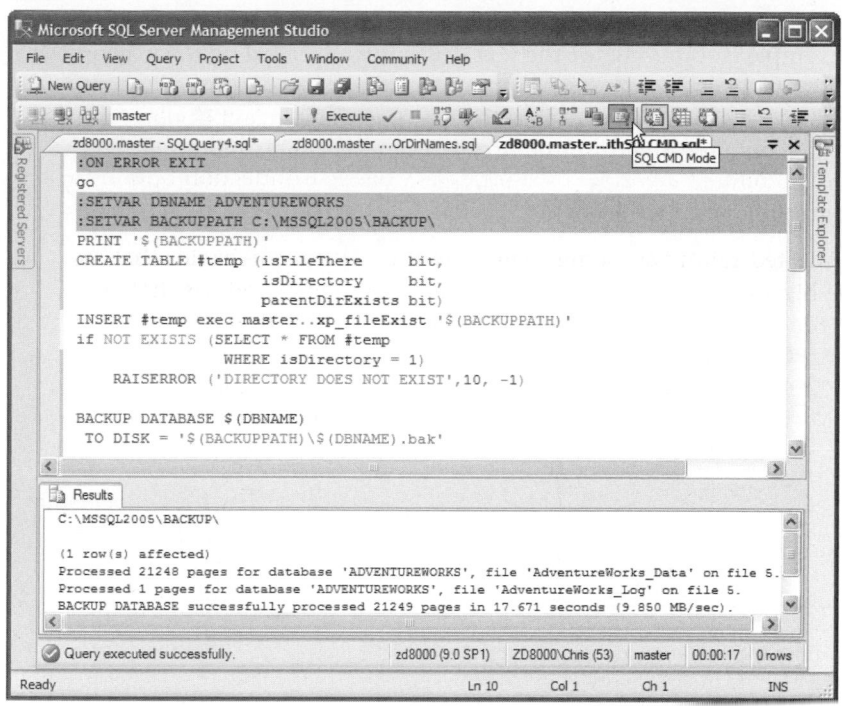

```
:ON ERROR EXIT
go
:SETVAR DBNAME ADVENTUREWORKS
:SETVAR BACKUPPATH C:\MSSQL2005\BACKUP\
PRINT '$(BACKUPPATH)'
CREATE TABLE #temp (isFileThere     bit,
                    isDirectory     bit,
                    parentDirExists bit)
INSERT #temp exec master..xp_fileExist '$(BACKUPPATH)'
if NOT EXISTS (SELECT * FROM #temp
              WHERE isDirectory = 1)
    RAISERROR ('DIRECTORY DOES NOT EXIST',10, -1)

BACKUP DATABASE $(DBNAME)
  TO DISK = '$(BACKUPPATH)\$(DBNAME).bak'
```

```
Results
C:\MSSQL2005\BACKUP\

(1 row(s) affected)
Processed 21248 pages for database 'ADVENTUREWORKS', file 'AdventureWorks_Data' on file 5.
Processed 1 pages for database 'ADVENTUREWORKS', file 'AdventureWorks_Log' on file 5.
BACKUP DATABASE successfully processed 21249 pages in 17.671 seconds (9.850 MB/sec).
```

FIGURE 3.13   Editing a SQLCMD script in SSMS.

SQLCMD scripts that are edited in SSMS can also be executed within SSMS. The results are displayed in the results window of the Query Editor window, just like any other script. After you test a script, you can execute it by using the SQLCMD command-line utility. The SQLCMD command-line utility is a very powerful tool that can help automate script execution. For more information on using SQLCMD in SSMS, refer to the Books Online topic "Editing SQLCMD Scripts with Query Editor." The SQLCMD command-line utility is discussed in more detail in Chapter 4, "SQL Server Command-Line Utilities."

Regular Expressions and Wildcards in SSMS

SSMS has a robust search facility that includes the use of regular expressions. Regular expressions provide a flexible notation for finding and replacing text, based on patterns within the text. Regular expressions are found in other programming languages and applications, including the Microsoft .NET Framework. The regular expressions in SSMS work in much the same way as these other languages, but there are some differences in the notation.

The option to use regular expressions is available whenever you are doing a find or replace within an SSMS script. You can use the find and replace option in the code pane or the results window. You can use the Find and Replace option from the Edit menu or use press either the Ctrl+F or Ctrl+H shortcut keys to launch the Find and Replace dialog box. Figure 3.14 shows an example of the Find and Replace dialog that utilizes a regular expression. This example is searching for the text Customer, preceded by the @ character and not followed by the Id characters. This kind of search could be useful for searching a large stored procedure where you want to find the customer references but don't want to see the variables that contain *customer* in the first part of the variable name.

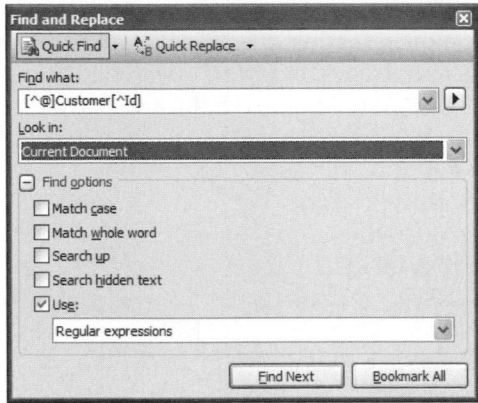

FIGURE 3.14   A find and replace with regular expressions.

You use regular expressions only when the Use check box in the Find and Replace dialog is selected. When this option is selected, you can choose either Regular Expressions or Wildcards. Wildcard searches work much the same way in SSMS as they do in file searches. For example, if you wanted to find any references to the word *zip*, you could enter *zip* in the Find What text box. The wildcard options are limited but very effective for simple searches.

Regular expressions have a much more extensive number of available search options. When you choose the option to use regular expressions, the arrow button is enabled to the right of the text box where you enter your search text. If you click this button, you are given an abbreviated list of regular expression characters that you can use in your searches. A brief description of what each character represents in the search is listed next to the character. For a complete list of characters, you can choose the Complete Character List option at the bottom of the list. This option brings you to the Books Online topic "How to: Search with Regular Expressions," which gives a comprehensive review of all the characters.

Enhanced Performance Output
The Query Editor in SSMS has an extended set of options available for capturing and distributing performance-related data. It contains many of the familiar performance features that you may have grown accustomed to in SQL Server 2000 Query Analyzer—plus more.

Changes in the collection of performance data include a new Execution Plan tab that is displayed in the results window, along with the Results and Messages tab. The Execution Plan tab can be populated with two different types of plans: estimated plans and actual plans. The actual execution plan is a new display for SQL Server 2005; it shows the plan that was used in generating the actual query results. The actual plan is generated along with the results when the Include Actual Execution Plan option is selected. This option can be selected from the SSMS toolbar or from the Query menu. Figure 3.15 shows an example of an actual execution plan generated for a query against the AdventureWorks database. It uses the familiar treelike structure that was also present in SQL Server 2000, but the display has been enhanced for SQL Server 2005. The ToolTips that are displayed when you mouse over a node in the execution plan include additional information; you can see that information in a more static form in the Properties window if you right-click the node and select Properties. The icons in the graphical plan have changed, and the display is generally easier to read in SQL Server 2005.

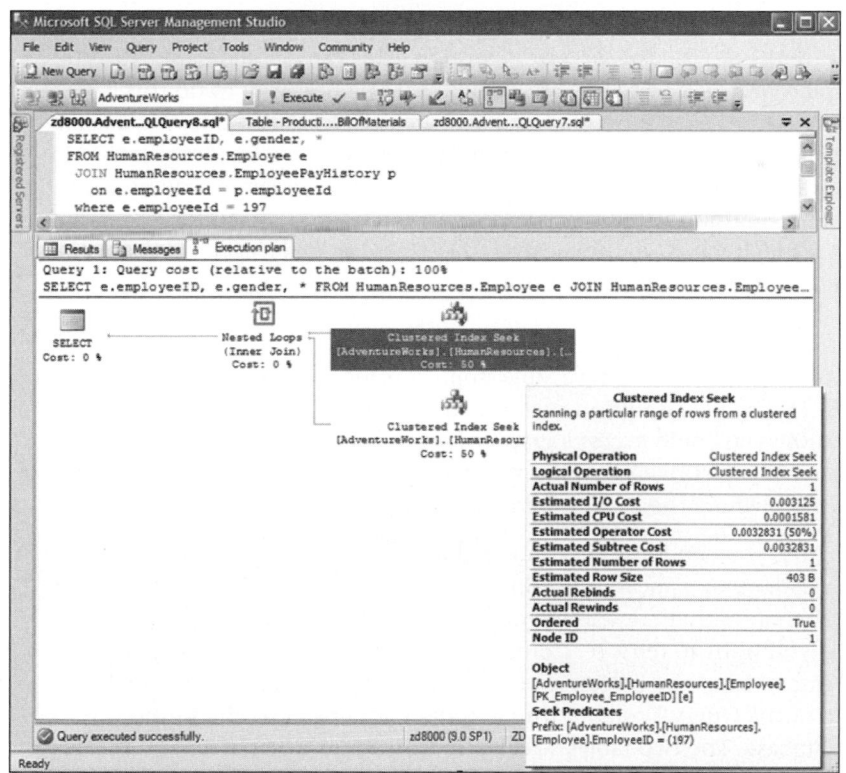

FIGURE 3.15   Displaying an actual execution plan in Query Editor.

NOTE

The Manage Indexes and Manage Statistics options that were available in the SQL Server 2000 Query Analyzer are not present in the Query Editor in SQL Server 2005. Those options in Query Analyzer were accessible by right-clicking a node in the query plan. You can use the Database Engine Tuning Advisor (DTA) in SQL Server 2005 to analyze the Query Editor statements or open the Table Designer to manage the indexes on a specific table.

Query plans generated in the Query Editor are easier to distribute in SQL Server 2005. You have several options for capturing query plan output so that you can save it or send it to someone else for analysis. If you right-click an empty section of the Execution Plan window, you can select the Save Execution Plan As option, which allows you to save the execution plan to a file. By default, the file has the extension .sqlplan. This file can be opened using SSMS on another machine to display the graphical output.

The query plan can also be output in XML format and distributed in this form. You make this happen by using the SET SHOWPLAN_XML ON option. This option generates the estimated execution plan in a well-defined XML document. The best way to do this is to turn off the display of the actual execution plan and execute the SET SHOWPLAN_XML ON statement in the code pane window. Next, you set the Query Editor to return results in grid format and then execute the statements for which you want to generate a query plan. If you double-click the grid results, they are displayed in the SSMS XML editor. You can also save the results to a file. If you save the file with the .sqlplan extension, the file will display the graphical plan when opened in SSMS.

Using the Query Designer in the Query Editor

A graphical query design tool is now accessible from the Query Editor window where you write your queries. This is a great option that was missing in prior versions of SQL Server. With SQL Server 2000, you could access a graphical query designer by opening a table in Enterprise Manager and selecting Query, but this option was disconnected from the Query Analyzer environment, where the queries were authored.

With SQL Server 2005, you can right-click in the Query Editor window and choose Design Query in Editor. A dialog box appears, allowing you to add tables to the graphical query designer surface. The tables that are selected are shown in a window that allows you to select the columns you want to retrieve. Columns that are selected appear in a SELECT statement that is displayed at the bottom of the Query Designer window. Figure 3.16 shows an example of the Query Designer window that contains two tables from the AdventureWorks database. The two tables selected in this figure are related, as indicated by the line between them.

The T-SQL statements are generated automatically as you select various options on the Query Designer screen. If you select Sort Type, an ORDER BY clause is added. If you choose an alias for a column, it is reflected in the T-SQL. If tables are related, the appropriate joins are generated.

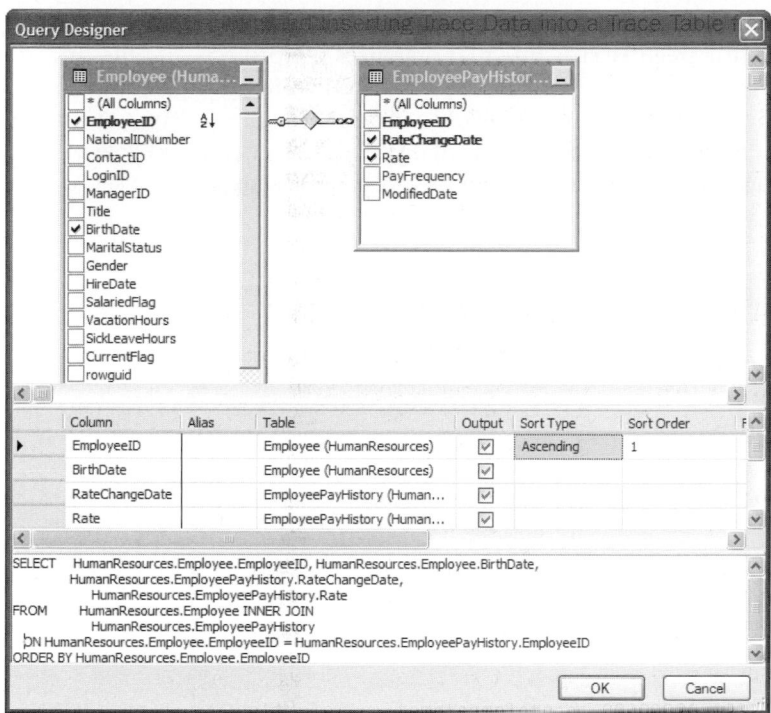

FIGURE 3.16   Designing queries in the Query Editor.

When you click OK on the Query Designer window, the related T-SQL is automatically placed in the Query Editor window. You can edit the T-SQL as needed or use it as is. You can imagine the time savings you can achieve by using this tool.

> **TIP**
>
> The Query Designer has a very impressive feature that allows you to view a T-SQL query visually. If you copy a valid T-SQL statement, open the Query Designer, and paste the T-SQL into the SQL pane at the bottom of the Query Designer, it tries to resolve the T-SQL into a graphical display. The tables in the FROM clause are shown in the designer panel, and information related to the selected columns is listed as well. The Query Designer cannot resolve all T-SQL statements and may fail to generate a visual display for some complex T-SQL.

Managing Projects in SSMS

Project management capabilities like those available in Visual Studio are now available in SSMS. Queries, connections, and other files that are related can be grouped into projects. A project or set of projects is further organized or grouped as a solution. This type of organization is the same as in the Visual Studio environment.

Projects and solutions are maintained and displayed with the Solution Explorer. The Solution Explorer contains a tree-like structure that organizes the projects and files in the solution. It is a component window within SSMS that you launch by selecting View, Solution Explorer. Figure 3.17 shows an example of the Solution Explorer. The solution in this example is named EmployeeUpgrade, and it contains two projects, named Phase1 and Phase2. Each project contains a set of connections, a set of T-SQL scripts, and a set of miscellaneous files.

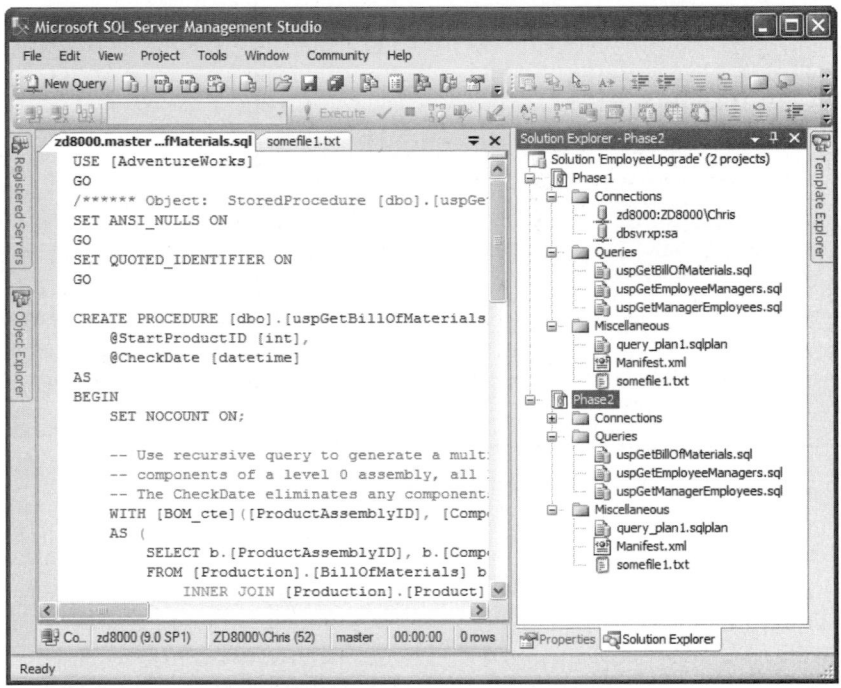

FIGURE 3.17   Solutions and projects listed in the Solution Explorer.

The first thing to do when using the project management capabilities in SSMS is to add a project. To do this, you select File, New, and when the New dialog appears, you select project to add a new project. It is a bit odd, but you must create the project before you can create the solution. When adding the new project, you are given a choice of the type of project, and you must select either SQL Server Scripts, Analysis Services Scripts, or SQL Mobile Scripts. Each one of these project types is geared toward the respective SQL Server technology.

After the project is added, you can add the related connections and files. To add a new connection, you simply right-click the Connections node. The Connections entries allow you to store SQL Server connection information that relates to the project you are working on. For example, you could have a connection to your test environment and another connection to the production environment that relates to the project. When a connection is included in the project, you can double-click it, and a new query window for that connection is established.

SQL script files are added to a project in a similar fashion to connections: You right-click the Queries node and select the New Query option. A new Query Editor window appears, allowing you to enter the T-SQL commands. Any T-SQL script is viable for this category, including those that relate to database objects such as stored procedures, triggers, and tables.

You can also add existing files to a project. To do this, you right-click the project node, select Add, and then select Existing Item. The file types listed in the drop-down at the bottom of the Add Existing Item dialog include SQL Server files (*.sql), SQL deadlock files (*.xdl), XML files (*.xml), and execution plan files (*.sqlplan). SQL Server files are added, by default, to the Queries node. All the other file types are added to the Miscellaneous node. The connection entries are not stored in a separate file but are contained in the project file itself.

Integrating SSMS with Source Control

SSMS has the capability to integrate database project files into a source control solution. Source control provides a means for protecting and managing files. Source control applications typically contain features that allow you to track changes to files, control and track who uses the files, and provide a means for tagging the files with a version stamp so that the files can be retrieved at a later time, by version.

SSMS can integrate with a number of different source control applications. Visual SourceSafe is Microsoft's basic source control solution, but other source control applications can be used instead. The source control client application must be installed on the machine on which SSMS is running. When this is complete, you can set the source control application that SSMS will use within SSMS. To do this, you select Tools, Options and navigate to the Source Control node. The available source control clients are listed in the Current Source Control Plug-in drop-down.

The link between SSMS and the source control application is the database solution. After a solution has been created, it can be added to source control. To add a solution to a source control application, you open the Solution Explorer and right-click the solution or any of the projects in the solution. You then see the Add Solution to Source Control option. You must then log in to the source control application and select a source control project to add the solution to.

When the solution has been added to a source control application, all the related projects and project files are added as well. The projects and files that are in the source control application have additional options available in the Solution Explorer. Figure 3.18 shows a sample solution that has been added to a source control application. A subset of the source control options that are available when right-clicking project files are shown in this figure as well.

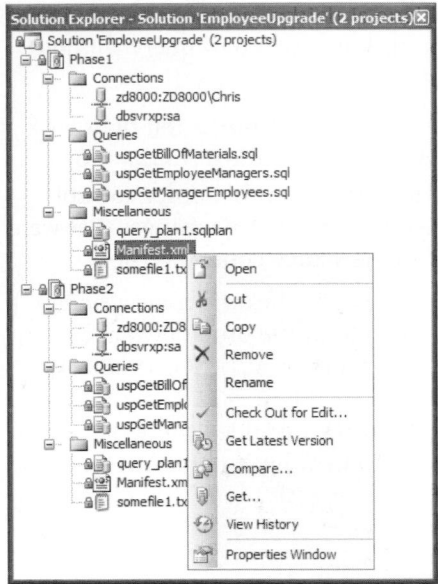

FIGURE 3.18   Source control options in the Solution Explorer.

The options that relate to source control are listed toward the bottom of the options list. The options that are available depend on the status of the selected file. For example, if a file has been checked out, additional options are displayed that relate to checking the file back in. The following are some of the common source control options:

▶ **Check Out for Edit**—This option allows you get a copy of the file from the source control application so that you can modify the file. When you check out the file, the source control provider can keep track of the user who has checked out the file, and it can also prevent other users from checking the file out.

▶ **Check In**—This option copies the locally modified file into the source control solution. The file must first be checked out for editing before you can use the Check In option. A new version for the file is established, and any prior versions of the file are retained as well.

▶ **Get Latest Version**—This option gets a read-only copy of the latest version of the project file from the source control application. The file is not checked out with this option.

▶ **Compare**—This option enables you to compare version of source control files. The default comparison that is shown is between the file in the source control application and the local file on your machine.

▶ **Get**—This option is similar to the Get Latest Version option, but it retrieves a read-only copy of the file. With this option, a dialog box appears, allowing you to select the file(s) that you want to retrieve.

▶ **View History**—This option lists all versions of the files that have been checked into the source control application. The History dialog box has many options that you can use with the different versions of the file. You can view differences between versions of the files, view the contents of a specific version, generate reports, or get an older version of the file.

▶ **Undo Checkout**—This option changes the checkout status in the source control application and releases the file to other source control users. Any changes that were made to the local copy of the file are not added to the source control version.

Other source control options are available via the Source Control menu in SSMS. You select an item in the Solution Explorer and then select File, Source Control. You can use this menu to check the status of a file by using the SourceSafe Properties option, set source control properties, launch the source control application, and perform other source control operations.

Using SSMS Templates

Templates provide a framework for the creation of database objects in SSMS. They are essentially boilerplate files that help generate scripts for common database objects. They can speed up the development of these scripts and help enforce consistency in the generation of the underlying database objects.

SQL Server 2005 has expanded the features available for generating templates. One substantial change is the addition of the Template Explorer. The Template Explorer is a component window that is available in SSMS and replaces the Template tab that was available in the SQL Server 2000 Query Analyzer. Figure 3.19 shows the Template Explorer and the available SQL Server template folders. Separate templates also exist for Analysis Services and SQL Server Mobile Edition. You can view them by selecting the related icon at the top of the Template Explorer.

You access the available templates by expanding the template folder in the Template Explorer tree. For example, if you expand the Index folder, you see six different types of index templates. If you double-click one of the templates, a new Query Editor window appears, populated with the template script. Figure 3.20 shows the template script that is displayed when you open the Create Index Basic template.

The template script contains template parameters that have the following format within the script:

```
<parameter_name, data_type, value>.
```

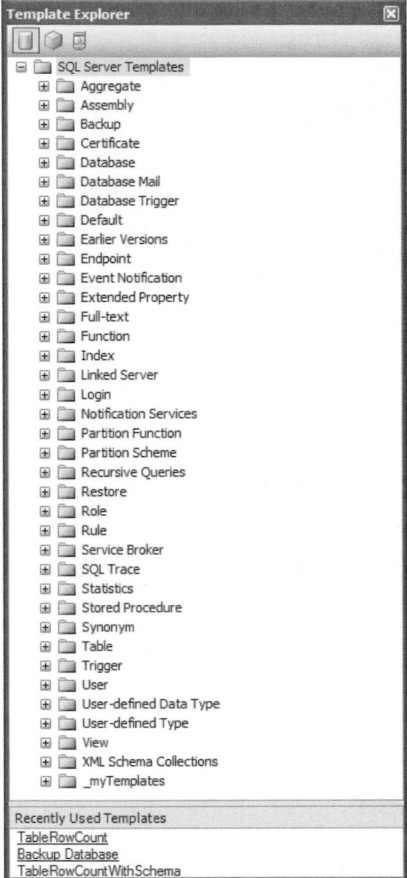

FIGURE 3.19   The SSMS Template Explorer.

You can manually replace these parameters in the script, or you can use the Specify Values for Template Parameters option from the Query menu to globally replace the parameters in the script with the desired values. Selecting Query, Specify Values for Template Parameters launches the Specify Values for Template Parameters dialog box, which enables you to enter the parameter values (see Figure 3.21).

> **TIP**
>
> When you use the Specify Values for Template Parameters option, some parameters may be missed if the parameter text has been altered. For example, if you add a carriage return after *parameter_name*, the Parameters dialog box does not list that parameter. It is best to leave the template script unchanged before you specify values for the parameters. You should make changes to the script after the values have been specified.

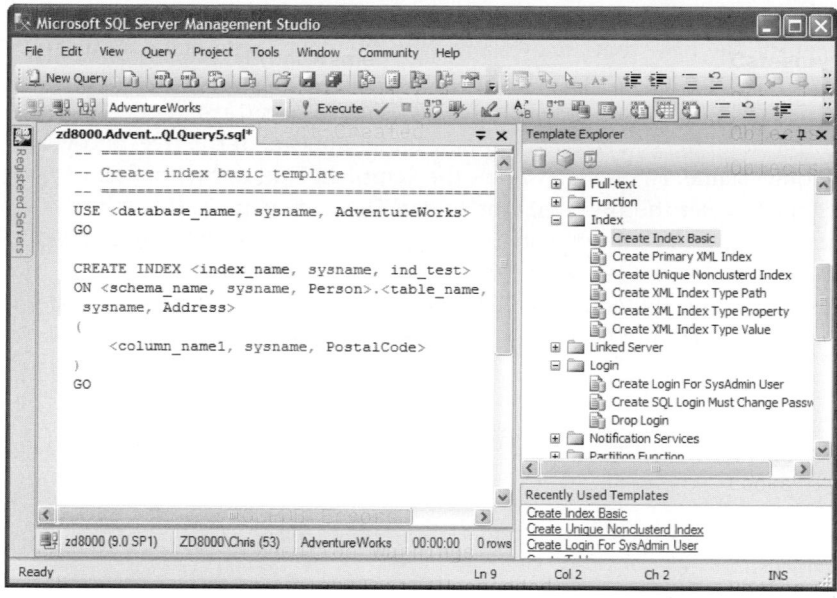

FIGURE 3.20   The template script for creating a basic index.

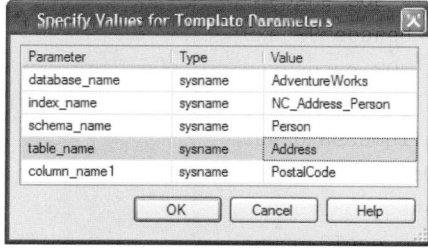

FIGURE 3.21   The Specify Values for Template Parameters dialog box.

After you have entered the parameter values and clicked OK, the values are reflected in the script. For example, the values shown in Figure 3.21 for the basic index template result in the following script:

```
-- =============================================
-- Create index basic template
-- =============================================
USE AdventureWorks
GO
CREATE INDEX NC_Address_Person
ON Person.Address
(
    PostalCode
)
GO
```

You also have the option of creating your own custom templates. These templates can contain parameters just like those that are available with the default templates. You can also create your own template folder that will be displayed in the Template Explorer tree. To create a new template folder, you right-click the SQL Server Templates node in the Template Explorer tree and select New, Folder. A new folder appears in the tree, and you can specify a new folder name. Figure 3.22 shows the Template Explorer with a set of custom templates found under the _mytemplates folder. The code pane in this figure shows the contents of a new custom template named sys.objectSelectWithParameters. This custom template contains two parameter declarations: object_type and modify_ date. When you select the Specify Values for Template Parameters options for this custom template, you have the opportunity to change the values, just as you can with the default templates.

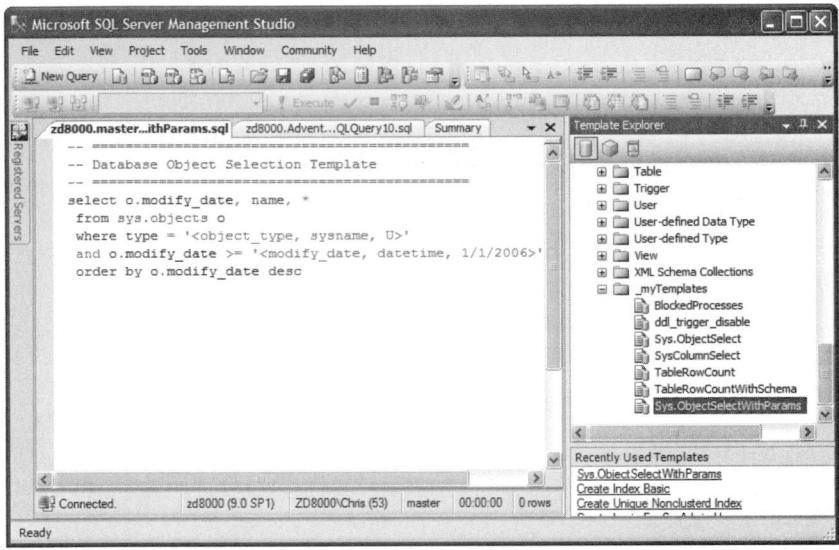

FIGURE 3.22   A custom template example.

> **NOTE**
>
> When you double-click a template in the Template Explorer tree, you create a script that is based on the template. Changes made to the script do not affect the template; they affect only the script that was generated from the template. To change the actual template, you need to right-click the template and select Edit. When you have completed your changes, you need to make sure to save the template.
>
> Also, keep in mind that there is no requirement to have parameters in your templates. Templates are handy tools for accessing any code snippet you might use. After the code snippet is added as a template, you can open a new Query Editor window based on the template or simply drag and drop the template from the Template Explorer to an existing Query Editor window, and the code for the template is pasted into the window.

Summary

The number of tools and features available in SSMS is extensive and can be daunting when you first enter the environment. Remember that you can customize this environment and hide many of the windows that are displayed. You can start with a fairly simple SSMS configuration that includes the Object Explorer and a Query Editor window. This allows you to accomplish a majority of your SQL Server tasks. As you become more familiar with the environment, you can introduce new tools and features to help improve your overall productivity.

The discussion of SSMS does not end with this chapter. Further details related to SSMS are covered throughout this book. You can use the new features described in this chapter as a starting point and look to other chapters for more detailed discussion of database features that are accessible through SSMS.

Chapter 4 looks at the SQL Server utilities that can be run from the command prompt. These tools allow you to perform some of the same tasks that are available in SSMS. The ability to launch these utilities from the command line can be useful when you're automating tasks or accessing SQL Server when graphical user interface tools such as SSMS are not available.

SQL Server Command-Line Utilities

IN THIS CHAPTER

▶ What's New in SQL Server Command-Line Utilities

▶ The `sqlcmd` Command-Line Utility

▶ The `dta` Command-Line Utility

▶ The `tablediff` Command-Line Utility

▶ The `sac` Command-Line Utility

▶ The `bcp` Command-Line Utility

▶ The `sqldiag` Command-Line Utility

▶ The `sqlservr` Command-Line Utility

▶ Removed or Deprecated Utilities in SQL Server 2005

This chapter explores various command-line utilities that ship with SQL Server. These utilities give administrators a different way to access the database engine and its related components. In some cases, they provide functionality that is also available with SQL Server's graphical user interface (GUI). Other command-line utilities provide functionality that is available only from the command prompt. For each utility, this chapter provides the command syntax along with the most commonly used options. For the full syntax and options available for the utility, see SQL Server Books Online.

> **NOTE**
>
> The focus of this chapter is on command-line utilities that are core to SQL Server and the SQL Server database engine. Several other command-line utilities, geared toward other SQL Server services, are not covered in this chapter. These utilities include `dtexec` and `dtutil`, which can be used with SQL Server Integration Services (SSIS). Reporting Services has the `rs`, `rsconfig`, and `rskeymgmt` command-line utilities, and Notification Services has the `nscontrol` utility. These utilities are beyond the scope of this chapter, but they are worth mentioning.

Table 4.1 lists the command-line utilities that are discussed in this chapter. This table lists the physical location of each utility's executable. The location is needed to execute the utility in most cases, unless the associated path has been added to the `Path` environmental variable.

TABLE 4.1   Command-Line Utility Installation Locations

Utility	Install Location
sqlcmd	x:\Program Files\Microsoft SQL Server\90\Tools\Binn
dta	x:\Program Files\Microsoft SQL Server\90\Tools\Binn
tablediff	x:\Program Files\Microsoft SQL Server\90\COM
sac	x:\Program Files\Microsoft SQL Server\90\Shared
bcp	x:\Program Files\Microsoft SQL Server\90\Tools\Binn
sqldiag	x:\Program Files\Microsoft SQL Server\90\Tools\Binn
sqlservr	x:\Program Files\Microsoft SQL Server\MSSQL.1\MSSQL\Binn

When testing many of these utilities, it is often easiest to set up a batch file (.BAT) that contains a command to change the directory to the location shown in Table 4.1. After you make this directory change, you can enter the command-line utility with the relevant parameters. Finally, you should enter a PAUSE command so that you can view the output of the utility in the command-prompt window. The following is an example that can be used to test the sac utility (which is discussed in more detail later in this chapter):

```
cd "C:\Program Files\Microsoft SQL Server\90\Shared
sac out c:\SAC_Features_output.xml -I MSSQLSERVER -F
pause
```

After you save the commands in a file with a .BAT extension, you can simply double-click the file to execute it. This is much easier than retyping the commands many times during the testing process.

What's New in SQL Server Command-Line Utilities

SQL Server 2005 offers a number of new command-line utilities that augment the capabilities available with the SQL Server 2005 graphical tools and in some cases provide functionality that is available only from the command prompt. The following new tools are discussed in detail later in this chapter:

- ▶ **sqlcmd**—The sqlcmd utility allows you to execute Transact-SQL (T-SQL) statements and scripts from the command prompt. It provides the same type of functionality that was available in isql and osql in previous versions of SQL Server, but it offers a number of new script execution options that go beyond what was available before.

- ▶ **dta**—The graphical Database Engine Tuning Advisor (DTA) has a related command-line utility named dta. dta is used to analyze a database workload and provide physical design recommendations that can be used to optimize performance.

- ▶ **tablediff**—This utility allows you to compare the data contained within two different tables. This utility was designed to help troubleshoot replication differences, but it can be used in many scenarios where differences in table data must be identified.

▶ **sac**—This utility can be used to import or export settings that related to surface area configuration. It can be a real timesaver and a means for ensuring consistency across a number of SQL Server installations.

Several other command-line utilities that are also new to SQL Server 2005 can be used to launch the graphical tools that come with SQL Server:

▶ **profiler90**—This utility launches the SQL Server Profiler application.

▶ **sqlwb**—This utility launches SQL Server Management Studio (SSMS).

▶ **dtswizard**—This utility launches the SQL Server Import/Export Wizard, which allows you to move data to and from SQL Server data sources. This is the same tool that is launched from SSMS by right-clicking a database and choosing Tasks, Export Data or Import Data.

These tools are not discussed in detail in this chapter, but they are handy alternatives to launching the GUI tools. You simply click Start, Run and enter the utility name or type in the utility name at a command prompt and press Enter.

The `sqlcmd` **Command-Line Utility**

The `sqlcmd` command-line utility is the next generation of the `isql` and `osql` utilities that you may have used in prior versions of SQL Server. It provides the same type of functionality as `isql` and `osql`, including the ability to connect to SQL Server from the command prompt and execute T-SQL commands. The T-SQL commands can be stored in a script file, entered interactively, or specified as command-line arguments to `sqlcmd`.

> **NOTE**
>
> The `isql` and `osql` command-line utilities are not covered in this chapter. `isql` is no longer supported in SQL Server 2005. The `osql` utility is still supported but will be removed in a future version of SQL Server. Make sure to use `sqlcmd` in place of `isql` or `osql`.

The syntax for `sqlcmd` follows:

```
sqlcmd
[{ { -U login_id [ -P password ] } ¦ –E trusted connection }]
[ -z new password ] [ -Z new password and exit]
[ -S server_name [ \ instance_name ] ] [ -H wksta_name ] [ -d db_name ]
[ -l login time_out ] [ -A dedicated admin connection ]
[ -i input_file ] [ -o output_file ]
[ -f < codepage > ¦ i: < codepage > [ < , o: < codepage > ] ]
[ -u unicode output ] [ -r [ 0 ¦ 1 ] msgs to stderr ]
[ -R use client regional settings ]
[ -q "cmdline query" ] [ -Q "cmdline query" and exit ]
```

```
[ -e echo input ] [ -t query time_out ]
[ -I enable Quoted Identifiers ]
[ -v var = "value"...] [ -x disable variable substitution ]
[ -h headers ][ -s col_separator ] [ -w column_width ]
[ -W remove trailing spaces ]
[ -k [ 1 ¦ 2 ] remove[replace] control characters ]
[ -y display_width ] [-Y display_width ]
[ -b on error batch abort ] [ -V severitylevel ] [ -m error_level ]
[ -a packet_size ][ -c cmd_end ]
[ -L [ c ] list servers[clean output] ]
[ -p [ 1 ] print statistics[colon format]]
[ -X [ 1 ] ] disable commands, startup script, environment variables [and exit]
[ -? show syntax summary ]
```

The number of options available for sqlcmd is extensive, but many of the options are not necessary for basic operations. To demonstrate the usefulness of this tool, we will look at several different examples of the sqlcmd utility, from fairly simple (using few options) to more extensive.

Executing the sqlcmd utility

Before getting into the examples, it is important to remember that sqlcmd can be run in several different ways. It can be run interactively from the command prompt, from a batch file, or from a Query Editor window in SSMS. When run interactively, the sqlcmd program name is entered at the command prompt with the required options to connect to the database server. When the connection is established, a numbered row is made available to enter the T-SQL commands. Multiple rows of T-SQL can be entered in a batch; they are executed only after the GO command has been entered. Figure 4.1 shows an example with two simple SELECT statements that were executed interactively with sqlcmd. The connection in this example was established by simply typing sqlcmd at the command prompt to establish a trusted connection to the default instance of SQL Server running on the machine on which the command prompt window is opened.

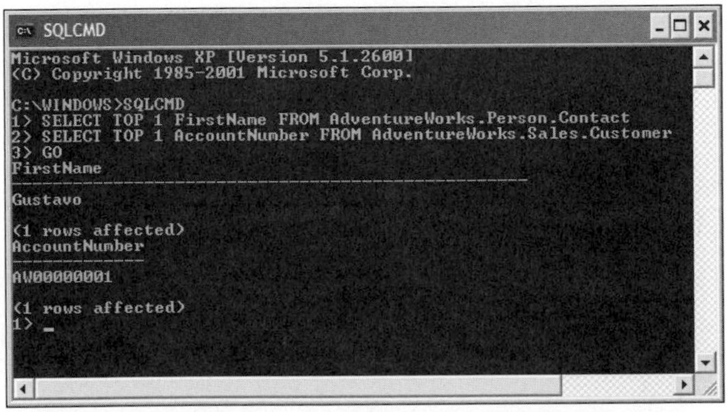

FIGURE 4.1   Executing sqlcmd interactively.

The ability to edit and execute sqlcmd scripts within SSMS is new to SQL Server 2005. A sqlcmd script can be opened or created in a Query Editor window within SSMS. To edit these scripts, you must place the editor in sqlcmd mode. You do so by selecting Query, sqlcmd Mode or by clicking the related toolbar button. When the editor is put in sqlcmd mode, it provides color coding and the ability to parse and execute the commands within the script. Figure 4.2 shows a sample sqlcmd script that is opened in SSMS in a Query Editor window that has been set to sqlcmd mode. The shaded lines are sqlcmd commands.

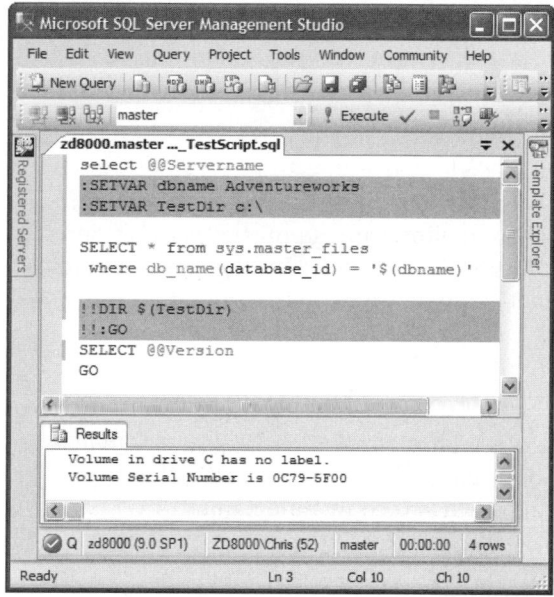

FIGURE 4.2   Executing and editing sqlcmd scripts in SSMS.

The most common means for executing sqlcmd utility is via a batch file. This method can provide a great deal of automation because it allows you to execute a script or many scripts by launching a single file. The examples shown in this section are geared toward the execution of sqlcmd in this manor. The following example illustrates the execution of sqlcmd, using a trusted connection to connect to the local database, and the execution of a simple query that is set using the -Q option:

```
sqlcmd -S (local) -E -Q"select getdate()"
```

You can expand this example by adding an output file to store the results of the query and add the -e option, which echoes the query that was run in the output results:

```
sqlcmd -S (local) -E -Q"select getdate()" -o c:\TestOutput.txt -e
```

The contents of the `c:\TestOutput.txt` file should look similar to this:

```
select getdate()
----------------------
2006-09-13 20:27:25.343
 (1 rows affected)
```

Using a trusted connection is not the only way to use `sqlcmd` to connect to a SQL Server instance. You can use the –U and –P command-line options to specify the SQL Server user and password to use to connect to the server. `sqlcmd` also provides an option to specify the password in an environmental variable named `sqlcmdPASSWORD`, which can be assigned prior to the `sqlcmd` execution and eliminates the need to hard-code the password in a batch file.

`sqlcmd` also provides a means for establishing a dedicated administrator connection (DAC) to the server. The DAC, which is new to SQL Server 2005, is typically used for troubleshooting on a server that is having problems. It allows an administrator to get onto the server when others may not be able to. If the DAC is enabled on the server, a connection can be established with the –A option and a query can be run, as shown in the following example:

```
sqlcmd -S (local) -A -Q"select getdate()"
```

To manage more complex T-SQL execution, it is typically easier to store the T-SQL in a separate input file. The input file can then be referenced as a `sqlcmd` parameter. For example, let's say that you have the following T-SQL stored in a file named `C:\TestsqlcmdInput.sql`:

```
BACKUP DATABASE Master
 TO DISK = 'c:\master.bak'

BACKUP DATABASE Model
 TO DISK = 'c:\model.bak'

BACKUP DATABASE MSDB
 TO DISK = 'c:\msdb.bak'
```

The `sqlcmd` execution, which accepts the `C:\TestsqlcmdInput.sql` file as input and executes the commands within the file, looks like this:

```
sqlcmd -S (local) -E -i"C:\TestsqlcmdInput.sql" -o c:\TestOutput.txt –e
```

The execution of the previous example backs up three of the system databases and writes the results to the output file specified.

Using scripting variables with `sqlcmd`

`sqlcmd` provides a means for utilizing variables within `sqlcmd` input files or scripts. These scripting variables can be assigned as `sqlcmd` parameters or set within the `sqlcmd` script.

To illustrate the use of scripting variables, let's change our previous backup example so that the database that is going to be backed up is a variable. A new input file named `c:\BackupDatabase.sql` should be created, and it should contain the following command:

```
BACKUP DATABASE $(DatabaseToBackup)
 TO DISK = 'c:\$(DatabaseToBackup).bak'
```

The variable in the previous example is named `DatabaseToBackup`. Scripting variables are referenced using the $( ) designators. These are resolved at the time of execution, and a simple replacement is performed. This allows variables to be specified within quotes, if necessary. The –v option is used to assign a value to a variable at the command prompt, as shown in the following example, which backs up the `model` database:

```
sqlcmd -S (local) -E -i"C:\BackupDatabase.sql" -v DatabaseToBackup = model
```

If multiple variables exist in the script, they can all be assigned after the –v parameter and should not be separated by a delimiter, such as a comma or semicolon. Scripting variables can also be assigned within the script, using the `:SETVAR` command. The input file from the previous backup would be modified as follows to assign the `DatabaseToBackup` variable within the script:

```
:SETVAR DatabaseToBackup Model
BACKUP DATABASE $(DatabaseToBackup)
 TO DISK = 'c:\$(DatabaseToBackup).bak'
```

Scripts that utilize variables, `sqlcmd` commands, and the many available options can be very sophisticated and can make your administrative life easier. The examples in this section illustrate some of the basic features of `sqlcmd`, including some of the new features in SQL Server 2005 that go beyond what was available in ISQL or OSQL.

The `dta` Command-Line Utility

`dta` is the command-line version of the graphical Database Engine Tuning Advisor. They both provide performance recommendations based on the workload provided to them. The syntax for `dta` is as follows:

```
        Dta [ -? ] ¦
    [
        [ -S server_name[ \instance ] ]
        {
            { -U login_id [-P password ] }
            ¦ –E                }
            { -D database_name [ ,...n ] }
              [-d database_name ]
              [ -Tl table_list ¦ -Tf table_list_file ]
            { -if workload_file ¦ -it workload_trace_table_name }
```

```
            { -s session_name ¦ -ID session_ID }
               [ -F ]
                      [ -of output_script_file_name ]
                      [ -or output_xml_report_file_name ]
                      [ -ox output_XML_file_name ]
                      [ -rl analysis_report_list [ ,...n ] ]
                      [ -ix input_XML_file_name ]
                      [ -A time_for_tuning_in_minutes ]
                      [ -n number_of_events ]
               [ -m minimum_improvement ]
                      [ -fa physical_design_structures_to_add ]
                      [ -fp partitioning_strategy ]
                      [ -fk keep_existing_option ]
                      [ -fx drop_only_mode ]
               [ -B storage_size ]
               [ -c max_key_columns_in_index ]
               [ -C max_columns_in_index ]
                      [ -e ¦ -e tuning_log_name ]
                      [ -N online_option]
                      [ -q ]
                  [ -u ]
                  [ -x ]
                  [ -a ]

      ]
```

There are an extensive number of options available with this utility, but many of them are not required to do basic analysis. At a minimum, you need to use options that provide connection information to the database, a workload to tune, a tuning session identifier, and the location to store the tuning recommendations. The connection options include –S for the server name, –D for the database, and either –E for a trusted connection or –U and –P, which can be used to specify the user and password.

The workload to tune is either a workload file or a workload table. The –if option is used to specify the workload file location, and the –it option is used to specify a workload table. The workload file must be a Profiler trace file (.trc), a SQL script (.sql) that contains T-SQL commands, or a SQL Server trace file (.log). The workload table is a table that contains output from a workload trace. The table is specified in the form *database_name.owner_name.table_name*.

The tuning session must be identified with either a session name or a session ID. The session name is character based and is specified with the –s option. If the session name is not provided, a session ID must be provided instead. The session ID is numeric and is set using the –ID option. If the session name is specified instead of the session ID, the dta generates an ID anyway.

The last options that are required for a basic dta execution identify the destination to store the dta performance recommendations. The performance recommendations can be

stored in a script file or in XML. The -of option is used to specify the output script filename. XML output is generated when the -or or -ox options are used. The -or option
generates a filename if one is not specified, and the -ox option requires a filename. The
-F option can be used with any of the output options to force an overwrite of a file with
the same name, if one exists.

To illustrate the use dta with the basic options, let's look at an example of tuning a
simple SELECT statement against the AdventureWorks database. To begin, you use the
following T-SQL, which is stored in a workload file named c:\myScript:

```
USE AdventureWorks ;
GO
select *
 from Production.transactionHistory
 where TransactionDate = '9/1/04'
```

The following example shows the basic dta execution options that can be used to acquire
performance recommendations:

```
dta -S zd8000 -E -D AdventureWorks -if c:\MyScript.sql
-s MySessionX -of C:\MySessionOutputScript.sql -F
```

> **NOTE**
>
> dta and other utilities that are executed at the command prompt are executed with all
> the options on a single line. The previous example and any others in this chapter that
> are displayed on more than one line should actually be executed at the command
> prompt or in a batch file on a single line. They are broken here only because the
> printed page can only accommodate a fixed number of characters.

The previous example utilizes a trusted connection against the AdventureWorks database,
a workload file named c:\MyScript.sql, and a session named MySessionX, and it outputs
the performance recommendations to a text file named c:\MySessionOutputScript.sql.
The -F option is used to force a replacement of the output file if it already exists. The
output file contains the following performance recommendations:

```
use [AdventureWorks]
go

CREATE NONCLUSTERED INDEX [_dta_index_TransactionHistory_6]
 ON [Production].[TransactionHistory]
(
    [TransactionDate] ASC
)
INCLUDE ( [TransactionID],
[ProductID],
[ReferenceOrderID],
```

```
[ReferenceOrderLineID],
[TransactionType],
[Quantity],
[ActualCost],
[ModifiedDate]) WITH (SORT_IN_TEMPDB = OFF,
DROP_EXISTING = OFF, IGNORE_DUP_KEY = OFF,
ONLINE = OFF) ON [PRIMARY]
go
```

In short, the `dta` output recommends that a new index be created on the `TransactionDate` column in the `TransactionHistory` table. This is a viable recommendation, considering that there was no index on the `TransactionHistory.TransactionDate` column, and it was used as a search argument in the workload file.

Many other options (that go beyond basic execution) can be used to manipulate the way `dta` makes recommendations. For example, a list can be provided to limit which tables the `dta` looks at during the tuning process. Options can be set to limit the amount of time that the `dta` tunes or the number of events. These options go beyond the scope of this chapter, but you can gain further insight about them by looking at the graphical DTA, which contains many of the same types of options. You can refine your tuning options in the DTA, export the options to an XML file, and use the `-ix` option with the `dta` utility to import the XML options and run the analysis.

The `tablediff` Command-Line Utility

The `tablediff` utility is a new addition to SQL Server 2005. This utility enables you to compare the contents of two tables. It was originally developed for replication scenarios to help troubleshoot nonconvergence, but it is also very useful in other scenarios. When data in two tables should be the same or similar, this tool can help determine whether they are the same, and if they are different, it can identify what data in the tables is different.

The syntax for `tablediff` is as follows:

```
tablediff
[ -? ] ¦
{
        -sourceserver source_server_name[\instance_name]
        -sourcedatabase source_database
        -sourcetable source_table_name
    [ -sourceschema source_schema_name ]
    [ -sourcepassword source_password ]
    [ -sourceuser source_login ]
    [ -sourcelocked ]
        -destinationserver destination_server_name[\instance_name]
        -destinationdatabase subscription_database
        -destinationtable destination_table
```

```
    [ -destinationschema destination_schema_name ]
    [ -destinationpassword destination_password ]
    [ -destinationuser destination_login ]
    [ -destinationlocked ]
    [ -b large_object_bytes ]
    [ -bf number_of_statements ]
    [ -c ]
    [ -dt ]
    [ -et table_name ]
    [ -f [ file_name ] ]
    [ -o output_file_name ]
    [ -q ]
    [ -rc number_of_retries ]
    [ -ri retry_interval ]
    [ -strict ]
    [ -t connection_timeouts ]
}
```

The tablediff syntax requires source and destination connection information in order to perform a comparison. This information includes the servers, databases, and tables that will be compared. Connection information must be provided for SQL Server authentication but can be left out if Windows authentication can be used. The source and destination parameters can be for two different servers or the same server, and the tablediff utility can be run on a machine that is neither the source nor the destination.

To illustrate the usefulness of this tool, let's look at a sample comparison in the AdventureWorks database. The simplest way to create some data for comparison is to select the contents of one table into another and then update some of the rows in one of the tables. The following SELECT statement makes a copy of the AddressType table in the AdventureWorks database to the AddressTypeCopy table:

```
select *
 into Person.AddressTypeCopy
 from Person.AddressType
```

In addition, the following statement updates two rows in the AddressTypeCopy table so that you can use the tablediff utility to identify the changes:

```
UPDATE Person.AddressTypeCopy
 SET Name = 'Billing New'
 WHERE AddressTypeId = 1

UPDATE Person.AddressTypeCopy
 SET Name = 'Shipping New',
  ModifiedDate = '20060918'
 WHERE AddressTypeId = 5
```

The `tablediff` utility can be executed with the following parameters to identify the differences in the `AddressType` and `AddressTypeCopy` tables:

```
tablediff -sourceserver "(local)" -sourcedatabase "AdventureWorks"
-sourceschema "Person" -sourcetable "AddressType"
-destinationserver "(local)" -destinationdatabase "AdventureWorks"
-destinationschema "Person" -destinationtable "AddressTypeCopy"
-f c:\TableDiff_Output.txt
```

The destination and source parameters are the same as in the previous example, except for the table parameters, which have the source `AddressType` and the destination `AddressTypeCopy`. The execution of the utility with these parameters results in the following output to the command prompt window:

```
User-specified agent parameter values:
-sourceserver (local)
-sourcedatabase AdventureWorks
-sourceschema Person
-sourcetable AddressType
-destinationserver (local)
-destinationdatabase AdventureWorks
-destinationschema Person
-destinationtable AddressTypeCopy
-f c:\TableDiff_Output


Table [AdventureWorks].[Person].[AddressType] on (local)
and Table [AdventureWorks].[Person].[AddressTypeCopy] on (local)
have 2 differences.
Fix SQL written to c:\TableDiff_Output.sql.
Err       AddressTypeID    Col
Mismatch          1        Name
Mismatch          5        ModifiedDate Name
The requested operation took 0.296875 seconds.
```

The output first displays a summary of the parameters used and then shows the comparison results. In this example, it found the two differences that are due to updates that were performed on `AddressTypeCopy`. In addition, the –f parameter that was used in the example caused the `tablediff` utility to output a SQL file that can be used to fix the differences in the destination table. The output file from this example looks as follows:

```
-- Host: (local)
-- Database: [AdventureWorks]
-- Table: [Person].[AddressTypeCopy]
SET IDENTITY_INSERT [Person].[AddressTypeCopy] ON
UPDATE [Person].[AddressTypeCopy]
```

```
SET [Name]='Billing'
WHERE [AddressTypeID] = 1
UPDATE [Person].[AddressTypeCopy]
 SET [ModifiedDate]='1998-06-01 00:00:00.000',
 [Name]='Shipping' WHERE [AddressTypeID] = 5
SET IDENTITY_INSERT [Person].[AddressTypeCopy] OFF
```

> **NOTE**
>
> The tablediff utility requires the source table to have at least one primary key, iden-
> tity, or ROWGUID column. This gives the utility a key that it can use to try to match a
> corresponding row in the destination table. If the -strict option is used, the destina-
> tion table must also have a primary key, identity, or ROWGUID column.

Keep in mind that several different types of comparisons can be done with the tablediff
utility. The -q option causes a quick comparison that compares only record counts and
looks for differences in the schema. The -strict option forces the schemas of each table
to be the same when the comparison is run. If this option is not used, the utility allows
some columns to be of different data types, as long as they meet the mapping requirements for the data type (for example, INT can be compared to BIGINT).

The tablediff utility can be used for many different types of comparisons. How you use
this tool depends on several factors, including the amount and type of data you are
comparing.

The sac **Command-Line Utility**

The sac utility allows you to import or export settings that are also available in the GUI
Surface Area Configuration (SAC) tool. Typically, you define these settings with the GUI
tool, and then you can use the sac utility to export those settings to a file. This file can
then be deployed to other machines so that you end up with a consistent set of sac
settings.

The syntax for the sac utility follows:

```
sac {in | out} filename [-S computer_name]
   [-U SQL_login [-P SQL_ password]]
   [-I instance_name ]
   [-DE] [-AS] [-RS] [-IS] [-NS] [-AG] [-BS] [-FT] [-AD]
   [-F] [-N] [-T] [-O]
   [-H | -?]
```

Table 4.2 gives a brief explanation of each of the sac parameters.

TABLE 4.2   sac Parameters

Option	Description
in	Used to import settings.
out	Used to export settings.
-S	Specifies the target computer name.
-U	Specifies the SQL Server login. If this option is not used, Windows authentication is used.
-P	Specifies the SQL Server password associated with the login set with the –U parameter.
-I	Specifies the name of the SQL Server instance to connect to. If it is not specified, all instances are targeted.
-DE	Used to import or export database engine settings.
-AS	Used to import or export Analysis Services settings.
-RS	Used to import or export Reporting Services settings.
-IS	Used to import or export SSIS settings.
-NS	Used to import or export Notification Services settings.
-AG	Used to import or export SQL Server Agent settings.
-BS	Used to import or export SQL Server Browser settings.
-FT	Used to import or export Full-Text Search settings.
-F	Used to import or export feature settings.
-N	Used to import or export network protocols for remote connectivity.
-T	Used to import or export service settings for SQL Server components.
-O	Used to set the name of the file that the command-line output will be written to.
-H -?	Used to get help on sac syntax.

The –S, –U and –P, and –I parameters define the connection information to the target or destination server. Most of the remaining options determine which settings will be imported or exported. These settings are broken down into two main categories: Surface Area Configuration for Services and Connections and Surface Area Configuration for Features. These same two categories are also displayed in the SQL Server 2005 SAC GUI application, as shown at the bottom of Figure 4.3.

When the –F option is used with the sac utility, all the feature options are imported or exported. These are the same features that can be defined with the Surface Area Configuration for Features selection in the GUI application. These features bridge several different components and are either enabled or disabled:

▶ **Database engine features**—Database engine features include ad hoc remote queries, CLR integration, DAC, Database Mail, Native XML Web services, OLE automation, Service Broker, SQL Mail, Web Assistant, and Xp_cmdshell.

▶ **Analysis Services features**—Analysis Services features include ad hoc mining queries, anonymous connections, linked objects, and user-defined functions.

▶ **Reporting Services features**—Reporting Services features include scheduled event and report delivery, Web service and HTTP access, and Windows integrated security.

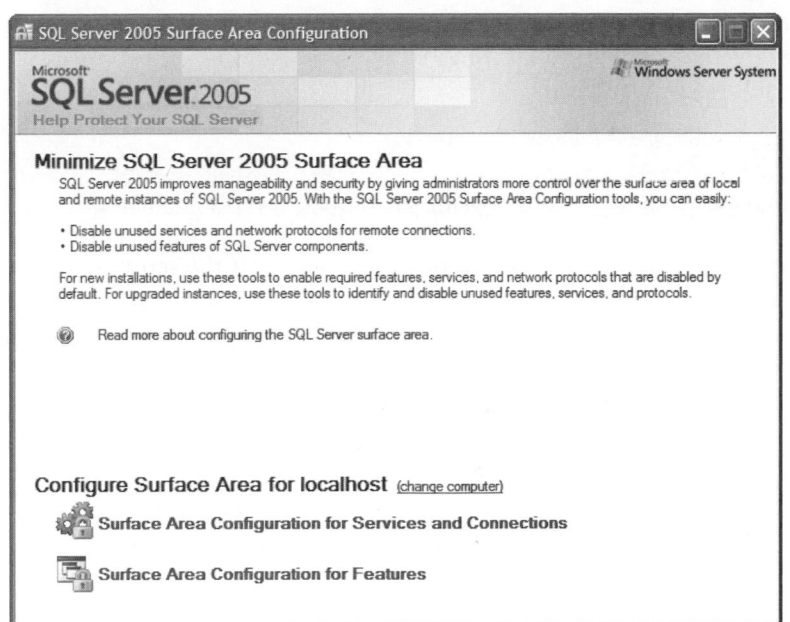

FIGURE 4.3   Configuration options on the SAC GUI.

The following is a sample execution of the sac utility, which exports all the features for the default instance on the local computer on which the sac utility is run:

```
sac out c:\SAC_Features_output.xml -I MSSQLSERVER –F
```

The output file is in XML format and contains a named pair for each feature listed previously. You can transfer this same output file to another machine and execute it with the in clause in order to import the settings to that machine, as shown in the following example:

```
sac in c:\SAC_Features_output.xml -I MSSQLSERVER –F
```

The other category of settings that can be imported or exported with sac relate to services and connections. Each service (for example, the database engine or Integration Services) has a number of settings, including how it will start and the status of the service. In addition, the database engine and Analysis Services have settings that relate to the state of the network protocols for remote connectivity. You can isolate the service settings by using the –T parameter, and you can use the –N option to isolate the settings related to network protocols. The following example gets all settings related to services and connections:

```
sac out c:\SAC_ServicesAndConnections_output.xml -I MSSQLSERVER -T -N
```

If the sac utility is run without the –F parameter or any other setting-specific parameters, all the settings will be targeted, including all settings for features, services, and connections, as shown in the following example:

```
sac in c:\SAC_Features_output.xml -I MSSQLSERVER
```

Many of the remaining parameters are used to isolate settings for specific services or components. For example, the –DE parameter causes sac to focus only on the database engine settings. The –RS parameter causes sac to only import or export the settings related to Reporting Services. More than one of these types of parameters can be used on a single sac execution, as shown in the following example, which exports all settings for the database engine and the SQL Server Agent:

```
sac out c:\SAC_dbAndAgent_output.xml -I MSSQLSERVER -DE -AG
```

The sac parameters provide a great deal of flexibility in choosing the settings that you want to work with. After you determine which settings you want to isolate, you can export them and then import them in the database environments that you want to make consistent.

The bcp **Command-Line Utility**

You use the bcp (bulk copy program) tool to address the bulk movement of data. The utility is bidirectional, allowing for the movement of data into and out of a SQL Server database.

The SQL Server 2005 and SQL Server 2000 versions of bcp utilize the ODBC bulk copy API instead of the DB-LIB API that was used in earlier versions of SQL Server. The ODBC bulk copy API is used to support new data types that the DB-LIB API does not support. Backward compatibility options are provided with the SQL Server 2005 bcp utility to allow bulk copy of data types supported in earlier versions.

bcp uses the following syntax:

```
bcp {[[database_name.][owner].]{table_name ¦ view_name} ¦ "query"}
    {in ¦ out ¦ queryout ¦ format} data_file
    [-mmax_errors] [-fformat_file] [-x] [-eerr_file]
    [-Ffirst_row] [-Llast_row] [-bbatch_size]
    [-n] [-c] [-N] [-w] [-V (60 ¦ 65 ¦ 70 ¦ 80)] [-6]
    [-q] [-C { ACP ¦ OEM ¦ RAW ¦ code_page } ] [-tfield_term]
    [-rrow_term] [-iinput_file] [-ooutput_file] [-apacket_size]
    [-Sserver_name[\instance_name]] [-Ulogin_id] [-Ppassword]
    [-T] [-v] [-R] [-k] [-E] [-h"hint [,...n]"]
```

Some of the commonly used options—other than the ones used to specify the database, such as user ID, password, and so on—are the –F and –L options. These options allow you to specify the first and last row of data to be loaded from a file, which is especially helpful in large batches. The –t option allows you to specify the field terminator that separates data elements in an ASCII file. The –E option allows you to import data into SQL Server fields that are defined with identity properties.

TIP

The BULK INSERT T SQL statement and SSIS are good alternatives to bcp. The BULK INSERT statement is limited to loading data into SQL Server, but it is an extremely fast tool for loading data. SSIS is a sophisticated GUI that allows for both data import and data export, and it has capabilities that go well beyond those that were available in SQL Server 2000's Data Transformation Services (DTS).

This section barely scratches the surface when it comes to the capabilities of bcp. For a more detailed look at bcp, refer to the section, "Using bcp" in Chapter 40, "SQL Server Integration Services."

The sqldiag **Command-Line Utility**

sqldiag is a diagnostic tool that you can use to gather diagnostic information regarding various SQL Server services. It is intended for use by Microsoft support engineers, but you might also find the information it gathers useful in troubleshooting a problem. sqldiag collects the information into files that are written, by default, to a folder named SQLDIAG, where the file sqldiag.exe is located (for example, C:\Program Files\Microsoft SQL Server\90\Tools\binn\SQLDIAG\). The folder holds files that contain information about the machine on which SQL Server is running in addition to the following types of diagnostic information:

- ▶ SQL Server configuration information

- ▶ SQL Server blocking output

- ▶ SQL Server Profiler traces

- ▶ Windows performance logs

- ▶ Windows event logs

The syntax for sqldiag has changed quite a bit in SQL Server 2005, and some of the options that were used in prior versions of sqldiag are not compatible with the current version. The full syntax for sqldiag is as follows:

```
sqldiag
    { [/?] }
    :
    :
    { [/I configuration_file]
      [/O output_folder_path]
      [/P support_folder_path]
      [/N output_folder_management_option]
      [/C file_compression_type]
```

```
    [/B [+]start_time]
    [/E [+]stop_time]
    [/A SQLdiag_application_name]
    [/Q] [/G] [/R] [/U] [/L] [/X] }
  ┊
  ┊
{ [START ¦ STOP ¦ STOP_ABORT] }
  ┊
  ┊
{ [START ¦ STOP ¦ STOP_ABORT] /A SQLdiag_application_name }
```

> **NOTE**
>
> Keep in mind that many of the new options for `sqldiag` identify how and when the `sqldiag` utility will be run. The utility can now be run as a service, scheduled to start and stop at a specific time of day, and it can be configured to change the way the output is generated. The details about these options are beyond the scope of this chapter but are covered in detail in SQL Server Books Online. This section is intended to give you a taste of the useful information that this utility can capture.

By default, the `sqldiag` utility must be run by a member of the Windows Administrators group, and this user must also be a member of the sysadmin fixed SQL Server role. To get a flavor for the type of information that `sqldiag` outputs, you should open a command prompt window, change the directory to the location of the `sqldiag.exe` file, and type the following command:

`sqldiag`

No parameters are needed in order to generate the output. The command prompt window scrolls status information across the screen as it collects the diagnostic information. You see the message "SQLDIAG Initialization starting..." followed by messages that indicate what information is being collected. The data collection includes a myriad of system information from `MSINFO32`, default traces, and SQLDumper log files. When you are ready to stop the collection, you can press Ctrl+C.

If you navigate to the `sqldiag` output folder, you find the files that were created during the collection process. You should find a file with a name containing `MSINFO32` in this output folder. It contains the same type of information that you see when you launch the System Information application from Accessories or when you run `MSINFO32.EXE`. This is key information about the machine on which SQL Server is running. This information includes the number of processors, the amount of memory, the amount of disk space, and a slew of other hardware and software data.

You also find a file named *xxx*`_sp_sqldiag_Shutdown.out`, where *xxx* is the name of the SQL Server machine. This file contains SQL Server–specific information, including the SQL Server error logs, output from several key system stored procedures, including `sp_helpdb` and `sp_configure`, and much more information related to the current state of SQL Server.

You find other files in the sqldiag output directory as well. Default trace files, log files related to the latest sqldiag execution, and a copy of the XML file containing configuration information are some of them. Microsoft documentation on these files is limited, and you may find that the best way to determine what they contain is simply to open the files and review the wealth of information they contain.

The sqlservr **Command-Line Utility**

The sqlservr executable is the program that runs when SQL Server is started. You can use the sqlservr executable to start SQL Server from a command prompt. When you do that, all the startup messages are displayed at the command prompt, and the command prompt session becomes dedicated to the execution of SQL Server.

CAUTION

If you start SQL Server from a command prompt, you cannot stop or pause it by using SSMS, Configuration Manager, or the Services applet in the Control Panel. You should stop the application only from the command prompt window in which SQL Server is running. If you press Ctrl+C, you are asked whether you want to shut down SQL Server. If you close the command prompt window in which SQL Server is running, SQL Server is automatically shut down.

The syntax for the sqlserver utility is as follows:

```
sqlservr [-sinstance_name] [-c] [-dmaster_path] [-f]
    [-eerror_log_path] [-lmaster_log_path] [-m]
    [-n] [-Ttrace#] [-v] [-x] [-gnumber] [-h]
```

Most commonly, you start SQL Server from the command prompt if you need to troubleshoot a configuration problem. The –f option starts SQL Server in minimal configuration mode. This allows you to recover from a change to a configuration setting that prevents SQL Server from starting. You can also use the –m option when you need to start SQL Server in single-user mode, such as when you need to rebuild one of the system databases.

SQL Server functions when started from the command prompt in much the same way as it does when it is started as a service. Users can connect to the server, and you can connect to the server by using SSMS. What is different is that the SQL Server instance running in the command prompt appears as if it is not running in some of the tools. SSMS and SQL Server Service Manager show SQL Server as being stopped because they are polling the SQL Server service, which is stopped when running in the command prompt mode.

> **TIP**
>
> If you simply want to start the SQL Server service from the command prompt, you can use the NET START and NET STOP commands. These commands are not SQL Server specific but are handy when you want to start or stop SQL Server, especially in a batch file. The SQL Server service name must be referenced after these commands. For example, NET START MSSQLSERVER starts the default SQL Server instance.

Removed or Deprecated Utilities in SQL Server 2005

A significant number of command-line utilities have been removed or deprecated in SQL Server 2005. Utilities that have been removed are no longer supported. Those that have been deprecated are still supported but will be removed in a future version of SQL Server. These utilities are not covered in detail in this chapter but are worth noting. You may have used these utilities in prior versions of SQL Server, and you certainly need to know what their status is now. Table 4.3 provides an alphabetic list of the utilities that have been removed or deprecated and provides a brief description of the function of each.

TABLE 4.3   Removed or Deprecated Command-Line Utilities

Utility	Description	Status
isql	This utility was used to execute SQL statements, stored procedures, and script files from the command prompt. You should use sqlcmd instead.	Removed
makepipe	This utility is used to verify a client's connectivity to SQL Server through named pipes.	Deprecated
odbcping	This utility is used to test a client machine's ODBC connectivity to the database server.	Deprecated
osql	This utility is used to execute SQL statements, stored procedures, and script files from the command prompt. You can use sqlcmd instead.	Deprecated
readpipe	This utility is used to verify a client's connectivity to SQL Server through named pipes.	Deprecated
rebuildm	This utility was used was used to rebuild the master database. You can use the REBUILDDATABASE option in the setup.exe file to achieve the same result.	Removed
regrebld	This utility was used to back up and restore the SQL Server Registry entries.	Removed
sqlmaint	This utility is used to execute maintenance plans that were created in previous versions of SQL Server.	Deprecated

Summary

SQL Server provides a set of command-line utilities that allow you to execute some of the SQL Server programs from the command prompt. Much of the functionality housed in these utilities is also available in graphical tools, such as SSMS. However, the ability to initiate these programs from the command prompt is invaluable in certain scenarios.

Chapter 5, "SQL Server Profiler," covers a tool that is critical for performance tuning in SQL Server 2005. SQL Server Profiler provides critical insight by monitoring and capturing the activity occurring on a SQL Server instance.

4

SQL Server Profiler

IN THIS CHAPTER

▶ What's New with SQL Server Profiler

▶ SQL Server Profiler Architecture

▶ Creating Traces

▶ Executing Traces and Working with Trace Output

▶ Saving and Exporting Traces

▶ Replaying Trace Data

▶ Defining Server-Side Traces

▶ Profiler Usage Scenarios

This chapter explores the SQL Server Profiler, one of SQL Server's most powerful auditing and analysis tools. The SQL Server Profiler gives you a basic understanding of database access and helps you answer questions such as these:

▶ Which queries are causing table scans on my invoice history table?

▶ Am I experiencing deadlocks, and, if so, why?

▶ What SQL queries is each application submitting?

▶ Which were the 10 worst-performing queries last week?

▶ If I implement this alternative indexing scheme, how will it affect my batch operations?

SQL Server Profiler records activity that occurs on a SQL Server instance. The tool has a great deal of flexibility and can be customized for your needs. You can direct SQL Server Profiler to record output to a window, a file, or a table. You can specify which events to trace, the information to include in the trace, how you want it grouped, and what filters you want to apply.

What's New with SQL Server Profiler

There are many new features in and changes to the SQL Server 2005 Profiler. These changes pervade the application and include the following:

▶ **New Profiler GUI**—The changes to the Profiler GUI application are dramatic. The way that a trace is created, the selection of events, and the general look and feel of the application are quite different than in previous versions.

▶ **New events**—Many new traceable events have been added to the Profiler. These new events include those that are included in entirely new event categories, such as Broker (Service Broker), CLR, Full Text, and OLE DB. In addition, many new events have been added to categories that existed in past versions, such as Deadlock graph, which can be selected from the Locks category.

▶ **New columns**—More than 20 new data columns are available with the SQL Server 2005 Profiler. New columns such as LineNumber and RowCounts help provide additional insight into what is occurring during a trace.

▶ **XML enhancement**—Trace, showplan, and deadlock results can now be stored in XML format. Trace results that are saved in XML can be edited and loaded back into the SQL Profiler for replay. Showplan results that are saved in XML can be opened in an SSMS Query Editor window, and the graphical execution plans will be rendered. Deadlock results that are captured in XML can be opened and viewed with a graphical display that helps easily identify the processes involved in the deadlock.

▶ **Performance Monitor integration**—You can now view trace file output and Performance Monitor files together. The integrated display is synchronized in such a way that you can correlate performance problems with specific activity in your trace output.

SQL Server Profiler Architecture

SQL Server 2005 has both a server and a client-side component for tracing activity on a server. The SQL trace facility is the server-side component that manages queues of events that are initiated by event producers on the server. Extended stored procedures can be used to define the server-side events that are to be captured. These procedures, which define a SQL trace, are discussed later in this chapter, in the section, "Defining Server-Side Traces."

The SQL Profiler is the client-side tracing facility. It comes with a fully functional GUI that allows for real-time auditing of SQL Server events. When it is used to trace server activity, events that are part of a trace definition are gathered at the server. Any filters that are defined as part of the trace definition are applied and the event data is queued for its final destination. The SQL Profiler application is the final destination when client-side tracing is used. The basic elements involved in this process are shown in Figure 5.1.

This figure illustrates the following four steps in the process when tracing from the SQL Server Profiler:

1. Event producers, such as the Query Processor, Lock Manager, ODS, and so on, raise events for the SQL Server Profiler.

2. The filters define the information to submit to SQL Server Profiler. A producer will not send events if the event is not included in the filter.

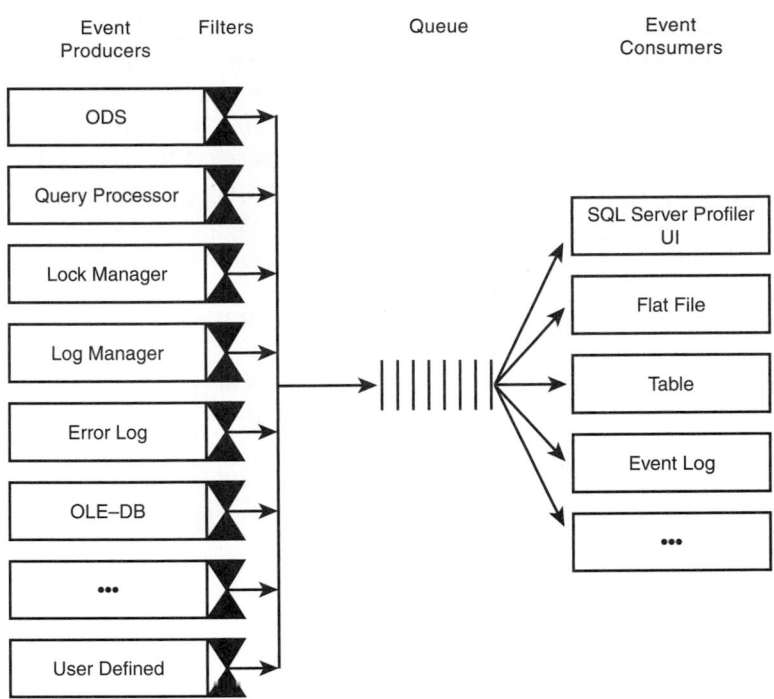

FIGURE 5.1   SQL Server Profiler's architecture.

3. SQL Server Profiler queues all the events.

4. SQL Server Profiler writes the events to each defined consumer, such as a flat file, a table, the Profiler client window, and so on.

In addition to obtaining its trace data from the event producers listed in step 1, you can also configure SQL Profiler so that it obtains its data from a previously saved location. This includes trace data that was saved in a file or table. The "Saving and Exporting Traces" section, later in this chapter, covers using trace files and trace tables in more detail.

Creating Traces

Because SQL Server Profiler can trace numerous events, it is easy to get lost when reading the trace output. You need to roughly determine the information you need and how you want the information grouped. For example, if you want to see the SQL statements that each user is submitting through an application, you could trace incoming SQL statements and group them by user and by application.

Once you have an idea about what you want to trace you should launch the SQL Server Profiler. The Profiler can be launched by selecting Start then SQL Server 2005 then Performance Tools and finally SQL Server Profiler. It can also be launched from within SSMS from the Tools menu. When you launch the Profiler, you are presented with an application window that is basically empty. To start a new trace, you select the File menu and choose New Trace. A connection dialog box is displayed that enables you to enter the connectivity information for the server you want to trace. After the connection is established, the General tab of the Trace Properties window (see Figure 5.2) is displayed.

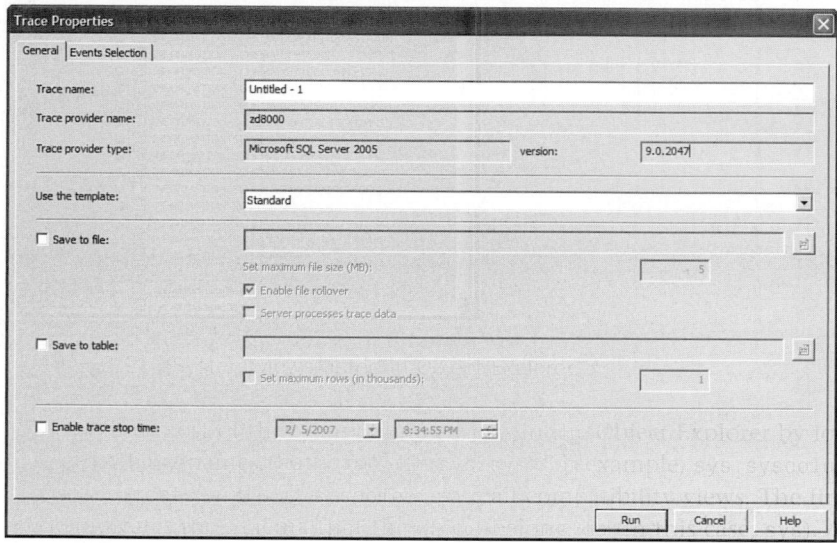

FIGURE 5.2   General trace properties.

The first place you should look when creating a new trace is at the trace templates. These templates contain predefined trace settings that address some common auditing needs. These templates have preset events, data columns, and filters that are targeted at specific profiling scenarios. The available trace templates are found in the template drop-down on the General Properties page and are listed in Table 5.1.

TABLE 5.1   SQL Profiler Templates

Template	Description
SP_Counts	Tracks all the stored procedures as they start. No event except for the stored procedure starting is traced.
Standard	Traces the completion of SQL statements and remote procedure calls (RPCs) as well as key connection information.
TSQL	Traces the start of SQL statements and RPCs. This template is useful for debugging client applications where some of the statements are not completing successfully.

TABLE 5.1   Continued

Template	Description
TSQL_Duration	Traces the total execution time for each completed SQL statement or RPC.
TSQL_Grouped	Traces the start of SQL statements and RPCs, grouped by `Application`, `NTUser`, `LoginName`, and `ClientProcessId`.
TSQL_Replay	Captures profiling information that is useful for replay. It contains the same type of information as the standard template, but it adds more detail, including cursor and RPC output details.
TSQL_SPs	Traces detailed stored procedures, including the start and completion of each stored procedure. The SQL statements within each procedure are traced as well.
Tuning	A streamlined trace that only tracks the completion of SQL statements and RPCs. The completion events provide duration details that can be useful for performance tuning.

Keep in mind that the templates that come with SQL Server 2005 are not actual traces. They simply provide a foundation for you in creating your own traces. After you select a template, you can modify the trace setting and customize it for your own needs. You can then save the modified template as its own template file that will appear in the template drop-down list for future trace creation.

Trace Name is another property that you can modify on the General tab. Trace Name is a relatively unimportant trace property for future traces. When you create a new trace, you can specify a name for the trace; however, this trace name will not be used again. For instance, if you have a trace definition you like, you can save it as a template file. If you want to run the trace again in the future, you can create a new trace and select the template file that you saved. You will not be selecting the trace to run based on the trace name you entered originally. Trace Name is useful only if you are running multiple traces simultaneously and need to distinguish between them more easily.

TIP

Do yourself a favor and save your favorite trace definitions in your own template. The default set of templates that come with SQL Server are good, but you will most likely want to change the position of a column or add an event that you find yourself using all the time. It is not hard to adjust one of the default templates to your needs each time, but if you save your own template with exactly what you need, it makes it all the more easy. Once you save your own template, you can set it as the default template, and it will be executed by default every time you start the Profiler.

The Save to File and Save to Table options on the General Properties page allow you to define where the trace output is stored. You can save the output to a flat file or a SQL Server table. These options are discussed in more detail later in the chapter, in the section "Saving and Exporting Traces."

The last option on the General Properties screen is the Enable Trace Stop Time option. This scheduling-oriented feature allows you to specify a date and time at which you want to stop tracing. This is handy if you want to start a trace in the evening before you go home. You can set the stop time so that the trace will run for a few hours but won't affect any nightly processing that might occur later in the evening.

Events

The events and data columns that will be captured by your Profiler trace are defined on the Events Selection tab. An example of the Events Selection tab is shown in Figure 5.3.

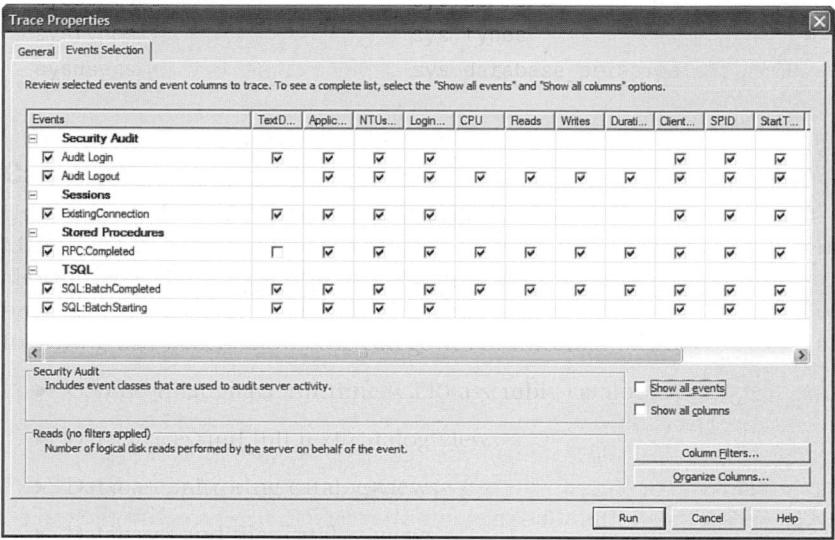

FIGURE 5.3   The Events Selection tab.

The Events Selection tab has changed dramatically in SQL Server 2005. It consolidates the selection of events, data columns, and filters on one tab. In SQL Server 2000, there were three separate tabs for each of these elements. One of the biggest advantages of the SQL Server 2005 Events Selection tab is that you can easily determine which data columns will be populated for each event by looking at the columns that have check boxes available for the event. For example, the Audit Login event has check boxes for Text Data, ApplicationName, and others but does not have a check box available for CPU, Reads, Writes, and other data columns that are not relevant to the event. For those data columns that have check boxes, you have the option of unchecking the box so that the data column will not be populated for the event when the trace is run.

In SQL Server 2000, if was not obvious what columns would be populated for a particular event. All the data columns were available for selection, regardless of the events chosen. You could determine the columns that were going to be populated for the event by looking at Books Online, but this was more time-consuming and less intuitive than the SQL Server 2005 approach.

On the flip side, you may find that adding events in SQL Server 2005 is less intuitive than it was in SQL Server 2000. When you select a template, the event categories, the selected events in those categories, and the selected columns are displayed in the Events Selection tab. Now, if you want to add additional columns, how do you do it? The answer to this question lies in the Show All Events check box in the lower-right corner of the Events Selection tab. When you click this check box, all the available event categories are listed on the screen. The events and columns that you had previously selected may or may not be visible on the screen. They are not lost, but you may need to scroll down the Events Selection tab to find the event categories that contain the events that you had selected prior to selecting the Show All Events check box.

You will also notice that all the events in the categories in which you had events selected are displayed. In other words, if you had only 2 events selected in the Security Audit category and then selected the Show All Events check box, you see all 42 events listed. The only 2 events that are selected are the ones that you had selected previously, but you need to wade through many events to see them. One upside to this kind of display is that you can easily view all the events for a category and the columns that relate to the events. One possible downside is that the Events Selection tab can be very busy, and it may take a little extra time to find what you are looking for.

TIP

If you capture too many events in one trace, the trace becomes difficult to review. Instead, you can create several traces, one for each type of information that you want to examine, and run them simultaneously. You can also choose to add or remove events after the trace has started. New to SQL Server 2005 is the ability to pause a running trace, change the selected events, and restart the trace without losing the output that was there prior to pausing the trace. In SQL Server 2000, if you didn't want to lose the prior output, you had to save the results to a file or table in this situation.

The selection and viewing of events is made easier by using the tree control that is available on each event. The tree control allows you to expand or compress an event category. When you click the + icon next to a category, all the events are displayed. When you click the - icon, the event category is collapsed to a single row on the display. When an event has been selected for use within a category, the category name is shown in bold. If you want to add all the events in a category to your trace, you can simply right-click the category name and choose the Select Event Category option. You can also remove all events in a category by right-clicking the category name and choosing the Deselect Event Category option.

Understanding what each of the events captures can be a challenging task. You can refer to "SQL Server Event Class Reference" in Books Online for a detailed description, or you can use the simple Help facility available on the Events Selection tab. The Events Selection tab has a Help facility that describes each of the events and categories. The Help text is displayed on the Events Selection tab below the list of available events. When you mouse over a particular event or event category, a description of that item is shown. This puts the information you need at your fingertips.

> **NOTE**
>
> If you are going to use SQL Server Profiler, you should spend some time getting to know the events first and the type of output that Profiler generates. You should do this first in a development environment or standalone environment where the Profiler's effect on performance does not matter. It's a good idea to start a trace with a few events at a time and execute some relevant statements to see what is displayed for each event. You will soon realize the strength of the SQL Server Profiler and the type of valuable information it can return.

Data Columns

The columns of information that are captured in a Profiler trace are determined by the Data Columns selected. The Events Selection tab has the functionality you need to add columns, organize the columns, and apply filters on the data that is returned in these columns. As mentioned earlier, you can select and deselect the available columns for a particular event by using the check boxes displayed for the listed events. To understand what kind of information a column is going to return, you can simply mouse over the column, and Help for that item is displayed in the second Help box below the event list. Figure 5.4 shows an example of the Help output. In this particular case, the mouse pointer is over the `ApplicationName` column that is returned for the `SQL:BatchCompleted` event. The first Help box displays information about the `SQL:BatchCompleted` event. The second Help box shows information about the data column.

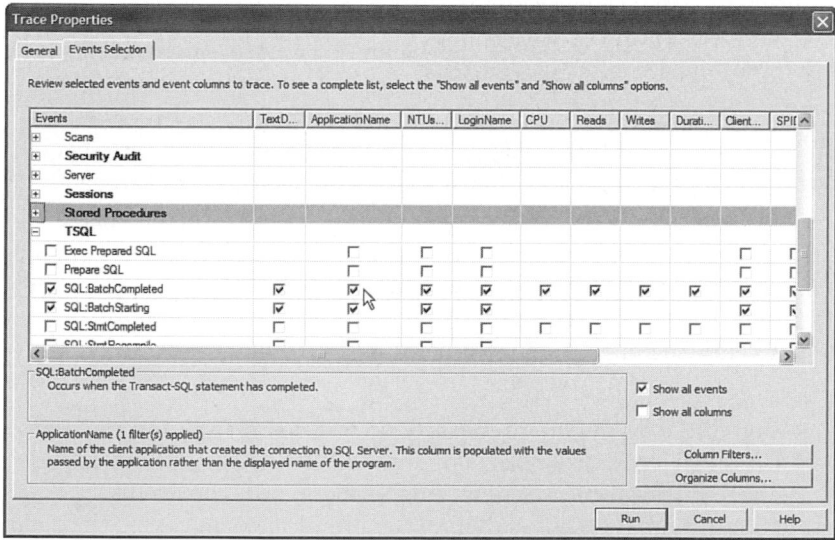

FIGURE 5.4   Help for data columns on the Events Selection tab.

Keep in mind that there is a default set of columns that is displayed for each event. You can view additional columns by selecting the Show All Columns check box. When you choose this option, an additional set of columns is displayed in the Events Selection tab. The additional columns are shown with a dark gray background, and you may need to scroll to the right on the Events Selection tab in order to see them. Figure 5.5 shows an example of the additional columns that are displayed for the Cursors event when the Show All Columns option is used. Some of the additional columns that are available for selection in this example are DatabaseID and DatabasedName.

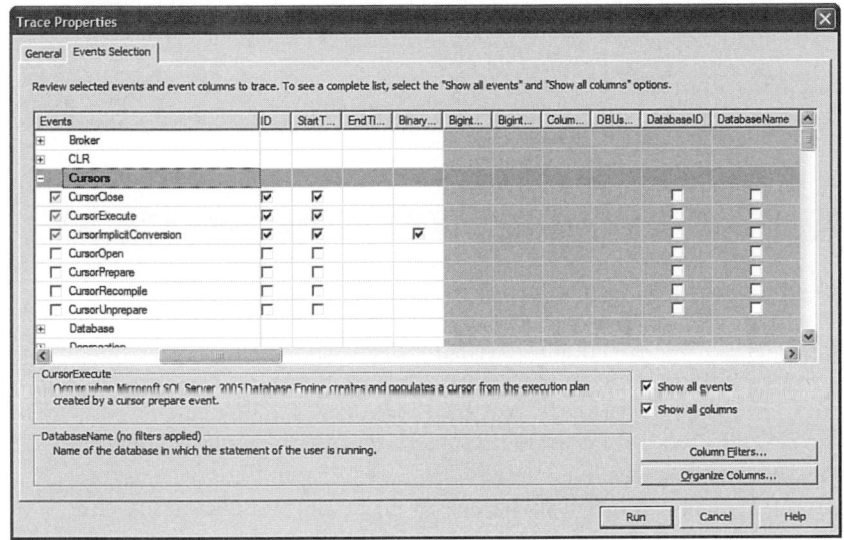

FIGURE 5.5   Additional columns displayed with the Show All Columns option.

To organize the columns that you have selected, you can choose the Organize Columns selection on the Events Selection tab. This Organize Columns window allows you to change the order of the columns in the trace output as well as group the data by selected columns. Figure 5.6 shows an example of the Organize Columns window with the groups and columns that are selected by default when you use the TSQL_Grouped template.

To change the order of a column, you simply select the column in the list and use the Up or Down buttons to move it. The same movement can be done with columns that have been selected for grouping. You add columns to groups by selecting the column in the data list and clicking the Up button until the column is moved out of the Columns list and into the Groups list. For example, in Figure 5.6, you can group the SPID column by selecting it and clicking the Up button one time, which places it in the Groups tree structure instead of the Columns tree structure.

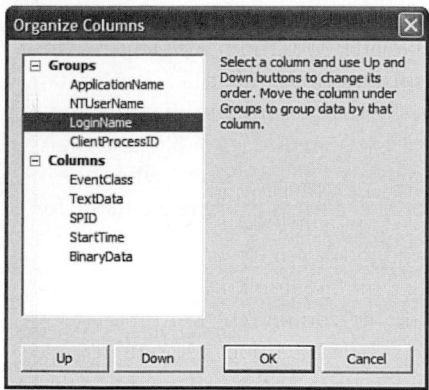

FIGURE 5.6   Organizing columns in the Events Selection tab.

> **TIP**
>
> You can select a particular column for all events by right-clicking the column header in the Events Selection tab and choosing the Select Column option. This causes all the check boxes on the grid to be selected. To remove a column from all events, you right-click the column header and choose Deselect Column.

The number of columns selected for grouping and the order of the columns are both important factors in the way the trace data will be displayed. If you choose only one column for grouping, the trace window displays events grouped by the values in the grouped data column and collapses all events under it. For example, if you group by DatabaseId, the output in the trace window grid displays DatabaseId as the first column, with a + sign next to each DatabaseId that has received events. The number displayed to the right of the event in parentheses shows the number of collapsed events that can be viewed by clicking on the + sign. Figure 5.7 shows an example of the trace output window that has been grouped by DatabaseId only. The database with a DatabaseId equal to 6 is shown at the bottom of the grid in this example. The grid has been expanded and some of the 20 events that were captured for this DatabaseId are shown.

If you select multiple columns for grouping, the output in the trace window is ordered based on the columns in the grouping. The events are not rolled up like a single column, but the trace output grid automatically places the incoming events in the proper order in the output display.

> **TIP**
>
> The organization of columns in a trace can happen after a trace has been defined and executed. If you save the trace to a file or a table, you can open it later and specify whatever ordering or grouping you want to reorganize the output. This flexibility gives you almost endless possibilities for analyzing the trace data.

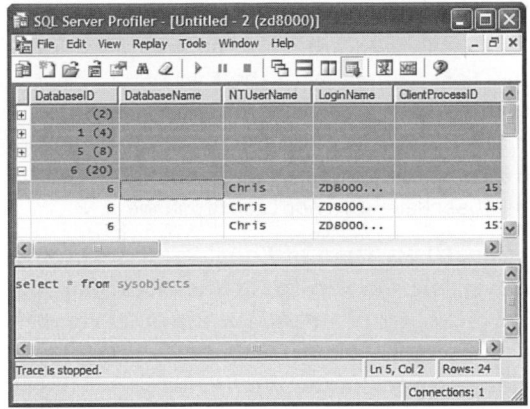

FIGURE 5.7   Grouping on a single column.

Filters

Filters restrict the event data that is returned in your trace output. You can filter the events that are captured by the SQL Profiler via the Column Filters button on the Events Selection tab. The SQL Server 2005 Edit Filter window that is displayed is much different than that which was used in SQL Server 2000. An example of the new window is shown in Figure 5.8. All the available columns for the trace are shown on the right side of the Edit Filter window, along with any defined filters. Those columns that have filters on them have a filter icon displayed next to the column in the column list.

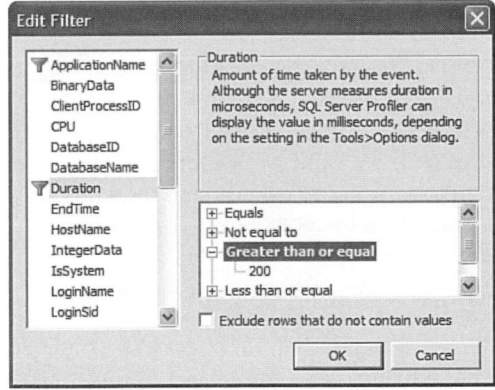

FIGURE 5.8   Editing filter properties.

The filtering options in SQL Server 2005 are similar to those available in SQL Server 2000. Which options are available depends on the type of column you are filtering on. The following list describes the different filtering options:

▶ **Like/Not Like**—This gives you the ability to include or exclude events based on a wildcard. You should use the % character as your wildcard character and press Enter to create an entry space for another value. For example, with the `ApplicationName` filter, you can specify `Like Microsoft%`, and you will get only those events related to applications that match the wildcard, such as Microsoft SQL Server Management Studio. This filtering option is available for text data columns and data columns that contain name information, such as `NTUserName` and `ApplicationName`.

▶ **Equals/Not Equal To/Greater Than or Equal/Less Than or Equal**—Filters with this option have all four of these conditions available. For the Equals and Not Equal To conditions, you can specify a single value or a series of values. For the other conditional types, a single value is supplied. For example, you can filter on `DataBaseID` and input numeric values under the `Equals To` node of the filtering tree. This filtering option is available for numeric data columns such as `Duration`, `IndexId`, and `ObjectId`.

▶ **Greater Than/Less Than**—This type of filtering option is available only on time-based data columns. This includes `StartTime` and `EndTime` filters. These filters expect date formats of the form YYYY-MM-DD or YYYY-MM-DD HH:MM:SS.

Each data column can use one of these three filtering options. When you click the data column that is available for filtering, you see the filtering options for that column displayed in the right pane of the Edit Filter window. You enter the values on which you want to filter in the data entry area on the filter tree. This input area is shown when you select a specific filtering option. For multiple filter values, you press the Enter key after you enter each value. This causes a new data entry area to appear below the value you were on.

> **CAUTION**
>
> Filters that are applied to columns that are not available or selected for an event do not prevent the event data from being returned. For example, if you place a filter on the `ObjectName` column and choose the `SQL:StmtStarting` event as part of your trace, the event data is not filtered because `ObjectName` is not a valid column for that event. This may seem relatively intuitive, but it is something to consider when you are receiving output from a trace that you believe should have been filtered out.
>
> Also, be careful when specifying multiple filter values and consider the Boolean logic that is applied to them. When specifying multiple values for the `Like` filter, the values are evaluated with an `OR` condition. For example, if you create a filter on `ObjectName` and have a `Like` filter with values of A%, B%, and C%, the filter will return object names that start with A or B or C. When you use the `Not Like` filter, the `AND` condition is used on multiple values. For example, `Not Like` filter values for `ObjectName` of A% and C% results in objects with names that do not start with A and object names that do not start with C.

Executing Traces and Working with Trace Output

After you have defined the events and columns that you want to capture in a trace, you can execute the Profiler trace. To do so, you click the Run button on the Trace Properties window, and the Profiler GUI starts capturing the events you have selected. The GUI contains a grid that is centrally located on the Profiler window, and newly captured events are scrolled on the screen as they are received. Figure 5.9 shows a simple example of the Profiler screen with output from an actively running trace.

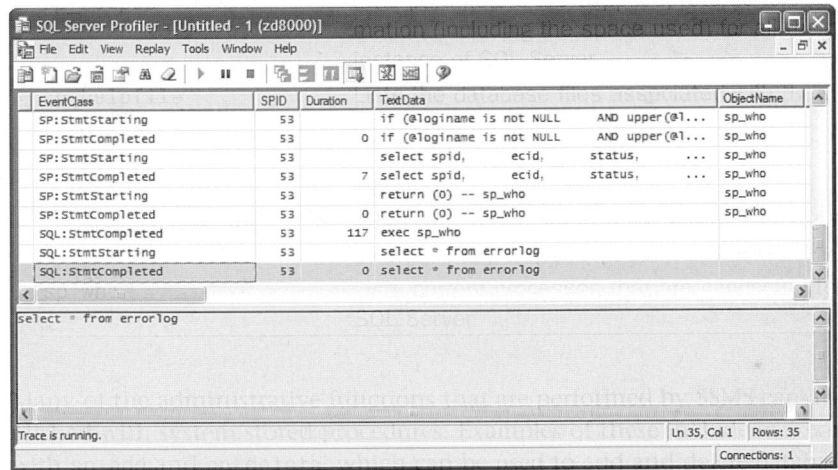

FIGURE 5.9   The Profiler GUI with an active trace.

The Profiler GUI provides many different options for dealing with an actively running trace. You can turn off scrolling on the trace, pause the trace, stop the trace, and view the properties of an actively running trace. You can find strings within the trace output, and you can even move the columns around in the display so that they are displayed in a different order. These options provide a great deal of flexibility and allow you to focus on the output that is most important to you.

Saving and Exporting Traces

In many cases, you will want to save or export the trace output generated by a Profiler trace. The output can be analyzed, replayed, imported, or manipulated at a later time after it has been saved. Trace output can be saved as the trace is running or saved after it has been generated to the Profiler GUI. The Trace Properties window provides options for saving trace output while the trace is running. The options are defined using the Save to File and Save to Table options on the General tab of the Trace Properties dialog. You can save to a file, a table, or both a table and a file. Figure 5.10 shows an example of a trace that will save to both a file and a table while it is executing.

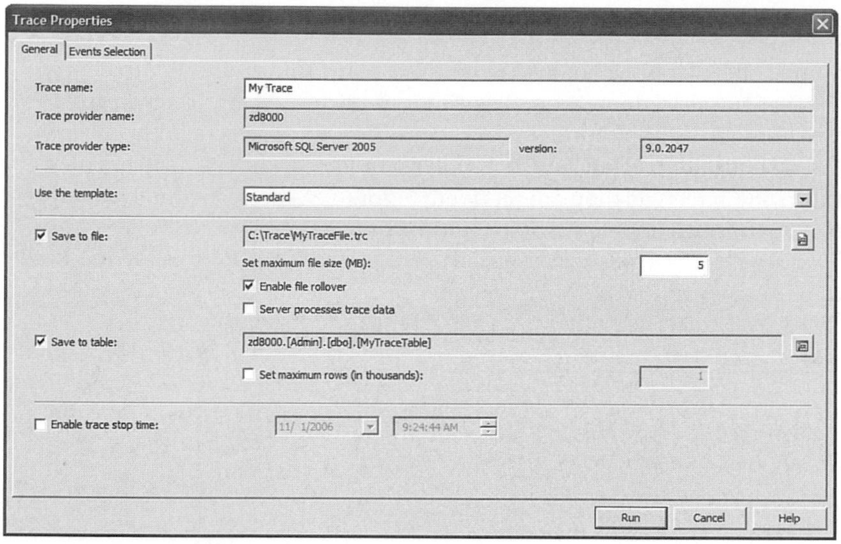

FIGURE 5.10   Saving trace output while a trace is running.

Saving Trace Output to a File

When you save a running trace to a file, you have several options for controlling the output. One option you should always consider is the Set Maximum File Size (MB) option. This option prevents a trace output file from exceeding the specified size. This helps make the file more manageable and, more importantly, it can save you from having a trace file gobble up all the disk space on the drive you are writing to. Remember that the amount of trace data that is written to a file on a busy production system can be extensive. You can also use this file size option in conjunction with the Enable File Rollover option. When the Enable File Rollover option is used, the trace does not stop when the file size maximum is met. Instead, a new trace file is created, and the output is generated to that file until it reaches the file size maximum.

Saving Trace Output to a Table

The Save to Table option writes the trace output directly to a SQL Server table as the trace is running. Having the data in a SQL table provides a great deal of flexibility for analyzing the data. You can use the full power of Transact-SQL against the table, including sorting, grouping, and more complex search conditions than are not available through the SQL Profiler filters.

You need to consider both the disk space requirements and the impact on performance when the Save to Table option is used. The Profiler provides an option, Set Maximum Rows (in Thousands), to limit the amount of output generated from the trace. The performance impact depends on the volume of data that is being written to the table. Generally, writing the trace output to a table should be avoided with high-volume SQL servers. The best option for high-volume servers is to first write the trace output to a file and then import the file to a trace table at a later time.

Saving the Profiler GUI Output

Another option for saving trace output occurs after trace output has been generated to the Profiler GUI and the trace has been stopped. Similar to the save options for an executing trace, the GUI output can be saved to a file or table. You access the options to save the GUI output by selecting File, Save As. The Trace File and Trace Table options are used to save to a file or table consecutively. With SQL Server 2005, you can also save the output to an XML file. The Trace XML File and Trace XML File for Replay options generate XML output that can be edited or used as input for replay with the SQL Server Profiler.

NOTE

Two distinct save operations are available in the SQL Profiler. You can save trace events to a file or table as just described, or you can save a trace definition in a template file. The Save As Trace Table and Save As Trace File options are for saving trace events to a file. The Save As Trace Template option saves the trace definition. Saving a trace template saves you the trouble of having to go through all the properties each time to set up the events, data columns, and filters for your favorite traces.

An alternative to saving all the event data associated with a particular trace is to select specific event rows from the SQL Profiler windows. You can capture all the trace information associated with a trace row by selecting a row in the trace output window of Profiler and choosing Edit, Copy. Or, you can just copy the event text (typically a SQL statement) by selecting the row, highlighting the text in the lower pane, and using the Copy option. You can then paste this data into SSMS or the tool of your choice for further execution and more detailed analysis. This can be particularly useful during performance tuning. After you identify the long-running statement or procedure, you can copy the SQL, paste it into SSMS, and display the query plan to determine why the query was running so long.

Importing Trace Files

A trace saved to a file or table can be read back into SQL Profiler at a later time for more detailed analysis or to replay the trace on the same SQL Server or another SQL Server instance. You can import data from a trace file or trace table by choosing File, Open and then selecting either a trace file or trace table. If you choose to open a trace file, you are presented with a dialog box to locate the trace file on the local machine. If you choose to import a trace table, you are first presented with a connection dialog box to specify the SQL Server name, the login ID, and the password to connect to it. When you are successfully connected, you are presented with a dialog box to specify the database and the name of the trace table you want to import from. After you specify the trace file or trace table to import into Profiler, the entire contents of the file or table are read in and displayed in a Profiler window.

You may find that large trace files or trace tables are difficult to analyze, and you may just want to analyze events associated with a specific application or table, or a specific types of queries. To limit the amount of information displayed in the Profiler window, you can filter out the data displayed via the Properties dialog. You can choose which events and data columns you want to display and also specify conditions in the Filters tab to limit the rows displayed from the trace file or trace table. These options do not affect the information stored in the trace file or trace table—only what information is displayed in the Profiler window.

Importing a Trace File into a Trace Table

Although you can load a trace file directly into Profiler for analysis, very large files can be difficult to analyze. Profiler loads an entire file. For large files, this can take quite a while, and the responsiveness of Profiler might not be the best. Multiple trace output files for a given trace can also be cumbersome and difficult to manage when those files are large.

You can use the trace filters to limit which rows are displayed but not which rows are imported into Profiler. You often end up with a bunch of rows displayed with no data in the columns you want to analyze. In addition, while the filters allow you to limit which rows are displayed, they don't really provide a means of running more complex reports on the data, such as generating counts of events or displaying the average query duration.

Fortunately, SQL Server 2005 provides a way for you to selectively import a trace file into a trace table. When importing a trace file into a trace table, you can filter the data before it goes into the table as well as combine multiple files into a single trace table. Once the data is in a trace table, you can load the trace table into Profiler or write your own queries and reports against the trace table for more detailed analysis than is possible in Profiler.

Microsoft SQL Server includes some built-in user-defined functions for working with Profiler traces. The `fn_trace_gettable` function is used to import trace file data into a trace table. The following is the syntax for this function:

```
fn_trace_gettable( [ @filename = ] filename , [ @numfiles = ] number_files )
```

This function returns the contents of the specified file as a table result set. You can use the result set from this function just as you would any table. By default, the function returns all possible Profiler columns, even if no data was captured for the column in the trace. To limit the columns returned, you specify the list of columns in the query. If you want to limit the rows retrieved from the trace file, you specify your search conditions in the WHERE clause. If your Profiler trace used rollover files to split the trace across multiple files, you can specify the number of files you want it to read in. If the default value of `default` is used, all rollover files for the trace are loaded. Listing 5.1 provides an example of creating and populating a trace table from a trace file, using SELECT INTO, and then adding rows by using an INSERT statement. Note that this example limits the columns and rows returned by specifying a column list and search conditions in the WHERE clause.

LISTING 5.1   Creating and Inserting Trace Data into a Trace Table from a Trace File

```
/********************************************************************
** NOTE - you will need to edit the path/filename on your system if
**        you use this code to load your own trace files
********************************************************************/

select EventClass,
       EventSubClass,
       TextData = convert(varchar(8000), TextData),
       BinaryData,
       ApplicationName,
       Duration,
       StartTime,
       EndTime,
       Reads,
       Writes,
       CPU,
       ObjectID,
       IndexID,
       NestLevel
    into TraceTable
    FROM ..fn_trace_gettable('c:\temp\sampletrace_20060826_0232.trc', default)
    where TextData is not null
       or EventClass in (16, --  Attention
                         25, -- Lock:Deadlock
                         27, -- Lock:Timeout
                         33, -- Exception
                         58, -- Auto Update Stats
                         59, -- Lock:Deadlock Chain
                         79, -- Missing Column Statistics
                         80, -- Missing Join Predicate
                         92, -- Data File Auto Grow
                         93, -- Log File Auto Grow
                         94, -- Data File Auto Shrink
                         95) -- Log File Auto Shrink

Insert into TraceTable (EventClass, EventSubClass,
            TextData, BinaryData,
            ApplicationName, Duration, StartTime, EndTime, Reads, Writes,
            CPU, ObjectID, IndexID, nestlevel)
     select EventClass, EventSubClass,
            TextData = convert(varchar(7900), TextData), BinaryData,
            ApplicationName, Duration, StartTime, EndTime, Reads, Writes,
            CPU, ObjectID, IndexID, nestlevel
        FROM ::fn_trace_gettable('c:\temp\sampletrace_20060826_0108.trc', -1)
```

LISTING 5.1   Continued

```
        where TextData is not null
            or EventClass in (16, -- Attention
                              25, -- Lock:Deadlock
                              27, -- Lock:Timeout
                              33, -- Exception
                              58, -- Auto Update Stats
                              59, -- Lock:Deadlock Chain
                              79, -- Missing Column Statistics
                              80, -- Missing Join Predicate
                              92, -- Data File Auto Grow
                              93, -- Log File Auto Grow
                              94, -- Data File Auto Shrink
                              95) -- Log File Auto Shrink
go
```

Once the trace file is imported into a trace table, you can open the trace table in Profiler or run your own queries against the trace table from a Query Editor window in SSMS. For example, the following query returns the number of lock timeouts encountered for each table during the period the trace was running:

```
select object_name(ObjectId), count(*)
    from TraceTable
    where EventClass = 27 -- Lock:Timout Event
    group by object_name(ObjectId)
go
```

Analyzing Trace Output with the Database Engine Tuning Advisor

In addition to being able to manually analyze traces in Profiler, you can also use the new Database Engine Tuning Advisor to analyze the queries captured in a trace and recommend changes to your indexing scheme. The Database Engine Tuning Advisor is a replacement for the Index Tuning Wizard. You can invoke it from the Tools menu in SQL Profiler. The Database Engine Tuning Advisor can read in a trace that was previously saved to a table or a file. This allows you to capture a workload, tune the indexing scheme, and rerun the trace to determine whether the index changes improved performance as expected.

Because the Database Engine Tuning Advisor analyzes SQL statements, you need to make sure that the trace includes one or more of the following events:

```
SP:StmtCompleted
SP:StmtStarting
SQL:BatchCompleted
SQL:BatchStarting
```

```
SQL:StmtCompleted
SQL:StmtStarting
```

One of each class (one `SP:` and one `SQL:`) is sufficient to capture dynamic SQL statements and statements embedded in stored procedures. You should also make sure that the trace includes the text data column, which contains the actual queries.

The Database Engine Tuning Advisor analyzes the trace and gives you recommendations, along with an estimated improvement-in-execution time. You can choose to create indexes now or at a later time, or you can save the `CREATE INDEX` commands to a script file.

Replaying Trace Data

To replay a trace, you must have a trace saved to a file or a table. The trace must be captured with certain trace events to enable playback. The required events are captured by default if you use the Profiler template `TSQL_Replay`. You can define a trace to be saved when you create or modify the trace definition. You can also save the current contents of the trace window to a file or table by using the Save As Trace File or Save As Trace Table options in the File menu.

To replay a saved trace, you use the File, Open menu to open a trace file or a trace table. After you select the type of trace to replay, a grid with the trace columns selected in the original trace is displayed. At this point, you can either start the replay of the trace step-by-step or complete execution of the entire trace. The options for replaying the trace are found under the Replay menu. When you start the replay of the trace, the Connect to Server dialog is displayed, enabling you to choose the server that you want to replay the traces against. Once you are connected to a server, a Replay Configuration dialog box like the one shown in Figure 5.11 is displayed.

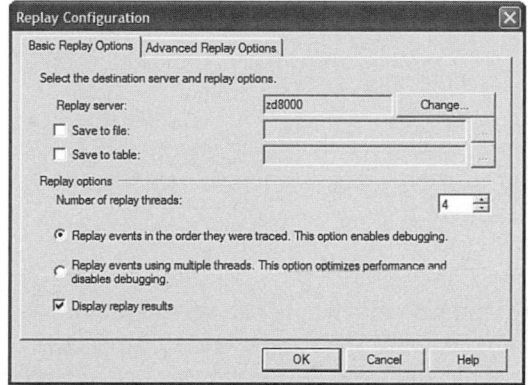

FIGURE 5.11   Basic replay options.

The first replay option, which is enabled by default, replays the trace in the same order in which it was captured and allows for debugging. The second option takes advantage of multiple threads; it optimizes performance but disables debugging. A third option involves specifying whether to display the replay results. You would normally want to see the results, but for large trace executions, you might want to forgo displaying the results and send them to an output file instead.

If you choose the option that allows for debugging, you can execute the trace in a manner similar to many programming tools. You can set breakpoints, step through statements one at a time, or position the cursor on a statement within the trace and execute the statements from the beginning of the trace to the cursor position.

> **NOTE**
>
> Automating testing scripts is another important use of the SQL Profiler Save and Replay options. For instance, a trace of a heavy production load can be saved and rerun against a new release of the database to ensure that the new release has similar or improved performance characteristics and returns the same data results. The saved traces can help make regression testing much easier.

You also have the option of specifying advanced replay options in SQL Server 2005. These are new options that are found on the Advanced Replay Options tab of the Replay Configuration dialog box (see Figure 5.12).

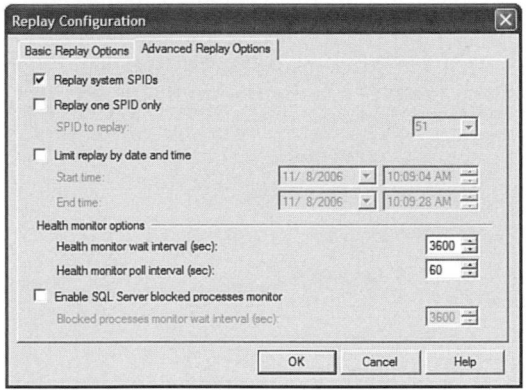

FIGURE 5.12   Advanced replay options.

The first two options on the Advanced Replay Options tab relate to the system process IDs (SPIDs) that will be targeted for replay. If the Replay System SPIDs option is selected, then the trace events for every SPID in the trace file will be replayed. If you want to target activity for a specific SPID, you should choose the Replay One SPID Only option and select the SPID from the drop-down menu. You can also limit the events that will be replayed based on the timing of the events. If you want to replay a specific time-based section of the trace, you can use the Limit Replay by Date and Time option. Only those trace events that fall between the data range you specify will be replayed.

The last set of advanced options are geared toward maintaining the health of the server on which you are replaying the trace. The Health Monitor Wait Interval (sec) option determines the amount of time a thread can run during replay before being terminated. This helps avoid an excessive drain on the server's resources. The Health Monitor Poll Interval (sec) option determines how often the health monitor will poll for threads that should be terminated. The last advanced option on the screen relates to blocked processes. When it is enabled, the monitor will poll for blocked processes according to the interval specified.

Defining Server-Side Traces

Much of the SQL Server Profiler functionality can also be initiated through a set of system stored procedures. Through these procedures, you can define a server-side trace that can be run automatically or on a scheduled basis, such as via a scheduled job, instead of through the Profiler GUI. Server-side traces are also useful if you are tracing information over an extended period of time or are planning on capturing a large amount of trace information. The overhead of running a server-side trace is less than that of running a client-side trace with Profiler.

To start a server-side trace, you need to define the trace by using the trace-related system procedures. These procedures can be called from within a SQL Server stored procedure or batch. You define a server-side trace by using the following four procedures:

- ▶ **sp_trace_create**—This procedure is used to create the trace definition. It sets up the trace and defines the file to store the captured events. sp trace create returns a trace ID number that you'll need to reference from the other three procedures to further define and manage the trace.

- ▶ **sp_trace_setevent**—You need to call this procedure once for each data column of every event that you want to capture.

- ▶ **sp_trace_setfilter**—You call this procedure once for each filter you want to define on an event data column.

- ▶ **sp_trace_setstatus**—After the trace is defined, you call this procedure to start, stop, or remove the trace. You must stop and remove a trace definition before you can open and view the trace file.

You will find that manually creating procedure scripts for tracing can be rather tedious. Much of the tedium is due to the fact that many numeric parameters drive the trace execution. For example, the sp_trace_setevent procedure accepts an eventid and a columnid that determine what event data will be captured. Fortunately, SQL Server 2005 provides a set of catalog views that contain these numeric values and what they represent. The sys.trace_categories catalog view contains the event categories. The sys.trace_ events catalog view contains the trace events, and sys.trace_columns contains the trace columns. The following SELECT statement utilizes two of these system views to return the available events and their related categories:

```
select e.trace_event_id, e.name 'Event Name', c.name 'Category Name'
 from sys.trace_events e
  join sys.trace_categories c on e.category_id = c.category_id
 order by e.trace_event_id
```

The results of this SELECT statement are shown in Table 5.2.

TABLE 5.2   Trace Events and Their Related Categories

trace_event_id	Event Name	Category Name
10	RPC:Completed	Stored Procedures
11	RPC:Starting	Stored Procedures
12	SQL:BatchCompleted	TSQL
13	SQL:BatchStarting	TSQL
14	Audit Login	Security Audit
15	Audit Logout	Security Audit
16	Attention	Errors and Warnings
17	ExistingConnection	Sessions
18	Audit Server Starts And Stops	Security Audit
19	DTCTransaction	Transactions
20	Audit Login Failed	Security Audit
21	EventLog	Errors and Warnings
22	ErrorLog	Errors and Warnings
23	Lock:Released	Locks
24	Lock:Acquired	Locks
25	Lock:Deadlock	Locks
26	Lock:Cancel	Locks
27	Lock:Timeout	Locks
28	Degree of Parallelism (7.0 Insert)	Performance
33	Exception	Errors and Warnings
34	SP:CacheMiss	Stored Procedures
35	SP:CacheInsert	Stored Procedures
36	SP:CacheRemove	Stored Procedures
37	SP:Recompile	Stored Procedures
38	SP:CacheHit	Stored Procedures
39	Deprecated	Stored Procedures
40	SQL:StmtStarting	TSQL
41	SQL:StmtCompleted	TSQL
42	SP:Starting	Stored Procedures
43	SP:Completed	Stored Procedures
44	SP:StmtStarting	Stored Procedures

TABLE 5.2   Continued

trace_event_id	Event Name	Category Name
45	SP:StmtCompleted	Stored Procedures
46	Object:Created	Objects
47	Object:Deleted	Objects
50	SQLTransaction	Transactions
51	Scan:Started	Scans
52	Scan:Stopped	Scans
53	CursorOpen	Cursors
54	TransactionLog	Transactions
55	Hash Warning	Errors and Warnings
58	Auto Stats	Performance
59	Lock:Deadlock Chain	Locks
60	Lock:Escalation	Locks
61	OLEDB Errors	OLEDB
67	Execution Warnings	Errors and Warnings
68	Showplan Text (Unencoded)	Performance
69	Sort Warnings	Errors and Warnings
70	CursorPrepare	Cursors
71	Prepare SQL	TSQL
72	Exec Prepared SQL	TSQL
73	Unprepare SQL	TSQL
74	CursorExecute	Cursors
75	CursorRecompile	Cursors
76	CursorImplicitConversion	Cursors
77	CursorUnprepare	Cursors
78	CursorClose	Cursors
79	Missing Column Statistics	Errors and Warnings
80	Missing Join Predicate	Errors and Warnings
81	Server Memory Change	Server
82	UserConfigurable:0	User configurable
83	UserConfigurable:1	User configurable
84	UserConfigurable:2	User configurable
85	UserConfigurable:3	User configurable
86	UserConfigurable:4	User configurable
87	UserConfigurable:5	User configurable
88	UserConfigurable:6	User configurable
89	UserConfigurable:7	User configurable
90	UserConfigurable:8	User configurable
91	UserConfigurable:9	User configurable
92	Data File Auto Grow	Database

TABLE 5.2   Continued

trace_event_id	Event Name	Category Name
93	Log File Auto Grow	Database
94	Data File Auto Shrink	Database
95	Log File Auto Shrink	Database
96	Showplan Text	Performance
97	Showplan All	Performance
98	Showplan Statistics Profile	Performance
100	RPC Output Parameter	Stored Procedures
102	Audit Database Scope GDR Event	Security Audit
103	Audit Schema Object GDR Event	Security Audit
104	Audit Addlogin Event	Security Audit
105	Audit Login GDR Event	Security Audit
106	Audit Login Change Property Event	Security Audit
107	Audit Login Change Password Event	Security Audit
108	Audit Add Login to Server Role Event	Security Audit
109	Audit Add DB User Event	Security Audit
110	Audit Add Member to DB Role Event	Security Audit
111	Audit Add Role Event	Security Audit
112	Audit App Role Change Password Event	Security Audit
113	Audit Statement Permission Event	Security Audit
114	Audit Schema Object Access Event	Security Audit
115	Audit Backup/Restore Event	Security Audit
116	Audit DBCC Event	Security Audit
117	Audit Change Audit Event	Security Audit
118	Audit Object Derived Permission Event	Security Audit
119	OLEDB Call Event	OLEDB
120	OLEDB QueryInterface Event	OLEDB
121	OLEDB DataRead Event	OLEDB
122	Showplan XML	Performance
123	SQL:FullTextQuery	Performance
124	Broker:Conversation	Broker
125	Deprecation Announcement	Deprecation
126	Deprecation Final Support	Deprecation
127	Exchange Spill Event	Errors and Warnings
128	Audit Database Management Event	Security Audit
129	Audit Database Object Management Event	Security Audit
130	Audit Database Principal Management Event	Security Audit

TABLE 5.2   Continued

trace_event_id	Event Name	Category Name
131	Audit Schema Object Management Event	Security Audit
132	Audit Server Principal Impersonation Event	Security Audit
133	Audit Database Principal Impersonation Event	Security Audit
134	Audit Server Object Take Ownership Event	Security Audit
135	Audit Database Object Take Ownership Event	Security Audit
136	Broker:Conversation Group	Broker
137	Blocked process report	Errors and Warnings
138	Broker:Connection	Broker
139	Broker:Forwarded Message Sent	Broker
140	Broker:Forwarded Message Dropped	Broker
141	Broker:Message Classify	Broker
142	Broker:Transmission	Broker
143	Broker:Queue Disabled	Broker
144	Broker:Mirrored Route State Changed	Broker
146	Showplan XML Statistics Profile	Performance
148	Deadlock graph	Locks
149	Broker:Remote Message Acknowledgement	Broker
150	Trace File Close	Server
152	Audit Change Database Owner	Security Audit
153	Audit Schema Object Take Ownership Event	Security Audit
155	FT:Crawl Started	Full text
156	FT:Crawl Stopped	Full text
157	FT:Crawl Aborted	Full text
158	Audit Broker Conversation	Security Audit
159	Audit Broker Login	Security Audit
160	Broker:Message Undeliverable	Broker
161	Broker:Corrupted Message	Broker
162	User Error Message	Errors and Warnings
163	Broker:Activation	Broker
164	Object:Altered	Objects
165	Performance statistics	Performance
166	SQL:StmtRecompile	TSQL
167	Database Mirroring State Change	Database
168	Showplan XML For Query Compile	Performance

5

TABLE 5.2   Continued

trace_event_id	Event Name	Category Name
169	Showplan All For Query Compile	Performance
170	Audit Server Scope GDR Event	Security Audit
171	Audit Server Object GDR Event	Security Audit
172	Audit Database Object GDR Event	Security Audit
173	Audit Server Operation Event	Security Audit
175	Audit Server Alter Trace Event	Security Audit
176	Audit Server Object Management Event	Security Audit
177	Audit Server Principal Management Event	Security Audit
178	Audit Database Operation Event	Security Audit
180	Audit Database Object Access Event	Security Audit
181	TM: Begin Tran starting	Transactions
182	TM: Begin Tran completed	Transactions
183	TM: Promote Tran starting	Transactions
184	TM: Promote Tran completed	Transactions
185	TM: Commit Tran starting	Transactions
186	TM: Commit Tran completed	Transactions
187	TM: Rollback Tran starting	Transactions
188	TM: Rollback Tran completed	Transactions
189	Lock:Timeout (timeout > 0)	Locks
190	Progress Report: Online Index Operation	Progress Report
191	TM: Save Tran starting	Transactions
192	TM: Save Tran completed	Transactions
193	Background Job Error	Errors and Warnings
194	OLEDB Provider Information	OLEDB
195	Mount Tape	Server
196	Assembly Load	CLR
198	XQuery Static Type	TSQL
199	QN: Subscription	Query Notifications
200	QN: Parameter table	Query Notifications
201	QN: Template	Query Notifications
202	QN: Dynamics	Query Notifications

The numeric IDs for the trace columns can be obtained from the sys.trace_columns catalog view, as shown in the following example:

```
select trace_column_id, name 'Column Name', type_name 'Data Type'
 from sys.trace_columns
 order by trace_column_id
```

Table 5.3 shows the results of this SELECT statement and lists all the available trace columns.

TABLE 5.3   Trace Columns Available for a Server-Side Trace

trace_column_id	Column Name	Data Type
1	TextData	text
2	BinaryData	image
3	DatabaseID	int
4	TransactionID	bigint
5	LineNumber	int
6	NTUserName	nvarchar
7	NTDomainName	nvarchar
8	HostName	nvarchar
9	ClientProcessID	int
10	ApplicationName	nvarchar
11	LoginName	nvarchar
12	SPID	int
13	Duration	bigint
14	StartTime	datetime
15	EndTime	datetime
16	Reads	bigint
17	Writes	bigint
18	CPU	int
19	Permissions	bigint
20	Severity	int
21	EventSubClass	int
22	ObjectID	int
23	Success	int
24	IndexID	int
25	IntegerData	int
26	ServerName	nvarchar
27	EventClass	int
28	ObjectType	int
29	NestLevel	int
30	State	int
31	Error	int
32	Mode	int
33	Handle	int
34	ObjectName	nvarchar
35	DatabaseName	nvarchar
36	FileName	nvarchar
37	OwnerName	nvarchar

5

TABLE 5.3   Continued

trace_column_id	Column Name	Data Type
38	RoleName	nvarchar
39	TargetUserName	nvarchar
40	DBUserName	nvarchar
41	LoginSid	image
42	TargetLoginName	nvarchar
43	TargetLoginSid	image
44	ColumnPermissions	int
45	LinkedServerName	nvarchar
46	ProviderName	nvarchar
47	MethodName	nvarchar
48	RowCounts	bigint
49	RequestID	int
50	XactSequence	bigint
51	EventSequence	int
52	BigintData1	bigint
53	BigintData2	bigint
54	GUID	uniqueidentifier
55	IntegerData2	int
56	ObjectID2	bigint
57	Type	int
58	OwnerID	int
59	ParentName	nvarchar
60	IsSystem	int
61	Offset	int
62	SourceDatabaseID	int
63	SqlHandle	image
64	SessionLoginName	nvarchar
65	PlanHandle	image

You have to call the sp_trace_setevent procedure once for each data column you want captured for each event in the trace. Based on the number of events and number of columns, you can see that this can result in a lot of executions of the sp_trace_setevent procedure for a larger trace.

To set up filters, you must pass the column ID, the filter value, and numeric values for the logical operator and the column operator to the sp_trace_setfilter procedure. The logical operator can be either 0 or 1. A value of 0 indicates that the specified filter on the column should be ANDed with any other filters on the column, while a value of 1 indicates that the OR operator should be applied. Table 5.4 describes the values allowed for the column operators.

TABLE 5.4   Column Operator Values for `sp_trace_setfilter`

Value	Comparison Operator
0	= (equal)
1	<> (not equal)
2	> (greater than)
3	< (less than)
4	>= (greater than or equal)
5	<= (less than or equal)
6	LIKE
7	NOT LIKE

Fortunately, there is an easier way of generating a trace definition script. You can set up your traces by using the SQL Profiler GUI and script the trace definition to a file. When you have the trace defined and have specified the events, data columns, and filters you want to use, you select File, Export, Script Trace Definition. The SQL commands (including calls to the aforementioned system stored procedures) to define the trace, start the trace, and write the trace to a file are generated into one script file. You have the option to generate a script for either SQL Server 2000 or 2005. Listing 5.2 shows an example of a trace definition that was exported from the Profiler. It contains the trace definitions for the TSQL trace template. You must replace the text InsertFileNameHere with an appropriate filename, prefixed with its pathname, before running this script.

LISTING 5.2   A SQL Script for Creating and Starting a Server-Side Trace

```
/******************************************************/
/* Created by: SQL Server Profiler 2005           */
/* Date: 11/12/2006  09:55:24 AM          */
/******************************************************/

-- Create a Queue
declare @rc int
declare @TraceID int
declare @maxfilesize bigint
set @maxfilesize = 5

-- Please replace the text InsertFileNameHere, with an appropriate
-- filename prefixed by a path, e.g., c:\MyFolder\MyTrace. The .trc extension
-- will be appended to the filename automatically. If you are writing from
-- remote server to local drive, please use UNC path and make sure server has
-- write access to your network share

exec @rc = sp_trace_create @TraceID output, 0, N'InsertFileNameHere',
   @maxfilesize, NULL
if (@rc != 0) goto error
```

LISTING 5.2   Continued

```
-- Client side File and Table cannot be scripted

-- Set the events
declare @on bit
set @on = 1
exec sp_trace_setevent @TraceID, 14, 1, @on
exec sp_trace_setevent @TraceID, 14, 14, @on
exec sp_trace_setevent @TraceID, 14, 12, @on
exec sp_trace_setevent @TraceID, 15, 14, @on
exec sp_trace_setevent @TraceID, 15, 12, @on
exec sp_trace_setevent @TraceID, 17, 12, @on
exec sp_trace_setevent @TraceID, 17, 1, @on
exec sp_trace_setevent @TraceID, 17, 14, @on
exec sp_trace_setevent @TraceID, 11, 2, @on
exec sp_trace_setevent @TraceID, 11, 14, @on
exec sp_trace_setevent @TraceID, 11, 12, @on
exec sp_trace_setevent @TraceID, 13, 12, @on
exec sp_trace_setevent @TraceID, 13, 1, @on
exec sp_trace_setevent @TraceID, 13, 14, @on


-- Set the Filters
declare @intfilter int
declare @bigintfilter bigint

-- Set the trace status to start
exec sp_trace_setstatus @TraceID, 1

-- display trace id for future references
select TraceID=@TraceID
goto finish

error:
select ErrorCode=@rc

finish:
go
```

> **TIP**
>
> If you want to always capture certain trace events when SQL Server is running, such as auditing-type events, you can create a stored procedure that uses the sp_trace stored procedures to create a trace and specify the events to be captured. You can use the code in Listing 5.2 as a basis to create the stored procedure. Then you can mark the procedure as a startup procedure by using the sp_procoption procedure to set the autostart option. The trace automatically starts when SQL Server is started, and it continues running in the background.
>
> Just be aware that although using server-side traces is less intrusive than using the SQL Profiler client, some overhead is necessary to run a trace. You should try to limit the number of events captured to minimize the overhead as much as possible.

Monitoring Running Traces

SQL Server 2005 provides some additional built-in user-defined functions to get information about currently running traces. Like the fn_trace_gettable function discussed previously, these functions return the information as a tabular result. The available functions are as follows:

▶ **fn_trace_getinfo(*trace_id*)**—This function is passed a traceid, and it returns information about the specified trace. If passed the value of default, it returns information about all existing traces. An example of the output from this function is shown in Listing 5.3.

▶ **fn_trace_geteventinfo(*trace_id*)**—This function returns a list of the events and data columns being captured for the specified trace. Only the event and column ID values are returned. You can use the information provided in Tables 5.2 and 5.3 to map the IDs to the more meaningful event names and column names.

▶ **fn_trace_getfilterinfo(*trace_id*)**—This function returns information about the filters being applied to the specified trace. Again, the column ID and logical and comparison operator values are returned as integer IDs that you need to decipher. See Table 5.4 for a listing of the column operator values.

LISTING 5.3   An Example of Using the Built-in User-Defined Functions for Monitoring Traces

```
SELECT * FROM ::fn_trace_getinfo(default)


traceid     property     value
----------  -----------  --------------------------------------------
1           1            2
1           2            C:\Program Files\Microsoft SQL Server\MSSQL.1\
                           MSSQL\LOG\log_375.trc
1           3            20
1           4            NULL
```

LISTING 5.3   Continued

```
1          5          1
2          1          0
2          2          c:\trace\mytrace.trc.trc
2          3          5
2          4          NULL
2          5          1


select * from ::fn_Trace_getfilterinfo(2)

columnid   logical_operator comparison_operator value
---------- ---------------- ------------------- ----------
3          0                0                   6
10         0                7                   Profiler
10         0                7                   SQLAgent
```

> **NOTE**
>
> You may be wondering why there is always a `traceid` with a value of 1 running when you run the `fn_trace_getinfo` procedure. This is the default trace that SQL Server automatically initiates when it starts. The default trace is enabled by default. You can identify which trace is the default by selecting from the `sys.traces` catalog view and examining the `is_default` column. The default trace captures a number of different types of events, including object creates and drops, errors, memory and disk changes, security changes, and more. You can disable this default trace, but it is generally lightweight and should be left enabled.

The output from the functions that return trace information is relatively cryptic because many of the values returned are numeric. For example, the property values returned by `fn_trace_getinfo` are specified as integer IDs. Table 5.5 describes of each of these property IDs.

TABLE 5.5   Description of Trace Property ID Values

Property ID	Description
1	Trace options specified in `sp_trace_create`
2	Trace filename
3	Maximum size of trace file, in MB
4	Date and time the trace will be stopped
5	Current trace status

Stopping Server-Side Traces

It is important to keep track of the traces you have running and to ensure that "heavy" traces are stopped. Heavy traces are typically traces that capture a lot of events and are run on a busy SQL Server. These traces can affect the overall performance of your SQL Server machine and write a large amount of information to the trace output file. If you specified a stop time when you started the trace, it will automatically stop and close when the stop time is reached. For example, in the SQL script in Listing 5.2, if you wanted the trace to run for 15 minutes instead of indefinitely, you'd set the value for the `stoptime` variable at the beginning of the script, using a command similar to the following:

```
set @stoptime = dateadd(minute, 15, getdate())
```

To otherwise stop a running server-side trace, you use the `sp_trace_setstatus` stored procedure and pass it the trace ID and a status of 0. Stopping a trace only stops gathering trace information and does not delete the trace definition from SQL Server. Essentially, it pauses the trace. You can restart the trace by passing `sp_trace_setstatus` a status value of 1.

Once you've stopped a trace, you can close the trace and delete its definition from SQL Server by passing `sp_trace_setstatus` the ID of the trace you want to stop and a status value of 2. After you close the trace, you must redefine it before you can restart it.

If you don't know the ID of the trace you want to stop, you can use the `fn_trace_getinfo` function to return a list of all running traces and select the appropriate trace ID. The following is an example of stopping and closing a trace with a trace ID of 2:

```
-- Set the trace status to stop
exec sp_trace_setstatus 2, 0
go

-- Close and Delete the trace
exec sp_trace_setstatus 2, 2
go
```

If you want to stop and close multiple traces, you must call `sp_trace_setstatus` twice for each trace. Listing 5.4 provides an example of a system stored procedure that you can create in SQL Server to stop a specific trace or automatically stop all currently running traces.

LISTING 5.4   A Sample System Stored Procedure to Stop Profiler Traces

```
use master
go
if object_id ('sp_stop_profiler_trace') is not null
    drop proc sp_stop_profiler_trace
go
```

5

LISTING 5.4   Continued

```
create proc sp_stop_profiler_trace @TraceID int = null
as

if @TraceID is not null
begin
    -- Set the trace status to stop
    exec sp_trace_setstatus @TraceID, 0

    -- Delete the trace
    exec sp_trace_setstatus @TraceID, 2
end
else
begin
--cg 2/8/06 - added a WHERE clause to eliminate a stop of the default trace
    declare c1 cursor for
    SELECT distinct traceid FROM :: fn_trace_getinfo (DEFAULT)
        WHERE traceId not in (select ID from sys.traces where is_default = 1)
    open c1
    fetch c1 into @TraceID
    while @@fetch_status = 0
    begin
        -- Set the trace status to stop
        exec sp_trace_setstatus @TraceID, 0

        -- Delete the trace
        exec sp_trace_setstatus @TraceID, 2
        fetch c1 into @TraceID
    end
    close c1
    deallocate c1
end
```

Profiler Usage Scenarios

This chapter has already covered many of the technical aspects of SQL Profiler, but what about some practical applications? Beyond the obvious uses of identifying what SQL statements an application is submitting, this section takes a look at a few scenarios in which the SQL Profiler can be useful. These scenarios are presented to give you some ideas about how SQL Profiler can be used. You'll see that the monitoring and analysis capabilities of SQL Profiler are limited only by your creativity and ingenuity.

Analyzing Slow Stored Procedures or Queries

After you have identified that a particular stored procedure is running slowly, what should you do? You might want to look at the estimated execution plan for the stored procedure, looking for table scans and sections of the plan that have a high cost percentage. But what if the execution plan has no obvious problems? This is when you should consider using the SQL Profiler.

You can set up a trace on the stored procedure that captures the execution of each statement within it, along with its duration, in milliseconds. Here's how:

1. Create a new trace, using the `TSQL_Duration` template.

2. Add the `SP:StmtCompleted` event from the stored procedure event class to the trace.

3. Add a filter on the `Duration` column with the duration not equal to `0`. You can also set the filter to a larger number to exclude more of the short-running statements.

If you are going to run the procedure from SSMS, you might want to add a filter on the `SPID` column as well. Set it equal to the process ID for your session; the SPID is displayed at the bottom of the SSMS window next to your username, in parentheses. This will trace only those commands that are executed from your SSMS Query Editor window.

When you run the trace and execute the stored procedure, you see only those statements in the procedure that have nonzero duration. The statements are listed in ascending duration order. You need to look to the bottom of the Profiler output window to find your longer-running statements. You can isolate these statements, copy them to SSMS, and perform a separate analysis on them to determine your problem.

You can also add showplan events to your Profiler trace to capture the execution plan as the trace is running. SQL Server now has showplan events that capture the showplan results in XML format. Traces with this type of XML output can have a significant impact on server performance while they are running but make the identification of poorly performing statements much easier. When tracing stored procedure executions, it is a good idea to add a filter on the specific stored procedure you are targeting to help minimize the impact on performance.

After you have run a trace with an XML showplan event, you can choose to extract the showplan events to a separate file. To do so, in the SQL Server Profiler you select File, Export, Extract SQL Server Events, Extract Showplan Events. At this point, you can save the showplan events in a single file or to a separate file for each event. The file(s) is saved with a `SQLPlan` file extension. This file can then be opened in SSMS, and the graphical query execution plan will be displayed.

Deadlocks

Deadlocks are a common occurrence in database management systems (DMBSs). In simple terms, deadlocks occur when a process (for example, SPID 10) has a lock on a resource that another process (for example, SPID 20) wants. In addition, the second process (SPID

20) wants the resource that the first process has locked. This cyclic dependency causes the DBMS to kill one of the processes in order to resolve the deadlock situation.

Resolving deadlocks and identifying the deadlock participants can be difficult. In SQL Server 2005 and past versions, trace flag 1204 can be set to capture the processes involved in the deadlock. The output is text based but provides valuable information about the types of locks and the statements that were executing at the time of the deadlock. In addition to this approach, SQL Server 2005 offers the ability to capture detailed deadlock information via the SQL Server Profiler. This type of tracing can be accomplished as follows:

1. Create a new trace, using a `Blank` template; this leaves the selection of all the events, data columns, and filters to you.

2. Add the `Locks:Deadlock graph` event to the trace from the `Locks` category. An additional tab appears on the Trace Properties window, named Event Extraction Settings.

3. Click the Save Deadlock XML Events Separately check box. This causes the deadlock information to be written to a separate file. You could also export the results after the trace has been run by using the File, Export option.

When you run this trace, it captures any deadlock event that occurs and writes it to the XML file specified. To test this, you can open two Query Editor windows and execute the following statements, in the order listed, and in the query window specified:

```
-- In Query Window # 1
--Step1
USE ADVENTUREWORKS
GO
BEGIN TRAN
   UPDATE HumanResources.Employee SET ModifiedDate = GETDATE()


-- In Query Window # 2
--Step2
USE ADVENTUREWORKS
GO
BEGIN TRAN
   UPDATE HumanResources.Department SET ModifiedDate = GETDATE()
   SELECT * FROM  HumanResources.Employee


-- In Query Window # 1
--Step3
   SELECT * FROM  HumanResources.Department
```

When the deadlock occurs, the results pane for one of the query windows contains a message similar to the following:

```
Msg 1205, Level 13, State 51, Line 3
Transaction (Process ID 55) was deadlocked on lock resources with another
process and has been chosen as the deadlock victim. Rerun the transaction.
```

When the row with the `Deadlock graph` event is selected in the Profiler output grid, a graph like the one shown in Figure 5.13 is displayed.

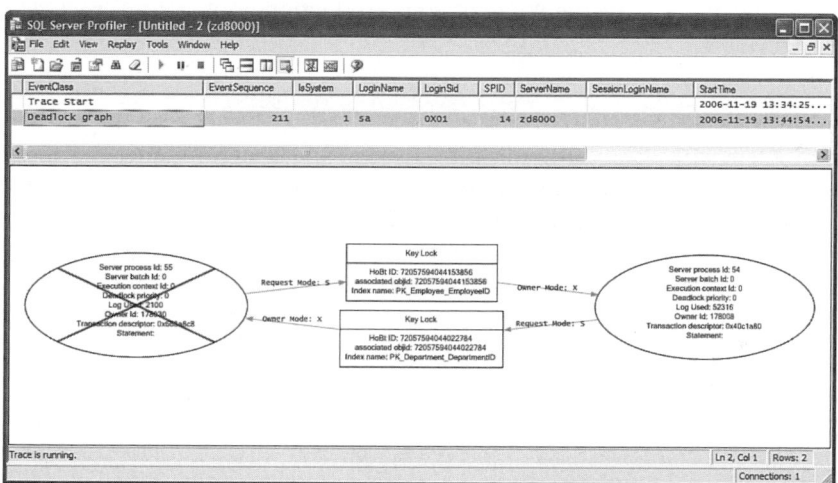

FIGURE 5.13   Output from the `Deadlock graph` event.

The `Deadlock graph` event contains a wealth of information about the deadlock occurrence. The oval nodes represent the processes involved in the deadlock. The oval with an X mark across it is the deadlock victim that had its process killed. The other oval represents the process that was allowed to complete when the deadlock was resolved. The boxes in the middle of the graph display lock information about the specific objects involved in the deadlock.

The graph is interactive and displays relevant information about the processes that were running when the deadlock occurred. For example, when you mouse over the oval nodes, pop-up text appears, displaying the SQL statement that was executing at the time of the deadlock. This is the same type of information that is displayed when the aforementioned trace flag is used, but the graph tends to be easier to decipher.

Identifying Ad Hoc Queries

One problem that can plague a production system is the execution of ad hoc queries against the production database. If you want to identify ad hoc queries, the application, and the users that are running them, SQL Profiler is your tool. You can create a trace as follows:

1. Create a new trace, using the `SQLProfilerStandard` template.

2. Add a new `ApplicationName` filter with `Like Microsoft%`.

When this trace is run, you can identify database access that is happening via SSMS or Microsoft Access. The user, the duration, and the actual SQL statement are captured. An alternative would be to change the `ApplicationName` filter to trace application access for all application names that are not like the name of your production applications, such as `Not Like MyOrderEntryApp%`.

Identifying Performance Bottlenecks

Another common problem with database applications is identifying performance bottlenecks. For example, say that an application is running slow, but you're not sure why. You tested all the SQL statements and stored procedures used by the application, and they were relatively fast. Yet you find that some of the application screens are slow. Is it the database server? Is it the client machine? Is it the network? These are all good questions, but what is the answer? SQL Profiler can help you find out.

You can start with the same trace definition that was used in the previous section. For this scenario, you need to specify an `ApplicationName` filter with the name of the application that you want to trace. You might also want to apply a filter to a specific `NTUserName` to further refine your trace and avoid gathering trace information for users other than the one that you have isolated.

After you have started your trace, you use the slow-running application's screens. You need to look at the trace output and take note of the duration of the statements as they execute on the database server. Are they relatively fast? How much time was spent on the execution of the SQL statements and stored procedures relative to the response time of the application screen? If the total database duration is 1,000 milliseconds (1 second), and the screen takes 10 seconds to refresh, then you need to examine other factors, such as the network or the application code.

With SQL Server 2005, you also combine Windows System Monitor (Perfmon) output with trace output to identify performance bottlenecks. This new feature helps unite system-level metrics (for example, CPU utilization, memory usage) with SQL Server performance metrics. The result is a very impressive display that is synchronized based on time so that a correlation can be made between system-level spikes and the related SQL Server statements.

To try out this powerful new feature, you open the Perfmon application and add a new performance counter log. For simplicity, you can just add one counter, such as `% Processor Time`. Then you choose the option to manually start the log and click OK. Now, you want to apply some kind of load to the SQL Server system. The following script does index maintenance on two tables in the `AdventureWorks` database and can be used to apply a sample load:

```
USE [AdventureWorks]
GO
ALTER INDEX [PK_SalesOrderDetail_SalesOrderID_SalesOrderDetailID]
 ON [Sales].[SalesOrderDetail]
 REORGANIZE WITH ( LOB_COMPACTION = ON )
GO


PRINT 'FIRST INDEX IS REBUILT'

WAITFOR DELAY '00:00:05'

USE [AdventureWorks]
GO
ALTER INDEX [PK_Individual_CustomerID]
 ON [Sales].[Individual] REBUILD WITH
  ( PAD_INDEX  = OFF, STATISTICS_NORECOMPUTE  = OFF,
    ALLOW_ROW_LOCKS  = ON, ALLOW_PAGE_LOCKS  = ON,
    SORT_IN_TEMPDB = OFF, ONLINE = OFF )
GO

PRINT 'SECOND INDEX IS REORGANIZED'
```

Next, you open the script in SSMS, but you don't run it yet. You open SQL Profiler and create a trace by using the Standard Profiler template. This template captures basic SQL Server activity and also includes the StartTime and EndTime columns that are necessary in order to correlate with the Perfmon counters. Now you are ready to start the performance log and the SQL Server Profiler trace. When they are running, you can run the sample load script. When the script has completed, you stop the performance log and the Profiler trace. You save the Profiler trace to a file and then open the file in the Profiler application.

The correlation of the Perfmon log to the trace output file is accomplished from within the Profiler application. To do this, you select File, Import Performance Data. Then you select the performance log file that was just created; these files are located by default in the c:\perflogs folder. Once you import the performance data, a new performance graph and associated grid with the performance counters is displayed in the Profiler, as shown in Figure 5.14

Now the fun begins! If you click one of the statements that was captured in the Profiler grid, a vertical red line appears in the Perfmon graph that reflects the time at which the statement was run. Conversely, if you click a location in the graph, the corresponding SQL statement that was run at that time is highlighted in the grid. If you see a spike in CPU in the Perfmon graph, you can click the spike in the graph and find the statement that may have caused the spike. This can help you quickly and efficiently identify bottlenecks and the processes that are contributing to it.

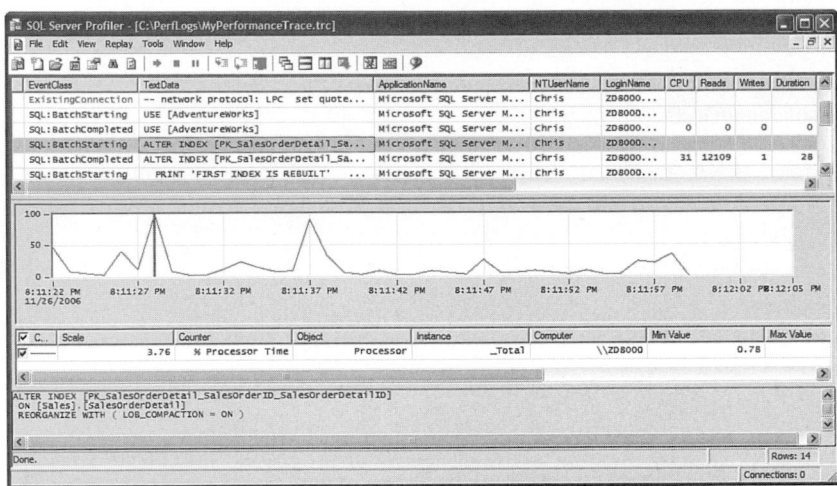

FIGURE 5.14   System Monitor counters correlated within a Profiler trace.

Monitoring Auto-Update Statistics

As discussed in Chapter 30, "Understanding Query Optimization," SQL Server updates index statistics automatically as data is changed in a table. In some environments, excessive auto-updating of statistics can affect system performance while the statistics are being updated. SQL Profiler can be used to monitor auto-updating of statistics as well as automatic statistics creation.

To monitor auto-updating of statistics, you create a trace and include the AutoStats event from the Performance event category. Then you select the TextData, Integer Data, Success, and Object ID columns. When the AutoStats event is captured, the Integer Data column contains the number of statistics updated for a given table, the Object ID is the ID of the table, and the TextData column contains names of the columns together with either an Updated: or Created: prefix. The Success column contains potential failure indication.

If you see an excessive number of AutoStats events on a table or index, and the duration is high, it could be affecting system performance. You might want to consider disabling auto-update for statistics on that table and schedule statistics to be updated periodically during non-peak periods. You may also want to utilize the new AUTO_UPDATE_STATISTICS_ ASYNC database setting, which allows queries that utilize affected statistics to compile without having to wait for the update of statistics to complete.

Monitoring Application Progress

The 10 user-configurable events can be used in a variety of ways, including for tracking the progress of an application or procedure. For instance, perhaps you have a complex procedure that is subject to lengthy execution. You can add debugging logic in this procedure to allow for real-time benchmarking via SQL Profiler.

The key to this type of profiling is the use of the sp_trace_generateevent stored procedure, which enables you to launch the User configurable event. The procedure needs to reference one of the User configurable event IDs (82 to 91) that correspond to the User configurable event 0 to 9. If you execute the procedure with eventid = 82, then User configurable event 0 catches these events.

Listing 5.5 contains a sample stored procedure that (in debug mode) triggers the trace events that SQL Profiler can capture.

LISTING 5.5   A Stored Procedure That Raises User configurable Events for SQL Profiler

```
CREATE PROCEDURE SampleApplicationProc (@debug bit = 0)
as
declare @userinfoParm nvarchar(128)
select @userinfoParm = getdate()

--if in debug mode, then launch event for Profiler
--     indicating Start of Application Proc
if @debug =1
begin
       SET @userinfoParm = 'Proc Start: ' + convert(varchar(30),getdate(),120)
       EXEC sp_trace_generateevent @eventid = 83, @userinfo = @userinfoparm
end

--Real world would have complex proc code executing here
--The WAITFOR statement was added to simulate processing time
WAITFOR DELAY '00:00:05'

---if debug mode, then launch event indicating next significant stage
if @debug =1
begin
       SET @userinfoParm = 'Proc Stage One Complete: '
                            + convert(varchar(20),getdate(),120)
       EXEC sp_trace_generateevent @eventid = 83, @userinfo = @userinfoparm
end

--Real world would have more complex proc code executing here
--The WAITFOR statement was added to simulate processing time
WAITFOR DELAY '00:00:05' --5 second delay

---if debug mode, then launch event indicating next significant stage
if @debug =1
begin
       SET @userinfoParm = 'Proc Stage Two Complete: '
                            + convert(varchar(30),getdate(),120)
       EXEC sp_trace_generateevent @eventid = 83, @userinfo = @userinfoparm
end
```

LISTING 5.5   Continued
--You get the idea

GO

Now you need to set up a new trace that includes the `UserConfigurable:1` event. To do so, you choose the `TextData` data column to capture the `User configurable` output and any other data columns that make sense for your specific trace. After this is complete, you can launch the sample stored procedure from Listing 5.5 and get progress information via SQL Profiler as the procedure executes. You can accumulate execution statistics over time with this kind of trace and summarize the results. The execution command for the procedure follows:

EXEC SampleApplicationProc @debug = 1

The resulting SQL Profiler results are shown in Figure 5.15.

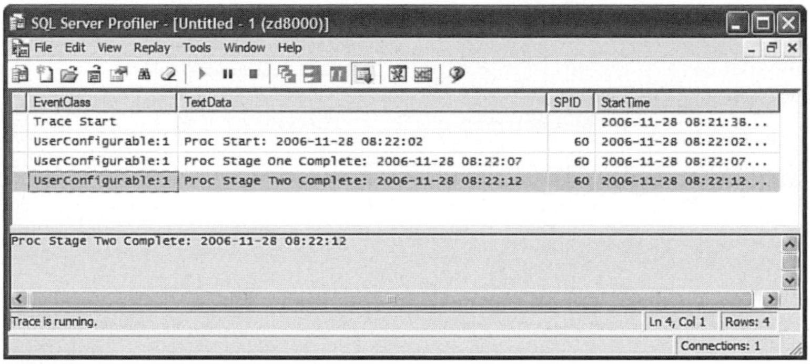

FIGURE 5.15   `User configurable` trace results.

There are many other applications for `User configurable` events. How you use them depends on your specific need. As is the case with many Profiler scenarios, there are seemingly endless possibilities.

Summary

Whether you are a developer or a database administrator, you should not ignore the power of the SQL Profiler. It is often one of the most underused applications in the SQL Server toolkit, yet it is one of the most versatile. Its auditing capabilities and ability to unravel complex server processes define its value.

This chapter wraps up the introduction to the tools and utilities available with SQL Server. Now you should be equipped to start administering and working with SQL Server.

The chapters in the next section focus on the overall administration of SQL, using some of the tools that you have been exposed to thus far. Chapter 6, "SQL Server System and Database Administration," gives you some insight into the inner workings of SQL Server and what it takes to effectively administer a SQL Server instance.

PART III

SQL Server Administration

IN THIS PART

CHAPTER 6   SQL Server System and Database
             Administration   155

CHAPTER 7   Installing SQL Server 2005   173

CHAPTER 8   Upgrading to SQL Server 2005   197

CHAPTER 9   Client Installation and
             Configuration   221

CHAPTER 10   Security and User Administration   247

CHAPTER 11   Database Backup and Restore   291

CHAPTER 12   Database Mail   339

CHAPTER 13   SQL Server Scheduling and
             Notification   361

CHAPTER 14   SQL Server High Availability   393

CHAPTER 15   Replication   415

CHAPTER 16   Database Mirroring   481

CHAPTER 17   SQL Server Clustering   515

CHAPTER 6

SQL Server System and Database Administration

IN THIS CHAPTER

▶ What's New in SQL Server System and Database Administration

▶ System Administrator Responsibilities

▶ System Databases

▶ System Tables

▶ System Views

▶ System Stored Procedures

This chapter outlines the role of a SQL Server system administrator and explores some of the methods that an administrator can use to query important system data. As with any other job, understanding the roles and responsibilities of an administrator is critical to doing the job well. You also need the right tools and the right information to do the job well and to do it efficiently.

The system data covered in this chapter provides some of the key information, and the methods discussed to access this information are some of the tools. System data discloses information that can be invaluable when assessing your SQL Server environment and is an essential part of administering a SQL Server database.

What's New in SQL Server System and Database Administration

The means for accessing system information has changed quite a bit in SQL Server 2005. Many of the system tables that you may have used in past versions are no longer system tables. You can still select from these tables (for example, sysobjects), but they exist in SQL Server 2005 as views. These views, which are discussed in much more detail later in this chapter, are called *compatibility views*. You can use compatibility views in much the same way as the system tables in past versions, but it is important to realize that they are now views. Microsoft has decided to hide from the SQL Server user the actual system tables that these compatibility views represent. This presents some benefits for Microsoft because they can change the underlying system tables while still maintaining consistency for the end user through the views.

In addition to compatibility views, two other view types for selecting system information have been added to SQL Server 2005: catalog views and dynamic management views (DMVs). Catalog views provide access to metadata in the SQL Server environment. Using catalog views is the preferred method for accessing the metadata (as defined by Microsoft) and should be used instead of compatibility views in most instances. DMVs are a new tool for assessing the health of the SQL Server environment. DMVs provide a fast and easy method for getting diagnostic information about a server and can be used to provide information that may have been available in past versions only through system stored procedures, DBCC commands, or Profiler traces.

The great news about all these new views is that they can be used in a SELECT statement the same way as a table. Compare this to data that is returned in a system stored procedure: The system stored procedure provides valuable information, but you can't easily join the results to other tables or views, and you can't be selective with the data that is returned. The system views provide a great deal of flexibility and allow you easy access to a wealth of system-level information.

System Administrator Responsibilities

A system administrator is responsible for the integrity and availability of the data in a database. This is a simple concept, but it is a huge responsibility. Some large corporations place a valuation on their data as high as $1 million per 100MB. The investment in dollars is not the only issue; many companies that lose mission-critical data simply never recover.

The job descriptions for system administrators vary widely. In small shops, the administrator might lay out the physical design, install SQL Server, implement the logical design, tune the installation, and then manage ongoing tasks, such as backups. Larger sites might have tasks broken out into separate job functions. Managing users and backing up data are common examples of this. However, a lead administrator should still be in place to define policy and coordinate efforts.

Whether performed by an individual or as a team, the core administration tasks are as follows:

- Install and configure SQL Server.
- Plan and create databases.
- Manage data storage.
- Control security.
- Tune the database.
- Perform backup and recovery.

Another task that is sometimes handled by administrators is managing stored procedures. Because stored procedures for user applications often contain complex Transact-SQL (T-SQL) code, they tend to fall into the realm of the application developer. However, because stored procedures are stored as objects in the database, they are also the responsibility of the administrator. If your application calls custom stored procedures, you as the system administrator must be aware of this and coordinate with the application developers.

The system administration job can be stressful, frustrating, and demanding, but it is a highly rewarding, interesting, and respected position. As a system administrator, you are expected to know all, see all, and predict all, but you are well compensated for your efforts.

System Databases

SQL Server uses system databases to support different parts of the database management system (DBMS). Each database serves a specific role and stores information that SQL Server needs to do its job. The system databases are much like the user databases created in SQL Server. They store data in tables and contain views, stored procedures, and other database objects that you also see in user databases. They also have associated database files (that is, .mdf and .ldf files) that are physically located on the SQL Server machine. Table 6.1 lists the system database and the related database filenames.

TABLE 6.1   System Databases and Their Associated Database Files

Database	.mdf Filename	.ldf Filename
master	master.mdf	mastlog.ldf
resource	mssqlsystemresource.mdf	mssqlsystemresource.ldf
model	model.mdf	modellog.ldf
msdb	msdbdata.mdf	msdblog.ldf
distribution	distmdl.ldf	distmdl.mdf
tempdb	tempdb.mdf	templog.ldf

TIP

You can use the new sys.master_files catalog view to list the physical locations of the system database files as well as the user database files. This catalog view contains a myriad of information, including the logical name, current state, and size of each database file.

The folder that each of these database files is located in depends on the SQL Server installation. By default, the installation process places these files in a folder named <drive>:\Program Files\Microsoft SQL Server\MSSQL.1\MSSQL\Data\. You can move these files after the installation by using special procedures that are documented in the SQL Server Books Online topic "Moving System Databases."

The following sections describe the function of each system database.

The `master` **Database**

The `master` database contains serverwide information about the SQL Server system. This serverwide information includes logins, linked server information, configuration information for the server, and information about user databases that have been created in the SQL Server instance. The actual locations of the database files and key properties that relate to each user database are stored in the `master` database.

SQL Server cannot start without a `master` database. This is not surprising, given the type of information that it contains. Without the `master` database, SQL Server does not know the location of the databases that it services and does not know how the server is configured to run.

One change to the `master` database in SQL Server 2005 is the removal of system objects from the database. A new database, the `resource` database, now contains this information.

The `resource` **Database**

The `resource` database contains all the system objects that are deployed with SQL Server 2005. These system objects include the system stored procedures and system views that logically appear in each database but are physically stored in the `resource` database. Microsoft moved all the system objects to the `resource` database to simplify the upgrade process. When a new release of the software is made available, the updated system objects need only be updated in one spot—the `resource` database.

You do not see the `resource` database in the list of databases shown in SQL Server Management Studio (SSMS). For the most part, you should not be aware of the existence of the `resource` database. It has database files named mssqlsystemresources.mdf and mssqlsystemresources.ldf that are found in the same location as the `master` database files, but you cannot access the database directly. In addition, you do not see the database listed when selecting databases using system views or with system procedures, such as sp_helpdb.

The `model` **Database**

The `model` database is a template on which all user-created databases are based. All databases must contain a base set of objects known as the *database catalog*. When a new database is created, the model is copied to populate the requisite objects. Conveniently, objects can be added to the `model` database. For example, if you want a certain table created in all your databases, you can create the table in the `model` database, and it is then propagated to all subsequently created databases.

The `msdb` **Database**

The `msdb` database is used to store information for the SQL Server Agent, the Service Broker, Database Mail, log shipping, and more. When you create and schedule a SQL Server Agent job, the job's parameters and execution history are stored in `msdb`. Backups and maintenance plan information are stored in `msdb` as well. If log shipping is implemented, critical information about the servers and tables that are involved in this process are stored in `msdb`.

The `distribution` **Database**

The `distribution` database is utilized during replication. It stores metadata and history information for all types of replication. It is also used to store transactions when transactional replication is utilized. By default, replication is not set up, and you do not see the `distribution` database listed in SSMS. However, the actual data files for the `distribution` database are installed by default.

Refer to Chapter 15, "Replication," for a more detailed discussion of the intricacies of replication.

The `tempdb` **Database**

The `tempdb` database stores temporary data and data objects. The temporary data objects include temporary tables, temporary stored procedures, and any other objects you want to create temporarily. The longevity of data objects in the temporary database depends on the type of object created. Ultimately, all temporary database objects are removed when the SQL Server service is restarted. The `tempdb` database is re-created, and all objects and data added since the last restart of SQL Server are lost.

`tempdb` can also be used for some of SQL Server's internal operations. Large sort operations are performed in `tempdb` before the result set is returned to the client. Certain index operations can be performed in `tempdb` to offload some of the space requirements. SQL Server also uses `tempdb` to store row versions that are generated from database modifications in databases that use row versioning or snapshot isolation transactions.

Maintaining System Databases

You should give system databases the same attention that you give your user databases. These databases should be backed up on a regular basis and secured in the event that one of them needs to be restored. All the system databases, with the exception of `tempdb` and the `resource` database, can be backed up. These same databases can also be restored to bring them back to a previous state.

It's important that you monitor the size of your system databases. The amount of data that accumulates in these databases can be significant. This is particularly true for the `tempdb`, `msdb`, and `distribution` databases. Large sort or index operations can increase the size of your `tempdb` database in a short period of time. The `msdb` and `distribution` databases contain a great deal of historical information. Take, for example, a server with hundreds of databases that have log backups occurring every 15 minutes. The information captured for each one of the backups is not significant, but the number of databases and the frequency of the backups causes many rows to be stored in the `msdb` database. Cleanup tasks and similar activities that remove older historical data can help keep the database size manageable.

System Tables

System tables contain data about objects in the SQL Server databases (that is, metadata) as well as information that SQL Server components use to do their job. Many of the system tables are now hidden and are no longer available for direct access by end users. In SQL Server 2005, compatibility views, which are discussed later in this chapter, have the same names as the system tables available in prior versions. For example, if you had a query in SQL Server 2000 that selected from syscolumns, this query continues to work in SQL Server 2005, but the results come from a view instead of a system table.

The system tables that you can view are now found in system databases, such as msdb or master. You can use the Object Explorer in SSMS to view the system tables in each database. Figure 6.1 shows the system tables listed for the master database in the Object Explorer:

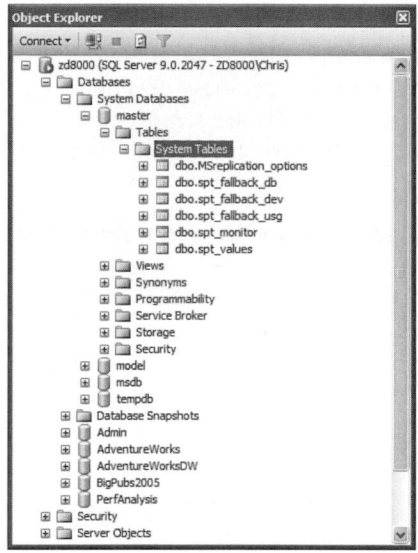

FIGURE 6.1   System tables listed in Object Explorer.

The most significant number of viewable system tables is found in the msdb system database. The system tables there support backup and restore, log shipping, maintenance plans, Notification Services, the SQL Server Agent, and more. You can retrieve a tremendous amount of information from these system tables if you know what you are looking for. The following example shows a query that selects from the system tables in msdb to report on recent restores for the AdventureWorks database:

```
select destination_database_name 'database', h.restore_date, restore_type,
   cast((backup_size/1024)/1024 as numeric(8,0)) 'backup_size MB',
   f.physical_device_name
```

```
from msdb..restorehistory h (NOLOCK)
    LEFT JOIN msdb..backupset b (NOLOCK)
        ON h.backup_set_id = b.backup_set_id
    LEFT JOIN msdb..backupmediafamily f (NOLOCK)
        ON b.media_set_id = f.media_set_id
where h.restore_date > getdate() - 5
    and UPPER(h.destination_database_name) = 'AdventureWorks'
order by UPPER(h.destination_database_name), h.restore_date desc
```

One of the challenges with using system tables is determining the relationships between them. Some vendors offer diagrams of these tables, and you can also determine the relationships by reviewing the foreign keys on these tables and by referring to SQL Server 2005 Books Online, which describes what each column in the system table is used for.

CAUTION

Microsoft does not recommend querying system tables directly. It does not guarantee the consistency of system tables across versions and warns that queries that may have worked against system tables in past versions may no longer work. Catalog views or information schema views should be used instead, especially in production code.

Queries against system tables are best used for ad hoc queries. The values in system tables should never be updated, and an object's structure should not be altered, either. Making changes to the data or structure could cause problems and cause SQL Server or one of its components to fail.

System Views

System views are virtual tables that expose metadata that relates to many different aspects of SQL Server. There are several different types of views that target different data needs. SQL Server 2005 offers an extended number of system views and view types that should meet most, if not all, your metadata needs.

The available system views can be shown in the Object Explorer in SSMS. Figure 6.2 shows the Object Explorer with the System Views node highlighted. There are far too many views to cover in detail in this chapter but we will cover each type of view and provide an example of each to give you some insight into their value. Each of the system views is covered in detail in SQL Server Books Online, including descriptions of each column.

Compatibility Views

Compatibility views were added to SQL Server 2005 for backward compatibility. Many of the system tables that were available in prior versions of SQL Server have now been implemented as compatibility views. These views have the same name as the system tables from prior versions and return the same metadata that was available in SQL Server 2000. They do not contain information that is new to SQL Server 2005.

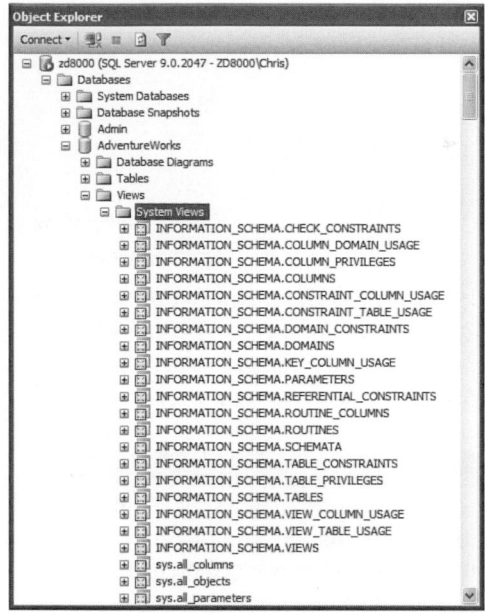

FIGURE 6.2   System views listed in Object Explorer.

You can find most of the compatibility views in the Object Explorer by looking for system views that have names that start with sys.sys. For example, sys.syscolumns, sys.syscomments, and sys.sysobjects are all compatibility views. The first part of the name indicates the schema that the object belongs to (in this case, sys). All system objects are part of this sys schema or the INFORMATION_SCHEMA schema. The second part of the name is the view name, which corresponds to the name of a system table in SQL Server 2000.

TIP

To see a list of compatibility views, you use the index lookup in SQL Server 2005 Books Online and look for sys.sys. The index is placed at the beginning of a list of compatibility views, starting with sys.sysaltfiles. Objects in the list that are compatibility views have the text "compatibility view" following the object name, so it is easy to identify them and get help.

You should transition from the use of compatibility views to the use of other system views, such as catalog views. The scripts that were created in SQL Server 2000 and reference SQL Server 2000 system tables should continue to function in SQL Server 2005, but this is strictly for backward compatibility. Table 6.2 provides a list of SQL Server 2000 system tables and alternative SQL Server 2005 system views that can be used instead.

TABLE 6.2   SQL Server 2005 Alternatives for SQL Server 2000 System Tables

SQL Server 2000 System Table	SQL Server 2005 System View	View Type
sysaltfiles	sys.master_files	Catalog view
syscacheobjects	sys.dm_exec_cached_plans	DMV
	sys.dm_exec_plan_attributes	DMV
	sys.dm_exec_sql_text	DMV
syscharsets	sys.syscharsets	Compatibility view
syscolumns	sys.columns	Catalog view
syscomments	sys.sql_modules	Catalog view
sysconfigures	sys.configurations	Catalog view
sysconstraints	sys.check_constraints	Catalog view
	sys.default_constraints	Catalog view
	sys.key_constraints	Catalog view
	sys.foreign_keys	Catalog view
syscurconfigs	sys.configurations	Catalog view
sysdatabases	sys.databases	Catalog view
sysdepends	sys.sql_dependencies	Catalog view
sysdevices	sys.backup_devices	Catalog view
sysfilegroups	sys.filegroups	Catalog view
sysfiles	sys.database_files	Catalog view
sysforeignkeys	sys.foreign_keys	Catalog view
sysfulltextcatalogs	sys.fulltext_catalogs	Catalog view
sysindexes	sys.indexes	Catalog view
	sys.partitions	Catalog view
	sys.allocation_units	Catalog view
	sys.dm_db_partition_stats	DMV
sysindexkeys	sys.index_columns	Catalog view
syslanguages	sys.syslanguages	Compatibility view
syslockinfo	sys.dm_tran_locks	DMV
syslocks	sys.dm_tran_locks	DMV
syslogins	sys.sql_logins (transact-sql)	Catalog view
sysmembers	sys.database_role_members	Catalog view
sysmessages	sys.messages	Catalog view
sysobjects	sys.objects	Catalog view
sysoledbusers	sys.linked_logins	Catalog view
sysopentapes	sys.dm_io_backup_tapes	DMV
sysperfinfo	sys.dm_os_performance_counters	DMV
syspermissions	sys.database_permissions	Catalog view
	sys.server_permissions	Catalog view

6

TABLE 6.2   Continued

SQL Server 2000 System Table	SQL Server 2005 System View	View Type
sysprocesses	sys.dm_exec_connections	DMV
	sys.dm_exec_sessions	DMV
	sys.dm_exec_requests	DMV
sysprotects	sys.database_permissions	Catalog view
	sys.server_permissions	Catalog view
sysreferences	sys.foreign_keys	Catalog view
sysremotelogins	sys.remote_logins	Catalog view
sysservers	sys.servers	Catalog view
systypes	sys.types	Catalog view
sysusers	sys.database_principals	Catalog view

Catalog Views

Using catalog views is the preferred method for returning information that is used by the Microsoft SQL Server database engine. There is a catalog view to return information about almost every aspect of SQL Server. The number of catalog views is far too large to list here, but you can gain some insight into the range of information available by looking at the following list, which shows the categories of information covered by catalog views:

► Common language runtime (CLR) assembly catalog views

► Data spaces and full-text catalog views

► Database mirroring catalog views

► Databases and files catalog views

► Endpoint catalog views

► Extended properties catalog views

► Linked servers catalog views

► Messages (for errors) catalog views

► Objects catalog views

► Partition function catalog views

► Scalar type catalog views

► Schemas catalog views

► Security catalog views

► Server-wide configuration catalog views

► Service Broker catalog views

► XML schemas (XML type system) catalog views

Some of the catalog views return information that is new to SQL Server 2005 or information that was not provided in prior versions. Examples of these include the CLR assembly catalog views and the database mirroring catalog views. Other catalog views provide information that may have been available in prior versions via system tables, system procedures, and so on, but the new catalog views expand on the information that is returned and include elements that are new to SQL Server 2005.

To demonstrate the use of a catalog view, let's compare a simple SQL Server 2000 SELECT statement that returns object information to a SELECT statement in SQL Server 2005 that returns similar information. The following example shows a SELECT statement that was written in SQL Server 2000 to return any stored procedure created after a given date:

```
select crdate, name
 from sysobjects o
 where type = 'p'
  and crdate > '1/1/05'
 order by crdate, name
```

Now, compare this SELECT statement to one that uses a SQL Server 2005 catalog view. The sys.objects catalog view is a new alternative to the SQL Server 2000 sysobjects system table. The following SELECT uses the sys.objects catalog view to return the same type of information as the previous example:

```
select o.create_date, o.modify_date, name
 from sys.objects o
 where type = 'p'
 and (create_date > '1/1/05'
   or o.modify_date >= '1/1/05')
 order by  1, 2, 3
```

As you can see, the modify_date column has been added to the SELECT statement. This column did not exist with the sysobjects system table. The addition of this column allows you to identify objects that were created as well as objects that were modified or altered.

Let's look at an example of using a catalog view to return the same kind of information returned in prior versions with a system procedure. The sp_helpfile system procedure is a handy procedure that returns information about database files that are associated with a given database. This procedure exists in SQL Server 2000 and is still available in SQL Server 2005. An alternative to this procedure is the new sys.master_files catalog view. This view returns all the information that sp_helpfile returns and more. The following example shows a SELECT statement using the sys.master_files catalog view to return the database files for the AdventureWorks database:

```
select *
 from sys.master_files
 where db_name(database_id) = 'adventureworks'
```

You have the distinct advantage of being able to select the database files for all the databases on your server by using this catalog view. You can also tailor your SELECT statement to isolate database files based on the size of the database or the location of the physical database files. For example, to return all database files that are found somewhere on your C drive, you could use the following SELECT:

```
select db_name(database_id), physical_name
 from sys.master_files
 where physical_name like 'c:\%'
```

There are plenty of catalog views that provide information about SQL Server that were not available before. When you are looking to return information about SQL Server components, you should look to the catalog views first. These views provide a great deal of flexibility and allow you to isolate the specific information you need.

Information Schema Views

Information schema views provide another system table–independent option for accessing SQL Server metadata. This type of view, unlike a catalog view, was available in prior versions of SQL Server. Using information schema views is a viable alternative for accessing SQL Server metadata from a production application. The information schema views enable an application that uses them to function properly even though the underlying system tables may have changed. Changes to the underlying system tables are most prevalent when a new version of SQL Server is released (such as SQL Server 2005), but changes can also occur as part of service packs to an existing version.

The information schema views also have the advantage of being SQL-92 compatible. Compliance with the SQL-92 standard means that SQL statements that are written against these views also work with other DBMSs that also adhere to the SQL-92 standard. The SQL-92 standard supports a three-part naming convention, which SQL Server has implemented as *database.schema.object*.

In SQL Server 2005, all the information schema views are in the same schema, named INFORMATION_SCHEMA. The following information schema views or objects are available:

- ▶ CHECK_CONSTRAINTS
- ▶ COLUMN_DOMAIN_USAGE
- ▶ COLUMN_PRIVILEGES
- ▶ COLUMNS
- ▶ CONSTRAINT_COLUMN_USAGE
- ▶ CONSTRAINT_TABLE_USAGE
- ▶ DOMAIN_CONSTRAINTS
- ▶ DOMAINS

- ▶ KEY_COLUMN_USAGE

- ▶ PARAMETERS

- ▶ REFERENTIAL_CONSTRAINTS

- ▶ ROUTINE_COLUMNS

- ▶ ROUTINES

- ▶ SCHEMATA

- ▶ TABLE_CONSTRAINTS

- ▶ TABLE_PRIVILEGES

- ▶ TABLES

- ▶ VIEW_COLUMN_USAGE

- ▶ VIEW_TABLE_USAGE

- ▶ VIEWS

When you refer to information schema views in a SQL statement, you must use a qualified name that includes the schema name. For example, the following statement returns all the tables and columns in a given database, using the tables and columns information schema views.

```
select t.TABLE_NAME, c.COLUMN_NAME
 from INFORMATION_SCHEMA.TABLES t
  join INFORMATION_SCHEMA.COLUMNS c on t.TABLE_NAME = c.TABLE_NAME
 order by t.TABLE_NAME, ORDINAL_POSITION
```

TIP

You can expand the Views node in a given database in the Object Explorer and open the System Views node to see a list of the available information schema views. The information schema views are listed at the top of the System Views node. If you expand the Column node under each information schema view, you see the available columns to select from the view. You can then drag the column into a query window for use in a SELECT statement.

Fortunately, the names of the information schema views are fairly intuitive and reflect the kind of information they contain. The relationships between the information schema views can be derived from the column names shared between the tables.

Dynamic Management Views

Dynamic management views (DMVs), which are new to SQL Server 2005, provide a simple means for assessing the state of a server. These views provide a lightweight means for gathering diagnostic information without the heavy burden associated with tools available in SQL Server 2000. The SQL Server 2000 diagnostic tools, such as heavy Profiler traces, PerfMon, dbcc executions, and pssdiag, are still available, but oftentimes, the information returned from the DMVs is enough to determine what may be ailing a SQL Server machine.

An extensive number of DMVs are available in SQL Server 2005. Some DMVs are scoped at the server level, and others are scoped at the database level. They are all found in the sys schema and have names that start with dm_. Table 6.3 lists the different types of DMVs. The DMVs in Table 6.3 are categorized based on function as well as the starting characters in the DMV names. The naming convention gives you an easy means for identifying the type of each DMV.

TABLE 6.3   Types of DMVs

Category	Name Prefix	Information Captured
Execution	dm_exec	Execution of user code
Operating system	dm_os	Low-level operating system information, including memory and locking information
Transaction	dm_tran	Transactions and isolation-level information
I/O	dm_io	Input and output on network disks
Database	dm_db	Databases and database objects
CLR	dm_clr	CLR information, including the CLR loaded assemblies
Replication	dm_repl	Replication information, including the articles, publications, and transaction involved in replication
Service Broker	dm_broker	Server Broker statistics, including activated tasks and connections
Full-Text	dm_fts	Full-Text Search information
Query Notification	dm_qn	Active Query Notification subscriptions

TIP

You can expand the Views node in a given database in the Object Explorer and open the System Views node to see a list of the available DMVs. The DMVs are all listed together and start with dm_ . If you expand the Column node under each DMV, you see the available columns to select from the view. You can then drag the column into a query window to be included in a SELECT statement.

To illustrate the value of the DMVs, let's look at a performance scenario and compare the SQL Server 2000 approach to a SQL Server 2005 approach using DMVs. A common performance-related question is "What stored procedures are executing most frequently on my server?" With SQL Server 2000, the most likely way to find out is to run a Profiler trace. You must have a Profiler trace that has already been running to capture the stored procedure executions, or you must create a new trace and run it for a period of time to answer the performance question. The trace takes time to create and can affect server performance while it is running.

With SQL Server 2005, you can use one of the DMVs in the execution category to answer the same performance question. The following example uses the `sys.dm_exec_query_stats` DMV along with a dynamic management function named `dm_exec_sql_text`. It returns the object IDs of the five most frequently executed stored procedures, along with the actual text associated with the procedure:

```
select top 5 q.execution_count, q.total_worker_time,
 s.dbid, s.objectid, s.text
 from sys.dm_exec_query_stats q
 CROSS APPLY sys.dm_exec_sql_text (q.sql_handle) s
 ORDER BY q.execution_count desc
```

The advantage of using a DMV is that it can return past information without having to explicitly create a trace or implement some other performance tool. SQL Server automatically caches the information so that you can query it at any time. The collection of the data starts when the SQL Server instance is started, so you can get a good cross-section of information. Keep in mind that your results can change as the server continues to collect information over time.

Many of the performance scenarios such as those that relate to memory, CPU utilization, blocking, and recompilation can be investigated using DMVs. You should consider using DMVs to address performance problems before using other methods in SQL Server 2005. In many cases, you may be able to avoid costly traces and glean enough information from the DMV to solve your problem.

NOTE

Dynamic management functions return the same type of information as DMVs. The dynamic management functions also have names that start with dm_ and reside in the sys schema. You can find the dynamic management functions listed in the Object Explorer within the `master` database. If you select Function, System Functions, Table-Valued Functions, you see the dynamic management functions listed at the top.

DMVs are also a great source of information that does not relate directly to performance. For example, you can use the `dm_os_sys_info` DMV to gather important server information, such as the number of CPUs, the amount of memory, and so on. The following example demonstrates the use of the `dm_os_sys_info` DMV to return CPU and memory information:

```
select cpu_count, hyperthread_ratio, physical_memory_in_bytes
 from sys.dm_os_sys_info

/* Results from prior select
```

```
cpu_count   hyperthread_ratio physical_memory_in_bytes
----------- ----------------- ------------------------
2           2                 2146357248
*/
```

The cpu_count column returns the number of logical CPUs, hyperthread_ratio returns the ratio between physical CPUs and logical CPUs, and the last column selected returns the physical memory on the SQL Server machine.

System Stored Procedures

System stored procedures have been a favorite of SQL Server DBAs since the inception of SQL Server. They provide a rich set of information that covers many different aspects of SQL Server. They can return some of the same types of information as system views, but they generally return a fixed set of information that cannot be modified using a SELECT statement. That is not to say that they are not valuable; they are valuable, and they are particularly useful for people who have been using SQL Server for a long time. System stored procedures such as sp_who, sp_lock, and sp_help are tools for a database professional that are as basic as a hammer is to a carpenter.

System stored procedures have names that start with sp_, and they are found in the sys schema. They are global in scope, which allows you to execute them from any database, without qualifying the stored procedure name. They also run in the context of the database you are in. In other words, if you execute sp_helpfile in the AdventureWorks database, the database files for the AdventureWorks database will be returned. This same type of behavior exists for any stored procedure that is created in the master database with a name that starts with sp_. For example, if you create a procedure named sp_helpme in the master database and execute that procedure in the AdventureWorks database, SQL Server ultimately looks for and finds the procedure in the master database.

System stored procedures are listed in the Object Explorer, in the Programmability node within Stored Procedures and then System Stored Procedures. There are far too many system stored procedures to list or discuss them all in this section. A quick check of the master database lists well over 1,000 procedures. SQL Server Books Online provides detailed help on these procedures, which it groups into 18 different categories.

Useful System Stored Procedures

You are likely to use only a handful of system stored procedures on a regular basis. What procedures you use depends on the type of work you do with SQL Server and your capacity to remember their names. Table 6.4 contains a sample set of system stored procedures that you may find useful.

TABLE 6.4   Useful System Stored Procedures

System Stored Procedure	Description
sp_configure	Displays or changes serverwide configuration settings.
sp_createstats	Creates statistics that are used by the Query Optimizer for all tables in a database.
sp_help	Provides details about the object that is passed to it. If a table name is passed to this procedure, it returns information on the columns, constraints, indexes, and more.
sp_helpdb	If no parameters are supplied, returns relevant database information (including the space used) for all the databases on an instance of SQL Server.
sp_helpfile	Lists the database files associated with the database you are connected to.
sp_lock	Displays current locking information for the entire SQL Server instance.
sp_spaceused	Provides the number of rows and disk space used by the table, indexed view, or queue passed to it.
sp_who	Lists current processes that are connected to an instance of SQL Server.

Many of the administrative functions that are performed by SSMS can also be accomplished with system stored procedures. Examples of these include procedures that start with sp_add and sp_delete, which can be used to add and delete database objects. In addition, there are approximately 90 system stored procedures that start with sp_help, which return help information on database objects.

TIP

You can use the sys.all_objects catalog view to search for available system stored procedures. This catalog view lists objects that are schema scoped as well as system objects. For example, the query SELECT * FROM sys.all_objects WHERE name LIKE 'sp_help%' returns all the system stored procedures that start with sp_help. You can turn to Books Online for detailed help on any of the system stored procedures. Just enter sp_ in the index search, and you see a list of them all.

It is well worth your while to become familiar with some of the system stored procedures. Using them is a very fast and effective means for gathering information from SQL Server. They do not require the creation of a SELECT statement, and using them is often the easiest way to get information via a query window.

Summary

Administering SQL Server can be a complex and time-consuming job. Understanding the SQL Server internals and some of the easy ways to obtain information about a SQL Server instance benefits you in the long run. Taking the time to learn what makes SQL Server tick expands your knowledge of this comprehensive DBMS and helps you make better decisions when working with it.

Chapter 7, "Installing SQL Server 2005," guides you through the installation of a SQL Server instance.

Installing SQL Server 2005

IN THIS CHAPTER

▶ What's New in Installing SQL Server 2005

▶ Installation Requirements

▶ Installation Walkthrough

▶ Unattended Installation

▶ Installing SP1

Installing SQL Server is the first and one of the easiest tasks you'll accomplish as an administrator. And even though it may take as little as 15 minutes to get SQL Server 2005 up and running by clicking through the install screens and accepting the defaults (Next, Next, Next...), it is crucial to first understand the meaning of each install option and its ramifications for your environment.

What's New in Installing SQL Server 2005

The installation process has been completely revised and updated for SQL Server 2005. Like most other new Microsoft applications, the installer now relies on the latest edition of the Windows Installer, rather than InstallShield, providing a robust, option-rich and feedback-rich experience with maximum rollback capabilities.

The goal of this chapter is to magnify the details hidden behind the well-polished surface of the installer to help you make informed decisions every step of the way.

Installation Requirements

Before installing SQL Server 2005 on your server, it's a good idea (even if you own the latest-and-greatest system) to review the hardware and software requirements. The next two sections gather all the fine print into a few conveniently organized tables.

> **NOTE**
>
> The SQL Server 2005 installer helps determine whether your system meets the minimum requirements by running the new System Configuration Checker (SCC) early in the install. SCC conveniently provides a savable (via a button click) textual report on its results (as well as displaying them onscreen). SCC is covered in detail later in this chapter.

Hardware Requirements

To install SQL Server 2005, your system must possess a few basic components:

▶ A pointing device

▶ A display device with resolution of at least 1024×768 (required by SQL Server Management Studio [SMSS])

▶ A DVD-ROM or CD-ROM drive (for installation from disc)

Table 7.1 lists server environment hardware requirements, by SQL Server edition, with reference to processor type and/or word length. This table lists the recommended configurations, rather than the base minimums, based on the assumption that you won't try to run SQL Server 2005 on outdated hardware. In addition, it goes without saying that installation to a redundant array of disks (RAID) on production systems is highly recommended.

Wherever you see a service pack (SP) designation in the table, you can assume that any later-released SPs are also supported. Of course, faster editions of processors, increased RAM, and more disk space won't negatively impact any installation. One final (and perhaps obvious) note: The more SQL Server components you install, the more disk space you need. Analysis Services, for example, requires an additional 157MB of disk space for the install.

TABLE 7.1   SQL Server 2005 Hardware Requirements, by Edition

SQL Server Editions	Memory (RAM)	Processors (CPU)	Free Hard Disk Space
Enterprise, Standard, and Developer (32-bit)	512MB	1GHz Pentium	600MB
Enterprise, Standard, and Developer (64-bit)	512MB	1GHz AMD Opteron, AMD Athlon 64, Intel Xeon with Intel EM64T support, or Intel Pentium IV with EM64T support	600MB
Enterprise, Standard, and Developer (Itanium)	512MB	1GHz Itanium	600MB
Workgroup (32-bit)	512MB	1GHz Pentium	600MB
Express (32-bit)	512MB	1GHz Pentium	600MB
Mobile (32-bit, server environment)	512MB	1GHz Pentium	250MB

> **NOTE**
>
> Licensing for dual-core processors is the same as for single-core processors: Only a single license is required for one dual-core processor. Another way of saying this is licensing is per CPU socket, not per processor core. Thanks, Microsoft!

Software Requirements

The following software prerequisites must be installed on any server running any SQL Server edition:

▶ Microsoft Internet Explorer 6.0 SP1 (required because it is a dependency of SMSS, Books Online, Business Intelligence Development Studio [for Analysis Services], and the Report Designer)

▶ Windows Installer 3.1 (sometimes distributed by Microsoft Windows Update services)

▶ Internet Information Server (IIS) 5.0 or later (required by Reporting Services [SSRS])

> **NOTE**
>
> IIS is not required for SQL Server 2005 endpoints.

▶ ASP.NET 2.0 (required by SRSS and enabled by the SQL Server 2005 installer if SRSS is a selected feature)

▶ NTFS filesystem

Table 7.2 lists the software and operating system requirements for SQL Server 2005, by edition.

TABLE 7.2   SQL Server 2005 Software Requirements, by Edition

SQL Server Editions	Supported Operating Systems	Additional Software Requirements	Must Install .NET Framework 2.0 Prior to Installation?
Enterprise (32-bit)	Windows 2000 Server SP4; Windows Server 2003 Standard, Enterprise, and Datacenter Editions w/SP1; and Windows Small Business Server 2003 SP1	(none)	No
Enterprise (64-bit)	Windows Server 2003 Standard, Enterprise, and Datacenter x64 Editions with SP1	(none)	No
Enterprise (Itanium)	Windows Server 2003 Enterprise and Datacenter Editions for Itanium-based systems with SP1	(none)	No

TABLE 7.2   Continued

SQL Server Editions	Supported Operating Systems	Additional Software Requirements	Must Install .NET Framework 2.0 Prior to Installation?
Standard and Developer (32-bit)	Windows 2000 Professional and Server Editions SP4; Windows XP SP2; Windows Server 2003 Enterprise, Standard, and Datacenter Editions with SP1; and Windows Small Business Server 2003 SP1	(none)	No
Standard and Developer (64-bit)	Windows Server 2003 Standard, Enterprise, and Datacenter x64 Editions with SP1; and Windows XP Professional x64 Edition	(none)	No
Standard and Developer (Itanium)	Windows Server 2003 Enterprise and Datacenter Editions for Itanium-based systems with SP1	(none)	No
Workgroup (32-bit)	Windows 2000 Server and Professional Editions SP4; Windows XP SP2; Windows Server 2003 Standard, Enterprise, and Datacenter Editions with SP1; and Windows Small Business Server 2003 SP1	(none)	No
Express (32-bit)	Windows XP (Home, Tablet, Professional, and Media Editions) SP2; Windows 2000 Professional, Server, Advanced, and Datacenter Editions SP4; Windows Server 2003 (Web, Standard, Enterprise, and Datacenter Editions (32 bit—or 64 bit, if running on Windows on Windows) with SP1; Windows Small Business Server (Standard or Premium) 2003 SP1; and MS Virtual PC & Virtual Server	(none)	Yes
Mobile (32-bit, client-side requirements)	Microsoft Windows CE 5.0; Microsoft Windows XP Tablet PC Edition; Windows Mobile 2003 Software for Pocket PC; and Windows Mobile 5.0	(none)	N/A
Mobile (32-bit, developers' system requirements)	Microsoft Windows Server 2003; Windows XP Media Center, Professional, and Tablet PC editions; and Windows 2000 Professional, Server SP4	Microsoft ActiveSync 4.0 (for debugging & deployment); and Microsoft Visual Studio 2005	Yes

TABLE 7.2   Continued

SQL Server Editions	Supported Operating Systems	Additional Software Requirements	Must Install .NET Framework 2.0 Prior to Installation?
Mobile (32-bit, server environment)	Windows Server 2003; Windows XP; and Windows 2000 SP4	Microsoft SQL Server 2000 SP3a; IIS 5.0 or later; ActiveSync 4.0 (for SMSS on connected devices); Internet Explorer 6.0 or later; and Outlook 98 (or later) for synchronization of email, calendar, contacts, tasks, and notes	N/A

Windows Service Requirements

In addition to the requirements listed in the preceding section, the following Windows services must be enabled for SQL Server 2005 to be installed (and run all features) successfully:

▶ Cryptographic Services (a.k.a. the Cryptographic Service Provider)

▶ Task Scheduler

▶ Windows Management Instrumentation (WMI) services

Finally, for distributed transactions to successfully enlist SQL Server 2005, Microsoft's Distributed Transaction Coordinator (MSDTC) service must be enabled. A distributed transaction can be defined as a transaction that traverses the boundary between program code and Transact-SQL (T-SQL), as in the case of a COM+ transaction (via .NET Enterprise Services), or a transaction that spans more than one SQL Server instance (including transactions that invoke T-SQL across linked servers).

Network Protocol Support

The following network protocols are supported for all editions (where applicable):

▶ Shared memory (but not for failover clusters)

▶ Named pipes

▶ TCP/IP (required for SQL Server endpoint communications)

▶ Virtual Interface Adapter (VIA)

The following (non–Microsoft-embraced) protocols are not supported:

▶ Banyan VINES

▶ Sequenced Packet Protocol (SPP)

▶ Multiprotocol

▶ AppleTalk

▶ NWLink IPX/SPX

Failover Cluster and Windows Vista Support

SQL Server 2005 failover clusters require Microsoft Cluster Service (MSCS) to be installed on one or more nodes. When you install SQL Server 2005 on a cluster, the installer detects that MSCS is running and provides the option to install SQL Server as a virtual server. The Components to Install screen has its Create a SQL Server Failover Cluster and Create an Analysis Server Failover Cluster check boxes enabled. All other options for installation are the same. Please see Chapters 14, "SQL Server High Availability," through 17, "SQL Server Clustering," for more details on configuring high-availability SQL Server solutions.

As for Windows Vista, the official word from Microsoft is that only SQL Server 2005 Express Edition SP1 is supported. All other editions are unsupported until the release of SQL Server 2005 SP2.

How to Handle Previously Installed Community Technology Preview (CTP) Editions of SQL Server 2005

If you installed any beta or CTP editions of either the .NET Framework 2.0, SQL Server 2005, or Visual Studio 2005, the installer may prompt to remove all previous beta editions of these products. You must accomplish this on your own because the installer will not do it for you.

When you open the Add or Remove Programs Control Panel to find your beta components, you might be surprised by the large number of individual SQL Server or Visual Studio components that must be uninstalled.

You can speed up the removal process by removing the main installations first—those reporting the largest size on disk, such as Microsoft SQL Server 2005 - September CTP—although you might find some leftovers that merely require a click of the Remove button to be cleaned up. (Your mileage may vary, depending on what you have installed.)

You can uninstall your beta components with some confidence because the SQL Server installer installs the appropriate version of the .NET Framework 2.0, as well as the new Premier Partner Edition of Visual Studio 2005, which allows for the creation of Visual Studio SQL Server database projects.

The only caveat is that uninstalling previous editions of the 2.0 .NET Framework may break other installed applications that rely on them. On the other hand, if you have a version of the .NET Framework later than that being installed by SQL Server 2005, this should not present an issue.

Running Multiple Simultaneous Editions

Believe it or not, you can install multiple editions of SQL Server 2005 on the same machine and run them simultaneously. This comes in handy when you need to test code or other feature functionality on one edition versus another, as when your development and deployment environments differ. In fact, you can even install and run SQL Server 2005 Enterprise Evaluation Edition on XP SP2 (not supported for the non–Evaluation Enterprise edition) if you need to test an Enterprise Edition feature on a non–Windows Server 2003 desktop.

> **NOTE**
>
> You can quickly ascertain the version you're running by executing this T-SQL query:
>
> ```
> select serverproperty('edition')
> ```

Installation Walkthrough

This section walks you through a typical installation scenario step-by-step. Important points of information are brought up along the way, providing a real-world perspective on the process. No past experience with SQL Server is required to understand this section.

For the example setup described here, the destination machine has a Pentium 4 processor (2.4GHz), 1GB of RAM, and 120GB of available hard disk space (quite a bit more than needed). The operating system is a fresh install of Windows 2003 Server, Standard Edition, with SP1.

This example shows installation of a copy of SQL Server 2005, 32-bit Standard Edition because this is the most widely used version of the product. When you're done, you'll also install SQL Server SP1.

> **NOTE**
>
> SQL Server 2005 is actually version 9 of the product, just as SQL Server 2000 is version 8, which succeeded SQL Server 7. Although versioning by year *seems* straightforward, it may obfuscate the reasoning behind the naming convention used for many installed items, such as folder names (for example, `Microsoft SQL Server\90`), application names (`DatabaseMail90.exe`), and so on. In addition, SQL Server 2000 servers appear as version 8 when registered in SMSS (and elsewhere). You can administer many aspects of SQL Server 2000 instances via the 2005 management tools.

Install Screens, Step-by-Step

The first step in installing SQL Server 2005 is, of course, to launch the installer's main Start window (or splash screen). You do this by simply inserting the install DVD in the drive (if autoplay is enabled) or by right-clicking the DVD drive letter in Windows Explorer and clicking the Autoplay menu option. If you're installing from a decompressed .iso file, double-click the file in the root folder splash.hta. Figure 7.1 shows the resulting Start window.

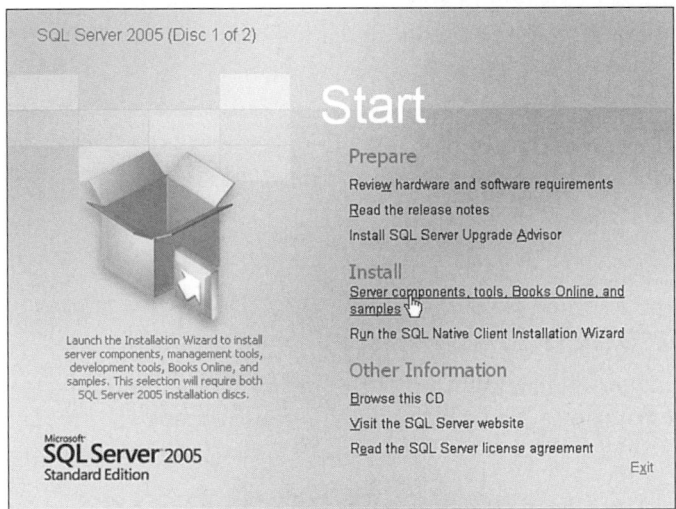

FIGURE 7.1   SQL Server 2005 installation Start window.

> **NOTE**
>
> To skip the Start screen and jump directly to the SQL Server install program, you can navigate to [*DVD-ROM Drive Letter*]:\Servers and run setup.exe.

The first thing you'll notice is that there is a great deal of content immediately available from the Start screen, including requirements documentation, the license agreement, release notes, web links, and the opportunity to install either SQL Server 2005, the SQL Server Upgrade Advisor (covered in Chapter 8, "Upgrading to SQL Server 2005"), and the new SQL Native Client (SNAC).

> **NOTE**
>
> SNAC succeeds MDAC as the primary library for the latest OLE DB and ODBC drivers whose APIs allows clients to interact with SQL Server 2005. It is a necessary install for clients who wish to utilize such hot new ADO.NET features as user-defined SQL data types (UDTs), multiple active result sets (MARS), query notifications, and, of

course, the xml data type. All these features are covered in either Chapter 36, "SQL Server and the .NET Framework," or Chapter 37, "Using XML in SQL Server."

SNAC is installed by default in a typical SQL Sever 2005 install, and it provides several benefits over MDAC, including side-by-side driver versioning, which means that versioning of the SNAC drivers is controlled at the SQL Server (rather than at the OS) level.

On the Start screen, under Install, click the Server Components, Tools, Books Online, and Samples link. (Note that you need to accept the license agreement that follows, or you can't proceed.) The next screen takes you into the component update phase of the install, during which some requisite software items must be installed:

▶ The .NET Framework 2.0 (Required because SQL Server 2005 is a Common Language Runtime [CLR] host, allowing developers to write managed code executed in a T-SQL context. It is also required by Reporting Services, SMSS, and so on.)

▶ SQL Server Native Client

▶ SQL Server 2005 Setup support files (used by the installer)

If all goes well upon completion of this stage, your install screen should look something like Figure 7.2. Even if there is a failure during install (such as an error you may encounter after terminating an install via Task Manager), simply rerunning the install from the Start screen may resolve the issue.

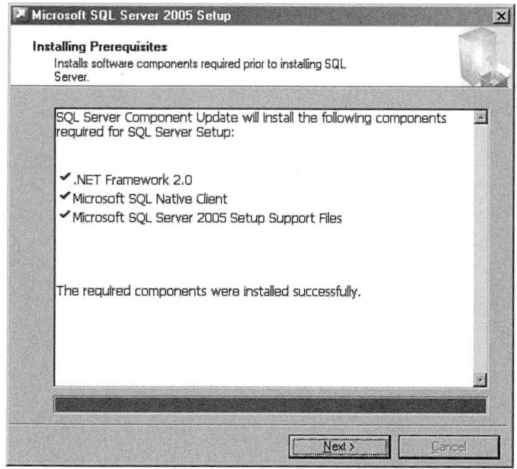

FIGURE 7.2   The component update phase of SQL Server 2005 install is complete.

When you click the Next button, the Microsoft SQL Server 2005 Setup (InstallShield) Installation Wizard is launched. Click Next, and the install application invokes the SCC.

SCC's job is to ensure that every aspect of SQL Server 2005 compatibility is met, including the following:

▶ Operating system (including word-length [32-bit and 64-bit]) and service pack compatibility

▶ Installed service (particularly WMI) and other software compatibility (including a check for Internet Explorer 6 SP1 or later)

▶ Whether the logged-in user is a system administrator (a must)

▶ Whether no other instances of the installer are running and no reboots are pending from other installers

▶ Whether the destination drive is formatted, writable, and uncompressed

NOTE

When you install SQL Server 2005 on a remote share, the administrative share (that is, admin$) of that cluster node or machine must be enabled (SCC alerts you if it is not).

SCC scans the environment, checking compatibility and also for previous editions of related software, such as MSXML (which happens to be upgraded to version 6 during the install) and previous editions of SQL Server. SCC also builds a list of available features, based on these results. Figure 7.3 illustrates the process.

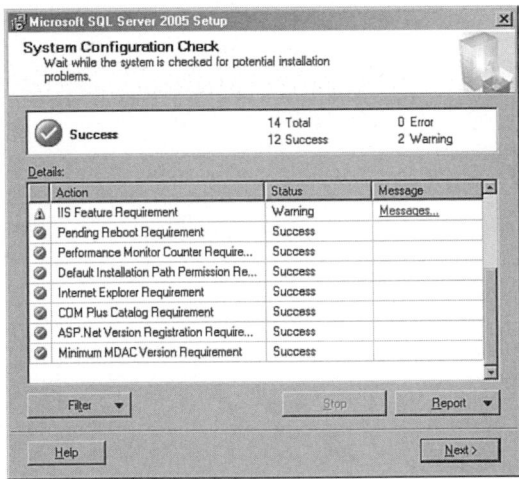

FIGURE 7.3   SCC results.

When the SCC scan is complete, you can click the Report button to view or save its detailed report, which notes any issues and offers suggestions for their resolution. There are several scenarios where the list of available features is affected by the results of SCC's scan. For example: IIS might not be set up on the target machine (as shown in Figure 7.3). A warning is indicated in SCC's results grid, and later, when we reach the Components to Install screen (which presents the list of available features) the Reporting Services (SSRS) check box will be disabled because SSRS depends on IIS. Figure 7.4 illustrates the Components to Install screen in this scenario.

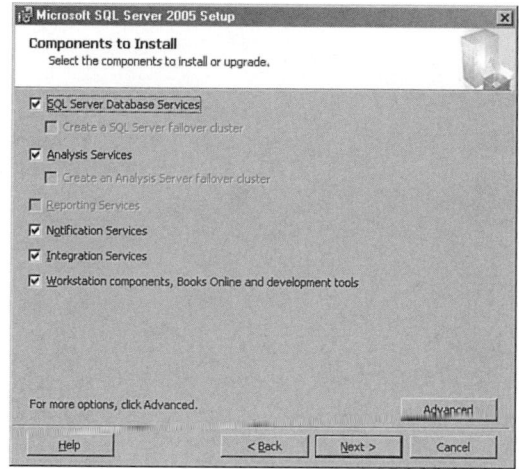

FIGURE 7.4   The Reporting Services install option is disabled when IIS is not configured.

NOTE

Installing Reporting Services on a separate machine from the rest of SQL Server 2005 (i.e., performing a second install on another box) requires an additional license.

One major change from previous editions of SQL Server is the downright helpfulness of SCC. The filterable, three-column grid format (Action, Status, and Message columns) breaks down issue success or failure on a per-task basis.

If any particular task fails or indicates warnings, a hyperlink appears in the message column, which pops up a detailed report when clicked. Overall success is detailed at the top of the main window for clarity's sake, and many install screens also have context-specific Help buttons.

When you have resolved any issues on your system, you click the Next button, launching the third phase of the install. At this point, you enter your personal name, company name, and security key data (this key is auto-entered for MSDN subscription–licensed versions of SQL Server 2005).

If you click the Advanced button at the bottom right of the screen, you can customize your installation by choosing from several subfeatures. Figure 7.5 illustrates the advanced feature selection options, with some typically desirable selections.

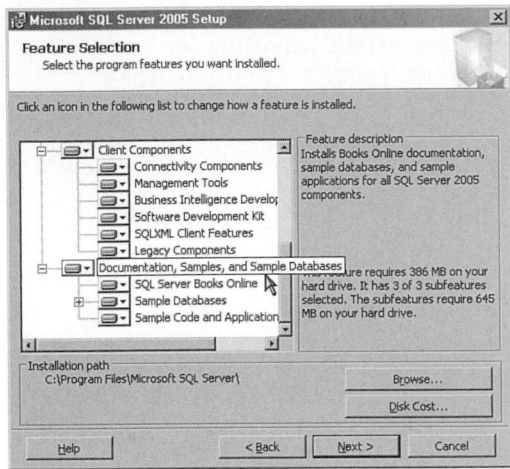

FIGURE 7.5   Advanced feature selection options.

The following are the most commonly available features (detailed in subsequent chapters of this book):

▶ **Database services**—Including the database engine and shared tools (discussed in multiple chapters), replication (see Chapter 15, "Replication"), and Full-Text Search (see Chapter 49, "SQL Server Full-Text Search").

▶ **Analysis Services**—Including the engine used to create business intelligence solutions that rely on OLAP and data mining (see Chapter 39, "SQL Server Analysis Services").

▶ **Reporting Services**—Including the engine and tools used to generate and deploy data-centric reports (see Chapter 41, "SQL Server Reporting Services").

▶ **Integration Services (SSIS)**—Including the engine and tools for performing data import/export/transfer with (or without) transformation (see Chapter 40, "SQL Server Integration Services").

▶ **Notification Services**—Including a framework (based on the publisher/subscriber paradigm) for providing notifications when specific events occur (see Chapter 47, "SQL Server Notification Services"). Note that Notification Services also provides the backbone for Service Broker (see Chapter 48, "SQL Server Service Broker").

▶ **Client Components**—Including all the new connectivity, development, and server management tools (discussed in multiple chapters).

> **NOTE**
>
> As a new SQL Server 2005 user, you'll probably want to install the sample AdventureWorks database. It is not installed by default and must be selected by clicking the Advanced button on the Components to Install setup screen. Then, in the Feature Selection screen that appears, you expand the Documentation, Samples, and Sample Databases node and select Sample Databases.

> **NOTE**
>
> If you're a former (or current) SQL Server 2000 user and you have created DTS packages (or if you wish to use SQL-DMO to connect to SQL Server 2005), you must make sure to leave the Legacy Components option, located under the Client Components node, selected. SQL Server 2000 DTS packages are executable as steps in new SSIS packages; however, the DTS Runtime is required to do so. SQL Server 2000 packages, however, are not editable using SQL Server 2005 tools.

The Feature Selection screen illustrates that installation is now completely component based. This means that each component is actually installed from its own MSI package and can be configured and removed separately from others. In addition, multiple instances of each component can be installed separately. This means, for example, that you can have five named instances of Analysis Server, two named instances of the database engine, three named instances of Reporting Services, and so on. It's completely up to you.

Now that you've made your selections, click Next. At the Instance Name screen (see Figure 7.6), you can install SQL Server 2005 as the default instance (if a SQL Server 2000 or 7 default instance is not present) or as a new named instance. (Upgrading from SQL Server 2000 or 7 is covered in Chapter 8.) Only one default instance of any version of SQL Server is possible on a given server.

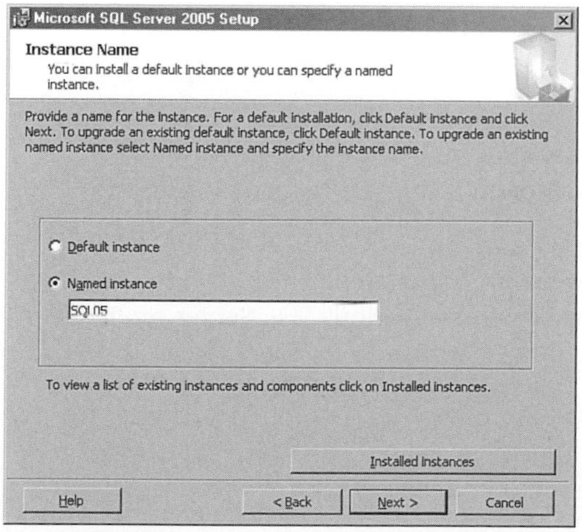

FIGURE 7.6   Instance installation options.

The verbiage on this screen is somewhat opaque. Basically, it attempts to convey the following information:

▶ If a previous edition of SQL Server is currently installed (such as SQL Server 2000) and the Default Instance radio button is selected, that previous edition will be upgraded to SQL Server 2005.

▶ If a previous edition of SQL Server is currently installed (such as SQL Server 2000) and the Default Instance radio button is *not* selected, that previous edition will be left alone, and you must provide a name for your new instance of SQL Server 2005 in the text box. The default instance on the server will remain a SQL Server 2000 instance.

▶ If Default Instance is selected and no previous edition of SQL Server is currently installed, the default instance of SQL Server 2005 is installed (no previous instance means no upgrade).

When installing a new named instance on a server that houses multiple SQL Server versions, it's a good idea to name the new instance something similar to SQL05. This helps to alleviate any confusion among clients as to which version of SQL they are connecting to. In addition, it's a good idea to change the TCP/IP port used to reach this new instance to a fixed port number (other than 1433). (SQL Server uses a range of dynamic port numbers by default.)

NOTE

When SQL Server 2005 Express Edition is installed by the Visual Studio 2005 installer, the instance name is always SQLEXPRESS.

You can also view a list of currently installed instances, either of SQL Server or Analysis Services, by clicking the Installed Instances button at the bottom right of the screen shown in Figure 7.6. Note again that SQL Server 2000 instances will be reported as version 8.*n*.

If this not your first install of SQL Server 2005 on the destination machine, the next dialog is Existing Components, which exists merely to tell you that some of the components already installed (such as SMSS and SQL Browser), will not be installed again because only one instance of each is needed.

Click Next, and you reach the Service Account screen (illustrated in Figure 7.7), which requires you to specify the user accounts under which the various SQL Server services will run.

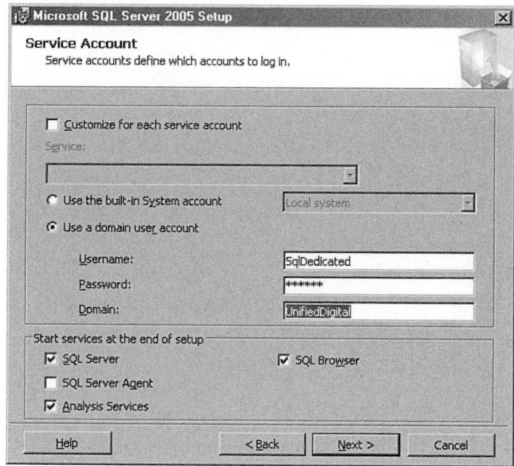

FIGURE 7.7   Service account options.

One recommendation is to create a single local or domain account for dedicated SQL Server 2005 use and assign it to all services or, for finer-grained control, create multiple accounts, one for each service. This helps reinforce the least-privileged user account approach, which states that a user should have only the privileges required to get the job done—and no more. It also makes it clearer for network administrators as to when SQL Server services (as opposed to the multitude of other running services) are requesting access to a resource. And, in some scenarios, the Local system or Network service accounts may be endowed with more privileges than desirable since they are shared.

Also on the Service Account screen, you can select to start various SQL Server services after install by checking the check boxes at the screen bottom. It is highly recommended to auto-start both the SQL Server and SQL Browser services, as they represent the database engine and the service that makes it accessible (via network name resolution), respectively. (You can change auto-start later, using the SQL Server Configuration Manager.) Make your selections and click Next.

NOTE

The SQL Server Browser service is installed only once, no matter how many instances you install.

The following screen (Authentication Mode; see Figure 7.8) provides the authentication options for SQL Server (Windows-only or mixed-mode).

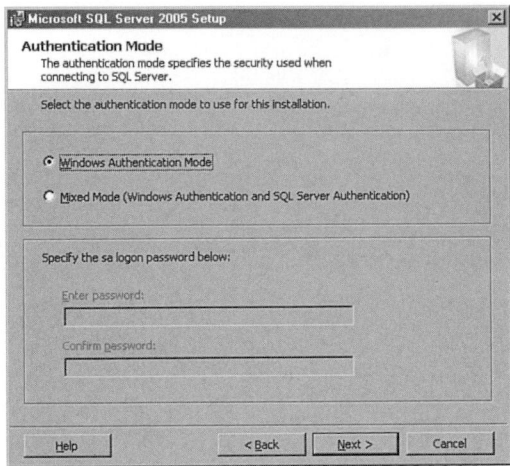

FIGURE 7.8   Authentication mode.

Note that mixed-mode authentication is required for any feature wherein non-Windows clients will be authenticating to SQL Server 2005. A strong sa password is recommended. Note also that if you select Windows authentication, the sa password is randomly generated. You can change it using SMSS after the install (recommended).

Click Next, and the Collation Settings screen appears, where you can set the collation for each SQL Server service (see Figure 7.9).

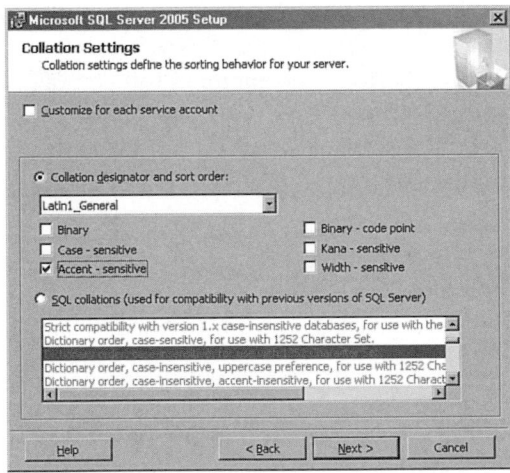

FIGURE 7.9   Collation settings.

Collations are important because they are used to determine case-sensitivity of textual data for comparisons, sort order in indexes, and so on.

You can create and customize your own collation by clicking the Collation Designator and Sort Order radio button and then checking the desired collation options.

NOTE

If you create your own collation, be aware that it may not be compatible when you attach SQL 2000 databases or when you replicate data from SQL Server 2005 to databases created in previous SQL Server editions.

If you're running Windows in the United States, the collation selection defaults to the SQL Server collation (Dictionary Order, Case-Insensitive, for use with 1252 Character Set), and this is a fine choice.

To achieve the same collation when designating your own collation, select the Collation Designator and Sort Order radio button, select Latin1_General from the drop-down box, and then check the Accent - Sensitive check box. (This is also the collation compatible when you're doing string comparisons using SQL code developed in .NET [that is, SQLCLR code]).

An excellent Books Online topic that discusses the many considerations when choosing a collation is titled Using SQL Collations.

If you've chosen to install Reporting Services, clicking Next takes you to the Report Server screen (shown in Figure 7.10), which has one related option: Install and configure (Install the Default Configuration) or just install.

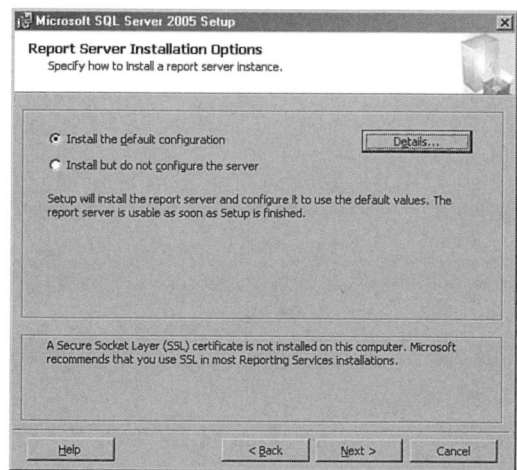

FIGURE 7.10   Reporting Services settings.

If you choose to install and configure, the Details button is enabled. Clicking Details shows the database, virtual directory, and SSL settings that SQL Server will use by default (see Figure 7.11).

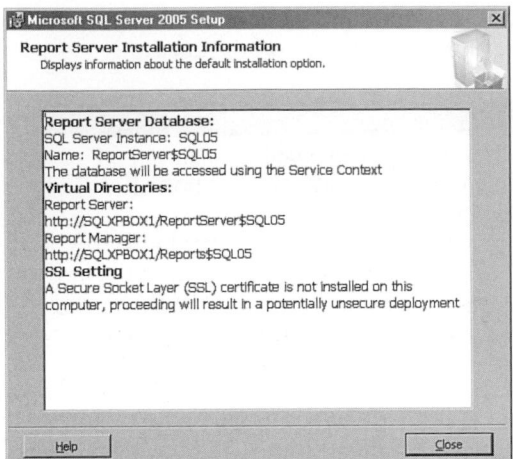

FIGURE 7.11   Reporting Services default configuration.

Click Next to reach the Error and Usage Report Settings screen. Here, you have the option to send error and feature usage data to Microsoft headquarters. This process is colloquially known as "phoning home," and you may be inclined to keep both options unchecked. Note that doing so reduces Microsoft's ability to gather important statistics helpful when debugging for the next service pack release.

The final screen (Ready to Install) provides a summary of your chosen install options and the Finished button you've been waiting to press.

Viewing the Installation Log Files

If you're interested in seeing the log files generated by the setup program, just look in the local folder [*Install Drive Letter*]:\Program Files\Microsoft SQL Server\90\Setup Bootstrap\LOG\Files. Summary.txt provides the log file listing for each installed instance.

Installation Paths

The installation path for SQL Server 2005 defaults to the system drive of the machine to which you are installing, followed by the root default folder: [*system drive letter*]:\Program Files\Microsoft SQL Server. From here, two main subfolders branch out:

▶ **90**—This is the parent folder for Integration Services (under DTS); Notification Services (under Notification Services); and client tools (under Tools); SQL Server Browser, shared tools, and WMI providers (under Shared); and COM components (under COM).

▶ **MSSQL.*n***—This is the parent folder for database engine components (under MSSQL/Binn), data files (under MSSQL/Data), Analysis Services (under OLAP), and Reporting Services (under Reporting Services).

> **NOTE**
>
> The *.n* in the MSSQL.*n* folder name indicates a new naming convention used by SQL Server 2005: Every new instance install is incremented by one, so the first is MSSQL.1, the second MSSQL.2, and so on. This differs from the naming convention used by SQL Server 2000, which used MSSQL$*InstanceName* instead.

Many of the install destination paths are configurable via the installer. To change the defaults, click on the Advanced button on the Components to Install screen and then, on the Feature Selection screen, click the tree node of the individual component whose path you wish to change. Then click the Browse button at the lower right of the screen.

Unattended Installation

If you need to install SQL Server 2005 to more than a few machines, you'll want to do so without having to be present to select the same options over and over. Unattended installs provide this much-needed time-saving feature. The setup.exe program found in the [DVD-ROM Drive]:\Servers directory doubles as a console application for just this purpose.

Unattended install options are either passed to setup.exe directly on the command line (as name/value pairs), or they can be stored in an .ini (initialization) text file, specified on the command line. setup.exe can also be used to add or change installed components.

Many unattended install samples are listed in a special example file called template.ini, located on the install DVD under both the Servers and Tools root folders.

To create your own .ini file, first, you need to specify a single Options .ini section, followed by a set of name/value pairs that supply the installer with the needed answers. Note that for any option for which you want to specify the default value, you need to simply leave that option out of the script.

Many of the .ini names correspond to the screens and screen options you'd see during an attended install. Here are some examples:

- ▶ **INSTANCENAME**—Specify a named instance name for the value or specify the special value MSSQLSERVER to install the default instance.

- ▶ **ADDLOCAL and REMOVE**—Specify values indicating which components you'd like to add (or remove), such as SQL_Engine for the database engine, Analysis_Server for Analysis Services, or SQL_AdventureWorksASSamples for the sample databases. The special value ALL installs all possible components.

- ▶ **INSTALLSQLDIR**—Specify a new path value to change the default install path for the SQL Server binaries.

- ▶ **SQLCOLLATION or ASCOLLATION**—Specify values to set the collation for SQL Server or Analysis Services.

▶ **SECURITYMODE**—Specify the special value SQL here to override the default of Windows-only authentication.

An example .ini file would look like this:

```
[Options]
USERNAME="Alex T. Silverstein"
COMPANYNAME="Unified Digital"
ADDLOCAL=ALL
INSTANCENAME=SQL05Test
SQLBROWSERACCOUNT=[dedicated user account]
SQLBROWSERPASSWORD=[user pw]
SQLACCOUNT=[dedicated user account]
SQLPASSWORD=[user pw]
AGTACCOUNT=[dedicated user account]
AGTPASSWORD=[user pw]
ASACCOUNT=[dedicated user account]
ASPASSWORD=[user pw]
RSACCOUNT=[dedicated user account]
RSPASSWORD=[user pw]
SQLCOLLATION=SQL_Latin1_General_CP1_CI_AS
ASCOLLATION=SQL_Latin1_General_CP1_CI_AS
```

Of course, there are many more options (too many to list here), some of which are designed solely for clustered installs, some for reinstalls, and some for repair installs. Template.ini provides full documentation on each option (inline in comments), and you can also refer to the comprehensive Books Online article "How to: Install SQL Server 2005 from the Command Prompt" for further detail.

To test your simple script, you can run it from a command prompt. The following command-line parameters are available for setup.exe:

▶ **/settings**—You specify your .ini filename after this parameter (and a single space).

▶ **/qn**—Specifies quiet mode (no GUI displayed).

▶ **/qb**—Specifies quiet mode (minimal GUI displayed, with no user interaction required). This option only shows the Setup Progress screens and is useful when you're getting started and troubleshooting.

You can execute your installation templates from a command prompt using the following syntax:

```
Start /wait [full path to setup.exe]
↪/settings [full path to .ini file--use quotes if there are spaces] /qb
```

Note that you don't have to use an .ini file; you can simply specify the same name/value pairs directly on the command line following the last (rightmost) parameter (for example, after /qb). Here's an example:

```
Start /wait [full path to setup.exe]
➥/qn [list of name value pairs, separating each pair by a space]
```

Remote Installation

The only supported method of performing a remote, unattended installation is via the console-install features, described in the previous section.

Remote installation requires a Windows domain, and you must have administrator privileges on the destination computer. If you install SQL Server 2005 from a remote folder, you must use a domain account that has read as well as execute permissions on the remote share. Also, as noted earlier, the administrative share (admin$) of the server or cluster node or machine must also be enabled.

Installing SP1

SQL Server 2005 SP1 addresses all publicly issued security bulletins released prior to February 15, 2006. (Microsoft Knowledge Base article 913090 lists all the fixes.) SP1 upgrades all SQL Server services and components, and it requires an additional 1.9GB disk space (about half of which is needed only for the duration of the install).

Before installing SP1, make sure to back up all user-created databases, as well as the system databases master, model, msdb, and any replicated databases. If you have installed Analysis Services, back up the entire OLAP directory (as discussed earlier in this chapter, in the "Installation Paths" section) and all its subdirectories.

Make sure to close all open connections to the instance to which you are applying SP1 (including any connections via the management tools; setup should prompt you to close them) and make sure the various SQL Server services are started in the Services Control Panel. Also, be sure master and msdb each have 500KB free (or that they are auto-grow enabled).

When you're ready, log on to the machine as an admin and start the SP1 executable. The Welcome screen shown in Figure 7.12 appears. As you can see from this window, SP1 upgrades all the features shown in the listbox. Clicking each feature merely shows a product description in the details text box.

Click Next, accept the license agreement, and then click Next again. The ensuing Feature Selection window lists (again) the features to be updated, organized in tree fashion, by instance name. You can uncheck the features you do not want to have upgraded, except for SNAC and the setup files, which are required. Figure 7.13 shows this screen.

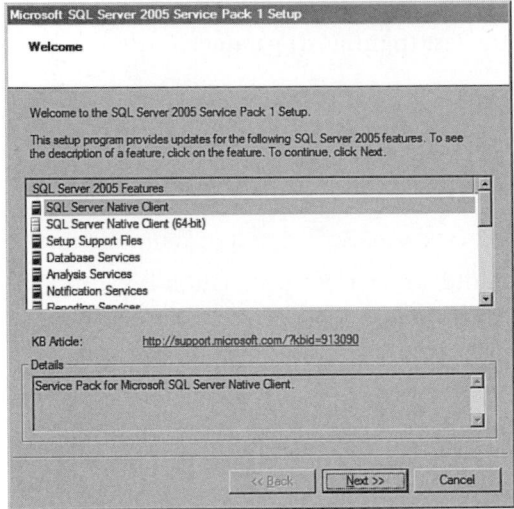

FIGURE 7.12   SQL Server 2005 SP1 Welcome screen.

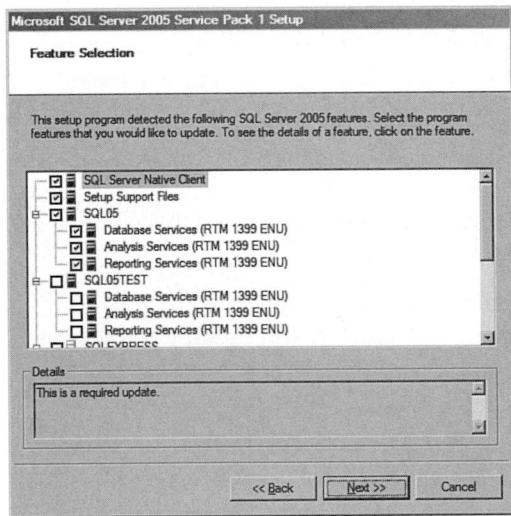

FIGURE 7.13   SQL Server 2005 SP1 Feature Selection screen.

Click Next to reach the Authentication Mode dialog. Provide here the necessary logon information so that SP1 can connect to SQL Server. After this is verified, the Ready to Install screen appears, and you can click Finish. When SP1 is finished, restart all the SQL Server services. Log files for the install are saved to the %windir%/Hotfix directory (and subdirectories, such as SQL9 and OLAP9).

> **NOTE**
>
> As of this writing, SP1 cannot be uninstalled. You must uninstall and reinstall SQL Server and then restore your backed-up databases and OLAP folder, as noted earlier.

Unattended SP1 Installation

Like the SQL Server 2005 main install, SP1 can also be installed from the command-line with no user interaction. To accomplish this for all installed instances, run the SP1 .exe from a command prompt, using the /quiet and /allinstances options, as in this example:

`[SQL Server SP1 Executable Name.exe] /quiet /allinstances`

There are, of course, some additional command-line options:

- ▶ **/?**—Displays help.

- ▶ **/instancename**—Installs SP1 for all components of a particular instance name.

- ▶ **/norestart**—Prevents SP1 from rebooting the computer (if required) when complete.

- ▶ **/user and /password**—Allows you to pass in the user name and password for the remote administrator.

- ▶ **/reportonly**—Does not apply SP1—merely lists the local instances that would be upgraded.

- ▶ **/sapwd**—Allows you to pass in the sa password (under SQL authentication).

- ▶ **/rsupgradedatabaseaccount and /rsupgradepassword**—This is for Reporting Services only. When upgrading a remote SSRS database, you might need to authenticate differently to the remote machine than to the local machine. If this is the case, use these parameters to specify the privileged remote account; otherwise, use only the SSRS components (no databases will be upgraded).

Summary

This chapter provides a fairly detailed overview of the SQL Server 2005 install process from start to finish. You've seen how the new, componentized Windows Installer–based setup makes it easy to install as many instances as you like, with whatever feature sets, and in whatever configuration you choose.

You've seen how the installer reports progress, failure, and success on an individual task basis rather than with one seemingly endless progress bar, making it a lot easier to rectify problems without calling Microsoft or scouring the newsgroups to figure out what went wrong.

Chapter 8 takes a similar approach to examining the process of upgrading from SQL Server 2000 (or SQL Server 7) to SQL Server 2005.

Upgrading to SQL Server 2005

IN THIS CHAPTER

▶ What's New in Upgrading SQL Server

▶ Using the SQL Server Upgrade Advisor (UA)

▶ Destination: SQL Server 2005

▶ Unattended Upgrades

SQL Server 2005 offers an array of new functionality that makes upgrading an irresistible proposition. And whether you're a gung-ho developer or the most conservative of administrators, there's an upgrade path to suit your comfort level. This chapter provides the best practices you need to upgrade without a hitch.

What's New in Upgrading SQL Server

For the simplest setups, most of your existing SQL Server 7 or 2000 components can be automatically upgraded in-place without negatively affecting existing applications. For more complex environments, you can install SQL Server 2005 alongside your existing SQL Server 7 or 2000 instances, and then you can migrate your content over when you're ready.

In-place upgrades and fresh installations rely on a new setup program that provides several value-added benefits, including component-based installation, configuration, and instancing; pre-upgrade system and content analysis; issue reporting and resolution assistance; and plentiful documentation.

Microsoft also provides a new, freely downloadable utility called the SQL Server Upgrade Advisor (UA) that can examine all your existing SQL Server 7 or 2000 components and provide pertinent advice *before you upgrade* so that when you do so, the process flows along smoothly. We'll take a look at the UA first.

Using the SQL Server Upgrade Advisor (UA)

It would be a daunting task indeed to try to test every stored procedure and function, every table and view, every online analytical processing (OLAP) cube, every Data Transformation Services (DTS) package, and so on that your team has built to make sure they still work after you migrate them to SQL Server 2005.

Thanks to the release of the SQL Server UA, you can relax a bit and let the combined experience and testing of early adopters and the SQL Server development team go to work for you.

> **NOTE**
>
> Even though the UA is a great tool, if you have the resources to do so, it is a good idea to set up an additional test environment just for SQL Server 2005. Also, you should thoroughly test your upgraded objects and code *after the upgrade* on a dry run, just to be sure you don't miss anything. Remember to make full backups!

The UA shows you exactly which aspects of your current setup need to be changed to become compatible with SQL Server 2005. Let's take a look at how it works.

Getting Started with the UA

When you pop your new SQL Server 2005 DVD in the drive, one of the first things listed on the Start screen is the UA, which can scan any local or remote SQL Server instance and then report on any potential upgrade compatibility issues.

Similar to SQL Server 2005 itself, the UA has the following prerequisites:

- ▶ Microsoft Windows Installer 3.1

- ▶ Microsoft .NET Framework 2.0

- ▶ One of the following operating systems: Windows 2000 with Service Pack 4 (SP4), Windows Server 2003 with SP1, or Windows XP with SP2

- ▶ SQL Server 2000 Decision Support Objects (DSO), required for scanning Analysis Services instances and installed by default with SQL Server 2000 Analysis Services; also installed when SQL Server Integration Services (SSIS) is installed

- ▶ SQL Server 2000 Client Tools (for scanning DTS packages)

- ▶ An administrative login that works for all components to be analyzed

- ▶ 20MB of free disk space

> **NOTE**
>
> The UA can be installed on any machine that has connectivity to a SQL Server instance. This means you don't have to install it directly on the machine where SQL Server resides.

As described in the following sections, the UA has two main functional areas: the Analysis Wizard and the Report Viewer.

The Analysis Wizard

You'll be glad to know that the analysis process does not modify any code or data; that is left to you to do (or not do) at a later time. As an example, let's run the UA's Analysis Wizard against all the SQL Server components of a locally installed SQL Server 2000 instance.

To start the process, you click the Launch Upgrade Advisor Analysis Wizard hyperlink at the bottom of the main screen. When the Analysis Wizard's welcome screen appears, click Next. When you reach the SQL Server Components screen, choose all the components to be analyzed by checking their corresponding check boxes (see Figure 8.1).

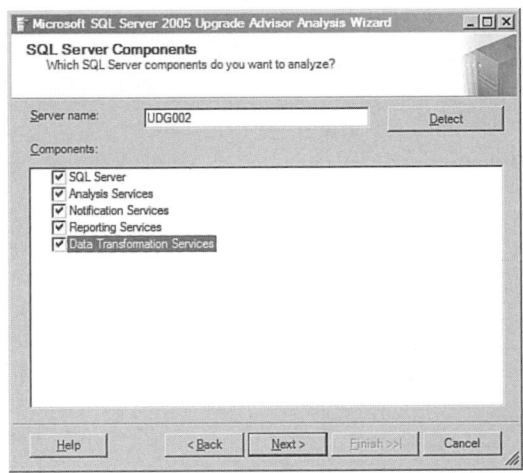

FIGURE 8.1   Choosing the components to be analyzed by the UA's Analysis Wizard.

When the Connection Parameters screen appears, choose the target server, select an authentication method, and enter your user name and password so that the UA can connect to your instance. Click Next, and the SQL Server Parameters screen, shown in Figure 8.2, appears. Choose which (if any) databases to analyze.

You can also use this screen to ask the UA to analyze one or more SQL Profiler trace (.trc) files; this is a useful method for scanning any "dynamic" Transact-SQL (T-SQL) that is compiled into application code and has been traced using SQL Profiler. You can also scan T-SQL batch files (scripts, procedures, functions, triggers, and so on), which is a tremendously useful capability all by itself.

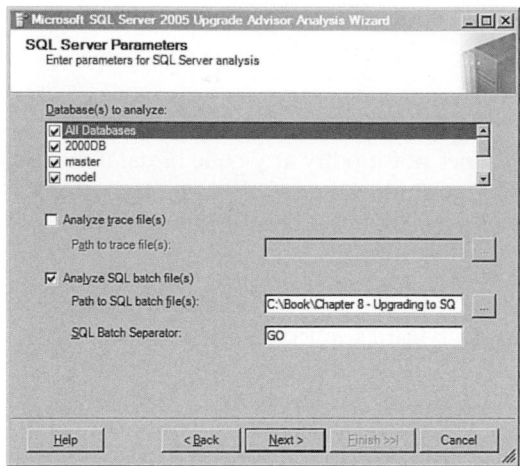

FIGURE 8.2   Choosing the databases and files for the UA to analyze.

For this example, you should add a batch file that contains the following T-SQL commands, most of which are deprecated in SQL Server 2005, just to test the UA:

```
EXEC sp_configure 'set working set size'

SELECT * FROM master.dbo.syslocks

DECLARE @ptr varbinary(16)

SELECT @ptr = TEXTPTR(TextContent)
FROM Store
WHERE StoreId = 1

SELECT *
FROM Store s, Store s2
WHERE s.StoreId *= s2.StoreId
AND s.Name <> s2.Name

READTEXT Store.TextContent @ptr 0 25
--note: My database [2000DB] contains a simple example table called Store
```

When you're ready, click Next, and the Notification Services Parameters screen appears. If you are upgrading from Notification Services 2.0, select that instance by name and enter the required authentication credentials here. If you know you haven't installed Notification Services 2.0, go back to the previous screen and uncheck the Notification Services check box.

The following screen, DTS Parameters (shown in Figure 8.3), gives you the option to analyze all the DTS packages on the target instance or to specify one or more structured storage files individually.

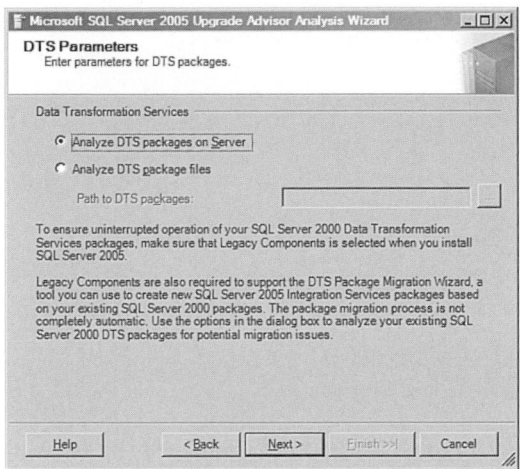

FIGURE 8.3   Choosing the DTS packages to analyze.

The DTS Parameters screen advises (as does Chapter 7, "Installing SQL Server 2005") that you must install the Legacy Components feature from the advanced options of the Feature Selection screen during the SQL Server 2005 installation, or SQL Server 2005 will not be able to run your DTS packages (unless they are upgraded to the new SSIS format). (To upgrade your DTS packages, you use the DTS Migration Wizard, which is installed with SSIS and discussed later in this chapter, in the section "Migrating DTS Packages.")

When you're all set with your DTS selections, click Next to reach the summary screen. Make sure that all your SQL Server 7 or 2000 services are running and (if you're happy with your selections) click the Run button to begin the analysis.

As you can see from the Upgrade Advisor Progress screen that appears (see Figure 8.4), the wizard performs a task-based study of each component, providing per-step reportage, just like the installer and the System Configuration Checker (both discussed in Chapter 7).

8

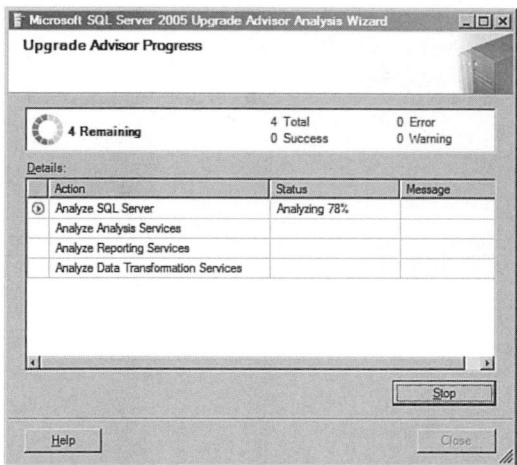

FIGURE 8.4   The Upgrade Advisor Progress screen.

The final output of the wizard is actually an XML report that you can view via the second major component of the UA, the Report Viewer, described in the following section.

> **NOTE**
>
> You can view your last generated report by using the Report Viewer; you can find the link to launch it on the main screen. If you run the UA more than once, however, you must save your previously generated reports to a directory other than the default output directory, or the most recently generated one will be overwritten.
>
> UA reports are saved by default to the folder My Documents\SQL Server 2005 Upgrade Advisor Reports*Servername*, and then they are broken down into separate XML files by component (for example, AS.xml for Analysis Services, DE.xml for the Database Engine).

You can launch the Report Viewer to figure out what to do about the issues the UA may have uncovered. Click the Launch Report button to proceed.

The Report Viewer

The Report Viewer is one of the most important tools in the upgrade process because it provides per-issue messaging, resolution tracking, and (in many cases) hyperlinks to the compiled help documentation that is distributed with the UA.

Issues are organized in the Report Viewer on a per-server and then per-component basis. They can be filtered by type (that is, all issues, all upgrade issues, pre-upgrade issues, all migration issues, and resolved issues), and you can track your resolution progress by checking the This Issue Has Been Resolved check boxes. Figure 8.5 shows the main user interface of the Report Viewer.

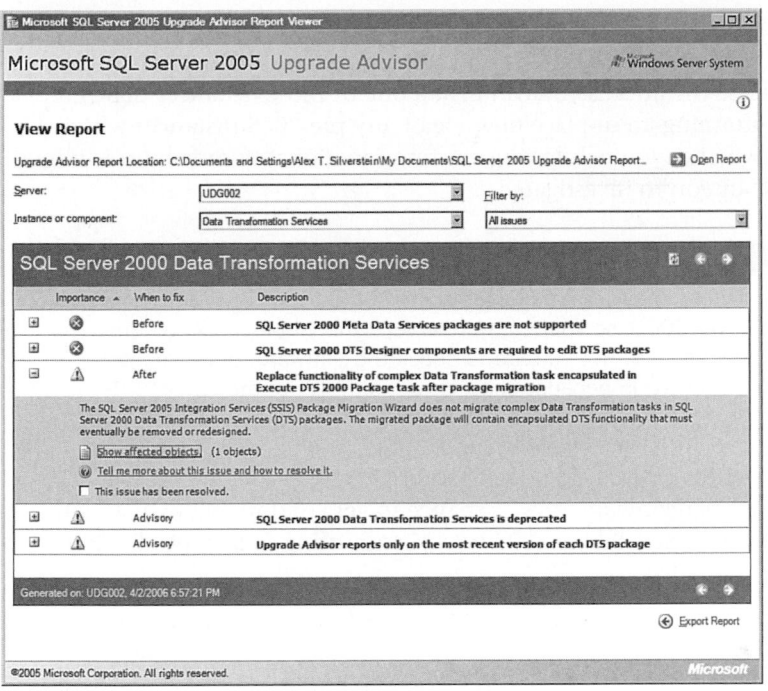

FIGURE 8.5   SQL Server UA's Report Viewer.

Destination: SQL Server 2005

Now that you have become familiar with how to use the helpful UA, you're ready to begin your extensive pre-upgrade testing phase. After you resolve all the issues you can, it's time to take the next step: install SQL Server 2005 (in your test environment first, of course).

Two different paths lead from SQL Server 7 or 2000 to SQL Server 2005:

▶ You can upgrade your current SQL Server 7 or 2000 instances automatically and in-place, using the Setup installation program.

▶ You can install SQL Server 2005 side-by-side with your current SQL Server 7 or 2000 instances and then migrate your data and other content to SQL Server 2005.

The path you choose depends primarily on two factors: your comfort level with the new platform and the scope of feature use in your current environment. When you have become familiar with what it takes to travel either path, you'll find it much easier to make your decision. The first approach we'll explore is the more conservative side-by-side migration path.

Side-by-Side Migration

SQL Server 2005 can coexist without a problem on the same servers as any existing SQL Server 2000 or 7 instances. This means you can install one or more instances of SQL Server 2005 without performing an in-place upgrade of any pre-2005 instances without having to worry about whether you're breaking existing functionality. Side-by-side migration is therefore an easy option to investigate.

> **NOTE**
>
> As detailed in Chapter 7, the hardware requirements for SQL Server 2005 are roughly the same as for SQL Server 2000, so your current servers should probably be sufficient for a side-by-side installation. But be sure to check the software requirements before you install SQL Server 2005 because they are definitively not the same.

Many administrators favor the side-by-side track because it gives everyone on the development team (including eager software folks) a chance to get comfortable with all (and there is a lot) that is new with SQL Server 2005 *before* committing to it in production environments.

In addition, it is far easier to roll back to your previous-version SQL Server components because installing side-by-side leaves them intact (unlike upgrading in-place, which removes them). When you are reasonably comfortable with SQL Server 2005, you can go confidently forward in migrating all your objects (presuming that, if you're leaving previous versions intact, you're also ready to perform necessary tasks, such as changing connection strings, server aliases, and so on).

Avoiding an Unintentional In-Place Upgrade During Setup

If you do intend to go ahead with a side-by-side installation, there's a small gotcha you need to watch out for when installing a new instance of SQL Server 2005. (Chapter 7 mentions this gotcha, but it's worth noting again for those who skipped ahead.)

When you run the Setup program, the Instance Name screen is somewhat lengthy in its header's verbiage, and if you don't take the time to read it closely, you might unintentionally upgrade all your components. This is the lowdown:

▶ If you choose the Default Instance radio button and you already have a SQL Server 7 or 2000 default instance, that default instance will be upgraded.

▶ If you the choose the Named Instance radio button, you need to make sure to enter a name that you know is not in use as an instance name for any pre-2005 instance; otherwise, that pre-2005 named instance will be upgraded.

Figure 8.6 shows a good example of how to make the right choice and use a name, SQL05, that makes it abundantly clear that you are installing a new 2005 instance.

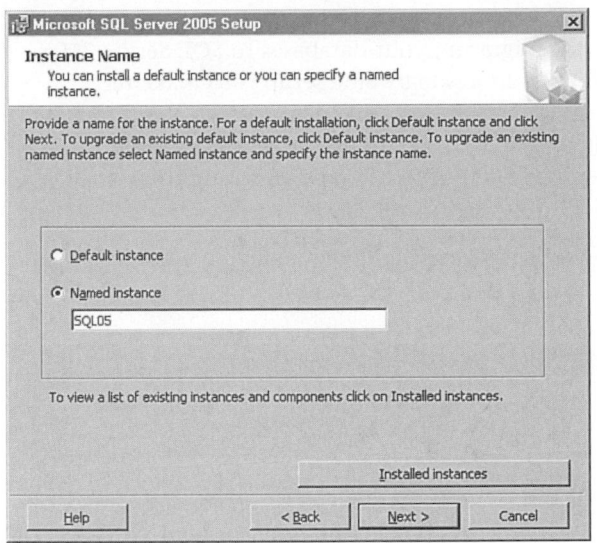

FIGURE 8.6   Installing a new named SQL Server 2005 instance.

Using the SQL Server Client Tools

It is important to understand client tool compatibility with the different editions of SQL Server. You can use SQL Server 2000 Service Manager to stop and start SQL Server 2005 instances. Likewise, you can use SQL Server 2005's Configuration Manager to control pre-2005 instances.

You can also execute T-SQL code and use the Object Browser in SQL Server Management Studio (SSMS) when working with SQL Server 2000 databases. You cannot, however, administer SQL Server 2005 using Enterprise Manager if you are using SQL Server 2000 SP4 (although SP3 is rumored to work). Query Analyzer (QA), on the other hand, works quite well with SQL Server 2005 instances. Note also that you can continue to use QA at the command line (that is, as isqlw.exe), although it has officially been replaced by the new SQLCMD utility.

> **NOTE**
>
> If you are using SQL Server 2005 Express Edition, be sure not to uninstall the SQL Server 2000 client tools when upgrading, or you will lose the ability to run your DTS packages because Express Edition does not include SSIS.

For further information regarding these and other client tools and the changes surrounding them, please see the chapters in Part II, "SQL Server Tools and Utilities."

8

Migrating Databases

Now it's time for the most important task: migrating your databases to SQL Server 2005. One great way to test your existing databases in a side-by-side setup is to make full backup copies of your pre-2005 databases, detach them, and then reattach them to a SQL Server 2005 instance (using either SSMS or T-SQL). You can also achieve the same outcome by backing up your SQL Server 7 or 2000 databases and restoring them to SQL Server 2005.

But a step easier than both of these methods is to use the revamped Copy Database Wizard.

TIP

Before using any of these methods, Microsoft recommends that you run the appropriate DBCC consistency checks to make sure all is well with your content.

The Copy Database Wizard   Using SSMS, connect the Object Explorer to your previous SQL Server version's instance. Next, you right-click the database you want to copy (or move) into SQL Server 2005, and then you select Tasks, Copy Database.

The first few wizard screens are fairly easy to navigate and may remind you of the DTS Import Wizard from SQL Server 2000's Enterprise Manager. This is because the Copy Database Wizard actually creates an SSIS package behind the scenes to accomplish its goal.

You click Next at the wizard's initial welcome screen, and then you select your source server (the 2000 or 7 instance). You click Next again and select your destination server (your newly installed SQL Server 2005 instance). Then you click Next again. The Select the Transfer Method screen that appears provides two options for copying or moving your databases:

- **Detach and Attach**—This option is fast, but it takes the database offline.

- **Use the SQL Server Management Objects (SMO) to Import the Database**—This option is slower, but it keeps the source database online during the process.

NOTE

When you use the detach and attach method, SSIS uses the service account of SQL Server Agent that is running on the 2005 (destination) instance. This account must be able to access the file systems of both servers, or the wizard will fail.

Select the option that works best for you and then click Next. The Select Databases screen appears, and, as Figure 8.7 shows, you should check the Copy (not Move) check boxes for the databases you want to import.

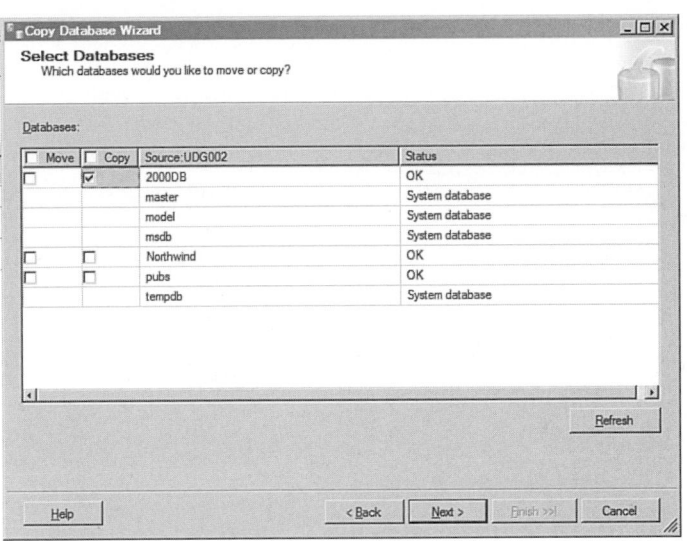

FIGURE 8.7   Selecting the databases to copy to SQL Server 2005.

CAUTION

After a pre-2005 database is upgraded (in case you choose the Move Database option or you perform an attach or restore and delete the original), it cannot be downgraded back to its former version—not even if you attempt to detach/attach or restore it to SQL 2000 or 7. Thus it is especially important to create full backup copies of all your objects before you upgrade. It's actually a good idea to back up the entire `Program Files/Microsoft SQL Server` directory tree.

After you make your database selections, click Next, and the Configure Destination Database screen appears, allowing you to rename the database on the destination server if you so desire. It also provides options to overwrite any existing MDF (data) and LDF (log) files on the destination server or to create new ones in the folders of your choice. Make your selections and click Next.

The Select Database Objects screen that appears next (see Figure 8.8) provides some real power because it allows the serverwide objects (those stored in the system tables and the source database) to be imported. These include stored procedures residing in `master`, SQL Server Agent jobs, custom-defined error messages, and SQL Server logins. You need to click the ellipsis button to choose the specific ones you want to import (rather than choosing them all, which is the default).

You can multiselect the objects you want brought over and then click the double arrow button. When you're finished, you click Next again. The Configure the Package screen that appears next illustrates how your import selections are built into an SSIS package, which you can name and save. You can schedule and log the execution of this package (specify any needed credentials). You click Finish when you're ready to fire it off.

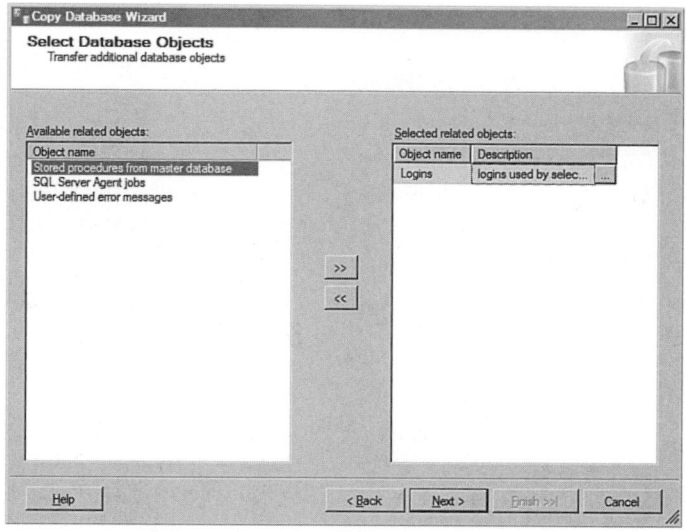

FIGURE 8.8   Importing serverwide objects, using the Copy Database Wizard.

As stated earlier, instead of using the wizard, you can simply detach any SQL Server 7 or 2000 databases and attach them to SQL Server 2005, although this doesn't take into account any objects residing in master or msdb. You can detach by using either the right-click menu in SQL Server 7 or 2000's Enterprise Manager or via the sp_detach_db system stored procedure. One thing has changed in the T-SQL syntax for accomplishing the attach to SQL Server 2005: You now need to use the new FOR ATTACH clause of the CREATE DATABASE statement. Here's an example:

```
CREATE DATABASE [DatabaseName]
ON
(
    FILENAME = N'Path To mdf file'
)
LOG ON
(
    FILENAME = N'Path To ldf file'
)
FOR ATTACH
```

NOTE

You might be wondering how the wizard handles your full-text catalogs. Rest assured, they are imported by default during either a restore, an attach, or via the Copy Database Wizard. For more information on Full-Text indexing, please see Chapter 49, "SQL Server Full-Text Search" (on the CD-ROM).

Database Compatibility Levels   Migrating pre-2005 databases into SQL Server 2005 brings up the question of *compatibility levels*. The compatibility level is a per-database setting that controls T-SQL execution behavior with regard to SQL Server's versioning system.

If you create a new database in SQL Server 2000, for example, it inherits compatibility level 80 (because that is the underlying version number for 2000) unless you manually change it (which you can do, at your discretion). The T-SQL execution engine is flexible insofar as it has the capacity to switch between varying, version-dependent behaviors according to the current compatibility level.

Databases imported to SQL Server 2005 retain their pre-import compatibility level, which usually corresponds to their source SQL Server instance, unless you've otherwise changed it. This is important to understand because many of the changes introduced in T-SQL for level 90 (SQL Server 2005) don't work with previous levels. Some examples include new keyword support (for example, PIVOT, REVERT, QUEUE, SERVICE), deprecation of the =* and *= join operators, differences in the results of the FOR XML and ORDER BY clauses, and changes in numeric type comparisons. You cannot take advantage of these changes unless you change the compatibility level to 90.

You can find a full list of the compatibility level differences in the Books Online article associated with the system stored procedure sp_dbcmptlevel, which you use to set or get the level for a particular database.

To discover a database's compatibility level, you execute sp_dbcmptlevel as follows:

```
EXEC sp_dbcmptlevel 'database name'
go
The current compatibility level is 80.
```

Migrating Analysis Services

Now that you've seen how to migrate databases, jobs, logins, custom error messages, and full-text catalogs, let's move on to discuss how you can migrate the rest of your SQL Server objects. First, let's look at Analysis Services.

The first task is to install a new named instance of SQL Server 2005 Analysis Services (SSAS) by using the Setup program. When this is complete, you can use the new Analysis Services Migration Wizard to import your Analysis Services content. This wizard re-creates your existing OLAP structures on the new instance, without altering the original source material. This is a good thing; however, it doesn't show you how to exploit the new features of SSAS's Unified Dimensional Model (UDM) in your existing cubes. To fully explore that topic, check out Chapter 39, "SQL Server 2005 Analysis Services."

To launch the Analysis Services Migration Wizard, you open the Object Browser and connect to Analysis Services. Then you navigate to the top-level Analysis Services node to find the wizard. You can also simply select Start, Run and then enter the command MigrationWizard.exe. You need to make sure that MSSQLServerOLAPService is running before you begin; you can verify this by using the SQL Server Service Manager.

8

You click Next on the Welcome screen, and the Specify Source and Destination screen appears (see Figure 8.9). You need to enter the name of your SQL Server 2000 Analysis Services server as the source. Then you have two options:

▶ **Server**—You can choose this radio button and enter the name of your new SSAS instance in order to immediately migrate your OLAP databases.

▶ **Script File**—If you select this radio button and enter a filename, the wizard can generate an XML for Analysis (XMLA) script, which you can later run to perform the same migration.

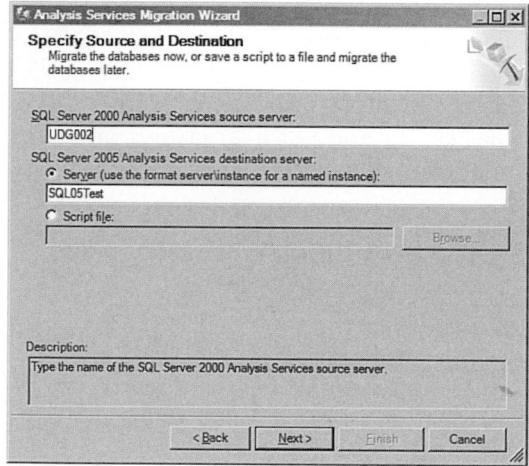

FIGURE 8.9   The Analysis Services Migration Wizard's Specify Source and Destination Screen.

Click Next, and the Select Databases to Migrate screen appears; this screen is fairly self-explanatory. Make your selections and then click Next. The Validating Databases screen appears. At this point, the wizard performs the migration and reports on its progress, noting any issues along the way.

When the wizard is done, click Next, and the Completing the Wizard screen appears, showing a summary report.

NOTE

According to Microsoft, there are three OLAP constructs that the Analysis Services Migration Wizard is unable to migrate: linked cubes, drill-through options, and remote partitions. You need to manually re-create these.

When your migration is complete, you need to remember to reprocess your cubes, or you will be unable to query the new database. You can perform this and all other relevant Analysis Services tasks by using the new SSIS Business Intelligence Development Studio.

> **NOTE**
>
> If you want to later change your new named SSAS instance to become the default instance, you use the new SSAS Rename Tool (which is not supported for clusters) by running the command `ASInstanceRename.exe` from the Run dialog box or a command prompt.

Migrating DTS Packages

To migrate your DTS packages to SSIS, you need to be sure to install SSIS when you install your new SQL Server 2005 instance.

You need to be sure the SSIS service is in the running state, and then you open SSMS's Object Explorer and navigate to the Legacy node, under Management. Then you right-click the Data Transformation Services (DTS) node. You have three options for how to deal with your existing packages:

▶ You can open any existing DTS-structured storage file (that is, `.dts` file) and edit it by using the DTS 2000 Package Designer. (You can even add connections to SQL Server 2005 instances.) Note that DTS packages built using SQL Server 7 or 2000 cannot be modified by using the SSIS tools, but they can be run as SSIS DTS execution tasks.

▶ You can import any existing DTS-structured file into the 2005 environment (SSMS) without altering it. (You can migrate it to SSIS at a later date by using the right-click menu for the package.)

▶ You can run the Package Migration Wizard to migrate one or more packages (those stored on a server or as files) to SSIS.

The first and second options are fairly self-explanatory, so let's just do a quick walk-through of the Package Migration Wizard. Click the Migration Wizard right-click menu option to begin.

> **NOTE**
>
> The Package Migration Wizard is not included with the Workgroup Edition of SQL Server 2005.

First, you need to select the source and destination servers (the source must be a SQL Server 7 or 2000 instance, and the destination must be a 2005 instance with SSIS running) on the Choose Source Location and Choose Destination Location screens.

You click Next to reach the List Packages screen (see Figure 8.10), where you check the check boxes for the packages you want to bring over. The name for each imported package is listed in the Destination Package column, and you can click there to edit it.

8

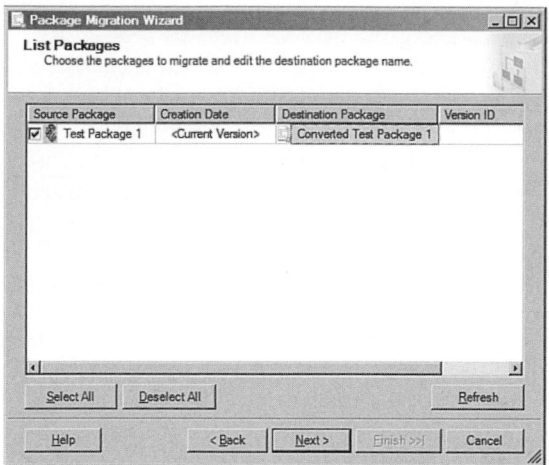

FIGURE 8.10   The Package Migration Wizard's List Packages screen.

At the next screen, you can specify a log file for the process. You click Next again and then click Finish to complete the migration.

As with all the other wizards provided with SQL Server 2005, the Package Migration Wizard reports progress and any issues on a per-package basis, offering an exportable report at the end.

After migration is complete, the original DTS package is still available on the SQL Server 7 or 2000 instance, in unmodified form. You can find imported packages in SSMS by connecting to SSIS in the Object Explorer and then navigating to the Stored Packages node and then the MSDB node.

Migrating Reporting Services

Migrating to a new side-by-side installation of Reporting Services is a multistep, manual task. It is recommended for installations that have been highly customized since the installation occurred.

Before you begin this migration process, you need to back up the following:

▶ The symmetric key (via the RSKEYMGMT tool)

▶ The Report Server database

▶ Configuration files (which end in .config)

▶ Reports

▶ Virtual directory settings

You perform the installation of Reporting Services by using Setup. You need to ensure that you do not upgrade your existing instance of SQL Server 2000 Reporting Services. When you reach the Reporting Services screen, you need to be sure to select the radio button Install but Do Not Configure the Server. When Setup is complete, you need to restore the database backup to your new SQL Server 2005 instance.

Next, you launch the new Reporting Services Configuration tool and create your virtual directories and specify the accounts to be used. Then you follow the link to the Database Setup screen, where you choose the Upgrade Database feature and perform the requested setup steps. Next, you link to the Encryption Keys screen and restore your backed-up symmetric key. Finally, you start Internet Information Services (IIS).

In terms of upgrading the reports themselves, all you need to do is open them using the Business Intelligence Development Studio, which then prompts you to convert them to the new Report Definition Language (RDL) format. (For detailed information on the changes to RDL and its object model, see Chapter 41, "SQL Server 2005 Reporting Services.")

Migrating Notification Services

The process of migrating Notification Services 2.0 (for SQL Server 2000) to SQL Server 2005 Notification Services (SSNS) is slightly different from the process you use for other components because it requires the combined use of the command prompt, the Setup program, and SSMS.

Before installing SSNS, you open a Notification Services 2.0 command prompt and disable the current instances via the `nscontrol` program:

```
nscontrol disable -name [InstanceName]
```

Next, you stop the service on all machines that are running it by using `net stop` or the Services Control Panel. Next, you unregister the 2.0 instances by using `nscontrol` again (you'll re-register these later):

```
nscontrol unregister -name [InstanceName]
```

Next, you install your new instance of Notification Services 2005 on each participating server, using SQL Server 2005 Setup. When that is complete, you open the newly installed SSNS 2005 command prompt and repair the server metadata by using the `nscontrol` `repair` command.

Next, you switch over to SSMS and expand the Notification Services node in the Object Explorer. Then you right-click your instance and choose Upgrade from the Tasks menu. Finally, you re-register the instance by using `nscontrol`:

```
nscontrol register -name [InstanceName]
```

You can also re-register the instance using SSMS, by right-clicking and then selecting Tasks, Register.

The scenario described here does not take into account any application-specific changes your Notification Services code may require (for example, changes in the `Notify()` function) for forward compatibility.

8

Upgrading In-Place

Now that you've seen how to migrate all your components by following the side-by-side migration path, let's take a look at the alternative: upgrading in-place. You achieve an in-place upgrade by running Setup and selecting your SQL Server 2000 (SP3 or greater only) instance on the Instance Name screen. Setup upgrades either the default instance or a named instance, based on your choice on the Instance Name screen. (The installation process and all its screens are described in Chapter 7 under the heading, "Install Screens, Step-By-Step.")

You need to be aware that this type of upgrade permanently modifies the SQL Server components, data, and metadata objects, and there is no going back. Of course, it's worth reiterating here that making a complete backup of all server components and content is recommended before you move forward.

You will likely be more comfortable taking the side-by-side migration path than doing an in-place upgrade, unless you have very few SQL Server features in use or you are confident about the upgrade process because you've done extensive issue resolution with the assistance of the UA.

> **NOTE**
>
> In-place upgrading is designed to be a high-availability solution, meaning that during the upgrade process, downtime for your instances is kept at an absolute minimum. But remember: If your code stops working because you haven't worked with the UA or done other testing prior to upgrading, you could end up having a low-availability result.

The SQL Server 2005 Upgrade Matrix

No software upgrade section would be complete without an illustrative table. But before you examine the one here, it's important to note the SQL Server versions from which you are allowed to upgrade to SQL Server 2005.

First, upgrading from SQL Server 6.5 or earlier versions is not supported. It is possible, however, to upgrade your 6.5 (or earlier) databases to SQL Server 7 or 2000. Then you can apply the latest service packs to these instances and upgrade from there.

For the two supported version upgrades—SQL Server 7 and 2000—you must first apply SP3 or later to 2000 or SP4 or later to 7.

Table 8.1 illustrates the supported upgrades from previous versions to SQL Server 2005, by edition.

TABLE 8.1   Supported Upgrades to SQL Server 2005

Previous SQL Server Edition	Can Be Upgraded to SQL Server 2005 Edition
SQL Server 6.5 (any SP) or earlier SQL Server versions	(none)
SQL Server 7 Enterprise Edition with SP4	SQL Server 2005 Enterprise Edition

TABLE 8.1   Continued

Previous SQL Server Edition	Can Be Upgraded to SQL Server 2005 Edition
SQL Server 7 Developer Edition with SP4	SQL Server 2005 Developer Edition or Enterprise Edition
SQL Server 7 Standard Edition with SP4	SQL Server 2005 Standard Edition or Enterprise Edition
SQL Server 7 Desktop Edition with SP4	SQL Server 2005 Workgroup Edition or Standard Edition
SQL Server 7 Evaluation Edition with SP4	(none)
MSDE 7 with SP4	SQL Server 2005 Express Edition
SQL Server 2000 Enterprise Edition with SP3	SQL Server 2005 Enterprise Edition
SQL Server 2000 IA64 Enterprise Edition	SQL Server 2005 IA64 Enterprise Edition
SQL Server 2000 Developer Edition with SP3	SQL Server 2005 Developer Edition
SQL Server 2000 IA64 Developer Edition	SQL Server 2005 IA64 Enterprise Edition or Developer Edition
SQL Server 2000 Standard Edition with SP3	SQL Server 2005 Enterprise Edition, Standard Edition, or Developer Edition
SQL Server 2000 Workgroup Edition	SQL Server 2005 Enterprise Edition, Standard Edition, Developer Edition, or Workgroup Edition
SQL Server 2000 Personal Edition	SQL Server 2005 SE, Workgroup Edition, or Express Edition
SQL Server 2000 Evaluation Edition with SP3	SQL Server 2005 Evaluation Edition
MSDE 2000	SQL Server 2005 Workgroup Edition or Express Edition
SQL Server 2005 Community Technology Preview (CTP) Editions (any)	(none—these must all be removed from the system prior to SQL Server 2005 installation [any edition])

To upgrade to SQL Server 2005 automatically, you use the same Setup program you would for a fresh installation. The installation process is the same for both installing and upgrading (with the exception of the Instance Name screen), so they don't bear repeating. Instead, the following sections detail automatic upgrade considerations for each SQL Server component.

NOTE

Upgrading has the following prerequisites for your previous version of SQL Server Agent:

▶ It must be configured to work under Windows authentication.

▶ Its service account must be a member of the sysadmin role.

Other Installed, Upgraded, and Discontinued Components
Let's take a quick look at a couple of the components that Setup upgrades:

▶ **MSXML 6.0**—This is installed by Setup but runs side-by-side with MSXML 3 and 4.

▶ **.NET Framework 2.0**—This is installed by Setup but runs side-by-side with previous editions. It is not compatible, however, with beta editions of itself; you must uninstall beta versions prior to installing SQL Server 2005.

NOTE

Microsoft English Query has been discontinued, and there is no upgrade path for it. If you need it, you may continue to use your SQL Server 2000 version or seek an alternative solution.

Upgrading Databases
Let's begin the upgrade walkthrough with the most important aspect, databases and the database engine. Before upgrading the database engine, it is strongly recommended that you do the following:

▶ Create full, verified backups of your SQL Server 7 or 2000 databases.

▶ Run the appropriate DBCC consistency checks (for example, DBCC CHECKDB, DBCC CHECKFILEGROUP, and DBCC CHECKTABLE).

▶ Make sure the system databases on your pre-2005 instances (for example, master, msdb, tempdb, and model) are all set to auto-grow.

▶ Disable any stored procedures that get kicked off when the SQL Server service starts. (Check the registered SQL Server properties in Enterprise Manager.)

▶ Disable database replication and empty the replication log.

After you perform all these actions, you are ready to begin the process.

Setup automatically upgrades all objects that are common to all databases, including the following:

▶ Tables, views, indexes, relationships, and constraints

▶ Stored procedures, functions, and triggers

▶ User-defined types (unless you've named the type xml, which is now a native SQL Server 2005 type), rules, and defaults

▶ Logins (unless you have one named sys, which is now a schema in SQL Server 2005), users, and permissions

▶ Database diagrams

> **NOTE**
>
> One caveat: Databases that use filegroups other than PRIMARY cannot be upgraded if the filegroup is set to read-only. You should review the Database Engine Upgrade Issues topic in the compiled help for the UA before going forward; it lists many other issues such as this.

You need to run the installer and make selections. When you reach the Instance Name screen, you can choose to install SQL Server 2005 as the default instance (replacing your SQL Server 7 or 2000 default instance) or as a new named instance (replacing any named instance with the same name). (Note that only one default instance of any version of SQL Server is possible on a given server.)

You need to make your selections and complete the installation, referring to the per-screen instructions detailed in Chapter 7. When your upgrade of the database engine is complete, it is recommended that you perform the following on all databases (also recommend for side-by-side migration):

▶ Repopulate your full-text catalogs. (This is automatically done for databases where Full-Text indexing was enabled prior to the upgrade.)

▶ Run the sp_updatestats system stored procedure to update statistics.

▶ Run the DBCC UPDATEUSAGE command to fix table and index rowcounts

▶ Make sure to set your databases' compatibility level to 90 if you want to take advantage of the latest and greatest T-SQL features.

> **Upgrading Replicated Databases**
>
> The replication security model has changed quite a bit since SQL Server 2000, and you should read Chapter 15, "Replication," to get a feel for what's new.
>
> If you disable replication prior to the upgrade, you'll need to enable it after Setup completes. You'll also need to run the Snapshot and Merge Agents to update your metadata.

The sections that follow examine how in-place upgrading works with all the other SQL Server components.

Upgrading Analysis Services

During Setup you need to choose to install the Analysis Services component. When you reach the Components to Upgrade screen, Setup prompts you to choose your existing instance of Analysis Services. Here, the instance name (which is also visible by clicking the Installed Instances button) is likely the server name itself because SQL Server 2000 Analysis Services does not support named instances (only a single default instance). The Setup program then automatically upgrades your OLAP databases to SQL Server 2005 by re-creating them in the new SSAS format. When this is complete, you should reprocess them all.

> **NOTE**
>
> 64-bit users must upgrade Analysis Services *before* upgrading the SQL Server database engine. You can, of course, run Setup more than once, so it is recommended in this situation that you upgrade Analysis Services first (separately) and then upgrade your other components on subsequent runs.

Upgrading DTS

SSIS is a complete rewrite of the DTS runtime, and this is why your DTS packages are not automatically migrated to SQL Server 2005 while Setup is running. Essentially, you have the same options you have when traveling the migration path. For this reason, you should see the section "Migrating DTS Packages," earlier in this chapter.

> **The Meta Data Services Repository**
>
> As the UA indicates, SQL Server 2005 does not support or use the Meta Data Services Repository (it is officially deprecated). However, in SQL Server 2005 you can still run DTS packages saved thereby using the SQL Server 2000 DTS runtime utility *if* they were saved to the local filesystem and you have imported them so that they appear in SSMS. See Chapter 40, "SQL Server Integration Services," for more details on executing a DTS 2000 package task in SSIS.

Upgrading Reporting Services

You can perform an in-place upgrade of any instance of SQL Server 2000 Reporting Services. However, there is one (perhaps major) caveat: Your team cannot have changed any of the initially installed configuration settings from their defaults. If any changes have been made since installation to either the virtual directory properties, service accounts used (including ASPNET), or file extensions (and related security), the UA should warn you that these must be changed back or the upgrade will fail.

Before upgrading Reporting Services, you need to back up the following:

- ▶ The symmetric key (by using the RSKEYMGMT tool)
- ▶ The Report Server database (whose table structures are changed during upgrade)
- ▶ Configuration files
- ▶ Reports

You need to stop IIS and the Report Services Windows service on each machine on which you will be running Setup. (For a Web farm [now known as a *scale-out* implementation], Setup must be run on every node.) Then you run Setup and select your existing instance at the appropriate screen. The Setup program upgrades the instance in-place, including all its components and any published reports and snapshots.

When Setup completes, you can upgrade your reports by opening them in Business Intelligence Development Studio (which prompts you to do so). They are also upgraded automatically when published to an instance of Reporting Services 2005. This upgrade is permanent.

The upgrade process removes the following components:

▶ Report Designer (which it replaces with Business Intelligence Development Studio)

▶ Reporting Services Books Online (because new docs are included in Books Online)

▶ Sample files and command-line tools

Upgrading Notification Services

Notification Services 2.0 (for SQL Server 2000) components are automatically upgraded during the automated Setup program. For details on how to migrate 2.0 instances after Setup runs, please see the section "Migrating Notification Services," earlier in this chapter.

Upgrading Clusters

If you want to join a nonclustered pre-2005 instance to a 2005 failover cluster, you must first install the new SQL Server 2005 cluster and then import your databases as described earlier. This is because only an existing SQL Server 7 or 2000 failover cluster can be upgraded to a SQL Server 2005 failover cluster.

Unattended Upgrades

If you've never used the unattended setup feature of SQL Server, you should refer to the "Unattended Installations" section in Chapter 7 to get a feel for the process.

The following are a few of the setup settings relevant to upgrades:

▶ **UPGRADE**—This setting specifies the SQL Server component to be upgraded (for example, UPGRADE=SQL_Engine).

▶ **INSTANCENAME**—This setting names the existing instance to be upgraded. For the default instance, you use the special value MSSQLSERVER.

▶ **SAVESYSDB**—This setting specifies that pre-2005 system databases are not to be deleted from their current folder (for example, SAVESYSDB=1).

▶ **USESYSDB**—This setting specifies the path to the data folder where the new system databases should stored (for example, USESYSDB="c:\Program Files\Microsoft SQL Server\MSSQL.1\MSSQL").

You need to be sure to review the special example file `template.ini` to learn about all the other possible upgrade settings. Then you can run `setup.exe` as described in Chapter 7 when you're ready to go.

Summary

Now that you've taken in a great deal of information to help your organization transition to SQL Server 2005, it's time to put that knowledge to work by actively taking the plunge.

If you need even more documentation, you can look to the many other chapters in this book and even more resources on the Web that can assist you. Of course, there's an abundance of content on Microsoft's website (after all, it's in Microsoft's interests that customers upgrade to SQL Server 2005), including webcasts, TechNet, and online learning courses available to MSDN subscribers.

When your new environment is ready to go, you can move on to Chapter 9, "Client Installation and Configuration," to learn how to get your clients up and running with your new installation of SQL Server 2005.

Client Installation and Configuration

IN THIS CHAPTER

▶ What's New in Client Installation and Configuration

▶ Client/Server Networking Considerations

▶ Client Installation

▶ Client Configuration

▶ Client Data Access Technologies

SQL Server 2005 provides vast improvements in its client/server architecture that improve speed and security, simplify configuration and maintenance, and enhance management capabilities.

This chapter contains the latest information on how to install, configure, and connect to SQL Server 2005 from the client side, and it offers key server-side insights in an effort to provide a complete understanding.

What's New in Client Installation and Configuration

SQL Server 2005 introduces a powerful new net-library known as SQL Native Client (SNAC). The release of SNAC heralds a shift in Microsoft's data access component distribution strategy: This latest SQL Server net-library is no longer bundled into Microsoft Data Access Components (MDAC). This has freed Microsoft to develop SNAC (and thus, the client-connectivity aspects of SQL Server) on a separate track from MDAC.

SNAC provides clients with access to the hottest database engine features, such as database mirroring, data types such as xml and user-defined types (UDTs), encrypted communications, Multiple Active Result Sets (MARS), query notifications, snapshot isolation, bulk copy operations, password expiration, and more.

This chapter examines the role of SNAC in the overall client/server architecture and also describes how to connect using several of the existing (and updated) providers, drivers, and tools.

Client/Server Networking Considerations

Before delving into all that's new on the client side in SQL Server, it's important that you take note of a few server-side changes. This will help you gain an understanding of which networking features are initially configured on the server (after an installation or upgrade) as well as how incoming connections are dealt with. Such knowledge can be invaluable in diagnosing connectivity issues.

If you've been following along chapter-by-chapter, you've just learned how to install or upgrade an instance of SQL Server 2005. In order to get your clients up and running fast, it's crucial to be sure the database engine is listening for them.

The following sections describe how to set up the server's basic network configuration, including configuring it to accept remote connections, learning which protocols it supports, and understanding how it listens for and responds to client requests.

Server Network Protocols

The first and most basic step after a SQL Server installation or upgrade is to make sure the appropriate network protocols are configured on the server.

> **NOTE**
>
> Note that the term *server* is used here to refer to an instance of the SQL Server 2005 database engine. The term *client* is used generally to mean any program that needs to communicate with a server. The server and client may reside on the same physical machine (especially when using SQL Server Mobile and Express editions).

First, you should ensure that the protocols your clients once used to connect to SQL Server 7 or 2000 (or that your clients would like to use) are both supported by SQL Server 2005 and configured.

It might surprise you to learn that the following protocols are no longer supported by SQL Server 2005:

- ▶ AppleTalk
- ▶ Banyan VINES
- ▶ Multiprotocol
- ▶ NW Link IPX/SPX

If you were using these protocols and you've just upgraded, your clients will no longer be able to connect. The following are the only protocols that SQL Server 2005 supports:

- ▶ Named pipes
- ▶ Shared memory

▶ TCP/IP

▶ Virtual Interface Adapter (VIA)

If you were using any of these protocols and you just upgraded, Setup will have copied your pre-upgrade settings over to SQL Server 2005, including the enabled state, IP addresses, TCP ports, pipe names, and so on. Clients can simply test their connections to be sure the upgrade was successful, and in most cases, no changes need to be made.

If you've just installed a new SQL Server 2005 instance, you might be surprised to learn that (in keeping with Microsoft's secure-by-default strategy), by default, shared memory is the only protocol enabled.

NOTE

Shared memory is new, and it works only for connections both to and from the same machine hosting the database engine. Shared memory is used by client tools such as SQL Server Management Studio (SSMS) and SQLCMD, and it's also a good choice for use by locally running custom applications because it is secure by design. (It is the default protocol used by local applications that do not specify otherwise.)

All remote connections to SQL Server are thus disabled by default. The following is an extremely common client-side error message illustrating connection failure due to disabled remote connectivity:

```
An error has occurred while establishing a connection to the server.
When connecting to SQL Server 2005, this failure may be caused by the fact that
under the default settings SQL Server does not allow remote connections.
```

The exact wording of this message varies slightly, depending on the particular client or connection method used. The same error also occurs when the database engine service is stopped.

To enable remote connections, you launch the Surface Area Configuration (SAC) tool and then, on the main screen, click the Surface Area Configuration for Services and Connections hyperlink. On the SQL Server 2005 Surface Area screen (see Figure 9.1) that appears, you click the Database Engine node located under your instance name, and then you click the Remote Connections node. Finally, you select a radio button on the right according to your preference. Keep in mind that these changes take effect only after you restart the database engine service.

When this step is complete, you (or your administrator) can launch SQL Server Configuration Manager (SSCM) to complete the server network configuration. This process is covered in detail in Chapter 6, "SQL Server System and Database Administration."

6

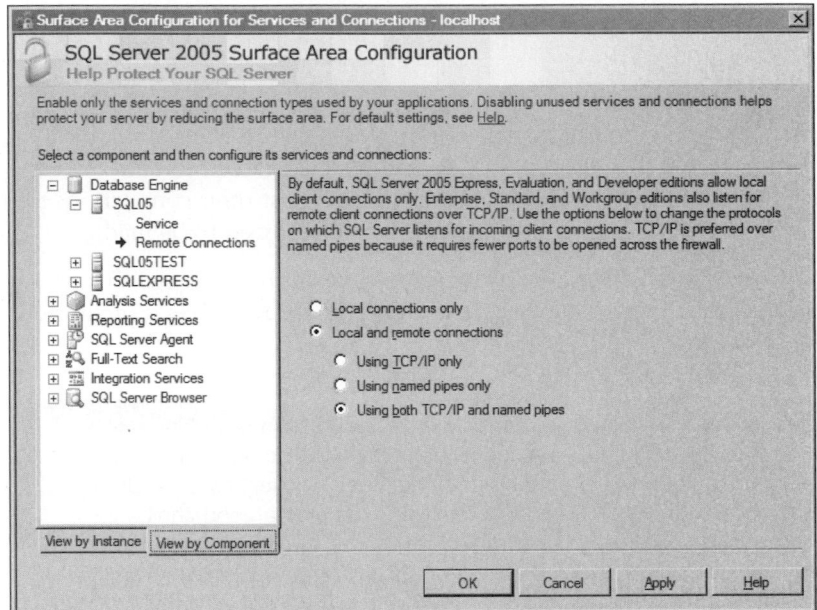

FIGURE 9.1   Enabling remote connections over TCP/IP and named pipes using SAC.

Note that SSCM is triple-purpose in that it is a replacement for SQL Server 2000's Server Network Utility, Client Network Utility, and Service Manager.

> **NOTE**
>
> SQL Server listens on all configured protocols simultaneously, giving no preference or priority to any. This is in contrast to the explicitly prioritized manner in which clients attempt to connect via all configured protocols, as you'll soon see.

The Server Endpoint Layer

A new networking feature in SQL Server 2005 adds an additional layer to the client/server network structure: Tabular Data Stream (TDS) endpoints. When you install (or upgrade to) SQL Server 2005, a single, nondroppable, default system endpoint is created on the server for each protocol, even if that protocol is disabled or otherwise unavailable.

> **NOTE**
>
> The term *endpoint* in this context refers to the combination of a protocol selection, one or more IP addresses (or pipe names), and any associated port numbers.

These are the default system endpoints:

- ▶ `TSQL Local Machine` (for shared memory)

- ▶ `TSQL Named Pipes`

- ▶ `TSQL Default TCP`

- ▶ `TSQL Default VIA`

- ▶ `Dedicated Admin Connection` (also known as the DAC)

You can view these endpoints and check their status by executing the following T-SQL statement:

```
Use Master
GO
SELECT * FROM sys.endpoints WHERE principal_id = 1
```

By default, all users are granted access to these endpoints (except the DAC, covered in Chapter 6, which is only for members of the `sysadmin` role). Administrators can create new endpoints on the server to increase connection security by stopping (or disabling) the default system endpoints and then creating new user-defined endpoints that only specific clients can access. (Creating a new system endpoint automatically revokes permission on the default endpoint of the same protocol to the `public` group.)

NOTE

Only one named pipe and one shared memory endpoint can exist per instance, but multiple VIA or TCP endpoints (with different port and address settings) can coexist.

Each endpoint communicates with clients via TDS packets, which are formatted on the server side by SNAC and on the client side by SNAC or another of the net-libraries.

Administrators have the option of stopping and starting endpoints while sessions are still active, preventing new connections from being made while still supporting existing ones.

An administrator can grant or revoke endpoint access to specific users or groups (for example, preventing backdoor access through client tools). It is therefore important for clients to both know that this structure exists and to learn how they receive permission to connect to endpoints through a server-side process known as *provisioning*.

Client Access Provisioning

There are three fairly straightforward rules of access provisioning. If any of these rules is met by an incoming client, that client may access the endpoint. If none are met, the client is denied access. These are the rules:

- ▶ If the client specifies an IP address and a TCP port that match those of a specific endpoint, the client may connect to it, if the client has permission to do so.

▶ If only the TCP port specified by the client matches that of a specific endpoint, and the endpoint is configured to listen on all IP addresses, the client may connect to it, if the client has permission to do so.

▶ If neither the TCP port nor IP address is specified, but the default endpoint for the protocol is enabled, the client may attempt to connect to the endpoint.

NOTE

If the endpoint to which access is successfully provisioned is currently stopped, or if the user does not have permission to connect to it, no further endpoints are tried and the client cannot continue.

For example, let's say a server has three TCP/IP endpoints defined:

▶ The default (TSQL Default TCP), which listens on all IP addresses and Port 1433 (a default SQL Server 2005 instance)

▶ A user-created endpoint called TCP_UserCreated 101_91, configured to listen on IP address 192.168.1.101 and Port 91

▶ A second user-created endpoint, called TCP_UserCreated Any_91, which is configured to listen on all IP addresses and Port 91

A client attempts to connect specifically to 192.168.1.101:91. Because this is an exact address and port match, the client can try to connect to TCP_UserCreated 101_91. Having an exact address and port match meets the first provisioning rule.

A second client attempts to connect to any IP address on Port 91. Because there is no exact address match, the client cannot attempt to connect to TCP_UserCreated 101_91. However, the client can attempt to connect to TCP_UserCreated Any_91 because it is configured to listen on all IP addresses. This meets the second provisioning rule.

A third client attempts to connect on any port and any address. If TSQL Default TCP is started, the client is granted permission to attempt to connect. This meets the third provisioning rule.

NOTE

Settings such as IP addresses and TCP ports are used to implicitly connect to specific endpoints. These values are specified by clients in connection strings, data source names (DSNs), and server aliases, all of which are discussed later in this chapter in the "Client Configuration" section.

If at any time you want to discover which protocol and endpoint a connected client is currently using, all you need is the SPID number to run the following T-SQL:

```
Use Master
GO
DECLARE @SPID int

SELECT name, net_transport, session_id, e.endpoint_id
FROM sys.dm_exec_connections d
JOIN sys.endpoints e
ON e.endpoint_id = d.endpoint_id
WHERE session_id = @SPID
go
name                        net_transport       session_id    endpoint_id
TSQL Local Machine          Shared memory       53            2
```

The following is an example of the client-side error message that results if the TSQL Default TCP endpoint is stopped and you try to connect to it:

```
A connection was successfully established with the server, but then an error
occurred during the login process
```

Now that you know a bit about endpoints, let's go a bit deeper and explore how client connections are facilitated on the server.

The Role of SQL Browser

You might be surprised to learn that when clients try to connect to SQL Server 2005, their first network access is made over UDP Port 1434 to the new SQL Browser service.

Regardless of the encryption status of the connection itself, login credentials are always encrypted when passed to SQL Server 2005 (to foil any malicious packet sniffing). If a certificate signed by an external authority (such as VeriSign) is not installed on the server, SQL Server automatically generates a self-signed certificate for use in encrypting login credentials.

6

SQL Browser is the upgrade to the SQL Server Resolution Protocol (SSRP) and its job is to hand out instance names, version numbers, and connection information for each (nonhidden) instance of the database engine (and Analysis Services) residing on a server—not only for SQL Server 2005 instances, but for SQL Server 7 and 2000 instances as well.

When clients connect by name, SQL Browser searches for that name in its list and then hands out the connection data for that instance.

Ports, Pipes, and Instances

Default instances of SQL Server 2005 are automatically configured (just as in previous editions) to listen on all IP addresses and TCP Port 1433.

Named instances, on the other hand, are automatically configured to listen on all IP addresses, using dynamic TCP port numbers that change when the database engine is restarted. (Most often, these change only when the port number last used by the service is in use by a different application.)

If the SQL Browser service is not running and a named instance is not using a fixed TCP port number, clients must specify the current port number in order to connect. SQL Browser, therefore, is configured to auto-start on servers that contain one or more named instances because clients connecting by name or address only need to tell them the new port number; they cannot keep track of it themselves. SQL Browser is also required for enumerating the server lists used to connect with client tools such as SMSS.

> **NOTE**
>
> If named instances have fixed port numbers known to clients, or if a pipe name is well known, SQL Browser is not required to connect.

> **NOTE**
>
> For named pipes, the default instance's pipe name is `\sql\query`; for named instances, the pipe name is `MSSQL$instancename\sql\query`.

When a link is made, endpoint provisioning kicks in to finalize (or reject) the connection.

Client Installation

Now that you have acquired some knowledge about the most important server-side networking considerations, it's time to learn how to install and configure the client-side half of the equation.

Installation Requirements

All SQL Server 2005 installations (including client-tools-only or SNAC-only installations) require Windows Installer 3.1, which is freely downloadable from Microsoft and included in Windows XP Service Pack 2 (SP2) and Windows Server 2003 SP1.

The same operating system requirements for server installations apply to client tools and SNAC installations, with one exception: When you install SNAC by itself on top of Windows XP, only SP1 is required, and when you install SNAC on top of Windows Server 2003, SP1 is not required. You can review the complete list of requirements in Chapter 7, "Installing SQL Server 2005," in the section "Installation Requirements."

Note that SNAC and the client tools both depend on the presence of the .NET Framework 2.0, and the client tools in turn depend on SNAC. Setup automatically installs both Framework 2.0 and SNAC, when required, on the target machine. If incompatible or beta versions exist that must be uninstalled first, Setup lets you know.

Installing the Client Tools

To install the SQL Server 2005 client tools, you start Setup normally and follow the prompts as described in Chapter 7. When the Components to Install screen appears, you check only the Workstation Components check box, as shown in Figure 9.2.

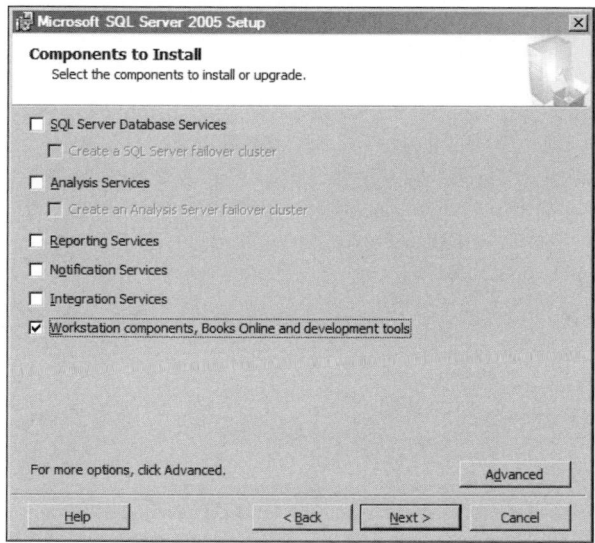

FIGURE 9.2   Performing a client-tools-only installation.

To perform the same kind of install by using the command-line (Setup doubles as a command-line application), you can run the following:

```
driveletter:\Servers\Setup>start /Wait setup.exe
➥ADDLOCAL=Client_Components,Connectivity,SQL_Tools90,SQL_BooksOnline
```

That's all there is to it!

You will be happy to learn that the SQL Server 2005 client tools can safely be installed side-by-side with your SQL Server 7 or 2000 client tools. You can even access databases and other objects created in either edition (with a few notable exceptions, such as database diagrams) by using either toolset.

The sections that follow describe how to install and use a few of the new client tools for client configuration and testing.

Installing SNAC

This section shows how easy it is to install SNAC, the key net-library for SQL Server 2005 and beyond.

As mentioned earlier, both the SQL Server 2005 database engine and the client tools depend on SNAC. You can launch the SNAC installer from the Install SQL Native Client hyperlink on the Autoplay screen of Setup, or you can simply launch it on its own from the SQL Server installation medium by running *driveletter:*\Servers\Setup\ sqlncli.msi.

Table 9.1 describes the files that the Microsoft Installer (MSI) package installs.

TABLE 9.1   Files Installed by the SNAC MSI Package

Filename	Purpose	Installed To
sqlncli.h	C++ header file (replaces sqloledb.h)	*Program Files*\Microsoft SQL Server\90\SDK
sqlncli.lib	C++ library file for calling BCP functions (replaces odbcbcp.lib)	*Program Files*\Microsoft SQL Server\90\SDK
sqlncli.dll	Main library, containing both the ODBC driver and OLE DB provider (houses all functionality)	*WINDIR*\system32
sqlnclir.rll	Resource file	*WINDIR*\system32
sqlncli.chm	Compiled help file for creating data sources using SNAC	*WINDIR*\system32

TIP

For detailed information on how to write C++ code by using the header and library files included in the SNAC software development kit (SDK), see the Books Online article "Using the SQL Native Client Header and Library Files."

The SNAC installer has two primary options (shown in Figure 9.3):

▶ Install SNAC by itself

▶ Install the SNAC SDK files along with it

NOTE

By default, all network protocols except for VIA are enabled on the client during installation.

That's all there is to installing SNAC!

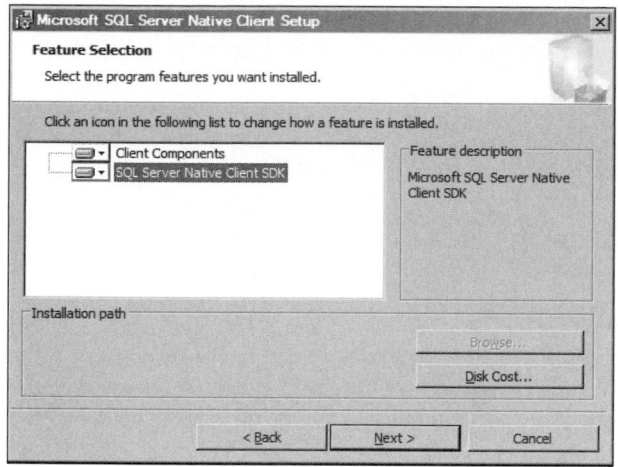

FIGURE 9.3   SNAC's installation options.

Redistributing SNAC with Custom Client Applications

If you build an application that relies on SNAC, you need to be aware that there are two ways it can be redistributed:

▶ As part of any SQL Server 2005 installation or upgrade

▶ As a custom application installation dependency

When building MSI files for an application, it is important that you register `sqlncli.msi` as a package dependency (and, of course, to install it as well, if it is not present on the destination machine). This helps ensure that SNAC will not be accidentally uninstalled from the destination machine without first flashing a warning to users, indicating that any application that relies on it will break. To do this, you execute the following command line early on in your application's installation process:

```
msiexec /i sqlncli.msi APPGUID={unique identifier for your product}
```

NOTE

The program name for SNAC found in the Add or Remove Programs Control Panel applet is Microsoft SQL Server Native Client, not SQL Native Client, as it is commonly known.

Client Configuration

Client configuration is a many-leveled beast, consisting of operating system tasks such as installing protocols, application tasks such as choosing or coding to a specific application programming interface (API), provider, or driver, and maintenance tasks such as configuring network settings, building connection strings, and so on. The following sections cover a broad range of these tasks, focusing on the most common. Many examples utilize TCP/IP both because it is the default protocol for remote clients and because it is the most widely used.

No chapter can cover all the possible ways of connecting, but this one is designed to give you the tools you need to get set up right from the start and to navigate your way in case specific issues arise.

The first client configuration tool we'll look at is SSCM.

Client Configuration Using SSCM

The Client Network Utility of previous SQL Server editions has been decommissioned, and all its functionality is now built into SSCM. This includes the ability to create server aliases, to enable and prioritize network protocols, to control the various SQL Server services, and more.

NOTE

One thing Microsoft is keen on including in Books Online is that neither Setup nor sqlncli.msi installs the actual network protocols themselves, nor do they enable them at the operating system level. This means that if you do not have TCP/IP installed and you need to start using it, you have to first set it up by using the Network Connections Control Panel applet (if you're using Windows, that is).

You can launch SSCM directly from its Start menu icon, or you can access it in the Services and Applications node of the Computer Management console. When you have SSCM up and running, to access its client-side functionality you expand its top-level node (SQL Server Configuration Manager (*servername*)) and then you click the SQL Native Client Configuration node. Below it, you click the Client Protocols node to reveal the enabled state and priority order of each protocol, in grid format, in the right pane (see Figure 9.4).

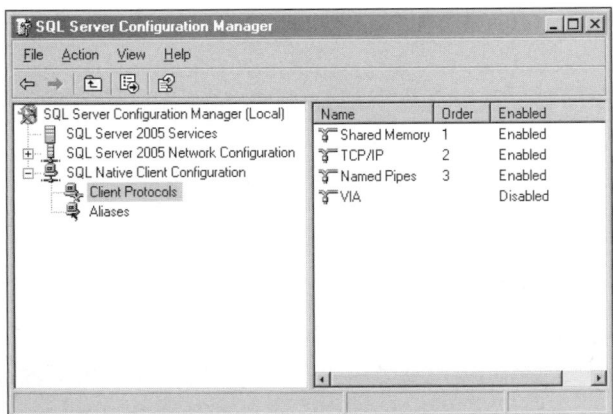

FIGURE 9.4   SSCM's Client Protocols screen.

From this screen, you can right-click any of the protocols to change their enabled state, view properties pages, or change the default connection order (except that of shared memory, which is always tried first and whose order cannot be changed). The following is the default connection order for clients connecting without the benefit of a server alias, connection string, or other means:

1. Shared memory

2. TCP/IP

3. Named pipes

(As the grid shows, VIA is disabled by default.) When connecting remotely, TCP/IP is the first protocol attempted because shared memory is local only.

> **NOTE**
>
> When a client does not specify a connection protocol, SNAC automatically tries each protocol in the list in sequence, according to the Order column. The first protocol to connect successfully wins.
>
> If the winning connection is subsequently rejected by the server for any reason, no other protocols are tried.
>
> Note also that local clients using MDAC 2.8 or lower cannot connect using shared memory, and they are automatically switched to named pipes if they attempt to do so.

Let's examine one of the protocols. To start, you need to double-click TCP/IP under the Name column to open the TCP/IP Properties screen (see Figure 9.5).

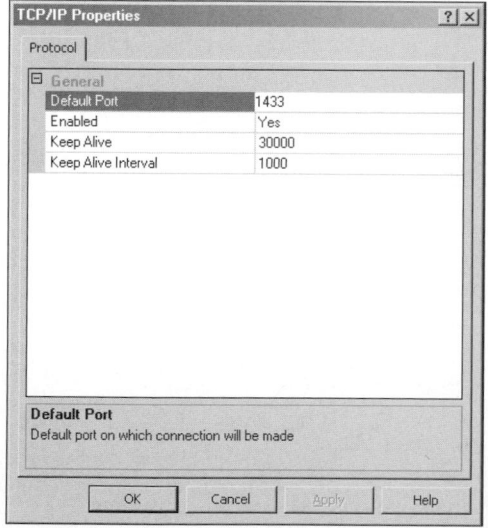

FIGURE 9.5   The TCP/IP Properties screen.

The values stored here are used by TCP/IP clients as default connection values, and they are applied only when a specific server alias or other configuration mechanism is not in use. They are also used by the SQL Server 2005 client tools (but not the SQL Server 7 or 2000 client tools) when shared memory is not available.

As you can see, the default port, 1433, is set up to connect to the more commonly configured default instances of SQL Server. By editing the values on this page, you can change the default port number, enabled state, keep-alive values, and other settings (when editing other protocols). You should edit and enable the protocols according to your specific needs.

Server Aliases

A *server alias* is a name that is used like a server name that represents a group of server settings for use by connecting clients. Server aliases are very handy because of the way they simplify connection parameters: Clients need only specify the alias name, and SNAC pulls the rest of the information (such as the IP address, TCP port number, and pipe name) from SSCM at connection time.

To create a server alias, you right-click the `Aliases` node under `SQL Native Client Configuration` and choose New Alias. On the Alias - New screen that appears (see Figure 9.6), you specify the alias name, protocol (except shared memory, for which you cannot create an alias), and server name. (`local`, `.`, and `localhost` also work for local connections over TCP/IP or named pipes.).

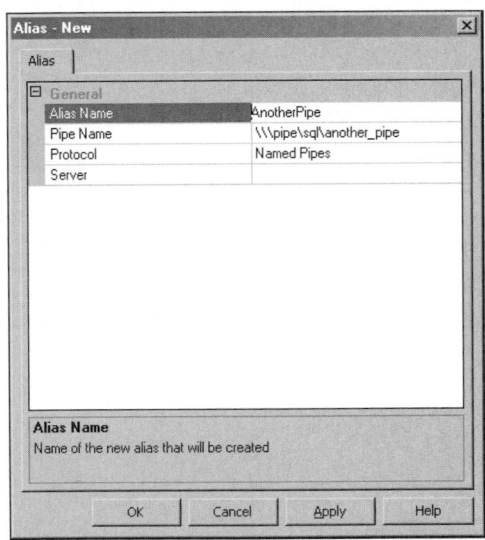

FIGURE 9.6   Alias properties for a new named pipe server alias.

When you make your protocol selection, the grid rows change to dynamically reveal the settings particular to that protocol. When you are finished, you click OK, and your alias is ready for use.

Connection Encryption

With SQL Server 2005, it is easy to set up Secure Sockets Layer (SSL) encrypted client/server communication over all protocols. The SNAC net-library handles the tasks of encryption and decryption on both the server and client ends. (Note that this process does cause a slight decrease in performance.) Setting it up requires both server-side and client-side configuration changes; this section covers only the client-side changes in detail.

SQL Server 2005 enables encryption using two types of certificates:

▶ Certificates generated by and obtained from an external certification authority such as VeriSign

▶ Certificates generated by SQL Server 2005 (known as *self-signed certificates*)

The bit strength of the encryption (40-bit or 128-bit) depends on the bit strength of the operating systems of the computers involved in the connection.

To set up the server for encryption, your administrator registers a certificate on the server operating system (using the Certificates Management console) and then installs it in the database engine.

If an externally signed certificate is not installed on the server, SQL Server uses its built-in self-signed certificate. (A server administrator may also create and save a self-signed certificate by using SQL Server 2005 via the new `CREATE CERTIFICATE` and `BACKUP CERTIFICATE` T-SQL syntax.) It is also up to the server to decide whether encryption is required or optional for connecting clients.

The client's half of the job is to have installed what is known as a *root-level certificate* that is issued by the same certification authority as the server's certificate. To install a root-level certificate, you right-click the certificate itself (a `.cer` or `.crt` file) and select Install Certificate to launch the Certificate Import Wizard. You click Next on the welcome screen to reach the Certificate Store screen (see Figure 9.7). Then you select the first radio button (Automatically Select the Certificate Store) and then click Next. Finally, you click Finish.

Next, you launch SSCM, right-click the `SQL Native Client Configuration` node and then select Properties. The Flags tab appears (see Figure 9.8) in the Properties window.

You set the `Force Protocol Encryption` property value to `Yes`. This causes clients to request an SSL-encrypted connection when communicating with the database engine. If the server does not respond in kind, the connection is killed.

The `Trust Server Certificate` property gives clients a choice in how they deal with server certificates:

▶ To use a self-signed certificate, you set the property value to `Yes`. This option prevents SNAC from validating the server's certificate.

▶ To use an externally signed certificate, you set the property value to `No`, which causes SNAC to validate the server's certificate.

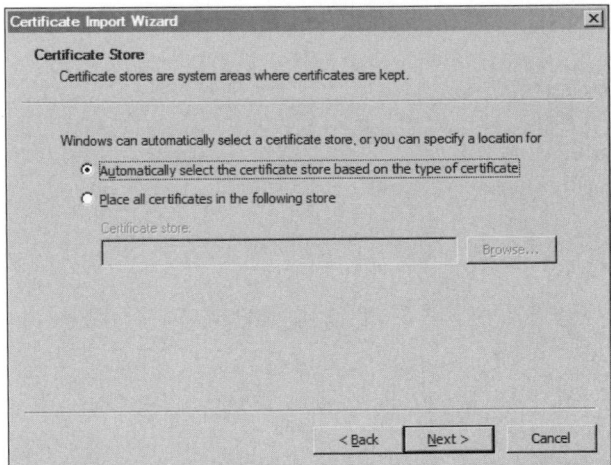

FIGURE 9.7   Importing a certificate on the client computer using the Certificate Import Wizard.

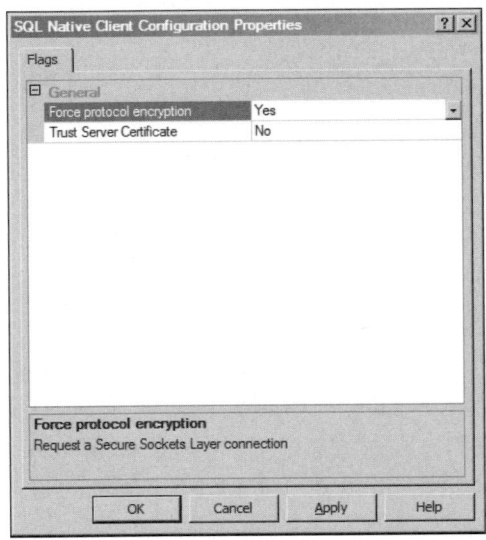

FIGURE 9.8   Forcing clients to request an encrypted connection using SSCM.

SSMS can also connect over an encrypted connection. When connecting using the Connect to Server dialog, you click the Options button and then click the Connection Properties tab. Then you choose your database and protocol and, at the bottom left, check the Encrypt Connection check box.

Client Data Access Technologies

The question of which data access technology to use with SQL Server 2005 is a common one, with a seemingly easy answer: Use SNAC because it has all the latest and greatest functionality, all rolled into one. (You'll learn how to use SNAC in the sections that follow.) A more correct answer is that it depends on which software technologies your clients currently use and what their specific needs are.

Your data access options consist of providers and drivers, whose functionality is often encapsulated inside code libraries known as *net-libraries* (such as SNAC's `sqlncli.dll`). In addition to these net-libraries, supporting services such as MDAC's OLE DB Core Services are also available, providing useful functionality not found in the net-libraries, such as connection pooling. (ADO.NET also functions as a service, to a certain degree.)

Provider Choices

A *provider* is software used for accessing various data stores in a consistent manner conforming to a specification, such as OLE DB. A provider may contain an API. Clients that use providers are known as *consumers*. SMSS and SQLCMD, for example, are consumers of the SNAC OLE DB provider.

You can choose from the following providers:

- ▶ **SQL Native Client OLE DB provider**—This is the latest OLE DB provider, and it is built into SNAC; it is also known as `SQLNCLI`. COM applications might want to switch to this provider to access the latest functionality; doing so also provides access to SQL Server 7 and 2000 databases.

- ▶ **.NET Framework data provider for SQL Server**—This data provider is built into the `System.Data.SqlClient` namespace in the .NET Framework. Managed code applications should use it to access the latest SQL Server 2005 functionality from .NET 2.0 applications. .NET 1.0 and 1.1 applications do not have access to all the latest SQL Server 2005 functionality through this provider.

- ▶ **Microsoft OLE DB provider for SQL Server**—This OLE DB provider, known as `SQLOLEDB`, is specialized for accessing SQL Server data and is distributed with MDAC. COM applications may continue to use it to access SQL Server 2005, or they can switch to SQLNCLI for the latest functionality.

- ▶ **Microsoft OLE DB provider for ODBC**—This deprecated OLE DB provider, known as `MSDASQL`, is distributed with MDAC. ADO applications can continue to use it to access SQL Server 2005, but SQL Server does not support the latest SNAC-specific OLE DB functionality.

Microsoft has also made available a few implementation-specific OLE DB providers, such as the OLE DB provider for DB2, a COM component for integrating IBM DB2 and SQL Server 2005 data.

6

Driver Choices

A *driver* in this context can be defined as software that conforms to a standard such as Open Database Connectivity (ODBC) and provides an API for accessing a specific type of data store. osql.exe is a good example of an application that uses an ODBC driver (the SNAC driver).

These are the available drivers:

▶ **SQL Native Client ODBC driver**—This is the latest ODBC driver, and it is built into SNAC. COM applications might want to switch to this driver to access the latest functionality.

▶ **Microsoft ODBC driver for SQL Server**—This is the ODBC driver distributed with MDAC for accessing SQL Server databases. COM applications can continue to use it to access SQL Server 2005, or they can switch to the SNAC ODBC driver for the latest functionality. This driver also provides access to SQL Server 7 and 2000 databases.

▶ **Java Database Connectivity (JDBC) driver**—The JDBC driver was built specifically for accessing SQL Server data from Java code.

CAUTION

Although it is still possible to connect to SQL Server 2005 by using DB-Library and Embedded SQL, Microsoft has deprecated them both, and they will not be supported in future editions.

Connecting Using the Various Providers and Drivers

Now that you know what your options are in terms of providers and drivers, the following sections detail them one by one, with a special focus on putting the new features in SQL Server 2005 to work.

Using SNAC

SNAC is a net-library that contains both the latest OLE DB provider and ODBC driver for using the rich features in SQL Server 2005 databases. It is compatible for accessing SQL Server 7 and 2000 databases as well.

The code for SNAC is contained in the single dynamic link library sqlncli.dll, and it serves as provider, driver, and API for applications that call its underlying COM functions from unmanaged code (that is, from C or C++).

The bottom line with SNAC is that if you're building applications that need to exploit the latest features of SQL Server 2005, you need to use its APIs. If you don't, your application will continue to work without SNAC.

> **NOTE**
>
> A large number of new connection keywords are available for use with SNAC connections. A few of them are illustrated in the examples that follow, but for a complete reference, see the Books Online topic "Using Connection String Keywords with SQL Native Client."

Using OLE DB with SNAC   Applications that call the COM APIs for OLE DB need to have the connection provider value changed from `SQLOLEDB` to `SQLNCLI`. In addition, the class ID (or GUID) for the OLE DB provider has to be changed from the constant `CLSID_SQLOLEDB` to `CLSID_SQLNCLI` (for use with the `CoCreateInstance` method, used to access the SNAC OLE DB provider). You also need to use the new SNAC header file, as in the following example:

```
include "sqlncli.h";
```

`sqlncli.h` contains the latest function prototypes and other definitions for use with SNAC. For more information on building COM applications that utilize SNAC, see the Books Online topic "Creating a SQL Native Client ODBC Driver Application."

> **NOTE**
>
> The SNAC OLE DB provider is OLE DB version 2.0 compliant.

Using ODBC with SNAC   To connect to SQL Server 2005 using ODBC, you use a connection string or a DSN that is accessible to the client application at runtime. The previous ODBC driver (simply called SQL Server) can still be used. But to get the latest SNAC functionality, you must use the driver called SQL Native Client (for example, `Provider={SQL Native Client}`).

To create a SNAC ODBC DSN, you run the Data Sources (ODBC) applet found in your operating system's administrative tools. You create a system, file, or user DSN, and you need to be sure to select the SQL Native Client driver on the Create New Data Source screen that appears. At this screen, you click the Advanced button to enter any SNAC-specific connection string keyword-value pairs, as shown in Figure 9.9.

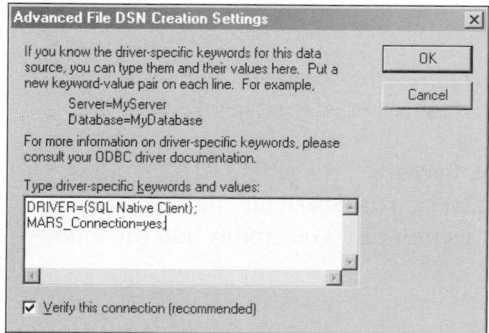

FIGURE 9.9   Using the Data Sources (ODBC) tool to configure MARS with a SNAC ODBC DSN.

You finish the wizard by entering the configuration data as you normally would, and you can use you new DSN just as you would any other.

Using ADO with SNAC   Of course, the first recommendation is that if you're still using ADO, you should switch to ADO.NET if you can. If that isn't feasible, you can still access SQL Server 2005 from your ADO applications. But you should do so only if you need the new features; in this case, you need to start using the SNAC OLE DB provider in your code. To do so, you first install SNAC, and then you update your connection strings (or DSNs) to use the new SQLNCLI value for the Provider connection string keyword. Then you set the DataTypeCompatibility keyword to 80. Here's an example (in Visual Basic 6 code):

```
Dim MyConnection As New ADODB.Connection
Dim MyFirstOpenRecordset As New ADODB.Recordset
Dim MySecondOpenRecordset As New ADODB.Recordset
Dim ConnString As String
Dim SelectResultsCount As Integer

Connstring =
    "Provider=SQLNCLI; DataTypeCompatibility=80; Database=MyAppsDB;" & _
    "Server=.\SQLEXPRESS; AttachDBFileName=c:\MyDBs\MyAppsDB.mdf;" & _
    "MARS Connection=true; Integrated Security=SSPI;"
MyConnection.ConnectionString = ConnString
MyConnection.Open
' Using 2 open recordsets on one connection puts MARS to work:
Set MyFirstOpenRecordset =
    MyConnection.Execute(
        "SELECT TOP 10 * FROM MyTable",
        SelectResultsCount,
        adCmdText
    )
Set MySecondOpenRecordset =
    MyConnection.Execute("SELECT TOP 10 * FROM MySecondTable", _
        SelectResultsCount, adCmdText)

' and so on...
```

Note the use of the new AttachDBFileName connection string keyword, which instructs SQL Server 2005 to attach the specified Microsoft data file (MyAppsDB.mdf).

Using the .NET Framework Data Provider for SQL Server
.NET applications that use the System.Data.SqlClient namespace rely on the .NET Framework data provider and ADO.NET. To use this provider, you simply add the following statement to your C# code file:

```
using System.Data.SqlClient;
```

For VB.NET, you use this:

```
Imports System.Data.SqlClient
```

And for JScript .NET, you use this:

```
import System.Data.SqlClient;
```

Note that the .NET provider supports a variety of connection string styles, including ODBC, OLE DB, and OLE DB/SNAC, and you can mix and match some of their respective connection string keywords. For example, `Database` and `Initial Catalog` mean the same thing to ADO.NET, and so do `Server` and `Data Source`. But don't let this fool you: Under the covers, only the .NET provider is always in use. (This is probably why changing the value passed to the `Provider` keyword seems to have no noticeable effect.)

Applications built on .NET Framework 1.0 and 1.1 can access SQL Server 2005 databases without issue. The only caveat is that those earlier versions of ADO.NET can't make use of certain new SQL Server 2005 features, such as asynchronous command execution, cache synchronization, bulk copy, and the new data types. (However, implicit conversions such as from `varchar` to `xml` and from UDTs to `varbinary` allow their use as T-SQL input from .NET Framework 1.1 applications.) ADO.NET 2.0 applications, however, have access to the full gamut of new functionality in SQL Server 2005.

The following is an example of two connection strings (in different styles) that both turn on the MARS feature for ADO.NET 2.0 applications:

The following is in ODBC style:

```
Driver={SQL Native Client}; Database=AdventureWorks; Server=MyServer/SQL05;
➥Encrypt=yes; Trusted_Connection=yes; MARS_Connection=yes
```

The following is in OLE DB style:

```
Provider=SQLNCLI; Database=AdventureWorks; Server=MyServer/SQL05;
➥Encrypt=yes; Trusted_Connection=yes; MultipleActiveResultSets=true
```

Notice the use of the new keywords `MARS_Connection` (`MultipleActiveResultSets` also works) and Encrypt (which requests connection encryption from the server).

The SQLCLR Context Connection   When you need to connect to SQL Server 2005 from within a managed stored procedure, function, or trigger (known as *SQLCLR code*), which is possible only with .NET 2.0, you use a special type of connection, known as a context connection. This feature prevents you from having to open a new connection because the code itself is already running within the context of an open connection.

The connection string for context connections is extremely easy to use (`"context connection=true"`), as the C# example in Listing 9.1 illustrates.

LISTING 9.1   Using the Context Connection from a Managed Stored Procedure

```csharp
using System;
using System.Data;
using System.Data.SqlClient;
using System.Data.SqlTypes;
using Microsoft.SqlServer.Server;

public partial class StoredProcedures
{
    [Microsoft.SqlServer.Server.SqlProcedure]
    public static void ContextConnectionTest()
    {
        using (SqlConnection Context =
            new SqlConnection("context connection=true"))
        {
            using (SqlCommand TestCommand =
                new SqlCommand("SELECT TOP 10 * FROM Person.Contact", Context))
            {
                using (SqlDataAdapter Adapter =
                    new SqlDataAdapter(TestCommand))
                {
                    using (DataSet MyData = new DataSet())
                    {
                        Adapter.Fill(MyData);
                    }
                }
            }
        }
    }
}
```

For more information on building SQLCLR client libraries, see Chapter 36, "SQL Server and the .NET Framework."

Using MDAC

MDAC contains the OLE DB provider for SQL Server (SQLOLEDB) and the ODBC driver for SQL Server. MDAC is officially part of the operating system, and, as mentioned earlier, MDAC and SNAC will be distributed and developed on separate tracks: MDAC with the operating system, and SNAC with SQL Server. They do interrelate, however, in that applications that use SNAC can make use of the core services provided by MDAC, including support for connection pooling, client-side cursors, ADO support, and memory management. As mentioned earlier, in order to make use of the latest SQL Server 2005 functionality, you need to use SNAC.

MDAC 2.6 is the earliest version you can use with SQL Server 2005, but it is better to use MDAC 2.8 SP1, which comes with Windows XP SP2 and Windows 2003 Server SP1.

TIP

If at any time you want to discover which version of MDAC is installed on a machine, you can simply check the value of the following registry key (using `regedit.exe` or from code):

`HKEY_LOCAL_MACHINE\SOFTWARE\Microsoft\DataAccess\Version`

Note also that the planned MDAC version 9.0 release has been killed and superseded by SNAC.

If you choose to upgrade from MDAC to SNAC, it's important to note some key differences between the two that could affect you applications:

▶ Return values from SQL Server 2005 to MDAC applications are implicitly type-converted, as shown in Table 9.2:

TABLE 9.2   Implicit type conversions for SQL Server 2005 data types.

SQL Server 2005 Data Type	Converted to Data Type
varbinary(MAX)	Image
xml	ntext
nvarchar(MAX)	ntext
varchar(MAX)	text
UDTs	varbinary

▶ Warning and error messages and message handling differ between MDAC and SNAC.

▶ SNAC requires that T-SQL parameters begin with the @ character; MDAC does not.

▶ SNAC, unlike MDAC, is not compatible with Visual Studio Analyzer or PerfMon.

For further details, see the Books Online article "Updating an Application to SQL Native Client from MDAC."

Using ODBC with MDAC   You can configure an ODBC connection by using a connection string or DSN that specifies the Microsoft ODBC driver for SQL Server.

For connection strings, you use the keyword-value pair `Provider={SQL Server}`.

To use a DSN, you run the Data Sources (ODBC) applet as mentioned earlier. When choosing a driver, you select the one simply named SQL Server.

Using OLE DB with MDAC   You can access SQL Server 2005 databases by using the Microsoft OLE DB provider for SQL Server (`SQLOLEDB`). In connection strings or property values, you use the `Provider` keyword and the value `SQLOLEDB`.

> **NOTE**
>
> Unlike with SNAC's OLE DB provider, with SQLOLEDB you can access both SQL Server data and data from non–SQL Server data sources. Also, SNAC is not dependent on any particular version of MDAC because it expects that a compatible MDAC version will be present on the operating system, as enforced by its own installation requirements.

Using JDBC

Microsoft recently released a new, freely downloadable, JDBC 3.0-compliant, Type 4 driver for use with SQL Server 2005. It can be used from all types of Java programs and servers via the J2EE connection API.

The following is the basic syntax for a JDBC connection string:

```
jdbc:sqlserver://ServerName\InstanceName:port;property=value[;property=value]
```

> **NOTE**
>
> The JDBC driver does not currently support MARS, although some somewhat inefficient "MARS-like" behavior is possible using client-side data caching.

For complete details on using JDBC, check out Microsoft's JDBC driver homepage at http://msdn.microsoft.com/data/ref/jdbc. You might also find the newsgroup microsoft.public.sqlserver.jdbcdriver helpful.

General Networking Considerations and Troubleshooting

This section provides guidelines for solving some common connectivity issues. Take the following steps as a first line of defense when your connections fail:

1. Check whether the server is configured (via SAC, as detailed earlier in this chapter, in the section "Server Network Protocols") to accept remote connections.

2. Ensure that the SQL Browser service is started.

3. Determine whether clients are specifying the correct port (for using fixed ports with named instances) in the server alias or connection string.

4. Check whether the client's network protocols are enabled and configured to correctly handshake with those of the server. They should use SSCM on both sides, as explained earlier in this chapter, in the section "Client Configuration Using SSCM."

5. Be sure you have permission to connect on the server's endpoints.

6. When using encryption, be sure the server and client certificates match (that is, check their *Common Name* (CN) and any other relevant attributes) and are installed and configured correctly on both sides. (See the section "Connection Encryption," earlier in this chapter.)

7. Make certain that your firewalls are configured to permit the required network traffic. (See the section "Firewall Considerations," later in this chapter.)

8. Check to see whether your users have permission to log in to the server and access the specified database.

9. Make sure that your clients' choices of providers support the SQL Server 2005 features they are trying to use.

10. Make sure the provider, driver, DSN, server alias, or other connection mechanism is still valid and hasn't been altered or removed from the system.

Firewall Considerations

In order for clients to successfully connect through a firewall, it must be configured to allow the following:

▶ **Bidirectional traffic on UDP Port 1434**—This is required only for communications to and from the SQL Browser service; when SQL Browser is not in use, you can close this port.

▶ **Bidirectional traffic on any TCP port used by SQL Server**—Be sure to open port 1433 for default instances, and also open any fixed ports assigned to your named or default instances. (TCP high port numbers must be opened only when dynamic ports are used by named instances. Using dynamic port numbers for named instances is not recommended.) You can determine the ports currently in use via SSCM.

When using Windows Firewall, you can easily open these ports. To do this, you run Windows Firewall from the Control Panel, and on the main screen that appears, you click the Exceptions tab. Then you click the Add Port button and enter the required names (either SQL Server or SQL Browser, for example) and port numbers, one at a time, on the Add a Port screen that appears (see Figure 9.10).

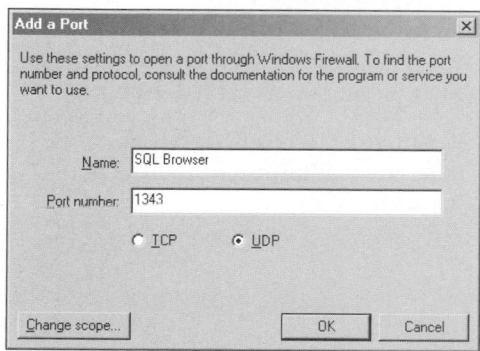

FIGURE 9.10   Creating port exceptions for SQL Server 2005, using Windows Firewall.

Tools for Testing Connections

It's always helpful to have a few tools on your belt for testing client connectivity.

SSCM is a tool that is usually easily accessible, and you can use its Connect to Server dialog to select a protocol to test (as described earlier in this chapter, in the section "Client Data Access Technologies"). You can also use SQLCMD with the -S parameter to connect to a particular server. This is the syntax:

```
SQLCMD -Sprotocol_prefix:ServerName,PortNumber -E
```

In this syntax, *protocol_prefix* takes one of the following values:

- np (for named pipes)
- tcp (for TCP/IP)
- lpc (for shared memory)
- via (for VIA)

In the following example, -E indicates trusted connection use:

```
SQLCMD –Stcp:.\SQL05,1435 -E
```

When all else fails, you can use telnet to test the openness of a port on the firewall. Here's an example:

```
telnet IP_Address Port_Number
```

Summary

This chapter covers a lot of ground regarding client-side (and even a bit of server-side) communication with SQL Server 2005. Some of the sections are admittedly dense enough to bear rereading, and you probably have questions about your specific setup. You can always refer to the sections presented in this chapter to pick up tips on how to best configure and troubleshoot the varying environments you may encounter. And you can (and should) use the extremely helpful Usenet groups that are devoted to the subject (for example, microsoft.public.sqlserver.clients or microsoft.public.sqlserver.programming).

Now that your client configuration is complete, you can move on to Chapter 10, "Security and User Administration," to learn how to securely administer the database engine.

Security and User Administration

IN THIS CHAPTER

▶ What's New in Security and User Administration

▶ An Overview of SQL Server Security

▶ Authentication Methods

▶ Managing Principals

▶ Managing Securables

▶ Managing Permissions

▶ Managing SQL Server Logins

▶ Managing SQL Server Users

▶ Managing Database Roles

▶ Managing SQL Server Permissions

▶ The Execution Context

Securing your database environment and providing the right type of access to your users is a critical administrative task. This chapter examines the security features in SQL Server 2005 that relate to user administration and the objects that users can access.

What's New in Security and User Administration

There have been some significant changes to the security model in SQL Server 2005. These changes are geared toward providing a more secure database environment that allows manageability at a very granular level. Many of the familiar security features that you may be accustomed to, such as logins and users, are still an integral part of the security paradigm, but you should pay careful attention to the following new features:

▶ **SQL login password policies**—SQL Server logins can now be governed by a more rigid password policy. This is implemented with new CHECK_POLICY and CHECK_EXPIRATION options that can be selected for a SQL Server login. These options facilitate stronger passwords and cause passwords to expire. The password policy is only enforced on Windows 2003 Server and above.

▶ **User/schema separation**—In prior versions, the fully qualified name for every object was directly tied to the object owner. With SQL Server 2005, schema names are used in the object namespace instead. This user/schema separation provides more flexibility in the object model and allows for object owners to be changed without affecting the code that references the objects.

▶ **Module execution context**—The EXECUTE AS option can be used to set the execution context for SQL statements. This allows a user to impersonate another user and is particularly useful for testing permissions.

▶ **Permission granularity**—The security model in SQL Server 2005 provides a much more granular level of control. This granular control provides some new types of security and allows you to apply security to a new set of database objects.

An Overview of SQL Server Security

Some significant changes have been made to security in SQL Server 2005. Many of the same basic security elements that were available in prior versions are still there, but many new features and concepts have been added.

The SQL Server 2005 security model is the best place to start to understand the changes. The model is based on three categories that separate the basic elements of security:

▶ **Principals**—Principals are the entities that request security to SQL Server resources. Principals include Windows users, SQL Server users, and database users.

▶ **Securables**—Securables are the SQL Server resources that permissions can be granted to.

▶ **Permissions**—The permissions link principals with securables.

Table 10.1 shows the security components contained in each tier of the SQL Server 2005 security model. The columns are ordered from left to right, based on the way security is established.

TABLE 10.1   SQL Server 2005 Security Components

Principals	Permissions	Securables
Windows:	GRANT/REVOKE/DENY	Server Scope
▶ Groups	▶ CREATE	▶ Login
▶ Domain Login	▶ ALTER	▶ Endpoint
▶ Local Login	▶ DROP	▶ Database
SQL Server:	▶ CONTROL	Database Scope
▶ SQL Login	▶ CONNECT	▶ User
▶ Server Role	▶ SELECT	▶ Role
Database:	▶ EXECUTE	▶ Application role
▶ User	▶ UPDATE	▶ Assembly
▶ Database Role	▶ DELETE	▶ Message Type
▶ Application Role	▶ INSERT	▶ Route
	▶ REFERENCES	▶ Service

TABLE 10.1   Continued

Principals	Permissions	Securables
	▶ RECEIVE	▶ Remote Service Binding
	▶ VIEW DEFINITION	▶ Fulltext Catalog
	▶ TAKE OWNERSHIP	▶ Certificate
	▶ CONTROL	▶ Asymmetric Key
		▶ Symmetric Key
		▶ Contract Schema
		Schema Scope
		▶ Table
		▶ View
		▶ Function
		▶ Procedure
		▶ Queue
		▶ Type
		▶ Synonym
		▶ Aggregate
		▶ XML Schema Collection

The implementation of the new security model is relatively straightforward: You choose the principal from Column 1, the desired permission from Column 2, and the securable to assign the permission from Column 3. For example, a SQL LOGIN (the principal) needs to CREATE (the permission) databases (the securable). Together, these three elements represent a complete security assignment.

Some complexity has been introduced, based on the hierarchical nature of some of the security components. Security can be established on these hierarchical components, which in turn cascades the security to the underlying components. In addition, not all the permission components apply to every securable. Many of the securables have a select number of permissions that apply to them; conversely, many permissions apply only to a select number of securables. For example, SELECT permission is applicable to securables such as tables and views but would not be appropriate for the procedures.

The following sections discuss the tiers of the security model and their underlying components.

Authentication Methods

The first level of security encountered when accessing SQL Server is known as *authentication*. The authentication process performs the validation needed to allow a user or client machine to connect to SQL Server. This connection can be granted via a Windows login or a SQL Server login.

Windows Authentication Mode

Windows Authentication mode validates the account name and password, using information that is stored in the Windows operating system. A Windows account or group must be established first, and then security can be established for that account in SQL Server. This mode has the advantage of providing a single login account and the ability to leverage domain security features, such as password length and expiration, account locking, encryption, and auditing. Microsoft recommends this approach.

Mixed Authentication Mode

Mixed authentication allows for both Windows authentication and SQL Server authentication. SQL Server authentication is based on a login that is created in SQL Server and lives in SQL Server only. No Windows account is involved with SQL Server authentication. The account and password are established and maintained in SQL Server. Fortunately, there have been some security enhancements in SQL Server 2005 related to SQL Server authentication. SQL Server logins can now be created with stronger password enforcement. This is discussed in more detail in the section "Managing SQL Server Logins," later in this chapter.

SQL Server authentication is useful in environments in which a Windows domain controller does not control network access. It can also be useful for Web applications or legacy applications, where it may be cumbersome to establish a Windows user account for every connection to the database server.

Setting the Authentication Mode

You can select the authentication mode when you install SQL Server, and you can change it after the installation. To change the authentication mode after installation, you right-click the server node in the Object Explorer and choose the Properties option. When the Server Properties dialog appears, you select the Security page (see Figure 10.1). The Security page allows you to specify Windows Authentication mode or SQL Server and Windows Authentication mode (that is, mixed authentication). Any changes to the authentication mode requires a restart of SQL Server to make the change effective.

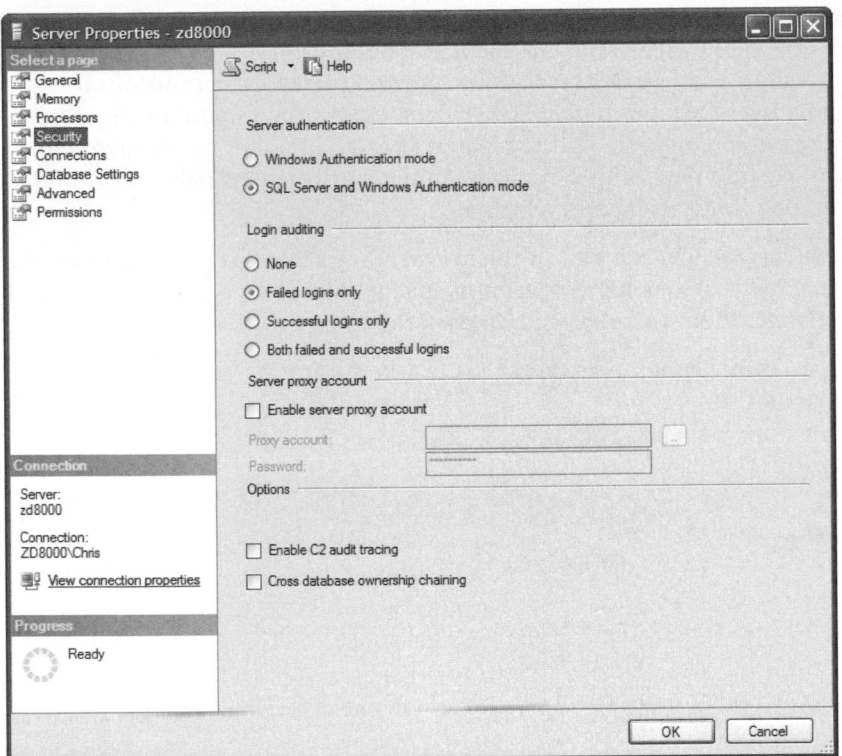

FIGURE 10.1   Changing the authentication mode.

Managing Principals

Principals are the entities that can request permission to SQL Server resources. They are made up of groups, individuals, or processes. Each principal has its own unique identifier on the server and is scoped at the Windows, server, or database level. The principals at the Windows level are Windows users or groups. The principals at the SQL Server level include SQL Server logins and server roles. The principals that are scoped at the database level include database users, data roles, and application roles.

Logins

Every principal that is granted security to SQL Server must have an associated login. The login provides access to SQL Server and can be associated with principals that are scoped at the Windows and server levels. These logins can be associated with Windows accounts, Windows groups, or SQL Server logins.

Logins are stored in the master database and can be granted permission to resources that are scoped at the server level. Logins provide the initial permission needed to access a SQL Server instance and allow you to grant access to the related databases. Permissions to specific database resources must be granted via a database user. The important thing to remember is that logins and users are directly related to each other but are different entities. It is possible to create a new login without creating an associated database user, but a new database user must have an associated login.

To better understand logins, you can look at the `sys.server_principals` catalog view. This view contains a row for every server-level principal, including each server login. The following example selects from this view and displays the results:

```
select left(name,25) name, type, type_desc
 from sys.server_principals AS log
WHERE (log.type in ('U', 'G', 'S', 'R'))
 order by 3,1


/*Results from previous query
name                      type type_desc
------------------------- ---- -----------
bulkadmin                  R    SERVER_ROLE
dbcreator                  R    SERVER_ROLE
diskadmin                  R    SERVER_ROLE
processadmin               R    SERVER_ROLE
public                     R    SERVER_ROLE
securityadmin              R    SERVER_ROLE
serveradmin                R    SERVER_ROLE
setupadmin                 R    SERVER_ROLE
sysadmin                   R    SERVER_ROLE
sa                         S    SQL_LOGIN
BUILTIN\Administrators     G    WINDOWS_GROUP
DBSVRXP\LocalUser1         U    WINDOWS_LOGIN
HOME\Administrator         U    WINDOWS_LOGIN
NT AUTHORITY\SYSTEM        U    WINDOWS_LOGIN
*/
```

The results from the `sys.server_principals` selection include the name of the server principal as well as the type of principal. The rows that have a type_desc value of SQL LOGIN, WINDOWS GROUP, or WINDOWS LOGIN are all logins that have been established on the SQL Server instance. A login with a type_desc of SQL_LOGIN represents a login that was created with SQL Server authentication. Logins with a type_desc of WINDOWS_GROUP or WINDOWS_LOGIN are Windows groups or individual Windows users that have been granted logins to SQL Server. The other entries with type_desc of SERVER_ROLE are fixed-server roles that are discussed later in this chapter.

The logins that are established for Windows logins or groups can be part of the local domain of the SQL Server machine, or they can be part of another domain. In the previous example, DBSVRXP\LocalUser1 is a login that was established for a local user on a database server named DBSVRXP. The HOME\Administrator login is also a Windows login, but it is part of a network domain named HOME. Both logins are preceded by the domain that they are part of and are displayed this way in SQL Server.

> **NOTE**
>
> In SQL Server 2000, logins were stored in the syslogins system table in the master database. The syslogins table is still available for selection as a view, but it is available only for backward compatibility. The catalog views (including sys.server_principals) are recommended for use instead.

You might have noticed in the earlier sys.server_principals output that three other logins are listed that we have not discussed yet. These logins (SA, BUILTIN\Administrators, and NT AUTHORITY\SYSTEM) are system accounts that are installed by default at installation time. Each of these accounts serves a special purpose in SQL Server.

The SA account is a SQL LOGIN that is assigned to the sysadmin fixed-server role. The SA account and members of the sysadmin fixed-server role have permission to perform any activity within SQL Server. The SA account cannot be removed, and it can always be used to gain access to SQL Server. The SA account should always have a strong password to prevent malicious attacks, and it should be used only by database administrators. Users or logins that require full administrative privileges can be assigned a separate SQL Server login that is assigned to the sysadmin fixed-server role. This improves the audit trail and limits the amount of use on the SA account.

The BUILTIN\Administrators login is a Windows group that corresponds to the local administrators group for the machine that SQL Server is running on. The BUILTIN\Administrators group is added as a SQL Server login during installation. The login is made a member of the sysadmin fixed-server role and thus has the same full administrative rights on the SQL Server instance as the SA account.

> **NOTE**
>
> The existence of the BUILTIN\Administrators login may worry some database administrators. The concern is that any member of the local administrators group on the SQL Server machine will by default have full administrative privileges to the SQL Server instance. Domain administrators and anyone else who has been added to the local administrators group will have full access, as well. The BUILTIN\administrators login can be removed as a login from SQL Server in situations in which network administrators must be restricted from SQL Server access.

The last special account is the NT AUTHORITY\SYSTEM login. This account is related to the local system account that SQL Server services can run under. It is also added as a member of the sysadmin fixed-server role and has full administrative privileges in SQL Server. This account can also be removed if the SQL Server services are not running with the local system account. This should be done with caution, however, because it can affect applications such as Reporting Services.

SQL Server Security: Users

Database users are principals that are scoped at the database level. Database users establish a link between logins (which are stored at the server level) and users (which are stored at the database level). Database users are required to use the database and are also required to access any object stored in the database.

Generally, the login name and the database user name are the same, but this is not a requirement. If desired, you could add a login named Chris and assign it to a user named Kayla. This type of naming convention would obviously cause some confusion and is not recommended, but SQL Server has the flexibility to allow you to do it. In addition, a user can be associated with a single person or a group of people. This is tied to the fact that a login can be related to a single account or a group. For example, a login named training could be created and tied to a Windows group (that is, *domain*\training) that contains all the training personnel. This login could then be tied to a single database user. That single database user would control database access for all the users in the Windows group.

> **TIP**
>
> The relationship between logins and users can be broken when databases are moved or copied between servers. This is based on the fact that a database user contains a reference to the associated login. Logins are referenced based on a unique identifier called a security identifier (SID). When a database is copied from one server to another, the users in that database contain references to logins that may not exist on the destination server or that may have different SIDs.
>
> You can use the sp_change_users_login system stored procedure to identify and fix these situations. You can run the following command against a newly restored or attached database to check for orphaned users:
>
> ```
> EXEC sp_change_users_login 'Report'
> ```
>
> If orphaned users are shown in the results, then you can rerun the procedure and fix the problems. For example, if the results indicate that a user named Chris is orphaned, the following command can be run to add a new login named Chris and tie the orphaned database user to this newly created login:
>
> ```
> EXEC sp_change_users_login 'Auto_Fix', 'Chris', NULL, 'pw'
> ```
>
> Refer to SQL Server Books Online for full documentation on the sp_change_users_login system stored procedure.

You can use the sys.database_principals catalog view to list all the users in a given database. The following example shows a SELECT using this view and the results from the SELECT:

```
SELECT
left(u.name,25) AS [Name],
type,
left(type_desc,15) as type_desc
FROM
sys.database_principals AS u
WHERE
(u.type in ('U', 'S', 'G'))
ORDER BY 1

/*Results from previous query
Name                        type type_desc
------------------------    ---- ---------------
dbo                         S    SQL_USER
DBSVRXP\LocalUser1          U    WINDOWS_USER
guest                       S    SQL_USER
INFORMATION_SCHEMA          S    SQL_USER
sys                         S    SQL_USER
*/
```

The SELECT in this example returns five rows (that is, five users). This SELECT was run against the AdventureWorks database, and the only user explicitly added to the database was the Windows user DBSVRXP\LocalUser1. The other users are special users that are added by default to each database. These users do not have corresponding server logins that are named the same. These users are discussed in the following sections.

The dbo User

The dbo user is the database owner and cannot be deleted from the database. Members of the Sysadmin server role are mapped to the dbo user in each database, which allows them to administer all databases. Objects owned by dbo that are part of the dbo schema can be referenced by the object name alone. When an object is referenced without a schema name, SQL Server first looks for the object in the default schema for the user that is connected. If the object is not in the user's default schema, the object is retrieved from the dbo schema. Users can have a default schema that is set to dbo.

Schemas and their relationship to users are discussed in more detail in the section "User/Schema Separation," later in this chapter.

The guest User

The guest user is created by default in each database when the database is created. This account allows users that do not have a user account in the database to access the database. By default, the guest user does not have permission to connect to the database. To allow logins without a specific user account to connect to the database, you need to grant

CONNECT permission to the guest account. You can run the following command in the target database to grant the CONNECT permission:

GRANT CONNECT TO GUEST

When the guest account is granted CONNECT permission, any login can use the database. This opens a possible security hole. The default permissions for the guest account are limited by design. You can change the permissions for the guest account, and all logins that use it will be granted those permissions. Generally, you should create new database users and grant permissions to these users instead of using the guest account.

If you want to lock down the guest account, you can. You cannot drop the guest user, but you can disable it by revoking its CONNECT permission. The following example demonstrates how to revoke the CONNECT permission for the guest user:

REVOKE CONNECT FROM guest

If you decide to grant additional access to the guest account, you should do so with caution. The guest account can be used as a means for attacking your database.

TIP

The Database User screen in SQL Server Management Studio generates an error message if you try to change the permissions for the guest account. The error message states "Login Name must be specified."

The guest account is a special account and does not have an associated login. You can change the access for the guest account by using T-SQL commands instead. For example, if you wanted to add the guest account to the db_datareader role, you could run the following command in the database to which you want to allow access:

```
EXEC sp_addrolemember N'db_datareader', N'guest'
```

The INFORMATION_SCHEMA User

The INFORMATION_SCHEMA user owns all the information schema views that are installed in each database. These views provide an internal view of the SQL Server metadata that is independent of the underlying system tables. Some examples of these views include INFORMATION_SCHEMA.COLUMNS and INFORMATION_SCHEMA.CHECK_CONSTRAINTS. The INFORMATION_SCHEMA user cannot be dropped from the database.

The sys User

The sys account gives users access to system objects such as system tables, system views, extended stored procedures, and other objects that are part of the system catalog. The sys user owns these objects. Like the INFORMATION_SCHEMA user, it cannot be dropped from the database.

> **TIP**
>
> If you are interested in viewing the specific objects that are owned by any of the special users discussed in this section, you can use a SELECT statement like the following:
>
> ```
> --Find all objects owned by a given user
> SELECT name, object_id, schema_id, type_desc
> FROM sys.all_objects
> WHERE OBJECTPROPERTYEX(object_id, N'OwnerId') = USER_ID(N'sys')
> ORDER BY 1
> ```
>
> The SELECT in this example shows all the objects that are owned by the sys user. To change the user, you simply change the parameter of the USER_ID function in the SELECT statement from 'sys' to whatever user you want.

User/Schema Separation

One of the biggest changes to security in SQL Server 2005 relates to schemas. Prior versions of SQL Server had schemas, but they did not conform to the American National Standards Institute (ANSI) definition of schemas. ANSI defines a schema as a collection of database objects that one user owns and that forms a single namespace. A single namespace is one in which each object name is unique and there are no duplicates. So, for example, if you have two tables named customer, they cannot exist in the same namespace.

To fully understand the user/schema changes in SQL Server 2005, you need to understand how schemas were used in prior versions of SQL Server. In SQL Server 7.0 and 2000, a default schema was created for each user, and it had the same name as the user. For example, if you created a new user named Rachael, a corresponding schema named Rachael would be created as well. There was no option in those releases to change the default schema for a user, and each user was forever bound to a schema with the same name. When the user created new objects, the objects were created by default in that user's schema, which is always the name of the user. So, if Rachael created an object named customer, it was placed in the Rachael schema, and the object was owned by Rachael. When Rachael wanted to reference the object, she could use a three-part name with the format *database.owner.object*. If a linked server was used, according to the SQL Server 2000 documentation, the object in the linked server could be referenced with the four-part name *linked_server.catalog.schema.object*. You can see that the schema name is used prior to the object name when the object is outside the local server. The bottom line is that the schema and owner were basically the same thing in SQL Server 7.0 and 2000.

With SQL Server 2005, the owner and schema have been separated. This is made possible in part by allowing a database user to have a default schema that is different from the name of the user. For example, our sample user Rachael could be assigned the default schema Sales. When Rachael creates objects in the database, her objects are created, by

10

default, in the Sales schema. If Rachael wants to reference an object that she created, she can use the full four-part name (*server.database.schema.object*) that includes the Sales schema name, or she can simply refer to the object with the object name alone, and the Sales schema will be searched first for the object. If the object name is not found in the Sales schema, the dbo schema will be searched.

The important thing to remember is that owners and schemas are different from one another in SQL Server 2005. For example, you can have a customer table that is created in the Sales schema, and that table can be owned by a user named Chris. The object should be referenced with the schema name qualifier, such as Sales.Customer, not Chris.Customer. This has the distinct advantage of allowing object ownership to change without affecting the code that references the object. This is based on the fact that database code that references an object uses the schema name instead of the object owner.

The schema enhancements in SQL Server 2005 go well beyond the user/schema separation. Schemas are an integral part of all the database objects that exist in SQL Server. As we delve into more details about SQL Server security and the assignment of permissions, you will see that schemas play a very important role.

Roles

Roles provide a consistent yet flexible model for security administration. Roles are similar to the groups used in administering networks. Permissions are applied to a role, and then members are added to the role. Any member of the role has all the permissions that the role has.

The use of roles simplifies the administrative work related to security. Roles can be created based on job function, application, or any other logical group of users. With roles, you do not have to apply security to each individual user. Any required changes to permissions for the role can be made to the role security, and the members of the role receive those changes.

SQL Server has the following three types of roles:

▶ **Fixed-server and fixed-database roles**—These roles are installed by default and have a predefined set of permissions.

▶ **User-defined roles**—These roles are created in each database, with a custom set of permissions for each set of users assigned to it.

▶ **Application roles**—These roles are a special roles that can be used to manage database access for an application.

These roles are discussed in the following sections.

Fixed-Server Roles

Fixed-server roles are scoped at the server level, which means that the permissions for these roles are oriented toward server-level securables. These roles contain a variety of fixed permissions that are geared toward common administrative tasks. Logins (not users) are assigned to these roles.

The same fixed-server roles that were available in SQL Server 2000 are also available in SQL Server 2005. These roles and their related permissions are listed in Table 10.2.

TABLE 10.2   Fixed-Server Roles

Role	Permission
bulkadmin	Allowed to run the BULK INSERT statement.
dbcreator	Allowed to CREATE, ALTER, DROP, and RESTORE any database.
diskadmin	Allowed to manage disk files that are used by SQL Server.
processadmin	Allowed to terminate SQL Server processes.
securityadmin	Allowed to GRANT, DENY, and REVOKE permissions for logins at the server and database levels. Members of this role can reset passwords for SQL Server logins.
serveradmin	Allowed to change serverwide configuration properties and shut down the server, if needed.
setupadmin	Allowed to add and remove linked servers and execute some system stored procedures.
sysadmin	Allowed to perform any activity in the server.

A single login can be assigned to one or more of these fixed-server roles. When multiple roles are assigned, the combination of permissions is allocated to the login.

NOTE

Keep in mind that when a login is assigned to certain fixed-server roles, they have implied permissions that cascade to the database level. For example, if a login is assigned to the sysadmin role, that login can perform any activity on the server, and it can also perform any action on any database on that server. Similarly, if a login is added to the securityadmin role, the login can change permissions at the database level as well as the server level.

All the fixed-server roles are listed in the SQL Server Management Studio (SSMS) Object Explorer. Figure 10.2 shows the Object Explorer with the Server Roles node expanded. You can right-click any of the roles and select Properties to display the logins that are currently members of the role.

Fixed-Database Roles

SQL Server provides fixed roles that define a common set of permissions at the database level. These fixed-database roles are assigned to database users. As with the fixed-server roles, the permissions that are defined for the fixed-database roles cannot be changed. Table 10.3 shows the fixed-database roles and their permissions.

10

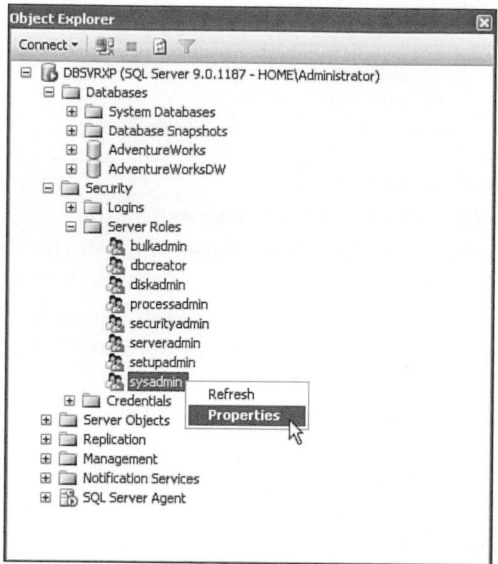

FIGURE 10.2   Fixed-server roles in Object Explorer.

TABLE 10.3   Fixed-Database Roles

Role	Permission
db_accessadmin	Allowed to add or remove database access for logins.
db_backupoperator	Allowed to back up the database.
db_datareader	Allowed to read all user table data.
db_datawriter	Allowed to change the data in all user tables.
db_ddladmin	Allowed to run any Data Definition Language (DDL) command against the database. This includes commands to create, alter, and drop database objects.
db_denydatareader	Denied the right to read all user table data.
db_denydatawriter	Denied the right to change the data in any of the user tables.
db_owner	Allowed to perform any action on the database. Members of the sysadmin fixed–server role are mapped to this database role.
db_securityadmin	Allowed to manage permissions for database users, including membership in roles.

NOTE

You can find a more granular breakdown of permissions associated with fixed-database roles in the SQL Server Books Online documentation. Look for the subject "Permissions of Fixed Database Roles." The extensive table in this documentation defines the specific permissions for each role. For example, the table shows that the db_backupoperator role is granted the CREATE SCHEMA, BACKUP DATABASE, and

BACKUP LOG permissions. This gives you more insight into what the members of this role can do. Some fixed-database roles have a large number of permission defined for them, such as db_ddladmin which has more than 40 individual permissions. The types of permissions and the improved granularity available with SQL Server 2005 are discussed in the "Managing Permissions" section, later in this chapter.

You can also find a list of fixed-database roles in the Object Explorer. Figure 10.3 shows the fixed-database roles for the AdventureWorks database. The roles are found under the Security node within each database. You can right-click a fixed-database role and select Properties to view the member users.

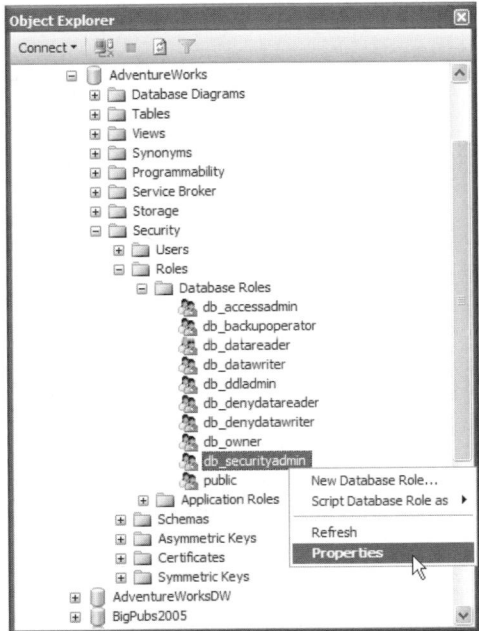

FIGURE 10.3   The fixed-database roles in Object Explorer.

Fixed-database roles and schemas are related. Figure 10.3 shows the expanded Schemas node for the AdventureWorks database. You can see that there is a corresponding schema for each of the fixed-database roles. These schemas are automatically created, and each is owned by the related database role.

The public Role   The public role is a special database role that is like a fixed-database role except that its permissions are not fixed. The permissions for this role can be altered. Every user in a database is automatically made a member of the public role and in turn receives any permissions that have been granted to the public role. Database users cannot be removed from the public role.

The public role is similar in function to the guest user that is installed by default in each database. The difference is that the permissions granted to the guest user are used by any login that does not have a user account in the database. In this case, the login is allowed to enter the database via the `guest` account. In the case of the `public` role, the login has been added as a user of the database and in turn picks up any permissions that have been granted to the `public` role.

To view the permissions associated with the `public` role, you can use a `SELECT` like the following:

```
SELECT top 5 g.name,
    object_name(major_id) as 'Object',
    permission_name
 from sys.database_permissions p
 join sys.database_principals g
  on p.grantee_principal_id = g.principal_id
    and g.name = 'public'
order by 1,2


/*Results from the previous select
name     Object           permission_name
------   --------------   ----------------
public   all_columns      SELECT
public   all_objects      SELECT
public   all_parameters   SELECT
public   all_sql_modules SELECT
public   all_views        SELECT
*/
```

This `SELECT` utilizes two catalog views that contain security information. The `SELECT` returns only the first five permissions for the `public` role, but the `TOP` clause can be removed to return all the permissions.

User-Defined Roles

SQL Server gives you the ability to create your own custom database roles. Like the fixed roles, user-defined roles can be used to provide a common set of permissions to a group of users. The key benefit behind using user-defined roles is that you can define your own set of custom permissions that fit your needs. User-defined roles can have a broad range of permissions, including the more granular set of permissions made available with SQL Server 2005.

To demonstrate the power of a user-defined database role, let's look at a simple example. Let's say that you have a group of users who need to read all the tables in a database but should be granted access to update only one table. If you look to the fixed-database roles, you have the db_datareader and db_datawriter roles, which give you a partial solution. You can use the db_datareader role to allow the read capability you need, but the db_datawriter role gives write permission to all the tables—not just one.

One possible solution would be to give every user in the group membership to the db_datareader group and assign the specific UPDATE permission to each user as well. If the group contains hundreds of users, you can see that this would be rather tedious. Another solution might be to create a Windows group that contains every user who needs the permissions. You can then assign a login and database user to this group and grant the appropriate permissions. The Windows group is a viable solution but can sometimes be difficult to implement in a complex Windows domain.

Another approach to this challenge is to use a user-defined database role. You can create the role in the database that contains the tables in question. After you create the role, you can include it in the db_datareader role, and you can establish the UPDATE permission to the single table. Finally, you can assign the individual users or group of users to the role. Any future permission changes for this set of users can be administered through the user-defined database role. The script in Listing 10.1 steps through a process that demonstrates and tests the addition of a database role. This is similar to the example we just walked through. Parts of the script need to be run by an administrator and other parts should be run in a Query Editor window that is connected to the database with the newly created testuser.

LISTING 10.1   An Example of User-Defined Database Roles

```
--The following statements must be run by an administrator to add
--a login and database user with no explicit permissions granted
CREATE LOGIN [TestUser] WITH PASSWORD=N'pw',
DEFAULT_DATABASE=[master], CHECK_EXPIRATION=OFF, CHECK POLICY=OFF
GO

GO
USE [AdventureWorks]
GO
CREATE USER [TestUser] FOR LOGIN [TestUser]
go
--the following statement fails when executed by the TestUser
--which has no explicit permissions defined in the AdventureWorks database
select top 5 * from person.contact
UPDATE person.contact SET suffix = 'Jr.'
 WHERE ContactID = 1
--The following statement is run by an administrator to:
--1)add a new TestDbRole with permission to UPDATE
--2)grant UPDATE permission on the Person.Contact table
--3)add the TestUser to the TestDbRole database role
USE [AdventureWorks]
GO
--1)
CREATE ROLE [TestDbRole] AUTHORIZATION [dbo]
--2)
GRANT UPDATE ON [Person].[Contact] TO [TestDbRole]
GRANT SELECT ON [Person].[Contact] TO [TestDbRole]
```

10

LISTING 10.1   Continued

```
--3)
EXEC sp_addrolemember N'TestDbRole', N'TestUser'

--the following statements now succeed when executed
--by the TestUser because the role that it
--was added to has SELECT and UPDATE permission
--on that table
select top 5 * from person.contact
UPDATE person.contact SET suffix = 'Jr.'
 WHERE ContactID = 1

--the following select fails because 'testdbrole'
--does not permit SELECT on any table but person.contact
select * from person.ContactType
--The following statement is run by an administrator
--to add the TestDbRole database role to the db_datareader
--fixed-database role
EXEC sp_addrolemember N'db_datareader', N'TestDbRole'
GO
--Finally, the testuser can update the Person.Contact table
-- and select from any other table in the database
select * from person.ContactType
```

Database roles and permissions are discussed in more detail later in this chapter, in the sections "Managing Database Roles" and "Managing Permissions."

Application Roles

Unlike other roles, application roles contain no database users. When an application role is created (see the section "Managing Database Roles," later in this chapter), rather than add a list of users who belong to the role, you specify a password. To obtain the permissions associated with the role, the connection must set the role and supply the password. This is done using the stored procedure sp_setapprole. You set the role to the sales application role (with the password PassW0rd) as follows:

```
EXEC sp_setapprole 'sales', 'PassW0rd'
```

You can also encrypt the password:

```
EXEC sp_setapprole 'sales', {ENCRYPT N ' PassW0rd'}, 'odbc'
```

When an application role is set, all permissions from that role apply, and all permissions inherited from roles other than public are suspended until the session is ended.

So why is it called an application role? The answer is in how it is used. An application role is used to provide permissions on objects through an application, *and only through the application.* Remember that you must use `sp_setapprole` and provide a password to activate the role; this statement and password are not given to the users; rather, they are embedded in the application's `CONNECT` string. This means that the user can get the permissions associated with the role only when running the application. The application can have checks and balances written into it to ensure that the permissions are being used for the forces of good and not evil.

Managing Securables

Securables are the entities in SQL Server that permissions can be granted on. In other words, principals (for example, users, logins) obtain permission to securables. This chapter has talked about many examples of securables, including tables, databases, and many entities that have been part of the SQL Server security model in past versions. The difference in SQL Server 2005's new security model is that there is now a more granular set of securables for applying permissions.

Securables are hierarchical in nature and are broken down into nested hierarchies of named scopes. Three scopes are defined: at the server, database, and schema levels. Table 10.4 list the securables for each scope.

TABLE 10.4   SQL Server 2005 Securables

Server	Database	Schema
Logins	User	Table
Endpoints	Role	View
Databases	Application role	Function
	Assembly	Procedure
	Message Type	Queue
	Route	Type
	Service	Synonym
	Remote Service Binding	Aggregate
	Fulltext Catalog	XML Schema Collection
	Certificate	
	Asymmetric Key	
	Symmetric Key	
	Contract	
	Schema Assemblies	
	Schemas	

As mentioned earlier, there is a hierarchy within each scope; in addition, there are relationships that cross scope boundaries. Servers contain databases, databases contain schemas, and schemas contain a myriad of objects that are also hierarchical. When certain permissions are granted on a securable at the server level, implied permission is granted at the database and schema levels. For example, if a login is granted `control` permission at the server level, then `control` is implicitly granted at the database and schema levels. The relationships between securables and permissions can be complicated. The next section details the different types of permissions and sheds some light on how these permissions affect securables.

Managing Permissions

Database security is mainly about managing permissions. Permissions are the security mechanisms that tie principals (for example, logins) to securables (for example, tables). With SQL Server 2005, permissions can be applied at a much more granular level than in previous versions. This provides a great deal of flexibility and control.

Permissions in SQL Server 2005 revolve around three commands: `GRANT`, `REVOKE`, and `DENY`. These three commands were also used in SQL Server 2000. When permission is granted, the user or role is given permission to perform an action, such as creating a table. The `DENY` statement denies permission on an object and prevents the principal from gaining `GRANT` permission based on membership in a group or role. The `REVOKE` statement removes a permission that was previously granted or denied.

When specifying permissions, you need to carefully consider the hierarchy that exists between `GRANT`, `REVOKE`, and `DENY`. This is particularly important when the principal (for example, user, login) is part of a group or role and permissions have been granted on securables at different scopes of the security model. The following are some examples of the precedence that exists between these statements:

▶ A `GRANT` of a permission removes any `REVOKE` or `DENY` on a securable. For example, if a table has `SELECT` permission denied on it and then the `SELECT` permission is granted, the `DENY` permission will then be removed on that table.

▶ `DENY` and `REVOKE` remove any `GRANT` permission on a securable.

▶ `REVOKE` removes any `GRANT` or `DENY` permission on a securable.

▶ Permissions denied at a higher scope in the security model override grants on that permission at a lower scope. Keep in mind that the security model has the server scope at the highest level, followed by database and schema. So, if `INSERT` permission is denied on tables at the database level, and `INSERT` on a specific table in that database is granted at the schema level, the result is that `INSERT` is denied on all tables. In this example, a database-level `DENY` overrides any `GRANT` at the lower schema level.

▶ Permissions granted at a higher scope in the security model are overridden by a `DENY` permission at a lower level. For example, if `INSERT` permission is granted on all tables at the database scope, and `INSERT` is denied on a specific table in the database (schema scope), `INSERT` is then denied on that specific table.

The assignment of a permission includes the `GRANT`, `DENY`, or `REVOKE` statements plus the permission that these statements will affect. The number of available permissions has increased in SQL Server 2005. Familiar permissions such as `EXECUTE`, `INSERT`, and `SELECT` that were available in SQL Server 2000 are still around in SQL Server 2005, but several new types of permissions have been added. The following are some of the new types:

▶ **CONTROL**—This type confers all defined permissions on the securable. This ownership-like capability also cascades to any lower level objects in the security hierarchy.

▶ **ALTER**—This type confers the ability to change the securable's properties but does not include the ability to make ownership changes. If ALTER is applied on a scope such as a database or a schema, the ability to use ALTER, CREATE, or DROP on any object in the scope is allocated as well.

▶ **IMPERSONATE**—This type allows the principal to impersonate another user or login.

▶ **VIEW DEFINITION**—This type allows access to SQL Server metadata. This type of data is no longer granted by default in SQL Server 2005; therefore, the VIEW DEFINITION permission was added to manage access.

The combination of available permissions and the securables that they can be applied to is extensive. The permissions that are applicable depend on the particular securable. SQL Server Books Online lists the permissions for specific securables. You can use the index feature at Books Online to look for "permissions [SQL Server]." You will find a section in this reference named "Permissions Applicable to Specific Securables" as well as a section named "SQL Server 2005 Permissions" that lists each securable and its related permissions.

You can also view the available permissions by using system functions and catalog views. The following example uses the sys.fn_builtin_permissions function to retrieve a partial listing of all the available permissions:

```
SELECT top 5 class_desc, permission_name, parent_class_desc
 FROM sys.fn_builtin_permissions(default)
order by 1,2
/* Results from previous query
class_desc              permission_name parent_class_desc
---------------         --------------- -----------------
APPLICATION ROLE        ALTER           DATABASE
APPLICATION ROLE        CONTROL         DATABASE
APPLICATION ROLE        VIEW DEFINITION DATABASE
ASSEMBLY                ALTER           DATABASE
ASSEMBLY                CONTROL         DATABASE
*/
```

The granularity with which permissions can be applied with SQL Server 2005 is impressive and, to some degree, challenging. You will see when you look at all the available permissions that some planning is needed to manage them. In the past, fixed-database roles were simple to use but in many cases provided permissions that went beyond what the user needed. Microsoft has now supplied the tools to facilitate the concept of "least privileges," which means providing only the privileges that are needed and nothing more.

10

The tools to help you manage permissions are discussed later in this chapter, in the section "Managing SQL Server Permissions."

Managing SQL Server Logins

You can easily create and administer logins easily through the SSMS. You can use T-SQL as well, but the GUI screens are often the best choice. The GUI screens present the configurable properties for a login including the available options, databases and securables that can be assigned to a login. The number of configurable options is extensive and can be difficult to manage with TSQL.

Using SSMS to Manage Logins

The visual tools for managing logins in SSMS are accessible via the Object Explorer. You need to expand the Security node in Object Explorer and right-click the Logins node. Then you select the New Login option, and the new login screen, shown in Figure 10.4, appears.

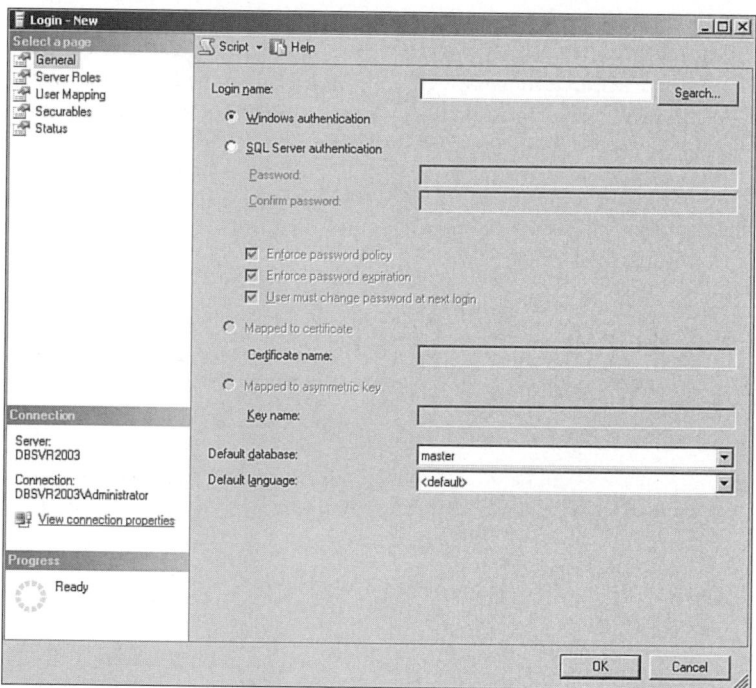

FIGURE 10.4   Creating a login in SSMS with Windows Authentication.

The default authentication mode for a new login is Windows Authentication. If you want to add a login with Windows Authentication, you need to type the name of your Windows user or group in the Login Name text box. You can also click the Search button to search for Windows logins. In either case, the login entered for Windows Authentication should be in the form *<DOMAIN>\<UserName>* (for example, `mydomain\Chris`) or in the form `user@company.com`.

With Windows Authentication, you have an option to restrict access to the server for the new login when it is created. If you select Deny Server Access, a command to deny access to SQL Server is issued immediately after the login is created (for example, `DENY CONNECT SQL TO [DBSVRXP\Chris]`). This can be useful for staging new logins and waiting until all the appropriate security has been applied prior to allowing the login to access your SQL Server instance. When you have completed the security setup for the login, you can select the login properties and choose the `GRANT SERVER ACCESS` option.

You can use the same new login screen shown in Figure 10.4 to add a login with SQL Server Authentication. Again, you need to provide a login name, but with the standard SQL Server login, there is no domain associated with the user. The login is independent of any Windows login and can be named as desired. The login and password for SQL Server Authentication are stored in SQL Server and maintained in SQL Server.

When SQL Server Authentication is selected, several new options related to passwords are enabled. These options, as shown in Figure 10.5, include Enforce Password Expiration, Enforce Password Policy, and User Must Change Password at Next Login. These options are all associated with a more rigid password policy. They are similar to options that are available with Windows accounts and provide a more robust security solution for SQL Server logins. The catch is that the new password options are enforced only on the Windows 2003 Server operating system and versions above. You can select these options when running SQL Server on a machine that has an operating system that is lower than Windows 2003 Server, but the hooks between SQL Server and the operating system are not in place to enforce the password policy.

The default database and default language are the final options located on the General page of the new login screen. These options are available regardless of the authentication method selected. The default database is the database that the login will connect to by default. `master` is the database that is selected, but it is generally not the best database to select for your default. You should choose the default database that your login will use most often and avoid using any of the system databases as your default. This will help prevent database users from executing statements against the wrong database, and it will also remove the step of having to change the database every time the user connects. Make sure that the login is given access to whatever database you select as the default. (The Database Access page is discussed later in this chapter.)

The default language determines the default language that will be used by the login. If no default language is specified and the <default> entry is left in the Language drop-down, the server's default language is used. The default language for the server can be retrieved or set by using the `sp_configure` system stored procedure. The language selection affects many things, including date formats, month names, and names of days. To see a list of languages available on the server and the related options, you use the `sys.syslanguages` catalog view.

10

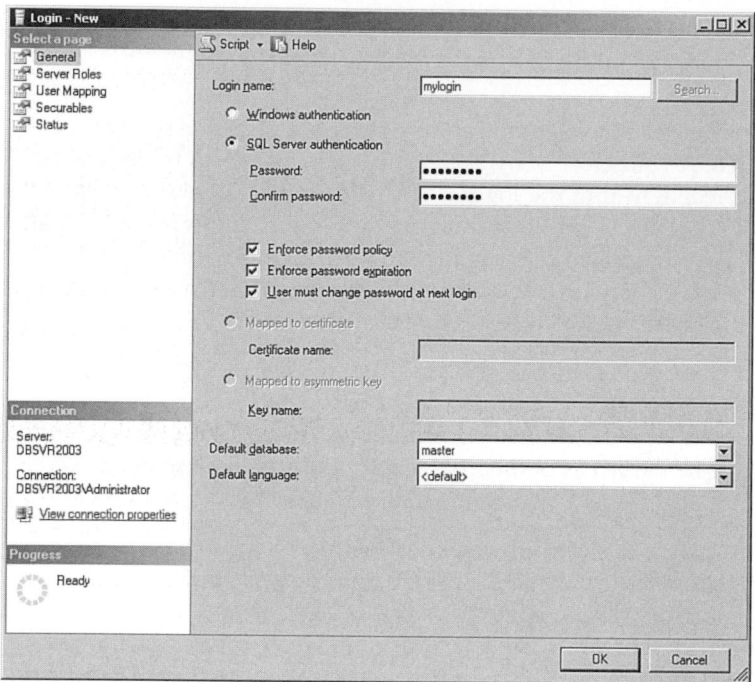

FIGURE 10.5   Creating a login in SSMS with SQL Server Authentication.

The new login screen has three other pages that are available for selection when creating your new login: Server Roles, Database Access, and Permissions.

The Server Roles page allows you to select one or more fixed-server roles for the login to participate in. Figure 10.6 shows the new login screen with the Server Roles page selected. For a more detailed review of the permissions related to each server role, refer to the section "Fixed-Server Roles," earlier in this chapter.

The Database Access page allows you to select the databases that the login will have access to. When the Permit check box is selected for a database, the Default Schema and User cells are enabled. The default schema is the schema that will contain the database objects that are created by the login. The login can create objects in schemas other than the default if the login has permission to use the other schemas. If no schema is specified, the default schema is used. The default schema also comes into play when you're retrieving database objects. If no schema is specified on database retrievals, then the default schema is searched first for the database object. If no Default Schema is specified on the Database Access screen, the default schema is set to dbo. The User data entry area allows you to enter a database user name that is different from the login name. By default, the database user name is the same as the login name, but you can change it.

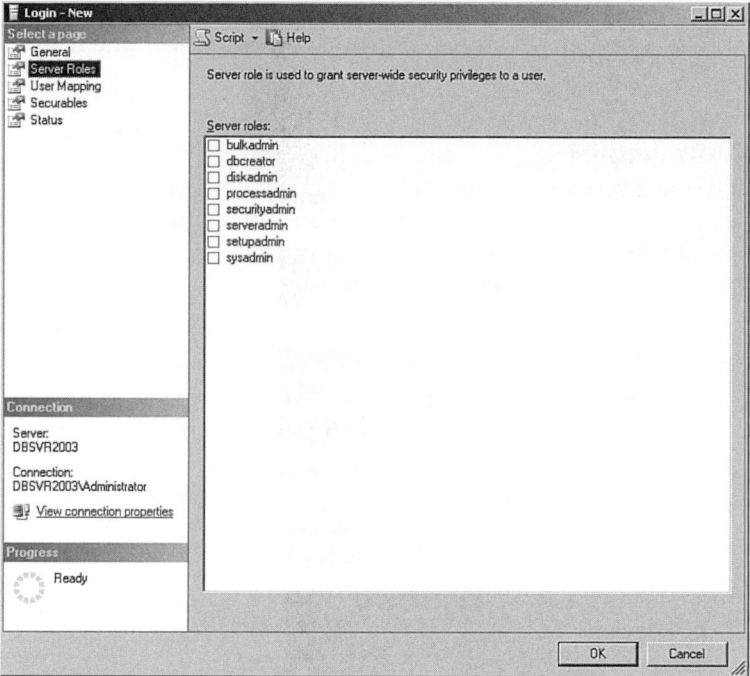

FIGURE 10.6   Choosing a server role.

The other thing that happens when you select the Permit check box on the database is that the list of database roles is enabled in the bottom portion of the screen. You can select one or more database roles for the login. Both fixed and user-defined database roles are available for selection. The `public` database role is selected by default and cannot be deselected.

The Permissions page is the last page that is available for selection on the new login screen. This page allows you to select server objects for login permissions. The server objects are limited to object types that are scoped at the server level. This includes `Servers`, `Endpoints`, `Logins`, and `Server Roles` object types. The management of all permissions, including those for `Logins`, is discussed in detail in the "Managing Permissions" section, later in the chapter.

To modify a login, you right-click the login in the `Security` node and select Properties. The same set of property pages that are available when you create a new login are displayed. You cannot change the authentication mode after the login has been created, but you can change all the other settings, if desired.

To delete a login, you right-click the login and select Delete. The Delete Object screen appears, and you can click OK to delete the login. A warning message appears, stating that "Deleting server logins does not delete the database users associated with the logins."

If the login has associated database users, and the login deletion is performed, database users are orphaned, and you have to manually delete the users associated with the login in each database.

Using T-SQL to Manage Logins

You can manage logins by using T-SQL statements. This is generally not as easy as using the user-friendly GUI screens that come with SSMS, but there are times when T-SQL is better. For example, with installations and upgrades that involve changes to logins, you can use T-SQL to script the changes and produce a repeatable process.

SQL Server 2005 includes system stored procedures and a new ALTER LOGIN statement that you can use to manage logins. The same system stored procedures that were available in SQL Server 2000 are still available in SQL Server 2005, but they have been deprecated and will not be available in a future version. Table 10.5 lists the available system stored procedures and the basic function and current state of each one. The state indicates whether the procedure has been deprecated and whether an alternative exists in SQL Server 2005.

TABLE 10.5   System Stored Procedures for Managing Logins

Store Procedure	Function	Status
sp_addlogin	Add a SQL Server login.	Deprecated; use CREATE LOGIN instead.
sp_defaultdb	Change the default database.	Deprecated; use ALTER LOGIN instead.
sp_defaultlanguage	Change the default language.	Deprecated; use ALTER LOGIN instead.
sp_denylogin	Deny server access to a Windows login.	Deprecated.
sp_droplogin	Drop a SQL Server login.	Deprecated; use DROP LOGIN instead.
sp_grantlogin	Add a Windows login.	Deprecated.
sp_password	Change a login's password.	Deprecated; use ALTER LOGIN instead.
sp_revokelogin	Drop a Windows login.	Deprecated; use DROP LOGIN instead.

The system stored procedures have a variety of parameters, which are documented in Books Online. Because they have been deprecated, they are not the focus of this section. Instead, this section focuses on a number of examples that utilize the new CREATE, ALTER, and DROP statements. The following example creates a SQL Server login with a password that must be changed the first time the login connects:

```
CREATE LOGIN Laura WITH PASSWORD=N'mypassw0rd$'
   MUST_CHANGE, CHECK_EXPIRATION=ON
```

You can then use the following ALTER LOGIN statement to change the default database, language, and password for the new Laura login:

```
ALTER LOGIN [Laura] WITH
 DEFAULT_DATABASE=[AdventureWorks],
 DEFAULT_LANGUAGE=[British],
 PASSWORD=N'myStr0ngPW'
```

Finally, you can drop the Laura login by using the following:

```
DROP LOGIN [Laura]
```

As you can see, the new T-SQL statements for Logins are relatively easy to use. To simplify matters, you can generate T-SQL statements from SSMS. To do so, you click the Script button that is available on the screen that appears after you specify a login action. For example, if you right-click a login and select Delete, the Delete Object screen appears. At the top of this screen is a Script button. When you click this button, SSMS scripts the related T-SQL statements into a Query Editor window for you to review and execute.

Managing SQL Server Users

The SSMS has a set of friendly user interfaces to manage SQL Server users as well. The screens are similar to the screens for logins and are also launched from the Object Explorer. You can also use a set of T-SQL statements to manage users.

Using SSMS to Manage Users

To manage users via SSMS, you open the Object Explorer and expand the Security node followed by the Users node. The Users node contains a list of the current database users. To add a new database user, you can right-click the Users node and select New User. Figure 10.7 shows the Object Explorer window with the option to create a new user selected for the AdventureWorks database.

Figure 10.8 shows the new database user screen that is displayed after you select the New User option. In this figure, a login named Chris is used, and the database user name is Chris as well. These two names do not need to match but are often the same for consistency. The login must exist before you can create the user. You can click the ellipsis next to the login name to view a list of available logins. You can click the Browse button to see the logins that have been added to SQL Server.

The biggest difference between the SQL Server 2000 and SQL Server 2005 new user screens is the addition of schemas. You can see in Figure 10.8 that there is now a new section dedicated to schemas owned by the user as well as the user's default schema. These changes are directly related to the user/schema separation described earlier in the chapter.

The default schema must be a valid schema that was created in the database. If the default schema is left blank, it defaults to dbo. After the default schema has been set, it is used as the default location for storing and retrieving database objects.

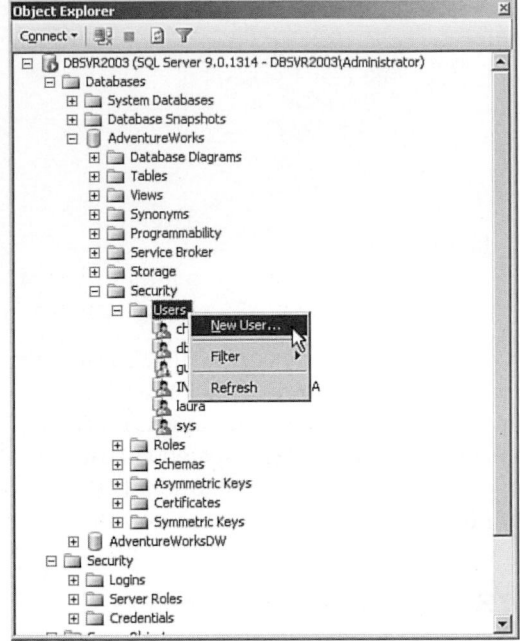

FIGURE 10.7   The New User option in Object Explorer.

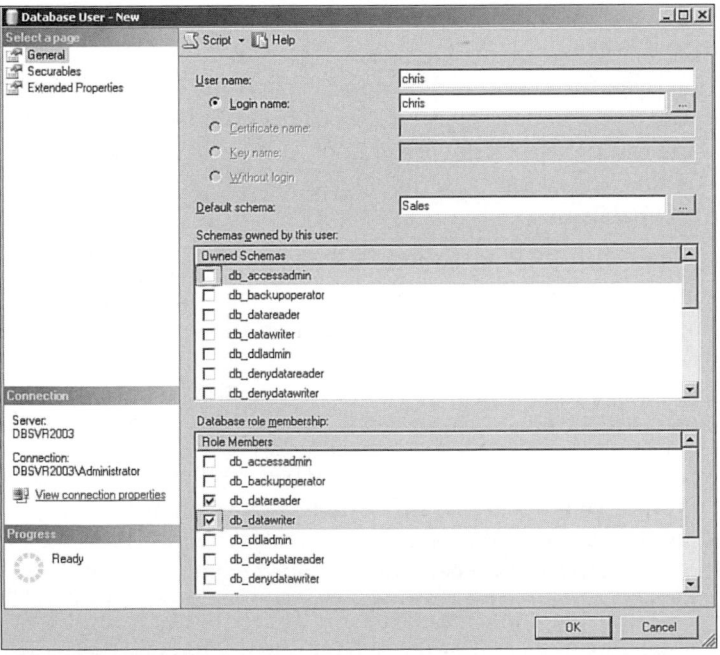

FIGURE 10.8   Using SSMS to create a new user.

You can select one or more schemas to be owned by the user, but a given schema can be owned by only one user in the database. When a schema is selected for ownership for a user, the previous owner loses ownership, and the new user gains ownership. The following example shows the type of T-SQL statement that you can run to accomplish the ownership change. This example changes the ownership on the Person schema to the user Laura:

```
ALTER AUTHORIZATION ON SCHEMA::[Person] TO [Laura]
```

When you select the Permissions page, you can assign permissions to securables scoped at the database and schema levels. The management of all permissions, including those for users, is discussed in detail in the "Managing Permissions" section, later in the chapter.

To modify or delete an existing database user, you can right-click the user in the Object Explorer and choose the related option. To modify the user, you select Properties, and a screen similar to the one you use to add the user is displayed. To delete the user, you select the Delete option.

Using T-SQL to Manage Users

CREATE USER, ALTER USER, and DROP USER are the T-SQL commands you use most often to manage database users. These commands are new to SQL Server 2005 and are replacements for the system stored procedures used in prior versions. The system stored procedures, such as sp_adducor, op_dropuser, sp_grantdbaccess, and sp_revokedbaccess, have been deprecated and will be removed in a future version. They are still available for use now, but you should avoid them when possible.

The following example demonstrates the use of the CREATE USER statement to create a new database user named Laura, with a default schema Sales:

```
CREATE USER Laura FOR LOGIN Laura
    WITH DEFAULT_SCHEMA = Sales
```

You can use the ALTER USE statement to change the default schema or the user name. The following example uses the ALTER USER statement to change the name of the database user currently named Laura to LauraG:

```
ALTER USER Laura WITH NAME = LauraG
```

If you want to delete a database user, you use the DROP USER command. The following example demonstrates how to delete the LauraG from the previous example:

```
DROP USER [LauraG]
```

When dropping database users, keep in mind that you cannot drop them if they are the owners of database objects. An object's ownership must be transferred to another database user before that object can be deleted. This applies to schemas that can be owned by the user as well.

10

Managing Database Roles

Database roles are custom roles that you can define to group your users and simplify the administration of permissions. Fixed roles are predefined, and you basically manage them by assigning logins and users to them. (The assignment of logins and users to fixed-server and fixed-database roles is covered earlier in this chapter.)

Using SSMS to Manage Database Roles

You can find database roles in the Object Explorer for each database, under the `Security` node, which contains a `Roles` node. The `Roles` node contains a `Database Roles` node, which lists both fixed and non–fixed-database roles. To add a new custom database role (non-fixed), you right-click the `Database Roles` node and select New Database Role. A new database role dialog box appears, as shown in Figure 10.9.

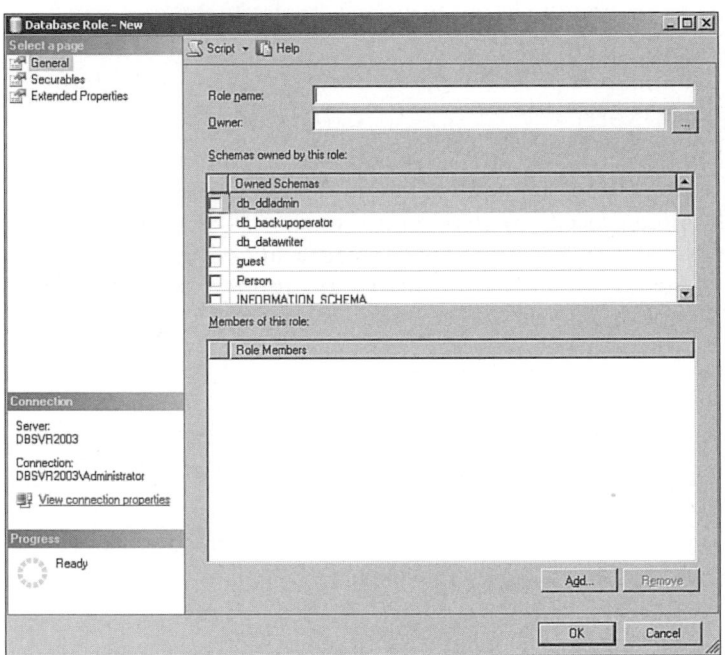

FIGURE 10.9   The new database role dialog box.

You need to enter a name for the role and a name for the owner of the role. Like a database user, a database role can also own schemas. If you click the Add button, you can add database users from the current database to the role.

If you select the Permissions page, you can define the permission for the database role. This definition includes the selection of database objects that are scoped at the database and schema levels. These permissions are discussed in detail in the "Managing Permissions" section, later in this chapter.

Using T-SQL to Manage Database Roles

Some of the T-SQL system stored procedures used in SQL Server 2000 to manage roles have been deprecated, including sp_addrole and sp_droprole. The sp_addrolemember and sp_droprolemember procedures have not been deprecated and are still good choices for adding members to a role.

The CREATE ROLE and DROP ROLE statements are the new replacements for sp_addrole and sp_droprole. The following example uses the CREATE ROLE statement to create a new database role named DevDbRole:

```
CREATE ROLE [DevDbRole]
```

To assign a user named Chris to the new DevDbRole role, you can use the following:

```
EXEC sp_addrolemember N'DevDbRole', N'chris'
```

Role membership is not limited to database users. It is possible to assign database roles as members of another role. The following adds the TestDbRole database role to the DevDbRole role created in the previous example:

```
EXEC sp_addrolemember N'DevDbRole', N'TestDbRole'
```

You cannot use sp_addrolemember to add a fixed-database role, a fixed-server role, or dbo to a role. You can, however, add a non fixed-database role as a member of a fixed-database role. If, for example, you want to add the DevDbRole database role as a member of the fixed-database role db_dataread, you use the following command:

```
EXEC sp_addrolemember N'db_datareader', N'DevDbRole'
```

The ALTER ROLE statement exists but is limited to changing the name of a role. To drop a database role, you use the DROP ROLE statement. Keep in mind that all role members must be dropped before a role can be dropped.

Managing SQL Server Permissions

You can use T-SQL or the visual tools available in SSMS to manage permissions. Based on the number of available permissions and their complexity, it is recommended that you use the SSMS tools. The following sections cover these tools from several different angles and look at the management of permissions at different levels of the security model. You'll learn how to use T-SQL to manage the permissions as well.

Using SSMS to Manage Permissions

The Object Explorer in SSMS gives you the ability to manage permissions at many different levels of the permission hierarchy. You can manage permissions at a high level, such as the entire server, or you can manage permissions at the very lowest level, including a specific object, such as a table or stored procedure. The degree of granularity you use for

10

permissions depends on your security needs. To demonstrate the scope of permissions, let's look at managing permissions at several different levels, starting at a high level and working down to the object level.

> **NOTE**
>
> There are many different ways to achieve a security goal in SSMS. For example, you can manage permissions for a database user from the database or from the user. You can apply permissions on schema objects for the entire schema or to the individual objects. You should always try to choose the permission solution that will allow you to achieve your security goals with the least amount of administrative overhead.

Using SSMS to Manage Permissions at the Server Level

Logins can be granted explicit permissions at the server level. Earlier we looked at fixed-server roles as one means for assigning permissions, but you can manage individual server-level securables as well. Figure 10.10 shows the Login Properties window for a login named `Chris`. You launch this window by right-clicking the login and selecting Properties. Figure 10.10 shows the Securables page, which allows you to add specific securables to the grid.

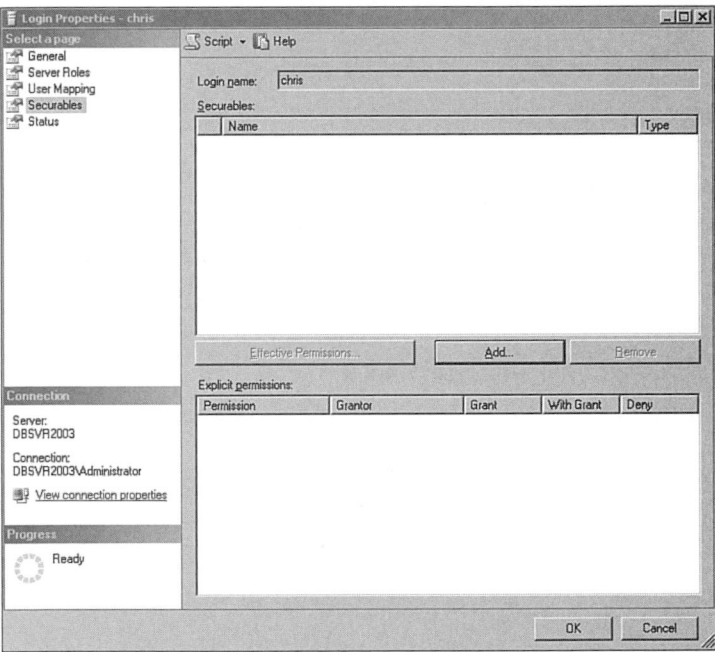

FIGURE 10.10   Server-level permissions.

> **NOTE**
>
> You can open a permission page like the one shown in Figure 10.10 from many differ-
> ent places in the Object Explorer. The title of the dialog box and the content of the grid
> vary, depending on the object selected, but the screen is generally the same, no
> matter where it is launched. This provides consistency and simplifies the overall
> management of permissions.

You can click the Add button shown in the middle of Figure 10.10 to add objects to the
securables grid. When you click this button, the Add Objects window shown in Figure
10.11 is displayed. This window allows you to choose the type of objects you want to add.
If you select Specific Objects, then you are taken directly to the Select Objects window. If
you choose All Objects of the Types, you are taken to an intermediate screen that allows
you to select the type of objects you want to assign permissions to.

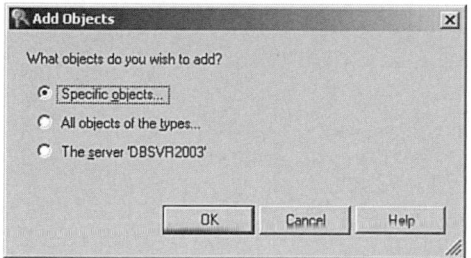

FIGURE 10.11   The Add Objects window.

Again, the Add button and the means for adding objects is fairly consistent for all permissions. What varies is the object types that are available for selection. For example, at the
server level, the types of objects available to assign permissions are scoped at the server
level. Figure 10.12 shows the Select Object Types window that is displayed when you
choose the All Objects of the Types option at the server level. You can see that the available objects are all scoped at the server level.

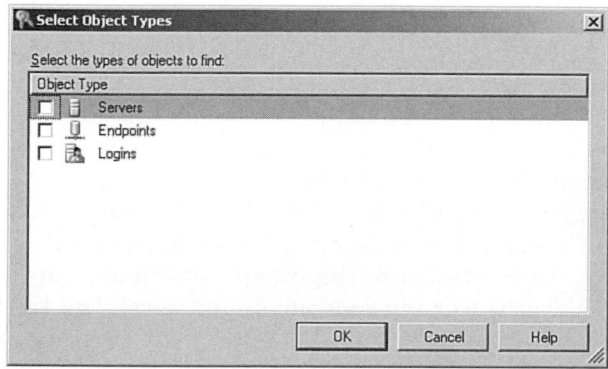

FIGURE 10.12   Server-level object types.

If the `endpoints` objects are selected, the securables grid is populated with all the available endpoints that have permissions to manage. Figure 10.13 shows the Login Properties window with the `endpoints` securables populated. The T-SQL `Named Pipes` securable is selected, which allows you to specify the explicit permissions for the securable in the bottom grid. In this example, the Grant and With Grant check boxes have been selected. This gives the login named `Chris` the right to control the `Named Pipes` endpoint and also allows him to grant this right (because `With Grant` is selected) to other logins.

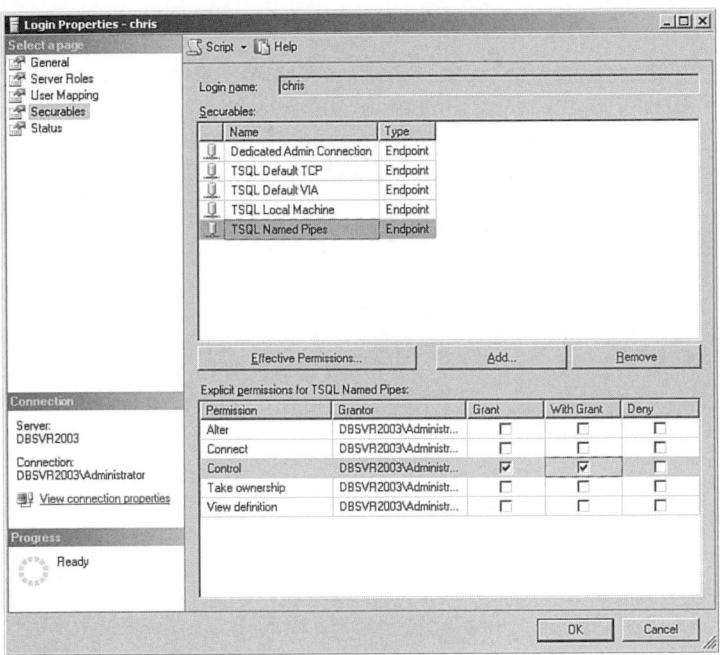

FIGURE 10.13   Server-level securables.

The examples we just walked through are related to the assignment of explicit permission on a specific instance of a securable. You can also apply server permissions at a more macro level. For example, you may want to specify permissions for a login to allow that login to control all server endpoints instead of specific endpoints. You can accomplish this in several ways. One way to do it is to select the `Server` object from the list of object types when adding permissions for a specific login. Another way is to right-click the server name in the Object Explorer and select Properties. The Server Properties window that appears has a Permission page that lists all the logins for the server, along with the macro-level permissions that are scoped for the server. Figure 10.14 shows the Server Properties window with the login `Chris` selected. The explicit permissions listed in this case are at a higher level and are not just for one instance. The example shown in Figure 10.14 allows the login `Chris` to alter any database or any endpoint on the server. This is based on the Grant check boxes selected.

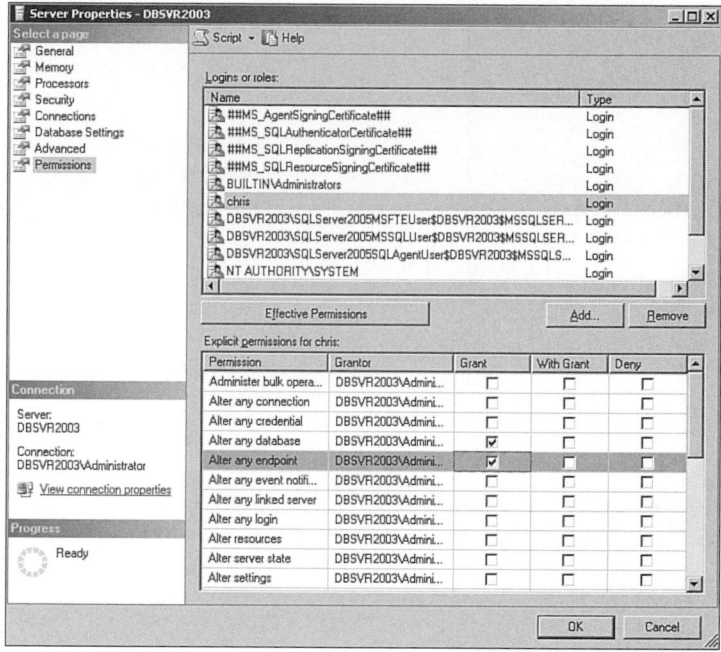

FIGURE 10.14   The Server Properties window's Permission page.

Using SSMS to Manage Permissions at the Database Level

The same type of hierarchy exists with permissions at the database level as at the server level. You can apply permissions at a high level to affect many objects of a particular type, or you can apply them on a specific object. You can also manage the permissions at the database level on a specific database user, or you can manage them on the database across many users.

To demonstrate the differences between object types that are available at the database level, let's first look at managing permissions for a specific database user. As with logins, you can right-click a database user and select Properties. On the Properties window that appears, you select the Securables page, and you get a screen to assign permissions that is very similar to the login permissions screen. The difference at the database level is in the object types available for selection. Figure 10.15 shows the object types available when you choose the All Objects of Types choice during the addition of securables for a database user.

When a low-level object type such as a table or stored procedure is selected, you have the ability to apply explicit permissions to a specific object instance. Figure 10.16 shows an example of low-level securables that are available when the Table object type is selected.

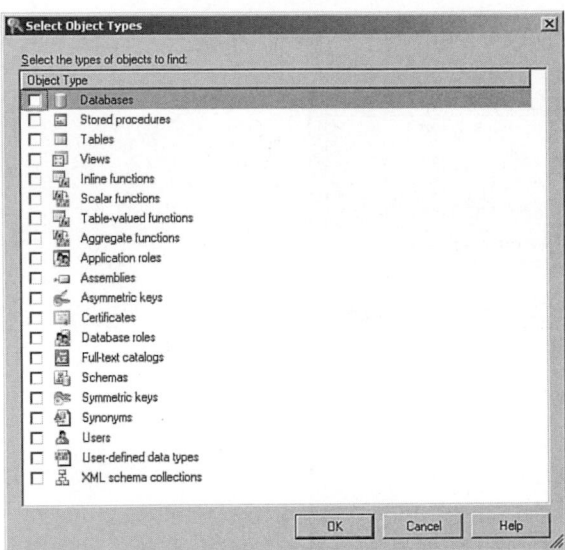

FIGURE 10.15   Database-level object types.

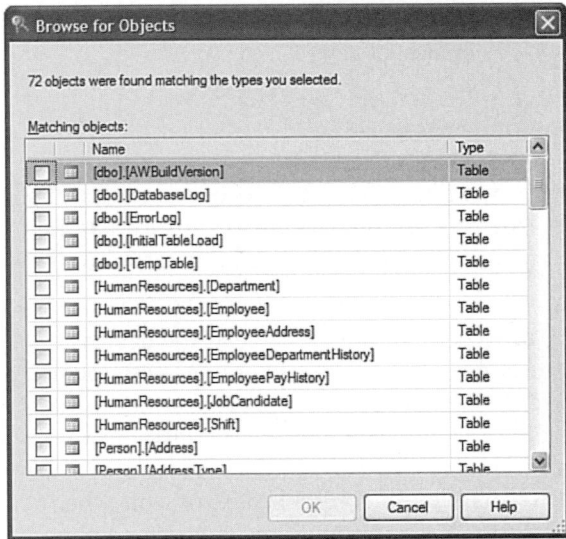

FIGURE 10.16   Low-level database securables.

To apply permissions at a higher level in the database, you choose the object type of Databases. With this securable added to the permissions grid, you can apply permissions to a group of objects by selecting a single permission. Figure 10.17 shows the AdventureWorks database selected as the securable and the related permissions available.

In this example, the login Chris has been granted INSERT, SELECT, and UPDATE permissions to all the tables in the AdventureWorks database.

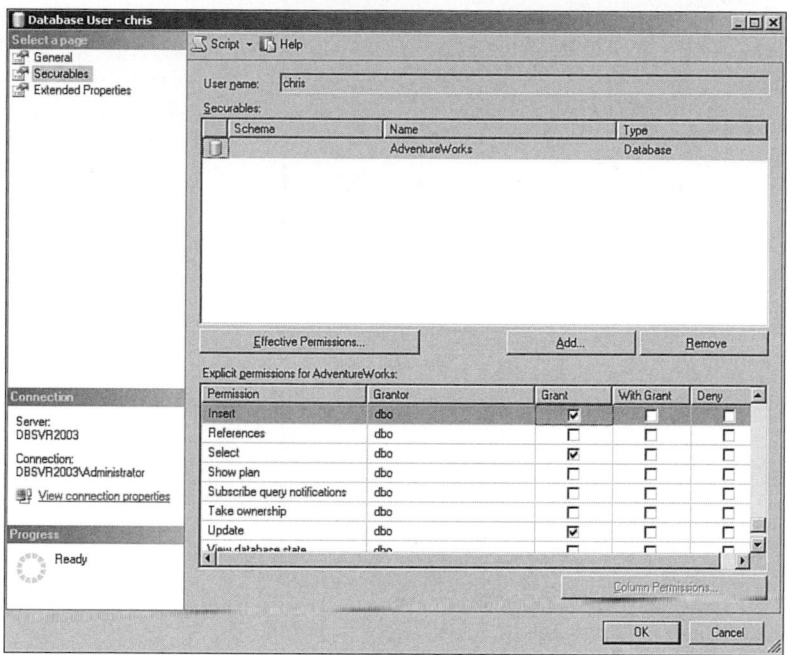

FIGURE 10.17   High-level database securables.

Using SSMS to Manage Permissions at the Object Level

The last permission assignment we will look at is the object level. SSMS gives you the ability to select a specific object instance in the Object Explorer and assign permissions to it. This method allows you to navigate to the object you want via the Object Explorer tree and assign permissions accordingly. Figure 10.18 shows the Object Explorer tree expanded to the Stored Procedures node. A specific stored procedure has been right-clicked, and the Properties option has been selected.

The Properties window has a page dedicated to permissions. You can select the Permissions page and then select the users or roles you want to add for the specific object, such as a stored procedure. Figure 10.19 shows the Permissions page with a user named Chris added to the Users or Roles window at the top of the page. The bottom portion of the page shows explicit permissions for the user Chris, which includes a DENY permission on the stored procedure selected.

10

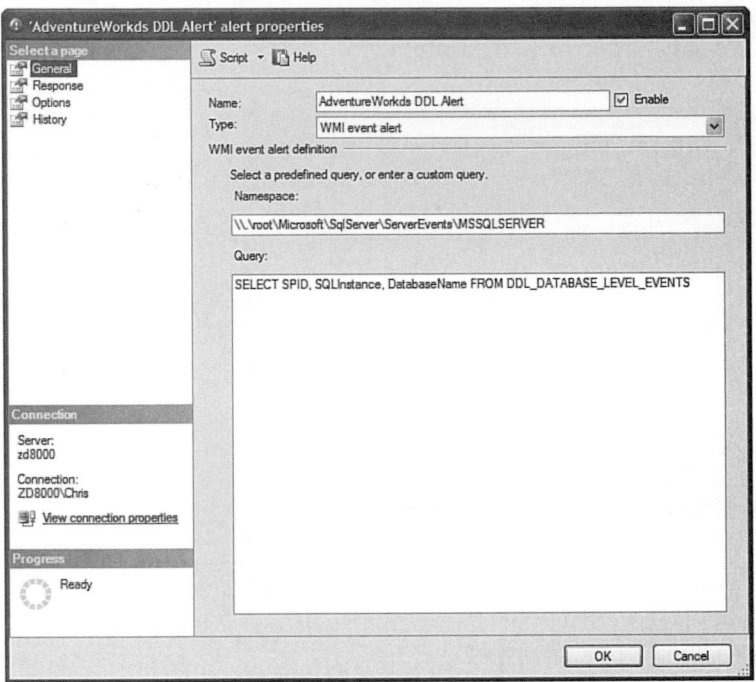

FIGURE 10.18   Object-level permissions selected via Object Explorer.

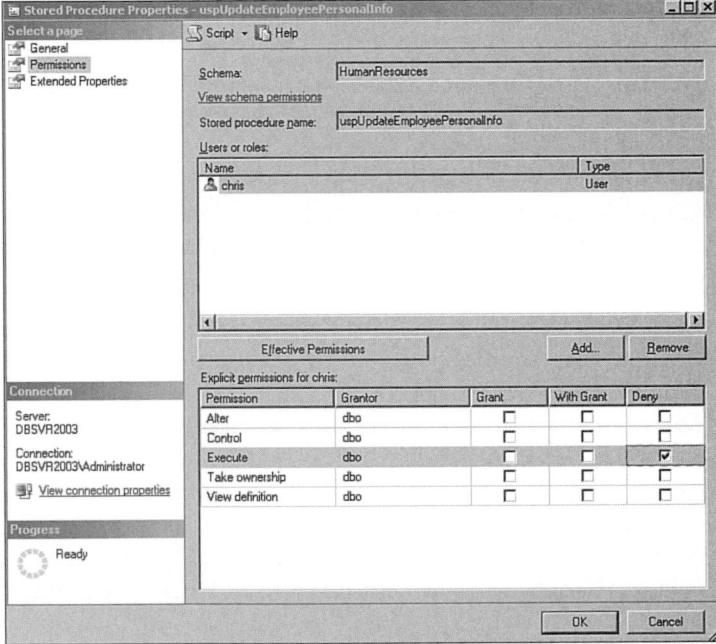

FIGURE 10.19   Object-level permissions.

> **NOTE**
>
> The methods described here for managing permissions in SSMS are by no means the only ways you can manage permissions in SSMS. You will find that the assignment of permissions pervades SSMS and that SSMS allows you to assign permissions in many different ways. The thing to keep in mind is that database roles, application roles, schemas, and other objects in the security model all have similar methods for assigning permissions.

Using T-SQL to Manage Permissions

As you saw in the SSMS Permissions pages, three options exist for assigning every permission: GRANT, DENY, and REVOKE. Each of these three options has its own T-SQL statements that can be used to manage permissions as well. The simplified syntax for the GRANT command is as follows:

```
GRANT { ALL [ PRIVILEGES ] }
      ¦ permission [ ( column [ ,...n ] ) ] [ ,...n ]
      [ ON [ class :: ] securable ] TO principal [ ,...n ]
      [ WITH GRANT OPTION ] [ AS principal ]
```

This basic GRANT syntax is similar to that in SQL Server 2000, but the addition of many new permissions and securables has expanded the scope of the command. The WITH GRANT option is new to SQL Server; it allows a permission to be granted to a principal and allows the principal to grant that permission to another principal.

The simplified syntax for the DENY and REVOKE commands is as follows:

```
DENY { ALL [ PRIVILEGES ] }
      ¦ permission [ ( column [ ,...n ] ) ] [ ,...n ]
      [ ON [ class :: ] securable ] TO principal [ ,...n ]
      [ CASCADE] [ AS principal ]


REVOKE [ GRANT OPTION FOR ]
      {
        [ ALL [ PRIVILEGES ] ]
        ¦
                permission [ ( column [ ,...n ] ) ] [ ,...n ]
      }
      [ ON [ class :: ] securable ]
      { TO ¦ FROM } principal [ ,...n ]
      [ CASCADE] [ AS principal ]
```

You can see that the simplified syntax for DENY and REVOKE is similar in structure to the GRANT statement. All the statements must identify the permission, the securable, and the principal that will receive the permission.

10

The ALL clause has been deprecated in SQL Server 2005. If ALL is specified, it does not affect all permissions on the object; it affects only a subset of the permissions related to the securable. The subset of permissions is dependent on the securable.

The following examples demonstrate several different types of permissions you can manage by using T-SQL commands:

```
--Grant permissions to create a table
-- to a user named Chris
GRANT CREATE TABLE TO Chris


--Grant ALL permissions on a stored procedure
-- to a database role named TestDBRole
GRANT ALL ON dbo.uspGetBillOfMaterials TO TestDBRole


--DENY UPDATE permission on the Customer table
-- to user named Laura
DENY UPDATE ON OBJECT::sales.customer TO Laura


--REVOKE UPDATE permissions on the Customer table
-- to user named Laura.
REVOKE UPDATE ON OBJECT::sales.customer TO Laura
```

There are many different flavors of the GRANT, DENY, and REVOKE statements, depending on the securable they are affecting. Books Online outlines the syntax for each securable and the permissions that can be applied.

Remember that you can use the Script option to generate the T-SQL from SSMS. The Script button is available when you're managing permissions, and using it is a great way to familiarize yourself with the T-SQL that is used to affect changes. You can select the permissions you want to apply via the GUI screen and then click the Script button to generate the T-SQL.

The Execution Context

The execution context determines what permissions will be checked when statements are executed or actions are performed on the database server. By default, the execution context is set to the principal that is connected to the server or database. If a user named Chris connects to the AdventureWorks database, the permissions assigned to Chris will be checked.

In SQL Server 2005, you can change the execution context so that permissions are checked for a principal other than that which you are connected. You can make this change in execution context (called *context switching*) explicitly or implicitly.

Explicit Context Switching

With explicit context switching, you can use the EXECUTE AS statement to change the user or login used to check permissions. This is similar to the SET USER statement that was available in SQL Server 2000. It is extremely useful for administrators who are testing the permissions they have set for users or logins. The following example demonstrates the use of the explicit EXECUTE AS statement:

```
--Assume that you are connected as an administrator (DBO)
--and want to prevent members of the Public role from
--selecting from the Sales.Customer table
DENY SELECT ON sales.customer TO Public

--We can check that user Laura cannot select from the
-- Sales.Customer table using the EXECUTE AS statement
EXECUTE AS USER = 'laura'
SELECT TOP 1 * FROM sales.customer

-- Revert to the previous execution context.
REVERT
```

You can also do explicit context switching at the login level. You can use the EXECUTE AS statement to switch the execution context to another login instead of a user.

Context switching is linked to the IMPERSONATE permission. As an administrator, you can grant IMPERSONATE to a login or user to enable that user to execute as that user. For example, an administrator can temporarily enable another login to run in the same execution context by using the IMPERSONATE permission and EXECUTE AS statement. The following example demonstrates the assignment of the IMPERSONATE permission to a login named Laura:

```
--Chris grants the right to Laura to impersonate
GRANT IMPERSONATE ON LOGIN::[chris] TO [laura]
GO

--Laura can then connect with her login and use
-- the EXECUTE AS command to run commands that
-- normally only Chris has permission to run
EXECUTE AS Login = 'Chris'
DBCC CHECKDB (AdventureWorks)
SELECT USER_NAME()
--Revert back to Laura's execution context
REVERT
SELECT USER_NAME()
```

Laura can now use EXECUTE as Chris, who is an administrator. This can be particularly useful when a user or login has many custom permissions that would take a lot of time to establish for another user or login.

10

Implicit Context Switching

With implicit context switching, the execution context is set within a module such as a stored procedure, trigger, or user-defined function. The EXECUTE AS clause is placed in the module and is set to the user that the module will be run as. The context switch is implicit because the user who runs the module does not have to explicitly specify the context before running the module. The context is set within the module.

The EXECUTE AS clause has several different options to establish the execution context. All modules have the ability to set the context to a specific user or login. Functions, stored procedures, and Data Manipulation Language (DML) triggers can also execute as CALLER, SELF, or OWNER. DDL triggers can run as CALLER or SELF. Queues can run as SELF or OWNER. The CALLER option is the default, and it runs the module in the context of the user who called the module. The SELF option causes the module to run in the context of the user or login that created the procedure. The OWNER option causes the module to run in the context of the current owner of the module.

The following example demonstrates the creation and execution of a stored procedure with the EXECUTE AS clause on a specific user named Chris:

```
CREATE PROCEDURE dbo.usp_TestExecutionContext
WITH EXECUTE AS 'chris'
AS SELECT USER_NAME() as 'User'

--Set the user to someone other than chris to test the
-- implicit EXECUTE AS
SETUSER 'DBO'
EXEC usp_TestExecutionContext

/*Results of the prior execution
User
------
chris
*/
```

This example shows that the USER_NAME retrieved in the stored procedure is Chris, regardless of who executed the procedure.

Implicit execution context can be particularly useful in situations in which permissions cannot be granted to a user directly. For example, TRUNCATE TABLE permissions cannot be granted explicitly to a user, but a database owner can run this command. Instead of granting dbo rights to a user needing TRUNCATE permissions, you can create a stored procedure that does the truncation. You can create the stored procedure with the execution context of dbo, and you can grant the user rights to execute the stored procedure that does the truncation. When you use this method, the user can perform the truncation but does not have any of the other permissions related to a database owner.

Summary

SQL Server 2005 delivers a phenomenal number of security enhancements in this release. These enhancements include a security scheme that allows for the administration of permissions at a very granular level. The granularity of the permissions and the other security-related features covered in this chapter allow you to keep your SQL Server environment safe.

Chapter 11, "Database Backup and Restore," looks at another aspect of SQL Server that helps secure your database environment. Chapter 11 describes in detail the backup and restore methods and the important part that they play in protecting your data.

10

CHAPTER 11

Database Backup and Restore

IN THIS CHAPTER

▶ What's New in Database Backup and Restore

▶ Developing a Backup and Restore Plan

▶ Types of Backups

▶ Recovery Models

▶ Backup Devices

▶ Backing Up a Database

▶ Backing Up the Transaction Log

▶ Backup Scenarios

▶ Restoring Databases and Transaction Logs

▶ Restore Scenarios

▶ Additional Backup Considerations

Y ou need to perform database backups in order to protect your investment in data. Backups may seem like mundane tasks, but consider Murphy's Law ("If anything can go wrong, it will") when you are considering your backup plan. For example, if you forget to add a new database to your backup plan, that database will crash. If you neglect to run a test restore of your backups, those backups will not restore properly. This type of thinking may seem a bit defeatist, but it can help you create a backup solution that is robust and that will allow you to sleep comfortably, knowing that you have a good plan.

Fortunately SQL Server comes with many different backup and restore options that you can use to develop a robust backup plan and avoid those worst-case scenarios. This chapter covers the key considerations in developing a backup and restore plan and then covers the options that are available with SQL Server in order to implement that plan.

What's New in Database Backup and Restore

Many of the backup and restore features that existed in SQL Server 2000 also exist in SQL Server 2005. SQL Server 2005 builds on those features and comes with enhancements that include the following:

▶ **Online restores**—You can restore a filegroup that is offline while keeping the rest of the database online. This does not mean that you can restore a database while users are in it, but it does allow you to keep most of your database up and running while restoring part of it that is offline.

▶ **Copy-only backups**—You can make copy-only backups without disrupting the sequencing of other backups. Sometimes you might just want a backup of your database that will not be used in conjunction with any other backup; this new backup option allows you to create one.

▶ **Mirrored backups**—SQL Server 2005 adds the ability to create additional copies of database backups via mirrored backups. Mirrored backups provide redundancy so that you can overcome the failure of a single backup device or media by utilizing the mirrored copy of the backup. This feature is not tied directly to hardware mirroring (for example, RAID 0) but instead allows you to specify from two to four alternate locations for your database to be backed up.

▶ **Partial backups**—A partial backup contains all the data in the primary filegroup, any filegroup that is not read-only, and any filegroup that has been explicitly identified for backup. The elimination of read-only filegroups from partial backups saves space, saves time, and reduces the server overhead that is required while performing the backup. Partial backups are best utilized with databases that have large amount of static data stored in read-only filegroups.

▶ **Database snapshots**—Database snapshots allow for the creation of a read-only static view of a database that is captured at a point in time. The snapshot database is transactionally consistent with the database from which the snapshot was taken (that is, the source database) and is often used for reporting purposes. These snapshots are not strictly for backup and restore, but they can be used to revert a source database back to the state it was in when the snapshot was taken. Refer to Chapter 27, "Database Snapshots," for a detailed discussion of this technology.

Developing a Backup and Restore Plan

Developing a solid backup and restore plan for SQL Server is one of the most critical tasks an administrator performs. Simply put, if you are a database administrator (DBA) and have a significant loss of data in a database that you are responsible for, your job may be on the line. You need to carefully examine the backup needs of your organization, document those needs, and deliver a plan that defines how your backup and restore plan will meet those needs.

The best place to start in identifying the backup requirements is to ask the right questions. The following are a series of questions that will help drive out the answers you need:

▶ How much data loss is acceptable? For example, if you choose to do only full database backups each night, would it be acceptable to lose all the data added to the database during the next day? This could happen if you had a failure and had to restore to the last full backup.

▶ What is the nature of the database? For example, is the database used for a data warehouse, or is it used for a high-volume transaction processing system?

▶ How often does the data in the database change? Some databases may change very little or not at all during the day but sustain heavy batch updates during the evening.

▶ What is the acceptable recovery time in the event that a database must be restored from previous backups? This question is directly related to the amount of downtime that is acceptable for the applications that use the database.

▶ Is there a maintenance window for the application/database? The maintenance window is typically a period of time when the database or server can be taken offline. What are the exact times of the maintenance windows?

▶ What is the size of the database(s) that needs to be backed up?

▶ What media is available for backup, and where is the media located?

▶ What is the budget for database backup and recovery? If no budget has been established, the answers to some of the prior questions drive the cost of the solution.

Some of the questions that need to be asked in order to come up with a good backup and restore plan may raise some eyebrows. For example, you may find that the answer you get for the question, "How much data loss is acceptable?" is "None!" Don't panic. There are sensible responses for these types of answers. The reality is that you can deliver a solution that virtually eliminates the possibility of data loss—but that comes at a cost. The cost may come in the form of real dollars as well as other costs, such as performance or disk space. As with many other technical solutions, trade-offs need to be considered in order to come up with the right plan.

> **NOTE**
>
> Many of the questions that relate to database backup and restore are related to system backups as well. Systemwide backups, which happen independently of SQL Server backups, capture all or most of the files on a server and write them to appropriate media. These server backups are often performed by DBAs, system administrators, and the like. You should consider having the person or persons responsible for the system backups present when asking the database backup and restore questions. This will help with the coordination and timing of the backups.

When you have the answers to these questions, you need to document them, along with your recommended solution. You should identify any assumptions and make sure to outline any portion of the plan that has not met the requirements.

The good news is that the implementation of the plan is often less difficult than coming up with the plan itself. Microsoft provides a myriad of tools to create database backups that can meet the needs of your organization. The remainder of this chapter focuses on the details required to finalize a solid backup and recovery plan.

Types of Backups

SQL Server offers a variety of different types of backups that can be used to restore a database to a former state. Each of these backups uses a file or set of files to capture the database state. The files are found outside the SQL Server database and can be stored on media such as tape or hard disk.

As described in the following sections, these backup types are available with SQL Server 2005:

- ▶ Full database backups
- ▶ Differential database backups
- ▶ Partial backups
- ▶ Differential partial backups
- ▶ File and filegroup backups
- ▶ Copy-only backups
- ▶ Transaction log backups

Full Database Backups

A full database backup is an all-inclusive backup that captures an entire database in one operation. This full backup can be used to restore a database to the state it was in when the database backup completed. The backup is transactionally consistent, contains the entire database structure, and contains the related data that is stored in these structures.

As with many other backups, SQL Server allows for updates to the database while a full backup is running. It keeps track of the changes that are occurring during the backup by capturing a portion of the transaction log in the database backup. The backup also records the log sequence number (LSN) when the database backup is started, as well as the LSN when the database backup completes. The LSN is a unique sequential number that can be used to determine the order in which updates occur in the database. The LSNs recorded in the backup are used in the restore process to recover the database to a point in time that has transactional consistency.

A full database backup is often used in conjunction with other backup types and it establishes a base when a restore operation is needed. The other backup types are discussed in the following sections, but it is important not to forget about the full backup that must be restored first in order to utilize other backup types. For example, say you are making hourly transaction log backups. If the database is to be recovered using those transaction log backups, the last full database backup must be restored first, and then the subsequent log backups can be applied.

Differential Database Backups

Differential database backups capture changes to any data extent that happened since the last full database backup. The last full database backup is referred to as the *differential base* and is required in order to make the differential backup useful. Each data extent that is monitored consists of eight physically contiguous data pages. As changes are made to the pages in an extent, a flag is set to indicate that a change has been made to the extent. When the differential database backup is executed, only those extents that have had pages modified are written to the backup.

Differential database backups can save backup space and improve the overall speed of recovery. The savings in space and time are directly related to the amount of change that occurs in the database. The amount of change in the database depends on the amount of time between differential backups. When the number of database changes since the last backup is relatively small, you achieve the best results. If, however, a significant number of changes occur to the data between differential backups, the value of this type of backup is diminished.

Partial Backups

Partial backups, which are new to SQL Server 2005, provide a means for eliminating read-only data from a backup. In some implementations, a portion of the data in a database may not change and is strictly used for inquiry. If this data is placed on a read-only file-group, you can use partial backups to back up everything except the read-only data. This reduces the size of your backup and reduces the time it takes to complete the backup. The read-only filegroups should still be backed up, but this needs to occur only after the read-only data is loaded.

Differential Partial Backups

Differential partial backups work like differential database backups but are focused on the same type of data as partial backups. The extents that have changed in filegroups that are not read-only are captured in this type of backup. This includes the primary filegroup and any read/write filegroups that are defined at the time of the backup. Like differential database backups, these backups also require a differential base, but it must be a single differential base.

File and Filegroup Backups

File and filegroup backups are targeted at databases that contain more than one filegroup. In these situations, the filegroup or files in the filegroups can be backed up independently. If a filegroup is backed up, then all the files defined in the filegroup are backed up.

File and filegroup backups are often used for larger databases where the creation time for a full database backup takes too long or the resulting backup is too large. In these situations, you can stagger the backups of the files or filegroups and write them to different locations.

The main disadvantage of this type of backup is the increase in administrative overhead. Each of the files in the database must be backed up, and a complete set of these files must be retained in order to restore the database. For a full recovery model, the transaction log backups must also be retained.

> **NOTE**
>
> SQL Server 2005 supports file and filegroup backups for all recovery models, including simple recovery. The catch with simple recovery is that the files and filegroups are limited to read-only secondary filegroups. SQL Server 2000 did not allow these types of backups with simple recovery.

Copy-Only Backups

Copy-only backups are new to SQL Server 2005. They allow a backup of any type to be taken without affecting any other backups. Normally, a database backup is recorded in the database itself and is identified as part of a chain that can be used for restore. For example, if a full database backup is taken, any subsequent differential database backups use this full database backup as their base. A restore process utilizing the differential database backups would have a reference to the full database backup, and that backup would have to be available.

Copy-only backups do not affect the restore chain. They are useful in situations in which you simply want to get a copy of the database for testing purposes or things of this nature. Copy-only backups are not supported via SQL Server Management Studio (SSMS) and must be performed via the Transact-SQL (T-SQL) BACKUP command. An example of the copy-only backup is provided later in this chapter, in the section, "Backing Up a Database."

Transaction Log Backups

Transaction log backups capture records that have been written to the transaction log file or files that have been defined for a database. The full and bulk logged recovery models are the only models that support transaction log backups. These models cause transaction events to be retained in the transaction log so that they can be backed up. Simple recovery mode causes the transaction log to be truncated prior to backup and thus invalidates the usefulness of the transaction log backups.

The transaction log backups and their strong ties to the recovery model are discussed in more detail in the next section.

Recovery Models

Each database has a recovery model that determines how transactions will be written to the transaction log. The recovery model you choose has a direct impact on your ability to recover from a media failure. These are the three recovery models available with SQL Server 2005:

- ▶ Full recovery
- ▶ Bulk logged
- ▶ Simple

You set the recovery model via T-SQL or the Database Properties window in SSMS. The following example shows the T-SQL command that can be used to change the AdventureWorks database to the bulk-logged model:

```
ALTER DATABASE [AdventureWorks] SET RECOVERY BULK_LOGGED WITH NO_WAIT
```

Figure 11.1 shows the Options page on the Database Properties window, which also allows you to select a recovery model.

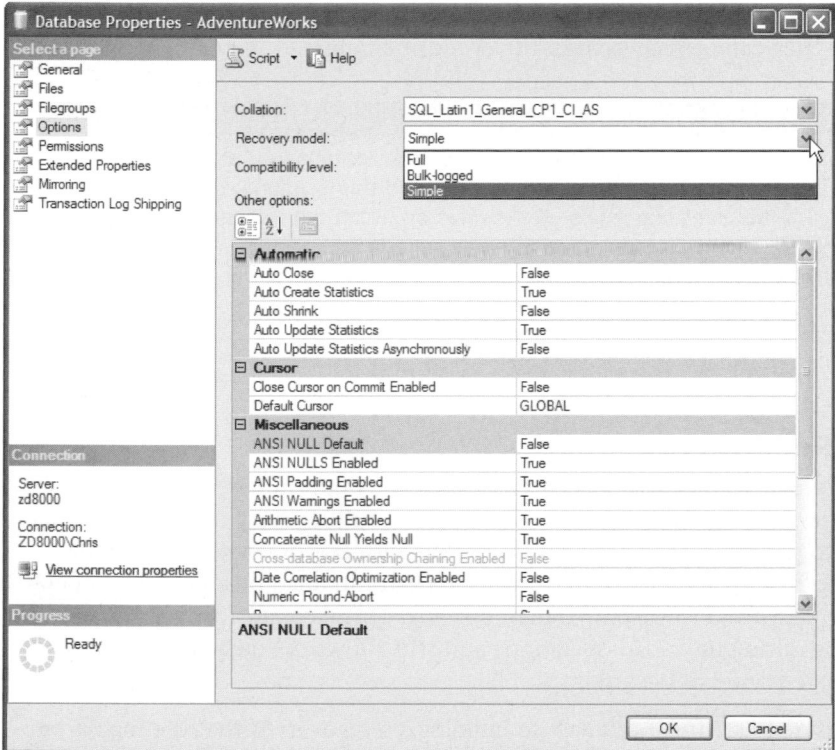

FIGURE 11.1   Setting the recovery model in SSMS.

Full Recovery

The full recovery model gives you the most protection against data loss. A database that is set to full recovery will have all database operations written to the transactions log. These operations include insertions, updates, and deletions, as well as any other statements that change the database. In addition, the full recovery model captures any database inserts that are the result of a BCP command or a BULK INSERT statement.

In the event of a media failure, a database that is in full recovery can be restored to the point in time at which the failure occurred. Your ability to restore to a point in time is dependent on your database backup plan. If a full database backup is available, along with the transaction log backups that occurred after the full database backup, you can recover to the point of the last transaction log backup. In addition, if your current transaction log is available, you can restore up to the point of the last committed transaction in the transaction log.

This is the most comprehensive recovery model, but in some respects, it is the most expensive. It is expensive in terms of the transaction log space needed to capture all the database operations. The space can be significant with databases that have a lot of update activity or with databases that have large bulk load operations. It is also expensive in terms of server overhead because every transaction is captured and retained in the transaction log so that they can be recovered in the event of a failure.

TIP

A common problem in SQL Server environments involves a database that is set to full recovery but whose transaction log is never backed up. In this scenario, the transaction log can grow to the point that it fills up the drive on which the transaction log is located. You need to ensure that you have regularly scheduled backups of the transaction log if you have set your database to full recovery. The transaction log backups allow you to recover from a media failure and also remove the inactive portion of the transaction log so that it does not need to grow.

Bulk-Logged Recovery

The bulk-logged recovery model is similar to full recovery, but it differs in the way that bulk operations are captured in the transaction log. With full recovery mode, SQL Server writes every row to the transaction log that is inserted with BCP or BULK INSERT. Bulk-logged recovery keeps track of the extents that have been modified by a bulk load operation but does not write each row to the transaction log. This reduces the overall size of the transaction log during bulk load operations and still allows the database to recover after a bulk load operation has occurred.

The biggest downside to setting a database to bulk logged recovery is that the log backups for the databases can be large. The log backups are large due to the fact that SQL Server copies all the data extents that have been affected by bulk load operations since the last backup of the transaction log. Remember that data extents consist of eight data pages each, and each page is 8KB in size. This may not seem like much by today's standards, but it can be significant when you're bulk loading a large table. For example, consider a table that occupies 1GB of space that is truncated each week and reloaded with a bulk insert. The bulk insert operation goes relatively fast because the rows are not being written to the transaction log, but the backup of the transaction log is much larger.

11

> **NOTE**
>
> In testing we did on a table with approximately 2.4 million rows (that occupied 500MB of space), the log file grew over 2GB during a bulk insert operation that reloaded all rows in a full recovery mode database. In contrast, the same bulk insert operation on the database with bulk logged recovery grew the log by only 9MB. However, the backup of the 9MB transaction log was approximately 500MB. This is much larger than the actual log itself because the bulk operation occurred and caused all the modified extents from the bulk insert operation to be stored in the log backup as well.

The other downside to bulk-logged recovery is that with it, you may sacrifice the ability to restore to the most recent point in time. This situation occurs if a bulk insert operation has occurred since the last database backup and a media failure occurs. In this case, the restores can occur for any backups that were taken that do not contain a bulk insert operation, but any outstanding changes that were retained in the transaction log cannot be applied. This is due to the fact that that bulk operations are not written to the log directly in this model and cannot be recovered. Only bulk operations that have been captured in a backup can be restored.

If transactions have occurred in a database since the last backup, and no bulk insert operations have occurred, you can recover those pending transactions as long as the media containing the transaction log is still available. The tail of the transaction log can be backed up and applied during a restore operation. The tail of the log and other restore scenarios are discussed in the "Restore Scenarios" section, later in this chapter.

Simple Recovery

The simple recovery model is the easiest to administer, but it is the option that has the greatest possibility for data loss. In this mode, your transactions log is truncated automatically based on a checkpoint in the database. These checkpoints happen often, and they cause the data in the transaction log to be truncated frequently.

> **NOTE**
>
> Prior to SQL Server 2000, the `trunc. log on checkpoint` database option was used to truncate the log on a checkpoint and produce the same type of behavior as simple recovery. This same database option is still available with SQL Server 2000 and 2005. Setting the option to `TRUE` with the `sp_dboption` system stored procedure implicitly places a database in simple recovery mode.

The most important thing to remember about the simple recovery model is that with it, you cannot back up the transaction log that captures changes to your database. If a media failure occurs, you are not able to recover the database activity that has occurred since the last database backup. This is a major exposure, so simple recovery is not recommended for production databases. However, it can be a good option for development databases where the loss of some transactions is acceptable. In these types of environments, simple recovery can equate to saved disk space because the transaction log is constantly truncated.

The administration in these environments is reduced as well because the transaction log backups are not an option and thus do not need to be managed.

For a more detailed discussion of the transaction log, see Chapter 26, "Transaction Management and the Transaction Log."

Backup Devices

A backup device is used to provide a storage destination for the database backups that are created with SQL Server. Backups can be written to logical or physical devices. A logical device is essentially an alias to the physical device and makes it easier to refer to the device when performing database backups. The physical backup devices that SQL Server can write to include files on local disks, tape, and network shares.

Disk Devices

A disk device is generally stored in a folder on a local hard drive. This should not be the same hard drive that your data is stored on! Disk devices have several advantages, including speed and reliability. If you have ever had a backup fail because you forgot to load a tape, you can appreciate the advantage of disk backups. On the other hand, if backups are done to a local disk and the server is destroyed, you lose your backups as well.

> **NOTE**
>
> Disks have become increasingly popular media as the prices have fallen. Storage area networks (SANs) and other large-scale disk solutions have entered mainstream usage and offer a large amount of storage at a relatively inexpensive price. They also offer redundancy and provide fault tolerance in order to mitigate the chance of losing data on a disk. Finally, increased network bandwidth across LANs and WANs has allowed for the movement of backups created on disk to alternate locations to add additional fault tolerance.

Tape Devices

Tape devices are used to back up to tape. Tape devices must be directly connected to the server, and parallel backups to multiple drives are supported to increase throughput. Tape backups have the advantage of being scalable, portable, and secure. Scalability is important as a database grows; available disk space often precludes the use of disk backups for large databases. Because tapes are removable media, they can easily be transported offsite, where they can be secured against theft and damage.

SQL Server supports the Microsoft Tape Format (MTF) for backup devices, which means that SQL Server backups and operating system backups can share the same tape. This is convenient for small sites with shared use servers and only one tape drive. You can schedule your SQL Server backups and file backups without having to be onsite to change the tape.

Network Shares

SQL Server 2005 allows the use of both mapped network drives and Universal Naming Convention (UNC) paths in the backup device filename. A mapped network drive must be mapped as a network drive in the session in which SQL Server is running. This is prone to error and generally not recommended. UNC paths are much simpler to administer. With UNC backup devices, the SQL Server service account must be able to see the UNC path on the network. This is accomplished by granting the service account full control permission on the share or by making the service account a member of the Administrators group on the remote computer.

Keep in mind that backups done on a network share should be done on a dedicated or high-speed network connection, and the backup should be verified to avoid potential corruption introduced by network error. The time it takes a backup to complete over the network depends on network traffic, so you need to take this into consideration when planning your backups.

Media Sets and Families

When you're backing up to multiple devices, the terms *media set* and *media family* are used to describe the components of the backup. A *media set* is the target destination of the database backup and comprises several individual media. All media in a media set must be of the same type (for example, all tape or all disk). A *media family* is the collection of media associated with an individual backup device. For example, a media family could be a collection of five tapes that are contained in a single tape device.

The first tape in the media family is referred to as the *initial* media, and the subsequent tapes are referred to as *continuation* media. All the media families combined are referred to as the *media set*. If, for example, a backup is written to 3 backup devices (each with 4 tapes), the media set would contain 3 media families and consist of a total of 12 tapes. It is recommended to use the MEDIANAME parameter of the BACKUP command to specify a name for the media set. This associates the multiple devices as members of the media set. The MEDIANAME parameter can then be referenced in future backup operations.

Creating Backup Devices

You can create logical backup devices by using T-SQL or SSMS. The T-SQL command for creating these logical backup devices is sp_adddumpdevice, which has the following syntax:

```
sp_addumpdevice [ @devtype = ] 'device_type'
        , [ @logicalname = ] 'logical_name'
        , [ @physicalname = ] 'physical_name'
    [ , { [ @cntrltype = ] controller_type ¦
        [ @devstatus = ] 'device_status' }
    ]
```

The following sample script demonstrates the creation of the different types of backup devices:

```
-- Local Disk
EXEC sp_addumpdevice 'disk', 'diskdev1',
    'c:\mssql2005\backup\AdventureWorks.bak'
-- Network Disk
EXEC sp_addumpdevice 'disk', 'networkdev1',
    '\\myserver\myshare\AdventureWorks.bak'
-- Tape
EXEC sp_addumpdevice 'tape', 'tapedev1', '\\.\tape0'
```

To create backup devices with SSMS, you navigate to the Server Objects node in the Object Explorer and right-click Backup Devices and then New Backup Device; the Backup Device screen appears. This screen includes a text box for the device name, along with a section to select the destination for the device. This is the physical location, and you can select either Tape or File.

Backing Up a Database

Now that you know the types of backups, the recovery models that they relate to, and the devices you can write to, you are ready to back up your database. You can create backups with SQL Server 2005 by using either the SSMS or T-SQL. Some backups are supported only through T-SQL, but the vast majority can be accomplished with either tool.

Creating Database Backups with SSMS

The backup options in SSMS are accessible through the Object Explorer. You right-click the AdventureWorks database in the SSMS Object Explorer, select Tasks and Backup, and a backup window like the one shown in Figure 11.2 appears.

The Source section on the Back Up Database screen contains information relative to the database that is going to be backed up. The target database is displayed in the first drop-down, along with the recovery model that has been set for the database. The backup types that are available in the drop-down are dependent on the recovery model. For simple recovery, only full and differential backup types are available. The full recovery and bulk logged recovery models have all backup types available in the drop-down.

The Backup Set section allows you to give the backup a meaningful name and specify when the backup set will expire. When the backup set expires, the backup can be over-written and is no longer retained. If the backup is set to expire after 0 days, it will never expire.

The Destination section identifies the disk or tape media that will contain the backup. You can specify multiple destinations in this section by clicking the Add button. For disk media, you can specify a maximum of 64 disk devices. The same limit applies to tape media. If multiple devices are specified, the backup information is spread across those devices. All the devices must be present in order for you to be able to restore the database. If there are no tape devices attached to the database server, the Tape option is disabled.

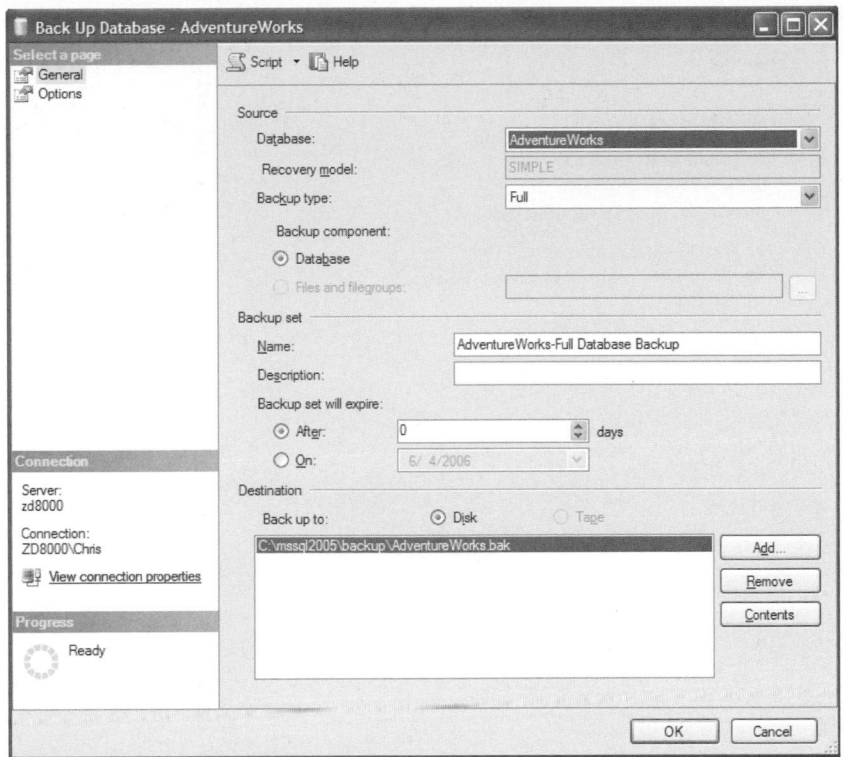

FIGURE 11.2   The Back Up Database window in SSMS.

You can select several different types of options for a database backup. Figure 11.3 shows the options page that is available when you back up a database by using SSMS.

The Overwrite Media section allows you to specify options relative to the destination media for the backup. Keep in mind that a given media set can contain more than one backup. This can occur if the Append to the Existing Backup Set options is selected. With this option, any prior backups that were contained on the media set are preserved, and the new backup is added to it. With the Overwrite All Existing Backup Sets option, the media set contains only the latest backup, and no prior backups are retained.

You can use the options in the Reliability section to ensure that the backup that has been created can be used reliably in a restore situation. Verifying the backup when finished is highly recommended but causes the backup time to be extended during the backup verification. Similarly, the Perform Checksum Before Writing to Media option helps ensure that you have a sound backup, but again, it causes the database backup to run longer.

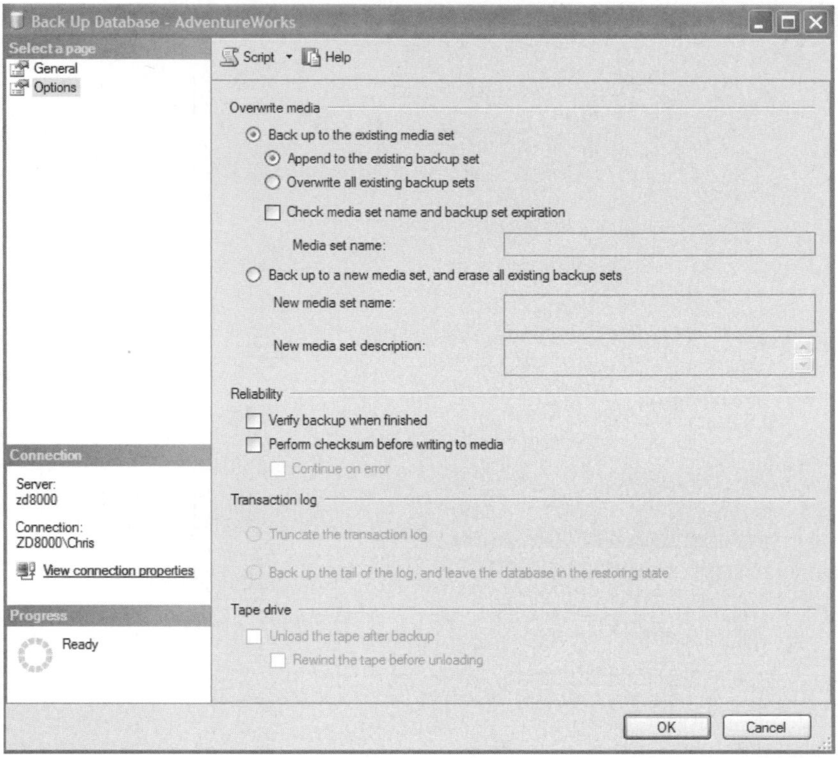

FIGURE 11.3   The Back Up Database Options page in SSMS.

The options in the Transaction Log section are available for databases in the full recovery or bulk-logged model. These options are disabled in the simple recovery model. The Truncate the Transaction Log option causes any inactive portion of the transaction log to be removed after the database backup is complete. This is the default option and helps keep the size of the transaction log manageable. The Back Up the Tail of the Log option is related to point-in-time restores and is discussed in more detail in the "Restore Scenarios" section later in this chapter.

The last set of options, in the Tape Drive section, are enabled only when tape has been selected for the destination media. Selecting the Unload the Tape After Backup option causes the media tape to be ejected when the backup completes. This can help identify the end of a backup and prevent the tape from being overwritten the next time the backup runs. The Rewind the Tape Before Unloading is self-explanatory; it causes the tape to be released and rewound before you unload the tape.

NOTE

Keep in mind that all backups can be performed while the database is in use. SQL Server has the ability to keep track of the changes that are occurring during the backup and can maintain transactional consistency as of the end of the backup. You need to consider some performance overhead during the actual backup, but the backup can occur during active database hours. However, it is still a good idea to schedule your database backups during off-hours, when database activity is at a minimum.

Creating Database Backups with T-SQL

The T-SQL BACKUP command offers a myriad of options to perform all the backup operations are available in SSMS. There are also some backup operations that can be performed only with T-SQL that SSMS does not support.

The BACKUP command comes in three different flavors. The first flavor involves the backup of a database. The command syntax starts with BACKUP DATABASE, followed by the relevant parameters and options. The second flavor involves the backup of a file or filegroup that is part of the database. The command syntax for this type of backup also utilizes the BACKUP DATABASE command, but a file or filegroup is specified after the database name to identify which parts of the database should be backed up. The last flavor involves the backup of the database's transaction log. The syntax for backing up the transaction log starts with BACKUP LOG. Each flavor shares many of the same options. The basic syntax for backing up a database follows:

```
BACKUP DATABASE { database_name | @database_name_var }
TO < backup_device > [ ,,,,n ]
[ [ MIRROR TO < backup_device > [ ,...n ] ] [ ...next-mirror ] ]
[ WITH
    [ BLOCKSIZE = { blocksize | @blocksize_variable } ]
    [ [ , ] { CHECKSUM | NO_CHECKSUM } ]
    [ [ , ] { STOP_ON_ERROR | CONTINUE_AFTER_ERROR } ]
    [ [ , ] DESCRIPTION = { 'text' | @text_variable } ]
    [ [ , ] DIFFERENTIAL ]
    [ [ , ] EXPIREDATE = { date | @date_var }
    | RETAINDAYS = { days | @days_var } ]
    [ [ , ] PASSWORD = { password | @password_variable } ]
    [ [ , ] { FORMAT | NOFORMAT } ]
    [ [ , ] { INIT | NOINIT } ]
    [ [ , ] { NOSKIP | SKIP } ]
    [ [ , ] MEDIADESCRIPTION = { 'text' | @text_variable } ]
    [ [ , ] MEDIANAME = { media_name | @media_name_variable } ]
    [ [ , ] MEDIAPASSWORD = { mediapassword | @mediapassword_variable } ]
    [ [ , ] NAME = { backup_set_name | @backup_set_name_var } ]
    [ [ , ] { NOREWIND | REWIND } ]
    [ [ , ] { NOUNLOAD | UNLOAD } ]
    [ [ , ] RESTART ]
    [ [ , ] STATS [ = percentage ]
 ] ]
    [ [ , ] COPY_ONLY ]
]
```

The number of options is extensive, but many of them are optional. A BACKUP DATABASE command can be as simple as the following example:

```
BACKUP DATABASE [AdventureWorks]
 TO  DISK = N'C:\mssql2005\backup\AdventureWorks_COPY.bak'
```

The first part of the BACKUP command is related to the database you want to back up (database_name), followed by the location to which you want to write the backup (backup_device). The remainder of the syntax relates to the options that can be specified following the WITH clause. These options determine how your backup will be created and the properties of the resulting backup. Table 11.1 outlines these options.

TABLE 11.1   BACKUP DATABASE Options

Option	Description
BLOCKSIZE	The physical block size that will be used to create the backup. The default is 64KB.
CHECKSUM ¦ NO_CHECKSUM	When CHECKSUM is specified, a checksum is calculated before the backup is written to validate that the backup is not corrupt. The default is NO_CHECKSUM.
STOP_ON_ERROR ¦ CONTINUE_AFTER_ERROR	This option is used in conjunction with the CHECKSUM option. The STOP_ON_ERROR option (which is the default) causes the backup to fail if the checksum cannot be validated.
DESCRIPTION	This is a 255-character description of the backup set.
DIFFERENTIAL	This option causes a differential backup to occur, which only captures changes since the last backup.
EXPIREDATE	This option specifies the date on which the backup set will expire and be overwritten.
RETAINDAYS	This option specifies the number of elapsed days before the backup set can be overwritten.
PASSWORD	This is a password that must be specified when restoring the backup set.
FORMAT ¦ NOFORMAT	FORMAT causes the existing media header and backup set to be overwritten. The default is NOFORMAT.
INIT ¦ NOINIT	The INIT option causes a backup set to be overwritten. The backup set is not overwritten if the backup set has not expired or if it does not match the media name specified with the NAME option. NOINIT (which is the default) causes the backup set to be appended to the existing media.

TABLE 11.1   Continued

Option	Description
NOSKIP ┊ SKIP	NOSKIP (which is the default) allows backup sets to be overwritten if they have expired. The SKIP option skips expiration and media name checks and is used to prevent the overwriting of backup sets.
MEDIADESCRIPTION	This is a 255-character description for the entire backup media containing the backup sets.
MEDIANAME	This is a 128-character name for the backup media. If it is specified, the target media must match this name.
MEDIAPASSWORD	This is a password for the media set. When media is created with this password, the password must be supplied in order to create a backup set on that media or to restore from that media.
NAME	This is a 128-character name for the backup set.
NOREWIND ┊ REWIND	This option is used for tape operations. REWIND (which is the default) causes the tape to be released and rewound after it fills.
NOUNLOAD ┊ UNLOAD	This option is used for tape operations. NOUNLOAD (which is the default) causes the tape to remain in the tape drive after a backup completes. UNLOAD causes the tape to be rewound and unloaded when the backup completes.
RESTART	This option has no effect and is in place only for backward compatibility.
STATS	This option causes completion statistics to be displayed at the specified interval to assess progress.
COPY_ONLY	This option allows a backup to be made without affecting the normal sequence of backups.

The "Backup Scenarios" section, later in this chapter, provides some examples of how to use these options.

Backing Up the Transaction Log

As discussed, the full and bulk-logged recovery models cause transactions to be written to the database's transaction log. These transactions should be backed up periodically for two main reasons. First, the transaction log backups can be used in case of a media failure to restore work that was completed in the database. These backups limit your exposure to data loss and give you the ability to reapply changes that have occurred.

The second reason for backing up the transaction log is to keep the size of the log manageable. Keep in mind that SQL Server is a write-ahead database management system (DBMS) and thus writes most changes to the transaction log first, before it updates the actual data files. This type of DBMS is great for recovery purposes, but it can be a real headache if you do not periodically clear those transactions from the log. Without a backup or manual truncation, the log can fill to a point where it will use up all the space on your disk.

Creating Transaction Log Backups with SSMS

The same backup screen that is utilized for database backups in SSMS can also be used for transaction log backups. Figure 11.4 shows the Back Up Database screen with Transaction Log selected as the backup type. A device must be selected to write the backup to, and some additional options on the Option page that relate to the transaction log are enabled.

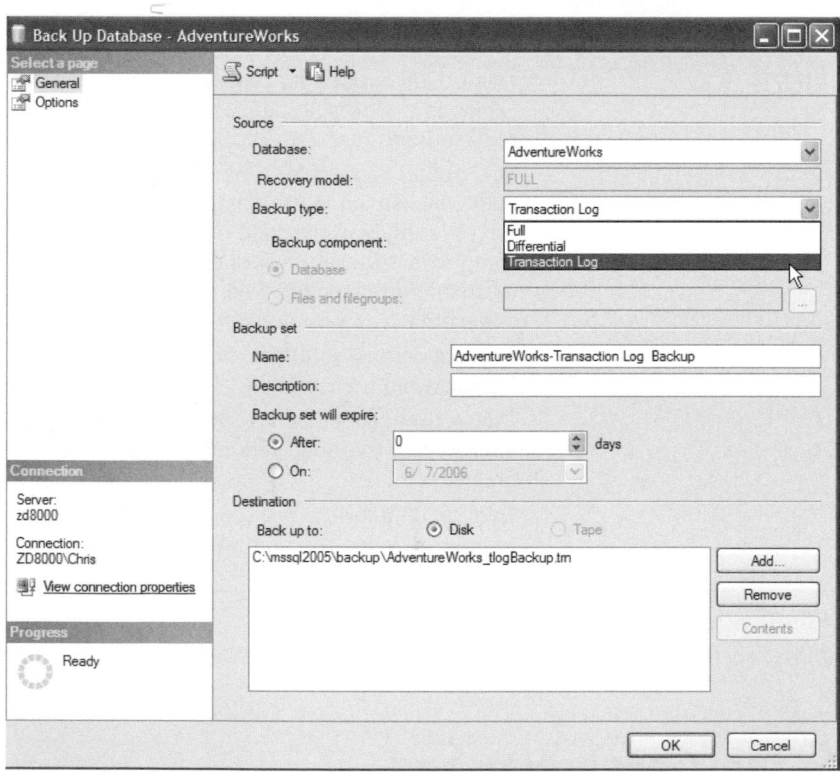

FIGURE 11.4   Backing up the transaction log in SSMS.

Creating Transaction Log Backups with T-SQL

When you back up a transaction log by using T-SQL, you use the BACKUP LOG command, which includes all the previously listed options except the DIFFERENTIAL option. (Differential backups do not apply to transaction logs.) Several additional options are available for transaction log backups. The following abbreviated syntax for the BACKUP LOG command shows the options that are exclusively for backing up transaction logs:

```
BACKUP LOG { database_name ¦ @database_name_var }
TO < backup_device > [ ,...n ]
[ [ MIRROR TO < backup_device > [ ,...n ] ] [ ...next-mirror ] ]
[ WITH
......
    [ [ , ] NO_TRUNCATE ]
    [ [ , ] { NORECOVERY ¦ STANDBY = undo_file_name } ]
```

In addition, one other variant of the BACKUP LOG command does not actually back up the transaction log but only truncates the inactive portion of the log. The syntax for this type of BACKUP LOG command follows:

```
BACKUP LOG { database_name ¦ @database_name_var }
    WITH
        { NO_LOG ¦ TRUNCATE_ONLY
```

The options that are specific to BACKUP LOG are discussed in detail in the following sections.

The NO_TRUNCATE Option

You use the NO_TRUNCATE option when the log is available but the database is not. Its function is actually the opposite of NO_LOG and TRUNCATE_ONLY. Under normal circumstances, the BACKUP LOG command not only writes to the transaction log but also signals a checkpoint for the database to flush any dirty buffers from memory to the database files. This becomes a problem when the media containing the database is unavailable and you must capture the current contents of a log to a backup file for recovery. If the last time you did a log backup was four hours ago, this would mean the loss of all the input since then. If your log is on a separate disk that is not damaged, you have those four hours of transactions available to you, but BACKUP LOG fails because it can't checkpoint the data files. You run BACKUP LOG with the NO_TRUNCATE option, and the log is backed up, but the checkpoint is not run because the log is not actually cleared. You now have this new log backup to restore as well, enabling recovery to the time of failure. The only transactions lost are those that were not yet committed.

The NORECOVERY ¦ STANDBY= undo_file_name Options

The NORECOVERY option causes the tail of the log to be backed up and leaves the database in a RESTORING state, which allows additional transaction logs to be applied, if necessary. The tail of the log is the active portion of the log that contains transactions that have not yet been backed up. This "tail" is critical in restore situations in which all committed transactions are reapplied. Typically, the NORECOVERY option is used with the NO_TRUNCATE option to retain the contents of the log.

The STANDBY option also backs up the tail of the log, but it leaves the database in a read-only/standby state. The read-only state allows inquiry on the database and allows additional transaction logs to be applied to the database as well. *undo_file_name* must be supplied with the STANDBY command so that transactions that were not committed and rolled back at the time of the backup can be reapplied if additional transaction logs are applied to the database. This STANDBY option produces the same results as executing BACKUP LOG WITH NORECOVERY followed by a RESTORE WITH STANDBY command.

The NO_LOG ¦ TRUNCATE_ONLY Options

The NO_LOG and TRUNCATE_ONLY options are synonymous: They cause the inactive portion of the transaction log to be discarded. When that is discarded, the transactions that are in the inactive portion of the log are not recoverable. You should use these options with extreme caution, and you should generally not use them in production systems. An example of the command follows:

```
BACKUP LOG AdventureWorks WITH TRUNCATE_ONLY
```

After this command is run, you should do a full backup or a differential backup of your database to ensure the best recoverability. If a full backup or differential backup has not yet been taken and a media failure occurs, you need to revert to the prior full or differential backup.

> **NOTE**
>
> Microsoft has indicated that the NO_LOG and TRUNCATE_ONLY options will be removed in a future version of SQL Server.

Backup Scenarios

Typically, several different types of backups are used in a comprehensive backup plan. These backups are often combined to produce maximum recoverability while balancing the load on the system and the amount of time to recover a database. The following backup scenarios outline some of the ways that SQL Server backups are used.

> **NOTE**
>
> Many of the examples that follow utilize a backup directory named c:\mssql2005\ backup. If you are interested in running some of these examples on your own system, you need to create this directory on the database server first before running the scripts that reference this directory. You can use backup and data directories that are different from the default directory to simplify the directory structure for the SQL Server files. Typically these directories should not be on the C: drive, but the C: drive is used here for simplicity.

Full Database Backups Only

A full database backup, without the use of other database backups, is often found in non-production environments where the loss of transactional data is relatively unimportant. Some development environments are good examples of this. In these environments, a nightly full backup is sufficient to ensure that recent Data Definition Language (DDL) changes and the related development data for the day are captured. If a catastrophic failure occurs during the day and causes a restore to occur, the database can be restored from the prior night's backup. The following example shows a full backup of the AdventureWorks database:

```
--Full Database Backup to a single disk device
BACKUP DATABASE [AdventureWorks]
 TO  DISK = N'C:\mssql2005\backup\AdventureWorks.bak'
 WITH NOFORMAT, INIT,  NAME = N'AdventureWorks-Full Database Backup',
 SKIP, NOREWIND, NOUNLOAD,  STATS = 10
```

The sole use of full database backups needs to be carefully considered. The benefits of limited administration and limited backup space requirements have to be weighed against the costs of losing an entire day's transactions.

Full Database Backups with Transaction Log Backups

Compared to making a full database backup only, a more comprehensive approach to database backups includes the use of transaction log backups to augment the recoverability of full database backups. Transaction log backups that are taken periodically capture incremental database activity that can be applied to a full database backup during database restore.

You need to measure the frequency of the transaction log backup against the tolerance for data loss. For example, if the requirement is to prevent no more than one hour's worth of work, then the transaction log backups should be taken hourly. If the media that the backup is stored on is accessible, you should loose no more than one hour's worth of data.

As mentioned earlier, the database must be placed in full or bulk logged recovery mode in order to capture transaction log backups. Listing 11.1 shows the commands necessary to place the AdventureWorks database in full recovery mode, the required backup to establish a base, followed by the command to perform the actual transaction log backup.

LISTING 11.1   Full Backups with Transaction Logs

```
--First need to change the recovery model from simple to full
--so that the tlogs are available for backup
ALTER DATABASE [AdventureWorks] SET RECOVERY FULL WITH NO_WAIT

--*** A Full database backup must be taken after the
--*** recovery mode has been changed
--*** in order set a base for future tlog backups.
```

LISTING 11.1   Continued

```
--*** If the full backups is not taken
--*** then tlog backups will fail.
--The Following full backup utilizes two devices on the same drive.
--Often times multiple devices are backed up to different drives.
--Backing up to different drives
-- can speed up the overall backup
time and help when you are running low on space on a drive
-- where your backups are written.

BACKUP DATABASE [AdventureWorks]
  TO  DISK = N'C:\mssql2005\backup\AdventureWorks_Full_Dev1.bak',
      DISK = N'C:\mssql2005\backup\AdventureWorks_Full_Dev2.bak'
  WITH NOFORMAT, NOINIT, SKIP, NOREWIND, NOUNLOAD,  STATS = 10


--Transaction log backups can be taken now that a base has been established
--The following tlog backup is written to a single file
BACKUP LOG [AdventureWorks]
  TO  DISK = N'C:\mssql2005\backup\log\AdventureWorks_FirstAfterFull.trn'
  WITH NOFORMAT, INIT,  NAME = N'AdventureWorks-Transaction Log  Backup',
  SKIP, NOREWIND, NOUNLOAD,  STATS = 10, CHECKSUM
```

Differential Backups

Differential backups can be used to reduce the amount of time required to restore a database and can be particularly useful in environments where the amount of data that changes is limited. Differential backups capture only the database extents that have changed since the last database backup—typically a full database backup.

The addition of differential backups to a plan that includes full database backups and transaction log backups can significantly improve the overall recovery time. The differential database backup eliminates the need to apply any transaction log backups that have occurred from the time of the last full backup up until the completion of the differential backup. Figure 11.5 depicts a backup plan that includes full database backups, transaction log backups, and differential backups. The differential backups are executed on a daily basis between the full backups.

It is important to remember that differential backups are cumulative and contain all changes since the last differential base. There is no need to apply previous differential backups if the new differential base has not been established. For example, in the backup plan shown in Figure 11.5, if a media failure occurred in the middle of the day on January 3, the differential backup that would be used is that which was taken at the beginning of the day on January 3; the differential backup that occurred on January 2 would not be needed. The full backup from January 1, the differential from January 3, and any transaction log backups that had occurred since the differential on January 3 would be used to restore the database.

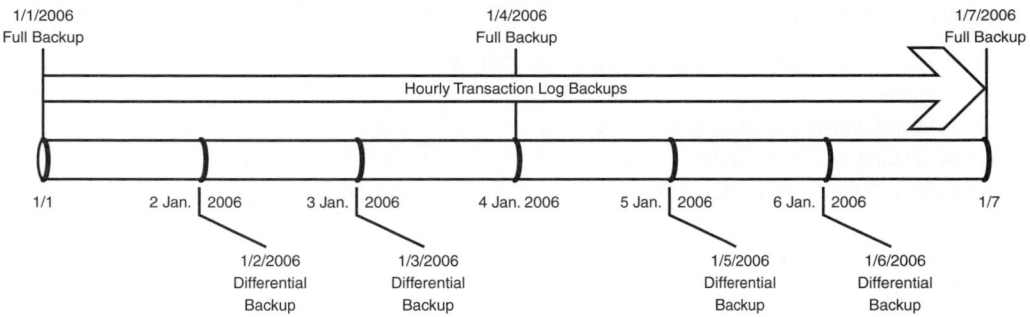

FIGURE 11.5   A backup plan that includes differential backup.

You can create differential backups by using SSMS or T-SQL. The following example demonstrates the creation of the differential backup for the AdventureWorks database using T-SQL:

```
BACKUP DATABASE [AdventureWorks]
TO  DISK = N'C:\mssql2005\backup\Adventureworks_Diff2.bak'
WITH  DIFFERENTIAL , NOFORMAT, INIT,
NAME = N'AdventureWorks-Differential Database Backup',
SKIP, NOREWIND, NOUNLOAD,  STATS = 10
```

Partial Backups

Partial backups are useful when read-only files or filegroups are part of a database. Listing 11.2 contains the commands necessary to add a read-only filegroup to the AdventureWorks database. The commands in Listing 11.2 do not perform a partial backup, but they do modify a sample database so that a partial database would make sense.

LISTING 11.2   Adding a Read-Only Filegroup to a Database

```
--Need to add a read only filegroup first to demonstrate
ALTER DATABASE AdventureWorks
ADD FILEGROUP ReadOnlyFG1
GO
-- Add a file to the Filegroup
ALTER DATABASE AdventureWorks
ADD FILE
(    NAME = AdventureWorks_ReadOnlyData,
     FILENAME = 'C:\mssql2005\data\AdventureWorks_ReadOnlyData.ndf',
     SIZE = 5MB,
     MAXSIZE = 100MB,
     FILEGROWTH = 5MB) TO FILEGROUP ReadOnlyFG1
go
--Create a table on the ReadOnly filegroup
```

LISTING 11.2   Continued

```
CREATE TABLE Adventureworks.dbo.MyReadOnlyTable
  ( FirstName varchar(50),
    LastName varchar(50),
    EMailAddress char(1000) )
ON ReadOnlyFG1

--Insert some data into the new read only Filegroup
insert Adventureworks.dbo.MyReadOnlyTable
 select LastName, FirstName, 'xxx'
 from Adventureworks.person.contact

--Make the filegroup readonly
ALTER DATABASE [AdventureWorks] MODIFY FILEGROUP [ReadOnlyFG1] READONLY
```

When you have a filegroup that contains read-only data, a partial backup can be valuable. The partial backup by default excludes any read-only filegroups and backs up only the read/write data that could have changed.

Listing 11.3 contains three separate backup commands that relate to the partial backup. The first backup command is not a partial backup but instead backs up the read-only filegroup. If the read-only filegroup is not backed up prior to the partial backup, the read-only filegroup is backed up, as is part of the partial backup. The second backup command creates the actual partial backup. The key parameter in this backup is READ_WRITE_FILEGROUPS, which causes the backup to skip the read-only data. The third backup command in Listing 11.3 shows that it is possible to perform a partial backup that includes the read-only data as well. This command includes a specific reference to the read-only filegroup, which causes it to be backed up as well.

LISTING 11.3   Making a Partial Backup

```
--Need to backup the readonly filegroup the was created
-- or it will be included in the partial backup
BACKUP DATABASE [AdventureWorks]
 FILEGROUP = N'ReadOnlyFG1'
 TO  DISK = N'C:\mssql2005\backup\AdventureWorks_ReadOnlyFG.bak'
 WITH NOFORMAT, NOINIT,  NAME = N'AdventureWorks-Full Filegroup Backup',
 SKIP, NOREWIND, NOUNLOAD,  STATS = 10

--Create the Partial Database Backup
--It will not contain the data from readonly filegroup
--The partial database backup can be restored without affecting
-- the data in the readonly filegroup
BACKUP DATABASE [AdventureWorks] READ_WRITE_FILEGROUPS
 TO  DISK = N'C:\mssql2005\backup\AdventureWorks_Partial.bak'
 WITH NOFORMAT, INIT,  NAME = N'AdventureWorks-Partial Database Backup',
```

LISTING 11.3   Continued

```
SKIP, NOREWIND, NOUNLOAD,  STATS = 10

--It is possible to backup the readonly filegroup(s) as well
--by listing the readonly filegroups in the backup command as shown in the
--following backup command
BACKUP DATABASE [AdventureWorks] FILEGROUP = 'ReadOnlyFG1', READ_WRITE_FILEGROUPS
 TO  DISK = N'C:\mssql2005\backup\AdventureWorks_Partial_WithReadOnly.bak'
 WITH NOFORMAT, INIT,  NAME = N'AdventureWorks-Partial Database Backup',
 SKIP, NOREWIND, NOUNLOAD,  STATS = 10
```

File/Filegroup Backups

Much of our discussion thus far has focused on backing up an entire database, but it is possible to only back up particular files or a group of files in a filegroup. A SQL Server database, by default, has only two files: the data file (with the file extension .MDF) and the log file (with the extension .LDF). You can add additional files and filegroups that contain these files to extend the database beyond the original two files. These additional files are often data files that are added to larger databases that require additional space. With very large databases, a full backup that contains all the database files can take too much time. In such a case, the individual files or filegroups can be backed up separately, enabling the backup to be spread out.

Listing 11.4 shows the T-SQL command that can be used to back up the read-only file you added to the AdventureWorks database in Listing 11.3.

LISTING 11.4   Creating a File Backup

```
BACKUP DATABASE [AdventureWorks] FILE = 'AdventureWorks_ReadOnlyData'
 TO  DISK = N'C:\mssql2005\backup\AdventureWorks_ReadOnlyData.bak'
 WITH NOFORMAT, INIT,  NAME = N'AdventureWorks-Readonly File Backup',
 SKIP, NOREWIND, NOUNLOAD,  STATS = 10
```

There is some additional administrative overhead associated with file and filegroup backups. Unlike a full database backup that produces one file that contains the entire database, the file backups do not stand by themselves and require other backups in order to create the entire database. You need to keep the following in mind when performing file and filegroup backups:

▶ A file or filegroup backup does not back up any portion of the transaction log. In order to restore a file or filegroup backup, you must have the transaction log backups since the last file or filegroup backup, including the tail of the log, in order for the database system to ensure transactional consistency. This also implies that the database must be in full or bulk-logged recovery because these are the only models that support transaction log backups.

- ▶ Individual file or filegroup backups can be restored from a full database backup.

- ▶ Point-in-time recovery is not permitted with file or filegroup backups.

- ▶ Differential backups can be combined with file or filegroup backups. These differential backups capture only those extents that have changed since the file or filegroup backup was made.

File and filegroup backups can be very powerful options for very large databases, but you need to ensure that the relevant backups can be accounted for. In all backup situations, the key to a successful plan is testing your backup strategy; this is particularly true with file and filegroup backups.

Mirrored Backups

The use of mirrored backups can help diminish the possibility of losing a database backup. Database backups can be your lifeline to recovery, and you do not want to lose them. Mirrored backups simultaneously write the backup information to more than one media set. You can mirror the backup to two, three, or four different media sets. Listing 11.5 gives an example of a mirrored backup that writes two different media sets.

LISTING 11.5   Creating a Mirrored Backup

```
BACKUP DATABASE AdventureWorks
TO disk = 'C:\mssql2005\backup\AdventureWorks_Mirror1a.bak',
    disk = 'C:\mssql2005\backup\AdventureWorks_Mirror1b.bak'
MIRROR TO disk = 'c:\mssql2005\backup\AdventureWorks_Mirror2a.bak',
    disk = 'C:\mssql2005\backup\AdventureWorks_Mirror2b.bak'
WITH FORMAT,
    MEDIANAME = 'AdventureWorksMirrorSet'
```

The example in Listing 11.5 is simplistic and only demonstrates the ability of the backup to write to two different locations. At the end of the backup example, four files will exist. Each pair of files can be used to restore the database. In the real world, a backup like that in Listing 11.5 would write to two different disk or tape drives. Storing the media on the same drive is very risky and does not give you all the advantages a mirror can afford.

Copy-Only Backups

If you want a backup that will not affect future or past backups, copy-only backups are for you. The copy-only backup allows you to make a database or log backup without identifying the backup as one that should be included in a restore sequence.

Contrast this with a full database backup: If a full database backup is taken, the information related to this backup is captured in the system tables. This backup can form the base for other backups, such as transaction log backups or differential backups, and must be retained in order to restore the backups that depend on the base.

The following example shows an example of a copy-only backup; the COPY_ONLY parameter is the key to creating this kind of backup:

```
BACKUP DATABASE [AdventureWorks]
 TO  DISK = N'C:\mssql2005\backup\AdventureWorks_COPY.bak'
 WITH COPY_ONLY
```

System Database Backups

The system databases are the master, model, msdb, resource, tempdb, and distribution databases. These are the databases that SQL Server uses as part of its internal workings. All these databases should be part of your backup plan, except for resource and tempdb. You can find detailed descriptions of these databases in Chapter 6, "SQL Server System and Database Administration." The key to remember about all these databases is that they contain key information about your SQL Server environment. The msdb database contains information about backups and scheduled jobs. The master database contains information about all the users' databases that are stored on the server. This information can change over time.

To ensure that you do not lose the information the system databases contain, you should back up these databases as well. Typically, nightly full database backups of these databases will suffice. You can use the same T-SQL syntax or SSMS screens as for a user database to accomplish this task.

Restoring Databases and Transaction Logs

A database restore allows a database or part of a database to be recovered to a state that it was in previously. This state includes the physical structure of the database, configuration options, and the data contained in the database. The options you have for recovery are heavily dependent on the backup plan that you have in place and the way you have configured your database. Databases that are set to simple recovery mode have limited options for database restore. Databases that are in full recovery mode and have frequent backups have many more restore options. The following are the basic options for restore:

▶ Restore an entire database.

▶ Perform a partial restore.

▶ Restore a file or a page from a backup.

▶ Restore a transaction log.

▶ Restore a database to a point in time by using a database snapshot.

The following sections delve further into the restore options listed here. They focus on the means for accomplishing these restores and some of the common restore scenarios you might encounter.

Restores with T-SQL

The command to restore a database in SQL Server is aptly named RESTORE. The RESTORE command is similar to the BACKUP command in that it can be used to restore a database, part of a database, or a transaction log. You restore an entire database or part of a database by using the RESTORE DATABASE syntax. You do transaction log restores by using the RESTORE TRANSACTION syntax.

Database Restores with T-SQL

Listing 11.6 shows the full syntax for RESTORE DATABASE.

LISTING 11.6   RESTORE DATABASE Syntax

```
--To Restore an Entire Database from a Full database backup (a Complete Restore):
RESTORE DATABASE { database_name ¦ @database_name_var }
[ FROM <backup_device> [ ,...n ] ]
[ WITH
   [ { CHECKSUM ¦ NO_CHECKSUM } ]
   [ [ , ] { CONTINUE_AFTER_ERROR ¦ STOP_ON_ERROR } ]
   [ [ , ] ENABLE_BROKER ]
   [ [ , ] ERROR_BROKER_CONVERSATIONS ]
   [ [ , ] FILE = { file_number ¦ @file_number } ]
   [ [ , ] KEEP_REPLICATION ]
   [ [ , ] MEDIANAME = { media_name ¦ @media_name_variable } ]
   [ [ , ] MEDIAPASSWORD = { mediapassword ¦
                  @mediapassword_variable } ]
   [ [ , ] MOVE 'logical_file_name' TO 'operating_system_file_name' ]
               [ ,...n ]
   [ [ , ] NEW_BROKER ]
   [ [ , ] PARTIAL ]
   [ [ , ] PASSWORD = { password ¦ @password_variable } ]
   [ [ , ] { RECOVERY ¦ NORECOVERY ¦ STANDBY =
          {standby_file_name ¦ @standby_file_name_var }
   } ]
   [ [ , ] REPLACE ]
   [ [ , ] RESTART ]
   [ [ , ] RESTRICTED_USER ]
   [ [ , ] { REWIND ¦ NOREWIND } ]
   [ [ , ] STATS [ = percentage ] ]
   [ [ , ] { STOPAT = { date_time ¦ @date_time_var }
    ¦ STOPATMARK = { 'mark_name' ¦ 'lsn:lsn_number' }
               [ AFTER datetime ]
    ¦ STOPBEFOREMARK = { 'mark_name' ¦ 'lsn:lsn_number' }
               [ AFTER datetime ]
   } ]
   [ [ , ] { UNLOAD ¦ NOUNLOAD } ]
]
```

Once again, there are many available options for restoring a database, but a simple restore is fairly simple. The following example demonstrates a full restore of the AdventureWorks database:

```
RESTORE DATABASE [AdventureWorks]
FROM  DISK = N'C:\mssql2005\backup\AdventureWorks_FullRecovery.bak'
WITH  FILE = 1,  NOUNLOAD,  REPLACE,  STATS = 10
```

For more sophisticated restores, you can specify options following the WITH clause. Table 11.2 lists and briefly describes these options. Many of the options are the same as for the BACKUP command and provide similar functionality.

TABLE 11.2   RESTORE DATABASE Options

Option	Description
CHECKSUM ¦ NO_CHECKSUM	When CHECKSUM is specified, a checksum is calculated before the backup is restored. If the checksum validation fails, the restore fails as well. The default is NO_CHECKSUM.
STOP_ON_ERROR ¦ CONTINUE_AFTER_ERROR	The STOP_ON_ERROR option (which is the default) causes the backup to fail if an error is encountered. CONTINUE_AFTER_ERROR allows the restore to continue if an error is encountered.
ENABLE_BROKER	This option starts the Service Broker so that messages can be received.
ERROR_BROKER_CONVERSATIONS	Service Broker conversations with the database being restored are ended, with an error stating that the database is attached or restored.
FILE = { file_number ¦ @file_number }	This option identifies the backup set number to be restored from the backup media. The default is 1, which indicates the latest backup set.
KEEP_REPLICATION	This option prevents replication settings from being removed during a restore operation. This is important when setting up replication to work with log shipping.
MEDIANAME	This is a 128-character name for the backup media. If it is specified, the target media must match this name.
MEDIAPASSWORD	This is a password for the media set. If the media was created with a password, the password must be supplied in order to restore from that media.
MOVE	This option causes the specified logical_file_name to be moved from its original file location to another location.

TABLE 11.2   Continued

Option	Description
NEW_BROKER	This option creates a new *service_broker_ guid*.
PARTIAL	This option causes a partial restore to occur that includes the primary filegroup and any specified secondary filegroup(s).
PASSWORD	This password is specific to the backup set. If a password was used when creating the backup set, a password must be used to restore from the media set.
RECOVERY ¦ NORECOVERY ¦ STANDBY	The RECOVERY option (which is the default) restores the database so that it is ready for use. NORECOVERY renders the database inaccessible but able to restore additional transaction logs. The STANDBY option allows additional transaction logs to be applied but the database to be read. These options are discussed in more detail later in this section.
REPLACE	This option causes the database to be created with the restore, even if the database already exists.
RESTART	This option allows a previously interrupted restore to restart where it was stopped.
RESTRICTED_USER	This option restricts access to the database after it has been restored. Only members of the db_owner, dbcreator, or sysadmin role can access it.
REWIND ¦ NOREWIND	This option is used for tape operations. REWIND (which is the default) causes the tape to be released and rewound.
STATS	This option causes completion statistics to be displayed at the specified interval to assess progress.
STOPAT ¦ STOPATMARK ¦ STOPBEFOREMARK	This option causes a restore to recover to a specified date/time or to recover to a point defined by a specific transaction. The STOPAT option restores the database to the state is was in at the date and time. The STOPATMARK and STOPBEFOREMARK options restore based on the specified marked transaction or LSN.
UNLOAD ¦ NOUNLOAD	This option is used for tape operations. NOUNLOAD cause the tape to remain in the tape drive after a restore completes. UNLOAD (which is the default) causes the tape to be rewound and unloaded when the restore completes.

A cross-section of these options are utilized in the "Restore Scenarios" section, later in this chapter. Those restore scenarios provide a frame of reference for the options and further meaning about what they can accomplish.

Transaction Log Restores with T-SQL

The syntax details and options for restoring a transaction log backup are similar to those for RESTORE BACKUP. The options that are not available with RESTORE LOG include ENABLE_BROKER, ERROR_BROKER_CONVERSATIONS, NEW_BROKER, and PARTIAL.

The RECOVERY ¦ NORECOVERY ¦ STANDBY options are particularly important when performing transaction log restores and also when restoring a database that will have transaction logs applied. If these options are used incorrectly, you can render your database inaccessible or unable to restore subsequent transaction log backups. With the RECOVERY option, any uncommitted transactions are rolled back, and the database is made available for use. When a restore (of either a database or transaction log) is run with this option, no further transaction logs can be applied. The NORECOVERY and STANDBY options do allow subsequent transaction logs to be applied. When the NORECOVERY option is specified, the database is completely unavailable after the restore and is left in a restoring state. In this state, you cannot read the database, update the database, or obtain information about the database, but you can restore transaction logs.

With the STANDBY option, the database is left in a read-only state that allows some database access. standby_file_name must be specified with the STANDBY option. standby_file_name contains uncommitted transactions that were rolled back to place the database in a consistent state for read operations. If subsequent transaction log backups are applied to the STANDBY database, the uncommitted transactions in the standby file are reapplied to the database.

CAUTION

Take note of the standby_file_name name that is used when restoring with the STANDBY option and make sure that the file is secure. If another restore operation is performed and the same standby_file_name is used, the previous standby file is overwritten. The database cannot be fully recovered without the standby file, so you have to perform all the restore operations again.

We speak from personal experience on this one. During a data recovery drill, for a large database (approximately 1TB), hours were spent restoring the transaction logs on a set of log-shipped databases. The last log to be applied was manually restored to place the database in STANDBY mode. Another database that was also in the data recovery drill was also placed in STANDBY, and unfortunately, the same standby file was used. This caused more than one person a very long night. Be careful!

Some of the other options of the RESTORE DATABASE command are covered in the "Restore Scenarios" section, later in this chapter. Once again, many of these options are not required for most types of restores. A simple example of restoring a log to the AdventureWorks database follows:

```
RESTORE LOG [AdventureWorks] FROM
DISK =
N'C:\mssql2005\backup\AdventureWorks\AdventureWorks_backup_200606091215.trn'
WITH  FILE = 1,  NOUNLOAD,  STATS = 10, NORECOVERY
```

> **NOTE**
>
> Restores can be performed on a database snapshot. The following is the syntax to revert a database to a database snapshot:
>
> ```
> RESTORE DATABASE { database_name ¦ @database_name_var }
> FROM DATABASE_SNAPSHOT = database_snapshot_name
> ```
>
> Database snapshots are discussed in more detail in Chapter 33, "Database Design and Performance."

Restoring by Using SSMS

The restore capabilities in SSMS are comprehensive and can reduce the amount of time it takes to perform a restore and limit the number of errors. This is partly due to the fact that SSMS keeps track of the backups that have occurred on a server. When a restore operation is requested for a database, SQL Server reads from its own system tables and presents a list of backups that it knows about that can be restored. In situations in which many files need to be restored, SSMS can be an invaluable tool.

You access the restore functions in SSMS by right-clicking the database in the Object Explorer and selecting Tasks and then Restore. The options available for restore include Database, File and Filegroups, and Transaction Log. Which restore options are enabled depends on the state of the database being restored. The Transaction Log option is disabled for databases that were restored with the RECOVERY option or are set to simple recovery mode. Figure 11.6 shows an example of the restore screen that is displayed when you select a database restore for the AdventureWorks database.

The Restore Database window can show more than one type of backup, depending on what is available. The first backup shown in Figure 11.6 is a full backup, followed by a series of transaction log backups. The beauty of this screen is that the backups are shown in the order in which they should be applied. This is very important with restores because they must be applied in the order in which they occurred. You can choose to apply all the backups or selectively choose the backups you want to apply. If you uncheck the first full database backup, all subsequent log backups are unchecked as well. If you recheck the full database backup and click one of the transaction log backups toward the bottom of the list, all the required backups that happened prior to the backups selected are also selected.

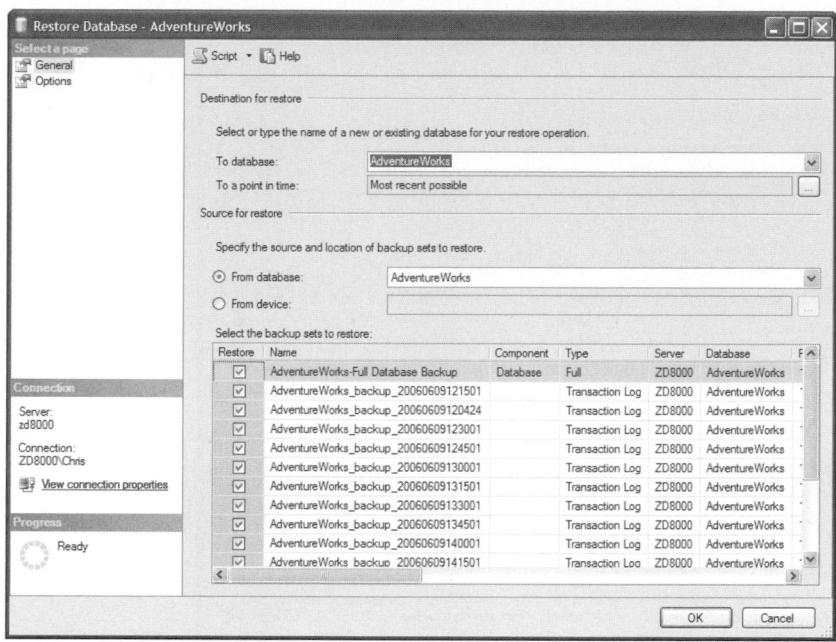

FIGURE 11.6   A database restore with SSMS.

Figure 11.7 shows an example or the Options screen of the Restore Database window for the AdventureWorks database. The Options page allows you to specify many of the T-SQL RESTORE options that were reviewed previously. The Overwrite the Existing Database option is equivalent to the REPLACE parameter and forces a replacement of the restored database if it exists already. The Preserve the Replication Settings option is equivalent to KEEP_REPLICATION. The Restrict Access to the Restored Database option is the same as using the RESTRICTED_USER option with the T-SQL RESTORE command. The Prompt Before Restoring Each Backup option does not have a T-SQL equivalent; it displays a prompt before restoring each backup set to ask whether you want to restore it.

The last three options on the Options page relate the recovery state of the last backup set restored. The first option is synonymous with the RECOVERY option, the second option is the same as NORECOVERY, and the last option is equivalent to the STANDBY option. The standby filename must be supplied with the STANDBY option and defaults to the default backup directory for the server. By default, the name of the file contains the name of the database being restored.

TIP

You should click the Script button that is available on the Restore Database screen if you want to see what is going on under the hood of the SSMS restores or want to run a restore later. You can learn a lot about the T-SQL options and how they work by scripting out the commands.

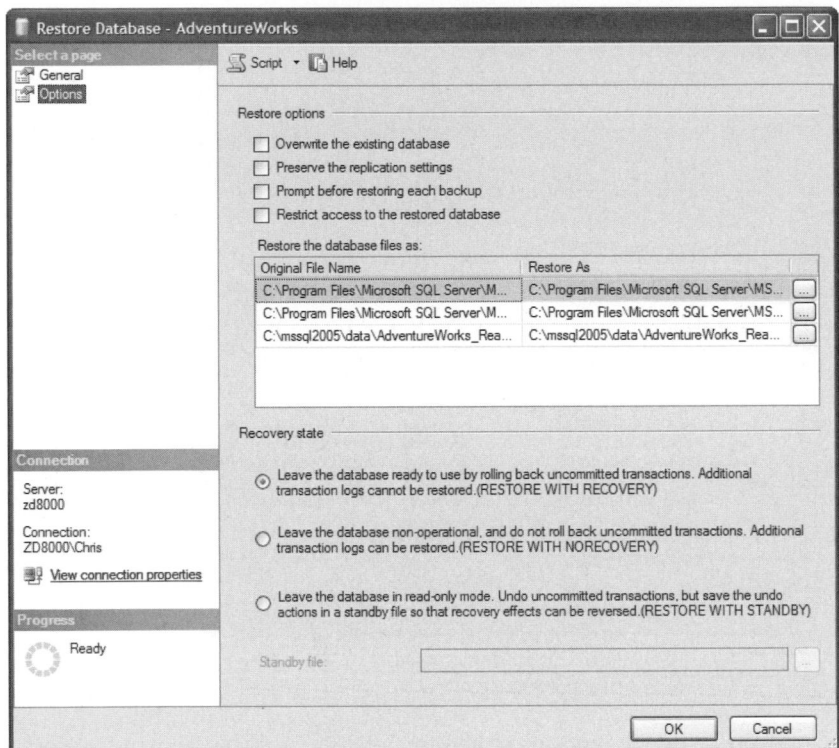

FIGURE 11.7   Restore options with SSMS.

Restore Information

Backup files and system tables contain a wealth of information about what can be restored or already has been restored. You can retrieve information from the backup files by using variations of the RESTORE command. These variations do not actually perform the restore operation but provide information about the backups that can be restored. The RESTORE commands and some useful system tables are detailed in the following sections.

The RESTORE FILELISTONLY Command

The RESTORE FILELISTONLY command returns a result set that contains a list of the database and log files contained in the backup. An example of this command follows:

```
RESTORE FILELISTONLY
FROM DISK = 'C:\mssql2005\backup\AdventureWorks_Partial.bak'
```

The results from this type of restore include the logical and physical filenames, the type of each file, and the size of each file.

The RESTORE HEADERONLY Command
The RESTORE HEADERONLY command returns a result set that contains the backup header data for all backup sets on the specified backup device. This command is useful when multiple backup sets are written to the same device. An example of this command follows:

```
RESTORE HEADERONLY
FROM DISK = 'C:\mssql2005\backup\AdventureWorks_Partial.bak'
```

More than 50 columns are returned in the result set. Some particularly useful pieces of information include the start and finish time for the backup, the recovery mode when the backup was taken, the type of backup, and the name of the computer from which the backup was performed.

The RESTORE VERIFYONLY Command
The RESTORE VERIFYONLY command verifies that a backup set is complete and readable. The restore does not attempt to verify the structure of the data in the backups, but it has been enhanced to run additional checks on the data. The checks are designed to increase the probability of detecting errors. An example of this command follows:

```
RESTORE VERIFYONLY
FROM DISK = 'C:\mssql2005\backup\AdventureWorks_Partial.bak'

/*Result from the prior RESTORE VERIFYONLY command
The backup set on file 1 is valid.
*/
```

The results from the prior example show that the RESTORE VERIFYONLY command does not contain much output, but the value of this command is in helping ensure that the backups are sound.

Backing Up and Restoring System Tables
The system tables for backups and restores are found in the msdb system database. These system tables are used to keep historical information about the backups and restores that have occurred on the server. These tables are listed in Table 11.3.

TABLE 11.3   Backing Up and Restoring System Tables

MSDB System Table	Description
backupfile	Contains one row for each data or log file of a database.
backupfilegroup	Contains one row for each filegroup in a database at the time of backup.
backupmediafamily	Contains a row for each media family.
backupmediaset	Contains one row for each backup media set.
backupset	Contains a row for each backup set.
logmarkhistory	Contains one row for each marked transaction that has been committed.
restorefile	Contains one row for each restored file. These include files restored indirectly, by filegroup name.

TABLE 11.3   Continued

MSDB System Table	Description
restorefilegroup	Contains one row for each restored filegroup.
restorehistory	Contains one row for each restore operation.
suspect_pages	Contains one row per page that failed with an 824 error (with a limit of 1,000 rows).
sysopentapes	Contains one row for each currently open tape device.

Refer to "Backup and Restore Tables" in the "System Tables" section of SQL Server Books Online for a detailed description of each table, including each column that can be retrieved.

It is possible to query these tables to obtain a variety of information related to backups and restores. You can tailor these queries to look at a specific database or a specific time-frame. The following example retrieves restore information for the AdventureWorks database:

```
select destination_database_name 'database', h.restore_date, restore_type,
 cast((backup_size/1024)/1024 as numeric(8,0)) 'backup_size MB',
  f.physical_device_name
 from msdb..restorehistory h (NOLOCK)
   LEFT JOIN msdb..backupset b (NOLOCK)
   ON h.backup_set_id = b.backup_set_id
   LEFT JOIN msdb..backupmediafamily f (NOLOCK)
   ON b.media_set_id = f.media_set_id
 where h.restore_date > getdate() - 5
    and UPPER(h.destination_database_name) = 'AdventureWorks'
 order by UPPER(h.destination_database_name), h.restore_date desc
```

This example displays information related to restores that have been executed in the past five days for the AdventureWorks database. The restore date, the type of restore, the size of the backup, and the physical location of the file used for the Restore are displayed when you run this query.

CAUTION

Queries against system tables are acceptable and can provide a wealth of information, but you need to exercise caution whenever you are dealing with a system table. SQL Server uses these tables, and problems can occur if the values in them are changed or their physical structure is altered.

Restore Scenarios

Restore scenarios are as varied as the backup scenarios that drive them. The number of scenarios is directly related to the types of backups that are taken and the frequency of those backups. If a database is in simple recovery mode and full database backups are taken each night, your restore options are limited. Conversely, full recovery databases that have multiple filegroups and take a variety of different types of backups have a number of different options that can be used to restore the database.

The following sections describe a number of restore scenarios to give you a taste of the types of restores you may encounter. The scenarios include some restores that are performed with T-SQL and others that are performed with SSMS.

Restoring to a Different Database

You can restore a database backup to a different database. The database being restored to can be on the same server or a different server, and the database can be restored to a different name, if needed. These types of restores are common in development environments where a production backup is recovered on a development server or multiple copies of the same development database are restored to different database names for use by different groups.

Listing 11.7 shows the T-SQL RESTORE command that can be used to create a new database named AdventureWorks_COPY from the backup of the AdventureWorks database. Take note of the MOVE options that specify where the database files for the new AdventureWorks_COPY database will exist. Each MOVE option must refer to the logical name for the file and include a physical file location that is a valid location on the server. In addition, the file that is referenced cannot be used by another database. The only exception is when you are restoring to the database that is using the files and the REPLACE option is used.

LISTING 11.7   Restore to a Different Database

```
RESTORE DATABASE [AdventureWorks_COPY]
 FROM  DISK = N'C:\mssql2005\backup\AdventureWorks.bak'
 WITH  FILE = 1,
 MOVE N'AdventureWorks_Data' TO N'C:\mssql2005\data\AdventureWorks_Copy.mdf',
 MOVE N'AdventureWorks_Log' TO N'C:\mssql2005\data\AdventureWorks_Copy_log.ldf',
 NOUNLOAD,  STATS = 10
```

TIP

A restore of a database backup taken from another server can cause problems after the restore completes. The problems are caused by broken relationships between the database users captured in the backup file and the associated logins on the server to which the backup is restored. The relationships are broken because each login receives a unique ID that is assigned to it when it is added. These unique IDs can and will be different across servers, even though the logins may have the same name. The unique ID from the login is stored with each database user in order to identify the login that the user is associated with. When the unique ID for the login is different or not found, you get spurious errors when trying to connect to the database with these users or when trying to administer these users in SSMS.

The `sp_change_users_login` system stored procedure is designed to correct these broken relationships. You can run this procedure with the `"report"` option in the database in question to help identify any problems. (that is, `sp_change_users_login "report"`). The stored procedure also has options to fix the broken relationships. For example, `sp_change_users_login "autofix", "myuser"` fixes the relationship for the `"myuser"` database user. You should check SQL Server Books Online for further options and details on this stored procedure.

Another quick-and-dirty means for fixing orphaned database users is to delete the users from the database and then re-create them. Of course, the login must exist on the server, and all the permissions associated with the database user must be reestablished. Permissions can be overlooked or missed with this method, so it is safer to stick with the `sp_change_users_login` procedure.

Restoring a Transaction Log

Transaction log restores deserve special attention because of their dependency on other backup types. Typical transaction log restores occur after a full or differential database restore has occurred. After this base is established, the transaction log restores must be done in the same sequential order as the backups that were taken.

Fortunately, SSMS does a good job of presenting the available backups in the order in which they must be applied. You can do the entire restore sequence with SSMS, including a full restore followed by a restore of any other backups, including transaction log backups. To restore transaction log backups (independent of other backups), you can select the Transaction Log option. Figure 11.8 shows a sample screen for restoring transaction logs in the AdventureWorks database.

The transaction logs shown in Figure 11.8 are listed in the order in which they were taken and the order in which they need to be applied. You can uncheck some of the available backups, but you are not allowed to select backups that are not in the correct sequence. In other words, you can uncheck backups from the bottom of the list, but if you uncheck backups toward the top of the list, all backups found below that item are unchecked as well.

It is important to remember that you can only restore transaction log backups to a database that is in the NORECOVERY or STANDBY state. Make sure that every restore prior to the last one uses one of these options. When you restore the last transaction log, you should use the RECOVERY option so that the database is available for use.

Restoring to the Point of Failure

A disk failure on a drive that houses some database files is a reality that some database administrators must deal with. This situation can give pause to the most seasoned administrators, but it is a situation that can be addressed with little or no data loss. Don't panic! You need to first identify the backups that are available.

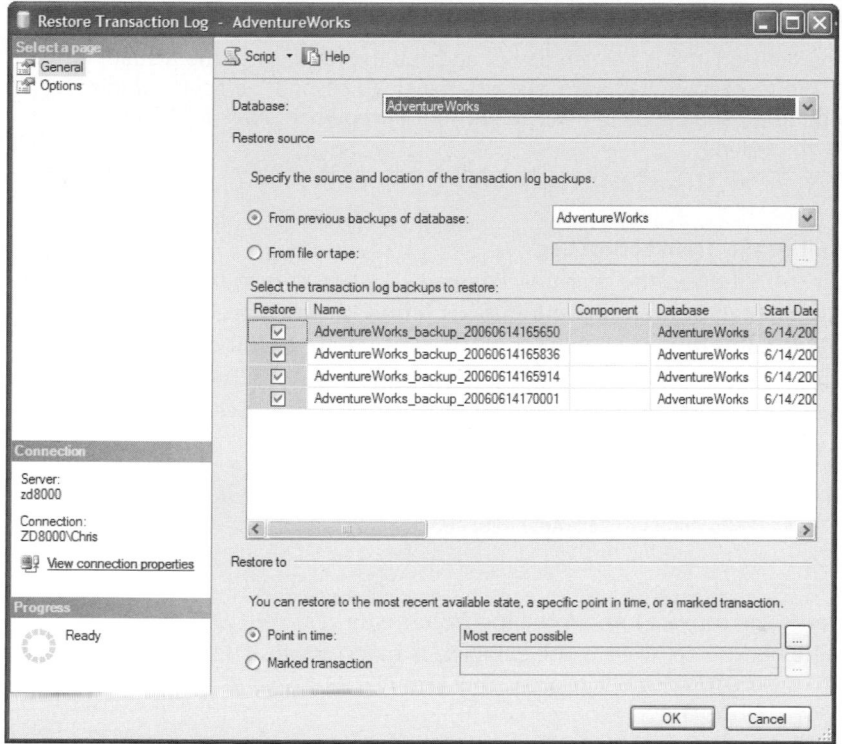

FIGURE 11.8   Transaction Log Restore.

> **NOTE**
>
> Hopefully, the disk that experienced a failure is not the same disk that houses your backups. Database backups should always be stored on separate media. One of the best approaches is to write the backups to a drive that does not contain any other SQL Server files and write the contents of that drive to tape. This minimizes the possibility of losing one of those all-important backups.

The backup components that you need to restore to the point of failure include the following:

▶ A backup of the tail of the transaction log

▶ A full database backup or file/filegroup backup to establish a base

▶ The full sequence of transaction log backups created since the full database backup

The following sections describe the detailed steps for recovery that relate to these backup components.

> **NOTE**
>
> The restore steps outlined in this section do not address the recovery of the actual disk that failed. The recovery of hardware, such as a disk, is beyond the scope of this book, but it needs to be addressed in order to get your environment back to the state it was in prior to the failure.

Backing Up the Tail of the Transaction Log

The first thing you should do in the event of a damaged database is to back up the tail of the transaction log. The tail of the transaction log is found in the active SQL Server transaction log file(s). This tail is only available for databases that are in full or bulk-logged recovery mode. This tail contains transactions that have not been backed up yet. The following example shows how to back up the tail of the log for the AdventureWorks database using T-SQL:

```
BACKUP LOG [AdventureWorks]
 TO  DISK = N'C:\mssql2005\backup\log\AdventureWorks_Tail.trn'
 WITH  NO_TRUNCATE
```

NO_TRUNCATE prevents the transactions in the log from being removed and allows the transaction log to be backed up, even if the database is inaccessible. This type of backup is possible only if the transaction log file is accessible and was not on the disk that had the failure.

Recovering the Full Database Recovery

After you have backed up the tail of the transaction log, you are ready to perform a full database Restore. This restore is based on a full database backup or a file/filegroup backup. This restore overwrites the existing database. It is imperative that the full database restore be done with the NORECOVERY option so that the transaction log backups and the tail of the log can be applied to the database as well. The following example restores a full backup of the AdventureWorks database, using the T-SQL RESTORE command:

```
RESTORE DATABASE [AdventureWorks]
 FROM  DISK = N'C:\mssql2005\backup\AdventureWorks.bak'
 WITH  FILE = 1,  NORECOVERY,  NOUNLOAD,  REPLACE,  STATS = 10
```

Upon completion of this type of restore, the database appears in the SSMS Object Explorer with "(Restoring...)" appended to the end of the database name. The database is now ready for transaction log backups to be applied.

Restoring the Transaction Log Backup

The final step in recovery is to apply the transaction log backups. These backups include all the transaction log backups since the last full backup plus the tail of the log that you backed up after the media failure. If differential backups were taken since the last full backup, you can apply the last differential backup and only apply those transaction log backups that have occurred since the last differential backup.

You can restore transaction log backups by using T-SQL or SSMS. To restore with SSMS, you can right-click the database that is in the restoring state and select the Transaction Log Restore option. The Restore Transaction Log screen lists the available transaction log backups, including the backup of the transaction log tail. You need to select all the transaction logs, including the tail. You should make sure to go to the Options tab and select the Recovery option so that your database is available after the restore completes.

Alternatively, you can use T-SQL to perform the transaction log backup restores. The following example shows a series of transaction log restores. The first two restores are done with the NORECOVERY option. The last command restores the tail of the log and uses the RECOVERY option to make the database available for use:

```
RESTORE LOG [AdventureWorks]
 FROM  DISK =
N'C:\mssql2005\backup\AdventureWorks_backup_200606180922.trn'
 WITH  FILE = 1,  NORECOVERY,  NOUNLOAD,  STATS = 10
GO
RESTORE LOG [AdventureWorks]
 FROM  DISK =
  N'C:\mssql2005\backup\AdventureWorks_backup_200606180923.trn'
 WITH  FILE = 1,  NORECOVERY,  NOUNLOAD,  STATS = 10
GO
RESTORE LOG [AdventureWorks]
 FROM  DISK =
  N'C:\mssql2005\backup\log\AdventureWorks_Tail.trn'
 WITH  FILE = 3,  NOUNLOAD,  STATS = 10
GO
```

When many transaction log backups are involved, using T-SQL to perform the restores can be challenging. The restores must occur in the proper order and refer to the proper location of the backup file(s). Restores done with SSMS are typically less prone to error.

Restoring to a Point in Time

Databases that are in the full or bulk-logged recovery models can be restored to a point in time. This type of restore is similar to the point-of-failure scenario covered previously, but it allows for a more precise restore operation. These restores allow the database to be recovered to a time prior to a particular event. Malicious attacks or erroneous updates are some examples of events that would justify a point-in-time restore.

NOTE

There are some limitations on point-in-time restores of databases that are set to the bulk-logged recovery model. Point-in-time restores are not possible on transaction log backups that contain bulk load operations. Point-in-time restores can occur using transaction log backups that occurred prior to the bulk load operation, as long as a bulk load did not occur during the time of these backups.

A point-in-time restore can be done using one of the following:

▶ A specific date/time within the transaction log backup

▶ A specific transaction name that was inserted in the log

▶ An LSN

Point-in-time restores can be done with T-SQL or SSMS. Figure 11.9 shows the General page that allows you to specify Point in Time parameters. The Restore To section at the bottom of the page allows you to select the type of point-in-time restore. The default is to restore to the most recent time possible, but you can click on the ellipsis to display the Point in Time Restore dialog box. This dialog box is shown in the middle of Figure 11.9. You can select the date to restore to using the date drop-down and enter the time to restore to as well.

Online Restores

Online restores are new to SQL Server 2005. They allow a filegroup, a file, or a specific page within a file to be restored while the rest of the database is online. The file or filegroup that is being restored to must be offline during the duration of the online restore.

> **TIP**
>
> You should take a full backup of a database immediately before taking a read-only file offline. This simplifies the online restore process and eliminates the need to apply a bunch of transaction log backups prior to the online restore. This applies only to databases that are in full or bulk-logged recovery.

The following example demonstrates how to take a read-only file offline:

```
ALTER DATABASE AdventureWorks
MODIFY FILE (NAME = 'AdventureWorks_ReadOnlyData', OFFLINE)
```

When the file is offline, you can perform a restore to that file without affecting the rest of the database. The following example shows an example of an online restore of a read-only file to the AdventureWorks database:

```
RESTORE DATABASE [AdventureWorks]
 FILE = N'AdventureWorks_ReadOnlyData'
 FROM  DISK = N'C:\mssql2005\backup\AdventureWorks_ReadOnlyData.bak'
 WITH  FILE = 1,  NOUNLOAD,  STATS = 10, RECOVERY
```

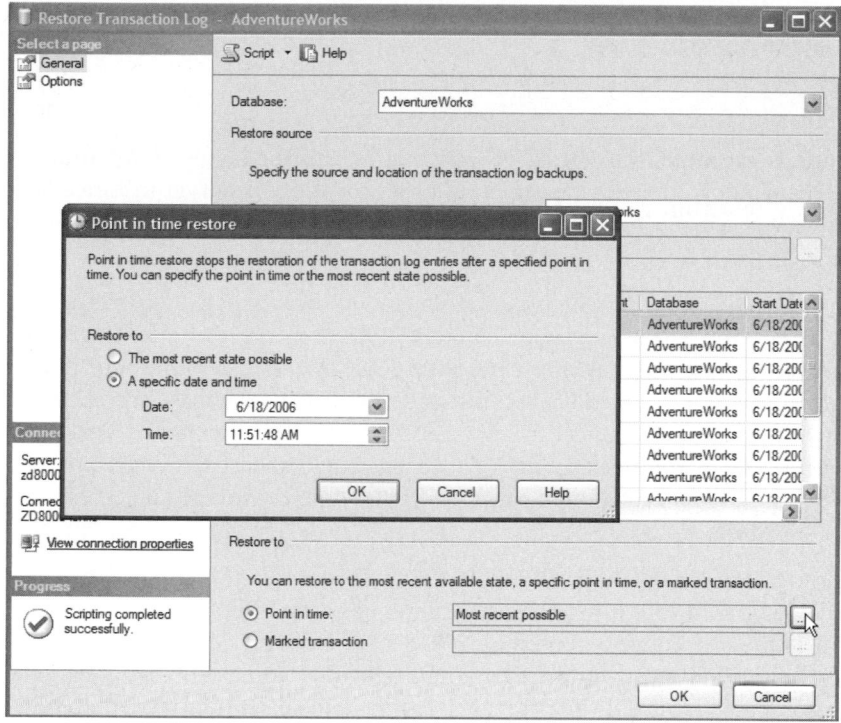

FIGURE 11.9   A point-in-time restore.

Restoring the System Databases

The SQL Server 2005 system databases that can be restored are the master, msdb, model, and distribution databases. Each of these databases performs an essential role in the operation of SQL Server. If these databases are damaged or lost, they can be restored from database backup files in a similar fashion to user databases.

The master database, which contains information about other databases and is required to start SQL Server, has some special restore considerations. It must be operational before restores of other system databases can be considered. When restoring the master database, there are two basic scenarios. The first scenario involves a restore of the master database when the master database currently used by SQL Server is operational. In the second scenario, the master database is unavailable, and SQL Server is unable to start.

The first master database restore scenario is less involved and typically less stressful than the second. In the first scenario, your SQL Server can be up and running until the time you want to do the restore. When you are ready to do the restore, the SQL Server instance must be running in single-user mode. The server can be started in single-user mode via a command prompt window. You stop the currently running SQL Server service, open a command prompt window, navigate to the directory where the sqlservr.exe file exists (typically `C:\Program Files\Microsoft SQL Server\MSSQL.1\MSSQL\Binn\`), and run the following command:

```
sqlservr.exe -m
```

When this command is executed, the SQL Server instance is running in the command prompt window. This window must be kept open in order for the SQL Server instance to keep running. The service for SQL Server appears as stopped, but the database engine is truly running.

The `-m` parameter places the server in single-user mode and allows a single administrator connection to the server. You can use that one connection to connect to the server to use the Object Explorer, a database query window in SSMS, SQLCMD, or any other tool that allows you to establish a connection and run commands against the database server. If you use the SSMS Object Explorer connection, you can right-click on the `master` database and select the Restore option. You need to enter `master` for the database to restore and select the overwrite option. You can instead run a T-SQL `RESTORE` command to achieve the same result.

When the restore of the `master` database is complete, SQL Server is automatically shut down. If you performed the restore using Object Explorer, you can expect to get an error message at the end of the restore process because SQL Server was shut down. You can simply close the command prompt window that you used earlier and establish a new connection to the database server. All the databases, logins, and so on that were present prior to the backup are reestablished.

In the second scenario, the `master` database is damaged or unavailable, and SQL Server cannot start. If SQL Server is unable to start, you must reestablish a base environment like that which existed when SQL Server was initially installed. Using the `REBUILDDATABASE` option in `setup.exe` is one way to re-create all the system databases and reestablish this base environment. The `REBUILDDATABASE` parameter is part of a SQL Server installation that is done from the command prompt. You need the installation media for the edition of SQL Server that is installed on the machine. After you insert the disk and when you have access to the installation files, you can use the following syntax to launch the Setup program from a command prompt window:

```
start /wait <CD or DVD Drive>\setup.exe /qn
INSTANCENAME=<InstanceName> REINSTALL=SQL_Engine
REBUILDDATABASE=1 SAPWD=<NewStrongPassword>
```

InstanceName should be set to `MSSQLSERVER` for a default instance of SQL Server or the name of the instance, if it is not the default. In addition, a new `SA` password needs to be supplied for the `SAPWD` parameter. The `/qn` parameter suppresses all the setup dialog boxes and error messages and causes the installation to run silently. If you want to receive more information during the installation, you can specify the `/qb` parameter.

NOTE

If you get a message about a missing Windows Installer, you can find that software on the SQL Server media in the Redist folder. You may also find that the setup.exe file is not found on the root of your installation media. If this is the case, you need to change the directory in the command prompt window to the location of the setup.exe file on the installation media prior to executing the command to launch the setup program. Finally, remember to reinstall any service packs or patches that you may have installed. The execution of the command prompt setup reverts the server back to the original software release.

At the end of the installation, all the system database files are installed to their original locations. This includes the original master.mdf, mastlog.ldf, msdbdata.mdf, and msdblog.ldf files, as well as the related database files for the other system databases. Any of the user databases that you may have added to the server are no longer known by the master database and in turn are not available in the Object Explorer or other database tools.

If you have a backup of the master database, you can restore it after the command prompt installation is complete. You follow the procedures outlined in the first scenario, earlier in this section, to restore the master database from a backup. At the completion of the restore, any user databases that were present at the time of the master database backup are now available. You can also run restores for other system databases at this time, including the Msdb database, which contains all your scheduled jobs and history.

If you do not have a backup of the master database, this is not the end of the world. You still have the option of manually attaching your user databases or restoring them from backup files. Attaching the database is typically much faster than restores from backup files and is the preferred method. You must also reestablish logins, backup devices, server triggers, and any other server-level objects that are stored in the master database. Depending on your environment, this can be a lengthy operation, but you can easily avoid it by making those all-important system database backups.

Additional Backup Considerations

A sound backup plan goes beyond the commands and tools described thus far in this chapter. There are several other considerations, detailed in this section, that should be considered as well:

Frequency of Backups

How often you back up your databases depends on many factors, including the following:

- The size of your databases and your backup window (that is, the time allocated to complete the task of backing up the database)

- The frequency of changes to the data and the method by which it is changed

▶ The acceptable amount of data loss in the event of a failure

▶ The acceptable recovery time in the event of a failure

First, you must establish what your backup window will be. Because SQL Server allows dynamic backups, users can still access the database during backups; however, this affects performance. This means you should still schedule backups for low-activity periods and have them complete in the shortest possible time.

After you have established your backup window, you can determine your backup method and schedule. For example, if it takes 4 hours for a full backup to complete, and the database is quiescent between midnight and 6:00 a.m., you have time to perform a full backup each night. On the other hand, if a full backup takes 10 hours, and you have a 2-hour window, you should consider monthly or weekly backups, perhaps in conjunction with filegroup, differential, and transaction log backups. In many decision-support databases that are populated with periodic data loads, it might suffice to back up once after each data load.

Backup frequency is also directly tied to acceptable data loss. In the event of catastrophic failure, such as a fire in the server room, you can recover data only up to the point of the last backup that was moved offsite. If it is acceptable to lose a day's worth of data entry, nightly backups might suffice. If your acceptable loss is an hour's worth of data, then hourly transaction log backups would have to be added to the schedule.

Your backup frequency affects your recovery time. In some environments, a weekly full backup plus transaction log backups taken every 10 minutes is an acceptable data loss factor. A failure a few days after backup would require a full database restore and the application of hundreds of transaction logs. Adding a daily differential backup in this case would vastly improve restore time. The full and differential backups would be restored, and then six logs would be applied for each hour between the differential backup and the time of failure.

Using a Standby Server

If the ability to quickly recover from failure is crucial to your operation, you might consider implementing a standby server. Implementing a standby server involves backing up the production server and then restoring it to the standby server, leaving it in recovery mode. As transaction logs are backed up on the production server, they are applied to the standby server. If there is a failure on the production server, the standby server can be recovered and used in place of the production server. If the production server is still running, you should not forget to back up the current log with the NO_TRUNCATE option and restore it to the standby server as well before bringing it online.

> **NOTE**
>
> Another advantage of restoring backups to a standby server is that it immediately validates your backups so you can be assured of whether they are valid. There is nothing worse than finding out during a recovery process that one of the backup files is damaged or missing.

The STANDBY =*undo_file_name* option plays a key role in the application of transaction logs to the standby server. When the database and subsequent log backups are restored to the standby server with this option, the database is left in recovery mode but is available as a read-only database. Now that the standby database is available for queries, it can actually reduce load on the production database by acting as a decision support system (DSS). Database Consistency Checks (DBCC) can be run on it as well, further reducing the load on the production system.

For the database to be available for reads, the data must be in a consistent state. This means that all uncommitted transactions must be rolled back. This is usually handled by the RECOVERY option during a restore. In the case of a standby server, this would cause a problem because you would intend to apply more logs, which could, in fact, commit those transactions. This is handled by the *undo_file_name* clause of the STANDBY option. The file specified here holds a copy of all uncommitted transactions rolled back to bring the standby server to a consistent, read-only state. If those transactions subsequently commit a log restore, this undo information can be used to complete the transaction.

The application of hundreds or thousands of transaction logs to the standby server can be challenging. Fortunately, SQL Server 2005 includes log shipping, which automates the transfer of logs to the standby server. Log shipping, which can be configured in SSMS, uses SQL Server Agent jobs on the primary server to back up the transaction log and copy it to a folder on the standby server. SQL Server Agent on the standby server then executes a load job to restore the log. Automating your standby server with log shipping reduces administration and helps to ensure that the standby database is up-to-date. For further details on log shipping, see Chapter 15, "Replication." Log shipping isn't a form of replication but is covered in Chapter 15 as an alternative to replication.

Snapshot Backups

Snapshot backups are developed in conjunction with independent hardware and software vendors. These backups are not related to SQL Server database snapshots and are not accessible from any of the SQL Server tools. They utilize backup and restore technology and can provide relatively fast backup and restore operations. Snapshot backups are typically utilized on very large databases that are unable to perform database backups and restores in a timely fashion using SQL Server's conventional backup and restore resources.

Considerations for Very Large Databases

When it comes to backup and recovery, special consideration must be given to very large databases, which are known as VLDBs. A VLDB has the following special requirements:

▶ **Storage**—Size might dictate the use of tape backups over the network or a disk.

▶ **Time**—As your backup window grows, the frequency of backups might have to be adjusted.

▶ **Method**—How you back up your database is affected by its size. Differential or file and filegroup backups might have to be implemented.

▶ **Recovery**—Partial database recovery, such as restoring a file or filegroup, might be required due to the prohibitive time required to restore the entire database.

When designing a VLDB, your backup plan must be integrated with storage, performance, and availability requirements. For a complete discussion of large databases, including information specific to backup and recovery, see Chapter 44, "Administering Very Large SQL Server Databases" (on the CD-ROM).

Maintenance Plans

SQL Server includes maintenance plans that provide database maintenance tasks, including optimization, integrity checks, and backups. The backup options available in the maintenance plans are comprehensive and include the ability to regularly schedule full, differential, and transaction log backups. This type of automations is essential to ensure that your backups are taken with a reliable tool at regular intervals.

You can create maintenance plans from within SSMS. If you open the `Management` node in the Object Explorer, you see a node named `Maintenance Plans`. If you right-click this node, you can select New Maintenance Plan to create a plan from scratch or you can select Maintenance Plan Wizard to have a wizard guide you through the creation of a new maintenance plan. The following options that relate to backups are available as part of a maintenance plan:

▶ Back Up Database (Full)

▶ Back Up Database (Differential)

▶ Back Up Database (Transaction Log)

Using these tasks in a maintenance plan is a great start to a solid backup and recovery plan. Refer to Chapter 28, "Database Maintenance," for further details about creating a maintenance plan.

Summary

A database environment without a solid backup and recovery plan is like owning a home without an insurance policy to protect it. If you develop a plan to minimize the possibility of losing a database, you have essentially bought an insurance policy for your data. In the event of a problem, you can call on the backups that you have invested in and recover the loss with a minimal amount of cost.

Chapter 12, "Database Mail," explores a new mail feature that is offered with SQL Server 2005. Database Mail allows you to send email notifications from SQL Server. These notifications can be tied to scheduled jobs and alerts within SQL Server, including jobs that perform those all-important database backups.

Database Mail

IN THIS CHAPTER

▶ What's New in Database Mail

▶ Setting Up Database Mail

▶ Sending and Receiving with Database Mail

▶ Using SQL Server Agent Mail

▶ Related Views and Procedures

Database Mail (formerly called *SQLiMail*) is SQL Server 2005's emailing component, built as the replacement for SQL Mail. Although SQL Mail can still be enabled in SQL Server 2005 (for backward compatibility), it's a simple task to convert all your existing SQL Mail code and SQL Agent Mail notifications to Database Mail. And you'll surely want to.

What's New in Database Mail

Database Mail is an enterprise-class implementation designed with all the features you'd expect from this next-generation database server, most of which are not available in SQL Mail. These include support for multiple email profiles and accounts, asynchronous (queued) message delivery via a dedicated process in conjunction with Service Broker, cluster-awareness, 64-bit compatibility, greater security options (such as governing of mail attachment size and prohibition of file extensions), and simplified mail auditing. Database Mail also utilizes industry-standard Simple Mail Transfer Protocol (SMTP), signaling the end of reliance on Extended Messaging Application Programming Interface (Extended MAPI).

Database Mail has more capabilities and is more scalable and reliable than SQL Mail, especially when stressed with the heavier usage scenarios common today. And, thankfully, it's a good deal easier to successfully configure than its predecessor.

Setting Up Database Mail

Unlike with SQL Mail, setting up profiles and accounts for use with Database Mail is easy to accomplish, thanks mainly to the new Database Mail Configuration Wizard, found in the SQL Server Management Studio (SSMS) Object Browser. You can use this wizard both to set up and manage Database Mail. Before using it, you need to switch on the Database Mail feature, which is off by default, in keeping with Microsoft's security-minded approach. Follow these steps to do so:

1. Log on to the machine running SQL Server 2005.

2. From the Windows Start menu, select Microsoft SQL Server 2005, Configuration Tools, SQL Server Surface Area Configuration.

3. Click the Surface Area Configuration for Features hyperlink at the bottom of the program window.

4. In the dialog that opens, expand the node corresponding to the relevant SQL Server 2005 instance and then expand the `Database Engine` node below it.

5. Next, click the `Database Mail` node and check the Enable Database Mail Stored Procedures check box (see Figure 12.1). This enables the Database Mail stored procedures, found in the `msdb` system database, which is known as the mail host database. `msdb` contains the stored procedures, views, tables, and Service Broker objects that support Database Mail.

6. Click the Apply button and then click OK. You can then close the Surface Area Configuration tool because you will not be needing it further.

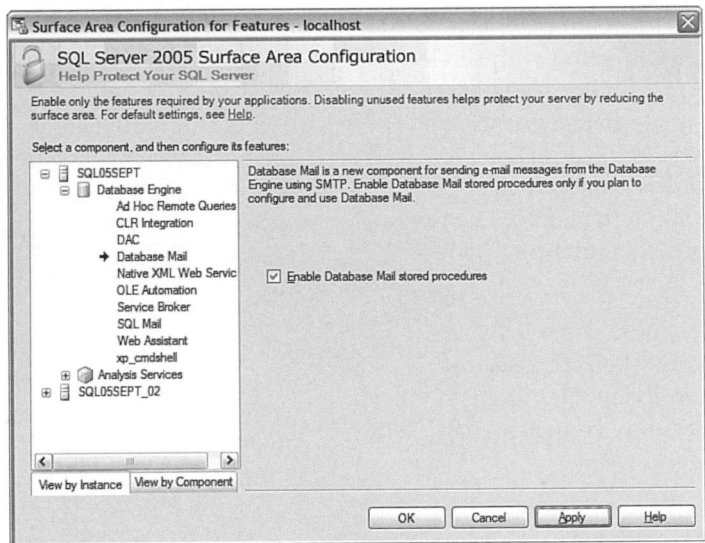

FIGURE 12.1   Using the new SQL Server Surface Area Configuration tool to enable Database Mail.

Instead of using the Surface Area Configuration tool, you can achieve the same effect by using the `Database Mail XPs` configuration option by running the following T-SQL code in a query window (while logged in as `sysadmin`, of course):

```
use Master
GO
sp_configure 'show advanced options', 1;
GO
RECONFIGURE;
GO
sp_configure 'Database Mail XPs', 1;
GO
RECONFIGURE
GO
Configuration option 'show advanced options' changed from 0 to 1. Run the
RECONFIGURE statement to install.
Configuration option 'Database Mail XPs' changed from 0 to 1. Run the
RECONFIGURE statement to install.
```

If you ever want to disable Database Mail, you can run this:

```
sp_configure 'Database Mail XPs', 0;
```

This prevents Database Mail from starting in response to a call to sysmail_start_sp (discussed later in this chapter). If Database Mail is running when you make this call, it sends unsent queued mail until the mail sending process (DatabaseMail90.exe) has been idle for the duration of the DatabaseMailExeMinimumLifeTime configuration setting (discussed later in this chapter); then it stops.

It is also necessary to enable Service Broker in msdb (if not done already) because Database Mail relies on it as part of its implementation. To do this, you stop the SQL Server Agent service and then execute the following script:

```
USE master
GO
ALTER DATABASE msdb SET ENABLE_BROKER
```

You can check the status of Service Broker on msdb by using the following code:

```
Use Master
GO
SELECT is_broker_enabled
FROM sys.databases
WHERE name = 'msdb'
GO
is_broker_enabled
-----------------
1
(1 row(s) affected)
```

To receive message send requests from outside the SQL Server instance, it is necessary to create an endpoint (preferably a certificate-secured one) associated with Service Broker. To accomplish this, please refer to the "Service Broker Routing and Security" section in Chapter 48, "SQL Server Service Broker" (on the CD-ROM), or consult the Books Online "Create Endpoint" topic.

To complete this configuration, you need to return to SSMS and establish a connection to the same SQL Server instance for which you just enabled Database Mail. You connect the Object Browser to that instance and expand the Management folder to reveal the `Database Mail` node. Then you right-click the `Database Mail` node and select the Configure Database Mail menu option to launch the Database Mail Configuration Wizard.

Creating Mail Profiles and Accounts

After you pass the Database Mail Configuration Wizard's welcome screen, you are presented with the opportunity to set up Database Mail ("for the first time"). You can achieve this by creating the required profiles, profile security settings, SMTP accounts, and systemwide mail settings. You should leave the first radio button (Set Up Database Mail by Performing the Following Tasks) selected and then click Next.

> **NOTE**
>
> In Database Mail, you use mail profiles. A *mail profile* is simply a securable container for a group of SMTP accounts that is used when sending mail. In contrast to SQL Mail, with Database Mail, you can set up multiple profiles containing multiple accounts, allowing for finer-grained administrative control. You can create one profile for admins and another for regular users, for example, or create distinct profiles dedicated to various software applications.
>
> Note also that in order to use Database Mail, it is no longer necessary to run the SQL Server or SQL Server Agent Windows services under user accounts (rather than using the default, `LocalSystem`), nor is it necessary to install Microsoft Outlook (or any other Extended MAPI client) on the machine hosting SQL Server 2005.

In the New Database Mail Account screen that appears (see Figure 12.2), you name (using a valid sysname) and describe your first profile in the provided text boxes, and then you click Add to add your first SMTP account. This process is much like the process of setting up the SMTP (or sending) portion of your email accounts with your regular email client software. To create the SMTP account, you specify a name, an optional description, a user display name, an email address, an optional reply address, a server name, a port, and an authentication mode, which is used to authenticate to the specified SMTP server (as required by your SMTP provider). For many non-Windows SMTP providers, anonymous (no authentication) or basic (simple user name/password) authentication is usually required. If your provider requires Windows Authentication, the credentials under which the SQL Server Windows service runs are supplied to the SMTP server at runtime.

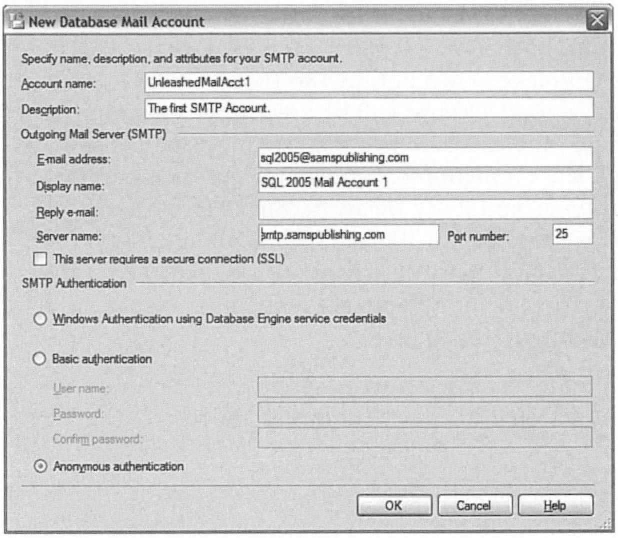

FIGURE 12.2   Using the Database Mail Configuration Wizard to set up SMTP accounts.

Instead of using the wizard, you can add a new profile via T-SQL. For example, the following three examples introduce the new Database Mail stored procedures sysmail add profile_sp, sysmail_add_account_sp, and sysmail_add_profileaccount_sp.

The first script creates the new profile:

```
EXEC msdb.dbo.sysmail_add_profile_sp
    @profile_name = 'Default SQL 2005 Profile',
    @description = 'Used for general-purpose emailing.'
```

The second script creates the new SMTP account:

```
EXEC msdb.dbo.sysmail_add_account_sp
    @account_name = 'UnleashedMailAcct1',
    @description = 'The first SMTP Account.',
    @email_address = 'sql2005@samspublishing.com',
    @display_name = 'SQL 2005 Mail Account 1',
    @mailserver_name = 'smtp.samspublishing.com' ;
```

The third script associates this new account with the new profile:

```
EXEC msdb.dbo.sysmail_add_profileaccount_sp
    @profile_name = 'Default SQL 2005 Profile',
    @account_name = 'UnleashedMailAcct1',
    @sequence_number =1;
```

The great thing you'll find when adding SMTP accounts is that Database Mail allows you to provide more than one SMTP account for the same profile. You can order the SMTP accounts by priority (using the Move Up/Move Down buttons) so that if a mail send via the top-level (or first) account fails, the second account will be used to retry sending, and so on. This is called *SMTP failover priority*, and there are two mail settings that control how it works. These settings, found on the Configure System Parameters screen of the wizard, are Account Retry Attempts and Account Retry Delay. Account Retry Attempts specifies how many mail send retries Database Mail will make before failing over to the SMTP account of next-highest priority. Account Retry Delay specifies (in seconds) how long to wait between mail send retries. These features represent a big improvement in reliability over SQL Mail, which had no such retry capabilities.

After adding the new account to the profile, you click Next to set up the profile security settings on the Manage Profile Security screen. Database Mail profiles have two levels of security (with two corresponding tabs on the wizard screen):

▶ **Public**—The profile can be used by all `msdb` users.

▶ **Private**—The profile can be used only by specific users or members of a specific role. (Note that to send mail, users must have `DatabaseMailUserRole` membership in `msdb`. You use `sp_addrolemember` to accomplish this.) You specify these users on the Private Profiles tab of the Manage Profile Security screen.

In this case, you should check the check box under the Public column of the data grid on the Public tab, and then you should click the word No under the Default Profile column. A drop-down list appears, allowing you to make the profile the default profile (by changing the selection to Yes). The default profile on the server is used when you invoke `sp_send_dbmail` (the successor to `xp_sendmail`) without specifying any profile name for the `@profile_name` parameter. It's a good idea to have a default profile set up for general mailing purposes, especially when testing.

To set profile security using T-SQL, you run the following call to the new stored procedure `sysmail_add_principalprofile_sp`:

```
exec msdb.dbo.sysmail_add_principalprofile_sp
    @profile_name = 'Default SQL 2005 Profile',
    @principal_name = 'public',
    @is_default = 1 ;
```

A third way to configure all the previously mentioned mail objects (in the form of a T-SQL script) is to use an SMSS Database Mail query template. To do this, you open the new Template Explorer via the View menu (or by pressing Ctrl+Alt+T), and then you expand to the `Database Mail` folder and double-click Simple Mail Database Configuration. Then you connect to your SQL Server instance, and, from the Query menu, select the Specify Values for Template Parameters option (or press Ctrl+Shift+M) to fill in the desired parameter values, which correspond to the parameters of the stored procedures mentioned previously.

Using T-SQL to Update and Delete Mail Objects

To delete or update profiles, accounts, profile-account associations, and profile security settings (note: do so in reverse order), you use the stored procedures shown in Table 12.1:

TABLE 12.1

Stored Procedure Name	Purpose
`sysmail_delete_profile_sp`	Delete a profile
`sysmail_delete_account_sp`	Delete an account
`sysmail_delete_principalprofile_sp`	Delete the association between a profile and a user or role (revokes permission for the principal on use of the profile)
`sysmail_delete_profileaccount_sp`	Delete the association between a profile and an account
`sysmail_update_profile_sp`	Update a profile
`sysmail_update_account_sp`	Update an account
`sysmail_update_principalprofile_sp`	Update the association between a profile and a user or role
`sysmail_update_profileaccount_sp`	Update the association between a profile and an account

For example, to delete a profile, you execute this:

```
exec msdb.dbo.sysmail_delete_profile_sp @profile_name='Undesireable Profile Name'
```

To update a profile's security, changing it from the default to the non-default profile, you execute the following:

```
exec msdb.dbo.sysmail_update_principalprofile_sp
    @profile_name = 'Default SQL 2005 Profile',
    @principal_name = 'public',
    @is_default = 0;
```

Alternatively, you can simply return to the wizard and select one of the Manage options to alter or drop any of the settings or objects. (Of course, under the covers, the wizard probably uses all these stored procedures.)

Setting Systemwide Mail Settings

You use the Configure System Parameters screen in the Database Mail Configuration Wizard to configure the systemwide Database Mail settings. (You click Next on the Select Configuration Task screen to reach this screen, if you haven't already.) We've already discussed the first two settings that appear in the grid (AccountRetryAttempts and

AccountRetryDelay) in an earlier section (Creating Mail Profiles and Accounts) as they relate to SMTP failover priority. These are the other four:

▶ **Maximum File Size (Bytes)**—This setting specifies the maximum size of any one email attachment.

▶ **Prohibited Attachment File Extensions**—This setting specifies which potentially dangerous or undesirable attachment types to ban from exchanged emails.

▶ **Database Mail Executable Minimum Lifetime (seconds)**—This setting specifies how long (minimally) the database mail process (that is, `DatabaseMail90.exe`, which is activated by Service Broker) should run idly before closing after it finishes emptying the mail send queue.

▶ **Logging Level**—This setting specifies the quality of email auditing to use, and it can be set to Normal (errors only), Extended (errors, warnings, and informational messages; this is the default), or Verbose (the same as Extended, plus success messages and other messages that are useful when you debug problems with `DatabaseMail90.exe`). To view Database Mail's primary log, you right-click the `Database Mail` folder in the Object Browser and then click the View Database Mail Log menu option. You examine and maintain the log by using the Log File Viewer that is launched. You can also use the built-in stored procedure `sysmail_delete_log_sp` to clear the log, or you can query the `msdb sysmail_event_log` view to see its contents in tabular format.

To change any of these configuration settings via T-SQL script, you use the new `sysmail_configure_sp` stored procedure. `sysmail_configure_sp` takes two parameters: the name of the setting (minus any spaces) and its new value. The following example uses the `sysmail_configure_sp` procedure to change `Account Retry Delay` to two minutes:

```
exec msdb.dbo.sysmail_configure_sp 'AccountRetryDelay', 1200
```

Testing Your Setup

The final step in setting up Database Mail is to ask SQL Server to send a test email. To do this, you right-click the `Database Mail` folder in the Object Browser and then click the Send Test E-mail menu option.

If the test fails, you click Troubleshoot, and SMSS opens the "Troubleshooting Database Mail" Books Online topic, which provides a solid set of troubleshooting steps to get you started.

If the mail is sent by SQL Server and successfully received in your client software's inbox, you can proceed to the next section to learn how to use the new `sp_send_dbmail` stored procedure to send email from T-SQL. Otherwise, look for more troubleshooting help in the "Related Views and Procedures" section of this chapter.

Sending and Receiving with Database Mail

If you're building client applications that rely heavily on Database Mail, it's crucial to gain an in-depth understanding of its underlying architecture. The following sections provide detailed information on its inner workings.

The Service Broker Architecture

As noted earlier, SQL Server relies on Service Broker (SSB) to activate the Database Mail process (DatabaseMail90.exe) used to send mail. DatabaseMail90.exe uses ADO.NET to connect to SQL Server and to read from and write to SSB queues (found in msdb) that hold send requests and send statuses in the form of typed SSB messages. You can view these queues (InternalMailQueue and ExternalMailQueue) in the Object Browser by selecting Service Broker and then Queues folder. If you look a bit further in the Object Browser, you'll see how the mail transmission architecture is implemented (in part) as an SSB application, as you'll find the corresponding internal and external Database Mail SSB services (InternalMailService and ExternalMailService), SSB message types (SendMail and SendMailStatus), and a single SSB contract (SendMail/v1.0).

SSB's involvement with Database Mail works like this:

1. sp_send_dbmail (as the SSB *initiator*) is invoked and returns immediately. Under the covers, this adds an SSB message of type SendMail to the SSB mail queue, activating the undocumented internal stored procedure sp_ExternalMailQueueListener. Note that the mail message itself is saved to one or more of the msdb tables (such as sysmail_unsentitems and sysmail_attachments) if there are any attachments.

2. SSB launches DatabaseMail90.exe (running under the credentials of the SQL Server service), which, in turn, connects back to SQL Server, using Windows Authentication.

3. DatabaseMail90.exe reads the queued SSB send message, retrieves the mail message data, sends the email, and, finally (acting as the SSB *target*), places a message of type SendMailStatus in the mail status queue, reporting on the mail sending success or failure.

4. When there's nothing left in the outbound queue to be sent, and the maximum process idle time has been reached, DatabaseMail90.exe exits.

By using SSB, Database Mail inherits the reliability of the SSB message transmission architecture. If you want to learn more about Service Broker and how its constructs work, consult Chapter 48 (on the CD-ROM) for full details.

Sending Email

The SSB queues that Database Mail uses must first be enabled before you can send mail from a session. You do this by executing the new msdb stored procedure sysmail_start_sp. This procedure is similar to its predecessor, xp_startmail (as it must be called before sending), except that it has no parameters, and, of course, has nothing to do with

MAPI. It returns 0 or 1, indicating success or failure. If you don't call this procedure, you receive this error message:

```
Mail not queued. Database Mail is stopped. Use sysmail_start_sp to
start Database Mail.
```

To temporarily disable SSB's activation of the mail process, you execute `sysmail_stop_sp` (also with no parameters), which returns 0 or 1. Mail that is sent from code after this call is queued; however, the external process is not started until `sysmail_start_sp` is called again. To check on the status of Database Mail, you can execute the stored procedure `sysmail_help_status_sp` (with no parameters). To check on the status of the queues, you execute `sysmail_help_queues_sp`.

After you execute `sysmail_start_sp`, you're ready to begin sending mail using the new `sp_send_dbmail` stored procedure. It has 21 parameters, most of which are optional. As the query engine will tell you if you try to execute it with no or too few parameters, at least one of the following parameters must be specified: @body, @query, @file_attachments, or @subject, as well as one of the following: @recipients, @copy_recipients, or @blind_copy_recipients.

> **NOTE**
>
> In order for the following T-SQL examples to work, you must first configure a default profile using either the Database Mail Configuration Wizard or the Database Mail stored procedures, as detailed earlier.

A minimally parameterized test call might look like the following:

```
exec msdb.dbo.sp_send_dbmail @body='Testing...', @subject='A Test',
@recipients='test@samspublishing.com'
go
Mail Queued.
```

Table 12.2 describes the parameters, their types, and the `xp_sendmail` parameters to which they may correspond, to help you along in converting your existing T-SQL code.

TABLE 12.2   Parameters for Database Mail stored procedure `sp_send_dbmail`

Parameter	Description	xp_sendmail **Parameter to Which It Corresponds**
@profile_name	The sysname of the profile whose SMTP accounts will be used to send.	Not available in xp_sendmail.
@recipients	A varchar(max) semicolon-delimited list of the recipients' email addresses.	Same as xp_sendmail.

TABLE 12.2   Continued

Parameter	Description	xp_sendmail **Parameter to Which It Corresponds**
@copy_recipients	A varchar(max) semicolon-delimited list of the carbon copy recipients' email addresses.	Same as xp_sendmail.
@blind_copy_recipients	A varchar(max) semicolon-delimited list of the blind carbon copy recipients' email addresses.	Same as xp_sendmail.
@subject	The nvarchar(255) email subject.	Same as xp_sendmail.
@body	The nvarchar(max) email body.	Was @message in xp_sendmail.
@body_format	One of the two varchar (20) email format type strings, either 'HTML' or 'TEXT' (the default).	Not available in xp_sendmail.
@importance	One of the three varchar (6) email importance strings, either 'Low', 'Normal' (the default), or 'High'.	Not available in xp_sendmail.
@sensitivity	One of the four varchar (12) email sensitivity strings, either 'Normal' (the default), 'Personal', 'Private', or 'Confidential'.	Not available in xp_sendmail.
@file_attachments	An nvarchar(max) semicolon-delimited list of absolute paths to files to attach.	Was @attachments in xp_sendmail.
@query	An nvarchar(max) T-SQL code string to be executed when the message is sent. The code is executed in a different session than the calling session, so variable scope is a consideration.	Same as xp_sendmail.
@execute_query_database	The sysname of the database in which the T-SQL in query is to be executed.	Was @dbuse in xp_sendmail.
@attach_query_result_as_file	A bit value indicating whether the results of the T-SQL in query should be an attachment (1) or appended to the body (0; the default).	Was @attach_results in xp_sendmail.

12

TABLE 12.2   Continued

Parameter	Description	xp_sendmail **Parameter to Which It Corresponds**
@query_attachment_filename	The nvarchar(255) filename for the attached query results (as per @query and @attach_ query_result_as_file). If not specified, the generated filename is arbitrary (usually QueryResults [*some number*].txt).	In xp_sendmail, the first filename in @attachments was used.
@query_result_header	A bit value indicating whether the query result should (1; the default) include the column headers.	Was @no_header in xp_sendmail.
@query_result_width	An int value (defaulting to 256; you specify a number between 10 and 32767) indicating how wide a line in the query results should be before line wrapping occurs.	Was @width in xp_sendmail.
@query_result_separator	A char(1) value (defaulting to a space) that indicates the query results column separator.	Was @separator in xp_sendmail.
@exclude_query_output	A bit value that indicates whether to suppress the query output (such as rowcounts, print statements, and so forth) from being printed on the query console. 0 (do not suppress) is the default.	Was @no_output in xp_sendmail.
@append_query_error	A bit value that indicates whether to send the email if the query to be executed raises an error. If set to 1, the error message is appended to the query output, and the query window for the session also displays the error ("A severe error occurred on the current command. The results, if any, should be discarded."). If set to 0 (the default), the message is not sent, and sp_send_dbmail returns 1.	Not available in xp_sendmail, but similar to @echo_error.

TABLE 12.2   Continued

Parameter	Description	xp_sendmail **Parameter to Which It Corresponds**
@query_no_truncate	A bit value that indicates whether to truncate query results having long values (such as varchar(max), text, xml, and so on) greater than 256. It defaults to 0 (off). Microsoft warns that using this can slow things down, but it is the only way to properly send these types.	Not available in xp_sendmail.
@mailitem_id	An output parameter, an int value indicating the unique mailitem_id of the message. You see this as a column in the views discussed in the section "Related Views and Procedures," later in this chapter.	Not available in xp_sendmail.

Note that xp_sendmail's @type and @set_user parameters are not available. @type, of course, is obsolete because it is MAPI specific. @set_user is also obsolete because the content of the T-SQL to be executed may contain an EXECUTE AS statement.

Now that you're familiar with the flurry of mail sending options, let's take a look at a few examples and then examine how to track your sent messages by using the system views. Both of the following examples rely on sending via the default profile of the current user context. If the user has a default private profile assigned, that is used. If not, the default public profile is used (as in these examples). If there is no default public profile, an error is raised.

The example shown in Listing 12.1 sends an email containing an xml result to a recipient as an attached Scalar Vector Graphics (SVG) document, retrieved from the AdventureWorks.Production.Illustration column.

LISTING 12.1   Sending XML as an Attachment with Database Mail

```
USE AdventureWorks
GO
DECLARE
    @subject nvarchar(255),
    @body varchar(max),
    @query nvarchar(max),
    @IllustrationId int,
    @query_attachment_filename nvarchar(255),
    @mailitem_id int
```

LISTING 12.1   Continued

```
SELECT
    @IllustrationId = pi.IllustrationId,
    @subject = 'SVG for "' + pm.Name + '" attached. '
FROM Production.Illustration pi
JOIN Production.ProductModelIllustration pmi
ON pmi.IllustrationId = pi.IllustrationId
JOIN Production.ProductModel pm
ON pm.ProductModelID = pmi.ProductModelID

SELECT
    @body =
        N'Attached, please find the SVG diagram for illustration #' +
        CAST(@IllustrationId as nvarchar(10)) +
        '. An SVG browser plug-in is required to view this file.'

SELECT @query =
    N'SELECT Diagram FROM Production.Illustration
    WHERE IllustrationId = ' + CAST(@IllustrationId as nvarchar(10))

SELECT @query_attachment_filename = N'PM_' +
    CAST(@IllustrationId as nvarchar(10)) + '.svg'

exec msdb.dbo.sp_send_dbmail
    @subject=@subject,
    @body=@body,
    @recipients='test@samspublishing.com',
    @query=@query,
    @execute_query_database='AdventureWorks',
    @attach_query_result_as_file=1,
    @query_attachment_filename=@query_attachment_filename,
    @query_no_truncate=1,
    @exclude_query_output=1,
    @query_result_width=32767,
    @mailitem_id=@mailitem_id OUTPUT

SELECT sent_status, sent_date
FROM msdb.dbo.sysmail_allitems
WHERE mailitem_id = @mailitem_id
GO
sent_status sent_date
----------- ---------
unsent      NULL
(1 row(s) affected)
```

Note that you must set @query_no_truncate to 1 and @query_result_width to the maximum (to be safe) value in order for the attached query results to contain consistently well-formed XML. In addition, you should not include any carriage returns or line feeds in the body of the message, or the SMTP servers may not be able to send it.

The example in Listing 12.2 sends some query results as a comma-separated value (CSV) file that can be imported into programs such as Microsoft Excel. (You need to use the Get External Data command to accomplish this with Excel 9.)

LISTING 12.2   Sending CSV Data as an Attachment with Database Mail

```
USE AdventureWorks
GO
DECLARE @mailitem_id int, @tab char(1)
SET @tab = char(13)

exec msdb.dbo.sp_send_dbmail
    @subject='C. Adams, Contact Info',
    @body='Attached is Carla Adams contact info, in CSV format.',
    @recipients='test@samspublishing.com',
    @query=N'SELECT ContactID, Title, FirstName, MiddleName, LastName, Phone
        FROM Person.Contact
        WHERE ContactId = 8',
    @execute_query_database='AdventureWorks',
    @attach_query_result_as_file=1,
    @query_attachment_filename='CAdams.csv',
    @exclude_query_output=1,
    @query_result_separator=',',
    @mailitem_id=@mailitem_id OUTPUT

SELECT sent_status, sent_date
FROM msdb.dbo.sysmail_allitems
WHERE mailitem_id = @mailitem_id
GO
sent_status sent_date
----------- ---------
unsent      NULL
(1 row(s) affected)
```

Notice that in both of these code listings, the values selected from the sent_status and sent_date columns of sysmail_allitems indicate that the mail has not yet been sent. This is because mail sending (like all other SSB messaging) is asynchronous: The message is immediately queued, and the Mail process later picks it up and sends it. To find out more about system views such as sysmail_allitems, see the section "Related Views and Procedures," later in this chapter.

Receiving Email

The only way for SQL Server 2005 to receive email is by using the legacy stored procedures, such as sp_processmail, with SQL Mail. Database Mail does not support receiving incoming messages because there is no IMAP or POP3 support. This may have something to do with the fact that receiving email can represent a major security risk. Imagine what a denial-of-service attack on a database cluster could do to an organization. Or consider the danger of an incoming email request resulting in the execution of a query such as DROP DATABASE X. Most SQL Server data is too precious to jeopardize in this manner. Microsoft has also made it clear that SQL Mail will be phased out in the next release of SQL Server. Plus, there are many better new alternatives to using this methodology, such as using native Web services (as discussed in Chapter 38, "SQL Server Web Services"), using .NET CLR-integrated assembly code (as discussed in Chapter 36, "SQL Server and the .NET Framework"), or building a dedicated Service Broker application (as discussed in Chapter 48).

Using SQL Server Agent Mail

As with SQL Server 2000, SQL Server 2005's Agent has the ability to send email notifications. These may be triggered by alerts or scheduled task completions, such as jobs. SQL Server 2005 provides the option of using either SQL Mail or Database Mail to do the sending, but SQL Mail will soon be phased out, and Database Mail is by far the more robust choice. As with Database Mail, SQL Server Agent Mail is off by default, and you must configure it via SMSS or T-SQL, as described in the following sections.

Job Mail Notifications

The following sections show an example in which you create a SQL Server Agent mail operator that SQL Server Agent will notify when a job completes.

Creating an Operator

First, you need to create an operator. To do so, using the Object Browser, you expand the SQL Server Agent node and then right-click the Operators folder and select New Operator. Then you should name this new operator Test Database Mail Operator and then provide an email address for testing purposes in the Email Name text box. You can use any valid email address you can access with your email client software. You click OK to save the new operator.

Enabling SQL Agent Mail

Next, you need to enable SQL Server Agent to use Database Mail. You right-click the SQL Server Agent node and then select Properties. On the left side of the Properties dialog that appears (see Figure 12.3), you click the Alert System link. Under the Mail Session group, you check the Enable Mail Profile check box. In the Mail System drop-down list, you select Database Mail (this is also where you can choose SQL Mail, if you desire). In the Mail Profile drop-down list, you select the default SQL 2005 profile you created earlier, and then you click OK. By doing this, you are telling SQL Server Agent to use the SMTP servers in your default profile to send email. You need to restart SQL Server Agent by using the right-click menu.

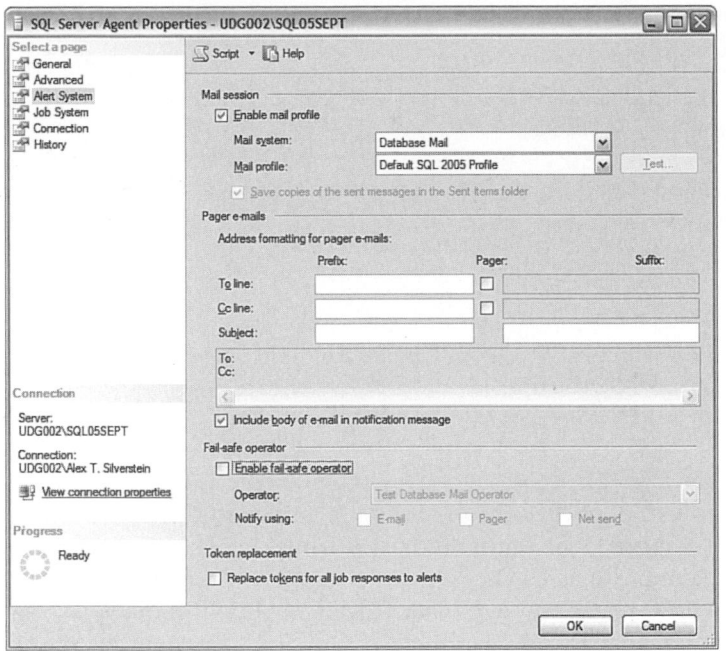

FIGURE 12.3   Using the SQL Server Agent Properties dialog to configure Database Mail.

Creating the Job

Next, you need to create the job. You begin by right-clicking the Jobs folder and then selecting New Job. You should name the job Database Mail Test Job and select an owner. Then you should check the Enabled check box near the bottom of the dialog and then click the Steps link on the left side of the dialog. Next, you click the New button and add a step named Test Mail Step 1. You should leave the type as Transact-SQL and then change the database selection to AdventureWorks. In the Command text box, you enter the following code:

```
RAISERROR('This is simply a test job.', 10, 1)
```

Next, you click the Advanced link on the left side of the dialog, and in the On Success Action drop-down list, you select Quit the Job Reporting Success. Then you click the Notifications link on the left side of the dialog. Then, under Actions to Perform When the Job Completes, you check the Email check box and select the operator you just created. On the drop-down to the right, you select When the Job Completes, and then you click OK to save the job.

Testing the Job-Completion Notification

To test the email configuration and notification you just set up, you right-click the job name under the Jobs folder and then select Start Job. If everything is set up properly, an email message appears in your inbox, indicating the job's successful completion. Its body text may look something like this:

```
JOB RUN:     'Database Mail Test Job' was run on 11/7/2005 at 8:37:22 PM
DURATION:    0 hours, 0 minutes, 0 seconds
STATUS:      Succeeded
MESSAGES:    The job succeeded.  The Job was invoked by User [TestUser].
    The last step to run was step 1 (Test Mail Step 1).
```

Alert Mail Notifications

As another example, in the following sections, you'll create a simple user-defined alert that you can trigger directly from T-SQL script.

Creating an Alert

You start by creating an alert. To do this, you use the Object Browser to expand the SQL Server Agent node, and then you right-click the Alerts node and select New Alert. In the alert properties dialog that appears (see Figure 12.4), you name the new alert Database Mail Test Alert and make sure the Enabled check box is checked. For the Event type, you leave the selection on SQL Server Event Alert. Under Event Alert Definition, you select AdventureWorks from the Database Name drop-down list, and then you click the Severity option button and choose 010 - Information. Next, you check the Raise Alert When Message Contains check box and type the phrase This is a Test in the Message Text text box.

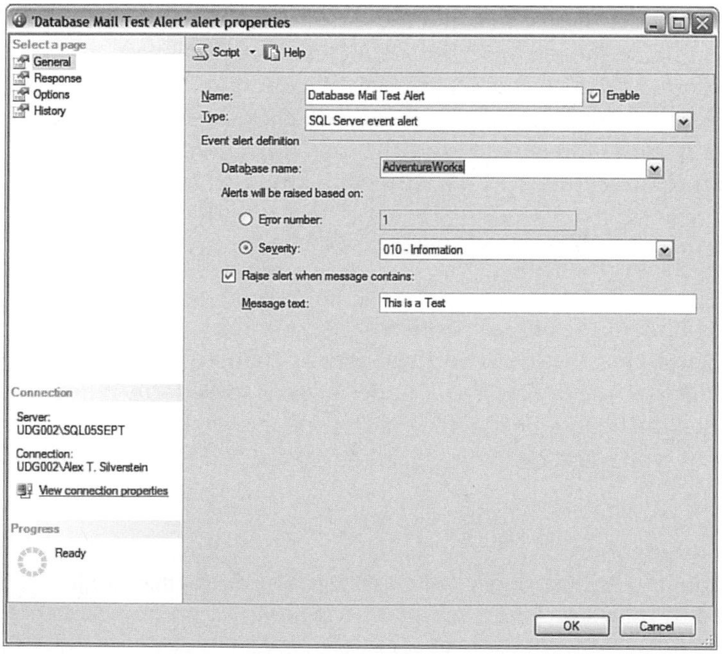

FIGURE 12.4   Creating a SQL Server event alert with a Database Mail notification.

On the left side of the alert properties dialog, you click the Response link. Then you check the Notify Operators check box, and, in the Operator list, you check the Email check box to the right of the Test Database Mail Operator grid row. Finally, you click OK to close and save the new custom alert.

Testing the Alert Notification
To test your new alert notification, you open a new query window in SMSS and enter the following code:

```
USE AdventureWorks
go
RAISERROR('This is an alert mail test', 10, 1) WITH LOG
go
'This is an alert mail test'
```

Because you specified WITH LOG, this simple statement writes an event to the Windows Event log, which in turn triggers the alert because the database context, message text, and severity all match the conditions of the alert. An email message should have appeared in your inbox, indicating the alert's successful triggering. This message should contain body text such as this:

```
DATE/TIME:    11/7/2005 9:00:45 PM
DESCRIPTION:    Error: 50000 Severity:  10 State; 1 This is an alert
    mail test
COMMENT:    (None)
JOB RUN:    (None)
```

Related Views and Procedures

To report on the status of all your Database Mail objects without relying on wizards and properties pages, you need some tabular views and stored procedures. msdb contains many system tables, views, and corresponding stored procedures that make this task easy. The following section lists the tables (or views) and their columns, noting the stored procedure (if any) that you can use to read from them.

Viewing the Mail Configuration Objects

The first set of msdb objects we'll review are those related to system objects such as profiles, profile security, and accounts:

▶ **sysmail_profile**—Contains basic profile data, including the unique profile_id, name, description, last_mod_datetime, and last_mod_user name. You execute sysmail_help_profile_sp to retrieve this data by @profile_name or @profile_id.

▶ **sysmail_principalprofile**—Contains profile security settings, including the profile_id, associated principal (or user) (principal_SID), profile default status (is_default: 1 for yes or 0 for no), last_mod_datetime, and last_mod_user name.

You execute `sysmail_help_principalprofile_sp` to retrieve this data by `@profile_name`, `@profile_id`, `@principal_name`, or `@principal_id` (not principal SID). Here's an example:

```
exec msdb.dbo.sysmail_help_principalprofile_sp
    @profile_name='Default SQL 200 Profile'
```

▶ **sysmail_account**—Contains basic account data, including the unique `account_id`, `name`, `description`, `email_address`, `display_name`, `replyto_address`, `last_mod_datetime`, and `last_mod_user` name. You execute `sysmail_help_account_sp` to retrieve this data by `@account_id` or `@account_name`.

▶ **sysmail_server**—Contains account SMTP server data, including the unique related `account_id` and `servertype`, `servername`, `port`, server `username`, server authentication data (`credential_id`), SSL status (`enable_SSL`), `last_mod_datetime`, and `last_mod_user` name. (`sysmail_help_account_sp` returns data from this table as well.)

▶ **sysmail_servertype**—Contains `servertype` data for accounts' servers. (SMTP is the only currently supported type, although it seems this system was built for extensibility, as the columns `is_incoming` and `is_outgoing` may leave the door open for adding POP or IMAP servers sometime in the future.) Also includes `last_mod_datetime` and `last_mod_user` name. (`sysmail_help_account_sp` returns data from this table as well.)

To join `sysmail_account`, `sysmail_server`, and `sysmail_servertype` (as `sysmail_help_account_sp` seems to do), you can try a query such as the following:

```
SELECT *
FROM msdb.dbo.sysmail_account a
JOIN msdb.dbo.sysmail_server s
ON a.account_id = s.account_id
JOIN msdb.dbo.sysmail_servertype st
ON st.servertype = s.servertype
```

▶ **sysmail_profileaccount**—Maintains the profile-account relationship, including the `profile_id`, `account_id`, account priority `sequence_number`, `last_mod_datetime`, and `last_mod_user` name. You execute `sysmail_help_profileaccount_sp` to retrieve this data by `@account_id`, `@account_name`, `@profile_id`, or `@profile_name`.

▶ **sysmail_configuration**—Contains the systemwide mail configuration settings (`paramname`, `paramvalue`, `description`), and when and by whom each was last modified (`last_mod_datetime` and `last_mod_user` name). You execute `sysmail_help_configure_sp` to query this data by `@parameter_name`. Here's an example:

```
exec msdb.dbo.sysmail_help_configure_sp
    @parameter_name='accountretrydelay'
```

Viewing Mail Message Data

The second set of msdb objects (and perhaps the more important ones) we'll review are those used to discover the status of mail messages.

The first thing you need to do is to check on the status of the mail messages you've attempted to send, without relying on inboxes to tell you if they've been received. Several views in msdb enable this, most of which may be filtered by mail account, sending user, send date, status, and more. To begin this process, you query the view sysmail_allitems, which contains all the data about your messages (subjects, recipients, importance, and so on) as well as send_request_date, sent_date, and sent_status. Here's an example:

```
SELECT mailitem_id, subject, sent_status
FROM msdb.dbo.sysmail_allitems
go
mailitem_id    subject                                          sent_status
- - - - - - - - - - - - - - - - - - - - - - - - - - - - - - - - - - - - - - - - - - - - - -

1              Database Mail Test                               sent
2              C. Adams, Contact Info                           sent
3              SVG for HL Touring Seat/Saddle attached.         sent
4              SQL Server Job System: 'Database Mail Test Job'  sent

(4 row(s) affected)
```

Because all these messages have a sent_status of sent, the contents of this recordset are analogous to what you'd find if you queried the view sysmail_sentitems. But suppose your sent_status column read failed. In that case, you'd start by querying the sysmail_faileditems view (a subset of sysmail_allmailitems) in conjunction with sysmail_event_log (which contains the detailed textual reasons why failures have occurred). Here's an example:

```
SELECT f.subject, f.mailitem_id, l.description
FROM msdb.dbo.sysmail_event_log l
JOIN msdb.dbo.sysmail_faileditems f
ON f.mailitem_id = l.mailitem_id
WHERE event_type = 'error'
ORDER BY log_date
go
subject              mailitem_id    description
- - - - - - - - - - - - - - - - - - - - - - - - - - - - - - - - - - - - - - - - - - - - - - - - -
Database Mail Test    3              The mail could not be sent because[...]the
➥string is not in the form required for an e-mail address

(1 row(s) affected)
```

Note that the quality of the contents of `sysmail_event_log` depends on the `Log Level` systemwide mail configuration setting (discussed earlier in this chapter, in the section "Setting Systemwide Mail Settings"). The Log File Viewer also uses this table's contents. To permanently delete its contents, you use the stored procedure `sysmail_delete_log_sp`.

To query how many messages are queued (waiting to be sent) and for how long, you use the `sysmail_unsentitems` view. Here's an example:

```
SELECT
    mailitem_id,
    subject,
    DATEDIFF(hh, send_request_date, GETDATE()) HoursSinceSendRequest
FROM msdb.dbo.sysmail_unsentitems
```

If you're unsure why messages aren't being sent, you can try the following:

▶ Execute `sysmail_help_queue_sp`, whose resulting `state` column tells the state of the mail transmission queues: `INACTIVE` (off) or `RECEIVES_OCCURRING` (on). To see the status for only the `mail` (outbound) or `status` (send status) queues, you use the `@queue_type` parameter.

▶ Execute `sysmail_help_status_sp`, whose resulting `Status` column tells you the state of Database Mail itself: `STOPPED` or `STARTED`.

Summary

In this chapter, you've seen how Database Mail has elevated the status of emailing with SQL Server from somewhat difficult to use to enterprise class. Microsoft has achieved this by relying on cross-platform industry standards, by making configuration easy, by providing a comprehensive set of system objects for storage and tracking, by adding failover capability, and by utilizing the Service Broker infrastructure. In short, the difficulties and limitations once experienced with SQL Mail are gone for good, with much applause.

Chapter 13, "SQL Server Scheduling and Notification," digs much deeper into configuring SQL Server Agent jobs and alerts, as well as using Database Mail for job and alert notifications.

CHAPTER 13

SQL Server Scheduling and Notification

IN THIS CHAPTER

▶ What's New in Scheduling and Notification

▶ Configuring the SQL Server Agent

▶ Viewing the SQL Server Agent Error Log

▶ SQL Server Agent Security

▶ Managing Operators

▶ Managing Jobs

▶ Managing Alerts

▶ Scripting Jobs and Alerts

▶ Multiserver Job Management

▶ Event Forwarding

Automation is the key to efficiency, and the SQL Server Agent is your automation tool in SQL Server 2005. This chapter delves into the administrative capabilities of the SQL Server Agent and its ability to schedule server activity and respond to server events.

The SQL Server Agent, which runs as a Windows service, is responsible for running scheduled tasks, notifying operators of events, and responding with predefined actions to errors and performance conditions. The SQL Server Agent can perform these actions without user intervention, using the following:

▶ **Alerts**—*Alerts* respond to SQL Server or user-defined errors, and they can also respond to performance conditions. An alert can be configured to run a job as well as notify an operator.

▶ **Jobs**—A *job* is a predefined operation or set of operations, such as transferring data or backing up a transaction log. A job can be scheduled to run on a regular basis or called to run when an alert is fired.

▶ **Operators**—An *operator* is a user who should be notified when an alert fires or a job requests notification. The operator can be notified by email, by pager, or via the NET SEND command.

What's New in Scheduling and Notification

Microsoft has continued to improve the capabilities of the SQL Server Agent. It has maintained a consistent basis for automation while enriching the feature set. The following are some of the key new features:

- ▶ **New Job Activity Monitor**—A new auto-refreshing tool called the Job Activity Monitor has been added to help monitor the execution of scheduled jobs. You can adjust the refresh rate of the screen and specify filtering criteria in order to isolate a job or set of jobs.

- ▶ **Shared job schedules**—A job schedule can now be shared among jobs that have the same job owner.

- ▶ **Enhanced SQL Server Agent security**—Several new roles have been added that provide enhanced security management for the SQL Server Agent. In addition, a separate proxy account can now be defined for each type of subsystem that the SQL Server Agent can interact with.

- ▶ **Performance improvements**—New thread pooling and reduced job execution delays have improved the performance of the SQL Server Agent.

Configuring the SQL Server Agent

The primary configuration settings for the SQL Server agent are found within the Object Explorer and the SQL Server Configuration Manager. The majority of the settings that define how the SQL Server Agent will execute are defined via the SQL Server Agent Properties that are accessible from the Object Explorer. The SQL Server Configuration Manager contains settings that are related to the SQL Server Agent's service. The service settings are limited but contain important properties such as the Startup Account for the SQL Server Agent.

Configuring SQL Server Agent Properties

Figure 13.1 shows the SQL Server Agent Properties dialog that appears when you right click on the SQL Server Agent node which is found on the root of the Object Explorer tree and select Properties.

You can set several different types of properties in the SQL Server Agent Properties dialog box. The General options are displayed by default, and they include the ability to set the Auto restart options and define an error log for the SQL Server Agent. Selecting the option Auto Restart SQL Server Agent if It Stops Unexpectedly is best for most installations. There is usually a heavy dependency on the Agent performing its actions, and you probably want the service to be restarted if it has been inadvertently stopped.

The Advanced page contains options for event forwarding and idle CPU conditions. The event forwarding options are discussed in detail in the section "Event Forwarding," later in this chapter. The idle CPU options define conditions related to the execution of jobs that have been set up to run when the CPU is idle. You can define idle CPU conditions such as the average CPU percentage that the CPU must be below in order to be considered idle.

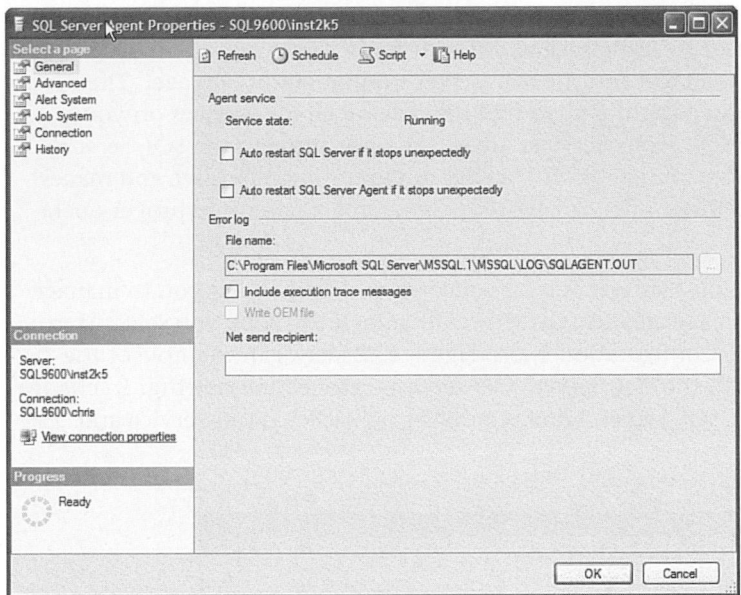

FIGURE 13.1   SQL Server Agent properties.

The Alert System page is related to configuring email notification and is discussed in the "Configuring Email Notification" section, later in this chapter.

The Job System page has an option to set the shutdown time-out interval. This option determines the amount of time that the SQL Server Agent waits for jobs to complete before finalizing the shutdown process. There is also an option related to proxy accounts that is discussed in the "SQL Server Agent Proxy Account" section, later in this chapter.

The Connection page has an option to set an alias for the local host server. This is useful if you cannot use the default connection properties for the local host and need to define an alias instead.

The History page options are related to the amount of job history you can retain. You have the option to limit the size of the job history log and/or remove job history that is older than a set period of time.

Configuring the SQL Server Agent Startup Account

The startup account defines the Microsoft Windows account that the SQL Server Agent service will run with. The selection of this account is critical in defining the level of security that the SQL Server Agent will have. Access to resources on the server that SQL Server is running on and access to network resources are determined by the startup account. This is particularly important in cases in which the Agent needs to access resources on other machines. Examples of network access that the SQL Server Agent might need include jobs that write backups to a drive on another machine and jobs that look for files that are found on other servers on the network.

The startup account for the SQL Server Agent is set initially during the installation of SQL Server, but you can change it by using several different tools. These tools include the Windows Service Control Manager and the SQL Server Configuration Manager. The Windows Service Control Manager is a good tool for viewing all the services on your server, but changes to the SQL Server services are better made through the SQL Server Configuration Manager. The Configuration Manager is more comprehensive and makes additional configuration settings, such as registry permissions, that ensure proper operation.

The SQL Server Configuration Manager is a consolidated tool that allows you to manage network options and services related to SQL Server. To launch this tool, you select Start, Microsoft SQL Server 2005, Configuration Tools. Figure 13.2 shows an example of the Configuration Manager with the SQL Server 2005 services selected for viewing. To change the startup account for the SQL Server Agent, you must right-click on its service and select Properties.

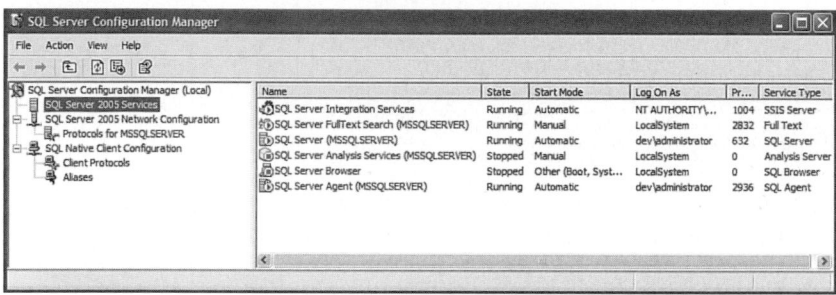

FIGURE 13.2   SQL Server Agent service properties.

The default logon or startup account is set to the local system account. This account provides the Agent with access only to the local resources of the machine that SQL Server is running on. It is a member of the administrators group on the local machine but has no domain access to network resources. It is included in SQL Server 2005 for backward compatibility, but for security reasons it is not the recommended account.

The recommended startup account for the SQL Server Agent is a Windows account. You specify a Windows startup account for SQL Server Agent by using the This Account option on the Service Properties window. The Windows account can be a local user account or a domain user account. It must be a member of the SQL Server sysadmin fixed server role on the local SQL Server instance. The use of this type of startup account provides the most flexibility and allows you to tailor the network and local resources that the SQL Server Agent has permission to access.

The Windows account does not have to be a member of the Windows administrators group. In fact, exclusion from the administrators group is recommended in most cases. This approach adheres to the principle of least privileges, which says that you should limit the amount of security provided to only that which is needed. In many cases, inclusion in the `administrators` group is not needed and only increases exposure to security threats.

The Windows account chosen with the This Account option must have certain security rights in order to function as the startup account for SQL Server. The account must have permission to log on as a service. You can set this permission and others by using the Local Security Policy application, which can be found under Administrative Tools. You can select the `Local Policies` node and then select `User Rights Assignment` to display a list of all the security settings, including Log On as a Service Policy. You should make sure the account you chose or the group that it is in is included in this policy.

TIP

SSMS is the best place to specify the startup account for the SQL Server Agent because it automatically assigns the appropriate rights and permissions for the account specified. If you have trouble assigning the startup account via SSMS, you can use the Windows Service Control Manager to make the assignment. In some situations, you may not be able to change the startup account in SSMS, but you may be able to make the change via the Windows Service Control Manager.

Configuring Email Notification

The SQL Server Agent has the ability to send email notifications. It can send email via SQL Mail or Database Mail. SQL Mail was retained for backward compatibility. It utilizes an Extended Messaging Application Programming Interface (Extended MAPI) interface to send email and requires that you install an email application (such as Outlook) that supports Extended MAPI communication on the computer that is running SQL Server.

Database Mail is now the recommended mail solution for the SQL Server Agent, and it is the focus of this section. It is new to SQL Server 2005, and it utilizes Simple Mail Transfer Protocol (SMTP) instead of Extended MAPI to send mail. This simplifies email setup and has many benefits over SQL Mail, including the following:

▶ There is no requirement that an email client be installed on the SQL Server machine.

▶ Email is queued for later delivery if the mail server stops or fails.

▶ Multiple SMTP servers can be specified so that mail can continue to be delivered in the event that one of the SMTP servers stops.

▶ Database Mail is cluster aware.

Database Mail is disabled by default in SQL Server 2005. You must explicitly enable Database Mail by using the SQL Server Surface Area Configuration tools or the Database Mail Configuration Wizard. Figure 13.3 shows the Surface Area Configuration tools screen for enabling Database Mail stored procedures.

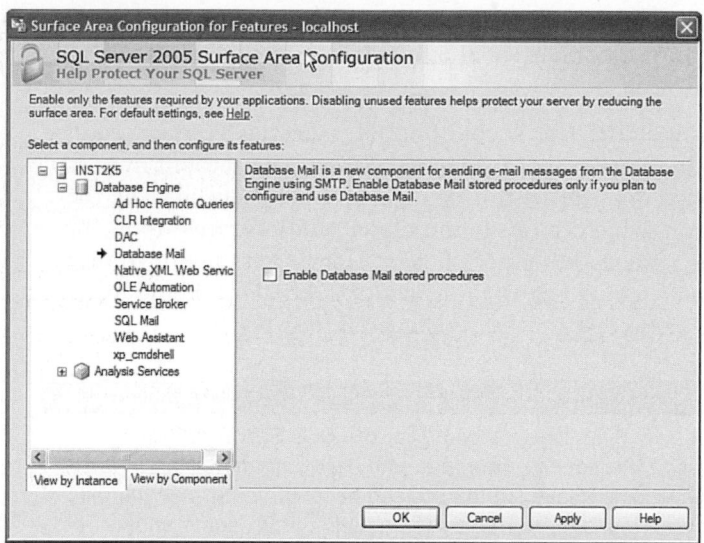

FIGURE 13.3   Surface Area Configuration tool screen for enabling Database Mail.

The Database Mail Configuration Wizard provides a more comprehensive means for configuring Database Mail. The Database Mail Configuration Wizard is not launched from the SQL Server Agent node of the Object Explorer tree. Instead, you can launch it by expanding the Management node, right-clicking Database Mail, and selecting Configure Database Mail. This wizard guides you through the configuration of mail profiles, SMTP accounts, and other options relevant to Database Mail. The Configuration Wizard and many other details related to Database Mail are discussed in detail in Chapter 12, "Database Mail."

After you have set up Database Mail and confirmed that it is working properly, you can select it as your mail system for the SQL Server Agent to send mail. You do this by right-clicking the SQL Server Agent node and selecting Properties. Then you select the Alert System page in the SQL Server Agent Properties dialog, and a screen similar to the one shown in Figure 13.4 appears. Figure 13.4 has Database Mail selected as the mail system, along with the mail profile for Database Mail that was created with the Database Mail Configuration Wizard. The mail profile that is selected can have multiple SMTP accounts assigned to it. This allows for redundancy in the event that the mail cannot be sent to one of the SMTP accounts.

To ensure proper functioning of the alert system, you should restart the SQL Server Agent service after the alert system has been configured. If you experience problems sending notifications via the SQL Server Agent, you should check the service account that SQL Server is running under. If the SQL Server Agent is running with the local system account, then resources outside the SQL Server machine will be unavailable; this includes mail servers that are on other machines. You should change the service account for the SQL Server Agent to a domain account to resolve this issue. Chapter 12 provides more information on using Database Mail in SQL Server 2005.

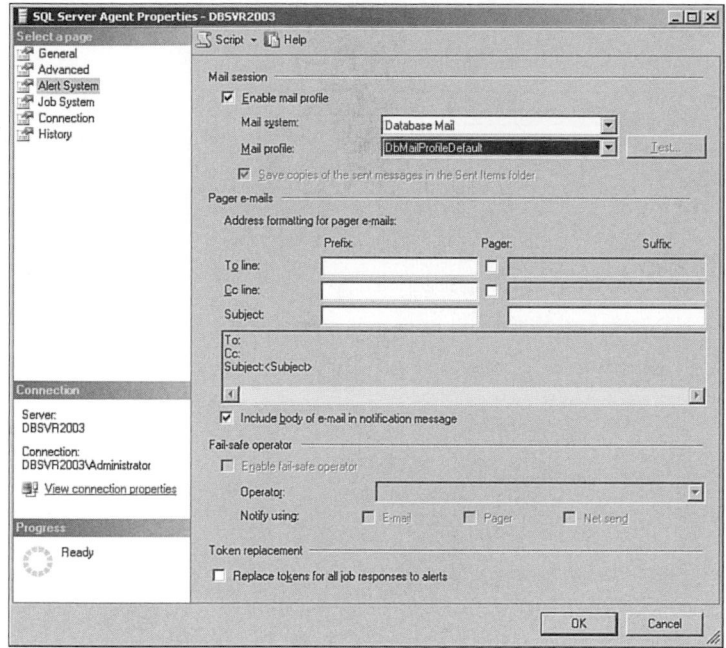

FIGURE 13.4   The Alert System page of the SQL Server Agent Properties dialog.

SQL Server Agent Proxy Account

Proxy accounts allow non–Transact-SQL (non–T-SQL) jobs steps to execute under a specific security context. By default, only users in the sysadmin role can execute these job steps. Non-sysadmin users can be assigned to a proxy account to allow them to run the special job steps. In SQL Server 2000, a single proxy account was provided for this function. With SQL Server 2005, multiple proxy accounts can be established, each of which can be assigned to a different SQL Server Agent subsystem.

To establish a proxy account for the SQL Server Agent, you must first create a credential. A *credential* contains the authentication information necessary to connect to a resource outside SQL Server. The credential is typically linked to a Windows account that has the appropriate rights on the server. To create a credential, you open the Security node in the Object Explorer, right-click the Credentials node, and select New Credential. You give the credential a name, enter an identity value that corresponds to a valid Windows account, and provide a password for the account.

After a credential is created, you can create a new proxy account and link it to the credential. To create a new proxy account, you expand the SQL Server Agent node in the Object Explorer tree, right-click Proxies, and select New Proxy Account. Figure 13.5 shows an example of the New Proxy Account dialog. In this example, the proxy name and credential name are the same, but they do not need to be. The only subsystem selected for the sample proxy account in Figure 13.5 is the operating system, but a proxy account can be linked to multiple subsystems.

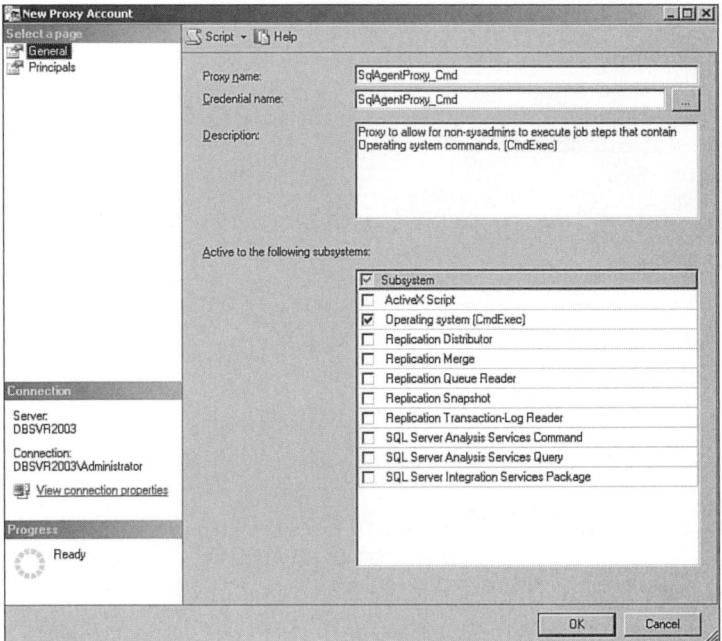

FIGURE 13.5   Creating a new proxy account.

After a proxy account is created, a sysadmin can assign one or more SQL logins, msdb roles, or server roles to the proxy. You do this by using the Principals page of the New Proxy Account dialog. A proxy account can have zero or many principals assigned to it. Conversely, a principal can be assigned to many different proxies. Linking non-admin principals to the proxy allows the principal to create job steps for subsystems that have been assigned to the proxy.

Proxy accounts are referenced within a SQL Server Agent job step. The General page of the Job Step Properties dialog contains a Run As drop-down that lists valid accounts or proxies that can be used to run the particular job step. After you add a proxy account, you see it in this drop-down list. Keep in mind that the account is not visible for a T-SQL job step that does not utilize a proxy account. Steps that utilize the T-SQL subsystem execute under the job owner's context, as they did in SQL Server 2000, and they do not utilize a proxy account.

Viewing the SQL Server Agent Error Log

The SQL Server Agent maintains an error log that records information, warnings, and error messages concerning its operation. A new node named Error Logs has been added to the SQL Server Agent tree in the Object Explorer. The Error Logs node contains multiple versions of the SQL Server Agent error log. By default, a maximum of 10 versions of the error log are displayed under the Error Logs node. The versions displayed include the current error log and the last 9 versions. Each time the SQL Server Agent is restarted, a new error log is generated, with a name that includes a timestamp. The current version is named with Current as the first part of the name. Older logs have a name that starts with Archive #, followed by a number. The newer logs have lower numbers. The SQL Server error log works in much the same way as the SQL Server Agent's error log.

TIP

You can cycle the error log at any time without stopping and starting the SQL Server Agent. To do so, you right-click the Error Logs node in the Object Explorer and select Recycle; a new error log is then generated. You can also use the msdb.dbo.sp_ cycle_agent_errorlog stored procedure to cycle the error log. You need to remember to also select the Refresh option to show the latest available error logs.

To view the contents of any of the logs, you need to double-click the particular log. Double-clicking a particular log file launches the Log File Viewer. The Log File Viewer contains the SQL Server Agent error logs in addition to logs that are associated with other SQL Server components, including Database Mail, SQL Server, and Windows NT. Figure 13.6 shows a sample Log File Viewer screen with the current SQL Server Agent error log selected for display. The Log File Viewer has filtering capabilities that allow you to focus on a particular type of error message, along with other viewing capabilities that are common to all the logs available for viewing.

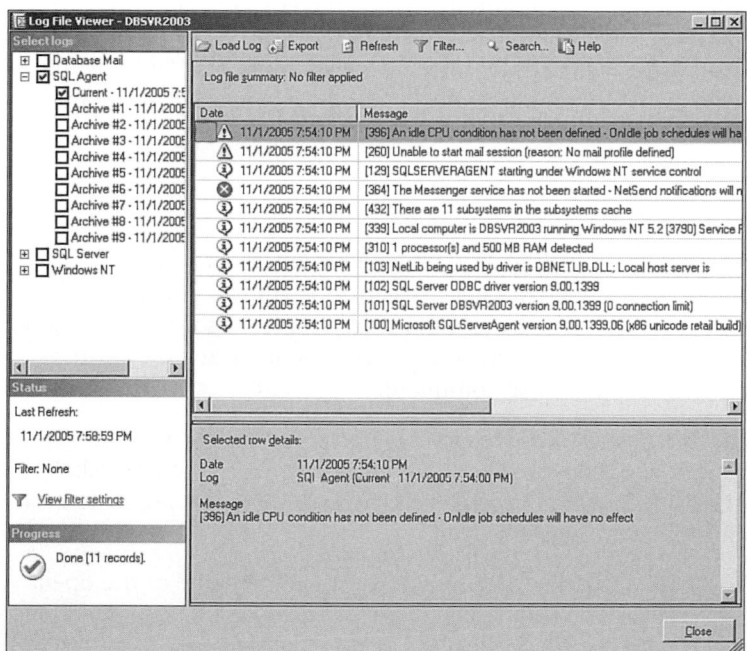

FIGURE 13.6   The SQL Server Agent error log.

SQL Server Agent Security

Many changes have been made to the security model related to the SQL Server Agent in SQL Server 2005. In the past, everyone could view the SQL Server Agent. In SQL Server 2005, logins must be a part of the sysadmin server role or assigned to one of three new msdb database roles in order to view and modify the SQL Server Agent. The SQL Server Agent node does not appear in the Object Explorer tree if the login does not have the appropriate permissions. These are the new msdb database roles and their basic permissions:

> ▶ **SQLAgentUserRole**—Users with this permission can create and manage local jobs and job schedules that they own. They cannot create multiserver jobs or manage jobs that they do not own.

> ▶ **SQLAgentReaderRole**—Users with this permission can view jobs that belong to other users in addition to all the permissions associated with SQLAgentUserRole.

> ▶ **SQLAgentOperatorRole**—Users with this permission can view operators and alerts and control jobs owned by other users. The job control on jobs owned by other users is limited to stopping or starting and enabling or disabling those jobs. SQLAgentOperatorRole also has all the permissions available to SQLAgentUserRole and SQLAgentReaderRole.

SQLAgentUserRole has the least privileges, and each subsequent role has increasing levels of security. In addition, each subsequent role inherits the permissions of the roles with lesser permissions. For example, SQLAgentReaderRole can do everything that SQLAgentUserRole can do and more. Refer to the topic "Implementing SQL Server Agent Security" in SQL Server Books Online for a detailed list of all the permissions related to the new database roles.

Managing Operators

Operators are accounts that can receive notification when an event occurs. These accounts are not linked directly to the user and login accounts that are defined on the server. They are basically aliases for people who need to receive notification based on job execution or alerts. Each operator can define one or more electronic means for notification, including email, pager, and the NET SEND command.

To add a new operator, you expand the SQL Server Agent node in the Object Explorer and right-click the Operators node. Then you select New Operator from the right-click menu. Figure 13.7 shows the New Operator screen, with many of the fields populated for the creation of a new operator named LauraG.

The General page of the New Operator screen allows you to enter the name of the operator, the notification options, and the "on duty" scheduled for the operator. The operator name can be any name, but it must be unique within the SQL Server instance and must be no more than 128 characters. The operator name can be the same as another login or user on the server, but this is not required.

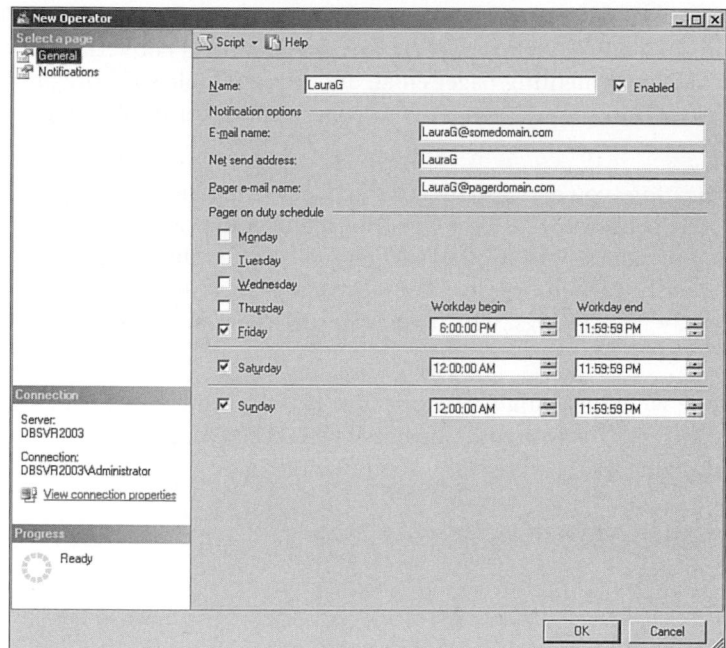

FIGURE 13.7   Creating a new operator.

The notifications options are the key to operators. You create operators so that you can then define notification options and have messages sent from SQL Server.

If you use the email notification option, the email address you specify must be a valid address that can be reached via Database Mail or SQL Mail. One of the two mail options must be configured before the email functionality will work. If Database Mail is configured, then the email will be sent via an SMTP server. To send email with SQL Mail, SQL Server must be able to access a Microsoft Exchange server, and you must have the Extended MAPI client installed on the SQL Server machine.

The NET SEND notification option causes a pop-up window to appear on the recipient's computer that contains the notification text. In the Net Send Address text box, you specify the name of the computer or user that is visible on the network to the SQL Server machine. In order for NET SEND to work, the Messenger service on SQL Server must be started. This Messenger service must also be started on the machine that is receiving the NET SEND message. You can test the basic NET SEND capabilities by executing NET SEND at the command prompt. The basic syntax for NET SEND follows:

```
NET SEND {name ¦ * ¦ /domain[:name] ¦ /users} message
```

The following example uses the NET SEND command to send the message "Test net send message" to the operator LauraG:

```
NET SEND LauraG "Test net send message"
```

The final notification option is via a pager email address. Pager email requires that third-party software be installed on the mail server to process inbound email and convert it to a pager message. The methods for implementing pager email and the available software are dependent on the pager provider. You should contact your pager vendor for implementation details.

If you implement pager notification, you can also define the pager schedule for the operator. The Pager on Duty Schedule section of the New Operator dialog allows you to define the days and times when the operator will be available to receive a page. The General page includes a check box for each day the operator can receive a page. It also includes the Workday Begin and Workday End settings, which you can use to define the valid time periods to receive a page.

The other page that is available when defining a new operator is the Notifications page. This page displays the alerts and jobs for which the operator will receive notifications. For a new operator, the Alert List or the Job List is empty, as shown in Figure 13.8.

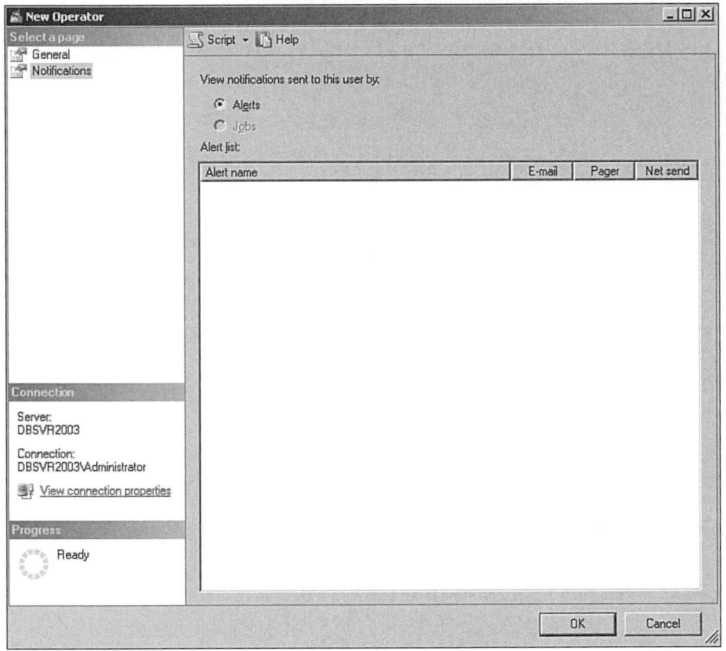

FIGURE 13.8   The Notifications page of the New Operator dialog.

You'll have a better understanding of the usefulness of operators after you read the following discussions of jobs and alerts. Jobs and alerts can have operators linked to them for notification purposes.

Managing Jobs

A job is a container for operations that can be executed by the SQL Server Agent. Jobs can be run once or scheduled to run on a regular basis. Jobs provide the basis for SQL Server automation and allow for the execution of many different types of operations, including T-SQL, SQL Server Integration Services (SSIS) packages, and operating system commands.

Defining Job Properties

The Jobs node is found under SQL Server Agent in the Object Explorer. You right-click the Jobs node and select New Job to create a new SQL Server Agent job. A New Job dialog like the one shown in Figure 13.9 appears.

> **NOTE**
>
> Only logins that are part of one of the new msdb fixed database roles or are members of the sysadmin fixed server role are able to create or modify jobs.

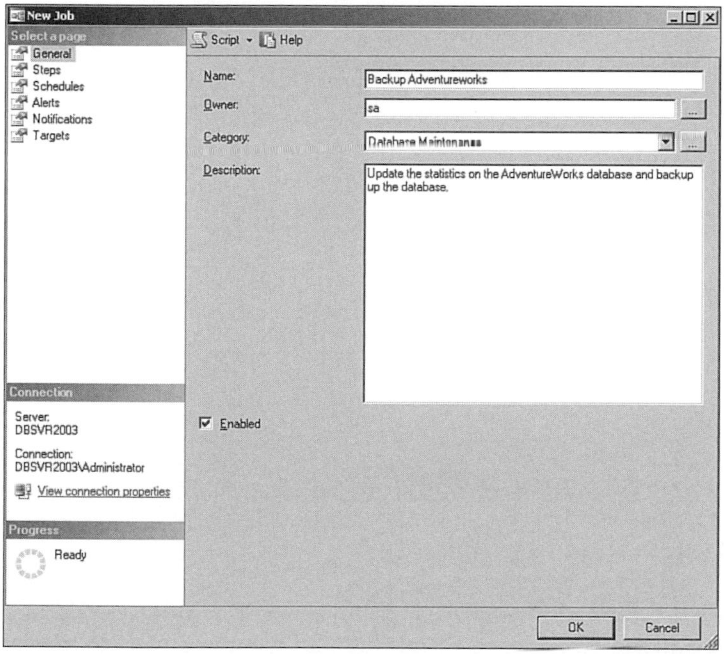

FIGURE 13.9   The New Job dialog.

The General properties page shown in Figure 13.9 contains the basic information about the job, including the name and description. The owner of the job defaults to the login for the person creating the job; however, if the login of the person creating the job is part of the sysadmin fixed server role, the default can be changed. You use the Category selection to group or organize jobs. There are several predefined categories for selection, including Database Maintenance and Log Shipping. The default category is set to [Uncategorized(local)].

Defining Job Steps

After you add the general information for a new job, you are ready to add the job steps that actually perform the work. To do this, you select the Steps page on the left side of the New Job screen, and the job steps for this job are listed. To create a new job step, you click the New button, and a New Job Step dialog like the one shown in Figure 13.10 appears.

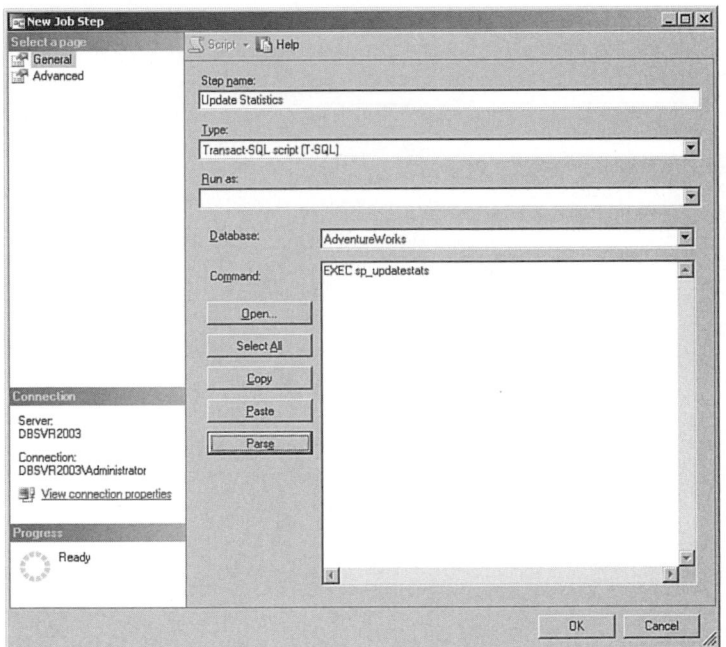

FIGURE 13.10   The New Job Step dialog.

A step name is the first piece of information you need to provide for the job step. It can be up to 128 characters long and must be unique within the job. Then you need to select a job step type. The SQL Server Agent can run a variety of types of job steps, including the following:

► ActiveX script (Visual Basic, Java, Perl script)

► Operating System (CmdExec)

► Replication Distributor

▶ Replication Merge

▶ Replication Queue Reader

▶ Replication Snapshot

▶ Replication Transaction Log Reader

▶ SQL Server Analysis Services Command

▶ SQL Server Analysis Services Query

▶ SQL Server Integration Services Package

▶ Transact-SQL script (T-SQL)

SQL Server Analysis Services Command, the Server Analysis Services Query, and SQL Server Integration Services Package are new types in SQL Server 2005. They provide integration with SQL Server Analysis Services (SSAS) and SSIS. Chapters 39, "SQL Server Analysis Services," and 40, "SQL Server Integration Services," provide detailed discussions of these technologies.

The Step properties page displays different information, depending on the type of step selected. When the Transact-SQL script (T-SQL) type is selected, you see a window similar to the one shown in Figure 13.10. If you choose the SQL Server Integration Services Package type, the Step properties page changes to allow you to enter all the relevant information needed to execute an SSIS package.

In many cases (including with T-SQL), a command window is available to input the step commands. With a T-SQL command, you can enter the same type of commands you would enter in Query Analyzer. You click the Parse button to validate the SQL and ensure proper syntax. The Operating system (CmdExec) type allows you to enter the same type of commands that you can enter in a command prompt window. Each step type has it own command syntax that you can test in the native environment to ensure proper operation.

You can select the Advanced page to configure job flow information and other information related to the job step. On Success Action allows you to specify the action to perform when the current job step completes. Actions include the execution of the next job step (if one exists) and the ability to set job status based on the step completion. The same selection options also exist for On Failure Action.

The Retry options define the options that relate to retrying the job step in the event that the job step fails. Retry Attempts defines the number of times the job step will be re-executed if it fails. Retry Intervals (Minutes) defines the amount of time (in minutes) between retry attempts.

TIP

The Retry options are useful for polling scenarios. For example, you might have a job step that tests for the existence of a file during a given period of the day. The job can be scheduled to start at a time of day when the file is expected. If the file is not there and the step fails, Retry Attempts can be set to poll again for the file. Retry Interval determines how often it retries, and the combination of Retry Attempts and Retry Interval determines the total polling window. For example, if you want to check for the file for 2 hours, you can set Retry Attempts to 24 with a Retry Interval of 5 minutes. If the job step fails more than the number of retries, the step completes in failure.

The last set of options on the Advanced page relate to the output from the job step. Job step output can be saved to an output file that can be overwritten each time the job step is run, or the output can be appended each time. SQL Server 2005 has introduced a new option to save the step output to a SQL Server table. The Log to Table option writes the job step output to the `sysjobstepslogs` table in the `msdb` database. The table contains one row for each job step, with the Log to Table option enabled. If Append Output to Existing Entry in Table is enabled, the `sysjobstepslogs` data row for the step can contain output for more than one execution. If this option is not selected, the table contains only execution history for the last execution of the step.

CAUTION

If you choose the Append Output to Existing Entry in Table option, the size of the `sysjobstepslogs` table will grow over time. You should consider using the `sp_delete_jobsteplog` stored procedure to remove data from the `sysjobstepslogs` table. This stored procedure has several different parameters that allow you to filter the data that will be removed. You can use these parameters to remove log data by job, job step, date, or the size of the log for the job step.

Defining Multiple Jobs Steps

You can define multiple jobs steps in a single job. This allows you to execute multiple dependent job actions. The jobs steps run one at a time (or serially), and you can specify the order of the job steps. The job order and the related dependencies are called *control of flow*.

Figure 13.11 shows an example of a job that has multiple dependent job steps. Take note of the On Success and On Failure columns, which define the control of flow. For example, if step 1 succeeds, the next step occurs. If step 1 fails, no further steps are executed, and the job quits, reporting a job failure. The control of flow is slightly different for the second step, whereby the control of flow passes to the next step on success but flows to the fourth step if a failure occurs.

FIGURE 13.11   Multiple job steps.

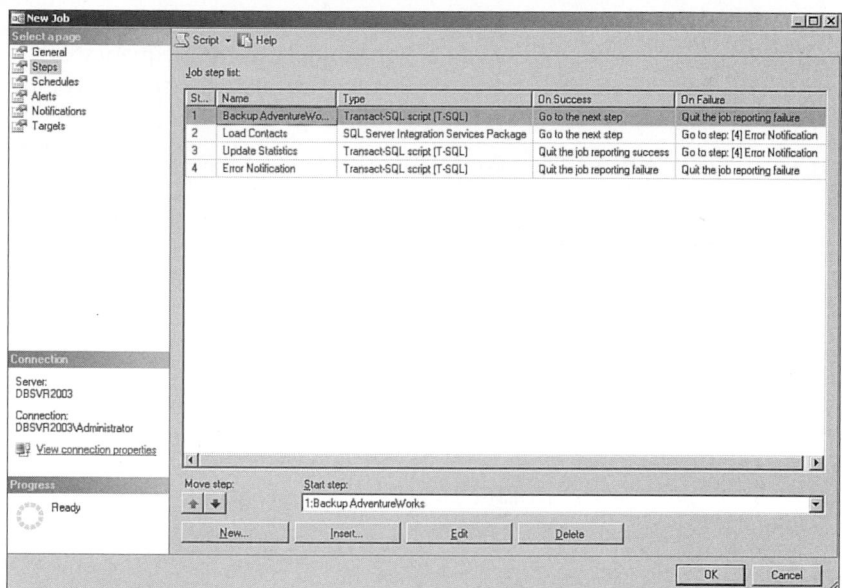

The control of flow is defined on each job step. As discussed earlier in this chapter, the Advanced tab of the New Job Step dialog provides drop-down lists that allow you to specify the actions to take on success and on failure. In addition, the Steps page that lists all of a job's steps allows you to specify the start step for the job. The drop-down box at the bottom of the Steps page provides this function. You can also use the Move Step arrows to change the start step. Manipulating the start step is useful when you're restarting a job manually, as in the case of a job failure; in this situation, you might want to set the job to start on a step other than the first step.

> **NOTE**
>
> SSIS provides the same type of flow control capabilities as the SQL Server Agent. In fact, maintenance plans that contain multiple related actions (such as optimization, backup, and reporting) utilize SSIS packages. A scheduled job starts an SSIS package, which executes the package in a single step, but the actual maintenance steps are defined within the package. The SSIS Designer utilizes a graphical tool that depicts the flow of control and allows you to modify the individual steps.

Defining Job Schedules

The SQL Server Agent contains a comprehensive scheduling mechanism you can use to automate the execution of your jobs. A job can have zero, one, or more schedules assigned to it. You can view the schedules associated with a job by selecting the Schedules page of the Job Properties screen. To create a new schedule for a job, you can click the New button at the bottom of the Schedules page. Figure 13.12 shows the Job Schedule

Properties screen, with a sample schedule and options defined. The options on this screen vary, depending on the frequency of the job schedule. For example, if the frequency of the schedule shown in Figure 13.12 were changed from daily to weekly, the screen would change to allow for the selection of specific days during the week to run the job.

FIGURE 13.12   The Job Schedule Properties page.

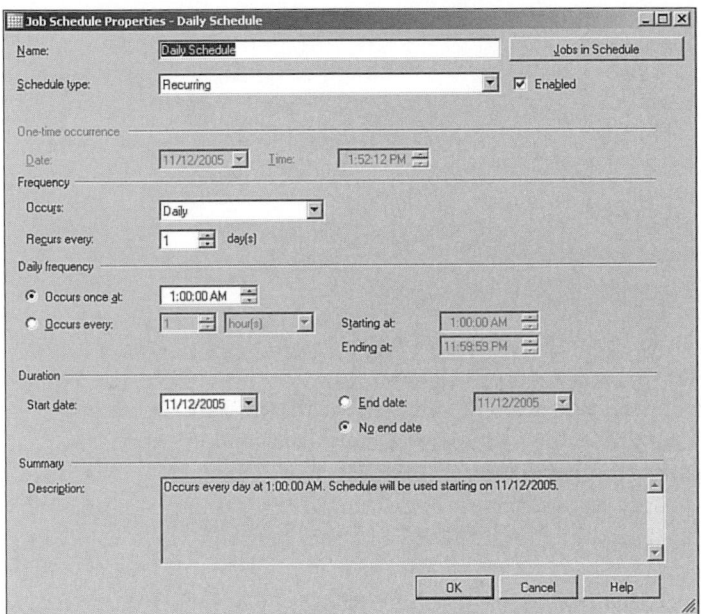

New to SQL Server 2005 is the ability to share job schedules so that one job schedule can be utilized by more than one job. When you select the Schedule page, a Pick button is available at the bottom of the page. If you click the Pick button, a screen appears, showing all the defined schedules. If you highlight one of the schedules in the list and click OK, the schedule is linked to the related job. You can also view all the jobs associated with a particular schedule by editing the schedule and clicking the Jobs in Schedule button in the top-right portion of the Job Schedule Properties screen.

Tracking multiple job schedules and schedule execution can be challenging in an environment that has many jobs and schedules. The sp_helpjobschedule, sp_help_jobs_in_schedule, and sp_help_jobactivity stored procedures are helpful system stored procedures that are found in the msdb database. The sp_helpjobschedule and sp_help_jobs_in_schedule stored procedures provide information about the relationship between jobs and schedules. The sp_help_jobactivity stored procedure provides point-in-time information about the runtime state of SQL Server jobs. This stored procedure returns a bulk of information, including recent job executions, the status of those executions, and the next scheduled run date.

Defining Job Notifications

The Notifications page of the Job Properties dialog (see Figure 13.13) allows you to define the notification actions to perform when a job completes..

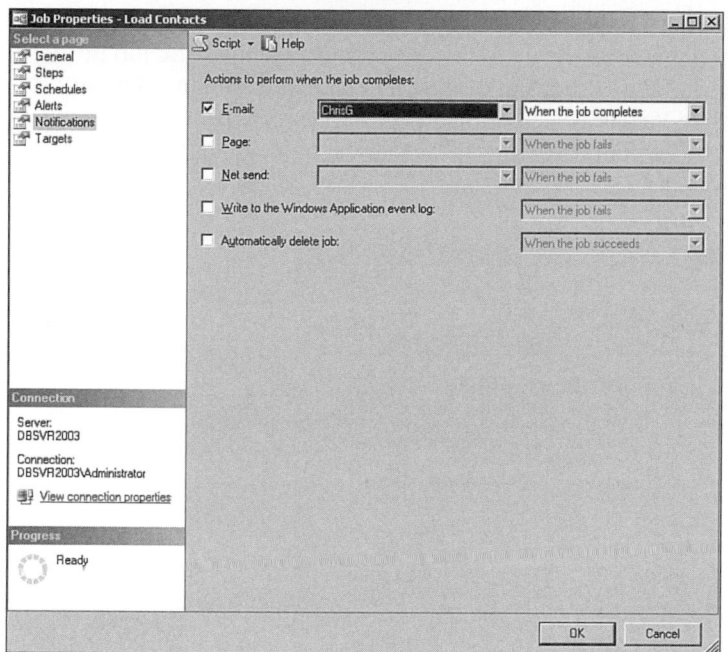

FIGURE 13.13   The Notifications page of the Job Properties dialog.

As discussed earlier in this chapter, notifications can be sent via email, pager, or NET SEND command. The notifications for a Schedule Job can be sent based on the following events:

▸ When the job succeeds

▸ When the job fails

▸ When the job completes

Each of these events can have a different notification action defined for it. For example, a notification might send an email if the job succeeds but page someone if it fails.

You also have the option of writing notification information into the Windows Application event log or automatically deleting the job when it completes. These two options are also available on the Notifications page. Writing events to the Application log is a useful tracking mechanism. Monitoring software is often triggered by events in the application log. The automatic job deletion options are useful for jobs that will be run only once. As with the other notification options, you can set up the delete job action such that it is deleted only when a specific job event occurs. For example, you might want to delete the job only if the job succeeds.

Viewing Job History

The means for viewing job history has changed in SQL Server 2005. You now view job history via the Log File Viewer. You still view job history by right-clicking the job in the SQL Server Agent and selecting History, but the display mechanism is much different than it used to be. The Log File Viewer is a comprehensive application that allows for many different types of logs to be viewed. Figure 13.14 shows the Log File Viewer with several examples of job history selected for viewing.

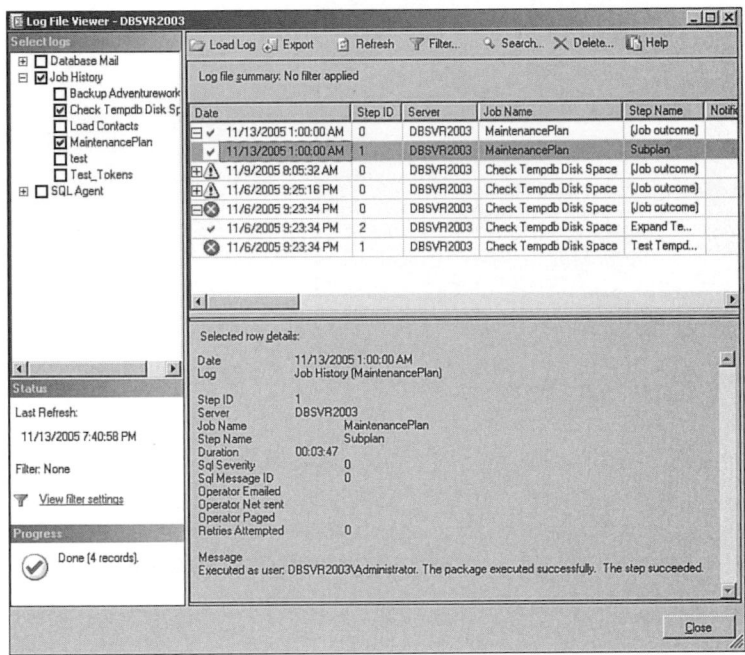

FIGURE 13.14   Job history shown in the Log File Viewer.

Compared to viewing job history in previous SQL Server versions, the Log File Viewer has some distinct advantages for viewing job history. In the Log File Viewer, you can select multiple jobs for viewing at one time. To view job step details, you expand the job entries and select a job step. You can use the row details shown below the log file summary to troubleshoot job errors and isolate problems. The Log File Viewer also has filtering capabilities that allow you to isolate the jobs to view. You can filter jobs by using a number of different settings, including User, Start Date, and Message Text. You must click the Apply Filter button in order for the selected filtering option to take effect.

The amount of history that is kept is based on the history settings defined for the SQL Server Agent. You access the history settings by right-clicking the SQL Server Agent node, selecting Properties, and then selecting the History page on the left part of the screen. The settings available on the History page are shown in Figure 13.15. By default, the job history log is limited to 1,000 rows, with a maximum of 100 rows per job. You can also select the Automatically Remove Agent History option and select a period of time to retain history. This will cause the SQL Server Agent to periodically remove job history from log. This is a good approach for keeping the size of the log manageable.

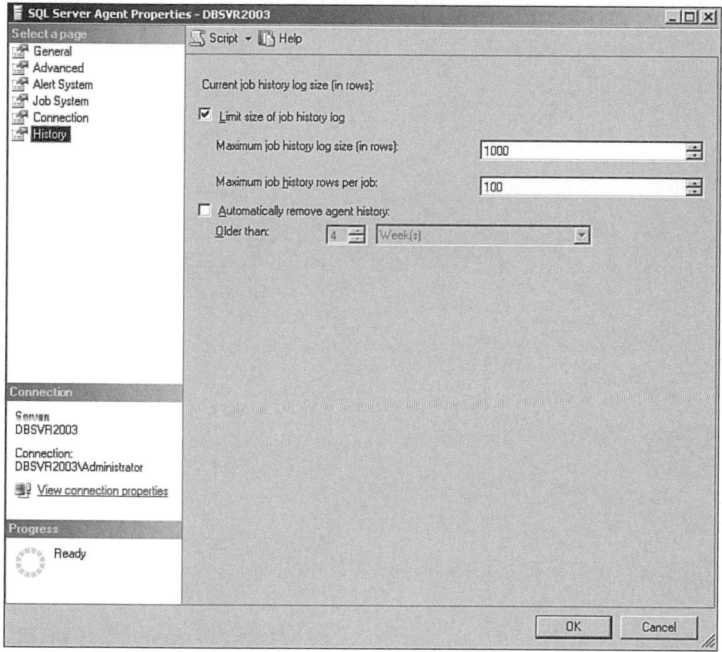

FIGURE 13.15   Job history settings.

Managing Alerts

The SQL Server Agent can monitor events that occur on the database server and automatically respond to these events with alerts. Alerts can be fired based on SQL Server events, performance conditions, and Windows Management Instrumentation (WMI) events. After an alert is fired, the SQL Server Agent can respond by notifying an operator or executing a job. This provides a proactive means for identifying and reacting to critical conditions on a database server.

Defining Alert Properties

To define alerts, you select the SQL Server Agent node in the Object Explorer tree and then right-click on the Alerts node and select New Alert. Figure 13.16 shows an example of the New Alert dialog that appears.

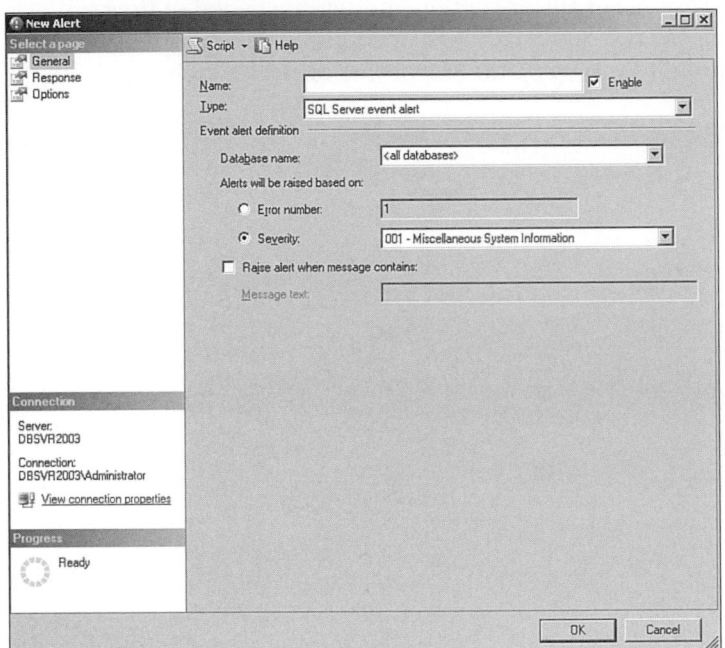

FIGURE 13.16   The General page of the New Alert dialog.

The General page that is selected in Figure 13.16 allows you to define the basic alert properties, including the name of the alert and the type of event you want the alert to respond to. The default type of alert is the SQL Server event alert. This type of alert is triggered by SQL Server events that write to the Windows Application event log. SQL Server writes to the Application event log when the following events occur:

▶ When sysmessages errors with a severity of 19 or higher are generated. You can use the sys.sysmessages catalog view to view all the sysmessages that are stored in the server. You can create new user-defined messages by using the sp_addmessage stored procedure; they must have a msg_id (or error number) that is greater than 50000. The error message must be created before you can reference the error number in an alert.

▶ When sysmessages errors are generated by the database engine. These messages have error numbers lower than 50000 and are installed by default.

▶ When any RAISERROR statement is invoked with the WITH LOG option. The WITH LOG statement forces the event to be written to the Application event log. Messages generated with RAISERROR that have a severity level greater than 18 are required to write to the Application event log.

▶ When sysmessages have been altered with the sp_altermessage statement to write to the application log. The sp_altermessage command has a write_to_log parameter that you can use to modify error numbers found in sys.messages. When the write_to_log parameter is set to WITH_LOG, these message automatically write to the Application event log, regardless of whether the WITH_LOG option is used when the error is raised.

▶ When application calls are made to xp_logevent to log an event to the application log.

The bottom portion of the General page of the New Alert dialog allows you to define which events in the Application event log the alert should respond to. You can have the event respond to a specific error number, the error severity level, or specific text that is contained in the error message. The sys.sysmessages catalog view contains a complete list of all the error message details for all the supported languages. You can use the following SELECT statement to list the error messages for the English language:

```
SELECT * FROM SYS.SYSMESSAGES
where msglangid = 1033
order by msglangid, error
```

You can define an alert for hundreds of messages. For example, you can define an alert that responds to changes to database options. You do this by selecting error number 5084, which is triggered whenever a change is made to the database options. You can also narrow the scope of the alert to look at a specific database by using the Database Name drop-down. This limits the alert to errors that occur in the specific database you choose. The default option is to look at all databases.

The two other types of alerts you can define are SQL Server performance condition alerts and the new WMI event alerts. A SQL Server performance condition alert reacts to performance conditions on the server. Figure 13.17 shows an example of this type of alert.

When you select a SQL Server performance condition alert, you need to select the performance object and counter for that object to monitor. The SQL Server performance objects and counters that are available on the General page of the New Alert dialog are a subset of those available in the Windows Performance Monitor application. These performance metrics encompass key indicators, such as memory, CPU, and disk space.

After you have selected the object and the counter, you need to define the performance threshold for the alert. You define the threshold at the bottom of the General page, below the Alert if Counter label. In the example shown in Figure 13.17, the alert is monitoring the transaction log file for the AdventureWorks database. The threshold has been set such that the alert will fire if the transaction log for this database rises above 2MB.

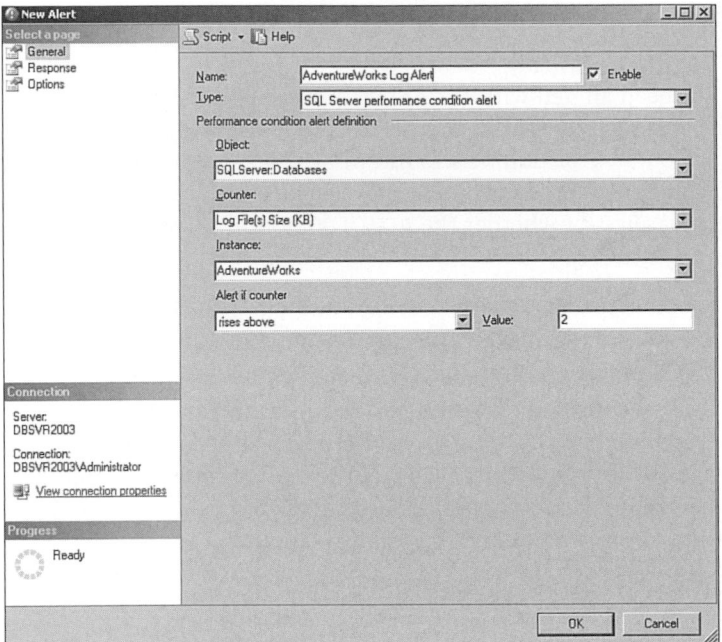

FIGURE 13.17   A SQL Server performance condition alert on the General page.

The WMI event alerts use WMI to monitor events in an instance of SQL Server. The SQL Server Agent can access SQL Server events by using the WMI provider for server events by issuing WMI Query Language (WQL) statements. WQL is a scaled-down version of SQL that contains some WMI-specific extensions. When a WMI query is run, it essentially creates an event notification in the target database so that a related event will fire. The number of WMI events is extensive. Refer to the "WMI Provider for Server Events Classes and Properties" section in SQL Server Books Online for a complete list.

Figure 13.18 shows an example of a WMI event alert. This example uses a WQL query that detects any Data Definition Language (DDL) changes to any of the databases on the server. After the alert is created, you can test it by running a DDL statement against the database (for example, `alter table Person.address add newcol int null`).

Defining Alert Responses

The definition of an alert has two primary components. As discussed earlier in this chapter, the first component involves the identification of the event or performance condition that will trigger the alert. The second part of an alert definition involves the desired response when the alert condition is met. You can define an alert response by using the Response page on the alert's Properties screen. Figure 13.19 shows a sample response that has been configured to use `NET SEND` on a message to the operator named ChrisG.

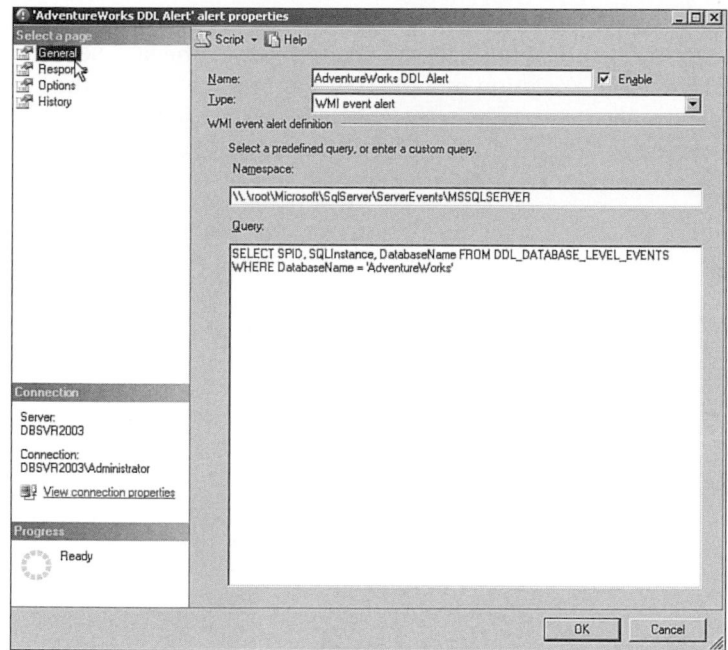

FIGURE 13.18   The General page showing a WMI event alert.

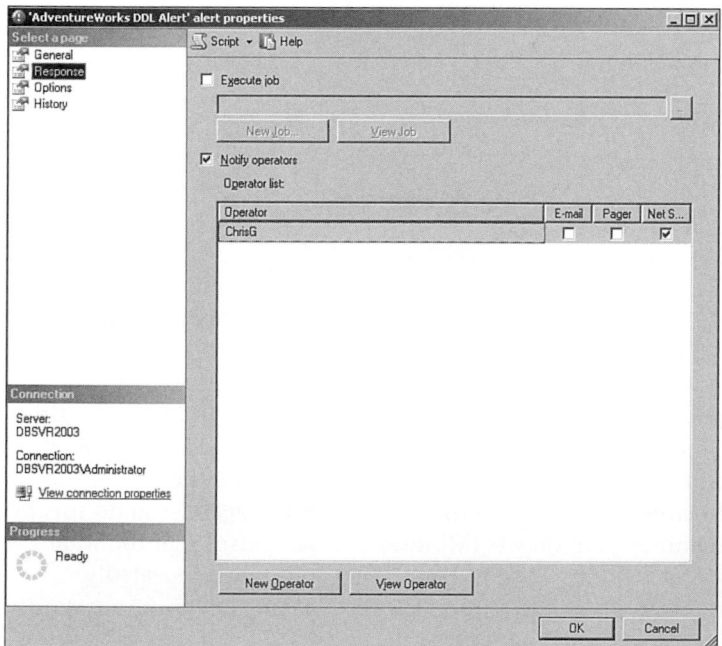

FIGURE 13.19   Configuring an alert response.

Operator notification and job execution are the two responses to an alert. Operator notification allows for one or more operators to be notified via email, pager, or the NET SEND command. Job execution allows for the execution of a job that has been defined in the SQL Server Agent. For example, you could execute a job that does a database backup for an alert that is triggered based on database size. You can define both job execution and operator notification in a single alert; they are not mutually exclusive.

You can further define an alert response by using the Options page of an alert's Properties window (see Figure 13.20).

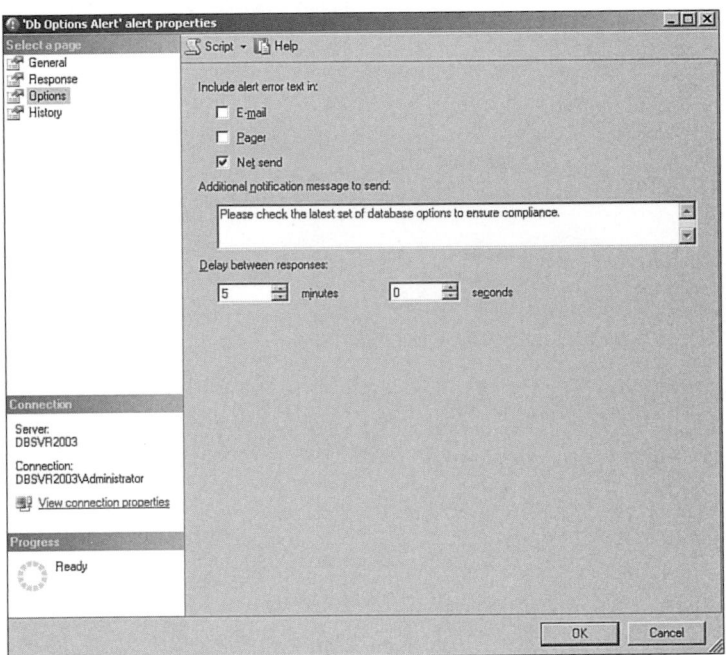

FIGURE 13.20   Alert options.

You can include an alert's error text in the operator notification message on this page. This alert error text provides further details about why the alert was fired. For example, if you have an alert that is triggered by changes to database options, the alert error text would include the actual option that was changed. You can also define additional notification text that is included when the message is sent. This message could include directives for the operators or additional instructions. Finally, you can define the amount of time that the alert will wait before responding to the alert condition again. You do this by using the Delay Between Responses drop-downs (Minutes and Seconds) to set the wait time. This is useful in situations in which an alert condition can happen repeatedly within a short period of time. You can define a response delay to prevent an unnecessarily large number of alert notifications from being sent.

Scripting Jobs and Alerts

SQL Server has options that allow for the scripting of jobs and alerts. As with many of the other objects in SQL Server, you might find that it is easier and more predictable to generate a script that contains the jobs and alerts on the server. You can use these scripts to reinstall the jobs and alerts or deploy them to another server. You can right-click the job or alert you want to script and choose a scripting option to generate the T-SQL for the individual object. You can also select the Job node or the Alerts node to view the Summary page that lists all the objects. You can also display the Summary page via the View menu or by selecting it as the active tab. When the Summary page is selected, you have the option of selecting one or more jobs to script. You can select multiple by holding down the Ctrl key and clicking the jobs you want to script.

Figure 13.21 shows a sample Summary page for jobs, with several of the jobs selected for scripting. To generate the script, you simply right-click one of the selected jobs and select the Script Job As menu option to generate the desired type of script.

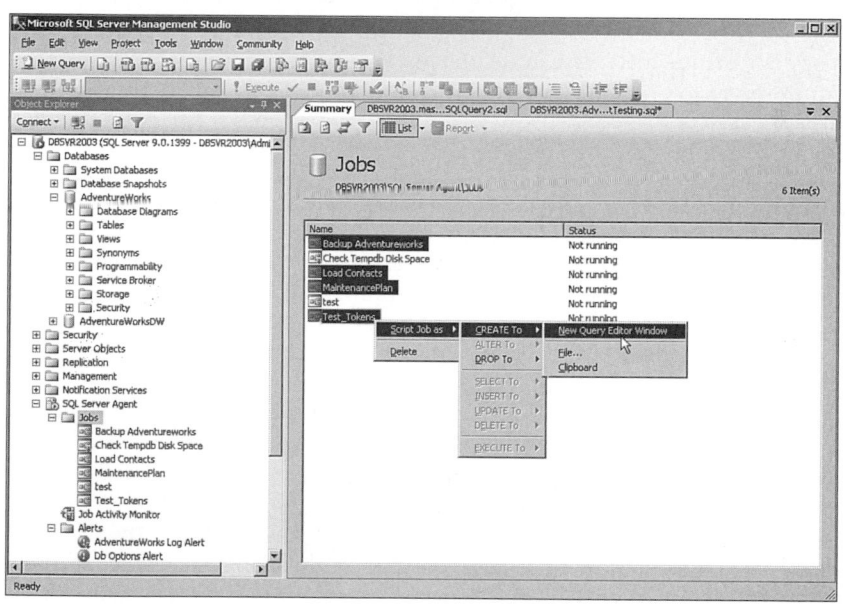

FIGURE 13.21   Script generation for jobs.

NOTE

The ability to selectively script jobs and alerts from the SQL Server 2005 Summary page is an improvement over SQL Server 2000. In SQL Server 2000, scripting of jobs and alerts was limited to one or all of the jobs. In other words, you could script an individual job, or you could script all of the jobs. You did not have the option to selectively choose the objects you wanted to script.

With SQL Server 2005, you can also filter the jobs you want to script by using the filtering capabilities that are available on the Summary page. For example, you can filter on jobs whose names contain specific text. After you filter the jobs, you can script the jobs that are displayed. The filtering options and the ability to selectively script jobs are particularly useful in environments in which many jobs and alerts exist.

Multiserver Job Management

Multiserver job management allows you to centralize the administration of multiple *target* servers on a single *master* server. The master server is a SQL Server instance that contains the job definitions and status information for all of the enlisted target servers. The target servers are SQL Server instances that obtain job information from the master server and continually update the master server with job statistics.

Multiserver job management is beneficial in SQL Server environments in which there are many instances to manage. You can establish jobs, operators, and execution schedules one time on the master server and then deploy them to all the target servers. This promotes consistency across the enterprise and can ease the overall administrative burden. Without multiserver job management, administrative jobs must be established and maintained on each server.

NOTE

By default, SQL Server 2005 utilizes Secure Sockets Layer (SSL) encryption to communicate between servers involved in multiserver job administration. With SSL communication, a certificate must be purchased from a public certification authority. This certificate must be assigned to the SQL Server instance and is used to validate communication between the servers that are involved in multiserver job administration. For a more detailed discussion of SSL encryption see the Books Online topic named "Encrypting Connections to SQL Server."

Service Pack 1 (SP1) for SQL Server 2005 comes with a new registry switch that can be used to control encryption between servers in multiserver job administration. The new registry key is `\HKEY_LOCAL_MACHINE\SOFTWARE\Microsoft\Microsoft SQL Server\`
`<instance_name>\SQLServerAgent\MsxEncryptChannelOptions(REG_DWORD)`. The value for the registry key can be set to 0 to disable encryption, 1 to enable encryption without certificate validation or 2 to enable full SSL encryption and certificate validation. The value of 2 is the default but you can manually edit the registry and change it to one of the other values. Keep in mind that you must use caution when changing any registry setting. Incorrectly editing the registry can cause serious problems on your server.

Creating a Master Server

The first step in creating a multiserver environment involves the creation of a master server. SQL Server 2005 provides the Master Server Wizard, which simplifies this task. You launch the Master Server Wizard by right-clicking the SQL Server Agent node in the

Object Explorer and selecting Multi Server Administration and Make This a Master. The Master Server Wizard then guides you through the creation of an operator to receive multiserver job notifications and allows you to specify the target servers for SQL Server Agent jobs.

Figure 13.22 shows the Master Server Wizard screen that allows you to add information related to the master server's operator. The operator that is created on the master server is named MSXOperator. MSXOperator is the only operator that can receive notifications for multiserver jobs.

FIGURE 13.22   The Master Server Wizard.

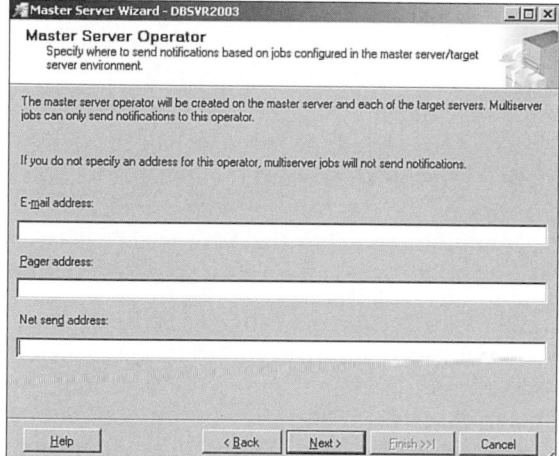

The Master Server Wizard also validates the service accounts that the SQL Server Agent uses on the target servers. These accounts are typically Windows domain accounts that are in the same domain as the master server. The service accounts are important because the target servers utilize Windows security to connect to the master server and download jobs for the SQL Server Agent. The validation process and security considerations are simplified if the master server and target servers are run with the same domain account.

Enlisting Target Servers

The Master Server Wizard allows you to enlist one or more target servers. Enlisting a target server identifies it to the master server and allows the master server to manage the administration of its jobs. You can also enlist additional target servers after the wizard completes. You do this by right-clicking the SQL Server Agent node of the target server, and then selecting Multi Server Administration and then Make This a Target. This launches the Target Server Wizard, which guides you through the addition of another target server. The Target Server Wizard performs some of the same actions as the Master Server Wizard, including the following:

▶ It ensures that the SQL Server versions on the two servers are compatible.

▶ It ensures that the SQL Server Agent on the master server is running.

▶ It ensures that the Agent Startup account has rights to log in as a target server.

▶ It enlists the target server.

Creating Multiserver Jobs

After the master and target servers are set up, you can create jobs on the master server and specify which target servers they should run on. Periodically, the target servers poll the master server. If any jobs defined for them have been scheduled to run since the last polling interval, the target server downloads the jobs and runs them. When a job completes, the target server uploads the job outcome status to the master server.

Event Forwarding

Event forwarding is another multiserver feature that allows a single SQL Server instance to process events for other servers in your SQL Server environment. This involves the designation of an alerts management server that other servers can forward their events to. You enable the alerts management server by right-clicking the SQL Server Agent node and selecting Properties. When the Properties pages appears, you click the Advanced page (see Figure 13.23).

To configure event forwarding, you select the Forward Events to a Different Server option on the Advanced page. You can then select the SQL Server instance you want as the alerts management server by using the Server drop-down. The servers that are shown in the drop-down are those that have been registered in SSMS. If the server you want does not appear in the drop-down, you need to choose Registered Servers from the View menu and ensure that the server is registered.

You can choose to forward all events to the alerts management server or send only a subset of the events. The default is to send all events, but you can restrict the event forwarding to events that are not handled on the source server. You can further limit the messages that are forwarded by specifying the severity level that the message must have in order to be forwarded. For example, you can configure the servers to forward only fatal error messages that have a severity greater than or equal to Level 19. In this scenario, you could define alerts on the alerts management server that respond to these fatal errors and notify operators that specialize in their resolution.

You need to consider a number of trade-offs when using event forwarding. You need to weigh the benefits of central administration and a lack of redundancy against the disadvantages of having a single point of failure and increased network traffic. The available network bandwidth, number of servers involved in event forwarding, and the stability of the alerts management server are some of the key factors you need to think about in making your decision.

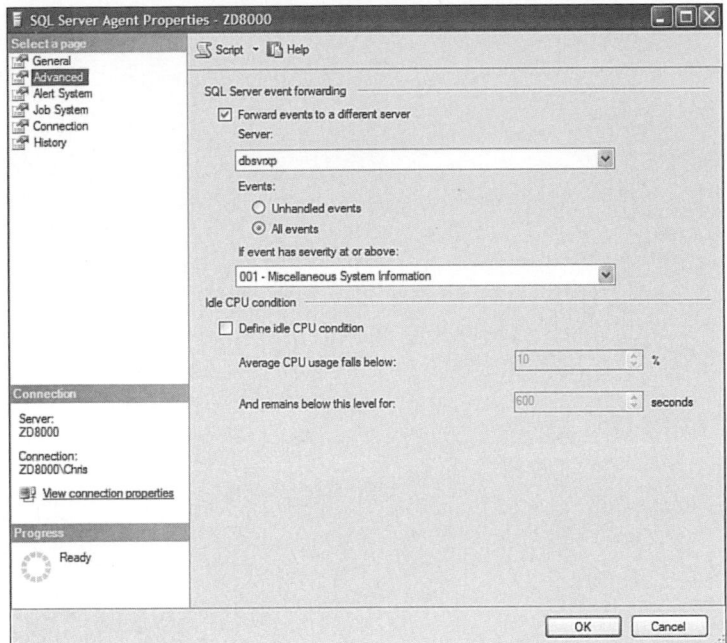

FIGURE 13.23   Configuring event forwarding.

Summary

The SQL Server Agent in SQL Server 2005 delivers a powerful set of tools to make your administrative life easier. It provides automation in the form of jobs, operators, and alerts that help you deliver a consistent and healthy database environment. After you have set up the appropriate automation with the SQL Server Agent, you can rest assured that you have been proactive in managing your environment.

If you work with multiple database servers, you should continue to Chapter 42, "Managing Linked and Remote Servers" (on the CD-ROM). Linked servers and remote servers provide the glue that allows different SQL Server machines to communicate with each other.

CHAPTER 14

SQL Server High Availability

IN THIS CHAPTER

▶ What's New in High Availability

▶ What Is High Availability?

▶ The Fundamentals of HA

▶ Building Solutions with One or More HA Options

▶ Other HA Techniques That Yield Great Results

▶ High Availability from the Windows Server Family Side

With SQL Server 2005, Microsoft has set the bar much higher in its quest to offer a variety of solid high-availability (HA) options. These options, coupled with extensive Windows server family enhancements, provide organizations their first real chance at achieving the mythical "five-nines" (that is, 99.999%) uptime.

Understanding your high-availability requirements is only the first step in implementing a successful high-availability application. Knowing what technical options exist is equally as important. Then, by following a few basic design guidelines, you can match your requirements to the best high-availability technical solution.

This chapter introduces a variety of fundamental HA options—such as redundant hardware configurations, RAID, and MSCS clustering—as well as more high-level options—such as SQL clustering, data replication, and database mirroring—that should lead you to a solid high-availability foundation. Microsoft has slowly been moving in the direction of trying to make SQL Server (and the Windows operating systems) as continuously available as possible for as many of its options as possible. Remember that Microsoft is competing with the UNIX/Linux-based worlds that have offered (and achieved) much higher uptime levels for years. The SQL Server RDBMS engine itself and the surrounding services, such as Analysis Services, Notification Services, and Reporting Services, have all taken big steps toward higher availability.

What's New in High Availability

In general, Microsoft SQL Server 2005 is shifting very strongly to a goal of providing a database engine foundation that can be highly available 7 days a week, 365 days a year. Microsoft's sights are set on being able to achieve five-nines reliability with almost everything it builds. An internal breakthrough that has enabled Microsoft to greatly enhance several new features is called "copy-on-write" technology, which is explored in detail later in this chapter.

Here are a few of the most significant enhancements and new features that have direct or indirect effects on increasing high availability for a SQL Server 2005–based implementation:

- ▶ **Increased number of nodes in a SQL cluster**—You can create a SQL cluster of up to eight nodes on Windows 2003 Data Center and up to four nodes on Windows 2003 Enterprise Edition.

- ▶ **Ability to do unattended cluster setup**—Instead of having to use wizards to set up SQL clustering, you can use the Unattended Cluster Setup mode. This is very useful for fast re-creation or remote creation of SQL clustering configurations.

- ▶ **Full SQL Server 2005 services as cluster managed resources**—All SQL Server 2005 services are cluster aware.

- ▶ **SQL Server 2005 database mirroring**—Database mirroring essentially extends the old log shipping feature of SQL Server 2000 and creates an automatic failover capability to a "hot" standby server. (Chapter 16, "Database Mirroring," covers database mirroring in detail.)

- ▶ **SQL Server 2005 peer-to-peer replication**—a new option of data replication that uses a publisher-to-publisher model (hence peer-to-peer).

- ▶ **SQL Server 2005 fast recovery**—Administrators can reconnect to a recovering database after the transaction log has been rolled forward (and before the rollback processing has finished).

- ▶ **Online restore**—Database administrators can perform a restore operation while the database is still online.

- ▶ **Online indexing**—The online index option allows concurrent modifications (updates, deletes, and inserts) to the underlying table or clustered index data and any associated indexes during index creation time.

- ▶ **Database snapshot**—SQL Server 2005 allows for the generation and use of a read-only, stable view of a database. The database snapshot is created without the overhead of creating a complete copy of the database or having completely redundant storage.

- ▶ **Data partitioning improvements**—Data partitioning has been enhanced with native table and index partitioning, which essentially allow you to manage large tables and indexes at a lower level of granularity.

▶ **Addition of a snapshot isolation level**—A new snapshot isolation (SI) level is being provided at the database level. With SI, users can access the last committed row, using a transactionally consistent view of the database.

▶ **Dedicated administrator connection**—SQL Server 2005 introduces a dedicated administrator connection that administrators can use to access a running server even if the server is locked or otherwise unavailable. This capability enables administrators to troubleshoot problems on a server by executing diagnostic functions or Transact-SQL statements without having to take down the server.

At the operating system level, Microsoft has introduced Virtual Server 2005 to start moving into the realm of virtualization. This will someday (in a few years) allow production systems to run on a completely virtual operating system footprint that will never bring down the physical server.

NOTE

Microsoft has announced that log shipping will be deprecated soon. Although it has been functionally replaced with database mirroring, log shipping remains available in SQL Server 2005.

Keep in mind that Microsoft already has an extensive capability in support of high availability. The new HA features add significant gains to the already feature-rich offering.

What Is High Availability?

The availability continuum depicted in Figure 14.1 shows a general classification of availability based on the amount of downtime an application can tolerate without impacting the business. You would write your service-level agreements (SLAs) to support and try to achieve one of these continuum categories.

Topping the chart is the category extreme availability, so named to indicate that this is the least tolerant category and is essentially a zero (or near zero) downtime requirement (that is, sustained 99.5% to 100% availability). The mythical five-nines falls at the high end of this category. Next is the high availability category, which has a minimal tolerance for downtime (that is, sustained 95% to 99.4% availability). Most "critical" applications would fit into this category of availability need. Then comes the standard availability category, with a more normal type of operation (that is, sustained 83% to 94% availability). The acceptable availability category is for applications that are deemed noncritical to a company's business, such as online employee benefit package self-service applications. These can tolerate much lower availability ranges (sustained 70% to 82% availability) than the more critical services. Finally, the marginal availability category is for nonproduction custom applications, such as marketing mailing label applications, that can tolerate significant downtime (that is, sustained 0% to 69% availability). Again, remember that availability is measured by the planned operation times of the application.

Availability Continuum

	Characteristic	Availability Range
Extreme Availability	Near zero downtime!	(99.5% - 100%)
High Availability	Minimal downtime	(95% - 99.4%)
Standard Availability	With some downtime tolerance	(83% - 94%)
Acceptable Availability	Non-critical Applications	(70% - 82%)
Marginal Availability	Non-production Applications	(up to 69%)

Availability Range describes the percentage of time relative to the "planned" hours of operations

8,760 hours/year | 168 hours/week | 24 hours/day

525,600 minutes/year | 7,200 minutes/week | 1,440 minutes/day

FIGURE 14.1   Availability continuum.

> **NOTE**
>
> Another featured book from Sams Publishing, called *Microsoft SQL Server High Availability*, can take you to the depths of high availability from every angle. This landmark offering provides a complete guide to high availability, beginning with how to gather and understand your HA requirements, assess your HA needs, and completely build out high-availability implementations for the most common business scenarios in the industry. Pick up this book if you are serious about achieving five-nines of reliability.

Achieving the mythical five-nines (that is, a sustained 99.999% availability) falls into the extreme availability category. In general, the computer industry calls this high availability, but we push this type of near-zero downtime requirement into its own extreme category, all by itself. Most applications can only dream about this level of availability because of the costs involved, the high level of operational support required, the specialized hardware that must be in place, and many other extreme factors.

The Fundamentals of HA

Every minute of downtime you have today translates into losses that you cannot well afford. You must fully understand how the hardware and software components work together and how, if one component fails, the others will be affected. High availability of an application is a function of all the components together, not just one by itself. Therefore, the best approach for moving into supporting high availability is to work on shoring up the basic foundation components of hardware, backup/recovery, operating system upgrading, ample vendor agreements, sufficient training, extensive quality assurance/testing, rigorous standards and procedures, and some overall risk-mitigating strategies, such as spreading out critical applications over multiple servers. By addressing these first, you add a significant amount of stability and high-availability capability across your hardware/system stack. In other words, you are moving up to a necessary level before you completely jump into a particular high-availability solution. If you do nothing further from this point, you will have already achieved a portion of your high availability goals.

Hardware

You need to start by addressing your basic hardware issues for high availability and fault tolerance. This includes redundant power supplies, UPS systems, redundant network connections, and ECC memory (error correcting). Also available are "hot-swappable" components, such as disks, CPUs, and memory. In addition, most servers are now using multiple CPUs, fault-tolerant disk systems such as RAID, mirrored disks, storage area networks (SANs), Network Attached Storage (NAS), redundant fans, and so on.

Cost may drive the full extent of what you choose to build out. However, you should start with the following:

▶ Redundant power supplies (and UPSs)

▶ Redundant fan systems

▶ Fault-tolerant disks, such as RAID (1 through 10), preferably "hot swappable"

▶ ECC memory

▶ Redundant Ethernet connections

Backup

After you consider hardware, you need to look at the basic techniques and frequency of your disk backups and database backups. For many companies, the backup plan isn't what it needs to be to guarantee recoverability and even the basic level of high availability. At many sites, database backups are not being run, are corrupted, or aren't even considered necessary. You would be shocked by the list of Fortune 1000 companies where this occurs.

Operating System

You need to make sure that all upgrades to your OS are applied and also that the configuration of all options is correct. This includes making sure you have antivirus software installed (if applicable), along with the appropriate firewalls for external-facing systems.

Vendor Agreements

Vendor agreements come in the form of software licenses, software support agreements, hardware service agreements, and both hardware and software service-level agreements. Essentially, you are trying to make sure you can get all software upgrades and patches for your OS and for your application software at any time, as well as get software support, hardware support agreements, and both software and hardware SLAs in place to guarantee a level of service within a defined period of time.

Training

Training is multifaceted, in that it can be for software developers to guarantee that the code they write is optimal, for system administrators who need to administer applications, and even for end users themselves to make sure they use the system correctly. All these types of training play into the ultimate goal of achieving high availability.

Quality Assurance

Testing as much as possible and doing it in a very formal way is a great way to guarantee a system's availability. Dozens of studies over the years have clearly shown that the more thoroughly you test (and the more formal your QA procedures), the fewer software problems you will have. Many companies foolishly skimp on testing, which has a huge impact on system reliability and availability.

Standards/Procedures

Standards and procedures are interlaced tightly with training and QA. Coding standards, code walkthroughs, naming standards, formal system development life cycles, protection of tables from being dropped, use of governors, and so on all contribute to more stable and potentially more highly available systems.

Server Instance Isolation

By design, you may want to isolate applications (such as SQL Server's applications and their databases) away from each other in order to mitigate the risk of such an application causing another to fail.

Plain and simple, you should never put applications in each other's way if you don't have to. The only things that might force you to load up a single server with all your applications would be expensive licensing costs for each server's software, and perhaps hardware scarcity (strict limitations to the number of servers available for all applications). A classic example of this is when a company loads up a single SQL Server instance with between two and eight applications and their associated databases. The problem is that the applications are sharing memory, CPUs, and internal work areas, such as `tempdb`. Figure 14.2 shows a loaded-up SQL Server instance that is being asked to service four major applications (Appl 1 DB through Appl 4 DB).

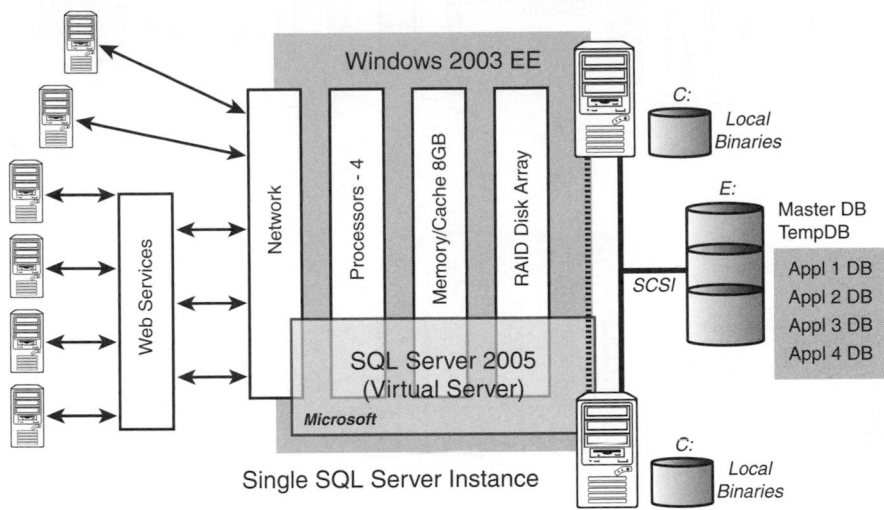

FIGURE 14.2   High risk: Many applications sharing a single SQL Server 2005 instance.

This single SQL Server instance in Figure 14.2 is sharing memory (cache) and critical internal working areas, such as `tempdb`, with all four major applications. Everything runs along fine until one of these applications submits a runaway query and all other applications being serviced by that SQL Server instance come to a grinding halt. Most of this built-in risk could be avoided by simply putting each application (or perhaps two applications) onto their own SQL Server instance, as shown in Figure 14.3. This fundamental design approach greatly reduces the risk of one application affecting another.

Many companies make this very fundamental error. The trouble is that they keep adding new applications to their existing server instance without a full understanding of the shared resources that underpin the environment. It is often too late when they finally realize that they are hurting themselves "by design." You have now been given proper warning of the risks. If other factors, such as cost or hardware availability, dictate otherwise, then at least it is a calculated risk that is entered into knowingly (and is properly documented as well).

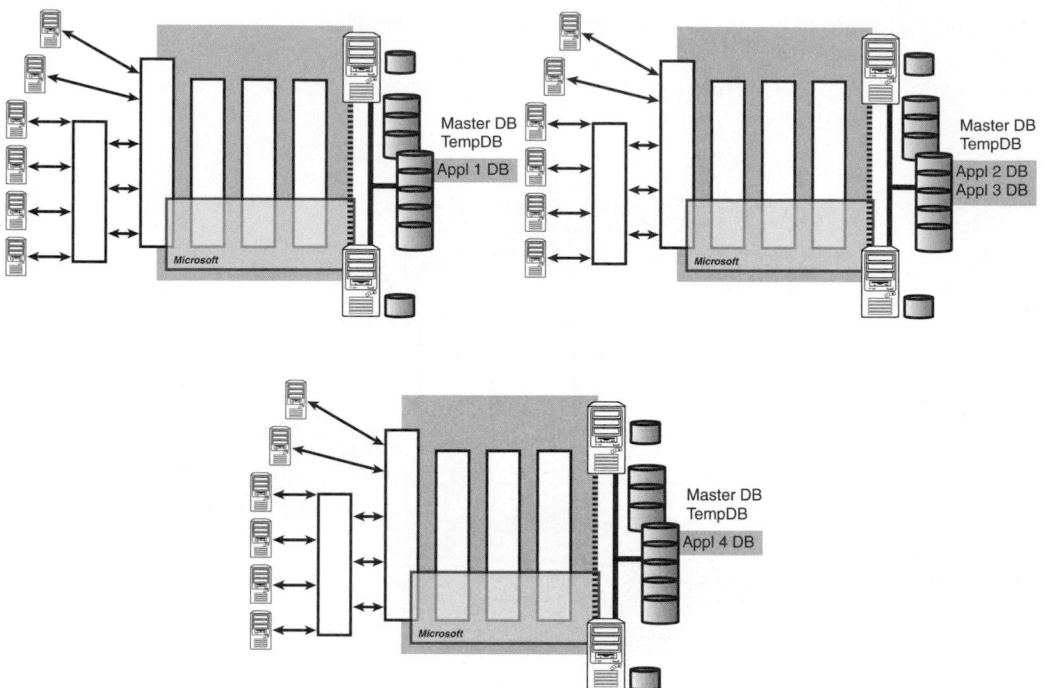

FIGURE 14.3   Mitigated risk: Isolating critical applications away from each other.

Building Solutions with One or More HA Options

When you have the fundamental foundation in place, as described in the preceding section, you can move on to building a tailored software-driven high-availability solution. Which HA option(s) you should be using really depends on your HA requirements. The following high-availability options are used both individually and, very often, together to achieve different levels of HA:

- ▶ Microsoft Cluster Services (non–SQL Server based)

- ▶ SQL clustering

- ▶ Data replication (including peer-to-peer configurations)

- ▶ Log shipping

- ▶ Database mirroring

All these options are readily available "out of the box" from Microsoft, from the Windows Server family of products and from Microsoft SQL Server 2005.

It is important to understand that some of these options can be used together, but not all go together. For example, you might use Microsoft Cluster Services (MSCS) along with

Microsoft SQL Server 2005's SQL Clustering to implement the SQL clustering database configuration, whereas, you wouldn't necessarily need to use MSCS with database mirroring.

Microsoft Cluster Services (MSCS)

MSCS could actually be considered a part of the basic HA foundation components described earlier, except that it's possible to build a high-availability system without it (for example, a system that uses numerous redundant hardware components and disk mirroring or RAID for its disk subsystem). Microsoft has made MSCS the cornerstone of its clustering capabilities, and MSCS is utilized by applications that are cluster enabled. A prime example of a cluster-enabled technology is Microsoft SQL Server 2005.

What is MSCS? MSCS is the advanced Windows operating system (OS) configuration that defines and manages between two and eight servers as "nodes" in a cluster. These nodes are aware of each other and can be set up to take over cluster-aware applications from any node that fails (for example, a failed server). This cluster configuration also shares and controls one or more disk subsystems as part of its high-availability capability. Figure 14.4 illustrates a basic two-node MSCS configuration.

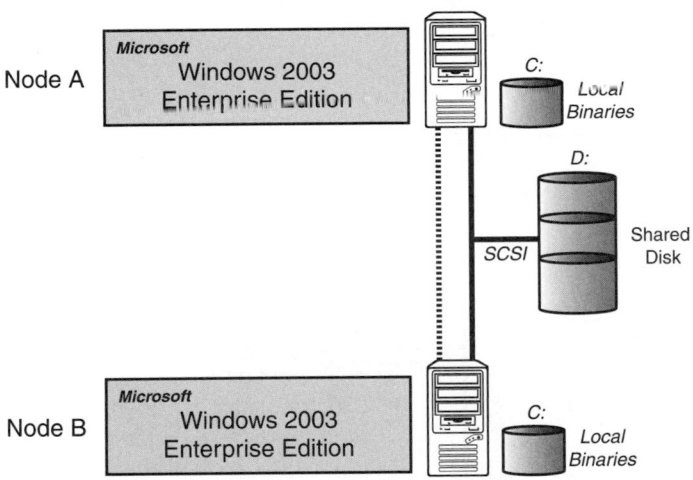

FIGURE 14.4   Basic two-node MSCS configuration.

MSCS is available only with Microsoft Windows Enterprise Edition, Advanced Server, and Data Center operating system products. Don't be alarmed, though. If you are looking at a high-availability system to begin with, there is a great probability that your applications are already running with these enterprise-level OS versions.

MSCS can be set up in an active/passive or active/active mode. Essentially, in an active/passive mode, one server sits idle (that is, is passive) while the other is doing the work (that is, is active). If the active server fails, the passive one takes over the shared disk and the cluster-aware applications instantaneously.

SQL Clustering

If you want a SQL Server instance to be clustered for high availability, you are essentially asking that this SQL Server instance (and the database) be completely resilient to a server failure and completely available to the application without the end user ever even noticing that there was a failure (or at least with minimal interruption). Microsoft provides this capability through the SQL Clustering option. SQL Clustering is built on top of MSCS for its underlying detection of a failed server and for its availability of the databases on the shared disk (which is controlled by MSCS). SQL Server is said to be a "cluster-aware/ enabled" technology.

Creating a SQL Server instance that is clustered is done by actually creating a virtual SQL Server instance that is known to the application (the constant in the equation) and then two physical SQL Server instances that share one set of databases. In an active/passive configuration, only one SQL Server instance is active at a time and just goes along and does its work. If that active server fails (and with it, the physical SQL Server instance), the passive server (and the physical SQL Server instance on that server) simply takes over instantaneously. This is possible because MSCS also controls the shared disk where the databases are. The end user (and application) pretty much never know which physical SQL Server instance they are on or whether one failed. Figure 14.5 illustrates a typical SQL Clustering configuration that is built on top of MSCS.

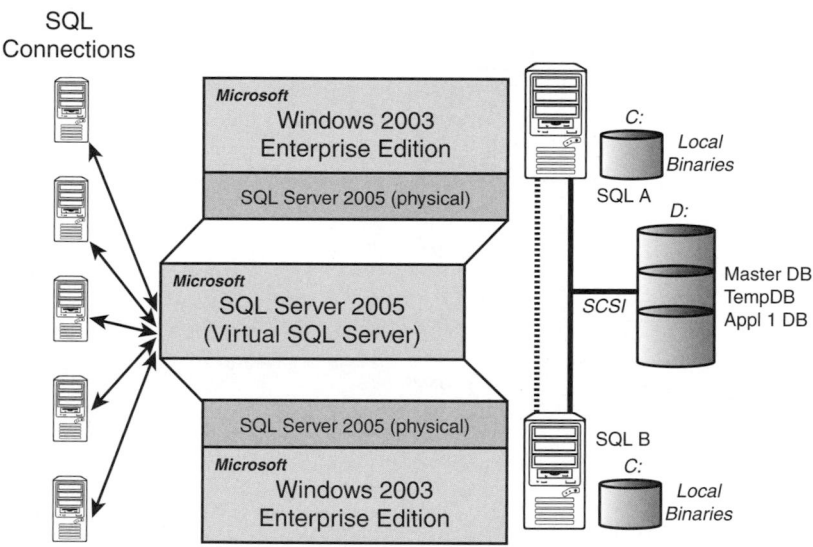

FIGURE 14.5   Basic SQL Clustering two-node configuration (active/passive).

Setup and management of this type of configuration is much easier than you might think. More and more, SQL Clustering is the method chosen for most high-availability solutions. Later in this chapter, you will see that other methods may also be viable for achieving high availability (based on the application's HA requirements). SQL Server Clustering is covered in detail in Chapter 17, "SQL Server Clustering."

Extending the clustering model to include Network Load Balancing (NLB) pushes this particular solution even further into higher availability—from client traffic high availability to back-end SQL Server high availability. Figure 14.6 shows a four-host NLB cluster architecture acting as a virtual server to handle the network traffic coupled with a two-node SQL cluster on the back end. This setup is resilient from top to bottom.

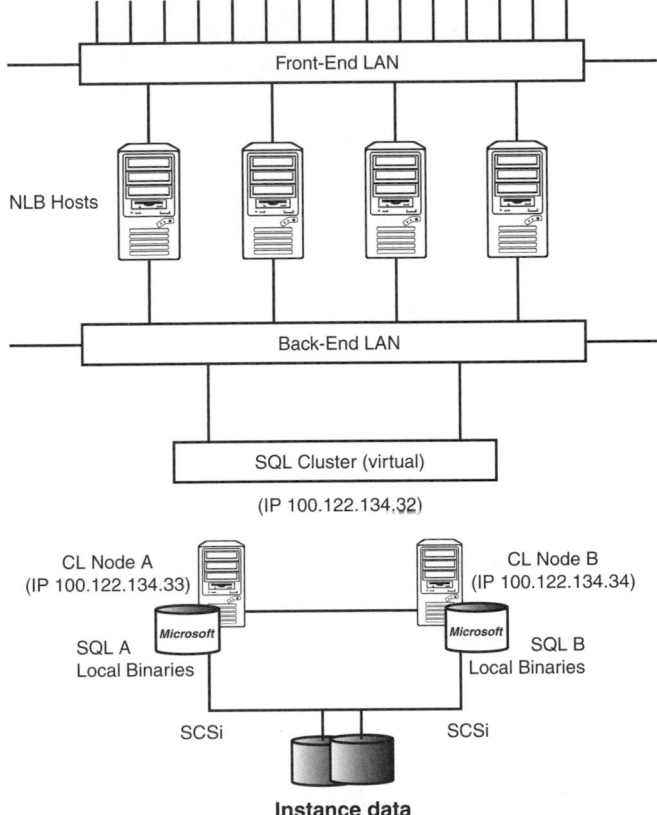

FIGURE 14.6   An NLB host cluster with a two-node server cluster.

The four NLB hosts work together, distributing the work efficiently. NLB automatically detects the failure of a server and repartitions client traffic among the remaining servers.

The following are a few enhancements to SQL Clustering in SQL Server 2005:

▶ **Full SQL Server 2005 Services as cluster-managed resources**—All SQL Server 2005 services, including the following, are cluster aware:

    ▶ SQL Server DBMS engine

    ▶ SQL Server Agent

    ▶ SQL Server Full-Text Search

- ▶ Analysis Services

- ▶ Notification Services

- ▶ Reporting Services

- ▶ Service Broker

Now, you can extend this fault-tolerant solution to embrace more SQL Server instances and *all* of SQL Server's related services. This is a big deal because things like Analysis Services previously had to be handled with separate techniques to achieve near high availability. Not anymore; each SQL Server service is now cluster aware.

Data Replication

The next technology option that can be utilized to achieve high availability is data replication. Originally, data replication was created to offload processing from a very busy server (such as an OLTP application that must also support a big reporting workload) or to geographically distribute data for different, very distinct user bases (such as worldwide product ordering applications). As data replication (transactional replication) became more stable and reliable, it started to be used to create "warm" (almost "hot") standby SQL Servers that could also be used to fulfill basic reporting needs. If the primary server ever failed, the reporting users would still be able to work (hence a higher degree of availability achieved for them), and the replicated reporting database could be used as a substitute for the primary server, if needed (hence a warm-standby SQL Server). When doing transactional replication in the "instantaneous replication" mode, all data changes were replicated to the replicate servers extremely quickly. With SQL Server 2000, updating subscribers allowed for even greater distribution of the workload and, overall, increased the availability of the primary data and distributed the update load across the replication topology. There are plenty of issues and complications involved in using the updating subscribers approach (for example, conflict handlers, queues).

With SQL Server 2005, Microsoft introduced peer-to-peer replication, which is not a publisher/subscription model but a publisher-to-publisher model (hence peer-to-peer). It is a lot easier to configure and manage than other replication topologies, but it still has its nuances to deal with. This peer-to-peer model allows excellent availability for this data and great distribution of workload along geographic (or other) lines. This may fit some companies' availability requirements and also fulfill their distributed reporting requirements as well.

The top of Figure 14.7 shows a typical SQL data replication configuration of a central publisher/subscriber using continuous transactional replication. This can serve as a basis for high availability and also fulfills a reporting server requirement at the same time. The bottom of Figure 14.7 shows a typical peer-to-peer continuous transactional replication model that is also viable.

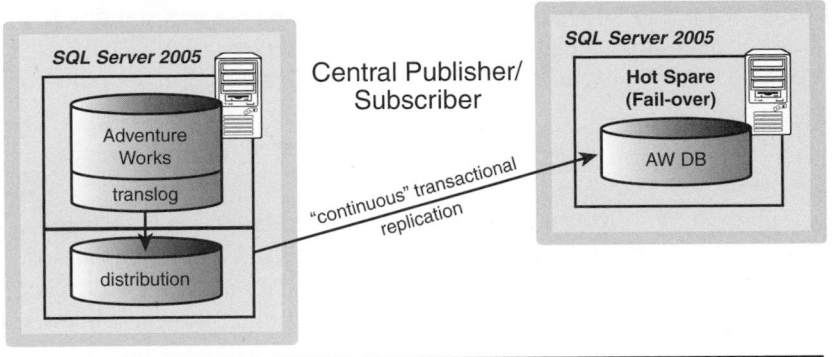

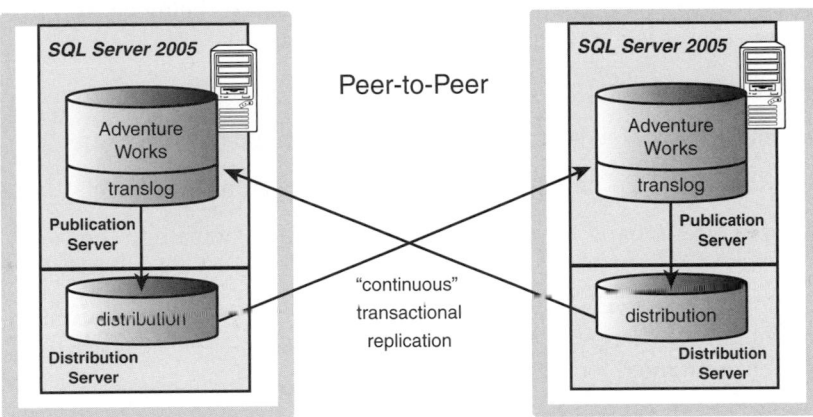

FIGURE 14.7   Basic data replication configurations for HA.

The downside of peer-to-peer replication comes into play if ever the subscriber (or the other peer) needs to become the primary server (that is, take over the work from the original server). This takes a bit of administration that is *not* transparent to the end user. Connection strings have to be changed, ODBC data sources need to be updated, and so on. But this may take minutes as opposed to hours of database recovery time, and it may well be tolerable to end users. Peer-to-peer configurations handles recovery a bit better in that much of the workload is already distributed to either of the nodes. So, at most, only part of the user base will be affected if one node goes down. Those users can easily be redirected to the other node (peer), with the same type of connection changes described earlier.

With either the publisher/subscriber or peer-to-peer replication approach, there is a risk of not having all the transactions from the publishing server. However, often, a company is willing to live with this small risk in favor of availability. Remember that a replicated database is an approximate image of the primary database (up to the point of the last update that was successfully distributed), which makes it very attractive as a warm standby. For publishing databases that are primarily read-only, using a warm standby is a great way to distribute the load and mitigate the risk of any one server failing. Chapter 15, "Replication," covers data replication and all the various implementation scenarios that you might ever need to use.

Log Shipping

Another, more direct, method of creating a completely redundant database image is to utilize log shipping. Microsoft "certifies" log shipping as a method of creating an "almost hot" spare. Some folks even use log shipping as an alternative to data replication (it has been referred to as "the poor man's data replication"). There's just one problem: Microsoft has formally announced that log shipping (as we know and love it) will be deprecated in the near future. The reasons are many, but the primary one it that is being replaced by database mirroring (referred to as *real-time log shipping*, when it was first being conceived). If you still want to use log shipping, it is perfectly viable—for now.

Log shipping does three primary things:

▶ Makes an exact image copy of a database on one server from a database dump

▶ Creates a copy of that database on one or more other servers from that dump

▶ Continuously applies transaction log dumps from the original database to the copy

In other words, log shipping effectively replicates the data of one server to one or more other servers via transaction log dumps. Figure 14.8 shows a source/destination SQL Server pair that has been configured for log shipping.

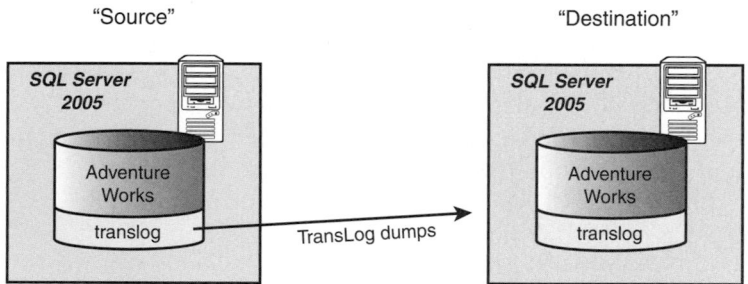

FIGURE 14.8   Log shipping in support of high availability.

Log shipping is a great solution when you have to create one or more failover servers. It turns out that, to some degree, log shipping fits the requirement of creating a read-only subscriber as well. The following are the gating factors for using log shipping as a method of creating and maintaining a redundant database image:

▶ Data latency lag is the time that exists between the transaction log dumps on the source database and when these dumps get applied to the destination databases.

▶ Sources and destinations must be the same SQL Server version.

▶ Data is read-only on the destination SQL Server until the log shipping pairing is broken (as it should be to guarantee that the transaction logs can be applied to the destination SQL Server).

The data latency restriction might quickly disqualify log shipping as an instantaneous high-availability solution (if you need rapid availability of the failover server). However, log shipping might be adequate for certain situations. If a failure ever occurs on the primary SQL Server, a destination SQL Server that was created and maintained via log shipping can be swapped into use fairly quickly. The destination SQL Server would contain exactly what was on the source SQL Server (right down to every user ID, table, index, and file allocation map, except for any changes to the source database that occurred after the last log dump was applied). This directly achieves a level of high availability. It is still not completely transparent, though, because the SQL Server instance names are different, and the end user may be required to log in again to the new server instance.

> **NOTE**
>
> Log shipping is not covered further in this book because of its limited life going forward. The *SQL Server 2000 Unleashed* version of this book covers log shipping in extensive detail. Remember that log shipping is not data replication and uses a completely different technology than data replication.

Database Mirroring

The newest failover option with SQL Server is database mirroring. Database mirroring essentially extends the old log shipping feature of SQL Server and creates an automatic failover capability to a "hot" standby server. Database mirroring is being billed as creating a fault-tolerant database that is an "instant" standby (ready for use in less than three seconds).

At the heart of database mirroring is the new "copy-on-write" technology. Copy-on-write means that transactional changes are shipped to another server as the logs are written. All logged changes to the database instance become immediately available for copying to another location. Database mirroring utilizes a witness server as well as client components to insulate the client applications from any knowledge of a server failure.

Chapter 16 dives much more deeply into database mirroring setup, configuration, and architecture. It is sufficient to say here that with database mirroring, an application can possibly be failed over to the mirrored database in three seconds or less, with nearly complete client transparency. You can also leverage this mirrored database for offloading reporting by creating a snapshot off of it. Again, that is covered in Chapter 16.

14

Combining Failover with Scale-Out Options

SQL Server 2005 pushes combinations of options to achieve higher availability levels. A prime example of this would be to combine data replication with database mirroring to provide maximum availability of data, scalability to users, and fault tolerance via failover, potentially at each node in the replication topology. By starting with the publisher and perhaps the distributor, you make them both database mirror failover configurations.

Building up a combination of both options together is essentially the best of both worlds: the super-low latency of database mirroring for fault-tolerance and high availability (and scalability) of data through replication.

Other HA Techniques That Yield Great Results

Microsoft has been revisiting (and architecting) several operations that previously required a table or whole database to be offline. For several critical database operations (such as recovery operations, restores, indexing, and others), Microsoft has either made the data in the database available earlier in the execution of an operation or made the data in the database completely available simultaneously with the operation. The following primary areas are now addressed:

▶ **Fast recovery**—This is a new faster recovery option that directly improves the availability of SQL Server databases. Administrators can reconnect to a recovering database after the transaction log has been rolled forward (and before the rollback processing has finished). Figure 14.9 illustrates how Microsoft makes a SQL Server 2005 database available earlier than would SQL Server 2000.

In particular, a database in SQL Server 2005 becomes available when committed transaction log entries are rolled forward (termed "redo") and no longer have to wait for the "in flight" transactions to be rolled back (termed "undo").

▶ **Online restore**—Now, database administrators can perform a restore operation while the database is still online. Online restore improves the availability of SQL Server because only the data being restored is unavailable; the rest of the database remains online and available to users. In addition, the granularity of the restore has changed to be at the filegroup level and even at the page level, if needed. The remainder of the database remains available.

▶ **Online indexing**—Concurrent modifications (updates, deletes, and inserts) to the underlying table or clustered index data and any associated indexes can now be done during index creation time. For example, while a clustered index is being rebuilt, you can continue to make updates to the underlying data and perform queries against the data.

▶ **Database snapshots**—You can now create a read-only, stable view of a database. A database snapshot is created without the overhead of creating a complete copy of the database or having completely redundant storage. A database snapshot is simply a reference point of the pages used in the database (that is defined in the system catalog). When pages are updated, a new page chain is started that contains the data pages changed since the database snapshot was taken, as illustrated in Figure 14.10.

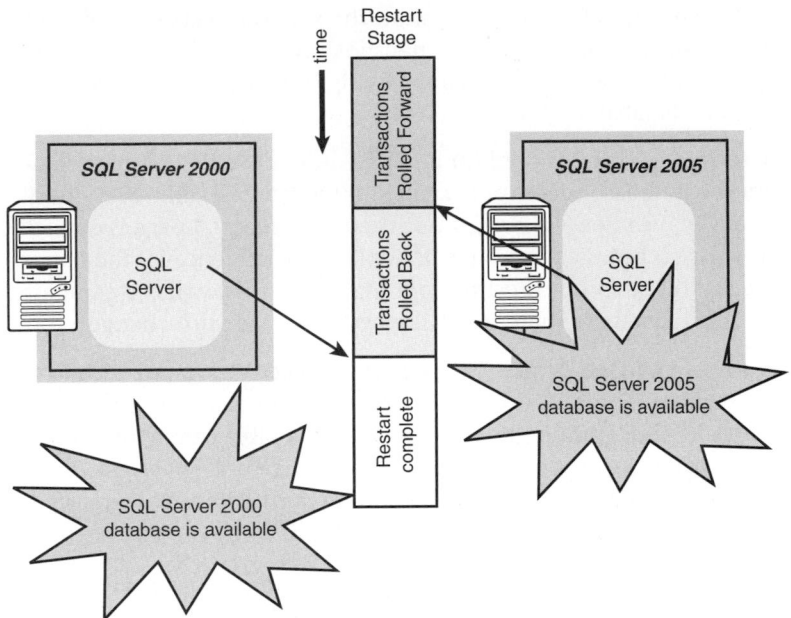

FIGURE 14.9   SQL Server 2005 databases become available earlier than databases with SQL Server 2000 database recovery (fast recovery).

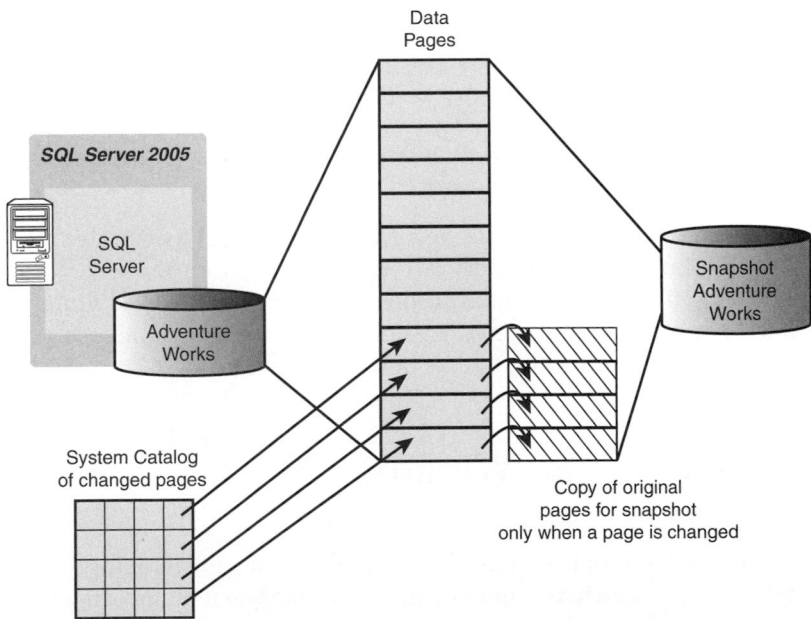

FIGURE 14.10   Database snapshots and the original database share pages and are managed within the system catalog of SQL Server 2005.

As the original database diverges from the snapshot, the snapshot gets its own copy of original pages when they are modified. The snapshot can even be used to recover an accidental change to a database by simply reapplying the pages from the snapshot back to the original database.

The copy-on-write technology that is used for database mirroring also enables database snapshots. When a database snapshot is created on a database, all writes check the system catalog of "changed pages" first; if not there, the original page is copied (using the copy-on-write technique) and is put in a place for reference by the database snapshot (because this snapshot must be kept intact). In this way, the database snapshot and the original database share the data pages that have not changed.

▶ **Data partitioning improvements**—Data partitioning has been enhanced with native table and index partitioning. It essentially allows you to manage large tables and indexes at a lower level of granularity. In other words, a table can be defined that identifies distinct partitions (such as by date or by a range of key values). This effectively defines a group of data rows that are unique to a partition. These partitions can be taken offline, restored, or loaded independently while the rest of the table is available.

▶ **Addition of a snapshot isolation level**—This new snapshot isolation (SI) level is a database level capability that allow users can access the last committed row, using a transactionally consistent view of the database. This capability provides improved scalability and availability by not blocking data access of this previously unavailable data state. This new isolation level essentially allows data reading requests to see the last committed version of data rows, even if they are currently being updated as part of a transaction (for example, they see the rows as they were at the start of the transaction without being blocked by the writers, and the writers are not blocked by readers as the readers do not lock the data). This new isolation level is probably best used for databases that are read-mostly (with few writes/updates) due to the potential overhead in maintaining this isolation level.

▶ **Dedicated administrator connection**—This new feature introduces a dedicated administrator connection that administrators can use to access a running server even if the server is locked or otherwise unavailable. This capability enables administrators to troubleshoot problems on a server by executing diagnostic functions or Transact-SQL statements without having to take down the server.

High Availability from the Windows Server Family Side

To enhance system uptimes, there have been numerous system architecture enhancements in Windows 2000 and 2003, such as improved memory management and driver verification, that directly reduce unplanned downtime. New file protection capabilities prevent new software installations from replacing essential system files and causing failures. In addition, device driver signatures identify drivers that may destabilize a system. And, perhaps another major step towards stabilization is the usage of virtual servers.

Microsoft Virtual Server 2005

Virtual Server 2005 is much more cost-effective virtual machine solution designed on top of Windows Server 2003 to increase operational efficiency in software testing and development, application migration, and server consolidation scenarios. Virtual Server 2005 is designed to increase hardware efficiency and help boost administrator productivity, and it is a key Microsoft deliverable toward the Dynamic Systems Initiative (eliminating reboots of servers—which directly affects downtime!). As shown in Figure 14.11, the host operating system—Windows Server 2003 in this case—manages the host system (at the bottom of the stack).

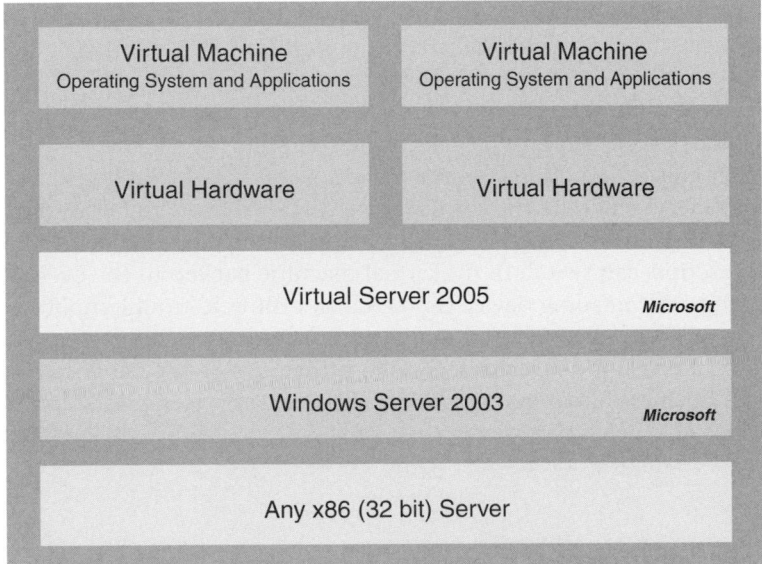

FIGURE 14.11   Microsoft Virtual Server 2005 server architecture.

Virtual Server 2005 provides a Virtual Machine Monitor (VMM) virtualization layer that manages virtual machines and provides the software infrastructure for hardware emulation. As you move up the stack, each virtual machine consists of a set of virtualized devices, the virtual hardware for each virtual machine.

A guest operating system and applications run in the virtual machine—unaware, for example, that the network adapter they interact with through Virtual Server is only a software simulation of a physical Ethernet device. When a guest operating system is running, the special-purpose VMM kernel takes mediated control over the CPU and hardware during virtual machine operations, creating an isolated environment in which the guest operating system and applications run close to the hardware at the highest possible performance.

Virtual Server 2005 is a multithreaded application that runs as a system service, with each virtual machine running in its own thread of execution; I/O occurs in child threads. Virtual Server derives two core functions from the host operating system: The underlying host operating system kernel schedules CPU resources, and the device drivers of the host operating system provide access to system devices. The Virtual Server VMM provides the software infrastructure to create virtual machines, manage instances, and interact with guest operating systems. An often discussed example of leveraging Virtual Server 2005 capabilities would be to use it in conjunction with a disaster recovery implementation.

Virtual Server 2005 and Disaster Recovery

Virtual Server 2005 enables a form of server consolidation for disaster recovery. Rather than maintaining redundancy with costly physical servers, customers can use Virtual Server 2005 to back up their mission-critical functionality in a cost-effective way by means of virtual machines. The Virtual Machine Monitor (VMM) and Virtual Hard Disk (VHD) technologies in Virtual Server 2005, coupled with the comprehensive COM API, can be used to create similar failover functionality as standard, hardware-driven disaster recovery solutions. Customers can then use the Virtual Server COM API to script periodic duplication of physical hard disks containing vital business applications to virtual machine VHDs. Additional scripts can switch to the virtual machine backup in the event of catastrophic failure. In this way, a failing device can be taken offline to troubleshoot, or the application or database can be moved to another physical or virtual machine. Moreover, because VHDs are a core Virtual Server technology, they can be used as a disaster recovery agent, wherein business functionality and data can be easily archived, duplicated, or moved to other physical machines.

Summary

As you come to completely understand and assess your application's high-availability requirements, you can create a matching high-availability solution that will serve you well for years to come. The crux of high availability is laying a fundamentally sound foundation that you can count on when failures occur; then, when failures do occur, determining how much data loss you can tolerate, how much downtime is possible, and what the downtime is costing you.

The overall future seems to be improving greatly in all the basic areas of your Microsoft platform foot print including:

- ▶ Cheaper and more reliable hardware components that are highly swappable

- ▶ The advent of virtual server capabilities (with Windows Virtual Server 2005) to insulate software failures from affecting hardware

- ▶ Enhancements that Microsoft is making to SQL Server 2005 that address availability

The critical enhancements to the cornerstone availability capabilities of SQL Clustering will help this fault-tolerant architecture grow more reliable for years to come. The big bonuses come with the new features of database mirroring as another fault-tolerant solution at the database level and the new database snapshots feature to make data more available to more users more quickly than the older method of log shipping.

To top it all off, Microsoft is making great strides in the areas of online maintenance operations (online restores, online index creates, and so on) and leaping into the realm of one or more virtual server machines (with Virtual Server 2005) that will not bring down a physical server that houses them (which is very UNIX-like).

Chapter 15 delves into the complexities of the major data replication options available with SQL Server 2005.

CHAPTER 15

Replication

There is no such thing as a typical configuration or application anymore. Companies now have to support numerous hardware and software configurations in multitiered, distributed environments. These diverse configurations and applications (and users of the applications) come in all sizes and shapes. And, of course, you need a way to deal with varied data access requirements for these different physical locations; these remote or mobile users over a local area network, wide area network, wireless connections, and dial-up connections; and any needs over the Internet. Microsoft's data replication facility allows for a great breadth of capability to deal with many of these demands. However, to build a proper data replication implementation that meets many of these user requirements, you must have a thorough understanding of the business requirements and the technical capabilities of data replication. Data replication is a set of technologies for storing and forwarding data and database objects from one database to another and then synchronizing this data between databases to maintain consistency. With SQL Server 2005, the data replication feature set offers numerous improvements in manageability, availability, programmability, mobility, scalability, and performance.

This chapter does the following:

- ▶ Helps you understand what data replication is.

- ▶ Shows you how to understand and analyze user requirements of data.

- ▶ Allows you to choose which replication configuration best meets these requirements (if any).

- ▶ Demonstrates how to implement a replication configuration.

- ▶ Describes how to administer and monitor a data replication implementation.

IN THIS CHAPTER

- ▶ What's New in Data Replication
- ▶ What Is Replication?
- ▶ The Publisher, Distributor, and Subscriber Metaphor
- ▶ Replication Scenarios
- ▶ Subscriptions
- ▶ Replication Agents
- ▶ Planning for SQL Server Data Replication
- ▶ SQL Server Replication Types
- ▶ Basing the Replication Design on User Requirements
- ▶ Setting Up Replication
- ▶ Scripting Replication
- ▶ Monitoring Replication

What's New in Data Replication

Much of what's new for Microsoft SQL Server data replication revolves around simplifying setup, administration, and monitoring of a data replication topology. This is the result of years of practical experience and thousands of production replication implementations around the globe. The overall data replication approach that Microsoft has developed (since its inception back in SQL Server 6.5 days) has been so solid that competitors, such as Oracle (with its Oracle Streams technology), have tried to mimic this architectural approach.

Among many others, the following are some of the new replications features and enhancements that make SQL Server 2005 data replication one of the best data distributions tools on the market:

▶ **Tracer tokens**—A token (that is, a small amount of data) is inserted into the publisher and replicated to subscribers. Statistics are gathered as the tracer token moves through the system.

▶ **Parallel snapshot preparation**—Parallel snapshot preparation involves processing of multiple articles while scripting schema or bulk copying data within the Snapshot Agent, allowing snapshot preparation to occur with greater speed and efficiency.

▶ **Initializing a transactional subscription from a backup**—Setting up replication between databases that initially contain large volumes of data can be time-consuming and require large amounts of storage. SQL Server 2005 provides a new publication option that allows any backup taken after the creation of a transactional publication to be restored at the subscriber rather than through the use of a snapshot to initialize the subscription.

▶ **Improved identity range management**—Identity range management has been improved: For transactional replication, identity columns can be replicated as identity columns rather than as int data types.

▶ **New Replication Monitor**—Replication Monitor has been completely redesigned for SQL Server 2005. It now allows you to monitor the overall health of a replication topology, providing detailed information about the status and performance of publications and subscriptions.

▶ **Replication security enhancements**—The replication security model has changed, allowing more control over the accounts under which replication agents run.

▶ **Simplification of the user interface**—Replication wizards and dialog boxes have been redesigned for SQL Server 2005 to simplify the setup of a replication topology. There are now 40% fewer wizard dialogs.

▶ **Scripting integrated into the wizards**—You can pretty much completely script replication setup or breakdown during or after wizard executions.

▶ **Replication of schema changes**—A much broader range of schema changes can be replicated without the use of special stored procedures. DDL statements are issued at the publisher and are automatically propagated to all subscribers.

▶ **Resumable snapshot delivery**—Improvements have been made to snapshot generation and application, including the automatic resumption of snapshots interrupted
during delivery.

▶ **Peer-to-peer transactional replication**—A new peer-to-peer model has been introduced that allows replication between identical participants in the topology (a
master/master or symmetric publisher concept).

▶ **Logical record replication**—By default, merge replication processes change on a
row-by-row basis. The logical records feature allows merge replication to treat a set of
related rows (such as a parent row and its child rows) as a single unit of work.

▶ **Heterogeneous replication**—Enhancements have been made for publishing data
from an Oracle database with transactional and snapshot replication and improved
support for many non–SQL Server subscribers.

▶ **Replication mobility**—Merge replication provides the ability to replicate data over
HTTPS with the web synchronization option, which is useful for synchronizing data
from mobile users over the Internet or synchronizing data between Microsoft SQL
Server databases across a corporate firewall.

Many of these terms and references might be new or foreign to you now, but they are all
explained in this chapter. At the end of this chapter, when you review these new features,
you'll be able to appreciate much more readily their significance.

What Is Replication?

Long before you ever start setting up and using SQL Server data replication, you need to
have a solid grasp of what data replication is and how it can be used to meet your
company's needs. In its classic definition, data replication is based on the "store-and-
forward" data distribution model, as shown in Figure 15.1. In other words, data that is
stored in one location (inserted) is automatically forwarded to one or more distributed
locations.

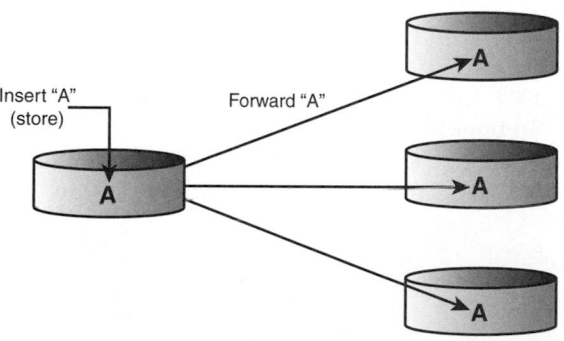

FIGURE 15.1   The store-and-forward data distribution model.

Of course, the data distribution model addresses all the other complexities of updates, deletes, data latency, autonomy, and so on. It is this data distribution model that Microsoft's data replication facility serves to implement. It has come a long way since the early days of Microsoft SQL Server replication (earlier than 6.5) and is now easily categorized as "production worthy." Numerous worldwide data replication scenarios have been implemented for some of the biggest companies in Silicon Valley without a hitch. These scenarios fall into four typical areas:

▸ You may need to deliver data to different locations to eliminate network traffic and unnecessary loads on a single server (for example, when you need to isolate reporting activity away from your online transaction processing).

▸ You might need to move data off a single server onto several other servers to provide for high availability and decentralization of data (or partitioning of data). This might be the basis of serving customer call centers around the globe.

▸ You might have regional ownership of data (for example, customers and their orders). In this case, it is possible to set up data replication to replicate data bidirectionally from two or more publishers of the same data.

▸ You could be replicating all data on a server to another server (that is, a failover server) so that if the primary server crashes, users can switch to the failover server quickly and continue to work with little downtime or data loss.

Figure 15.2 illustrates the topology of some of these replication variations.

You can use data replication for many reasons. A few of them are discussed later in this chapter. First, however, you need to understand some of the common terms and metaphors Microsoft uses in relationship to data replication.

The Publisher, Distributor, and Subscriber Metaphor

Any SQL Server can play up to three distinct roles in a data replication environment:

▸ **Publication server**—The publication server (or publisher) contains the database or databases that are going to be published. This is the source of the data that is to be replicated to other servers. In Figure 15.3, the Customer table in the AdventureWorks database is the data to be published. To publish data, the database that contains the data that is going to be published must first be enabled for publishing. Full publishing configuration requirements are discussed later in this chapter, in the section "Setting Up Replication."

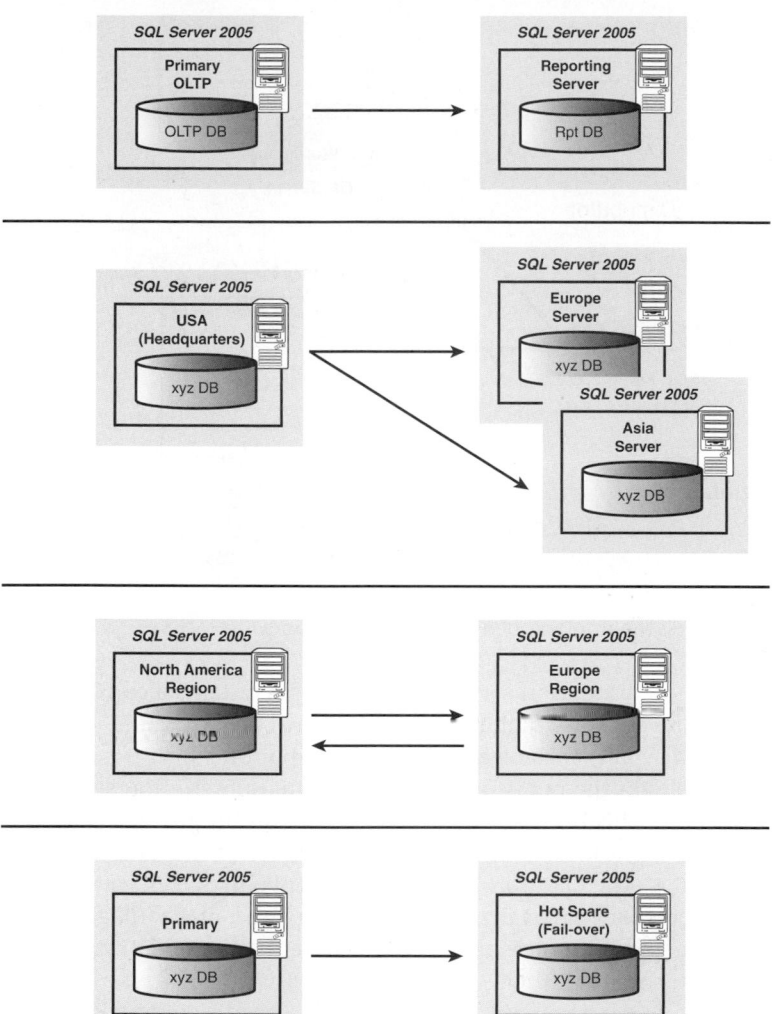

FIGURE 15.2   Data replication scenarios.

▶ **Distribution server**—The distribution server (or distributor) can either be on the same server as the publication server or on a different server (in which case it is a remote distribution server). This server contains the distribution database. This database, also called the store-and-forward database, holds all the data changes that are to be forwarded from the published database to any subscription servers that subscribe to the data. A single distribution server can support several publication servers. The distribution server is truly the workhorse of data replication.

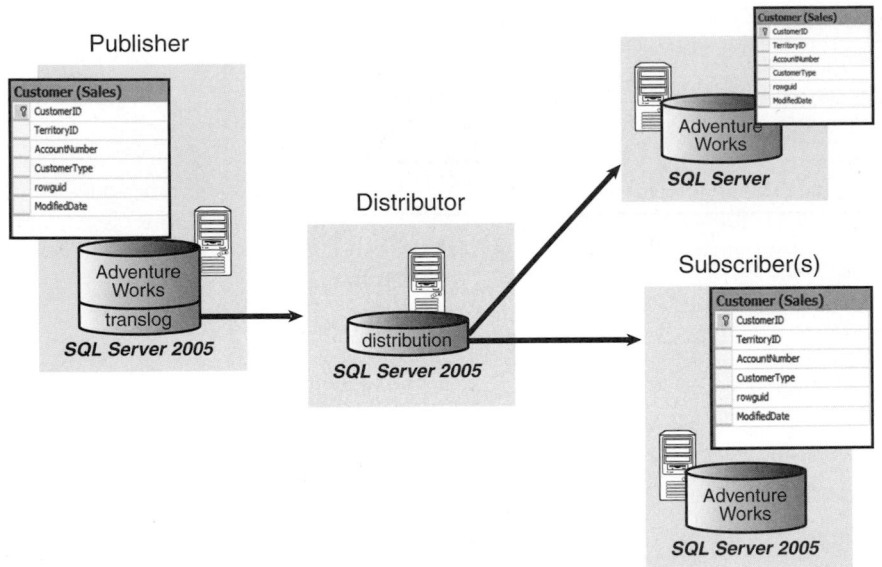

FIGURE 15.3   The publisher, distributor, and one or more subscribers.

> ▶ **Subscription server**—The subscription server (or subscriber) contains a copy of the database or portions of the database that are being published, (for example, the Customer table in the AdventureWorks database). The distribution server sends any changes made to this table (in the published database) to the subscription server's copy of the Customer table. This is known as store-and-forward. In previous versions of SQL Server, many data replication approaches would only send the data to the subscription server and then the data was treated as read-only. In SQL Server 7.0, 2000, and 2005, subscribers (known as updating subscribers) can make updates, which are returned to the publisher. It is important to note that an updating subscriber is not the same as a publisher.

However, a new variation of this update subscriber option is called *peer-to-peer*. Peer-to-peer allows for more than one publisher of the same data (table) and, at the same time, each publisher is also a subscriber (hence, peer-to-peer). This chapter provides more information on updating subscribers and peer-to-peer configurations in the "Updating Subscribers" section, later on.

Along with enabling distinct server roles (publisher, distributor, and subscriber), Microsoft utilizes a few more metaphors, including publications and articles. A *publication* is a group of one or more *articles* and is the basic unit of data replication. An *article* is simply a pointer to a single table, or a subset of rows or columns out of a table, that will be made available for replication.

Publications and Articles

A single database can contain more than one publication. You can publish data from tables, from database objects, from the execution of stored procedures, and even from schema objects, such as referential integrity constraints, clustered indexes, nonclustered indexes, user triggers, extended properties, and collation. Regardless of what you plan to replicate, all articles in a publication are synchronized at the same time. Figure 15.4 shows an example of a publication with three articles. You can choose to replicate whole tables or just parts of tables via filtering.

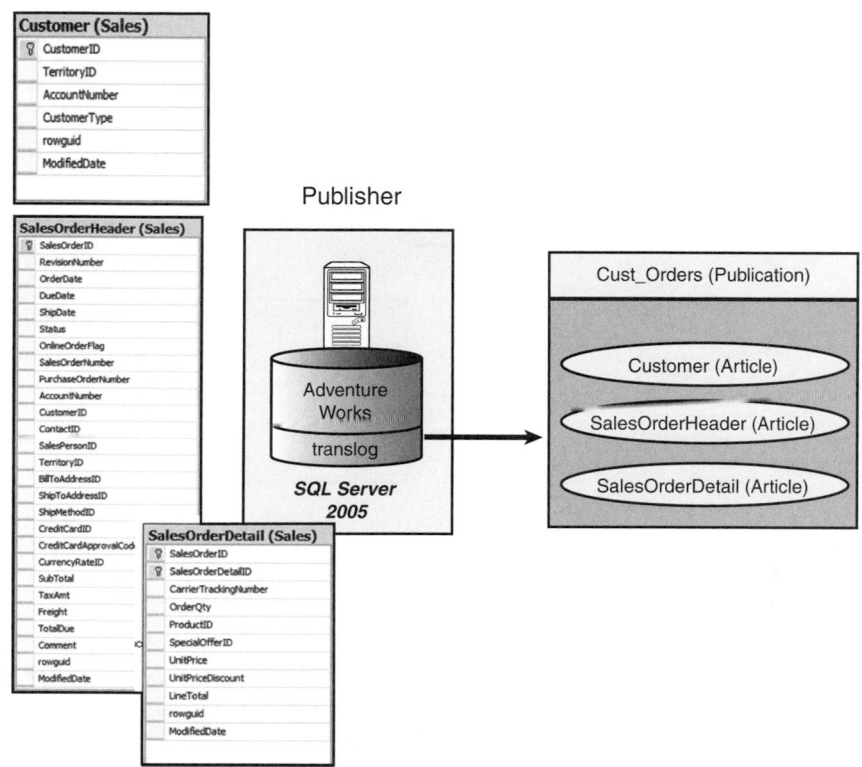

FIGURE 15.4   The Cust_Orders publication (in the AdventureWorks database).

Filtering Articles

You can create articles on SQL Server in several different ways. The basic way to create an article is to publish all the columns and rows that are contained in a table. Although this is the easiest way to create articles, your business needs might require that you publish only certain columns or rows of a table. This is referred to as *filtering vertically* or *horizontally*. When you filter vertically, you filter only specific columns, whereas with horizontal filtering, you filter only specific rows. In addition, SQL Server 2005 provides the added functionality of join filters and dynamic filters.

As Figure 15.5 shows, you might only need to replicate a customer's `CustomerID`, `TerritoryID`, and `CustomerType` to various subscribing servers around your company. In your company, the other data, such as `AccountNumber`, may be restricted information that should not be replicated for general use. You can create an article for data replication that contains a subset of the `Customer` table that will be replicated to these other locations that excludes `AccountNumber` (and `rowguid` and `ModifiedDate` as well).

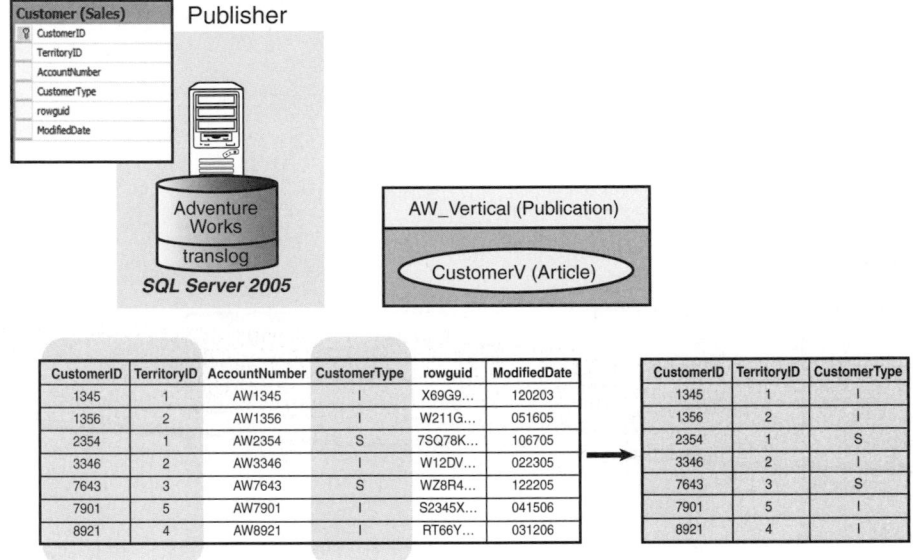

FIGURE 15.5   Vertical filtering is the process of creating a subset of columns from a table to be replicated to subscribers.

As another example, you might need to publish only the `Customer` table data for a specific customer type, such as individual customers ((for example, `CustomerType = 'I'`) or customers that are stores (for example, `CustomerType = 'S'`). This process, as shown in Figure 15.6, is known as horizontal filtering.

It is possible to combine horizontal and vertical filtering, as shown in Figure 15.7. This way, you can weed out unneeded columns and rows that aren't required for replication (that is, are not needed by the subscribers). For example, you might only need the customers who are stores and only require `CustomerID`, `TerritoryID`, and `CustomerType` data to be published.

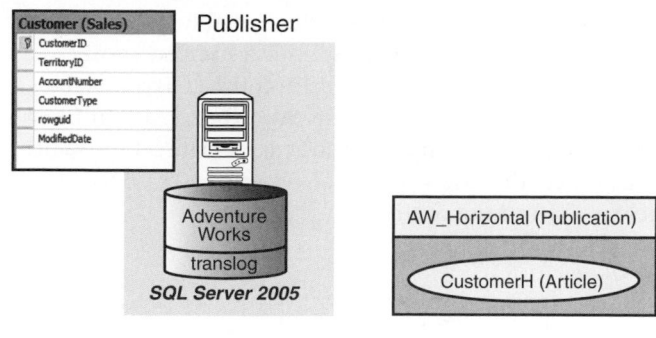

CustomerID	TerritoryID	AccountNumber	CustomerType	rowguid	ModifiedDate
1345	1	AW1345	I	X69G9...	120203
1356	2	AW1356	I	W211G...	051605
2354	1	AW2354	S	7SQ78K...	106705
3346	2	AW3346	I	W12DV...	022305
7643	3	AW7643	S	WZ8R4...	122205
7901	5	AW7901	I	S2345X...	041506
8921	4	AW8921	I	RT66Y...	031206

CustomerID	TerritoryID	AccountNumber	CustomerType	rowguid	ModifiedDate
2345	1	AW2345	S	7SQ78K...	106705
7643	3	AW7643	S	WZ8R4...	122205

FIGURE 15.6   Horizontal filtering is the process of creating a subset of rows from a table to be replicated to subscribers.

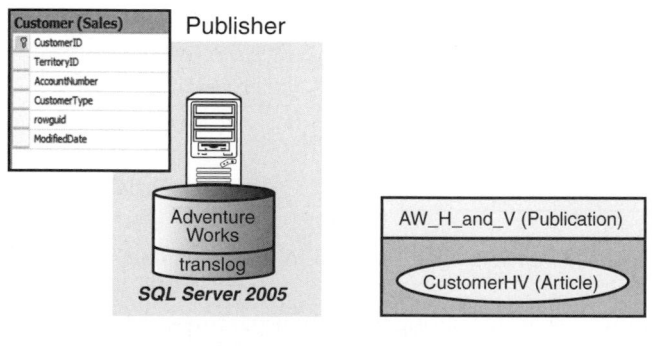

CustomerID	TerritoryID	AccountNumber	CustomerType	rowguid	ModifiedDate
1345	1	AW1345	I	X69G9...	120203
1356	2	AW1356	I	W211G...	051605
2354	1	AW2354	S	7SQ78K...	106705
3346	2	AW3346	I	W12DV...	022305
7643	3	AW7643	S	WZ8R4...	122205
7901	5	AW7901	I	S2345X...	041506
8921	4	AW8921	I	RT66Y...	031206

CustomerID	TerritoryID	CustomerType
2354	1	S
7643	3	S

FIGURE 15.7   Combining horizontal and vertical filtering allows you to pare down the information in an article to only the important information needed by the subscribers.

As mentioned earlier, it is now possible to use join filters. Join filters enable you to use the values of one article (that is, table) to determine what gets replicated from another article (that is, table) via a join. In other words, if you are publishing the `Customer` table data based on the customers who are stores, you can extend filtering (that is, a join filter) to replicate only those orders for these types of customers (as shown in Figure 15.8). This way, you replicate only orders for customers that are stores to a subscriber that needs to see only this data. This can be efficient if it is done well.

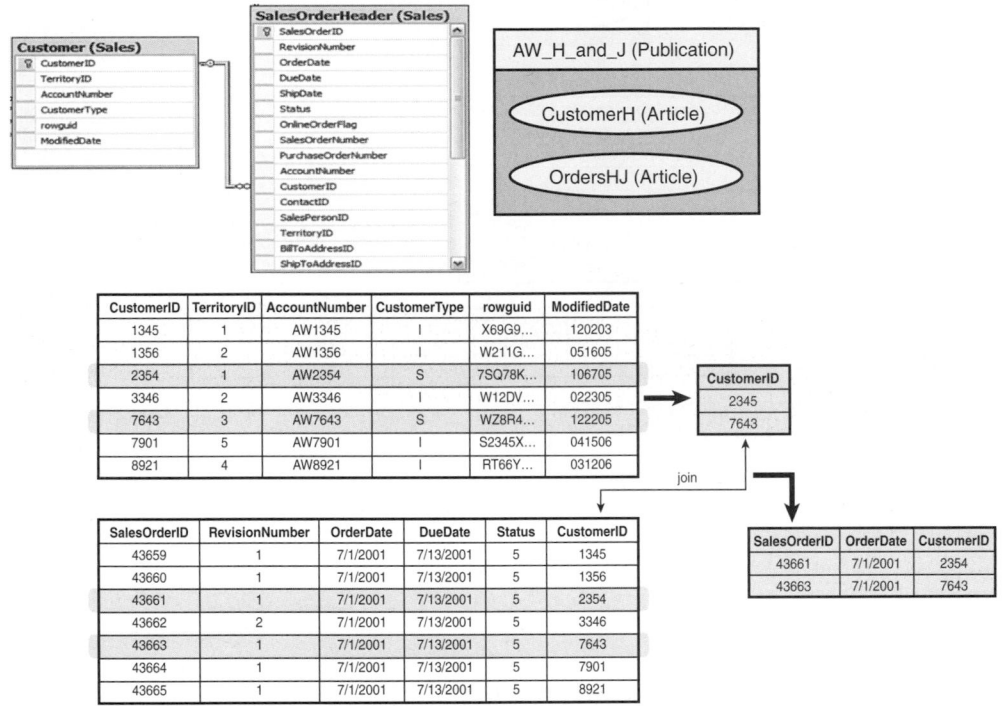

FIGURE 15.8   Horizontal and join publication: Joining `Customers` to `SalesOrderHeader`.

You also can publish stored procedure executions, along with their parameters, as articles. This can be either a standard procedure execution article or a serializable procedure execution article. The difference is that the latter is executed as a serializable transaction, and the former is not. This stored procedure execution approach gives you a major reduction in the amount of SQL statements being replicated across the network.

For instance, if you wanted to update the `Customer` table for every customer via a stored procedure, the resulting `Customer` table updates would be replicated as a large multistep transaction involving at least 5,000 steps at a minimum. This would significantly bog down your network. However, with stored procedure execution articles, only the execution of the stored procedure is replicated to the subscription server, and the stored procedure—not the numerous update statements—is executed on that subscription server.

Figure 15.9 illustrates the difference in execution described earlier. Some subtleties when utilizing this type of data replication processing can't be overlooked, such as making sure the published stored procedure behaves the same on the subscribing server side.

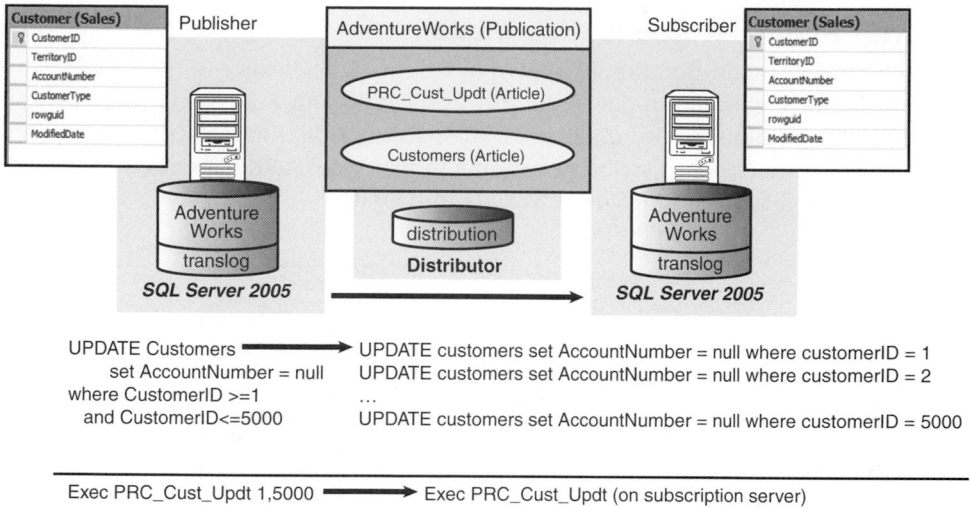

FIGURE 15.9   Comparison of stored procedure execution and default SQL statement replication.

Many more data replication terms are presented in this chapter, but it is essential that you first learn about the different types of replication scenarios that can be built and the reasons any of them would be desired over the others. It is also worth noting that Microsoft SQL Server 2005 supports replication to and from many different "heterogeneous" data sources. In other words, OLE DB and ODBC data sources can subscribe to SQL Server publications, and they can receive data replicated from a number of data sources, including Microsoft Exchange, Microsoft Access, Oracle, and DB2.

Replication Scenarios

In general, depending on your business requirements, one of several different data replication models can be implemented, including the following:

▶ Central publisher

▶ Central publisher with a remote distributor

▶ Publishing subscriber

▶ Central subscriber

▶ Multiple publishers or multiple subscribers

▶ Multiple publishers or multiple subscribers

- ▶ Updating subscribers
- ▶ Peer-to-peer

The Central Publisher Replication Model

The central publisher replication model, shown in Figure 15.10, is Microsoft's default scenario and the most common model used. In this scenario, one SQL Server performs the function of both publisher and distributor. The publisher/distributor can have any number of subscribers. These subscribers can come in many different varieties, such as SQL Server 2005, SQL Server 2000, SQL Server 7.0, and Oracle.

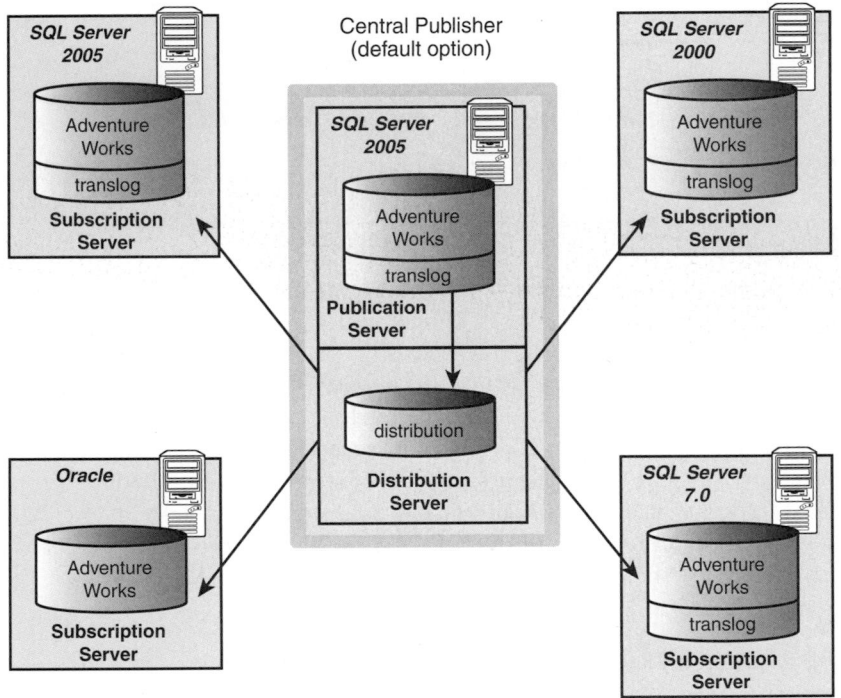

FIGURE 15.10   The central publisher scenario is fairly simple and is the replication model used most often.

The central publisher scenario can be used in the following situations:

- ▶ Creation of a copy of a database for ad hoc queries and report generation (classic use)

- ▶ Publication of master lists to remote locations, such as master customer lists or master price lists

- ▶ Maintenance of a remote copy of an online transaction processing (OLTP) database that could be used by the remote sites during communication outages

▶ Maintenance of a spare copy of an OLTP database that could be used as a "hot spare" in case of server failure

However, it's important to consider the following for this replication model:

▶ If your OLTP server's activity is substantial and affects greater than 10% of your total data per day, this scenario is not for you. Other scenarios or configurations will better fit your needs.

▶ If your OLTP server is maximized on CPU, memory, and disk utilization, you should also consider another data replication scenario because this one is not for you either.

The Central Publisher with Remote Distributor Replication Model

The central publisher with remote distributor scenario, as shown in Figure 15.11, is similar to the central publisher scenario and would be used in the same general situations. The major difference between the two is that in the central publisher with remote distributor scenario, a second server is used to perform the role of distributor. This is highly desirable when you need to free the publishing server from having to perform the distribution task from a CPU, disk, and memory point of view. This is also the best scenario from which to expand the number of publishers and subscribers. Remember that a single distribution server can distribute changes for several publishers. The publisher and distributor must be connected to each other via a reliable, high-speed data link. This remote distributor scenario is proving to be one of the best data replication configurations due to its minimal impact on the publication server and maximum distribution capability to any number of subscribers.

As mentioned previously, the central publisher/remote distributor approach can be used for all the same purposes as the central publisher scenario, and it also provides the added benefit of having minimal resource impact on the publication servers. If your OLTP server's activity affects more than 10% of your total data per day, this scenario can usually handle it without much issue. If your OLTP server has overburdened CPU, memory, and disk utilization, implementing this model easily solves these issues as well. The central publisher/remote distribution model is useful for the vast majority of all the data replication configurations due to its optimal characteristics.

The Publishing Subscriber Replication Model

In the publishing subscriber scenario, as shown in Figure 15.12, the publication server also has to act as a distribution server to one subscriber. This subscriber, in turn, immediately publishes the data to any number of other subscribers. The configuration depicted here does not use a remote distribution configuration option but serves the same distribution model purpose. This scenario is best used when a slow or expensive network link exists between the original publishing server and all the other potential subscribers. This allows the initial (critical) publication of the data to be distributed from the original publishing server to that single subscriber across the slow, unpredictable, or expensive network line. Then, each of the many other subscribers can subscribe to the data, using faster, more predicable, "local" network lines that they would have with the publishing subscriber server.

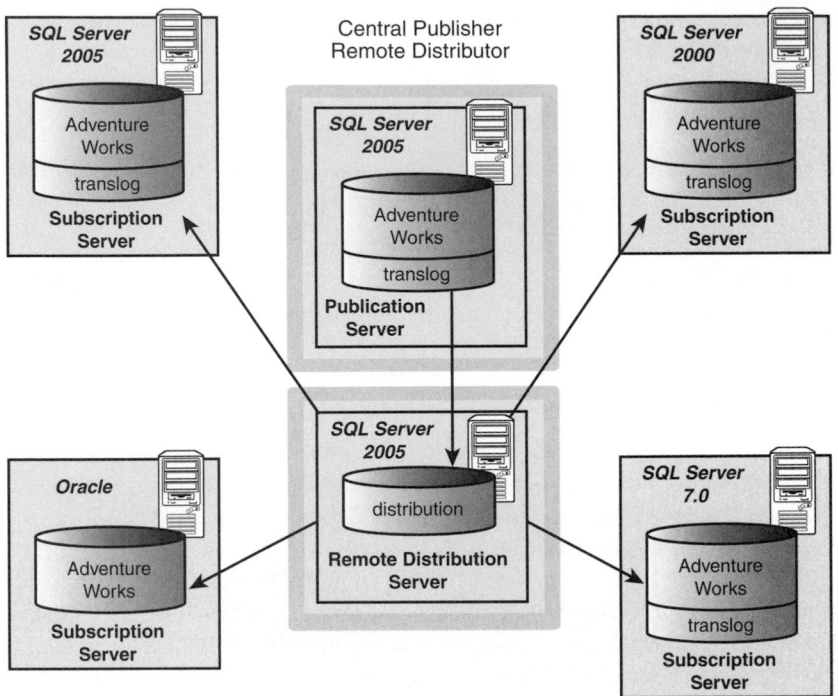

FIGURE 15.11   You use the central publisher with remote distributor scenario when you need to offload the distribution work to another server (to minimize the impact to the publishing server).

A classic example of this model is a company whose main office is in San Francisco and has several branch offices in Europe. Instead of replicating changes to all the branch offices in Europe, it replicates the updates to a single publishing subscriber server in Paris. This publishing subscriber server in Paris then replicates the updates to all other subscriber servers around Europe.

The Central Subscriber Replication Model

In the central subscriber scenario, as shown in Figure 15.13, several publishers replicate data to a single, central subscriber. Basically, this supports the concept of consolidating data at a central site. An example of this might be consolidating all new orders from regional sales offices to company headquarters. In such a situation, you now have several publishers of the Orders table, and you need to take some form of precaution, such as filtering by region. This would guarantee that no one publisher could update another region's orders.

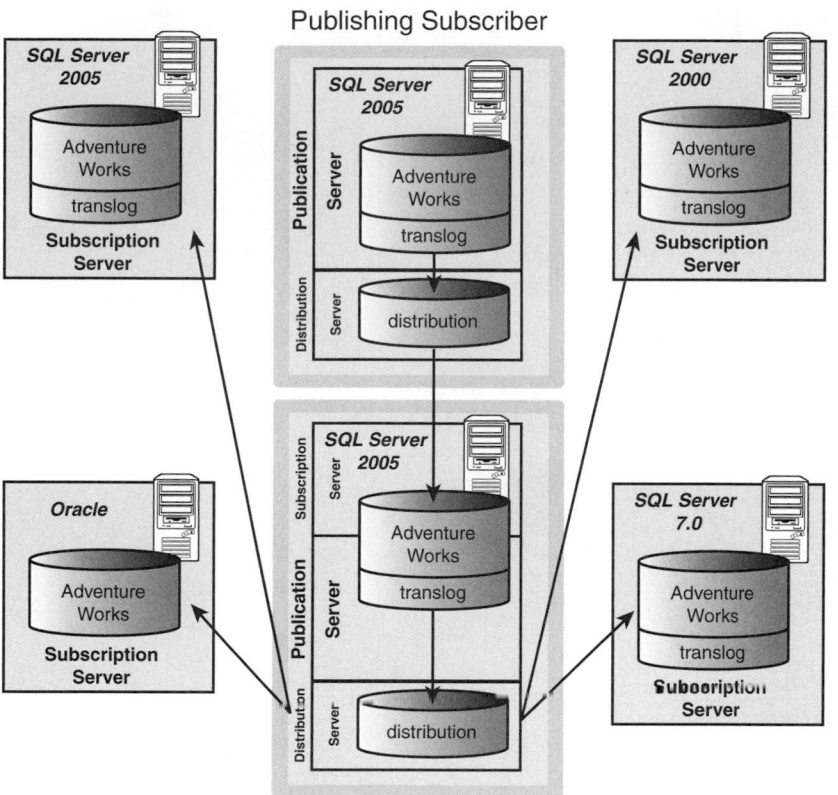

FIGURE 15.12   The publishing subscriber scenario works well when having to deal with slow, unpredictable, or expensive network links in diverse geographic situations.

The Multiple Publishers or Multiple Subscribers Replication Model

In the multiple publishers or multiple subscribers scenario, as shown in Figure 15.14, a common table (such as the Customer table) is maintained on every server participating in the scenario. Each server publishes a particular set of rows (for example, the customer rows in a customer's own territory) that pertain to it—usually via filtering on something that identifies that site to the data rows it owns—and subscribes to the rows that all the other servers are publishing. The result is that each server has all the data at all times and can make changes to its data only. You must be careful when implementing this scenario to ensure that all sites remain synchronized. The most frequently used applications of this system are regional order processing systems and reservation tracking systems. When setting up this type of system, you need to make sure that only local users update local data. This check can be implemented through the use of stored procedures, restrictive views, or a check constraint.

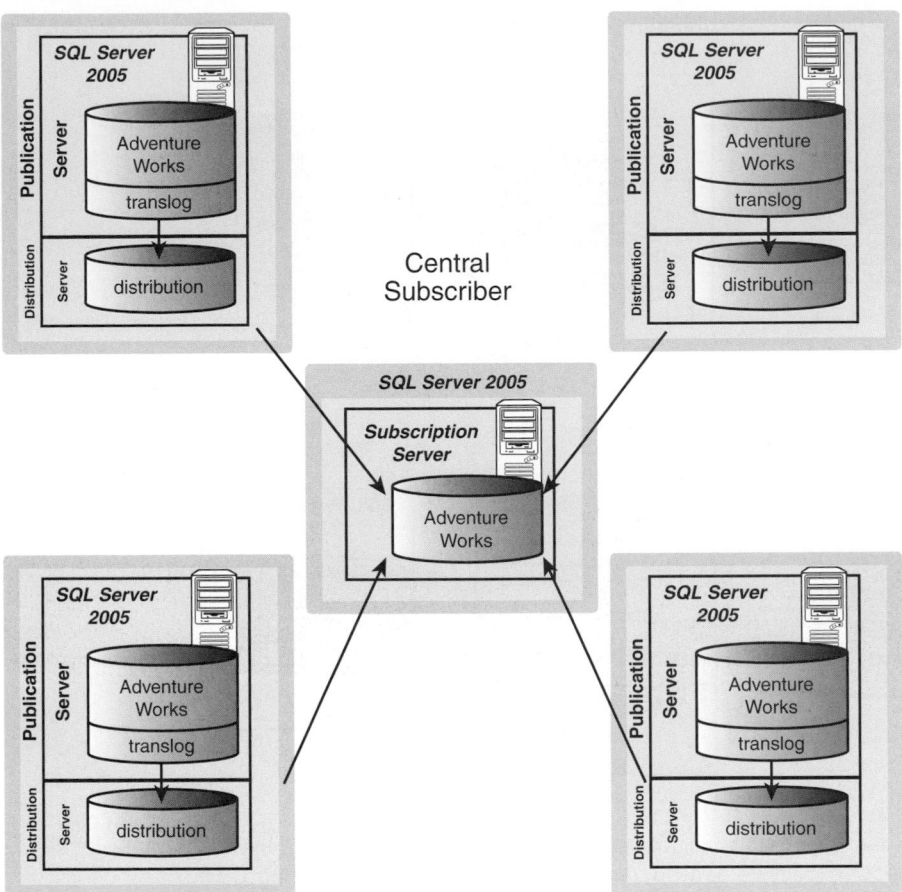

FIGURE 15.13   With the central subscriber scenario, several publishers send data to a single, central subscriber.

The Updating Subscribers Replication Model

SQL Server 2005 has built-in functionality that allows the subscriber to update data in a table to which it subscribes and have those updates automatically made back to the publisher through either immediate or queued updates. This model, called the updating subscribers model, utilizes a two-phase commit process to update the publishing server as the changes are made on the subscribing server. These updates are then replicated to any other subscribers, but not to the subscriber that made the update.

Immediate updating allows subscribers to update data only if the publisher will accept these updates immediately. If the changes are accepted at the publisher, they are propagated to the other subscribers. The subscribers must be continuously and reliably connected to the publisher to make changes at the subscriber.

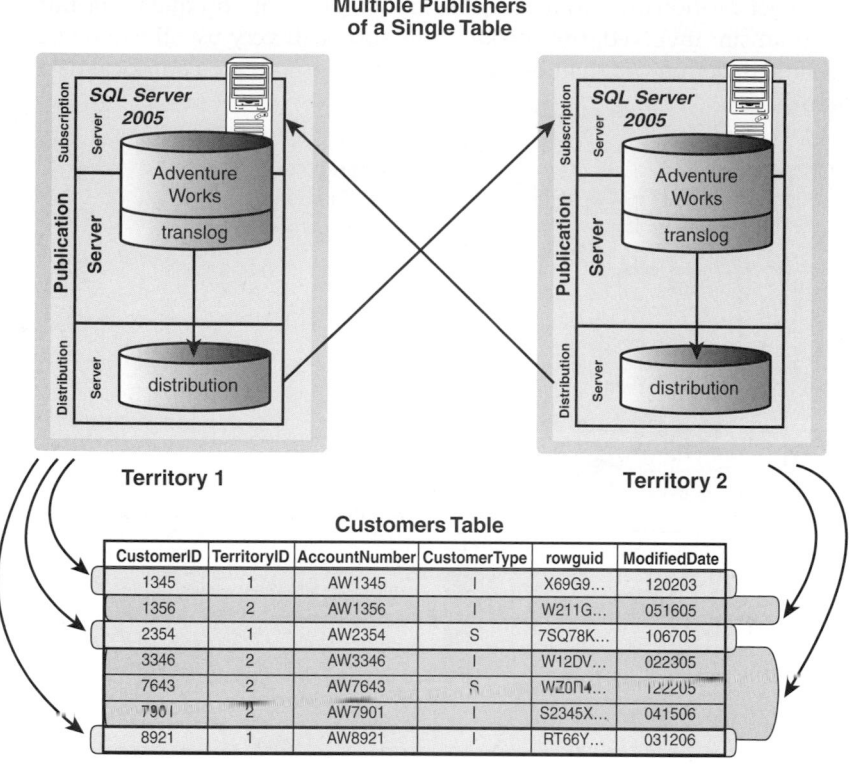

**Multiple Publishers
of a Single Table**

FIGURE 15.14   In the multiple publishers of a single table scenario, every server in the scenario maintains a common table.

Queued updating allows subscribers to update data and then store those updates in a queue while disconnected from the publisher. When the subscriber reconnects to the publisher, the updates are propagated to the publisher. This functionality utilizes SQL Server 2005 queues and the queue reader agent or Microsoft Message Queuing (MSMQ).

A combination of immediate updating with queued updating allows the subscriber to use immediate updating but switch to queued updating if a connection cannot be maintained between the publisher and subscribers. After switching to queued updating, reconnecting to the publisher, and emptying the queue, the subscriber can switch back to immediate updating mode. An updating subscriber is shown in Figure 15.15.

The Peer-to-Peer Replication Model

In SQL Server 2005, Microsoft has introduced a simpler way for all nodes to have the same data and update this data independently. Peer-to-peer replication is different from subscriber updating in that there is no publisher/subscriber hierarchical relationship. Each peer is equal in level. Peers do not subscribe to each other's data; they share each other's data. There are several limitations with peer-to-peer replication, most of which are to

protect this peer-to-peer relationship from being corrupted. There are no queues or immediate updating mechanisms involved, thus making this approach very useful when you
need to have the same data in more than one place and need to update your local data to
your heart's content.

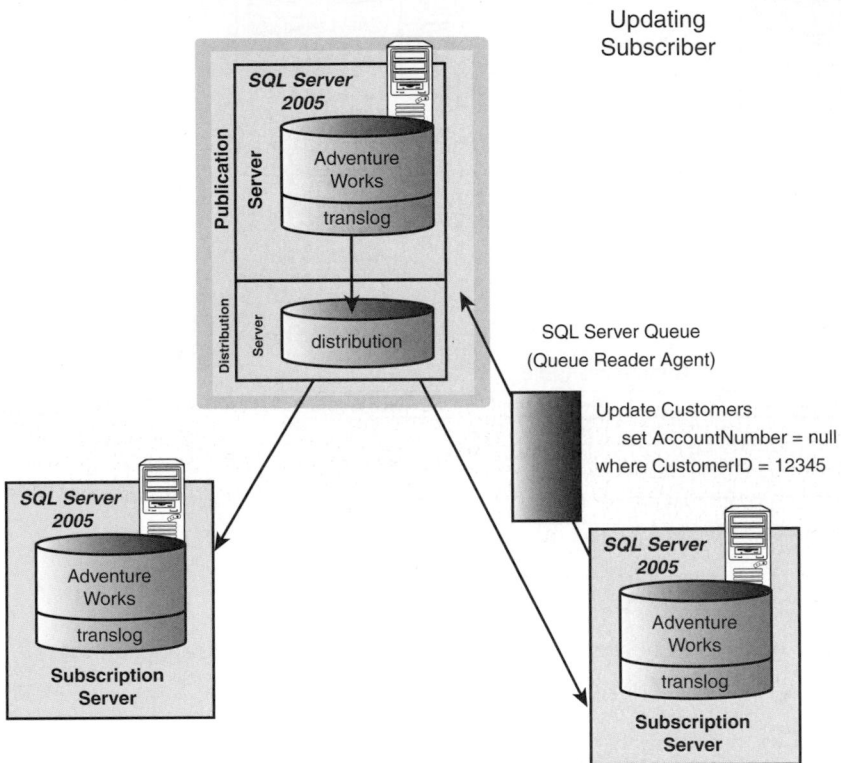

FIGURE 15.15   An updating subscriber updating its copy of a customer table and queuing
the changes back to the publisher.

Figure 15.16 illustrates a typical peer-to-peer configuration with each peer using its own
distribution server. It's best not to use a single distributor in this model because doing so
would create a single point of failure that would affect more than one node. Also note
that with peer-to-peer replication, you should not try to update the other nodes' data by
putting into place some type of stored procedure or view restrictions that allow the local
node to update only its own local data. The example in Figure 15.16 shows that North
American users can update customers with customer IDs between 1 and 3000, while Asian
users can update customers with customer IDs between 3001 and 9000.

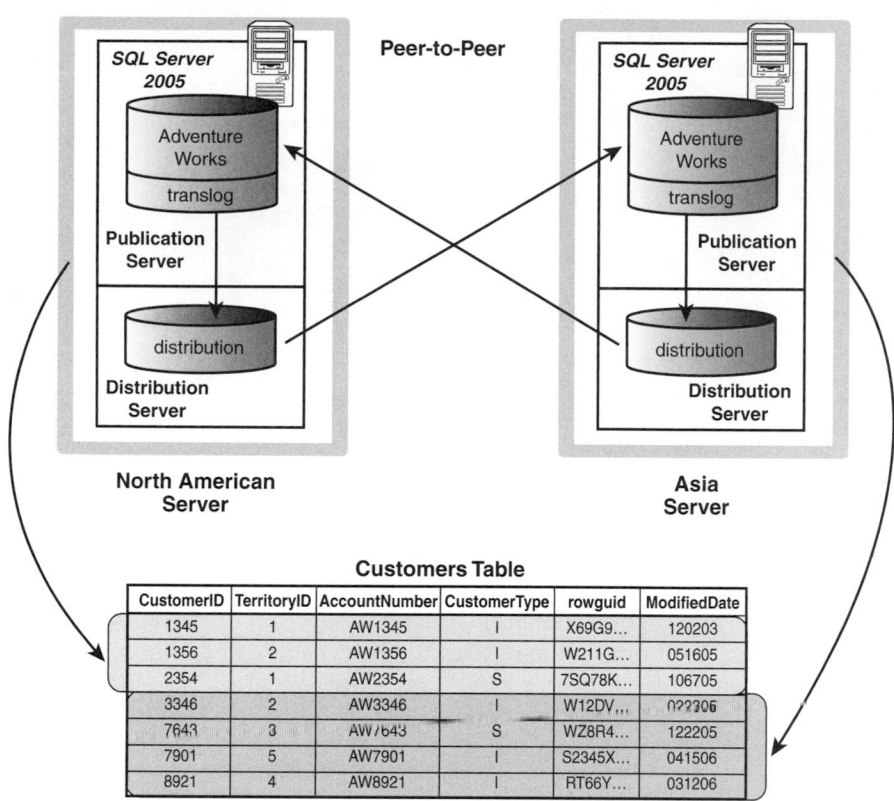

FIGURE 15.16   Peer-to-peer replication.

Subscriptions

A *subscription* is essentially a formal request and registration of that request for data that is being published. By definition, you subscribe to all articles of a publication.

When a subscription is being set up, you have the option of either having the data "pushed" to the subscriber server or "pulling" the data to the subscription server when it is needed. This is referred to as either a *push subscription* or a *pull subscription*.

As shown in Figure 15.17, a pull subscription is set up and managed by the subscription server. The biggest advantage here is that pull subscriptions allow the system administrators of the subscription servers to choose what publications they will receive and when they receive them. With pull subscriptions, publishing and subscribing are separate acts and are not necessarily performed by the same user. In general, pull subscriptions are best when the publication does not require high security or if subscribing is done intermittently when the subscriber's data needs to be periodically brought up to date.

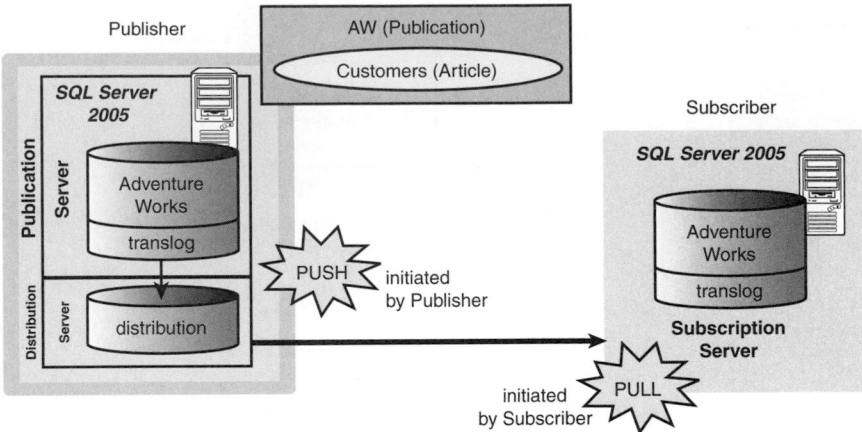

FIGURE 15.17   Push and pull subscriptions.

As you can also see in Figure 15.17, a push subscription is created and managed by the publication server. In effect, the publication server is pushing the publication to the subscription server. The advantage of using push subscriptions is that all the administration takes place in a central location (on the publication server side). In addition, publishing and subscribing happen at the same time, and many subscribers can be set up at once. This is also recommended when dealing with heterogeneous subscribers because of the lack of pull capability on the subscription server side.

Anonymous Subscriptions (Pull Subscriptions)

It is possible to have "anonymous" subscriptions. An anonymous subscription is a special type of pull subscription that can be used in the following circumstances:

▶ When you are publishing data to the Internet

▶ When you have a huge number of subscribers

▶ When you don't want the overhead of maintaining extra information at the publisher or distributor

▶ When all the rules of your pull subscriptions apply to all your anonymous subscribers

Normally, information about all the subscribers, including performance data, is stored on the distribution server. Therefore, if you have a large number of subscribers or you do not want to track detailed information about the subscribers, you might want to allow anonymous subscriptions to a publication. Then little is kept at the distribution server, but it then becomes the responsibility of the subscriber to initiate the subscription and to keep synchronized.

The Distribution Database

The distribution database is a special type of database installed on the distribution server. This database, which is as a store-and-forward database, holds all transactions waiting to be distributed to any subscribers. This database receives transactions from any published databases that have designated it as their distributor. The transactions are held here until they are sent to the subscribers successfully. After a period of time, these transactions are purged from the distribution database. In some special situations, the transactions might not be purged for a longer period, enabling anonymous subscribers ample time to synchronize. The distribution database is the heart of the data replication facility. As you can see in Figure 15.18, the distribution database has several MS tables, such as MSarticles. These tables contain all the necessary information for the distribution server to fulfill the distribution role. The following are some of these tables:

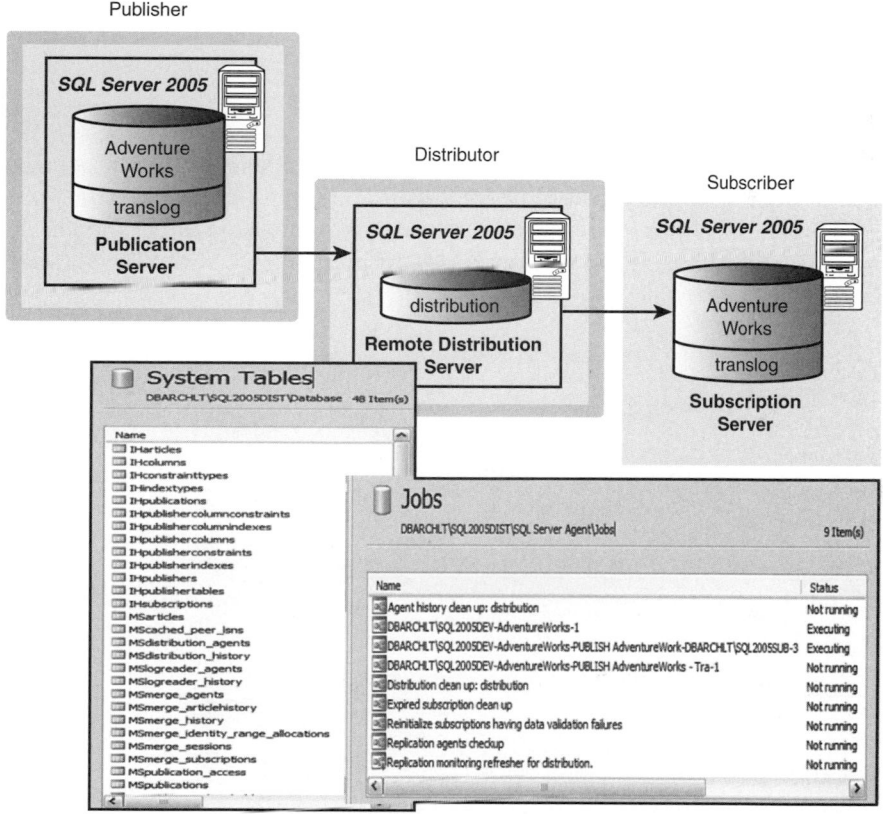

FIGURE 15.18   Tables of the distribution database and the distribution agents.

▶ **All the different publishers who will use this distribution server**—Stored in the MSpublisher_databases and MSpublication_access tables.

▶ **The publications and articles that will be distributed**—Stored in the `MSpublications` and `MSarticles` tables.

▶ **The complete information for all the distribution agents to perform their tasks**—Stored in the `MSdistribution_agents` table.

▶ **The complete information of the executions of these agents**—Stored in the `MSdistribution_history` table.

▶ **The subscribers**—Stored in `MSsubscriber_info`, `MSsubscriptions`, and other related tables.

▶ **Any errors that occur during replication and synchronization states**—Stored in `MSrepl_errors`, `MSsync_state`, and related tables.

▶ **The actual commands and transactions that are to be replicated**—Stored in the `MSrepl_commands` and `MSrepl_transactions` tables.

Replication Agents

SQL Server utilizes replication agents to do different tasks during the replication process. These agents are constantly waking up at some frequency and fulfilling specific jobs. As you can see in Figure 15.19, several replication agent categories are listed under the Job Activity Monitor when you expand the SQL Server Agents branch (SQL Server Agent, Job Activity Monitor branch).

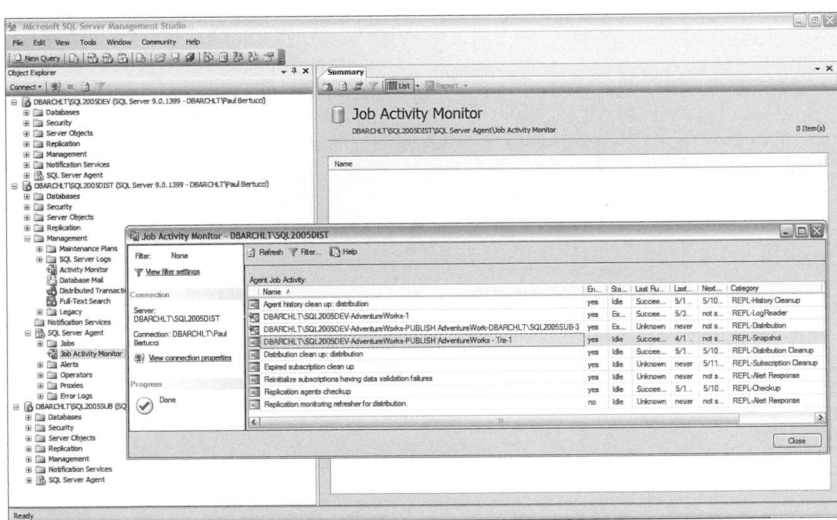

FIGURE 15.19   Replication agent jobs. Replication job category entries are prefixed with REPL-.

Let's look at the main replication agent categories:

- ▶ Snapshot Agent

- ▶ Log Reader Agent

- ▶ Distribution Agent

- ▶ Merge Agent (for updating subscribers)

- ▶ History Cleanup Agent

- ▶ Distribution Cleanup Agent

- ▶ Expired Subscription Cleanup Agent

- ▶ Reinitialize Subscription Having Data Validation Failures Agent

- ▶ Replication Agent Cleanup Agent

The Snapshot Agent

The snapshot agent is responsible for preparing the schema and initial data files of published tables and stored procedures, storing the snapshot on the distribution server, and recording information about the synchronization status in the distribution database. Each publication has its own snapshot agent that runs on the distribution server. It takes on the name of the publication within the publishing database within the machine on which it executes (that is, [Machine][Publishing database][Publication Name]).

Figure 15.19 shows what this snapshot agent looks like under the SQL Server Agent, Job Activity Monitor branch in SQL Server Management Studio. The snapshot agent is named DBARCHLT\SQL2005DEV-AdventureWorks-PUBLISH AdventureWorks - Tra-1. In addition, these agents can be referenced from the Replication Monitor option (when you launch the Replication Monitor via right-mouse click from the Replication branch in SQL Server Management Studio). You are likely to most often use the SQL Server Agent path to these agents.

It's worth noting that the snapshot agent might not even be used if the initialization of the subscriber's schema and data is done manually.

The Snapshot Agent Synchronizaton

The snapshot agent is the process that ensures that both databases start on an even playing field. This process is known as *synchronization*. The synchronization process is performed whenever a publication has a new subscriber. Synchronization happens only one time for each new subscriber. It ensures that database schema and data are exact replicas on both servers. After the initial synchronization, all updates are made via replication.

When a new server subscribes to a publication, synchronization is performed. When synchronization begins, a copy of the table schema is copied to a file with the .sch extension. This file contains all the information necessary to create the table and any indexes

15

on the tables, if they are requested. Next, a copy is made of the data in the table to be synchronized and written to a file with the .bcp extension. The data file is a BCP, or bulk copy file. Both files are stored in the temporary working directory on the distribution server.

After the synchronization process has started and the data files have been created, any inserts, updates, and deletes are stored in the distribution database. These changes are not replicated to the subscription database until the synchronization process is complete.

When the synchronization process starts, only new subscribers are affected. Any subscriber that has been synchronized already and has been receiving modifications is unaffected. The synchronization set is applied to all servers that are waiting for initial synchronization. After the schema and data have been re-created, all transactions that have been stored in the distribution server are sent to the subscriber.

When you set up a subscription, it is possible to manually load the initial snapshot onto the server. This is known as *manual synchronization*. For extremely large databases, it is frequently easier to dump the database to tape and then reload the database on the subscription server. If you load the snapshot this way, SQL Server assumes that the databases are already synchronized and automatically begins sending data modifications.

Snapshot Agent Processing

Figure 15.20 shows the details of the snapshot agent execution for a typical push subscription. You can see the execution history by simply right-clicking the snapshot job and choosing View History.

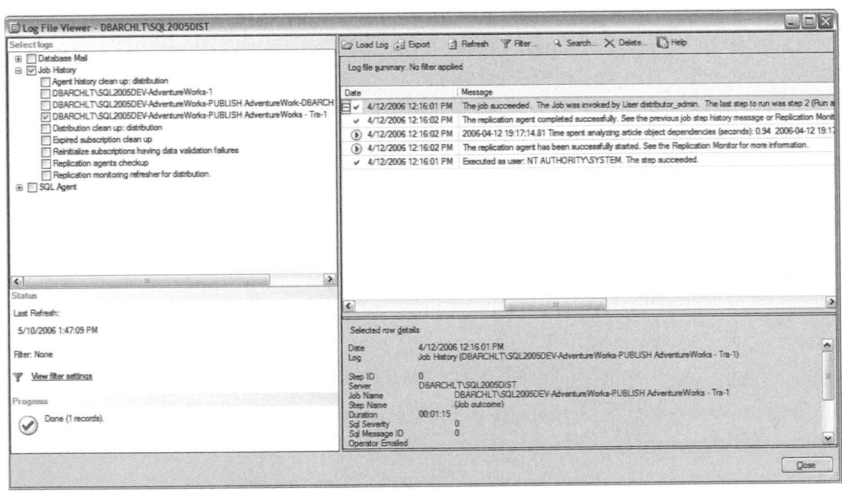

FIGURE 15.20   Snapshot agent execution job history.

The following sequence of tasks occurs with the snapshot agent:

1. The snapshot agent is initialized. This initialization can be immediate or at a designated time in the company's nightly processing window.

2. The agent connects to the publisher.

3. The agent generates schema files with the .sch file extension for each article in the publication. These schema files are written to a temporary working directory on the distribution server. These are the create table statements and such that will be used to create all objects needed on the subscription server side. They exist only for the duration of the snapshot processing.

4. All the tables in the publication are locked (held). The lock is required to ensure that no data modifications are made during the snapshot process.

5. The agent extracts a copy of the data in the publication and writes it to the temporary working directory on the distribution server. If all the subscribers are SQL Server machines, the data will be written using a SQL Server native format, with the .bcp file extension. If you are replicating to databases other than SQL Server, the data will be stored in standard text files with the .txt file extension. The .sch file and the .txt files/.bmp files are known as a *synchronization set*. Every table or article has a synchronization set.

CAUTION

It's important to make sure you have enough disk space on the drive that contains the temporary working directory. The snapshot data files will potentially be huge, and this size is the most common reason for snapshot failure.

---

6. As you can see in Figure 15.21, the agent executes the object creations and bulk copy processing at the subscription server side, in the order in which they were generated (or it skips the object creation part if the objects have already been created on the subscription server side and you have indicated this during setup). This takes a while, so it is best to do this in an off time so as not to impact the normal processing day. Network connectivity is critical here. Snapshots often fail at this point.

7. The snapshot agent posts the fact that a snapshot has occurred and what articles/publications were part of the snapshot to the distribution database. This is the only thing that is sent to the distribution database.

8. When all the synchronization sets have finished being executed, the agent releases the locks on all the tables of this publication. The snapshot is now considered finished.

The Log Reader Agent

The log reader agent is responsible for moving transactions marked for replication from the transaction log of the published database to the distribution database. Each database published using transactional replication has its own log reader agent that runs on the distribution server. It is easy to find because it takes on the name of the publishing database whose transaction log it is reading ([*Machine name*][*Publishing DB name*]) and the REPL-LogReader category. Figure 15.19 shows the log reader agent for the AdventureWorks database. It is named DBARCHLT\SQL2005DEV-AdventureWorks-1.

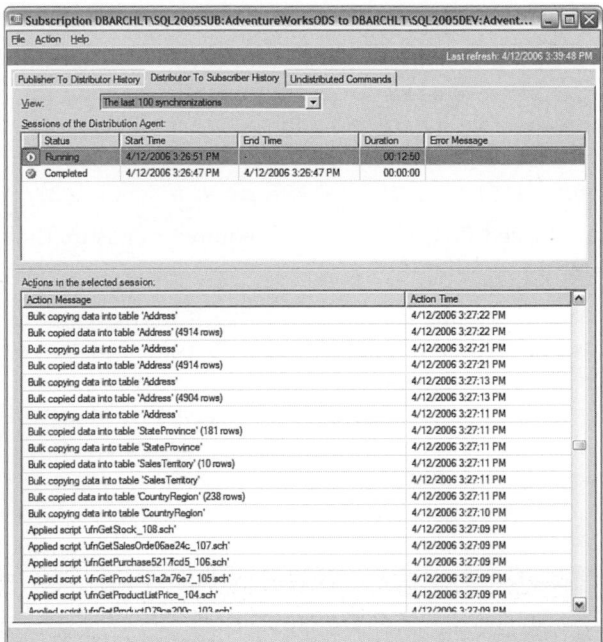

FIGURE 15.21   Snapshot agent delivering the snapshot to the subscriber (most recent operation on the top).

After initial synchronization has taken place, the log reader agent begins to move transactions from the publication server to the distribution server. All actions that modify data in a database are logged to the transaction log in that database. Not only is this log used in the automatic recovery process, it is also used in the replication process. When an article is created for publication and the subscription is activated, all entries about that article are marked in the transaction log. For each publication in a database, a log reader agent reads the transaction log and looks for any marked transactions. When the log reader agent finds a change in the log, it reads the changes and converts them to SQL statements that correspond to the action taken in the article. The SQL statements are then stored in a table on the distribution server, waiting to be distributed to subscribers.

Because replication is based on the transaction log, several changes are made in the way the transaction log works. During normal processing, any transaction that has either been successfully completed or rolled back is marked inactive. When you are performing replication, completed transactions are not marked inactive until the log reader process has read them and sent them to the distribution server.

Truncating and fast bulk-copying into a table are non-logged processes. In tables marked for publication, you cannot perform non-logged operations unless you temporarily turn off replication on that table.

> **NOTE**
>
> One of the major changes in the transaction log comes when you have the Truncate Log on Checkpoint option turned on. When this option is on, SQL Server truncates the transaction log every time a checkpoint is performed, which can be as often as every several seconds. With replication, the inactive portion of the log is not truncated until the log reader process has read the transaction.

The Distribution Agent

A distribution agent moves transactions and snapshot jobs held in the distribution database out to the subscribers. This agent isn't created until a push subscription is defined to a subscriber. The distribution agent takes on the name of what the publication database is along with the subscriber information ([*Machine name*][*Publication DB name*] [*Subscriber machine name*]). If you look back at Figure 15.19, you see a distribution agent (the REPL-Distribution Category entry) for the AdventureWorks database to a subscriber. It is named DBARCHLT\SQL2005DEV-AdventureWorks - PUBLISH AdventureWork - DBARCHLT\SQL2005SUB-3.

Those not set up for immediate synchronization share a distribution agent that runs on the distribution server. Pull subscriptions, to either snapshot or transactional publications, have a distribution agent that runs on the subscriber. Merge publications do not have a distribution agent at all. Rather, they rely on the merge agent, discussed next.

In transactional replication, the transactions have been moved into the distribution database, and the distribution agent either pushes out the changes to the subscribers or pulls them from the distributor, depending on how the servers are set up. All actions that change data on the publishing server are applied to the subscribing servers in the same order they were incurred. Figure 15.22 shows the latest history of the distribution agent and the total duration of the current subscription (00:31:55:3581744 minutes in this example).

15

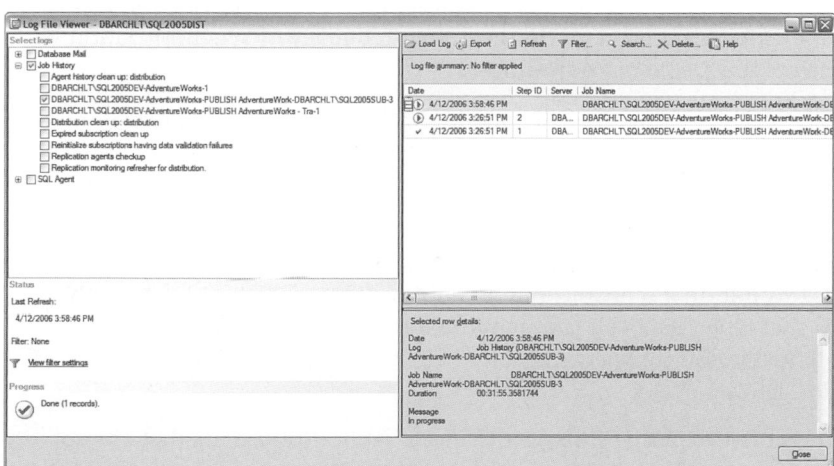

FIGURE 15.22   Distribution agent job history.

The Merge Agent

When dealing with merge publications, the merge agent moves and reconciles incremental data changes that occur after the initial snapshot was created. Each merge publication has a merge agent that connects to the publishing server and the subscribing server and updates both as changes are made. In a full merge scenario, the agent first uploads all changes from the subscriber where the generation is 0 or greater than the last generation sent to the publisher. The agent gathers the rows in which changes were made, and the rows without conflicts are applied to the publishing database.

A conflict can arise when changes are made at both the publishing server and the subscription server to a particular row(s) of data. A conflict resolver handles these conflicts. Conflict resolvers are associated with an article in the publication definition. These conflict resolvers are sets of rules or custom scripts that can handle any complex conflict situation that might occur. The agent then reverses the process by downloading any changes from the publisher to the subscriber. Push subscriptions have merge agents that run on the publication server, whereas pull subscriptions have merge agents that run on the subscription server. Snapshot and transactional publications do not use merge agents.

Other Specialized Agents

In Figure 15.19, you can see that several other agents have been set up to do house cleaning around the replication configuration:

▶ **Agent History Clean Up: Distribution**—This agent clears out agent history from the distribution database every 10 minutes (by default). Depending on the size of the distribution, you might want to vary the frequency of this agent.

▶ **Distribution Clean Up: Distribution**—This agent clears out replicated transactions from the distribution database every 72 hours by default. This agent is used for snapshot and transactional publications only. If the volume of transactions is high, the frequency of this agent will want to be adjusted downward so you don't have too large of a distribution database. However, the frequency of synchronization with subscribers drives this frequency adjustment.

▶ **Expired Subscription Clean Up**—This agent detects and removes expired subscriptions from the published databases. As part of the subscription setup, an expiration date is set. This agent usually runs once per day by default. You don't need to change this.

▶ **Reinitialize Subscriptions Having Data Validation Failures**—This agent is manually invoked. It is not on a schedule, but it could be. It automatically detects the subscriptions that failed data validation and marks them for re-initialization. This can then potentially lead to a new snapshot being applied to a subscriber that had data validation failures.

▶ **Replication Agents Checkup**—This agent detects replication agents that are not actively logging history. This is critical because debugging replication errors is often dependent on an agent's history that has been logged.

Planning for SQL Server Data Replication

You must consider many factors when choosing a method to distribute data. Your business requirements determine which is the right method for you. In general, you need to understand the timing and latency of your data, its independence at each site, and your specific need to filter or partition the data.

Autonomy, Timing, and Latency of Data

Distributed data implementations can be accomplished using a few different facilities in Microsoft: Integration Services (IS), Distributed Transaction Coordinator (DTC), and Data Replication. The trick is to match the right facility to the type of data distribution you need to get done.

In some applications, such as online transaction processing and inventory control systems, data must be synchronized at all times. This requirement, called *immediate transactional consistency*, was known as tight consistency in previous versions of SQL Server.

SQL Server implements immediate transactional consistency data distribution in the form of two-phase commit processing. *A two-phase commit*, sometimes known as *2PC*, ensures that transactions are committed on all servers, or the transaction is rolled back on all servers. This ensures that all data on all servers is 100% in sync at all times. One of the main drawbacks of immediate transactional consistency is that it requires a high-speed LAN to work. This type of solution might not be feasible for large environments with many servers because occasional network outages can occur. These types of implementations can be built with DTC and IS.

In other applications, such as decision support and report generation systems, 100% data synchronization all the time is not terribly important. This requirement, called *latent transactional consistency*, was known as loose consistency in previous versions of SQL Server.

Latent transactional consistency is implemented in SQL Server via data replication. Replication allows data to be updated on all servers, but the process is not a simultaneous one. The result is "real-enough-time" data. This is known as latent transactional consistency because a lag exists between the data updated on the main server and the replicated data. In this scenario, if you could stop all data modifications from occurring on all servers, all the servers would eventually have the same data. Unlike the two-phase consistency model, replication works over both LANs and WANs, as well as slow or fast links.

When planning a distributed application, you must consider the effect of one site's operation on another. This is known as *site autonomy*. A site with complete autonomy can continue to function without being connected to any other site. A site with no autonomy cannot function without being connected to all other sites. For example, applications that utilize two-phase commits rely on all other sites being able to immediately accept changes that are sent to them. In the event that any one site is unavailable, no transactions on any server can be committed. In contrast, sites using merge replication can be completely disconnected from all other sites and continue to work effectively, not guaranteeing data consistency. Luckily, some solutions combine both high data consistency and site autonomy.

15

Methods of Data Distribution

After you have determined the amount of transactional latency and site autonomy needed, based on your business requirements, you need to select the data distribution method that corresponds. Each different type of data distribution has a different amount of site autonomy and latency. With these distributed data systems, you can choose from several methods:

▶ **Distributed transactions**—Distributed transactions ensure that all sites have the same data at all times. You pay a certain amount of overhead cost to maintain this consistency. (We do not discuss this non-data replication method here.)

▶ **Transactional replication with updating subscribers**—Users can change data at the local location, and those changes are applied to the source database at the same time. The changes are then eventually replicated to other sites. This type of data distribution combines replication and distributed transactions because data is changed at both the local site and source database. A variation on this theme is peer-to-peer replication, which is essentially full transactional replication between two (or more) sites, but is publisher-to-publisher (not update subscriber).

▶ **Transactional replication**—With transactional replication, data is changed only at the source location and is sent out to the subscribers. Because data is changed at only a single location, conflicts cannot occur.

▶ **Snapshot replication with updating subscribers**—This method is much like transactional replication with updating subscribers; users can change data at the local location, and those changes are applied to the source database at the same time. The entire changed publication is then replicated to all subscribers. This type of replication provides higher autonomy than transactional replication.

▶ **Snapshot replication**—A complete copy of the publication is sent out to all subscribers. This includes both changed and unchanged data.

▶ **Merge replication**—All sites make changes to local data independently and then update the publisher. It is possible for conflicts to occur, but they can be resolved.

SQL Server Replication Types

Microsoft has narrowed the field to three major types of data replication approaches within SQL Server: snapshot, transactional, and merge. Each replication type applies to only a single publication. However, it is possible to have multiple replication types per database.

Snapshot Replication

Snapshot replication makes an image of all the tables in a publication at a single moment in time and then moves that entire image to the subscribers. Little overhead on the server is incurred because snapshot replication does not track data modifications as the other forms of replication do. It is possible, however, for snapshot replication to require large amounts of network bandwidth, especially if the articles being replicated are large. Snapshot replication is the easiest form of replication to set up and is used primarily with smaller tables for which subscribers do not have to perform updates. An example of this might be a phone list that is to be replicated to many subscribers. This phone list is not considered to be critical data, and the frequency of it being refreshed is more than enough to satisfy all its users.

The primary agents used for snapshot replication are the snapshot agent and the distribution agent.

- ▶ The snapshot agent creates files that contain the schema of the publication and the data. The files are temporarily stored in the snapshot folder of the distribution server, and then the distribution jobs are recorded in the distribution database.

- ▶ The distribution agent is responsible for moving the schema and data from the distributor to the subscribers.

A few other agents are also used that deal with other needed tasks for replication, such as cleanup of files and history. In snapshot replication, after the snapshot has been delivered to all the subscribers, these agents delete the associated .bcp and .sch files from the distributor's working directory.

Transactional Replication

Transactional replication is the process of capturing transactions from the transaction log of the published database and applying them to the subscription databases. With SQL Server transactional replication, you can publish all or part of a table, views, or one or more stored procedures as an article. All data updates are then stored in the distribution database and sent and applied to any number of subscribing servers. Obtaining these updates from the publishing database's transaction log is extremely efficient. No direct reading of tables is required except during initial snapshot, and only the minimal amount of traffic is generated over the network. This has made transactional replication the most often used method.

As data changes are made, they are propagated to the other sites at nearly real time—you determine the frequency of this propagation. Because changes are usually made only at the publishing server, data conflicts are avoided for the most part. As an example, push subscribers usually receive updates from the publisher in a minute or less, depending on the speed and availability of the network. Subscribers also can be set up for pull subscriptions. This is useful for disconnected users who are not connected to the network at all times.

The primary agents used for transactional replication are the snapshot agent, log agent, and distribution agent:

- ▶ The snapshot agent creates files that contain the schema of the publication and the data. The files are stored in the snapshot folder of the distribution server, and the distribution jobs are recorded in the distribution database.

15

▶ The log reader agent monitors the transaction log of the database that it is set up to service. Each database published has its own log reader agent set up for replication and it will copy the transactions from the transaction log of that published database into the distribution database.

▶ The distribution agent is responsible for moving the schema and data from the distributor to the subscribers for the initial synchronization and then moving all the subsequent transactions from the published database to each subscriber as they come in. These transactions are stored in the distribution database for a certain length of time and are eventually purged.

A few other agents deal with the other housekeeping issues surrounding data replication, such as schema files cleanup, history cleanup, and transaction cleanup.

Merge Replication

Merge replication involves getting the publisher and all subscribers initialized and then allowing data to be changed at all sites involved in the merge replication at the publisher and at all subscribers. All these changes to the data are subsequently merged at certain intervals so that, again, all copies of the database have identical data.

Occasionally, data conflicts have to be resolved. The publisher does not always win in a conflict resolution. Instead, the winner is determined by whatever criteria you establish.

The primary agents used for merge replication are the snapshot agent and the merge agent:

▶ The snapshot agent creates files that contain the schema of the publication and the data. The files are stored in the snapshot folder of the distribution server, and the distribution jobs are recorded in the distribution database. This is essentially the same behavior as with all other types of replication methods.

▶ The merge agent takes the initial snapshot and applies it to all the subscribers. It then reconciles all changes made on all the servers, based on the rules you configure.

Preparing for Merge Replication

When you set up a table for merge replication, SQL Server performs three schema changes to the database. First, it must either identify or create a unique column for each row that is going to be replicated. This column is used to identify the different rows across all the different copies of the table. If the table already contains a column with the ROWGUIDCOL property, SQL Server automatically uses that column for the row identifier. If not, SQL Server adds a column called rowguid to the table. SQL Server also places an index on this rowguid column.

Next, SQL Server adds triggers to the table to track changes that occur to the data in the table and record them in the merge system tables. The triggers can track changes at either the row or the column level, depending on how you set it up. SQL Server supports multiple triggers of the same type on a table, so merge triggers do not interfere with user-defined triggers on the table.

Finally, SQL Server adds new system tables to the database that contains the replicated tables. The `MSMerge_contents` and `MSMerge_tombstone` tables track the updates, inserts, and deletes. These tables rely on `rowguid` to track which rows have actually been changed.

The merge agent is responsible for moving changed data from the site where it was changed to all other sites in the replication scenario. When a row is updated, the triggers that were added by SQL Server fire off and update the new system tables, setting the generation column equal to `0` for the corresponding `rowguid`. When the merge agent runs, it collects the data from the rows where the generation column is `0` and then resets the generation values to values higher than the previous generation numbers. This allows the merge agent to look for data that has already been shared with other sites without having to look through all the data. The merge agent then sends the changed data to the other sites.

When the data reaches the other sites, the data is merged with existing data according to rules that you have defined. These rules are flexible and highly extensible. The merge agent evaluates existing and new data and resolves conflicts based on priorities or which data was changed first. Another available option is that you can create custom resolution strategies using the Component Object Model (COM) and custom stored procedures. After conflicts have been handled, synchronization occurs to ensure that all sites have the same data.

The merge agent identifies conflicts using the `MSMerge_contents` table. In this table, a column called `lineage` is used to track the history of changes to a row. The agent updates the `lineage` value whenever a user makes changes to the data in a row. The entry into this column is a combination of a site identifier and the last version of the row created at the site. As the merge agent is merging all the changes that have occurred, it examines each site's information to see whether a conflict has occurred. If a conflict has occurred, the agent initiates conflict resolution based on the criteria mentioned earlier.

Basing the Replication Design on User Requirements

As mentioned earlier, the business requirements drive your replication configuration and method. In addition, nailing down all the details of the business requirement is the hardest part of a data replication design process. After you have completed the requirements gathering, the replication design usually just falls out from it easily. The requirements gathering is highly recommended to get a prototype up and running as quickly as possible to measure the effectiveness of one approach over the other. You must understand several key aspects to make the right design decisions, including the following:

▶ What is the number of sites and what is the site autonomy in the scope (location)?

▶ Which sites have the master data (data ownership)?

- ▶ What is the data latency requirement (by site)?
- ▶ What type of data accesses are being made (by site)?
  - ▶ Reads
  - ▶ Writes
  - ▶ Updates
  - ▶ Deletes

  This needs to include exactly what data and data subsets that drive filtering are needed for the data accesses (by site).

- ▶ What is the volume of activity/transactions, including the number of users (by site)?
- ▶ How many machines do you have to work with (by site)?
- ▶ What are the available processing power (CPU and memory) and disk space on each of these machines (by site)?
- ▶ What are the stability, speed, and saturation level of the network connections between machines (by site)?
- ▶ What is the dial-in, Internet, or other access mechanism requirement for the data?
- ▶ What potential subscriber or publisher database engines are involved?

Figure 15.23 shows the factors that contribute to replication designs and the possible data replication configuration that would best be used. It is only a partial table because of the numerous factors and the many replication configuration options available. However, it gives a good idea of the general design approach described here. Perhaps 95% of user requirements can be classified fairly easily. The other 5% might take some imagination in determining the best overall solution. Depending on the requirements that need to be supported, you might even end up with a solution using something like log shipping (which is discussed later in this chapter).

Data Characteristics

You need to analyze the underlying data types and characteristics thoroughly. Issues such as collation or character set and data sorting come into play. You must be aware of what these are set to on all nodes of your replication configuration. SQL Server 2005 does not convert the replicated data and might even mistranslate the data as it is replicated because it is impossible to map all characters between character sets. It is best to look up the character set "mapping chart" for SQL Server replication to all other data target environments. Most are covered well, but problems arise with certain data types, such as image, timestamp, and identity. Sometimes, using the Unicode data types at all sites is best for consistency. The following is a general list of things to watch out for in this regard:

Data Access	Latency	Autonomy	Sites (locations)	Frequency	Network	Machines	Owner	Other	REPLICATION
Read Only Reporting	short	high	many	high	fast/ stable	1 server/site	1 OLTP site	Each site only needs regional data	Central Publisher Transactional repl filter by region
Read Only Reporting	long	high	many	low	fast/ stable	1 server/site	1 OLTP site	Each site only needs regional data	Central Publisher Snapshot repl filter by region
Read Mostly A few updates	short	high	<10	medium	fast/ stable	1 server/site	1 OLTP site	Regional updates on one table	Central Publisher Transactional repl Updating Subs
Read Mostly A few updates	medium	high	<10	medium	slow/ unreliable	1 server/site	All update	Regional update all tables	Central Publisher Merge repl
Read equal Equal updates	short	high	<10	medium	fast/ stable	1 server/site	All update	Regional update all tables	Peer-to-Peer Transactional repl
Inserts (new orders)	short	high	many	high	fast/ stable	1 server/site	1 report site	Each site only needs regional data	Central Subscriber Transactional repl
Hot/Warm Spare	very short	high	<2	high	fast/ stable	1 server/site	1 OLTP site	Fail-over	Central Publisher Remote Distributor Transactional repl

15

FIGURE 15.23   Replication design factors.

- ▶ Collation consistency across all nodes of replication.

- ▶ Timestamp column data in replication. It might not be what you think.

- ▶ `identity`, `uniqueidentifier`, and `guid` column behavior with data replication.

- ▶ `text` or `image` data types to heterogeneous subscribers.

- ▶ Missing or unsupported data types because of prior versions of SQL Server or heterogeneous subscribers as part of the replication configuration.

- ▶ Maximum row size limitations between merge replication and transactional replication.

Figure 15.24 lists further SQL Server 2005 replication object limitations.

NOTE

If you have triggers on your tables and you want them to be replicated along with your table, you might want to revisit them and add the line of code `NOT FOR REPLICATION` so that the trigger code isn't executed redundantly on the subscriber side.

Microsoft SQL Server 2005 Replication object	Maximum sizes/numbers (32-bit)	Maximum sizes/numbers (64-bit)
Articles (merge publication)	256	256
Articles (snapshot or transactional publication)	32,767	32,767
Columns in a table (merge publication)	246	246
Columns in a table (SQL Server snapshot or transactional publication)	1000	1000
Columns in a table (Oracle snapshot or transactional publication)	995	995
Bytes for a column used in a row filter (merge publication)	1024	1024
Bytes for a column used in a row filter (snapshot or transactional publication)	8000	8000

FIGURE 15.24   SQL Server 2005 replication object limitations.

Setting Up Replication

In general, SQL Server 2005 data replication is exceptionally easy to set up via SQL Server Management Studio wizards. However, if you use the wizards, you need to be sure to generate SQL scripts for every phase of replication configuration. In a production environment, you are likely to rely heavily on scripts and not have the luxury of having much time to set up and break down production replication configurations via wizards. Generating SQL scripts also eases the setup/breakdown process in development, test, and user acceptance environments.

You always have to define any data replication configuration in the following order:

1. Create or enable a distributor to enable publishing.

2. Enable publishing. (A distributor must be designated for a publisher.)

3. Create a publication and define articles within the publication.

4. Define subscribers and subscribe to a publication.

Figure 15.25 shows SQL Server Management Studio with three separate server connections. These three servers represent a possible replication topology.

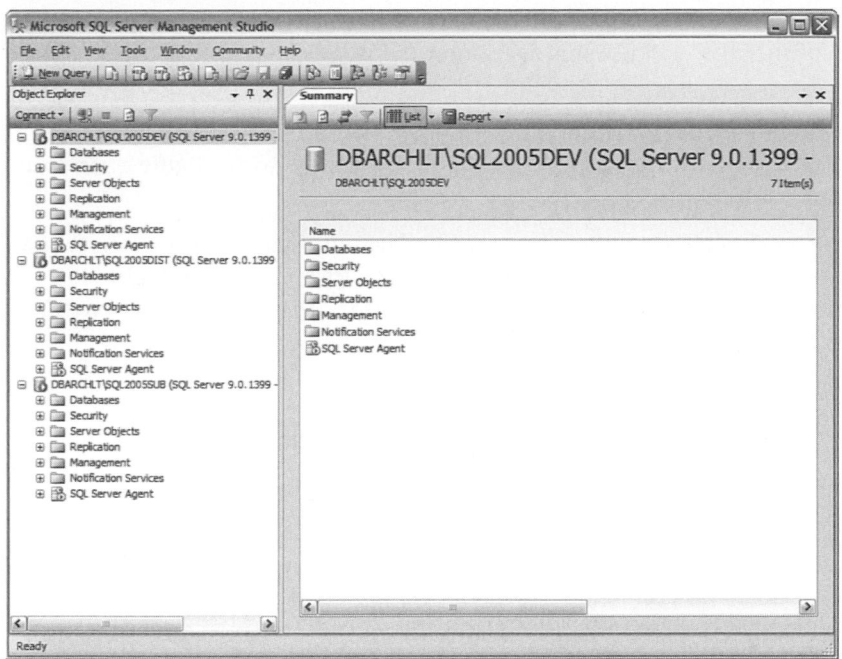

FIGURE 15.25   Three registered servers to be used in the replication topology (central publisher, remote distributor, and subscriber).

The following section takes you through the process of building up a typical central publisher/remote distribution data replication configuration. The following SQL Server named instances are used for different purposes (as shown in Figure 15.25):

▶ **Publisher**—A SQL2005DEV named instance

▶ **Distributor**—A SQL2005DIST named instance (remote distributor)

▶ **Subscriber**—A SQL2005SUB named instance

The following section highlights the different areas in SQL Server Management Studio that are needed to create this replication configuration.

Creating a Distributor and Enabling Publishing

Before setting up a publisher, you have to designate a distribution server to be used by that publisher. As discussed earlier, you can either configure the local server as the distribution server or choose a remote server as the distributor (not on the same machine as the publication server). You can configure the server as a distributor and publisher at the same time, or you can configure the server as a dedicated distributor on the remote server separately. In the sample topology described here, you will start by creating a remote distributor separately so you can orient yourself to what is happening on each server in the topology as it is being built up. You will also be able to enable a specific SQL Server instance as the publisher that will use this distributor (all in one wizard sequence). This is very efficient.

Before you can configure replication, you must be a member of the sysadmin server role, so you should ensure that now. Then you use the following steps to configure a server as a distributor (remote distributor):

1. In SQL Server Management Studio, locate the replication node under the server that will be the distributor (under the SQL2005DIST named instance node). Right-click the replication node and choose Configure Distribution. This starts you through the wizard, which provides three options:

    ▶ Configure this server to be a distributor.

    ▶ Configure this server to be both a publisher and distributor.

    ▶ Configure this server to be a publisher that uses another server as its distributor.

2. When the wizard starts, click past the initial Configure Distribution Wizard splash page. Then chose the first radio button, which should say 'DBARCHLT\ SQL2005DIST' Will Act As Its Own Distributor (as shown in Figure 15.26). This designates this server as a distributor for one or more publishers. The distribution database and log are created here as well (and not on the publication server).

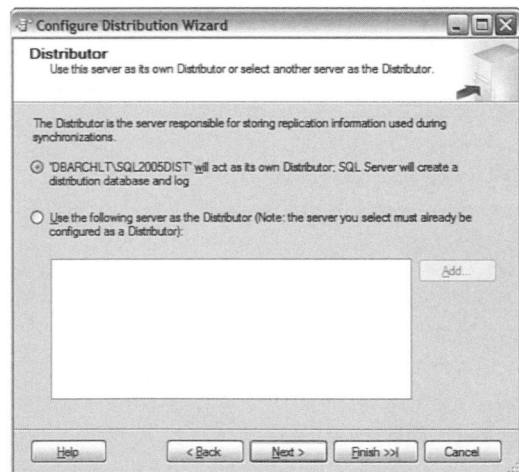

FIGURE 15.26   Configuring a separate distributor (remote) wizard.

3. When you are asked to specify a snapshot folder, give it the proper network full pathname. Remember that much data will be coming here, and it should be on a drive that can support the snapshot concept without filling up the drive.

4. When you are asked to configure the distribution database, select the default settings. Figure 15.27 shows all the distribution database name and location information.

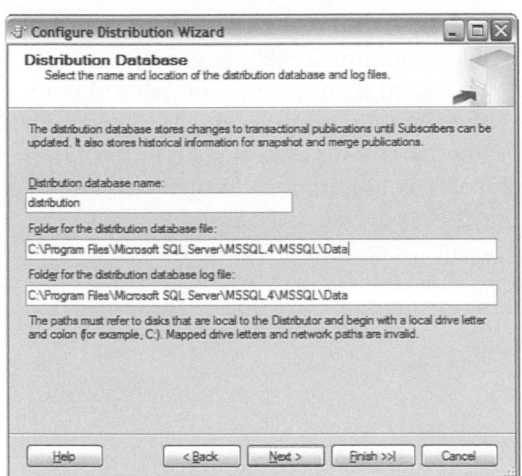

FIGURE 15.27   Specification of the distribution database name and location.

5. Identify the publisher if you know which SQL Server instance will be publishing the data that this distributor will distribute for. To do this, click the Add button at the bottom-left corner of the Publishers page to enable servers to use this distributor when they become publishers. You are prompted for the server name and authentication method for the distributor to reach this publisher. Specify DBARCHLT\SQL2005DEV as a publisher that will use this distributor. The end result, as shown in Figure 15.28, is SQL2005DEV designated (checked) as a publisher that will use this distribution database (distributor). Remember to uncheck the SQL Server named instance of the distribution server (the SQL2005DIST named instance). It will not be a publisher.

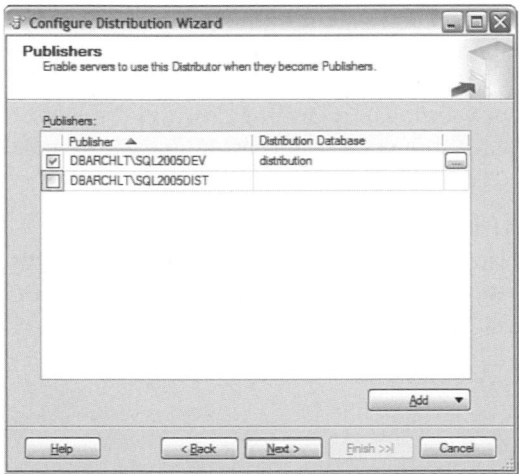

FIGURE 15.28   Designate a publisher that will use this remote distributor.

15

6. Specify a distributor password. This is the password that will be used by publishers to connect to the distributor. You will be able to administer this password through SQL Server Management Studio directly. The wizard then summarizes what actions you want to take place, such as configure the distribution server or generate a script file with steps to configure distribution. Choose both. It's always good to have the scripts created now so you can start script-based configurations immediately. A Complete the Wizard page is displayed, describing all the tasks that are about to happen, along with their configuration specifications. Figure 15.29 show this summary.

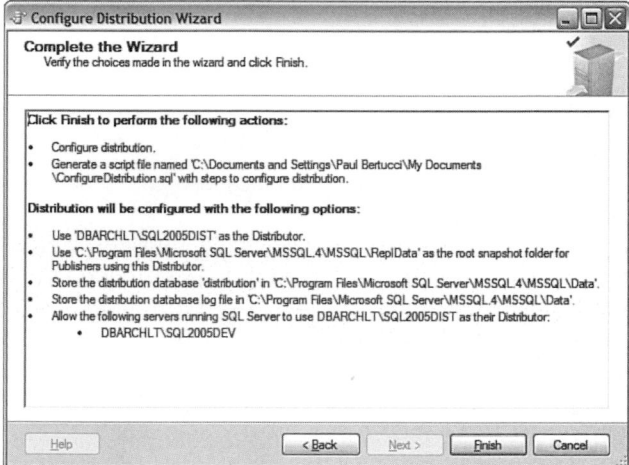

FIGURE 15.29   Completing the configuration of the distributor and enabling the publisher.

When you click Finish, several things begin to occur. First, a configuring dialog page comes up and spins its wheels through each step you have requested (as shown in Figure 15.30). A summary of steps, errors, and warnings is displayed on this page. When it completes, you can explore any issues (errors or warnings) by drilling down in the Report option (lower-right side of this dialog page). Make sure you see Success after each step of this configuration.

Now is probably a good time to locate that distributor setup and enabling publication script and drop it into your replication administrator folder. Figure 15.31 shows what this script looks like. Notice that the password is not displayed. The details of these scripts are described a bit later in this chapter, in the "Scripting Replication" section.

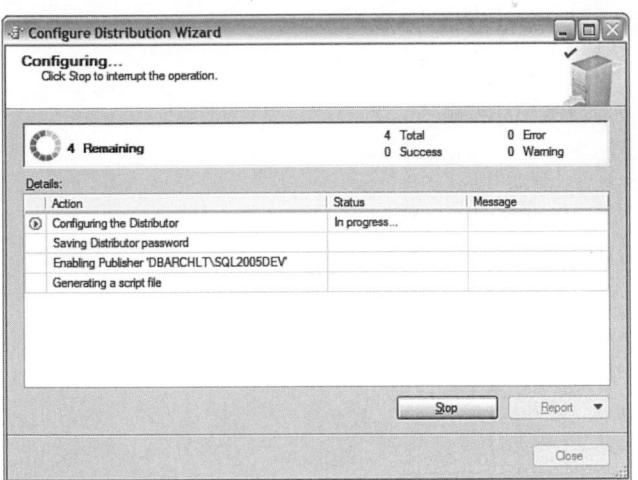

FIGURE 15.30   Configuring the distributor and enabling a publisher under way.

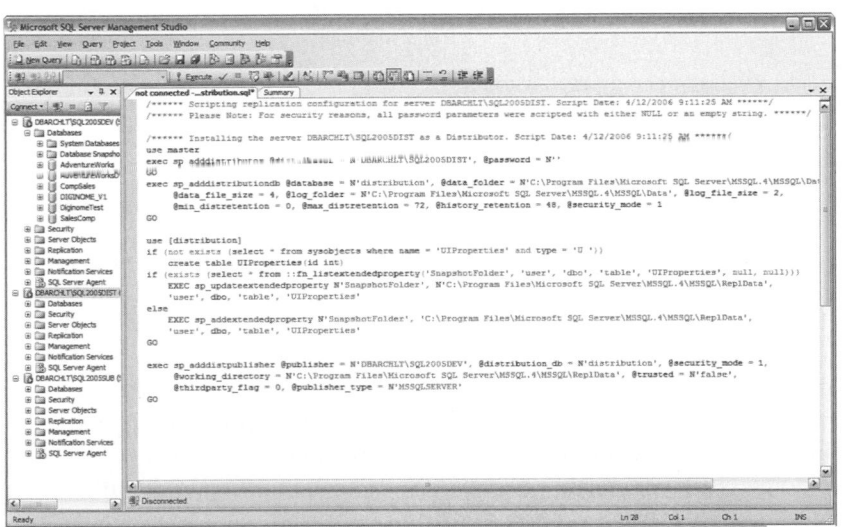

FIGURE 15.31   A script generated for creating the distributor and enabling a publisher.

When the distributor is configured and the distribution database is created, a series of replication agents (managed by SQL Server Agent) are created, with various duties, as described earlier in this chapter. Figure 15.32 shows the initial set of agents that are created on the distribution server. No agents exist yet that actually publish data or distribute data. Those are created later, as you start publishing and subscribing.

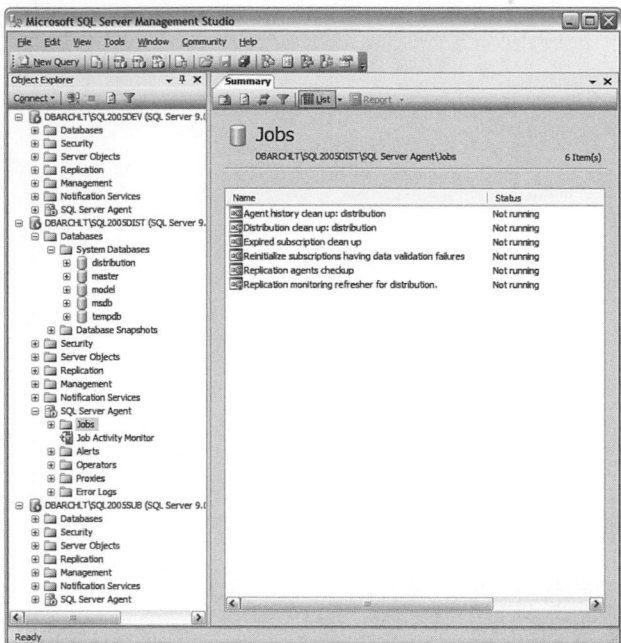

FIGURE 15.32   Initial replication agents on the distributor.

Creating a Publication

When the distribution database has been created and publishing has been enabled on the server, you can create and configure a publication. In SQL Server Management Studio, you start by locating the replication node under the publication server that you want to publish data from (the DBARCHLT\SQL2005DEV named instance in this example). Figure 15.33 shows the program item option when you right-click the replication node under what will be the publication server. As you can see, there are three options here: one to create a new publication, one to create an Oracle publication, and one to create a subscription. You should choose to create a new publication (the first option), and the New Publication Wizard is launched.

Here's how you create a new publication:

1. The first New Publication Wizard page outlines the two major things that can be done with this wizard. Select the data and database objects you want to replicate and filter the published data so that subscribers receive only the data they need. After this splash page, you need to specify how you want to distribute the data for this new publication. As you can see in Figure 15.34, you should use a remote distributor (the DBARCHLT\SQL2005DIST named instance) to distribute data for this new publication you are defining.

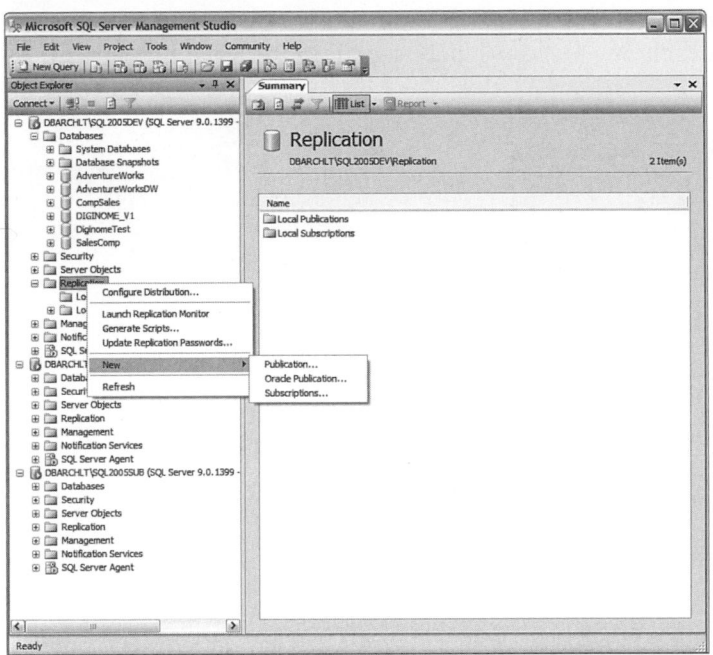

FIGURE 15.33   The Create a New Publication item option on the server that will be the publisher.

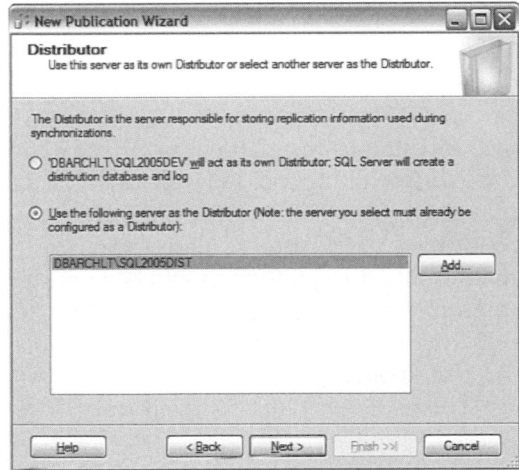

FIGURE 15.34   Specifying the distribution server for the new publication.

2. When you are asked to provide a password that will be used to establish the administrative link to the distributor, supply it. It should be the same thing you specified earlier when setting up the distribution server.

3. Identify the database on which you are going to set up a publication (see Figure 15.35). For this example, choose to create a publication on the AdventureWorks database.

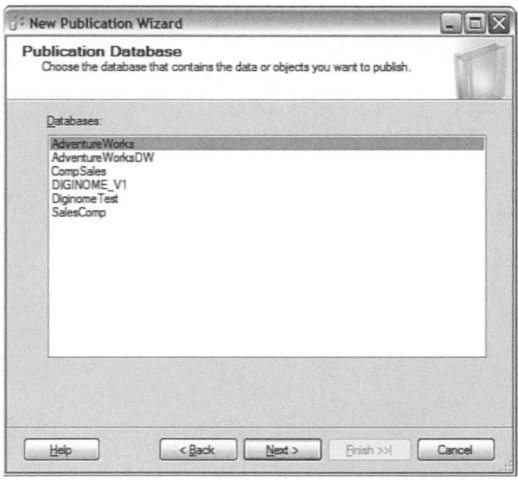

FIGURE 15.35   Choosing the database that contains the data or objects you want to publish.

4. Choose the type of replication method for this publication: Snapshot Publication, Transactional Publication, Transactional Publication with Updateable Subscriptions, or Merge Publication Method of Replication. For this example, select Transactional Publication.

5. Next you are presented with the place where you specify what tables and other objects to publish. These will become your articles. You can specify filtering of any selected articles, where appropriate. To keep this simple, just choose the primary stored procedures, views, indexed views, user-defined functions, and tables of the AdventureWorks database for this publication. (You do not select any filtering at this time.) Figure 15.36 shows the Articles specification page. Also in Figure 15.36, you can view the article properties that dictate how all article objects should be handled by replication (via the Article Properties button in the upper-right corner of this wizard screen). An example of this is specifying the delete delivery format behavior for this publication (for all tables) to be Do Not Replication Delete Statements or Use Stored Procedures to Do the Deletes and not individual delete statements.

    The next wizard screen carefully analyzes what you are asking to become articles and highlights any dependencies that must be considered as part of replication. A good example of this is that indexed views require the tables they are bound to be part of the replication.

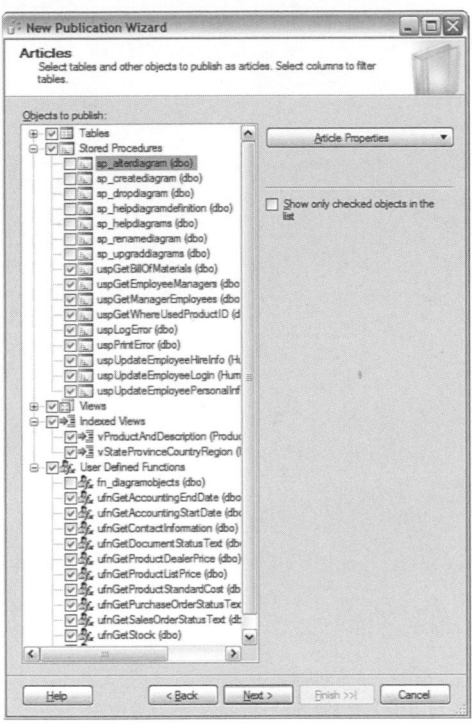

FIGURE 15.36   Choosing the tables and other objects that determine the articles to publish.

6. When the Snapshot Agent wizard configuration screen prompts you to either create a snapshot immediately or at some scheduled time and to keep the snapshot available to initialize subscriptions, select to create a snapshot immediately and keep it available to initialize the subscription. As part of this snapshot agent creation, you have to specify under what security credentials you want the agent security to run. In addition, you can specify if you want the log reader agent to use the same security settings as the snapshot agent. The rule of thumb here is to keep it simple and let these agents use the same security settings (as shown in Figure 15.37).

7. The wizard now has enough information to create the publication. When the wizard actions are summarized for you, choose to create the publication and generate a script file with all the steps to create the publication in it. Again, this script generation part is highly recommended. You certainly don't want to have to go through this wizard over and over. Once is enough.

8. When the summary of all choices made in the creation of a new publication is listed in the Complete the Wizard screen, name the publication appropriately. Your publication names should contain the type of publication method being used (for example, Snapshot, Transactional, Merge) and any other identifying qualifier that seems appropriate (usually reflecting the scope of the publication). Figure 15.38 shows this summary of actions and the publication name PUBLISH AdventureWorks - Transactional.

15

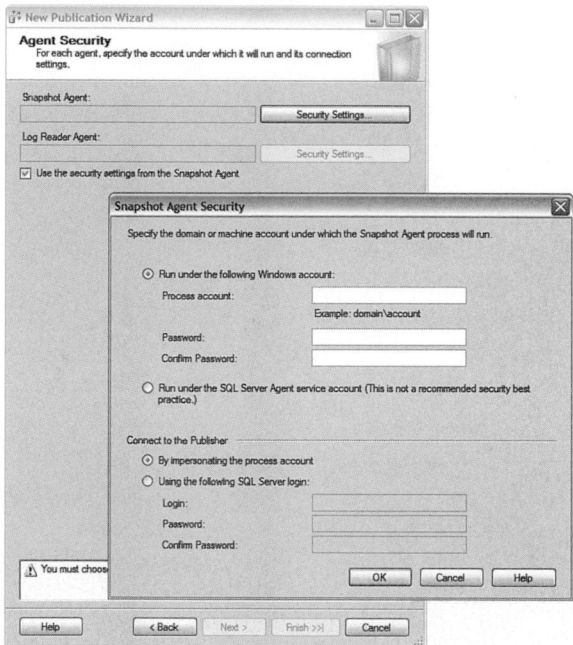

FIGURE 15.37   Agent security for snapshot agent and log reader agent.

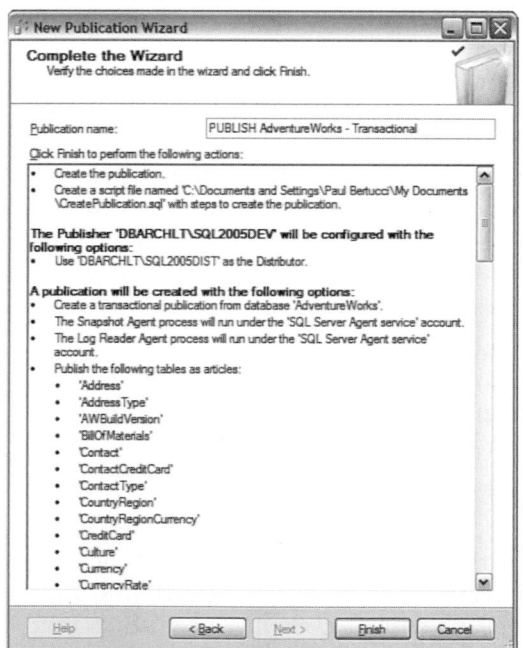

FIGURE 15.38   Publication action summary and naming the publication before it is created.

The actual creation of the publication is next. An action progress screen appears, showing each step (action) and indicating any errors or warnings occurring in the publication creation process. To view any errors or warnings, you simply click the Report button in the lower-right side after the processing completes. As you can see in Figure 15.39, this lists, by name, all articles created and that the snapshot agent is starting. This is where all the initial action takes place.

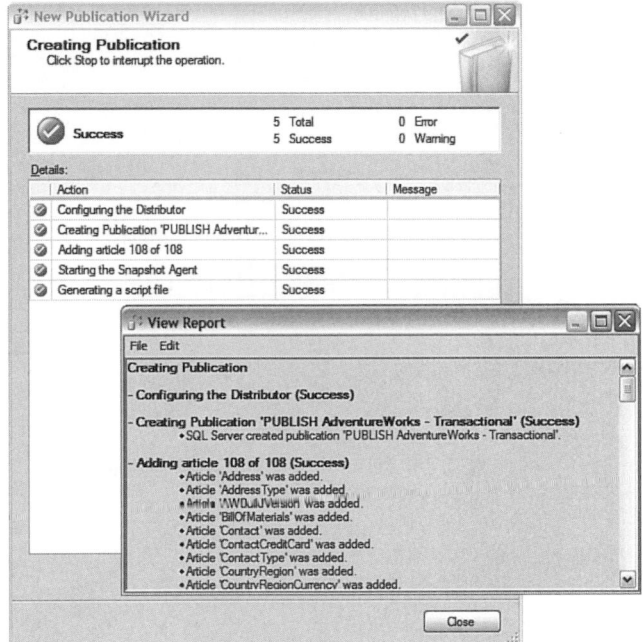

FIGURE 15.39   The publication steps and status, along with the report that is generated during this process.

As part of this process, several new agents (jobs) are added that implement this publication using the designated distributor. There are no subscribers yet; they come later. Figure 15.40 shows the new jobs (agents) and publication entries. You are now ready to create subscriptions against this publication.

As you can see in Figure 15.41, if you launch Replication Monitor (from the Replication node under the publication server), you can see the newly created publication and its status, and you have access to whomever is subscribing to it (none yet), along with the common replication jobs that are servicing this publication.

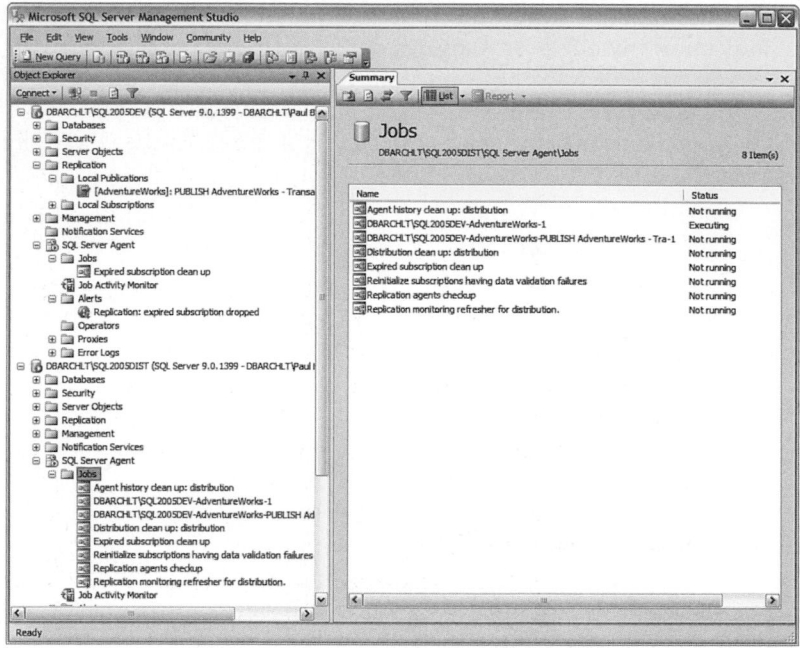

FIGURE 15.40   SQL Server Management Studio and the new publication agents (snapshot agent, distribution agent, and so on) and the new local publication.

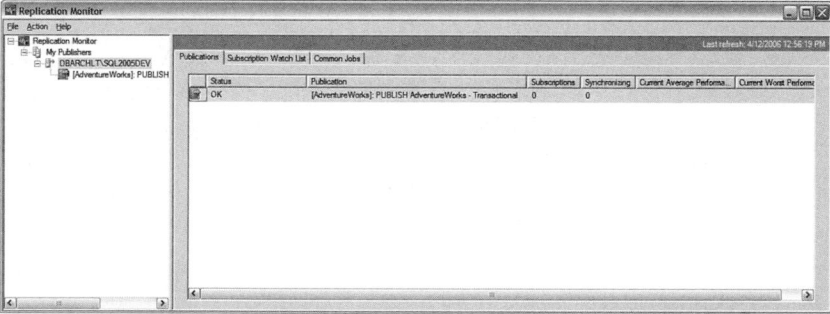

FIGURE 15.41   Replication Monitor, viewing the status of the newly created publication.

Because you chose to execute the snapshot immediately, the snapshot executes and utilizes the snapshot folder to generate the schema files (.sch files), data snapshot files (.bcp), and so on to fully enable a subscription when one is created. Figure 15.42 shows the contents of the snapshot folder being used for the publication of the AdventureWorks publication. Remember that this folder must be located in a place that is big enough to contain all the data that will be extracted and used for the snapshot; plan ahead.

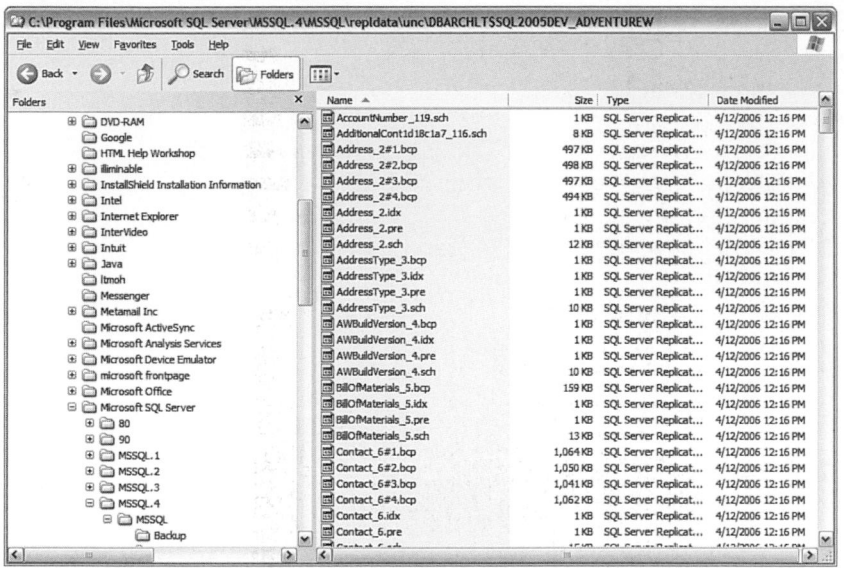

FIGURE 15.42   Contents of the snapshot folder produced for the publication.

Horizontal and Vertical Filtering

During the publication creation process, you could have done some further filtering of data, either horizontal or vertical (or both at the same time). The concept of filtering is covered earlier in this chapter. Figure 15.43 illustrates all you need to do to vertically filter (in terms of limiting what gets published to a subset of columns of a table). As you can see, you uncheck the AccountNumber column for the Customer table so that it isn't included in the article for that object in this publication. This might be done because account number information needs to be more tightly controlled within your company and shouldn't be part of what is viewed by any subscribing systems.

In addition, you can specify horizontal filters by using the Filter Rows option on a publication (publication properties). This allows you to specify horizontal filtering on any table you publish. Figure 15.44 shows a typical row filter on the Customer table that results in publishing North East Territory customers only (that is, those with TerritoryID values of 1 or 2).

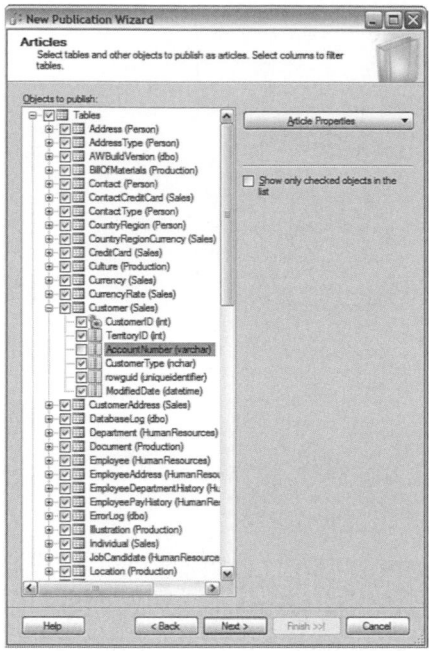

FIGURE 15.43   Specifying a vertical filter on the Customer table (limiting the columns to be published).

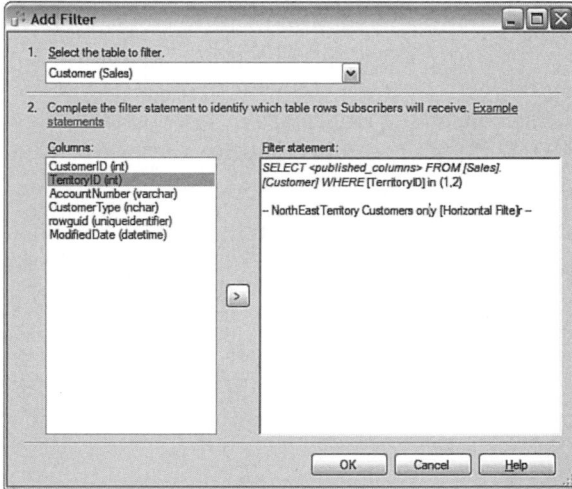

FIGURE 15.44   Specifying a horizontal filter on the Customer table (limiting the rows to be published).

Join filtering allows you to limit the rows you will publish, via a join criteria, to another table. Figure 15.45 shows a complex join that filters SalesOrderHeader rows that correspond to North East Territory customers only (that is, those with TerritoryID values of 1 or 2).

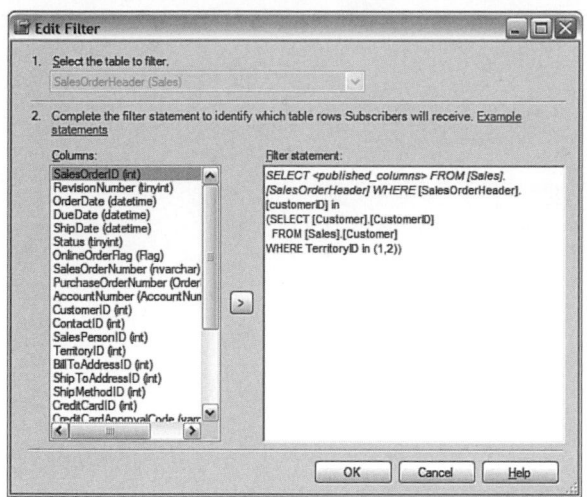

FIGURE 15.45   Specifying a join filter on the SalesOrderHeader table (limiting the sales rows that will be published by joining for the North East customers only).

Creating Subscriptions

Now that you have installed and configured the distributor, enabled publishing, and created a publication, you need to create subscriptions.

Remember that two types of subscriptions can be created: push or pull. Pull subscriptions allow remote sites to subscribe to any publication that they are allowed to, but for this to work, you must be confident that the administrators at the other sites have properly configured the subscriptions at their sites. Push subscriptions are easier to create because all the subscription processes are performed and administered from the publication/distributor point of view. This also makes them the most common approach.

At this point, you can use the New Subscription Wizard to create a push subscription:

1. In SQL Server Management Studio, locate the Replication node under the publication server (the DBARCHLT\SQL2005DEV named instance in this example). Open this node, navigate to the Local Publication branch, and right-click the newly created publication of the AdventureWorks database (that is, [AdventureWorks]:PUBLISH AdventureWorks - Transactional). As you can see in Figure 15.46, this launches the New Subscription Wizard, where you can create one or more subscriptions to a publication and specify where and when to run the agents that synchronize the subscription.

2. When you are presented with the option of where the replication agents will be run for the subscription, choose the first option—having the agents run at the distributor. This makes it a push subscription and is much easier to control and manage centrally than a pull subscription.

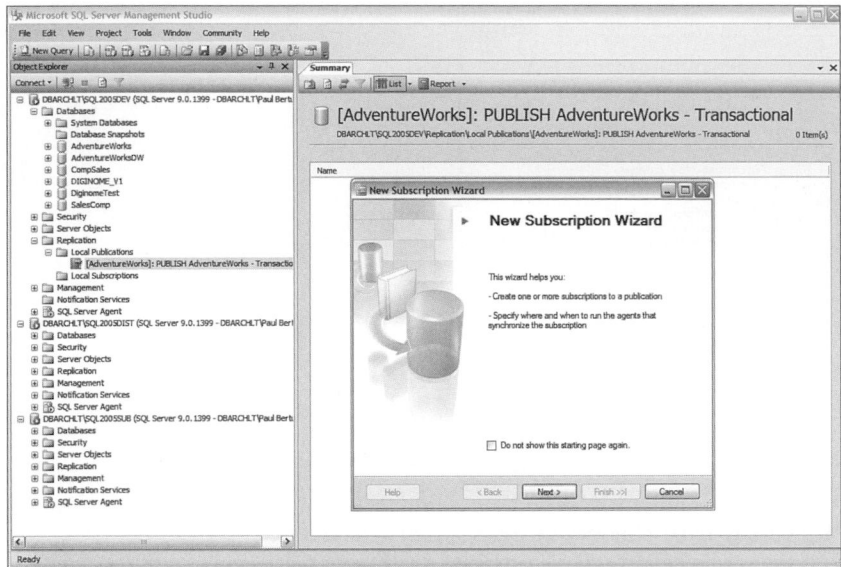

FIGURE 15.46   Launching the New Subscription Wizard from SQL Server Management Studio.

3. On the next wizard screen, identify the subscriber server by clicking the Add Subscriber button on the lower-left side of this screen and providing the connection information to that subscriber server (that is, server name and authentication information). The New Database dialog appears, asking you to identify the database target for the subscription and the physical database files for its allocation (assuming that you want to create this from scratch using this wizard process). Figure 15.47 shows this New Database screen, with the target database named AdventureWorksODS.

4. In the Subscribers screen, with the new entry for the target subscriber server (the DBARCHLT\SQL2005SUB named instance in this example), check the box for the target subscription server. Figure 15.48 shows this subscriber server and the subscription database target.

5. Specify the process account and connection options for the distribution agent (to connect to the subscription server). Typically, you choose the option to use a domain account or choose to impersonate the process account.

6. Specify the synchronization schedule for each agent. You want the distribution agent to run continuously, but you also have the options to run on a schedule and on demand.

7. Specify the initialization of the subscription. Again, you want the subscription to be initialized immediately, but, depending on the size of the database, this might be accomplished manually with a database backup of the publication database.

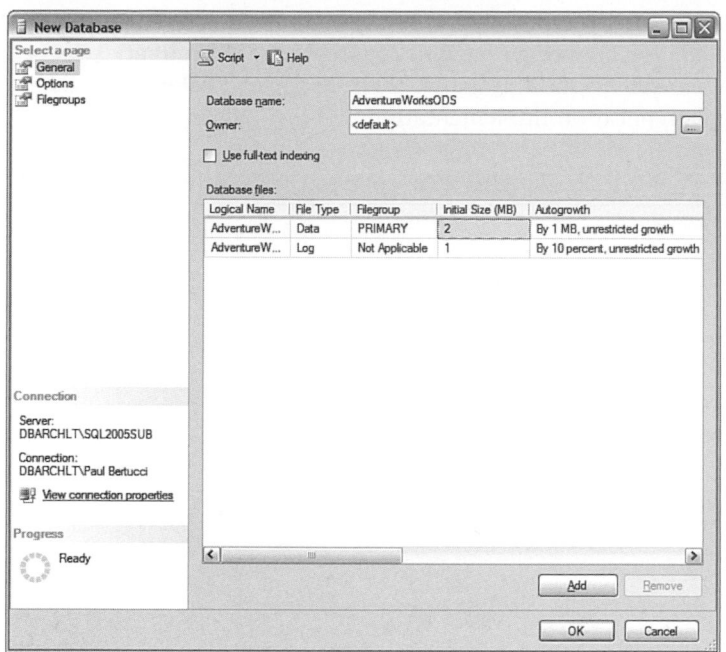

FIGURE 15.47   The New Database screen specifying the targot database.

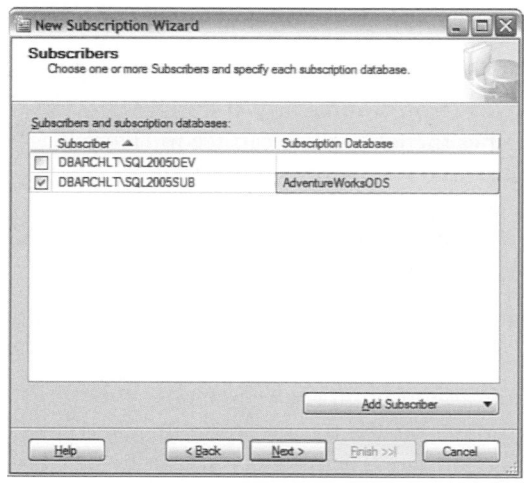

FIGURE 15.48   Specifying the subscription server target database.

8. On the next screen, which lists the New Subscription Wizard actions, choose to create the subscription and generate a script file with all the steps to create the subscription for use later.

9. On the next wizard dialog, identify the location of the script that will be generated. As shown in Figure 15.49, you are presented with the final wizard summary screen. Click Finish to create your subscription, initialize the subscription database, and enjoy a full transactional replication implementation.

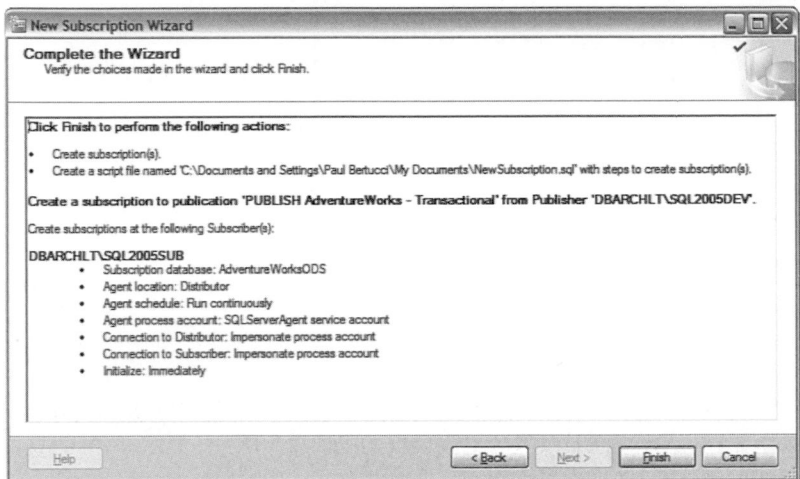

FIGURE 15.49   The New Subscription Wizard summary.

When you click Finish, the create subscription process starts and goes through each step. Remember to check for errors or warnings if any errors occur. When this completes, you wait for the agents to initialize the target database and start replication to the subscriber. If you have specified that the schema and data be created immediately, things start happening quickly. The distribution agent finishes the job. As you can see in Figure 15.50, the distribution agent applies the schemas to the subscriber (as viewed from the Replication Monitor's Distribute to Subscriber History tab). The bulk copying of the data into the tables on the subscriber side follows accordingly. After this bulk copying is done, the initialization step is completed, and active replication begins.

The complete replication buildup is finished, and you should be fully functional for replicating transactions to the subscriber.

Figure 15.51 shows what it looks like from Replication Monitor as transactions flow through the replication topology. This screenshot shows the transaction counts and commands being delivered on the last leg in the journey (from the distributor to a subscriber). You are in business!

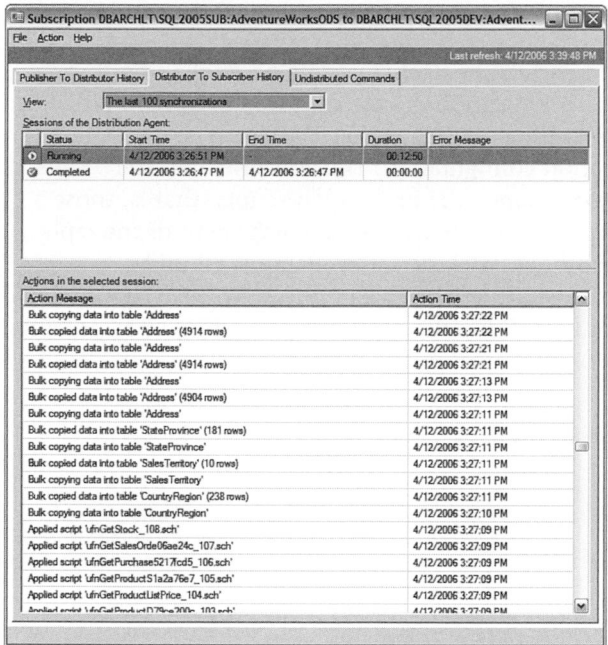

FIGURE 15.50   Applying schemas (.sch files) and bulk loading data to the subscriber.

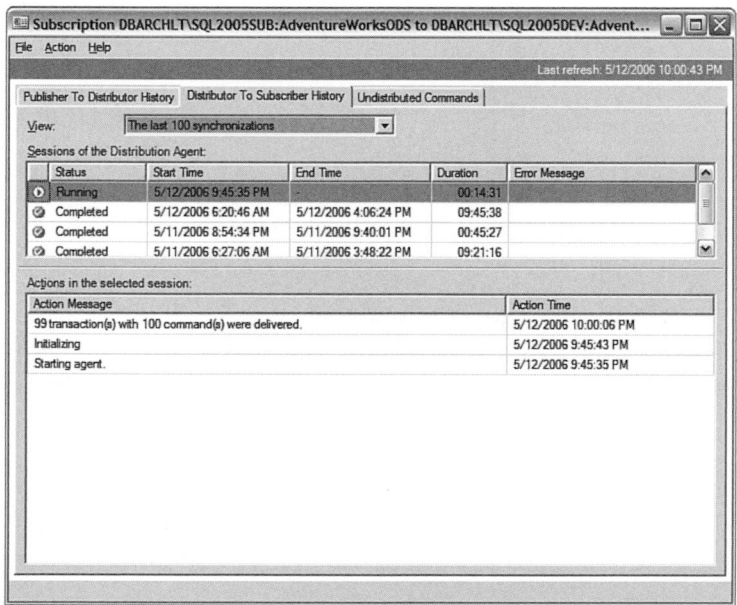

FIGURE 15.51   Transactions replicating to the subscriber (pushed).

Scripting Replication

Earlier, it was suggested to generate SQL scripts for all that you do because going through wizards every time you have to configure replication is a difficult way to run a production environment. In the example in the preceding section, you always chose to generate these scripts as you built up the replication configuration. This was only half the scripts that are needed, however. You must also generate the breakdown scripts (that is, those that drop and remove replication components) to remove each component of the replication topology in case you need to start from scratch or, as an example, rebuild a subscriber that is completely nonfunctional. As you can see in Figure 15.52, SQL Server Management Studio has a great feature that allows the complete generation of all aspects of replication topology (including disabling and removing replication).

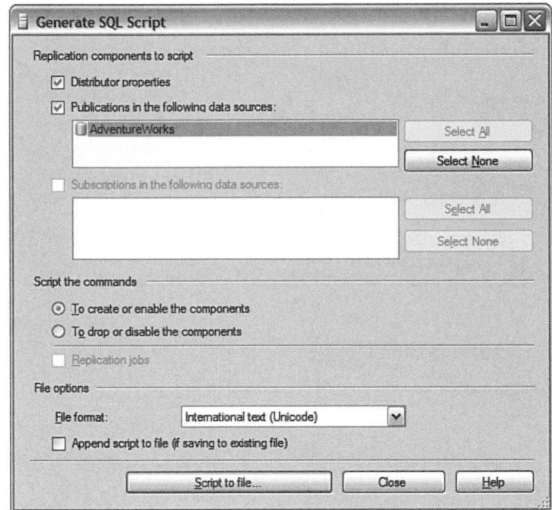

FIGURE 15.52   A script-generation feature for all replication topology components.

The following is an example of the SQL scripts needed to generate the part of the data replication configuration that you just built with the wizard:

> **NOTE**
>
> Remember that working from scripts minimizes the errors you make while supporting your data replication environments (especially at 3:00 a.m.).

```
use master
GO
/****** Scripting replication configuration for server DBARCHLT\SQL2005DIST.
Script Date: 4/12/2006 9:11:25 AM ******/
```

```
/****** Please Note: For security reasons, all password parameters were
scripted with either NULL or an empty string. ******/
/****** Installing the server DBARCHLT\SQL2005DIST as a Distributor.
Script Date: 4/12/2006 9:11:25 AM ******/
use master
exec sp_adddistributor @distributor = N'DBARCHLT\SQL2005DIST', @password = N''
GO
exec sp_adddistributiondb @database = N'distribution', @data_folder =
N'C:\Program Files\Microsoft SQL Server\MSSQL.4\MSSQL\Data',
@data_file_size = 4,
@log_folder = N'C:\Program Files\Microsoft SQL Server\MSSQL.4\MSSQL\Data',
@log_file_size = 2, @min_distretention = 0, @max_distretention = 72,
@history_retention = 48, @security_mode = 1
GO
use [distribution]
if (not exists (select * from sysobjects where name = 'UIProperties'
and type = 'U '))
    create table UIProperties(id int)
if (exists (select * from ::fn_listextendedproperty('SnapshotFolder',
'user', 'dbo', 'table', 'UIProperties', null, null)))
    EXEC sp_updateextendedproperty N'SnapshotFolder',
N'C:\Program Files\Microsoft SQL Server\MSSQL.4\MSSQL\ReplData',
'user', dbo, 'table', 'UIProperties'
else
    EXEC sp_addextendedproperty N'SnapshotFolder',
'C:\Program Files\Microsoft SQL Server\MSSQL.4\MSSQL\ReplData',
'user', dbo, 'table', 'UIProperties'
GO

exec sp_adddistpublisher @publisher = N'DBARCHLT\SQL2005DEV',
@distribution_db = N'distribution', @security_mode = 1,
@working_directory = N'C:\Program Files\MS SQL Server\MSSQL.4\MSSQL\ReplData',
@trusted = N'false', @thirdparty_flag = 0, @publisher_type = N'MSSQLSERVER'
GO
```

The complete set of buildup and breakdown scripts for the example used here are available on this book's CD-ROM.

Monitoring Replication

After replication is up and running, it is important for you to monitor it and see how things are running. You can do this in several ways, including using SQL statements, SQL Server Management Studio, and Windows Performance Monitor. You are interested in the agent's successes and failures, the speed at which replication is done, and the synchronization state of tables involved in replication. Other things to watch for are the sizes of the distribution database, the growth of the subscriber databases, and the available space on the distribution server's snapshot working directory.

Replication Monitoring SQL Statements

One way to look at the replication configuration and do things such as validate row counts is to use various replication stored procedures, including the following:

- ▶ **sp_helppublication**—Info on the publication server
- ▶ **sp_helparticle**—Article definition information
- ▶ **sp_helpdistributor**—Distributor information
- ▶ **sp_helpsubscriberinfo**—Subscriber server information
- ▶ **sp_helpsubscription**—Subscription information

These are all extremely useful for verifying exactly how the replication configuration is really configured. If you execute these stored procedures (from the publication database), you get a great documentation of your complete replication topology that can be included in run books or other system documentation. Here's what you might do to see how the current replication configuration has been built-out:

```
use AdventureWorks
go
exec sp_helppublication
exec sp_helparticle @publication='PUBLISH AdventureWorks - Transactional'
exec sp_helpdistributor
exec sp_helpsubscriberinfo
exec sp_helpsubscription
go
```

It yields this:

```
1 PUBLISH AdventureWorks - Transactional        0      1     1     0
- - - - - - - - - - - - - - - - - - - - - - - - - - - - - - - - - - - - - - - -
1  Address           [Person].[Address]             Address
2  AddressType       [Person].[AddressType]         AddressType
3  AWBuildVersion    [dbo].[AWBuildVersion]         AWBuildVersion
4  BillOfMaterials   [Production].[BillOfMaterials] BillOfMaterials
5  Contact           [Person].[Contact]             Contact
6  ContactCreditCard [Sales].[ContactCreditCard]    ContactCreditCard
7  ContactType       [Person].[ContactType]         ContactType
...
```

In addition, sp_replcounters shows the activity of this replication session. You can see the volume of traffic and the throughput here:

```
exec sp_replcounters
go
```

It yields this:

```
database repl_trans rate trans/sec latency (sec) etc.
AdventureWorks     0          1562.5     1.243
```

For actual row count validation, you can use sp_publication_validation, which goes through and checks the row counts of the publication and subscribers:

```
exec sp_publication_validation @publication
    = 'PUBLISH AdventureWorks - Transactional'
go
```

It yields this:

```
Generated expected rowcount value of 19614 for Address.
Generated expected rowcount value of 6 for AddressType.
Generated expected rowcount value of 1 for AWBuildVersion.
Generated expected rowcount value of 2679 for BillOfMaterials.
Generated expected rowcount value of 19972 for Contact.
Generated expected rowcount value of 19118 for ContactCreditCard.
Generated expected rowcount value of 20 for ContactType.
Generated expected rowcount value of 238 for CountryRegion.
Generated expected rowcount value of 109 for CountryRegionCurrency.
Generated expected rowcount value of 19118 for CreditCard.
Generated expected rowcount value of 8 for Culture.
```

Another way to monitor replication is to look at the actual data that is being replicated. To do this, you first run the SELECT count (*) FROM tblname statement against the table where data is being replicated. Then you verify directly whether the most current data available is in the database. If you make a change to the data in the published table, do the changes show up in the replicated tables? If not, you might need to investigate how replication was configured on the server.

If you are allowing updatable subscriptions, the replication queue comes into play. You need to learn all about the queueread command prompt utility. This utility configures and begins the queue reader agent, which reads messages stored in the SQL Server queue or a Microsoft message queue and applies those messages to the publisher.

To help you visualize how replication works, and to help you monitor replication, the following sample stored procedure, called REPL_ROWS_GENERATED, takes one parameter (the number of rows [new customers in the Customer table] you want to have inserted at a time) and generates new rows in the Customer table that can reflect different data activity that will be published:

```
Use AdventureWorks
Go
--------------------------------------------------------
-- generate 500 new customers for replication testing --
--------------------------------------------------------
exec REPL_ROWS_GENERATOR 500
go
```

This example shows how to execute this stored procedure to insert 500 new customers. If you don't supply any parameter, the default is 100 new customers. Try it out.

The following messages appear after you execute the REPL_ROWS_GENERATED stored procedure:

```
INSERTING ROW: 1
INSERTING ROW: 2
INSERTING ROW: 3
INSERTING ROW: 4
INSERTING ROW: 5
INSERTING ROW: 6
INSERTING ROW: 7
INSERTING ROW: 8
INSERTING ROW: 9
INSERTING ROW: 10
...
INSERTING ROW: 500
```

Figure 15.53 shows this stored procedure, which is included on the CD-ROM for this book.

Monitoring Replication within SQL Server Management Studio

As you can imagine, SQL Server Management Studio provides considerable information about the status of replication. Most of this is available via Replication Monitor. In Replication Monitor, you can see the activity for publishers, distributors, and subscribers; you can see all agent details; and you can configure alerts.

Through Replication Monitor, you also can invoke validation subscriptions processing to see if replication is in sync. You just navigate to the publication whose subscription you want to validate, right-click, and chose Validate Subscription option. This allows you to verify that the subscriber has the same number of rows of replicated data as the publisher. You can validate all subscriptions or just a particular one. Validation options are extensive and include using fast row count methods, actual row count methods, and even checksum comparisons of row data. This is a huge area of improvement for SQL Server 2005. Figure 15.54 shows the results of running a complete subscription validation.

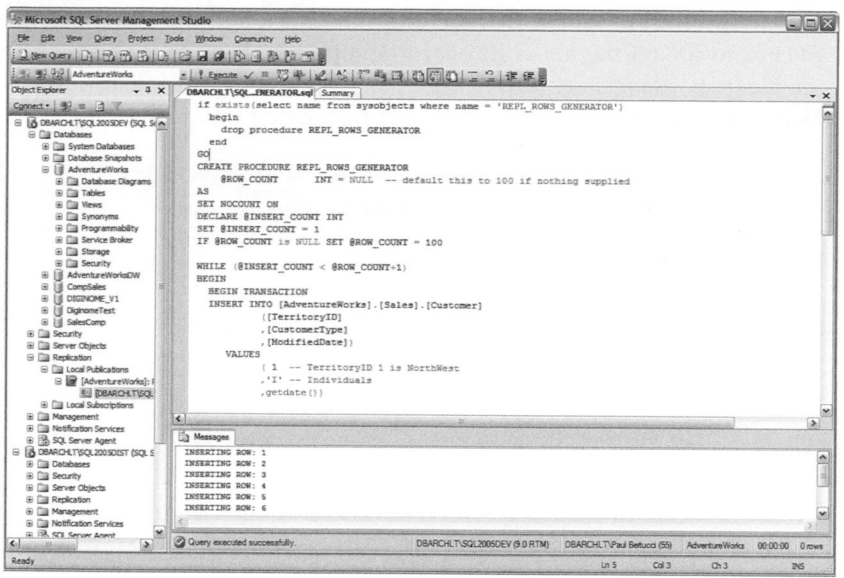

FIGURE 15.53   A sample row-generating stored procedure for testing data replication.

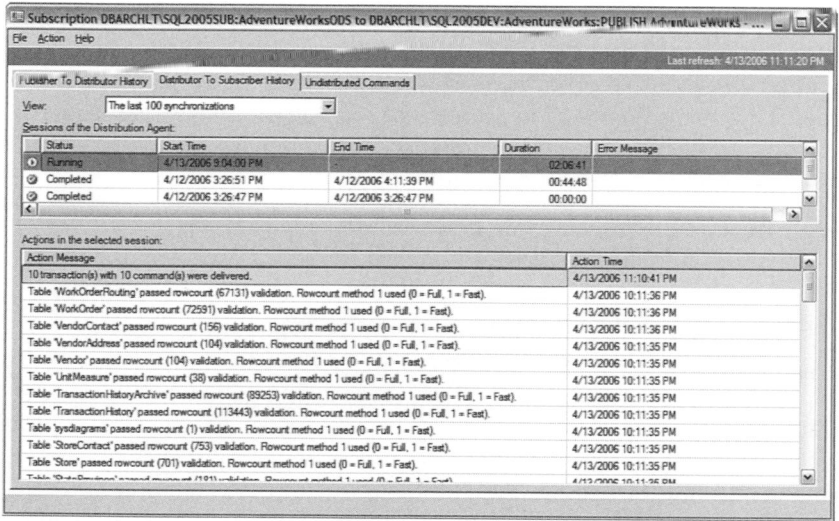

FIGURE 15.54   Validation of subscriptions via Replication Monitor.

Another new feature to help monitor replication is tracer tokens. Essentially, you create a marker (called a token) that flows through the full replication topology (from publisher to distributor to subscriber). It does not affect data tables! This flow is monitored and measured, down to the millisecond, and is for a specific publisher-to-subscriber path.

Figure 15.55 shows the Tracer Tokens tab of the Replication Monitor and the Insert Tracer button that you can click to fire off the token through the topology. You can click this button to quickly see where bottlenecks exist (for example, from publisher to distributor, from distributor to subscriber) and the latency of the data flow along the way.

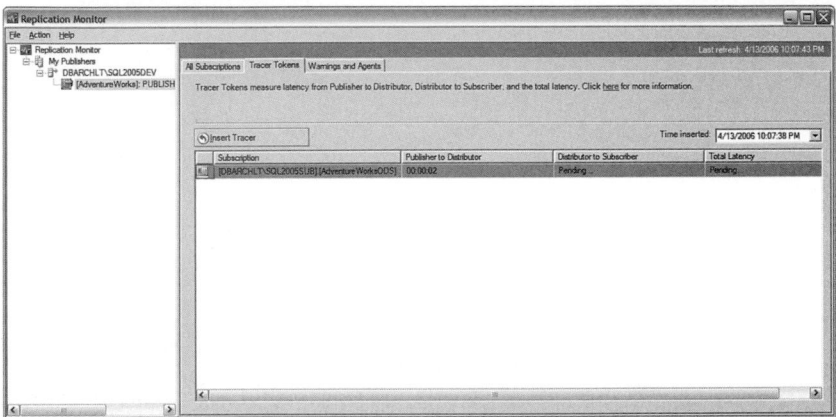

FIGURE 15.55   Tracer tokens for monitoring data replication throughput.

Troubleshooting Replication Failures

Configuring replication and monitoring for successful replication is pretty easy. The fun begins when failures start arising. Replication Monitor pays for itself quickly. Red flags begin appearing to indicate agent failures. Depending on how you have the alerts defined, you probably also get considerable emails or pages.

The following are the most common issues you find with data replication:

▶ Data row count inconsistencies, as discussed in the preceding section

▶ Subscriber/publisher schema change failures

▶ Connection failures

▶ Agent failures

For the conventional replication situations, if the problem is with the validation of subscriptions processing, it is usually best to resynchronize the subscription by dropping it and re-subscribing or by re-initializing the subscription.

Another common issue is that the SQL Server Agent service doesn't start. Manually attempting to restart this service usually shakes things loose. Sometimes an object on the subscriber becomes messed up. The solution is usually to create that object again and reload its data via BCP or IS. Then you can resynchronize the subscription. In such a case, the subscription included this object originally, but it has become invalid in some way. With a heterogeneous subscriber, you often see connection errors due to invalid login IDs used in the ODBC connection. The quick fix is usually to just redefine the ODBC data source connection information.

A much more complex failure can arise when the replication queue is stopped due to some type of SQL language failure in the command being replicated. This is extremely serious because it stops all replication from continuing, and the distribution database starts growing rapidly. Replication keeps trying to execute, but it fails each time. This situation is essentially a permanent roadblock. The solution is to locate the exact transaction in the distribution database and delete it physically from the transaction queue. This is highly unusual, but it is necessary when the circumstance presents itself. First, by looking at the error detail information in the distribution agent history, you can isolate the SQL statement on which it is choking. Then you have to find it in the distribution database. You start by executing the `sp_browsereplcmds` stored procedure from the distribution database. This gives you all the replication transactions (that is, each `xact_seqno`) along with the associated SQL command. You have to pump this to a text file for searching. You then search this data for the matching SQL command. When you locate it, you look for its associated transaction number (`xact_seqno`). You use this `xact_seqno` value to delete it from the `Msrepl_commands` table in the distribution database. This frees up the roadblock. You see this type of issue only about once every six months, if at all (hopefully).

The Performance Monitor

You can use Windows Performance Monitor to monitor the health of your replication scenario. When you install SQL Server, you get several new objects and counters in Performance Monitor:

- ▶ **SQLServer:Replication Agents**—This object contains counters used to monitor the status of all replication agents, including the total number running.

- ▶ **SQLServer:Replication Dist**—This object contains counters used to monitor the status of the distribution agents, including the latency and the number of transactions transferred per second.

- ▶ **SQLServer:Replication Logreader**—This object contains counters used to monitor the status of the log reader agent, including the latency and the number of transactions transferred per second.

- ▶ **SQLServer:Replication Merge**—This object contains counters used to monitor the status of the merge agents, including the number of transactions and the number of conflicts per second.

- ▶ **SQLServer:Replication Snapshot**—This object contains counters used to monitor the status of the snapshot agents, including the number of transactions per second.

Replication in Heterogeneous Environments

SQL Server 2005 allows for transactional and snapshot replication of data into and out of environments other than SQL Server. This is termed *heterogeneous* replication. The easiest way to set up this replication is to use ODBC or OLE DB and create a push subscription to the subscriber. This is much easier to make work than you might imagine. SQL Server can publish to the following database types:

▶ Microsoft Access

▶ Oracle

▶ Sybase

▶ IBM DB2/AS400

▶ IBM DB2/MVS

SQL Server can replicate data to any other type of database, provided that the following are true:

▶ The driver must be ODBC Level 1 compliant.

▶ The driver must be 32-bit, thread safe, and designed for the processor architecture on which the distribution process runs.

▶ The driver must support transactions.

▶ The driver and underlying database must support Data Definition Language (DDL).

▶ The underlying database cannot be read-only.

Backup and Recovery in a Replication Configuration

A replication-oriented backup strategy will reap major benefits for you after you have implemented a data replication configuration. You must realize that the scope of data and what you must back up together have changed. In addition, you must be aware of the recovery time frame and plan your backup/recovery strategy for this. You might not have multiple hours available to you to recover an entire replication topology. You now have databases that are conceptually joined, and you might need to back them up together in one synchronized backup. Figure 15.56 shows overall backup strategies for the most common recovery needs.

When backing up environments, you need to back up the following at each site:

▶ Publisher (published database, `msdb`, and `master`)

▶ Distributor (distribution database, `msdb`, and `master`)

▶ Subscribers (subscriber database, optionally `msdb`, and `master` when pull subscriptions are being done)

You should always make copies of your replication scripts and keep them handy. At a very minimum, you need to keep copies at the publisher and distributor and one more location, such as at one of your subscribers. You will use them for recovery someday.

Recovery Need	Backup Strategy
100% data, All sites, Small Recovery Window	Coordinated DB backups at all sites involved in the replication configuration (publisher, distributor and all subscribers). Somewhat complex to do.
100% data, All sites, Medium Recovery Window	Backup Publication DB and Distribution DB together. Replication can be recovered from this point very easily without reconfiguring anything. Just have to re-initialize the subscribers. This is the most common approach being used.
100% data, All sites, Big Recovery Window	Backup of Publication DB only. Can then reconfigure replication via scripts and reinitialize distribution, and all subscribers fairly easily.

FIGURE 15.56   Common backup strategies for different recovery needs.

You shouldn't forget to back up `master` and `msdb` when any new replication object is created, updated, or deleted.

If you have allowed updating of subscribers using queued updates, you need to expand your backup capability to include these queues.

In general, you will find that even when you walk up and pull the plug on your distribution server, publication server, or any subscribers, automatic recovery works well to get you back online and replicating quickly, without human intervention.

Some Thoughts on Performance

From a performance point of view, the replication configuration defaults err on the side of optimal throughput. That's the good news. The bad news is that everybody is different in some way, so you have to consider a bit of tuning of your replication configuration. In general, you can get your replication configuration working well by doing the following:

▶ Keeping the amount of data to be replicated at any one point small by running agents continuously, instead of at long, scheduled intervals.

▶ Setting a minimum amount of memory allocated to SQL Server by using the Min Server Memory option to guarantee ample memory across the board.

▶ Using good disk drive physical separation rules, such as keeping the transaction log on a separate disk drive from the data portion. Your transaction log is much more heavily used when you opt for transactional replication.

▶ Putting your snapshot working directory on a separate disk drive to minimize disk drive arm contention. You should use a separate snapshot folder for each publication.

▶ Publishing only what you need. By selectively publishing only the minimum amount of data required, you implement a much more efficient replication configuration, which is faster overall.

▶ Trying to run snapshots in non-peak times so your network and production environments aren't bogged down.

▶ Minimizing transformation of data involved with replication.

Log Shipping

If you have a small need to create a read-only (ad hoc query/reporting) database environment that can tolerate a high degree of data latency, you might be a candidate for using log shipping. Log shipping is still a feature for SQL Server 2005, but it will be deprecated by the next release. In other words, it might be easy to use and easy to manage, but it is being phased out as a feature of SQL Server. For this reason, we do not describe it in this book (it is described in detail in *SQL Server 2000 Unleashed*, though). For those who have current log shipping configurations, it is time to move to database mirroring. This will be an easy transition because the two capabilities are so much alike. (Actually, many aspects of database mirroring came from log shipping.)

Data Replication and Database Mirroring for Fault Tolerance and High Availability

SQL Server 2005 allows you to use combinations of options to achieve higher availability levels. A prime example of this is combining data replication with database mirroring to provide maximum availability of data, scalability to users, and fault tolerance via failover at potentially each node in the replication topology. You can start with the publisher and the distributor, making them both database mirror failover configurations. Building up a combination of both options together is the best of both worlds: the super low latency of database mirroring for fault tolerance and the high availability (and scalability) of data through replication. (For more information, see Chapter 16, "Database Mirroring.")

Summary

Replication is a powerful feature of SQL Server that can be used in many business situations. Companies can use replication for anything from roll-up reporting to relieving the main server from ad hoc queries and reporting. It is critical to let your company's requirements drive the type of replication technique to use. Determining the replication option and configuration to use is difficult, but actually setting it up is pretty easy. Microsoft has come a long way in this regard. Microsoft's overall architectural approach and implementation is the model for the industry. You should not be afraid to use this facility. It is more than production-worthy, and the flexibility it offers and the overall performance are just short of incredible, incredible, incredible (replication humor for you).

In Chapter 16 we delve into the ability to make an image of a database for failover purposes using the newest mechanism available within SQL Server 2005. This is a landmark addition for SQL Server.

Database Mirroring

IN THIS CHAPTER

▶ What's New in Database Mirroring

▶ What Is Database Mirroring?

▶ Roles of the Database Mirroring Configuration

▶ Setting Up and Configuring Database Mirroring

▶ Testing Failover from the Principal to the Mirror

▶ Client Setup and Configuration for Database Mirroring

▶ Using Replication and Database Mirroring Together

▶ Using Database Snapshots from a Mirror for Reporting

Finally, Microsoft has added a feature that makes it worth upgrading to this new version of SQL Server as fast as you possibly can. Database mirroring is such a huge technology jump in capabilities that even the smallest company can now provide near-real-time database failover without fancy, expensive hardware that is required with more complex configurations, such as with SQL Server Clustering (that is built on Microsoft Cluster Service [MSCS]). Remember that MSCS requires shared resources, separate network connections for internal heartbeat communication, and so on. In addition, multiple layers of software are involved (MSCS plus SQL Server). With database mirroring, you can set up a near-real-time database failover environment using all conventional, low-cost machines, without any complex hardware compatibility requirements, and database mirror can fail over in as little as 3 seconds! Wow!

This new feature allows anyone to immediately step up to nearly 99% availability at the database layer at a very low cost, and it is easily configured and managed.

What's New in Database Mirroring

As mentioned earlier, Microsoft SQL Server 2005 is shifting very strongly to a goal of providing a database engine foundation that can be highly available 7 days a week, 365 days a year. With database mirroring, Microsoft is providing the masses with the opportunity to achieve that dream much more quickly. Database mirroring is a completely new feature of SQL Server 2005. It was earlier known as Real–time Log Shipping (RLTS), and then had another name for a while, and it finally ended up being called database mirroring—which is what it really is. (We don't know why Microsoft had so much trouble naming it in the first place.)

The key breakthrough that has allowed Microsoft to offer database mirroring is "copy-on-write" technology. We will describe it in more detail in a bit. Suffice it to say that with copy-on-write technology, a transaction can be distributed (that is, written) to another completely separate SQL Server database immediately, and that other database can, in turn, be used as a hot spare (that is, it can be used to fail over to in less than 3 seconds).

What Is Database Mirroring?

When you mirror a database, you are essentially asking for a complete copy of a database to be created and maintained, with as much up-to-the-second completeness as possible; you are asking for a mirror image. Database mirroring is a database-level feature. This means that there is no support for filtering, subsetting, or any form of partitioning. You mirror a complete database or nothing at all. This actually keeps database mirroring simple and clean to implement. It also certainly provides some drawbacks, such as burning up twice the amount of disk storage, but what you get in return is well worth it.

When SQL Server 2005 was first released for general availability, database mirroring was available only for evaluation purposes and had to be enabled via trace flag 1400. With Service Pack 1 (SQL Server 2005 SP1, available as of May 1, 2006), database mirroring became completely supported as a general feature, with no restrictions.

Database mirroring works through the transaction log of the principal database (of the database that is to be mirrored). You can only mirror a database that is using the full database recovery model. Otherwise, it would not be possible to forward transaction log entries to another server. Utilizing the copy-on-write technology, a change to data in a primary server's database (as reflected in active transaction log entries) is first "copied" to the target server, and then it is "written" (that is, applied) to the target database server (that is, to the mirror server) transaction log. That is why it's called copy-on-write.

Database mirroring is very different from data replication. With replication, database changes are at the logical level (insert, update, delete statements, stored procedure executions, and so on), whereas database mirroring uses the actual physical log entries on both the primary database server side and the mirror database server side. Effectively, the physical "active" log records from the transaction log of the principal database are copied and written directly to the transaction log of the mirror database. These physical log record–level transactions can be applied extremely quickly. As these physical log records are being applied to the mirror database, even the data cache reflects the forward application of the log records. This makes the entire database and data cache ready for the principal to take over extremely quickly.

Figure 16.1 shows a typical database mirroring configuration that has three components:

> ▶ **Principal database server**—This is the source of the mirroring. You can mirror one or more databases on a single SQL Server instance to another SQL Server instance. You cannot mirror a database on one SQL Server instance to itself (that is, the same SQL Server instance).

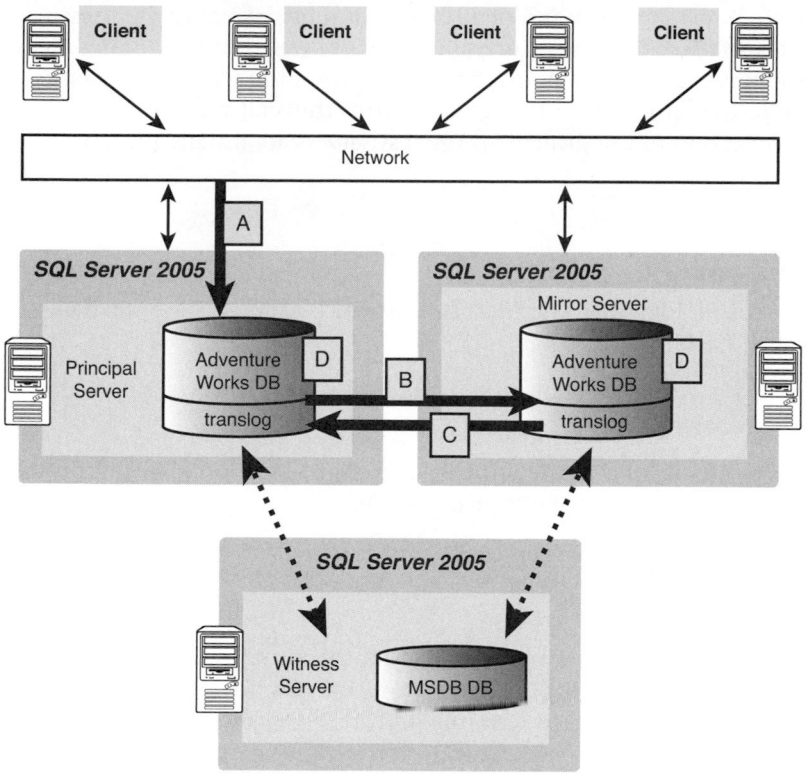

FIGURE 16.1   A basic database mirroring configuration with a principal server, mirror server, and witness server.

▶ **Mirror database server**—The mirror server is the recipient of the mirroring from the principal database server. This mirrored database is kept in hot standby mode and cannot be used directly in any way. In fact, once you have configured database mirroring, this database shows its status as being in continuous restore mode. This is because the physical transaction records are continuously applied to this mirror database. This database is essentially a hot standby database and is not available for direct database usage. The one exception to this non-usage scenario is creating database snapshots from the mirror database. (Taking database snapshots with database mirroring is described in more detail later in this chapter.)

▶ **Witness database server**—You use the witness database server, which is optional, when you want to be continuously checking to see whether any failures have occurred to the primary database server and to help make the decision to fail over to the mirror database server. Using a witness server is a sound way to configure database mirroring. If you do not identify a witness server, the principal and mirror are left on their own to decide whether to fail over. With the witness server, a quorum is formed (that is, two out of three servers), and it takes the quorum to make a failover decision. A typical scenario is that the principal server fails for some reason, the witness sees this failure, the mirror also sees the failure, and together they agree that the principal is lost and that the mirror must take over the principal role. If the witness still sees that the principal is alive and well, but the communication between the mirror and the principal has been broken, the witness does not agree to fail over to the mirror (even though the mirror thinks it must do this because it lost connection to the principal). Witness servers are usually put on separate physical servers.

Copy-on-Write Technology

The new copy-on-write technology that Microsoft has created is at the core of the database mirroring capability. Look back at Figure 16.1, and notice what happens:

1. A transaction from a client connection to the principal server (A) is written to the AdventureWorks database (D).

2. When the transaction is written to the principal server's transaction log, it is immediately copied (B) and written to the mirror server (D).

3. When this physical log record is written to the mirror server, it sends back an acknowledgement (C) to the principal of its write success.

This is the copy-on-write technology. The end result is that the mirror server is in exactly the same state as the principal server (if the physical log record has been successfully written on the mirror side). If failure occurs now, the mirror server can pick up immediately all processing from the clients extremely quickly and without data loss. Exceptional!

> **NOTE**
>
> Database mirroring cannot be used for any of SQL Server's internal databases—
> tempdb, masterdb, msdb, or modeldb. Also, database mirroring is fully supported in
> SQL Server Standard Edition, Developer Edition, and Enterprise Edition. Database
> mirroring is *not* supported in SQL Server Workgroup Edition or Express Edition.
> However, machines running these server editions could be used as witness servers.

When to Use Database Mirroring

As mentioned earlier in this chapter, database mirroring elevates the availability level of a SQL Server–based application to a very high level without any special hardware and extra administration staff skills. However, when you should use database mirroring varies depending on your true needs.

Basically, if you need to increase the availability of the database layer, need to have automatic data protection (that is, redundant storage of data), or need to decrease the downtime that would normally be required to do upgrades, you should use database mirroring. In addition, when you need to offload reporting (that is, periodic data snapshots) without affecting the transactional system, you can use database mirroring with database snapshots. Finally, if you need data distribution, high availability, and high data resiliency, using data replication with database mirroring is also a good idea. We discuss these latter two ideas a bit later in this chapter.

Roles of the Database Mirroring Configuration

As you have seen, a typical database mirroring configuration has a principal server, a mirror server, and a witness server. Each of these servers plays a role at some point. They may switch roles as well. It is important to understand what these roles are and when a server is playing a particular role.

Playing Roles and Switching Roles

A *role* corresponds to what a server is doing at a particular point in time. There are three possible roles:

▶ **Witness role**—If a server is playing a witness role, it is essentially standing alongside both partners of a database mirror configuration and is used to settle all arguments. It is getting together with any one of the other servers and forming a quorum to come up with decisions. The decision that it will participate in is to whether to fail over. That is it.

▶ **Principal role**—If a server is playing a principal role, it is the server that the application will be connected to and that is generating the transactions. One of the partners in the database mirror must start out as the principal. After a failure, the mirror server takes over the principal role, and the roles reverse.

▶ **Mirror role**—If a server is playing a mirror role, it is the server that is having transactions written to it. It is in a constant recovery state (that is, the database state that is needed in order to accept physical log records). One of the partners in the database mirroring configuration must start out in the mirror role. Then, if a failure occurs, the mirror server changes to the principal role.

Database Mirroring Operating Modes

With database mirroring, you have the option of deploying in one of three modes: high-availability mode, high-protection mode, and high-performance mode. Each of these modes has different failure and protection characteristics and uses the database mirroring configurations slightly differently. As you might expect, of these modes, the high-performance mode offers the least amount of protection; you must sacrifice levels of protection for performance.

Database mirroring runs with either asynchronous or synchronous operations:

▶ **Synchronous operations**—With synchronous operations, a committed transaction will be committed (that is, written) on both partners of the database mirroring pair. This obviously adds some latency cost to a complete transaction because it is across two servers. High-availability mode and high-protection mode use synchronous operations.

16

▶ **Asynchronous operations**—With asynchronous operations, transactions commit without waiting for the mirror server to write the log to disk. This can speed up performance significantly. High-performance mode uses asynchronous operations.

Whether the operations are asynchronous or synchronous depends on the transaction safety setting. You control this through the SAFETY option when configuring with Transact-SQL (T-SQL) commands. You set SAFETY to FULL for synchronous operations, and you set it to OFF for asynchronous operations. If you are using the mirroring wizard, this is set up for you automatically.

Of the three modes, only the high-availability mode requires the witness server. The others can operate fine without this third server in their configuration. Remember that the witness server is looking at both the principal and mirror server and will be utilized (in a quorum) for automatic failover.

Role switching is the act of transferring the principal role to the mirror server. It is the mirror server that is acting as the failover partner for the principal server. When a failure occurs, the principal role is switched to the mirror server, and its database is brought online as the principal database.

Failover variations are:

▶ **Automatic failover**—Automatic failover is enabled with a three-server configuration involving a principal, a mirror, and a witness server. Synchronous operations are required, and the mirror database must already be synchronized (that is, in sync with the transactions as they are being written to the principal). Role switching is done automatically. This is for high-availability mode.

▶ **Manual failover**—Manual failover is needed when there is no witness server and your are in synchronous operations. The principal and the mirror are connected to each other, and the mirror database must already be synchronized. Role switching is done manually. This is for either high-availability mode or high-protection mode.

▶ **Forced service**—In the case of a mirror server being available but possibly not synchronized, the mirror server can be forced to take over when the principal server has failed. This possibly means data loss because the transactions were not synchronized. This is for either high-protection mode or high-performance mode.

Setting Up and Configuring Database Mirroring

Microsoft has introduced several new concepts and technologies that are used in database mirroring. You have already learned about the copy-on-write technology. Microsoft also uses *endpoints*, which are assigned to each server in a database mirroring configuration. In addition, establishing connections to each server is much more tightly controlled and requires service accounts or integrated (domain-level) authentication. Within SQL Server, grants must also be given to the accounts that will be executing database mirroring.

You can completely setup database mirroring by using T-SQL scripts, or you can use the Database Mirroring Wizard within SQL Server Management Studio (SSMS). We always advise that you use something that is repeatable, such as SQL scripts, and you can easily generate SQL scripts by using the new wizard. It's not fun to have to re-create or manage a database mirroring configuration in the middle of the night. Having this whole process in a script reduces almost all errors.

Getting Ready to Mirror a Database

Before you get started in setting up and configuring a database mirroring environment, it is always best to run through a simple checklist of basic requirements:

1. Verify that all server instances are at the same service pack level. You must be on at least SP1 to even be able to use database mirroring. In addition, the SQL Server edition you have must support database mirroring.

2. Verify that you have as much or more disk space available on the mirror server as on the principal server. You also need the same room for growth on both.

3. Verify that you have connectivity to each server from the others. You can most easily do this by simply trying to register each SQL Server instance in SSMS. If you can register the server, the server will be able to be used for database mirroring. Do this for the principal, the mirror, and the witness server.

4. Verify that the principal server database that is to be mirrored is using the full database recovery model. If you try to start configuring database mirroring and the database recovery model is not full for the principal database, you get a nasty message to that effect (see Figure 16.2). Because database mirroring is transaction log based, it makes sense to be using the full database recovery model: All transactions are written to the transaction log and are not truncated, as with other database recovery models.

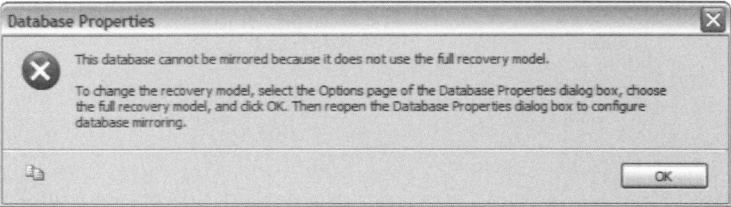

FIGURE 16.2   Trying to mirror a database that is not using the full database recovery model.

Before you go any further, you must establish the endpoints for each of the servers that will be a part of the database mirroring configuration. You can use the Configure Security option of the wizard to do this, but getting into the practice of using SQL scripts is really the best approach. Using SQL scripts is very easily done, as you will soon see.

Endpoints utilize TCP/IP addressing and listening ports for all communication between the servers. Within a server, the endpoint is given a specific name (that is, an endpoint name) for easy reference and to establish the partner roles that this server (endpoint) will possibly play. In addition, a connect GRANT is needed for access to be allowed from each server to the others. This account is usually a particular login that is known to the domain and is to be used for all connections in the database mirroring topology. Figure 16.3 shows the mirroring database properties of the AdventureWorks database on a SQL Server instance named SQL2005DEV. As you can see, there are no server network addresses set up for database mirroring of any kind, and the mirroring status says This Database Has Not Been Configured for Mirroring.

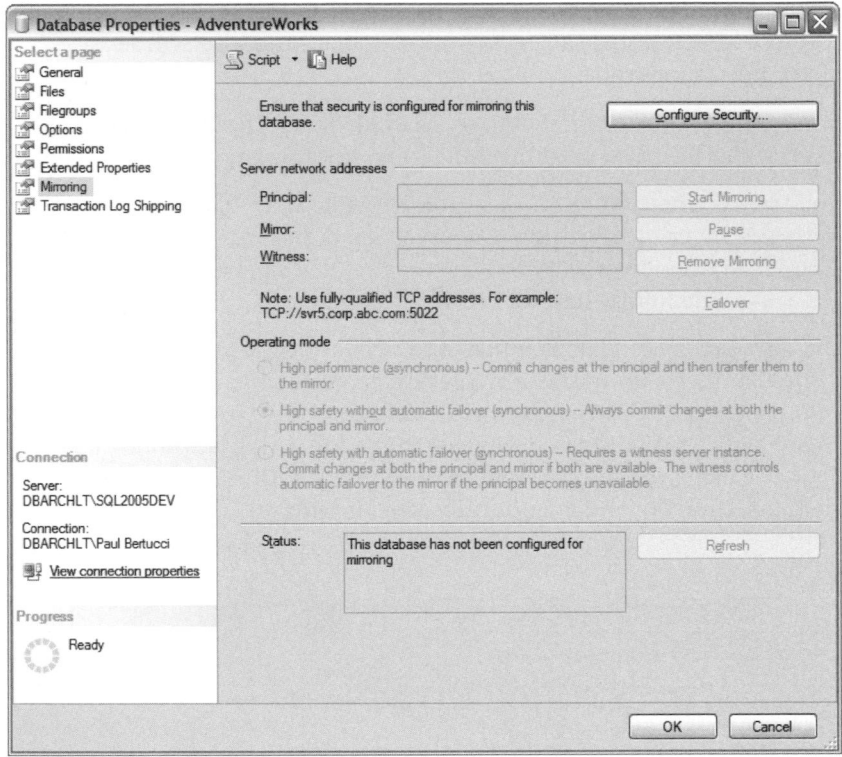

FIGURE 16.3   The Database Properties Mirroring page: mirroring network addressing and mirroring status.

Next, we'll look at how to set up full, high-availability mode database mirroring with a principal, a mirror, and a witness server. For this, you can mirror the old reliable AdventureWorks database that Microsoft provides with SQL Server 2005. Figure 16.4 illustrates the database mirroring configuration you will set up.

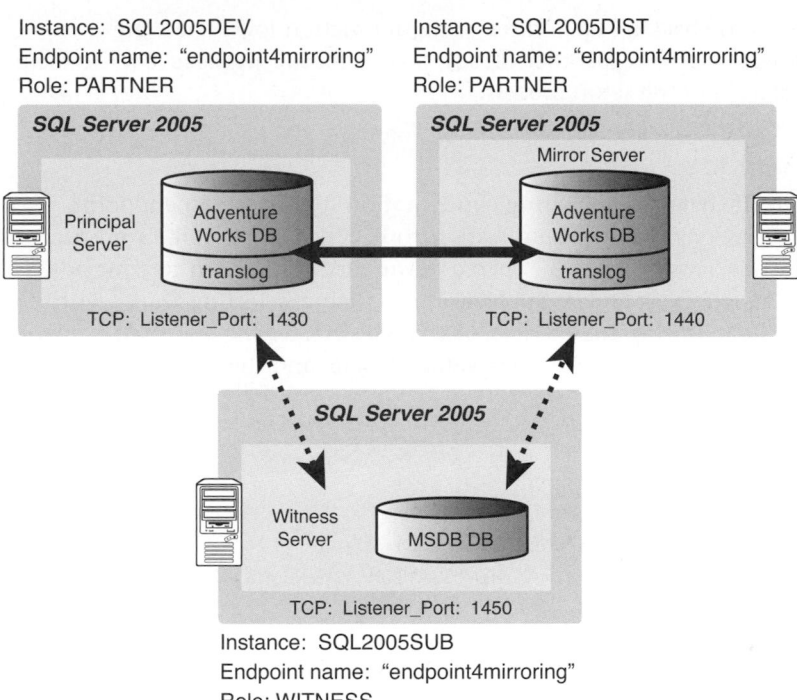

Instance: SQL2005DEV
Endpoint name: "endpoint4mirroring"
Role: PARTNER

Instance: SQL2005DIST
Endpoint name: "endpoint4mirroring"
Role: PARTNER

Instance: SQL2005SUB
Endpoint name: "endpoint4mirroring"
Role: WITNESS

FIGURE 16.4   A high-availability database mirroring configuration with the AdventureWorks database.

The initial principal server will be the SQL Server instance named SQL2005DEV, the initial mirror server will be the SQL Server instance named SQL2005DIST, and the witness server will be the SQL Server instance named SQL2005SUB.

You need to establish a local endpoint named endpoint4mirroring on each of these SQL Server instances, and you need to identify the TCP listening port that will be used for all database mirroring communication. The principal server will be listening on Port 1430, the mirror server on Port 1440, and the witness server on Port 1450. These port numbers must be unique within a single server machine, and the machine name and port combination must be unique within the network. An example of the fully qualified network address name of this server and the listing port is DBARCHLT:1430, where DBARCHLT is the machine name, and 1430 is the listening port that is created with the endpoint. In addition, each server's initial role needs to be specified. The SQL2005DEV instance can play any partner role (that is, a mirror and/or principal), the SQL2005DIST instance can play any partner role as well, and the SQL2005SUB instance should play the witness role only.

We have included three SQL script templates with this book (on the book's companion website at www.samspublishing.com, in the Chapter 18 code directory) that have working examples of creating the endpoints, granting connection permissions to a login for the endpoints, verifying that the endpoints were created, altering the endpoints, backing up and restoring databases, and backing up and restoring transaction logs. These are endpoint partner 1.sql, endpoint partner 2.sql, and endpoint witness.sql. You can leverage these to get started in the setup process.

Creating the Endpoints

Each server instance in the database mirroring configuration must have an endpoint defined so that the other servers can communicate with it. This is sort of like a private phone line to your friends. From SSMS, you open a new query connection to your principal database by selecting File, New and in the New Query dialog, selecting Query with Current Connection. The following CREATE ENDPOINT T-SQL creates the endpoint named endpoint4mirroring, the correct listener_port value of 1430, and the database mirroring role Partner:

```
-- create endpoint for principal server --
CREATE ENDPOINT [endpoint4mirroring]
    STATE=STARTED
    AS TCP (LISTENER_PORT = 1430, LISTENER_IP = ALL)
    FOR DATA_MIRRORING (ROLE = PARTNER, AUTHENTICATION = WINDOWS NEGOTIATE
, ENCRYPTION = REQUIRED ALGORITHM RC4)
```

After this runs, you should quickly run the following SELECT statements to verify that the endpoint has been correctly created:

```
select name,type_desc,port,ip_address from sys.tcp_endpoints
select name,role_desc,state_desc from sys.database_mirroring_endpoints
```

Figure 16.5 shows the desired result set from these queries.

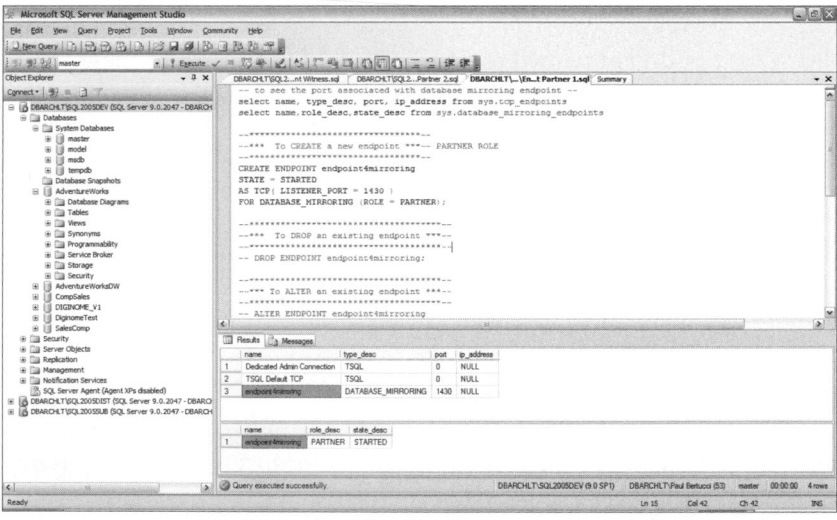

FIGURE 16.5   Verifying that endpoints are created for database mirroring.

If you look at the database properties for the AdventureWorks database on the principal server (SQL2005DEV, in this example), you see the server network address for the principal server automatically appear now when you look at the Mirroring page (see Figure 16.6).

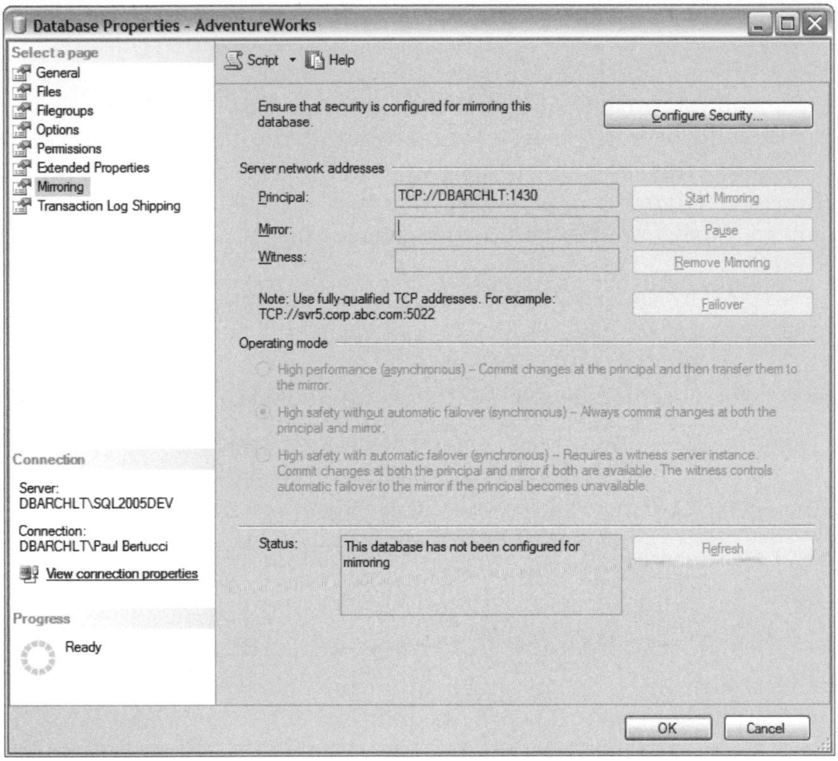

FIGURE 16.6   The Mirroring page of the AdventureWorks database on the principal server.

Now you need to repeat the endpoint creation process for the mirror server (using a listener_port value of 1440) and the witness server (using a listener_port value of 1450) by opening a query connection to each one of these servers and running the following CREATE ENDPOINT commands:

```
-- create endpoint for mirror server --
CREATE ENDPOINT [endpoint4mirroring]
    STATE=STARTED
    AS TCP (LISTENER_PORT = 1440, LISTENER_IP = ALL)
    FOR DATA_MIRRORING (ROLE = PARTNER, AUTHENTICATION = WINDOWS NEGOTIATE
, ENCRYPTION = REQUIRED ALGORITHM RC4)
```

For the witness server (notice that the role is now Witness), you run the following:

```
-- create endpoint for mirror server --
CREATE ENDPOINT [endpoint4mirroring]
```

```
    STATE=STARTED
    AS TCP (LISTENER_PORT = 1450, LISTENER_IP = ALL)
    FOR DATA_MIRRORING (ROLE = WITNESS, AUTHENTICATION = WINDOWS NEGOTIATE
, ENCRYPTION = REQUIRED ALGORITHM RC4)
```

Granting Permissions

It is possible to have an AUTHORIZATION [login] statement in the CREATE ENDPOINT command that establishes the permissions for a login account to the endpoint being defined. However, separating this out into a GRANT greatly stresses the point of allowing this connection permission. From each SQL query connection, you run a GRANT to allow a specific login account to connect on the ENDPOINT for database mirroring.

First from the principal server instance (SQL2005DEV), you run the following GRANT:

```
GRANT CONNECT ON ENDPOINT::endpoint4mirroring TO [DBARCHLT\Paul Bertucci];
```

Then, from the mirror server instance (SQL2005DIST), you run the following GRANT:

```
GRANT CONNECT ON ENDPOINT::endpoint4mirroring TO [DBARCHLT\Paul Bertucci];
```

Then, from the witness server instance (SQL2005SUB), you run the following GRANT:

```
GRANT CONNECT ON ENDPOINT::endpoint4mirroring TO [DBARCHLT\Paul Bertucci];
```

Identifying the Other Endpoints for Database Mirroring

It may be necessary to identify the endpoints and listener port values to the databases involved in the database mirroring configuration (the principal and the mirror). This requires altering the database by using either the SET PARTNER or SET WITNESS statements. The database mirroring wizard can also do this step for you, but doing it manually is easy. For this example, you can let the mirroring wizard do this. Even if you tried to alter the database right now, you would get an error indicating that the database is not enabled for mirroring yet.

We will identify unique endpoint listening port values for each endpoint that are unique within the server. These will be port values 1430, 1440, and 140. The following statements identify the mirror server endpoint and witness server endpoints to the principal server's database (you can do this only if the database is already enabled for mirroring):

```
-- From the Principal Server Database: identify the mirror server endpoint --
ALTER DATABASE AdventureWorks
    SET PARTNER = 'TCP://DBARCHLT:1440'
GO
-- From the Principal Server Database: identify the witness server endpoint --
ALTER DATABASE AdventureWorks
  SET WITNESS = 'TCP://DBARCHLT:1450'
GO
```

Remember that because you don't have the `AdventureWorks` database created on the mirror server yet, you can't alter it yet. After you create the database on the mirror server, however, you can run the following `ALTER DATABASE` command on the mirror server:

```
-- From the Mirror Server Database: identify the principal server endpoint --
ALTER DATABASE AdventureWorks
    SET PARTNER = 'TCP://DBARCHLT:1430'
GO
```

You do not have to alter any database from the witness server.

If you have issues or just want to start over, you can drop an endpoint or alter an endpoint quite easily. To drop and existing endpoint, you use the `DROP ENDPOINT` command. In this example, the following command would drop the endpoint you just created:

```
-- To DROP an existing endpoint --
DROP ENDPOINT endpoint4mirroring;
```

Altering an endpoint (for example, to change the `listerner_port` value) is just as easy as dropping one. The following is an example of altering the currently defined endpoint to a new `listener_port` value of 1435 because there was a conflict at the network level:

```
-- To ALTER an existing endpoint --
ALTER ENDPOINT endpoint4mirroring
    STATE = STARTED
    AS TCP( LISTENER_PORT = 1435 )
    FOR DATABASE_MIRRORING (ROLE = PARTNER)
```

Creating the Database on the Mirror Server

When the endpoints are configured and the roles are established, you can create the database on the mirror server and get it to the point of being able to mirror. You must first make a backup copy of the principal database (`AdventureWorks`, in this example). This backup will be used to create the database on the mirror server. You can use SSMS tasks or use SQL scripts to do this. The SQL scripts, which are easily repeatable, are used here.

On the principal server, you make a complete backup as follows:

```
BACKUP DATABASE [AdventureWorks]
    TO DISK = N'C:\Program Files\Microsoft SQL
Server\MSSQL.2\MSSQL\Backup\AdventureWorks4Mirror.bak'
    WITH FORMAT
GO
```

Next, you copy this backup file to a place where the mirror server can reach it on the network. When that is complete, you can issue the following database restore command

16

to create the `AdventureWorks` database on the mirror server (using the `WITH NORECOVERY` option):

```
-- use this restore database(with NoRecovery option)
to create the mirrored version of this DB --
RESTORE FILELISTONLY
    FROM DISK = 'C:\Program Files\Microsoft SQL
Server\MSSQL.2\MSSQL\Backup\AdventureWorks4Mirror.bak'
go
RESTORE DATABASE AdventureWorks
    FROM DISK = 'C:\Program Files\Microsoft SQL
              Server\MSSQL.2\MSSQL\Backup\AdventureWorks4Mirror.bak'
  WITH NORECOVERY,
      MOVE 'AdventureWorks_Data' TO 'C:\Program Files\Microsoft SQL
            Server\MSSQL.4\MSSQL\Data\AdventureWorks_Data.mdf',
      MOVE 'AdventureWorks_Log'  TO 'C:\Program Files\Microsoft SQL
            Server\MSSQL.4\MSSQL\Data\AdventureWorks_Log.ldf'
GO
```

Because you don't necessarily have the same directory structure on the mirror server, you use the `MOVE` option as part of this restore to place the database files in the location you desire.

The restore process should yield something that looks like the following result set when restoring the `AdventureWorks` database that is shipped with SQL Server 2005:

```
-- Processed 21200 pages for database 'AdventureWorks',
                  file 'AdventureWorks_Data' on file 1.
-- Processed 2 pages for database 'AdventureWorks',
                  file 'AdventureWorks_Log' on file 1.
-- RESTORE DATABASE successfully processed 21202 pages

                  in 14.677 seconds (11.833 MB/sec).
```

Basically, this says that you are not ready to get into the mirroring business yet. You must now apply at least one transaction log dump to the mirror database. This brings the mirror database to a point of synchronization with the principal and leaves the mirror database in the `Restoring` state. At this database recovery point, you can run through the mirroring wizard and start mirroring for high availability.

From the principal server, you dump (that is, back up) a transaction log as follows:

```
BACKUP LOG [AdventureWorks] TO
DISK = N'C:\Program Files\Microsoft SQL
Server\MSSQL.2\MSSQL\Backup\AdventureWorksLog.bak'
GO
```

Then you move this backup to a place where it can be reached by the mirror server. When that is done, you restore the log to the mirror database. From the mirror server, you restore the transaction log as follows:

```
RESTORE LOG [AdventureWorks]
   FROM  DISK = N'C:\Program Files\Microsoft SQL
         Server\MSSQL.4\MSSQL\Backup\AdventureWorksLog.bak'
   WITH  FILE = 4, NORECOVERY
GO
```

The restore log process should yield something that looks like the following result set:

```
Processed 0 pages for database 'AdventureWorks',
         file 'AdventureWorks_Data' on file 4.
Processed 39 pages for database 'AdventureWorks',
         file 'AdventureWorks_Log' on file 4.
RESTORE LOG successfully processed 39 pages

         in 0.034 seconds (9.396 MB/sec).
```

> **NOTE**
>
> You might need to update the FILE = xx entry in the RESTORE LOG command to correspond to the file value given during the log backup.

16

You are now ready to mirror the database in high-availability mode.

Configuring Database Mirroring by Using the Wizard

When the endpoints are configured, the roles are established, the connections to the endpoints are granted, and the mirror database is restored on the mirror server, you can run through the final short steps in the mirroring wizard to enable and start mirroring. Figure 16.7 shows the Mirror option from the AdventureWorks database (reached by right-clicking the database name) from what will be the principal server. Because this database is not enabled for mirroring yet, you must run through the Configure Security option on the top portion of the Mirroring page (refer to Figure 16.6). At this point, you can probably see only the network server address of the principal server. Don't worry; the rest (mirror and witness network server addresses) will all be established and identified during the Configure Database Mirroring Security Wizard steps.

You need to click the Configure Security button on the Mirroring page. This immediately launches the Configure Database Mirroring Security Wizard for the database you have selected (AdventureWorks, in this example). Figure 16.8 shows this initial wizard splash page.

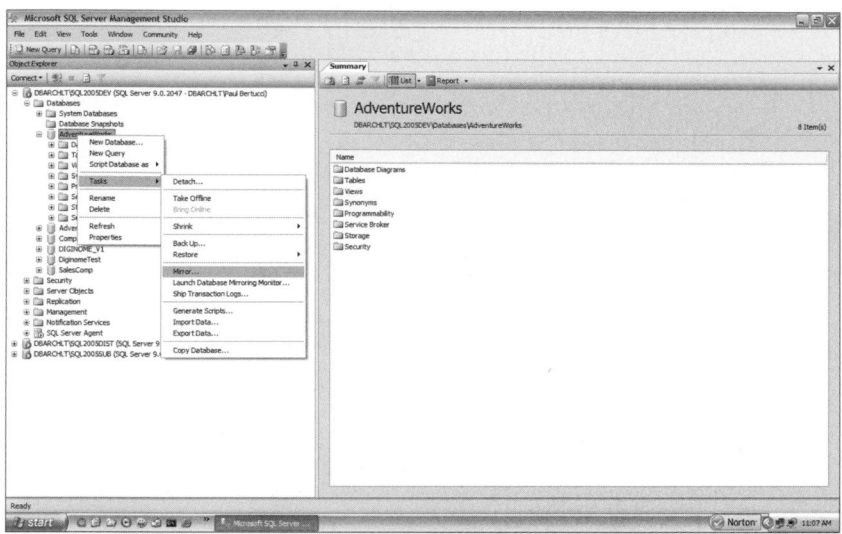

FIGURE 16.7   The Mirror option for the principal database server (`AdventureWorks`).

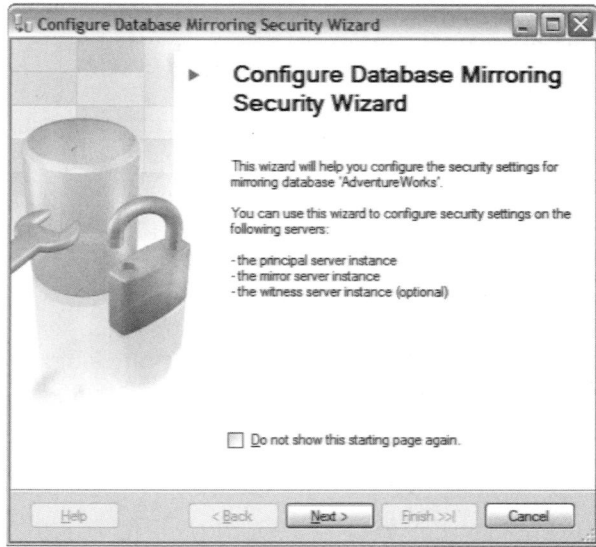

FIGURE 16.8   The Configure Database Mirroring Security Wizard for the `AdventureWorks` database.

You will be configuring all three server instances (principal, mirror, and witness servers) for the high-availability mode. The first option that must be indicated is whether you will include a witness server instance in your mirroring configuration. You are configuring a high-availability database mirroring configuration (synchronous mode with automatic failover), so you should select Yes on the dialog shown in Figure 16.9—since we want to create a full high availability mode for automated failover.

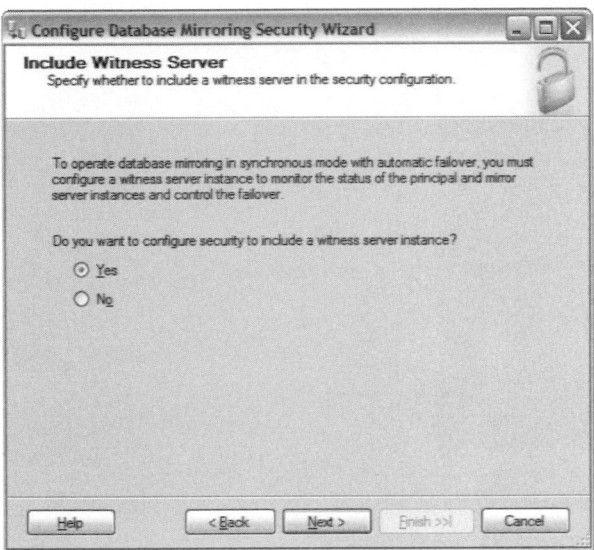

FIGURE 16.9   Including the witness server instance in the mirroring configuration.

The next page in the wizard prompts you to decide where to save the security configurations for database mirroring. You have no choice for the principal and mirror server instances; their security configuration information must be stored with them. You must also choose the default location for the witness server instance. The wizard then takes you through each server instance in the database mirroring configuration to establish all needed connection information to implement database mirroring. As you can see in Figure 16.10, this starts with the principal server instance. The wizard should be finding the endpoint and `listener_port` values you set up earlier (`listener_port` value `1430` and endpoint name `endpoint4mirroring`, in this example).

Next comes the specification of the listener and endpoint entry for the mirror server instance (where the mirror copy of the database will be located). Initially, this page lists all server instances available on your network (that is, possible mirror server instances) and does not have a listener port or endpoint name specified yet. You need to identify which server you want to use as the mirror server instance (`DBARCHLT\SQL2005DIST`, in this example) and click the Connect button to establish a valid (authorized) connection to the mirror server instance. Because you already set up the endpoint on this server (and granted connection permission, using a specific login ID), when you complete the connection dialog, the endpoint (`endpoint4mirroring`, in this example) and `listener_port` value (`1440`, in this example) should be disabled, as shown in Figure 16.11.

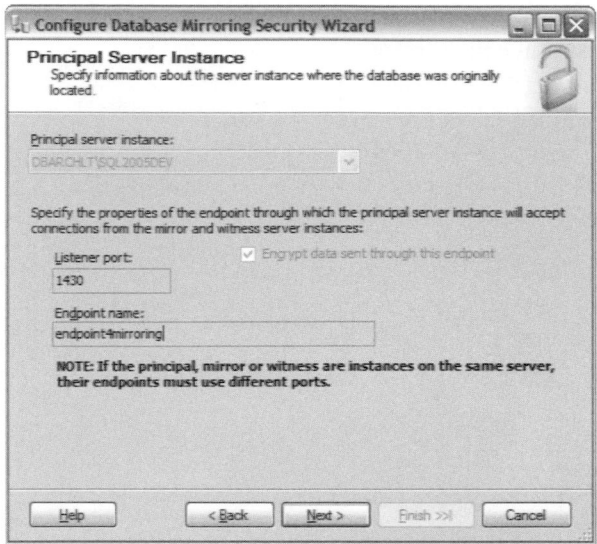

FIGURE 16.10   The Principal Server Instance screen of the Configure Database Mirroring Security Wizard.

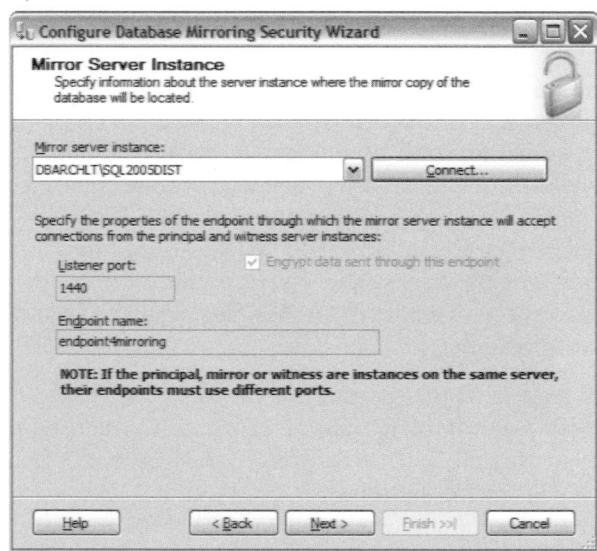

FIGURE 16.11   The Mirror Server Instance screen of the Configure Database Mirroring Security Wizard.

Finally, you need to specify the witness server instance. Again, this dialog page lists all server instances available on the network (that is, possible witness server instances) and does not have a listener port or an endpoint name specified yet. You need to identify which server you want to use as the witness server instance (`DBARCHLT\SQL2005SUB`, in this example) and click the Connect button to establish a valid (authorized) connection to the witness server instance. Because you already set up the endpoint on this server (and granted connection permission, using a specific login ID), when you complete the connection dialog, the endpoint (`endpoint4mirroring`, in our example) and `listener_port` value (`1450`, in this example) should be disabled, as shown in Figure 16.12.

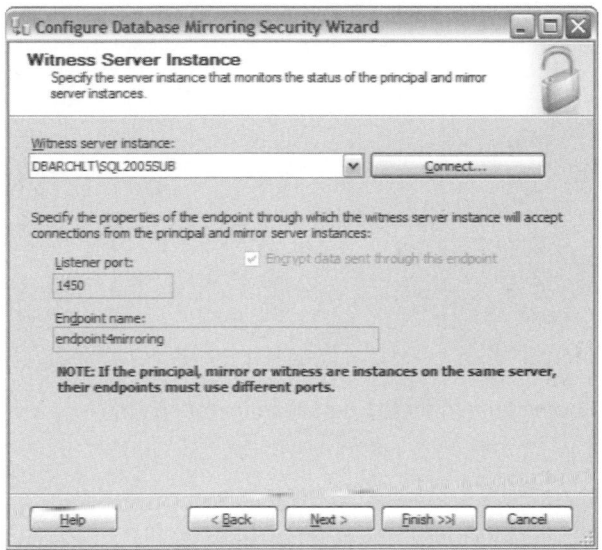

FIGURE 16.12   The Witness Server Instance screen of the Configure Database Mirroring Security Wizard.

The last step in the Configure Database Mirroring Security Wizard is to identify any service accounts that you want to use for the server instances in this database mirroring configuration. You are already using a single domain login ID for this purpose and explicitly granted connect permissions on each endpoint. Therefore, nothing more needs to be done here. If the server instances use different accounts in the same or a trusted domain as their service accounts for SQL Server, you can enter these accounts here. It is best to do this via scripts (as you saw earlier, when you created the endpoints on each server instance).

As you can see in Figure 16.13, the Configure Database Mirroring Security Wizard now presents a summary list of all the actions on each server instance that it will perform. You click Finish to have them executed.

FIGURE 16.13   Summary of actions to be performed for the database mirroring configuration.

A report is generated, telling the total number of actions taken (three, in this case) and the status of each action. If any errors or warnings result, you can drill down into the Report button option in the bottom-right corner of this summary of actions page to determine what has occurred. If each status shows success, then a Database Properties dialog box, as shown in Figure 16.14, appears when you close this report page. This dialog box gives you the option to start mirroring immediately or not start mirroring (because you will start mirroring at some other time). For this example, you want to start mirroring right away, so click the Start Mirroring button.

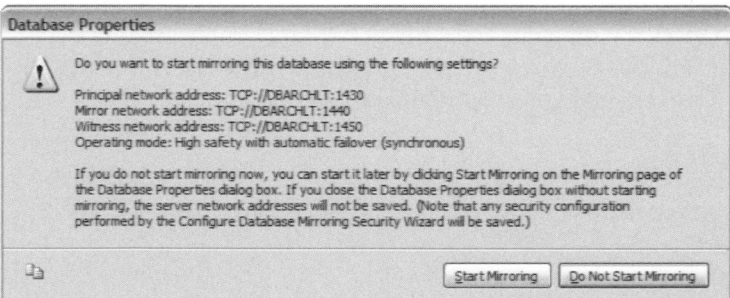

FIGURE 16.14   Specifying to start database mirroring for high safety with automatic failover.

Figure 16.15 shows the full Database Properties screen for the AdventureWorks database, all server network addresses, and the operating mode for mirroring.

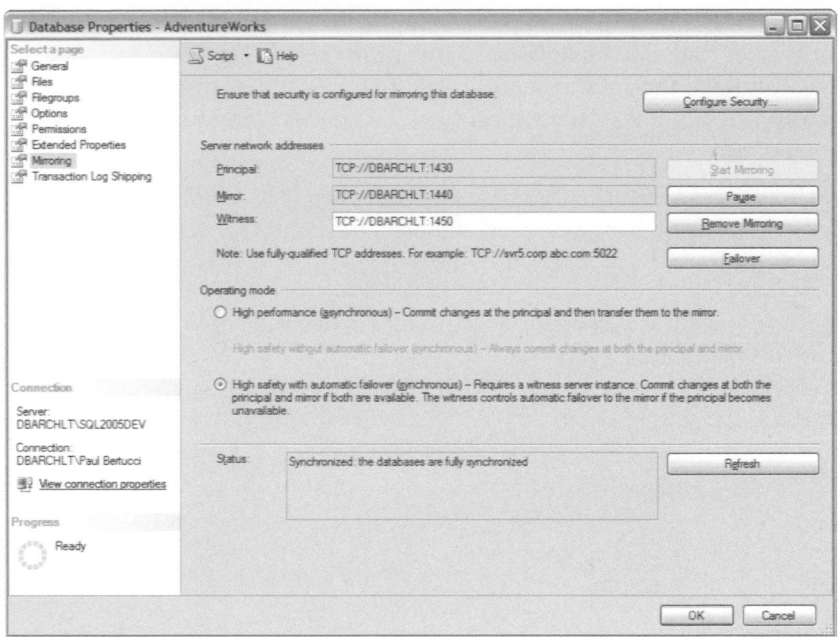

FIGURE 16.15   Fully configured properties and active mirroring for database mirroring.

If you take a look at the SQL Server log file (that is, the current log), you can see log entries indicating that database mirroring is active:

```
7/21/2006 22:33:33,spid21s,Unknown,Database mirroring is
        active with database 'AdventureWorks' as the
        principal copy. This is an informational message
        only. No user action is required.
7/21/2006 22:33:09,spid17s,Unknown,Starting up database 'AdventureWorks'.
7/21/2006 22:33:07,Server,Unknown,SQL Server is now
        ready for client connections. This is an
        informational message; no user action is required.
7/21/2006 22:33:00,spid12s,Unknown,The Database
        Mirroring protocol transport is now listening for connections.
7/21/2006 22:33:00,spid12s,Unknown,Server is
        listening on [ 'any' <ipv4> 1430].
```

Congratulations. You are now mirroring a database!

Monitoring a Mirrored Database Environment

After active mirroring has started, you have a few ways you can monitor the complete mirrored topology. You can start by registering the database that is being mirrored to a new facility within SSMS called Database Mirroring Monitor. Database Mirroring Monitor allows you to monitor roles of the mirroring partnership (that is, principal, mirror, and witness), see the history of transactions flowing to the mirror server, see the status and speed of this transaction flow, and set thresholds to alert you if failures or other issues occur. In addition, you can administer the logins/service accounts being used in the mirrored database topology.

Figure 16.16 shows how you launch the Database Mirroring Monitor from SSMS: You right-click the principal database being mirrored, choose Tasks, and then choose Launch Database Mirroring Monitor.

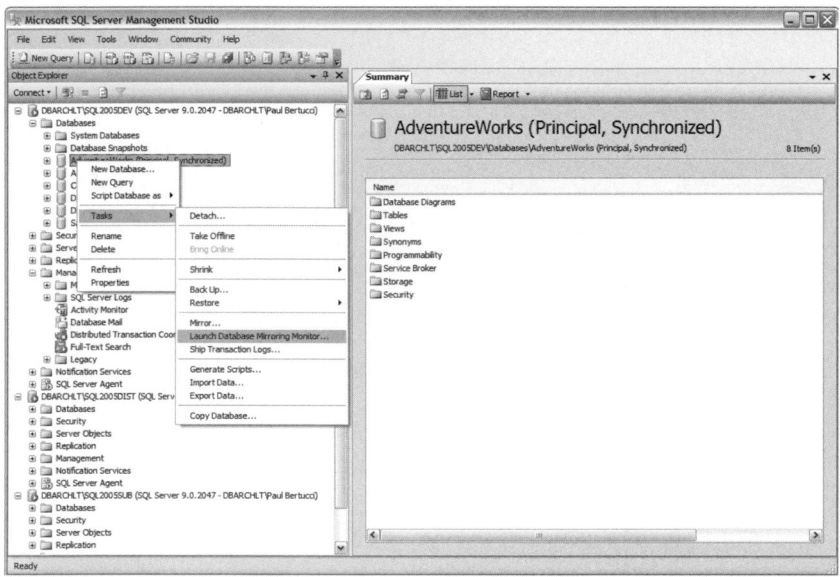

FIGURE 16.16   Launching Database Mirroring Monitor from SSMS.

You must register the database that is being mirrored. To do so, you select the principal or mirror server instance and set the Register check box for the database. Database Mirroring Monitor registers the database and both partner server instances, as shown in Figure 16.17.

After the database is registered, all partners and the witness server instances show up in the Database Mirroring Monitor, as shown in Figure 16.18.

At a glance, you can see which server is playing what role (principal or mirror) and whether each partner has defined and is connecting to a witness server. In addition, you can see the unsent log (in size), the un-restored log (in size), when the oldest unsent transaction occurred, the amount of time it took to send the transaction to the mirror server instance, the send rate (KB/second), the current rate at which the transactions get restored (KB/second), the mirror commit overhead (in milliseconds), the listener port of the witness server instance, and the operating mode of the mirroring (in this case, high safety with automatic failover—synchronous).

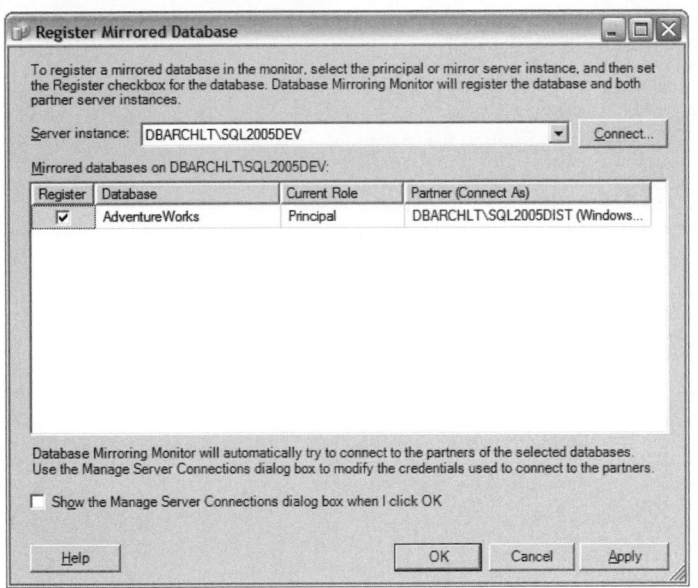

FIGURE 16.17   Registering the mirrored database within the Database Mirroring Monitor.

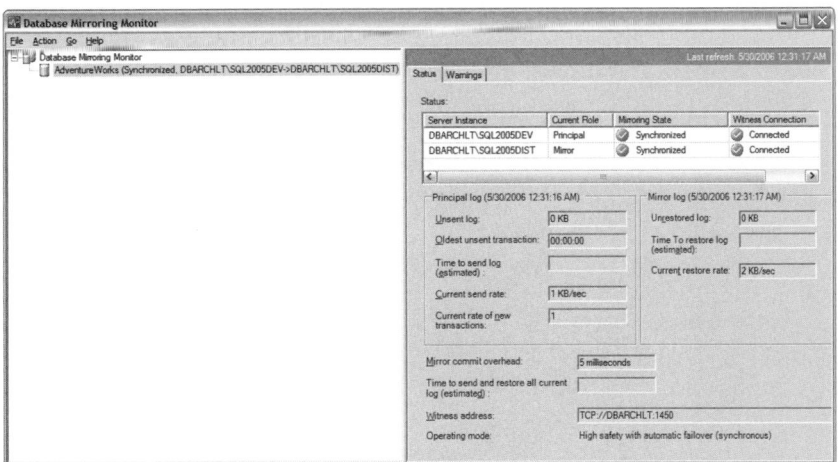

FIGURE 16.18   The registered database and the status of each mirroring partner.

Figure 16.19 shows the detailed transaction history for a particular part of the mirroring flow (either the copy-out of the principal part or the restore to the mirror part). You can click the appropriate partner to see all transaction history details of the mirrored copy and restore process.

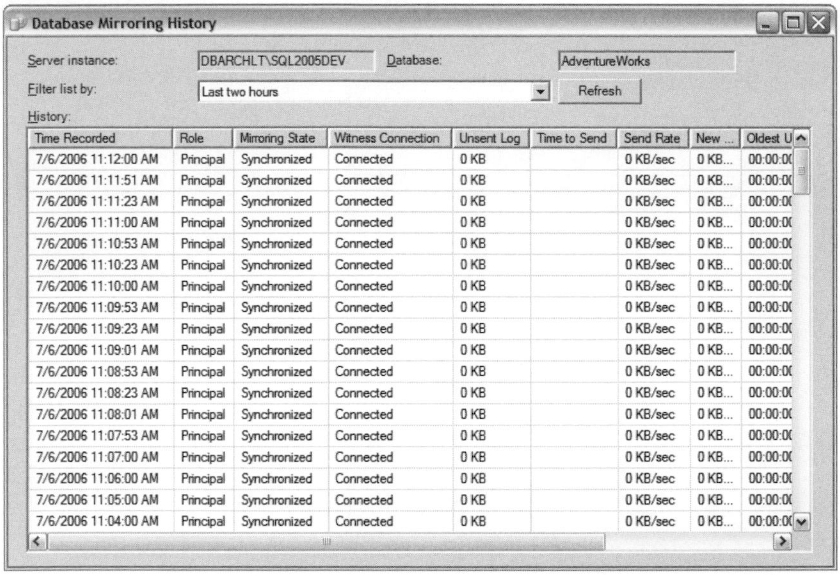

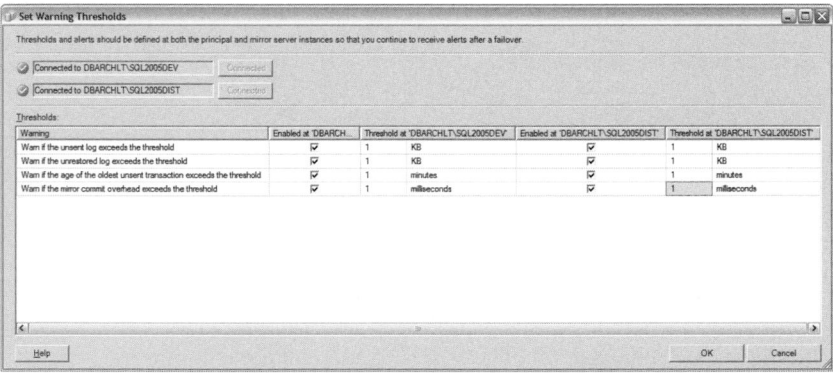

FIGURE 16.19   Transaction history of mirroring partners.

If you click the Warnings tab of the Database Mirroring Monitor, you can set various thresholds within the monitor to alert you when they have been reached (see Figure 16.20). Basically, you want to set thresholds that monitor the effectiveness of the mirroring operation.

FIGURE 16.20   Setting thresholds to monitor mirroring effectiveness.

If these key thresholds are ever exceeded, you want to be notified that something is very wrong and that failover may be in jeopardy. When a threshold is exceeded, an event is logged to the Application event log. You can configure an alert on this event by using SSMS or Microsoft Management Operations Manager (MOM). The threshold levels depend on your own failover tolerance. Our advice is to monitor the transaction and transfer rates for a peak period and then set the thresholds to be 100% higher than that. For example, if you see a peak mirror commit overhead value of 750 milliseconds, you should set the threshold to 1,500 milliseconds. This should be within the tolerance for commit overhead in your organization.

Figure 16.21 shows how easy it is to administer the service accounts/login IDs being used for database mirroring. You simply click an Edit button to change or set the login account you want to use for database mirroring at each instance in the mirroring topology.

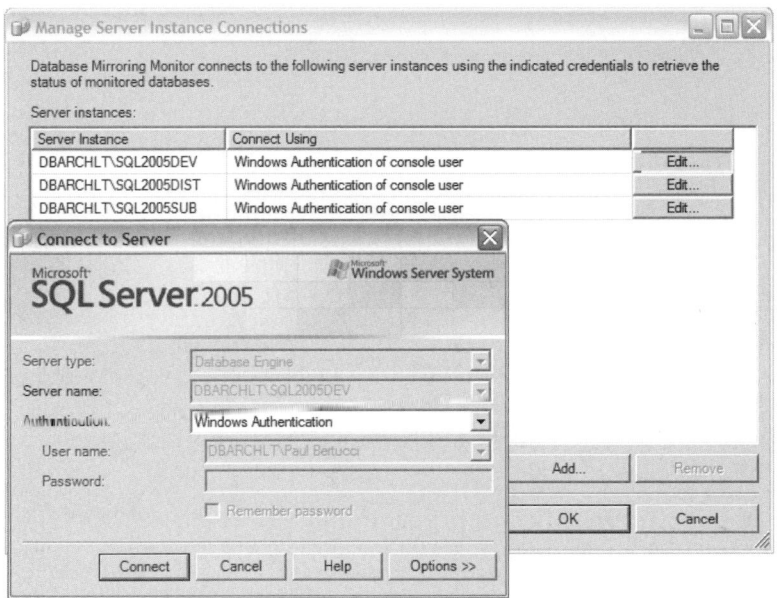

FIGURE 16.21   Setting service accounts/login IDs within the mirroring topology.

From the Database Properties Mirroring page, you can easily pause (and resume) database mirroring if you suspect that there are issues related to the mirroring operation. In addition, you can easily see what role each server instance is playing.

Removing Mirroring

Very likely, you will have to remove all traces of database mirroring from each server instance of a database mirroring configuration. This is actually pretty easy to do. Basically, you have to disable mirroring of the principal, drop the mirror server's database, and remove all endpoints from each server instance. You start from the Database Properties page and the Mirroring option. Then you choose to remove mirroring (from the principal server instance) as shown in Figure 16.22.

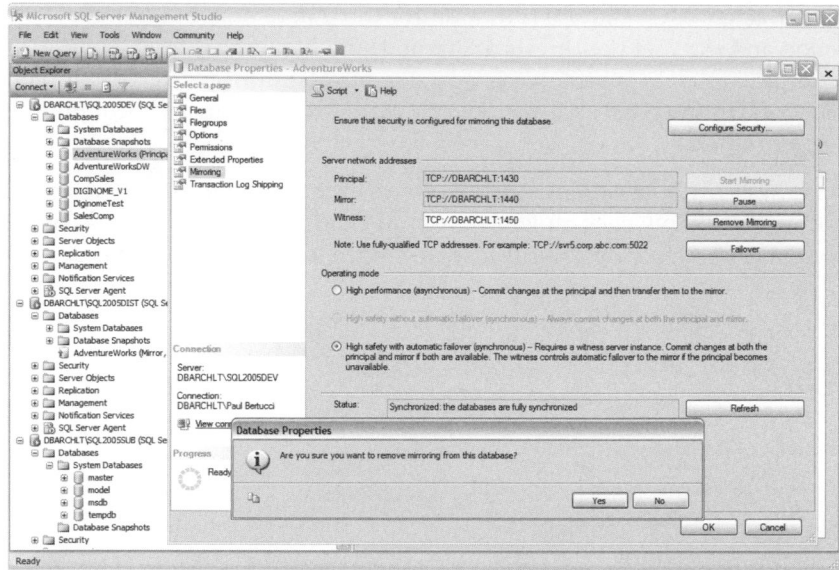

FIGURE 16.22   Removing database mirroring.

The mirroring process is immediately disabled. When mirroring is disabled, you can drop the database on the mirror server instance, remove the endpoints on each server instance (that is, principal, mirror, and witness instances), and be done. This is very straightforward.

From the mirror server instance (not the principal!), you run the DROP DATABASE SQL command and the DROP ENDPOINT SQL command, as follows:

```
DROP DATABASE AdventureWorks
go
DROP ENDPOINT endpoint4mirroring
go
```

From the witness server and principal server instances, you remove the endpoints as follows:

```
DROP ENDPOINT endpoint4mirroring
go
```

To verify that you have removed these endpoints from each server instance, you simply run the following SELECT statements:

```
select name,type_desc,port,ip_address from sys.tcp_endpoints
select name,role_desc,state_desc from sys.database_mirroring_endpoints
```

All references to the endpoints and roles will have been removed.

You can also take a peek at the SQL Server log entries being made as you remove database mirroring:

```
07/05/2006 13:06:42,spid55,Unknown,The Database
           Mirroring protocol transport is disabled or not configured.
07/05/2006 13:06:40,spid55,Unknown,The Database Mirroring
           protocol transport has stopped listening for connections.
07/05/2006 12:52:55,spid19s,Unknown,Database mirroring
           connection error 4 'An error occurred while receiving
           data: '64(The specified network name is no longer
           available.)'.' for 'TCP://DBARCHLT:1440'.
07/05/2006 12:52:55,spid19s,Unknown,Error: 1474
           <c/> Severity: 16<c/> State: 1.
07/05/2006 12:52:55,spid19s,Unknown,Database mirroring
           connection error 4 'An error occurred while
           receiving data: '64(The specified network name is
           no longer available.)'.' for 'TCP://DBARCHLT:1450'.
07/05/2006 12:52:55,spid19s,Unknown,Error: 1474
           <c/> Severity: 16<c/> State: 1.
07/05/2006 12:51:14,spid21s,Unknown,Database mirroring
           has been terminated for database 'AdventureWorks'.
```

These are all informational messages only. No user action is required. As you can see from these messages, you are now in a state of no database mirroring. You have to completely build up database mirroring again if you want to mirror the database again.

Testing Failover from the Principal to the Mirror

From the SSMS, you can easily fail over from the principal to the mirror server instance (and back again) by using the Failover button on the Database Properties Mirroring page, as shown in Figure 16.23.

You must test this failover at some point to guarantee that it works. When you click the Failover button for this database mirroring configuration, you are prompted to continue with the failover by clicking Yes or No in the dialog shown in Figure 16.24.

Remember that clicking Yes closes all connections to the principal server instance that are connected to this database. Later, we will show you how to make your clients aware of both the principal and mirror server instances so that they can just pick up and run against either server instance, by design.

Now, if you look at the Database Properties Mirroring page (see Figure 16.25), you see that the principal and mirror listener port values have switched: The principal instance is now port value 1440, and the mirror instance is port value 1430. The server instances have now completely switched their roles. You must now go to the server instance that is playing the principal role to fail over back to the original operating mode. If you try to open the current mirror server instance database, you get an error stating that you cannot access this database because it is in restore mode.

16

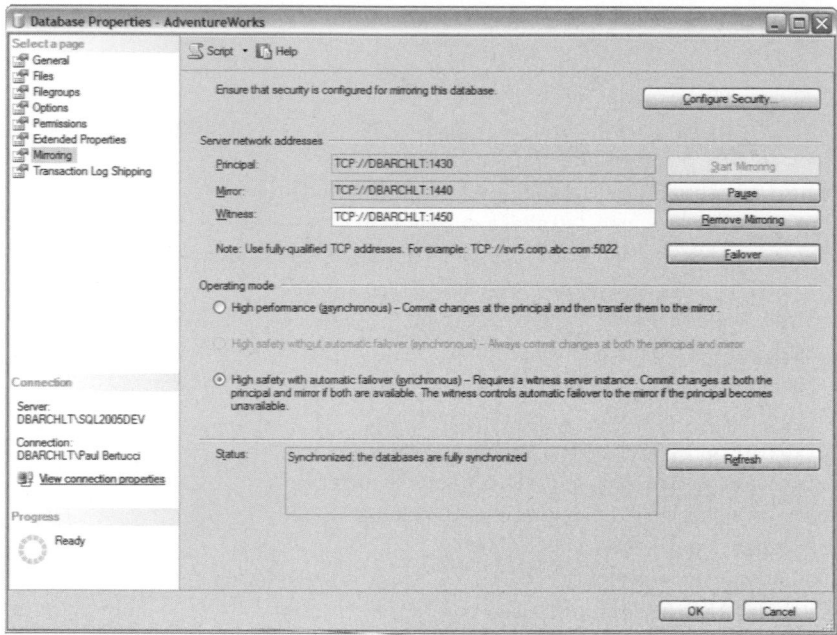

FIGURE 16.23   Testing failover of a mirrored database.

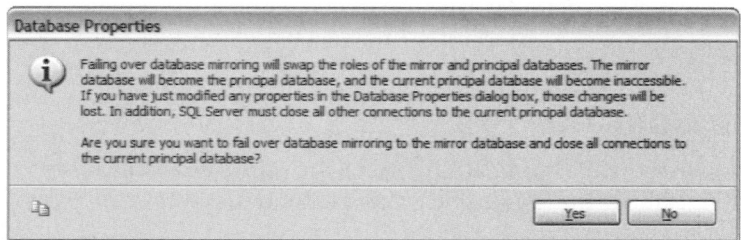

FIGURE 16.24   The failover dialog box for database mirroring.

When you are mirroring a database, you cannot bring the principal offline as you would be able to do in an un-mirrored configuration.

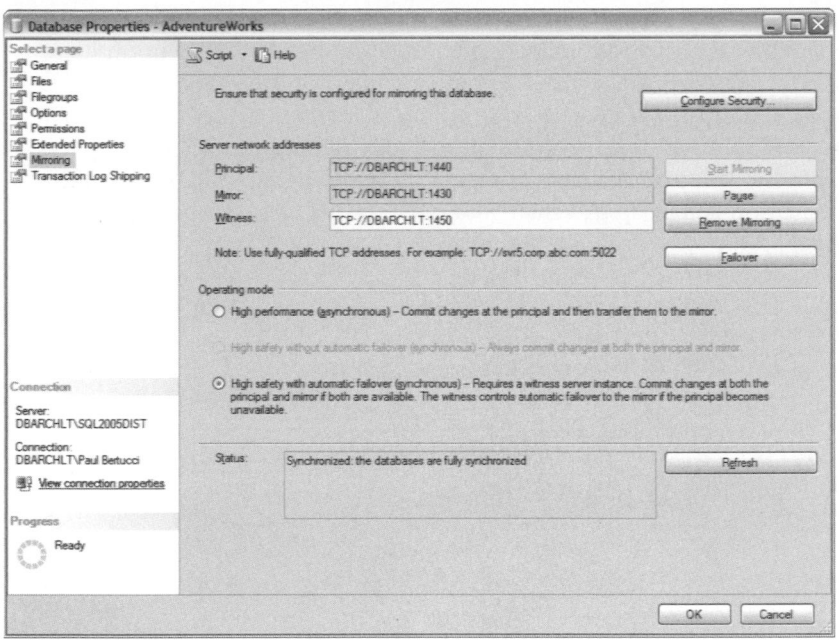

FIGURE 16.25   Server instances switch roles following a failover.

Client Setup and Configuration for Database Mirroring

Microsoft has enhanced the client connection capabilities to become mirroring aware. In other words, it is now possible for a client application to connect to either partner in a mirrored configuration. The client would, of course, only be connecting to the server instance that is the current principal. With the help of an extension to the client connection configuration file, all .NET applications can easily add both partners to their connection string information, and when a principal fails, they can automatically establish a connection to the new principal (in a mirrored configuration). Figure 16.26 shows the added connection string information that you provide in the configuration file (app.config) for your application. This enhancement uses the Failover Partner= addition that identifies the proper failover server instance for this mirrored configuration.

```
<?xml version="1.0" encoding="utf-8" ?>
<configuration>
    <configSections>
    </configSections>
    <connectionstrings>
        <add name="WindowsApplication4.Properties.Settings.AdventureworksConnectionString"
            connectionString="Server=DBARCHLT\SQL2005DEV;Failover Partner=DBARCHLT\SQL2005DIST;Database=Adventureworks;
            Integrated Security=True";providerName="System.Data.SqlClient" />
    </connectionstrings>
</configuration>
```

FIGURE 16.26   A client connection string configuration identifying the failover partner.

As a bonus, we have provided a small .NET C# client application that you can easily use to test client connections in a database mirroring configuration. This C# solution file, SQL Client DB Mirroring Test.zip, is on the book's companion website at www. samspublishing.com, under the Chapter 18 code samples. When you expand this file, it builds a complete .NET solution directory with all the code needed for this test application. With Visual Studio, you just open the WindowsApplication4.sln file (solution file), and the entire application comes up in Visual Studio. Figure 16.27 shows this simple application in Visual Studio.

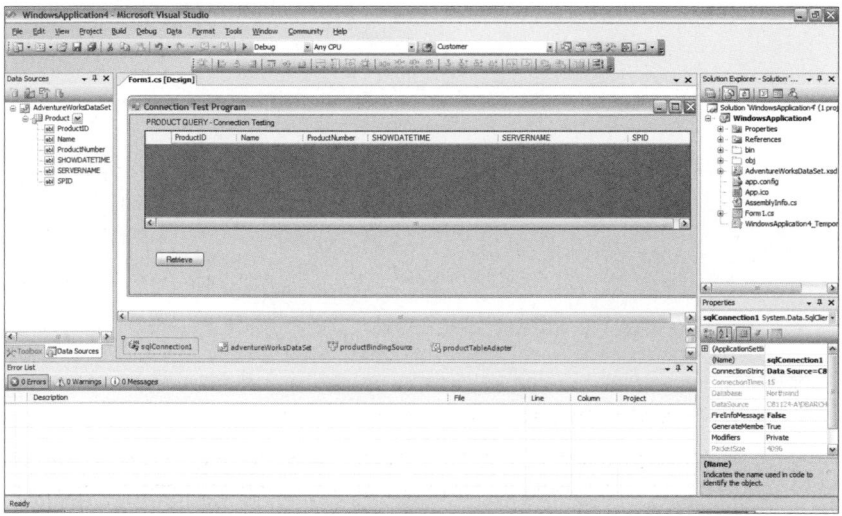

FIGURE 16.27   A SQL client test program for database mirroring in Visual Studio.

This simple test program displays data from the Product table in the AdventureWorks database (which you are mirroring), along with the exact date time of the data retrieval, the name of the server instance the data came from, and the SQL process ID (SPID) of the current server instance. This way, you can easily see where the data is coming from. If you are trying to use this program, all you have to do is update the app.config file connection string entry with your two partner server instance names (DBARCHLT\SQL2005DEV and DBARCHLT\SQL2005DIST, in this example):

```
ConnectionString=
"Server=DBARCHLT\SQL2005DEV;
 Failover Partner= DBARCHLT\SQL2005DIST;
 Database=AdventureWorks;...."
```

Then, you execute the test application. This application automatically connects to the current principal database (AdventureWorks on the DBARCHLT\SQL2005DEV server instance, in this example), as you can see in Figure 16.28.

Next, you can fail over the principal to the mirror server, using the Database Properties Mirroring page's Failover button (refer to Figure 16.23). After you have failed this server over to its mirror (that is, switched roles), you simple click the Retrieve button at the bottom of the client test program to access the data in the AdventureWorks database again. Figure 16.29 shows this subsequent data retrieval. The test application is showing the same data rows, along with the date and time of this data retrieval and the name of the server instance from which it got its data.

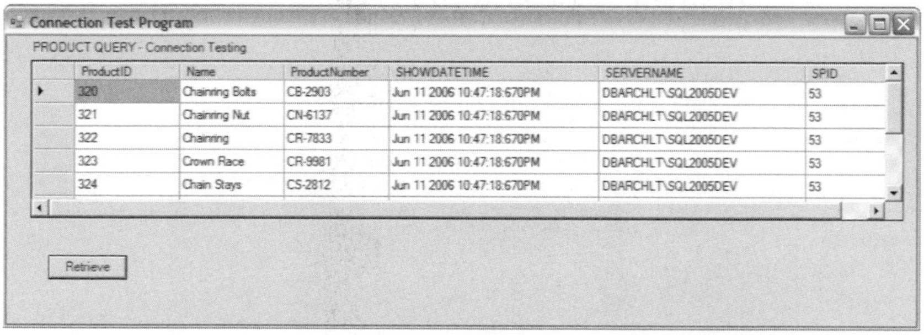

FIGURE 16.28   A SQL client test against the current principal server instance.

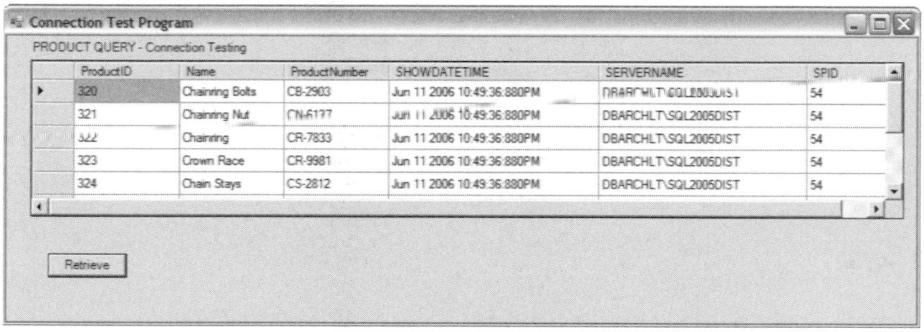

FIGURE 16.29   A SQL client test against the current principal server instance (formerly the mirror server) after failover.

In this case, the data came from the other partner server instance (AdventureWorks on the DBARCHLT\SQL2005DIST server instance, in this example). The test application is simply using the added connection information to reestablish its connection to the failed-over server instance (that is, the mirror server), completely transparently to the application. Exceptional!

Using Replication and Database Mirroring Together

SQL Server 2005 allows you to use combinations of options to achieve higher availability levels. A prime example of this would be to combine data replication with database mirroring to provide maximum availability of data, scalability to users, and fault tolerance via failover, potentially at each node in a replication topology. By starting with the publisher and perhaps the distributor, you make them both database mirror failover configurations. Figure 16.30 shows a possible data replication and database mirroring configuration (database mirroring of the publisher and database mirroring of the distributor). For further explanation of a transactional replication topology, see Chapter 15, "Replication."

Using database mirroring and replication together is essentially the best of both worlds: You get the super low latency of database mirroring for fault tolerance, and you get high availability (and scalability) of data through replication. The downside of this type of combined capability is that it requires additional servers (for mirroring of the databases). The upside is the increased scalability and resilience of your applications.

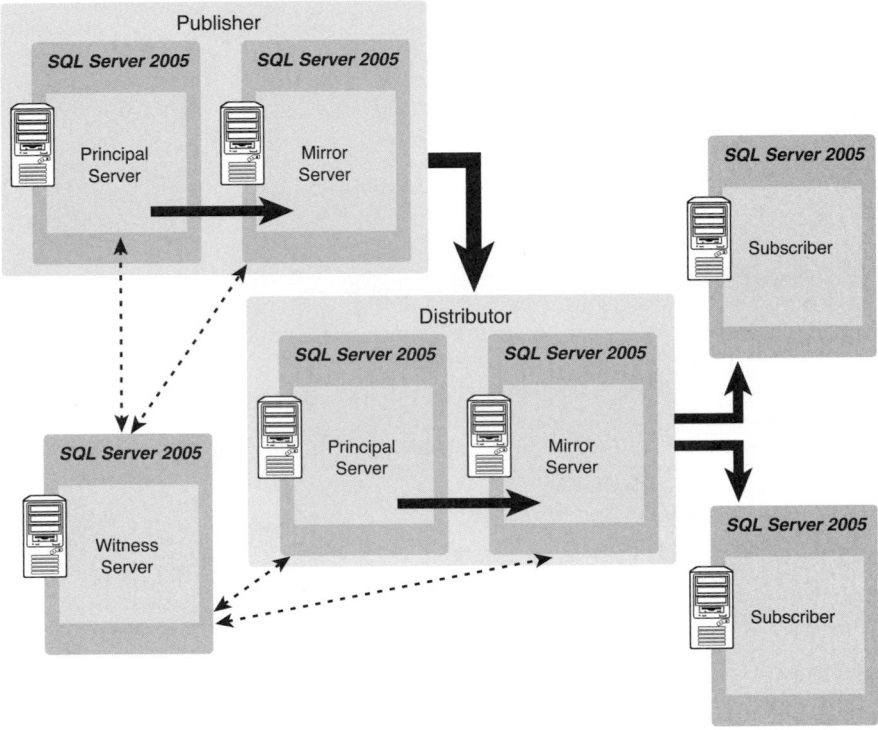

FIGURE 16.30   Rolling out database mirroring failover within data replication for scalability, availability, and fault tolerance.

Using Database Snapshots from a Mirror for Reporting

A powerful configuration to help offload reporting workload is to use database snapshots with database mirroring. A database snapshot is a highly efficient feature of SQL Server 2005 that allows for the generation and use of a read-only, stable view of a database at a moment in time (hence, it's called a snapshot). The database snapshot is also created without the overhead of creating a complete copy of the database or having completely redundant storage. A database snapshot is simply a reference point of the pages used in the database (that is defined in the system catalog). When pages are updated, a new page chain is started that contains the data pages changed since the database snapshot was taken, as illustrated in Figure 16.31.

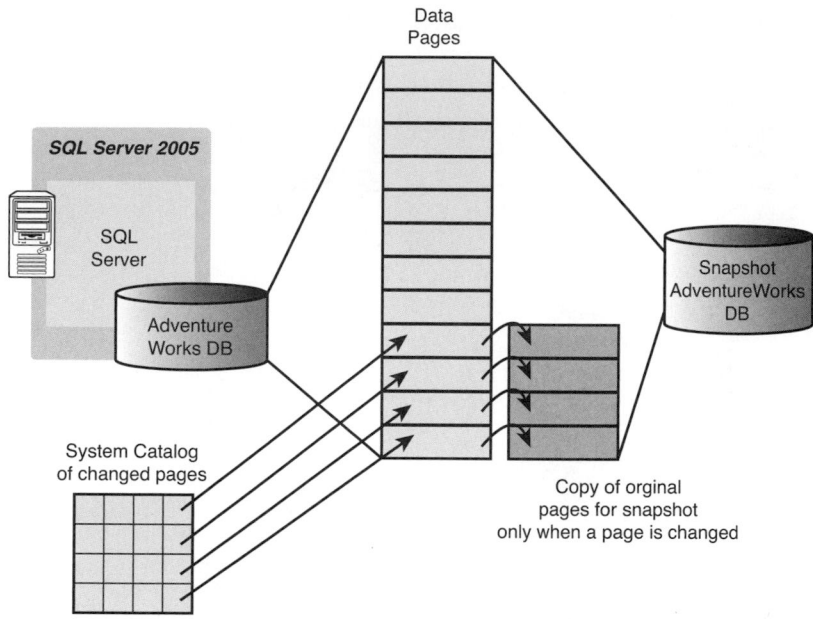

FIGURE 16.31   Database snapshots and the original database share pages and are managed within the system catalog of SQL Server 2005.

As the original database diverges from a snapshot, the snapshot gets its own copy of original pages when they are modified. The copy-on-write technology that is used for database mirroring also enables a database snapshot. When a database snapshot is created on a database (a mirror database, in this case), all writes check the system catalog of changed pages first; if the snapshot is not there, the original page is copied (using copy-on-write) and is put in a place for reference by the database snapshot (because the snapshot must be kept intact). In this way, a database snapshot and the original database share the data pages that have not changed.

Unlike a mirror database, a database snapshot can be accessed by a reporting client in read-only mode, as shown in Figure 16.32. As long as the mirror server is communicating to the principal, reporting clients can be accessing the snapshot database.

If the principal fails over to the mirror server, the connections to the snapshot database are disconnected during the database restart process (which makes the mirror server the new principal server). It is possible to reconnect the reporting clients to the database snapshot after a failover is completed, but remember that now both the transactional clients and the reporting clients are connected to a single SQL Server instance. This may not be acceptable from a performance point of view. Also, it is always a good idea to keep the number of snapshots to a minimum when creating them against a database mirror.

Chapter 27, "Database Snapshots," covers how to create database snapshots.

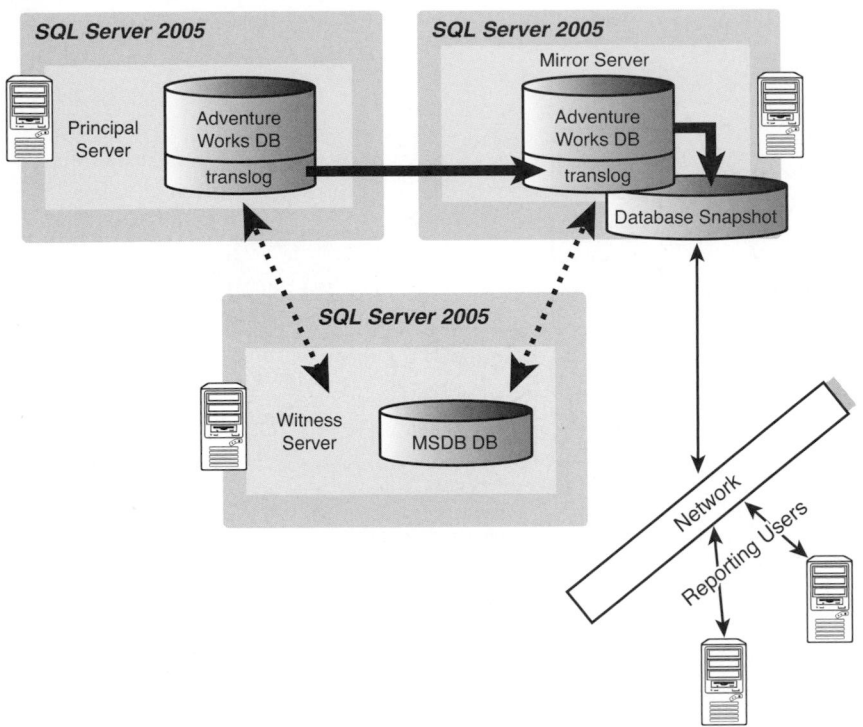

FIGURE 16.32   A database snapshot defined from a mirror server for reporting use.

Summary

Database mirroring is one of the most significant new SQL Server features to come along in a long time. This feature has provided a way for users to get to a minimum level of high availability for their databases and applications, without having to use complex hardware and software configurations (as are needed with MSCS and SQL Server Clustering configurations).

To mirror a database, you essentially ask for a complete copy of a database to be created and maintained up to the last committed transaction. The ease and simplicity of creating and monitoring database mirroring will quickly make it a configuration that many people use. Adding variations to this configuration, such as enhancing data replication or offloading reporting users, adds even more availability, resilience, and scalability possible than ever existed before. And, as you have seen, it is very easy to have your applications take advantage of database mirroring transparently.

Chapter 17, "SQL Server Clustering," delves into the complexities and significant benefits of building high-availability solutions by using SQL Server Clustering.

CHAPTER 17

SQL Server Clustering

IN THIS CHAPTER

▶ What's New in SQL Server Clustering

▶ How Microsoft SQL Server Clustering Works

▶ Installing SQL Server Clustering

Enterprise computing requires that the entire set of technologies you use to develop, deploy, and manage mission-critical business applications be highly reliable, scalable, and resilient. These technologies include the network, the entire technology stack, the operating systems on the servers, the applications you deploy, the database management systems, and everything in between.

An enterprise must now be able to provide a complete solution in regards to the following:

▶ **Scalability**—As organizations grow, so does the need for more computing power. The systems in place must enable an organization to leverage existing hardware and to quickly and easily add computing power as needs demand.

▶ **Availability**—As organizations rely more on information, it is critical that the information be available at all times and under all circumstances. Downtime is not acceptable. Moving to five-nines reliability (which means 99.999% uptime) is a must, not a dream.

▶ **Interoperability**—As organizations grow and evolve, so do their information systems. It is impractical to think that an organization will not have many heterogeneous sources of information. It is becoming increasingly important for applications to get to all the information, regardless of its location.

▶ **Reliability**—An organization is only as good as its data and information. It is critical that the systems providing that information be bulletproof.

It is assumed that you will provide a certain level of foundational capabilities in regard to network, hardware, and operating system resilience. The good news is that you can achieve many of your enterprise's demands easily and inexpensively by using Microsoft Cluster Service (MSCS), Network Load Balancing (NLB), and SQL Server Clustering (or combinations of these).

What's New in SQL Server Clustering

Much of what's new for MSCS and SQL Server Clustering has to do with the expanded number of nodes that can be managed together and several ease-of-use enhancements in MSCS, including the following:

- ▶ **Simpler MSCS setup**—Installing MSCS has become very easy (with Windows 2003 and above). And, as you will learn in this chapter, MSCS is a prerequisite for SQL Server Clustering.

- ▶ **Cleaner SQL Server Clustering installation wizard**—Running through the SQL Server installation wizard is almost as easy as making a peanut butter sandwich. The much-improved wizard detects and handles most prerequisites, and it provides for a single point of installation for multiple SQL Server node installations.

- ▶ **Increased instances per cluster**—SQL Server 2005 Enterprise Edition supports up to 50 SQL Server instances per cluster, and SQL Server Standard Edition supports up to 16 SQL Server instances per cluster.

- ▶ **More cluster aware applications**—many of the MS SQL Server 2005 products are now clusterware, such as Analysis Services, Full Text Search, and others, making these applications easily supported under clustering configurations.

- ▶ **Number of nodes in a cluster**—With Windows 2003 Enterprise Edition, you can now create up to 8 nodes in a single cluster.

These new features and enhancements combine to make setting up SQL Server Clustering an easy proposition. They take much of the implementation risk out of the equation and make this type of installation available to a broader installation base.

How Microsoft SQL Server Clustering Works

Put simply, SQL Server 2005 allows failover and failback to or from another node in a cluster. This is an immensely powerful tool for achieving higher availability virtually transparently. There are two approaches to implementing SQL Server Clustering: active/passive or active/active modes.

In an active/passive configuration, an instance of SQL Server actively services database requests from one of the nodes in a SQL Server cluster (that is, the active node). Another node is idle until, for whatever reason, a failover occurs (to the passive node). With a failover situation, the secondary node (the passive node) takes over all SQL Server resources (for example, databases and the Distributed Transaction Coordinator [DTC]) without the end user ever knowing that a failover has occurred. The end user might experience a brief transactional interruption because SQL Server Clustering cannot take over in-flight transactions. However, the end user still just looks at a single (virtual) SQL Server and truly doesn't know which node is fulfilling their requests.

Figure 17.1 shows a typical two-node SQL Server Clustering configuration using active/passive mode, in which Node 2 is idle (that is, passive).

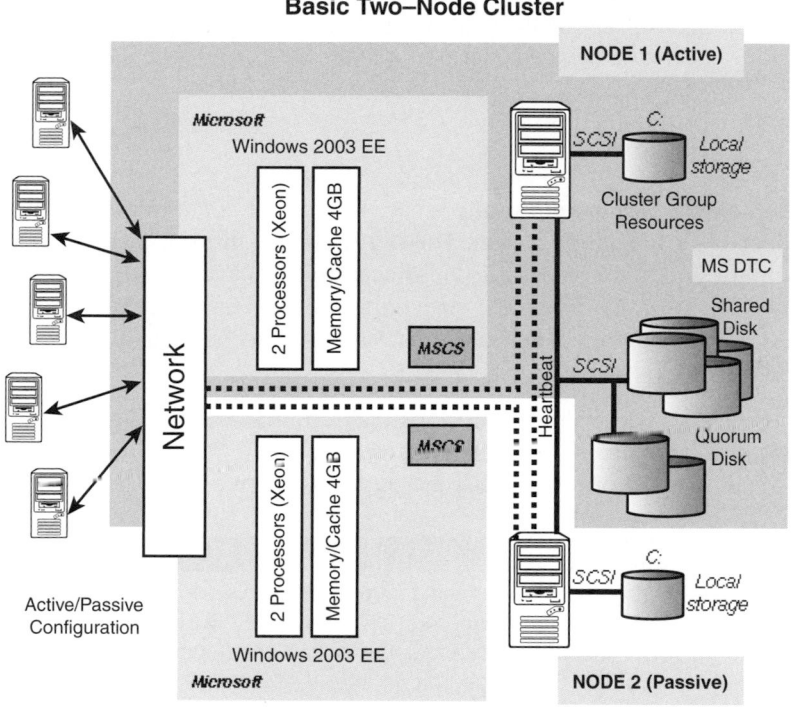

Basic Two–Node Cluster

FIGURE 17.1   A typical two-node active/passive SQL Server Clustering configuration.

In an active/active configuration, SQL Server runs multiple servers simultaneously, with different databases. This gives organizations with more constrained hardware requirements a chance to use a clustering configuration that can fail over to or from any node, without having to set aside idle hardware.

By taking advantage of the clustering capabilities of Windows 2003, SQL Server 2005 provides the high availability and reliability required of an enterprise-class database management system.

As previously mentioned, SQL Server Clustering is actually created within MSCS. MSCS, not SQL Server, is capable of detecting hardware or software failures and automatically shifting control of the managed resources to a healthy node. SQL Server 2005 implements failover clustering based on the clustering features of the Microsoft Clustering Service. In other words, SQL Server is a fully cluster-aware application and becomes a set of resources managed by MSCS. The failover cluster shares a common set of cluster resources (or cluster groups), such as clustered (that is, shared) disk drives.

NOTE

You can install SQL Server on as many servers as you want; the number is limited only by the operating system. However, MSCS (for Windows 2003) can manage only up to 16 instances of Microsoft SQL Server Standard Edition at a time and up to 50 instances of Microsoft SQL Server Enterprise Edition at a time.

Understanding MSCS

A *server cluster* is a group of two or more physically separate servers that are running MSCS and working collectively as a single system. The server cluster, in turn, provides high availability, scalability, and manageability for resources and applications. In other words, a group of servers is physically connected via communication hardware (network), shares storage (via SCSI or Fibre Channel), and uses MSCS software to tie them all together into managed resources.

Server clusters can preserve client access to applications and resources during failures and planned outages. If one of the servers in a cluster is unavailable due to failure or maintenance, resources and applications move to another available cluster node.

NOTE

You cannot do clustering with Windows 2000 Professional or older server versions. Clustering is available only on servers running Windows 2000 Advanced Server (which supports two-node clusters), Windows 2000 Datacenter Server (which supports up to four-node clusters), and Windows 2003 Enterprise Edition and Windows 2003 Datacenter Server (which support up to eight-node clusters).

Clusters use an algorithm to detect a failure, and they use failover policies to determine how to handle the work from a failed server. These policies also specify how a server is to be restored to the cluster when it becomes available again.

Although clustering doesn't guarantee continuous operation, it does provide availability sufficient for most mission-critical applications and is the building block of numerous high-availability solutions. MSCS can monitor applications and resources, automatically recognizing and recovering from many failure conditions. This provides great flexibility in managing the workload within a cluster, and it improves the overall availability of the system. Mechanisms that are "cluster aware"—such as SQL Server, Microsoft Message Queuing (MSMQ), and file shares—have already been programmed to work with MSCS.

MSCS is extremely sensitive to the hardware and network equipment you put in place. For this reason, it is imperative that you verify your own hardware's compatibility *before* you go any further in deploying MSCS.

As you can see in Figure 17.2, the *heartbeat* (named `ClusterInternal` in this figure) is a private network set up between the nodes of the cluster that checks whether a server is up and running. This occurs at regular intervals, known as *time slices*. If the heartbeat is not functioning, a failover is initiated, and another node in the cluster takes over for the failed node. In addition to the heartbeat private network, at least one public network (named `ClusterPublic` in this figure) must be enabled so that external connections can be made to the cluster.

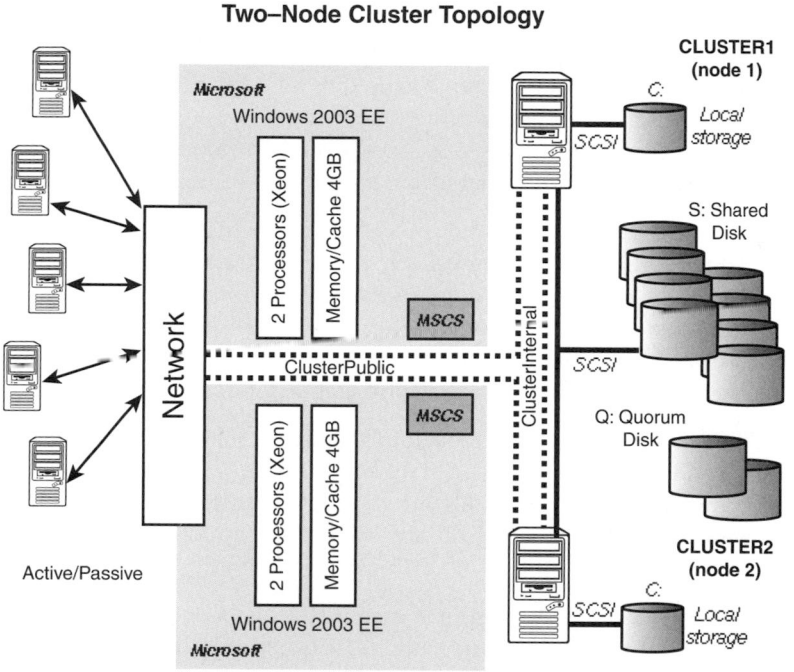

Two–Node Cluster Topology

FIGURE 17.2   A two-node active/passive MSCS cluster configuration.

The *shared disk* array is a collection of physical disks (SCSI RAID or Fibre Channel) that the cluster accesses. MSCS supports *shared nothing* disk arrays, in which only one node can own a given resource at any given moment. All other nodes are denied access until they own the resource. This protects the data from being overwritten when two computers have access to the same drives concurrently.

The *quorum drive* is a logical drive designated on the shared disk array for MSCS. This continuously updated drive contains information about the state of the cluster. If this drive becomes corrupt or damaged, the cluster installation also becomes corrupt or damaged.

NOTE

In general (and as part of a high-availability disk configuration), the quorum drive should be isolated to a drive all by itself and be mirrored to guarantee that it is available to the cluster at all times. Without it, the cluster doesn't come up at all, and you cannot access your SQL databases.

The MSCS architecture requires there to be a single quorum resource in the cluster that is used as the tie-breaker to avoid split-brain scenarios. A *split-brain scenario* happens when all the network communication links between two or more cluster nodes fail. In these cases, the cluster may be split into two or more partitions that cannot communicate with each other. MSCS guarantees that even in these cases, a resource is brought online on only one node. If the different partitions of the cluster each brought a given resource online, this would violate what a cluster guarantees and potentially cause data corruption. When the cluster is partitioned, the quorum resource is used as an arbiter. The partition that owns the quorum resource is allowed to continue. The other partitions of the cluster are said to have lost quorum, and MSCS and any resources hosted on nodes that are not part of the partition that has quorum are terminated.

The quorum resource is a storage-class resource and, in addition to being the arbiter in a split-brain scenario, is used to store the definitive version of the cluster configuration. To ensure that the cluster always has an up-to-date copy of the latest configuration information, the quorum resource should be deployed on a highly available disk configuration (using mirroring, triple-mirroring, or RAID 10, at the very least). On a Windows 2000 Server, the quorum device is typically a shared disk or physical disk resource type.

Starting with Windows 2003, a more durable approach of managing the quorum disks with clustering was created, called *majority node set*. It all but eliminates the single-point-of-failure weakness in the traditional quorum disk configuration that exists with Windows 2000 servers. However, even this new approach isn't always the best option for many clustered scenarios.

The notion of quorum as a single shared disk resource means that the storage subsystem has to interact with the cluster infrastructure to provide the illusion of a single storage device with very strict semantics. Although the quorum disk itself can be made highly available via RAID or mirroring, the controller port may be a single point of failure. In addition, if an application inadvertently corrupts the quorum disk or an operator takes down the quorum disk, the cluster becomes unavailable.

This can be solved by using a majority node set option as a single quorum resource from an MSCS perspective. In this set, the cluster log and configuration information are stored on multiple disks across the cluster. A new majority node set resource ensures that the cluster configuration data stored on the majority node set is kept consistent across the different disks.

The disks that make up the majority node set could, in principle, be local disks physically attached to the nodes themselves or disks on a shared storage fabric (that is, a collection of centralized shared storage area network [SAN] devices that are connected over a

switched-fabric or Fibre Channel arbitrated loop SAN). In the majority node set implementation that is provided as part of MSCS in Windows Server 2003, every node in the
cluster uses a directory on its own local system disk to store the quorum data, as shown in
Figure 17.3.

Windows 2003 Quorum disk option

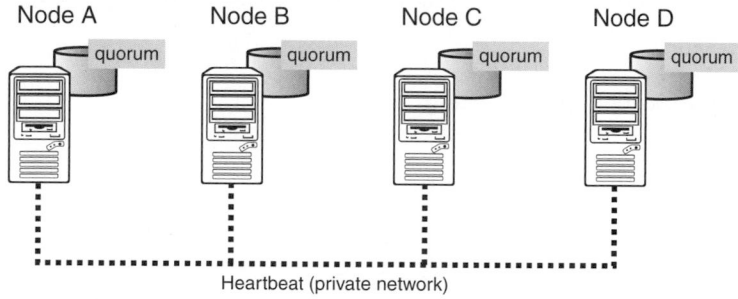

Node A   Node B   Node C   Node D

quorum   quorum   quorum   quorum

Heartbeat (private network)

The majority node set resource uses the
private network cluster connection between
nodes to transfer data to the shares

FIGURE 17.3   A majority node set.

If the configuration of the cluster changes, that change is reflected across the different
disks. The change is considered to have been committed (that is, made persistent) only if
that change is made to a majority of the nodes (that is, [Number of nodes configured in
the cluster]/2) + 1). In this way, a majority of the nodes have an up-to-date copy of the
data. MSCS itself starts up only if a majority of the nodes currently configured as part of
the cluster are up and running as part of MSCS.

If there are fewer nodes, the cluster is said *not* to have quorum, and therefore MSCS waits
(trying to restart) until more nodes try to join. Only when a majority (or quorum) of
nodes is available does MSCS start up and bring the resources online. This way, because
the up-to-date configuration is written to a majority of the nodes, regardless of node failures, the cluster always guarantees that it starts up with the most up-to-date configuration.

17

> **TIP**
>
> A quick check to see whether your hardware (server, controllers, and storage devices)
> is listed on Microsoft's Hardware Compatibility List will save you headaches later on.
> See www.microsoft.com/technet/prodtechnol/windows2000serv/default.mspx or, for
> the Windows 2003 server family, see www.microsoft.com/windows/catalog/server.

Extending MSCS with NLB

You can use a critical technology called NLB to ensure that a server is always available to handle requests. NLB works by spreading incoming client requests among a number of servers that are linked together to support a particular application. A typical example is to use NLB to process incoming visitors to your website. As more visitors come to your site, you can incrementally increase capacity by adding servers. This type of expansion is often referred to as *software scaling,* or *scaling out.* Figure 17.4 illustrates this extended clustering architecture with NLB.

MSCS with Network Load Balancing

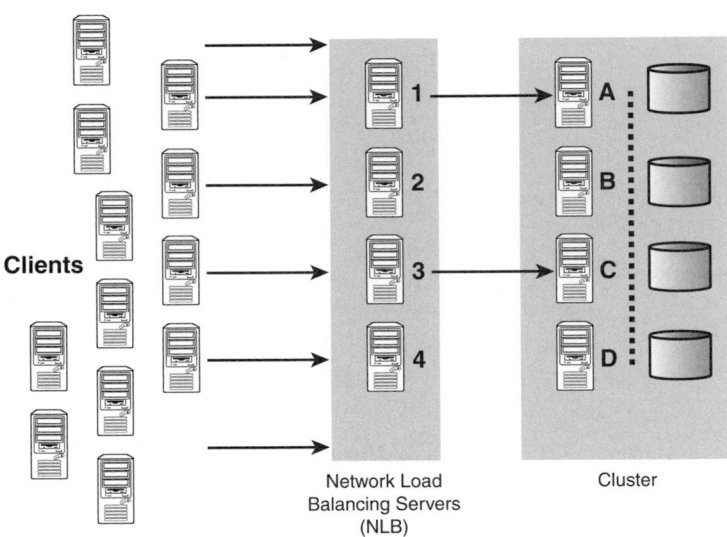

FIGURE 17.4   An NLB configuration.

By using both MSCS and NLB clustering technologies together, you can create an *n*-tier infrastructure. For instance, you can create an *n*-tiered e-commerce application by deploying NLB across a front-end web server farm and use MSCS clustering on the back end for your line-of-business applications, such as clustering your SQL Server databases. This gives you the benefits of near-linear scalability without server- or application-based single points of failure. This, combined with industry-standard best practices for designing high-availability networking infrastructures, can ensure that your Windows-based, Internet-enabled business will be online all the time and can quickly scale to meet demand. Other tiers could be added to the topology, such as an application-center tier that uses component load balancing. This further extends the clustering and scalability reach for candidate applications that can benefit from this type of architecture.

How MSCS Sets the Stage for SQL Server Clustering

Figure 17.5 shows an Excel spreadsheet that documents all the needed Internet Protocol (IP) addresses, network names, domain definitions, and SQL Server references to set up a two-node SQL Server Clustering configuration (configured in an active/passive mode). CLUSTER1 is the first node, CLUSTER2 is the second node, and the cluster group name is CLUSTER GROUP. (Very simple naming is used here to better illustrate the point.) The public network name is ClusterPublic, and the internal heartbeat network name is ClusterInternal. This spreadsheet has also been included in the download files for this book. It's a good idea to fill out this spreadsheet *before* you start installing and configuring your servers.

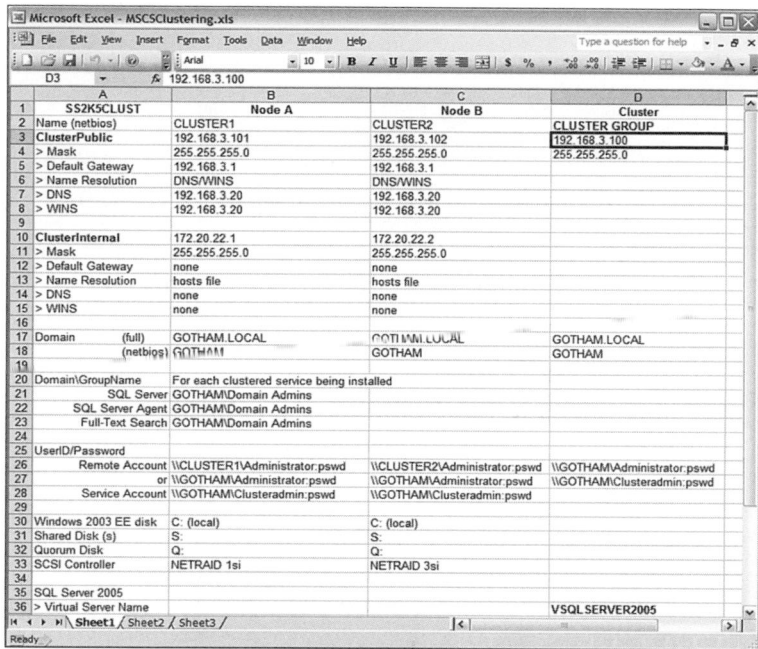

FIGURE 17.5   An Excel spreadsheet for a two-node cluster configuration.

The cluster controls the following resources:

▶ Physical disks (Q: is for the quorum disk, S: is for the shared disks, and so on)

▶ The cluster IP address

▶ The cluster name (network name)

▶ The DTC

▶ The SQL Server virtual IP address

▶ The SQL Server virtual name (network name)

▶ SQL Server

▶ SQL Server Agent

▶ The SQL Server Full-Text Search service instance (if installed)

After you have successfully installed, configured, and tested your cluster (MSCS), you are ready to add the SQL Server components as resources that will be managed by MSCS. This is where the magic happens. Figure 17.6 shows what the Cluster Administrator should look like after you have installed/configured MSCS. It doesn't have a SQL Server machine installed yet.

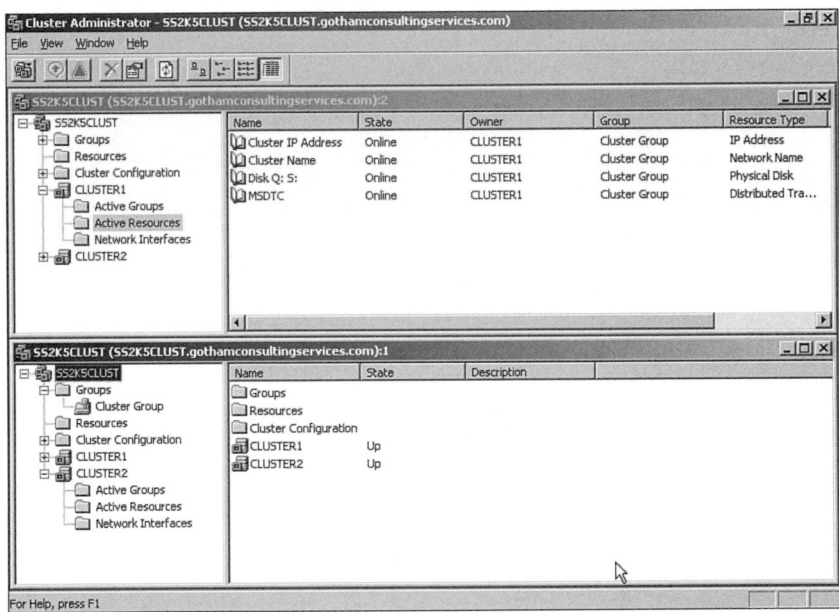

FIGURE 17.6   Cluster Administrator, showing managed resources prior to installing SQL Server.

Installing SQL Server Clustering

When you install SQL Server in a clustered server configuration, you create it as a virtual server. A virtual server is not tied to a specific physical server; it is associated with a virtualized SQL Server name that is assigned a separate IP address (not the IP address or name of the physical servers on which it runs). Handling matters this way allows for your applications to be completely abstracted away from the physical server level.

Figure 17.7 shows the same two-node cluster configuration as Figure 17.1, with all the SQL Server components identified. This virtual server is the only thing the end user will ever see. As you can also see in Figure 17.7, the virtual server name is VSQLSERVER2005, and the SQL Server instance name defaults to blank (you can, of course, give your instance a name). Figure 17.7 also shows the other cluster group resources that will be part of the SQL Server Clustering configuration: DTC, SQL Agent, SQL Server Full-Text Search, and the shared disk where the databases will live.

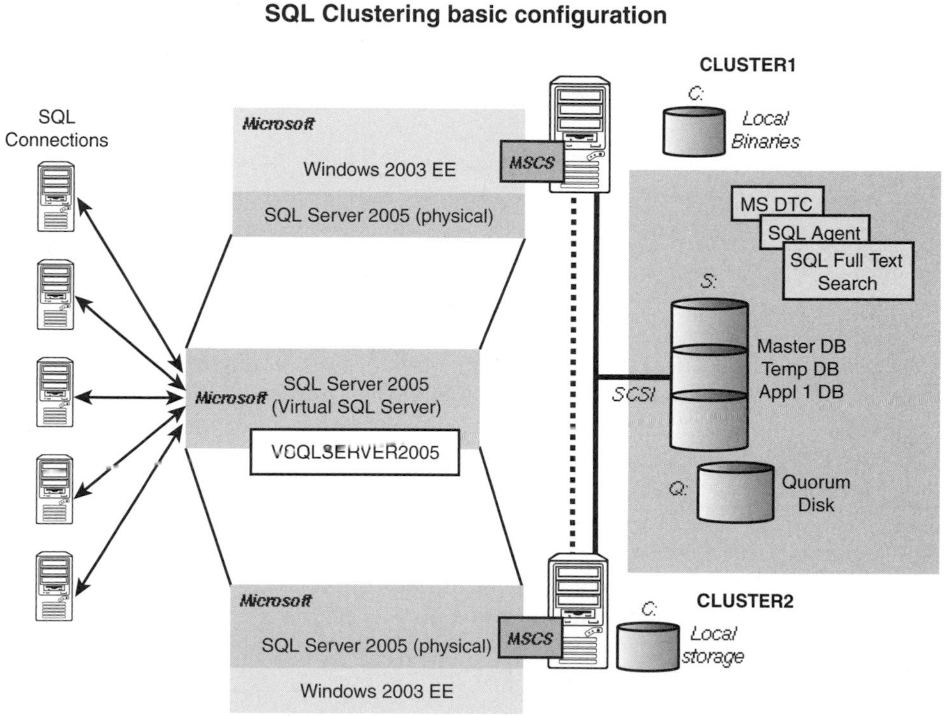

SQL Clustering basic configuration

FIGURE 17.7   A basic SQL Server Clustering configuration.

SQL Server Agent will be installed as part of the SQL Server installation process, and it is associated with the SQL Server instance it is installed for. The same is true for SQL Server Full-Text Search; it is associated with the particular SQL Server instance that it is installed to work with. The SQL Server installation process completely installs all software on all nodes you designate.

Configuring SQL Server Database Disks

Before we go too much further, we need to talk about how you should lay out a SQL Server implementation on the shared disks that are managed by the cluster. The overall usage intent of a particular SQL Server instance dictates how you might choose to have configured your shared disk and how it might be best configured for scalability and availability.

In general, RAID 0 is great for storage that doesn't need fault tolerance; RAID 1 or RAID 10 is great for storage that needs fault tolerance but doesn't have to sacrifice too much performance (as with most online transaction processing [OLTP] systems); and RAID 5 is great for storage that needs fault tolerance but whose data doesn't change that much (that is, low data volatility, as in many Decision Support Systems [DSSs]/read-only systems).

All this means that there is a time and place to use each of the different fault-tolerant disk configurations. Table 17.1 provides a very good rule of thumb to follow for deciding which SQL Server database file types should be placed on which RAID level disk configuration. (This would be true regardless of whether the RAID disk array was a part of a SQL Server cluster or not.)

TABLE 17.1   SQL Server Clustering Disk Fault Tolerance Recommendations

Device	Description	Fault Tolerance
Quorum drive	The quorum drive used with MSCS should be isolated to a drive by itself (often mirrored as well, for maximum availability).	RAID 1 or RAID 10
OLTP SQL Server database files	For OLTP systems, the database data/index files should be placed on a RAID 10 disk system.	RAID 10
DSS SQL Server database files	For DSSs that are primarily read-only, the database data/index files should be placed on a RAID 5 disk system.	RAID 5
tempdb	This is a highly volatile form of disk I/O (when not able to do all its work in the cache).	RAID 10
SQL Server transaction log files	The SQL Server transaction log files should be on their own mirrored volume for both performance and database protection. (For DSSs, this could be RAID 5 also.)	RAID 10 or RAID 1

TIP

A good practice is to balance database files across disk arrays (that is, controllers). In other words, if you have two (or more) separate shared disk arrays (both RAID 10) available within a cluster group's resources, you should put the data file of Database 1 on the first cluster group disk resource (for example, DiskRAID10-A) and its transaction log on the second cluster group disk resource (for example, DiskRaid10-B); then you should put the data file of Database 2 on the second cluster group disk resource of DiskRAID10-B and its transaction log on the first cluster group disk resource of DiskRAID10-A. In this way, you can stagger these allocations and in general balance the overall RAID controller usage, minimizing any potential bottlenecks that might occur on one disk controller.

Installing Network Interfaces

You might want to take a final glance at Cluster Administrator so that you can verify that both CLUSTER1 and CLUSTER2 nodes and their private and public network interfaces are completely specified and their state (status) is up. If you like, you should also double-check the IP addresses and network names against the Excel spreadsheet created for this cluster specification.

Installing MSCS

As you can see in Figure 17.8, MSCS is running and has been started by the ClusterAdmin login account for the GOTHAM domain.

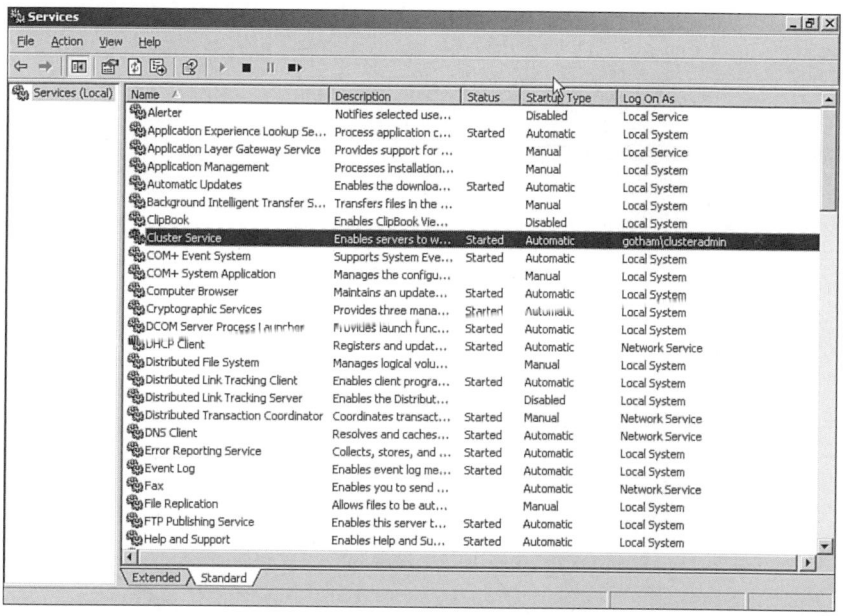

FIGURE 17.8   You need to make sure MSCS is running and started by the cluster account for the domain.

> **NOTE**
>
> If MSCS is not started and won't start, you cannot install SQL Server Clustering. You have to remove and then reinstall MSCS from scratch. You should browse the Event Viewer to familiarize yourself with the types of warnings and errors that can appear with MSCS.

Installing SQL Server

ForSQL Clustering, you must install a new SQL Server instance within a minimum two-node cluster. You should not move a SQL Server instance from a nonclustered configuration to a clustered configuration. If you already have SQL Server installed in a nonclustered environment, you need to make all the necessary backups (or detach databases) first, and then you need to uninstall the nonclustered SQL Server instance. You basically start from scratch.

With all MSCS resources running and in the online state, you run the SQL Server Setup program from the node that is online (for example, CLUSTER1). You are asked to install all software components required prior to installing SQL Server (.NET Framework 2.0, Microsoft SQL Native Client, and the Microsoft SQL Server 2005 Setup support files). After you do this, the standard Welcome to SQL Server Installation Wizard begins. It starts with a System Configuration check of all nodes in the cluster (CLUSTER1 and CLUSTER, in this case). Figure 17.9 shows the results of a successful system check.

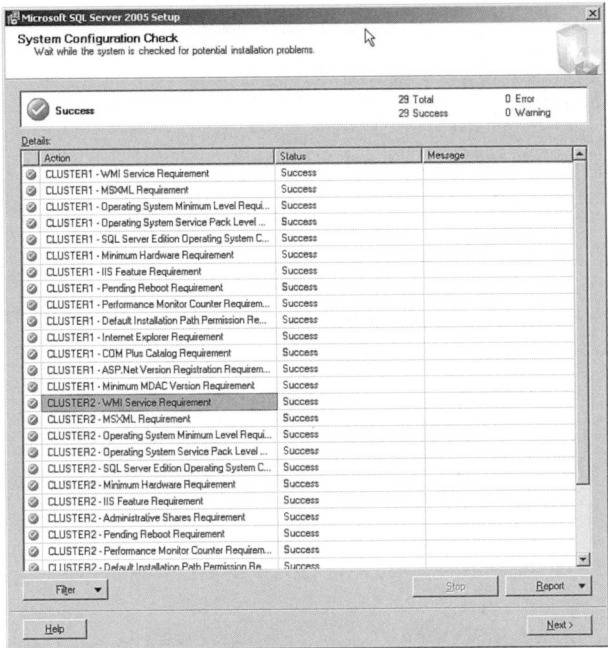

FIGURE 17.9   A Microsoft SQL Server Setup system check across two nodes in a cluster.

NOTE

SQL Server Clustering is available with SQL Server 2005 Standard Edition, Enterprise Edition, and Developer Edition. However, Standard Edition supports only a 2-node cluster. If you want to configure a cluster with more than 2 nodes, you might need to upgrade to SQL Server 2005 Enterprise Edition.

If the system check fails (warnings are acceptable), you must resolve them before you continue. If the system check is successful, you are then prompted for registration information and product keys for SQL Server, followed by the checklist of components you want to install. Figure 17.10 shows the Components to Install dialog box, with the Create a SQL Server Failover Cluster box checked.

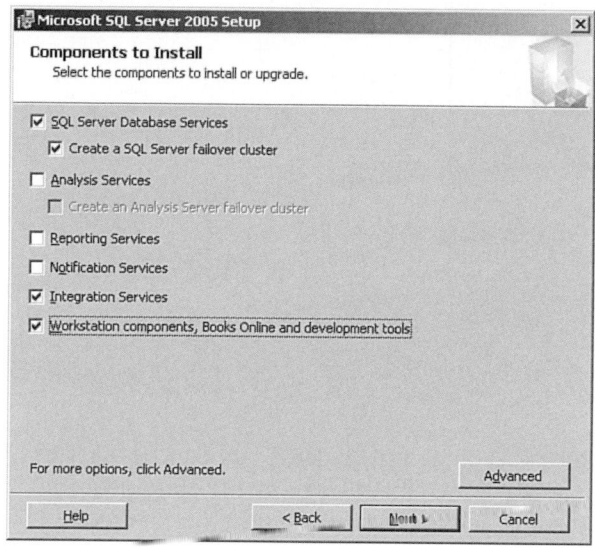

FIGURE 17.10   The SQL Server Setup Wizard Components to Install dialog, with the Create a SQL Server Failover Cluster box checked.

You then see a dialog box where you can either use the default SQL Server instance name (no name), or specify a unique SQL Server instance name.

The next dialog box you see is the Virtual Server Name dialog (see Figure 17.11). You need to provide a name for the virtual server that the client applications will see and to which they will connect. When an application attempts to connect to an instance of SQL Server 2005 that is running on a failover cluster, the application must specify both the virtual server name and the instance name (if an instance name was used), such as VSQLDBARCH\ VSQLSRV1 (virtual server name\SQL Server instance name) or VSQLSERVER2005 (just the virtual server name with the default SQL Server instance name). The virtual server name must be unique on the network.

> **NOTE**
>
> A good naming convention to follow is to preface all virtual SQL Server names and virtual SQL Server instance names with a V. This way, you can easily identify which SQL Server machines on your network are clustered. For example, you could use VSQLSERVER2005 as a virtual SQL Server name and VSQLSRV1 as an instance name.

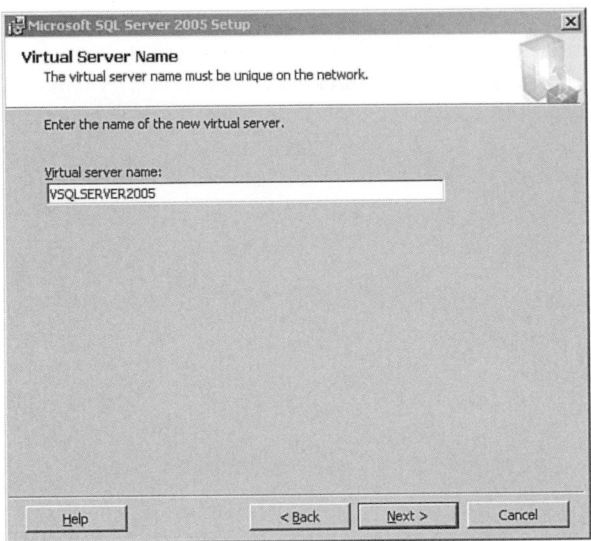

FIGURE 17.11   Specifying the virtual server name (VSQLSERVER2005).

You cannot access a SQL Server machine by specifying the machine name (CLUSTER1) and instance name because the SQL Server machine is not listening on the IP address of this "local" server. It is listening on the clustered IP addresses created during the setup of a virtual server.

The next thing you need to do for this new virtual server specification is to identify an IP address and which network it should use. As you can see in Figure 17.12, you simply type in the IP address (for example, 192.168.3.110) that is to be the IP address for this virtual SQL Server machine and identify which network to use (for example, ClusterPublic). Then you click the Add button. This specification now appears in the lower window of the Virtual Server Configuration dialog box. If the IP address that is being specified is already in use, an error occurs.

NOTE

Keep in mind that you use a separate IP address for the virtual SQL Server that is completely different from the cluster IP addresses. In a nonclustered installation of SQL Server the server can be referenced using the machine's IP address. In a clustered configuration, you do not use the IP addresses of the servers themselves; instead, you use this separately assigned IP address for the "virtual" SQL Server.

Next, you identify the cluster-managed disk(s) for the database files for SQL Server. For the current example, Figure 17.13 shows the cluster group and managed disks that are available. It contains an S: drive (that you want SQL Server to use) and a Q: drive that is being used for the quorum files (do not select this drive!). You simply select the available drive(s) that you want to put your SQL database files on (the S: drive in this example). If the quorum resource is in the cluster group you have selected, a warning message is issued, informing you of this fact. A general rule of thumb is to isolate the quorum resource to a separate cluster group, if possible.

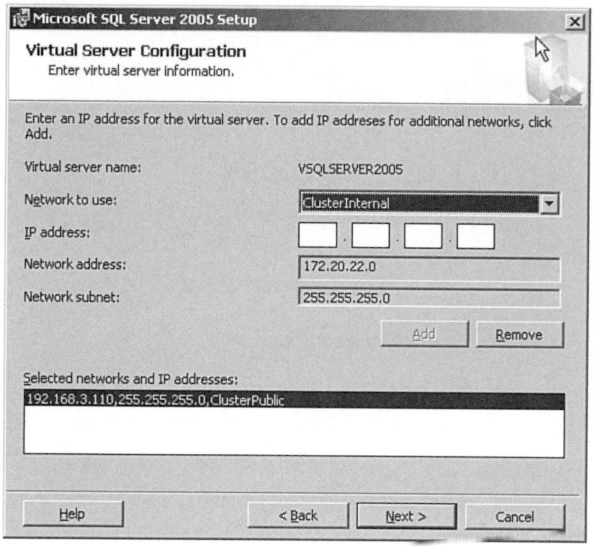

FIGURE 17.12   Specifying the virtual SQL Server IP address and which network to use.

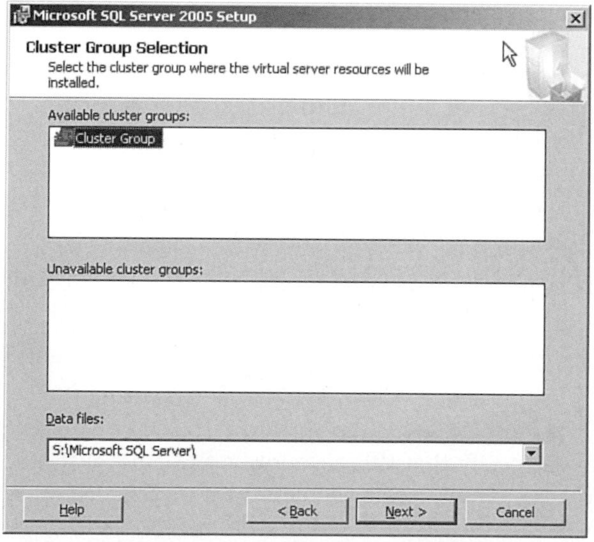

FIGURE 17.13   Specifying the SQL Server data files disks for SQL Server Clustering.

Now you must specify the nodes available to run SQL Server (see Figure 17.14). This allows any identified node to take over in the event of a node failure. The left side of the Cluster Node Configuration dialog box lists the required node (CLUSTER1 in this case) and any available nodes that you want to be a part of your SQL Server Clustering configuration. You select CLUSTER2 (that is, move it to the right side of the dialog box) to complete the two-node cluster configuration.

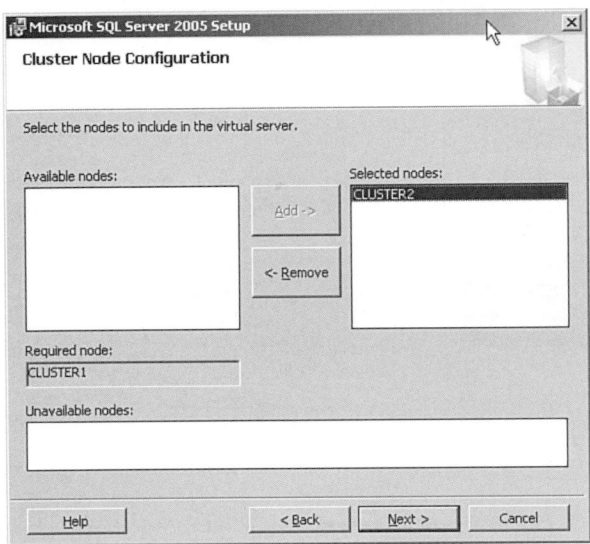

FIGURE 17.14   Selecting the nodes for the cluster node configuration.

You must now specify a remote account for all the remote setup operations for SQL Server Clustering. Figure 17.15 shows the Remote Account Information dialog box you use for this. As you can see in this dialog box, the remote account is an administrator account that is valid for all nodes in the cluster. If you are not sure which account to specify, you should use Administrator to be safe. This account is used during setup only.

The setup process installs SQL Server binaries locally on each node in the cluster (that is, in C:\Program Files\Microsoft SQL Server). The database files for the master, model, tempdb, and msdb databases are placed on the S: drive in this example. This is the shared disk location that must be available to all nodes in the SQL Server cluster.

In addition, you must be prepared to identify the user account that will be starting the services associated with SQL Server (SQL Server itself, SQL Agent, and SQL Server Full-Text Search service). As Figure 17.16 shows, you specify that this account be the ClusterAdmin account you set up for use within the cluster configuration. Remember, this account must have administrator rights within the domain and on each server (that is, it must be a member of the Administrators local group on any node in the cluster).

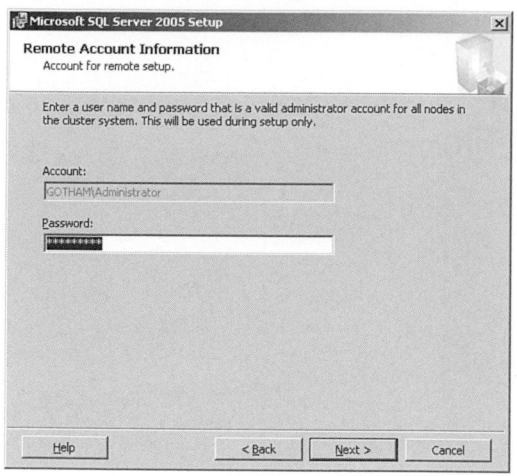

FIGURE 17.15   Specifying the remote account information for SQL Server Clustering setup.

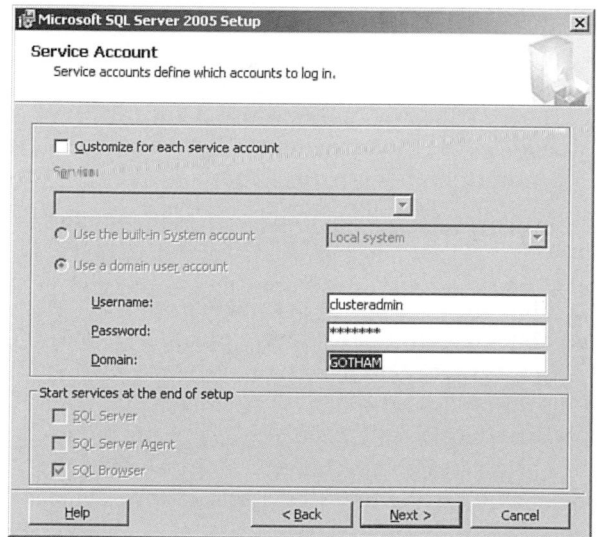

FIGURE 17.16   Specifying the Service Account for SQL Server Clustering.

You need to configure the domain group for these clustered services with the access controls. Figure 17.17 shows the domain groups that are to be used by each SQL Server service (SQL Server, SQL Server Agent, and Full-Text Search)—GOTHAM\Domain Admins in this case.

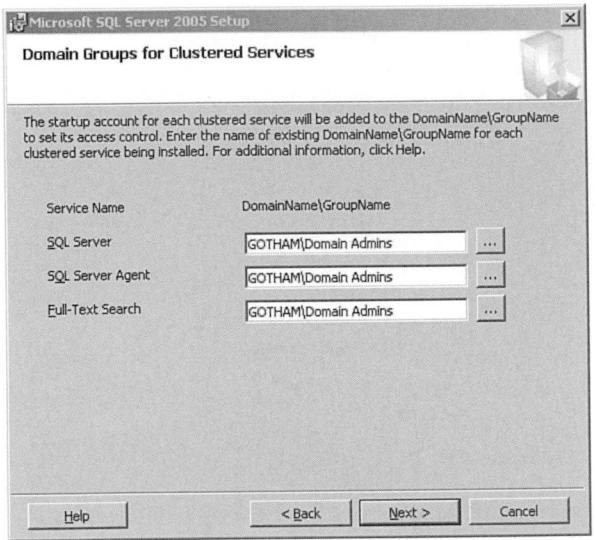

FIGURE 17.17   Specifying the domain group for each SQL Server service name.

You must specify what type of authentication mode you want for SQL Server access: Windows Authentication (only) or mixed mode (Windows Authentication and SQL Server Authentication). For this example, you should choose the mixed mode option and provide a password for the sa SQL Server administration login.

Finally, you must specify the collation settings used for sorting order and compatibility with previous versions of SQL Server.

The SQL Setup program now has enough information to do the complete installation of the SQL Server cluster, with the identified nodes. Figure 17.18 shows a dialog box that indicates that the setup is being done on each cluster node. This setup can take a while because quite a lot of things are being done. In particular, binaries are being installed locally, databases are being created on the shared disks, services are being created on each node for SQL Server, and SQL resources are being created and brought online within the cluster group. Eventually, you see a dialog box indicating that the virtual server resources have been installed.

You aren't done yet. You now need to apply the latest SQL Server service pack to this installation (if one exists). You should do it now. This is important because the time you take to apply this service pack application in the future counts against you for planned downtime and lowers your availability percentage. If you haven't done so already, you should download this service pack from Microsoft and run the Setup program.

As you can see in Figure 17.19, SQL Server has been successfully installed on the cluster, and Cluster Administrator shows the newly added online resources within the cluster group.

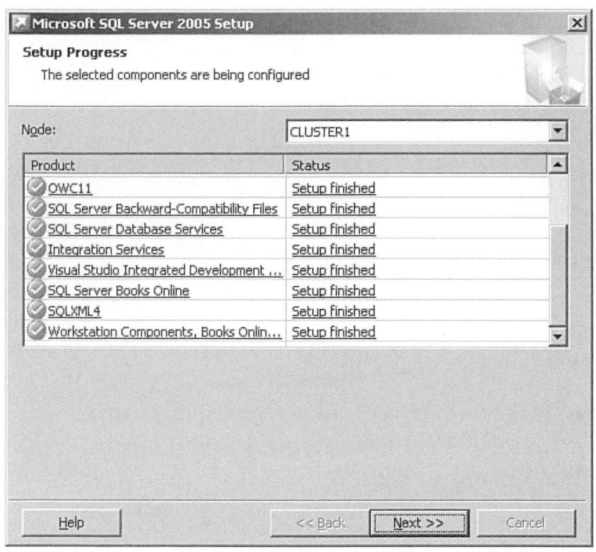

FIGURE 17.18   Setup progress for each node in the SQL Server cluster.

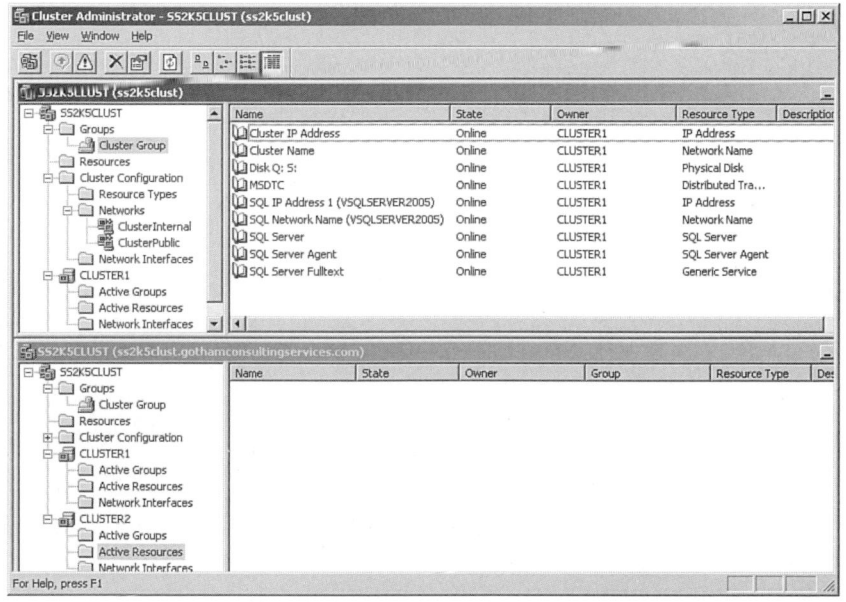

FIGURE 17.19   Cluster Administrator and the new online SQL Server resource entries.

These are the new SQL Server resource entries:

1. The SQL Server "virtual" IP address (for VSQLSERVER2005)

2. The SQL Server network name (of VSQLSERVER2005)

3. SQL Server (the instance itself)

4. SQL Server Agent (for the instance)

5. The SQL Server Full-Text Search service (for the instance)

Each resource entry should say Online in the State column and be owned by the same node (CLUSTER1 in this example).

You should now verify that the correct system services were set up by displaying the services selection (via the Administrative Tools section of the Control Panel) for the current node you are on (CLUSTER1). As you can see in Figure 17.20, these new services entries are SQL Server (MSSQLSERVER) for the SQL Server instance, SQL Server Agent (MSSQLSERVER) for the SQL Agent entry, and several other SQL Server services. Notice that the services that are managed by MSCS have the startup type "manual." MSCS is used to start them up. So when the cluster starts up, these services are started.

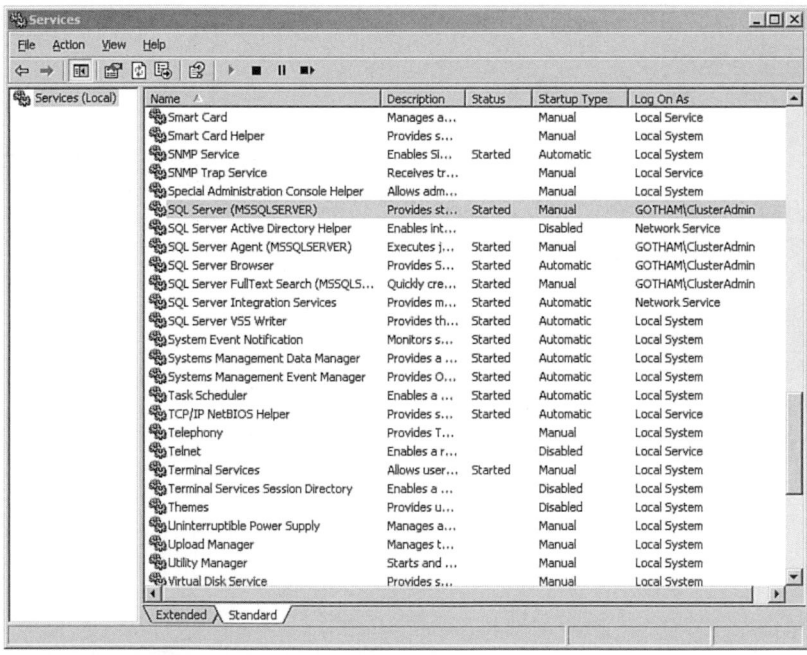

FIGURE 17.20   New SQL Server services entries.

In the Cluster Administrator, you can easily view the properties of each of the new SQL Server resources by right-clicking a resource and selecting Properties. Figure 17.21 shows the properties of the SQL IP Address (VSQLSERVER2005) resource for the newly created virtual SQL Server machine. The Parameters tab indicates the IP address (192.168.3.110) that it will have on the network, the subnet mask (255.255.255.0), and the network that it will use (ClusterPublic). This is where you change these parameters if and when you need to.

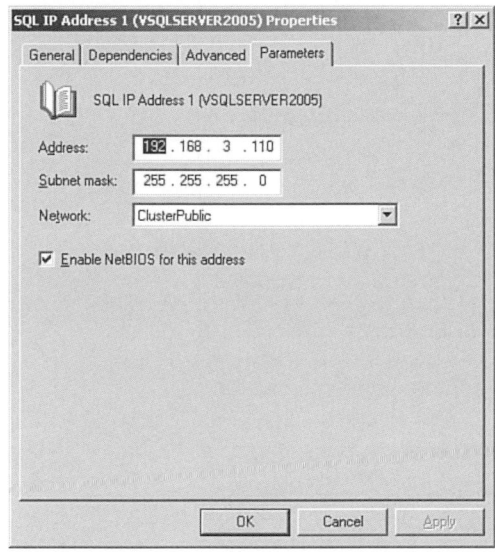

FIGURE 17.21   Properties of the SQL IP Address (VSQLSERVER2005) resource.

When you right-click a resource entry in the Cluster Administrator, you have an option to take the resource offline or to initiate a failure. You sometimes need to do this when you're trying to fix or test a SQL Server Clustering configuration. However, when you're initiating full SQL Server failover to another node (for example, from CLUSTER1 to CLUSTER2), you typically use the Move Group cluster group technique because you want all the resources for the cluster group to fail over—not just one specific resource. Figure 17.22 shows that you simply right-click the Cluster Group item entry and select Move Group). All resources then fail over to CLUSTER2.

Failure of a Node

As you can see in Figure 17.23, one of the nodes in the SQL Server cluster (CLUSTER1) has failed, and MSCS is in the middle of failing over to the other node in the cluster (CLUSTER2). As you can also see, the CLUSTER2 node item group has a red hourglass on it, indicating that an MSCS operation is under way. The states of the resources on CLUSTER2 are mostly online pending. In other words, these resources are in the middle of failing over to this node. As they come up successfully, Online Pending turns to Online.

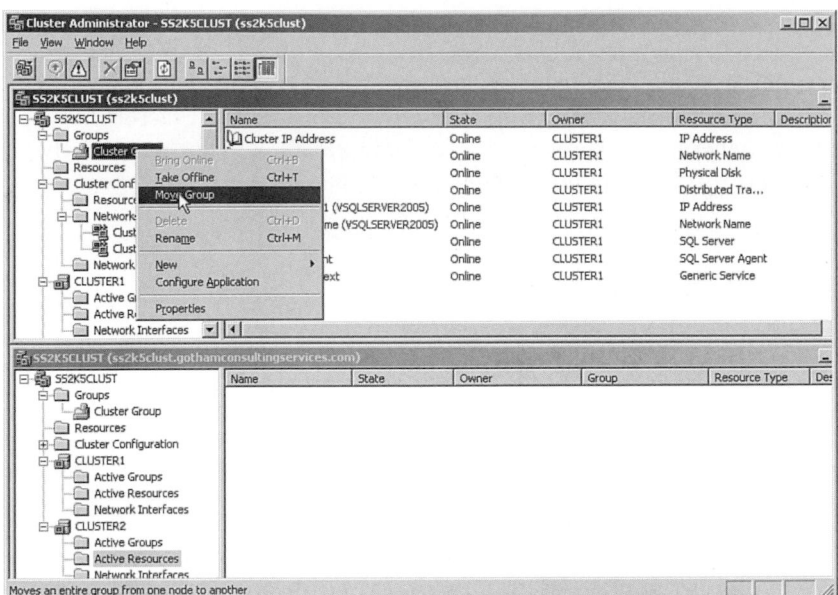

FIGURE 17.22   Using Move Group to fail over to another node in a cluster.

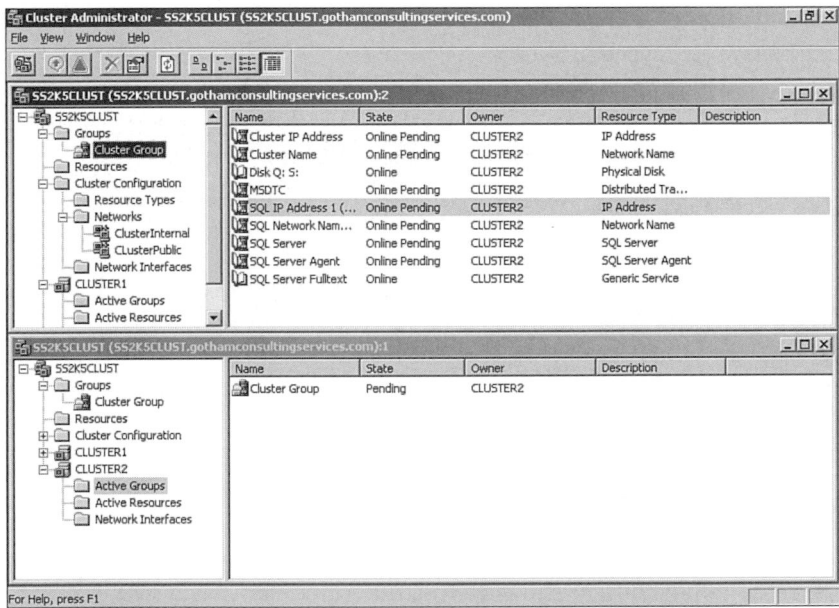

FIGURE 17.23   Failing over from one node to another.

In addition, the failure of a node (for any reason) is also written to the System event log.

This example shows an intentional failure of the SQL Server instance (VSQLSERVE2005) via the Cluster Administrator. SQL Server Clustering does the right thing by failing over to the other node. This serves to verify that SQL Server Clustering is working properly. The next section illustrates what this effect has on a typical client application point of view, using a custom client test program called Connection Test Program. Figure 17.24 shows the successful failing over onto the CLUSTER2 node. All resources are now online.

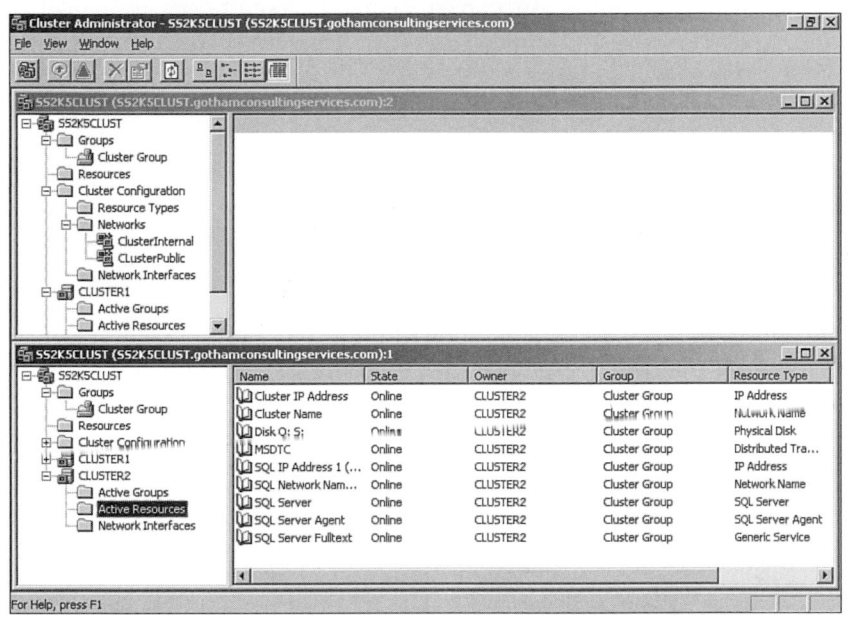

FIGURE 17.24   All SQL Server resources successfully failed over to CLUSTER2.

Congratulations! You are now up and running, with your SQL Server cluster intact, and should now be able to start achieving significantly higher availability for your end users. It is very easy to register this new virtual SQL Server (VSQLSERVER2005) within SQL Server Management Studio (SSMS) and completely manage it as you would any other SQL Server instance.

The Connection Test Program for a SQL Server Cluster

To help in visualizing exactly what effect a SQL Server failure and subsequent failover may have on an end-user application, we have created a small test program using Visual Studio 2005. This small C# test program accesses the AdventureWorks database that is included with SQL Server 2005, and it was created in about 10 minutes. It displays a few columns of data, along with a couple system variables that show connection information, including the following:

▶ **ProductID, Name, and ProductNumber**—This is a simple three-column display of data from the Product table in the AdventureWorks database.

▶ **SHOWDATETIME**—This shows the date and time (to the millisecond) of the data access being executed.

▶ **SERVERNAME**—This is the SQL Server name that the client is connected to.

▶ **SPID**—This is the SQL Server process ID (SPID) that reflects the connection ID to SQL Server itself by the client application.

This type of small program is very useful because the connection it makes is always to the virtual SQL Server. This enables you to see what effect a failover would have with your client applications.

To populate this display grid, you execute the following SQL statement:

```
SELECT ProductID, Name, ProductNumber,
CONVERT (varchar(32), GETDATE(), 9) AS SHOWDATETIME,
@@SERVERNAME AS SERVERNAME,
@@SPID AS SPID
FROM Production.Product WHERE (ProductID LIKE '32%')
```

You use Visual Studio 2005 to set up a simple Windows form like the one shown in Figure 17.25; build a simple button that will retrieve the data from the SQL Server database on the virtual server; and also show the date, time, server name, and SPID information for each access invocation.

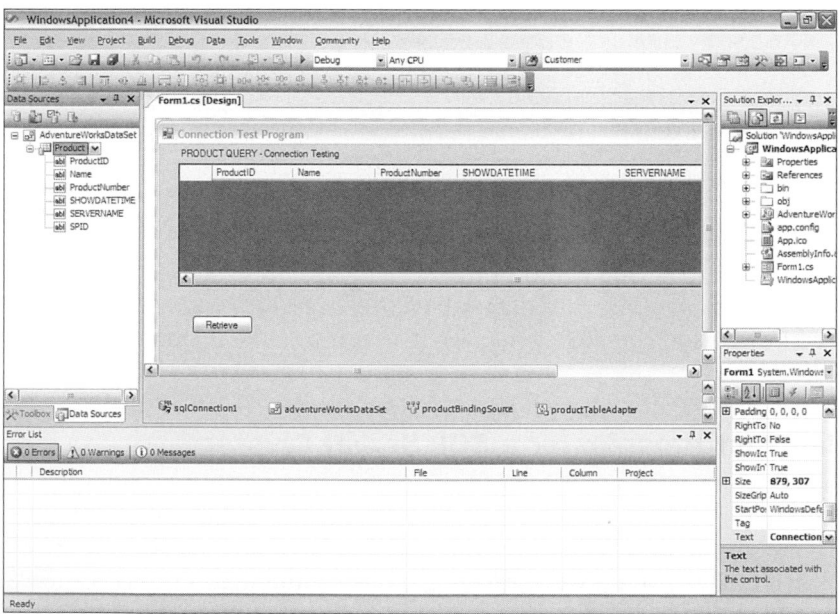

FIGURE 17.25   Visual Studio 2005 Windows form and data adapters needed for the test client C# program.

The Visual Studio 2005 project files for the Connection Test Program are available on the Sams website for this book (www.samspublishing.com). The program is called `WindowsApplication4.sln SQLClientTest4` Visual Studio 2005 project and is zipped up in a file named `SQLClientTest.zip`. If you want to install this program, you just unzip the `SQLClientTest.zip` file and locate the `WindowsApplication4.sln` solution file. You open this from your Visual Studio 2005 start page. Then you rebuild and deploy it after you have modified the connection string of the dataset adapter.

When you get this simple test program deployed, you simply execute it from anywhere on your network. As you can see in the `App.config` XML file for this application, shown here, the connection string references the `VSQLSERVER2005` virtual server name only:

```
<?xml version="1.0" encoding="utf-8" ?>
<configuration>
    <configSections>
    </configSections>
    <connectionStrings>
        <add name="WindowsApplication4.Properties.Settings.
        AdventureWorksConnectionString"
        connectionString="Data Source=VSQLSERVER2005;Initial Catalog=AdventureWorks;
Integrated Security=True"
            providerName="System.Data.SqlClient" />
    </connectionStrings>
</configuration>
```

Figure 17.26 shows the first execution of the Connection Test Program. If you click the Retrieve button, the program updates the data grid with a new data access to the virtual SQL Server machine, shows the name of the server that the client program is connecting to (`SERVERNAME`), shows the date and time information of the data access (in the `SHOWDATETIME` column), and displays the SQL SPID that it is using for the data access (in the `SPID` column). You are now executing a typical C# program against the virtual SQL Server. Note that the SPID value is 54. This represents the SQL connection to the virtual SQL Server machine that is servicing the data request.

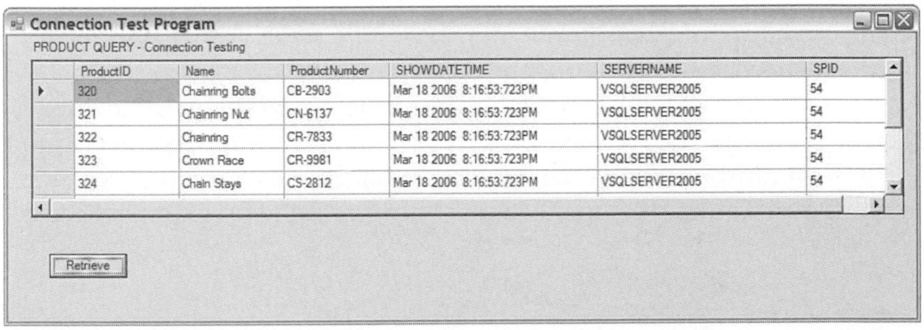

FIGURE 17.26   Executing the Connection Test Program with current connection information.

Now let's look at how this high-availability approach works, from the client application point of view. In order to simulate the failure of the active node, you simply turn off the machine (CLUSTER1 in this case). This is the best (and most severe) test case of all.

After you simulate this failure, you click the Retrieve button in the Connection Test Program again, and an unhandled exception occurs (see Figure 17.27). You can view the details of the error message, choose to quit the application, or choose to continue. You should click Continue for now.

What has happened is that the application can no longer connect to the failed SQL Server (because you turned off CLUSTER1), and it is still in the middle of failing over to CLUSTER2 in the two-node cluster.

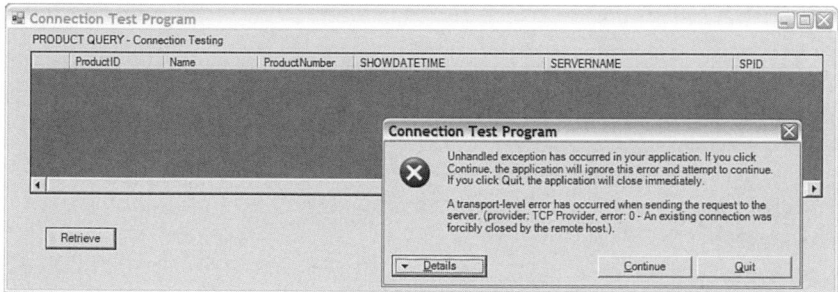

FIGURE 17.27   An unhandled exception has occurred; it is a transport-level error (that is, a TCP provider error).

A failover occurs in a short amount of time; the actual amount of time varies, depending on the power and speed of the servers implemented and the number of in-flight transactions that need to be rolled back or forward at the time of the failure. (A complete SQL failover often occurs in about 15 to 45 seconds. This is very minor and well within most service-level agreements and high-availability goals.) You then simply click the Retrieve button again in the Connection Test Program, and you are talking to SQL Server again, but now to CLUSTER2.

As you can see in Figure 17.28, the data connection has returned the customer data, SHOWDATETIME has been updated, and SERVERNAME still shows the same virtual SQL Server name that the application needs to connect to, but the SPID has changed from 54 to 53. This is due to the new connection of the Connection Test Program to the newly owned (failed-over) SQL Server machine. The Connection Test Program has simply connected to the newly started SQL Server instance on CLUSTER2. The unhandled exception (error) goes away, and the end user never knows a complete failover occurred; the user simply keeps processing as usual.

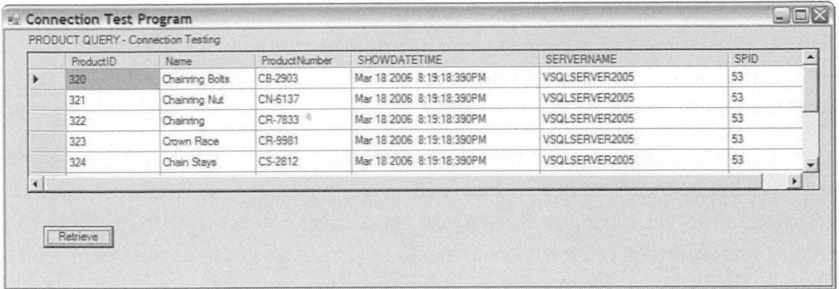

FIGURE 17.28   Executing the Connection Test Program again against the failed-over cluster node.

> **NOTE**
>
> You could program better error handling that would not show the "unhandled exception" error. You might want to display a simple error message, such as "database momentarily unavailable—please try again," which would be much more user friendly.

Potential Problems to Watch Out for with SQL Server Clustering

Many potential problems can arise during setup and configuration of SQL Server Clustering. The following are some items you should watch out for:

▶ SQL Server service accounts and passwords should be kept the same on all nodes, or a node will not be able to restart a SQL Server service. You can use `administrator` or a designated account (for example, `Cluster` or `ClusterAdmin`) that has administrator rights within the domain and on each server.

▶ Drive letters for the cluster disks must be the same on all nodes (servers). Otherwise, you might not be able to access a clustered disk.

▶ You might have to create an alternative method to connect to SQL Server if the network name is offline and you cannot connect using TCP/IP. You can use named pipes, specified as `\\.\pipe\$$\SQLA\sql\query`.

▶ It is likely that you will run into trouble getting MSCS to install due to hardware incompatibility. Be sure to check Microsoft's Hardware Compatibility List before you venture into this installation.

Summary

Building out your company's infrastructure with clustering technology at the heart is a huge step toward achieving five-nines reliability. If you do this, every application, system component, or database you deploy on this architecture has that added element of resilience. And, in many cases, the application or system component changes needed to take advantage of these clustering technologies are completely transparent. Utilizing a combination of NLB and MSCS allows you to not only fail over applications but to scale for increasing network capacity.

The two-node, active/passive node is one of the most common SQL Server Clustering configurations used. As you become more familiar with SQL Server Clustering and your high-availability requirements get closer to five-nines), you might need to put in place other, more advanced configurations, such as four-node SQL Server clusters and/or datacenter-class clusters (of up to eight-node SQL Server clusters and active/active variations). If you follow the basic guidelines of disk configurations and database allocations across these disk configurations, as described in this chapter, you can guarantee a certain level of stability, performance, and scalability. SQL Server Clustering is one of the best, most cost-effective solutions, and it is literally "out of the box" with SQL Server and the Windows family of servers.

Remember that SQL Server 2005 supports other concepts related to high availability, such as data replication, log shipping (soon to be deprecated), and database mirroring. You might use these solutions rather than SQL Server Clustering, depending on your requirements.

Clustering is a very complex subject. The information contained in this chapter is sufficient to start you in this area, but for a much more complete and thorough understanding of how to assess your high-availability needs, to evaluate what you should build for high availability, and to implement a high-availability platform that uses MSCS and SQL Server Clustering, you should find a copy of *Microsoft SQL Server High Availability* by Paul Bertucci (Sams Publishing). This book is loaded with full explanations, a formal approach to achieving five-nines reliability, and numerous live examples.

Chapter 45, "SQL Server Disaster Recovery Planning" (on the CD-ROM), covers many of the critical issues surrounding recovery in case of major failure.

PART IV

Database Administration

IN THIS PART

CHAPTER 18 Creating and Managing Databases 547

CHAPTER 19 Creating and Managing Tables 579

CHAPTER 20 Creating and Managing Indexes 623

CHAPTER 21 Implementing Data Integrity 641

CHAPTER 22 Creating and Managing Views
in SQL Server 667

CHAPTER 23 Creating and Managing Stored
Procedures 699

CHAPTER 24 Creating and Managing
User-Defined Functions 799

CHAPTER 25 Creating and Managing Triggers 833

CHAPTER 26 Transaction Management and the
Transaction Log 873

CHAPTER 27 Database Snapshots 919

CHAPTER 28 Database Maintenance 945

CHAPTER **18**

Creating and Managing Databases

IN THIS CHAPTER

▶ What's New in Creating and Managing Databases

▶ Data Storage in SQL Server

▶ Database Files

▶ Creating Databases

▶ Setting Database Options

▶ Managing Databases

A *database* is a collection of tables and related objects that helps protect and organize data. It must exist before you can create all database objects, including tables, indexes, and stored procedures. This chapter focuses on how to create a sound database that can house database objects and how to manage the database after the objects are created. The creation and management of the various database objects is discussed in the remaining chapters in Part IV, "SQL Server Database Administration."

NOTE

It is important to remember that SQL Server actually uses its own set of databases that are installed by default when SQL Server is installed. These databases are referred to as system databases. The databases that users create are aptly named user databases. The system databases include the master, model, msdb, tempdb and resource databases. Each of these databases perform a key function in the operation of SQL Server. For example, the master database contains an entry for every user database that is created and contains serverwide information that is critical to the operation of SQL Server. The model database is basically a template database for any newly created databases. Each of these system databases are based on a structure similar to user databases and contain database objects like those contained in user databases. The system databases are discussed in detail in Chapter 6, "SQL Server System and Database Administration."

What's New in Creating and Managing Databases

Several new database-specific features have been added to SQL Server 2005. These changes are primarily related to the database engine. The following are some of the most important enhancements:

▶ **Instant file initialization**—New or expanded database files are made available much faster now because the initialization of the file with binary zeros is deferred until the file is accessed by SQL queries.

▶ **ATTACH_REBUILD_LOG**—A new ATTACH_REBUILD_LOG option has been added that allows a database to be attached without the log files. The log files are created on-the-fly.

▶ **Partial availability**—In the event of database file corruption, a database can still be brought online if the primary filegroup is available.

▶ **Database file movement**—You can now use the ALTER DATABASE command to move a database file. You must manually move the physical file. This feature was available in SQL Server 2000, but it only worked on tempdb.

Data Storage in SQL Server

A database is a storage structure for database objects. It is made up of at least two files. One file is referred to as a *data file*, and it stores the database objects, such as tables and indexes. The second file is the *transaction log file*, and it records changes to the data. A data file or log file can belong to only one database.

SQL Server stores data on the data file in 8 KB blocks, known as pages. A *page* is the smallest unit of input/output (I/O) that SQL Server uses to transfer data to and from disk. An 8KB page is equal to 1024 bytes × 8, or 8192 bytes. There is some overhead associated with each data page, so the maximum number of bytes of data that can be stored on a page is 8060 bytes. The overhead on a data page includes a 96-byte page header that contains system information about the page. This system information includes the page number, the page type, and the amount of free space on the page.

Generally, a row of data in a SQL Server database is limited to the 8060-byte maximum. With SQL Server 2005, there are some exceptions to this 8060 limit if the table contains columns that have the data types text/image, varchar, nvarchar, varbinary, or sql variant. With these data types, SQL Server can store the data in a separate data structure when the size of the row exceeds the 8060-byte limit. When the 8060-byte limit is exceeded, SQL Server stores a pointer to the separate data structure so that the information in these columns can be accessed.

In an effort to reduce internal operations and increase I/O efficiency, SQL Server, when allocating space to a table or an index, allocates space in extents. An *extent* is eight contiguous pages, or 64KB of storage. There are actually two types of extents. Every table or index is initially allocated space in a *mixed extent*. As the name implies, mixed extents store pages from more than one object. When an index or a table is first created, it is assigned an index allocation map (IAM), which is used to track space usage for the object, and at least one data page. The IAM and data page are assigned to a mixed extent in an effort to save space because dedicating an extent to a table with a few small rows would be wasteful. Up to eight initial pages are assigned this way. When an object requires more than eight pages of storage, all further space is allocated from uniform extents. A *uniform extent* stores pages for only a single index or table. This allows SQL Server to optimize read and write operations and reduce fragmentation because the data will be stored in units of 64KB (that is, eight pages) as opposed to individual 8KB pages being scattered throughout the data file.

For more detailed information on the internal storage structures and how to manage them in SQL Server databases, see Chapter 33, "Database Design and Performance."

Database Files

SQL Server maps a database over a set of operating system files that are visible to the SQL Server machine. Microsoft recommends that the files be located on a storage area network (SAN), on an iSCSI-based network, or on a locally attached disk. These three storage options provide the best performance and reliability for a SQL Server database. You have an option of storing database files on a network, but this option is turned off by default. You can use the trace flag 1807 to enable network-based database files, but it is generally not recommended that you do so.

Each database can contain a maximum of 32,726 files. Each of the database files serves a different purpose for the database engine. These files have a standard layout that allows SQL Server to organize and read the data within the files. SQL Server needs to keep track of the allocated space in each data file; it does so by allocating special pages in the first extent of each file. Because the data stored on these pages is dense and the files are accessed often, they are usually found in memory; therefore, they can be retrieved quickly.

The first page (page 0) in every file is the file header page. This page contains information about the file, such as the database to which the file belongs, the filegroup it is in, the minimum size, and its growth increment.

The second page (page 1) in each file is the page free space (PFS) page. The PFS page keeps track of the other pages in the database file. The PFS uses 1 byte for each page. This byte keeps track of whether the page is allocated, whether it is empty, and, if it is not empty, how full the page is. A single PFS page can keep track of 8,000 contiguous pages. Additional PFS pages are created as needed.

The third page (page 2) in each file is the global allocation map (GAM) page. This page tracks allocated extents. Each GAM page tracks 63,904 extents, and additional GAM pages are allocated as needed. The GAM page contains 1 bit for each extent, which is set to 0 if the extent is allocated to an object and to 1 if it is free.

The fourth page (page 3) is the secondary GAM (SGAM) page. The SGAM page tracks allocated mixed extents. Each SGAM page tracks 63,904 mixed extents, and additional SGAM pages are allocated as needed. A bit set to 1 for an extent indicates a mixed extent with pages available.

Primary Files

The *primary data file* is the data file that keeps track of all the other data files that are used by the database. It is an operating system file that typically has a file extension of .mdf. SQL Server does not require that it have this .mdf extension, but it is recommended for consistency. The primary data file is the first file created for a database. Each database must have one and only one primary file. This file stores data for any database objects mapped to it, and it contains references to any other database files that are created.

In many cases, the primary data file is the only data file. There is no requirement to have more than one data file, and oftentimes, a database contains only one primary data file (for example, C:\mssql\mydb.mdf) and only one log file (for example, C:\mssql\mydb_log.ldf).

Secondary Files

You can create zero or more secondary data files in a database. These files, by default, are identified with an .ndf extension, but the extension can be different. Secondary data files provide an opportunity to spread the data that SQL Server stores over more than one physical file. This can be particularly useful for larger databases and can help with performance and management of database files. Take, for example, a situation in which a database server has four physical drives that are available for the data file(s). Each drive is 1GB in size, but the database you are creating is 2GB. In this example, the database will not fit on one drive. A solution to this is to create a primary data file on one of the drives and a secondary data file on each of the three remaining drives. SQL Server automatically spreads the 2GB database across the four data files that are located on four separate drives.

Secondary files also provide some added flexibility for backing up or copying databases. This is most apparent with large database. For example, let's say you have a database that is 100GB, and it contains only a primary data file. If you want to move this database to another environment, you must have a drive that is at least 100GB to store the primary data file. If you want to copy the database to a server that has 10 50GB drives, you cannot do it. You have the space across all 10 drives, but you do not have a single drive that can hold the primary data file. If, however, you create the database with several secondary files, you have the option of placing each of the secondary files on a separate drive.

TIP

You can use the new sys.master_files catalog view to list the database files for all the databases. For example, SELECT db_name(database_id),* from sys.master_files order by 1 returns all the database files, ordered by the name of the database they belong to. You can change the sort order for the SELECT and order it by physical_name to quickly locate a database file and find which database is using that file.

Using Filegroups

Filegroups allow you to align certain database objects with specific data files. Tables, indexes, and large object (LOB) data can be assigned to a filegroup. A filegroup can be associated with one or more data files. The alignment of data and indexes to filegroups can provide performance benefits and improve manageability. Each database has at least one filegroup, called the primary filegroup. This filegroup, by default, contains the primary data file and any other secondary data files that have not been specifically aligned with another filegroup. Any database object that you create without specifying a filegroup is created in the primary filegroup.

Additional filegroups can be created and aligned with secondary data files. There is no requirement to have more than one filegroup, but additional filegroups give you added flexibility. Filegroups can be aligned with data files that are contained on separate disk drives to improve data access. This improvement is facilitated by concurrent disk access across the disk drives that are assigned to the filegroups.

TIP

If too many outstanding I/Os are causing bottlenecks in the disk I/O subsystem, you might want to consider spreading the files across more disk drives. Performance Monitor can identify I/O bottlenecks by monitoring the `PhysicalDisk` object and `Disk Queue Length` counter. You should consider spreading the files across multiple disk drives if the `Disk Queue Length` counter is greater than two times the number of spindles on the disk. For more information on monitoring SQL Server performance, see Chapter 34, "Monitoring SQL Server Performance."

For example, you could create a filegroup called `UserData_FG`, consisting of three files spread over three physical drives. You could create another filegroup named `Index_FG`, with a single file, on a fourth drive. Then, when you create the tables, you can create them on the `UserData_FG` filegroup. You can create indexes on the `Index_FG` filegroup. This reduces contention between tables because the data is spread over three disks and can be accessed independently of the indexes. If more storage is required in the future, you can easily add additional files to the index or data filegroup, as appropriate.

You can create filegroups at the time the database is created, or you can add them after the database is created. When you create filegroups along with the database, the definition for the filegroup is contained in the `CREATE DATABASE` statement. The following is an example of a `CREATE DATABASE` statement with filegroup definitions:

```
CREATE DATABASE [mydb] ON  PRIMARY
( NAME = N'mydb',
    FILENAME = N'C:\mssql2005\data\mydb.mdf' ,
    SIZE = 2048KB , FILEGROWTH = 1024KB ),
 FILEGROUP [Index_FG]
( NAME = N'mydb_index1',
    FILENAME = N'I:\mssql2005\data\mydb_index1.ndf' ,
    SIZE = 2048KB , FILEGROWTH = 1024KB ),
```

18

```
  FILEGROUP [UserData_FG]
( NAME = N'mydb_userdata1',
     FILENAME = N'D:\mssql2005\data\mydb_userdata1.ndf' ,
     SIZE = 2048KB , FILEGROWTH = 1024KB ),
( NAME = N'mydb_userdata2',
     FILENAME = N'E:\mssql2005\data\mydb_userdata2.ndf' ,
     SIZE = 2048KB , FILEGROWTH = 1024KB ),
( NAME = N'mydb_userdata3',
     FILENAME = N'F:\mssql2005\data\mydb_userdata3.ndf' ,
     SIZE = 2048KB , FILEGROWTH = 1024KB )
  LOG ON
( NAME = N'mydb_log',
     FILENAME = N'L:\mssql2005\log\mydb_log.ldf' ,
     SIZE = 1024KB , FILEGROWTH = 10%)
```

This example creates a database named mydb that has three filegroups. The first filegroup is the PRIMARY filegroup, which contains the .mdf file. Index_FG contains one file: I:\mssql2005\data\mydb_index1.ndf. The third filegroup, UserData_FG, contains three data files that are located on the D:, E:, and F: drives. This example demonstrates the relationship between databases, filegroups, and the underlying operating system files. (The T-SQL for creating a database is discussed in detail later in this chapter.)

After you create a database with multiple filegroups, you can then create a database object on a specific filegroup. In the previous example, you could use the filegroup named UserData_FG to hold user-defined tables, and you could use the filegroup named Index_FG for the database indexes. You assign database objects at the time that you create the object. The following example demonstrates the creation of a user-defined table on the UserData_FG filegroup and the creation of an index for that table on the Index_FG filegroup:

```
CREATE TABLE dbo.Table1
    (TableId int NULL,
    TableDesc varchar(50) NULL)
  ON [UserData_FG]

CREATE CLUSTERED INDEX [CI_Table1_TableID] ON [dbo].[Table1]
( [TableId] ASC)
  ON [Index_FG]
```

Any objects that are not explicitly created on a filegroup are created on the default filegroup. The PRIMARY filegroup is the default filegroup when a database is created. You can change the default filegroup, if necessary. If you want to change the default group to another group, you can use the ALTER DATABASE command. For example, the following command changes the default filegroup for the mydb database:

```
ALTER DATABASE [mydb] MODIFY FILEGROUP [UserData_FG] DEFAULT
```

You can also change the default filegroup by right-clicking the database in the Object Explorer, choosing Properties, and selecting the Filegroups page. Then you select the check box labeled Default to make the given filegroup the default. Figure 18.1 shows the filegroups for the AdventureWorks database, with the primary filegroup selected as the default.

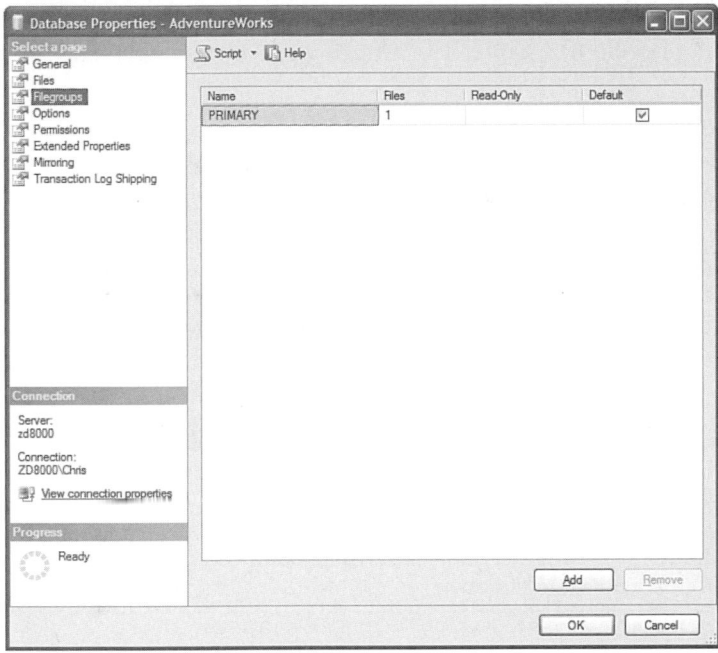

FIGURE 18.1   Setting the default filegroup in SQL Server Management Studio (SSMS).

When creating filegroups, you should keep in mind the following restrictions:

▶ You can't move a data file to another filegroup after it has been added to the database.

▶ Filegroups apply only to data files and not to log files.

▶ A data file can be part of only one filegroup and cannot be spread across multiple filegroups.

▶ You can have a maximum of 32,767 filegroups for each database.

NOTE

Using SANs and RAID arrays for the database disk subsystem diminishes the need for filegroups. SAN and RAID systems typically have many disks that are mapped to a single data drive. This inherently allows for concurrent disk access without requiring the creation of a filegroup with multiple data files.

18

Using Partitions

Partitioning has been enhanced in SQL Server 2005 so that a single table or index can be aligned to more than one filegroup. In the past, you could use filegroups to isolate a table or an index to a single filegroup, but the table or index could not be spread across multiple filegroups or data files. The ability to spread a table or an index across multiple filegroups is particularly useful for large tables. You can partition a table across multiple filegroups and have data files live on separate disk drives to improve performance. Table partitioning is discussed in more detail in Chapter 19, "Creating and Managing Tables."

Transaction Log Files

A *transaction* is a mechanism for grouping a series of database changes into one logical operation. SQL Server keeps track of each transaction in a file called the *transaction log*. This log file usually has the extension .ldf, but it can have a different extension. Typically, there is only one log file. You can specify multiple log files, but these files are accessed sequentially. If multiple files are used, SQL Server fills one file before moving to the next. You realize no performance benefit by using multiple files, but you can use them to extend the size of the log.

> **NOTE**
>
> The transaction log file is not a text file that can be read by opening the file in a text editor. The file is proprietary, and you cannot easily view the transactions or changes within it. However, you can use the undocumented DBCC LOG (*database name*) command to list the log contents. The output is relatively cryptic, but it can give you some idea of the type of information that is stored in the log file.

Because the transaction log file keeps track of all changes that are applied to a database, it is very important for database recovery. The transaction log is your friend: It can prevent significant data loss and provide recovery that is not possible without it. Take, for example, a case in which a database is put in simple recovery mode. In short, this causes transaction detail to be automatically removed from the transaction log. This option is often selected because the transaction log is seen as taking too much disk space. The problem with simple mode is that it limits your ability to recover transactions. If a catastrophic failure occurs, you can restore your last database backup, but that may be it. If that backup was taken the night before, then all the database work done that day is lost.

If your database is not in simple mode (full or bulk logged), and the transaction log is intact, then you have much better recovery options. For example, if you back up your transaction log periodically (for example, every hour) and a catastrophic error occurs, your data loss is limited. You still need to restore your last database backup, but you have the option of applying all the database changes that are stored in your transaction log. With hourly backups, you should lose no more than an hour of work. This topic is covered in detail in Chapter 11, "Database Backup and Restore."

How the Transaction Log Works

SQL Server utilizes a write-ahead log. As changes are made to data through transactions, those changes are written immediately to the transaction log when the transaction is complete. The write-ahead log guarantees that all data modifications are written to the log prior to being written to disk. By writing each change to the transaction log before it is written to the database, SQL Server can increase I/O efficiency to the data files and ensure data integrity in case of system failure.

To fully understand the write-ahead log, you must first understand the role of SQL Server's cache or memory as it relates to database updates. SQL Server does not write updates directly to the data page on disk. Instead, SQL Server writes a change to a copy of the data page that has been placed in memory. Pages that are changed in memory and not yet written to disk are called *dirty pages*. The same basic approach is used for transaction log updates. The update to the log is performed in the log cache first, and it is written to disk at a later time. The time when the updates are actually written from cache to disk is called a *checkpoint*. The checkpoint occurs periodically, and SQL Server ensures that dirty pages are not written to disk before the corresponding log entry is written to disk.

The write-ahead log was designed for performance reasons and it is critical for the recovery process after a system failure. If the system fails, an automatic recovery process is initiated when SQL Server restarts. This recovery process can use the checkpoint marker in the log file as a starting point for recovery. SQL Server examines all transactions after the checkpoint. If they are committed transactions, they are rolled forward; if they are incomplete transactions, they are rolled back, or undone.

> **NOTE**
>
> Changes in SQL Server 2005 improve the availability of the database during the recovery process. In prior versions of SQL Server, the database was not available until it was completely recovered and the roll forward and roll back processes were complete. With SQL Server 2005, the database is made available right after the roll forward process. The roll back or undo process can occur while users are in the database.

18

For more detailed information on transaction management and the transaction log, see Chapter 26, "Transaction Management and the Transaction Log."

Creating Databases

Database creation is a relatively straightforward operation that you can perform by using T-SQL statements or SSMS. Because the data and log files are created at the time the database is created, the time it takes for the database to be created depends on the size and number of files you specify when you create the database. If there is not enough disk space to create any of the files specified, SQL Server returns an error, and none of the files are created.

> **NOTE**
>
> Fortunately, some enhancements in SQL Server 2005 have reduced the amount of time it takes to create a database. The reduction in creation time is attributed to a change in the way that the database files are initialized. The initialization of the file with binary zeros is now deferred until the file is accessed via SQL queries. This results in much faster database creation and expansion. For example, we created a database with a 1GB data file on a machine running SQL Server 2005. The database was created in approximately 1 second. The same database was then created in SQL Server 2000, running on the same machine. The creation of the database on SQL Server 2000 took approximately 38 seconds. This new feature will make a lot of folks who create and support large databases very happy.

Using SSMS to Create a Database

The Object Explorer in SSMS makes creating a database very simple. You right-click the Databases node and select New Database. The New Database dialog appears, as shown in Figure 18.2. The General page is selected by default. It allows you to select the essential information needed to create a database, including the database name, the database owner, and the location of the database files.

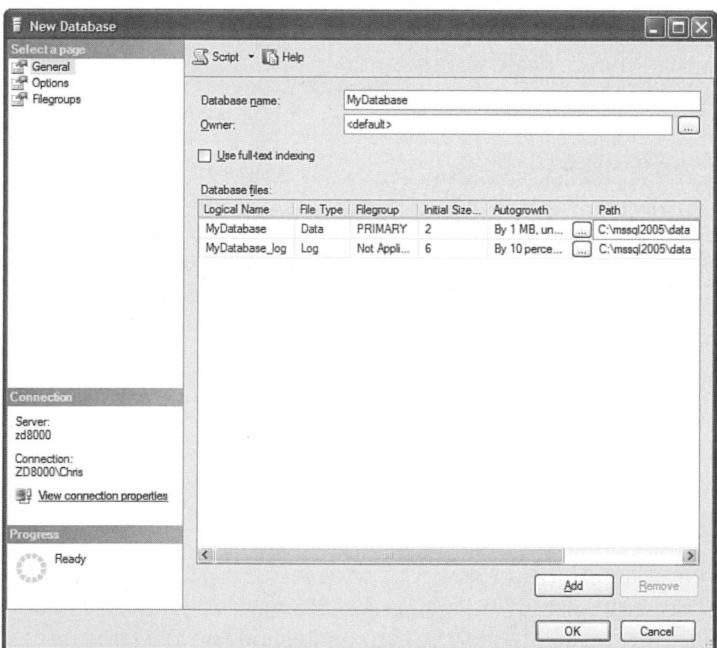

FIGURE 18.2   Creating a database by using SSMS.

Some related information is populated when you enter the database name. For example, the logical name of the database files is populated using the database name. The data file (which is identified with the file type `Data`) is named the same as the database. The log file (file type `Log`) has a database name with the suffix `_log`. The logical filename can be changed, but it must be unique within the database.

The location of the database files is an important decision. The location for each file is entered in the Path column in the Database Files grid. This column is found on the right side of the Database Files grid and includes an ellipses that can help you navigate the directory structure on your server. When you select the location of these files, you should keep in mind the following:

▶ **Disk space**—Databases, by nature, grow over time. You need to make sure the location where you place your database files has sufficient space for growth.

▶ **Performance**—The location of your database files can affect performance. Generally, the data and log files should be placed on separate disk drives (with separate controllers) in order to maximize performance.

▶ **Organization**—Choosing a common location or directory for your database files can help keep things organized. For example, you could choose to place your data files in directories named `\mssql\data\` and `\mssql\log` instead of using the long pathname that SQL Server uses by default.

There are several restrictions related to the database files specified. Each filename must be unique and cannot be used by another database. The files specified for a database must be located on a local drive of the machine SQL Server is installed on, a SAN drive, or an iSCSI-based network drive. Finally, you need to make sure the path specified exists on the drive prior to creating the database.

NOTE

The default path for the database files is populated based on database settings values that are specified in the Server Properties dialog. To open this dialog, you right-click the server in the Object Explorer and choose Properties. When the Server Properties dialog appears, you choose the Database Settings page, and you see the database default locations. If the database default locations for the log and data files are not specified, then the paths to the `master` database files are used. You can determine the paths to the `master` database files by looking at the startup parameters for the SQL Server instance. You can view these startup parameters within the SQL Server Configuration Manager. After you open this application, you right-click the SQL Server service and select Properties. On the Advanced tab of the Properties dialog that appears, you find the setting named Startup Parameters. The –d parameter identifies the location of the data file for the `master` database. The –l parameter identifies the location of the log file for the `master` database.

The remaining pages in the New Database dialog allow you to set database options, utilize filegroups, and set extended properties. The Options page contains many settings that are discussed in the "Setting Database Options" section later in this chapter. Three settings at the top of the Options page deserve special attention: Collation, Recovery Model, and Compatibility Level. Figure 18.3 shows the Options page.

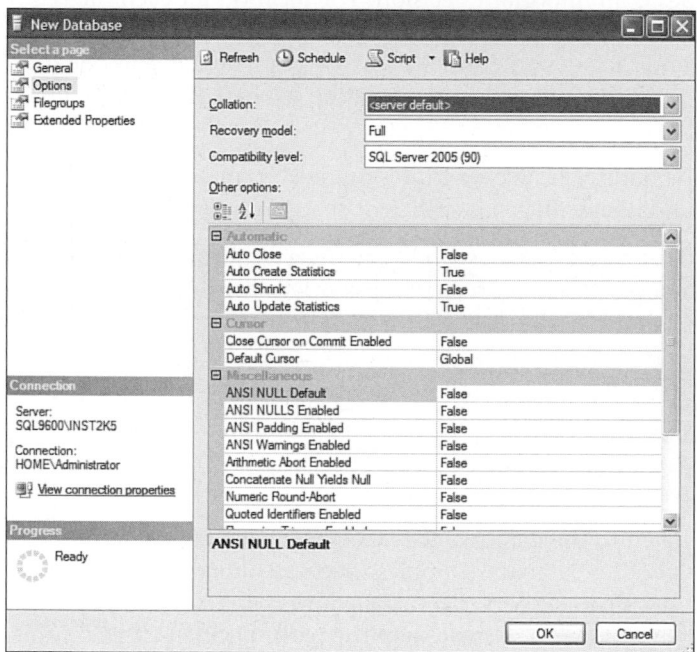

FIGURE 18.3   The Options page for creating a database.

Collation specifies how strings are sorted and compared. The selection of collation is language dependent and addresses differences in the way that characters are ordered. The default collation for a database is based on the server default, which is set during the installation of SQL Server. The server default for many U.S.-based installations is SQL_Latin1_General_CP1250_CI_AS. Different parts of the collation name mean different things. For example, CP1250 refers to Code Page 1250, CI is an acronym for Case Insensitive, and AS indicates a default sort of ascending. In most cases, you will not want to change the collation from the server default.

The Recovery Model setting is critical in determining how much data can be recovered in the event of a media failure. The default is Full, which provides the greatest level of recovery. With Full recovery, all changes to the database (inserts, updates, and deletions) are written to the transaction log, and so are any changes that may have occurred using BCP or BULK INSERT. If there is a failure on one of the database files, you can restore the database by using the last full backup. All the changes captured in the transaction log since the last full backup can be reapplied to the database as well.

The Bulk-Logged recovery setting is very similar to Full recovery but has some differences in the way that operations (BCP or BULK INSERT) are logged. With Bulk-Logged recovery, you can still restore all the transaction log backups to recover your database to a point in time.

> **NOTE**
>
> When either Full recovery or Bulk-Logged settings is selected, it is important to set up a job or maintenance plan that performs periodic backups of the transaction log. A backup of the transaction log removes data from the log and keeps the size of the transaction log manageable. If regular backups of the transaction log are not made, the transaction log will continue to grow as every change in the database is written to it.

Simple recovery mode offers the simplest backup/recovery model but the greatest possibility of losing changes to the database. This is based on the fact that changes recorded in the transaction log are automatically truncated when the database is placed in Simple recovery mode. Recovery with Simple mode is limited to using full or differential database backups that have been taken. Simple recovery mode is a good option for read-only databases and for development databases that can afford the loss of changes since the last database backup. All the recovery models are discussed in detail in Chapter 11.

The last settings on the Options page that deserves special attention is Compatibility Level. The compatibility level determines the level of backward compatibility that the database engine uses. For many newly created databases in SQL Server 2005, the default of SQL Server 2005 (90) will suffice. With this setting, all the new features available with SQL Server 2005 are utilized. There are some situations in which you might want a SQL Server 2005 database to behave as though it were a SQL Server 2000 database or a SQL Server 7.0 database. You can accomplish this by setting Compatibility Level to SQL Server 2000 (80) or SQL Server 7.0 (70). Generally, you select older compatibility levels to allow code that was developed for prior versions of SQL Server to work as it did with prior versions.

Using T-SQL to Create Databases

Instead of using SSMS, you can use T-SQL to create a database. The T-SQL command to do this is CREATE DATABASE. The CREATE DATABASE syntax is extensive and is best illustrated with an example. Listing 18.1 shows an example script to create a database called mydb. This script was generated using the Script option that is available on the New Database screen.

LISTING 18.1   Using T-SQL to Create a Database

```
CREATE DATABASE [mydb] ON  PRIMARY
( NAME = N'mydb', FILENAME = N'C:\mssql2005\data\mydb.mdf' ,
    SIZE = 2048KB , FILEGROWTH = 1024KB )
 LOG ON
( NAME = N'mydb_log', FILENAME = N'C:\mssql2005\log\mydb_log.ldf',
    SIZE = 1024KB , FILEGROWTH = 10%)
GO
```

The database created in Listing 18.1 is relatively simple. It is named mydb and contains one data file and one log file. The data file is created on the PRIMARY filegroup; it is named mydb.mdf and is created in the C:\mssql2005\data folder. The mydb.mdf file is initially created with a size of 2048KB, or 2MB. If the database utilizes the entire 2MB, the file can be expanded by the amount specified in the FILEGROWTH parameter. In this case, the file can grow in 1MB increments. (Managing file growth is discussed in the section "Managing Databases," later in this chapter.)

The log file is defined using the LOG ON clause in the CREATE DATABASE command. The mydb database created in Listing 18.1 has a log file named mydb_log.ldf that is also created in the C:\mssql2005\data folder. The initial size of the file is 1MB, and it can expand by 10% of the current log file size. You need to use caution with large databases when using a percentage to define FILEGROWTH. For example, you may have problems if you have a large database that has a 30GB log file and a FILEGROWTH of 10%. If the database file is set to autogrow, and the 30GB log file is full, it will expand the log file by 3GB. An expansion of this size could be detrimental to performance and the disk drive that the log file is on might not have that much space left.

You can specify many of the other options that define a database after the database is created. You can do this by using the ALTER DATABASE statement. The T-SQL scripting option that is available on the CREATE DATABASE screen generates the basic CREATE DATABASE syntax shown in Listing 18.1, and then it generates a series of ALTER DATABASE commands that further define the database. These options are discussed in the next section.

Setting Database Options

You can use an abundance of database options to refine the behavior of a database. These options fall into the following categories, which are part of the option specification:

    db_state_option

    db_user_access_option

    db_update_option

    external_access_option

    cursor_option

    auto_option

    sql_option

    recovery_option

    database_mirroring_option

    supplemental_logging_option

    service_broker_option

    date_correlation_optimization_option

    parameterization_option

For each category, you can set one or more options. You can find a full list of options for each category in SQL Server Books Online. Some of the options are discussed in further detail in the chapters of this book that relate to the database options. For example, the recovery options are discussed in detail in Chapter 11, the Service Broker options are discussed in Chapter 48, "SQL Server Service Broker" (on the CD-ROM), and database mirroring options are discussed in Chapter 16, "Database Mirroring."

The following sections focus on the database options that are displayed on the Options page in the SSMS.

The Database Options

You can access many of the most common database options via the Options page of the Database Properties dialog. To get to this dialog, you right-click a database in the SSMS Object Explorer and select Properties. When the dialog appears, you select the Options page from the list on the left side of the Database Properties dialog. Figure 18.4 shows the Options page for the AdventureWorks database. The options listed under Other Options can be listed alphabetically or by category. The default display mode is by category.

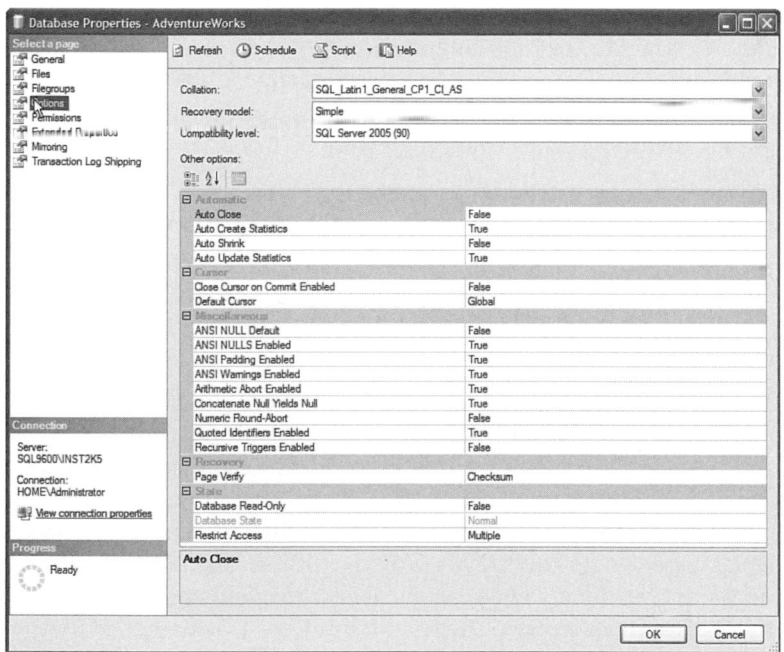

FIGURE 18.4   Database options in SSMS.

The default settings for these options suffice for most installations. However, some options deserve special attention. The options listed under the Automatic category are some of these options. The Auto Close could cause problems in prior versions of SQL

Server. This option is intended for desktop implementations in which the database does not need to be online all the time. When users are not accessing the database and this option is selected, the database files are closed. When the first user accesses the database, the database is brought back online. The problem in prior versions was that the synchronous operation of opening and closing the database files caused performance problems. This has been addressed in SQL Server 2005 because the operations are now performed asynchronously. The Auto Close option defaults to `true` only for SQL Server 2005 Express and should generally be left set to `false` for all other versions.

The Auto Create Statistics and Auto Update Statistics options also deserve special attention in situations in which the creation or updating of statistics is affecting performance. Generally, the creation and updating of statistics improves performance. These statistics enable the Query Optimizer to make the best decisions when determining the access path to the data. In some rare circumstances, there may be performance problems at the time that statistics are created or updated automatically. When these situations arise, you can turn off the Auto Statistics options and schedule the statistics operations to occur during off-hours.

Enabling the Auto Shrink option is a good idea for keeping a non-production database as small as possible. This option automatically performs a database shrink operation against the database files when more than 25% of a file contains unused space. The default setting is `false` because this option can cause performance problems (related to the timing of the shrink operation) in a production database. Because the operation is automatic, it can run at any time, including times when there may be heavy production load.

The Page Verify option in the Recovery category has been enhanced in SQL Server 2005. The enhancement comes in the form of a new `CHECKSUM` option. This new `CHECKSUM` option is the default; it causes a checksum calculation to occur across the entire database page. Prior to the availability of the `CHECKSUM` option, page verification was done with `TORN_PAGE_DETECTION`. Both of these options help detect damaged database pages, but `CHECKSUM` is the method that Microsoft recommends.

The Database Read-Only and Restrict Access options are two other options in the State category that are commonly used. You can set Database Read-Only to `true` to prevent updates from occurring in the database. Databases that are used for reference and are not updated are perfect candidates for this option. The Restrict Access options are handy when you're executing system maintenance or mass updates in which you want to restrict users from accessing the database. Single User allows only one user to access the database. The Restricted option allows only members of `db_owner`, `dbcreator`, and `sysadmin` to access the database. With the Restricted option, there is no limit on the number of users in these groups that can access the database.

You can easily set up the options reviewed in this section as well as the other options mentioned by using the Database Properties dialog. The current value for each option is shown in the right-hand column. To set an option to another value, you click the current value, and a drop-down arrow appears. When you click the drop-down arrow, you can select from the list of valid values for the option. When you have made all your option changes, you can click OK for the changes to take effect immediately, or you can click the Script button to generate the T-SQL code to change the options. The T-SQL code used to change the options is discussed in the next section.

Using T-SQL to Set Database Options

If you prefer to use T-SQL, or if the option you need to set doesn't appear in the Database Properties dialog, you can use the ALTER DATABASE command to set options. For example, the following command sets AUTO_UPDATE STATISTICS to OFF in the AdventureWorks database:

```
ALTER DATABASE [AdventureWorks] SET AUTO_UPDATE_STATISTICS OFF WITH NO_WAIT
```

You can also change some of the options by using the system stored procedure sp_dboption. This feature is scheduled to be removed in a future release of SQL Server but is still available in this release. You might still be using this procedure based on prior releases, and old habits are hard to break. The following is an example of one of the sp_dboption commands that many people have been using for years:

```
EXEC sp_dboption 'AdventureWorks', 'single user', 'TRUE'
```

This sets the AdvenureWorks database to single-user mode. Setting a database to single-user mode is useful when you're performing certain database operations. For example, you might use sp_dboption to set a database to single-user mode prior to renaming the database with the sp_renamedb system procedure. It is important to break old habits and move on to using the ALTER DATABASE command. The single-user option and the database name change have both been integrated into the ALTER DATABASE syntax. The following example shows how to set the single-user mode option and change the database name by using ALTER DATABASE:

```
ALTER DATABASE [AdventureWorks] SET  SINGLE_USER WITH NO_WAIT
GO
ALTER DATABASE [AdventureWorks] MODIFY NAME = [AdventureWorks_New]
GO
```

As you can see, using ALTER DATABASE is fairly straightforward and offers a consistent approach for modifying a database and its options.

18

TIP

Databases can be brought offline in SQL Server 2005 using SSMS or the T-SQL ALTER DATABASE command. For example, you use the following T-SQL command to take the AdventureWorks database offline:

```
ALTER DATABASE [AdventureWorks] SET OFFLINE WITH NO_WAIT
```

You can also specify an option with the ALTER DATABASE command that sets the database into an emergency state. This state marks the database as READ_ONLY, logging is disabled and access to the database is limited to members of the sysadmin fixed server role. This option quickly prevents normal users from getting at the database but leaves the database available for inquiry for administrators. An example of setting a database to the emergency state follows: ALTER DATABASE [AdventureWorks] SET emergency WITH NO_WAIT.

Retrieving Option Information

You can retrieve database settings by using several different methods. You can use the Database Properties dialog in SSMS (as described in the previous section) to display commonly accessed options. You can also use the DATABASEPROPERTYEX function or the sp_dboption system stored procedure to display individual database options. As mentioned previously, sp_dboption is slated for removal in a future release, so the DATABASEPROPERTYEX function is preferred. This function accepts input values for the database name and the option for which you want to retrieve the value. The following is an example of a SELECT statement you can use to retrieve the Auto Shrink option for the AdventureWorks database:

```
SELECT DATABASEPROPERTYEX ('AdventureWorks', 'IsAutoShrink')
```

This function returns a value of 1 or 0 for Boolean values—with 1 being "on" or "true"—and returns the actual value for non-Booleans. Table 18.1 lists the valid properties for the DATABASEPROPERTYEX function.

TABLE 18.1   DATABASEPROPERTYEX properties

Property	Explanation
Collation	This is the default collation name for the database.
ComparisonStyle	This is the Windows comparison style of the collation.
IsAnsiNullDefault	The database follows SQL-92 rules for allowing null values.
IsAnsiNullsEnabled	All comparisons to a null evaluate to unknown.
IsAnsiPaddingEnabled	Strings are padded to the same length before comparison or insertion.
IsAnsiWarningsEnabled	Error or warning messages are issued when standard error conditions occur.
IsArithmeticAbortEnabled	Queries are ended when an overflow or divide-by-zero error occurs during query execution.
IsAutoClose	The database shuts down cleanly and frees resources after the last user exits.
IsAutoCreateStatistics	Existing statistics are automatically updated when the statistics become out-of-date because the data in the tables has changed.
IsAutoShrink	Database files are candidates for automatic periodic shrinking.
IsAutoUpdateStatistics	The AUTO_UPDATE_STATISTICS database option is enabled.

TABLE 18.1   Continued

Property	Explanation
IsCloseCursorsOnCommitEnabled	Cursors that are open when a transaction is committed are closed.
IsFulltextEnabled	The database is full-text enabled.
IsInStandBy	The database is online as read-only, with the restore log allowed.
IsLocalCursorsDefault	Cursor declarations default to LOCAL.
IsMergePublished	The tables in a database can be published for merge replication, if replication is installed.
IsNullConcat	The null concatenation operand yields NULL.
IsNumericRoundAbortEnabled	Errors are generated when loss of precision occurs in expressions.
IsParameterizationForced	The PARAMETERIZATION database SET option is FORCED.
IsPublished	The tables of the database can be published for snapshot or transactional replication, if replication is installed.
IsQuotedIdentifiersEnabled	Double quotation marks can be used on identifiers.
IsRecursiveTriggersEnabled	Recursive firing of triggers is enabled.
IsSubscribed	The database is subscribed to a publication.
IsSyncWithBackup	The database is either a published database or a distribution database and can be restored without disrupting transactional replication.
IsTornPageDetectionEnabled	The SQL Server database engine detects incomplete I/O operations caused by power failures or other system outages.
LCID	This is the Windows locale ID (LCID) for the collation.
Recovery	This is the recovery model for the database.
SQLSortOrder	The SQL Server sort order ID that is supported in earlier versions of SQL Server.
Status	This is the database status.
Updateability	This indicates whether data can be modified.
UserAccess	This indicates which users can access the database.
Version	This is the internal version number of the SQL Server code with which the database was created. It is for internal use only by SQL Server tools and in upgrade processing.

18

If you would like to retrieve all the options that have been set for a database, you have a couple options. The option that has been around for a while is sp_helpdb. You can pass to this system stored procedure the database name, and it returns several pieces of information about the database, including the options set. The database options are returned in the first result set from `sp_helpdb` in a column named Status. The database options are displayed in a comma-delimited format in the Status column. All Boolean options that are set to `ON` are returned in the Status column, and all non-Boolean values are returned with the value to which they are set.

The syntax for `sp_helpdb` is as follows:

```
sp_helpdb database_name
```

A new option in SQL Server 2005 for listing all the database options utilizes the `sys.databases` catalog view. The `sys.databases` catalog view has a separate column for each of the database options and is much easier to read than the `sp_helpdb` output. The view also has the added flexibility of allowing you to choose a set of options to return. The following example shows a `SELECT` statement that uses the `sys.databases` catalog view to return a common set of options:

```
select name, is_auto_close_on, is_auto_shrink_on,
    is_auto_create_stats_on, is_auto_update_stats_on
from sys.databases
where name = 'AdventureWorks'
```

The results from this `SELECT` return Boolean values in each column, indicating whether the option is set to on or off. The number of columns available for selection is extensive and similar to those options available with the `DATABASEPROPERTYEX` function.

TIP

Selecting columns from the `sys.databases` catalog view is easier when you use the Object Explorer. You go to the `master` database and expand the `Views` node, followed by the `System Views` node. You see the `sys.databases` view listed under `System Views`. Next, you expand the columns for the `sys.databases` view to see a list of all the available columns. You can then drag the options you want to view into a database query window for use in a `SELECT` statement.

Managing Databases

After you create a database, you have the ongoing task of managing it. At the database level, this generally involves manipulating the file structure and setting options appropriate for the usage of the database.

Managing File Growth

As discussed earlier in this chapter, SQL Server manages file growth by automatically growing files by preset intervals when a need for additional space arises. However, this is a very loose definition of the word *manages*. What actually happens is that when the database runs out of space, it suspends all update activity, checks whether it is allowed additional space, and if space is available, it increases the file size by the value defined by `FILEGROWTH`. When the database fills up again, the whole process starts over.

When all the files in a filegroup are full and they are configured to autogrow, SQL Server automatically expands one file at a time in a round-robin fashion to accommodate more data. For example, if a filegroup consists of multiple files, and no free space is available in any file in the filegroup, the first file is expanded by the specified file-growth setting. When the first file is full again, and there is no more free space elsewhere in the filegroup, the second file is expanded. When the second file is full, and there is no more free space elsewhere in the filegroup, the third file is expanded, and so on.

Because `FILEGROWTH` can be defined as small as 64KB, automatically increasing the file size can be detrimental to performance if it happens too frequently. When you think of managing file growth, you can think of the database administrator proactively monitoring the size of files and increasing the size before SQL Server runs out of space when allocating new extents. That's not to say automatic file growth is a bad thing; it is, in fact, a great "safety valve" to accommodate unpredictable data growth or a lack of attention on the part of the administrator.

Expanding Databases

As previously discussed, databases can be expanded automatically, or you can intervene and expand them manually. The manual expansion can be accomplished by adding more files to the database or by increasing the size of the existing files. The database expansions can be accomplished with either SSMS or T-SQL.

To expand the size of the data files using SSMS, you right-click the database in the Object Explorer and select Properties. When the Database Properties dialog appears, you select the Files page to list all the files associated with the database. The Initial Size (MB) column displays the current disk allocation for each file. You can enter the new size directly into the column or use the up arrow to increase the size. When you have established the new size, you can simply click OK to expand the database file, or you can script the change by using the Script button at the top of the Database Properties window.

You can use the Files page of the Database Properties dialog in SSMS to add files to a database. You do this by clicking the Add button, which adds a new file entry row into the Database Files grid. You must supply a logical name for the new file, which typically contains the database name. In addition, you must supply the other data values in the row, including the file type, filegroup, initial size, autogrowth parameters, and path to the file.

You can also expand a database by using the T-SQL `ALTER DATABASE` command. Listing 18.2 shows an `ALTER DATABASE` example that increases the size of a data file in the AdventureWorks database to 200MB.

LISTING 18.2   Using T-SQL to Increase the Size of a Database File

```
ALTER DATABASE [AdventureWorks]
 MODIFY FILE ( NAME = N'AdventureWorks_Data', SIZE = 200MB )
GO
```

You can also use the ALTER DATABASE command to add a new file to a database. Listing 18.3 shows an example that adds a new data file to the AdventureWorks database.

LISTING 18.3   Using T-SQL to Add a New Database File

```
ALTER DATABASE [AdventureWorks]
 ADD FILE ( NAME = N'AdventureWorks_Data2',
 FILENAME = N'C:\Program Files\Microsoft SQL
Server\MSSQL.1\MSSQL\DATA\AdventureWorks_Data2.ndf',
  SIZE = 2048KB , FILEGROWTH = 1024KB ) TO FILEGROUP [PRIMARY]
GO
```

Shrinking Databases

Shrinking database files is a bit more involved than expanding them. Generally, you do database shrink operations manually, using DBCC commands. SQL Server does have the AUTOSHRINK database option, but it is usually reserved for development databases and should not be used in production. The reason it is not recommended for production is that the AUTOSHRINK operation can run at peak usage time and affect performance. AUTOSHRINK is executed when more than 25% of a file contains unused space. This event can occur, for example, after a large deletion.

If you want to shrink a database manually, you can do so by using DBCC SHRINKDATABASE, DBCC SHRINKDATAFILE, or SSMS. The following sections describe these three methods.

> **NOTE**
>
> Generally, you should avoid shrinking database files if you believe that the files are going to grow to the same larger size again. The continual expansion of a database can affect performance while the expansion is occurring. Also, if a database file is repeatedly shrunk and expanded, the database file itself can become fragmented within the file system, which can degrade I/O performance for the file.

Using DBCC SHRINKDATABASE to Shrink Databases

The DBCC SHRINKDATABASE statement attempts to shrink all the files in a database and leave a specified target percentage of free space. The following is an example of the DBCC SHRINKDATABASE syntax and running the command against the AdventureWorks database:

```
DBCC SHRINKDATABASE
( 'database_name' ¦ database_id ¦ 0
    [ ,target_percent ]
    [ , { NOTRUNCATE ¦ TRUNCATEONLY } ]
)
[ WITH NO_INFOMSGS ]
--Shrink Example
DBCC SHRINKDATABASE (AdventureWorks, 25)
```

The first parameter of the DBCC SHRINKDATABASE command is the *database_name* or *database_id*, and the second parameter is the desired percentage that will be left free. In the preceding example, an attempt will be made to shrink the database file and leave 25% free space in the files. This operation is done one data file at a time, and the log files are treated as one unit and shrunk together.

There are quite a few things to consider when you use the DBCC SHRINKDATABASE command. The following are some of the most important considerations:

▶ DBCC SHRINKDATABASE does not shrink a file smaller than its minimal size. The minimal size is the size of the file when it was initially created or the size of the file after it was explicitly resized. Explicit resizing can be accomplished with the DBCC SHRINKFILE command.

▶ The TRUNCATEONLY option frees any unused space at the end of a file but does not attempt any page movement within the file. The target percentage is ignored when this option is specified.

▶ The NOTRUNCATE option attempts to move pages in the files in order to push all free space to the end of the file. This option does not actually return the space to the operating system, and the physical file does not end up smaller when this option is used.

▶ If neither the NOTRUNCATE nor TRUNCATEONLY options are specified, this is equivalent to running DBCC SHRINKDATABASE WITH NOTRUNCATE followed by DBCC SHRINKDATABASE WITH TRUNCATEONLY. The first part attempts to push all the free space to the end of the file; then the free space is released to the operating system, and the file ends up smaller.

▶ The database files can never be shrunk to a size smaller than the data contained within them.

For smaller databases, the DBCC SHRINKFILE command is often considered to be a good choice because it is all inclusive and applies to all the database files. For larger databases or situations in which you need more control, you should consider using the DBCC SHRINKFILE command, which is discussed in the next section.

Using `DBCC SHRINKFILE` **to Shrink Databases**

The `DBCC SHRINKFILE` command operates on individual database files. For databases that contain many database files, you must execute multiple commands in order to shrink the entire database. This requires some extra work, but the increased control is often worth it. This, combined with the fact that you can shrink a file below its minimum specified size, makes it a very good option.

The following example shows the syntax for the `DBCC SHRINKFILE` command and a simple example for the AdventureWorks database:

```
DBCC SHRINKFILE
(
    { ' file_name ' ¦ file_id }
    { [ , EMPTYFILE]
    ¦ [ [ , target_size ] [ , { NOTRUNCATE ¦ TRUNCATEONLY } ] ]
    }
)
[ WITH NO_INFOMSGS ]
-- sample shrink command
USE [AdventureWorks]
GO
DBCC SHRINKFILE (N'AdventureWorks_Data' , 180)
GO
DBCC SHRINKFILE (N'AdventureWorks_Log' , 10)
GO
```

Note that with this option, a filename or an ID is supplied, rather than the database name. `DBCC SHRINKFILE` must be run in the database that the file belongs to. You specify `TARGET_SIZE` in megabytes; this is the desired size for the file after the shrink completes. If `TARGET_SIZE` is not specified or the target size is too small, the command tries to shrink the file as much as possible. The `EMPTYFILE` option migrates all data in the file to other files in the same filegroup. No further data can be placed on the file. The file can subsequently be dropped from the database. This can be useful when you want to migrate a data file to a new disk. The `NOTRUNCATE` and `TRUNCATEONLY` options for `DBCC SHRINKDATAFILE` work the same way as with `DBCC SHRINKDATABASE`. Refer to the previous section for details.

> **TIP**
>
> If you would like to shrink every database file by using the `DBCC SHRINKFILE` command, you can generate the commands by using a `SELECT` statement. The following `SELECT` is an example of this:
>
> ```
> SELECT 'PRINT ''LOGICAL NAME: ' + rtrim(name) +
>     ' FILENAME: ' + rtrim(filename) + '''' + char(10) +
>     'go' + char(10) +
>     ' DBCC SHRINKFILE (' + convert(varchar(8),fileid) + ',1)' +
> ```

```
      char(10) + 'go' + char(10)
      from sysfiles   order by fileid
```

The results from this SELECT produce the DBCC SHRINKFILE commands for all the files in the database that it is run against. You can then paste the results into another query window and execute them. This particular example uses a fixed target size of 1MB, but you can adjust this in the SELECT statement. You could also modify this SELECT statement so that it uses the new sys.master_files catalog view instead of using sysfiles.

Shrinking the Log File

The data file that is most likely to grow beyond a normal size and require periodic shrinking is the transaction log file. If a user process issues a large update transaction, the log file grows to the size needed to hold the records generated by the transaction. This could be significantly larger than the normal growth of the transaction log.

As with data files, shrinking of the log file in SQL Server 2000 can take place only from the end of the log file. However, you must first back up or truncate the log to remove the inactive log records and reduce the size of the logical log. You can then run the DBCC SHRINKFILE or DBCC SHRINKDATABASE command to release the unused space in the log file.

Transaction log files are divided logically into segments, called virtual log files. Transaction log files can only be shrunk to a virtual log file boundary. It is therefore not possible to shrink a log file to a size smaller than the size of a virtual log file, even if the space is not being used. The size of the virtual log files in a transaction log increase as the size of the log file increases. For example, a database defined with a log file of 1GB may have virtual log files 128MB in size. Therefore, the log can be shrunk to only about 128MB.

Because of the overhead incurred when the autoshrink process attempts to shrink database files, it is not recommended that you enable this option for the transaction log because it could be triggered numerous times during the course of a business day. It is better to schedule the shrinking of the log file to be performed during normal daily maintenance, when production system activity is at a minimum.

Using SSMS to Shrink Databases

In addition to shrinking a database by using T-SQL, you can do so through SSMS. In the Object Explorer, you right-click the database you want to shrink, and then you choose Tasks, followed by Shrink. You can then select either Database or Files. Selecting the Database option displays the Shrink Database dialog (see Figure 18.5). The currently allocated size and the free space for the database are shown. You have the option of selecting the Shrink Action and checking the Reorganize Files Before Releasing Unused Space check box.

18

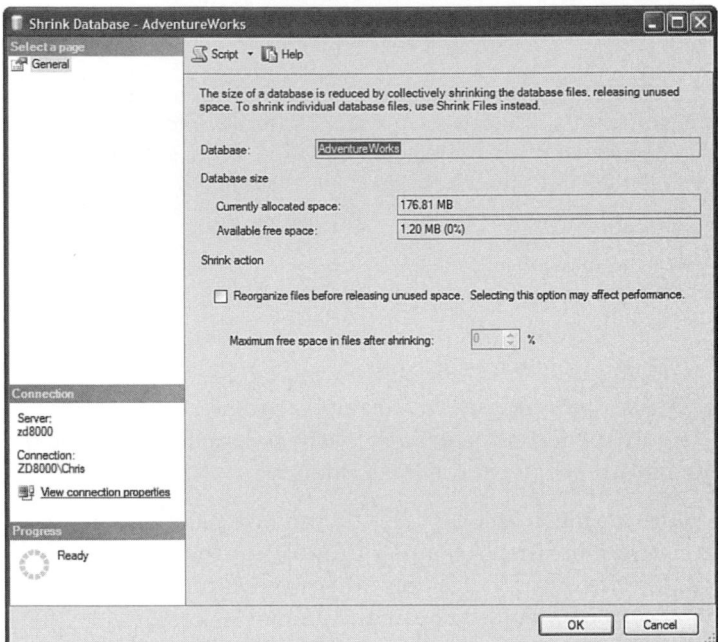

FIGURE 18.5   Shrinking an entire database using SSMS.

You can click the Script button to generate the T-SQL that will be used to perform the database shrink operation. When you do, a DBCC SHRINKDATABASE command is generated.

If you want to shrink database files, you choose the Files option instead of Database. Figure 18.6 shows the Shrink File dialog that is displayed when you select Files. You can shrink one database file at a time with this window. If you choose the shrink option Release Unused Space, SMSS uses the DBCC SHRINKFILE command with the TRUNCATEONLY option. If you choose the Reorganize Pages Before Releasing Unused Space option, SMSS uses the DBCC SHRINKFILE command without the TRUNCATEONLY or NOTRUNCATE option. As mentioned earlier, this causes page movement in order to free as much space as possible. A TRUNCATE operation then releases the free space back to the operating system.

Moving Databases

It is sometimes necessary to move a database or a database file. There are several ways to accomplish this:

▶ Make a database backup and then restore it to a new location.

▶ Alter the database, specifying a new location for the database file.

▶ Detach the database and then reattach the database, specifying an alternate location.

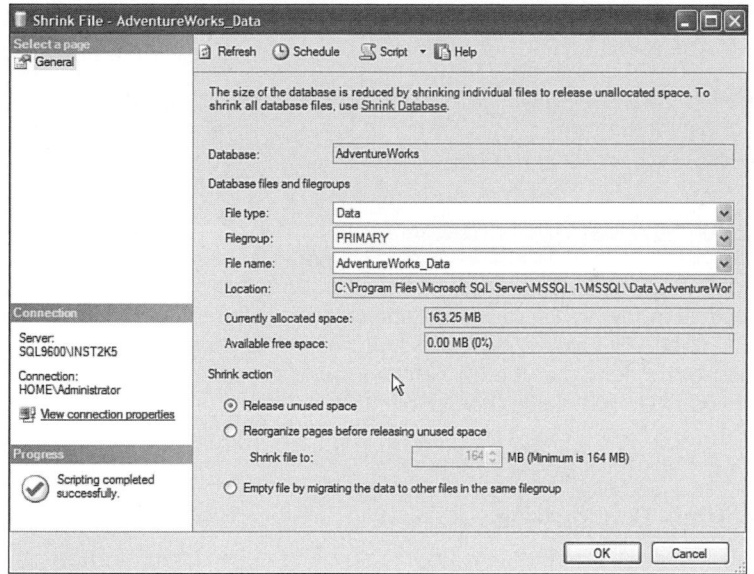

FIGURE 18.6   Shrinking database files in SSMS.

Restoring a Database Backup to a New Location

The database backup option is fairly straightforward. You make a backup of the database and then write it to a file or files. The file is restored, and any changes to the location of the database files are made at that time. Backup and restoration are discussed in detail in Chapter 11.

You can easily detach a database by right-clicking the database in the Object Explorer and choosing Tasks and then Detach. When the database is detached, you can move the file(s) to the desired location. You can then right-click on the database's node and select Attach. The Attach Databases screen that appears allows you to select the .mdf file and change the file location for any of the related database files. Attaching and detaching a database is discussed in detail in the later section, "Detaching and Attaching Databases."

Using ALTER DATABASE

The ALTER DATABASE option for moving user database files is new to SQL Server 2005. This option involves the following steps:

1. Take the database offline.

2. Manually move the file(s) to the new location.

3. Run the ALTER DATABASE command to set the FILENAME property to the new file location.

4. Bring the database online.

18

The following example uses the ALTER DATABASE command to move the log file for the AdventureWorks database to the root of the C: drive.

```
ALTER DATABASE AdventureWorks
 MODIFY FILE (NAME = AdventureWorks_Log,
  FILENAME = 'C:\AdventureWorks_log.ldf')
```

> **CAUTION**
>
> Use caution when specifying the FILENAME parameter to move a database log file. If the FILENAME setting specified in the ALTER DATABASE command is incorrect and the file does not exist, the command still completes successfully. When the database is brought back online, a message stating that the file can't be found appears, and a new log file is created for you. This invalidates the old log file.

Detaching and Attaching Databases

Detaching and attaching databases is a convenient way to move or copy database files. Detaching database files removes the database from an instance of SQL Server but leaves the database files intact. When the database has been detached, the files associated with the database (that is, .mdf, .ndf, and .ldf files) can be copied or moved to an alternate location. You can then reattach the relocated files by using the CREATE DATABASE command with the FOR ATTACH option.

> **TIP**
>
> Detaching and attaching a database is extremely fast. It is therefore a good alternative to BACKUP and RESTORE when you're copying a database to another environment. The catch with detaching a database is that all users must be disconnected from the database, and the database is unavailable during the detach and copy of the database files.

To detach a database, you right-click the database in Object Explorer and select Tasks and then Detach. Figure 18.7 shows an example of the Detach Database dialog box for detaching the AdventureWorks database. You can specify several options, including a handy option (called Drop Connections) to kill any users that may still be connected to the database when the detach operation is running. If you do not select the Drop Connections option, and users are still connected to the database, the detach operation fails.

Other options available during the detach operation are also useful. The Update Statistics option updates out-of-date statistics for all the database tables before you detach the database. The statistics update can take some time on larger databases, so this slows down the overall detach operation. The other option, Keep Full Text Catalogs, is new to SQL Server 2005. It allows you to detach any full-text catalogs that are associated with the database. These detached full-text catalogs are then reattached along with the database when the files are attached.

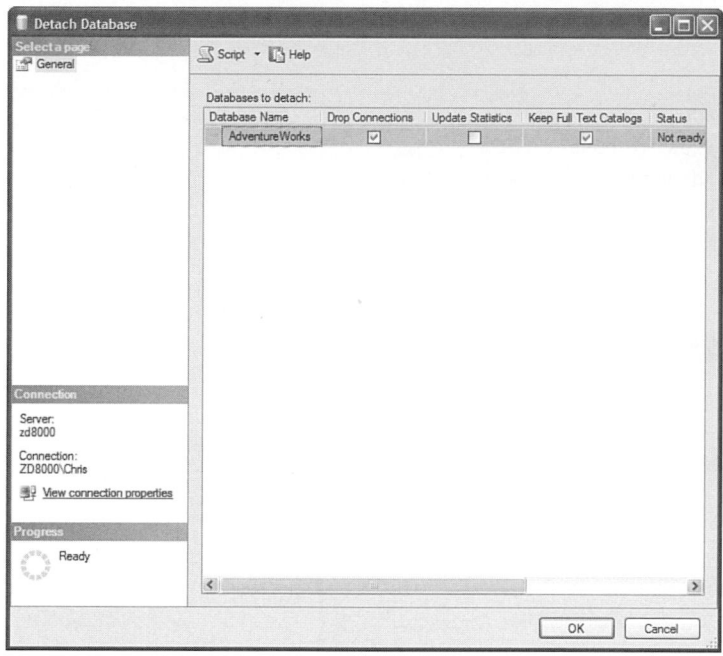

FIGURE 18.7   Detaching a database by using SSMS.

The attach operation is simple to execute through SMSS. In Object Explorer, you simply right-click the database's node and select the Attach option. The Attach Databases dialog box appears, allowing you to specify the database file(s) you want to attach. You need to click the Add button in order to select a database file for restoration. When you select the main .mdf file associated with the database, the associated file information for the other related database files is populated as well.

Figure 18.8 shows the Attach Databases dialog box for the AdventureWorks database. The top portion of the dialog box lists the main (.mdf) database file that was selected for the AdventureWorks database. The bottom portion lists the related files. You have an option to attach the database with a different name by changing the Attach As name located at the top of the screen. You can also edit the database details at the bottom of the screen and enter the location of the database files that will be attached. The Current File Path column displays the original file locations determined from the .mdf file. If the files were moved to a new location, this is the place to change the current file path to the new location.

You can also accomplish the detach and attach operations by using T-SQL. You perform the detach operation with the sp_detach_db system stored procedure. You perform the attach operation with the CREATE DATABASE command, using the FOR ATTACH option. The following is an example of T-SQL commands for detaching and attaching the Adventure Works database:

```
--Detach the database
EXEC master.dbo.sp_detach_db
```

18

```
@dbname = N'AdventureWorks', @keepfulltextindexfile=N'false'
GO
--Attach the database
CREATE DATABASE [AdventureWorks] ON
( FILENAME = 'C:\Program Files\Microsoft SQL
Server\MSSQL.1\MSSQL\Data\AdventureWorks_Data.mdf' ),
( FILENAME = 'C:\Program Files\Microsoft SQL
Server\MSSQL.1\MSSQL\Data\AdventureWorks_log.LDF' )
 FOR ATTACH
```

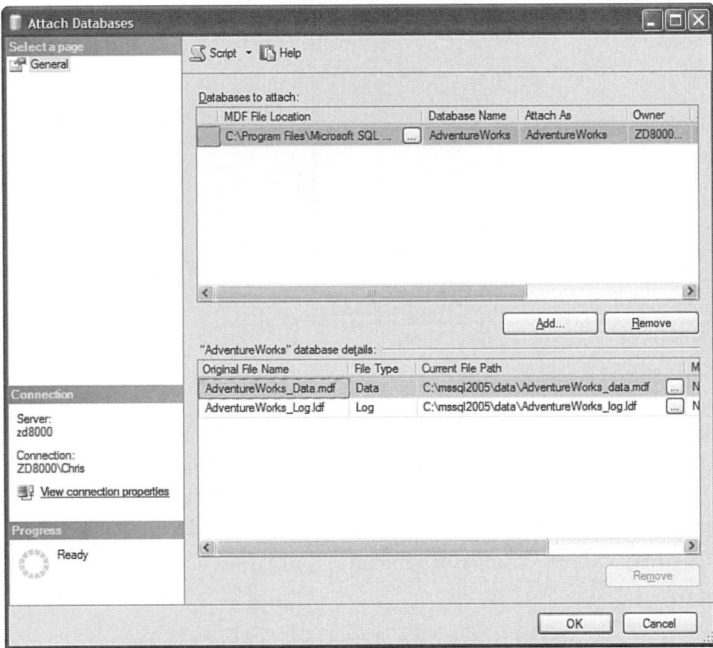

FIGURE 18.8   Attaching a database by using SSMS.

> **NOTE**
>
> You can also use the sp_attach_db procedure to attach a database, but Microsoft
> recommends that you use the CREATE DATABASE ... FOR ATTACH command instead.
> The sp_attach_db procedure has been deprecated and is slated for removal in a
> future release of SQL Server.

Another new feature with SQL Server 2005 is the ability to attach a database without all
the log files. You do this by using the ATTACH_REBUILD_LOG clause when creating the database. When you use this clause, SQL Server rebuilds the log files for you. This is useful on
large databases that may have large logs that are not needed in the environment where

the database files are attached. For example, a READ_ONLY database would not need the log files that may be associated with its production counterpart. The following example uses the ATTACH_REBUILD_LOG clause to create a copy of the AdventureWorks database:

```
CREATE DATABASE [AdventureWorksTemp] ON
( FILENAME = 'C:\Temp\AdventureWorks_Data.mdf' )
 FOR ATTACH_REBUILD_LOG
```

Summary

Creating and managing databases is by no means limited to the topics in this chapter. A database consists of many database objects and has a myriad of other features that are discussed throughout this book. The next chapter, "Creating and Managing Tables," delves into one of the most basic elements of a database: the table.

18

CHAPTER 19

Creating and Managing Tables

IN THIS CHAPTER

▶ What's New in Creating and Managing Tables

▶ Creating Tables

▶ Defining Columns

▶ Defining Table Location

▶ Defining Table Constraints

▶ Modifying Tables

▶ Dropping Tables

▶ Partitioned Tables

▶ Creating Temporary Tables

T*ables* are logical constructs used for the storage and manipulation of data in databases. Tables contain *columns*, which describe data, and *rows*, which are instances of table data. Basic relational database design determines the table and column names as well as the distribution of columns within tables.

This chapter gives you the administrative knowledge you need to create tables and manage them within your enterprise. It focuses on the basic constructs for tables and the table-level features that can make your tables robust and efficient objects to house your data.

What's New in SQL Server 2005

Most of the new table-oriented features available with SQL Server 2005 are related to the database engine. Some of these features define how the data in tables is stored in the database. The following are some of the key new features:

▶ **Partitioned tables**—Data within a table can now be divided so that portions of the table can be stored on more than one filegroup. The data is split horizontally so that groups of rows can be mapped to individual partitions.

▶ **Large rows**—Enhancements in SQL Server 2005 allow for the storage of rows that are larger than 8060 bytes. The 8060-byte limitation that existed with SQL Server 2000 has been relaxed, and SQL Server 2005 allows the storage of certain data types (such as varchar and nvarchar) on a row overflow data page.

▶ **Large-value data types**—Three new large data types

have been added that allow you to store up to 2^{31} bytes of data (or 2^{30} for Unicode). These data types have the (MAX) designator and include varchar(max), nvarchar(max), and varbinary(max).

▶ **Stored computed columns**—Computed columns that were calculated on-the-fly in prior versions can now be stored in the table structure. You do this by specifying the PERSISTED keyword as part of the computed column definition.

Many other enhancements have been made to the supporting structures for tables, such as indexes, constraints, and triggers. These enhancements are discussed in the chapters that are dedicated to those specific areas.

Creating Tables

SQL Server 2005 supports the creation of tables using T-SQL, the SSMS Object Explorer and the SSMS Database Diagram Editor. Regardless of the tool you choose, creating a table involves naming the table, defining the columns, and assigning properties to the columns. The visual tools (such as Object Explorer and database diagrams) are usually the best starting point for creating tables. These tools offer drop-down boxes that allow you to choose the data types for your columns and check boxes that allow you to define their nullability.

This chapter first looks at the visual tools and then delves into the specific parameters related to the underlying T-SQL statements that ultimately create a table.

Using Object Explorer to Create Tables

The Object Explorer in SSMS has a Tables node under each database listed. You can add tables via the Object Explorer by right-clicking this Tables node. Figure 19.1 shows the New Table option that is displayed after you right-click the Tables node in Object Explorer. The top-right side of the screen shown in Figure 19.1 shows the table creation screen that allows you to enter the column name and the data type and to set the Allow Nulls option.

The data entry area under Column Name is a free-form area where you can define a column name. You can select the data type from the Data Type drop-down, which displays the data types that are available with SQL Server. The Allow Nulls option is Boolean in nature and is either checked or not checked. For each column selected, a Column Properties section is displayed in SSMS, providing a myriad of additional properties that you can assign to each column. These properties are discussed in more detail in the "Defining Columns" section, later in this chapter.

Using Database Diagrams to Create Tables

You can use the database diagrams for a more robust visual representation of your tables. You view them from within SSMS, and they give you the distinct advantage of being able to display multiple tables and the relationships between them. The Database Diagram Editor behaves similarly to other data modeling tools that allow you to move related tables around in the diagram and group them accordingly.

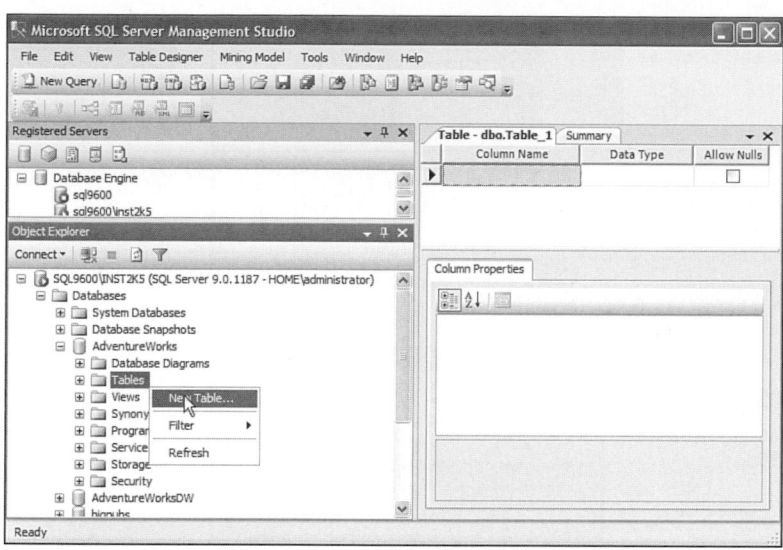

FIGURE 19.1   Using Object Explorer to create a table.

Figure 19.2 shows several screens related to database diagrams. The left side of Figure 19.2 shows the Object Explorer and the resulting New Database Diagram option that is displayed if you right-click the Database Diagrams node. The right side of the screen shows the diagram design window. In this example, the existing Department table from the AdventureWorks database was added to the diagram, and a new Printer table was added as well. The printer table was added by right-clicking in the diagram design window and selecting the New Table option.

The column names and related attributes for the new Printer table in Figure 19.2 were added using the table entry fields. The data entry screen for the table is very similar to that which is provided with the Object Explorer. You enter column names, along with their associated data types and nullability option.

The advantage of database diagrams is that you can define relationships and show them with a visual representation. This visual view provides a much easier way to view the table structures in a database. In the example shown in Figure 19.2, the line drawn between the Department and Printer tables represents a relationship between these two tables. You define such a foreign key relationship in the database diagram by right-clicking one of the related tables and selecting the Relationships option. Table relationships and constraints are discussed later in this chapter, in the section "Defining Table Constraints."

19

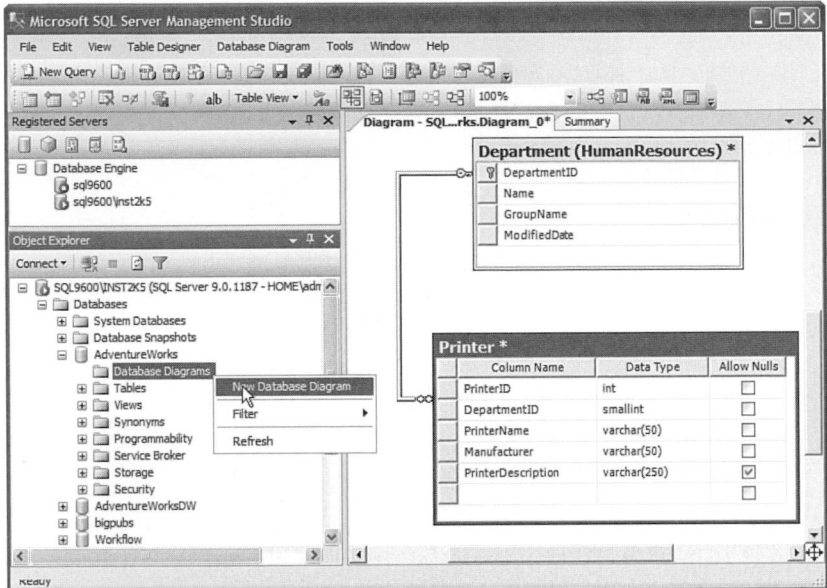

FIGURE 19.2   Using database diagrams to create a table.

Using T-SQL to Create Tables

Ultimately, all the tables created with the visual tools can also be created by using T-SQL. As with many of the SSMS tools, database objects can be resolved or scripted into TSQL statements. Let's examine the T-SQL syntax in order to better understand some of the table creation options, then we can discuss the definition of the columns in each table.

The full T-SQL CREATE TABLE syntax is extensive. It includes options to define table constraints, indexes, and index options. SQL Server Books Online shows the full syntax and describes each of these options in detail. Listing 19.1 shows the basic T-SQL syntax, the first part of the syntax listed in Books Online. This syntax is enough to enable you to create a table with its associated column definitions.

LISTING 19.1   Basic T-SQL CREATE TABLE Syntax

```
CREATE TABLE
    [ database_name . [ schema_name ] . ¦ schema_name . ] table_name
        ( { <column_definition> ¦ <computed_column_definition> }
        [ <table_constraint> ] [ ,...n ] )
    [ ON { partition_scheme_name ( partition_column_name ) ¦ filegroup
        ¦ "default" } ]
    [ { TEXTIMAGE_ON { filegroup ¦ "default" } ]
[ ; ]
```

LISTING 19.1   Continued

```
<column_definition> ::=
column_name <data_type>
    [ COLLATE collation_name ]
    [ NULL ¦ NOT NULL ]
    [
        [ CONSTRAINT constraint_name ] DEFAULT constant_expression ]
      ¦ [ IDENTITY [ ( seed ,increment ) ] [ NOT FOR REPLICATION ] ]
    ]
    [ ROWGUIDCOL ] [ <column_constraint> [ ...n ] ]

<data type> ::=
[ type_schema_name . ] type_name
    [ ( precision [ , scale ] ¦ max ¦
        [ { CONTENT ¦ DOCUMENT } ] xml_schema_collection ) ]
```

The number of options in this basic syntax can be daunting, but the reality is that you can exclude many of the options and execute a relatively simple statement. Listing 19.2 is an example of a simple statement you can use to create a table. This listing shows a CREATE TABLE statement that you can use to create the Printers table shown in Figure 19.2.

LISTING 19.2   A Basic T-SQL CREATE TABLE Example

```
CREATE TABLE Printer
    (
    PrinterID int NOT NULL,
    DepartmentID smallint NOT NULL,
    PrinterName varchar(50) NOT NULL,
    Manufacturer varchar(50) NOT NULL,
    PrinterDescription varchar(250) NULL
    )
```

The CREATE TABLE statement in Listing 19.2 specifies the table to create, followed by an ordered list of columns to add to the table. The following section describes the specifics related to defining the columns.

19

TIP

SSMS provides several methods for generating the T-SQL code to create tables. Therefore, you rarely need to type the CREATE TABLE statements from scratch. Instead, you can use the friendly graphical user interface (GUI) screens that enable you to define the table, and then you can generate the T-SQL script. For example, you can right-click a new table in the database diagram and select Generate Change Script to generate the associated T-SQL for the table.

One of the important considerations during table creation is schema assignment. *Schemas* allow you to logically group objects (including tables) and define ownership, independent of the individual users in the database. Schemas have been enhanced with SQL Server 2005 and can play a significant role in the definition of tables in a database. Take, for example, the AdventureWorks database that ships with SQL Server 2005. The tables in this database have been assigned to schemas that group the tables according to their functional areas. The schemas in the AdventureWorks database include Sales, Purchasing, Person, Production, HumanResources, and dbo. Some sample tables in the Person schema include the Contact and Address tables. The Purchasing schema includes tables that related to purchasing, including the PurchaseOrderHeader and Vendor tables.

The designation of a schema in the CREATE TABLE statement is relatively simple. Listing 19.3 includes a three-part table name for the creation of a Printer table in the HumanResources schema. The database name (AdventureWorks) is the first part of the name, followed by a schema name (HumanResources). The last part of Listing 19.3 shows a sample SELECT statement against the Printer table that is owned by the HumanResources schema. The schema name must precede the table, when referenced. The only exception to this rule is tables that belong to the default schema assigned to the user executing the query.

LISTING 19.3   Using T-SQL CREATE TABLE in a Schema

```
CREATE TABLE AdventureWorks.HumanResources.Printer
    (
    PrinterID int NOT NULL,
    DepartmentID smallint NOT NULL,
    PrinterName varchar(50) NOT NULL,
    Manufacturer varchar(50) NOT NULL,
    PrinterDescription varchar(250) NULL
    )
go
select * from HumanResources.Printer
```

The creation of schemas and the assignment of tables to schemas requires some forethought. This task, which is permission oriented, is discussed in more detail in Chapter 10, "Security and User Administration."

Defining Columns

A table is defined as a collection of columns. Each column represents an attribute of the database table and has characteristics that define its scope and the type of data it can contain. In defining a column, you must assign a name and a data type. For consistency and readability, the column names should adhere to a naming convention that you define for your environment. Naming conventions often use a set of standard suffixes that indicate the type of data the column will contain. For example, you can add the Date suffix to a column name (for example, `OrderDate`) to identify it as a column that contains date/time data, or you can add the suffix `ID` (for example, `PrinterID`) to indicate that the column contains a unique identifier.

When creating and naming columns, you need to keep the following restrictions in mind:

- ▶ You can define up to 1,024 columns for each table.

- ▶ Column names must be unique within a table.

- ▶ A row can hold a maximum of 8060 bytes. Some data types can be stored off the 8KB data page to allow a row to exceed this limit.

- ▶ A data type must be assigned to each column.

These restrictions provide a framework for a column definition. The next consideration in defining a column is the data type. The following section discusses the various data types.

Data Types

SQL Server 2005 has an extensive list of data types to choose from, including some that are new to SQL Server 2005. New data types include the `xml` data type and the large object data types `varchar(max)`, `nvarchar(max)`, and `varbinary(max)`. Each data type is geared toward a specific type of data that will be stored in the column. Table 19.1 provides a complete list of the available data types.

TABLE 19.1   Table Data Types

Data Type	Range/Description	Storage
bigint	-2^{63} (-9,223,372,036,854,775,808) to 2^{63-1} (9,223,372,036,854,775,807)	8 bytes
binary (n)	Binary data with a length of n bytes	The number of bytes defined by n, up to 8,000
bit	An integer data type that can take a value of 1, 0, or NULL.	1 byte for every eight columns that are defined as bits on the table
char	Up to 8,000 characters	1 byte per character
datetime	January 1, 1753, through December 31, 9999	8 bytes; accurate to 3.33 milliseconds
decimal	-10^{38+1} to 10^{38-1}	Based on the precision
float	-1.79E + 38 to -2.23E - 38, 0 and 2.23E -38 to 1.79E + 38	4 or 8 bytes, depending on the mantissa allocation
image	Variable-length binary data	Up to 2^{31-1} (2,147,483,647) bytes
int	-2^{31} (-2,147,483,648) to 2^{31-1} (2,147,483,647)	4 bytes
money	-922,337,203,685,477.5808 to 922,337,203,685,477.5807	8 bytes

19

TABLE 19.1   Continued

Data Type	Range/Description	Storage
nchar	Up to 4,000 Unicode characters	Two times the number of characters entered
ntext	Up to 2^{30-1} (1,073,741,823) characters	Two times the number of characters entered
numeric (p,s)	-10^{38+1} through 10^{38-1}	Based on the precision
nvarchar(n)	Up to 4,000 Unicode characters	Two times the number of characters entered
nvarchar(max)	Unicode characters up to the maximum storage capacity	Two times the number of characters entered plus 2 bytes, up to 2^{30-1}
real	-1.18E - 38, 0 and 1.18E - 38 to 3.40E + 38	4 bytes
smalldatetime	January 1, 1900, through June 6, 2079	4 bytes; accurate to 1 minute
smallint	-2^{15} (-32,768) to 2^{15-1} (32,767)	2 bytes
smallmoney	-214,748.3648 to 214,748.3647	4 bytes
sql_variant	A data type that stores values of various SQL Server 2005–supported data types, except text, ntext, image, timestamp, and sql_variant	Up to 8016 bytes
text	Up to 2^{31-1} (2,147,483,647) characters	Up to 2,147,483,647 bytes
timestamp	Automatically generated, unique binary numbers within a database; generally used for version stamping rows	8 bytes
tinyint	0 to 255	1 byte
uniqueidentifier	A 16-byte globally unique identifier (GUID)	16 bytes
varbinary(n)	Binary data with a length of n bytes	The number of bytes defined by n, up to 8000
varbinary(max)	Binary data up to the maximum storage capacity	Two times the number of characters entered plus 2 bytes, up to 2^{30-1}
varchar (n)	Up to 8,000 characters	1 byte per character
varchar (max)	Non-Unicode characters up to the maximum storage capacity	1 byte per character; maximum 2^{31-1} bytes
xml	XML instances or a variable of XML type	2GB

The data type you select is important because it provides scope for the column. For example, if you define a column as type int, you can be assured that only integer data will be stored in the column and that character data will not be allowed. The advantages of data typing are fairly obvious but sometimes overlooked.

You should avoid defining most of your columns with a single data type, such as varchar. As mentioned earlier in this chapter, the visual tools provide a great way for you to select a data type: You simply select a data type from a drop-down selection box that lists the available data types.

TIP

The Object Explorer has a categorized list of all the system data types. To get to it, you open the Programmability node under your database and then expand the Types node. You then see a node named System Data Types that lists all the data type categories, including Exact Numbers, Approximate Numbers, and Date and Time. The data types for each category are listed under each category node. If you mouse over the particular data type, you see a brief description, including the valid range of values.

Several data types in SQL Server 2005 deserve special attention. Some of these data types are new to SQL Server 2005, and with others, enhancements have been made to improve flexibility. The following sections discuss these new and enhanced data types.

New Large-Value Data Types

Three new large-value data types have been added that allow you to store a significant amount of data in a single column. They allow you to store up to 2^{31} bytes of non-Unicode data and 2^{30} bytes of Unicode data. All these new data types have the (max) designator: varchar(max), nvarchar(max), and varbinary(max). The varchar, nvarchar, and varbinary data types were available in previous versions, but the max parameter is new.

The great thing about these new data types is that they are much easier to work with than large object (LOB) data types. LOB data types (which include text, ntext, and image) require special programming when retrieving and storing data. The large-value data types do not have these restrictions. They can be used much like their smaller counterparts varchar(n), nvarchar(n), and varbinary(n) that are defined without the max keyword. So if you want to select data from a varchar(max) column, you can simply execute a SELECT statement against it, regardless of the amount of data that is stored in it. Take, for example, the following SELECT statement, executed against a varchar(max) column named DocumentSummary in the AdventureWorks.Production.Document table:

```
select Title, substring(DocumentSummary,1,30) 'DocumentSummary'
from production.document
where LEFT(DocumentSummary,30) like 'Reflector%'


/* results from previous select statement
Title                                        DocumentSummary
-------------------------------------------  ------------------------------
Front Reflector Bracket Installation         Reflectors are vital safety co
*/
```

19

This works fine with the varchar(max) column, but the LEFT function used in the WHERE clause would cause an error if the column were a text column instead.

The large-value data types can be stored in the data row or in a separate data page, based on the setting of the sp_tableoption 'large value types out of row' option. If the option is set to OFF, then up to 8,000 characters can be stored in this column in the actual data row. If the option is set to ON, data for this column is stored in a separate data page if its length would result in the data row exceeding 8060 bytes. The actual location of the column data is transparent to any user accessing the table.

Large Row Support

In SQL Server 2000, there was a strict limit of 8060 bytes that could be stored in a single row. If the total amount of data exceeded this limit, the update or insert would fail. In SQL Server 2005, enhancements have been made to dynamically manage rows that exceed the 8060-byte limit. This dynamic behavior is designed for columns that are defined as varchar, nvarchar, varbinary, or sql_variant. If the values in these columns cause the total size of the row to go beyond the 8060-byte limit, SQL Server moves one or more of the variable-length columns to pages in the ROW_OVERFLOW_DATA allocation unit. A pointer to this separate storage location, rather than the actual data, is kept in the data row. If the data row shrinks below the 8060-byte limit at a later time, SQL Server dynamically moves the data from the ROW_OVERFLOW_DATA allocation unit back into the data page.

The following example creates a table that has columns that could exceed the 8060-byte limit, with a total of 9,000 characters:

```
CREATE TABLE t1
(col1 varchar(4000), col2 varchar(5000))

insert t1
select replicate('x', 4000),replicate('x', 5000)
```

If you execute the CREATE TABLE statement, you do not get any warning message related to the 8060-byte limit. After the table is created, you can execute an insert into the table that exceeds the 8060-byte limit. The insert succeeds, and the dynamic allocation previously described is handled automatically.

The xml Data Type

SQL Server 2005 has introduced a new xml data type that can store XML documents and XML fragments in a SQL Server database. (An XML fragment is an XML instance that is missing a single top-level element.) The xml data type is discussed in more detail in Chapter 37, "Using XML in SQL Server 2005."

User-Defined Data Types

User-defined data types allow you to create custom data types that are based on the existing system data types. These data types are also called *alias data types* in SQL Server 2005. You create a user-defined data type and give it a unique name that you can then use in the definitions of tables. For example, you can create a user-defined data type named

ShortDescription, defined as varchar(20), and assign it to any column. This promotes data type consistency across your tables.

You can create user-defined data types by using T-SQL in a couple different ways. Using the sp_addtype system stored procedure and using the new CREATE TYPE command are two possibilities. The sp_addtype system stored procedure is slated to be removed in a future version of SQL Server, so using the CREATE TYPE command is preferred. The following example shows how to create the ShortDescription user-defined data type:

```
CREATE TYPE [dbo].[ShortDescription] FROM [varchar](20) NOT NULL
```

After a user-defined data type is created, you can use it in the definition of tables. The following is an example of a table created with the new ShortDescription user-defined data type:

```
CREATE TABLE [dbo].CodeTable
 (TableId int identity,
  TableDesc ShortDescription)
```

When you look at the definition of the CodeTable table in Object Explorer, you see the TableDesc column displayed with the ShortDescription data type as well as the underlying data type varchar(20).

You can use the Object Explorer to create user-defined data types as well. To do so, you right-click the User-Defined Data Types node then select Programmability then select Types. Then you choose the New User-Defined Data Type option, and you can create a new user-defined data type through a friendly GUI screen. If you create a user-defined data type in the model database, then this user-defined data type is created in any newly created database.

CLR User-Defined Types

SQL Server 2005 introduces support for user-defined types (UDTs) implemented with the Microsoft .NET Framework common language runtime (CLR). CLR UDTs enable you to extend the type system of the database and also enable you to define complex structured types.

A UDT may be simple or structured and of any degree of complexity. A UDT can encapsulate complex, user-defined behaviors. You can use CLR UDTs in all contexts where you can use a system type in SQL Server, including in columns in tables, in variables in a batches, in functions or stored procedures, as arguments of functions or stored procedures, or as return values from functions.

A UDT must first be implemented as a managed class or structure in any one of the CLR languages and compiled into a .NET Framework assembly. You can then register it with SQL Server by using the CREATE ASSEMBLY command, as in the following example:

```
CREATE ASSEMBLY latlong FROM 'c:\samplepath\latlong.dll'
```

After the assembly has been registered, you can create the CLR UDTs by using a variation of the CREATE TYPE command shown previously:

```
CREATE TYPE latitude EXTERNAL NAME latlong.latitude
CREATE TYPE longitude EXTERNAL NAME latlong.longitude
```

When a CLR UDT is created, you can use it in the definition of tables. The following is an example of a table created with the new latitude and longitude UDTs:

```
CREATE TABLE [dbo].StoreLocation
 (StoreID int NOT NULL,
  StoreLatitude latitude,
  StoreLongitude longitude)
```

For more details on programming and defining CLR UDTs, see Chapters 35, "What's New for Transact-SQL in SQL Server 2005," and 36, "SQL Server and the .NET Framework."

Column Properties

Name and data type are the most basic properties of a column, but many other properties can be defined for a column. You do not have to specify these properties in order to create the columns, but you can use them to further refine the type of data that can be stored within a column. Note that many of the available column properties relate to indexes and constraints that are beyond the scope of this section. The following sections describe some of the column properties you are most likely to encounter.

The NULL and NOT NULL Keywords

When defining tables, it is always good idea to explicitly state whether a column should or should not contain nulls. You do this by specifying the NULL or NOT NULL keywords after the column data type. If the nullability option is not specified, the SQL Server default is to allow nulls unless the ANSI_NULL_DFLT_OFF option is enabled for the session or no setting is specified for the session, and the ANSI_NULL_DEFAULT option for the database is set to OFF. Because of this uncertainty, it is best to always explicitly specify the desired nullability option for each column. Listing 19.4 creates a new table named PrinterCartridge that has the NULL or NOT NULL property specified for each column.

LISTING 19.4   Defining Column NULL Properties by Using CREATE TABLE

```
CREATE TABLE dbo.PrinterCartridge
    (
    CartridgeId int NOT NULL,
    PrinterID int NOT NULL,
    CartridgeName varchar(50) NOT NULL,
    CartridgeColor varchar(50) NOT NULL,
    CartrideDescription varchar(255) NULL,
    InstallDate datetime NOT NULL
    )
GO
```

NOTE

It is beyond the scope of this section to debate whether columns should ever allow nulls. In some organizations, nulls are heavily used, and in others they are not allowed. There is no right answer, but it is important for a development team to be aware of the existence of nulls so that it can create appropriate code to handle them.

Identity Columns

A property that is commonly specified when creating tables is the IDENTITY property. This property automatically generates a unique sequential value when it is assigned to a column. It can be assigned only to columns that are of the following types:

▶ decimal

▶ int

▶ numeric

▶ smallint

▶ bigint

▶ tinyint

Only one identity column can exist for each table, and that column cannot allow nulls.

When implementing the IDENTITY property, you supply a seed and an increment. The *seed* is the starting value for the numeric count, and the *increment* is the amount by which it grows. A seed of 10 and an increment of 10 would produce values of 10, 20, 30, 40, and so on. If not specified, the default seed value is 1, and the increment is 1. Listing 19.5 adds an IDENTITY value to the PrinterCartridge table used in the previous example.

LISTING 19.5   Defining an Identity Column by Using CREATE TABLE

```
IF  EXISTS (SELECT * FROM dbo.sysobjects
WHERE id = OBJECT_ID(N'dbo.PrinterCartridge')
AND OBJECTPROPERTY(id, N'IsUserTable') = 1)
DROP TABLE dbo.PrinterCartridge

CREATE TABLE dbo.PrinterCartridge
    (
    CartridgeId int IDENTITY (1000, 1) NOT NULL,
    PrinterID int NOT NULL,
    CartridgeName varchar(50) NOT NULL,
    CartridgeColor varchar(50) NOT NULL,
    CartrideDescription varchar(255) NULL,
    InstallDate datetime NOT NULL
```

19

LISTING 19.5   Continued

```
    )
GO

insert PrinterCartridge
 (PrinterID, CartridgeName, CartridgeColor, CartrideDescription, InstallDate)
values (1, 'inkjet', 'black','laser printer cartridge', '8/1/05')

select CartridgeId, PrinterID, CartridgeName
 from PrinterCartridge

/* results from previous SELECT statement
CartridgeId PrinterID    CartridgeName
----------- -----------  -----------------------------------------------------
1000        1            inkjet
*/
```

In this listing, the seed value has been set to 1000, and the increment has been set to 1. An insert into the PrinterCartridge table and a subsequent SELECT from that table follows the CREATE TABLE statement in the listing. Notice that the results of the SELECT show a value of 1000 for the identity column CartridgeID. This is the seed or starting point that is defined.

ROWGUIDCOL Columns

An alternative to an identity column is a column that is defined with the ROWGUIDCOL property. Like the IDENTITY property, the ROWGUIDCOL property is auto-generating and unique. The difference is that the ROWGUIDCOL option generates column values that will be unique on any networked database anywhere in the world. The identity column generates values that are unique only within the table that contains the column.

You can have only one ROWGUIDCOL column per table. You must create this ROWGUIDCOL column with the uniqueidentifier data type, and you must assign a default of NEWID()to the column in order to generate the unique value. Keep in mind that users can manually insert values directly into columns defined as ROWGUIDCOL. These manual inserts could cause duplicates in the column so a UNIQUE constraint should be added to the column as well to ensure uniqueness.

Listing 19.6 shows the creation of a table with a ROWGUIDCOL column. Several rows are inserted into the newly created table, and those rows are selected at the end of the listing.

LISTING 19.6   Defining a ROWGUIDCOL Column

```
CREATE TABLE SomeUniqueTable
   (UniqueID   UNIQUEIDENTIFIER      DEFAULT NEWID(),
   EffectiveDate datetime )
GO
```

LISTING 19.6   Continued

```
INSERT INTO SomeUniqueTable (EffectiveDate) VALUES ('7/1/05')
INSERT INTO SomeUniqueTable (EffectiveDate) VALUES ('8/1/05')
GO
select * from SomeUniqueTable
/* Results from previous select statement
UniqueID                               EffectiveDate
------------------------------------   -----------------------
614181BC-D7B9-4108-B2BD-C2F39E999424 2005-07-01 00:00:00.000
62368A2D-3557-4727-9DD3-FBCA38705B1B 2005-08-01 00:00:00.000
*/
```

You can see that the ROWGUIDCOL values are fairly large. They are 16-byte binary values that are significantly larger than most of the data types that are used for identity columns. For example, an identity column that is defined as data type int occupies only 4 bytes. You need to consider the storage requirements for ROWGUIDCOL when you select this data type.

Computed Columns

A *computed column* is a column whose value is calculated based on other columns. Generally speaking, the column is a virtual column because it is calculated on-the-fly, and no value is stored in the database table. With SQL Server 2005, you have an option of actually storing the calculated value in the database. You do so by marking the column as persisted. If the computed column is persisted, you can create an index on this column as well.

Listing 19.7 includes several statements that relate to the creation of a computed column. It starts with an ALTER TABLE statement that adds a new computed column named SetRate to the Sales.CurrencyRate table in the AdventureWorks database. The new rate column is based on an average of two other rate columns in the table. A SELECT statement is executed after that; it returns several columns, including the new SetRate computed column. The results are shown after the SELECT. Finally, an ALTER TABLE statement is used to change the newly added column so that its values are stored in the database. This is accomplished with the ADD PERSISTED option.

LISTING 19.7   Defining a Computed Column

```
--Add a computed column to the Sales.CurrencyRate Table named SetRate
ALTER TABLE Sales.CurrencyRate
 ADD SetRate AS ( (AverageRate + EndOfDayRate) / 2)
go
--Select several columns including the new computed column
select top 5 AverageRate, EndOfDayRate , SetRate
 from sales.currencyrate

/*Results from previous SELECT statement
```

LISTING 19.7   Continued

AverageRate	EndOfDayRate	SetRate
1.00	1.0002	1.0001
1.5491	1.55	1.5495
1.9379	1.9419	1.9399
1.4641	1.4683	1.4662
8.2781	8.2784	8.2782

```
*/

--Alter the computed SetRate column to be PERSISTED
ALTER TABLE Sales.CurrencyRate
 alter column SetRate ADD PERSISTED
```

> **NOTE**
>
> You can use the sp_spaceused stored procedure to check the space allocated to the
> Sales.CurrencyRate table. You need to check the size before the column is
> persisted, and then you need to check the space allocated to the table after the
> column is persisted. As you would expect, the space allocated to the table is
> increased only after the column is persisted.

Defining Table Location

As databases scale in size, the physical location of database objects, particularly tables and indexes, becomes crucial. Consider two tables, Authors and Titles, that are always queried together. If they are located on the same physical disk, contention for hardware resources may slow performance. SQL Server addresses this issue by enabling you to specify where a table (or an index) is stored.

The mechanism for specifying the physical table location is the filegroup. Filegroups are aligned to physical data files. By default, each database has a primary filegroup and a data file that matches the name of the database. You can create additional filegroups and align them to other data files. When these filegroups are created, SQL Server enables you to create your database tables on a specific filegroup.

> **NOTE**
>
> Using partitioned tables is a way to specify table location. This new SQL Server 2005
> feature allows you to divide a table into partitions and align those partitions with file-
> groups. This concept is discussed in detail in the "Partitioned Tables" section, later in
> this chapter.

The placement of tables on separate filegroups has some distinct advantages, including performance benefits. You can achieve performance improvements by storing filegroups on different disks. You can also achieve some manageability improvements by using filegroups because you can back up and manipulate filegroups separately. This is particularly important for large tables.

You specify the location of a table by using the ON clause during table creation. Listing 19.8 shows an example of creating two filegroups in the BigPubs2005 database, followed by the creation of two new tables on those filegroups. Note that the filegroups must exist before the tables are created. For more information on filegroups, see Chapter 18, "Creating and Managing Databases."

LISTING 19.8   An Example of Creating Tables on Specific Filegroups

```
--Add the filegroups
ALTER DATABASE BigPubs2005 ADD FILEGROUP FG1
ALTER DATABASE BigPubs2005 ADD FILEGROUP FG2
GO
--Add files to the filegroups
ALTER DATABASE BigPubs2005 ADD FILE
(   NAME = FG1_File,
    FILENAME = 'c:\BigPubs2005FG1.ndf',
    SIZE = 2MB) TO FILEGROUP FG1
go

ALTER DATABASE BigPubs2005 ADD FILE
(   NAME = FG2_File,
    FILENAME = 'c:\BigPubs2005FG2.ndf',
    SIZE = 2MB) TO FILEGROUP FG2
go

CREATE TABLE [dbo].[authors_NEW](
    [au_id] [dbo].[id] NOT NULL,
    [au_lname] [varchar](40) ,
    [au_fname] [varchar](20) ,
    [phone] [char](12),
    [address] [varchar](40)  NULL,
    [city] [varchar](20)  NULL,
    [state] [char](2)  NULL,
    [zip] [char](5)  NULL,
    [contract] [bit] NOT NULL,
) ON FG1
go

CREATE TABLE [dbo].[titles_NEW](
    [title_id] [dbo].[tid] NOT NULL,
```

19

LISTING 19.8   Continued

```
    [title] [varchar](80)  NOT NULL,
    [type] [char](12)  NOT NULL,
    [pub_id] [char](4)  NULL,
    [price] [money] NULL,
    [advance] [money] NULL,
    [royalty] [int] NULL,
    [ytd_sales] [int] NULL,
    [notes] [varchar](400)  NULL,
    [pubdate] [datetime] NOT NULL,
) ON FG2
```

Defining Table Constraints

Constraints provide a means to enforce data integrity. In addition to NULL/NOT NULL, discussed earlier in this chapter, SQL Server provides five constraint types: PRIMARY KEY, FOREIGN KEY, UNIQUE, CHECK, and DEFAULT. These constraints help further define the type of data you can store in tables.

Constraints are covered in detail in Chapter 21, "Implementing Data Integrity." This chapter introduces the basic means for adding constraints to a table. You can add constraints at the time of table creation, or you can add them after a table has been created, by using the ALTER TABLE statement.

Listing 19.9 shows a CREATE TABLE statement that has an example of each one of the five constraint types listed. The PRIMARY KEY constraint is created at the bottom of the script and is named PK_TitleHistory. The FOREIGN KEY constraint is created on the title_id column and is named FK_titles_titleHistory. The UNIQUE constraint is part of the primary key and can be identified with the UNIQUE keyword. The CHECK constraint is created on the price column; it checks to make sure the price is greater than zero. Finally, a DEFAULT constraint is created on the modify_user column; it sets the user to the value of system if no explicit value is specified.

LISTING 19.9   Example of Creating Constraints with CREATE TABLE

```
CREATE TABLE dbo.TitleHistory(
    title_id dbo.tid
        CONSTRAINT FK_titles_titleHistory
        REFERENCES titles (title_id)NOT NULL ,
    change_date datetime NOT NULL,
    title varchar(80) NOT NULL,
    type char(12)  NOT NULL,
    price money NULL
        CONSTRAINT CK_TitleHistory_Price CHECK  (Price>0),
    modify_user nchar(10) NOT NULL
        CONSTRAINT DF_TitleHistory_modify_user  DEFAULT (N''system''),
```

LISTING 19.9   Continued

```
 CONSTRAINT PK_TitleHistory UNIQUE CLUSTERED
( title_id ASC,
  change_date ASC ) )
```

You can create the same constraints as in Listing 19.9 by using the ALTER TABLE statement. This means you can first create the table (without the constraints) and then add
the constraints afterward. Listing 19.10 shows the creation of the same titleHistory
table, with the constraints added later via the ALTER TABLE statement.

LISTING 19.10   Example of Creating Constraints with ALTER TABLE

```
IF  EXISTS (SELECT * FROM dbo.sysobjects
WHERE id = OBJECT_ID(N'[dbo].[TitleHistory]')
AND OBJECTPROPERTY(id, N'IsUserTable') = 1)
DROP TABLE [dbo].[TitleHistory]

CREATE TABLE dbo.TitleHistory(
   title_id dbo.tid NOT NULL,
   change_date datetime NOT NULL,
   title varchar(80) NOT NULL,
   type char(12) NOT NULL,
   price money NULL,
   modify_user nchar(10) NOT NULL )
GO


--PRIMARY KEY/UNIQUE CONSTRAINT
ALTER TABLE dbo.TitleHistory
   ADD  CONSTRAINT PK_TitleHistory UNIQUE CLUSTERED
   (
     title_id ASC,
     change_date ASC
   )WITH (SORT_IN_TEMPDB = OFF, ONLINE = OFF)
go
--FOREIGN KEY CONSTRAINT
ALTER TABLE dbo.TitleHistory  WITH CHECK
   ADD  CONSTRAINT FK_titles_titleHistory FOREIGN KEY(   title_id)
     REFERENCES dbo.titles (title_id)
GO
--CHECK CONSTRAINT
ALTER TABLE dbo.TitleHistory  WITH CHECK
   ADD  CONSTRAINT CK_TitleHistory_Price CHECK  ((Price>(0)))
GO
--DEFAULT CONSTRAINT
ALTER TABLE dbo.TitleHistory
```

19

LISTING 19.10   Continued

```
  ADD  CONSTRAINT DF_TitleHistory_modify_user
    DEFAULT (N''system'') FOR modify_user
```

Modifying Tables

You will often need to modify database tables after you create them. Fortunately, you can use several tools to accomplish this task. These tools are the same set of tools you can use to add, modify, and delete tables: the SSMS Object Explorer, the Table Designer, the Database Diagram Editor, and T-SQL. The following sections touch on each of these tools but focus most heavily on the use of T-SQL.

Regardless of the method you use, you must always exercise caution when modifying tables, particularly in a production environment. Table relationships and the impact to data that may already exist in a table are key considerations in modifying a table. A visual tool such as a database diagram can assist you in determining the impact to related tables and can be used to generate the T-SQL script. The following section looks at the underlying T-SQL that can be used to modify a table, and then we'll delve into the visual tools that can simplify your life and generate some of the T-SQL for you.

Using T-SQL to Modify Tables

You can modify tables in many different ways, including making changes to the columns, constraints, and indexes associated with a table. Some of the changes have a bigger impact on the database than others. Some modifications require that the modified table be dropped and re-created in order to effect the change. Fortunately, you can use the T-SQL ALTER TABLE statement to mitigate the database impact and help streamline many of the most common modifications. You can make the following types of changes by using the ALTER TABLE statement:

▶ Change a column property, such as a data type or NULL property.

▶ Add new columns or drop existing columns.

▶ Add or drop constraints.

▶ Enable or disable CHECK and FOREIGN KEY constraints.

▶ Enable or disable triggers.

▶ Reassign partitions.

▶ Alter an index associated with a constraint.

The following sections discuss a few examples of these types of changes to familiarize you with the ALTER TABLE command. The full syntax for the ALTER TABLE command is extensive, and you can find it in SQL Server Books Online.

Changing a Column Property

You can use the ALTER COLUMN clause of the ALTER TABLE command to modify column properties, including the NULL property or the data type of a column. Listing 19.11 shows an example of changing the data type of a column.

LISTING 19.11   Changing the Data Type of a Column by Using ALTER TABLE

```
alter table titles
 alter column notes varchar(400) null
```

You must be aware of several restrictions when you modify the data type of a column. The following rules apply when altering columns:

- ▶ You cannot modify a text, image, ntext, or timestamp column.

- ▶ The column cannot be the ROWGUIDCOL for the table.

- ▶ The column cannot be a computed column or be referenced by a computed column.

- ▶ The column cannot be a replicated column.

- ▶ If the column is used in an index, the column length can only be increased in size. In addition, it must be of varchar, nvarchar, or varbinary data type, and the data type cannot change.

- ▶ If statistics have been generated using CREATE STATISTICS, the statistics must first be dropped before the column can be altered.

- ▶ The column cannot have a PRIMARY KEY or FOREIGN KEY constraint or be used in a CHECK or UNIQUE constraint. The exception is that a column with a CHECK or UNIQUE constraint, if defined as variable length, can have the length altered.

- ▶ A column with a default defined for it can have only the length, nullability, or precision and scale altered.

- ▶ If a column has a schema-bound view defined on it, the same rules that apply to columns with indexes apply.

19

TIP

Changing some data types can result in changing the data. For example, changing from nchar to char could result in any extended characters being converted. Similarly, changing precision and scale could result in data truncation. Other modifications, such as changing from char to int, might fail if the data doesn't match the restrictions of the new data type. Before you change data types, you should always validate that the data conforms to the desired new data type.

Adding and Dropping Columns
You add columns to a table by using the ADD COLUMN clause. Listing 19.12 illustrates the addition of a new column named ISBN to the titles table.

LISTING 19.12   Adding a Column by Using ALTER TABLE

```
ALTER TABLE titles
 add ISBN int null
```

When you use the ALTER TABLE statement to add a column, the new column is added at the end of the table. In most cases, this is acceptable. The location of the column in the table generally has no bearing on the use of the table. There are, however, situations in which it is desired to have the new column added in the middle of the table. The ALTER TABLE statement does not work for this situation. In order to do this, you need to create a new version of the table with a different name and the columns in the desired order, copy the data from the old table, drop the old table, and rename the new table with the old table name. Alternatively, you can also accomplish this by using SSMS, as described in the following section.

There are also some things you need to consider with regard to the null option specified for a new column. In the case of a column that allows nulls, there is no real issue: SQL Server adds the column and allows a NULL value for all rows. If NOT NULL is specified, however, the column must be an identity column or have a default specified. Note that even if a default is specified, if the column allows nulls, the column does not be populated with the default. You use the WITH VALUES clause as part of the default specification to override this and populate the column with the default.

With some restrictions, columns can also be dropped from a table. Listing 19.13 shows the syntax for dropping a column. You can specify to drop multiple columns, separated by commas.

LISTING 19.13   Dropping a Column by Using ALTER TABLE

```
alter table titles
 drop column ISBN
```

The following columns cannot be dropped:

- ▶ A column in a schema-bound view
- ▶ An indexed column
- ▶ A replicated column
- ▶ A column used in a CHECK, FOREIGN KEY, UNIQUE, or PRIMARY KEY constraints
- ▶ A column that is associated with a default or bound to a default object
- ▶ A column that is bound to a rule

> **NOTE**
>
> Be careful when using ALTER TABLE to modify columns that hold existing data. When you add, drop, or modify columns, SQL Server places a schema lock on the table, preventing any other access until the operation completes. Changes to columns in tables that have many rows can take a long time to complete and generate a large amount of log activity.

As mentioned earlier, the ALTER TABLE statement is not the only T-SQL statement you can use to modify tables. You accomplish some table changes by using T-SQL that drops and re-creates the tables that are being modified. The following sections look at some examples of these types of changes.

Using Object Explorer and the Table Designer to Modify Tables

The Object Explorer in SSMS is your window into the various tables that are available for modification in a database. You expand the Tables node in the Object Explorer tree and right-click the table you would like to modify. Then you select the Modify option, and a Table Designer window appears, showing all the table columns. In addition, a new Table Designer menu option appears at the top of the SSMS window. The Table Designer menu includes many options, including Insert Columns, Delete Columns, and Remove Primary Key. The full list of available options is shown in Figure 19.3. A Table Designer window for the BigPubs2005.Authors table is shown as the active tab on the right side of Figure 19.3.

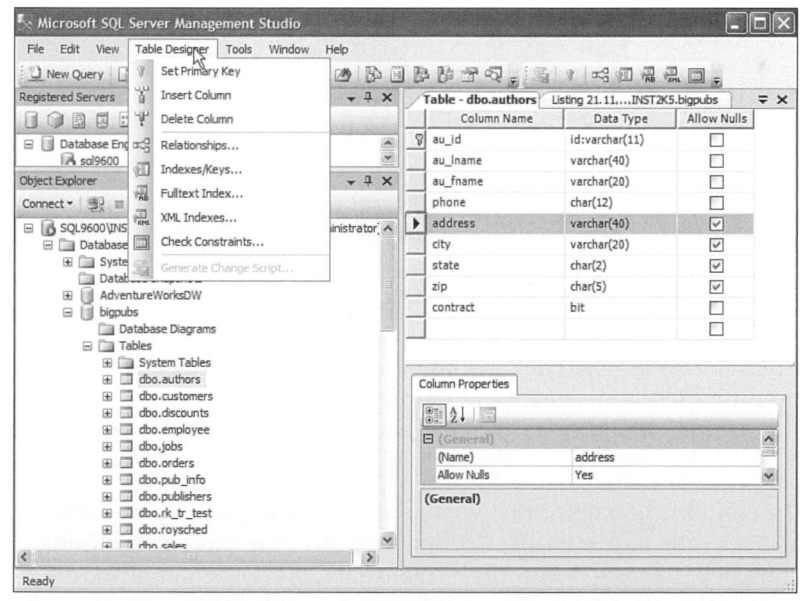

FIGURE 19.3   The Table Designer.

19

To illustrate the power of the Table Designer, let's add a new column to the authors table. You should add the column to the middle of the table, just prior to the address column. You do this by highlighting the entire address row in the Table Designer grid and then selecting Table Designer, Insert Column. A new data entry row is added to the Table Designer grid, where you can specify the name of the new column, the data type, and a null option. For this example, you should name the new column Gender, with a data type of char(1) and the setting ALLOW NULLS. Figure 19.4 shows the Table Designer grid with the newly added Gender column highlighted. In addition, the figure shows the Table Designer menu options with the newly enabled Generate Change Script option selected.

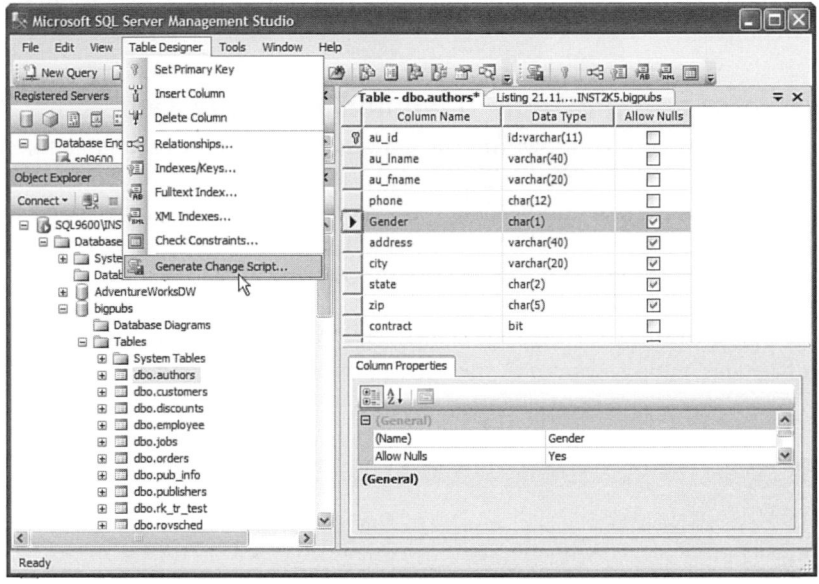

FIGURE 19.4   Inserting a column in Table Designer.

You do not need to use the Generate Change Script option for changes you make in the Table Designer. You can close the Table Designer tab where you made your changes, and the Table Designer makes the changes for you behind-the-scenes. Sometimes, though, you might want to script the changes and see exactly what is going to happen to the database. Clicking the Script button is also the preferred method for deploying changes to other environments. You can save a script in a change repository and execute it in your target environments. This ensures that you have a repeatable, well-documented means for making table changes.

Listing 19.14 shows the contents of a script that would be generated based on the new Gender column you added to the authors table. For the sake of space, some of the initial script options and the triggers associated with the authors table have been removed from the script. The important thing to note is how extensive this script is. A new temporary authors table is created, and it includes the new column; the data from the authors table is copied into the temporary table; and then the table is renamed. In addition, the script must manage the constraints, indexes, and other objects associated with the authors table. The good news is that Table Designer does most of the work for you.

LISTING 19.14   Changing Script Generated from the Table Designer

```
ALTER TABLE dbo.authors
   DROP CONSTRAINT DF__authors__phone__04C4C0F4
GO
CREATE TABLE dbo.Tmp_authors
   (
   au_id dbo.id NOT NULL,
   au_lname varchar(40) NOT NULL,
   au_fname varchar(20) NOT NULL,
   phone char(12) NOT NULL,
   Gender char(1) NULL,
   address varchar(40) NULL,
   city varchar(20) NULL,
   state char(2) NULL,
   zip char(5) NULL,
   contract bit NOT NULL
   ) ON [PRIMARY]
GO
ALTER TABLE dbo.Tmp_authors ADD CONSTRAINT
   DF__authors__phone__04C4C0F4 DEFAULT (''UNKNOWN'') FOR phone
GO
IF EXISTS(SELECT * FROM dbo.authors)
    EXEC(''INSERT INTO dbo.Tmp_authors (au_id, au_lname,
      au_fname, phone, address, city, state, zip, contract)
      SELECT au_id, au_lname, au_fname, phone, address,
         city, state, zip, contract
      FROM dbo.authors WITH (HOLDLOCK TABLOCKX)'')
GO
ALTER TABLE dbo.titleauthor
   DROP CONSTRAINT FK__titleauth__au_id__14070484
GO
DROP TABLE dbo.authors
GO
EXECUTE sp_rename N''dbo.Tmp_authors'', N''authors'', ''OBJECT''
GO
ALTER TABLE dbo.authors ADD CONSTRAINT
   UPKCL_auidind PRIMARY KEY CLUSTERED
   (
   au_id
   ) WITH( STATISTICS_NORECOMPUTE = OFF, IGNORE_DUP_KEY = OFF,
      ALLOW_ROW_LOCKS = ON, ALLOW_PAGE_LOCKS = ON) ON [PRIMARY]
GO
```

19

LISTING 19.14   Continued

```
CREATE NONCLUSTERED INDEX aunmind ON dbo.authors
   (
   au_lname,
   au_fname
   ) WITH( STATISTICS_NORECOMPUTE = OFF, IGNORE_DUP_KEY = OFF,
      ALLOW_ROW_LOCKS = ON, ALLOW_PAGE_LOCKS = OFF) ON [PRIMARY]
GO
ALTER TABLE dbo.authors WITH NOCHECK ADD CONSTRAINT
   CK__authors__au_id__03D09CBB
      CHECK (([au_id] like
      ''[0-9][0-9][0-9]-[0-9][0-9]-[0-9][0-9][0-9][0-9]''))
GO
ALTER TABLE dbo.authors WITH NOCHECK ADD CONSTRAINT
   CK__authors__zip__05B8E52D
      CHECK (([zip] like ''[0-9][0-9][0-9][0-9][0-9]''))
GO
```

You will find that you can make most of the changes you want to make by using the Table Designer. To make other changes, you can use the same approach you just used to add a column. This approach involves making the changes via the Table Designer menu options and then using the option to script the change. This is a great way to evaluate the impact of your changes and to save those changes for later execution.

Using Database Diagrams to Modify Tables

Database diagrams offer an excellent visual view of your database tables that you can also use to modify tables. You do this by adding the table you want to modify to a new or existing database diagram. Oftentimes, it is best to also add all the related tables to the diagram as well. You can easily do this by right-clicking the table and choosing the Add Related Tables option.

With a database diagram, you have the same options that you have with the Table Designer, plus you have diagramming options. Both the Table Designer and Database Diagrams menus are shown when a database diagram is in focus. These menus disappear if you change the tabbed window to a database engine query window, so remember that you must select the diagram window in order to display the menu options.

Figure 19.5 shows a database diagram for the HumanResouces.Department table, along with its related table. The Table Designer menu is selected to show that it is available when you work with a database diagram. You must have one of the tables selected in order to enable all the menu options. In Figure 19.5, the Department table has been high-lighted, and a new ModifiedUser column has been added to the end of the table. Figure 19.5 also shows that the Database Diagram menu is available for selection. This menu includes options to add tables to the diagram and manipulate the tables within the diagram.

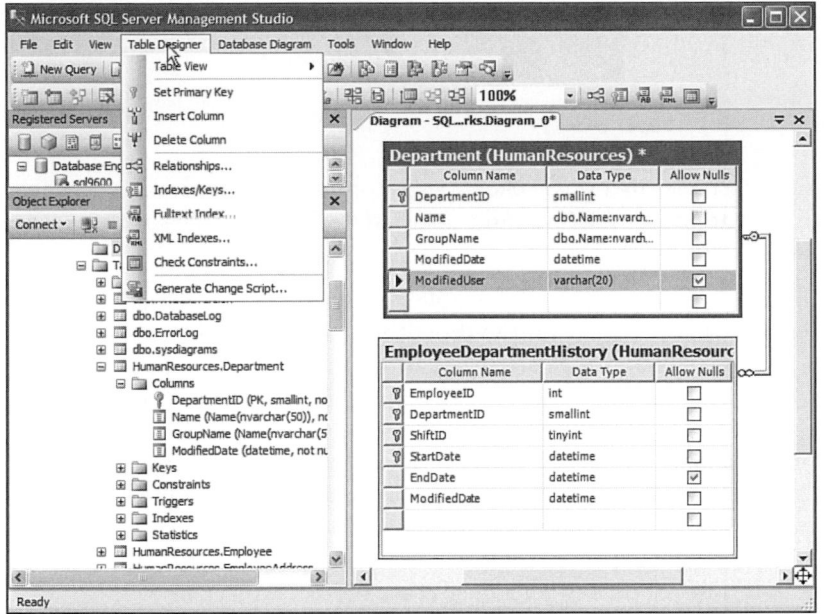

FIGURE 19.5   Modifying tables by using a database diagram.

The same scripting options are available with a database diagram as are available in the Table Designer. You can make your changes from within the diagram and then choose the Generate Change Script menu option. Listing 19.15 shows the change script that is generated based on the addition of the `ModifiedUser` column to the end of the `Department` table. As expected, this change is accomplished with an `ALTER TABLE` statement.

LISTING 19.15   The Change Script Generated from a Database Diagram

```
ALTER TABLE HumanResources.Department ADD
    ModifiedUser varchar(20) NULL
GO
```

The use of the `ALTER TABLE` statement in this listing brings us full circle, back to our initial method for making table modifications. Using all the tools discussed in this section together will usually give you the best results.

Dropping Tables

There are several different methods for dropping (or deleting) a table. You can right-click the table in the SSMS Object Explorer and select Delete, you can right-click a table in a database diagram and choose Delete Tables from Database, or you can use the old-fashioned method of utilizing T-SQL. Here's an example of the T-SQL DROP TABLE statement:

```
DROP TABLE [HumanResources].[Department]
```

You can reference multiple tables in a single DROP TABLE command by separating the table names with commas. Any triggers and constraints associated with the table are also dropped when the table is dropped.

A big consideration when dropping a table is the table's relationship to other tables. If a foreign key references the table that you want to drop, the referencing table or foreign key constraint must be dropped first. In a database that has many related tables, this can get complicated. Fortunately, a few tools can help you through this. The system stored procedure sp_helpconstraint is one of the tools. This procedure lists all the foreign key constraints that reference a table. Listing 19.16 shows an execution of this stored procedure for the Sales.Store table in the AdventureWorks database. The procedure results include information about all the constraints on the table. The results to focus on are those that follow the heading Table Is Referenced by Foreign Key. The partial results shown in Listing 19.16 for the Sales.Store table indicate that FK_StoreContact_Store_CustomerID must be dropped first before you can drop the Sales.Store table.

LISTING 19.16   Using sp_helpconstraint to Find Foreign Key References

```
sp_helpconstraint [Sales.Store]

/*partial results of sp_helpconstraint execution
Table is referenced by foreign key
----------------------------------------------------------------
AdventureWorks.Sales.StoreContact: FK_StoreContact_Store_CustomerID
*/
```

Two other approaches are useful for identifying foreign key references prior to dropping a table. The first is using a database diagram. You can create a new database diagram and add the table that you are considering for deletion. After the table is added, you right-click the table in Object Explorer and select Add Related Tables. The related tables, including those that have foreign key references, are then added. You can then right-click the relationship line connecting two tables and select Delete Relationships from Database. When you have deleted all the foreign key relationships from the diagram, you can right-click the table you want to delete and select Generate Change Script to create a script that can be used to remove the foreign key relationship(s).

The other approach is to right-click the table in Object Explorer and choose View Dependencies. The dialog that appears gives you the option of viewing the objects that depend on the table or viewing the objects on which the table depends. If you choose the option to view the objects that depend on the table, all the dependent objects are displayed, but you can focus on the objects that are tables.

Partitioned Tables

In SQL Server 2005, tables are stored in one or more partitions. *Partitions* are organizational units that allow you to divide data into logical groups. By default, a table has only a single partition that contains all the data. The power of partitions comes into play when you define multiple partitions for a table that is segmented based on a key column. This column allows the data rows to be horizontally split. For example, a date/time column can be used to divide each month's data into a separate partition. These partitions can also be aligned to different filegroups for added flexibility and ease of maintenance.

The important thing to remember is that you access tables with multiple partitions (which are called *partitioned tables*) the same way you access tables with a single partition. Data Manipulation Language (DML) operations such as INSERT and SELECT statements reference the table the same way, regardless of partitioning. The difference between these types of tables has to do with the back-end storage and the organization of the data.

Generally, partitioning is most useful for large tables. *Large* is a relative term, but these tables typically contain millions of rows and take up gigabytes of space. Oftentimes, the tables targeted for partitioning are large tables that are experiencing performance problems because of their size. Partitioning has several different applications, including the following:

▶ **Archival**—Table partitions can be moved from a production table to another archive table that has the same structure. When done properly, this partition movement is very fast and allows you to keep a limited amount of recent data in the production table while keeping the bulk of the older data in the archive table.

▶ **Maintenance**—Table partitions that have been assigned to different filegroups can be backed up and maintained independently of each other. With very large tables, maintenance activities on the entire table (such as backups) can take a prohibitively long time. With partitioned tables, these maintenance activities can be performed at the partition level. Take, for example, a table that is partitioned by month—all the new activity (updates and insertions) occurs in the partition that contains the current month's data. In this scenario, the current month's partition would be the focus of the maintenance, thus limiting the amount of data you need to process.

▶ **Query performance**—Partitioned tables that are joined on partitioned columns can experience improved performance because the Query Optimizer can join to the table based on the partitioned column. The caveat is that joins across partitioned tables that are not joining on the partitioned column may actually experience some performance degradation. Queries can also be parallelized along the partitions.

19

Now that we have discussed some of the reasons to use partitioned tables, let's take a look at how to set up partitions. There are three basic steps:

1. Create a partition function that maps the rows in the table to partitions based on the value of a specified column.

2. Create a partition scheme that outlines the placement of the partitions in the partition function to filegroups.

3. Create a table that utilizes the partition scheme.

These steps are predicated on a good partitioning design, based on an evaluation of the data within the table and the selection of a column that will effectively split the data. If multiple filegroups are used, those filegroups must also exist before you execute the three steps in partitioning. The following sections look at the syntax related to each step, using a simple example. These examples utilize the BigPubs2005 database, which can be found on the Sams website (www.samspublishing.com).

Creating a Partition Function

A partition function identifies values within a table that will be compared to the column on which you partition the table. As mentioned previously, it is important that you know the distribution of the data and the specific range of values in the partitioning column before you create the partition function. The following query provides an example of determining the distribution of data values in the `sales_big` table by year:

```
--Select the distinct yearly values
SELECT year(ord_date) as 'year', count(*) 'rows'
 FROM sales_big
 GROUP BY year(ord_date)
 ORDER BY 1
go


year          rows
----------- -----------
      1992          30
      1993      613560
      1994      616450
      1995      457210
```

You can see from the results of the `SELECT` statement that there are four years of data in the `sales_big` table. Because the values specified in the `CREATE PARTITION FUNCTION` statement are used to establish data ranges, at a minimum, you would need to specify at least three data values when defining the partition function, as shown in the following example:

```
--Create partition function with the yearly values to partition the data
CREATE PARTITION FUNCTION SalesBigPF1 (datetime)
```

```
AS RANGE RIGHT FOR VALUES
('01/01/1993', '01/01/1994',
   '01/01/1995')
GO
```

In this example, four ranges, or partitions, would be established by the three range right values specified in the statement:

- ▶ **values < 01/01/1993**—This partition includes any rows prior to 1993.

- ▶ **values >= 01/01/1993 AND values < 01/01/1994**—This partition includes all rows for 1993.

- ▶ **values >= 01/01/1994 AND values < 01/01/1995**—This partition includes all rows for 1994.

- ▶ **values > 01/01/1995**—This includes any rows for 1996 or later.

This method of partitioning would be more than adequate for a static table that is not going to be receiving any additional data rows for different years than already exist in the table. However, if the table is going to be populated with additional data rows after it has been partitioned, it is good practice to add additional range values at the beginning and end of the ranges to allow for the insertion of data values less than or greater than the existing range values in the table. To create these additional upper and lower ranges, you would want to specify five values in the VALUES clause of the CREATE PARTITION FUNCTION as shown in Listing 19.17. The advantages of having these additional partitions will be demonstrated later in this section.

LISTING 19.17   Creating a Partition Function

```
if exists (select 1 from sys.partition_functions where name = 'SalesBigPF1')
   drop partition function SalesBigPF1
go
--Create partition function with the yearly values to partition the data
Create PARTITION FUNCTION SalesBigPF1 (datetime)
   AS RANGE RIGHT FOR VALUES
   ('01/01/1992', '01/01/1993', '01/01/1994',
      '01/01/1995',  '01/01/1996')
GO
```

In this example, six ranges, or partitions, are established by the five range values specified in the statement:

- ▶ **values < 01/01/1992**—This partition includes any rows prior to 1992.

- ▶ **values >= 01/01/1992 AND values < 01/01/1993**—This partition includes all rows for 1992.

▶ **values >= 01/01/1993 AND values < 01/01/1994**—This partition includes all rows for 1993.

▶ **values >= 01/01/1994 AND values < 01/01/1995**—This partition includes all rows for 1994.

▶ **values >= 01/01/1995 AND values < 01/01/1996**—This partition includes all rows for 1995.

▶ **values >= 01/01/1996**—This partition includes any rows for 1996 or later.

An alternative to the RIGHT clause in the CREATE PARTITION FUNCTION statement is the LEFT clause. The LEFT clause is similar to RIGHT, but it changes the ranges such that the < operands are changed to <=, and the >= operands are changed to >.

TIP

It is usually best to use RANGE RIGHT partitions for datetime values because this makes it easier to specify the limits of the ranges. The datetime data type can store values only with accuracy to 3.33 milliseconds. The largest value it can store is 0.997 milliseconds. A value of 0.998 milliseconds rounds down to 0.997, and a value of 0.999 milliseconds rounds up to the next second.

If you used a RANGE LEFT partition, the maximum time value you could include with the year to get all values for that year would be 23:59:59.997. For example, if you specified 12/31/1993 23:59:59.999 as the boundary for a RANGE LEFT partition, it would be rounded up so that it would also include rows with datetime values less than or equal to 01/01/1994 00:00:00.000, which is probably not what you would want. Redefining the example shown in Listing 19.17 as a RANGE LEFT partition function would be as follows:

```
CREATE PARTITION FUNCTION SalesBigPF1 (datetime)
    AS RANGE LEFT FOR VALUES
    ('12/31/1991 23:59:59.997', '12/31/1992 23:59:59.997',
     '12/31/1993 23:59: 59.997', '12/31/1994 23:59:59.997',
     '12/31/1995 23:59:59.997')
```

As you can see, it's a bit more straightforward and probably less confusing to use RANGE RIGHT partition functions when dealing with datetime values or any other continuous-value data types, such as float or numeric.

Creating a Partition Scheme

After you create a partition function, the next step is to associate a partition scheme with the partition function. A partition scheme can be associated with only one partition function, but a partition function can be shared across multiple partition schemes.

The core function of a partition scheme is to map the values defined in the partition function to filegroups. When creating the statement for a partition scheme, you need to keep in mind the following:

▶ A single filegroup can be used for all partitions, or a separate filegroup can be used for each individual partition.

▶ Any filegroup referenced in the partition scheme must exist before the partition scheme is created.

▶ There must be enough filegroups referenced in the partition scheme to accommodate all the partitions. The number of partitions is one more than the number of values specified in the partition function.

▶ The number of partitions is limited to 1,000.

▶ The filegroups listed in the partition scheme are assigned to the partitions defined in the function based on the order in which the filegroups are listed.

Listing 19.18 creates a partition schema that references the partition function created in Listing 19.17. This example assumes that the referenced filegroups have been created for each of the partitions. (For more information on creating filegroups and secondary files, see Chapter 18, "Creating and Managing Databases.")

NOTE

If you'd like to create the same filegroups and files used by the examples in this section, there is a script file on the Sams website (www.samspublishing.com) in the code listings directory for this chapter called `Create_Filegroups_and_Files_for_ Partitioning.sql`. If you run this script, it will create all the necessary file groups and files referenced in the examples. Note that you will need to edit the script to change the `FILENAME` value if you need the files to be created in a directory other than `C:\MSSQL2005\DATA`.

LISTING 19.18   Creating a Partition Scheme

```
--Create a partition scheme that is aligned with the partition function
CREATE PARTITION SCHEME SalesBigPS1
    AS PARTITION SalesBigPF1
    TO ([Older_data], [1992_data], [1993_data],
        [1994_data], [1995_data], [1996_data])
GO
```

Alternatively, if all partitions are going to be on the same filegroup, such as the PRIMARY filegroup, you could use the following:

```
Create PARTITION SCHEME SalesBigPS1
    as PARTITION SalesBigPF1
    ALL to ([PRIMARY])
go
```

19

Notice that `SalesBifPF1` is referenced as the partition function in Listing 19.18. This ties together the partition scheme and the partition function. Figure 19.6 shows how the partitions defined in the function would be mapped to the filegroup(s). At this point, you have made no changes to any table, and you have not even specified the column in the table that you will partition. The next section discusses those details.

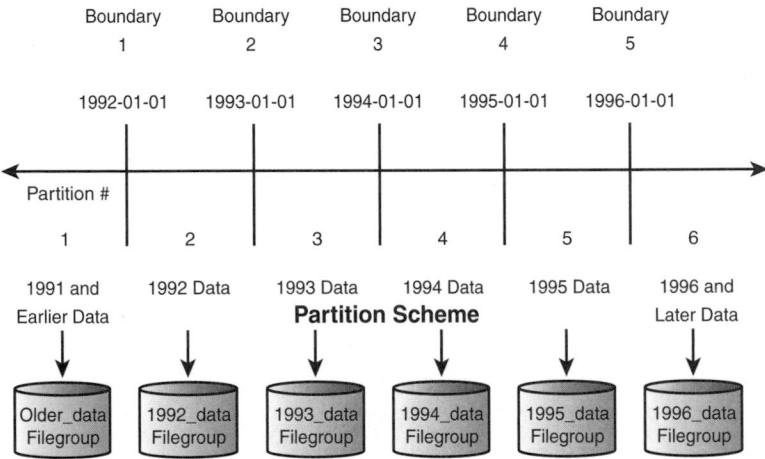

FIGURE 19.6   Mapping of partitions to filegroups, using a `RANGE RIGHT` partition function.

Creating a Partitioned Table

Tables are partitioned only when they are created. This is an important point to keep in mind when you are considering adding partitions to a table that already exists. Sometimes, performance issues or other factors may lead you to determine that a table you have already created and populated may benefit from being partitioned.

The re-creation of large tables in a production environment requires some forethought and planning. The data in the table must be retained in another location in order to re-create the table. Bulk copying the data to a flat file or renaming the table are two possible solutions for retaining the data. After you determine the data retention method, you can re-create the table, with the new partition scheme. For simplicity's sake, the example in Listing 19.19 creates a new table named `sales_big_Partitioned` instead of using the original `sales_big` table. The second part of Listing 19.19 copies the data from the `sales_big` table into the `sales_big_Partitioned` table.

LISTING 19.19   Creating a Partitioned Table

```
CREATE TABLE dbo.sales_big_Partitioned(
        sales_id int IDENTITY(1,1) NOT NULL,
        stor_id char(4) NOT NULL,
```

LISTING 19.19   Continued

```
        ord_num varchar(20) NOT NULL,
        ord_date datetime NOT NULL,
        qty smallint NOT NULL,
        payterms varchar(12) NOT NULL,
        title_id dbo.tid NOT NULL
) ON SalesBigPS1 (ord_date)  --this statement is key to Partitioning the table
GO


GO


--Insert data from the sales_big table into the new sales_big_partitioned table
SET IDENTITY_INSERT sales_big_Partitioned ON
GO
INSERT sales_big_Partitioned with (TABLOCKX)
 (sales_id, stor_id, ord_num, ord_date, qty, payterms, title_id)
 SELECT sales_id, stor_id, ord_num, ord_date, qty, payterms, title_id
  FROM sales_big
go
SET IDENTITY_INSERT sales_big_Partitioned OFF
GO
```

The key clause to take note of in this listing is ON SalesBigPS1 (ord_date). This clause identifies the partition scheme on which to create the table (SalesBigPS1) and the column within the table to use for partitioning (ord_date).

After you create the table, you might wonder whether the table was partitioned correctly. Fortunately, there are some catalog views related to partitions that you can query for this kind of information. Listing 19.20 shows a sample SELECT statement that utilizes the sys.partitions view. The results of the statement execution are shown immediately after the SELECT statement. Notice that there are six numbered partitions and that the estimated number of rows for each partition corresponds to the number of rows you saw when you selected the data from the unpartitioned SalesBig table.

LISTING 19.20   Viewing Partitioned Table Information

```
select convert(varchar(16), ps.name) as partition_scheme,
       p.partition_number,
       convert(varchar(10), ds2.name) as filegroup,
       convert(varchar(19), isnull(v.value, ''), 120) as range_boundary,
       str(p.rows, 9) as rows
  from sys.indexes i
  join sys.partition_schemes ps on i.data_space_id = ps.data_space_id
  join sys.destination_data_spaces dds
       on ps.data_space_id = dds.partition_scheme_id
  join sys.data_spaces ds2 on dds.data_space_id = ds2.data_space_id
```

19

LISTING 19.20   Continued

```
join sys.partitions p on dds.destination_id = p.partition_number
                and p.object_id = i.object_id and p.index_id = i.index_id
    join sys.partition_functions pf on ps.function_id = pf.function_id
    LEFT JOIN sys.Partition_Range_values v on pf.function_id = v.function_id
            and v.boundary_id = p.partition_number - pf.boundary_value_on_right
    WHERE i.object_id = object_id('sales_big_partitioned')
       and i.index_id = 0
    order by p.partition_number

/* Results from the previous SELECT statement
partition_scheme partition_number filegroup  range_boundary        rows
---------------- ---------------- ---------- -------------------- ---------

SalesBigPS1                     1 Older_Data                             0
SalesBigPS1                     2 1992_Data  1992-01-01 00:00:00        30
SalesBigPS1                     3 1993_Data  1993-01-01 00:00:00    613560
SalesBigPS1                     4 1994_Data  1994-01-01 00:00:00    616450
SalesBigPS1                     5 1995_Data  1995-01-01 00:00:00    457210
SalesBigPS1                     6 1996_Data  1996-01-01 00:00:00         0
*/
```

Adding and Dropping Table Partitions

One of the most useful features of partitioned tables is that you can add and drop entire partitions of table data in bulk. If the table partitions are set up properly, these commands can take place in seconds, without the expensive input/output (I/O) costs of physically copying or moving the data. You can add and drop table partitions by using the SPLIT RANGE and MERGE RANGE options of the ALTER PARTITION FUNCTION command:

```
ALTER PARTITION FUNCTION partition_function_name()
{ SPLIT RANGE ( boundary_value ) ¦ MERGE RANGE ( boundary_value ) }
```

Adding a Table Partition

The SPLIT RANGE option adds a new boundary point to an existing partition function and affects all objects that use this partition function. When this command is run, one of the function partitions is split in two. The new partition is the one that contains the new boundary point. The new partition is created to the right of the boundary value if the partition is defined as a RANGE RIGHT partition function or to the left of the boundary if it is a RANGE LEFT partition function. If the partition is empty, the split is instantaneous.

If the partition being split contains data, any data on the new side of the boundary is physically deleted from the old partition and inserted into the new partition. In addition to being I/O intensive, a split also is also log intensive, generating log records that are four times the size of the data being moved. In addition, an exclusive table lock is held for the duration of the split. To avoid this costly overhead when adding a new partition to the end of the partition range, it is recommended that you always keep an empty partition available at the end and split it before it is populated with data. If the partition is empty, SQL Server does not need to scan the partition to see whether there is any data to be moved.

Before you split a partition, a filegroup must be marked to be the NEXT USED partition by the partition scheme that uses the partition function. You initially allocate filegroups to partitions by using a CREATE PARTITION SCHEME statement. If a CREATE PARTITION SCHEME statement allocates more filegroups than there are partitions defined in the CREATE PARTITION FUNCTION statement, one of the unassigned filegroups is automatically marked as NEXT USED by the partition scheme, and it will hold the new partition.

If there are no filegroups currently marked NEXT USED by the partition scheme, you must use ALTER PARTITION SCHEME to either add a filegroup or designate an existing filegroup to hold the new partition. This can be a filegroup that already holds existing partitions. Also, if a partition function is used by more than one partition scheme, all the partition schemes that use the partition function to which you are adding partitions must have a NEXT USED filegroup. If one or more do not have a NEXT USED filegroup assigned, the ALTER PARTITION FUNCTION statement fails, and the error message displays the partition scheme or schemes that lack a NEXT USED filegroup.

The following SQL statement adds a NEXT USED filegroup to the SalesBigPS1 partition scheme. Note that in this example, the filegroup specified is a new filegroup, 1997_DATA:

```
ALTER PARTITION SCHEME SalesBigPS1 NEXT USED '1997_Data'
```

Now that you have specified a NEXT USED filegroup for the partition scheme, you can go ahead and add the new range for 1997 and later data rows to the partition function, as in the following example:

```
--Alter partition function with the yearly values to partition the data
ALTER PARTITION FUNCTION SalesBigPF1 () SPLIT RANGE ('01/01/1997')
GO
```

Figure 19.7 shows the effects of splitting the 1996 table partition.

19

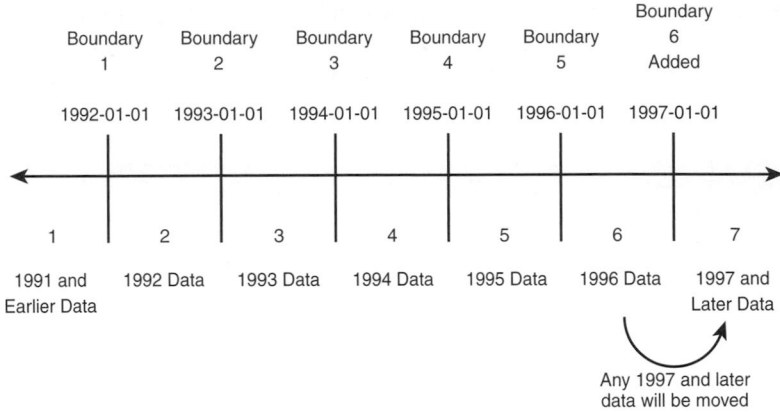

FIGURE 19.7   The effects of splitting a `RANGE RIGHT` table partition.

You can also see the effects of splitting the partition on the system catalogs by running the same query as shown earlier, in Listing 19.20:

```
/* New results from the SELECT statement in Listing 19.20
partition_scheme partition_number filegroup  range_boundary      rows
---------------- ---------------- ---------- ------------------- ---------
SalesBigPS1                     1 Older_Data                             0
SalesBigPS1                     2 1992_Data  1992-01-01 00:00:00        30
SalesBigPS1                     3 1993_Data  1993-01-01 00:00:00    613560
SalesBigPS1                     4 1994_Data  1994-01-01 00:00:00    616450
SalesBigPS1                     5 1995_Data  1995-01-01 00:00:00    457210
SalesBigPS1                     6 1996_Data  1996-01-01 00:00:00         0
SalesBigPS1                     7 1997_Data  1997-01-01 00:00:00         0
*/
```

Dropping a Table Partition

You can drop a table partition by using the `ALTER PARTITION FUNCTION ... MERGE RANGE` command. This command essentially removes a boundary point from a partition function as the partitions on each side of the boundary are merged into one. The partition that held the boundary value is removed. The filegroup that originally held the boundary value is removed from the partition scheme unless it is used by a remaining partition or is marked with the `NEXT USED` property.

Any data that was in the removed partition is moved to the remaining neighboring partition. If a `RANGE RIGHT` partition boundary was removed, the data that was in that boundary's partition is moved to the partition to the left of boundary. If it was a `RANGE LEFT` partition, the data is moved to the partition to the right of the boundary.

The following command merges the 1992 partition into the Old_Data partition for the sales_big_partitioned table:

```
ALTER PARTITION FUNCTION SalesBigPF1 () MERGE RANGE ('01/01/1992')
```

Figure 19.8 demonstrates how the 1992 RANGE RIGHT partition boundary is removed and the data is merged to the left, into the Old_Data partition.

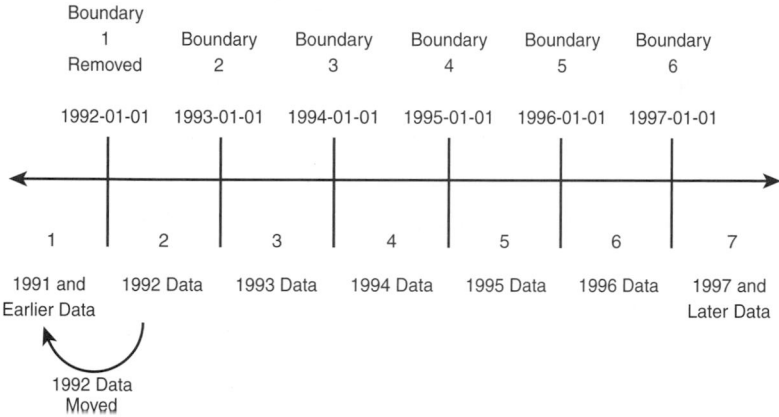

FIGURE 19.8   The effects of merging a RANGE RIGHT table partition.

CAUTION

Splitting or merging partitions for a partition function affects all objects using that partition function.

You can also see the effects of merging the partition on the system catalogs by running the same query as shown in Listing 19.20:

```
/* New results from the SELECT statement in Listing 19.20
partition_scheme partition_number filegroup  range_boundary        rows
---------------- ---------------- ---------- -------------------- ---------
SalesBigPS1                     1 Older_Data                             30
SalesBigPS1                     3 1993_Data  1993-01-01 00:00:00     613560
SalesBigPS1                     4 1994_Data  1994-01-01 00:00:00     616450
SalesBigPS1                     5 1995_Data  1995-01-01 00:00:00     457210
SalesBigPS1                     6 1996_Data  1996-01-01 00:00:00          0
SalesBigPS1                     7 1997_Data  1997-01-01 00:00:00          0
*/
```

Like the split operation, the merge operation occurs instantaneously if the partition being merged is empty. The process can be very I/O intensive if the partition has a large amount of data in it. Any rows in the removed partition are physically moved into the remaining partition. This operation is also very log intensive, requiring log space approximately four times the size of data being moved. An exclusive table lock is held for the duration of the merge.

If you no longer want to keep the data in the table for a partition you are merging, you can move the data in the partition to another empty table or empty table partition by using the SWITCH PARTITION option of the ALTER TABLE command. This is discussed in more detail in the following section.

Switching Table Partitions

One of the great features of table partitions is that they enable you to instantly swap the contents of one partition to an empty table, the contents from a partition on one table to a partition in another table, or an entire table's contents into another table's empty partition. This operation performs changes only to metadata in the system catalogs for the affected tables/partitions, with no actual physical movement of data.

In order for you to switch data from a partition to a table or from a table into a partition, the following criteria must be met:

▶ The source table and target table must both have the same structure (that is, the same columns in the same order, with the same names, data types, lengths, precisions, scales, nullabilities, and collations). The tables must also have the same primary key constraints and settings for ANSI_NULLS and QUOTED_IDENTIFIER.

▶ The source and the target of the ALTER TABLE...SWITCH statement must reside in the same filegroup.

▶ If you are switching a partition to a single, nonpartitioned table, the table receiving the partition must already be created, and it must be empty.

▶ If you are adding a table as a partition to an already existing partitioned table or moving a partition from one partitioned table to another, the receiving partition must exist, and it must be empty.

▶ If you are switching a partition from one partitioned table to another, both tables must be partitioned on the same column.

▶ The source must have all the same indexes as the target, and the indexes must also be in the same filegroup.

▶ If you are switching a nonpartitioned table to a partition of an already existing partitioned table, the nonpartitioned table must have a constraint defined on the column corresponding to the partition key of the target table to ensure that the range of values fits within the boundary values of the target partition.

▶ If the target table has any FOREIGN KEY constraints, the source table must have the same foreign keys defined on the corresponding columns, and those foreign keys must reference the same primary keys that the target table references.

If you are switching a partition of a partitioned table to another partitioned table, the boundary values of the source partition must fit within those of the target partition. If the boundary values do not fit, there must be a constraint defined on the partition key of the source table to make sure all the data in the table fits into the boundary values of the target partition.

> **CAUTION**
>
> If the tables have `IDENTITY` columns, partition switching can result in the introduction of duplicate values in `IDENTITY` columns of the target table and gaps in the values of `IDENTITY` columns in the source table. You can use `DBCC_CHECKIDENT` to check the identity values of tables and correct them if necessary.

When you switch a partition, data is not physically moved. Only the metadata information in the system catalogs about where the data is stored is changed. In addition, all associated indexes are automatically switched, along with the table or partition.

To switch table partitions, you use the `ALTER TABLE` command:

```
ALTER TABLE table_name SWITCH [ PARTITION source_partition_number_expression ]
    TO target_table [ PARTITION target_ partition_number_expression ]
```

You can use the `ALTER TABLE...SWITCH` command to switch an unpartitioned table into a table partition, switch a table partition into an empty unpartitioned table, or switch a table partition into another table's empty table partition. The code shown in Listing 19.21 creates a table to hold the data from the 1993 partition and then switches the 1993 partition from the `sales_big_partitioned` table to the new table.

LISTING 19.21   Switching a Partition to an Empty Table

```
CREATE TABLE dbo.sales_big_1993(
        sales_id int IDENTITY(1,1) NOT NULL,
        stor_id char(4) NOT NULL,
        ord_num varchar(20) NOT NULL,
        ord_date datetime NOT NULL,
        qty smallint NOT NULL,
        payterms varchar(12) NOT NULL,
        title_id dbo.tid NOT NULL
) ON '1993_data'  -- required in order to switch the partition to this table
go
alter table sales_big_partitioned
    switch partition $PARTITION.SalesBigPF1 ('1/1/1993')
    to sales_big_1993
go
```

19

Note that Listing 19.21 uses the $PARTITION function. You can use this function with any partition function name to return the partition number that corresponds with the specified partitioning column value. This prevents you from having to query the system catalogs to determine the specific partition number for the specified partition value.

You can now run the query from Listing 19.20 to show that the 1993 partition is now empty:

```
partition_scheme partition_number filegroup  range_boundary        rows
---------------- ---------------- ---------- -------------------- ---------

SalesBigPS1                     1 Older_Data                           30
SalesBigPS1                     2 1993_Data  1993-01-01 00:00:00        0
SalesBigPS1                     3 1994_Data  1994-01-01 00:00:00   616450
SalesBigPS1                     4 1995_Data  1995-01-01 00:00:00   457210
SalesBigPS1                     5 1996_Data  1996-01-01 00:00:00        0
SalesBigPS1                     6 1997_Data  1997-01-01 00:00:00        0
```

Now that the 1993 data partition is empty, you can merge the partition without incurring the I/O cost of moving the data to the Older_data partition:

```
ALTER PARTITION FUNCTION SalesBigPF1 () merge RANGE ('1/1/1993')
```

Rerunning the query in Listing 19.20 now returns the following result set:

```
partition_scheme partition_number filegroup  range_boundary        rows
---------------- ---------------- ---------- -------------------- ---------

SalesBigPS1                     1 Older_Data                           30
SalesBigPS1                     2 1994_Data  1994-01-01 00:00:00   616450
SalesBigPS1                     3 1995_Data  1995-01-01 00:00:00   457210
SalesBigPS1                     4 1996_Data  1996-01-01 00:00:00        0
SalesBigPS1                     5 1997_Data  1997-01-01 00:00:00        0
```

To demonstrate switching a table into a partition, you can update the date for all the rows in the sales_big_1993 table to 1996 and switch it into the 1996 partition of the sales_big_partitioned table. Note that before you can do this, you need to copy the data to a table in the 1996_data filegroup and also put a check constraint on the ord_date column to make sure all rows in the table are limited to values that are valid for the 1996_data partition. Listing 19.22 shows the commands you use to create the new table and switch it into the 1996 partition of the sales_big_partitioned table.

LISTING 19.22   Switching a Table to an Empty Partition

```
CREATE TABLE dbo.sales_big_1996(
      sales_id int IDENTITY(1,1) NOT NULL,
      stor_id char(4)  NOT NULL,
      ord_num varchar(20)  NOT NULL,
      ord_date datetime NOT NULL
        constraint CK_sales_big_1996_ord_date
```

LISTING 19.22   Continued

```
               check (ord_date >= '1/1/1996' and ord_date < '1/1/1997'),
        qty smallint NOT NULL,
        payterms varchar(12)  NOT NULL,
        title_id dbo.tid NOT NULL
) ON '1996_data'  -- required to switch the table to the 1996 partition
go
set identity_insert sales_big_1996 on
go
insert sales_big_1996 (sales_id, stor_id, ord_num,
                       ord_date, qty, payterms, title_id)
   select sales_id, stor_id, ord_num,
          dateadd(yy, 3, ord_date),
          qty, payterms, title_id
     from sales_big_1993
go
set identity_insert sales_big_1996 off
go
alter table sales_big_1996
  switch to sales_big_partitioned
  partition $PARTITION.SalesBigPF1 ('1/1/1996')
go
```

Rerunning the query from Listing 19.20 now returns the following result:

```
partition_scheme partition_number filegroup  range_boundary        rows
---------------- ---------------- ---------  ------------------    ---------
SalesBigPS1                      1 Older_Data                            30
SalesBigPS1                      2 1994_Data 1994-01-01 00:00:00     616450
SalesBigPS1                      3 1995_Data 1995-01-01 00:00:00     457210
SalesBigPS1                      4 1996_Data 1996-01-01 00:00:00     613560
SalesBigPS1                      5 1997_Data 1997-01-01 00:00:00          0
```

> **TIP**
>
> Switching data into or out of partitions provides a very efficient mechanism for archiving old data from a production table, importing new data into a production table, or migrating data to an archive table. You can use SWITCH to empty or fill partitions very quickly. As you've seen in this section, split and merge operations occur instantaneously if the partitions being split or merged are empty first. If you must split or merge partitions that contain a lot of data, you should empty them first by using SWITCH before you perform the split or merge.

19

Creating Temporary Tables

A temporary table is a special type of table that is automatically deleted when it is no longer used. Temporary tables have many of the same characteristics as permanent tables and are typically used as work tables that contain intermediate results.

You designate a table as temporary in SQL Server by prefacing the table name with a pound sign (#). Temporary tables are created in tempdb; if a temporary table is not explicitly dropped, it is dropped when the session that created it ends or the stored procedure it was created in finishes execution.

If a table name is prefaced with a single pound sign (for example, #table1), it is a *private* temporary table, available only to the session that created it.

A table name prefixed with a double pound sign (for example, ##table2) indicates that it is a *global* temporary table, which means it is accessible by all database connections. A global temporary table exists until the session that created it terminates. If the creating session terminates while other sessions are accessing the table, the temporary table is available to those sessions until the last session's query ends, at which time the table is dropped.

> **NOTE**
>
> Table variables are a good alternative to temporary tables. These variables are also temporary in nature and have some advantages over temporary tables. Table variables are easy to create, are automatically deleted, cause fewer recompilations, and use fewer locking and logging resources. Generally speaking, you should consider using table variables instead of temporary tables when the temporary results are relatively small. Parallel query plans are not generated with table variables, and this can impede overall performance when you are accessing a table variable that has a large number of rows.
>
> For more information on using temporary tables and table variables, see Chapter 46, "Transact-SQL Programming Guidelines, Tips, and Tricks."

Tables created without the # prefix but explicitly created in tempdb are also considered temporary, but they are a more permanent form of a temporary table. They are not dropped automatically until SQL Server is restarted and tempdb is reinitialized.

Summary

Tables are the key to a relational database system. When you create tables, you need to pay careful attention in choosing the proper data types to ensure efficient storage of data, adding appropriate constraints to maintain data integrity, and scripting the creation and modification of tables to ensure that they can be re-created, if necessary.

Good table design includes the creation of indexes on a table. Tables without indexes are generally inefficient and cause excessive use of resources on your database server. Chapter 20, "Creating and Managing Indexes," covers indexes and how they improve the performance of database tables.

Creating and Managing Indexes

IN THIS CHAPTER

► What's New in Creating and Managing Indexes

► Types of Indexes

► Creating Indexes

► Managing Indexes

► Dropping Indexes

► Online Indexing Operations

► Indexes on Views

Just like the index in this book, an index on a table or view allows you to efficiently find the information you are looking for in a database. SQL Server does not require indexes in order to retrieve data from tables because it can perform a full table scan to retrieve a result set. However, doing a table scan is analogous to scanning every page in this book to find a word or reference you are looking for.

This chapter introduces the different types of indexes that are available in SQL Server 2005 to keep your database access efficient. It focuses on creating and managing indexes by using the tools Microsoft SQL Server 2005 provides. For a more in-depth discussion of the internal structures of indexes and designing and managing indexes for optimal performance, see Chapter 29, "Indexes and Performance."

What's New in Creating and Managing Indexes

The creation and management of indexes is one of the most important performance activities in SQL Server. Because of this, Microsoft continually provides new and improved product features related to indexing. The following are some of the most important new features that are available with SQL Server 2005:

► **Online index operations**—High availability requirements have been addressed with new indexing options that allow concurrent user access to a table while indexes on that table are being rebuilt, created, or dropped.

▶ **Included columns**—Non-key columns can now be added to an index for improved performance. The performance gains are achieved with covering indexes that allow the Query Optimizer to locate all the column values referenced in the query within the leaf rows of the index.

▶ **XML indexes**—Indexes can now be created on columns that are XML data types.

▶ **Altering indexes**—Similarly to other database objects such as tables and databases, indexes can now be modified with an `ALTER` statement. Index operations that were previously performed with DBCC commands or system stored procedures can now be accomplished with the `ALTER INDEX` command.

▶ **Parallel index operations**—Scan and sort activities associated with index operations can now be done in parallel. You can control the number of processors that are used in parallel index operations by using the `MAXDOP` options.

Types of Indexes

SQL Server has two main types of indexes: clustered and nonclustered. They both help the query engine get at data faster, but they have different effects on the storage of the underlying data. The following sections describe these two main types of indexes and provide some insight into when to use each type.

Clustered Indexes

Clustered indexes sort and store the data rows for a table, based on the columns defined in the index. For example, if you were to create a clustered index on the `LastName` and `FirstName` columns in a table, the data rows for that table would be organized or sorted according to these two columns. This has some obvious advantages for data retrieval. Queries that search for data based on the clustered index keys have a sequential path to the underlying data, which helps reduce I/O.

A clustered index is analogous to a filing cabinet where each drawer contains a set of file folders stored in alphabetical order, and each file folder stores the files in alphabetical order. Each file drawer contains a label that indicates which folders it contains (for example, folders A–D). To locate a specific file, you first locate the drawer containing the appropriate file folders, then locate the appropriate file folder within the drawer, and then scan the files in that folder in sequence until you find the one you need.

A clustered index is structured as a balanced tree (B-tree). Figure 20.1 shows a simplified diagram of a clustered index defined on a last name column.

The top, or root, node is a single page where searches via the clustered index are started. The bottom level of the index is the leaf nodes. With a clustered index, the leaf nodes of the index are also the data pages of the table. Any levels of the index between the root and leaf nodes are referred to as *intermediate nodes*. All index key values are stored in the clustered index levels in sorted order. To locate a data row via a clustered index, SQL Server starts at the root node and navigates through the appropriate index pages in the intermediate levels of the index until it reaches the data page that should contain the desired data row(s). It then scans the rows on the data page until it locates the desired value.

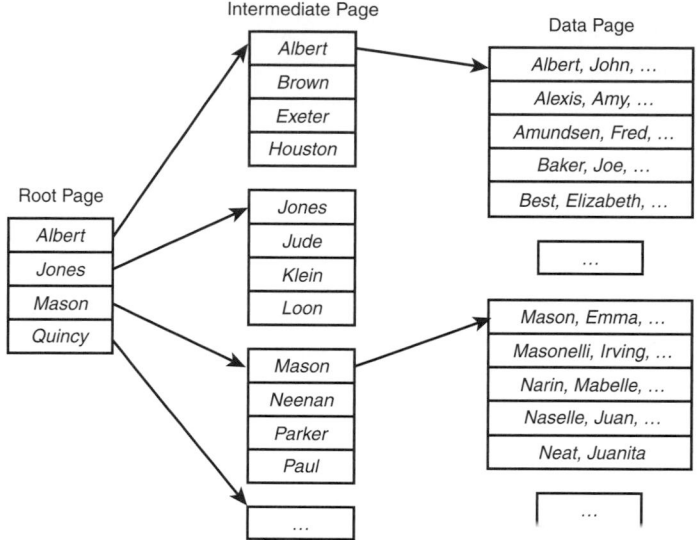

FIGURE 20.1   A simplified diagram of a clustered index.

There can be only one clustered index per table. This is driven by the fact that the underlying data rows can be sorted and stored in only one way. With very few exceptions, every table in a database should have a clustered index. The selection of columns for a clustered index is very important and should be driven by the way the data is most commonly accessed in the table. You should consider using the following types of columns in a clustered index:

- ▶ Those that are often accessed sequentially

- ▶ Those that contain a large number of distinct values

- ▶ Those that are used in range queries that use operators such as BETWEEN, >, >=, <, or <= in the WHERE clause

- ▶ Those that are frequently used by queries to join or group the result set

When using these criteria, it is important to focus on the most critical data access—the queries that are run most often or that must have the best performance. This can be challenging but ultimately reduces the number of data pages and related I/O for the queries that matter.

20

Nonclustered Indexes

A nonclustered index is a separate index structure, independent of the physical sort order of the data rows in the table. You are therefore not restricted to creating only 1 nonclustered index per table; in fact, you can create up to 249 nonclustered indexes per table.

A nonclustered index is analogous to an index in the back of a book. To find the pages on which a specific subject is discussed, you look up the subject in the index and then go to the pages referenced in the index. With nonclustered indexes, you may have to jump around to many different nonsequential pages in order find all the references.

A nonclustered index is also structured as a B-tree. Figure 20.2 shows a simplified diagram of a nonclustered index defined on a first name column.

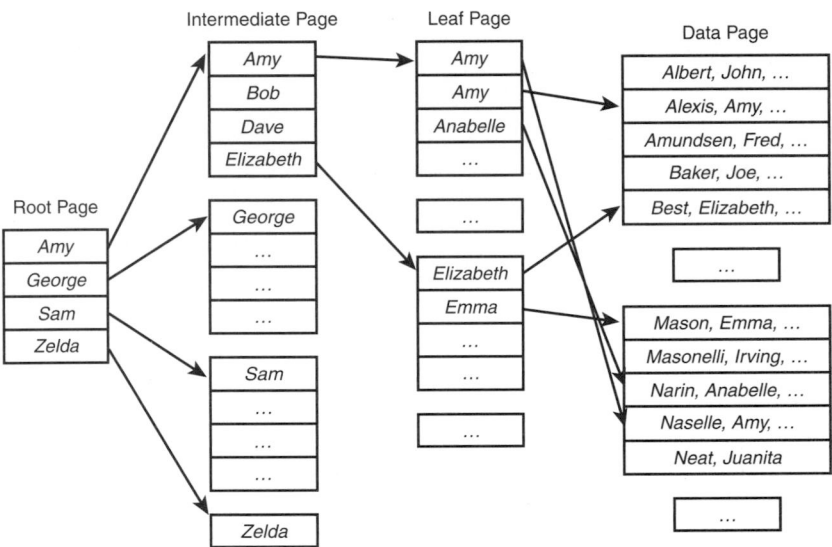

FIGURE 20.2   A simplified diagram of a nonclustered index.

As with a clustered index, in a nonclustered index, all index key values are stored in the nonclustered index levels in sorted order, based on the index key(s). This sort order is typically different from the sort order of the table itself. The main difference between a nonclustered index and a clustered index is that the leaf row of a nonclustered index is independent of the data rows in the table. The leaf level of a nonclustered index contains a row for every data row in the table, along with a pointer to locate the data row. This pointer is either the clustered index key for the data row, if the table has a clustered index on it, or the data page ID and row ID of the data row if the table is stored as a heap structure (that is, if the table has no clustered index defined on it).

To locate a data row via a nonclustered index, SQL Server starts at the root node and navigates through the appropriate index pages in the intermediate levels of the index until it reaches the leaf page, which should contain the index key for the desired data row. It then scans the keys on the leaf page until it locates the desired index key value. SQL

Server then uses the pointer to the data row stored with the index key to retrieve the corresponding data row.

> **NOTE**
>
> For a more detailed discussion of clustered tables versus heap tables (that is, tables with no clustered indexes) and more detailed descriptions of clustered and nonclustered index key structures and index key rows, as well as how SQL Server internally maintains indexes, see Chapter 29.

The efficiency of the index lookup and the types of lookups should drive the selection of nonclustered indexes. In the book index example, a single page reference is a very simple lookup for the book reader and requires little work. If, however, there are many pages referenced in the index, and those pages are spread throughout the book, the lookup is no longer simple, and much more work is required to get all the information.

You should choose your nonclustered indexes with the book index example in mind. You should consider using nonclustered indexes for the following:

▶ Queries that do not return large result sets

▶ Columns that are frequently used in the WHERE clause that return exact matches

▶ Columns that have many distinct values (that is, high cardinality)

▶ All columns referenced in a critical query (A special nonclustered index called a *covering index* that eliminates the need to go to the underlying data pages.)

Having a good understanding of your data access is essential to creating nonclustered indexes. Fortunately, SQL Server comes with tools such as the SQL Server Profiler and the Database Engine Tuning Advisor that can help you evaluate your data access and determine which columns are the best candidates. SQL Profiler is discussed in more detail in Chapter 5, "SQL Server Profiler," and using SQL Profiler and the Database Engine Tuning Advisor to assist in developing an optimal indexing strategy are discussed in Chapter 29.

Creating Indexes

The following sections examine the most common means for creating indexes in SQL Server. Microsoft provides several different methods for creating indexes, each of which has advantages. The method used is often a matter of personal preference, but there are situations in which a given method has distinct advantages.

Creating Indexes with T-SQL

Transact-SQL (T-SQL) is the most fundamental means for creating an index. This method was available in all previous versions of SQL Server. It is a very powerful option for creating indexes because the T-SQL statements that create indexes can be stored in a file and run as part of a database installation or upgrade. In addition, T-SQL scripts that were used in prior SQL Server versions to create indexes can be reused with very little change.

You can create indexes by using the T-SQL CREATE INDEX command. Listing 20.1 shows the basic CREATE INDEX syntax. Refer to SQL Server 2005 Books Online for the full syntax.

LISTING 20.1   CREATE INDEX Syntax

```
CREATE [ UNIQUE ] [ CLUSTERED ¦ NONCLUSTERED ] INDEX index_name
    ON <object> ( column [ ASC ¦ DESC ] [ ,...n ] )
    [ INCLUDE ( column_name [ ,...n ] ) ]
    [ WITH ( <relational_index_option> [ ,...n ] ) ]
```

Table 20.1 lists the CREATE INDEX arguments.

TABLE 20.1   Arguments for CREATE INDEX

Argument	Explanation
UNIQUE	Indicates that no two rows in the index can have the same index key values. Inserts into a table with a UNIQUE index will fail if a row with the same value already exists in the table.
CLUSTERED ¦ NON-CLUSTERED	Defines the index as clustered or nonclustered. NON-CLUSTERED is the default. Only one clustered index is allowed per table.
index_name	Specifies the name of the index to be created.
object	Specifies the name of the table or view to be indexed.
column_name	Specifies the column or columns that are to be indexed.
ASC ¦ DESC	Specifies the sort direction for the particular index column. ASC causes and ascending sort order and is the default. The DESC option causes the index to be created in descending order.
INCLUDE (column [,... n])	Allows a column to be added to the leaf level of an index without being part of the index key. This is a new argument.
relational_index_option	Specifies the index option to use when creating the index.

The following is a simple example using the basic syntax of the CREATE INDEX command:

```
CREATE NONCLUSTERED INDEX [nc_titles_pub_id] ON [dbo].[titles] ([pub_id] ASC
```

This example creates a nonclustered index on the titles table, based on the pub_id column. The NONCLUSTERED and ASC keywords are not necessary because they are the defaults. Because the UNIQUE keyword is not specified, duplicates are allowed in the index (that is, multiple rows in the table can have the same pub_id).

Unique indexes are more involved because they serve two roles: They provide fast access to the data via the index's columns, but they also serve as a constraint by allowing only one row to exist on a table for the combination of column values in the index. They can be clustered or nonclustered. Unique indexes are also defined on a table whenever you define a unique or primary key constraint on a table. The following example shows the creation of a clustered unique index:

```
CREATE UNIQUE NONCLUSTERED INDEX [AK_Authors_Name]
    ON [dbo].[authors] ([au_lname] , [au_fname] )
```

This creates a nonclustered index named AK_Authors_Name on the authors table. This index is based on a composite index key that includes the author's last name (au_lname) and first name (au_fname). When it is created, this index prevents authors with the same last name and first name from being inserted into the authors table.

The relational index options listed in Table 20.2 allow you to define more sophisticated indexes or specify how an index is to be created.

TABLE 20.2   Relational Index Options for CREATE INDEX

Argument	Explanation
PAD_INDEX = {ON	OFF}	Determines whether free space is allocated to tho non leaf level pages of an index. The percentage of free space is determined by FILLFACTOR.
FILLFACTOR = *fillfactor*	Determines the amount of free space left in the leaf level of each index page. The *fillfactor* values represent a percentage, from 0 to 100. The default value is 0. If *fillfactor* is 0 or 100, the index leaf-level pages are filled to capacity, leaving only enough space for at least one more row to be inserted.
SORT_IN_TEMPDB = {ON ¦ OFF}	Specifies whether intermediate sort results that are used to create the index are stored in tempdb. Using them can speed up the creation of the index (if tempdb is on a separate disk), but it requires more disk space.
IGNORE_DUP_KEY = {ON ¦ OFF}	Determines whether multi-row inserts will fail when duplicate rows in the insert violate a unique index. When this option is set to ON, duplicate key values are ignored, and the rest of the multi-row insert succeeds. When it is OFF (the default), the entire multi-row insert fails if a duplicate is encountered.
STATISTICS_NO_RECOMPUTE = {ON ¦ OFF}	Determines whether distribution statistics used by the Query Optimizer are recomputed. When ON, the statistics are not automatically recomputed.

20

TABLE 20.2   Continued

Argument	Explanation
DROP_EXISTING = {ON ¦ OFF}	Determines whether an index with the same name is dropped prior to re-creation. This can provide some performance benefits over dropping the existing index first and then creating. Clustered indexes see the most benefit.
ONLINE = {ON ¦ OFF}	Determines whether the index is built such that the underlying table is still available for queries and data modification during the index creation. This new feature is discussed in more detail in the "Online Indexing Operations" section, later in this chapter.
ALLOW_ROW_LOCKS = {ON ¦ OFF}	Determines whether row locks are allowed when accessing the index. The default for this new feature is ON.
ALLOW_PAGE_LOCKS = {ON ¦ OFF}	Determines whether page locks are allowed when accessing the index. The default for this new feature is ON.
MAXDOP = number of processors	Determines the number of processors that can be used during index operations. The default for this new feature is 0, which causes an index operation to use the actual number of processors or fewer, depending on the workload on the system. This can be a useful option for index operations on large tables that may impact performance during the operation. For example, if you have four processors, you can specify MAXDOP = 2 to limit the index operation to use only two of the four processors.

The following example creates a relatively complex index that utilizes several of the index options described in Table 20.2:

```
CREATE UNIQUE CLUSTERED INDEX [employee_ind]
  ON [dbo].[employee] ([lname], [fname], [minit])
  WITH (PAD_INDEX = ON, DROP_EXISTING = ON, IGNORE_DUP_KEY = ON, FILLFACTOR = 80)
```

This example creates a composite unique index on the employee's last name (lname), first name (fname), and middle initial (minit). It utilizes some of the commonly used options and demonstrates how multiple options can be used in a single CREATE statement.

> **TIP**
>
> SQL Server Management Studio (SSMS) has several methods for generating the T-SQL code that creates indexes. You therefore rarely need to type index CREATE statements from scratch. Instead, you can use the friendly GUI screens that enable you to specify the common index options, and then you can generate the T-SQL script that can be executed to create the index.

Additional syntax options (not listed here) relate to backward compatibility and the creation of indexes on XML columns. Refer to Chapter 37, "Using XML in SQL Server 2005," and the SQL Server Books Online documentation for further details.

Creating Indexes with SSMS

SQL Server 2005 has expanded on the means for creating indexes within SSMS. You can create indexes within SSMS via the Database Engine Tuning Advisor, database diagrams, the Table Designer, and several places within the Object Explorer. The means available from the Object Explorer are the simplest to use and are the focus of this section. The other options are discussed in more detail in related chapters of this book.

Index creation in the Object Explorer is facilitated by the New Index screen. You can launch this screen from SMSS by expanding the database tree in the Object Explorer and navigating to the Indexes node of the table that you want to add the index to. Then you right-click the Indexes node and select New Index. A screen like the one shown in Figure 20.3 is displayed.

The name and options that are populated in Figure 20.3 are based on the author index created in the previous T-SQL section. The au_lname and au_fname columns were selected and added as part of this new index by clicking the Add button, which displays a screen with all the columns in the table that are available for the index. You simply select the column(s) you want to include on the index. This populates the Index Key Columns grid on the default General page.

> **TIP**
>
> The functionality in the Add Index screen is very similar to that which was available via the Manage Indexes tool in the SQL Server 2000 Query Analyzer. The Manage Indexes tool is no longer available, but the same ease of use is still available via the Add Index screen.

You can select other options for an index by changing the Select a Page options available on the top-left side of the Add Index screen. The Options, Included Columns, Storage, and Extended Properties pages each provide a series of options that relate to the corresponding category and are utilized when creating the index.

20

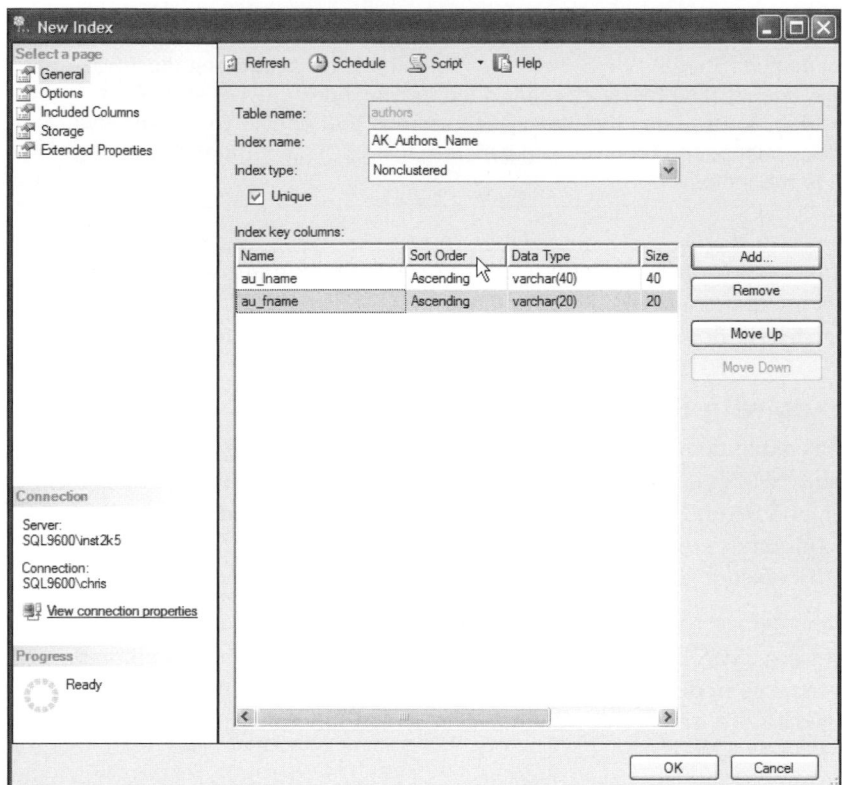

FIGURE 20.3   Using Object Explorer to create indexes.

Of particular interest is the Included Columns page. This page allows you to select columns that you want to include in the leaf-level pages of the index but don't need as part of the index key. For example, you could consider using included columns if you have a critical query that often selects last name, first name, and address from a table but uses only the last name and first name as search arguments in the WHERE clause. This may be a situation in which you would want to consider the use of a covering index that places all the referenced columns from the query into a nonclustered index. In the case of our critical query, the address column can be added to the index as an included column. It is not included in the index key, but it is available in the leaf-level pages of the index so that the additional overhead of going to the data pages to retrieve the address is not needed.

After you have selected all the options that you want for your index via the Add Index screen, you have several options for actually creating the index. You can script the index, schedule the index creation for a later time, or simply click OK to allow the Add Index screen to add the index immediately. As mentioned in an earlier tip, it is a good idea to use this Add Index screen to specify the index options, and then you can click the Script button to generate all the T-SQL statements needed to create the index. You can then save this script to a file to be used for generating a database build script or for maintaining a record of the indexes defined in a database.

Managing Indexes

There are two different aspects to index management. The first aspect is the management of indexes by the SQL Server database engine. Fortunately, the engine does a good job of managing the indexes internally so that limited manual intervention is required. This is predicated on a well-designed database system and the use of SQL Server features, such as automatic updates to distribution statistics.

The other aspect of index management typically comes into play when performance issues arise. Index adjustments and maintenance of these indexes make up the bulk of this effort.

Managing Indexes with T-SQL

One of the new features available with SQL Server 2005 is the ALTER INDEX statement. This new T-SQL statement simplifies many of the tasks associated with managing indexes. Index operations such as index rebuilds and changes to fill factor that were previously handled with DBCC commands are now available via the ALTER INDEX statement. The basic syntax for ALTER INDEX is as follows:

```
ALTER INDEX {index_name ¦ ALL}
    ON [{database_name.[schema_name]. ¦ schema_name.}]
      {table_or_view_name}
    { REBUILD [WITH(<rebuild_index_option>[,...n])]
    ¦ REORGANIZE [ WITH( LOB_COMPACTION = {ON ¦ OFF})]
    ¦ DISABLE
    ¦ SET (<set_index_option>[,...n]) }
```

Let's look at a few examples that demonstrate the power of the ALTER INDEX statement. The first example simply rebuilds the primary key index on the authors table:

```
ALTER INDEX [UPKCL_auidind] ON [dbo].[authors] REBUILD
```

This is an offline operation that is equivalent to the DBCC DBREINDEX command. The specified index is dropped and re-created, removing all fragmentation from the index pages. This is done dynamically, without the need to drop and re-create constraints that reference any of the affected indexes. If it is run on a clustered index, the data pages of the table are defragmented as well. If you specify the ALL option for the ALTER INDEX command, all indexes as well as the data pages of the table (if the table has a clustered index) are defragmented.

20

> **NOTE**
>
> If the REBUILD option is run on a heap table (that is, a table with no clustered index), the rebuild operation does not affect the underlying table. Only the specified nonclustered indexes are rebuilt.

For added flexibility, you can also specify index options as part of the REBUILD operation. The options available with the REBUILD command are the same options that are available when you are creating indexes. The only exception is that the DROP EXISTING option is not available with the REBUILD operation. (Table 20.2, earlier in this chapter, provides detailed descriptions of the options.) The following example rebuilds the clustered index on the authors table and specifies several of the available REBUILD options:

```
ALTER INDEX [UPKCL_auidind] ON [dbo].[authors]
 REBUILD WITH ( PAD_INDEX  = OFF, STATISTICS_NORECOMPUTE  = OFF,
 ALLOW_ROW_LOCKS  = ON, ALLOW_PAGE_LOCKS  = ON, SORT_IN_TEMPDB = OFF,
 ONLINE = OFF )
```

An alternative to the REBUILD operation is the REORGANIZE operation. The REORGANIZE operation is equivalent to the DBCC INDEX DEFRAG option that was available in prior versions of SQL Server. During the REORGANIZE operation, the leaf-level pages of the index are physically reordered to match the logical order of the index keys. The indexes are not dropped. The REORGANIZE operation is always an online operation and does not require long-term table locks to complete.

> **TIP**
>
> The REORGANIZE operation can generate a large number of transactions during its execution. You need to be sure to carefully evaluate the amount of space available in the transaction log and monitor the free space during this operation. If the transaction log is set to AUTOGROW, you need to make sure you have adequate free space on the drive where your transaction log lives. This is especially true for very large tables.

The REORGANIZE operation has just one option: LOB_COMPACTION. When the LOB_COMPACTION option is set to ON, the data for columns with large object (LOB) data types is compacted. This consolidates the data and frees disk space. LOB data types include image, text, ntext, varchar(max), nvarchar(max), varbinary(max), and xml. The following example performs a REORGANIZE operation on the clustered index of the authors table with the LOB_COMPACTION option set to OFF:

```
ALTER INDEX [UPKCL_auidind] ON [dbo].[authors]
REORGANIZE WITH ( LOB_COMPACTION = OFF )
```

Disabling an index is another new feature that can be accomplished with the ALTER INDEX statement. When the DISABLE option is used on an index, the index is no longer available to be used for retrieving data from a table. If a clustered index is disabled, the entire table is made unavailable. The data remains in the table, but no Data Manipulation Language (DML) operations can be performed on the table until the index is dropped or rebuilt. Unlike dropping an index, when an index is disabled, SQL Server retains the index definition in metadata so it can easily be re-enabled; index statistics are still maintained for nonclustered indexes that have been disabled.

Once an index is disabled, you can re-enable it only by re-creating the index. This can be accomplished with the ALTER INDEX REBUILD command or the CREATE INDEX WITH DROP_EXISTING command.

Disabling indexes can be particularly useful for testing purposes. Let's say you have a nonclustered index on a table that you believe is used very little. You can disable the index initially before removing it to evaluate the change. The definition of the index is still contained in the database. If you ultimately determine that the index is still needed, you can rebuild the index to make it available again.

> **TIP**
>
> Another reason for disabling a nonclustered index is to reduce the space requirements when rebuilding the index. If an index to be rebuilt is not disabled, SQL Server requires enough temporary disk space in the database to store both the old and new versions of the index. However, if the index is disabled first, SQL Server can reuse the space required for the disabled index to rebuild it. No additional disk space is necessary except for temporary space required for sorting, which is only about 20% of the index size.

The following example disables a nonclustered index on the authors table:

```
ALTER INDEX [aunmind] ON [dbo].[authors] DISABLE
```

You can also easily change options on an index with the ALTER INDEX statement. The following example sets all the available options for a nonclustered index on the authors table:

```
ALTER INDEX [aunmind] ON [dbo].[authors]
 SET (
    ALLOW_PAGE_LOCKS = ON,
    ALLOW_ROW_LOCKS = OFF,
    IGNORE_DUP_KEY = ON,
    STATISTICS_NORECOMPUTE = ON

    )
```

Other options exist for managing indexes with T-SQL, but the ALTER INDEX statement provides the bulk of what you need. Many of the other T-SQL options that you may have used for managing indexes in SQL Server 2000, such as DBCC DBREINDEX, are still available in SQL Server 2005 for backward compatibility.

20

For more information and guidelines on managing indexes for performance, such as why and when to rebuild an index, see Chapter 29.

Managing Indexes with SSMS

There are several tools available in SSMS for managing indexes. You can use tools such as the Database Engine Tuning Advisor, database diagrams, and the Table Designer to view indexes and make modifications. These tools have many features that are geared toward specific tasks, but again, the Object Explorer provides the simplest means for managing indexes.

Figure 20.4 shows the index options that are available by right-clicking an index in the Object Explorer. Many of these options are geared toward index management, including the options Rebuild, Reorganize, and Disable.

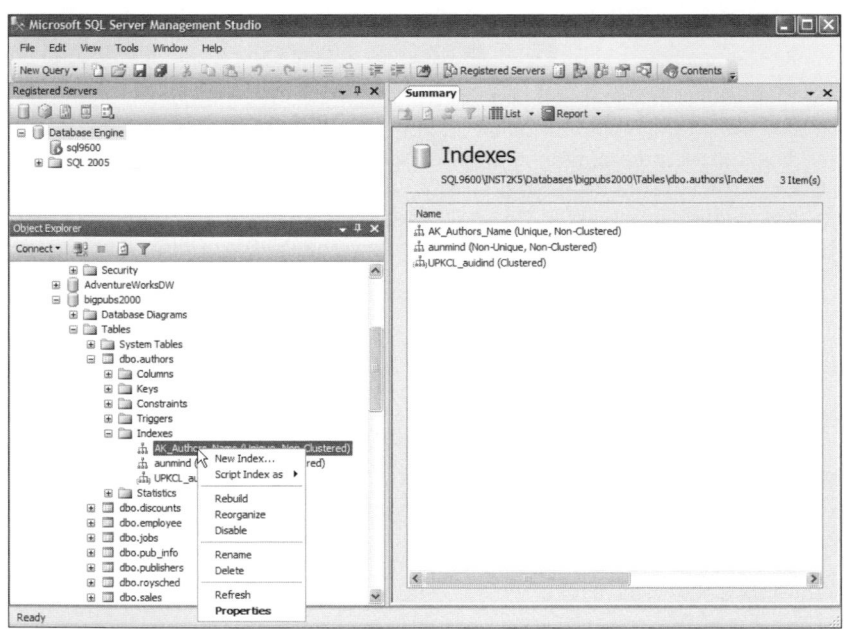

FIGURE 20.4   Using Object Explorer to manage indexes.

Similar options are also available in the Indexes node of the Object Explorer that enable you to rebuild, reorganize, or disable all the indexes for the table.

> **TIP**
>
> You can right-click an index in the Object Explorer and choose Properties to display the index columns and other relevant information. This option was not available with the SQL Server 2000 Object Explorer. You can also run the SP_HELPINDEX command on any table in a database to list all the indexes on the table and their related columns. This command must be run in a database engine query window.

Dropping Indexes

You can drop indexes by using T-SQL or via tools in the SSMS. To drop indexes with T-SQL you use the DROP INDEX command, a simple example of which follows:

```
DROP INDEX [dbo].[authors].[aunmind]
```

This command drops the index named aunmind on the authors table.

Using the Object Explorer in SSMS is the simplest alternative for dropping indexes. In the Object Explorer, you simply right-click the index you want to drop and then select Delete. The same execution options that are available for adding and modifying indexes are also available after you select Delete. This includes the option to script the T-SQL statements like that which is shown in the earlier DROP INDEX example.

Dropping indexes that are referenced by other tables requires some additional work. For example, indexes created for primary key or unique key constraints that are referenced by a foreign key can be dropped only if those references are removed first. This can get very involved when you have a table that is referenced by many foreign keys. You can identify the foreign keys that reference a table by using the sp_helpconstraint system stored procedure or a query similar to the one shown in Listing 20.2, which uses the new sys.foreign_keys view to display the foreign key constraints that reference the Person.StateProvince table in the Northwind database.

LISTING 20.2   Identifying Foreign Key References for a Table

```
select cast(object_name(parent_object_id) as varchar(20)) as TableName,
       cast(name as varchar(50)) as ForeignKey
  from sys.foreign_keys
  where referenced_object_id = objecT_id('Person.StateProvince')
go

TableName            ForeignKey
-------------------  -------------------------------------------------
SalesTaxRate         FK_SalesTaxRate_StateProvince_StateProvinceID
Address              FK_Address_StateProvince_StateProvinceID
```

Online Indexing Operations

One of the great new features available with SQL Server 2005 is online indexing. This feature allows you to create, rebuild, or drop indexes without having exclusive access to the index or table. What this means is that users can have concurrent access to the underlying tables and indexes while the index operation is in progress. This bodes well for high-availability applications and databases that have limited downtime available for offline operations.

20

The following is an example of the T-SQL syntax for an online index operation:

```
ALTER INDEX [AK_Authors_Name] ON [dbo].[authors]
   REBUILD WITH (FILLFACTOR = 80, ONLINE = ON)
```

The ONLINE = ON parameter is the key to making the index operation an online operation.

To accomplish online indexing, SQL Server must maintain the old and new versions of the affected indexes during the operation. The old version (referred to as the *source*) includes any table or indexes that are affected by the index operation. For example, if a clustered index is part of the online operation, the clustered index and all the nonclustered indexes that reference the clustered index are maintained as part of the source. The new version (referred to as the *target*) is the new index or indexes that are being created or rebuilt. In the case of a table without a clustered index, a structure known as a heap is used as the source and target.

During online index operations, the following three phases occur:

▶ **Preparation**—Concurrent activity is temporarily suspended while a snapshot of the source index structure is taken and written as an empty structure to the target.

▶ **Building**—The source index structures are scanned, sorted, merged, and inserted into the target. User SELECT statements are satisfied via the source. Insertions, updates, and deletions to the affected table are written to both the source and the target.

▶ **Final**—Concurrent activity is temporarily suspended while the source is replaced by the newly created structures (target).

When the final phase is complete, all the query and update plans that were using the old structures are invalidated. Future queries utilize the newly created index structures after this point.

When using online indexing, you need to consider the following:

▶ **Disk space**—Generally, the disk space requirements for online operations are the same as those for offline operations. The exception to this is online index operations on clustered indexes. These operations use a temporary mapping index that requires additional disk space. The temporary mapping index contains one row for each record in the table.

▶ **Performance**—Online index operations are generally slower and take more system resources than offline operations. This is primarily because the old and new index structures are maintained during the index operation. Heavy updates to the tables involved in the index operation can cause an overall decrease in performance and a spike in CPU utilization and I/O as the two index structures are maintained.

▶ **Transaction log**—Online index operations are fully logged. You may therefore encounter a heavy burden on your transaction log during online index operations for large tables. This can cause your transaction log to fill quickly. The transaction log can be backed up, but it cannot be truncated during online index operations. You need to make sure you have enough space for your log to grow, or the online index operation could fail.

Indexes on Views

SQL Server 2005 supports the creation of indexes on views. Like indexes on tables, indexes on views can dramatically improve the performance of the queries that reference the views. By nature, a view is a virtual table and does not have a separate data structure as does a table, even though it can be reference like a table. After an index is created on a view, the result set of the view is stored in the database, just as it would be for a table. The indexed view is no longer virtual because it requires maintenance as rows are added to, deleted from, or modified in the tables referenced by the view. Refer to Chapter 22, "Creating and Managing Views," for a more detailed discussion of views.

The first index that is created on a view must be a unique clustered index. After that is created, other nonclustered indexes can be built on the view for additional performance gains.

The most difficult part of the index creation process is identifying a view that is valid for index creation. Many requirements that must be met in order for a view to qualify. Refer to the SQL Server Books Online documentation for a complete list of all the restrictions. The following is a partial list of the most common requirements:

▶ All the tables in the view must be in the same database as the view and have the same owner as the view.

▶ The view must not reference any other views.

▶ The view must be created with SCHEMABINDING, and any function referenced in the view must also be created with SCHEMABINDING.

▶ A two-part name with the schema prefix must be used for every table or user-defined function referenced in the view.

▶ Many SET options, including ANSI_NULLS, ANSI_PADDING, ANSI_WARNINGS, CONCAT_NULL_YIELDS_NULL, and QUOTED_IDENTIFIER must be set to ON.

▶ Any functions referenced in the view must be deterministic. (See Chapter 24, "Creating and Managing User-Defined Functions," for more information on deterministic functions.)

▶ Views with aggregate functions must also include COUNT_BIG(*).

The following example shows the creation of a view that can have an index created on it:

```
CREATE VIEW titleview
 WITH SCHEMABINDING AS
```

20

```
select title, au_ord, au_lname, price, ytd_sales, pub_id
  from dbo.authors, dbo.titles, dbo.titleauthor
  where authors.au_id = titleauthor.au_id
    AND titles.title_id = titleauthor.title_id
```

The SCHEMABINDING clause and the database schema qualifier (dbo) for each table are necessary in the view definition in order to make the view valid for index creation. The following example creates an index on the titleview view:

```
CREATE UNIQUE CLUSTERED INDEX [AK_TitleView] ON [dbo].[titleview]
  ( [au_lname] ASC, [au_ord] ASC, [title] ASC )
```

After the index is created, you can manage it in much the same way that you manage the indexes on tables. You can use both T-SQL and SSMS to manage these indexes.

For more information and guidelines on creating and using indexed views, see Chapter 22.

Summary

Index creation is an important part of managing a database. Creating useful indexes can vastly improve query performance, but you must also consider the impact that indexes can have on disk space and other data manipulation operations, such as updates and insertions. In Chapter 21, you will see how you can use indexes to enforce data integrity. Subsequent chapters cover the internal working of indexes and give you more insight into their role in performance.

Implementing Data Integrity

IN THIS CHAPTER

▸ What's New in Data Integrity

▸ Types of Data Integrity

▸ Enforcing Data Integrity

▸ Using Constraints

▸ Rules

▸ Defaults

The value of your data is determined by its integrity. You may have heard the phrase "garbage in, garbage out." In the database world, "garbage in" refers to data that has been loaded into a database without validation or without data integrity. This "garbage" data can then be retrieved ("garbage out"), and erroneous decisions can result because of it.

Implementing good data integrity measures is your best defense against the "garbage in, garbage out" scenario. This involves identifying valid values for tables and columns and deciding how to enforce the integrity of those values. This chapter covers the different types of data integrity and the methods for enforcing them.

What's New in Data Integrity

Much of the functionality related to data integrity has remained the same in SQL Server 2005. However, there have been a few changes:

▸ **New cascading integrity constraints**—There are two new additions to the REFERENCES clause for defining a cascading referential integrity constraint. You can now specify the SET NULL and SET DEFAULT options to cause foreign key values on referencing tables to be set to NULL or set to the default value that has been defined on the foreign key column.

▸ **Bound default deprecation**—The CREATE DEFAULT statement has been slated for removal in a future version of SQL Server. For now, you can still use this statement to create a default that is bound to one or more columns. Microsoft recommends using the DEFAULT keyword with ALTER TABLE or CREATE TABLE instead.

Types of Data Integrity

How integrity is enforced depends on the type of integrity being enforced. As described in the following sections, the types of data integrity are domain, entity, and referential integrity.

Domain Integrity

Domain integrity controls the validation of values for a column. You can use domain integrity to enforce the type, format, and possible values of data stored in a column. SQL Server provides several mechanisms to enforce domain integrity:

▶ You can control the type of data stored in a column by assigning data type to the column.

▶ You can use CHECK constraints and rules to control the format of the data.

▶ You can control the range of values stored in a column by using FOREIGN KEY constraints, CHECK constraints, default definitions, nullability, and rules.

Entity Integrity

Entity integrity requires that all rows in a table be unique. You can enforce entity integrity in SQL Server by using PRIMARY KEY constraints, UNIQUE constraints, and IDENTITY properties.

Referential Integrity

Referential integrity preserves the defined relationships between tables. You can define such a relationship in SQL Server by relating foreign key columns on one table to the primary key or unique key of another table. When it is defined, referential integrity ensures that values inserted in the foreign key columns have corresponding values in the primary table. It also controls changes to the primary key table and ensures that related foreign key rows are not left orphaned.

Enforcing Data Integrity

You can enforce data integrity by using declarative or procedural methods. Implementing declarative data integrity requires little or no coding. Implementing procedural data integrity is more flexible but requires more custom coding.

Implementing Declarative Data Integrity

Declarative integrity is enforced within the database, using constraints, rules, and defaults. This is the preferred method of enforcing integrity because it has low overhead and requires little or no custom programming. It can be centrally managed in the database, and it provides a consistent approach for ensuring the integrity of data. Declarative integrity utilizes constraints, rules, and defaults, which are the primary focus of this chapter.

Implementing Procedural Data Integrity

Procedural integrity can be implemented with stored procedures, triggers, and application code. It requires custom programming that defines and enforces the integrity of the data. The biggest benefits of implementing procedural data integrity are flexibility and control. You can implement the custom code in many different ways to enforce the integrity of your data. The custom code can also be a detriment; the lack of consistency and potential inefficiencies in the way the data integrity is performed can be a real problem.

In general, declarative data integrity should be used as the primary means for control. Procedural data integrity can be used to augment declarative data integrity, if needed.

Using Constraints

Constraints—including PRIMARY KEY, FOREIGN KEY, UNIQUE, CHECK, and DEFAULT—are the primary method used to enforce data integrity. You can implement defaults as constraints or as objects in a database; for more information, see the "Defaults" section, later in this chapter.

The PRIMARY KEY Constraint

The PRIMARY KEY constraint is one of the key methods for ensuring entity integrity. When this constraint is defined on a table, it ensures that every row can be uniquely identified with the primary key value(s). The primary key can have one or more columns as part of its definition. None of the columns in the primary key definition can allow nulls. When multiple columns are used in the definition of the primary key, the combination of the values in all the primary key columns must be unique. Duplication can exist in a single column that is part of a multicolumn primary key.

There can be only one primary key defined for each table. When a primary key is defined on a table, a unique index is automatically created as well. This index contains all the columns in the primary key and ensures that the rows in this index are unique. Generally, every table in a database should have a primary key. The primary key and its associated unique index provide fast access to a database table.

Figure 21.1 shows the AdventureWorks database Employee table, which is an example of a table that has a primary key defined. The primary key in this table is EmployeeID, and it is denoted in the dialog shown in Figure 21.1 with a key symbol in the leftmost column.

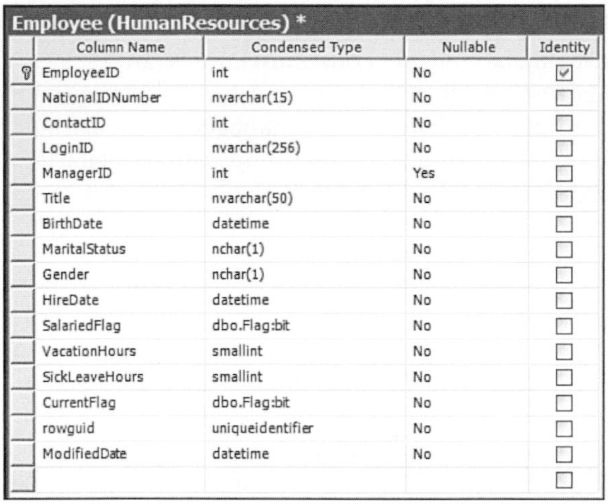

Employee (HumanResources) *			
Column Name	Condensed Type	Nullable	Identity
🔑 EmployeeID	int	No	☑
NationalIDNumber	nvarchar(15)	No	☐
ContactID	int	No	☐
LoginID	nvarchar(256)	No	☐
ManagerID	int	Yes	☐
Title	nvarchar(50)	No	☐
BirthDate	datetime	No	☐
MaritalStatus	nchar(1)	No	☐
Gender	nchar(1)	No	☐
HireDate	datetime	No	☐
SalariedFlag	dbo.Flag:bit	No	☐
VacationHours	smallint	No	☐
SickLeaveHours	smallint	No	☐
CurrentFlag	dbo.Flag:bit	No	☐
rowguid	uniqueidentifier	No	☐
ModifiedDate	datetime	No	☐
			☐

FIGURE 21.1   A primary key example.

The existing primary key on the Employee table in the AdventureWorks database can be generated as a T-SQL script as shown in the following example:

```
ALTER TABLE [HumanResources].[Employee]
   ADD  CONSTRAINT [PK_Employee_EmployeeID] PRIMARY KEY CLUSTERED
( EmployeeID ASC )
```

In general, you try to choose a primary key that is relatively short. EmployeeID, for example, is a good choice because it is an integer column and takes only 4 bytes of storage. This is particularly important when the primary key is CLUSTERED, as in the case of PK_Employee_EmployeeID. The key values from the clustered index are used by all nonclustered indexes as lookup keys. If the clustered key is large, this consumes more space and affects performance.

Surrogate keys are often good choices for primary keys. The EmployeeID column in the Employee table is an example of a surrogate key. Surrogate keys consist of a single column that automatically increments and is inherently unique, as in the case of an identity column. Surrogate keys are good candidates for primary keys because they are implicitly unique and relatively short in length. You should avoid using large, multicolumn indexes as primary keys. They can impede performance because fewer index rows can be stored on each index page. The performance implications related to primary key indexes and other indexes are discussed in more detail in Chapter 29, "Indexes and Performance."

NOTE

Over the years, there has been much debate over the use of surrogate keys for primary keys. One school of thought is to avoid surrogate keys because insertions always occur at the end of the primary key index and are not distributed. This can lead to "hot spots" in the index because the insert activity is always on the last page of the index. In addition, surrogate keys have no real meaning and are less intuitive than primary keys that have meaning, such as `lastname` and `firstname`.

The other school of thought, in favor of using surrogate keys for primary keys, emphasizes the importance of defining primary keys that are not based on meaningful columns. If meaningful columns are used and the definitions of those columns change, this can have a significant impact on the table that contains the primary key and any tables related to it. Those in favor of using surrogate keys as primary keys also focus on the relatively small key size, which is good for performance and reduces pages splits because the values are always inserted into the index sequentially.

The UNIQUE Constraint

The UNIQUE constraint is functionally similar to PRIMARY KEY. It also uses a unique index to enforce uniqueness, but unlike PRIMARY KEY, it allows nulls in the columns that participate in the UNIQUE constraint. The definition of a UNIQUE constraint with columns that are nulls is generally impractical. The value of NULL is considered a unique value, so you are limited to the number of rows that can be inserted with NULL values. For example, only one row with a NULL value in the constraint column can be inserted if the UNIQUE constraint is based on a single column. UNIQUE constraints with multiple nullable columns can have more than one row with null values in the constraint keys, but the number of rows is limited to the combination of unique values across all the columns.

You generally use a UNIQUE constraint when a column other than the primary key must be guaranteed to be unique. For example, consider the Employee table example used in the previous section. The primary key on the identity column EmployeeID ensures that a unique value will be assigned to each employee row, but it does not prevent duplication in any of the other columns. For example, every row in the Employee table could have the same LoginID setting if no other UNIQUE constraints were found on this table. Generally, each employee should have his or her own unique LoginID. You can enforce this policy by adding a UNIQUE constraint on the LoginID column. The following example demonstrates the creation of a UNIQUE constraint on the EmployeeID column:

```
ALTER TABLE [HumanResources].[Employee]
 ADD CONSTRAINT AK_Employee_LoginID
  UNIQUE NONCLUSTERED (LoginID ASC)
```

As with PRIMARY KEY constraints, a unique index is created whenever a UNIQUE constraint is created. If you drop the UNIQUE constraint, you drop the unique index as well. Conversely, if you drop the unique index, you indirectly drop the UNIQUE constraint, too. You can implement a UNIQUE constraint as a constraint or an index. To illustrate this, the following example shows the creation of the same UNIQUE constraint on Employee_LoginID as before, this time using an index:

```
CREATE UNIQUE NONCLUSTERED INDEX [AK_Employee_LoginID]
 ON [HumanResources].[Employee]
(LoginID ASC)
```

> **NOTE**
>
> Although `UNIQUE` constraints and unique indexes achieve the same goal, they must be managed based on how they were created. In other words, if you create a `UNIQUE` constraint on a table, you cannot directly drop the associated unique index. If you try to drop the unique index directly, you get a message stating that an explicit `DROP INDEX` is not allowed and that it is being used for unique key constraint enforcement. To drop the `UNIQUE` constraint, you must use the `DROP CONSTRAINT` syntax associated with the `ALTER TABLE` statement. Similarly, if you create a unique index, you cannot drop that index by using a `DROP CONSTRAINT` statement; you must use `DROP INDEX` instead.

You can have more than one unique constraint per table. When creating unique constraints, you have all the standard index-creation options available. These options include how the underlying index is clustered, the fill factor, and a myriad of other index options.

The `FOREIGN KEY` **Referential Integrity Constraint**

The basic premise of a relational database is that tables are related. These relationships are maintained and enforced via referential integrity. `FOREIGN KEY` constraints are the declarative means for enforcing referential integrity in SQL Server. You implement `FOREIGN KEY` constraints by relating one or more columns in a table to the columns in a primary key or unique index. The columns in the referencing table can be referred to as *foreign key columns*. The table with the primary key or unique index can be referred to as the *primary table*. Figure 21.2 shows a relationship between the `Employee` table and the `JobCandidate` table. The foreign key in this example is `EmployeeID` on the `JobCandidate` table. `EmployeeID` on this table is related to the primary key on the `Employee` table. The foreign key relationship in this diagram is denoted by the line between these two tables.

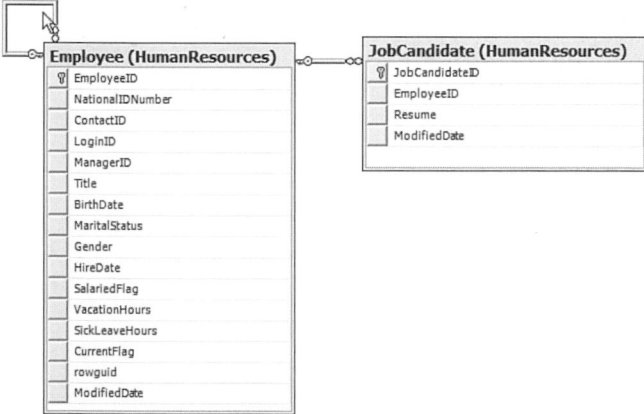

FIGURE 21.2   A foreign key constraint on the `JobCandidate` table.

Once defined, a foreign key, by default, enforces the relationship between the tables in the following ways:

- ▶ Values in the foreign key columns must have a corresponding value in the primary table. If the new values in the foreign key columns do not exist in the primary table, the insert or update operation fails.

- ▶ Values in the primary key or unique index that are referenced by the foreign key table cannot be deleted. If an attempt is made to delete a referenced value in the primary table, the delete fails.

- ▶ Values in the primary key or unique index that are referenced by the foreign key table cannot be modified. If an attempt is made to change a referenced value in the primary table, the update fails.

In the case of the Employee/JobCandidate relationship shown in Figure 21.2, any EmployeeID used in the JobCandidate table must have a corresponding value in the Employee table. Listing 21.1 shows an INSERT statement in the JobCandidate table that does not have a valid EmployeeID entry in the Employee table. The statement fails, and the resulting message is shown after the INSERT statement. A similar error message is displayed if an attempt is made to delete or update values in the primary key or unique index.

LISTING 21.1   A Foreign Key Conflict with INSERT

```
INSERT HumanResources.JobCandidate
 (EmployeeID, Resume, ModifiedDate)
 VALUES (-1,NULL,GETDATE())

/* RESULTS OF INSERT FOLLOW
Msg 547, Level 16, State 0, Line 1
The INSERT statement conflicted with the FOREIGN KEY
constraint "FK_JobCandidate_Employee_EmployeeID".
The conflict occurred in database "AdventureWorks",
table "Employee", column 'EmployeeID'.
The statement has been terminated.
*/
```

The following example shows the T-SQL needed to create the foreign key relationship between the Employee and JobCandidate tables:

```
ALTER TABLE [HumanResources].[JobCandidate]
 ADD  CONSTRAINT [FK_JobCandidate_Employee_EmployeeID]
  FOREIGN KEY(    [EmployeeID])
 REFERENCES [HumanResources].[Employee] ([EmployeeID])
```

When you create a FOREIGN KEY constraint, the related primary key or unique index must exist first. In the case of the Employee/JobCandidate relationship, the Employee table and the primary key on EmployeeID must exist before you can create the FK_JobCandidate_Employee_EmployeeID foreign key. In addition, the data types of the related columns must be the same. The related columns in the two tables can actually have different names, but in practice the columns are usually named the same. Naming the columns the same makes your database much more intuitive.

> **NOTE**
>
> In addition to relating two different tables with a foreign key, you can also relate a table to itself. An example of this self-referencing relationship can be found in the AdventureWorks database, in the Employee table. In this case, ManagerID on the Employee table has a relationship to the primary key index on EmployeeID. The manager is an employee, so it makes sense that he should have a valid EmployeeID. The FK_Employee_Employee_ManagerID foreign key on the Employee table enforces this relationship.

Cascading Referential Integrity

Cascading referential integrity was introduced with SQL Server 2000. This type of integrity allows for updates and deletions on the primary table to be cascaded to the referencing foreign key tables. By default, a FOREIGN KEY constraint prevents updates and deletions to any primary key or unique index values that are referenced by a foreign key. With cascading referential integrity, you can bypass this restriction and are able to define the type of action you want to occur when the updates and deletions happen.

You define the cascading actions on the FOREIGN KEY constraint, using the ON DELETE and ON UPDATE clauses. The ON DELETE clause defines the cascading action for deletions to the primary table, and the ON UPDATE clause defines the actions for updates. These clauses are used with the CREATE TABLE or ALTER TABLE statements and are part of the REFERENCES clause of these statements.

You can specify the same cascading actions for updates and deletions:

- **NO ACTION**—This is the default action. It causes deletions and updates to the primary table to fail if the rows are referenced by a foreign key.

- **CASCADE**—This option causes updates and deletions to cascade to any foreign key records that refer to the affected rows in the primary table. If the CASCADE option is used with the ON DELETE clause, then any records in the foreign key table that refer to the deleted rows in the primary table are also deleted. When CASCADE is used with the ON UPDATE clause, any updates to the primary table records are also made in the related rows of the foreign key table.

- **SET NULL**—This option is new in SQL Server 2005. It is similar to the CASCADE option except that the affected rows in the foreign key table are set to NULL when deletions or updates are performed on the related primary table. The value of NULL is assigned

21

to every column that is defined as part of the foreign key and requires that each column in the foreign key allow null values.

▶ **SET DEFAULT**—This option is new in SQL Server 2005. It is similar to the CASCADE option except that the affected rows in the foreign key table are set to the default values defined on the columns when deletions or updates are performed on the related primary table. In order to set this option, each column in the foreign key must have a default definition assigned to it, or it must be defined as nullable. If no default definition is assigned to the column, NULL is used as the default value. It is imperative that the primary table have related records for the default or null entries that can result from the cascading action. For example, if you have a two-column foreign key, and each column has a default of 1, a corresponding record with the key values of 1 and 1 needs to exist in the primary table, or the cascade action fails. The integrity of the relationship must be maintained.

To illustrate the power of cascading actions, consider the Employee/JobCandidate relationship used in previous examples. Let's say you want to remove the associated JobCandidate records when an Employee record is deleted. The addition of the ON DELETE CASCADE clause at the bottom of the following foreign key definition achieves this result:

```
ALTER TABLE [HumanResources].[JobCandidate]
 ADD  CONSTRAINT [FK_JobCandidate_Employee_EmployeeID]
FOREIGN KEY([EmployeeID])
REFERENCES [HumanResources].[Employee] ([EmployeeID])
ON DELETE CASCADE
```

Keep in mind that other factors affect the successful execution of a cascading deletion. If other foreign keys exist on the table, and they do not have ON DELETE CASCADE specified, the cascading actions do not succeed if a foreign key violation occurs on these tables. In addition, you need to consider the existence of triggers. In the case of the Employee table, a delete trigger prevents deletions from occurring. Also, you need to consider that a series of cascading actions can be initiated by a single DELETE statement. This happens when you have many related tables that each have cascading actions defined. This works fine as long as there are no circular references that cause one of the tables in the cascading tree to be affected by a table lower in the tree.

If you want to specify the cascading action for updates, you can add an additional ON UPDATE clause, along with the ON DELETE clause. For example, you can change the foreign key in the previous example so that JobCandidate records are set to NULL when an update is made to the related key on the primary table. This can be accomplished with the following foreign key definition:

```
ALTER TABLE [HumanResources].[JobCandidate]
 ADD  CONSTRAINT [FK_JobCandidate_Employee_EmployeeID]
  FOREIGN KEY([EmployeeID])
 REFERENCES [HumanResources].[Employee] ([EmployeeID])
 ON DELETE CASCADE
 ON UPDATE SET NULL
```

NOTE

There is one catch in the previous example. The foreign key can be defined as shown with the `ON UPDATE` clause without error, but updates to the `EmployeeID` column on the `Employee` table can then never happen. The reason updates can never happen is that the `EmployeeID` column is defined as an identity column. Direct updates to identity columns are not allowed, so the update cascading action can never be used.

You can see that cascading referential integrity is a powerful tool. However, it must be used with caution. Consider the fact that foreign keys without cascading actions may prevent erroneous actions. For example, if a `DELETE` statement is mistakenly executed against the entire `Employee` table, the deletion would fail before the records could be deleted because foreign key tables are referencing the `Employee` table. This failure would be a good thing. If, however, the `ON DELETE CASCADE` clause were used in the foreign key definitions, the erroneous deletion would succeed, and all the foreign key records would be deleted as well.

The CHECK Constraint

You can use the `CHECK` constraint to enforce domain integrity and to provide a means for restricting the values that can be entered in a column. A `CHECK` constraint is implemented as a Boolean expression, and it must not be `FALSE` if the insertion or update is to proceed. The Boolean expression can reference other columns in the same table, but it cannot reference other tables. Foreign keys and triggers can be used to reference columns in other tables, if needed. The expression can also include functions that do not return results. A `CHECK` constraint that is defined on a specific column can only reference the values in the column.

`CHECK` constraints are good for ensuring the format of data inserted in a column and for defining a list of acceptable values. Columns with phone numbers or Social Security numbers are good candidates for `CHECK` constraints that enforce formatting restrictions. Columns that have the data types `money` or `integer` can use `CHECK` constraints to ensure that the values are always greater than or equal to zero. A column that has a small fixed number of valid values is also a good candidate for a `CHECK` constraint. A fixed number of values can be defined in the `CHECK` constraint, and no additional table lookup or coding is necessary to ensure that the valid values are inserted. The following example shows a `CHECK` constraint on the `Employee` table that checks the values for the `Gender` column:

```
ALTER TABLE [HumanResources].[Employee]  WITH CHECK
 ADD  CONSTRAINT [CK_Employee_Gender]
 CHECK  ((upper([Gender])='F' OR upper([Gender])='M'))
```

The `CHECK` constraint in this example ensures that only `F` or `M` is inserted in this column. These types of `CHECK` constraints are relatively fast and are preferred over `FOREIGN KEY` constraints when the values are fixed.

> **NOTE**
>
> Be careful with CHECK constraint expressions that can evaluate to NULL. CHECK constraints allow insertions and updates to the table to proceed when the CHECK constraint expression does not evaluate to FALSE. A NULL value is considered to be unknown and does not evaluate to FALSE, so the insertion or update succeeds. For example, if you have a nullable column that has a constraint specifying that the value must be greater than or equal to zero, this constraint will not prevent a NULL value from being inserted into the column.

Keep in mind that the creation of a CHECK constraint on a table that already has data in it may fail. This is due to a validation that is performed when the constraint is created. If existing data violates the constraint, the constraint is not created. The only exception is to create the constraint by using the NOCHECK option. When this option is used, the existing data is not checked, but any future updates or insertions are. The following example shows the creation of a CHECK constraint on the Employee table:

```
ALTER TABLE [HumanResources].[Employee]  WITH NOCHECK
ADD  CONSTRAINT [CK_Employee_Gender_F]
CHECK  ((upper([Gender])='F'))
```

The constraint is on the Gender column that already has a check constraint on it, which ensures that the data values are only F or M. The new constraint on the Gender column specifies that the value must be F. The existing data has values of F and M, but the NOCHECK option allows you to add the constraint anyway.

Any new rows added to the Employee table after the new CK_Employee_Gender_F CHECK constraint has been added are then checked. With multiple CHECK constraints defined on a column, the constraints are evaluated in the order in which they were added to the table. In the preceding example, the CK_Employee_Gender constraint is evaluated first, and then the new CK_Employee_Gender_F constraint is evaluated. If a Gender value of F is entered, both constraints evaluate to TRUE, and the change is accepted. If a value of M is inserted in the Gender column, the CK_Employee_Gender constraint succeeds, but the CK_Employee_Gender_F constraint fails, and the change is rejected.

Creating Constraints

You can define constraints on a single column or on multiple columns. Single-column constraints are referred to as *column-level* constraints. You can define this type of constraint when you create the column on the table. Constraints that reference multiple columns must be defined on the table and are considered *table-level* constraints. Table-level constraints must be defined after all the referenced columns in the table are created.

Using T-SQL to Create Constraints

You can create constraints with T-SQL by using the CREATE TABLE statement or the ALTER TABLE statement. When you create a column-level constraint by using the CREATE TABLE statement, the CONSTRAINT keyword and the constraint definition are included immediately after the column definition. Table-level constraints that are defined with the CREATE TABLE statement are specified after the column list in the table definition.

The Customer table in the AdventureWorks database is a good example of a table that has several different types of constraints. Listing 21.2 shows the CREATE TABLE command, along with the constraint definitions for a table named Customer2 that is modeled after the Customer table. All the constraints in this example have been included in the CREATE TABLE statement. The constraints on this table include a PRIMARY KEY constraint, a FOREIGN KEY constraint, and a CHECK constraint. You can find all the constraints in the CREATE TABLE statement by looking for the CONSTRAINT keyword.

LISTING 21.2   Creating Constraints by Using a CREATE TABLE Statement

```
CREATE TABLE [Sales].[Customer2](
    [CustomerID] [int] IDENTITY(1,1) NOT FOR REPLICATION NOT NULL,
    [TerritoryID] [int] NULL,
    [AccountNumber]  AS
      (isnull('AW'+[dbo].[ufnLeadingZeros]([CustomerID]),'')),
    [CustomerType] [nchar](1) NOT NULL
       CONSTRAINT CK_Customer_CustomerType2 CHECK
       ((upper([CustomerType])='I' OR upper([CustomerType])='S')),
    [rowguid] [uniqueidentifier] ROWGUIDCOL  NOT NULL
       CONSTRAINT [DF_Customer_rowguid2]  DEFAULT (newid()),
    [ModifiedDate] [datetime] NOT NULL
       CONSTRAINT [DF_Customer_ModifiedDate2]  DEFAULT (getdate()),
 CONSTRAINT [PK_Customer_CustomerID2] PRIMARY KEY CLUSTERED
    ([CustomerID] ASC),
 CONSTRAINT FK_Customer_SalesTerritory_TerritoryID2 FOREIGN KEY
    ([TerritoryID])
    REFERENCES [Sales].[SalesTerritory] ([TerritoryID])
)
GO
```

Generally, it is easier to manage constraints by using the ALTER TABLE statement than by integrating them into the CREATE TABLE statement. One of the biggest reasons is that the scripting capability in SQL Server Management Studio (SSMS) generates ALTER TABLE statements for many of the constraints. You can easily script a table and its constraints by using SSMS, and you will find that SSMS uses the ALTER TABLE statement extensively. Listing 21.3 includes a statement to remove the Customer2 table and a subsequent set of statements that re-creates the Customer2 table and utilizes the ALTER TABLE statement to create several of the constraints. The statements to re-create the Customer2 table were generated using the Object Explorer in SSMS. You will see that some of the constraints are created within the initial CREATE TABLE statement, and some are created with the ALTER TABLE statement.

LISTING 21.3   Creating Constraints by Using ALTER TABLE

```
IF  EXISTS (SELECT * FROM dbo.sysobjects WHERE id
   = OBJECT_ID(N'[Sales].[Customer2]') AND OBJECTPROPERTY(id, N'IsUserTable') = 1)
 DROP TABLE [Sales].[Customer2]
go

CREATE TABLE [Sales].[Customer2](
   [CustomerID] [int] IDENTITY(1,1) NOT FOR REPLICATION NOT NULL,
   [TerritoryID] [int] NULL,
   [AccountNumber]  AS (isnull('AW'+[dbo].[ufnLeadingZeros]([CustomerID]),'')),
   [CustomerType] [nchar](1) COLLATE SQL_Latin1_General_CP1_CI_AS NOT NULL,
   [rowguid] [uniqueidentifier] ROWGUIDCOL  NOT NULL
    CONSTRAINT [DF_Customer_rowguid2]  DEFAULT (newid()),
   [ModifiedDate] [datetime] NOT NULL
    CONSTRAINT [DF_Customer_ModifiedDate2]  DEFAULT (getdate()),
 CONSTRAINT [PK_Customer_CustomerID2] PRIMARY KEY CLUSTERED
(
   [CustomerID] ASC
) ON [PRIMARY]
) ON [PRIMARY]

GO
ALTER TABLE [Sales].[Customer2]  WITH CHECK
 ADD  CONSTRAINT [FK_Customer_SalesTerritory_TerritoryID2]
  FOREIGN KEY(   [TerritoryID])
   REFERENCES [Sales].[SalesTerritory] (   [TerritoryID])
GO
ALTER TABLE [Sales].[Customer2]  WITH CHECK
 ADD  CONSTRAINT [CK_Customer_CustomerType2]
  CHECK  ((upper([CustomerType])='I' OR upper([CustomerType])='S'))
```

Using SSMS to Create Constraints

Most of the examples used so far in this chapter use T-SQL to demonstrate constraints. SSMS simplifies the administration of constraints by providing a user-friendly interface that allows you to view and manage constraints. The visual tools available for managing constraints in SSMS include the Object Explorer, the Database Diagram Editor, and the Table Designer.

Figure 21.3 shows the Object Explorer with the Constraints node expanded for the Employee table and the New Constraint option selected. The Constraints node contains the CHECK and DEFAULT constraints for the table. Notice in the Object Explorer that some of the constraints (PRIMARY KEY, UNIQUE and FOREIGN KEY) are actually contained under the Keys node.

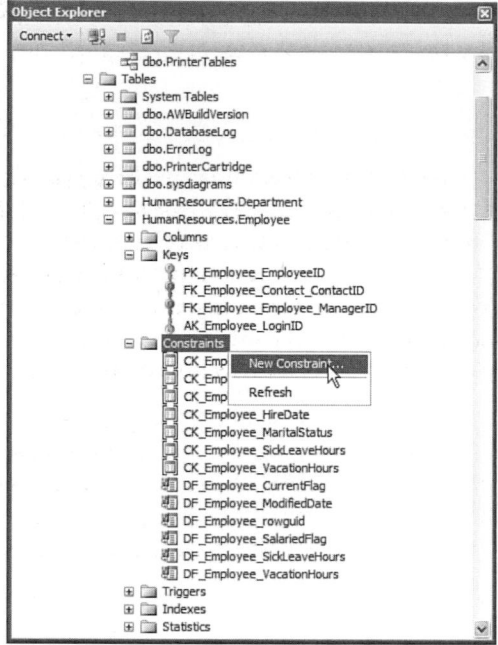

FIGURE 21.3   Constraints in Object Explorer.

When you select the New Constraint option from the Object Explorer, the Check Constraint dialog, shown in Figure 21.4, appears. This dialog gives you the option to define a new CHECK constraint on the table selected. You simply fill in a valid expression for the constraint, give it a unique name, and select the options you want.

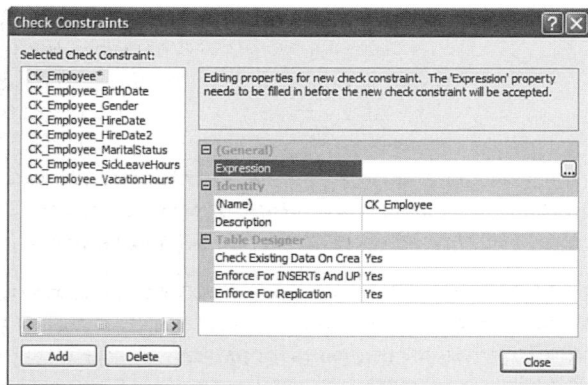

FIGURE 21.4   A new CHECK constraint in Object Explorer.

Similarly, you can right-click the Keys node and select New Foreign Key to add a new FOREIGN KEY constraint. Figure 21.5 shows the Foreign Key Relationships dialog that is displayed after selecting New Foreign Key. You click the ellipsis to the right of Tables and Columns Specification, and you can select the primary key table you want the foreign key to relate to. Finally, you select the desired options, and you are ready to add your new FOREIGN KEY constraint.

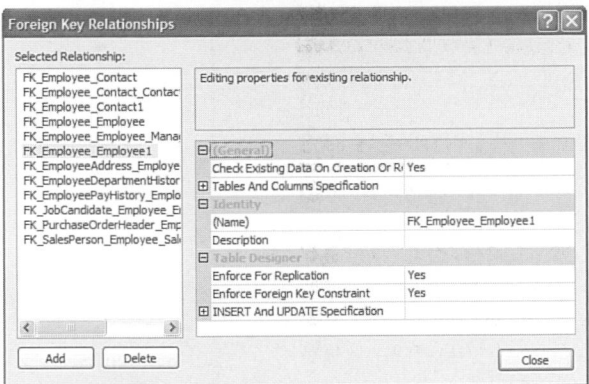

FIGURE 21.5   A new FOREIGN KEY constraint in Object Explorer.

TIP

When you use the Object Explorer to add or modify constraints, two windows are important to this process. The first window is the Constraint window, which allows you to input the constraint information. The Table Designer window that displays the column properties for the table is the other window that is important to the change process. It is launched in the background, and you can view it on the tabbed display of SSMS. When you make changes using the Constraint window, those changes are not applied via SSMS until the Table Designer window is closed. This may cause some confusion because even though you close your Constraint window with your changes, those changes may not be reflected in the database. You must close the Table Designer window in order to actually make the changes to the table. When you close the Table Designer window, a prompt appears, asking whether you want to save the changes to the table. If you click Yes, your constraint changes are applied to the database. If you click No, none of the constraint changes you have made are applied. You can also use the Table Designer menu to script out the related changes and apply them manually via a database engine query window.

The Database Diagram Editor is another great visual tool for adding constraints. This tool is particularly useful for viewing and adding foreign key relationships to tables. Take, for example, the database diagram shown in Figure 21.6. This diagram shows the Employee and JobCandidate tables and the relationships that exist between them. To add a new relationship, you right-click the table you want to add the foreign key to and select the Relationships option. After you fill in the appropriate information for the relationship, you can generate a change script by using the Table Designer menu, or you can simply close the database diagram window and respond to the prompt to save changes. You can also see options to add other constraints, such as CHECK constraints, by right-clicking the table in the database diagram and selecting the desired option.

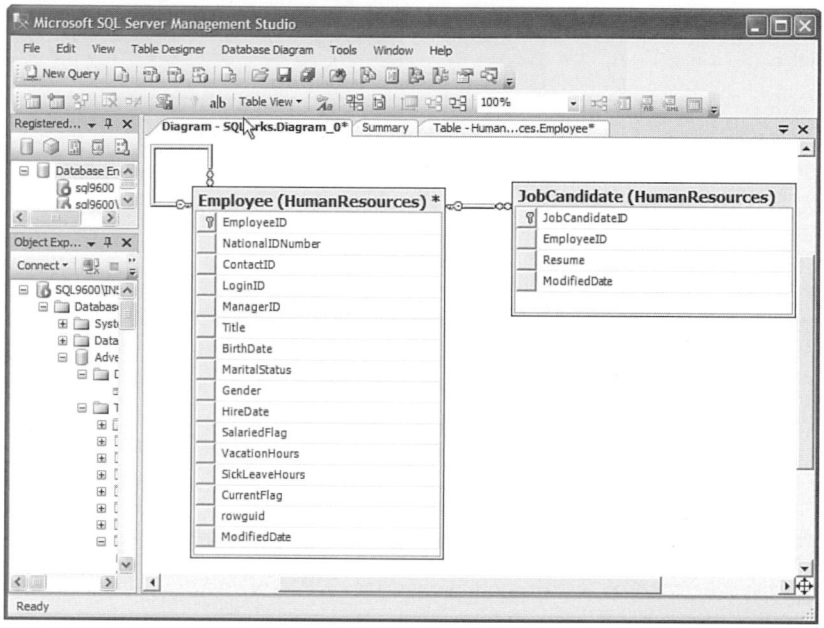

FIGURE 21.6   Adding constraints by using a database diagram.

You can launch windows for adding constraints from the Table Designer menu. To enable the Table Designer menu, you right-click the table you want to add constraints to and select the Modify option. The table and column properties are displayed, and the Table Designer menu is enabled. The Table Designer menu includes options to manage relationships, indexes/keys, and CHECK constraints.

> **TIP**
>
> It is a good idea to generate a script to implement changes that are made using SSMS visual tools. You can review the script for accuracy, run it at a later time, and save it in a file to keep track of the changes. You can also apply the saved script to other environments, if needed.

Managing Constraints

Managing constraints consists of gathering information about constraints, disabling and re-enabling constraints, and dropping constraints. These actions are discussed in the following sections.

Gathering Constraint Information

You can obtain information about constraints by using the visual tools, system stored procedures, and information_schema views. The visual tools (including the Object Explorer, Table Designer, and database diagrams) are introduced in the previous section. These tools offer a simple, user-friendly means for obtaining information related to constraints. These tools allow you to view a table's constraints and display the relative information.

The sp_help and sp_helpconstraint system stored procedures are another good source of information about constraints. Like the visual tools, these procedures allow you to gather constraint information about a specific table. The sp_helpconstraint procedure provides the most concise information related to constraints. Figure 21.7 shows the sp_helpconstraint output for the Sales.Customer table. You need to make sure to enclose the table name in brackets, as shown here, when the schema name is included. The output from sp_helpconstraint includes all the constraints for the table, and it supplies a list of tables that have foreign key references to the table.

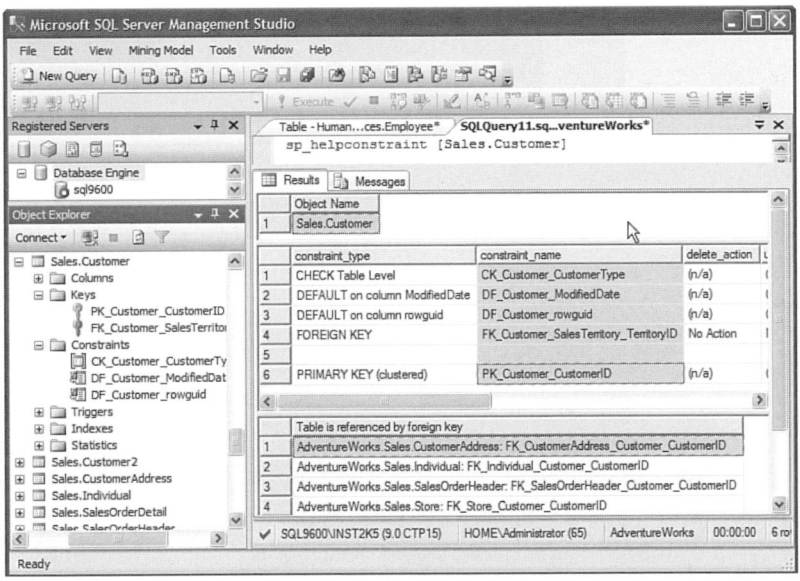

FIGURE 21.7   Executing sp_helpconstraint on the Customer table.

Keep in mind that the sp_helpconstraint system stored procedure is slated to be removed in a future version of SQL Server. SQL Server Books Online recommends using the sys.key_constraints, sys.check_constraints, and sys.default_constraints catalog views instead. These catalog views allow you to obtain constraint information for more than one table at a time. They are very flexible and allow you to customize the type of data you want to return simply by adjusting the selection criterion.

Listing 21.4 shows a sample SELECT statement for each of the catalog views related to constraints and the resulting output. The SELECT statements in this example have a WHERE clause in them that limits the results to the Customer table, but you can remove this clause to retrieve constraints for all the tables.

LISTING 21.4   Using Catalog Views to Display Constraint Information

```
select LEFT(name,30) NAME, type from sys.key_constraints
    where object_name(parent_object_id) = 'Customer'
    order by 1

select LEFT(name,30) NAME, type from sys.check_constraints
    where object_name(parent_object_id) = 'Customer'
    order by 1

select LEFT(name,30) NAME, type from sys.default_constraints
    where object_name(parent_object_id) = 'Customer'
    order by 1

/* Results of the previous SELECT statements
NAME                            type
------------------------------- ----
PK_Customer_CustomerID          PK

(1 row(s) affected)

NAME                            type
------------------------------- ----
CK_Customer_CustomerType        C

(1 row(s) affected)

NAME                            type
------------------------------- ----
DF_Customer_ModifiedDate        D
DF_Customer_rowguid             D

(2 row(s) affected)
*/
```

Dropping Constraints

You can drop constraints by using the visual tools or by using T-SQL. You can right-click a constraint in the Object Explorer and select the Delete option to drop that constraint. The Object Explorer also offers a script option that generates the T-SQL statements used to drop the constraint. The ALTER TABLE command is the T-SQL command you use to make

the change. For example, to drop the CK_Customer_CustomerType constraint on the
Customer table, you can use the following command:

```
ALTER TABLE [Sales].[Customer]
DROP CONSTRAINT [CK_Customer_CustomerType]
```

You should use caution when dropping constraints because some constraints affect other
tables. For example, if you drop the PRIMARY KEY constraint on a table and that table is
referenced by foreign keys, the drop statement fails.

Disabling Constraints

You can disable CHECK and FOREIGN KEY constraints by using the NOCHECK clause. This
allows you to stop the constraints from being checked without removing the constraints
from your database. The following example shows the ALTER TABLE command that you
can use to disable the FK_Customer_SalesTerritory_TerritoryID foreign key constraint
on the Customer table:

```
ALTER TABLE Sales.Customer
    NOCHECK CONSTRAINT FK_Customer_SalesTerritory_TerritoryID
```

When the constraint is disabled, it no longer performs validation. You should disable
constraints with caution because the integrity of your data can be compromised. In the
previous example, for example, disabling the FOREIGN KEY constraint would allow an
invalid TerritoryID to be inserted in the Customer table.

Why would you disable constraints? One possible reason would be to disable the
constraints during large data loads. The execution of constraints can slow the load
process. To facilitate the fastest load speed, you can disable constraints and then reenable
them when the data load is complete. To reenable a constraint, you use the CHECK
keyword in the ALTER TABLE statement. The following example reenables the FOREIGN KEY
constraint for the Customer table:

```
ALTER TABLE Sales.Customer
    CHECK CONSTRAINT FK_Customer_SalesTerritory_TerritoryID
```

Rules

You can use rules as another method to enforce domain integrity. Rules are similar to
CHECK constraints but have some limitations. The biggest advantage when using a rule is
that one rule can be bound to multiple columns or user-defined data types. This can be
useful for columns that contain the same type of data and are found in multiple tables in
a database. The syntax for creating a rule is as follows:

```
CREATE RULE [ schema_name . ] rule_name
AS condition_expression
[ ; ]
```

condition_expression can include any statement that can be placed in a WHERE clause. It includes one variable that is preceded with the @ symbol. This variable contains the value of the bound column that is supplied with the INSERT or UPDATE statement. The name of the variable is not important, but the conditions and formatting within the expression are. Only one variable can be referenced per rule. The following example illustrates the creation of a rule that could be used to enforce the format of data inserted in phone number columns:

```
CREATE RULE phone_rule AS
@phone LIKE '([0-9][0-9][0-9]) [0-9][0-9][0-9]-[0-9][0-9][0-9][0-9]'
```

The variable in the condition expression is @phone, and it contains the inserted or updated value for any column that the rule is bound to. The following example binds the phone_rule rule to the phone column in the person.contact table:

```
sp_bindrule phone_rule, 'person.contact.phone'
```

When a rule is bound to a column, any future insertions or updates to data in the bound column are constrained by the rule. Existing data is not affected at the time the rule is bound to the column. For example, many different phone number formats in the person.contact table do not conform to phone_rule, but phone_rule can be bound to this table successfully. To illustrate this point, the following UPDATE statement can be run against the person.contact table after the phone_rule rule is bound to the phone column:

```
update person.contact
  set phone = phone
```

The preceding update sets the phone value to itself, but this causes phone_rule to execute. The following error message is displayed after the update is run because the existing data in the person.contact table violates the phone_rule rule:

```
Msg 513, Level 16, State 0, Line 2
A column insert or update conflicts with a rule imposed
by a previous CREATE RULE statement.
The statement was terminated.
The conflict occurred in database 'AdventureWorks',
table 'Contact', column 'Phone'.
The statement has been terminated.
```

Although rules are powerful objects, Microsoft has slated them for removal in a future version of SQL Server. Microsoft recommends using CHECK constraints on each column instead of rules. CHECK constraints provide more flexibility and a consistent approach, and multiple CHECK constraints can be applied to a single column.

Defaults

A default provides a value for a column when a value is not supplied. Defaults can be anything that evaluates to a constant, such as a constant, a built-in function, or a mathematical expression. Defaults are of two types: declarative and bound. The two types are functionally the same; the difference is in how they are implemented.

Declarative Defaults

A *declarative default* is a constraint that is defined as part of the table definition. Using declarative defaults is the preferred method for assigning default values to columns. You can use the CREATE TABLE or ALTER TABLE statement to create a default and assign it to a column. Declarative defaults are assigned to a single column and cannot be reused for other columns in the database. The following example shows the creation of a default on the CustomerType column in the Customer table:

```
ALTER TABLE Sales.Customer ADD CONSTRAINT
    DF_Customer_CustomerType DEFAULT 'I' FOR CustomerType
```

It is important to remember that a default constraint only stores the default value when a value is not provided during the insertion of a row into the table. The creation of a default constraint does not affect the existing data in the table. UPDATE statements do not utilize the values specified in the default constraint, either, unless the DEFAULT keyword is explicitly referenced; this is discussed later in this chapter, in the section "When a Default Is Applied." Generally, the only time a default comes into play is when the row is initially inserted. The following example shows an INSERT statement that causes the default value defined in the DF_Customer_CustomerType constraint to be used:

```
INSERT Sales.Customer
 (TerritoryID)
 SELECT TOP 1 TerritoryID from Sales.SalesTerritory

select CustomerID, CustomerType from Sales.Customer
 where CustomerID = @@identity

/*Results from previous select statement
CustomerID  CustomerType
----------- -----------
29484       I
*/
```

The Sales.Customer table in the AdventureWorks database is an interesting table because most of the columns have defaults defined or are identity columns. This table has six columns, but only one value is supplied in the previous example. The rest of the columns, including the CustomerType column, have default definitions that automatically populate the values upon insertion.

One common misconception with defaults is that a default value is stored when a NULL value is supplied for a column on insertion. However, NULL is considered a value, so the default value is not used in this situation. This is demonstrated in the following example, where the CustomerType column is altered to accept NULLs and then a NULL value is specified in the INSERT statement:

```
ALTER TABLE Sales.Customer
 ALTER COLUMN CustomerType nchar(1) null

INSERT Sales.Customer
 (TerritoryID, CustomerType)
 SELECT TOP 1 TerritoryID, null
  from Sales.SalesTerritory
```

The insertion in this example succeeds, and the Null value is stored in the CustomerType column that has a default defined on it.

To remove a declarative default constraint, you use ALTER TABLE with the DROP CONSTRAINT clause. The following example removes the DF_Customer_CustomerType constraint from the Sales.Customer table.

```
ALTER TABLE Sales.Customer DROP CONSTRAINT DF_Customer_CustomerType
```

Bound Defaults

Bound defaults are similar to rules in that you first create a bound default and then bind it to a column or set of columns. Bound defaults are also similar to rules in that they are slated for removal in a future version of SQL Server. This section covers the basics of bound defaults, but keep in mind that Microsoft recommends that you avoid using them for new development work.

You use the CREATE DEFAULT command to establish a default that can be bound to a column at a later time. The CREATE DEFAULT syntax is as follows:

```
CREATE DEFAULT [ schema_name . ] default_name
AS constant_expression [ ; ]
```

constant_expression can include any constant, built-in function, or mathematical expression. It cannot include user-defined functions. Character and data values that are part of the expression should be enclosed in single quotes. Monetary, integer, and floating-point constants do not require the single quotes.

The following example creates a default named password_df that can be used to supply a default password for any password-oriented columns:

```
CREATE DEFAULT password_df AS 'defaultpw'
```

After you create a default, you can bind it to a column. The following example binds the password_df default to the passwordSalt column on the person.contact table:

```
sp_bindefault password_df, 'person.contact.PasswordSalt'
```

As you can see, a bound default appears to require an extra step, but after it is created, it offers an advantage: You can bind it to other columns. This provides some consistency across all the columns that the default is bound to and reduces the overall number of database objects.

When a Default Is Applied

Defaults are applied only when no value is specified for a column during an insertion. They can also be applied during insertions and updates when the DEFAULT keyword is used. To demonstrate the application of defaults, consider the following examples:

```
CREATE TABLE test_default
(id int IDENTITY NOT NULL,
 tmstmp timestamp NOT NULL,
 password char(13) NOT NULL DEFAULT 'defaultpw',
 Shortdesc VARCHAR(50) NULL)
```

The table in this example has a unique characteristic: Each of the columns has some sort of default value associated with it. One column has a default of NULL because it is nullable. The IDENTITY and TIMESTAMP columns automatically generate values because of their data type, and the password column has an explicit default definition. In this scenario, you can supply the keywords DEFAULT VALUES in the INSERT statement to insert a row of data, as shown in the following example:

```
INSERT test_default DEFAULT VALUES
select * from test_default
/* results from previous select statement
id          tmstmp             password      Shortdesc
----------- ------------------ ------------- ------------------------
1           0x00000000000007D1 defaultpw     NULL
*/
```

You can see from the results of the SELECT statement in this example that a row was inserted in the new table, and this row includes default values for all the columns. If you want to supply values for some of the columns and allow the defaults to be used for other columns, you can simply exclude the columns with defaults from the column listing in the INSERT statement. The following example demonstrates how to do this:

```
INSERT test_default (ShortDesc)
 VALUES('test default insertion')
SELECT * FROM test_default
 where ShortDesc = 'test default insertion'
```

21

```
/* results from previous select statement
id  tmstmp              password   Shortdesc
--- ------------------- ---------- ----------------------
2   0x00000000000007D2 defaultpw  test default insertion
*/
```

The DEFAULT keyword can also be listed explicitly in the VALUE listing of the INSERT statement, as shown in the following example:

```
INSERT test_default (tmstmp, password, ShortDesc)
 VALUES(DEFAULT, DEFAULT, DEFAULT)
SELECT * FROM test_default where id = @@identity
/*
(1 row(s) affected)
id  tmstmp              password     Shortdesc
--- ------------------- ------------- ----------
3   0x00000000000007D5 defaultpw      NULL
*/
```

All the examples so far have dealt with INSERT statements, but there is one scenario in
which a default value can be applied with an UPDATE statement. This scenario is similar to
the preceding example and requires the use of the DEFAULT keyword. The following
example demonstrates the use of the DEFAULT keyword in an UPDATE statement:

```
UPDATE top (1) test_default
 SET PASSWORD = DEFAULT
GO
SELECT top 1 * from test_default
/*
id          tmstmp              password      Shortdesc
----------- ------------------- ------------- -----------
1           0x00000000000007DE defaultpw      NULL
*/
```

Keep in mind that default values are *not* used for updates unless the DEFAULT keyword is
explicitly referenced in the SET clause of the UPDATE statement.

Restrictions on Defaults

When creating defaults, you need to keep in mind the following restrictions:

▶ A default cannot be created on columns that have been defined with TIMESTAMP,
  IDENTITY, or ROWGUIDCOL properties.

▶ Only one default can be assigned to a given column. This restriction applies to both
  declarative and bound defaults, and only one of these can exist per column.

▶ The default value must be compatible with the data type of the column.

▶ Defaults that are bound cannot be dropped if the default is currently bound to a column. The default must be unbound from the column first.

▶ The expression in a default cannot include the names of any columns or other database objects.

There are also some considerations related to the interaction of rules, defaults, and constraints:

▶ If a column has both a rule and a default, the default is not inserted if it violates the rules.

▶ If a default value violates a CHECK constraint, the default is not inserted. Ultimately, all the rules, defaults, and constraints that are active will be validated. If the change to the data violates any of them, it is rejected.

Summary

This chapter covers the basic tools you can use to ensure the integrity of the data in a database. The integrity of data is directly related to its value; remember the concept of "garbage in, garbage out." If you take the time to implement constraints and the other methods discussed in this chapter, you will provide a solid foundation for the storage of data and avoid the headaches related to "garbage" data.

Chapter 22, "Creating and Managing Views," discusses a means for virtually accessing the data in tables. Virtual tables, or views, allow you to selectively choose the data elements on one or more tables that you want to present as a single window into your data.

Creating and Managing Views in SQL Server

IN THIS CHAPTER

▶ What's New in Creating and Managing Views

▶ Definition of Views

▶ Using Views

▶ Creating Views

▶ Managing Views

▶ Data Modifications and Views

▶ Partitioned Views

▶ Indexed Views

Views offer a window into your data that does not require physical storage. They are essentially virtual tables that are defined by a SELECT statement. This chapter describes the benefits and advantages of these powerful database objects.

What's New in Creating and Managing Views

Much of the core functionality associated with standard views has remained unchanged in SQL Server 2005. There have, however, been some significant changes related to indexed views. These changes include an expanded set of views that can be indexed. In addition, views that contain scalar aggregates, user-defined functions, and imprecise columns can now be indexed with SQL Server 2005.

SQL Server 2005 also provides support for views that are defined with the new common language runtime (CLR) types. CLR User-Defined Type (UDT) columns or expressions derived from these columns can now be included in the definition of a view. CLR user-defined functions that are scalar can be included in a view as well. Indexed views can be defined on these new CLR types provided that they are deterministic and meet several other criteria.

Definition of Views

Views are a logical way of viewing data in the underlying physical tables. They are tied to a SELECT statement that retrieves data from one or more tables or views in the same database or a different database. In most cases there is no physical storage of data associated with the view and the SELECT that is associated with the view is run dynamically whenever the view is referenced.

The following example shows a T-SQL statement that can be used to create a simple view in the AdventureWorks database:

```
CREATE VIEW [dbo].[vw_CustomerAddress]
AS
SELECT Sales.Customer.CustomerID, Sales.Customer.AccountNumber,
Person.Address.AddressLine1,
 Person.Address.StateProvinceID, Person.Address.City, Person.Address.PostalCode
FROM Sales.Customer
 INNER JOIN  Sales.CustomerAddress
  ON Sales.Customer.CustomerID = Sales.CustomerAddress.CustomerID
 INNER JOIN Person.Address
  ON Sales.CustomerAddress.AddressID = Person.Address.AddressID
```

The vw_CustomerAddress view in this example selects from three different tables in the AdventureWorks database: Sales.Customer, Sales.CustomerAddress, and Person.Address. Once the view is created, it can be used in the FROM clause of another SELECT statement. The following is an example of data retrieval using the newly created view:

```
select c.AccountNumber, s.OrderDate, c.city , c.StateProvinceId
  from vw_CustomerAddress c
   INNER JOIN Sales.SalesOrderHeader s
   ON c.CustomerID = s.CustomerID
 WHERE StateProvinceId = 14
  AND s.OrderDate = '9/21/01'
 ORDER BY c.city
```

```
AccountNumber OrderDate                       city                   StateProvinceId
AW00020060    2001-09-21 00:00:00.000  Runcorn                14
AW00011333    2001-09-21 00:00:00.000  Newcastle upon Tyne 14
```

You can see from the sample SELECT that the view is treated much like a table that is referenced in a SELECT statement. The view can be joined to other tables, individual columns from the view can be selected, and those columns can be included in the ORDER BY clause. All the retrieval is done dynamically when the view is referenced, and the underlying tables that are part of the view definition are implicitly accessed, without the need to know the underlying structure of the view.

Using Views

Views are useful in many scenarios. Some of the most common scenarios include the following:

- ▶ Simplifying data manipulation
- ▶ Focusing on specific data
- ▶ Data abstraction
- ▶ Controlling access to data

Simplifying Data Manipulation

Views can be used to simplify data access. Common queries that utilize complex joins, UNION queries, and more involved SQL can be defined as views. This minimizes the amount of complex code that must be written or rewritten and provides a simple way of organizing your common data access.

SQL Server 2005 comes with a set of system views that demonstrate the views' ability to mask complex queries and simplify data manipulation. These system views include catalog views, information schema views, and compatibility views. In many cases, the definition of these views is hidden but some of them can be analyzed using the sp_ helptext system procedure. For example, sys.triggers is a new catalog view that has been defined in SQL Server 2005, and has the following definition associated with it:

```
CREATE VIEW sys.triggers AS
   SELECT o.name,
    object_id = o.id,
    parent_class = o.pclass,
    parent_class_desc = pc.name,
    parent_id = o.pid,
    type = o.type,
    type_desc = n.name,
    create_date = o.created,
    modify_date = o.modified,
    is_ms_shipped = sysconv(bit, o.status & 1),        -- OBJALL_MSSHIPPED
    is_disabled = sysconv(bit, o.status & 256),        -- OBJTRG_DISABLED
    is_not_for_replication = sysconv(bit, o.status & 512),    -- OBJTRG_NOTFORREPL
    is_instead_of_trigger = sysconv(bit, o.status & 1024)    -- OBJTRG_INSTEADOF
   FROM sys.sysschobjs o
   LEFT JOIN sys.syspalnames n ON n.class = 'OBTY' AND n.value = o.type
   LEFT JOIN sys.syspalvalues pc ON pc.class = 'UNCL' AND pc.value = o.pclass
   WHERE o.type IN ('TA','TR') AND o.pclass <> 100
      AND has_access('TR', o.id, o.pid, o.nsclass) = 1
```

To select the relevant data from the sys.triggers view, you need only reference the columns in the view that are of interest, and the complexity of the view is hidden. The following query demonstrates the simplicity of a SELECT against the sys.triggers view:

```
select name, type, create_date
 from sys.triggers
 where name like 'i%'
```

You can see from the sys.triggers example why the folks at Microsoft are big proponents of views. Complex queries such as the sys.triggers view can be written and tested once, and subsequent data retrieval can be accomplished by selecting from the view.

Focusing on Specific Data

Views allow users or developers to focus on the specific data elements that they need to work with. Tables that contain hundreds of columns or columns that have limited value for the end user can be filtered with a view such that only the relevant data elements are returned.

The HumanResources.vEmployee view in the AdventureWorks database is a good example of a view that focuses on specific data and simplifies data access. The view definition follows:

```
SELECT     e.EmployeeID, c.Title, c.FirstName, c.MiddleName,
    c.LastName, c.Suffix, e.Title AS JobTitle, c.Phone, c.EmailAddress,
c.EmailPromotion, a.AddressLine1, a.AddressLine2, a.City,
sp.Name AS StateProvinceName, a.PostalCode, cr.Name AS CountryRegionName,
    c.AdditionalContactInfo
FROM  HumanResources.Employee AS e INNER JOIN
    Person.Contact AS c ON c.ContactID = e.ContactID INNER JOIN
    HumanResources.EmployeeAddress AS ea ON e.EmployeeID = ea.EmployeeID INNER JOIN
    Person.Address AS a ON ea.AddressID = a.AddressID INNER JOIN
    Person.StateProvince AS sp ON sp.StateProvinceID = a.StateProvinceID INNER JOIN
      Person.CountryRegion AS cr ON cr.CountryRegionCode = sp.CountryRegionCode
```

The HumanResources.vEmployee view filters out much of the data that is sensitive or superfluous when gathering the basic information about an employee.

Data Abstraction

Data abstraction, in its simplest form, isolates the client code from changes to the underlying structure. A view can be used to implement data abstraction within your database schema. If for example, you have client code that is going to retrieve data from a database table that is likely to change, then you can implement a view that retrieves data from the underlying table. The client code will then reference the view and never access the underlying table directly. If the underlying tables change or the source of the data for the view changes, then these changes can be isolated from the referencing client code.

To demonstrate this, take a look at the following SELECT statement, which retrieves data directly from the Sales.SalesOrderHeader table:

```
select TerritoryID, sum(TotalDue)
 from Sales.SalesOrderHeader
  group by TerritoryID
order by TerritoryID
```

The client code could certainly utilize this kind of query to retrieve the territory data. You may find, however, that the data retrieval would be better placed within a view if the summarized territory data were slated to be rolled up into an aggregate table at a later time. In this scenario, a view like the following could be created initially:

```
CREATE VIEW vw_TerritoryOrders AS
select TerritoryID, sum(TotalDue) 'TotalSales'
 from Sales.SalesOrderHeader
  group by TerritoryID
```

The client code that needs the territory data would then reference the vw_TerritoryOrders view. If the source of the territory data changes and it is rolled up in an aggregate table, then the view can be changed to reflect the new source for the data, but the client code remains unchanged. The following example alters the vw_TerritoryOrders view such that the source of the data is changed:

```
ALTER VIEW vw_TerritoryOrders AS
select TerritoryID, SalesYTD 'TotalSales'
 from Sales.SalesTerritory
```

Changing a single view in these types of scenarios can be much easier than changing the client code that has direct references to the table. This type of abstraction also applies to partitioned views, which are discussed later on in this chapter.

Controlling Access to Data

Views can be used as a security mechanism to limit a user's access to specific data. This type of view security can be used to limit the columns that a user has access to or the rows that the user has access to. A view that limits the accessible columns can be referred to as vertical security, or column-level security. A view that restricts the rows that are returned is referred to as horizontal security, or row-level security.

With vertical security, a view is created that contains only the data elements or columns that you want to make visible. Columns that are sensitive in nature (for example, payroll data) can be excluded from a view so that they are not seen when the user selects from the view.

Once the view is created, security can be granted on the view. If the owner of the objects referenced in the view is the same as the owner of the view itself, the user that is granted permission to the view does not need to have permission granted to the underlying objects. Listing 22.1 gives an example of this scenario.

LISTING 22.1   Security with Views

```
USE adventureWorks
go
CREATE LOGIN OwnerLogin WITH PASSWORD = 'pw'
CREATE USER OwnerLogin FOR LOGIN OwnerLogin
EXEC sp_addrolemember N'db_owner', N'OwnerLogin'

CREATE LOGIN NonOwnerLogin WITH PASSWORD = 'pw'
CREATE USER NonOwnerLogin FOR LOGIN NonOwnerLogin

--Connect as the OwnerLogin at this point
Go

CREATE VIEW OwnerView as
 select EmployeeID, Title, BirthDate, Gender, HireDate, SalariedFlag
  from HumanResources.Employee
go

GRANT SELECT ON [dbo].[OwnerView] TO [NonOwnerLogin]

--Connect as the NonOwnerLogin at this point

--The following select succeeds because the owner of the
--view that was granted permission is the same as the underlying
--table in the view
select * from OwnerView

--The following SELECT against the underlying table fails
--because the NonOwnerLogin does not have permission to
--select from the table.  He can only select through the view
select * from HumanResources.Employee
```

Listing 22.1 outlines a scenario where one login creates a view that selects specific columns from the HumanResources.Employee table. The Employee table is part of the HumanResources schema, and it is owned by DBO. The view that is created is also owned by DBO because the login (OwnerLogin) that created the view is a member of the db_owner role. Ultimately, NonOwnerLogin is granted permission to the view. When the NonOwnerLogin user connects to the database, that user can select rows from the view and will see only the columns in the employee table that have been selected in the view. If that user tries to select rows directly from the underlying `HumanResources.Employee` table, a permission-related error fires. Ownership chaining is the key to making this scenario work.

With ownership chaining, SQL Server automatically authorizes a user to the underlying tables, views, or functions referenced in the view. This happens only if the view has the same owner as the underlying objects and the user has been granted permission to the view. If, however, you have various owners of the underlying objects that a view references, permissions must be checked at each level. If access is denied at any level, access to the view is denied. Ownership chaining was available in SQL Server 2000 and is still available in SQL Server 2005 for backward compatibility.

Horizontal security can also be implemented with a view. With horizontal security, a `WHERE` clause is included in the view's `SELECT` statement to restrict the rows that are returned. The following example demonstrates a simple view that utilizes horizontal security:

```
CREATE VIEW EmpViewHorizontal
  as
 select EmployeeID, BirthDate, Gender, HireDate, SalariedFlag
  from HumanResources.Employee
 where HireDate >  '3/1/03'


--Sample SELECT results from the view:

EmployeeID  BirthDate               Gender HireDate
----------- ----------------------- ------ -----------------------
288         1965-02-11 00:00:00.000 M      2003-04-15 00:00:00.000
289         1965-08-09 00:00:00.000 F      2003-07-01 00:00:00.000
290         1961-04-18 00:00:00.000 F      2003-07-01 00:00:00.000
```

Only the rows in the `Employee` table with a `HireDate` value greater than March 1, 2003, are returned when you select everything from the view. Separate views can be created based on geography, demographics, or any other data element that requires a different set of security.

Keep in mind that additional conditions can be applied when selecting from a view. You can utilize another `WHERE` clause in the `SELECT` statement that uses a view. This is demonstrated in the following example:

```
select * from EmpViewHorizontal
 where HireDate >= '7/1/03'
  and BirthDate > '1/1/65'


EmployeeID  BirthDate               Gender HireDate
----------- ----------------------- ------ -----------------------
289         1965-08-09 00:00:00.000 F      2003-07-01 00:00:00.000
```

As you can see, a view with horizontal security restricts your initial result set but does not prevent you from applying additional conditions to obtain the desired result.

Creating Views

You can create several different types of views in SQL Server 2005, including standard views, indexed views, and partitioned views. Standard views are like those that have been discussed thus far in this chapter; they let you achieve most of the benefits associated with views. An indexed view has a unique clustered index defined on it that causes the view to be materialized. In other words, the creation of the index causes physical storage of the data related to the view's index. Partitioned views join horizontally partitioned data from a set of distinct tables. They can be locally partitioned, meaning that the tables are on the same server or they can be distributed meaning that some of the tables exist on other servers. Partitioned views and indexed views are discussed in detail later in this chapter.

All types of views share a common set of restrictions:

▶ Every column (including derived columns) must have a name.

▶ The SELECT statement used in the view cannot include the COMPUTE BY clause or the INTO keyword.

▶ The SELECT statement used in the view cannot include the ORDER BY clause.

▶ The SELECT statement used in the view cannot contain temporary tables.

▶ You cannot associate AFTER triggers with views, but you can associate INSTEAD OF triggers.

▶ You cannot associate rules or default definitions with a view.

▶ You cannot define a full-text index on a view.

A view can have a maximum of 1,024 columns. You can select all the columns for a view by using a SELECT * statement, but you need to use some caution when doing this. In particular, keep in mind that the view will not display columns that have been added to the view's underlying tables after the view has been created. The fact that the new columns are not displayed can be a good thing but is sometimes overlooked. You can prevent changes to the underlying objects (for example, tables) by creating the view with SCHEMABINDING. SCHEMABINDING is discussed in the next section.

If you want the changes to the underlying objects to be reflected in the views, then you can use the sp_refreshview stored procedure. This stored procedure updates the metadata for the specified non-schema-bound view.

TIP

SQL Server Books Online lists a handy script that can be used to update any view that has a dependency on an object. The script is shown in the `sp_refreshview` examples. The script is listed below and is coded such that it will generate output that can be run to generate the `sp_refreshview` statements for the `Person.Contact` table in the AdventureWorks database:

```
SELECT DISTINCT 'EXEC sp_refreshview ''' + name + ''''
FROM sys.objects so INNER JOIN sys.sql_dependencies sd
ON so.object_id = sd.object_id
WHERE type = 'V'
AND sd.referenced_major_id = object_id('Person.Contact')
```

To generate the executions for another object, you simply change the name of the object (that is, `Person.Contact`) found at the end of the script to the name of the object you want to investigate.

With these guidelines in mind, you are now ready to create your view. Views can be created in SQL Server 2005 using T-SQL or SQL Server Management Studio (SSMS).

Creating Views Using T-SQL

The `CREATE VIEW` statement is used to create views with T-SQL. The syntax for the `CREATE VIEW` statement follows:

```
CREATE VIEW [ schema_name . ] view_name [ (column [ ,...n ] ) ]
[ WITH <view_attribute> [ ,...n ] ]
AS select_statement [ ; ]
[ WITH CHECK OPTION ]


<view_attribute> ::=
{
    [ ENCRYPTION ]
    [ SCHEMABINDING ]
    [ VIEW_METADATA ]     }
```

This statement and the related options are essentially the same in SQL Server 2005 as they were in SQL Server 2000. The schema name has replaced the database owner, but the rest remains the same. We will first look at a simple example for creating a view with T-SQL, and then we will delve into several other examples that utilize the view attributes. Listing 22.2 shows a sample T-SQL statement for creating a simple view:

LISTING 22.2   Creating a Simple View with T-SQL

```
CREATE VIEW Sales.vw_OrderSummary as
select datepart(yy, orderdate) as 'OrderYear',
    datepart(mm, orderdate) as 'OrderMonth',
    sum(TotalDue) as 'OrderTotal'
 from Sales.SalesOrderHeader
 group by datepart(yy, orderdate), datepart(mm, orderdate)
```

There are several important things to notice in the example in Listing 22.2. First, all the columns in the SELECT statement are derived columns and do not simply reference a column in a table. You do not need to have a derived column in your view, but if you do, the derived column(s) must have a name or an alias assigned to it in order to create the view. The column name allows you to reference the derived column when selecting from the view. If the derived columns in the SELECT statement are not named, then the CREATE VIEW statement will fail.

Another notable characteristic of the simple view example is that an aggregate is used in the SELECT statement. Aggregates are allowed in views and are common implementations of views. Views with aggregates can be used instead of summary tables that de-normalize data and use additional disk space. Keep in mind that the results of any view (including those with aggregates) are not returned in any particular order. Views cannot be created with the ORDER BY clause, but the ORDER BY clause can be utilized in a SELECT statement that references the view. The following example shows the first five rows of the vw_OrderSummary view created in Listing 22.2:

```
select top 5 * from Sales.vw_OrderSummary
```

```
OrderYear    OrderMonth    OrderTotal
-----------  -----------   --------------------
2003         5             4449886.2315
2001         11            3690018.6652
2003         8             6775857.0745
2002         7             3781879.0708
2003         11            5961182.6761
```

You can see from the results of the SELECT that the summarized order information is not returned in any particular order. If you want to sort the results, you can treat the view like a table in a SELECT statement and use the ORDER BY clause to produce the desired results. The following example shows a SELECT statement from the vw_OrderSummary view and the ordered results:

```
select top 5 *
 from Sales.vw_OrderSummary
 where OrderYear >= 2004
 order by OrderYear, OrderMonth
```

OrderYear	OrderMonth	OrderTotal
2004	1	3691013.2227
2004	2	5207182.5122
2004	3	5272786.8106
2004	4	4722890.7352
2004	5	6518825.2262

> **TIP**
>
> In many cases, it is best to create views with primary key columns that allow the views to be joined to other tables. Take, for example, a view that is created on the `Employee` table in the `AdventureWorks` database. If you want to join that view to another table (such as `EmployeeAddress`), you need the primary key of the table (that is, `Employee.EmployeeID`) in the view.

Views can also be created with special view attributes, including `ENCRYPTION`, `SCHEMABINDING`, and `VIEW_METADATA`. Each of these attributes and some other specialized views are discussed in the following sections.

ENCRYPTION

The `ENCRYPTION` attribute causes the view definition to be stored as encrypted text in `sys.syscomments`. This feature is also available for stored procedures and other database code that you may want to protect. One thing to consider when you create a view using the `ENCRYPTION` option is that this option prevents the view from being published as part of SQL Server replication.

The following example shows the creation of one of our prior views with the `ENCRYPTION` attribute:

```
IF  EXISTS (SELECT * FROM sys.views WHERE
object_id = OBJECT_ID(N'[Sales].[vw_OrderSummary]'))
DROP VIEW [Sales].[vw_OrderSummary]
GO

CREATE VIEW Sales.vw_OrderSummary
    WITH ENCRYPTION AS
select datepart(yy, orderdate) as 'OrderYear',
    datepart(mm, orderdate) as 'OrderMonth',
    sum(TotalDue) as 'OrderTotal'
 from Sales.SalesOrderHeader
 group by datepart(yy, orderdate), datepart(mm, orderdate)
go
```

The following `SELECT` statement from `sys.syscomments` retrieves the text related to the encrypted view and shows that the view definition is not visible in the `Text` column:

```
SELECT id, OBJECT_NAME(ID) 'ViewName', text
FROM SYS.sysCOMMENTS
 WHERE OBJECT_NAME(ID) LIKE '%vw_OrderSummary%'

id            ViewName                 text
-----------   ---------------------    ---------------------
919674324     vw_OrderSummary          NULL
```

SCHEMABINDING

The `SCHEMABINDING` attribute binds a view to the schema of the underlying table(s) referenced in the view's `SELECT` statement. This binding action prevents any changes to the underlying tables that would affect the view definition. For example, if you have a view that includes the `Employee.Title` column, then this column could not be altered or dropped in the `Employee` table. If schema changes are attempted on the underlying tables, an error message is returned, and the change is not allowed. The only way to make the change is to drop the view or alter the view to remove the `SCHEMABINDING` attribute.

> **TIP**
>
> Views created with `SCHEMABINDING` have been used in prior versions to simply prevent changes to the underlying schema. Any table for which you wanted to prevent schema changes would be included in a view, and this essentially locked the definition of the table. With SQL Server 2005, this approach is no longer needed because you can accomplish the same thing with DDL triggers that can react to schema changes and prevent them, if desired.

VIEW_METADATA

When the `VIEW_METADATA` option is specified, SQL Server returns information about the view, as opposed to the base tables. This happens when browse-mode metadata is requested for a query that references the view via a database API. Browse-mode metadata is additional information returned by SQL Server to client-side DBLIB, ODBC, and OLE DB APIs, which allows them to implement client-side updatable cursors.

WITH CHECK OPTION

`WITH CHECK OPTION` forces all data modifications made through a view to adhere to the conditions in the view. The example shown in Listing 22.3 shows a view created using `WITH CHECK OPTION`.

LISTING 22.3   View WITH CHECK OPTION

```
CREATE VIEW HumanResources.vw_MaleEmployees
 AS
```

LISTING 22.3   Continued

```
SELECT EmployeeID, LoginID, Gender
 FROM HumanResources.Employee
 WHERE Gender = 'M'
 WITH CHECK OPTION
```

The following UPDATE statement fails when executed against the view created in Listing 22.3 because the Gender change would cause it to no longer be seen by the view:

```
UPDATE HumanResources.vw_MaleEmployees
 SET Gender = 'F'
 WHERE LoginId = 'adventure-works\taylor0'
```

Updates and other modifications though a view are discussed further in the "Data Modifications and Views" section, later in this chapter.

Creating Views Using the View Designer

SQL Server 2005 provides a graphical tool that can be used to create views. The graphical tool is called the View Designer, and it can be an invaluable aid when creating or modifying a view. The View Designer is equipped with four panes that provide the information relative to the view. Figure 22.1 shows the View Designer display for the Person. vStateProvinceCountryRegion view that is installed in the AdventureWorks database. To create a new view via the View Designer, right-click the Views node in the Object Explorer and select New. An empty View Designer is displayed.

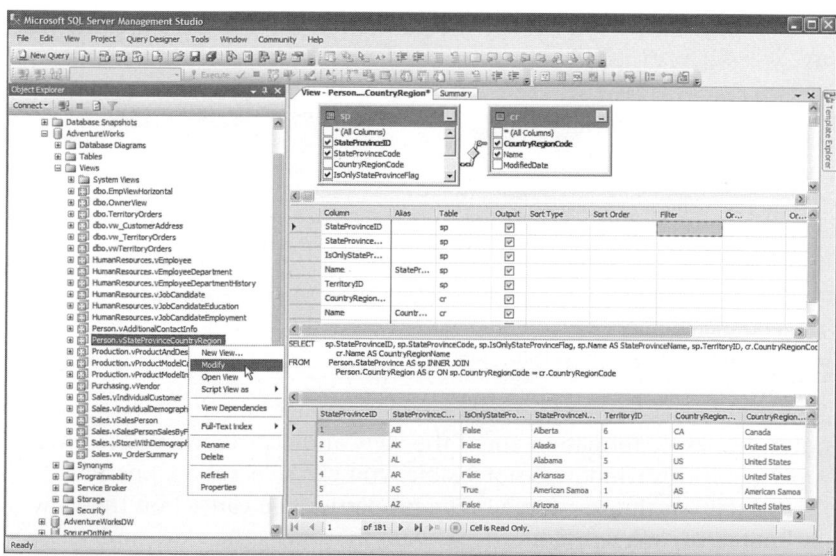

FIGURE 22.1   The View Designer window.

The View Designer has four panes:

▶ **Diagram pane**—Gives a graphical view of the tables that are part of the view. This includes the columns in the tables and relationships between the tables contained in the view.

▶ **Criteria pane**—Displays all the columns that are selected in the view and allows for sorting, filtering, and other related column-oriented criteria.

▶ **SQL pane**—Renders the T-SQL associated with the view.

▶ **Results pane**—Shows the SELECT statement that defines the view and the results of that SELECT.

The panes in the View Designer are dependent on each other. If you add a WHERE clause in the SQL pane, then the corresponding Filter value will be added in the Criteria pane. Similarly, if you right-click in the Diagram pane and add a table to the view, then the Criteria pane and SQL pane will be updated to reflect this change.

TIP

One of the most amazing features of the View Designer is the ability to render a SQL statement into its graphical form. You can copy T-SQL into the SQL pane, and the View Designer will reverse engineer the tables into the Diagram pane, giving you a graphical display of the query. Some complex SQL statements cannot be rendered, but many of them can.

You can control the View Designer via the Query Designer menu option as well. Options to add a new table, verify the T-SQL, and change the panes that are displayed are just some of the options available via this menu.

NOTE

The View Designer does not allow you to set every attribute of a view. It is a great starting point for creating a view, but some attributes need to be set with T-SQL after the view has been created. For example, you cannot specify WITH CHECK OPTION in the View Designer, but you can set it by altering the view after it has been created.

There is also no option to script a view from the View Designer. You must close the View Designer first, and then you are asked if you want to save the view. If you click Yes, you are given a prompt that allows you to specify a name.

The Properties window displays information about the view and also allows you to enter additional view properties. If this window is not visible, you can select the Properties window from the View menu or simply press F4. The properties you can set on the view include (but are not limited to) a description, the schema that owns the view, and whether to bind it to the schema. Figure 22.2 shows the Properties window for the Person.vStateProvinceCountryRegion view that we looked at earlier.

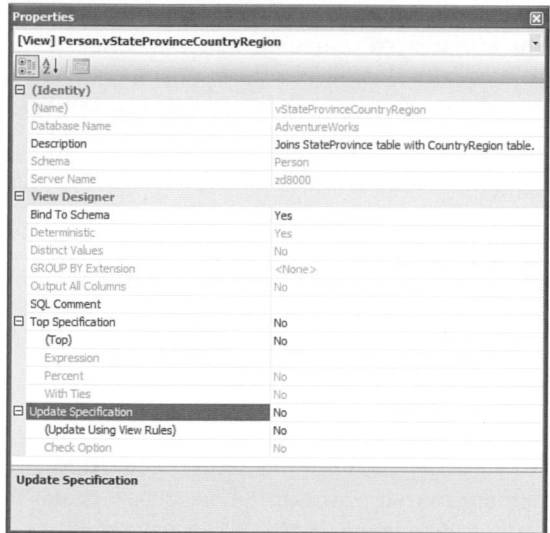

FIGURE 22.2   The view Properties window.

Once you have defined a view using the panes in the View Designer and set its properties, you can save the view, and are prompted to give it a name. After it is saved, the view appears in the Object Explorer tree.

Managing Views

Once your view is created, you can manage the view via T-SQL or the View Designer. The T-SQL commands for managing views are the ALTER VIEW and DROP VIEW statements. The ALTER VIEW statement is used to modify the properties or definition of the view, and the DROP VIEW statement is used to remove the view from the database.

Altering Views with T-SQL

The ALTER VIEW syntax follows:

```
ALTER VIEW [ schema_name . ] view_name [ ( column [ ,...n ] ) ]
[ WITH <view_attribute> [ ,...n ] ]
AS select_statement [ ; ]
[ WITH CHECK OPTION ]

<view_attribute> ::=
{
    [ ENCRYPTION ]
    [ SCHEMABINDING ]
    [ VIEW_METADATA ]
}
```

The ALTER VIEW statement utilizes the same set of options and parameters as the CREATE VIEW statement. You should consider using the ALTER VIEW statement when making changes to your view instead of dropping and re-creating the view. Views that are altered retain their associated permissions and do not affect dependent stored procedures or triggers.

An example of the ALTER VIEW statement follows:

```
ALTER VIEW [dbo].[vw_employee]
with SCHEMABINDING
AS
SELECT TITLE, GENDER
   FROM HumanResources.Employee
WITH CHECK OPTION
```

The entire definition of the view, including any attributes or options, must be listed in the ALTER VIEW statement. This behavior is similar to that of the ALTER PROCEDURE statement and some of the other ALTER statements. You can generate the ALTER VIEW statement from the Object Explorer by right-clicking the view and selecting Script View As and then choosing Alter To. This allows you to script the ALTER statement to a new Query Editor window, a file, or the Clipboard.

Dropping Views with T-SQL

You can drop views from a database by using the DROP VIEW statement. The syntax for DROP VIEW follows:

```
DROP VIEW [ schema_name . ] view_name [ ...,n ] [ ; ]
```

You can drop more than one view by using one DROP VIEW statement and listing all the targeted views, separated by commas. You should consider running the sp_depends stored procedure against the targeted views before dropping them. This procedure lists the objects that are dependent on the view you are dropping.

TIP

You can also drop more than one view via SSMS. Simply select the Views node in Object Explorer and then activate the Summary window. The Summary window displays all the views and allows you to select multiple views that are displayed. Once you have the views that you want to delete selected, you can right-click a selection and choose Delete to remove all the views selected.

Managing Views with SSMS

You can use the Object Explorer in SQL Server Management Studio to alter or drop views as well. To do so, you right-click a view in the Object Explorer and choose Modify to launch the View Designer. The View Designer allows you to modify a view in an easy-to-use graphical interface. Refer to the "Creating Views Using the View Designer" section, earlier in this chapter, for a detailed review of the View Designer.

To drop a view, you right-click the view in the Object Explorer and choose Delete. You can drop the view by clicking OK on the Delete Object screen, or you can script the drop statement for later execution.

Data Modifications and Views

Data modifications are allowed through a view under certain circumstances. Views that meet these criterions are sometimes called *updatable views*. Updatable views can be referenced in an INSERT, UPDATE, or DELETE statement, and these statements ultimately affect the underlying table(s) in the view.

The following example contains a SQL statement to create a view that is updatable, followed by an UPDATE statement that performs a data modification using the view:

```
CREATE VIEW vw_CreditCard
AS
SELECT     CreditCardID, CardType, CardNumber, ExpMonth, ExpYear
FROM       Sales.CreditCard

UPDATE vw_CreditCard
 SET ExpYear = ExpYear + 1
 WHERE ExpYear < 2006
```

In general, views that are updatable are similar to the previous example but are less complex. The following specific conditions allow a view to be updatable:

▶ Any data modification via a view must reference columns from a single base table. This does not restrict a view to only one table, but the columns referenced in the data modification can only be for one of the tables defined in the view.

▶ The columns affected by the data modification must directly reference the underlying tables. They cannot be derived through an aggregate function (for example, AVG, COUNT, SUM) and cannot contain computations from an expression that utilizes columns from another table.

▶ The TOP clause cannot be part of the SELECT statement that defines the view when the WITH CHECK OPTION clause is used.

▶ The columns affected by the data modification cannot be affected by a GROUP BY, HAVING, or DISTINCT clauses in the view definition.

You can overcome these restrictions by using INSTEAD OF triggers to perform the data modifications. You can create INSTEAD OF triggers on a view, and the logic within the triggers performs the actual database updates. INSTEAD OF triggers are discussed in detail in Chapter 25, "Creating and Managing Triggers."

Partitioned views are another means for performing data modifications via a view. Partitioned views can be updatable and are not subject to all the restrictions that are listed for conventional views. There are, however, some additional restrictions that apply to partitioned views. These additional restrictions and other details about partitioned views are discussed in the next section.

Partitioned Views

Partitioned views are used to access data that has been horizontally split, or partitioned, across multiple tables. These tables can be in the same or different databases—or even spread across multiple servers. Partitioning of tables is done to spread the I/O and processing load of large tables across multiple disks or servers.

You combine the tables in a partitioned view by using a UNION ALL statement that causes the data from the separate tables to appear as if they were one table. These separate tables are referred to as *member tables* or *base tables*. The member tables in a SELECT statement of the view must all be structured in the same way, and the view must adhere to the following restrictions:

- ▶ All the columns from the member tables should be included in the view definition.

- ▶ Columns with the same ordinal position in the SELECT list should have the same data type.

- ▶ The same column cannot be used multiple times in the SELECT list.

- ▶ A partitioning column that segments the data must be identified and needs to have the same ordinal position across all the member table SELECT statements.

- ▶ The partitioning column cannot be a computed column, an identity, a default, or a timestamp.

- ▶ The data values in the partitioning column cannot overlap in the underlying tables.

- ▶ The partitioning column must be part of the primary key of the member table.

- ▶ The member tables in the partitioned view need a CHECK constraint on the partitioning column.

- ▶ A table can appear only once as part of the UNION ALL statement.

- ▶ The member tables cannot have indexes created on computed column in the table.

- ▶ The number of columns in the member table primary key constraints should be the same.

- ▶ All member tables should have the same ANSI PADDING setting when created.

The list of restrictions for creating partitioned views is extensive, but the creation of a partitioned view is relatively straightforward and intuitive. Take, for example, the Sales.SalesOrderHeader table in the AdventureWorks database. This table is relatively small, but it is the type of table that could have a large number of rows and experience heavy utilization. To balance the workload against this table, you could use a partitioned view that utilizes base tables that each contain a separate year's data. Listing 22.4 shows the CREATE TABLE statements to create the base tables for each year. The yearly tables are intended to hold summarized daily numbers, and each contains only a subset of the columns in the Sales.SalesOrderHeader table.

LISTING 22.4   Creating the Base Tables for a Partitioned View

```
CREATE TABLE Sales.Sales_2001
(
    OrderDay datetime NOT NULL
        CHECK (OrderDay BETWEEN '20010101' AND '20011231'),
    SubTotal money NOT NULL ,
    TaxAmt money not null,
    Freight money not null,
 CONSTRAINT PK_Sales_2001_OrderDay PRIMARY KEY CLUSTERED (OrderDay ASC)
)


CREATE TABLE Sales.Sales_2002
(
    OrderDay datetime NOT NULL,
        CHECK (OrderDay BETWEEN '20020101' AND '20021231'),
    SubTotal money NOT NULL ,
    TaxAmt money not null,
    Freight money not null,
 CONSTRAINT PK_Sales_2002_OrderDay PRIMARY KEY CLUSTERED (OrderDay ASC)
)


CREATE TABLE Sales.Sales_2003
(
    OrderDay datetime NOT NULL
        CHECK (OrderDay BETWEEN '20030101' AND '20031231'),
    SubTotal money NOT NULL ,
    TaxAmt money not null,
    Freight money not null,
 CONSTRAINT PK_Sales_2003_OrderDay PRIMARY KEY CLUSTERED (OrderDay ASC)
)


CREATE TABLE Sales.Sales_2004
(
    OrderDay datetime NOT NULL
        CHECK (OrderDay BETWEEN '20040101' AND '20041231'),
```

LISTING 22.4   Continued

```
    SubTotal money NOT NULL ,
    TaxAmt money not null,
    Freight money not null,
 CONSTRAINT PK_Sales_2004_OrderDay PRIMARY KEY CLUSTERED (OrderDay ASC)
)
```

Notice that each table has a primary key on OrderDay, the partitioning column. Also notice that a CHECK constraint is defined for each table; it ensures that only orders for the given year can be stored in the table.

To demonstrate the power of a partitioned view, it is best to populate the base tables that will be used by the view. Listing 22.5 contains a series of INSERT statements that select from the Sales.SalesOrderHeader table and populate the base tables. The SELECT statements summarize several key columns by day and contain a WHERE clause that limits the result to orders for the respective years.

LISTING 22.5   Populating the Base Tables for a Partitioned View

```
INSERT Sales.Sales_2001
    SELECT CONVERT(VARCHAR(8),OrderDate,112),
        SUM(SubTotal), SUM(TaxAmt), SUM(Freight)
     FROM Sales.SalesOrderHeader
     WHERE OrderDate between '20010101' AND '20011231'
     GROUP BY CONVERT(VARCHAR(8),OrderDate,112)

INSERT Sales.Sales_2002
    SELECT CONVERT(VARCHAR(8),OrderDate,112),
        SUM(SubTotal), SUM(TaxAmt), SUM(Freight)
     FROM Sales.SalesOrderHeader
     WHERE OrderDate between '20020102' AND '20021231'
     GROUP BY CONVERT(VARCHAR(8),OrderDate,112)

INSERT Sales.Sales_2003
    SELECT CONVERT(VARCHAR(8),OrderDate,112),
        SUM(SubTotal), SUM(TaxAmt), SUM(Freight)
     FROM Sales.SalesOrderHeader
     WHERE OrderDate between '20030101' AND '20031231'
     GROUP BY CONVERT(VARCHAR(8),OrderDate,112)

INSERT Sales.Sales_2004
    SELECT CONVERT(VARCHAR(8),OrderDate,112),
        SUM(SubTotal), SUM(TaxAmt), SUM(Freight)
     FROM Sales.SalesOrderHeader
     WHERE OrderDate between '20040102' AND '20041231'
     GROUP BY CONVERT(VARCHAR(8),OrderDate,112)
```

Now that you have the populated base table, you can create a partitioned view and ensure that the view is selecting only from the base tables that it needs.

Two types of partitioned views are discussed in this chapter: local and distributed. A local partitioned view utilizes base tables that are found on the same server. A distributed partitioned view contains at least one base table that resides on a different (remote) server. The focus in the section is on local partitioned views; distributed partitioned views are discussed later in this chapter. The T-SQL for creating a local partitioned view named Sales.vw_Sales_Daily is shown in Listing 22.6.

LISTING 22.6   Creating a Local Partitioned View

```
Create View Sales.vw_Sales_Daily
 as
      SELECT * FROM Sales.Sales_2001
       UNION ALL
      SELECT * FROM Sales.Sales_2002
       UNION ALL
      SELECT * FROM Sales.Sales_2003
       UNION ALL
      SELECT * FROM Sales.Sales_2004
```

The best way to validate that a partitioned view is working properly is to run a conditional SELECT against the view and display the execution plan. If the partitioned view is functioning properly, it should only be accessing the base tables it needs to satisfy the SELECT and should not access all the tables in the view unless it needs to. The following example shows a sample SELECT against the new partitioned view:

```
SELECT * FROM Sales.vw_Sales_Daily
 WHERE OrderDay > '20040701'
   and SubTotal > 2000
```

If you execute this statement and review the actual execution plan, you will see that an index seek is performed against the Sales.Sales_2004 table. This is the correct result, given that the SELECT statement is targeting order data from 2004.

> **NOTE**
>
> Local partitioned views are included in SQL Server 2005 for backward compatibility. The recommended method for partitioning data on a local server in SQL Server 2005 is through the use of partitioned tables and indexes. Partitioned tables and indexes, which are new to SQL Server 2005, are discussed in Chapter 19, "Creating and Managing Tables."

Modifying Data Through a Partitioned View

You can modify data via a partitioned view if the SQL statement performing the modification meets certain conditions, as described here:

▶ All columns in the partitioned view must be specified in the INSERT statement. Columns that include a DEFAULT constraint or allow nulls are also subject to this requirement.

▶ The DEFAULT keyword cannot be used on inserts to partitioned views or on updates to partitioned views.

▶ UPDATE statements cannot modify PRIMARY KEY columns if the member tables have text, ntext, or image columns.

▶ Inserts and updates to a partitioned view are not allowed if the view contains a timestamp.

▶ Identity columns in a partitioned view cannot be modified by an INSERT or UPDATE statement.

▶ INSERT, UPDATE, and DELETE statements are not allowed against a partitioned view if there is a self-join with the same view or with any of the member tables in the statement.

> **NOTE**
>
> Data can be modified through partitioned views only in the Enterprise and Developer Editions of SQL Server 2005

In addition to the conditions shown in this list, you must also satisfy any restrictions that apply to the member tables. Check constraints, foreign key constraints, and any other table-level restrictions must be accounted for in the modification statement. The user executing the modification against the partitioned view must have the appropriate INSERT, UPDATE, or DELETE permissions on the member tables in order for the update to succeed.

Distributed Partitioned Views

Microsoft provides distributed partitioned views (DPVs) as a primary means to scale out a database server. Scalability allows an application or a database to utilize additional resources, which allows it to perform more work. There are two kinds of scalability: scaleup and scaleout. A scaleup solution focuses on a single server that is scaled to provide more processing power than its predecessor. An example of scaleup would be migrating from a server with a four-way processor to a 16-processor machine. Scaleout solutions include the addition of servers to augment the overall processing power.

DPVs are similar to local partitioned views, but they utilize one or more tables located on a remote server. The placement of partitioned data on remote servers allows the processing power of more than one server to be utilized. The partitioning is intended to be transparent to the application and allow for additional partitions and servers as the application's needs scale.

The following list outlines the basic requirements for creating a DPV:

▶ A linked server definition is added to each member server that will contain the partitioned data. The linked server contains the connection information required to run distributed queries on another member server.

▶ The `lazy schema validation` option is set to `true` on each of the member servers, using `sp_serveroption`. This option is set for performance reasons and allows the query processor to skip schema checking of remote tables if the query can be satisfied on a single member server.

▶ A DPV is created on each member server. This DPV references the local tables in addition to the tables found on the other member servers.

Listing 22.7 shows sample SQL commands for satisfying the requirements in the prior list. The DPV that is created in the last portion of the script is similar to the local partitioned view created in the prior section. The key difference in this DPV example is the inclusion of a distributed query that retrieves records for `Sales.Sales_2002` from a remote server. The remote server in this example is named `DbSvrXP`.

LISTING 22.7   Creating a Distributed Partitioned View

```
Exec sp_addlinkedserver @server='dbsvrxp',
      @srvproduct='',
      @provider='MSDASQL',
      @provstr='DRIVER={SQL Server};
SERVER=dbsvrxp;UID=linklogin;PWD=pw;Initial Catalog=AdventureWorks'

--Set the server option for improved DPV performance
exec sp_serveroption dbsvrxp, 'lazy schema validation', true

Create View Sales.vw_Sales_Daily
 as
      SELECT * FROM Sales.Sales_2001
        UNION ALL
      SELECT * FROM dbsvrxp.AdventureWorks.Sales.Sales_2002
        UNION ALL
      SELECT * FROM Sales.Sales_2003
        UNION ALL
      SELECT * FROM Sales.Sales_2004
```

The DPV created in Listing 22.7 contains only one remote table. The example could be further expanded to have each table in the UNION clause on a different remote server. Keep in mind that the DPV CREATE statement needs to be adjusted when run on the remote server(s). The tables that are local on one server are now remote on the other server, and those that are remote can now be local.

If they are properly defined, SQL Server 2005 attempts to optimize the performance of DPVs by minimizing the amount of data transferred between member servers. The query processor retrieves the CHECK constraint definitions from each member table. This allows the query processor to map the specified search arguments to the appropriate table(s). The query execution plan then accesses only the necessary tables and retrieves only the remote rows needed to complete the SQL statement.

Data can be modified through a DPV as well. Updatable DPVs, which where introduced in SQL Server 2000, are still available in SQL Server 2005. Data modifications are performed against a view, allowing true transparency. The view is accessed as if it were a base table, and the user or application is unaware of the actual location of the data. If it is configured properly, SQL Server determines via the WHERE clause specified in the update query which partition defined in the view must be updated rather than updating all tables in the join.

NOTE

Data can be modified through distributed partitioned views only in the Enterprise and Developer Editions of SQL Server 2005.

Indexed Views

You establish indexed views by creating a unique clustered index on the view itself, independent of the member tables that it references. The creation of this unique index transforms a view from an object that is virtual in nature to one that has physical storage associated with it. Like all other indexes, the index on a view takes up physical storage, requires maintenance, and, most importantly, can provide performance benefits that justify its creation.

Creating Indexed Views

Indexed views were first available for creation in SQL Server 2000 and continue to be a viable means for improving query performance in SQL Server 2005. An index can be created on a view in all versions of SQL Server 2005, but there are limitations on some of the versions. The Developer and Enterprise Editions of SQL Server 2005 are the only editions that support the use of indexed views for queries that don't specifically reference the views. Other editions of SQL Server must reference the view by name in the SQL statements and must also use the NOEXPAND keyword in the query. The details of NOEXPAND are discussed in the section "To Expand or Not to Expand," later in this chapter.

Regardless of the edition of SQL Server you are running, some basic requirements must be satisfied in order to create an indexed view. These requirements are detailed in SQL Server 2005 Books Online and shown in the following list:

▶ The ANSI_NULLS and QUOTED_IDENTIFIER options must be set to ON when the CREATE VIEW statement is executed.

▶ The ANSI_NULLS option must be set to ON for the execution of all CREATE TABLE statements that create tables referenced by the view.

▶ The view must not reference any other views—only base tables.

▶ All base tables referenced by the view must be in the same database as the view and have the same owner as the view.

▶ The view must be created with the SCHEMABINDING option. Schema binding binds the view to the schema of the underlying base tables.

▶ User-defined functions referenced in the view must be created with the SCHEMABINDING option.

▶ Tables and user-defined functions must be referenced via two-part names in the view. One-part, three-part, and four-part names are not allowed.

▶ All functions referenced by expressions in the view must be deterministic.

▶ If the view definition uses an aggregate function, the SELECT list must also include COUNT_BIG (*).

▶ The DATA ACCESS property of a user-defined function must be NO SQL, and the EXTERNAL ACCESS property must be NO.

▶ CLR functions can appear only in the SELECT list of the view and can only reference fields that are not part of the clustered index key. They cannot appear in the WHERE clause of the view or the ON clause of a JOIN operation in the view.

▶ CLR functions and methods of CLR user-defined types used in the view definition must have the properties set as DETERMINISTIC = TRUE, PRECISE = TRUE, DATA ACCESS = NO SQL, and EXTERNAL ACCESS = NO.

▶ If GROUP BY is specified, the view SELECT list must contain a COUNT_BIG(*) expression, and the view definition cannot specify HAVING, CUBE, or ROLLUP.

▶ The view cannot contain any of the T-SQL elements shown in the following list.

xxx	xxx	xxx
* or tablename.*	An expression on a column that is found in the GROUP BY clause	A derived table
A common table expression (CTE)	A rowset function	The UNION, EXCEPT, or INTERSECT operators
Subqueries	Outer joins or self-joins	The TOP clause
The ORDER BY clause	The DISTINCT keyword	COUNT (COUNT_BIG is allowed)
AVG, MAX, MIN, STDEV, STDEVP, VAR, or VARP	A SUM function that references a nullable expression	A CLR user-defined aggregate function
The full text predicate CONTAINS or FREETEXT	COMPUTE or COMPUTE BY	CROSS APPLY or OUTER APPLY operators
Table hints	Join hints	

You can see from this list that the number of requirements is extensive. It can therefore be difficult to determine whether all the requirements have been met for a particular view. To simplify this determination, you can query the `IsIndexable` property, using the `OBJECTPROPERTY` function. The following example demonstrates the use of the `IsIndexable` property against the `sys.views` catalog view:

```
SELECT name AS ViewName
  ,SCHEMA_NAME(schema_id) AS SchemaName
  ,OBJECTPROPERTYEX(object_id,'IsIndexed') AS IsIndexed
  ,OBJECTPROPERTYEX(object_id,'IsIndexable') AS IsIndexable
  ,create_date
  ,modify_date
FROM sys.views;
```

The `IsIndexable` property returns a 1 (or `TRUE`) if an index can be created on the view and a 0 if it is not indexable. Most of the views in the `AdventureWorks` database are not indexable, but the database does contain a couple examples of views that have been indexed. The following example shows the `CREATE` statement for an index on the vProductAndDescription view. The `SET` options that are required when creating the index are included in the example as well:

```
SET ARITHABORT ON   -- for 80 compatibility or earlier
GO
SET CONCAT_NULL_YIELDS_NULL ON
GO
SET QUOTED_IDENTIFIER ON
GO
SET ANSI_NULLS ON
GO
SET ANSI_PADDING ON
GO
SET ANSI_WARNINGS ON
GO
SET NUMERIC_ROUNDABORT OFF
GO

CREATE UNIQUE CLUSTERED INDEX [IX_vProductAndDescription]
 ON [Production].[vProductAndDescription]
(
      [CultureID] ASC,
      [ProductID] ASC
)
```

The following example shows the `Production.vProductAndDescript` view that the index was created on:

```
CREATE VIEW [Production].[vProductAndDescription]
WITH SCHEMABINDING
AS
View (indexed or standard) to display products
--and product descriptions by language.
SELECT
    p.[ProductID]
    ,p.[Name]
    ,pm.[Name] AS [ProductModel]
    ,pmx.[CultureID]
    ,pd.[Description]
FROM [Production].[Product] p
    INNER JOIN [Production].[ProductModel] pm
    ON p.[ProductModelID] = pm.[ProductModelID]
    INNER JOIN [Production].[ProductModelProductDescriptionCulture] pmx
    ON pm.[ProductModelID] = pmx.[ProductModelID]
    INNER JOIN [Production].[ProductDescription] pd
    ON pmx.[ProductDescriptionID] = pd.[ProductDescriptionID];
```

Indexed Views and Performance

Adding indexes to tables is a generally accepted means for improving database performance. Indexes provide a keyed lookup to rows of data that can improve database access and avoid the performance nightmare of a table scan where the entire contents of a table are searched. The same basic principles apply to indexes on views but indexed views are best utilized to increase performance in the following scenarios:

▶ Aggregations such as SUM or AVG can be precomputed and stored in the index to minimize the potentially expensive computations during query execution.

▶ Large table joins can be persisted to eliminate the need for a join.

▶ A combination of aggregations and large table joins can be stored.

The performance improvements from the aforementioned scenarios can be significant and can justify the use of an index. The Query Optimizer can use the precomputed results that are stored in the view's index and avoid the cost of aggregating or joining the underlying tables. Keep in mind that the Query Optimizer may still use the indexes that are found on the member tables of the view instead of the index on the view. The Query Optimizer uses the following conditions in determining whether the index on the view can be utilized:

▶ The tables in the query FROM clause must be a superset of the tables in the indexed view's FROM clause. In other words, the query must contain all the tables in the view. The query can contain additional tables that are not contained in the view.

▶ The join conditions in the query must be a superset of the view's join conditions.

▶ The aggregate columns in the query must be derivable from a subset of the aggregate columns in the view.

▶ All expressions in the query SELECT list must be derivable from the view SELECT list or from the tables not included in the view definition.

▶ All columns in the query search condition predicates that belong to tables in the view definition must appear in the GROUP BY list, the SELECT list if there is no GROUP BY, or the same or equivalent predicate in the view definition.

NOTE

Predicting the Query Optimizer's use of an indexed view can be complicated and depends on the complexity of the view that is indexed and the complexity of the query that may utilize the view. A detailed discussion of these scenarios is beyond the scope of this chapter, but the Microsoft TechNet article "Improving Performance with SQL Server 2005 Indexed Views" provides that detail. This article includes more than 20 examples that illustrate the use of indexed views and the conditions the Query Optimizer uses in selecting an indexed view.

The flip side of performance with indexes (including those on views) is that there is a cost in maintaining an index. This cost can adversely affect the performance of data modifications against objects that have these indexes. Generally speaking, indexes should *not* be placed on views that have underlying data sets that are frequently updated. Caution must be exercised when placing indexes on views that support online transaction processing (OLTP) applications. A balance must be struck between improving the performance of database modification and improving the performance of database inquiry. Indexed views improve database inquiry. Databases that are used for data warehousing and decision support are usually the best candidates for indexed views.

The impact of data modifications on indexed views is exacerbated by the fact that the complete result set of a view is stored in the database. When the clustered index is created on a view, you specify the clustered index key(s) in the CREATE UNIQUE CLUSTERED INDEX statement, but more than the columns in the key are stored in the database. As in a clustered index on a base table, the B-tree structure of the clustered index contains only the key columns, but the data rows contain all the columns in the view's result set.

The increased space utilized by the index view is demonstrated in the following examples. This first example creates a view and an associated index view similar to the AdventureWorks Production.vProductAndDescription view used in a prior example:

```
result setCREATE VIEW [Production].[vProductAndDescription_2]
WITH SCHEMABINDING
AS
```

```
View (indexed or standard) to display products and
-- product descriptions by language.
SELECT
    p.[ProductID]
    ,pmx.[CultureID]
FROM [Production].[Product] p
    INNER JOIN [Production].[ProductModel] pm
    ON p.[ProductModelID] = pm.[ProductModelID]
    INNER JOIN [Production].[ProductModelProductDescriptionCulture] pmx
    ON pm.[ProductModelID] = pmx.[ProductModelID]
    INNER JOIN [Production].[ProductDescription] pd
    ON pmx.[ProductDescriptionID] = pd.[ProductDescriptionID];
go
CREATE UNIQUE CLUSTERED INDEX [IX_vProductAndDescription_2]
  ON [Production].[vProductAndDescription_2]
(
      [CultureID] ASC,
      [ProductID] ASC
)
```

The difference with this new view is that the result set returns only the two columns in the clustered index; there are no additional columns in the result set.

When the new view and associated index are created, you can compare the amount of physical storage occupied by each. The following example shows the sp_spaceused commands for each view and the associated results:

```
exec sp_spaceused 'Production.vProductAndDescription'
/* results
name                            rows     reserved     data      index_size  unused
---------------------           ----     --------     ------    ----------  ------
vProductAndDescription          1764     592 KB       560 KB    16 KB       16 KB
*/
exec sp_spaceused 'Production.vProductAndDescription_2'
/* results
name                            rows     reserved     data      index_size  unused
---------------------           ----     --------     ------    ----------  ------
vProductAndDescription_2        1764     64 KB        48 KB     16 KB       0 KB
*/
```

Take note of the reserved space and data results for each view. The view that was created with only two result columns takes much less space than the view that has an index with five result columns. You need to consider the overhead of storing these additional result columns along with the index when creating the view and the related index. Changes that are made to any of the columns in the view's bases tables that are part of the view results must also be maintained for the index view as well.

Nonclustered indexes can be created on a view, and they can also provide added query performance benefits when used properly. Typically, columns that are not part of the clustered index on a view are added to the nonclustered index. Like nonclustered indexes on tables, the nonclustered indexes on the view provide additional options for the Query Optimizer when it is choosing the best query path. Common search arguments and foreign key columns that may be joined in the view are common targets for nonclustered indexes.

To Expand or Not to Expand

The expansion of a view to its base tables is a key consideration when evaluating the use of indexes on views. The SQL Server Query Optimizer can expand a view to its base tables or decide to utilize indexes that are found on the view itself. The selection of an index on a view is directly related to the edition of SQL Server 2005 that you are running and the expansion options selected for a related query.

As mentioned earlier, the Enterprise and Developer Editions are the only editions that allow the Query Optimizer to use an indexed view to solve queries that structurally match the view, even if they don't refer to the view by name. For other editions of SQL Server 2005, the view must be referenced in the query, and the NOEXPAND hint must be used as well in order for the Query Optimizer to consider the index on the view. The following example demonstrates the use of the NOEXPAND hint:

```
SELECT *
FROM Production.vProductAndDescription (NOEXPAND)
 WHERE cultureid = 'he'
```

When this example is run against the AdventureWorks database, the execution plan indicates that a clustered index seek will be performed, using the index on the view. If the NOEXPAND hint is removed from the query, the execution plan will ignore the index on the view and return the results from the base table(s). The only exception to this is when the Enterprise or Developer Editions are used. These editions can always consider indexed views but may or may not choose to use them.

SQL Server also has options to force the Query Optimizer to use the expanded base tables and ignore indexed views. The (EXPAND VIEWS) query hint ensures that SQL Server will process a query by accessing data directly from the base tables. This option may seem counterproductive, but it can be useful in situations in which contention exists on an indexed view. It is also handy for testing indexed views and determining overall performance with and without the use of indexed views.

The following example, which utilizes the same view as the previous example, demonstrates the use of the (EXPAND VIEWS) query hint:

```
SELECT *
FROM Production.vProductAndDescription
 WHERE cultureid = 'he'
 OPTION (EXPAND VIEWS)
```

The query plan in this example shows the use of the base tables, and the index on the view is ignored. For more information on query optimization and indexes, see Chapter 29, "Indexes and Performance."

Summary

Views provide a broad spectrum of functionality, ranging from simple organization to improved overall query performance. They can simplify life for developers and users by filtering the complexity of a database. They can help organize data access and provide a security mechanism that helps keep a database safe. Finally, they can provide performance improvements via the use of partitioned views and indexed views that help keep a database fast.

Some of the same benefits, including performance and security benefits, can also be achieved through the use of stored procedures. Chapter 23, "Creating and Managing Stored Procedures," delves into these useful and powerful database objects.

Creating and Managing Stored Procedures

IN THIS CHAPTER

▶ What's New in Creating and Managing Stored Procedures

▶ Advantages of Stored Procedures

▶ Creating Stored Procedures

▶ Executing Stored Procedures

▶ Deferred Name Resolution

▶ Viewing Stored Procedures

▶ Modifying Stored Procedures

▶ Using Input Parameters

▶ Using Output Parameters

▶ Returning Procedure Status

▶ Using Cursors in Stored Procedures

▶ Nested Stored Procedures

▶ Using Temporary Tables in Stored Procedures

▶ Using Remote Stored Procedures

▶ Debugging Stored Procedures Using Microsoft Visual Studio .NET

▶ Using System Stored Procedures

▶ Stored Procedure Performance

▶ Using Dynamic SQL in Stored Procedures

▶ Startup Procedures

▶ T-SQL Stored Procedure Coding Guidelines

▶ Creating and Using CLR Stored Procedures

▶ Using Extended Stored Procedures

A *stored procedure* is one or more SQL commands stored in a database as an executable object. Stored procedures can be called interactively, from within client application code, from within other stored procedures, and from within triggers. Parameters can be passed to and returned from stored procedures to increase their usefulness and flexibility. A stored procedure can also return a number of result sets and a status code.

What's New in Creating and Managing Stored Procedures

The most significant new feature in SQL Server 2005 for stored procedures is the ability to create stored procedures in the CLR, taking advantage of the power and capabilities of the .NET languages. Being able to define procedures in the CLR significantly extends the capabilities of what you can do in stored procedures beyond what is achievable using Transact-SQL (T-SQL) alone. Later in this chapter, we'll introduce you to writing stored procedures in the CLR and provide some general guidelines on when to use the CLR for stored procedures versus when to create them in T-SQL.

> **NOTE**
>
> This chapter focuses primarily on creating T-SQL–based stored procedures. This chapter touches on how to install CLR procedures into SQL Server and some guidelines on using CLR procedures versus T-SQL stored procedures, but for more information and examples on creating CLR procedures, see Chapter 36, "SQL Server and the .NET Framework."

SQL Server 2005 also provides a new way of specifying the security context in which a stored procedure should run, with the addition of the EXECUTE AS clause. The use of this clause is discussed in the "Executing Stored Procedures" section of this chapter.

Within SQL Server Management Studio (SSMS), you can now manage stored procedure source code in a source code control product such as Visual SourceSafe. This feature is covered in the "T-SQL Stored Procedure Coding Guidelines" section of this chapter.

SQL Server 2005 also has a new TRY...CATCH construct that can be used for exception handling within stored procedure code. When an error condition is detected in a T-SQL statement that is inside a TRY block, control is passed to a CATCH block, where the error can be processed. This is covered in more detail in the "T-SQL Stored Procedure Coding Guidelines" section of this chapter.

Advantages of Stored Procedures

Using stored procedures provides many advantages over executing large and complex SQL batches from client applications. The following are some of them:

▶ **Modular programming**—Subroutines and functions are often used in ordinary 3GL and 4GL languages (such as C, C++, and Microsoft Visual Basic) to break code into smaller, more manageable pieces. The same advantages are achieved when using stored procedures, with the difference that the stored procedure is stored in SQL Server and can be called by any client application.

▶ **Restricted, function-based access to tables**—Someone can have access to execute a stored procedure without having permissions to operate directly on the underlying tables.

▶ **Reduced network traffic**—Stored procedures can consist of many individual SQL statements but can be executed with a single statement. This allows you to reduce the number and size of calls from the client to the server.

▶ **Faster execution**—Stored procedures' query plans are kept in memory after the first execution. The code doesn't have to be reparsed and reoptimized on subsequent executions.

▶ **Enforced consistency**—If users modify data only through stored procedures, problems that often result from ad hoc modifications (such as omitting a crucial WHERE clause) are eliminated.

▶ **Reduced operator and programmer errors**—Because less information is being passed, complex tasks can be executed more easily, with less likelihood of SQL errors.

▶ **Automating complex or sensitive transactions**—If all modifications of certain tables take place in stored procedures, you can guarantee the data integrity on those tables.

Some of the disadvantages of using stored procedures (depending on the environment) are as follows:

▶ **Increase in server processing requirements**—Using stored procedures can increase the amount of processing that takes place on the server. In a large user environment with considerable activity in the server, it may be more desirable to offload some of the processing to the client workstation.

▶ **Less cross-DBMS portability**—Although the ANSI-99 SQL standard provides a standard for stored procedures in database management systems (DBMS), the format and structure are different from those of SQL Server stored procedures. These procedures would all have to be rewritten to be compatible with another DBMS environment.

Should you use stored procedures? The answer is (as it often is), that it depends.

If you are working in a two-tier environment, using stored procedures is often advantageous. The trend is shifting to three- (or more) tier environments. In such environments, business logic is often handled in some middle tier (possibly ActiveX objects managed by Microsoft Transaction Server). If you operate in that type of environment, you might want to restrict the stored procedures to performing basic data-related tasks, such as retrievals, insertions, updates, and deletions.

> **NOTE**
>
> You can use stored procedures to make a database sort of a "black box" as far as the developers and the application code are concerned. If all database access is managed through stored procedures, the applications are shielded from possible changes to the underlying database structures.
>
> For example, one organization found the need to split one table across multiple databases. By simply modifying the existing stored procedures to handle the multiple tables and by using distributed partitioned views, the company was able to make this change without requiring any changes to the front-end application code.

Creating Stored Procedures

To create a stored procedure, you need to give the procedure a unique name within the schema and then write the sequence of SQL statements to be executed within the procedure. The following is the basic syntax for creating stored procedures:

```
CREATE { PROC ¦ PROCEDURE } [schema_name.]procedure_name [ ; number ]
    [ { @parameter [ schema_name.]data_type }
        [ VARYING ] [ = default ] [ OUT ¦ OUTPUT ]
    ] [ ,...n ]
[ WITH  {  [ ENCRYPTION ]
        , [ RECOMPILE ]
        , [ EXECUTE_AS_Clause ]
        [ ,...n ] ]
```

```
[ FOR REPLICATION ]
   SQL_Statements
[   RETURN scalar_expression ]
```

It is good programming practice to always end a procedure with the RETURN statement and to specify a return status other than 0 when an error condition occurs. Listing 23.1 shows a simple stored procedure that returns book titles and the names of the authors who wrote them.

LISTING 23.1   A Sample Stored Procedure

```
use bigpubs2005
go
IF EXISTS ( SELECT * FROM INFORMATION_SCHEMA.ROUTINES
               WHERE SPECIFIC_SCHEMA = N'dbo'
                  AND SPECIFIC_NAME = N'title_authors')
   DROP PROCEDURE dbo.title_authors
GO
CREATE PROCEDURE title_authors
AS
BEGIN
   SELECT a.au_lname, a.au_fname, t.title
      FROM titles t INNER JOIN
            titleauthor ta ON t.title_id = ta.title_id RIGHT OUTER JOIN
            authors a ON ta.au_id = a.au_id
   RETURN
END
```

> **NOTE**
>
> Unless stated otherwise, all examples in this chapter run in the context of the
> bigpubs2005 database.

Creating Procedures in SSMS

To create a stored procedure in SSMS, you open the object tree for the database in which you want to create the procedure, open the Programmability folder, right-click the Stored Procedures folder, and from the context menu choose New Stored Procedure. SSMS opens a new query window, populated with code that is based on a default template for stored procedures. Listing 23.2 shows an example of the default template code for a stored procedure that would be opened into a new query window.

LISTING 23.2   An Example of a New Stored Procedure Creation Script Generated by SSMS

```
-- =================================================
-- Template generated from Template Explorer using:
-- Create Procedure (New Menu).SQL
--
-- Use the Specify Values for Template Parameters
-- command (Ctrl-Shift-M) to fill in the parameter
-- values below.
--
-- This block of comments will not be included in
-- the definition of the procedure.
-- =================================================
SET ANSI_NULLS ON
GO
SET QUOTED_IDENTIFIER ON
GO
-- =============================================
-- Author:          <Author,,Name>
-- Create date: <Create Date,,>
-- Description:     <Description,,>
-- =============================================
CREATE PROCEDURE <Procedure_Name, sysname, ProcedureName>
-- Add the parameters for the stored procedure here
<@Param1, sysname, @p1> <Param1_Datatype, , int> = <Param1_Default_Value, , 0>,
<@Param2, sysname, @p2> <Param2_Datatype, , int> = <Param2_Default_Value, , 0>
AS
BEGIN
    -- SET NOCOUNT ON added to prevent extra result sets from
    -- interfering with SELECT statements.
    SET NOCOUNT ON;

    -- Insert statements for procedure here
    SELECT <@Param1, sysname, @p1>, <@Param2, sysname, @p2>
END
GO
```

You can modify the template code as necessary to name the procedure and to specify the parameters, return value, and function body. When you are finished, you can execute the contents of the query window to create the procedure. When you have created the procedure successfully, it is recommended that you save the source code to a file by choosing the Save or Save As option from the File menu. This way, you can re-create the stored procedure from the file if it is accidentally dropped from the database.

TIP

When you create a new stored procedure in SSMS, the procedure does not show up in the `Stored Procedures` folder in the Object Browser unless you right-click the `Stored Procedures` folder and choose the Refresh option.

One thing you might notice about the stored procedure template is that it contains template parameters for things like parameter names, procedure name, author name, create date, and so on. These template parameters are in the format *<parameter, type, value>*:

▶ *parameter_name* is the name of the template parameter in the script.

▶ *data_type* is the optional data type of the template parameter.

▶ *value* is the default value to be used to replace every occurrence of the template parameter in the script

You can auto substitute values for template parameters by selecting Query, Specify Values for Template Parameters or by pressing Ctrl+Shift+M. This brings up the dialog box shown in Figure 23.1

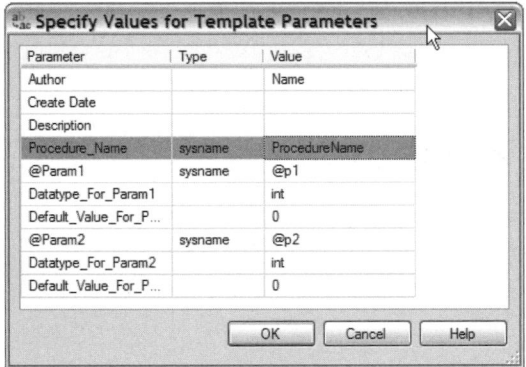

FIGURE 23.1   Using the Specify Values for Template Parameters dialog in SSMS.

You enter the values for the template parameters in the Value column and then click OK. SSMS then substitutes any values you specified wherever the template parameter is used within the template.

An alternative way to create a stored procedure from a template is to use the Template Explorer in SSMS. You can open the Template Explorer by selecting View, Template Explorer in SSMS or by pressing Ctrl+Alt+T. The Template Explorer window appears in SSMS, as shown in Figure 23.2.

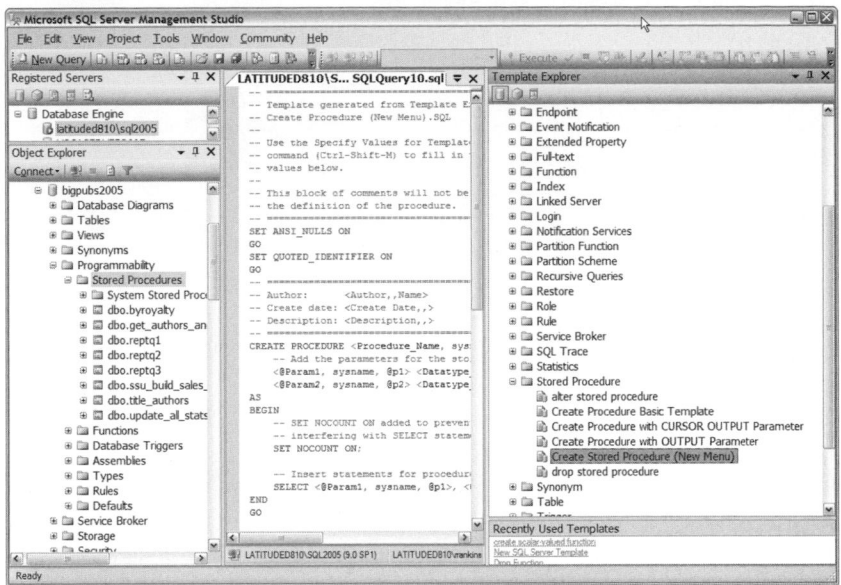

FIGURE 23.2   Using the Template Explorer for creating stored procedures in SSMS.

You can double-click the name of the stored procedure template you want to use or right-click the desired template and then select Open. SSMS opens a new query window, populated with the template code.

NOTE

It is also possible to edit the provided stored procedure templates available in the Template Explorer by right-clicking them and selecting the Edit option. You can then customize the templates to include code fragments, comments, or structure that is more to your preference and save the changes to the template file. However, it is generally recommended that you not modify the provided templates and instead create your own custom templates.

Creating Custom Stored Procedure Templates

To create a custom stored procedure template, you right-click the `Stored Procedure` folder in the Template Explorer and select New. SSMS then creates an entry in the Template Explorer, and you can specify the name for the template.

To begin adding code to the template, you right-click the template and select Edit. This opens a query window in which you can start entering the new template code. Probably the best way to get started is to copy the template code from one of the templates provided with SQL Server 2005 and then modify it as you desire. You then select File, Save to save the template code to the file.

Listing 23.3 shows an example of a new stored procedure template.

LISTING 23.3   An Example of Custom Stored Procedure Template

```
-- ==========================================
-- Create basic stored procedure template
-- ==========================================

-- Drop stored procedure if it already exists
IF EXISTS (
  SELECT *
    FROM INFORMATION_SCHEMA.ROUTINES
   WHERE SPECIFIC_SCHEMA = N'<Schema_Name, sysname, dbo>'
     AND SPECIFIC_NAME = N'<Proc_Name, sysname, myproc>'
)
   DROP PROCEDURE <Schema_Name, sysname, dbo>.<Proc_Name, sysname, myproc>
GO


-- ==========================================
-- Author:          <Author,,Name>
-- Create date: <Create Date,,>
-- Description:     <Description,,>
-- ==========================================
CREATE PROCEDURE <Schema_Name, sysname, dbo>.<Proc_Name, sysname, myproc>
    -- Add the parameters for the stored procedure here
    <@param1, sysname, @p1> <param1_type, , int> = <param1_default, , 0>,
    <@param2, sysname, @p2> <param2_type, , int> = <param2_default, , 0>,
    <@param3, sysname, @p3> <param3_type, , int>  OUTPUT
AS
BEGIN
    -- SET NOCOUNT ON added to prevent extra result sets from
    -- interfering with SELECT statements.
    SET NOCOUNT ON;

    DECLARE @trancnt int
    SELECT @trancnt = @@TRANCOUNT

    if @trancnt = 0
        BEGIN TRAN <Proc_Name, sysname, myproc>
    else
        SAVE TRAN <Proc_Name, sysname, myproc>

    /* Insert processing code here */

    if (@@error != 0) -- check for error condition
    begin
```

LISTING 23.3   Continued

```
        -- rollback to savepoint, or begin tran
        rollback tran <Proc_Name, sysname, myproc>
        -- return error code indicating rollback
        return -101
    end

    /* Insert more processing here if required */



    -- set value of output parameter
    set <@param3,sysname, @p3> = <@param1,sysname, @p1> + <@param2,sysname, @p2>

    if @trancnt = 0      -- this proc issued begin tran
      -- commit tran, decrement @@trancount to 0
      commit tran <Proc_Name, sysname, myproc>
    -- commit not required with save tran

    return 0 /* successful return */

END
GO



-- ============================================
-- Example to execute the stored procedure
-- ============================================
DECLARE <@output_variable, sysname, @p3_output> <output_datatype, , int>

EXECUTE <Schema_name, sysname, dbo>.<Proc_name, sysname, myproc>
        <@param1, sysname, @p1> = <param1_value, , 1>,
        <@param2, sysname, @p2> = <param2_value, , 1>,
        <@param3, sysname, @p3> = <@output_variable, sysname, @p3_output> OUTPUT

SELECT <@output_variable, sysname, @p3_output>
GO
```

After you define a custom stored procedure template, you can use it as you would use the built-in templates. You can double-click it or right-click and select Open, and SSMS opens a new query window with a new stored procedure creation script based on the custom template. If you use the default values for the template parameters, after the parameter substitution, the CREATE PROCEDURE script looks like the one in Listing 23.4.

LISTING 23.4   An Example of a CREATE PROCEDURE Script Generated from the Custom Stored Procedure Template

```
-- ===========================================
-- Create basic stored procedure template
-- ===========================================

-- Drop stored procedure if it already exists
IF EXISTS (
  SELECT *
    FROM INFORMATION_SCHEMA.ROUTINES
   WHERE SPECIFIC_SCHEMA = N'dbo'
     AND SPECIFIC_NAME = N'myproc'
)
    DROP PROCEDURE dbo.myproc
GO


-- ===========================================
-- Author:          Name
-- Create date:
-- Description:
-- ===========================================
CREATE PROCEDURE dbo.myproc
    -- Add the parameters for the stored procedure here
    @p1 int = 0,
    @p2 int = 0,
    @p3 int  OUTPUT
AS
BEGIN
    -- SET NOCOUNT ON added to prevent extra result sets from
    -- interfering with SELECT statements.
    SET NOCOUNT ON;

    DECLARE @trancnt int
    SELECT @trancnt = @@TRANCOUNT

    if @trancnt = 0
        BEGIN TRAN myproc
    else
        SAVE TRAN myproc

    /* Insert processing code here */

    if (@@error != 0) -- check for error condition
    begin
        -- rollback to savepoint, or begin tran
```

LISTING 23.4   Continued

```
        rollback tran myproc
        -- return error code indicating rollback
        return -101
    end

    /* Insert more processing here if required */


    -- set value of output parameter
    set @p3 = @p1 + @p2

    if @trancnt = 0      -- this proc issued begin tran
      -- commit tran, decrement @@trancount to 0
      commit tran myproc
    -- commit not required with save tran

    return 0 /* successful return */

END
GO



-- ============================================
-- Example to execute the stored procedure
-- ============================================
DECLARE @p3_output int

EXECUTE dbo.myproc
        @p1 = 1,
        @p2 = 1,
        @p3 = @p3_output OUTPUT

SELECT @p3_output
GO
```

Temporary Stored Procedures

SQL Server provides the ability to create private and global temporary stored procedures. Temporary stored procedures are analogous to temporary tables in that they can be created with the # and ## prefixes added to the procedure name. The # prefix denotes a local temporary stored procedure; ## denotes a global temporary stored procedure. A local temporary stored procedure can be executed only by the connection that created it, and the procedure is automatically deleted when the connection is closed. A global temporary stored procedure can be accessed by multiple connections and exists until the connection used by the user who created the procedure is closed and any currently executing versions of the procedure by any other connections are completed.

If a stored procedure not prefixed with # or ## is created directly in the `tempdb` database, the stored procedure exists until SQL Server is shut down. Procedures created directly in `tempdb` continue to exist even after the creating connection is terminated.

Temporary stored procedures are provided for backward compatibility with earlier versions of SQL Server that did not support the reuse of execution plans for T-SQL statements or batches. Applications connecting to SQL Server 2000 and higher should use the `sp_executesql` system stored procedure instead of temporary stored procedures.

TIP

It is strongly recommended that `sp_executesql` be used instead of temporary stored procedures. Excessive use of temporary stored procedures can lead to locking contention on the system tables in `tempdb`, which can adversely affect overall system performance.

Executing Stored Procedures

To execute a stored procedure, you simply invoke it by using its name (the same way you probably have already executed system stored procedures, such as `sp_help`). If the execution of the stored procedure isn't the first statement in a batch, you need to precede the procedure name with the EXEC keyword. The following is the basic syntax for executing stored procedures:

```
[EXEC[UTE]] [@status =] [schema].procedure_name[; number]
  [[@param_name =] expression [output][, ... ]]
[WITH RECOMPILE]
```

NOTE

The reason you need the EXEC keyword when invoking a stored procedure in a batch or other stored procedure is quite simple. SQL Server parses the commands sent to it in a batch by searching for keywords. Stored procedure names aren't keywords. If SQL Server finds a procedure name among the SQL statements, chances are that SQL Server will return an error message because it tries to treat it as part of the preceding command. Sometimes the execution is successful, but SQL Server doesn't execute what you want. Consider this example:

```
SELECT * FROM titles
sp_help
```

The SELECT statement runs fine, but the procedure is not executed. The reason is that sp_help ends up being used as a table alias for the titles table in the SELECT statement.

However, if you precede the procedure name with EXEC, like this, you get the expected behavior:

```
SELECT * FROM titles
EXEC sp_help
```

Why don't you have to put EXEC in front of the procedure name if the procedure is the first statement in a batch? If SQL Server doesn't recognize the first string in a batch, it simply assumes that it is a name of a stored procedure. For example, execute the following string and notice the error message:

```
Dsfdskgkghk
go


Msg 2812, Level 16, State 62, Line 1
Could not find stored procedure 'Dsfdskgkghk'.
```

As good programming practice, it is best to always precede stored procedures with the EXEC keyword. This way, it will always work as expected, whether it's the first statement in a batch or not.

Executing Procedures in SSMS

To execute a stored procedure in SSMS, you open the object tree for the database, open the Programmability folder, and open the Stored Procedures folder. Then you right-click the stored procedure and from the context menu choose Execute Stored Procedure. SSMS then presents you with the Execute Procedure dialog, as shown in Figure 23.3. In this window, you can enter values for any parameters contained in the stored procedure. If you want to pass a NULL value to a parameter, you need to be sure to place a check mark in the Pass Null Value check box for that parameter.

After you specify values for all the parameters, SSMS opens up a new query window with the generated execute statement and automatically executes it. It displays any results in the Results window. If the stored procedure contains output parameters, SSMS generates local variables for the output paramaters and uses a SELECT statement to display the values returned to the output paramaters. Listing 23.5 shows an example of the execute script and its results for the procedure invoked in Figure 23.3 (this procedure is the one generated from the customer procedure template, as shown in Listing 23.4).

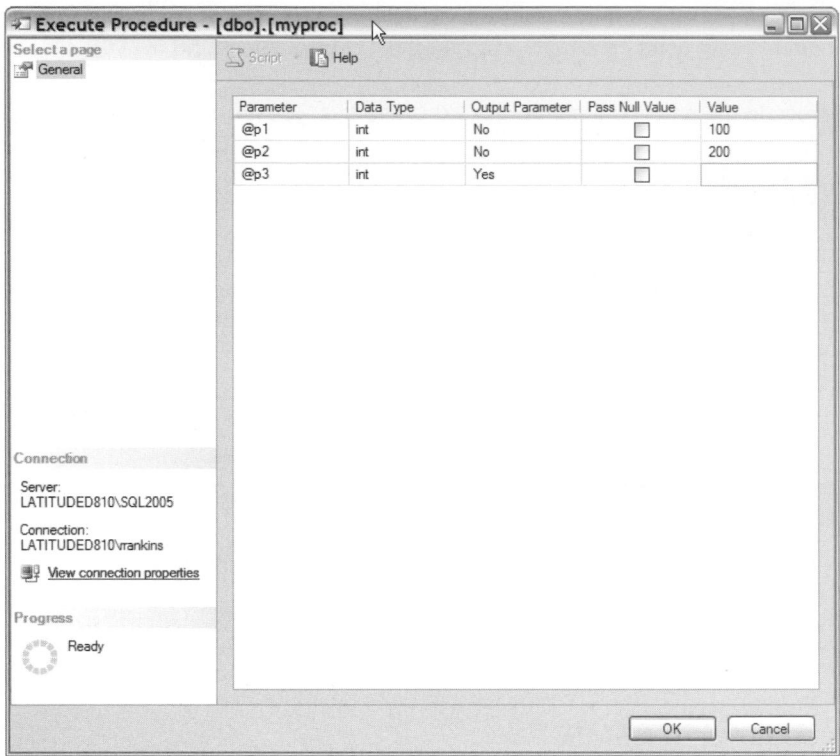

FIGURE 23.3   Using the Execute Procedure dialog in SSMS.

LISTING 23.5   A Procedure Execution Script Generated by SSMS

```
USE [bigpubs2005]
GO

DECLARE @return_value int,
        @p3 int

EXEC @return_value = [dbo].[myproc]
        @p1 = 100,
        @p2 = 200,
        @p3 = @p3 OUTPUT

SELECT @p3 as N'@p3'

SELECT 'Return Value' = @return_value

GO
```

LISTING 23.5   Continued

```
@p3
-----------
300


Return Value
-----------
0
```

Execution Context and the EXECUTE AS **Clause**

Normally, stored procedures execute within the security context of the current user. The exception to this is when the objects referenced by a stored procedure are owned by the same user who created the stored procedure. In this case, permissions on the referenced objects in the stored procedure are dependent on the ownership chain that exists between the calling procedure and the referenced objects. For example, if the creator of a stored procedure also owns the table that it references, the user executing the stored procedure inherits the rights on the referenced table from the owner within the context of the stored procedure, without having to be granted explicit rights on the table by the table owner.

However, there are limitations to using ownership chaining alone for inheriting access permissions:

 ▶ The rights inherited by ownership chaining apply only to DML statements: SELECT, INSERT, UPDATE, and DELETE.

 ▶ The owners of the calling and the called objects must be the same.

 ▶ The rights inherited by ownership chaining do not apply to dynamic queries inside the stored procedure.

In SQL Server 2005, you can implicitly define the execution context of functions (except inline table-valued functions), stored procedures, queues, and triggers by specifying the EXECUTE AS clause. The EXECUTE AS clause allows you to go beyond ownership chaining to specify the security context under which a stored procedure will execute and what access rights the user will have on the referenced objects. The EXECUTE AS clause allows you to specify explicitly the security context under which the stored procedure will execute. In other words, it allows you to specify which user account SQL Server should use to validate permissions on the database objects that are referenced by the stored procedure. The user executing the stored procedure, in effect, impersonates the user specified in the EXECUTE AS clause within the context of the execution of the stored procedure.

The EXECUTE AS clause can be specified when the stored procedure is created to set the default security context for all users when executing the stored procedure. Alternatively, the EXECUTE AS clause can be specified explicitly within the stored procedure code or within each individual user session. When specified in a user session, the security context switches to that specified until the connection is closed, a REVERT statement is run, or another EXECUTE AS statement is run. The syntax of the EXECUTE AS clause for stored procedures is as follows:

```
{ EXEC ¦ EXECUTE } AS { CALLER ¦ SELF ¦ OWNER ¦ 'user_name' }
```

You can specify the following security context options when using the EXECUTE AS clause:

- ▶ **CALLER**—This option specifies that the statements inside the stored procedure are executed in the context of the caller of the module (that is, the current user). The user executing the stored procedure must have execute permission on the stored procedure and also permissions on any database objects that are referenced by the stored procedure that are not owned by the procedure creator. CALLER is the default behavior for all stored procedures, and it is the same as SQL Server 2000 behavior.

- ▶ **SELF**—This option is equivalent to EXECUTE AS *user_name*, where the specified user is the person creating or modifying the stored procedure.

- ▶ **OWNER**—This option specifies that the statements inside the stored procedure execute in the context of the current owner of the stored procedure. If the procedure does not have a specified owner, the owner of the schema in which the procedure was created is used. OWNER must map to a single user account and cannot be a role or group.

- ▶ **'user_name'**—This option specifies that the statements inside the stored procedure execute in the context of the *user_name* specified. Permissions for any objects within the stored procedure are verified against this user. The user specified must exist in the current database and cannot be a group, role, certificate, key, or built-in account.

To determine the execution context of a stored procedure, you can query the *execute_as_principal_id* column in either the sys.sql_modules or sys.assembly_modules catalog view.

Specifying an execution context for a stored procedure can be very useful when you want to define custom permission sets. For example, some actions, such as TRUNCATE TABLE, cannot be explicitly granted to other users. However, if you use the EXECUTE AS clause to set the execution context of a stored procedure to a user who does have truncate table permissions (for example, a user who has permissions to alter the table), you can then incorporate the TRUNCATE TABLE statement within the procedure. Any user to whom you then grant EXECUTE permission on the stored procedure is then able to run it to execute the TRUNCATE TABLE command contained in it.

TIP

When using the EXECUTE AS clause to customize the permission set for a stored procedure, try to specify a login or user that has the least privileges required to perform the operations defined in the stored procedure. Do not specify an account such as a database owner account unless those permissions are required.

To specify the EXECUTE AS clause when you create or modify a stored procedure and specify a user account other than your own, you must have impersonate permissions on the specified user account in addition to having permissions to create or alter the stored procedure. When no execution context is specified or EXECUTE AS CALLER is specified, impersonate permissions are not required.

The following is an example that demonstrates how the user context changes when you use the EXECUTE AS clause in the creation of a stored procedure:

```
use bigpubs2005
go
sp_addlogin fred, fred2005
go
sp_grantdbaccess fred
go

create proc test_execute_as
with EXECUTE AS 'fred'
as
select user_name() as 'User context within proc'
go


select user_name() as 'User context before EXEC'
exec test_execute_as


User context before EXEC
-------------------------------
dbo

User context within proc
-------------------------------
Fred
```

Deferred Name Resolution

In SQL Server 2005, the object names that a stored procedure references do not have to exist at the time the procedure is created. SQL Server 2005 checks for the existence of database objects at the time the stored procedure is executed and returns an error message at runtime if the referenced object doesn't exist. The only exception is when a stored procedure references another stored procedure that doesn't exist. In that case, a warning message is issued, but the stored procedure is still created (see Listing 23.6).

LISTING 23.6   Procedure Name Resolution During Stored Procedure Creation

```
create proc p2
as
exec p3
go
```

```
Cannot add rows to sysdepends for the current object because it depends on the
 missing object 'p3'. The object will still be created.
```

When a table or view *does* exist at procedure creation time, the column names in the referenced table are validated. If a column name is mistyped or doesn't exist, the procedure is not created (see Listing 23.7).

LISTING 23.7   Column Name Validation in Stored Procedures

```
IF EXISTS ( SELECT * FROM INFORMATION_SCHEMA.ROUTINES
            WHERE SPECIFIC_SCHEMA = N'dbo'
              AND SPECIFIC_NAME = N'get_authors_and_titles')
   DROP PROCEDURE dbo.get_authors_and_titles
GO
create proc get_authors_and_titles
as

select a.au_lname, au_fname, title, isbn_number
   from authors a join titleauthor ta on a.au_id = ta.au_id
   join titles t on t.title_id = ta.title_id
return
go
```

```
Server: Msg 207, Level 16, State 1, Procedure get_authors_and_titles, Line 4
Invalid column name 'isbn_number'.
```

One advantage of delayed (or deferred) name resolution is the increased flexibility when creating stored procedures; the order of creating procedures and the tables they reference does not need to be exact. Delayed name resolution is an especially useful feature when a stored procedure references a temporary table that isn't created within that stored procedure. However, at other times, it can be frustrating for a stored procedure to create successfully only to have it fail when it runs due to a missing table, as shown in Listing 23.8.

LISTING 23.8   Runtime Failure of a Stored Procedure with an Invalid Object Reference

```
create proc get_authors_and_titles
as
```

LISTING 23.8   Continued

```
select a.au_lname, au_fname, title, pub_date
    from authors a join titleauthor ta on a.au_id = ta.au_id
    join books t on t.title_id = ta.title_id

go

EXEC get_authors_and_titles
go

Server: Msg 208, Level 16, State 1, Procedure get_authors_and_titles, Line 4
Invalid object name 'books'.
```

Another issue to be careful of with deferred name resolution is that you can no longer rename objects referenced by stored procedures and have the stored procedure continue to work. In versions of SQL Server prior to 7.0, after the stored procedure was created, object references within the stored procedure were made via the object ID rather than the object name. This allowed stored procedures to continue to function properly if a referenced object was renamed. However, now that object names are resolved at execution time, the procedure fails at the statement referencing the renamed object. For the stored procedure to execute successfully, it needs to be altered to specify the new object name.

Identifying Objects Referenced in Stored Procedures

Because changing the name of a table can cause stored procedures to no longer work, you might want to identify which stored procedures reference a specific table so you know which stored procedures will be affected. You can view the dependencies between database objects by querying the sys.sql_dependencies object catalog view. Unfortunately, all you really see if you query the sys.sql_dependencies view is a bunch of numbers—just the IDs of the objects and columns that have a dependency relationship, along with some additional status information.

The better way to display a list of stored procedures that reference a specific table or view, or to display a list of objects referenced by a stored procedure, is to use the sp_depends system procedure:

```
EXEC sp_depends {[[database_name.]schema_name.]object_name}
```

For example, to display the stored procedures, triggers, functions, and views that reference the titles table, you would execute the following:

```
EXEC sp_depends titles
go
```

```
In the current database, the specified object is referenced by the following:
name                                     type
---------------------------------------  ----------------
dbo.reptq1                               stored procedure
dbo.reptq3                               stored procedure
dbo.title_authors                        stored procedure
dbo.titleview                            view
```

To display the objects referenced by the title_authors stored procedure, you would execute the following:

```
exec sp_depends title_authors
go
```

```
In the current database, the specified object references the following:
name                  type            updated selected column
--------------------  --------------- ------- -------- ----------------
dbo.titleauthor       user table      no      yes      au_id
dbo.titleauthor       user table      no      yes      title_id
dbo.authors           user table      no      yes      au_id
dbo.authors           user table      no      yes      au_lname
dbo.authors           user table      no      yes      au_fname
dbo.titles            user table      no      yes      title_id
dbo.titles            user table      no      yes      title
```

You can also see dependency information in SSMS by right-clicking an object and choosing View Dependencies. This brings up the Object Dependencies window, as shown in Figure 23.4. You can view either the objects that depend on the selected object or objects on which the selected object depends. You can also expand the dependency tree for the objects listed in the Dependencies pane.

NOTE

Unfortunately, dependency information is generated only when a stored procedure is created. If a table is dropped and re-created with the same name, the stored procedure continues to work, but the dependency information is deleted when the table is dropped. Another way to identify any stored procedures or other objects that reference a table is to search the text of the stored procedure with a query similar to the following (replacing *tablename* with the name of the object or other text for which you want to search):

```
select * from information_schema.routines
where specific_catalog = 'bigpubs2005'
and specific_schema = 'dbo'
and routine_type = 'Procedure'
and routine_definition like '%tablename%'
```

This query searches the `routine_definition` column of the `routines` information schema view to identify any stored procedures whose code contains the string specified in the `LIKE` clause.

This method is not foolproof, either, because the `routines` information schema view stores only the first 4,000 bytes of a stored procedure. If a stored procedure is larger than 4,000 bytes, *tablename* may not be in the `routine_definition` column and wouldn't match the search argument. The better approach would be to query the `sys.sql_modules` object catalog view, which stores the text of the stored procedure in the `definition` column, which is defined as a `varchar(max)`, so the text will not be truncated:

```
select distinct object_name(object_id)
    from sys.sql_modules
    where definition like '%tablename%'
```

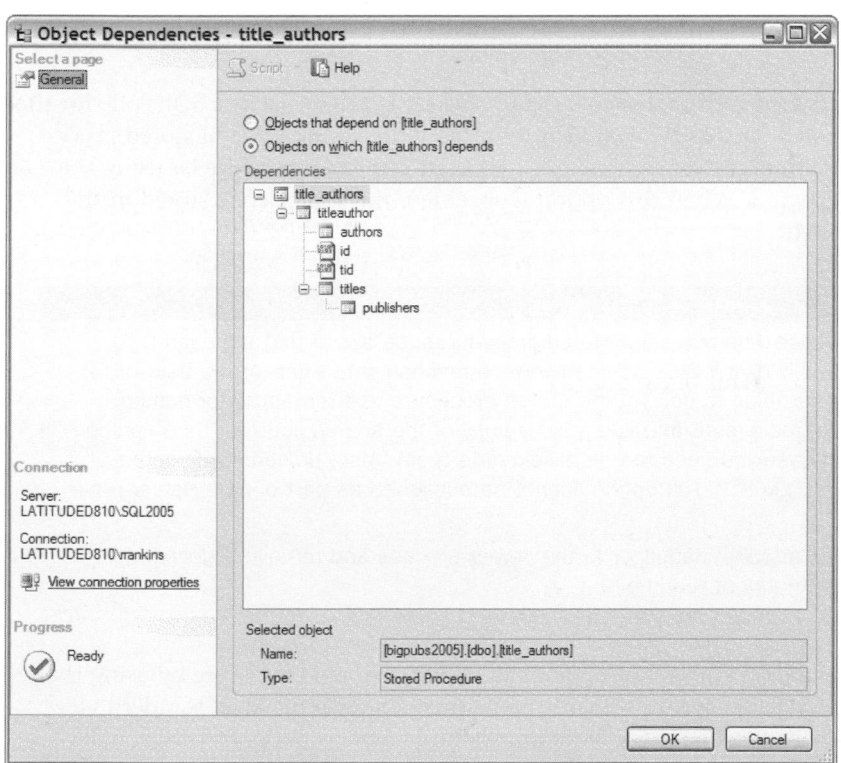

FIGURE 23.4   Viewing object dependencies in SSMS.

Viewing Stored Procedures

As stated in the previous section, you can view the source code for stored procedures in SQL Server 2005 by querying the `definition` column of the object catalog view `sys.sql_modules` or by using the system procedure `sp_helptext` (see Listing 23.9).

LISTING 23.9   Viewing Code for a Stored Procedure by Using sp_helptext

```
exec sp_helptext title_authors
go

Text
-------------------------------------------------------------
CREATE PROCEDURE title_authors
AS
BEGIN
   SELECT a.au_lname, a.au_fname, t.title
      FROM titles t INNER JOIN
           titleauthor ta ON t.title_id = ta.title_id RIGHT OUTER JOIN
           authors a ON ta.au_id = a.au_id
   RETURN
END
```

By default, all users have permission to execute sp_helptext to view the SQL code for the stored procedures in a database. If you want to protect the source code of stored procedures and keep its contents from prying eyes, you can create a procedure by using the WITH ENCRYPTION option. When this option is specified, the source code stored in the database is encrypted.

> **NOTE**
>
> If you use encryption when creating stored procedures, be aware that although SQL Server can internally decrypt the source code, no mechanisms exist for the user or for any of the end-user tools to decrypt the stored procedure text for display or editing. With this in mind, make sure that you store a copy of the source code for those procedures in a file in case you need to edit or re-create them. Also, procedures created by using the WITH ENCRYPTION option cannot be published as part of SQL Server replication.
>
> You can, however, attach a debugger to the server process and retrieve a decrypted procedure from memory at runtime.

As mentioned previously, you can also view the text of a stored procedure by using the ANSI INFORMATION_SCHEMA view routines. The routines view is an ANSI standard view that provides the source code for the stored procedure in the routine_description column. The following example uses the INFORMATION_SCHEMA.routines view to display the source code for the title_authors stored procedure:

```
select routine_definition
from INFORMATION_SCHEMA.routines
where specific_catalog = 'bigpubs2005'
  and specific_schema = 'dbo'
```

```
  and routine_type = 'Procedure'
  and routine_name = 'title_authors'
go


routine_definition
----------------------------------------------------------------------
CREATE PROCEDURE title_authors
AS
BEGIN
   SELECT a.au_lname, a.au_fname, t.title
      FROM titles t INNER JOIN
           titleauthor ta ON t.title_id = ta.title_id RIGHT OUTER JOIN
           authors a ON ta.au_id = a.au_id
   RETURN
END
```

However, as also mentioned previously, the routine_description column is limited to only the first 4,000 characters of the stored procedure code. A better way to view the code with a query is to use the sys.sql_modules object catalog view:

```
select definition
    from sys.sql_modules
    where object_id = object_id('title_authors')
go


CREATE PROCEDURE title_authors
AS
BEGIN
   SELECT a.au_lname, a.au_fname, t.title
      FROM titles t INNER JOIN
           titleauthor ta ON t.title_id = ta.title_id RIGHT OUTER JOIN
           authors a ON ta.au_id = a.au_id
   RETURN
END
```

Finally, one other method of displaying the source code for a stored procedure is to use the new object_definition() function. This function takes the object ID as a parameter. If you, like most other people, do not know the object ID of the procedure in question, you can use the object_id() function. The following is an example of using the object_definition() function:

```
select object_definition(object_id('dbo.title_authors'))
go


----------------------------------------------------------------------
CREATE PROCEDURE title_authors @state char(2) = '%'
```

```
AS
BEGIN
    SELECT a.au_lname, a.au_fname, t.title
        FROM titles t INNER JOIN
            titleauthor ta ON t.title_id = ta.title_id RIGHT OUTER JOIN
            authors a ON ta.au_id = a.au_id
    RETURN
END
```

TIP

If you are running these queries to display the procedure code in SSMS, you probably need to modify the query results options to have the procedures display correctly. From the Query menu, select Query Options. Expand the Results item and select Text. Enter a value up to 8192 for the Maximum Number of Characters Displayed in Each Column setting and click OK.

You probably also want to have the results displayed as text rather than in the grid. To make this change, under the Query menu, select the Results To submenu and then select Results to Text. As a shortcut, you can press Ctrl+T to switch to Results to Text. You can press Ctrl+D to switch back to Results to Grid.

Modifying Stored Procedures

You can modify the text of a stored procedure by using the ALTER PROCEDURE statement. The syntax for ALTER PROCEDURE is the same as for CREATE PROCEDURE (see Listing 23.10). Using ALTER PROCEDURE has a couple advantages over dropping and re-creating a procedure to modify it. The main advantage is that you don't have to drop the procedure first to make the change. The second advantage is that because you don't have to drop the procedure, you don't have to worry about reassigning permissions to it or losing any object dependency information.

LISTING 23.10   Modifying a Stored Procedure by Using ALTER PROCEDURE

```
ALTER PROCEDURE title_authors @state char(2) = '%'
AS
BEGIN
    SELECT a.au_lname, a.au_fname, t.title, t.pubdate
        FROM titles t
        INNER JOIN titleauthor ta ON t.title_id = ta.title_id
        RIGHT OUTER JOIN authors a ON ta.au_id = a.au_id
        where state like @state
    RETURN
END
```

Modifying Stored Procedures with SSMS

You can also use SSMS to create, view, and modify stored procedures.

To edit a stored procedure in SSMS, you expand the `Programmability` folder and then the `Stored Procedures` folder, right-click the name of the procedure you want to modify, and select Modify (see Figure 23.5).

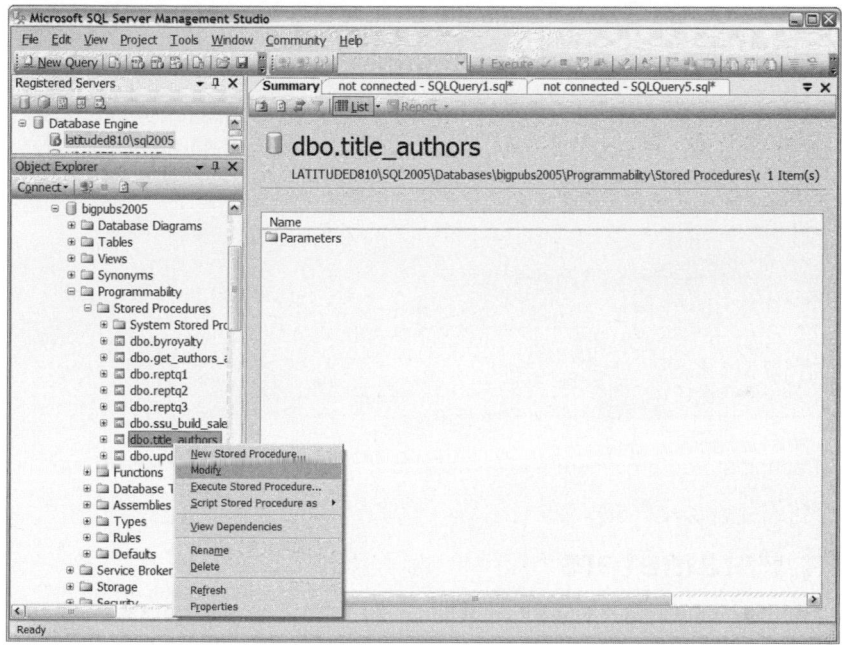

FIGURE 23.5   Modifying stored procedures in SSMS.

SSMS then extracts the `ALTER PROCEDURE` statement for the selected procedure into a new query window. Here you can edit the procedure code as needed and then execute the contents of the query window to modify the procedure. In addition, the Object Browser in SSMS provides other options for extracting the stored procedure source code. It can generate code to create, alter, or drop the selected stored procedure. You can script the stored procedure source code to a new window, to a file, or to the Windows Clipboard by right-clicking the stored procedure name in the Object Browser and choosing the appropriate option (see Figure 23.6).

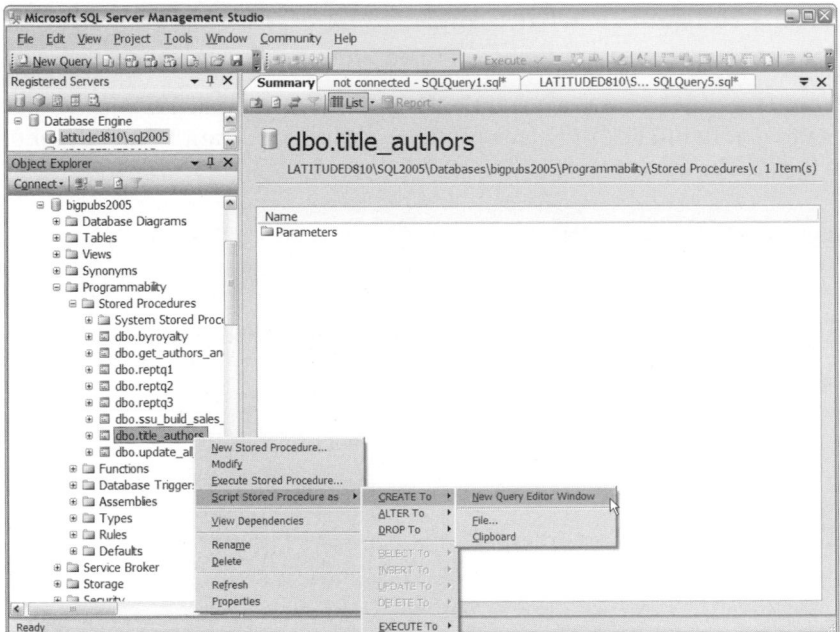

FIGURE 23.6   Extracting stored procedure source code to a new query window.

Using Input Parameters

To increase the flexibility of stored procedures and perform more complex processing, you can pass parameters to procedures. The parameters can be used anywhere that local variables can be used within the procedure code.

The following is an example of a stored procedure that requires three parameters:

```
CREATE PROC myproc
 @parm1 int, @parm2 int, @parm3 int
AS
-- Processing goes here
RETURN
```

To help identify the data values for which the parameters are defined, it is recommended that you give your parameters meaningful names. Parameter names, like local variables, can be up to 128 characters in length, including the @ sign, and they must follow SQL Server rules for identifiers. Up to 2,100 parameters can be defined for a stored procedure.

When you execute a procedure, you can pass the parameters by position or by name:

```
--Passing parameters by position
EXEC myproc 1, 2, 3
--Passing parameters by name
```

```
EXEC myproc @parm2 = 2, @parm1 = 1, @parm3 =3
--Passing parameters by position and name
EXEC myproc 1, @parm3 =3, @parm2 = 2
```

After you've specified one parameter by name, you must pass all subsequent parameters for the procedure in that EXECUTE statement by name as well. You cannot pass any of the subsequent parameters by position. If you want to skip parameters that are not the last parameter(s) in the procedure and have them take default values, you also need to pass parameters by name or use the DEFAULT keyword in place of the parameter value.

TIP

When embedding calls to stored procedures in client applications and script files, it is advisable to pass parameters by name. Reviewing and debugging the code becomes easier that way. Half a day was spent one time debugging a set of nested stored procedures to figure out why they weren't working correctly, only to find the problem was due to a missed parameter; all the parameter values were shifted over one place and the wrong values ended up being passed to the wrong parameters. This resulted in the queries not finding any matching values. Had the parameters been passed by name, this would not have occurred. This was a lesson learned the hard way!

Input parameter values passed in can only be explicit constant values or local variables or parameters. You cannot specify a function or another expression as an input parameter value. You would have to store a return value from the function or expression value in a local variable and pass the local variable as the input parameter. Likewise, you cannot use a function or another expression as a default value for a parameter.

Setting Default Values for Parameters

You can assign a default value to a parameter by specifying a value in the definition of the parameter, as shown in Listing 23.11.

LISTING 23.11   Assigning a Default Value for a Parameter in a Stored Procedure

```
ALTER PROCEDURE title_authors @state char(2) = '%'
AS
SELECT a.au_lname, a.au_fname, t.title
   FROM titles t
   INNER JOIN titleauthor ta ON t.title_id = ta.title_id
   RIGHT OUTER JOIN authors a ON ta.au_id = a.au_id
    WHERE a.state like @state
RETURN
GO
```

You can have SQL Server apply the default value for a parameter during execution by not specifying a value or by specifying the DEFAULT keyword in the execution of the parameter, as shown in Listing 23.12.

LISTING 23.12   Applying a Default Value for a Parameter When Executing a Stored Procedure

```
EXEC title_authors
EXEC title_authors DEFAULT
EXEC title_authors @state = DEFAULT
```

TIP

If you are involved in creating stored procedures that other people will use, you probably want to make the stored procedures as easy to use as possible.

If you leave out a parameter that is required, SQL Server presents an error message. The myproc procedure, shown earlier in this section, requires three parameters: @parm1, @parm2, and @parm3:

```
EXEC myproc

Server: Msg 201, Level 16, State 4, Procedure myproc, Line 0
Procedure 'myproc' expects parameter '@parm1', which was not
 supplied.
```

Note that SQL Server only complains about the first missing parameter. The programmer passes the first parameter, only to find out that more parameters are required. This is a good way to annoy a programmer or an end user.

When you execute a command-line program, you probably expect that you can use /? to obtain a list of the parameters the program expects. You can program stored procedures in a similar manner by assigning NULL (or some other special value) as a default value to the parameters and checking for that value inside the procedure. The following is an outline of a stored procedure that presents the user with information about the parameters expected if the user doesn't pass parameters:

```
CREATE PROC MyProc2
 @parm1 int = NULL, @parm2 int = 32, @parm3 int = NULL
AS
IF (@parm1 IS NULL or @parm1 NOT BETWEEN 1 and 10) OR
   @parm3 IS NULL
PRINT 'Usage:
 EXEC MyProc2
 @parm1 int,    (Required: Can be between 1 and 10)
 @parm2 = 32,   (Optional: Default value of 32)
 @parm3 int,    (Required: Any number within range)'
-- Processing goes here
RETURN
GO

EXEC MyProc2
GO

Usage:
 EXEC MyProc2
```

```
@parm1 int,    (Required: Can be between 1 and 10)
@parm2 = 32,   (Optional: Default value of 32)
@parm3 int,    (Required: Any number within range)
```

You can develop a standard for the way the message is presented to the user, but
what is important is that the information is presented at all.

To display the parameters defined for a stored procedure, you can view them in the SSMS
Object Explorer (see Figure 23.7) or by executing the sp_help stored procedure, as shown
in Listing 23.13. (Note that the output has been edited to fit the page.)

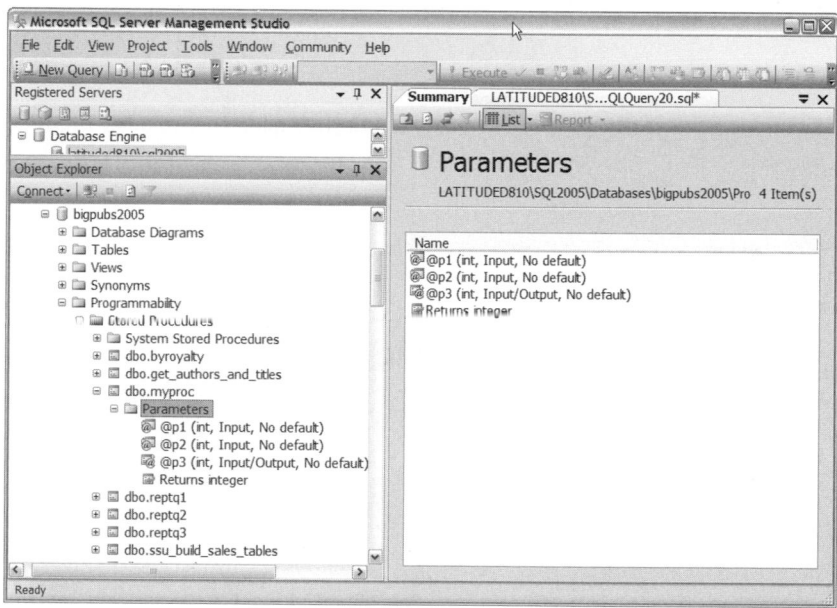

FIGURE 23.7   Displaying stored procedure parameters in SSMS.

LISTING 23.13   Displaying Stored Procedure Parameters by Using sp_help

```
exec sp_help title_authors
Name              Owner     Type              Created_datetime
----------------  --------  ----------------  ------------------------------
title_authors     dbo       stored procedure  2001-04-15 21:15:06.540




Parameter_name Type  Length Prec Scale Param_order Collation
-------------- ----- ------ ---- ----- ----------- ----------------------------
@state         char  2      2    NULL              1 SQL_Latin1_General_CP1_CI_AS
```

You can also display the stored procedure parameters by running a query against the INFORMATION_SCHEMA view parameters:

```
select substring(Parameter_NAME,1, 30) as Parameter_name,
       substring (DATA_TYPE, 1, 20) as Data_Type,
       CHARACTER_MAXIMUM_LENGTH as Length,
       ordinal_position as param_order,
       Collation_name
from INFORMATION_SCHEMA.parameters
where specific_name = 'title_authors'
  and specific_schema = 'dbo'
order by ordinal_position

go


Parameter_name    Data_Type     Length  param_order Collation_name
----------------  ------------  ------- ----------- ----------------------------
@state            char               2            1 SQL_Latin1_General_CP1_CI_AS
```

Passing Object Names As Parameters

You cannot pass object names as parameters to be used in place of an object name in a stored procedure unless the object name is used as an argument in a where clause or in a dynamically built query, using the EXEC statement. For example, the code in Listing 23.14 generates an odd error message when you try to create the stored procedure.

LISTING 23.14   Attempting to Create a Stored Procedure by Using a Parameter to Pass in a Table Name

```
CREATE  proc find_data @table varchar(128)
as

select * from @table

GO

Server: Msg 137, Level 15, State 2, Procedure find_data, Line 6
Must declare the variable '@table'.
```

This error seems odd because the variable @table is declared as a parameter. However, SQL Server is expecting the variable to be defined as a table variable. (Using table variables in stored procedures is discussed later in this chapter.) Listing 23.15 shows a possible approach to this problem using the exec() command.

LISTING 23.15   Passing a Table as a Parameter to a Stored Procedure for Dynamic Query Execution

```
CREATE  proc find_data @table varchar(128)
as

exec ('select * from ' + @table)
return
go

exec find_data @table = 'publishers'
go
```

pub_id	pub_name	city	state	country
0736	New Moon Books	Boston	MA	USA
0877	Binnet & Hardley	Washington	DC	USA
1389	Algodata Infosystems	Berkeley	CA	USA
1622	Five Lakes Publishing	Chicago	IL	USA
1756	Ramona Publishers	Dallas	TX	USA
...				
9952	Scootney Books	New York	NY	USA
9999	Lucerne Publishing	Paris	NULL	France

Using Wildcards in Parameters

Wildcards can be included in varchar-based input parameters and used in a LIKE clause in a query to perform pattern matching. However, you should not use the char data type for parameters that will contain wildcard characters because SQL Server pads spaces onto the value passed into the parameter to expand it to the specified size of the char datatype. For example, if you declared an @lastname parameter as char(40) and passed in 'S%', SQL Server would search not for a string starting with 'S' but for a string starting with 'S', any characters, and ending with up to 38 spaces. This would likely not match any actual data values.

Also, to increase the flexibility of a stored procedure that searches for character strings, you can default the parameter to '%', as in the following example:

```
IF EXISTS ( SELECT * FROM INFORMATION_SCHEMA.ROUTINES
            WHERE SPECIFIC_SCHEMA = N'dbo'
              AND SPECIFIC_NAME = N'find_authors')
   DROP PROCEDURE dbo.find_authors
GO
 create proc find_authors @lastname varchar(40) = '%'
as
    select au_id, au_lname, au_fname
        from authors
```

```
        where au_lname like @lastname
        order by au_lname, au_fname
```

This procedure, if passed no parameter, returns data for all authors in the `authors` table. If passed a string containing wildcard characters, this procedure returns data for all authors matching the search pattern specified. If a string containing no wildcards is passed, the query performs a search for exact matches against the string value.

Unfortunately, wildcard searches can only be performed against character strings. If you want to have similar flexibility searching against a numeric value, such as an integer, you can default the value to `NULL` and when the parameter is `NULL`, compare the column with itself, as shown in the following example:

```
IF EXISTS ( SELECT * FROM INFORMATION_SCHEMA.ROUTINES
             WHERE SPECIFIC_SCHEMA = N'dbo'
               AND SPECIFIC_NAME = N'find_titles_by_sales')
   DROP PROCEDURE dbo.find_titles_by_sales
GO
create proc find_titles_by_sales @ytd_sales int = null
as
    select title_id, title, ytd_sales
        from titles
        where ytd_sales = isnull(@ytd_sales, ytd_sales)
```

However, the problem with this approach is that the procedure returns all rows from the `titles` table except those in which `ytd_sales` contains a `NULL` value. This is because `NULL` is never considered equal to `NULL`; you cannot compare an unknown value with another unknown value. To return all rows, including those in which `ytd_sales` is `NULL`, you need to implement a dual-query solution, as in the following example:

```
IF EXISTS ( SELECT * FROM INFORMATION_SCHEMA.ROUTINES
             WHERE SPECIFIC_SCHEMA = N'dbo'
               AND SPECIFIC_NAME = N'find_titles_by_sales')
   DROP PROCEDURE dbo.find_titles_by_sales
GO
create proc find_titles_by_sales @ytd_sales int = null
as
if @ytd_sales is null
    select title_id, title, ytd_sales
        from titles
else
    select title_id, title, ytd_sales
        from titles
        where ytd_sales= @ytd_sales
```

Using Output Parameters

If a calling batch passes a variable as a parameter to a stored procedure and that parameter is modified inside the procedure, the modifications are not passed to the calling batch unless you specify the OUTPUT keyword for the parameter when creating and executing the stored procedure.

If you want a procedure to be able to pass parameters out from the procedure, you need to use the keyword OUTPUT when creating and calling the procedure. The following example accepts two parameters, one of which is used as an output parameter:

```
IF EXISTS ( SELECT * FROM INFORMATION_SCHEMA.ROUTINES
              WHERE SPECIFIC_SCHEMA = N'dbo'
                AND SPECIFIC_NAME = N'ytd_sales')
   DROP PROCEDURE dbo.ytd_sales
GO
CREATE PROC ytd_sales
@title varchar(80), @ytd_sales int OUTPUT
AS
SELECT @ytd_sales = ytd_sales
   FROM titles
   WHERE title = @title
RETURN
```

The calling batch (or stored procedure) needs to declare a variable to store the returned value. The execute statement must include the OUTPUT keyword as well, or the modifications won't be reflected in the calling batch's variable:

```
DECLARE @sales_up_to_today  int
EXEC ytd_sales 'Life Without Fear', @sales_up_to_today OUTPUT
PRINT 'Sales this year until today''s date: ' +
      CONVERT(VARCHAR(10), @sales_up_to_today) + '.'
```

```
Sales this year until today's date: 111.
```

You can also pass the output parameter by name:

```
DECLARE @sales_up_to_today  int
EXEC ytd_sales 'Life Without Fear',
     @ytd_sales = @sales_up_to_today OUTPUT
PRINT 'Sales this year until today''s date: ' +
      CONVERT(VARCHAR(10), @sales_up_to_today) + '.'
```

Note that when you pass an output parameter by name, the parameter name (@ytd_sales, in this example) is listed on the left side of the expression, and the local variable (@sales_up_to_today), which is set equal to the value of the output paramater, is on the right side of the expression. An output parameter can also serve as an input parameter.

23

Output parameters can also be passed back and captured in a client application by using ADO, ODBC, OLE DB, and so on.

Returning Procedure Status

Most programming languages have the ability to pass a status code to the caller of a function or a subroutine. A value of 0 generally indicates that the execution was successful. SQL Server stored procedures are no exception.

SQL Server automatically generates an integer status value of 0 after successful completion of a stored procedure. If SQL Server detects an error, a status value between -1 and -99 is returned. You can use the RETURN statement to explicitly pass a status value less than -99 or greater than 0. The calling batch or procedure can set up a local variable to retrieve and check the return status.

In Listing 23.16, you want to return the year-to-date sales for a given title as a result set. If the title does not exist, you do not want to return an empty result set. Therefore, you perform a check inside the procedure and return the status value -101 if the title does not exist.

In the calling batch or stored procedure, you need to create a variable to hold the return value. The variable name is passed after the EXECUTE statement.

LISTING 23.16   Returning a Status Code from a Stored Procedure

```
IF EXISTS ( SELECT * FROM INFORMATION_SCHEMA.ROUTINES
            WHERE SPECIFIC_SCHEMA = N'dbo'
               AND SPECIFIC_NAME = N'ytd_sales2')
    DROP PROCEDURE dbo.ytd_sales2
GO
--Create the procedure
CREATE PROC ytd_sales2 @title varchar(80)
AS
IF NOT EXISTS (SELECT * FROM titles WHERE title = @title)
    RETURN -101
SELECT ytd_sales
    FROM titles
    WHERE title = @title
RETURN
GO


-- Execute the procedure
DECLARE @status int
EXEC @status = ytd_sales2 'Life without Fear'
IF @status = -101
    PRINT 'No title with that name found.'
```

LISTING 23.16   Continued

```
go

ytd_sales
-----------
111

-- Execute the procedure
DECLARE @status int
EXEC @status = ytd_sales2 'Life without Beer'
IF @status = -101
    PRINT 'No title with that name found.'
go

No title with that name found.
```

Return values can also be passed back and captured by the client application through ADO, ODBC, OLE DB, and so on.

Using Cursors in Stored Procedures

When using cursors in stored procedures in SQL Server 2005, you need to be aware of the scope of the cursor and how it can be accessed within calling or called procedures. Cursors in SQL Server can be declared as local or global. A global cursor defined in a stored procedure is available until it is deallocated or when the connection closes. A local cursor goes out of scope when the stored procedure that declared it terminates or the procedure scope changes.

If neither the GLOBAL nor LOCAL option is specified when the cursor is declared in a stored procedure, the default cursor type is determined by the database option CURSOR_DEFAULT, which is set with the ALTER DATABASE statement. The default value for the option is_local_cursor_default is FALSE, which defaults cursors as global, to match the behavior of earlier versions of SQL Server. If this value in the sys.databases catalog view is set to TRUE, T-SQL cursors default to local cursors.

> **TIP**
>
> The default setting in SQL Server 2005 is for all cursors to be global if neither GLOBAL nor LOCAL is specified, which provides backward compatibility for versions of SQL Server prior to 7.0, in which all cursors were global. The default setting for cursors might change in future versions, so it is recommended that you explicitly specify the LOCAL or GLOBAL option when declaring your cursors so your code will not be affected by changes to the default setting.

If stored procedures are nested, they can access cursors declared in higher-level stored procedures in the call tree, only if the cursors are declared as global. If the cursor is declared as local, it can only be referenced within the scope of the stored procedure it is declared in. It cannot be accessed from a called or calling procedure. If the cursor is declared as global, it can be accessed in a called procedure or even from within the calling procedure.

In the following example, procedure p1 creates a cursor defined as global which can then be accessed by procedure p2:

```
if object_id('p1') is not null
    drop proc p1
go
if object_id('p2') is not null
    drop proc p2
go
create proc p2
as
set nocount on
-- fetch from global cursor defined in calling proc p1
fetch c1
return
go

create proc p1
as
set nocount on
-- Declare global cursor
declare c1 cursor global for
   select title_id, type from titles
open c1
fetch c1
exec p2
close c1
deallocate c1
go


exec p1
go


title_id type
-------- ------------
BI0194   biography

title_id type
-------- ------------
BI1408   biography
```

As you can see in the preceding example, the cursor c1 is defined as global in procedure p1 and can be accessed from within procedure p2.

> **TIP**
>
> To clean up the output when using cursors within stored procedures, specify the `set nocount on` option within the stored procedure to disable the *n* `rows(s) affected` that would normally be displayed after each invocation of the `fetch` statement.

Now, look what happens if you modify procedure p1 to declare the cursor as local:

```
alter proc p1
as
set nocount on
-- Declare local cursor
declare c1 cursor local for
    select title_id, type from titles
open c1
fetch c1
exec p2
close c1
deallocate c1
go
exec p1
go


title_id type
-------- ------------
BI0194   biography

Msg 16916, Level 16, State 1, Procedure p2, Line 5
A cursor with the name 'c1' does not exist.
```

Notice in this example that the cursor c1 was not available to the procedure p2. This is because the cursor was defined as local and is only accessible within the scope of procedure p1. Because the cursor is localized to the scope of p1, this allows you to define a cursor with the same name within the scope of procedure p2:

```
alter proc p2
as
set nocount on
-- Declare another local cursor with same name 'c1'
declare c1 cursor local for
    select au_id, au_lname from authors
open c1
fetch c1
```

23

```
close c1
deallocate c1
return
go
exec p1
go

title_id type
-------- ------------
BI0194   biography

au_id        au_lname
----------   ---------------------------------------
047-43-0360 Michener
```

Notice that by defining the scope of both cursors as local, each procedure can create a cursor with the same name without any conflict between them. You can take advantage of this feature if you have a recursive stored procedure that uses a cursor as demonstrated in the "Recursive Stored Procedures" section later in this chapter.

In addition to a global cursor defined in a calling procedure being available within a called procedure, the reverse is possible as well. A global cursor defined in a called procedure is available to the calling procedure as demonstrated in the following example:

```
alter proc p2
as
set nocount on
-- declare global cursor c2
declare c2 cursor global for
    select au_id, au_lname from authors
open c2
--do not close/deallocate cursor so it can be used by calling proc p1
return
go
alter proc p1
as
set nocount on
declare c1 cursor local for
    select title_id, type from titles
open c1
fetch c1
exec p2
-- fetch from global cursor declared in proc p2
fetch c2
close c1
deallocate c1
```

```
close c2
deallocate c2
return
go
exec p1
go


title_id type
-------- -----------
BI0194   biography


au_id       au_lname
----------- ---------------------------------------
047-43-0360 Michener
```

As you can see in this last example, the global cursor defined in the called procedure p2 is available for use by the calling procedure p1 as long as the cursor is left open by the called procedure p2.

<table>
<tr><td>NOTE</td></tr>
</table>

Remember that global cursors persist beyond the scope of the procedure they are defined in. If you are going to declare global cursors in called procedures to be accessed by the calling procedure, be sure the calling procedure closes and deallocates the cursor declared in the called procedure before it returns. Otherwise, the cursor will remain open and defined until the end of the user session. The following example demonstrates this behavior:

```
alter proc p1
as
set nocount on
declare c1 cursor local for
   select title_id, type from titles
open c1
fetch c1
exec p2
-- fetch from global cursor declared in proc p2
fetch c2
close c1
deallocate c1
-- Cursor c2 is not closed/deallocated before return
return
go
exec p1
go
--Cursor c2 should still be open here so the following fetch will work
```

```
fetch c2
go


title_id type
........ ............
BI0194   biography


au_id       au_lname
.......... ........................................
047-43-0360 Michener


au_id       au_lname
.......... ........................................
052-04-3539 Gray
```

Using CURSOR **Variables in Stored Procedures**

Another method available in SQL Server 2005 for passing cursor result sets between stored procedures is using the cursor data type. The cursor data type can be used to bind a cursor result set to a local variable and that variable can then be used to manage and access the cursor result set. Cursor variables can be referenced in any of the cursor management statements: OPEN, FETCH, CLOSE, and DEALLOCATE.

A stored procedure can pass cursor variables as output parameters only; cursor variables cannot be passed as input parameters. When defining a CURSOR output parameter, the VARYING keyword must also be specified.

When assigning a cursor to a cursor variable, you must use the SET command because an assignment select is not allowed. Cursor data types can either be the source or the target in a SET statement.

The following stored procedure declares a cursor, opens it, and passes it back as an output parameter using the cursor data type:

```
IF EXISTS ( SELECT * FROM INFORMATION_SCHEMA.ROUTINES
            WHERE SPECIFIC_SCHEMA = N'dbo'
              AND SPECIFIC_NAME = N'cursor_proc')
   DROP PROCEDURE dbo.cursor_proc
GO
create proc cursor_proc @cursor CURSOR VARYING OUTPUT
as
declare curs1 cursor global for
   select cast(title as varchar(30)) as title , pubdate from titles
set @cursor = curs1
open curs1
return
```

A cursor variable and the declared cursor name can be used interchangeably in cursor commands. You can use either the variable name or the declared name to open, fetch, close, and deallocate the cursor. Fetching using either the cursor name or the cursor variable fetches the next row in the cursor result set. Listing 23.17 illustrates how each fetch gets the next row in the result set.

LISTING 23.17   Fetching Cursor Rows by Using the Declared Cursor Name and a Cursor Variable

```
set nocount on
declare @curs CURSOR
exec cursor_proc @cursor = @curs output
fetch curs1
fetch @curs
fetch curs1
fetch @curs
go
```

title	pubdate
Samuel Johnson	1995-09-19 00:00:00.000

title	pubdate
Freud, Dora, and Vienna 1900	1995-02-25 00:00:00.000

title	pubdate
Freud: A Life for Our Time	1995-06-21 00:00:00.000

title	pubdate
For Love of the World	1993-01-06 00:00:00.000

One of the problems with a cursor declared as a global cursor in the procedure is that you cannot invoke the procedure again within the same session unless the cursor is closed and deallocated. This can be a problem if you need to get the cursor into a cursor variable again. If you try to invoke the procedure again, and the cursor hasn't been closed or deallocated, you get error messages, as shown in the following example:

```
set nocount on
declare @curs CURSOR
exec cursor_proc @cursor = @curs output
go
```

Msg 16915, Level 16, State 1, Procedure cursor_proc, Line 4

```
A cursor with the name 'curs1' already exists.
Msg 16905, Level 16, State 1, Procedure cursor_proc, Line 6
The cursor is already open.
```

```
close curs1
deallocate curs1
go
```

One way to work around this issue is to use the CURSOR_STATUS function in the procedure to check whether the cursor exists yet before declaring it and also to check whether the cursor is already open before opening it. Thus, it declares the cursor only if it doesn't exist and opens the cursor only if it's closed, but it always returns the cursor in the cursor output parameter. Keeping this in mind, take a look at a revised version of the cursor_proc stored procedure:

```
IF EXISTS ( SELECT * FROM INFORMATION_SCHEMA.ROUTINES
              WHERE SPECIFIC_SCHEMA = N'dbo'
                AND SPECIFIC_NAME = N'cursor_proc')
   DROP PROCEDURE dbo.cursor_proc
GO
go
create proc cursor_proc @cursor CURSOR VARYING OUTPUT
as
if CURSOR_STATUS('global', 'curs1') = -3  -- cursor does not exist
    declare curs1 cursor global for
        select cast(title as varchar(30)) as title , pubdate from titles
if CURSOR_STATUS('global', 'curs1') = -1  -- cursor is not open
    open curs1
set @cursor = curs1
return
```

When the procedure is written this way, you can now safely call the procedure at any time, even if the cursor is already open. If the cursor is open, you only need to get the cursor into the cursor variable.

If you want to close the cursor, you can do so by using either the cursor variable or the declared cursor name. When it is closed, however, you cannot fetch more rows from the cursor or the cursor variable until it is reopened:

```
set nocount on
declare @curs CURSOR
exec cursor_proc @cursor = @curs output
fetch curs1
fetch @curs
-- close the cursor
close curs1
-- try to fetch from the cursor variable
```

```
fetch @curs
go
```

```
title                           pubdate
----------------------------    ----------------------
Samuel Johnson                  1995-09-19 00:00:00.000
```

```
title                           pubdate
----------------------------    ----------------------
Freud, Dora, and Vienna 1900    1995-02-25 00:00:00.000
```

```
Msg 16917, Level 16, State 2, Line 7
Cursor is not open.
```

However, if the cursor has been assigned to a cursor variable, it cannot be fully deallo-cated until the last remaining reference to the cursor issues the DEALLOCATE command. Until all references to the cursor issue the DEALLOCATE command, the cursor can be reopened, but only by using the remaining cursor reference(s) that hasn't issued the DEALLOCATE command. An example of this behavior is shown in Listing 23.18. If the cursor has not been closed, only the last deallocation of the cursor closes it.

LISTING 23.18   Deallocating a Cursor by Cursor Name and Cursor Variable

```
declare @curs CURSOR
exec cursor_proc @cursor = @curs output

print 'FETCH VIA NAME:'
fetch curs1
print 'FETCH VIA VARIABLE:'
fetch @curs

print 'CLOSE BY NAME'
close curs1
print 'DEALLOCATE BY NAME'
deallocate curs1
print 'ATTEMPT FETCH VIA VARIABLE (CURSOR SHOULD BE CLOSED):'
fetch @curs
print 'ATTEMPT TO OPEN VIA VARIABLE (CURSOR SHOULD OPEN, NOT DEALLOCATED YET)'
open @curs
print 'ATTEMPT FETCH VIA VARIABLE (SHOULD START FROM BEGINNING AGAIN):'
fetch @curs
print 'CLOSE AND DEALLOCATE VIA VARIABLE'
close @curs
deallocate @curs
print 'ATTEMPT TO OPEN VIA VARIABLE (SHOULD FAIL, SINCE NOW FULLY DEALLOCATED):'
open @curs
```

23

LISTING 23.18   Continued

```
go

FETCH VIA NAME:
TITLE                           PUBDATE
------------------------------  ----------------------
SAMUEL JOHNSON                  1995-09-19 00:00:00.000

FETCH VIA VARIABLE:
TITLE                           PUBDATE
------------------------------  ----------------------
FREUD, DORA, AND VIENNA 1900    1995-02-25 00:00:00.000

CLOSE BY NAME

DEALLOCATE BY NAME

ATTEMPT FETCH VIA VARIABLE (CURSOR SHOULD BE CLOSED):
MSG 16917, LEVEL 16, STATE 2, LINE 15
CURSOR IS NOT OPEN.

ATTEMPT TO OPEN VIA VARIABLE (CURSOR SHOULD OPEN, NOT DEALLOCATED YET)

ATTEMPT FETCH VIA VARIABLE (SHOULD START FROM BEGINNING AGAIN):
TITLE                           PUBDATE
------------------------------  ----------------------
SAMUEL JOHNSON                  1995-09-19 00:00:00.000


CLOSE AND DEALLOCATE VIA VARIABLE
ATTEMPT TO OPEN VIA VARIABLE (SHOULD FAIL, SINCE NOW FULLY DEALLOCATED):
MSG 16950, LEVEL 16, STATE 2, LINE 27
The variable '@curs' does not currently have a cursor allocated to it.
```

If the cursor is declared as a local cursor within a stored procedure, it can still be passed back in an output variable to a cursor variable, but it is accessible only through the cursor variable, as shown in Listing 23.19.

LISTING 23.19   Assigning a Local Cursor to a Cursor Output Parameter

```
IF EXISTS ( SELECT * FROM INFORMATION_SCHEMA.ROUTINES
            WHERE SPECIFIC_SCHEMA = N'dbo'
                AND SPECIFIC_NAME = N'cursor_proc2')
    DROP PROCEDURE dbo.cursor_proc2
GO
```

LISTING 23.19   Continued

```
create proc cursor_proc2 @cursor CURSOR varying output
as
declare curs1 cursor local for
    select cast(title as varchar(30)) as title , pubdate from titles
set @cursor = curs1
open curs1
go
declare @curs CURSOR
exec cursor_proc2 @cursor = @curs output

print 'ATTEMPT FETCH VIA NAME:'
fetch next from curs1
print 'ATTEMPT FETCH VIA VARIABLE:'
fetch next from @curs
go

ATTEMPT FETCH VIA NAME:
Msg 16916, Level 16, State 1, Line 4
A cursor with the name 'curs1' does not exist.
ATTEMPT FETCH VIA VARIABLE:
title                          pubdate
----------------------------   ----------------------
Samuel Johnson                 1995-09-19 00:00:00.000
```

Nested Stored Procedures

Stored procedures can call other stored procedures, and any of those procedures can call other procedures, up to a maximum nesting level of 32 levels deep. If you exceed the 32-level nesting limit, an error message is raised, the batch is aborted, and any open transaction in the session is rolled back. The nesting level limit prevents a recursive procedure from calling itself repeatedly in an infinite loop until a stack overflow occurs. To check the depth to which a procedure is nested, you use the system function @@NESTLEVEL (see Listing 23.20).

LISTING 23.20   Checking @@NESTLEVEL in Nested Stored Procedures

```
create proc main_proc
as
print 'Nesting Level in main_proc before sub_proc1 = ' + str(@@NESTLEVEL, 1)
exec sub_proc1
print 'Nesting Level in main_proce after sub_proc1 = ' + str(@@NESTLEVEL, 1)
exec sub_proc2
print 'Nesting Level in main_proc after sub_proc2 = ' + str(@@NESTLEVEL, 1)
return
```

LISTING 23.20   Continued

```
go

create proc sub_proc1
as
print 'Nesting Level in sub_proc1 before sub_proc2 = ' + str(@@NESTLEVEL, 1)
exec sub_proc2
print 'Nesting Level in sub_proc1 after sub_proc2 = ' + str(@@NESTLEVEL, 1)
return
go

create proc sub_proc2
as
print 'Nesting Level in sub_proc2 = ' + str(@@NESTLEVEL, 1)
return
go

print 'Nesting Level before main_proc = ' + str(@@NESTLEVEL, 1)
exec main_proc
print 'Nesting Level after main_proc = ' + str(@@NESTLEVEL, 1)
go

Cannot add rows to sysdepends for the current object because it depends on the
 missing object 'sub_proc1'. The object will still be created.
Cannot add rows to sysdepends for the current object because it depends on the
 missing object 'sub_proc2'. The object will still be created.
Cannot add rows to sysdepends for the current object because it depends on the
 missing object 'sub_proc2'. The object will still be created.
Nesting Level before main_proc = 0
Nesting Level in main_proc before sub_proc1 = 1
Nesting Level in sub_proc1 before sub_proc2 = 2
Nesting Level in sub_proc2 = 3
Nesting Level in sub_proc1 after sub_proc2 = 2
Nesting Level in main_proce after sub_proc1 = 1
Nesting Level in sub_proc2 = 2
Nesting Level in main_proc after sub_proc2 = 1
Nesting Level after main_proc = 0
```

Although a limit exists for the number of levels to which procedures can be nested, the
number of stored procedures that can be called from within a single procedure is limitless.
The main-level procedure can call potentially hundreds of other procedures. As long
as the other procedures never invoke another procedure, the nesting level never
exceeds two.

Any stored procedure that is called from within another procedure should always return a status code if an error condition occurs. Depending on the severity of the error, failure within a nested procedure does not always cause the calling procedure or batch to be aborted. Checking the error condition from a nested procedure allows you to conditionally determine whether to continue processing.

Recursive Stored Procedures

A stored procedure can call itself up to the maximum nesting level of 32. This is referred to as *recursion*. Be aware that when you create a recursive procedure, it generates the following warning message:

```
Cannot add rows to sysdepends for the current object because it depends on the
 missing object 'procname'. The stored procedure will still be created.
```

This error occurs simply because the procedure is trying to add a dependency to itself, which it cannot do because the procedure doesn't exist yet. This does not affect the functionality of the stored procedure in any way; the procedure correctly resolves the reference to itself at runtime, so you can ignore the warning message.

When might you want a stored procedure to be recursive? One common example is when you need to expand a tree relationship. Although a Common Table Expression (CTE) can be used to recursively expand a tree relationship, internally it builds the entire tree before applying any filters to display the tree, starting at a specific level. It is also somewhat limited in how the tree is displayed (see Listing 23.21).

LISTING 23.21   Using a Self-Join to Expand a Tree Relationship

```
WITH PartsTree (PartID, PartName, parentPartID, Level)
AS
(
-- Anchor member definition
    SELECT PartID, PartName, ParentPartID,
        0 AS Level
    FROM Parts AS parent
        where Parent.parentpartid is null
    UNION ALL
-- Recursive member definition
    SELECT child.PartID, child.PartName, child.ParentPArtID,
        Level + 1
    FROM Parts AS Child
    INNER JOIN PartsTree AS parent
        ON child.ParentPartID = parent.PArtID
)
-- Statement that executes the CTE
select * from PArtsTree
go
```

LISTING 23.21   Continued

PartID	PartName	parentPartID	Level
22	Car	NULL	0
1	DriveTrain	22	1
23	Body	22	1
24	Frame	22	1
2	Engine	1	2
3	Transmission	1	2
4	Axle	1	2
12	Drive Shaft	1	2
9	Flywheel	3	3
10	Clutch	3	3
16	Gear Box	3	3
15	Reverse Gear	16	4
17	First Gear	16	4
18	Second Gear	16	4
19	Third Gear	16	4
20	Fourth Gear	16	4
5	Radiator	2	3
6	Intake Manifold	2	3
7	Exhaust Manifold	2	3
8	Carburetor	2	3
13	Piston	2	3
14	Crankshaft	2	3
21	Piston Rings	13	4
11	Float Valve	8	4

A recursive procedure can provide a somewhat more elegant solution to expanding a tree relationship from any level in the tree. This solution also provides more control over formatting of the output. For example, the procedure in Listing 23.22 formats the output so that the child parts are indented within the parent part.

LISTING 23.22   Expanding a Tree Relationship by Using a Recursive Procedure

```
IF EXISTS ( SELECT * FROM INFORMATION_SCHEMA.ROUTINES
            WHERE SPECIFIC_SCHEMA = N'dbo'
              AND SPECIFIC_NAME = N'SHOW_PARTS_LIST')
   DROP PROCEDURE dbo.SHOW_PARTS_LIST
GO
CREATE PROC SHOW_PARTS_LIST @partid varchar(50)
as
set nocount on

declare @treelevel int,
```

LISTING 23.22   Continued

```
        @partname varchar(50),
        @childpartid int,
        @parentpartid int

select @treelevel = @@NESTLEVEL -- keep track of nesting level for indenting

if @@nestlevel = 1  -- this is the top of the tree
begin
    select @partname = PArtName from Parts where Partid = @partid
    print 'Expanded parts list for ' + @partname
end

if @@NESTLEVEL < 32  -- Make sure we don't exceed the maximum nesting level
begin
    -- set up cursor to find all child parts for the current part
    declare c1 cursor local for
        select PartId, PartName from Parts
            where parentpartid = @partid
    open c1
    fetch c1 into @childpartid, @partname
    while @@fetch_Status = 0
    begin
        -- use the current tree level to set the indenting when
        --  we print out this record
        print replicate('-', @treelevel * 3) + '> '
                + @partname + ', Part Number: ' + ltrim(str(@childpartid))
        -- Now, call the procedure again to find all the child parts
        --  for the current part
        exec show_parts_list @childpartid
        fetch c1 into @childpartid, @partname
    end
    close c1
    deallocate c1
end
else
begin
    -- We are at maximum nesting level, print out message to indicate this
    print 'Nesting level at 32. Cannot expand tree further.'
end
return
go
-- show the whole parts tree
declare @car_partid int
select @car_partid = partid from Parts where PartName = 'Car'
exec show_parts_list @partid = @car_partid
```

23

LISTING 23.22   Continued

```
go


Expanded parts list for Car
---> DriveTrain, Part Number: 1
------> Engine, Part Number: 2
---------> Radiator, Part Number: 5
---------> Intake Manifold, Part Number: 6
---------> Exhaust Manifold, Part Number: 7
---------> Carburetor, Part Number: 8
------------> Float Valve, Part Number: 11
---------> Piston, Part Number: 13
------------> Piston Rings, Part Number: 21
---------> Crankshaft, Part Number: 14
------> Transmission, Part Number: 3
---------> Flywheel, Part Number: 9
---------> Clutch, Part Number: 10
---------> Gear Box, Part Number: 16
------------> Reverse Gear, Part Number: 15
------------> First Gear, Part Number: 17
------------> Second Gear, Part Number: 18
------------> Third Gear, Part Number: 19
------------> Fourth Gear, Part Number: 20
------> Axle, Part Number: 4
------> Drive Shaft, Part Number: 12
---> Body, Part Number: 23
---> Frame, Part Number: 24


-- show the parts tree for 'Engine'
declare @car_partid int
select @car_partid = partid from Parts where PartName = 'Engine'
exec show_parts_list @partid = @car_partid
go

Expanded parts list for Engine
---> Radiator, Part Number: 5
---> Intake Manifold, Part Number: 6
---> Exhaust Manifold, Part Number: 7
---> Carburetor, Part Number: 8
------> Float Valve, Part Number: 11
---> Piston, Part Number: 13
------> Piston Rings, Part Number: 21
---> Crankshaft, Part Number: 14
```

Using Temporary Tables in Stored Procedures

Temporary tables are commonly used in stored procedures when intermediate results need to be stored in a worktable for additional or more advanced processing. You need to keep a few things in mind when using temporary tables in stored procedures.

In versions of SQL Server prior to 7.0, if a subprocedure referenced a temporary table created externally, a temporary table with the same name and structure had to exist at the time the stored procedure was created. This is no longer the case now that SQL Server performs deferred name resolution. The existence of the temporary table is not checked until the stored procedure is executed.

Local temporary tables created in a stored procedure are automatically dropped when the stored procedure exits. Global temporary tables created in a stored procedure still exist after the stored procedure exits until they are explicitly dropped (see Listing 23.23) or the user session in which they were created disconnects from SQL Server.

LISTING 23.23   Using Local and Global Temporary Tables in Stored Procedures

```
set nocount on
go
create proc temp_test2
as
select pub_id, pub_name, city, state
into ##temp
from publishers
where State in ('MA', 'DC', 'CA')

select pub_id, pub_name, city, state
into #temp
from publishers
where State in ('MA', 'DC', 'CA')
go

exec temp_test2
go

select * from ##temp
go

pub_id pub_name                               city                 state
------ -------------------------------------- -------------------- -----
0736   New Moon Books                         Boston               MA
0877   Binnet & Hardley                       Washington           DC
1389   Algodata Infosystems                   Berkeley             CA
9912   Landlocked Books                       Boston               MA
9913   Blackberry's                           Cambridge            MA
```

23

LISTING 23.23   Continued

```
select * from #temp
go

Server: Msg 208, Level 16, State 0, Line 1
Invalid object name '#temp'.
```

Note what happens if you try to run the stored procedure again:

```
exec temp_test2
go
Server: Msg 2714, Level 16, State 6, Procedure temp_test2, Line 3
There is already an object named '##temp' in the database.
```

> **TIP**
>
> The general consensus is that there is not much need for using global temporary tables in stored procedures. The typical reason for using temporary tables in stored procedures is that you need a work area within the stored procedure only. You normally wouldn't want it sticking around after the procedure finishes. Creating a global temporary table in a stored procedure requires an explicit drop of the table before the procedure exits if you no longer need it. If that's the case, what's the benefit of using a global temporary table? Any subprocedures will be able to see and reference a local temporary table created in the calling procedure, so global temporary tables are not needed in that case.
>
> Only if you need to create and populate a worktable and have it available after the procedure exits should you consider using a global temporary table. However, you have to remember to explicitly drop it at some point before attempting to run the procedure again. But if an error occurs that aborts processing of the stored procedure, the explicit drop might not be executed.
>
> You might want to include a check for the global temporary table in your stored procedure and drop it automatically before attempting to create it again, as in the following code snippet:
>
> ```
> create proc myproc
> as
> if exists (select 1 from tempdb..sysobjects where name = '##global_temp'
>                                            and type = 'U')
>     drop table ##global_Temp
>
> select * into  ##global_temp from ...
> ```

Temporary Table Performance Tips

All users in SQL Server share the same `tempdb` database for worktables and temporary tables, regardless of the database in which they are working. This makes `tempdb` a potential bottleneck in any multiuser system. The primary bottleneck in tempdb is disk I/O, but locking contention may also occur between processes on the tempdb system catalogs.

SQL Server 2005 solves the disk I/O problem a bit by logging just enough information to allow rollback of transactions without logging all the additional information that would be necessary to recover those transactions. The recovery information is needed only when recovering a database at system startup or when restoring from a backup. Because tempdb is rebuilt during SQL Server startup (and no one in their right mind would restore tempdb from a backup), it's unnecessary to keep this recovery information. By reducing the logging in tempdb, data modification operations on tables in tempdb can be up to four times faster than the same operations in other databases.

On the other hand, locking in tempdb is still a potential performance bottleneck. If you create a table in tempdb within a transaction, locks are held on rows in the system catalogs. These locks being held on the system tables could lead to locking contention with other processes that are trying to read or update the tempdb system catalogs.

To minimize the potential for locking contention on the system tables in tempdb, you should consider creating your temporary tables before starting the transaction so that locks are released immediately and not held on the system catalogs until the end of the transaction. If the table must be created in a transaction, you should commit your transaction as soon as possible.

Also, you need to be aware that even if it's not in a transaction, creating a temporary table by using SELECT INTO holds locks on the system catalogs in tempdb until the SELECT INTO completes. If locking contention in tempdb becomes a problem, you should consider replacing SELECT INTO with CREATE TABLE, followed by an INSERT using a SELECT statement. Although this might run a bit more slowly than SELECT INTO, the system table locks are held only for the brief moment it takes for CREATE TABLE to complete.

Another way to speed up temporary table creation/population is to keep temporary tables as small as possible so they are created and populated more quickly. You should select only the required columns, rather than use SELECT *, and you should only retrieve the rows from the base table that you actually need to reference. The smaller the temporary table, the faster it is to create the table; smaller temporary tables also help speed up queries against the temporary table.

If a temporary table is of sufficient size and is going to be accessed multiple times within a stored procedure, it might be cost-effective to create an index on it on the column(s) that will be referenced in the search arguments of queries against the temporary table. If the time it takes to create the index plus the time the queries take to run using the index is less than the sum total of the time it takes the queries against the temporary table to run without the index, you probably want to consider creating an index on the temporary table.

The following example demonstrates the creation of an index on a temporary table:

```
use bigpubs2005
go
create proc ptemp1 WITH RECOMPILE
as
select title_id, type, pub_id, ytd_sales
   into #temp_titles
   from titles

create index tmp on #temp_titles(pub_id)

select sum(ytd_sales)
   from #temp_titles
   where pub_id = '0736'
select min(ytd_sales)
   from #temp_titles
   where pub_id = '0736'

return
go
```

The following are some other final tips for using temporary tables in stored procedures:

▶ Don't use temporary tables to combine result sets together when a UNION or UNION ALL will suffice. UNION ALL is the fastest because no worktable in tempdb is required to merge the result sets.

▶ Drop temporary tables as soon as possible to free up space in tempdb.

▶ Consider using the table data type to avoid using tempdb altogether.

Using the table Data Type

The table data type can be used to define table variables in stored procedures and elsewhere in SQL code. Table variables are defined similarly to regular tables, except they are defined in a DECLARE statement, rather than using CREATE TABLE:

```
DECLARE @table_variable  TABLE ({ column_definition ¦ table_constraint }
                                  [ ,...n ])
```

The following is a simple example that shows how to use a table variable in a stored procedure:

```
-- proc to get year-to-date sales for all books published since specified date
-- with ytd_sales greater than specified threshold
create proc tab_var_test @pubdate datetime = null,
                         @sales_minimum int = 0
```

```
as

declare @ytd_sales_tab TABLE (title_id char(6),
                              title varchar(50),
                              ytd_sales int)

if @pubdate is null
    -- if no date is specified, set date to last year
    set @pubdate = dateadd(month, -12, getdate())

insert @ytd_sales_tab
    select title_id, convert(varchar(50), title), ytd_sales
      from titles
      where pubdate > @pubdate
        and ytd_sales > @sales_minimum
select * from @ytd_sales_tab
return
go

exec tab_var_test '6/1/1991', 10000
go

title_id title                                             ytd_sales
-------- ------------------------------------------------- ----------
BU2075   You Can Combat Computer Stress!                   18722
MC3021   The Gourmet Microwave                             22246
TC4203   Fifty Years in Buckingham Palace Kitchens         15096
```

You can use table variables in user-defined functions, stored procedures, and batches. You should consider using table variables instead of temporary tables whenever possible because they provide the following benefits:

- ▶ Table variables are memory resident and require no space in tempdb.

- ▶ When table variables are used in stored procedures, fewer recompilations of the stored procedures occur than when temporary tables are used.

- ▶ Transactions involving table variables last only for the duration of an update on the table variable. Thus, table variables require fewer locking and logging resources.

- ▶ A table variable behaves like a local variable, and its scope is limited to the stored procedure in which it is declared. It is cleaned up automatically at the end of the function, stored procedure, or batch in which it is defined.

A table variable can be used like a regular table in SELECT, INSERT, UPDATE, and DELETE statements. However, a table variable cannot be used in the following statement:

```
SELECT select_list INTO table_variable ...
```

You need to keep a couple other limitations in mind when considering using table variables in stored procedures. First, table variables cannot be used as stored procedure parameters. You cannot pass a table variable as an input or output parameter for a stored procedure, nor can you access a table variable declared outside the currently executing stored procedure. If you need to share result sets between stored procedures, you have to use temporary tables or cursor variables. Second, you cannot create indexes on table variables by using the CREATE INDEX command. You can, however, define a primary or unique key on the table variable when it is declared.

TIP

One solution to the inability of stored procedures to pass table variables as output parameters is to convert a stored procedure to a user-defined function if possible. User-defined functions can return a table result set that can be referenced in a SELECT statement just like a regular table. Thus, you can include a user-defined function in an insert ... select ... statement and insert the results into a local table variable (something you cannot do with a result set from a stored procedure). For example, the following is an example of the tab_var_test stored procedure converted to a user-defined function:

```
-- function to get year to date sales for all books published since specified
-- date with ytd_sales greater than specified threshold
create function tab_function (@pubdate datetime = NULL,
                              @sales_minimum int = 0)
returns @ytd_sales_tab TABLE (title_id char(6),
                              title varchar(50),
                              ytd_sales int)
as
begin

if @pubdate is null
    -- if no date is specified, set date to last year
    set @pubdate = dateadd(month, -12, getdate())

insert @ytd_sales_tab
    select title_id, convert(varchar(50), title), ytd_sales
      from titles
      where pubdate > @pubdate
        and ytd_sales > @sales_minimum
return
end
go

declare @local_tab table (title_id char(6), title varchar(50), ytd_sales int)
insert @local_tab select * from tab_function('6/1/1991', 10000)
```

```
select * from @local_tab
go
```

```
title_id  title                                        ytd_sales
--------  -------------------------------------------- -----------
BU2075    You Can Combat Computer Stress!              18722
MC3021    The Gourmet Microwave                        22246
TC4203    Fifty Years in Buckingham Palace Kitchens    15096
```

For more information on defining and using user-defined functions, see Chapter 24, "Creating and Managing User-Defined Functions."

Using Remote Stored Procedures

You can execute a stored procedure residing on another server by using a four-part naming scheme:

```
EXEC server_name.db_name.owner_name.proc_name
```

This concept is called remote stored procedures. The name implies that the procedure called on the other server is a special type of stored procedure, but it is not. Any stored procedure can be called from another server, as long as the remote server has been configured and the appropriate login mapping has been done. The method used to set up servers to allow remote procedure calls (RPCs) is described in Chapter 42, "Managing Linked and Remote Servers" (on the CD-ROM).

The processing done by the remote stored procedure is, by default, not done in the local transaction context. If the local transaction rolls back, modifications performed by the remote stored procedure are not undone. However, you *can* get the remote stored procedures to execute within the local transaction context by using distributed transactions, as in the following example:

```
BEGIN DISTRIBUTED TRANSACTION
EXEC purge_old_customers  --A local procedure
EXEC LONDON.customers.dbo.purge_old_customers -- a remote procedure
COMMIT TRANSACTION
```

SQL Server also automatically promotes a local transaction to a distributed transaction if the remote proc trans option is enabled and a remote stored procedure is invoked in a transaction. This option can be configured globally in SQL Server via sp_configure, or it can be set explicitly at the connection level with the SET REMOTE_PROC_TRANSACTIONS command. If the remote proc trans option is enabled, remote stored procedure calls in local transactions are automatically protected as part of distributed transactions, without requiring you to rewrite applications to specifically issue BEGIN DISTRIBUTED TRANSACTION instead of BEGIN TRANSACTION.

Distributed transactions and the Microsoft Distributed Transaction Coordinator service are also discussed in Chapter 42.

Debugging Stored Procedures Using Microsoft Visual Studio .NET

One of the great tools that was available in the SQL Server 2000 Query Analyzer, the built-in SQL Debugger, is gone in SQL Server 2005. SSMS does not provide a built-in mechanism for debugging stored procedures. Your only option for debugging stored procedures is to use the T-SQL debugger provided with the Visual Studio .NET development suite.

> **NOTE**
>
> Unfortunately, the version of Visual Studio that is installed with SQL Server 2005 for developing Integration Services and Analysis Services solutions does not have the ability to debug T-SQL procedures. You need to acquire and install Visual Studio 2005 Professional or Team Edition if you want to debug T-SQL procedures.

If you are using Visual Studio to create and develop database projects, you can define T-SQL stored procedures within those projects and create and debug them from there. However, you don't have to go to all the trouble to put your T-SQL stored procedures in database projects in order to debug them. The easiest way to debug T-SQL procedures in Visual Studio is through the Server Explorer. This is similar to the way you can debug stored procedures with Query Analyzer in SQL Server 2000. Perform the following steps to debug a procedure in Visual Studio:

1. If the Server Explorer is not visible, you can press Ctrl+Alt+S or select View, Server Explorer.

2. When the Server Explorer is visible, expand the Data Connections node.

3. If the database that contains the stored procedure you want to debug is not listed, you need to add it. To do so, you right-click the Data Connections node and select Add Connection.

4. In the Connection dialog that appears (see Figure 23.8), enter the server name, login information, and database name and click Test Connection to verify the connection information

5. Then click OK.

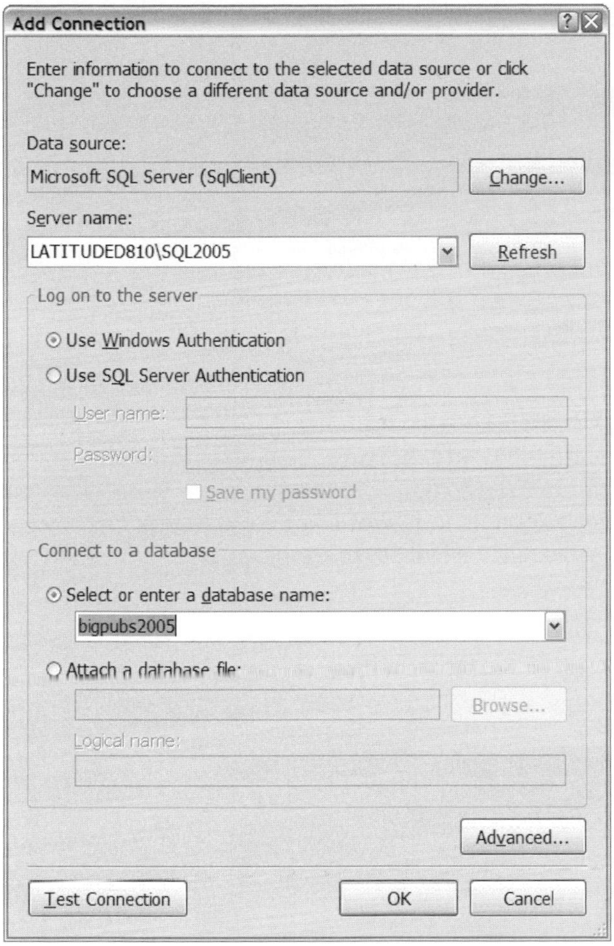

FIGURE 23.8   Adding a database connection in Visual Studio 2005.

After you make the connection to the database, you can expand the database connection and expand the Stored Procedures folder. Then you locate the stored procedure you want to debug, right-click it, and select Step into Stored Procedure (see Figure 23.9).

If the procedure does not contain any parameters, the stored procedure is loaded directly into the debugger (see Figure 23.10). If the stored procedure does take any parameters, you are first presented with the Run Stored Procedure dialog, as shown in Figure 23.11. You supply any values for the parameters or select <DEFAULT> or <NULL>.

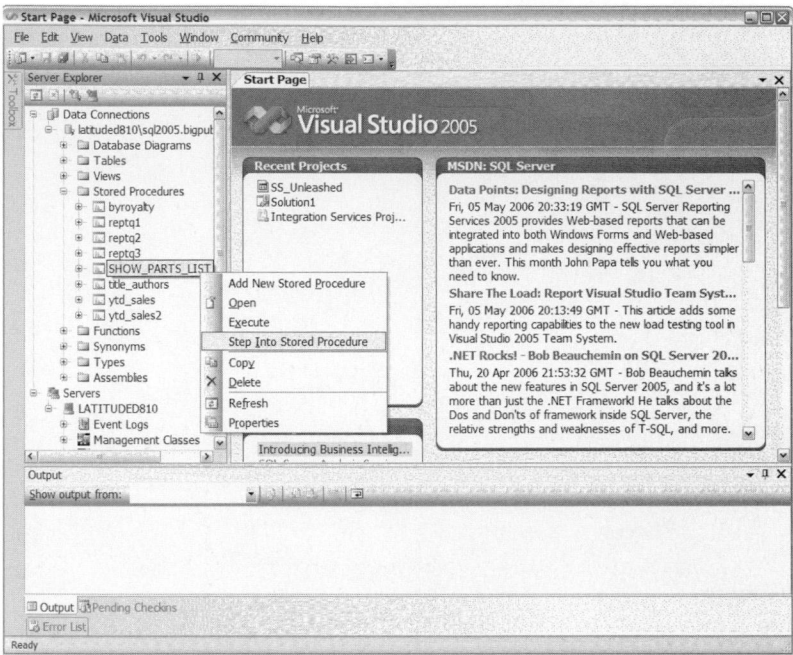

FIGURE 23.9   Invoking the T-SQL debugger in Visual Studio 2005.

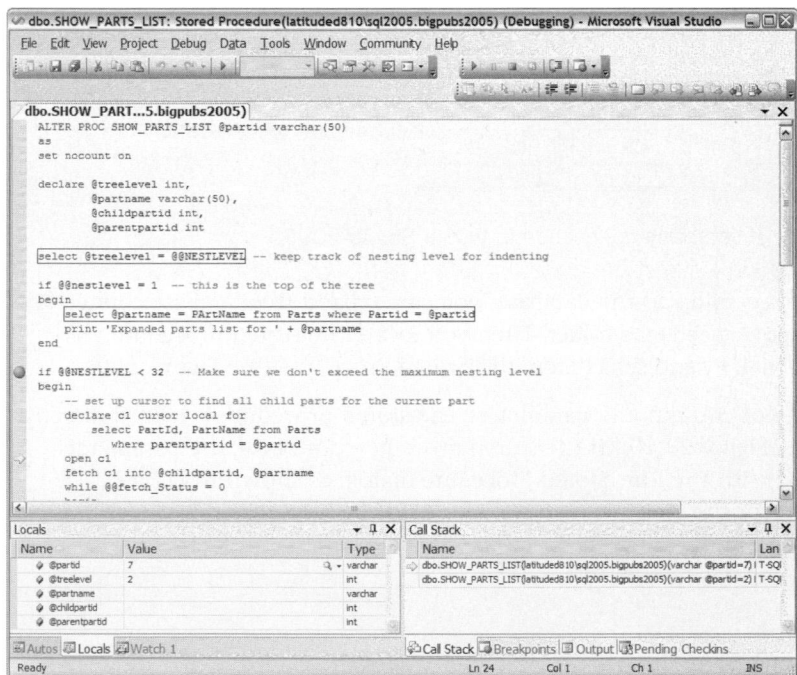

FIGURE 23.10   Debugging a T-SQL stored procedure in Visual Studio 2005.

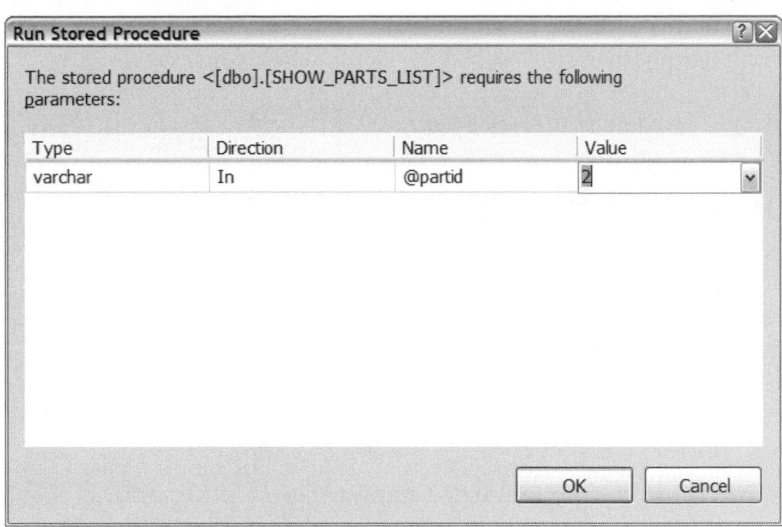

FIGURE 23.11   Supplying procedure parameter values in the Run Stored Procedure dialog.

After you supply all the parameter values, you click OK, and you are presented with the debugger window, as shown in Figure 23.10.

The debugger initially stops on the first line of code in the stored procedure. You can then set any breakpoints and run to the breakpoints or step through the procedure code one line at a time. You can press F10 to step through the code one line at a time. If your stored procedure calls another stored procedure, you can press F11 to step into the called procedure.

Near the bottom of the debugger window are some useful information windows. The first group of windows is the Variables windows, which consists of the Autos, Locals, and Watch windows. The Autos window displays variables in use in the current statement. The Locals window displays the current values in all the local variables within the current scope. You can also modify the values of the variables in the Locals and Autos windows to test various scenarios or to adjust data values so the code executes differently. The Watch window is where you can add variables whose values you want to watch, such as the global variables @@NESTLEVEL, @@FETCH_STATUS, or @@ROWCOUNT.

The second group of windows is the Call Stack, Breakpoints, and Output windows. The Call Stack window shows the procedure that's currently executing, where you can also monitor the nesting of the stored procedures. The Breakpoints window lets you view the breakpoints you have set, and from this window you can jump to the code where the breakpoint is set, display the location of the breakpoint, display the breakpoint hit count, or perform an action when the breakpoint is hit, such as display a message or invoke a macro. Finally, the Output window is where any output generated by the procedure (or the debugger itself) is displayed.

Although it is unfortunate that there is no debugger built into SSMS and you have to acquire and install Visual Studio to perform T-SQL debugging, when you start working with the debugger in Visual Studio, you will find that is does have more capabilities and flexibility than the debugger provided with SQL Server 2000.

Using System Stored Procedures

A system stored procedure is a stored procedure that has some special characteristics. These procedures, created when SQL Server is installed or upgraded, are generally used to administer SQL Server. They shield a DBA from accessing the system catalogs directly. Some system stored procedures are used to present information from the system catalog, and others modify the system catalogs. Information about login IDs, for instance, can be viewed with the `sp_helplogins` procedure and modified with `sp_addlogin`, `sp_droplogin`, and so on.

The earliest versions of SQL Server had no GUI-based administration tools, so a DBA had to have knowledge of the system stored procedures. Today, the system stored procedures are not an absolute must to administer SQL Server, but it is still a good idea to be familiar with the basic system stored procedures. There are currently more than 500 documented system stored procedures in SQL Server 2005, so it would be a tough job to learn the names and syntax for all of them. The total number of system stored procedures is over 1,200. Some of the undocumented stored procedures are called by other procedures, and others are called from SSMS or other SQL Server tools and utility programs.

The following attributes characterize a system stored procedure:

▶ The stored procedure name begins with `sp_`.

▶ The stored procedure resides in the `Resource` database.

▶ The procedure is defined in the `sys` schema.

These attributes make the procedure *global*, which means you can execute the procedure from any database without qualifying the database name. The procedure executes within the current database context.

Although system stored procedures reside in the `Resource` database, they also run in any database context when fully qualified with a database name, regardless of the current database context. For instance, `sp_helpfile` shows information about the files configured for the current database. In the following example, when not qualified, `sp_helpfile` returns file information for the `master` database, and when qualified with `bigpubs2005..`, it returns file information for the `bigpubs2005` database:

```
exec sp_helpfile
go
```

```
name     fileid filename                                    filegroup size
 maxsize    growth usage
```

```
-------- ------ ---------------------------------------------- ---------- --------
--------- ------ ---------
master   1      C:\MSSQL2005\DATA\MSSQL.1\MSSQL\DATA\master.mdf   PRIMARY    4096 KB
 Unlimited 10%    data only
mastlog  2      C:\MSSQL2005\DATA\MSSQL.1\MSSQL\DATA\mastlog.ldf NULL        512 KB
 Unlimited 10%    log only


exec bigpubs2005..sp_helpfile
go

name           fileid filename                             filegroup size
 maxsize    growth usage
--------------- ------ --------------------------------------- ---------- ---------
---------- ------ ---------
bigpubs2005    1       C:\MSSQL2005\DATA\bigpubs2005.mdf     PRIMARY    214912 KB
 Unlimited 10%    data only
bigpubs2005_log 2      C:\MSSQL2005\DATA\bigpubs2005_log.LDF NULL        504 KB
 Unlimited 10%    log only
```

Table 23.1 describes the categories of system stored procedures.

TABLE 23.1   System Stored Procedure Categories

Category	Description
Catalog stored procedures	Used to implement ODBC data dictionary functions and isolate ODBC applications from changes to underlying system tables.
Cursor stored procedures	Used to implement cursor variable functionality.
Database engine stored procedures	Used for general maintenance of the SQL Server Database Engine.
Database mail stored procedures	Used to perform email operations from within an instance of SQL Server.
Database maintenance plan procedures	Used to set up core database maintenance tasks.
Distributed queries stored procedures	Used to link remote servers and manage distributed queries.
Full-text search stored procedures	Used to implement and query full-text indexes.
Log shipping stored procedures	Used to configure, modify, and monitor log shipping configurations.
Automation stored procedures	Allow OLE automation objects to be used within a T-SQL batch.
Notification services stored procedures	Used to manage SQL Server 2005 Notification Services.
Replication stored procedures	Used to manage replication.

TABLE 26.1　Continued

Category	Description
Security stored procedures	Used to manage security, such as login IDs, usernames, and so on.
SQL Server Profiler stored procedures	Used by SQL Server Profiler to monitor performance and activity.
SQL Server Agent stored procedures	Used by SQL Server Agent to manage scheduled and event-driven activities.
Web task stored procedures	Used for creating Web pages.
XML stored procedures	Used for XML text management.
General extended stored procedures	Provide an interface from an instance of SQL Server to external programs for various maintenance activities (e.g., xp_sqlmaint)

Some of the most useful system stored procedures are listed in Table 23.2.

TABLE 23.2　Useful System Stored Procedures

Procedure Name	Description
sp_who and sp_who2	Returns information about current connections to SQL Server.
sp_help [object_name]	Lists the objects in a database or returns information about a specified object.
sp_helpdb [db_name]	Returns a list of databases or information about a specified database.
sp_helptext [object_name]	Returns the CREATE statement for stored procedures, views, and so on.
sp_configure	Lists or changes configuration settings.

Stored Procedure Performance

As stated at the beginning of this chapter, using stored procedures can provide a number of benefits to SQL Server applications. One performance benefit is reduced network traffic because stored procedures minimize the number of round trips between client applications and SQL Server. Stored procedures can consist of many individual SQL statements but can be executed with a single statement. This allows you to reduce the number and size of calls from the client to the server. If you have to take different actions based on data values, you can specify to have these decisions made directly in the procedure, avoiding the need to send data back to the application to determine what to do with the data values.

By default, SQL Server sends a message back to the client application after each statement is completed within the stored procedure to indicate the number of rows affected by the statement. To further reduce the amount of "chatter" between the client and server and to therefore further improve stored procedure performance, you can eliminate these

DONE_IN_PROC messages by issuing the set nocount on command at the beginning of the stored procedure. Be aware that if you turn this option on, the number of rows affected by the commands in the procedure is not available to the ODBC SQLRowCount function or its OLE DB equivalent. You can still issue select @@rowcount after a statement executes to determine the number of rows affected.

Another performance benefit of using stored procedures is potentially faster execution due to the caching of stored procedure query plans. Stored procedure query plans are kept in cache memory after the first execution. The code doesn't have to be reparsed and reoptimized on subsequent executions.

Query Plan Caching

When a batch of SQL statements is submitted to SQL Server, SQL Server performs a number of steps, including the following, before the data can be returned to the client:

1. Parse the SQL statements and build a query tree (the internal format on which SQL Server operates).

2. Optimize the SQL statements and generate an execution plan.

3. Check for permissions for access to the underlying objects.

4. Execute the execution plan for the SQL statements.

The first time a stored procedure executes, SQL Server loads the SQL code for the stored procedure from the system catalog into the procedure cache and optimizes and compiles an execution plan.

The optimization of SQL statements is based on the parameters passed, the index distribution statistics, the number of rows in each table, and other information available at the time of the first execution. The compiled plan is then saved in cache memory. For subsequent executions, all SQL Server has to do is find the plan in cache and execute it, essentially skipping steps 1 and 2. Parsing and compilation always add some overhead, and depending on the complexity of the stored procedure code, they can sometimes be as expensive as the actual execution. Just by skipping these two steps, you can achieve a performance gain by using stored procedures.

The SQL Server Procedure Cache

SQL Server uses the same buffer area for storing data and index pages and procedure query plans. The portion of the buffer pool that is used to store execution plans is referred to as the *procedure cache*. The percentage of the memory pool allocated to execution plans fluctuates dynamically, depending on the state of the system. Also, SQL Server can keep query plans in cache for ad hoc queries. This means that even dynamic SQL queries might be able to reuse a cached execution plan and skip recompilation. The cache space is dynamically allocated as needed.

With the ability to keep query plans in memory for ad hoc queries, it is not as critical in SQL Server 2005 for applications to use stored procedures to achieve performance benefits of using precompiled plans. However, when and how the plans are stored and reused for ad hoc queries is not nearly as predictable as with stored procedures. The query plans for stored procedures remain in cache memory more persistently. In addition, you have little explicit control over the recompilation of ad hoc queries.

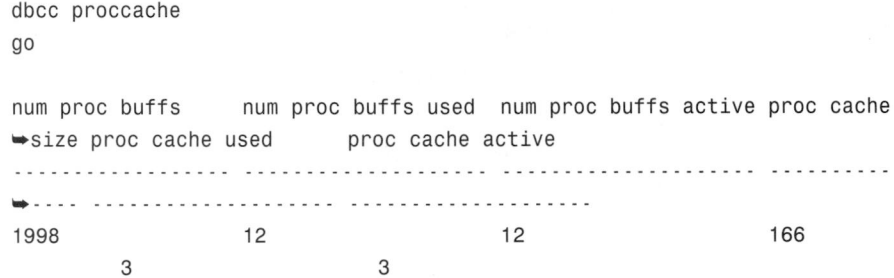

> ## TIP
>
> You can get a summary of the amount of memory used by the procedure cache by using the DBCC PROCCACHE command. DBCC PROCCACHE returns the current size of the procedure cache. (SQL Server grows and shrinks this size automatically.) Here's an example of how you use it:
>
> ```
> dbcc proccache
> go
>
> num proc buffs    num proc buffs used  num proc buffs active proc cache
> ➥size proc cache used    proc cache active
> ---------------- -------------------- -------------------- ----------
> ➥---- -------------------- --------------------
> 1998             12                   12                   166
>         3                    3
> ```
>
> The information in the DBCC PROCCACHE output is as follows:
>
> - ▸ num_proc_buffs is the total number of query plans that could be in the procedure cache.
> - ▸ num proc buffs used is the number of cache slots currently holding query plans.
> - ▸ num proc buffs active is the number of cache slots holding query plans that are currently executing.
> - ▸ proc cache size is the total size of the procedure cache, in number of pages.
> - ▸ proc cache used is the amount of memory, in number of pages, used in the procedure cache to hold query plans.
> - ▸ proc cache active is the amount of memory, in number of pages, being used in the procedure cache for currently executing query plans.
>
> You can get more detailed information about what is currently in the procedure cache via the dm_exec_cached_plans, dm_exec_plan_attributes, and dm_exec_sql_text dynamic management views. These views return the current server state information regarding the procedure cache.

Shared Query Plans

SQL Server 2005 execution plans consist of two main components: a query plan and an execution context. The query plan is the bulk of the execution plan. Query plans are re-entrant, read-only data structures used by any number of users. There are at most ever only two copies of the query plan in memory: one copy for all serial executions and another for all parallel executions. The parallel copy covers all parallel executions, regardless of their degree of parallelism. When a SQL statement is executed, the database engine searches the procedure cache to see whether an execution plan for the same SQL statement is already in the procedure cache. If a query plan does exist, the database engine reuses it, saving the overhead of recompiling the SQL statement. However, if no existing query plan is found, SQL Server 2005 generates a new execution plan for the query and saves it into the procedure cache.

For each user that is currently executing a query, there is a data structure that holds information specific to that user's execution, such as parameter values. This data structure is referred to as the *execution context*. Execution context data structures are also reusable if they are not currently in use. When a user executes a query, SQL Server looks for an execution context structure that is not being used, and it reinitializes the structure with the context for the new user. If no free execution context structures exist, SQL Server creates a new one. Thus, there can potentially be multiple execution context structures in the procedure cache for the same query.

For more information on the `syscacheobjects` table and how query plans are cached and managed in SQL Server, see Chapter 30, "Understanding Query Optimization" and Chapter 31, "Query Analysis."

Automatic Query Plan Recompilation

SQL Server attempts to reuse existing execution plans for stored procedures, but certain operations cause the execution plans to become inefficient or invalid. In these cases, a new execution plan needs to be recompiled on the next execution of the stored procedure. The following conditions cause a plan to be invalidated:

▶ Whenever there is a change to the schema of a referenced table or view

▶ When an index for a referenced table is dropped or changed

▶ When the statistics used by an execution plan have been updated, either explicitly or automatically

▶ When `sp_recompile` has been run on a table referenced by a stored procedure

▶ When a sufficient amount of data changes in a table that is referenced by the stored procedure

▶ For tables with triggers, when the number of rows in the inserted and deleted tables grows significantly

In addition to these reasons, other events that can cause stored procedures to recompile new query plans include the following:

▶ When SQL Server activity is heavy enough to cause query plans to be flushed from cache memory

▶ When the `WITH RECOMPILE` option has been specified in the `CREATE PROCEDURE` or `EXEC` command

▶ When shutting down and restarting SQL Server because this flushes all query plans from memory

In SQL Server 2000, whenever an execution plan was invalidated, the entire batch or stored procedure was recompiled. In SQL Server 2005, only the statement, the batch, or the stored procedure that caused the query plan to be invalidated has to be recompiled. Because often only a small number of statements in batches or stored procedures are the reason a plan becomes invalidated, statement-level recompilation improves performance in terms of CPU time and locks by avoiding the need to have to recompile all the other statements in the batch whose execution plans are still valid.

Monitoring Stored Procedure Recompilation

You can monitor when stored procedures or statements are automatically recompiled by using SQL Profiler. The two events you want to monitor are the `SP:Recompile` and `SQL:StmtRecompile` trace events (see Figure 23.12). In SQL Server 2005, the `TextData` column of these events is filled in with information about the query that caused the recompile, so it is not necessary to also trace the `SP:StmtStarting` or `SP:StmtCompleted` events in order to capture the query information.

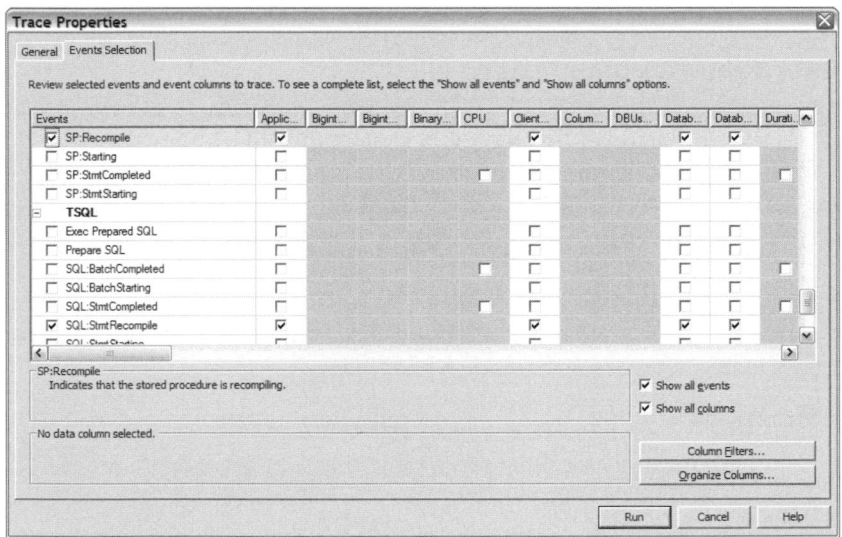

FIGURE 23.12   Adding events in SQL Profiler to monitor stored procedure recompilation.

If a stored procedure or statement is automatically recompiled during execution, SQL Profiler displays the `SP:Recompile` event and/or the `SQL:StmtRecompile` event. For example, you can create the following stored procedure to create and populate a temporary table:

```
create proc recomp_test
as
create table #titles (title_id varchar(6), title varchar(80), pubdate datetime)
insert #titles select title_id, title, pubdate from titles
where pubdate >  '10/1/1991'
select * from #titles
go
```

Say you turn on SQL Profiler and then execute the following SQL, which executes the procedure (which in turn results in the initial compilation), and then add an index on pubdate to the titles table:

```
exec recomp_test
go
create index idx1 on titles (pubdate)
go
exec recomp_test
go
drop index titles.idx1
go
```

When you do this, you capture the events shown in Figure 23.13.

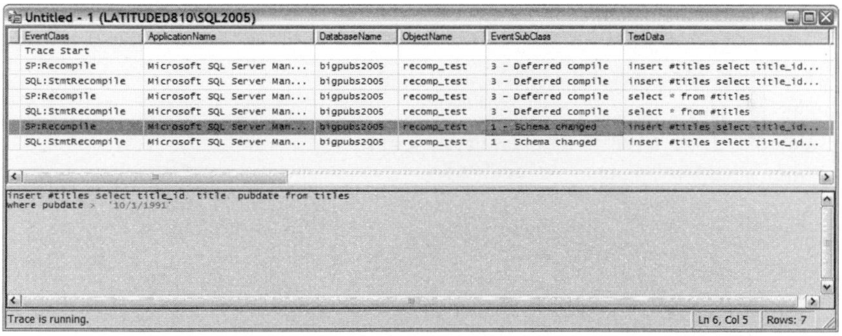

FIGURE 23.13   Recompile events captured for a stored procedure in SQL Profiler.

The key columns to focus on in the Profiler trace are ObjectName, EventSubclass, and TextData. The TextData column shows which statements were recompiled. You can see in Figure 23.13 that on the subsequent execution, only the statement affected by the new index on the titles table was recompiled. The EventSubclass column provides the reason for the recompile. These reasons are summarized in Table 23.3

TABLE 23.3   SQL Profiler `EventSubClass` Values for Recompile Events

EventSubClass **Value**	**Description**
1	Schema changed.
2	Statistics changed.
3	Deferred compile.
4	SET option changed.
5	Temporary table changed.
6	Remote rowset changed.
7	FOR BROWSE permission changed.
8	Query notification environment changed.
9	Partitioned view changed.
10	Cursor options changed.
11	OPTION (RECOMPILE) requested.

For more information on using SQL Profiler to monitor SQL Server performance, see Chapter 5, "SQL Server Profiler."

Forcing Recompilation of Query Plans

In some situations, a stored procedure might generate different query plans, depending on the parameters passed in. At times, depending on the type of query and the parameter values passed in, it can be difficult to predict the best query plan for all executions. Consider the following stored procedure:

```
IF EXISTS ( SELECT * FROM INFORMATION_SCHEMA.ROUTINES
              WHERE SPECIFIC_SCHEMA = N'dbo'
                AND SPECIFIC_NAME = N'advance_range')
   DROP PROCEDURE dbo.advance_range
GO
create proc advance_range
    (@low money, @high money)
as
select * from dbo.titles
  where advance between @low and @high
return
```

Assume that a nonclustered index exists on the advance column in the `titles` table. A search in which advance is between 1,000 and 2,000 might be highly selective, and the index statistics might indicate that fewer than 5% of the rows fall within that range, and thus an index would be the best way to find the rows. If those were the values passed on the first execution, the cached query plan would indicate that the index should be used.

Suppose, however, that if on a subsequent execution, search values of 5,000 and 10,000 were specified. These values match against 90% of the rows in the table, and if optimized normally, SQL Server would likely use a table scan because it would have to visit almost all rows in the table anyway. Without recompiling, however, it would use the index as specified in the cached query plan, which would be a suboptimal query plan because it would likely be accessing more pages using the index than would a table scan.

When a lot of variance exists in the distribution of data values in a table or in the range of values passed as parameters, you might want to force the stored procedure to recompile and build a new execution plan during execution and not use a previously cached plan. Although you incur the overhead of compiling a new query plan for each execution, it is typically much less expensive than executing the wrong query plan.

You can force recompilation of the query plan for a stored procedure by specifying the WITH RECOMPILE option when creating or executing a stored procedure. Including the WITH RECOMPILE option in the create procedure command causes the procedure to generate a new query plan for each execution:

```
IF EXISTS ( SELECT * FROM INFORMATION_SCHEMA.ROUTINES
              WHERE SPECIFIC_SCHEMA = N'dbo'
                AND SPECIFIC_NAME = N'advance_range')
   DROP PROCEDURE dbo.advance_range
GO
create proc advance_range
    (@low money, @high money)
    WITH RECOMPILE
as
select * from dbo.titles
  where advance between @low and @high
return
```

If the procedure is not created with the WITH RECOMPILE option, you can generate a new query plan for a specific execution by including the WITH RECOMPILE option in the EXEC statement:

```
exec advance_range 5000, 10000 WITH RECOMPILE
```

Because of the performance overhead of recompiling query plans, you should try to avoid using WITH RECOMPILE whenever possible. One approach is to create different subprocedures and execute the appropriate one based on the passed-in parameters. For example, you could have a subprocedure to handle small-range retrievals that would benefit from an index and a different subprocedure to handle large-range retrievals. The queries in each procedure would be identical; the only difference would be in the parameters passed to them. This is controlled in the top-level procedure. An example of this approach is demonstrated in Listing 23.24.

23

LISTING 23.24   Using Multiple Stored Procedures As an Alternative to Using WITH
RECOMPILE

```
IF EXISTS ( SELECT * FROM INFORMATION_SCHEMA.ROUTINES
            WHERE SPECIFIC_SCHEMA = N'dbo'
              AND SPECIFIC_NAME = N'advance_range')
   DROP PROCEDURE dbo.advance_range
GO
go

create proc get_titles_smallrange
   @low money, @high money
as
select * from titles
  where advance between @low and @high
return
go
create proc get_titles_bigrange
   @low money, @high money
as
select * from titles
  where advance between @low and @high
return
go
create proc advance_Range
   @low money, @high money
as
if @high - @low >= 1000
-- if the difference is over 5000
    exec get_titles_bigrange @low, @high
else
-- execute the small range procedure
    exec get_titles_smallrange @low, @high
```

Obviously, this solution would require substantial knowledge of the distribution of data
in the table and where the threshold is on the range of search values that results in different query plans.

Another type of stored procedure that can sometimes generate different query plans based
on initial parameters is a multipurpose procedure, which usually performs different
actions based on conditional branching, as in the following example:

```
IF EXISTS ( SELECT * FROM INFORMATION_SCHEMA.ROUTINES
            WHERE SPECIFIC_SCHEMA = N'dbo'
              AND SPECIFIC_NAME = N'get_titles_data')
   DROP PROCEDURE dbo.get_titles_data
GO
```

```
create proc get_titles_data (@flag tinyint, @value money)
as
if @flag = 1
    select * from titles where price = @value
else
    select * from titles where advance = @value
```

At query compile time, the Query Optimizer doesn't know which branch will be followed because the `if...else` construct isn't evaluated until runtime. On the first execution of the procedure, the Query Optimizer generates a query plan for all `select` statements in the stored procedure, regardless of the conditional branching, based on the parameters passed in on the first execution. A value passed into the parameter intended to be used for searches against a specific table or column (in this example, `price` versus `qty`) might not be representative of normal values to search against another table or column.

Again, a better approach would be to break the different `select` statements into separate subprocedures and execute the appropriate stored procedure for the type of query to be executed, as in the following example:

```
IF EXISTS ( SELECT * FROM INFORMATION_SCHEMA.ROUTINES
            WHERE SPECIFIC_SCHEMA = N'dbo'
              AND SPECIFIC_NAME = N'get_titles_data')
   DROP PROCEDURE dbo.get_titles_data
GO
drop proc get_titles_data
go
create proc get_titles_data_by_price (@value money)
as
    select * from titles where price = @value
go
create proc get_titles_data_by_advance (@value money)
as
    select * from titles where advance = @value
go
create proc get_titles_data (@flag tinyint, @value money)
as
if @flag = 1
    exec get_titles_data_by_price @value
else
    exec get_titles_data_by_advance @value
```

Using sp_recompile

In versions of SQL Server prior to 7.0, it was necessary to use the `sp_recompile` system stored procedure when you wanted to force all stored procedures that referenced a specific table to generate a new query plan upon the next execution. This was necessary if you had added new indexes to a table or had run UPDATE STATISTICS on the table. However,

23

the usefulness of this command in SQL Server 2005 is questionable because new query
plans are generated automatically whenever new indexes are created or statistics are
updated on a referenced table. It appears that sp_recompile is available primarily for
backward compatibility or for times when you want the recompilations to occur explicitly
for all procedures referencing a specific table.

Using Dynamic SQL in Stored Procedures

SQL Server allows the use of the EXEC statement in stored procedures to execute dynamic
SQL statements. This capability allows you to do things such as pass in object names as
parameters and dynamically execute a query against the table name passed in, as in the
following example:

```
IF EXISTS ( SELECT * FROM INFORMATION_SCHEMA.ROUTINES
              WHERE SPECIFIC_SCHEMA = N'dbo'
                AND SPECIFIC_NAME = N'get_order_data')
   DROP PROCEDURE dbo.get_order_data
GO
create proc get_order_data
 (@table varchar(30), @column varchar(30), @value int)
as
declare @query varchar(255)

select @query = 'select * from ' + @table
         + ' where ' + @column
         + ' = ' + convert(varchar(10), @value)

EXEC (@query)

return
```

This feature is especially useful when you have to pass a variable list of values into a
stored procedure. The string contains a comma-separated list of numeric values or character strings, just as they would appear inside the parentheses of an IN clause. If you are
passing character strings, you need to be sure to put single quotes around the values, as
shown in Listing 23.25.

LISTING 23.25   Passing a Variable List of Values into a Stored Procedure

```
IF EXISTS ( SELECT * FROM INFORMATION_SCHEMA.ROUTINES
              WHERE SPECIFIC_SCHEMA = N'dbo'
                AND SPECIFIC_NAME = N'find_books_by_type')
   DROP PROCEDURE dbo.find_books_by_type
GO
create proc find_books_by_type @typelist varchar(8000)
```

LISTING 23.25   Continued

```
as

exec ('select title_id, title = substring(title, 1, 40), type, price
        from titles where type in ('
     + @typelist + ') order by type, title_id')
go

set quoted_identifier off
exec find_books_by_type "'business', 'mod_cook', 'trad_cook'"
go
```

title_id	title	type	price
BU1032	The Busy Executive's Database Guide	business	14.9532
BU1111	Cooking with Computers: Surreptitious Ba	business	14.595
BU2075	You Can Combat Computer Stress!	business	15.894
BU7832	Straight Talk About Computers	business	14.9532
MC2222	Silicon Valley Gastronomic Treats	mod_cook	14.9532
MC3021	The Gourmet Microwave	mod_cook	15.894
TC3218	Onions, Leeks, and Garlic: Cooking Secre	trad_cook	0.0017
TC4203	Fifty Years in Buckingham Palace Kitchen	trad_cook	14.595
TC7777	Sushi, Anyone?	trad_cook	14.3279

When using dynamic SQL in stored procedures, you need to be aware of a few issues:

▶ Any local variables that are declared and assigned values in the constructed string within an EXEC statement are not available to the stored procedure outside the EXEC command. The lifespan of a local variable is limited to the context in which it is declared, and the context of the EXEC command ends when it completes. For a solution to passing values back out from a dynamic query, see the section "Using Output Parameters with sp_executesql," later in this chapter.

▶ Any local variables that are declared and assigned values in the stored procedure can be used to build the dynamic query statement, but the local variables cannot be referenced by any statements within the EXEC string. The commands in the EXEC statement run in a different context from the stored procedure, and you cannot reference local variables declared outside the current context.

▶ Commands executed in an EXEC string execute within the security context of the user executing the procedure, not that of the user who created the procedure. Typically, if a user has permission to execute a stored procedure, that user also has implied permission to access all objects referenced in the stored procedure that are owned by the same person who created the stored procedure. However, if a user has permission to execute the procedure but hasn't explicitly been granted the permissions necessary to perform all the actions specified in the EXEC string, a permission violation occurs at runtime.

▶ If you issue a USE command to change the database context in an EXEC statement, it is in effect only during the EXEC string execution. It does not change the database context for the stored procedure (see Listing 23.26).

LISTING 23.26   Changing Database Context in an EXEC Statement

```
use bigpubs2005
go
create proc db_context as
print db_name()
exec ('USE AdventureWorks print db_name()')
print db_name()
go

exec db_context
go

bigpubs2005
AdventureWorks
bigpubs2005
```

Using sp_executesql

If you want to have the flexibility of dynamic SQL but better persistence of stored query plans, you should consider using sp_executesql instead of EXEC in your stored procedures. The syntax for sp_executesql is as follows:

```
sp_executesql @SQL_commands, @parameter_definitions, param1,...paramN
```

sp_executesql operates just as the EXEC statement with regard to the scope of names, permissions, and database context. However, sp_executesql is more efficient for executing the same SQL commands repeatedly when the only change is the values of the parameters. Because the SQL statement remains constant and only the parameters change, SQL Server is more likely to reuse the execution plan generated for the first execution and simply substitute the new parameter values. This saves the overhead of having to compile a new execution plan each time.

Listing 23.27 provides an example of a stored procedure that takes up to three parameters and uses sp_executesql to invoke the dynamic queries.

LISTING 23.27   Invoking Dynamic Queries in a Procedure by Using `sp_executesql`

```
IF EXISTS ( SELECT * FROM INFORMATION_SCHEMA.ROUTINES
              WHERE SPECIFIC_SCHEMA = N'dbo'
                AND SPECIFIC_NAME = N'find_books_by_type2')
   DROP PROCEDURE dbo.find_books_by_type2
GOgo
create proc find_books_by_type2 @type1 char(12),
                                @type2 char(12) = null,
                                @type3 char(12) = null
as

exec sp_executesql N'select title_id, title = substring(title, 1, 40),
     type, price from bigpubs2005.dbo.titles where type = @type',
     N'@type char(12)',
     @type = @type1
if @type2 is not null
    exec sp_executesql N'select title_id, title = substring(title, 1, 40),
         type, price from bigpubs2005.dbo.titles where type = @type',
         N'@type char(12)',
         @type = @type2
if @type3 is not null
    exec sp_executesql N'select title_id, title = substring(title, 1, 40),
         type, price from bigpubs2005.dbo.titles where type = @type',
         N'@type char(12)',
         @type = @type3
go

set quoted_identifier off
exec find_books_by_type2 'business', 'mod_cook', 'trad_cook'
go

title_id title                                        type        price
-------- -------------------------------------------- ----------- ----------------
BU1032   The Busy Executive's Database Guide          business    14.9532
BU1111   Cooking with Computers: Surreptitious Ba     business    14.595
BU2075   You Can Combat Computer Stress!              business    15.894
BU7832   Straight Talk About Computers                business    14.9532

title_id title                                        type        price
-------- -------------------------------------------- ----------- ----------------
MC2222   Silicon Valley Gastronomic Treats            mod_cook    14.9532
MC3021   The Gourmet Microwave                        mod_cook    15.894
```

LISTING 23.27   Continued

title_id	title	type	price
TC3218	Onions, Leeks, and Garlic: Cooking Secre	trad_cook	0.0017
TC4203	Fifty Years in Buckingham Palace Kitchen	trad_cook	14.595
TC7777	Sushi, Anyone?	trad_cook	14.3279

Note that the SQL command and parameter definition parameters to `sp_executesql` must be of type `nchar`, `nvarchar`, or `ntext`. Also, to ensure that the query plans is reused, the object names should be fully qualified in the SQL command.

Using Output Parameters with `sp_executesql`

The important concept to remember about dynamic SQL is that it runs in a separate scope from the stored procedure that invokes it. This is similar to when a stored procedure executes another stored procedure. Because local variables are available only within the current scope, a nested procedure cannot access a local variable declared in the calling procedure. Similarly, you cannot access a local variable declared outside the scope of a dynamic SQL statement. With stored procedures, you can work around this limitation by using input and output parameters to pass values into and out of a nested stored procedure.

If you use `sp_executesql` to execute dynamic SQL, you can use output parameters to pass values both into and out of the dynamic SQL query through local variables. As described in the previous section, the second parameter to `sp_executesql` is a comma-separated list that defines the parameters you will be using within the dynamic SQL statement. As with parameter definitions for a stored procedure, some of these parameters can be defined as output parameters. To get the values back out, you define the parameter as an output parameter in the parameter list and then specify the `OUTPUT` keyword when passing the variable in the corresponding argument list for `sp_executesql`.

Listing 23.28 shows an example of a stored procedure that uses `sp_executesql` to execute a dynamic SQL query and return a value via an output parameter. You can use the parameters inside the dynamic SQL–like parameters inside a stored procedure. Any values assigned to output parameters within the dynamic SQL query are passed back to the local variable in the calling procedure.

LISTING 23.28   Using Output Parameters in `sp_executesql`

```
IF EXISTS ( SELECT * FROM INFORMATION_SCHEMA.ROUTINES
            WHERE SPECIFIC_SCHEMA = N'dbo'
              AND SPECIFIC_NAME = N'get_avg_price')
    DROP PROCEDURE dbo.get_avg_price
GO
create proc get_avg_price @dbname sysname,
                    @type varchar(12) = '%'
```

LISTING 23.28   Continued

```
as

declare @dsql nvarchar(500),
        @avgval float

/***********************************************************
** build the dynamic query using the @avg and @type as
** variables, which will be passed in via sp_executesql
***********************************************************/
select @dsql = 'select @avg = avg(isnull(price, 0)) from '
                + @dbname+ '..titles '
                + 'where type like @type'

/************************************************************
** submit the dynamic query using sp_executesql, passing type
**   as an input parameter, and @avgval as an output parameter
**   The value of @avg in the dynamic query will be passed
**   back into @avgval
************************************************************/
exec sp_executesql @dsql, N'@avg float OUT, @type varchar(12)',
                   @avgval OUT, @type
print 'The avg value of price for the titles table'
     + ' where type is like ''' + @type
     + ''' in the ' + @dbname + ' database'
     + ' is ' + ltrim(str(@avgval, 9,4))

go

exec get_avg_price @dbname = 'bigpubs2005',
                   @type = 'business'
go

The avg value of price for the titles table where type is like 'business'
 in the bigpubs2005 database is 15.0988


exec get_avg_price @dbname = 'bigpubs2005',
                   @type = DEFAULT
go

The avg value of price for the titles table where type is like '%' in the
  bigpubs2005 database is 0.3744
```

Startup Procedures

A SQL Server administrator can create stored procedures that are marked for execution automatically whenever SQL Server starts. They are often referred to as *startup procedures*. Startup procedures are useful for performing housekeeping-type tasks or starting up a background process when SQL Server starts. Some possible uses for startup procedures include the following:

▶ Automatically perform system or maintenance tasks in tempdb, such as creating a global temporary table.

▶ Enable custom SQL Profiler traces automatically whenever SQL Server is running. (For more information on SQL Profiler traces, see Chapter 5.)

▶ Automatically start other external processes on the SQL Server machine, using xp_cmdshell. (Using xp_cmdshell is discussed in the section "Using Extended Stored Procedures," later in this chapter.)

▶ Prime the data cache with the contents of your critical, frequently used tables.

▶ Prime the procedure cache by executing procedures or functions you want to have compiled and cached before applications start using them.

To create a startup procedure, you log in as a system administrator and create the procedure in the master database. Then you set the procedure startup option to true by using sp_procoption:

```
sp_procoption procedure_name, startup, true
```

If you no longer want the procedure to run at startup, you remove the startup option by executing the same procedure and changing the value to false.

A startup procedure runs in the context of the system administrator, but it can use SETUSER to impersonate another account, if necessary. If you need to reference objects in other databases from within a startup procedure, you need to fully qualify the object with the appropriate database and owner names.

Startup procedures are launched asynchronously; that is, SQL Server doesn't wait for them to complete before continuing with additional startup tasks. This allows a startup procedure to execute in a loop for the duration of the SQL Server process, or it allows several startup procedures to be launched simultaneously. While a startup procedure is running, it runs as a separate worker thread.

TIP

If you need to execute a series of stored procedures in sequence during startup, you can nest the stored procedure calls within a single startup procedure. This consumes only a single worker thread.

Any error messages or print statements generated by a startup procedure are written to the SQL Server error log. For example, consider the following whimsical but utterly useless startup procedure:

```
use master
go
create procedure good_morning
as
print 'Good morning, Dave'
return
go
sp_procoption good_morning, startup, true
go
```

When SQL Server is restarted, the following entries would be displayed in the error log:

```
2006-06-12 13:21:00.04 spid5s      Recovery is complete. This is an
 informational message only. No user action is required.
2006-06-12 13:21:00.15 spid5s      Launched startup procedure 'good_morning'.
2006-06-12 13:21:00.15 spid51s     Good morning, Dave
```

Any result sets generated by a startup procedure vanish into the infamous bit bucket. If you need to return result sets from a startup procedure, you write a procedure to insert the results into a table. The table needs to be a permanent table and not a temporary table because a temporary table would be automatically dropped when the startup procedure finished executing.

The following startup procedure is an example of a procedure that could preload all tables within the bigpubs2005 database into data cache memory on SQL Server startup:

```
use master
go
create procedure prime_cache
as
declare @tablename varchar(128)

declare c1 cursor for select name from pubs.dbo.sysobjects where type = 'U'
open c1
fetch c1 into @tablename
while @@fetch_status = 0
begin
    print 'Loading ''' + @tablename + ''' into data cache'
    exec ('select * from pubs.dbo.' + @tablename)
    fetch c1 into @tablename
end
close c1
deallocate c1
```

```
return
go

sp_procoption prime_cache, startup, true
go
```

The error log output from this startup procedure would be as follows:

```
2006-06-12 13:27:44.03 spid5s      Launched startup procedure 'prime_cache'.
2006-06-12 13:27:44.17 spid51s     Loading 'sales_big' into data cache
2006-06-12 13:27:50.32 spid51s     Loading 'roysched' into data cache
2006-06-12 13:27:50.37 spid51s     Loading 'titleauthor' into data cache
2006-06-12 13:27:50.40 spid51s     Loading 'publishers' into data cache
2006-06-12 13:27:50.43 spid51s     Loading 'PARTS' into data cache
2006-06-12 13:27:50.43 spid51s     Loading 'authors' into data cache
2006-06-12 13:27:50.43 spid51s     Loading 'jobs' into data cache
2006-06-12 13:27:50.43 spid51s     Loading 'pub_info' into data cache
2006-06-12 13:27:50.45 spid51s     Loading 'sales' into data cache
2006-06-12 13:27:51.51 spid51s     Loading 'stores' into data cache
2006-06-12 13:27:51.73 spid51s     Loading 'titles' into data cache
2006-06-12 13:27:51.78 spid51s     Loading 'discounts' into data cache
2006-06-12 13:27:51.78 spid51s     Loading 'employee' into data cache
2006-06-12 13:27:51.78 spid51s     Loading 'sales_noclust' into data cache
```

If you want to disable the automatic execution of all startup procedures, you can use sp_configure to disable the scan for startup procs configuration option. Setting this option to 0 disables the running of startup procedures on subsequent SQL Server restarts.

If SQL Server is not currently running and you want to skip running the startup procedures, you can specify Trace Flag 4022 as a startup parameter. You can set the trace flag for a SQL Server instance by using the SQL Server Configuration Manager. In SQL Server Configuration Manager, perform the following steps:

1. Click on SQL Server 2005 Services.

2. In the right pane, right-click the SQL Server instance you want to set the trace flag for and select Properties.

3. Go to the Advanced tab and select the the Startup Parameters box.

4. Click the expand arrow to the right of the input field to expand the entire field.

5. Place your cursor at the end of the value and type a semicolon (;).

6. Type -T4022 (see Figure 23.14).

7. Finally, click OK.

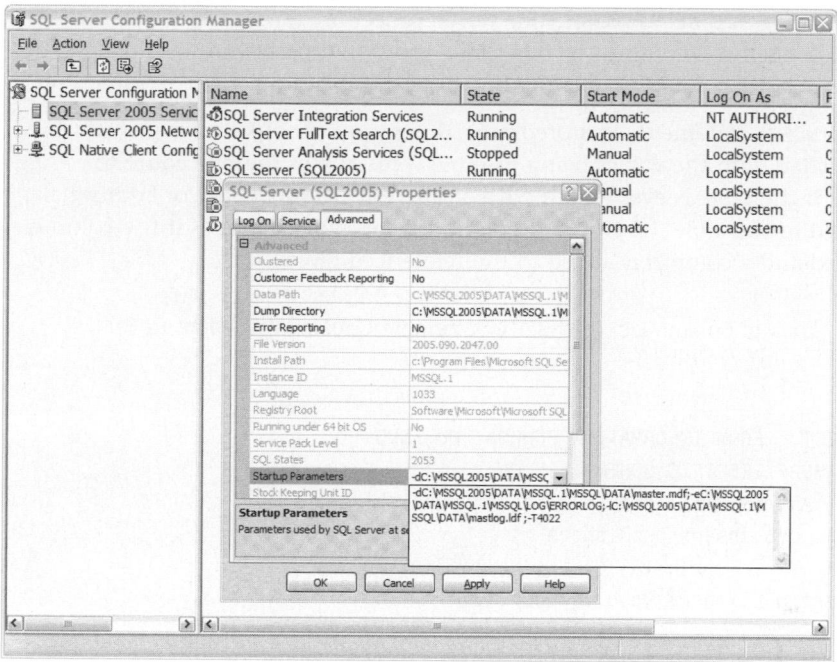

FIGURE 23.14   Setting Trace Flag 4022 to prevent startup procedures from executing.

Also, if you start SQL Server with minimal configuration (by using the `-f` flag), the startup stored procedures are not executed.

T-SQL Stored Procedure Coding Guidelines

Stored procedures should be treated just like reusable application code. You should follow these suggested guidelines to ensure that your stored procedures are solid and robust:

▶ Check all parameters for validity and return an error message if a problem exists.

▶ Be sure that the parameter data types match the column data types they are compared against to avoid data type mismatches and poor query optimization.

▶ Check the `@@error` system function after each SQL statement, especially `insert`, `update`, and `delete`, to verify that the statements executed successfully. Return a status code other than `0` if a failure occurs.

▶ Be sure to comment your code so that when you or others have to maintain it, the code is self-documenting.

▶ Consider using a source code management system, such as Microsoft Visual Studio SourceSafe or Serena PVCS, to maintain versions of your stored procedure source code.

You should avoid using select * ... in your stored procedure queries. If someone were to add columns to or remove columns from a table, the stored procedure would generate a different result set, which could potentially break the application code.

Whenever using INSERT statements in stored procedures, you should always provide the column list associated with the values being inserted. This allows the procedure to continue to work if the table is ever rebuilt with a different column order or additional columns are added to the table. Listing 23.29 demonstrates what happens if the column list is not provided and a column is added to the referenced table.

LISTING 23.29   Lack of Column List in INSERT Statement Causing Procedure to Fail

```
use bigpubs2005
go
IF EXISTS ( SELECT * FROM INFORMATION_SCHEMA.ROUTINES
              WHERE SPECIFIC_SCHEMA = N'dbo'
                 AND SPECIFIC_NAME = N'insert_publishers')
   DROP PROCEDURE dbo.insert_publishers
GO
create proc insert_publishers @pub_id char(4),
                              @pub_name varchar(40),
                              @city varchar(20),
                              @state char(2),
                              @country varchar(30)
as
INSERT INTO bigpubs2005.dbo.publishers
VALUES(@pub_id, @pub_name, @city, @state, @country)
if @@error = 0
    print 'New Publisher added'
go

exec insert_publishers '9950', 'Sams Publishing', 'Indianapolis', 'IN', 'USA'
go

New Publisher added


alter table publishers add street varchar(80) null
go

exec insert_publishers '9951', 'Pearson Education', 'Indianapolis', 'IN', 'USA'
go

Msg 213, Level 16, State 1, Procedure insert_publishers, Line 7
Insert Error: Column name or number of supplied values does not match table
 definition.
```

A stored procedure cannot directly create schemas, views, triggers, defaults, rules, aggregates, functions, or stored procedures. You can, however, execute dynamic SQL that creates the object:

```
CREATE PROC create_other_proc AS
  EXEC ('CREATE PROC get_au_lname AS
        SELECT au_lname from authors
        RETURN')
```

> **TIP**
>
> If you are using dynamic SQL to create objects in stored procedures, be sure to qualify each object with the name of the object schema if users other than the stored procedure owner will be executing the stored procedure.

You can create tables in stored procedures. Generally, only temporary tables are created in stored procedures. Temporary tables created in stored procedures are dropped automatically when the procedure terminates. Global temporary tables, however, exist until the connection that created them terminates.

If you don't qualify object names within a stored procedure, they default to the schema of the stored procedure. It is recommended that objects in stored procedures be qualified with the appropriate schema name to avoid confusion.

You cannot drop a table and re-create another table with the same name within the procedure unless you use dynamic SQL to execute a string that creates the table.

A stored procedure cannot issue the USE statement to change the database context in which it is running; the database context for execution is limited to a single database. If you need to reference an object in another database, you should qualify the object name with the database name in your procedure code.

Calling Stored Procedures from Transactions

Stored procedures can be called from within a transaction, and they can also initiate transactions. SQL Server notes the transaction nesting level, which is available from the @@trancount function, before calling a stored procedure. If the value of @@trancount when the procedure returns is different from the value of @@trancount when it was executed, SQL Server displays error message 266: Transaction count after EXECUTE indicates that a COMMIT or ROLLBACK TRAN is missing. This message indicates that transaction nesting is out of balance. Because a stored procedure does not abort the batch on a rollback transaction statement, a rollback transaction statement inside the procedure could result in a loss of data integrity if subsequent statements are executed and committed.

A rollback transaction statement rolls back all statements to the outermost transaction, including any work performed inside nested stored procedures that have not been fully committed. A commit tran within the stored procedure decreases the value of @@trancount by only one. Because the transaction is not fully committed until @@trancount returns to zero, the work can be completely rolled back at any time prior to that. Essentially, the nested transaction inside the stored procedure is largely ignored. The modifications within the procedure are committed or rolled back based on the final action taken for the outermost transaction.

To avoid transaction nesting issues, you need to develop a consistent error-handling strategy for failed transactions or other errors that occur in transactions within your stored procedures and implement that strategy consistently across all procedures and applications. Within stored procedures that might be nested, you need to check whether the procedure is already being called from within a transaction before issuing another begin tran statement. If a transaction is already active, you can issue a save tran statement so that the procedure can roll back only the work that it has performed and allow the calling procedure that initiated the transaction to determine whether to continue or abort the overall transaction.

To maintain transaction integrity when calling procedures that involve transactions, follow these guidelines:

▶ Make no net change to @@trancount within your stored procedures.

▶ Issue a begin tran only if no transaction is already active.

▶ Set a savepoint if a transaction is already active so that a partial rollback can be performed within the stored procedure.

▶ Implement appropriate error handling and return an error status code if something goes wrong and a rollback occurs.

▶ Issue a commit tran only if the stored procedure issued the begin tran statement.

Listing 23.30 provides a template for a stored procedure that can ensure transactional integrity whether it is run as part of an ongoing transaction or independently.

LISTING 23.30   Template Code for a Stored Procedure That Can Run as Part of a Transaction or Run As Its Own Transaction

```
/* proc to demonstrate no net change to @@trancount
** but rolls back changes within the proc
** VERY IMPORTANT: return an error code
** to tell the calling procedure rollback occurred */

create proc ptran1
as
declare @trncnt int

select @trncnt = @@trancount  -- save @@trancount value
```

LISTING 23.30   Continued

```
if @trncnt = 0    -- transaction has not begun
   begin tran ptran1  -- begin tran increments nest level to 1

else              -- already in a transaction
   save tran ptran1   -- save tran doesn't increment nest level

/* do some processing */

if (@@error != 0) -- check for error condition
begin
    rollback tran ptran1  -- rollback to savepoint, or begin tran
    return 25            -- return error code indicating rollback
end

/* more processing if required */

if @trncnt = 0       -- this proc issued begin tran
   commit tran ptran1   -- commit tran, decrement @@trancount to 0
                  -- commit not required with save tran

return 0 /* successful return */
```

Listing 23.31 provides a template for the calling batch that might execute the stored procedure shown in Listing 23.30. The main problem you need to solve is handling return codes properly and responding with the correct transaction handling.

LISTING 23.31   Template Code for a Calling Batch or Stored Procedure That Might Execute a Stored Procedure Built with the Template in Listing 23.30

```
/* Retrieve status code to determine if proc was successful */

declare @status_val int, @trncnt int

select @trncnt = @@trancount   -- save @@trancount value

if @trncnt = 0    -- transaction has not begun
   begin tran t1  -- begin tran increments nest level to 1
else              -- otherwise, already in a transaction
   save tran t1   -- save tran doesn't increment nest level

/* do some processing if required */

if (@@error != 0) -- or other error condition
begin
```

LISTING 23.31   Continued

```
      rollback tran t1   -- rollback to savepoint,or begin tran
      return             -- and exit batch/procedure
end

execute @status_val = ptran1 --exec procedure, begin nesting

if @status_val = 25 -- if proc performed rollback
begin          -- determine whether to rollback or continue
    rollback tran t1
    return
end

/* more processing if required */

if @trncnt = 0     -- this proc/batch issued begin tran
  commit tran t1   -- commit tran, decrement @@trancount to 0
return             -- commit not required with save tran
```

Handling Errors in Stored Procedures

SQL Server 2005 introduces the TRY...CATCH construct, which you can use within your T-SQL stored procedures to provide a more graceful mechanism for exception handling than was available in previous versions of SQL Server with checking @@ERROR (and often the use of GOTO statements) after each SQL statement.

A TRY...CATCH construct consists of two parts: a TRY block and a CATCH block. When an error condition is detected in a T-SQL statement that is inside a TRY block, control is immediately passed to a CATCH block, where the error is processed. T-SQL statements in the TRY block that follow the statement that generated the error are not executed.

If an error occurs and processing is passed to the CATCH block, after the statements in the CATCH block are executed, control is then transferred to the first T-SQL statement that follows the END CATCH statement. If there are no errors inside the TRY block, control is passed to the statement immediately after the associated END CATCH statement, essentially skipping over the statements in the CATCH block.

A TRY is initiated with the BEGIN TRY statement and ended with the END TRY statement and can consist of one or more T-SQL statements between the BEGIN TRY and END TRY statements. The TRY block must be followed immediately by a CATCH block. A CATCH block is indicated with the BEGIN CATCH statement and ended with the END CATCH statement and can consist of one or more SQL statements. In SQL Server, each TRY block can be associated with only one CATCH block.

The syntax of the TRY...CATCH construct is as follows:

```
BEGIN TRY
    one_or_more_sql_statements
END TRY
BEGIN CATCH
    one_or_more_sql_statements
END CATCH
```

When in a CATCH block, you can use the following error functions to capture information about the error that invoked the CATCH block:

▶ **ERROR_NUMBER()**—Returns the error number.

▶ **ERROR_MESSAGE()**—Returns the complete text of the error message.

▶ **ERROR_SEVERITY()**—Returns the error severity.

▶ **ERROR_STATE()**—Returns the error state number.

▶ **ERROR_LINE()**—Returns the line number inside the procedure that caused the error.

▶ **ERROR_PROCEDURE()**—Returns the name of the stored procedure or trigger where the error occurred.

Unlike @@error, which is reset by each statement that is executed, the error information retrieved by the error functions remains constant anywhere within the scope of the CATCH block of a TRY...CATCH construct. Error functions can also be referenced inside a stored procedure and can be used to retrieve error information when the stored procedure is executed within a CATCH block. This allows you to modularize the error handling into a single procedure so you do not have to repeat the error-handling code in every CATCH block. Listing 23.32 shows an example of an error-handling procedure that you can use in your CATCH blocks.

LISTING 23.32   An Example of a Standard Error-Handling Procedure

```
create proc dbo.error_handler
as
begin
    Declare @errnum int,
            @severity int,
            @errstate int,
            @proc nvarchar(126),
            @line int,
            @message nvarchar(4000)
    -- capture the error information that caused the CATCH block to be invoked
    SELECT @errnum = ERROR_NUMBER(),
           @severity = ERROR_SEVERITY(),
           @errstate = ERROR_STATE(),
           @proc = ERROR_PROCEDURE(),
```

LISTING 23.32   Continued

```
            @line = ERROR_LINE(),
            @message = ERROR_MESSAGE()
    -- raise an error message with information on the error
    RAISERROR ('Failed to add new publisher for the following reason:
 Error: %d, Severity: %d, State: %d, in proc %s at line %d, Message: "%s"',
                16, 1, @errnum, @severity, @errstate, @proc, @line, @message)
    Return
end
```

Listing 23.33 provides an example of the use of the TRY...CATCH construct in a stored procedure, modifying the insert_publishers procedure created in Listing 23.29. Note that this CATCH block uses the dbo.error_handler procedure defined in Listing 23.32.

LISTING 23.33   Using a TRY...CATCH Construct for Error Handling in a Stored Procedure

```
use bigpubs2005
go
alter proc insert_publishers @pub_id char(4),
                             @pub_name varchar(40),
                             @city varchar(20),
                             @state char(2),
                             @country varchar(30)
as
BEGIN TRY
    INSERT INTO bigpubs2005.dbo.publishers
            (pub_id, pub_name, city, state, country)
        VALUES(@pub_id, @pub_name, @city, @state, @country)
    -- if no error occurs, we should see this print statement
    print 'New Publisher added'
END TRY
BEGIN CATCH
    -- invoke the error_handler procedure
    exec error_handler
    -- return a non-zero status code
    RETURN -101
END CATCH
-- if successful execution, return 0
RETURN 0
go

exec insert_publishers '9951', 'Pearson Education', 'Indianapolis', 'IN', 'USA'
exec insert_publishers '9950', 'Sams Publishing', 'Indianapolis', 'IN', 'USA'
go
```

LISTING 23.33   Continued

```
New Publisher added

Msg 50000, Level 16, State 1, Procedure insert_publishers, Line 18
Failed to add new publisher for the following reason:
Error: 2627, Severity: 14, State: 1, in proc insert_publishers at line 8,
 Message: "Violation of PRIMARY KEY constraint 'UPKCL_pubind'. Cannot insert
 duplicate key in object 'dbo.publishers'."
```

If you want to capture and handle any errors that may occur within a CATCH block, you can incorporate another TRY...CATCH block within the CATCH block itself.

Also note that some errors with severity 20 or higher that cause SQL Server to close the user connection cannot be handled by the TRY...CATCH construct. However, severity level 20 or higher errors that do not result in the connection being closed are captured and handled by the CATCH block. Any errors with a severity level of 10 or less are considered warnings or informational messages and not really errors and thus are not handled by the TRY...CATCH construct. Also, any compile errors (such as syntax errors) or object name resolution errors that happen during deferred name resolution also do not invoke a CATCH block. These errors are returned to the application or batch that called the error-generating routine.

Using Source Code Control with Stored Procedures

When you can, it's generally a good idea to use source code control for your stored procedure scripts. Stored procedures are as much a part of an application as the application code itself and should be treated as such. When using source code control, you can link versions of your procedures and other object creation scripts with specific versions of your applications. Using source code control systems also provides a great way to keep track of the changes to your stored procedures and other object creation scripts, enabling you to go back to a previous version if the modifications lead to problems with the applications or data.

SSMS provides a feature similar to Visual Studio that lets you organize your SQL scripts into solutions and projects. A *project* is a collection of one or more script files that are stored in the Windows file system, usually in a folder with the same name as the project. A *solution* is a collection of one or more projects.

In addition to providing a way to manage and organize your scripts, SSMS can also integrate with source code control software if the source code control system provides a compatible plug-in. If you are using Visual Studio, it's likely that you are also using Visual SourceSafe. Visual SourceSafe provides a one-to-one mapping between SSMS projects and Visual SourceSafe projects. After you create an SSMS solution, you can check the entire SSMS solution into Visual SourceSafe and then check out individual script files or projects. You can also specify that a solution be added to source code control when you create a new solution. In SSMS, you select File, New and then select New Project. In the New

Project dialog, you can specify the name for the project and the solution, and you can also specify whether to add to solution to source code control, as shown in Figure 23.15.

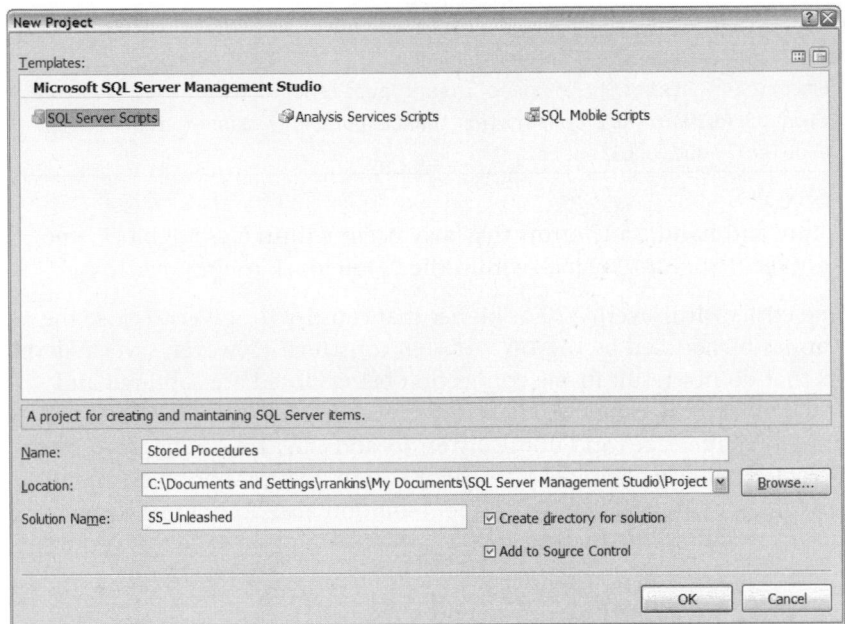

FIGURE 23.15   Creating a new project/solution and adding it to source control.

When you add a solution to Visual SourceSafe, it prompts you for the login ID and password to use to access Visual SourceSafe. After you provide that information, Visual SourceSafe then prompts you for the Visual SourceSafe project to add the SMSS project to, or it allows you to create a new project in Visual SourceSafe.

Within a project, you can specify the database connection(s) for the project and add SQL script files to the Queries folder. After creating a new script file, you can add it into the source code control system by right-clicking the script file in the Solutions Explorer and selecting Check In (see Figure 23.16).

After you check in a script file, you can right-click the file and perform source code control tasks such as checking the script out for editing, getting the current version, comparing versions, and viewing the check-in history. If you check out the script for editing, you can then open it in a new query window, where you can make changes to the script and then execute it in the database. When you are satisfied with the changes, you can check the new version back into the source code control system.

For more information on working with solutions and projects in SSMS, see Chapter 3, "SQL Server Management Studio."

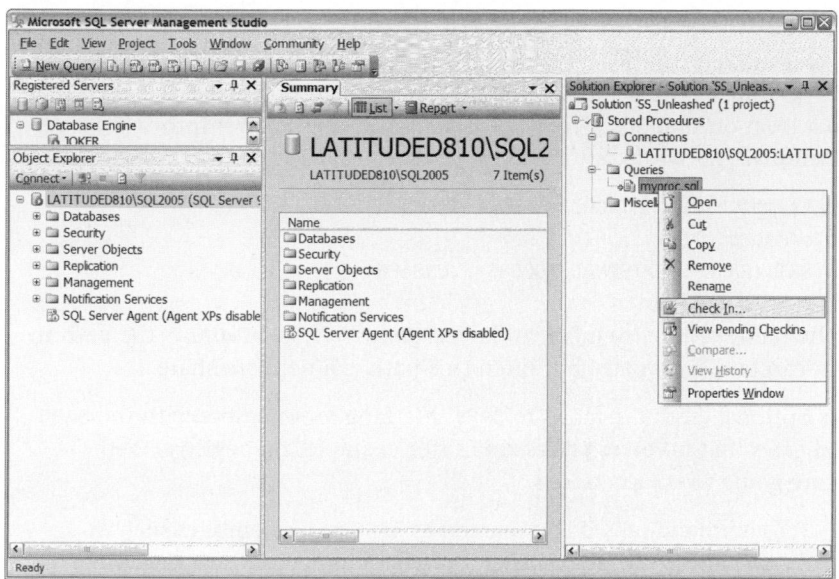

FIGURE 23.16   Checking in a new script file.

Creating and Using CLR Stored Procedures

Prior to SQL Server 2005, the only way to extend the functionality of SQL Server beyond what was available using the T-SQL language was to create extended stored procedures or COM components. The main problems with these types of extensions were that if not written very carefully, they could have an adverse impact on the reliability and security of SQL Server. Besides extended stored procedures and COM components, in SQL Server, the only language the stored procedures could be written in was T-SQL. Unfortunately, T-SQL has a somewhat limited command set for things such as complex string comparison and manipulation and complex numeric computations.

In SQL Server 2005, you can now create stored procedures in any Microsoft .NET Framework programming language, such as Microsoft Visual Basic .NET or Microsoft Visual C#. Stored procedures written in the CLR are much more secure and reliable than extended stored procedures or COM components.

For information on the methods and tools for actually creating and compiling CLR stored procedures, see Chapter 36. In this chapter, we focus only on how to install and use CLR procedures in a SQL Server database.

> **NOTE**
>
> The CLR procedure examples presented subsequently in this chapter are provided as illustrations only. The sample code will not execute successfully as the underlying CLR assemblies have not been provided.

Adding CLR Stored Procedures to a Database

If you've already created and compiled a CLR stored procedure, the next thing to do is to install that CLR procedure in the database. The first step in this process is to copy the .NET assembly to a location that SQL Server can access and then load it into SQL Server by creating an assembly. The syntax for the CREATE ASSEMBLY command is as follows:

```
CREATE ASSEMBLY AssemblyName [AUTHORIZATION LoginName]
FROM  StringPathToAssemblyDll
[WITH PERMISSION_SET (SAFE ¦ EXTERNAL_ACCESS ¦ UNSAFE) ]
```

AssemblyName is the name of the assembly, and StringPathToAssemblyDll is the path to the DLL. The path can be a local path, but often this path is a network share.

The WITH clause is optional, and it defaults to SAFE. Marking an assembly with the SAFE permission set indicates that no external resources (for example, the registry, Web services, file I/O) are going to be accessed.

The CREATE ASSEMBLY command fails if it is marked as SAFE and assemblies such as System.IO are referenced, and anything causing a permission demand for executing similar operations results in an exception being thrown at runtime.

Marking an assembly with the EXTERNAL_ACCESS permission set tells SQL Server that it will be using resources such as networking, files, and so forth. Assemblies such as System.Web.Services (but not System.Web) may be referenced with this set. To create an EXTERNAL_ACCESS assembly, the creator must have EXTERN_ACCESS permission.

Marking an assembly with the UNSAFE permission set tells SQL Server that not only might external resources be used, but unmanaged code may be invoked from managed code. An UNSAFE assembly can potentially undermine the security of either SQL Server or the CLR. Only members of the sysadmin role can create UNSAFE assemblies.

After an assembly has been created, the next step is to associate the method within the assembly with a stored procedure. This is done with the CREATE PROCEDURE command, using the following syntax:

```
CREATE PROCEDURE [ schema_name. ] procedure_name
    ( [ { @parameter_name [AS] [ schema_name.]scalar_datatype [ = default ] }
    [ ,...n ] ] )
 [ AS ] EXTERNAL NAME assembly_name.class_name.method_name
```

After the CLR procedure has been created successfully, it can be used just like a T-SQL stored procedure. The following is an example of manually deploying a CLR stored procedure:

```
CREATE ASSEMBLY pr_address_verify
FROM 'F:\assemblies\address_routines\address_procs.dll'
WITH PERMISSION_SET = SAFE
GO
```

```
CREATE PROCEDURE pr_address_verify (@address1 nvarchar(100),
                                    @address2 nvarchar(100),
                                    @city varchar(50),
                                    @state char(2),
                                    @zip char(9))
AS
EXTERNAL NAME [SQLCLR].[Routines.StoredProcedures].[address_verify]
go
```

> **NOTE**
>
> The preceding examples show the manual steps of registering an assembly and creating the CLR function. If you are using Visual Studio's new Deploy feature, Visual Studio automatically issues the CREATE/ALTER ASSEMBLY and the CREATE PROCEDURE commands. For more details on using Visual Studio to create and deploy user-defined CLR functions, see Chapter 36.

T-SQL or CLR Stored Procedures?

One question that often comes up about SQL Server 2005 is whether it's better to develop stored procedures in T-SQL or in the CLR. The best answer is that it really depends on the situation and what functionality the procedure needs to implement.

The general rule of thumb is that if the stored procedure will be performing data access or large set-oriented operations with little or no complex procedural logic, it's better to create it in T-SQL for best performance. This is because T-SQL works more closely with the data and doesn't require multiple transitions between the CLR and the SQL OS.

On the other hand, most benchmarks have shown that the CLR performs better than T-SQL for procedures that require a high level of computation or text manipulation. The CLR offers much richer APIs that provide capabilities not available in T-SQL for operations such as text manipulation, cryptography, I/O operations, data formatting, and invocation of Web services. For example, T-SQL provides only rudimentary string manipulation capabilities, whereas .NET supports capabilities such as regular expressions, which are much more powerful for pattern matching and replacement than the T-SQL replace() function.

In a nutshell, performance tests have generally shown that T-SQL generally performs better for standard CRUD (create, read, update, delete) operations, whereas CLR code performs better for complex math, string manipulation, and other tasks that go beyond data access.

Using Extended Stored Procedures

If you've worked with SQL Server for a while, you are probably familiar with extended stored procedures. These are stored procedures that reside in the master database and have names that begin with xp_. Extended stored procedures are invoked and managed similarly to regular stored procedures. You can grant and revoke permissions on extended stored procedures as you do for normal stored procedures. Although extended stored procedures reside in the `master` database like system procedures, the procedure name has to be fully qualified with the `master` database name when it is invoked from a database other than `master`, as in the following example:

```
use bigpubs2005
go
exec master..xp_fixeddrives
```

Extended stored procedures are not built with T-SQL commands; instead, they map to a function stored in a DLL. Historically, extended stored procedures were the mechanism available to extend SQL Server functionality. However, the introduction of CLR procedures provides a much easier, safer way to extend the functionality of SQL Server 2005.

Extended stored procedures are typically written in Microsoft C or Visual C++, using the Microsoft Extended Stored Procedure API, and coding them can be quite complex. In addition, extended stored procedures run under the same security context as SQL Server and within the same address space. A poorly written extended stored procedure could bring down the SQL Server service. CLR procedures, on the other hand, are written in .NET code that is type safe and runs within the `Appdomain` boundary so it cannot access random SQL Server memory locations. In other words, it is much easier and safer to create and deploy CLR procedures than extended stored procedures.

TIP

Because of the unsafe nature of extended stored procedures, and the greater security and capabilities of CLR stored procedures, extended stored procedures are a feature that will very likely be removed in some future version of Microsoft SQL Server. For new development efforts, you should use CLR procedures instead of extended stored procedures. For any existing extended stored procedures, you should make plans to convert any applications that currently use extended stored procedures to use CLR procedures instead.

Adding Extended Stored Procedures to SQL Server

If you do happen to have a DLL that contains one or more extended stored procedures that you need to add to SQL Server, you can use the `sp_addextendedproc` system stored procedure. Only SQL Server system administrators can add extended stored procedures to SQL Server. The syntax is as follows:

```
sp_addextendedproc [ @functname = ] 'procedure' , [ @dllname = ] 'dll'
```

Extended stored procedures are added only in the `master` database. The `sp_addextended` procedure adds an entry for the extended stored procedure to the system catalogs and registers the DLL with SQL Server. You must provide the complete path for the DLL when registering it with SQL Server.

To remove an extended procedure from SQL Server, you use `sp_dropextendedproc`:

```
sp_dropextendedproc [ @functname = ] 'procedure'
```

CAUTION

Because extended stored procedure DLLs and SQL Server share the same address space, poorly written extended procedure code can adversely affect SQL Server functioning. Any memory access violations or exceptions thrown by an extended stored procedure could possibly damage SQL Server data areas. For this reason, it is strongly recommended that CLR procedures be considered as an alternative to extended stored procedures. If there is some compelling reason to use extended stored procedures, they should be very thoroughly tested and verified before they are installed.

Obtaining Information on Extended Stored Procedures

To obtain information on the extended stored procedures in SQL Server, you use `sp_helpextendedproc` as follows:

```
sp_helpextendedproc [ [@funcname = ] 'procedure' ]
```

If the procedure name is specified, `sp_helpextendedproc` lists the procedure name along with the DLL that is invoked when the extended stored procedure is executed. If no procedure name is passed in, `sp_helpextendedproc` lists all extended stored procedures that are defined in SQL Server and their associated DLLs.

Extended Stored Procedures Provided with SQL Server

Most of the extended stored procedures that ship with SQL Server are undocumented. All extended stored procedures (or rather, the references to them) are stored in the `master` database. You can display them in SSMS under the `master` database. To do so, you open the `Programmability` folder for the `master` database and then open the `Extended Stored Procedures` folder. The provided extended stored procedures are listed in the `System Extended Stored Procedures` folder.

If you plan to use an undocumented extended stored procedure, be careful. First, you have to find out what it does and what parameters it takes. You should also be aware that Microsoft does not support the use of undocumented extended stored procedures. Moreover, an undocumented procedure might not be included in a later version of SQL Server, or if it is included, it might behave differently than it does now.

Table 23.4 lists the general categories of extended stored procedures.

TABLE 23.4   Extended Stored Procedures Categories

Category	Description
General extended procedures	General functionality. Perhaps the most useful is xp_cmdshell, which executes external programs and returns the output from them as a result set.
SQL Mail extended procedures	Used to perform email operations from within SQL Server.
SQL Server Profiler extended procedures	Used by SQL Server Profiler. These can also be used directly, for instance, to create a trace queue and start the trace from within a stored procedure.
OLE automation procedures	Allows SQL Server to create and use OLE automation objects.
API system stored procedures	Undocumented extended stored procedures used by the API libraries. The server cursor functionality, for instance, is implemented as a set of extended stored procedures.

Using xp_cmdshell

One of the most useful, and potentially dangerous, extended stored procedures provided with SQL Server 2005 is xp_cmdshell. xp_cmdshell can execute any operating system command or program that is available on the SQL Server system, as long as it is a console program that doesn't require user input. xp_cmdshell accepts a varchar(8000) (or nvarchar(4000)) value as the command string to be executed, and it returns the results of the command as a single nvarchar(255) column. The full syntax of xp_cmdshell is as follows:

```
xp_cmdshell { 'command_string' } [ , no_output ]
```

If the no_output option is specified, the results from the command are not displayed.

The following example uses xp_cmdshell to list the files in a directory on the SQL Server computer's hard disk:

```
EXEC xp_cmdshell 'DIR c:\*.*'
```

xp_cmdshell runs synchronously. Control is not returned to the SQL Server user session until the shell command completes. This is why you have to ensure that the shell command invoked via xp_cmdshell does not prompt for user input. Commands invoked via xp_cmdshell do not run interactively, so there is no way to respond to the user input prompt. The SQL Server session waits indefinitely for a command invoked via xp_cmdshell to return.

> **CAUTION**
>
> After SQL Server passes off the xp_cmdshell command to the operating system, SQL Server cannot interact with the command. If the command requires user input, the process waits indefinitely, and it usually doesn't go away without a fight. Killing the process in SQL Server usually just leaves it in a KILLED/ROLLBACK state. Closing the session that invoked the xp_cmdshell statement doesn't help either. Sometimes, you may have to stop and restart SQL Server to make the process finally go away.

If xp_cmdshell is invoked from another database, it has to be fully qualified as master..xp_cmdshell. Unlike with system procedures, SQL Server doesn't automatically look for extended stored procedures in the master database.

Because of the potentially dangerous nature of xp_cmdshell (it essentially allows a user to run operating system-level commands on the SQL Server machine), it is disabled by default. To enable xp_cmdshell, you must run the following commands:

```
EXEC sp_configure 'show advanced options', 1
GO
RECONFIGURE
GO
-- To enable the feature.
EXEC sp_configure 'xp_cmdshell', 1
GO
RECONFIGURE
GO
```

As an additional security measure in SQL Server 2005, by default, permission to execute xp_cmdshell is limited to users with CONTROL SERVER permission. The Windows process spawned by xp_cmdshell runs within the security context of the account under which the SQL Server service is running. Essentially, it has the same security rights as the SQL Server service account.

When xp_cmdshell is invoked by a user who is not a member of the sysadmin fixed server role, it fails unless a proxy account has been set up. A *proxy account* is a Windows account that a system administrator defines and sets a security context for within the Windows environment. When a user who is not a member of the sysadmin group runs xp_cmdshell, the commands are run within the security context of the defined proxy account.

The proxy account for xp_cmdshell can be created by executing sp_xp_cmdshell_ proxy_account. The syntax of this command is as follows:

```
sp_xp_cmdshell_proxy_account [ NULL ¦ { 'account_name' , 'password' } ]
```

23

For example, the following command creates a proxy credential for the Windows domain user Developer\tom that has the Windows password ss2k5Unl:

```
sp_xp_cmdshell_proxy_account 'Developer/tom' , 'ss2k5Unl'
```

If NULL is passed as *account_name*, the proxy credential is deleted.

CAUTION

Because of the potential havoc that could be wreaked on your database server if xp_cmdshell got into the wrong hands, it is recommended that the ability to run xp_cmdshell be left disabled. If you must use xp_cmdshell, be very careful about who has access to it by limiting it to only those with sysadmin permissions if at all possible. If for some reason xp_cmdshell must be made available to all users, be sure that the permissions granted to the proxy account are restricted to the minimum permissions required to perform the commands that need to be invoked via xp_cmdshell.

Summary

Stored procedures are one of the premier features of Microsoft SQL Server. They provide a number of benefits over using ad hoc SQL, including faster performance; restricted, function-based access to tables; protection of application code from database changes; and the ability to simplify complex tasks into a simple stored procedure call. With the introduction of the CLR in SQL Server 2005, you can write even more powerful stored procedures in languages other than T-SQL to further expand the capability and power of the stored procedures that reside in SQL Server.

It is important to understand the various capabilities and limitations of stored procedures before writing much stored procedure code. Poorly written procedures make the server appear to run sluggishly and inefficiently. Well-written procedures run efficiently and solidly. Following the guidelines and tips presented in this chapter should help you write efficient and solid stored procedures.

CHAPTER 24

Creating and Managing User-Defined Functions

IN THIS CHAPTER

▶ What's New in SQL Server 2005

▶ Why Use User-Defined Functions?

▶ Types of User-Defined Functions

▶ Creating and Managing User-Defined Functions

▶ Systemwide Table-Valued Functions

▶ Rewriting Stored Procedures as Functions

▶ Creating and Using CLR Functions

SQL Server provides a number of predefined functions that are built in to T-SQL. The supplied functions help extend the capabilities of T-SQL, providing the ability to perform string manipulation, mathematical calculations, data type conversions, and so on within T-SQL code. Although SQL Server provides a pretty extensive set of functions, you might sometimes wish you had a function that is not provided. You could create a stored procedure to perform custom processing, but you can't use the result of a stored procedure in a WHERE clause or as a column in a SELECT list. For this type of situation, SQL Server 2005 provides user-defined functions.

A user-defined function can return a single scalar value, like the majority of the built-in functions, or it can return a result set as a table result, similarly to a table variable.

This chapter takes a look at how to create and manage user-defined functions as well as when it may be better to rewrite stored procedures as functions.

What's New in SQL Server 2005

The most significant new feature in SQL Server 2005 for user-defined functions is the ability to define functions in the common language runtime (CLR) in addition to T-SQL–based functions. Being able to define functions in the CLR significantly extends what you can do in user-defined functions by opening up the power and capabilities of the .NET Framework languages. This means you can develop functions in SQL Server that are either impossible or very difficult to achieve using T-SQL alone. Later in this chapter, in the section "Creating and Using CLR Functions," you'll learn about CLR functions and some general guidelines on when to use CLR functions versus T-SQL functions.

> **NOTE**
>
> This chapter focuses primarily on creating T-SQL functions. For more information about creating and coding examples of CLR functions, see Chapter 36, "SQL Server and the .NET Framework."

Also along the lines of expanding the capability of user-defined functions, SQL Server 2005 now allows most of the nondeterministic built-in functions to be used in user-defined T-SQL functions. For example, the getdate() function, which is nondeterministic, can now be used in the code inside a user-defined function. You'll learn about this capability and the differences between deterministic and nondeterministic functions in the "Creating and Managing Functions" section, later in this chapter.

SQL Server 2005 provides additional ways of specifying the security context in which a user-defined function should run, with the addition of the EXECUTE AS clause. The use of this clause is discussed in the "Creating and Managing Functions" section, later in this chapter.

Why Use User-Defined Functions?

The main benefit of user-defined functions is that they mean you are not limited to just the functions SQL Server provides. You can develop your own functions to meet your specific needs or to simplify complex SQL code. For example, the getdate() function returns the current system date and time. It always includes both a date component and a time component, with accuracy down to the milliseconds. What if you wanted to return just the date and have the time always set to midnight? To strip the time off the result from getdate(), you would have to pass the result from getdate() through some other functions to zero out the time component. The following is one possible solution:

```
select convert(datetime, convert(char(10), getdate(), 110))
```

Each time you wanted just the date, with the time always set to midnight, you would have to perform this same conversion operation on the result of the getdate() function. As an alternative, you could create a user-defined function that performs the operations on getdate() automatically and always returns the current date, with a time value of midnight. You could then use the user-defined function in your SQL code in place of the getdate() function, instead of having to perform the more complex conversion each time. You can use user-defined functions, like the built-in system functions, in SELECT lists, SET clauses of UPDATE statements, VALUES clauses of INSERT statements, as default values, and so on. For example, the following query uses a user-defined function, getonlydate(), to return the current date, with a time of midnight:

```
select dbo.getonlydate()
```

You'll learn how to define the `getonlydate()` function later in this chapter, in the section "Using T-SQL to View Functions."

The following examples show how you can use the `getonlydate()` function in other statements:

```
CREATE TABLE Orders (
        OrderID int IDENTITY (1, 1) NOT NULL Primary Key,
        CustomerID nchar (5) COLLATE SQL_Latin1_General_CP1_CI_AS NULL ,
        EmployeeID int NULL ,
        OrderDate datetime NULL default dbo.getonlydate(),
        RequiredDate datetime NULL ,
        ShippedDate datetime NULL
)
go

insert Orders (CustomerID, EmployeeID, RequiredDate)
    values ('BERGS', 3, dbo.getonlydate() + 7)
go

update Orders
    set ShippedDate = dbo.getonlydate()
    where OrderID = 1
go

select OrderDate,
       RequiredDate,
       ShippedDate
    from Orders
  where OrderDate = dbo.getonlydate()
go

OrderDate               RequiredDate            ShippedDate
----------------------- ----------------------- -----------------------
2006-06-03 00:00:00.000 2006-06-10 00:00:00.000 2006-06-03 00:00:00.000
```

If you use the new `getonlydate()` function consistently when you want to store only dates, searching against `datetime` columns is easier because you don't have to concern yourself with the time component. For example, if you used `getdate()` instead of `getonlydate()`, you would have to account for the time component in your queries against `OrderDate` to ensure that you find all records for a particular day:

```
SELECT OrderDate,
       RequiredDate,
```

```
        ShippedDate
    from Orders
  where OrderDate >= convert(varchar(10), getdate(), 110)
    and OrderDate < convert(varchar(10), getdate() + 1, 110)
```

From this example, you can see how much using the `getonlydate()` user-defined function can simplify your queries.

In addition to functions that return scalar values, you can also define functions that return table results. You can use functions that return table results anywhere in queries that a table or view can be used, including joins, subqueries, and so on. The following are a couple examples of using a table-valued function that returns a list of valid book types:

```
select * from dbo.valid_book_types()
go
insert titles
select * from newtitles
where type in (select * from dbo.valid_book_types())
```

Essentially, you have reduced a query to a simple function that you can now use anywhere a table can be referenced.

With a few restrictions—which are covered later in this chapter, in the "Creating and Managing Functions" section—you can write all types of functions in SQL Server to perform various calculations or routines. For example, you could create a T-SQL function that returns a valid list of code values, a function to determine the number of days that items are backordered, a function to return the average price of all books, and so on. Plus, with the ability to now create CLR-based functions, you can create significantly more powerful functions than what can be accomplished using T-SQL alone. Examples of CLR-based functions might include a more robust `soundex()` function, a function to return the factorial of a number, and an address comparison function. The possibilities are nearly endless. As you have seen, user-defined functions significantly increase the capabilities and flexibility of T-SQL.

Types of User-Defined Functions

SQL Server supports three types of user-defined functions:

▶ Scalar functions

▶ Inline table-valued functions

▶ Multistatement table-valued functions

The next few sections take an in-depth look at the differences between the function types and how and where you can use them.

Scalar Functions

A scalar function is like the standard built-in functions provided with SQL Server. It returns a single scalar value that can be used anywhere a constant expression can be used in a query. (You saw an example of this in the earlier example of the `getonlydate()` function.)

A scalar function typically takes one or more arguments and returns a value of a specified data type. Every T-SQL function must return a result using the `RETURN` statement. The value to be returned can be contained in a local variable defined within the function, or the value can be computed in the `RETURN` statement. The following two functions are variations of a function that returns the average price for a specified type of book from the `titles` table:

```
use bigpubs2005
go
CREATE FUNCTION AverageBookPrice(@booktype varchar(12) = '%')
RETURNS money
AS
BEGIN
    DECLARE @avg money
    SELECT @avg = avg(price)
    FROM titloo
    WHERE type like @booktype

    RETURN @avg
END
go


CREATE FUNCTION AverageBookPrice2(@booktype varchar(12) = '%')
RETURNS money
AS
BEGIN
    RETURN ( SELECT avg(price)
             FROM titles
             WHERE type like @booktype)
END
```

As mentioned earlier in this chapter, a scalar function can be used anywhere a constant expression can be used. For example, SQL Server doesn't allow aggregate functions in a `WHERE` clause unless they are contained in a subquery. The `AvgBookPrice()` function lets you compare against the average price without having to use a subquery:

```
select title_id, type, price from titles
where price > dbo.AverageBookPrice('popular_comp')
go
```

```
title_id type         price
-------- ------------ ---------------------
PC1035   popular_comp 17.1675
PS2091   psychology   17.0884
```

When invoking a user-defined scalar function, you must include the schema name. If you omit the schema name, you get the following error, even if the function is created in your default schema or exists in the dbo schema in the database:

```
select AverageBookPrice('popular_comp')
go

Server: Msg 195, Level 15, State 10, Line 1
'AverageBookPrice' is not a recognized function name.
```

You can return the value from a user-defined scalar function into a local variable in two ways. You can assign the result to a local variable by using the SET statement or an assignment select, or you can use the EXEC statement. The following commands are functionally equivalent:

```
declare @avg1 money,
        @avg2 money,
        @avg3 money
select @avg1 = dbo.AverageBookPrice('popular_comp')
set @avg2 = dbo.AverageBookPrice('popular_comp')
exec @avg3 = dbo.AverageBookPrice 'popular_comp'
select @avg1 as avg1, @avg2 as avg2, @avg3 as avg3
go

Warning: Null value is eliminated by an aggregate or other SET operation.
avg1                 avg2                 avg3
-------------------- -------------------- --------------------
16.0643              16.0643              16.0643
```

Notice, however, that when you use a function in an EXEC statement, you invoke it similarly to the way you invoke a stored procedure, and you do not use parentheses around the function parameters. Also, when you invoke a function in the EXEC statement, the function generates the warning message, Warning: Null value is eliminated by an aggregate or other SET operation. This warning isn't generated when the function is invoked in the SET or SELECT statement. To avoid confusion, you should stick to using the EXEC statement for stored procedures and invoke scalar functions as you would normally invoke a SQL Server built-in function.

Table-Valued Functions

A table-valued user-defined function returns a rowset instead of a single scalar value. You can invoke a table-valued function in the FROM clause of a SELECT statement, just as you would a table or view. In some situations, a table-valued function can almost be thought of as a view that accepts parameters, so the result set is determined dynamically. A table-valued function specifies the keyword TABLE in its RETURNS clause.

Table-valued functions are of two types: inline and multistatement. The two types of table-valued functions return the same thing, and they are also invoked the same way. The only real difference between them is the way the function is written to return the rowset. The next couple sections look at each of these types of table-valued functions.

Inline Table-Valued Functions

An inline table-valued function specifies only the TABLE keyword in the RETURNS clause, without table definition information. The code inside the function is a single RETURN statement that invokes a SELECT statement. For example, you could create an inline table-valued function that returns a rowset of all book types and the average price for each type, where the average price exceeds the value passed into the function:

```
use bigpubs2005
go
CREATE FUNCTION AveragePricebyType (@price money = 0.0)
RETURNS table
AS

    RETURN ( SELECT type, avg(isnull(price, 0)) as avg_price
             FROM titles
             group by type
             having avg(isnull(price, 0)) > @price)
```

You can invoke the function by referencing it in a FROM clause as you would a table or view:

```
select * from AveragePricebyType (15.00)
go


type          avg_price
------------  --------------------
business      15.0988
mod_cook      15.4236
```

Notice that when you invoke a table-valued function, you do not have to specify the schema name as you do with a user-defined scalar function.

Multistatement Table-Valued Functions

Multistatement table-valued functions differ from inline functions in two major ways:

▶ The RETURNS clause specifies a table variable and its definition.

▶ The body of the function contains multiple statements, at least one of which populates the table variable with data values.

You define a table variable in the RETURNS clause by using the TABLE data type. The syntax to define the table variable is similar to the CREATE TABLE syntax. Note that the name of the table variable comes before the TABLE keyword:

```
RETURNS @variable TABLE ( column definition ¦ table_constraint [, ...] )
```

The scope of the table variable is limited to the function in which it is defined. Although the contents of the table variable are returned as the function result, the table variable itself cannot be accessed or referenced outside the function.

Within the function in which it is defined, a table variable can be treated like a regular table. You can perform any SELECT, INSERT, UPDATE, or DELETE statement on the rows in a table variable, except for SELECT INTO. Here's an example:

```
INSERT INTO table_variable EXEC stored_procedure
```

The following example defines the inline table-valued function AveragePricebyType() as a multistatement table-valued function called AveragePricebyType2():

```
use bigpubs2005
go
CREATE FUNCTION AveragePricebyType2 (@price money = 0.0)
RETURNS @table table (type varchar(12) null, avg_price money null)
AS
begin
    insert @table
        SELECT type, avg(isnull(price,0)) as avg_price
            FROM titles
            group by type
            having avg(isnull(price, 0)) > @price
    return
end
```

Notice the main differences between this version and the inline version: In the multistatement version, you have to define the structure of the table rowset you are returning and also have to include the BEGIN and END statements as wrappers around the multiple statements that the function can contain. Other than that, both functions are invoked the same way and return the same rowset:

```
select * from AveragePricebyType2 (15.00)
go

type          avg_price
-----------   --------------------
business      15.0988
mod_cook      15.4236
```

Why use multistatement table-valued functions instead of inline table-valued functions? Generally, you use multistatement table-valued functions when you need to perform further operations (for example, inserts, updates, or deletes) on the contents of the table variable before returning a result set. You would also use them if you need to perform additional processing on the input parameters of the function before invoking the query to populate the table variable.

Creating and Managing User-Defined Functions

The preceding sections of this chapter have already shown some examples of creating functions. This section discusses in more detail the CREATE FUNCTION syntax and what types of operations are allowed in functions. This section also shows how to create and manage T-SQL functions by using SQL Server Management Studio (SSMS).

Creating User-Defined Functions

You create T-SQL functions by using T-SQL statements. You can enter the T-SQL code in sqlcmd, SSMS, or any other third-party query tool that allows you to enter ad hoc T-SQL code. The following sections first look at the basic syntax for creating functions and then look at how you can create functions by using the features of SSMS.

Creating T-SQL Functions

User-defined functions can accept 0–1,024 input parameters but can return only a single result: either a single scalar value or a table result set.

The T-SQL syntax for the CREATE FUNCTION command for scalar functions is as follows:

```
CREATE FUNCTION [ schema_name. ] function_name
    ( [ { @parameter_name [AS] [ schema_name.]scalar_datatype [ = default ] }
      [ ,...n ] ] )
RETURNS scalar_datatype
[ WITH { [ ENCRYPTION ]
        [ , SCHEMABINDING ]
        [ , RETURNS NULL ON NULL INPUT ¦ CALLED ON NULL INPUT ]
        [ , EXECUTE_AS_Clause ]
      } ]
 [ AS ]
BEGIN
    SQL_Statements
```

```
    RETURN scalar_expression
END
```

The syntax for the CREATE FUNCTION command for inline table-valued functions is as follows:

```
CREATE FUNCTION [ schema_name. ] function_name
    ( [ { @parameter_name [AS] [ schema_name.]scalar_datatype [ = default ] }
      [ ,...n ] ] )
RETURNS TABLE
[ WITH { [ ENCRYPTION ]
        [ , SCHEMABINDING ]
        [ , RETURNS NULL ON NULL INPUT ¦ CALLED ON NULL INPUT ]
        [ , EXECUTE_AS_Clause ]
      } ]
[ AS ]
RETURN [ ( ] select-stmt [ ) ]
```

The syntax for the CREATE FUNCTION command for multistatement table-valued functions is as follows:

```
CREATE FUNCTION [ schema_name. ] function_name
    ( [ { @parameter_name [AS] [ schema_name.]scalar_datatype [ = default ] }
      [ ,...n ] ] )
RETURNS @table_variable TABLE ( { column_definition ¦ table_constraint }
                                [ ,...n ] )
[ WITH { [ ENCRYPTION ]
        [ , SCHEMABINDING ]
        [ , RETURNS NULL ON NULL INPUT ¦ CALLED ON NULL INPUT ]
        [ , EXECUTE_AS_Clause ]
      } ]
 [ AS ]
BEGIN
    SQL_Statments
    RETURN
END
```

The types of SQL statements that are allowed in a function include the following:

- ▶ DECLARE statements to define variables and cursors that are local to the function.

- ▶ Assignments of values to variables that are local to the function, using the SET command or an assignment select.

- ▶ Cursor operations on local cursors that are declared, opened, closed, and deallocated within the function. FETCH statements must assign values to local variables by using the INTO clause.

- ▶ Control-of-flow statements such as `IF`, `ELSE`, `WHILE`, `GOTO`, and so on, excluding the `TRY...CATCH` statements.

- ▶ `UPDATE`, `INSERT`, and `DELETE` statements that modify table variables that are defined within the function.

- ▶ `EXECUTE` statements that call an extended stored procedure. (Any results returned by the extended stored procedure are discarded.)

- ▶ Other user-defined functions, up to a maximum nesting level of 32.

If you specify the `ENCRYPTION` option, the SQL statements used to define the function are stored encrypted in the `syscomments` table. This prevents anyone from viewing the function source code in the database.

> **NOTE**
>
> If you choose to encrypt the function code, you should be sure to save a copy of the script used to create the function to a file outside the database, in case you ever need to modify the function or re-create it. After the source code for the function is encrypted, you cannot extract the original unencrypted source code from the database.

If a function is created with the `SCHEMABINDING` option, the database objects that the function references cannot be altered or dropped unless the function is dropped first or the schema binding of the function is removed, using the `ALTER FUNCTION` command and without specifying the `SCHEMABINDING` option. A `CREATE FUNCTION` statement with the `SCHEMABINDING` option specified fails unless all the following conditions are met:

- ▶ Any user-defined functions and views referenced within the function are also schema bound.

- ▶ Any objects referenced by the function are referenced using a two-part name (`schema.object_name`).

- ▶ The function and the objects it references belong to the same database.

- ▶ The user executing the `CREATE FUNCTION` statement has `REFERENCES` permission on all database objects that the function references.

You can specify the `SCHEMABINDING` option only for T-SQL functions. The following example modifies the `AveragePricebyType2` function by specifying the `SCHEMABINDING` option:

```
ALTER FUNCTION AveragePricebyType2 (@price money = 0.0)
RETURNS @table table (type varchar(12) null, avg_price money null)
with schemabinding
AS
```

```
begin
    insert @table
        SELECT type, avg(price) as avg_price
                FROM dbo.titles
                group by type
                having avg(price) > @price
    return
end
```

The following example shows what happens if you try to modify a column in the `titles` table that is referenced by the function:

```
alter table titles alter column price smallmoney null
go

Msg 5074, Level 16, State 1, Line 1
The object 'AveragePricebyType2' is dependent on column 'price'.
Msg 5074, Level 16, State 1, Line 1
The statistics 'price' is dependent on column 'price'.
Msg 4922, Level 16, State 9, Line 1
ALTER TABLE ALTER COLUMN price failed because one or more objects access this
➥column.
```

If the `RETURNS NULL ON NULL INPUT` option is specified, the function automatically returns `NULL` as a result, without invoking the function body. If this option is not specified, the default option of `CALLED ON NULL INPUT` is applied. The following example shows the difference between these two options:

```
CREATE FUNCTION striptime (@datetimeval datetime)
RETURNS datetime
AS
BEGIN
    DECLARE @dateval datetime
    SELECT @dateval = convert(char(10), isnull(@datetimeval, getdate()), 110)
    RETURN @dateval
END
GO




CREATE FUNCTION striptime2(@datetimeval datetime)
RETURNS datetime
WITH RETURNS NULL ON NULL INPUT
AS
BEGIN
    DECLARE @dateval datetime
    SELECT @dateval = convert(char(10), isnull(@datetimeval, getdate()), 110)
```

```
    RETURN @dateval

END
GO

select dbo.striptime(NULL), dbo.striptime2(NULL)

----------------------- ----------------------
2006-06-05 00:00:00.000 NULL
```

The EXECUTE AS clause allows you to specify the security context under which the user-defined function will execute. This allows you to control which user account SQL Server uses to validate permissions on any database objects that are referenced by the function. This option cannot be specified for inline table-valued functions.

Another key restriction on user-defined functions is that SQL statements within a function cannot generate side effects; that is, a user-defined function cannot generate permanent changes to any resource whose scope extends beyond the function. For example, a function cannot modify data in a table, operate on cursors that are not local to the function, create or drop database objects, issue transaction control statements, or generate a result set other than the defined function result via a SELECT statement or an extended stored procedure that would be returned to the user. The only changes that can be made by the SQL statements in a function are to the objects that are local to the function, such as local cursors or variables.

A new feature in SQL Server 2005 is that you can now include most built-in system functions within a user-defined function, even ones that are non-deterministic (that is, functions that can return different data values on each call). For example, the getdate() function is considered nondeterministic because even though it is always invoked with the same argument, it returns a different value each time it is executed. However, the following nondeterministic built-in functions are still not allowed in user-defined functions:

▶ newid()

▶ newsequentialid()

▶ rand()

▶ textptr()

User-defined functions can also call other user-defined functions, with a limit of 32 levels of nesting. Nesting of functions can help improve the modularity and reusability of function code. For example, the following is a version of the getonlydate() function that uses the striptime() function example shown earlier in this chapter:

```
CREATE FUNCTION dbo.getonlydate()
RETURNS datetime
as
```

```
BEGIN
DECLARE @date datetime
SET @date = dbo.striptime( getdate())
RETURN @date
end
```

Using SSMS to Create Functions

To create a function by using SSMS, you open the Object Explorer to the database in which you want to create the function. Then you select the Programmability node, right-click the Functions node, select New, and then choose one of the three available options:

- Inline Table-Valued Function
- Multi-statement Table-Valued Function
- Scalar-Valued Function

SSMS opens a new query window that is populated with a template for that type of function (see Figure 24.1).

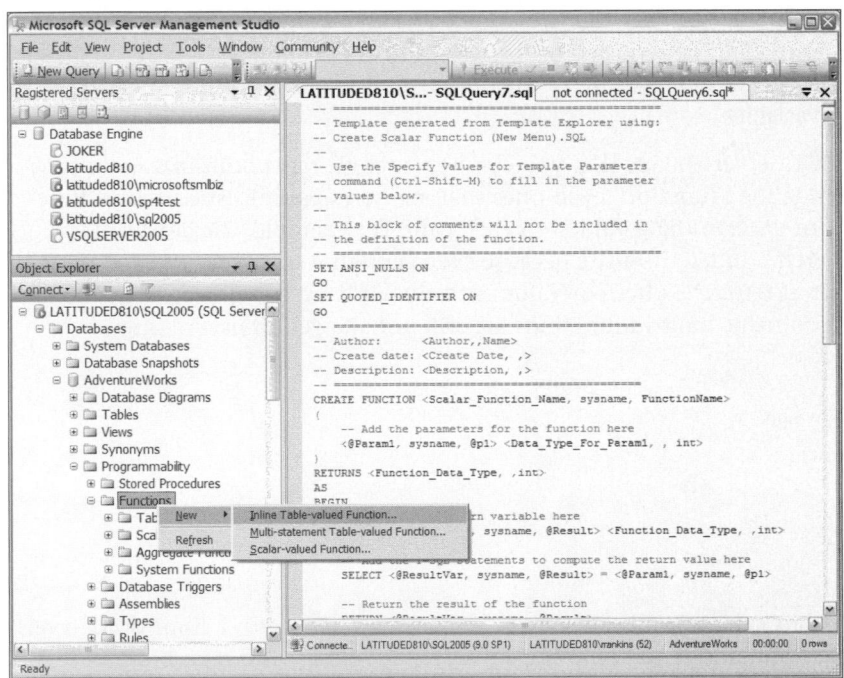

FIGURE 24.1   Creating a new function from the Object Browser in SSMS.

Listing 24.1 shows an example of the default template code for an inline table-valued function that would be opened into a new query window.

LISTING 24.1   An Example of a New Function Creation Script Generated by SSMS

```
-- =================================================
-- Template generated from Template Explorer using:
-- Create Inline Function (New Menu).SQL
--
-- Use the Specify Values for Template Parameters
-- command (Ctrl-Shift-M) to fill in the parameter
-- values below.
--
-- This block of comments will not be included in
-- the definition of the function.
-- =================================================
SET ANSI_NULLS ON
GO
SET QUOTED_IDENTIFIER ON
GO
-- =================================================
-- Author:          <Author,,Name>
-- Create date: <Create Date,,>
-- Description:     <Description,,>
-- =================================================
CREATE FUNCTION <Inline_Function_Name, sysname, FunctionName>
(
    -- Add the parameters for the function here
    <@param1, sysname, @p1> <Data_Type_For_Param1, , int>,
    <@param2, sysname, @p2> <Data_Type_For_Param2, , char>
)
RETURNS TABLE
AS
RETURN
(
    -- Add the SELECT statement with parameter references here
    SELECT 0
)
GO
```

You can modify the template code as necessary to name the function and to specify the parameters, return value, and function body. When you are finished, you execute the contents of the query window to create the function. When you have created a function successfully, you should save the source code to a file by choosing File, Save or File, Save As. This way, you can re-create the function from the file if it is accidentally dropped from the database.

24

One thing you might notice about the function templates is that they contain template parameters for things such as parameter names and function names. These template parameters are in the format *<parameter_name, data_type, value>*:

- ▶ *parameter_name* is the name of the template parameter in the script.

- ▶ *data_type* is the optional data type of the template parameter.

- ▶ *value* is the default value to be used to replace every occurrence of the template parameter in the script.

You can automatically substitute values for template parameters by selecting Query, Specify Values for Template Parameters or by pressing Ctrl+Shift+M. The Specify Values for Template Parameters dialog box, shown in Figure 24.2, appears.

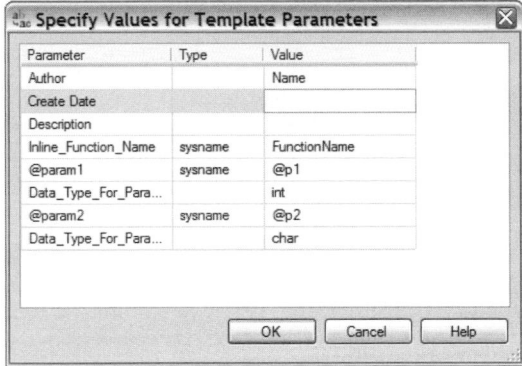

FIGURE 24.2   Using the Specify Values for Template Parameters dialog box when functions in SSMS.

You enter the values for the template parameters in the Value column and then click OK. SSMS then substitutes any values you specified wherever the template parameter is defined within the template.

An alternative way to create a function from a template is to use the Template Explorer in SSMS. You can open the Template Explorer by selecting View, Template Explorer in SSMS or by pressing Ctrl+Alt+T. The Template Explorer window appears in SSMS, as shown in Figure 24.3.

You double-click the template for the type of function you want to create or right-click the desired template and then select Open. SSMS opens a new query window that is populated with the template code.

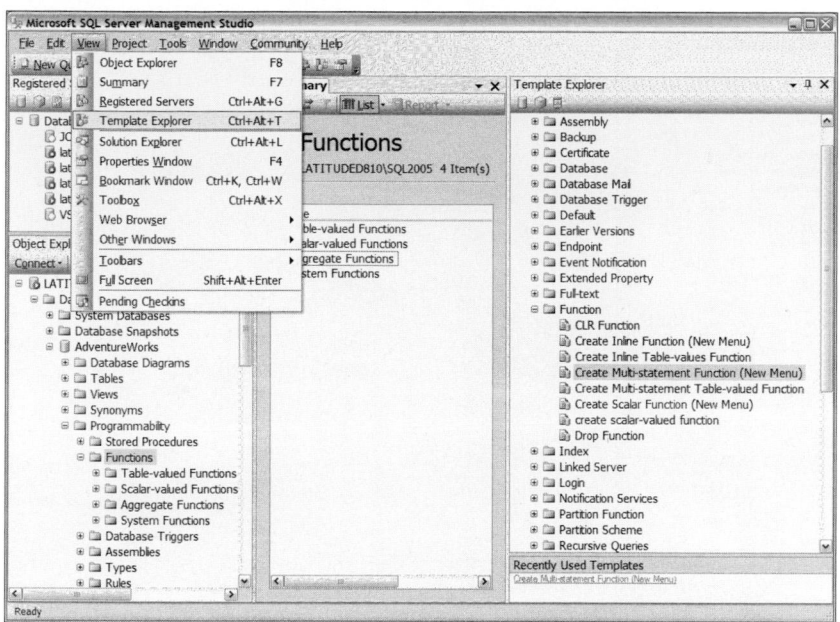

FIGURE 24.3   Using the Template Explorer to create functions in SSMS.

NOTE

It is also possible to edit the provided function templates available in the Template Explorer by right-clicking them and selecting Edit option. You can then customize the templates to include code fragments, comments, or structure that is more to your preferences and save the changes to the template file. However, it is generally recommended that you not modify the provided templates alone and instead create your own custom templates.

Creating Custom Function Templates

To create a custom function template, you right-click the Function folder in the Template Explorer and select New. SSMS then creates an entry in the Template Explorer, and you can specify the name for the template, as shown in Figure 24.4.

To begin adding code to the template, you double-click it or right-click and select Open. A blank query window appears, and you can use it to enter the new template code. Probably the best way to get started is to copy the template code from one of the templates provided with SQL Server 2005.

FIGURE 24.4   Creating a new function template in SSMS.

Listing 24.2 shows an example of a new function template.

LISTING 24.2   An Example of Custom Function Template

```
--==========================================
-- SQL Server 2005 Unleashed Sample
--  Create scalar-valued function template
--==========================================


USE <database_name, sysname, bigpubs2005>
GO


IF OBJECT_ID (N'<schema_nm, sysname, dbo>.<func_nm, sysname, fn_myfunc>')
      IS NOT NULL
    DROP FUNCTION <schema_nm, sysname, dbo>.<func_nm, sysname, fn_myfunc>
GO


CREATE FUNCTION <schema_nm, sysname, dbo>.<func_nm, sysname, fn_myfunc>
    (<parameter1, sysname, @param1> <parameter1_datatype,, int>,
      <parameter2, sysname, @param2> <parameter2_datatype,, int>,
      <parameter3, sysname, @param3> <parameter3_datatype,, int>)
RETURNS <return_value_datatype,,int>
```

LISTING 24.2   Continued

```
WITH EXECUTE AS CALLER
AS
-- place the body of the function here
BEGIN
    DECLARE <variable1, sysname, @var1> <variable1_datatype,, int>,
            <variable2, sysname, @var2> <variable2_datatype,, int>

    select <variable1, sysname, @var1> = isnull(<parameter1, sysname, @param1> )
    <T-SQL_Body,,>

    RETURN <variable1, sysname, @var1>
END
GO
```

After you define a custom function template, you can use it as you do the built-in templates. You can double-click it or right-click and select Open, and SSMS opens a new query window with a new function creation script that is based on the custom template. If you use the default values for the template parameters, after the parameter substitution, your CREATE FUNCTION script should look like the one in Listing 24.3.

LISTING 24.3   An Example of CREATE FUNCTION Script Generated from a Custom Function Template

```
--==========================================
-- SQL Server 2005 Unleashed Sample
--   Create scalar-valued function template
--==========================================

USE bigpubs2005
GO


IF OBJECT_ID (N'dbo.fn_myfunction') IS NOT NULL
    DROP FUNCTION dbo.fn_myfunction
GO

CREATE FUNCTION dbo.fn_myfunction
    (@param1 int,
     @param2 int,
     @param3 int)
RETURNS int
WITH EXECUTE AS CALLER
AS
-- place the body of the function here
BEGIN
```

LISTING 24.3   Continued

```
    DECLARE @var1 int,
            @var2 int

    select @var1 = isnull(@param1 )


    RETURN @var1
END
GO
```

Viewing and Modifying User-Defined Functions

Besides using T-SQL commands to create functions, you can also use them to view and modify functions. You can get information by using the provided system procedures and queries against the INFORMATION_SCHEMA.routines view. The following sections describe these methods.

Using T-SQL to View Functions

To view the source code for a user-defined function, you can use the sp_helptext procedure:

```
use bigpubs2005
go
exec sp_helptext getonlydate
go

Text
---------------------------------------------------------------------------

create function getonlydate()
returns datetime
as
begin
declare @date datetime
set @date = convert(datetime, convert(char(10), getdate(), 110))
return @date
end
```

> **NOTE**
>
> To display the source code for the functions clearly, configure the SSMS query window to display results as text rather than in the grid by pressing Ctrl+T.

In addition to sp_helptext, you can write queries against the INFORMATION_SCHEMA. routines view to display the source code for a function:

```
SELECT routine_definition
from INFORMATION_SCHEMA.routines
where routine_name = 'getonlydate'
and specific_schema = 'dbo'
and specific_catalog = 'bigpubs2005'


routine_definition
-----------------------------------------------------------------------------
create function getonlydate()
returns datetime
as
begin
declare @date datetime
set @date = convert(datetime, convert(char(10), getdate(), 110))
return @date

end
```

If you want to display information about the input parameters for a function, you use the INFORMATION_SCHEMA.parameters view. For scalar functions, the view also displays information for the return parameter, which has an ordinal position of 0 and no parameter name:

```
select substring(parameter_name,1,20) as parameter_name,
       substring(data_type, 1, 20) as data_type,
       Parameter_mode,
       ordinal_position
from INFORMATION_SCHEMA.parameters
where specific_name = 'striptime'
and specific_schema = 'dbo'
and specific_catalog = 'bigpubs2005'
order by ordinal_position
go
```

parameter_name	data_type	Parameter_mode	ordinal_position
	datetime	OUT	0
@datetimeval	datetime	IN	1

If you want to display information about the result columns returned by a table-valued function, you use the INFORMATION_SCHEMA.routine_columns view:

```
select substring(column_name, 1, 20) as column_name,
       substring (data_type, 1, 12)
            + case when character_maximum_length is not null
               then '(' + cast(character_maximum_length as varchar(4)) + ')'
                    else ''
                    end
              as datatype,
       numeric_precision as 'precision',
       numeric_scale as scale,
       ordinal_position
from INFORMATION_SCHEMA.routine_columns
where table_name = 'AveragePricebyType'
order by ordinal_position
go
```

column_name	datatype	precision	scale	ordinal_position
type	char(12)	NULL	NULL	1
avg_price	money	19	4	2

In addition, SQL Server provides the OBJECTPROPERTY function, which you can use to get information about functions. One of the things you can find out is whether a function is a multistatement table function, an inline function, or a scalar function. The OBJECTPROPERTY function accepts an object ID and an object property parameter, and it returns the value 1 if the property is true, 0 if it is false, or NULL if an invalid function ID or property parameter is specified. The following property parameters are appropriate for functions:

- ▶ **IsTableFunction**—Returns 1 if the function is a table-valued function but not an inline function.

- ▶ **IsInlineFunction**—Returns 1 if the function is an inline table-valued function.

- ▶ **IsScalarFunction**—Returns 1 if the function is a scalar function.

- ▶ **IsSchemaBound**—Returns 1 if the function was created with the SCHEMABINDING option.

- ▶ **IsDeterministic**—Returns 1 if the function is deterministic (that is, it always returns the same result each time it is called with a specific set of input values).

The following example demonstrates a possible use of the OBJECTPROPERTY function with the INFORMATION_SCHEMA.routines view:

```
select convert(varchar(10), specific_Schema) as 'schema',
  convert(varchar(20), specific_name) as 'function',
```

```
    case objectproperty(object_id(specific_name), 'IsScalarFunction')
        when 1 then 'Yes' else 'No' end as IsScalar,
    case objectproperty(object_id(specific_name), 'IsTableFunction')
        when 1 then 'Yes' else 'No' end as IsTable,
    case objectproperty(object_id(specific_name), 'IsInlineFunction')
        when 1 then 'Yes' else 'No' end as IsInline,
    case objectproperty(object_id(specific_name), 'IsSchemaBound')
        when 1 then 'Yes' else 'No' end as IsSchemaBnd,
    case objectproperty(object_id(specific_name), 'IsDeterministic')
        when 1 then 'Yes' else 'No' end as IsDtrmnstc
from information_Schema.routines
where routine_type = 'FUNCTION'
order by specific_name
go
```

schema	function	IsScalar	IsTable	IsInline	IsSchemaBnd	IsDtrmnstc
dbo	AverageBookPrice	Yes	No	No	No	No
dbo	AverageBookPrice2	Yes	No	No	No	No
dbo	AveragePricebyType	No	Yes	Yes	No	No
dbo	AveragePricebyType2	No	Yes	No	Yes	Yes
dbo	getdateonly	Yes	No	No	No	No
dbo	getonlydate	Yes	No	No	No	No
dbo	striptime	Yes	No	No	No	No
dbo	striptime2	Yes	No	No	No	No

Using T-SQL to Modify Functions

You can use the ALTER FUNCTION command to change a function's definition without having to drop and re-create it. The syntax for the ALTER FUNCTION command is identical to the syntax for CREATE FUNCTION, except that you replace the CREATE keyword with the ALTER keyword. The following example modifies the AveragePricebyType2 function:

```
ALTER FUNCTION AveragePricebyType2 (@price money = 0.0)
RETURNS @table table (type varchar(12) null, avg_price money null)
with schemabinding
AS
begin
    insert @table
        SELECT type, avg(price) as avg_price
            FROM dbo.titles
            group by type
            having avg(price) > @price
        order by avg(price) desc
    return
end
```

Using the `ALTER FUNCTION` command has a couple advantages over dropping and re-creating a function to modify it. The main advantage, as mentioned earlier, is that you don't have to drop the function first to make the change. The second advantage is that, because you don't have to drop the function, you don't have to worry about reassigning permissions to the function. To determine whether a function has been altered since it was created, you can query the `LAST_ALTERED` column in the `INFORMATION_SCHEMA.` routines view for that function.

One limitation of the `ALTER FUNCTION` command is that you cannot use this command to change a table-valued function to a scalar function or to change an inline function to a multistatement function. You have to drop and re-create the function.

Using SSMS to View and Modify Functions

To view or edit a function within SSMS, open the Object Explorer to the database in which you want to create the function. Then you select the `Programmability` node, right-click the `Functions` node, and then select either the Table-Valued Functions folder or the Scalar-Valued Functions folder. SSMS then displays a list of the functions of that type defined in that database within the Object Explorer as well as in the Summary window.

NOTE

If the function you want to view or edit is not showing in the list, it was probably created after the list of functions in the Object Explorer was populated. You might need to refresh the function list in Object Explorer. To do this, you right-click the `Functions` folder and choose Refresh.

When you right-click a function name in either the Object Explorer or the Summary window, you are presented with a number of options for viewing or modifying the function, as shown in Figure 24.5.

You can view or edit the function properties, view the function dependencies, delete the function, rename it, modify it, or script the function definition. If you choose to edit the function by clicking Modify, SSMS opens a new query window with the source code of the function extracted from the database as an `ALTER FUNCTION` command. You can edit the function as needed and execute the code in the query window to modify the function.

There are also options for scripting a function as a `CREATE`, `ALTER`, `DROP`, or `SELECT` command to either a new query window, a file, or the Clipboard, as shown in Figure 24.6.

You can also view the function properties by selecting the Properties option from the context menu. The Properties dialog appears, as shown in Figure 24.7. Unfortunately, except for the function permissions and extended properties, the properties shown are read-only.

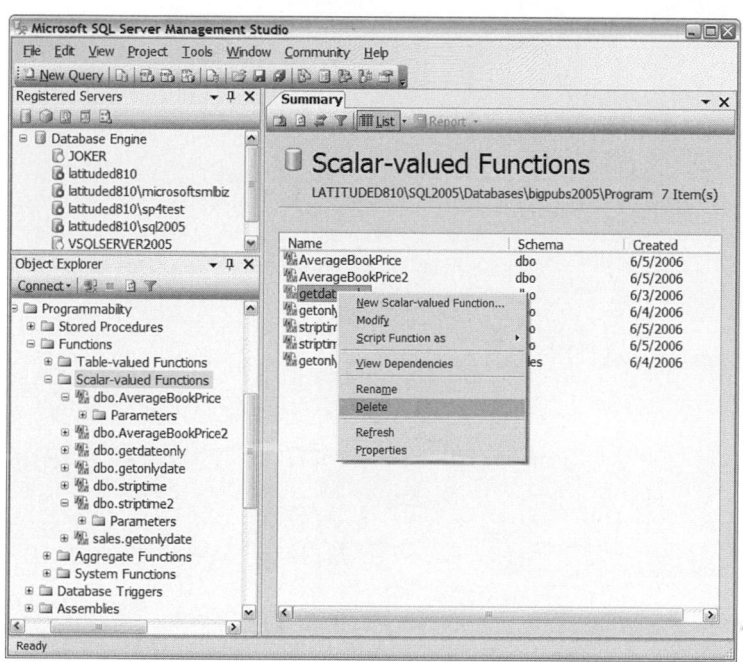

FIGURE 24.5   The Options menu for viewing and editing functions in SSMS.

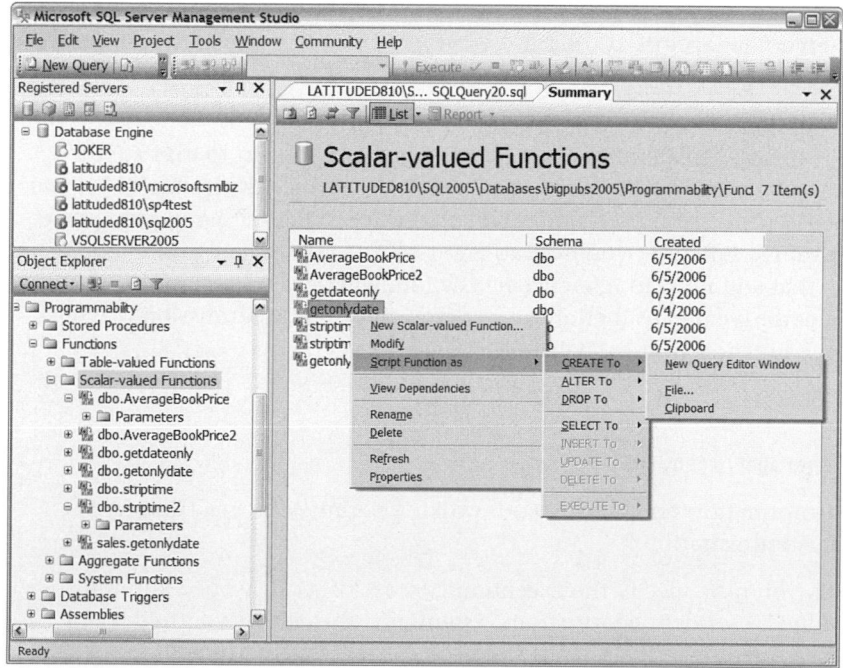

FIGURE 24.6   Options for scripting functions in SSMS.

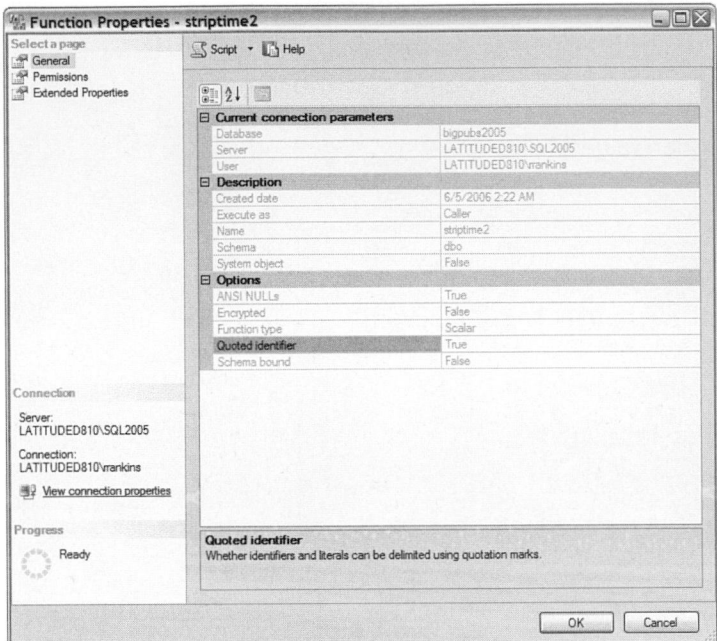

FIGURE 24.7   The Function Properties dialog in SSMS.

For more information on the features and options for SSMS and for scripting objects, see Chapter 3, "SQL Server Management Studio."

Managing User-Defined Function Permissions

When a function is initially created, the only user who has permission to execute the function is the user who created it. To allow other users to execute a scalar function, you need to grant EXECUTE permission on the function to the appropriate user(s), group(s), or role(s). For a table-valued function, you need to grant SELECT permission to the user(s), group(s), or role(s) that will need to reference it. The following example grants EXECUTE permission on the getonlydate() function to everyone and SELECT permission on the AveragePriceByType function to the database user fred:

```
GRANT EXECUTE on dbo.getonlydate to public
```

```
GRANT SELECT on AveragePricebyType to fred
```

For more detailed information on granting and revoking permissions, see Chapter 10, "Security and User Administration."

In SQL Server 2005, you now specify the execution context of scalar-valued and multi-statement, table-valued, user-defined functions. Essentially, this allows you to control which user account is used to validate permissions on objects that are referenced by the function, regardless of what user is actually executing the function. This provides additional flexibility and control in managing permissions for user-defined functions and the objects they reference. Only EXECUTE or SELECT permissions need to be granted to users on the function itself; you do not have to grant them explicit permissions on the referenced objects. Only the user account which is defined as the execution context for the function by the EXECUTE AS clause must have the necessary permissions on the objects that the function accesses.

For example, in the following SQL script, the AverageBookPrice2 function is being modified to run within the context of the dbo user. Any user who invokes this function essentially inherits the permissions of the dbo user on any objects accessed within the scope of the function temporarily for the execution of the function:

```
ALTER FUNCTION [dbo].[AverageBookPrice2](@booktype varchar(12) = '%')
RETURNS money
WITH EXECUTE AS 'dbo'
AS
BEGIN
    RETURN ( SELECT avg(price)
             FROM titles
             WHERE type like @booktype)
END
GO
```

Systemwide Table-Valued Functions

In addition to the built-in scalar functions, SQL Server 2005 also provides a set of systemwide table-valued functions that can be invoked from any database. Usually, when you invoke a user-defined, table-valued function that is not local to the current database context, you have to fully qualify the function name with the database name. This is not required for systemwide table-valued functions. Special syntax is used to invoke systemwide table-valued funcions. You must precede the function name with two colons (::), as shown in the following example:

```
SELECT * FROM ::fn_servershareddrives()
go


DriveName
---------
Q
S
```

SQL Server 2005 provides a number of documented and undocumented table-valued functions. The following are the documented functions:

▶ **fn_get_sql(*sqlhandle*)**—Returns the text of the SQL statement for the specified SQL handle.

▶ **fn_helpcollations()**—Lists all collations supported by SQL Server 2005.

- **fn_listextendedproperty(*propertyname,level0objecttype, level0objectname, level1objecttype, level1objectname, level2objecttype, level2objectname*)**— Lists extended property values for a database or objects stored in a database.

- **fn_serversharedrives()**—Returns the names of shared drives used by a clustered server.

- **fn_trace_geteventinfo(*traceID*)**—Returns information about the events being traced for the trace specified.

- **fn_trace_getfilterinfo(*traceID*)**—Returns information about the filters applied to the trace specified.

- **fn_trace_getinfo(*traceID*)**—Returns information about the specified trace.

- **fn_trace_gettable(*filename*, *numfiles*)**—Returns trace file information from the specified file, in table format.

- **fn_virtualfilestats(*dbid*, *fileid*)**—Returns file I/O information for the file of the specified database.

- **fn_virtualservernodes()**—Returns a list of nodes on which a virtual server can run. This information is useful in failover clustering environments.

The trace-related functions are discussed in more detail in Chapter 5, "SQL Server Profiler."

The majority of the undocumented systemwide table-valued functions are used in SQL Server replication and are not intended for end-user execution.

Rewriting Stored Procedures as Functions

In releases of SQL Server prior to SQL Server 2000, if you wanted to do custom processing within SQL code, your only real option was to create stored procedures to do things that often would have worked much better as functions. For example, you couldn't use the result set of a stored procedure in a WHERE clause or to return a value as a column in a select list. Using a stored procedure to perform calculations on columns in a result set often required using a cursor to step through each row in a result set and pass the column values fetched, one at a time, to the stored procedure as parameters. This procedure then typically returned the computed value via an output parameter, which had to be mapped to another local variable. Another alternative was to retrieve the initial result set into a temporary table and then perform additional queries or updates against the temporary table to modify the column values, which often required multiple passes. Neither of these methods was an efficient means of processing the data, but prior to SQL Server 2000, few alternatives existed. If you needed to join against the result set of a stored procedure, you had to insert the result set into a temporary table first and then join against the temporary table, as shown in the following code fragment:

```
...
insert #results exec result_proc
select * from other_Table
   join #results on other_table.pkey = #results.keyfield
...
```

Now that SQL Server supports user-defined functions, you might want to consider rewriting some of your old stored procedures as functions to take advantage of the capabilities of functions and improve the efficiency of your SQL code. You mainly want to do this in situations in which you would like to be able to invoke a stored procedure directly from within a query. If the stored procedure returns a result set, it is a candidate for being written as a table-valued function. If it returns a scalar value, usually via an output parameter, it is a candidate for being written as a scalar function. However, the following criteria also are indications that a procedure a good candidate for being rewritten as a function:

▶ The procedure logic is expressible in a single SELECT statement; however, it is written as a stored procedure, rather than a view, because of the need for it to be parameter driven.

▶ The stored procedure does not perform update operations on tables, except against table variables.

▶ There are no dynamic SQL statements executed via the EXECUTE statement or sp_executesql.

▶ The stored procedure returns no more than a single result set.

▶ If the stored procedure returns a result set, its primary purpose is to build an intermediate result that is typically loaded into a temporary table, which is then queried in a SELECT statement.

The result_proc stored procedure, used earlier in this section, could possibly be rewritten as a table-valued function called fn_result(). The preceding code fragment could then be rewritten as follows:

```
SELECT *
   FROM fn_results() fn
   join other_table o.pkey = fn.keyfield
```

Creating and Using CLR Functions

Prior to SQL Server 2005, the only way to extend the functionality of SQL Server beyond what was available using the T-SQL language was to create extended stored procedures or Component Object Model (COM) components. The main problems with these types of extensions was that if not written very carefully, they could have an adverse impact on the reliability and security of SQL Server. In addition, neither of these options allowed you to create custom user-defined functions that could be written in any programming language other than T-SQL, which has a limited command set for operations such as complex string comparison and manipulation and complex numeric computations.

Now, in SQL Server 2005, you can write custom user-defined functions in any Microsoft .NET Framework programming language, such as Microsoft Visual Basic .NET or Microsoft Visual C#. SQL Server supports both scalar and table-valued CLR functions, as well as CLR user-defined aggregate functions. These extensions written in the CLR are much more secure and reliable than extended stored procedures or COM components.

For information on the methods and tools to actually create and compile CLR user-defined functions, see Chapter 36, "SQL Server and the .NET Framework." This chapter focuses only on how to install and use CLR functions in a SQL Server database.

> **NOTE**
>
> The CLR function examples presented in the following sections are provided as illustrations only. The sample code will not execute successfully because the underlying CLR assemblies have not been provided.

Adding CLR Functions to a Database

If you've already created and compiled a CLR function, the next thing to do is to install that CLR function in the database. The first step in this process is to copy the .NET assembly to a location that SQL Server can access, and then you need to load it into SQL Server by creating an assembly. The syntax for the CREATE ASSEMBLY command is as follows:

```
CREATE ASSEMBLY AssemblyName [AUTHORIZATION LoginName]
FROM  StringPathToAssemblyDll
[WITH PERMISSION_SET (SAFE ¦ EXTERNAL_ACCESS ¦ UNSAFE) ]
```

AssemblyName is the name of the assembly, and StringPathToAssemblyDll is the path to the DLL. The path can be a local path, but often the path is a network share.

The WITH clause is optional, and it defaults to SAFE. Marking an assembly with the SAFE permission set indicates that no external resources (for example, the Registry, Web services, file I/O) are going to be accessed.

The CREATE ASSEMBLY command fails if it is marked as SAFE and assemblies like System.IO are referenced. Also, if anything causes a permission demand for executing similar operations, an exception is thrown at runtime.

Marking an assembly with the EXTERNAL_ACCESS permission set tells SQL Server that it will be using resources such as networking, files, and so forth. Assemblies such as System.Web.Services (but not System.Web) can be referenced with this set. To create an EXTERNAL_ACCESS assembly, the creator must have EXTERN ACCESS_permission.

Marking an assembly with the UNSAFE permission set tells SQL Server that not only might external resources be used, but unmanaged code may be invoked from managed code. An UNSAFE assembly can potentially undermine the security of either SQL Server or the CLR. Only members of the sysadmin role can create UNSAFE assemblies.

After the assembly is created, the next step is to associate the method within the assembly with a user-defined function. You do this with the CREATE FUNCTION command, using the following syntax:

```
CREATE FUNCTION [ schema_name. ] function_name
    ( [ { @parameter_name [AS] [ schema_name.]scalar_datatype [ = default ] }
    [ ,...n ] ] )
RETURNS { return_data_type ¦ TABLE ( { column_name data_type } [ ,...n ] ) }
[ WITH { [ , RETURNS NULL ON NULL INPUT ¦ CALLED ON NULL INPUT ]
        [ , EXECUTE_AS_Clause ] } ]
[ AS ] EXTERNAL NAME assembly_name.class_name.method_name
```

When the CLR function has been created successfully, you can use it just as you would a T-SQL function. The following is an example of manually deploying a table-valued CLR function:

```
CREATE ASSEMBLY fn_EventLog
FROM 'F:\assemblies\fn_EventLog\fn_eventlog.dll'
WITH PERMISSION_SET = SAFE
GO
CREATE FUNCTION ShowEventLog(@logname nvarchar(100))
RETURNS TABLE (logTime datetime,
                Message nvarchar(4000),
                Category nvarchar(4000),
                InstanceId bigint)
AS
EXTERNAL NAME fn_EventLog.TabularEventLog.InitMethod
GO
SELECT * FROM dbo.ReadEventLog(N'System') as T
go
```

NOTE

The preceding examples show the steps involved in manually registering an assembly and creating a CLR function. If you use Visual Studio's new Deploy feature, the CREATE/ALTER ASSEMBLY and the CREATE FUNCTION commands are issued automatically by Visual Studio. For more details on using Visual Studio to create and deploy user-defined CLR functions, see Chapter 36.

24

Deciding Between Using T-SQL or CLR Functions

One question that often comes up about SQL Server 2005 is whether it's better to develop functions in T-SQL or in the CLR. It really depends on the situation and what the function will be doing.

The general rule of thumb is that if the function will be performing data access or large set-oriented operations with little or no complex procedural logic, it's better to create it in T-SQL to get the best performance. This is because T-SQL works more closely with the data and doesn't require multiple transitions between the CLR and the SQL Server engine.

On the other hand, most benchmarks have shown that the CLR performs better than T-SQL for functions that require a high level of computation or text manipulation. The CLR offers much richer APIs that provide capabilities not available in T-SQL for operations such as text manipulation, cryptography, I/O operations, data formatting, and invoking of Web services. For example, T-SQL provides only rudimentary string manipulation capabilities, whereas the .NET Framework supports capabilities such as regular expressions, which are much more powerful for pattern matching and replacement than the T-SQL replace() function.

Another good candidate for CLR functions is user-defined aggregate functions. User-defined aggregate functions cannot be defined in T-SQL. To compute an aggregate value over a group in T-SQL, you would have to retrieve the values as a result set and then enumerate over the result set, using a cursor to generate the aggregate. This results in slow and complicated code. With CLR user-defined aggregate functions, you only need to implement the code for the accumulation logic. The query processor manages the iteration, and any user-defined aggregates referenced by the query are automatically accumulated and returned with the query result set. This approach can be orders of magnitude faster than using cursors, and it is comparable to using SQL Server built-in aggregate functions. For example, the following shows how you might use a user-defined aggregate function that aggregates all the authors for a specific BookId into a comma-separated list:

```
use bigpubs2005
go
SELECT t.Title_ID, count(*), dbo.CommaList(a.au_lname) as AuthorNames
   FROM Authors a
   JOIN titleauthor ta on a.au_id = ta.au_id
   JOIN Titles t on ta.title_id = t.title_id
GROUP BY t.title_id
having count(*) > 2
go


Title_ID AuthorNames
-------- -----------------------------------------------------------------
TC7777    O'Leary, Gringlesby, Yokomoto
```

> **NOTE**
>
> Please note that the preceding example will not execute successfully as we have not created the CommaList() CLR function. It is provided merely as an example of how such a function could be used if it was created.

In a nutshell, performance tests have generally shown that T-SQL generally performs better for standard CRUD (create, read, update, delete) operations, whereas CLR code performs better for complex math, string manipulation, and other tasks that go beyond data access.

Summary

User-defined functions are a very useful feature in SQL Server 2005. User-defined functions allow you to create reusable routines that can help make your SQL code more straightforward and efficient.

In this chapter, you have seen how to create and modify scalar functions and inline and multistatement table-valued functions and how to invoke and use them in queries. Scalar functions can be used to perform more complex operations than those provided by the built-in scalar functions. Table-valued functions provide a way to create what are essentially parameterized views, and you can include them inline in your queries, just as you would in a table or view.

With the introduction of CLR-based functions, SQL Server 2005 greatly increases the power and capabilities of user-defined functions, and CLR functions can also provide performance improvements over T-SQL functions that need to perform complex computations or string manipulations.

CHAPTER 25

Creating and Managing Triggers

IN THIS CHAPTER

▶ What's New in Creating and Managing Triggers

▶ Using DML Triggers

▶ Using DDL Triggers

▶ Using CLR Triggers

▶ Using Nested Triggers

▶ Using Recursive Triggers

A *trigger* is a special type of stored procedure that is executed automatically based on the occurrence of a database event. In previous versions of SQL Server, the database events that fired triggers were based on data manipulations, such as insertions, updates, or deletions. Triggers in SQL Server 2005 can also fire on events that are related to the definition of database objects. The two triggering events are referred to as Data Manipulation Language (DML) and Data Definition Language (DDL) events.

Most of the benefits derived from triggers are based on their event-driven nature. Once created, triggers automatically fire (without user intervention) based on an event in the database. This differs from other database code, which must be called explicitly in order to execute.

Say, for example, that you would like to keep track of historical changes to the data in several key tables in a database. Whenever a change is made to the data in the tables, you would like to put a copy of the data in a historical table before the change is made. You could accomplish this via the application code that is making the change to the data. The application code could copy the data to the history table before the change occurs and then execute the actual change. You could also manage this in other ways, such as by using stored procedures that are called by the application and subsequently insert records into the history tables.

These solutions work, but a trigger-based solution has some distinct advantages over them. With a trigger-based solution, a trigger can act on any modifications to the key tables. In the case of the history table example, triggers would automatically insert records into the history table whenever a modification was made to the data. This would all happen within the scope of the original transaction and would write history records for any changes made to these tables, including ad hoc changes that may have been made directly to the tables outside the application.

This is just one example of the benefits and uses of triggers. This chapter discusses the different types of triggers and further benefits they can provide.

What's New in Creating and Managing Triggers

Microsoft has expanded the capabilities of triggers in SQL Server 2005. The bulk of this expansion is delivered in two new types of triggers:

- **DDL triggers**—DDL triggers fire when DDL statements are executed. These triggers are administrative in nature and are great for auditing and regulating database operations.

- **CLR triggers**—Triggers can now be written based on the common language runtime (CLR). The CLR integration in SQL Server 2005 allows triggers to be written using any .NET language (such as C# or Visual Basic .NET) that the CLR supports.

Using DML Triggers

DML triggers are invoked when a DML event occurs in the database. DML events manipulate or modify the data in a table or view. These events include insertions, updates, and deletions.

DML triggers are powerful objects for maintaining database integrity and consistency. They are able to evaluate data before it has been committed to the database. During this evaluation period, these triggers can perform a myriad of actions, including the following:

- Compare before and after versions of data.
- Roll back invalid modifications.
- Read from other tables, including those in other databases.
- Modify other tables, including those in other databases.
- Execute local and remote stored procedures.

Based on the nature of these actions, triggers were originally used in many cases to enforce referential integrity. Triggers were used when foreign key columns in one table had to be validated against primary keys or unique index values in another table. The triggers could fire when data was modified, and validations could be performed to ensure that referential integrity was maintained.

The advent of declarative referential integrity (DRI) diminished the need for referential integrity triggers. DRI is implemented with database objects such as foreign key constraints that perform the referential integrity validation internally. Because of this, triggers generally handle more complex integrity concepts and enforce restrictions that cannot be handled through data types, constraints, defaults, or rules. The following are some examples of trigger uses:

▶ **Maintenance of duplicate and derived data**—A denormalized database generally introduces data duplications (that is, redundancy). Instead of exposing this redundancy to end users and programmers, you can keep the data in sync by using triggers. If the derived data is allowed to be out of sync, you might want to consider handling refreshes through batch processing or some other method instead.

▶ **Complex column constraints**—If a column constraint depends on other rows within the same table or rows in other tables, using a trigger is the best method for that column constraint.

▶ **Complex defaults**—You can use a trigger to generate default values based on data in other columns, rows, or tables.

▶ **Inter-database referential integrity**—When related tables are found in two different databases, you can use triggers to ensure referential integrity across the databases.

You can use stored procedures for all these tasks, but the advantage of using triggers is that they can fire on all data modifications. Stored procedure code or SQL in application code is executed only when it makes the data modifications. With triggers, all data modifications are subject to the trigger code, except for bulk copy and a few other non-logged actions. Even if a user utilizes an ad hoc tool, such as Query Analyzer, the integrity rules cannot be bypassed after the trigger is in place.

NOTE

Triggers and stored procedures are not mutually exclusive. You can have both triggers and stored procedures that perform modifications and validation on that same table. If desired, you can perform some tasks via triggers and other tasks via stored procedures.

Creating DML Triggers

You can create and manage triggers in SQL Server Management Studio (SSMS) or directly via Transact-SQL (T-SQL) statements. The Object Explorer in SSMS provides a simple means of creating triggers that you can use to generate the underlying T-SQL code. You expand the Object Explorer tree to the user table level and then right-click the Triggers node. When you select the New Trigger option, as shown in Figure 25.1, the trigger template shown in the right pane of Figure 25.1 appears.

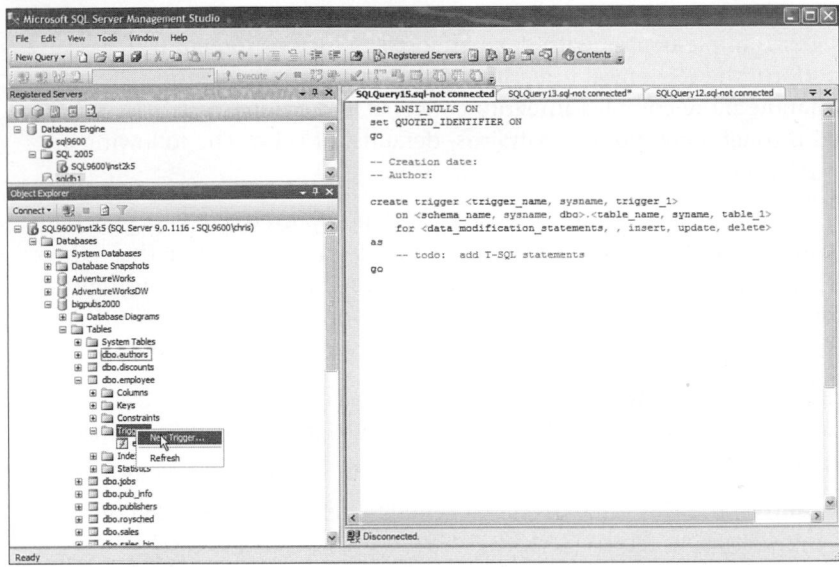

FIGURE 25.1   Using SSMS to create triggers.

You can populate the trigger template manually or by selecting the Query menu option then Specify Values for Template Parameters. When you select Specify Values for Template Parameters, a screen appears, allowing you to fill in the basic values for the trigger, including the table that the trigger will be on and the events to respond to.

You can launch the New Trigger template and other templates related to triggers via the Template Explorer, which you open by selecting View, Template Explorer in SSMS. Figure 25.2 shows a partial list of the available templates, including those related to triggers.

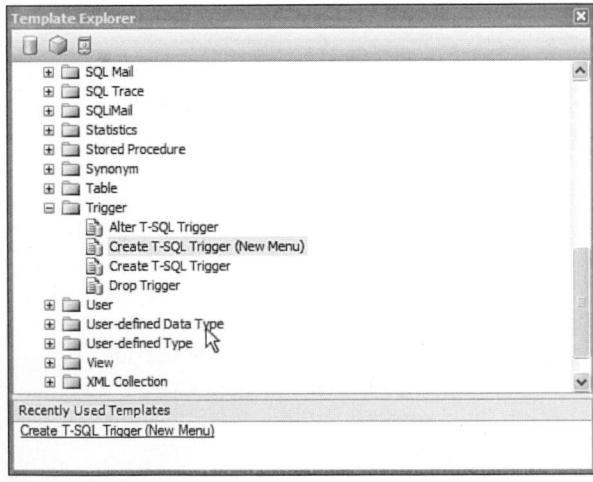

FIGURE 25.2   The Template Explorer.

All the trigger templates provide a basic framework for you to create a trigger, but the core logic is up to you. Existing triggers or sample triggers are often good alternatives to the templates because they offer more of the core logic. You can right-click a trigger in the Object Explorer and select the Script Trigger As option. This option contains several different methods to script the trigger. After you script a trigger, you can modify it as necessary to meet the needs your needs.

TIP

Using the new sys.triggers catalog view is a good way to list all the triggers in a database. To use it, you simply open a new Query Editor window in SSMS and select all the rows from the view as shown in the following example:

```
SELECT * FROM sys.triggers
```

After you have a basic trigger template, you can code the trigger, with limited restrictions. Almost every T-SQL statement you would use in a SQL batch or stored procedure is also available for use in the trigger code. However, you cannot use the following commands in a DML trigger:

▶ ALTER DATABASE

▶ CREATE DATABASE

▶ DISK RESIZE

▶ DROP DATABASE

▶ LOAD DATABASE and LOAD LOG

▶ RECONFIGURE

▶ RESTORE DATABASE and RESTORE LOG

The following sections describe the different types of DML triggers that can be coded and some of their common uses.

Using AFTER Triggers

An AFTER trigger is the original mechanism that SQL Server created to provide an automated response to data modifications. Prior to the release of SQL Server 2000, the AFTER trigger was the only type of trigger, and the word AFTER was rarely used in its name. Any trigger written for prior versions of SQL Server or documentation referring to these triggers is for AFTER triggers.

SQL Server 2000 introduced a new type of trigger called an INSTEAD OF trigger. This trigger is discussed later in this chapter (see the later section titled, "INSTEAD OF Triggers"). The introduction of that new trigger and the inclusion of the word AFTER in the name of the old trigger has helped accentuate the behavior of the AFTER trigger: The AFTER trigger executes *after* a data modification has taken place.

> **NOTE**
>
> Throughout the rest of this chapter, if the trigger type is not specified, you can assume that it is an AFTER trigger.

The fact that an AFTER trigger fires *after* a data modification might seem like a simple concept, but it is critical to understanding how it works. The AFTER trigger fires after the data modification statement completes but before the statement's work is committed to the databases. The statement's work is captured in the transaction log but not committed to the database until the trigger has executed and performed its actions.

The trigger has the ability to roll back its actions as well as the actions of the modification statement that invoked it. This is possible because an implicit transaction exists that includes both the modification statement and the trigger it fires. If the trigger does not issue a rollback, then an implicit COMMIT of all the work is issued when the trigger completes.

The basic syntax for creating an AFTER trigger is as follows:

```
CREATE TRIGGER trigger_name
ON table_name
AFTER { INSERT ¦ UPDATE ¦ DELETE }
AS
SQL statements
```

The AFTER trigger is the default type of DML trigger, so the AFTER keyword is optional.

Listing 25.1 shows the code you use to create a trigger in the BigPubs2005 database. (Instructions for creating the BigPubs2005 database are found on this book's website at www.samspublishing.com) This new trigger prints a message, stating the number of rows updated by an UPDATE statement. You then execute a couple UPDATE statements to see whether the trigger works.

LISTING 25.1   An Example of a Simple AFTER Trigger

```
CREATE TRIGGER tr_au_upd ON authors
AFTER UPDATE
AS
PRINT 'TRIGGER OUTPUT: ' +CONVERT(VARCHAR(5), @@ROWCOUNT)
+ ' rows were updated.'
GO

UPDATE authors
SET au_fname = au_fname
WHERE state = 'UT'
GO
--TRIGGER OUTPUT: 1 rows were updated.
```

LISTING 25.1   Continued

```
UPDATE authors
SET au_fname = au_fname
WHERE state = 'CA'
GO
--TRIGGER OUTPUT: 37 rows were updated.
```

Even though you do not actually change the contents of the au_fname column (because you set it to itself), the trigger fires anyway. This is not a typical use of a trigger, but it gives you some insight into how and when a trigger fires. The fact that the trigger fires, regardless of what is updated, causes many developers to test the @@rowcount value at the beginning of the trigger code. If @@rowcount is equal to zero, then the trigger can return without executing the remainder of the trigger code. This is a good tactic for optimizing the performance of triggers.

> **NOTE**
>
> Triggers are meant to guarantee the integrity of data. Although you can return result sets and messages in triggers, doing so is not recommended. The programmers who write applications that perform modifications on a table are probably not prepared to get result sets or messages when they submit data modification statements.
>
> The exception is returning an error with the RAISERROR command. If a trigger performs ROLLBACK TRAN, it should also execute RAISERROR to communicate the failure to the application.

Executing AFTER Triggers

You know that the AFTER trigger fires when a data modification (such as an insertion, an update, or a deletion) takes place. What about the trigger's execution in relationship to other events, including the execution of constraints? The following events take place before an AFTER trigger executes:

▶ **Constraint processing**—This includes CHECK constraints, UNIQUE constraints, and PRIMARY KEY constraints.

▶ **Declarative referential actions**—These are the actions defined by FOREIGN KEY constraints that ensure the proper relationships between tables.

▶ **Triggering action**—This is the data modification that caused the trigger to fire. The action occurs before the trigger fires, but the results are not committed to the database until the trigger completes.

You need to consider this execution carefully when you design triggers. For example, if you have a constraint and a trigger defined on the same column, any violations to the constraint abort the statement, and the trigger execution does not occur.

25

Specifying Trigger Firing Order

You can create more than one trigger on a table for each data modification action. In other words, you can have multiple triggers responding to an INSERT, an UPDATE, or a DELETE command. This can be useful in certain situations, but it can generate confusion because you might not know the order in which the triggers fire for the particular action.

Some of the confusion has been alleviated by the fact that SQL Server 2005 allows you to specify the first and last trigger that fire for a particular action. If you have four triggers responding to updates on a given table, you can set the order for two of the triggers (first and last), but the order of the remaining two triggers remains unknown.

The sp_settriggerorder procedure is the tool you use to set the trigger order. This procedure takes the trigger name, order value (FIRST, LAST, or NONE), and action (INSERT, UPDATE, or DELETE) as parameters. For example, you could use the following to set the firing order on the trigger used in this chapter's simple example:

```
sp_settriggerorder tr_au_upd, FIRST, 'UPDATE'
```

The execution of this command sets the tr_au_upd trigger as the first trigger to fire when an update happens to the table on which this trigger has been placed. If an ALTER statement is executed against the trigger after the trigger order has been defined, the firing order is lost. The sp_settriggerorder procedure must be run again to reestablish the firing order.

> **NOTE**
>
> It is recommended that you avoid defining multiple triggers for the same event on the same table when possible. Oftentimes, it is possible to include all the logic in one trigger defined for an action. This can simplify your database and avoid the uncertainty of the firing order.

Special Considerations with AFTER Triggers

Following are a few other considerations for AFTER triggers:

- ▶ AFTER triggers can be used on tables that also have cascading referential integrity constraints. The cascading feature, which was new to SQL Server 2000, allows you to define cascading actions when a user updates or deletes a primary key to which a foreign key points. This new feature is discussed in more detail in Chapter 19, "Creating and Managing Tables."

- ▶ WRITETEXT and TRUNCATE TABLE do not fire triggers. BCP by default does not fire triggers either, but the FIRE_TRIGGERS bulk copy hint can be specified to cause both AFTER and INSTEAD OF triggers to execute.

- ▶ Triggers are objects, so they must have unique names within the database. If you try to add a trigger with a name that already exists, you get an error message. You can, however, use ALTER on an existing trigger.

The following restrictions apply to AFTER triggers:

- ▶ AFTER triggers can be placed only on tables, not on views.

- ▶ An AFTER trigger cannot be placed on more than one table.

- ▶ The text, ntext, and image columns cannot be referenced in the AFTER trigger logic.

Using inserted and deleted Tables

In most trigger situations, you need to know what changes were made as part of the data modification. You can find this information in the inserted and deleted tables. For the AFTER trigger, these tables are temporary memory-resident tables that contain the rows that were modified by the statement. With the INSTEAD OF trigger, the inserted and deleted tables are actually temporary tables that are created on-the-fly.

The inserted and deleted tables have identical column structures and names as the tables that were modified. Consider running the following statement against the BigPubs2005 database:

```
UPDATE titles
 SET price = $15.05
 WHERE type LIKE '%cook%'
```

When this statement is executed, a copy of the rows to be modified is recorded, along with a copy of the rows after the modification. These copies are available to the trigger in the deleted and inserted tables.

If you want to be able to see the contents of the deleted and inserted tables for testing purposes, you can create a copy of the table and then create a trigger on that copy (see Listing 25.2). You can perform data modification statements and view the contents of these tables without the modification actually taking place.

LISTING 25.2   Viewing the Contents of the inserted and deleted Tables

```
--Create a copy of the titles table in the BigPubs2005 database
SELECT *
 INTO titles_copy
 FROM titles
GO
--add an AFTER trigger to this table for testing purposes
CREATE TRIGGER tc_tr ON titles_copy
 FOR INSERT, UPDATE, DELETE
 AS
 PRINT 'Inserted:'
 SELECT title_id, type, price FROM inserted
 PRINT 'Deleted:'
 SELECT title_id, type, price FROM deleted
 ROLLBACK TRANSACTION
```

25

The `inserted` and `deleted` tables are available within the trigger after INSERT, UPDATE, and DELETE. Listing 25.3 shows the contents of `inserted` and `deleted`, as reported by the trigger when executing the preceding UPDATE statement.

LISTING 25.3   Viewing the Contents of the `inserted` and `deleted` Tables When Updating the `titles_copy` Table

```
UPDATE titles_copy
 SET price = $15.05
 WHERE type LIKE '%cook%'

Inserted:
title_id type          price
-------- ------------  --------------------
TC7777   trad_cook     15.05
TC4203   trad_cook     15.05
TC3218   trad_cook     15.05
MC3021   mod_cook      15.05
MC2222   mod_cook      15.05

Deleted:
title_id type          price
-------- ------------  --------------------
TC7777   trad_cook     14.3279
TC4203   trad_cook     14.595
TC3218   trad_cook     0.0017
MC3021   mod_cook      15.894
MC2222   mod_cook      14.9532
```

> **NOTE**
>
> In SQL Server 2005, an error message is displayed after a rollback is initiated in a trigger. The error message indicates that the transaction ended in the trigger and that the batch has been aborted. Previous versions of SQL Server did not display an error message when a rollback was encountered in the trigger.

The nature of the `inserted` and `deleted` tables enables you to determine the action that fired the trigger. For example, when an INSERT occurs, the `deleted` table is empty because there were no previous values prior to the insertion. Table 25.1 shows the DML triggering events and the corresponding contents in the `deleted` and `inserted` tables.

TABLE 25.1   Determining the Action That Fired a Trigger

Statement	Contents of `inserted`	Contents of `deleted`
INSERT	Rows added	Empty
UPDATE	New rows	Old rows
DELETE	Empty	Rows deleted

NOTE

Triggers do not fire on a row-by-row basis. One common mistake in coding triggers is to assume that only one row is modified. However, triggers are set based. If a single statement affects multiple rows in the table, the trigger needs to handle the processing of all the rows that were affected, not just one row at a time.

One common approach to dealing with the multiple rows in a trigger is to place the rows in a cursor and then process each row that was affected, one at a time. This works, but it can have an adverse effect on the performance of the trigger. To keep your trigger execution fast, you should try to use rowset-based logic instead of cursors in triggers when possible.

25

Checking for Column Updates

The UPDATE() function is available inside INSERT and UPDATE triggers. UPDATE() allows a trigger to determine whether a column was affected by the INSERT or UPDATE statement that fired the trigger. By testing whether a column was actually updated, you can avoid performing unnecessary work.

For example, suppose a rule mandates that you cannot change the city for an author (a silly rule, but it demonstrates a few key concepts). Listing 25.4 creates a trigger for both INSERT and UPDATE that enforces this rule on the authors table in the BigPubs2005 database.

LISTING 25.4   Using the UPDATE() Function in a Trigger

```
CREATE TRIGGER tr_au_ins_upd ON authors
FOR INSERT, UPDATE
AS
IF UPDATE(city)
 BEGIN
 RAISERROR ('You cannot change the city.', 15, 1)
 ROLLBACK TRAN
 END
GO
UPDATE authors
SET city = city
```

LISTING 25.4   Continued

```
WHERE au_id = '172-32-1176'

Server: Msg 50000, Level 15, State 1, Procedure
 tr_au_ins_upd, Line 5
You cannot change the city.
```

Listing 25.4 shows how you generally write triggers that verify the integrity of data. If the modification violates an integrity rule, an error message is returned to the client application, and the modification is rolled back.

The UPDATE() function evaluates to TRUE if you update the column in the UPDATE statement. You do not actually change the value for city (you set it to itself), but you update the column in the query.

> **NOTE**
>
> If you created the tr_au_upd trigger on the authors table as part of the AFTER trigger example earlier in this chapter, you might have also seen the TRIGGER OUTPUT: 1 rows were updated message. This trigger was set to be the first trigger to fire, and it executes in addition to the new ins_upd trigger that was added in the example from this section.

Now you can try a couple INSERTs on the authors table:

```
INSERT authors (au_id, au_lname, au_fname, city, contract)
VALUES('111-11-1111', 'White', 'Johnson','Menlo Park', 1)

--Results from the previous insert
Server: Msg 50000, Level 15, State 1
You cannot change the city.
```

The UPDATE() function evaluates to TRUE and displays the error message. This is expected because the trigger was created for INSERT as well, and the IF UPDATE condition is evaluated for both insertions and updates.

Now you can see what happens if you change the INSERT statement so that it does not include the city column in the INSERT:

```
INSERT authors (au_id, au_lname, au_fname, contract)
VALUES('111-11-2222', 'White', 'Johnson', 1)

Server: Msg 50000, Level 15, State 1
You cannot change the city.
```

The error message is still displayed, even though the insertion was performed without the city column. This might seem counterintuitive, but the IF UPDATE condition always returns a TRUE value for INSERT actions. This is because the columns have either explicit default values or implicit (NULL) values inserted, even if they are not specified. The IF UPDATE conditions see this as a change and evaluate to TRUE.

If you change the tr_au_ins_upd trigger to be for UPDATE only (not INSERT and UPDATE), then the insertions can take place without error.

Enforcing Referential Integrity by Using DML Triggers

Several options, including foreign key constraints and stored procedures are available to enforce referential integrity, but using a trigger is still a viable alternative. A trigger provides a great deal of flexibility and allows you to customize your referential integrity solution to fit your needs. Some of the other alternatives such as foreign keys do not provide the same degree of customization.

> **TIP**
>
> In a database environment in which multiple databases are used with related data, a trigger can be invaluable for enforcing referential integrity. The trigger can span databases, and it can ensure that data rows that are inserted into a table in one database are valid based on rows in another database.

Listing 25.5 shows how to re-create and populate the customers and orders tables in the sample BigPubs2005 database.

LISTING 25.5   Creating and Populating the customers and orders Tables

```
if exists (select * from sysobjects
    where id = object_id('orders') and sysstat & 0xf = 3)
        drop table orders
GO
if exists (select * from sysobjects
    where id = object_id('customers') and sysstat & 0xf = 3)
        drop table customers
GO

CREATE TABLE customers
(customer_id INT PRIMARY KEY NOT NULL,
customer_name NVARCHAR(25) NOT NULL,
customer_comments NVARCHAR(22) NULL)
CREATE TABLE orders
(order_id INT  PRIMARY KEY NOT NULL,
customer_id INT,
order_date DATETIME,
```

25

LISTING 25.5   Continued

```
CONSTRAINT FK_orders_customers
      FOREIGN KEY (customer_id) REFERENCES customers (customer_id))

INSERT customers (customer_id, customer_name, customer_comments)
VALUES(1, 'Hardware Suppliers AB','Stephanie is contact.')
INSERT customers (customer_id, customer_name, customer_comments)
VALUES(2, 'Software Suppliers AB','Elisabeth is contact.')
INSERT customers (customer_id, customer_name, customer_comments)
VALUES(3, 'Firmware Suppliers AB','Mike is contact.')

INSERT orders (order_id, customer_id, order_date)
VALUES(100, 1, GETDATE())
INSERT orders (order_id, customer_id, order_date)
VALUES(101, 1, GETDATE())
INSERT orders (order_id, customer_id, order_date)
VALUES(102, 1, GETDATE())

SELECT * FROM customers
SELECT * FROM orders
customer_id customer_name                customer_comments
----------- -------------------------    ---------------------
1           Hardware Suppliers AB        Stephanie is contact.
2           Software Suppliers AB        Elisabeth is contact.
3           Firmware Suppliers AB        Mike is contact.

order_id    customer_id order_date
----------- ----------- ---------------------
100         1           2005-06-17 05:16:49.233
101         1           2005-06-17 05:16:49.233
102         1           2005-06-17 05:16:49.233
```

The FOREIGN KEY constraint FK_orders_customers on the orders table prohibits the
following:

▶ Inserting rows into the orders table for customer numbers that don't exist in the
  customers table

▶ Updating the orders table by changing the customer number to values that don't
  exist in the customers table

▶ Deleting rows in the customers table for which orders exist

▶ Updating the customers table by changing the customer number for which
  orders exist

You might want a cascading action instead of prohibiting the deletion or update of rows on the customers table. This would include automatically cascading the DELETE or UPDATE statement executed on the customers table to the related orders table. You can do this by using triggers.

Cascading Deletes

TIP

SQL Server 2000 added a new feature that allows you to define cascading actions on a FOREIGN KEY constraint. When defining the constraints on a table, you can use the ON UPDATE CASCADE clause or the ON DELETE CASCADE clause, which cause changes to the primary key of a table to cascade to the related foreign key tables. Refer to Chapter 21, "Implementing Data Integrity," for further information on this option.

A cascading delete is relatively simple to create. Listing 25.6 shows a cascading delete trigger for the customers table.

LISTING 25.6   A Cascading Delete for the customers Table

```
CREATE TRIGGER cust_del_orders ON customers
FOR DELETE
AS
IF @@ROWCOUNT = 0
 RETURN
DELETE orders
 FROM orders o , deleted d
 WHERE o.customer_id = d.customer_id
IF @@ERROR <> 0
 BEGIN
  RAISERROR ('ERROR encountered in cascading trigger.', 16, 1)
  ROLLBACK TRAN
  RETURN
 END
```

The following DELETE statement deletes the row for Customer 1, so all three rows for that customer in the orders table should be deleted by the trigger:

```
DELETE customers WHERE customer_id = 1
```

```
Server: Msg 547, Level 16, State 1
The DELETE statement conflicted with COLUMN REFERENCE
constraint 'FK_orders_customers'.
The conflict occurred in database 'BigPubs2005',
table 'orders', column 'customer_id'.
The statement has been terminated.
```

This might not be what you expected. The FOREIGN KEY constraint here restricts the
DELETE statement, so the trigger never fires. The trigger in this example is an AFTER trigger.
Therefore, the trigger never fires, and the cascading action never takes place. You have
several options to get around this:

▶ Remove the FOREIGN KEY constraint from orders to customers.

▶ Disable the FOREIGN KEY constraint from orders to customers.

▶ Keep the FOREIGN KEY constraint and perform all cascading actions in stored procedures.

▶ Keep the FOREIGN KEY constraint and perform all cascading actions in the application.

▶ Use an INSTEAD OF trigger in place of the AFTER trigger.

▶ Use the new cascading referential integrity constraints.

Listing 25.7 shows how you can disable the FOREIGN KEY constraint so that a cascading
delete can occur.

LISTING 25.7   Disabling the FOREIGN KEY Constraint to the customers Table So That a
Cascading Delete Can Occur

```
ALTER TABLE orders
 NOCHECK CONSTRAINT FK_orders_customers
GO

GO
DELETE customers WHERE customer_id = 1
SELECT * FROM customers
SELECT * FROM orders
customer_id customer_name          customer_comments
----------- ---------------------- ----------------------
2           Software Suppliers AB   Elisabeth is contact.
3           Firmware Suppliers AB   Mike is contact.


order_id    customer_id order_date
----------- ----------- --------------------------
```

In Listing 25.7, the cascading deletes occur via the trigger because the FOREIGN KEY
constraint is disabled. Compared to a trigger for cascading deletes, a trigger for cascading
updates is more complex and not as common. This is discussed in more detail in the next
section.

If you disable the FOREIGN KEY constraint, you have a potential integrity problem. If rows
are inserted or updated in the orders table, there are no constraints to ensure that the

customer number exists in the `customer` table. You can take care of this by using an `INSERT` and `UPDATE` trigger on the `orders` table (see Listing 25.8). This trigger tests for the existence of a customer before the order is inserted or updated.

LISTING 25.8   Handling a Restriction by Using a Trigger on the `orders` Table

```
if exists (select * from sysobjects where id = object_id('dbo.ord_ins_upd_cust')
        and sysstat & 0xf = 8)
        drop trigger dbo.ord_ins_upd_cust
GO


CREATE TRIGGER ord_ins_upd_cust ON orders
FOR INSERT, UPDATE
AS
IF EXISTS (SELECT * FROM inserted
            WHERE customer_id NOT IN
          (SELECT customer_id FROM customers))
 BEGIN
  RAISERROR('No customer with such customer number', 16, 1)
  ROLLBACK TRAN
  RETURN
 END
```

Cascading Updates

A cascading update is tricky to achieve. Modifying a primary key, per definition, really involves deleting a row and inserting a new row. The problem is that you lose the connection between the old row and the new row in the `customers` table. How do you know which changes to cascade to which rows?

This situation is simpler if you can restrict the changes to one row (see Listing 25.9) because you have only one row in the `deleted` and `inserted` tables. You know the customer number before and after the modification.

LISTING 25.9   A Cascading Update in a Trigger

```
if exists (select * from sysobjects where id = object_id('dbo.cust_upd_orders')
        and sysstat & 0xf = 8)
        drop trigger dbo.cust_upd_orders
GO


CREATE TRIGGER cust_upd_orders ON customers
FOR UPDATE
AS
DECLARE @rows_affected int, @c_id_before int, @c_id_after int
SELECT @rows_affected = @@ROWCOUNT
IF @rows_affected = 0
```

LISTING 25.9   Continued

```
 RETURN -- No rows changed, exit trigger
IF UPDATE(customer_id)
BEGIN
 IF @rows_affected = 1
 BEGIN
   SELECT @c_id_before = customer_id FROM deleted
   SELECT @c_id_after = customer_id FROM inserted
   UPDATE orders
    SET customer_id = @c_id_after
    WHERE customer_id = @c_id_before
 END
ELSE
  BEGIN
     RAISERROR ('Cannot update more than 1 row.', 16, 1)
     ROLLBACK TRAN
     RETURN
  END
END
```

If several rows are updated, it's not easy to know which order belongs to which customer. You can easily modify the trigger shown in Listing 25.9 to handle a situation in which several rows change to the same value; however, this is not allowed because of the primary key on the customers table. Modifying several rows and changing the primary key value is rare, and you are not likely to encounter it.

> **NOTE**
>
> The cascading FOREIGN KEY constraints are an excellent alternative to triggers, and they are efficient. If you choose not to use the cascading feature, you might still want to enjoy the simplicity of constraints. Then you only need to handle cascading actions in stored procedures or in client applications.
>
> Stored procedures are often a good choice because they essentially give application developers a function-based interface for modifications. If the implementation details (for example, the table structure or rules) change, client applications can be isolated from the changes, as long as the interfaces to the stored procedures stay the same. The question of how to handle a cascade is a matter of personal preference, however.
>
> Handling cascading updates in a client application or stored procedure is a chicken-and-egg situation: You cannot change the primary key table first because other tables reference it. You also cannot change the referencing table because no row exists in the primary key table with a corresponding value. The solution is to insert in the referenced table a new row that contains the new primary key value, change the referencing rows, and then delete the old row from the referenced table.

INSTEAD OF **Triggers**

SQL Server 2000 introduced a new type of trigger called an INSTEAD OF trigger. This type of trigger extends SQL Server's trigger capabilities and provides an alternative to the AFTER trigger that was heavily utilized in prior versions of SQL Server.

The name of the trigger gives you some insight into how this new trigger operates: This trigger performs its actions *instead of* the action that fired it. This is much different from the AFTER trigger, which performs its actions *after* the statement that caused it to fire has completed. This means you can have an INSTEAD OF update trigger on a table that successfully completes but does not include the actual update to the table.

The basic syntax for creating an INSTEAD OF trigger is as follows:

```
CREATE TRIGGER trigger_name
ON table_name
INSTEAD OF { INSERT ¦ UPDATE ¦ DELETE }
AS
SQL statements
```

Listing 25.10 shows how to create a trigger that prints a message stating the number of rows updated by an UPDATE statement. It then executes an UPDATE against the table that has the trigger on it. Finally, it selects the rows from the table for review.

LISTING 25.10   A Simple INSTEAD OF Trigger

```
if exists (select * from sysobjects where id = object_id('dbo.cust_upd_orders')
        and sysstat & 0xf = 8)
        drop trigger dbo.cust_upd_orders
GO
CREATE TRIGGER trI_au_upd ON authors
INSTEAD OF UPDATE
AS
PRINT 'TRIGGER OUTPUT: '
+CONVERT(VARCHAR(5), @@ROWCOUNT) + ' rows were updated.'
GO

UPDATE authors
SET au_fname = 'Rachael'
WHERE state = 'UT'
GO
TRIGGER OUTPUT: 1 rows were updated.

SELECT au_fname, au_lname FROM authors
WHERE state = 'UT'
GO
au_fname              au_lname
------------------    -------------------------------------
Johann Wolfgang       von Goethe
```

As you can see from the results of the SELECT statement, the first name (au_fname) column is not updated to 'Rachael'. The UPDATE statement is correct, but the INSTEAD OF trigger does not apply the update from the statement as part of its INSTEAD OF action. The only action the trigger carries out is to print its message.

The important point to realize is that after you define an INSTEAD OF trigger on a table, you need to include all the logic in the trigger to perform the actual modification as well as any other actions that the trigger might need to carry out.

Executing INSTEAD OF Triggers

To gain a complete understanding of the INSTEAD OF trigger, you must understand its execution in relationship to the other events that are occurring. The following key events are important when the INSTEAD OF trigger fires:

▶ **Triggering action**—The INSTEAD OF trigger fires *instead of* the triggering action. As shown earlier, the actions of the INSTEAD OF trigger replace the actions of the original data modification that fired the trigger.

▶ **Constraint processing**—Constraint processing—including CHECK constraints, UNIQUE constraints, and PRIMARY KEY constraints—happens *after* the INSTEAD OF trigger fires.

Listing 25.11 demonstrates the trigger execution order.

LISTING 25.11   INSTEAD OF Trigger Execution

```
CREATE TRIGGER employee_insInstead
ON employee
INSTEAD OF insert
AS

DECLARE @job_id smallint

--Insert the jobs record for the employee if it does not already exist
IF NOT EXISTS
(SELECT 1
   FROM jobs j, inserted i
  WHERE i.job_id = j.job_id)
BEGIN
   INSERT jobs
       (job_desc, min_lvl, max_lvl)
      SELECT 'Automatic Job Add', i.job_lvl, i.job_lvl
      FROM inserted i

--Capture the identify value for the job just inserted
--This will be used for the employee insert later
```

LISTING 25.11   Continued

```
    SELECT @job_id = @@identity

    PRINT 'NEW job_id ADDED FOR NEW EMPLOYEE:' + convert(char(3),@job_id)

END

--Execute the original insert action with the newly added job_id
INSERT employee
        (emp_id, fname, minit, lname, job_id, job_lvl, pub_id, hire_date)
    SELECT emp_id, fname, minit, lname, @job_id, job_lvl, pub_id, hire_date
      FROM Inserted


GO
```

The trigger in Listing 25.11 can be created in BigPubs2005. The key feature of this INSTEAD OF trigger is that it can satisfy a referential integrity constraint that was not satisfied before the INSERT was executed. Note the FOREIGN KEY constraint on the employee table that references job_id on the jobs table. The trigger first checks whether the jobs record associated with the job_id of the employee being inserted exists. If the jobs record does not exist for the inserted employee's job_id, the trigger inserts a new jobs record and uses it for the insertion of the employee record.

If you execute the following INSERT statement, which has a job_id that does not exist, it succeeds:

```
INSERT EMPLOYEE
        (emp_id, fname, minit, lname, job_id, job_lvl, pub_id, hire_date)
  VALUES ('KNN33333F', 'Kayla', 'N', 'Nicole', 20, 100, 9952, getdate())
Go
```

This statement succeeds because the constraint processing happens after the INSTEAD OF trigger completes its actions. Conversely, if you were to create the same trigger as an AFTER trigger, the FOREIGN KEY constraint would execute before the AFTER trigger, and the following error message would be displayed:

```
INSERT statement conflicted with COLUMN FOREIGN KEY constraint
'FK__employee__job_id__1BFD2C07'. The
conflict occurred in database 'BigPubs2005', table 'jobs', column 'job_id'.
-->The statement has been terminated.
```

Notice with the previous INSTEAD OF trigger example that the last action that the trigger performs is the actual insertion of the employee record. The trigger was created to fire when an employee was inserted, so the trigger must perform the actual insertion. This insertion occurs in addition to any other actions that justify the trigger's creation.

Using AFTER **Versus** INSTEAD OF **Triggers**

Now that you have seen some of the key differences between AFTER and INSTEAD OF triggers, you need to decide which trigger to use. In the previous example (Listing 25.11), the INSTEAD OF trigger is the only trigger option for this kind of functionality. However, you can oftentimes use either trigger type to attain the same result.

Something you should consider when choosing one of these triggers is the efficiency of the overall modification. For example, if you have a modification that will cause a trigger to fire and often reject the modification, you might want to consider using the INSTEAD OF trigger. The rationale is that the INSTEAD OF trigger does not perform the actual modification until after the trigger completes, so you do not need to undo the modification. If you were to use an AFTER trigger in the same scenario, any modifications that were rejected would need to be rolled back because they have already been written to the transaction log by the time the AFTER trigger fires.

Conversely, if you have a situation in which the vast majority of the updates are not rejected, the AFTER trigger might be your best choice.

The particular situation dictates the preferred trigger, but keep in mind that INSTEAD OF triggers tend to be more involved than AFTER triggers because an INSTEAD OF trigger must perform the actual data modification that fired it.

Using AFTER **and** INSTEAD OF **Triggers Together**

An important consideration when coding an INSTEAD OF trigger is that it can exist on the same table as an AFTER trigger. INSTEAD OF triggers can also execute based on the same data modifications as AFTER triggers.

Take, for example, the INSTEAD OF trigger from Listing 25.11 that you placed on the employee table in the BigPubs2005 database. An AFTER trigger already existed on the employee table. Listing 25.12 shows the syntax for the existing AFTER trigger on the employee table.

LISTING 25.12   An AFTER Trigger Placed on the Same Table as an INSTEAD OF Trigger

```
if exists (select * from sysobjects where id = object_id('dbo.employee_insupd')
        and sysstat & 0xf = 8)
        drop trigger dbo.employee_insupd
GO

CREATE TRIGGER employee_insupd
ON employee
FOR INSERT, UPDATE
AS
--Get the range of level for this job type from the jobs table.
declare @min_lvl tinyint,
   @max_lvl tinyint,
   @emp_lvl tinyint,
   @job_id smallint
```

LISTING 25.12   Continued

```
select @min_lvl = min_lvl,
    @max_lvl = max_lvl,
    @emp_lvl = i.job_lvl,
    @job_id = i.job_id
from employee e, jobs j, inserted i
where e.emp_id = i.emp_id AND i.job_id = j.job_id
IF (@job_id = 1) and (@emp_lvl <> 10)
begin
    raiserror ('Job id 1 expects the default level of 10.',16,1)
    ROLLBACK TRANSACTION
end
ELSE
IF NOT (@emp_lvl BETWEEN @min_lvl AND @max_lvl)
begin
    raiserror ('The level for job_id:%d should be between %d and %d.',
        16, 1, @job_id, @min_lvl, @max_lvl)
    ROLLBACK TRANSACTION
End
go
```

This AFTER trigger checks whether the job level assigned to the employee falls within a valid range for the job_id assigned to the employee. It is fired for both insertions and updates, and it can exist on the same table as the employee_insInstead INSTEAD OF trigger described earlier. The combined effect on an employee insertion with both the triggers on the employee table is to have the following actions happen:

1. The INSERT data modification is executed.

2. The INSTEAD OF trigger fires, completes its validation, and ultimately does the employee insertion that is written to the transaction log.

3. Constraint processing completes.

4. The AFTER trigger fires, performing its actions on the employee record inserted by the INSTEAD OF trigger.

5. The AFTER trigger completes and commits the transaction to the database.

One of the key points in this example is that the AFTER trigger performs its actions on the row inserted by the INSTEAD OF trigger. It does not use the record from the original INSERT that started the trigger execution. Therefore, in this chapter's example, where the INSTEAD OF trigger generates a new job_id, the new job_id value—not the job_id that was originally inserted—is used in the AFTER trigger.

You need to consider rollback and recovery in this scenario as well, but they are beyond the scope of this discussion. This example simply shows that INSTEAD OF and AFTER triggers can be combined and that you need to consider the order of execution when designing a trigger solution.

Using Views with INSTEAD OF Triggers

One of the most powerful applications of an INSTEAD OF trigger is to a view. The INSTEAD OF trigger, unlike the AFTER trigger, can be applied to a view and triggered based on modifications to the view. For more information on views, see Chapter 22, "Creating and Managing Views."

The reason this is so important is that data modifications have many restrictions when made via a view. The list is extensive, but the following are a few examples:

▶ You cannot use data modification statements that apply to more than one table in the view in a single statement.

▶ All columns defined as NOT NULL in the underlying tables that are being inserted must have the column values specified in the INSERT statement.

▶ If the view was defined with the WITH CHECK OPTION clause, rows cannot be modified in a way that will cause them to disappear from the view.

You can use the INSTEAD OF trigger to overcome some of these restrictions. In particular, the first restriction (related to making a single table modification) can be addressed with the INSTEAD OF trigger. The INSTEAD OF trigger fires before the actual modification takes place, so it can resolve the modifications to the underlying tables associated with the view. It can then execute the modification directly against those base tables. The following example demonstrates this capability:

```
Use BigPubs2005
go
CREATE VIEW employeeJobs
AS
select j.min_lvl, j.max_lvl, j.job_id, j.job_desc, e.job_lvl, e.emp_id
 from employee e, jobs j
where e.job_id = j.job_id
GO
```

This creates a view in the BigPubs2005 database that joins data from the employee and jobs tables. It retrieves the job types and the associated levels, the employees assigned to the job types, and each employee's current job level. The following is a sample set of rows from the view:

min_lvl	max_lvl	job_id	job_desc	job_lvl	emp_id
25	100	14	Designer	35	ENL44273F
25	100	14	Designer	89	PSA89086M
25	100	14	Designer	100	KFJ64308F
25	100	12	Editor	32	Y-L77953M
25	100	12	Editor	35	H-B39728F
25	100	12	Editor	100	HAS54740M

Say you want to change the minimum job level (min_lvl) for the Designer job to 40 and at the same time set the job level (job_lvl) for any employees who have this job to 40. If you execute the following update—without an INSTEAD OF trigger—against the view, you get the message shown:

```
UPDATE employeeJobs
   SET min_lvl = 40,
       job_lvl = 40
 WHERE job_id = 12
GO
View or function 'employeeJobs' is not updateable
because the modification affects multiple base tables.
```

To get around this problem, you can use an INSTEAD OF trigger. The trigger can decipher the update to the view and apply the updates to the base table without causing the error. This functionality is demonstrated in the INSTEAD OF trigger shown in Listing 25.13.

LISTING 25.13   A Basic View with an INSTEAD OF Trigger

```
CREATE TRIGGER employeeJobs_updInstead
ON employeeJobs
INSTEAD OF UPDATE
AS
IF @@ROWCOUNT = 0 RETURN
--update the data related to the jobs table
UPDATE jobs
   SET jobs.min_lvl = i.min_lvl,
       jobs.max_lvl = i.max_lvl,
       jobs.job_desc = i.job_desc
  FROM inserted i
 WHERE jobs.job_id = i.job_id
   AND (jobs.min_lvl <> i.min_lvl
       OR jobs.max_lvl <> i.max_lvl
       OR jobs.job_desc <> i.job_desc)

--update the data related to the employee table
UPDATE employee
```

25

LISTING 25.13   Continued

```
    SET employee.job_lvl = i.min_lvl
  FROM inserted i
 WHERE employee.emp_id = i.emp_id
GO
```

Listing 25.13 has a section that checks the fields related to the jobs table and updates the base table if any of the values have changed. It also has a section that updates the employee table for the employee fields that have been changed in the view.

> **NOTE**
>
> You could enhance the trigger in Listing 25.13 to include logic to check for specific updates or to update only those employees who are assigned to the job and have a job level below the new minimum. These enhancements are not included in the listing to keep the example simple.

If you now execute the same UPDATE statement, you don't get an error message:

```
UPDATE employeeJobs
   SET min_lvl = 40,
       job_lvl = 40
 WHERE job_id = 12
GO
```

The following results show values selected from the employeeJobs view after the update is executed successfully:

min_lvl	max_lvl	job_id	job_desc	job_lvl	emp_id
25	100	14	Designer	35	ENL44273F
25	100	14	Designer	89	PSA89086M
25	100	14	Designer	100	KFJ64308F
25	100	13	Sales Representative	35	PMA42628M
25	100	13	Sales Representative	64	CGS88322F
25	100	13	Sales Representative	100	TP055093M
40	100	12	Editor	40	Y-L77953M
40	100	12	Editor	40	H-B39728F
40	100	12	Editor	40	HAS54740M

Notice that the Editor job now has a minimum level (min_lvl) equal to 40 and that all the employees who have that job level (job_lvl) are also set to 40.

You can see the added flexibility that you get by using the INSTEAD OF trigger on a basic view. This flexibility is also applicable to a more sophisticated view called a *distributed partitioned view*. With this type of view, data for the view can be partitioned across different servers. This gives you the ability to scale a database solution and still have a single view of the data that appears as one table.

You can make data modifications via a distributed partitioned view, but some restrictions exist. If you do not meet the requirements for updating the view, you can use the INSTEAD OF trigger to bypass these restrictions; this is similar to adding an INSTEAD OF trigger on a non-partitioned view.

For a more in-depth discussion of distributed partitioned views, see Chapter 44, "Administering Very Large SQL Server Databases" (on the CD-ROM).

INSTEAD OF **Trigger Restrictions**

INSTEAD OF triggers have many capabilities, but they also have limitations. The following are some of them:

▶ INSTEAD OF triggers do not support recursion. This means they cannot call themselves, regardless of the setting of the Recursive Triggers database option. For example, if an INSERT is executed on a table that has an INSTEAD OF trigger, and the INSTEAD OF trigger performs an INSERT on this same table, the INSTEAD OF trigger for this INSERT does not fire a second time. Any AFTER triggers defined on the same table for INSERT fire based on the INSTEAD OF trigger INSERT.

▶ You can define only one INSTEAD OF trigger for each action on a given table. Therefore, you can have a maximum of three INSTEAD OF triggers for each table: one for INSERT, one for UPDATE, and one for DELETE.

▶ A table cannot have an INSTEAD OF trigger and a FOREIGN KEY constraint with CASCADE defined for the same action. For example, you cannot have an INSTEAD OF trigger defined for DELETE on a given table as well as a foreign key with a CASCADE DELETE definition. You get an error if you attempt to do this. In this situation, you could have INSTEAD OF triggers defined on INSERT and UPDATE without receiving errors.

Using DDL Triggers

DDL triggers are a new feature in SQL Server 2005. These triggers focus on changes to the definition of database objects as opposed to changes to the actual data. The definition of database objects is dictated by the DDL events that these new triggers respond to.

The DDL events that these triggers fire on can be broken down into two main categories. The first category includes DDL events that are scoped at the database level and affect the definition of objects such as tables, indexes, and users. The second category of DDL triggers is scoped at the server level. These triggers apply to server objects, such as logins.

The number of DDL events at the database level far exceeds the number at the server level. Table 25.2 lists the DDL statements that DDL triggers can fire on.

25

TABLE 25.2   DDL Statements

Create/Grant Statements	Alter/Update/Deny Statements	Drop/Revoke Statements
Statements with Database-Level Scope		
CREATE_APPLICATION_ROLE	ALTER_APPLICATION_ROLE	DROP_APPLICATION_ROLE
CREATE_ASSEMBLY	ALTER_ASSEMBLY	DROP_ASSEMBLY
	ALTER_AUTHORIZATION_ DATABASE	
CREATE_CERTIFICATE	ALTER_CERTIFICATE	DROP_CERTIFICATE
CREATE_CONTRACT		DROP_CONTRACT
CREATE_DATABASE	ALTER_DATABASE	DROP_DATABASE
GRANT_DATABASE	DENY_DATABASE	REVOKE_DATABASE
CREATE_EVENT_ NOTIFICATION		DROP_EVENT_ NOTIFICATION
CREATE_FUNCTION	ALTER_FUNCTION	DROP_FUNCTION
CREATE_INDEX	ALTER_INDEX	DROP_INDEX
CREATE_MESSAGE_TYPE	ALTER_MESSAGE_TYPE	DROP_MESSAGE_TYPE
CREATE_PARTITION_FUNCTION	ALTER_PARTITION_FUNCTION	DROP_PARTITION_ FUNCTION
CREATE_PARTITION_SCHEME	ALTER_PARTITION_SCHEME	DROP_PARTITION_SCHEME
CREATE_PROCEDURE	ALTER_PROCEDURE	DROP_PROCEDURE
CREATE_QUEUE	ALTER_QUEUE	DROP_QUEUE
CREATE_REMOTE_SERVICE_ BINDING	ALTER_REMOTE_SERVICE_ BINDING	DROP_REMOTE_SERVICE_ BINDING
CREATE_ROLE	ALTER_ROLE	DROP_ROLE
CREATE_ROUTE	ALTER_ROUTE	DROP_ROUTE
CREATE_SCHEMA	ALTER_SCHEMA	DROP_SCHEMA
CREATE_SERVICE	ALTER_SERVICE	DROP_SERVICE
CREATE_STATISTICS	UPDATE_STATISTICS	DROP_STATISTICS
CREATE_SYNONYM		DROP_SYNONYM
CREATE_TABLE	ALTER_TABLE	DROP_TABLE
CREATE_TRIGGER	ALTER_TRIGGER	DROP_TRIGGER
CREATE_TYPE		DROP_TYPE
CREATE_USER	ALTER_USER	DROP_USER
CREATE_VIEW	ALTER_VIEW	DROP_VIEW
CREATE_XML_SCHEMA_ COLLECTION	ALTER_XML_SCHEMA_ COLLECTION	DROP_XML_SCHEMA_ COLLECTION
Statements with Server-Level Scope		
ALTER_AUTHORIZATION_SERVER		
CREATE_ENDPOINT		DROP_ENDPOINT
CREATE_LOGIN	ALTER_LOGIN	DROP_LOGIN
GRANT_SERVER	DENY_SERVER	REVOKE_SERVER

Triggers created on the DDL events are particularly important for auditing purposes. In the past, it was very difficult to isolate changes to the definition of a database or to secure them from change. With DDL triggers, you have the tools necessary to manage these changes.

Creating DDL Triggers

The basic syntax for creating a DDL trigger follows:

```
CREATE TRIGGER trigger_name
ON { ALL SERVER ¦ DATABASE }
[ WITH <ddl_trigger_option> [ ,...n ] ]
{ FOR ¦ AFTER } { event_type ¦ event_group } [ ,...n ]
AS { sql_statement  [ ; ] [ ...n ] ¦ EXTERNAL NAME < method specifier >  [ ; ] }
```

The best way to illustrate the use of the DDL trigger syntax and the power of these triggers is to look at a few examples. The example shown in Listing 25.14 illustrates the creation of a DDL trigger that is scoped at the database level and prevents table-level changes.

LISTING 25.14   A Database-Scoped DDL Trigger for Tables

```
CREATE TRIGGER ti_TableAudit
ON DATABASE
FOR CREATE_TABLE, ALTER_TABLE, DROP_TABLE
AS
    PRINT 'You must disable the TableAudit trigger in order
       to change any table in this database'
    ROLLBACK
GO
```

This trigger is fired whenever the CREATE, ALTER, or DROP TABLE statements are executed. Take, for example, the following statements that can be run against the BigPubs2005 database:

```
ALTER table titles
 add new_col int null
alter table titles
 drop column new_col
```

```
You must disable the TableAudit trigger in order to change any table in this
➥database
Msg 3609, Level 16, State 2, Line 1
The transaction ended in the trigger. The batch has been aborted.
```

These `ALTER` statements add a column to the `titles` table and then remove the column. With the tr_TableAudit trigger in place on the `BigPubs2005` database, the error message is displayed after the first `ALTER` statement is executed.

This type of trigger is useful for controlling development and production database environments. It goes beyond the normal security measures and helps manage unwanted change. For development environments, this type of trigger gives the database administrator the ability to lock down an environment and focus all changes through that person.

The previous examples include events that are scoped at the database level. Let's take a look at an example that applies to server-level events. The script in Listing 25.15 creates a trigger that is scoped at the server level. It prevents changes to the server logins. When this trigger is installed, it displays a message and rolls back any login changes that are attempted.

LISTING 25.15   A Server-Scoped DDL Trigger for Logins

```
CREATE TRIGGER tr_LoginAudit
ON ALL SERVER
FOR CREATE_LOGIN, ALTER_LOGIN, DROP_LOGIN
AS
    PRINT 'You must disable the tr_LoginAudit trigger before making login changes'
    ROLLBACK
```

The DDL trigger examples we have looked at thus far have targeted specific events listed in Table 25.2. These individual events can also be referenced via an event group. Event groups are hierarchical in nature and can be referenced in DDL triggers instead of the individual events. For example, the table-level trigger from Listing 25.14 can be changed as shown in Listing 25.16 to accomplish the same result. In Listing 25.16, the DDL_TABLE_EVENTS group reference replaces the individual event references to CREATE_TABLE, ALTER_TABLE, and DROP_TABLE.

LISTING 25.16   An Example of a DDL Trigger Referencing an Event Group

```
USE [BigPubs2005]
IF  EXISTS (SELECT * FROM sys.triggers
    WHERE name = N'tr_TableAudit' AND parent_class=0)
DROP TRIGGER [tr_TableAudit] ON DATABASE
go

CREATE TRIGGER tr_TableAudit
ON DATABASE
FOR DDL_TABLE_EVENTS
AS
    PRINT 'You must disable the TableAudit trigger in
        order to change any table in this database'
    ROLLBACK
GO
```

SQL Server Books Online has an excellent diagram that lists all the event groups that can be used to fire DDL triggers. Refer to the "Event Groups for Use with DDL Triggers" topic in Books Online, which shows the event groups and the related DDL events they contain. Event groups simplify administration and allow for auditing at a high level.

The DDL trigger examples we have looked at thus far have executed simple print statements. To further extend the functionality of DDL triggers, you can code them to capture event information related to the DDL trigger execution. You do this by using the EVENTDATA function. The EVENTDATA function returns an XML string that includes the time of the event, the server process ID (SPID), and the type of event that fired the trigger. For some events, additional information, such as the object name or T-SQL statement, is included in the XML string as well.

The EVENTDATA function is essentially the replacement for the inserted and deleted tables that are available with DML triggers but not available with DDL triggers. It gives you information you can use to implement an auditing solution that captures changes to a data definition. This is particularly useful in situations in which you do not want to prevent changes to your definition but you want a record of the changes that occur.

Listing 25.17 shows an auditing solution with a DDL trigger that utilizes the EVENTDATA function to capture any changes to indexes in the BigPubs2005 database. Several event data elements are selected from the EVENTDATA XML string and displayed whenever a change is made to an index.

LISTING 25.17   An Example of a DDL Trigger That References an Event Group

```
CREATE TRIGGER tr_ddl_IndexAudit
ON DATABASE
FOR CREATE_INDEX, ALTER_INDEX, DROP_INDEX
AS
  DECLARE @EventData XML
-- Capture event data from the EVENTDATA function
  SET @EventData = EVENTDATA()
-- Select the auditing info from the XML stream
  SELECT    @EventData.query (''data(/EVENT_INSTANCE/PostTime)'')
            AS [Event Time],
          @EventData.query (''data(/EVENT_INSTANCE/EventType)'')
            AS [Event Type],
          @EventData.query (''data(/EVENT_INSTANCE/ServerName)'')
            AS [Server Name],
          @EventData.query (''data(/EVENT_INSTANCE/TSQLCommand/CommandText)'')
            AS [Command Text]
GO
```

To test the DDL trigger in Listing 25.17, you can run the following statement to create an index on the `titles` table in the `BigPubs2005` database:

```
CREATE NONCLUSTERED INDEX [nc_titles_type] ON [dbo].[titles] ( [type] ASC )
```

The `INDEX CREATE` statement completes successfully, and the event-specific information appears in the Results pane.

You can further extend the auditing capabilities of this type of DDL trigger by writing the results to an audit table. This would give you a quick way of tracking changes to database objects. This type of approach dramatically improves change control and reporting on database changes.

> **NOTE**
>
> DDL triggers can also execute managed code that is based on the CLR. This is discussed in the section "Using CLR Triggers," later in this chapter.

Managing DDL Triggers

The administration of DDL triggers is similar to the administration of DML triggers, but DDL triggers are located in a different part of the Object Explorer tree. This is because DDL triggers are scoped at the server or database level, not at the table level. Figure 25.3 shows the Object Explorer tree and the nodes related to DDL triggers at both the server and database levels. The `tr_TableAudit` trigger that you created earlier in this chapter is shown under the `Database Triggers` node. Figure 25.3 shows the options that are available when you right-click a database trigger in the Object Explorer tree.

The DDL triggers that are scoped at the server level are found in the `Triggers` node under the `Server Objects` node of the Object Explorer tree. (The `Server Objects` node is near the bottom of Figure 25.3.)

You can obtain information about DDL triggers by using catalog views. These views provide a convenient and flexible means for querying database objects, including DDL triggers. Table 25.3 lists the catalog views that relate to triggers. The table includes the scope of the trigger that the view reports on and a brief description of what it returns.

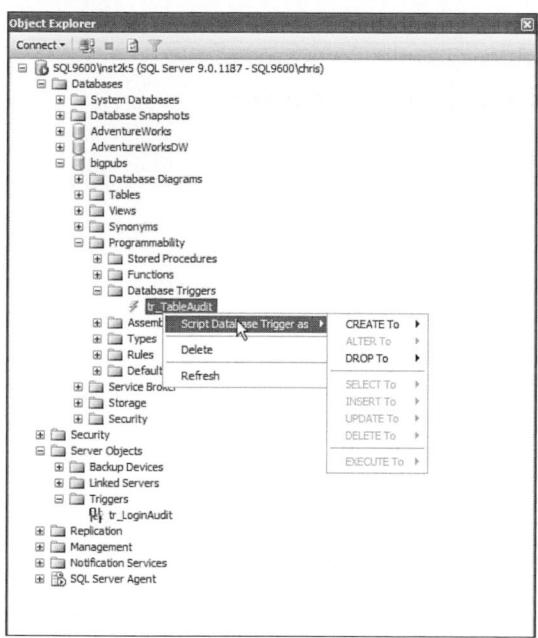

FIGURE 25.3   Using SSMS to manage DDL triggers.

TABLE 25.3   Catalog Views for DDL Triggers

Catalog View	Description
Statements with Database-Level Scope	
sys.triggers	All triggers, including DDL database-scoped triggers
sys.trigger_events	All trigger events, including those that fire DDL database-scoped triggers
sys.sql_modules	All SQL-defined modules, including trigger definitions
sys.assembly_modules	All CLR-defined modules, including database-scoped triggers
Statements with Server-Level Scope	
sys.server_triggers	Server-scoped DDL triggers
sys.server_trigger_events	Events that fire server-scoped triggers
sys.sql_modules	DDL trigger definitions for server-scoped triggers
sys.server_assembly_modules	CLR trigger definitions for server-scoped triggers

Listing 25.18 shows sample SELECT statements that utilize the catalog views. These statements use the sys.triggers and sys.server_triggers views. The SELECT against the sys.triggers table uses a WHERE clause condition that checks the parent_class column in order to retrieve only DDL triggers. The SELECT from sys.server_triggers does not need a WHERE clause because it inherently returns only DDL triggers. The results of each statement are shown below each SELECT in the listing.

LISTING 25.18   Viewing DDL Triggers with Catalog Views

```
--DATABASE SCOPED DDL TRIGGERS
select left(name,20) 'Name', create_date, modify_date, is_disabled
 from sys.triggers
 where parent_class = 0


--Name                    create_date             modify_date             is_disabled
-------------------       --------------------    --------------------    -----------
--tr_TableAudit           2005-06-18 12:48:43.140 2005-06-18 12:48:43.140 0
--tr_ddl_IndexAudit       2005-06-22 06:35:10.233 2005-06-22 06:35:10.233 0


--SERVER SCOPED DDL TRIGGERS
select left(name,20) 'Name', create_date, modify_date, is_disabled
 from sys.server_triggers


--Name                    create_date             modify_date             is_disabled
-------------------       --------------------    --------------------    -----------
--tr_LoginAudit           2005-06-18 12:13:46.077 2005-06-18 12:13:46.077 0
```

Using CLR Triggers

CLR triggers are triggers that are based on the CLR. CLR integration, which was added with SQL Server 2005, allows for database objects (such as triggers) to be coded in one of the supported .NET languages, including Visual Basic .NET and C#.

The decision to code triggers and other database objects by using the CLR depends on the type of operations in the trigger. Typically, objects that have heavy computations or require references to objects that are outside SQL are coded in the CLR. Triggers that are strictly geared toward database access should continue to be coded in T-SQL.

You can code both DDL or DML triggers by using a supported CLR language. Generally speaking, it is much easier to code a CLR trigger in the Visual Studio .NET integrated development environment (IDE) but they can be created outside the IDE as well. Visual Studio .NET provides a development environment that offers IntelliSense, debugging facilities, and other user-friendly capabilities that come with a robust IDE. The .NET Framework and the development environment are discussed in more detail in Chapter 36, "SQL Server and the .NET Framework."

The following basic steps are required to create a CLR trigger:

1. Create the CLR class. You code the CLR class module with references to the namespaces that are required to compile CLR database objects.

2. Compile the CLR class into an assembly or a DDL file, using the appropriate language compiler.

3. Load the CLR assembly into SQL Server so that it can be referenced.

4. Create the CLR trigger that references the loaded assembly.

The following listings provide examples of each of these steps.

> **NOTE**
>
> The CLR must be enabled on your server before you can add CLR components. The CLR option is disabled by default. To enable the CLR, you use the `sp_configure 'clr enabled', 1` T-SQL command followed by the `RECONFIGURE` command. You can also enable CLR integration by using SQL Server 2005 Surface Area Configuration then choosing the Surface Area Configuration for Features and selecting the Enable CLR Integration option.

Listing 25.19 contains C# code that can be used for the first step: creating the CLR class. It is a simple example that selects rows from the `inserted` table.

LISTING 25.19   A CLR Trigger Class Created with C#

```csharp
using System;
using System.Data;
using System.Data.Sql;
using Microsoft.SqlServer.Server;
using System.Data.SqlClient;
using System.Data.SqlTypes;
using System.Xml;
using System.Text.RegularExpressions;

public class clrtriggertest
{
    public static void showinserted()
    {
        SqlTriggerContext triggContext = SqlContext.TriggerContext;
        SqlConnection conn = new SqlConnection ("context connection = true");
        conn.Open();
        SqlCommand sqlComm = conn.CreateCommand();
        SqlPipe sqlP = SqlContext.Pipe;
        SqlDataReader dr;
                sqlComm.CommandText = "SELECT pub_id, pub_name from inserted";
                dr = sqlComm.ExecuteReader();
                while (dr.Read())
                        sqlP.Send((string)dr[0] + ", " + (string)dr[1]);

    }
}
```

The CLR class in Listing 25.19 needs to be compiled in order to be used by SQL Server. The compiler for C# is located in the .NET Framework path, which is `C:\WINDOWS\Microsoft.NET\Framework\`*version* by default. The last part of the path, *version*, is the number of the latest version installed on your machine. For simplicity's sake, you can add the full .NET Framework path to your path variable in the Advanced tab of your System Properties dialog. If you add the .NET Framework path to your path variable then you will be able to run the executable for the compiler without navigating to that location.

You can save the code from Listing 25.19 in a text file named `clrtriggertesting.cs`. Then you can open a command prompt window and navigate to the folder where you saved the `clrtriggertesting.cs` file. The command shown in Listing 25.20 compiles the `clrtriggertesting.cs` file into `clrtriggertesting.dll`. This command can be run from any directory if you have added the .NET Framework path to your path variable. Without the additional path entry you will need to naviagate to the .NET Framework path prior to executing the command.

LISTING 25.20   A CLR Trigger Class Compilation

```
csc /target:library clrtriggertesting.cs
```

After you have compiled `clrtriggertesting.dll`, you need to load the assembly into SQL Server. Listing 25.21 shows the T-SQL command you can execute to create the assembly for `clrtriggertesting.dll`.

LISTING 25.21   Using CREATE ASSEMBLY in SQL Server

```
CREATE ASSEMBLY triggertesting
 from 'c:\clrtrigger\clrtriggertesting.dll'
WITH PERMISSION_SET = SAFE
```

The final step is to create the trigger that references the assembly. Listing 25.22 shows the T-SQL commands to add a trigger on the `publishers` table in the `BigPubs2005` database.

LISTING 25.22   Creating a CLR Trigger

```
CREATE TRIGGER tri_publishers_clr
ON publishers
FOR INSERT
AS
EXTERNAL NAME triggertesting.clrtriggertest.showinserted
```

Listing 25.23 contains an `INSERT` statement to the `publishers` table that fires the newly created CLR trigger.

LISTING 25.23   Using an INSERT Statement to Fire a CLR Trigger

```
INSERT publishers
 (pub_id, pub_name)
 values ('9922','Sams Publishing')
```

The trigger simply echoes the contents of the inserted table. The output from the trigger based on the insertion in Listing 25.23 is as follows:

```
9922, Sams Publishing
```

The tri_publishers trigger demonstrates the basic steps for creating a CLR trigger. The true power of CLR triggers lies in adding complex calculations and things of this nature that the CLR can do much more efficiently than T-SQL.

> **NOTE**
>
> For more detailed information and examples of CLR triggers, see Chapter 36.

Using Nested Triggers

Triggers can be nested up to 32 levels. If a trigger changes a table on which another trigger exists, the second trigger is fired and can then fire a third trigger, and so on.

If any trigger in the chain sets off an infinite loop, the nesting level is exceeded, the trigger is canceled, and the transaction is rolled back.

The following error message is returned if the nesting level is exceeded:

```
Server: Msg 217, Level 16, State 1, Procedure ttt2, Line 2
Maximum stored procedure nesting level exceeded (limit 32).
```

You can disable nested triggers by setting the nested triggers option of sp_configure to 0 (off):

```
EXEC sp_configure 'nested triggers', 0
GO
RECONFIGURE WITH OVERRIDE
GO
```

After the nested triggers option has been turned off, the only triggers to fire are those that are part of the original data modification: the top-level triggers. If updates to other tables are made via the top-level triggers, those updates are completed, but the triggers on those tables do not fire. For example, say you have an UPDATE trigger on the jobs table in the BigPubs2005 database and an UPDATE trigger on the employee table as well. The trigger on the jobs table updates the employee table. If an update is made to the jobs table, the jobs trigger fires and completes the updates on the employee table. However, the trigger on the employee table does not fire.

The default configuration is to allow nested triggers.

Using Recursive Triggers

Recursive triggers were introduced in SQL Server 7.0. If a trigger modifies the same table where the trigger was created, the trigger does not fire again unless the recursive triggers option is turned on. recursive triggers is a database option that is turned off by default.

The first command in the following example checks the setting of recursive triggers for the BigPubs2005 database, and the second sets recursive triggers to TRUE:

```
EXEC sp_dboption BigPubs2005, 'recursive triggers'

EXEC sp_dboption BigPubs2005, 'recursive triggers', TRUE
```

If you turn off nested triggers, recursive triggers are automatically disabled, regardless of how the database option is set. The maximum nesting level for recursive triggers is the same as for nested triggers: 32 levels.

You should use recursive triggers with care. It is easy to create an endless loop, as shown in Listing 25.24, which creates a recursive trigger on a new test table in the BigPubs2005 database.

LISTING 25.24   The Error Message Returned for an Endless Loop with Recursive Triggers

```
--The first statement is used to disable the previously created
--DDL trigger which would prevent any changes.
DISABLE TRIGGER ALL ON DATABASE
EXEC sp_configure 'nested triggers', 1
RECONFIGURE WITH OVERRIDE
EXEC sp_dboption BigPubs2005, 'recursive triggers', TRUE
CREATE TABLE rk_tr_test (id int IDENTITY)
GO
CREATE TRIGGER rk_tr ON rk_tr_test FOR INSERT
AS INSERT rk_tr_test DEFAULT VALUES
GO
INSERT rk_tr_test DEFAULT VALUES

Server: Msg 217, Level 16, State 1, Procedure rk_tr, Line 2
Maximum stored procedure nesting level exceeded (limit 32).
```

The recursion described thus far is known as *direct recursion*. Another type of recursion exists as well: indirect recursion. With *indirect recursion*, a table that has a trigger fires an update to another table, and that table, in turn, causes an update to happen to the original table on which the trigger fired. This causes the trigger on the original table to fire again.

With indirect recursion, setting the `recursive triggers` database setting to FALSE does not prevent the recursion from happening. The only way to prevent this type of recursion is to set the `nested triggers` setting to FALSE, which, in turn, prevents all recursion.

Summary

Triggers are one of the most powerful tools for ensuring the quality of the data in a database. The range of commands that can be executed from within triggers and their ability to automatically fire give them a distinct role in defining sound database solutions.

Chapter 26, "Transaction Management and the Transaction Log," takes a look at the methods for defining and managing transactions within SQL Server 2005.

25

Transaction Management and the Transaction Log

IN THIS CHAPTER

▶ What's New in Transaction Management

▶ What Is a Transaction?

▶ How SQL Server Manages Transactions

▶ Defining Transactions

▶ Transaction Logging and the Recovery Process

▶ Transactions and Batches

▶ Transactions and Stored Procedures

▶ Transactions and Triggers

▶ Transactions and Locking

▶ Coding Effective Transactions

▶ Long-Running Transactions

▶ Bound Connections

▶ Distributed Transactions

Transaction management is an important area in database programming. The transactions you construct and issue can have a huge impact on the performance of SQL Server and the consistency of your databases. This chapter takes a look at the methods for defining and managing transactions in SQL Server 2005.

What's New in Transaction Management

Not much has really changed in SQL Server 2005 related to transactions, transaction logging, and transaction management. However, there are a couple of new features.

One new feature is a new checkpoint duration option available for the CHECKPOINT statement: `checkpoint_duration` sets the desired duration for SQL Server 2005 to perform a checkpoint. When this parameter is omitted, SQL Server 2005 automatically adjusts the checkpoint duration to minimize the performance impact on database applications. Checkpoints and the new `checkpoint_duration` option are discussed in more detail later in this chapter, in the section "Transaction Logging and the Recovery Process."

SQL Server 2005 also introduces row-level versioning, also called snapshot isolation. Snapshot isolation allows for SQL Server to keep versions of data rows so that a user transaction sees a snapshot of the committed data as it existed at the start of the transaction rather than being blocked by locks held by current transactions. This feature is described in the "Transactions and Locking" section of this chapter.

What Is a Transaction?

A *transaction* is one or more SQL statements that must be completed as a whole or, in other words, as a single logical unit of work. Transactions provide a way of collecting and associating multiple actions into a single all-or-nothing multiple-operation action. All operations within the transaction must be fully completed or not performed at all.

Consider a bank transaction in which you move $1,000 from your checking account to your savings account. This transaction is, in fact, *two* operations: a decrement of your checking account and an increment of your savings account. Consider the impact on your finances if the bank's server went down after it completed the first step and never got to the second! By combining the two operations together, as a transaction, they either both succeed or both fail as a single, complete unit of work.

A transaction is a logical unit of work that has four special characteristics, known as the ACID properties:

- ▶ **Atomicity**—Associated modifications are an all-or-nothing proposition; either all are done or none are done.

- ▶ **Consistency**—After a transaction finishes, all data is in the state it should be in, all internal structures are correct, and everything accurately reflects the transaction that has occurred.

- ▶ **Isolation**—One transaction cannot interfere with the processes of another transaction.

- ▶ **Durability**—After the transaction has finished, all changes made are permanent.

The responsibility for enforcing the ACID properties of a transaction is split between T-SQL developers and SQL Server. The developers are responsible for ensuring that the modifications are correctly collected together and that the data is going to be left in a consistent state that corresponds with the actions being taken. SQL Server ensures that the transaction is isolated and durable, undertakes the atomicity requested, and ensures the consistency of the final data structures. The transaction log of each database provides the durability for the transaction. As you will see in this chapter, you have some control over how SQL Server handles some of these properties.

How SQL Server Manages Transactions

SQL Server uses the database's transaction log to record the modifications that occur within the database. Each log record is labeled with a unique log sequence number (LSN), and all log entries that are part of the same transaction are linked together so that they can be easily located if the transaction needs to be undone or redone. The primary responsibility of logging is to ensure transaction durability—either ensuring that the completed changes make it to the physical database files or ensuring that any unfinished transactions are rolled back in the event of an error or a server failure.

What is logged? Obviously, the start and end of a transaction are logged, but SQL Server also logs the actual data modification, page allocations and deallocations, and changes to indexes. SQL Server keeps track of a number of pieces of information, all with the aim of ensuring the ACID properties of the transaction.

After a transaction has been committed, it cannot be rolled back. The only way to undo a committed transaction is to write another transaction to reverse the changes made. A transaction can be rolled back before it is committed, however.

SQL Server provides transaction management for all users, using the following components:

▶ Transaction-control statements to define the logical units of work

▶ A write-ahead transaction log

▶ An automatic recovery process

▶ Data-locking mechanisms to ensure consistency and transaction isolation

Defining Transactions

You can carry out transaction processing with Microsoft SQL Server in three ways:

▶ **AutoCommit**—Every T-SQL statement is its own transaction and automatically commits when it finishes. This is the default mode in which SQL Server operates.

▶ **Explicit**—This approach provides programmatic control of the transaction, using the BEGIN TRAN and COMMIT/ROLLBACK TRAN/WORK commands.

▶ **Implicit**—In this mode, when you issue certain SQL commands, SQL Server automatically starts a transaction. You must finish the transaction by explicitly issuing the COMMIT/ROLLBACK TRAN/WORK commands.

Each of these methods is discussed in the following sections.

> **NOTE**
>
> The terms for explicit and implicit transactions can be somewhat confusing. The way to keep them straight is to think of how a multistatement transaction is initiated, not how it is completed. AutoCommit transactions are in a separate category because they are both implicitly started and committed.
>
> Implicit and explicit transactions have to be explicitly ended, but explicit transactions must also be explicitly started with the BEGIN TRAN statement, whereas no BEGIN TRAN is necessary to start a multistatement transaction when in implicit transaction mode.

AutoCommit Transactions

AutoCommit is the default transaction mode for SQL Server. Each individual T-SQL command automatically commits or rolls back its work at the end of its execution. Each SQL statement is considered to be its own transaction, with begin and end control points implied. The following is an example:

```
[implied begin transaction]
UPDATE account
   SET balance = balance + 1000
   WHERE account_no = "123456789"
[implied commit or rollback transaction]
```

If an error is present in the execution of the statement, the action is undone (that is, rolled back); if no errors occur, the action is completed, and the changes are saved.

Now let's consider the banking transaction mentioned at the beginning of this chapter that involved moving money from a savings account to a checking account. Assume that it is written as follows in T-SQL:

```
declare @checking_account char(10),
        @savings_account char(10)
select @checking_account = '0003456321',
       @savings_account = '0003456322'
update account
   set balance = balance - $1000
   where account_number = @checking_account
update savings_account
   set balance = balance + $1000
   where account_number = @savings_account
```

What would happen if an error occurred in updating the savings account? With AutoCommit, each statement is implicitly committed after it completes successfully, so the update for the checking account has already been committed. You would have no way of rolling it back except to write another separate update to add the $1,000 back to the account. If the system crashed during the updates, how would you know which updates, if any, completed, and whether you need to undo any of the changes because the subsequent commands were not executed? You would need some way to group the two commands together as a single logical unit of work so they can complete or fail as a whole. SQL Server provides transaction control statements that allow you to explicitly create multistatement user-defined transactions.

Explicit User-Defined Transactions

To have complete control of a transaction and define logical units of work that consist of multiple data modifications, you need to write explicit user-defined transactions. Any SQL Server user can make use of the transaction control statements; no special privileges are required.

To start a multistatement transaction, use the `BEGIN TRAN` command, which optionally takes a transaction name:

```
BEGIN TRAN[SACTION] [transaction_name [WITH MARK ['description']]]
```

The transaction name is essentially meaningless as far as transaction management is concerned, and if transactions are nested (which is discussed later in this chapter), the name is useful only for the outermost `BEGIN TRAN` statement. Rolling back to any other name, besides a savepoint name, generates an error message similar to the following error message and does not roll back the transaction:

```
Msg 6401, Level 16, State 1, Line 5
Cannot roll back t2. No transaction or savepoint of that name was found.
```

Naming transactions is really useful only when you use the `WITH MARK` option. If the `WITH MARK` option is specified, a transaction name must be specified. `WITH MARK` allows for restoring a transaction log backup to a named mark in the transaction log. (For more information on restoring database and log backups, see Chapter 11, "Database Backup and Restore.") This option allows you to restore a database to a known state or to recover a set of related databases to a consistent state. However, you need to be aware that `BEGIN TRAN` records are written to the log only if an actual data modification occurs within the transaction.

You complete an explicit transaction by issuing either a `COMMIT TRAN` or `COMMIT [WORK]` statement, and you can undo an explicit transaction by using either `ROLLBACK TRAN` or `ROLLBACK [WORK]`. The syntax of these commands is as follows:

```
COMMIT [TRAN[SACTION] [transaction_name]] ¦ [WORK]
```

```
ROLLBACK [TRAN[SACTION] [transaction_name ¦ savepointname]] ¦ [WORK]
```

The `COMMIT` statement marks the successful conclusion of a transaction. This statement can be coded as `COMMIT`, `COMMIT WORK`, or `COMMIT TRAN`. The only difference is that the first two versions are SQL-92 ANSI compliant.

The `ROLLBACK` statement unconditionally undoes all work done within the transaction. This statement can also be coded as `ROLLBACK`, `ROLLBACK WORK`, or `ROLLBACK TRAN`. The first two commands are ANSI-92 SQL compliant and do not accept user-defined transaction names. `ROLLBACK TRAN` is required if you want to roll back to a savepoint within a transaction.

The following is an example of how you could code the previously mentioned banking example as a single transaction in SQL Server:

```
declare @checking_account char(10),
        @savings_account char(10)
select @checking_account = '0003456321',
       @savings_account = '0003456322'
begin tran
```

```
update account
   set balance = balance - $1000
   where account_number = @checking_account
if @@error != 0
begin
    rollback tran
    return
end
update savings_account
   set balance = balance + $1000
   where account_number = @savings_account
if @@error != 0
begin
    rollback tran
    return
end
commit tran
```

Certain commands cannot be specified within a user-defined transaction, primarily because they cannot be effectively rolled back in the event of a failure. In most cases, because of their long-running nature, you would not want them to be specified within a transaction anyway. The following are the commands you cannot specify in a user-defined transaction:

```
ALTER DATABASE

BACKUP DATABASE

BACKUP LOG

CREATE DATABASE

DROP DATABASE

RESTORE DATABASE

RECONFIGURE

RESTORE LOG

UPDATE STATISTICS
```

Savepoints

A savepoint allows you to set a marker in a transaction that you can roll back to undo a portion of the transaction but commit the remainder of the transaction. The syntax is as follows:

```
SAVE TRAN[SACTION] savepointname
```

Savepoints are not ANSI-SQL 92 compliant, so you must use the SQL Server–specific transaction management commands that allow you to specify a named point within the transaction and then recover back to it.

The following code illustrates the differences between the two types of syntax when using the SAVE TRAN command:

SQL-92 Syntax	SQL Server–Specific Syntax
BEGIN TRAN mywork	BEGIN TRAN mywork
UPDATE table1...	UPDATE table1...
SAVE TRAN savepoint1	SAVE TRAN savepoint1
INSERT INTO table2...	INSERT INTO table2...
DELETE table3...	DELETE table3...
IF @@error = -1	IF @@error = -1
ROLLBACK WORK	ROLLBACK TRAN savepoint1
COMMIT WORK	COMMIT TRAN

Note the difference between the SQL-92 syntax on the left and the SQL Server–specific syntax on the right. In the SQL-92 syntax, when you reach the ROLLBACK WORK command, the *entire* transaction is undone rather than undoing only to the point marked by the savepoint. You have to use the SQL Server–specific ROLLBACK TRAN command and specify the savepoint name to roll back the work to the savepoint and still be able to subsequently roll back or commit the rest of the transaction.

Nested Transactions

As a rule, you can't have more than one active transaction per user session within SQL Server. However, suppose you have a SQL batch that issues a BEGIN TRAN statement and then subsequently invokes a stored procedure, which also issues a BEGIN TRAN statement. Because you can only have one transaction active, what does the BEGIN TRAN inside the stored procedure accomplish? In SQL Server, this leads to an interesting anomaly referred to as *nested transactions*.

To determine whether transactions are open and how deep they are nested within a connection, you can use the global function @@trancount. If no transaction is active, the transaction nesting level is 0. As a transaction is initiated, the transaction nesting level is incremented; as a transaction completes, the transaction nesting is decremented. The overall transaction remains open and can be entirely rolled back until the transaction nesting level returns to 0.

You can use the @@trancount function to monitor the current status of a transaction. For example, what would SQL Server do when encountering the following transaction (which produces an error because of the reference constraint on the titles table)?

```
BEGIN TRAN
    DELETE FROM publishers
    WHERE pub_id = '0736'
go
```

26

```
Msg 547, Level 16, State 0, Line 2
The DELETE statement conflicted with the REFERENCE constraint
 "FK__pub_info__pub_id__2BDE8E15". The conflict occurred in database
 "bigpubs2005", table "dbo.pub_info", column 'pub_id'.
The statement has been terminated.
```

Is the transaction still active? You can find out by using the @@trancount function:

```
select @@trancount
go


-----------
          1
```

In this case, @@trancount returns a value of 1, which indicates that the transaction is still open and in progress. This means that you can still issue commands within the transaction and commit the changes, or you can roll back the transaction. Also, if you were to log out of the user session from SQL Server before the transaction nesting level reached 0, SQL Server would automatically roll back the transaction.

Although nothing prevents you from coding a BEGIN TRAN within another BEGIN TRAN, doing so has no real benefit, even though such cases might occur. However, if you nest transactions in this manner, you must execute a COMMIT statement for each BEGIN TRAN statement issued. This is because SQL Server modifies the @@trancount with each transaction statement and considers the transaction finished only when the transaction nesting level returns to 0. Table 26.1 shows the effects that transaction control statements have on @@trancount.

TABLE 26.1   Transaction Statements' Effects on @@trancount

Statement	Effect on @@trancount
BEGIN TRAN	+1
COMMIT	−1
ROLLBACK	Sets to 0
SAVE TRAN savepoint	No effect
ROLLBACK TRAN savepoint	No effect

Following is a summary of how transactional control relates to the values reported by @@trancount:

▶ When you log in to SQL Server, the value of @@trancount for your session is initially 0.

▶ Each time you execute begin transaction, SQL Server increments @@trancount.

▶ Each time you execute commit transaction, SQL Server decrements @@trancount.

▶ Actual work is committed only when @@trancount reaches 0 again.

▶ When you execute ROLLBACK TRANSACTION, the transaction is canceled and @@trancount returns to 0. Notice that ROLLBACK TRANSACTION cuts straight through any number of nested transactions, canceling the overall main transaction. This means that you need to be careful how you write code that contains a ROLLBACK statement. You need to be sure to check for the return status up through all levels and exit accordingly so you don't continue executing data modifications that were meant to be part of the larger overall transaction.

▶ Setting savepoints and rolling back to a savepoint do not affect @@trancount or transaction nesting in any way.

▶ If a user connection is lost for any reason when @@trancount is greater than 0, any pending work for that connection is automatically rolled back. SQL Server requires that multistatement transactions be explicitly committed.

▶ Because the BEGIN TRAN statement increments @@trancount, each BEGIN TRAN statement must be paired with a COMMIT for the transaction to complete successfully.

Let's take a look at some sample code to show the values of @@trancount as the transaction progresses. This first example is a simple explicit transaction with a nested BEGIN TRAN:

SQL Statement	@@trancount Value
SELECT "Starting....."	0
BEGIN TRAN	1
DELETE FROM table1	1
BEGIN TRAN	2
INSERT INTO table2	2
COMMIT	1
UPDATE table3	1
COMMIT	0

Transactions are nested *syntactically only.* The only commit tran statement that has an impact on real data is the last one, the statement that returns @@trancount to 0. That statement fully commits the work done by the initial transaction and the nested transactions. Until that final COMMIT TRAN is encountered, all the work can be rolled back with a ROLLBACK statement.

As a general rule, if a transaction is already active, you shouldn't issue another BEGIN TRAN statement. You should check the value of @@trancount to determine whether a transaction is already active. If you want to be able to roll back the work performed within a nested transaction without rolling back the entire transaction, you can set a savepoint instead of issuing a BEGIN TRAN statement. Later in this chapter, you will see an example of how to check @@trancount within a stored procedure to determine whether the stored procedure is being invoked within a transaction and then issue a BEGIN TRAN or SAVE TRAN, as appropriate.

Implicit Transactions

AutoCommit transactions and explicit user-defined transactions in SQL Server are not ANSI-92 SQL compliant. ANSI-92 SQL standard states that any data retrieval or modification statement issued should implicitly begin a multistatement transaction that remains in effect until an explicit ROLLBACK or COMMIT statement is issued.

To enable implicit transactions for a connection, you need to turn on the IMPLICIT_TRANSACTIONS session setting, whose syntax is as follows:

```
SET IMPLICIT_TRANSACTIONS {ON ¦ OFF}
```

After this option is turned on, transactions are implicitly started, if they are not already in progress, whenever any of the following commands are executed:

```
ALTER TABLE
CREATE
DELETE
DROP
FETCH
GRANT
INSERT
OPEN
REVOKE
SELECT
TRUNCATE TABLE
UPDATE
```

Note that neither the ALTER VIEW nor ALTER PROCEDURE statement starts an implicit transaction.

You must explicitly complete implicit transactions by issuing a COMMIT or ROLLBACK; a new transaction is started again on the execution of any of the preceding commands. If you plan to use implicit transactions, the main thing to be aware of is that locks are held until you explicitly commit the transaction. This can cause problems with concurrency and the ability of the system to truncate the transaction log.

Even when using implicit transactions, you can still issue the BEGIN TRAN statement and create transaction nesting. In the following example, IMPLICIT_TRANSACTIONS ON has been turned on to see the effect this has on the value of @@trancount.

SQL Statements	@@trancount Value
SET IMPLICIT_TRANSACTIONS ON	0
go	0
INSERT INTO table1	1
UPDATE table2	1
COMMIT	0
go	
SELECT * FROM table1	1
BEGIN TRAN	2
DELETE FROM table1	2
COMMIT	1
go	
DROP TABLE table1	1
COMMIT	0

As you can see in this example, if a BEGIN TRAN is issued while a transaction is still active, transaction nesting occurs, and a second COMMIT is required to finish the transaction. The main difference between this example and the preceding one is that here, a BEGIN TRAN was *not* required to start the transaction. The first INSERT statement initiated the transaction. When you are running in implicit transaction mode, you don't need to issue a BEGIN TRAN statement; in fact, you should avoid it to prevent transaction nesting and the need for multiple commits.

The following is an example of the previous banking transaction, using implicit transactions:

```
set implicit_transactions on
go

declare @checking_account char(10),
        @savings_account char(10)
select @checking_account = '0003456321',
       @savings_account = '0003456322'
update account
   set balance = balance - $1000
   where account_number = @checking_account
if @@error != 0
begin
    rollback
    return
end
update savings_account
   set balance = balance + $1000
```

26

```
     where account_number = @savings_account
if @@error != 0
begin
     rollback
     return
end
commit
```

This example is nearly identical to the explicit transaction example except for the lack of a BEGIN TRAN statement. In addition, when in implicit transaction mode, you cannot roll back to a named transaction because no name is assigned when the transaction is invoked implicitly. You can, however, still set savepoints and roll back to savepoints to partially roll back work within an implicit transaction.

> **TIP**
>
> If you need to know within your SQL code whether implicit transactions are enabled so you can avoid issuing explicit BEGIN TRAN statements, you can check the @@options function. @@options returns a bitmap that indicates which session-level options are enabled for the current session. If bit 2 is on, implicit transactions are enabled. The following code snippet can be used in stored procedures or SQL batches to check this value and decide whether to issue a BEGIN TRAN statement:
>
> ```
> if @@options & 2 != 2 -- if bit 2 is not turned on
>    BEGIN TRAN --a begin tran can be issued since implicit transactions
> ➥are off
>    ...
> ```

Implicit Transactions Versus Explicit Transactions

When would you want to use implicit transactions versus explicit transactions? If you are porting an application from another database environment, such as DB2 or Oracle, that uses implicit transactions, that application will convert over to SQL Server more easily and with fewer code changes if you run in implicit transaction mode. Also, if the application you are developing needs to be ANSI compliant and run across multiple database platforms with minimal code changes, you might want to use implicit transactions.

If you use implicit transactions in your applications, you need to be sure to issue COMMIT statements as frequently as possible to prevent leaving transactions open and holding locks for an extended period of time, which can have an adverse impact on concurrency and overall system performance.

If an application is only going to be hosted on SQL Server, it is recommended that you use AutoCommit and explicit transactions so that changes are committed as quickly as possible and so that only those logical units of work that are explicitly defined contain multiple commands within a transaction.

Transaction Logging and the Recovery Process

Every SQL Server database has its own transaction log that keeps a record of all data modifications in a database (for example, insert, update, delete), in the order in which they occur. This information is stored in one or more log files associated with the database. The information stored in these log files cannot be modified or viewed effectively by any user process.

SQL Server uses a write-ahead log. The buffer manager guarantees that changes are written to the transaction log before the changes are written to the database. The buffer manager also ensures that the log pages are written out in sequence so that transactions can be recovered properly in the event of a system crash.

The following is an overview of the sequence of events that occurs when a transaction modifies data:

1. Writes a BEGIN TRAN record to the transaction log in buffer memory.

2. Writes data modification information to transaction log pages in buffer memory.

3. Writes data modifications to the database in buffer memory.

4. Writes a COMMIT TRAN record to the transaction log in buffer memory.

5. Writes transaction log records to the transaction log file(s) on disk.

6. Sends a COMMIT acknowledgement to the client process.

The end of a typical transaction is indicated by a COMMIT record in the transaction log. The presence of the COMMIT record indicates that the transaction must be reflected in the database or be redone, if necessary. A transaction that is aborted during processing by an explicit rollback or a system error will have its changes automatically undone.

Notice that the data records are not written to disk when a COMMIT occurs. This is done to minimize disk I/O. All log writes are done synchronously to ensure that the log records are physically written to disk and in the proper sequence. Because all modifications to the data can be recovered from the transaction log, it is not critical that data changes be written to disk right away. Even in the event of a system crash or power failure, the data can be recovered from the log if it hasn't been written to the database.

SQL Server ensures that the log records are written before the affected data pages by recording the log sequence number (LSN) for the log record making the change on the modified data page(s). Modified, or "dirty," data pages can be written to disk only when the LSN recorded on the data page is less than the LSN of the last log page written to the transaction log.

When and how are the data changes written to disk? Obviously, they must be written out at some time or it could take an exceedingly long time for SQL Server to start up if it had to redo all the transactions contained in the transaction log. Also, how does SQL Server know during recovery which transactions to reapply, or roll forward, and which transactions to undo, or roll back? The following section looks at the mechanisms involved in the recovery process.

The Checkpoint Process

During recovery, SQL Server examines the transaction log for each database and verifies whether the changes reflected in the log are also reflected in the database. In addition, it examines the log to determine whether any data changes were written to the data that were caused by a transaction that didn't complete before the system failure.

As discussed earlier, a COMMIT writes the log records for a transaction to the transaction log (see Figure 26.1). Dirty data pages are written out either by the Lazy Writer process or the checkpoint process. The Lazy Writer process runs periodically to check whether the number of free buffers has fallen below a certain threshold, reclaims any unused pages, and writes out any dirty pages that haven't been referenced recently.

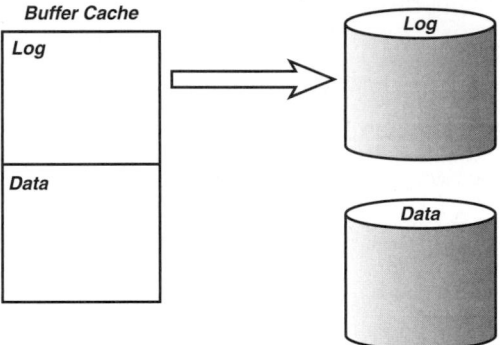

FIGURE 26.1   A commit writes all "dirty" log pages from cache to disk.

The checkpoint process also scans the buffer cache periodically and writes all dirty log pages and dirty data pages to disk (see Figure 26.2). The purpose of the checkpoint is to sync up the data stored on disk with the changes recorded in the transaction log. Typically, the checkpoint process finds little work to do because most dirty pages have been written out previously by the worker threads or Lazy Writer process.

SQL Server performs the following steps during a checkpoint:

1. Writes a record to the log file to record the start of the checkpoint.

2. Stores information recorded for the checkpoint in a chain of checkpoint log records.

3. Records the minimum recovery LSN (MinLSN), which is the first log image that must be present for a successful databasewide rollback. The MinLSN is either the LSN of the start of the checkpoint, the LSN of the oldest active transaction, or the LSN of the oldest transaction marked for replication that hasn't yet been replicated to all subscribers.

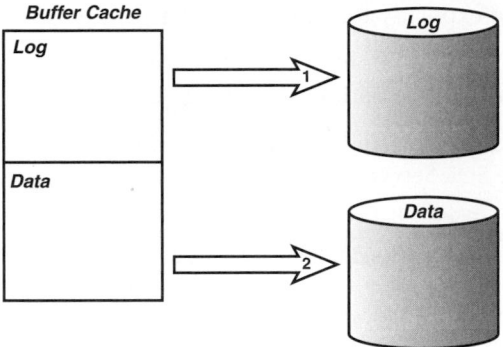

FIGURE 26.2   A checkpoint writes log pages from cache to disk, and then writes all "dirty" data pages.

4. Writes a list of all outstanding, active transactions to the checkpoint records.

5. Writes all modified log pages to the transaction log on disk.

6. Writes all dirty data pages to disk. (Data pages that have not been modified are not written back to disk to save I/O.)

7. Writes a record to the log file, indicating the end of the checkpoint.

8. Writes the LSN of the start of the checkpoint log records to the database boot page. (This is so SQL Server can find the last checkpoint in the log during recovery.)

Figure 26.3 shows a simplified version of the contents of a transaction log after a checkpoint. (For simplicity, the checkpoint records are reflected as a single log entry.)

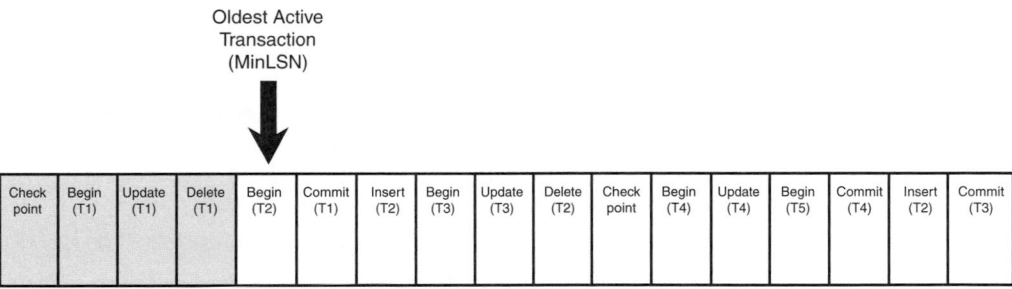

FIGURE 26.3   A simplified view of the end of the transaction log with various completed and active transactions, as well as the last checkpoint.

The primary purpose of a checkpoint is to reduce the amount of work the server needs to do at recovery time to redo or undo database changes. A checkpoint can occur under the following circumstances:

▶ When a checkpoint statement is executed explicitly for the current database.

▶ When ALTER DATABASE is used to change a database option. ALTER DATABASE automatically checkpoints the database when database options are changed.

▶ When an instance of SQL Server is shut down gracefully either due to the execution of the SHUTDOWN statement or because the SQL Server service was stopped.

NOTE

The SHUTDOWN WITH NOWAIT statement does not perform what is considered a graceful shutdown of SQL Server. This statement forces a shutdown of SQL Server without waiting for current transactions to complete and *without* executing a checkpoint of each database. This may cause the subsequent restart of SQL Server to take a longer time to recover the databases on the server.

▶ When SQL Server periodically generates automatic checkpoints in each database to reduce the amount of time the instance would take to recover the database.

Automatic Checkpoints

The frequency of automatic checkpoints is determined by the setting of the recovery interval for SQL Server. However, the decision to perform a checkpoint is based on the number of records in the log, not a specific period of time. The time interval between the occurrence of automatic checkpoints can be highly variable. If few modifications are made to the database, the time interval between automatic checkpoints could be quite long. Conversely, automatic checkpoints can occur quite frequently if the update activity on a database is high.

The recovery interval does not state how often automatic checkpoints should occur. The recovery interval is actually related to an estimate of the amount of time it would take SQL Server to recover the database by applying the number of transactions recorded since the last checkpoint. By default, the recovery interval is set to 0, which means SQL Server determines the appropriate recovery interval for each database. It is recommended that you keep this setting at the default value unless you notice that checkpoints are occurring too frequently and are impairing performance. You should try increasing the value in small increments until you find one that works well. You need to be aware that if you set the recovery interval higher, fewer checkpoints will occur, and the database will likely take longer to recover following a system crash.

If the database is using either the full or bulk-logged recovery model, an automatic checkpoint occurs whenever the number of log records reaches the number that SQL Server estimates it can process within the time specified by the recovery interval option.

If the database is using the simple recovery model, an automatic checkpoint occurs whenever the number of log records reaches the number that SQL Server estimates it can process during the time specified by the recovery interval option or the log becomes 70%

full and the database is in log truncate mode. A database is considered to be in log truncate mode when the database is using the simple recovery model and one of the following events has occurred since the last full backup of the database:

▶ A minimally logged operation is performed in the database, such as a minimally logged bulk copy operation or a minimally logged WRITETEXT statement.

▶ An ALTER DATABASE statement is executed that adds or deletes a file in the database.

▶ A BACKUP LOG statement referencing the database is executed with either the NO_LOG or TRUNCATE_ONLY option.

When a database is configured to use the simple recovery model, the automatic checkpoint also truncates the unused portion of the transaction log prior to the oldest active transaction.

Manual Checkpoints

In addition to automatic checkpoints, a checkpoint can be explicitly initiated by members of the sysadmin fixed server role or the db_owner or db_backupoperator fixed database roles. The syntax for the CHECKPOINT command is as follows:

```
CHECKPOINT [ checkpoint_duration ]
```

To minimize the performance impact on other applications, SQL Server 2005 by default adjusts the frequency of the writes that a checkpoint operation performs. SQL Server uses this strategy for automatic checkpoints and for any CHECKPOINT statement that does not specify the *checkpoint_duration* value.

You can use the *checkpoint_duration* option to request the amount of time, in seconds, for the checkpoint to complete. When *checkpoint_duration* is specified, SQL Server attempts to perform the checkpoint within the requested duration. The performance impact of using *checkpoint_duration* depends on the number of dirty pages, the activity on the system, and the actual duration specified. For example, if the checkpoint would normally complete in 120 seconds, specifying a *checkpoint_duration* of 60 seconds causes SQL Server to devote more resources to the checkpoint than would be assigned by default in order to complete the checkpoint in half the time. In contrast, specifying a *checkpoint_duration* of 240 seconds causes SQL Server to assign fewer resources than would be assigned by default. In other words, a short *checkpoint_duration* increases the resources devoted to the checkpoint, and a longer *checkpoint_duration* reduces the resources devoted to the checkpoint.

Regardless of the checkpoint duration specified, SQL Server always attempts to complete a checkpoint when possible. In some cases, a checkpoint may complete sooner than the specified duration, and at times it may run longer than the specified duration.

The Recovery Process

When SQL Server is started, it verifies that completed transactions recorded in the log are reflected in the data and that incomplete transactions whose changes are reflected in the

26

data are rolled back out of the database. This is the recovery process. Recovery is an auto-matic process performed on each database during SQL Server startup. Recovery must be completed before the database is made available for use.

The recovery process guarantees that all completed transactions recorded in the transac-tion log are reflected in the data and all incomplete transactions reflected in the data are rolled back. During recovery, SQL Server looks for the last checkpoint record in the log. Only the changes that occurred or were still open since the last checkpoint need to be examined to determine the need for any transactions to be redone (that is, rolled forward) or undone (that is, rolled back). After all the changes are rolled forward or rolled back, as necessary, the database is checkpointed, and recovery is complete.

The recovery algorithm has three phases that are centered around the last checkpoint record in the transaction log, as shown in Figure 26.4.

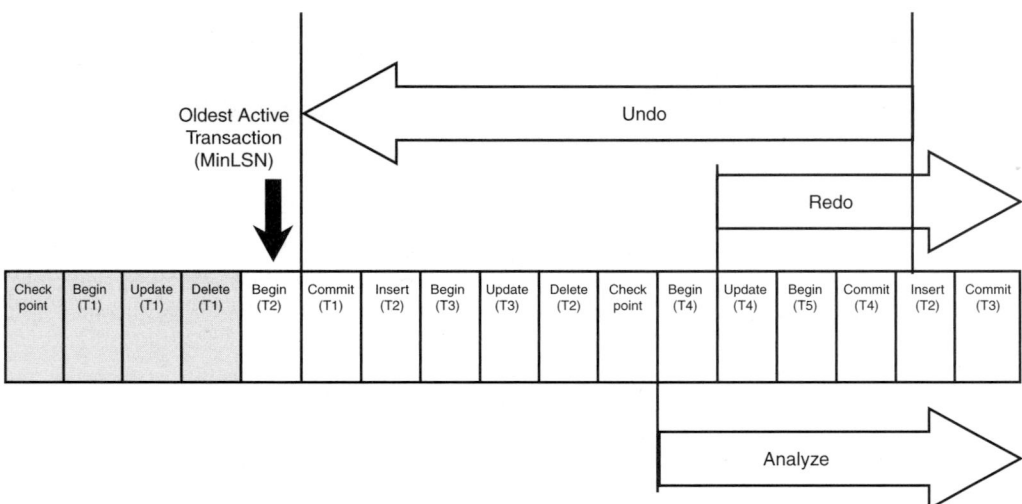

FIGURE 26.4   The phases of the recovery process.

These phases are described as follows:

1. **Analysis phase**—SQL Server reads forward from the last checkpoint record in the transaction log. This pass identifies a list of pages (the dirty page table [DPT]) that might have been dirty at the time of the system crash or when SQL Server was shut down, as well as a list of the uncommitted transactions at the time of the crash.

2. **Redo (roll-forward) phase**—During this phase, SQL Server rolls forward all the committed transactions recorded in the log since the last checkpoint. This phase returns the database to the state it was in at the time of the crash. The starting point for the redo pass is the LSN of the oldest committed transaction within the DPT, so that only changes that were not previously checkpointed (only the committed dirty pages) are reapplied.

3. **Undo (rollback) phase**—This phase moves backward from the end of the log to the oldest active transaction at the time of the system crash or shutdown. All transactions that were not committed at the time of the crash but that had pages written to the database are undone so that none of their changes are actually reflected in the database.

Now let's examine the transactions in the log in Figure 26.4 and determine how they will be handled during the recovery process:

▶ Transaction T1 is started and committed prior to the last checkpoint. No recovery is necessary.

▶ Transaction T2 started before the last checkpoint but had not completed at the time of the system crash. The changes written out by the checkpoint process for this transaction have to be rolled back.

▶ Transaction T3 started before the last checkpoint was issued and committed after that checkpoint but prior to the system crash. The changes made to the data after the checkpoint need to be rolled forward.

▶ Transaction T4 started and committed after the last checkpoint. This entire transaction needs to be rolled forward.

▶ Transaction T5 started after the last checkpoint, but no changes to the data were recorded in the log, so no data changes were written to the data. (Remember that changes must be written to the log before they can be written to the data.) No undo action is required for this transaction.

In a nutshell, this type of analysis is pretty much the same analysis the recovery process would do. To identify the number of transactions rolled forward or rolled back during recovery, you can examine the SQL Server error log and look at the recovery startup messages for each database. The following is a sample fragment of the recovery messages you might see in the SQL Server error log:

```
2006-08-05 23:49:42.37 spid9s      Clearing tempdb database.
2006-08-05 23:49:43.35 spid12s     Starting up database 'msdb'.
2006-08-05 23:49:43.35 spid13s     Starting up database 'BigPubs2005'.
2006-08-05 23:49:43.37 spid15s     Starting up database 'AdventureWorksDW'.
2006-08-05 23:49:43.37 spid14s     Starting up database 'AdventureWorks'.
2006-08-05 23:49:44.07 spid12s     1 transactions rolled forward in database
 'msdb' (4). This is an informational message only. No user action is required.
2006-08-05 23:49:44.29 spid5s      0 transactions rolled back in database 'msdb'
 (4). This is an informational message only. No user action is required.
2006-08-05 23:49:44.29 spid5s      Recovery is writing a checkpoint in database
 'msdb' (4). This is an informational message only. No user action is required.
2006-08-05 23:49:44.54 spid14s     1 transactions rolled forward in database
 'AdventureWorks' (6). This is an informational message only. No user action is
 required.
```

26

```
2006-08-05 23:49:44.70 spid15s     1 transactions rolled forward in database
 'AdventureWorksDW' (7). This is an informational message only. No user action
 is required.
2006-08-05 23:49:44.79 spid5s      0 transactions rolled back in database
 'AdventureWorks' (6). This is an informational message only. No user action
 is required.
2006-08-05 23:49:44.79 spid5s      Recovery is writing a checkpoint in database
 'AdventureWorks' (6). This is an informational message only. No user action is
 required.
2006-08-05 23:49:44.93 spid12s     0 transactions rolled back in database
 'AdventureWorksDW' (7). This is an informational message only. No user action
 is required.
2006-08-05 23:49:44.93 spid12s     Recovery is writing a checkpoint in database
 'AdventureWorksDW' (7). This is an informational message only. No user action
 is required.
2006-08-05 23:49:45.29 spid14s     Starting up database 'bigpubs2005'.
2006-08-05 23:49:47.32 spid14s     1 transactions rolled forward in database
 'bigpubs2005' (10). This is an informational message only. No user action is
 required.
2006-08-05 23:49:47.79 spid5s      0 transactions rolled back in database
 'bigpubs2005' (10). This is an informational message only. No user action is
 required.
2006-08-05 23:49:47.79 spid5s      Recovery is writing a checkpoint in database
 'bigpubs2005' (10). This is an informational message only. No user action is
 required.
2006-08-05 23:49:47.85 spid9s      Starting up database 'tempdb'.
2006-08-05 23:49:52.96 spid5s      Recovery is complete. This is an informational
 message only. No user action is required.
```

Managing the Transaction Log

Each database in SQL Server has at least one transaction log file. The transaction log file contains the transaction log records for all changes made in that database. By default, transaction log files have the file extension .ldf.

A database can have several log files, and each log file can have a maximum size of 32TB. A log file cannot be part of a filegroup. No information other than transaction log records can be written to a log file.

Regardless of how many physical files have been defined for the transaction log, SQL Server treats it as one contiguous file. The transaction log for a database is actually managed as a set of virtual log files (VLFs). VLFs have no fixed size, and there is no fixed number of VLFs for a physical log file. The size and number of VLFs is not configurable. SQL Server determines the size of the VLFs dynamically, based on the total size of all the log files and the growth increment specified for the log. Figure 26.5 shows an example of a physical log file divided into multiple virtual log files.

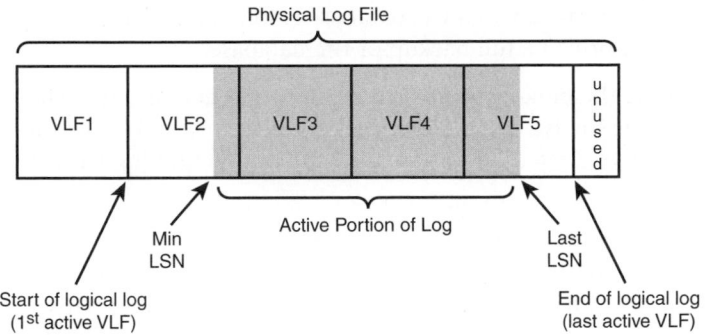

FIGURE 26.5   The structure of a physical log file showing VLFs.

The transaction log is essentially a wrap-around file. Initially, the logical log file begins at the start of the physical log file. As transactions are committed, new log records are added to the end of the logical log, and the logical log expands toward the end of the physical log. When the logical log reaches the end of the physical log file, SQL Server attempts to wrap around and start writing log records back at the beginning of the physical log file, as shown in Figure 26.6.

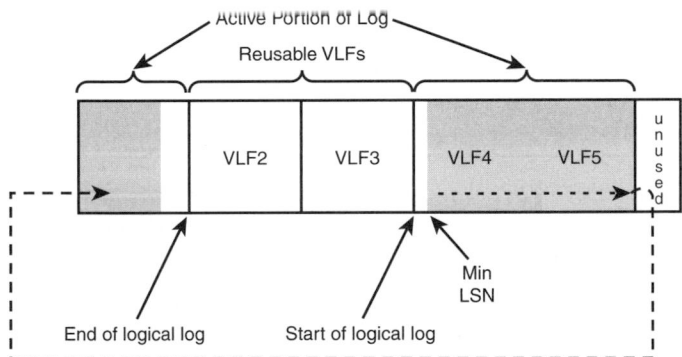

FIGURE 26.6   An example of the active portion of a log cycling around to reusable VLF at the beginning of log file.

However, SQL Server can reuse only the first VLF if it is no longer part of the logical log—that is, the VLF does not contain any active log records, and the contents of the inactive VLFs have been truncated. Log truncation frees any virtual logs whose records all appear in front of the MinLSN. The MinLSN is the log sequence number of the oldest log record that is required for a successful database recovery.

In environments where the log is not being maintained, SQL Server automatically truncates and reuses the space in the VLFs at the beginning of the log file as soon as it reaches the end of the log file. This can occur as long as the VLFs at the beginning of the log file do not contain the MinLSN. SQL Server assumes that the log is not being maintained when the log has been manually truncated, when the database is in simple recovery mode, or when you have never performed a full backup of the database.

If the database is configured to use the bulk-logged or full recovery models and the database has been backed up so that the log is being maintained, the reusable portion of the log prior to the MinLSN cannot be truncated or purged until the transaction log has actually been backed up.

If the first VLF cannot be reused because it contains the MinLSN or it hasn't been truncated yet, SQL Server needs to expand the log file. This is done by adding a new VLF to the end of the physical log (as long as the log file is still configured to grow automatically). SQL Server can then continue writing log records to the new VLF. However, if the log file is not configured to auto-grow, a 9002 error is generated, indicating that the log file is out of space.

Certain conditions can cause log records to remain active, preventing the MinLSN from moving out of the first VLF, which in turn prevents the VLFs at the beginning of the physical log file from being reused. Some of the conditions that can lead to the log space not being reused include, but are not limited to, the following:

- No checkpoint has taken place yet since the log was last truncated, and the log records are needed for database recovery.

- A database or log backup is in progress.

- A long-running transaction is still active.

- Database mirroring is paused. (For more information, see Chapter 16, "Database Mirroring.")

- The database is the primary database for transactional replication, and transactions relevant to the publications have not yet been delivered to the distribution database. (For more information on replication, see Chapter 15, "Replication.")

- A database snapshot is being created (for more information, see Chapter 27, "Database Snapshots").

If something is preventing the log from being truncated, SQL Server 2005 provides some new information in the system catalogs to determine what is preventing log truncation. This information is available in the log_reuse_wait_desc column of the sys.databases catalog view, which you can display by using a query similar to the following:

```
select name, log_reuse_wait_desc
   from sys.databases
   where name = db_name()
```

When a log file is configured to auto-grow and there is significant update activity against the database and the inactive portion of the transaction log is not being truncated frequently enough (or at all) to allow for the reuse of VLFs, the log file size can become excessive. This can lead to insufficient disk space in the file system that contains the log file. This can subsequently also lead to a 9002 out-of-space error if the log file needs to grow and there is not enough disk space available. At times, it may be necessary to shrink the log file to reduce its size.

Shrinking the Log File

After the log has been backed up and the active portion of the log has wrapped around to the beginning of the log file, the VLFs at the end of the physical log can be deleted from the log file, and the log file can be reduced in size.

When you shrink a log file, the space freed can only come from the end of the log file. The unit of size reduction is the size of the virtual log file. For example, if you have a 1GB log file that has been divided into five 200MB virtual log files, the log file can only be shrunk in 200MB increments. The file size can be reduced to sizes such as 800MB or 400MB, but the file cannot be reduced to sizes such as 333MB or 750MB.

SQL Server 2005 provides the DBCC SHRINKFILE command for shrinking the transaction log file. Its syntax is as follows:

```
DBCC SHRINKFILE ( { 'file_name' } { [ ,EMPTYFILE] ¦ [ ,target_size ] } )
    [ WITH NO_INFOMSGS ]
```

If no target size is specified for the DBCC SHRINKFILE command, SQL Server removes as many of the inactive virtual log files from the end of the physical log file as possible to restore the transaction log file to its default size. The default size of the transaction log file is the size specified when the log file was created or the last size set by using the ALTER DATABASE command.

If a target size is specified for DBCC SHRINKFILE, SQL Server attempts to remove as many VLFs from the end of the log file as possible to reduce the log file to as close to the target size as possible without making the log smaller than the specified target size. After shrinking, the log file is typically somewhat larger than the target size, especially if the target size is not a multiple of the VLF size.

If no VLFs beyond the target_size mark contain an active portion of the log, all the VLFs that come after the target_size mark are freed, and the DBCC SHRINKFILE statement completes successfully, with no messages. However, if any VLF beyond the target_size mark does contain an active portion of the log, SQL Server frees from the end of the physical log file as many of the VLFs as possible that do not contain active portions of the log. When this occurs, the DBCC SHRINKFILE command returns an informational message indicating that not all the requested space was freed. When the active portion of the log moves off the VLF(s) at the end of the physical log file, you can reissue the DBCC SHRINKFILE statement again to free the remaining space.

You can also use SQL Server Management Studio (SSMS) to shrink the transaction log file. In the Object Browser, expand the Databases folder and right-click the target database. Then select Tasks, Shrink, and Files. The Shrink File dialog appears, as shown in Figure 26.7.

26

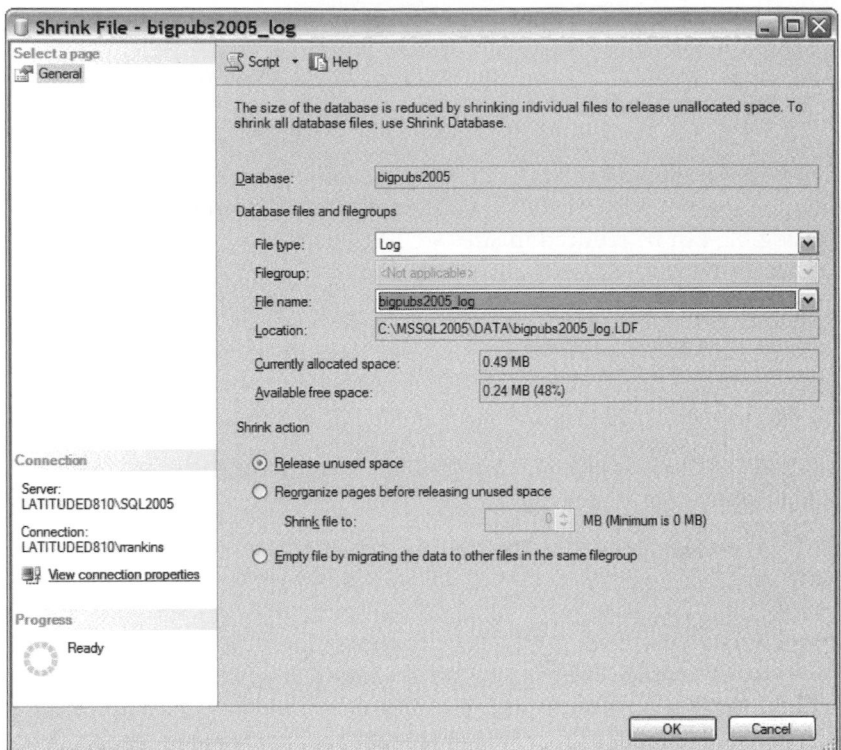

FIGURE 26.7   The SSMS Shrink File dialog.

In the File Type drop-down list, select Log. To shrink the log file to its default size, click the radio button next to Release Unused Space in the Shrink Action area of the dialog box. To shrink the log file to a desired size, click the radio button next to Reorganize Pages Before Releasing Unused Space and specify the desired target size. After you choose the desired shrink option, click OK.

In addition to manually shrinking the transaction log, SQL Server also provides a database option, AUTO_SHRINK, that can be enabled to shrink the log and database files automatically when space is available at the end of the file. If you are regularly backing up or truncating the log, the AUTO_SHRINK option keeps the size of the log file in check. The auto-shrink process runs periodically and determines whether the log file can be shrunk. The Log Manager keeps track of how much log space has been used since the auto-shrink process last ran. The auto-shrink process then shrinks the log to the larger of 125% of the maximum log space used since auto-shrink last ran or the default size of the transaction log file.

> **TIP**
>
> Repeated growing and shrinking of the log file can lead to excessive file fragmentation, which can have an adverse impact on the file I/O performance. It is recommended that instead of using `AUTO_SHRINK`, you set the transaction log to the size it is expected to grow to during normal processing and enable the auto-grow option so that it doesn't run out of space if something prevents the log from being truncated. This helps avoid the need for the log file to be constantly expanded during normal processing and also avoids excessive fragmentation of the log file. If something causes the log file to auto-grow and exceed the normal log file size, you can always manually shrink the file back to its normal size.

Transactions and Batches

There is no inherent transactional quality to batches. As you have seen already, unless you provide the syntax to define a single transaction made up of several statements, each individual statement in a batch is its own separate transaction, and each statement is carried to completion or fails individually.

The failure of a transaction within a batch does not cause the batch to stop processing. In other words, transaction flow does not affect process flow. After a `ROLLBACK TRAN` statement, processing continues with the next statement in the batch or stored procedure. For this reason, you want to be sure to check for error conditions after each data modification within a transaction and exit the batch or stored procedure, as appropriate.

Consider the banking transaction again, this time removing the `RETURN` statements:

```
declare @checking_account char(10),
        @savings_account char(10)
select @checking_account = '0003456321',
       @savings_account = '0003456322'
begin tran
update account
   set balance = balance - $1000
   where account_number = @checking_account
if @@error != 0
    rollback tran
update savings_account
   set balance = balance + $1000
   where account_number = @savings_account
if @@error != 0
    rollback tran
commit tran
```

26

Assume that a check constraint on the account prevents the balance from being set to a value less than 0. If the checking account has less than $1,000 in it, the first update fails, and the T-SQL code catches the error condition and rolls back the transaction. At this point, the transaction is no longer active, but the batch still contains additional statements to execute. Without a return after the rollback, SQL Server continues with the next statement in the batch, which in this case is the update to the savings account. However, this now executes as its own separate transaction, and it automatically commits if it completes successfully. This is not what you want to happen because now that second update is its own separate unit of work, so you have no way to roll it back.

The key concept to keep in mind here is that transaction flow does not affect program flow. In the event of an error within a transaction, you need to make sure you have the proper error checking and a means to exit the transaction in the event of an error. This prevents the batch from continuing with any remaining modifications that were meant to be a part of the original transaction. As a general rule, a RETURN statement should almost always follow a rollback.

Although you can have multiple transactions within a batch, you can also have transactions that span multiple batches. For example, you could write an application that begins a transaction in one batch and then asks for user verification during a second batch. The SQL might look like this:

First batch:

```
begin transaction
insert publishers (pub_id, pub_name, city, state)
    values ('1111', 'Joe and Marys Books', 'Northern Plains', 'IA')
if @@error = 0
    print 'publishers insert was successful. Please go on.'
else
    print 'publisher insert failed. Please roll back'
```

Second batch:

```
update titles
    set pub_id = '1111'
    where pub_id = '1234'
delete authors
    where state = 'CA'
commit transaction
```

Writing transactions that span multiple batches is almost always a bad idea. The locking and concurrency problems can become complicated, with awful performance implications. What if the application prompted for user input between batches, and the user went out to lunch? Locks would be held until the user got back and continued the transaction. In general, you want to enclose each transaction in a single batch, using conditional programming constructs to handle situations like the preceding example. The following is a better way to write that code:

```
begin transaction
insert publishers (pub_id, pub_name, city, state)
    values ('1111', 'Joe and Marys Books', 'Northern Plains', 'IA')
if @@error = 0
begin
    print 'publishers insert was successful. Continuing.'
    update titles
        set pub_id = '1111'
        where pub_id = '1234'
    delete authors
        where state = 'CA'
    commit transaction
end
else
begin
    print 'publisher insert failed. rolling back transaction'
    rollback transaction
end
```

The important point in this example is that the transaction now takes place within a single batch for better performance and consistency. As you will see in the next section, it is usually best to encode transactions in stored procedures for even better performance and to avoid the possibility of unfinished transactions.

Transactions and Stored Procedures

Because SQL code in stored procedures runs locally on the server, it is recommended that transactions be coded in stored procedures to speed transaction processing. The less network traffic going on within transactions, the faster they can finish.

Another advantage of using stored procedures for transactions is that it helps avoid the occurrence of partial transactions—that is, transactions that are started but not fully committed. It also avoids the possibility of user interaction within a transaction. The stored procedure keeps the transaction processing completely contained because it starts the transaction, carries out the data modifications, completes the transaction, and returns the status or data to the client.

Stored procedures also provide the additional benefit that if you need to fix, fine-tune, or expand the duties of the transaction, you can do all this at one time, in one central location. Your applications can share the same stored procedure, providing consistency for the logical unit of work across your applications.

Although stored procedures provide a useful solution to managing transactions, you need to know how transactions work within stored procedures and code for them appropriately. Consider what happens when one stored procedure calls another, and they both do their own transaction management. Obviously, they now need to work in concert with each other. If the called stored procedure has to roll back its work, how can it do so correctly without causing data integrity problems?

The issues you need to deal with go back to the earlier topics of transaction nesting and transaction flow versus program flow. Unlike a rollback in a trigger (see the next section), a rollback in a stored procedure does not abort the rest of the batch or the calling procedure.

For each BEGIN TRAN encountered in a nested procedure, the transaction nesting level is incremented by 1. For each COMMIT encountered, the transaction nesting level is decremented by 1. However, if a rollback other than to a named savepoint occurs in a nested procedure, it rolls back all statements to the outermost BEGIN TRAN, including any work performed inside the nested stored procedures that has not been fully committed. It then continues processing the remaining commands in the current procedure as well as the calling procedure(s).

To explore the issues involved, you can work with the sample stored procedure shown in Listing 26.1. The procedure takes a single integer argument, which it then attempts to insert into a table (testable). All data entry attempts—whether successful or not—are logged to a second table (auditlog). Listing 26.1 contains the code for the stored procedure and the tables it uses.

LISTING 26.1   Sample Stored Procedure and Tables for Transaction Testing

```
CREATE TABLE testable (col1 int)
go
CREATE TABLE auditlog (who varchar(128), valuentered int null)
go
CREATE PROCEDURE trantest @arg INT
AS
BEGIN TRAN
   IF EXISTS( SELECT * FROM testable WHERE col1 = @arg )
   BEGIN
      RAISERROR ('Value %d already exists!', 16, -1, @arg)
      ROLLBACK TRANSACTION
   END
   ELSE
   BEGIN
      INSERT INTO testable (col1) VALUES (@arg)
      COMMIT TRAN
   END

INSERT INTO auditlog (who, valuentered) VALUES (USER_NAME(), @arg)
return
```

Now explore what happens if you call this stored procedure in the following way and check the values of the two tables:

```
set nocount on
EXEC trantest 1
EXEC trantest 2
SELECT * FROM testable
SELECT valuentered FROM auditlog
go
```

The execution of this code gives the following results:

```
col1
-----------
1
2


valuentered
-----------
1
2
```

These would be the results you would expect because no errors would occur, and nothing would be rolled back.

Now, if you were to run the same code a second time, testable would still have only two rows because the procedure would roll back the attempted insert of the duplicate rows. However, because the procedure and batch are not aborted, the code would continue processing, and the rows would still be added to the auditlog table. The result would be as follows:

```
set nocount on
EXEC trantest 1
EXEC trantest 2
SELECT * FROM testable
SELECT valuentered FROM auditlog
go

Msg 50000, Level 16, State 1, Procedure trantest, Line 6
Value 1 already exists!

Msg 50000, Level 16, State 1, Procedure trantest, Line 6
Value 2 already exists!

col1
-----------
1
2
```

```
valuentered
-----------
1
2
1
2
```

Now explore what happens when you execute the stored procedure from within a transaction:

```
set nocount on
BEGIN TRAN
EXEC trantest 3
EXEC trantest 1
EXEC trantest 4
COMMIT TRAN
SELECT * FROM testable
SELECT valuentered FROM auditlog
go
```

The execution of this code gives the following results:

```
Msg 50000, Level 16, State 1, Procedure trantest, Line 6
Value 1 already exists!

Msg 266, Level 16, State 2, Procedure trantest, Line 0
Transaction count after EXECUTE indicates that a COMMIT or ROLLBACK TRANSACTION
 statement is missing. Previous count = 1, current count = 0.

Msg 3902, Level 16, State 1, Line 5
The COMMIT TRANSACTION request has no corresponding BEGIN TRANSACTION.

col1
-----------
1
2
4

valuentered
-----------
1
2
1
2
1
4
```

A number of problems are occurring now. For starters, you get a message telling you that the transaction nesting level was messed up. More seriously, the results show that the value 4 made it into the `testable` table anyway and that the `auditlog` table picked up the inserts of 1 and the 4 but lost the fact that you tried to insert a value of 3. What happened?

Let's take this one step at a time. First, you start the transaction and insert the value 3 into `trantest` . The stored procedure starts its own transaction, adds the value to `testable`, commits that, and then adds a row to `auditlog`. Next, you execute the procedure with the value 1. This value already exists in the table, so the procedure raises an error and rolls back the transaction. Remember that a `ROLLBACK` undoes work to the outermost `BEGIN TRAN`—which means the start of this batch. This rolls back everything, including the insert of 3 into `trantest` and `auditlog`. The `auditlog` entry for the value 1 *is* inserted and not rolled back because it occurred after the transaction was rolled back and is a standalone, automatically committed statement now.

You then receive an error regarding the change in the transaction nesting level because a transaction should leave the state of a governing procedure in the same way it was entered; it should make no net change to the transaction nesting level. In other words, the value of `@@trancount` should be the same when the procedure exits as when it was entered. If it is not, the transaction control statements are not properly balanced.

Also, because the batch is not aborted, the value 1 is inserted into `trantest`, an operation that completes successfully and is automatically committed. Finally, when you try to commit the transaction, you receive the last error regarding a mismatch between `BEGIN TRAN` and `COMMIT TRAN` because no transaction is currently in operation.

The solution to this problem is to write the stored procedures so that transaction nesting doesn't occur and so the stored procedure rolls back only its own work. When a rollback occurs, it should return an error status so that the calling batch or procedure is aware of the error condition and can choose to continue or abort the work at that level. You can manage this by checking the current value of `@@trancount` and determining what needs to be done. If a transaction is already active, the stored procedure should not issue a `BEGIN TRAN` and nest the transaction; rather, it should set a savepoint. This allows the procedure to perform a partial rollback of its work. If no transaction is active, the procedure can safely begin a new transaction. The following SQL code fragment is an example of using this approach:

```
DECLARE @trancount INT
/* Capture the value of the transaction nesting level at the start */
SELECT @trancount = @@trancount
IF (@trancount = 0)   -- no transaction is current active, start one
   BEGIN TRAN mytran
ELSE                  -- a transaction is active, set a savepoint only
   SAVE TRAN mytran
.
.
/* This is how to trap an error. Roll back either to your
```

```
   own BEGIN TRAN or roll back to the savepoint. Return an
   error code to the caller to indicate an internal failure.
   How the caller handles the transaction is up to the caller.*/
IF (@@error <> 0)
BEGIN
   ROLLBACK TRAN mytran
   RETURN -1969
END
.
.
.
/* Once you reach the end of the code, you need to pair the BEGIN TRAN,
   if you issued it, with a COMMIT TRAN. If you executed the SAVE TRAN
   instead, you have nothing else to do...end of game! */
IF (@trancount = 0)
  COMMIT TRAN

RETURN 0
```

If you apply these concepts to all stored procedures that need to incorporate transaction processing as well as the code that calls the stored procedures, you should be able to avoid problems with transaction nesting and inconsistency in your transaction processing. You just need to be sure to check the return value of the stored procedure and determine whether the whole batch should be failed or whether that one call is of little importance to the overall outcome and the transaction can continue.

For additional examples of and discussion about coding guidelines for stored procedures in transactions, see Chapter 23, "Creating and Managing Stored Procedures."

Transactions and Triggers

SQL Server 2005 provides two types of Data Manipulation Language (DML) triggers: AFTER triggers and INSTEAD OF triggers. INSTEAD OF triggers perform their actions before any modifications are made to the actual table the trigger is defined on.

Whenever a trigger is invoked, it is *always* invoked within another transaction, whether it's a single-statement AutoCommit transaction or a user-defined multistatement transaction. This is true for both AFTER triggers and INSTEAD OF triggers. Even though an INSTEAD OF trigger fires before, or "instead of," the data modification statement itself, if a transaction is not already active, an AutoCommit transaction is still automatically initiated as the data modification statement is invoked and prior to the invocation of the INSTEAD OF trigger. (For more information on AFTER and INSTEAD OF triggers, see Chapter 25, "Creating and Managing Triggers.")

NOTE

Although the information presented in this section applies to both AFTER and INSTEAD OF triggers, the examples presented pertain primarily to AFTER triggers.

Because the trigger is already operating within the context of a transaction, the only transaction control statements you should ever consider using in a trigger are ROLLBACK and SAVE TRAN. You don't need to issue a BEGIN TRAN because a transaction is already active; a BEGIN TRAN would only serve to increase the transaction nesting level, and that would complicate things further.

Triggers and Transaction Nesting

To demonstrate the relationship between a trigger and the transaction nesting level, you can use the following SQL code to create a trigger on the employee table:

```
use bigpubs2005
go
CREATE TRIGGER tD_employee ON employee
FOR DELETE
AS
   DECLARE @msg VARCHAR(255)

   SELECT @msg = 'Trancount in trigger = ' + CONVERT(VARCHAR(2), @@trancount)

   PRINT @msg

   RETURN
go
```

The purpose of this trigger is simply to show the state of the @@trancount within the trigger as the deletion is taking place.

If you now execute code for an implied and an explicit transaction, you can see the values of @@trancount and the behavior of the batch. First, here's the implied transaction:

```
set nocount on
print 'Trancount before delete = ' + CONVERT(VARCHAR(2), @@trancount)
DELETE FROM employee WHERE emp_id = 'PMA42628M'
print 'Trancount after delete = ' + CONVERT( VARCHAR(2), @@trancount)
go
```

The results of this are as follows:

```
Trancount before delete = 0
Trancount in trigger = 1
Trancount after delete = 0
```

Because no transaction starts until the DELETE statement executes, the first value of @@trancount indicates this with a value of 0. Within the trigger, the transaction count has a value of 1; you are now inside the implied transaction caused by the DELETE. After the trigger returns, the DELETE is automatically committed, and the transaction is finished, and @@trancount returns to 0 to indicate that no transaction is currently active.

Now explore what happens within an explicit transaction:

```
begin tran
print 'Trancount before delete = ' + CONVERT(VARCHAR(2), @@trancount)
DELETE FROM employee WHERE emp_id = 'PMA42628M'
print 'Trancount after delete = ' + CONVERT( VARCHAR(2), @@trancount)
commit tran
print 'Trancount after commit = ' + CONVERT( VARCHAR(2), @@trancount)
go
```

This code gives the following results:

```
Trancount before delete = 1
Trancount in trigger = 1
Trancount after delete = 1
Trancount after commit = 0
```

In this example, a transaction is already active when the DELETE is executed. The BEGIN TRAN statement initiates the transaction, and @@trancount is 1 before the DELETE is executed. The trigger becomes a part of that transaction, which is not committed until the COMMIT TRAN statement is executed.

What would happen, however, if the trigger performed a rollback? You can find out by modifying the trigger to perform a rollback as follows:

```
ALTER TRIGGER tD_employee ON employee
FOR DELETE
AS
print 'Trancount in trigger = ' + CONVERT(VARCHAR(2), @@trancount)

ROLLBACK TRAN

return
```

Now rerun the previous batch. The outcome this time is as follows:

```
Trancount before delete = 1
Trancount in trigger = 1
Msg 3609, Level 16, State 1, Line 3
The transaction ended in the trigger. The batch has been aborted.
```

Notice in this example that the batch did not complete, as evidenced by the missing output from the last two print statements. When a rollback occurs within a trigger, SQL Server aborts the current transaction, continues processing the commands in the trigger, and after the trigger returns, aborts the rest of the batch and returns error message 3609 to indicate that the batch has been aborted because the transaction was ended within the trigger. A ROLLBACK TRAN statement in a trigger rolls back all work to the first BEGIN TRAN statement. It is not possible to roll back to a specific named transaction, although you can roll back to a named savepoint, as will be discussed later in this section.

Again, the batch and transaction are aborted when the trigger rolls back; any subsequent statements in the batch are not executed. The key concept to remember is that the trigger becomes an integral part of the statement that fired it and of the transaction in which that statement occurs.

However, it is important to note that although the batch is aborted immediately after the trigger that performed a rollback returns, any statements within the trigger that follow the ROLLBACK TRAN statement but before it returns are executed. For example, you can modify the previous trigger further to include a print statement after the ROLLBACK TRAN statement:

```
ALTER TRIGGER tD_employee ON employee
FOR DELETE
AS
print 'Trancount in trigger = ' + CONVERT(VARCHAR(2), @@trancount)

ROLLBACK TRAN

print 'Trancount in trigger after rollback = ' + CONVERT(VARCHAR(2), @@trancount)

return
```

Now, if you rerun the previous batch, you can see the print statement after the ROLLBACK TRAN but before the RETURN statement is executed:

```
Trancount before delete = 1
Trancount in trigger = 1
Trancount in trigger after rollback = 0
Msg 3609, Level 16, State 1, Line 3
The transaction ended in the trigger. The batch has been aborted.
```

Notice that the Trancount after the ROLLBACK TRAN in the trigger is now 0. If the trigger subsequently performed any data modifications following the ROLLBACK TRAN, they would now be running as AutoCommit transactions. For this reason, you must be careful to be sure you issue a RETURN statement to exit the trigger after a ROLLBACK TRAN is issued to avoid the trigger performing any operations that would then be automatically committing, leaving no opportunity to roll them back.

Triggers and Multistatement Transactions

Now let's look at another example. First, you need to create a trigger to enforce referential integrity between the titles table and the publishers table:

```
--The first statement is used to disable any previously created
--DDL triggers in the database which would prevent creating a new trigger.
```

```
DISABLE TRIGGER ALL ON titles
go
create trigger tr_titles_i on titles for insert as
declare @rows int  -- create variable to hold @@rowcount
select @rows = @@rowcount
if @rows = 0 return
if update(pub_id) and (select count(*)
        from inserted i, publishers p
        where p.pub_id = i.pub_id ) != @rows
  begin
        rollback transaction
        raiserror ('Invalid pub_id inserted', 16, 1)
  end
return
go
```

Next, for the trigger to take care of the referential integrity, you might first need to disable the foreign key constraint on the `titles` table with a command similar to the following:

```
alter table titles nocheck constraint FK__titles__pub_id__0F424F67
```

> **NOTE**
>
> The system-generated name for the foreign key constraint may possibly be different on your database. You can use `sp_helpconstraint titles` to verify the name of the foreign key constraint on the `pub_id` column of the `titles` table and use it in place of the constraint name specified in this example.

Now, run a multistatement transaction with an invalid `pub_id` in the second insert statement:

```
/* transaction inserts rows into a table */
begin tran add_titles
insert titles (title_id, pub_id, title)
        values ('XX1234', '0736', 'Tuning SQL Server')
insert titles (title_id, pub_id, title)
        values ('XX1235', 'abcd', 'Tuning SQL Server')
insert titles (title_id, pub_id, title)
        values ('XX1236', '0877', 'Tuning SQL Server')
commit tran
go


Msg 50000, Level 16, State 1, Procedure tr_titles_i, Line 10
Invalid pub_id inserted
Msg 3609, Level 16, State 1, Line 4
The transaction ended in the trigger. The batch has been aborted.
```

How many rows are inserted if `'abcd'` is an invalid pub_id? In this example, no rows are inserted because the `rollback tran` in the trigger rolls back all modifications made by the trigger, including the insert with the bad pub_id and all statements preceding it within the transaction. After the `RETURN` statement is encountered in the trigger, the rest of the batch is aborted.

CAUTION

You should never issue a `begin tran` statement in a trigger because a transaction is already active at the time the trigger is executed. Rolling back to a named transaction in a trigger is illegal and generates a runtime error, rolling back the transaction and immediately terminating processing of the trigger and the batch. The only transaction control statements you should ever consider including in a trigger are `ROLLBACK TRAN` and `SAVE TRAN`.

Using Savepoints in Triggers

While `BEGIN TRAN` statements are not recommended within a trigger, you can set a savepoint in a trigger and roll back to the savepoint. This rolls back only the operations within the trigger subsequent to the savepoint. The trigger and the transaction it is a part of are still active until the transaction is subsequently committed or rolled back. The batch continues processing.

Savepoints can be used to avoid a trigger arbitrarily rolling back an entire transaction. You can roll back to the named savepoint in the trigger and then issue a `raiserror` and return immediately to pass the error code back to the calling process. The calling process can then check the error status of the data modification statement and take appropriate action, either rolling back the transaction, rolling back to a savepoint in the transaction, or ignoring the error and committing the data modification.

The following is an example of a trigger that uses a savepoint:

```
alter trigger tr_titles_i on titles for insert as
declare @rows int  -- create variable to hold @@rowcount
select @rows = @@rowcount
if @rows = 0 return
save tran titlestrig
if update(pub_id) and (select count(*)
        from inserted i, publishers p
        where p.pub_id = i.pub_id ) != @rows
  begin
      rollback transaction titlestrig
      raiserror ('Invalid pub_id inserted', 16, 1)
  end
return
```

This trigger rolls back all work since the savepoint and returns an error number of 50000. In the transaction, you can check for the error number and make the decision about whether to continue the transaction, roll back the transaction, or, if savepoints were set in the transaction, roll back to a savepoint and let the transaction continue. The following example rolls back the entire transaction if either of the first two inserts fail, but it only rolls back to the named savepoint if the third insert fails, allowing the first two to be committed:

```
begin tran add_titles
insert titles (title_id, pub_id, title)
      values ('XX1234', '0736', 'Tuning SQL Server')
if @@error = 50000 -- roll back entire transaction and abort batch
   begin
   rollback tran add_titles
   return
   end
insert titles (title_id, pub_id, title)
      values ('XX1236', '0877', 'Tuning SQL Server')
 if @@error = 50000 -- roll back entire transaction and abort batch
   begin
   rollback tran add_titles
   return
   end
save tran keep_first_two  -- set savepoint for partial rollback
insert titles (title_id, pub_id, title)
      values ('XX1235', 'abcd', 'Tuning SQL Server')
 if @@error = 50000  -- roll back to save point, continue batch
   begin
   rollback tran keep_first_two
   end
commit tran
```

> **TIP**
>
> When you use a savepoint inside a trigger, the trigger is not rolling back the transaction. Therefore, the batch is not automatically aborted. You must explicitly return from the batch after rolling back the transaction to prevent subsequent statements from executing.

> **NOTE**
>
> Don't forget to reenable the constraint on the `titles` table when you are finished testing:
>
> ```
> alter table titles check constraint FK__titles__pub_id__0F424F67
> ```

Transactions and Locking

SQL Server issues and holds on to locks for the duration of a transaction to ensure the isolation and consistency of the modifications. Data modifications that occur within a transaction acquire exclusive locks, which are then held until the completion of the transaction. Shared locks, or read locks, are held for only as long as the statement needs them; usually, a shared lock is released as soon as data has been read from the resource (for example, row, page, table). You can modify the length of time a shared lock is held by using keywords such as HOLDLOCK in a query or setting the REPEATABLE_READ or SERIALIZABLE lock isolation levels. If one of these options is specified, shared locks are held until the completion of the transaction.

What this means for you as a database application developer is that you should try to hold on to as few locks or as small a lock as possible for as short a time as possible to avoid locking contention between applications and to improve concurrency and application performance. The simple rule when working with transactions is to keep them short and keep them simple. In other words, you should do what you need to do in the most concise manner, in the shortest possible time. You should keep any extraneous commands that do not need to be part of the logical unit of work—such as SELECT statements, commands for dropping temporary tables, commands for setting up local variables, and so on—outside the transaction.

To modify the manner in which a transaction and its locks can be handled by a SELECT statement, you can issue the SET TRANSACTION ISOLATION LEVEL statement. This statement allows the query to choose how much it is protected against other transactions modifying the data being used. The SET TRANSACTION ISOLATION LEVEL statement has the following mutually exclusive options:

▶ **READ COMMITTED**—This setting is the default for SQL Server. Modifications made within a transaction are locked exclusively, and the changes cannot be viewed by other user processes until the transaction completes. Commands that read data only hold shared locks on the data for as long as they are reading it. Because other transactions are not blocked from modifying the data after you have read it within your transaction, subsequent reads of the data within the transaction might encounter nonrepeatable reads or phantom data.

▶ **READ UNCOMMITTED**—With this level of isolation, one transaction can read the modifications made by other transactions prior to being committed. This is, therefore, the least restrictive isolation level, but it is one that allows the reading of dirty and uncommitted data. This option has the same effect as issuing NOLOCK within SELECT statements, but it has to be set only once for your connection. This should never be used in an application in which accuracy of the query results is required.

▶ **REPEATABLE READ**—When this option is set, as data is read, locks are placed and held on the data for the duration of the transaction. These locks prevent other transactions from modifying the data you have read so that you can carry out multiple passes across the same information and get the same results each time. This isolation level is obviously more restrictive than READ COMMITTED and READ UNCOMMITTED, and it can block other transactions. However, although it prevents nonrepeatable reads, it does not prevent the addition of new rows or *phantom rows* because only *existing* data is locked.

▶ **SERIALIZABLE**—This option is the most restrictive isolation level because it places a range lock on the data. This prevents any modifications to the data being read from until the end of the transaction. It also avoids phantom reads by preventing rows from being added or removed from the data range set.

▶ **SNAPSHOT**—Snapshot isolation is a new isolation level available in SQL Server 2005. Snapshot isolation specifies that data read by any statement will only see data modifications that were committed before the start of the transaction. The effect is as if the statements in a transaction see a snapshot of the committed data as it existed at the start of the transaction. The ALLOW_SNAPSHOT_ISOLATION database option must be set to ON for a transaction to specify the SNAPSHOT isolation level.

READ_COMMITTED_SNAPSHOT **Isolation**

In addition to the new SNAPSHOT isolation level, SQL Server also supports a special form of read-committed isolation, referred to as READ_COMMITTED_SNAPSHOT. This form of isolation is similar to snapshot isolation, but unlike snapshot isolation, which sees the version of the data at the start of the transaction, read committed snapshot queries see the version of the data at the start of the statement.

To enable the READ_COMMITTED_SNAPSHOT isolation level for queries, you need to enable the READ_COMMITTED_SNAPSHOT database option. Any queries that normally would run at the standard READ_COMMITTED isolation level automatically run at the READ_COMMITTED_SNAPSHOT isolation level, without requiring any code changes.

For more information on transaction isolation levels and their effect on lock types, locking behavior, and performance, see Chapter 32, "Locking and Performance."

Coding Effective Transactions

Poorly written or inefficient transactions can have a detrimental effect on concurrency of access to data and overall application performance. SQL Server can hold locks on a number of resources while the transaction is open; modified rows acquire exclusive locks, and other locks might also be held, depending on the isolation level used. To reduce locking contention for resources, transactions should be kept as short and efficient as possible. During development, you might not even notice that a problem exists; the problem might become noticeable only after the system load is increased and multiple users are executing transactions simultaneously. Following are some guidelines to consider when coding transactions to minimize locking contention and improve application performance:

▶ Do not return result sets within a transaction. Doing so prolongs the transaction unnecessarily. Perform all data retrieval and analysis outside the transaction.

▶ *Never* prompt for user input during a transaction. If you do, you lose all control over the duration of the transaction. (Even the best programmers miss this one on occasion.) On the failure of a transaction, be sure to issue the rollback before putting up a message box telling the user that a problem occurred.

▶ Keep the start and end of a transaction together in the same batch or, better yet, use a stored procedure for the operation.

▶ Keep the transaction short. Start the transaction at the point where you need to do the modifications. Do any preliminary work beforehand.

▶ Make careful use of different locking schemes and transaction isolation levels.

▶ If user input is unavoidable between data retrieval and modification and you need to handle the possibility of another user modifying the data values read, use optimistic locking strategies rather than acquiring and holding locks by using HOLDLOCK or other locking options. Chapter 32 covers optimistic locking methods in more detail.

▶ Collect multiple transactions into one transaction, or batch transactions together, if appropriate. This might seem to go against some of the other suggestions, but it reduces the amount of overhead SQL Server will encounter to start, finish, and log the transactions.

Long-Running Transactions

As you have already seen, transaction information is recorded in each database's transaction log. However, long-running transactions can be a cause of consternation to a system administrator who is attempting to back up and prune the transaction log. Only the inactive portion of the log can be truncated during this operation. The inactive portion of the log is the pages that contain log records for all completed transactions prior to the first log record of the oldest still-active transaction (see Figure 26.8). Even if completed transactions follow the first record of the oldest active transaction, they cannot be removed from the log until the oldest active transaction completes. This is because the log is pruned by clearing out entire pages of information prior to the oldest active transaction. Pages after that point cannot be cleared because they might contain records for the active transaction that would be needed in the event of a rollback or database recovery.

In addition to preventing the log from being pruned, long-running transactions can degrade concurrency by holding locks for an extended period of time, preventing other users from accessing the locked data.

To get information about the oldest active transaction in a database, you can use the DBCC OPENTRAN command, whose syntax is as follows:

```
DBCC OPENTRAN [('DatabaseName' ¦ DatabaseId)]
[WITH TABLERESULTS [, NO_INFOMSGS]]
```

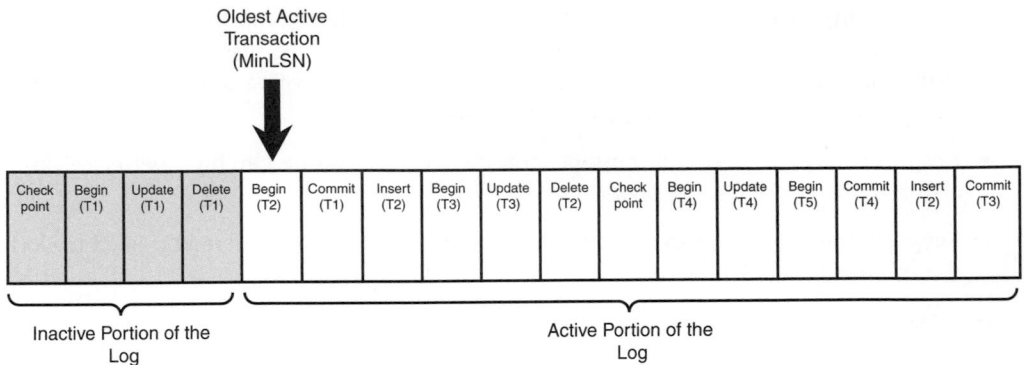

FIGURE 26.8   The inactive portion of the log is the pages in the log prior to the oldest active transaction.

The following example displays a sample of the oldest active transaction for the bigpubs2005 database:

```
DBCC OPENTRAN (bigpubs2005)
go
```

```
Transaction information for database 'bigpubs2005'.
```

```
Oldest active transaction:
    SPID (server process ID): 51
    UID (user ID) : -1
    Name          : add_titles
    LSN           : (1839:343:386)
    Start time    : Aug  7 2006 10:58:03:467PM
    SID           : 0x01050000000000051500000000919eeef679f7411a88d4a16ded030000
DBCC execution completed. If DBCC printed error messages, contact your system
 administrator.
```

DBCC OPENTRAN returns the server process ID (SPID) of the process that initiated the transaction, the user ID, the name of the transaction (this is when naming transactions are helpful because the names might help you identify the SQL code that initiated the transaction), the LSN of the page containing the initial BEGIN TRAN statement for the transaction, and, finally, the time the transaction was started.

If you specify the TABLERESULTS option, this information is returned in two columns that you can load into a table for logging or comparison purposes. The NO_INFOMSGS option suppresses the display of the 'DBCC execution completed...' message. The following example runs DBCC OPENTRAN and inserts the results into a temp table:

```
CREATE TABLE #opentran_results
( result_label VARCHAR(30), result_value VARCHAR(46))
```

```
insert #opentran_results
    exec ('dbcc opentran (bigpubs2005) WITH TABLERESULTS, no_infomsgs')

select * from #opentran_results
go
```

result_label	result_value
OLDACT_SPID	51
OLDACT_UID	-1
OLDACT_NAME	add_titles
OLDACT_LSN	(1839:343:386)
OLDACT_STARTTIME	Aug 7 2006 10:58:03:467PM
OLDACT_SID	0x01050000000000051500000919eeef679f7411a88d4

If no open transactions exist for the database, you receive the following message from
DBCC OPENTRAN:

```
No active open transactions.
DBCC execution completed. If DBCC printed error messages, contact your
 system administrator.
```

DBCC OPENTRAN provides a means for you to identify which transactions are potential problems, based on their longevity. If you capture the process information at the same time, using sp_who, you can identify who or what application is causing the longest-running transaction(s). Using this information, you can terminate the process, if necessary, or you can just have a quiet word with the user if the query is ad hoc or with the application developers if it is SQL code generated by a custom application.

Bound Connections

During the course of a transaction, the process that initiated the transaction acquires exclusive locks on the data that is modified. These locks prevent other user processes or connections from seeing any of these changes until they are committed. However, it is common for some SQL Server applications to have multiple connections to SQL Server. Even though each connection might be for the same user, SQL Server treats each connection as an entirely separate SQL Server process, and by default, one connection cannot see the uncommitted changes of another nor modify records locked by the other connection.

Bound connections provide a means of linking multiple connections together to share the same lock space and participate in the same transaction. This can be useful, especially if an application makes use of extended stored procedures. Extended stored procedures, although invoked from within a user session, run externally in a separate session. An extended stored procedure might need to call back into the database to access data. Without bound connections between the original process and the extended stored procedure, the extended stored procedure would be blocked by the locks held on the data by the originating process.

> **NOTE**
>
> In earlier versions of SQL Server, bound sessions were primarily used in developing extended stored procedures that needed to execute T-SQL statements on behalf of the process calling them. In SQL Server 2005, it is recommended that extended stored procedures be replaced with stored procedures written using the CLR. CLR stored procedures are more secure, scalable, and stable than extended stored procedures. In addition, CLR-stored procedures use the `SqlContext` object to join the context of the calling session rather than bound connections.

Bound connections are of two types: local and distributed. Local bound connections are two or more connections within a single server that are bound into a single transaction space. Distributed bound connections make use of the Microsoft Distributed Transaction Coordinator (MS DTC; described in more detail later in this chapter, in the section "Distributed Transactions") to share a transaction space across connections from more than one server. The following sections discuss how to set up and use local bound connections.

Creating Bound Connections

Binding connections together is actually fairly simple and requires the acquisition of a token by the first process that can be passed to another connection that identifies the lock space to be shared.

A bind token is acquired using the stored procedure `sp_getbindtoken`. This stored procedure creates a bound connection context and returns the unique identifier for this through an output parameter:

```
sp_getbindtoken @TokenVariable OUTPUT [, @for_xp_flag]
```

`@TokenVariable` is a variable defined as a `varchar(255)` and is used to receive the bind token from the stored procedure. If you pass the `@for_xp_flag` argument a 1, the stored procedure creates a bind token that extended stored procedures can use to call back into SQL Server.

> **NOTE**
>
> Only the owner of a connection can gain the bind token for it.

After you have the bind token, you have to pass it to the intended co-client, which then uses a different stored procedure, `sp_bindsession`, to participate in your transaction context:

```
sp_bindsession [@TokenVariable ¦ NULL]
```

`@TokenVariable` is the value created in the previous step. The NULL value is used to unbind a connection from another. You can also unbind a connection by executing `sp_bindsession` without arguments.

To illustrate the use of these procedures together, consider the following code:

```
begin tran
DECLARE @token VARCHAR(255)
EXECUTE sp_getbindtoken @token OUTPUT
select @token


----------------------------------
14I`RN1.6QCd>hFgOl18;]5---0I@=--
```

Each call to `sp_getbindtoken` results in a different value. Depending on who the intended recipient is, you must find some way to programmatically communicate this value to the recipient, which the recipient then uses in the call:

```
EXEC sp_bindsession '14I`RN1.6QCd>hFgOl18;]5---0I@=--'
```

In addition to sharing lock space, bound connections also share the same transaction space. If you execute a ROLLBACK TRAN from a bound connection, it rolls back the transaction initiated in the orginating session. It is recommeded that all transaction control statements be kept in the initial connection. If an error occurs in a bound connection, it should return an error code to the originating session so that it can perform the appropriate rollback.

Binding Multiple Applications

If you bind connections across applications, you have to find a way of communicating the bind token so that it can be used with `sp_bindsession`. SQL Server does not provide a simple solution to this problem, but you can consider mechanisms like these:

▶ Using an interprocess communication (IPC) mechanism such as remote procedure calls, dynamic data exchange (DDE), or Net-DDE.

▶ Placing the bind token in a file that is accessible to each application.

▶ Storing the bind token in a SQL Server table. You might also create a stored procedure to manage the assignment of the token to the requesting applications.

▶ If the applications are local, you might be able to pass the token through global or shared memory, or directly, using a function call.

Using bound connections has an important downside: sequential processing. Only one connection out of all the connections bound together can actually be doing any work at any given time. This means that during a result set retrieval, either the entire result set must be retrieved or the command must be canceled before a participating connection can do any other work. Any attempt to perform an operation while another operation is in process results in an error that should be trapped so that you can resubmit the work after a certain time interval.

26

Distributed Transactions

Typically, transaction management controls only the data modifications made within a single SQL Server instance. However, the increasing interest and implementation of distributed systems brings up the need to access and modify data distributed across multiple SQL Server instances within a single unit of work.

What if in the banking example, the checking accounts reside on one SQL Server instance and the savings accounts on another? Moving money from one account to another would require updates to two separate instances. How do you modify data on two different instances and still treat it as a single unit of work? You need some way to ensure that the distributed transaction retains the same ACID properties as a local transaction. To provide this capability, SQL Server ships with the MS DTC service, which provides the ability to control and manage the integrity of multiserver transactions. MS DTC uses the industry-standard two-phase commit protocol to ensure the consistency of all parts of any distributed transaction passing through SQL Server and any referenced linked servers.

Chapter 42, "Managing Linked and Remote Servers" (on the CD-ROM), covers the process of configuring servers and writing SQL code to support distributed transactions.

Summary

A transaction is a logical unit of work as well as a unit of recovery. The successful control of transactions is of the utmost importance to the correct modification of related information. In this chapter, you have learned how to define and control transactions, examined different transaction-management schemes, learned how the recovery process works, and discovered how to correctly code transactions within triggers and stored procedures. You have also learned methods for optimizing transactions to improve application performance, and you have gotten an overview of locking and distributed transactions. Locking is covered in more detail in Chapter 32, and distributed transactions are covered in more detail in Chapter 42. In addition, this chapter introduces you to the new snapshot isolation options available in SQL Server 2005. Snapshot isolation provides the ability to keep versions of row data that existed prior to the start of a transaction.

Chapter 27 discusses the concept of database snapshots, which provide a way to keep a read-only, static view of a database.

Database Snapshots

IN THIS CHAPTER

▶ What's New with Database Snapshots

▶ What Are Database Snapshots?

▶ Limitations and Restrictions of Database Snapshots

▶ Copy-on-Write Technology

▶ When to Use Database Snapshots

▶ Setup and Breakdown of a Database Snapshot

▶ Reverting to a Database Snapshot for Recovery

▶ Setting Up Snapshots Against a Database Mirror

▶ Database Snapshots Maintenance and Security Considerations

Can it be true? Microsoft has finally added database snapshots to its database arsenal. Database snapshots have been a part of competing products (Oracle and DB2) for years. This is no doubt a concerted effort to level the playing field with these other two database engine titans. Database snapshots are great for fulfilling point-in-time reporting requirements, reverting a database back to a point in time (recoverability and availability), and for potentially reducing the processing impact of querying against your primary transactional databases (via database mirroring and database snapshots).

Keep in mind that database snapshots are point-in-time and read-only. Database snapshots are not materialized views. Materialized views become part of the data object (table) that they are touching (that is, that are bound to them); when data changes in the base tables, materialized views change (that is, are updated). Database snapshots are scheduled and are not bound to the underlying database objects that they pull their data from. They provide a full, read-only copy of the database at a specific point in time. Because of this point-in-time aspect, data latency must be well understood for all users of this feature: Snapshot data is only as current as the last time the snapshot was made.

Database snapshots make huge use of Microsoft's copy-on-write technology. In fact, the copy-on-write technology is the primary enabling mechanism for snapshots. If you recall from Chapter 16, "Database Mirroring," the copy-on-write technology is what enables database mirroring. Database snapshots can also be used in conjunction with database mirroring to provide a highly available transactional system and a reporting platform that is created from the database mirror and not the primary transactional database, without any data loss impact whatsoever. This is a very powerful reporting and availability configuration.

What's New with Database Snapshots

Everything about database snapshots is new because this is a completely new feature for SQL Server. There will be new data definition statements introduced, data latency considerations to understand, and some new, much more complex database configurations that are possible. The database snapshot feature is available only with the Enterprise Edition of SQL Server 2005! With this new database snapshot feature, you will see:

▶ What the DDL additions for the snapshots are

▶ How to do database snapshots against transactional databases

▶ How to revert to a database snapshot for recovery

▶ How to make database snapshots against database mirrors (database mirroring is also new)

▶ How database snapshots can safeguard against mass changes

▶ How database snapshots can be used for testing (or for QA purposes)

This is truly a feature that will solve many a company's reporting, data safeguarding, and performance issues and may also directly contribute to higher availability of all of their systems. Be aware, there are plenty of restrictions with doing database snapshots. In fact, these may prohibit you from using snapshots at all. We will talk about these restrictions and when you can safely do database snapshots in a bit.

What Are Database Snapshots?

With SQL Server 2005, Microsoft has shifted very strongly to a goal of providing a database engine foundation that can be highly available 7 days a week, 365 days a year. Database snapshots contribute to this goal in several ways:

▶ They decrease recovery time of a database because you can restore a troubled database with a database snapshot—referred to as *reverting*.

▶ They create a security blanket (safeguard) prior to running mass updates on a critical database. If something goes wrong with the update, the database can be reverted in a very short amount of time.

▶ They provide a read-only, point-in-time reporting database for ad hoc or canned reporting needs quickly (hence increasing reporting environment availability).

▶ They create a read-only, point-in-time reporting and off-loaded database for ad hoc or canned reporting needs quickly from a database mirror (again, increasing reporting environment availability and also offloading reporting impact away from your production server/principal database server).

▶ As a bonus, database snapshots can be used to create testing or QA synchronization points to enhance and improve all aspects of critical testing (hence decreasing bad code from going into production that directly affects the stability and availability of that production implementation).

A database snapshot is simply a point-in-time full database view. It's not a copy—at least not a full copy when it is originally created. We will talk about this more in a moment. Figure 27.1 shows conceptually how a database snapshot can be created from a source database on a single SQL Server instance.

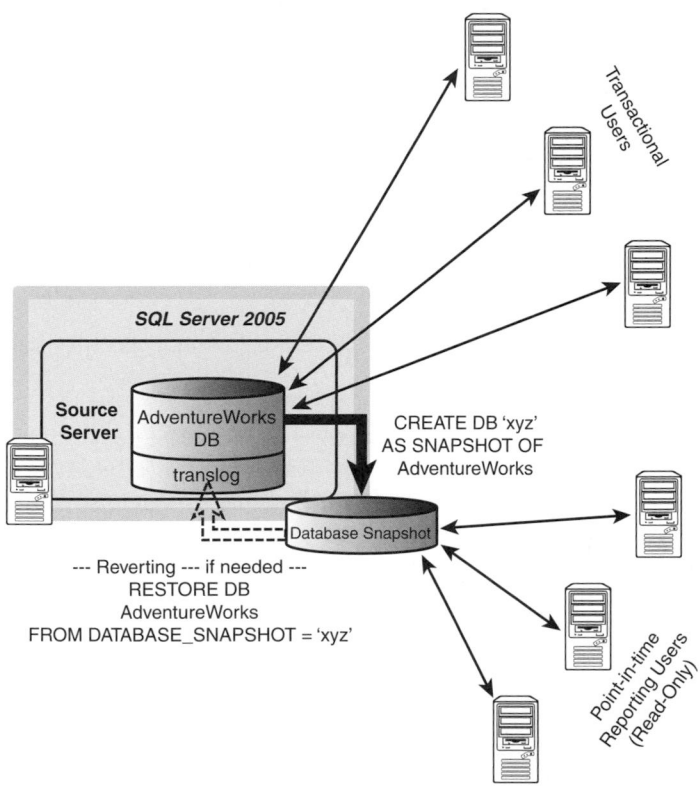

FIGURE 27.1   Basic database snapshot concept: a source database and its database snap-shot, all on a single SQL Server instance.

This point-in-time view of a database's data never changes, even though the data (data pages) in the primary database (the source of the database snapshot) may change. It is truly a snapshot at a point in time. For a snapshot, it always simply points to data pages in the source database that were present at the time the snapshot was created. If a data page is updated in the source database, a copy of the original source data page is moved to a new page chain termed the *sparse file*. This utilizes copy-on-write technology. Figure 27.2 shows this new sparse file that is created, alongside the source database itself.

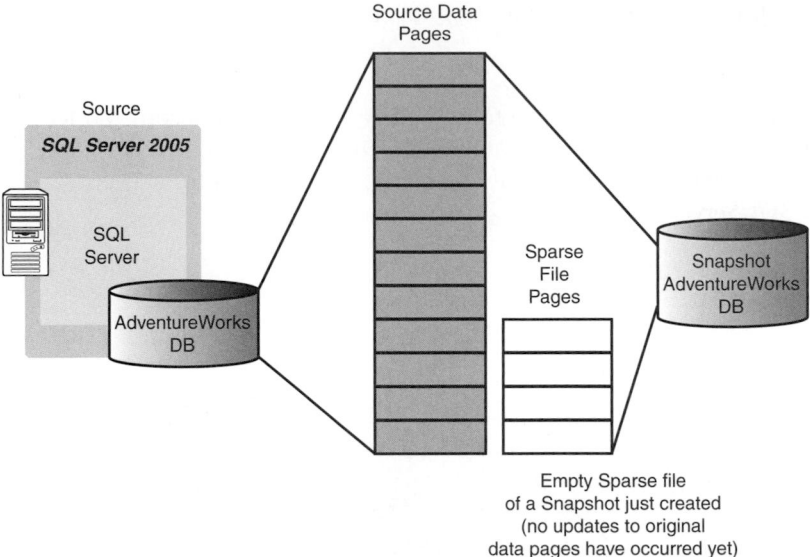

FIGURE 27.2   Source database data pages and the sparse file data pages that comprise the database snapshot.

A database snapshot really uses the primary database's data pages up until the point that one of these data pages is updated (changed in any way). As already mentioned, if a data page is updated in the source database, the original copy of the data page (which is referenced by the database snapshot) is written to a sparse file page chain as part of an update operation, using the copy-on-write technology. It is this new data page in the sparse file that still provides the correct point-in-time data to the database snapshot that it serves. Figure 27.3 illustrates that as more data changes (updates) occur in the source database, the sparse file gets larger and larger with the old original data pages.

Eventually a sparse file could contain the entire original database if all data pages in the primary database were changed. As you can also see in Figure 27.3, what data pages the database snapshot uses from the original (source) database and from the sparse file are all managed in the system catalog for the database snapshot. This is incredibly efficient and represents a major breakthrough of providing data to others. Because SQL Server is using the copy-on-write technology, a certain amount of overhead is used during write operations. This is one of the critical factors you must sort through if you plan on using database snapshots. Nothing is free. The overhead includes the copying of the original data page, the writing of this copied data page to the sparse file, and then the subsequent metadata updating to the system catalog that manages the database snapshot data page list. Because of this sharing of data pages, it should also be clear why database snapshots must be within the same instance of a SQL Server: Both the source database and the snapshot start out as the same data pages and then diverge as source data pages are updated. In addition, when a database snapshot is created, SQL Server rolls back any uncommitted transactions for that database snapshot; only the committed transactions will be part of a newly created database snapshot. And, as you might expect of something that shares data pages, database snapshots become unavailable if the source database becomes unavailable (for example, if it is damaged or goes offline).

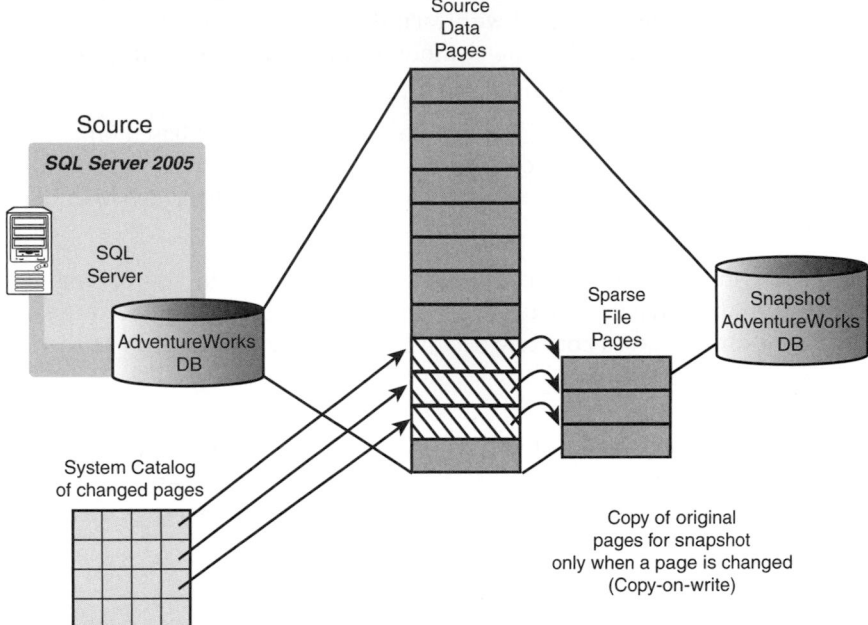

FIGURE 27.3   Data pages being copied to the sparse file for a database snapshot as pages are being updated in the source database.

27

> **NOTE**
>
> You might want to plan to do a new snapshot after about 30% of the source database has changed to keep overhead and file sizes in the sparse file at a minimum. The most frequent problem that occurs with database snapshots is related to sparse file sizes and available space. Remember, the sparse file has the potential of being as big as the source database itself (if all data pages in the source database eventually get updated). Plan ahead for this.

There are, of course, alternatives to database snapshots, such as data replication, log shipping, and even materialized views, but none are as easy to manage and to use as database snapshots.

The most common terms associated with database snapshots are:

▶ **Source database**—This is the database on which the database snapshot will be based. A database is a collection of data pages. It is the fundamental data storage mechanism that SQL Server uses.

▶ **Snapshot databases**—There can be one or more database snapshots defined against any one source database. All snapshots must reside in the same SQL Server instance.

▶ **Database snapshot sparse file**—This is a new data page allocation that contains the original source database data pages when updates occur to the source database data pages. There is one sparse file associated with each database data file. If you have a source database that is allocated with one or more separate data files, you have corresponding sparse files of each of these as well.

▶ **Reverting to a database snapshot**—If you restore a source database based on a particular database snapshot that was done at a point in time, you are reverting. You are actually doing a database RESTORE operation with a FROM DATABASE_SNAPSHOT statement.

▶ **Copy-on-write technology**—As part of an update transaction in the source database, a copy of the source database data page is written to a sparse file so that the database snapshot can be served correctly (that is, still see the data page as of the snapshot point-in-time).

As Figure 27.4 illustrates, any data query using the database snapshot looks at both the source database data pages and the sparse file data pages at the same time. And these data pages always reflect the unchanged data pages at the point in time the snapshot was created.

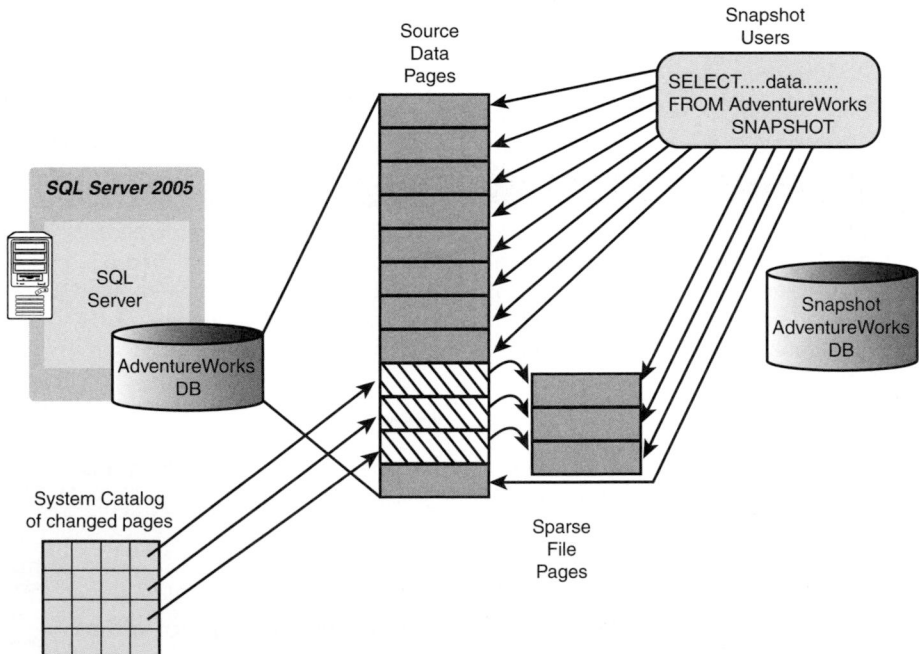

FIGURE 27.4   A query using the database snapshot touches both source database data pages and sparse file data pages to satisfy a query.

Limitations and Restrictions of Database Snapshots

There are many restrictions or limitations involved with using database snapshots in SQL Server. Some of these are pretty restrictive and may determine whether you can consider using snapshots. With the current release of SQL Server Management Studio, you cannot even set up database snapshots with this GUI or a wizard; it must all be done using T-SQL statements (which is not that bad of a deal). The following are some of the other restrictions:

▶ You must drop all other database snapshots when using a database snapshot to revert a source database.

▶ You lose visibility to the source database uncommitted transactions in the database snapshot when it is created.

▶ The more updates to pages in the source database, the bigger your database snapshot sparse files become.

▶ A database snapshot can only be done for an entire database, not for a subset of the database.

▶ No additional changes can be made to a database snapshot. It is read-only and can't even have additional indexes created for it to make reporting queries run faster.

▶ Additional overhead is incurred on update operations on the source database due to the copy-on-write technique (only when something changes, though).

▶ If you're using a database snapshot to revert (restore) a source database, both the snapshot and the source database are not available.

▶ The source database cannot be dropped, detached, or restored until the database snapshot is dropped first.

▶ Files on the source database or the snapshot cannot be dropped.

▶ In order for the database snapshot to be used, the source database must also be online (unless the source database is a mirrored database).

▶ The database snapshot must be on the same SQL Server instance as the source database.

▶ Snapshots are read-only.

▶ Database snapshot files must be on NTFS only (not FAT 32 or RAW partitions).

▶ Full-text indexing is not supported.

▶ If a source database ever goes into a `RECOVERY_PENDING` status, the database snapshot also becomes unavailable.

▶ If a database snapshot ever runs out of disk space, it must be dropped; it is actually marked as `SUSPECT`.

27

This may seem like a lot of restrictions—and it is. But look to Microsoft to address many of these restrictions in future releases. These current restrictions may disqualify many folks from getting into the database snapshot business. Others will thrive in its use out of the box.

Copy-on-Write Technology

The new copy-on-write technology that Microsoft has introduced with SQL Server 2005 is at the core of both database mirroring and database snapshot capabilities. How it is used in database mirroring is explained in Chapter 16. In this section, we walk through a typical transactional user's update of data in a source database.

As you can see in Figure 27.5, an update transaction is initiated against the AdventureWorks database (labeled A). As the data is being updated in the source database's data page and the change is written to the transaction log (labeled B), the copy-on-write technology also copies the original source database data page in its unchanged state to the sparse data file (also labeled B) and updates the metadata page references in the system catalog (also labeled B) with this movement.

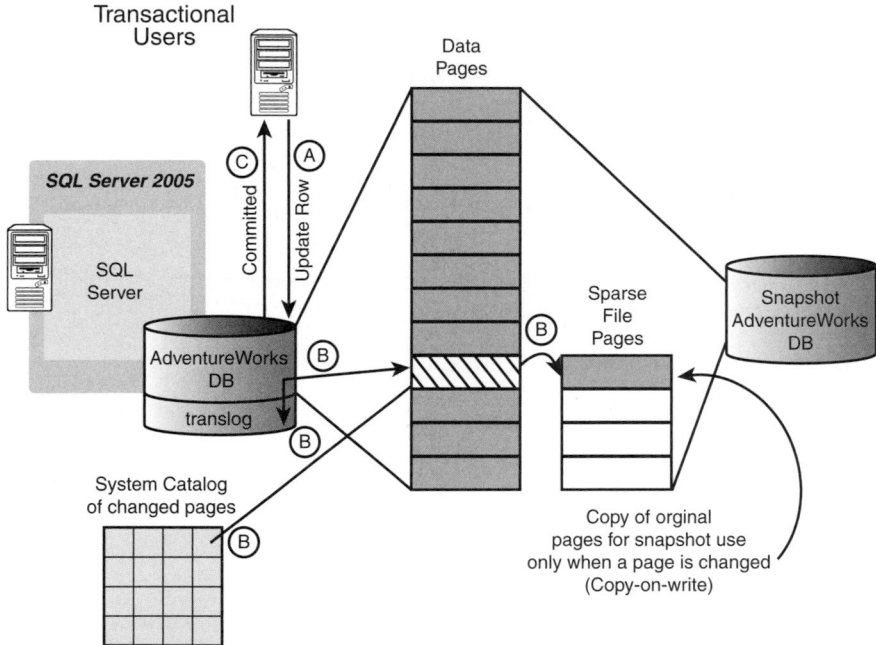

FIGURE 27.5   Using the copy-on-write technology with database snapshots.

The original source data page is still available to the database snapshot. This adds extra overhead to any transaction that updates, inserts, or deletes data from the source database, but this is known overhead that may far outweigh any usability impact this may have. Once the copy-on-write technology finishes its write on the sparse file, the original update transaction is properly committed, and acknowledgement is sent back to the user (labeled C).

NOTE

Database snapshots cannot be used for any of SQL Server's internal databases— tempdb, master, msdb, or model. Also, database snapshots are supported only in the Enterprise Edition of SQL Server 2005.

When to Use Database Snapshots

As mentioned previously, there are a few basic ways you can use database snapshots effectively. Each use is for a particular purpose, and each has its own benefits. When you have factored in the limitations and restrictions mentioned earlier, you can consider these uses. Let's look at each of them separately.

Reverting to a Snapshot for Recovery Purposes

This is probably the most basic usage of database snapshots: decreasing recovery time of a database by restoring a troubled database with a database snapshot—referred to as *reverting*. As Figure 27.6 shows, one or more regularly scheduled snapshots can be generated during a 24-hour period that effectively provide you with data recovery milestones that can be rapidly used. As you can see in this example, four database snapshots are six hours apart (6:00 a.m., 12:00 p.m., 6:00 p.m., and 12:00 a.m.). Each is dropped and re-created once per day, using the same snapshot name. Any one of these snapshots can rapidly be used to recovery the source database in the event of a logical data error (such as rows deleted or a table being dropped). This technique is not supposed to take the place of a good maintenance plan that includes full database backups and incremental transaction log dumps. However, it can be extremely fast to get a database back to a particular milestone.

To revert to a particular snapshot interval, you simply use the RESTORE DATABASE command with the FROM DATABASE_SNAPSHOT statement. This is a complete database restore; you cannot limit it to just a single database object. In addition, you must drop all other database snapshots before you can use one of them to restore a database.

As you can also see in Figure 27.6, a targeted SQL statement variation from a complete database restore from a snapshot could be used instead if you knew exactly what you wanted to restore at the table and row level. You could simply use SQL statements (such as an UPDATE SQL statement or an INSERT SQL statement) from one of the snapshots to selectively apply only the fixes you are sure need to be recovered (reverted). In other words, you don't restore the whole database from the snapshot, you only use some of the snapshots data with SQL statements and bring the messed-up data row values back in line with the original values in the snapshot. This is at the row and column level and usually requires quite a bit of detail analysis before it can be applied to a production database.

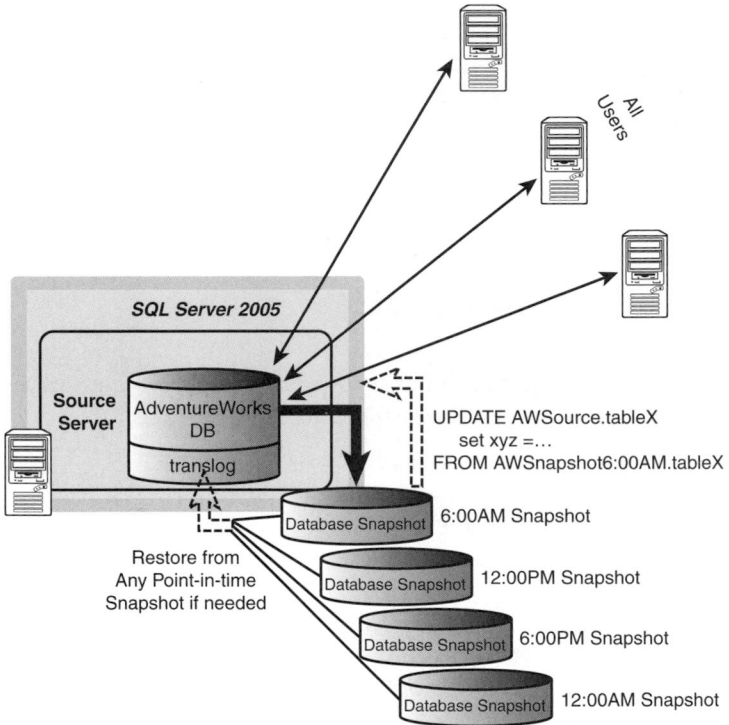

FIGURE 27.6   Basic database snapshot configuration: a source database and one or more database snapshots at different time intervals.

It is also possible to use a snapshot to recover a table that someone accidentally dropped. There is a little data loss since the last snapshot, but it is a simple INSERT INTO statement from the latest snapshot before the table drop. So be careful here, but consider the value as well.

Safeguarding a Database Prior to Making Mass Changes

Often, you plan regular events against your database tables that result in some type of mass update being applied to big portions of the database. If you do a quick database snapshot *before* any of these types of changes, you are essentially creating a nice safety net for rapid recovery in the event that you are not satisfied with the mass update results. Figure 27.7 illustrates this type of safeguarding technique.

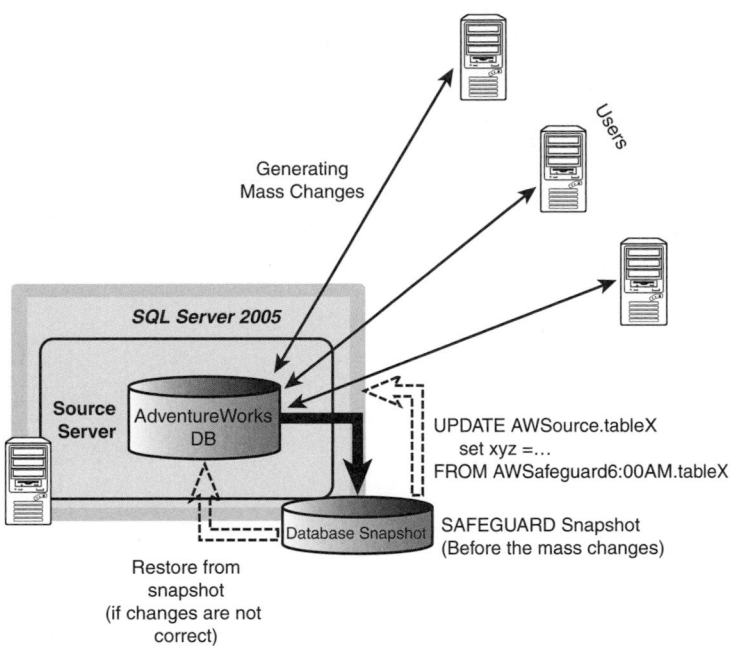

FIGURE 27.7   Creating a before database snapshot prior to scheduled mass updates to a database.

If you are not satisfied with the entire update operation, you can do a RESTORE DATABASE from the snapshot and revert it to this point. Or, if you are happy with some updates but not others, you can use the SQL statement technique to selectively UPDATE (restore) particular values back to their original values using the snapshot.

Providing a Testing (or Quality Assurance) Starting Point (Baseline)

In testing and the QA phases of your development life cycle, you often need to conduct tests over and over. These are either logic tests or even performance tests. To aid testing and QA, database snapshots can be made of a test database prior to full testing (create a testing baseline database snapshot) and then the test database can be reverted back to its original state at a moment's notice, using that baseline snapshot. This can be done any number of times. Figure 27.8 shows how easy it is to simply create a testing reference point (or synchronization point) with a database snapshot.

You then just run your test scripts or do any manual testing—as much as you want—and then revert back to this starting point rapidly. Then you run more tests again.

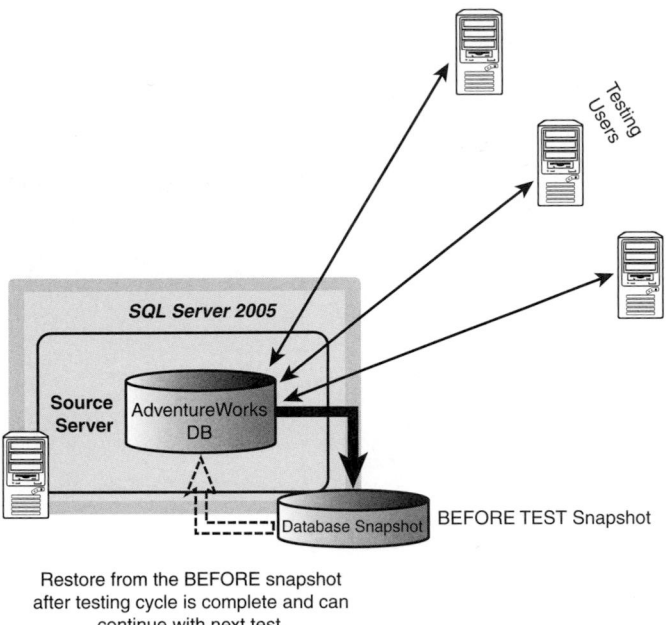

FIGURE 27.8   Establishing a baseline testing database snapshot before running tests and then reverting when finished.

Providing a Point-in-Time Reporting Database

If what you really need is a true point-in-time reporting database to run ad hoc or canned reports from, often a database snapshot can serve this purpose much more easily than resorting to log shipping or data replication. Key to determining when you can use this database snapshot technique is whether the reporting load on this database server instance can easily support the reporting workload and whether the update transactions against this database are adversely affected by the database snapshot overhead of each transaction. Figure 27.9 shows the typical database snapshot configuration for one (or more) database snapshots that are to be used for reporting.

Remember, this is a point-in-time snapshot of the source database. How frequently you need to create a new snapshot is dictated by your reporting requirements for data latency (how old the data can be in these reports).

Providing a Highly Available and Offloaded Reporting Database from a Database Mirror

If you are using database mirroring to improve your high availability, you can also create a database snapshot against this mirrored database and expose the snapshot to your reporting users. Even though the mirrored database is not usable for any access whatsoever (it is in constant restore mode), SQL Server allows a snapshot to be created against it (as shown in

Figure 27.10). This is a very powerful configuration in that a database snapshot against a mirror does not impact the load of the principal server—guaranteeing high performance against the principal server. Also, by isolating the database snapshot over to the mirror server, the performance of the reporting users is also more predictable because they are not competing with the transactional users for resources on the principal server. Only real issues arise when the principal server fails over to the mirror database. You now have both transactional and reporting users using the same database server instance, and performance of them all is affected.

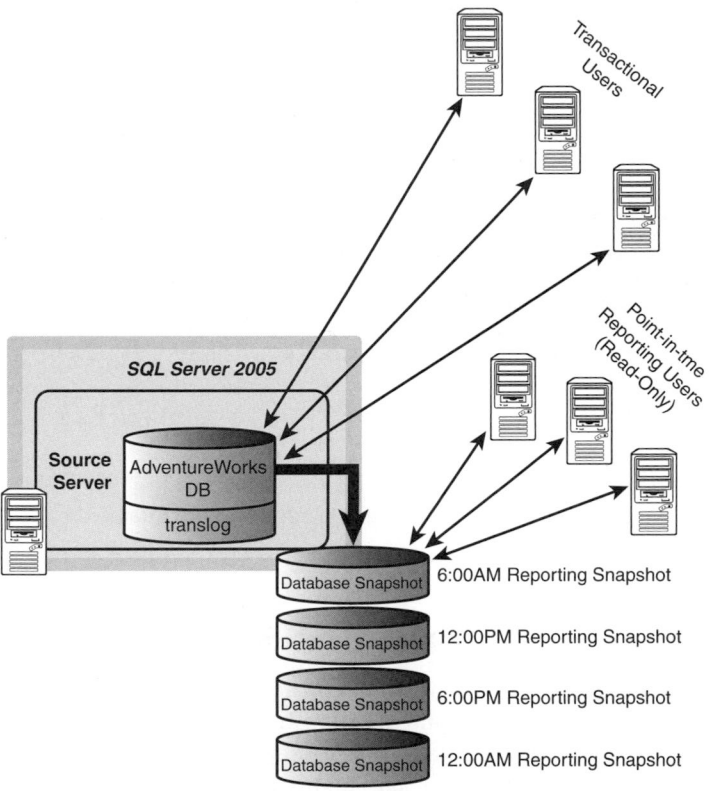

FIGURE 27.9   A point-in-time reporting database via a database snapshot.

A possible solution to this would be to automatically (or manually) drop the database snapshot on the mirror server if it becomes the principal and create a new snapshot on the old principal server if it is available (it is now the mirror). You then just point all your reporting users to this new database snapshot. This can be handled fairly easily in an application server layer. This is basically a reciprocal principal/mirror reporting configuration approach that always tries to get the database snapshot that is used for reporting to be on the server that is the mirror server. You would never really want to have active database snapshots on both the principal server and the mirror server at the same time. This is way too much overhead for both servers. You want just the database snapshots to be on the mirror server. For a full explanation of all the capabilities of a database mirroring configuration, please refer to Chapter 16.

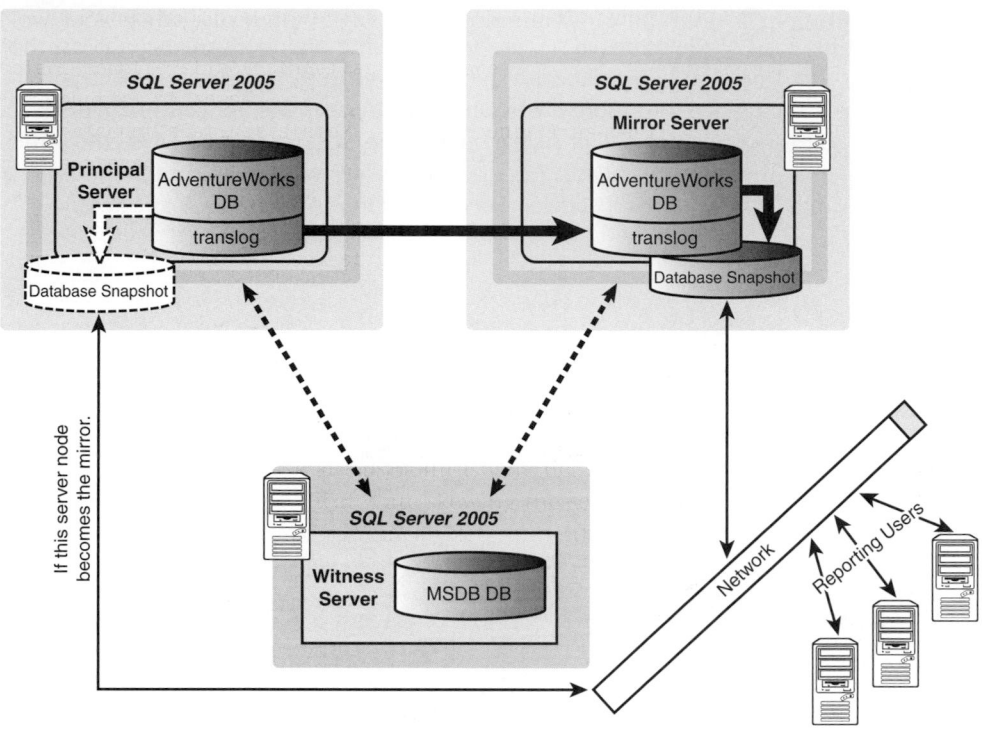

FIGURE 27.10   Creating a database snapshot for reporting against a mirrored database to offload the reporting impact on the principal server.

Setup and Breakdown of a Database Snapshot

You might actually be surprised to find out how easy it is to set up a database snapshot. This simplicity is partly due to the level at which database snapshots are created—at the database level and not at the table level. Setting up a database snapshot only entails running a CREATE DATABASE with the AS SNAPSHOT OF statement. You cannot create database snapshots from SQL Server Management Studio or from any other GUI or wizard for that matter. All must be done using SQL scripts. All SQL scripts for this chapter are available to you as a download from the Sams Publishing website for this book title (www.samspublishing.com). The script file, named DBSnapshotSQL.sql, also contains a variety of other useful SQL statements to help you better manage a database snapshot environment.

Creating a Database Snapshot

One of the first things you must figure out before you create a database snapshot is whether your source database data portion has more than one physical file in its allocation. All these file references must be accounted for in the snapshot. You execute the system stored procedure sp_helpdb with the source database name as the parameter as done here:

```
EXEC SP_HELPDB AdventureWorks
Go
```

The following shows the detailed file allocations of this database:

```
Name                 FileID  File Name
AdventureWorks_Data1  1      C:\Server\MSSQL.4\MSSQL\DATA\Unleashed_Data1.mdf
AdventureWorks_Data2  2      C:\Server\MSSQL.4\MSSQL\DATA\Unleashed_Data2.mdf
```

You need to worry about only the data portion of the database for the snapshot. As you can see, if you have two data files that comprise the data portion of a source database, you must have two both data file references present in the database snapshot as well (as shown here):

```
CREATE DATABASE SNAP_AdventureWorks_6AM
ON
 ( NAME = AdventureWorks_Data1,
   FILENAME= 'C:\Server\MSSQL.4\MSSQL\DATA\SNAP_AW_data1_6AM.snap'),
( NAME = AdventureWorks_Data2,
   FILENAME= 'C:\Server\MSSQL.4\MSSQL\DATA\SNAP_AW_data2_0AM.snap')
AS SNAPSHOT OF AdventureWorks
go
```

It is really that easy. Now let's walk through a simple example of creating a series of four database snapshots against the AdventureWorks source database that represent snapshots that are six hours apart (as shown in Figure 27.6). The following is the next snapshot to be run at 12:00 p.m.:

```
CREATE DATABASE SNAP_AdventureWorks_12PM
ON
 ( NAME = AdventureWorks_Data1,
   FILENAME= 'C:\Server\MSSQL.4\MSSQL\DATA\SNAP_AW_data1_12PM.snap'),
( NAME = AdventureWorks_Data2,
   FILENAME= 'C:\Server\MSSQL.4\MSSQL\DATA\SNAP_AW_data2_12PM.snap')
AS SNAPSHOT OF AdventureWorks
go
```

These will represent snapshots at equal time intervals and can be used for reporting or for reverting.

27

NOTE

We use a simple naming convention for the database names for snapshots and for the snapshot files themselves. The database snapshot name is the word SNAP, followed by the source database name, followed by a qualifying description of what this snapshot represents, all separated with underscores. For example, a database snapshot that represents a 6:00 a.m. snapshot of the AdventureWorks database would have this name:

```
"SNAP_AdventureWorks_6AM"
```

The snapshot file-naming convention is similar. The name would start with the word SNAP, followed by the database name that the snapshot is for (AdventureWorks, in our example), followed by the data portion indication (for example, data, data1), a short identification of what this snapshot represents (for example, 6AM), and then the filename extension .snap to distinguish it from .mdf and .ldf files. For example, the snapshot filename for the preceding database snapshot would look like this:

```
"SNAP_AdventureWorks_data_6AM.snap"
```

We will use the AdventureWorks database for this example. AdventureWorks is currently only using a single data file allocation for its data portion. Here's how you create the first snapshot, to reflect a 6:00 a.m. snapshot:

1. Create the snapshot on the source database AdventureWorks:

```
Use [master]
go
CREATE DATABASE SNAP_AdventureWorks_6AM
ON ( NAME = AdventureWorks_Data, FILENAME= 'C:\Program Files\
    Microsoft SQL Server\MSSQL.2\MSSQL\DATA\
    SNAP_AdventureWorks_data_6AM.snap')
AS SNAPSHOT OF AdventureWorks
Go
```

2. Look at this newly created snapshot from the SQL Server instance point of view, using a SQL query against the sys.databases system catalog, as follows:

```
Use [master]
go
SELECT name,
       database_id,
       source_database_id, -- source DB of the snapshot
       create_date,
       snapshot_isolation_state_desc
FROM sys.databases
Go
```

This shows the existing source database and the newly created database snapshot:

name	database_id	source_database_id	create_date	snapshot_isolation_state_desc
AdventureWorks	6	NULL	2006-02-17 23:37:02.763	OFF
SNAP_AdventureWorks_6AM	13	6	2006-12-05 08:18:36.597	ON

Note that source_database_id for the newly created database snapshot contains the database ID of the source database. Of course you can also look at this database snapshot properties by using SQL Server Management Studio, as shown in Figure 27.11:

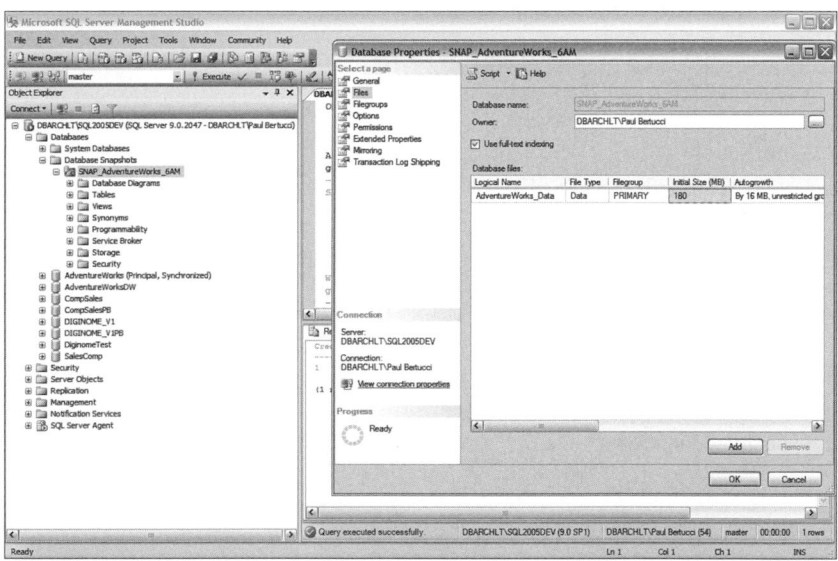

FIGURE 27.11   Using SQL Server Management Studio to view the database snapshot properties.

3. Look at the newly created physical file for the sparse file (for the database snapshot) by querying the sys.master_files system catalog:

```
SELECT database_id, file_id, name, physical_name
FROM sys.master_files
WHERE Name = 'AdventureWorks_data'
and is_sparse = 1
go
```

Note that we are focusing on only the sparse files for the newly created database snapshot (that is, the is_sparse = 1 qualification). This query results in the following:

database_id	file_id	name	physical_name
13	1	AdventureWorks_Data	C:\Prog...\DATA\ SNAP_AdventureWorks_data_6AM.snap

4. To see the number of bytes that a snapshot sparse file is burning up, you can issue a series of SQL statements against system catalog views/tables by using fn_virtualfilestats and sys.master_files. However, the following is a quick-and-dirty stored procedure that should make this task much easier. Just create this stored procedure on your SQL Server instance (in the master database), and you can use it to see the sizes of any database snapshot sparse file on your server (also available in the downloadable SQL script file for this chapter):

```
CREATE PROCEDURE SNAP_SIZE_UNLEASHED
        @DBDATA varchar(255) = NULL
AS
if @DBDATA is not null
    BEGIN
        SELECT B.name as 'Sparse files for Database Name',
              A.DbId, A.FileId, BytesOnDisk      FROM fn_virtualfilestats
➥(NULL, NULL) A,
              sys.master_files B
        WHERE A.DbID = B.database_id
          and A.FileID = B.file_id
          and B.is_sparse = 1
          and B.name = @DBDATA
    END
ELSE
    BEGIN
        SELECT B.name as 'Sparse files for Database Name',
              A.DbId, A.FileId, BytesOnDisk
        FROM fn_virtualfilestats (NULL, NULL) A,
              sys.master_files B
        WHERE A.DbID = B.database_id
          and A.FileID = B.file_id
          and B.is_sparse = 1
    END
Go
```

When the SNAP_SIZE_UNLEASHED stored procedure is created, you run it with or without the name of the data portion of the database that you have created a snapshot for. If you do not supply the data portion name, you see all sparse files and their sizes on the SQL Server instance. The following is an example of executing this stored procedure to see the sparse file current size for the `AdventureWorks_data` portion:

```
EXEC SNAP_SIZE_UNLEASHED 'AdventureWorks_Data'
Go
```

This results in the detail bytes that the sparse file is using on disk:

```
Sparse files for Database Name  DbId   FileId   BytesOnDisk
-------------------------------------------------------------------
AdventureWorks_Data              13      1       196608
```

Right now, the sparse file is very small (196kb) because it was recently created. Little to no source data pages have changed, so it is basically empty right now. It will start growing as data is updated in the source database and data pages are copied to the sparse file (by the copy-on-write mechanism). You can use the `SNAP_SIZE_UNLEASHED` stored procedure to keep an eye on the sparse file size.

5. Believe it or not, the database snapshot is ready for you to use. The following is an example of a SQL statement that is selecting rows from this newly created database snapshot for a typical point-in-time based query against the `CreditCard` table:

```
Use [SNAP_AdventureWorks_6AM]
go
SELECT [CreditCardID]
      ,[CardType]
      ,[CardNumber]
      ,[ExpMonth]
      ,[ExpYear]
      ,[ModifiedDate]
  FROM [SNAP_AdventureWorks_6AM].[Sales].[CreditCard]
WHERE CreditCardID = 1
go
```

This delivers the correct, point-in-time result rows from the database snapshot:

```
CreditCardID CardType        CardNumber          ExpMonth ExpYear
                                                          ModifiedDate
------------ ----------------------------------------------------
                                                          ----------------
1            SuperiorCard    33332664695310      1        2010
                                                          2006-12-03 00:00:39.560
```

You are now in the database snapshot business.

27

Breaking Down a Database Snapshot

If you want to get rid of a snapshot or overlay a current snapshot with a more up-to-date snapshot, you simple use the DROP DATABASE command and then create it again. The DROP DATABASE command immediately removes the database snapshot entry and all sparse file allocations associated with the snapshot. It's very simple indeed. The following is an example of dropping the database snapshot just created:

```
Use [master]
go
DROP DATABASE SNAP_AdventureWorks_6AM
go
```

If you'd like, you can also drop (delete) a database snapshot from SQL Server Management Studio by right-clicking the database snapshot entry and choosing the Delete option. However, it's best to do everything with scripts so that you can accurately reproduce the same action over and over.

Reverting to a Database Snapshot for Recovery

If you have a database snapshot defined for a source database, you can use that snapshot to revert the source database to that snapshot's point-in-time milestone. In other words, you consciously overlay a source database with the point-in-time representation of that database (which you got when you created a snapshot). You must remember that you will lose all data changes that had occurred from that point-in-time moment and the current state of the source database. However, this may be exactly what you are intending.

Reverting a Source Database from a Database Snapshot

Reverting is just a logical term for using the DATABASE RESTORE command with the FROM DATABASE_SNAPSHOT statement. It effectively causes the point-in-time database snapshot to become the source database. Under the covers, much of this is managed from the system catalog metadata level. However, the results are that the source database will be in exactly the same state as the database snapshot. When you use a database snapshot as the basis of a database restore, all other database snapshots that have the same source database must first be dropped. Again, to see what database snapshots may be defined for a particular database, you can execute the following query:

```
Use [master]
go
SELECT name,
       database_id,
       source_database_id, -- source DB of the snapshot
       create_date,
       snapshot_isolation_state_desc
FROM sys.databases
Go
```

This shows the existing source database and the newly created database snapshot:

```
name               database_id source_database_id  create_date  snapshot_isolation_
                                                                 state_desc
--------------------------------------------------------------------------
                                                                 ------------

AdventureWorks            6      NULL         2006-02-17 23:37:02.763
                                                                 OFF

SNAP_AdventureWorks_6AM   13      6           2006-12-05 06:01:36.597
                                                                 ON

SNAP_AdventureWorks_12PM  14      6           2006-12-05 12:00:36.227
                                                                 ON
```

In this example, there are two snapshots against the AdventureWorks database. The one you don't want to use when reverting must be dropped first. Then you can proceed to restore the source database with the remaining snapshot that you want. These are the steps:

1. Drop the unwanted snapshot(s):

```
Use [master]
go
DROP DATABASE SNAP_AdventureWorks_12PM
go
```

2. Issue the RESTORE DATABASE command with the remaining snapshot:

```
USE [master]
go
RESTORE DATABASE AdventureWorks FROM DATABASE_SNAPSHOT =
➥'SNAP_AdventureWorks_6AM'
go
```

When this is complete, the source database and the snapshot are essentially the same point-in-time database. But the source database quickly diverges, as updates begin to flow in again.

Using Database Snapshots with Testing and QA

Reverting to a "golden" copy of a database via a database snapshot is going to be popular going forward because of the simplicity that creating and reverting provides. Testing and QA groups will thrive on this feature, and this will directly affect the velocity of testing in your organization. With the increase in the frequency and stability of your testing and QA environments, a direct improvement in the quality of your application should be attainable. Essentially, these are the steps:

27

1. Create the golden database snapshot *before* you run your testing:

```
Use [master]
go
CREATE DATABASE SNAP_AdventureWorks_GOLDEN
ON ( NAME = AdventureWorks_Data, FILENAME= 'C:\Program Files\
    Microsoft SQL Server\MSSQL.2\MSSQL\DATA\
              SNAP_AdventureWorks_data_GOLDEN.snap')
AS SNAPSHOT OF AdventureWorks
Go
```

2. Run your tests or QA to your heart's content.

3. Revert to the golden copy when the testing is completed so that the process can be repeated again, or regression testing can be run, or stress testing be done, or performance testing started, or further application testing can be done:

```
USE [master]
go
RESTORE DATABASE AdventureWorks
FROM DATABASE_SNAPSHOT = 'SNAP_AdventureWorks_GOLDEN'
go
```

Setting Up Snapshots Against a Database Mirror

If you are using database mirroring to improve your high availability, you can also create a database snapshot against this mirrored database and expose the snapshot to your reporting users. This further enhances the overall database availability to all end users (transactional and reporting users). In addition, it serves to isolate the reporting users from the transactional users. The reporting users are connected to the mirror server's version of the database (via a database snapshot of the mirrored database), and their reporting queries do not impact the principal server in any way. Remember that the mirrored database is not usable for any access whatsoever (it is in constant restore mode). SQL Server allows a snapshot to be created against it (as shown in Figure 27.10). As mentioned before, the only real issues arise when the principal server fails over to the mirror database. When the mirror server takes over for the principal, the database snapshot terminates its reporting user connections. The reporting users only need to reconnect to pick up where they left off. However, you now have both transactional and reporting users using the same database server instance and performance of all will be affected.

A possible solution to this would be to automatically (or manually) drop the database snapshot on the mirror server if it becomes the principal and create a new snapshot on the old principal server if it is available (it is now the mirror). You then just point all your reporting users to this new database snapshot. This can be handled fairly easily in an application server layer. This is basically a reciprocal principal/mirror reporting configuration approach that always tries to get the database snapshot that is used for reporting to be on the server that is the mirror server. You would never really want to have active database snapshots on both the principal server and the mirror server at the same time.

Reciprocal Principal/Mirror Reporting Configuration

The following steps outline the method to create the snapshot on the mirror, drop it when the mirror becomes the principal, and create a new snapshot against the old principal (now the mirror):

1. Create the database snapshot on a mirrored database server for reporting on the mirror server (DBARCHLT\SQL2005DIST):

```
Use [master]
go
CREATE DATABASE SNAP_AdventureWorks_REPORTING
ON ( NAME = AdventureWorks_Data, FILENAME= 'C:\Program Files\
    Microsoft SQL Server\MSSQL.2\MSSQL\DATA\
        SNAP_AdventureWorks_data_REPORTING.snap')
AS SNAPSHOT OF AdventureWorks
Go
```

As you can see in Figure 27.12, this would be the live configuration of the principal server (DBARCHLT\SQL2005DEV), the mirror server (DBARCHLT\SQL2005DIST), and the reporting database snapshot (SNAP_AdventureWorks_REPORTING), as shown from SQL Server Management Studio.

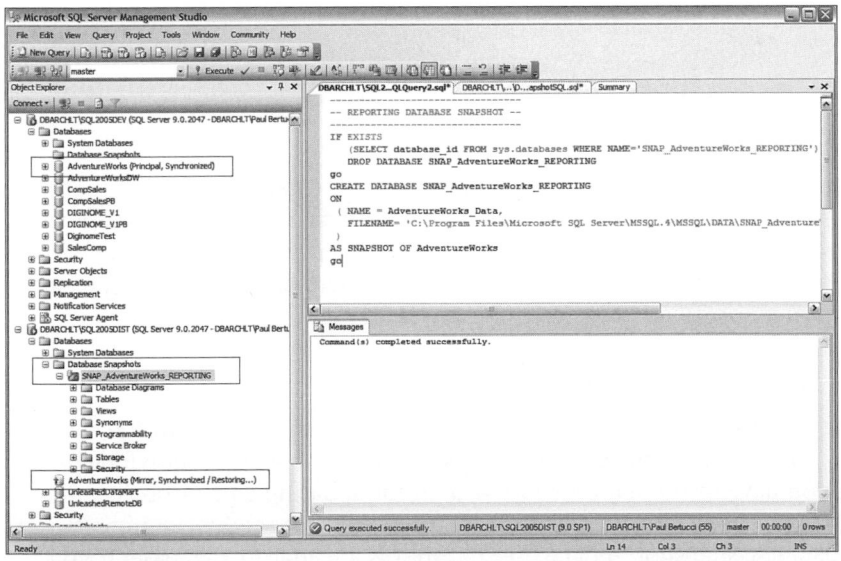

FIGURE 27.12   SQL Server Management Studio, showing database mirroring with a database snapshot for reporting configuration.

If the principal fails over to the mirror, you would drop the database snapshot that is currently created off that database and create a new one on the old principal (now the mirror), as follows:

2. Drop the reporting database snapshot on the new principal server (the principal is now DBARCHLT\SQL2005DIST):

```
Use [master]
go
DROP DATABASE SNAP_AdventureWorks_REPORTING
go
```

3. Create the new reporting database snapshot on the new mirrored database server (the mirror is now DBARCHLT\SQL2005DEV):

```
Use [master]
go
CREATE DATABASE SNAP_AdventureWorks_REPORTING
ON ( NAME = AdventureWorks_Data, FILENAME= 'C:\Program Files\
    Microsoft SQL Server\MSSQL.4\MSSQL\DATA\
        SNAP_AdventureWorks_data_REPORTING.snap')
AS SNAPSHOT OF AdventureWorks
Go
```

That's it. You have now gotten your reporting users completely isolated away from your principal server (and the transactional users) again. Life can return to normal very quickly.

Database Snapshots Maintenance and Security Considerations

There are several things that need to be highly managed with regard to database snapshots: snapshot sparse file size management, data latency management that corresponds to your user's needs, the location of the sparse files within your physical deployment, the sheer number of database snapshots that you are willing to support against a single database instance, and the security and access needs of users of database snapshots.

Security for Database Snapshots

By default, you get the security roles and definitions that you have created in the source database available to you within the database snapshot *except* for roles or individual permissions that you have in the source database used for updating data or objects. This is referred to as "inherited from the source database." These updating rights are not available to you in a database snapshot. A database snapshot is a read-only database! If you have specialized roles or restrictions you want to be present in the database snapshot, you need to define them in the source database, and you will get them instantly. You manage from a single place, and everyone is happy.

Snapshot Sparse File Size Management

Sparse file size is probably the most critical thing to deal with when managing database snapshots. It is imperative that you keep a close watch on the growing size of any (and all) database snapshot sparse files you create. If your snapshot runs out of space because you didn't manage this well, it becomes suspect and is not available to use. The only path out of this scenario is to drop the snapshot and re-create it. The following are some things to consider for sparse files:

▶ Monitor sparse files regularly. Make use of stored procedures such as the `SNAP_SIZE_UNLEASHED` stored procedure to help with this.

▶ Pay close attention to the volatility of the source database. This rate of change directly translates to the size of the sparse file and how fast it grows. The rule of thumb is to match your drop and re-create of a database snapshot frequency to when the sparse file is at around 30% of the size of the source database. Your data latency user requirements may demand a faster rate of drop/re-create.

▶ Isolate sparse files away from the source database data files. You do not want to compete with disk arm movement in any way. Always work to get disk I/O as parallel as possible.

Number of Database Snapshots per Source Database

In general, you shouldn't have too many database snapshots defined on a database because of the copy-on-write overhead each snapshot requires. However, this all depends on the volatility of the source database and a server's capacity. If there is low volatility and the server is not using much CPU, memory, and disk capacity, then this database could more readily support many separate database snapshots at once. If the volatility is high and CPU, memory, and perhaps disk capacity are saturated, you should minimize drastically the number of database snapshots.

Summary

Database snapshots can be thought of as an enabling capability with many purposes. They are great for fulfilling point-in-time reporting requirements easily, reverting a database to a point in time (recoverability and availability), insulating a database from issues that may arise during mass updates, and potentially reducing the processing impact of querying against the primary transactional databases (via database mirroring and database snapshots). You must remember that database snapshots are point-in-time and read-only. The only way to update a snapshot is to drop it and re-create it. Data latency of this point-in-time snapshot capability must always be made very clear to any of its users.

Database snapshots are snapshots of the entire database, not a subset. This clearly makes data snapshots very different from alternative data access capabilities such as data replication and materialized views. This feature has been made possible via a major breakthrough from Microsoft called copy-on-write technology. This is certainly an exciting

27

extension to SQL Server but is not to be used as a substitute for good old database backups and restores. This is one capability that we would recommend you consider using as soon as possible. It also appears to be rock solid in its implementation. Thanks, Microsoft.

Chapter 28, "Database Maintenance," provides a detailed explanation of the best practices surrounding maintaining a database.

CHAPTER **28**

Database Maintenance

IN THIS CHAPTER

▶ What's New in Database Maintenance

▶ The Maintenance Plan Wizard

▶ Managing Maintenance Plans Without the Wizard

▶ Executing a Maintenance Plan

▶ Maintenance Without a Maintenance Plan

Database maintenance is an essential part of database administration that is needed to keep databases healthy. It includes tasks that are performed after your database is created to ensure the integrity of the data in the database, provide performance improvements, and help keep the database safe.

This chapter examines some of the key tasks that should be included in your database maintenance plan. It discusses the means for creating these plans, including tools such as the Maintenance Plan Wizard that is part of SQL Server 2005. These tools make the creation of a solid database maintenance plan easier and provide a framework that allows you to create the plan once and let automation do the rest of the work.

What Needs to Be Maintained

The core tasks related to the maintenance of a SQL Server database are backing up the database and log, rebuilding indexes, updating statistics, and running integrity checks against the database. These ongoing, repetitive tasks are best run on a scheduled basis and are the backbone of the maintenance plan. Other tasks related to maintenance involve managing access by the users, maintaining data files, and monitoring performance. These tasks are more apt to be performed on an ad hoc basis when the need arises.

What's New in Database Maintenance

The required database maintenance tasks in SQL Server 2005 have remained the same as in earlier versions, but the tools that are included with SQL Server 2005 to produce and execute a plan have changed dramatically. These changes include the following:

▶ **Maintenance plans**—The database maintenance plans that are created using SQL Server Management Studio (SSMS) are now referred to as *maintenance plans*. In SQL Server 2000, they were called *database maintenance plans*. This is a small change but one worth noting to avoid any confusion.

▶ **SQL Server Integration Services (SSIS)**—SSIS is the replacement for Data Transformation Service (DTS), which came with SQL Server 2000. It is an integral part of maintenance plans that are created in SQL Server 2005. SSIS provides better control of workflow related to maintenance plans and provides much more flexibility than was available with database maintenance plans created in SQL Server 2000.

▶ **Log shipping**—Log shipping plans are no longer created using the maintenance plan tools. You create log shipping plans in SQL Server 2005 by selecting the properties for the database in SSMS and choosing the Transaction Log Shipping properties page to configure the appropriate settings.

▶ **SQLMAINT deprecation**—The SQLMAINT utility is the backbone for database maintenance plans created in SQL Server 2000. This utility is still available in SQL Server 2005 in order to execute plans that were created in SQL Server 2000, but it has been deprecated and is scheduled to be removed in a future version of the product.

The Maintenance Plan Wizard

The Maintenance Plan Wizard is a tool that you access from the Management node in SSMS. It provides an automated means for creating the basic tasks needed to maintain a database. It does not include all the tasks that are available for use in a maintenance plan but is a great starting point that allows you to quickly generate the basic elements of a good plan.

> **NOTE**
>
> The creation of a comprehensive maintenance plan requires that you manually edit the plan that is created with the Maintenance Plan Wizard. For example, the wizard can generate a plan that includes a full backup of your databases, but this plan does not include a task to remove older backups. The removal of older backups is essential in order to ensure that you do not use up all your disk space. The section "Managing Maintenance Plans Without the Wizard," later in this chapter, covers how to do this.

You launch the Maintenance Plan Wizard by expanding the Management node in SSMS and then right-clicking Maintenance Plans and selecting Maintenance Plan Wizard. The Maintenance Plan Wizard is like most other Microsoft wizards in that it presents sequential dialog boxes that allow you to incrementally provide the information needed to create the wizard's objective.

The Maintenance Plan Wizard first displays an introductory dialog box. When you click Next, it displays a dialog box (like the one shown in Figure 28.1) that allows you to specify the target server that the maintenance plan will be run against. You can also specify the name of your maintenance plan on this screen. You should choose a naming convention that will allow you to easily identify a maintenance plan and the type of maintenance it is performing.

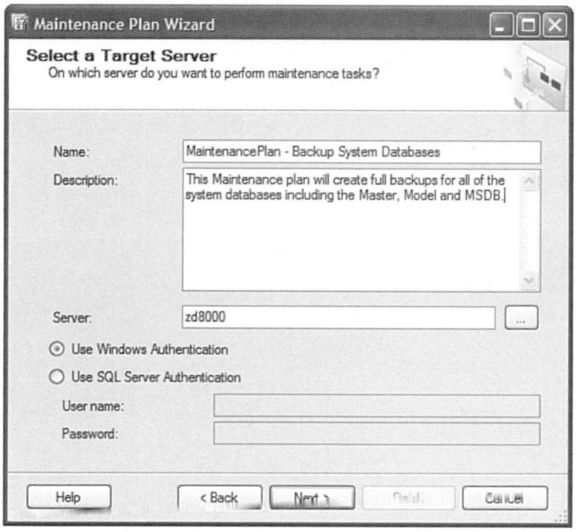

FIGURE 28.1   Setting the target server in the Maintenance Plan Wizard.

After you name the maintenance plan and select the target server, you can click Next. The dialog box that appears next allows you to select the maintenance tasks you would like to perform on the server. Figure 28.2 shows the Select Maintenance Tasks dialog, with the tasks that are available from the wizard. You can select more than one task for a given plan. As mentioned earlier, the tasks listed in the wizard are not all the tasks available in a maintenance plan.

The dialog box that appears next allows you to specify the order in which the tasks are executed (see Figure 28.3). Obviously, the order of the tasks can be a critical factor and is dependent on the type of tasks you are running. You can click the Move Up and Move Down buttons to change the order of the tasks.

The dialog boxes that have been discussed so far are consistent for all the maintenance plans. The dialog boxes that follow are dependent on the tasks selected for the plan. Each task has a relevant set of properties that are displayed for entry in a subsequent dialog box. The following sections cover some of the common maintenance tasks and the wizard screens that relate to them.

28

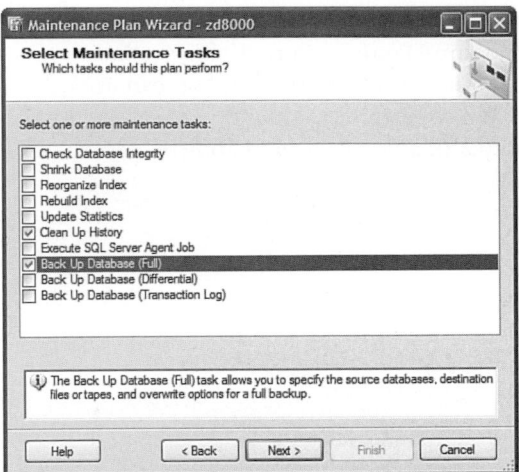

FIGURE 28.2   Selecting maintenance tasks in the Maintenance Plan Wizard.

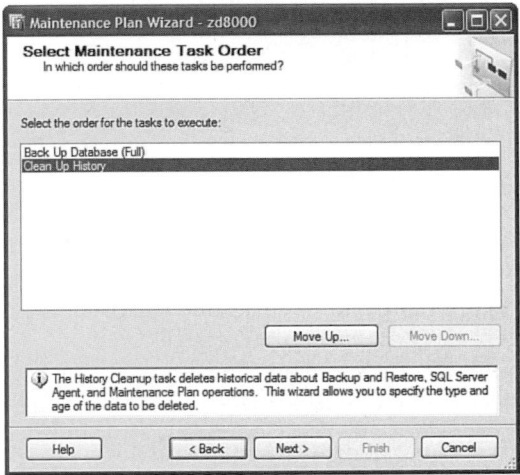

FIGURE 28.3   Selecting the order of the maintenance tasks in the Maintenance Plan Wizard.

Backing Up Databases

Backing up databases is the most basic element of a maintenance plan—and probably the most important part. The importance of backups and the role they play are discussed in detail in Chapter 11, "Database Backup and Restore," but basically, backups are needed to help limit the amount of data loss. For example, in the event of a disk drive failure, database backups can be used to restore the database data that was located on that drive.

The database backup options that are available via a maintenance plan include full, differential, and transaction log backups. Full and transaction log backups were available in SQL Server 2000's database maintenance plans, but differential backups are new to SQL Server 2005's maintenance plans. The type of backups you select for a plan is heavily dependent on the type of environment you are maintaining and the type of database you are backing up. Databases that have very few changes may only need a nightly full backup and do not require transaction log or differential backups.

In most cases, it is a good idea to take a full backup of your system and user databases each night. Figure 28.4 shows the backup options that the wizard displays for a full backup.

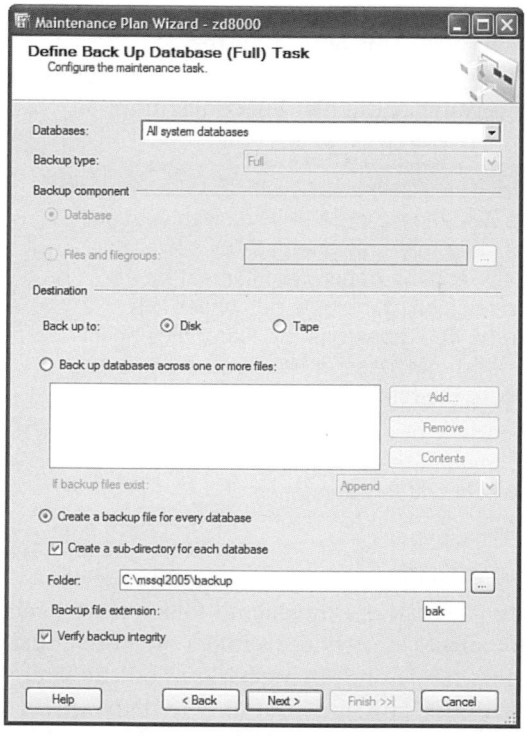

FIGURE 28.4   Full backup options in the Maintenance Plan Wizard.

To set the properties for a full backup, you need to first define the databases you want to back up. You select the databases by using the Databases drop-down at the top of the screen. This drop-down is unique in that it gives you a variety of radio button options rather than just a simple list. You can choose to back up all databases, all system databases, or all user databases or you can select specific databases.

After you select the database(s) that you want to back up, you must select a destination for the backup files. The destination includes the type of media (that is, tape or disk) and the file or files on that medium. The option Back Up Databases Across One or More Files allows you to specify one or more fixed files that the database backup will always be written to. With this option, you can choose to append each backup to the file(s) or overwrite the contents of the file(s) each time the backup is performed. If you choose to overwrite the backup each time, you will have only the latest backup available for restoration. If you choose to append to the file, older backups will be retained on this file, and the file will continue to grow with each subsequent backup.

The preferred option for creating full backups with the wizard is the option Create a Backup File for Every Database. This option creates a separate file for each database in the maintenance plan. The backup file that is created has the database name as the first part of the filename, followed by _backup_ and then a timestamp that indicates when the backup was created. For example, a backup named AdventureWorks_backup_ 200608231402.bak would be a backup file created using this option for the AdventureWorks database. Multiple versions of backups can be retained with this option, and the identification of the backup is simple because of the naming convention.

TIP

You should use the option Back Up Databases Across One or More Files with caution. The pitfall with overwriting the file with this option is that only one backup is available for restoration. When this option is used with the Append option, you can eat up all your disk space if the file is not cleaned up. In addition, if multiple databases are backed up with the plan, all these backups will be spread across the file or files specified for the destination. A separate backup for each database is not created with this option. This can lead to confusion and complicate the restoration process.

Generally speaking, you should steer clear of backing up the database to a single file or set of files. Instead, you should choose the option Create a Backup File for Every Database. This option has fewer pitfalls and requires little attendance.

When you use the Create a Backup File for Every Database option, you need to specify a folder for the database backups to be written to. You can use the default folder, or you can change it to a folder of your choice. It is a good practice to choose a folder on a drive that is different than the drive that your database files reside on. Having backups on the same drive as your data could be a big problem if that drive fails and your only backups are on that drive. If you select the option Create a Sub-directory for Each Database, each database will have a separate subfolder under the folder specified for the backup.

CAUTION

The main pitfall associated with the option Create a Backup File for Every Database is that many backup files can be created and are not automatically deleted by default. This has been mentioned already, but it is a critical consideration. The good news is that you can add the deletion of the older backups to the maintenance plan after it has been created. You do this by adding the maintenance cleanup task to your plan, as discussed later in this chapter, in the section "Managing Maintenance Plans Without the Wizard."

The last option on the Define Back Up Database screen is Verify Backup Integrity. If you select this option, SQL Server checks the integrity of the backup files that were written as part of the backup operation. Selecting this option extends the execution time for the backup plan but is generally a good idea to ensure that you have a viable backup for recovery. It is particularly useful when backups have been written across multiple files. Unfortunately, the backup task does not allow you to utilize the new checksum options that are available with the SQL Server 2005 BACKUP command, but the basic VERIFY option suffices in most instances.

Checking Database Integrity

The Define Database Check Integrity Task screen of the Maintenance Plan Wizard (see Figure 28.5) allows you to schedule the database consistency command DBCC CHECKDB, which checks the data pages for inconsistencies and is a good tool for ensuring that a database is healthy. The integrity checks can be made before each backup or on an independent schedule.

The options available for checking database integrity via the wizard are limited.

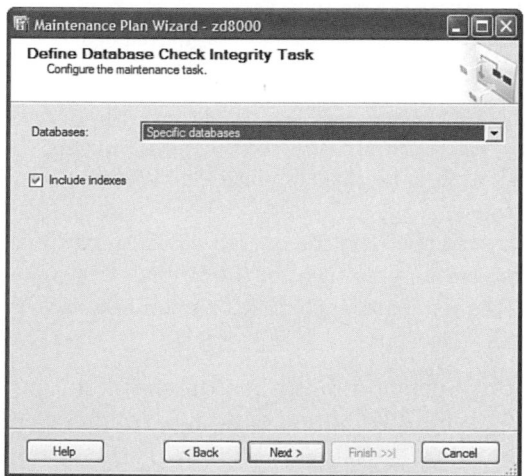

FIGURE 28.5   The Define Database Check Integrity Task screen of the Maintenance Plan Wizard.

Checking the Include Indexes check box causes integrity checks to be performed on the index pages as well. Checking the index pages for each table extends the amount of time that the task runs, but it is the most thorough way to perform an integrity check. If problems are found, you can run the DBCC CHECKDB command manually with additional options to repair the problems. For more information on resolving DBCC errors, see Chapter 45, "SQL Server Disaster Recovery Planning" (on the CD-ROM). In some cases, the problems cannot be fixed without the possibility of data loss. You should consider contacting Microsoft support if you receive consistency errors in a critical database.

Shrinking Databases

The Define Shrink Database Task page of the Maintenance Plan Wizard (see Figure 28.6) can be useful for keeping the size of your databases manageable. As its name implies, this task is used to reduce the overall size of a database. This task's execution is essentially the equivalent to running the DBCC SHRINKDATABASE command, and it contains task options that mirror the options available with the DBCC command.

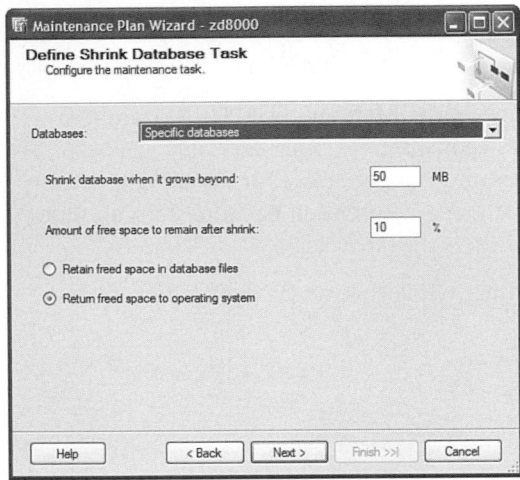

FIGURE 28.6   The Define Shrink Database Task page of the Maintenance Plan Wizard.

The setting Shrink Database When It Grows Beyond specifies the overall database size that must be exceeded in order for the shrink operation to occur. You set the size in megabytes, and it must be a whole number. If the database, including data and log files, is smaller than this size, the shrink operation does not occur.

The remaining options determine how the shrink operation runs when the shrink threshold is exceeded. The Amount of Free Space to Remain After Shrink option determines how much space is left in the database files after the shrink operation is finished. This is a target percentage and may not be feasible if the amount of disk space is limited. SQL Server does its best to achieve the target percentage, but it is not guaranteed. Generally, in environments where you have abundant disk space, it is best to leave at least 10% free after the operation so that the database can grow without the need for expanding the size of the database files.

The last settings on the screen determine how free space beyond the target percentage is handled. For example, let's assume that a large number of rows were deleted from a database and the target free space percentage is set to 10%. The shrink operation is run and is able to shrink the database such that 40% is now free. You can choose to retain in the database files the 30% beyond the target that is free by selecting the Retain Freed Space in the Database Files option. Choosing this option is the same as running the DBCC SHRINK

DATABASE command with the NOTRUNCATE option. With this option, you do not see any changes to the size of the database files, and the free space on the disk remains unchanged.

The other option, Return Freed Space to Operating System, can reduce the size of the database files and return that space to the operating system. This option utilizes the TRUNCATEONLY option that comes with the DBCC SHRINK DATABASE command and is the option needed to free up disk space on a server.

TIP

It is not necessarily a good idea to run the Shrink Database task for every database. With the Shrink Database task, the database is condensed so that the data is located on contiguous pages in the database data file(s). This involves the movement of pages from one part of the file to another. This movement can cause fragmentation in tables and indexes. The fragmentation can, in turn, cause performance problems and undo work that may have been done with other tasks, such as rebuilding the indexes.

The other problem with shrinking the database relates to the cost of expanding the database at a later time. For example, let's say you have a database that has grown to 1GB. You shrink the database so that it is now only 800MB, but normal use of the database causes it to expand again. The expansion of the database files can be expensive and cause performance problems during the actual expansion, especially on high-volume production systems. The best solution is to purchase the appropriate amount of disk space and size the database so that database files do not need to expand frequently and the shrink operation is not needed. This is easier said than done, but it is the right answer nonetheless.

Maintaining Indexes and Statistics

Maintaining indexes and statistics is essential in most database environments, including those that have frequent changes to the data. These changes can cause tables and their indexes to become fragmented and inefficient. These types of environments can also lead to outdated statistics on indexes. Outdated statistics can cause the query engine to make less-than-optimal choices when determining the best access path to the data.

The maintenance of indexes and statistics is facilitated through the use of three different tasks in the Maintenance Plan Wizard: Reorganize Index, Rebuild Index, and Update Statistics. Using the Reorganize Index task is equivalent to running the ALTER INDEX REORGANIZE command. This task defragments and compacts clustered and nonclustered indexes on tables and views. This helps improve index-scanning performance and should improve overall response time. The operation is always done online and is also equivalent to running the DBCC INDEXDEFRAG command.

Figure 28.7 shows the screen you use to define the Reorganize Index task. This screen allows you select tables, views, or tables and views. You can also select specific tables or views that you want to reorganize. The Compact Large Objects option is equivalent to ALTER INDEX LOB_COMPACTION = ON. It causes data in large object (LOB) data types, such as image or text objects, to be compacted.

28

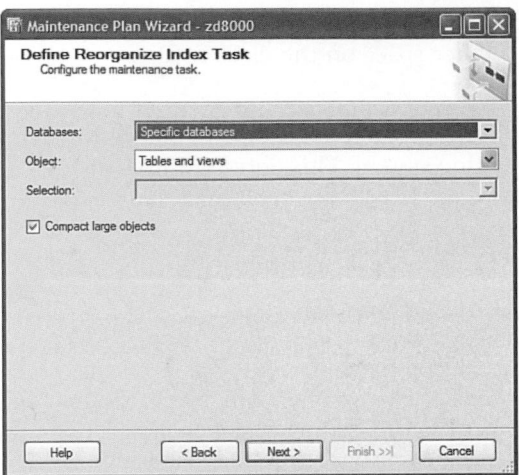

FIGURE 28.7   The Reorganize Index task options in the Maintenance Plan Wizard.

The Reorganize Index task moves the leaf-level pages so that they match the logical order-ing of the index. This improves performance but it is not as extensive as the Rebuild Index task, which is equivalent to the new `ALTER INDEX REBUILD` command in SQL Server 2005. It is also equivalent to the `DBCC DBREINDEX` command available with SQL Server 2000. When the Rebuild Index task is executed, it rebuilds the indexes from scratch. This can achieve the best performance results, but it also has the most impact on users of the database.

Figure 28.8 shows the options that are available for rebuilding an index with the Maintenance Plan Wizard.

There is an expanded set of available options for rebuilding an index. The Free Space Options section pertains to the amount of free space left in the index pages. This free space is defined by the fill factor for the index. When the Reorganize Pages with the Default Amount of Free Space option is used, the fill factor is reset to the value used when the index was created. The other option, Change Free Space per Page Percentage To, allows you to choose a new fill factor value to be used for all indexes that have been selected for the rebuild operation.

The following advanced Rebuild Index task options are available:

▶ **Pad Index**—This is equivalent to the `PAD_INDEX` option for the index. This option sets the percentage of free space in the intermediate pages (non-leaf level) to the value specified. If this option is not selected, the intermediate pages are filled, leaving room for only one additional row.

▶ **Sort Results in tempdb**—This is equivalent to the `SORT_IN_TEMPDB` option for the index. This option causes `tempdb` to be used to store intermediate results while rebuilding the index. If this option is not used, these intermediate results are stored in the database in which the index resides. Storing the results in `tempdb` can help prevent unnecessary growth of the user database in which the index is being rebuilt.

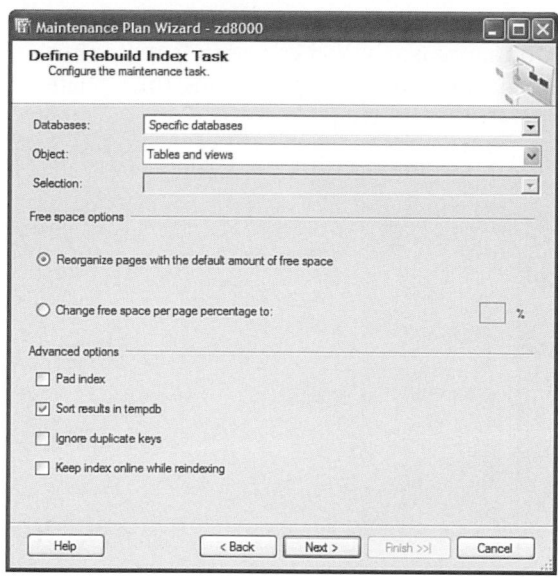

FIGURE 28.8   The Rebuild Index task options in the Maintenance Plan Wizard.

▶ **Ignore Duplicate Keys**—This is equivalent to the IGNORE_DUP_KEY option for the index. This option determines the insert behavior of a unique index after it has been rebuilt. When this option is checked, inserts that would cause a duplicate row are rejected, but any other nonduplicate inserts in the transaction are allowed to complete. When this option is unchecked, any duplicate row cause all inserts in a multirow INSERT transaction to fail.

▶ **Keep Index Online While Reindexing**—This is equivalent to the ONLINE option for the index. This option allows users to access the underlying table and the associated indexes during the index rebuild operation. If this option is not used, the index rebuild is on offline operation, and a table lock is held on the table that is having its indexes rebuilt.

These index options and further information regarding indexes are discussed in Chapter 20, "Creating and Managing Indexes." Refer to Chapter 29, "Indexes and Performance," for details on the performance impact of some of the index options discussed.

The maintenance of statistics can be just as important as the maintenance of indexes on a table. Statistics contain information about the distribution of data in tables and indexes and provide valuable information to the SQL Server query engine. When the statistics are outdated, the query engine may not make the best decisions for getting the data.

Fortunately, there are database options that cause statistics to be automatically updated. The AUTO UPDATE STATISTICS and AUTO UPDATE STATISTICS ASYNCHRONOUSLY options cause index statistics to be created automatically. However, there are situations in which the automatic update of statistics is not happening often enough or the update is happening at inopportune times and can cause performance issues. You can address these situations by scheduling the updating of statistics via a maintenance plan, using the Update Statistics task.

Figure 28.9 shows the Maintenance Plan Wizard screen for setting the Update Statistics task options.

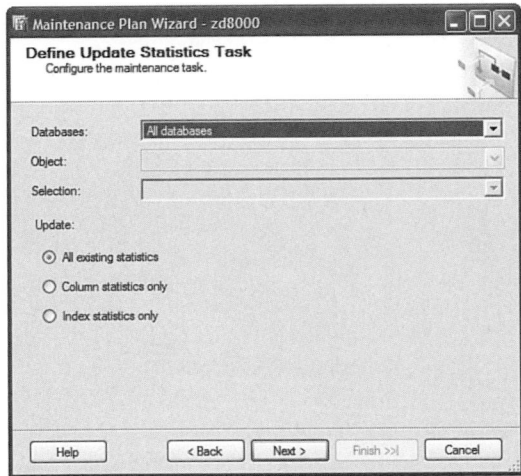

FIGURE 28.9   The Update Statistics task options in the Maintenance Plan Wizard.

The top portion of the Define Update Statistics Task screen is much like the option screens for maintaining indexes. You can choose the type of objects (tables or views) on which you want to update statistics, or you can focus on specific tables or views. The Update options at the bottom of the screen identify the type of statistics that are to be updated. If the All Existing Statistics option is selected, statistics for both indexes and columns are updated. Statistics on columns exists if the AUTO CREATE STATISTICS option has been set to ON or the statistics were manually created. The other two update options on the screen allow you to focus the update of statistics on columns only or indexes only.

Scheduling a Maintenance Plan

One of the greatest features of a maintenance plan is that you can schedule it. Scheduling takes manual work off your plate and provides consistency that might be missed if the plan had to be run manually. History is kept for each of the scheduled executions, which provides an audit trail, and notifications can be tied to the scheduled plans to allow a person to respond to failures or other results from the plan.

The screen to set scheduling options, the Job Schedule Properties dialog box (see Figure 28.10), appears after you have defined the options for each task. This screen contains the same flexible scheduling features that are available in the SQL Server Agent.

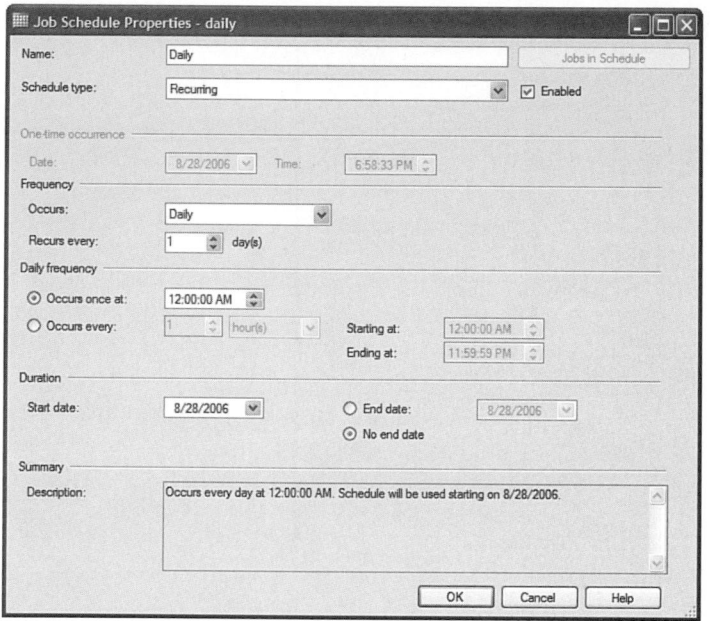

FIGURE 28.10   Scheduling options in the Maintenance Plan Wizard.

When a maintenance plan is saved, a scheduled job with the same name as the maintenance plan is created. The job schedule that is defined for the maintenance plan is
applied to the scheduled job, and the SQL Server Agent manages the execution of the job,
based on the schedule. Scheduling changes that are made to the maintenance plan are
automatically reflected in the scheduled job. In addition, if the name of the maintenance
plan is changed, the name of the scheduled job is changed as well. If an attempt is made
to delete the scheduled job related to the maintenance plan, an error is returned, disal-
lowing the deletion.

With a scheduled job for a maintenance plan in SQL Server 2005, the scheduled job
executes an SSIS package. In comparison, the scheduled job in SQL Server 2000 utilized
the SQLMAINT utility instead. Figure 28.11 shows an example of the scheduled job step for
a SQL Server 2005 maintenance plan.

The utilization of SSIS in the execution of maintenance plans is a significant change for
SQL Server 2005. The use of SSIS provides added workflow capabilities and extends the
feature set for maintenance plans. The scheduled job step that executes an SSIS package
for the maintenance plan shows some of the options and flexibility of SSIS, but the real
power is in the maintenance plan editor and the Business Intelligence Design Studio
(BIDS) that is used to manage all SSIS packages. Chapter 40, "SQL Server Integration
Services," provides further detail on SSIS. The maintenance plan editor is discussed in the
following section.

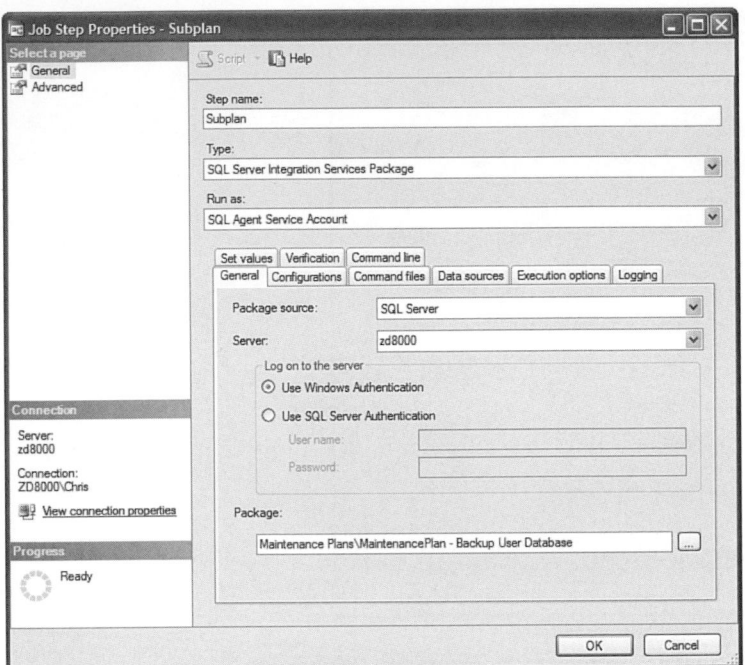

FIGURE 28.11   Scheduling jobs for a maintenance plan.

TIP

Scheduling in the Maintenance Plan Wizard is limited to one schedule. You can surpass this limitation by adding additional schedules to the scheduled job that is associated with the maintenance plan. To do so, you simply open the associated scheduled job that is found in the SQL Server Agent node in SSMS and create the additional schedules. This is handy when you want a varied execution, such as a weekly schedule combined with daily executions of the same plan.

An integral part of a scheduled maintenance plan is the notification and reporting capabilities. The Select Report Options screen is displayed at the end of the Maintenance Plan Wizard (see Figure 28.12).

The option Write a Report to a Text File provides details about the execution of each maintenance plan. This option should be selected for most plans, and it provides excellent information for researching past executions and diagnosing any maintenance plan failures.

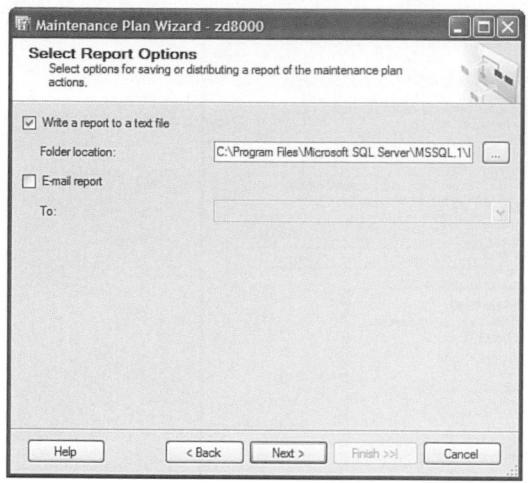

FIGURE 28.12   Reporting options in the Maintenance Plan Wizard.

The E-mail Report option provides a means for notifying a SQL Server operator when a task fails. You must have Database Mail enabled in order to use this option, and the agent selected must have a valid email address in order to receive the notification. You can also edit the job associated with the maintenance plan after it has been created and set up notification there. The notification options on the scheduled job are more extensive than those in the Maintenance Plan Wizard.

CAUTION

If you have a maintenance plan generate a report, you need to make sure you have a means for cleaning up the files. The wizard does not create a plan that deletes the older report files. You can address this by modifying the plan after the wizard has created it and adding a Maintenance Cleanup task. This is the same task that can be used to delete old database backup files. The modification of a maintenance plan and the addition of the Maintenance Cleanup task are discussed in the following section.

Managing Maintenance Plans Without the Wizard

You can create or modify maintenance plans in SQL Server 2005 without using the Maintenance Plan Wizard. To create a new maintenance plan without the wizard, you right-click the `Maintenance Plan` node and select New Maintenance Plan. You are prompted for a maintenance plan name and then taken to the Design tab for the mainte-nance plan. The Design tab consists of a properties section at the top of the screen and a plan designer surface that is empty for a new maintenance plan.

Existing maintenance plans display in the Design tab when you right-click the plan and select Modify. Figure 28.13 shows the Design tab for a maintenance plan that was created with the Maintenance Plan Wizard to back up the system databases.

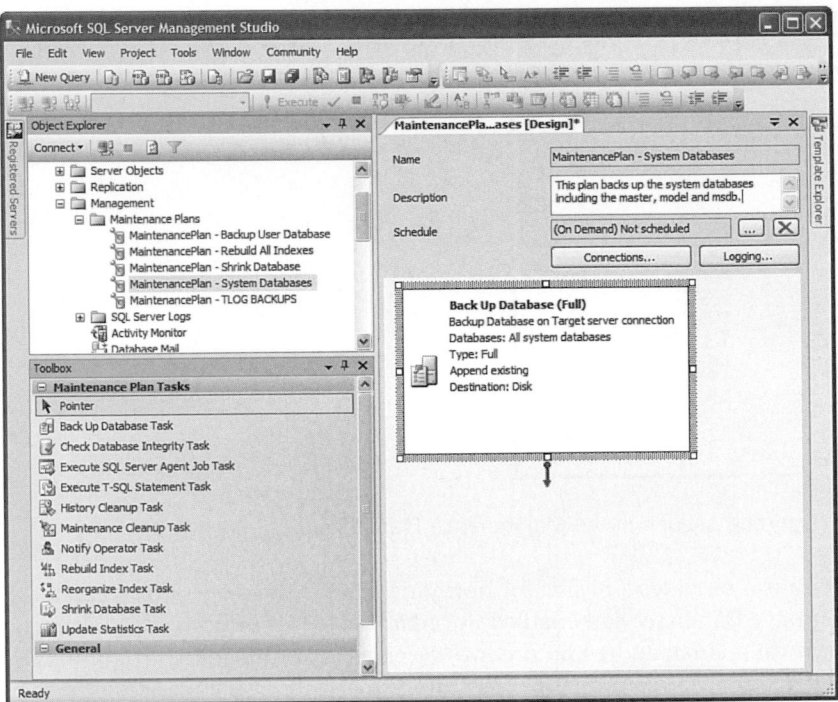

FIGURE 28.13   The maintenance plan Design tab.

The Design tab represents a significant difference from the way maintenance plans were managed in SQL Server 2000. The plan designer surface on the Design tab has drag-and-drop capabilities that allow you to add maintenance tasks to your plan. The tasks that are available are found in the Toolbox component. The Toolbox and the related tasks are shown in Figure 28.13 in the bottom-left portion of the screen. To add a tool from the Toolbox, you drag the item from the toolbox to the plan designer surface. Or you can double-click the task, and the task appears on the plan designer surface.

On the plan designer surface, you can move each of the tasks around, link them to other tasks, and edit them by double-clicking them. You can also right-click a task to edit it, group it with other tasks, autosize it, and gain access to other task options. You can right-click an empty section of the plan designer surface to add annotations or comments that provide additional information about the task or the overall plan.

NOTE

The dialog boxes that are displayed when you edit a task are unique for each task. Tasks that are available in the Maintenance Plan Wizard display an options screen like the one that is displayed during the execution of the wizard.

Adding a task to an existing maintenance plan is a good starting point to become familiar with the working of the Design tab. Take, for example, the maintenance plan shown in Figure 28.13. This plan, which was initially created with the Maintenance Plan Wizard, is used to create full database backups of all the system databases. One critical thing that is missing from this plan is a task to remove older database backups. The task that can help you with this is the Maintenance Cleanup task. If you double-click that task in the Toolbox, the task is added to the plan designer surface, as shown in Figure 28.14.

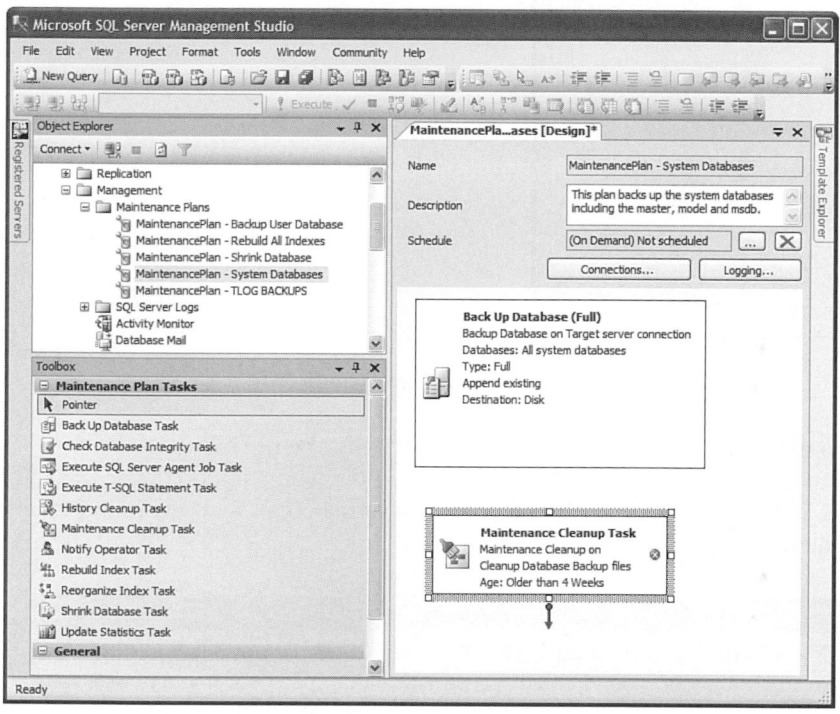

FIGURE 28.14   Adding a task to the plan designer surface.

After you add a task to the plan designer surface, you need to configure it. Note that a small red X icon appears on the right side of the task if the task has not yet been configured. To configure the Maintenance Cleanup task, you double-click it on the plan designer surface. Figure 28.15 shows the screen that appears so you can configure the Maintenance Cleanup task.

You can use the Maintenance Cleanup task to clean up old backup files or maintenance plan text reports. The deletion of older backup files is particularly important because database backups tend to be large files and can use up a significant amount of disk space. The File Location section of the screen enables you to delete a specific file, or you can delete files in a folder based on search criteria. In most cases, you want to search the folder to delete older files.

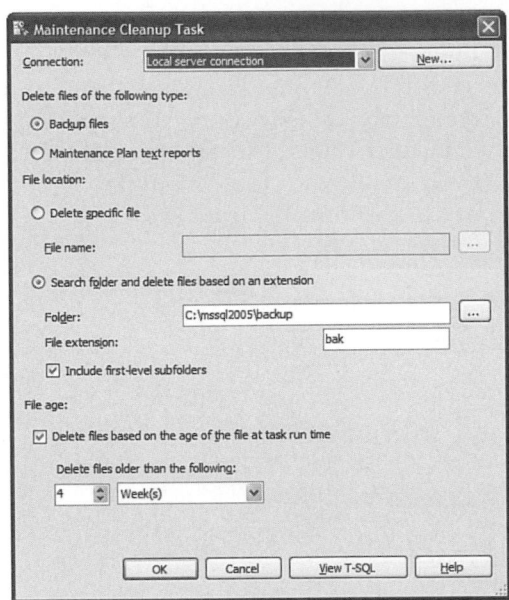

FIGURE 28.15   Configuring the Maintenance Cleanup task.

When cleaning up database backup files, you typically specify the file extension .bak. If you want to write each database's backups to a separate folder, you should choose the Include First-Level Subfolders options, which allows you to search all first-level subfolders that exist under the folder specified.

CAUTION

The Release To Manufacturing (RTM) version of SQL Server 2005 did not allow for the deletion of files in the subfolders found under the parent folder specified. If you chose to create a separate subfolder for each database in your backup plan, the Maintenance Cleanup task would not delete the backup in the subfolders of the parent subfolder specified. The workaround for the RTM version is to write all backups for all databases to the same folder and not use the option to create a subfolder for each database in your backup plan. You can then configure the Maintenance Cleanup task to point at that folder.

Fortunately, this problem was fixed with the Service Pack 1 release. The check box named Include First-Level Subfolders was added to the configuration screen for the Maintenance Cleanup task; when this is selected, SQL Server searches the first-level subfolders and removes older backups.

In the last section of the configuration screen for the Maintenance Cleanup task, you specify how old a file must be in order to be deleted. The default is four weeks, but you can adjust this to the desired time frame by using the related drop-downs. If you uncheck Delete Files Based on the Age of the File at Task Run Time, all files in the folder or subfolders are deleted, regardless of age.

The deletion of database backup files is not based on the file dates or the name of the backup file. The Maintenance Cleanup task uses a procedure named `xp_delete_file` that examines the database backup and the time that the backup was created. Renaming the database backup file does not affect its inclusion in the deletion process.

After you have configured the options for the Maintenance Cleanup task, you can click the View T-SQL button at the bottom of the screen. This is a nice new feature that reveals what is going on behind the scenes when the plan executes. With prior versions of SQL Server, you had to obtain this kind of information by using the Profiler.

When you click OK, the task is ready to use in the maintenance plan. The task runs in parallel with the other tasks defined in the plan unless a precedence or link is established between the tasks. To establish a link between the tasks, you select the first task that you want to execute. When the task is selected, a green arrow is shown at the bottom of the task's box in the plan designer surface. You click the green arrow and drag it to the task that you want to run next. The green arrow is then connected to the other task. If you double-click the green arrow (or right-click and choose Edit), the Precedence Constraint Editor appears (see Figure 28.16).

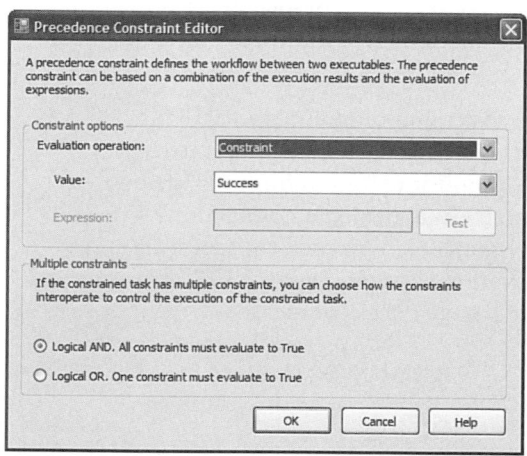

FIGURE 28.16   The Precedence Constraint Editor.

The paragraph at the top of the Precedence Constraint Editor gives a good description of what a precedence constraint is. In short, it can link tasks together based on the results of their execution. For example, if a backup database task succeeds, a Maintenance Cleanup task can be defined to run next. You can also set the constraint value so that the next task will run only if the first task fails, or you can have the next task run based on the prior task's completion, regardless of whether if succeeds or fails. In addition, you can link multiple tasks together with precedence. You define the logical relationship between tasks in the Multiple Constraints section of the Precedence Constraint Editor.

The workflow and relationships that can be defined between tasks for a maintenance plan is extensive and beyond the scope of this chapter. Many of the workflow concepts are similar to those of the DTS designer in SQL Server 2000 and the SSIS designer in SQL Server 2005.

Executing a Maintenance Plan

Maintenance plans that have been scheduled run automatically according to the schedule defined. You can also run maintenance plans manually by right-clicking a maintenance plan and selecting Execute or by selecting the SQL Server Agent job that is associated with the maintenance plan and starting the job. The execution behavior is different, depending on the means you use. If you choose to run the maintenance plan from the Management node, the SSIS package is launched, and the Execute Maintenance Plan window indicates a status of Success almost immediately after the execution starts. This does not mean that the entire plan has completed successfully; it just indicates that the SSIS package was started successfully.

If you run the SQL Server Agent job to execute the maintenance plan, a dialog box indicating the execution status of the plan appears. The dialog does not indicate success for the maintenance plan until the entire maintenance plan has completed. This method causes less confusion than the one just described because it is more obvious when the entire plan has completed.

There are two other means for monitoring the execution of maintenance plans. The Job Activity Monitor shows a status of executing while a maintenance plan is executing. You can set the refresh settings on the Job Activity Monitor to auto-refresh for the desired increment. You can also monitor the execution by establishing a connection to the SSIS server in SSMS. To establish an SSIS connection in SSMS, you click the Connect drop-down in the Object Explorer and choose Integration Services. Figure 28.17 shows an example of the Object Explorer with an Integration Services connection.

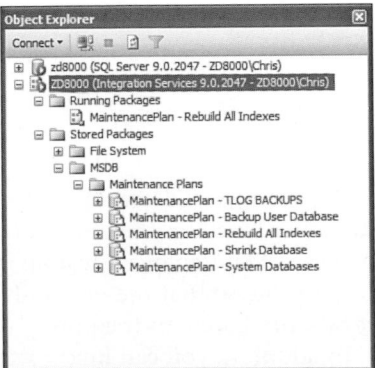

FIGURE 28.17   The Object Explorer with an Integration Services connection.

The Integration Services connection in the Object Explorer shows the packages that are running in addition to the packages that have been created. If you expand the Stored Packages node and navigate to the MSDB node, you see a node named Maintenance Plans that shows all the SSIS packages that have been created. You can also edit the package with BIDS, but that is beyond the scope of this chapter. See Chapter 40, "SQL Server Integration Services" for more information.

> **NOTE**
>
> SSIS must be installed on the SQL Server machine in order to create and execute maintenance plans. The SSIS services must be running as well. If the services are stopped, they are automatically started when you access a maintenance plan or execute it.

Maintenance Without a Maintenance Plan

You can perform database maintenance without the use of the built-in maintenance plans that come with SQL Server. The additional complexity related to SSIS integration in SQL Server 2005 may steer some people away from the use of these plans. In addition, there are maintenance plans that have been developed for past versions of SQL Server that can be used independently of those versions.

Database maintenance that is performed without a maintenance plan is often performed with custom scripts or stored procedures that execute the T-SQL commands to perform the maintenance. Other plans manually execute the SQLMAINT utility to perform the maintenance tasks. These are viable options, but they require additional development work and may lack the integration with other SQL Server components that is offered with the SQL Server 2005 maintenance plans.

Summary

As you have learned in this chapter, it is important to establish a database maintenance plan. Just like your car or your home, a database needs maintenance to keep working properly. The powerful new features available with the SQL Server 2005 maintenance plans and the Maintenance Plan Wizard make the creation of a robust maintenance plan easy. If you establish your maintenance plans early in the life of your databases, you will save yourself time and aggravation in the long run.

Chapter 29 delves further into the importance of indexes and their relationship to performance. It expands on the optimization of indexes discussed in this chapter and describes the role that indexes play in keeping databases running fast.

28

PART V

SQL Server Performance and Optimization

IN THIS PART

CHAPTER 29   Indexes and Performance   969

CHAPTER 30   Understanding Query
             Optimization   1027

CHAPTER 31   Query Analysis   1115

CHAPTER 32   Locking and Performance   1151

CHAPTER 33   Database Design and
             Performance   1213

CHAPTER 34   Monitoring SQL Server
             Performance   1233

CHAPTER 29

Indexes and Performance

IN THIS CHAPTER

▶ What's New for Indexes and Performance

▶ Understanding Index Structures

▶ Index Utilization

▶ Index Selection

▶ Evaluating Index Usefulness

▶ Index Statistics

▶ SQL Server Index Maintenance

▶ Index Design Guidelines

▶ Indexed Views

▶ Indexes on Computed Columns

▶ Choosing Indexes: Query Versus Update Performance

There can be a number of reasons why SQL Server performance might be less than optimal, but in many cases, it comes down to poor index design or simply a lack of appropriate indexes. You can often realize substantial performance gains in SQL Server based applications by creating the proper indexes to support the queries and operations being performed in SQL Server. The great benefit here is that the applications immediately reap the benefits of the indexes without having to rewrite the code in any way.

You need to closely examine the indexes defined on the tables to ensure that the appropriate indexes exist for the Query Optimizer to use to avoid table scans and reduce the I/O costs of resolving queries. You also need to have a good understanding of the criteria SQL Server uses to determine when to use an index.

It's also important to keep in mind that although many indexes on a table can help improve response time for queries and reports, too many indexes can hurt the performance of inserts, updates, and deletes. At other times, other index design decisions, such as which column(s) to create a clustered index on, might be influenced as much by how the data is inserted and modified and what the possible locking implications might be as it is by the query response time alone.

Clearly, proper index design is a key issue in achieving optimum SQL Server application performance. In this chapter, you'll learn about the structure of an index and how SQL Server maintains indexes because this provides a basis for understanding the performance if indexes. This chapter then discusses how SQL Server evaluates and uses indexes to improve query response time. Using this information, you should have a better understanding of the issues and factors that influence index design.

What's New for Indexes and Performance

SQL Server provides a number of new features related to indexes and performance. One of these new features is included columns. The included columns feature provides a way to add columns to the leaf level of a nonclustered index for the purpose of index covering without having to add them as part of the index key.

SQL Server also provides the ability to disable indexes. When an index is disabled, the definition of the index is maintained in the system catalogs, but the index itself contains no index key rows.

SQL Server 2005 also provides some improvements in the area of index statistics. One of these enhancements is the introduction of string summary statistics. String summary statistics help the Query Optimizer estimate the selectivity of query predicates when LIKE conditions are present in a query—even when the leading character of the string pattern begins with a wildcard, such as WHERE ProductName LIKE '%Bike' or WHERE Name LIKE '[CS]heryl'.

SQL Server 2005 also provides the new database option AUTO_UPDATE_STATISTICS_ASYNC, which provides asynchronous statistics updating. When this option is set to ON, queries no longer need to wait for the statistics to be updated before compiling.

> **NOTE**
>
> This chapter assumes that you already have an understanding of the different types of indexes and how to define them. For more information on index types and how to create indexes, see Chapter 20, "Creating and Managing Indexes."

Understanding Index Structures

When you run a query against a table that has no indexes, SQL Server has to read every page of the table, looking at every row on each page to find out whether each row satisfies the search arguments. SQL Server has to scan all the pages because there's no way of knowing whether any rows found are the only rows that satisfy the search arguments. This search method is referred to as a *table scan*.

Needless to say, a table scan is not an efficient way to retrieve data unless you really need to retrieve all rows. The Query Optimizer in SQL Server always calculates the cost of performing a table scan and uses that as a baseline when evaluating other access methods. The various access methods and query plan cost analysis are discussed in more detail in Chapter 30, "Understanding Query Optimization."

Suppose that a table is stored on 10,000 pages; even if only one row is to be returned or modified, all the pages must be searched, resulting in a scan of approximately 80MB of data (that is, 10,000 pages × 8KB per page = 80,000KB).

Indexes are structures stored separately from the actual data pages; they contain pointers to data pages or data rows. Indexes are used to speed up access to the data; they are also the mechanism used to enforce the uniqueness of key values.

Indexes in SQL Server are balanced trees (B-trees; see Figure 29.1). There is a single root page at the top of the tree, which branches out into N pages at each intermediate level until it reaches the bottom (leaf level) of the index. The leaf level has one row stored for each row in the table. The index tree is traversed by following pointers from the upper-level pages down through the lower-level pages. Each level of the index is linked as a doubly linked list.

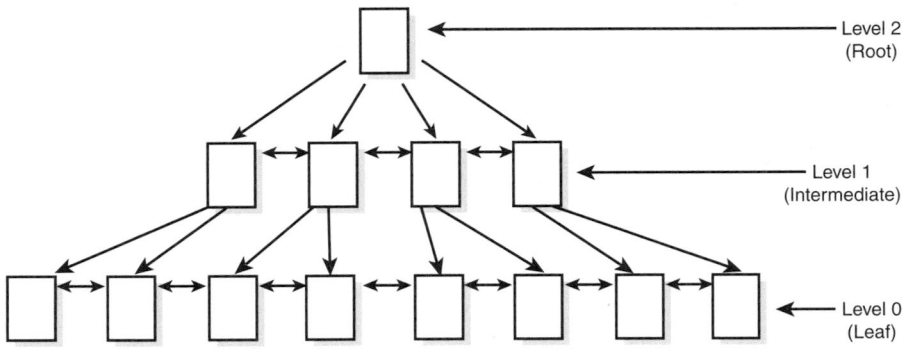

Level 2
(Root)

Level 1
(Intermediate)

Level 0
(Leaf)

FIGURE 29.1   The basic structure of a B-tree index.

An index can have many intermediate levels, depending on the number of rows in the table, the index type, and the index key width. The maximum number of columns in an index is 16; the maximum width of and index row is 900 bytes.

To provide a more efficient mechanism to identify and locate specific rows within a table quickly and easily, SQL Server supports two types of indexes: clustered and nonclustered.

Clustered Indexes

When you create a clustered index, all rows in the table are sorted and stored in the clustered index key order. Because the rows are physically sorted by the index key, you can have only one clustered index per table. You can think of the structure of a clustered index as being similar to a filing cabinet: The data pages are like folders in a file drawer in alphabetical order, and the data rows are like the records in the file folder, also in sorted order.

You can think of the intermediate levels of the index tree as the file drawers, also in alphabetical order, that assist you in finding the appropriate file folder. Figure 29.2 shows an example of a clustered index tree structure.

29

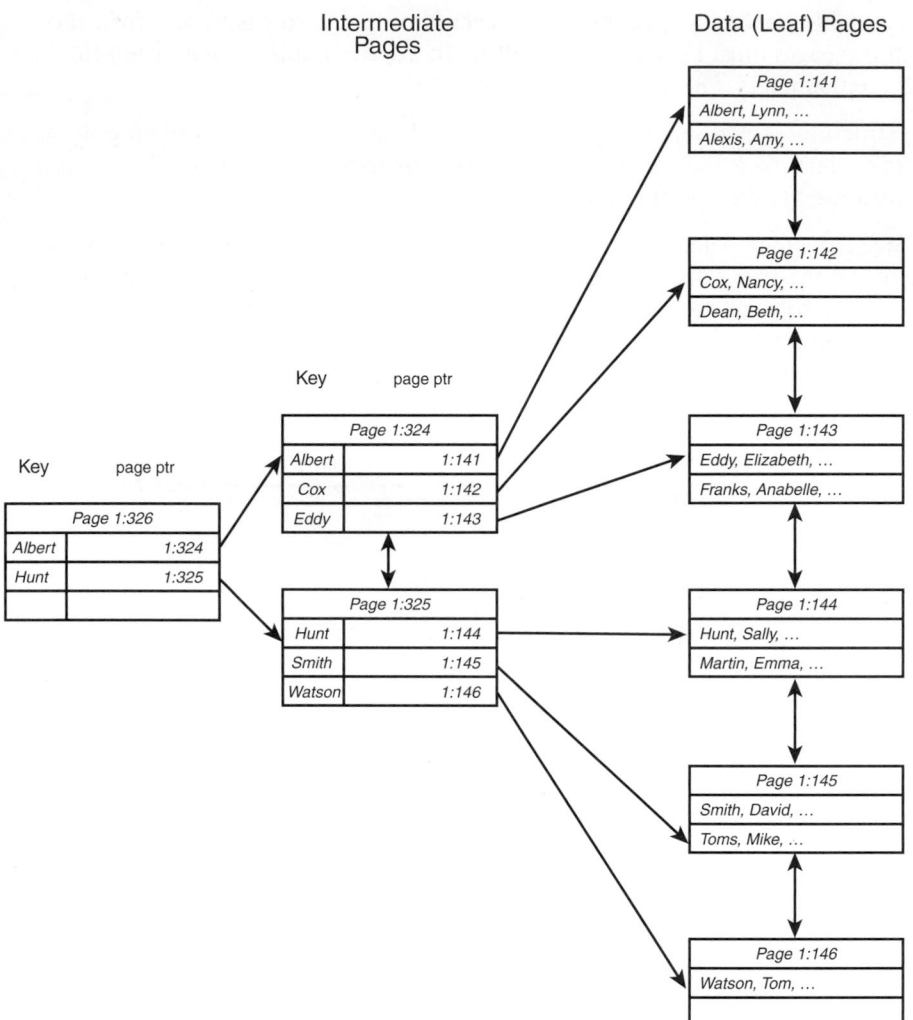

FIGURE 29.2   The structure of a clustered index.

In Figure 29.2, note that the data page chain is in clustered index order. However, the rows on each page might not be physically sorted in clustered index order, depending on when rows were inserted or deleted in the page. SQL Server still keeps the proper sort order of the rows via the row IDs. A clustered index is useful for range-retrieval queries or searches against columns with duplicate values because the rows within the range are physically located in the same page or on adjacent pages.

The data pages of the table are also the leaf level of a clustered index. To find all clustered index key values, SQL Server must eventually scan all the data pages.

SQL Server performs the following steps when searching for a value using a clustered index:

1. Queries the system catalogs for the page address for the root page of the index.

2. Compares the search value against the key values stored on the root page.

3. Finds the highest key value on the page where the key value is less than or equal to the search value.

4. Follows the page pointer stored with the key to the appropriate page at the next level down in the index.

5. Continues following page pointers (that is, repeats steps 3 and 4) until the data page is reached.

6. Searches the rows on the data page to locate any matches for the search value. If no matching row is found on that data page, the table contains no matching values.

Nonclustered Indexes

A nonclustered index is a separate index structure, independent of the physical sort order of the data rows in the table. You can have up to 249 nonclustered indexes per table.

A nonclustered index is similar to the index in the back of a book. To find the pages on which a specific subject is discussed, you look up the subject in the index and then go to the pages referenced in the index. This is an efficient method, as long as the subject is discussed on only a few pages. If the subject is discussed on many pages, or if you want to read about many subjects, it can be more efficient to read the entire book.

A nonclustered index works similarly to the book index. From the index's perspective, the data rows are randomly spread throughout the table. The nonclustered index tree contains the index key values, in sorted order. There is a row at the leaf level of the index for each data row in the table. Each leaf-level row contains a data row locator to locate the actual data row in the table.

If no clustered index is created for the table, the data row locator for the leaf level of the index is an actual pointer to the data page and the row number within the page where the row is located (see Figure 29.3).

Versions of SQL Server prior to 7.0 stored only the row locators (the RowIds) in nonclustered indexes to identify the data rows that the index key referenced. If a table had a clustered index defined on it, and one or more rows moved to another page (as a result of an INSERT or UPDATE), all corresponding rows in the nonclustered indexes had to be modified to reflect the new row IDs. This made insertions and updates costly.

In SQL Server 7.0 and later, nonclustered indexes on clustered tables no longer include the data row ID as part of the index. Instead, the data row locator for the nonclustered index is the associated clustered index key value for the record. When SQL Server reaches the leaf level of a nonclustered index, it uses the clustered index key to start searching through the clustered index to find the actual data row (see Figure 29.4). This adds some I/O to the search itself, but the benefit is that if a page split occurs in a clustered table, or if a row is moved (for example, as a result of an update), the nonclustered indexes stay the same. As long as the clustered index key is not modified, no data row locators in the index have to be updated.

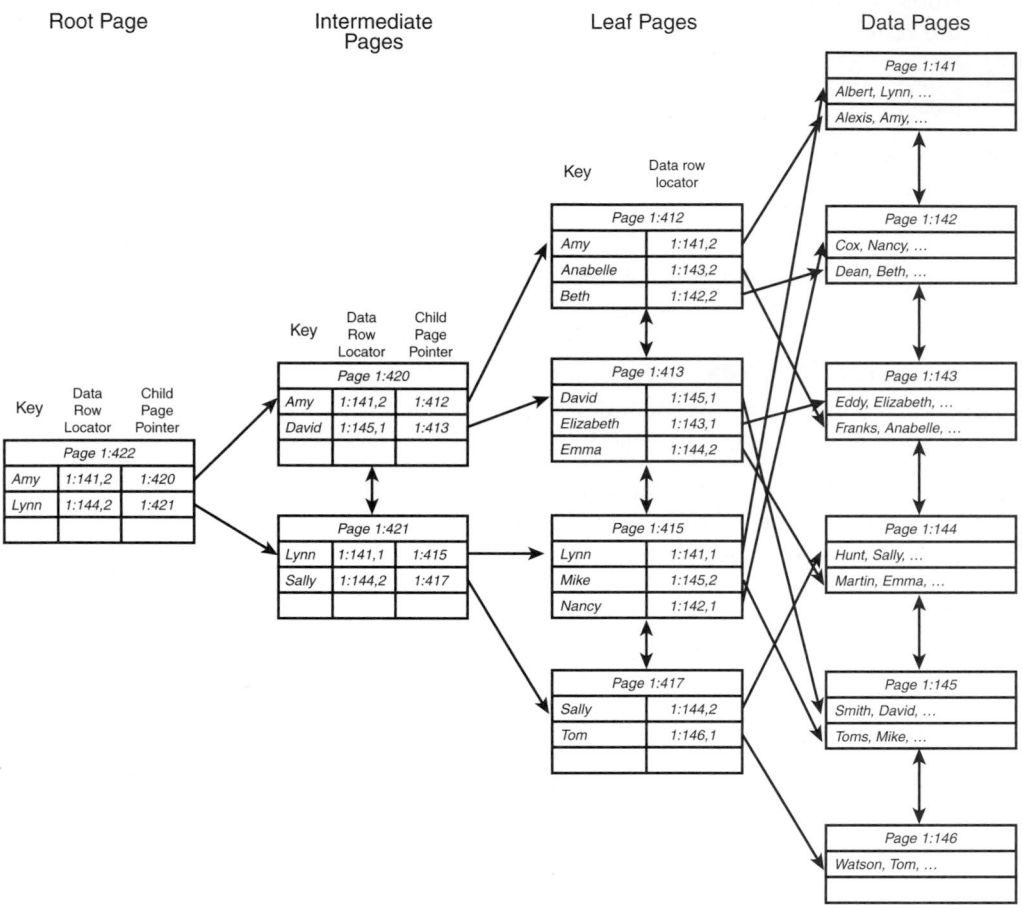

FIGURE 29.3   A nonclustered index on a heap table.

SQL Server performs the following steps when searching for a value by using a nonclustered index:

1. Queries the system catalog to determine the page address for the root page of the index.

2. Compares the search value against the index key values on the root page.

3. Finds the highest key value on the page where the key value is less than or equal to the search value.

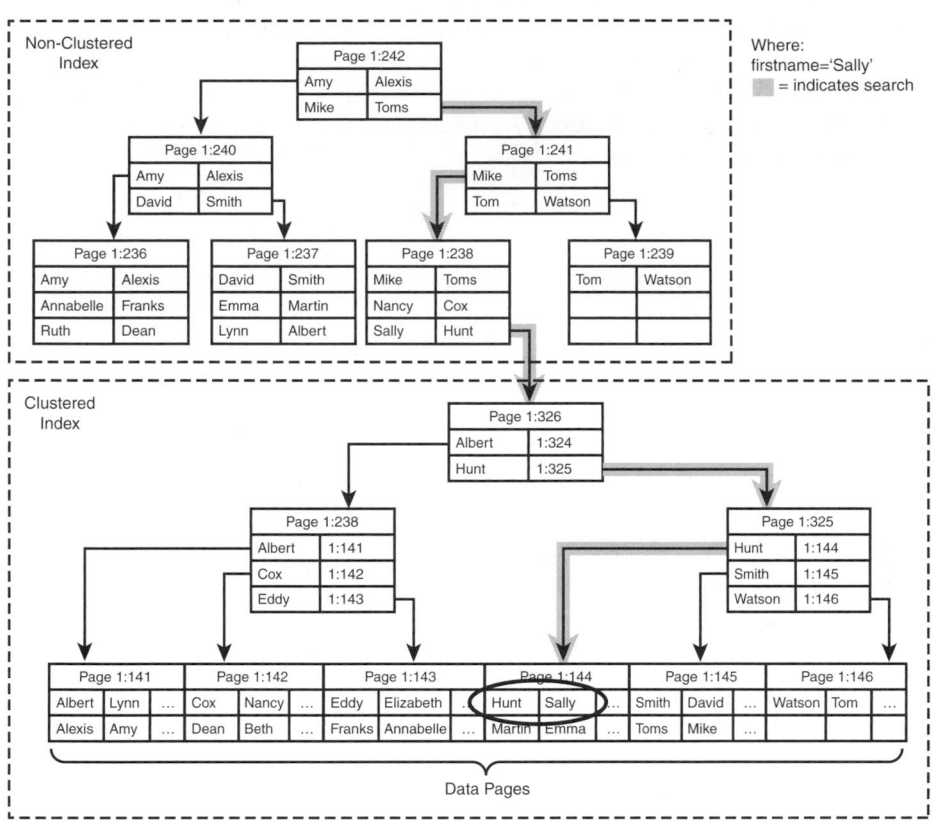

FIGURE 29.4   A nonclustered index on a clustered table.

4. Follows the down-page pointer to the next level down in the nonclustered index tree.

5. Continues following page pointers (that is, repeats steps 3 and 4) until the non-clustered index leaf page is reached.

6. Searches the index key rows on the leaf page to locate any matches for the search value. If no matching row is found on the leaf page, the table contains no matching values.

7. If a match is found on the leaf page, SQL Server follows the data row locator to the data row on the data page.

Index Utilization

To effectively determine the appropriate indexes that should be created, you need to determine whether they'll actually be used by the SQL Server Query Optimizer. If an index isn't being used effectively, it's just wasting space and creating unnecessary overhead during updates.

29

The main criterion to remember is that SQL Server does not use an index for the more efficient bookmark lookup if at least the first column of the index is not included in a valid search argument (SARG) or join clause. You should keep this in mind when choosing the column order for composite indexes. For example, consider the following index on the `stores` table in the bigpubs2005 database:

```
create index nc1_stores on stores (city, state, zip)
```

> **NOTE**
>
> Unless stated otherwise, all sample queries in this chapter are run in the bigpubs2005 database which is available via download from this book's website at www.samspublishing.com.

Each of the following queries could use the index because they include the first column, `city`, of the index as part of the SARG:

```
select stor_name from stores
   where city = 'Frederick'
     and state = 'MD'
     and zip = '21702'

select stor_name from stores
   where city = 'Frederick'
     and state = 'MD'

select stor_name from stores
   where city = 'Frederick'
     and zip = '21702'
```

However, the following queries do not use the index for a bookmark lookup because they don't specify the `city` column as a SARG:

```
select stor_name from stores
   where state = 'MD'
     and zip = '21702'

select stor_name from stores
   where zip = '21702'
```

For the index `nc1_stores` to be used for a bookmark lookup in the last query, you would have to reorder the columns so that `zip` is first—but then the index wouldn't be useful for any queries specifying only `city` and/or `state`. Satisfying all the preceding queries in this case would require additional indexes on the `stores` table.

For the two preceding queries, if you were to display the execution plan information (as described in Chapter 31, "Query Analysis"), you might see that the queries actually use the `nc1_stores` index to retrieve the result set. However, if you look closely, you can see the queries are not using the index in the most efficient manner; the index is being used to perform an index scan rather than an index seek. An index seek is what we are really after. (Alternative query access methods are discussed in more detail in Chapter 30). In an index *seek*, SQL Server searches for the specific SARG by walking the index tree from the root level down to the specific row(s) with matching index key values and then uses the bookmark value stored in the index key to directly retrieve the matching row(s) from the data page(s); the bookmark is either a specific row identifier or the clustered key value for the row.

For an index *scan*, SQL Server searches all the rows in the leaf level of the index, looking for possible matches. If any are found, it then uses the bookmark to retrieve the data row.

Although both seeks and scans use an index, the index scan is still more expensive in terms of I/O than an index seek but slightly less expensive than a table scan, which is why it is used. However, in this chapter you'll learn to design indexes that result in index seeks, and when this chapter talks about queries using an index, index seeks are what it refers to (except for the section on index covering, but that's a horse of a slightly different color).

You might think that the easy solution to get bookmark lookups on all possible columns is to index all the columns on a table so that any type of search criteria specified for a query can be helped by an index. This strategy might be somewhat appropriate in a read-only decision support system (DSS) environment that supports ad hoc queries, but it is not likely because many of the indexes probably still wouldn't even be used. As you'll see in the section "Index Selection," later in this chapter, just because an index is defined on a column doesn't mean that the Query Optimizer is necessarily always going to use it if the search criteria are not selective enough. Also, creating that many indexes on a large table could take up a significant amount of space in the database, increasing the time required to back up and run DBCC checks on the database. As mentioned earlier, too many indexes on a table in an online transaction processing (OLTP) environment can generate a significant amount of overhead during inserts, updates, and deletes and have a detrimental impact on performance.

A common design mistake often made is too many indexes defined on tables in OLTP environments. In many cases, some of the indexes are redundant or are never even considered by the SQL Server Query Optimizer to process the queries used by the applications. These indexes end up simply wasting space and adding unnecessary overhead to data updates.

A case in point was one client who had eight indexes defined on a table, four of which had the same column, which was a unique key, as the first column in the index. That column was included in the WHERE clauses for all queries and updates performed on the table. Only one of those four indexes was ever used.

Hopefully, by the end of this chapter, you'll understand why all these indexes were unnecessary and be able to recognize and determine which columns benefit from having indexes defined on them and which indexes to avoid.

Index Selection

To determine which indexes to define on a table, you need to perform a detailed query analysis. This involves examining the search clauses to see what columns are referenced, knowing the bias of the data to determine the usefulness of the index, and ranking the queries in order of importance and frequency of execution. You have to be careful not to examine individual queries and develop indexes to support one query, without considering the other queries that are executed on the table as well. You need to come up with a set of indexes that works for the best cross-section of your queries.

TIP

A useful tool to help you identify your frequently executed and critical queries is SQL Server Profiler. I've found SQL Server Profiler to be invaluable when going into a new client site and having to identify the problem queries that need tuning. SQL Server Profiler allows you to trace the procedures and queries being executed in SQL Server and capture the runtime, reads and writes, execution plans, and other processing information. This information can help you identify which queries are providing substandard performance, which ones are being executed most often, which indexes are being used by the queries, and so on.

You can analyze this information yourself manually or save a trace to analyze with the Database Engine Tuning Advisor. The features of SQL Server Profiler are covered in more detail in Chapter 5, "SQL Server Profiler." The Database Engine Tuning Advisor is discussed in more detail in Chapter 37, "Configuring, Tuning, and Optimizing SQL Server Options."

Because it's usually not possible to index for everything, you should index first for the queries most critical to your applications or those run frequently by many users. If you have a query that's run only once a month, is it worth creating an index to support only that query and having to maintain it throughout the rest of the month? The sum of the additional processing time throughout the month could conceivably exceed the time required to perform a table scan to satisfy that one query.

TIP

If, due to query response time requirements, you must have an index in place when a query is run, consider creating the index only when you run the query and then dropping the index for the remainder of the month. This is a feasible approach as long as the time it takes to create the index and run the query that uses the index doesn't exceed the time it takes to simply run the query without the index in place.

Evaluating Index Usefulness

SQL Server provides indexes for two primary reasons: as a method to enforce the uniqueness of the data in the database tables and to provide faster access to data in the tables. Creating the appropriate indexes for a database is one of the most important aspects of physical database design. Because you can't have an unlimited number of indexes on a table, and it wouldn't be feasible anyway, you should create indexes on columns that have high selectivity so that your queries will use the indexes. The selectivity of an index can be defined as follows:

Selectivity ratio = Number of unique index values / Number of rows in table

If the selectivity ratio is high—that is, if a large number of rows can be uniquely identified by the key—the index is highly selective and useful to the Query Optimizer. The optimum selectivity would be 1, meaning that there is a unique value for each row. A low selectivity means that there are many duplicate values and the index would be less useful. The SQL Server Query Optimizer decides whether to use any indexes for a query based on the selectivity of the index. The higher the selectivity, the faster and more efficiently SQL Server can retrieve the result set.

For example, say that you are evaluating useful indexes on the authors table in the bigpubs2005 database. Assume that most of the queries access the table either by author's last name or by state. Because a large number of concurrent users modify data in this table, you are allowed to choose only one index—author's last name or state. Which one should you choose? Let's perform some analysis to see which one is a more useful, or selective, index.

First, you need to determine the selectivity based on the author's last name with a query on the authors table in the bigpubs2005 database:

```
select count(distinct au_lname) as '# unique',
   count(*) as '# rows',
   str(count(distinct au_lname) / cast (count(*) as real),4,2) as 'selectivity'
from authors
go

# unique    # rows      selectivity
----------- ----------- -----------
160         172         0.93
```

The selectivity ratio calculated for the au_lname column on the authors table, 0.93, indicates that an index on au_lname would be highly selective and a good candidate for an index. All but 12 rows in the table contain a unique value for last name.

Now, look at the selectivity of the state column:

```
select count(distinct state) as '# unique',
    count(*) '# rows',
    str(count(distinct state) / cast (count(*) as real),4,2) as 'selectivity'
from authors
go
```

```
# unique    # rows     selectivity
----------- ---------- -----------
38          172        0.22
```

As you can see, an index on the state column would be much less selective (0.22) than an index on the au_lname column and possibly not as useful.

One of the questions to ask at this point is whether a few values in the state column that have a high number of duplicates are skewing the selectivity or whether there are just a few unique values in the table. You can determine this with a query similar to the following:

```
select state,
        count(*) as numrows,
        count(*)/b.totalrows * 100 as percentage
from authors a,
    (select convert(numeric(6,2), count(*)) as totalrows from  authors) as b
group by state, b.totalrows
having count(*) > 1
order by 2 desc
go
```

```
state numrows    percentage
----- ---------- --------------------------------------
CA    37         21.5116200
NY    18         10.4651100
TX    15         8.7209300
OH    9          5.2325500
FL    8          4.6511600
IL    7          4.0697600
NJ    7          4.0697600
WA    6          3.4883700
PA    6          3.4883700
CO    5          2.9069700
LA    5          2.9069700
MI    5          2.9069700
MN    3          1.7441800
MO    3          1.7441800
OK    3          1.7441800
```

```
AZ    3         1.7441800
AK    2         1.1627900
IN    2         1.1627900
GA    2         1.1627900
MA    2         1.1627900
NC    2         1.1627900
NE    2         1.1627900
SD    2         1.1627900
VA    2         1.1627900
WI    2         1.1627900
WV    2         1.1627900
```

As you can see, most of the state values are relatively unique, except for one value, 'CA', which accounts for more than 20% of the values in the table. Therefore, state is probably not a good candidate for an indexed column, especially if most of the time you are searching for authors from the state of California. SQL Server would generally find it more efficient to scan the whole table rather than search via the index.

As a general rule of thumb, if the selectivity ratio for a nonclustered index key is less than .85 (in other words, if the Query Optimizer cannot discard at least 85% of the rows based on the key value), the Query Optimizer generally chooses a table scan to process the query rather than a nonclustered index. In such cases, performing a table scan to find all the qualifying rows is more efficient than seeking through the B-tree to locate a large number of data rows.

NOTE

You can relate the concept of selectivity to a hypothetical example. Say that you needed to find every instance of the word *SQL* in this book. Would it be easier to do it by using the index and going back and forth from the index to all the pages that contain the word, or would it be easier just to scan each page from beginning to end to locate every occurrence? What if you had to find all references to the word *squonk*, if any? Squonk would definitely be easier to find via the index (actually, the index would help you determine that it doesn't even exist). Therefore, the selectivity for *Squonk* would be high, and the selectivity for *SQL* would be much lower.

29

How does SQL Server determine whether an index is selective and which index, if it has more than one to choose from, would be the most efficient to use? For example, how would SQL Server know how many rows the following query might return?

```
select * from table
    where key between 1000000 and 2000000
```

If the table contains 10,000,000 rows with values ranging between 0 and 20,000,000, how does the Query Optimizer know whether to use an index or a table scan? There could be 10 rows in the range, or 900,000. How does SQL Server estimate how many rows are between 1,000,000 and 2,000,000? The Query Optimizer gets this information from the index statistics, as described in the next section.

Index Statistics

As mentioned earlier, the selectivity of a key is an important factor that determines whether an index will be used to retrieve the data rows that satisfy a query. SQL Server stores the selectivity and a histogram of sample values of the key; based on the statistics stored for the key columns for the index and the SARGs specified for the query, the Query Optimizer decides which index to use.

To see the statistical information stored for an index, use the `DBCC SHOW_STATISTICS` command, which returns the following pieces of information:

▶ A histogram that contains an even sampling of the values for the first column in the index key. SQL Server stores up to 200 sample values in the histogram.

▶ Index densities for the combination of columns in the index. Index density indicates the uniqueness of the index key(s) and is discussed later in this section.

▶ The number of rows in the table at the time the statistics were computed.

▶ The number of rows sampled to generate the statistics.

▶ The number of sample values (steps) stored in the histogram.

▶ The average key length.

▶ Whether the index is defined on a string column.

▶ The date and time the statistics were generated.

The syntax for `DBCC SHOW_STATISTICS` is as follows:

```
DBCC SHOW_STATISTICS (tablename, index)
```

Listing 29.1 displays the abbreviated output from `DBCC SHOW_STATISTICS`, showing the statistical information for the `aunmind` nonclustered index on the `au_lname` and `au_fname` columns of the `authors` table.

LISTING 29.1   `DBCC SHOW_STATISTICS` Output for the aunmind Index on the authors Table

```
dbcc show_statistics (authors, aunmind )
go


Name     Updated                  Rows  Rows Sampled Steps  Density Average key length
➥ String Index
-------- -------------------- ----- ------------ ----- ------- ------------------
➥ -----------
aunmind  Jul  2 2006  9:45PM 172   172          148   1       24.06977
➥ YES
```

LISTING 29.1   Continued
_____

```
All density   Average Length Columns
------------  -------------- --------------------------
0.00625       6.406977       au_lname
0.005813953   13.06977       au_lname, au_fname
0.005813953   24.06977       au_lname, au_fname, au_id


RANGE_HI_KEY        RANGE_ROWS     EQ_ROWS   DISTINCT_RANGE_ROWS  AVG_RANGE_ROWS
------------------- -------------- --------- -------------------- --------------
Ahlberg             0              2         0                    1
Alexander           0              1         0                    1
Amis                0              1         0                    1
Arendt              0              1         0                    1
Arnosky             0              1         0                    1
Bate                0              1         0                    1
Bauer               0              1         0                    1
Benchley            0              1         0                    1
Bennet              0              1         0                    1
Blotchet-Halls      0              1         0                    1
...
DeFrance            0              1         0                    1
del Castillo        0              1         0                    1
Dillard             0              1         0                    1
Doctorow            0              1         0                    1
Doyle               0              1         0                    1
Durrenmatt          2              1         2                    1
Eastman             0              1         0                    1
...
Gringlesby          0              1         0                    1
Grisham             0              1         0                    1
Gunning             0              1         0                    1
Hill                0              1         0                    1
Hutchins            3              2         3                    1
Ionesco             0              1         0                    1
...
Van Allsburg        0              1         0                    1
Van der             0              1         0                    1
Van der Meer        0              1         0                    1
von Goethe          0              1         0                    1
Walker              0              1         0                    1
Warner              0              1         0                    1
White               0              2         0                    1
Wilder              0              1         0                    1
Williams            0              2         0                    1
```

29

LISTING 29.1   Continued

Wilson	0	1	0	1
Yates	0	1	0	1
Yokomoto	0	1	0	1
Young	0	1	0	1

Looking at the output, you can determine that the statistics were last updated on July 2, 2006. At the time the statistics were generated, the table had 172 rows, and all 172 rows were sampled to generate the statistics. The average key length is 24.06977 bytes. From the All density information, you can see that this index is highly selective. (A low density means high selectivity; index densities are covered shortly.)

After the general information and the index densities, the index histogram is displayed.

The Statistics Histogram

Up to 200 sample values can be stored in the statistics histogram. Each sample value is called a *step*. The sample value stored in each step is the endpoint of a range of values. Three values are stored for each step:

- ▶ **RANGE_ROWS**—This indicates how many other rows are inside the range between the current step and the step prior, not including the step values themselves.

- ▶ **EQ_ROWS**—This is the number of rows that have the same value as the sample value. In other words, it is the number of duplicate values for the step.

- ▶ **Range density**—This indicates the number of distinct values within the range. The range density information is actually displayed in two separate columns, DISTINCT_RANGE_ROWS and AVG_RANGE_ROWS:

  - ▶ DISTINCT_RANGE_ROWS is the number of distinct values between the current step and the step prior, not including the step values itself.

  - ▶ AVG_RANGE_ROWS is the average number of rows per distinct value within the range of the step.

In the output in Listing 29.1, distinct key values in the first column of the index are stored as the sample values in the histogram. Because most of the values for au_lname are unique, most of the range values are 0. You can see that there is a duplicate in the index key for the last name of Hutchins (EQ_ROWS is 2). For comparison purposes, Listing 29.2 shows a snippet of the DBCC SHOW_STATISTICS output for the titleidind index on the sales table in bigpubs2005.

LISTING 29.2   DBCC SHOW_STATISTICS Output for the titleidind Index on the sales Table
in the bigpubs2005 Database

```
dbcc show_statistics (sales, 'titleidind')
go


Name        Updated              Rows   Rows Sampled Steps  Density
➥ Average key length String Index
---------- ------------------- ------ ------------ ----- ----------
➥ ----------------- ------
titleidind Jul  2 2006  9:45PM 168725       43629   200  0.01239928
➥ 26.4007            YES


All density   Average Length Columns
------------- -------------- -------------------------------------------------
0.001858736   6              title_id
5.99844E-06   10             title_id, stor_id
5.926804E-06  26.4007        title_id, stor_id, ord_num


RANGE_HI_KEY RANGE_ROWS    EQ_ROWS       DISTINCT_RANGE_ROWS  AVG_RANGE_ROWS
------------ ------------- ------------- -------------------- --------------
BI0194       0             273.7798      0                    1
BI1953       309.9226      327.7646      1                    308.7705
BI2790       840.6651      293.0601      3                    279.5264
BI3224       364.1591      277.6359      1                    362.8053
BI4717       662.4596      296.9161      2                    330.3054
BI6450       337.0408      335.4767      1                    335.7879
BI9506       922.0198      250.6435      3                    306.5773
BU2075       573.3568      401.0296      2                    285.8784
CH0000       309.9226      320.0525      1                    308.7705
CH0249       662.4596      285.348       2                    330.3054
CH0623       588.853       343.1888      2                    293.6048
CH0649       302.1746      281.4919      1                    301.0512
CH0741       914.2717      308.4843      3                    304.001
CH0960       600.475       354.7569      2                    299.3997
CH1248       371.9071      374.0372      1                    370.5246
CH1305       573.3568      254.4995      2                    285.8784
CH1488       340.9149      327.7646      1                    339.6475
CH1568       255.6862      304.6282      1                    254.7357
CH1692       918.1458      339.3327      3                    305.2892
CH2080       309.9226      277.6359      1                    308.7705
CH2240       724.4441      262.2116      2                    361.2112
CH2288       685.7038      354.7569      2                    341.8951
CH2360       278.9304      323.9085      1                    277.8934
CH2436       294.4265      273.7798      1                    293.332
CH2485       635.3414      366.3251      2                    316.7841
```

29

LISTING 29.2   Continued

CH2666	922.0198	358.613	3	306.5773
CH2730	418.3955	312.3403	1	416.8401
CH2867	360.285	374.0372	1	358.9457
...				
FI9620	654.7115	339.3327	2	326.4422
FI9890	615.9712	285.348	2	307.1261
FI9968	654.7115	343.1888	2	326.4422
LC4930	984.0043	254.4995	3	327.1875
MC3021	794.1767	289.204	3	264.0687
NF2924	650.8375	293.0601	2	324.5106
NF8918	674.0817	343.1888	2	336.1003
PS1372	906.5236	320.0525	3	301.4247
PS3333	627.5933	277.6359	2	312.9209
TC4203	654.7115	362.469	2	326.4422
TC7777	0.585101	381.7493	0	313.6142

As you can see in this example, there are a greater number of rows per range and a greater number of duplicates for each step value. Also, all 200 steps in the histogram are used, and the sample values for the 168,725 rows in the table are distributed across those 200 step values. Also, in this example, 43,629 rows, rather than the whole table, were sampled to generate the statistics.

How the Statistics Histogram Is Used

The histogram steps are used for SARGs only when a constant expression is compared against an indexed column and the value of the constant expression is known at query compile time. The following are examples of SARGs where histogram steps can be used:

▶ where col_a = getdate()

▶ where cust_id = 12345

▶ where monthly_sales < 10000 / 12

▶ where l_name like "Smith" + "%"

Some constant expressions cannot be evaluated until query runtime. These include search arguments that contain local variables or subqueries and also join clauses, such as the following:

▶ where price = @avg_price

▶ where total_sales > (select sum(qty) from sales)

▶ where titles.pub_id = publishers.pub_id

For these types of statements, you need some other way of estimating the number of matching rows. In addition, because histogram steps are kept only on the first column of the index, SQL Server must use a different method for determining the number of matching rows for SARGs that specify multiple column values for a composite index, such as the following:

```
select * from sales
   where title_id = 'BI3976'
     and stor_id = 'P648'
```

When the histogram is not used or cannot be used, SQL Server uses the index density values to estimate the number of matching rows.

Index Densities

SQL Server stores the density values of each column in the index for use in queries where the SARG value is not known until runtime or when the SARG is on multiple columns of the index. For composite keys, SQL Server stores the density for the first column of the composite key; for the first and second columns; for the first, second, and third columns; and so on. This information is shown in the All density section of the DBCC SHOW_STATISTICS output in Listings 32.1 and 32.2.

Index density essentially represents the inverse of all unique key values of the key. The density of each key is calculated by using the following formula:

Key density = 1.00 / Count of distinct key values in the table

Therefore, the density for the au_lname column in the authors table in the bigpubs2005 database is calculated as follows:

```
Select Density = 1.00/ (select count(distinct au_lname) from authors)
go
Density
----------------------------------------
0.0062500000000
```

The density for the combination of the columns au_lname and au_fname is as follows:

```
Select Density = 1.00/ (select count(distinct au_lname + au_fname) from authors)
go
Density
----------------
0.0058139534883
```

Notice that, unlike with the selectivity ratio, a *smaller* index density indicates a more selective index. As the density value approaches 1, the index becomes less selective and essentially useless. When the index selectivity is poor, the Query Optimizer might choose to do a table scan or a leaf-level index scan rather than perform an index seek because it is more cost-effective.

29

> **TIP**
>
> Watch out for database indexes that have poor selectivity. Such indexes are often more of a detriment to the performance of the system than they are a help. Not only are they usually not used for data retrieval, but they also slow down your data modification statements because of the additional index overhead. You should identify such indexes and consider dropping them.

Typically, the density value should become smaller (that is, more selective) as you add more columns to the key. For example, in Listing 29.2, the densities get progressively smaller (and thus, more selective) as additional columns are factored in, as shown in Table 29.1.

TABLE 29.1   Index Densities for the `titleidind` Index on the `sales` Table

Key Column	Index Density
title_id	0. 001858736
title_id, stor_id	5. 99844E-06 (.00000599844)
title_id, stor_id, ord_num	5. 926804E-06 (.000005926804)

Estimating Rows Using Index Statistics

How does the Query Optimizer use the index statistics to estimate the number of rows that match the SARGs in a query?

SQL Server uses the histogram information when searching for a known value being compared to the leading column of the index key column, especially when the search spans a range or when there are duplicate values in the key. Consider this query on the sales table in the `bigpubs2005` database:

```
select * from sales
    where title_id = 'BI1953'
```

Because there are duplicates of `title_id` in the table, SQL Server uses the histogram on `title_id` (refer to Listing 32.2) to estimate the number of matching rows. For the value of BI1953, it would look at the EQ_ROWS value, which is 327.7646. This indicates that there are approximately 327.765 rows in the table that have a `title_id` value of BI1953.

When an exact match for the search argument is not found as a step in the histogram, SQL Server uses the AVG_RANGE_ROWS value for the next step greater than the search value. For example, SQL Server would estimate that for a search value of 'BI2184', on average, it would match approximately 279.5264 rows because that is the AVG_RANGE_ROWS value for the step value of 'BI2790', which is the next step greater than 'BI2184'.

When the query is a range retrieval that spans multiple steps, SQL Server sums up the RANGE_ROWS and EQ_ROWS values between the endpoints of the range retrieval. For example, using the histogram in Listing 32.2, if the search argument were where title_id <= 'BI3224', the row estimate would be 273.7798 + 309.9226 + 327.7646 + 840.6651 + 293.0601 + 364.1591 + 277.6359, or 2686.99 rows.

As mentioned previously, when the histogram cannot be used, SQL Server uses just the index density to estimate the number of matching rows. The formula is straightforward for an equality search; it looks like this:

Row Estimate = Number of Rows in Table [ts] Index Density

For example, to estimate the number of matching rows for any given title_id in the sales table, multiply the number of rows in the sales table by the index density for the title_id key (0.001858736), as follows:

```
select count(*) * 0.001858736 as 'Row Estimate'
from sales
go

Row Estimate
------------------
313.615231600
```

If a query specifies both the title_id and stor_id as SARGs, and if the SARG for title_id is a constant expression that can be evaluated at optimization time, SQL Server uses both the index density on title_id and stor_id as well as the histogram on title_id to estimate the number of matching rows. For some data values, the estimated number of matching rows for title_id and stor_id calculated using the index density could be greater than the estimated number of rows that match the specific title_id, as determined by the histogram. SQL Server uses whichever is the smaller of the two to gcalculate the row estimate.

Multiplying the number of rows in the sales table by the index density for title_id, stor_id (5.99844E-06), you can see that it is nearly unique, essentially matching only a single row:

```
select count(*) * 5.99844E-06 as 'Row Estimate'
from sales

Row Estimate
-------------
1.012086789
```

In this example, SQL Server would use the index density on title_id and stor_id to estimate the number of matching rows. In this case, it is estimated that the query will return, on average, one matching row.

29

Generating and Maintaining Index and Column Statistics

At this point, you might ask, "How do the index statistics get created?" and "How are they maintained?" The index statistics are first created when you create the index on a table that already contains data rows or when you run the UPDATE STATISTICS command. Index statistics can also be automatically updated by SQL Server. SQL Server can be configured to constantly monitor the update activity on the indexed key values in a database and update the statistics through an internal process, when appropriate.

Auto-Update Statistics

To automatically update statistics, an internal SQL Server process monitors the updates to a table's columns to determine when statistics should be updated. SQL Server internally keeps track of the number of modifications made to a column via column modification counters (colmodctrs). SQL Server uses information about the table and the colmodctrs to determine whether statistics are out of date and need to be updated. Statistics are considered out of date in the following situations:

▶ When the table size has gone from 0 to >0 rows

▶ When the number of rows in the table at the time the statistics were gathered was 500 or fewer and the colmodctr of the leading column of the statistics object has changed by more than 500

▶ When the table had more than 500 rows at the time the statistics were gathered and the colmodctr of the leading column of the statistics object has changed by more than 500 + 20% of the number of rows in the table

If the statistics are defined on a temporary table, there is an additional threshold for updating statistics every six column modifications if the table contains fewer than 500 rows.

The colmodctrs are incremented in the following situations:

▶ When a row is inserted into the table

▶ When a row is deleted from the table

▶ When an indexed column is updated

Whenever the index statistics have been updated for a column, the colmodctr for that column is reset to 0.

> **NOTE**
>
> SQL Server 2005's auto-update statistics behavior is very different from that in SQL Server 2000. In SQL Server 2000, when the rowmodctr triggered a statistics update due to the number of updates to the data row, all index statistics for that table were updated. By refining the granularity to the number of modifications to a column, SQL Server 2005 updates only the statistics on the columns that have undergone modifications.

When SQL Server generates an update of the column statistics, it generates the new statistics based on a sampling of the data values in the table. Sampling helps minimize the overhead of the AutoStats process. The sampling is random across the data pages, and the values are taken from the table or the smallest nonclustered index on the columns needed to generate the statistics. After a data page containing a sampled row has been read from disk, all the rows on the data page are used to update the statistical information.

> **CAUTION**
>
> Having up-to-date statistics on tables helps ensure that optimum execution plans are being generated for queries at all times. In most cases, you would want SQL Server to automatically keep the statistics updated. However, it is possible that Auto-Update Statistics can cause an update of the index statistics to run at inappropriate times in a production environment or in a high-volume environment to run too often. If this problem is occurring, you might want to turn off the AutoStats feature and set up a scheduled job to update statistics during off-peak periods. Do not forget to update statistics periodically, or the resulting performance problems might end up being much worse than the momentary ones caused by the AutoStats process.

To determine how often the AutoStats process is being run, you can use SQL Server Profiler to determine when an automatic update of index statistics is occurring by monitoring the Auto Stats event in the Performance event class. (For more information on using SQL Server Profiler, see Chapter 5.)

If necessary, it is possible to turn off the AutoStats behavior by using the sp_autostats system stored procedure. This stored procedure allows you to turn the automatic updating of statistics on or off for a specific index or all the indexes of a table. The following command turns off the automatic update of statistics for an index named aunmind on the authors table:

```
Exec sp_autostats 'authors', 'OFF', 'aunmind'
go

Automatic statistics maintenance turned OFF for 1 indices.
```

When you run sp_autostats and simply supply the table name, it displays the current setting for the table as well as the database. Following are the settings for the authors table:

```
Exec sp_autostats 'authors'
go

Global statistics settings for [bigpubs2005]:
  Automatic update statistics: OFF
  Automatic create statistics: ON

Settings for table [authors]
```

29

Index Name	AUTOSTATS	Last Updated
[UPKCL_auidind]	ON	2006-07-03 17:24:23.170
[aunmind]	OFF	2006-07-03 17:24:23.263
[_WA_Sys_state_4AB81AF0]	ON	2006-07-03 17:24:23.263
[au_fname]	ON	2006-07-03 17:24:23.263
[phone]	ON	2006-07-03 17:24:23.310
[address]	ON	2006-07-03 17:24:23.310
[city]	ON	2006-07-03 17:24:23.340
[zip]	ON	2006-07-03 17:24:23.387
[state_idx]	ON	2006-07-03 17:24:23.387

There are three other ways to disable auto-updating of statistics for an index:

▶ Specify the STATISTICS_NORECOMPUTE clause when creating the index.

▶ Specify the NORECOMPUTE option when running the UPDATE STATISTICS command.

▶ Specify the NORECOMPUTE option when creating statistics with the CREATE STATISTICS command. (You'll learn more on this command a bit later, in the "Creating Statistics" section.)

You can also turn AutoStats on or off for the entire database by setting the database option in SQL Server Management Studio (SSMS); to do this, you right-click the database to bring up the Database Properties dialog box, select the Options page, and set the Auto Update Statistics option to False. You can also disable or enable the AutoStats option for a database by using the ALTER DATABASE command:

```
ALTER DATABASE dbname SET AUTO_UPDATE_STATISTICS { ON | OFF }
```

NOTE

What actually happens when you execute sp_autostats or use the NORECOMPUTE option in the UPDATE STATISTICS command to turn off auto-update statistics for a specific index or table? SQL Server internally sets a flag in the system catalog to inform the internal SQL Server process not to update the index statistics for the table or index that has had the option turned off using any of these commands. To re-enable Auto Update Statistics, you either run UPDATE STATISTICS without the NORECOMPUTE option or execute the sp_autostats system stored procedure and specify the value 'ON' for the second parameter.

Asynchronous Statistics Updating

In previous versions of SQL Server, when SQL Server determined that the statistics being examined to optimize a query were out of date, the query would wait for the statistics update to complete before compilation of the query plan would continue. This is still the default behavior in SQL Server 2005. However, in SQL Server 2005, a new database option, AUTO_UPDATE_STATISTICS_ASYNC, can be enabled to support asynchronous statistics updating.

When the AUTO_UPDATE_STATISTICS_ASYNC option is enabled, queries do not have to wait for the statistics to be updated before compiling. Instead, SQL Server puts the out-of-date statistics on a queue to be updated by a worker thread, which runs as a background process. The query and any other concurrent queries compile immediately by using the existing out-of-date statistics. Because there is no delay for updated statistics, query response times are more predictable, even if the out-of-date statistics may cause the Query Optimizer to choose a less-efficient query plan. Queries that start after the updated statistics are ready use the updated statistics.

Manually Updating Statistics

Whether you've disabled AutoStats or not, you can still manually update index statistics by using the UPDATE STATISTICS T-SQL command, whose syntax is as follows:

```
UPDATE STATISTICS table ¦ view
    [ { { index ¦ statistics_name }
          ¦ ( { index ¦statistics_name } [ ,...n ] ) } ]
    [ WITH [ [ FULLSCAN ]
             ¦ SAMPLE number { PERCENT ¦ ROWS } ]
             ¦ RESAMPLE
       [ [ , ] [ ALL ¦ COLUMNS ¦ INDEX ]
       [ [ , ] NORECOMPUTE ] ]
```

If neither the FULLSCAN nor SAMPLE options are specified, the default behavior is to perform a sample scan to calculate the statistics, and SQL Server automatically computes the appropriate sample size.

The FULLSCAN option forces SQL Server to perform a full scan of the data in the table or index to calculate the statistics. This generates more accurate statistics than using sampling but is also the most time-consuming and I/O-intensive method. When you use the SAMPLE option, you can specify a fixed number of rows or a percentage of rows to sample to build or update the index statistics. If the sampling ratio specified ever results in too few rows being sampled, SQL Server automatically corrects the sampling, based on the number of existing rows in the table or view. At a minimum, approximately 1,000 data pages are sampled.

The RESAMPLE option specifies that the statistics be generated using the previously defined sampling ratio. This RESAMPLE option is useful for indexes or column statistics that were created with different sampling values. For example, if the index statistics were created using FULLSCAN, and the column statistics were created using a 50% sample, specifying the RESAMPLE option would update the statistics using FULLSCAN on the indexes and using the 50% sample for the others.

Specifying ALL, COLUMNS, or INDEX specifies whether the UPDATE STATISTICS command affects all existing statistics or only column or index statistics. By default, if no option is specified, the UPDATE STATISTICS statement affects all statistics.

As previously discussed, SQL Server automatically updates the index statistics by default. If you specify the NORECOMPUTE option with UPDATE STATISTICS, it disables AutoStats for the table or index.

When the automatic update statistics option is turned off, you should run the UPDATE STATISTICS command periodically, when appropriate. To determine the last time statistics were updated, you run the following command:

```
select STATS_DATE(tableid, indexid)
```

The following is an example:

```
select STATS_DATE(object_id('authors'), 1)
go
```

```
- - - - - - - - - - - - - - - - - - - - - -
2006-07-03 17:24:23.170
```

TIP

You can get the index ID from sys.indexes for each index on a table by using the following query:

```
select name, index_id from sys.indexes
    Where object_id = object_id('table_name') and index_id > 0
```

Column-Level Statistics

In addition to statistics on indexes, SQL Server can also store statistics on individual columns that are not part of any indexes. Knowing the likelihood of a particular value being found in a non-indexed column can help the Query Optimizer better estimate the number of matching rows for SARGs on the non-indexed columns. This helps it determine the optimal execution plan, whether or not SQL Server is using an index to actually locate the rows.

For example, consider the following query:

```
select stor_name
   from stores st
   join sales s on (st.stor_id = s.stor_id)
   where s.qty <= 100
```

SQL Server knows the density of the stor_id column in both the sales and stores tables because of indexes on the column in those tables. There is no index on qty. However, if the Query Optimizer were to know how many rows in the sales table had a qty less than 100, it would be better able to choose the most efficient query plan for joining between sales and stores. For example, assume that, on average, there are approximately 500 sales per store. However, there are only approximately 5 sales per store where the qty is less than 100. With the statistics on qty, SQL Server has the opportunity to determine this, and knowing there might be only 5 matching rows per store in sales versus 500, it might choose a different, more efficient, join strategy between the two tables.

Being able to keep statistics on the qty column without having to add it to an existing index with stor_id or create a separate index on qty provides SQL Server with the selectivity information it needs for optimization. By not having to create an index on qty to generate statistics on the column, you avoid incurring the overhead of having to maintain the index key rows for each insert, update, and delete that occurs on the table. Only the index statistics on qty need to be maintained, which is required only after many modifications to the data have occurred.

By default, SQL Server generates column statistics automatically when queries are optimized and the column is specified in a SARG or join clause. If no column statistics exist and the Query Optimizer needs to estimate the approximate density or distribution of column values, SQL Server automatically generates statistics for that column. This rule has two exceptions:

- ▶ Statistics are not automatically created for columns when the cost of creating the statistics exceeds the cost of the query plan itself.

- ▶ Statistics are not automatically created when SQL Server is too busy (that is, when there are too many outstanding query compilations in progress).

If you want to disable or re-enable the database option to auto-create statistics in the database, you use the ALTER DATABASE command:

```
ALTER DATABASE dbname SET AUTO_CREATE_STATISTICS { ON | OFF }
```

You can also turn the Auto Create Statistics option on or off for the entire database by setting the database option in SSMS. You right-click the database to bring up the Database Properties dialog box, select the Options page, and set the Auto Create Statistics option to True or False.

Column statistics are stored in the system catalogs. General information about them can be viewed in the sys.stats catalog view. Auto-generated statistics have a name in the format _WA_Sys_colname_systemgeneratednumber. You can retrieve a list of auto-generated column statistics with a query similar to the following:

```
SELECT cast(object_name(object_id) as varchar(30)) as 'table',
       cast (name as varchar(30)) as autostats
  FROM sys.stats
  WHERE auto_created = 1
    AND objectproperty (object_id, 'IsUserTable') = 1
go
table                         autostats
----------------------------- -----------------------------
PARTS                         _WA_Sys_00000003_24285DB4
authors                       _WA_Sys_state_4AB81AF0
```

29

stores_noCI	_WA_Sys_00000005_57A801BA
stores_noCI	_WA_Sys_00000006_57A801BA
sales	_WA_Sys_ord_num_628FA481
sales	_WA_Sys_qty_628FA481
stores	_WA_Sys_state_6477ECF3
stores	_WA_Sys_zip_6477ECF3
titles	_WA_Sys_type_6A30C649

Creating Statistics

If you want finer control over how the column statistics are generated, you can use the CREATE STATISTICS command. Its syntax is similar to that of UPDATE STATISTICS, with the exception that you specify a column or list of columns instead of an index on which to create statistics:

```
CREATE STATISTICS statistics_name ON table (column [,...n])
    [    WITH  [ [ FULLSCAN ¦ SAMPLE number { PERCENT ¦ ROWS } ] [,] ]
         [ NORECOMPUTE]       ]
```

Any column that can be specified as an index key can also be specified for statistics, except for XML columns or when the maximum allowable size of the combined column values exceeds the 900-byte limit on an index key. New for SQL Server 2005, statistics can be created on computed columns if the ARITHABORT and QUOTED_IDENTIFIER database options are set to ON. In addition, statistics can be created on CLR user-defined type columns if the CLR type supports binary ordering.

If you want to create single-column statistics on all eligible columns in a database, you can use the sp_createstats system procedure:

```
sp_createstats [[@indexonly =] 'indexonly']
        [,[@fullscan =] 'fullscan']
        [,[@norecompute =] 'norecompute']
```

The created statistics have the same name as the column on which they are created. Statistics are not created on columns that already have statistics on them (for example, the first column of an index or a column that already has explicitly created statistics).

To display a list of all column statistics, whether auto-generated or manually created, you use a query similar to the previous one, but you include user-created statistics as well:

```
SELECT cast(object_name(object_id) as varchar(30)) as 'table',
       cast (name as varchar(30)) as name,
       stats_id
   FROM sys.stats
   WHERE objectproperty (object_id, 'IsUserTable') = 1
     and (auto_created = 1 or user_created = 1)
order by 1, 3
go
```

table	name	stats_id
authors	_WA_Sys_state_4AB81AF0	3
authors	au_fname	4
authors	phone	5
authors	address	6
authors	city	7
authors	zip	8
discounts	discounttype	2
discounts	stor_id	3
discounts	lowqty	4
discounts	highqty	5
discounts	discount	6
employee	fname	3
employee	minit	4
employee	job_id	5
employee	job_lvl	6
employee	pub_id	7
employee	hire_date	8
jobs	job_desc	2
jobs	min_lvl	3
jobs	max_lvl	4
PARTS	_WA_Sys_00000003_24285DB4	3
publishers	pub_name	2
publishers	city	3
publishers	state	4
publishers	country	5
roysched	lorange	3
roysched	hirange	4
roysched	royalty	5
sales	_WA_Sys_ord_num_628FA481	3
sales	ord_date	4
sales	_WA_Sys_qty_628FA481	5
sales	payterms	6
stores	_WA_Sys_state_6477ECF3	3
stores	_WA_Sys_zip_6477ECF3	4
stores	stor_name	5
stores	stor_address	6
stores_noCI	_WA_Sys_00000005_57A801BA	3
stores_noCI	_WA_Sys_00000006_57A801BA	4
titleauthor	au_ord	4
titleauthor	royaltyper	5
titles	_WA_Sys_type_6A30C649	3
titles	pub_id	4
titles	price	5

29

titles	advance	6
titles	royalty	7
titles	ytd_sales	8
titles	notes	9
titles	pubdate	10

To remove a collection of statistics on one or more columns for a table in the current database, you use the DROP STATISTICS command, which has the following syntax:

```
DROP STATISTICS {table | view}.statistics_name
```

Be aware that dropping the column statistics could affect how your queries are optimized, and less efficient query plans might be chosen. Also, if the Auto Create Statistics option is enabled for the database, SQL Server is likely to automatically create statistics on the columns the next time they are referenced in a SARG or join clause for a query.

String Summary Statistics

SQL Server 2005 includes a new type of statistics for estimating the selectivity of LIKE conditions. SQL Server now creates string summary statistics, which are statistical summaries of substring frequency distribution for character columns. String summary statistics can be created on columns of type text, ntext, char, varchar, and nvarchar. String summary statistics allow SQL Server to estimate the selectivity of LIKE conditions, where the search string may have any number of wildcards in any combination, including LIKE conditions where the first character is a wildcard. In previous versions of SQL Server, row estimates could not be accurately obtained when the leading character of a search string was a wildcard character. SQL Server 2005 can now estimate the selectivity of any of the following predicates:

▶ Column LIKE 'string%'

▶ Column LIKE '%string'

▶ Column LIKE '%string%'

▶ Column LIKE 'str[abc]ing'

▶ Column LIKE '%abc%xy'

String summary statistics include additional information beyond what is displayed by DBCC SHOW_STATISTICS for the histogram. You can determine whether string summary statistics have been created for a column or an index by examining the String Index column returned by DBCC SHOW_STATISTICS. If the value is YES, then the statistics for that column or index also includes a string summary. However, DBCC SHOW_STATISTICS does not display the actual contents of the string summary.

SQL Server Index Maintenance

SQL Server indexes are self-maintaining, which means that any time a data modification (such as an update, a delete, or an insert) takes place on a table, the index B-tree is automatically updated to reflect the correct data values and current rows. Generally, you do not have to do any maintenance of the indexes, but indexes and tables can become fragmented over time. There are two types of fragmentation: external fragmentation and internal fragmentation.

External fragmentation occurs when the logical order of pages does not match the physical order or the extents allocated to the table are not contiguous. These situations occur typically with clustered tables as a result of page splits and pages being allocated and linked into the page chain from other extents. External fragmentation is usually not much of an issue for most queries that are performing small result set retrievals via an index. It's more of a performance issue for ordered scans of all or part of a table or index. If the table is heavily fragmented and the pages are not contiguous, scanning the page chain is more expensive.

Internal fragmentation occurs when an index is not using up all the space within the pages in the table or index. Fragmentation within an index page can happen for the following reasons:

▶ As more records are added to a table, space is used on the data page and on the index page. As a result, the page eventually becomes completely full. If another insert takes place on that page and there is no more room for the new row, SQL Server splits the page into two, each page now being about 50% full. If the clustered key values being inserted are not evenly distributed throughout the table (as often happens with clustered indexes on sequential keys), this extra free space might not be used.

▶ Frequent update statements can cause fragmentation in the database at the data and index page level as the updates cause rows to move to other pages. Again, if future clustered key values inserted into the table are not evenly distributed throughout the table, the empty slots left behind might not be used.

▶ As rows are deleted, space becomes freed up on data and index pages. If no new rows within the range of deleted values on the page are inserted, the page remains sparse.

NOTE

Internal fragmentation is not always a bad thing. Although pages that are not completely full use up more space and require more I/O during retrieval, free space within a page allows for rows to be added without having to perform an expensive page split. For some environments where the activity is more insert intensive than query intensive, you might want more free space in pages. This can be accomplished by applying the fill factor when creating the index on the table. Applying the fill factor is described in more detail in the next section.

Usually in a system, all these factors contribute to the fragmentation of data within the data pages and the index pages. In an environment that is subject to a lot of data modification, you might see a lot of fragmentation on the data and index pages over a period of time. These sparse and fragmented pages remain allocated to the table or index even if they have only a single row or two, and the extent containing the page remains allocated to the table or index.

Data fragmentation can adversely affect performance for table or index scanning operations because the data is spread across more pages than necessary. More I/Os are required to retrieve the data. SQL Server provides a DBCC command to monitor the level of fragmentation in the database. The syntax for this command is as follows:

```
DBCC SHOWCONTIG({table ¦ view}[,index])
   [ WITH { [ , [ ALL_INDEXES ] ]
            [ , [ TABLERESULTS ] ]
            [ , [ FAST ] ]
            [ , [ ALL_LEVELS ] ]
            [ NO_INFOMSGS ]
          }
   ]
```

You can use the TABLERESULTS option to receive the output from DBCC SHOWCONTIG as a table result set, which could be inserted into a table for historical or analysis purposes.

The following is a sample scan of the sales table, which in this case has a fair amount of internal and external fragmentation:

```
DBCC SHOWCONTIG(sales)
go

DBCC SHOWCONTIG scanning 'sales' table...
Table: 'sales' (1653580929); index ID: 1, database ID: 10
TABLE level scan performed.
- Pages Scanned................................: 1818
- Extents Scanned..............................: 232
- Extent Switches..............................: 1816
- Avg. Pages per Extent........................: 7.8
- Scan Density [Best Count:Actual Count].......: 12.55% [228:1817]
- Logical Scan Fragmentation ..................: 99.12%
- Extent Scan Fragmentation ...................: 5.60%
- Avg. Bytes Free per Page.....................: 2582.7
- Avg. Page Density (full).....................: 68.09%
```

Notice that Avg. Page Density (full) is 68.09%, and Avg. Bytes Free per Page is 2582.7 bytes. This indicates that the majority of the pages in the table are only about two-thirds full. This is wasting space and costing extra I/O during data retrieval. Scan Density is also rather low, so the page chain is fairly fragmented as well. You can also see that Logical Scan Fragmentation is 99.12%. Logical Scan Fragmentation indicates the percentage of pages for the leaf level of a clustered index that are out of order. An out-of-order page is a page for which the next physical page allocated to the index is not the page pointed to by the next-page pointer in the current leaf page.

Although DBCC SHOWCONTIG can still be used in SQL Server 2005, it is being deprecated and will not be supported in a future release of SQL Server. In its place is the new dynamic management function sys.dm_db_index_physical_stats, which is a multistatement table-valued function that returns size and fragmentation information for the data and indexes of a specified table or view. One of the advantages of the dynamic management function over the DBCC SHOWCONTIG command is that the results are returned by a normal SELECT statement and thus can be saved to a table for reporting purposes and historical analysis. The syntax of dm_db_index_physical_stats is as follows:

```
sys.dm_db_index_physical_stats (
    { database_id ¦ NULL ¦ 0 ¦ DEFAULT }
    , { object_id ¦ NULL ¦ 0 ¦ DEFAULT }
    , { index_id ¦ NULL ¦ 0 ¦ -1 ¦ DEFAULT }
    , { partition_number ¦ NULL ¦ 0 ¦ DEFAULT }
    , { mode ¦ NULL ¦ DEFAULT } )
```

The parameters for dm_db_index_physical_stats are summarized in Table 29.2.

TABLE 29.2   dm_db_index_physical_stats Parameters

Parameter	Description
database_id	The ID of the database. The default is 0, which returns information for all databases. NULL, 0, and DEFAULT are equivalent values in this context. If you specify NULL, or 0, for database_id, you must specify NULL for object_id, index_id, and partition_number.
object_id	The object ID of the table or view the index is on. Valid inputs are the ID number of a table or view, NULL, 0, or DEFAULT. The default is 0, which returns information for all tables and views in the specified database. NULL, 0, and DEFAULT are equivalent values in this context.

Parameter	Description
index_id	The ID of the index. Valid inputs are the ID number of an index, 0 if object_id is a heap, NULL, -1, or DEFAULT. The default is -1, which returns information for all indexes for a table or view. NULL, -1, and DEFAULT are equivalent values in this context. If you specify NULL for index_id, you must also specify NULL for partition_number.
partition_number	The partition number in the object. Valid inputs are the partition_number of an index or a heap, NULL, 0, or DEFAULT. The default is 0, which returns information for all partitions of the object. NULL, 0, and DEFAULT are equivalent values in this context. Use a partition_number of 1 for a nonpartitioned index or heap.
mode	The scan level that is used to obtain physical index statistics. Valid inputs are DEFAULT, NULL, LIMITED, SAMPLED, or DETAILED. The default mode is LIMITED. NULL and DEFAULT are equivalent values in this context.

29

Unlike DBCC SHOWCONTIG, which requires a shared table lock when invoked, the sys.dm_db_index_physical_stats function requires only an Intent-Shared table lock, regardless of the mode in which it runs. This provides for the capability to run the `sys.dm_db_index_physical_stats` function online without blocking all update activity on a table.

The scan-level mode determines the level of scanning performed by the function to obtain the physical statistics for the index. The `LIMITED` mode is the fastest and scans the smallest number of pages. It scans all data pages for a heap but scans only leaf-level pages for an index. It also returns only a subset of the data columns, as shown in Table 29.3. The `SAMPLED` mode returns statistics based on a 1% sample of all the pages in the index or heap. If the index or heap has fewer than 10,000 pages, `DETAILED` mode is used instead of `SAMPLED`. The `SAMPLED` scan mode displays information for only data pages of a heap and leaf-level pages of an index. The `DETAILED` mode scans all pages and returns all statistics for all data and index levels.

> **TIP**
>
> The scan modes get progressively slower from `LIMITED` to `DETAILED` because more work is performed in each mode. To quickly gauge the size or fragmentation level of a table or an index, you first use the `LIMITED` mode. It is the fastest and does not return a row for each non-leaf level in the `IN_ROW_DATA` allocation unit of the index.

Table 29.3 describes the result columns returned by the `dm_db_index_physical_stats` table-valued function.

TABLE 29.3   `dm_db_index_physical_stats` Result Columns

Column Name	Data Type	Description	Displayed in `LIMITED` Scan Mode
`database_id`	Smallint	A database ID database containing the table or view.	Yes
`object_id`	int	The object ID of the table or view that the index is on.	Yes
`index_id`	int	The index ID of the index. 0 indicates a heap.	Yes
`partition_number`	int	A partition number within the owning table, view, or index.	Yes
`index_type_desc`	nvarchar(60)	The index type. Values are HEAP, CLUSTERED INDEX, NONCLUSTERED INDEX, PRIMARY XML INDEX, and XML INDEX.	Yes
`alloc_unit_type_desc`	nvarchar(60)	A description of the allocation unit type. Values are IN_ROW_DATA, LOB_DATA, and ROW_OVERFLOW_DATA.	Yes
`index_depth`	tinyint	The number of index levels.	Yes
`index_level`	tinyint	The current level of the index. 0 indicates index leaf levels, heaps, and LOB_DATA or ROW_OVERFLOW_DATA allocation units.	Yes

TABLE 29.3   Continued

Column Name	Data Type	Description	Displayed in LIMITED Scan Mode
avg_fragmentation_in_percent	float	The percentage of logical fragmentation (out-of-order pages in the index).	Yes
fragment_count	bigint	The number of fragments (physically consecutive leaf pages) in the index.	Yes
avg_fragment_size_in_pages	float	The average number of pages in one fragment in an index.	Yes
page_count	bigint	The total number of index or data pages at the current level.	Yes
avg_page_space_used_in_percent	Float	The average percentage of available data storage space used in all pages.	No
record_count	Bigint	The total number of records at the current level.	No
ghost_record_count	Bigint	The number of ghost records ready for removal by the ghost cleanup task.	No
version_ghost_record_count	Bigint	The number of ghost records retained by an outstanding snapshot isolation transaction in an allocation unit.	No
min_record_size_in_bytes	Int	The minimum record size, in bytes.	No
max_record_size_in_bytes	Int	The maximum record size, in bytes.	No
avg_record_size_in_bytes	Float	The average record size, in bytes.	No
forwarded_record_count	Bigint	The number of forwarded records in a heap.	No

Listing 29.3 shows examples of running sys.dm_db_index_physical_stats on the sales table, using both LIMITED and DETAILED scan modes.

LISTING 29.3   sys.dm_db_index_physical_stats Examples

```
use bigpubs2005
go
select str(index_id,3,0) as indid,
     left(index_type_desc, 20) as index_type_desc,
     index_depth as idx_depth,
     index_level as idx_level,
     str(avg_fragmentation_in_percent, 5,2) as avg_frgmnt_pct,
     str(page_count, 10,0) as pg_cnt
  FROM sys.dm_db_index_physical_stats
     (db_id(), object_id('sales'),null, 0, 'LIMITED')
```

LISTING 29.3   Continued

```
select str(index_id,3,0) as indid,
      left(index_type_desc, 20) as index_type_desc,
      index_depth as idx_depth,
      index_level as idx_level,
      str(avg_fragmentation_in_percent, 5,2) as avg_frgmnt_pct,
      str(page_count, 10,0) as pg_cnt
  FROM sys.dm_db_index_physical_stats
    (db_id(), object_id('sales'),null, 0, 'DETAILED')
go
```

indid	index_type_desc	idx_depth	idx_level	avg_frgmnt_pct	pg_cnt
1	CLUSTERED INDEX	3	0	99.12	1818
2	NONCLUSTERED INDEX	3	0	99.32	740

indid	index_type_desc	idx_depth	idx_level	avg_frgmnt_pct	pg_cnt
1	CLUSTERED INDEX	3	0	99.12	1818
1	CLUSTERED INDEX	3	1	100.0	16
1	CLUSTERED INDEX	3	2	0.00	1
2	NONCLUSTERED INDEX	3	0	99.32	740
2	NONCLUSTERED INDEX	3	1	85.71	7
2	NONCLUSTERED INDEX	3	2	0.00	1

> **NOTE**
>
> In SQL Server 2005, the algorithm for calculating fragmentation is more precise than it was in SQL Server 2000. For example, in SQL Server 2000, a table was not considered fragmented if it included pages 32 and 34 from the same extent but not page 33. However, in SQL Server 2005, accessing pages 32 and 34 would require two physical I/O operations, so SQL Server counts this as fragmentation. As a result, the fragmentation values may appear higher in SQL Server 2005 than for an equivalent index in SQL Server 2000.

Again you can see from the output in Listing 29.3 that the logical fragmentation (avg_frgmnt_pct) is 99.12% for the leaf level of the clustered index (idx_level = 0). This indicates that the data pages are out of order in relation to the data values. If you want to improve the performance of table scans or clustered index scans for the sales table, you need to decide whether to rebuild the index or simply defragment the index.

The degree of fragmentation helps you decide which defragmentation method to use. A rough guideline to use to help decide is to examine the avg_fragmentation_in_percent value returned by the sys.dm_db_index_physical_stats function. If the avg_fragmentation_in_percent value is greater than 5% but less than 30%, you should reorganize the index. If the avg_fragmentation_in_percent value is greater than 30%, you should rebuild the index. If you also have a dedicated maintenance window large enough to perform a rebuild instead of simply reorganizing the index, you may as well run a rebuild because it performs a more thorough defragmentation than reorganizing the index.

Another factor in determining whether an index needs to be defragmented is how the data is accessed. If your applications are performing primarily single-row lookups, randomly accessing individual rows of data, the internal or external fragmentation is not a factor when it comes to query performance. Accessing one row from a fragmented table is just as easy as from an unfragmented table. However, if your applications are performing ordered range scan operations and reading all or large numbers of the pages in a table, excessive fragmentation can greatly slow down the scan. The more contiguous and full the pages, the better the performance of the scanning operations will be.

> **TIP**
>
> If you have very low levels of fragmentation (less than 5%), it is recommended that you not bother with either a reorganization or a rebuild because the benefit of removing such a small amount of fragmentation is not enough to justify the cost of reorganizing or rebuilding the index.

SQL Server provides a couple different methods for reorganizing or rebuilding an index. SQL Server 2005 still supports the DBCC DBREINDEX and DBCC INDEXDEFRAG commands that were available in SQL Server 2000 for backward compatibility purposes. However, in SQL Server 2005, the ALTER INDEX command replaces the DBCC DBREINDEX and DBCC INDEXDEFRAG commands for defragmenting an index. The following is the syntax for the ALTER INDEX command in SQL Server 2005:

```
ALTER INDEX { index_name ¦ ALL }
    ON [ [database_name.][schema_name.]] table_or_view_name
    { REBUILD
        [ [ WITH ( <rebuild_index_option> [ ,...n ] ) ]
          ¦ [ PARTITION = partition_number
              [ WITH ( <single_partition_rebuild_index_option> [ ,...n ] ) ]
            ]
        ]
    ¦ DISABLE
    ¦ REORGANIZE [ PARTITION = partition_number ]
                 [ WITH ( LOB_COMPACTION = { ON ¦ OFF } ) ]
    ¦ SET ( <set_index_option> [ ,...n ] )   }

<rebuild_index_option > ::=
{ PAD_INDEX  = { ON ¦ OFF }
  ¦ FILLFACTOR = fillfactor
  ¦ SORT_IN_TEMPDB = { ON ¦ OFF }
  ¦ IGNORE_DUP_KEY = { ON ¦ OFF }
  ¦ STATISTICS_NORECOMPUTE = { ON ¦ OFF }
```

29

```
¦ ONLINE = { ON ¦ OFF }
¦ ALLOW_ROW_LOCKS = { ON ¦ OFF }
¦ ALLOW_PAGE_LOCKS = { ON ¦ OFF }
¦ MAXDOP = max_degree_of_parallelism }

<single_partition_rebuild_index_option> ::=
{ SORT_IN_TEMPDB = { ON ¦ OFF } ¦ MAXDOP = max_degree_of_parallelism }

<set_index_option>::=
{   ALLOW_ROW_LOCKS= { ON ¦ OFF }
  ¦ ALLOW_PAGE_LOCKS = { ON ¦ OFF }
  ¦ IGNORE_DUP_KEY = { ON ¦ OFF }
  ¦ STATISTICS_NORECOMPUTE = { ON ¦ OFF } }
```

In SQL Server 2005, the REORGANIZE option is always performed online, regardless of which edition of SQL Server 2005 you are running. This allows for other users to continue to update and query the underlying data in the table while the REORGANIZE process is running. The REBUILD option can be executed online only if you are running SQL Server 2005 Enterprise Edition. In all other editions of SQL Server 2005, the REBUILD option is executed offline. When it is executed offline, SQL Server acquires exclusive locks on the underlying data and associated indexes so any data modifications to the table are blocked until the rebuild completes.

Reorganizing an index uses minimal system resources to defragment only the leaf level of clustered and nonclustered indexes of tables and views. The first phase of the reorganization process compacts the rows on the leaf pages, reapplying the current fill factor value to reduce the internal fragmentation. To view the current fill factor setting, you can run a query such as the following against the sys.indexes system catalog view:

```
select cast(name as varchar(30)) as name, index_id, fill_factor
   from sys.indexes
   where object_id = object_id('sales')
go
name                             index_id    fill_factor
-----------------------------    ---------   -----------
UPKCL_sales                      1           0
titleidind                       2           0
```

For more information on fill factor and how to set it, see the "Setting the Fill Factor" section, later in this chapter.

The second phase of the reorganization process involves the rearranging of the leaf-level pages so that the logical and physical order of the pages match, thereby reducing the external fragmentation of the leaf level of the index. SQL Server 2005 runs a REORGANIZATION of an index online because the second phase processes only two pages at a time, in an operation similar to a bubble sort. When defragmenting the index, SQL Server 2005 determines the first physical page belonging to the leaf level and the first logical page in the leaf level, and it swaps the data on those two pages. It then identifies the next logical and physical page and swaps them, and so on, until no more swaps need to be made. At this point, the logical page ordering matches the physical page ordering. While swapping the logical and physical pages, SQL Server uses an additional new page as a temporary storage area. After each page swap, SQL Server releases all locks and latches and saves the key of the last moved page.

The following example uses ALTER TABLE to reorganize the clustered index on the sales table:

```
ALTER INDEX UPKCL_sales on sales REORGANIZE
```

After running this command, you can run a query similar to the query in Listing 29.3 to display the fragmentation of the UPKCL_sales index on the sales table:

```
select str(s.index_id,3,0) as indid,
      left(i.name, 20) as index_name,
      left(index_type_desc, 20) as index_type_desc,
      index_depth as idx_depth,
      index_level as level,
      str(avg_fragmentation_in_percent, 5,2) as avg_frgmnt_pct,
      str(page_count, 10,0) as pg_cnt
  FROM sys.dm_db_index_physical_stats
      (db_id('bigpubs2005'), object_id('sales'),1, 0, 'DETAILED') s
    join sys.indexes i on s.object_id = i.object_id and s.index_id = i.index_id
go
```

indid	index_name	index_type_desc	idx_depth	level	avg_frgmnt_pct	pg_cnt
1	UPKCL_sales	CLUSTERED INDEX	3	0	2.32	1251
1	UPKCL_sales	CLUSTERED INDEX	3	1	100.0	16
1	UPKCL_sales	CLUSTERED INDEX	3	2	0.00	1

As you can see, the average fragmentation percentage is down to 2.32% from 99.32%, indicating that the index is now mostly defragmented. In addition, the page count is down to 1251 pages from 1818 pages as a result of the compaction of the data rows. However, the average fragmentation percentage of the intermediate level of the index (level = 1) is still 100%, indicating that it is completely fragmented. In order to defragment the non-leaf levels of the index, you need to rebuild the index. The following example shows how to rebuild the index using the ALTER INDEX command:

```
ALTER INDEX UPKCL_sales on sales REBUILD
```

After running this command, you can again run a query similar to the query in Listing 29.3 to display the fragmentation of the UPKCL_sales index on the sales table:

```
select str(s.index_id,3,0) as indid,
      left(i.name, 20) as index_name,
```

29

```
      left(index_type_desc, 20) as index_type_desc,
      index_depth as idx_depth,
      index_level as level,
      str(avg_fragmentation_in_percent, 5,2) as avg_frgmnt_pct,
      str(page_count, 10,0) as pg_cnt
   FROM sys.dm_db_index_physical_stats
      (db_id('bigpubs2005'), object_id('sales'),1, 0, 'DETAILED') s
   join sys.indexes i on s.object_id = i.object_id and s.index_id = i.index_id
go
```

indid	index_name	index_type_desc	idx_depth	level	avg_frgmnt_pct	pg_cnt
1	UPKCL_sales	CLUSTERED INDEX	3	0	0.00	1243
1	UPKCL_sales	CLUSTERED INDEX	3	1	0.00	7
1	UPKCL_sales	CLUSTERED INDEX	3	2	0.00	1

You can see from these results that the REBUILD option performs a more thorough defragmentation of the UPKCL_sales index than REORGANIZE. The average fragmentation percentage of both the leaf and intermediate levels is now 0%.

> **NOTE**
>
> When you rebuild a nonclustered index, the rebuild operation requires enough temporary disk space to store both the old and new indexes. However, if the index is disabled before being rebuilt, the disk space made available by disabling the index can be reused by the subsequent rebuild or any other operation. No additional space is required except for temporary disk space for sorting, which is typically only about 20% of the index size.
>
> Therefore, if disk space is limited, it may be helpful to disable a nonclustered index before rebuilding it. For more information on disabling indexes, see the "Disabling Indexes" section, later in this chapter.

One of the other options to the CREATE INDEX and ALTER INDEX commands is the FILL-FACTOR option. The fill factor allows you to specify, as a percentage, the fullness of the pages at the data and leaf index page levels.

Setting the Fill Factor

Fill factor is a setting you can use when creating an index to specify, as a percentage, how full you want your data pages or leaf-level index pages to be when the index is created. A lower fill factor has the effect of spreading the data and leaf index rows across more pages by leaving more free space in the pages. This reduces page splitting and dynamic reorganization of index and data pages, which can improve performance in environments where there are a lot of inserts and updates to the data. A higher fill factor has the effect of packing more data and index rows per page by leaving less free space in the pages. This is useful in environments where the data is relatively static because it reduces the number of pages required for storing the data and its indexes, and it helps improve performance for queries by reducing the number of pages that need to be accessed.

By default, when you create an index on a table, if you don't specify a value for FILLFACTOR, the default value is 0. With a FILLFACTOR setting of 0, or 100, the data pages for a clustered index and the leaf pages for a nonclustered index are created completely full. However, space is left within the non-leaf nodes of the index for one or two more rows. The default fill factor to be used when creating indexes is a server-level configuration option. If you want to change the serverwide default for the fill factor, you use the sp_configure command:

```
sp_configure 'fill factor',N
```

It is generally recommended that you leave the serverwide default for fill factor as 0 because, typically, you specify the fill factor to be used for an index within the index creation statement.

You can override the default fill factor value by specifying the FILLFACTOR option for the CREATE INDEX statement:

```
CREATE [UNIQUE] [CLUSTERED ¦ NONCLUSTERED] INDEX index_name
   ON [ [database_name.][schema_name.]] table_or_view_name
    [ WITH ( <relational_index_option> [ ,...n ] ) ]
<relational_index_option> ::=
{ PAD_INDEX  = { ON ¦ OFF }
  ¦ FILLFACTOR = fillfactor
  ¦ SORT_IN_TEMPDB = { ON ¦ OFF }
  ¦ IGNORE_DUP_KEY = { ON ¦ OFF }
  ¦ STATISTICS_NORECOMPUTE = { ON ¦ OFF }
  ¦ DROP_EXISTING = { ON ¦ OFF }
  ¦ ONLINE = { ON ¦ OFF }
  ¦ ALLOW_ROW_LOCKS = { ON ¦ OFF }
  ¦ ALLOW_PAGE_LOCKS = { ON ¦ OFF }
  ¦ MAXDOP = max_degree_of_parallelism }
```

The FILLFACTOR option for the CREATE INDEX command allows you to specify, as a percentage, how full the data or leaf-level index pages should be when you create an index on a table. The specified percentage can be from 1 to 100. Specifying a value of 80 would mean that each data or leaf page would be filled approximately 80% full at the time you create the index. It is important to note that as more data gets modified or added to a table, the fill factor is not maintained at the level specified during the CREATE INDEX command. Over a period of time, you will find that each page has a different percentage of fullness as rows are added and deleted.

29

> **TIP**
>
> A fill factor setting specified when creating a nonclustered index affects only the nonclustered index pages and doesn't affect the data pages. To apply a fill factor to the data pages in a table, you must provide a fill factor setting when creating a clustered index on the table. Also, it is important to remember that the fill factor is applied only at index creation time and is *not* maintained by SQL Server. When you begin updating and inserting data, the fill factor is eventually lost. Therefore, specifying a fill factor when creating your indexes is useful only if the table already contains data or if you simply want to set a default fill factor for the index other than 0 that will be used when indexes are rebuilt or reorganized by ALTER INDEX.

If you specify only the FILLFACTOR option, only the data or leaf-level index pages are affected by the fill factor. To specify the level of fullness for non-leaf pages, you use the PAD_INDEX option together with FILLFACTOR. This option allows you to specify how much space to leave open on each node of the index, which can help to reduce page splits within the non-leaf levels of the index. You don't specify a value for PAD_INDEX; it uses the same percentage value that is specified with the FILLFACTOR option. For example, to apply a 50% fill factor to the leaf and non-leaf pages in a nonclustered index on title_id in the titles table, you execute the following:

```
CREATE INDEX title_id_index on titles (title_id)
        with (FILLFACTOR = 50, PAD_INDEX = ON)
```

> **TIP**
>
> When you use PAD_INDEX, the value specified by FILLFACTOR cannot be such that the number of rows on each index node falls below two. If you do specify such a value, SQL Server internally overrides it so that the number of rows on an intermediate index page is never less than two.

Reapplying the Fill Factor

When might you need to reestablish the fill factor for your indexes or data? As data gets modified in a table, the value of FILLFACTOR is not maintained at the level specified in the CREATE INDEX statement. As a result, each page can reach a different level of fullness. Over a period of time, this can lead to heavy fragmentation in the database if insert/delete activity is not evenly spread throughout the table, and it could affect performance. In addition, if a table becomes very large and then very small, rows could become isolated within data pages. This space will likely not be recovered until the last row on the page is deleted and the page is marked as unused. To either spread rows out or to reclaim space by repacking more rows per page, you need to reapply the fill factor to your clustered and nonclustered indexes.

In environments where insert activity is heavy, reapplying a low fill factor might help performance by spreading out the data and leaving free space on the pages, which helps to minimize page splits and possible page-locking contention during heavy OLTP activity. You can use Performance Monitor to monitor your system and determine whether excessive page splits are occurring. (See Chapter 34, "Monitoring SQL Server Performance" for more information on using Performance Monitor.)

A DBA must manually reapply the fill factor to improve the performance of the system. This can be done by using the `ALTER INDEX` command discussed earlier or by dropping and re-creating the index. `ALTER INDEX` is preferred because, by default, it applies the original fill factor specified when the index was created, or you can provide a new fill factor to override the default. The original fill factor for an index is stored in `sys.indexes` in the `fill_factor` column. In addition, if you use the `ALTER INDEX` command to reorganize or rebuild your table or index, it attempts to reapply the index's original fill factor when it compacts the pages.

Disabling Indexes

A new feature available in SQL Server 2005 is the ability to set an index as disabled. When an index is disabled, the definition of the index is maintained in the system catalogs, but the index itself contains no index key rows. Disabling an index prevents user access to the index. Disabling a clustered index also prevents access to the underlying table data.

You can manually disable an index at any time by using the `ALTER INDEX DISABLE` statement:

```
ALTER INDEX titleidind ON sales DISABLE
```

The reasons you might want to disable an index include the following:

▶ Correcting a disk I/O or allocation error on an index page and then rebuilding the index later

▶ Temporarily removing the index for troubleshooting purposes

▶ Saving temporary disk space while rebuilding nonclustered indexes

When you disable an index, the index is not maintained while it is disabled, and the Query Optimizer does not consider the index when creating query execution plans. However, statistics on a disabled nonclustered index remain in place and are updated automatically if the AutoStats option is in effect.

If you disable a clustered index, all nonclustered indexes on the table are automatically disabled as well. The nonclustered index cannot be re-enabled until the clustered index is either enabled or dropped. After you enable the clustered index, the nonclustered indexes must be explicitly enabled unless the clustered index was enabled by using the `ALTER INDEX ALL REBUILD` statement. Because the data rows of the table cannot be accessed while the clustered index is disabled, the following operations cannot be performed on the table:

▶ SELECT, UPDATE, DELETE, and INSERT

▶ CREATE INDEX

▶ CREATE STATISTICS

▶ UPDATE STATISTICS

▶ ALTER TABLE statements that modify table columns or constraints

After an index is disabled, it remains in a disabled state until it is rebuilt or dropped. You can enable a disabled index by rebuilding it by using one of the following methods:

▶ ALTER INDEX statement with the REBUILD clause

▶ CREATE INDEX with the DROP_EXISTING clause

▶ DBCC DBREINDEX

To determine whether an index is currently disabled, you can use the INDEXPROPERTY function (a value of 1 indicates the index is disabled):

```
select indexproperty(object_id('sales'), 'titleidind', 'IsDisabled')
```

1

Managing Indexes with SSMS

So far, you've seen the commands necessary for index management. In addition to these commands, SSMS provides tools for managing indexes.

To reorganize or rebuild an index using SSMS, in the Object Explorer, you connect to an instance of the SQL Server 2005 database engine and then expand that instance. Then you expand Databases, expand the database that contains the table with the specified index, and expand Tables. Next, you expand the table in which the index belongs and then expand Indexes. Finally, you right-click the index to rebuild and then click Rebuild or Reorganize. To rebuild or reorganize all indexes on a table, you right-click Indexes and select Rebuild All or Reorganize All.

You can also disable indexes in SSMS. In the Object Explorer, you right-click the index you want to disable and then select the Disable option. To disable all indexes on a table, you right-click on Indexes and select Disable All.

You can also use SSMS to modify indexes. In the Object Explorer, you right-click the index you want to modify and then click Properties. In the Properties dialog that appears (see Figure 29.5), you can add or remove columns from the index, change the uniqueness setting, set the index option, set the fill factor, rebuild the index, view the index fragmentation, reorganize the index, and so on.

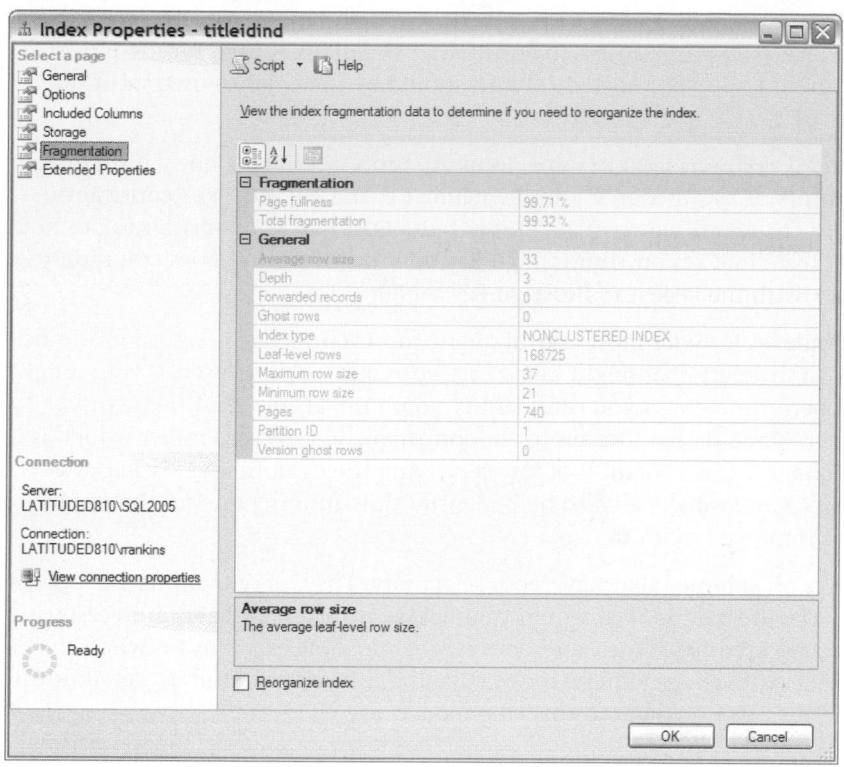

FIGURE 29.5   Setting and viewing index properties in SSMS.

Index Design Guidelines

SQL Server indexes are mostly transparent to end users and T-SQL developers. Indexes are typically not specified in queries unless you use table hints to force the Query Optimizer to use a particular index. (Although forcing indexes is generally not advised, using Query Optimizer table hints is covered in more detail in Chapter 30, "Understanding Query Optimization.") Normally, based on the index key histogram or density values, the SQL Server cost-based Query Optimizer automatically chooses the index that is least expensive from an I/O standpoint.

Chapter 30 goes into greater detail on how the Query Optimizer estimates I/O and determines the most efficient query plan. In the meantime, the following are some of the main guidelines to follow in creating useful indexes that the Query Optimizer can use effectively:

▶ For composite indexes, try to keep the more selective columns leftmost in the index. The first element in the index should be the most unique (if possible), and index column order in general should be from most to least unique. However,

29

remember that selectivity doesn't help if the first ordered index column is not specified in your SARGs or join clauses. To ensure that the index is used for the largest number of queries, the first ordered column should be the column used most often in your queries.

▶ Be sure to index columns used in joins. Joins are processed inefficiently if no index on the column(s) is specified in a join. Remember that a PRIMARY KEY constraint automatically creates an index on a column, but a FOREIGN KEY constraint does not. You should create indexes on your foreign key columns if your queries commonly join between the primary key and foreign key tables.

▶ Tailor your indexes for your most critical queries and transactions. You cannot index for every possible query that might be run against your tables. However, your applications will perform better if you can identify your critical and most frequently executed queries and design indexes to support them. SQL Server Profiler, which is covered in Chapter 5, is a useful tool for identifying the most frequently executed queries. SQL Server Profiler can also help identify slow-running queries that might benefit from improved index design.

▶ Avoid indexes on columns that have poor selectivity. The Query Optimizer is not likely to use the indexes, so they would simply take up space and add unnecessary overhead during inserts, updates, and deletes. One possible exception is when the index can be used to cover a query. Index covering is discussed in more detail in the "Index Covering" section, later in this chapter.

▶ Choose your clustered and nonclustered indexes carefully. The next two sections discuss tips and guidelines for choosing between clustered or nonclustered indexes, based on the data contained in the columns and the types of queries executed against the columns.

Clustered Index Indications

Searching for rows via a clustered index is almost always faster than searching for rows via a nonclustered index—for two reasons. One reason is that a clustered index contains only pointers to pages rather than pointers to individual data rows; therefore, a clustered index is more compact than a nonclustered index. Because a clustered index is smaller and doesn't require an additional bookmark lookup to find the matching rows, the rows can be found with fewer page reads than with a similarly defined nonclustered index. The second reason is that because the data in a table with a clustered index is physically sorted on the clustered key, searching for duplicate values or for a range of clustered key values is faster; the rows are adjacent to each other, and SQL Server can simply locate the first qualifying row and then search the rows in sequence until the last qualifying row is found. However, because you are only allowed to create one clustered index per table, you must judiciously choose the column or columns on which to define the clustered index.

If you require only a single index on a table, it's typically advantageous to make it a clustered index; the resulting overhead of maintaining clustered indexes during updates, inserts, and deletes can be considerably less than the overhead incurred by nonclustered indexes.

By default, the primary key on a table is defined as a clustered unique index. In most applications, the primary key column on a table is almost always retrieved in single-row lookups. For single-row lookups, a nonclustered index usually costs you only a few more I/O than a similar clustered index. Are you or the users really going to notice a difference between three page reads to retrieve a single data row versus four- to six-page reads to retrieve a single data row? Not at all. However, if you have to perform a range retrieval, such as a lookup on last name, will you notice a difference between scanning 10% of the table versus having to find the rows using a full table scan? Most definitely. With this in mind, you might want to consider creating your primary key as a unique nonclustered index and choosing another candidate for your clustered index.

The following are guidelines to consider for other potential candidates for clustered indexes:

▶ **Columns with a number of duplicate values that are searched frequently (for example, `WHERE last_name = 'Smith'`)**   Because the data is physically sorted, all the duplicate values are kept together. Any query that tries to fetch records against such keys finds all the values, using a minimum of I/O. SQL Server locates the first row that matches the SARG and then scans the data rows in order until it finds the last row matching the SARG.

▶ **Columns that are often specified in the `ORDER BY` clause**—Because the data is already sorted, SQL Server can avoid having to re-sort the data if the `ORDER BY` is on the clustered index key and the data is retrieved in clustered key order. Remember that even for a table scan, the data is retrieved in clustered key order because the data in the table is in clustered key order. The only exception is if a parallel query operation is used to retrieve the data rows; in that case, the results needs to be re-sorted when the result sets from each parallel thread are merged. (For more information on parallel query strategies, see Chapter 30.)

▶ **Columns that are often searched for within a range of values (for example, `WHERE price between $10 and $20`)**—A clustered index can be used to locate the first qualifying row in the range of values. Because the rows in the table are in sorted order, SQL Server can simply scan the data pages in order until it finds the last qualifying row within the range. When the result set within the range of values is large, a clustered index scan is significantly more efficient in terms of total logical I/O performed than repeated bookmark lookups via a nonclustered index.

▶ **Columns, other than the primary key, that are frequently used in join clauses**— Clustered indexes tend to be smaller than nonclustered indexes; the amount of page I/O required per lookup is generally less for a clustered index than for a nonclustered index. It can be a significant difference when joining many records. An extra page read or two might not seem like much for a single-row retrieval, but add those additional page reads to 100,000 join iterations, and you're looking at a total of 100,000 to 200,000 additional page reads.

29

When you consider columns for a clustered index, you might want to try to keep your clustered indexes on relatively static columns to minimize the re-sorting of data rows when an indexed column is updated. Any time a clustered index key value changes, the entire data row has to be moved to keep the clustered data values in physical sort order. In addition, all nonclustered indexes using the clustered key as the bookmark to that row also need to be updated.

You should also avoid creating clustered indexes on wide keys that are made up of several columns, especially several large-size columns. This is because the clustered key values are incorporated in all nonclustered indexes as the bookmark lookup keys. Because the nonclustered index entries contain the clustering key in addition to the key columns defined for that nonclustered index, the nonclustered indexes end up being significantly larger and less efficient in terms of I/O.

Because you can physically sort the data in a table in only one way, you can have only one clustered index per table. Any other columns you want to index have to be defined with nonclustered indexes.

Nonclustered Index Indications

SQL Server allows you to create a maximum of 249 nonclustered indexes on a table. Until tables become extremely large, the actual space taken by a nonclustered index is a minor expense compared to the increased access performance. You need to keep in mind, however, that as you add more indexes to the system, database modification statements get slower due to the index maintenance overhead.

Also, when defining nonclustered indexes, you typically want to define indexes on columns that are more selective (that is, columns with low density values) so that they can be used effectively by the Query Optimizer. A high number of duplicate values in a nonclustered index can often make it more expensive (in terms of I/O) to process the query using the nonclustered index than a table scan. Let's look at a hypothetical example:

```
select title from titles
    where price between $5. and $10.
```

Assume that you have 1 million rows within the range; those 1 million rows could be randomly scattered throughout the table. Although the index leaf level has all the index rows in sorted order, reading all data rows one at a time would require a separate bookmark lookup for each row in the worst-case scenario.

Thus, the worst-case I/O estimate for range retrievals using a nonclustered index is as follows:

Number of levels in the nonclustered index

+ Number of index pages scanned to find all matching rows

+ (Number of matching rows × Number of pages per bookmark lookup)

If you have no clustered index on the table, the bookmark is simply a page and row pointer and requires one data page read to find the matching data row. If 1 million rows are in the range, the worst-case cost estimate to search via the nonclustered index with no clustered index on the table would be as follows:

Number of index page reads to find all the bookmarks

+ (1 million matching rows × 1 data page read)

= 1 million+ I/O

If you have a clustered index on the table, the bookmark is a clustered index key for the data row. Using the bookmark to find the matching row requires searching the clustered index tree to locate the data row. Assuming that the clustered index has two non-leaf levels, it would cost three pages to find each qualifying row on a data page. If the range has 1million rows, the worst-case cost estimate to search via the nonclustered index with a clustered index on the table would be as follows:

Number of index page reads to find all the bookmarks

+ (1 million matching rows × 3 pages per bookmark lookup)

= 3 million+ I/O

Contrast each of these scenarios with the cost of a table scan. If the entire table takes up 50,000 pages, a full table scan would cost only 50,000 in terms of I/O. Therefore, in this example, doing a table scan would actually be more efficient than using the nonclustered index.

The following guidelines help you identify potential candidates for nonclustered indexes for your environment:

▶ Columns referenced in SARGs or join clauses that have a relatively high selectivity (the density value is low).

▶ Columns referenced in both the WHERE clause and the ORDER BY clause. When the data rows are retrieved using a nonclustered index, they are retrieved in nonclustered index key order. If the result set is to be ordered by the nonclustered index key(s) as well, SQL Server can avoid having to re-sort the result set, resulting in a more efficient query. The following query is an example in which SQL Server can avoid the extra step of sorting the result set if a nonclustered index is on state and the index is used to retrieve the matching rows:

```
select * from authors
    where state like 'C%'
    order by state
```

In general, nonclustered indexes are useful for single-row lookups, joins, queries on columns that are highly selective, or queries with small range retrievals. Also, when considering your nonclustered index design, don't overlook the benefits of index covering, as described in the following section.

29

Index Covering

Index covering is a situation where all the information required by the query in the SELECT and WHERE clauses can be found entirely within the nonclustered index itself. Because the nonclustered index contains a leaf row corresponding to every data row in the table, SQL Server can satisfy the query from the leaf rows of the nonclustered index. This results in faster retrieval of data because all the information can come directly from the index page, and SQL Server avoids lookups of the data pages.

Because the leaf pages in a nonclustered index are linked together, the leaf level of the index can be scanned just like the data pages in a table. Because the leaf index rows are typically much smaller than the data rows, a nonclustered index that covers a query will be faster than a clustered index on the same columns because fewer pages would need to be read.

In the following example, a nonclustered index on the au_lname and au_fname columns of the authors table would cover the query because the result columns and the SARGs can all be derived from the index itself:

```
Select au_lname, au_fname
   From authors
   Where au_lname like 'M%'
Go
```

Many other queries that use an aggregate function (such as MIN, MAX, AVG, SUM, and COUNT) or simply check for existence of criteria also benefit from index covering. The following queries are examples of aggregate queries that can take advantage of index covering:

```
select count(au_lname) from authors where au_lname like 'M%'
```

```
select count(*) from authors where au_lname like 'M%'
```

```
select count(*) from authors
```

You might be wondering how the last query, which doesn't even specify a SARG, can use an index. SQL Server knows that by its nature, a nonclustered index contains a row for every data row in the table; it can simply count all the rows in any of the nonclustered indexes instead of scanning the whole table. For the last query, SQL Server chooses the smallest nonclustered index—that is, the one with the smallest number of leaf pages.

Index covering can sometimes occur when you are not be expecting it. As discussed previously in this chapter, when you have a clustered index defined on a table, the clustered key is carried into all the nonclustered indexes to be used as the bookmark to locate the actual data row. Having the additional clustered key column values in the nonclustered index provides more data values that can be used in index covering.

For example, assume that the authors table has a clustered index on au_lname and au_fname and a nonclustered primary key defined on au_id. Each row in the nonclustered index on au_id would contain the clustered key values for au_lname and au_fname for its corresponding data row. Because of this, the following query would actually be covered by the nonclustered index on au_id:

```
select au_lname, au_fname
   from authors
   where au_id like '123%'
```

Explicitly adding additional columns to nonclustered indexes to promote the occurrence of index covering has historically been a common method of improving query response time. Consider the following query:

```
select royalty from titles
   where price between $10 and $20
```

If you create an index on only the price column, SQL Server can find the rows in the index where price is between $10 and $20, but it has to access the data rows to retrieve royalty. With 100 rows in the range, the worst-case I/O cost to retrieve the data rows would be as follows:

> Number of index levels
>
> + Number of index pages to find 100 the matching rows
>
> + (100 × Number of pages per bookmark lookup)

If the royalty column were added to the index on the price column, SQL Server could scan the index to retrieve the results instead of having to perform the bookmark lookups against the table, resulting in faster query response. The I/O cost using index covering would be lower, as follows:

> Number of index levels
>
> + Number of index pages to scan to find the 100 matching rows

If you are considering padding your indexes to take advantage of index covering, beware of making an index too wide. As index row width approaches data row width, the benefits of covering are lost as the number of pages in the leaf level increases. As the number of leaf-level index pages approaches the number of pages in the table, the number of index levels also increases, increasing the I/O cost of using the index to locate data.

You should also avoid adding to the index columns that are frequently updated. Remember that any changes to the columns in the data rows cascades into the indexes as well. This increases the index maintenance overhead, which can adversely affect update performance.

As an alternative to adding columns to the nonclustered index key to encourage index covering, you might want to consider taking advantage of the new included columns feature in SQL Server 2005.

Included Columns

A new feature introduced for nonclustered indexes in SQL Server 2005 is included columns. Included columns allow you to add non-key columns to the leaf level of a nonclustered index for the purpose of index covering.

One advantage of included columns is that because the non-key columns are stored only in the leaf level of the index, the non-leaf rows of the index are smaller, which helps reduce the overall size of the index, thereby helping reduce the I/O cost of using the index. Another advantage is that this feature allows you to exceed the SQL Server limits for number of index key column and index key size limits of a maximum of 16 key columns and a maximum index key size of 900 bytes. The included non-key columns are not factored in when calculating the number of index key columns or index key size. All data types are allowed as included columns except for the text, ntext, and image data types.

To add included columns to an index, you specify the INCLUDE clause to the CREATE INDEX statement:

```
CREATE INDEX NC_titles_price on titles (price) INCLUDE (royalty)
```

> **TIP**
>
> If you have existing nonclustered indexes with a large index key size, you should consider redesigning them so that only columns used for searching and lookups are key columns. You should make all other columns that were added for index covering into included columns. This way, you still have all columns needed to cover your queries, but the index key itself is smaller and more efficient.

You still want to be careful to avoid adding unnecessary columns as included columns of an index. Adding too many index columns, key or non-key, can adversely affect performance for the following reasons:

▶ Fewer index leaf rows fit on a page, which can increase I/O costs to search the leaf level of the index and also reduce data cache efficiency.

▶ Because of the increased leaf row size, more disk space is required to store the index, especially if you are adding varchar(max), nvarchar(max), varbinary(max), or xml data types as non-key index columns. Because the column values are also copied into the index leaf level, you are essentially storing the data values twice.

▶ Changes to the included columns in the data rows cascade into the leaf rows of the index as well. This increases the index maintenance overhead, which can adversely affect performance of data modifications.

Wide Indexes Versus Multiple Indexes

As an index key gets wider, the selectivity of the key generally becomes higher as well. It might seem that creating wide indexes would result in better performance. This is not necessarily true. The reason is that the wider the key, the fewer rows SQL Server stores on the index pages, requiring more pages at each level; this results in a higher number of levels in the index B-tree. To get to specific rows, SQL Server must perform more I/O.

To get better performance from queries, instead of creating a few wide indexes, you should consider creating multiple narrower indexes. The advantage here is that with smaller keys, the Query Optimizer can quickly scan through multiple indexes to create the most efficient access plan. SQL Server has the option of performing multiple index lookups within a single query and merging the result sets together to generate an intersection of the indexes. Also, with more indexes, the Query Optimizer can choose from a wider variety of query plan alternatives.

If you are considering creating a wide key, you should individually check the distribution of values for each member of the composite key. If the selectivity on the individual columns is high, you might want to break up the index into multiple indexes. If the selectivity of individual columns is low but is high for combined columns, it makes sense to have wider keys on the table. To get to the right combination, you can populate your table with real-world data, experiment with creating multiple indexes, and check the distribution of values for each column. Based on the histogram steps and index density, you can make the decisions for an index design that works best for your environment.

Indexed Views

As discussed in Chapter 22, "Creating and Managing Views," SQL Server 2005 allows you to create indexed views. An *indexed view* is any view that has a clustered index defined on it. When a CREATE INDEX statement is executed on a view, the result set for the view is materialized and stored in the database with the same structure as a table with a clustered index. Changes made to the data in the underlying tables of the view are automatically reflected in the view the same way any changes to a table are reflected in its indexes. In addition to a clustered index, you can create additional nonclustered indexes on indexed views to provide additional query performance. Additional indexes on views might provide more options for the Query Optimizer to choose from during the optimization process.

In the Developer and Enterprise Editions of SQL Server 2005, when an indexed view exists on a table and you access the view directly within a query, the Query Optimizer automatically considers using the index on the view to improve query performance, just as an index on a table is used to improve performance. The Query Optimizer also considers using the indexed view, even for queries that do not directly name the view in the FROM clause. In other words, when a query might benefit from using the indexed view, the Query Optimizer can use the indexed view to satisfy the query in place of an existing index on the table itself. (For more information on how indexed views are used in query plans, see Chapter 30.)

It is important to note that although indexed views can be created in all editions of SQL Server 2005, only the Developer and Enterprise Editions automatically use indexed views to optimize queries. In the other editions, indexed views are not used to improve query performance unless the view is explicitly specified in the query and the NOEXPAND hint is specified as well. Without the NOEXPAND hint, SQL Server expands the view to its underlying base tables and optimizes based on the table indexes. The following example shows the use of the NOEXPAND option to force SQL Server to use the indexed view specified in the query:

```
select * from sales_Qty_Rollup WITH (NOEXPAND)
   where stor_id between 'B914' and 'B999'SET ARITHABORT ON
```

Indexed views add overhead and can be more complex for SQL Server to maintain over time than normal indexes. Each time an underlying table of a view is modified, SQL Server has to update the view result set and potentially the index on that view. The scope of a view's index can be larger than that of any single table's index, especially if the view is defined on several large tables. The overhead associated with maintaining a view and its index during updates can negate any benefit that queries gain from the indexed view. Because of this additional maintenance overhead, you should create indexes only on views where the advantage provided by the improved speed in retrieving the results outweighs the increased maintenance overhead.

The following are some guidelines to consider when you design indexed views:

▶ Create indexes on views where the underlying table data is relatively static.

▶ Create indexed views that will be used by several queries.

▶ Keep the indexes small. As with table indexes, a smaller index allows SQL Server to access the data more efficiently.

▶ Create indexed views that will be significantly smaller than the underlying table(s). An indexed view might not provide significant performance gains if its size is similar to the size of the original table.

▶ You need to specify the NOEXPAND hint in editions of SQL Server other than the Developer and Enterprise Editions of SQL Server, or the indexed view is not used to optimize the query.

Indexes on Computed Columns

SQL Server 2005 allows you to build indexes on computed columns in your tables. Computed columns can participate at any position of an index, along with your other table columns, including in a PRIMARY KEY or UNIQUE constraint. To create an index on computed columns, the following SET statements must be set as shown:

▶ SET ARITHABORT: ON

▶ SET CONCAT_NULL_YIELDS_NULL: ON

▶ SET QUOTED_IDENTIFIER: ON

▶ SET ANSI_NULLS: ON

▶ SET ANSI_PADDING: ON

▶ SET ANSI_WARNINGS: ON

▶ SET NUMERIC_ROUNDABORT: OFF

If any of these seven SET options were not in effect when you created the table, you get the following message when you try to create an index on the computed column:

```
Server: Msg 1934, Level 16, State 1, Line 2
CREATE INDEX failed because the following SET options
 have incorrect settings: '<OPTION NAME>'.
```

In addition, the functions in the computed column must be deterministic. A *deterministic* function is one that returns the same result every time it is called with the same set of input parameters.

When you create a clustered index on a computed column, it is no longer a virtual column in the table. The computed value for the column is stored in the data rows of the table. If you create a nonclustered index on a computed column, the computed value is stored in the nonclustered index rows but not in the data rows, unless you also have a clustered index on the computed column.

Be aware of the overhead involved with indexes on computed columns. Updates to the columns that the computed columns are based on result in updates to the index on the computed column as well.

Indexes on computed columns can be useful when you need an index on large character fields. As discussed earlier, the smaller an index, the more efficient it is. You could create a computed column on the large character field by using the CHECKSUM() function. CHECKSUM() generates a 4-byte integer that is relatively unique for character strings but not absolutely unique. (Different character strings can generate the same checksum, so when searching against the checksum, you need to include the character string as an additional search argument to ensure that you are matching the right row.) The benefit is that you can create an index on the 4-byte integer generated by the CHECKSUM() that can be used to search against the character string instead of having to create an index on the large character column itself. Listing 29.4 shows an example of applying this solution.

LISTING 29.4   Using an Index on a Computed Checksum Column

```
--The first statement is used to disable any previously created
--DDL triggers in the database which would prevent creating a new constraint.
DISABLE TRIGGER ALL ON DATABASE
go
-- First add the computed column to the table
alter table titles add title_checksum as CHECKSUM(title)
go
```

LISTING 29.4   Continued

```
-- Next, create an index on the computed column
create index NC_titles_titlechecksum on titles(title_checksum)
go

-- In your queries, include both the checksum column and the title column in
--   your search argument
select title_id, ytd_sales
  from titles
  where title_checksum = checksum('Fifty Years in Buckingham Palace Kitchens')
    and title = 'Fifty Years in Buckingham Palace Kitchens'
```

SQL Server 2005 also supports persisted computed columns. With persisted computed columns, SQL Server stores the computed values in the table without requiring an index on the computed column. Like indexed computed columns, persisted computed columns are updated when any other columns on which the computed column depends are updated.

Persisted computed columns allow you to create an index on a computed column that is defined with a deterministic, but imprecise, expression. This option enables you to create an index on a computed column when SQL Server cannot determine with certainty whether a function that returns a computed column expression—for example, a CLR function that is created in the Microsoft .NET Framework—is both deterministic and precise.

Choosing Indexes: Query Versus Update Performance

I/O is the primary factor in determining query performance. The challenge for a database designer is to build a physical data model that provides efficient data access. Creating indexes on database tables allows SQL Server to access data with fewer I/O. Defining useful indexes during the logical and physical data modeling step is crucial. The SQL Server Query Optimizer relies heavily on index key distribution and index density to determine which indexes to use for a query. The Query Optimizer in SQL Server can use multiple indexes in a query (through index intersection) to reduce the I/O required to retrieve information. In the absence of indexes, the Query Optimizer performs a table scan, which can be costly from an I/O standpoint.

Although indexes provide a means for faster access to data, they slow down data modification statements due to the extra overhead of having to maintain the index during inserts, updates, and deletes.

In a DSS environment, defining many indexes can help your queries and does not create much of a performance issue because the data is relatively static and doesn't get updated frequently. You typically load the data, create the indexes, and forget about it until the next data load. As long as you have the necessary indexes to support the user queries and they're getting decent response time, the penalties of having too many indexes in a DSS environment are the space wasted for indexes that possibly won't be used, the additional time required to create the excessive indexes, and the additional time required to back up and run DBCC checks on the data.

In an OLTP environment, on the other hand, too many indexes can lead to significant performance degradation, especially if the number of indexes on a table exceeds four or five. Think about it for a second. Every single-row insert is at least one data page write and one or more index page writes (depending on whether a page split occurs) for every index on the table. With eight nonclustered indexes, that would be a minimum of nine writes to the database for a single-row insert. Therefore, for an OLTP environment, you want as few indexes as possible—typically only the indexes required to support the update and delete operations and your critical queries, and to enforce your uniqueness constraints.

The natural solution, in a perfect world, would be to create a lot of indexes for a DSS environment and as few indexes as possible in an OLTP environment. Unfortunately, in the real world, you typically have an environment that must support both DSS and OLTP applications. How do you resolve the competing indexing requirements of the two environments? Meeting the indexing needs of DSS and OLTP applications requires a bit of a balancing act, with no easy solution. It often involves making hard decisions as to which DSS queries might have to live with table scans and which updates have to contend with additional overhead.

One solution is to have two separate databases—one for DSS applications and another for OLTP applications. Obviously, this method requires some method of keeping the databases in sync. The method chosen depends on how up-to-date the DSS database has to be. If you can afford some lag time, you could consider using a dump-and-load mechanism, such as Log Shipping or periodic full database restores. If the DSS system requires up-to-the-minute concurrency, you might want to consider using replication or database mirroring.

Another possible alternative is to have only the required indexes in place during normal processing periods to support the OLTP requirements. At the end of the business day, you can create the indexes necessary to support the DSS queries and reports, and they can run as batch jobs after normal processing hours. When the DSS reports are complete, you can drop the additional indexes, and you're ready for the next day's processing. Note that this solution assumes that the time required to create the additional indexes is offset by the time saved by the faster running of the DSS queries. If the additional indexes do not result in substantial time savings, they are probably not necessary and need not be created in the first place. The queries need to be more closely examined to select the appropriate indexes to best support your queries.

As you can see, it is important to choose indexes carefully to provide a good balance between data search and data modification performance. The application environment usually governs the choice of indexes. For example, if the application is mainly OLTP with transactions requiring fast response time, creating too many indexes might have an adverse impact on performance. On the other hand, the application might be a DSS with few transactions doing data modifications. In that case, it makes sense to create a number of indexes on the columns that are frequently used in queries.

Summary

One of the most important aspects of improving SQL Server performance is proper index design. Choosing the appropriate indexes for SQL Server to use to process queries involves thoroughly understanding the queries and transactions being run against the database, understanding the bias of the data, understanding how SQL Server uses indexes, and staying aware of the performance implications of overindexing tables in an OLTP environment. In general, you should consider using clustered indexes to support range retrievals or when data needs to be sorted in clustered index order; you should use nonclustered indexes for single- or discrete-row retrievals or when you can take advantage of index covering.

To really make good index design choices, it helps to have an understanding of the SQL Server Query Optimizer to know how it uses indexes and index statistics to develop query plans. This would be a good time to continue on and read Chapter 30.

CHAPTER 30

Understanding Query Optimization

IN THIS CHAPTER

▶ What's New in Query Optimization

▶ What Is the Query Optimizer?

▶ Query Compilation and Optimization

▶ Query Analysis

▶ Row Estimation and Index Selection

▶ Join Selection

▶ Execution Plan Selection

▶ Query Plan Caching

▶ Other Query Processing Strategies

▶ Parallel Query Processing

▶ Common Query Optimization Problems

▶ Managing the Optimizer

Query optimization is the process SQL Server goes through to analyze individual queries and determine the best way to process them. To achieve this end, SQL Server uses a cost-based Query Optimizer. As a cost-based Query Optimizer, the Query Optimizer's purpose is to determine the query plan that will access the data with the least amount of processing time in terms of logical and physical I/O. The Query Optimizer examines the parsed SQL queries and, based on information about the objects involved (for example, number of pages in the table, types of indexes defined, index statistics), generates a query plan. The query plan is the set of steps to be carried out to execute the query.

To allow the Query Optimizer to do its job properly, you need to have a good understanding of how the Query Optimizer determines query plans for queries. This will help you to understand what types of queries can be optimized effectively and to learn techniques to help the Query Optimizer choose the best query path. This knowledge will help you write better queries, choose better indexes, and detect potential performance problems.

> **NOTE**
>
> To better understand the concepts presented in this chapter, you should have a reasonable understanding of how indexes affect performance. If you haven't already read Chapter 29, "Indexes and Performance," it is recommended that you review it now.

> **NOTE**
>
> Occasionally throughout this chapter, graphical execution plans are used to illustrate some of the principles discussed. Chapter 31, "Query Analysis," provides a more detailed discussion of the graphical execution plan output and describes the information contained in the execution plans and how to interpret it. In this chapter, the execution plans are provided primarily to give you an idea of what you can expect to see for the different types of queries presented when you are doing your own query analysis.

What's New in Query Optimization

SQL Server 2005 introduces a number of new features and capabilities to improve query optimization and query performance. Some of these changes are not immediately visible as they involve modifications to the internal algorithms and strategies employed by the Query Optimizer to help it generate more efficient query plans. For example, some of the general Query Optimizer enhancements available in SQL Server 2005 include better optimization for inequality operators and computed columns.

SQL Server also provides some enhancements and improvements to the index and column statistics that help the Query Optimizer perform more accurate cost analysis of queries, resulting in more appropriate query plans. One of these changes is the introduction of string summary statistics, which help the Query Optimizer better estimate and optimize search arguments involving a LIKE clause that contains leading or midstring wildcard characters.

To help keep the improved index and column statistics up-to-date, with less impact on the performance of your queries, SQL Server 2005 introduces the AUTO_UPDATE_ STATISTICS_ASYNC database option. If this option is enabled, when a query causes an automatic statistics update to be invoked, the query is allowed to run with the existing statistics, and the statistics are updated by a background task so the query is not held up by the update statistics task itself.

SQL Server 2005 includes improved support for statistics on computed columns and also can perform automatic matching of computed columns to matching expressions in search arguments. This enables you to create and exploit computed columns without having to change the actual queries in your application to use the computed columns explicitly.

The SQL Server 2005 Query Optimizer can now match more queries to indexed views than in previous versions, including queries that contain scalar expressions, scalar aggregate and user-defined functions, interval expressions, and equivalency conditions. Unfortunately, automatic matching of indexed views to queries is still only available in the Enterprise Edition of SQL Server 2005.

In addition to new features to help the Query Optimizer generate better query plans, SQL Server also provides improved query plan caching strategies, which help queries match existing query plans already in cache more effectively and efficiently and also reduce the need for query plan compilation.

If a query plan needs to be recompiled for a batch or a stored procedure, SQL Server 2005 can now perform statement-level recompiles, recompiling only the statements that require a recompile rather than the entire batch or stored procedure. Depending on the complexity of the stored procedures and the data events in the database, this can potentially provide significant out-of-the-box performance enhancements for SQL Server–based applications.

While there have been improvements to the Query Optimizer in SQL Server 2005 that should result in better and more appropriate query plans being generated automatically, SQL Server 2005 also provides four additional query hints that can be specified to provide even more control over how the queries are optimized:

▶ RECOMPILE

▶ OPTIMIZE FOR

▶ USE PLAN

▶ PARAMETERIZATION

SQL Server 2005 also provides a new plan guide feature, which is available to optimize the performance of queries by attaching specific query hints to them when it is not possible or desirable to change the text of the query directly. Plan guides can be useful when a small subset of queries in a database application deployed from a third-party vendor are not performing as expected. For more information on plan guides and the new query hints, see the "Managing the Optimizer" section in this chapter.

Finally, in addition to the new options available for overriding the Query Optimizer, SQL Server 2005 introduces a number of new tools and system objects for monitoring the Query Optimizer and the plan cache. One of the new features is the improved SHOWPLAN commands and the ability to view and save query plans as XML documents. Also, SQL Server 2005 provides a number of dynamic management views (DMVs) that provide some insight into the operations of the Query Optimizer and the plan cache. Some of the useful DMVs discussed in this chapter include the following:

▶ sys.dm_exec_cached_plans

▶ sys.dm_exec_sql_text

▶ sys.dm_exec_query_stats

▶ sys.dm_exec_plan_attributes

30

NOTE

There have been a number of internal changes and enhancements to the Query Optimizer in SQL Server 2005. Many of the internal changes to the Query Optimizer and its costing algorithms are considered proprietary and have not been made public. Much of the information provided here is based on analysis and observation of query plans generated for various queries and search values.

The intent of this chapter is therefore not so much to describe the specific steps, algorithms, and calculations implemented by the Query Optimizer as to provide a general overview of the query optimization process in SQL Server 2005 and what goes into estimating and determining an efficient query plan.

In addition to new algorithms and optimization strategies, the number of possible ways SQL Server can optimize and process queries has increased as well. The examples presented in this chapter focus on some of the more common optimization strategies.

What Is the Query Optimizer?

For any given SQL statement, the source tables can be accessed in many ways to return the desired result set. The Query Optimizer analyzes all the possible ways that the result set can be generated and chooses the most appropriate method, called the *query execution plan*. SQL Server uses a cost-based Query Optimizer. The Query Optimizer assigns a cost to every possible execution plan in terms of CPU resource usage and disk I/O. The Query Optimizer then chooses the execution plan with the least associated cost.

Thus, the primary goal of the Query Optimizer is to find the least expensive execution plan that minimizes the total time required to process a query. Because I/O is the most significant factor in query processing time, the Query Optimizer analyzes the query and primarily searches for access paths and techniques to minimize the number of logical and physical page accesses as much as possible. The lower the number of logical and physical I/Os performed, the faster the query should run.

The process of query optimization in SQL Server is extremely complicated and is based on sophisticated costing models and data access algorithms. It is beyond the scope of a single chapter to explain in detail all the various costing algorithms that the Query Optimizer currently employs. This chapter is intended to help you better understand some of the concepts related to how the Query Optimizer chooses an execution strategy and provide an overview of the query optimization strategies employed to improve query processing performance.

Query Compilation and Optimization

Query compilation is the complete process from the submission of a query to its actual execution. There are many steps involved in query compilation—one of which is optimization. All T-SQL statements are compiled, but not all are optimized. Primarily, only the standard SQL Data Manipulation Language (DML) statements—SELECT, INSERT, UPDATE, and DELETE—require optimization. The other procedural constructs in T-SQL (IF, WHILE, local variables, and so on) are compiled as procedural logic but do not require optimization. DML statements are set-oriented requests that the Query Optimizer must translate into procedural code that can be executed efficiently to return the desired results.

> **NOTE**
>
> SQL Server also optimizes some Data Definition Language (DDL) statements, such as CREATE INDEX or ALTER TABLE, against the data tables. For example, a displayed query plan for the creation of an index shows optimization steps for accessing the table, sorting data, and inserting into the index tree. However, the focus in this chapter is on optimization of DML statements.

Compiling DML Statements

When SQL Server compiles an execution plan for a DML statement, it performs the following basic steps:

1. The query is parsed and checked for proper syntax, and the T-SQL statements are parsed into keywords, expressions, operators, and identifiers to generate a query tree. The query tree (sometimes referred to as the *sequence tree*) is an internal format of the query that SQL Server can operate on. It is essentially the logical steps needed to transform the query into the desired result.

2. The query tree is then normalized and simplified. During normalization, the tables and columns are verified, and the metadata (data types, null properties, index statistics, and so on) about them is retrieved. In addition, any views are resolved to their underlying tables, and implicit conversions are performed (for example, an integer compared with a float value). Also during this phase, any redundant operations (for example, unnecessary or redundant joins) are removed, and the query tree is simplified.

3. The Query Optimizer analyzes the different ways the source tables can be accessed and selects the series of steps that returns the results fastest while typically using the fewest resources. The query tree is updated with the optimized series of steps, and an execution plan (also referred to as query plan) is generated from the final, optimized version of the sequence tree.

4. After the optimized execution plan is generated, SQL Server stores the optimized plan in the procedure cache.

5. SQL Server reads the execution plan from the procedure cache and executes the query plan, returning the result set (if any) to the client.

The optimized execution plan is then left in the procedure cache. If the same query or stored procedure is executed again and the plan is still available in the procedure cache, the steps to optimize and generate the execution plan are skipped, and the stored query execution plan is reused to execute the query or stored procedure.

Optimization Steps

When the query tree is passed to the Query Optimizer, the Query Optimizer performs a series of steps to break down the query into its component pieces for analysis in order to generate an optimal execution plan:

1. **Query analysis**—The query is analyzed to determine search arguments and join clauses. A search argument is defined as a WHERE clause that compares a column to a constant. A join clause is a WHERE clause that compares a column from one table to a column from another table.

2. **Row estimation and index selection**—Indexes are selected based on search arguments and join clauses (if any exist). Indexes are evaluated based on their distribution statistics and are assigned a cost.

3. **Join selection**—The join order is evaluated to determine the most appropriate order in which to access tables. In addition, the Query Optimizer evaluates the most appropriate join algorithm to match the data.

4. **Execution plan selection**—Execution costs are evaluated, and a query execution plan is created that represents the most efficient solution.

The next four sections of this chapter examine each of these steps in more detail.

> **NOTE**
>
> Unless stated otherwise, the examples presented in this chapter operate on the tables in the bigpubs2005 database. A copy of the bigpubs2005 database is available on the CD included with this book. Instructions on how to install the database are presented in the Introduction.

Query Analysis

The first step in query optimization is to analyze each table in the query to identify all search arguments (SARGs), OR clauses, and join clauses. The SARGs, OR clauses, and join clauses are used in the second step, index selection, to select useful indexes to satisfy a query.

Identifying Search Arguments

A SARG is defined as a WHERE clause that compares a column to a constant. The format of a SARG is as follows:

```
Column operator constant_expression [and...]
```

SARGs provide a way for the Query Optimizer to limit the rows searched to satisfy a query. The general goal is to match a SARG with an index to avoid a table scan. Valid operators for a SARG are =, >, <, >=, and <=, BETWEEN, and LIKE. Multiple SARGs can be combined with the AND clause. (A single index might match some or all of the SARGs ANDed together.) The following are examples of SARGs:

- ▶ `flag = 7`

- ▶ `salary > 100000`

- ▶ `city = 'Saratoga' and state = 'NY'`

- ▶ `price between $10 and $20` (the same as `price > = $10 and price <= $20`)

- ▶ `100 between lo_val and hi_val` (the same as `lo_val <= 100 and hi_val >= 100`)

- ▶ `au_lname like 'Sm%'` (the same as `au_lname >= 'Sm' and au_lname < 'Sn'`)

In some cases, the column in a SARG might be compared with a constant expression rather than a single constant value. The constant expression can be an arithmetic operation, a built-in function, a string concatenation, a local variable, or a subquery result. As long as the left side of the SARG contains a column, it's considered an optimizable SARG.

Identifying OR Clauses

The next statements the Query Optimizer looks for in the query are OR clauses. OR clauses are SARGable expressions combined with an OR condition rather than an AND condition and are treated differently than standard SARGs. The format of an OR clause is as follows:

SARG or *SARG* [or ...]

with all columns involved in the OR belonging to the same table.

The following IN statement:

`column in ( constant1, constant2, ...)`

is also treated as an OR clause, becoming this:

`column = constant1 or column = constant2 or ...`

Some examples of OR clauses are as follows:

```
where au_lname = 'Smith'  or au_fname = 'Fred'
where (type = 'business' and price > $25) or pub_id = "1234"
where au_lname in ('Smith', 'Jones', 'N/A')
```

An OR clause is a disjunction; all rows matching either of the two criteria appear in the result set. Any row matching both criteria should appear only once.

The main issue is that an OR clause cannot be satisfied by a single index search. Consider the first example just presented:

`where au_lname = 'Smith'  or au_fname = 'Fred'`

An index on au_lname and au_fname helps SQL Server find all the rows where au_lname = 'Smith' AND au_fname = 'Fred', but searching the index tree does not help SQL Server efficiently find all the rows where au_fname = 'Fred' and the last name is any value. Unless an index on au_fname exists as well, the only way to find all rows with au_fname = 'Fred' is to search every row in the table or scan every row in a nonclustered index that contains au_lname as a nonleading index key.

An OR clause can typically be resolved by either a table scan or by using the OR strategy. Using a table scan, SQL Server reads every row in the table and applies each OR criteria to each row. Any row that matches any one of the OR criteria is put into the result set.

A table scan is an expensive way to process a query, so the Query Optimizer looks for an alternative for resolving an OR. If an index can be matched against all SARGs involved in the OR clause, SQL Server evaluates the possibility of applying the index union strategy described later in this chapter, in the section "Using Multiple Indexes."

Identifying Join Clauses

The next type of clause the Query Optimizer looks for during the query analysis phase is the join clause. A join condition is specified in the FROM clause using the JOIN keyword, as follows:

```
FROM table1 JOIN table2  on table1.column = table2.column
```

Alternatively, join conditions can be specified in the WHERE clause using the old-style join syntax, as shown in the following example:

Table1.Column Operator Table2.Column

A join clause always involves two tables, except in the case of a self-join, but even in a self-join, you must specify the table twice in the query. Here's an example:

```
select employee = e.LastName + ', ' + e.FirstName,
       manager = m.LastName + ', ' + m.FirstName
    from Northwind..Employees e left outer join Northwind..Employees m
    on e.ReportsTo = m.EmployeeID
    order by 2, 1
```

SQL Server treats a self-join just like a normal join between two different tables.

In addition to join clauses, the Query Optimizer also looks for subqueries, derived tables, and common table expressions and makes the determination whether they need to be flattened into joins or processed using a different strategy. Subquery optimization is discussed later in this chapter.

Row Estimation and Index Selection

When the query analysis phase of optimization is complete and all SARGs, OR clauses, and join clauses have been identified, the next step is to determine the selectivity of the expressions (that is, the estimated number of matching rows) and to determine the cost of finding the rows. The costs are measured primarily in terms of logical and physical I/O, with the goal of generating a query plan that results in the lowest estimated I/O and processing cost. Primarily, the Query Optimizer attempts to identify whether an index exists that can be used to locate the matching rows. If multiple indexes or search strategies can be considered, their costs are compared with each other and also against the cost of a table or clustered index scan to determine the least expensive access method.

An index is typically considered useful for an expression if the first column in the index is used in the expression and the search argument in the expression provides a means to effectively limit the search. If no useful indexes are found for an expression, typically a table or clustered index scan is performed on the table. A table or clustered index scan is the fallback tactic for the Query Optimizer to use if no lower-cost method exists for returning the matching rows from a table.

Evaluating SARG and Join Selectivity

To determine selectivity of a SARG, which helps in determining the most efficient query plan, the Query Optimizer uses the statistical information stored for the index or column, if any. If no statistics are available for a column or index, SQL Server automatically creates statistics on non-indexed columns specified in a SARG if the AUTO_CREATE_STATISTICS option is enabled for the database. SQL Server also automatically generates and updates the statistics for any indexed columns referenced in a SARG if the AUTO_UPDATE_STATISTICS option is enabled. In addition, you can explicitly create statistics for a column or set of columns in a table or an indexed view by using the CREATE STATISTICS command. Both index statistics and column statistics (whether created automatically or manually with the CREATE STATISTICS command) are maintained and kept up-to-date, as needed, if the AUTO_UPDATE_STATISTICS option is enabled or if the UPDATE STATISTICS command is explicitly run for a table, index, or column statistics. Available and up-to-date statistics allow the Query Optimizer to more accurately assess the cost of different query plans and choose a high-quality plan.

If no statistics are available for a column or an index and the AUTO CREATE STATISTICS and AUTO UPDATE STATISTICS options have been disabled for the database or table, SQL Server cannot make an informed estimate of the number of matching rows for a SARG and resorts to using some built-in percentages for the number of matching rows for various types of expressions. These percentages currently are as follows:

Operator	Row Estimate
=	5%
between, > and <	9% (closed-range search)
>, <, >=, <=	30% (open-range search)

Using these default percentages almost certainly results in inappropriate query execution plans being chosen. You should always try to ensure that you have up-to-date statistics available for any columns referenced in your SARGs and join clauses.

When the value of a SARG can be determined at the time of query optimization, the Query Optimizer uses the statistics histogram to estimate the number of matching rows for the SARG. The histogram contains a sampling of the data values in the column and stores information on the number of matching rows for the sampled values, as well as for values that fall between the sampled values. If the statistics are up-to-date, this is the most accurate estimate of the number of matching rows for a SARG. (For a more detailed discussion of index and column statistics and the information contained in them, see Chapter 29.)

If the SARG contains an expression that cannot be evaluated until runtime but is an equality expression (=), the Query Optimizer uses the density information from the statistics to estimate the number of matching rows. The density value reflects the overall uniqueness of the data values in the column or index. Density information does not estimate the number of matching rows as accurately as the histogram because its value is determined across the entire range of values in a column or an index key and can be skewed higher by one or more values that have a high number of duplicates. Expressions that cannot be evaluated until runtime include comparisons against local variables or function expressions that cannot be evaluated until query execution.

If an expression cannot be evaluated at the time of optimization and the SARG is not an equality search but a closed- or open-range search, the density information cannot be used. The same percentages are used for the row estimates as when no statistics are available (9% for a closed-range search and 30% for an open-range search).

As a special case, if a SARG contains the equality (=) operator and a unique index exists that matches the SARG, based on the nature of a unique index, the Query Optimizer knows, without having to analyze the index statistics, that one and only one row can match the SARG.

If the query contains a join clause, SQL Server determines whether any usable indexes or column statistics exist that match the column(s) in the join clause. Because the Query Optimizer has no way of determining what value(s) will join between rows in the table at optimization time, it can't use the statistics histogram on the join column to estimate the number of matching rows. Instead, it uses the density information, as it does for SARGs that are unknown during optimization.

A lower density value indicates a more selective index. As the density approaches 1, the join condition becomes less selective. For example, if a nonclustered index has a high density value, it will likely be more expensive in terms of I/O to retrieve the matching rows using the nonclustered index than to perform a table scan or clustered index scan and the index likely will not be used.

> **NOTE**
>
> For a more thorough and detailed discussion of indexes and index and column statistics, see Chapter 29.

SARGs and Inequality Operators

In previous versions of SQL Server, when a SARG contained an inequality operator (!= or <>), the selectivity of the SARG could not be determined effectively for the simple reason that index or column statistics can help you estimate only the number of matching rows for a specific value, not the number of nonmatching rows. However, for some SARGs with inequality operators, if index or column statistics are available, SQL Server 2005 has the ability to estimate the number of matching rows. For example, consider the following SARG:

```
WHERE qty <> 1000
```

Without any available index or column statistics on the qty column, SQL Server would treat the inequality SARG as a SARG with no available statistics. Potentially every row in the table could satisfy the search criteria, so it would estimate the number of matching rows as all rows in the table.

However, if index or column statistics were available for the qty column, the Query Optimizer would look up the search value (1000) in the statistics and estimate the number of matching rows for the search value and then determine the number of matching rows for the query as the total number of rows in the table minus the estimated number of matching rows for the search value. For example, if there are 150,000 rows in the table and the statistics indicate that 1,570 rows match, where qty = 1000, then the number of matching rows would be calculated as follows:

```
    150,000  rows
  – 1,570  rows (where qty = 1000)
= 148,430 rows (where qty <> 1000)
```

In this example, with the large number of estimated rows where qty <> 1000, SQL Server would likely end up performing a table scan to resolve the query. However, if the Query Optimizer estimates that there is a very small number of rows where qty <> 1000, the Query Optimizer might determine that it would be more efficient to use an index to find the nonmatching rows. You may be wondering how SQL Server efficiently searches the index for the rows where qty <> 1000 without having to look at every row. In this case, internally, it converts the inequality SARG into two range retrievals by using an OR condition:

```
WHERE qty < 1000 OR qty > 1000
```

30

> **NOTE**
>
> Even if an inequality SARG is optimizable, that doesn't necessarily mean an index will be used. It simply allows the Query Optimizer to make a more accurate estimate of the number of rows that will match a given SARG. More often than not, an inequality SARG will result in a table or clustered index scan. You should try to avoid using inequality SARGs whenever possible.

SARGs and `LIKE` Clauses

In previous versions of SQL Server, the Query Optimizer would estimate the selectivity of a `LIKE` clause only if the first character in the string was a constant. Every row would have to be examined to determine if it was a match. SQL Server 2005 introduces a new type of statistics for estimating the selectivity of `LIKE` conditions: string summary statistics.

String summary statistics provide a statistical summary of substring frequency distribution for character columns. String summary statistics can be created on columns of type `text`, `ntext`, `char`, `varchar`, and `nvarchar`. String summary statistics allow SQL Server to estimate the selectivity of `LIKE` conditions where the search string may have any number of wildcards in any combination, including when the first character is a wildcard. In previous versions of SQL Server, row estimates could not be accurately obtained when the leading character of a search string was a wildcard character. SQL Server 2005 can now estimate the selectivity of `LIKE` predicates similar to the following:

▶ `au_lname LIKE 'Smith%'`

▶ `stor_name LIKE '%Books'`

▶ `title LIKE '%Cook%'`

▶ `title_id LIKE 'BU[1234567]001'`

▶ `title LIKE '%Cook%Chicken'`

The new string summary statistics result in fairly accurate row estimates and are a significant improvement over the SQL Server 2000 Query Optimizer, which uses a guess for selectivity of any `LIKE` clause when there are wildcards specified in the string pattern other than a trailing wildcard at the end of the pattern. However, if there is a user-specified escape character in a `LIKE` pattern (for example, `stor_name LIKE '%abc#_%'` `ESCAPE '#'`), SQL Server 2005 also guesses the selectivity of the SARG.

The values generated for string summary statistics are not visible via `DBCC SHOW_STATISTICS`. However, `DBCC SHOW_STATISTICS` does indicate if string summary statistics have been calculated; if the value `YES` is specified in the `String Index` field in the first rowset returned by `DBCC SHOW_STATISTICS`, the statistics also includes a string summary. Also, if the strings are more than 80 characters in length, only the first and last 40 characters are used for creating the string summary statistics. Accurate frequency estimates cannot be determined for substrings that do not appear in the first and last 40 characters of a string.

SARGS on Computed Columns

In previous versions of SQL Server, for a SARG to be optimizable, there had to be no computations on the column itself in the SARG. In SQL Server 2005, expressions involving computations on a column might be treated as SARGs during optimization if SQL Server can simplify the expression into a SARG. For example, this SARG:

```
ytd_sales/12 = 1000
```

can be simplified to this:

```
ytd_sales = 12000
```

The simplified expression is used only during optimization to determine an estimate of the number of matching rows and the usefulness of the index. During actual execution, the conversion is not done while traversing the index tree as it won't be able to do the repeated division by 12 for each row while searching through the tree. However, doing the conversion during optimization and getting a row estimate from the statistics helps the Query Optimizer decide on other strategies to consider, such as index scanning versus table scanning, or it might help to determine an optimal join order if it's a multitable query.

SQL Server 2005 supports the creation, update, and use of statistics on computed columns. The Query Optimizer can make use of the computed column statistics even when a query doesn't reference the computed column by name but rather contains an expression that matches the computed column expression. This feature avoids the need to rewrite the SARGs in queries with expressions that match a computed column expression to SARGs that explicitly contain the computed column itself.

When the SARG has a more complex operation performed on it, such as a function, it can potentially prevent effective optimization of the SARG. If you cannot avoid using a function or complex expression on a column in the search expression, you should consider creating a computed column on the table and creating an index on the computed column. This will materialize the function result into an additional column on the table that can be indexed for faster searching, and the index statistics can be used to better estimate the number of matching rows for the SARG expression that references the function.

An example of using this approach would be for a query that has to find the number of orders placed in a certain month, regardless of the year. The following is a possible solution:

```
select distinct stor_id
   from sales
   where datepart(month, ord_date) = 6
```

This query gets the correct result set but ends up having to do so with a full table or index scan because the function on the ord_date column prevents the Query Optimizer from using an index seek against any index that might exist on the ord_date column.

If this query is used frequently in the system and quick response time is critical, you could create a computed column on the function and index it as follows:

```
alter table sales add ord_month as datepart(month, ord_date)
create index nc_sales_ordmonth on sales(ord_month)
```

Now, when you run the query on the table again, if you specify the computed column in the WHERE clause, the Query Optimizer can use the index on the computed column to accurately estimate the number of matching rows and possibly use the nonclustered

30

index to find the matching rows and avoid a table scan, as it does for the following query:

```
select distinct stor_id
    from sales
    where ord_month = 6
```

Even if the query still ends up using a table scan, it now at least has statistics available to know how many rows it can expect to match where the month matches the value specified. In addition, if a computed column exists that exactly matches the SARG expression, SQL Server 2005 can still use the statistics and index on the computed column to optimize the query, even if the computed column is not specified in the query itself. For example, with the ord_month column defined on the sales table and an index created on it, the following query can also use the statistics and the index to optimize the query:

```
select distinct stor_id
    from sales
    where datepart(month, ord_date) = 6
```

TIP

The automatic matching of computed columns in SQL Server 2005 enables you to create and exploit computed columns without having to change the queries in your application. Be aware, though, that computed column matching is based on identical comparison. For example, a computed column of the form A + B + C will not match an expression of the form A + C + B.

Estimating Access Path Cost

After the selectivity of each of the SARGs, OR clauses, and join clauses is determined, the next phase of optimization is estimating the access path cost of the query. The Query Optimizer attempts to identify the total cost of various access paths to the data and determine which path results in the lowest cost to return the matching rows for an expression.

The primary cost of an access path, especially for single-table queries, is the number of logical I/Os required to retrieve the data. Using the available statistics and the information stored in SQL Server regarding the average number of rows per page and the number of pages in the table, the Query Optimizer estimates the number of logical page reads necessary to retrieve the estimated number of rows using a table scan or any of the candidate indexes. It then ranks the candidate indexes to determine which access path would retrieve the matching data rows with the lowest cost, typically the access path that requires the fewest number of logical and physical I/Os.

> **NOTE**
>
> A logical I/O occurs every time a page is accessed. If the page is not in cache, a physical I/O is first performed to bring the page into cache memory, and then a logical I/O is performed against the page. The Query Optimizer has no way of knowing whether a page will be in memory when the query actually is executed, so the total number of logical I/Os is the primary factor in determining the cost of the access path. Physical I/Os are a key performance factor that needs to be monitored by watching the overall cache hit ratio for SQL Server.

> **TIP**
>
> The rest of this section assumes a general understanding of SQL Server index structures. If you haven't already, now is a good time to read through Chapter 29.

Clustered Index Cost

Clustered indexes are efficient for lookups because the rows that match the SARGs are clustered on the same page or over a range of adjacent pages. SQL Server needs only to find its way to the first page and then read the rows from that page and any subsequent pages in the page chain until no more matching rows are found.

Therefore, the I/O cost estimate for a clustered index is calculated as follows:

> Number of index levels in the clustered index
>
> + Number of pages to scan within the range of values

The number of pages to scan is based on the estimated number of matching rows divided by the number of rows per page. For example, if SQL Server can store 250 rows per page for a table, and 600 rows are within the range of values being searched, SQL Server would estimate that it would require at least three page reads to find the qualifying rows. If the index is three levels deep, the logical I/O cost would be as follows:

> 3 (index levels to find the first row)
>
> + 3 (data pages: 600 rows divided by 250 rows per page)
>
> = 6 logical page I/Os

For a unique clustered index and an equality operator, the logical I/O cost estimate is one data page plus the number of index levels that need to be traversed to access the data page.

When a clustered index is used to retrieve the data rows, you see a query plan similar to the one shown in Figure 30.1.

30

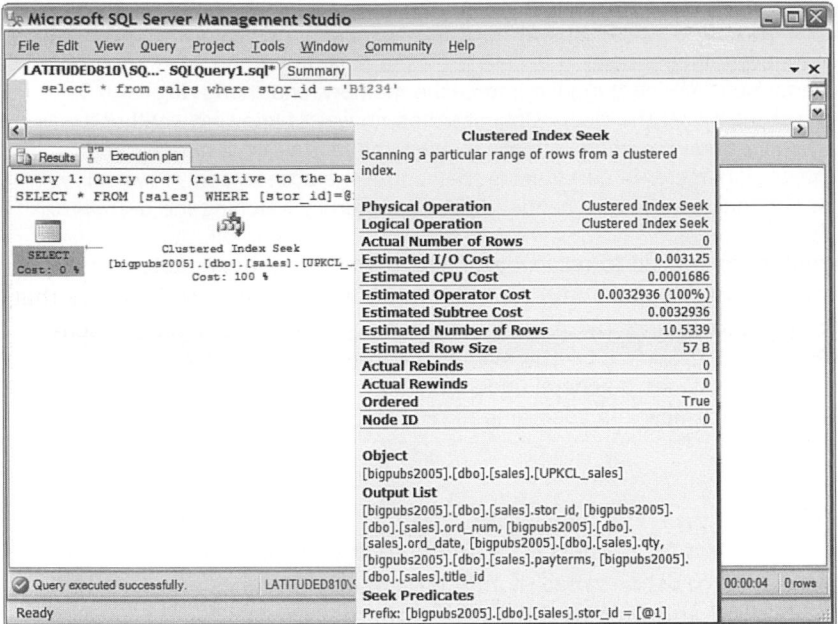

FIGURE 30.1   An execution plan for a clustered index seek.

Nonclustered Index Cost

When searching for values using a nonclustered index, SQL Server reads the index key values at the leaf level of the index and uses the bookmark to locate and read the data row. SQL Server has no way of knowing if matching search values are going to be on the same data page until it has read the bookmark. It is possible that while retrieving the rows, SQL Server might find all data rows on different data pages, or it might revisit the same data page multiple times. Either way, a separate logical I/O is required each time it visits the data page.

The I/O cost is therefore based on the depth of the index tree, the number of index leaf rows that need to be scanned to find the matching key values, and the number of matching rows. The cost of retrieving each matching row depends on whether the table is clustered or is a heap table (that is, a table with no clustered index defined on it). For a heap table, the nonclustered row bookmark is the page and row pointer (the row ID [RID]) to the actual data row. A single I/O is required to retrieve the data row. Therefore, the worst-case logical I/O cost for a heap table can be estimated as follows:

> Number of nonclustered index levels
>
> + Number of leaf pages to be scanned
>
> + Number of qualifying rows (each row represents a separate data page read)

> **NOTE**
>
> This estimate assumes that the data rows have not been forwarded. In a heap table, when a row has been forwarded, the original row location contains a pointer to the new location of the data row; therefore, an additional page read is required to retrieve the actual data row. The actual I/O cost would be one page greater per row than the estimated I/O cost for any rows that have been forwarded.

When a nonclustered index is used to retrieve the data rows from a heap table with a clustered index, you see a query plan similar to the one shown in Figure 30.2. Notice that in SQL Server 2005, the bookmark lookup operator is replaced by a RID lookup, essentially as a join with the RIDs returned by the nonclustered index seek.

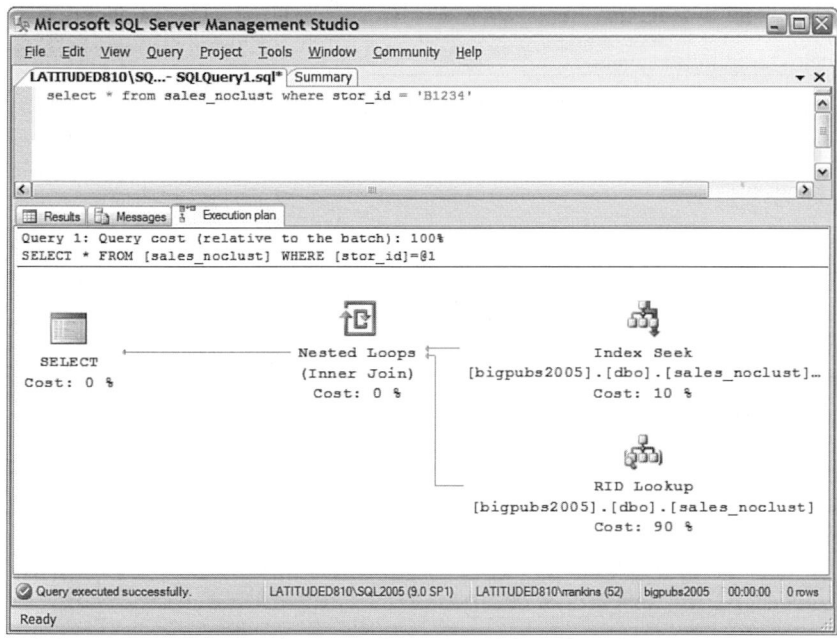

FIGURE 30.2   An execution plan for a nonclustered index seek against a heap table.

If the table is clustered, the row bookmark is the clustered key for the data row. The number of I/Os to retrieve the data row depends on the depth of the clustered index tree, as SQL Server has to use the clustered index to find each row. The logical I/O cost of finding a row using the nonclustered index on a clustered table is therefore as follows:

    Number of nonclustered index levels

+ Number of leaf pages to be scanned

+ Number of qualifying rows × Number of page reads to find a single row via the clustered index

For example, consider a heap table with a nonclustered index on last name. Assume that the index holds 800 rows per page (they're really big last names!), and 1,700 names are within the range you are looking for. If the index is three levels deep, the estimated logical I/O cost for the nonclustered index would be as follows:

    3 (index levels)
  + 3 (leaf pages: 1,700 leaf rows/800 rows per page)
 + 1,700 (data page reads)
 = 1,706 total logical I/Os

Now, assume that the table has a clustered index on it, and the size of the nonclustered index is the same. If the clustered index is three levels deep, including the data page, the estimated logical I/O cost of using the nonclustered index would be as follows:

    3 (nonclustered index levels)
  + 3 (leaf pages: 1,700 leaf rows/800 rows per page)
 + 5,100 (1,700 rows × 3 clustered page reads per row)
 = 5,106 (total logical I/Os)

> **NOTE**
>
> Although the I/O cost is greater for bookmark lookups in a nonclustered index when a clustered index exists on the table, the cost savings during row inserts, updates, and deletes using the clustered index as the bookmark are substantial, whereas the couple extra logical I/Os per row during retrieval do not substantially impact query performance.

For a unique nonclustered index using an equality operator, the I/O cost is estimated as the number of index levels traversed to access the bookmark plus the number of I/Os required to access the data page via the bookmark.

When a nonclustered index is used to retrieve the data rows on a table with a clustered index, you see a query plan similar to the one shown in Figure 30.3. Notice that in SQL Server 2005, the bookmark lookup operator is replaced by a clustered index seek, essentially as a join between the clustered index and the clustered index keys returned by the nonclustered index seek.

Covering Nonclustered Index Cost

When analyzing a query, the Query Optimizer considers any possibility to take advantage of index covering. *Index covering* is a method of using the leaf level of a nonclustered index to resolve a query when all the columns referenced in the query (in both the column list and WHERE clause, as well as any GROUP BY columns) are included in the index leaf row as either index key columns or included columns.

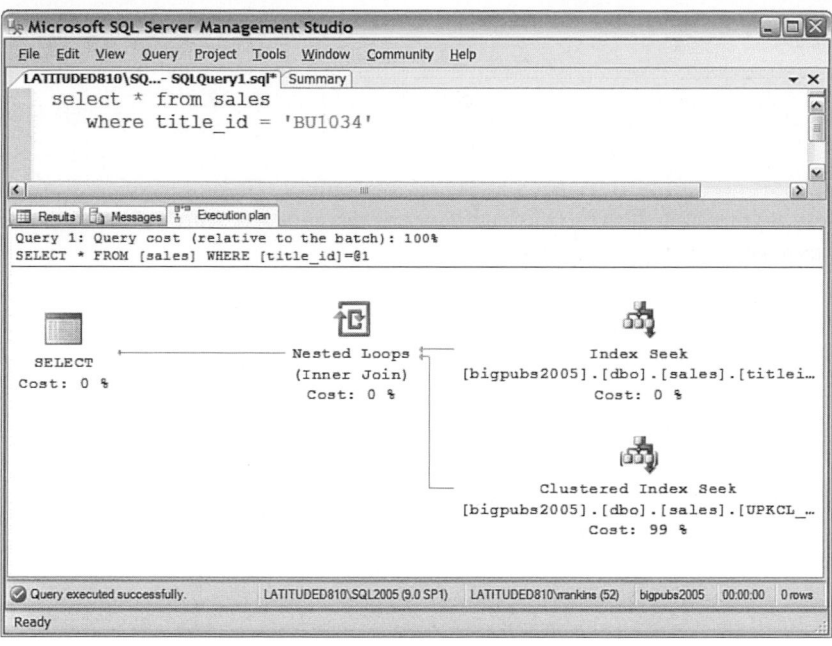

FIGURE 30.3   An execution plan for a nonclustered index seek against a table with a clustered index.

Index covering can save a significant amount of I/O because the query doesn't have to access the data page to return the requested information. In most cases, a nonclustered index that covers a query is faster than a similarly defined clustered index on the table because of the greater number of rows per page in the index leaf level compared to the number of rows per page in the table itself. (As the nonclustered leaf row size approaches the data row size, the I/O cost savings are minimal, if any.)

If index covering can take place in a query, the Query Optimizer considers it and estimates the I/O cost of using the nonclustered index to cover the query. The estimated I/O cost of index covering is as follows:

> Number of index levels
>
> + Number of leaf level index pages to scan

The number of leaf-level pages to scan is based on the estimated number of matching rows divided by the number of leaf index rows per page. For example, if index covering could be used on the nonclustered index on title_id for the query in the previous example, the I/O cost would be the following:

> 3 (nonclustered index levels)
>
> + 3 (leaf pages: 1,700 leaf rows/800 rows per page)
>
> = 6 total logical I/Os

30

> **TIP**
>
> For more information on index covering and when it can take place, as well as the included columns feature introduced in SQL Server 2005, see Chapter 29.

When index covering is used to retrieve the data rows, you might see a query plan similar to the one shown in Figure 30.4. If the entire leaf level of the index is searched, it displays as an index scan, as shown in this example.

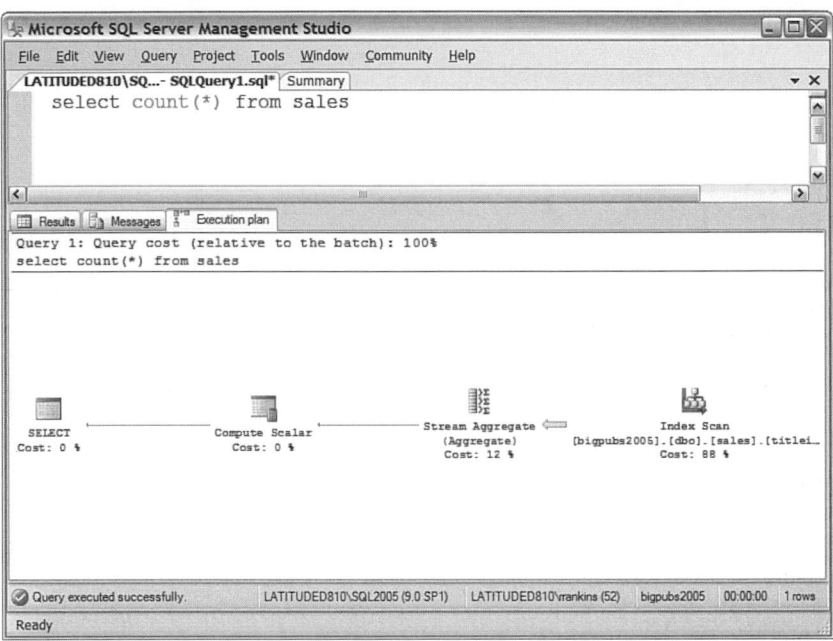

FIGURE 30.4   An execution plan for a covered index scan without limits on the search.

Other times, if the index keys can be searched to limit the range, you might see an index seek used, as shown in Figure 30.5. Note that the difference here from a normal index lookup is the lack of the RID or clustered index lookup because SQL Server does not need to go to the data row to find the needed information.

Table Scan Cost

If no usable index exists that can be matched with a SARG or a join clause, the Query Optimizer's only option is to perform a table scan. The estimate of the total I/O cost is simply the number of pages in the table, which is stored in the system catalogs and can be viewed by querying the used_page_count column of the sys.dm_db_partition_stats DMV:

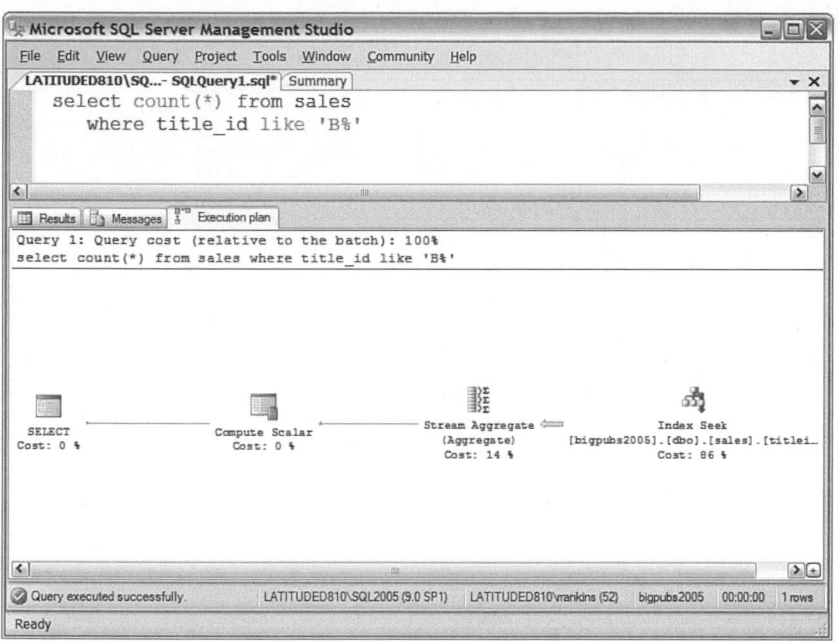

FIGURE 30.5   An execution plan for a covered index seek with limits on the search.

```
select used_page_count
   from sys.dm_db_partition_stats
   where object_id = object_id('sales_noclust')
     and (index_id = 0      -- data pages for heap table
          or index_id = 1) -- data pages for clustered table
go

used_page_count
-------------------
1244
```

Keep in mind that there are instances (for example, large range retrievals on a nonclus-tered index column) in which a table scan might be cheaper than a candidate index in terms of total logical I/O. For example, in the previous nonclustered index example, if the index does not cover the query, it costs between 1,706 and 5,106 logical I/Os to retrieve the matching rows using the nonclustered index, depending on whether a clustered index exists on the table. If the total number of pages in the table is less than either of these values, a table scan would be more efficient in terms of total logical I/Os than using a nonclustered index.

When a table scan is used to retrieve the data rows from a heap table, you see a query plan similar to the one shown in Figure 30.6.

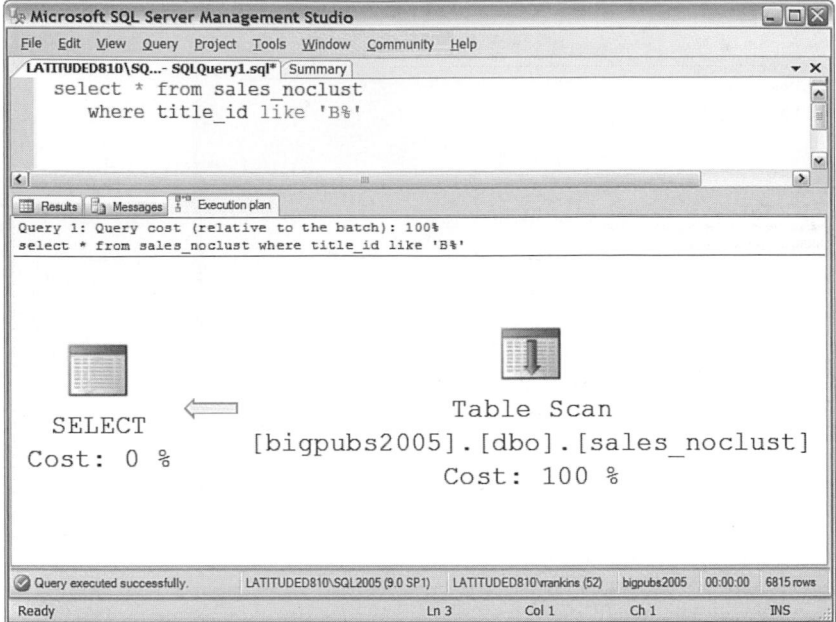

FIGURE 30.6   A table scan on a heap table.

When a table scan is used to retrieve the data rows from a clustered table, you see a query plan similar to the one shown in Figure 30.7. Notice that it displays as a clustered index scan because the table is the leaf level of the clustered index.

Using Multiple Indexes

SQL Server allows the creation of multiple indexes on a table. If there are multiple SARGs in a query that can each be efficiently searched using an available index, the Query Optimizer in SQL Server can make use of multiple indexes via intersection of the indexes or using the index union strategy.

Index Intersection

Index intersection is a mechanism that allows SQL Server to use multiple indexes on a table when you have two or more SARGs in a query and each can be efficiently satisfied using an index as the access path. Consider the following example:

```
--First, create 2 additional indexes on sales to support the query
create index ord_date_idx on sales(ord_date)
create index qty_idx on sales(qty)
go
select * from sales
   where qty = 816
     and ord_date = '1/2/1995'
```

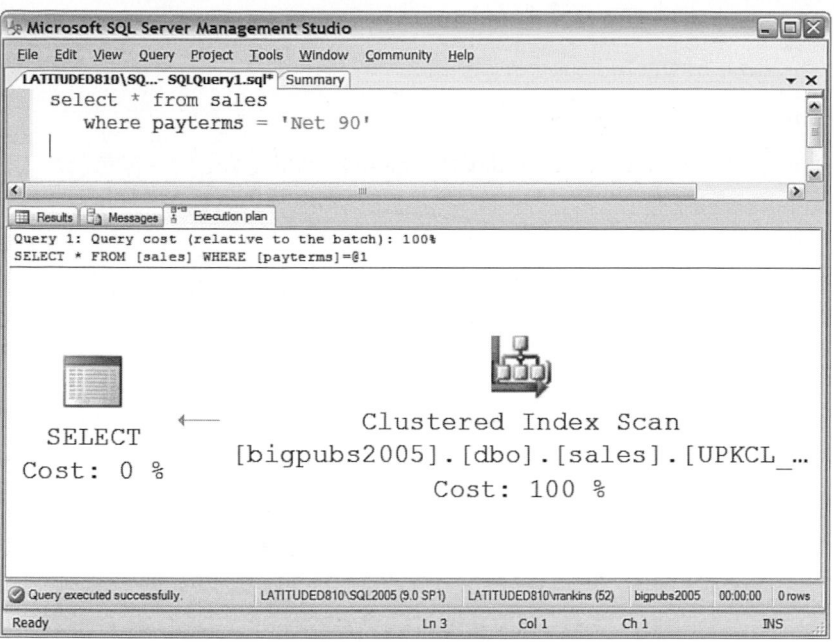

FIGURE 30.7   A table scan on a clustered table.

In this example, two additional nonclustered indexes are created on the Sales table: one on the qty column and one on the ord_date column. In this example, the Query Optimizer considers the option of searching the index leaf rows of each index to find the rows that meet each of the search conditions and joining on the matching bookmarks (either the clustered index key or RIDs if it's a heap table) for each result set. It then performs a merge join on the bookmarks and uses the output from that to retrieve the actual data rows for all the bookmarks that are in both result sets.

The index intersection strategy is applied only when the cost of retrieving the bookmarks for both indexes and then retrieving the data rows is less than that of retrieving the qualifying data rows using only one of the indexes or using a table scan.

You can go through the same analysis as the Query Optimizer to determine whether an index intersection makes sense. For example, the Sales table has a clustered index on stor_id, ord_num, and title_id, and this clustered index is the bookmark used to retrieve the data rows for the matching data rows found via the nonclustered indexes. Assume the following statistics:

▶ 1,200 rows are estimated to match where qty = 816.

▶ There are approximately 215 index rows per leaf page for the index on qty.

▶ 212 rows are estimated to match where ord_date = '1/2/1995'.

▶ There are approximately 185 index rows per leaf page for the index on ord_date.

▶ The Query Optimizer estimates that the overlap between the two result sets is 1 row.

▶ The number of levels in the index on qty is 3.

▶ The number of levels in the index on ord_date is 3.

▶ The number of levels in the clustered index on the sales table is 3.

▶ The sales table is 1,252 pages in size.

Using this information, you can calculate the I/O cost for the different strategies the Query Optimizer can consider.

A table scan would cost 1,836 pages.

A standard data row retrieval via the nonclustered index on qty would have the following approximate cost:

    2 index page reads (root and intermediate pages to locate first leaf page)

  + 6 leaf page reads (1200 rows / 215 rows per page)

 + 3600 (1,200 rows × 3 pages per bookmark lookup via the clustered index)

= 3,608 pages

A standard data row retrieval via the nonclustered index on ord_date would have the following approximate cost:

    2 nonclustered index page reads (root and intermediate pages)

  + 2 nonclustered leaf page reads (212 rows / 185 rows per page)

 + 636 (212 rows × 3 pages per bookmark lookup via clustered index)

= 640 pages

The index intersection is estimated to have the following cost:

    8 pages (1 root page + 1 intermediate page + the 6 leaf pages to find all the bookmarks for the 1,200 matching index rows on qty)

  + 4 pages (1 root page + 1 intermediate page + 2 leaf pages to find all the bookmarks for the 212 matching index rows on ord_date)

  + 3 page reads to find the 1 estimated overlapping row between the two indexes using the clustered index

= 15 pages

As you can see from these examples, the index intersection strategy is definitely the cheapest approach. If at any point the estimated intersection cost reaches 640 pages, SQL Server just uses the single index on ord_date and checks both search criteria against the 212 matching rows for ord_date. If the estimated cost of using an index in any way ever exceeds 1,836 pages, a table scan is likely to be performed, with the criteria checked against all rows.

When an index intersection is used to retrieve the data rows from a table with a clustered index, you see a query plan similar to the one shown in Figure 30.8.

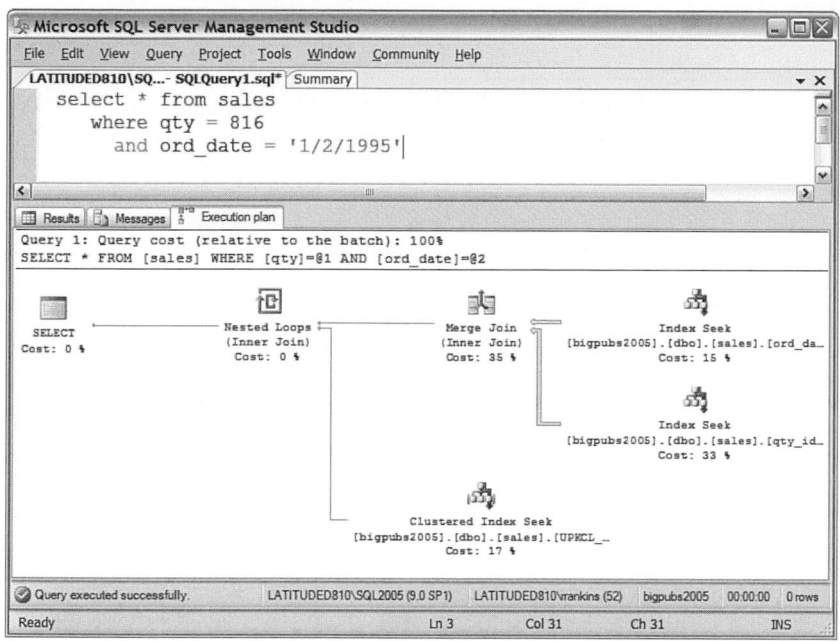

FIGURE 30.8   An execution plan for an index intersection on a clustered table.

If the table does not have a clustered index (that is, a heap table) and has supporting nonclustered indexes for an index intersection, you see a query plan similar to the one shown in Figure 30.9.

Notice that in the example shown in Figure 30.9, the Query Optimizer performs a hash join rather than a merge join on the RIDs returned by each nonclustered index seek and uses the results from the hash join to perform an RID lookup to retrieve the matching data rows.

NOTE

To duplicate the query plan shown in Figure 30.9, you need to create the following two additional indexes on the `sales_noclust` table:

```
create index ord_date_idx on sales_noclust(ord_date)
create index qty_idx on sales_noclust(qty)
```

30

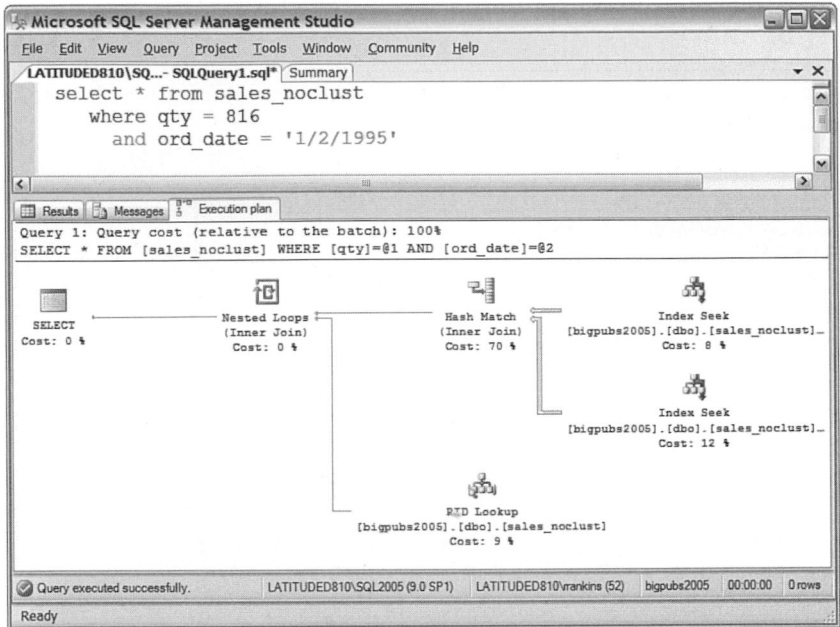

FIGURE 30.9   An execution plan for an index intersection on a heap table.

The Index Union Strategy

You see a strategy similar to an index intersection applied when you have an OR condition between your SARGs, as in the following query:

```
select * from sales
  where title_id = 'DR8514'
      or ord_date = '1993-01-01 00:00:00.000'
```

The index union strategy (often referred to as the OR strategy) is similar to an index intersection, with one slight difference. With the index union strategy, SQL Server executes each part separately, using the index that matches the SARG, but after combining the results with a merge join, it removes any duplicate bookmarks for rows that match both search arguments. It then uses the unique bookmarks to retrieve the result rows from the base table.

When the index union strategy is used on a table with a clustered index, you see a query plan similar to the one shown in Figure 30.10. Notice the addition of the stream aggregation step, which differentiates it from the index intersection query plan. The stream aggregation step performs a grouping on the bookmarks returned by the merge join to eliminate the duplicate bookmarks.

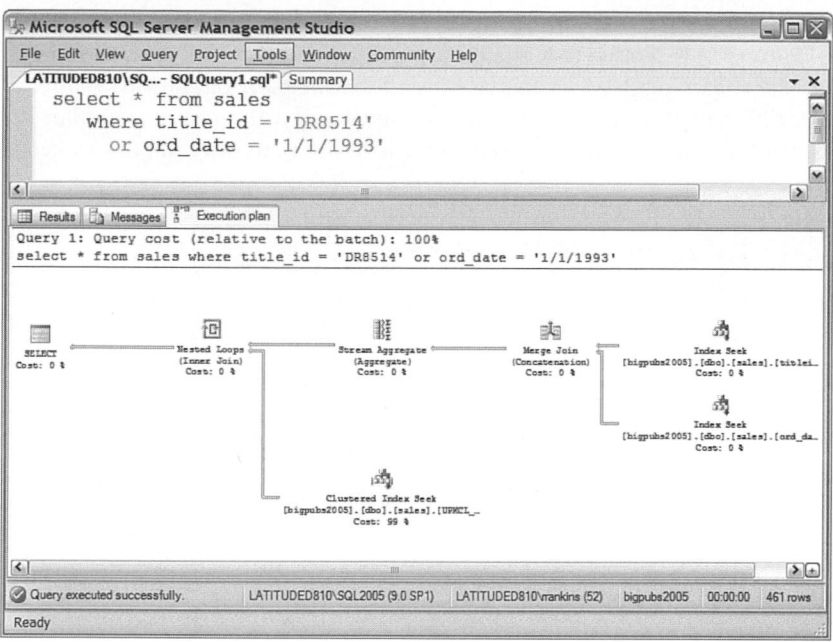

FIGURE 30.10   An execution plan for *an* index union strategy on a clustered table.

The following steps describe how SQL Server determines whether to use the index union strategy:

1. Estimate the cost of a table scan and the cost of using the index union strategy. If the cost of the index union strategy exceeds the cost of a table scan, stop here and simply perform a table scan. Otherwise, continue with the succeeding steps to perform the index union strategy.

2. Break the query into multiple parts, as in this example:

```
select * from sales where title_id = 'DR8514'
select * from sales where ord_date = '1993-01-01 00:00:00.000'
```

3. Match each part with an available index.

4. Execute each piece and perform a join on the row bookmarks.

5. Remove any duplicate bookmarks.

6. Use the resulting list of unique bookmarks to retrieve all qualifying rows from the base table.

If any one of the OR clauses needs to be resolved via a table scan for any reason, SQL Server simply uses a table scan to resolve the whole query rather than applying the index union strategy.

When the index union strategy is used on a heap table, you see a query plan similar to the one shown in Figure 30.11. Notice that the merge join is replaced with a concatenation operation, and the stream aggregate is replaced with distinct sort operation. While the steps are slightly different than the index intersection strategy, the result is similar: A list of unique RIDs is returned, and they are used to retrieve the matching data rows in the table itself.

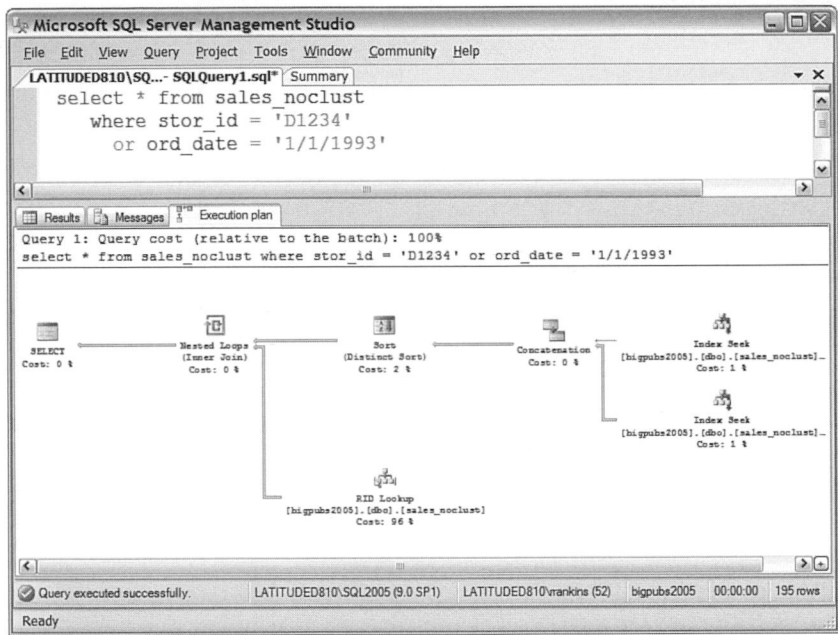

FIGURE 30.11   An execution plan for an index union strategy on a heap table.

When the OR in the query involves only a single column and a nonclustered index exists on the column, the Query Optimizer in SQL Server 2005 typically resolves the query with an index seek against the nonclustered index and then a bookmark lookup to retrieve the data rows. Consider the following query:

```
select title_id from titles
    where title_id in ('BU1032', 'BU1111', 'BU2075', 'BU7832')
```

This query is the same as the following:

```
select title_id from titles
    where title_id = 'BU1032'
    or title_id = 'BU1111'
    or title_id = 'BU2075'
    or title_id = 'BU7832'
```

To process this query, SQL Server performs a single index seek that looks for each of the search values and then joins the list of bookmarks returned with either the clustered index or the RIDs of the target table. No removal of duplicates is necessary because each OR condition matches a distinct set of rows. Figure 30.12 shows an example of the query plan for multiple OR conditions against a single column.

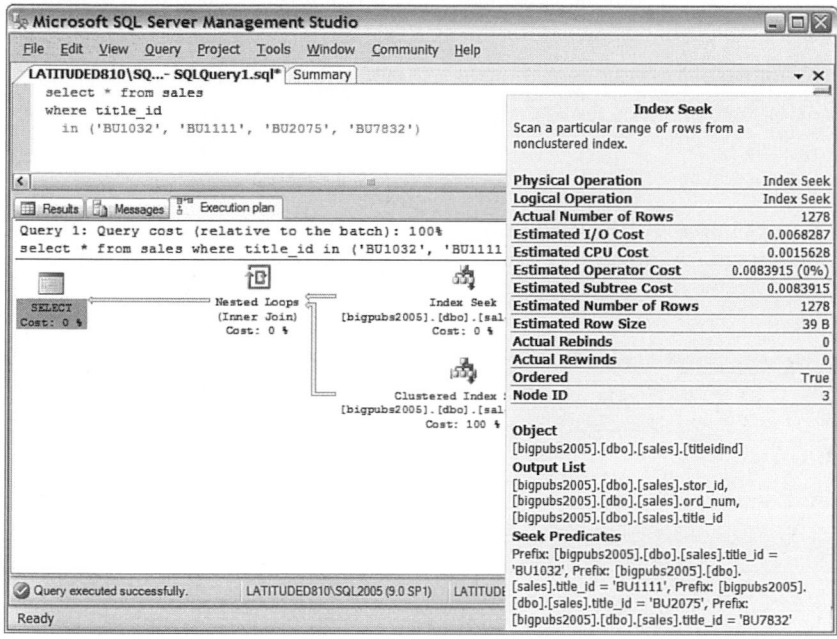

FIGURE 30.12   An execution plan using index seek to retrieve rows for an OR condition on a single column.

Index Joins

Besides using the index intersection and index union strategies, another way of using multiple indexes on a single table is to join two or more indexes to create a covering index. This is similar to an index intersection, except that the final bookmark lookup is not required because the merged index rows contain all the necessary information. Consider the following example:

```
select stor_id from sales
   where qty = 816
     and ord_date = '1/2/1995'
```

Again, the sales table contains indexes on both the qty and ord_date columns. Each of these indexes contains the clustered index as a bookmark, and the clustered index contains the stor_id column. In this instance, when the Query Optimizer merges the two indexes using a merge join, joining them on the matching clustered indexes, the index rows in the merge set have all the information needed to resolve the query because

30

stor_id is part of the nonclustered indexes. There is no need to perform a bookmark lookup on the data page. By joining the two index result sets, SQL Server creates the same effect as having one covering index on qty, ord_date, and stor_id on the table. Using the same numbers as in the "Index Intersection" section presented earlier, the cost of the index join would be as follows:

> 8 pages (1 root page + 1 intermediate page + the 6 leaf pages to find all the book-marks for the 1,200 matching index rows on qty)

> + 4 pages (1 root page + 1 intermediate page + 2 leaf pages to find all the bookmarks for the 212 matching index rows on ord_date)

> = 12 pages

Figure 30.13 shows an example of the execution plan for an index join. Notice that it does not include the bookmark lookup present in the index intersection execution plan (refer to Figure 30.8).

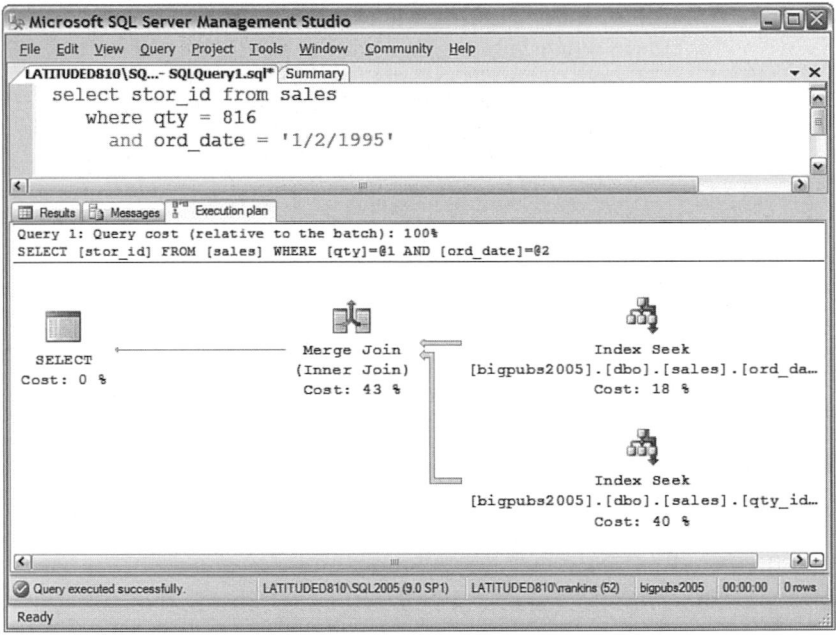

FIGURE 30.13   An execution plan for an index join.

Optimizing with Indexed Views

In SQL Server 2005, when you create a unique clustered index on a view, the result set for the view is materialized and stored in the database with the same structure as a table that has a clustered index. Changes made to the data in the underlying tables of the view are automatically reflected in a view the same way as changes to a table are reflected in its indexes. In the Developer and Enterprise Editions of SQL Server 2005, the Query Optimizer automatically considers using the index on the view to speed up access for queries run directly against the view. The Query Optimizer in the Developer and Enterprise Editions of SQL Server 2005 also looks at and considers using the indexed view for searches against the underlying base table, when appropriate.

NOTE

While indexed views can be created in any edition of SQL Server 2005, they are considered for query optimization only in the Developer and Enterprise Editions of SQL Server 2005. In other editions of SQL Server 2005, indexed views are not used to optimize the query unless the view is explicitly referenced in the query and the NOEXPAND Query Optimizer hint is specified. For example, to force the Query Optimizer to consider using the sales_Qty_Rollup indexed view in the Standard Edition of SQL Server 2005, you execute the query as follows:

```
select * from sales_Qty_Rollup WITH (NOEXPAND)
    where stor_id between 'B914' and 'B999'
```

The NOEXPAND hint is allowed only in SELECT statements, and the indexed view must be referenced directly in the query. (Only the Developer and Enterprise Editions consider using an indexed view that is not directly referenced in the query.) As always, you should use Query Optimizer hints with care. When the NOEXPAND hint is included in the query, the Query Optimizer cannot consider other alternatives for optimizing the query.

Consider the following example, which creates an indexed view on the sales table, containing stor_id and sum(qty) grouped by stor_id:

```
set quoted_identifier on
go

if object_id('sales_Qty_Rollup') is not null
    drop view sales_Qty_Rollup
go
create view sales_qty_rollup
with schemabinding
as
    select stor_id, sum(qty) as total_qty, count_big(*) as id
        from dbo.sales
        group by stor_id
go

create unique clustered index idx1 on sales_Qty_Rollup (stor_id)
go
```

30

The creation of the clustered index on the view essentially creates a clustered table in the database with the three columns `stor_id`, `total_qty`, and `id`. As you would expect, the following query on the view itself uses a clustered index seek on the view to retrieve the result rows from the view instead of having to scan or search the sales table itself:

```
select * from sales_Qty_Rollup
    where stor_id between 'B914' and 'B999'
```

However, the following query on the `sales` table uses the indexed view `sales_qty_rollup` to retrieve the result set as well:

```
select stor_id,  sum(qty)
    from sales
    where stor_id between 'B914' and 'B999'
    group by stor_id
```

Essentially, the Query Optimizer recognizes the indexed view as an index on the `sales` table that covers the query. The execution plan in Figure 30.14 shows the indexed view being searched in place of the table.

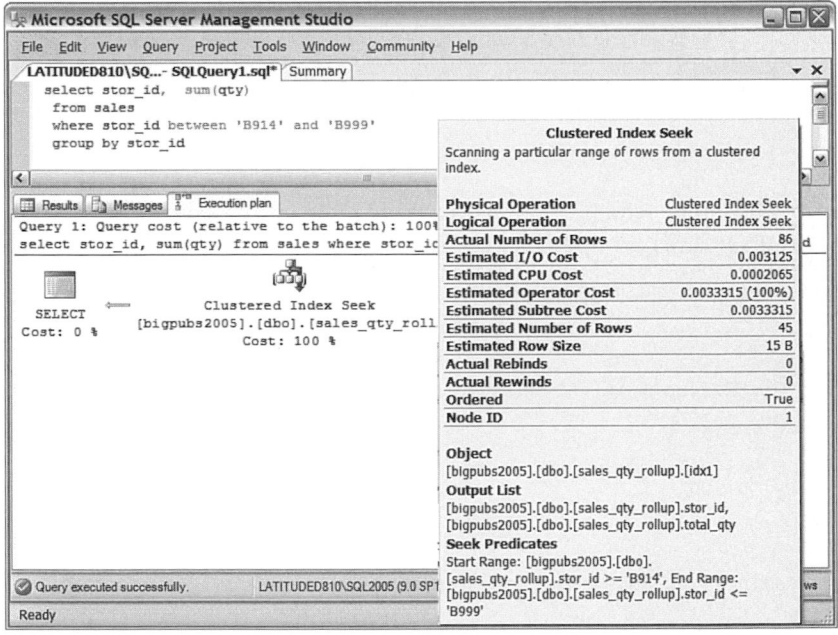

FIGURE 30.14   An execution plan showing an indexed view being searched to satisfy a query on a base table.

> **NOTE**
>
> In addition to the seven required SET options that need to be set appropriately when the indexed view is created, they must also be set the same way for a session to be able to use the indexed view in queries. The required SET option settings are as follows:
>
> ```
> SET ARITHABORT ON
> SET CONCAT_NULL_YIELDS_NULL ON
> SET QUOTED_IDENTIFIER ON
> SET ANSI_NULLS ON
> SET ANSI_PADDING ON
> SET ANSI_WARNINGS ON
> SET NUMERIC_ROUNDABORT OFF
> ```
>
> If these SET options are not set appropriately for the session running a query that could make use of an indexed view, the indexed view is not used, and the table is searched instead.
>
> For more information on indexed views, see Chapters 22 and 29.

You might find rare situations when using the indexed view in the Enterprise or Developer Editions of SQL Server 2000 leads to poor query performance, and you might want to avoid having the Query Optimizer use the indexed view. To force the Query Optimizer to ignore the indexed view(s) and optimize the query using the indexes on the underlying base tables, you specify the EXPAND VIEWS query option, as follows:

```
select * from sales_Qty_Rollup
   where stor_id between 'B914' and 'B999'
   OPTION (EXPAND VIEWS)
```

Join Selection

The job of the Query Optimizer is incredibly complex. The Query Optimizer can consider literally thousands of options when determining the optimal execution plan. The statistics are simply one of the tools that the Query Optimizer can use to help in the decision-making process.

In addition to examining the statistics to determine the most efficient access paths for SARGs and join clauses, the Query Optimizer must consider the optimum order in which to access the tables, the appropriate join algorithms to use, the appropriate sorting algorithms, and many other details too numerous to list here. The goal of the Query Optimizer during join selection is to determine the most efficient join strategy.

As mentioned at the beginning of this chapter, delving into the detailed specifics of the various join strategies and their costing algorithms is beyond the scope of a single chapter on optimization. In addition, some of these costing algorithms are proprietary and not publicly available. The goal of this section, then, is to present an overview of the most

30

common query processing algorithms that the Query Optimizer uses to determine an efficient execution plan.

Join Processing Strategies

If you are familiar with SQL, you are probably very familiar with using joins between tables in creating SQL queries. A join occurs any time the SQL Server Query Optimizer has to compare two inputs to determine an output. The join can occur between one table and another table, between an index and a table, or between an index and another index (as described previously, in the section "Index Intersection").

The SQL Server Query Optimizer uses three primary types of join strategies when it must compare two inputs: nested loops joins, merge joins, and hash joins. The Query Optimizer must consider each one of these algorithms to determine the most appropriate and efficient algorithm for a given situation.

Each of the three supported join algorithms could be used for any join operation. The Query Optimizer examines all the possible alternatives, assigns costs to each, and chooses the least expensive join algorithm for a given situation. Merge and hash joins often greatly improve the query processing performance for very large data tables and data warehouses.

Nested Loops Joins

The nested loops join algorithm is by far the simplest of the three join algorithms. The nested loops join uses one input as the "outer" loop and the other input as the "inner" loop. As you might expect, SQL Server processes the outer input one row at a time. For each row in the outer input, the inner input is searched for matching rows.

Figure 30.15 illustrates a query that uses a nested loops join.

Note that in the graphical showplan, the outer loop is represented as the top input table, and the inner loop is represented as the bottom input table. In most instances, the Query Optimizer chooses the input table with the fewest number of qualifying rows to be the outer loop to limit the number of iterative lookups against the inner table. However, the Query Optimizer may choose the input table with the greater number of qualifying rows as the outer table if the I/O cost of searching that table first and then performing the iterative loops on the other table is lower than the alternative.

The nested loop join is the easiest join strategy for which to estimate the I/O cost. The cost of the nested loop join is calculated as follows:

Number of I/Os to read in outer input

+ Number of matching rows × Number of I/Os per lookup on inner input

= Total logical I/O cost for query

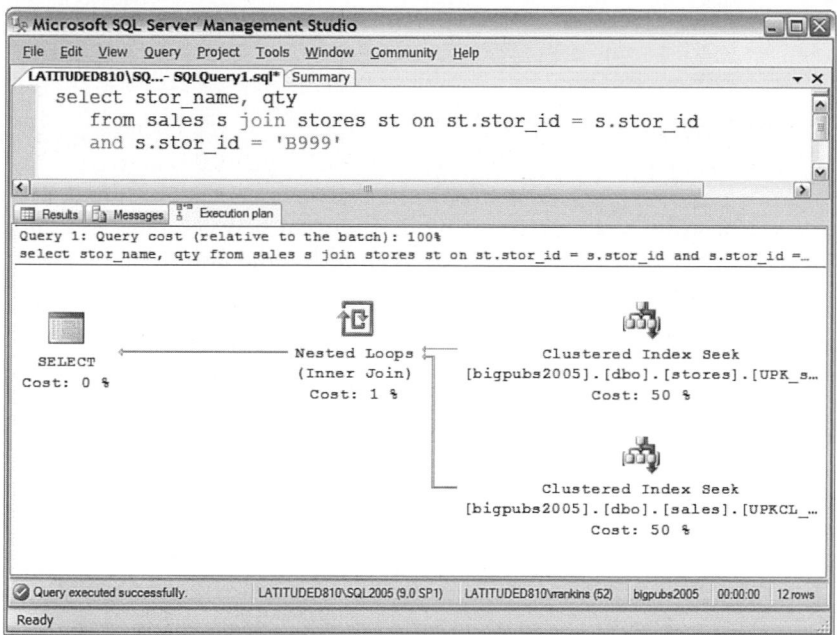

FIGURE 30.15   An execution plan for a nested loops join.

The Query Optimizer evaluates the I/O costs for the various possible join orders as well as the various possible access paths and indexes available to determine the most efficient join order. The nested loops join is efficient for queries that typically affect only a small number of rows. As the number of rows in the outer loop increases, the effectiveness of the nested loops join strategy diminishes. This is because of the increased number of logical I/Os required as the number of qualifying rows increases.

Also, if there are no useful indexes on the join columns, the nested loop join is not an efficient join strategy as it requires a table scan lookup on the inner table for each row in the outer table. Lacking useful indexes for the join, the Query Optimizer often opts to perform a merge or hash join.

Merge Joins

The merge join algorithm is much more effective than the nested loops join for dealing with large data volumes or when the lack of limiting SARGs or useful indexes on SARGs leads to a table scan of one or both tables involved in the join. A merge join works by retrieving one row from each input and comparing them, matching on the join column(s). Figure 30.16 illustrates a query that uses a merge join.

30

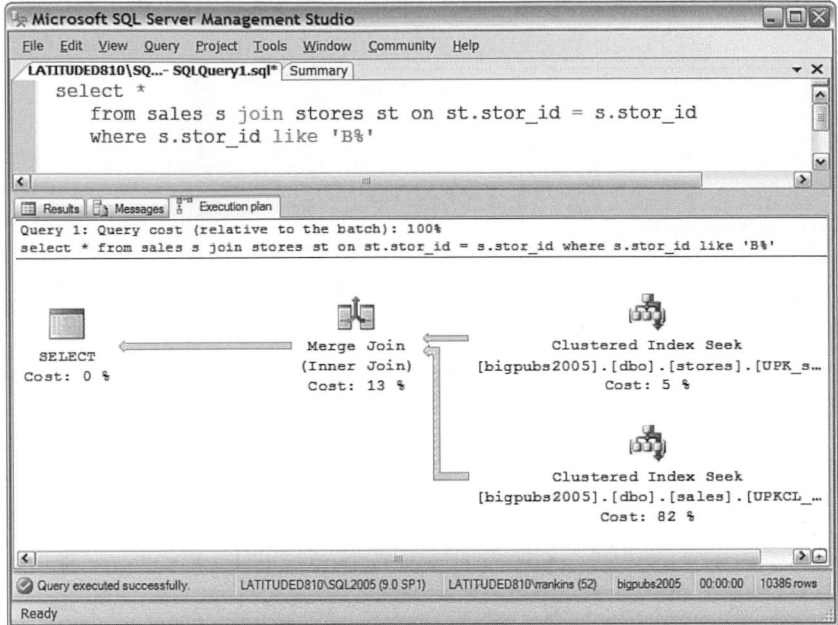

FIGURE 30.16   An execution plan for a merge join.

A merge join requires that both inputs be sorted on the merge columns—that is, the columns specified in the equality (ON) clauses of the join predicate. A merge join does not work if both inputs are not sorted. In the query shown in Figure 30.16, both tables have a clustered index on stor_id, so the merge column (stor_id) is already sorted for each table. If the merge columns are not already sorted, a separate sort operation may be required before the merge join operation. When the input is sorted, the merge join opera-tion retrieves a row from each input and compares them, returning the rows if they are equal. If the inputs are not equal, the lower-value row is discarded, and another row is obtained from that input. This process repeats until all rows have been processed.

Usually, the Query Optimizer chooses a merge join strategy, as in this example, when the data volume is large and both columns are contained in an existing presorted index, such as a clustered primary key. If either of the inputs is not already sorted, the Query Optimizer has to perform an explicit sort before the join. Figure 30.17 shows an example of a sort being performed before the merge join is performed.

In the query in Figure 30.17, the titles table is already sorted on the primary key on title_id, but the rows being returned from the sales table are being returned initially in stor_id order. (stor_id is the leading column in the clustered primary key on sales.) The resulting rows matching the search criteria on ord_date via the clustered index scan on the sales table are then re-sorted by title_id, and then the merge join is performed with the rows retrieved from the titles table.

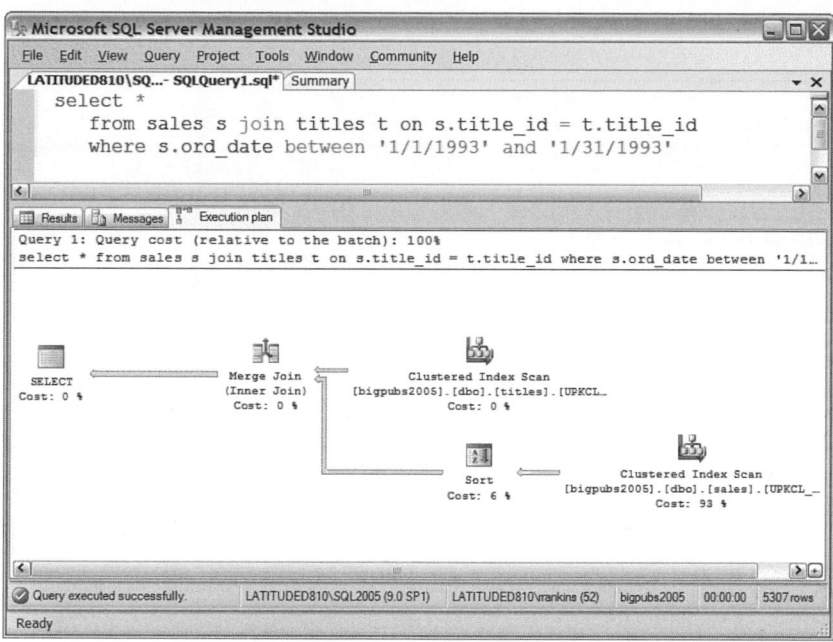

FIGURE 30.17   An execution plan for a merge join with a preliminary sort step.

If one or more of the inputs to the merge join is not sorted, and the additional sorting causes the merge join to be too expensive to perform, the Query Optimizer may consider using the hash join strategy instead.

Hash Joins

The final—and most complicated—join algorithm is the hash join. The hash join is an effective join strategy for dealing with large data volumes where the inputs might not be sorted and when no useful indexes exist on your tables for performing the join. Figure 30.18 illustrates a query that uses a hash join.

The basic hash join algorithm involves separating the two inputs into a build input and a probe input. The Query Optimizer usually attempts to assign the smaller input as the build input. The hash join scans the build input and creates a hash table. Each row from the build input is inserted into the hash table based on a hash key value, which is computed. The probe input is then scanned, one row at a time. A hash key value is computed for each row in the probe, and the hash table is scanned for matches. The hash join is an effective join strategy when dealing with large data volumes and unsorted data inputs.

In a hash join, the keys that are common between the two tables are hashed into a hash bucket, using the same hash function. This bucket usually starts out in memory and then moves to disk, as needed. The type of hashing that occurs depends on the amount of memory required. Hashing is commonly used for inner and outer joins, intersections, unions, and differences. The Query Optimizer often uses hashing for intermediate processing.

30

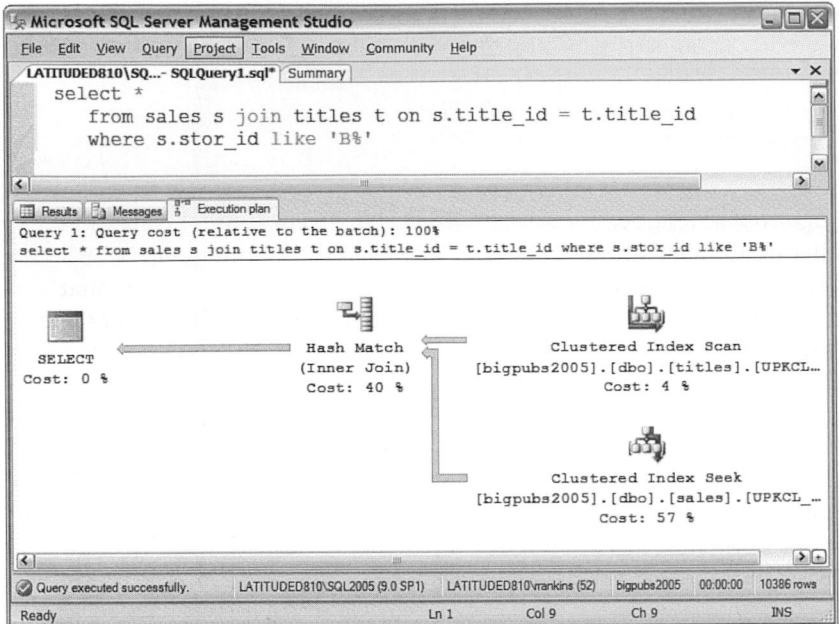

FIGURE 30.18   An execution plan for a hash join.

Pseudocode for a simple hash join might look like this:

```
create an empty hash table
for each row in the input table
    read the row
    hash the key value
    insert the hashed key into the hash bucket
for each row in the larger table
    read the row
    hash the key value
    if hashed key value is found in the hash bucket
        output hash key and both row identifiers
drop the hash table
```

Although hashing is useful when no useful indexes are on the tables for a join, the Query Optimizer still might not choose it as the join strategy if it has a high cost in terms of memory required. If the entire hash table doesn't fit in memory, SQL Server has to split both the build and probe inputs into partitions, each containing a different set of hash keys, and write those partitions out to disk. As each partition is needed, it is brought into memory. This increases the amount of I/O and general processing time for the query.

To use the hashing strategy efficiently, it is best if the smaller input is used as the build input. If, during execution, SQL Server discovers that the build input is actually larger than the probe input, it might switch the roles of the build and probe input midstream. The Query Optimizer usually doesn't have a problem determining which input is smaller if the statistics on the columns involved in the query are current. Column-level statistics can also help the Query Optimizer determine the estimated number of rows matching a SARG, even if no actual index will be used.

Grace Hash Joins   If the two inputs are too large to fit into memory for a normal hash join, SQL Server might use a modified method, called the *grace hash join*. This method partitions the smaller input table (also referred to as the *build input*) into a number of buckets. The total number of buckets is calculated by determining the bucket size that will fit in memory and dividing it into the number of rows in the table. The larger table (also referred to as the *probe input*) is then also partitioned into the same number of buckets. Each bucket from each input can then be read into memory and the matches made.

A *hybrid join* is a join method that uses elements of both a simple in-memory hash and a grace hash.

> **NOTE**
>
> Hash and merge join strategies can be applied only when the join is an equijoin—that is, when the join condition compares columns from two inputs with the equality (=) operator. If the join is not based on an equality, (for example, using a BETWEEN clause), using nested loop joins is the only strategy that can be employed.

Determining the Optimal Join Order

In addition to determining the best join strategies, the Query Optimizer also evaluates and determines the optimal join order that would result in the most efficient query plan. In the query's execution plan, you might find that the order of the tables in the execution plan is a different order than specified in the query. Regardless of the join strategy used, the Query Optimizer needs to determine which table is the outer input and which is the inner input to the join strategy chosen. For example, consider the following query:

```
select a.au_lname, t.title, pubdate
   from authors a
   join titleauthor ta on a.au_id = ta.au_id
   join titles t on ta.title_id = t.title_id
```

In addition to the possible access paths and join strategies available, the server can consider the following pool of possible join orders:

authors → titleauthor → titles

titles → titleauthor → authors

titleauthor → titles → authors

titleauthor → authors → titles

```
authors → titles → titleauthor
titles → authors → titleauthor
```

For each of these join orders, the Query Optimizer considers the various access paths available for each table as well as the different join strategies available. For example, the Query Optimizer could consider the following possible join strategies:

▶ Perform a table scan on the authors table and for each row perform an index seek against the auidind index on titleauthor to find the matching rows by au_id. And for each matching row in titleauthor, perform an index seek against the primary key of the titles table to find the matching rows in titles by title_id.

▶ Perform a table scan on the titles table and for each row perform an index seek against the titleidind index on titleauthor to find the matching rows by title_id. And for each matching row in titleauthor, perform an index seek against the primary key of the authors table to find the matching rows in authors by au_id.

▶ Perform an index scan of the titleidind of the titleauthor table and use a hash join to match it with a clustered index scan of the titles table. And for each of the qualifying rows from this hash join, perform another hash join with and index scan of the aunmind index of the authors table.

> **NOTE**
>
> If you run this query yourself and examine the query plan, you'll likely see that the third alternative is the one chosen by the Query Optimizer. Index scans are performed on the authors and titleauthor tables because the nonclustered indexes on those tables cover the join query. That is, the nonclustered indexes contain all the columns necessary to satisfy the join conditions as well as the requested result columns.

These are just three of the possibilities. There are many more options for the Query Optimizer to consider as execution plans for processing this join. For example, for each of the three options, there are other indexes to consider, and there are other possible join orders and strategies to consider as well.

As you can see, there can be a large number of execution plan options for the Query Optimizer to consider for procession a join, and this example is a relatively simple three-table join. The number of options increases exponentially as the number of tables involved in the query increases. The "Execution Plan Selection" section, later in this chapter, describes how the Query Optimizer deals with the large number of possible execution plan options.

Subquery Processing

SQL Server optimizes subqueries differently, depending on how they are written. For example, SQL Server attempts to flatten some subqueries into joins when possible, to allow the Query Optimizer to select the optimal join order rather than be forced to process the query inside-out. This section examines the different types of subqueries and how SQL Server optimizes them.

IN, ANY, and EXISTS Subqueries

In SQL Server, any query that contains a subquery introduced with an IN, = ANY, or EXISTS predicate is usually flattened into an existence join unless the outer query also contains an OR clause or unless the subquery is correlated or contains one or more aggregates.

An existence join is optimized the same way as a regular join, with one exception: With an existence join, as soon as a matching row is found in the inner table, the value TRUE is returned, and SQL Server stops looking for further matches for that row in the outer table and moves on to the next row. A normal join would continue processing to find all matching rows. The following query is an example of a subquery that would be converted to an existence join:

```
select pub_name from publishers
    where pub_id in (select pub_id from titles where type = 'business')
```

Figure 30.19 shows an example of the execution plan for this quantified predicate subquery being flattened into an existence join.

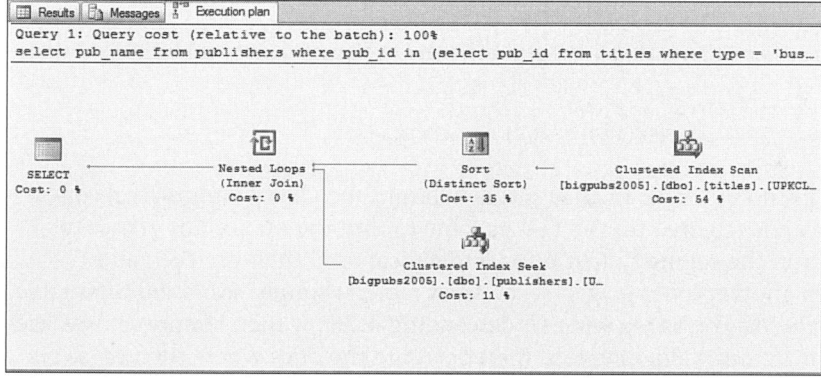

FIGURE 30.19   An execution plan for a quantified predicate subquery flattened into an existence join.

Materialized Subqueries

If an outer query is comparing a column against the result of a subquery using any of the comparison operators (=, >, <, >=, <=, !=), and the subquery is not correlated, the results of the subquery are often resolved—that is, materialized—before comparison against the outer table column. For these types of queries, the Query Optimizer processes the query inside-out.

30

An example of this type of query is as follows:

```
select title from titles
    where ytd_sales = (select max(qty) from sales)
```

In this example, the subquery is resolved first to find the maximum qty value from the sales table to compare against ytd_sales in the outer query. Figure 30.20 shows an example of a query plan for this materialized subquery.

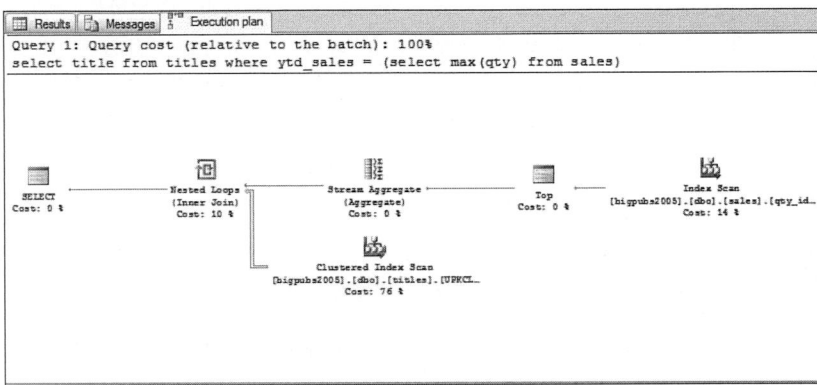

FIGURE 30.20   An execution plan for a materialized subquery.

The following query is an interesting case in which the subquery is not materialized first:

```
select title from titles
    where ytd_sales = (select max(ytd_sales) from titles)
```

In this example, with no index on the ytd_sales column, the Query Optimizer recognizes that a table scan is required on the titles table to find the maximum ytd_sales value. Rather than run the subquery first using a table scan and then use the value returned to perform another lookup against the titles table, it simply scans the titles table and returns and sorts the ytd_sales value in descending order. It then simply returns the rows with the top matching values because these rows are the ones where the ytd_sales value is the maximum. Figure 30.21 shows an example of a query plan for this subquery processing strategy.

Correlated Subqueries

A correlated subquery contains a reference to an outer table in a join clause in the subquery. The following is an example of a correlated subquery:

```
SELECT title_id, price
FROM titles
WHERE ytd_sales IN
    (SELECT qty
    FROM sales
    WHERE titles.title_id = sales.title_id)
```

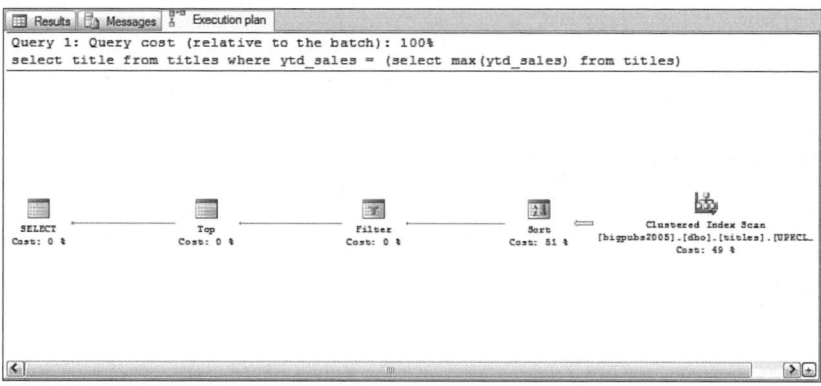

FIGURE 30.21   An execution plan for a subquery flattened into a table scan with sort.

Because correlated subqueries depend on values from the outer query for resolution, they cannot be processed independently. Instead, SQL Server usually processes correlated subqueries repeatedly, once for each qualifying outer row. Often, a correlated subquery looks like a nested loop join. An example of an execution plan for the preceding correlated subquery example is shown in Figure 30.22. Notice that an inner join using a left semi join is performed. *Semi joins* are joins that return rows from one table based on the existence of related rows in the other table. A *left semi join* operation returns each row from the first (top or left) input when there is a matching row in the second (bottom or right) input. If the attributes are returned from the bottom (or right) table, it's referred to as a *right semi join*.

> **NOTE**
>
> The inverse of a semi join is an anti–semi join. An anti–semi join looks for rows in one table based on their nonexistence in the other, such as for a NOT IN or NOT EXISTS type subquery, or for some outer join queries.

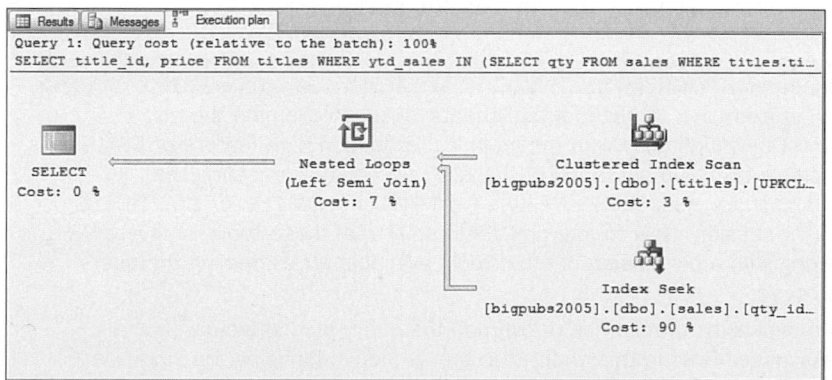

FIGURE 30.22   An execution plan for a correlated subquery.

30

However, if there is no useful index on the correlated columns to find the matching rows, the Query Optimizer may choose to perform a single search against each table separately and perform a hash join against the results.

Execution Plan Selection

At this point in the query optimization process, the Query Optimizer has examined the entire query and estimated the costs of all possible access paths for the SARGs and join clauses and also the various join orders and query-processing strategies. It now needs to choose which plan to pass on to SQL Server for execution.

For a single table query, choosing the best query plan typically involves choosing the access path and query processing strategy that results in the most efficient execution plan—usually this will be the plan that requires the fewest number of logical I/Os and typically requiring the least resources to process the query on that table. However, sometimes the Query Optimizer may choose a plan that returns rows faster to the user but with a greater, but reasonable, cost in resources (I/O plus CPU and memory). For example, processing a query in parallel (that is, using multiple CPUs simultaneously for the same query) typically requires more resources than processing it via a single CPU, but the query may complete much faster when processed in parallel. The Query Optimizer may choose to use such a parallel plan for execution if the load on the server is not adversely affected.

For a multitable query, choosing the best plan involves not only determining the cheapest access path and query processing strategy for each table individually but also determining the best access paths in conjunction with the optimal join strategy that results in the lowest estimated query cost, as discussed in the earlier section on join selection.

In addition, if any ORDER BY, GROUP BY, or DISTINCT clauses are present, the Query Optimizer chooses the most efficient method to process them.

For all its options, the overriding factor in selecting a plan is primarily the overall I/O cost. The Query Optimizer usually selects a query plan that results in the least amount of I/O processing as I/O is often the most expensive aspect of a query. After the plan is selected, it's passed to the database engine for execution.

NOTE

As you have seen in examples throughout this chapter, you can examine the query plan chosen by the Query Optimizer with the graphical execution plan feature of SSMS. You can also display a text representation of the execution plan by enabling the SHOWPLAN_TEXT, SHOWPLAN_ALL, SHOWPLAN_XML, STATISTICS PROFILE, or STATISTICS XML option in a user session. How to interpret the output from these tools is covered in Chapter 31, along with a discussion of other tools available for examining the query plan selection process.

You also have the capability to influence or override the query plan selection process, using methods discussed later in this chapter, in the section "Managing the Optimizer."

The Query Optimizer can choose from many possible execution plans, especially when a large number of tables are involved in the query—and an even greater number of permutations of join strategies and index usage is possible. The number of permutations grows exponentially as the number of tables involved in the query grows. Some complex queries could potentially have millions of possible execution plans. In these cases, the Query Optimizer does not analyze all possible plan combinations. Instead, it tries to find an execution plan that has a cost reasonably close to the theoretical minimum.

Initially, SQL Server tries to determine whether only one viable plan for a query exists. This is called *trivial plan optimization*. For simple queries, this can save the Query Optimizer a lot of work. The idea behind trivial plan optimization is that cost-based optimization can be expensive to initialize and run. The Query Optimizer can try many possible variations in looking for the cheapest plan and the time required to find the optimal query plan could potentially be longer than the time required to execute the query itself. If the Query Optimizer can determine by investigating the query and the relevant metadata that there is only one viable plan for a query, it can avoid a lot of the work required to initialize and perform cost-based optimization.

An example of a trivial query plan is a single table SELECT statement with a SARG on a unique key or a SELECT on a table with no indexes or GROUP BY clause. Another example is an INSERT statement using a VALUES clause into a table that doesn't participate in indexed views: There is only one way to insert this record. For each of these examples, the query plans are fairly obvious plans that are typically very inexpensive, so the Query Optimizer generates the plan without trying to find something better. If the Query Optimizer tried to consider every possible plan, the optimization cost could actually exceed the query processing time, outweighing any benefit provided by well-optimized queries.

If a trivial plan is not available, the Query Optimizer next performs some query simplifications, usually syntactic transformations of the query itself, such as commutative properties and operations that can be rearranged. An example of simplification is evaluation of simple single-table SARG filters before processing the joins. While the filters are logically evaluated after the joins, evaluating the filters before the joins still produces the correct result and is more efficient because it removes unqualified rows before the join operation is performed, resulting in fewer iterations and subsequently, fewer I/Os.

After any attempts at query simplification, the Query Optimizer begins a more thorough optimization process. To avoid just running through all the possibilities that would cause the optimization process to take a long time, the optimization is broken up into three phases. After each phase, the Query Optimizer applies a set of rules to evaluate the cost of any resulting plan. If, according to these rules, the plan is cheap enough, it chooses and submits that plan for execution. If, according to the rules, no plan is cheap enough, the Query Optimizer continues on to the next phase, with its own set of (usually more complex) rules to apply. In the vast majority of cases, the Query Optimizer finds a viable execution plan in the preliminary phases.

30

The first phase of optimization, Phase 0, contains a limited set of rules and is applied to queries with at least four tables. As you've seen previously, join reordering alone generates many potential plan candidates, so the Query Optimizer uses a limited number of join orders in Phase 0 and considers using only the hash or nested-loop join strategies. If at the end of this phase the Query Optimizer finds a plan with an estimated cost below the threshold for Phase 0, the optimization ends. Phase 0 is also referred to as the *transaction processing phase* as the final query plans produced by Phase 0 are typically found in transaction processing applications.

The next phase is Phase 1, or quick plan optimization. This phase applies additional transformation rules and examines different possible join orders than were considered in Phase 0. If at the end of Phase 1, the Query Optimizer finds a best plan with a cost less than the threshold for Phase 1, optimization ends and the best plan identified is returned.

Up to this point, the Query Optimizer has considered only nonparallel query plans. If more than one CPU is available to SQL Server and the cost of the least expensive plan produced by Phase 1 is greater than the Cost Threshold for Parallelism configuration setting, the Query Optimizer runs the Phase 1 optimization again, this time looking for the best parallel query plan. The costs of the nonparallel and parallel plans generated by Phase 1 are then compared and the Query Optimizer enters the last phase of optimization, Phase 2, for the cheaper of the two.

Phase 2 is also referred to as the full optimization phase. If the cost of the best nonparallel plan found so far is still below the parallelism threshold, or there is only a single CPU available, the full optimization phase continues using a brute-force method to find the best serial plan, checking additional combinations of indexes and processing strategies such as outer join reordering and automatic indexed view substitution for multitable views. In this phase, the Query Optimizer examines every possible execution plan and eventually chooses the cheapest one. The number of execution plans it considers during Phase 2 is restricted by a time limit. When the designated time limit for Phase 2 is reached, the Query Optimizer returns the cheapest plan found thus far.

Eventually, an execution plan is determined to be the most efficient. After this is determined, the execution plan is passed on to the SQL Server query processor to be executed.

Query Plan Caching

SQL Server 2005 has a pool of memory that is used to store both execution plans and data. The amount of memory allocated to execution plans or data changes dynamically, depending on the needs of the system. The portion of memory used to store execution plans is often referred to as the *plan cache*.

The first time a cacheable query is submitted to SQL Server, the query plan is compiled and put into the plan cache. Query plans are read-only re-entrant structures that are shared by multiple users. At most, there are two instances of a query plan at any time in the plan cache: a serial execution plan and a parallel query execution plan. The same parallel execution plan is used for all parallel executions, regardless of the degree of parallelism.

When you execute subsequent SQL statements, the database engine first checks to see whether an existing execution plan for the same SQL statement already resides in the plan cache. If it finds one, SQL Server 2005 attempts to reuse the matching execution plan, thereby saving the overhead of having to recompile an execution plan for each ad hoc SQL statement issued. If no matching execution plan is found, SQL Server 2005 is forced to generate a new execution plan for the query.

The ability to reuse query plans for ad hoc queries in addition to caching query plans for stored procedures can help improve the performance for complex queries that are executed frequently because SQL Server can avoid having to compile a query plan every time it's executed if a matching query plan is found in memory first.

Query Plan Reuse

Query plan reuse for stored procedures is pretty straightforward. The whole idea behind stored procedures is to promote plan reuse. For stored procedures and triggers, plan reuse is simply based on the procedure or trigger name. The first time a stored procedure is executed, the query plan is generated based on the initial parameters. On subsequent executions, SQL Server checks the plan cache to see whether a query plan exists for a procedure with the same name, and if one is found, it simply substitutes the new parameter values into the existing query plan for execution.

Another method that promotes query plan reuse is using the sp_executesql stored procedure for executing dynamic SQL statements. When using sp_executesql, typically you specify a dynamic query with explicitly identified parameters for SARGs. Here's an example:

```
sp_executesql N'select t.title, pubdate from bigpubs2005.dbo.authors a
join bigpubs2005.dbo.titleauthor ta on a.au_id = ta.au_id
join bigpubs2005.dbo.titles t on ta.title_id = t.title_id
where a.au_lname = @name', N'@name varchar(30)', 'Smith'
```

When the same query is executed again via sp_executesql, SQL Server reuses the existing query plan (if it is still in the plan cache) and simply substitutes the different parameter values.

While SQL Server can also match query plans for ad hoc SQL statements, there are some limitations as to when a plan can be reused. In order for SQL Server to match SQL statements to existing execution plans in the plan cache for ad hoc queries, all object references in the query must be qualified with at least the schema name, and fully qualified object names (database plus schema name) provide increased likelihood of plan reuse. In addition, plan caching for ad hoc queries requires an exact text match between the queries. The text match is both case sensitive and space sensitive. For example, the

30

following two queries are logically identical, but because they are not textually identical, they would not share the same query plan:

```
select a.au_lname, t.title, pubdate
from authors a
join titleauthor ta on a.au_id = ta.au_id
join titles t on ta.title_id = t.title_id

select a.au_lname,
       t.title,
       pubdate
from authors a
join titleauthor ta on a.au_id = ta.au_id
join titles t on ta.title_id = t.title_id
```

Another factor that can prevent query plan reuse by matching queries is differences in certain SET options, database options, or configuration options that are in effect for the user session when the query is invoked. For example, a query might optimize differently for one session if the ANSI_NULLS option is turned on than it would if it were turned off. The following list of SET options must match for a query plan to be reused by a session:

- ► ANSI_PADDING
- ► FORCEPLAN
- ► CONCAT_NULL_YIELDS_NULL
- ► ANSI_WARNINGS
- ► ANSI_NULLS
- ► QUOTED_IDENTIFIER
- ► ANSI_NULL_DFLT_ON
- ► ANSI_NULL_DFLT_OFF

If any one of these setting values does not match the setting options for a cached plan, the session generates a new query plan. Likewise, if the session is using a different language or DATEFORMAT setting than a cached plan, it needs to generate a new execution plan. As you can see, sometimes fairly subtle differences can prevent plan reuse.

Simple Query Parameterization

For certain simple queries executed without parameters, SQL Server 2005 automatically replaces constant literal values with parameters and compiles the query plan. This simple parameterization of the query plan increases the possibility of query plan matching for subsequent queries. If a subsequent query differs in only the values of the constants, it will match with the parameterized query plan and reuse the query plan.

Consider this query:

```
SELECT * FROM AdventureWorks.Production.Product WHERE ProductSubcategoryID = 1
```

The search value 1 at the end of the statement can be treated like a parameter. When the query plan is generated for this query, the Query Optimizer replaces the search value with a placeholder parameter, such as @p1. This process is called *simple parameterization*. (In SQL Server 2000, the process was referred to as auto-parameterization.) Using the method of simple parameterization, SQL Server 2005 recognizes that the following two statements generate essentially the same execution plan and reuses the first plan for the second statement:

```
SELECT * FROM AdventureWorks.Production.Product WHERE ProductSubcategoryID = 9
```

NOTE

You can determine whether simple parameterization has been used for a query by examining the showplan information for the query. If the showplan information contains such placeholders as @p1 and @p2 in the search predicates when literal values were specified in the actual query, you know simple parameterization has been applied for the query.

Query Plan Aging

A query plan is saved in cache along with a cost factor that reflects the cost of actually creating the plan when compiling the query. For ad hoc query plans, SQL Server sets its cost to 0, which indicates that the plan can be removed from the plan cache immediately if space is needed for other plans. For other query plans, such as for a stored procedure, the query plan cost is a measure of the amount of resources required to produce it. This cost is calculated in "number of ticks." The maximum plan cost is 31. The plan cost is determined as follows:

> Every 2 I/Os required by the plan = 1 tick (with a maximum of 19 ticks)
>
> Every 2 context switches in the plan = 1 tick (with a maximum of 8 ticks)
>
> Every 16 pages (128KB) of memory required for the plan = 1 tick (with a maximum of 4 ticks)

All reusable query plans remain in cache until space is needed in the plan cache for a new plan. When space is needed, SQL Server removes the oldest unused execution plan from the plan cache that has the lowest plan cost.

As plans age in cache, the plan cost is not decremented until the size of the plan cache reaches 50% of the buffer pool size. When this occurs, the next access of the plan cache results in the plan cost for all query plans being decremented by 1. As plans reside in the plan cache over a period of time and are not reused, they eventually reach a plan cache

30

cost of 0 and thus become eligible to be removed from cache the next time plan cache space is needed. However, when a query plan is reused, its plan cost is reset back to its initial value. This helps ensure that frequently accessed query plans remain in the plan cache.

Recompiling Query Plans

Certain changes in a database over time can cause existing execution plans to become either inefficient or invalid, based on the new state of the database. SQL Server detects the changes that invalidate an execution plan and marks the plan as not valid. A new plan is then automatically recompiled the next time the query that uses that query plan is invoked. Most query plan recompilations are required either for statement correctness or to obtain potentially faster query execution plans. The types of conditions that can invalidate a query plan include the following:

▶ Modifications made to the definition of a table or view referenced by the query using ALTER TABLE and ALTER VIEW

▶ Changes made to any indexes used by the execution plan

▶ Updates to the statistics used by the execution plan via either the UPDATE STATISTICS command or automatically

▶ Dropping of an index used by the execution plan

▶ Execution of sp_recompile on a table referenced by the query plan

▶ Large numbers of changes to keys (generated by INSERT or DELETE statements from other users that modify a table referenced by the query)

▶ When the number of rows in the inserted or deleted tables grows significantly within a trigger defined on a table referenced in the query plan

▶ Execution of a stored procedure with the WITH RECOMPILE option specified

In SQL Server 2000, whenever a statement within a batch or stored procedure required recompilation, the entire batch or stored procedure would be recompiled. To avoid the unnecessary recompilation of statements that do not require it, SQL Server 2005 introduces the concept of statement-level recompilation. In SQL Server 2005, only the statement inside the batch or stored procedure that requires recompilation is recompiled. Statement-level recompilation helps improve query performance because, in most cases, only a small number of statements within a batch or stored procedure cause recompilations and their associated penalties, in terms of CPU time and locks. These penalties are therefore avoided for the other statements in the batch that do not have to be recompiled.

Forcing Query Plan Recompiles

If you suspect that a query plan that is being reused is not appropriate for the current execution of a query, you can also manually force the query plan to be recompiled for the query. This can be especially useful for parameterized queries. Query parameterization provides a performance benefit by minimizing compilation overhead, but a parameterized query often provides less specific costing information to the Query Optimizer and can result in the creation of a more general plan, which can be less efficient than a more specific plan created for a specific set of literal values.

If the initial parameterized query plan generated for the query was not based on a representative set of parameters, or if you are invoking an instance of the query with a nonrepresentative set of search values, you may find it necessary to force the Query Optimizer to generate a new query plan. You can force query recompilation for a specific execution of a query by specifying the RECOMPILE query hint. For more information on specifying the RECOMPILE query hint, see the "Managing the Optimizer" section, later in this chapter.

Monitoring the Plan Cache

You can view and get information about the query plans currently in plan cache memory by using some of the new DMVs available in SQL Server 2005. The following are some of the useful ones related to monitoring the plan cache:

- ▶ **sys.dm_exec_cached_plans**—Returns general information about the query execution plans that are currently in the plan cache.

- ▶ **sys.dm_exec_query_stats**—Returns aggregate performance statistics for cached query plans.

- ▶ **sys.dm_exec_sql_text**—Returns the text of the SQL statement for a specified plan handle.

- ▶ **sys.dm_exec_plan_attributes**—Returns one row per attribute associated with the plan for a specified plan handle.

NOTE

In SQL Server 2000, the plan cache could be examined using the syscacheobjects table. While this table is available in SQL Server 2005 as the sys.syscacheobjects compatibility view, it is provided for backward-compatibility purposes only and will not be supported in future releases of SQL Server. It is recommended that you use the new DMVs instead.

---

sys.dm_exec_cached_plans

The sys.dm_exec_cached_plans DMV provides information on all the execution plans currently in the plan cache. Because there can be a large number of plans in the cache, you usually want to limit the results returned from sys.dm_exec_cached_plans by using a filter on the cacheobjtype column and also using the TOP clause. For example, the query shown in Listing 30.1 returns the top 10 compiled plans currently in the plan cache, sorted in descending order by the number of times the plan has been reused (usecounts).

LISTING 30.1   Returning the Top 10 Compiled Plans, by Usage Count

```
select top 10 objtype, usecounts, size_in_bytes, plan_handle
   from sys.dm_exec_cached_plans
   where cacheobjtype = 'Compiled Plan'
   order by usecounts desc
go
```

objtype	usecounts	size_in_bytes	plan_handle
Adhoc	60	24576	0x06000A00BA188505B8C17D0F0000000000000000000000000
Adhoc	58	24576	0x06000A000C6F501CB861950F0000000000000000000000000
Proc	4	385024	0x0500FF7FE4F8E01CB8611D110000000000000000000000000
Adhoc	4	24576	0x060006000C6F501CB861B6110000000000000000000000000
Adhoc	4	40960	0x06000A00B38AE915B8816A120000000000000000000000000
Adhoc	3	73728	0x06000A00EAAC3123B881940F0000000000000000000000000
Adhoc	3	40960	0x06000A00A456F32DB8A18811000000000000000000000000
Adhoc	3	24576	0x06000600BA188505B8C1B2110000000000000000000000000
Proc	2	1187840	0x0500FF7F39114733B8012A110000000000000000000000000
Proc	2	81920	0x0500FF7FC9638000B8C1C7100000000000000000000000000

The types of plans in the plan cache are listed under the `cacheobjtype` column and can be any of the following:

► **Compiled Plan**—The actual compiled plan generated that can be shared by sessions running the same procedure or query.

► **Executable Plan**—The actual execution plan and the environment settings for the session that ran the compiled plan. Caching the environment settings for an execution plan makes subsequent executions more efficient. Each concurrent execution of the same compiled plan will have its own executable plan. All executable plans are associated with a compiled plan having the same `plan_handle`, but not all compiled plans have an associated executable plan.

► **Parse Tree**—The internal parsed form of a query generated before compilation and optimization.

► **Extended stored procedure**—The cached information for an extended stored procedure.

The type of object or query for which a plan is cached is stored in the `objtype` column. This column can contain one of the following values:

► **Proc**—The cached plan is for a stored procedure or inline function.

► **Prepared**—The cached plan is for queries submitted using `sp_executesql` or for queries using the prepare and execute method.

► **Adhoc**—The cached plan is for queries that don't fall into any other category.

- ▶ **ReplProc**—The cached plan is for replication agents.

- ▶ **Trigger**—The cached plan is for a trigger.

- ▶ **View**—The cached plan is for a view or a non-inline function. You typically see a parse tree only for a view or non-inline function, not a compiled plan. The view or function typically does not have its own separate plan because it is expanded as part of another query.

- ▶ **UsrTab or SysTab**—The cached plan is for a user or system table that has computed columns. This is typically associated with a parse tree.

- ▶ **Default, Check, or Rule**—The cached plan is simply a parse tree for these types of objects because they are expanded as part of another query in which they are applied.

To determine how often a plan is being reused, you can examine the value in the usecounts columns. The usecounts value is incremented each time the cached plan is looked up and reused.

sys.dm_exec_sql_text

Overall, the information returnd by sys.dm_exec_cached_plans is not overly useful unless you know what queries or stored procedures these plans refer to. You can view the SQL text of these query plans by writing a query that joins sys.dm_exec_cached_plans with the sys.dm_exec_sql_text DMV. For example, the query shown in Listing 30.2 can be used to return the SQL text for the top 10 largest ad hoc query plans currently in the plan cache.

LISTING 30.2   Returning the Top 10 Largest Ad Hoc Query Plans

```
select top 10 objtype, usecounts, size_in_bytes,  plan_handle,
       -- the following removes newline and carriage return from the sql text
       replace(replace( text, char(13), ' '), char(10), ' ') as sqltext
   from sys.dm_exec_cached_plans as p
   cross apply sys.dm_exec_sql_text (p.plan_handle)
   where cacheobjtype = 'Compiled Plan'
     and objtype = 'Adhoc'
   order by size_in_bytes desc, usecounts desc
```

sys.dm_exec_query_stats

The plan cache also keeps track of useful statistics about each cached plan, such as the amount of CPU or the number of reads and writes performed by the query plan since it was placed into the plan cache. This information can be examined using the sys.dm_exec_query_stats DMV. The sys.dm_exec_query_stats DMV returns statistics for each statement in a stored procedure or a SQL batch. To provide statistics for the procedure or batch as a whole, you need to summarize the data. Listing 30.3 provides a sample query that returns the I/O, CPU, and elapsed time statistics for the 10 most recently executed stored procedures.

LISTING 30.3   Returning Query Plan Stats for the 10 Most Recently Executed Procedures

```
select TOP 10 usecounts, size_in_bytes,
   max(last_execution_time) as last_execution_time,
   sum(total_logical_reads) as total_logical_reads,
   sum(total_physical_reads) as total_physical_reads,
   sum(total_worker_time/1000) as total_CPU_time,
   sum(total_elapsed_time/1000) as total_elapsed_time,
   replace(substring (text,
                      patindex('%create procedure%', text),
                      datalength(text)),
         'create procedure', '') as procname
   from sys.dm_exec_query_stats s
   join sys.dm_exec_cached_plans p on s.plan_handle = p.plan_handle
   CROSS APPLY sys.dm_exec_sql_text(p.plan_handle) as st
   where p.objtype = 'Proc' and p.cacheobjtype = 'Compiled Plan'
   group by usecounts, size_in_bytes, text
   order by max(last_execution_time) desc
```

Table 30.1 describes some of the most useful columns returned by the sys.dm_exec_query_stats DMV.

TABLE 30.1   Description of Columns for sys.dm_exec_query_stats

Column Name	Description
statement_start_offset	Indicates, in bytes, beginning with 0, the starting position of the query that the row describes within the text of its batch or stored procedure.
statement_end_offset	The ending position of the query that the row describes within the text of its batch or stored proc. A value of -1 indicates the end of the batch.
plan_generation_num	The number of times the plan has been recompiled while it has remained in the cache.
plan_handle	A pointer to the plan. This value can be passed to the dm_exec_query_plan dynamic management function.
creation_time	The time that the plan was compiled.
last_execution_time	The last time that the plan was executed.
execution_count	The number of times that the plan has been executed since it was last compiled.
total_worker_time	The total amount of CPU time, in microseconds, consumed by executions of this plan for the statement.
last_worker_time	The CPU time, in microseconds, consumed the last time the plan was executed.

TABLE 30.1   Continued

Column Name	Description
min_worker_time	The minimum CPU time, in microseconds, that this plan has ever consumed during a single execution.
max_worker_time	The maximum CPU time, in microseconds, that this plan has ever consumed during a single execution.
total_physical_reads	The total number of physical reads performed by executions of this plan since it was compiled.
last_physical_reads	The number of physical reads performed the last time the plan was executed.
min_physical_reads	The minimum number of physical reads that this plan has ever performed during a single execution.
max_physical_reads	The maximum number of physical reads that this plan has ever performed during a single execution.
total_logical_writes	The total number of logical writes performed by executions of this plan since it was compiled.
last_logical_writes	The number of logical writes performed the last time the plan was executed.
min_logical_writes	The minimum number of logical writes that this plan has ever performed during a single execution.
max_logical_writes	The maximum number of logical writes that this plan has ever performed during a single execution.
total_logical_reads	The total number of logical reads performed by executions of this plan since it was compiled.
last_logical_reads	The number of logical reads performed the last time the plan was executed.
min_logical_reads	The minimum number of logical reads that this plan has ever performed during a single execution.
max_logical_reads	The maximum number of logical reads that this plan has ever performed during a single execution.
total_elapsed_time	The total elapsed time, in microseconds, for completed executions of this plan.
last_elapsed_time	The elapsed time, in microseconds, for the most recently completed execution of this plan.
min_elapsed_time	The minimum elapsed time, in microseconds, for any completed execution of this plan.
max_elapsed_time	The maximum elapsed time, in microseconds, for any completed execution of this plan.

30

sys.dm_exec_plan_attributes

If you want to get information about specific attributes of a specific query plan, you use
sys.dm_exec_plan_attributes. This DMV takes a plan_handle as an input parameter and
returns one row for each attribute associated with the query plan. These attributes include
information such as the ID of the database context the query plan was generated in, the

ID of the user that generated the query plan, session SET options in effect at the time the plan was generated, and so on. Many of these attributes are used as part of the cache lookup key for the plan (indicated by a value 1 in the is_cache_key_column). The following is an example of the output for sys.dm_exec_plan_attributes:

```
select convert(varchar(30), attribute) as attribute,
       convert(varchar(12), value) as value,
       is_cache_key
from
sys.dm_exec_plan_attributes (0x06000A00C201DB23B80107110000000000000000000000000)
where is_cache_key = 1
go
```

attribute	value	is_cache_key
set_options	4347	1
objectid	601555394	1
dbid	10	1
dbid_execute	0	1
user_id	1	1
language_id	0	1
date_format	1	1
date_first	7	1
status	0	1
required_cursor_options	0	1
acceptable_cursor_options	0	1

Note the attributes that are flagged as cache keys for the plan. If one of these properties does not match the state of the current user session, the plan cannot be reused for that session, and a new plan must be compiled and stored in the plan cache. If you see multiple plans in cache for what appears to be the same query, you can determine the key differences between them by comparing the columns associated with the plan's cache keys to see where the differences lie.

> **TIP**
>
> If SQL Server has been running for a while, with a lot of activity, the number of plans in the plan cache can become quite large, resulting in a large number of rows being returned by the plan cache DMVs. To run your own tests to determine which query plans get cached and when specific query plans are reused, you should clear out the cache occasionally. You can use the DBCC FREEPROCCACHE command to clear all cached plans from memory. If you want to clear only the cached plans for objects or queries in a specific database, you execute the following command:
>
> ```
> DBCC FLUSHPROCINDB (dbid)
> ```
>
> Keep in mind that you should run these commands only in a test environment. Running these commands in production servers could impact the performance of the currently running applications.

Other Query Processing Strategies

In addition to the optimization strategies covered so far, SQL Server also has some additional strategies it can apply for special types of queries. These strategies are used to help further reduce the cost of executing various types of queries.

Predicate Transitivity

You might be familiar with the transitive property from algebra. The transitive property simply states that if A=B and B=C then A=C. SQL Server supports the transitive property in its query predicates. Predicate transitivity enables SQL Server to infer a join equality from two given equalities. Consider the following example:

```
SELECT *
   FROM table1 t1
   join table2 t2 on t1.column1 = t2.column1
   join table3 t3 on t2.column1 = t3.column1
```

Using the principle of predicate transitivity, SQL Server is able to infer that `t1.column1` is equal to `t3.column1`. This provides the Query Optimizer with another join strategy to consider when optimizing this query. This might result in a much cheaper execution plan.

The transitive property can also be applied to SARGs used on join columns. Consider the following query:

```
select *
   from sales s
   join stores st on s.stor_id = st.stor_id
   and s.stor_id = 'B199'
```

Again, using transitive closure, it follows that `st.stor_id` is also equal to `'B199'`. SQL Server recognizes this and can compare the search value against the statistics on both tables to more accurately estimate the number of matching rows from each table.

GROUP BY Optimization

One way SQL Server can process GROUP BY results is to retrieve the matching detailed data rows into a worktable and then sort the rows and calculate the aggregates on the groups formed. In SQL Server 2005, the Query Optimizer also may choose to use hashing to organize the data into groups and then compute the aggregates.

The hash aggregation strategy uses the same basic method for grouping and calculating aggregates as for a hash join. At the point where the probe input row is checked to determine whether it already exists in the hash bucket, the aggregate is computed if a hash match is found. The following pseudocode summarizes the hash aggregation strategy:

```
create a hash table
for each row in the input table
```

30

```
    read the row
    hash the key value
    search the hash table for matches
    if match found
        aggregate the value into the old record
    else
        insert the hashed key into the hash bucket
scan and output the hash table contents
drop the hash table
```

For some join queries that contain GROUP BY clauses, SQL Server might perform the grouping operation before processing the join. This could reduce the size of the input table to the join and lower the overall cost of executing the query.

> **NOTE**
>
> One important point to keep in mind is that regardless of the GROUP BY strategy employed, the rows are not guaranteed to be returned in sorted order by the grouping column(s) as they were in earlier releases. If the results must be returned in a specific sort order, you need to use the ORDER BY clause with GROUP BY to ensure ordered results. You might want to get into the habit of doing this regularly.

Queries with DISTINCT

When the DISTINCT clause is specified in a query, SQL Server can eliminate duplicate rows by the sorting the result set in a worktable to identify and remove the duplicates, similar to how a worktable is used for GROUP BY queries. In SQL Server 2005, the Query Optimizer can also employ a hashing strategy similar to that used for GROUP BY to return only the distinct rows before the final result set is determined.

In addition, if the Query Optimizer can determine at compile time that there will be nonduplicate rows in the result set (for example, each row contains the table's primary key), the strategies for removing duplicate rows are skipped altogether.

Queries with UNION

When you specify UNION in a query, SQL Server merges the result sets, applying one of the merge or concatenation operators with sorting strategies to remove any duplicate rows. Figure 30.23 shows an example very similar to the OR strategy where the rows are concatenated and then sorted to remove any duplicates.

If you specify UNION ALL in a query, SQL Server simply appends the result sets together. No intermediate sorting or merge step is needed to remove duplicates. Figure 30.24 shows the same query as in Figure 30.23, except that a UNION ALL is specified.

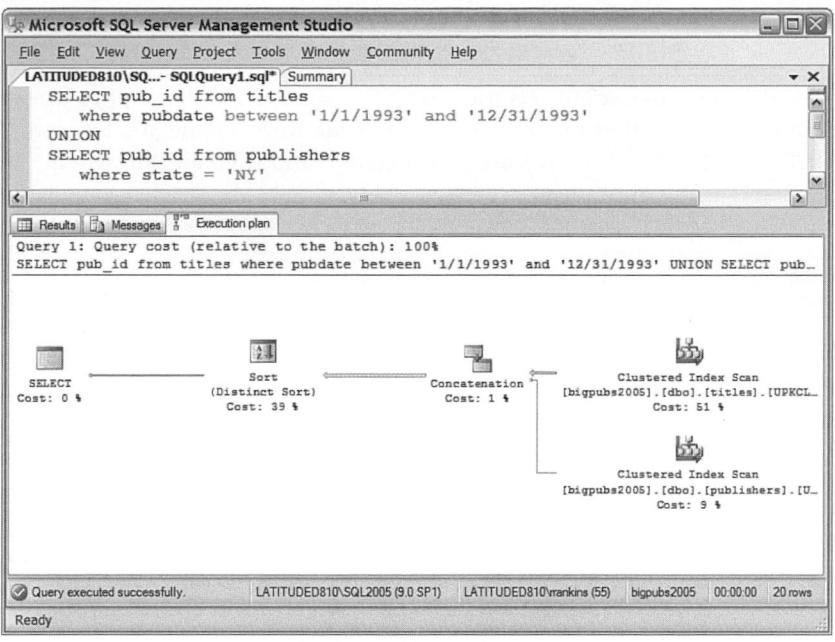

FIGURE 30.23   An execution plan for a UNION query.

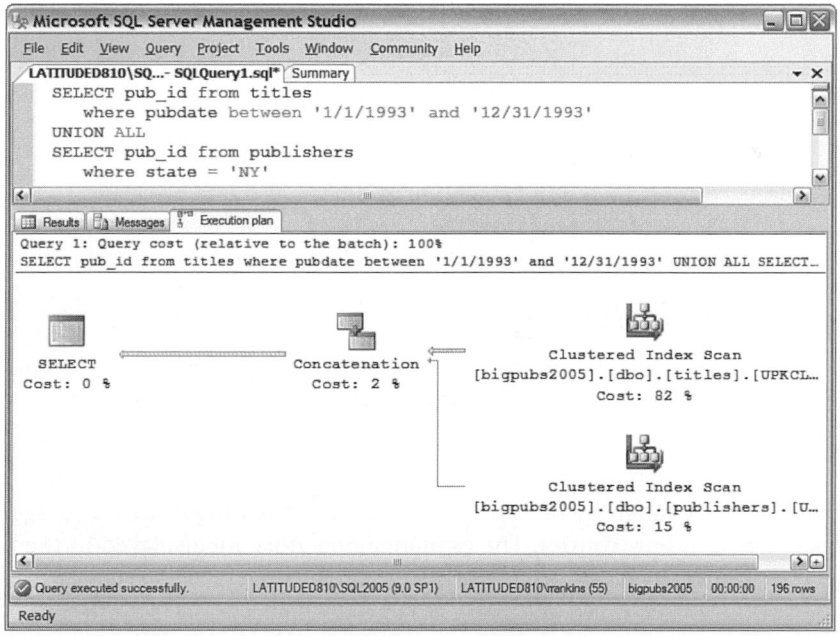

FIGURE 30.24   An execution plan for a UNION ALL query.

30

When you know that you do not need to worry about duplicate rows in a UNION result set, always specify UNION ALL to eliminate the extra overhead required for sorting.

When using a UNION to merge large result sets together, SQL Server 2005 may opt to use a merge join or a hash match operation to remove any duplicate rows. Figure 30.25 shows an example of a UNION query where the rows are concatenated and then a hash match operation is used to remove any duplicates.

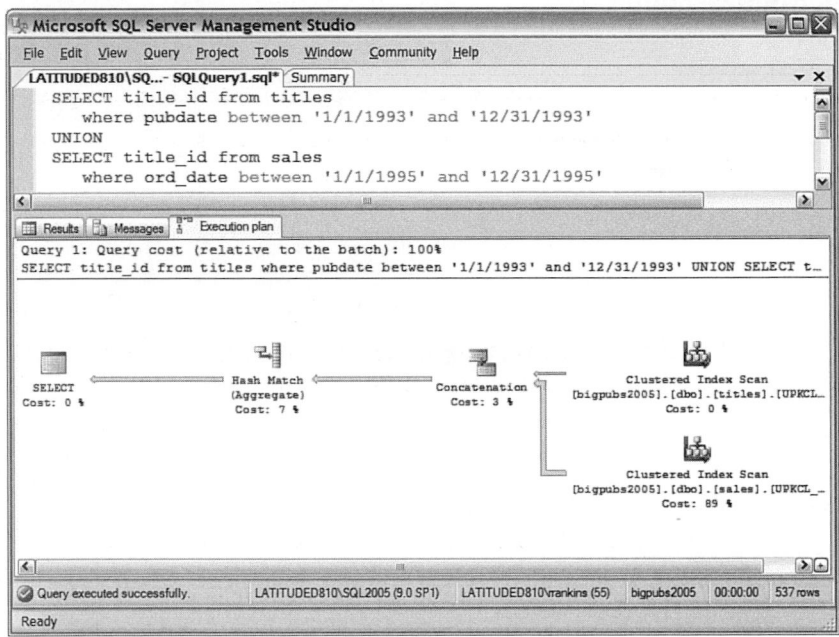

FIGURE 30.25   An execution plan for a UNION query, using a hash match to eliminate duplicate rows.

Parallel Query Processing

The query processor in SQL Server 2005 includes parallel query processing—an execution strategy that can improve the performance of complex queries on computers with more than one processor.

SQL Server inserts exchange operators into each parallel query to build and manage the query execution plan. The exchange operator is responsible for providing process management, data redistribution, and flow control. The exchange operators are displayed in the query plans as the Distribute Streams, Repartition Streams, and Gather Streams logical operators. One or more of these can appear in the showplan output of a query plan for a parallel query.

Whereas a parallel query execution plan can use more than one thread, a serial execution plan, used by a nonparallel query, uses only a single thread for its execution. Prior to query execution time, SQL Server determines whether the current system state and configuration allow for parallel query execution. If parallel query execution is justified, SQL Server determines the optimal number of threads, called the degree of parallelism, and distributes the query workload execution across those threads. The parallel query uses the same number of threads until the query completes. SQL Server reexamines the optimal degree of parallelism each time a query execution plan is retrieved from the procedure cache. Individual instances of the same query could be assigned a different degree of parallelism.

SQL Server calculates the degree of parallelism for each instance of a parallel query execution by using the following criteria:

▶ How many processors does the computer running SQL Server have?

   If your computer has two or more processors, it can use parallel queries.

▶ What is the number of concurrent active users?

   The degree of parallelism is inversely related to CPU usage. The Query Optimizer assigns a lower degree of parallelism if the CPUs are already busy.

▶ Is sufficient memory available for parallel query execution?

   Queries, like other processes, require resources to execute, particularly memory. Obviously, a parallel query demands more memory than a serial query. More importantly, as the degree of parallelism increases, so does the amount of memory required. The Query Optimizer carefully considers this in developing a query execution plan. The Query Optimizer could either adjust the degree of parallelism or use a serial plan to complete the query.

▶ What is the type of query being executed?

   Queries that use several CPU cycles justify using a parallel execution plan. Some examples are joins of large tables, substantial aggregations, and sorting large result sets. The Query Optimizer determines whether to use a parallel or serial plan by checking the value of the cost threshold for parallelism.

▶ Are a sufficient number of rows processed in the given stream?

   If the Query Optimizer determines that the number of rows in a stream is too low, it does not execute a parallel plan. This prevents scenarios where the costs exceed the benefits of executing a parallel plan.

Regardless of the answers to the previous questions, the Query Optimizer does not use a parallel execution plan for a query if any one of the following conditions is true:

▶ The serial execution cost of the query is not high enough to consider an alternative parallel execution plan.

30

▶ A serial execution plan exists that is estimated to be faster than any possible parallel execution plan for the particular query.

▶ The query contains scalar or relational operators that cannot be run in parallel.

Parallel Query Configuration Options

Two server configuration options— `maximum degree of parallelism` and `cost threshold for parallelism`—affect the consideration for a parallel query. Although doing so is not recommended, you can change the default settings for each. For single processor machines, these settings are ignored.

The `maximum degree of parallelism` option limits the number of threads to use in a parallel plan execution. The range of possible values is 0 to 32. This value is configured to 0 by default, which allows the Query Optimizer to use up to the actual number of CPUs allocated to SQL Server. If you want to suppress parallel processing completely, set the value to 1.

The `cost threshold for parallelism` option establishes a ceiling value the Query Optimizer uses to consider parallel query execution plans. If the calculated value to execute a serial plan is greater than the value set for the cost threshold for parallelism, a parallel plan is generated. This value is defined by the estimated time, in seconds, to execute the serial plan. The range of values for this setting is 0 to 32767. The default value is 5. If the maximum degree of parallelism is set to 1, or if the computer has a single processor, the cost threshold for parallelism value is ignored.

You can modify the settings for the `maximum degree of parallelism` and the `cost threshold for parallelism` server configuration options either by using the sp_configure system stored procedure or through SSMS. To set the values for these options use the sp_configure system stored procedure via SSMS or via SQLCMD, as follows:

```
USE master
go
exec sp_configure 'show advanced options', 1
GO
RECONFIGURE
GO
exec sp_configure 'max degree of parallelism', 2
GO

Configuration option 'max degree of parallelism' changed from 0 to 2.
 Run the RECONFIGURE statement to install.
exec sp_configure 'cost threshold for parallelism', 15
GO

Configuration option 'cost threshold for parallelism' changed from 5 to 15.
 Run the RECONFIGURE statement to install.
RECONFIGURE
GO
```

To set these configuration options via SSMS, you right-click the SQL Server instance in the Object Explorer and then click Properties. In the Server Properties dialog, you select the Advanced page. The parallelism options are near the bottom, as shown in Figure 30.26.

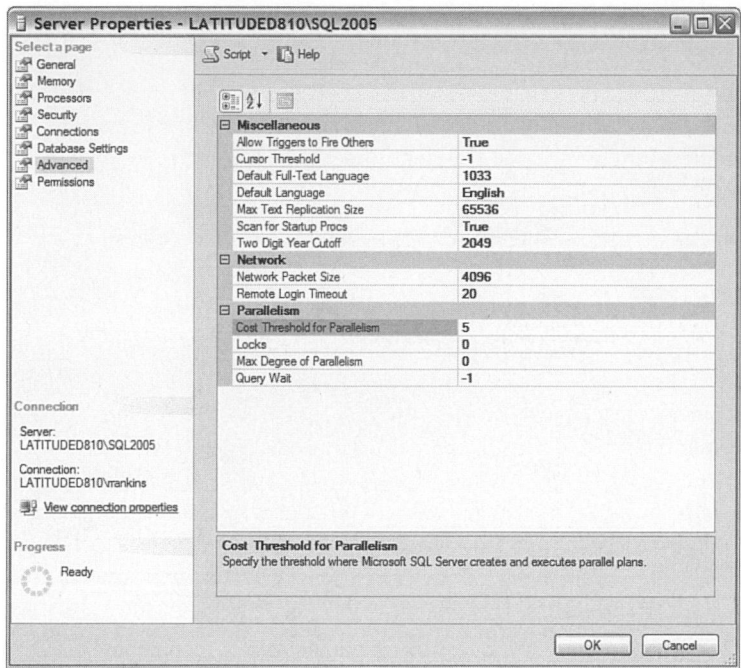

FIGURE 30.26   Setting SQL Server parallelism options.

Identifying Parallel Queries

You can identify when a parallel execution plan is being chosen by displaying the graphical execution plan in SSMS. The graphical execution plan uses icons to represent the execution of specific statements and queries in SQL Server. The showplan output for every parallel query will have at least one of these three logical operators:

▶ **Distribute Streams**—Receives a single input stream of records and distributes multiple output streams. The contents and form of the record are unchanged. All records enter through the same single input stream and appear in one of the output streams, preserving the relative order.

▶ **Gather Streams**—Assembles multiple input streams of records and yields a single output stream. The relative order of the records, contents, and form is maintained.

▶ **Repartition Streams**—Accepts multiple input streams and produces multiple streams of records. The record contents and format are unchanged.

30

Figure 30.27 provides an example of a portion of a query plan that uses parallel query techniques—both repartition streams and gather streams.

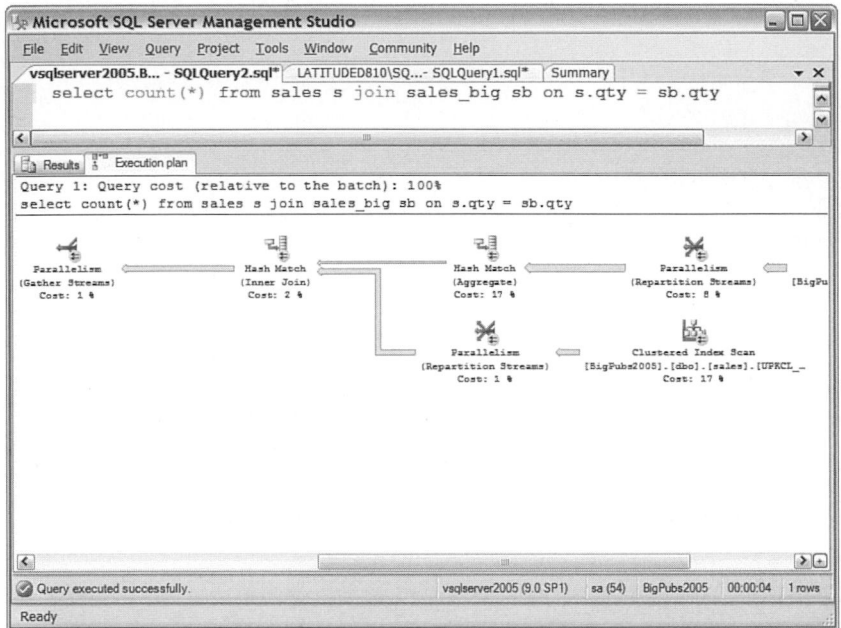

FIGURE 30.27   A graphical execution plan of a query using parallel query techniques.

Common Query Optimization Problems

So you've written a query and examined the query plan, and performance isn't what you expected. It might appear that SQL Server isn't choosing the appropriate query plan that you expect. Is something wrong with the query or with the Query Optimizer? Before delving into a detailed discussion about how to debug and analyze query plans (covered in detail in Chapter 31), this section takes a look at some of the most common problems and SQL coding issues that can lead to poor query plan selection.

Out-of-Date or Unavailable Statistics

Admittedly, out-of-date or unavailable statistics is not as big a problem as it was in SQL Server releases prior to 7.0. Back in those days, the first question asked when someone was complaining of poor performance was, "When did you last update statistics?" If the answer was "Huh?" we usually found the culprit.

With the Auto-Update Statistics and Auto-Create Statistics features in SQL Server 2005, this problem is not as prevalent as it used to be. If a query detects that statistics are out of date or missing, it causes them to be updated or created and then optimizes the query plan based on the new statistics.

> **NOTE**
>
> If statistics are missing or out of date, the first query to run that detects this condition might run a bit more slowly as it updates or creates the statistics first, especially if the table is relatively large, and also if it has been configured for FULLSCAN when indexes are updated.
>
> However, SQL Server 2005 introduces the new AUTO_UPDATE_STATISTICS_ASYNC database option. When this option is set to ON, queries do not wait for the statistics to be updated before compiling. Instead, the out-of-date statistics are put on a queue for updating by a worker thread in a background process, and the query and any other concurrent queries compile immediately, using the existing out-of-date statistics. Although there is no delay for updated statistics, the out-of-date statistics may cause the Query Optimizer to choose a less efficient query plan, but the response times are more predictable. Any queries invoked after the updated statistics are ready use the updated statistics in generating a query plan. This may cause the recompilation of any cached plans that depend on the older statistics.
>
> You should consider setting the AUTO_UPDATE_STATISTICS_ASYNC option to ON when any of your applications have experienced client request timeouts caused by queries waiting for updated statistics or when it is acceptable for your application to run queries with less efficient query plans due to outdated statistics in order to maintain predictable query response times.

You should not assume that you always have up-to-date statistics, however. Because of the possible query performance issues in SQL Server 2000 when auto-update statistics were invoked, some DBAs got into the habit of disabling the AUTO_UPDATE and AUTO_CREATE statistics options, choosing instead to run update statistics periodically via scheduled jobs. If the update statistics jobs are not run frequently enough (or possibly not run at all for some reason), valid, up-to-date statistics will not be available to effectively optimize the queries. It is not recommended that the AUTO_UPDATE and AUTO_CREATE statistics options be turned off arbitrarily; you should use SQL Server Profiler and other statistics monitoring tools to confirm that these options are causing a performance problem before turning them off. If you turn them off, you need to do additional performance testing to see if performance improves or degrades with these options disabled, and you need to make sure jobs are scheduled to ensure that statistics are being kept updated frequently enough. The AutoStats option was implemented to ensure that you have up-to-date statistics all the time, and it serves a useful purpose.

Another case where you could have insufficient statistics to properly optimize a query is if the sample size used when the statistics were generated wasn't large enough. Depending on the nature of your data and the size of the table, the statistics might not accurately reflect the actual data distribution and cardinality. If you suspect that this is the case, you can update statistics by specifying the FULLSCAN option or a larger sample size, so SQL Server examines more records to derive the statistics.

For more information on understanding and managing index statistics, see Chapter 29.

Poor Index Design

Poor index design is another reason—often a primary reason—why queries might not optimize as you expect them to. If no supporting indexes exist for a query, or if a query contains SARGs that cannot be optimized effectively to use the available indexes, SQL Server end ups performing either a table scan, an index scan, or another hash or merge join strategy that is less efficient. If this appears to be the problem, you need to reevaluate your indexing decisions or rewrite the query so it can take advantage of an available index. For more information on designing useful indexes, see Chapter 29.

Search Argument Problems

It's the curse of SQL that there are a number of ways to write a query and get the same result set. Some queries, however, might not be as efficient as others. A good understanding of the Query Optimizer can help you avoid writing search arguments that SQL Server can't optimize effectively. This section highlights some of the common "gotchas" encountered in SQL Server SARGs that can lead to poor or unexpected query performance.

Using Optimizable SARGs

As mentioned previously, in the section "Identifying Search Arguments," the Query Optimizer uses search arguments to help it narrow down the set of rows to evaluate. The search argument is in the form of a WHERE clause that equates a column to a constant. SARGs that optimize most effectively are SARGs that compare a column with a constant value that is not an expression or a variable, and with no operation performed against the column itself. The following is an example:

```
SELECT column1
   FROM table1
   WHERE column1 = 123
```

You should try to avoid using any negative logic in your SARGs (for example, !=, <>, not in) or performing operations on, or applying functions to, the columns in the SARG.

No SARGs

You need to watch out for queries in which the SARG might have been left out inadvertently, such as this:

```
select title_id from titles
```

A SQL query with no search argument (that is, no WHERE clause) always performs a table or clustered index scan unless a nonclustered index can be used to cover the query. (See Chapter 29 for a discussion of index covering.) If you don't want the query to affect the entire table, you need to be sure to specify a valid SARG that matches an index on the table to avoid table scans.

Unknown Values in WHERE Clauses

You need to watch out for expressions where the search value in the SARG cannot be evaluated until runtime. These often are expressions where the search value is a local variables or subquery that can be materialized to a single value.

SQL Server treats these expressions as SARGs but can't use the statistics histogram to estimate the number of matching rows because it doesn't have a value to compare against the histogram values during query optimization. The values for the expressions aren't known until the query is actually executed. In this situation, the Query Optimizer uses the index density information. The Query Optimizer is generally able to better estimate the number of rows affected by a query when it can compare a known value against the statistics histogram than when it has to use the index density to estimate the average number of rows that match an unknown value. This is especially true if the data in a table isn't distributed evenly. When you can, you should try to avoid using constant expressions that can't be evaluated until runtime so that the statistics histogram can be used rather than the density value.

To avoid using constant expressions in WHERE clauses that can't be evaluated until runtime, you should consider putting the queries into stored procedures and passing in the constant expression as a parameter. Because the Query Optimizer evaluates the value of a parameter prior to optimization, SQL Server evaluates the expression prior to optimizing the stored procedure.

For best results when writing queries inside stored procedures, you should use stored procedure parameters rather than local variables in your SARGs whenever possible. This strategy allows the Query Optimizer to optimize the query by using the statistics histogram, comparing the parameter value against the statistics histogram to estimate the number of matching rows. If you use local variables as SARGs in stored procedures, the Query Optimizer is restricted to using index density, even if the local variable is assigned the value of a parameter.

Other types of constructs for which it is difficult for the Query Optimizer to accurately estimate the number of qualifying rows or the data distribution using the statistics histogram include aggregations in subqueries, scalar expressions, user-defined functions, and non-inlined table-valued functions.

Data Type Mismatches

Another common problem is data type mismatches. If you attempt to join tables on columns of different data types, the Query Optimizer might not be able to effectively use indexes to compute the join. This can result in a less efficient join strategy because SQL Server has to convert all values first before it can process the query. You should avoid this situation by maintaining data type consistency across the join key columns in your database.

Large Complex Queries

For complex queries with a large number of tables and join conditions, the number of possible execution plans can be enormous. The full optimization phase of the Query Optimizer has a time limit to restrict how long it spends analyzing all the possible query plans. There is no known general and effective shortcut to arrive at the optimal plan. To deal with such a large selection of plans, SQL Server 2005 implements a number of heuristics to deal with very large queries and attempt to come up with an efficient query plan within the time available. When it is not possible to analyze the entire set of plan alternatives and the heuristics are applied, it is not uncommon to encounter suboptimal query plans being chosen.

When is your query large enough to be a concern? This is a difficult question to answer because it depends on the number of tables involved, the form of filter and join predicates, and the operations performed. If a query involves more than 12 tables, it is likely that the Query Optimizer is having to rely on heuristics and shortcuts to generate a query plan and may miss some optimal strategies.

In general, you get more optimal query plans if you can simplify your queries as much as possible.

Triggers

If you are using triggers on INSERT, UPDATE, or DELETE, it is possible that your triggers can cause performance problems. You might think that INSERT, UPDATE, or DELETE is performing poorly when actually it is the trigger that needs to be tuned. In addition, you might have triggers that fire other triggers. If you suspect that you are having performance problems with the triggers, you can monitor the SQL they are executing and the response time, as well as execution plans generated for statements within triggers using SQL Server Profiler. For more information on monitoring performance with SQL Server Profiler, see Chapter 5, "SQL Server Profiler." You can also see the query plans for statements executed in triggers by using SSMS if you enable the Include Actual Execution Plan option. For more information on using SSMS to view and analyze query plans, see Chapter 31.

Managing the Optimizer

Because the Query Optimizer might sometimes make poor decisions as to how to best process a query, you need to know how and when you may need to override the Query Optimizer and force SQL Server to process a query in a specific manner.

How often does SQL Server require manual intervention to execute a query optimally? Considering the overwhelming number of query types and circumstances in which those queries are run, SQL Server does a surprisingly effective job of query optimization in most instances. For all but the most grueling, complex query operations, experience has shown that SQL Server's Query Optimizer is quite clever—and very, very good at wringing the best performance out of any hardware platform. For this reason, you should treat the material covered in this chapter as a collection of techniques to be used only where other methods of getting optimal query performance have already failed.

Before indiscriminately applying the techniques discussed in this section, remember one very important point: Use of these features can effectively hide serious fundamental design or coding flaws in your database, application, or queries. In fact, if you're tempted to use these features (with a few moderate exceptions), it should serve as an indicator that the problems might lie elsewhere in the application or queries.

If you are satisfied that no such flaws exist and that SQL Server is choosing the wrong plan to optimize your query, you can use the methods discussed in this section to override two of the three most important decisions the Query Optimizer makes:

- ▶ Choosing which index, if any, to resolve the query

- ▶ Choosing the join strategy to apply in a multitable query

The other decision made by the Query Optimizer is the locking strategy to apply. Using table hints to override locking strategies is discussed in Chapter 32, "Locking and Performance."

Throughout this section, one point must remain clear in your mind: These options should be used only in *exception cases* to cope with specific optimization problems in specific queries in specific applications. There are therefore no standard or global rules to follow because the application of these features, by definition, means that normal SQL Server behavior isn't taking place.

The practical result of this idea is that you should test every option in *your* environment, with *your* data and *your* queries, and use the techniques and methods discussed in this chapter and the other performance-related chapters to optimize and fine-tune the performance of your queries. The fastest-performing query wins, so you shouldn't be afraid to experiment with different alternatives—but you shouldn't think that these statements and features are globally applicable or fit general categories of problems, either! There are, in fact, only three rules: *Test*, *test*, and *test*!

TIP

As a general rule, Query Optimizer and table hints should be used only as a last resort, when all other methods to get the Query Optimizer to generate a more efficient query plan have failed. Always try to find other ways to rewrite the queries to encourage the Query Optimizer to choose a better plan. This includes adding additional SARGs, substituting unknown values for known values in SARGS or trying to replace unknown values with known values, breaking up queries, converting subqueries to joins or joins to subqueries, and so on. Essentially, you should try other coding variations on the query itself to get the same result in a different way and try to see if one of the variations ends up using the more efficient query plan that you expect it to.

In reality, about the only time you should use these hints is when you're testing the performance of a query and want to see if the Query Optimizer is actually choosing the best execution plan. You can enable the various query analysis options, such as STATISTICS PROFILE and STATISTICS IO, and then see how the query plan and statistics change as you apply various hints to the query. You can examine the output

30

to determine whether the I/O cost and/or runtime improves or gets worse if you force one index over another or if you force a specific join strategy or join order.

The problem with hard-coding table and Query Optimizer hints into application queries is that the hints prevent the Query Optimizer from modifying the query plan as the data in the tables changes over time. Also, if subsequent service packs or releases of SQL Server incorporate improved optimization algorithms or strategies, the queries with hard-coded hints will not be able to take advantage of them.

If you find that you must incorporate any of these hints to solve query performance problems, you should be sure to document which queries and stored procedures contain Query Optimizer and table hints. It's a good idea to periodically go back and test the queries to determine whether the hints are still appropriate. You might find that, over time, as the data values in the table have changed, the query plan generated because of the hints is no longer the most efficient query plan, and the Query Optimizer now generates a more efficient query plan on its own.

Optimizer Hints

You can specify three types of hints in a query to override the decisions made by the Query Optimizer:

▶ Table hints

▶ Join hints

▶ Query hints

The remainder of this section examines and describes each type of table hints.

Forcing Index Selection with Table Hints

In addition to locking hints that can be specified for each table in a query, SQL Server 2005 allows you to provide table-level hints that enable you to specify the index SQL Server should use for accessing the table. The syntax for specifying an index hint is as follows:

```
SELECT column_list FROM tablename WITH (INDEX (indid ¦ index_name [, ...]) )
```

This syntax allows you to specify multiple indexes. You can specify an index by name or by ID. It is recommended that you specify indexes by name as the IDs for nonclustered indexes can change if they are dropped and re-created in a different order than that in which they were created originally. You specify an index ID of 0 to force a table scan.

When you specify multiple indexes in the hint list, all the indexes listed are used to retrieve the rows from the table, forcing an index intersection or index covering via an index join. If the collection of indexes listed does not cover the query, a regular row fetch is performed after all the indexed columns are retrieved.

To get a list of indexes on a table, you can use sp_helpindex. However, the stored procedure doesn't display the index ID. To get a list of all user-defined tables and the names of the indexes defined on them, you can execute a query against the sys.indexes catalog view similar to the one shown in Listing 30.4, which was run against the bigpubs2005 database.

LISTING 30.4   Query Against sys.indexes Catalog View to Get Index Names and IDs

```
select 'Table name' = convert(char(20), object_name(object_id)),
       'Index name' = convert(char(30), name),
       'Index ID' = index_id,
       'Index Type' = convert(char(15), type_desc)
  from sys.indexes where object_id > 99 --only system tables have id less than 99
   and index_id between 1 and 254    /* do not include rows for text columns
                              or tables without a clustered index*/
     /* do not include auto statistics */
   and is_hypothetical = 0
   and objectproperty(object_id, 'IsUserTable') = 1
order by 1, 3
go
```

Table name	Index name	Index ID	Index Type
authors	UPKCL_auidind	1	CLUSTERED
authors	aunmind	2	NONCLUSTERED
employee	employee_ind	1	CLUSTERED
employee	PK_emp_id	2	NONCLUSTERED
jobs	PK__jobs__job_id__25319086	1	CLUSTERED
PARTS	PK__PARTS__0880433F	1	CLUSTERED
PARTS	UQ__PARTS__09746778	2	NONCLUSTERED
pub_info	UPKCL_pubinfo	1	CLUSTERED
publishers	UPKCL_pubind	1	CLUSTERED
roysched	titleidind	2	NONCLUSTERED
sales	UPKCL_sales	1	CLUSTERED
sales	titleidind	2	NONCLUSTERED
sales_big	ci_sales_big	1	CLUSTERED
sales_big	idx1	2	NONCLUSTERED
sales_noclust	idx1	2	NONCLUSTERED
stores	UPK_storeid	1	CLUSTERED
stores	nc1_stores	2	NONCLUSTERED
titleauthor	UPKCL_taind	1	CLUSTERED
titleauthor	auidind	2	NONCLUSTERED
titleauthor	titleidind	3	NONCLUSTERED
titles	UPKCL_titleidind	1	CLUSTERED
titles	titleind	2	NONCLUSTERED

30

Forcing Join Strategies with Join Hints

Join hints let you force the type of join that should be used between two tables. The join hints correspond with the three types of join strategies:

- ▶ LOOP
- ▶ MERGE
- ▶ HASH

You can specify join hints only when you use the ANSI-style join syntax—that is, when you actually use the keyword JOIN in the query. The hint is specified between the type of join and the keyword JOIN, which means you can't leave out the keyword INNER for an inner join. Thus, the syntax for the FROM clause when using join hints is as follows:

```
FROM table1 {INNER ¦ OUTER} [LOOP ¦ MERGE ¦ HASH} JOIN table2
```

The following is an example of forcing SQL Server to use a hash join:

```
select st.stor_name, ord_date, qty
   from stores st INNER HASH JOIN sales s on st.stor_id = s.stor_id
   where st.stor_id between 'B100' and 'B599'
```

You can also specify a global join hint for all joins in a query by using a query processing hint.

Specifying Query Processing Hints

SQL Server 2005 enables you to specify additional query hints to control how your queries are optimized and processed. You specify query hints at the very end of a query by using the OPTION keyword. There can be only one OPTION clause per query, but you can specify multiple hints in an OPTION clause, as shown in the following syntax:

```
OPTION (hint1 [, ...hintn])
```

Query hints are grouped into four categories: GROUP BY, UNION, join, and miscellaneous.

GROUP BY **Hints**

GROUP BY hints specify how GROUP BY or COMPUTE operations should be performed. The following GROUP BY hints can be specified:

- ▶ **HASH GROUP**—This option forces the Query Optimizer to use a hashing function to perform the GROUP BY operation.
- ▶ **ORDER GROUP**—This option forces the Query Optimizer to use a sorting operation to perform the GROUP BY operation.

Only one GROUP BY hint can be specified at a time.

UNION **Hints**

The UNION hints specify how UNION operations should be performed. The following UNION hints can be specified:

- ▶ **MERGE UNION**—This option forces the Query Optimizer to use a merge operation to perform the UNION operation.

- ▶ **HASH UNION**—This option forces the Query Optimizer to use a hash operation to perform the UNION operation.

- ▶ **CONCAT UNION**—This option forces the Query Optimizer to use the concatenation method to perform the UNION operation.

Only one UNION hint can be specified at a time, and it must come after the last query in the UNION. The following is an example of forcing concatenation for a UNION:

```
select stor_id from sales where stor_id like 'B19%'
UNION
select title_id from titles where title_id like 'C19%'
OPTION (CONCAT UNION)
```

Join Hints

The join hint specified in the OPTION clause specifies that all join operations in the query are performed as the type of join specified in the hint. The join hints that can be specified in the query hints are the same as the table hints:

- ▶ LOOP JOIN

- ▶ MERGE JOIN

- ▶ HASH JOIN

If you've also specified a join hint for a specific pair of tables, the table-level hints specified must be compatible with the query-level join hint.

Miscellaneous Hints

The following miscellaneous hints can be used to override various query operations:

- ▶ **FORCE ORDER**—This option tells the Query Optimizer to join the tables in the order in which they are listed in the FROM clause and not to determine the optimal join order.

- ▶ **FAST *n***—This hint instructs SQL Server to optimize the query to return the first *n* rows as quickly as possible, even if the overall throughput is reduced. In other words, it improves response time at the expense of total query execution time. This option generally influences the Query Optimizer to retrieve data using a nonclustered index that matches the ORDER BY clause of a query instead of using a different access method that would require a sort operation first to return rows in the specified order. After *n* number of rows have been returned, the query continues execution normally to produce its full result set.

- ▶ **ROBUST PLAN**—This option forces the Query Optimizer to attempt a plan that works for the maximum potential row size, even if it means degrading performance. If you have very wide VARCHAR columns, some types of query plans might create intermediate tables, and if any of the internal operations need to store and process rows in

30

these intermediate tables, some rows might exceed SQL Server's row size limit. If this happens, SQL Server generates an error during query execution. When the ROBUST PLAN hint is specified, the Query Optimizer does not consider any plans that might encounter this problem.

▶ **MAXDOP** *number*—This hint overrides the server-level configuration setting for max degree of parallelism for the current query in which the hint is specified.

▶ **KEEP PLAN**—When this hint is specified, it forces the Query Optimizer to relax the estimated recompile threshold for a query. The estimated recompile threshold is the point at which a query is automatically recompiled when the estimated number of indexed column changes have been made to a table by updates, inserts, or deletes. Specifying KEEP PLAN ensures that the query is not recompiled as frequently when there are multiple updates to a table. This option is useful primarily for queries whose execution plan stays in memory, such as for stored procedures. An example of when you might want to specify this option is for a stored procedure that does a lot of work with temporary tables, which can lead to frequent recompilations of the execution plan for the stored procedure.

▶ **KEEPFIXED PLAN**—This query hint tells the Query Optimizer not to recompile the query plan when there are changes in statistics or modifications to indexed columns used by the query via updates, deletes, or inserts. When this option is specified, the query is recompiled only if the schema of the underlying tables is changed or sp_recompile is executed against those tables.

▶ **EXPAND VIEWS**—The hint tells the Query Optimizer not to consider any indexed view as a substitute for any part of the query and to force the view to be expanded into its underlying query. This hint essentially prevents direct use of indexed views in the query plan.

▶ **MAXRECURSION** *number*—This hint specifies the maximum number of recursions allowed for the common table expression query, where *number* is an integer between 0 and 32767. When 0 is specified, no limit is applied. If this option is not specified, the default limit for the server is 100. For more information on common table expressions and recursive queries, see Chapter 35, "What's New for Transact-SQL in SQL Server 2005."

▶ **RECOMPILE**—This hint forces SQL Server to not keep the execution plan generated for the query in the plan cache after it executes. This forces a new plan to be generated the next time the same or a similar query plan is executed. RECOMPILE is useful for queries with variable values that vary widely each time they are compiled and executed. This hint can be used for individual statements within a stored procedure in place of the global WITH RECOMPILE option when you only want a subset of queries inside the stored procedure to be recompiled rather than all of them.

▶ **OPTIMIZE FOR (@***variable_name*** =** ***literal_constant*** [, ...***n***])**—This hint instructs SQL Server to use a specified value to optimize the SARGs for a local variable that is otherwise unknown when the query is compiled and optimized. The value is used only during query optimization and not during query execution. `OPTIMIZE FOR` can help improve optimization by allowing the Query Optimizer to use the statistics histogram rather than index densities to estimate the rows that match the local variable. or can be used when you create plan guides.

▶ **USE PLAN N'*xml_plan*'**—This hint instructs SQL Server to use an existing query plan for a query as specified by the designated *xml_plan*. The USE PLAN query hint can be used for queries whose plans result in slow execution times but for which you know better plans exist.

> **NOTE**
>
> Optimizer hints are not always executed. For example, the Query Optimizer is likely to ignore a HASH UNION hint for a query using the UNION ALL statement. Because UNION ALL means to return all rows whether there are duplicates or not, you don't need to hash these values to determine uniqueness and remove duplicates, so the normal concatenation is likely to still take place.

Using the USE PLAN **Query Hint**

The new USE PLAN query hint in SQL Server 2005 can be used to encourage the Query Optimizer to use the specified XML query plan for processing the query. This option provides more control over influencing the execution of a query than is possible with the other available query hints, such as FORCE ORDER, LOOP JOIN, and KEEP PLAN. None of these options individually are powerful enough to influence the Query Optimizer to consistently choose a particular query plan, especially when the referenced table row counts, statistics, indexes, and other attributes of the environment change.

You specify the USE PLAN query hint in the OPTION clause and provide it with a showplan in XML format. Listing 30.5 provides an example of the USE PLAN hint being specified to for a merge join for a simple query that consists of a join between two tables. (Note: For the sake of space, the full XML plan has been truncated.)

LISTING 30.5   Specifying the USE PLAN Query Option

```
select st.stor_name, s.ord_date
   from sales s join stores st on s.stor_id = st.stor_id
   WHERE st.state = 'NY'
OPTION (USE PLAN N'
<ShowPlanXML xmlns:xsi="http://www.w3.org/2001/XMLSchema-instance"
xmlns:xsd="http://www.w3.org/2001/XMLSchema" Version="1.0" Build="9.00.2047.00"
xmlns="http://schemas.microsoft.com/sqlserver/2004/07/showplan">
  <BatchSequence>
    <Batch>
      <Statements>
        <StmtSimple StatementCompId="1" StatementEstRows="10723.8" StatementId="1"
```

30

LISTING 30.5   Continued

```
StatementOptmLevel="FULL" StatementSubTreeCost="5.01066"
 StatementText="select st.stor_name, s.ord_date&#xD;&#xA;
   from sales s inner merge join stores st on s.stor_id = st.stor_id&#xD;&#xA;
   and st.state = ''NY''&#xD;&#xA;" StatementType="SELECT">
        <StatementSetOptions ANSI_NULLS="false" ANSI_PADDING="false"
ANSI_WARNINGS="false" ARITHABORT="true" CONCAT_NULL_YIELDS_NULL="false"
NUMERIC_ROUNDABORT="false" QUOTED_IDENTIFIER="false" />
        <QueryPlan DegreeOfParallelism="0" CachedPlanSize="11">
          <RelOp AvgRowSize="39" EstimateCPU="0.439461" EstimateIO="0.319573"
EstimateRebinds="0" EstimateRewinds="0" EstimateRows="10723.8"
LogicalOp="Inner Join" NodeId="0" Parallel="false"
PhysicalOp="Merge Join" EstimatedTotalSubtreeCost="5.01066">
…
            </Merge>
          </RelOp>
        </QueryPlan>
      </StmtSimple>
    </Statements>
   </Batch>
  </BatchSequence>
</ShowPlanXML>')
```

To obtain an XML-formatted query plan, which you can provide to the USE PLAN query hint, SQL Server 2005 provides the following methods:

▶ Using the SET SHOWPLAN_XML and SET STATISTICS XML session options

▶ Querying the plan column of the sys.dm_exec_query_plan dynamic management view for a cached query plan

▶ Using SQL Server Profiler and capturing either the Showplan XML, Showplan XML Statistics Profile, or Showplan XML For Query Compile event classes

---

NOTE

When the XML query plan contains a character string in single quotation marks ('), the quotation marks must be escaped by a second quotation mark before using the plan with the USE PLAN query hint. For example, a plan that contains WHERE A.varchar = 'This is a string' must be escaped by modifying the code to WHERE A.varchar = ''This is a string'', or it will generate a syntax error when submitted for execution.

You may choose to use the USE PLAN hint for queries where the execution plan chosen leads to slow execution times but for which you know a better plan exists. A common scenario where this may occur is for queries that might have executed well in an earlier version of SQL Server but that perform poorly under an upgraded version. Another scenario could be a complex query that involves multiple tables where the compiled or recompiled query plan generated is occasionally not optimal possibly as a result of out-of-date or missing statistics in any of the underlying tables or because of complex constructs in the query that cause the Query Optimizer to inaccurately estimate the size of the intermediate query results.

The USE PLAN query hint can be specified only for SELECT and SELECT INTO statements. Also, you can force only query plans that can be produced by the Query Optimizer's normal optimization strategy.

Because the USE PLAN option requires that the XML showplan be hard-coded in the SQL statement itself, it is not a viable solution for deployed or third-party applications where it may not be possible or feasible to modify the queries directly. It's really useful only as a tool for troubleshooting poorly running queries. To force query plans to apply query hints to queries when you cannot or do not want to directly change the application or SQL code, you should consider using plan guides.

Using Plan Guides

At times, you may find it necessary to use query hints to improve the performance of queries for a particular query or a small set of queries. While this may be easy to do when you have access to the application code, often, the particular queries to be modified are embedded within a third-party application, and alteration of the queries themselves is virtually impossible. Also, if you start hard-coding query hints in your application code, changing them as necessary when data volumes change or when upgrading to a new version of SQL Server can be a difficult undertaking.

The new plan guides feature in SQL Server 2005 provides an ideal solution for such scenarios by offering another mechanism for injecting query hints into the original query without having to modify the query itself. The plan guides mechanism uses an internal lookup system table, based on information in the sys.plan_guides catalog view, to map the original query to a substitute query or query template.

As described earlier in this chapter, when a SQL statement is submitted, it is first compared against the cached plans to check for a match. If a match exists, the cached query plan is used to execute the query. If no cached plan exists for the query, the Query Optimizer next looks for a match against the set of existing plan guides, if any, stored in the current database for a match. If an active plan guide is found that matches the SQL statement, the original matching statement is substituted with the one from the plan guide, the query plan is compiled and cached, and the query is executed using the plan generated from the plan guide.

Queries that can benefit from plan guides are generally queries that are parameter based and those that are likely performing poorly because they use cached query plans whose parameter values do not represent a more representative scenario.

30

The plan guides feature essentially consists of two stored procedures to create, drop, enable, and disable plan guides and the sys.plan_guides metadata view that describes the stored plan guides. Plan guides are created and administered by using the two system stored procedures:

▶ sp_create_plan_guide

▶ sp_control_plan_guide

The syntax for these procedures is as follows:

```
sp_create_plan_guide [ @name = ] N'plan_guide_name'
    , [ @stmt = ] N'statement_text'
    , [ @type = ] N'{ OBJECT ¦ SQL ¦ TEMPLATE }'
    , [ @module_or_batch = ]
    {
                    N'[ schema_name. ] object_name'
        ¦ N'batch_text'
        ¦ NULL
    }
    , [ @params = ] { N'@parameter_name data_type [ ,...n ]' ¦ NULL }
    , [ @hints = ] { N'OPTION ( query_hint [ ,...n ] )' ¦ NULL }

sp_control_plan_guide [ @operation = ] N'<control_option>'
  [ , [ @name = ] N'plan_guide_name' ]

<control_option>::=
{
    DROP
  ¦ DROP ALL
  ¦ DISABLE
  ¦ DISABLE ALL
  ¦ ENABLE
  ¦ ENABLE ALL
}
```

Creating Plan Guides

Plan guides can be created to match queries that are executed in the following contexts:

▶ An OBJECT plan guide matches queries that execute in the context of T-SQL stored procedures, scalar functions, or multistatement table-valued functions.

▶ A SQL plan guide matches queries that execute in the context of ad hoc T-SQL statements and batches that are not part of a stored procedure or other compiled database object.

▶ A TEMPLATE plan guide matches ad hoc queries that parameterize to a specified form. These plan guides are used to override the current SET PARAMETERIZATION database option.

In the sp_create_plan_guide statement, you specify the query that you want optimized and provide the OPTION clause with the query hints necessary to optimize the query in the manner desired. When the query executes, SQL Server matches the query to the plan guide and applies the OPTION clause to the query at runtime.

The plan guide can specify any of the following query hints individually or combined with others, when applicable:

▶ {HASH ¦ ORDER} GROUP

▶ {CONCAT ¦ HASH ¦ MERGE} UNION

▶ {LOOP ¦ MERGE ¦ HASH} JOIN

▶ FAST *n*

▶ FORCE ORDER

▶ MAXDOP *number_of_processors*

▶ OPTIMIZE FOR (*@variable_name* = *literal_constant*) [,...*n*]

▶ RECOMPILE

▶ ROBUST PLAN

▶ KEEP PLAN

▶ KEEPFIXED PLAN

▶ EXPAND VIEWS

▶ MAXRECURSION *number*

▶ USE PLAN *<xmlplan>*

▶ PARAMETERIZATION { SIMPLE ¦ FORCED }

The PARAMETERIZATION { SIMPLE ¦ FORCED } query hint can be used only within a plan guide, and it specifies whether a query is parameterized as part of compiling a query plan. This option overrides the current setting of the PARAMETERIZATION option set at the database level.

Listing 30.6 provides an example of a plan guide created for a simple SQL statement.

30

LISTING 30.6   Creating a Plan Guide for a Simple SQL Statement

```
sp_create_plan_guide @name = N'PlanGuide1',
@stmt = N'SELECT COUNT(*) AS Total
FROM dbo.sales s, dbo.titles t
WHERE s.title_id = t.title_id
and t.pubdate BETWEEN ''1/1/1992'' AND ''1/1/1994''
',
@type = N'SQL',
@module_or_batch = NULL,
@params = NULL,
@hints = N'OPTION (HASH JOIN)'
```

In order for plan guides of type 'SQL' or 'TEMPLATE' to match a query successfully, the values for *batch_text* and *@parameter_name data_type [,…n]* must be provided in exactly the same format as their counterparts submitted by the application. Specifically, they must match character-for-character, including comments and whitespaces.

TIP

When creating plan guides, be careful to specify the query in the @stmt parameter and any parameter names and values in the @params parameter exactly as they are received from the application. The best way to ensure this is by capturing the batch or statement text from SQL Server Profiler. (See Chapter 5 for more information on using SQL Server Profiler to capture SQL queries.) Also, as with the XML query plans passed to the USE PLAN query hint, single-quoted literal values, such as '1/1/2000', need to be delimited with single quotes escaped by additional single quotes, as shown in Listing 30.6.

Managing Plan Guides

You use the sp_control_plan_guide stored procedure to enable, disable, or drop a plan guide. The following example drops the plan guide created in Listing 30.6:

```
sp_control_plan_guide N'DROP', N'PlanGuide1'
```

To execute sp_control_plan_guide on a plan guide of type OBJECT (for example, a plan guide created for a stored procedure), you must have at least ALTER permission on the object that is referenced by the plan guide. For all other plan guides, you must have at least ALTER DATABASE permission. Attempting to drop or alter a function or stored procedure that is referenced by a plan guide results in an error.

The sys.plan_guides Catalog View

All plan guides are stored in the sys.plan_guides database system catalog view. You can get information about the plan guides defined in a database by running a query against the sys.plan_guides catalog view, as in the following example:

```
select name, is_disabled, scope_type_desc, scope_object_id,
       parameters, hints, query_text from sys.plan_guides
```

Table 30.2 describes the columns in the `sys.plan_guides` catalog view.

TABLE 30.2   `sys.plan_guides` Columns

Column Name	Description
plan_guide_id	Unique identifier of the plan guide.
Name	Name of the plan guide.
create_date	Date and time the plan guide was created.
modify_date	Date the plan guide was last modified.
is_disabled	1 = disabled and 0 = enabled.
query_text	Text of the query on which the plan guide is created.
scope_type	Identifies the scope of the plan guide: 1 = OBJECT, 2 = SQL, and 3 = TEMPLATE.
scope_type_desc	Description of scope of the plan guide: OBJECT, SQL, or TEMPLATE.
scope_object_id	If the scope type is OBJECT, the object_id of the object defining the scope of the plan guide; otherwise, NULL.
scope_batch	If scope_type is SQL, the text of the SQL batch. If NULL, either batch type is not SQL or scope_type is SQL, and the value of query_text applies.
parameters	The string defining the list of parameters associated with the plan guide. If NULL, no parameter list is associated with the plan guide.
hints	The query OPTION hints associated with the plan guide.

Plan Guide Best Practices

Following are some of the recommended best practices for using the USE PLAN query hint and the plan guides feature:

▶ The USE PLAN query hint and plan guides should be used only when other standard query tuning options, such as index tuning and ensuring current statistics, have been extensively tried and have failed to produce the necessary results. Once a query plan is forced by using either the USE PLAN query hint or a plan guide, it prevents the Query Optimizer from adapting to changing data distributions, new indexes, or improved query execution algorithms in successive SQL Server releases or service packs.

▶ You need to be sure to have a full understanding of query optimization and of the implications and long-term ramifications of forcing query plans.

▶ You should try to force only a small fraction of the workload. If you find you are forcing more than a few dozen queries, you should check whether there are other issues with the configuration that could be limiting performance, including insufficient system resources, incorrect database configuration settings, missing indexes, poorly written queries, and other factors.

30

▶ It is not advisable to attempt to code by hand or modify the XML showplan that is specified in the USE PLAN query hint. You should capture and use a plan produced by SQL Server itself. The XML showplan is a lengthy and complex listing, and improper changes could prevent it from identically matching one of the Query Optimizer generated plans which would result in the USE PLAN hint being ignored.

▶ The USE PLAN query hint should not be directly embedded into the application code because that would make the maintenance of the application across query plan and SQL Server version changes difficult to manage. Also, embedding USE PLAN directly into the query generally prevents the plan for the query from being cacheable. The USE PLAN hint is intended primarily for ad-hoc performance tuning and test purposes, and for use with the plan guides feature.

▶ The plan guides created for an application should be well documented and regularly backed up because they constitute an integral part of the application's performance tuning. You should also retain the scripts that you used to create plan guides and treat them as you would other source code for an application.

▶ After being created, a plan guide should be tested to make sure that it is being applied to the intended queries.

Verifying That a Plan Guide Is Being Applied

When you have a plan guide defined, you might want to verify that the application query is making use of the plan guide. The following steps describe a method of confirming whether a plan guide is being used:

1. After creating the plan guide, run SQL Server Profiler and configure it to capture the query text and XML execution plan for the application and the query in question and start the Profiler trace.

2. Run your application and cause it to invoke the query in question.

3. Stop the profiler trace and collect the query plan by right-clicking the Showplan XML Statistics Profile event that corresponds to the query and then selecting the Extract Event Data option.

4. Save the event data to a file.

5. Open the Showplan.xml file in any text file viewer or Internet Explorer to examine the XML code.

6. If the plan guide was used to generate the query plan, the XML showplan output contains the PlanGuideDB and PlanGuideName tags, as shown in the following example:

```
<ShowPlanXML xmlns=
"http://schemas.microsoft.com/sqlserver/2004/07/showplan"
 Version="1.0" Build="9.00.1282.00">
  <BatchSequence>
```

```
<Batch>
  <Statements>
    <StmtSimple PlanGuideDB="bigpubs2005"
PlanGuideName="PlanGuide1">
…
    </StmtSimple>
  </Statements>
</Batch>
  </BatchSequence>
</ShowPlanXML>
```

Forced Parameterizaion

In SQL Server 2005, if a SQL statement is executed without parameters, the Query Optimizer parameterizes the statement internally to increase the possibility of matching it against an existing execution plan. This process is called *simple parameterization*, sometimes referred to as auto-parameterization. Simple parameterization is somewhat limited in that it can only parameterize a relatively small number of queries which match a small number of very simple and strictly defined query templates. For example, simple parameterization is not possible for queries that contain any of the following query elements:

▶ References to more than one table

▶ IN clauses or OR expressions

▶ UNION

▶ Any query hints

▶ DISTINCT

▶ TOP

▶ Subqueries

▶ GROUP BY

▶ Not equal (<> or !=) comparisons

▶ References to functions

SQL Server 2005 provides the ability to override the default simple parameterization behavior of SQL Server and provide parameterization for more complex queries by specifying that all SELECT, INSERT, UPDATE, and DELETE statements in a database be implicitly parameterized when they are compiled by the Query Optimizer. This is enabled by setting the PARAMETERIZATION option to FORCED in the ALTER DATABASE statement:

```
ALTER DATABASE dbname SET PARAMETERIZATION {FORCED ¦ SIMPLE}
```

Setting the PARAMETERIZATION option is an online operation that can be issued at any time and requires no database-level exclusive locks.

30

Forced parameterization may improve the performance of queries for certain databases by reducing the frequency of query compilations and recompilations. Essentially, forced parameterization provides the query plan reuse benefits of parameterized queries without requiring you to rewrite a single line of application code. Databases that may benefit from forced parameterization are generally databases that support OLTP-type applications that experience high volumes of concurrent queries, such as point-of-sale applications.

When the PARAMETERIZATION FORCED option is enabled, any literal value that appears in a SELECT, INSERT, UPDATE, or DELETE statement, submitted in any form, is converted to a parameter during query compilation. The exceptions are literals that appear in the following query constructs:

- ▶ INSERT...EXECUTE statements

- ▶ Statements inside the bodies of stored procedures, triggers, or user-defined functions (SQL Server already reuses query plans for these routines.)

- ▶ Prepared statements that have already been parameterized by the client-side application

- ▶ Statements inside a T-SQL cursor

- ▶ Any statement that is run in a context where ANSI_PADDING or ANSI_NULLS is set to OFF

- ▶ Statements that contain more than 2,097 literals that are eligible for parameterization

- ▶ Statements that reference variables, such as WHERE st.state = @state

- ▶ Statements that contain the RECOMPILE or OPTIMIZE FOR query hints

- ▶ Statements that contain a COMPUTE clause

- ▶ Statements that contain a WHERE CURRENT OF clause

If an execution plan for a query is cached, you can determine whether the query was parameterized by referencing the sql column of the sys.syscacheobjects DMV. If a query is parameterized, the names and data types of parameters are listed in this column before the text of the submitted SQL (for example, @1 tinyint).

Guidelines for Using Forced Parameterization

Consider the following guidelines when determining whether to enable forced parameterization for a database:

- ▶ Forced parameterization, in effect, changes the literal constants in a query to parameters when the query is compiled, and thus, the Query Optimizer might choose suboptimal plans for queries. For example, the Query Optimizer may be less likely to match the query to an indexed view or an index on a computed column. It may also choose suboptimal plans for queries posed on partitioned tables and distributed partitioned views. Forced parameterization should not be used for environments that rely heavily on indexed views and indexes on computed columns.

▶ Enabling the PARAMETERIZATION FORCED option causes all query plans for the database to be flushed from the plan cache.

▶ Generally, the PARAMETERIZATION FORCED option should only be used by experienced database administrators after determining that doing this does not adversely affect performance.

If forced parameterization is enabled and you want to override this behavior and have simple parameterization used for a single query and any others that are syntactically equivalent but differ only in their parameter values, you can use plan guides and specify PARAMETERIZATION SIMPLE when creating the plan guide. Conversely, rather than enabling PARAMETERIZATION FORCED for an entire database, you can use plan guides and specify the PARAMETERIZATION FORCED query option only for a specific set of syntactically equivalent queries that you have determined would benefit from forced parameterization.

Limiting Query Plan Execution with the Query Governor

An interesting tool available in SQL Server 2005 is the query governor. Because SQL Server uses a cost-based Query Optimizer, the cost of executing a given query is always estimated before the query is actually executed. The query governor enables you to set a cost threshold to prevent certain long-running queries from being executed. This is not so much a tuning tool as it is a performance problem prevention tool.

For example, if you have an application with an ad hoc reporting front end, you have no way of controlling what the user is going to request from the database and the type of query generated. The query governor allows you to prevent a runaway query from executing and using up valuable CPU and memory resources by processing a poorly formed query. You can set the query governor cost limit for the current user session by setting the session-level property QUERY_GOVERNOR_COST_LIMIT:

```
SET QUERY_GOVERNOR_COST_LIMIT value
```

The value specified is the maximum length of time, in seconds, a query is allowed to run. If the Query Optimizer estimates that the query would take longer than the specified value, SQL Server does not execute it.

Although the option is specified in seconds, it is a relative value that corresponds to the estimated subtree cost, as calculated by the Query Optimizer. In other words, if you set the query governor cost limit to 100, it prevents the execution of any queries whose estimated subtree cost is greater than 100 seconds. The estimated subtree cost time is based on the query cost algorithm in SQL Server and might not map exactly to how long the query actually takes to run on your own system. The actual runtime depends on a number of factors—CPU speed, I/O speed, network speed, the number of rows returned over the network, and so on. You need to correlate the Query Optimizer runtime estimate to how long the query actually takes to run on your system to set the query governor cost limit to a value related to actual query runtime.

The best way to figure out how to set the query governor is to run your queries with the STATISTICS PROFILE and STATISTICS TIME session settings enabled. (These settings are discussed in more detail in Chapter 31.) You then compare the values in the TotalSubtree Cost column for the first row of the STATISTICS PROFILE output with the elapsed time displayed by STATISTICS TIME for your query. If you do this for a number of your queries, you may be able to come up with an average correlation of the actual runtimes with the Query Optimizer's estimated query cost. For example, if the average cost estimate is 30 seconds and the actual runtimes are 15 seconds, you may need to double the setting for query governor cost limit to correspond to the actual execution time threshold; in other words, if you want the threshold to be 60 seconds for this example, you would want to set the query governor threshold to 120.

To configure a query governor threshold for all user connections, you can also set it at the server level. In SSMS, you right-click the server in the Object Browser and choose Properties from the menu. In the Server Properties dialog, you select the Connections page. Then you enable the Use Query Governor to Prevent Long-Running Queries check box and specify the desired cost threshold (see Figure 30.28). The cost threshold is specified in the same units as specified for the QUERY_GOVERNOR_COST_LIMIT session setting.

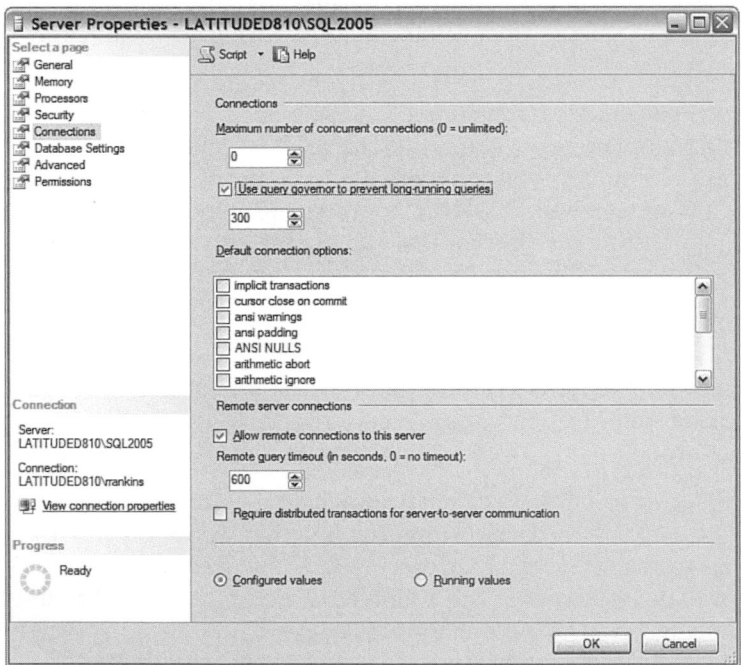

FIGURE 30.28   Configuring the query governor settings in the SQL Server Properties dialog box.

Alternatively, you can configure the serverwide query governor setting by using `sp_configure`:

```
sp_configure query governor cost limit, 100
```

Summary

The SQL Server Query Optimizer has continuously improved over the years, taking advantage of new techniques and algorithms to improve its capability to find the most efficient execution plan. Understanding how queries are optimized and what information the Query Optimizer uses to generate and select an execution plan will help you write more efficient queries and choose better indexes. To help the Query Optimizer, you should at least try to write queries that can be optimized effectively by avoiding the common query optimization problems discussed in this chapter.

The majority of the time, the Query Optimizer chooses the most efficient query plan. When it doesn't, it might be because of problems with the way the query itself is written, out-of-date or unavailable statistics, poor index design, or other common query performance problems, as discussed in this chapter. Still, on occasion, the Query Optimizer may make the wrong choice for an execution plan. When you suspect that the Query Optimizer is making the wrong decision, you can use SQL Server's table and Query Optimizer hints and the new plan guide feature to override the Query Optimizer's decisions. However, before arbitrarily applying these hints, you should analyze the queries fully to try to determine why the Query Optimizer is choosing a particular plan. To aid you in this effort, SQL Server provides a number of tools to analyze the query plans generated and determine the source of the problem. These tools are described in Chapter 31.

Query Analysis

IN THIS CHAPTER

▶ What's New in Query Analysis

▶ Query Analysis in SSMS

▶ SSMS Client Statistics

▶ Using the SHOWPLAN SET Statement Options

▶ Using sys.dm_exec_query_plan

▶ Query Statistics

▶ Query Analysis with SQL Server Profiler

SQL Server's cost-based Query Optimizer typically does a good job of determining the best query plan for processing a query. At times, however, you might be a little bit skeptical about the plan that the Query Optimizer generates or want to understand why it is choosing a specific plan. At the least, you will want to know the specifics about the query plans the Query Optimizer is generating, such as the following:

▶ Is the Query Optimizer using the indexes you have defined, or is it performing table or index scans?

▶ Are work tables being used to process the query?

▶ What join strategy is being applied?

▶ What join order is the Query Optimizer using?

▶ What statistics and cost estimates is the Query Optimizer using to make its decisions?

▶ How do the Query Optimizer's estimates compare to actual I/O costs and row counts?

Fortunately, SQL Server provides some tools to help you answer these questions. The primary tool is SQL Server Management Studio (SSMS). SSMS provides a number of features for monitoring the estimated or actual execution plan as well as viewing the actual runtime statistics for your queries. This chapter looks at the following features:

▶ Displaying the graphical execution plan

▶ Displaying the server trace

▶ Displaying client statistics

Although SSMS is a powerful and useful tool for query analysis, SQL Server still provides some text-based query analysis utilities as well. These tools are also described in this chapter, along with tips on how to use them most effectively.

> **NOTE**
>
> Note that the examples presented in this chapter use the `bigpubs2005` database as most examples require sufficient data to demonstrate many of the more interesting query plans. A copy of the `bigpubs2005` database is available on the web (www.samspublishing.com). Instructions on how to obtain and install the database are presented in the Introduction.

What's New in Query Analysis

The biggest change in query analysis for SQL Server 2005 is the replacement of SQL Server 2000's Query Analyzer with SSMS. While SSMS provides the same capabilities as Query Analyzer, along with some new features, some of the features and settings you may be familiar with in Query Analyzer are available under different settings or may function slightly differently in SSMS.

One of the key new features provided by SSMS is the ability to save graphical execution plans as XML files. This provides the ability to keep a history of your query performance and execution plans over time; you can use these plans to compare performance differences as the data volumes and SQL Server activity levels change over time. You can also share your graphical plans with others who can load the XML files into SSMS to view the graphical execution plans and assist in the query analysis.

In addition to the new graphical query plans available in SSMS, SQL Server 2005 also provides two new SET options that can be specified to generate showplan information: `SET SHOWPLAN_XML` and `SET STATISTICS XML`. These are the new counterparts to the `SET SHOWPLAN ALL` and `SET STATISTICS PROFILE` options. The key difference is that the information is generated as a well-formed XML document, which, like the graphical execution plans, can be saved to a file and then viewed as a graphical execution plan in SSMS.

SQL Server Profiler has also undergone a major facelift in SQL Server 2005, and one of the improvements related to query analysis is the ability to capture the XML showplan information during a SQL trace. SQL Server Profiler provides the ability to view the graphical execution plans in Profiler itself, as well as the ability to save the XML execution plans to a file that can be loaded back into SSMS for further query analysis.

Another new feature provided by SQL Server is dynamic management views (DMVs). DMVs return server state information that can be used monitor and diagnose database engine issues and help tune performance. One DMV that is particularly useful for query analysis is `sys.dm_exec_query_plan`. This DMV returns the showplan information for any T-SQL batch whose query execution plan currently resides in the plan cache. The `sys.dm_exec_query_plan` DMV is most useful for retrieving the execution plan information for currently long-running processes to help diagnose why they may be running slowly.

Query Analysis in SSMS

The main tool for query analysis in SQL Server 2005 is the Query Editor available in SSMS. The SSMS Query Editor can produce a graphical execution plan that provides analysis information in an intuitive and easy-to-view manner. You can display the execution plan in one of two ways: the estimated execution plan or the actual execution plan.

You can display an estimated execution plan for the entire contents of the query window, or for any highlighted SQL code in the query window, by choosing Display Estimated Execution Plan from the Query menu. You can also invoke it by using the Ctrl+L keyboard shortcut. This feature is useful for displaying and analyzing execution plans for long-running queries or queries with large result sets without having to actually run the query and wait for the results to be returned.

You can also display the actual execution plans for queries as they are executed by selecting the Include Actual Execution Plan option from the Query menu or by using the Ctrl+M keyboard shortcut. This option is a toggle that remains on until you select it again to disable it. When this option is enabled, your query results are displayed, along with an Execution Plan tab in the Results panel. You click the Execution Plan tab to display the execution plan for the query or queries that are executed. This option is especially useful when you want to execute commands and compare the actual runtime and I/O statistics with the execution plan estimates. (These statistics can be displayed with the SET STATISTICS options described in the "Statistics" section, later in this chapter.)

The graphical execution plans display a series of nodes that are connected by lines. Each node is represented by an icon, which indicates the logical and physical operator executed for that node. The execution plan flows from right to left and top to bottom, eventually ending at a statement icon, which indicates the type of query that generated the execution plan. This query might be a SELECT, INSERT, UPDATE, TABCREATE, and so on. The arrows between the icons indicate the movement of rows between operators. If the query window contains multiple statements, multiple query execution plans are displayed in the Execution Plan tab. For each query in the batch that is analyzed and displayed, the relative cost of the query is displayed as a percentage of the total cost of the batch.

To interpret and analyze the execution plan output, you start with the farthest icon on the right and read each ToolTip as you move left and down through the tree. Each icon in the query tree is called a *node*, and icons displayed under each other participate in the same level of the execution tree.

> **NOTE**
>
> The displayed width of each of the arrowhead lines in the graphical execution plan can indicate the relative cost, in estimated number of rows, and the row size of the data moving through the query. The smaller the width of the arrow, the smaller the estimated row count or row size. Moving the cursor over the line displays a ToolTip that indicates the estimated row count and row size.

Figure 31.1 shows a sample SSMS graphical execution plan window.

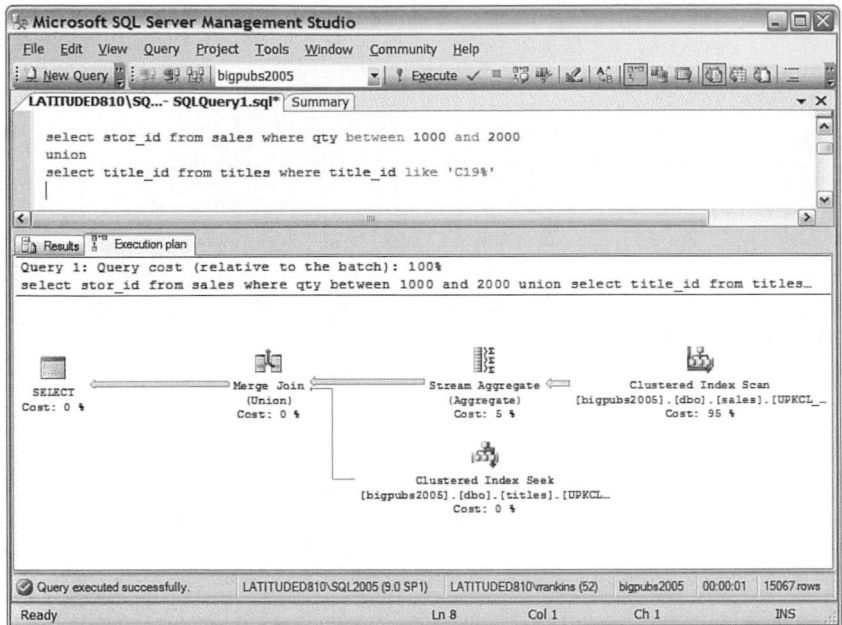

FIGURE 31.1   SSMS graphical execution plan.

The remainder of this section describes the icons and information provided in the graphical execution plan.

Execution Plan ToolTips

When a graphical execution plan is presented in the Query Analyzer, you can get more information about each node in the execution plan by moving the mouse cursor over one of the icons. ToolTips for estimated execution plans are slightly different from the ToolTips displayed for an execution plan that is generated when a query is actually executed. The ToolTip that is displayed for an estimated execution plan provides the following information:

▶ **Physical Operation**—Lists the physical operation that is being performed for the node, such as a Clustered Index Scan, Index Seek, Aggregate, Hash or Nested Loop Join, and so on.

▶ **Logical Operation**—Lists the logical operation that corresponds with the physical operation, such as the logical operation of a union being physically performed as a merge join. The logical operator, if different from the physical operator, is listed in parentheses below the physical operator in the icon text in the graphical execution plan. Essentially, the logical operators describe the relational operation used to process a statement, while the physical operation describes how it is being performed.

31

▶ **Estimated I/O Cost**—The estimated relative I/O cost for the operation. Preferably, this value should be as low as possible.

▶ **Estimated CPU Cost**—The estimated relative CPU cost for the operation.

▶ **Estimated Operator Cost**—The estimated cost to execute the physical operation. For best performance, you want this value as low as possible.

▶ **Estimated Number of Rows**—The estimated number of rows to be output by the operation and passed on to the parent operation.

▶ **Estimated Row Size**—The estimated average row size of the rows being passed through the operator.

▶ **Estimated Subtree Cost**—The estimated cumulative total cost of this operation and all child operations preceding it in the same subtree.

▶ **Object**—Indicates which database object is being accessed by the operation being performed by the current node.

▶ **Predicate**—Indicates the search predicate specified for the object in the original query.

▶ **Seek Predicates**—When an index seek is being performed, this indicates the search predicate that is being used in the seek against the index.

▶ **Output List**—Indicates which columns of data are being returned by the operation.

▶ **Ordered**—Indicates whether the rows are being retrieved via an index in sorted order.

▶ **Node ID**—Unique identifier of the node within the execution plan.

Some operators may also include the Actual Rebinds and Actual Rewinds counts. When an operator is on the outer side of a loop join, Actual Rebinds equals 1 and Actual Rewinds equals 0. If an operator is on the inner side of a loop join, the sum of the number of rebinds and rewinds should equal the number of rows returned by the table on the outer side of the join. A rebind means that one or more of the correlated parameters of the join changed and the inner side must be reevaluated. A rewind means that none of the correlated parameters changed and the prior inner result set may be reused.

> **NOTE**
>
> Depending on the type of operator and other query characteristics, not all the preceding items are displayed in the ToolTip.

The ToolTips for an execution plan that is generated when the query is actually executed display the same information as the estimated execution plan, but the ToolTip also displays the actual number of rows returned by the operation. This information is useful in determining the effectiveness of the statistics on the column or index because it helps you compare how closely the estimated row count matches the actual row count. If a significant difference exists (significant being a relative term), you might need to update the statistics and possibly increase the sample size used when the statistics are updated to generate more accurate statistics.

Figure 31.2 displays a sample ToolTip. Notice the difference between the Estimated Number of Rows value (8325.01) and the Actual Number of Rows value (195). This indicates an obvious issue with missing or out-of-date statistics.

Table Scan	
Scan rows from a table.	
Physical Operation	Table Scan
Logical Operation	Table Scan
Actual Number of Rows	195
Estimated I/O Cost	0.923125
Estimated CPU Cost	0.185754
Estimated Operator Cost	1.10888 (81%)
Estimated Subtree Cost	1.10888
Estimated Number of Rows	8325.01
Estimated Row Size	51 B
Actual Rebinds	0
Actual Rewinds	0
Ordered	False
Node ID	2

Predicate
[bigpubs2005].[dbo].[new_sales].[ord_date] as
[s].[ord_date]='1993-01-01 00:00:00.000'
Object
[bigpubs2005].[dbo].[new_sales] [s]
Output List
[bigpubs2005].[dbo].[new_sales].stor_id,
[bigpubs2005].[dbo].[new_sales].ord_num,
[bigpubs2005].[dbo].[new_sales].ord_date,
[bigpubs2005].[dbo].[new_sales].qty,
[bigpubs2005].[dbo].[new_sales].payterms,
[bigpubs2005].[dbo].[new_sales].title_id
Warnings
Columns With No Statistics: [bigpubs2005].[dbo].
[new_sales].ord_date

FIGURE 31.2   A ToolTip example.

NOTE

In order to achieve the large difference between the actual row count and the estimated row count as shown in Figure 31.2, the AUTO-CREATE STATISTICS option was disabled for the database. If this option is not disabled, SQL Server will automatically generate the missing statistics on the ord_date column before generating the execution plan. With the column statistics generated, it would likely come up with a better row estimate.

In this example, the ToolTip displays the information for a Table Scan physical operation. The Estimated I/O Cost and Estimated CPU Cost provide critical information about the relative performance of this query. You want these numbers to be as low as possible.

31

The Estimated Subtree Cost displays cumulated costs for this node and any previous nodes that feed into it. This number increases as you move from right to left in the execution plan diagram. For the next-to-last icon for a query execution path (the icon leading into the statement icon), the ToolTip displays the Total Estimated Subtree Cost for the entire query.

> **NOTE**
>
> The total Estimated Subtree Cost that is displayed for the statement icon is the cost that is compared against the Query Governor cost threshold setting, if enabled, to determine whether the query will be allowed to run. For more information on configuring the Query Governor, see Chapter 30, "Understanding Query Optimization."

The Predicate section outlines the predicates and parameters that the query uses. This information is useful in determining how the Query Optimizer is interpreting your search arguments (SARGs) and if they are being interpreted as SARGs that can be optimized effectively.

Putting all the ToolTip information together provides the key to understanding each operation and its potential cost. You can use this information to compare various incarnations of a query to determine whether changes to the query result in improved query plans, and whether the estimated values are consistent with actual values.

> **NOTE**
>
> If the Query Optimizer has issued a warning about one of the execution plan operators, such as missing column statistics or missing join predicates, the icon is displayed with a yellow warning triangle (see Figure 31.3). These warnings indicate a condition that can cause the Query Optimizer to choose a less efficient query plan than otherwise expected. The ToolTip for the operation with the warning icon includes a Warnings item that indicates why the warning was generated.

If you prefer to view the information about a node in an execution tree in more detail and with something more stable than a ToolTip, you can right-click the node and select Properties. This brings up the Properties window, as shown in Figure 31.4.

The Properties window provides all the same information that is available in the ToolTip, and it also provides some more detailed information, along with descriptions of the types of information provided.

Logical and Physical Operator Icons

To better understand the graphical execution plans displayed in SSMS, it helps to be able to recognize what each of the displayed icons represents. This is especially valuable when you need to quickly locate operations that appear out of place for the type of query being executed. The following sections cover the more common logical and physical operators displayed in the Query Analyzer execution plans.

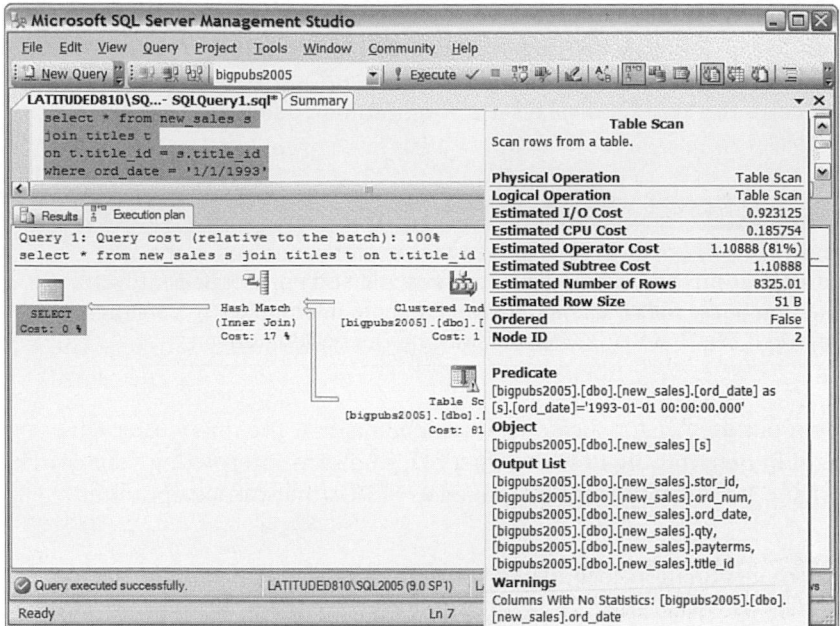

FIGURE 31.3   An example of an execution plan with warnings.

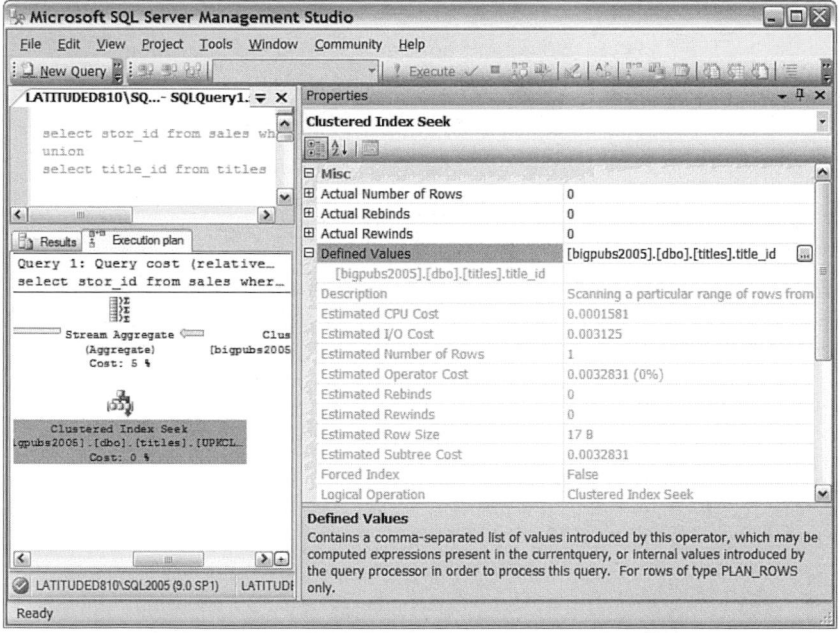

FIGURE 31.4   The query execution plan node properties.

> **NOTE**
>
> For more examples of graphical execution plans, see Chapter 30. In the sections that discuss the different query strategies are examples of the graphical showplans that correspond to the strategies. Many of these provide various examples of the operator icons that are discussed in this session.

Assert

Assert is used to verify a condition, such referential integrity (RI) or check constraint, or to ensure that a scalar subquery returns only a single row. It sort of acts as a roadblock, allowing a result stream to continue only if the check being performed is satisfied. The argument that is displayed in the Assert ToolTip spells out each check being performed.

For example, a deletion from the `titles` table in the `bigpubs2005` database has to be verified to ensure that it doesn't violate referential integrity with the `sales` and `titleauthors` table. The reference constraints need to check that the `title_id` being deleted does not exist in either the `sales` or `titleauthors` tables. If the result of the Assert returns a `NULL`, the stream continues through the query. Figure 31.5 shows the estimated execution plan and ToolTip of the Assert that appears for a delete on `titles`. The Predicate indicates that the reference constraint rejects any case in which the matching foreign key expression that returns from both child tables is `NOT NULL`. Notice that it returns a different value (0 or 1), depending on the table on which the foreign key violation occurs so that the appropriate error message can be displayed.

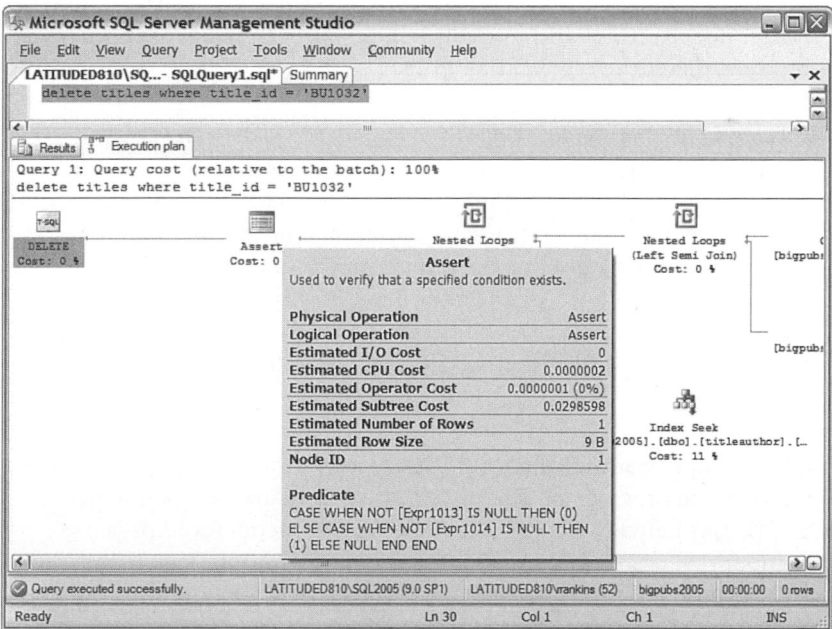

FIGURE 31.5   An Assert example.

Clustered Index Delete [icon], Insert [icon], and Update [icon]

The Clustered Index physical operators Delete, Insert, and Update indicate that one or more rows in the specified clustered index are being deleted, inserted, or updated. The index or indexes affected by the operation are specified in the Object item of the ToolTip. The Predicate indicates which rows are being deleted or which columns are being updated.

Nonclustered Index Delete [icon], Insert [icon], and Update [icon]

Similar to the Clustered Index physical operators Delete, Insert, and Update, the Nonclustered Index physical operators Delete, Insert, and Update indicate that one or more rows in the specified nonclustered index are being deleted, inserted, or updated.

Clustered Index Seek [icon] and Scan [icon]

A Clustered Index Seek is a logical and physical operator that indicates the Query Optimizer is using the clustered index to find the data rows via the index pointers. A Clustered Index Scan (also a logical and physical operator) indicates whether the Query Optimizer is scanning all or a subset of the table or index rows. Note that a table scan against a table with a clustered index displays as a Clustered Index Scan; the Query Optimizer is performing a full scan against all data rows in the table, which are in clustered key order.

Figure 31.6 shows a Clustered Index Seek ToolTip. The ToolTip indicates that the seek is being performed against the UPK_Storeid index on the stores table. The Seek Predicates item indicates the search predicate being used for the lookup against the clustered index, and the Query Optimizer determines that the results will be output in clustered index order, as indicated by the Ordered item indicating true.

Nonclustered Index Scan [icon] and Seek [icon]

A Nonclustered Index Seek is a logical and physical operator that indicates the Query Optimizer is using the nonclustered index to find the data rows via the index pointers. A Nonclustered Index Scan (also a logical and physical operator) indicates whether the Query Optimizer is scanning all or a subset of the nonclustered index rows. The Seek Predicates item in a Nonclustered Index Seek operator identifies the search predicate being used for the lookup against the nonclustered index. The Ordered item in the ToolTip indicates true if the rows will be returned in nonclustered index key order.

Split [icon] and Collapse [icon]

A Split physical and logical operator indicates that the Query Optimizer has decided to break the rows' input from the previous update optimization step into a separate delete and insert operation. The Estimated Number of Rows in the Split icon ToolTips is normally double the input row count, reflecting this two-step operation. If possible, the Query Optimizer might choose later in the plan to collapse those rows, grouping by a key value. The collapse typically occurs if the query processor encounters adjacent rows that delete and insert the same key values.

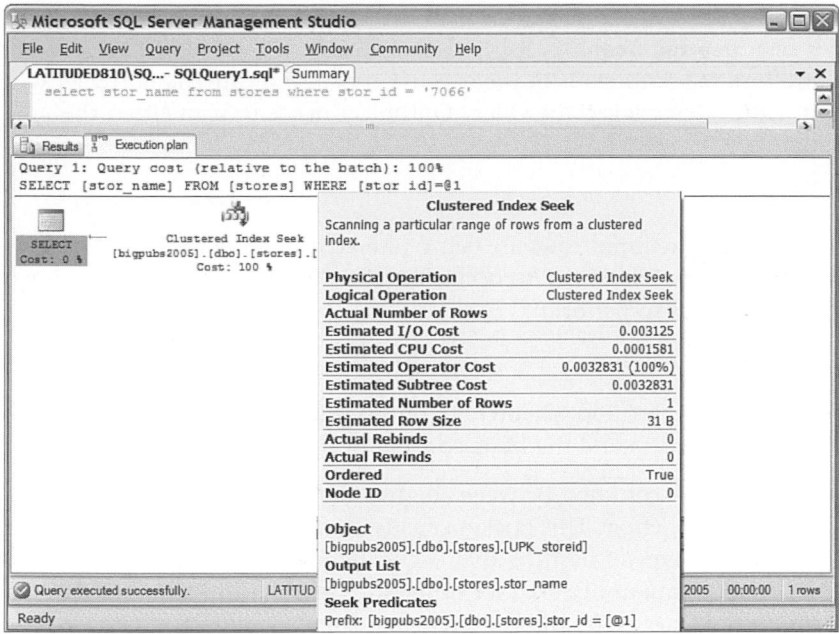

FIGURE 31.6   Clustered Index Seek ToolTip example.

Compute Scalar

The Query Optimizer uses the Compute Scalar operator to output a computed scalar value. This is a value that might be returned in the result set or used as input to another operation in the query, such as a Filter operator. You might see this operator when data values that are feeding an input need to be converted to a different data type first.

Concatenation

The Concatenation operator indicates that the result sets from two or more input sources are being concatenated into a single output. You often see this when a UNION ALL is being used. You can force a concatenation union strategy by using the OPTION clause in the query and specifying a CONCAT UNION. Optimization of UNION queries, with examples of the execution plan outputs, is covered in Chapter 30.

Constant Scan

The Constant Scan operator introduces one or more constant rows into a query. A Compute Scalar operation sometimes is used to provide input to the constant scan operator. A Compute Scalar operator often follows a Constant Scan operator to add columns to any rows produced by the Constant Scan operator.

Deleted Scan and Inserted Scan

The Deleted Scan and Inserted Scan icons in the execution plan indicate that a trigger is being fired and that within that trigger, the Query Optimizer needs to scan either the deleted or inserted tables.

Filter

The Filter icon indicates that the input rows are being filtered according to the predicate that is indicated in the ToolTip. This seems to occur primarily for intermediate operations that the Query Optimizer needs to perform.

Hash Match

Hash joins are covered in more detail in Chapter 30, but to understand the Hash Match physical operator, you must understand the basic concept of hash joins to some degree.

In a hash join, the keys that are common between the two tables are hashed into a hash bucket, using the same hash function. This bucket usually starts out in memory and then moves to disk, as needed. The type of hashing that occurs depends on the amount of memory required. Hashing is commonly used for inner and outer joins, intersections, unions, and differences. The Query Optimizer often uses hashing for intermediate processing.

A hash join requires at least one equality clause in the predicate, which includes the clauses used to relate a primary key to a foreign key. Usually, the Query Optimizer selects a hash join when the input tables are unsorted or are different in size, when no appropriate indexes exist, or when specific ordering of the result is not required. Hash joins help provide better query performance for large databases, complex queries, and distributed tables.

A hash match operator uses the hash join strategy and might also include other criteria to be considered a match. The other criteria are indicated in the `Probe Residual` clause shown in the Hash Match ToolTip.

Nonclustered Index Spool , Row Count Spool , and Table Spool

An Index Spool, Row Count Spool, or Table Spool icon indicates that the rows are being stored in a hidden spool table in the tempdb database which exists only for the duration of the query. Generally, this spool is created to support a nested iteration operation because the Query Optimizer might need to use the rows again. If the operator is rewound (for example, by a Nested Loops operator) but no rebinding is needed, the spooled data is used instead of rescanning the input data.

Often, you see a Spool icon under a Nested Loops icon in the execution plan. A Table Spool ToolTip does not show a predicate because no index is used. An Index Spool ToolTip shows a `SEEK` predicate. A temporary work table is created for an index spool, and then a temporary index is created on that table. These temporary work tables are local to the connection and live only as long as the query.

31

The Row Count Spool operator counts how many rows are present in the input and returns just the number of rows. This operator is used when checking for the existence of rows, rather than the actual data contained in the rows (for example, an existence subquery or an outer join when the actual data from the inner side is not needed).

Eager Spool or Lazy Spool

The Query Optimizer selects to use either an Eager or Lazy method of filling the spool, depending on the query. The Eager method means that the spool table is built all at once upon the first request for a row from the parent operator. The Lazy method builds the spool table as a row is requested by its parent operator.

Log Row Scan

The Log Row Scan icon indicates that the transaction log is being scanned.

Merge Join

The merge join is a strategy requiring that both the inputs be sorted on the common columns, defined by the predicate. The Merge Join operator may be preceded by an explicit sort operation in the query plan. A merge join performs one pass through each input table, matching the columns defined in the WHERE or JOIN clause as it steps through each input. A merge join looks similar to a simple nested loop but uses only a single pass of each table. Occasionally, you might see an additional sort operation prior to the merge join operation when the initial inputs are not sorted properly. Merge joins are often used to perform inner joins, left outer joins, left semi-joins, left anti-semi-joins, right outer joins, right semi-joins, right anti-semi-joins, and union logical operations.

Nested Loops

Nested loop joins are also known as nested iteration. Basically, in a nested iteration, every qualifying row in the outer table is compared to every qualifying row in the inner table. This is why you may at times see a Spool icon of some sort providing input to a Nested Loop icon. This allows the inner table rows to be reused (that is, rewound). When every row in each table is being compared, it is called a naïve nested loops join. If an index is used to find the qualifying rows, it is referred to as an index nested loops join. Nested loops can be used to perform inner joins, left outer joins, left semi-joins, and left anti-semi-joins.

The number of comparisons performed for a nested loop join is the calculation of the number of outer rows times the estimated number of matching inner rows for each lookup. This can become expensive. Generally, a nested loop join is considered to be most effective when both input tables are relatively small.

Parameter Table Scan

The Parameter Table Scan icon indicates that a table is acting as a parameter in the current query. Typically, this is displayed when INSERT queries exist in a stored procedure.

Remote Delete  **, Remote Insert** , **Remote Query** , **Remote Scan** ,

and Remote Update

The Remote Delete, Remote Insert, Remote Query, Remote Scan, and Remote Update operators indicate that the operation is being performed against a remote object such as a linked table.

RID Lookup

The RID Lookup operator indicates that a bookmark lookup is being performed on a heap table using a row identifier (RID). The ToolTip will indicate the bookmark label used to look up the row and the name of the table in which the row is being looked up. The RID Lookup operator is always accompanied by a Nested Loop Join operator.

Sequence

The Sequence operator executes each operation in its child node, moving from top to bottom in sequence, and returns only the end result from the bottom operator. You see this most often in the updates of multiple objects.

Sort

The Sort operator indicates that the input is being sorted. The sort order is displayed in the ToolTip's Order By item.

Stream Aggregate

You most often see the Stream Aggregate operation when you are aggregating a single input, such as a DISTINCT clause or a SUM, COUNT, MAX, MIN, or AVG operator. The output of this operator may be referenced by later operators in the query, returned to the client, or both.

Since the Stream Aggregate operator requires input ordered by the columns within its groups, a Sort operator often precedes the Stream Aggregate operator unless the data is already sorted due to a prior Sort operator or due to an ordered index seek or scan.

Table Delete , **Table Insert** , **Table Scan** , **and Table Update**

You see the Table Delete, Table Insert, Table Scan, and Table Update operators when the indicated operation is being performed against that table as a whole. This does not always mean that a problem exists, although a table scan can be an indicator that you may need some indexes to support the query. A table scan may be performed on small tables even if appropriate indexes exist, especially when the table is only a single page or two in size.

Table-valued Function

The Table-valued Function operator is displayed for queries with calls to table-valued functions. The Table-valued Function operator evaluates the table-valued function, and the resulting rows are stored in the tempdb database. When the parent operators request the rows, the Table-valued Function operator returns the rows from tempdb.

Top

The Top operator indicates a limit that is set, either by number of rows or a percentage, on the number of results to be returned from the input. The ToolTip may also contain a list of the columns that are being checked for ties if the WITH TIES option has been specified.

Parallelism Operators

The Parallelism operators indicate that parallel query processing is being performed. The associated logical operator displayed is one of the Distribute Streams, Gather Streams, or Repartition Streams logical operators.

Distribute Streams   The Distribute Streams operator takes a single input stream of records and produces multiple output streams. Each record from the input stream appears in one of the output streams. Hashing is typically used to decide to which output stream a particular input record belongs.

Gather Streams   The Gather Streams operator consumes several input streams and produces a single output stream of records by combining the input streams. If the output is ordered, the ToolTip will contain an Order By item indicating the columns being ordered.

Repartition Streams   The Repartition Streams operator consumes multiple streams and produces multiple streams of records. Each record from an input stream is placed into one output stream. If the output is ordered, the ToolTip contains an Order By item indicating the columns being ordered.

> **NOTE**
>
> Parallel query processing strategies are covered in more detail in Chapter 30.

Analyzing Stored Procedures

When displaying the estimated execution plan for a stored procedure, you see multiple statement operators as inputs to the Stored Procedure operator, especially if you have any conditional branching in the stored procedure. One operator exists for each statement that is defined in the stored procedure. When there is conditional branching in the stored procedure, SQL Server does not know at query optimization time which statements in the stored procedure will actually be executed, so it has to estimate a query plan for each individual statement. An example is shown in Figure 31.7.

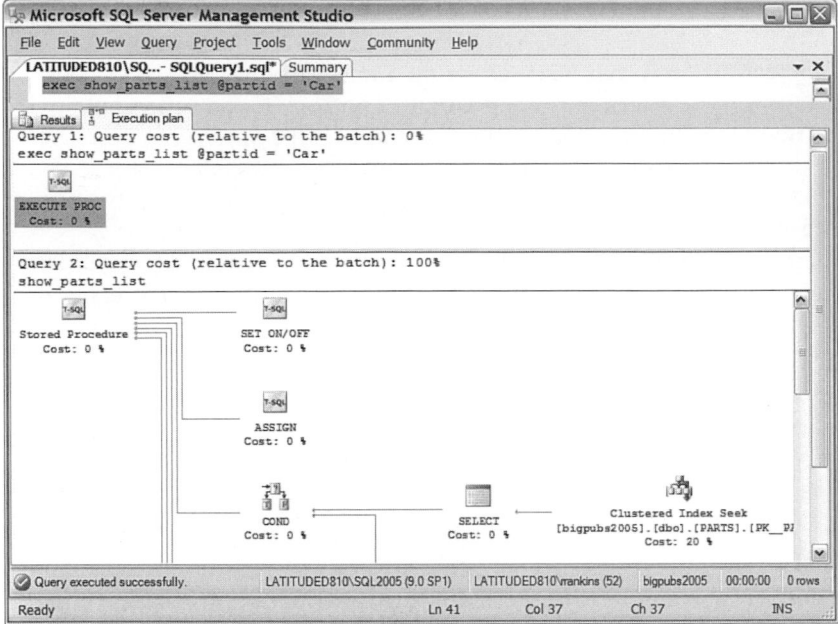

FIGURE 31.7   Estimated execution plan for a stored procedure.

When you execute the stored procedure with the Show Execution Plan option enabled, SSMS displays only the execution plans for the path or statements that are actually executed, as shown in Figure 31.8.

In addition, because stored procedures can become quite complex, with multiple SQL statements, seeing the graphical execution plan in the SSMS Execution Plan window can be difficult. You might find it easier to break up the stored procedure into smaller batches or individual queries and analyze it a bit at a time.

Saving and Viewing Graphical Execution Plans

One of the biggest problems with graphical execution plans in SQL Server 2000 was that there was no way to save them for future analysis, nor was there any easy way to send the execution plans to someone else to view and analyze. All you could do to save a graphical query plan was to print it out, which didn't work very well for large query plans that couldn't fit on a single page. Also, a printed graphical query plan didn't have the ability to display detailed information about the execution plan operators. Fortunately, this limitation has been removed in SQL Server 2005.

SQL Server 2005 provides the ability to save an execution plan as an XML file. To save a graphical execution plan in SSMS, you right-click anywhere on the graphical execution plan and choose Save Execution Plan As to bring up the Save As dialog (alternatively, you can also choose the Save Execution Plan As option from the File menu).

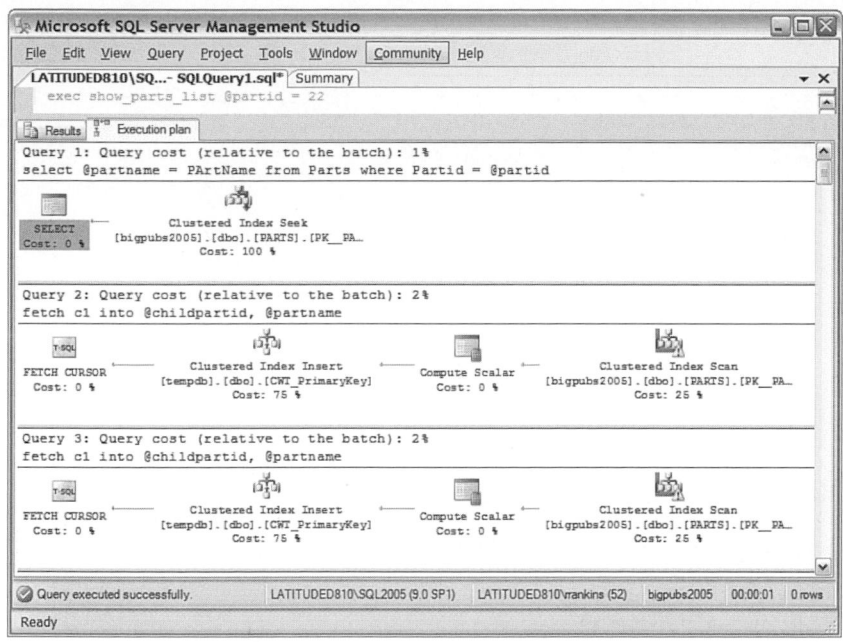

FIGURE 31.8   Actual execution plan used for a stored procedure.

When you save the execution plan to a file, the graphical execution plan is saved as an XML, file with the `.sqlplan` file extension. To view a saved execution plan, you click on the File menu, then select Open, and File. In the Open File dialog, you select Execution Plan files in the Files of Type drop-down to limit the files displayed to just Execution Plan Files (see Figure 31.9). Once you've identified the file you want to load, you click the Open button, and SSMS opens a new window with the selected execution plan displayed. Just like when the execution plan was originally generated, you can mouse over the operators and display the detailed information contained in the ToolTips.

NOTE

If there are multiple execution plans displayed in the Execution Plan tab in SSMS (for example, for a multistatement batch or stored procedure), only the currently selected execution plan is saved. To save all the execution plans for each query, you have to save them each individually.

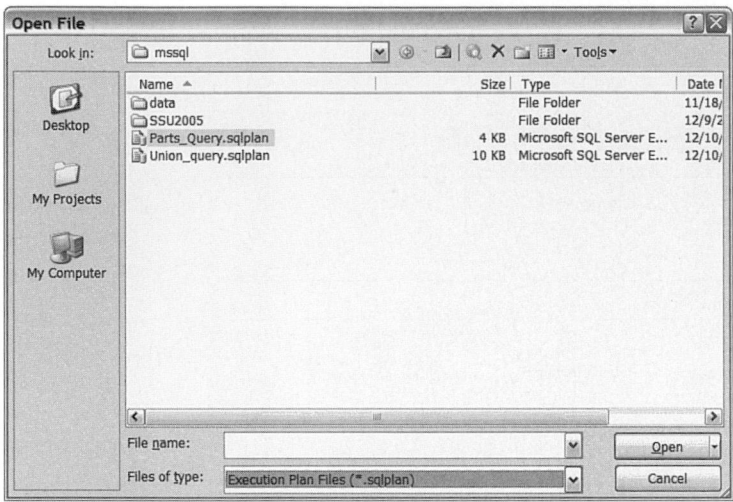

FIGURE 31.9   Loading an Execution Plan into SSMS

SSMS Client Statistics

You can use SSMS to get some additional information related to the client-side performance of the query by toggling the Include Client Statistics option in the Query menu. When turned on, the Client Statistics tab is added to the Results panel. This tab displays useful performance statistics in a tabular format that is related to how much work the client had to do to submit the query and process the results, including statistics about the network packets and the elapsed time of the query.

One of the enhancements of the SSMS client statistics over SQL Server 2000 Query Analyzer client statistics is that SSMS keeps track of the statistics for previous executions within a session so that you can compare the statistics between different query executions. It also keeps track of the overall average statistics across all executions. Figure 31.10 shows an example of the client statistics displayed after three separate query executions.

The first line in the Client Statistics tab displays the actual time the query was executed. The Time Statistics values are specified in number of milliseconds. Some of the most useful pieces of information include the number of rows returned by SELECT statements, the total client processing time, the total execution time, and the number of bytes sent and received across the network.

The Average column contains the cumulative average since the Include Client Statistics option was enabled. Turning the option off and back on clears out all the historical statistics and resets the averages. Alternatively, you can also reset the client statistics by selecting the Reset Client Statistics option from the Query menu.

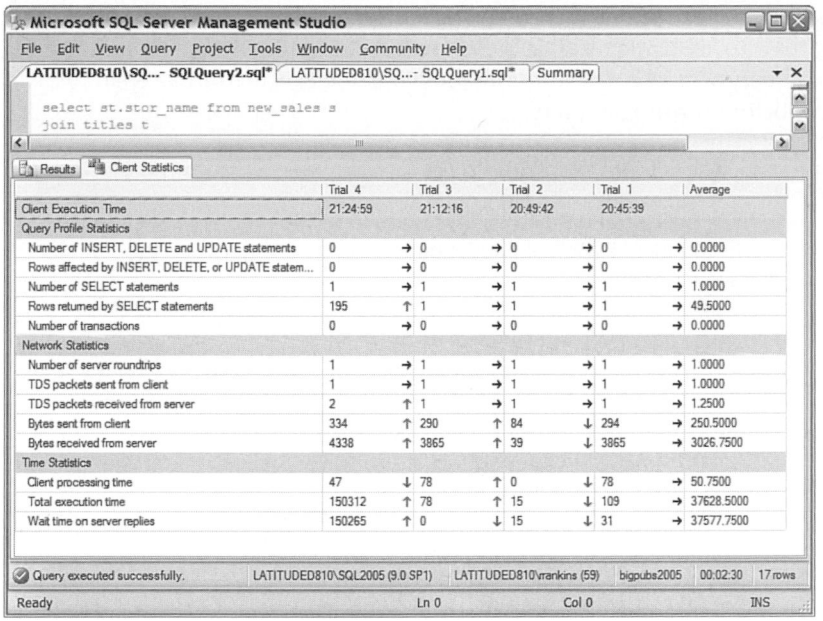

FIGURE 31.10   SSMS client statistics.

One of the most helpful features of the client statistics is the arrow indicators provided for the different executions, which makes it easy to identify which values increased, decreased, or stayed this same. This makes it easy to compare the runtime statistics between different queries or different executions of the same query.

TIP

Unlike the graphical execution plans, SSMS does not provide a way to save the client statistics. Fortunately, the statistics are displayed using a standard grid control. You can right-click the client statistics and choose Select All. Then you right-click and select Copy. You can then paste the information into a spreadsheet program such as Excel, which allows you to save the information or perform further statistical analysis on it.

Using the SET SHOWPLAN Options

In addition to the graphical execution plans available in SSMS, SQL Server 2005 provides three SET SHOWPLAN options to display the execution plan information in a text format. These options are SET SHOWPLAN_TEXT, SET SHOWPLAN_ALL, and SET SHOWPLAN_XML. When one of these options is enabled, SQL Server returns the execution plan that is generated for the query, but no results are returned because the query is not executed. It's similar to the Display Estimated Execution Plan option in SSMS.

You can turn on the textual execution plan output in a couple ways. One way is to issue the SET SHOWPLAN_TEXT ON, SET SHOWPLAN_ALL ON, or SET SHOWPLAN_XML ON command directly in the SSMS query window. These commands must be executed in a separate batch by themselves before running a query.

TIP

Before enabling SHOWPLAN_TEXT or SHOWPLAN_ALL options in a Query Editor session in SSMS, be sure to disable the Include Actual Execution Plan option; otherwise, the SHOWPLAN options will have no effect.

SHOWPLAN_TEXT

Typing the following command in a SSMS query window turns on the SHOWPLAN_TEXT option:

```
SET SHOWPLAN_TEXT ON
GO
```

Setting this option causes the textual showplan output to be displayed in the results panel but does not execute the query. You can also enable the SHOWPLAN_TEXT option by choosing the Query Options item from the Query menu. In the Query Options dialog, you click the Advanced item and check the SET SHOWPLAN_TEXT option.

The SHOWPLAN_TEXT option displays a textual representation of the execution plan. Listing 31.1 shows an example for a simple inner join query.

TIP

When displaying the SHOWPLAN_TEXT information in SSMS, it is usually easiest to view if you configure SSMS to return results to text rather than as a grid.

LISTING 31.1   An Example of SHOWPLAN_TEXT Output

```
set showplan_text on
go
select st.stor_name, ord_date, qty
from stores st join sales_noclust s on st.stor_id = s.stor_id
where st.stor_id between 'B100' and 'B199'
go
StmtText
--------------------------------------------------------------------------------
select st.stor_name, ord_date, qty
from stores st join sales_noclust s on st.stor_id = s.stor_id
where st.stor_id between 'B100' and 'B199'
```

LISTING 31.1   Continued

```
StmtText
----------------------------------------------------------------
  ¦--Nested Loops(Inner Join, OUTER REFERENCES:([Bmk1002], [Expr1006])
➡ WITH UNORDERED PREFETCH)
      ¦--Nested Loops(Inner Join, OUTER REFERENCES:([st].[stor_id]))
      ¦     ¦--Clustered Index Seek(OBJECT:([bigpubs2005].[dbo].[stores].
➡[UPK_storeid] AS [st]), SEEK:([st].[stor_id] >= 'B100' AND [st].[stor_id]
➡ <= 'B199') ORDERED FORWARD)
      ¦     ¦--Index Seek(OBJECT:([bigpubs2005].[dbo].[sales_noclust].[idx1]
➡ AS [s]), SEEK:([s].[stor_id]=[bigpubs2005].[dbo].[stores].[stor_id] as
➡ [st].[stor_id]),  WHERE:([bigpubs2005].[dbo].[sales_noclust].[stor_id]
➡ as [s].[stor_id]>='B100' AND [bigpubs2005].[dbo].[sales_noclust].[stor_id]
➡ as [s].[stor_id]<='B199') ORDERED FORWARD)
      ¦--RID Lookup(OBJECT:([bigpubs2005].[dbo].[sales_noclust] AS [s]),
➡ SEEK:([Bmk1002]=[Bmk1002]) LOOKUP ORDERED FORWARD)
```

The output is read from right to left, similarly to the graphical execution plan. Each line represents a physical/logical operator. The text displayed matches the logical and physical operator names displayed in the graphical execution plan. If you can read the graphical query plan, you should have no trouble reading the SHOWPLAN_TEXT output.

In the example in Listing 31.1, SQL Server is performing a clustered index seek on the stores table, using the UPK_storeid index, and a nonclustered index seek on sales_noclust, using index idx1. The inputs are combined using a nested loop join. Finally, a RID lookup is being performed to retrieve the ord_date and qty information from the sales_noclust table.

Once the SHOWPLAN_TEXT option is set to ON, execution plan information about all subsequent SQL Server 2005 statements is returned until the option is set to OFF. Also, all subsequent commands are optimized but not executed. To turn off the textual showplan output and allow execution of commands again, you type the following command:

```
SET SHOWPLAN_TEXT OFF
GO
```

TIP

To switch from one SET SHOWPLAN option to another, remember that no commands are executed until the SET SHOWPLAN option is turned off. This includes setting the SET SHOWPLAN options. For example, to switch from SHOWPLAN_TEXT to either SHOWPLAN_ALL or SHOWPLAN_XML, you have to turn off SHOWPLAN_TEXT first with the SET SHOWPLAN_TEXT OFF command.

SHOWPLAN_ALL

The SHOWPLAN_ALL option displays the same textual execution plan information as the SHOWPLAN_TEXT option, and it also provides additional columns of output for each row of textual showplan output. These columns provide much of the same information that is available in the graphical execution ToolTips, and the column headings correspond to the ToolTip items listed in the "Execution Plan ToolTips" section, earlier in this chapter. Table 31.1 describes the information provided in the data columns returned by the SHOWPLAN_ALL option.

TABLE 31.1   Data Columns Returned by SHOWPLAN_ALL

Column Name	Description
StmtText	The text of the T-SQL statement and also each of the physical operators in the execution plan. (It may optionally also contain the logical operators.)
StmtId	The number of the statement in the current batch.
NodeId	The ID of the node in the current query.
Parent	The node ID of the parent operator for the current operator.
PhysicalOp	Physical operator description for the current node.
LogicalOp	Logical operator description for the current node.
Argument	Supplemental information about the operation being performed.
DefinedValues	A comma-separated list of values introduced by this operator. These may be either computed expressions that were present in the current query or internal values introduced by the query processor in order to process this query.
EstimateRows	Estimated number of rows of output produced by the operator.
EstimateIO	Estimated I/O cost for the operator.
EstimateCPU	Estimated CPU cost for the operator.
AvgRowSize	Estimated average row size (in bytes) of the row being passed through the operator.
TotalSubtreeCost	Estimated (cumulative) cost of this operation and all child operations.
OutputList	A comma-separated list of columns being projected by the current operation.
Warnings	A comma-separated list of warning messages relating to the current operation (for example, missing statistics).
Type	The type of node (either PLAN_ROW or the type of T-SQL statement).
Parallel	Whether the operator is running in parallel (1) or not (0).
EstimateExecutions	Estimated number of times this operator will be executed while running the current query.

TIP

When displaying the SHOWPLAN_ALL information in SSMS, it is usually easiest to view if you configure SSMS to return results to grid rather than as text.

SHOWPLAN_XML

When the SET SHOWPLAN_XML is set to ON, SQL Server does not execute the query but returns execution information for each T-SQL batch as an XML document. The execution plan information for each T-SQL batch is contained in a single XML document. Each XML document contains the text of the statements in the batch, followed by the details of the execution steps and operators. The document includes the estimated costs, numbers of rows, indexes used, join order, and types of operators performed.

The SHOWPLAN_XML option generates the same XML schema as the Show Estimated Execution Plan option in SSMS. In essence, you are looking at the same information, just without the pretty pictures. As a matter of fact, you can save the output from the SHOWPLAN_XML option to a file and open it back into SSMS as a SQL plan file. The recommended approach is to configure the query window to return results to a grid. If you return the results as text or to a file, the maximum output size for a character column in SSMS is 8,192 bytes. If the XML document exceeds this length, it is truncated and does not load correctly. In the grid results, the maximum size of XML data is 2MB.

After you run the query and generate the grid results, you can right-click on the result row and choose the Save Results As option to specify the file to save the results to. If all goes well, you end up with a .sqlplan file that you can then load back into SSMS for further analysis at a later date.

> **NOTE**
>
> The document containing the XML schema for the SET SHOWPLAN_XML output is available in the same directory as the SQL Server installation, which by default is Program Files\Microsoft SQL Server\90\Tools\Binn\schemas\sqlserver\2004\07\showplan\showplanxml.xsd.

Using sys.dm_exec_query_plan

Dynamic Management Views are a new feature in SQL Server 2005 that can return server state information that can be used to monitor and diagnose database engine issues and help tune performance. One of the new DMVs provided is sys.dm_exec_query_plan. This DMV returns the showplan information for a T-SQL batch whose query execution plan resides in the plan cache. This can be any SQL batch, not just the batch executed by the current user session. The sys.dm_exec_query_plan DMV provides the ability to get the showplan for currently long-running processes to help diagnose why they may be running slowly.

The showplan information provided by sys.dm_exec_query_plan is returned in a column called query_plan, which is of the xml data type. This column provides the same information as SET SHOWPLAN XML. The syntax of sys.dm_exec_query_plan is

```
sys.dm_exec_query_plan ( plan_handle )
```

In SQL Server 2005, the query plans for various types of T-SQL batches are cached in an area of memory called the *plan cache*. Each cached query plan is identified by a unique identifier called a *plan handle*. To view the showplan for one of these batches, you provide the plan handle for the batch to the sys.dm_exec_query_plan DMV.

The tricky part about using sys.dm_exec_query_plan is determining the plan handle to use. First, you need to determine the SPID for the process with the long-running query. This is usually accomplished using sp_who.

Once you have the SPID, you can use the sys.dm_exec_requests DMV to obtain the plan handle (assume in this case that the SPID is 58):

```
select plan_handle from sys.dm_exec_requests where session_id = 58
go


plan_handle
---------------------------------------------------------------------------
0x06000A00E96E6D2CB8A1F50500000000000000000000000000000
```

Once you have the plan handle, you can pass it on to the sys.dm_exec_query_plan DMV to return the query plan:

```
SELECT query_plan
FROM sys.dm_exec_query_plan (0x06000A00E96E6D2CB8A1F50500000000000000000000000000000)
```

Alternatively, to prevent having to copy and paste the plan handle from the sys.dm_exec_requests query into the query against sys.dm_exec_query_plan, you can use the CROSS APPLY clause, as in the following query:

```
SELECT query_plan FROM sys.dm_exec_requests cp
    CROSS APPLY sys.dm_exec_query_plan(cp.plan_handle)
    where cp.session_id = 58
```

If you return the results to grid, you can right-click the data in the query_plan column and save it to a file, which can then be loaded into SSMS to view the graphical execution plan, just like the output from the SET SHOWPLAN_XML option.

To return the query plan for all currently running T-SQL batches, you can run the following:

```
SELECT query_plan FROM sys.dm_exec_requests cp
    CROSS APPLY sys.dm_exec_query_plan(cp.plan_handle)
```

In addition to returning the query plans for the currently running T-SQL batches, SQL Server 2005 also provides the sys.dm_exec_query_stats and sys.dm_exec_cached_plans DMVs. The sys.dm_exec_cached_plans DMV can be used to return information about all query plans currently residing in the plan cache. For example, to retrieve a snapshot of all query plans residing in the plan cache, you use the CROSS APPLY operator to pass the plan handles from sys.dm_exec_cached_plans to sys.dm_exec_query_plan, as follows:

```
SELECT * FROM sys.dm_exec_cached_plans cp
    CROSS APPLY sys.dm_exec_query_plan(cp.plan_handle)
```

To retrieve a snapshot of all query plans that currently reside in the plan cache for which the server has gathered statistics, use the CROSS APPLY operator to pass the plan handles from sys.dm_exec_query_stats to sys.dm_exec_query_plan as follows:

```
SELECT * FROM sys.dm_exec_query_stats qs
    CROSS APPLY sys.dm_exec_query_plan(qs.plan_handle)
```

Because sys.dm_exec_query_plan provides the ability to view the query plan for any session, a user must be a member of the sysadmin fixed server role or have the VIEW SERVER STATE permission on the server in order to invoke it.

Query Statistics

SQL Server 2005 still provides the SET STATISTICS IO option and the SET STATISTICS TIME option, which display the actual logical and physical page reads incurred by a query and the CPU and elapsed time, respectively. These two SET options return actual execution statistics, as opposed to the estimates returned by SSMS and the SHOWPLAN options discussed previously. These two tools are invaluable for determining the actual cost of a query.

In addition to the IO and TIME statistics, SQL Server also provides the SET STATISTICS PROFILE option and the new SET STATISTICS XML options. These options are provided to display execution plan information while still allowing the query to run.

STATISTICS IO

You can set the STATISTICS IO option for individual user sessions, and you can turn it on in an SSMS query window by typing the following:

```
SET STATISTICS IO ON
GO
```

You can also set this option for the query session in SSMS by choosing the Options item in the Query menu. In the Query Options dialog, click the Advanced item and check the SET STATISTICS IO check box, as shown in Figure 31.11.

The STATISTICS IO option displays the scan count (that is, the number of iterations), the logical reads (from cached data), the physical reads (from physical storage), and the read-ahead reads.

Listing 31.2 displays the STATISTICS IO output for the same query executed in Listing 31.1. (Note that the result set has been deleted to save space.)

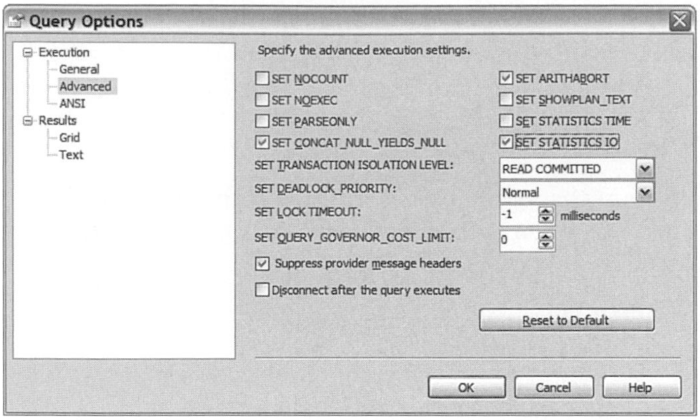

FIGURE 31.11   Enabling the STATISTICS IO Option in SSMS.

LISTING 31.2   An Example of STATISTICS IO Output

```
set statistics io on
go
select st.stor_name, ord_date, qty
from stores st join sales_noclust s on st.stor_id = s.stor_id
where st.stor_id between 'B100' and 'B199'
go

-- output deleted

Table 'sales_noclust'. Scan count 100, logical reads 1383, physical reads 0,
   read-ahead reads 0, lob logical reads 0, lob physical reads 0,
   lob read-ahead reads 0.
Table 'stores'. Scan count 1, logical reads 3, physical reads 0,
   read-ahead reads 0, lob logical reads 0, lob physical reads 0,
   lob read-ahead reads 0.
```

Scan Count

The Scan count value indicates the number of times the corresponding table was accessed during query execution. The outer table of a nested loop join typically has a scan count of 1. The scan count for the inner tables typically reflects the number of times the inner table is searched, which is usually the same as the number of qualifying rows in the outer table. The number of logical reads for the inner table is equal to the scan count multiplied by the number of pages per lookup for each scan. Note that the scan count for the inner table might sometimes be only 1 for a nested join if SQL Server copies the needed rows from the inner table into a work table in cache memory and reads from the work table for subsequent iterations (for example, if it uses the Table Spool operation). The scan count for hash joins and merge joins will typically be 1 for both tables involved in the join, but the logical reads for these types of joins will usually be substantially higher.

Logical Reads

The `logical reads` value indicates the total number of page accesses necessary to process the query. Every page is read from cache memory, even if it first has to be read from disk. Every physical read always has a corresponding logical read, so the number of physical reads will never exceed the number of logical reads. Because the same page might be accessed multiple times, the number of logical reads for a table could exceed the total number of pages in the table.

Physical Reads

The `physical reads` value indicates the actual number of pages that were read from disk. The value for physical reads can vary greatly and should decrease, or drop to zero, with subsequent executions of the query because the data will be loaded into the data cache by the first execution. The number of physical reads will also be lowered by pages that are brought into memory by the read-ahead mechanism.

Read-Ahead Reads

The `read-ahead reads` value indicates the number of pages that were read into cache memory using the read-ahead mechanism while the query was processed. Pages read by the read-ahead mechanism will not necessarily be used by the query. When a page that was read by the read-ahead mechanism is accessed by the query, it counts as a logical read, but not as a physical read.

The read-ahead mechanism can be thought of as an optimistic form of physical I/O, reading the pages into cache memory that it expects the query will need before the query needs them. When scanning a table or index, the table's index allocation map pages (IAMs) are looked at to determine which extents belong to the object. An extent consists of eight data pages. The eight pages in the extent are read with a single read and the extents are read in the order that they are stored on disk. If the table is spread across multiple files, the read-ahead mechanism attempts parallel reads from up to eight files at a time instead of sequentially reading from the files.

LOB Reads

If the query retrieves text, ntext, image, or large value type (varchar(max), nvarchar(max), varbinary(max)) data, the `lob logical reads`, `lob physical reads`, and `lob read-ahead reads` values provide the logical, physical, and read-ahead read statistics for the LOB I/Os.

Analyzing STATISTICS IO Output

The output shown in Listing 31.2 indicates that the sales_noclust table was scanned 100 times, with no physical reads (that is, no physical I/Os were performed). The stores table was scanned once, with all reads coming from cache as well.

You can use the STATISTICS IO option to evaluate the effectiveness of the size of the data cache and to evaluate, over time, how long a table will stay in cache. The lack of physical reads is a good sign, indicating that memory is sufficient to keep the data in cache. If you keep seeing many physical reads when you are analyzing and testing your queries, you might want to consider adding more memory to the server to improve the cache hit ratio. You can estimate the cache hit ratio for a query by using the following formula:

Cache hit ratio = (Logical reads – Physical reads) / Logical reads

The number of physical reads appears lower than it actually is if pages are preloaded by read-ahead activity. Because read-ahead reads lower the physical read count, they give the indication of a good cache hit ratio, when in actuality, the data is still being physically read from disk. The system could still benefit from more memory so that the data remains in cache and the number of read-ahead reads is reduced. STATISTICS IO is generally more useful for evaluating individual query performance than for evaluating overall cache hit ratio. The pages that reside and remain in memory for subsequent executions are determined by the data pages being accessed by other queries executing at the same time, and the number of data pages that are being accessed by the other queries. If no other activity is occurring, you are likely to see no physical reads for subsequent executions of the query if the amount of data being accessed fits in the available cache memory. Likewise, if the same data is being accessed by multiple queries, the data tends to stay in cache, and the number of physical reads for subsequent executions tends to be low. However, if other queries executing at the same time are accessing large volumes of data from different tables or ranges of values, the data needed for the query you are testing might end up being flushed from cache, and the physical I/Os will increase. Depending on the other ongoing SQL Server activity, the physical reads you see displayed by STATSITICS IO can be inconsistent.

When you are evaluating individual query performance, examining the logical reads value is usually more helpful because the information is consistent across all executions, regardless of other SQL Server activity. Generally speaking, the queries with the fewest logical reads will be the fastest queries. If you want to monitor the overall cache hit ratio for all SQL Server activity to evaluate the SQL Server memory configuration, use Performance Monitor, which is discussed in Chapter 34, "Monitoring SQL Server Performance."

STATISTICS TIME

You can set the STATISTICS TIME option for individual user sessions. In a SSMS query window, you type the following:

```
SET STATISTICS TIME ON
```

You can also set this option for the query session in SSMS by choosing the Options item in the Query menu. In the Query Options dialog, you click the Advanced item and check the SET STATISTICS TIME check box.

The STATISTICS TIME option displays the total CPU and elapsed time that it takes to actually execute a query. The STATISTICS TIME output for the query in Listing 31.1 returns the output shown in Listing 31.3. (Again, the data rows returned have been deleted to save space.)

LISTING 31.3   An Example of STATISTICS TIME Output

```
set statistics io on
set statistics time on
go

select st.stor_name, ord_date, qty
from stores st join sales_noclust s on st.stor_id = s.stor_id
where st.stor_id between 'B100' and 'B199'
go


SQL Server parse and compile time:
   CPU time = 0 ms, elapsed time = 1 ms.

--output deleted

Table 'sales_noclust'. Scan count 100, logical reads 1383, physical reads 0,
  read-ahead reads 0, lob logical reads 0, lob physical reads 0,
  lob read-ahead reads 0.
Table 'stores'. Scan count 1, logical reads 3, physical reads 0,
  read-ahead reads 0, lob logical reads 0, lob physical reads 0,
  lob read-ahead reads 0.

SQL Server Execution Times:
   CPU time = 0 ms,   elapsed time = 32 ms.
```

Here, you can see that the total execution time, denoted by the elapsed time, was relatively low and not significantly higher than the CPU time. This is due to the lack of any physical reads and the fact that all activity is performed in memory.

NOTE

In some situations, you might notice that the parse and compile time for a query is displayed twice. This happens when the query plan is being added to the plan cache for possible reuse. The first set of information output is the actual parse and compile before placing the plan in cache, and the second set of information output appears when SQL Server is retrieving the plan from cache. Subsequent executions still show the same two sets of output, but the parse and compile time is 0 when the plan is reused because a query plan is not being compiled.

If elapsed time is much higher than CPU time, the query had to wait for something, either I/O or locks. If you want to see the effect of physical versus logical I/Os on the performance of a query, you need to flush the pages accessed by the query from memory. You can use the DBCC DROPCLEANBUFFERS command to clear all clean buffer pages out of memory. Listing 31.4 shows an example of clearing the pages from cache and rerunning the query with the STATISTICS IO and STATISTICS TIME options enabled.

TIP

To ensure that none of the table is left in cache, make sure all pages are marked as clean before running the DBCC DROPCLEANBUFFERS command. A buffer is dirty if it contains a data row modification that has either not been committed yet or has not been written out to disk yet. To clear the greatest number of buffer pages from cache memory, make sure all work is committed, checkpoint the database to force all modified pages to be written out to disk, and then execute the DBCC DROPCLEANBUFFERS command.

LISTING 31.4   An Example of Clearing the Clean Pages from Cache to Generate Physical I/Os

```
USE bigpubs2005
go
CHECKPOINT
go
DBCC DROPCLEANBUFFERS
go

SET STATISTICS IO ON
SET STATISTICS TIME ON
go
select st.stor_name, ord_date, qty
from stores st join sales_noclust s on st.stor_id = s.stor_id
where st.stor_id between 'B100' and 'B199'
go


SQL Server parse and compile time:
   CPU time = 0 ms, elapsed time = 1 ms.

--output deleted

Table 'sales_noclust'. Scan count 100, logical reads 1383, physical reads 5,
 read-ahead reads 8, lob logical reads 0, lob physical reads 0,
 lob read-ahead reads 0.
Table 'stores'. Scan count 1, logical reads 3, physical reads 2,
 read-ahead reads 0, lob logical reads 0, lob physical reads 0,
```

31

LISTING 31.4 Continued

```
lob read-ahead reads 0.

SQL Server Execution Times:
   CPU time = 16 ms,  elapsed time = 118 ms.
```

Notice that this time around, the CPU time was only slightly higher, but the elapsed time was 118 milliseconds (ms), nearly 4 times slower, due to the physical I/Os that had to be performed during this execution.

You can use the STATISTICS TIME and STATISTICS IO options together in this way as a useful tool for benchmarking and comparing performance.

Using datediff() to Measure Runtime

While the STATISTICS TIME option works fine for displaying the runtime of a single query, it is not as useful for displaying the total CPU time and elapsed time for a stored procedure. The STATISTICS TIME option generates time statistics for every command executed within the stored procedure. This makes it difficult to read the output and determine the total elapsed time for the stored procedure.

Another way to display runtime for a stored procedure is to capture the current system time right before it starts, capture the current system time as it completes, and display the difference between the two, specifying the appropriate-sized datepart parameter to the datediff() function, depending on how long your procedures typically run. For example, if a procedure takes minutes to complete, you probably want to display the difference in seconds or minutes, rather than milliseconds. If the time to complete is in seconds, you likely want to specify a datepart of seconds or milliseconds. Listing 31.5 displays an example of using this approach.

LISTING 31.5 Using datediff() to Determine Stored Procedure Runtime

```
set statistics time off
set statistics io off
go
declare @start datetime
select @start = getdate()
exec sp_help
select datediff(ms, @start, getdate()) as 'runtime(ms)'
go


-- output deleted

runtime(ms)
-----------
      233
```

STATISTICS PROFILE

The SET STATISTICS PROFILE option is similar to the SET SHOWPLAN_ALL option but allows the query to actually execute. It returns the same execution plan information that is displayed with the SET SHOWPLAN_ALL statement, with the addition of two columns that display actual execution information. The Rows column displays the actual number of rows that is returned in the execution step, and the Executions column shows the actual number of executions for the step. The Rows column can be compared to the EstimatedRows column, and the Execution column can be compared to the EstimatedExecution column to determine the accuracy of the execution plan.

You can set the STATISTICS PROFILE option for individual query sessions. In an SSMS query window, you type the following:

```
SET STATISTICS PROFILE ON
GO
```

STATISTICS XML

Similar to the STATISTICS PROFILE option, the SET STATISTICS XML option allows a query to execute while also returning the execution plan information. The execution plan information returned is similar to the XML document displayed with the SET SHOWPLAN_XML statement.

To set the STATISTICS XML option for individual query sessions in SSMS or another query tool, you type the following:

```
SET STATISTICS XML ON
GO
```

> **NOTE**
>
> With all the fancy graphical tools available, why would you want to use the text-based analysis tools? Although the graphical tools are useful for analyzing individual queries one at a time, they can be a bit tedious if you have to perform analysis on a number of queries. As an alternative, you can put all the queries you want to analyze in a script file and set the appropriate options to get the query plan and statistics output you want to see. You can then run the script through a tool such as sqlcmd and route the output to a file. You can then quickly scan the file or use an editor's Find utility to look for the obvious potential performance issues, such as table scans or long-running queries. Next, you can copy the individual problem queries you identify from the output file into SSMS, where you can perform a more thorough analysis on them.
>
> You could also set up a job to run this SQL script periodically to constantly capture and save performance statistics. This gives you a means to keep a history of the query performance and execution plans over time. This information can be used to compare performance differences as the data volumes and SQL Server activity levels change over time.

Another advantage of the textual query plan output over the graphical query plans is that for very complex queries, the graphical plan tends to get very big and spread out so much that it's difficult to read and follow. The textual output is somewhat more compact and easier to see all at once.

Query Analysis with SQL Server Profiler

SQL Server Profiler serves as another powerful tool available for query analysis. When you must monitor a broad range of queries and database activity and analyze the performance, it is difficult to analyze all those queries manually. For example, if you have a number of stored procedures to analyze, how would you know which ones to focus on as problem procedures? You would have to identify sample parameters for all of them and manually execute them individually to see which ones were running too slowly and then, after they were identified, do some query analysis on them.

With SQL Server Profiler, you can simply define a trace to capture performance-related statistics on-the-fly while the system is being used normally. This way, you can capture a representative sample of the type of activity your database will receive and capture statistics for the stored procedures as they are being executed with real data values. Also, to avoid having to look at everything, you can set a filter on the Duration column so that it only displays items with a runtime longer than the specified threshold.

The events you want to capture to analyze query performance are listed under the Performance events. They include Showplan All, Showplan Statistics Profile, Showplan Text, Showplan Text (Unencoded), Showplan XML, and Showplan XML Statistics Profile. The data columns that you want to be sure to include when capturing the showplan events are TextData, CPU, StartTime, Duration, and Reads and Writes. Also, for the Showplan Statistics and Showplan All events, you must also select the BinaryData data column.

Capturing the showplan performance information with SQL Server Profiler provides you with all the same information you can capture with all the other individual tools discussed in this chapter. You can easily save the trace information to a file or a table for replaying the sequence to test index or configuration changes, or simply for historical analysis. If you choose any of the Showplan XML options, you have the option of saving the XML Showplan events separately from the overall trace file. You can choose to save all XML Showplan events in a single file or a separate file for each event (see Figure 31.12). You can then load the Showplan XML file into SSMS to view the graphical execution plans to perform your query analysis.

When you run a SQL Server Profiler trace with the Showplan XML event enabled, SQL Server Profiler displays the graphical execution plans captured in the bottom display panel of the Profiler window when you select a record with a Showplan XML EventClass. The graphical execution plans displayed in SQL Server Profiler are just like the ones displayed in SSMS, and they also include the same detailed information available via the ToolTips. Figure 31.13 shows an example of a graphical execution plan being displayed in SQL Server Profiler.

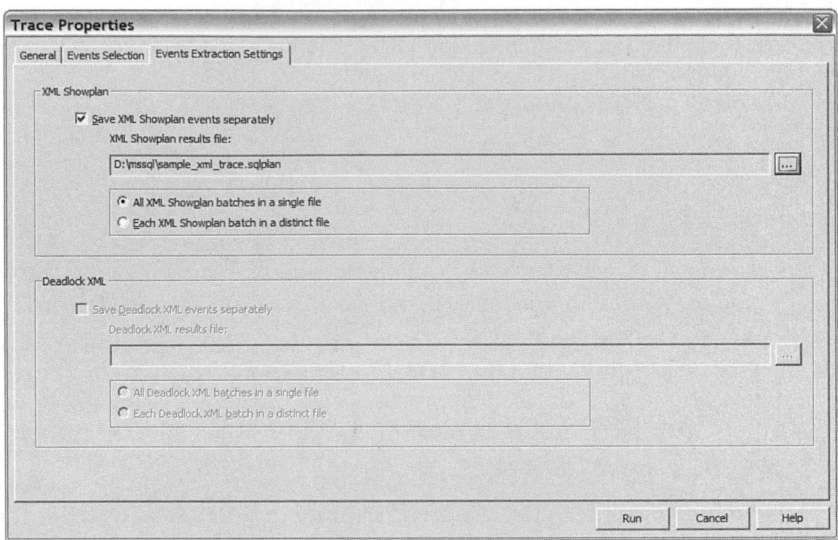

FIGURE 31.12   Saving XML Showplan events to a single file.

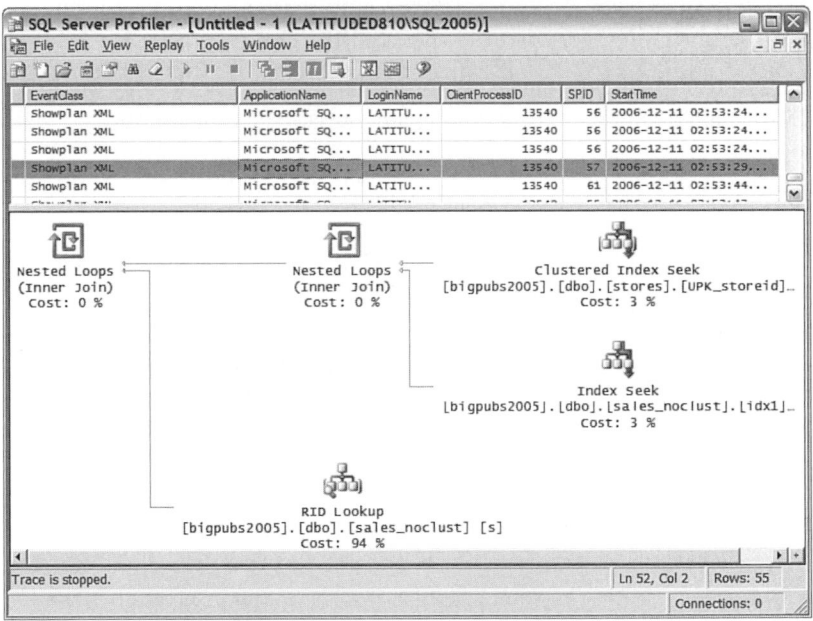

FIGURE 31.13   Displaying an XML Showplan event in SQL Server Profiler.

For more information on using SQL Server Profiler, see Chapter 5, "SQL Server Profiler."

> **NOTE**
>
> Because of the ability to view the graphical execution plans in SQL Server Profiler as well as the ability to save the XML Showplan events to a separate file, which you can bring into SSMS for analysis, the XML Showplan events provide a significant benefit over the other, older-style showplan events provided. As a matter of fact, these other showplan events are provided primarily for backward compatibility purposes. In a future version of SQL Server, the Showplan All, Showplan Statistics Profile, Showplan Text, and Showplan Text (Unencoded) event classes will be deprecated. It is recommended that you switch to using the newer XML event classes instead.

Summary

Between the features of SSMS and the text-based query analysis tools, SQL Server 2005 provides a number of powerful utilities to analyze and understand how your queries are performing and also to help you develop a better understanding of how queries in general are processed and optimized in SQL Server 2005. Such an understanding can help ensure that the queries you develop will be optimized more effectively by SQL Server.

The tools discussed in this chapter are useful for analyzing individual query performance. However, in a multiuser environment, query performance is often affected by more than just how a single query is optimized. One of those factors is locking contention. Chapter 32 delves into locking in SQL Server, its impact on query and application performance, and how to minimize locking performance issues in SQL Server systems.

Locking and Performance

IN THIS CHAPTER

▶ What's New in Locking and Performance

▶ The Need for Locking

▶ Transaction Isolation Levels in SQL Server

▶ The Lock Manager

▶ Monitoring Lock Activity in SQL Server

▶ SQL Server Lock Types

▶ SQL Server Lock Granularity

▶ Lock Compatibility

▶ Locking Contention and Deadlocks

▶ Table Hints for Locking

▶ Optimistic Locking

This chapter examines locking and its impact on transactions and performance in SQL Server. It also reviews locking hints that you can specify in queries to override SQL Server's default locking behavior.

What's New in Locking and Performance

One of the key new features of SQL Server 2005 related to locking and performance is the new row version–based isolation levels, such as Read Committed Snapshot and Snapshot Isolation. Snapshot Isolation provides the benefit of repeatable reads without acquiring and holding shared locks on the data that is read. To provide this capability, SQL Server maintains versions of each row that is modified in tempdb. This can help minimize locking and blocking problems between read operations and update operations. Read operations do not have to wait for write operations, and writes don't have to wait for reads. For more information on snapshot isolation, see "Transaction Isolation Levels in SQL Server," later in this chapter.

SQL Server 2005 also provides improved tools for monitoring locking in SQL Server. SQL Server Management Studio (SSMS) provides the Activity Monitor for monitoring locks. This tool is much improved over what was available in SQL Server 2000 Enterprise Manager. It provides the ability to apply filters to the monitored data as wall as an auto-refresh capability. In addition, SQL Server 2005 provides two new data management views for monitoring locking and blocking processes: sys.dm_tranlocks and sys.dm_os_waiting_tasks. These new tools are covered in the section, "Monitoring Lock Activity in SQL Server."

SQL Server 2005 also provides improved deadlock monitoring. The 1204 trace flag is still available, and SQL Server 2005 introduces the 1222 trace flag, which provides deadlock information, first by processes and then by resources. The information is returned in an XML-like format. For even easier analysis of deadlocks in SQL Server 2005, SQL Server Profiler provides the ability to capture a Deadlock Graph event. The Deadlock Graph provides a graphical representation of the deadlocks encountered. These can be saved to a file and viewed in SSMS. For more information on Deadlock Graphs and deadlock analysis, see the later section, "Locking Contention and Deadlocks."

In SQL Server 2005, the `tsequal()` function is no longer supported for use by applications that want to use optimistic locking. This chapter discusses a T-SQL alternative along with information on using snapshot isolation for optimistic locking purposes.

The Need for Locking

In any multiuser database, there must be a consistent set of rules for making changes to the data. For a true transaction-processing database, the database management system (DBMS) is responsible for resolving potential conflicts between two different processes that are attempting to change the same piece of information at the same time. Such a situation cannot occur because the consistency of a transaction cannot be guaranteed. For example, if two users were to change the same data at approximately the same time, whose change would be propagated? Theoretically, the results would be unpredictable because the answer is dependent on whose transaction completed last. Because most applications try to avoid "unpredictability" with data wherever possible (imagine a banking system returning "unpredictable" results, and you'll get the idea), some method must be available to guarantee sequential and consistent data changes.

Any relational database must support the ACID properties for transactions, as discussed in Chapter 26, "Transaction Management and the Transaction Log":

- ▶ Atomicity
- ▶ Consistency
- ▶ Isolation
- ▶ Durability

These ACID properties ensure that data changes in a database are correctly collected together and that the data is going to be left in a consistent state that corresponds with the actions being taken.

The main role of locking is to provide the isolation that transactions need. Isolation ensures that individual transactions don't interfere with one another, that a given transaction does not read or modify the data being modified by another transaction. In addition, the isolation that locking provides helps ensure consistency within transactions. Without locking, consistent transaction processing is impossible. Transactions are logical units of work that rely on a constant state of data, almost a "snapshot in time" of what they are modifying, to guarantee their successful completion.

Although locking provides isolation for transactions and helps ensure their integrity, it can also have a significant impact on the performance of the system. To keep your system performing well, it is necessary to keep transactions as short, concise, and non-interfering as possible. This chapter explores the locking features of SQL Server that provide isolation for transactions. You'll come to understand the performance impact of the various levels and types of locks in SQL Server and how to define transactions to minimize locking performance problems.

Transaction Isolation Levels in SQL Server

Isolation levels determine the extent to which data being accessed or modified in one transaction is protected from changes to the data by other transactions. In theory, each transaction should be fully isolated from other transactions. However, in practice, for practical and performance reasons, this might not always be the case. In a concurrent environment in the absence of locking and isolation, the following four scenarios can happen:

▶ **Lost update**—In this scenario, no isolation is provided to a transaction from other transactions. Multiple transactions can read the same copy of data and modify it. The last transaction to modify the data set prevails, and the changes by all other transactions are lost.

▶ **Dirty reads**—In this scenario, one transaction can read data that is being modified by other transactions. The data read by the first transaction is inconsistent because the other transaction might choose to roll back the changes.

▶ **Nonrepeatable reads**—In this scenario, which is somewhat similar to zero isolation, a transaction reads the data twice, but before the second read occurs, another transaction modifies the data; therefore, the values read by the first read are different from those of the second read. Because the reads are not guaranteed to be repeatable each time, this scenario is called nonrepeatable reads.

▶ **Phantom reads**—This scenario is similar to nonrepeatable reads. However, instead of the actual rows that were read changing before the transaction is complete, additional rows are added to the table, resulting in a different set of rows being read the second time. Consider a scenario in which Transaction A reads rows with key values within the range of 1 through 5 and returns three rows with key values 1, 3, and 5. Before Transaction A reads the data again within the transaction, Transaction B adds two more rows with the key values 2 and 4 and commits the changes. Assuming that Transaction A and Transaction B both can run independently without blocking each other, when Transaction A runs the query a second time, it now gets five rows with key values 1, 2, 3, 4, and 5. This phenomenon is called *phantom reads* because in the second pass, you get records you did not expect to retrieve.

Ideally, a DBMS must provide levels of isolation to prevent these types of scenarios. Sometimes, for practical and performance reasons, databases relax some of the rules. The American National Standards Institute (ANSI) has defined four transaction isolation levels, each providing a different degree of isolation to cover the previous scenarios. ANSI SQL-92 defines the following four standards for transaction isolation:

- Read Uncommitted (Level 0)
- Read Committed (Level 1)
- Repeatable Read (Level 2)
- Serializable (Level 3)

SQL Server 2005 supports all the ANSI isolation levels; in addition, SQL Server 2005 also supports two new transaction isolation levels that use row versioning. One is a new implementation of Read Committed isolation called Read Committed Snapshot, and the other is the new Snapshot transaction isolation level.

You can set the default transaction isolation for a user session by using the SET TRANSACTION ISOLATION LEVEL T-SQL command, or for individual SELECT statements, you can specify table-level isolation hints within the query. Using table-level hints is covered later in this chapter, in the section "Table Hints for Locking."

Read Uncommitted Isolation

If you set the Read Uncommitted mode for a session, no isolation is provided to the SELECT queries in that session. A transaction that is running with this isolation level is not immune to dirty reads, nonrepeatable reads, or phantom reads.

To set the Read Uncommitted mode for a session, you run the following statements from the client:

- **T-SQL**—Use SET TRANSACTION ISOLATION LEVEL READ UNCOMMITTED.
- **ODBC**—Use the function call SQLSetConnectAttr with Attribute set to SQL_ATTR_TXN_ISOLATION and ValuePtr set to SQL_TXN_READ_UNCOMMITTED.
- **OLE DB**—Use the function call ITransactionLocal::StartTransaction with the isoLevel set to ISOLATIONLEVEL_READUNCOMMITTED.
- **ADO**—Set the IsolationLevel property of the Connection object to adXactReadUncommitted.
- **ADO.NET**—For applications using the System.Data.SqlClient managed namespace, call the SqlConnection.BeginTransaction method and set the IsolationLevel option to ReadUncommitted.

You need to be careful when running queries at Read Uncommitted isolation; it is possible to read changes that have been made to data that are subsequently rolled back. In essence, the accuracy of the results cannot be guaranteed. You should use this mode only when you need to get information quickly from an online transaction processing (OLTP) database, without affecting or being affected by the ongoing updates and when the accuracy of the results is not critical.

32

Read Committed Isolation

The Read Committed mode is the default locking-isolation mode for SQL Server. With Read Committed as the transaction isolation level, read operations can only read pages for transactions that have already been committed. No "dirty reads" are allowed. Locks acquired by update transactions are held for the duration of the transaction. However, in this mode, read requests within the transaction release locks as soon as the query finishes reading the data. Although this improves concurrent access to the data for updates, it does not prevent nonrepeatable reads or phantom reads. For example, within a transaction, a process could read one set of rows early in the transaction and then, before reading the information again, another process could modify the result set, resulting in a different result set being read the second time.

Because Read Committed is the default isolation level for SQL Server, you do not need to do anything to set this mode. If you need to set the isolation level back to Read Committed mode for a session, you run the following statements from the client:

- ▶ **T-SQL**—Use `SET TRANSACTION ISOLATION LEVEL READ COMMITTED`.

- ▶ **ODBC**—Use the function call `SQLSetConnectAttr` with `Attribute` set to `SQL_ATTR_TXN_ISOLATION` and `ValuePtr` set to `SQL_TXN_READ_COMMITTED`.

- ▶ **OLE DB**—Use the function call `ITransactionLocal::StartTransaction` with `isoLevel` set to `ISOLATIONLEVEL_READCOMMITTED`.

- ▶ **ADO**—Set the `IsolationLevel` property of the `Connection` object to `adXactReadcommitted`.

- ▶ **ADO.NET**—For applications using the `System.Data.SqlClient` managed namespace, call the `SqlConnection.BeginTransaction` method and set the `IsolationLevel` option to `ReadCommitted`.

Read Committed Snapshot Isolation

When the `READ_COMMITTED_SNAPSHOT` database option is set to `ON`, sessions running with the Read Committed isolation mode use row versioning to provide statement-level read consistency. When this database option is enabled and a transaction runs at the Read Committed isolation level, all statements within the transaction see a snapshot of the data as it exists at the start of the statement.

When the `READ_COMMITTED_SNAPSHOT` option is enabled for a database, SQL Server maintains versions of each row that is modified. Whenever a transaction modifies a row, an image of the row before modification is copied into a page in the version store, which is a collection of data pages in `tempdb`. If multiple transactions modify a row, multiple versions of the row are linked in a version chain. Queries running with Read Committed Snapshot isolation retrieve the last version of each row that had been committed when the statement started, providing a statement-level snapshot of the data.

In the Read Committed Snapshot isolation mode, read operations do not acquire shared page or row locks on the data. Therefore, readers using row versioning do not block other processes modifying the same data, and, similarly, processes modifying the data do not block the readers. In addition, because the read operations do not acquire locks, locking overhead is reduced. However, processes modifying data still block other processes modifying data because two operations cannot modify the same data at the same time. Exclusive locks on modified data are still acquired and held until the end of the transaction.

While locking overhead is reduced for read operations when using Read Committed Snapshot isolation, it does introduce overhead to maintain the row versions in tempdb. In addition, tempdb must have sufficient space to hold the row versions in addition to the space required for normal tempdb operations.

You might want to consider enabling the READ_COMMITTED_SNAPSHOT database option when blocking between read and write operations affects performance to the point that the overhead of creating and managing row versions is offset by the concurrency benefits. You may also consider using Read Committed Snapshot isolation when an application requires absolute accuracy for long-running aggregations or queries where data values must be consistent to the point in time that the query starts.

> **NOTE**
>
> You can use Read Committed Snapshot isolation mode with most existing SQL Server 2000–based applications without making any change to the application code itself if the applications are written to use the default Read Committed isolation level. The behavior of Read Committed, whether to use row versioning or not, is determined by the database option setting, and this can be enabled or disabled without requiring any changes to the application code.

Repeatable Read Isolation

In Repeatable Read mode, SQL Server provides the same level of isolation for updates as in Read Committed mode, but it also allows the data to be read many times within the same transaction and guarantees that the same values will be read each time. Repeatable Read isolation mode prevents other users from updating data that has been read within the transaction until the transaction in which it was read is committed or rolled back. This way, the reading transaction does not pick up changes to the rows it read previously within the transaction. However, this isolation mode does not prevent additional rows (that is, phantom reads) from appearing in the subsequent reads.

Although preventing nonrepeatable reads is desirable for certain transactions, it requires holding locks on the data that has been read until the transaction is completed. This reduces concurrent access for multiple update operations and causes performance degradation due to lock waits and locking contention between transactions. It can also potentially lead to deadlocks. (Deadlocking is discussed in more detail in the "Deadlocks" section, later in this chapter.)

To set Repeatable Read mode for a session, you run the following statements from the client:

- ▶ **T-SQL**—Use `SET TRANSACTION ISOLATION LEVEL REPEATABLE READ`.

- ▶ **ODBC**—Use the function call `SQLSetConnectAttr` with `Attribute` set to `SQL_ATTR_TXN_ISOLATION` and `ValuePtr` set to `SQL_TXN_REPEATABLEREAD`.

- ▶ **OLE DB**—Use the function call `ITransactionLocal::StartTransaction` with `isoLevel` set to `ISOLATIONLEVEL_REPEATABLEREAD`.

- ▶ **ADO**—Set the `IsolationLevel` property of the `Connection` object to `adXact REPEATABLEREAD`.

- ▶ **ADO.NET**—For applications using the `System.Data.SqlClient` managed namespace, call the `SqlConnection.BeginTransaction` method and set the `IsolationLevel` option to `RepeatableRead`.

Serializable Read Isolation

Serializable Read mode is similar to repeatable reads but adds to it the restriction that rows cannot be added to a result set that was read previously within a transaction. This prevents phantom reads. In other words, Serializable Read locks the existing data being read as well as rows that do not yet exist. It accomplishes this by locking the data being read. In addition, SQL Server puts locks on the range of values being read so that additional rows cannot be added to the range.

For example, say you run a query in a transaction that retrieves all records for the `Sales` table in the `Pubs` database for a store with the `stor_id` of `7066`. To prevent additional sales records from being added to the sales table for this store, SQL Server locks the range of values with `stor_id` of `7066`. It accomplishes this by using key-range locks, which are discussed in the "Serialization and Key-Range Locking" section, later in this chapter.

Although preventing phantom reads is desirable for certain transactions, Serializable Read mode, like Repeatable Read, reduces concurrent access for multiple update operations and can cause performance degradation due to lock waits and locking contention between transactions, and it can potentially lead to deadlocks.

To set Serializable Read mode for a session, you run the following statements from the client:

- ▶ **T-SQL**—Use `SET TRANSACTION ISOLATION LEVEL SERIALIZABLE`.

- ▶ **ODBC**—Use the function call `SQLSetConnectAttr` with `Attribute` set to `SQL_ATTR_TXN_ISOLATION` and `ValuePtr` set to `SQL_TXN_SERIALIZABLE`.

- ▶ **OLE DB**—Use the function call `ITransactionLocal::StartTransaction` with `isoLevel` set to `ISOLATIONLEVEL_SERIALIZABLE`.

- ▶ **ADO**—Set the `IsolationLevel` property of the `Connection` object to `adXact SERIALIZABLE`.

▶ **ADO.NET**—For applications using the `System.Data.SqlClient` managed namespace, call the `SqlConnection.BeginTransaction` method and set the `IsolationLevel` option to `Serializable`.

Snapshot Isolation

Snapshot Isolation is a new isolation level available in SQL Server 2005. Similar to Read Committed Snapshot, Snapshot Isolation mode uses row versioning to take a point-in-time snapshot of the data. However, unlike Read Committed Snapshot isolation, which provides a statement-level snapshot of the data, Snapshot Isolation maintains a snapshot of the data for the duration of the transaction. A data snapshot is taken when the transaction starts and the snapshot remains consistent for the duration of the transaction.

Snapshot Isolation mode provides the benefit of repeatable reads without acquiring and holding shared locks on the data that is read. This can help minimize locking and blocking problems between read operations and update operations. Read operations do not have to wait for write operations and writes don't have to wait for reads.

To set the Snapshot Isolation mode for a session, you run the following statement:

```
SET TRANSACTION ISOLATION LEVEL SNAPSHOT
```

In addition, in order to be able to request the Snapshot Isolation mode in a session, the database option `ALLOW_SNAPSHOT_ISOLATION` must be enabled with the `ALTER DATABASE` command:

```
ALTER DATABASE dbname SET ALLOW_SNAPSHOT_ISOLATION ON
```

When Snapshot Isolation mode is enabled, SQL Server assigns a transaction sequence number to each transaction that manipulates data using row versioning. When either the `READ_COMMITTED_SNAPSHOT` or `ALLOW_SNAPSHOT_ISOLATION` database options is set to `ON`, SQL Server stores a version of the previously committed image of the data row in `tempdb` whenever the row is modified by a transaction. Each of these versions is marked with the transaction sequence number of the transaction that made the change. The versions of the modified rows are linked together in a chain, with the most recent version of the row always stored in the current database and the versioned rows stored in `tempdb`.

When a transaction requests a read of data, it searches the version chain to locate the last committed version of the data row with a lower transaction sequence number than the current transaction. Row versions are kept in `tempdb` only long enough to satisfy the requirements of any transactions running under row versioning–based isolation levels. SQL Server keeps track of the sequence number of the oldest outstanding transaction and periodically deletes all row versions stamped with transaction sequence numbers that are lower than that.

You might consider using snapshot isolation in the following instances:

▶ When you want optimistic concurrency control

▶ When it is unlikely that your transaction would have to be rolled back because of an update conflict

▶ When an application generates reports based on long-running, multistatement queries that must have point-in-time consistency

▶ With systems that are incurring a high number of deadlocks because of read/write contention

There is a risk to using snapshot isolation, however. If two client applications both retrieve the same data and then both attempt to write changes to the data back to the database, the second application could potentially overwrite the first application's changes. This is called a *lost update error*. Fortunately, SQL Server 2005 resolves this problem by blocking the second transaction's writes. So, while snapshot isolation provides benefits for resolving conflicts between read and write operations, there can still be conflicts between multiple write operations. For systems with heavy read and insert activity and with little concurrent updating of the same resource, snapshot isolation can provide a solution for concurrency issues.

Another cost of snapshot isolation is that it can make heavy use of `tempdb`. For this reason, you should locate `tempdb` on its own high-performance drive system.

NOTE

Only one of the transaction isolation levels can be active at any given time for a user session. The isolation level you set within an application is active for the duration of the connection or until it is manually reset. To check the current transaction isolation level settings, you run the DBCC USEROPTIONS command and examine the value for isolation level, as in the following example:

```
DBCC USEROPTIONS
go
```

Set Option	Value
textsize	2147483647
language	us_english
dateformat	mdy
datefirst	7
lock_timeout	-1
quoted_identifier	SET
arithabort	SET
ansi_null_dflt_on	SET
ansi_warnings	SET
ansi_padding	SET
ansi_nulls	SET
concat_null_yields_null	SET
isolation level	snapshot

The Lock Manager

The responsibility for ensuring lock conflict resolution between user processes falls on the SQL Server Lock Manager. SQL Server automatically assigns locks to processes to guarantee that the current user of a resource (for example, a data row or page, an index row or page, a table, an index, or a database) has a consistent view of that resource, from the beginning to the end of a particular operation. In other words, what you start with is what you work with throughout your transaction. Nobody can change what you are working on in midstate, thereby ensuring the consistency of your transaction.

The Lock Manager is responsible for deciding the appropriate lock type (for example, shared, exclusive, update) and the appropriate granularity of locks (for example, row, page, table), according to the type of operation being performed and the amount of data being affected. Based on the type of transaction, the SQL Server Lock Manager chooses different types of lock resources. For example, a CREATE INDEX statement might lock the entire table, whereas an UPDATE statement might lock only a specific row.

The Lock Manager also manages compatibility between lock types attempting to access the same resources, resolves deadlocks, and escalates locks to a higher level, if necessary.

The Lock Manager manages locks for both shared data and internal system resources. For shared data, the Lock Manager manages row locks, page locks, and table locks on tables, as well as data pages, text pages, and leaf-level index pages. Internally, the Lock Manager uses latches to manage locking on index rows and pages, controlling access to internal data structures, and in some cases, for retrieving individual rows of data. Latches provide better system performance because they are less resource intensive than locks. Latches also provide greater concurrency than locks. Latches are typically used for operations such as page splits, deletion of index rows, movement of rows in an index, and so on. The main difference between a lock and a latch is that a lock is held for the duration of the transaction, and a latch is held only for the duration of the operation for which it is required. Locks are used to ensure the logical consistency of data, whereas latches are used to ensure the physical consistency of the data and the data structures.

The remainder of this chapter examines how the Lock Manager determines the type and level of lock to assign, based on the type of command being executed, the number of rows affected, and the lock isolation level in effect.

Monitoring Lock Activity in SQL Server

To monitor the performance of a system, it is necessary to keep track of locking activity in SQL Server. The following are the most commonly used methods to do so:

- ▶ Querying the sys.dm_tran_locks dynamic management view directly
- ▶ Viewing locking activity with SSMS
- ▶ Viewing locking activity with SQL Server Profiler
- ▶ Monitoring locks with System Monitor

▶ Using the `sp_lock` stored procedure

▶ Querying the `syslockinfo` view directly

As you read through the rest of this chapter, you might want to examine or monitor the locking activity for the examples presented. To assist you in that effort, the remainder of this section describes the methods of examining lock activity in SQL Server 2005.

> **NOTE**
>
> The `sp_lock` system procedure and `syslockinfo` view are still supported in SQL Server 2005, but for backward compatibility only. Both are features that are being deprecated in future releases of SQL Server. To obtain information about locks in the SQL Server 2005 database engine, you should use the `sys.dm_tran_locks` dynamic management view instead. For this reason, this chapter does not cover the `sp_lock` stored procedure or the `syslockinfo` view.

Querying the `sys.dm_tran_locks` View

The `sys.dm_tran_locks` dynamic management view returns information about all the locks currently granted or waiting to be granted in SQL Server. (The information is populated from the internal lock management structures in SQL Server 2005.) This view provides no historical information; rather, the data in this view corresponds to live Lock Manager information. This data can change at any time for subsequent queries of the view as locks are acquired and released.

The information returned by the view can be divided into two main groups: resource information and lock request information. The resource information describes the resource on which the lock request is being made, and the request information provides details on the lock request itself. Table 32.1 describes the most useful data columns returned by the `sys.dm_tran_locks` view.

TABLE 32.1   Useful Columns Returned by the `sys.dm_tran_locks` View

Column Name	Description
`resource_type`	Indicates the type of resource the lock is being held or requested on.
`resource_subtype`	Indicates a subtype of the `resource_type`, if any.
`resource_database_id`	Indicates the database ID of the database the resource resides in.
`resource_description`	Provides information about the resource that is not available from other resource columns.
`resource_associated_entity_id`	Indicates the ID of the entity in a database that the resource is associated with.
`resource_lock_partition`	Indicates the ID of the associated partition for a resource that is partitioned.

TABLE 32.1   Continued

Column Name	Description
request_mode	Indicates the lock mode of the request that has been granted or is being waited on.
request_type	Indicates the request type. (The value is LOCK.)
request_status	Indicates the current status of this request (GRANTED, CONVERT, or WAIT).
request_reference_count	Returns an approximate number of times the same requestor has requested this resource.
request_session_id	Indicates the ID of the session that generated the corresponding request.
request_exec_context_id	Indicates the ID of the execution context of the process that generated the lock request.
request_request_id	Indicates the batch ID of the process that generated the request.
request_owner_type	Indicates the type of entity that owns the request. Possible values include, but are not limited to, TRANSACTION, CURSOR, and SESSION.
request_owner_id	Indicates the user ID of the specific owner of the lock request.

Table 32.2 lists the possible lock request modes that can be displayed in the request_mode column of the sys.dm_tran_locks view.

TABLE 32.2   Lock Request Modes

Value	Lock Type	Description	Request Mode
1	N/A	No access provided to the requestor	NULL
2	Schema	Schema stability lock	Sch-S
3	Schema	Schema modification lock	Sch-M
4	Shared	Acquisition of a shared lock on the resource	S
5	Update	Acquisition of an update lock on the resource	U
6	Exclusive	Exclusive lock granted on the resource	X
7	Intent	Intent for a shared lock	IS
8	Intent	Intent for an update lock	IU
9	Intent	Intent for an exclusive lock	IX
10	Intent	Shared lock with intent for an update lock on subordinate resources	SIU
11	Intent	Shared lock with intent for an exclusive lock on subordinate resources	SIX
12	Intent	Update lock with an intent for an exclusive lock on subordinate resources	UIX
13	Bulk	BULK UPDATE lock used for bulk copy operations	BU

TABLE 32.2   Continued

Value	Lock Type	Description	Request Mode
14	Key-Range	Shared lock on the range between keys and shared lock on the key at the end of the range; used for serializable range scan	Range_S_S
15	Key-Range	Shared lock on the range between keys, with an update lock on the key at the end of the range	Range_S_U
16	Key-Range	Exclusive lock used to prevent inserts into a range between keys	RangeIn-N
17	Key-Range	Key-range conversion lock created by overlap of RangeIn-N and shared (S) locks	RangeIn-S
18	Key-Range	Key-range conversion lock created by overlap of RangeIn-N and update (U) locks	RangeIn-U
19	Key-Range	Key-range conversion lock created by overlap of RangeIn-N and exclusive (X) locks	RangeIn-X
20	Key-Range	Key-range conversion lock created by overlap of RangeIn-N and RangeS_S locks	RangeX-S
21	Key-Range	Key-Range conversion lock created by overlap of RangeIn-N and RangeS_U locks	RangeX-U
22	Key-Range	Exclusive lock on range between keys, with an exclusive lock on the key at the end of the range	RangeX-X

Listing 32.1 provides an example of a query against the sys.dm_tran_locks view.

LISTING 32.1   An Example of a Query Against the sys.dm_tran_locks View

```
select str(request_session_id, 4,0) as spid,
     convert (varchar(12), db_name(resource_database_id)) As db_name,
     case when resource_database_id = db_id() and resource_type = 'OBJECT'
          then convert(char(20), object_name(resource_Associated_Entity_id))
          else convert(char(20), resource_Associated_Entity_id)
          end as object,
     convert(varchar(12), resource_type) as resource_type,
     convert(varchar(12), request_type) as request_type,
     convert(char(1), request_mode) as mode,
     convert(varchar(8), request_status) as status
  from sys.dm_tran_locks
order by request_session_id, 3 desc
go

spid db_name     object               resource_type request_type mode status
---- ----------- -------------------- ------------- ------------ ---- --------
  52 bigpubs2005 0                    DATABASE      LOCK         S    GRANT
  53 bigpubs2005 titles               OBJECT        LOCK         I    GRANT
  53 bigpubs2005 72057594038910976    KEY           LOCK         X    GRANT
```

LISTING 32.1   Continued

53	bigpubs2005	72057594038910976	KEY	LOCK	X	GRANT
53	bigpubs2005	72057594038910976	KEY	LOCK	X	GRANT
53	bigpubs2005	72057594038910976	KEY	LOCK	X	GRANT
53	bigpubs2005	72057594038910976	PAGE	LOCK	I	GRANT
53	bigpubs2005	72057594038910976	PAGE	LOCK	I	GRANT
53	bigpubs2005	72057594038910976	KEY	LOCK	X	GRANT
53	bigpubs2005	72057594038910976	KEY	LOCK	X	GRANT
53	bigpubs2005	72057594038910976	KEY	LOCK	X	GRANT
53	bigpubs2005	72057594038910976	KEY	LOCK	X	GRANT
53	bigpubs2005	72057594038910976	KEY	LOCK	X	GRANT
53	bigpubs2005	72057594038910976	KEY	LOCK	X	GRANT
53	bigpubs2005	72057594038910976	KEY	LOCK	X	GRANT
53	bigpubs2005	72057594038910976	KEY	LOCK	X	GRANT
53	bigpubs2005	72057594038779904	KEY	LOCK	X	GRANT
53	bigpubs2005	72057594038779904	KEY	LOCK	X	GRANT
53	bigpubs2005	72057594038779904	KEY	LOCK	X	GRANT
53	bigpubs2005	72057594038779904	KEY	LOCK	X	GRANT
53	bigpubs2005	72057594038779904	PAGE	LOCK	I	GRANT
53	bigpubs2005	72057594038779904	PAGE	LOCK	I	GRANT
53	bigpubs2005	72057594038779904	KEY	LOCK	X	GRANT
53	bigpubs2005	72057594038779904	KEY	LOCK	X	GRANT
53	bigpubs2005	72057594038779904	PAGE	LOCK	I	GRANT
53	bigpubs2005	0	DATABASE	LOCK	S	GRANT

Note that the query in Listing 32.1 contains a CASE expression for displaying the object name. If the resource type is OBJECT and the database ID of the locked resource is the same as the current database context, it returns the object name; otherwise, it returns the object ID because the object_name() function operates only in the current database context.

> **TIP**
>
> To save yourself the trouble of having to type in the query listed in Listing 32.1, or having to read it in from a file each time you want to run it, you might want to consider creating your own stored procedure that invokes this query. You can then use that stored procedure to monitor locks, similarly to using the sp_lock system procedure.

Viewing Locking Activity with SSMS

In addition to querying the sys.dm_tran_locks system catalog view, you can also use SSMS to display locking information. To see this information within SSMS, you expand the server items in the Object Explorer, expand the Management folder, and double-click Activity Monitor. By default, the Activity Monitor displays the process info. You can select either the Locks by Process or Locks by Object page to display lock info.

The Locks by Process page displays a list of the locks currently held by the process specified in the Selected Processes drop-down list (see Figure 32.1).

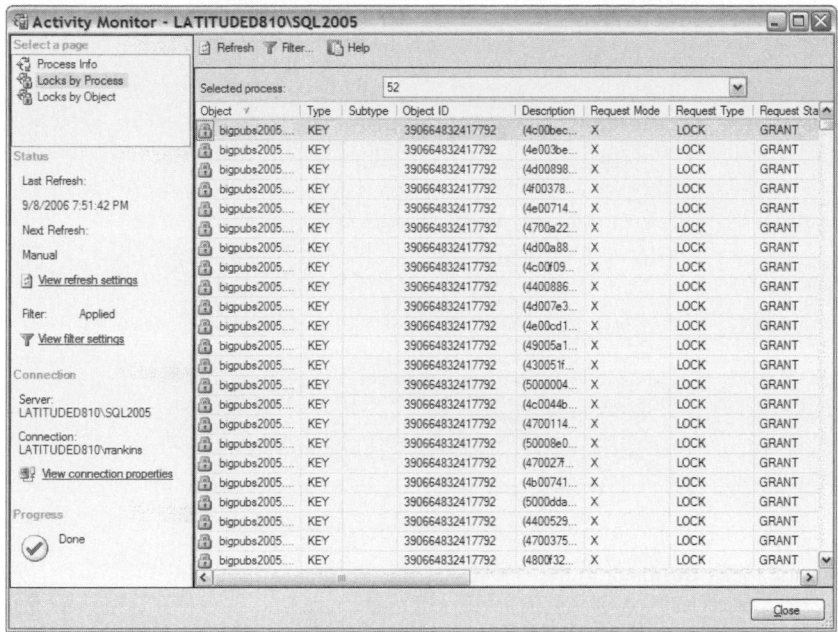

FIGURE 32.1   Viewing locks by process in the SSMS Activity Monitor.

The Locks by Object page displays a list of the locks currently held on the object specified in the Selected Object drop-down list (see Figure 32.2).

To manually refresh the information displayed in the SSMS Activity Monitor, you click the Refresh icon at the top of the Activity Monitor window or press the F5 key. You can also configure the Activity Monitor to auto-refresh at a specified interval. You click the View Refresh Settings hyperlink in the Status pane to bring up the Refresh Settings dialog, as shown in Figure 32.3. You click the Auto-Refresh Every check box to enable the auto-refresh interval. The default auto-refresh interval is 60 seconds, but you can set it to anything greater than 0. However, it's recommended you don't set it too low because the overhead of querying the lock information too frequently can affect the overall system performance.

You can also fine-tune the filters used to display the lock information in the SSMS Activity Monitor. To do so, you click the View Filter Settings hyperlink in the Status pane to bring up the Filter Settings dialog, as shown in Figure 32.4. You can choose to filter based on connection information, such as process ID, application name, hostname, username, and process status, as well as by blocking status, waiting status, database name, transaction status, and process memory use.

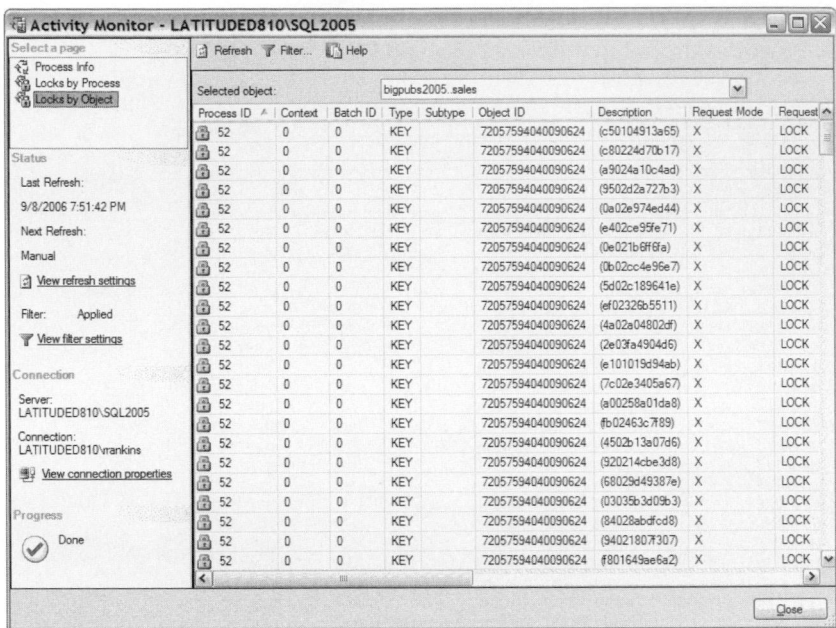

FIGURE 32.2   Viewing locks by object in the SSMS Activity Monitor.

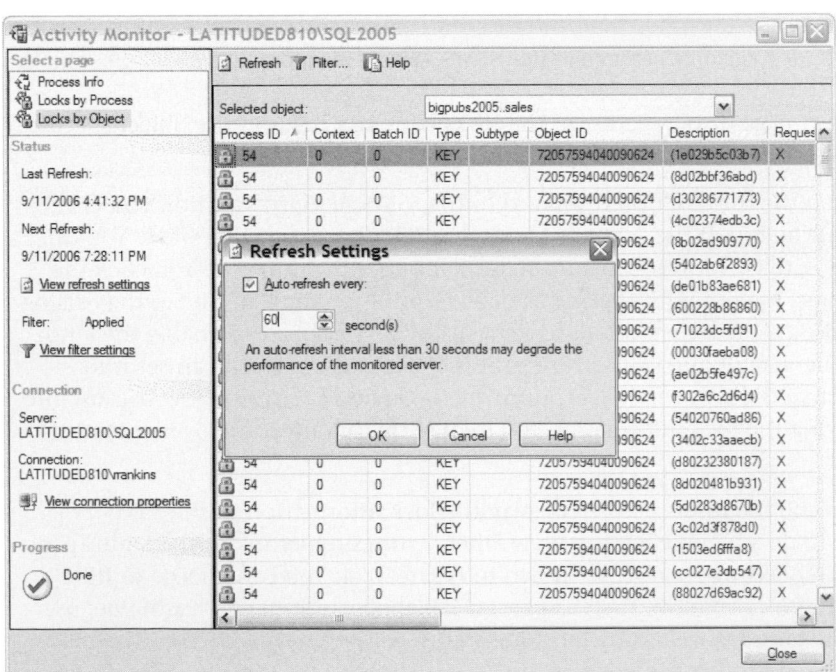

FIGURE 32.3   Setting the auto-refresh interval in the SSMS Activity Monitor.

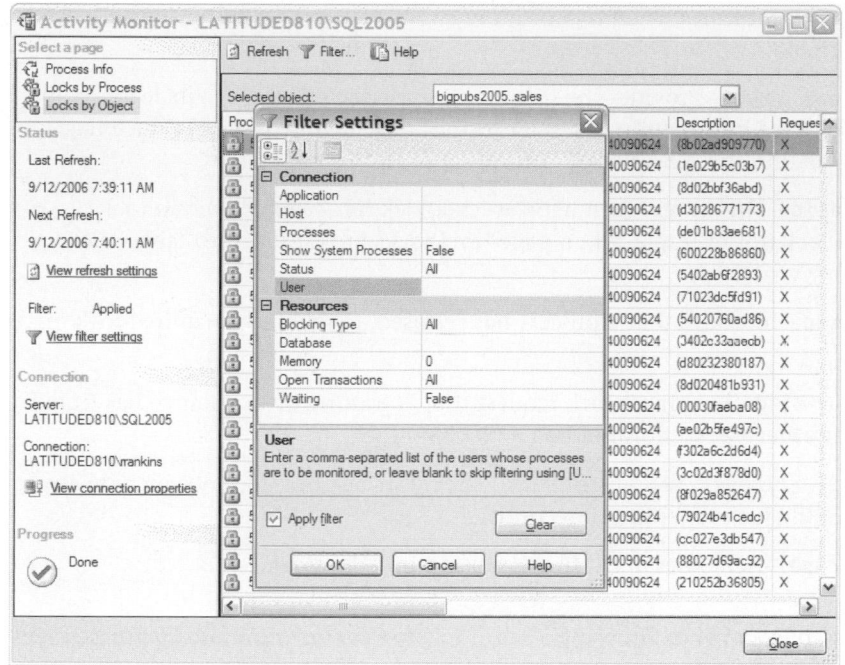

FIGURE 32.4   Setting filters in the SSMS Activity Monitor.

Viewing Locking Activity with SQL Server Profiler

Another tool to help you monitor locking activity in SQL Server 2005 is SQL Server Profiler. SQL Server Profiler provides a number of lock events that you can capture in a trace. The trace information can be viewed in real-time or saved to a file or database table for further analysis at a later date. Saving the information to a table allows you to run different reports on the information to help in the analysis.

> **NOTE**
>
> This chapter provides only a brief overview of how to capture and view locking informa-
> tion using SQL Server Profiler. For more information on the features and capabilities of
> SQL Server Profiler and how to use it, see Chapter 5, "SQL Server Profiler."

SQL Profiler provides the following lock events that can be captured in a trace:

▶ **Lock:Acquired**—Indicates when a lock on a resource, such as a data page or a row, has been acquired.

▶ **Lock:Cancel**—Indicates when the acquisition of a lock on a resource has been canceled (for example, as the result of a deadlock).

▶ **Lock:Deadlock**—Indicates when two or more concurrent processes have deadlocked with each other.

▶ **Lock:Deadlock Chain**—Provides the information for each of the events leading up to a deadlock. This information is similar to that provided by the 1204 trace flag, which is covered in the "Deadlocks" section, later in this chapter.

▶ **Lock:Escalation**—Indicates when a lower-level lock has been converted to a higher-level lock (for example, when page-level locks are escalated to table-level locks).

▶ **Lock:Released**—Indicates that a process has released a previously acquired lock on a resource.

▶ **Lock:Timeout**—Indicates that a lock request that is waiting on a resource has timed out due to another transaction holding a blocking lock.

▶ **Lock:Timeout (timeout >0)**—Is similar to Lock:Timeout but does not include any events where the lock timeout is 0 seconds.

▶ **Deadlock Graph**—Generates an XML description of a deadlock.

Figure 32.5 shows an example of choosing a set of locking events to monitor with SQL Server Profiler.

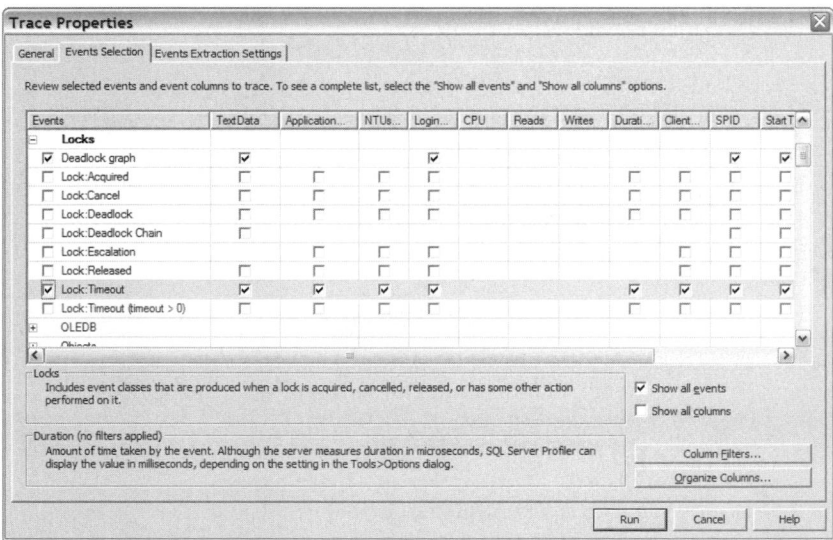

FIGURE 32.5   Choosing lock events in SQL Server Profiler.

SQL Server Profiler also provides a number of data values to display for the events being monitored. You might find the following data columns useful when monitoring locking activity:

- ► **spid**—The process ID of the process that generated the event.

- ► **EventClass**—The type of event that is being captured.

- ► **Mode**—For lock monitoring, the type of lock that is involved in the captured event.

- ► **ObjectID**—The ID of the object that is involved in the locking event—that is, the object that the lock is associated with.

- ► **ObjectName**—The name of the object involved in the locking event.

- ► **IndexID**—The ID of the index that the lock is associated with.

- ► **TextData**—The query that generated the lock event.

- ► **LoginName**—The login name associated with the process.

- ► **ApplicationName**—The name of the application that is generating the lock event.

Keep in mind that many internal system processes also acquire locks in SQL Server. If you want to filter out those processes and focus on specific processes, users, or applications, you use the filters in SQL Server Profiler to include the information you want to trace or exclude the information you don't want to trace (see Figure 32.6).

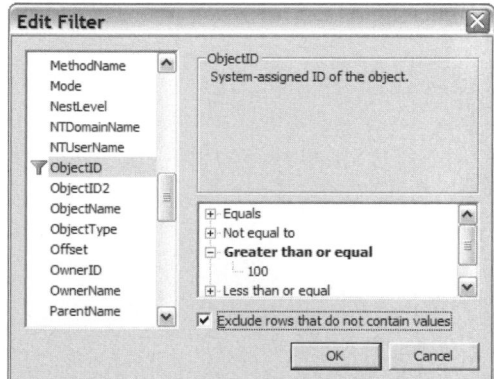

FIGURE 32.6   Filtering out unwanted information in SQL Server Profiler.

After you have set up your events, data columns, and filters, you can begin the trace. Figure 32.7 shows an example of the type of information captured.

Monitoring Locks with Performance Monitor

Another method of monitoring locking in SQL Server is through the Performance Monitor. The sys.dm_tran_locks view and SSMS Activity Monitor provide a snapshot of the actual locks currently in effect in SQL Server. If you want to monitor the locking activity as a whole on a continuous basis, you can use the Windows Performance Monitor and monitor the counters that are available for the SQLServer:Locks performance object (see Figure 32.8).

FIGURE 32.7   Lock information captured in a SQL Server Profiler trace.

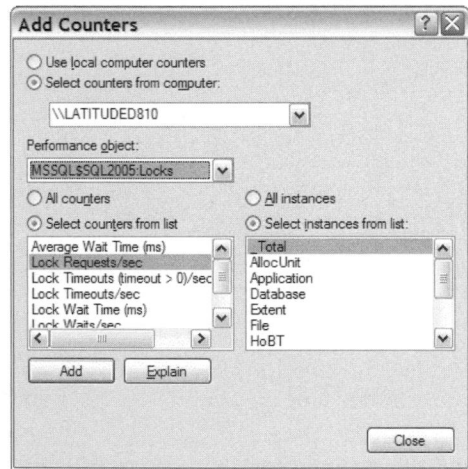

FIGURE 32.8   Choosing counters for the SQLServer:Locks performance object in Performance Monitor.

NOTE

If you are monitoring a SQL Server 2005 named instance rather than a default instance of SQL Server 2005, the SQL Server performance counters are listed under the name of the SQL Server instance rather than under the generic SQLServer performance counters.

You can use the SQLServer:Locks object to help detect locking bottlenecks and contention points in the system as well as to provide a summary of the overall locking activity in SQL Server. You can use the information that Performance Monitor provides to identify whether locking problems are the cause of any performance problems. You can then take appropriate corrective actions to improve concurrency and the overall performance of the system. The counters that belong to the SQLServer:Locks object are as follows:

▶ **Average Wait Time**—This counter represents the average wait time (in milliseconds) for each lock request. A high value is an indication of locking contention which could be affecting performance of concurrent processes.

▶ **Lock Requests/sec**—This counter represents the total number of new locks and lock conversion requests made per second. A high value for this counter is not necessarily a cause for alarm; it might simply indicate a system with a high number of concurrent users.

▶ **Lock Timeouts/sec**—This counter represents the total number of lock timeouts per second that occur for lock requests on a resource that cannot be granted before the lock timeout interval is exceeded. By default, a blocked process waits indefinitely unless the application specifies a maximum timeout limit, using the SET LOCK_ TIMEOUT command. A high value for this counter might indicate that the timeout limit is set to a low value in the application or that you are experiencing excessive locking contention.

▶ **Lock Wait Time**—This counter represents the cumulative wait time for each lock request. It is given in milliseconds. A high value here indicates that you might have long-running or inefficient transactions that are causing blocking and locking contention.

▶ **Lock Waits/sec**—This counter represents the total number of lock requests generated per second for which a process had to wait before a lock request on a resource was granted. A high value might indicate inefficient or long-running transactions or a poor database design that is causing a large number of transactions to block one another.

▶ **Number of Deadlocks/sec**—This number represents the total number of lock requests per second that resulted in deadlocks. Deadlocks and how to avoid them are discussed in the "Deadlocks" section, later in this chapter.

For more information on using Windows Performance Monitor for monitoring SQL Server performance, see Chapter 34, "Monitoring SQL Server Performance."

SQL Server Lock Types

Locking is handled automatically in SQL Server. The Lock Manager chooses the type of locks, based on the type of transaction (such as SELECT, INSERT, UPDATE, or DELETE). Lock Manager uses the following types of locks:

- ▶ Shared locks

- ▶ Update locks

- ▶ Exclusive locks

- ▶ Intent locks

- ▶ Schema locks

- ▶ Bulk update locks

In addition to choosing the type of lock, the Lock Manager in SQL Server 2005 automatically adjusts the granularity of the locks (for example, row, page, table), based on the nature of the statement that is executed and the number of rows that are affected.

Shared Locks

By default, SQL Server uses shared locks for all read operations. A shared lock is, by definition, not exclusive. Theoretically, an unlimited number of shared locks can be held on a resource at any given time. In addition, shared locks are unique in that, by default, a process locks a resource only for the duration of the read on the resource (row, page, or table). For example, the query SELECT * from authors locks the first row in the authors table when the query starts. After the first row is read, the lock on that row is released, and a lock on the second row is acquired. After the second row is read, its lock is released, and a lock on the third row is acquired, and so on. In this fashion, a SELECT query allows other data rows that are not being read to be modified during the read operation. This increases concurrent access to the data.

Shared locks are compatible with other shared locks as well as with update locks. A shared lock does not prevent the acquisition of additional shared locks or an update lock by other processes on a given row or page. Multiple shared locks can be held at any given time, for a number of transactions or processes. These transactions do not affect the consistency of the data. However, shared locks do prevent the acquisition of exclusive locks. Any transaction that is attempting to modify data on a page or a row on which a shared lock is placed is blocked until all the shared locks are released.

NOTE

It is important to note that within a transaction running at the default isolation level of Read Committed, shared locks are not held for the duration of the transaction or even the duration of the statement that acquires the shared locks. Shared lock resources (row, page, table, and so on) are normally released as soon as the read operation on the resource is completed. SQL Server provides the HOLDLOCK clause for the SELECT statement, which you can use if you want to continue holding the shared lock for the duration of the transaction. HOLDLOCK is explained later in this chapter, in the section "Table Hints for Locking." Another way to hold shared locks for the duration of a transaction is to set the isolation level for the session or the query to Repeatable Read or Serializable Reads.

Update Locks

Update locks are used to lock rows or pages that a user process would like to modify. When a transaction tries to update a row, it must first read the row to ensure that it is modifying the appropriate record. If the transaction were to put a shared lock on the resource initially, it would eventually need to get an exclusive lock on the resource to modify the record and prevent any other transaction from modifying the same record. The problem is that this could lead to deadlocks in an environment in which multiple transactions are trying to modify data on the same resource at the same time. Figure 32.9 demonstrates how deadlocks can occur if lock conversion takes place from shared locks to exclusive locks. When both processes attempt to escalate the shared lock they both hold on a resource to an exclusive lock, it results in a deadlock situation.

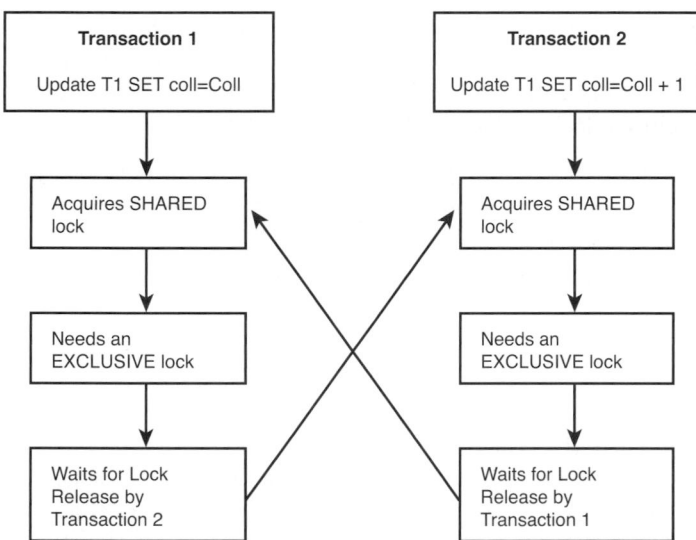

FIGURE 32.9   A deadlock scenario with shared and exclusive locks.

Update locks in SQL Server are provided to prevent this kind of deadlock scenario. Update locks are partially exclusive in that only one update lock can be acquired at a time on any resource. However, an update lock is compatible with shared locks, in that both can be acquired on the same resource simultaneously. In effect, an update lock signifies that a process wants to change a record, and it keeps out other processes that also want to change that record. However, an update lock allows other processes to acquire shared locks to read the data until the UPDATE or DELETE statement is finished locating the records to be affected. The process then attempts to escalate each update lock to an exclusive lock. At this time, the process waits until all currently held shared locks on the same records are released. After the shared locks are released, the update lock is escalated to an exclusive lock. The data change is then carried out, and the exclusive lock is held for the remainder of the transaction.

> **NOTE**
>
> Update locks are not used just for update operations. SQL Server uses update locks any time a search for data is required prior to performing the actual modification, such as with qualified updates and deletes (that is, when a WHERE clause is specified). Update locks are also used for insertions into a table with a clustered index because SQL Server must first search the data and the clustered index to identify the correct position at which to insert the new row to maintain the sort order. After SQL Server has found the correct location and begins inserting the record, it escalates the update lock to an exclusive lock.

Exclusive Locks

As mentioned earlier, an exclusive lock is granted to a transaction when it is ready to perform data modifications. An exclusive lock on a resource makes sure no other transaction can interfere with the data locked by the transaction that is holding the exclusive lock. SQL Server releases the exclusive lock at the end of the transaction.

Exclusive locks are incompatible with other lock types. If an exclusive lock is held on a resource, any other read or data modification requests for the same resource by other processes is forced to wait until the exclusive lock is released. Likewise, if a resource currently has read locks held on it by other processes, the exclusive lock request is forced to wait in a queue for the resource to become available.

Intent Locks

Intent locks do not really constitute a locking mode; rather, they act as a mechanism to indicate at a higher level of granularity the type of locks held at a lower level. The types of intent locks mirror the lock types previously discussed: shared intent locks, exclusive intent locks, and update intent locks. SQL Server Lock Manager uses intent locks as a mechanism to indicate that a shared, update, or exclusive lock is held at a lower level. For example, a shared intent lock on a table by a process signifies that the process currently holds a shared lock on a row or page within the table. The presence of the intent lock prevents other transactions from attempting to acquire a table level lock that would be incompatible with the existing row or page locks.

Intent locks improve locking performance by allowing SQL Server to examine locks at the table level to determine the types of locks held on the table at the row or page level rather than searching through the multiple locks at the page or row level within the table. Intent locks also prevent two transactions that are both holding locks at a lower level on a resource from attempting to escalate those locks to a higher level while the other transaction still holds the intent lock. This prevents deadlocks during lock escalation.

You typically see three types of intent locks when monitoring locking activity: intent shared (IS) locks, intent exclusive (IX) locks, and shared with intent exclusive (SIX) locks. An IS lock indicates that the process currently holds, or has the intention of holding, shared locks on lower-level resources (row or page). An IX lock indicates that the process currently holds, or has the intention of holding, exclusive locks on lower-level resources. An SIX (pronounced as the letters *S-I-X*, not like the number six) lock occurs under special circumstances when a transaction is holding a shared lock on a resource, and later in the transaction, an IX lock is needed. At that point, the IS lock is converted to an SIX lock.

In the following example, the SELECT statement running at the serializable level acquires a shared table lock. It then needs an exclusive lock to update the row in the sales_big table:

```
SET TRANSACTION ISOLATION LEVEL serializable
go
BEGIN TRAN
 select sum(qty) FROM sales_big
UPDATE sales_big
    SET qty = 0
    WHERE sales_id = 1001
COMMIT TRAN
```

Because the transaction initially acquired a shared (S) table lock and then needed an exclusive row lock, which requires an intent exclusive (IX) lock on the table within the same transaction, the S lock is converted to an SIX lock.

> **NOTE**
>
> If only a few rows were in sales_big, SQL Server might only acquire individual row or key locks rather than a table-level lock. SQL Server would then have an intent shared (IS) lock on the table rather than a full shared (S) lock. In that instance, the UPDATE statement would then acquire a single exclusive lock to apply the update to a single row, and the X lock at the key level would result in the IS locks at the page and table levels being converted to an IX lock at the page and table level for the remainder of the transaction.

Schema Locks

SQL Server uses schema locks to maintain structural integrity of SQL Server tables. Unlike other types of locks that provide isolation for the data, schema locks provide isolation for the schema of database objects, such as tables, views, and indexes within a transaction. The Lock Manager uses two types of schema locks:

▶ **Schema stability locks**—When a transaction is referencing either an index or a data page, SQL Server places a schema stability lock on the object. This ensures that no other process can modify the schema of an object—such as dropping an index or dropping or altering a stored procedure or table—while other processes are still referencing the object.

▶ **Schema modification locks**—When a process needs to modify the structure of an object (for example, alter the table, recompile a stored procedure), the Lock Manager places a schema modification lock on the object. For the duration of this lock, no other transaction can reference the object until the changes are complete and committed.

Bulk Update Locks

Bulk update locks are a special type of lock used only when bulk copying data into a table using the bcp utility or the BULK INSERT command. This special lock is used for these operations only when either the TABLOCK hint is specified to bcp or the BULK INSERT command or when the table lock on bulk load table option has been set for the table. Bulk update locks allow multiple bulk copy processes to bulk copy data into the same table in parallel, while preventing other processes that are not bulk copying data from accessing the table.

SQL Server Lock Granularity

Lock granularity is essentially the amount of data that is locked as part of a query or update to provide complete isolation and serialization for the transaction. The Lock Manager needs to balance the concurrent access to resources versus the overhead of maintaining a large number of lower-level locks. For example, the smaller the lock size, the greater the number of concurrent users who can access the same table at the same time but the greater the overhead in maintaining those locks. The greater the lock size, the less overhead required to manage the locks, but concurrency is also less. Figure 32.10 demonstrates the trade-offs between lock size and concurrency.

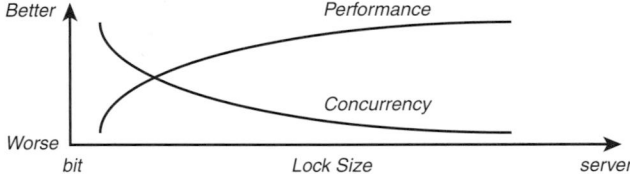

FIGURE 32.10   Trade-offs between performance and concurrency, depending on lock granularity.

Currently, SQL Server balances performance and concurrency by locking at the row level or higher. Based on a number of factors, such as key distribution, number of rows, row density, search arguments (SARGs), and so on, the Query Optimizer makes lock granularity decisions internally, and the programmer does not have to worry about such issues. SQL Server provides a number of T-SQL extensions that give you better control over query behavior from a locking standpoint. These Query Optimizer overrides are discussed in the "Table Hints for Locking" section, later in this chapter.

SQL Server provides the following locking levels:

▶ **Database**—Whenever a SQL Server process is using a database other than `master`, the Lock Manager grants a database lock to the process. These are always shared locks, and they are used to keep track of when a database is in use to prevent another process from dropping the database, setting the database offline, or restoring the database. Note that because `master` and `tempdb` cannot be dropped or set offline, database locks are not required on those databases.

▶ **File**—A file lock is a lock acquired on a database file.

▶ **Extent**—Extent locks are used for locking extents, usually only during space allocation and deallocation. An extent consists of eight contiguous data or index pages. Extent locks can be shared extent or exclusive extent locks.

▶ **AllocUnit**—This type of lock is acquired on a database allocation unit.

▶ **Table**—With this type of lock, the entire table, inclusive of data and indexes, is locked. Examples of when table-level locks may be acquired include selecting all rows from a large table at the serializable level and performing unqualified updates or deletes on a table.

▶ **Heap or B-Tree (HOBT)**—This type of lock is acquired on a heap of data pages or on the B-Tree structure of an index.

▶ **Page**—With a page lock, the entire page, consisting of 8KB of data or index information, is locked. Page-level locks might be acquired when all rows on a page need to be read or when page-level maintenance needs to be performed, such as updating page pointers after a page split.

▶ **Row ID (RID)**—With an RID lock, a single row within a page is locked. RID locks are acquired whenever efficient and possible to do so in an effort to provide maximum concurrent access to the resource.

▶ **Key**—SQL Server uses two types of key locks. The one that is used depends on the locking isolation level of the current session. For transactions that run in Read Committed or Repeatable Read isolation modes, SQL Server locks the actual index keys that are associated with the rows being accessed. (If a clustered index is on the table, the data rows are the leaf level of the index. You see key locks instead of row locks on those rows.) When in Serializable Read isolation mode, SQL Server prevents phantom rows by locking a range of key values so that no new rows can be inserted into the range. These are referred to as *key-range locks*. Key-range locks associated with a particular key value lock that key and the previous one in the index to indicate that all values between them are locked. Key-range locks are covered in more detail in the next section.

▶ **Metadata**—This type of lock is acquired on system catalog information

32

▶ **Application**—An application lock allows users to essentially define their own locks by specifying a name for the resource, a lock mode, an owner, and a timeout interval. Using application locks is discussed later in this chapter, in the section "Using Application Locks."

Serialization and Key-Range Locking

As mentioned in the previous section, SQL Server provides serialization (Isolation Level 3) through the SET TRANSACTION ISOLATION SERIALIZABLE command. One of the isolations that is provided by this isolation level is the prevention against phantom reads. Preventing phantom reads means that the recordset that a query obtains within a transaction must return the same result set when it is run multiple times within the same transaction. That is, while a transaction is active, another transaction should not be allowed to insert new rows that would appear in the recordset of a query that were not in the original recordset retrieved by the transaction. SQL Server provides this capability though key-range locking.

As described earlier in this chapter, key-range locking in SQL Server provides isolation for a transaction from data modifications made by other transactions. This means that a transaction should return the same recordset each time. The following sections show how key-range locking works with various lock modes. Key-range locking covers the scenarios of a range search that returns a result set as well as searches against nonexistent rows.

Key-Range Locking for a Range Search

In a scenario that involves key-range locking for a range search, SQL Server places locks on the index pages for the range of data covered in the WHERE clause of the query. (For a clustered index, the rows would be the actual data rows in the table.) Because the range is locked, no other transaction can insert new rows that fall within the range. In Figure 32.11, for example, Transaction B tries to insert a row into the sales table with a key value (stor_id = 7200) that falls within the range being retrieved by Transaction A (stor_id between 6000 and 7500).

Listing 32.2 shows the locks acquired when using the sys.dm_tran_locks catalog view. (In this sample output, spid 52 is executing the SELECT statement, and spid 53 is attempting the INSERT.)

LISTING 32.2   Viewing Key-Range Locks Using the sys.dm_tran_locks View

```
select str(request_session_id, 4,0) as spid,
       convert (varchar(12), db_name(resource_database_id)) As db_name,
       case when resource_database_id = db_id() and resource_type = 'OBJECT'
            then convert(char(20), object_name(resource_Associated_Entity_id))
            else convert(char(20), resource_Associated_Entity_id)
            end as object,
       convert(varchar(12), resource_type) as resource_type,
       convert(varchar(10), request_mode) as mode,
```

LISTING 32.2   Continued

```
        convert(varchar(8), request_status) as status
    from sys.dm_tran_locks
order by request_session_id, 3 desc
go

spid db_name       object                  resource_type mode         status
---- -----------    --------------------    ------------- ----------   --------
  52 bigpubs2005   stores                  OBJECT        IS           GRANT
  52 bigpubs2005   391941215944704         KEY           RangeS-S     GRANT
  52 bigpubs2005   391941215944704         KEY           RangeS-S     GRANT
  52 bigpubs2005   391941215944704         KEY           RangeS-S     GRANT
  52 bigpubs2005   391941215944704         PAGE          IS           GRANT
  52 bigpubs2005   391941215944704         KEY           RangeS-S     GRANT
  52 bigpubs2005   391941215944704         KEY           RangeS-S     GRANT
  52 bigpubs2005   0                       DATABASE      S            GRANT
  53 bigpubs2005   stores                  OBJECT        IX           GRANT
  53 bigpubs2005   391941215944704         PAGE          IX           GRANT
  53 bigpubs2005   391941215944704         KEY           RangeI-N     WAIT
  53 bigpubs2005   0                       DATABASE      S            GRANT
  54 bigpubs2005   0                       DATABASE      S            GRANT
```

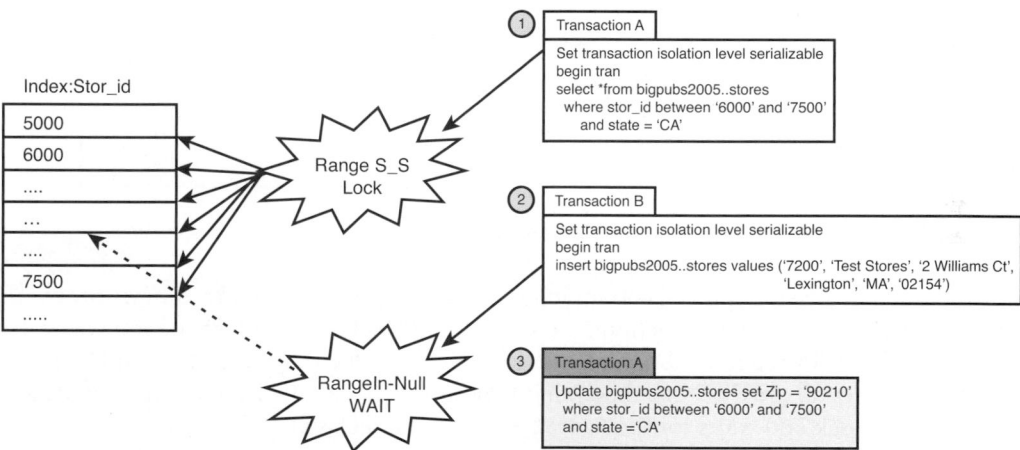

FIGURE 32.11   Key-range locking with a range search.

To provide key-range isolation, SQL Server places RangeS-S locks (that is, a shared lock on
the key range and a shared lock on the key at the end of the range) on the index keys for
the rows with the matching values. It also places intent share (IS) locks on the page(s)
and the table that contain the rows. The insert process acquires intent exclusive (IX) locks
on the destination page(s) and the table. In this case, the insert process is waiting for a

RangeIn-Null lock on the key range until the RangeS-S locks in the key range are released. The RangeIn-Null lock is an exclusive lock on the range between keys, with no lock on the key. This is acquired because the insert process is attempting to insert a new store ID that has no associated key value.

Key-Range Locking When Searching Nonexistent Rows

In a scenario that involves key-range locking when searching nonexistent rows, if a transaction is trying to delete or retrieve a row that does not exist in the database, it still should not find any rows at a later stage in the same transaction with the same query. For example, in Figure 32.12, Transaction A is trying to fetch a nonexistent row with the key value 7200, and another concurrent transaction (Transaction B) is trying to insert a record with the same key value (stor_id = 7200).

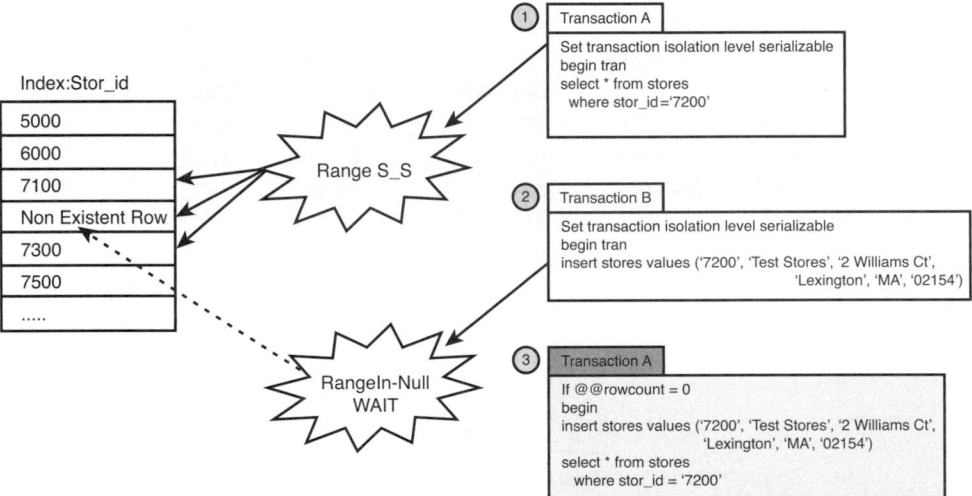

FIGURE 32.12   Key-range locking with a nonexistent data set.

In this mode, SQL Server prevents Transaction B (spid 53) from inserting a new row by using a RangeS-S lock for Transaction A (spid 52). This lock is placed on the index key rows for the rows in the range between MAX(stor_id) < 7200 (key value 7100 in Figure 32.12) and MIN(stor_id) > 7200 (key value 7300 in Figure 32.12). Transaction B holds a RangeIn-Null lock and waits for the RangeS-S lock to be released.

Listing 32.3 provides an example of the query against the sys.dm_tran_locks catalog view for these two transactions.

LISTING 32.3   Viewing Key-Range Locks on Nonexistent Row

```
select str(request_session_id, 4,0) as spid,
       convert (varchar(12), db_name(resource_database_id)) As db_name,
       case when resource_database_id = db_id() and resource_type = 'OBJECT'
            then convert(char(20), object_name(resource_Associated_Entity_id))
            else convert(char(20), resource_Associated_Entity_id)
            end as object,
       convert(varchar(12), resource_type) as resource_type,
       convert(varchar(10), request_mode) as mode,
       convert(varchar(8), request_status) as status
    from sys.dm_tran_locks
order by request_session_id, 3 desc
go
```

spid	db_name	object	resource_type	mode	status
52	bigpubs2005	stores	OBJECT	IS	GRANT
52	bigpubs2005	391941215944704	PAGE	IS	GRANT
52	bigpubs2005	391941215944704	KEY	RangeS-S	GRANT
52	bigpubs2005	0	DATABASE	S	GRANT
53	bigpubs2005	stores	OBJECT	IX	GRANT
53	bigpubs2005	391941215944704	KEY	RangeI-N	WAIT
53	bigpubs2005	391941215944704	PAGE	IX	GRANT
53	bigpubs2005	0	DATABASE	S	GRANT
54	bigpubs2005	0	DATABASE	S	GRANT

Using Application Locks

The SQL Server Lock Manager knows nothing about the object or the structure of the object it is locking. The Lock Manager simply checks whether two processes are trying to obtain incompatible locks on the same resource. If so, blocking occurs.

SQL Server allows you to extend the resources that can be locked beyond the ones automatically provided. You can define your own custom locking resources and let the Lock Manager control the access to those resources as it would for any resource in a database. This essentially allows you to choose to lock anything you want. These user-defined lock resources are called *application locks*. To define an application lock, you use the sp_getapplock stored procedure and specify a name for the resource you are locking, a mode, an optional lock owner, and an optional lock timeout interval. The syntax for sp_getapplock is as follows:

```
sp_getapplock [ @Resource = ] 'resource_name',
    [ @LockMode = ] 'lock_mode'
    [ , [ @LockOwner = ] { 'transaction' ¦ 'session' } ]
    [ , [ @LockTimeout = ] 'value' ]
    [ , [ @DbPrincipal = ] 'database_principal' ]
```

Two resources are considered to be the same resource and are subject to lock contention if they have the same name and the same lock owner in the same database. The resource name used in these procedures can be any identifier up to 255 characters long. The lock owner can be specified as either `transaction` or `session`. Multiple requests for locks on the same resource can be granted only if the locking modes of the requests are compatible. (See the "Lock Compatibility" section, later in this chapter, for a lock compatibility matrix.) The possible modes of the lock allowed are shared, update, exclusive, intent exclusive, and intent shared. The database principal is the user, role, or application role that has permissions to an object in a database. The default is `public`.

For what purpose can you use application locks, and how do you use them? Suppose you have a table that contains a queue of items to be processed by the system. You need a way to serialize the retrieval of the next item from the queue so that the multiple concurrent processes do not grab the same item at the same time. In the past, one way this could be accomplished was by forcing an exclusive lock on the table. (The use of table hints to override default locking behavior is covered in the "Table Hints for Locking" section, later in this chapter.) Only the first process to acquire the exclusive lock would be able to retrieve the next item from the queue. The other processes would have to wait until the exclusive lock was released. The problem with this approach is that the exclusive lock would also block other processes that might need to simply retrieve data from the table.

You can use application locks to avoid having to place an exclusive lock on the entire table. By using `sp_getapplock`, you can define and lock a custom lock resource for a transaction or session. Locks that are owned by the current transaction are released when the transaction commits or rolls back. Locks that are owned by the session are released when the session is closed. Locks can also be explicitly released at any time, with the `sp_releaseapplock` stored procedure. The syntax for `sp_releaseapplock` is as follows:

```
sp_releaseapplock [ @Resource = ] 'resource_name'
    [ , [ @LockOwner = ] { 'transaction' | 'session' }]
    [ , [ @DbPrincipal = ] 'database_principal' ]
```

NOTE

If a process calls `sp_getapplock` multiple times for the same lock resource, `sp_releaseapplock` must be called the same number of times to fully release the lock. In addition, if `sp_getapplock` is called multiple times on the same lock resource but specifies different lock modes each time, the resulting lock on the resource is a union of the different lock modes. Generally, the lock mode ends up being promoted to the more restrictive level of the existing lock mode and the newly requested mode. The resulting lock mode is held until the last lock release call is made to fully release the lock. For example, assume that a process initially called `sp_getapplock` requested a shared lock. If it subsequently called `sp_getapplock` again and requested an exclusive lock, an exclusive lock would be held on the resource until `sp_releaseapplock` was executed twice.

In the following example, you first request an exclusive lock on an application lock called
'QueueLock' by using sp_getapplock. You then invoke the procedure to get the next item
in the queue. After the procedure returns, you call sp_releaseapplock to release the
application lock called 'QueueLock' to let another session acquire the application lock:

```
sp_getapplock 'QueueLock', 'Exclusive', 'session'
exec get_next_item_from_queue
sp_releaseapplock 'QueueLock', 'session'
```

As long as all processes that need to retrieve items from the queue execute this same
sequence of statements, no other process can execute the get_next_item_from_queue
process until the application lock is released. The other processes block attempts to
acquire the exclusive lock on the resource 'QueueLock'. For example, Listing 32.4 shows
an example of a query against the sys.dm_tran_locks view, showing one process (spid
55) holding an exclusive lock on QueueLock, while another process (spid 53) is waiting
for an exclusive lock on QueueLock. (The hash value generated internally for QueueLock is
shown as 18fb067e in the Resource_Desc field.)

LISTING 32.4   Viewing Application Locks Using sys.dm_tran_locks

```
select str(request_session_id, 4,0) as spid,
       convert (varchar(12), db_name(resource_database_id)) As db_name,
       case when resource_database_id = db_id() and resource_type = 'OBJECT'
            then convert(char(6), object_name(resource_Associated_Entity_id))
            else convert(char(6), resource_Associated_Entity_id)
            end as object,
       convert(varchar(12), resource_type) as resource_type,
       convert(varchar(4), request_mode) as mode,
       convert(varchar(24), resource_description) as resource_desc,
       convert(varchar(6), request_status) as status
   from sys.dm_tran_locks
order by request_session_id, 3 desc
go
```

spid	db_name	object	resource_type	mode	resource_desc	status
53	bigpubs2005	0	DATABASE	S		GRANT
53	bigpubs2005	0	APPLICATION	X	0:[QueueLock]:(18fb067e)	WAIT
54	bigpubs2005	0	DATABASE	S		GRANT
55	bigpubs2005	0	DATABASE	S		GRANT
55	bigpubs2005	0	APPLICATION	X	0:[QueueLock]:(18fb067e)	GRANT

> **CAUTION**
>
> This method of using application locks to control access to the queue works only if all processes that are attempting to retrieve the next item in the queue follow the same protocol. The get_next_item_from_queue procedure itself is not actually locked. If another process attempts to execute the get_next_item_from_queue process without attempting to acquire the application lock first, the Lock Manager in SQL Server does not prevent the session from executing the stored procedure.

Index Locking

As with locks on data pages, SQL Server manages locks on index pages internally. There is the opportunity for greater locking contention in index pages than in data pages. Contention at the root page of the index is the highest because the root is the starting point for all searches via the index. Contention usually decreases as you move down the various levels of the B-tree, but it is still higher than contention at the data page level due to the typically greater number of index rows per index page than data rows per data page.

If locking contention in the index becomes an issue, you can use ALTER INDEX to manage the locking behavior at the index level. The syntax of this command is as follows:

```
ALTER INDEX { index_name ¦ ALL } ON object
{   ALLOW_ROW_LOCKS = { ON ¦ OFF }
  ¦ ALLOW_PAGE_LOCKS = { ON ¦ OFF }
```

The default for both ALLOW_ROW_LOCKS and ALLOW_PAGE_LOCKS is ON. When both of these options are enabled, SQL Server automatically makes the decision whether to apply row or page locks on the indexes and can escalate locks from the row or page level to the table level. When ALLOW_ROW_LOCKS is set to OFF, row locks on indexes are not used. Only page- or table-level locks are applied. When ALLOW_PAGE_LOCKS is set to OFF, no page locks are used on indexes, and only row- or table-level locks are applied. When ALLOW_ROW_LOCKS and ALLOW_PAGE_LOCK are both set to OFF, only a table-level lock is applied when the index is accessed.

> **NOTE**
>
> When ALLOW_PAGE_LOCKS is set to OFF for an index, the index cannot be reorganized.

SQL Server usually makes good choices for the index locks, but based on the distribution of data and nature of the application, you might want to force a specific locking option on a selective basis. For example, if you are experiencing a high level of locking contention at the page level of an index, you might want to force SQL Server to use row-level locks by turning off page locks.

As another example, if you have a lookup table that is primarily read-only (for example, one that is only refreshed by a weekly or monthly batch process), it may be more efficient to turn off page and row locking so that all readers simply acquire shared table-level locks, thereby reducing locking overhead. When the weekly or monthly batch update runs, the update process acquires an exclusive table-level lock when refreshing the table.

To display the current locking option for a given index, you use the INDEXPROPERTY function:

```
select INDEXPROPERTY(object_ID , index_name,
                 { 'IsPageLockDisallowed' ¦ 'IsRowLockDisallowed' } )
```

> **CAUTION**
>
> SQL Server generally makes the correct decision in choosing the appropriate locking granularity for a query. It is generally not recommended that you override the locking granularity choices that the Query Optimizer makes unless you have good reason to do so and have evaluated all options first. Setting the inappropriate locking level can adversely affect the concurrency for a table or index.

Row-Level Versus Page-Level Locking

For years, it was often debated whether row-level locking was better than page-level locking. That debate still goes on in some circles. Many people argue that if databases and applications are well designed and tuned, row-level locking is unnecessary. This is borne out somewhat by the number of large and high-volume applications that were developed when row-level locking wasn't even an option. (Prior to SQL Server version 7, the smallest unit of data that SQL Server could lock was the page.) However, at that time, the page size in SQL Server was only 2KB. With page sizes expanded to 8KB, a greater number of rows (four times as many) can be contained on a single page. Page-level locks on 8KB pages could lead to greater page-level contention because the likelihood of the data rows being requested by different processes residing on the same page is greater. Using row-level locking increases the concurrent access to the data.

On the other hand, row-level locking consumes more resources (memory and CPU) than page-level locks simply because there is a greater number of rows than pages in a table. If a process needed to access all rows on a page, it would be more efficient to lock the entire page than acquire a lock for each individual row. This would result in a reduction in the number of lock structures in memory that the Lock Manager would have to manage.

Which is better—greater concurrency or lower overhead? As shown earlier, in Figure 32.10, it's a trade-off. As lock size decreases, concurrency improves, but performance degrades due to the extra overhead. As the lock size increases, performance improves due to less overhead, but concurrency degrades. Depending on the application, the database design, and the data, either page-level or row-level locking can be shown to be better than the other in different circumstances.

SQL Server makes the determination automatically at runtime—based on the nature of the query, the size of the table, and the estimated number of rows affected—of whether to initially lock rows, pages, or the entire table. In general, SQL Server attempts to first lock at the row level more often than the page level, in an effort to provide the best concurrency. With the speed of today's CPUs and the large memory support, the overhead of managing row locks is not as expensive as in the past. However, as the query processes and the actual number of resources locked exceed certain thresholds, SQL Server might attempt to escalate locks from a lower level to a higher level, as appropriate.

At times, SQL Server might choose to do both row and page locking for the same query. For example, if a query returns multiple rows, and if enough contiguous keys in a nonclustered index page are selected to satisfy the query, SQL Server might place page locks on the index while using row locks on the data. This reduces the need for lock escalation.

Lock Escalation

When SQL Server detects that the locks acquired by a query are using too much memory and consuming too many system resources for the Lock Manager to manage the locks efficiently, it automatically attempts to escalate row, key, or page locks to table-level locks. For example, because a query on a table continues to acquire row locks and every row in the table will eventually be accessed, it makes sense for SQL Server to escalate the row locks to a table-level lock. After the table-level lock is acquired, the row-level locks are released. This helps reduce locking overhead and keeps the system from running out of available lock structures. Recall from earlier sections in this chapter that the potential need for lock escalation is reflected in the intent locks that are acquired on the table by the process locking at the row or page level.

> **NOTE**
>
> If another process is also holding locks at the page or row level on the same table (indicated by the presence of that process's intent lock on the table), lock escalation cannot take place if the lock types are not compatible until the lower-level locks are released by the other processes. In this case, SQL Server continues acquiring locks at the row or page level until the table lock becomes available.

What are the lock escalation thresholds? SQL Server attempts lock escalation whenever a single T-SQL statement acquires at least 5,000 locks on a single reference of a table or index, or when the number of locks acquired exceeds memory or configuration thresholds. If locks cannot be escalated because of lock conflicts, SQL Server reattempts lock escalation when every 1,250 additional locks are acquired. The memory threshold depends on the setting of the locks configuration option.

The locks Configuration Setting

The total number of locks available in SQL Server is dependent on the amount of memory available for the lock structures. This is controlled by the locks configuration option for

SQL Server. By default, the locks option is set to 0, which allows SQL Server to allocate and deallocate lock structures dynamically, based on ongoing system requirements. Initially, SQL Server allocates enough memory for a pool of 2,500 locks. Each lock structure consumes 96 bytes of memory.

As the pool of locks is exhausted, additional lock structures are allocated, up to a maximum of 40 percent of the memory currently allocated to SQL Server. If more memory is required for locks than is currently available to SQL Server, and if more server memory is available, SQL Server allocates additional memory from the operating system dynamically. Doing so satisfies the request for locks as long as the allocation of the additional memory does not cause paging at the operating system level. If allocating more lock structures would lead to paging, more lock space is not allocated. In addition, the dynamic lock pool will not acquire more than 60% of the total memory allocated to the database engine.

If no more memory is available or if the lock pool has reached 60% of the memory acquired by an instance of the database engine, further requests for locks generate an error. When this occurs, the transaction is aborted, and the user sees a message like the following:

```
Server: Msg 1204, Level 19, State 1, Line 1
The instance of the SQL Server Database Engine cannot obtain a LOCK resource
 at this time. Rerun your statement when there are fewer active users. Ask
 the database administrator to check the lock and memory configuration for
 this instance, or to check for long-running transactions.
```

It is recommended that you leave the locks configuration setting at 0 to allow SQL Server to allocate lock structures dynamically. If you repeatedly receive error messages that you have exceeded the number of available locks, you might want to override SQL Server's ability to allocate lock resources dynamically by setting the locks configuration option to a value large enough for the number of locks needed. Because each lock structure requires 96 bytes of memory, be aware that setting the locks option to a high value might result in an increase in the amount of memory dedicated to the SQL Server instance. For more information on changing SQL Server configuration options, see Chapter 43, "Configuring, Tuning, and Optimizing SQL Server Options" (on the CD-ROM).

Lock Compatibility

If a process has already locked a resource, the granting of lock requests by other transactions on the same resource is governed by the lock compatibility matrix within SQL Server. Table 32.3 shows the lock compatibility matrix for the locks most commonly acquired by the SQL Server Lock Manager, indicating which lock types are compatible and which lock types are incompatible when requested on the same resource.

TABLE 32.3   SQL Server Lock Compatibility Matrix

Requested Lock Type	Existing Lock Type								
	IS	S	U	IX	SIX	X	Sch-S	SCH-M	BU
Intent shared	Yes	Yes	Yes	Yes	Yes	No	Yes	No	No
Shared	Yes	Yes	Yes	No	No	No	Yes	No	No
Update	Yes	Yes	No	No	No	No	Yes	No	No
Intent exclusive	Yes	No	No	Yes	No	No	Yes	No	No
Shared with intent exclusive	Yes	No	No	No	No	No	Yes	No	No
Exclusive	No	No	No	No	No	No	Yes	No	No
Schema stability	Yes	Yes	Yes	Yes	Yes	Yes	Yes	No	Yes
Schema modify	No	No	No	No	No	No	No	No	No
Bulk update	No	No	No	No	No	No	Yes	No	Yes

For example, if a transaction has acquired a shared lock on a resource, the possible lock types that can be acquired on the resource by other transactions are intent shared, shared, update, and schema stability locks. Intent exclusive, SIX, exclusive, schema modification, and bulk update locks are incompatible with a shared lock and cannot be acquired on the resource until the shared lock is released.

Locking Contention and Deadlocks

In the grand scheme of things, the most likely culprits of SQL Server application performance problems are typically poorly written queries, poor database and index design, and locking contention. Whereas the first two problems result in poor application performance, regardless of the number of users on the system, locking contention becomes more of a performance problem as the number of users increases. It is further compounded by increasingly complex or long-running transactions.

Locking contention occurs when a transaction requests a lock type on a resource that is incompatible with an existing lock type on the resource. By default, the process waits indefinitely for the lock resource to become available. Locking contention is noticed in the client application through the apparent lack of response from SQL Server.

Figure 32.13 demonstrates an example of locking contention. Process 1 has initiated a transaction and acquired an exclusive lock on page 1:325. Before Process 1 can acquire the lock that it needs on page 1:341 to complete its transaction, Process 2 acquires an exclusive lock on page 1:341. Until Process 2 commits or rolls back its transaction and releases the lock on Page 1:341, the lock continues to be held. Because this is not a deadlock scenario (which is covered in the "Deadlocks" subsection, later in this section), by default, SQL Server takes no action. Process 1 simply waits indefinitely.

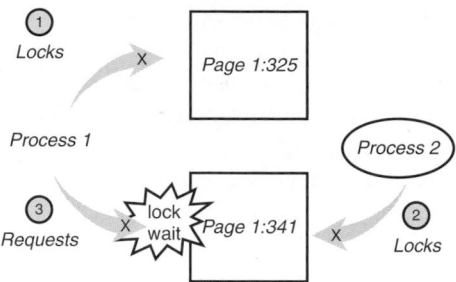

FIGURE 32.13   Locking contention between two processes.

Identifying Locking Contention

When a client application appears to freeze after submitting a query, this is often due to locking contention. To identify locking contention between processes, you can use the SSMS Activity Monitor, as discussed earlier in this chapter, in the "Monitoring Lock Activity in SQL Server" section, use the sp_who stored procedure, or query the sys.dm_tran_locks system catalog view.

To identify whether a process is being blocked, you can examine the blk column returned by sp_who:

```
exec sp_who
go
```

spid	ecid	status	loginame	hostname	blk	dbname	cmd	request_id
1	0	background	sa		0	NULL	RESOURCE MONITOR	0
2	0	background	sa		0	NULL	LAZY WRITER	0
3	0	suspended	sa		0	NULL	LOG WRITER	0
4	0	background	sa		0	NULL	LOCK MONITOR	0
5	0	background	sa		0	master	SIGNAL HANDLER	0
6	0	sleeping	sa		0	master	TASK MANAGER	0
7	0	background	sa		0	master	TRACE QUEUE TASK	0
8	0	sleeping	sa		0	NULL	UNKNOWN TOKEN	0
9	0	background	sa		0	master	BRKR TASK	0
10	0	background	sa		0	master	TASK MANAGER	0
11	0	suspended	sa		0	master	CHECKPOINT	0
12	0	background	sa		0	master	BRKR EVENT HNDLR	0
13	0	background	sa		0	master	BRKR TASK	0
14	0	sleeping	sa		0	master	TASK MANAGER	0
15	0	sleeping	sa		0	master	TASK MANAGER	0
16	0	sleeping	sa		0	master	TASK MANAGER	0
17	0	sleeping	sa		0	master	TASK MANAGER	0
18	0	sleeping	sa		0	master	TASK MANAGER	0

```
19   0   sleeping    sa               0   master     TASK MANAGER    0
20   0   sleeping    sa               0   master     TASK MANAGER    0
21   0   sleeping    sa               0   master     TASK MANAGER    0
51   0   sleeping    rrankins  LD810  0   master     AWAITING COMMAND 0
52   0   suspended   rrankins  LD810  53  bigpubs2005 SELECT         0
53   0   sleeping    rrankins  LD810  0   bigpubs2005 AWAITING COMMAND 0
54   0   runnable    rrankins  LD810  0   bigpubs2005 SELECT         0
```

If the value in the blk column is 0, then no blocking is occurring for that session. If the value is anything other than 0, the session is being blocked, and the number in the blk column is the server process ID (SPID) of the process that is causing the blocking. In the previous example, you can see that Process 53 is blocking Process 52.

To determine what table, page, or rows are involved in blocking and at what level the blocking is occurring, you can query the sys.dm_tran_locks catalog view, as shown in Listing 32.5.

LISTING 32.5   Viewing Locking Contention by Using the sys.dm_tran_locks View

```
select str(request_session_id, 4,0) as spid,
       convert (varchar(12), db_name(resource_database_id)) As db_name,
       case when resource_database_id = db_id() and resource_type = 'OBJECT'
           then convert(char(12), object_name(resource_Associated_Entity_id))
           else convert(char(16), resource_Associated_Entity_id)
           end as object,
       convert(varchar(12), resource_type) as resource_type,
       convert(varchar(8), request_mode) as mode,
       convert(varchar(14), resource_description) as resource_desc,
       convert(varchar(6), request_status) as status
   from sys.dm_tran_locks
order by request_session_id, 3 desc
go
```

```
spid db_name     object            resource_type mode     resource_desc status
---- ----------- ----------------- ------------- -------- ------------- ------
  52 bigpubs2005 stores            OBJECT        IS                     GRANT
  52 bigpubs2005 391941215944704   PAGE          S        1:280         WAIT
  52 bigpubs2005 0                 DATABASE      S                      GRANT
  53 bigpubs2005 stores            OBJECT        IX                     GRANT
  53 bigpubs2005 673416192655360   KEY           X        (5102cbc7a46c) GRANT
  53 bigpubs2005 673416192655360   PAGE          IX       1:167         GRANT
  53 bigpubs2005 391941215944704   PAGE          IX       1:280         GRANT
  53 bigpubs2005 391941215944704   KEY           X        (37005ad7376d) GRANT
  53 bigpubs2005 0                 DATABASE      S                      GRANT
  54 bigpubs2005 0                 DATABASE      S                      GRANT
```

From this output, you can see that Process 52 is waiting for a shared (S) lock on page 1:280 of the stores table. Process 53 has an intent exclusive (IX) lock on that page because it has an exclusive (X) lock on a key on that page. (Both have the same resource_Associated_Entity_id of 391941215944704.)

As an alternative to sp_who and the sys.dm_tran_locks view, you can also get specific information on any blocked processes by querying the sys.dm_os_waiting_tasks system catalog view, as shown in Listing 32.6.

LISTING 32.6   Viewing Blocked Processes by Using the sys.dm_os_waiting_tasks View

```
select convert(char(4), session_id) as spid,
       convert(char(8), wait_duration_ms) as duration,
       convert(char(8), wait_type) as wait_type,
       convert(char(3), blocking_session_id) as blk,
       resource_description
from sys.dm_os_waiting_tasks
where blocking_session_id is not null
go


spid duration wait_type blk  resource_description
---- -------- --------- ---- -------------------------------------------------
52   359344   LCK_M_S   53   pagelock fileid=1 pageid=280 dbid=10 id=lock175a9ec0
                             mode=IX associatedObjectId=391941215944704
```

Setting the Lock Timeout Interval

If you do not want a process to wait indefinitely for a lock to become available, SQL Server allows you to set a lock timeout interval by using the SET LOCK_TIMEOUT command. You specify the timeout interval in milliseconds. For example, if you want your processes to wait only 5 seconds (that is, 5,000 milliseconds) for a lock to become available, you execute the following command in the session:

```
SET LOCK_TIMEOUT 5000
```

If your process requests a lock resource that cannot be granted within 5 seconds, the statement is aborted, and you get the following error message:

```
Server: Msg 1222, Level 16, State 52, Line 1
Lock request time out period exceeded.
```

To examine the current LOCK_TIMEOUT setting, you can query the system function @@lock_timeout:

```
select @@lock_timeout
go
```

```
- - - - - - - - - - -
      5000
```

If you want processes to abort immediately if the lock cannot be granted (in other words, no waiting at all), you set the timeout interval to 0. If you want to set the timeout interval back to infinity, execute the SET_LOCK_TIMEOUT command and specify a timeout interval of -1.

Minimizing Locking Contention

Although setting the lock timeout prevents a process from waiting indefinitely for a lock request to be granted, it doesn't address the cause of the locking contention. In an effort to maximize concurrency and application performance, you should minimize locking contention between processes as much as possible. Some general guidelines to follow to minimize locking contention include the following:

▶ Keep transactions as short and concise as possible. The shorter the period of time locks are held, the less chance for lock contention. Keep commands that are not essential to the unit of work being managed by the transaction (for example, assignment selects, retrieval of updated or inserted rows) outside the transaction.

▶ Keep statements that comprise a transaction in a single batch to eliminate unnecessary delays caused by network input/output (I/O) between the initial BEGIN TRAN statement and the subsequent COMMIT TRAN commands.

▶ Consider coding transactions entirely within stored procedures. Stored procedures typically run faster than commands executed from a batch. In addition, because they are server resident, stored procedures reduce the amount of network I/O that occurs during execution of the transaction, resulting in faster completion of the transaction.

▶ Commit updates in cursors frequently and as soon as possible. Cursor processing is much slower than set-oriented processing and causes locks to be held longer.

NOTE

Even though cursors might run more slowly than set-oriented processing, cursors can sometimes be used to minimize locking contention for updates and deletions of a large number of rows from a table, which might result in a table lock being acquired. The UPDATE or DELETE statement itself might complete faster; however, if it is running with an exclusive lock on the table, then no other process can access the table until it completes. By using a cursor to update a large number of rows one row at a time and committing the changes frequently, the cursor uses page- or row-level locks rather than a table-level lock. It might take longer for the cursor to complete the actual update or delete, but while the cursor is running, other processes are still able to access other rows or pages in the table that the cursor doesn't currently have locked.

▶ Use the lowest level of locking isolation required by each process. For example, if dirty reads are acceptable and accurate results are not imperative, consider using transaction Isolation Level 0. Use the Repeatable Read or Serializable Read isolation levels only if absolutely necessary.

▶ Never allow user interaction between a BEGIN TRAN statement and a COMMIT TRAN statement because doing so may cause locks to be held for an indefinite period of time. If a process needs to return rows for user interaction and then update one or more rows, consider using optimistic locking or Snapshot Isolation in your application. (Optimistic locking is covered in the "Optimistic Locking" section, later in this chapter.)

▶ Minimize "hot spots" in a table. Hot spots occur when the majority of the update activity on a table occurs within a small number of pages. For example, hot spots occur for concurrent insertions to the last page of a heap table or the last pages of a table with a clustered index on a sequential key. You can often eliminate hot spots by creating a clustered index in a table on a column or columns to order the rows in the table in such a way that insert and update activity is spread out more evenly across the pages in the table.

Deadlocks

A *deadlock* occurs when two processes are each waiting for a locked resource that the other process currently holds. Neither process can move forward until it receives the requested lock on the resource, and neither process can release the lock it is currently holding until it can receive the requested lock. Essentially, neither process can move forward until the other one completes, and neither one can complete until it can move forward.

Two primary types of deadlocks can occur in SQL Server:

▶ **Cycle deadlocks**—A cycle deadlock occurs when two processes acquire locks on different resources, and then each needs to acquire a lock on the resource that the other process has. Figure 32.14 demonstrates an example of a cycle deadlock.

In Figure 32.14, Process 1 acquires an exclusive lock on page 1:201 in a transaction. At the same time, Process 2 acquires an exclusive lock on page 1:301 in a transaction. Process 1 then attempts to acquire a lock on page 1:301 and begins waiting for the lock to become available. Simultaneously, Process 2 requests an exclusive lock on page 1:201, and a deadlock, or "deadly embrace," occurs.

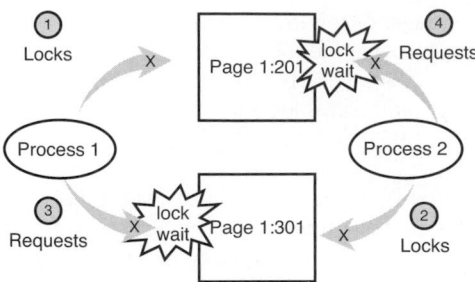

FIGURE 32.14   An example of a cycle deadlock.

▶ **Conversion deadlocks**—A conversion deadlock occurs when two or more processes each hold a shared lock on the same resource within a transaction and each wants to promote the shared lock to an exclusive lock, but neither can do so until the other releases the shared lock. An example of a conversion deadlock is shown in Figure 32.15.

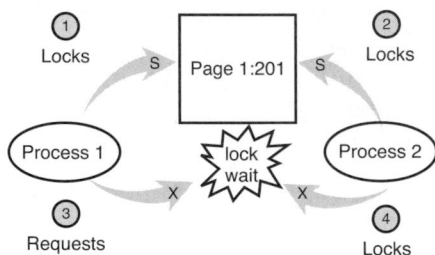

FIGURE 32.15   An example of a conversion deadlock.

It is often assumed that deadlocks happen at the data page or data row level. In fact, deadlocks often occur at the index page level. Figure 32.16 depicts a scenario in which a deadlock occurs due to contention at the index page level.

SQL Server automatically detects when a deadlock situation occurs. A separate process in SQL Server, called LOCK_MONITOR, checks the system for deadlocks roughly every 5 seconds. In the first pass, this process detects all the processes that are waiting on a lock resource. The LOCK_MONITOR thread checks for deadlocks by examining the list of waiting lock requests to see if any circular lock requests exist between the processes that are holding locks and the processes that are waiting for locks. When the LOCK_MONITOR detects a deadlock, SQL Server aborts the transaction of one of the involved processes. How does SQL Server determine which process to abort? It attempts to choose as the deadlock victim the transaction that it estimates would be least expensive to roll back. If both processes involved in the deadlock have the same rollback cost and the same deadlock priority, the deadlock victim is chosen randomly.

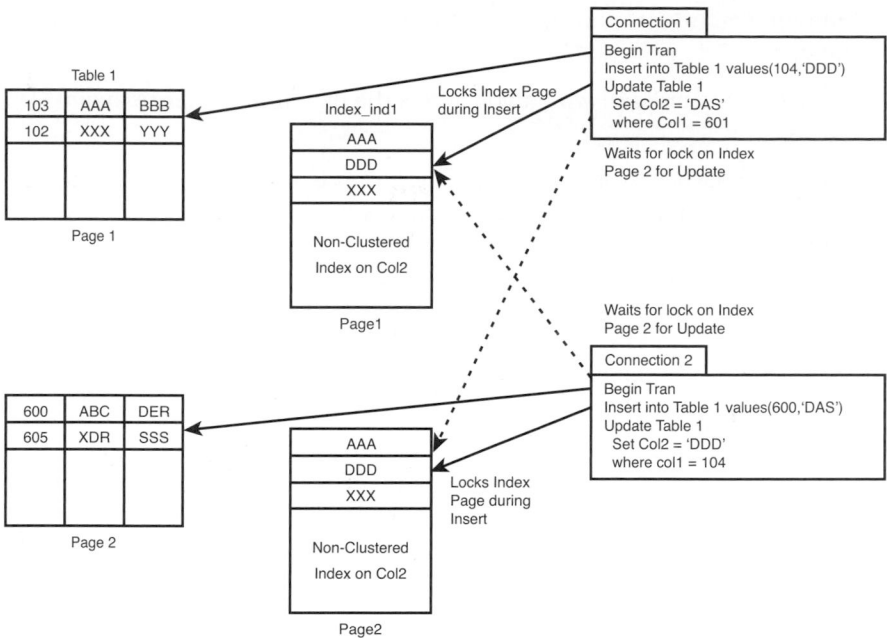

FIGURE 32.16   Deadlocks due to locks on index pages.

You can influence which process will be the deadlock victim by using the SET DEADLOCK_
PRIORITY statement. DEADLOCK_PRIORITY can be set to LOW, NORMAL, or HIGH. Alternatively,
DEADLOCK_PRIORITY can also be set to any integer value from -10 to 10. The default deadlock priority is NORMAL. When two sessions deadlock, and the deadlock priority has been
set to something other than the default, the session with the lower priority is chosen as
the deadlock victim. If you have lower-priority processes that you would prefer always be
chosen as the deadlock victims, you might want to set the process's deadlock priority to
LOW. Alternatively, for critical processes, you might want to set the deadlock priority to
HIGH to specify processes that should always come out as the winners in a deadlock
scenario.

Avoiding Deadlocks

Although SQL Server automatically detects and handles deadlocks, you should try to
avoid deadlocks in your applications. When a process is chosen as a deadlock victim, it
has to resubmit its work because it has been rolled back. Frequent deadlocks create performance problems if you have to keep repeating work.

You can follow a number of guidelines to minimize, if not completely eliminate, the
number of deadlocks that occur in your application(s). Following the guidelines presented
earlier to minimize locking contention and speed up your transactions also helps to eliminate deadlocks. The less time for which a transaction is holding locks, the less likely the
transition will be around long enough for a conflicting lock request to be requested at the

same time. In addition, you might want to follow this list of additional guidelines when designing applications:

▶ Be consistent about the order in which you access the data from tables to avoid cycle deadlocks.

▶ Minimize the use of HOLDLOCK or queries that are running using Repeatable Read or Serializable Read isolation levels. This helps avoid conversion deadlocks. If possible, perform UPDATE statements before SELECT statements so that your transaction acquires an update or exclusive lock first. This eliminates the possibility of a conversion deadlock. (Later, in the "Table Hints for Locking" section in this chapter, you will see how to use table-locking hints to force SELECT statements to use update or exclusive locks as another strategy to avoid conversion deadlocks.)

▶ Choose the transaction isolation level judiciously. You might be able to reduce deadlocks by choosing lower isolation levels.

Handling and Examining Deadlocks

SQL Server returns error number 1205 to the client when it aborts a transaction as a result of deadlock. The following is an example of a 1205 error message:

```
Msg 1205, Level 13, State 51, Line 1
Transaction (Process ID 53) was deadlocked on lock resources with another process
 and has been chosen as the deadlock victim. Rerun the transaction.
```

Because a deadlock is not a logical error but merely a resource contention issue, the client can resubmit the entire transaction. To handle deadlocks in applications, be sure to trap for message 1205 in the error handler. When a 1205 error occurs, the application can simply resubmit the transaction automatically. It is considered bad form to allow end users of an application to see the deadlock error message returned from SQL Server.

Earlier in this chapter, you learned how to use sp_who and the sys.dm_tran_locks and sys.dm_os_waiting_tasks system catalog views to monitor locking contention between processes. However, when a deadlock occurs, one transaction is rolled back, and one is allowed to continue. If you examine the output from sp_who and the system catalog views after a deadlock occurs, the information likely will not be useful because the locks on the resources involved will have since been released.

Fortunately, SQL Server provides a couple trace flags to monitor deadlocks within SQL Server. These are trace flag 1204 and trace flag 1222. When enabled, they print deadlock information to the SQL Server error log. Trace flag 1204 provides deadlock information generated by each process involved in the deadlock. Trace flag 1222 provides deadlock information by processes and by resources. Both trace flags can be enabled to capture a complete representation of a deadlock event.

You use the DBCC TRACEON command to turn on the trace flags and DBCC TRACEOFF to turn them off. The 1204 and 1222 trace flags are global trace flags. Global trace flags are set at the server level and are visible to every connection on the server. They cannot be set for a specific session only. They enable or disable a global trace flag, and the `-1` option must be specified as the second argument to the `DBCC TRACEON` and `DBCC TRACEOFF` commands. The following example shows how to globally enable the 1204 trace flag:

```
dbcc traceon(1204, -1)
```

If possible, it is best to set global trace flags whenever SQL Server is started up by adding the `-T` option with the appropriate trace flag value to the SQL Server startup parameters. For example, to have SQL Server turn on the 1204 trace flag automatically on startup, you use the SQL Server Configuration Manager. In the SQL Server Configuration Manager window, you click SQL Server 2005 Services; in the right pane, right-click the SQL Server service for the appropriate SQL Server instance name, and then click Properties. On the Advanced tab, expand the Startup Parameters box and type a semicolon (;) and `-T1204` after the last startup parameter listed (see Figure 32.17), then click OK to save the changes. You then need to stop and restart SQL Server for the trace flag to take effect.

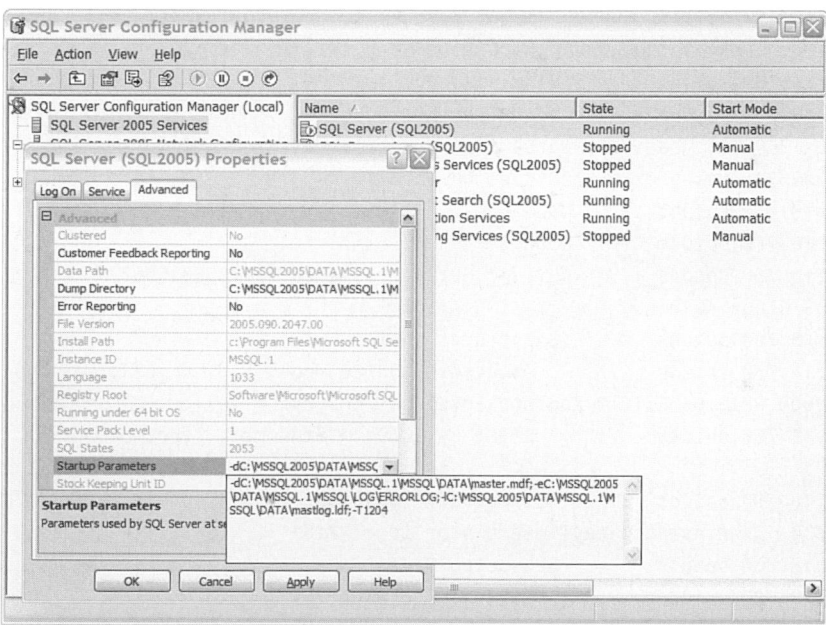

FIGURE 32.17   Setting the 1204 trace flag to be enabled on SQL Server startup.

CAUTION

The 1204 and 1222 trace flags may incur some additional processing overhead in SQL Server. They should be used only when debugging and tuning SQL Server performance, and they should not be left on indefinitely in a production environment. You should turn them off after you have diagnosed and fixed the problems.

The 1204 Trace Flag   Trace flag 1204 prints useful information to the SQL Server error log when a deadlock is detected. The following is a sample of the output from the error log for this trace flag:

```
2006-09-22 19:51:18.760 spid4s        Deadlock encountered .... Printing deadlock
 information
2006-09-22 19:51:18.760 spid4s        Wait-for graph
2006-09-22 19:51:18.760 spid4s        NULL
2006-09-22 19:51:18.760 spid4s        Node:1
2006-09-22 19:51:18.760 spid4s        KEY: 10:391941215944704 (3700560a5b33)
 CleanCnt:4 Mode:S Flags: 0x0
2006-09-22 19:51:18.760 spid4s         Grant List 0:
2006-09-22 19:51:18.760 spid4s          Owner:0x03B57D40 Mode: S       Flg:0x0
 Ref:0 Life:02000000 SPID:53 ECID:0 XactLockInfo: 0x176F4D6C
2006-09-22 19:51:18.760 spid4s          SPID: 53 ECID: 0 Statement Type: UPDATE
 Line #: 1
2006-09-22 19:51:18.760 spid4s          Input Buf: Language Event: update stores
 set stor_address = '24-A Avocado Way' where stor_id = '7131'
2006-09-22 19:51:18.760 spid4s         Requested By:
2006-09-22 19:51:18.760 spid4s          ResType:LockOwner
 Stype:'OR'Xdes:0x176F5960 Mode: X SPID:54 BatchID:0 ECID:0
 TaskProxy:(0x18242374) Value:0x3b58720 Cost:(0/0)
2006-09-22 19:51:18.760 spid4s        NULL
2006-09-22 19:51:18.760 spid4s        Node:2
2006-09-22 19:51:18.760 spid4s        KEY: 10:391941215944704 (3700560a5b33)
 CleanCnt:4 Mode:S Flags: 0x0
2006-09-22 19:51:18.760 spid4s         Grant List 0:
2006-09-22 19:51:18.760 spid4s          Owner:0x03B58780 Mode: S       Flg:0x0
 Ref:0 Life:02000000 SPID:54 ECID:0 XactLockInfo: 0x176F5984
2006-09-22 19:51:18.760 spid4s          SPID: 54 ECID: 0 Statement Type: UPDATE
 Line #: 1
2006-09-22 19:51:18.760 spid4s          Input Buf: Language Event: update stores
 set stor_address = '24-A Avocado Way' where stor_id = '7131'
2006-09-22 19:51:18.760 spid4s         Requested By:
2006-09-22 19:51:18.760 spid4s          ResType:LockOwner
 Stype:'OR'Xdes:0x176F4D48 Mode: X SPID:53 BatchID:0 ECID:0
 TaskProxy:(0x1670A374) Value:0x3b58700 Cost:(0/0)
2006-09-22 19:51:18.760 spid4s        NULL
2006-09-22 19:51:18.760 spid4s        Victim Resource Owner:
2006-09-22 19:51:18.760 spid4s          ResType:LockOwner Stype:'OR'Xdes:0x176F4D48
 Mode:X SPID:53 BatchID:0 ECID:0 TaskProxy:(0x1670A374) Value:0x3b58700 Cost:(0/0)
```

Although the 1204 output is somewhat cryptic, it is not too difficult to read if you know what to look for. If you look through the output, you can see where it lists the SPIDs of the processes involved in the deadlock (in this example, SPIDs 53 and 54) and indicates which process was chosen as the deadlock victim (SPID:53). The type of statement involved is indicated by Statement Type. In this example, both processes were running an UPDATE statement. You can also examine the actual text of the query (Input Buf) that each process was executing at the time the deadlock occurred. The output also displays the locks granted to each process (Grant List), the lock types (Mode:) of the locks held, and the lock resources requested by the deadlock victim.

The 1222 Trace Flag   Trace flag 1222 provides deadlock information, first by processes and then by resources. The information is returned in an XML-like format that does not conform to an XML schema definition. The output has three major sections:

▶ The first section declares the deadlock victim.

▶ The second section describes each process involved in the deadlock

▶ The third section describes the resources involved

The following is an example of the 1222 trace flag output for the same deadlock scenario displayed by the 1204 trace flag output in the previous section:

```
2006-09-22 20:13:20.200 spid14s      deadlock-list
2006-09-22 20:13:20.200 spid14s       deadlock victim=process6b9798
2006-09-22 20:13:20.200 spid14s       process-list
2006-09-22 20:13:20.200 spid14s        process id=process6b9798 taskpriority=0
 logused=0 waitresource=KEY: 10:391941215944704 (3700560a5b33) waittime=62
 ownerId=381197 transactionname=user_transaction
 lasttranstarted=2006-09-22T20:13:08.340 XDES=0x176f4d48 lockMode=X schedulerid=1
 kpid=3168 status=suspended spid=53 sbid=0 ecid=0 priority=0 transcount=2
 lastbatchstarted=2006-09-22T20:13:20.077
 lastbatchcompleted=2006-09-22T20:13:08.340
 clientapp=Microsoft SQL Server Management Studio - Query
 hostname=LATITUDED810 hostpid=4764 loginname=LATITUDED810\rrankins
 isolationlevel=read committed (2) xactid=381197 currentdb=10
 lockTimeout=4294967295 clientoption1=671090784 clientoption2=390200
2006-09-22 20:13:20.200 spid14s          executionStack
2006-09-22 20:13:20.200 spid14s           frame procname=adhoc line=1 stmtstart=70
 sqlhandle=0x0200000034026231e81bb557465ef1132a2e0522acbc1e58
2006-09-22 20:13:20.200 spid14s      UPDATE [stores] set [stor_address] = @1
  WHERE [stor_id]=@2
2006-09-22 20:13:20.200 spid14s           frame procname=adhoc line=1
 sqlhandle=0x02000000570d0403c6777d9cc0ac24355eb68fc216b25765
2006-09-22 20:13:20.200 spid14s      update stores set stor_address =
 '24-A Avocado Way' where stor_id = '7131'
2006-09-22 20:13:20.200 spid14s          inputbuf
2006-09-22 20:13:20.200 spid14s      update stores set stor_address =
```

```
'24-A Avocado Way' where stor_id = '7131'
2006-09-22 20:13:20.200 spid14s                  process id=process6b9978 taskpriority=0
 logused=0 waitresource=KEY: 10:391941215944704 (3700560a5b33) waittime=5000
 ownerId=381212 transactionname=user_transaction
 lasttranstarted=2006-09-22T20:13:12.700 XDES=0x176f5960 lockMode=X schedulerid=1
 kpid=4500 status=suspended spid=54 sbid=0 ecid=0 priority=0 transcount=2
 lastbatchstarted=2006-09-22T20:13:15.140
 lastbatchcompleted=2006-09-22T20:13:12.700
 clientapp=Microsoft SQL Server Management Studio - Query
 hostname=LATITUDED810 hostpid=4764 loginname=LATITUDED810\rrankins
 isolationlevel=read committed (2) xactid=381212 currentdb=10
 lockTimeout=4294967295 clientoption1=671090784 clientoption2=390200
2006-09-22 20:13:20.200 spid14s                  executionStack
2006-09-22 20:13:20.200 spid14s                  frame procname=adhoc line=1 stmtstart=70
 sqlhandle=0x0200000034026231e81bb557465ef1132a2e0522acbc1e58
2006-09-22 20:13:20.200 spid14s       UPDATE [stores] set [stor_address] = @1
  WHERE [stor_id]=@2
2006-09-22 20:13:20.200 spid14s                  frame procname=adhoc line=1
 sqlhandle=0x02000000570d0403c6777d9cc0ac24355eb68fc216b25765
2006-09-22 20:13:20.200 spid14s       update stores set stor_address =
 '24-A Avocado Way' where stor_id = '7131'
2006-09-22 20:13:20.200 spid14s                  inputbuf
2006-09-22 20:13:20.200 spid14s       update stores set stor_address =
 '24-A Avocado Way' where stor_id = '7131'
2006-09-22 20:13:20.200 spid14s            resource-list
2006-09-22 20:13:20.200 spid14s             keylock hobtid=391941215944704 dbid=10
 objectname=bigpubs2005.dbo.stores indexname=UPK_storeid id=lock17708840 mode=S
 associatedObjectId=391941215944704
2006-09-22 20:13:20.200 spid14s              owner-list
2006-09-22 20:13:20.200 spid14s              owner id=process6b9978 mode=S
2006-09-22 20:13:20.200 spid14s              owner id=process6b9798 mode=S
2006-09-22 20:13:20.200 spid14s            waiter-list
2006-09-22 20:13:20.200 spid14s              waiter id=process6b9978 mode=X
 requestType=convert
2006-09-22 20:13:20.200 spid14s              waiter id=process6b9798 mode=X
 requestType=convert
```

Monitoring Deadlocks with SQL Server Profiler

If you still find the 1204 and 1222 trace flag output too difficult to interpret, you'll be pleased to know that SQL Server Profiler provides a much more user-friendly way of capturing and examining deadlock information. As discussed in the "Monitoring Lock Activity in SQL Server" section, earlier in this chapter, SQL Profiler provides three deadlock events that can be monitored:

▶ Lock:Deadlock

▶ Lock:Deadlock Chain

▶ Deadlock Graph

The Lock:Deadlock and Lock:Deadlock Chain events aren't really very useful in SQL Server 2005. The Lock:Deadlock event generates a simple trace record that indicates when a deadlock occurs between two processes. The SPID column indicates what process was chosen as the deadlock victim. The Lock:Deadlock Chain event generates a trace record for each process involved in the deadlock. Unfortunately, neither of these trace events provides any detailed information, such as the queries involved in the deadlock. (You would need to also trace the T-SQL commands executed to capture this information, but you would then be capturing all SQL statements, not just those involved in the deadlock.)

Fortunately, SQL Server Profiler provides the new Deadlock Graph event. When this event is enabled, SQL Server Profiler populates the TextData data column in the trace with XML data about the process and objects that are involved in the deadlock. This XML data can then be used to display a Deadlock Graph in SQL Server Profiler itself, or the XML can be extracted to a file, which can be read in and viewed in SSMS. Figure 32.18 shows an example of a Deadlock Graph being displayed in SQL Server Profiler.

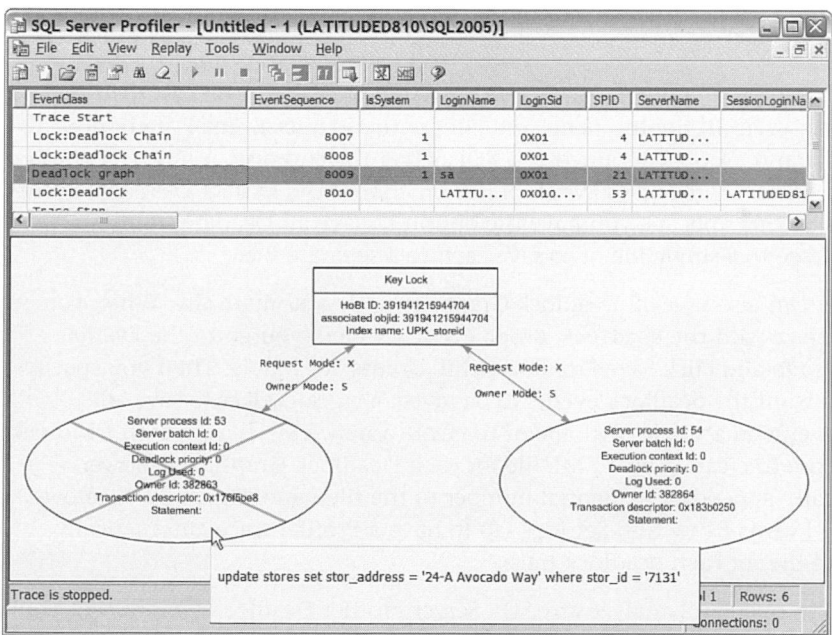

FIGURE 32.18   Displaying a Deadlock Graph in SQL Server Profiler.

The Deadlock Graph displays the processes, the resources, and the relationships between the processes and the resources. The following components make up a Deadlock Graph:

▶ **Process node**—An oval containing information about each thread that performs a task involved in the deadlock (for example, INSERT, UPDATE, or DELETE).

▶ **Resource node**—A rectangle containing information about each database object being referenced (for example, a table, an index, a page, a row, or a key).

▶ **Edge**—A line representing a relationship between a process and a resource. A request edge occurs when a process waits for a resource. An owner edge occurs when a resource waits for a process. The lock mode is included in the edge description.

Figure 32.18 displays the deadlock information for the processes involved in the deadlocks displayed by the 1204 and 1222 trace flag output listed in the previous sections. You can see that it displays the resource(s) involved in the deadlock in the Resource node (Key Lock), the lock type held on the resource by each process (Owner Mode: S), the lock type being requested by each process (Request Mode: X), and general information about each process (for example, SPID, deadlock priority) displayed in each process node. The process node of the process chosen as the deadlock victim has an X through it. If you place the mouse pointer over a process node, a ToolTip displays the SQL statement for that process involved in the deadlock. If the graph appears too large or too small for the profiler window, you can right-click anywhere within the graph to bring up a context menu that allows you to increase or decrease the size of the graph.

To save a Deadlock Graph to a file for further analysis at a later date, you can right-click the Deadlock Graph event in the top panel and choose the Extract Event Data option. To save all Deadlock Graph events contained in a SQL Server trace to one or more files, you select File, Export, Extract SQL Server Events and then choose the Extract Deadlock Events option. In the dialog that appears, you have the option to save all Deadlock Graphs contained in the trace to a single file or to save each to a separate file.

SQL Server Profiler can also save all Deadlock Graphs to a file automatically. When you are configuring a trace with the Deadlock Graph event selected, you go to the Events Extraction Settings tab and click Save Deadlock XML Events Separately. Then you specify the file where you want the deadlock events to be saved. You can select to save all Deadlock Graph events in a single XML file or to create a new XML file for each Deadlock Graph. If you choose to create a new XML file for each Deadlock Graph, SQL Server Profiler automatically appends a sequential number to the filename. Figure 32.19 shows an example of the Events Extraction Settings tab to have a Profiler trace automatically generate a separate file for each deadlock trace.

You can use SSMS to open and analyze any SQL Server Profiler Deadlock Graphs that you have saved to a file. To do so, in SSMS you choose File, Open and then click File. In the Open File dialog box, you select the .xdl file type as the type of file. You now have a filtered list of only deadlock files (see Figure 32.20). After you select the file or files, you are able to view them in SSMS.

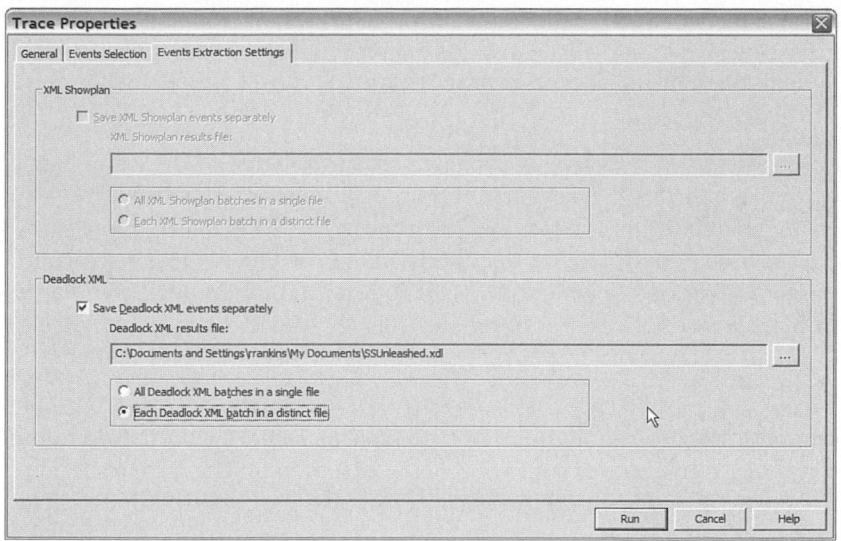

FIGURE 32.19   Configuring SQL Server Profiler to export Deadlock Graphs to individual files.

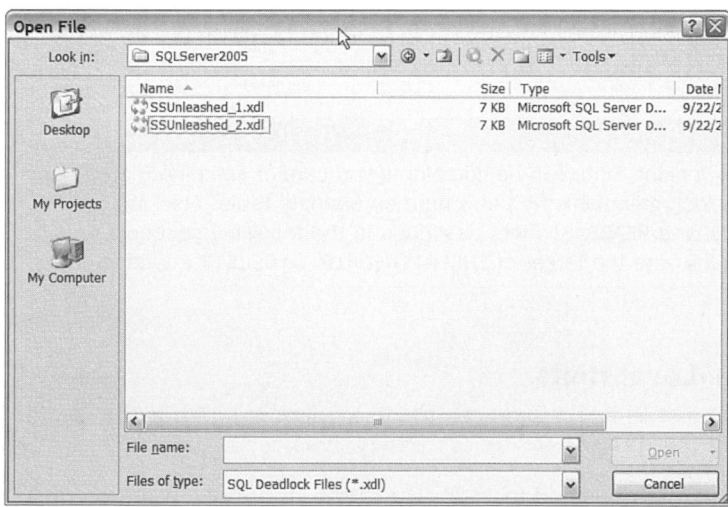

FIGURE 32.20   Opening a Deadlock Graph file in SSMS.

Table Hints for Locking

As mentioned previously in this chapter, in the "Transaction Isolation Levels in SQL
Server" section, you can set an isolation level for your connection by using the SET
TRANSACTION ISOLATION LEVEL command. This command sets a global isolation level for
an entire session, which is useful if you want to provide a consistent isolation level for an

application. However, sometimes you might want to specify different isolation levels for specific queries or for different tables within a single query. SQL Server allows you to do this by supporting table hints in the SELECT, UPDATE, INSERT, and DELETE statements. In this way, you can override the isolation level that is currently set at the session level.

In this chapter, you have seen that locking is dynamic and automatic in SQL Server. Based on certain factors (for example, SARGs, key distribution, data volume), the Query Optimizer chooses the granularity of the lock (that is, row, page, or table level) on a resource. Although it is usually best to leave such decisions to the Query Optimizer, you might encounter certain situations in which you want to force a different lock granularity on a resource than what the optimizer has chosen. SQL Server provides additional table hints that you can use in the query to force lock granularity for various tables that are participating in a join.

SQL Server also automatically determines the lock type (SHARED, UPDATE, EXCLUSIVE) to use on a resource, depending on the type of command being executed on the resource. For example, a SELECT statement uses a shared lock. SQL Server also provides additional table hints to override the default lock type.

The table hints to override the lock isolation, granularity, or lock type for a table can be provided using the WITH operator of the SELECT, UPDATE, INSERT, and DELETE statements.

The following sections discuss the various locking hints that can be passed to an optimizer to manage isolation levels and the lock granularity of a query.

NOTE

Although many of the table-locking hints can be combined, you cannot combine more than one isolation level or lock granularity hint at a time on a single table. Also, the NOLOCK, READUNCOMMITTED, and READPAST hints described in the following sections cannot be used on tables that are the target of INSERT, UPDATE, or DELETE queries.

Transaction Isolation–Level Hints

SQL Server provides a number of hints that you can use in a query to override the default transaction isolation level:

▶ **HOLDLOCK**—HOLDLOCK maintains shared locks for the duration of the entire statement or for the entire transaction, if the statement is in a transaction. This option is equivalent to the Serializable Read isolation level. The following hypothetical example demonstrates the usage of the HOLDLOCK statement within a transaction:

```
declare @seqno int
begin transaction
-- get a UNIQUE sequence number from sequence table
SELECT @seqno = isnull(seq#,0) + 1
from sequence WITH (HOLDLOCK)
```

```
-- in the absence of HOLDLOCK, shared lock will be released
-- and if some other concurrent transaction ran the same
-- command, both of them could get the same sequence number

UPDATE sequence
set    seq# = @seqno

--now go do something else with this unique sequence number
commit tran
```

NOTE

As discussed earlier in this chapter, in the "Deadlocks" section, using HOLDLOCK in this manner leads to potential deadlocks between processes that are executing the transaction at the same time. For this reason, the HOLDLOCK hint, as well as the REPEATABLEREAD and SERIALIZABLE hints, should be used sparingly, if at all. In this example, it might be better for the SELECT statement to use an update or an exclusive lock on the sequence table, using the hints discussed later in this chapter, in the section "Lock Type Hints." Another option would be to use an application lock, as discussed previously in this chapter, in the section "Using Application Locks."

▶ **NOLOCK**—You can use this option to specify that no shared lock be placed on the resource. This option is similar to running a query at Isolation Level 0 (Read Uncommitted), which allows the query to ignore exclusive locks and read uncommitted changes. The NOLOCK option is a useful feature in reporting environments, where the accuracy of the results is not critical.

▶ **READUNCOMMITTED**—This is the same as specifying the Read Uncommitted mode when using the SET TRANSACTION ISOLATION LEVEL command, and it is the same as the NOLOCK table hint.

▶ **READCOMMITTED**—This is the same as specifying the Read Committed mode when you use the SET TRANSACTION ISOLATION LEVEL command. The query waits for exclusive locks to be released before reading the data. This is the default locking isolation mode for SQL Server. If the database option READ_COMMITTED_SNAPSHOT is ON, SQL Server does not acquire shared locks on the data and uses row versioning.

▶ **READCOMMITTEDLOCK**—This option specifies that read operations acquire shared locks as data is read and release those locks when the read operation is completed, regardless of the setting of the READ_COMMITTED_SNAPSHOT database option.

▶ **REPEATABLEREAD**—This is the same as specifying Repeatable Read mode with the SET TRANSACTION ISOLATION LEVEL command. It prevents nonrepeatable reads within a transaction and behaves similarly to the HOLDLOCK hint.

▶ **SERIALIZABLE**—This is the same as specifying Serializable Read mode with the SET TRANSACTION ISOLATION LEVEL command. It prevents phantom reads within a transaction, and behaves similarly to using the HOLDLOCK hint.

▶ **READPAST**—This hint specifies that the query skip over the rows or pages that are locked by other transactions, returning only the data that can be read. Read operations specifying READPAST are not blocked. When specified in an UPDATE or DELETE statement, READPAST is applied only when reading data to identify which records to update. READPAST can be specified only in transactions operating at the Read Committed or Repeatable Read isolation levels. This lock hint is useful when reading information from a SQL Server table used as a work queue. A query using READPAST skips past queue entries locked by other transactions to the next available queue entry, without having to wait for the other transactions to release their locks.

Lock Granularity Hints

You can use the following optimizer hints to override lock granularity:

▶ **ROWLOCK**—You can use this option to force the Lock Manager to place a row-level lock on a resource instead of a page-level or a table-level lock. You can use this option in conjunction with the XLOCK lock type hint to force exclusive row locks.

▶ **PAGLOCK**—You can use this option to force a page-level lock on a resource instead of a row-level or table-level lock. You can use this option in conjunction with the XLOCK lock type hint to force exclusive page locks.

▶ **TABLOCK**—You can use this option to force a table-level lock instead of a row-level or a page-level lock. You can use this option in conjunction with the HOLDLOCK table hint to hold the table lock until the end of the transaction.

▶ **TABLOCKX**—You can use this option to force a table-level exclusive lock instead of a row-level or a page-level lock. No shared or update locks are granted to other transactions as long as this option is in effect. If you are planning maintenance on a SQL Server table and you don't want interference from other transactions, using this option is one of the ways to essentially put a table into a single-user mode.

Lock Type Hints

You can use the following optimizer hints to override the lock type that SQL Server uses:

▶ **UPDLOCK**—This option is similar to HOLDLOCK except that whereas HOLDLOCK uses a shared lock on the resource, UPDLOCK places an update lock on the resource for the duration of the transaction. This allows other processes to read the information, but not acquire update or exclusive locks on the resource. This option provides read repeatability within the transaction while preventing deadlocks that can result when using HOLDLOCK.

▶ **XLOCK**—This option places an exclusive lock on the resource for the duration of the transaction. This prevents other processes from acquiring locks on the resource.

Optimistic Locking

With many applications, clients need to fetch the data to browse through it, make modifications to one or more rows, and then post the changes back to the database in SQL Server. These human-speed operations are slow in comparison to machine-speed operations, and the time lag between the fetch and post might be significant. (Consider a user who goes to lunch after retrieving the data.)

For these applications, you would not want to use normal locking schemes such as SERIALIZABLE or HOLDLOCK to lock the data so it can't be changed from the time the user retrieves it to the time he or she applies any updates. This would violate one of the key rules for minimizing locking contention and deadlocks that you should not allow user interaction within transactions. You would also lose all control over the duration of the transaction. In a multiuser OLTP environment, the indefinite holding of the shared locks could significantly affect concurrency and overall application performance due to blocking on locks and locking contention.

On the other hand, if the locks are not held on the rows being read, another process could update a row between the time it was initially read and when the update is posted. When the first process applies the update, it would overwrite the changes made by the other process, resulting in a lost update.

So how do you implement such an application? How do you allow users to retrieve information without holding locks on the data and still ensure that lost updates do not occur?

Optimistic locking is a technique used in situations in which reading and modifying data processes are widely separated in time. Optimistic locking helps a client avoid overwriting another client's changes to a row without holding locks in the database.

One approach for implementing optimistic locking is to use the timestamp data type. Another approach is to take advantage of the optimistic concurrency features of snapshot isolation.

Optimistic Locking Using the timestamp Data Type

SQL Server provides a special data type called timestamp that can be used for optimistic locking purposes within applications. The purpose of the timestamp data type is to serve as a version number in optimistic locking schemes. SQL Server automatically generates the value for a timestamp column whenever a row that contains a column of this type is inserted or updated. The timestamp data type is an 8-byte binary data type, and other than guaranteeing that the value is unique and monotonically increasing, the value is not meaningful; you cannot look at the individual bytes and make any sense of them. Despite the name of the data type, the value has no relationship to the time that the record was modified. A synonym for the timestamp data type is rowversion.

In an application that uses optimistic locking, the client reads one or more records from the table, being sure to retrieve the primary key and the current value of the timestamp column for each row, along with any other desired data columns. Because the query is not run within a transaction, any locks acquired for the SELECT are released after the data has been read. At some later time, when the client wants to update a row, it must ensure that no other client has changed the same row in the intervening time. The UPDATE statement must include a WHERE clause that compares the timestamp value retrieved with the original query, with the current timestamp value for the record in the database. If the timestamp values match—that is, if the value that was read is the same as the value currently in the database—then no changes to that row have occurred since it was originally retrieved. Therefore, the change attempted by the application can proceed. If the timestamp value in the client application *does not* match the value in the database, then that particular row has been changed since the original retrieval of the record. As a result, the state of the row that the application is attempting to modify is not the same as the row that currently exists in the database. As a result, the transaction should not be allowed to take place, to avoid the lost update problem.

To ensure that the client application does not overwrite the changes made by another process, the client needs to prepare the T-SQL UPDATE statement in a special way, using the timestamp column as a versioning marker. The following pseudo-code represents the general structure of such an update:

```
UPDATE theTable
   SET theChangedColumns = theirNewValues
   WHERE primaryKeyColumns = theirOldValues
     AND timestamp = itsOldValue
```

Because the WHERE clause includes the primary key, the UPDATE can only apply to exactly one row or to no rows; it cannot apply to more than one row because the primary key is unique. The second part of the WHERE clause provides the optimistic "locking." If another client has updated the row, the timestamp no longer has its old value (remember that the server changes the timestamp value automatically with each update), and the WHERE clause does not match any rows. The client needs to check whether any rows were updated. If the number of rows affected by the update statement is zero, the row has been modified since it was originally retrieved. The application can then choose to reread the data or do whatever recovery it deems appropriate. This approach has one problem: How does the application know whether it didn't match the row because the timestamp was changed, because the primary key had changed, or because the row had been deleted altogether?

In SQL Server 2000, there was an undocumented tsequal() function (which was documented in prior releases) that could be used in a WHERE clause to compare the timestamp value retrieved by the client application with the timestamp value in the database. If the timestamp values matched, the update would proceed. If not, the update would fail, with error message 532, to indicate that the row had been modified. Unfortunately, this function is no longer provided in SQL Server 2005. Any attempt to use it now results in a syntax error. As an alternative, you can programmatically check whether the update modified any rows, and if not, you can check whether the row still exists and return the appropriate message. Listing 32.7 provides an example of a stored procedure that implements this strategy.

32

LISTING 32.7   An Example of a Procedure for Optimistic Locking

```
create proc optimistic_update
      @id int, -- provide the primary key for the record
      @data_field_1 varchar(10), -- provide the data value to be updated
      @timestamp timestamp -- pass in the timestamp value retrieved with
                         --  the initial data retrieval
as
-- Attempt to modify the record
update data_table
   set data_field_1 = @data_field_1
   where id = @id
     and timestamp = @timestamp
-- Check to see if no rows updated
IF @@ROWCOUNT=0
BEGIN
   if exists (SELECT * FROM data_table WHERE id=@id)
   -- The row exists but the timestamps don't match
   begin
      raiserror ('The row with id "%d" has been updated since it was read',
                10, 1, @id)
      return -101
   end
   else  -- the row has been deleted
   begin
      raiserror ('The row with id "%d" has been deleted since it was read',
                10, 2, @id)
      return -102
   end
end
ELSE
   PRINT 'Data Updated'
return 0
```

Using this approach, if the update doesn't modify any rows, the application receives an error message and knows for sure that the reason the update didn't take place is because either the timestamp values didn't match or the row was deleted. If the row is found and the timestamp values match, then the update proceeds normally.

Optimistic Locking with Snapshot Isolation

SQL Server 2005's Snapshot Isolation mode provides another mechanism for implementing optimistic locking through its automatic row versioning. If a process reads data within a transaction when Snapshot Isolation mode is enabled, no locks are acquired or held on the current version of the data row. The process reads the version of the data at the time of the query. Because no locks are held, it doesn't lead to blocking, and another process can modify the data after it has been read. If another process does modify a data row read by the first process, a new version of the row is generated. If the original process then attempts to update that data row, SQL Server automatically prevents the lost update problem by checking the row version. In this case, because the row version is different, SQL Server prevents the original process from modifying the data row. When it attempts to modify the data row, the following error message appears:

```
Msg 3960, Level 16, State 4, Line 1
Snapshot isolation transaction aborted due to update conflict. You cannot use
 snapshot isolation to access table 'dbo.data_table' directly or indirectly in
 database 'bigpubs2005' to update, delete, or insert the row that has been
 modified or deleted by another transaction. Retry the transaction or change the
 isolation level for the update/delete statement.
```

To see how this works, you can create the following table:

```
use bigpubs2005
go
--The first statement is used to disable any previously created
--DDL triggers in the database which would prevent creating a new table.
DISABLE TRIGGER ALL ON DATABASE
go
create table data_table
    (id int identity,
     data_field_1 varchar(10),
     timestamp timestamp)
go
insert data_table (data_field_1) values ('foo')
go
```

Next, you need to ensure that bigpubs2005 is configured to allow snapshot isolation:

```
ALTER DATABASE bigpubs2005 SET ALLOW_SNAPSHOT_ISOLATION ON
```

In one user session, you execute the following SQL statements:

```
SET TRANSACTION ISOLATION LEVEL SNAPSHOT
go
begin tran
select * from data_table
go


id          data_field_1 timestamp
----------- ------------ ------------------
1           foo          0x0000000000000BC4
```

Now, in another user session, you execute the following UPDATE statement:

```
update data_table set data_field_1 = 'bar'
   where id = 1
```

Then you go back to the original session and attempt the following update:

```
update data_table set data_field_1 = 'fubar'
   where id = 1
go
```

```
Msg 3960, Level 16, State 4, Line 1
Snapshot isolation transaction aborted due to update conflict. You cannot use
  snapshot isolation to access table 'dbo.data_table' directly or indirectly in
  database 'bigpubs2005' to update, delete, or insert the row that has been
  modified or deleted by another transaction. Retry the transaction or change the
  isolation level for the update/delete statement.
```

Note that for the first process to hold on to the row version, the SELECT and UPDATE statements must be run in the same transaction. When the transaction is committed or rolled back, the row version acquired by the SELECT statement is released. However, because the SELECT statement run at the Snapshot Isolation level does not hold any locks, there are no locks being acquired or held by that SELECT statement within the transaction, so it avoids the problems that would normally be encountered by using HOLDLOCK or the Serializable Read isolation level. Because no locks were held on the data row, the other process was allowed to update the row after it was retrieved, generating a new version of the row. The automatic row versioning provided by SQL Server's Snapshot Isolation mode prevented the first process from overwriting the update performed by the second process, thereby preventing a lost update.

CAUTION

Locking contention is prevented in the previous example only because the transaction performed only a SELECT before attempting the UPDATE. A SELECT run with Snapshot Isolation mode enabled reads the current version of the row and does not acquire or hold locks on the actual data row. However, if the process were to perform any other modification on the data row, the update or exclusive locks acquired would be held until the end of the transaction, which could lead to locking contention, especially if user interaction is allowed within the transaction after the update or exclusive locks are acquired.

Also, be aware of the overhead generated in tempdb when Snapshot Isolation mode is enabled for a database, as described in the section "Transaction Isolation Levels in SQL Server," earlier in this chapter.

Because of the overhead incurred by snapshot isolation and the cost of having to roll back update conflicts, you should consider using Snapshot Isolation mode only to provide optimistic locking for systems where there is little concurrent updating of the same resource so that it is unlikely that your transactions have to be rolled back because of an update conflict.

Summary

Locking is critical in a multiuser environment for providing transaction isolation. SQL Server supports all ANSI-defined transaction isolation levels, and SQL Server 2005 also provides the new Snapshot Isolation level for applications that can benefit from optimistic concurrency. The Lock Manager in SQL Server automatically locks data at the row level or higher, as necessary, to provide the appropriate isolation while balancing the locking overhead with concurrent access to the data. It is important to understand how locking works and what its effect is on application performance to develop efficient queries and applications.

SQL Server provides a number of tools for monitoring and identifying locking problems and behavior. In addition, SQL Server provides a number of table-locking hints that give the developer better control over the default lock types and granularity used for certain queries.

Although following the guidelines to minimize locking contention in applications is important, another factor that affects locking behavior and query performance is the actual database design. Chapter 33, "Database Design and Performance," discusses database design and its effect on database performance and provides guidelines to help ensure that transactions and T-SQL code run efficiently.

Database Design and Performance

IN THIS CHAPTER

▶ What's New in Database Design and Performance

▶ Basic Tenets of Designing for Performance

▶ Logical Database Design Issues

▶ Denormalizing a Database

▶ Database Filegroups and Performance

▶ RAID Technology

Various factors contribute to the optimal performance of a database application. Some of these factors include logical database design (rules of normalization), physical database design (denormalization, indexes, data placement), choice of hardware (SMP servers/multiprocessor servers), network bandwidth (LAN versus WAN), client and server configuration (memory, CPU), data access techniques (ODBC, ADO, OLEDB), and application architecture (two-tier versus n-tier). This chapter helps you understand some of the key database design issues to ensure that you have a reliable high-performance application.

> **NOTE**
>
> Index design is often considered part of physical database design. Because index design guidelines and the impact of indexes on query and update performance are covered in detail in Chapter 29, "Indexes and Performance," this chapter does not discuss index design. It focuses instead on other aspects of database design and performance.

What's New in Database Design and Performance

Many of the database design and performance consideration that applied to previous version of SQL Server still apply to SQL Server 2005. These principles are basic in nature and are not affected by the version of the database management system. This chapter focuses on those relatively unchanged principles.

There are, however, some new features in SQL Server 2005 that will augment these basic principles. Table partitions, new indexing options, and other table-oriented features are just a few things that should be considered when designing your database for performance. These features are discussed in detail in Chapter 19 "Creating and Managing Tables," Chapter 29 "Indexes and Performance," and other chapters in Part V, "SQL Server Performance and Optimization."

Basic Tenets of Designing for Performance

Designing for performance requires making trade-offs. For example, to get the best write performance out of a database, you must sacrifice read performance. Before tackling database design issues for an application, it is critical to understand your goals. Do you want faster read performance? faster write performance? a more understandable design?

Following are some basic truths about physical database design for SQL Server 2005 and the performance implications of each:

▶ It's important to keep table row sizes as small as possible. This is not about saving disk space. Having smaller rows means more rows fit on a single 8KB page, which means fewer physical disk reads are required to read a given number of rows.

▶ You should use indexes to speed up read access. However, the more indexes a table has, the longer it takes to insert, update, and delete rows from the table.

▶ Using triggers to perform any kind of work during an insert, an update, or delete exacts a performance toll and decreases concurrency by lengthening transaction duration.

▶ Implementing declarative referential integrity (via primary and foreign keys) helps maintain data integrity, but enforcing foreign key constraints requires extra lookups on the primary key table to ensure existence.

▶ Using ON DELETE CASCADE referential integrity constraints helps maintain data integrity but requires extra work on the server's part.

Keeping tables as narrow as possible—that is, ensuring that the row size is as small as possible—is one of the most important things you can do to ensure that a database performs well. To keep your tables narrow, you should choose column data types with size in mind. You shouldn't use an int data type if a tinyint will do. If you have zero-to-one relationships in tables, you should consider vertically partitioning the tables. (See the "Vertical Data Partitioning" section, later in this chapter, for details on this scenario.)

Cascading deletes (and updates) cause extra lookups to be done whenever a delete runs against the parent table. In many cases, the optimizer uses worktables to resolve delete and update queries. Enforcing these constraints manually, from within stored procedures, for example, can give better performance. This is not a wholehearted endorsement against referential integrity constraints. In most cases, the extra performance hit is worth the saved aggravation of coding everything by hand. However, you should be aware of the cost of this convenience.

Logical Database Design Issues

A good database design is fundamental to the success of any application. Logical database design for relational databases follows rules of normalization. As a result of normalization, you create a data model that is usually, but not necessarily, translated into a physical data model. A logical database design does not depend on the relational database you intend to use. The same data model can be applied to Oracle, Sybase, SQL Server, or any other relational database. On the other hand, a physical data model makes extensive use of the features of the underlying database engine to yield optimal performance for the application. Physical models are much less portable than logical models.

> **TIP**
>
> If portability is a big concern to you, consider using a third-party data modeling tool, such as ERwin or ERStudio. These tools have features that make it easier to migrate your logical data models to physical data models on different database platforms. Of course, this just gets you started; to get the best performance out of your design, you need to tweak the physical design for the platform you have chosen.

Normalization Conditions

Any database designer must address two fundamental issues:

▶ Designing the database in a simple, understandable way that is maintainable and makes sense to its developers and users

▶ Designing the database such that data is fetched and saved with the fastest response time, resulting in high performance

Normalization is a technique used on relational databases to organize data across many tables so that related data is kept together based on certain guidelines. Normalization results in controlled redundancy of data; therefore, it provides a good balance between disk space usage and performance. Normalization helps people understand the relationships between data and enforces rules to ensure that the data is meaningful.

> **TIP**
>
> Normalization rules exist, among other reasons, to make it easier for people to understand the relationships between data. But a perfectly normalized database sometimes doesn't perform well under certain circumstances, and it may be difficult to understand. There are good reasons to deviate from a perfectly normalized database.

Normalization Forms

Five normalization forms exist, represented by the symbol 1NF for first normal form, 2NF for second normal form, and so on. If you follow the rules for the first rule of normalization, your database can be described as "in first normal form."

Each rule of normalization depends on the previous rule for successful implementation, so to be in second normal form (2NF), your database must also follow the rules for first normal form.

A typical relational database used in a business environment falls somewhere between second and third normal forms. It is rare to progress past the third normal form because fourth and fifth normal forms are more academic than practical in real-world environments.

Following is a brief description of the first three rules of normalization.

First Normal Form

The first rule of normalization requires removing repeating data values and specifies that no two rows in a table can be identical. This means that each table must have a logical primary key that uniquely identifies a row in the table.

Consider a table that has four columns—`PublisherName`, `Title1`, `Title2`, and `Title3`—for storing up to three titles for each publisher. This table is not in first normal form due to the repeating `Title` columns. The main problem with this design is that it limits the number of titles associated with a publisher to three.

Removing the repeating columns so there is just a `PublisherName` column and a single `Title` column puts the table in first normal form. A separate data row is stored in the table for each title published by each publisher. The combination of `PublisherName` and `Title` becomes the primary key that uniquely identifies each row and prevents duplicates.

Second Normal Form

A table is considered to be in second normal form if it conforms to the first normal form and all non-key attributes of the table are fully dependent on the entire primary key. If the primary key consists of multiple columns, non-key columns should depend on the entire key and not just on a part of the key. A table with a single column as the primary key is automatically in second normal form if it satisfies first normal form as well.

Assume that you need to add the publisher address to the database. Adding it to the table with the `PublisherName` and `Title` column would violate second normal form. The primary key consists of both `PublisherName` and `Title`, but the `PublisherAddress` attribute is an attribute of the publisher only. It does not depend on the entire primary key.

To put the database in second normal form requires adding an additional table for storing publisher information. One table consists of the `PublisherName` column and `PublisherAddress`. The second table contains the `PublisherName` and `Title` columns. To retrieve the `PublisherName`, `Title`, and `PublisherAddress` information in a single result would require a join between the two tables on the `PublisherName` column.

Third Normal Form

A table is considered to be in third normal form if it already conforms to the first two normal forms and if none of the non-key columns are dependent on any other non-key columns. All such attributes should be removed from the table.

Let's look at an example that comes up often during database architecture. Suppose that an employee table has four columns: `EmployeeID` (the primary key), `salary`, `bonus`, and `total_salary`, where `total_salary = salary + bonus`. Existence of the `total_salary` column in the table violates the third normal form because a non-key column (`total_salary`) is dependent on two other non-key columns (`salary` and `bonus`). Therefore, for the table to conform to the third rule of normalization, you must remove the `total_salary` column from the employee table.

Benefits of Normalization

The following are the major advantages of normalization:

▶ Because information is logically kept together, normalization provides improved overall understanding of the system.

▶ Because of controlled redundancy of data, normalization can result in fast table scans and searches (because less physical data has to be processed).

▶ Because tables are smaller with normalization, index creation and data sorts are much faster.

▶ With less redundant data, it is easier to maintain referential integrity for the system.

▶ Normalization results in narrower tables. Because you can store more rows per page, more rows can be read and cached for each I/O performed on the table. This results in better I/O performance.

Drawbacks of Normalization

One result of normalization is that data is stored in multiple tables. To retrieve or modify information, you usually have to establish joins across multiple tables. Joins are expensive from an I/O standpoint. Multitable joins can have an adverse impact on the performance of the system. The following sections discuss some of the denormalization techniques you can use to improve the performance of a system.

> **TIP**
>
> An old adage for normalization is "Normalize 'til it hurts; denormalize 'til it works." To put this into use, try to put your database in third normal form initially. Then, when you're ready to implement the physical structure, drop back from third normal form, where excessive table joins are hurting performance. A common mistake is that developers make too many assumptions and over-denormalize the database design before even a single line of code has been written to even begin to assess the database performance.

33

1218   CHAPTER 33   Database Design and Performance

Denormalizing a Database

After a database has been normalized to the third form, database designers intentionally backtrack from normalization to improve the performance of the system. This technique of rolling back from normalization is called *denormalization*. Denormalization allows you to keep redundant data in the system, reducing the number of tables in the schema and reducing the number of joins to retrieve data.

TIP

Duplicate data is more helpful when the data does not change very much, such as in data warehouses. If the data changes often, keeping all "copies" of the data in sync can create significant performance overhead, including long transactions and excessive write operations.

Denormalization Guidelines

When should you denormalize a database? Consider the following points:

- Be sure you have a good overall understanding of the logical design of the system. This knowledge helps in determining how other parts of the application are going to be affected when you change one part of the system.

- Don't attempt to denormalize the entire database at once. Instead, focus on the specific areas and queries that are accessed most frequently and are suffering from performance problems.

- Understand the types of transactions and the volume of data associated with specific areas of the application that is having performance problems. You can resolve many such issues by tuning the queries without denormalizing the tables.

- Determine whether you need virtual (computed) columns. Virtual columns can be computed from other columns of the table. Although this violates third normal form, computed columns can provide a decent compromise because they do not actually store another exact copy of the data in the same table.

- Understand data integrity issues. With more redundant data in the system, maintaining data integrity is more difficult, and data modifications are slower.

- Understand storage techniques for the data. You may be able to improve performance without denormalization by using RAID, SQL Server filegroups, and table partitioning.

- Determine the frequency with which data changes. If data is changing too often, the cost of maintaining data and referential integrity might outweigh the benefits provided by redundant data.

- Use the performance tools that come with SQL Server (such as SQL Server Profiler) to assess performance. These tools can help isolate performance issues and give you possible targets for denormalization.

> **TIP**
>
> If you are experiencing severe performance problems, denormalization should *not* be the first step you take to rectify the problem. You need to identify specific issues that are causing performance problems. Usually, you discover factors such as poorly written queries, poor index design, inefficient application code, or poorly configured hardware. You should try to fix these types of issues *before* taking steps to denormalize database tables.

Essential Denormalization Techniques

You can use various methods to denormalize a database table and achieve desired performance goals. Some of the useful techniques used for denormalization include the following:

- Keeping redundant data and summary data
- Using virtual columns
- Performing horizontal data partitioning
- Performing vertical data partitioning

Redundant Data

From an I/O standpoint, joins in a relational database are inherently expensive. To avoid common joins, you can add redundancy to a table by keeping exact copies of the data in multiple tables. The following example demonstrates this point. This example shows a three-table join to get the title of a book and the primary author's name:

```
select c.title,
       a.au_lname,
       a.au_fname
  from   authors a join titleauthor b on a.au_id = b.au_id
  join titles c on b.title_id = c.title_id
  where  b.au_ord = 1
  order by c.title
```

You could improve the performance of this query by adding the columns for the first and last names of the primary author to the titles table and storing the information in the titles table directly. This would eliminate the joins altogether. Here is what the revised query would look like if this denormalization technique were implemented:

```
select title,
       au_lname,
       au_fname
  from  titles
  order by title
```

As you can see, the `au_lname` and `au_fname` columns are now redundantly stored in two places: the `titles` table and the `authors` table. It is obvious that with more redundant data in the system, maintaining referential integrity and data integrity is more difficult. For example, if the author's last name changed in the `authors` table, to preserve data integrity, you would also have to change the corresponding `au_lname` column value in the `titles` table to reflect the correct value. You could use SQL Server triggers to maintain data integrity, but you should recognize that update performance could suffer dramatically. For this reason, it is best if redundant data is limited to data columns whose values are relatively static and are not modified often. In the example just presented, it is highly unlikely that an author's last name for a published book would change.

Computed Columns

A number of queries calculate aggregate values derived from one or more columns of a table. Such computations can be CPU intensive and can have an adverse impact on performance if they are performed frequently. One of the techniques to handle such situations is to create an additional column that stores the computed value. Such columns are called *virtual columns*, or *computed columns*. Since SQL Server 7.0, computed columns have been natively supported. You can specify such columns in `create table` or `alter table` commands. The following example demonstrates the use of computed columns:

```
create table emp (
        empid int not null primary key,
        salary money not null,
        bonus money not null default 0,
        total_salary as ( salary+bonus )
        )
go
insert emp (empid, salary, bonus) values (100, $150000.00, $15000)
go
select * from emp
go
empid       salary         bonus                total_salary
----------- -------------- -------------------- ----------------
100         150000.0000    15000.0000           165000.0000
```

By default, virtual columns are not physically stored in SQL Server tables. SQL Server internally maintains a column property named `iscomputed` that can be viewed from the `sys.columns` system view. It uses this column to determine whether a column is computed. The value of the virtual column is calculated at the time the query is run. All columns that are referenced in the computed column expression must come from the table on which the computed column is created. You can, however, reference a column from another table by using a function as part of the computed column's expression. The function can contain a reference to another table, and the computed column calls this function.

Since SQL Server 2000, computed columns have been able to participate in joins to other tables, and they can be indexed. Creating an index that contains a computed column creates a physical copy of the computed column in the index tree. Whenever a base column participating in the computed column changes, the index must also be updated, which adds overhead and may possibly slow down update performance.

In SQL Server 2005, you also have the option of defining a computed column so that its value is physically stored. This is accomplished with the new `ADD PERSISTED` option, as shown in the following example:

```
--Alter the computed SetRate column to be PERSISTED
ALTER TABLE Sales.CurrencyRate
 alter column SetRate ADD PERSISTED
```

SQL Server automatically updates the persisted column values whenever one of the columns that the computed column references is changed. Indexes can be created on these columns, and they can be used just like non-persisted columns. One advantage of using a computed column that is persisted is that it has fewer restrictions than a non-persisted column. In particular, a persisted column can contain an imprecise expression, which is not possible with a non-persisted column.

Summary Data

Summary data is most helpful in a decision support environment, to satisfy reporting requirements and calculate sums, row counts, or other summary information and store it in a separate table. You can create summary data in a number of ways:

- ▶ **Real-time**—Every time your base data is modified, you can recalculate the summary data, using the base data as a source. This is typically done using stored procedures or triggers.

- ▶ **Real-time incremental**—Every time your base data is modified, you can recalculate the summary data, using the old summary value and the new data. This is more complex than the real-time option, but it could save time if the increments are relatively small compared to the entire dataset. This, too, is typically done using stored procedures or triggers.

- ▶ **Delayed**—You can use a scheduled job to recalculate summary data on a regular basis. This is the recommended method to use in an OLTP system to keep update performance optimal.

Horizontal Data Partitioning

As tables grow larger, data access time also tends to increase. For queries that need to perform table scans, the query time is proportional to the number of rows in the table. Even when you have proper indexes on such tables, access time slows as the depth of the index trees increases. The solution is splitting the table into multiple tables such that each table has the same table structure as the original one but stores a different set of data.

Figure 33.1 shows a billing table with 90 million records. You can split this table into 12 monthly tables (all with the identical table structure) to store billing records for each month.

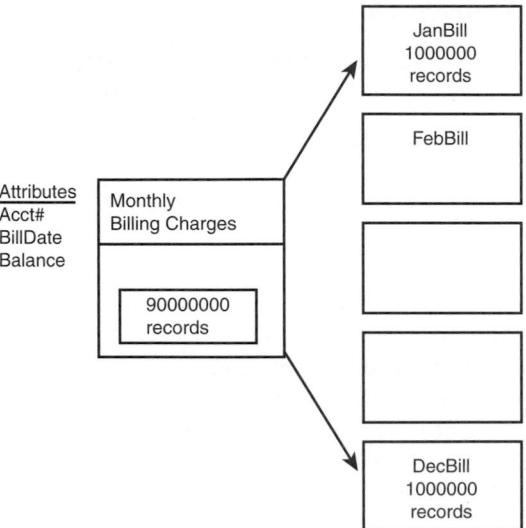

FIGURE 33.1   Horizontal partitioning of data.

You should carefully weigh the options when performing horizontal splitting. Although a query that needs data from only a single month gets much faster, other queries that need a full year's worth of data become more complex. Also, queries that are self-referencing do not benefit much from horizontal partitioning. For example, the business logic might dictate that each time you add a new billing record to the billing table, you need to check any outstanding account balance for previous billing dates. In such cases, before you do an insert in the current monthly billing table, you must check the data for all the other months to find any outstanding balance.

TIP

Horizontal splitting of data is useful where a subset of data might see more activity than the rest of the data. For example, say that in a health care provider setting, 98% of the patients are inpatients, and only 2% are outpatients. In spite of the small percentage involved, the system for outpatient records sees a lot of activity. In this scenario, it makes sense to split the patient table into two tables—one for the inpatients and one for the outpatients.

When splitting tables horizontally, you must perform some analysis to determine the optimal way to split the table. You need to try to find a logical dimension along which to split the data. The best choice takes into account the way your users use your data. In the example that involves splitting the data among 12 tables, date was mentioned as the optimal split candidate. However, if the users often did ad hoc queries against the billing table for a full year's worth of data, they would be unhappy with the choice to split that data among 12 different tables. Perhaps splitting based on a customer type or another attribute would be more useful.

> **NOTE**
>
> You can use partitioned views to hide the horizontal splitting of tables. The benefit of using partitioned views is that multiple horizontally split tables appear to the end users and applications as a single large table. When this is properly defined, the optimizer automatically determines which tables in the partitioned view need to be accessed, and it avoids searching all tables in the view. The query runs as quickly as if it were run only against the necessary tables directly. For more information on defining and using partitioned views, see Chapter 22, "Creating and Managing Views."
>
> In SQL Server 2005, you also have the option of physically splitting the rows in a single table over more than one partition. This new feature, called *partitioned tables*, utilizes a partitioning function that splits the data horizontally and a partitioning scheme that assign the horizontally partitioned data to different filegroups. When a table is created, it references the partitioned schema, which causes the rows of data to be physically stored on different filegroups. There are no additional tables needed, and the table is still referenced with the original table name. The horizontal partitioning happens at the physical storage level and is transparent to the user.

Vertical Data Partitioning

As you know, a database in SQL Server consists of 8KB pages, and a row cannot span multiple pages. Therefore, the total number of rows on a page depends on the width of the table. This means the wider the table, the smaller the number of rows per page. You can achieve significant performance gains by increasing the number of rows per page, which in turn reduces the number of I/Os on the table. Vertical splitting is a method of reducing the width of a table by splitting the columns of the table into multiple tables. Usually, all frequently used columns are kept in one table, and others are kept in the other table. This way, more records can be accommodated per page, fewer I/Os are generated, and more data can be cached into SQL Server memory. Figure 33.2 illustrates a vertically partitioned table. The frequently accessed columns of the authors table are stored in the author_primary table, whereas less frequently used columns are stored in the author_secondary table.

> **TIP**
>
> Make the decision to split data very carefully, especially when the system is already in production. Changing the data structure might have a systemwide impact on a large number of queries that reference the old definition of the object. In such cases, to minimize risks, you might want to use SQL Server views to hide the vertical partitioning of data. Also, if you find that users and developers are frequently joining between the vertically split tables because they need to pull data together from the two tables, you might want to reconsider the split point or the splitting of the table itself. Doing frequent joins between split tables with smaller rows requires more I/Os to retrieve the same data than if the data resided in a single table with wider rows.

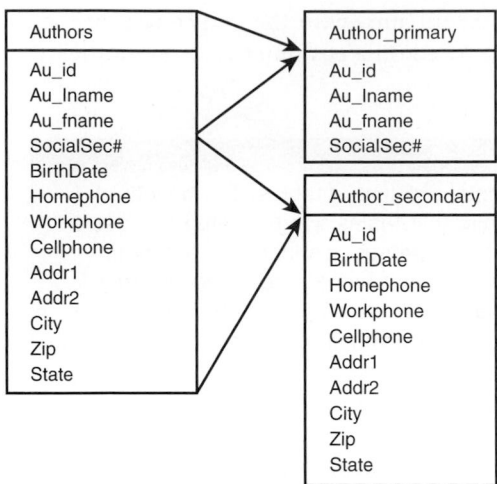

FIGURE 33.2   Vertical partitioning of data.

Performance Implications of Zero-to-One Relationships

Suppose that one of the development managers in your company, Bob, approaches you to discuss some database schema changes. He is one of several managers whose groups all use the central User table in your database. Bob's application makes use of about 5% of the users in the User table. Bob has a requirement to track five yes/no/undecided flags associated with those users. He would like you to add five one-character columns to the User table to track this information. What do you tell Bob?

Bob has a classic zero-to-one problem. He has some data he needs to track, but it applies to only a small subset of the data in the table. You can approach this problem in one of three ways:

> ▶ **Option 1: Add the columns to the User table**—95% of your users will have NULL values in those columns, and the table will become wider for everybody.

> ▶ **Option 2: Create a new table with a vertical partition of the User table**—The new table will contain the User primary key and Bob's five flags. 95% of your users will still have NULL data in the new table, but the User table is protected against the effects of this. Because other groups don't need to use the new partition table, this is a nice compromise.

> ▶ **Option 3: Create a new vertically partitioned table as in Option 2 but populate it only with rows that have at least one non-NULL value for the columns in the new partition**—This is great for database performance, and searches in the new table will be wonderfully fast. The only drawback to this is that Bob's developers will have to add additional logic to their applications to determine whether a row exists during updates. Bob's folks will need to use an outer join to the table to cover the possibility that a row doesn't exist.

Depending on the goals of the project, any one of these options can be appropriate. Option 1 is simple and is the easiest to code for and understand. Option 2 is a good compromise between performance and simplicity. Option 3 gives the best performance in certain circumstances but impacts performance in certain other situations and definitely requires more coding work to be done.

Database Filegroups and Performance

Filegroups allow you to decide where on disk a particular object should be placed. You can do this by defining a filegroup within a database, extending the database onto a different drive or set of drives, and then placing a database object on the new filegroup.

Every database has a primary filegroup that contains the primary data file. There can be only one primary filegroup. If you don't create any other filegroups or change the default filegroup to a filegroup other than the primary filegroup, all files are in the primary file-group unless they are specifically placed in other filegroups.

In addition to the primary filegroup, you can add one or more additional filegroups to the database, and each of those filegroups can contain one or more files. The main purpose of using filegroups is to provide more control over the placement of files and data on the server. When you create a table or an index, you can map it to a specific file-group, thus controlling the placement of data. A typical SQL Server database installation generally uses a single RAID array to spread I/O across disks and create all files in the primary filegroup; more advanced installations or installations with very large databases spread across multiple array sets can benefit from the finer level of control of file and data placement afforded by additional filegroups.

For example, for a simple database such as AdventureWorks, you can create just one primary file that contains all data and objects and a log file that contains the transaction log information. For a larger and more complex database, such as a securities trading system, where large data volumes and strict performance criteria are the norm, you might create the database with one primary file and four secondary files. You can then set up filegroups so you can place the data and objects within the database across all five files. If you have a table that itself needs to be spread across multiple disk arrays for performance reasons, you can place multiple files in a filegroup, each of which resides on a different disk, and create the table on that filegroup. For example, you can create three files (Data1.ndf, Data2.ndf, and Data3.ndf) on three disk arrays and then assign them to the filegroup called spread_group. Your table can then be created specifically on the spread_group filegroup. Queries for data from the table are then spread across the three disk arrays, thereby improving I/O performance.

Filegroups are most often used in high-performance environments to isolate key tables or indexes on their own set of disks, which are in turn typically part of a high-performance RAID array. Assuming that you start with a database that has just a PRIMARY filegroup (the default), the following example shows how you would add an index filegroup on a new drive and move some nonclustered indexes to it:

```
-- add the filegroup
alter database Grocer
      add filegroup FG_INDEX

-- Create a new database file and add it to the FG_INDEX filegroup
alter database Grocer
add file(
    NAME = Grocer_Index,
        FILENAME = 'g:\Grocer_Index.ndf',
        SIZE = 2048MB,
        MAXSIZE = 8192MB,
        FILEGROWTH = 10%
) to filegroup FG_INDEX

create nonclustered index xOrderDetail_ScanDT
    on OrderDetail(ScanDT)
    on FG_INDEX
```

Moving the indexes to a separate RAID array minimizes I/O contention by spreading out the I/O generated by updates to the data that affect data rows and require changes to index rows as well.

> **NOTE**
>
> Because the leaf level of a clustered index is the data page, if you create a clustered index on a filegroup, the entire table moves from the existing filegroup to the new filegroup. If you want to put indexes on a separate filegroup, you should reserve that space for nonclustered indexes only.

Having your indexes on a separate filegroup gives you the following advantages:

▶ Index scans and index page reads come from a separate disk, so they need not compete with other database processes for disk time.

▶ Inserts, updates, and deletes on the table are spread across two separate disk arrays. The clustered index, including all the table data, is on a separate array from the nonclustered indexes.

▶ You can target your budget dollars more precisely because the faster disks improve system performance more if they are given to the index filegroup rather than the database as a whole.

The next section gives specific recommendations on how to architect a hardware solution based on using separate filegroups for data and indexes.

RAID Technology

Redundant array of inexpensive disks (RAID) is used to configure a disk subsystem to provide better performance and fault tolerance for an application. The basic idea behind using RAID is that you spread data across multiple disk drives so that I/Os are spread across multiple drives. RAID has special significance for database-related applications, where you want to spread random I/Os (data changes) and sequential I/Os (for the transaction log) across different disk subsystems to minimize disk head movement and maximize I/O performance.

The four significant levels of RAID implementation that are of most interest in database implementations are as follows:

- RAID 0 is data striping with no redundancy or fault tolerance.

- RAID 1 is mirroring, where every disk in the array has a mirror (copy).

- RAID 5 is striping with parity, where parity information for data on one disk is spread across the other disks in the array. The contents of a single disk can be re-created from the parity information stored on the other disks in the array.

- RAID 10, or 1+0, is a combination of RAID 1 and RAID 0. Data is striped across all drives in the array, and each disk has a mirrored duplicate, offering the fault toler-ance of RAID 1 with the performance advantages of RAID 0.

RAID Level 0

RAID Level 0 provides the best I/O performance among all other RAID levels. A file has sequential segments striped across each drive in the array. Data is written in a round-robin fashion to ensure that data is evenly balanced across all drives in the array. However, if a media failure occurs, no fault tolerance is provided, and all data stored in the array is lost. RAID 0 should not be used for a production database where data loss or loss of system availability is not acceptable. RAID 0 is occasionally used for `tempdb` to provide the best possible read and (especially) write performance. RAID 0 is helpful for random read requirements, such as those that occur on `tempdb` and in data segments.

TIP

Although the data stored in `tempdb` is temporary and noncritical data, failure of a RAID 0 stripeset containing `tempdb` results in loss of system availability because SQL Server requires a functioning `tempdb` to carry out many of its activities. If loss of system avail-ability is not an option, you should not put `tempdb` on a RAID 0 array. You should use one of the RAID technologies that provides redundancy.

If momentary loss of system availability is acceptable in exchange for the improved I/O and reduced cost of RAID 0, recovery of `tempdb` is relatively simple. The `tempdb` data-base is re-created each time the SQL Server instance is restarted. If the disk that contained your `tempdb` was lost, you could replace the failed disk, restart SQL Server, and the files would automatically be re-created. This scenario is complicated if the failed disk with the `tempdb` file also contains your `master` database or other system databases. See Chapter 11, "Database Backup and Restore," for a more detailed discussion of restoring system databases.

33

RAID 0 is the least expensive of the RAID configurations because 100% of the disks in the array are available for data, and none are used to provide fault tolerance. Performance is also the best of the RAID configurations because there is no overhead required to maintain redundant data.

Figure 33.3 depicts a RAID 0 disk array configuration.

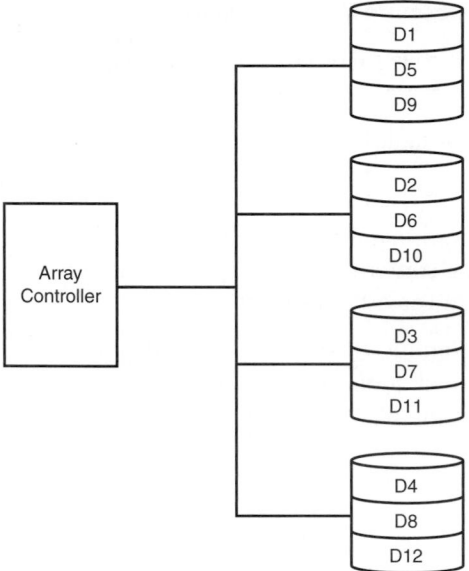

FIGURE 33.3   RAID Level 0.

RAID Level 1

With RAID 1, known as disk mirroring, every write to the primary disk is written to the mirror set. Either member of the set can satisfy a read request. RAID 1 devices provide excellent fault tolerance because in the event of a media failure, either on the primary disk or the mirrored disk, the system can still continue to run. Writes are much faster than with RAID 5 arrays because no parity information needs to be calculated first. The data is simply written twice.

RAID 1 arrays are best for transaction logs and for index filegroups. RAID 1 provides the best fault tolerance and the best write performance, which is critical to log and index performance. Because log writes are sequential write operations and not random access operations, they are best supported by a RAID 1 configuration.

RAID 1 arrays are the most expensive RAID configurations because only 50% of total disk space is available for actual storage. The rest is used to provide fault tolerance.

Figure 33.4 shows a RAID 1 configuration.

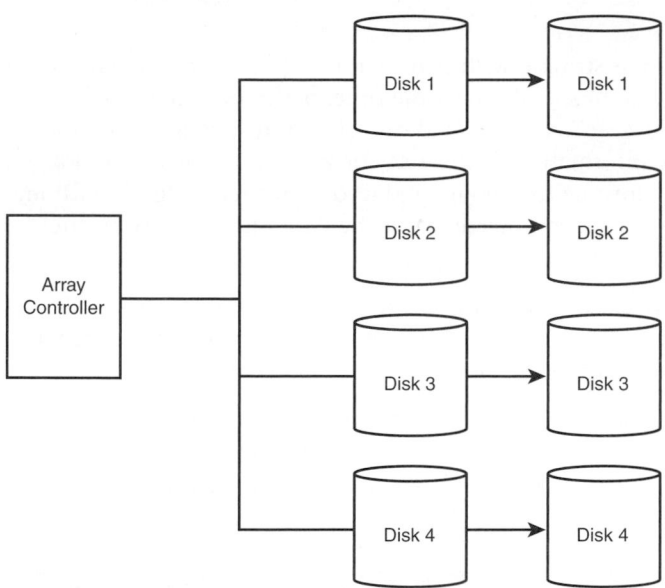

FIGURE 33.4 RAID Level 1.

Because RAID 1 requires that the same data be written to two drives at the same time, write performance is slightly less than when writing data to a single drive because the write is not considered complete until both writes have been done. Using a disk controller with a battery-backed write cache can mitigate this write penalty because the write is considered complete when it occurs to the battery-backed cache. The actual writes to the disks occur in the background.

RAID 1 read performance is often better than that of a single disk drive because most controllers now support split seeks. Split seeks allow each disk in the mirror set to be read independently of each other, thereby supporting concurrent reads.

RAID Level 10

RAID 10, or RAID 1+0, is a combination of mirroring and striping. It is implemented as a stripe of mirrored drives. The drives are mirrored first, and then a stripe is created across the mirrors to improve performance. This should not be confused with RAID 0+1, which is different and is implemented by first striping the disks and then mirroring.

Many businesses with high-volume OLTP applications opt for RAID 10 configurations. The shrinking cost of disk drives and the heavy database demands of today's business applications are making this a much more viable option. If you find that your transaction log or index segment is pegging your RAID 1 array at 100% usage, you can implement a RAID 10 array to get better performance. This type of RAID carries with it all the fault tolerance (and cost!) of a RAID 1 array, with all the performance benefits of a RAID 0 striping.

33

RAID Level 5

RAID 5 is most commonly known as striping with parity. In this configuration, data is striped across multiple disks in large blocks. At the same time, parity bits are written across all the disks for a given block. Information is always stored in such a way that any one disk can be lost without any information in the array being lost. In the event of a disk failure, the system can still continue to run (at a reduced performance level) without downtime by using the parity information to reconstruct the data that was lost on the missing drive.

Some arrays provide "hot-standby" disks. The RAID controller uses the standby disk to rebuild a failed drive automatically, using the parity information stored on all the other drives in the array. During the rebuild process, performance is markedly worse.

The fault tolerance of RAID 5 is usually sufficient, but if more than one drive in the array fails, you lose the entire array. It is recommended that a spare drive be kept on hand in the event of a drive failure, so the failed drive can be replaced quickly before any other drives fail.

NOTE

Many of the RAID solutions available today support "hot-spare" drives. A hot-spare drive is connected to the array but doesn't store any data. When the RAID system detects a drive failure, the contents of the failed drive are re-created on the hot-spare drive, and it is automatically swapped into the array in place of the failed drive. The failed drive can then be manually removed from the array and replaced with a working drive, which becomes the new hot spare.

RAID 5 provides excellent read performance but expensive write performance. A write operation on a RAID 5 array requires two writes: one to the data drive and one to the parity drive. After the writes are complete, the controller reads the data to ensure that the information matches (that is, that no hardware failure has occurred). A single write operation causes four I/Os on a RAID 5 array. For this reason, putting log files or `tempdb` on a RAID 5 array is not recommended. Index filegroups, which suffer worse than data filegroups from bad write performance, are also poor candidates for RAID 5 arrays. Data filegroups where more than 10% of the I/Os are writes are also not good candidates for RAID 5 arrays.

Note that if write performance is not an issue in your environment—for example, in a DSS/data warehousing environment—you should, by all means, use RAID 5 for your data and index segments.

In any environment, you should avoid putting `tempdb` on a RAID 5 array. `tempdb` typically receives heavy write activity, and it performs better on a RAID 1 or RAID 0 array.

RAID 5 is a relatively economical means of providing fault tolerance. No matter how many drives are in the array, only the space equivalent to a single drive is used to support fault tolerance. This method becomes more economical with more drives in the array. You must have at least three drives in a RAID 5 array. Three drives would require that 33% of available disk space be used for fault tolerance, four would require 25%, five would require 20%, and so on.

Figure 33.5 shows a RAID 5 configuration.

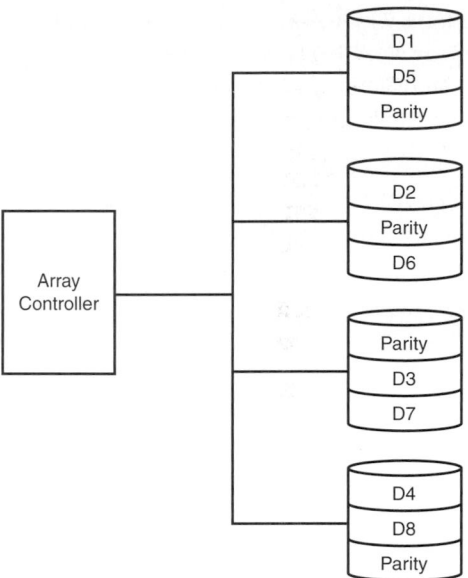

FIGURE 33.5   RAID Level 5.

Summary

A good database design is the best place to start to ensure a smoothly running system. You can take steps to ensure a solid design. If you inherit a database with an inadequate design, you can still take steps to ensure good performance. The primary goals of a database designer should be to index the database effectively and keep table row sizes as narrow as possible. A good database design goes a long way toward ensuring excellent performance. In addition, Chapter 44, "Administering Very Large SQL Server Databases," is dedicated to very large database designs and the maintenance issues that must be considered when dealing with huge data sizes.

The next chapter, "Monitoring SQL Server Performance," delves into another key aspect of database design and performance. Optimal database performance is achieved and sustained by monitoring your database environment. Changes in that environment, including more data, new stored procedures and the like can affect the way that your server performs.

CHAPTER 34

Monitoring SQL Server Performance

IN THIS CHAPTER

▶ What's New in Monitoring SQL Server Performance

▶ A Performance Monitoring Approach

▶ Performance Monitor

▶ Windows Performance Counters

▶ SQL Server Performance Counters

▶ Using DBCC to Examine Performance

▶ The Top 100 Worst-Performing Queries

▶ Other SQL Server Performance Considerations

No SQL Server implementation is perfect out of the box. As you build and add SQL Server-based applications to your server, you should take an active approach to monitoring performance. You also need to keep reevaluating things as more and more load is placed on your servers. This chapter focuses on SQL Server monitoring and leaves the other types of servers (including application servers, backup servers, domain controllers, file and print servers, mail/messaging servers, and web servers) for those specialists.

You can monitor many things on your SQL Server platform, ranging from physical and logical I/O to network packets being handled by the server. To make this monitoring task a little cleaner, this chapter classifies the key monitoring handles into network, processors, memory/cache, and disk systems. Figure 34.1 shows how these key elements interrelate with SQL Server 2005 and Windows. The aspect of utilization—whether CPU utilization, memory utilization, or something else—is at the center of most of the discussions in this chapter. The important concept to remember is how to monitor or measure utilization and how to make changes to improve this utilization because you are still not in a perfect world of infinite CPU power, infinite disk space, infinite network load capability, and infinite memory.

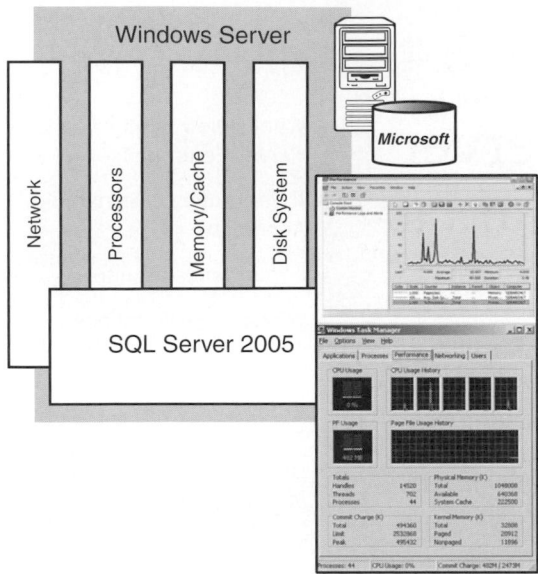

FIGURE 34.1   Key elements of SQL Server 2005 performance monitoring: network, processors, memory/cache, and disks.

It is essential that you know which tools you can use to get this valuable information. The tools you can use include Windows Performance Monitor and its various counters, a few SQL Server DBCC options, SQL Profiler, and even a variety of SQL Server dynamic management views (DMVs) that are new with SQL Server 2005. Many other third-party products are also available that you might already have in-house. But first, let's take a look at what's new with SQL Server 2005 for monitoring performance.

What's New in Monitoring SQL Server Performance

With SQL Server 2005, many aspects of the kernel itself have been rewritten and re-architected. This has allowed Microsoft to expose many internal structures and much of the statistical data critical to performance for the user. Many of these are now available in the new DMVs, which are systemwide internal views. You might be used to poking around SQL Server 2000 using various system stored procedures or various systems tables (such as sysprocesses or sysdatabases). You really don't have to do this anymore. Other areas in SQL Server 2005 have also been added to help in the performance-monitoring realm:

▶ Many new performance counters that add granularity to the operating system, network, devices, processors, memory, and numerous SQL Server instance-related counters.

▶ Microsoft has introduced some new twists to DBCC as well: DBCC MEMORYSTATUS, a few FREE CACHE mechanisms (for freeing up session cache, system cache, and procedure cache), and modifications to DBCC SQLPERF.

- ▶ `DBCC SHOWCONTIG` improvements help to shed light on data and index structures and their issues.

- ▶ More detailed and consistent "wait" information (session waits, OS waits, latch waits, so on). This is critical for spotting bottlenecks of various kinds.

- ▶ More granularity in analyzing how `tempdb` is operating (`tempdb: Version Store` information).

- ▶ As mentioned earlier, the addition of DMVs to expose the critical internal structures and statistics of SQL Server usage.

- ▶ A number of the changes have been made to the caching framework (the uniform caching framework) that are relevant for overall SQL Server performance.

A Performance Monitoring Approach

If you take a closer look at the performance monitoring areas depicted in Figure 34.1, you can see that SQL Server spans them all. SQL Server must process requests submitted to it via the network, service those requests with one or more processors, and rely on accessing a request's data from both memory/cache and the disk system. If you maximize utilization on these resources from the point of view of SQL Server and the operating system, you will end up with a well-tuned database server. This doesn't mean you have a good database design or are using optimal index strategies. The whole picture is important to tuning your SQL Server implementation, but the database, table designs, indexing strategy, and SQL statement tuning are described in much detail in other chapters. This chapter focuses on the SQL Server instance as it sits on the OS and the hardware along with the major monitoring capabilities available to you.

One area of interest is the amount of network traffic handled by SQL Server and the size of these network requests. Another area of interest is the ability of the available processors to service the load presented to them by SQL Server without exceeding certain CPU saturation. This chapter looks at the overall memory utilization of what is available on the server and how effectively SQL Server is utilizing the disk system.

In general, you want to start from the bottom, with the network, and work your way up into the SQL Server-specific elements. This allows you to quickly isolate certain issues that are paramount in performance tuning. In each of these areas, this chapter provides a list of minimum detail performance handles or counters that can be examined. This approach can be summarized into the following steps:

1. Understand and monitor network request characteristics as they relate to SQL Server and the machine on which SQL Server has been installed. This means a complete profile of what is coming into and sent back out over the network from SQL Server.

2. Understand processor utilization. It might be that the processing power is the biggest issue. You need to get a handle on this early.

3. Understand and monitor memory and cache utilization. This is the next detail step into the overall memory usage at the operating system point of view and into the memory that SQL Server is using for such things as data caching, procedure caching, and so on.

4. Understand and monitor disk system utilization. You are often rewarded for a simple disk configuration or data storage approach. And you often don't know you have a problem unless you look for it. Techniques that are often used include disk striping, isolation of logs from data, and so on.

You need to repeat steps 1 through 4 on a regular basis. Your continued success and salary increases will reflect your diligence here. For each step, certain tools and facilities will be available to you to use that gather all that is needed to identify and monitor performance issues. Let's explore the Performance Monitor facility of the Windows server family first.

Performance Monitor

Performance Monitor is a graphical tool supplied as part of the installation of any Windows server or workstation that monitors various performance indicators. Hundreds of counters are organized within performance objects. These counters can be monitored on the local machine or over the network, and they can be set up to monitor any object and counter on multiple systems at once from one session. A small subset of performance information is also available via the Windows Task Manager Performance tab. However, all this information and more is available using the Performance Monitor facility.

Performance Monitor can be launched from many different points. From SQL Profiler, choose the Tools menu option and choose the Performance Monitor item. Figure 34.2 shows this menu option from SQL Profiler. You can also launch it from the Administrative Tools window in Windows.

Performance Monitor Views

You can switch the Performance Monitor display modes to one of three different representations:

▶ **Graphic chart**—This is the default view. It shows the selected counters as colored lines with the y-axis representing the value and the x-axis representing time. You can also add grid lines (horizontal and vertical).

▶ **Histogram chart**—This view shows the selected counters as colored horizontal bars (as in a histogram). These histogram bars are dynamically changed to reflect the data sampling values. With this view, you often lose site of the trends of activity.

▶ **Report display**—In this mode, you see the current values for counters collected under their parent object in a textual display format. Again, this cannot show you the activity trends, just the current sampling value, but it is great for showing what counters you are collecting data with.

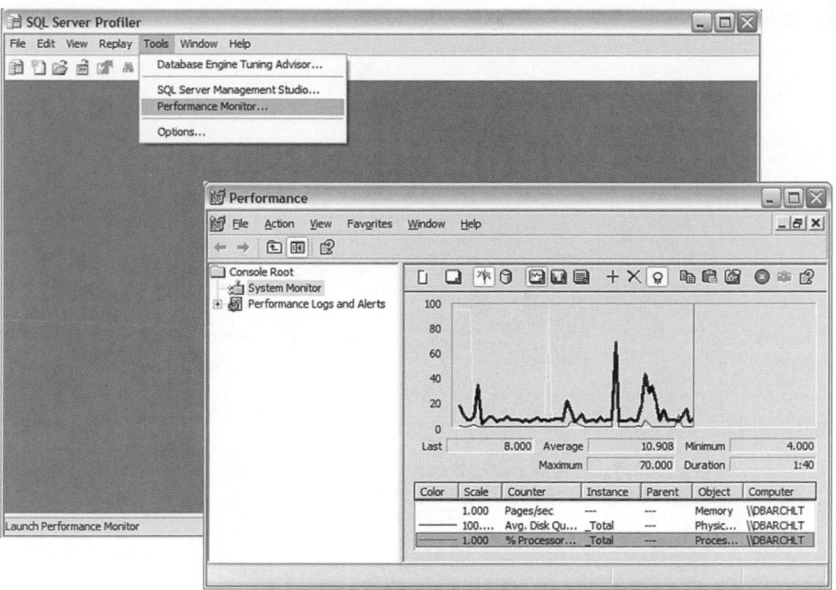

FIGURE 34.2   Launching Performance Monitor from SQL Profiler.

A couple other features of Performance Monitor are that you can use it to set alerts when your counter values exceed certain thresholds and that you can capture the performance counter information into logs that can be viewed in detail after they are captured:

▶ **Alerts**—You can set thresholds for counters, and Performance Monitor maintains a visual log of when they are reached.

▶ **Performance logs**—This option allows you to capture counter values, with times, to a file. This gives you a set of values that you can load back into the Performance Monitor facility at a later time. That way, you can monitor the system after-hours and capture statistical data.

Figure 34.3 shows the basic graphical user interface for Performance Monitor using the default chart view and several tasty system counters that are explained later in this chapter.

Monitoring Values

When you open Performance Monitor (from the Administrative Tools group or from within SQL Profiler), you see three default performance counters (Memory: Pages/sec, PhysicalDisk:Avg.Disk Queue Length, and Processor:% Processor Time). These are a good start, but you really want to see many other counters that reflect the complete picture of how your server is behaving. This chapter explains the right ones for SQL Server, in the "SQL Server Performance Counters" section.

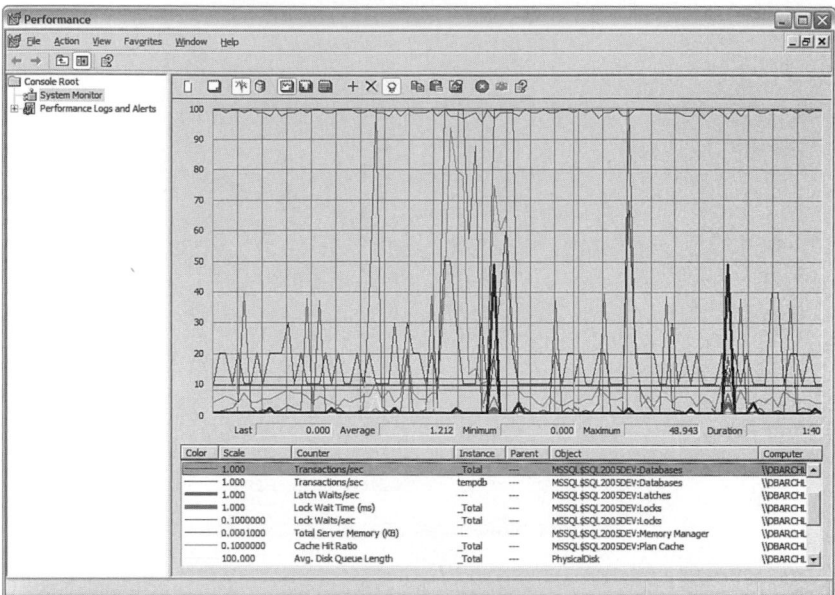

FIGURE 34.3   Performance Monitor chart view, with various counters.

You add a counter by clicking the large plus sign toolbar button near the top. The Add Counters dialog box that appears (see Figure 34.4) allows you to select a computer (either locally or for monitoring remotely), a performance object, any specific counters, and an instance of the counter, if applicable.

You can customize the look of the line in the chart view by specifying color, width, and style from the Data tab of the System Monitor Properties dialog. The default counter you are presented with is the %Processor Time counter from the Processor performance object. This counter indicates the percentage of time that the processor (CPU instance 0) is executing a non-idle thread and is the primary indicator of processor activity.

By clicking the Explain button, you can get a simple explanation of the counter. You can change the scale of a counter's value as well. In this case, you don't need to change the scale because it is a percentage, and the chart's y-axis is numbered to 100.

To remove a counter, you simply highlight the line in the bottom area of the Chart view window and press the Delete key or click on the X button in the toolbar.

You follow the same process whether you're adding the counter to chart view, histogram view, or report view. The next section discusses some of the counters and when you want to use them.

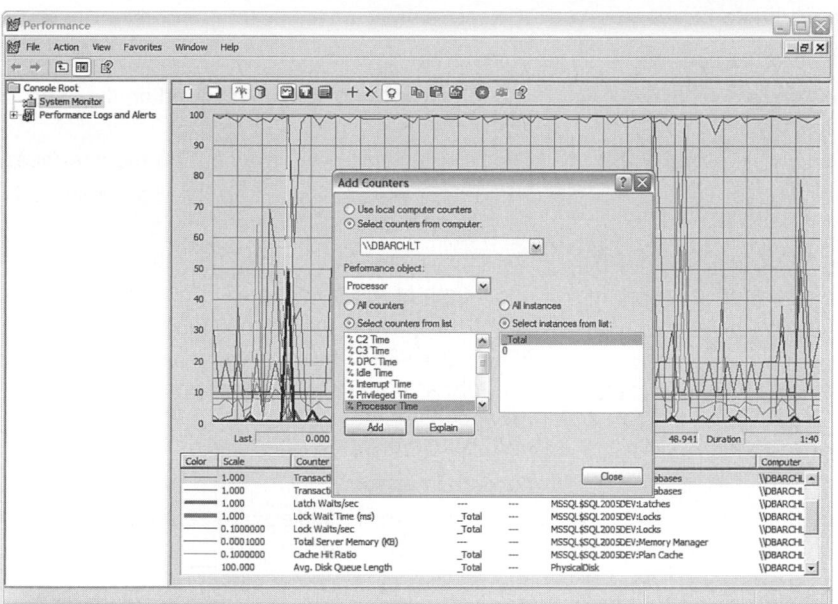

FIGURE 34.4   Adding a counter in the Performance Monitor.

Windows Performance Counters

You need to be able to tell how the Windows server is reacting to the presence of SQL Server running within it: how SQL Server is using memory, the processors, and other important system resources. A large number of objects and counters relate to Windows and the services it is running. The next few sections look at the objects and counters that provide useful information in investigating certain areas of the system and focus on the ones you need for monitoring SQL Server.

Monitoring the Network Interface

One area of possible congestion is the network card or network interface; it does not matter how fast the server's work is if it has to queue up to go out through a small pipe. Remember: Any activity on the server machine might be consuming some of the bandwidth of the network interface card. You can see the total activity via Performance Monitor.

Table 34.1 shows the typical network performance object and counters you use to measure the total network interface activity.

TABLE 34.1   Network Interface Performance Objects and Counters

Performance Monitor Object	Description
Network Inter: Bytes Received	The rate at which bytes are received on the interface.
Network Inter: Bytes Sent	The rate at which bytes are sent on the interface.
Network Inter: Bytes Total	The rate at which all bytes are sent and received on the interface.
Network Inter: Current Bandwidth	The bits per second (bps) of the interface card.
Network Inter: Output Queue Length	The length of the output packet queue (in packets). If this is longer than 2, delays are occurring, and a bottleneck exists.
Network Inter: Packets Received	The rate at which packets are received on the network interface.
Network Inter: Packets Sent	The rate at which packets are sent on the network interface.
Network Inter: Packets	The rate at which packets are sent and received on the network interface.
Server: Bytes Received	The number of bytes the server has received from the network. This is the big-picture indicator of how busy the server is.
Server: Bytes Transmitted	The number of bytes the server has sent/transmitted to the network. Again, this is a good overall picture of how busy the server is.

Figure 34.5 illustrates a pretty low-usage picture for a particular network interface. Microsoft allows you to save any selected counters in an .MSC file for future use. We have provided a sample file that contains the primary network-related counters for download from the Sams Publishing website for this book (www.samspublishing.com). The filename is NETWORKperfmon.msc. For the SQL Server–oriented counters, we have provided another file, named SQLperfmon.msc. Both of these are good references for setting up the same set of counters on your SQL Server platform. You just double-click the file and choose to add counters for your local machine. For each counter, you do the same thing for your target machine (that you are trying to monitor). When you finish identifying each of these counters for your own environment, you can delete the original ones. Then, save your selected counters to some folder location where you can recall it easily. You are ready to go now.

> **NOTE**
>
> Under previous versions of SQL Server (6.5 and earlier), a counter called SQLServer:Network Reads/sec indicated SQL Server's contribution to network traffic. With SQL Server 2005, you need to use the DBCC PERFMON command to find similar information (for network reads and writes, down to the bytes level) or use sp_monitor (for packet reads and writes, in and out of SQL Server).

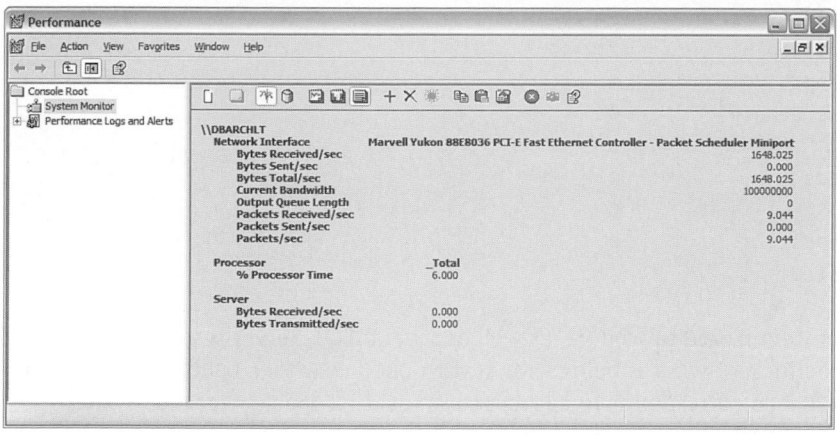

FIGURE 34.5   A network interface's performance object and counters.

In general, if the SQL Server packet sends or receives are grossly lower than the overall server's counter, then other activity on the server is occurring that is potentially bogging down this server or not allowing SQL Server to be used optimally. The rule of thumb here is to isolate all other functionality to other servers if you can and let SQL Server be the main application on a machine.

You need to pay strict attention to how many requests are queuing up, waiting to make use of the network interface. You can see this by using the DBCC PERFMON command and looking at the Command Queue Length value. This number should be 0. If it is 2 or more, then the network interface has a bottleneck. You should check the bus width of the card. Obviously, a 32-bit PCI card is faster than an 8-bit ISA one. You should also check that you have the latest drivers from the hardware vendor.

When you use DBCC PERFMON, the detail information of actual bytes read and written allows you to understand the size of this network activity. A quick calculation of reads/bytes gives you an average size of reads from the network. If this is large, you might want to question what the application is doing and whether the network as a whole can handle this big of a bandwidth request. Here's an execution of DBCC PERFMON:

```
DBCC PERFMON
Go
Statistic                         Value
--------------------------------  ------------
Reads Outstanding                 0
Writes Outstanding                0
(2 row(s) affected)
Statistic                         Value
--------------------------------  ------------
Network Reads                     15170
Network Writes                    15179
```

```
Network Bytes Read            3477044
Network Bytes Written         2021400
Command Queue Length          0
Max Command Queue Length      0
Worker Threads                0
Max Worker Threads            0
Network Threads               0
Max Network Threads           0
(10 row(s) affected)
```

The Sp_monitor system stored procedure, as well as several SQL Server system variables, can be used to see much of what is being shown with DBCC PERFMON. DBCC PERFMON:Network Reads corresponds to sp_monitor's (or the @@pack_received system variable) packets_
received, and DBCC PERFMON:Network Writes corresponds to sp_monitor's (or the @@pack_sent system variable) packets_sent.

The following SELECT statement retrieves a current picture of what is being handled by SQL Server from a network packet's point of view:

```
SELECT  @@connections as Connections,
        @@pack_received as Packets_Received,
        @@pack_sent as Packets_Sent,
        getdate() as 'As of datetime'
go
Connections    Packets Received       Packets Sent    As of datetime
39             992228                 17468999        2006-09-01 14:11:56.660

(1 row(s) affected)
```

The Sp_monitor system stored procedure provides packets sent and received as a running total and since the last time it was run (difference in seconds). Here's an example of what would result (the network- and packets-related results):

```
EXEC sp_monitor
GO
last_run                    current_run              seconds
----------------------      ----------------------   -----------
2006-12-15 12:22:40.003 2006-12-15 12:22:41.353      1
packets_received            packets_sent             packet_errors
----------------------      ----------------------   -------------
16008(121)                  1060121(18011)           0(0)
```

The values within the parentheses are the amounts since the last time sp_monitor was run last, and the seconds column shows how long that period was. You can actually see the rate at which traffic is coming into and out of SQL Server.

Dynamic Management Views or System Views for Monitoring Network Items

Performance Monitor and sp_monitor are far better than any of the newly introduced DMVs for seeing the characteristics of a network. Just two DMVs help to shed a little light on how many and what type of session connections are being serviced by a particular SQL Server instance. In particular they show the characteristics of the network connection and the status of that connection. The following is an example of using sys.dm_exec_connections:

```
SELECT session_id, protocol_type, num_reads, num_writes, net_packet_size
FROM sys.dm_exec_connections
GO
session_id protocol_type              num_reads   num_writes  net_packet_size
---------- ---------------------      ----------  ----------- ---------------

NULL       Database Mirroring         5           9123        16384
NULL       TSQL                       9127        5           16384
NULL       TSQL                       9092        5           16384
NULL       Database Mirroring         5           9085        16384
51         TSQL                       17          17          4096
52         TSQL                       307         307         4096
53         TSQL                       67          89          4096
54         TSQL                       33          223         4096
```

The next example uses sys.dm_exec_requests to show the specific command and usage of all connections to that SQL Server instance, and its output is much like what you would see when looking at current activity within SSMS:

```
SELECT session_id, command, database_id, user_id, cpu_time, reads,
       writes, logical_reads
FROM sys.dm_exec_requests
GO
session_id command       database_id user_id     cpu_time reads writes  logical_reads
---------- ---------------- ----------- ----------- ---------- ----------- -------------------
-
1          RESOURCE MONITOR 0           1           0        0     0       0
2          LAZY WRITER    0           1           650      0     0       0
4          LOCK MONITOR   0           1           0        0     0       0
5          SIGNAL HANDLER 1           1           0        0     0       0
6          TASK MANAGER   1           1           0        0     0       0
7          TRACE QUEUE TASK 1         1           150      0     0       0
10         TASK MANAGER   1           1           0        0     0       0
12         BRKR TASK      1           1           40       2     0       148
13         TASK MANAGER   1           1           0        0     1       3334
14         TASK MANAGER   1           1           0        0     0       176
15         TASK MANAGER   1           1           0        0     0       2685
18         BRKR EVENT HNDLR 1         1           0        6     27      377
```

34

19	BRKR TASK	1	1	0	0	0	0
20	BRKR TASK	1	1	0	0	0	0
21	TASK MANAGER	1	1	0	0	0	101
22	TASK MANAGER	1	1	0	0	0	176
23	BRKR TASK	1	1	20	44	4	1978
24	TASK MANAGER	1	1	0	0	0	552
54	SELECT	1	1	0	0	0	195

Monitoring the Processors

The main processors of a server do the majority of the hard work, executing the operating system code and all applications. This is the next logical place to start looking at the performance of a system. With SQL Server 2005, you can identify the number of CPUs that you want to utilize on your physical machine. If your physical machine has 32 CPUs, it doesn't mean that you want to make all 32 CPUs available to SQL Server. In fact, in some cases, this would be a detriment; some CPU processing should be reserved to the OS and the network management on heavily loaded servers (5% of the CPUs). SQL Server allows you to identify how many CPUs it can use from what is available on the physical machine. In Figure 34.6, you can see the number of CPUs that are available to SQL Server on a typical server from SSMS server properties. In this example, all CPUs are being made available to SQL Server.

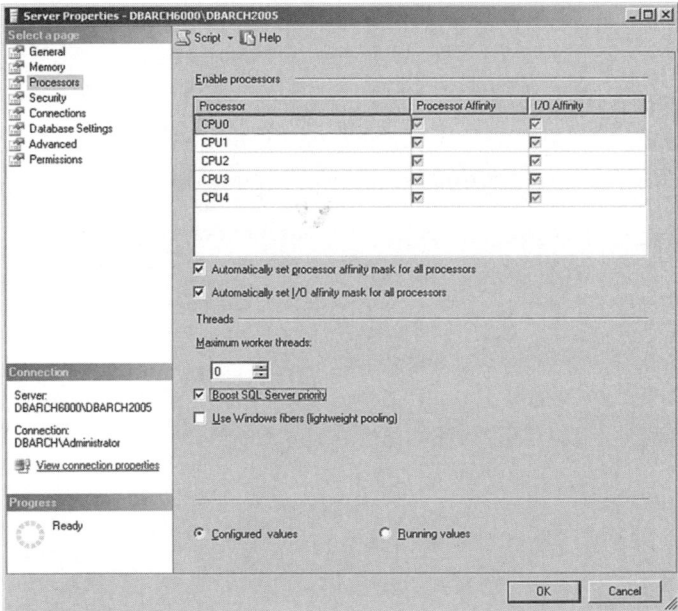

FIGURE 34.6   Processor (CPU) properties of a SQL Server instance.

In a 32-CPU server example and using the 5% number just mentioned, you should let SQL Server use 30 of the CPUs and reserve 2 CPUs for dedicated network- and OS-related activity (.05 × 32 = 1.6, rounded up to 2 CPUs). This also allows SQL Server to utilize SQL parallelism effectively.

Keep in mind that from a multitasking point of view, Windows servers often move process threads among different processors. This process thread movement activity can reduce Microsoft SQL Server performance under heavy system loads, as each processor cache is repeatedly reloaded with data. It is possible to assign processors to specific threads, which can improve performance under these types of conditions by eliminating processor reloads. This association between a thread and a processor is called *processor affinity*. SQL Server 2005 supports processor affinity by means of two affinity mask options: affinity mask (also known as CPU affinity mask) and affinity I/O mask. If you do nothing, SQL Server will be allowed to use each CPU for all its processing, with no affinity whatsoever. The operating system distributes threads from instances of SQL Server evenly among these CPUs.

If you want to specify the SQL Server affinity mask option, you must use it in conjunction with the affinity I/O mask option; it is represented as a binary bit mask that you read from right to left. Any binary bit mask has a decimal value equivalent. Table 34.2 shows a simple processing-to-CPU affinity masking for a four-CPU server, where CPU 0 corresponds to the rightmost bit. Keep in mind that you wouldn't want to enable the same CPU in both the processor affinity mask and the affinity I/O mask options. That would defeat the affinity capability. The bits corresponding to each CPU should be in one of the following three states:

▶ 0 in both the processor affinity mask option and the affinity I/O mask option

▶ 1 in the processor affinity mask option and 0 in the affinity I/O mask option

▶ 0 in the processor affinity mask option and 1 in the affinity I/O mask option

These bit patterns indicate the CPUs that are used to run threads for an instance of SQL Server.

TABLE 34.2   Processing Thread-to-CPU Affinity Masking

Decimal Value	Binary Bit Mask	CPU Allowed to Service Threads
1	0001	0
3	0011	0 and 1
7	0111	0, 1, and 2
15	1111	0, 1, 2, and 3

For example, an affinity mask value of 14 represents the bit pattern 1110. On a computer that has four CPUs, this indicates that threads from that instance of SQL Server can be scheduled on CPUs 3, 2, and 1, but not on CPU 0. To assign set the affinity masking advanced option values, you would use the `sp_configure` system stored procedure as follows (first to see what the values are and then to set them):

```
sp_configure 'show advanced options', 1;
RECONFIGURE;
GO
name                               minimum     maximum     config_value run_value
---------------------------------- ----------- ----------- ------------ -----------
Ad Hoc Distributed Queries         0           1           0            0
affinity I/O mask                  -2147483648 2147483647  0            0
affinity mask                      -2147483648 2147483647  0            0


-----------------------------------------------------------------
-- SETS Processing Threads to an affinity with CPU 3, 2, and 1 --
-----------------------------------------------------------------
EXEC SP_CONFIGURE 'affinity mask', 14
RECONFIGURE
GO
----------------------------------------------------------------
-- SETS I/O Thread processing to an affinity with CPU 0 --
----------------------------------------------------------------
EXEC SP_CONFIGURE 'affinity I/O mask', 1
RECONFIGURE
GO
```

The `affinity I/O mask` option binds SQL Server disk I/O to a specified subset of CPUs. In high-end SQL Server online transaction processing (OLTP) environments, this extension can enhance the performance of SQL Server threads issuing high number of I/Os. This enhancement does not support hardware affinity for individual disks or disk controllers, though. Perhaps this will be a SQL Server 2005 future enhancement.

> **NOTE**
>
> A side effect of specifying the `affinity mask` option is that the operating system does *not* move threads from one CPU to another. Most systems obtain optimal performance by letting the operating system schedule the threads among the available CPUs, but there are exceptions to this approach. The only time we have used this affinity setting was to isolate CPUs to specific SQL Server instances on the same box that had numerous CPUs to utilize.

From a Performance Monitor point of view, the emphasis is on seeing if the processors that are allocated to the server are busy enough to maximize performance but not so saturated as to create a bottleneck. The rule of thumb here is to see if your processors are working at between 20% and 50%. If this usage is consistently above 80% to 95%, you should consider splitting off some of the workload or adding processors. Table 34.3 indicates some of the key performance objects and counters for measuring processor utilization.

TABLE 34.3   Processor-Related Performance Objects and Counters

Performance Monitor Object	Description
Processor: % Processor Time	The rate at which bytes are received on the interface.
System: Processor Queue Length	The number of threads in the processor queue. A sustained processor queue of greater than two threads indicates a processor bottleneck.
System: Threads	The number of threads executing on the machine. A thread is the basic executable entity that can execute instructions in a processor.
System: Context Switches	The rate at which the processor and SQL Server had to change from executing on one thread to executing on another. This costs CPU resources.
Processor: % Interrupt Time	The percentage of time that the processor spends receiving and servicing hardware interrupts.
Processor: Interrupts/sec	The average number of hardware interrupts the processor is receiving and servicing.

The counters System: % Total Processor Time, System: Processor Queue Length, and Processor: % Processor Time are the most critical to watch. If the percentages are consistently high (above that 80%–95% level), you need to identify which specific processes and threads are consuming so many CPU cycles. For the SQL Server CPU-oriented counters, we have provided another file, named CPUperfmon.msc (shown in Figure 34.7), that you can download from the Sams Publishing website for this book (www.samspublishing.com). It contains these primary Performance Monitor processor-oriented counters.

No one should use a SQL Server box as a workstation because using the processor for client applications can cause SQL Server to starve for processor time. The ideal Windows setup is to run SQL Server on a standalone member server to the Windows domain. You should not install SQL Server on a primary domain controller (PDC) or backup domain controller (BDC) because the PDC and BDCs run additional services that consume memory, CPU, and network resources.

Before you upgrade to the latest processor just because the % Processor Time counter is constantly high, you might want to check the load placed on the CPU by your other devices. By checking Processor: % Interrupt Time and Processor: Interrupts/Sec, you can tell whether the CPU is interrupted more than normal by devices such as disk controllers.

The % Interrupt Time value should be as close to 0 as possible; controller cards should handle any processing requirements. The optimum value of Interrupts/Sec varies with the CPU used; for example, DEC Alpha processors generate a nonmaskable interrupt every 10 milliseconds (ms), whereas Intel processors interrupt every 15ms. The lowest absolute values are 100 interrupts per second and 67 interrupts per second, respectively.

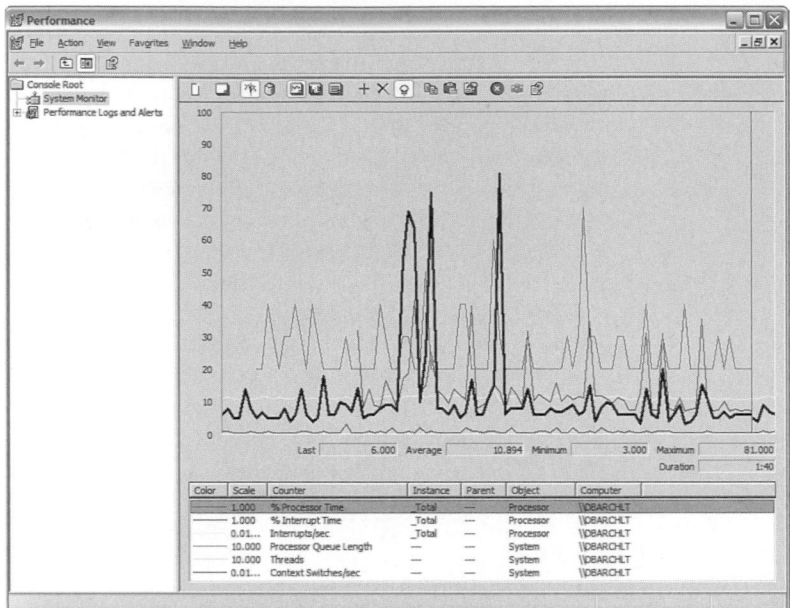

FIGURE 34.7   Processor-oriented counters in Performance Monitor.

The System: Context Switches counter can reveal when excessive context switching occurs, which usually directly affects overall performance. In addition, the System: Threads counter can give a good picture of the excessive demand on the CPU of having to service huge numbers of threads. In general, you should look at these counters only if processor queuing is happening.

By upgrading inefficient controllers to bus-mastering controllers, you can take some of the load from the CPU and put it back on the adapter. You should also keep the controller patched with the latest drivers from the hardware vendor.

Dynamic Management Views or System Views for Monitoring Processor Items

Within SQL Server, you can execute a simple SELECT statement that yields the SQL Server processes and their corresponding threads:

```
SELECT spid, lastwaittype, dbid, uid, cpu, physical_io, memusage,status,
       loginame, program_name
from sys.sysprocesses
ORDER BY cpu desc
GO
```

This lists the top CPU resource hogs that are active on SQL Server. After you identify which processes are causing a burden on the CPU, you can check whether they can be either turned off or moved to a different server. If they cannot be turned off or moved, then you might want to consider upgrading the processor. The same information is available via the new DMV:

```
SELECT session_id, command, database_id, user_id, cpu_time, reads,
      writes, logical_reads
from sys.dm_exec_requests
order by cpu_time desc
GO
```

Taking a peek at the SQL Server schedulers (using the `sys.dm_os_schedulers` DMV) also shows whether the number of runnable tasks is getting bogged down. If the `runnable_tasks_count` values are nonzero, there aren't enough CPU time slices available to run the current SQL Server workload. The following is how you query the "dm_os_schedulers" view for this information:

```
SELECT scheduler_id, current_tasks_count, runnable_tasks_count
FROM Sys.dm_os_schedulers
GO
scheduler_id current_tasks_count runnable_tasks_count
------------ ------------------- --------------------
0            20                  0
257          1                   0
255          2                   0
```

And finally, to get an idea of the top CPU hogs in SQL Server cached SQL and stored procedures, you can query the `sys.dm_exec_query_stats` DMV and aggregate on `total_worker_time` to get the total CPU consumption, as follows:

```
SELECT top 50 sum(total_worker_time) as Total_CPU,
              sum(execution_count) as Total_Count,
              count(*) as Total_Statements,
              plan_handle
FROM   sys.dm_exec_query_stats
GROUP BY plan_handle
Order by 1 desc
GO
```

To actually see the SQL code that is behind the `plan_handle`, you can execute the `dm_exec_sql_text` function to get your "hog" list:

```
SELECT total_worker_time, b.text
FROM sys.dm_exec_query_stats A
CROSS APPLY sys.dm_exec_sql_text (A.plan_handle) AS B
order by 1 desc
GO
```

34

Monitoring Memory

Memory, like a processor, is divided into segments for each process running on the server. If memory has too much demand, the operating system has to use virtual memory to supplement the physical memory. Virtual memory is storage allocated on the hard disk; it is named PAGEFILE.SYS under Windows. Table 34.4 reflects the main performance objects and counters that are best utilized to monitor memory for SQL Server.

TABLE 34.4   Memory-Related Performance Objects and Counters

Performance Monitor Object	Description
Process: Working Set¦sqlservr	The set of memory pages touched recently by the threads in the process (SQL Server, in this case).
MSSQL$ Buffer Manager: Buffer cache hit ratio	The percentage of pages were found in the buffer pool without having to incur a read from disk.
MSSQL$ Buffer Manager: Total Pages	The total number of pages in the buffer pool, including database pages, free pages, and stolen pages.
MSQL$ Memory Manager: Total Server Memory (KB)	The total amount of dynamic memory the server is currently consuming.
MSQL$ Memory Manager: SQL Cache Memory (KB)	The total amount of dynamic memory SQL Server cache is currently consuming.
Memory: Pages/sec	The number of pages read from or written to disk to resolve hard page faults. This usually gives a direct indication of memory issues.
Memory: Pages Read/sec	The number of times the disk was read to resolve hard page faults.
Memory: Page Faults	The overall rate at which faulted pages are handled by the processor.
Process: Page Faults¦sqlservr	The rate of page faults occurring in the threads associated with a process (SQL Server, in this case).

Numerous goals can be achieved related to memory and SQL Server. Figure 34.8 shows a typical monitoring of memory under way.

It is important to remember that when the operating system or SQL Server isn't able to use memory to find something and has to use virtual memory stored on the disk, performance degrades. You need to work on minimizing this situation, known as *swapping* or *page faulting*.

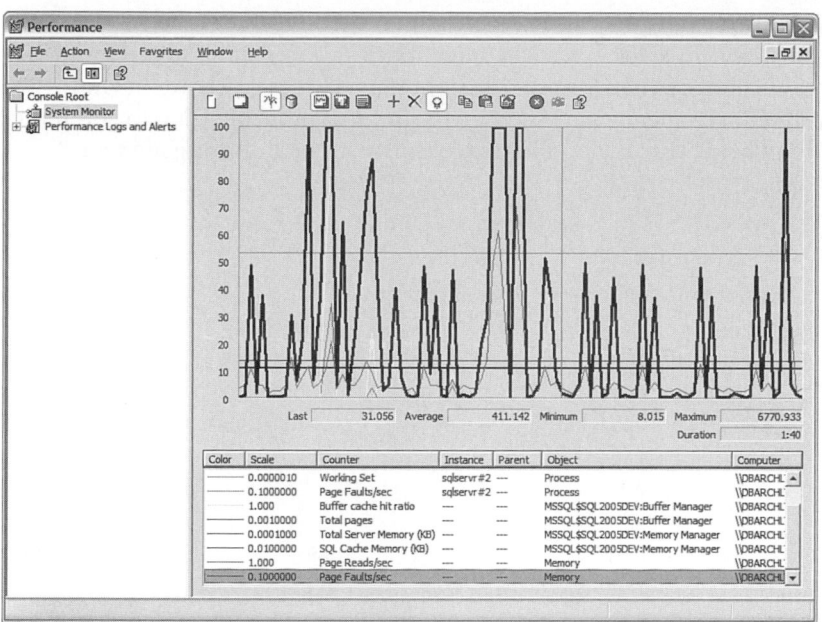

FIGURE 34.8   Memory performance object and counters.

To observe the level of the page faulting, you can look at the Memory: Page Faults/sec and Process: Page Faults (for a SQL Server instance) counters. Next in line are the MSSQL Buffer Manager: Buffer Cache hit ratio and MSSQL Buffer Manager: Total Pages counters. These directly indicate how well SQL Server is finding data in its controlled memory (cache). You need to achieve a near 90% or higher ratio here. DBCC PERFMON also has the cache hit ratio and cache size information.

If the Memory: Pages/sec counter is greater than 0 or the Memory: Page Reads counter is greater than 5, the operating system is being forced to use the disk to resolve memory references. These are called *hard faults*. The Memory: Page counter is one of the best indicators of the amount of paging that Windows is doing and the adequacy of SQL Server's current memory configuration.

Because the memory used by SQL Server 2000 dynamically grows and shrinks, you might want to track the exact usage by using either Process: Working Set: SQLServr or MSSQL: Memory Manager: Total Server Memory (KB) counters. These counters indicate the current size of the memory used by the SQL Server process. If these are consistently high, compared to the amount of physical memory in the machine, you are probably ready to install more memory on this box. If you see a performance degradation because SQL Server must continually grow and shrink its memory, you should either remove some of the other services or processes running or use the configuration option Use a Fixed Memory Size.

Using the new MEMORYSTATUS option of DBCC, you can get a good feel for how memory has been distributed for use within SQL Server. The target buffer counts should correspond with committed buffer counts. When you see target buffers decrease, you are having issues with the distribution of memory in SQL Server, and it is probably time to add more memory or figure out where other issues might be occurring. The following are two sections of DBCC MEMORYSTATUS:

```
DBCC MEMORYSTATUS
GO
 Buffer Counts              Buffers
-----------------------------  --------
Committed                  24661
Target                     26488
Hashed                     4514
Stolen Potential           112142
External Reservation       0
Min Free                   32
Visible                    26488
Available Paging File      189349

(8 row(s) affected)

Procedure Cache            Value
-----------------------------  -----------
TotalProcs                 1228
TotalPages                 9194
InUsePages                 13
```

There are several other sections to this DBCC command, but these are the ones to focus on.

> **NOTE**
>
> One of the big differences in regard to memory in SQL Server 2005 is the method in which caching is implemented. A uniform caching framework was put into place to implement a clock algorithm (an internal clock and an external clock). The internal clock controls the size of a cache relative to other caches. It kicks in when the framework predicts that the cache is about to reach its max. The external clock kicks in when SQL Server as a whole is nearing full memory.

Dynamic Management Views or System Views for Monitoring Memory Items

The DMVs associated with memory are numerous. The ones you'll most likely utilize are memory clerks, memory pools, and cache counters.

To find out a bit more of how SQL Server has allocated memory using any AWE memory, you can use the following:

```
SELECT sum(awe_allocated_kb) / 1024
FROM sys.dm_os_memory_clerks
Go
```

You can find memory allocations by type by using the sys.dm_os_memory_clerks DMV
view:

```
SELECT type, sum(multi_pages_kb) from sys.dm_os_memory_clerks
WHERE multi_pages_kb <> 0
GROUP BY type
GO
type
------------------------------------------------------------     ---------------------
MEMORYCLERK_SQLSTORENG                                           56
OBJECTSTORE_SNI_PACKET                                           288
MEMORYCLERK_SQLOPTIMIZER                                         72
MEMORYCLERK_SQLGENERAL                                           1624
MEMORYCLERK_SQLBUFFERPOOL                                        256
MEMORYCLERK_SOSNODE                                              8088
CACHESTORE_STACKFRAMES                                           16
MEMORYCLERK_SQLSERVICEBROKER                                     192
CACHESTORE_OBJCP                                                 16
MEMORYCLERK_SNI                                                  32
MEMORYCLERK_SQLUTILITIES                                         2384
```

To see how the cache is being used, you can query sys.dm_os_memory_cache_counters:

```
SELECT substring(name,1,25) AS Name, single_pages_kb,
       single_pages_in_use_kb
FROM sys.dm_os_memory_cache_counters
GO
Name                          single_pages_kb     single_pages_in_use_kb
--------------------------     --------------------     ---------------------
SOS_StackFramesStore          0                   8
EventNotificationCache        16                  0
Object Plans                  3528                0
SQL Plans                     76880               128
Bound Trees                   944                 0
Extended Stored Procedure     24                  0
Temporary Tables & Table      16                  0
XMLDBCACHE                    8                   0
XMLDBCACHE                    8                   0
XMLDBCACHE                    8                   0
View Definition Cache         16                  0
Notification Store            16                  0
Service broker routing ca     8                   0
Service broker mapping ta     8                   0
```

Finally, when you want to see the total pages allocated to the different objects in memory, you use the sys.dm_os_memory_objects DMV:

```
SELECT substring(type,1,25) as Type,
       sum(pages_allocated_count) as Total_Memory_Allocated
FROM sys.dm_os_memory_objects
group by type
order by 2 desc
GO
Type                        Total_Memory_Allocated
- - - - - - - - - - - - - - - - - - - - - - - - -    - - - - - - - - - - - - - - - - - - - - - -
MEMOBJ_STATEMENT            43264
MEMOBJ_COMPILE_ADHOC        32932
MEMOBJ_XSTMT                26081
MEMOBJ_QUERYEXECCNTXTFORS   1983
MEMOBJ_EXECUTE              1352
MEMOBJ_SOSNODE              1028
MEMOBJ_PLANSKELETON         999
MEMOBJ_DBMIRRORING          306
MEMOBJ_SQLMGR               166
MEMOBJ_RESOURCE             145
MEMOBJ_PARSE                117
MEMOBJ_SOSSCHEDULER         76
MEMOBJ_PERDATABASE          76
MEMOBJ_CACHESTORESQLCP      72
MEMOBJ_METADATADB           70
MEMOBJ_SERVICEBROKER        65
MEMOBJ_SESCHEMAMGR          56
```

Monitoring the Disk System

By monitoring the portion of the system cache used for the server services (synchronous) and related to SQL Server (asynchronous), you can see how much disk access is related to SQL Server. Not all asynchronous disk activity is SQL Server activity, but on a dedicated box, it should be. You can watch a number of different synchronous and asynchronous counters, depending on the type of activity you want to monitor. SQL Server performance depends heavily on the I/O subsystem. SQL Server is constantly reading and writing pages to disk via the data cache. Focusing on the database data files, transaction log files, and especially tempdb can yield great performance for your SQL Server platform. Table 34.5 lists the essential performance objects and counters related to monitoring the disk system.

TABLE 34.5   Disk Usage-Related Performance Objects and Counters

Performance Monitor Object	Description
Physical Disk: Current Disk Queue Length	The number of outstanding requests (read/write) for a disk.
Physical Disk: Avg. Disk Queue Length	The average number of both read and write requests queued for disks.
Physical Disk: Disk Read Bytes	The rate at which bytes are transferred from the disk during read operations.
Physical Disk: Disk Write Bytes	The rate at which bytes are transferred to the disk during write operations.
Physical Disk: % Disk Time	The percentage of elapsed time that the selected disk drive is busy servicing read or write requests.
Logical Disk: Current Disk Queue Length	The number of outstanding requests (read/write) for a disk.
Logical Disk: Avg. Disk Queue Length	The average number of both read and write requests queued for disks.
Logical Disk: Disk Read Bytes	The rate at which bytes are transferred from the disk during read operations.
Logical Disk: Disk Write Bytes	The rate at which bytes are transferred to the disk during write operations.
Logical Disk: % Disk Time	The percentage of elapsed time that the selected disk drive is busy servicing read or write requests.

34

Slow disk I/O causes a reduction in the transaction throughput. To identify which disks are receiving all the attention, you should monitor both the Physical Disk and Logical Disk performance objects. You have many more opportunities to tune at the disk level than with other components, such as processors. This has long been the area where database administrators and system administrators have been able to get better performance. You can start by looking at the behavior of the Physical Disk: Current Disk Queue Length and Physical Disk: Avg. Disk Queue Length counters for all disks or for each particular disk. This way, you can identify where much of the attention is, from a disk-usage point of view.

As you monitor each individual disk, you might see that some drives are not as busy as others. You can relocate heavily used resources to minimize these long queue lengths that you have uncovered and spread out the disk activity. Common techniques for this are to relocate indexes away from tables, isolate read-only tables away from volatile tables, and so on. You need to take special care with tempdb. The best practice is to isolate it away from all other disk I/O processing.

The Physical Disk: % Disk Time counter for each physical disk drive shows the percentage of time that the disk is active; a continuously high value could indicate an underperforming disk subsystem.

Of course, the monitoring up to this point show only half the picture if drives are partitioned into multiple logical drives. To see the work on each logical drive, you need to examine the logical disk counters; in fact, you can monitor read and write activity separately with `Logical Disk: Disk Write Bytes/sec` and `Logical Disk: Disk Read Bytes/sec`. You should be looking for average times below 20ms. If the averages are over 50ms, the disk subsystem is in serious need of replacement, reconfiguration, or redistribution.

If you use RAID, it is necessary to know how many physical drives are in each RAID array to figure out the monitored values of disk queuing for any one disk. In general, you just divide the disk queue value by the number of physical drives in the disk array. This gives you a fairly accurate number for each physical disk's queue length.

Dynamic Management Views or System Views for Monitoring Disk System Items

There are several I/O-related DMVs and functions. They cover backup tape I/O, pending I/O requests, I/O on cluster shared drives, and virtual file I/O statistics.

The best of these is the `sys.dm_io_virtual_file_stats` function, which allows you to see the file activity within a database allocation. You supply the database ID as the first parameter, along with the file ID of the database file as the second parameter. This yields an accumulating set of statistics that can be used to isolate and characterize heavy I/O:

```
SELECT database_id, file_id, num_of_reads, num_of_bytes_read,
       num_of_bytes_written, size_on_disk_bytes
FROM sys.dm_io_virtual_file_stats (1,1)
GO
database_id file_id num_of_reads num_of_bytes_read num_of_bytes_written
                                                   size_on_disk_bytes

----------- ------- ------------ -----------------
                                                   -----------------
1           1       38           2375680           24576
                                                   4194304

(1 row(s) affected)
```

In addition, the OS wait stats for I/O latch waits are great for identifying when reading or writing of a page is not available from data cache. These latch waits account for the physical I/O waits when a page is accessed for reading or writing. When the page is not found in cache, an asynchronous I/O gets posted. If there is any delay in the I/O, the `PAGEIOLATCH_EX` or the `PAGEIOLATCH_SH` latch waits are affected. An increased number of latch waits indicates that an I/O bottleneck exists. The following is the query that reveals this latch wait information:

```
SELECT substring(wait_type,1,15) AS Latch_Waits, waiting_tasks_count, wait_time_ms
FROM sys.dm_os_wait_stats
WHERE wait_type like 'PAGEIOLATCH%'
ORDER BY wait_type
GO
```

```
Latch_Waits      waiting_tasks_count  wait_time_ms
---------------  -------------------  ------------
PAGEIOLATCH_DT  0                    0
PAGEIOLATCH_EX  22                   771
PAGEIOLATCH_KP  0                    0
PAGEIOLATCH_NL  0                    0
PAGEIOLATCH_SH  328                  28470
PAGEIOLATCH_UP  159                  891


(6 row(s) affected)
```

SQL Server Performance Counters

For each SQL Server instance that is installed, Performance Monitor has a number of SQL Server–specific performance objects added to it, each with a number of associated counters. Because you can now have multiple SQL Server instances on a single machine, each has separate monitoring objects. You certainly wouldn't want to mix monitoring values across multiple instances. You have already seen a few of these as you were monitoring each major component of network, processors, memory, and disk systems. When SQL Server is being installed, these objects are added to the available performance objects and use the naming convention MSSQL$ followed by the instance name (for example, MSSQL$SQL2005DEV:General Statistics). Table 34.6 shows a list of the primary SQL Server performance objects.

TABLE 34.6   SQL Server Performance Objects

Performance Monitor Object	Description
MSSQL$:Access Methods	Information on searches and allocations of database objects.
MSSQL$:Backup Device	Information on throughput of backup devices.
MSSQL$:Buffer Manager	Memory buffers used by SQL Server.
MSSQL$:Buffer Partition	Buffer free list page request information.
MSSQL$:Plan Cache	Information on any cacheable objects, such as stored procedures, triggers, and query plans.
MSSQ$L:Databases	Database-specific information, such as the log space usage or active transactions in the database.
MSSQL$:General Statistics	Serverwide activity, such as number of logins started per second.
MSSQL$:Latches	Information regarding latches on internal resources.
MSSQL$:Locks	Individual lock information, such as lock timeouts and number of deadlocks.
MSSQL$:Memory Manager	SQL Server's memory usage, including counters such as the connection and lock memory use.
MSSQL$:Replication Agents	Information about the SQL Server replication agents that are currently running.

34

TABLE 34.6   Continued

`MSSQL$:Replication Dist.`	Commands and transactions that are read from the distribution database and delivered to the subscriber databases by the distribution agent and latency information.
`MSSQL$:Replication Logreader`	Commands and transactions that are read from the published databases and delivered to the distribution database by the log reader agent.
`MSSQL$:Replication Merge`	Information about merge replication.
`MSSQL$:Replication Snapshot`	Information about snapshot replication.
`MSSQL$:SQL Statistics`	Query statistics, such as the number of batches of SQL received by SQL Server.
`MSSQL$:User Settable`	Counters that return anything you might want to monitor.

In addition, there are a host of new SQL Server performance objects. The following sections look at some of the most relevant performance objects and counters.

MSSQL$:Plan Cache Object

For finding information about the operation of SQL Server's caches, the `MSSQL$:Cache Manager` object holds a number of useful counters that measure such things as data cache, procedure, and trigger cache operations.

These cache counters allow you to watch how each of the caches is used and what each one's upper limit is. These useful counters help indicate whether additional physical memory would benefit SQL Server:

▶ **Cache Pages**—The number of pages used by the cache

▶ **Cache Object Counts**—The number of objects using the cache pages

▶ **Cache Objects in Use Counts/sec**—The object usage

▶ **Cache Hit Ratio**—The difference between cache hits and lookup

You can display each of these counters for specific cache instances, ranging from ad hoc SQL plans to procedure plans and trigger plans.

A few related cache counters provide more of an overview on the cache operations: `MSSQL$:Memory Manager:SQL Cache Memory` and `MSSQL$:Memory Manager:Optimizer Memory`.

The `MSSQL$:Buffer Manager` object also contains a counter that pertains to the operation of Read Ahead Manager: `Readahead Pages/sec`. The information returned by this counter indicates how much work is done populating the page cache due to sequential scans of data. This might indicate the need to optimize certain queries, add more physical memory, or even consider pinning a table into the cache.

Monitoring SQL Server's Disk Activity

In the section "Monitoring the Disk System," earlier in this chapter, you saw how to monitor disk activity. Here, we will examine what SQL Server's contribution is to all this disk activity. Disk activity can be categorized into reads and writes. SQL Server carries out writes to the disk for the following processes:

▶ Logging records

▶ Writing dirty cache pages at the end of a transaction

▶ Freeing space in the page cache

Logging is a constant occurrence in any database that allows modifications, and SQL Server attempts to optimize this process by batching a number of writes together. To see how much work is done on behalf of the database logs, you can examine the `MSSQL$:Databases:Log Bytes Flushed` and `MSSQL$:Databases:Log Flushes/sec` counters. The first tells you the quantity of the work, and the second tells you the frequency.

The third kind of write occurs to make space within the page cache. This is carried out by the Lazy Writer process, which you can track with the counter `MSSQL$:Buffer Manager:Lazy Writes`.

It is easy to monitor the amount of reading SQL Server is doing by using the counter `MSSQL$:Buffer Manager:Page Reads`. All read and write counter values are combined server-level values.

Locks

One of the often overlooked areas of performance degradation is locking. You need to ensure that the correct types of locks are issued and that the worst kind of lock, a blocking lock, is kept to a minimum. A blocking lock, as its name implies, prevents other users from continuing his or her own work. An easy way to identify the level of blocking locks is to use the counter `MSSQL$:Memory Manager:Lock Blocks`. If this counter frequently indicates a value greater than 0, you need to examine the queries being executed or even revisit the database design.

Users

Even though you cannot always trace performance problems directly to the number of users connected, it is a good idea to occasionally monitor how this number fluctuates. It is fairly easy to trace one particular user who is causing a massive performance problem.

The leverage point here is to see the current number of user connections with the `MSSQL$: General Statistics:User Connections` counter in conjunction with other objects and counters. It is easy to say that the disk subsystem is a bottleneck, but how many users is SQL Server supporting at the time?

The Procedure Cache

Another area of memory used by SQL Server exclusively is the procedure cache, and a large number of counters correspond to the procedure cache and provide insight on its utilization.

The procedure cache maintains pointers to the procedure buffer, which is where the executable from the stored procedures is actually kept. You can separately monitor the amount of memory used by the procedure buffers and cache.

For the procedure buffers, you can use `MSSQL$:Plan Cache:Object Counts:Procedure Plans` to track how many are currently in use. SQL Server also maintains a separate set of counters for the parts of the cache that are active as opposed to only in use. You can also track the total size of the procedure cache by using the `MSSQL$:Plan Cache:Cache Pages:Procedure Plans` counter, which is in 8KB pages. This counter value fluctuates with the execution of each new stored procedure and other server activity.

User-Defined Counters

You can extend the range of information that the Performance Monitor displays by creating up to 10 of your own counters. These user-defined counters appear under the `MSSQL$:User Settable:Query` object, which contains the 10 counters as instances, starting with User Counter 1. You define your own counters by calling stored procedures with the names `sp_user_counter1` through `sp_user_counter10`, which are located in the `master` database.

These counters work differently than they did under previous versions of SQL Server and require you to call the stored procedures to update the information they return to the Performance Monitor. To make any real use of these stored procedures, you now need to call them within a loop or as part of a job that is scheduled on some recurring basis.

Using these counters allows you to monitor any information you want, whether it is system, database, or even object specific. The only restriction is that the stored procedure can take only a single integer value argument.

The following sample procedure sets the average connection time for all user connections. Processes that have a `session_id` less than 27 are system ones (checkpoint, Lazy Writer, and so on):

```
DECLARE @value INT

SELECT @value = AVG( DATEDIFF( mi, login_time, GETDATE()))
FROM sys.dm_exec_sessions
WHERE session_id > 26

EXEC sp_user_counter1 @value
```

You could further extend this information by creating additional user procedures for returning the minimum and maximum times connected, as well as database usage. Your only limitation is that you can monitor only 10 pieces of information at one time.

Dynamic Management Views or System Views: Access to Perfmon Counters

Most of the SQL Server–oriented performance counter values can also be seen at any point in time via a new system view named sys.sysperfinfo. As you can see in the following example, this view shows the performance object name, the counter name, and the current counter value as of the time the system view is executed:

```
SELECT * from sys.sysperfinfo
GO
```

object_name	counter_name	cntr_value	cntr_type
MSSQL$SQL2005DEV:Buffer Manager	Buffer cache hit ratio	779	537003264
MSSQL$SQL2005DEV:Buffer Manager	Total pages	11730	65792
MSSQL$SQL2005DEV:General Statistics	Active Temp Tables	8	65792
MSSQL$SQL2005DEV:General Statistics	Logins/sec	689	272696576
MSSQL$SQL2005DEV:General Statistics	SOAP WSDL Requests	0	272696576
MSSQL$SQL2005DEV:Locks	Number of Deadlocks/sec	0	272696576
MSSQL$SQL2005DEV:Locks	Lock Wait Time (ms)	0	272696576
MSSQL$SQL2005DEV:Databases	Data File(s) Size (KB)		
	AdventureWorks	184256	65792
MSSQL$SQL2005DEV:Databases	Log File(s) Size (KB)		
	AdventureWorks	18424	65792
MSSQL$SQL2005DEV:Databases	Transactions/sec		
	AdventureWorks	180	272696576
MSSQL$SQL2005DEV:Database Mirroring	_Total	0	272696576
MSSQL$SQL2005DEV:Latches	Latch Waits/sec	973	272696576
MSSQL$SQL2005DEV:Latches	Average Latch Wait Time	34363	1073874176
MSSQL$SQL2005DEV:Memory Manager	SQL Cache Memory (KB)	792	65792
MSSQL$SQL2005DEV:Memory Manager	Target Server Memory(KB)	209096	65792
MSSQL$SQL2005DEV:Memory Manager	Total Server Memory (KB)	93840	65792

Keep in mind that many of these are accumulation counters, and you have to run this at intervals and determine the difference (change) from one interval to the next. Others are current values of things such as transaction rates, memory usage, and hit ratios.

Using DBCC to Examine Performance

Microsoft might have targeted the DBCC command for extinction, but DBCC can still provide useful information on the current state of SQL Server. The next several sections detail the available options. Many of the same commands are used and presented in a more friendly format by the SQL tools; however, you can capture information from these DBCC commands into tables for historical statistics.

SQLPERF

The DBCC SQLPERF command has been drastically altered from previous versions and now reports only transaction log space usage for all databases and active threads on the server. The following is the DBCC command to see the transaction log information:

```
DBCC SQLPERF( LOGSPACE )
Go
Database Name        Log Size (MB) Log Space Used (%) Status
master               0.4921875     47.61905           0
tempdb               0.9921875     53.59252           0
model                0.4921875     48.4127            0
msdb                 2.492188      42.63323           0
AdventureWorksDW     1.992188      20.19608           0
AdventureWorks       17.99219      42.48806           0
```

The results of this command are tabular and can be captured into a database table to maintain historical statistics on log usage on the server. The following information is returned:

- **Database Name**—Name of the database

- **Log Size (MB)**—Current size of the log file

- **Log Space Used (%)**—Percentage of the log file currently used

- **Status**—Status of the log file (always contains 0)

For the active threads information, the command is as follows:

```
DBCC SQLPERF(THREADS)
Go
Spid   Thread ID   Status      LoginName IO    CPU   MemUsage
------ ----------- ----------- -----------------------------
1      2308        background  sa        0     0     0
53     NULL        sleeping    DBA\Paul  18    120   2
54     1568        running     DBA\Paul  2901  1226  29
```

The results of this command are also tabular and can be captured into a database table to maintain historical statistics on the threads used and for what purpose. The following information is returned:

- **Spid**—Server process ID

- **Thread ID**—Thread ID at the operating system level

- **Status**—Status of the process (sleeping, background, and so on)

- **LoginName**—SQL Server login associated with the SPID

▶ **IO**—Amount of I/O accumulated

▶ **CPU**—Amount of CPU accumulated

▶ **MemUsage**—Amount of memory touched

Overall, DBCC SQLPERF is great for corresponding SQL Server processes back to the operating system thread information.

PERFMON

Another DBCC command that is useful for finding performance information on SQL Server is DBCC PERFMON:

```
DBCC PERFMON
Go
Statistic                        Value
-------------------------------- -------------
Reads Outstanding                0
Writes Outstanding               0

(2 row(s) affected)

Statistic                        Value
-------------------------------- -------------
Network Reads                    11606
Network Writes                   11641
Network Bytes Read               2669226
Network Bytes Written            1669399
Command Queue Length             0
Max Command Queue Length         0
Worker Threads                   0
Max Worker Threads               0
Network Threads                  0
Max Network Threads              0

(10 row(s) affected)
```

This command returns information about the I/O work that SQL Server has been performing, the page cache state and operation, and network statistics. The system-stored procedure equivalent is sp_monitor. PERFMON might be left out of future SQL Server releases, so use caution when embedding its use in your activities.

SHOWCONTIG

The DBCC SHOWCONTIG command has been discussed in other chapters and is mentioned here only for completeness. The DBCC SHOWCONTIG command illustrates the internal state of extents and pages of each table and index for a database and is helpful in determining how SQL Server is likely to perform when reading data from a table:

```
USE dbname
Go
DBCC SHOWCONTIG
Go
DBCC SHOWCONTIG scanning 'ProductProductPhoto' table...
Table: 'ProductProductPhoto' (18099105); index ID: 0, database ID: 6
TABLE level scan performed.
- Pages Scanned................................: 2
- Extents Scanned..............................: 1
- Extent Switches..............................: 0
- Avg. Pages per Extent........................: 2.0
- Scan Density [Best Count:Actual Count].......: 100.00% [1:1]
- Extent Scan Fragmentation ...................: 0.00%
- Avg. Bytes Free per Page.....................: 1544.0
- Avg. Page Density (full).....................: 80.92%
DBCC SHOWCONTIG scanning 'StoreContact' table...
Table: 'StoreContact' (30623152); index ID: 1, database ID: 6
TABLE level scan performed.
```

This can be valuable information when you're trying to determine the level of fragmentation and the page density of table allocations.

PROCCACHE

The DBCC PROCCACHE command returns the following information on the procedure cache:

▶ **num proc buffs**—The number of possible cache slots in the cache

▶ **num proc buffs used**—The number of cache slots in use by procedures

▶ **num proc buffs active**—The number of cache slots that have currently executing procedures

▶ **proc cache size**—The total size of the procedure cache

▶ **proc cache used**—The amount of the procedure cache holding stored procedures

▶ **proc cache active**—The amount of the procedure cache holding stored procedures that are currently executing

The following is the DBCC command to see this procedure cache information:

```
DBCC PROCCACHE
GO
num proc buffs num proc buffs used num proc buffs active proc cache size proc
------------------ -------------------- -------------------- -------------
4113             21                    21                    517              5        5
```

Even though SQL Server 2005 grows and shrinks the procedure cache size as required, you should still monitor how much of the memory allocated to SQL Server is in use by the procedure cache. This need makes the DBCC command quite useful. You can also use the DBCC FREEPROCCACHE command to remove all elements from the procedure cache. This, for example, causes an ad hoc SQL statement to be recompiled rather than reused from the cache.

INPUTBUFFER **and** OUTPUTBUFFER

You use the DBCC INPUTBUFFER/OUTPUTBUFFER command to examine the statements sent by a client to the SQL Server. The syntax for these commands is as follows:

```
DBCC INPUTBUFFER(spid)
DBCC OUTPUTBUFFER(spid)
```

INPUTBUFFER shows the last statement sent from the specified client, and OUTPUTBUFFER shows the results sent back from the SQL Server.

SQL tools use INPUTBUFFER and OUTPUTBUFFER to display current activity, and you can also use them to examine the commands sent by certain processes that are affecting system performance.

To actually see the SQL code that is behind plan_handle, you execute the dm_exec_sql_text function to get your hog list:

```
SELECT total_worker_time, b.text
FROM sys.dm_exec_query_stats A
CROSS APPLY sys.dm_exec_sql_text (A.plan_handle) AS B
order by 1 desc
GO
```

The Top 100 Worst-Performing Queries

One of the things we are asked to do whenever we show up on a customer's SQL Server site is to quickly identify the top 100 worst-performing SQL queries on a problem SQL Server installation. This can be done in a number of ways, but the best way is to utilize the SQL Profiler tracing capabilities, along with some slick queries against what is captured. The other method is to utilize the newly introduced DMVs and functions to identify and display the current worst performers.

Using SQL Server Profiler, you can start a trace against the desired SQL Server instance and even limit your trace to consider only a specific database (such as AdventureWorks). You simply start up the SQL Profiler from the SSMS toolbar or from the Microsoft SQL Server 2005 program group under the Performance Tools Program item. Then you choose to create a new trace and name the trace something like "Top100Trace," and choose the Tuning trace template (as shown in Figure 34.9).

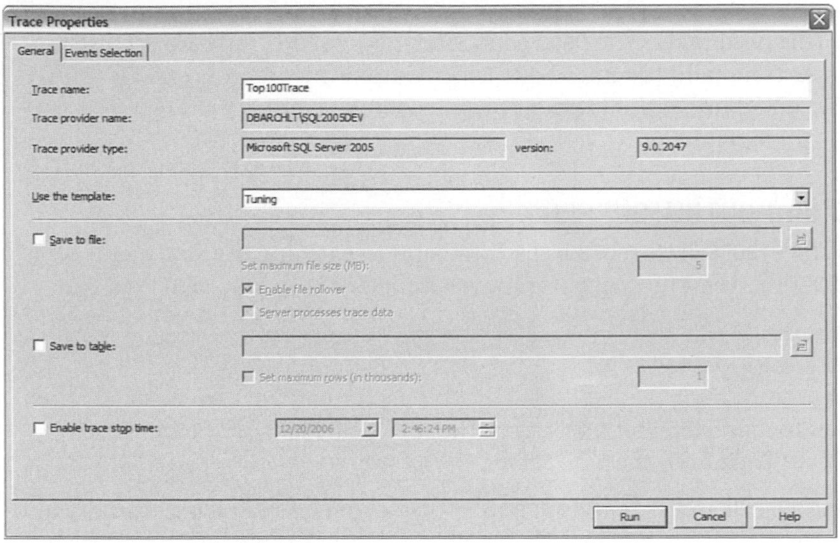

FIGURE 34.9   A new SQL Server Profiler trace, using the Tuning trace template.

Next, you click the Events Selection tab and click the Show All Columns option at the bottom right. Then you put a check mark on the individual entries you want to see like CPU, Reads, and Writes additional columns for this trace. Then uncheck the Show All Columns option, as shown in Figure 34.10.

Now you simply start the trace (by clicking the Run button). After you have captured a reasonable amount of SQL hitting the server that represents a good sampling of the SQL queries, you can stop the trace. Figure 34.11 shows what this trace looks like. When the trace is stopped, you choose to save the trace in a trace table in a working database somewhere by using File, Save As.

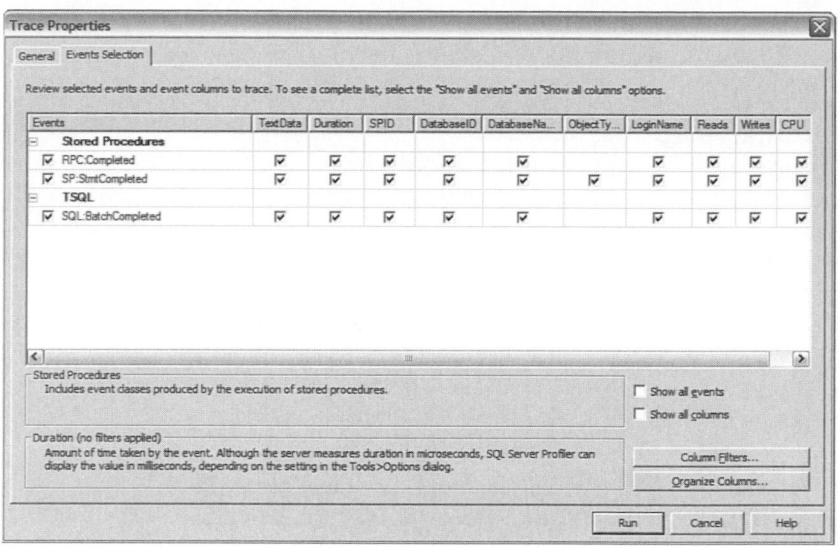

FIGURE 34.10   A new SQL Server Profiler trace with events selection.

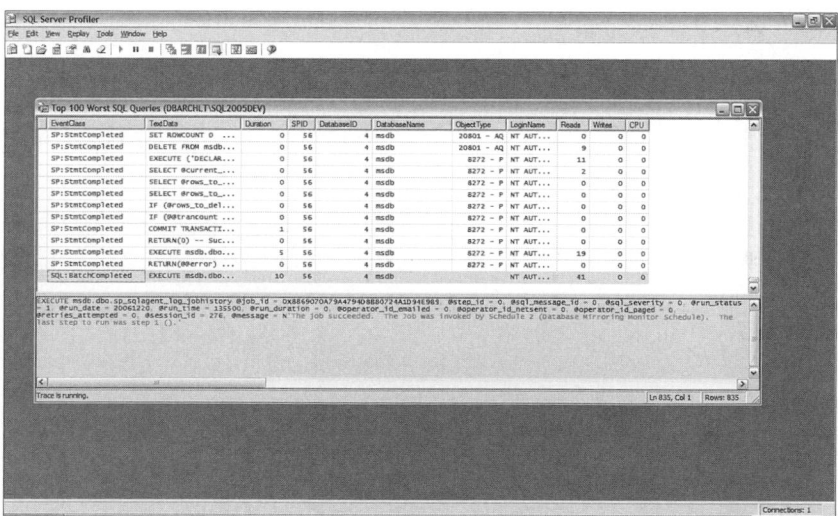

FIGURE 34.11   A new SQL Server Profiler trace's execution results.

After this is saved as a table, you can run the following SQL statement to have this data ordered into the top 100 worst-performing SQL queries in this particular trace sample:

```
SELECT TOP 100 RowNumber,
               TextData,
               LoginName,
               spid,
               Reads,
               Writes,
               CPU,
               Duration
FROM Top100TraceTable
WHERE Reads is not null
ORDER BY Reads DESC
GO
```

Text_Data	LoginName	Spid	Reads	Writes	CPU	Duration
insert into	NT AUTHORITY\SYSTEM	56	2152	0	20	20200
insert into @	NT AUTHORITY\SYSTEM	56	2148	0	20	21484
dbcc dbtable	NT AUTHORITY\SYSTEM	56	1351	0	10	16514
SELECT Contact	DBARCHLT\PaulBert	57	630	0	41	2345731

Via dynamic management views, you can use the dm_exec_sql_text function along with the sys.dm_exec_query_stats DMV to show the top 100 worst SQL statements, based on total worker time:

```
SELECT Top 100 A.total_worker_time, b.text
FROM sys.dm_exec_query_stats A
CROSS APPLY sys.dm_exec_sql_text (A.plan_handle) AS B
order by 1 desc
GO
```

total_worker_time	text
2076330	create procedure

```
sys.sp_dbmmonitorMSgetthelatestlsn@database_name sysname,
➥@end_of_log_lsn numeric(25,0)=null output
Asbegin   set nocount on
   if (is_srvrolemember(N'sysadmin') <> 1 )
   begin
       raiserror(21089, 16, 1)
       return 1
```

| 1017504 | SELECT b.text |

```
FROM sys.dm_exec_query_stats A
CROSS APPLY sys.dm_exec_sql_text (A.plan_handle) AS B
order by 1 desc
```

| 934647 | SELECT A.total_worker_time, b.text |

```
FROM sys.dm_exec_query_stats A
CROSS APPLY sys.dm_exec_sql_text (A.plan_handle) AS B
order by 1 desc
653272                 SELECT a.*,A.total_worker_time, b.text
FROM sys.dm_exec_query_stats A
CROSS APPLY sys.dm_exec_sql_text (A.plan_handle) AS B
order by 1 desc
```

Other SQL Server Performance Considerations

As mentioned earlier in this chapter, many opportunities exist for SQL Server performance tuning in the area of disk usage. The classic server-level configuration typically tries to separate certain SQL Server items across different hard drives, RAID controllers, and PCI channels. This results in a physical I/O segregation with minimal confusion and maximum value. The main items to try to segregate are transaction logs, tempdb, databases, certain tables, and even nonclustered indexes.

You can easily segregate (that is, isolate) transaction logs away from the data files simply by specifying a different location during database creation. You shouldn't have transaction logs located on the same physical device as the data files.

Segregating tempdb is a bit more difficult in that you must use an Alter DB command to change the physical file location of the SQL Server logical filename associated with tempdb. However, by isolating tempdb away from the data files of your other databases, you can almost achieve minimal disk arm contention for one of the most heavily used databases in SQL Server.

Database partitioning can be accomplished using files and filegroups. In general, you can segregate databases with high volatility away from other database with high volatility by defining the files/filegroups on physically separate devices and not sharing a single device.

For tables and nonclustered indexes, you can reference the filegroups from within their create statements (the ON statement) to physically segregate these objects away from others. This can be extremely powerful for heavily used tables and indexes.

> **NOTE**
>
> As a bonus to this chapter, we provide a Performance Monitor analysis example that we did at a live customer site. It identifies the primary performance counters to focus on and then goes through a live customer monitoring exercise. The document also highlights the findings and suggests solutions to this customer's issues. This document can be found on the Sams Publishing website for this book (www.samspublishing.com); it is named PerfMon Analysis SQL Server Sample.doc. All SQL code run in this chapter is also available at the website, in a file called SQL2005Perf.sql.

34

Summary

Attacking SQL Server performance is not a simple task because so many variables are involved. Tuning queries and proper database design are a huge part of this, but dealing with SQL Server as an engine that consumes resources and the physical machine are equally important. This is why it is so critical to take an orderly, methodical approach when undertaking this task. As pointed out in this chapter, you need to basically peel apart the box on which SQL Server has been installed, one component at a time (network, CPU, memory, and disk). This allows you to explore the individual layer or component in a clear and concise manner. Within a short amount of time, you will be able to identify the biggest performance offenders and resolve them.

Chapter 35, "What's New for Transact-SQL in SQL Server 2005," opens up the covers on many of the new features and options introduced with SQL Server 2005.

PART VI

SQL Server Application Development

IN THIS PART

CHAPTER 35	What's New for Transact-SQL in SQL Server 2005	1273
CHAPTER 36	SQL Server and the .NET Framework	1319
CHAPTER 37	Using XML in SQL Server 2005	1377
CHAPTER 38	SQL Server Web Services	1439

What's New for Transact-SQL in SQL Server 2005

IN THIS CHAPTER

▶ The xml Data Type

▶ The max Specifier

▶ TOP Enhancements

▶ The OUTPUT Clause

▶ Common Table Expressions

▶ Ranking Functions

▶ PIVOT and UNPIVOT

▶ The APPLY Operator

▶ TRY...CATCH Logic for Error Handling

▶ The TABLESAMPLE Clause

SQL Server 2005 introduces some new features and changes to the Transact-SQL (T-SQL) language. The focus in this chapter is primarily on the new and modified Data Manipulation Language (DML) commands and programming constructs built into T-SQL. The various new and updated Data Definition Language (DDL) commands are covered in other chapters, primarily those in Part IV, "Database Administration."

SQL Server 2005 doesn't really provide many new Transact-SQL DML statements over what was available in 2000. However, it offers the following new features:

▶ The xml data type

▶ The max specifier for the varchar and varbinary data types

▶ TOP enhancements

▶ The OUTPUT clause

▶ Common table expressions (CTEs)

▶ Ranking functions

▶ PIVOT and UNPIVOT

▶ The APPLY operator

▶ TRY-CATCH logic for error handling

▶ The TABLESAMPLE clause

> **NOTE**
>
> Unless stated otherwise, all examples in this chapter make use of tables in the
> bigpubs2005 database.

The xml Data Type

SQL Server 2005 introduces a new xml data type that supports storing XML documents and fragments in database columns or variables. The xml data type can be used with local variable declarations, as the output of user-defined functions, as input parameters to stored procedures and functions, and much more. The results of a FOR XML statement can now easily be stored in a column, stored procedure parameter, or local variable. XML data is stored in an internal binary format and can be up to 2GB in size. XML instances stored in xml columns can contain up to 128 levels of nesting.

xml columns can also be used to store code files such as XSLT, XSD, XHTML, and any other well-formed content. These files can then be retrieved by user-defined functions written in managed code hosted by SQL Server. (See Chapter 36, "SQL Server and the .NET Framework," for a full review of SQL Server managed hosting.)

For more information and detailed examples on using the xml data type, see Chapter 37, "Using XML in SQL Server 2005."

The max Specifier

In SQL Server 2000, the most data that could be stored in a varchar, nvarchar, or varbinary column was 8,000 bytes. If you needed to store a larger value in a single column, you had to use the large object (LOB) data types: text, ntext, or image. The main disadvantage of using the LOB data types is that they cannot be used in many places where varchar or varbinary data types can be used (for example, as local variables, as arguments to SQL Server string manipulation functions such as REPLACE, and in string concatenation operations).

SQL Server 2005 introduces the new max specifier for varchar and varbinary data types. This specifier expands the storage capabilities of the varchar and varbinary data types to store up to 2^31-1 bytes of data, which is the same maximum size of text and image data types. The main difference is that these new large value data types can be used just like the smaller varchar, nvarchar, and varbinary data types. The large value data types can be used in functions where LOB objects cannot (such as the REPLACE function), as data types for Transact-SQL variables, and in string concatenation operations. They can also be used in the DISTINCT, ORDER BY, and GROUP BY clauses of a SELECT statement as well as in aggregates, joins, and subqueries.

The following example shows a local variable being defined using the varchar(max) data type:

```
declare @maxvar varchar(max)
go
```

However, a similar variable cannot be defined using the text data type:

```
declare @textvar text
go
```

```
Msg 2739, Level 16, State 1, Line 2
The text, ntext, and image data types are invalid for local variables.declare
 @maxvar varchar(max)
```

The remaining examples in this section make use of the following table to demonstrate the differences between a varchar(max) column and a text column:

```
create table maxtest (maxcol varchar(max),
                      textcol text)
go
-- populate the columns with some sample data
insert maxtest
   select replicate('1234567890', 1000), replicate('1234567890', 1000)
go
```

In the following example, you can see that the substring function works with both varchar(max) and text data types:

```
select substring (maxcol, 1, 10),
       substring (textcol, 1, 10)
   from maxtext
go
```

```
maxcol     textcol
---------- ----------
1234567890 1234567890
```

However, in this example, you can see that while a varchar(max) column can be used for string concatenation, the text data type cannot:

```
select substring('xxx' + maxcol, 1, 10) from maxtest
go
```

```
----------
xxx1234567
```

```
select substring('xxx' + textcol, 1, 10) from maxtest
go
```

```
Msg 402, Level 16, State 1, Line 1
The data types varchar and text are incompatible in the add operator.
```

With the introduction of the max specifier, the large value data types have the ability to store data with the same maximum size as the LOB data types, but with the ability to be used just as their smaller varchar, nvarchar, and varbinary counterparts. It is recommended that the max data types be used instead of the LOB data types as the LOB data types are being deprecated in future releases of SQL Server.

TOP **Enhancements**

The TOP clause allows you to specify the number or percentage of rows to be returned by a SELECT statement. SQL Server 2005 allows the TOP clause to also be used in INSERT, UPDATE, and DELETE statements and enhances the syntax to allow the use of a numeric expression for the number value rather than having to be a hard-coded number.

The new syntax for the TOP clause is as follows:

```
SELECT [TOP (numeric_expression) [PERCENT] [WITH TIES]]
    FROM table_name ...[ORDER BY...]
DELETE [TOP (numeric_expression) [PERCENT]] FROM table_name ...
UPDATE [TOP (numeric_expression) [PERCENT]] table_name SET ...
INSERT [TOP (numeric_expression) [PERCENT]] INTO table_name ...
```

numeric_expression must be specified in parentheses. Specifying constants without parentheses is only supported in SELECT queries for backward compatibility. The parentheses around the expression are always required when TOP is used in UPDATE, INSERT, or DELETE statements.

If you do not specify the PERCENT option, the numeric expression must be implicitly convertible to the bigint data type. If you specify the PERCENT option, the numeric expression must be implicitly convertible to float and fall within the range of 0 to 100. The WITH TIES option with the ORDER BY clause is supported only with SELECT statements.

The following example shows the use of a local variable as the numeric expression for the TOP clause to limit the number of rows returned by a SELECT statement:

```
declare @rows int
select @rows = 5
select top (@rows) * from sales
go
```

stor_id	ord_num	ord_date	qty	payterms	title_id
6380	6871	1994-09-14 00:00:00.000	5	Net 60	BU1032
6380	722a	1994-09-13 00:00:00.000	3	Net 60	PS2091
6380	ONFFFFFFFFFFFFFFFFFFFF	1994-08-09 00:00:00.000	852	Net 30	FI1980
7066	A2976	1993-05-24 00:00:00.000	50	Net 30	PC8888
7066	ONAAAAAAAAAA	1994-01-13 00:00:00.000	948	Net 60	CH2480

Allowing the use of a numeric expression rather than a constant for the TOP command is especially useful when the number of requested rows is passed as a parameter to a stored procedure or function. When you use a subquery as the numeric expression, it must be self-contained; it cannot refer to columns of a table in the outer query. Using a self-contained subquery allows you to more easily develop queries for dynamic requests, such as "calculate the average number of titles published per week and return that many titles which were most recently published":

```
SELECT TOP(SELECT COUNT(*)/DATEDIFF(month, MIN(pubdate), MAX(pubdate))
          FROM titles)
       title_id, pub_id, pubdate
FROM titles
ORDER BY pubdate DESC
go
```

title_id	pub_id	pubdate
CH9009	9903	1996-05-31 00:00:00.000
PC9999	1389	1996-03-31 05:27:00.000
FI0375	9901	1995-09-24 00:00:00.000
DR4250	9904	1995-09-21 00:00:00.000
BI4785	9914	1995-09-20 00:00:00.000
BI0194	9911	1995-09-19 00:00:00.000
BI3224	9905	1995-09-18 00:00:00.000
FI0355	9917	1995-09-17 00:00:00.000
FI0792	9907	1995-09-13 00:00:00.000

NOTE

Be aware that the TOP keyword does not speed up a query if the query also contains an ORDER BY clause. This is because the entire result set is selected into a worktable and sorted before the top *N* rows in the ordered result set are returned.

When using the TOP keyword, you can also add the WITH TIES option to specify that additional rows should be returned from the result set if duplicate values of the columns specified in the ORDER BY clause exist within the last values returned. The WITH TIES option can be specified only if an ORDER BY clause is specified. The following query returns the top four most expensive books:

```
SELECT TOP 4 price, title
   FROM titles
   ORDER BY price DESC
go
```

```
price                 title
-------------------   ---------------------------------------
17.1675               But Is It User Friendly?
17.0884               Is Anger the Enemy?
15.9329               Emotional Security: A New Algorithm
15.894                You Can Combat Computer Stress!
```

If you use WITH TIES, you can see that there is an additional row with the same price (15.894) as the last row returned by the previous query:

```
SELECT TOP 4 WITH TIES price, title
   FROM titles
   ORDER BY price DESC
go
```

```
price                 title
-------------------   ---------------------------------------
17.1675               But Is It User Friendly?
17.0884               Is Anger the Enemy?
15.9329               Emotional Security: A New Algorithm
15.894                The Gourmet Microwave
15.894                You Can Combat Computer Stress!
```

In previous versions of SQL Server, if you wanted to limit the number of rows affected by an UPDATE statement or a DELETE statement, you had to use the SET ROWCOUNT statement:

```
set rowcount 100
DELETE sales where ord_date < (select dateadd(year, 1, min(ord_date)) from sales)
set rowcount 0
```

Using SET ROWCOUNT in this way was often done to allow backing up and pruning of the transaction log during a purge process and also to prevent lock escalation. The problem with SET ROWCOUNT is that it applies to the entire current user session. You have to remember to set the rowcount back to 0 to be sure you don't limit the rows affected by subsequent statements. With TOP, you can now more easily specify the desired number of rows for each individual statement:

```
DELETE top (100) sales
   where ord_date < (select dateadd(year, 1, min(ord_date)) from sales)
```

```
UPDATE top (100) titles
   set royalty = royalty * 1.25
```

You may be thinking that using TOP in INSERT statements is not really necessary because you can always specify it in a SELECT query, as shown in Listing 35.1.

LISTING 35.1   Limiting Rows for Insert with TOP in a SELECT Statement

```
CREATE TABLE top_sales
   (stor_id char(4),
    ord_num varchar(20),
    ord_date datetime NOT NULL,
    qty smallint NOT NULL,
    payterms varchar(12) ,
    title_id dbo.tid NOT NULL)
go
insert top_sales
   select top 100 * from sales
      where qty > 1700
      order by qty desc
```

However, you may find using the TOP clause in an INSERT statement useful when inserting the result of an EXEC command or the result of a UNION operation, as shown in Listing 35.2.

LISTING 35.2   Using TOP in an Insert with a UNION ALL Query

```
insert top (50) into top_sales
   select stor_id, ord_num, ord_date, qty, payterms, title_id from sales
      where qty >= 1800
   union all
   select stor_id, ord_num, ord_date, qty, payterms, title_id from sales_big
      where qty >= 1800
   order by qty desc
```

When a TOP (*n*) clause is used with DELETE, UPDATE, or INSERT, the selection of rows the operation is performed on is not guaranteed. If you want the TOP(*n*) clause to operate on rows in a meaningful chronological order, you must use TOP together with ORDER BY in a subselect statement. The following query deletes the 10 rows of the sales_big table that have the earliest order dates:

```
delete from sales_big
   where sales_id in (select top 10 sales_id
                         from sales_big order by ord_date)
```

To ensure that only 10 rows are deleted, the column specified in the subselect statement (sales_id) is the primary key of the table. Using a non-key column in the subselect statement could result in the deletion of more than 10 rows if the specified column matched duplicate values.

NOTE

SQL Server Books Online states that when you use TOP (*n*) with INSERT, UPDATE, and DELETE operations, the rows affected should be a random selection of the TOP(*n*) rows from the underlying table. In practice, this behavior has not been observed. Using TOP (*n*) with INSERT, UPDATE, and DELETE appears to affect only the first *n* matching rows. However, because the row selection is not guaranteed, it is still recommended that you use TOP together with ORDER BY in a subselect to ensure the expected result.

The OUTPUT Clause

By default, the execution of a DML statement such as INSERT, UPDATE, or DELETE does not produce any results that indicate what rows changed except for checking @@ROWCOUNT to determine the number of rows affected.

In SQL Server 2005, the INSERT, UPDATE, and DELETE statements have been enhanced to support an OUTPUT clause to be able to identify the actual rows affected by the DML statement. The OUTPUT clause allows you to return data from a modification statement (INSERT, UPDATE, or DELETE). This data can be returned as a result set to the caller or returned into a table variable or an output table. To capture information on the affected rows, the OUTPUT clause provides access to the inserted and deleted virtual tables that are normally accessible only in a trigger. The inserted and deleted tables provide access to the new/old images of the modified rows; this is similar to how they provide the information in triggers. In an INSERT statement, you are only allowed to access the inserted table. In a DELETE statement, you are only allowed to access the deleted table. In an UPDATE statement, you are allowed to access both the inserted and the deleted tables.

The following is the general syntax of the new OUTPUT clause:

```
UPDATE [ TOP ( expression ) [ PERCENT ] ] tablename
    SET { column_name = { expression ¦ DEFAULT ¦ NULL }
          ¦ @variable = expression
          ¦ @variable = column = expression [ ,...n ]
        } [ ,...n ]
    OUTPUT
    { DELETED ¦ INSERTED ¦ from_table_name}.{* ¦ column_name} ¦ scalar_expression
            [ INTO { @table_variable ¦ output_table } [ ( column_list ) ] ] }
    [ FROM { table_name } [ ,...n ] ]
    [ WHERE search_conditions ]
```

```
DELETE [ TOP ( expression ) [ PERCENT ] ] tablename
    OUTPUT { DELETED ¦ from_table_name}.{* ¦ column_name} ¦ scalar_expression
            [ INTO { @table_variable ¦ output_table } [ ( column_list ) ] ] ] }
    [ FROM ] table_name
    [ FROM table_name [ ,...n ] ]
    [ WHERE search_conditions ]

INSERT [ TOP ( expression ) [ PERCENT ] ] [ INTO ] tablename
{
    [ ( column_list ) ]
    [ OUTPUT { INSERTED ¦ from_table_name}.{* ¦ column_name} ¦ scalar_expression
            [ INTO { @table_variable ¦ output_table } [ ( column_list ) ] ] ] }
    { VALUES ( { DEFAULT ¦ NULL ¦ expression } [ ,...n ] )
      ¦ SELECT_statement
    }
}
```

The output table (*output_table*) may be a table variable, a permanent table, or a temporary table. If *column_list* is not specified, the output table must have the same number of columns as the OUTPUT result set. If *column_list* is specified, any omitted columns must either allow null values or have default values assigned to them. Any identity or computed columns in the output table must be skipped. In addition, *output_table* cannot have any enabled triggers defined on it, participate on either side of a foreign key constraint, or have any check constraints or enabled rules.

One use of the OUTPUT clause is to verify the rows being deleted, updated, or inserted:

```
begin tran
delete from sales_big output deleted.*
where sales_id in (select top 10 sales_id from sales_big order by ord_date)
rollback
go
```

sales_id	stor_id	ord_num	ord_date	qty	payterms	title_id
168745	7067	P2121	1992-06-15 00:00:00.000	40	Net 30	TC3218
168746	7067	P2121	1992-06-15 00:00:00.000	20	Net 30	TC4203
168747	7067	P2121	1992-06-15 00:00:00.000	20	Net 30	TC7777
20	7067	P2121	1992-06-15 00:00:00.000	40	Net 30	TC3218
21	7067	P2121	1992-06-15 00:00:00.000	20	Net 30	TC4203
22	7067	P2121	1992-06-15 00:00:00.000	20	Net 30	TC7777
337470	7067	P2121	1992-06-15 00:00:00.000	40	Net 30	TC3218
337471	7067	P2121	1992-06-15 00:00:00.000	20	Net 30	TC4203
337472	7067	P2121	1992-06-15 00:00:00.000	20	Net 30	TC7777
506195	7067	P2121	1992-06-15 00:00:00.000	40	Net 30	TC3218

35

Another possible use of the OUTPUT clause is as a purge/archive solution. Suppose you want to periodically purge historic data from the sales_big table but also want to copy the purged data into an archive table called sales_big_archive. Rather than writing a process that has to select the rows to be archived before deleting them, or putting a delete trigger on the table, you could use the OUTPUT clause to insert the deleted rows into the archive table.

On approach would be to implement a loop to delete historic data (for example, delete rows for the oldest month in the sales_big table) in chunks, using the TOP clause to specify the chunk size. The OUTPUT clause can be specified to copy the deleted rows into the sales_big_archive table, as shown in Listing 35.3.

LISTING 35.3   Implementing a Purge/Archive Scenario, Using the OUTPUT Clause

```
declare @purge_date datetime,
        @rowcount int
-- find the oldest month in the sales_big table
select @purge_date = dateadd(day, - (datepart(day, min(ord_date))) + 1,
                          dateadd(month, 1, min(ord_date))),
        @rowcount = 1000
    from sales_big
while @rowcount = 1000
begin
    delete top (1000) sales_big
        output deleted.* into sales_big_archive
        where ord_date < @purge_date
    set @rowcount = @@rowcount
end
```

In addition to referencing columns in the table being modified by using the INSERTED or DELETED qualifier, you can also retrieve information from another table included in the FROM clause of a DELETE or an UPDATE statement that is used to specify the rows to update or delete:

```
begin tran
delete top (5) sales
  output t.title_id
  from sales s
  join titles t on t.title_id = s.title_id
  where t.pub_id = '9906'
rollback
go

title_id
--------
FI9620
```

```
CH2080
BI7178
CH8924
FI2680
```

When used with an UPDATE command, OUTPUT produces both a deleted and an inserted table. The deleted table contains the values before the UPDATE command, and the inserted table has the values after the UPDATE command. The OUTPUT clause is also useful for retrieving the value of identity or computed columns after an INSERT or an UPDATE operation. Listing 35.4 shows an example of OUTPUT being used to capture the computed column as the result of an UPDATE.

LISTING 35.4   Using OUTPUT to Capture a Computed Column

```
create table UpdateOutputTest
(col1 tinyint,
 col2 tinyint,
 computed_col3 as convert(float, col2/convert(float, col1)))
go

insert UpdateOutputTest (col1, col2)
  output inserted.computed_col3
  values (10, 20)
insert UpdateOutputTest (col1, col2)
  output inserted.computed_col3
  values (10, 25)
go


computed_col3
---------------------
2
computed_col3
---------------------
2.5


declare @output_table TABLE (del_col1 int, ins_col1 int,
                    del_col2 int, ins_col2 int,
                    del_computed_col3 float, ins_computed_col3 float,
                    mod_date datetime)
update UpdateOutputTest
   set col2 = col2/5.0
   output deleted.col1, inserted.col1,
        deleted.col2, inserted.col2,
        deleted.computed_col3, inserted.computed_col3,
        getdate()
     into @output_table
```

LISTING 35.4   Continued

```
   output deleted.computed_col3,
          inserted.computed_col3,
          getdate() as mod_date
select del_col1, ins_col1, del_col2, ins_col2,
       del_computed_col3 as del_col3,  ins_computed_col3 as ins_col3,
       mod_date from @output_table
go

computed_col3          computed_col3          mod_date
---------------------  ---------------------  ----------------------
2                      0.4                    2006-11-19 20:13:42.077
2.5                    0.5                    2006-11-19 20:13:42.077


del_col1 ins_col1 del_col2 ins_col2 del_col3 ins_col3 mod_date
-------- -------- -------- -------- -------- -------- ----------------------
10       10       20       4        2        0.4      2006-11-19 20:13:42.077
10       10       25       5        2.5      0.5      2006-11-19 20:13:42.077
```

The UPDATE statement in Listing 35.4 also demonstrates the ability to use OUTPUT to both insert values into a table and return values to the caller.

Note that the OUTPUT clause is not supported in DML statements that reference local partitioned views, distributed partitioned views, remote tables, or INSERT statements that contain an execute_statement. Columns returned from OUTPUT reflect the data as it is after the INSERT, UPDATE, or DELETE statement has completed but before any triggers on the target table are executed.

Common Table Expressions

A common table expression (CTE) is an ANSI SQL-99 expression that produces a table that is referred to by name within the context of a single query. The general syntax for a CTE is as follows:

```
WITH expression_name [ ( column_name [ ,...n ] ) ]
    AS ( CTE_query_definition )
```

The WITH clause, in effect, defines a table and its columns. Note that the syntax of the WITH clause is very similar to that of a view. You can think of a CTE as a temporary view that lasts only for the life of the query that defines the CTE. Listing 35.5 shows an example of a simple CTE. This CTE is used to return the average and maximum sales quantities for each store. The CTE is then joined to the sales table to return the average and maximum sales quantity for the store, along with sales records for a specific title_id.

LISTING 35.5   An Example of a Simple CTE

```
with sales_avg (stor_id, avg_qty, max_qty)
   as (select stor_id, avg(qty), max(qty)
        from sales
        group by stor_id)
select top 5 s.stor_id, s.ord_num,
           convert(varchar(10), ord_date, 101) as ord_date,
           qty, title_id, avg_qty, max_qty
    from sales s
    join sales_avg a on s.stor_id = a.stor_id
    where s.title_id = 'DR8514'
go
```

stor_id	ord_num	ord_date	qty	title_id	avg_qty	max_qty
A004	ONGGGGGGGGGGGGGGG	09/13/1993	1224	DR8514	1008	1716
A068	ONEEEEEEEEEEE	09/02/1994	1572	DR8514	961	1572
A071	ONWWWWWWWWWWWWWWWWWWW	08/20/1993	1728	DR8514	948	1728
A161	ONDDDDDDDDDDDD	05/25/1993	624	DR8514	829	1668
A203	ONGGGGGGGGGGGGGGGGGGG	11/16/1993	1572	DR8514	1056	1692

35

> **NOTE**
>
> If the WITH clause for a CTE is not the first statement in the batch, you should delimit it from the preceding statement by placing a semicolon (;) in front of it. The semicolon is used to avoid ambiguity with other uses of the WITH clause (for example, for table hints). Including a semicolon is not necessary in all cases, but it is recommended that you use it consistently to avoid problems.

It is also possible to define multiple CTEs in a single query, with each CTE delimited by a comma. Each CTE has the ability to refer to previously defined CTEs. Listing 35.6 shows an example of a nested CTE that calculates the minimum, maximum, and difference of counts of store orders.

LISTING 35.6   An Example of Multiple CTEs in a Single Query

```
WITH store_orders(stor_id, cnt)
AS ( SELECT stor_id, COUNT(*) FROM sales
    GROUP BY stor_id ),
MinMaxCTE(MN, MX, Diff)
AS ( SELECT MIN(Cnt), MAX(Cnt), MAX(Cnt)-MIN(Cnt)
     FROM store_orders )
SELECT * FROM MinMaxCTE
go
```

LISTING 35.6   Continued

```
MN          MX          Diff
----------- ----------- -----------
1           22          21
```

A CTE must be followed by a single SELECT, INSERT, UPDATE, or DELETE statement that references some or all of the CTE columns. A CTE can also be specified in a CREATE VIEW statement as part of the defining SELECT statement of the view.

Listing 35.7 shows an example of a CTE used in a DELETE statement.

LISTING 35.7   An Example of a CTE in a DELETE

```
with oldest_sales (stor_id, ord_num, ord_date)
  as (select top 1000 stor_id, ord_num, ord_date from sales_big order by ord_date)
delete sales_big from sales_big s, oldest_sales o
  where s.stor_id = o.stor_id
    and s.ord_num = o.ord_num
    and s.ord_date = o.ord_date
go
```

Most valid SELECT statement constructs are allowed in a CTE, except the following:

- ► COMPUTE or COMPUTE BY

- ► ORDER BY (except when a TOP clause is specified)

- ► INTO

- ► OPTION clause with query hints

- ► FOR XML

- ► FOR BROWSE

When a CTE is not the first statement in a batch, the statement before it must be followed by a semicolon.

Recursive Queries with CTEs

Nonrecursive CTEs are ANSI SQL-99 compliant expressions that provide T-SQL coding flexibility. However, for each nonrecursive CTE, there is usually another T-SQL construct that can be used to achieve the same results (for example, derived tables). The real power and capability of CTEs is revealed when you use CTEs to create recursive queries.

A recursive CTE can help simplify the code required to run a recursive query within a SELECT, INSERT, UPDATE, DELETE, or CREATE VIEW statement. Recursive queries are often useful for expanding a hierarchy stored in a relational table (for example, displaying employees in an organizational chart). In previous versions of SQL Server, a recursive query usually required using temporary tables, cursors, and logic to control the flow of the recursive steps.

A CTE is considered recursive when it refers to itself in the CTE definition. Recursive CTEs are constructed from at least two queries. One is a nonrecursive query, also referred to as the anchor member (AM). The other is the recursive query, also referred to as the recursive member (RM). The queries are combined using the UNION ALL operator.

The following pseudocode defines the basic structure of a recursive CTE:

```
WITH cte_name ( column_name [,...n] )
AS
( CTE_query_definition1 -- Anchor member (AM) is defined.
UNION ALL
CTE_query_definition2 -- Recursive member (RM) is referencing cte_name.
)
-- Statement using the CTE
SELECT col_list FROM cte_name
...
```

Logically, you can think of the algorithm implementing the recursive CTE as follows:

1. The anchor member is activated, and the initial result set (R) is generated.

2. The recursive member is activated, using the initial result set (Rn) as input and generating result set Rn+1.

3. The logic of step 2 is run repeatedly, incrementing the step number (n) until an empty set is returned.

4. The outer query is executed, getting the cumulative (UNION ALL) result of all of the previous steps when referring to the recursive CTE.

You can have more than two members in a recursive CTE, but only the UNION ALL operator is allowed between a recursive member and another recursive or nonrecursive member. Other operators, such as UNION, are only allowed between nonrecursive members. Recursive CTEs also require an exact match of the columns in all members, including the same data type, length, and precision.

Listing 35.8 shows a simple recursive CTE that simply generates a list of sequential numbers. Note that the AM generates the base result, and the RM following the UNION ALL controls the recursion. It is important in this example that a valid endpoint be defined to avoid infinite recursion.

LISTING 35.8   An Example of a Simple Recursive CTE

```
with numlist (val)
  as (select 1
  union all
  select val + 1
   from numlist
   where val < 10)
select * from numlist
go

val
-----------
1
2
3
4
5
6
7
8
9
10
```

The following sections present some examples and uses of recursive CTEs.

Using Recursive CTEs for Expanding a Hierarchy

For this hierarchy example, we use the PARTS table in the bigpubs2005 database. This table contains a simplified hierarchy of car parts, as shown in Figure 35.1.

In the PARTS table, any part that is a subpart of another part has the parent part ID stored in the parentpartid column. The parentpartid column is a foreign key that references the partid column. Therefore, the parentpartid must either correspond to a valid partid within the table or be NULL. For example, the car itself has NULL in the parentpartid column.

The following are some common requests that might be run on the PARTS table:

▶ Return all the parts for the engine.

▶ Show me all parts that are two levels below the drivetrain.

▶ Show me all the parts in such a way that it will be easy to see their hierarchical dependencies.

The first request is probably the most common one: returning a part (for example, the engine, which has partid = 2) and all subparts. The recursive CTE shown in Listing 35.9 provides a solution to this request.

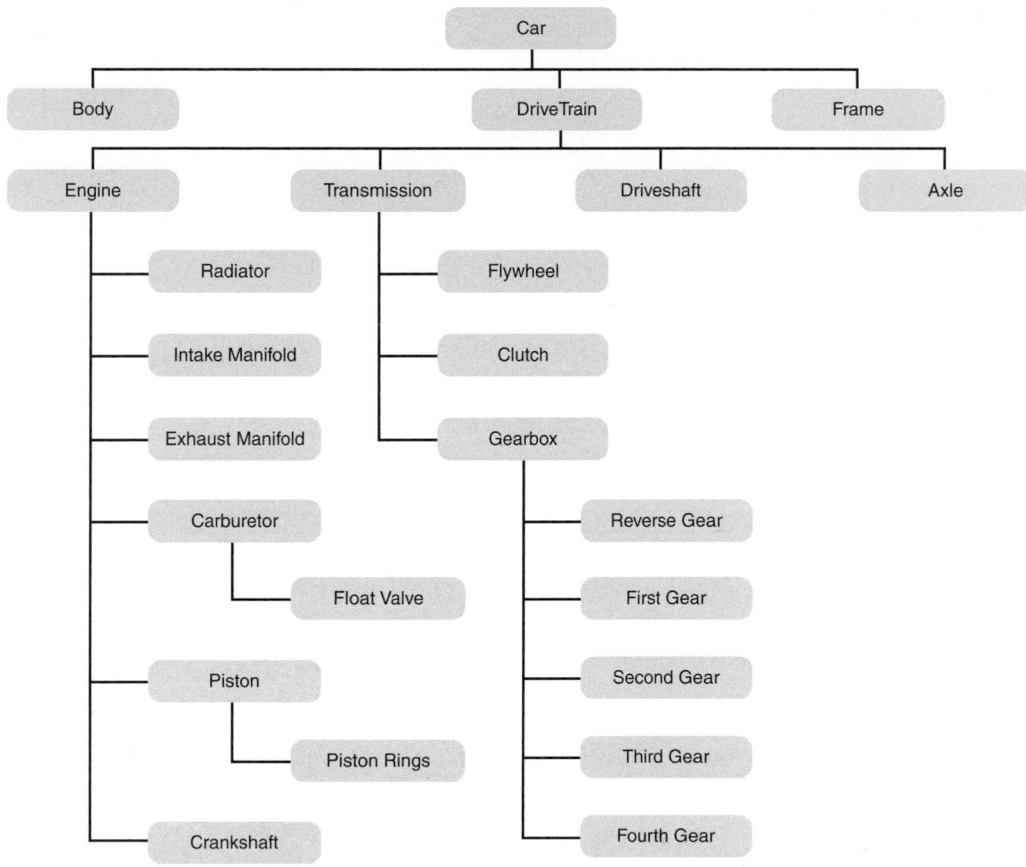

FIGURE 35.1   Parts table hierarchy.

LISTING 35.9   A Recursive CTE to Return a Part and All Subparts

```
WITH PartsCTE(partid, partname, parentpartid, lvl)
AS
(
  SELECT partid, partname, parentpartid, 0
  FROM PARTS
  WHERE partid = 2 -- Engine
  UNION ALL

  SELECT P.partid, P.partname, P.parentpartid, PP.lvl+1
  FROM Parts as P
    JOIN PartsCTE as PP
      ON P.parentpartid = PP.Partid
)
```

35

LISTING 35.9   Continued

```
SELECT PartID, Partname, ParentPartid, lvl
FROM PartsCTE
go
```

PartID	Partname	ParentPartid	lvl
2	Engine	1	0
5	Radiator	2	1
6	Intake Manifold	2	1
7	Exhaust Manifold	2	1
8	Carburetor	2	1
13	Piston	2	1
14	Crankshaft	2	1
21	Piston Rings	13	2
11	Float Valve	8	2

Notice that the lvl value is repeatedly incremented with each recursive invocation of the CTE. You can use this level counter to limit the number of iterations in the recursion. For example, Listing 35.10 is an example of a CTE that returns all parts that are two levels below the drivetrain.

LISTING 35.10   A Recursive CTE to Return All Subparts Two Levels Below a Part

```
WITH PartsCTE(partid, partname, parentpartid, lvl)
AS
(
  SELECT partid, partname, parentpartid, 0
  FROM PARTS
  WHERE partid = 1 -- Drivetrain
  UNION ALL

  SELECT P.partid, P.partname, P.parentpartid, PP.lvl+1
  FROM Parts as P
    JOIN PartsCTE as PP
      ON P.parentpartid = PP.Partid
    where lvl < 2
)
SELECT PartID, Partname, ParentPartid, lvl
FROM PartsCTE
where lvl = 2
go
```

LISTING 35.10   Continued

PartID	Partname	ParentPartid	lvl
9	Flywheel	3	2
10	Clutch	3	2
16	Gear Box	3	2
5	Radiator	2	2
6	Intake Manifold	2	2
7	Exhaust Manifold	2	2
8	Carburetor	2	2
13	Piston	2	2
14	Crankshaft	2	2

In Listing 35.10, the filter WHERE lvl < 2 in the recursive member is used as a recursion termination check; recursion stops when lvl = 2. The filter on the outer query (WHERE lvl = 2) is used to remove all parts up to the second level. Logically, the filter in the outer query (lvl = 2) is sufficient by itself to return only the desired rows, but for performance reasons, you should include the filter in the recursive member to stop the recursion as soon as two levels below the drivetrain are returned.

SQL Server allows the use of local variables in a CTE to help make the query more generic. For example, you can use variables instead of constants for the part ID and level, as shown in Listing 35.11.

LISTING 35.11   Using Local Variables in a Recursive CTE

```
DECLARE @partid AS INT, @lvl AS INT;
SET @partid = 22; -- Car
SET @lvl = 2; -- two levels
WITH PartsCTE(partid, partname, parentpartid, lvl)
AS
(
  SELECT partid, partname, parentpartid, 0
  FROM PARTS
  WHERE partid = @partid
  UNION ALL

  SELECT P.partid, P.partname, P.parentpartid, PP.lvl+1
  FROM Parts as P
    JOIN PartsCTE as PP
      ON P.parentpartid = PP.Partid
  WHERE lvl < @lvl
)
SELECT PartID, Partname, ParentPartid, lvl
FROM PartsCTE
```

35

LISTING 35.11   Continued

PartID	Partname	ParentPartid	lvl
22	Car	NULL	0
1	DriveTrain	22	1
23	Body	22	1
24	Frame	22	1
2	Engine	1	2
3	Transmission	1	2
4	Axle	1	2
12	Drive Shaft	1	2

You can also use recursive CTEs to perform aggregations, such as counting the total number of subparts that make up each parent part, as shown in Listing 35.12.

LISTING 35.12   Performing Aggregation with a Recursive CTE

```
WITH PartsCTE(parentpartid, lvl)
AS
(
  SELECT parentpartid, 0
  FROM PARTS
  WHERE parentpartid is not null
  UNION ALL
  SELECT P.parentpartid, lvl+1
  FROM Parts as P
    JOIN PartsCTE as PP
      ON PP.parentpartid = P.Partid
  WHERE P.parentpartid is not null
)
SELECT C.parentpartid, P.PartName, COUNT(*) AS cnt
FROM PartsCTE C
JOIN PArts P on C.ParentPartID = P.PartID
GROUP BY C.parentpartid, P.PArtName
go
```

parentpartid	PartName	cnt
1	DriveTrain	20
2	Engine	8
3	Transmission	8
8	Carburetor	1
13	Piston	1
16	Gear Box	5
22	Car	23

In the example in Listing 35.12, the anchor member returns a row with the `parentpartid` for each part, being sure to filter out the `NULL` value in the `parentpartid` column because it is essentially the top of the hierarchy and represents no parent part. The recursive member returns the `parentpartid` of each parent of the previously returned parts, again excluding any `NULL` values. Eventually, the CTE contains, for each part, as many occurrences as their direct or indirect number of subparts. The outer query is then left with the tasks of grouping the results by `parentpartid` and returning the count of occurrences. A join to `Parts` is included to get the corresponding `partname` for each parent part to provide more meaningful results.

Suppose you want to generate a report that is a bit more readable, with the subparts sorted and indented according to hierarchical dependencies. Listing 35.13 provides an example of a way you could accomplish this.

LISTING 35.13   Generating a Formatted Report with a Recursive CTE

```
WITH PartsCTE(partid, partname, parentpartid, lvl, sortcol)
AS
(
  SELECT partid, partname, parentpartid, 0, cast(partid as varbinary(max))
  FROM Parts
  WHERE partid = 22
  UNION ALL
  SELECT P.partid, P.partname, P.parentpartid, PP.lvl+1,
         CAST(sortcol + CAST(P.partid AS BINARY(4)) AS VARBINARY(max))
  FROM Parts AS P
    JOIN PartsCTE AS PP
      ON P.parentpartID = PP.PartID
)
SELECT
  REPLICATE('--', lvl)
    + right('>',lvl)
    + partname AS partname
FROM PArtsCTE
order by sortcol
go


partname
----------------------------------
Car
-->DriveTrain
---->Engine
------>Radiator
------>Intake Manifold
------>Exhaust Manifold
------>Carburetor
```

LISTING 35.13   Continued

```
-------->Float Valve
------>Piston
-------->Piston Rings
------>Crankshaft
---->Transmission
------>Flywheel
------>Clutch
------>Gear Box
-------->Reverse Gear
-------->First Gear
-------->Second Gear
-------->Third Gear
-------->Fourth Gear
---->Axle
---->Drive Shaft
-->Body
-->Frame
```

In this example, you use a `varbinary` string as the `sortcol` in order to sort subparts according to the `partid` value. The anchor member is the starting point, generating a binary value for the `partid` of the root part. In each iteration, the recursive member appends the current part ID, converted to a binary value, to the parent part ID's `sortcol`. The outer query then sorts the result by `sortcol`, which groups the subparts under each immediate parent part.

Setting the MAXRECURSION Option

To help avoid infinite recursion in CTEs, SQL Server by default sets a `MAXRECURSION` value of `100`. If a recursive CTE attempts to perform more than 100 recursions, it is aborted, with the following error message:

```
Msg 530, Level 16, State 1, Line 1
The statement terminated. The maximum recursion 100 has been exhausted before
 statement completion.
```

You can override the default `MAXRECURSION` setting by using the `OPTION(MAXRECURSION value)` query hint to force termination of the query after a specific number of recursive iterations have been invoked. Listing 35.14 shows an example.

LISTING 35.14   Controlling the Number of Recursions with MAXRECURSION

```
WITH PartsCTE(partid, partname, parentpartid, lvl)
AS
(
  SELECT partid, partname, parentpartid, 0
  FROM PARTS
```

LISTING 35.14   Continued

```
  WHERE partid = 22 -- Car
  UNION ALL

  SELECT P.partid, P.partname, P.parentpartid, PP.lvl+1
  FROM Parts as P
    JOIN PartsCTE as PP
      ON P.partid = PP.Partid
)
SELECT PartID, Partname, ParentPartid, lvl
FROM PartsCTE
OPTION (MAXRECURSION 10)
go

Msg 530, Level 16, State 1, Line 2
The statement terminated. The maximum recursion 10 has been exhausted before
 statement completion.
```

Keep in mind that if you use MAXRECURSION to control the number of levels of recursion in a CTE, your application receives the error message. It is not considered good programming practice to use code that returns errors in valid situations. Certain applications may discard query results if an error message is received. Instead, it is recommended that you use the level counter to limit recursion, as shown earlier in this chapter, in Listing 35.10. You should use the MAXRECURSION hint as a safeguard against infinite loops due to bad data or as a coding safeguard.

Ranking Functions

SQL Server 2005 introduces four new ranking functions: ROW_NUMBER, RANK, DENSE_RANK, and NTILE. These new functions allow you to analyze data and provide ranking values to result rows of a query. For example, you might use the new ranking functions for assigning sequential integer row IDs to result rows or for presentation, paging, or scoring purposes.

All four ranking functions follow a similar syntax pattern:

```
function_name() OVER(
  [PARTITION BY partition_by_list]
  ORDER BY order_by_list)
```

The ROW_NUMBER Function

The ROW_NUMBER function allows you to provide sequential integer values to the result rows of a query, based on the order of the rows in the result. The result set must be ordered using an OVER clause, with an ORDER BY clause as a variable.

The ROW_NUMBER function has been a feature long-desired by SQL Server developers. For example, suppose you wanted to return the publishers and the total number of titles per publisher and list the result rows, in descending order, with a numeric score assigned to each row. The query shown in Listing 35.15 generates the desired results by using the ROW_NUMBER function, specifying ordering over the num_titles column, in descending order.

LISTING 35.15   Using ROW_NUMBER to Rank Publishers by Number of Titles

```
select top 10 WITH TIES p.pub_id, pub_name, count(*) as num_titles,
ROW_NUMBER () OVER (order by count(*) DESC) as Rank
from publishers p join titles t on p.pub_id = t.pub_id
group by p.pub_id, p.pub_name
order by count(*) desc
go
```

pub_id	pub_name	num_titles	Rank
9911	Jones Jones and Johnson	44	1
9904	Strawberry Publications	34	2
9907	Incandescent Imprints	33	3
9905	Gooseberry Titles	32	4
9909	North American Press	30	5
9912	Landlocked Books	30	6
9913	Blackberry's	28	7
9914	Normanskill Printing Company	28	8
9910	Sidney's Books and More	28	9
9906	Tomato Books	28	10
9903	Kumquat Technical Publishing	28	11

In this example, the publishers with the highest number of titles got row number 1, and the publisher with the tenth-highest number of titles got row number 10. The ROW_NUMBER function always generates a distinct row number for each row, according to the requested sort.

If the ORDER BY list specified within the OVER() option is not on a unique key, the ordering of the row numbers is nondeterministic. For publishers that may have the same number of titles, each row would be assigned a different unique row number. The sequence of the row numbers assigned to those publishers could be different in different invocations of the query. In the results for Listing 35.15, for example, five different publishers have the same number of titles (28). Because SQL Server has to assign different row numbers to the different publishers, you should assume that the row numbers were assigned in arbitrary order among those publishers.

To ensure that the result is always deterministic, specify a unique ORDER BY list. For example, adding pub_id to the ORDER BY list ensures that in the case of a tie between publishers, the lowest pub_id is always assigned the lower row number, as shown in Listing 35.16.

LISTING 35.16   Using a Unique ORDER BY List for Deterministic ROW_NUMBER Results

```
select top 10 WITH TIES p.pub_id, pub_name, count(*) as num_titles,
ROW_NUMBER () OVER (order by count(*) DESC, p.pub_id) as Rank
from publishers p join titles t on p.pub_id = t.pub_id
group by p.pub_id, p.pub_name
order by count(*) desc
go
```

pub_id	pub_name	num_titles	Rank
9911	Jones Jones and Johnson	44	1
9904	Strawberry Publications	34	2
9907	Incandescent Imprints	33	3
9905	Gooseberry Titles	32	4
9909	North American Press	30	5
9912	Landlocked Books	30	6
9903	Kumquat Technical Publishing	28	7
9906	Tomato Books	28	8
9910	Sidney's Books and More	28	9
9913	Blackberry's	28	10
9914	Normanskill Printing Company	28	11

In the previous two examples, the sequence of row numbers is generated across the entire result set as one group. You can also have ranking values calculated within groups of rows independently as opposed to being calculated for all table rows as one group by using the PARTITION BY clause.

Partitioning by ROW_NUMBER()

PARTITION BY allows you to specify a list of expressions that identify the groups of rows for which ranking values should be calculated independently. For example, the query in Listing 35.17 assigns row numbers within each type of book separately, in num_titles and pub_id order.

LISTING 35.17   Using PARTITION BY to Rank Rows Within Groups

```
select top 20 WITH TIES p.pub_id, pub_name, type, count(*) as num_titles,
ROW_NUMBER () OVER (partition by type order by count(*) DESC, p.pub_id) as Rank
from publishers p join titles t on p.pub_id = t.pub_id
group by p.pub_id, p.pub_name, type
order by type, count(*) desc
go
```

35

LISTING 35.17   Continued

pub_id	pub_name	type	num_titles	Rank
9906	Tomato Books	biography	4	1
9911	Jones Jones and Johnson	biography	4	2
9905	Gooseberry Titles	biography	2	3
9900	Boysenberry Books	biography	1	4
9903	Kumquat Technical Publishing	biography	1	5
9904	Strawberry Publications	biography	1	6
9909	North American Press	biography	1	7
9913	Blackberry's	biography	1	8
9914	Normanskill Printing Company	biography	1	9
9916	Nordome Titles	biography	1	10
9918	Significant Titles Company	biography	1	11
1389	Algodata Infosystems	business	3	1
0736	New Moon Books	business	1	2
9911	Jones Jones and Johnson	children	21	1
9914	Normanskill Printing Company	children	13	2
9905	Gooseberry Titles	children	12	3
9901	GGG&G	children	11	4
9903	Kumquat Technical Publishing	children	11	5
9915	Beanplant General	children	9	6
9900	Boysenberry Books	children	8	7
9913	Blackberry's	children	8	8

The RANK and DENSE_RANK Functions

The RANK and DENSE_RANK functions are similar to the ROW_NUMBER function in the sense that they also provide ranking values according to a specified sort. The difference is that rather than assign a unique ranking value to each row, RANK and DENSE_RANK assign the same ranking value to rows with the same values in the specified sort columns when the ORDER BY list is not unique.

The difference between RANK and DENSE_RANK is that with the DENSE_RANK function, there are no gaps in the ranking. The RANK function skips the next number if there is a tie in the ranking value. Listing 35.18 modifies the query shown in Listing 35.15 by replacing the ROW_NUMBER function with RANK and DENSE_RANK and provides a good example of the differences between the two.

LISTING 35.18   Using RANK and DENSE_RANK

```
select top 10 WITH TIES p.pub_id, pub_name, count(*) as num_titles,
RANK() OVER (order by count(*) DESC) as Rank,
DENSE_RANK() OVER (order by count(*) DESC) as Dense_Rank
from publishers p join titles t on p.pub_id = t.pub_id
```

LISTING 35.18   Continued

```
group by p.pub_id, p.pub_name
order by count(*) desc
go
```

pub_id	pub_name	num_titles	Rank	Dense_Rank
9911	Jones Jones and Johnson	44	1	1
9904	Strawberry Publications	34	2	2
9907	Incandescent Imprints	33	3	3
9905	Gooseberry Titles	32	4	4
9909	North American Press	30	5	5
9912	Landlocked Books	30	5	5
9913	Blackberry's	28	7	6
9914	Normanskill Printing Company	28	7	6
9910	Sidney's Books and More	28	7	6
9906	Tomato Books	28	7	6
9903	Kumquat Technical Publishing	28	7	6

Notice that in this result set, all publishers with the same number of titles get the same RANK and DENSE_RANK values.

NOTE

If the ORDER BY list for a ranking function is unique, ROW_NUMBER, RANK, and DENSE_RANK produce exactly the same values.

The NTILE Function

The NTILE function assigns a ranking value by separating the result rows of a query into a specified number of approximately even-sized groups. Each group of rows is assigned the same ranking number, starting with 1 for the first group, 2 for the second, and so on. You specify the number of groups you want the result set divided into as the argument to the NTILE function. The number of rows in a group is determined by dividing the total number of rows in the result set by the number of groups. If there's a remainder, n, the first n groups have an additional row assigned to them. Listing 35.19 provides an example of using the NTILE function, so you can compare it to the ROW_NUMBER function.

LISTING 35.19   Using the NTILE Function

```
select p.pub_id, pub_name, count(*) as num_titles,
NTILE(3) OVER (order by count(*) DESC) as NTILE,
ROW_NUMBER() OVER (order by count(*) DESC) as RowNum
from publishers p join titles t on p.pub_id = t.pub_id
```

LISTING 35.19   Continued

```
group by p.pub_id, p.pub_name
order by count(*) desc
go
```

pub_id	pub_name	num_titles	NTILE	RowNum
9911	Jones Jones and Johnson	44	1	1
9904	Strawberry Publications	34	1	2
9907	Incandescent Imprints	33	1	3
9905	Gooseberry Titles	32	1	4
9909	North American Press	30	1	5
9912	Landlocked Books	30	2	6
9913	Blackberry's	28	2	7
9914	Normanskill Printing Company	28	2	8
9910	Sidney's Books and More	28	2	9
9906	Tomato Books	28	2	10
9903	Kumquat Technical Publishing	28	3	11
9902	Lemon Legal Publishing	27	3	12
9901	GGG&G	25	3	13
9908	Springfield Publishing	25	3	14
9900	Boysenberry Books	23	4	15
9916	Nordome Titles	22	4	16
9915	Beanplant General	21	4	17
9917	BFG Books	17	4	18
9918	Significant Titles Company	17	5	19
0877	Binnet & Hardley	6	5	20
1389	Algodata Infosystems	6	5	21
0736	New Moon Books	5	5	22

In this example, NTILE is used to divide the result set into five groups. Because there are 22 rows in the publishers table, there are 4 rows in each group, with 2 left over. The 2 extra rows are added to the first two groups.

The NTILE function provides a way to generate a histogram with an even distribution of items for each step. In the previous example, the first step represents the publishers with the highest number of titles, and the last step represents the publishers with the lowest number of titles. You can use this information in a CASE expression to provide descriptive meaningful alternatives to the ranking numbers, as shown in Listing 35.20.

LISTING 35.20   Using a CASE Expression to Provide Meaningful Labels to Ranking Values

```
select p.pub_id, pub_name, count(*) as num_titles,
    case NTILE(5) OVER (order by count(*) DESC)
        when 1 then 'Highest'
        when 2 then 'Above Average'
        when 3 then 'Average'
        when 4 then 'Below Average'
        when 5 then 'Lowest'
        end as Ranking
from publishers p join titles t on p.pub_id = t.pub_id
group by p.pub_id, p.pub_name
order by pub_id
go
```

pub_id	pub_name	num_titles	Ranking
0736	New Moon Books	5	Lowest
0877	Binnet & Hardley	6	Lowest
1389	Algodata Infosystems	6	Lowest
9900	Boysenberry Books	23	Below Average
9901	GGG&G	25	Average
9902	Lemon Legal Publishing	27	Average
9903	Kumquat Technical Publishing	28	Average
9904	Strawberry Publications	34	Highest
9905	Gooseberry Titles	32	Highest
9906	Tomato Books	28	Above Average
9907	Incandescent Imprints	33	Highest
9908	Springfield Publishing	25	Average
9909	North American Press	30	Highest
9910	Sidney's Books and More	28	Above Average
9911	Jones Jones and Johnson	44	Highest
9912	Landlocked Books	30	Above Average
9913	Blackberry's	28	Above Average
9914	Normanskill Printing Company	28	Above Average
9915	Beanplant General	21	Below Average
9916	Nordome Titles	22	Below Average
9917	BFG Books	17	Below Average
9918	Significant Titles Company	17	Lowest

35

Using Row Numbers for Paging Results

Typical uses for row numbers are for paging through the results of a query and for selecting a specific subset of rows from within the result set. Essentially, given a page size in terms of number of rows, and a page number, you can return the rows that belong to that given page.

For example, suppose you want to return the second page of rows from a query similar to the one shown in Listing 35.16. Assuming a page size of five rows, the query shown in Listing 35.21 uses a CTE to first calculate the row numbers according to the ranking by number of titles, and then only those rows with numbers 6 through 10, which belong to the second page, are returned.

LISTING 35.21   Using `ROW_NUMBER` to Page Through Results

```
with pub_titles as
(
select p.pub_id, pub_name, count(*) as num_titles,
ROW_NUMBER () OVER (order by count(*) DESC, p.pub_id) as Rank
from publishers p join titles t on p.pub_id = t.pub_id
group by p.pub_id, p.pub_name
)
select * from pub_titles
where Rank between 6 and 10
go
```

```
pub_id pub_name                                          num_titles  Rank
------ -------------------------------------------       ----------- --------------------
9912   Landlocked Books                                  30          6
9903   Kumquat Technical Publishing                      28          7
9906   Tomato Books                                      28          8
9910   Sidney's Books and More                           28          9
9913   Blackberry's                                      28          10
```

You could make this query more generic by using local variables for the page number and page size and using them to calculate the proper set of rows to return, as shown in Listing 35.22.

LISTING 35.22   Using Local Variables for Determining Page Size When Paging Through Results

```
declare @pagesize tinyint,
        @pagenum tinyint;
set @pagesize = 6;
set @pagenum = 2;

with pub_titles as
(
select p.pub_id, pub_name, count(*) as num_titles,
ROW_NUMBER () OVER (order by count(*) DESC, p.pub_id) as Rank
from publishers p join titles t on p.pub_id = t.pub_id
group by p.pub_id, p.pub_name
)
```

LISTING 35.22   Continued

```
select * from pub_titles
where Rank between ((@pagenum - 1) * @pagesize) + 1
            and @pagenum * @pagesize
go
```

pub_id	pub_name	num_titles	Rank
9903	Kumquat Technical Publishing	28	7
9906	Tomato Books	28	8
9910	Sidney's Books and More	28	9
9913	Blackberry's	28	10
9914	Normanskill Printing Company	28	11
9902	Lemon Legal Publishing	27	12

The example in Listing 35.22 is adequate for ad hoc requests when you're only interested in retrieving one specific page of the result set. However, this approach is not adequate for most applications that would issue multiple requests for individual pages of data because each invocation of the query would require a complete scan of the table in order to calculate the row numbers. A more efficient method for when the user might repeatedly request different pages would be to first populate a temporary table with all the base table rows, including the calculated row numbers, and then create a clustered index on the column in the temp table that contains the row numbers. An example is presented in Listing 35.23.

LISTING 35.23   Using a Temp Table for Paging Through Results

```
select p.pub_id, pub_name, count(*) as num_titles,
       ROW_NUMBER () OVER (order by count(*) DESC, p.pub_id) as Rank
   into #paging_table
   from publishers p join titles t on p.pub_id = t.pub_id
   group by p.pub_id, p.pub_name
go
create unique clustered index idx1 on #paging_table(Rank)
go
declare @pagesize tinyint,
        @pagenum tinyint;
set @pagesize = 6;
set @pagenum = 2;
SELECT *
FROM #paging_table
WHERE Rank BETWEEN (@pagenum-1)*@pagesize+1 AND @pagenum*@pagesize
ORDER BY Rank
set @pagesize = 6;
set @pagenum = 4;
```

LISTING 35.23   Continued

```
SELECT *
FROM #paging_table
WHERE Rank BETWEEN (@pagenum-1)*@pagesize+1 AND @pagenum*@pagesize
ORDER BY Rank
go
```

pub_id	pub_name	num_titles	Rank
9903	Kumquat Technical Publishing	28	7
9906	Tomato Books	28	8
9910	Sidney's Books and More	28	9
9913	Blackberry's	28	10
9914	Normanskill Printing Company	28	11
9902	Lemon Legal Publishing	27	12

pub_id	pub_name	num_titles	Rank
9918	Significant Titles Company	17	19
0877	Binnet & Hardley	6	20
1389	Algodata Infosystems	6	21
0736	New Moon Books	5	22

If you are limiting the result set to a specific number of rows and are using a fixed page size, an alternative to using ROW_NUMBER would be to use the NTILE function to calculate the actual page numbers. For example, if you are using TOP to limit the result set to the first 500 rows and each page contains 10 rows, the total number of pages would be 500 / 10, or 50 pages. If you use 50 as the argument to the NTILE function, the query generates 50 distinct ranking values with 10 rows each. An example of this solution is presented in Listing 35.24.

LISTING 35.24   Using NTILE to Generate Page Numbers

```
select TOP 500 t.title_id,
       left(title, 20) as title,
       sum(qty) as total_sales,
       NTILE(50) OVER(ORDER BY sum(qty) desc) AS pagenum
   into #title_list
   from titles t join sales s on t.title_id = s.title_id
   group by t.title_id, title
go
create clustered index page_index on #title_list(pagenum)
go
select * from #title_list
where pagenum = 11
```

LISTING 35.24   Continued

```
go
```

title_id	title	total_sales	pagenum
FI1704	Journey	295872	11
FI2784	Rhoda: A Life in Sto	295836	11
FI4524	The Unconsoled	295584	11
FI4554	The Spy Who Came in	295500	11
FI0897	Polar Star	295308	11
CH0126	Little Bear	295296	11
FI5040	The Tombs of Atuan	295284	11
PS1372	Computer Phobic AND	295172	11
FI7820	Tinker, Tailor, Sold	295092	11
FI2816	Zuckerman Unbound	294960	11
CH0623	The Black Cauldron	294960	11

PIVOT **and** UNPIVOT

SQL Server 2005 adds the PIVOT clause to T-SQL. A typical analytical use of the PIVOT command is to convert temporal data into categorized data in order to make the data easier to view and analyze.

The first, and simplest, option for returning the temporal data is to query the data, grouping the fact information in such a way that it answers the questions being asked. For example, Listing 35.25 retrieves data from the titles tables and provides the total number of business books sold, by year. Note that it's difficult to see trends of the number of titles sold between years. It is also even more difficult to answer questions about how sales of one title compared to sales of other titles in the same year.

LISTING 35.25   A Standard Query to Return Total Sales of Titles, by Year

```
select t.title_id,
       datepart(year, ord_date) as year,
       sum(qty) as total_sales
from sales s join titles t on s.title_id = t.title_id
where t.type = 'business'
group by t.title_id, datepart(year, ord_date)
go
```

title_id	year	total_sales
BU7832	1993	102975
BU1111	1993	104149
BU1032	1994	97131

LISTING 35.25   Continued

BU1032	1995	59772
BU2075	1993	108995
BU1111	1995	72336
BU1032	1993	95556
BU2075	1994	117888
BU7832	1994	104616
BU2075	1995	84588
BU1111	1994	88116
BU7832	1995	78240

You could visualize and answer these questions more easily if you could pivot the YEAR column to create columns of TOTAL_SALES for each year. The resulting table is generally referred to as a *crosstab*. The PIVOT clause provides this capability.

The syntax of the PIVOT expression is as follows:

```
pivoted_table ::=
      table_source PIVOT ( aggregate_function ( value_column )
         FOR pivot_column
         IN ( column_list ) table_alias
```

To use the PIVOT feature, you first decide which column contains the important values for the query. In this example, the important piece of information is the total_sales amount. Next, you determine which field data becomes the columns you will pivot the data into. In this example, because you want to analyze sales over a period of time, you want to pivot the sales year field data into columns in the final result.

You start out by defining a CTE that returns the detail data on which you want to aggregate. This CTE might look like the following SQL code fragment:

```
with title_sales as
(select t.title_id,
       datepart(year, ord_date) as year,
       qty
from sales s join titles t on s.title_id = t.title_id
where t.type = 'business')
```

Drawing from the title_sales CTE, the value column is the qty column. Because you want to sum the qty values, you need to use the SUM() aggregate function in the PIVOT expression. The pivot column is YEAR. You need to define a list of YEAR columns that you want to see. For this example, the columns are 1993, 1994, and 1995. You specify these values as column headings in the select list in the SQL expression and also as the column list in the PIVOT expression. Putting all the pieces together, you end up with the SQL statement shown in Listing 35.26.

LISTING 35.26   Using PIVOT to Return Total Sales by Year

```
with title_sales as
(select t.title_id,
        datepart(year, ord_date) as year,
        qty as total_sales
from sales s join titles t on s.title_id = t.title_id
where t.type = 'business')
select ts_pivot.title_id,
        isnull([1993], 0) as [1993],
        isnull([1994], 0) as [1994],
        isnull([1995], 0) as [1995]
from title_sales
pivot (sum(total_sales) for year in ([1993], [1994], [1995])
) as ts_pivot
go
```

title_id	1993	1994	1995
BU1032	95556	97131	59772
BU1111	104149	88116	72336
BU2075	108995	117888	84588
BU7832	102975	104616	78240

Note that in this example, the SUM aggregate function is a required component of the PIVOT expression. If you think about it, the CTE could easily have been coded to perform the sum of the qty values, grouping them by year and simply have the PIVOT expression pivot using only the total_sales, without the need for the SUM function. Unfortunately, the PIVOT expression requires having an aggregate function included, so it must be coded this way.

Also note that the data specified in the IN column list for the PIVOT expression must explicitly include the names of all the values that will be pivoted into columns. Currently, the syntax does not allow for this column list to be dynamic.

The UNPIVOT expression is used to take data that is already in the form of a crosstab and rotate the data columns into data rows. You are likely to use UNPIVOT much less often than PIVOT.

For example, you can create a temporary table from the results of the PIVOT query in Listing 35.26:

```
with title_sales as
(select t.title_id,
        datepart(year, ord_date) as year,
        qty
from sales s join titles t on s.title_id = t.title_id
where t.type = 'business')
```

```
select ts_pivot.title_id,
       isnull([1993], 0) as [1993],
       isnull([1994], 0) as [1994],
       isnull([1995], 0) as [1995]
into #title_sales_by_year
from title_sales
pivot (sum(qty) for year in ([1993], [1994], [1995])
) as ts_pivot
go
select title_id, [1993], [1994], [1995]
    from #title_sales_by_year
go


title_id 1993          1994          1995
-------- ------------  ------------  -----------
BU1032   95556         97131         59772
BU1111   104149        88116         72336
BU2075   108995        117888        84588
BU7832   102975        104616        78240
```

To unpivot the #title_sales_by_year table, you start with the common table expression that returns the rows and columns that you want to unpivot:

```
with title_sales as
(select title_id, [1993], [1994], [1995]
    from #title_sales_by_year)
```

Drawing from the title_sales CTE, the year columns become a single column called year, and you rotate the current total_sales columns into a single column. This time around, the year column is the unpivot column. For this example, the columns you want to unpivot are 1993, 1994, and 1995. You specify these values as the column list in the UNPIVOT expression and rename it as a single column called total_sales. Putting all the pieces together, you end up with the SQL statement shown in Listing 35.27.

LISTING 35.27   Using UNPIVOT to Rotate Pivoted Data

```
with title_sales as
(select title_id, [1993], [1994], [1995]
    from #title_sales_by_year)
select title_id,
       cast(ts_unpivot.year as smallint) as year,
       ts_unpivot.total_sales
   from title_sales
   UNPIVOT (total_sales for year in ([1993], [1994], [1995])
          ) as ts_unpivot
```

LISTING 35.27   Continued

```
go

title_id year   total_sales
-------- ------  -----------
BU1032   1993    95556
BU1032   1994    97131
BU1032   1995    59772
BU1111   1993    104149
BU1111   1994    88116
BU1111   1995    72336
BU2075   1993    108995
BU2075   1994    117888
BU2075   1995    84588
BU7832   1993    102975
BU7832   1994    104616
BU7832   1995    78240
```

35

NOTE

Note that UNPIVOT is not the exact reverse of PIVOT. PIVOT performs an aggregation and, therefore, merges possible multiple rows into a single row in the output. UNPIVOT does not reproduce the original detail rows from the summary values.

The APPLY Operator

The APPLY relational operator allows you to invoke a table-valued function once per each row of an outer table expression. You specify APPLY in the FROM clause of a query, similarly to the way you use the JOIN operator. APPLY can take two forms: CROSS APPLY and OUTER APPLY.

CROSS APPLY

CROSS APPLY invokes a table-valued function for each row in an outer table expression, returning a unified result set out of all the results returned by the individual invocations of the table-valued function. The columns in the outer table are used as arguments to the table-valued function. If the table-valued function returns an empty set for a given outer row, that outer row is not returned in the result.

For example, the table-valued function in Listing 35.28 accepts stor_id and an integer as arguments and returns a list of the top *N* largest orders for that store. The number of rows returned is determined by the value passed to the second parameter. If you call this function with stor_id and a number of rows, it returns that many rows, ordered by the qty of the order, in descending order.

LISTING 35.28   A Table-Valued Function That Returns the Top *N* Orders for stor_id

```
CREATE FUNCTION dbo.fn_GetTopOrders(@stor_id AS char(4), @n AS INT)
  RETURNS TABLE
AS
RETURN
  SELECT TOP(@n) *
  FROM dbo.sales
  WHERE stor_id = @stor_id
  ORDER BY qty DESC
GO
```

The following is a sample invocation of the function in Listing 35.28:

```
select * from dbo.fn_GetTopOrders ('B251', 3)
go
```

stor_id	ord_num	ord_date	qty	payterms	title_id
B251	ONQQQQQQQQQQQQQQQQ	1995-01-23 00:00:00.000	1740	Net 60	CH6808
B251	ONKKKKKKKKKKKKKKKK	1994-11-04 00:00:00.000	1704	Net 60	FI9420
B251	ONTTTTTTTTTTTTTTTT	1995-02-22 00:00:00.000	1560	Net 60	FI8000

If you wanted to generate a result set that shows each store name and the top three largest orders for each store, you can use the CROSS APPLY function to join to the dbo.fn_GetTopOrders function for each stor_id in the outer query, as shown in Listing 35.29.

LISTING 35.29   Using CROSS APPLY

```
select st.stor_id, stor_name, s.ord_date, s.qty
from stores st
cross apply
dbo.fn_GetTopOrders (st.stor_id, 3) as s
where st.state = 'MI'
and st.stor_name in ('Barnes & Noble', 'B Dalton BookSeller', 'Waldenbooks')
order by stor_id, s.qty DESC
go
```

stor_id	stor_name	ord_date	qty
B251	B Dalton Bookseller	1995-01-23 00:00:00.000	1740
B251	B Dalton Bookseller	1994-11-04 00:00:00.000	1704
B251	B Dalton Bookseller	1995-02-22 00:00:00.000	1560
B510	Barnes & Noble	1995-08-13 00:00:00.000	1464
B510	Barnes & Noble	1994-10-08 00:00:00.000	1200

LISTING 35.29   Continued

B510	Barnes & Noble	1993-01-08 00:00:00.000 924
P963	Waldenbooks	1995-07-07 00:00:00.000 1668
P963	Waldenbooks	1993-12-30 00:00:00.000 1068
P963	Waldenbooks	1993-03-29 00:00:00.000 1032
Q017	Waldenbooks	1994-11-02 00:00:00.000 1776
Q017	Waldenbooks	1993-06-15 00:00:00.000 1704
Q017	Waldenbooks	1994-02-24 00:00:00.000 1548

CROSS APPLY only returns rows from the outer table that produce a result set from the table-valued function. If a store has no orders, it does not appear in the result set. To include all rows from the outer table, use OUTER APPLY.

OUTER APPLY

OUTER APPLY returns from the outer table both rows that produce a result set and rows that do not. Rows that do not produce a result set from the table-valued function return NULL values in the columns produced by the table-valued function.

The following example is similar to the query in Listing 35.29 but replaces CROSS APPLY with the OUTER APPLY clause:

```
select st.stor_id, stor_name, s.ord_date, s.qty
from stores st
outer apply
dbo.fn_GetTopOrders (st.stor_id, 3) as s
where st.state = 'MI'
and st.stor_name in ('Barnes & Noble', 'B Dalton BookSeller', 'Waldenbooks')
order by stor_id, s.qty DESC
go
```

stor_id	stor_name	ord_date	qty
B251	B Dalton Bookseller	1995-01-23 00:00:00.000	1740
B251	B Dalton Bookseller	1994-11-04 00:00:00.000	1704
B251	B Dalton Bookseller	1995-02-22 00:00:00.000	1560
B510	Barnes & Noble	1995-08-13 00:00:00.000	1464
B510	Barnes & Noble	1994-10-08 00:00:00.000	1200
B510	Barnes & Noble	1993-01-08 00:00:00.000	924
B511	Barnes & Noble	NULL	NULL
P963	Waldenbooks	1995-07-07 00:00:00.000	1668
P963	Waldenbooks	1993-12-30 00:00:00.000	1068
P963	Waldenbooks	1993-03-29 00:00:00.000	1032
Q017	Waldenbooks	1994-11-02 00:00:00.000	1776
Q017	Waldenbooks	1993-06-15 00:00:00.000	1704
Q017	Waldenbooks	1994-02-24 00:00:00.000	1548

35

TRY...CATCH **Logic for Error Handling**

SQL Server 2005 introduces the TRY...CATCH construct, which you can use within T-SQL code to provide a more graceful mechanism for exception handling than was available in previous versions of SQL Server. In previous versions, error handling was typically done by checking @@ERROR after each SQL statement and often using the GOTO statement to branch to an error-handling routine.

A TRY...CATCH construct consists of two parts: a TRY block and a CATCH block. When an error condition is detected in a T-SQL statement that is inside a TRY block, control is immediately passed to the CATCH block, where the error is processed. T-SQL statements in the TRY block that follow the statement that generated the error are not executed.

If an error occurs and processing is passed to the CATCH block, after the statements in the CATCH block are executed, control is transferred to the first T-SQL statement that follows the END CATCH statement. If there are no errors inside the TRY block, control is passed to the statement immediately after the associated END CATCH statement, essentially skipping over the statements in the CATCH block.

A TRY block is initiated with the BEGIN TRY statement and ended with the END TRY statement and can consist of one or more Transact-SQL statements between the BEGIN TRY and END TRY statements. The TRY block must be followed immediately by a CATCH block. A CATCH block is indicated with the BEGIN CATCH statement and ended with the END CATCH statement and can consist of one or more SQL statements. In SQL Server, each TRY block can be associated with only one CATCH block.

The syntax of the TRY...CATCH construct is as follows:

```
BEGIN TRY
    one_or_more_sql_statements
END TRY
BEGIN CATCH
    one_or_more_sql_statements
END CATCH
```

In a CATCH block, you can use the following error functions to capture information about the error that invoked the CATCH block:

- ► **ERROR_NUMBER()**—Returns the error number.

- ► **ERROR_MESSAGE()**—Returns the complete text of the error message.

- ► **ERROR_SEVERITY()**—Returns the error severity.

- ► **ERROR_STATE()**—Returns the error state number.

- ► **ERROR_LINE()**—Returns the line number inside the procedure that caused the error.

- ► **ERROR_PROCEDURE()**—Returns the name of the stored procedure or trigger where the error occurred.

Unlike @@ERROR, which is reset by each statement that is executed, the error information retrieved by the error functions remains constant anywhere within the scope of the CATCH block of a TRY...CATCH construct. Error functions can also be referenced from within a stored procedure that is invoked within a CATCH block. This allows you to modularize the error handling into a single stored procedure so you do not have to repeat the error-handling code in every CATCH block. Listing 35.30 shows an example of an error-handling procedure that you can use in your CATCH blocks.

LISTING 35.30   An Example of a Standard Error Handler Procedure

```
use bigpubs2005
go
create proc dbo.error_handler
as
begin
    Declare @errnum int,
            @severity int,
            @errstate int,
            @proc nvarchar(126),
            @line int,
            @message nvarchar(4000)
    -- capture the error information that caused the CATCH block to be invoked
    SELECT @errnum = ERROR_NUMBER(),
           @severity = ERROR_SEVERITY(),
           @errstate = ERROR_STATE(),
           @proc = ERROR_PROCEDURE(),
           @line = ERROR_LINE(),
           @message = ERROR_MESSAGE()
    -- raise an error message with information on the error
    RAISERROR ('Failed to add new publisher for the following reason:
 Error: %d, Severity: %d, State: %d, in proc %s at line %d, Message: "%s"',
               16, 1, @errnum, @severity, @errstate, @proc, @line, @message)
    Return
end
```

Listing 35.31 provides an example of the use of the TRY...CATCH construct in a T-SQL batch. Note that this CATCH block uses the dbo.error_handler procedure defined in Listing 35.30.

LISTING 35.31   Using a TRY...CATCH Construct for Error Handling in a T-SQL Batch

```
use bigpubs2005
go
BEGIN TRY
    INSERT INTO bigpubs2005.dbo.publishers
            (pub_id, pub_name, city, state, country)
```

LISTING 35.31   Continued

```
        VALUES('9950', 'Sams Publishing', 'Indianapolis', 'IN', 'USA')
    -- if no error occurs, we should see this print statement
    print 'New Publisher added'
END TRY
BEGIN CATCH
    -- invoke the error_handler procedure
    exec error_handler
    -- return a non-zero status code
END CATCH
-- if successful execution, return 0
go
Msg 50000, Level 16, State 1, Procedure error_handler, Line 18
Failed to add new publisher for the following reason:
 Error: 2627, Severity: 14, State: 1, in proc (null) at line 2,
 Message: "Violation of PRIMARY KEY constraint 'UPKCL_pubind'.
 Cannot insert duplicate key in object 'dbo.publishers'."
```

If you want to capture and handle any errors that may occur within a CATCH block, you can incorporate another TRY...CATCH block within the CATCH block.

> **NOTES**
>
> Note that some errors with severity 20 or higher that would cause SQL Server to close the user connection cannot be handled by the TRY...CATCH construct. However, severity level 20 or higher errors that do not result in the connection being closed can be captured and handled by the CATCH block. Any errors with a severity level of 10 or less are considered only warnings or informational messages and not really errors, and thus they are not handled by the TRY...CATCH construct. Also, any compile errors (such as syntax errors) or object name resolution errors that happen during deferred name resolution also do not invoke a CATCH block. These errors are returned to the application or batch that called the error-generating routine.

The TABLESAMPLE Clause

SQL Server 2005 introduces the TABLESAMPLE clause, which lets you query a random sample of data from a table (either an exact number of rows or a percentage of rows). You can use TABLESAMPLE to quickly return a sample from a large table when the sample does not have to be a truly random sample at the level of individual rows. This clause is also useful when you want to test your code against a random subset of data that you copy from a production environment or when you just want to test the validity of your solutions against a subset of data as opposed to the entire data set.

To return a random sample of data using the TABLESAMPLE clause, you specify it in a query's FROM clause, right after the table name or table alias. The TABLESAMPLE clause has the following syntax:

```
TABLESAMPLE [SYSTEM] (sample_number [ PERCENT ¦ ROWS ] )
[ REPEATABLE (repeat_seed) ]
```

Specifying the SYSTEM keyword is optional, but this option is currently the only sampling method available in SQL Server 2005 and is applied by default. SYSTEM specifies that an ANSI SQL implementation-dependent sampling method will be used. This means that individual database management system (DBMS) products can implement this method differently. In SQL Server 2005, the same sampling method that it uses to sample data to create statistics is used to generate the results for TABLESAMPLE.

The result set returned by a query using TABLESAMPLE and a specified percentage is created by generating a random value for each physical page in the table. Based on the random value generated for a page, that page is either included in the sample or excluded. When a page is included in the sample, all rows on that page are returned in the result set. For example, if you specify TABLESAMPLE SYSTEM 10 PERCENT, SQL Server returns all the rows from approximately 10% of the randomly selected data pages of the table.

When a specific number of rows rather than a percentage is specified, the requested number of rows is converted into a percentage of the total number of rows in the table and a percentage of the number of pages that should be returned. The TABLESAMPLE operation is then performed against the computed percentage of pages.

If the rows are evenly distributed on the pages of the table, the number of rows returned by a TABLESAMPLE query should be close to the requested sample size. However, if there is a mix of full and sparse pages in the table, the number of rows returned may vary widely for subsequent executions of the query. Consider the following query:

```
with sales_sample as
( select * from sales TABLESAMPLE (1 percent) )
select count(*) as numrows from sales_sample
go

numrows
-----------
2055
```

There are 168,715 rows in the sales table in the bigpubs2005 database. A 1% sample should return approximately 1,687 rows. However, as you can see from the previous example, it returned 2,055 rows.

NOTE

Note that each time this query is run, it is likely to return a different set of rows, so your row counts may not match those presented in these examples.

If you invoke the query again, it could return a different number of rows:

```
with sales_sample as
( select * from sales TABLESAMPLE (1 percent) )
select count(*) as numrows from sales_sample
go

numrows
-----------
1138
```

Note also that if you specify an actual number of rows, because the sampling is done at the page level, the pages sampled may have more or fewer rows than required to provide the requested sample size. For example, consider the following query, which requests a TABLESAMPLE of 1,000 rows:

```
with sales_sample as
( select * from sales TABLESAMPLE (1000 rows) )
select count(*) as numrows from sales_sample
go

numrows
-----------
683
```

A subsequent execution of the same query could return a different number of rows:

```
with sales_sample as
( select * from sales TABLESAMPLE (1000 rows) )
select count(*) as numrows from sales_sample
go

numrows
-----------
1371
```

If you run this query repeatedly, you are likely to get a different number of rows every time. However, the larger the table and the greater the number of rows you request, the more likely it is to get a closer percentage or number of requested rows returned. The smaller the table and the smaller the number or percentage of rows you request, the less likely the query is to return the number of rows close to the number or percentage you requested. With very small tables, you might not even get any rows.

To increase the likelihood of receiving the number of rows that you request, you should specify a greater number of rows than you actually need in the TABLESAMPLE clause and use the TOP option to specify the number of rows you actually want. For example, if you want a set of 1,000 random rows, you should request 2,000 rows in the TABLESAMPLE clause and then limit it to 1,000 rows with the TOP option, as in this example:

```
select top 1000 * from sales TABLESAMPLE (2000 rows)
```

When you do this, you may still get fewer than 1,000 rows returned, but the likelihood of that occurring is lower than if you request 1,000 rows in the TABLESAMPLE clause alone. Also, by specifying TOP(1000), you're guaranteed to not to get *more* than 1,000 rows. When you use a combination of TABLESAMPLE and TOP, the data you obtain is a more representative sampling of the data in your table than if you use TOP alone.

If you want to generate the same random sample each time you use the TABLESAMPLE clause, you can specify the REPEATABLE option with a specified *repeat_seed* value. The REPEATABLE option causes a selected sample to be returned again. When REPEATABLE is specified with the same *repeat_seed* value, SQL Server returns the same subset of rows, as long as no changes have been made to the table. For example, the following query uses *repeat_seed* of 1 and, in this case, returns 16,896 rows:

```
with sales_sample as
( select * from sales TABLESAMPLE (10 percent) repeatable (1) )
select count(*) as numrows from sales_sample
go

numrows
-----------
16896
```

When REPEATABLE is specified with a different *repeat_seed* value, SQL Server typically returns a different sample of the rows in the table. For example, the following query uses *repeat_seed* of 2 and gets a different set and number of rows:

```
with sales_sample as
( select * from sales TABLESAMPLE (10 percent) repeatable (2) )
select count(*) as numrows from sales_sample
go

numrows
-----------
19856
```

Running the query again with *repeat_seed* of 1 returns the same result rows as previously:

```
with sales_sample as
( select * from sales TABLESAMPLE (10 percent) repeatable (1) )
select count(*) as numrows from sales_sample
go

numrows
-----------
16896
```

35

The types of actions that are considered changes and could affect the repeatability of the TABLESAMPLE results include inserts, updates, deletes, index rebuilding, index defragmenting, restoration of a database, and attachment of a database.

You can use other techniques to request random data samples, but most of those techniques require scanning the entire table, which can be time-consuming and I/O intensive for very large tables. Using TABLESAMPLE for a specific table limits the Query Optimizer to performing only table scans on that table, but physical I/Os are performed only on the actual sampled pages that are included in the result set. Because of this, using TABLESAMPLE is usually a faster way of generating a random sampling of your data.

Summary

T-SQL has always been a powerful data access and data modification language, providing additional features, such as functions, variables, and commands, to control execution flow. SQL Sever 2005 further expands the power and capabilities of T-SQL with the addition of a number of new features. These new Transact-SQL features can be incorporated into the building blocks for creating even more powerful SQL Server database components, such as views, stored procedures, triggers, and user-defined functions.

In addition to these powerful new T-SQL features, SQL Server 2005 provides another way to increase the power and capabilities of your stored procedures, triggers, and functions. SQL Server 2005 provides the ability to define custom-managed database objects like stored procedures, triggers, functions, data types, and custom aggregates using .NET code. The next chapter, "SQL Server and the .NET Framework" provides an overview of using the .NET Common Language Runtion (CLR) to develop these custom-managed objects.

CHAPTER 36

SQL Server and the .NET Framework

IN THIS CHAPTER

▶ What's New in SQL Server 2005 and the .NET Framework

▶ Working with ADO.NET 2.0 and SQL Server

▶ Developing Custom Managed Database Objects

This chapter examines the deep integration of the .NET Framework with SQL Server 2005. It first covers how to program using ADO.NET 2.0, then it delves into SQL Server 2005's brand-new support for the creation of custom managed database objects.

What's New in SQL Server 2005 and the .NET Framework

SQL Server 2005 has the capability to use types and run routines written in C# or VB.NET. This is a huge extension of the T-SQL language: Stored procedures, functions, triggers, data types, and custom aggregates can now be written in .NET code and consumed in either a T-SQL or an ADO.NET context (or both).

This chapter gets into the details of creating and using managed database objects. In addition, we'll take a look at what's new in the ADO.NET classes.

Working with ADO.NET 2.0 and SQL Server

The following are the main .NET Framework namespaces you need to familiarize yourself with to program with SQL Server 2005:

▶ **System.Data**—This is the root namespace, which contains essential data access classes, such as DataSet, DataTable, and DataRow.

▶ **System.Data.SqlClient**—This namespace contains classes specialized for SQL Server access, such as SqlConnection, SqlCommand, and SqlParameter.

▶ **System.Xml**—This namespace holds most of the objects you need in order to work with SQL Server XML.

The easiest way to immerse ourselves in the code is to walk through some typical usage scenarios, which we do in the following sections.

ADO.NET: Advanced Basics

To get started coding with ADO.NET and SQL Server, you first need to connect to an instance of SQL Server. To do this, you need a connection string. A *connection string* is simply a string literal that contains all the parameters necessary to locate and log in to a server in a semicolon-delimited format. The following is an example:

```
"Data Source=(SQLServer001); Initial Catalog=AdventureWorks;Integrated
Security=True"
```

This connection string tells ADO.NET to connect to a server called SQLServer001, change to the AdventureWorks database context, and use integrated Windows security to connect—which means it should use the credentials of the currently authenticated user (in web applications, this is usually ASPNET, unless impersonation is used). You typically want to store this connection string in your application's .config file, preferably encrypted.

There are too many different connection string parameters to list here; you can check the MSDN "Connection Strings" topic for full information.

The managed object that represents a SQL Server connection is System.Data.SqlClient.SqlConnection.

This chapter uses as an example a C# Windows application in Visual Studio 2005. It contains every manager's dream: a form (MainForm.cs) with a big button (btnGo) that says Go on it that does everything you need. When you double-click btnGo in design mode, the IDE enters the C# source code block within the context of btnGo's OnClick event-handler.

To import the namespaces of the code libraries required for connecting to SQL Server into your C# class file, you add the following using statements to the list at the top:

```
using System.Data.SqlClient;
using System.Configuration;
```

Now you right-click the project and add an application configuration file to it (via Add New Item). Next, you open App.Config and enter the following lines, substituting your server name for (local) in the connection string:

```
<?xml version="1.0" encoding="utf-8" ?>
<configuration>
  <appSettings>
```

```
    <add
      key="SqlConn"
      value="Data Source=(local);Initial Catalog=AdventureWorks;
➥Integrated Security=True"/>
    </appSettings>
</configuration>
```

In addition to the Go button, you should add to the form a `DataGridView` control, which will hold the data returned from executing your `SqlCommand`. The `SqlCommand` object allows you to execute T-SQL statements, including stored procedures and functions, from within the context of an active connection.

`SqlCommand` has several execution methods, each of which behaves differently and returns a different type of object:

- ▶ **ExecuteNonQuery**—Executes the T-SQL statements and returns an `Int32`, that indicates the number of rows affected. It also populates any output parameters. This is especially useful when executing INSERT and UPDATE queries.

- ▶ **ExecuteScalar**—Executes the T-SQL statements and returns an object (of type `Object`) that contains the value of the first column of the first row returned. The object returned is castable to one of the native .NET types (for example, `Int32`, `String` [even for returned xml columns], `Boolean`).

- ▶ **ExecuteReader**—Executes the T-SQL statements and returns a `SqlDataReader` object. `SqlDataReader` objects are useful when you want to perform some behavior on the returned result set on a per-row and/or per-column basis (usually using a looping construct).

- ▶ **ExecuteXmlReader**—Executes the T-SQL statements and returns a `System.Xml.XmlReader`, which you can use to iterate through the nodes in selected XML (or to instantiate other `System.Xml` objects, such as `System.Xml.XPath.XPathDocument`), produced either via SELECT...FOR XML or from a column or variable of the new xml data type.

TIP

New for SQL Server 2005, `System.Data.SqlClient` now provides asynchronous versions of these method calls in begin call/end call pairs that take a handy callback method parameter, such as `BeginExecuteReader`, `EndExecuteReader`, `BeginExecuteNonQuery`, and `EndExecuteNonQuery`. Note that there is no `BeginExecuteScalar/EndExecuteScalar`.

To wire up the data returned from `SqlCommand` into a `System.Data.DataSet`, you use an object of type `System.Data.SqlClient.SqlDataAdapter`.

You frequently use `SqlDataAdapter` objects to map data from SQL Server to `DataSet` objects and back, using the `Fill()` and `Update()` methods, respectively.

36

You may also want your code to catch any `SqlException` objects in a `try-catch` block that may be thrown in the course of running the database access code.

To test the use of classes we've just discussed, add the code in Listing 36.1 to the `btnGo_Click()` event-handler.

LISTING 36.1   A Button Event Handler That Illustrates the Use of Several ADO.NET Objects

```
private void btnGo_Click(object sender, EventArgs e)
{
  using (SqlConnection Connection =
          new SqlConnection(ConfigurationManager.AppSettings["SqlConn"]))
  {
    using (SqlCommand Command =
            new SqlCommand(
            @"SELECT TOP 10 * FROM HumanResources.JobCandidate"
            , Connection))
    {
      try
      {
        using (SqlDataAdapter Adapter =
                new SqlDataAdapter(Command))
        {
          using (DataSet Set = new DataSet())
          {
            Connection.Open();
            Adapter.Fill(Set);
            GridView.DataSource = Set.Tables[0];
          }
        }
      }
      catch (SqlException SqlEx)
      {
        foreach (SqlError SqlErr in SqlEx.Errors)
        {
          MessageBox.Show(
            "The following SQL Error occurred: " + SqlErr.Message,
            "SqlError");
        }
      }
    }
  }
}
```

Next, you run the Windows application and click `btnGo`. Your form should look something like the form in Figure 36.1.

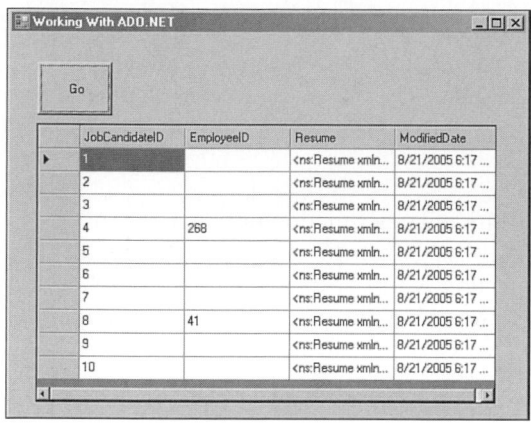

FIGURE 36.1   Using ADO.NET in a Windows application.

This code executes as follows: A connection to SQL Server is made via `SqlConnection` and the subsequent call to `Connection.Open()` (which, by the way, is unnecessary because `SqlDataAdapter.Fill()` implicitly opens the closed connection). The `SqlCommand` object `Command` is set to use this connection via its constructor. The constructor also takes a string parameter that contains the text of the query. It can also take the name of a stored procedure, for example. When using a stored procedure name, you change its `CommandType` property from the default of `CommandType.Text` to `CommandType.StoredProcedure`.

Next, you instantiate a `SqlDataAdapter` object that registers the `Command` object as what it will execute on the call to `Fill()`. You also create a `DataSet` object to hold the returned data. In the simplest respect, `DataSet` objects are collections of `DataTable` objects, which map directly to SQL Server query results. Each `DataTable` object, as you may guess, holds an array of `DataRow` objects, each of which in turn holds an array of `DataColumn` values accessible by indexers.

You bind the `DataGridView` object to the filled `DataSet` object's first table (`Tables[0]`), and you can rest assured that the catch block will notify you with a message box about each `SqlError` contained in the `Errors` collection of any raised `SqlException`.

NOTE

One convention used in the code in this chapter is the use of nested `using` statements with these objects. When you use this C# syntax convention, you don't have to set up a `finally` block that calls `Dispose()` for every object; `using` does that implicitly for you.

Many of the database classes provided in ADO.NET have a `Dispose()` method because, under the covers, they utilize unmanaged (COM) resources. The objects you most commonly use for database applications that provide `Dispose()` are `SqlConnection`, `SqlCommand`, `SqlDataAdapter`, `SqlDataReader`, and `DataSet`.

What's New in ADO.NET for SQL Server 2005

What's new in ADO.NET for SQL Server 2005? Well, a lot. In fact, there are more new features than this section has space to describe them. The following sections look at a few of the ones you're likely to use.

Multiple Active Result Sets (MARS)

The acronym MARS is goofy (I didn't make it up), but the functionality is not: MARS enables multiple SqlCommand objects to be executed against the same open SqlConnection while a SqlDataReader returned on that connection is still open. Using MARS, each subsequent SqlCommand object creates a new session with SQL Server, using the same connection.

In earlier versions of ADO.NET, attempting to execute a second SqlCommand while iterating through a SqlDataReader would raise a System.InvalidOperationException stating "There is already an open DataReader associated with this Command which must be closed first."

To enable MARS, you append the following to the connection string in the App.Config file:

```
MultipleActiveResultSets=True
```

> **NOTE**
>
> MSDN states that MARS is turned off by default. In our testing, however, we found the opposite to be true.

The code in Listing 36.2 shows how with MARS, you can execute a second SqlCommand object while reading data from a SqlDataReader object on the same connection. To test it out, you can replace the code from Listing 36.1 with that of Listing 36.2.

LISTING 36.2   Using MARS

```csharp
private void btnGo_Click(object sender, EventArgs e)
{
  using (SqlConnection Connection =
    new SqlConnection(ConfigurationSettings.AppSettings["SqlConn"]))
  {
    using (SqlCommand Command =
      new SqlCommand(
        @"SELECT TOP 10 *
          FROM HumanResources.JobCandidate", Connection))
    {
      try
      {
        Connection.Open();
        using (SqlDataReader Reader1 = Command.ExecuteReader())
```

LISTING 36.2   Continued

```csharp
    {
      while (Reader1.Read())
      {
        if (Reader1.GetInt32(0) == 4)
        {
          SqlCommand Command2 =
            new SqlCommand(
              @"SELECT *
                FROM HumanResources.Employee
                WHERE EmployeeId = " + Reader1.GetInt32(1), Connection);
          using (SqlDataReader Reader2 = Command2.ExecuteReader())
          {
            DataTable Table = new DataTable();
            Table.Columns.Add(
              new DataColumn("ContactId",Type.GetType("System.Int32")));
            while (Reader2.Read())
            {
              DataRow Row = Table.NewRow();
              Row[0] = Reader2.GetInt32(0);
              Table.Rows.Add(Row);
            }
            GridView.DataSource = Table;
          }
        }
      }
    }
  }
  catch (SqlException SqlEx)
  {
    foreach (SqlError SqlErr in SqlEx.Errors)
    {
      MessageBox.Show(
        "The following SQL Error occurred: " + SqlErr.Message,
        "SqlError");
    }
  }
}
}
}
}
```

If you run the Windows application and click btnGo, your form should (depending on your layout choices) look something like the form shown in Figure 36.2.

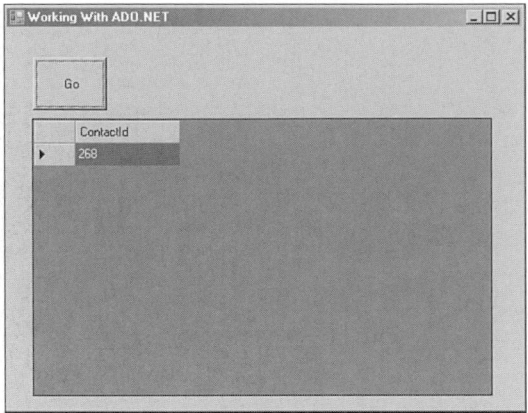

FIGURE 36.2   Using MARS in a Windows application.

Additions to System.Data.SqlTypes
The System.Data.SqlTypes namespace now contains the new xml data type, known as System.Data.SqlTypes.SqlXml.

To try it out, you add the following using statements to the form's C# file:

```
using System.Xml;
using System.Data.SqlTypes;
```

Then, you add a new button called btnGetXml to the form, as well as a new text box, txtSqlXml. Next, you double-click btnGetXml and add the code in Listing 36.3 to btnGetXml_Click().

LISTING 36.3   Using the New SqlXml Object

```
private void btnGetXML_Click(object sender, EventArgs e)
{
  using (SqlConnection Connection =
    new SqlConnection(ConfigurationSettings.AppSettings["SqlConn"]))
  {
    using (SqlCommand Command =
      new SqlCommand(
        @"SELECT Resume
          FROM HumanResources.JobCandidate
          WHERE JobCandidateId = 1", Connection))
    {
      try
      {
        Connection.Open();
        using (SqlDataReader Reader = Command.ExecuteReader())
        {
```

LISTING 36.3   Continued

```
      while (Reader.Read())
      {
        SqlXml SqlX = Reader.GetSqlXml(0);
        XmlDocument XDoc = new XmlDocument();
        XDoc.Load(SqlX.CreateReader());
        txtSqlXml.Text = XDoc.OuterXml;
      }
    }
  }
  catch (SqlException SqlEx)
  {
    foreach (SqlError SqlErr in SqlEx.Errors)
    {
      MessageBox.Show(
        "The following SQL Error occurred: " + SqlErr.Message,
        "SqlError");
    }
  }
  }
 }
}
}
```

As you can see in the try-catch block, the SqlDataReader object provides the new GetSqlXml method, returning a SqlXml object. (Note that using SqlDataReader.GetValue() actually returns the XML as a String.)

When you have the object (SqlX), you can use its handy CreateReader method to return an instance of XmlReader. Then, you can load that reader into an XmlDocument object and display its contents in txtSqlXml.Text. Figure 36.3 illustrates this.

In addition to SqlXml, you can access any user-defined managed types in ADO.NET. This is covered later in this chapter, in the section "Using Managed User-Defined Types (UDTs)."

Also new in SQL Server 2005 are the [n]varchar(max) and [n]varbinary(max) data types. You can access the content of these data types in ADO.NET via SqlDataReader by calling the methods GetSqlChars() (which returns an object of type SqlChars) and GetSqlBytes() (which returns an object of type SqlBytes), respectively.

In addition, you can slurp the entire contents of an [n]varbinary(max) column into a SqlBinary object via the method SqlDataReader.GetSqlBinary().

When varbinary data is returned from SQL Server to .NET DataTable objects (in DataRow columns), the value of these columns is of type byte[].

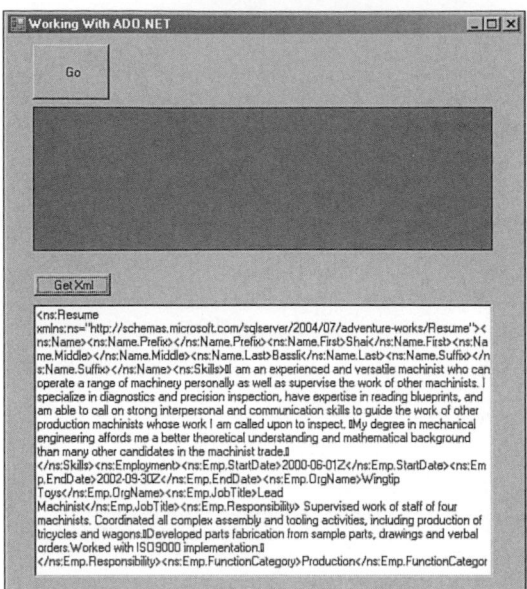

FIGURE 36.3   Using `SqlXml` in a Windows application.

Connection Pooling

Connection pools turned on for `SqlConnections` can now be cleared by using the new static (or *shared*, in VB .NET) `SqlConnection` methods `ClearAllPools()` (which clears all pools for all connections) and `ClearPool(SqlConnection)` (which clears the pool for a specific connection). This is helpful for applications that need greater pooling control than the built-in behind-the-scenes pool management.

Query Notification

In the past, applications that used cached data needed to periodically check the server for changes to the cached data and update the cache accordingly. With new Query Notifications, it's no longer necessary for the database client to perform the check: Applications (including ASP.NET applications) can now register to be notified of server-side changes to SQL Server data and can respond accordingly.

This feature is built on the new Service Broker functionality and uses the new QUEUE database object under the covers. For more information on Service Broker, see Chapter 48, "SQL Server Service Broker" (on the CD-ROM).

To work with Query Notifications, you need to familiarize yourself with the following new objects in the `System.Data.SqlClient` namespace:

> ▶ `SqlDependency`—Given a `SqlCommand` that returns data to be cached, you want to know whether that data has changed in the lifetime of the application. You execute the `SqlCommand`, cache your data, and provide a callback method to the `SqlDependency`'s `OnChange` event. Your callback is invoked when the data selected in

the original command has changed. Note that as of this writing, you cannot use
SELECT * in a SqlCommand that participates in a SqlDependency.

▶ **SqlNotificationRequest**—A more complex programming choice than
SqlDependency, SqlNotificationRequest allows client applications to process
request notification messages rather than having them be processed automatically
by the SqlQueryNotificationService in msdb.

▶ **SqlCacheDependency**—You use this object with ASP.NET applications that need to be
notified. ASP.NET notifications happen via System.Web.Caching.Cache object dependencies. SqlCacheDependency is a subclass of CacheDependency that works just like
SqlDependency.

To use SqlDependency from your Windows application, you add the following using statement:

```
using System.Security.Permissions;
```

This is needed because you want the application to demand the unrestricted
SqlClientPermission to make sure it can do this kind of thing. If the call to Demand() in
the code fails, a security exception is raised.

Next, you add the following call in the constructor of the form after the call to
InitializeComponent():

```
StartDependency();
```

Finally, you add to the class the code in Listing 36.4.

LISTING 36.4   Using the New SqlDependency Object

```
private static SqlConnection _connection =
  new SqlConnection(ConfigurationSettings.AppSettings["SqlConn"]);

private static SqlCommand _command =
  new SqlCommand(
    @"SELECT AddressId
      FROM Person.Address
      WHERE AddressId = 1", _connection);

private static SqlDependency SqlDep =
  new SqlDependency(_command);

private static SqlDataReader _reader = null;

public void StartDependency()
{
  SqlClientPermission SqlPerm =
```

LISTING 36.4   Continued

```
    new SqlClientPermission(PermissionState.Unrestricted);
  SqlPerm.Demand();
  SqlDep.OnChange += new OnChangeEventHandler(DepChange);
  connection.Open();
  reader = _command.ExecuteReader();
}


private void DepChange(object sender, SqlNotificationEventArgs e)
{
  MessageBox.Show(e.Info.ToString(), "SqlDependency");
}
```

Before running this application, you need to open a new query window in SQL Server Management Studio (SSMS), log in as sa or an equally privileged user, and run the following T-SQL statements:

```
use Adventureworks
GO
ALTER DATABASE AdventureWorks SET ENABLE_BROKER;
GO
use MSDB
GO
GRANT SEND
  ON SERVICE::[http://schemas.microsoft.com/SQL/Notifications/
➥QueryNotificationService]
  TO GUEST
GO
use AdventureWorks
GO
```

These statements turn on Service Broker in the AdventureWorks database and enable the sending of Query Notification messages to the example application. The SqlQueryNotificationService in msdb processes query notification messages.

Finally, you run the application and then execute the following query in the query window:

```
UPDATE Person.Address
SET AddressLine1 = AddressLine1
WHERE AddressId = 1
```

If everything is set up correctly, you will see a message box in the application with the word "Update" displayed, indicating that the data it originally requested changed on the server.

Developing Custom Managed Database Objects

SQL Server now hosts the Common Language Runtime (CLR), implementing what's known as the Hosting API (new in .NET 2.0). The Hosting API gives SQL Server 2005 full control over the execution of .NET code in a carefully managed environment that honors the shared resource usage of both SQL Server and the CLR. The CLR provides an execution context far safer than that of code you might formerly have run in an extended stored procedure or COM object under SQL Server 2000.

Compare the relative runtime safety of in-process objects created via sp_OACreate (which could easily crash the sqlserver.exe process) with that of verifiably type-safe code running in a permission-managed application domain, and you'll see why it's a great leap forward.

In the sections that follow, you'll create one of each of the new managed versions of database routines and types. You'll work with both the new SQL Server project type in Visual Studio 2005 and the new T-SQL Data Definition Language (DDL) syntax for managed objects.

Finally, you'll learn about advanced topics such as transaction control in mixed (T-SQL and managed) environments.

An Introduction to Custom Managed Database Objects

The ability to run managed code presents a world of possibilities, yet these features must be leveraged appropriately. The meaning of *appropriate* will ultimately be the result of ongoing dialogs between database administrators and the developers who want to use the .NET Framework in SQL Server.

Just like SQL Server's new ability to host web services (covered in Chapter 38, "SQL Server Web Services"), this new feature set begins to blur the line between SQL Server as a database server and SQL Server as a lightweight application server.

.NET assemblies are built using Visual Studio or the command-line compilers and then literally uploaded into the database and loaded into memory on the same physical server as the SQL Server instance. CLR objects may therefore consume valuable server and network resources. This presents a challenging new management paradigm that database administrators, managers, and developers have to negotiate. Administrators are just beginning to consider strategies for what kinds of .NET code should be allowed to be run and in which contexts. The following are a few general rules to consider as to when managed objects should and should not be used:

▶ Data selection and modification should always be performed using T-SQL because that's what it's optimized to do. You should not create a T-SQL wrapper in your .NET code.

▶ You should use managed code when you need to overcome the procedural limitations of T-SQL, such as avoiding the use of nested cursors that connect to multiple databases and other awkward constructs. (SQL was never developed to be a procedural language, only a set-based query language.)

▶ You should use managed code when you want to extend the per-row or per-set effects of routines to leverage managed resources, such as XML parsers, web services, and custom code libraries.

It's still up to the software development staff what to do, but, thankfully, SQL Server has some rules of its own for what kinds of operations can be called and under which permission sets, as discussed in the following section.

Managed Object Permissions

The first thing to know about managed object permissions is that SQL Server has only blessed a certain group of assemblies usable under each of the three SQL Server permission sets.

The screenshot in Figure 36.4, taken from the Add References dialog for a SQL Server project in Visual Studio 2005, shows the list of these .NET Framework assemblies. They are the only assemblies (aside from user-created assemblies) that can be referenced in SQL Server projects. Note that this list doesn't change in Visual Studio, regardless of the permission set used. Note also that SQL Server and/or Visual Studio walks down the reference chain to see if any referenced assemblies reference anything that is not blessed. So you shouldn't bother trying to get around this; there isn't even a Browse button on the dialog box as there is with the other project types.

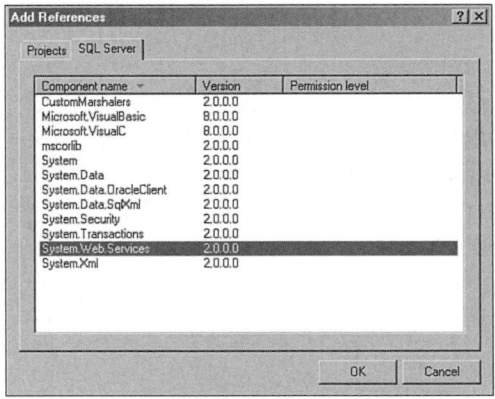

FIGURE 36.4   Blessed assemblies in the Add References dialog in Visual Studio 2005.

The Three Permission Sets

SQL Server has three built-in .NET Code Access Security (CAS) permission sets that define which kinds of operations can be executed at runtime. Using the CAS layer is a huge improvement over running extended stored procedures under default login credentials because it allows for fine-grained permission granting and revocation.

These are the permission sets, in increasing order of freedom:

- ▶ SAFE

- ▶ EXTERNAL_ACCESS

- ▶ UNSAFE

These keywords are used in the DDL syntax for assemblies.

Assuming that you have built an assembly targeted for SQL Server use (which you'll do in the next section), the following is the syntax for loading that assembly into your database of choice:

```
CREATE ASSEMBLY AssemblyName [AUTHORIZATION LoginName]
FROM  StringPathToAssemblyDll ¦ BinaryDataValue
[WITH PERMISSION_SET (SAFE ¦ EXTERNAL_ACCESS ¦ UNSAFE) ]
```

This syntax is reasonably self-explanatory: You tell SQL Server the name of the assembly and the path (using a UNC if needed) to it. If you're loading an assembly from a varbinary column, you supply the actual data that makes up the compiled code of the assembly instead of the path to it (Visual Studio does this).

NOTE

CREATE ASSEMBLY and ALTER ASSEMBLY are commands used by Visual Studio's new Deploy feature, which does the managed code DDL work for you.

The WITH PERMISSION SET clause is optional, and it defaults to SAFE. Marking an assembly with the SAFE permission set indicates that no external resources (for example, the registry, web services, file I/O) are going to be accessed. The DDL will fail if assemblies such as System.IO are referenced, and anything causing a permission demand for executing similar operations will result in an exception being thrown at runtime. Marking an assembly with the EXTERNAL_ACCESS permission set tells SQL Server that it will be using resources such as networking, files, and so forth. Assemblies such as System.Web.Services (but not System.Web) may be referenced with this set.

Marking an assembly with the UNSAFE permission set tells SQL Server that not only might external resources be used, but unmanaged code may even be invoked from managed code.

Some assemblies in the .NET Framework go so far as to tell the processes that ultimately host them (such as SQL Server or Internet Explorer) about their relative safety, using a specific .NET attribute: HostProtectionAttribute (HPA).

The enumeration flags of the HPA's parameter indicate to the host what kinds of operations the classes decorated with it may attempt. Because documentation of the HPA with regards to SQL Server is scant, it's unclear whether SQL Server ultimately relies on the

36

HPA to determine what may be loaded. (It seems to do so at runtime, but the blessed list is likely to be hard coded.)

The following are some of the operations you cannot perform with .NET code running under SQL Server's SAFE and EXTERNAL_ACCESS options (but possibly under UNSAFE):

- ▶ Thread synchronization
- ▶ External process management
- ▶ Framework security changes
- ▶ Use of non-read-only static fields

Only those in the sysadmin role can upload UNSAFE assemblies to SQL Server. (Just don't tell your DBA we told you how to do it.)

The EXTERNAL_ACCESS permission on master is required for uploading EXTERNAL_ACCESS assemblies. And anyone in the dbowner role may load SAFE assemblies.

Developing Managed Objects with Visual Studio 2005

When SQL Server 2005 is installed, it includes Microsoft.SqlServer.Server, the new assembly that contains the attributes and other classes needed for SQLCLR (the common acronym for managed code running in SQL Server) programming.

At this point, you should go ahead and create your first Visual Studio project. Start up Visual Studio 2005 and create a new SQL Server project named SQLCLR. Figure 36.5 shows the New Project dialog box.

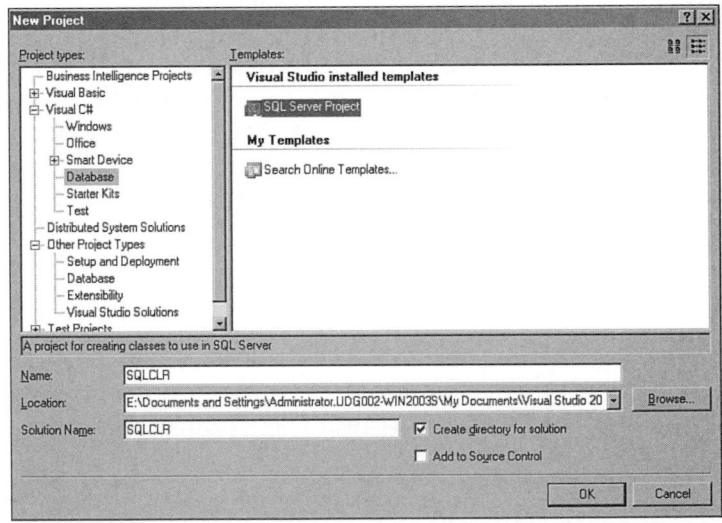

FIGURE 36.5   Using the New Project dialog in Visual Studio 2005.

The next thing Visual Studio asks you to do is create or add a database reference, as shown in Figure 36.6.

FIGURE 36.6   Adding a database reference for a SQL Server Visual Studio project.

This reference contains the connection to the SQL Server database to which your assembly (and with it, its types and routines) will be uploaded. Performing this step is fairly self-explanatory: You just need to be sure to choose the built-in AdventureWorks database, or the examples that follow won't work.

Next, you'll create your first managed SQL Server object, a stored procedure written in C#.

> **NOTE**
>
> This chapter assumes that you have intermediate .NET and basic T-SQL programming skills.

Using Managed Stored Procedures

Stored procedures are a great starting point for getting into SQLCLR because they are easy to implement. To do so, you right-click your project in the Visual Studio's Solution Explorer window and then select Add, Stored Procedure. A partial class called StoredProcedures opens in the code window. Note that Visual Studio automatically adds the required reference to Microsoft.SqlServer.Server and the associated using statement. Microsoft.SqlServer.Server contains the SqlProcedure attribute required for turning our first method into a SQLCLR stored procedure.

For this example, you need to change the default method name to GetSetIllustrationWebLinks. Next, if you're not working in Visual Studio, you need to decorate this method with the SqlProcedure attribute.

Attributes and the Implementation Contract

If you've never used attributes, you can think of them as metadata that tells the compiler, often through reflection, that the decorated element (known as the *target*) meets some criterion.

All the managed objects you'll create in this chapter require certain attributes to be applied, or they cannot be used in SQL Server.

The classes you build must also supply particular methods and/or method signatures in order to be deployed successfully. This is known as fulfilling the *implementation contract*. For stored procedures, fulfilling the contract requires that the method to be called is marked static. The return type and number and type of parameters is up to you. These are the only contract requirements to be filled for stored procedures.

> **NOTE**
>
> It makes sense that the method is marked as a static member because it is called by the runtime host via the class's type object rather than via an instance (for example, *AssemblyName.ClassName.StaticMethodName(Parameters)*).

Object-oriented (OO) purists might suggest that this way of creating managed SQL Server objects could have been done in a more OO-friendly way if the contract to be filled required overriding the methods of an abstract class or implementing interfaces. The static requirement, however, currently makes this impossible because static members are not inherited and cannot be used to implement interface members.

The constructor for the SqlProcedure attribute is overloaded to either take zero parameters or take one parameter that is actually a list of named parameters.

Having a list of named parameters in the attribute signature is common to most of the attributes used in this chapter, although the choice of named parameters pairs varies from attribute to attribute.

For stored procedures, only one named parameter exists: Name. You use Name when you want to name the method one thing but have the name it generates for use in a SQL Server context be another name.

The code in Listing 36.5 illustrates the use of named parameters in attributes and contains a complete program for creating scalar vector graphics (SVG) files on the local web server. It then generates and selects a result set of URLs that point back to the generated SVG files.

LISTING 36.5   A Managed Procedure That Creates SVG Files on a Local Web Server

```
using System;
using System.Data;
using System.Data.Sql;
using System.Data.SqlTypes;
using Microsoft.SqlServer.Server;
using System.Data.SqlClient; // added
using System.IO; // added
using System.Security.Permissions; // added
```

LISTING 36.5   Continued

```csharp
namespace Routines
{
  public partial class StoredProcedures
  {
    [Microsoft.SqlServer.Server.SqlProcedure(
      Name = "sp_GetSetIllustrationWebLinks"
    )]
    public static void GetSetIllustrationWebLinks(int ProductModelId)
    {
      using (SqlConnection c = new SqlConnection("Data Source=(local);Initial
➡Catalog=AdventureWorks;Integrated Security=True"))
      {
        using (SqlCommand scADO = new SqlCommand())
        {
          c.Open();
          scADO.Connection = c;
          scADO.CommandText = "Production.GetIllustrationsByProductModel";
          SqlParameter pmId = new SqlParameter("ProductModelId", ProductModelId);
          scADO.Parameters.Add(pmId);
          scADO.CommandType = CommandType.StoredProcedure;
          SqlDataReader reader = scADO.ExecuteReader();

          using (SqlConnection ContextConnection =
            new SqlConnection("context connection=true"))
          {
            SqlDataRecord record =
                new SqlDataRecord(
                    new SqlMetaData[]
                {
                  new SqlMetaData("IllustrationId",
                    SqlDbType.Int),
                  new SqlMetaData("SVGURL",
                    SqlDbType.VarChar, 1000)
                }
              );

            SqlContext.Pipe.SendResultsStart(record);

            while (reader.Read())
            {
              SqlXml x = reader.GetSqlXml(2);
              if (!x.IsNull)
              {
```

36

LISTING 36.5   Continued

```
          Int32 IllId = reader.GetInt32(0);

          string FileName = IllId.ToString() +
              "__" + reader.GetString(1) + ".svg";

          string SVGURL = "http://localhost/Illustrations/" +
            FileName;

          string FilePath = @"e:\inetpub\wwwroot\illustrations\";

          FileIOPermission fp = new FileIOPermission(
              FileIOPermissionAccess.Write,
              FilePath);

          fp.Demand();

          using (StreamWriter sw = new StreamWriter(
              FilePath + FileName))
          {
            sw.Write(x.Value);
          }

          using (SqlCommand scCLR = new SqlCommand())
          {
            scCLR.Connection = c;
            scCLR.CommandType = CommandType.StoredProcedure;
            scCLR.CommandText =
              "Production.InsertUpdateIllustrationWebLink";

            scCLR.Parameters.Add("@IllustrationId",
              SqlDbType.Int).Value = IllId;

            scCLR.Parameters.Add("@IllustrationURL",
              SqlDbType.VarChar, 1000).Value = SVGURL;

            scCLR.ExecuteNonQuery();
            record.SetInt32(0, IllId);
            record.SetString(1, SVGURL);
            SqlContext.Pipe.SendResultsRow(record);
          }
        }
      }
      SqlContext.Pipe.SendResultsEnd();
    }
```

LISTING 36.5   Continued

```
        }
      }
    }
  }
}
```

To create files on a local web server, it is necessary to add a reference to System.IO (a blessed assembly), write the corresponding using statement, and change the assembly's permission set from the default of SAFE to EXTERNAL_ACCESS. To do to latter in Visual Studio, you right-click the project in Solution Explorer and select Properties. Then, on the left side of the window, you select the Database tab. Note that the Database tab is where Visual Studio stores a connection string for your database reference. (You can change that here as well.)

Under the Permission Level drop-down, you need to change the value from Safe to External and save the project. (You can also access this functionality by using the IDE's property window, which you may open by pressing F4).

You can also type in the name of the SQL Server login (under Assembly Owner) that will be specified for the AUTHORIZATION parameter of CREATE ASSEMBLY during auto-deployment by Visual Studio.

The idea behind the code in Listing 36.5 is that, given a ProductModelId, you want to look up the illustrations belonging to that ProductModel and output them to a file on the web server. You then want to store and return a result set of links to those new files. The illustration data is stored as SVG XML in an xml column on Production.Illustration called Diagram.

To select the values you want, our example requires the following T-SQL stored procedure:

```
CREATE PROC Production.GetIllustrationsByProductModel
(
    @ProductModelId int
)
AS
SELECT
    pi.IllustrationId, pm.Name, pi.Diagram
FROM Production.Illustration pi
JOIN Production.ProductModelIllustration pmi
ON pmi.IllustrationId = pi.IllustrationId
JOIN Production.ProductModel pm
ON pm.ProductModelID = pmi.ProductModelID
WHERE pm.ProductModelId = @ProductModelId
```

The Context Connection

Back in your managed procedure, you use ADO.NET to create a connection to the AdventureWorks database. Why would you do this, if you know the managed code is destined to run from *within* the context of an active connection already?

In this case, you need to have two connections open simultaneously: The first executes GetIllustrationsByProductModel and returns a reader; the second uses the context connection to do insertions while looping through the reader's data. You can't both read from the context connection and write to it.

To use the context connection, you simply use the magic connection string "context connection=true".

The example also hints at the fact that you can connect to any other database server, even on a different platform, inside the running managed stored procedure.

Objects in Microsoft.SqlServer.Server

Your managed procedure uses a few brand-new objects to send data to the server through the active connection:

▶ **SqlContext**—This represents the server execution context for the managed routine. You can think of it as the line of communication between the .NET and SQL Server environments.

▶ **SqlContext.Pipe**—SqlContext holds the all-important Pipe property, which is used to send SqlDataRecord objects or text messages to the caller, which may be either another managed routine (via ADO.NET) or T-SQL user code.

▶ **SqlDataRecord**—This is an abstraction that represents a record in any table. The schema of the columns for a SqlDataRecord object is created by using SqlMetaData objects.

▶ **SqlMetaData**—An array of SqlMetaData objects is passed to the constructor of SqlDataRecord. Each SqlMetaData object defines the name, type, precision, scale, and so forth for the column via its overloaded constructors.

Pipe has a few methods you need to use to insert rows into a new table, required for our example, called Production.IllustrationWebLinks. Create this table in AdventureWorks as follows:

```
CREATE TABLE Production.IllustrationWebLinks
(
        IllustrationId int
        PRIMARY KEY CLUSTERED
        REFERENCES Production.Illustration(IllustrationId),
    IllustrationURL varchar(1000)
)
```

The example inserts rows into this table, using the following T-SQL stored procedure:

```
CREATE PROC Production.InsertUpdateIllustrationWebLink
(
    @IllustrationId int,
    @IllustrationURL varchar(1000)
)
AS
IF NOT EXISTS(
    SELECT DISTINCT IllustrationId
    FROM Production.IllustrationWebLinks
    WHERE IllustrationId = @IllustrationId
)
    INSERT Production.IllustrationWebLinks
    SELECT @IllustrationId, @IllustrationURL
ELSE
    UPDATE Production.IllustrationWebLinks
    SET IllustrationURL = @IllustrationURL
    WHERE IllustrationId = @IllustrationId
```

Returning to the code in Listing 36.5, before looping through our `SqlDataReader(Reader)`, you call `Pipe.SendResultsStart` and pass the `SqlDataRecord` object whose structure matches that of the new table. This tells SQL Server that the procedure is about to send back to the caller rows that have a specific structure.

Looping through the reader (using `while (reader.Read())`), you insert (or update) rows in the new table and then return the same inserted values to the caller. To do this, you use the `Set[DataTypeName]` methods on the `SqlDataRecord` object `record`. Once the values are set, you can call `SqlContext.Pipe.SendResultsRow(record)` to return the data.

After you're done returning values to the client, you clean up by calling `Pipe.SendResultsEnd`. The `Pipe` object also has an `ExecuteAndSend` method that takes a `SqlCommand` parameter, executes it, and sends all the results back to the caller, in one fell swoop.

In addition, you can query the status of the `Pipe` object by checking its `IsSendingResults` Boolean property. You can even send an informational text message (similar to T-SQL's print function) to the caller, using `Pipe.Send("Text")`. `Send()` is also overloaded to accept a `SqlDataRecord` object or a `SqlDataReader` object that contains the data to be returned.

Setting Up the Server for Managed Code Execution

Before you can test your managed database objects, you need to execute the following T-SQL commands in the context of the `master` database:

```
sp_configure 'clr enabled', 1
RECONFIGURE
go
```

This is necessary because SQL Server comes with managed code execution turned off by default.

Building and Deploying the Assembly

At this point, you can go ahead and build the Visual Studio project and then choose the new Deploy command from the Build menu. This is the part of the process where Visual Studio creates the T-SQL DDL scripts needed to upload the assembly into SQL Server and add the managed stored procedure to the AdventureWorks database.

You've already seen the CREATE ASSEMBLY DDL used by Visual Studio. For now, let's assume that you've already uploaded the assembly once. In this case, you (or Visual Studio) need to call the following to replace the assembly with a newly compiled version of the same:

```
ALTER ASSEMBLY AssemblyName
[AUTHORIZATION LoginName]
FROM  StringPathToAssemblyDll ¦ BinaryDataValue
[PERMISSION_SET = (SAFE ¦ EXTERNAL_ACCESS ¦ UNSAFE) ]
```

You can also use the ALTER ASSEMBLY statement to upload the C# class files to the server so that when you're debugging exceptions, you get the source code line numbers in the call stack dump. Here's an example:

```
ALTER ASSEMBLY AssemblyName ADD FILE FROM FilePath
```

> **TIP**
>
> Keep in mind that any user-defined types (covered later in this chapter) bound to database objects (as column data types, for example) will prevent an assembly from being dropped or altered until they themselves have first been dropped.

After the assembly is loaded, you use the following DDL to add our SQLCLR stored procedure to the AdventureWorks database:

```
CREATE PROCEDURE [dbo].[sp_GetSetIllustrationWebLinks]
    @ProductModelId [int]
WITH EXECUTE AS CALLER
AS
EXTERNAL NAME
[SQLCLR].[Routines.StoredProcedures].[GetSetIllustrationWebLinks]
```

The new WITH EXECUTE AS CALLER clause tells SQL Server that the permissions for executing the procedure should be those of its caller. (See the "EXECUTE AS" Books Online topic for more info.)

The new EXTERNAL NAME keywords tell SQL Server that the routines or types being created belong to a specific class in a loaded assembly. The dotted notation for EXTERNAL NAME's string parameter is as follows:

AssemblyName.ClassName.RoutineOrTypeName

You'll see this parameter again in the DDL of the other managed objects we'll soon create.

To view the objects created during script execution or Visual Studio deployment, you can open the Object Explorer in SSMS, expand the AdventureWorks database node, and then expand the Programmability node. There you will find the Assemblies node. (The managed objects in the assembly are kept in their respective folders.) If you right-click an assembly and view its properties, another window appears where you can view or change the assembly's permissions.

Debugging Managed Code

If you have all the needed permissions and have IIS installed locally as well, you're 90% ready to successfully run our managed stored procedure example. The only thing left to do is create a virtual directory called Illustrations in IIS and map it to a new empty physical folder of the same name under the web root (under wwwroot, for example). (You also need the Adobe SVG Viewer plug-in to actually see the illustration.)

Open a new query window in SSMS and test the stored procedure, just as you would any other. Try the following:

```
EXEC sp_GetSetIllustrationWebLinks 47
Go
IllustrationId    SVGURL
---------------------------------------------------------------------------
4                 http://localhost/Illustrations/4__LL Touring Handlebars.svg
5                 http://localhost/Illustrations/5__LL Touring Handlebars.svg
(2 rows(s) affected.)
```

Then, you can plug one of the SVGURL values into Internet Explorer's address bar and click Go. Who knew they put stuff like that in AdventureWorks?

Finally, you can try debugging with Visual Studio. By default, every Visual Studio SQL Server project is created with a Test Scripts folder and a file called Test.sql. Test.sql (or any other .sql files in a SQL Server project) is kind of like a hybrid of a code file and a query window. In this file you can execute a batch of arbitrary database commands, and you can also set breakpoints on each code line. The output of the commands appears in the Database Output section of the Output window.

You need to enter the same T-SQL in Test.sql that you just did in SSMS. Then you should set a breakpoint on the line. Press F5 or click the Run button, and you can now execute and step through your managed stored procedure in a single environment.

36

You may first need to acknowledge a dialog window that asks whether it's okay to enable SQLCLR debugging on the server. Answer in the affirmative, unless you're in a non-testing environment.

Using Managed User-Defined Functions (UDFs)

Using SQL Server 2005 and the .NET Framework, you can write both scalar (single-valued) and table-valued user-defined functions in managed code. Scalar functions are the easier of the two, so we'll look at them first.

Scalar UDFs

In Visual Studio, you should right-click your SQLCLR project in the Solution Explorer and select Add, Add New Function. Next, you should name this new class XSLT, and when it opens up in the code editor, you should rename its default method to XSLTransform because that's what it will be doing: transforming the XML content of an xml typed variable using XSLT with a stylesheet that is also stored in an xml column.

The xml data type lets you take advantage of server-side storage of XML, and why not leverage that technology to store XSLT stylesheets? You'll have the assurance that before you save your XSLTs to the table, they are well formed.

You need to add using statements to the newly created XSLT.cs for the namespaces System.IO, System.Xml, and System.Xml.Xsl. You need System.IO to use the streams it offers (not to write files), and you need the new XslCompiledTransform object to perform the transformation.

Listing 36.6 shows the code of our new scalar function.

LISTING 36.6   A Managed Scalar UDF for Transforming XML

```
using System;
using System.Data;
using System.Data.Sql;
using System.Data.SqlTypes;
using Microsoft.SqlServer.Server;
// added:
using System.IO;
using System.Xml;
using System.Xml.Xsl;

public class XSLT
{
    [Microsoft.SqlServer.Server.SqlFunction(
        DataAccess = DataAccessKind.None,
        IsDeterministic=false,
        IsPrecise=true,
        Name="XSLTransform",
        SystemDataAccess=SystemDataAccessKind.None
    )]
```

LISTING 36.6   Continued

```
    public static SqlXml XSLTransform(SqlXml InputXml, SqlXml XSLT)
    {
        MemoryStream ms = new MemoryStream();
        XslCompiledTransform xslcomp = new XslCompiledTransform(false);
        xslcomp.Load(XSLT.CreateReader());
        xslcomp.Transform(InputXml.CreateReader(), null, ms);
        ms.Seek(0, SeekOrigin.Begin);
        XmlTextReader xreader = new XmlTextReader(ms);
        return new SqlXml(xreader);
    }
};
```

Notice the use of the new `SqlFunction` attribute and its named parameter list. The implementation contract for managed scalar functions is just the same as for stored procedures: You just mark it as `static` and decorate it with the appropriate attribute.

The following named parameters are available for scalar UDFs:

- ▶ **DataAccess**—Tells SQL Server whether the function will access user table data on the server in its body. If you provide the enum value `DataAccessKind.None`, some optimizations may be made.

- ▶ **SystemDataAccess**—Tells SQL Server whether the function will access system table data on the server in its body. Again, if you provide the enum value `SystemDataAccessKind.None`, some optimizations may be made.

- ▶ **IsDeterministic**—Tells SQL Server whether the function will always return the same values, given the same input parameters.

  A common example of a nondeterministic function is `GETDATE()`, which always returns something different. A function is also said to be nondeterministic if any of the functions that it calls are nondeterministic. `ISNUMERIC()` is a good example of a deterministic function.

- ▶ **IsPrecise**—Tells SQL Server whether the function does floating-point arithmetic (in which case, you provide the value `false`). Precise functions can be indexed; nonprecise functions cannot.

- ▶ **Name**—Tells the deployment routine what to call the function when it is created in the database.

What's neat about the code in Listing 36.6 is that it performs the entire XML transformation without using file I/O (except for the I/O required for SQL Server's paging functionality). You should build and deploy the code in this listing to your instance of SQL Server.

36

To test this example, you should create the following table in `AdventureWorks` to hold XSLTs pertaining to the tables in the `HumanResources` schema:

```
CREATE TABLE HumanResources.XmlResources
(
    XmlResourceId int IDENTITY(1,1) PRIMARY KEY CLUSTERED,
    XmlResourceType int NOT NULL DEFAULT(1),
    XmlResourceName varchar(50) NOT NULL,
    XmlResource xml
)
```

You also need a stylesheet to test it. Listing 36.7 inserts into this table an XSLT which searches the XML in the Resume xml column of `JobCandidate` and pulls out the name and address info into a more simplified XML structure.

LISTING 36.7   Inserting the XSLT for a Managed Scalar UDF

```
INSERT HumanResources.XmlResources
SELECT
    1,
    'ResumeAddressTransformer',
    '<?xml version="1.0" ?>
<xsl:stylesheet
    xmlns:xsl="http://www.w3.org/1999/XSL/Transform"
    xmlns:ns="http://schemas.microsoft.com/sqlserver/2004/07/adventure-
➥works/Resume"
    version="1.0">
    <xsl:template match="ns:Resume">
        <NameAndAddress>
            <xsl:apply-templates/>
        </NameAndAddress>
    </xsl:template>

    <xsl:template match="ns:Name">
        <Name>
            <xsl:value-of select="ns:Name.First"/>
            <xsl:text disable-output-escaping="yes"> </xsl:text>
            <xsl:value-of select="ns:Name.Last"/>
        </Name>
    </xsl:template>

    <xsl:template match="ns:Address[ns:Addr.Type=''Home'']">
        <HomeAddress>
            <HomeStreet>
                <xsl:value-of select="ns:Addr.Street"/>
            </HomeStreet>
```

LISTING 36.7   Continued

```
          <HomeCity>
               <xsl:value-of
➥select="ns:Addr.Location/ns:Location/ns:Loc.City"/>
          </HomeCity>
          <HomeState>
               <xsl:value-of
➥select="ns:Addr.Location/ns:Location/ns:Loc.State"/>
          </HomeState>
          <HomeZip>
               <xsl:value-of select="ns:Addr.PostalCode"/>
          </HomeZip>
        </HomeAddress>
    </xsl:template>
    <xsl:template match="node()"/>
</xsl:stylesheet>
'
```

Now that you have your resource saved, you need to test it on some data. You should copy the code from Listing 36.7 into your code window and deploy your assembly. Then you need to copy the code in Listing 36.8 into an SSMS query window and execute it, preferably using the results-to-text (Ctrl+T) option.

You should use results-to-text here because the code in the listing executes the UDF and then, using query(), performs an XQuery against the results of the transformation (itself an instance of the xml data type) to reformat the content as textual output for use by a mail merge program.

LISTING 36.8   Running the XSLT UDF and Retransforming the Output

```
DECLARE @inputXML xml, @XSLT xml

SELECT @inputXML = Resume
FROM HumanResources.JobCandidate
WHERE Resume.exist('
    declare namespace
    ns="http://schemas.microsoft.com/sqlserver/2004/07/adventure-works/Resume";
    /ns:Resume/ns:Name[ns:Name.First="Shai"]
') = 1

SELECT @XSLT = XmlResource
FROM HumanResources.XmlResources
WHERE XmlResourceName = 'ResumeAddressTransformer'

SELECT dbo.XSLTransform(@inputXML, @XSLT).query('
    declare namespace
```

LISTING 36.8   Continued

```
    ns="http://schemas.microsoft.com/sqlserver/2004/07/adventure-works/Resume";

    text {(/NameAndAddress/Name/text())[1]},
    text {"&#10;"},
    text {(/NameAndAddress/HomeAddress/HomeStreet/text())[1]},
    text {"&#10;"},
    text {(/NameAndAddress/HomeAddress/HomeCity/text())[1]},
    text {", "},
    text {(/NameAndAddress/HomeAddress/HomeState/text())[1]},
    text {(/NameAndAddress/HomeAddress/HomeZip/text())[1]}
') AS StreetAddress
go
StreetAddress
------------
Shai Bassli
567 3rd Ave
Saginaw, MI 53900
(1 row(s) affected)
```

Table-Valued UDFs (TVFs)

Like scalar UDFs, table-valued UDFs (TVFs) use the SqlFunction attribute, except that for TVFs, two additional named parameters are available:

▶ **TableDefinition**—Because you'll be returning a table, you need to tell the compiler what the schema of that table will be. TableDefinition takes a string that corresponds to the column definition list used in the CREATE TABLE statement (that is, *ColumnName ColumnDataType Constraints (etc)*).

▶ **FillRowMethodName**—At execution time, each row in the returned table is represented in the class as an array of object (for example, in C#, Object[]). SQL Server needs to call a particular method of the TVF's class on a per-row basis that takes an empty array of object and fills each value of the array with an appropriate column value for the current row.

As you may have already surmised, SQL Server relies quite a bit on the .NET interfaces IEnumerable and IEnumerator to build a table of rows.

The main method of any TVF must be decorated with the SqlFunction attribute and also must implement IEnumerable. This simply means it must provide a parameterless method called GetEnumerator() that returns an instance of an object that implements IEnumerator.

The object that implements IEnumerator in turn implements the MoveNext() and Reset() methods and the Current property. To those who have used and implemented .NET Framework collections, this should seem like a straightforward approach.

It may be useful to think of SQL Server as the "user" that calls the implemented methods of the code. This is because the actual runtime caller only needs to specify the name of the SqlFunction object; the caller doesn't need to know (or care) how things actually get called under the covers at runtime.

One thing on everyone's wish list for T-SQL has always been the use of regular expressions because the LIKE operator just isn't powerful enough for many matches. The code in Listing 36.9 contains a set of classes for a TVF that acts as a regular expression evaluator. It's unique from many examples out there in a few respects:

- ▶ It takes an input string, a user-defined type (covered later in this chapter) that represents a regular expression pattern (the RegexPattern UDF provides built-in pattern validation and storage), and an Int32 that represents the .NET Framework System.Text.RegularExpressions.RegexOptions enum.

- ▶ It returns a two-column table of results, one row per match:

  - ▶ The first column is an incremental ID for the match.

  - ▶ The second column is an instance of the xml data type that contains the text of the match, the groups matched, and their respective captures.

The neat thing is that you can use this class just as you would the Regex.Match() method, options and all, and get a complete report of the matches on a per-match (think *per-row*) basis.

LISTING 36.9   A Table-Valued UDF for Pattern Matching

```
using System;
using System.Data;
using System.Data.Sql;
using System.Data.SqlTypes;
using Microsoft.SqlServer.Server;

//added
using System.Text.RegularExpressions;
using System.Collections;
using System.Xml;
using System.IO;
using System.Data.SqlClient;

public class RegexLibrary
{
  [Microsoft.SqlServer.Server.SqlFunction
  (
    IsDeterministic = true,
    IsPrecise = true,
    Name = "MatchAll",
```

LISTING 36.9   Continued

```
    DataAccess = DataAccessKind.None,
    SystemDataAccess = SystemDataAccessKind.None,
    FillRowMethodName = "FillMatchAll",
    TableDefinition =
        @"MatchIndex int,
          GroupList xml"
)]
public static IEnumerable MatchAll(string Input,
    RegexPattern Expression, Int32 Options)
{
  return new RegexReader(Input, Expression, Options);
}

public static void FillMatchAll(
    object row,
    out SqlInt32 MatchIndex,
    out SqlXml GroupList)
{
  Object[] RowArray = (Object[])row;
  MatchIndex = (SqlInt32)RowArray[0];
  GroupList = (SqlXml)RowArray[1];
}

public class RegexReader : IEnumerable
{
  public String input = string.Empty;
  public RegexPattern Expression;
  public Int32 Options = int.MinValue;

  public RegexReader(String Input, RegexPattern Expression, Int32 Options)
  {
    this.input = Input;
    this.Expression = Expression;
    this.Options = Options;
  }

  //Called by SS after initialization
  public IEnumerator GetEnumerator()
  {
    return new RegexEnumerator(this);
  }
}

public class RegexEnumerator : IEnumerator
```

LISTING 36.9   Continued

```csharp
{
  private Regex _rex = null;
  private Match _match = null;
  private Object[] _current = null;
  private RegexReader _reader = null;
  private int _matchIndex = 0;

  public RegexEnumerator(RegexReader Reader)
  {
    _reader = Reader;
    Reset();
  }

  public void Reset()
  {
    _rex = null;
    _matchIndex = 0;
    _current = null;
    _rex = new Regex(_reader.Expression.ToString(),
      (RegexOptions)_reader.Options);
    _match = _rex.Match(_reader.input);
  }

  public bool MoveNext()
  {
    if (_match.Success)
    {
      _matchIndex++;
      _current = new Object[6];
      _current[0] = (SqlInt32)_matchIndex;

      string GroupList = @"<matchlog pattern='" + _rex.ToString() +
              "' options='" + _rex.Options.ToString() + "' idx='" +
              _matchIndex.ToString() +
              "' matchtext='" + _match.ToString() + "'>";

      for (int g = 1; g < _match.Groups.Count; g++)
      {
        Group grp = _match.Groups[g];
        GroupList += "<group idx='" + g.ToString() +
              "' text='" + grp + "'>";

        string CaptureList = string.Empty;
        CaptureCollection caps = grp.Captures;
```

36

LISTING 36.9   Continued

```
        for (int c = 0; c < caps.Count; c++)
        {
          Capture cap = caps[c];
          CaptureList += "<capture idx='" + c + "' pos='" +
            cap.Index.ToString() + "' text='" + cap + "'/>";
        }

        GroupList += CaptureList + "</group>";
      }

      GroupList += "</matchlog>";
      _current[1] = new SqlXml(
                new XmlTextReader(
                  new StringReader(GroupList)));
      _match = _match.NextMatch();
      return true;
    }
    else
    {
      return false;
    }
  }

  public Object Current
  {
    get {
      return _current;
    }
  }
 }
}
```

When MatchAll() is invoked, it returns an instance of the RegexReader class. In its constructor, RegexReader sets the passed-in regular expression, input string, and options to its data members. Then, at initialization time, SQL Server invokes RegexReader's GetEnumerator() instance method, which returns an instance of RegexEnumerator, which does all the real work, utilizing the members of the RegexReader object that is passed into its constructor and set to its private _reader object.

Reset() is called in RegexEnumerator's constructor so that it can initialize its members in the following way:

▶ RegexEnumerator uses a private Regex object (_rex) for performing the match and stores the resulting array of Match (Match[]) in a private Regex.Match object (_match).

- The ordinal number of the match is kept in _matchIndex and initialized to 0 (in case there are no matches).

- When Reset() is complete, it is up to SQL Server to iterate through the matches by calling MoveNext().

MoveNext() does the work of re-creating the row (represented as a private array of object called _current) for every successful match stored in _match:

- _match[0] is set to the value of _matchIndex (incremented on a per-match basis) and corresponds to the output table column (defined in the TableDefinition named parameter) MatchIndex.

- _match[1] is set to the value of an XML document that is built for every match and contains subnodes for each group and group capture. This value corresponds to the output table column GroupList.

When SQL Server uses the RegexEnumerator, it first calls MoveNext() and then uses the Current property.

Next, execution passes to the method specified in FillRowMethodName (FillMatchAll()).

Finally, the CLR passes the latest value of _current to FillMatchAll() as the row parameter. Each out parameter of FillMatchAll() is set to the value for the columns in the output row.

> **NOTE**
>
> If this seems a daunting implementation, the best way to overcome that is by walking though the function line-by-line in debug mode, using Visual Studio 2005.

Deploy the code in listing 45.9 to SQL Server so you can test the example to see what it can do for you:

```
DECLARE @rp3 RegexPattern
SET @rp3 = '(sil)'
SELECT *
FROM dbo.MatchAll('Silly Sils', @rp3, 513);
go
MatchIndex   GroupList
-------------------------------------------------------------------------
1            <matchlog
               pattern="(sil)"
               options="IgnoreCase, CultureInvariant"
               idx="1"
               matchtext="Sil">
               <group
```

```
              idx="1"
              text="Sil">
              <capture
                idx="0"
                pos="0"
                text="Sil" />
            </group>
          </matchlog>
2         <matchlog
            pattern="(sil)"
            options="IgnoreCase, CultureInvariant"
            idx="2"
            matchtext="Sil">
            <group
              idx="1"
              text="Sil">
              <capture
                idx="0"
                pos="6"
                text="Sil" />
            </group>
          </matchlog>
(2 row(s) affected)
```

Using Managed User-Defined Types (UDTs)

In the preceding section, you used a managed UDT called RegexPattern to store the regular expression pattern. In this section, you'll explore how custom UDTs are built and used in SQL Server.

The first thing to note is that although the name *UDT* is the same as the extended data types built using SQL Server 2000, they are by no means the same in SQL Server 2005. SQL Server 2000's UDTs have actually been retronamed "alias data types" for SQL Server 2005. SQL Server 2005 UDTs are *structs* (value types) built using the .NET Framework.

To create a UDT of your own, you right-click your Visual Studio project and then select Add, User-Defined Type. Next, you should name both the class and its auto-generated method RegexPattern. Notice the attribute used to decorate the RegexPattern struct: SqlUserDefinedType. Its constructor has the following parameters:

▶ **Format**—Tells SQL Server how serialization (and its complement, deserialization) of the struct should be done. You specify Format.Native to let SQL Server handle serialization for you. You specify Format.UserDefined to do your own serialization.

When Format.UserDefined is specified, the struct must implement the IBinarySerialize interface to explicitly take the values from string (or int, or whatever the value passed into the constructor of the type is) back to binary and vice versa.

▶ **A named parameter list**—This list contains the following:

    ▶ **IsFixedLength**—Tells SQL Server that the byte count of the struct is the same for all its instances.

    ▶ **IsByteOrdered**—Tells SQL Server that the bytes of the struct are ordered so that it may be used in binary comparisons, as with `ORDER BY`, `GROUP BY`, or `PARTITION BY` clauses, in indexing, and when the UDT as a primary or foreign key.

    ▶ **MaxByteSize**—Tells SQL Server not to allow more than the specified number of bytes to be held in an instance of the UDT. The overall limit is 8KB. You must specify this when using `Format.UserDefined`.

    ▶ **Name**—Tells the deployment routine what to call the UDT when it is created in the database.

    ▶ **ValidationMethodName**—Tells SQL Server which method of the struct to use to validate it when it has been deserialized (in certain cases).

The implementation contract for any UDT is as follows:

▶ It must provide a static method called `Parse()`, used by SQL Server for conversion to the struct from a string.

▶ It must provide an instance method that overrides the default `ToString()` method for converting from the struct to a string.

▶ It must implement the `INullable` interface, providing a Boolean instance method called `IsNull`, used by SQL Server to determine whether an instance is null.

▶ It must have a static property called `Null` of the type of the struct. This property returns an instance of the struct whose value is `null` (that is, where `IsNull` is true for that instance). (This concept seems to be derived from the "null object" design pattern.)

Also, you need to be aware that UDTs can have only read-only static fields, they cannot use inheritance, and they cannot have overloaded methods (except the constructor, whose overloads are mainly used when ADO.NET is the calling context).

Given these fairly stringent requirements, Listing 36.10 provides an implementation of a UDT representing a regular expression pattern.

LISTING 36.10   A UDT Representing a Regular Expression Pattern

```
using System;
using System.Data;
using System.Data.Sql;
using System.Data.SqlTypes;
using Microsoft.SqlServer.Server;
```

LISTING 36.10   Continued

```
//added
using System.Text.RegularExpressions;

[Serializable]
[Microsoft.SqlServer.Server.SqlUserDefinedType(
  Format.UserDefined, // requires IBinarySerialize
  IsFixedLength=false,
  IsByteOrdered=true,
  MaxByteSize=250,
  ValidationMethodName = "RegexPatternValidator"
)]
public struct RegexPattern : INullable, IBinarySerialize
{
  //instance data fields
  private Regex _reg;
  private bool _null;

  //constructor
  public RegexPattern(String Pattern)
  {
    reg = new Regex(Pattern);
    null = (Pattern == String.Empty);
  }

  //instance method
  public override string ToString()
  {
    return _reg.ToString();
  }

  //instance property
  public bool IsNull
  {
    get
    {
      if (_reg == null || _reg.ToString() == string.Empty)
      {
        return true;
      }
      else
        return false;
    }
  }
```

LISTING 36.10   Continued

```csharp
//static method
public static RegexPattern Null
{
  get
  {
    RegexPattern NullInstance = new RegexPattern();
    NullInstance._null = true;
    return NullInstance;
  }
}

//static method
public static RegexPattern Parse(SqlString Pattern)
{
  if (Pattern.IsNull)
    return Null;
  else
  {
    RegexPattern u = new RegexPattern((String)Pattern);
    return u;
  }
}

//private instance method
private bool RegexPatternValidator()
{
  return (_reg.ToString() != string.Empty);
}

//instance method
public Int32 Match(String Input)
{
  Match m = _reg.Match(Regex.Escape(Input.ToString()));
  if (m != null)
    return Convert.ToInt32(m.Success);
  else
    return 0;
}

//instance property
public bool IsFullStringMatch
{
  get
  {
```

LISTING 36.10   Continued

```
      Match m = Regex.Match(_reg.ToString(), @"\^.+\$");
      if (m != null)
        return m.Success;
      else
        return false;
      }
    }

  //instance method
  [SqlMethod(
    DataAccess = DataAccessKind.None,
    IsMutator = false,
    IsPrecise = true,
    OnNullCall = false,
    SystemDataAccess = SystemDataAccessKind.None
  )]
  public Int32 MatchingGroupCount(SqlString Input)
  {
    Match m = _reg.Match(Regex.Escape(Input.ToString()));
    if (m != null)
      return m.Groups.Count;
    else
      return 0;
  }

  //static method
  [SqlMethod(
    DataAccess = DataAccessKind.None,
    IsMutator = false,
    IsPrecise = true,
    OnNullCall = false,
    SystemDataAccess = SystemDataAccessKind.None
  )]
  public static bool UsesLookaheads(RegexPattern p)
  // must be static to be called with :: syntax
  {
    Match m = Regex.Match(p.ToString(), @"\(\?[:¦!].+\)");
    if (m != null)
      return m.Success;
    else
      return false;
  }

  #region IBinarySerialize Members
```

LISTING 36.10   Continued

```
public void Read(System.IO.BinaryReader r)
{
  _reg = new Regex(r.ReadString());
}

public void Write(System.IO.BinaryWriter w)
{
  w.Write(_reg.ToString());
}

#endregion
}
```

As you can see by scanning this code, it meets the required implementation contract. In addition, it declares static and instance methods, as well as instance properties. Both static and instance methods can optionally be decorated with the `SqlMethod` attribute. By default, methods of UDTs are declared to be nondeterministic and non-*mutator*, meaning that they do not change the value of the instance.

You use the named parameters of `SqlMethod`'s constructor to override this and other behaviors. These are its named parameters:

- **DataAccess**—Tells SQL Server whether the method will access user table data on the server in its body. If you provide the `enum` value `DataAccessKind.None`, some optimizations may be made.

- **SystemDataAccess**—Tells SQL Server whether the method will access system table data on the server in its body. Again, if you provide the `enum` value `SystemDataAccessKind.None`, some optimizations may be made.

- **IsDeterministic**—Tells SQL Server whether the method always returns the same values, given the same input parameters.

- **IsMutator**—Must be set to true if the method changes the state of the instance.

- **Name**—Tells the deployment routine what to call the UDT when it is created in the database.

- **OnNullCall**—If any arguments to the method are null, returns null.

- **InvokeIfReceiverIsNull**—If the instance of the struct itself is null, indicates whether to invoke the method.

To create this type in SQL Server without using Visual Studio, you use the new CREATE TYPE DDL syntax, as follows:

```
CREATE TYPE RegexPattern EXTERNAL NAME SQLCLR.RegexPattern
```

Note that DROP TYPE *TypeName* is also available, but there is no ALTER TYPE statement.

A few words on the code in Listing 36.10: The constructor to RegexPattern validates the expression passed to it via the constructor of System.Text.RegularExpressions.Regex.

If you pass an invalid regex to the T-SQL SET statement (when declaring a variable of type RegexPattern) or when the UDT is used as a table column data type and a value is modified, the Regex class does its usual pattern validation, as it does in the .NET world.

Let's look at some of the ways you can use your UDT. The following example shows how to call all the public members (both static and instance) of RegexPattern:

```
DECLARE @rp RegexPattern
SET @rp = '(\w+)\s+?(?!bar)'

SELECT
    @rp.ToString() AS ToString,
    @rp.IsFullStringMatch AS FullStringMatch,
    @rp.Match('uncle freddie') AS Match,
    @rp.MatchingGroupCount('loves elken') AS GroupCount,
    RegexPattern::UsesLookaheads(@rp) AS UsesLH
go
ToString            FullStringMatch  Match  GroupCt   UsesLH
------------------------------------------------------------
(\w+)\s+?(?!bar)    0                1      2         1
(1 row(s) affected)
```

Note that static members can be called (without an instance, that is) by using the following new syntax:

TypeName::*MemberName*(*OptionalParameters*)

To try this, you can create a table and populate it as shown here:

```
CREATE TABLE dbo.RegexTest
(
  PatternId int IDENTITY(1,1),
  Pattern RegexPattern
)
GO
INSERT RegexTest SELECT '\d+'
INSERT RegexTest SELECT 'foo (?:bar)'
INSERT RegexTest SELECT '(\s+()'
Msg 6522, Level 16, State 2, Line 215
A .NET Framework error occurred during execution of user defined
routine or aggregate
➥ 'RegexPattern':
System.ArgumentException: parsing "(\s+()" - Not enough )'s.
```

```
System.ArgumentException:
   at System.Text.RegularExpressions.RegexParser.ScanRegex()
   at System.Text.RegularExpressions.RegexParser.Parse(String re,
➡RegexOptions op)
   at System.Text.RegularExpressions.Regex..ctor(String pattern,
➡RegexOptions options,
➡ Boolean useCache)
   at System.Text.RegularExpressions.Regex..ctor(String pattern)
   at RegexPattern..ctor(String Pattern)
   at RegexPattern.Parse(SqlString Pattern)
```

Whoops! Do you see what happens when you try to insert an invalid regex pattern into the `Pattern` column (the third insert statement)? The parenthesis count is off, so the CLR tells you so in the query window's output.

Because the UDT has the `IsByteOrdered` named parameter set to `true`, you can index this column (based on the struct's serialized value) and use it in `ORDER BY` statements. Here's an example:

```
CREATE NONCLUSTERED INDEX PatternIndex ON dbo.RegexTest(Pattern)
GO
SELECT
    Pattern.ToString(),
    RegexPattern::UsesLookaheads(Pattern)
FROM RegexTest
ORDER BY Pattern
go
PatString      UsesLookaheads
------------------------------
\d+            0
foo (?:bar)    1
(2 row(s) affected)
```

Back in ADO.NET land, you can access the UDT by using the new `SqlDbType.Udt` enum value. To try this, you can add a new C# Windows application to your sample solution. You can add a project reference to your sample project (`"SQLCLR"`) and then add a `using` statement for `System.Data.SqlClient`. Then you should add a list box to the form, called `lbRegexes`. Finally, you should add a button to the form, called `btnCallUDT`, double-click it, and add the code in Listing 36.11 to the body of its `OnClick` event handler.

LISTING 36.11   Using a UDT from ADO.NET in a Client Application

```
private void btnCallUDT_Click(object sender, EventArgs e)
{
    using (SqlConnection c =
    new SqlConnection(ConfigurationManager.AppSettings["connstring"]))
    {
```

LISTING 36.11   Continued

```
  using (SqlCommand s = new SqlCommand("SELECT Pattern FROM dbo.RegexTest", c))
  {
    c.Open();
    SqlDataReader r = s.ExecuteReader(CommandBehavior.CloseConnection);
    {
    while (r.Read())
    {
      RegexPattern p = (RegexPattern)r.GetValue(0);
      lbRegexes.Items.Add(p.ToString());
    }
    r.Close();
    }
  }
}
```

In this example, you selected all the rows from the sample table dbo.RegexText and then cast the Pattern column values into RegexPattern structs. Finally, you called the ToString() method of each struct, adding the text of the regex as a new item in the list box.

Figure 36.7 shows how your form might look as a finished product.

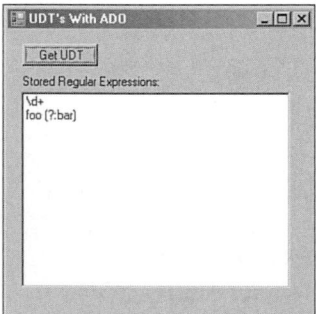

FIGURE 36.7   A test application for using managed UDTs with ADO.NET clients.

You can also create SqlParameter objects to be mapped to UDT columns by using code such as the following:

```
SqlParameter p = new SqlParameter("@Pattern", SqlDbType.Udt);
p.UdtTypeName = "RegexPattern";
p.Value = new RegexPattern("\d+\s+\d+");
command.Parameters.Add(p);
```

Finally, keep in mind that `FOR XML` does not implicitly serialize UDTs. You have to do that yourself, as in the following example:

```
SELECT Pattern.ToString() AS '@Regex'
FROM dbo.RegexTest
FOR XML PATH('Pattern'), ROOT('Patterns'), TYPE
go
<Patterns>
  <Pattern Regex="\d+" />
  <Pattern Regex="foo (?:bar)" />
</Patterns>
```

Using Managed User-Defined Aggregates (UDAs)

A highly specialized feature of SQL Server 2005, managed UDAs provide the ability to aggregate column data based on user-defined criteria built into .NET code. You can now extend the (somewhat small) list of aggregate functions usable inside SQL Server to include those you custom-define.

> **NOTE**
>
> If you've been following the examples in this chapter sequentially, at this point, you need to drop the sample table dbo.RegexTest to redeploy the assembly after creating the UDA example.

The implementation contract for a UDA requires the following:

- ▶ A static method called `Init()`, used to initialize any data fields in the struct, particularly the field that contains the aggregated value.

- ▶ A static method called `Terminate()`, used to return the aggregated value to the UDA's caller.

- ▶ A static method called `Aggregate()`, used to add the value in the current row to the growing value.

- ▶ A static method called `Merge()`, used when SQL Server breaks an aggregation task into multiple threads of execution (SQL Server actually uses a thread abstraction called a *task*), each of which needs to merge the value stored in its instance of the UDA with the growing value.

UDAs cannot do any data access, nor can they have any side-effects—meaning they cannot change the state of the database. They take only a single input parameter, of any type. You can also add public methods or properties other than those required by the contract (such as the `IsPrime()` method used in the following example).

Like UDTs, UDAs are structs. They are decorated with the `SqlUserDefinedAggregate` attribute, which has the following parameters for its constructor:

▶ **Format**—Tells SQL Server how serialization (and its complement, deserialization) of the struct should be done. This has the same possible values and meaning as described earlier for `SqlUserDefinedType`.

▶ A named parameter list—This list contains the following:

    ▶ **IsInvariantToDuplicates**—Tells SQL Server whether the UDA behaves differently with respect to duplicate values passed in from multiple rows.

    ▶ **IsInvariantToNulls**—Tells SQL Server whether the UDA behaves differently when null values are passed to it.

    ▶ **IsInvariantToOrder**—Tells SQL Server whether the UDA cares about the order in which column values are fed to it.

    ▶ **IsNullIfEmpty**—Tells SQL Server that the UDA will return null if its aggregated value is empty (that is, if its value is 0, or the empty string "", and so on).

    ▶ **Name**—Tells the deployment routine what to call the UDA when it is created in the database.

    ▶ **MaxByteSize**—Tells SQL Server not to allow more than the specified number of bytes to be held in an instance of the UDA. You must specify this when using `Format.UserDefined`.

For this example, you'll implement a very simple UDA that sums values in an integer column, but only if they are prime. Listing 36.12 shows the code to do this.

LISTING 36.12   A UDA That Sums Prime Numbers

```
using System;
using System.Data;
using System.Data.Sql;
using System.Data.SqlTypes;
using Microsoft.SqlServer.Server;

[Serializable]
[Microsoft.SqlServer.Server.SqlUserDefinedAggregate(
  Format.Native,
  IsInvariantToDuplicates=false,
  IsInvariantToNulls=true,
  IsInvariantToOrder=true,
  IsNullIfEmpty=true
)]
public struct SumPrime
{
```

LISTING 36.12   Continued

```
  SqlInt64 Sum;

  private bool IsPrime(SqlInt64 Number)
  {
    for (int i = 2; i < Number; i++)
    {
      if (Number % i == 0)
      {
        return false;
       }
     }
     return true;
  }

  public void Init()
  {
    Sum = 0;
  }

  public void Accumulate(SqlInt64 Value)
  {
    if (!Value.IsNull && IsPrime(Value) && Value > 1)
      Sum += Value;
  }

  public void Merge(SumPrime Prime)
  {
    Sum += Prime.Sum;
  }

  public SqlInt64 Terminate()
  {
      return Sum;
  }
}
```

In this code, SQL Server first calls Init(), initializing the private Sum data field to 0.

For each column value passed to the aggregate, the Accumulate() method is called, wherein Sum is increased by the value of the column, if it is prime.

When multiple threads converge, Merge() is called, adding the values stored in each instance (as the Prime parameter) to Sum.

When the rowset has been completely parsed, SQL Server calls `Terminate()`, wherein the accumulated value `Sum` is returned.

The following are the results of testing `SumPrime` on `Production.Product` (an existing AdventureWorks table):

```
SELECT TOP 10 dbo.SumPrime(p.ProductId) AS PrimeSum, p.Name
FROM Production.Product p
JOIN Production.WorkOrder o ON
o.ProductId = p.ProductId
WHERE Name LIKE '%Frame%'
GROUP BY p.ProductId, p.Name
ORDER BY PrimeSum DESC
go
PrimeSum   Name
------------------------------------------
360355     HL Mountain Frame - Black, 42
338462     HL Mountain Frame - Silver, 42
266030     HL Road Frame - Red, 48
214784     HL Road Frame - Black, 48
133937     HL Touring Frame - Yellow, 46
68338      LL Road Frame - Red, 52
54221      LL Mountain Frame - Silver, 48
15393      ML Road Frame - Red, 52
0          HL Mountain Frame - Black, 38
0          HL Road Frame - Black, 44
(10 row(s) affected.)
```

The following is the DDL syntax for this UDA:

```
CREATE AGGREGATE SumPrime(@Number bigint)
RETURNS bigint
EXTERNAL NAME SQLCLR.SumPrime
```

As with UDTs, with UDAs there is no `ALTER AGGREGATE`, but you can use `DROP AGGREGATE` to drop them.

Using Managed Triggers

Managed triggers are static methods of a .NET class decorated with the new `SqlTrigger` attribute. `SqlTrigger` has three named parameters:

- ▶ **Event**—A required string-valued parameter that tells SQL Server which type of trigger you're defining, as is done when defining T-SQL triggers.

- ▶ **Target**—A required string-valued parameter that tells SQL Server which schema and table you're attaching the trigger to.

- ▶ **Name**—An optional string parameter that tells the deployment routine what to call the trigger when it is created in the database.

The implementation contract for a managed trigger is only that it be a static method that returns void.

Inside the method body of a managed trigger, you need to get a reference to the execution context of the trigger so you can find out what Data Manipulation Language (DML) statement the trigger is responding to and which columns have been updated. You do this by using the `SqlContext.TriggerContext` object of type `SqlTriggerContext`. (Note that this object is null when used in non-trigger contexts.) It has the following members:

- ▶ **ColumnCount**—An integer property that indicates how many columns were affected by the operation.

- ▶ **IsUpdatedColumn**—A Boolean method that indicates whether the column at a specific position was updated during the operation.

- ▶ **TriggerAction**—Enum that indicates which operation caused the trigger to fire. For DML triggers, this is either `TriggerAction.Insert`, `TriggerAction.Update`, or `TriggerAction.Delete`. For DDL triggers, the list is quite a bit longer. Refer to MSDN to see all the possible values of the `TriggerAction` enumeration.

- ▶ **EventData**—In the case of a DDL trigger, an object of type `SqlXml` that contains an XML document whose content explains the DDL that just fired. (The XML content model for this object is the same as that returned by the `EVENTDATA()` built-in function.)

Have you ever wanted to be notified by email that some important column value in your tables has been created or updated? There are many ways to do this, including using Query Notifications (discussed earlier in this chapter, in the section "Query Notification"). You can also accomplish this by writing a managed trigger that calls a web service, which in turn sends an email.

Up until now, you haven't had to decrease the runtime safety of your assembly. But because certain aspects of web services use the `Synchronized` attribute (which means they do thread synchronization), we'll have to change our SQLCLR assembly's permission set to `UNSAFE`.

CAUTION

Only the `sysadmin` role can upload an `UNSAFE` assembly to SQL Server. You should allow this uploading only when you know the code being uploaded doesn't do anything that might compromise the integrity of the data, the server, or your job.

First, you need to create a simple web service routine that sends our email. To do this using Visual Studio 2005, you create a new local IIS website called `photoserve` and add to it a new web service called `PhotoService.asmx`. Then you replace the entire body of `PhotoService.cs` with the following C# code:

```
using System;
using System.Web.Services;
```

36

```
using System.Net.Mail;
using System.Configuration;

[WebService(Namespace = "urn:www-samspublishing-com:examples:sqlclr:triggers")]
[WebServiceBinding(ConformsTo = WsiProfiles.BasicProfile1_1)]
public class PhotoService : System.Web.Services.WebService
{
  [WebMethod]
  public void PhotoUpdateNotify(int ProductPhotoId)
  {
    MailMessage m = new MailMessage();
    m.Subject = "New Photo: " + ProductPhotoId.ToString();
    m.From = new MailAddress("ProductPhotoService@localservername");
    m.Body = "http://localhost:1347/photoserve/getphoto.aspx?ppid=" +
        ProductPhotoId.ToString();
    m.To.Add(new MailAddress("PhotoAdmin@ localservername "));
    SmtpClient s = new SmtpClient("localservername", 25);
    s.Send(m);
  }
}
```

Of course, you need to have SMTP and IIS correctly configured on your server for our
example to completely work. You also need to replace localhost and localservername
and the email account names shown in the code with values that work for you.

Next, you should add a new web form to the site, called getphoto.aspx. You replace the
entire contents of getphoto.aspx.cs with the code in Listing 36.13.

LISTING 36.13   A Web Form That Retrieves Photos from SQL Server

```
using System;
using System.Data;
using System.Configuration;
using System.Web;
//added:
using System.Data.SqlClient;
using System.IO;

public partial class getphoto : System.Web.UI.Page
{
  protected void Page_Load(object sender, EventArgs e)
  {
    if (Request.QueryString["ppid"] != null)
    {
      string ppid = Request.QueryString["ppid"].ToString();
      string FileName = "photos/" + ppid + ".jpeg";
```

LISTING 36.13   Continued

```csharp
      string MappedFileName = Server.MapPath(FileName);
      using (SqlConnection c =
        new SqlConnection(
          "Data Source=(local);Initial Catalog=AdventureWorks;
➡Integrated Security=True"
        )
      )
      {
        using (SqlCommand s = new SqlCommand(
            @"SELECT LargePhoto
              FROM Production.ProductPhoto
              WHERE ProductPhotoId = " + ppid, c))
        {
          c.Open();
          using (SqlDataAdapter a = new SqlDataAdapter(s))
          {
            using (DataSet d = new DataSet())
            {
              a.Fill(d);
              if (d.Tables.Count == 1 && d.Tables[0].Rows.Count == 1)
              {
                byte[] BigImg = (byte[])d.Tables[0].Rows[0]["LargePhoto"];
                FileStream f =
                  new FileStream(
                    MappedFileName,
                    FileMode.Create,
                    FileAccess.Write);
                f.Write(BigImg, 0, BigImg.GetUpperBound(0));
                f.Close();
                Response.Redirect(FileName, false);
              }
              else
              {
                Response.Write("<H2>Sorry, ProductPhotoId " + ppid
                  + " was not found.</H2>");
              }
            }
          }
        }
      }
    }
    else
    {
    Response.Write("<H2>A querystring value for ppid is required.</H2>");
```

36

LISTING 36.13   Continued

```
      }
    }
}
```

Next, you add a subfolder to the site called photos. This is where the web form will save product photos as JPEG files and redirect the email recipient. The main body of the code in Listing 36.13 illustrates how to save LOB values to file in a succinct manner, so it may prove useful for your other applications.

You need to either give your ASP.NET user file I/O permissions on photos or have the web application impersonate a user who has those permissions.

To recap, the website code so far consists of the following: a web service (PhotoService.asmx) that generates notification emails containing URLs. These URLs in turn point to a web form (getphoto.aspx) that saves the varbinary value of Production.ProductPhoto.LargePhoto (given a particular ProductPhotoId) to the photos folder as [ProductPhotoId].jpeg.

The last item you need is the reason you're writing this code in the first place: a managed trigger that invokes the web service to kick off the whole process. To add this, you right-click the SQLCLR project and then select Add, Trigger. Name this new trigger class Triggers.cs (the default). Then replace the entire content of Triggers.cs with the code in Listing 36.14.

LISTING 36.14   A Managed Trigger That Invokes a Web Service

```csharp
using System;
using System.Data;
using Microsoft.SqlServer.Server;

//added:
using System.Data.SqlClient;
using SQLCLR.photoserve;

public partial class Triggers
{
  [Microsoft.SqlServer.Server.SqlTrigger(
    Event = "FOR UPDATE",
    Name = "Production.PhotoUpdateTrigger",
    Target = "Production.ProductPhoto"
  )]
  public static void PhotoUpdateTrigger()
  {
    SqlTriggerContext stc = SqlContext.TriggerContext;
    if (stc.TriggerAction == TriggerAction.Update)
    {
```

LISTING 36.14   Continued

```
    if (stc.IsUpdatedColumn(3)) //The LargePhoto varbinary(max) column
    {
      using (SqlCommand s = new SqlCommand(
        "SELECT DISTINCT ProductPhotoId FROM INSERTED",
        new SqlConnection("context connection=true")))
      {
        s.Connection.Open();
        using (SqlDataReader r =
          s.ExecuteReader(CommandBehavior.CloseConnection))
        {
          PhotoService p = new PhotoService();
          while (r.Read())
          {
            SqlContext.Pipe.Send(
              "Notifying Web Service of Update for PPID: " +
              r.GetInt32(0).ToString());
            p.PhotoUpdateNotify(r.GetInt32(0));
          }
        }
      }
    }
  }
}
```

Now that all the code is in place, all that's left is an explanation of the code of PhotoUpdateTrigger(), and a test case.

In the code in Listing 36.14, you check to see whether the current TriggerAction is TriggerAction.Update, meaning that the trigger is firing due to an update. You declare this to be true by using the Event named parameter of the SqlTrigger attribute.

Next, you select the ProductPhotoId of the updated row from the INSERTED table and connect to the database by using the context connection.

You execute the command and get your SqlDataReader (r), then you instantiate the PhotoService web service. Using the overloaded method of the Pipe object, you send a string literal informational message (equivalent to T-SQL's print function), which tells any clients what's about to happen. You call the PhotoUpdateNotify method of the web service and pass in the ProductPhotoId, which in turn sends the email containing the link back to getphoto.aspx, which generates the photo JPEG for that ProductPhotoId.

To make the test case work, you need to make your local machine's Network Service user a SQL Server login and a user in AdventureWorks with at least db_datareader access. In addition, it may be necessary to use the Visual Studio `sgen.exe` tool to create a serialization assembly for `SQLCLR.dll` (which `sgen.exe` would, by default, name `SQLCLR.XmlSerializers.dll`).

You'll need to load this serialization assembly into `AdventureWorks` before loading the main assembly (using `CREATE ASSEMBLY`). (At the time of this writing, it was necessary to also load `System.Web.dll` and its dependencies into `AdventureWorks` before loading the application assemblies.)

To test the trigger, you simply update a value of `Production.ProductPhoto.LargePhoto`:

```
UPDATE Production.ProductPhoto
SET LargePhoto = LargePhoto
WHERE ProductPhotoId = 69
go
Notifying Web Service of Update for PPID: 69
(1 row(s) affected.)
```

If you get an email in your test inbox, you've done everything right. If not, don't fret; this is a challenging example developed mainly to show the power of managed code.

Using Transactions

When writing managed objects, just as with T-SQL, it's important to be aware of the current transaction context under which your code may be running.

Managed database objects have the option of making use of the classes in the new `System.Transactions` namespace to control transactions. The following are the main objects you use to do this:

- ▶ **Transaction.Current**—This is a static object of type `Transaction` that represents the current transaction. You use this object to explicitly roll back the current transaction (using `Rollback()`). It contains an `IsolationLevel` property that indicates the current transaction isolation level, as well as a `TransactionCompleted` event that your objects may subscribe to and a `TranactionInformation` property that indicates `TransactionStatus` and other attributes of the transaction. You can also use this object to manually enlist additional objects in the current transaction.

- ▶ **TransactionScope**—This object represents a transactional scope that is used to wrap managed code. Note that transactions automatically roll back unless they are explicitly committed using this object's `Complete()` method. It is enough to merely instantiate this object at the beginning of the managed code: If a current transaction is active, the instantiated object assumes that transaction; if not, a new transaction is initiated.

Note that it is not necessary to explicitly declare or even use transactions: If your managed code is already running in the scope of a transaction, it automatically participates in that transaction. (To turn this behavior off, you append `"enlist=false"` to your connection string.) In fact, even if your code opens additional connections on additional servers, the transaction context is not only preserved but is automatically promoted to a distributed transaction that enlists all the connections involved. (The MSDTC service must be running for distributed transactions to work.)

One thing you cannot do with managed transactions that you can with T-SQL is begin a new transaction and then just leave it open.

The code example in Listing 36.15 illustrates the use of the System.Transactions objects in a managed stored procedure. You need to add a new managed stored procedure to the SQLCLR project and call it SPTrans. Then you need to add the using statement using System.Transactions; and replace the autogenerated method with the code from Listing 36.15.

LISTING 36.15   Using Transactions in a Managed Stored Procedure

```
[SqlProcedure]
public static void SpTrans()
{
  TransactionScope ts = null;
  try
  {
    SqlContext.Pipe.Send("Proc Started");
    if (Transaction.Current != null)
    {
      SqlContext.Pipe.Send("A) Current tran is not null.");
      SqlContext.Pipe.Send("A) About to rollback current tran...");
      Transaction.Current.Rollback(
        new ApplicationException("I wanted to do this."));
      SqlContext.Pipe.Send("A) Rollback Complete.");
    }
    else
    {
      SqlContext.Pipe.Send("A) Current tran is null.");
    }

    ts = new System.Transactions.TransactionScope();
    SqlContext.Pipe.Send("New Tran Started");
    if (Transaction.Current != null)
      SqlContext.Pipe.Send("B) Current tran is not null.");
    else
      SqlContext.Pipe.Send("B) Current tran is null.");

    if (ts != null)
      ts.Complete();
      SqlContext.Pipe.Send("B) Complete() is Complete.");
  }
```

36

LISTING 36.15   Continued

```
finally
{
  if (ts != null)
    ts.Dispose();
  SqlContext.Pipe.Send("Proc Complete");
}
}
```

To test this code, you simply run the stored procedure from a query window (or use sqlcmd.exe) inside and outside a transactional scope and watch the results. Here's an example:

```
BEGIN TRAN
EXEC dbo.SpTrans
ROLLBACK TRAN
EXEC dbo.SPTrans
```

Using the Related System Catalogs

As with other database objects, SQL Server provides catalog views that enable you to view loaded managed assemblies, routines, and types. The base view for finding these objects is sys.assemblies.

To see which assemblies have been loaded (including the one you created in this chapter), you use the following query:

```
SELECT TOP 5
    name,
    assembly_id,
    permission_set_desc as permission_set
FROM sys.assemblies
ORDER BY assembly_id desc
go
name                           assembly_id    permission_set
------------------------------------------------------------
SQLCLR                         65719          UNSAFE_ACCESS
System.Configuration.Install   65705          UNSAFE_ACCESS
System.ServiceProcess          65704          UNSAFE_ACCESS
System.Web.RegularExpressions  65703          UNSAFE_ACCESS
System.Drawing.Design          65702          UNSAFE_ACCESS
```

Now that you have the `assembly_id` for your SQLCLR project (yours will not be the same value as shown here), you can look up its routines and classes in `sys.assembly_modules`:

```
SELECT TOP 5
    name,
    assembly_class as class,
    assembly_method as method
FROM sys.assembly_modules am
JOIN sys.assemblies a
ON am.assembly_id = a.assembly_id
WHERE a.assembly_id = 65719
GO
name         class                      method
------------------------------------------------------------------
SQLCLR       Routines.StoredProcedures  GetSetIllustrationWebLinks
SQLCLR       StoredProcedures           SpTrans
SQLCLR       RegexLibrary               MatchAll
SQLCLR       XSLT                       XSLTransform
SQLCLR       SumPrime                   NULL
```

Notice that the class holding your UDA (`SumPrime`) is listed, but your UDA itself is not listed. In addition, your UDT (`RegexPattern`) is not listed. To see everything, you right-click SQLCLR in the `Assemblies` node of the Object Browser and then select View Dependencies.

Summary

This chapter covered the development of SQLCLR code using ADO.NET and user-defined managed database objects. We've also reviewed advanced topics, such as transaction control and system catalog viewing.

If you've attempted the examples from start to finish, you will have upgraded your SQL Server and .NET programming arsenal and opened the doorway to a new world of integrated software.

Chapter 37, "Using XML in SQL Server 2005," delves into the ever-expanding world of SQL Server XML.

36

Using XML in SQL Server 2005

IN THIS CHAPTER

▶ What's New in Using XML in SQL Server 2005

▶ Understanding XML

▶ Relational Data as XML: The FOR XML Modes

▶ XML as Relational Data: Using OPENXML

▶ Using the New xml Data Type

▶ Indexing and Full-Text Indexing of xml Columns

SQL Server first planted its Extensible Markup Language (XML) roots with the introduction of the FOR XML and OPENXML keywords in SQL Server 2000, right around the time XML was growing in popularity as a markup format with seemingly unlimited uses.

With the release of SQL Server 2005, the bar has clearly been raised for XML support in relational databases.

What's New in Using XML in SQL Server 2005

XML and relational data may coexist side-by-side and are more interchangeable than ever, thanks to SQL Server's XML-centric features, such as the new xml data type, extensions to FOR XML, schema storage, content validation, indexing, XQuery support, and more.

The introduction of these features is both vital and timely because XML has become the standard for everything from traditional markup for publications to business-to-business data exchange, web services, application programming (with XAML), graphics display (with SVG), news syndication (with RSS), and the list goes on.

Before digging into the world of SQL Server XML, let's briefly take a look at what XML is.

Understanding XML

XML was first created as a solution to the complexity inherent in the Standard Generalized Markup Language (SGML), the granddaddy of all structured markup languages. What you may not know is that SGML actually contains the rules that define how to produce other markup languages, such as HTML. XML is just a subset or restriction of those rules, providing the specifications for producing markup for all kinds of content based on a few simple conventions.

XML documents are either *well formed*, meaning they contain a single root element that contains every other element (or none), or *valid*, meaning they are well formed, and all their elements adhere to all the constraints set forth in their associated Document Type Definition (DTD) or XML Schema Definition (XSD).

An XML document that adheres to the constraints of a particular DTD or schema is known as an *instance* of that DTD or schema. In some cases, an XML document is referred to as a *fragment*, meaning it contains more than one root element and/or text-only nodes.

XML documents are generally made up of elements (also called *tags*), attributes, instructions to the applications that use the document (known as *processing instructions*), comments, and text. Despite their variation in kind, all these structures are commonly known as *nodes*.

Keep in mind that there is no set list of predefined XML tags: They can be anything the XML specialist chooses. And just as HTML is considered to be an instance of SGML, the XML content model is also itself an instance of XML.

XML's only job is to provide the specification for how a document may be structured (or *marked up*). It contains no inherent information pertaining to data display or layout, content usage, or anything else.

In the pages that follow, you'll see many examples of XML, both simple and complex. We'll tour the many ways SQL Server can produce, store, load, and transform XML.

Relational Data as XML: The FOR XML Modes

One of the most important uses of XML is to provide a way of describing and encapsulating relational data. Doing so requires a mapping between two basic kinds of data structures: sets and trees. The techniques shown in this section thus have a single goal: converting the columns and rows that make up the sets derived from any SELECT statement into XML trees.

Note that before XML came along, selected result sets would most likely be exported to delimited text files for consumption by disparate systems. Today, most data interchange favors the use of XML. In response, developers have come to rely on XSL for Transformations (XSLT) as a companion skill for translating XML into HTML, PDF, RTF, or any other type of document.

Let's take a look at how the SELECT...FOR XML syntax can automatically mark up relational data in a variety of ways. The simplest approach uses FOR XML RAW.

RAW **Mode**

When specified at the end of a SELECT statement, the keywords FOR XML RAW tell SQL Server to generate a one-XML-element-per-row structure. The FOR XML statement has a few options that change its output from the default of document fragments to well-formed documents with a slightly (compared to a few other FOR XML options) reshaped structure. This is its syntax:

```
FOR XML RAW [ ('ElementName') ]
[
[ , BINARY BASE64 ]
[ , TYPE ]
[ , ROOT [ ('RootName') ] ]
]
[ , { XMLDATA ¦ XMLSCHEMA [ ('TargetNameSpaceURI') ]} ]
[ , ELEMENTS [ XSINIL ¦ ABSENT ] ]
```

Listing 37.1 illustrates the XML generated by the no-option version of FOR XML RAW. (Note that all the code in this chapter relies on the AdventureWorks sample database.)

LISTING 37.1   A SELECT Statement That Uses FOR XML RAW with No Additional Modifiers

```
SELECT Name, ListPrice, Color
FROM Production.Product [Product]
WHERE Name LIKE '%Chain%'
ORDER BY Name
FOR XML RAW
go
<row Name="Chain" ListPrice="20.2400" Color="Silver" />
<row Name="Chain Stays" ListPrice="0.0000" />
<row Name="Chainring" ListPrice="0.0000" Color="Black" />
<row Name="Chainring Bolts" ListPrice="0.0000" Color="Silver" />
<row Name="Chainring Nut" ListPrice="0.0000" Color="Silver" />
```

This kind of XML shape is known as *attribute-centric* XML because each column in the result set is mapped to an attribute rather than an element. Each row is mapped to an element named row, which holds these attributes.

Listing 37.2 illustrates how the resultant XML can be changed into an *element-centric* shape, where each selected column is converted to an XML element simply through the addition of the ELEMENTS keyword to FOR XML RAW. This is a new feature in SQL Server 2005.

LISTING 37.2   A SELECT Statement That Uses FOR XML RAW, ELEMENTS

```
SELECT Name, ListPrice, Color
FROM Production.Product [Product]
WHERE Name LIKE '%Chain%'
```

37

LISTING 37.2   Continued

```
ORDER BY Name
FOR XML RAW, ELEMENTS
go
<row>
  <Name>Chain</Name>
  <ListPrice>20.2400</ListPrice>
  <Color>Silver</Color>
</row>
<row>
  <Name>Chain Stays</Name>
  <ListPrice>0.0000</ListPrice>
</row>
<row>
  <Name>Chainring</Name>
  <ListPrice>0.0000</ListPrice>
  <Color>Black</Color>
</row>
<row>
  <Name>Chainring Bolts</Name>
  <ListPrice>0.0000</ListPrice>
  <Color>Silver</Color>
</row>
<row>
  <Name>Chainring Nut</Name>
  <ListPrice>0.0000</ListPrice>
  <Color>Silver</Color>
</row>
```

If the tag name row is undesirable, the element name can be changed by simply adding a string-valued parameter, in parentheses, to the RAW keyword.

Note that in contrast to FOR XML AUTO (discussed later in this chapter), in this case, aliasing the Production.Product table has no effect on the output. Here's an example:

```
SELECT Name, ListPrice, Color
FROM Production.Product [Product]
WHERE Name LIKE '%Chain%'
ORDER BY Name
FOR XML RAW('ChainElement'), ELEMENTS
```

Also new to SQL Server 2005 is the ability to return NULL column values in generated XML. Previously, when a NULL column value was returned in the result set when using FOR XML, the null value was simply omitted from the XML: no attribute or element was generated at all. In SQL Server 2005, by specifying the keyword XSINIL after ELEMENTS, you can ensure that all null values are represented in the XML.

Note how the xsi:nil="true" attribute is produced for elements representing null column values. In addition, SQL Server automatically adds the XML schema namespace declaration to each node of the resulting fragment. This is required under the rules of XML because this fragment is using a Boolean attribute called nil, which is declared in the XML schema located at the specified URL. This, as well as the effect of the ELEMENTS keyword, is illustrated in Listing 37.3.

LISTING 37.3   A SELECT Statement That Uses FOR XML RAW, ELEMENTS XSINIL

```
SELECT TOP 1 Name, ListPrice, Color, Weight
FROM Production.Product [Product]
WHERE Name LIKE '%Chain%'
ORDER BY Name
FOR XML RAW('ChainElement'), ELEMENTS XSINIL
go
<ChainElement xmlns:xsi="http://www.w3.org/2001/XMLSchema-instance">
  <Name>Chain</Name>
  <ListPrice>20.2400</ListPrice>
  <Color>Silver</Color>
  <Weight xsi:nil="true"/>
</ChainElement>
```

Note that the XML results in Listing 37.3 happen to produce a well-formed XML document only because a single row was selected: This one row acts as both the root of the document and its entire content. All other XML results (including all the previous listings) encapsulating two or more rows are actually just fragments.

To easily change these XML fragments to well-formed documents, you can apply the new ROOT keyword to add a root node to the output, as shown in Listing 37.4.

37

LISTING 37.4   A SELECT Statement That Uses FOR XML RAW and the ROOT Keyword

```
SELECT Name, ListPrice, Color, Weight
FROM Production.Product [Product]
WHERE Name LIKE '%Chain%'
ORDER BY Name
FOR XML RAW('ChainElement'), ELEMENTS XSINIL, ROOT('ChainDoc')
go
<ChainDoc xmlns:xsi="http://www.w3.org/2001/XMLSchema-instance">
  <ChainElement>
    <Name>Chain</Name>
    <ListPrice>20.2400</ListPrice>
    <Color>Silver</Color>
    <Weight xsi:nil="true" />
  </ChainElement>
  <ChainElement>
    <Name>Chain Stays</Name>
```

LISTING 37.4   Continued

```
      <ListPrice>0.0000</ListPrice>
      <Color xsi:nil="true" />
      <Weight xsi:nil="true" />
   </ChainElement>
   <ChainElement>
      <Name>Chainring</Name>
      <ListPrice>0.0000</ListPrice>
      <Color>Black</Color>
      <Weight xsi:nil="true" />
   </ChainElement>
   <ChainElement>
      <Name>Chainring Bolts</Name>
      <ListPrice>0.0000</ListPrice>
      <Color>Silver</Color>
      <Weight xsi:nil="true" />
   </ChainElement>
   <ChainElement>
      <Name>Chainring Nut</Name>
      <ListPrice>0.0000</ListPrice>
      <Color>Silver</Color>
      <Weight xsi:nil="true" />
   </ChainElement>
</ChainDoc>
```

Users (or applications) on the receiving side of RAW-produced XML may also require an inline XML schema (XSD) or an inline XML-Data Reduced (XDR) schema. Note that inline XDR schemas are considered to be deprecated in this release.

To produce these schemas, you add the XMLSCHEMA or XMLDATA keyword to the clause. The results are too long to be listed here, but to see how these schema types differ, compare the output of this:

```
SELECT Name, ListPrice, Color, Weight
FROM Production.Product [Product]
WHERE Name LIKE '%Chain%'
ORDER BY Name
FOR XML RAW, ELEMENTS XSINIL, XMLDATA
```

to the output of this:

```
SELECT Name, ListPrice, Color, Weight
FROM Production.Product [Product]
WHERE Name LIKE '%Chain%'
ORDER BY Name
FOR XML RAW('ChainElement'),
```

```
ELEMENTS XSINIL,
ROOT('ChainDoc'),
XMLSCHEMA ('urn:www-samspublishing-com:examples')
```

XML schemas are discussed in further detail later in this chapter, in the section "Using XML Schema Collections."

> **NOTE**
>
> The XMLDATA keyword is not permitted when ROOT is specified or when a tag name parameter has been passed to RAW (for example, RAW('ChainElement')).
>
> Note also that XMLSCHEMA takes an optional string-valued parameter, allowing you to specify a value for the target namespace of the produced XML (for example, XMLSCHEMA ('urn:www-samspublishing-com:examples)).

Working with Binary Columns

Even though XML is purely a text-based markup language, FOR XML still has the ability to generate XML that contains data selected from binary–data-typed columns, such as image, binary, and varbinary. To do this, SQL Server base-64 encodes the data, resulting in a long character string.

To implement this in a query, you add joins from the table Production.Product to Production.ProductProductPhoto and then to Production.ProductPhoto, which contains the varbinary(max)–data-typed ThumbNailPhoto column. Then, you add the keywords BINARY BASE64 to the FOR XML clause. Listing 37.5 illustrates this and also shows the schema generated by the XMLSCHEMA keyword. (Note that the base-64 character data is truncated in the listing for brevity with the character string {...}.)

LISTING 37.5   A SELECT Statement That Uses FOR XML RAW and the BINARY BASE64 Option

```
SELECT TOP 1 Name, ListPrice, Color, Weight, ThumbNailPhoto
FROM Production.Product [Product]
JOIN Production.ProductProductPhoto PhotoJunction ON
  [Product].ProductId = PhotoJunction.ProductId
JOIN Production.ProductPhoto Photo
ON Photo.ProductPhotoId = PhotoJunction.ProductPhotoId
WHERE Name LIKE '%Chain%'
ORDER BY Name
FOR XML RAW('ChainElement'),
  ELEMENTS XSINIL,
  ROOT('ChainDoc'),
  XMLSCHEMA('urn:www-samspublishing-com:examples'),
  BINARY BASE64
go
<ChainDoc xmlns:xsi="http://www.w3.org/2001/XMLSchema-instance">
  <xsd:schema targetNamespace="urn:www-samspublishing-com:examples"
```

37

LISTING 37.5   Continued

```
    xmlns:xsd="http://www.w3.org/2001/XMLSchema"
    xmlns:sqltypes="http://schemas.microsoft.com/sqlserver/2004/sqltypes"
    elementFormDefault="qualified">
    <xsd:import
      namespace=http://schemas.microsoft.com/sqlserver/2004/sqltypes
      schemaLocation="http://schemas.microsoft.com/sqlserver/2004/
➡sqltypes/sqltypes.xsd"
    />
    <xsd:element name="ChainElement">
      <xsd:complexType>
        <xsd:sequence>
          <xsd:element name="Name" nillable="1">
            <xsd:simpleType sqltypes:sqlTypeAlias="[AdventureWorks].[dbo].[Name]">
              <xsd:restriction base="sqltypes:nvarchar" sqltypes:localeId="1033"
                  sqltypes:sqlCompareOptions="IgnoreCase IgnoreKanaType
                  IgnoreWidth" sqltypes:sqlSortId="52">
                <xsd:maxLength value="50" />
              </xsd:restriction>
            </xsd:simpleType>
          </xsd:element>
          <xsd:element name="ListPrice" type="sqltypes:money" nillable="1" />
          <xsd:element name="Color" nillable="1">
            <xsd:simpleType>
              <xsd:restriction base="sqltypes:nvarchar" sqltypes:localeId="1033"
                  sqltypes:sqlCompareOptions="IgnoreCase IgnoreKanaType
                  IgnoreWidth" sqltypes:sqlSortId="52">
                <xsd:maxLength value="15" />
              </xsd:restriction>
            </xsd:simpleType>
          </xsd:element>
          <xsd:element name="Weight" nillable="1">
            <xsd:simpleType>
              <xsd:restriction base="sqltypes:decimal">
                <xsd:totalDigits value="8" />
                <xsd:fractionDigits value="2" />
              </xsd:restriction>
            </xsd:simpleType>
          </xsd:element>
          <xsd:element
              name="ThumbNailPhoto" type="sqltypes:varbinary" nillable="1"/>
        </xsd:sequence>
      </xsd:complexType>
    </xsd:element>
  </xsd:schema>
```

LISTING 37.5   Continued

```
  <ChainElement xmlns="urn:www-samspublishing-com:examples">
    <Name>Chain</Name>
    <ListPrice>20.2400</ListPrice>
    <Color>Silver</Color>
    <Weight xsi:nil="true" />
    <ThumbNailPhoto>R0lGODlhUAAxAPcAAKeamoyLj {…}</ThumbNailPhoto>
  </ChainElement>
</ChainDoc>
```

AUTO **Mode**

When RAW mode is not enough, FOR XML AUTO provides a few more ways to shape your XML output. Its usefulness derives from its ability to produce nested XML elements from rows derived by joining multiple tables, in contrast to the flat structure of RAW mode.

The ROOT keyword introduced earlier also applies with AUTO mode, and it is good practice to continue to use it in your queries. Like RAW mode, AUTO mode produces attribute-centric XML by default, but you can change this by using the ELEMENTS keyword. XSINIL and XMLSCHEMA are also applicable here, having the same effect as with RAW mode. Listing 37.6 illustrates these points.

LISTING 37.6   A SELECT Statement That Uses FOR XML AUTO, ELEMENTS XSINIL, ROOT

```
SELECT
    Color,
    Offer.SpecialOfferId Id,
    Product.ProductId Id,
    Name,
    Description [Desc],
    Size
FROM Sales.SpecialOffer Offer
JOIN Sales.SpecialOfferProduct OP ON
OP.SpecialOfferId = Offer.SpecialOfferId
JOIN Production.Product Product ON
Product.ProductId = OP.ProductId
WHERE Name LIKE 'Mountain Bike%'
FOR XML AUTO, ELEMENTS XSINIL, ROOT('MountainBikeSpecials')
go
<MountainBikeSpecials xmlns:xsi="http://www.w3.org/2001/XMLSchema-instance">
  <Product>
    <Color>White</Color>
    <Id>710</Id>
    <Name>Mountain Bike Socks, L</Name>
    <Size>L</Size>
    <Offer>
```

LISTING 37.6   Continued

```
      <Id>1</Id>
      <Desc>No Discount</Desc>
    </Offer>
  </Product>
  <Product>
    <Color>White</Color>
    <Id>709</Id>
    <Name>Mountain Bike Socks, M</Name>
    <Size>M</Size>
    <Offer>
      <Id>1</Id>
      <Desc>No Discount</Desc>
    </Offer>
    <Offer>
      <Id>2</Id>
      <Desc>Volume Discount 11 to 14</Desc>
    </Offer>
    <Offer>
      <Id>3</Id>
      <Desc>Volume Discount 15 to 24</Desc>
    </Offer>
    <Offer>
      <Id>4</Id>
      <Desc>Volume Discount 25 to 40</Desc>
    </Offer>
  </Product>
</MountainBikeSpecials>
```

With AUTO mode, the keywords BINARY BASE64 have the same effect as with RAW mode, with one major difference: RAW mode generates an error if binary data is selected and BINARY BASE64 is not specified; therefore, it is required. With AUTO mode, binary data may be selected without specifying BINARY BASE64, although SQL Server requires that the primary key of the table containing the binary data be selected. This is so that SQL Server can generate a path to the binary field, using the primary key to address the row (in place of the encoded data), of the form:

```
'dbobject/SchemaName.TableName[@PrimaryKeyName="PrimaryKeyValue"]/@ColumnName'
```

This special XPath-like output is unique to AUTO mode and is useful for applications that incorporate SQLXML's URL-based querying to return the desired binary data. Listing 37.7 illustrates this XML production.

LISTING 37.7   Addressing Binary Data That Uses FOR XML AUTO

```
SELECT Top 1
    Photo.ProductPhotoId, ThumbNailPhoto, Color, Offer.SpecialOfferId Id,
    Product.ProductId Id, Name, Description [Desc], Size
FROM Sales.SpecialOffer Offer
JOIN Sales.SpecialOfferProduct OP ON
OP.SpecialOfferId = Offer.SpecialOfferId
JOIN Production.Product Product ON
Product.ProductId = OP.ProductId
JOIN Production.ProductProductPhoto PhotoJunction ON
    Product.ProductId = PhotoJunction.ProductId
JOIN Production.ProductPhoto Photo ON
    Photo.ProductPhotoId = PhotoJunction.ProductPhotoId
WHERE Name LIKE 'Mountain Bike%'
FOR XML AUTO, ELEMENTS XSINIL, ROOT('MountainBikeSpecials')
go
<MountainBikeSpecials xmlns:xsi="http://www.w3.org/2001/XMLSchema-instance">
  <Photo>
    <ProductPhotoId>1</ProductPhotoId>
    <ThumbNailPhoto>
      dbobject/Production.ProductPhoto[@ProductPhotoID='1']/@ThumbNailPhoto
    </ThumbNailPhoto>
    <Product>
      <Color>White</Color>
      <Id>710</Id>
      <Name>Mountain Bike Socks, L</Name>
      <Size>L</Size>
      <Offer>
        <Id>1</Id>
        <Desc>No Discount</Desc>
      </Offer>
    </Product>
  </Photo>
</MountainBikeSpecials>
```

Notice how you can generate an additional level of nesting (with the Photo element) in the XML hierarchy simply by selecting a value from an additional table.

SQL Server has a set of rules it uses for nesting elements in AUTO mode. As rows are streamed to output, the XML engine studiously compares the values in adjacent columns to check for differences from the first row on down to the last. When one or more primary keys have been selected in the query, only the primary key values are used in the column comparison. When no primary keys have been selected, all column values are used in the comparison, except for columns of type ntext, text, image, or xml, whose values are always assumed to be different.

The following is an example that includes primary keys in the SELECT statement:

```
SELECT Offer.SpecialOfferId, Product.ProductId, Name
FROM Sales.SpecialOffer Offer
JOIN Sales.SpecialOfferProduct OP ON
OP.SpecialOfferId = Offer.SpecialOfferId
JOIN Production.Product Product ON
Product.ProductId = OP.ProductId
WHERE Name LIKE 'Mountain Bike%'
go
SpecialOfferId    ProductId    Name
---------------------------------------------------
1                 710          Mountain Bike Socks, L
1                 709          Mountain Bike Socks, M
2                 709          Mountain Bike Socks, M
3                 709          Mountain Bike Socks, M
4                 709          Mountain Bike Socks, M
 (5 row(s) affected)
```

As the XML engine works down this result set, it sees that SpecialOfferId has the same value in the first and second rows, but ProductId differs in the same rows. It therefore creates one Offer element and nests the two different Product values in Product subelements.

Column selection order is also a determining factor in AUTO mode XML composition. Notice that even though in Rows 2–5, the ProductId remains 709, the XML engine still nests Product under Offer because Offer.SpecialOfferId is specified first in the list of selected columns. When FOR XML AUTO is added to the preceding query, it results in the following:

```
<MountainBikeSpecials>
  <Offer SpecialOfferId="1">
    <Product ProductId="710" Name="Mountain Bike Socks, L" />
    <Product ProductId="709" Name="Mountain Bike Socks, M" />
  </Offer>
  <Offer SpecialOfferId="2">
    <Product ProductId="709" Name="Mountain Bike Socks, M" />
  </Offer>
  <Offer SpecialOfferId="3">
    <Product ProductId="709" Name="Mountain Bike Socks, M" />
  </Offer>
  <Offer SpecialOfferId="4">
    <Product ProductId="709" Name="Mountain Bike Socks, M" />
  </Offer>
</MountainBikeSpecials>
```

To tell the XML engine that you prefer to nest Offer under Product, you simply change the column order in the SELECT statement:

```
SELECT Product.ProductId, Offer.SpecialOfferId, Name
FROM Sales.SpecialOffer Offer
JOIN Sales.SpecialOfferProduct OP ON
OP.SpecialOfferId = Offer.SpecialOfferId
JOIN Production.Product Product ON
Product.ProductId = OP.ProductId
WHERE Name LIKE 'Mountain Bike%'
FOR XML AUTO, ROOT('MountainBikeSpecials')
go
<MountainBikeSpecials>
  <Product ProductId="710" Name="Mountain Bike Socks, L">
    <Offer SpecialOfferId="1" />
  </Product>
  <Product ProductId="709" Name="Mountain Bike Socks, M">
    <Offer SpecialOfferId="1" />
    <Offer SpecialOfferId="2" />
    <Offer SpecialOfferId="3" />
    <Offer SpecialOfferId="4" />
  </Product>
</MountainBikeSpecials>
```

EXPLICIT Mode

FOR XML EXPLICIT is a powerful, oft-maligned, somewhat daunting mode of SQL Server XML production. It allows for the shaping of row data in any desirable XML structure, but the SQL required to produce it can easily end up being hundreds (or, in some cases, thousands) of lines long, leading to a potential maintenance headache.

With EXPLICIT mode, the query author is responsible for making sure the XML is well formed and that the rowset generated behind the scenes corresponds to a very particular format.

The FOR XML PATH statement renders FOR XML EXPLICIT obsolete except when you need to output column values as CDATA. This section therefore briefly covers the required query structure for and provides an example of this particular case.

> **NOTE**
>
> It's not an easy task to understand EXPLICIT mode just by reading. Practice is essential. After you've succeeded in using it a few times, it will begin to feel like an intuitive, albeit complex, way of doing things.

Microsoft calls the relational structure behind EXPLICIT mode queries the *universal table*. The universal table has a hierarchical structure sometimes known as the *adjacency list*

37

model. Put simply, this means that the first column in the table is the primary key and the second column is a foreign key referencing it, creating a parent–child relationship between rows in the same table. XML similarly models this relationship through the nesting of elements because nodes contained inside other nodes also hold a parent–child relationship.

Each level of hierarchical depth in the universal table is created by a separate SELECT statement, and each SELECT is unioned to the next, producing the complete rowset. Some details on the table structure help make this clearer:

▶ The first column in the universal table (think of it as the primary key) must be named Tag and hold an integer value. The value of Tag can be thought of as representing the depth of the node that will be produced.

▶ The second column must be named Parent and must refer to a valid value of Tag, or null, in the case of the first branch.

▶ The rest of the selected columns in the query are mapped either to attributes, subelements, or CDATA nodes, or they may be selected but not produced in the resultant XML.

Listing 37.8 shows a query that returns a universal table. Later, you can change it so that it returns XML by adding FOR XML EXPLICIT.

LISTING 37.8   A Query That Generates the Universal Table Rowset Format

```
SELECT
    1 as Tag,
    NULL as Parent,
    Reason.ScrapReasonId 'ScrapReason!1!ScrapReasonId!element',
    Name 'ScrapReason!1!!cdata',
    WorkOrderId 'WorkOrder!2!WorkOrderId',
    NULL 'WorkOrder!2!ScrappedQuantity'
FROM Production.ScrapReason Reason
JOIN Production.WorkOrder WorkOrder
ON Reason.ScrapReasonId = WorkOrder.ScrapReasonID
WHERE Reason.ScrapReasonId = 12

UNION ALL

SELECT
    2 as Tag,
    1 as Parent,
    Reason.ScrapReasonId,
    NULL,
    WorkOrderId,
    ScrappedQty
FROM Production.ScrapReason Reason
```

LISTING 37.8   Continued

```
JOIN Production.WorkOrder WorkOrder
ON Reason.ScrapReasonId = WorkOrder.ScrapReasonID
WHERE Reason.ScrapReasonId = 12
```

The first SELECT statement in the union must use a special column alias syntax that tells the XML generator how to shape each column. This is the syntax:

element_name!corresponding_Tag_value!attribute_or_subelement_name[!directive]

The following list explains each part of the preceding syntax:

- ▶ **element_name**—The name of the generated element associated with each row.

- ▶ **corresponding_Tag_value**—The value of Tag for the context rowset.

- ▶ **attribute_or_subelement_name**—The name of the attribute or subelement associated with the column in the context row.

- ▶ **directive**—An optional directive to the XML generator. The possible values are:

  - ▶ **element**—When specified, tells the XML generator to produce the column associated with attribute_or_subelement_name as a subelement. (An attribute is produced by default.)

  - ▶ **hide**—Tells the XML generator not to show the associated column data at all in the produced XML. This may be needed if there is some side effect desired from selecting the column but the data is not needed to be shown.

  - ▶ **cdata**—Tells the XML generator to output the associated column data as a CDATA section.

  - ▶ **xml**—Disables entitization of text data. This can lead to non-well-formed XML because the XML special characters (&, ', ", <, >) are output directly.

In all subsequent SELECT statements, the columns corresponding to the rowsets identified by Tag are selected according to the layout specified in the first SELECT.

Notice how in Listing 37.8, NULL is selected for WorkOrder!2!ScrappedQuantity. This is done because the value for that column is going to be filled in by the SELECT statement having a Tag value of 2, as specified in corresponding_Tag_value. Likewise, ScrappedQty is selected only in the second SELECT statement (where NULL is supplied for ScrapReason!1!!cdata) because Name is selected in this column in the first SELECT. The primary key (ScrapReasonId) that is the common thread joining both sets of rows must be specified in both SELECT statements for this query to work.

Now that you have an understanding of the universal table structure that must be built, the only thing left to do is add FOR XML EXPLICIT to the query in Listing 37.8 and then order the output according to the desired element hierarchy. Listing 37.9 illustrates the final query and its result.

37

LISTING 37.9   Using FOR XML EXPLICIT

```
SELECT
    1 as Tag,
    NULL as Parent,
    Reason.ScrapReasonId 'ScrapReason!1!ScrapReasonId!element',
    Name 'ScrapReason!1!!cdata',
    WorkOrderId 'WorkOrder!2!WorkOrderId',
    NULL 'WorkOrder!2!ScrappedQuantity'
FROM Production.ScrapReason Reason
JOIN Production.WorkOrder WorkOrder
ON Reason.ScrapReasonId = WorkOrder.ScrapReasonID
WHERE Reason.ScrapReasonId = 12
UNION ALL
SELECT
    2 as Tag,
    1 as Parent,
    Reason.ScrapReasonId,
    NULL,
    WorkOrderId,
    ScrappedQty
FROM Production.ScrapReason Reason
JOIN Production.WorkOrder WorkOrder
ON Reason.ScrapReasonId = WorkOrder.ScrapReasonID
WHERE Reason.ScrapReasonId = 12
ORDER BY 'ScrapReason!1!ScrapReasonId!element', 'WorkOrder!2!WorkOrderId'
FOR XML EXPLICIT, ROOT('ScrappedWorkOrders')
go
<ScrappedWorkOrders>
    <ScrapReason>
      <ScrapReasonId>12</ScrapReasonId>
      <![CDATA[Thermoform temperature too high]]>
      <WorkOrder WorkOrderId="2573" ScrappedQuantity="14" />
    </ScrapReason>
    <ScrapReason>
      <ScrapReasonId>12</ScrapReasonId>
      <![CDATA[Thermoform temperature too high]]>
      <WorkOrder WorkOrderId="4972" ScrappedQuantity="1" />
    </ScrapReason>
    <ScrapReason>
      <ScrapReasonId>12</ScrapReasonId>
      <![CDATA[Thermoform temperature too high]]>
      <WorkOrder WorkOrderId="7771" ScrappedQuantity="6" />
    </ScrapReason>
    <ScrapReason>
      <ScrapReasonId>12</ScrapReasonId>
```

LISTING 37.9   Continued

```
        <![CDATA[Thermoform temperature too high]]>
        <WorkOrder WorkOrderId="9071" ScrappedQuantity="1" />
      </ScrapReason>
      <ScrapReason>
        <ScrapReasonId>12</ScrapReasonId>
        <![CDATA[Thermoform temperature too high]]>
        <WorkOrder WorkOrderId="10274" ScrappedQuantity="1" />
      </ScrapReason>
{...}
</ScrappedWorkOrders>
```

In the ORDER BY clause, you tell the XML generator to first produce ScrapReason elements and then nest the WorkOrder elements underneath them.

Like the other modes, FOR XML EXPLICIT supports the BINARY BASE64 keywords, although base-64 encoding is performed automatically by the parser, even if not specified.

The ROOT keyword can also be used, although not when specifying XMLDATA. XMLSCHEMA is not supported as of this writing. ELEMENTS and XSINIL are also not supported, probably because you can get along without them, thanks to the many shaping options available.

PATH **Mode**

PATH mode is the latest and best addition to the FOR XML syntax. It provides a straightforward way of using a limited XPath syntax to specify the shaping of query-produced XML. It is also a very compact syntax in comparison with some of the other modes, especially EXPLICIT.

Let's take a look at how PATH mode works by re-creating the XML produced in Listing 37.9, this time using PATH mode. Listing 37.10 illustrates this mode.

LISTING 37.10   Using FOR XML PATH to Simplify an EXPLICIT Query

```
SELECT
    Reason.ScrapReasonId,
    Name 'text()',
    WorkOrderId 'WorkOrder/@WorkOrderId',
    ScrappedQty 'WorkOrder/@ScrappedQuantity'
FROM Production.ScrapReason Reason
JOIN Production.WorkOrder WorkOrder
ON Reason.ScrapReasonId = WorkOrder.ScrapReasonID
WHERE Reason.ScrapReasonId = 12
FOR XML PATH('ScrapReason'), ROOT('ScrappedWorkOrders')
go
<ScrappedWorkOrders>
```

37

LISTING 37.10 Continued

```
    <ScrapReason>
      <ScrapReasonId>12</ScrapReasonId>
      Thermoform temperature too high
      <WorkOrder WorkOrderId="2573" ScrappedQuantity="14" />
    </ScrapReason>
    <ScrapReason>
      <ScrapReasonId>12</ScrapReasonId>
      Thermoform temperature too high
      <WorkOrder WorkOrderId="4972" ScrappedQuantity="1" />
    </ScrapReason>
    <ScrapReason>
      <ScrapReasonId>12</ScrapReasonId>
      Thermoform temperature too high
      <WorkOrder WorkOrderId="7771" ScrappedQuantity="6" />
    </ScrapReason>
    <ScrapReason>
      <ScrapReasonId>12</ScrapReasonId>
      Thermoform temperature too high
      <WorkOrder WorkOrderId="9071" ScrappedQuantity="1" />
    </ScrapReason>
{...}
</ScrappedWorkOrders>
```

The only difference between Listing 37.10 and Listing 37.9 is that here you aren't outputting a CDATA section—just a text node for the `ScrapReason.Name` column. Which `FOR XML` query would you rather maintain?

As the query in Listing 37.10 illustrates, the `PATH` keyword works like `RAW` in that all columns values are wrapped in a default element. Like `RAW`, `PATH` takes a parameter to specify the name of this default element. If a name is not specified, `row` is used, just as it is with `RAW`.

Unlike `RAW`, `PATH` mode is element-centric. When a column is not specified to be generated as an attribute (for example, using an XPath column alias, such as `WorkOrderId '@Id'`), it is produced as a subelement of the default tag.

You can also specify the `ROOT` keyword and the `ELEMENTS XSINIL` keywords in the same manner as `RAW`, although using `ELEMENTS` is somewhat redundant because `PATH` mode defaults to element-centric XML. Using `ELEMENTS XSINIL` is still the only way to produce null values in the XML.

`XMLSCHEMA` and `XMLDATA` are not allowed to be specified. `BINARY BASE64` may be specified, but it is not required because base-64 encoded data is automatically generated.

To build the XML, the engine first works down the column list to figure out the desired XML shape to be output. XML is then generated for each row, based on the shape specified by the column names or aliases. Columns can be aliased using the literal string XPath format, or they may have no alias at all.

In the example in Listing 37.10, the following structure is specified by the column selections:

▶ For `Reason.ScrapReasonId`, output a subelement of `ScrapReason` (specified by `PATH('ScrapReason')`) called `ScrapReasonId`. When no alias is specified, the default shape is element-centric.

▶ For `Name`, output the value as a text-only child node of `ScrapReason`.

▶ For `WorkOrderId`, output a child node of `ScrapReason` called `WorkOrder` and add an attribute called `WorkOrderId` to it.

▶ For `ScrappedQty`, output an attribute of `WorkOrder` called `ScrappedQuantity`.

Usually, when you set out to shape XML, you'll intuitively know where you want your values to be, so it's more a matter of practice and application than memorization. When you know the basics, the syntax is intuitive enough to create whatever XML you desire.

FOR XML PATH has a few other neat features, which Listing 37.11 illustrates in one fell swoop.

LISTING 37.11   Demonstrating Several Features of FOR XML PATH in a Single Query

```
SELECT
    Reason.ScrapReasonId '*',
    'Comment: Name = ' + Name 'comment()',
    ModifiedDate 'processing-instruction(ModDatePI)',
    (
        SELECT WorkOrderId 'data()'
        FROM Production.WorkOrder WorkOrder
        JOIN Production.ScrapReason Reason
        ON Reason.ScrapReasonId = WorkOrder.ScrapReasonID
        WHERE Reason.ScrapReasonId = 12
        ORDER BY WorkOrderId desc
        FOR XML PATH('')
    ) 'WorkOrders/@WorkOrderIds'
FROM Production.ScrapReason Reason
WHERE Reason.ScrapReasonId = 12
FOR XML PATH('ScrappedWorkOrder'), ROOT('ScrappedWorkOrders')
go
<ScrappedWorkOrders>
    <ScrapReason>12
    <!--Comment: Name = Thermoform temperature too high-->
    <?ModDatePI 1998-06-01T00:00:00?>
```

LISTING 37.11   Continued

```
    <WorkOrders WorkOrderIds="72370 72273 70875 69474 69173 68573 65970 60472
➡56975 56875 55275 53771 50370 47670 45773 42071 41975 39372 36673
➡36671 32872 32775 32770 31073 29370 27771 24174 22673 22670 17674
➡16073 13073 10274 9071 7771 4972 2573" />
    </ScrapReason>
</ScrappedWorkOrders>
```

Let's review the selected columns in Listing 37.11: The first is aliased with the asterisk (*) character. This tells SQL Server to inline-generate the data for that column (as text). (Using the text() node test would do the same in this case.)

Next, the comment() node test is specified for Name, telling the XML generator to output its value in a comment. For clarity's sake, we added a little syntactic sugar in this statement by prepending the text 'Comment: Name = ' to the value produced inside the comment.

Next, the processing-instruction() node test is specified to output each value of ModifiedDate to a new processing instruction called ModDatePI.

Finally, the fourth column is produced as a list of WorkOrderId values, using the magical data() keyword in a nested FOR XML PATH statement. data() tells SQL Server to generate a space-delimited list of atomic column values, one value for each row in the result set.

Note that the nested query is merely used to generate a list of WorkOrderId values. The empty string is given for the PATH keyword, telling the XML engine not to generate a default element at all, so no XML is generated whatsoever! You can extract and test the statement to see this in action.

The nested query applies the same WHERE clause as its parent to filter WorkOrderId values where the value of ScrapReasonId is 12. This ensures the relevancy of the nested data to the outer query.

The resulting list of values is grafted to the XML of the outer statement, using the column alias 'WorkOrders/@WorkOrderIds'.

FOR XML **and the New** xml **Data Type**

By default, the results of any FOR XML query (using all four modes) is streamed to output as a one-column/one-row dataset with a column named XML_F52E2B61-18A1-11d1-B105-00805F49916B of type nvarchar(max). (In SQL Server 2000, this was a stream of XML split into multiple varchar(8000) rows.)

One of the biggest limitations of SQL Server 2000's XML production was the inability to save the results of a FOR XML query to a variable or store it in a column directly without using some middleware code to first save the XML as a string and then insert it back into an ntext or nvarchar column and then select it out again.

Today, SQL Server 2005 natively supports column storage of XML, using the new xml data type. Be sure to read the section "Using the New xml Data Type," later in this chapter, for a complete overview.

You can easily convert FOR XML results to instances of xml by using the TYPE directive with all four modes (RAW, AUTO, EXPLICIT, and PATH). Listing 37.12 demonstrates the use of FOR XML PATH with the TYPE directive.

LISTING 37.12   Using FOR XML PATH, TYPE to Create an Instance of the xml Data Type

```
SELECT *
FROM Production.WorkOrder WorkOrder
WHERE ScrapReasonId = 12
AND WorkOrderId = 72370
FOR XML RAW('WorkOrder'), ELEMENTS XSINIL, ROOT('WorkOrders'), TYPE
go
<WorkOrders xmlns:xsi="http://www.w3.org/2001/XMLSchema-instance">
  <WorkOrder>
    <WorkOrderID>72370</WorkOrderID>
    <ProductID>329</ProductID>
    <OrderQty>48</OrderQty>
    <StockedQty>47</StockedQty>
    <ScrappedQty>1</ScrappedQty>
    <StartDate>2004-07-01T00:00:00</StartDate>
    <EndDate>2004-07-11T00:00:00</EndDate>
    <DueDate>2004-07-12T00:00:00</DueDate>
    <ScrapReasonID>12</ScrapReasonID>
    <ModifiedDate>2004-07-11T00:00:00</ModifiedDate>
  </WorkOrder>
</WorkOrders>
```

Notice that in contrast to the preceding FOR XML examples, in this example, the query window in SQL Server Management Studio (SSMS) no longer displays the lengthy XML column UUID in the results frame, nor on the window tab. The results have been cast to a single instance of the xml data type, ready for use in variables of type xml, in subsequent queries, inserted into xml columns, or returned to the client.

The five xml data type methods—value(), exist(), nodes(), query(), and modify(), discussed later in this chapter, in the section "The Built-in xml Data Type Methods"—can be intermixed with relational queries by using all FOR XML modes. This makes it even easier to shape your XML exactly the way you want.

Listing 37.13 demonstrates how you can nest XQuery queries inside regular FOR XML T-SQL to produce XML documents built from both relational and XML sources.

37

LISTING 37.13   Bridging the Gap Between Relational and XML Data by Using FOR XML PATH and the xml Data Type

```
SELECT
    FirstName,
    LastName,
    E.Title,
    Resume.query(
        'declare namespace ns="http://schemas.microsoft.com/sqlserver/2004/07/
➥adventure-works/Resume";
        //ns:Education
        '
    ) '*'
FROM HumanResources.Employee E
JOIN Person.Contact C on E.ContactId = C.ContactId
JOIN HumanResources.JobCandidate J on J.EmployeeId = E.EmployeeId
WHERE J.JobCandidateId = 8
FOR XML PATH('AWorthyJobCandidate'), TYPE
go
<AWorthyJobCandidate>
  <FirstName>Peng</FirstName>
  <LastName>Wu</LastName>
  <Title>Quality Assurance Supervisor</Title>
  <ns:Education xmlns:ns="http://schemas.microsoft.com/sqlserver/2004/07/adventure-
works/Resume">
    <ns:Edu.Level>学士</ns:Edu.Level>
    <ns:Edu.StartDate>1986-09-15Z</ns:Edu.StartDate>
    <ns:Edu.EndDate>1990-05-15Z</ns:Edu.EndDate>
    <ns:Edu.Degree>Bachelor of Science</ns:Edu.Degree>
    <ns:Edu.Major>贸易</ns:Edu.Major>
    <ns:Edu.Minor />
    <ns:Edu.GPA>3.3</ns:Edu.GPA>
    <ns:Edu.GPAScale>4</ns:Edu.GPAScale>
    <ns:Edu.School>Western University</ns:Edu.School>
    <ns:Edu.Location>
      <ns:Location>
        <ns:Loc.CountryRegion>US </ns:Loc.CountryRegion>
        <ns:Loc.State>WA </ns:Loc.State>
        <ns:Loc.City>Seattle</ns:Loc.City>
      </ns:Location>
    </ns:Edu.Location>
  </ns:Education>
</AWorthyJobCandidate>
```

In this example, the asterisk (*) is used as a column alias for the results of the nested query (on `HumanResources.JobCandidate.Resume`), telling SQL Server to simply inline the XML with the other nodes.

XML as Relational Data: Using OPENXML

This section covers what might be called the inverse of FOR XML: OPENXML. You use OPENXML in T-SQL queries to read XML data and *shred* (or decompose) it into relational result sets. OPENXML is part of the SELECT statement, and you use it to generate a table from an XML source.

The first step required in this process is a call to the system stored procedure sp_xml_preparedocument. sp_xml_preparedocument creates an in-memory representation of any XML document tree for use in querying. It takes the following parameters:

▶ An integer output parameter for storing a handle to the document tree

▶ The XML input data

▶ An optional XML namespace declaration, used in subsequent OPENXML queries

sp_xml_preparedocument is able to convert the following data types into internal XML objects: text, ntext, varchar, nvarchar, single-quoted literal strings, and untyped XML (data from an xml column having no associated schema collection). This is its syntax:

sp_xml_preparedocument *integer_variable* OUTPUT[, *xmltext*][, *xpath_namespaces*]

And here is an example of OPENXML in use:

```
DECLARE @XmlDoc XML, @iXml int
SET @XmlDoc = '
    <ex:ExampleDoc xmlns:ex="urn:www-samspublishing-com:examples">
      <ex:foo>hello</ex:foo>
      <ex:bar>sql!</ex:bar>
    </ex:ExampleDoc>'
EXEC sp_xml_preparedocument
    @iXml OUTPUT,
    @XmlDoc,
    '<ExampleDoc xmlns:ex="urn:www-samspublishing-com:examples"/>'
SELECT id, parentid, nodetype, localname, prefix
FROM OPENXML(@iXml, '/ex:ExampleDoc/ex:foo')
--WITH (foo varchar(10) '/ex:ExampleDoc/ex:foo')
EXEC sp_xml_removedocument @iXml
go
id     parentid    nodetype    localname    prefix
--------------------------------------------------
3      0           1           foo          ex
5      3           3           #text        NULL
```

37

Notice in the example that the WITH predicate has been commented out. This is to illustrate in the query results what is known as an *edge table:* the XML document in its relational form. *Edge* is a term taken from graph theory. It refers to what you might visualize as a depth line between two nodes.

If the edge table looks familiar, it's probably because it bears a resemblance to the *universal table* that must be created for EXPLICIT mode. As with the universal table, the edge table follows the adjacency list model for its hierarchical relationships. The node types of the input XML are marked in the nodetype column (1 = element, 2 = attribute, 3 = text). Namespaces are stored in namespaceuri, and the data of each node is stored in the text column.

If you uncomment the WITH predicate and change the query from SELECT * to SELECT foo, you get back a one-row/one-column table with a column called foo that has the varchar(10) value hello. This shows that the WITH predicate instructs OPENXML how to decompose the nodes to columns by using XPath syntax.

The syntax for OPENXML (including the WITH predicate) is as follows:

```
OPENXML(integer_document_handle_variable int, rowpattern nvarchar,[flags byte])
    [WITH (SchemaDeclaration ¦ TableName)]
```

Let's match this syntax with the values in the example:

- ▶ The first parameter is the local variable @iXml, which acts as a handle to the internal XML representation.

- ▶ The next parameter is a row pattern in XPath syntax that tells OPENXML how to select nodes into rows. OPENXML generates one row in the result set for each node that matches this row pattern. This is similar to the .NET XmlDocument object's SelectNodes() method, insofar as every matching node in rowpattern returns a row in the rowset.

- ▶ The result set's columns are then defined, using matching nodes as the context and the XPath in the column definitions of the WITH predicate to find the values relative to the node.

- ▶ The *flags* parameter is a combinable byte value that controls how the selected XML nodes are to be decomposed. The following values are possible:

  - ▶ 0—Uses attribute-centric decomposition. In this case, each attribute in the source XML is decomposed into a column. This is the default.

  - ▶ 1—Uses attribute-centric decomposition. May be combined with flag 2 (that is, the value 3 may be specified). Combining flags 1 and 2 tells the rowset generator how to deal with the values in the XML not yet accounted for in the downward parse of the XML document from nodes into rows. In other words, attribute-centric decomposition takes place before element-centric decomposition. This is important because without the combinability of the flags, only one or the other decomposition will happen, and (lacking a WITH predicate that captures all the nodes) some nodes would not make it into the rowset.

> ▶ **2**—Uses element-centric decomposition. Combinable with flag 1 (that is, specify 3).

> ▶ **8**—Tells the rowset generator how to deal with text data in the metaproperties (not covered in this chapter). Can be combined with flags 1, 2, or both.

Note that the column generation determined by the flags 0, 1, and 2 can all be overridden by the XPath expressions expressed in the lines of the WITH predicate. For example, if the 1 flag is specified to map a particular attribute to a column, but, in the line of the WITH predicate for that same column, the XPath maps the value from an XML element, the WITH predicate takes precedence. It's truly best to just set the value of *flags* to 3 in most cases, unless you care to ignore attributes or elements for some reason.

The syntax of the WITH predicate tells the rowset generator which column names and data types to use when mapping the XML to rows. If the structure of the input XML matches the schema of a particular table in your database, the name of that table may be specified. An example of this case is when the input XML has been produced from an existing table, using FOR XML. The values in the FOR XML-produced document have been updated, and the new values need to make it back into the table. The following code example illustrates this common scenario:

```
DECLARE @JobCandidateXmlDoc XML, @iXml int
SET @JobCandidateXmlDoc = '
    <JobCandidateUpdate>
      <ModifiedDate>
        10/5/2005 12:34PM
      </ModifiedDate>
    </JobCandidateUpdate>'
EXEC sp_xml_preparedocument
    @iXml OUTPUT,
    @JobCandidateXmlDoc,
    '<JobCandidateUpdate
      xmlns:ns="http://schemas.microsoft.com/sqlserver/2004/07/adventure-
➥works/Resume"/>';
UPDATE HumanResources.JobCandidate
SET ModifiedDate = OXML.ModifiedDate
FROM
(
    SELECT *
    FROM OPENXML(@iXml, '/JobCandidateUpdate', 2)
    WITH HumanResources.JobCandidate
) AS OXML
WHERE JobCandidateId = 8
EXEC sp_xml_removedocument @iXml
go
(1 row(s) affected)
```

37

If a table name is not specified, you need to specify a comma-separated list of lines, using the following syntax:

```
column_name datatype 'XPath'
```

The following list explains each part of the preceding syntax:

- ▶ *column_name*—Provides a relational name for the XML-produced column.

- ▶ *datatype*—Provides a T-SQL data type for the XML-produced column.

- ▶ *'XPath'*—Specifies a row pattern that matches the nodes in the XML whose values are to be mapped to the XML-produced column.

When you're done reading out the XML, it's important to free the memory used to hold the internal XML document. You accomplish this by calling the system stored procedure sp_xml_removedocument, as in the following example:

```
EXEC sp_xml_removedocument @iXml
```

Using the New xml Data Type

The new xml data type is a real problem solver for those who use both XML and SQL Server on a daily basis. For the first time, relational columns and XML data can be stored side-by-side in the same table, in an implementation that plays to the strengths of both. With SQL Server's powerful XML storage, validation, querying, and indexing capabilities, it's bound to cause quite a stir in the field of XML content management and beyond.

Some of the benefits of storing XML on the database tier can be realized immediately. Building middleware using the .NET Framework to manage XML stored in columns, rather than on the filesystem, is a far more robust solution than depending on the filesystem—plus, it's a lot easier to access the content from anywhere.

SQL Server inherently provides to stored XML the traditional DBMS benefits of backup and restoration, replication and failover, query optimization, granular locking, indexing, and content validation. The xml data type can be used with local variable declarations, as the output of user-defined functions, as input parameters to stored procedures and functions, and much more. XML instances containing up to 128 levels of nesting can be stored in xml columns; deeper instances cannot be inserted, nor may existing instances be made to increase beyond this depth via the modify() data type method.

xml columns can also be used to store code files such as XSLT, XSD, XHTML, and any other well-formed content. These files can then be retrieved by user-defined functions written in managed code hosted by SQL Server. (See Chapter 36, "SQL Server and the .NET Framework," for a full review of SQL Server–managed hosting.)

In some cases, it's still a perfectly valid scenario to store XML on the filesystem or in [n]varchar(max), [n]text, or [n]varbinary(max) columns. However, there are few cases when this is actually recommended. The following summary details some possible XML usage scenarios and makes suggestions for each.

XML data is stored in an internal binary format and can be up to 2GB in size.

Before we dig into the many uses of the xml data type, it's worthwhile to consider some of the different ways you can leverage your institution's XML with SQL Server:

▶ XML can be used solely as a temporary output format produced from relational data, using FOR XML. This applies in scenarios in which the relational tables hold the real-time data and XML is produced only for read-only application uses, as in the display of dynamic Web pages. In this scenario, the XML really just provides a DBMS-independent, easy-to-transform view of the data.

▶ XML can continue to be stored in relational (nvarchar and so on) columns. This might be the best option when your XML is sometimes not well formed or when the learning curve to XQuery is too high for an application-delivery time frame. This is also a valuable option when the byte-for-byte exactness of the XML must be preserved.

Note that the latter is a necessary option in some institutions because *typed XML* (that is, xml data type columns associated with a schema collection) storage disregards extra whitespace characters, namespace prefixes, attribute order, and the XML declaration in order to make way for query optimizations. This scenario also leverages fast data retrieval because, as far as SQL Server is concerned, XML is never brought into the mix (it's all relational). The data can still be converted to the xml data type, using the methods described earlier, and applications can use OPENXML to read it as well. To read XML into SQL Server from server-side accessible files, you call the T-SQL OPENROWSET function.

▶ The XML can be stored as untyped XML—that is, XML stored in an xml data type column lacking an associated schema collection. This provides the benefits of querying the XML using the new data type methods (discussed later in the section, "The Built-in xml Data Type Methods") and provides server-side well-formedness checks. This scenario also allows for the possibility that XML adhering to any (or no) schemas may reside in the column. A schema collection could be added later to provide validation on the existing data (although a few intermediate editing steps may be necessary if any documents fail to validate).

Safely armed with an understanding of some of the different options and uses, let's plunge into our discussion of xml.

37

Defining and Using xml Columns

You can add columns of type xml to any table by using a familiar Data Definition Language (DDL) syntax, with a few new twists. Much like their relational counterparts, xml columns, parameters, and variables may contain null or non-null values.

The following snippet shows the DDL used to create the table HumanResources.JobCandidate from AdventureWorks. The column you are concerned with is Resume:

```
CREATE TABLE [HumanResources].[JobCandidate](
    [JobCandidateID] [int] IDENTITY(1,1) NOT NULL,
    [EmployeeID] [int] NULL,
    [Resume] [xml](CONTENT [HumanResources].[HRResumeSchemaCollection]) NULL,
    [ModifiedDate] [datetime] NOT NULL
    CONSTRAINT [DF_JobCandidate_ModifiedDate] DEFAULT (getdate()),
    CONSTRAINT [PK_JobCandidate_JobCandidateID] PRIMARY KEY CLUSTERED
(
  [JobCandidateID] ASC
) ON [PRIMARY]
) ON [PRIMARY]
```

When defining objects of type xml, either of two *facets* may be applied:

- ▶ **CONTENT**—This facet specifies that well-formed XML documents as well as fragments may be inserted into the xml column or variable. (CONTENT is the default and may be omitted from the definition.)

  Fragments may have more than one top-level node (as is produced, by default, using FOR XML), and elements may be mixed with text-only nodes.

- ▶ **DOCUMENT**—This facet specifies that only well-formed, valid XML conforming to a specified schema collection may be stored. Updates to the column must also result in schema-valid, well-formed XML.

XML schema collections can be associated with xml variables, parameters, or columns. The name of the schema collection is specified directly after the chosen facet, as is done in JobCandidate.Resume.

The following code example defines a typed xml local variable that allows only valid Resume data to be stored in it:

```
DECLARE @ValidWellFormed xml (DOCUMENT HumanResources.HRResumeSchemaCollection)
```

Trying to insert the following well-formed but invalid document throws an error that says the first (and only) ThisBlowsUp element in the document is not declared in any of the schemas in HRResumeSchemaCollection:

```
SELECT @ValidWellFormed = '<ThisBlowsUp/>'
go
XML Validation: Declaration not found for element 'ThisBlowsUp'.
Location:/*:ThisBlowsUp[1]
```

When you change the facet to CONTENT (the default) and remove the schema association, the following is possible:

```
DECLARE @WellFormed xml
SELECT @WellFormed = '<ThisWorks/>'
go
Command(s) completed successfully.
```

When defining xml columns, you can specify defaults and constraints just as you do with relational columns. Consider the following example:

```
CREATE TABLE XmlExample
(
    XmlColumn xml NOT NULL DEFAULT CONVERT(xml,'<root/>',0)
)
```

This creates an xml column called XmlColumn that starts out having an empty root node. Notice how the string '<root/>' is converted to the xml type. This is actually not necessary because conversions from literal strings and from varchar to xml are implicit.

The next example adds a table-level constraint to XmlColumn to make sure the root node always exists. It depends on a scalar-valued user-defined function to do its validation work:

```
CREATE FUNCTION dbo.fn_XmlColumnNotNull
(
    @XmlColumnValue xml
)
RETURNS bit
AS
BEGIN
    RETURN @XmlColumnValue.exist('/root')
END
GO
CREATE TABLE XmlExample
(
    XmlColumn xml NOT NULL DEFAULT CONVERT(xml,'<root/>',0)
)
GO
ALTER TABLE XmlExample WITH CHECK
ADD CONSTRAINT CK_XmlExample_HasRoot
CHECK (dbo.fn_XmlColumnNotNull(XmlColumn) = 1)
```

37

The following statement thus fails:

```
INSERT XmlExample SELECT '<foo/>'
```

But this succeeds:

```
INSERT XmlExample SELECT '<root><foo/></root>'
```

Let's say you manage the data for a company that's just upgraded from SQL Server 2000 to 2005. You already store all your XML inside ntext columns, and it's time to convert those columns to xml. You can do this easily if the stored XML is well formed, as in the following example:

```
CREATE TABLE NTextXml
(
    NTextXmlColumn ntext NULL
)
GO
INSERT NTextXml
SELECT
    '<feedback_review>
      <parts_order id="106">
        <customer_comment>Lot&apos;s of Junk!</customer_comment>
      </parts_order>
    </feedback_review>'
GO
ALTER TABLE NTextXml
ALTER COLUMN NTextXmlColumn xml NULL
```

Next, you would like to ensure that all your XML validates against a schema. To change the column from typed to untyped XML by associating a schema, you execute the following:

```
ALTER TABLE NTextXml
ALTER COLUMN NTextXmlColumn xml
(DOCUMENT HumanResources.HRResumeSchemaCollection)
go
XML Validation: Declaration not found for element 'feedback_review'.
Location: /*:feedback_review[1]
The statement has been terminated.
```

Notice the error generated. This is because the tags used are not defined in the schemas of HRResumeSchemaCollection, so the XML does not validate, and the ALTER TABLE statement fails. What you really want is for the XML to validate against your own schema, which is described in the next section.

Using XML Schema Collections

In this section, you'll define a simple XML schema, add it to a new schema collection stored on the server, and create a table where you can store instances of this schema. You'll also add a check constraint to ensure that the value of the ProductId attribute of the XML's root node matches the value of the ProductId column, using the xml data type value() method (discussed later in this chapter, in the section, "The Built-in xml Data Type Methods"). The foreign key constraint you'll define on ProductId also serves to ensure that both ProductId values reference a primary key value in HumanResources. Product.

The real-world concept behind this sample schema is that it defines groups of customer feedback calls and subsequent corporate responses pertaining to different kinds of orders. Listing 37.14 shows the schema and the table definition.

LISTING 37.14   An XSD and Table for Modeling and Storing Customer Feedback Reviews

```
use AdventureWorks
go
CREATE XML SCHEMA COLLECTION Sales.FeedbackSchemaCollection AS
'<?xml version="1.0"?>
<xsd:schema
    xmlns:xsd="http://www.w3.org/2001/XMLSchema"
    targetNamespace="urn:www-samspublishing-com:examples:feedback_review_xsd"
    xmlns="urn:www-samspublishing-com:examples:feedback_review_xsd"
    elementFormDefault="qualified"
    attributeFormDefault="unqualified">
    <xsd:element name="feedback_review" type="feedbackReviewType"/>
    <xsd:complexType name="feedbackReviewType">
            <xsd:sequence minOccurs="1" maxOccurs="unbounded">
                <xsd:element name="order" type="orderType"/>
            </xsd:sequence>
            <xsd:attribute
                name="product_id"
                type="xsd:integer"
                use="optional"/>
    </xsd:complexType>
    <xsd:complexType name="feedbackType" mixed="true">
        <xsd:attribute name="id" type="xsd:integer" use="required"/>
    </xsd:complexType>
    <xsd:complexType name="orderType">
        <xsd:choice minOccurs="0" maxOccurs="unbounded">
            <xsd:element name="customer_comment" type="feedbackType"/>
            <xsd:element name="company_response" type="feedbackType"/>
        </xsd:choice>
        <xsd:attribute name="id" type="xsd:integer" use="required"/>
        <xsd:attribute name="type" use="required">
```

37

LISTING 37.14   Continued

```
            <xsd:simpleType>
                <xsd:restriction base="xsd:string">
                    <xsd:enumeration value="parts"/>
                    <xsd:enumeration value="product"/>
                    <xsd:enumeration value="service"/>
                </xsd:restriction>
            </xsd:simpleType>
        </xsd:attribute>
    </xsd:complexType>
</xsd:schema>'
GO
CREATE FUNCTION Sales.fnCheckProductId
(
  @FeedbackReviewXml xml
)
RETURNS int
AS
BEGIN
  DECLARE @ProductId int

  SELECT @ProductId = @FeedbackReviewXml.value('
          declare namespace
              fr="urn:www-samspublishing-com:examples:feedback_review_xsd";
              /fr:feedback_review[1]/@product_id', 'int')

  RETURN @ProductId
END
GO
CREATE TABLE Sales.FeedbackReview
(
    FeedbackReviewId int IDENTITY(1, 1) NOT NULL PRIMARY KEY,
    ProductId int NULL REFERENCES Production.Product,
    FeedbackReviewXml xml (DOCUMENT Sales.FeedbackSchemaCollection) NOT NULL,
    CONSTRAINT ProductIdMatches
    CHECK (Sales.fnCheckProductId(FeedbackReviewXml) = ProductId)
)
GO
```

Having created the xml column, you can now insert valid, well-formed documents into
FeedbackReview in the following manner:

```
INSERT Sales.FeedbackReview
SELECT
    NULL,
```

```
'<feedback_review
    xmlns="urn:www-samspublishing-com:examples:feedback_review_xsd">
    <order id="353" type="service">
        <customer_comment id="131">
                        You guys said you&apos;d be here on Monday.
                </customer_comment>
        <company_response id="242">I said Wednesday!</company_response>
    </order>
</feedback_review>'
GO
(1 row(s) affected)
```

Using INSERT, you can input XML into xml columns as varchar, xml, or literal string data, or you can insert the output of a subquery that returns these types.

The syntax used to create an XML schema collection is simple and straightforward:

```
CREATE SCHEMA COLLECTION schema_collection_name AS schema
```

The *schema* parameter can be either a string (as shown), or a variable that contains the text of the schema of type varchar, nvarchar, varbinary, nvarbinary, or xml.

Dropping a schema collection is just as easy:

```
DROP SCHEMA COLLECTION schema_collection_name
```

If you ever want to select your schema back out again, you simply call the system function xml_schema_namespace, as in the following example:

```
SELECT xml_schema_namespace(
    'Sales',
    'FeedbackSchemaCollection',
    'urn:www-samspublishing-com:examples:feedback_review_xsd'
)
```

To add additional schemas to the collection, you use ALTER XML SCHEMA COLLECTION:

```
ALTER XML SCHEMA COLLECTION
Sales.FeedbackSchemaCollection ADD another schema
```

To view some of the nodes in your stored XML schemas, you query sys.xml_schema_collection and its related catalog views. Here's an example:

```
use AdventureWorks
go
SELECT el.name, el.*, el.must_be_qualified
FROM sys.columns sc
JOIN sys.xml_schema_collections xs
ON sc.xml_collection_id = xs.xml_collection_id
```

```
JOIN sys.xml_schema_elements el
ON xs.xml_collection_id = el.xml_collection_id
WHERE sc.name = 'FeedbackReviewXml'
```

Given the name of the table's typed xml column (FeedbackReviewXml), you can find its associated schema collection by querying the catalog views as follows:

```
SELECT
    sc.name XmlColumnName,
    xs.name CollectionName,
    ns.name Namespace
from sys.columns sc
JOIN sys.xml_schema_collections xs
ON sc.xml_collection_id = xs.xml_collection_id
JOIN sys.xml_schema_namespaces ns
ON ns.xml_collection_id = sc.xml_collection_id
WHERE sc.name = 'FeedbackReviewXml'
go
XmlColumnName         CollectionName              Namespace
-------------------------------------------------------------------------

FeedbackReviewXml     FeedbackSchemaCollection    urn:www-samspublishing-
➥com:examples:feedback_review_xsd
```

You can accomplish the same thing by using the Object Browser in SSMS by viewing the properties of the xml column or by right-clicking the Modify menu choice on the table object, as shown in Figure 37.1.

You can control permissions on schema collections by using the standard ALTER, CONTROL, TAKE OWNERSHIP, REFERENCES, VIEW DEFINITION, and EXECUTE syntax. Here's an example:

```
GRANT ALTER ON XML SCHEMA COLLECTION::Sales.FeedbackSchemaCollection
TO some_login
```

There are a few unsupported XML schema features in schema collections. Check the Books Online article, "Guidelines and Limitations of XML Schema Collections on the Server" for the most up-to-date information. The following are some notable limitations:

▶ The XSD constraints key, keyref, and unique are not supported.

▶ XSD include and redefine are not supported.

▶ Lax validation is not supported.

You can also manage XML schema collections using SSMS. To do so, you open the Object Browser and expand the main tree to the following node: ServerName\Databases\ AdventureWorks\Programmability\Types\XML Schema Collections. Then you right-click a schema collection to drop it or to add new schemas. You can also easily script schemas out for review whenever needed. Figure 37.2 shows the expanded Object Browser tree.

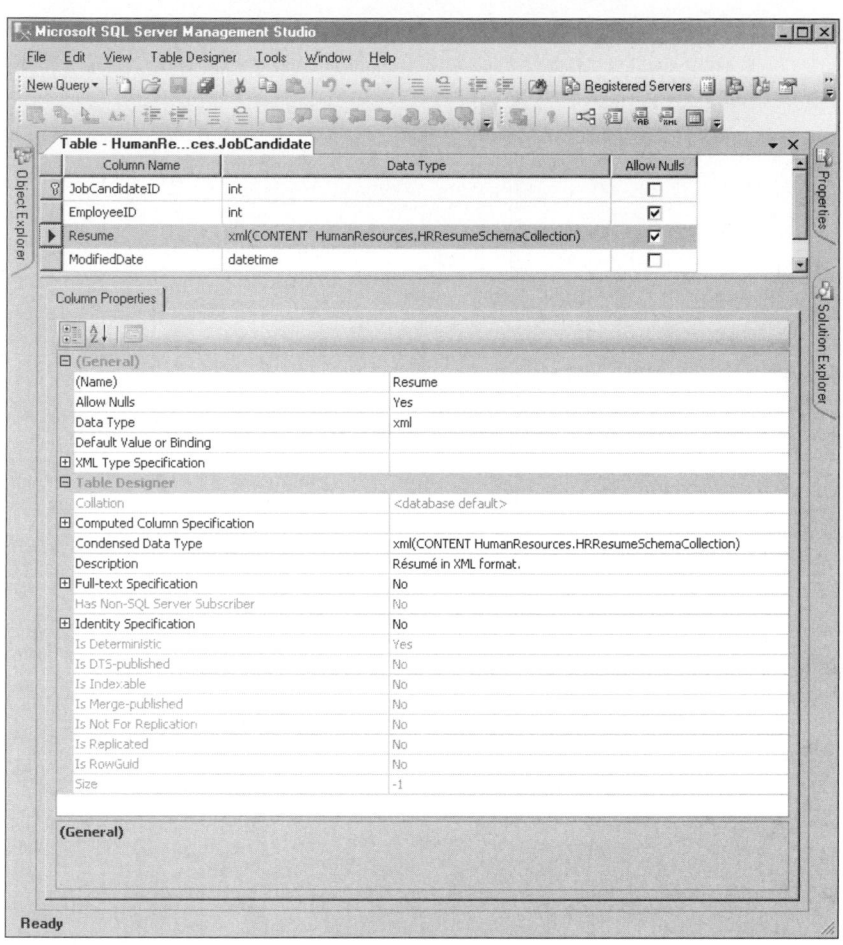

FIGURE 37.1   Viewing the properties of an xml column in SSMS.

The Built-in xml Data Type Methods

Now that you know how to create and manage typed and untyped xml columns, the next step is to learn how to query and modify stored XML content. Although SQL Server supports only a subset of the XQuery 1.0 recommendation, you'll soon see that it's plenty to get the job done.

Keep in mind that a mastery of XQuery is not a requirement for selecting out XML data; you can just specify the name of the xml column to select all the data back at once.

SQL Server provides five built-in methods on the xml data type: query(), exists(), value(), nodes(), and modify(). These methods are appended to the name of the xml column in question, using the *ColumnName.MethodName([MethodParameters])* syntax. These methods work on XML in the following ways:

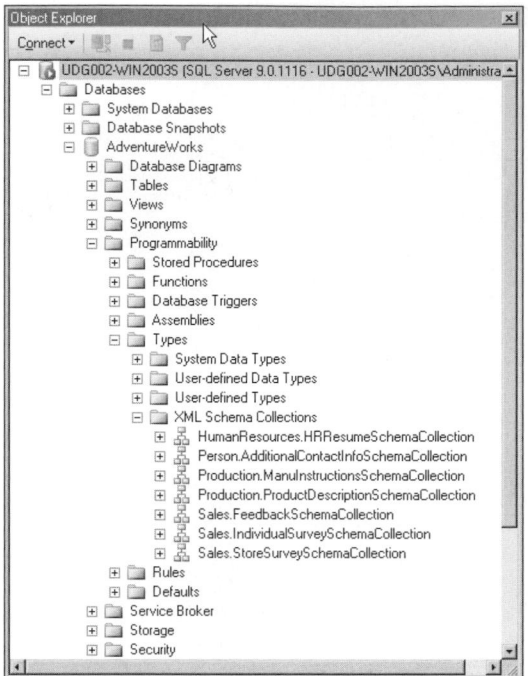

FIGURE 37.2   Using the Object Browser to manage XML schema collections.

- ▶ **query()**—Evaluates an XQuery expression into a node list, allowing for reshaping of the selected nodes. Results in untyped XML.

- ▶ **exists()**—Performs a Boolean test to see whether the result of an XQuery expression is empty (no matching nodes). Returns 1 (non-empty), or 0 (empty).

- ▶ **value()**—Extracts a single (that is, *scalar*) value from an XML node and casts it to a SQL Server relational data type (for example, int, varchar).

- ▶ **nodes()**—Uses an XQuery expression to decompose the XML input into a rowset; this is similar to the effect of OPENXML.

- ▶ **modify()**—Alters the content of an XML document using the insert, replace value of, and delete XQuery functions.

XQuery is a bit like T-SQL in that it uses similar SELECT-FROM-WHERE-ORDER BY semantics to find the required nodes. It also bears a resemblance to writing foreach loops with object iterators in a language such as C#. It is unique in that it combines the navigational power of XPath to locate nodes and (in the same expressions) allows for new XML generation on-the-fly, all in one tight syntax package built especially for processing XML.

To use XQuery effectively, it is essential that you have at least a rudimentary understanding of XPath. A great starting point is the World Wide Web Consortium's (W3C's) site, at www.w3.org/TR/xpath20/. The following subsections assume such basic knowledge.

Selecting XML by Using query()

The job of query() is to retrieve XML nodes by using XQuery expressions. The result of query() is an instance of untyped xml. It takes a single parameter, a string literal containing the XQuery code itself.

NOTE

Like all the other four xml data type methods (and unlike most other T-SQL keywords), query() is case-sensitive. This is in keeping with the case-sensitivity of XML itself.

NOTE

The parameter to query() cannot be a variable; it must be a string literal. This puts something of a hold on dynamic XQuery expressions. However, declared T-SQL variables and column values are available for use in XQuery, using the functions sql:variable() and sql:column() (described later in this chapter).

Each XQuery query is broken into two distinct parts, separated by a semicolon. The first part is known as the *prolog*. This is where any namespaces used in the XPath expressions and selected nodes are declared. The second part is known as the *body*, and this is where XPath and XQuery expressions are evaluated.

The following example declares the act namespace in its query prolog and then selects any act:eMail nodes from Person.Contact.AdditionalContactInfo in its body:

```
SELECT
    AdditionalContactInfo.query(
'
    declare namespace
        act="http://schemas.microsoft.com/sqlserver/2004/07/adventure-
➥works/ContactTypes";
    //act:eMail
'
)
FROM Person.Contact
WHERE ContactId = 2
go
<act:eMail
    xmlns:act="http://schemas.microsoft.com/sqlserver/2004/07/adventure-
➥works/ContactTypes">
    <act:eMailAddress>Joe@xyz.com</act:eMailAddress>
    <act:SpecialInstructions>
        Dont send emails for urgent issues. Use telephone instead.
    </act:SpecialInstructions>
</act:eMail>
```

Note that as with FOR XML, the result of query() can sometimes be an XML fragment (or an empty string). You can again use FOR XML RAW, ROOT to guarantee that this won't happen. Listing 37.15 illustrates this, as well as the new WITH XMLNAMESPACES statement:

LISTING 37.15   Using WITH XMLNAMESPACES with FOR XML and query()

```
WITH XMLNAMESPACES
(
    'http://schemas.microsoft.com/sqlserver/2004/07/adventure-works/ContactTypes'
      as act
)
SELECT
    FirstName,
    LastName,
    AdditionalContactInfo.query(
    '
    //act:eMail
    '
)
FROM Person.Contact
WHERE ContactId = 2
FOR XML RAW('ContactInfo'), ROOT('Contact')
go
<Contact xmlns:act="http://schemas.microsoft.com/sqlserver/2004/07/adventure-
➥works/ContactTypes">
  <ContactInfo FirstName="Catherine" LastName="Abel">
    <act:eMail xmlns:act="http://schemas.microsoft.com/sqlserver/2004/07/
➥adventure-works/ContactTypes">
      <act:eMailAddress>Joe@xyz.com</act:eMailAddress>
      <act:SpecialInstructions>
        Dont send emails for urgent issues. Use telephone instead.
      </act:SpecialInstructions>
    </act:eMail>
  </ContactInfo>
</Contact>
```

You can use WITH XMLNAMESPACES to declare namespaces for use in subsequent SELECT statements. This makes it possible to omit the prolog from the query(). It also has the desirable side effect of adding the act namespace declaration to the root Contact node in the resulting FOR XML RAW wrapper. It's a great keystroke saver and helps keep xml data type queries readable.

In addition to selecting nodes with simple XPath expressions, you can use query() to specify WHERE clause conditions on the selected nodes, iterate through the nodes using for-each semantics, order the nodes differently than in the original document, and return XML in any desired structure, based on the selection. This type of processing is known by its acronym FLWOR (pronounced *flower*), which stands for `for`, `let`, `where`, `order by`, `return`. (Note that SQL Server doesn't support the *let* part of this syntax.)

The `for` Clause   The `for` clause establishes a variable that is bound to a node list for the purpose of iterating over each node. In each iteration of the `for` loop, this bound variable takes the value of the context node. It may be optionally typed (using as *XML_Schema_TypeName)* to a schema-declared type, and it is followed by the XPath used to match the nodes to be selected. The bound variable in the following example is `$ContextNode`:

```
SELECT Instructions.query('
    declare default element namespace
    "http://schemas.microsoft.com/sqlserver/2004/07/adventure
    ➥-works/ProductModelManuInstructions";
    for $ContextNode in //Location
    return
        <LotSize>
            {$ContextNode/@LotSize}
        </LotSize>
') as Result
FROM   Production.ProductModel
WHERE ProductModelID = 10
Go
<LotSize xmlns="http://schemas.microsoft.com/sqlserver/2004/07/adventure-
➥works/ProductModelManuInstructions" LotSize="100" />
```

This example also shows the use of the `declare default element namespace` statement, which allows the specified XPath expressions that follow it to omit any namespace prefixes.

In place of an XPath expression, you can use the bound variable to iterate through a sequence of values, rather than nodes, as in the following example:

```
SELECT Instructions.query('
    for $ContextNode in (1, 2, 3)
    return
        <Number>
            {$ContextNode }
        </Number>
') as Result
FROM   Production.ProductModel
WHERE ProductModelID = 10
go
<Number>1</Number>
<Number>2</Number>
<Number>3</Number>
```

37

You can also specify more than one bound variable in the `for` clause. Bound variables subsequent to the first can be used in XPath queries against the first. In this manner, two related context nodes—one inner and one outer—can be created simultaneously. This is analogous to writing a nested `for` loop in a programming language, but here you need only declare both context variables by the simple use of a comma. Here's an example:

```
DECLARE @Xml xml
SET @Xml = '
    <outernode name="a">
        <innernode>1</innernode>
        <innernode>2</innernode>
        <innernode>3</innernode>
    </outernode>
    <outernode name="b">
        <innernode>4</innernode>
        <innernode>5</innernode>
        <innernode>6</innernode>
    </outernode>
'
SELECT @Xml.query('
    for $outer in /outernode,
        $inner in $outer/innernode
    return
        <Outside letter="{$outer/@name}">
            <Inside number="{$inner}"/>
        </Outside>
')
go
<Outside letter="a">
  <Inside number="1" />
</Outside>
<Outside letter="a">
  <Inside number="2" />
</Outside>
<Outside letter="a">
  <Inside number="3" />
</Outside>
<Outside letter="b">
  <Inside number="4" />
</Outside>
<Outside letter="b">
  <Inside number="5" />
</Outside>
<Outside letter="b">
  <Inside number="6" />
</Outside>
```

The where **Clause**   Just like the WHERE clause in T-SQL, XQuery's where clause restricts the nodes in the selected node list to those matching a certain expression. Here's an example:

```
SELECT TOP 1 Resume.query('
    declare namespace
    ns="http://schemas.microsoft.com/sqlserver/2004/07/adventure-works/Resume";

    for $ResumeNode in /ns:Resume
    where count($ResumeNode/ns:Employment) > 2
    return
        $ResumeNode/ns:Employment/ns:Emp.JobTitle
')
FROM HumanResources.JobCandidate
go
<ns:Emp.JobTitle
    xmlns:ns="http://schemas.microsoft.com/sqlserver/2004/07/adventure-
➥works/Resume">
      Lead Machinist
</ns:Emp.JobTitle>
<ns:Emp.JobTitle
    xmlns:ns="http://schemas.microsoft.com/sqlserver/2004/07/adventure-
➥works/Resume">
      Machinist
</ns:Emp.JobTitle>
<ns:Emp.JobTitle
    xmlns:ns="http://schemas.microsoft.com/sqlserver/2004/07/adventure-
➥works/Resume">
      Assistant Machinist
</ns:Emp.JobTitle>
```

Here, you use the T-SQL-analogous count() aggregate function to restrict the result set to ns:Resume nodes having three or more ns:Employment children. The standard aggregate functions are available in XQuery expressions. They are max(), min(), avg(), sum(), and count().

The order by **Clause**   Just like T-SQL's ORDER BY, XQuery's order by is used to reorder the selected nodes from the default document order to a new order, based on an expression. The order may be set to descending or ascending (the default).

The following example casts a node value to an instance of the xs:date type and orders the results from most to least recent date:

```
SELECT Resume.query('
    declare namespace
        ns="http://schemas.microsoft.com/sqlserver/2004/07/adventure-works/Resume";
    <Achievements>
    {
```

```
        for $EducationNode in //ns:Education
        order by xs:date(string($EducationNode/ns:Edu.EndDate[1])) descending
        return
            <Degree>
                <DateAwarded>
                { string($EducationNode/ns:Edu.EndDate[1]) }
                </DateAwarded>
                <Name>
                { string($EducationNode/ns:Edu.Degree[1]) }
                </Name>
            </Degree>
    }
    </Achievements>
')
FROM HumanResources.JobCandidate
WHERE JobCandidateId = 2
go
<Achievements>
  <Degree>
    <DateAwarded>1997-06-03Z</DateAwarded>
    <Name>Bachelor of Science</Name>
  </Degree>
  <Degree>
    <DateAwarded>1993-06-12Z</DateAwarded>
    <Name>Diploma</Name>
  </Degree>
</Achievements>
```

The expression xs:date(string($EducationNode/ns:Edu.EndDate[1])) requires some explanation. Working from the inside out: ns:Edu.EndDate is selected, using the child node of the node stored in the bound context variable $EducationNode. For the string() typecasting function to work, a *singleton*, or single node, must be specified; this is why the positional predicate [1] must be specified. Finally, the string is cast to xs:date. (Note that in the return statement, the string value of the same node is used.)

This example illustrates not only the type-related aspects of FLWOR expressions but also the ability to generate a root node without using FOR XML...ROOT. All that is required is that a root node (in this case, Achievements), followed by curly braces, surround the entire FLWOR statement.

The return Clause   Similar to T-SQL's SELECT statement, the return clause executes once for every selected context node. This is the section where you specify the structure and content of the resulting XML. The key aspect of it is the use of node *constructors*.

> **TIP**
>
> When using attribute constructors in the `return` clause, you need to make sure your curly braces are directly adjacent to the attribute's begin and end quotes, with no whitespace in between (for example, `attribute="{$Node}"`), or SQL Server raises an error. This is because string literals (even blank spaces) cannot be mixed with attribute constructors.

Put simply, constructors create the nodes and node values to be output. There are two types of constructors:

▶ **Computed constructors**—These are placed inside curly-braced expressions and evaluated against the context node (for example, `attribute="{$N}"`).

▶ **Direct constructors**—These are constant node strings used in the FLWOR statement (for example, `<Achievements>`). Listing 37.16 illustrates a variety of constructors.

LISTING 37.16   Using XQuery Constructors

```
SELECT Resume.query('
    declare namespace
        ns="http://schemas.microsoft.com/sqlserver/2004/07/adventure-works/Resume";

    for $N in //ns:Education
    return
        <NodeConstructor attributeConstructor="{string($N/ns:Edu.School[1])}">
            { $N/ns:Edu.Major }
            <?PI processing-instruction constructor PI?>
            <!-- comment constructor -->
        </NodeConstructor>
')
FROM HumanResources.JobCandidate
WHERE JobCandidateId = 1
go
<NodeConstructor attributeConstructor="Midwest State University">
    <ns:Edu.Major
      xmlns:ns="http://schemas.microsoft.com/sqlserver/2004/07/adventure-
➥works/Resume">
      Mechanical Engineering
    </ns:Edu.Major>
  <?PI processing-instruction constructor PI?>
  <!-- comment constructor -->
</NodeConstructor>
```

37

Exactly the same XML result can be generated a third way—using the alternative node-type-name constructors (for example, element, attribute, text) in a comma-delimited list within curly braces. Here's an example:

```
SELECT Resume.query('
    declare namespace
        ns="http://schemas.microsoft.com/sqlserver/2004/07/adventure-works/Resume";

    for $N in //ns:Education
    return
        element NodeConstructor
        {
            attribute attributeConstructor { string($N/ns:Edu.School[1])},
            text { string($N/ns:Edu.Major[1]) },
            <?PI processing-instruction constructor PI?>,
            <!-- comment constructor -->
        }
')
FROM HumanResources.JobCandidate
WHERE JobCandidateId = 1
```

> **TIP**
>
> Because query() returns an instance of xml, the xml data type methods can be stacked on its result, allowing for powerful XQuery subqueries, such as query('').query('').exist('').

Testing XML by Using exist()

A common task when working with XML is the need to check for the existence of a node or node value. The exist() method does just that, returning 1 if the node test returns non-empty, or 0 if empty.

Listing 37.17 tests whether the annual revenue of a surveyed store exceeds $100,000.

LISTING 37.17   Using exist() to Test for a Specific Node Value

```
WITH XMLNAMESPACES
(
    DEFAULT 'http://schemas.microsoft.com/sqlserver/2004/07/adventure-
➡works/StoreSurvey'
)
SELECT Demographics.query(
'
    for $N in /StoreSurvey
    order by $N/AnnualSales
    return
```

LISTING 37.17   Continued

```
    if ($N/AnnualSales >= 3000000)
    then
        <Money
          Bank="{$N/BankName}"
          AnnualRevenue="{$N/AnnualRevenue}"
          AnnualSales="{$N/AnnualSales}"
          Comments="really big bucks"/>
    else
        <Money
          AnnualRevenue="{$N/AnnualRevenue}"
          AnnualSales="{$N/AnnualSales}"
          Comments="big bucks"/>
')
FROM Sales.Store
WHERE Demographics.exist('
    (//AnnualRevenue[xs:integer(.)>100000])
') = 1
go
<p1:Money xmlns:p1="http://schemas.microsoft.com/sqlserver/2004/07/adventure-
➥works/StoreSurvey" AnnualRevenue="150000" AnnualSales="1500000"
➥Comments="big bucks" />
<p1:Money xmlns:p1="http://schemas.microsoft.com/sqlserver/2004/07/adventure-
➥works/StoreSurvey" AnnualRevenue="150000" AnnualSales="1500000"
➥Comments="big bucks" />
<p1:Money xmlns:p1="http://schemas.microsoft.com/sqlserver/2004/07/adventure-
➥works/StoreSurvey" AnnualRevenue="150000" AnnualSales="1500000"
➥Comments="big bucks" />
<p1:Money xmlns:p1="http://schemas.microsoft.com/sqlserver/2004/07/adventure-
➥works/StoreSurvey" AnnualRevenue="150000" AnnualSales="1500000"
➥Comments="big bucks" />
<p1:Money xmlns:p1="http://schemas.microsoft.com/sqlserver/2004/07/adventure-
➥works/StoreSurvey" Bank="International Bank" AnnualRevenue="300000"
➥AnnualSales="3000000" Comments="really big bucks" />
{...}
```

Listing 37.17 also illustrates the use of the XQuery if-then-else construct, which is used to conditionally generate the BankName attribute and change the value of the Comments attribute. In the WITH XMLNAMESPACES statement that precedes the query, you use the DEFAULT keyword to specify a default namespace for the selection.

Converting a Node Value to a T-SQL Data Type by Using value()

The value() function allows for a selected node value to be cast to a T-SQL–data typed value. It has two parameters: The first is a string-literal XPath expression that selects the desired node value. The second is a string-literal T-SQL data type name.

The code in Listing 37.18 queries a scalar vector graphics (SVG) document by using
value() to select the height attribute of the first svg node and cast it to a decimal. Notice
that the returned results are rows rather than XML.

LISTING 37.18   Using value() to Retrieve and Convert a Node Value

```
WITH XMLNAMESPACES
(
    'http://ns.adobe.com/Extensibility/1.0/' as x,
    'http://ns.adobe.com/AdobeIllustrator/10.0/' as i,
    'http://ns.adobe.com/Graphs/1.0/' as graph,
    'http://www.w3.org/1999/xlink' as xlink,
    'http://ns.adobe.com/AdobeSVGViewerExtensions/3.0/' as a,
     DEFAULT 'http://www.w3.org/2000/svg'
)
SELECT
    IllustrationID,
    Diagram.value('/svg[1]/@height', 'decimal(16,4)') SVGHeightAsSQLDecimal
FROM Production.Illustration
go
IllustrationID    SVGHeightAsSQLDecimal
--------------    ---------------------
3                 150.4220
4                 312.9940
5                 108.8500
6                 213.5410
7                 167.0700
(5 row(s) affected)
```

Accessing Relational Columns and T-SQL Variables in XQuery Expressions   Besides value(),
two other bridges between T-SQL and XQuery are the XQuery functions sql:column()
and sql:variable().

sql:column(), as the name implies, allows for the selection of a relational column value
in a FLWOR statement. In Listing 37.19, contact name data is pulled from
Person.Contact into an XQuery element constructor and then selected back out again as
a node value. In addition, the value of the declared T-SQL variable TotalPurchaseYTD is
compared against the value of the node of the same name in the XQuery where clause,
using sql:variable().

LISTING 37.19   Using sql:column() and sql:variable() in XQuery

```
DECLARE @TotalPurchaseYTD decimal(6,2)
SET @TotalPurchaseYTD = 8248.99
SELECT Demographics.query('
    declare default element namespace
```

LISTING 37.19   Continued

```
    "http://schemas.microsoft.com/sqlserver/2004/07/adventure-
➥works/IndividualSurvey";
    for $IS in /IndividualSurvey
    where $IS/TotalPurchaseYTD[.= sql:variable("@TotalPurchaseYTD")]
    return
    element Contact
    {
        attribute ID { sql:column("C.ContactID") },
        attribute YTDTotal { sql:variable("@TotalPurchaseYTD") },
        element FullName { concat(sql:column("FirstName"), " ",
          sql:column("LastName")) }
    }
')
FROM Sales.Individual I
JOIN Person.Contact C ON
C.ContactID = I.ContactID
AND C.ContactID = 12731
```

concat() is one of several string functions built into XQuery, in addition to contains(), substring(), and string-length().

Using the nodes() Method to Shred XML

In the section, "XML as Relational Data: Using OPENXML," earlier in this chapter, you learned how to decompose XML directly into relational rows that could be mapped to values in existing tables or used any other T-SQL way.

nodes() is kind of like OPENXML's big brother: Given an XML input document and an XQuery expression, it generates a table with an xml column against which subsequent XQuery queries can be run. nodes() can be applied to both xml variables and xml columns.

Each row in the generated table contains a copy of the original input content. The context node for each row is based on the XQuery expression parameter. It is possible to shred the input in multiple ways by running multiple XQuery queries on the generated column in the same SELECT statement. For example, one query might return a relational value from each context node, using the value() method. Another could transform and return each content node to a different XML schema.

Let's examine a simple example that shows how this works. Listing 37.20 illustrates how an XML document is shredded into relational rows and columns by applying six different XQuery queries on each generated row, each of which creates a new relational column.

37

LISTING 37.20   Shredding XML Six Ways, Using nodes()

```
DECLARE @XmlVar xml
SET @XmlVar = '
<alphnumerics>
    <item>
        <alph name="A" val="65"/>
    </item>
    <item>
        <alph name="B" val="66"/>
    </item>
    <item>
        <alph name="C" val="67"/>
    </item>
    <item>
        <num name="1" val="49"/>
    </item>
    <item>
        <num name="2" val="50"/>
    </item>
    <item>
        <num name="3" val="51"/>
    </item>
</alphnumerics>'
SELECT
    XmlTable.XmlColumn.query('alph') AS ANode,
    XmlTable.XmlColumn.value('alph[1]/@name', 'char(1)') AS AName,
    XmlTable.XmlColumn.value('alph[1]/@val', 'int') AS AVal,
    XmlTable.XmlColumn.query('num') AS NNode,
    XmlTable.XmlColumn.value('num[1]/@name', 'int') AS NName,
    XmlTable.XmlColumn.value('num[1]/@val', 'int') AS NVal
FROM @XmlVar.nodes('/alphnumerics/item') AS XmlTable(XmlColumn)
```

The syntax of nodes() is as follows:

```
nodes(XQuery) AS GeneratedTableName(GeneratedXmlColumnName)
```

Note that it is not possible to directly select the xml column generated by nodes without using one of the xml data type methods. Using the XML from the preceding example, the following code would raise an error:

```
SELECT XmlTable.XmlColumn
FROM @XmlVar.nodes('/alphnumerics/item') AS XmlTable(XmlColumn)
```

You can also use nodes() with CROSS APPLY or OUTER APPLY to execute nodes() once for every row returned in the outer table. In this way, you can combine relational data with multiple XQuery queries against a relational rowset. Listing 37.21 illustrates this technique.

LISTING 37.21   Using `nodes()` with `CROSS APPLY`

```
WITH XMLNAMESPACES(
    'http://schemas.microsoft.com/sqlserver/2004/07/adventure-works/Resume' as ns
)
SELECT
    JC.JobCandidateId,
    E.EmployeeId,
    ResumeTable.XmlColumn.value('ns:Emp.JobTitle[1]', 'nchar(50)') JobTitle
FROM HumanResources.JobCandidate JC
CROSS APPLY JC.Resume.nodes('
    /ns:Resume/ns:Employment[2]
') as ResumeTable(XmlColumn)
JOIN HumanResources.Employee E ON
E.EmployeeId = JC.EmployeeId
go
JobCandidateId    EmployeeId    JobTitle
----------------------------------------
4                 268           Sales Associate
8                 41            高级销售助理
 (2 row(s) affected.)
```

Using `modify()` to Insert, Update, and Delete XML

A frequent requirement when working with XML is the insertion, deletion, and modification of nodes and node values. These operations are known as *XML Data Modification Language* (XML DML) statements, and they are supported by the xml data type's `modify()` method.

When working with typed XML, `modify()` performs type and structural checks that allow operations to succeed only if they result in valid XML, so it's important to know your schema well.

When document order is important, it's also crucial to know the exact location and position of the nodes or values to be changed. In the case of untyped or loosely constrained typed XML, it may not matter all that much where a new node is placed.

XQuery provides a few functions and operators related to node order. `position()` returns the numeric position of a node (starting at 1). `last()` returns the numeric position of the last node in a selected node list. They are both performed against a context node.

In addition, you can use the node order comparison operators << and >> to compare the relative positions of two selected nodes. The Boolean `is` operator is also provided to test whether two selected nodes are actually the same node.

37

modify() allows for three main operations in its XQuery expression parameter: insert, replace value of, and delete. Let's look at delete first.

Removing XML Nodes by Using delete   delete uses its XPath parameter to locate the node to remove. In the example in Listing 37.22, any alph node that has a name attribute with a value of B is deleted. Then, the remaining values for alph/@name are selected, using nodes() to illustrate the success of the deletion.

LISTING 37.22   Deleting Nodes by Using delete

```
DECLARE @XmlVar xml
SET @XmlVar = '
<alphnumerics>
    <item>
        <alph name="A" val="65"/>
    </item>
    <item>
        <alph name="B" val="66"/>
    </item>
    <item>
        <alph name="C" val="67"/>
    </item>
    <item>
        <num name="1" val="49"/>
    </item>
    <item>
        <num name="2" val="50"/>
    </item>
    <item>
        <num name="3" val="51"/>
    </item>
</alphnumerics>'
SET @XmlVar.modify('delete(//item/alph[@name="B"])')
SELECT XmlTable.XmlCol.value('./@name', 'char(1)')
    as RemainingAlphNames
FROM @XmlVar.nodes('//item/alph') as XmlTable(XmlCol)
go
AlphNames
A
C
(2 row(s) affected)
```

Modifying XML with insert **and** replace value of   You can insert and update new nodes in document trees by using insert. This is where node position counts most. Let's look at a real-world example for the examples in this section: Say that a content author is building a structured document. Each node has both its respective level (or *depth*) and its order of appearance. Your DML operations must respect both. The markup and table storage for such a scenario might look something like the untyped XML in Listing 37.23.

LISTING 37.23   Simple Untyped XML Markup for a Book

```
CREATE TABLE SimpleBook
    (BookId int IDENTITY(1,1) PRIMARY KEY CLUSTERED, BookXml xml)
GO
INSERT SimpleBook
SELECT
'<book book_id="1">
    <title>A Great Work</title>
    <chapter chapter_id="1">
        <title>An Excellent Chapter</title>
        <section section_id="1">
            <title>A Boring Section</title>
            <paragraph para_id="1">
                Something boring.
            </paragraph>
        </section>
        <section section_id="2">
            <title>Another Fine Section</title>
            <paragraph para_id="2">
                Another fine paragraph.
            </paragraph>
        </section>
    </chapter>
</book>'
```

In this listing, notice that the XML element content in the first section seems out of place, considering the laudatory content of the chapter and book titles. You can fix this by using replace value of, which has the following syntax:

```
replace value of old_expression with new_expression
```

> **NOTE**
>
> When updating typed xml values, the value specified in new_expression must be of the same XSD-declared type as the value selected in old_expression.

Here is the update for the book's incongruous content:

```
UPDATE SimpleBook
SET BookXml.modify('
    replace value of (/book/chapter/section[@section_id="1"]/title/text())[1]
    with "A Fine Section"
```

```
')
WHERE BookId = 1
GO
UPDATE SimpleBook
SET BookXml.modify('
    replace value of (/book/chapter/section/paragraph[@para_id="1"]/text())[1]
    with "A Fine Paragraph"
')
WHERE BookId = 1
(1 row(s) affected)
(1 row(s) affected)
```

You can also add a new section to the document by using the `insert` function, which has the following syntax:

```
insert new_node_expression (
    {{{as first ¦ as last} into} ¦ after ¦ before}
    reference_node_expression )
```

`new_node_expression` is where you specify the nodes to be inserted, using the familiar direct or computed constructor syntax, discussed earlier in this chapter, in the section, "Selecting by XML Using `query()`."

What's different about `insert` is that it allows for the specification of where, with respect to the `reference_node_expression`, the constructed nodes are to be placed. To specify that the new nodes are to be inserted as children of the reference node, you use as `first into` when specifying the first child. You use as `last into` when specifying the last child.

To specify that the new node is to be inserted as a sibling of the reference node, you use `after` to specify the next sibling or `before` to specify that the new node is a previous sibling of the reference node (that is, the new node is now to be the leftmost sibling).

You can finish the sample document by adding a new `chapter` to the `book`, using the code in Listing 37.24.

LISTING 37.24   Inserting Nodes by Using `insert`

```
UPDATE SimpleBook
SET BookXml.modify('
    insert
        <chapter chapter_id="2">
            <title>This is Chapter 2</title>
        </chapter>
    after
    (/book/chapter[@chapter_id=1])[1]
')
```

LISTING 37.24   Continued

```
WHERE BookId = 1
GO
UPDATE SimpleBook
SET BookXml.modify('
    insert
        <section section_id="3">
            <title>This is Section 3</title>
        </section>
    as last into
    (/book/chapter[@chapter_id=2])[1]
')
WHERE BookId = 1
GO
SELECT BookXml FROM SimpleBook
GO
<book book_id="1">
  <title>A Great Work</title>
  <chapter chapter_id="1">
    <title>An Excellent Chapter</title>
    <section section_id="1">
      <title>A Fine Section</title>
      <paragraph para_id="1">A Fine Paragraph</paragraph>
    </section>
    <section section_id="2">
      <title>Another Fine Section</title>
      <paragraph para_id="2">
        Another fine paragraph.
      </paragraph>
    </section>
  </chapter>
  <chapter chapter_id="2">
    <title>This is Chapter 2</title>
    <section section_id="3">
      <title>This is Section 3</title>
    </section>
  </chapter>
</book>
```

The first call to modify() inserts a new chapter after the first chapter, as its right-most sibling. The second call to modify() inserts a new section as the last child of the new section.

> **TIP**
>
> Both *reference_node_expression* of insert and *new_expression* of replace
> value of require a singleton to be matched in their XPath expressions, or SQL Server
> will raise an error. This is sometimes hard to do because you have to think like an
> XML parser in terms of how many possible nodes may be matched.
>
> Even though you may know that there's only one node in the instance document
> matching a complex predicate such as /book/chapter/section/
> paragraph[@para_id="1"]/text(), the parser knows that more than one is possible
> because the position of the nodes has not been specified.
>
> It's usually best to enclose the matching XPath expression in parentheses and then
> apply the positional predicate (that is, [1]) to the entire sequence, as the examples
> illustrate. Otherwise, your XPath expressions need to look as ugly as the following,
> where the position is specified for every node in the sequence:
>
> ```
> /book[1]/chapter[1]/section[1]/paragraph[1]
> ➡[@para_id="1" and position() = 1]/text()[1]
> ```

All three XML DML functions that use modify() have the side effect of causing any XML
indexes on the xml column to be repropagated to reflect the changes, just as with relational indexes. The next section covers how to create and maintain primary and
secondary indexes on your xml columns.

Indexing and Full-Text Indexing of xml Columns

Just as with relational data, xml column data, whether typed or untyped, can be indexed.

Indexing xml Columns

Two levels of indexing are available for xml columns: primary and secondary. Three types
of secondary indexing are available, based on the different kinds of XQuery queries that
will be performed on the column: PATH for path-based querying, PROPERTY for property
bag scenarios, and VALUE for value-based querying.

To create a primary XML index on a table, a few requirements must be met:

- The table must have a clustered primary key (with fewer than 16 columns in it).
  This is because the primary XML index contains a copy of the primary key for back
  referencing. It is also required for table partitioning because it ensures that the
  primary XML index is partitioned in the same manner as the table. The primary key
  of the table thus cannot be modified unless all the XML indexes on the table are
  dropped.

- Your SET options must have the following values when you're creating or rebuilding
  XML indexes or when you're attempting to use the modify() xml data type method,
  which triggers index maintenance:

  ```
  SET ANSI_NULLS ON
  SET ANSI_PADDING ON
  ```

```
SET ANSI_WARNINGS ON
SET ARITHABORT ON
SET CONCAT_NULL_YIELDS_NULL ON
SET NUMERIC_ROUNDABORT OFF
SET QUOTED_IDENTIFIER ON
```

Note that these are the SET values in a default SQL Server installation. You can view them by calling DBCC USEROPTIONS in T-SQL.

As with many other operations, indexes can be created both by using the dialogs in SSMS and also in T-SQL. The following is the syntax for creating a primary XML index on an xml column:

```
CREATE PRIMARY XML INDEX IndexName ON TableName(XmlColumnName)
```

For example, using the SimpleBook table from the previous section, you would execute:

```
CREATE PRIMARY XML INDEX PrimaryXmlIndex_BookXml ON SimpleBook(BookXml)
```

To drop an XML index, you execute:

```
DROP INDEX IndexName ON TableName
```

To do the same thing in SSMS, you right-click the table name in Object Explorer, click Modify, and then right-click the xml column and select XML Indexes. Then you use the Add or Delete buttons to create or drop indexes.

> **NOTE**
>
> Dropping the primary XML index also drops all secondary indexes because they are dependent on the columns of the shredded Infoset's table of the primary XML index (discussed in the next section).

You can disable XML indexes using the following syntax:

```
ALTER INDEX XmlIndexName on TableName DISABLE
```

You can rebuild them using the following syntax:

```
ALTER INDEX XmlIndexName on TableName REBUILD
```

You can also query XML indexes like other indexes, using the catalog view sys.indexes.

XML indexes are different from relational indexes in a few important ways. Let's consider their underlying structure and how they work at runtime.

Understanding XML Indexes

XML indexes store the xml column data for a table in a compressed B⁺tree (pronounced *B plus tree*) data structure. The XML data is stored there in its shredded (rather than original XML format (remember the universal table?). XML Infoset *information items* (that is, nodes), the navigational paths used to find each item, and other crucial data are stored in the columns of the index.

> **NOTE**
>
> XML Infoset is a W3C recommendation defining an abstract data set and a corresponding set of terms used to refer to any item in any well-formed XML document. For example, each element in a document is considered to be an *element information item*, each attribute an *attribute information item*, and so forth.
>
> A B⁺tree is a tree data structure that stores content such that the values for every node in the tree are exclusively kept in its leaves; the branches contain only pointers to the leaves. B⁺trees are optimized for fast insertion and removal of nodes.

When retrieving xml, SQL Server builds a query plan that consists of both the relational and XML portions of the query. The XML portion is built using the primary XML index. Secondary indexes are chosen based on cost after the query is optimized.

The Primary XML Index   When the primary XML index is created, each xml column value is shredded into a relational representation of its Infoset and stored. The index itself is clustered on the column that contains the *ordpath*: a node labeling scheme that captures a document's order and hierarchy, which allows for insertion of new nodes without node relabeling and provides efficient access to nodes, using range scans.[1]

Let's look at an example of how ordpaths work. Assume that some node is labeled 1.1. All nodes are initially labeled in document order during index creation, using odd numbers, allowing inserted nodes to be labeled with even numbers without changing the existing node labels. The original children of 1.1 would be thus be labeled 1.1.1, 1.1.3, and so forth. Any children inserted after labeling would get an even number, such as 1.1.4. Each number in the ordpath represents a node, and each dot represents an edge of depth.

To see the actual columns of our primary XML index, you can run the following query:

```
SELECT *
FROM sys.columns sc
JOIN sys.indexes si ON
si.object_id = sc.object_id
AND si.name LIKE 'PrimaryXmlIndex_BookXml'
AND si.type = 1
```

---

[1] S. Pal, , S., I. Cseri, O. Seeliger, M. Rys, G. Schaller, W. Yu, D. Tomic, A. Baras, B. Berg, D. Churin, and E. Kogan. "XQuery Implementation in a Relational Database System," in *Proceedings of the 31st International Conference on Very Large Data Bases (VLDB 2005)*, 1175-1186. New York: ACM Press, 2005.

Given the XML document used in Listings 37.23 and 37.24, its shredded rows for it in the index might look something like those shown in Table 37.1. The real index's column names are underlined beside the conceptual names; conceptual names and values are supplied to make the table easy to understand.

TABLE 37.1   Shredded Infoset Rows for the XML Instance in Listing 37.23[2]

BookId (pk1)	Ordpath (id)	Tag (nid)	NodeType (tid)	Value (value)	PathId (hid)
1	1	1 (book)	1 (Element)	Null	#1
1	1.1	2 (book_id)	2 (Attribute)	1	#2#1
1	1.3	3 (title)	1	'A Great Work'	#3#1
1	1.5	4 (chapter)	1	Null	#4#1
1	1.5.1	5 (chapter_id)	2	1	#5#1
1	1.5.3	6 (title)	1	'An Excellent Chapter'	#6#4#1
1	1.5.5	7 (section)	1	Null	#7#4#1
1	1.5.5.1	8 (section_id)	1	1	#8#4#1
1	1.5.5.3	9 (title)	1	'A Boring Section'	#9#7#4#1
1	1.5.5.5	10 (paragraph)	1	'Something Boring'	#10#7#4#1
1	1.5.5.5.1	11 (para_id)	2	1	#11#7#4#1
1	1.5.7	7 (section)	1	Null	#7#4#1
1	1.5.7.1	8 (section_id)	2	2	#8#4#1
1	1.5.7.3	9 (title)	1	'Another Fine Section'	#9#7#4#1
1	1.5.7.5	10 (paragraph)	1	'Another Fine Paragraph'	#10#7#4#1
1	1.5.7.5.1	11 (para_id)	2	2	#11#7#4#1

The NodeType column holds an integer based on the Infoset type of the node. The Value column holds the value of the node (if any) or a pointer to that value. The Tag column holds a non-unique integer assigned to each Infoset item. These numbers repeat for similar items, as when a second section or para_id appears in the content. The PathId column is computed based on the path from the root to the current item. For example, the section element with Ordpath value 1.5.5 has the same Tag value as the section element with Ordpath value 1.5.7.

When calculating PathId, SQL Server recognizes that the path from either section back to the root is the same. That is to say, from either section (Tag = 7), through chapter (Tag = 4), to book (Tag = 1), the path is the same: #7#4#1. The Tag and PathId values for these

---

[2] S. Pal, I. Cseri, O. Seeliger, M. Rys, G. Schaller, W. Yu, D. Tomic, A. Baras, B. Berg, D. Churin, E. Kogan, "XQuery Implementation in a Relational Database System," Proceedings of the 31st International Conference on Very Large Data Bases (VLDB 2005), ACM Press, New York (2005), pp. 1175-1186.

groups of rows are thus the same. Another way of looking at this is to consider that the XPath /book/chapter/section would return both section nodes, regardless of their text values or positions.

The PathId value is stored with the path in reverse order for the purpose of optimizing when the descendant-or-self (//) XPath axis is specified in the queries; in that case, only the final node names in a path such as //section/title are known.

When XQuery queries are executed against the xml columns, they are translated into relational queries against this Infoset table. First, the primary key of the table (in this case, BookId) is scanned to find the group of rows that contains the nodes. Then the PathId and Value columns are used to find the matching paths and values requested in the XPath of the XQuery. When found, the resulting nodes are serialized up from the Infoset table and reassembled into XML.

The Secondary XML Indexes   Secondary XML indexes are useful when specific types of XQuery queries are run against the XML documents.

The syntax for creating a secondary XML index is as follows:

```
CREATE XML INDEX SecondaryXmlIndexName ON TableName(XmlColumnName)
USING XML INDEX PrimaryXmlIndexName FOR ( PROPERTY ¦ VALUE ¦ PATH)
```

Secondary XML indexes are dropped in the same way as primary XML indexes.

The PATH Secondary XML Index   Generally speaking, the PATH secondary index is useful when the bulk of your queries attempt to locate nodes via a simple path to the node (for example, /book/chapter/section/title).

At runtime, the XPath is translated to the value of PathId in the Infoset table, and then the matching PathId values are used to retrieve the unique Ordpath of the matching nodes. Note that Value is used secondarily to PathId in this type of index.

The VALUE Secondary XML Index   When many of the XPath queries to the XML are value based, meaning that the value of an element or attribute is specified in a predicate, a VALUE secondary index may improve seek times. In this case, the Value column of the Infoset table is primarily relied on during index searches, and then PathId.

The following is an example of a value-based XQuery:

```
SELECT BookXml.query('
/book[@book_id=1]/chapter[@chapter_id=1]//paragraph[contains(text()[1], "fine")]
')
FROM SimpleBook
WHERE BookId = 1
go
<paragraph para_id="2">Another fine paragraph.</paragraph>
(1 row(s) affected)
```

The* PROPERTY *Secondary XML Index   When the XML in the xml column is used to encapsulate multiple properties of a object (for example, in an object serialization scenario) and these properties are often retrieved together, it may be useful to create a PROPERTY secondary index.

For example, if your markup resembles the following:

```
DECLARE @objectXml xml
SET @objectXml =
'<object id="111">
    <name>MyObject</name>
    <value>Value 1</value>
    <coordinateX>24</coordinateX>
    <coordinateY>636</coordinateY>
</object>'
```

and your XQuery queries often retrieve multiple values simultaneously, such as the following:

```
SELECT
    @objectXml.value('(/object/name)[1]', 'varchar(20)') as OName,
    @objectXml.value('(/object/value)[1]', 'varchar(20)') as OValue,
    @objectXml.value('(/object/coordinateX)[1]', 'int') as X,
    @objectXml.value('(/object/coordinateY)[1]', 'int') as Y
WHERE @objectXml.exist('(/object[@id=111])[1]') = 1
```

the PROPERTY index should help to optimize index seek time. This is because PROPERTY indexes rely primarily on the Value column of the index and secondarily on PathId.

> **NOTE**
>
> Every call to value() requires an additional SELECT statement against the Infoset table, so it's important to try to index for this scenario, when applicable.

XML Index Performance Considerations

You know that indexing works well with untyped XML, but it actually works better with typed xml columns. When the XML is untyped, node values are stored internally as Unicode strings. Each time a value comparison must be made, those strings must typecast to the corresponding SQL for the XML type used in the XQuery. This type conversion must also be made for every possible value match in Infoset table, and this operation grows proportionally more costly as the number of rows of the table grows. It also prevents the value range scans possible when matching against typed values.

When the types of all the nodes are declared in an associated XML schema, the values are stored as the corresponding SQL type (not as strings), and runtime typecasting is not necessary.

37

The following are some other points for performance consideration:

▶ When retrieving an entire XML instance, it is faster to select the xml column by name, without using query() or nodes(), because serialization of the XML up from the shredded Infoset format is costly.

▶ XML indexes are not used during execution of check constraints on xml columns.

▶ You should use the exist() method whenever possible to restrict the range of data being scanned.

Full-Text Indexing

xml columns can be full-text indexed, just like relational columns. The big difference is that for xml columns, the word *boundary* is not whitespace but element delimiters (<, >). Element text is indexed; attribute values are ignored.

It's important to use exist() when using a full-text T-SQL function such as CONTAINS to reduce unnecessary scans on the XML columns that don't contain the text you are looking for.

> **NOTE**
>
> To generate a full-text index, a unique, non-null, single column index is required. The constraint name PK_ _SimpleBook_ _2F2FFC0C shown in the example below represents the automatically generated primary key index name for SimpleBook's primary key. Your instance of SQL Server will likely generate a different name for this index.

Here's an example of how to generate and utilize a full-text index on an xml column:

```
CREATE FULLTEXT CATALOG FullTextXmlCatalog
GO
CREATE FULLTEXT INDEX ON SimpleBook(BookXml)
KEY INDEX PK_ _SimpleBook_ _2F2FFC0C
ON FullTextXmlCatalog
GO
SELECT 'End of Chapter'
FROM SimpleBook
WHERE CONTAINS(BookXml, 'Excellent')
AND
BookXml.exist('(/book/chapter/title[contains(text()[1], "Excellent")])[1]')=1
GO
End of Chapter
```

Summary

Within reason, there's nothing you can't do with XML in SQL Server 2005. The Microsoft team has addressed nearly every XML complaint and wish-list item gathered from the days of SQL Server 2000 and has gone the extra mile by throwing in XQuery and indexing to boot.

For the beginner and expert alike, SQL Server 2005 offers much to master in the realm of XML processing. The sheer quantity of new features may seem challenging at first. Remember that you need only utilize those features that are appropriate to your current application needs. How your applications develop and grow from there is entirely up to you.

In Chapter 38, "SQL Server Web Services," we'll take a look at how the team has done it again by building native XML web services directly into SQL Server 2005.

37

SQL Server Web Services

IN THIS CHAPTER

▶ What's New in SQL Server Web Services

▶ Web Services History and Overview

▶ Building Web Services

▶ Examples: A C# Client Application

▶ Using Catalog Views and System Stored Procedures

▶ Controlling Access Permissions

W eb services address a problem domain that is crucial to business-driven programming: the need for application and platform-independent remote procedure calls (RPCs). They also provide one of the few ways in which non-Microsoft clients can consume SQL Server data over the Internet.

This chapter provides all the details necessary to get native web services up and running on your instance of SQL Server 2005. It includes examples of both the client- and server-side code needed to make things happen at runtime.

What's New in SQL Server Web Services

Microsoft first made it possible to expose T-SQL query batches, stored procedures, and scalar-valued functions as web services with the release of SQLXML 3.0, an add-on package for SQL Server 2000 that allowed for the interchange of relational data as Extensible Markup Language (XML).

Over the past few years, the SQLXML packages have addressed the growing dependence of data-driven, distributed applications on XML and have kept SQL Server 2000 current with the explosion of progress in the world of XML.

Today, we no longer need SQLXML to create SQL Server web services because SQL Server 2005 supports them natively.

Web Services History and Overview

Web services are supported on most major software platforms and can be built using integrated development environments (IDEs) that comply with a few key World Wide Web Consortium (W3C) recommendations:

▶ **Web Services Description Language (WSDL)**—WSDL is the XML grammar used to specify the functions and types (known as its *interface*) of a web service.

▶ **Simple Object Access Protocol (SOAP) 1.2**—SOAP is the network transport-layer protocol for web services.

The good news is that SQL Server 2005 supports web services natively.

Until now, Open Database Connectivity (ODBC) and Tabular Data Stream (TDS) (a proprietary protocol developed by Sybase) were the only means available for clients to access SQL Server data. But because the web service standards are nonproprietary (although there are proprietary extensions), web service clients don't need to install Microsoft Data Access Components (MDAC), ODBC, SQL Server Client Tools, or any open-source variants of these.

NOTE

Some of the examples in this chapter assume that you have a rudimentary knowledge of HTTP, a touch of coding savvy (some examples utilize Visual Studio 2005 and the C# .NET programming language), and a general understanding of how XML is used to describe and encapsulate data.

The Web Services Pattern

Web services follow a stateless request/response model that corresponds directly with the client/server model of Hypertext Transfer Protocol (HTTP). The following summary illustrates this programming pattern:

▶ A client application discovers that a server application hosts a web service that exposes one or more web methods. This process, known as *discovery*, is accomplished in one or more of the following ways:

▶ Microsoft's Universal Description, Discovery, and Integration (UDDI) service, an online catalog for publishing web services, facilitates this process.

▶ More commonly, the developer of the hosted web service provides the network address and web method descriptions to the developer of the client application that will consume it (that is, call its methods). This is still the dominant way web services are exposed because most provide data that is strictly confidential.

▶ The client then asks the discovered web service to describe its methods and their types, parameters, and return values, using the standard WSDL XML vocabulary. This is usually performed via an HTTP request to the web service in the form http[s]://*ServerDomainName/WebServiceName*?wsdl.

▶ The web service responds by providing the WSDL (an XML document).

▶ The client application (or, in some cases, the IDE of the client, such as Visual Studio) creates a code class based on the server-generated WSDL. This class is known as a *stub*, or *proxy*, because it merely contains callable references to the actual remote methods of the web service, wrapped in the formal language semantics of the client's software platform. (The actual implementation of those methods is held on the server application.)

▶ The client invokes a web service method over some protocol (usually HTTP). This invocation is an HTTP request encoded in the SOAP XML vocabulary.

▶ The web service responds (hopefully) with a SOAP-encoded response.

NOTE

Content and metadata pertaining to these stateless communications is always encoded in XML-tagged documents known as SOAP *envelopes*. For complete information on SOAP, visit the SOAP messaging framework specification, available online from the W3C, at www.w3.org.

The W3C is the organizational body responsible for creating and maintaining World Wide Web standards, including XML. The W3C website is a great place to get accurate and up-to-date information on Web standards.

To recap: UDDI or word-of-mouth provides a discovery mechanism for web services. WSDL provides the web methods, types, and metadata of the web service. Stateless requests and responses are invoked over HTTP (or perhaps TCP) and transmitted in SOAP-encoded format.

Before SQL Server 2005, developers had to use the Internet Information Services (IIS) Virtual Directory Management (IISVDM) for SQL Server utility to create SOAP-typed virtual names to expose their data. (Incidentally, this could also be accomplished using a language such as Visual Basic .NET with the SQLVDir object model that came with IISVDM.)

Today, it is far easier. SQL Server no longer relies on IISVDM or even IIS to publish web services. It ties directly in with operating-system–level (or *kernel-mode*) HTTP, listening by way of the HTTP API (sometimes referred to as http.sys). This means that under the covers, SQL Server registers the virtual paths (also known as URIs, such as www.myserver.com/urlpath) specified in endpoint creation syntax with http.sys in the same way that IIS 6 registers virtual directories. The operating system then farms out incoming HTTP requests to IIS or SQL Server, based on the path of the incoming request.

SQL Server also includes the entire SOAP messaging stack in its binaries. You might say that to a certain degree, SQL Server is now a web server with limited applications.

> **NOTE**
>
> It is possible to create SQL Server endpoints for use with database mirroring schemes, network connectivity, and SQL Server Service Broker. This chapter focuses strictly on web service endpoints.

Building Web Services

Let's delve right into the process of building a web service in SQL Server 2005.

The first step is to decide which data or T-SQL functionality to expose to the clients who will ultimately call the web methods.

For this first example, you should create the stored procedure shown in Listing 38.1, which returns a row of data from the AdventureWorks sample database. The purpose is to reveal a few attributes of an employee, given his or her unique EmployeeId.

LISTING 38.1   A Stored Procedure for Your First Web Service

```
CREATE PROC dbo.GetEmployeeBasics
(
    @EmployeeId int
)
AS
SELECT
    EmployeeId,
    FirstName,
    LastName,
    e.Title
FROM AdventureWorks.HumanResources.Employee e
JOIN AdventureWorks.Person.Contact p ON
    e.ContactId = p.ContactId
WHERE EmployeeId = @EmployeeId
```

To expose this procedure as a web method of your web service, you use the CREATE ENDPOINT T-SQL statement, which falls under the formal SQL category of Data Definition Language (DDL). An *endpoint* can be defined as simply an entity on one end of a connection over a communication protocol, such as HTTP. SOAP endpoints have an additional nickname: *nodes*. SOAP nodes consist of a SOAP *sender* and a SOAP *receiver*, following the request-response model.

To create a SOAP-based HTTP endpoint, you use the fairly complex T-SQL syntax shown in Listing 38.2.

LISTING 38.2   CREATE ENDPOINT T-SQL Syntax

```
CREATE ENDPOINT EndPointName [ AUTHORIZATION login ]
STATE = { STARTED ¦ STOPPED ¦ DISABLED }
AS HTTP
(
  PATH = 'url'
      , AUTHENTICATION =( { BASIC ¦ DIGEST ¦ INTEGRATED ¦ NTLM ¦ KERBEROS }
      [ ,...n ] )
      , PORTS = ( { CLEAR ¦ SSL} [ ,... n ] )
  [ SITE = {'*' ¦ '+' ¦ 'webSite' },]
  [, CLEAR_PORT = clearPort ]
  [, SSL_PORT = SSLPort ]
  [, AUTH_REALM = { 'realm' ¦ NONE } ]
  [, DEFAULT_LOGON_DOMAIN = { 'domain' ¦ NONE } ]
  [, RESTRICT_IP = { NONE ¦ ALL } ]
  [, COMPRESSION = { ENABLED ¦ DISABLED } ]
  [, EXCEPT_IP = ( { <4-part-ip> ¦ <4-part-ip>:<mask> } [ ,...n ] )
)
FOR SOAP
(
  [ { WEBMETHOD [ 'namespace' .] 'method_alias'
    (   NAME = 'database.owner.name'
      [ , SCHEMA = { NONE ¦ STANDARD ¦ DEFAULT } ]
      [ , FORMAT = { ALL_RESULTS ¦ ROWSETS_ONLY } ]
    )
  } [ ,...n ] ]
  [   BATCHES = { ENABLED ¦ DISABLED } ]
  [ , WSDL = { NONE ¦ DEFAULT ¦ 'sp_name' } ]
  [ , SESSIONS = { ENABLED ¦ DISABLED } ]
  [ , LOGIN_TYPE = { MIXED ¦ WINDOWS } ]
  [ , SESSION_TIMEOUT = timeoutInterval ¦ NEVER ]
  [ , DATABASE = { 'database_name' ¦ DEFAULT }
  [ , NAMESPACE = { 'namespace' ¦ DEFAULT } ]
  [ , SCHEMA = { NONE ¦ STANDARD } ]
  [ , CHARACTER_SET = { SQL ¦ XML }]
  [ , MAX_SOAP_HEADERS_SIZE = { int ¦ DEFAULT }]
)
```

Before running the examples that follow, you should create a dedicated Windows login to use in the authorization scheme; this user should own and be able to access the database objects you create. In the examples that follow, this user is indicated as *MyDomain\ SQLWebServicesClient*. Replace this name with your own.

Listing 38.3 contains the endpoint creation DDL that exposes dbo.GetEmployeeBasics to its web consumers.

LISTING 38.3   T-SQL for Creating a SQL Server Web Service Endpoint

```
CREATE ENDPOINT EPT_SQL2005UnleashedExamples
AUTHORIZATION [MyDomain\SQLWebServicesClient]
STATE = STARTED
AS HTTP
(
    AUTHENTICATION = (INTEGRATED),
    PATH = '/opensql/',
    PORTS = (CLEAR, SSL),
    CLEAR_PORT = 80,
    SSL_PORT = 443,
    SITE = '*',
    COMPRESSION = ENABLED
)
FOR SOAP
(
    WEBMETHOD 'urn:www-samspublishing-com:examples'.'WM_GetEmployeeBasics'
    (
        NAME = 'AdventureWorks.dbo.GetEmployeeBasics',
        SCHEMA = STANDARD,
        FORMAT = ALL_RESULTS
    ),
    WSDL = DEFAULT,
    BATCHES = DISABLED,
    SCHEMA = STANDARD,
    LOGIN_TYPE = WINDOWS,
    SESSION_TIMEOUT = 120,
    DATABASE = 'AdventureWorks',
    NAMESPACE = 'urn:www-samspublishing-com:examples',
    CHARACTER_SET = XML
)
```

In this listing, the name of the endpoint (EPT_SQL2005UnleashedExamples) immediately follows the keywords CREATE ENDPOINT.

> **NOTE**
>
> Using EPT_ as a prefix is a naming convention chosen to delineate endpoints from other types of user-created objects. Any valid database object name is acceptable here.

The endpoint name is also conveniently used to drop the endpoint from the server, as follows:

```
DROP ENDPOINT EPT_SQL2005UnleashedExamples
```

But don't drop the endpoint until you've finished trying out all the examples!

Next in the DDL, the AUTHORIZATION keyword is used to specify the name of the login (either of authorization type Windows or SQL Server) that owns the endpoint. You can change the name of the login later by using the ALTER AUTHORIZATION statement, as in the following example:

```
ALTER AUTHORIZATION ON ENDPOINT::EPT_SQL2005UnleashedExamples
TO MyDomain\SomeOtherUser
```

Next, the STATE keyword indicates the initial state of the endpoint.

Much as in Windows services, the possible states are STOPPED, STARTED, and DISABLED. (For security's sake, STOPPED is the default.)

To change the state of any endpoint, you again invoke the ALTER ENDPOINT syntax. The following example stops the endpoint:

```
ALTER ENDPOINT EPT_SQL2005UnleashedExamples STATE = STOPPED
```

Again, don't do this until you are done with the examples!

The AS HTTP Keyword Group

The AS HTTP statements describe the protocol, ports, virtual path, and TCP/IP bindings for the endpoint. This keyword group is of interest to security professionals because this is where you can implement IP restrictions, authentication, and other lock-down mechanisms.

In the example shown in Listing 38.3, HTTP is the transport protocol. But you could just as easily use TCP if your application demands it: When creating a TCP endpoint, you specify AS TCP instead of AS HTTP. Then, you add the following parameters:

▶ **LISTENER_PORT**—Specifies an integer-valued port number on which the server listens for incoming requests. The default is 4022.

▶ **LISTENER_IP**—Specifies an incoming IP address on which the TCP listener accepts connections. The default is the keyword ALL (that is, listening on all IP addresses).

Next, you specify that the AUTHENTICATION method is INTEGRATED. Microsoft recommends INTEGRATED (which includes both KERBEROS and NTLM) and KERBEROS as the securest ways of authenticating to endpoints, although they are not necessarily platform-independent ways. This is in contrast to using BASIC or DIGEST authentication. In case the endpoint consumer requires BASIC authentication, SQL Server requires that the HTTP port of the web service be secured via Secure Sockets Layer (SSL).

NOTE

Using BASIC authentication allows for the additional keyword DEFAULT_LOGON_DOMAIN to specify the domain under which users will authenticate.

38

DIGEST authentication is also available, but only a domain-level account may be used in the AUTHORIZATION section for the endpoint to be successfully created.

TIP

This is also true for all other authentication methods (KERBEROS, BASIC, INTEGRATED, and NTLM): SQL Server does not register the endpoint if authorization checks fail at DDL execution time.

Using DIGEST allows for the additional keyword AUTH_REALM, whose string value represents the challenge hint required by this type of authentication.

NOTE

In contrast to SQLXML 3.0, there is no way for web anonymous users (such as *I_USER_MACHINENAME*) to access SQL Server 2005 endpoints. This is an uncommonly proactive security move for Microsoft, and database administrators will applaud it.

Next, you specify the PATH (/opensql) to the web service. PATH is simply the part of the URL that follows the server and domain name portion of a URL (for example, *http://ServerDomainName/PATH*). Paths are sometimes also referred to as *virtual names*. Clients connecting to the HTTP endpoint will thus access it via the URL *http://ServerDomainName/opensql*.

This is similar to the way virtual directories are used with IIS, and this is because IIS and SQL Server register their endpoints similarly with the HTTP API. When the web service is called by a client, the HTTP API responds by farming the request out to SQL Server.

NOTE

You cannot register a value for PATH that is already registered by SQL Server, IIS, or any other application that uses the HTTP API. If you attempt to do so, SQL Server raises the following error:

```
The URL specified by endpoint 'ENDPOINTNAME' is already registered
to receive requests or is reserved for use by another service.
```

Next up in the syntax, you specify the PORTS on which SQL Server listens for requests for this endpoint. The example in Listing 38.3 specifies both CLEAR (the unsecured standard HTTP port, which defaults to 80) as well as SSL (the standard SSL port, which defaults to 443). You can also specify non-default numeric values for CLEAR_PORT and SSL_PORT, but this example simply restates the default for clarity.

Note that it is essential that you do not use port numbers owned by other network services (such as email, telnet, and so on), although SQL Server may allow you to do so. Only one port can be specified each for CLEAR_PORT and SSL_PORT.

In addition to specifying ports, you can restrict or grant endpoint access to specific IP addresses by using a combination of the keywords RESTRICT_IP and EXCEPT_IP. RESTRICT_IP defaults to NONE (that is, no IP addresses are restricted), but you can change this to ALL to prevent users from accessing the endpoint (which is useful during offline maintenance periods). For EXCEPT_IP, you can add specific client IP addresses in parentheses. Here's an example:

```
CREATE ENDPOINT EPT_SQL2005UnleashedIPExample
AUTHORIZATION [MyDomain\SQLWebServicesClient]
STATE = STARTED
AS HTTP
(
    AUTHENTICATION = (INTEGRATED),
    PATH = '/opensql2/',
    PORTS = (CLEAR, SSL),
    CLEAR_PORT = 80,
    SSL_PORT = 443,
    SITE = '*',
    COMPRESSION = ENABLED,
    RESTRICT_IP = ALL,
    EXCEPT_ID = 192.168.10.1
)
FOR SOAP
(
    WEBMETHOD 'urn:www-samspublishing-com:examples'.'WM_GetEmployeeBasics2'
    (
        NAME = 'AdventureWorks.dbo.GetEmployeeBasics',
        SCHEMA = STANDARD,
        FORMAT = ALL_RESULTS
    ),
    WSDL = DEFAULT,
    BATCHES = DISABLED,
    SCHEMA = STANDARD,
    LOGIN_TYPE = WINDOWS,
    SESSION_TIMEOUT = 120,
    DATABASE = 'AdventureWorks',
    NAMESPACE = 'urn:www-samspublishing-com:examples',
    CHARACTER_SET = XML
);
```

38

TIP

It is assumed that for most endpoints, you will want to implement some level of IP filtering. It is recommended that you use the modifiers described here to prevent broad access.

Next, you use the SITE keyword to specify the host name(s) used on the server hosting the endpoint. In this case, '*' restates the default (that is, all host names reserved by the local machine), but you can use a specific host name (such as 'hostname'), or all host names (that is, '+'). This is useful (and necessary) when multiple host headers are in play for the same IP address.

The NAMESPACE keyword indicates to clients that the web method originates from a specific organizational entity. This prevents confusion when comparing the XML generated by this web service with that of any other organization that might expose a web method of the same name on an endpoint of the same name (which is an entirely possible situation).

> **TIP**
>
> Specifying the company name in uniform resource name (URN) format is standard practice for namespace naming. A URN differs from a uniform resource locator (URL) in that it specifies just the name of a resource, independent of its location. This is useful because the name of a resource is usually valid longer than the lifetime of any particular URL.

COMPRESSION is an interesting optional keyword because, when specified, it tells SQL Server to decompress its incoming SOAP requests if they have been compressed using gzip; then, in turn, it tells SQL Server to use gzip on the outgoing responses. You might think that web services over SOAP are too slow for the average application because of the sheer byte-count of SOAP XML documents. However, using gzip on an XML file usually results in a compression ratio of greater than 80%.

When COMPRESSION is set to ENABLED, both the client and server must support gzip compression for web service compression to work properly, although the web service can still process uncompressed requests with uncompressed responses even with the setting turned on.

To enable compression on IIS 6 (on Windows 2003 Server, Standard Edition), you follow these steps:

1. Open the IIS Manager, expand the main tree, right-click the Web Sites node, and choose Properties.

2. When the Web Sites Properties dialog appears, click on the Service tab and check the Compress Application Files and Compress Static Files check boxes.

3. Add a web service extension for the .gzip file extension and edit the metabase appropriately, if necessary.

The Web Sites Properties dialog box should look something like Figure 38.1 when these steps are complete.

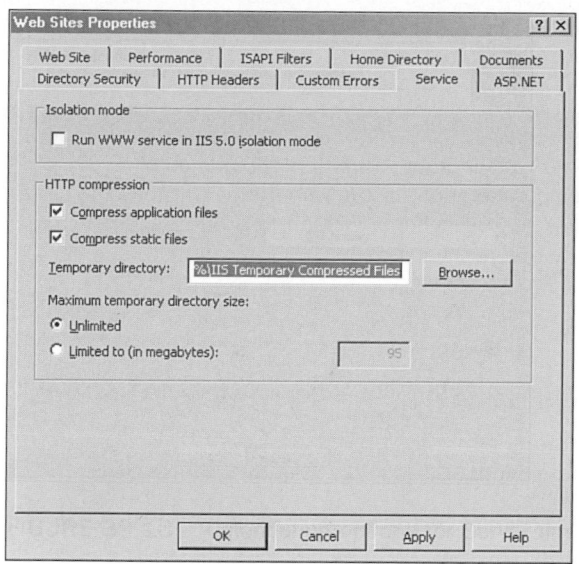

FIGURE 38.1   Enabling compression on IIS 6.

The FOR SOAP **Keyword Group**

The second major section of the DDL begins after the end parenthesis of the AS clause, with the FOR SOAP group, whose keywords appear in parentheses.

First, you assign the namespaced-name 'urn:www-samspublishing-com:examples'.'WM_ GetEmployeeBasics' to WEBMETHOD. This name is specified in two parts to ensure its uniqueness:

▶ A namespace as a string in URN format (followed by a period)

▶ The string name of the web method

NOTE

In Listing 38.3, the naming convention WM_ is used simply to differentiate the web method from other database objects. Later in this chapter, you'll see how this makes objects easy to pick out in query results on the endpoint catalog views in the section "Using Catalog Views and System Stored Procedures."

The following keyword options are used inside the parenthetical group following WEBMETHOD:

▶ **NAME**—The string value represents the SQL Server scalar-valued user-defined function (UDF) or stored procedure that will be executed via the web service.

▶ **SCHEMA**—This keyword choice describes the quality of XML schema produced to describe the transmitted XML data.

CAUTION

The SCHEMA keyword occurs twice in the FOR SOAP group. This first occurrence of SCHEMA relates specifically to inline schema generation for the web method. It tells the compiler how to generate (or not generate) an XSD schema within the SOAP response envelope that describes the types used by this particular WEBMETHOD.

These are the valid keyword values for SCHEMA:

▶ **NONE**—Do not include web method–specific schema information in the SOAP response.

▶ **STANDARD**—Generate a standard schema.

▶ **DEFAULT**—Use the value of the SCHEMA keyword that is specified (somewhat confusingly, a second time) after the end of the WEBMETHOD clause.

▶ **FORMAT**—This option specifies which kinds of objects are returned to the web method's caller. These are the valid keyword values for FORMAT:

   ▶ **ALL_RESULTS**—Include two or more objects in the SOAP response, including the following:

      ▶ The result set itself (in .NET, deserialized as DataSet; or, in the case of web methods that return XML, one or more sqlresultstream:SqlXml nodes deserialized as XmlElements)

      ▶ A row count of the result set (in .NET, deserialized as a SqlRowCount object; or, in the case of XML results, a sqlresultstream:SqlRowCount node deserialized as an XmlElement)

      ▶ A result code (in .NET, an integer; or, in the case of XML results, a sqlresultstream:SqlResultCode node deserialzed as an XmlElement)

      ▶ Any SQL Server errors or warnings, if generated at runtime (in .NET, deserialized as SqlMessage objects)

   ▶ **ROWSETS_ONLY**—Return just the result sets, if any.

   ▶ **NONE**—Do not mark up the output data in SOAP-typed envelope data. NONE is an advanced setting and should be used with the following caveat: No output parameters or UDFs are allowed with this option, and WSDL for the web method is not generated.

▶ **BATCHES**—Setting this switch to ENABLED or DISABLED allows or disallows ad hoc T-SQL statements to be executed on the endpoint. This means that any number of SQL statements (with associated parameters) may be run via the special sqlbatch() web service proxy method, explained later in this chapter.

Although it is convenient, the BATCHES feature has some security implications because a wide range of T-SQL may be executed; thus, many administrators want it kept off. (It is disabled by default.) There are, however, some valid situations for using it, including:

▶ During the design and testing phases of a website

▶ When implementing highly customized remote database administrative tools

▶ For ad hoc-query–dependent features

▶ **LOGIN_TYPE**—You use this setting to set the SQL Server Authentication mode for the endpoint to either MIXED (both Windows and SQL Server) or WINDOWS (the default). As with BASIC authentication, SSL is required to be both implemented on the server and specified after the PORTS keyword for the statement to compile.

▶ **WSDL**—You use this setting to determine whether SQL Server will generate WSDL for methods on the endpoint. You specify DEFAULT to do so or NONE. When you require specific WSDL to be generated, you specify a string value corresponding to the name of the custom stored procedure that generates the home-grown WSDL. Here's an example:

```
WSDL 'wsdl_generating_stored_procedure_name'
```

Note that in order for the C# web service client example later in this chapter to work, the value for WSDL must be DEFAULT. This is because the Visual Studio .NET IDE uses the generated WSDL to create web references as the basis for generating proxy classes used to call them.

The built-in system stored procedures that SQL Server uses to generate WSDL are sp_http_generate_wsdl_complex, sp_http_generate_wsdl_simple, sp_http_generate_wsdl_defaultcomplexorsimple, and sp_http_generate_wsdl_defaultsimpleorcomplex. You can test them by executing them with varying parameters to see how they work.

For more information on generating custom WSDL, see the Books Online topic "Implementing Custom WSDL Support."

WSDL on SQL Server comes in two different flavors: the default and simple. To see an example of simple WSDL, try the following URL (after you create the example endpoint by running the code in Listing 38.3): http[s]://ServerDomainName/opensql?wsdlsimple.

▶ **SESSIONS**—You use this setting to specify whether SOAP sessions managed by SQL Server are ENABLED or DISABLED (the default). Managing SOAP sessions on the client side requires a fair amount of programming in an environment such as Visual Studio 2005 for successful implementation. Not all SOAP clients require sessions.

38

▶ **SESSION_TIMEOUT**—You use this setting to specify how long (in seconds) before a SQL Server SOAP session times out.

▶ **DATABASE**—You use this setting to specify the database (named with a string value) in whose context the web methods of this endpoint are executed. Note that the keyword DEFAULT is also an option. Using it tells SQL Server to execute the web methods in the context of the default database of the login accessing the endpoint.

▶ **SCHEMA**—This is the second occurrence of this keyword in the CREATE ENDPOINT DDL. This time around, it applies to schema generation for all SOAP responses of all web methods on the endpoint, not merely of a particular web method. These are the possible values:

  ▶ **NONE**—Do not generate an inline XML schema in the SOAP response.

  ▶ **STANDARD**—Do generate an inline schema.

▶ **CHARACTER_SET**—The XML specification specifies a set of characters that are invalid in element and attribute values. They are <, >, ", ', and &. The reason for this is that XML parsers would have a hard time figuring out whether these characters represent markup or text values because they are used to delimit XML information items. For example, they are used in element tagging (for example, *<element>*), attribute naming (for example, *attribute="value"*), and entity naming (for example, *&entity;*).

The two keyword values for CHARACTER_SET treat these and other special characters (when found in markup) in distinct ways:

  ▶ **XML**—If a SOAP response is sent and the special XML characters are not escaped into their valid entity equivalents (<, >, ", ', and &) the response generates an error. This is the default.

  ▶ **SQL**—Any invalid XML characters are transformed into their respective entity representations (a process called *entitization*) before response transmission.

Other special characters are not permitted in the names of XML attributes or elements (known formally as *qualifying names,* or *QNames*) but may nevertheless end up in XML documents. SQL Server automatically escapes these by taking their Unicode hexadecimal values and preceding them with the string *#x[4-digit hex value]*. The asterisk (*) character, for example, would be converted to the character string *#x002A*.

NOTE

This character conversion may not be cross-platform compatible because not all parsers will approve of it, but it is far better to convert characters than have your SQL connection closed due to an XML parsing error.

One of the ways that such special character entitization may occur is when you use SQL column (or other object) aliases that, though legally named in T-SQL, are not valid QNames (for example, SELECT ColumnName AS '*' FROM TableName FOR XML RAW).

▶ `MAX_SOAP_HEADERS_SIZE`—Optionally, you can set the maximum size of the header section of each transmitted SOAP envelope. (The default is 8KB.) Transmitting a larger header than specified in this setting thus causes a server error.

As you can see, the `CREATE ENDPOINT` syntax offers a feast of options. Thankfully, it is easy to choose the ones you need, depending on your application's requirements.

Examples: A C# Client Application

After you execute the DDL in Listing 38.3, you can call your SOAP endpoint. In the following sections, you'll learn how to call the endpoint's web methods using a simple C# client application.

If you do not want to try your hand at C#, you can skip to the next section, but working through the following examples is recommended so that you have a complete understanding of both sides of the web service pattern.

Example 1: Running a Web Method Bound to a Stored Procedure from C#

Using Visual Studio 2005, create a new website and name it `SQLWebServicesClient`. Next, add a web reference to the SQL Server web service we created in Listing 38.3. To do this, you right-click the project name in the Server Explorer window and select Add Web Reference. In the dialog that appears, you type the following in the URL text box, replacing `ServerDomainName` with the server name of your SQL Server instance:

`http[s]://ServerDomainName/opensql?wsdl`

Next, you click the green Go arrow button. You may be required to Windows-authenticate to the machine that is hosting the SQL web service. After you do so, the Add Web Reference dialog should look something like the one shown in Figure 38.2.

Notice in the dialog that the browser box (directly below the URL text box) contains the endpoint name you used in the DDL (`EPT_SQL2005WebUnleashedExamples`), located on top and in quotation marks. It is followed by the name of the web method you added (`WM_GetEmployeeBasics`).

Also note how on the right side of the dialog, under the heading Web Services Found at This URL, the value you specified for `PATH` (`opensql`) is displayed. You need to type `openxml` in the Web Reference Name text box and click the Add Reference button. Next, you open the automatically created `default.aspx` file in design mode and add `GridView`, `TextBox`, `Label`, and `Button` controls to the form. Using the Properties dialog, you should name the label `lblResults`, the text box `txtEmployeeId`, the grid view `gvData`, and the button `btnGetValue`.

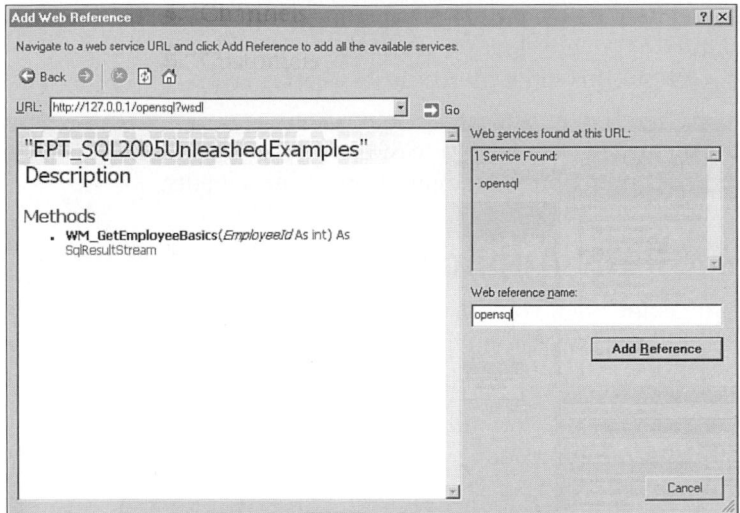

FIGURE 38.2   Adding a web reference by using Visual Studio 2005.

Next, you need to double-click btnGetValue. The IDE exits design mode and enters the code region of the C# partial class default.aspx.cs. The following empty event handler is auto-generated:

```
protected void btnGetValue_Click(object sender, EventArgs e) {}
```

At the top of this file, you type the following C# using statement:

```
using opensql;
```

This tells the compiler to import the names culled from the WSDL of the web service into this C# class. The namespace contains a C# stub class with the same name as the endpoint (EPT_SQL2005UnleashedExamples); the .NET runtime (CLR) uses this name to call the SQL Server HTTP endpoint.

At this point, you need to type the code in Listing 38.4 inside the empty body of btnGetValue_Click().

LISTING 38.4   Calling a SQL Server Web Method from C#

```
if (txtEmployeeId.Text != string.Empty)
{
    EPT_SQL2005UnleashedExamples SQLEndpointProxy =
        new EPT_SQL2005UnleashedExamples();
    SQLEndpointProxy.Credentials = System.Net.CredentialCache.DefaultCredentials;
    int EmployeeId = int.Parse(txtEmployeeId.Text);
    object[] ReturnArray = SQLEndpointProxy.WM_GetEmployeeBasics(EmployeeId);

    foreach (object Obj in ReturnArray)
```

LISTING 38.4   Continued

```
    {
        if (Obj is DataSet)
        {
            DataSet ds = (DataSet)Obj;
            if (ds.Tables.Count == 0)
            {
                lblResults.Text = "(No Results Found)";
            }
            else
            {
                lblResults.Text = "(" +
                    ((SqlRowCount)ReturnArray[1]).Count + " Result(s) Found)";
                gvData.DataSource = ds;
                gvData.DataBind();
            }
        }
    }
}
```

After you test whether the text box `txtEmployeeId` is non-empty, you instantiate the WSDL-based stub class `opensql.EPT_SQL2005UnleashedExamples` and name it `SQLEndpointProxy`. Next, you set the credentials used by the web service to those of the currently logged-on user.

> **NOTE**
>
> When using SQL Server (not Windows) Authentication, instead of assuming the default credentials, you need to add Web services security (WS-Security) username and password headers to the SOAP request. Note that the password will be sent in clear text, so SSL is required to be installed and turned on for your web service.

Anonymous web access is completely disabled for SQL Server web services, and Visual Studio turns on NTLM authentication by default for the sample web application's virtual directory.

Depending on your system's security policy configuration, the following line might be required in the configuration section of your `web.config` (or `machine.config`) file:

```
<identity impersonate="true" userName="SQLWebServicesClient" password="wsdl"/>
```

This tells the CLR to run the web application under the credentials of the user `SQLWebServicesClient` (created earlier and also specified after the `AUTHORIZATION` keyword in the DDL). The client application thus *impersonates* `SQLWebServicesClient` in its requests to the web service, regardless of the credentials of the logged-in Windows user.

When `btnGetValue` is clicked in the running browser window, the text typed into `txtEmployeeId` is typecast to an integer value. This value represents the `EmployeeId` of the employee about whom the web method's stored procedure returns data.

You pass this value into the call to the SQL Server web method with the code:

```
opensql.WM_GetEmployeeBasics(EmployeeId)
```

Notice that `WM_ GetEmployeeBasics` is exactly the same name you specified in `WEBMETHOD` (minus the namespace prefix). `EmployeeId` corresponds to the input parameter of the stored procedure `@EmployeeId`.

The next line of Listing 38.4 illustrates how the SOAP results returned from SQL Server are deserialized from XML into .NET Framework objects.

As mentioned earlier in this chapter, when `ALL_RESULTS` is specified for the `FORMAT` statement of the web method, you get back the array object `object[] ReturnArray` that has two or more elements:

▶ The result set (if any) of the stored procedure, deserialized by the CLR into `System.Data.DataSet`. `SELECT` queries on relational data (as opposed to XML data) are always returned as .NET `DataSets`

▶ An object of type `SqlRowCount`, representing the number of records in the result set

▶ Any errors or warnings (or the value `0`, if none occur), typed as `SqlMessage` objects

Also possible in the object array are the following objects (not returned in this example):

▶ The results of `SELECT...FOR` XML statements are deserialized into `System.Xml. XmlElement` objects.

▶ Output parameters of a SQL Server web method–bound stored procedure are deserialized as `SqlParameter` objects.

Because you don't always know at runtime which objects are in which position in an array, it is best to iterate through the objects, testing to see which class they are before using them. This is the purpose of the `foreach` loop in the code example.

At this point, you need to run the web application by clicking the IDE's Run toolbar button or by pressing F5. When the browser is up and running, you enter a number in `txtEmployeeId` and click `btnGetValue`. If any tables are returned in the `DataSet` (for example, if (ds.Tables.Count == 0)) the `DataSet` is bound to `GridView`, and the resulting data is displayed.

With a little visual sprucing up, your webpage should look a lot like Figure 38.3.

Listing 38.5 contains the HTML built in `default.aspx` so far. (You will be adding to this code as you continue through the examples.)

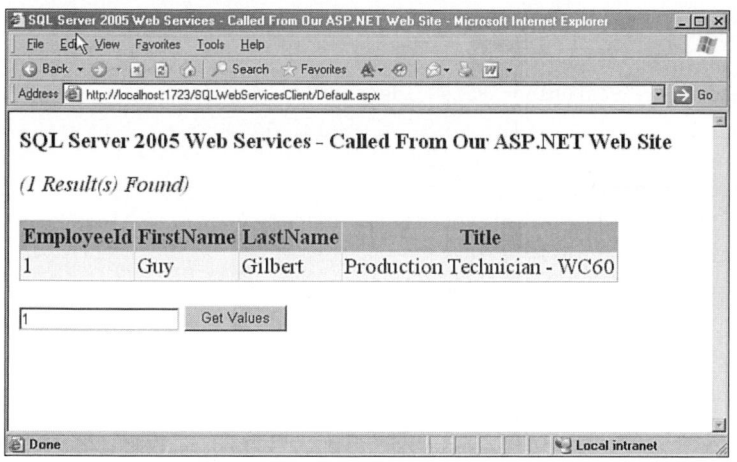

FIGURE 38.3   Calling a SQL Server web service from a C# web application.

LISTING 38.5   ASP.NET HTML Code in `default.aspx`

```
<%@ Page Language="C#" AutoEventWireup="true" CodeFile="Default.aspx.cs"
➥Inherits="_Default" %>
<!DOCTYPE html PUBLIC "-//W3C//DTD XHTML 1.1//EN"
"http://www.w3.org/TR/xhtml11/DTD/xhtml11.dtd">
<%@ Page Language="C#" AutoEventWireup="true" CodeFile="Default.aspx.cs"
➥Inherits="_Default" %>
<html xmlns="http://www.w3.org/1999/xhtml" >
<head runat="server">
    <title>SQL Server 2005 Web Services - Called From Our ASP.NET Web Site</title>
</head>
<body>
    <form id="form1" runat="server">
    <div>
        <h4>SQL Server 2005 Web Services - Called From Our ASP.NET Web Site</h4>
        <asp:Label ID="lblResults"
            runat="server" Text="" Font-Italic=true></asp:Label>
        <br />
        <br />
        <asp:GridView ID="gvData" runat=server
            BackColor="LightGoldenrodYellow"
            BorderColor="Tan" BorderWidth="1px"
            CellPadding="2" ForeColor="Black">
            <FooterStyle BackColor="Tan" />
            <PagerStyle BackColor="PaleGoldenrod"
                ForeColor="DarkSlateBlue" HorizontalAlign="Center" />
            <SelectedRowStyle BackColor="DarkSlateBlue" ForeColor="GhostWhite" />
```

38

LISTING 38.5   Continued

```
            <HeaderStyle BackColor="Tan" Font-Bold="True" />
            <AlternatingRowStyle BackColor="PaleGoldenrod" />
        </asp:GridView>
        <br />
        <h6>Run Stored Procedure:</h6>
        EmployeeID: <asp:TextBox ID="txtEmployeeId" runat="server">1</asp:TextBox>
        <asp:Button ID="btnGetValue" runat="server"
            OnClick="btnGetValue_Click" Text="Get Employee" /><br />
```

Example 2: Running Ad Hoc T-SQL Batches from a SQL Server Web Service

For this example, you need to execute a batch of T-SQL statements by adding a new web method to the endpoint and changing it to accept query batches.

The syntax for making changes to SOAP endpoints is similar to that for CREATE ENDPOINT. The differences are shown in Listing 38.6 in bold italics.

LISTING 38.6   ALTER ENDPOINT T-SQL Syntax

```
ALTER ENDPOINT endpointname
<same as above>
AS HTTP
(
    <same as above>
    <except>
        ADD EXCEPT_IP =  (ip-address)
        DROP EXCEPT_IP = ( { <4-part-ip> ¦ <4-part-ip>:<mask> } [ ,...n ] )
        ADD WEBMETHOD webmethodname
        ALTER WEBMETHOD webmethodname
        DROP WEBMETHOD webmethodname
)
FOR SOAP
(
    <same as above>
)
```

The following bullets explain the kewords used with ALTER ENDPOINT:

▶ ADD and DROP EXCEPT_IP allow you to update the list of IP addresses that are allowed to connect to the web service.

▶ ADD WEBMETHOD allows a new web method to be added to the web service.

▶ ALTER WEBMETHOD permits changes in the attributes of an existing web method.

▶ DROP WEBMETHOD permanently drops the named web method from the endpoint.

Now you can change your endpoint and set BATCHES to ENABLED so you can run ad hoc queries on the web service:

```
ALTER ENDPOINT EPT_SQL2005UnleashedExamples
FOR SOAP
(
    BATCHES = ENABLED
)
```

At this point, you need to return to Visual Studio and right-click the App_WebReferences node under the project name in the Solution Explorer. Then you select Update Web References from the context menu. This causes the IDE to re-request the WSDL from SQL Server to check for changes to the service description.

The .NET IDE recognizes that batching has been turned on by adding the sqlbatch() method to the proxy class. All the behind-the-scenes work for SQL batching is done via this magical .NET method. When BATCHES is enabled, SQL Server adds some special elements to the WSDL XML to make this happen.

A peek at the WSDL in opensql.wsdl (found under the App_WebReferenece node in Solution Explorer) serves to illustrate some of the special batching XML nodes:

```
<wsdl:message name="sqlbatchSoapIn">
    <wsdl:part name="parameters" element="s0:sqlbatch" />
</wsdl:message>
<wsdl:message name="sqlbatchSoapOut">
    <wsdl:part name="parameters" element="s0:sqlbatchResponse" />
</wsdl:message>
```

You should now open default.aspx once again in design mode and add an additional TextBox control to the form named txtSQLBatch. Then you set its TextMode property to MultiLine. Then you need to add a second Button control named btnRunBatch. Next, you double-click btnRunBatch and add the code in Listing 38.7 to the empty event handler (btnRunBatch_Click()) generated by the IDE.

LISTING 38.7   Calling Ad Hoc T-SQL Batches from C#

```
EPT_SQL2005UnleashedExamples SQLEndpointProxy =
    new EPT_SQL2005UnleashedExamples();

SQLEndpointProxy.Credentials = System.Net.CredentialCache.DefaultCredentials;
opensql.SqlParameter[] sqlParams =
    new opensql.SqlParameter[1];
// note: using opensql.SqlParameter avoids namespace collisions
```

38

LISTING 38.7   Continued

```
//        with System.Data.SqlClient.SqlParameter
sqlParams[0] = new opensql.SqlParameter();
sqlParams[0].name = "EmployeeId";
sqlParams[0].Value = int.Parse(txtEmployeeId.Text);
object[] ReturnArray = SQLEndpointProxy.sqlbatch(txtSQLBatch.Text, ref sqlParams);
if (ReturnArray.Length > 0)
{
    foreach (Object Obj in ReturnArray)
    {
        if (Obj is DataSet)
        {
            DataSet ds = (DataSet)Obj;
            if (ds.Tables.Count == 0)
            {
                lblResults.Text = "(No Results Found)";
            }
            else
            {
                gvData.DataSource = ds;
                gvData.DataBind();
            }
        }
    }
}
else
{
    lblResults.Text = "(No Results)";
}
```

As in the first example, the first and second code lines in Listing 38.7 create the proxy object and set its credentials. Next, an array of opensql.SqlParameter objects of length 1 is created, and its single parameter (EmployeeID) is assigned the value of txtEmployeeId. Text, typecast to an integer. You'll use this value as a declared parameter to your SQL batch.

Instead of calling any web method by name, you instead call SQLEndpointProxy. sqlbatch(), passing in the text of the T-SQL statement and the value of txtEmployeeId. Text. With a little visual sprucing up, the running webpage should look something like Figure 38.4.

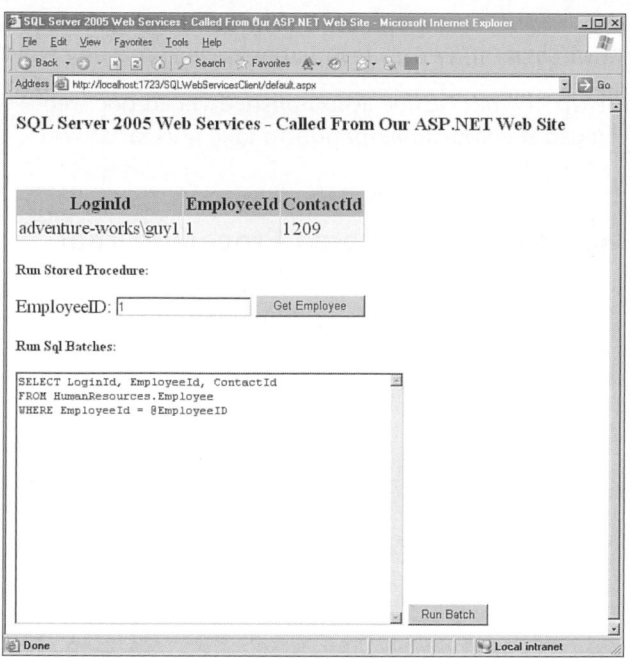

FIGURE 38.4   Running T-SQL batches on a web service by using `sqlbatch()`.

Now you need to append the HTML code in Listing 38.8 to `default.aspx` just below the last line entered.

LISTING 38.8   Additional ASP.NET HTML Code for `default.aspx`

```
<br />
<h6>Run Sql Batches:</h6>
<asp:TextBox
    ID="txtSQLBatch" runat="server"
    Height="280px" TextMode="MultiLine"
    Width="437px">SELECT LoginId, EmployeeId, ContactId
    FROM HumanResources.Employee
            WHERE EmployeeId = @EmployeeID
</asp:TextBox>
<asp:Button ID="btnRunBatch" runat="server" OnClick="btnRunBatch_Click"
 Text="Run Batch" />
```

When `btnRunBatch` is clicked at runtime, the text of the query stored in `txtSQLBatch.Text` is executed. The parameter `@EmployeeId` is populated from `txtEmployeeId.Text` (in this case, typecast to the integer value 1), and the batch is run. The web service responds with SOAP flowing over HTTP, and the envelope is deserialized into an array of objects.

38

The resulting `DataSet` is again bound to the `GridView` gvData. Any `SqlMessages` in the `ReturnArray` are appended to the text of `lblResults` for viewing on the page.

This type of querying just touches the tip of what can be accomplished via ad hoc web services queries using `sqlbatch()`. You can use your imagination to take it as far as you want.

Example 3: Calling a Web Method–Bound Stored Procedure That Returns XML

For your third and final web method, you'll create a stored procedure that returns XML from an `xml` column, using the new `FOR XML PATH` syntax. To do this, you need to create the stored procedure in Listing 38.9 in the context of the `AdventureWorks` database.

LISTING 38.9   A Stored Procedure That Returns XML

```
CREATE PROC dbo.GetJobCandidateResumeXml
(
    @JobCandidateId int
)
AS
SELECT
    Resume.query('
        declare namespace
        ns="http://schemas.microsoft.com/sqlserver/2004/07/adventure-works/Resume";
        /ns:Resume/ns:Name
    ') as "Name",
    Resume.query('
        declare namespace
        ns="http://schemas.microsoft.com/sqlserver/2004/07/adventure-works/Resume";
        /ns:Resume/ns:Skills
    ') as "Skills"
FROM AdventureWorks.HumanResources.JobCandidate
WHERE JobCandidateId = @JobCandidateId
FOR XML PATH('CandidateQuickView')
```

The `Resume` column of `HumanResources.JobCandidate` is of the new SQL data type `xml`. The `.query()` syntax used in `GetJobCandidateResumeXml` is part of the XQuery language, which is newly supported in SQL Server 2005. Chapter 37, "Using XML in SQL Server 2005," describes these features in detail.

Now you need to bind the stored procedure to the existing endpoint, using the T-SQL in Listing 38.10.

LISTING 38.10   ALTER ENDPOINT Syntax for Adding a Web Method That Returns XML

```
ALTER ENDPOINT EPT_SQL2005UnleashedExamples
FOR SOAP
(
    ADD WEBMETHOD
        'urn:www-samspublishing-com:examples '.'WM_GetJobCandidateResumeXml'
    (
        NAME = 'AdventureWorks.dbo.GetJobCandidateResumeXml',
        FORMAT = ALL_RESULTS,
        SCHEMA = STANDARD
    )
)
```

You need to return to Visual Studio and update the web reference of the project, as described in Example 1. Then you switch default.aspx to design mode and add another Button control, named btnGetXml, to the bottom of the page.

In the HTML Source view of default.aspx, you append to the page the lines of ASP.NET code found in Listing 38.11.

LISTING 38.11   The Final ASP.NET HTML Code in default.aspx

```
<h6>Run Xml-Based Stored Procedure:</h6>
    Job Candidate Id: <asp:TextBox ID="txtJobCandidateId" runat=server
        Text="1"></asp:TextBox>
<asp:Button ID="btnGetXml" runat="server" Text="Get Xml"
    OnClick="btnGetXml_Click" /></div>
<br />
<h6>res.Any[0].OuterXml (xsl-transformed): </h6>
<hr />
<asp:Literal ID="litXmlAsHTML" runat="server"></asp:Literal>
<hr />
<h6>res.Any[1] (SqlRowCount=<asp:Label ID="lblRowCount"
    runat=server></asp:Label>)</h6>
<h6>res.Any[2] (SqlResultCode=<asp:Label ID="lblResultCode"
    runat=server></asp:Label>)</h6>
```

At this point you should double-click btnGetXml. In btnGetXml_Click(), you type or copy the C# code found in Listing 38.12.

38

LISTING 38.12   Consuming a Web Method That Returns XML in C#

```csharp
opensql_simple.EPT_SQL2005UnleashedExamples SQLEndpointProxy =
        new opensql_simple.EPT_SQL2005UnleashedExamples();
SQLEndpointProxy.Credentials = System.Net.CredentialCache.DefaultCredentials;
WM_GetJobCandidateResumeXmlResponseWM_GetJobCandidateResumeXmlResult XmlResult =

SQLEndpointProxy.WM_GetJobCandidateResumeXml(int.Parse(txtJobCandidateId.Text));

if (XmlResult.Any.Length == 3)
{
    lblRowCount.Text = ((XmlElement)XmlResult.Any[1]).InnerText;
    lblResultCode.Text = ((XmlElement)XmlResult.Any[2]).InnerText;
    XmlElement CandidateQuickViewXmlElement = (XmlElement)XmlResult.Any[0];
    XmlNodeReader InputReader = new XmlNodeReader(CandidateQuickViewXmlElement);
    XslCompiledTransform xslt = new XslCompiledTransform();
    xslt.Load(Server.MapPath(@"xslt\defaultss.xslt"));
    MemoryStream OutputStream = new MemoryStream();
    xslt.Transform(InputReader, null, OutputStream);
    OutputStream.Seek(0, SeekOrigin.Begin);
    StreamReader OutputReader = new StreamReader(OutputStream);
    litXmlAsHTML.Text = OutputReader.ReadToEnd();
    InputReader.Close();
    OutputStream.Close();
    OutputReader.Close();
}
```

For this example to compile, you must add the following C# using statements to the top of default.aspx.cs:

```csharp
using System.IO;
using System.Text;
using System.Xml;
using System.Xml.Xsl;
```

Then you add a new folder to the root of the project and name it xslt.

Next, you need to run Internet Explorer from your desktop and request the following URL if you have MSXML 4 or greater installed on your desktop:

```
res://msxml/defaultss.xsl
```

If you are running MSXML 3, use this instead:

```
res://msxml3/defaultss.xsl
```

This URL produces Internet Explorer's secret default WD-XSL stylesheet, which is used to display .xml files in the browser window. You can use it in your project to display the XML output of your stored procedure in default.aspx. To do this, you select File, Save As in Internet Explorer and save the file to your Visual Studio project folder, xslt. If you have any problems getting this to save correctly, you can do a file search on your machine, and you will find the file as a temporary file that you can copy.

Because we defined your new web method to return ALL_RESULTS, the return value on the client side is declared to be of type WM_GetJobCandidateResumeXmlResponseWM_GetJobCandidateResumeXmlResult. This hideously long-named type is automatically generated and simply represents the name of the web method with the word Response or Result appended. You need to set a breakpoint at the top of the body of this method and run the project.

Next, you enter a value in txtJobCandidateId, and when the debugger kicks in, you examine the values returned from the web method in the object XmlResult.Any. Notice that the results are contained not in an Object array, as in the previous examples, but in an array of System.Xml.XmlElement because you are returning XML by using ALL_RESULTS.

You typecast the second element of XmlResult.Any (Any[1]) to an XmlElement and use its InnerText property to set the text of lblRowCount. This is possible because you know from examining the code (by using breakpoints and the watch window at runtime) that Any[1] contains the SqlRowCount object.

You typecast the third element of XmlResult.Any (Any[2]) to an XmlElement and use its InnerText property to set the text of lblResultCode. This is possible because you know from examining the code that Any[2] contains the SqlResultCode object.

The next line typecasts Any[0] (our result set) to XmlElement:

```
CandidateQuickViewXmlElement = (XmlElement)XmlResult.Any[0];
```

The XSLT stylesheet (defaultss.xsl) you borrowed from Internet Explorer is loaded into an XslCompiledTransform object you can use to transform the XML returned by WM_GetJobCandidateResumeXml into visually friendly XML for display on the page.

The following lines in Listing 38.12 use streams and readers of different kinds to manipulate the XML until it's ready to be displayed. The XML is then transformed into HTML by xslt.Transform(InputReader, null, OutputStream). Finally, before you close all readers and streams, you need to add the transformed XML to the Text property of the HTMLLiteral control litXmlAsHTML:

```
litXmlAsHTML.Text = OutputReader.ReadToEnd();
```

The final output should display the result of the GetJobCandidateResumeXml stored procedure, as shown in Figure 38.5.

38

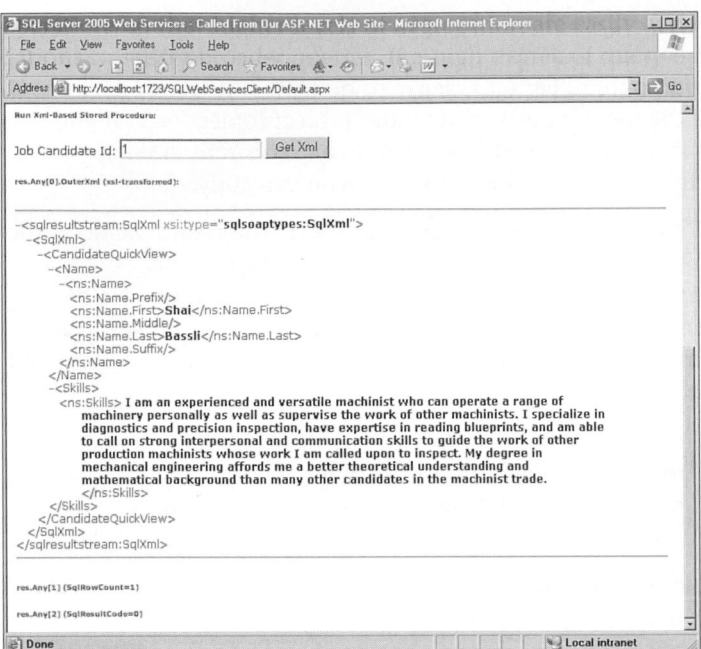

FIGURE 38.5   Returning XML from a stored procedure to a SQL Server web service C# client.

Using Catalog Views and System Stored Procedures

SQL Server provides a set of stored procedures and catalog views that are directly related to endpoint functionality. With these, you can find out anything you need to know about what endpoints exist on the server, the states they are in, the web methods associated with them, the settings used in their DDL, and so on.

To get a result set of all the registered endpoints for a server, you execute the following simple T-SQL statement against sys.endpoints in a new query window in the context of the master database:

```
SELECT name, endpoint_id, protocol_desc, type_desc, state_desc
FROM sys.endpoints
Go
name                         endpoint_id   protocol_desc   type_desc   state_desc
-------------------------------------------------------------------------------
Dedicated Admin Connection        1        TCP             TSQL        STARTED
TSQL Local Machine                2        SHARED_MEMORY   TSQL        STARTED
TSQL Named Pipes                  3        NAMED_PIPES     TSQL        STARTED
TSQL Default TCP                  4        TCP             TSQL        STARTED
```

```
TSQL Default VIA                      5            VIA        TSQL        STARTED
EPT_SQL2005UnleashedExamples   65536            HTTP       SOAP        STARTED
(6 row(s) affected)
```

As the result set illustrates, listeners for the basic SQL Server network protocols (for example, T-SQL named pipes, T-SQL default TCP) are also registered as endpoints.

After you ascertained the `endpoint_id` of the endpoint (65536), you can get all the details about it by querying the catalog view sys.`http_endpoints`:

```
SELECT name, site, url_path, clear_port, ssl_port
FROM sys.http_endpoints
WHERE endpoint_id = 65536
Go
name                             site      url_path   clear_port    ssl_port
------------------------------------------------------------------------------
EPT_SQL2005UnleashedExamples      *        /opensql/    80            443
(1 row(s) affected)
```

To see all of the endpoint's web methods and their DDL-defined settings, you can try the following query against the view sys.`endpoint_webmethods`:

```
SELECT
    method_alias,
    result_schema_desc as [schema],
    result_format_desc as [format]
FROM sys.endpoint_webmethods
WHERE namespace = 'urn:www-samspublishing-com:examples'
AND endpoint_id = 65536
Go
method_alias                     schema       format
----------------------------------------------------------
WM_GetEmployeeBasics             STANDARD     ALL_RESULTS
WM_GetJobCandidateResumeXml      STANDARD     ALL_RESULTS
(2 row(s) affected)
```

To see all endpoints defined using FOR SOAP and some of the settings used in their FOR SOAP clause, you can use the following:

```
SELECT name, principal_id, type_desc, login_type, header_limit
FROM sys.SOAP_endpoints
Go
name                         principal_id   type_desc    login_type   header_limit
-----------------------------------------------------------------------------------
EPT_SQL2005UnleashedExamples  259            SOAP         WINDOWS       4096
(1 row(s) affected)
```

38

Controlling Access Permissions

An important task in endpoint management is the granting, revoking, and denying of endpoint permissions. To control whether a login may connect to (and thus consume) an endpoint, you use the following syntax:

```
{ GRANT ¦ DENY ¦ REVOKE } CONNECT ON ENDPOINT:: <EndPointName> TO <login>
```

For example, to give a login called `MyDomain\MyUserName` connect permission on your endpoint, you would use this statement:

```
GRANT CONNECT ON ENDPOINT::EPT_SQL2005UnleashedExamples TO MyDomain\MyUserName
```

Note that whenever the login specified in the AUTHORIZATION keyword of the endpoint DDL isn't the same as the login consuming the service, you must grant connect permission to that login. To control whether a given login may create endpoints on your SQL Server instance, you use the following syntax:

```
{ GRANT ¦ DENY ¦ REVOKE } CREATE ENDPOINT TO <login>
```

For example, to prevent your test user from creating more endpoints, you execute the following statement:

```
REVOKE CREATE ENDPOINT TO [MyDomain\SQLWebServicesClient]
```

> **NOTE**
>
> The main difference between DENY and REVOKE is that REVOKE removes both currently granted and currently denied permissions, but DENY also prevents permissions from being inherited through role assignment.

To allow a login permission to alter endpoints, you use the following syntax:

```
{ GRANT ¦ DENY ¦ REVOKE } ALTER ANY ENDPOINT TO <login>
{ GRANT ¦ DENY ¦ REVOKE } ALTER ON ENDPOINT:: <EndPointName> TO <login>
{ GRANT ¦ DENY ¦ REVOKE } CONTROL ON ENDPOINT:: <EndPointName> TO <login>
```

For example, to allow serverwide endpoint altering to a login, you execute the following:

```
GRANT ALTER ANY ENDPOINT TO [MyDomain\MyUserLogin]
```

And to disallow ALTER permission on a specific endpoint, you execute the following statement:

```
DENY ALTER ON ENDPOINT::EPT_SQL2005UnleashedExamples TO [MyDomain\MyUserLogin]
```

The CONTROL keyword changes whether a given login may transfer ownership of, alter, drop, or connect to a specific endpoint. To revoke control for a specific endpoint, you execute the following:

```
REVOKE CONTROL ON ENDPOINT::EPT_SQL2005UnleashedExamples TO [MyDomain\MyUserLogin]
```

The following syntax controls the ability for a login to see the metadata of an endpoint via the catalog views:

```
{GRAND¦DENY¦REVOKE} VIEW DEFINITION ON ENDPOINT:: <EndPointName> TO <login>
```

Finally, you use the following syntax to allow a login the ability to take ownership of an endpoint, using the AUTHORIZATION keyword in endpoint DDL:

```
{ GRANT ¦ DENY ¦ REVOKE } TAKE OWNERSHIP ON ENDPOINT:: <EndPointName> TO <login>
```

To allow a given login the ability to take ownership of your endpoint, you execute the following:

```
GRANT TAKE OWNERSHIP ON ENDPOINT::EPT_SQL2005UnleashedExamples
    TO [MyDomain\MyUserLogin]
```

At the time of this writing, there are just a few limitations in SQL Server web services worth noting:

▶ Table-valued user-defined functions cannot be specified as web methods. However, you can solve this by simply calling a table-valued UDF inside a stored procedure exposed as a web method.

▶ SQL Server's SOAP engine allows for XML processing instructions embedded in SOAP envelopes (contrary to the SOAP specification). SQL Server ignores these processing instructions, so this shouldn't be an issue for most applications.

▶ SOAP over HTTP is simply slower (by up to 30%, according to Microsoft) than the native TDS protocol. So for applications in which speed is key, TDS is still the protocol of choice.

38

Summary

Using the new functionality in SQL Server 2005, applications built and running on varying software platforms can now communicate with SQL Server with little or no dependence on expensive, proprietary middleware. And they can do so with minimal client configuration. In providing custom HTTP endpoint support, SQL Server 2005 is also pushing the bounds of what it means to be a traditional database server.

Chapter 39, "SQL Server 2005 Analysis Services," takes on the topic of using Analysis Services to deeply mine data.

PART VII

SQL Server Business Intelligence Features

IN THIS PART

CHAPTER 39 SQL Server 2005 Analysis
            Services   1473

CHAPTER 40 SQL Server Integration Services 1539

CHAPTER 41 SQL Server 2005 Reporting
            Services   1607

SQL Server 2005 Analysis Services

IN THIS CHAPTER

▶ What's New in SSAS

▶ Understanding SSAS and OLAP

▶ Understanding the SSAS Environment Wizards

▶ An Analytics Design Methodology

▶ An OLAP Requirements Example: CompSales International

SQL Server 2005 Analysis Services (SSAS) is jam-packed with numerous data warehousing, data mining, and online analytical processing (OLAP)–rich tools and technologies. A complete overhaul and redeployment of SSAS was delivered by Microsoft and has launched SSAS into a new dimension in the business intelligence (BI) space. SSAS also has the distinction of beating SQL Server 2005 (then known as Yukon) to the general availability point (in fact, nearly a year ahead of Yukon). Other more traditional (and much more expensive) OLAP and BI platforms such as Cognos, Hyperion, Business Objects, and others will be challenged, if not completely replaced, by this new version of SSAS.

A data warehouse manager from a prominent Silicon Valley company said recently, "I can now build [using SSAS] sound, extremely usable, OLAP cubes myself, faster and smarter than my whole department could do only a few years ago." This is what Microsoft has brought to the table. In past SQL Server versions, it was much more difficult to turn OLAP requirements into viable and scalable OLAP cubes, let alone get a handle on complex data mining models. Things have gotten a lot better!

What's New in SSAS

It might actually be easier to describe what has stayed the same in SSAS than to list what's new in SSAS because everything has changed: the architecture, the development environment, the multidimensional languages supported, the wizards, and so on. Here are the highlights:

▶ SSAS is still the land of the wizards. Microsoft has greatly enhanced the wizards, though, to be more discrete and independent, but now the trick is to know when to use what wizard.

▶ Microsoft has introduced projects and a formal development platform for BI that is integrated into the Visual Studio development IDE.

▶ SSAS is now fully integrated with SQL Server Management Studio (SSMS). In fact, many of the same wizards and management aspects of the development studio are available in SSMS. You can also easily create queries from either place for such things as Multidimensional Expressions (MDX), Data Mining Extensions (DMX), and XML for Analysis (XMLA). It is rapidly becoming a fully integrated management and development platform.

▶ You can now have up to 50 separate instances of SSAS on one machine with Microsoft SQL Server 2005 Enterprise Edition or up to 16 separate instances with the Developer Edition and Standard Edition.

▶ Failover clustering is completely supported. SSAS has gone from no support whatsoever to four-node clusters (for 32-bit systems) and eight-node clusters (for 64-bit systems). In other words, SSAS is now a cluster-aware application. This is a big deal.

▶ SSAS provides support for the XML for SSAS 1.1 specification and Analysis Services Scripting Language (ASSL) for XML-based administration.

▶ SSAS enables proactive caching at the partition level, which pushes data that has changed into the cache for immediate access in SSAS. This is a big architectural change that directly addresses high-performance query execution of data in OLAP cubes that change frequently.

▶ SSAS allows utilization of the Universal Dimensional Model (UDM) paradigm, which provides a powerful metadata abstraction layer to use for all SSAS reference needs. It leverages concepts such as dimensions, measures, hierarchies, and so on and provides these simplified reference points to all interfaces and environments.

▶ Key performance indicators (KPIs) allow predefined common metric measurements and calculations within cubes.

▶ Perspectives simplify and control the end user's view into complex cubes.

▶ Several new data mining algorithms have appeared, such as the Naïve Bayes, Association, Sequence Clustering, Time Series/Linear Regression, and Neural Network algorithms.

▶ SSAS provides much more robust usage and integration with the new SQL Server Integration Services (SSIS) for complex data transformations, filtering of data mining, and so on.

Understanding SSAS and OLAP

Because OLAP is at the heart of SSAS, you need to understand what it is and how it solves the requirements of decision makers in a business. As you might already know, data warehousing requirements typically include all the capability needed to report on a business's transactional history, such as sales history. This transactional history is often organized into subject areas and tiers of aggregated information that can support some online querying and usually much more batch reporting. Data warehouses and data marts typically extract data from online transaction processing (OLTP) systems and serve data up to these business users and reporting systems. In general, these are all called decision support systems (DSS), or BI systems, and the latency of this data is determined by the business requirements it must support. Typically, this latency is daily or weekly, depending on the business needs, but more and more, we are seeing more real-time (or near-real-time) reporting requirements.

OLAP falls squarely into the realm of BI. The purpose of OLAP is to provide for a mostly online reporting environment that can support various end user reporting requirements. Typically, OLAP representations are of OLAP cubes. A *cube* is a multidimensional representation of basic business facts that can be accessed easily and quickly to provide you with the specific information you need to make a critical decision. It is useful to note that a cube can be comprised of from 1 to N dimensions. However, remember that the business facts represented in a cube must exist for all the dimensions being defined for the fact. In other words, all dimensional values (that is, intersections) have to be present in order for a fact value to be stored in the cube.

Figure 39.1 illustrates the `Sales_Units` historical business fact, which is the intersection of time, product, and geography dimensional data. For a particular point in time (February 2006), for a particular product (IBM laptop model 451D), and in a particular country (France), the sales units were 996 units. With an OLAP cube, you can easily see how many of these laptop computers were sold in France in February 2006.

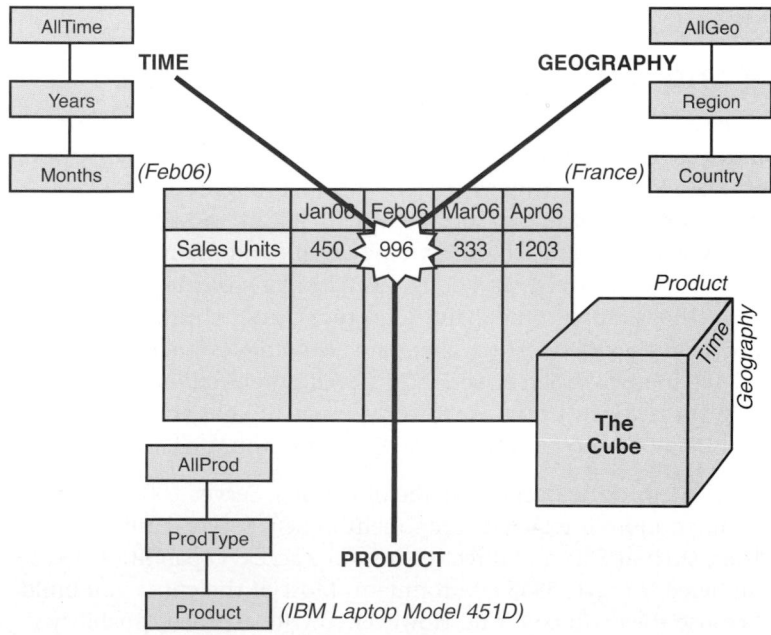

FIGURE 39.1   Multidimensional representation of business facts.

Basically, cubes enable you to look at business facts via well-defined and organized dimensions (time, product, and geography dimensions, in this example). Note that each of these dimensions is further organized into hierarchical representations that correspond to the way data is looked at from the business point of view. This provides for the capability to drill down into the next level from a higher, broader level (like drilling down into a specific country's data within a geographic region, such as France's data within the European geographic region).

SSAS directly supports this and other data warehousing capabilities. In addition, SSAS allows a designer to implement OLAP cubes using a variety of physical storage techniques that are directly tied to data aggregation requirements and other performance considerations. You can easily access any OLAP cube built with SSAS via the Pivot Table Service, you can write custom client applications by using MDX with OLE DB for OLAP or ActiveX Data Objects Multidimensional (ADO MD), and you can use a number of third-party "OLE DB for OLAP" compliant tools.

Microsoft utilizes something called the Unified Dimensional Model (UDM) to conceptualize all multidimensional representations in SSAS. It is also worth noting that many of the leading OLAP and statistical analysis software vendors have joined the Microsoft Data Warehousing Alliance and are building front-end analysis and presentation tools for SSAS. The data mining capabilities that are part of SSAS provide a new avenue for organized data discovery. This includes using SQL Server DMX.

This chapter takes you through the major components of SSAS, discusses a mini-methodology for OLAP cube design, and leads you through the creation and management of a robust OLAP cube that can easily be used to meet a company's BI needs.

Understanding the SSAS Environment Wizards

Welcome to the "land of wizards." This implementation of SSAS, as with older versions of SSAS, is heavily wizard oriented. SSAS has a Cube Wizard, a Dimension Wizard, a Partition Wizard, an Incremental Update Wizard, a Storage Design Wizard, a Usage Analysis Wizard, a Usage-Based Optimization Wizard, a Calculated Cells Wizard, a Mining Model Wizard, and a Security Roles Wizard. All of them are useful, and many of their capabilities are also available through editors and designers. Using a wizard is helpful for those who need to have a little structure in the definition process and who want to rely on the default for much of what they need. The wizards are also plug-and-play oriented and have been made available in all SQL Server and .NET development environments. In other words, you can access these wizards from wherever you need to, when you need to. All the wizard-based capabilities can also be coded in MDX, DMX, and ASSL.

Figure 39.2 shows how SSAS fits into the overall scheme of the SQL Server 2005 environment. SSAS has become a much more integrated component of SQL Server. Utilizing many different mechanisms, such as SSIS and direct data source access capabilities, a vast amount of data can be funneled into the SSAS environment. Most of the cubes you build will likely be read-only because they will be for BI. However, a write-enabled capability is available in SSAS for situations that meet certain data updatability requirements.

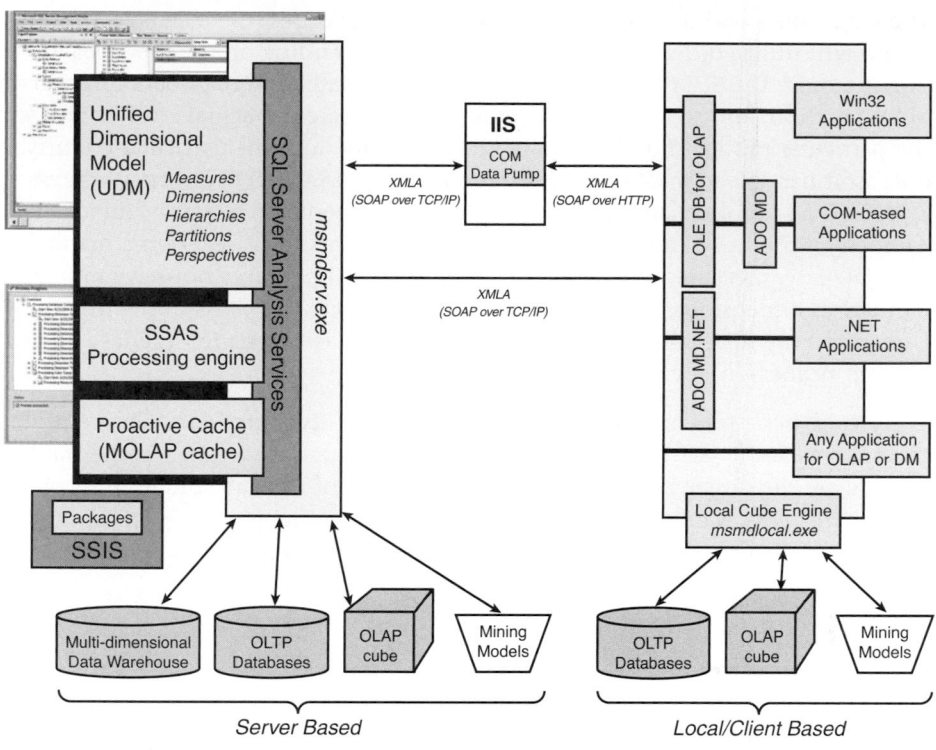

FIGURE 39.2   SSAS as part of the overall SQL Server 2005 environment.

As you can also see in Figure 39.2, the basic components in SSAS are all focused on building and managing data cubes. SSAS consists of the analysis server, processing services, integration services, and a number of data providers. SSAS has both server-based and client-/local-based SSAS capabilities. This essentially provides a complete platform for SSAS.

You create cubes by preprocessing aggregations (that is, precalculated summary data) that reflect the desired levels within dimensions and support the type of querying that will be done. These aggregations provide the mechanism for rapid and uniform response times to queries. You create them *before* the user uses the cube. All queries utilize either these aggregations, the cube's source data, a copy of this data in a client cube, data in cache, or a combination of these sources. A single Analysis Server can manage many cubes. You can have multiple SSAS instances on a single machine.

By orienting around UDM, SSAS allows for the definition of a cube that contains data measures and dimensions. Each cube dimension can contain a hierarchy of levels to specify the natural categorical breakdown that users need to drill down into for more details. Look back at Figure 39.1, and you can see a product hierarchy, time hierarchy, and geography hierarchy representation.

39

The data values within a cube are represented by measures (the facts). Each measure of data might utilize different aggregation options, depending on the type of data. Unit data might require the SUM (summarization) function, Date of Receipt data might require the MAX function, and so on. Members of a dimension are the actual level values, such as the particular product number, the particular month, and the particular country. Microsoft has solved most of the limitations within SSAS. SSAS can now address up to 2,147,483,647 of most anything within its environment (for example, dimensions in a database, attributes in a dimension, databases in an instance, levels in a hierarchy, cubes in a database, measures in a cube). In reality, you will probably not have more than a handful of dimensions. Remember that dimensions are the paths to the interesting facts. Dimension members should be textual and are used as criteria for queries and as row and column headers in query results.

Every cube has a schema from which the cube draws its source data. The central table in this schema is the fact table that yields the cube's data measures. The other tables in the schema are the dimension tables that are the source of the cube dimensions. A classic star-schema data warehouse design has this central fact table along with multiple dimension tables. This is a great starting point for OLAP cube creation, as you can see in Figure 39.3.

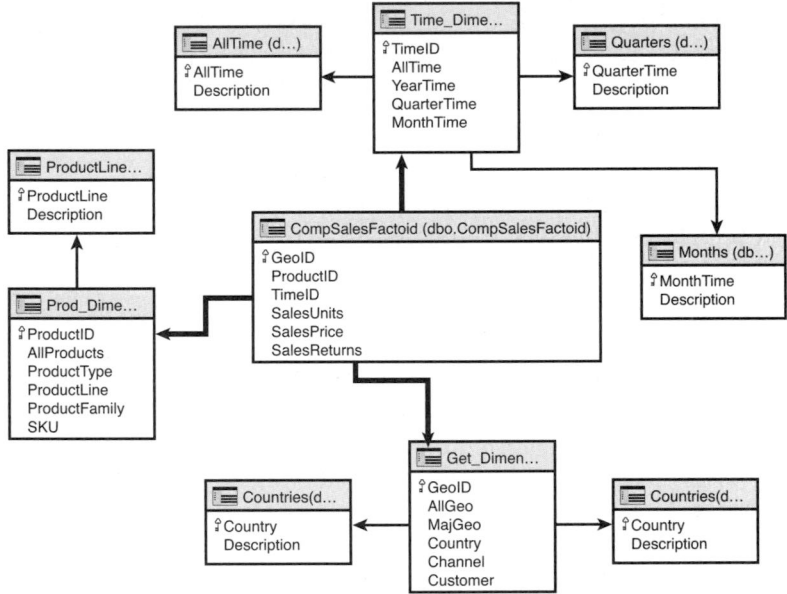

FIGURE 39.3   A star-schema data warehouse design with a central fact table and multiple dimensions of these facts as the source for an OLAP cube in SSAS.

SSAS allows you to build dimensions and cubes from heterogeneous data sources. It can access relational OLTP databases, multidimensional data databases, text data, and any other source that has an OLE DB provider available. You don't have to move all your data first; you just connect to its source.

Essentially, cubes can be regular or local cubes. Regular cubes are based on real tables as the data source, have aggregations, and occupy physical storage space of some kind. If a data source that contributes to this cube changes, the cube must be reprocessed. Figure 39.4 shows cube representations.

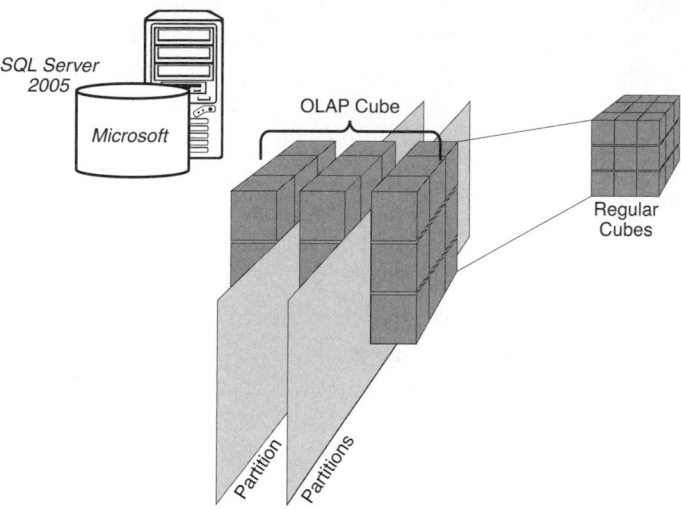

FIGURE 39.4   The SSAS cube representations—regular OLAP cubes and partitions.

Local cubes are entirely contained in portable SSAS files (that is, tables) and can be browsed without a connection to an SSAS instance. This is really like being in "disconnected" mode.

Write-enabled dimensions within a cube enable updates (that is, writes) of data that can be shared back (that is, written back) with the data sources.

The following is a quick summary of all the essential cube terms in SSAS:

- ▶ **Database**—A database is a logical container of one or more cubes. Cubes are defined within Analysis Server databases.

- ▶ **Cube**—A cube is a multidimensional representation of the business facts. Types of cubes are regular and local.

- ▶ **Data source**—The data source is the origin of a cube's data.

- ▶ **Measure group**—This group is a collection (or grouping) of one or more measures into some type of logical unit for business purposes. A measure group does not occupy any physical space. It is metadata only.

- ▶ **Measure**—A measure is a data fact representation. A measure is typically a data value fact, such as price, unit, or quantity.

39

▶ **Cell**—A cell is the part of a data measure that is at the intersection of the dimensions. The cell contains the data value. If an intersection (that is, cell) has no value yet, it does not physically exist until it is populated.

▶ **Dimension**—A cube's dimension is defined by the aggregation levels of the data that are needed to support the data requirements. A dimension can be shared with other cubes, or it can be private to a cube. The structure of a dimension is directly related to the dimension table columns, member properties, or structure of OLAP data mining models. This structure becomes the hierarchy and should be organized accordingly. You can also have strict parent/child dimensions in which two columns are identified as being parent and child and the dimension is organized according to them. In a regular dimension, each column in the dimension contributes a hierarchy level.

▶ **Level**—A level includes the nodes of the hierarchy or data mining model. Each level contains the members. Millions of members are possible for each level.

▶ **Partition**—One or more partitions comprise a cube. Using a partition is a way to physically separate parts of a cube. This separation essentially lets you deal with individual slices of a data cube separately, querying only the relevant data sources. If you partition by dimension, you can perform incremental updates to change that dimension independently of the rest of the cube. Consequently, you have to reprocess only the aggregations that are affected by those changes. This is an excellent feature for scalability.

▶ **Hierarchy**—A hierarchy is a set of members in a dimension and their position relative to each other. Hierarchies can either be balanced or unbalanced. Being balanced simply means that all branches of the hierarchy descend to the same level. An unbalanced hierarchy allows for branches to descend to different levels. It is also possible to define more than one hierarchy for a single dimension. A great example of this is "fiscal calendar time" and "Gregorian calendar time" being defined in one dimension—a Time dimension that contains both time.gregorian and time.fiscal.

As mentioned previously, SSAS has many wizards. Which wizards you use depends on what you need to create. The "Creating an OLAP Database" section, later in this chapter, outlines the order and path through these wizards.

OLAP Versus OLTP

One of the primary goals of OLAP is to increase data retrieval speed for business-related queries that are critical to decisions. Very often, there is a need to broaden the scope of a business query or to drill down into more granular details of the query. OLAP was created to facilitate this type of capability. A multidimensional schema is not a typical normalized relational database; redundant data is stored to facilitate quick retrieval. The data in a multidimensional database should be relatively static; in fact, data is not useful for decision support if it changes constantly. The information in a data warehouse is built out of carefully chosen snapshots of business data from OLTP systems. If you capture data at the right times for transfer to the data warehouse, you can quickly make accurate comparisons of important business activities over time.

In an OLTP system, transaction speed is paramount. Data modification operations must be quick, deal with concurrency (locking/holding of resources), and provide transactional consistency. An OLTP system is constantly changing; snapshots of the OLTP system, even if taken only a few seconds apart, are all different. Although historical information is certainly available in an OLTP system, it might be impractical to use it for BI-type analysis. Storing old data in an OLTP system becomes expensive, and you might need to reconstruct history dynamically from a series of transactions. In addition, OLTP designs and indexes usually don't support large-scale decision support querying.

SSAS supports three OLAP storage methods—MOLAP, ROLAP, and HOLAP—providing flexibility to the data warehousing solution and enabling powerful partitioning and aggregation optimization capabilities.

Figure 39.5 shows the MOLAP, HOLAP, and ROLAP storage continuum. MOLAP stores all data locally (to SSAS), and ROLAP is the opposite (storing all data in the relational database). MOLAP is by far the most often used storage approach. The following sections take a closer look at them.

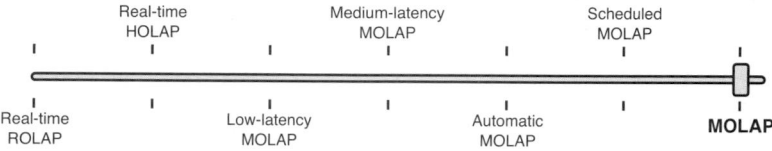

FIGURE 39.5   MOLAP, HOLAP, and ROLAP storage continuum.

MOLAP

Multidimensional OLAP (MOLAP) is an approach in which cubes are built directly from OLTP data sources or from dimensional databases and downloaded to a persistent store.

In SSAS, data is downloaded to the server, and the details and aggregations are stored in a native Microsoft OLAP format. No zero-activity records are stored.

The dimension keys in the fact tables are compressed, and bitmap indexing is used. A high-speed MOLAP query processor retrieves the data.

ROLAP

Relational OLAP (ROLAP) uses fact data in summary tables in the OLTP data source to make data much more current (real-time). The summary tables are populated by processes in the OLTP system and are not downloaded to SSAS. The summary tables are known as materialized views and contain various levels of aggregation, depending on the options you select when building data cubes with SSAS. SSAS builds the summary tables with a column for each dimension and each measure. It indexes each dimension column and creates an additional index on all the dimension columns.

39

HOLAP

SSAS implements a combination of MOLAP and ROLAP called hybrid OLAP (HOLAP). Here, the facts are left in the OLTP data source, and aggregations are stored in the SSAS server. You use SSAS to boost query performance. This approach helps avoid data duplication, but performance suffers a bit when you query fact data in the OLTP summary tables. The amount of performance degradation depends on the level of aggregation selected.

ROLAP and HOLAP are useful in situations where an organization wants to leverage its investment in relational database technology and existing infrastructure. The summary tables of facts are also accessible in the OLTP system via normal data access methods. However, when using SSAS, both ROLAP and HOLAP require more storage space because they don't use the storage optimizations of the pure MOLAP-compressed implementation.

An Analytics Design Methodology

A data warehouse can be built from the top down or from the bottom up. To build a top-down warehouse, you need to form a complete picture or logical data model for the entire organization (or all the subsystems within the scope of the project, such as all financial systems). In contrast, building a warehouse from the bottom up takes a much more departmental or specific business-area focus (for example, a sales order system only). This breaks the task of modeling the data into more manageable chunks. Such a departmental approach produces data marts that are potentially subsets of the overall data warehouse. The bottom-up approach can simplify implementation. It helps get departmental or business-area information to the people who need it, makes it easier to protect sensitive data, and results in better query response times because data marts deal with less data than a voluminous transactional system. The potential risk in the data mart approach is that disparity in data mart implementation can result in a logically disjointed enterprise data warehouse if efforts aren't carefully coordinated across the organization.

Before you embark on an OLAP database creation effort, the time you spend understanding the underlying requirements is the best time you can give your effort. If scope is set correctly, you will be able to achieve an industrial-strength OLAP design without much difficulty. First, you need to take care of some groundwork:

1. Carefully assess the scope of what you want to represent in the BI environment. Start small, as the bottom-up approach suggests. For instance, just tackle the sales data facts.

2. Coordinate your efforts with other related BI efforts. Let people know that you are carving out a specific subject area or departmental data and, when you finish, publish your design to everyone.

3. Seek out any shared dimensions that might have already been created for other cubes. You want to leverage these as much as possible for the sake of data consistency and nonredundant processing.

4. Understand your data sources. The OLAP cube you create will be only as good as the data you put into it. It's best to understand the dirty data issues of what you are about to touch long before you try to build an OLAP cube with it.

An Analytics Mini-Methodology

To successfully build OLAP solutions, you are advised to carefully assess the requirements of your end-users in as detailed fashion as is possible. A mini-methodology that focuses on the essential usages and characteristics of an Analytic solution can prove invaluable. The following sections outline a solid approach to nailing down your BI requirements and yielding optimal OLAP designs that solve your end users' needs.

Assumption: You are building a business area–focused OLAP cube.

Requirements Phase

1. Identify the processing requirements for this DSS. What analysis do you need to do? Are trend reporting, forecasting, and so on necessary? These can often be represented in use case form (via UML).

   a. Ask each user what business decision questions he or she needs to have answered.

   b. Ask each user how often he or she needs these questions answered and exactly when the questions must be answered.

   c. Ask each user how current the data must be to get accurate answers. (This speaks to data latency.)

2. Identify the data needed to fulfill these requirements. What data must be touched to provide answers? The best way to capture this type of information is a logical data model. Even a rough model is better than none at all. This is where you focus on the facts that need to be analyzed.

3. Identify all possible hierarchies and level representations (that is, aggregations). This is how the data is used. Most users are likely to tell you that they want to see product data in the product hierarchy structure that has already been set up (for example, product family, product groups).

4. Identify the time hierarchies that the users need. Because time is usually implicit, it just needs to be clarified in terms of levels of aggregation (for example, years, quarters, months, weeks, days) and whether it needs to be fiscal versus Gregorian calendar, both, or something else.

5. Understand the data that each user can view from a security point of view.

39

Design Phase

1. Analyze which data sources are needed to fulfill the requirements. See whether dimensions or OLAP cubes that already exist can be shared.

2. Understand what data transformations need to be done to the source data to provide it to the OLAP world. This might include pre-aggregation, reformatting, data integrity verifications, and so on.

3. Translate these requirements into an OLAP model design:

   a. Translate to MOLAP if your data sources are not going to be leveraged at all and you will be taking full advantage of OLAP storage.

   b. Translate to ROLAP if you are going to leverage an existing relational design and storage.

   c. Translate to HOLAP if you are going to partially utilize the source data storage and partially utilize OLAP storage. This is the most frequently used approach.

Construction Phase

1. Implement data extraction, transformation, and loading (ETL) logic (via T-SQL, SSIS, or other methods).

2. Create the data sources to be used.

3. Create the dimensions.

4. Create the cube.

5. Select data measures (that is, the data facts) for the cube.

6. Design the storage and aggregations.

7. Process the cube. This brings the data into the OLAP environment.

8. Verify data integrity.

Implementation Phase

1. Define the security roles in the cube.

2. Train the user to use the system.

3. Process the data into the OLAP environment (from production data sources).

4. Verify data integrity.

5. Allow users to use the OLAP cube.

Maintenance Phase

1. Evaluate access optimization in the OLAP cube via usage analysis.

2. Do data mining discovery, if desired.

3. Make schema changes/enhancements, as necessary.

An OLAP Requirements Example: CompSales International

Following is an abbreviated requirement that reflects an actual implementation that was done for a large Silicon Valley company. We will follow the mini-methodology as closely as possible to implement this requirement in SSAS, pointing out which facilities of SSAS should be used for which purpose along the way.

CompSales International Requirements

A large computer manufacturer named CompSales International needs to do basic analytical processing of its product data in a new BI environment. The main business issues at hand are related to minimizing channel inventory and better understanding market demand for the company's most popular products. The detailed data processing requirements are as follows:

1. You want to view sales unit actuals and sales returns for system and non-system products for the past two years via the product hierarchy (All Products, Product Types, Product Lines, Product Families, SKUs), geography hierarchy (All Geos, Major Geos, Countries, Channels, Customers), and different time levels (All Time, Years, Quarters, Months).

2. You want to view data primarily at the yearly and monthly levels, although the finance department also uses it a little bit at quarterly levels.

3. You want to view net sales (sales minus returns) at all levels of the hierarchy.

4. The fiscal and Gregorian calendar are the same for CompSales International.

5. One day past month-end processing, all "actuals" data from the prior month is available (sales units and returns).

You need to implement some general design decisions using SSAS, including the following:

▶ **Hierarchies (dimensions)**—This includes product, geography, and time.

▶ **Facts (measures)**—This includes sales units, sales returns, and net sales (units minus returns) calculated.

▶ **OLAP storage**—This will be MOLAP or HOLAP (if you want to use the star-schema data mart that already contains most of what you are after).

39

▶ **Physical tables that exist**—This includes Geo_Dimension, Prod_Dimension, Time_Dimension, and CompSalesFactoid (the fact table). This data is updated weekly. Each of these tables uses an artificial key into the main facts table for performance reasons (GeoID, ProductID, TimeID). In addition, there are several member/value description tables associated with each dimension table. Basically, there is one table for each level in a dimension. These description tables can be leveraged to make the result rows from OLAP queries much more user friendly.

Figure 39.6 illustrates the desired hierarchies and facts for CompSales International's requirements.

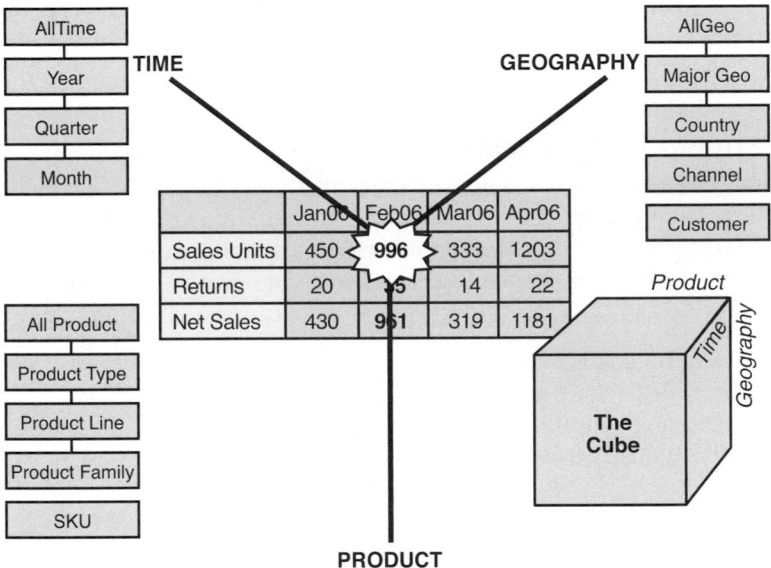

FIGURE 39.6   CompSales International's multidimensional OLAP requirements.

OLAP Cube Creation

A star schema data mart named CompSales is used as the basis of creating the OLAP cube example in this chapter. You can download this data mart, CompsSales.zip, from the Sams Publishing website for this book title at www.samspublishing.com. You can easily unzip and attach this database to any SQL Server 2005 database instance. This is not an SSAS database; it is a SQL Server database. You will be building the SSAS OLAP cube yourself (by following the steps outlined here).

You'll spend most of the construction phase using SQL Server Business Intelligence Development Studio (BIDS; also known as Visual Studio) and Microsoft SSMS. All wizards and editors are invoked from either BIDS or SSMS. As mentioned earlier, Microsoft has moved to a project orientation. For this reason, you need to start out in the BIDS (which actually invokes Visual Studio with the BI plug-ins). You must have already installed SSAS. In general, here's what you'll be doing in this example:

1. Create a BI project.

2. Identify data sources and data source views that you want to use for a new cube.

3. Define the basic dimensions for the cube (Time, Geography, Product) and their hierarchies.

4. Create the cube.

5. Define the measure groups/measures.

6. Define the hierarchies.

7. Process the cube.

8. Deploy the solution.

9. Use the cube.

Using SQL Server BIDS

The SQL Server BIDS (a.k.a. Visual Studio with the BI plug-ins) is launched from the SQL Server 2005 Program group on the Start menu. When this is open, you choose File, New Project, Business Intelligence Projects. Figure 39.7 shows the New Project dialog from which you should highlight the Analysis Services Project template option and specify a project name, project location, and solution name for this new BI project. In this case, the solution name is "CompSales Unleashed OLAP."

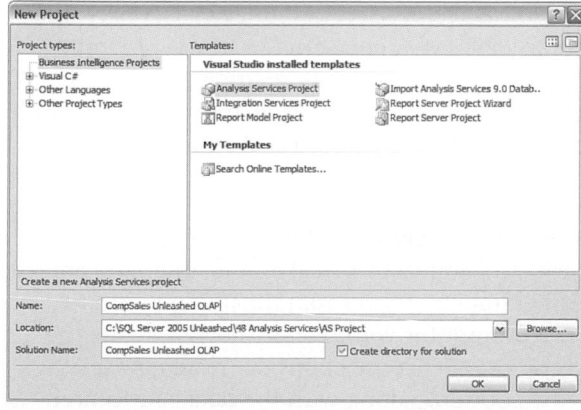

FIGURE 39.7   The SQL Server BIDS New Project dialog.

NOTE

You can also start a new project by leveraging any other existing SSAS database project. You can easily clone an existing project and tweak it a bit to fit your new needs. To do this, you use the Import Analysis Services 9.0 Database template option.

After you create a new project, a set of objects is presented to you in the upper-right pane, which is the Solution Explorer. Figure 39.8 shows the Solution Explorer for the new project. All OLAP project objects reside here—including data sources, dimensions, cubes, mining structures, and roles.

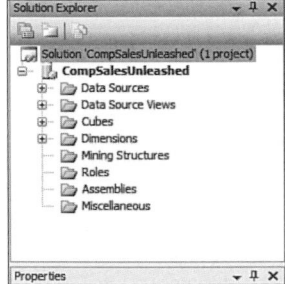

FIGURE 39.8   The Solution Explorer view for the new CompSalesUnleashed project.

Creating an OLAP Database

Remember that an OLAP database is made up of data sources, dimensions, and cubes. A data source is simply a pointer to data somewhere, such as via a Jet OLE DB provider, an OLE DB provider, SQL Native Client, Microsoft Directory Services, or even SSIS packages. Dimensions are constructed of columns from tables that you select to be used to build and filter data cubes. Cubes are combinations of dimensions whose intersections contain strategically significant measures of business performance, such as quantities, units, and so on. You need to identify any data sources on which your OLAP cube is to be based.

Adding a Data Source

To add data sources for a new database, you simply right-click the Data Sources object in the Solution Explorer or select Project, New Data Source in Visual Studio. The Data Source Wizard is then initiated. As mentioned earlier, much of SSAS administration is wizard based. The Data Source Wizard starts with a prompt for you to select how to define the connection to a data source. You can use any existing connections or create new ones from this dialog. Figure 39.9 shows these two options, along with the data connection properties. If you have attached the CompSales database (or any other database) already, you can easily create a new connection to this database for use in this example.

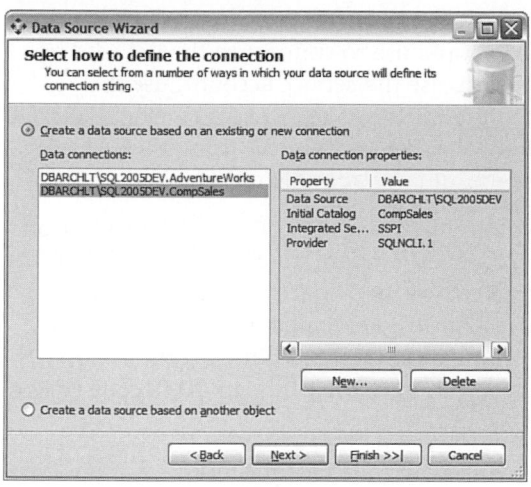

FIGURE 39.9   Defining a data source connection in the Data Source Wizard.

Figure 39.10 shows the Connection Manager dialog, where you specify the provider to use (for example, Native OLE DB\SQL Native Client), the name of the database to connect to, and the authentication method to use for the connection. You should go ahead and establish a connection to the CompSales database you just attached and click the Test Connection button in the lower-right corner to verify that it is valid. If you have referenced the CompSales database from Visual Studio before, it may already appear in the Data Connections list.

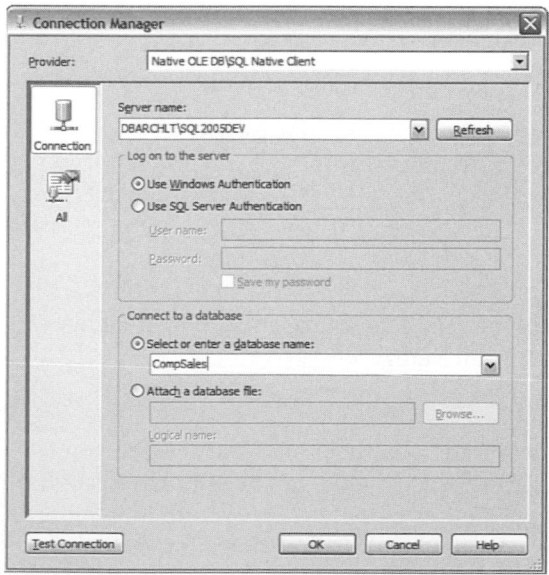

FIGURE 39.10   Connection Manager specification for a new data source.

As part of this connection specification, you must specify the impersonation information. That is, you must define what credentials SSAS should use to connect to the data source. You can specify a specific user name and password, use the service account, use the credentials of the current user, or use default authentication. You can also create a specialized domain account to use for all SSAS connections. We recommend using the service account approach, which is easily leveraged for most cube administration.

To finish, you must name the data source "Comp Sales" and then click the Finish button. Your data source then appears in the Solution Explorer, under Data Sources. As part of this process, an XML file is created, from which you can easily manage all connection properties for this data source (Comp Sales.ds in this example). Remember that you have just established connection information only—nothing more. If you right-click the Comp Sales.ds entry under the Data Sources object, you can view the complete XML code of this entry by selecting the View Code option.

The following is the XML code that represents this data source connection:

```
<DataSource xmlns:xsd="http://www.w3.org/2001/XMLSchema"
    xmlns:xsi="http://www.w3.org/2001/XMLSchema-instance"
    xmlns:dwd="http://schemas.microsoft.com/DataWarehouse/Designer/1.0"
    xsi:type="RelationalDataSource" dwd:design-time-name=
    "2d1509d1-ec6f-4002-9e15-3ee3fe7a7274"
    xmlns="http://schemas.microsoft.com/analysisservices/2003/engine">
  <ID>Comp Sales</ID>
  <Name>Comp Sales</Name>
  <CreatedTimestamp>0001-01-01T00:00:00Z</CreatedTimestamp>
  <LastSchemaUpdate>0001-01-01T00:00:00Z</LastSchemaUpdate>
  <ConnectionString>Provider=SQLNCLI.1;Data Source=DBARCHLT\SQL2005DEV;
    Integrated Security=SSPI;Initial Catalog=CompSales</ConnectionString>
  <ConnectionStringSecurity>Unchanged</ConnectionStringSecurity>
  <ImpersonationInfo>
    <ImpersonationMode>ImpersonateServiceAccount</ImpersonationMode>
    <ImpersonationInfoSecurity>Unchanged</ImpersonationInfoSecurity>
  </ImpersonationInfo>
  <Timeout>PT0S</Timeout>
</DataSource>
```

You can also choose the View Designer option on this data source entry, which allows you to view and modify the properties of the data source entry.

Creating Data Source Views
Because you will be basing your cube on a data warehouse/data mart star schema you already have available, you need to further define exactly what you need to have access to within that data source. Creating a data source view essentially allows you to look more deeply into the metadata of the data source and add additional relationships, create things like calculations, and set logical keys on the metadata of the data source. You start

by right-clicking the Data Source View object in the Solution Explorer and selecting New Data Source View (or choosing Project, New Data Source View). This starts the Data Source View Wizard, which you use to define what view of data to use for the cube. The first dialog box allows you to select a data source to use as the basis of the data source view. Figure 39.11 shows the data source CompSales that you defined earlier. Chose it and click Next.

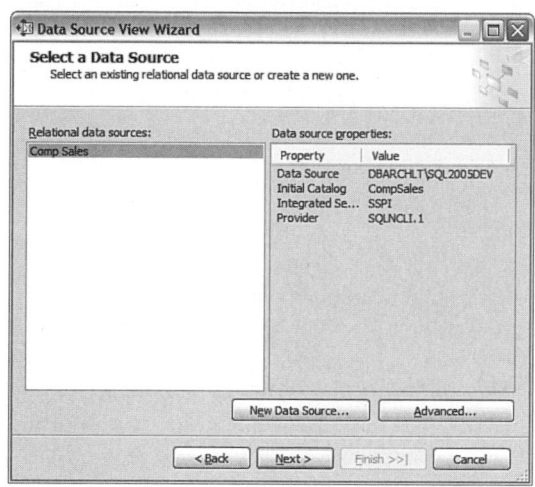

FIGURE 39.11   Identifying which data source to use for the view in the Data Source View Wizard.

If you need to limit the data source to a particular schema within the database, you can click the Advanced button and specify a schema (or schemas) to be restricted to. If your schema doesn't include foreign key specifications, you can use this wizard to try to discover foreign key relationships, using a few different types of column name matching. Figure 39.12 shows an example of using a simple primary key column name matching technique to identify any foreign key relationships with other tables in your schema. If you have used some type of common naming convention on your source tables, you can easily leverage this name-matching dialog.

You essentially can identify the following:

▶ Matches based on the exact column name match (as compared to the primary key column):

Order.**CustomerID** (foreign key) → Customer.**CustomerID** (primary key)

▶ Matches based on the column name being the primary key table name:

Order.**Customer** → **Customer**.CustomerID (primary key)

39

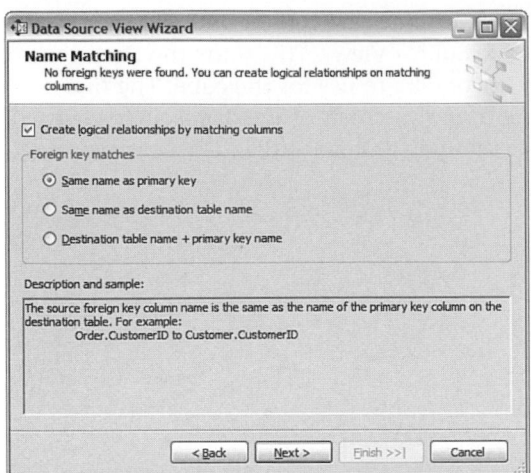

FIGURE 39.12   Logical relationship discovery, using column-naming matching in the Data Source View Wizard.

▶ Matches based on similar column name by comparing the table name concatenated with its primary key column name and then loosely comparing it to other column names of other tables:

Order.**CustomerID** → **Customer.ID**

(concatenated to Customer+ID=CustomerID)

Order.**Customer ID** → **Customer.ID**

Or Order.**Customer_ID** → Customer.ID

In this example, we have used some good naming conventions for columns, so you can simply specify the first option (match based on exact column match). This is the lead-in to select the tables (and/or views) you need to be included from your data source. As you can see in Figure 39.13, you can choose from any number of objects. You must select the base tables you need in your data source views. These are the CompSalesFactoid, Geo_Dimension, Prod_Dimension, and Time_Dimension tables. However, you should also click the Add Related Tables button to add all related tables, based on the matching technique you specified earlier. This completes the set of tables that comprise the data source views for your cube.

You now complete this wizard by naming the data source views (Comp Sales) and clicking Finish.

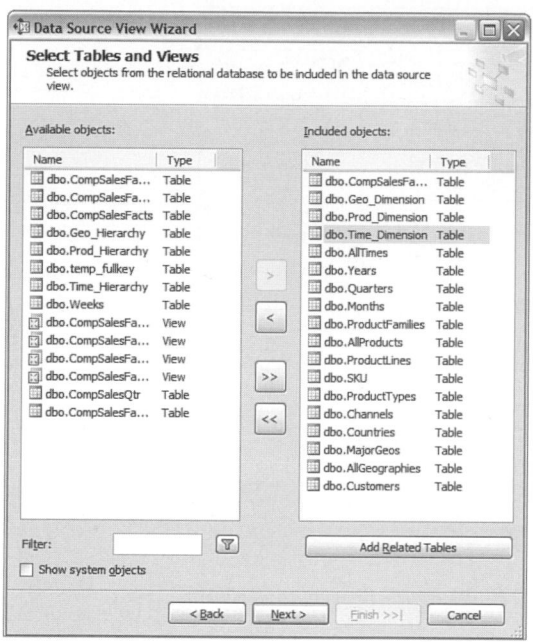

FIGURE 39.13   Available and included objects for your data source views in the Data Source View Wizard.

When you exit the wizard, you end up in the designer view in Visual Studio, with a graphical representation of the data source views that will be the basis of the cube you are building (see Figure 39.14). This figure highlights the primary fact table (CompSalesFactoid), the primary dimension tables (Time_Dimension, Prod_Dimension, Geo_Dimension), and all tables related to these dimensions (that contain the values/descriptions of the member entries for the hierarchies of the dimensions).

Now, because you have fully specified data source views, you can easily define a cube via the Cube Wizard. Or you can jump to defining your cube's dimensions and then use these dimensions in the Cube Wizard later. Because you know your source database well, you should go ahead and create your dimensions and hierarchies first.

Defining Dimensions and Hierarchies

You are now ready to start defining dimensions and hierarchies to your database. Dimensions are the building blocks for cubes in SSAS. You start by right-clicking the Dimension object in the Solution Explorer (or choosing Project, New Dimension). You can create a new (standard) dimension or define a dimension that is linked to another SSAS cube or database.

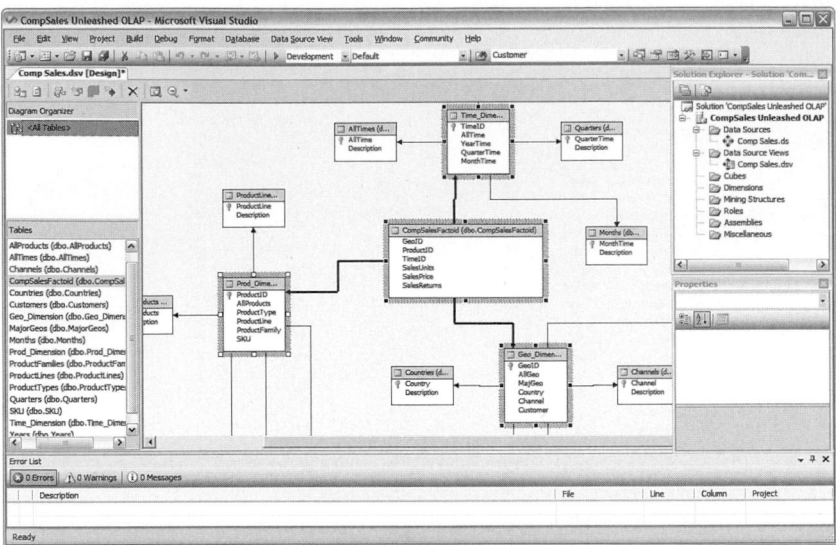

FIGURE 39.14   A designer graphical representation of the data source views.

For this example, you will be creating three new cube dimensions, based on the dimension tables you have in your data source views (Time_Dimension, Prod_Dimension, Geo_Dimension). When you choose the New Dim option, you are welcomed to the Dimension Wizard. You need to build the new dimensions by using your data source views. As you can see in Figure 39.15, the first wizard dialog prompts you to specify whether you will be using a data source to create a dimension. This is the wizard build method. If you haven't defined any data sources (and perhaps don't have them yet), you can use a template approach to define dimensions. This is the second option on this dialog. You do have a valid data source to use, but you don't want the wizard to auto build (because you know what your dimensions should look like already). Therefore, you need to specify that you want to create a dimension by using a data source but uncheck the Auto Build option (if it is selected) and click Next.

You are prompted to identify the data source views you want to use to provide data to the new dimension. Because you have already defined the data source views in a previous step (the Comp Sales data source views), it should be available for you to use. Figure 39.16 shows the Comp Sales data source views and all the tables available for your use. You should highlight this data source view and click Next.

As you can see in Figure 46.17, you must now specify what kind of dimension you are creating. This can be either a standard dimension (most dimensions are standard), a time dimension that Microsoft has defined for you already (Server Time Dimension), or a dimension that is based on data values in a table (Time Dimension with a table specified to base it on).

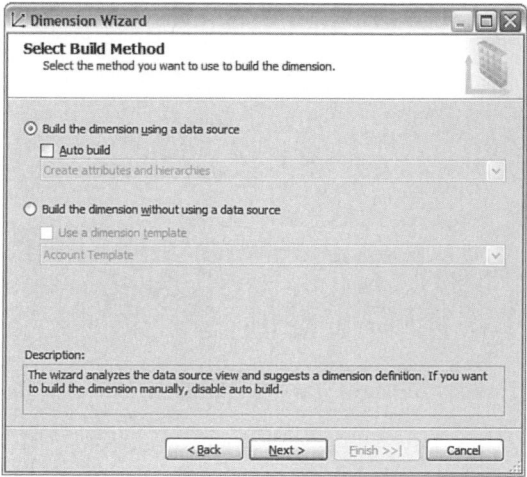

FIGURE 39.15   Creating a dimension by using a data source in the Dimension Wizard.

FIGURE 39.16   Identifying which data source views to use for a dimension in the Dimension Wizard.

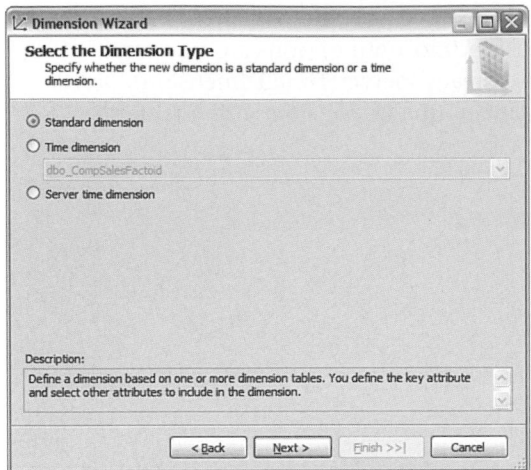

FIGURE 39.17   Specifying which kind of dimension to create in the Dimension Wizard.

The first dimension you should create is the Time dimension, but you already have a time dimension table and hierarchy in your data source views to base it on. Therefore, you need to define it as a standard dimension. If you didn't have such a well-defined dimension to use as your time dimension, you could use either of the other two kinds of time dimension options within this wizard.

Figure 39.18 shows the different Server Time Dimension options that Microsoft provides for your convenience. Microsoft has tried to cover the primary variations of time dimensions and calendars in the market: Fiscal, Reporting (for example, for Marketing, which also includes week-by-month patterns such as 4-4-5 calendars), Manufacturing, and even ISO 8601 calendars. The process is to first identify a time period and then select the calendar type to use. The wizard then creates a Server time dimension for you that meets your needs.

Figure 39.19 shows how to correspond an existing table to predefined time properties of a time dimension that Microsoft has defined. In other words, you can match columns in a table that you have in your data source views to these predefined time properties (for example, a Sales_Year column in a fact table to the Year time property). Then the wizard builds the corresponding time dimension for the cube. A limitation here is that these are the only time properties allowed. You might have defined other types of time columns in your fact table that have no correspondence to these standard time properties. In those cases, you should create standard time dimensions.

> **NOTE**
>
> Keep in mind that you might want to have multiple time dimensions in your cube to fulfill multiple business unit group needs. You can create as many as you need and then provide perspectives of the cube for each group that include only each group's specific time dimension for their needs.

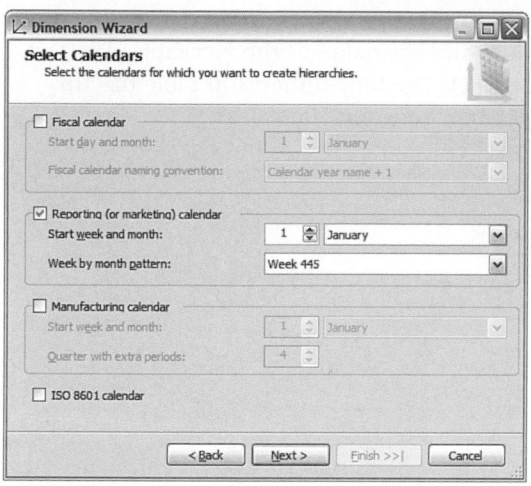

FIGURE 39.18   Calendaring options for Server time dimensions in the Dimension Wizard.

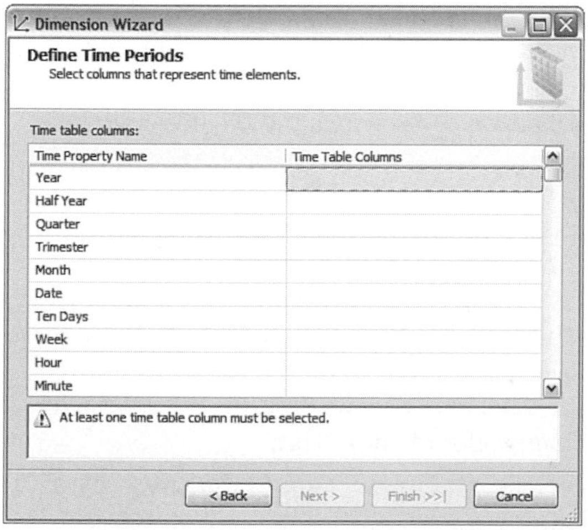

FIGURE 39.19   Time property associations to table columns for time dimension in the Dimension Wizard.

Standard dimensions are not predefined to SSAS. Most dimensions (for example, Product, Geography, Customer) are standard dimensions. In this example, you have a valid time dimension in your data source views already, and you simply need to create a standard cube dimension for it. You need to first define a standard time dimension, then a product dimension, and finally a geography dimension (per the requirements stated earlier).

You start by selecting the Standard Dimension option (refer to Figure 39.17) and click Next. Now you must identify the dimension table for the cube's time dimension. You use the pull-down menu to select dbo.Time_Dimension from the list. After you do this, all the columns in that table appear in the key columns list (as shown in Figure 39.20). You must identify which column here corresponds to the key value in the fact table. The fact table's time is keyed by a pseudo-key called TimeID. The time dimension table has this corresponding key column. You check its check box here and click Next.

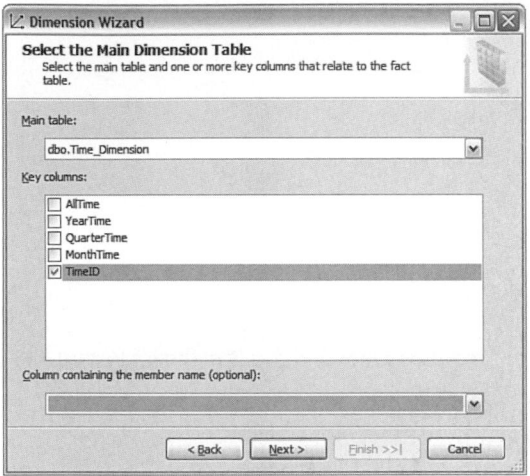

FIGURE 39.20   Specifying the key column for the time dimension in the Dimension Wizard.

You have probably noticed that the time dimension table has all the other levels of the time dimension hierarchy as separate columns as well. In addition, there are a few related tables to this time dimension table that hold the member value descriptions that correspond to each level in the hierarchy. It is really nice to have the member-level descriptions available in the cube for ease of use by the end user. It is pretty easy to include these in the next step of identifying any related tables to this dimension. Figure 39.21 shows the list of related tables identified earlier in the data source views. You need to check all the related tables for inclusion in the time dimension and click Next.

It is now time to select the attributes you want to include in the dimension. The Dimension Wizard presents a Dimension Attributes list, along with the attribute key column and attribute name column correspondences. You want to identify the correct key column value from your data source views for Attribute Key Column and use the Description column values from your data source views as Attribute Name Column in your dimension. So, for each dimension attribute, you need to indicate the appropriate data source views column origin. First, you check the check box for each dimension attribute that you need: All Times, Years, Quarters, and Months. Then, for the selected dimension attributes, you specify the correct attribute key column to use as the basis. The dimension attribute All Times should use the dbo.AllTimes.AllTime key column. Next, the Attribute name column for All Times should use the dbo.AllTimes.Description column. Figure 39.22 shows all the dimension attribute values for the time dimension you are building. After you have specified the desired dimension attributes, you click Next.

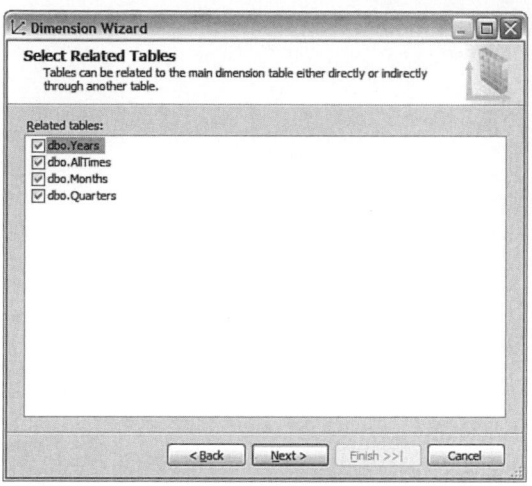

FIGURE 39.21   Including the related member description tables in the dimension in the Dimension Wizard.

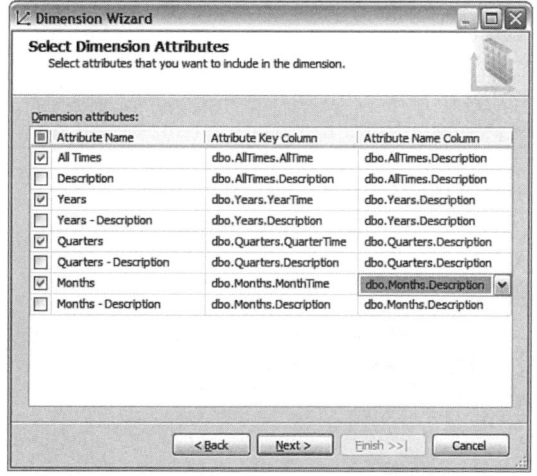

FIGURE 39.22   Selecting dimension attributes for the dimension in the Dimension Wizard.

Now you must identify the type of this dimension (regular or a specific type). Microsoft has predefined several types of dimensions in order to help map dimension attributes to some standard attribute types, such as Bill-of-Materials types, Channel types, and several others, as you can see in Figure 39.23. For the purposes of this example, you simply use the regular dimension type because all your dimensions are well formed already, so select Regular and then click Next.

39

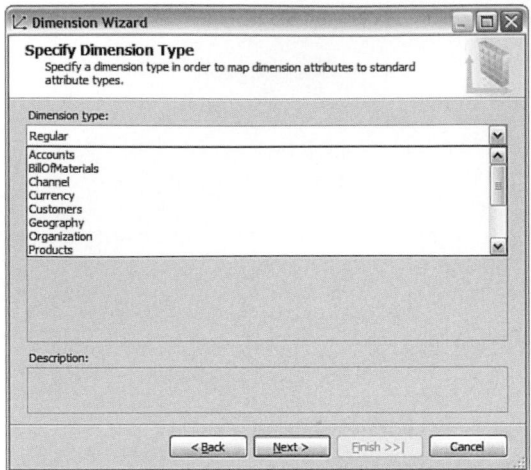

FIGURE 39.23   The Regular dimension type specification in the Dimension Wizard.

When this wizard completes, it places you in the dimension designer for the dimension you just created (the time dimension, in this example). In addition, a dimension entry is added to the Solution Explorer, and now you can easily create the hierarchical view for this dimension. This is quite easy because all the attributes that represent a level in a hierarchy are visible, and you can drag them into a hierarchy from within this designer. As you can see in Figure 39.24, you can click and drag any attribute listed in this dimension from the Attributes pane (on the far left) to the Hierarchies and Levels pane. A new hierarchy is created automatically when you pull your first attribute into this work area. Your goal is to create the following hierarchy for the time dimension (in this order, from top to bottom):

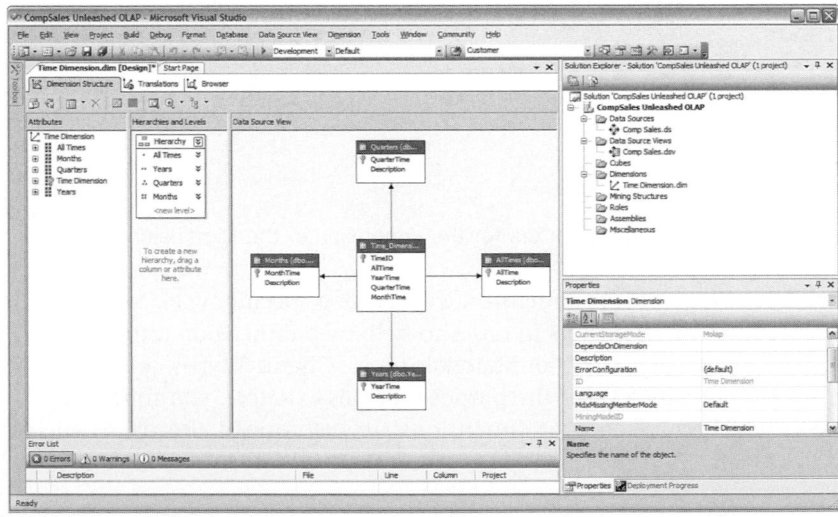

FIGURE 39.24   Creating the time hierarchy in the dimension designer.

1. All Time

2. Years

3. Quarters

4. Months

Now, you essentially need to go through the whole process of creating a dimension and a hierarchy for the other dimensions (product and geography). The process is as follows:

1. Invoke the Dimension Wizard (by right-clicking the Dimensions object in the Solution Explorer).

2. Build the dimension by using the data source approach. Remember, do not specify to auto-build (uncheck this box).

3. Select the Comp Sales data source views.

4. Create a standard dimension.

5. Select the main dimension table to use (db.Prod_Dimension for the product dimension and dbo.Geo_Dimension for the geography dimension).

6. Check the key column of each new dimension (ProductID for the product dimension, GeoID for the geography dimension).

7. Check all the relevant tables and specify the appropriate level description columns for the level attribute name column.

8. Specify the regular dimension type.

9. Finish the Dimension Wizard and move into the dimension designer.

10. Drag the dimension attributes to the Hierarchies and Levels pane to create the dimension hierarchy view:

    ▶ Use the following product hierarchy, in this order (see Figure 39.25):

        1. All Products

        2. Product Types

        3. Product Lines

        4. Product Families

        5. SKU

    ▶ Use the following geography hierarchy, in this order (see Figure 39.26):

        1. All Geographies

        2. Major Geos

        3. Countries

4. Channels

5. Customers

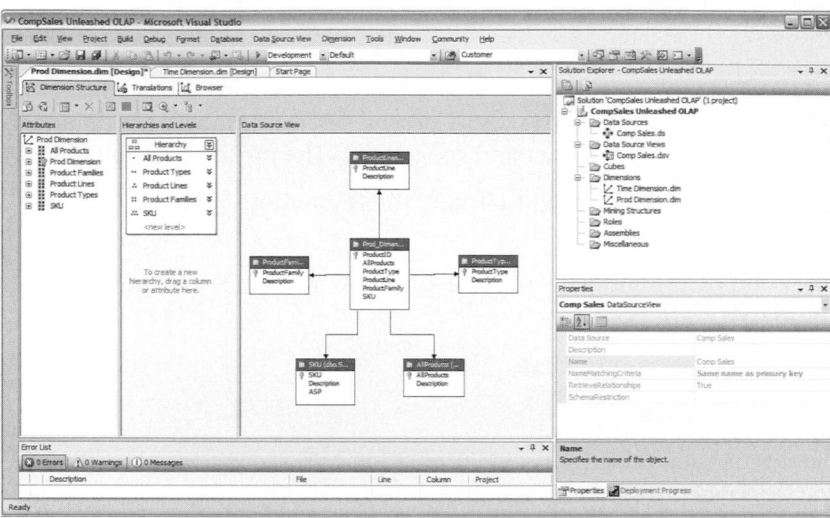

FIGURE 39.25   Creating the product hierarchy in the dimension designer.

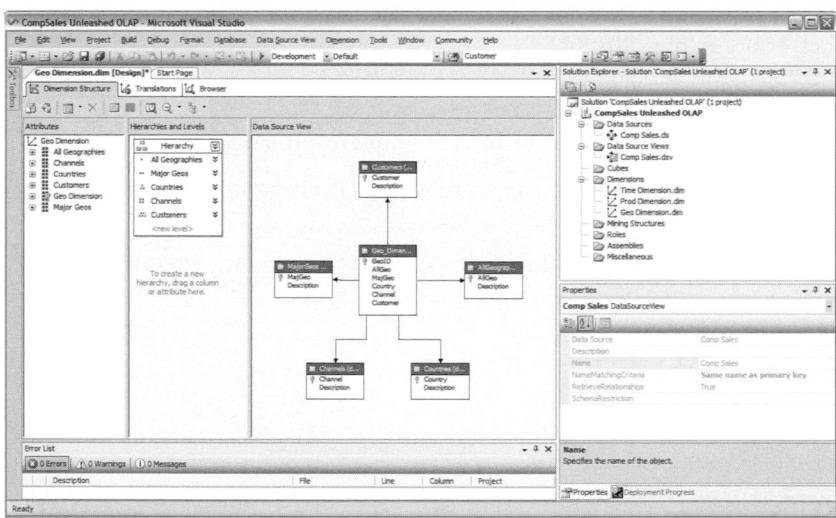

FIGURE 39.26   Creating the geography hierarchy in the dimension designer.

Creating the Cube

Most of the hard work in the CompSales International example is done. All that is left to do now is to create a cube that is based on the dimensions and hierarchies you just defined and then process it (that is, populate it with data). In the Solution Explorer, you right-click the Cube object and select New Cube. This invokes the Cube Wizard. Because you want to build the cube manually, you should not select the Auto Build option when prompted for the method to build the cube, as shown in Figure 39.27.

FIGURE 39.27   Selecting the build method for the cube in the Cube Wizard.

Next, you select the data source views to use to provide data to the cube. Available data source viewss are listed on the left side of this dialog. Because you have already defined a data source views (Comp Sales), you simple highlight it, as shown in Figure 39.28, and click Next.

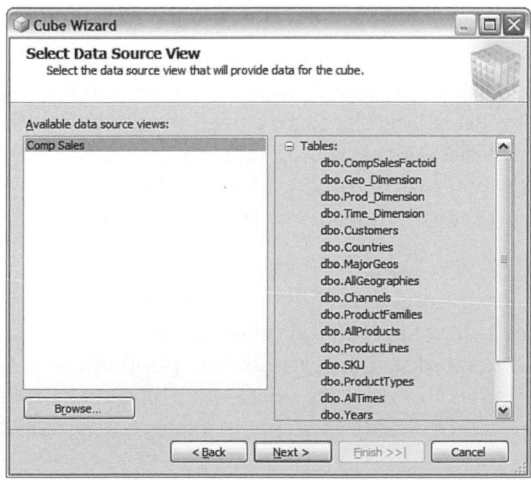

FIGURE 39.28   Selecting the data source views to use for the cube in the Cube Wizard.

39

When the data source views is selected, you must identify the facts and the dimensions for the cube (see Figure 39.29). To do so, you select the following:

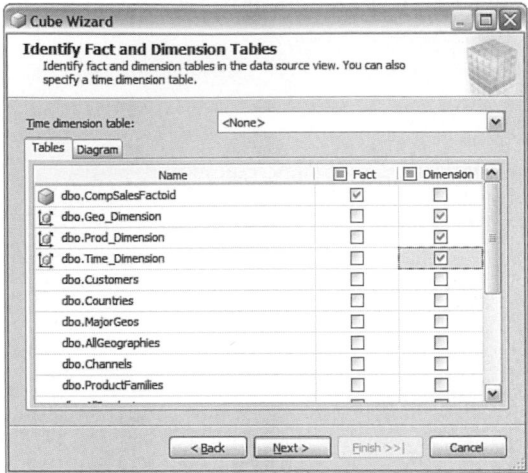

FIGURE 39.29   Selecting the fact and dimension tables for the cube in the Cube Wizard.

- ▶ dbo.CompSalesFactoid (Fact)
- ▶ dbo.Geo_Dimension (Dimension)
- ▶ dbo.Prod_Dimension (Dimension)
- ▶ And, dbo.Time_Dimension (Dimension)

You should check nothing else at this point. Then click Next.

If you have dimensions defined already (as you chose to do earlier), you want the new cube to use these definitions. The next wizard dialog lists any shared dimensions that have been created already. Your dimensions are listed there, and you need to select them by moving them from the Available Dimensions side of this dialog (left) to the Cube Dimensions side of the dialog (right). To do so, you just highlight all three of these dimensions (see Figure 39.30) and then click one of the right-arrow buttons. Then you click Next.

Now you get to select the measures and measure groups to include in the cube. You want all measures that are being identified, including an artificial measure called CompSalesFactoid Count (which the wizard generated so that various data population values can be kept in the cube). Figure 39.31 shows the measure selection. This is the first time you have seen the explicit measures that will be usable in the cube (Sales Units, Sales Price, and Sales Returns).

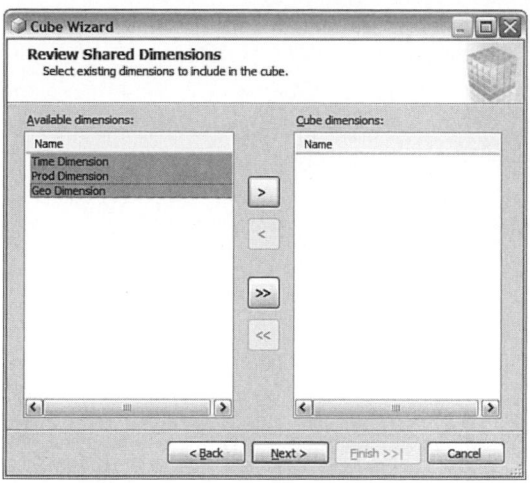

FIGURE 39.30   Using the available shared dimension for the new cube in the Cube Wizard.

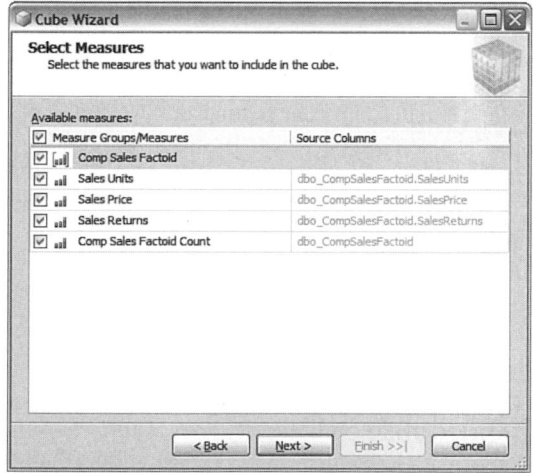

FIGURE 39.31   Selecting the measure group and measures to use for the cube in the Cube Wizard.

As you can see in Figure 39.32, the last dialog in this wizard shows a preview of your complete cube definition and provides you a place to name the cube (name it Comp Sales). The hierarchy definition of the time dimension is expanded to show you how this is represented. Because you didn't have the wizard detect hierarchies (you used the ones that you defined when you created the dimension definitions), the wizard still thinks it needs to do this (but it doesn't). (This bug has been reported to Microsoft.) Now you click Finish.

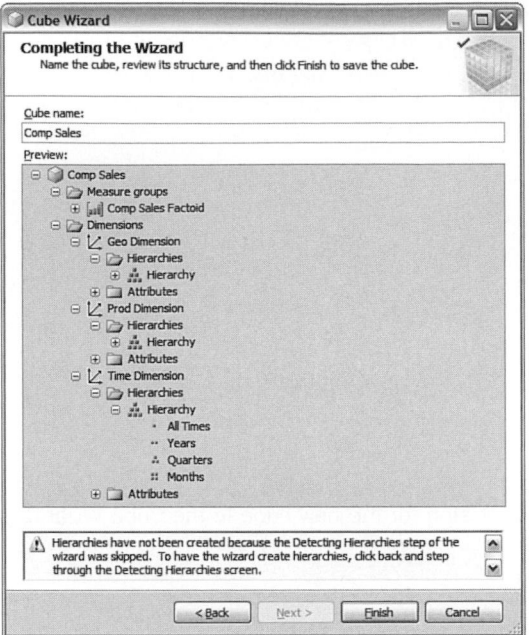

FIGURE 39.32   Naming the cube and previewing the cube definition in the Cube Wizard.

You are now put in the cube designer, which shows the completed cube design for Comp Sales. The cube designer provides all related cube information within the single IDE (Visual Studio). Figure 39.33 shows the cube designer and all related tabs that can be invoked from here (Dimension Usage, Calculations, KPIs, Actions, Partitions, Perspectives, Translations, and the cube data browser).

Building and Deploying the Cube
You basically have a cube definition now, but it is just an empty shell. You need to process it and then deploy it so that it is instantiated and populated with data (via the data source views). Remember that this cube definition is a solution project, just like a C# code project. It must be deployed before it can be used. First, you need to verify that the properties of the cube you are building are set correctly. You must have these properties correct before the cube can be processed. (*Process*, in this case, means build the cube structure and populate the measures and their associated dimensions.) You can assume that the properties will not be set correctly, so you should take a quick look and update them accordingly. You start by going to the Project menu item in Visual Studio and locating the Properties item entry (see Figure 39.34).

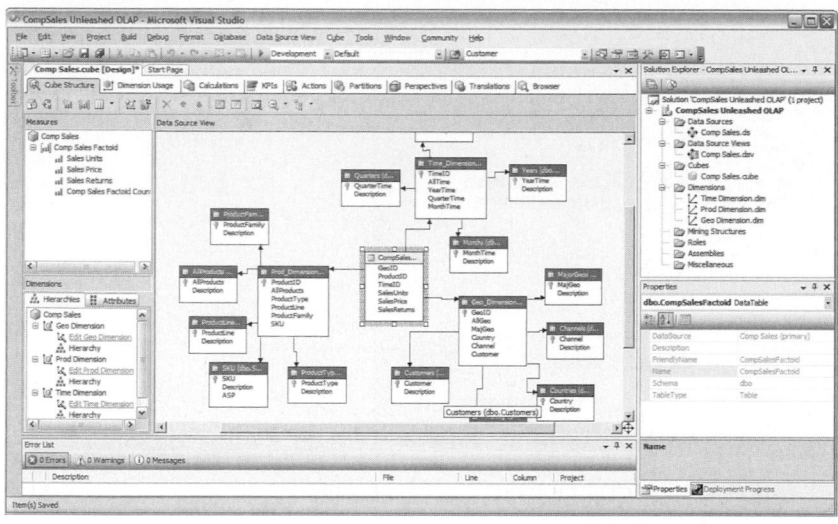

FIGURE 39.33   The Comp Sales cube definition in the cube designer.

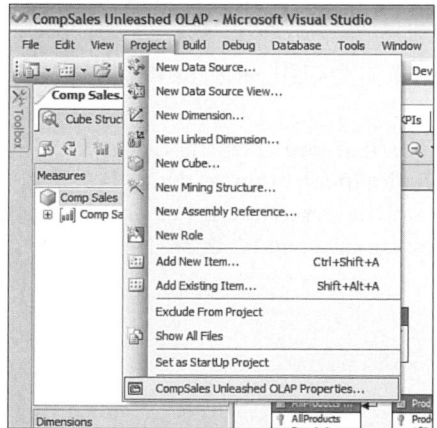

FIGURE 39.34   Selecting the cube properties for Comp Sales from the Project toolbar.

39

After you select this option, you navigate to the Deployment entry (the configuration property on the bottom). You need to focus on the Target (the target of the deployment) properties. As you can see in Figure 39.35, the Server property should be pointing to the location where you want this cube to be deployed. The Database property is simply the name under which you will deploy the database. For this example, you should make sure to specify a valid Server value; the default is (local). The default in this property usually is not what you want to happen and usually results in an error during the deployment step. Therefore, you should specify this explicitly (DBARCHLT\SQL2005DEV Analysis Services server). After the cube is deployed, you will be able to connect to this server (SSAS engine) with SSMS and administer the cube accordingly.

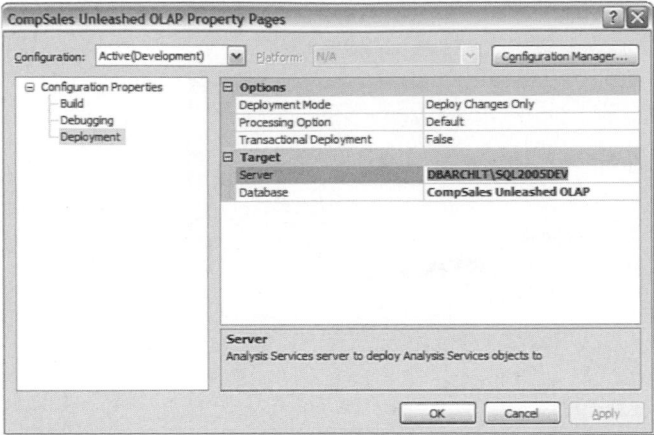

FIGURE 39.35   Deployment properties for the Comp Sales cube.

When you apply these property changes, you are ready to first do a build and then deploy your SSAS cube. You start by making sure you have a successful build by using the Build menu item on the toolbar or using the specific build option for the current SSAS solution: Build CompSales Unleashed OLAP. They both do the same thing. If you have no errors (and you have received a Build Succeeded message in the lower-left message bar of Visual Studio), you can deploy this SSAS solution.

Again, you should choose the Build menu item in the toolbar and click the Deploy Solution option to deploy this cube. Immediately, a Deployment Progress dialog box appears in the lower-right corner of Visual Studio. When the deployment has progressed, you receive a Deployment Completed Successfully message (see Figure 39.36).

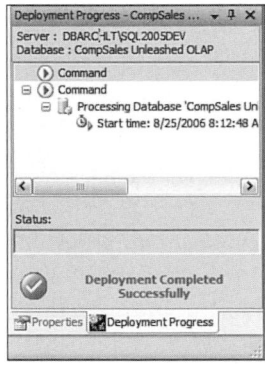

FIGURE 39.36   Deployment successful for Comp Sales.

Populating the Cube with Data

Now you can process actual data into your cube from the data source views. To do so, you right-click the CompSales Unleashed OLAP database entry in the Solution Explorer and choose the Process item. A Process Database dialog appears, with the object list of available OLAP databases to process. You select the CompSales Unleashed OLAP database (by highlighting it) and then click the Run button to start the processing of data (see Figure 39.37).

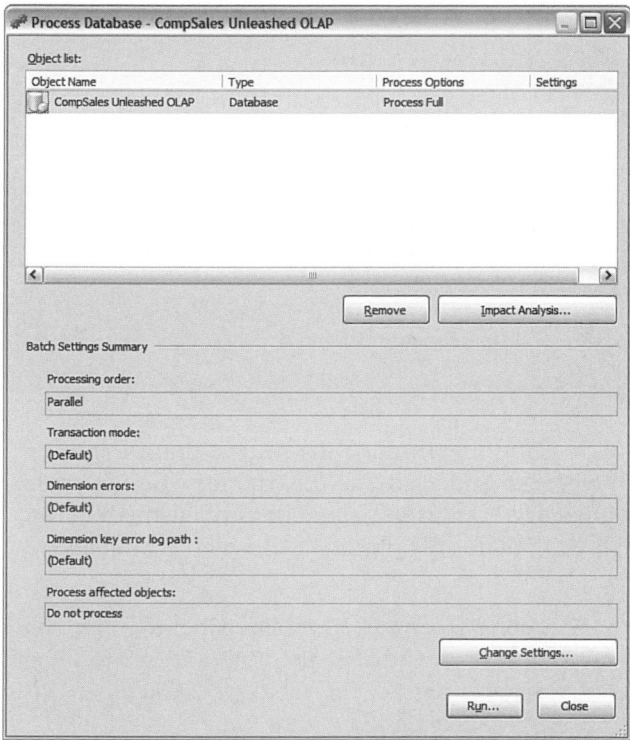

FIGURE 39.37   Process Database dialog for Comp Sales.

A Process Progress dialog box appears as the processing begins. Figure 39.38 shows the multistep process of processing through each dimension and the measure groups for the cube. Remember that this data is the dimension member values and the measure data values and has not been aggregated up through a complete cube representation (at all levels in the hierarchies). That will be done shortly, via the Aggregation Design Wizard. You can actually use your cube right now, but browsing would be challenging.

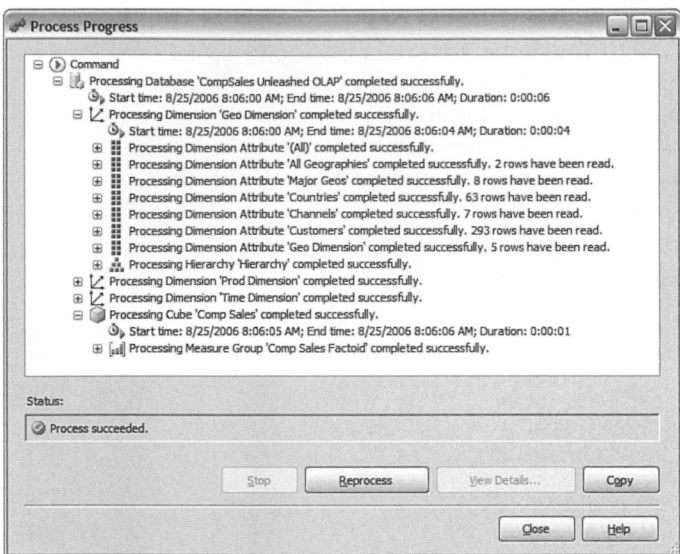

FIGURE 39.38   Dimension and measure group processing of data for the cube.

Aggregating Data Within the Cube

The last step of creating your OLAP cube is running through the Aggregation Design Wizard and determining how best to represent and aggregate the data for your users. This is where you must determine the optimal aggregation levels and the storage method for these aggregations (MOLAP, HOLAP, or ROLAP) for the optimal performance of queries against the cube.

You double-click the cube entry in the Solution Explorer (Comp Sales.cube) to bring up the cube designer for your newly created cube. Then you click the Partitions tab to see the current partition for Comp Sales. Just to the lower right of this tab is the Design Aggregations option, which invokes the Aggregation Design wizard (see Figure 39.39).

You need to indicate what type of storage mode and caching options you want for the partition that will contain your aggregations. (These storage modes are discussed earlier in this chapter.) You want to optimize performance and don't need real-time refreshes of the data. For these reasons, you specify the MOLAP (native SSAS storage) mode. Figure 39.40 shows this MOLAP specification in the Aggregation Design Wizard. This dialog works as a sliding scale. You just need to make sure the slider is positioned at the MOLAP storage option.

You also want to take advantage of the proactive caching capabilities that come with SSAS. You can activate this feature by clicking the Options button of this dialog and then checking the Enable Proactive Caching check box at the top of the Storage Options dialog that appears (see Figure 39.41). In addition, you use the option Update the Cache When Data Changes, as indicated in Figure 39.41.

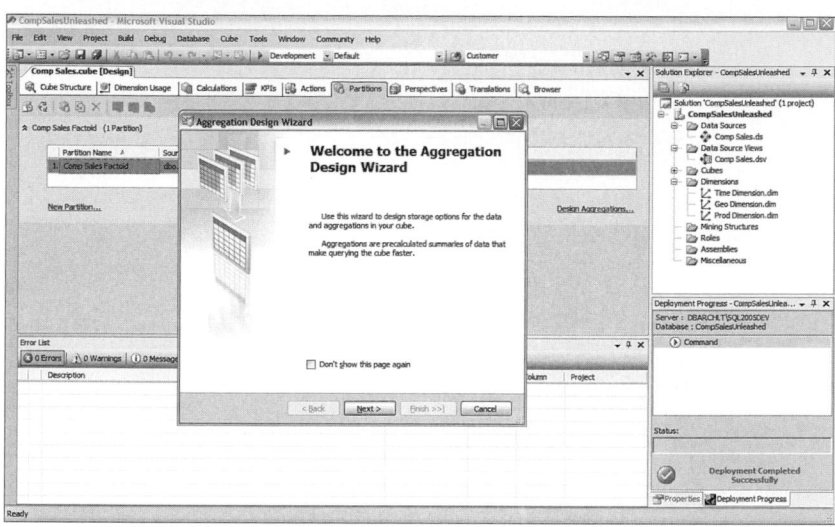

FIGURE 39.39   The Aggregation Design Wizard for the Comp Sales cube.

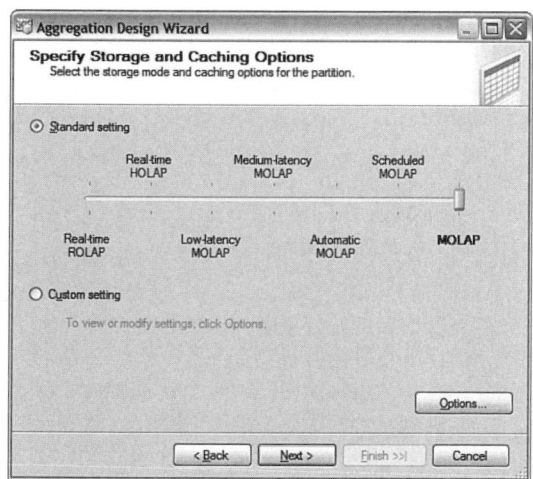

FIGURE 39.40   Specifying MOLAP storage mode for your cube in the Aggregation Design Wizard.

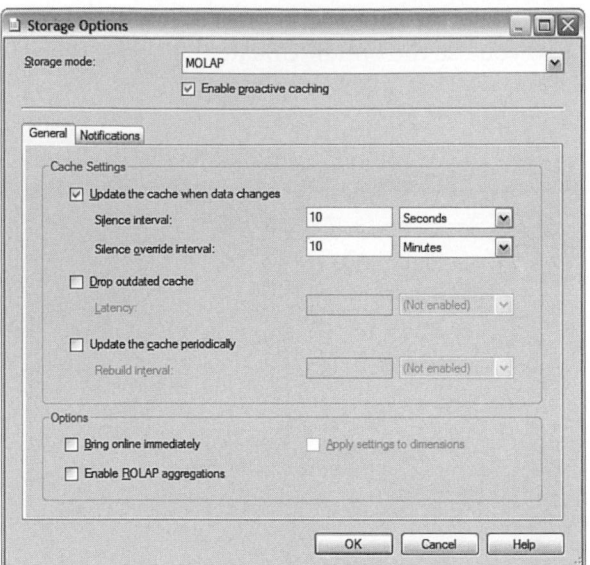

FIGURE 39.41   Enabling proactive caching for the cube.

A good rule of thumb is to refresh the cache interval based on response requirements and the volatility of the data from the data source views and whether the changes will have a dramatic effect on the BI query results.

The next step is to specify the object counts of the total population of facts and the number of values at each hierarchical level within each dimension. If you know what the full extent of counts will be for your cube, you can manually supply these count values in the Estimated Count column (see Figure 39.42). You typically do this when you have been able to load only a partial amount of data or the data will grow quite rapidly over time. If you are building a statically sized cube and have populated the data already, you just click the Count button to tell the wizard to use the actual data as the basis of the aggregation.

The next dialog optimizes the storage, based on the level of aggregation. You can specify a maximum storage approach (you create optimized storage based on the amount of disk space you can allocate to the cube), tell the wizard to simply optimize to achieve a certain percentage of performance gain (for example, 50%, 80%), specify to start the aggregation design process dynamically and stop when you feel the cube is optimized enough, or do no design aggregation at all. You really want to visually see the design aggregation process happen. Remember that the higher the performance you want, the more storage it will require (and the longer it will take to reprocess the aggregations). As you can see in Figure 39.43, you should select the I Click Stop option and stop the design aggregation when the optimization level starts to level off (right at 79% optimization level). Any further optimization would really just waste storage space.

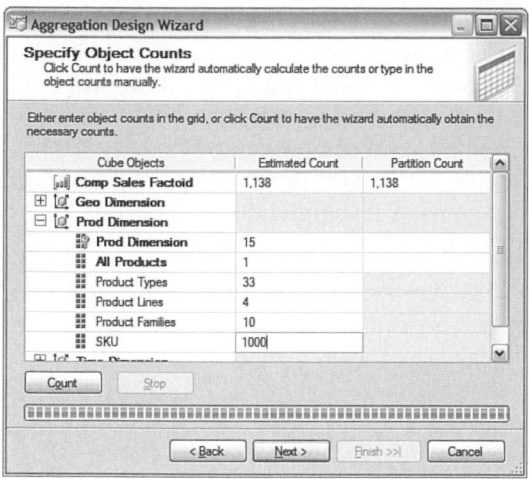

FIGURE 39.42   Specifying cube object counts for aggregation in the Aggregation Design Wizard.

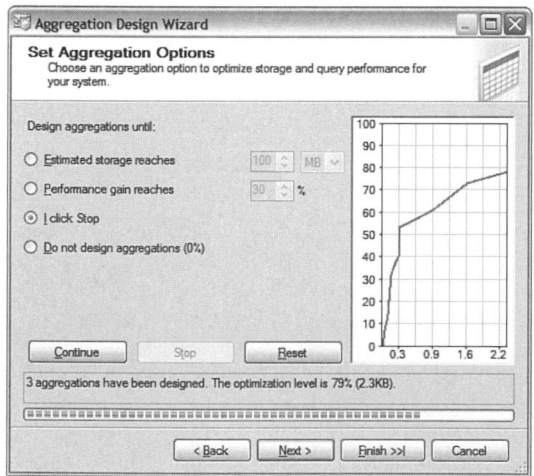

FIGURE 39.43   Setting the optimal storage and query performance level in the Aggregation Design Wizard.

If your company has sales transaction data for the past five years and 250 stores that sell an average of 1,000 items per day, the fact table will have 456,500,000 rows. This is obviously a challenge in terms of disk space by itself, without aggregation tables to go along with it. The control that SSAS provides here is important in balancing storage and retrieval speed (that is, performance vs. size). Aggregations are built to optimize rollup operations so that higher levels of aggregation are easily derived from the existing aggregations to satisfy broader queries. If a high degree of query optimization weren't possible due to limitations in storage space, SSAS might choose to build aggregates of monthly or quarterly data only. If a user queried the cube for yearly or multiyear data, those aggregations would be created dynamically from the highest level of pre-aggregated data. With disk storage becoming more and more inexpensive and servers becoming more powerful, the tendency is to opt for meeting performance gains. A recommended approach is to specify between an 80% and 90% performance gain here.

You are now ready to complete the Aggregation Design Wizard. The final step is to either process this aggregation or save your results and process it later. You should choose to process this aggregation now and then click Finish. The Process Progress dialog appears immediately, and you get to watch the full extent of the cube's aggregation partitions being built (that is, populated). Figure 39.44 shows the details of one of the SQL queries created to do the aggregations (which are implementing your design levels). It's nice to have Microsoft dynamically create these complex queries for this critical performance optimization step so you don't have to worry about it yourself.

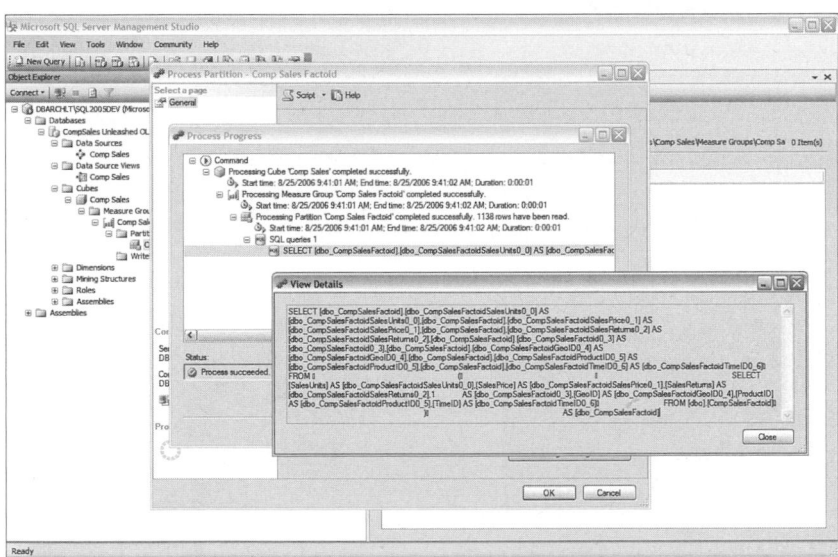

FIGURE 39.44   Processing the design aggregations for a cube in the Aggregation Design Wizard.

When this completes, you have a fully optimized cube that is ready for data browsing. Congratulations!

Browsing Data in the Cube

You're ready to browse some cube data now. There are several ways to view data in a multidimensional cube. OLE DB for OLAP and ADO MD expose interfaces to do this kind of data browsing, and many leading vendors have used these interfaces to build front-end analysis tools and ActiveX controls. These tools should prove useful for developers of user interfaces in data warehousing and data mart projects. You can also easily browse a cube's data from either Visual Studio or SSMS or via any tool or facility that uses the multidimensional extensions of SQL (that is, SQL with DMX and MDX extensions).

To browse your newly created cube from SSMS, you fire up SSMS and connect to the SSAS server on which you deployed your cube. You should not connect to the SQL Server database engine. These are two completely different servers. When you are connected, you expand the Databases tree on the left until you can see the cube you created (Comp Sales, in this example).

> **NOTE**
>
> In Visual Studio, you can simply click the Browse tab when you are in the cube designer. All browse functionality uses the same plug-ins, whether you are in Visual Studio or SSMS. In either Visual Studio or SSMS, you can browse the cube (the entire cube with all dimensions) or just a dimension (using the dimension browser).

In SSMS, you just right-click the Comp Sales cube entry and choose the Browse option. As you can see in Figure 39.45, a multipaned, drag-and-drop interface is your view into the data in your cube.

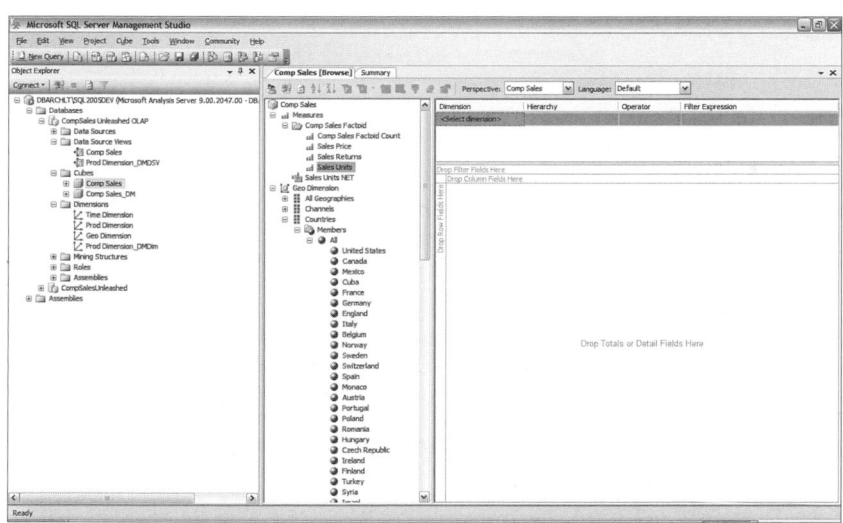

FIGURE 39.45   Browsing data in your cube in the SMSS data browser.

The middle pane lists all cube objects that you can drag into the data browsing pane (on the right). The data browser uses the Pivot Table Service to access and display your cube's

39

data. You can expand any of the cube hierarchy objects and see the actual member entries that are in your cube for each level. This is helpful when you want to further filter data in the browser (for example, focus on a particular SKU value or a particular geography, such as United States or France).

The data browsing pane is very easy to use. For example, say that you simply want to see all product sales and product returns for SKUs across all geographies, for each year in the cube. To do this, you expand the measures object until you see all the measures in the Comp Sales cube. Then you drag Sales Units to the center of the lower portion of the data browsing pane (into the Drop Totals or Fields Here section in the lower right). You do the same for the Sales Returns measure. Data values (totals) for these are already displayed immediately. These are the total (aggregated) values for sales returns and sales units across all products, all geographies, and all times. To see the product breakdown of these data measures, you drag the SKU object within the product dimension object to the Drop Column Fields Here section (just above where the data measures were dropped). You immediately see the data measure values being broken out by each product SKU value. Now, you drag the Year object within the time dimension to the Drop Row Fields Here section (just to the left of where the data measures were dropped). You now see the data broken out by the years along the left side (rows) in the cube that contains sales and return data for products, as shown in Figure 39.46.

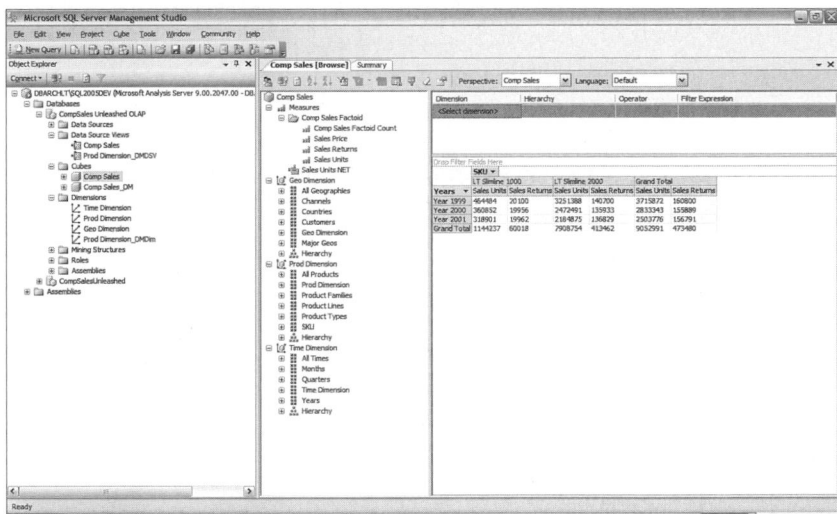

FIGURE 39.46   Sales units and sales returns for all SKUs by years in the SMSS data browser.

If you want much more drill-up and drill-down visibility into your data, you could build up a much more complicated representation in the data browser. Say that you want to see sales units and sales returns but across the full product dimension breakouts and full time dimension breakouts for the United States geographic region only. You also want to see all dimension levels, totals by levels, and grand totals by dimension. You start the same way as you did earlier and expand out the measures object until you see all the detail measures in the Comp Sales cube. If you still have the previous example in your data browser, you can simply locate the Clear Results icon in the data browser tab and clear the data browser pane. Then you drag Sales Units to the center of the lower portion of the data browsing pane (into the Drop Totals or Fields Here section in the lower right). You do the same for the Sales Returns measure. Then you drag the geography dimension to the upper-right section called Select Dimensions or just highlight Select Dimensions and choose the geography dimension. This is the dimension-level filtering capability within the data browser. You now just select (via the drop-downs of each section within a filter specification) the level and type of filtering you want to do for the dimension you are working with. You can specify any number of filters within any number of dimensions. To just filter on countries within the geography dimension, you select Countries within the hierarchies list of the geography dimension, and then the operator you want is Equal, and the filter expression is the data value that you want to filter on (the United States country value, in this case). These are all drop-down lists that you can easily select by either clicking the entry or indicting which ones to use via a check box entry. Figure 39.47 shows the fully specified Geo Dimension filter specified.

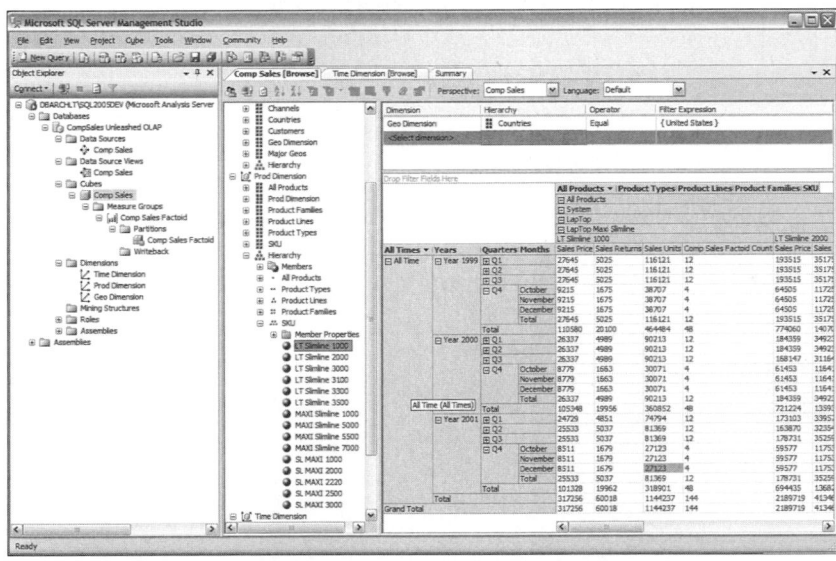

FIGURE 39.47   Complex data browsing with full dimensions and filtering in the SMSS data browser.

The data values you now see are only those of the United States. You now drag the product dimension object to the Drop Column Fields Here section (just above where the data measures were dropped). You immediately see the data measure values being broken out by the entire product dimension (you expand the plus sign of the product hierarchy all the way out to the SKU level). Then you drag the time dimension object to the Drop Row Fields Here section (just to the left of where the data measures were dropped). Then you expand out the time dimension (using the plus sign) of the time hierarchy all the way out to the month level. Figure 39.47 shows this robust data representation within the data browser. You can choose to view the data at any level within either the time or product hierarchies, and you can filter on any other dimension values. You can also just add a dimension or dimension level to the filter portion within the data browser or just drag off dimensions, measures, or filters from the data browser if you don't want to use them anymore. This is very easy indeed. The cube browser shows you what your cube has in it and also illustrates the utility of a dimensional database. Users can easily analyze data in meaningful ways.

SSIS allows you to browse individual dimension member data. You just right-click any dimension in the left pane of SSMS (for example, the time dimension) and choose Browse. As you can see in Figure 39.48, the dimension browser opens with All as the top node in the dimension. You simply expand the levels to see the actual member values within this cube dimension. Expanding each level gets you to more detailed information as you move down the dimension hierarchy.

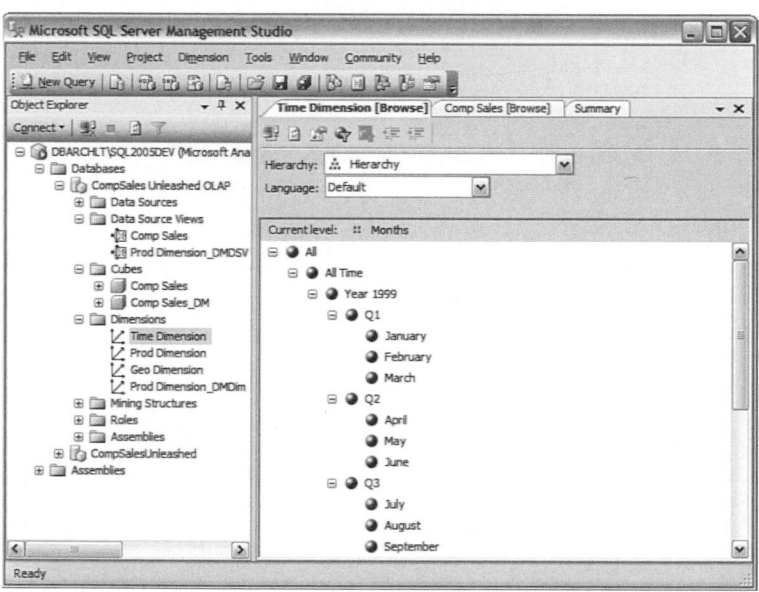

FIGURE 39.48   Browsing the Time dimension using SSMS.

Delivering Data to Users

SSAS provides a great deal of flexibility for building scalable OLAP solutions, but how do you present the data to users? The client-side components deliver much of the functionality of SSAS, using the same code base for the dimensional calculation engine, caching, and query processing. You can use the Pivot Table Service to manage client/server connections, and this is the layer for user interfaces to access SSAS cubes through the OLE DB for OLAP interface. ADO MD provides an application-level programming interface for development of OLAP applications. Third-party tools and future versions of Microsoft Excel and other Microsoft Office products will use the Pivot Table Service to access cubes.

The underlying Pivot Table Service shares metadata with SSAS, so a request for data on the client causes data and metadata to be downloaded to the client. The Pivot Table Service determines whether requests need to be sent to the server or can be satisfied at the client with downloaded data. If a user requests sales information for the first quarter of 1998 and then later decides to query that data for the first quarter of 1997 for comparison, only the request for 1997 data has to go to the server to get more data. The 1998 data is cached on the client.

Slices of data that are retrieved to the client computer can also be saved locally for analysis when the client computer is disconnected from the network. Users can download the data in which they are interested and analyze it offline. The Pivot Table Service can also create simple OLAP databases by accessing OLE DB–compliant data sources.

With the ADO MD interface, developers will be able to access and manipulate objects in an SSAS database, enabling web-based OLAP application development.

Many independent software vendors, such as Brio, Cognos, Business Objects, and Hyperion, are working with Microsoft to leverage the rich features of these OLAP services. They offer robust user interfaces that can access SSAS's cubes. Versions of Microsoft Office include the Pivot Table Service to enable built-in analysis in tools such as Excel. It is getting easier and easier to bring OLAP to the masses.

Multidimensional Expressions

The OLE DB for OLAP specification contains MDX syntax that is used to build datasets from cubes and is used to define cubes themselves. Developers of OLE DB OLAP providers can map MDX syntax to SQL statements or native query languages of other OLAP servers, depending on the storage techniques.

MDX statements build datasets by using information about cubes from which the data will be read. This includes the number of axes to include, the dimensions on each axis and the level of nesting, the members or member tuples and sort order of each dimension, and the dimension members used to filter, or slice, the data. (*Tuples* are combinations of dimensions such as time and product time that present multidimensional data in a two-dimensional dataset.)

An MDX statement has four basic parts:

- ▶ Member scope information, using the WITH MEMBER clause

- ▶ Dimension, measure, and axis information in the SELECT clause

- ▶ The source cube in the FROM clause

- ▶ Dimension slicing in the WHERE clause

39

Expressions in an MDX statement operate on numbers, strings, members, tuples, and sets. Numbers and strings mean the same thing here as they do in other programming contexts. Members are the values in a dimension, and levels are groups of members. Sets are collections of tuple elements to further combine facts. If the dimension were time, a particular year, quarter, or month would be a member, and month values would belong to the month level. You use the dimension browser in SSAS to view members of a dimension.

The following is an example of an MDX SQL expression:

```
WITH MEMBER [Measures].[Total Sales Units] AS 'Sum([Measures].[Sales Units])'
SELECT
    {[Measures].[Total Sales Units]} ON COLUMNS,
    {Topcount([Prod Dimension].[SKU].members,5,[Measures].[Total Sales Units])}
    ON ROWS
FROM [Comp Sales]
WHERE ([Time Dimension].[All Time].[Year 1999].[Q1])
```

You can download this simple query against the Comp Sales cube from Sams Publishing at www.samspublishing.com. It returns the sums of the sales units for products for the specific time period of the first quarter of 1999. Figure 39.49 shows the full execution of this query within a query window of SSMS. Notice that the metadata for the cube is also made available in the center pane of SSMS, along with an MDX functions tab that provides all the MDX functions that can be used. This is very helpful for building valid MDS queries within this environment. Also notice that the result set display area is very specialized in order to display multidimensional results.

FIGURE 39.49   Comp Sales MDX query execution in SSMS.

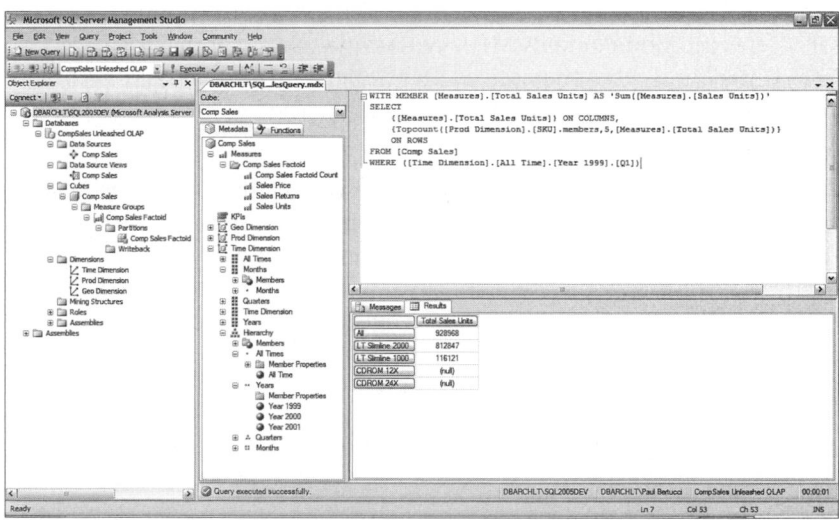

This simple MDX statement shows the basic parts of a working query. In this case, measures are displayed in columns, and the product dimension members make up the axes of this multidimensional query and are displayed in rows. The display of multiple dimensions in rows like this is how the term *tuple* is used in the context of SSAS.

Much more could be said about MDX syntax, and a complete discussion of MDX could fill its own chapter. For more information, see the OLE DB for OLAP Programmers Reference, which is available on the Microsoft website at http://msdn2.microsoft.com/en-us/library/ms145506.aspx. It contains detailed information about MDX expressions and grammar.

ADO MD

ADO MD is an easy-to-use access method for dimensional data via an OLE DB for OLAP provider. You can use ADO MD in Visual Basic, Visual C++, and Visual J++. Like ADO, ADO MD offers a rich application development environment that can be used for multi-tier client/server and web application development.

You can retrieve information about a cube, or metadata, and execute MDX statements by using ADO MD to create cellsets to return interesting data to a user. ADO MD is another subject too broad to cover in detail in this chapter. Specifications for OLE DB for OLAP and ADO MD are available on the Microsoft website at http://msdn2.microsoft.com/en-us/library/ms126037.aspx.

Calculated Members (Calculations)

Remember from the Comp Sales requirements that there was an additional user need to see the difference between sales units and sales returns (sales units minus sales returns) to yield net sales. One way to do this type of thing is to use the SSAS calculated members (calculations) capability. This creates an expression against existing measures that are treated the same as measures. Basically, you need to complete the requirements for the Comp Sales cube by adding a calculation measure to this cube for net sales units.

To create a calculation, you go back to Visual Studio and the cube designer. Then you click the Calculations tab and create a new calculation measure called Sales Units NET with the calculation expression of (Sales Units – Sales Returns), as shown in Figure 39.50. Many functions are available for use that should meet your individual calculation needs.

This fulfills the data measure requirements of CompSales. All that is left to do is to process the cube so others can use it. The following is an example MDX query that uses the newly created calculation measure:

```
WITH MEMBER [Measures].[Total Sales Units] AS 'Sum([Measures].[Sales Units NET])'
SELECT
    {[Measures].[Total Sales Units]} ON COLUMNS,
    {Topcount([Prod Dimension].[SKU].members,5,[Measures].[Sales Units NET])}
    ON ROWS
FROM [Comp Sales]
WHERE ([Time Dimension].[All Time].[Year 1999].[Q1])
```

39

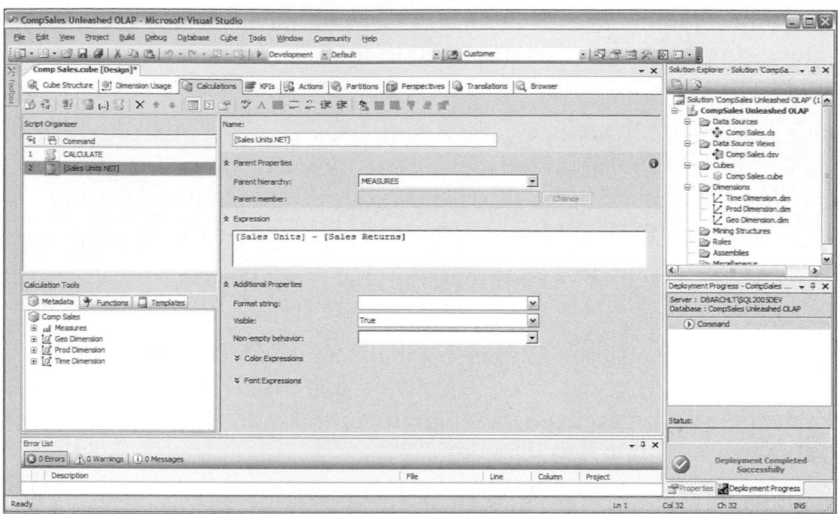

FIGURE 39.50   A new calculation measure of Sales Units NET in the Visual Studio cube designer.

Figure 39.51 shows this new calculation measure listed in the cube's metadata pane and how easy it is to use in the cube data browser. You might want to check the math to make sure the calculation is correct.

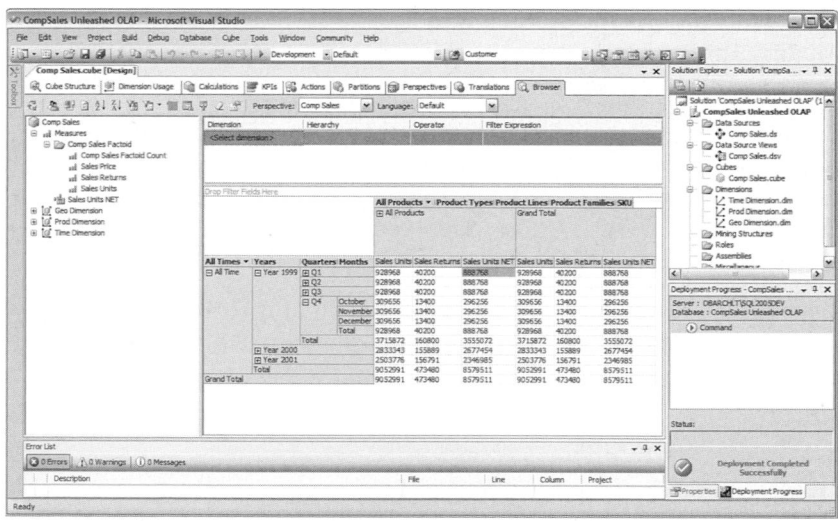

FIGURE 39.51   Data browsing using the Sales Units NET calculation in the SSMS cube data browser.

Query Analysis and Optimization

In SSAS, you can look at query utilization and performance in a cube. You can look at queries by user, frequency, and execution time to determine how to better optimize aggregations. If a slow-running query is used frequently by many users, or by the CEO, it might be a good candidate for individual tuning. A usage-based analysis capability can be used to change aggregations based on actual live queries that the cube must service. This adjusts aggregations based on a query to reduce response time. You start this wizard by right-clicking the cube's partition. Figure 39.52 shows the Usage-Based Optimization Wizard splash page.

FIGURE 39.52   The Usage-Based Optimization Wizard.

The Usage-Based Optimization Wizard allows you to filter queries by user, frequency of execution, time frame, and execution time. You see a record for each query you have run since the date you began, the number of times it was executed, and the average execution time, in seconds. This is like a SQL trace analysis of your OLAP queries.

Because aggregations already exist, the wizard asks whether you want to replace them or add new ones. If you replace the existing aggregations, the cube is reprocessed with this particular query in mind.

Generating a Relational Database

The examples you have worked with up to this point have been from a dimensional database that uses a star or snowflake schema (the CompSales database). Very often, however, you create cubes based on requirements only and do not have an existing data source (or sources) to draw on at design time. When you have completed your cube design, you can choose to generate a relational schema that can be used to retain (that is, stage) the cube's source data or that can be a data warehouse/data mart unto itself. Figure 39.53 shows the start of the Schema Generation Wizard for building a data warehouse/staging database from the top down.

FIGURE 39.53   Generating a relational schema from the cube and dimension definitions.

NOTE

Designing dimensional databases is an art form and requires not only sound dimensional modeling knowledge but also knowledge of the business processes with which you are dealing. Data warehousing has several design approaches. Regardless of which approach you take, having a good understanding of the approach's design techniques is critical to the success of a data warehouse project. Although Microsoft provides a powerful set of tools to implement data marts, astute execution of design methods is critical to getting the correct data—the truly business-significant business data—to the end users.

Limitations of a Relational Database

Even using a tool such as SSAS, you face limitations when dealing with a normalized database. Using a view can often solve (or mask) these issues. In some cases, however, more complicated facts and dimensions might require de-normalized tables or a dimensional database in the storage component of the data warehouse to bring information together. Data cleansing and transformation are also major considerations before you attempt to present decision makers with data from OLTP systems.

Cube Perspectives

A new feature in SSAS is cube perspectives. This is essentially a way to create working views of a complex cube that is focused on just what a particular user or group of users need. They don't need all the dimensions, calculations, levels, and KPIs that would other-wise be visible as part of a complex SSAS cube. Therefore, you need a method to tailor or limit a larger cube environment to be just what the users need and nothing more—hence, the cube perspective. Figure 39.54 shows the Perspectives tab in the cube designer, which allows you to very easily customize a view (perspective), which is what will be deployed or referenced to a target user group. In this example, you are creating a new perspective called Comp Sales wo Sales Price, which will exclude the extremely sensitive Sales Price data measure from whomever is given access to this perspective.

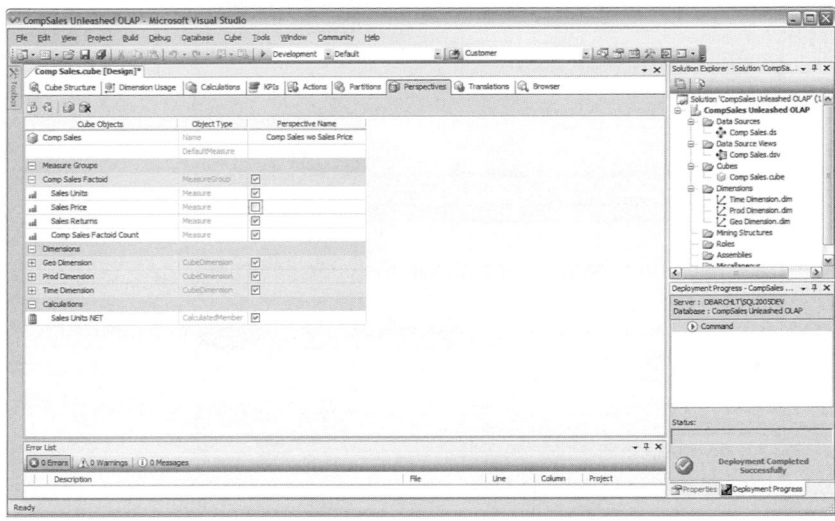

FIGURE 39.54   Creating cube perspectives within SSAS in the cube designer.

You can have any number of perspectives on a cube. Figure 39.55 shows what a cube user sees when trying to browse (or access) cube data via a perspective.

Using perspectives is a great way to simplify the user's life in an already complicated OLAP world.

KPIs

Figure 39.56 shows another new capability in SSAS: creating embedded KPIs. Just like calculations, KPIs allow you to define thresholds, goals, status indications, and trend expressions that become part of an OLAP cube. Each can then be graphically displayed in a variety of ways (for example, gauges, thermometers, traffic lights, trend indications such as up arrows, smiling faces). This is perfect for an executive dashboard or portal imple-mentation that has its basis in an SSAS cube. You can easily access KPIs via the cube designer's KPIs tab. What are you waiting for? It is now easier than ever before to create powerful KPIs with this simple yet rich interface.

39

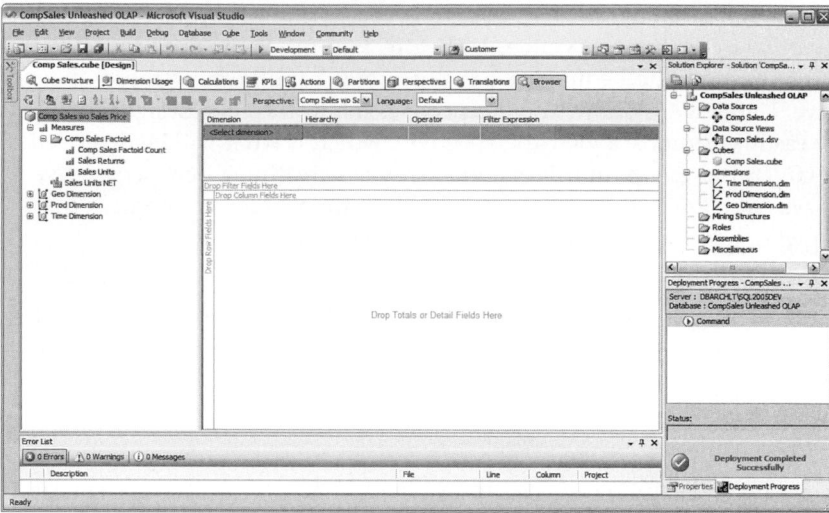

FIGURE 39.55   Browsing cube data via a perspective in the cube designer.

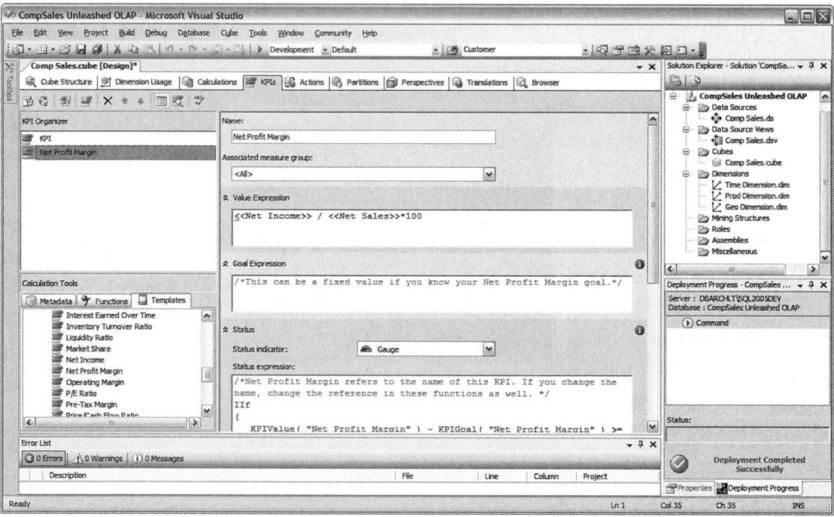

FIGURE 39.56   Creating KPIs in the cube designer.

Data Mining

With SSAS, defining OLAP data mining models has been taken to a new level. Its predecessor, Microsoft Analysis Services, was a bit limited in the types of data mining discovery techniques possible. With SSAS, a much more robust selection of capabilities has come bursting onto the scene.

Data mining is the process of understanding potentially undiscovered characteristics or distributions of data. Data mining can be extremely useful for OLAP database design in that patterns or values might define different hierarchy levels or dimensions that were not previously known. As you create dimensions, you can even choose a data mining model as the basis for a dimension.

Basically, a data mining model is a reference structure that represents the grouping and predictive analysis of relational or multidimensional data. It is composed of rules, patterns, and other statistical information of the data that it was analyzing. These are called *cases*. A *case set* is simply a means for viewing the physical data. Different case sets can be constructed from the same physical data. Basically, a case is defined from a particular point of view. If the algorithm you are using supports the view, you can use mining models to make predictions based on these findings.

Another aspect of a data mining model is using training data. This process determines the relative importance of each attribute in a data mining model. It does this by recursively partitioning data into smaller groups until no more splitting can occur. During this partitioning process, information is gathered from the attributes used to determine the split. Probability can be established for each categorization of data in these splits. This type of data can be used to help determine factors about other data utilizing these probabilities. This training data, in the form of dimensions, levels, member properties and measures, is used to process the OLAP data mining model and further define the data mining column structure for the case set.

In SSAS, Microsoft provides several data mining algorithms (or techniques):

▶ **Association Rules**—This algorithm builds rules that describe which items are most likely to appear together in a transaction. The rules help predict when the presence of one item is likely with another item (which has appeared in the same type of transaction before).

▶ **Clustering**—This algorithm uses iterative techniques to group records from a dataset into clusters that contain similar characteristics. This is one of the best algorithms, and it can be used to find general groupings in data.

▶ **Sequence Clustering**—This algorithm is a combination of sequence analysis and clustering, and it identifies clusters of similarly ordered events in a sequence. The clusters can be used to predict the likely ordering of events in a sequence, based on known characteristics.

▶ **Decision Trees**—This algorithm is a classification algorithm that works well for predictive modeling. It supports the prediction of both discrete and continuous attributes.

▶ **Linear Regression**—This algorithm is a regression algorithm that works well for regression modeling. It is a configuration variation of the Decision Trees algorithm, obtained by disabling splits. (The whole regression formula is built in a single root node.) The algorithm supports the prediction of continuous attributes.

39

▶ **Logistic Regression**—This algorithm is a regression algorithm that works well for regression modeling. It is a configuration variation of the Neural Network algorithm, obtained by eliminating the hidden layer. This algorithm supports the prediction of both discrete and continuous attributes.

▶ **Naïve Bayes**—This algorithm is a classification algorithm that is quick to build, and it works well for predictive modeling. It supports only discrete attributes, and it considers all the input attributes to be independent, given the predictable attribute.

▶ **Neural Network**—This algorithm uses a gradient method to optimize parameters of multilayer networks to predict multiple attributes. It can be used for classification of discrete attributes as well as regression of continuous attributes.

▶ **Time Series**—This algorithm uses a linear regression decision tree approach to analyze time-related data, such as monthly sales data or yearly profits. The patterns it discovers can be used to predict values for future time steps across a time horizon.

To create an OLAP data mining model, SSAS uses either an existing source OLAP cube or an existing relational database/data warehouse, a particular data mining technique/algorithm, case dimension and level, predicted entity, or, optionally, training data. The source OLAP cube provides the information needed to create a case set for the data mining model. You then select the data mining technique (decision tree, clustering, or one of the others). It uses the dimension and level that you choose in order to establish key columns for the case sets. The case dimension and level provide a certain orientation for the data mining model into the cube for creating a case set. The predicted entity can be either a measure from the source OLAP cube, a member property of the case dimension and level, or any member of another dimension in the source OLAP cube.

> **NOTE**
>
> The data mining wizard can also create a new dimension for a source cube and enables users to query the data mining data model data just as they would query OLAP data (using the SQL DMX extension or the mining structures browser).

In Visual Studio, you simply initiate the Data Mining Wizard by right-clicking the Mining Structures entry in the Solution Explorer. You cannot do this from SSMS (yet). When you are past the wizard's splash screen, you have the option of creating your mining model from either an existing relational database (or data warehouse) or an existing OLAP cube (as shown in Figure 39.57).

Say that you want to define a data mining model that can shed light on product (SKU) sales characteristics and that will be based on the data and structure you have created so far in your CompSales Unleashed OLAP cube. For this example, you choose to use the existing OLAP cube you already have.

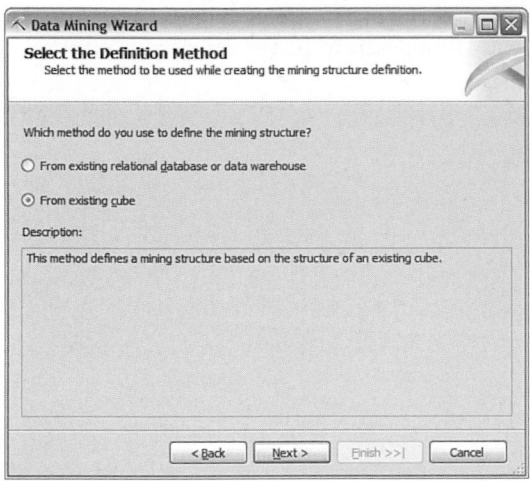

FIGURE 39.57   Selecting the definition method to used for the mining structure in the Data Mining Wizard.

You must now select the data mining technique you think will help you find value in your cube's data. Clustering is probably the best one to start from because it finds natural groupings of data in a multidimensional space. It is useful when you want to see general groupings in your data, such as hot spots. You are trying to find just such things with sales of products (for example, things that sell together or belong together). Figure 39.58 shows the data mining technique Microsoft Clustering being selected.

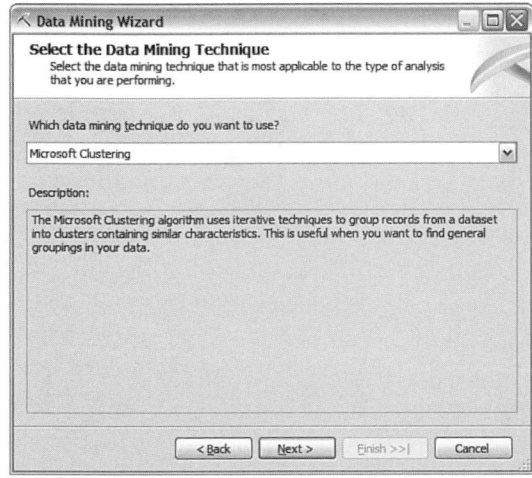

FIGURE 39.58   Using clustering to identify natural groups in the Data Mining Wizard.

Now you have to identify the source cube dimension to use to build the mining structure. As you can see in Figure 39.59, you choose Prod Dimension to fit the mining intentions stated earlier.

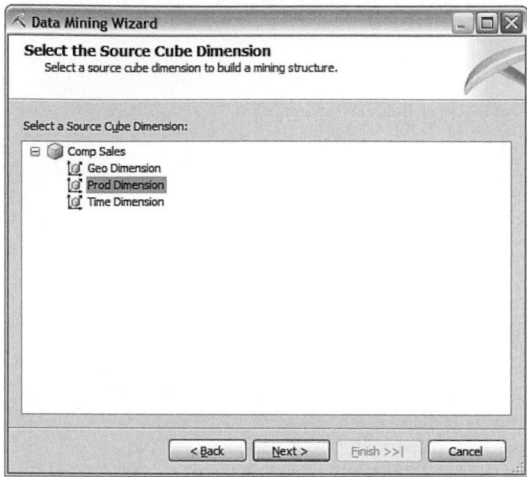

FIGURE 39.59   Identifying the product dimension as the basis for the mining structure in the Data Mining Wizard.

You then select the case key or point of view for the mining analysis. Figure 39.60 illustrates the case to be based on the product dimension and at the SKU level (that is, the individual product level).

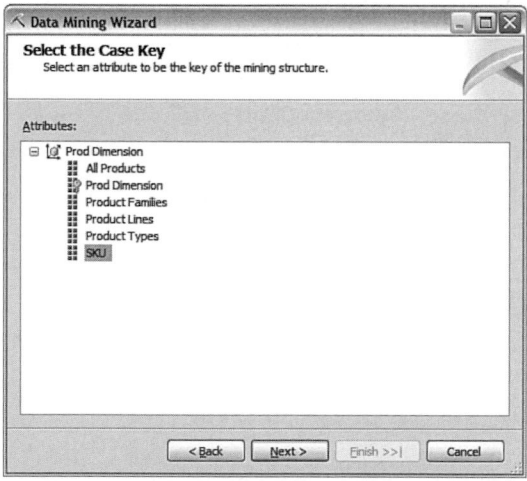

FIGURE 39.60   Identifying the basic unit of analysis for the mining model in the Data Mining Wizard.

You now specify the attributes and measures as case-level columns of the new mining structure. Figure 39.61 shows the possible selections. You can simply choose all the data measures for this mining structure. Then you click the Next button.

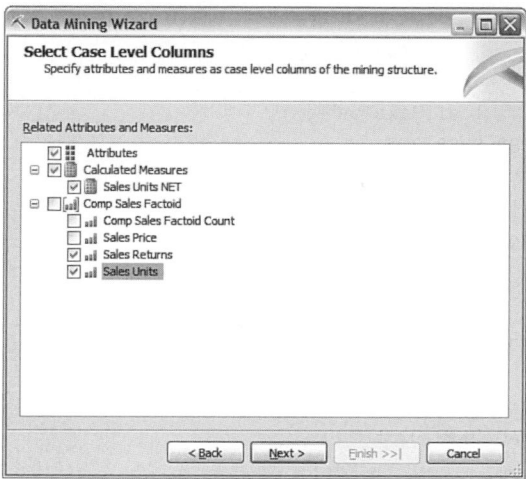

FIGURE 39.61   Specifying the measure for the mining model in the Data Mining Wizard.

The mining model is now specified and must be named and processed. Figure 39.62 shows what you have named the mining structure (Prod Dimension) and the mining model name (Prod Dimension). Also, you indicate the Allow Drill Through option so you can look further into the data in the mining model. Then you click the Next button.

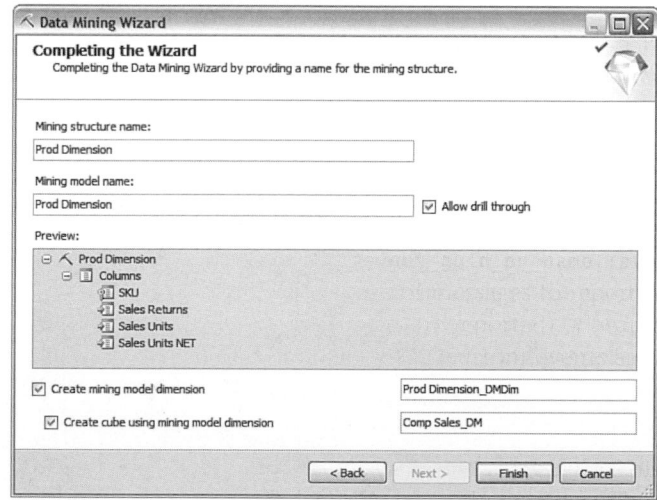

FIGURE 39.62   Naming the mining model and completing the Data Mining Wizard.

When the Data Mining Wizard is complete, the mining structure viewer pops up, with your mining structure case-level column's specification (on the center left) and its correlation to your cube (see Figure 39.63).

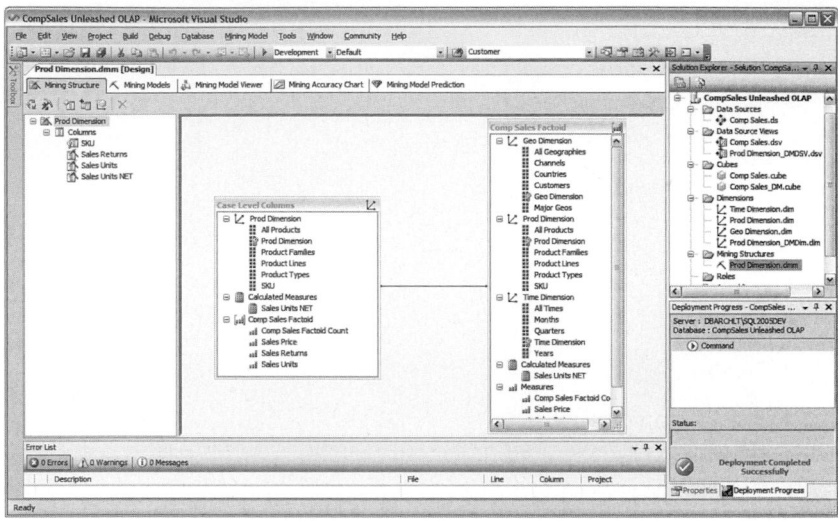

FIGURE 39.63   Your new mining structure in the mining structure viewer.

You must now process the mining structure to see what you come up with. You do this by selecting the Mining Model toolbar option and selecting the Process option. You then see the usual Process dialog screen, and you have to choose to run this (process the database). After the database processing completes, a whole new mining model viewer appears, showing the results of the clustering analysis (see Figure 39.64). Notice that because you selected to allow drill through, you can simply click any of the clusters identified and see the data that is part of the cluster. This viewer clearly shows that there is some clustering of SKU values that might indicate products that sell together or belong together.

If you click the Cluster Profiles tab of this viewer, you see the data value profile characteristics that were processed (see Figure 39.65).

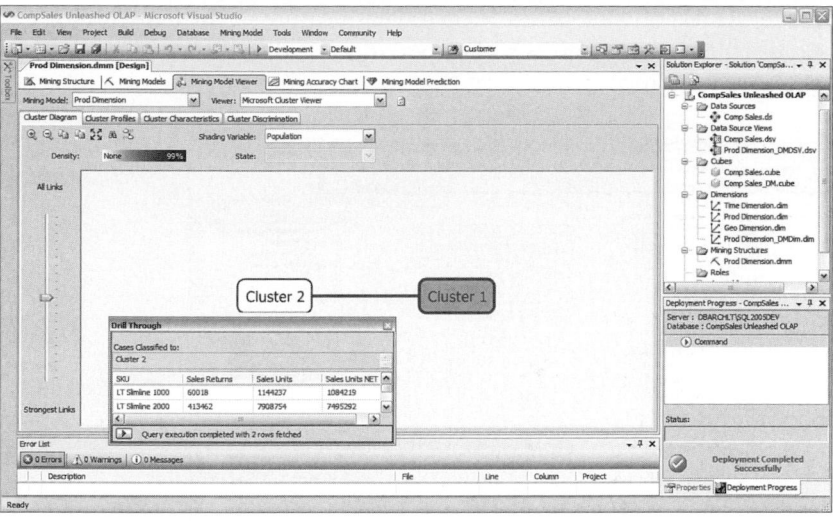

FIGURE 39.64   Clustering results and drilling through to the data in the mining model viewer.

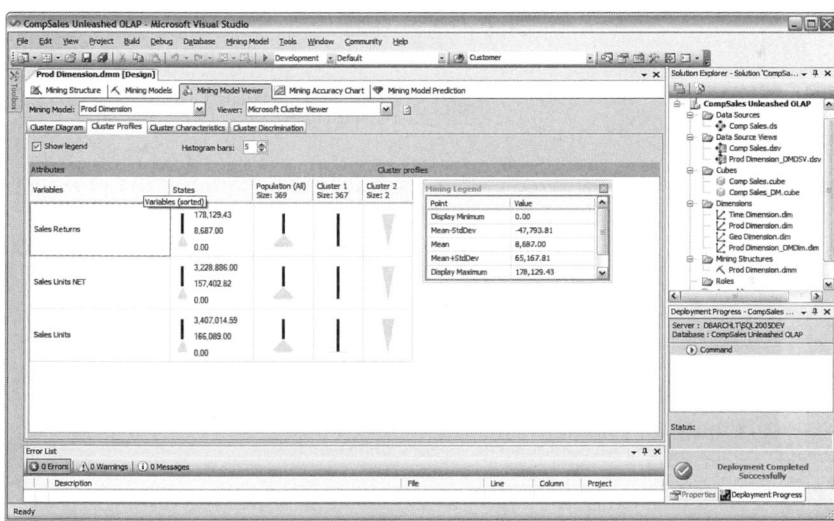

FIGURE 39.65   Cluster data profiles in the mining model viewer.

Figure 39.66 shows the clusters of data values of each data measure in the data mining model. This characteristic information gives you a good idea of what the actual data values are and how they cluster together.

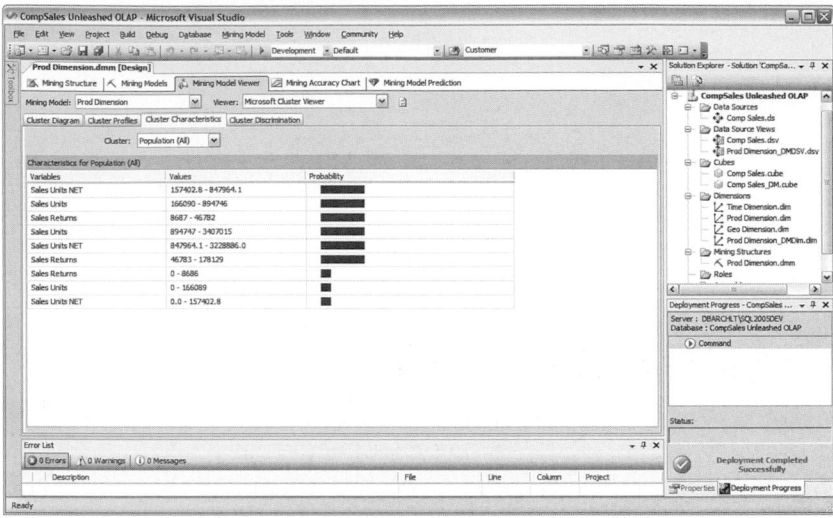

FIGURE 39.66   Cluster characteristics of the data values for each measure in the mining model viewer.

Finally, you can see the cluster node contents at the detail level by changing the mining model viewer type to Microsoft Mining Content Viewer, which is just below the Mining Model Viewer tab on top. Figure 39.67 shows the detail contents of each model node and its technical specification.

If you want, you can now build new cube dimensions that can help you do predictive modeling based on the findings of the data mining structures you just processed. In this way, you could predict sales units of one SKU and the number of naturally clustered SKUs quite easily (based on the past data mining analysis). This type of predictive modeling is very powerful.

SSIS

SSIS provides a robust means to move data between sources and targets. Data can be exported, validated, cleaned up, consolidated, transformed, and then imported into a destination of any kind. With any OLAP/SSAS implementation, you will undoubtedly have to transform, clean, or preprocess data in some way. You can now tap into SSIS capabilities from within the SSAS platform.

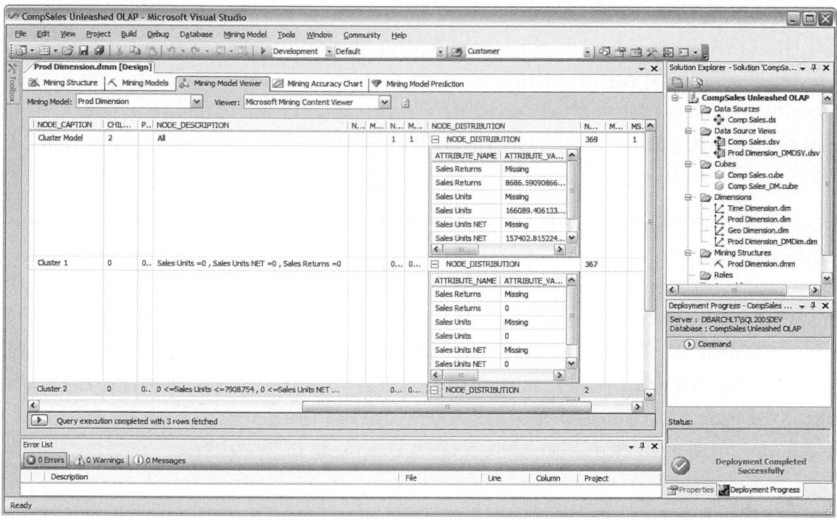

FIGURE 39.67   The Mining Model Content Viewer of the cluster nodes in the mining model viewer.

You can combine multiple column values into a single calculated destination column or divide column values from a single source column into multiple destination columns. You might need to translate values in operational systems. For example, many OLTP systems use product codes that are stored as numeric data. Few people are willing to memorize an entire collection of product codes. An entry of 100235 for a type of shampoo in a product dimension table is useless to a vice president for marketing who is interested in how much of that shampoo was sold in California in the past quarter.

Cleanup and validation of data is critical to the data's value in the data warehouse. The old saying "garbage in, garbage out" applies. If data is missing, redundant, or inconsistent, then high-level aggregations can be inaccurate, so you should at least know that these conditions exist. Perhaps data should be rejected for use in the warehouse until the source data can be reconciled. If the shampoo of interest to the vice president is called Shamp in one database and Shampoo in another, aggregations on either value would not produce complete information about the product.

The SSIS packages define the steps in a transformation workflow. You can execute the steps serially and in combinations of serially, in parallel, or conditionally. For more information on SSIS, refer to Chapter 40, "SQL Server Integration Services."

OLAP Performance

Performance has been a big emphasis of this release of SSAS. Usage-based aggregation is at the heart of much of what you can do to help in this area. In addition, the new proactive caching mechanism in SSAS has allowed much of what was previously a bottleneck (and a slowdown) to be circumvented.

39

When designing cubes for deployment, you should consider the data scope of all the data accesses (that is, all the OLAP queries that will ever touch the cube). You should only build a cube that is big enough to handle these known data scopes. If you don't have requirements for something, you shouldn't build it. This helps keep things a smaller, more manageable size (that is, smaller cubes), which translates into faster overall performance for those who use the cube.

You can also take caching to the extreme by relocating the OLAP physical storage components on a solid-state disk device (that is, a persistent memory device). This can give you tenfold performance gains. The price of this type of technology has been dramatically reduced within the past year or so, and the ease of transparently applying this type of solution to OLAP is a natural fit. It affects both the OLAP data population process and the day-to-day what-if usage by the end users. You should keep these types of surgical incisions in mind when you face OLAP performance issues in this platform. They are easy to apply, the gains are huge, and you quickly get a return on your investment.

Security and Roles

Security is straightforward in SSAS. For each database or cube, roles are identified with varying levels of granularity for users. Roles are used when accessing the data in cubes. It works like this: A role is defined, and then an individual user or group who is a member of that role is assigned that role. To create the roles you need for this data, you right-click on the Roles entry in the Solution Explorer and select New Role. Figure 39.68 shows the creation of a database role with process database and read definitions permissions.

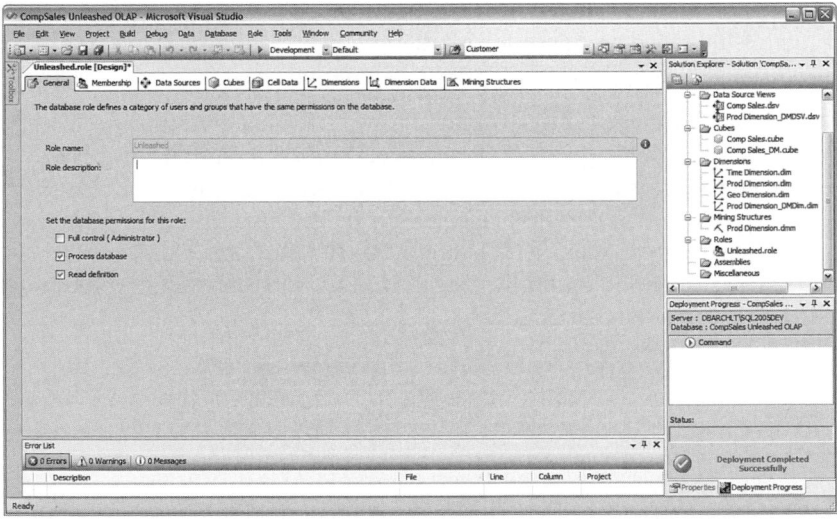

FIGURE 39.68   Creating a database role and permissions in the role designer.

The other tabs allow you to further specify the controls, such as which members you want to have this role (Membership tab), what data source access you want (Data Sources tab), which cubes can be used (Cubes tab), what specific cell data the role has access to (Cell Data tab), what dimensions can be accessed (Dimensions tab), what dimensional data can be accessed (Dimension Data tab), and what mining structures are allowed to be used (Mining Structures tab). These are additive. As you can see in Figure 39.69, you can also specify full MDX queries as part of the process of filtering what a member and role can have access to.

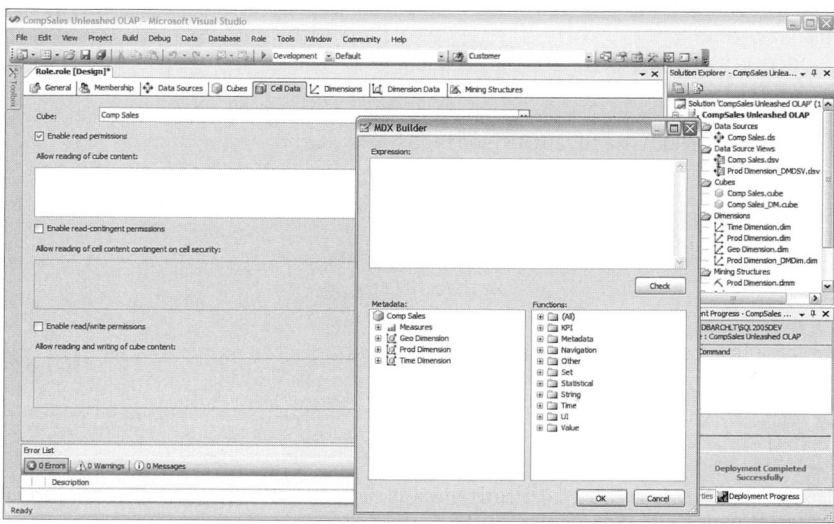

FIGURE 39.69   Specifying MDX-based filtering, using the role designer.

Summary

This chapter discusses the OLAP approach, SSAS terms, and the tools Microsoft provides to enable OLAP cubes. It presents a mini-methodology to follow that should help you get an OLAP project off the ground and running smoothly. These efforts are typically not simple, and a well-trained data warehouse analyst, BI specialist, or data architect is usually worth his or her weight in gold because of the end results (and value) that can be achieved through good OLAP cube design.

Sometimes it is difficult to engage end users and get them to use an OLAP cube successfully. Easy-to-use third-party tools can greatly help with this problem.

From an SSAS point of view, the ease of control of storage methods, dimension creation, degrees of aggregation, cube partitioning, and usage-based optimization are features that make this product a serious data warehousing tool. It is getting easier and easier to publish OLAP data via websites or other means. SSAS is truly the land of the wizards, but having a wizard lead you through a good OLAP cube design is critical. The wizards significantly reduce the expense and complexity of a data warehouse or data mart OLAP solution, enabling you to build many more much-needed solutions for your end users.

Chapter 40, "SQL Server 2005 Integration Services," ventures into the massively increased offering from Microsoft in regards to aggregating data for not only Analysis Service, but most other production platforms that require complex data transformations.

CHAPTER 40

SQL Server Integration Services

IN THIS CHAPTER

► What's New with SSIS

► SSIS Basics

► SSIS Architecture and Concepts

► SSIS Tools and Utilities

► A Data Transformation Requirement

► Running the SSIS Wizard

► The SSIS Designer

► The Package Execution Utility

► Using bcp

► Logged and Non-Logged Operations

Taking over the reins for Data Transformation Services (DTS) is SQL Server Integration Services (SSIS). It's actually a bit more than taking over the reins, though, because Microsoft has completely redeployed DTS and integrated it into the Business Intelligence (BI) Development Studio/ Visual Studio environments and SQL Server Management Studio (SSMS). This chapter describes the SSIS environment and how SSIS addresses complex data movement and integration needs.

SSIS focuses on importing, exporting, and transforming data from one or more data sources to one or more data targets. This is Microsoft's version of extraction, transformation, and loading (ETL) on steroids. Competing ETL products are Informatica and Data Junction, but Microsoft has simply bundled this functionality together with SQL Server, thus providing more reasons to purchase SQL Server and not have to buy more expensive competing products. Other Microsoft solutions exist for importing and exporting data, but SSIS can be used for a larger variety of data transformation purposes, and its strength is in direct data access and complex data transformation.

If you have existing DTS implementations (that is, DTS packages), you can convert them to SSIS packages with little to no effort, or you can simply execute them as-is.

For those who still use the Bulk Copy Program (bcp), a section at the end of this chapter describes this legacy SQL Server capability. bcp is still the workhorse of many production environments and cannot just be discarded every time a new version of SQL Server comes along. We estimate that bcp will be around for years to come.

The alternatives to SSIS and bcp in the Microsoft SQL Server 2005 environment include replication, distributed queries, BULK INSERT, and SELECT INTO/INSERT. This chapter helps you determine how and when to use both SSIS and bcp as opposed to these other alternatives.

What's New with SSIS

In SQL Server 2005, Microsoft has completely redeployed DTS into a much more comprehensive and robust data integration platform—with the emphasis on the word *platform*. In fact, everything about SSIS is new! SSIS has now been deployed from almost every angle of data movement and data transformation that is possible. The following are some of the highlights of SSIS:

▶ Graphical tools and wizards for building, debugging, and deploying SSIS packages

▶ Workflow functions, such as File Transfer Protocol (FTP), SQL statement execution, and more

▶ SSIS application programming interfaces (APIs)

▶ Complex data transformation for cleansing, aggregating, merging, and copying data

▶ An email messaging interface

▶ A service-based implementation (that is, the Integration Services service)

▶ Support for both native and managed code (C++ and any common language runtime (CLR)–compliant languages, such as C# and J#)

▶ The Integration Services object model

SSIS Basics

As the world becomes ever more data oriented, much greater emphasis is being placed on getting data from one place to another. To complicate matters, data can be stored in many different formats, contexts, filesystems, and locations. In addition, the data often requires significant transformation and conversion processing as it is being moved around. Whether you are trying to move data from Excel to SQL Server, create a data mart (or data warehouse), or distribute data to heterogeneous databases, you are essentially enabling someone with data.

This section describes the SSIS environment and how it is addressing these needs. As mentioned earlier, the focus is on importing, exporting, and transforming data from one or more data sources to one or more data targets.

Common requirements of SSIS might include the following:

▶ Exporting data out of SQL Server tables to other applications and environments (for example, ODBC or OLE DB data sources or via flat files)

▶ Importing data into SQL Server tables from other applications and environments (for example, ODBC or OLE DB data sources or via flat files)

▶ Initializing data in some data replication situations, such as initial snapshots

▶ Aggregating data (that is, data transformation) for distribution to/from data marts or data warehouses

▶ Changing the data's context or format before importing or exporting it (that is, data conversion)

Some typical business scenarios for SSIS might include the following:

▶ Enabling data marts to receive data from a master data warehouse through periodic updates (see Figure 40.1)

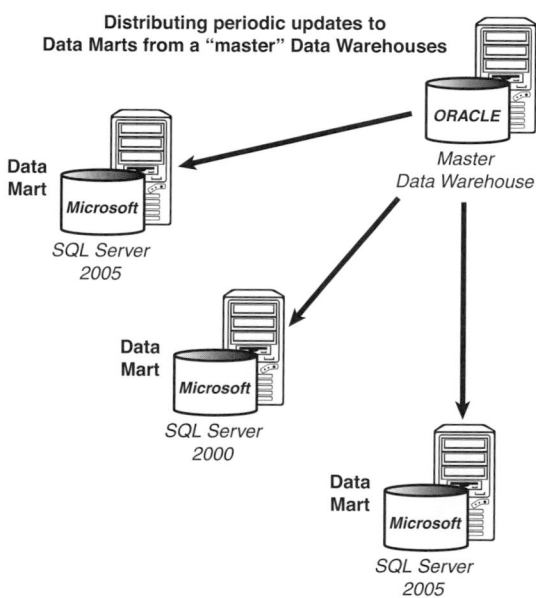

FIGURE 40.1   Distributing periodic updates to data marts.

▶ Populating a master data warehouse from legacy systems (see Figure 40.2)

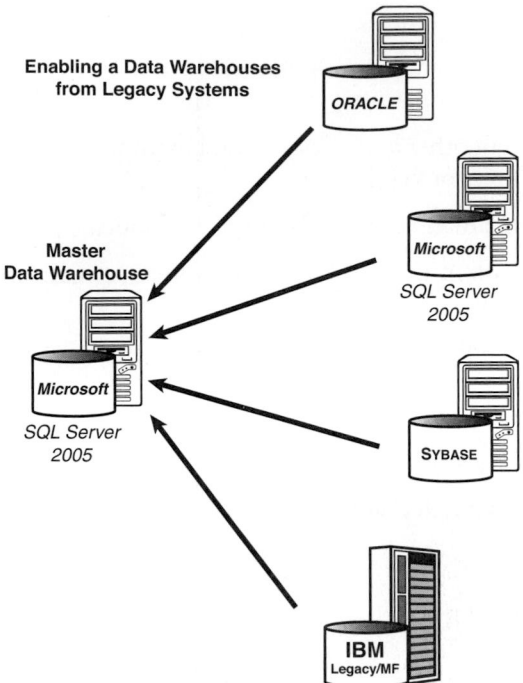

FIGURE 40.2   Populating a data warehouse from one or more data sources.

▶ Initializing heterogeneous replication subscriber tables on Oracle from a SQL Server 2005 Publisher (see Figure 40.3)

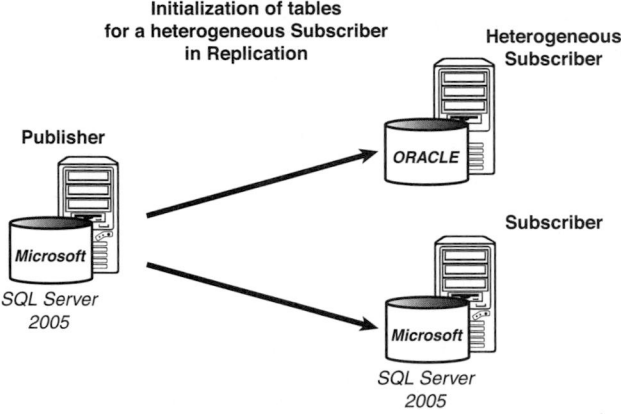

FIGURE 40.3   Initializing a heterogeneous replication subscriber (such as Oracle).

▶ Pulling sales data directly into SQL Server 2005 from an Access or Excel application (see Figure 40.4)

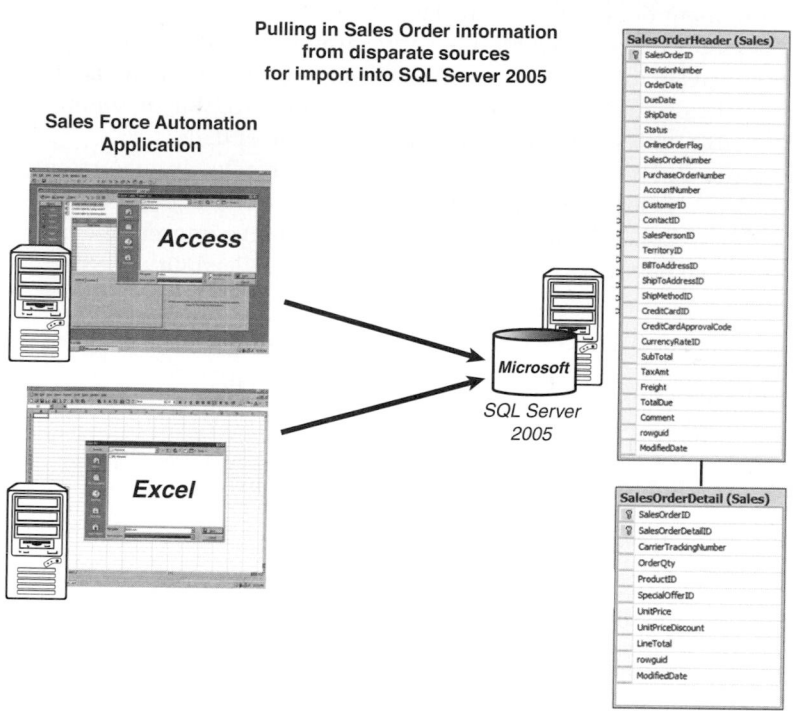

**Pulling in Sales Order information
from disparate sources
for import into SQL Server 2005**

**Sales Force Automation
Application**

Access

Excel

Microsoft

SQL Server
2005

SalesOrderHeader (Sales)
- SalesOrderID
- RevisionNumber
- OrderDate
- DueDate
- ShipDate
- Status
- OnlineOrderFlag
- SalesOrderNumber
- PurchaseOrderNumber
- AccountNumber
- CustomerID
- ContactID
- SalesPersonID
- TerritoryID
- BillToAddressID
- ShipToAddressID
- ShipMethodID
- CreditCardID
- CreditCardApprovalCode
- CurrencyRateID
- SubTotal
- TaxAmt
- Freight
- TotalDue
- Comment
- rowguid
- ModifiedDate

SalesOrderDetail (Sales)
- SalesOrderID
- SalesOrderDetailID
- CarrierTrackingNumber
- OrderQty
- ProductID
- SpecialOfferID
- UnitPrice
- UnitPriceDiscount
- LineTotal
- rowguid
- ModifiedDate

FIGURE 40.4   Pulling data from other disparate applications.

- ▶ Exporting static time-reporting data files (that is, flat files) for distribution to remote consultants

- ▶ Importing new orders directly or indirectly from a sales force or distributed sales systems

In general, you need SSIS if any of the following conditions exist:

- ▶ You need to import data directly into SQL Server from one or more ODBC data sources, .NET and OLE DB data providers, or via flat files.

- ▶ You need to export data directly out of SQL Server to one or more ODBC data sources, .NET and OLE DB data providers, or via flat files.

- ▶ You need to perform data conversions, data cleansing/data standardization, transformations, merges, or aggregations on data from one or more data sources for distribution to one or more data targets. You also need SSIS if you need to access the data directly via any ODBC data source, .NET or OLE DB data providers, or via flat files.

40

▶ Your bulk data movement doesn't have to be faster than the speed of light. Unfortunately, SSIS must utilize conventional connection techniques to these data sources. It must also create intermediate buffers to hold data during the transformation steps. This usually disqualifies SSIS on the high-performance side of requirements (at least for large, bulk data movements with any type of data transformations defined). However, many performance enhancements are present in SSIS and the new data providers that are now supported, which has resulted in about a 50% increase in bulk data movement speeds. Alternative importing/exporting facilities such as bcp offer better performance but lack the flexibility of SSIS.

The following additional SSIS data sources and destinations are now supported:

▶ An XML source for extracting data from XML documents directly

▶ Full insert and updating support SQL Server Mobile destinations

▶ Reading and writing to Raw data files (sources and destinations)

▶ Creating an in-memory ADO DB recordset via a destination

▶ Direct access to a number of Analysis Services object destinations (for example, mining models, cubes, and dimensions)

▶ The ADO.NET DataReader source and destination for reading and writing to any .NET framework data provider

SQL Server 2005 now supports the following additional SSIS data transformations:

▶ Data warehousing operations, such as the Aggregate, Pivot, Un-pivot, and Slowly Changing Dimension transformations

▶ Enhanced text data mining via the Term Extraction and Term Lookup transformations

▶ Enhancing data values from a lookup table via the Data Lookup and Fuzzy Lookup transformations

▶ The identification of similar data rows via the Fuzzy Grouping transformation

▶ Multiple downstream data flow component data distribution via the Conditional Split and Multicast transformations

▶ The merging and combining of data rows from multiple upstream data flow components via the Union All, Merge, and Merge Join transformations

▶ Extensive copying and modifying of column data values, using the Copy Column, Data Conversion, and Derived Column transformations

▶ Sample rowset extractions, using the Percentage Sampling and Row Sampling transformations

▶ Sorting of data and identification of duplicate data rows via the Sort transformation

SSIS includes a set of tools and features that support managing, editing, executing, and migrating DTS packages from earlier versions of SQL Server. You can see all available DTS packages in SSMS (in a separate branch). You can also choose to migrate old DTS packages (from SQL Server 2000) forward to SSIS packages (to SQL Server 2005) via the Package Migration Wizard. It's quite easy. If you can't migrate old DTS packages yet, you can directly execute DTS packages from SSIS packages. If you need to be able to design changes to existing DTS packages, you can either download the special DTS designer version for SQL Server 2005 from Microsoft's website, or just bite the bullet and migrate them forward. We recommend migration as rapidly as is feasible.

SSIS Architecture and Concepts

You can think of SSIS as a data import/export/transformation layer in the overall system architecture that you are deploying for at least most of your Microsoft-based applications and a few non-Microsoft applications (see Figure 40.5). SSIS allows you to "data enable" almost all the individual applications or systems that are part of an overall implementation, such as OLTP databases, multidimensional cubes, OLAP data warehouses, Excel files, Access databases, flat files, other heterogeneous database sources, and even web services. The Integration Services object model includes both native and managed APIs for doing most SSIS work. This includes APIs for any of the SSIS tools, the command-line utilities, and even custom applications. SSIS Designer and the Integration Services Wizard both use the Integration Services object model. SSIS includes the integration service itself (that is, the service that manages all SSIS packages), the Integration Services object model, the SSIS runtime and runtime executables, and the data flow task (which has data flow engine, source, transformation, and destination components).

Microsoft uses SSIS packages to implement any data movement/transformation. Basically, Microsoft is now treating SSIS packages as if they are managed code and now requires that you create Integration Services projects and deployment utilities as part of managing these SSIS packages. All in all, this is a very good approach that significantly reduces errors and allows you to go through a reasonably formal release to production (that is, development and deployment) cycle.

SSIS packages contain a collection of connections, control flow elements, data flow elements, event handlers, variables, and configurations. These take the form of tasks, containers, transformations, and workflows. SSIS packages go through one or more steps that are either executed sequentially or in parallel at package execution time. In a nutshell, when an SSIS package is executed, it does the following:

1. Connects to any identified data source

2. Copies data (and database objects, if needed)

3. Transforms data

4. Disconnects from the data sources

5. Notifies users, processes, and even other packages of events (such as sending an email when something is done or has errors)

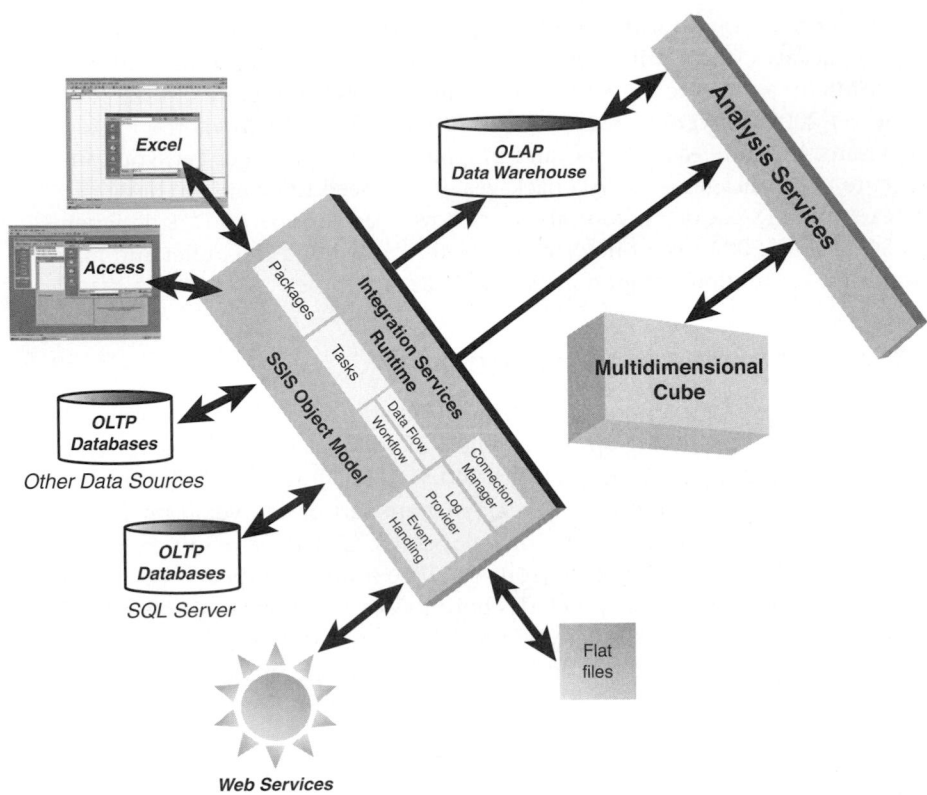

FIGURE 40.5   SSIS architecture.

The basic SSIS package consists of the following:

▶ **SSIS packages**—A package is a discrete, named collection of connections, control flow, and data flows that implement data movement/data transformation.

▶ **SSIS control flow and tasks**—One or more tasks and containers drive what the package does. You organize control flow based on what you want the package to do. *Tasks* are the actions taken to accomplish the desired data transformation and movement. A task can execute any SQL statement, send mail, bulk insert data, execute an ActiveX script, or launch another package or an external program.

▶ **SSIS containers**—A container groups one or more related tasks that you want to manage together (and reuse together).

▶ **Workflows**—Workflows are definable precedence constraints that allow you to link two tasks, based on whether the first task executes, executes successfully, or executes unsuccessfully. Workflow containers are the wrappers for the tasks and are the means for the flow of control. A task can run alone, parallel to another task, or sequentially, according to precedence constraints. Precedence constraints are of three types:

- ▶ **Unconditional**—It does not matter whether the preceding step failed or succeeded.

- ▶ **On success**—The preceding step must have been successful for the execution of the next step.

- ▶ **On failure**—Returns the appropriate error.

▶ **SSIS data flow**—The data flow identifies the sources and destinations that extract and load data, identifies the transformations that manipulate or enhance the data, and provides the paths that link sources, transformations, and destinations.

▶ **SSIS data flow task**—A data flow task creates, orders, and runs the data flows themselves, using a data flow engine.

▶ **SSIS transformations**—Transformations are one or more functions or operations applied against a piece of data before the data arrives at the destination.

In SSIS, everything is pretty much a task or a collection of tasks (one or more containers, tasks in containers), as you can see in Figure 40.6. Control flow determines the overall execution of the package and data flows that access the data, transform it, and write it. Precedence constraints determine the overall control flow—connecting the executables, containers, and tasks into an ordered control flow.

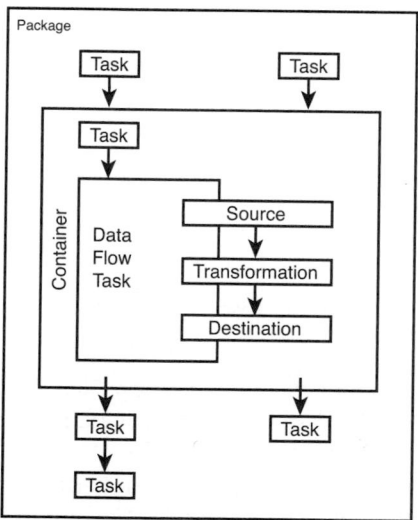

FIGURE 40.6   SSIS package elements.

40

SSIS also has several objects that extend package functionality:

▶ **SSIS event handlers**—These are workflow tasks that run in response to events raised by a package, task, or container. This is much the same as most programming languages, such as Java or C#. If a task (or package or container) has some issue (that is, raises an event), the event handler can be used to handle the issue appropriately. Typical events in data transformation processing that need to be handled with event handlers might include connections not being established, disk space issues, and so on. You can even have the event handlers write out emails or initiate other workflows.

▶ **SSIS configurations**—These are used to help parameterize many of the previously hard-bound characteristics of packages at runtime. When a package is run, the configuration information is loaded (updating the values of the package's properties), and then the package is run, using the new configuration values (all without having to modify the package). SSIS configurations use the classic property/value pair paradigm to represent the properties that are to be configurable. The following are the varied methods of representing configuration files:

  ▶ **XML configuration file**—This file identifies the configuration property/value pairs for any number of configuration values. The following is an example of this XML configuration file for a package named UnleasedPackage with a property of PKGVar:

```
<?xml version="1.0"?>
<DTSConfiguration>
    <DTSConfigurationHeading>
        <DTSConfigurationFileInfo
            GeneratedBy="DatabaseArchitects\PBertucci"
            GeneratedFromPackageName="UnleashedPackage"
            GeneratedFromPackageID="{3GV09721-816B-4E28-9878-0DE37A150234}"
            GeneratedDate="7/09/2006 7:12:22 AM"/>
    </DTSConfigurationHeading>
    <Configuration ConfiguredType="Property"
Path="\Package.Variables[User::PKGVar].Value"
ValueType="Int32">
        <ConfiguredValue>0</ConfiguredValue>
    </Configuration>
</DTSConfiguration>
```

  A configuration header contains information about the configuration file. This element includes attributes such as when the file was created and the name of the person who generated the file. In addition, a configuration element contains information about each configuration. This element includes attributes such as the property path and the configured value of a property.

▶ **Configuration table in SQL Server**—This table stores configuration entries for use by the packages.

▶ **Environment Variables (VARs)**—These can be referenced by the package.

▶ **Parent package VARs**—These can be used by child packages.

▶ **Entry in registry**—The registry can also contain the configuration values.

▶ **SSIS Logging**—Logging can be done from any task or package to write out any type of logging information desired. By using a supplied logging provider, a package can provide a rich runtime history. Logs are associated with packages (that is, the reference point), but any task (or container) can write to any package's log. In this way, it is possible to have consolidated logs of a driver package with the full execution history of all child packages. The log providers (out of the box) write to a flat file (text file) or to SQL Server tables. Other custom logging providers can be used, though. You can log what you need to log—start date/time, end date/time, records transformed, errors, and so on.

▶ **SSIS variables**—SSIS has both system variables and user-defined variables. System variables provide runtime package object information to tasks or other packages. This is helpful when you want to reference these system variables to help decide what to do next. (They can be used in expressions, scripts, and configurations.) User-defined variables are really for specialized variables that are not found as system variables and only have to be used within a package's scope. Again, these can be used in expressions, scripts, and configurations within a package.

SSIS packages can run other packages. This is very helpful when you want to granularly break out common data transformations for reuse by many different higher-level solutions (that is, higher-level packages that execute common-detail-level transformation packages).

> **NOTE**
>
> When an SSIS package is first created, it is given a globally unique identifier (GUID) that is added to the package's ID property and a name that is added to its NAME property. After these are created, they become part of the reference mechanism for the package itself. If you ever copy a package as the basis of a new package, you have to rename these two properties so they are unique (that is, new GUID and new NAME property). If you simply want to give an existing package a new NAME or ID value, you can do so directly or with the `dtutil` command-line utility.

You can also create packages that can be restarted. This is a super addition to SQL Server 2005. You can now create packages that can be restarted at a point of failure, including restarting specific tasks within a package (and not all the tasks in a package). If a package had more than one data flow tasks and one completed but the others didn't, you could restart just the data flow tasks that had not completed without rerunning the ones that worked fine. Long-running packages can also create checkpoints to provide milestones from which to restart. This will save many sleepless nights for the folks doing production support for data transformation processing.

SSIS Tools and Utilities

SSIS includes several tools that simplify package creation, execution, and management. These tools are available within the Visual Studio/BI Development Studio IDE (as shown in the drop-down list in Figure 40.7) or integrated into other component-based tools (such as SSMS, as shown in Figure 40.8).

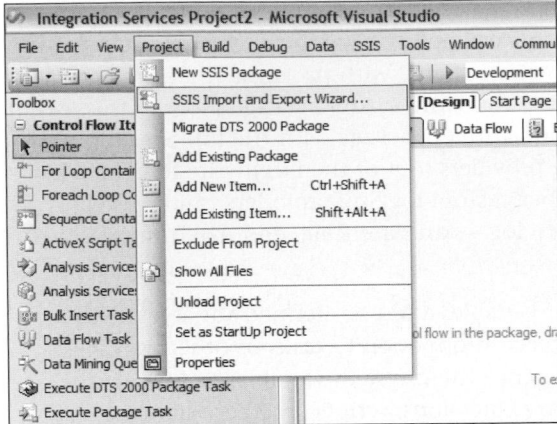

FIGURE 40.7   Package creation options within Visual Studio/BI Development Studio.

Equally as easily, you can invoke SSIS functionality (for example, the SSIS Import and Export Wizard) from within SSMS (see Figure 40.8).

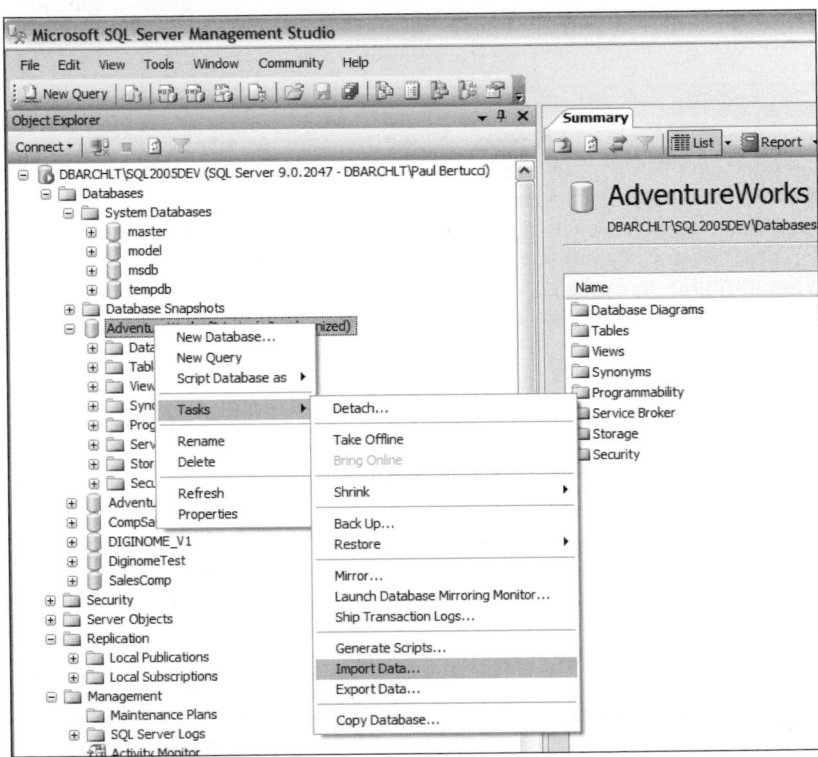

FIGURE 40.8   Invoking SSIS import/export data (package creation) capability from within SSMS.

Also, within SSMS, you can organize packages; execute packages (via the Execute Package utility); import and export packages to and from the SQL Server `msdb` database, the SSIS package store, and the filesystem (`.dtsx` files); and migrate DTS packages (older SQL Server version packages).

The following are the primary working environments for creating, managing, and deploying SSIS packages:

▶ **Import and Export Wizard**—You can use this wizard, available within Visual Studio/BI Development Studio or from SSMS, to build packages to import, export, and transform data or to copy database objects (see Figure 40.9). This is an easy way to create the basic SSIS packages that you need quickly and deploy them with great ease.

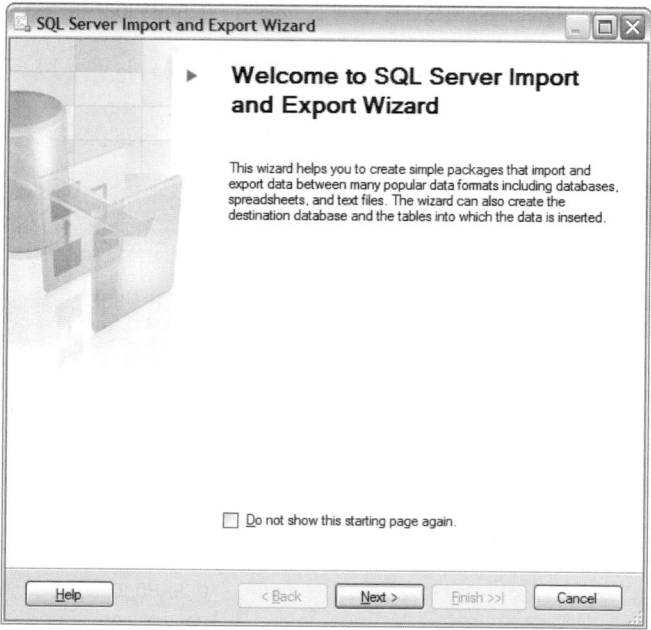

FIGURE 40.9   The Import and Export Wizard from Visual Studio/BI Development Studio.

▶ **SSIS Designer**—This standard GUI is available in the Visual Studio/BI Development Studio, as part of an SSIS project). It lets you construct/manipulate packages containing complex workflows, multiple connections to heterogeneous data sources, and even event-driven logic (see Figure 40.10). This is the same IDE that all code development uses in the .NET platform, making it extremely easy to get started and start developing right away.

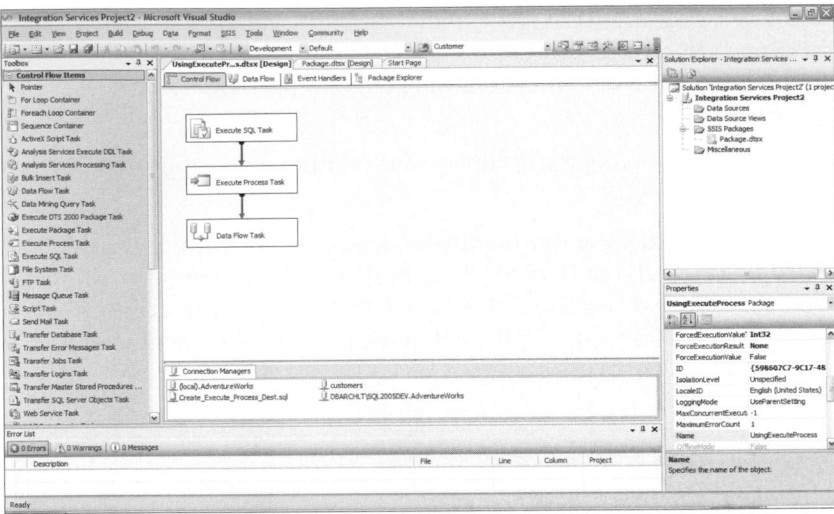

FIGURE 40.10   The SSIS Designer IDE.

- ▶ **SSIS command-prompt utilities**—A number of utilities are available within SSMS to aid you in running and managing SSIS packages (see Figure 40.11). One example is the Execute Package utility (which uses `dtexec` and `dtutil` command-line utilities). If the utility accesses a package that is stored in `msdb`, the command prompt may require a username and a password.

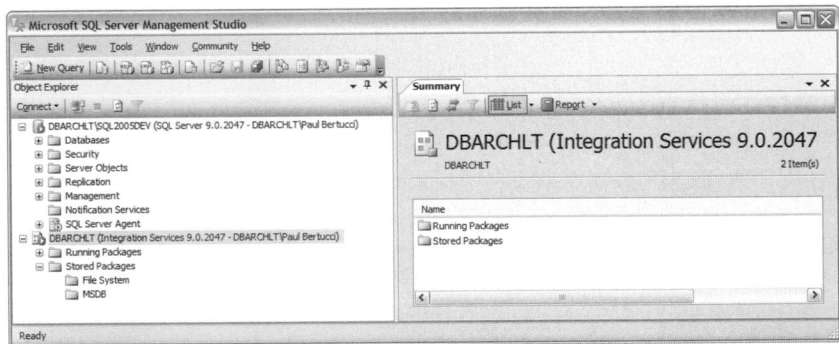

FIGURE 40.11   The Integration Services branch in SSMS.

- ▶ **SSIS Query Builder**—Query Builder provides a very easy-to-use GUI for quickly developing SQL queries, testing the queries, and embedding them into the SSIS packages that you are developing. It is sort of like a mini SQL Query Profiler. It is entirely point-and-click oriented. Figure 40.12 shows the point at which you can invoke the Query Builder as you add `Execute SQL Task` as part of an SSIS package to the SQL Task Editor.

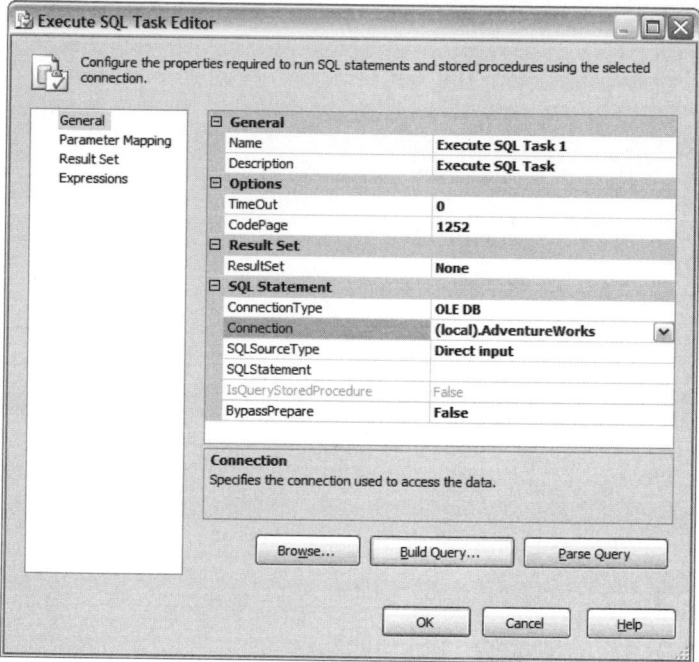

FIGURE 40.12   Invoking the Query Builder interface from the SQL Task Editor dialog.

Figure 40.13 shows the full Query Builder interface, along with a SQL statement that is being developed that retrieves address information from the AdventureWorks Person.Address table.

▶ **SSIS Expression Builder**—You can use Expression Builder to develop the simple or complex expressions that get used by a package (the expression property of the package configuration). These are things like validating working directories on a local machine where an SSIS package has been deployed and other complex evaluations that you want to have used by an SSIS package property. This is a graphical tool that enhances your ability to use these types of expressions for your SSIS packages. Not only does it help you develop the expressions, but it also evaluates them to make sure they are providing the proper results (much like what Query Builder does for SQL statements). Figure 40.14 shows a typical expression within SSIS Expression Builder for validating a working directory on a server that will be used by an SSIS package.

Finally, after you have created SSIS packages, you need to execute them via command-line execution, within SQL programs, or via other .NET-supported programming languages. You can easily do this by using the dtexec package execution utility. You manage packages by using the dtutil utility.

40

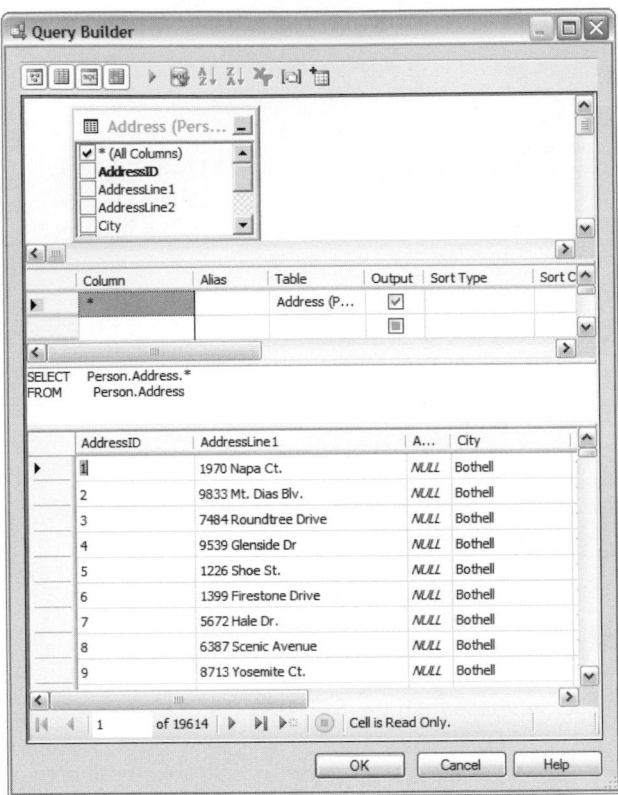

FIGURE 40.13   The Query Builder GUI for developing SQL queries.

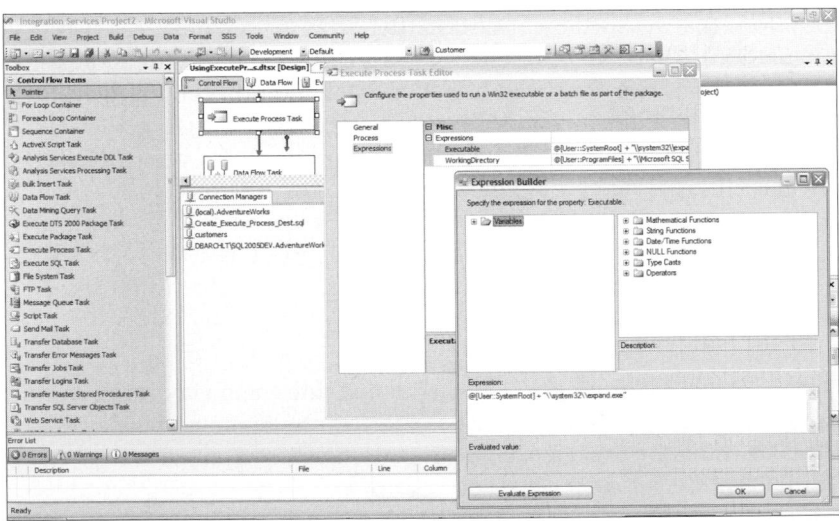

FIGURE 40.14   The SSIS Expression Builder GUI for developing expressions.

A Data Transformation Requirement

Let's consider a true-life data export requirement that is best served by using SSIS. The requirement is for a small business intelligence data mart (on SQL Server 2005) to be spun off each week from the main OLTP database (also on SQL Server 2005) that addresses a product sales manager's need to see the total year-to-date business that a customer has generated. This data mart is merely a standard SQL Server database and tables that have been transformed (that is, aggregated) for a targeted purpose. As an option, the manager would also like to spin off an Excel version of this, which will be distributed via email to all salespeople in the region. This overall requirement has been named "Hot Customers Plus" to indicate the emphasis on customers who are generating significant business for the company. The offloaded data mart is on a separate machine from the critical OLTP system for all of the right reasons; no reporting or ad hoc queries are done against the OLTP system. This process must be repeated on a weekly basis as a total refresh (see Figure 40.15).

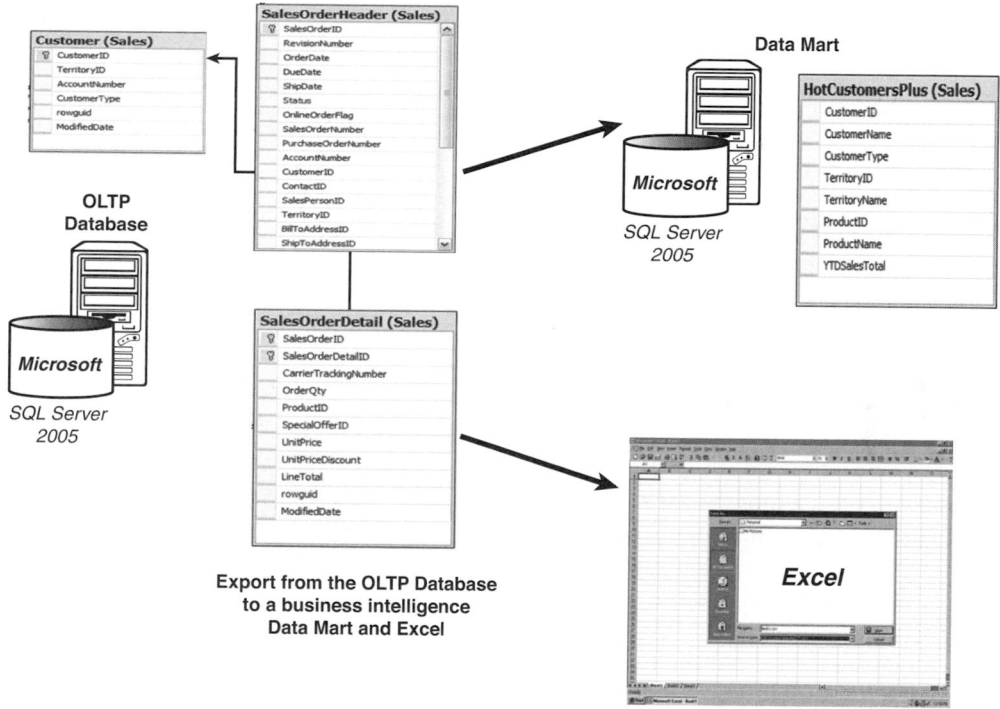

Export from the OLTP Database
to a business intelligence
Data Mart and Excel

FIGURE 40.15   Creating a data mart and an Excel file from an OLTP database, using SSIS.

Essentially, order data from the OLTP database (contained in the Customer, Product, Store, SalesTerritory, SalesOrderHeader, and SalesOrderDetails tables) must be aggregated for every order for each customer. In addition, the total amount to be stored in the YTDTotalSales column in the data mart has to be extended out to reflect the summary of each product for each customer. The manager is also interested only in customers who are ordering products that total $5,000 or more. After the data mart is repopulated on the weekend, an email notification must be sent to the primary business user. Although the requirements are many, SSIS should be able to handle all this with no problem.

So that you can get a good feel for the two main SSIS tool capabilities, this chapter takes you through generating the solution to this requirement using the SSIS Wizard first, and then we will walk through the same solution but using SSIS Designer.

Running the SSIS Wizard

The SSIS Wizard is a streamlined interface solely used to generate SSIS packages for importing or exporting data. It is really quite powerful and provides an easy but sophisticated way to move data from or to any OLE DB, ODBC, or text source to another OLE DB, ODBC, or text source. You can also define simple or complex data transformations, using the many options provided by the wizard or. The wizard can also copy database schema, but the transfer of all other database objects, such as indexes, constraints, users, permissions, stored procedures, and so on is supported only between SQL Server 7.0 and above SQL Servers.

The SSIS Import/Export Wizard takes the user through five basic steps for both imports and exports:

1. Select/identify the data source (source).

2. Select/identify the destination (target).

3. Select the data copy and transformation type. The options are to copy data with or without the schema, to move data based on a query, or to transfer objects and data between data stores.

4. Define any data transformations, if required.

5. Save, schedule, and execute the package.

Let's walk through a quick wizard sequence and create a package that fulfills the "Hot Customers Plus" data movement/transformation requirement. You need to have two SQL Server instances up and running, and you will be pulling and transforming data from the AdventureWorks database on one server instance (SQL2005DEV) and pushing it to another server instance (SQL2005DIST). You need to create a database named UnleashedDataMart on the target server to hold the new HotCustomersPlus table you will be creating with SSIS. Remember that, using the SSIS Wizard is for simple package creations (or data transfers). Nothing fancy here. To get started, here's what you do:

1. Fire up the SSIS Wizard from within SSMS by either right-clicking the database branch for the database from which you will be exporting data or right-clicking in the summary pane for that same database (as shown in Figure 40.16). If you select the Tasks option, you are given the option of either importing data or exporting data. You want to export data from this database, so choose the Export Data option.

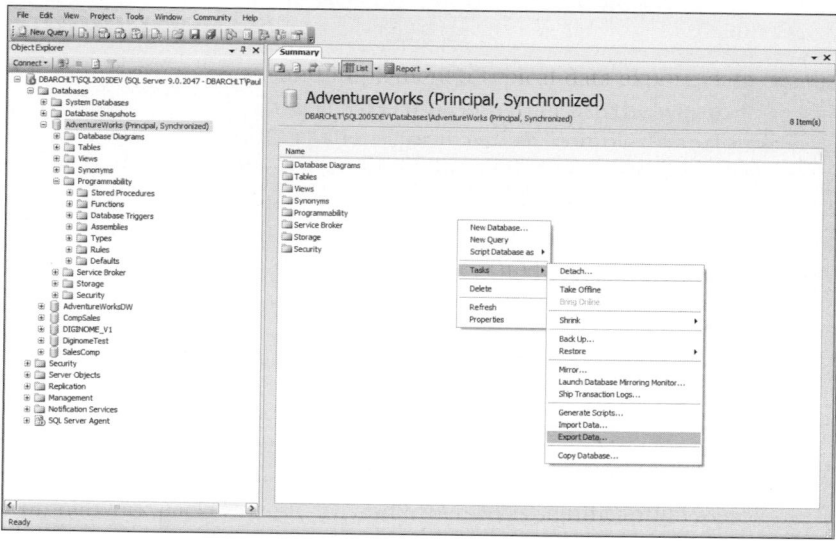

FIGURE 40.16   Invoking the Export Data Wizard.

2. Work through the steps of the SSIS Wizard. The initial step is identifying the source for the data. In this example, you need to choose a valid SQL Server and source database (In our example: DBARCHLT\SQL2005DEV for the server and AdventureWorks for the database). In addition, you must provide the appropriate access credentials (Windows authentication or SQL Server authentication) for this source SQL Server. You have a few options of exactly what access mechanism to use (to this data source). Choose the SQL Native Client connection method (see Figure 40.17).

3. Next is the data "destination" specification (the target). Because we will be targeting another SQL Server instance and database, we either specify its name and an existing Database location or we can create a new database from within this wizard. We had already created a new database (called UnleashedDataMart) for this purpose before we started and will use that for this example. Our example will use a SQL Server Instance of DBARCHLT\SQL2005DIST, using the connection method to this SQL Server instance of SQL Native Client, and the previously mentioned database of UnleashedDataMart (as shown in Figure 40.18). We will also be using Windows Authentication. You are finished with this window, so click Next.

4. The next step in the wizard asks you if you will be pulling source data from one or more tables (or views) or if you will be specifying a SQL query to pull data from the source. For our example, we will select the "Write a query to specify the data to transfer" option because this approach will best fit the requirement we specified earlier (see Figure 40.19).

40

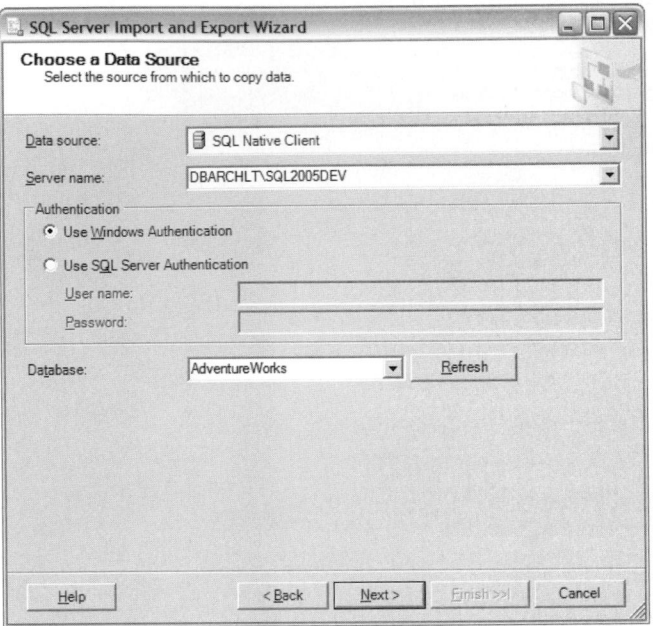

FIGURE 40.17   Identifying the SSIS source database and server locations.

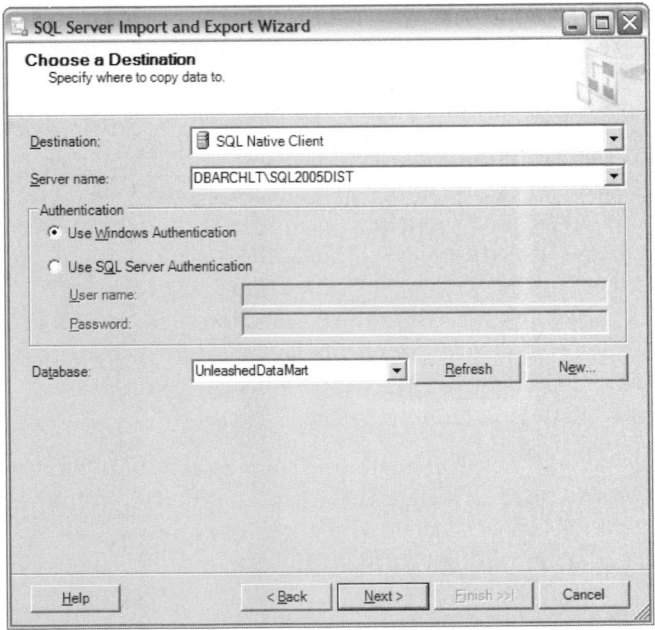

FIGURE 40.18   Identifying the SSIS destination database and server locations.

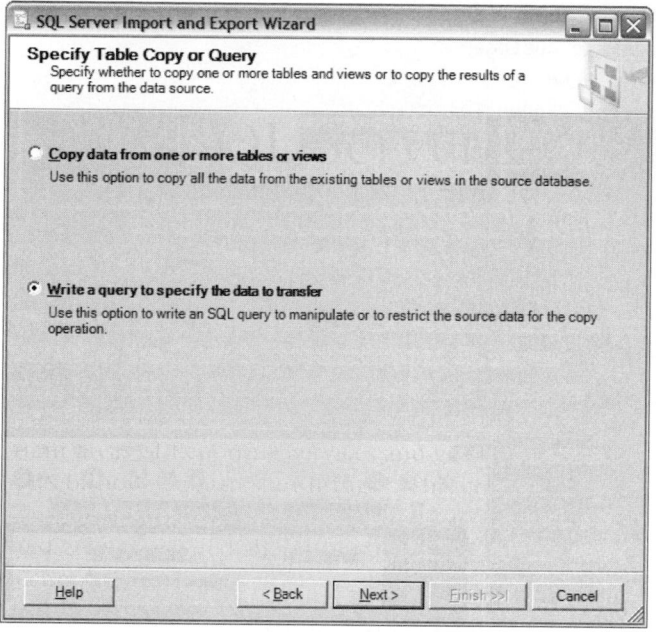

FIGURE 40.19   Specifying to use tables or a query for data transfer from the data source.

5. In the next step in the wizard, create your custom SQL statement that will be used to select data from the source database. We have provided you a fairly complex SQL query that selects (and joins) data from six tables in the AdventureWorks database that fulfills the data requirement for our example. This is also downloadable from the Sams website for this book title (www.samspublishing.com). In this step of the wizard, enter the following query:

```
select  a.CustomerID,
        e.name as CustomerName,
        a.CustomerType,
        a.TerritoryID,
        d.name as TerritoryName,
        c.ProductID,
        f.name as ProductName,
        sum(c.LineTotal) as YTDSalesTotal
FROM
    [sales].[Customer] a
    INNER JOIN [sales].[SalesOrderHeader] b
            ON a.customerid = b.customerid
    INNER JOIN [sales].[SalesOrderDetail] c
            ON b.SalesOrderID = c.SalesOrderID
    INNER JOIN [sales].[SalesTerritory] d
            ON a.TerritoryID = d.TerritoryID
```

```
            INNER JOIN [sales].[Store] e
                   ON a.customerid = e.customerid
            INNER JOIN [Production].[Product] f
                   ON c.productID = f.ProductID
    WHERE b.orderdate >= '2004-01-01 00:00:00.000'
    GROUP BY a.customerID,
             e.name,
             a.CustomerType,
             a.TerritoryID,
             d.name,
             c.ProductID,
             f.name
    HAVING sum(c.LineTotal) > 5000
    ORDER BY d.name,
             e.name
```

In this window, you can select a query from a file by clicking the Browse button to search for this file or you can simply start coding directly in the window. You can click the Parse button to guarantee that the SQL statement has valid syntax and form (see Figure 40.20). You can test it in the next wizard step.

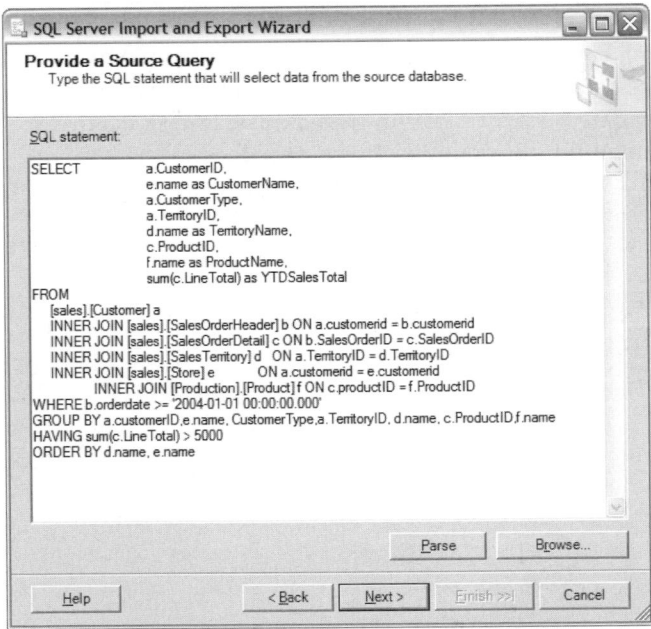

FIGURE 40.20   Providing a SQL query to select data from a data source.

If you had chosen to copy data directly from the database tables (and not use a SQL query), you would have been provided a list of tables and views from the source database and would have been able to map one or more of these tables to tables on the destination database. Figure 40.21 shows this Select Source Tables and Views window.

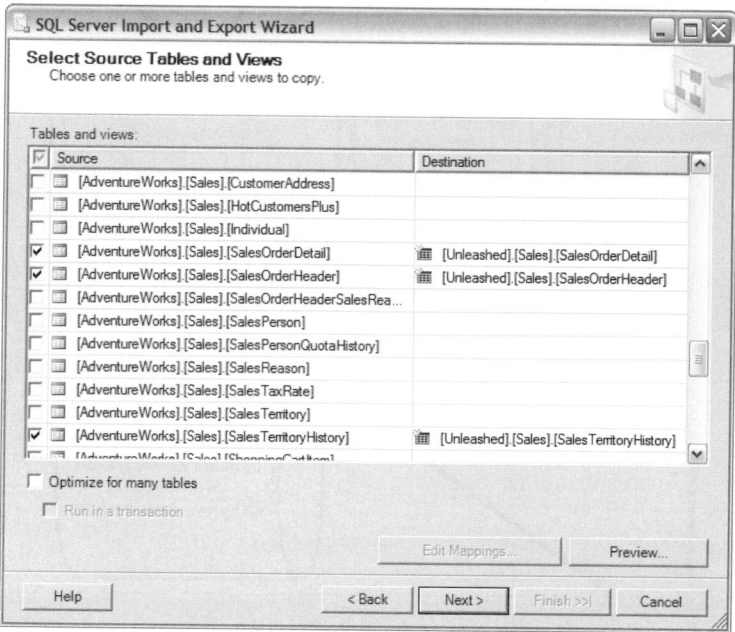

FIGURE 40.21   Mapping source tables and views to a destination.

6. Rename the destination table nameby changing [UnleashedDataMart].[dbo].[Query] to [UnleashedDataMart].[dbo].[HotCustomersPlus] (see Figure 40.22). All subsequent references to this destination target will be what you want.

7. Click the Preview button on this dialog to actually execute the SQL query specified in step 5. Figure 40.23 shows the Preview Data results of the custom SQL query. Close this data preview window when you are finished reviewing the data results.

8. Click the Edit Mappings button to see the details of the column-level mappings being defined. At this point, you can further subset the columns, change data types, use precision or scale change and/or not have a column mapped during the data transformation. As you can see in Figure 40.24, the Source and Destination columns are side-by-side, and when you click a column name, you can adjust what you want to occur. In addition, at the object level, you can have the table created at the destination, have it truncate the data in an existing table at the destination, or append data to existing data at the destination. For this example, choose to completely drop and re-create the destination table each time. You are basically done creating the logic and data mappings for this simple data transformation.

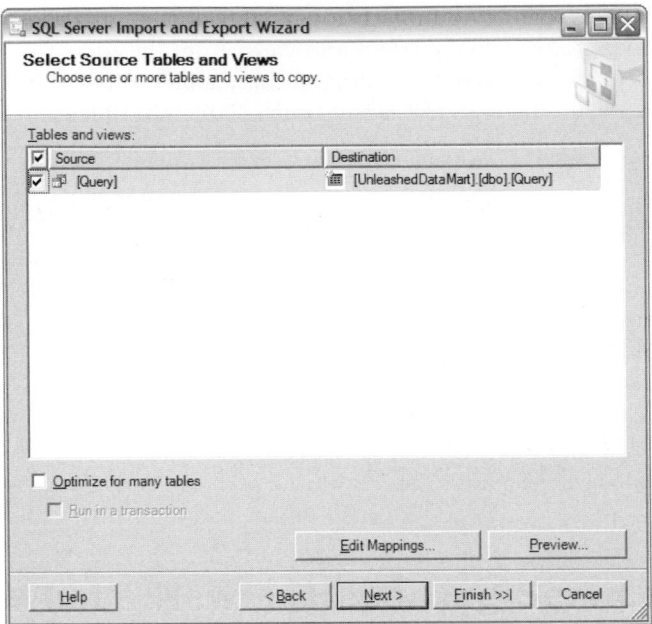

FIGURE 40.22   Source query mapping to a destination.

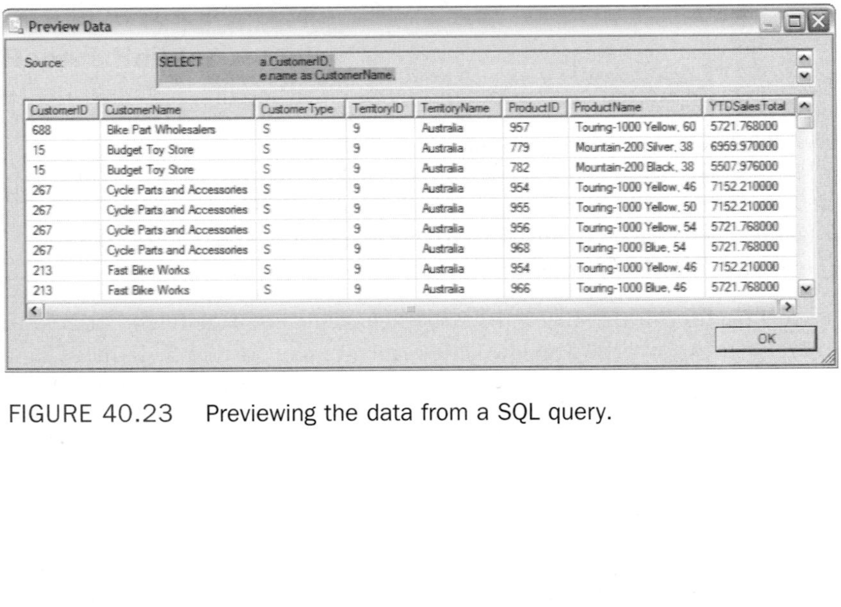

CustomerID	CustomerName	CustomerType	TerritoryID	TerritoryName	ProductID	ProductName	YTDSalesTotal
688	Bike Part Wholesalers	S	9	Australia	957	Touring-1000 Yellow, 60	5721.768000
15	Budget Toy Store	S	9	Australia	779	Mountain-200 Silver, 38	6959.970000
15	Budget Toy Store	S	9	Australia	782	Mountain-200 Black, 38	5507.976000
267	Cycle Parts and Accessories	S	9	Australia	954	Touring-1000 Yellow, 46	7152.210000
267	Cycle Parts and Accessories	S	9	Australia	955	Touring-1000 Yellow, 50	7152.210000
267	Cycle Parts and Accessories	S	9	Australia	956	Touring-1000 Yellow, 54	5721.768000
267	Cycle Parts and Accessories	S	9	Australia	968	Touring-1000 Blue, 54	5721.768000
213	Fast Bike Works	S	9	Australia	954	Touring-1000 Yellow, 46	7152.210000
213	Fast Bike Works	S	9	Australia	966	Touring-1000 Blue, 46	5721.768000

Source: SELECT   a.CustomerID,
                     e.name as CustomerName,

FIGURE 40.23   Previewing the data from a SQL query.

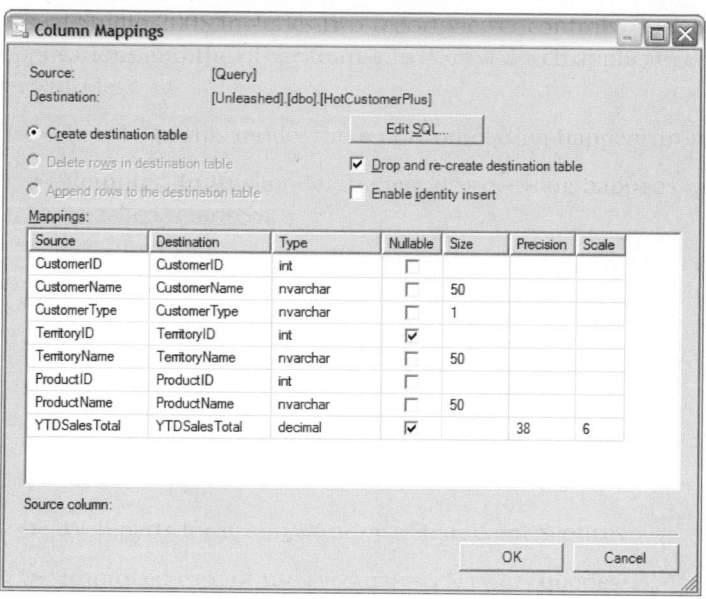

FIGURE 40.24   Column Mappings options.

9. Click the Edit SQL button in the Column Mappings dialog. A `CREATE TABLE` SQL statement appears, and you can modify if you want (see Figure 40.25). You don't need to do any further changes at this time.

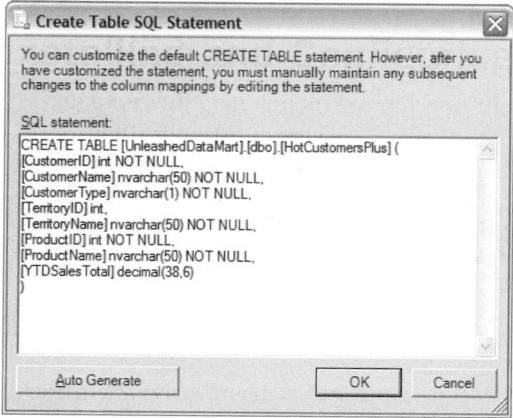

FIGURE 40.25   Manually customizing the default `CREATE TABLE` statement.

10. In the Save and Execute Package dialog that appears, choose Execute Immediately and Save SSIS Package. Save the SSIS package in SQL Server in the `msdb` SQL Server database (see Figure 40.26). It is also possible to save the SSIS package in a structured storage file at the file system level (in a ".dtsx" file).

40

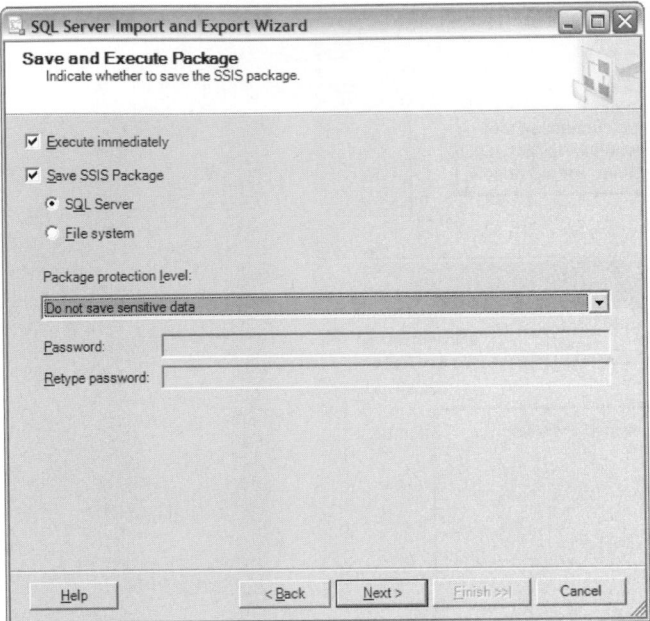

FIGURE 40.26   Options for executing and saving SSIS packages.

11. In the Save SSIS Package dialog, you will specify the name of the package, the description of the package, and the location of where the package is to be stored. For this example, specify a name of "HotCustomersPlus" for the SSIS package name. (as shown in Figure 40.27).

12. When the SSIS Wizard displays the Complete the Wizard dialog, summarizing all the actions to be taken, carefully review the list and then click Finish when you are ready to proceed. After you click Finish, the wizard's execution console appears (as shown in Figure 40.28). This shows all the steps taken, the status of these steps, and informational detail, as required. Note in Figure 40.28 the Copying to [Unleashed].[dbo].[HotCustomersPlus] table message that 943 rows were transferred. Following this particular "Copying" step will be the simple post execute and cleanup actions for the package.

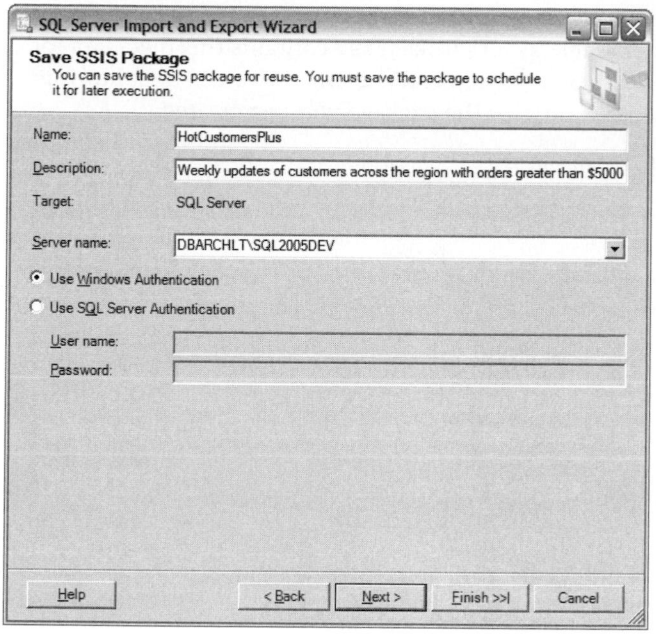

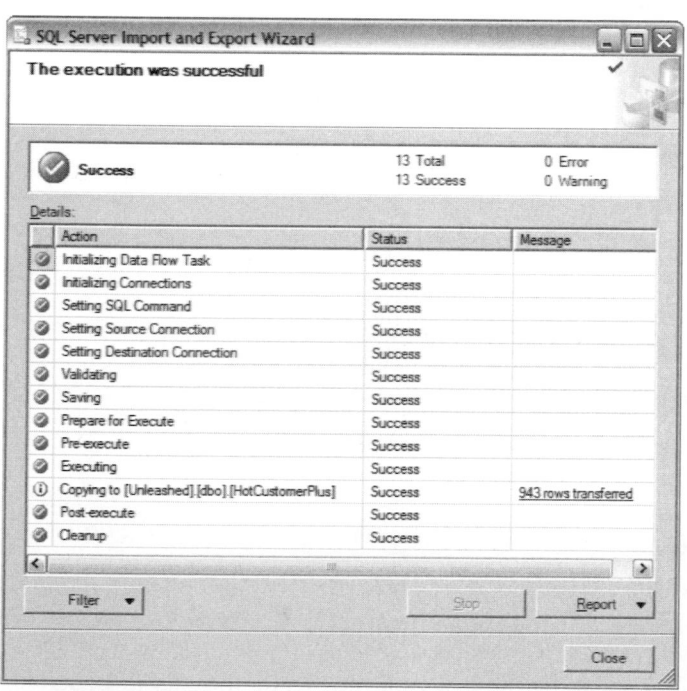

FIGURE 40.27   Saving a package for reuse.

FIGURE 40.28   SSIS package initialization, saving, and execution.

If you would like, you can also query the system catalog table that contains the metadata for packages. In this case, the system table sysdtspackages90 contains this metadata for SSIS packages starting with this release of SQL Server, and going forward. The following simple SQL query shows the metadata entry for the package you just created:

```
SELECT * FROM [msdb].[dbo].[sysdtspackages90]
```

The results look like this:

```
Name              ID        Description        Datetime
HotCustomersPlus  4BEDD...  Weekly updates...  2006-08-04 ...
```

Figure 40.29 shows the execution tasks for doing straight table copying (transferring) using SSIS packages of the tables to create a quick-and-dirty (refreshable) data mart. This is a very useful method of spinning off data quickly, and it fits out requirements.

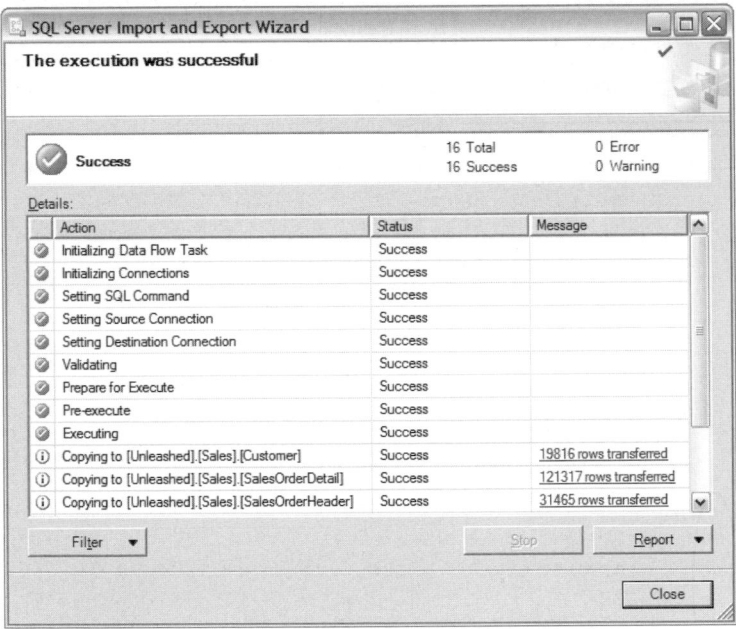

FIGURE 40.29   An SSIS package straight table copy/transfer example.

The SSIS Designer

The SSIS Designer is extremely easy to use and gives a user the flexibility of editing and manipulating any of the package properties in any order that is needed, as opposed to the strict sequential order of the SSIS Wizard. You will find that after you have mastered all the package concepts, you will be spending most of your time using the SSIS Designer instead of the wizard.

Because you have already created an SSIS package using the wizard, you can just open a version of this package (which you stored in the filesystem as a .dtsx file) with the SSIS Designer to see some of the SSIS Designer's capabilities (see Figure 40.30). You simply locate a .dtsx package file (such as HotCustomersPlus.dtsx) using the File Open option within (BI) Development Studio/Visual Studio.

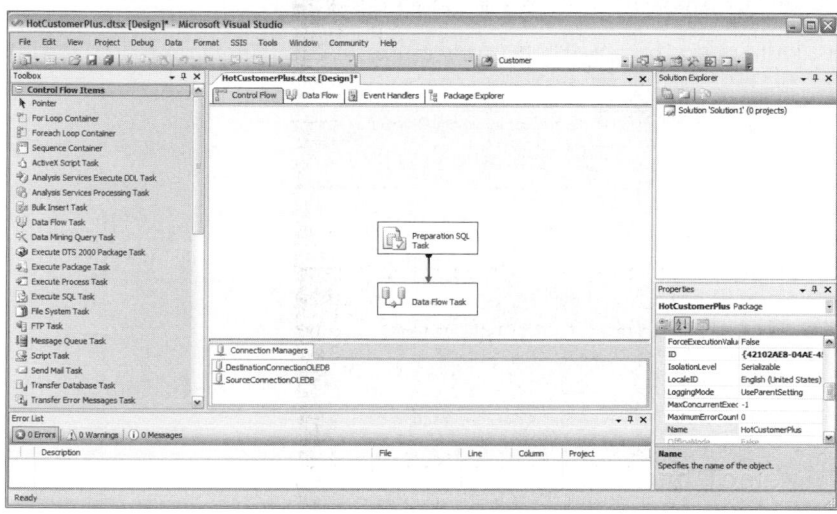

FIGURE 40.30   The SSIS Designer: opening the HotCustomersPlus.dtsx package.

As you can see with the SSIS Designer, you are within the common Visual Studio IDE environment for any type of managed code. SSIS package creation is now just another option of a code development project. The SSIS Designer includes a main designer pane, a palette of toolbox icons to the left, an error pane on the bottom, the Solution Explorer to the right, and Properties pane in the bottom right. The Connection Manager sits right below the designer pane, and there are four basic tabs in the designer pane for different purposes: The Control Flow pane is for overall task, control of flow, and constraint specification; the Data Flow pane is for generating and manipulating the data mapping and transformation itself; the Event Handlers pane is for defining what error handling needs to be part of this package; and the Package Explorer pane is for an overall view of the elements of the package.

The SSIS Designer is truly a point, click, and drag working environment. For anything in the workspace, you simply click the icon, such as DestinationConnectionOLEDB (in the Connection Managers pane) or the Preparation SQL Task icon in the Control Flow pane to see its properties, or you click the solid line between the Preparation SQL Task and Data Flow Task boxes to see the task constraints and workflow defined for the package. If you haven't created the HotCustomersPlus SSIS package, you should do so now with the wizard and save it to the filesystem as well (as a .dtsx file). You will use it in our next example.

40

At this point, you need to fire up Visual Studio 2005 or the BI Development Studio environment. Either way, the same IDE is started. The SSIS Designer is initiated within this IDE. When you have successfully started the Visual Studio 2005 IDE environment, you can easily open the SSIS package you just created and use it to get familiar with the SSIS Designer. Simply choose the File, Open in Visual Studio 2005 and locate the `HotCustomersPlus.dtsx` SSIS package you created earlier (see Figure 40.31). We are about to modify this SSIS package to more fully support the `HotCustomersPlus` data mart and Excel file creation requirements because the wizard could not completely do that.

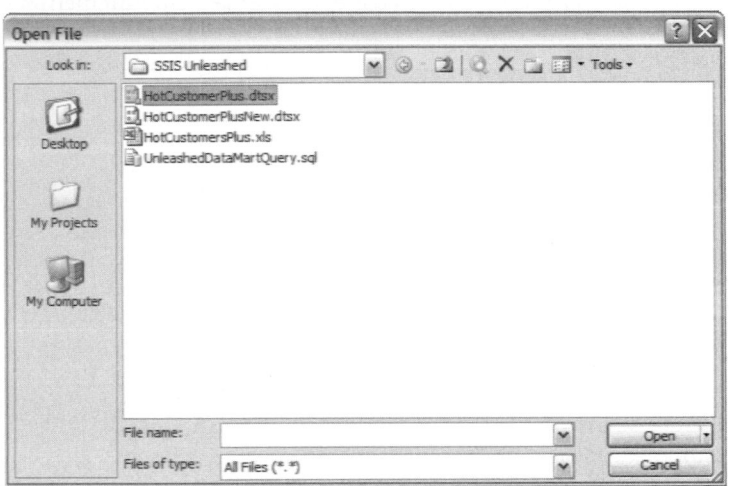

FIGURE 40.31   Opening the `HotCustomersPlus.dtsx` package.

When you open this package, you enter Visual Studio's development environment, where you can use the SSIS Designer capabilities. You will be using the SSIS Toolbox to the left to add functionality to this small SSIS package so that it will completely fulfill the data mart requirements outlined earlier. If you look back at Figure 40.30, you will see this simple SSIS package within the SSIS Designer. This is what you should have as well. Now, you can modify any existing tasks or add others to this SSIS package. If you recall, you originally set up this package to create a new destination table (on the other SQL Server instance) as the first step. Because you already executed this once, that table now exists (HotCustomersPlus on the destination SQL Server instance). Therefore, you need to change this first step to truncate the destination table instead of re-creating it each time. In addition, you need to add another task to this package that will spin off newly populated data (from the destination table) into an Excel file that can be easily distributed to the sales team. As you change this package, you will also re-label the tasks to be more reflective of what they are doing (and not use the default task naming that the wizard used).

The sales team is waiting, so follow these steps:

1. Right-click Preparation SQL Task, and choose Edit. The Execute SQL Task editor comes up, and in it you can see all aspects of this SQL task. Click the SQL statement

property within this window (where you see the CREATE TABLE statement) and then click the ... icon to the left of the CREATE TABLE statement. This opens up an editor window that contains the full SQL statement. Now, change this CREATE TABLE statement to a TRUNCATE TABLE statement for the same table on the destination SQL Server instance:

```
TRUNCATE TABLE [UnleashedDataMart].[dbo].[HotCustomersPlus]
GO
```

This is clearly shown in Figure 40.32. When you have updated the SQL statement to a TRUNCATE, click OK and then go ahead and click Parse Query to make sure the SQL statement is valid. You can now rename this task to something more appropriate by just clicking the Name property of this task and changing it to something like Clear out all rows in Destination Table. If all is well, click OK to exit this window. Now this task clears out the destination table before it re-populates it with new data instead of re-creating the destination table over and over.

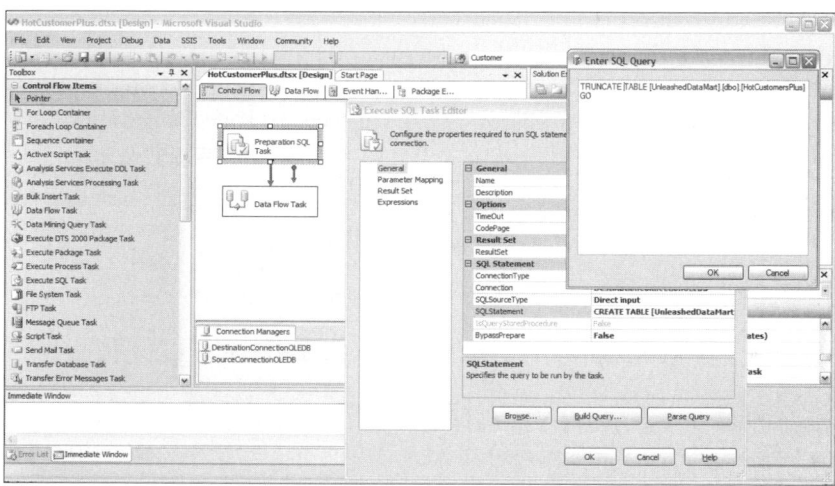

FIGURE 40.32   Modifying the Execute SQL Task from a CREATE TABLE statement to a TRUNCATE TABLE statement.

2. Rename the existing data flow task that pulls data out of the source SQL Server tables via a SELECT statement and populates the destination table the way it is. To do so, click this current data flow task and either right-click and choose Edit or just click the Data Flow tab in the IDE. You now see the multiple steps within this data flow. Locate the Name property of this data flow task and rename it from Data Flow Task to Extract from Source Tables, Populate to Destination table. Click the first step of the data flow (which has the name property Source - Query) and rename it Select orders from AdventureWorks. Now, click on the destination task (Destination - HotCustomersPlus) and rename it Populate Destination Table - HotCustomersPlus (as shown in Figure 40.33).

40

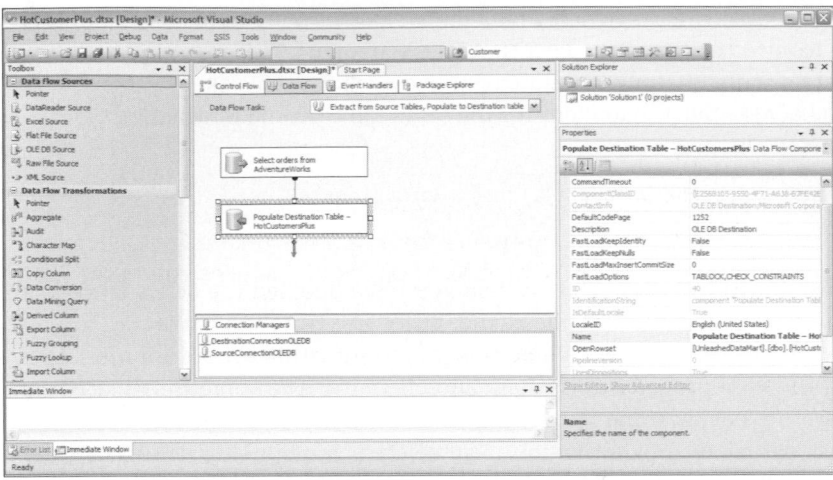

FIGURE 40.33 Modifying the data flow task within the SSIS package.

3. Add a new data flow task that will read the sales order data from the destination table that is being populated from the source tables and then write out an Excel file with this new data. From the Control Flow tab of this SSIS package, drag a new data flow task (from the Toolbox on the left) out to the Control Flow designer pane and then modify its name property to be Read from Destination table, Populate Excel file (as shown in Figure 40.34).

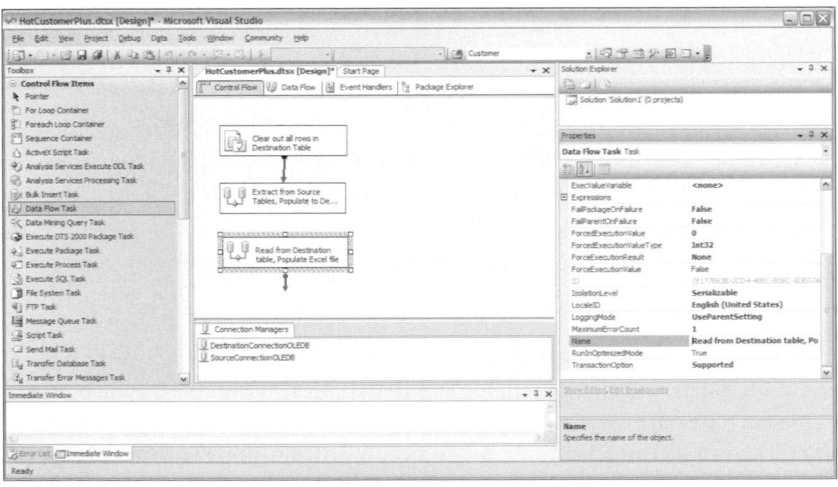

FIGURE 40.34 Creating a new data flow task to write data out to Excel.

4. Click the Data Flow tab, and you are in the Data Flow designer pane. Nothing is there yet (the Data Flow design space is empty). Also note that the Toolbox entries change when you click this tab (they are now all the data flow task items). Drag an

OLE DB Source item from the Toolbox over to the Data Flow designer pane. You will use this to get the data from the destination table. Rename this Data Flow step something like `Pull data from Destination Table` and then right-click this new Data Flow source task and choose Edit. This puts you in the OLE DB Source editor, where you can identify which connection manager to use (`DestinationConnectionOLEDB`, in this example) and what table you want to get data from (`HotCustomersPlus` table). You want the whole table, so specify the Table or View option for the access mode (see Figure 40.35). Click the Preview button at the bottom of this editor to verify that you will get all data from the destination table. Clicking OK returns you to the Data Flow designer pane.

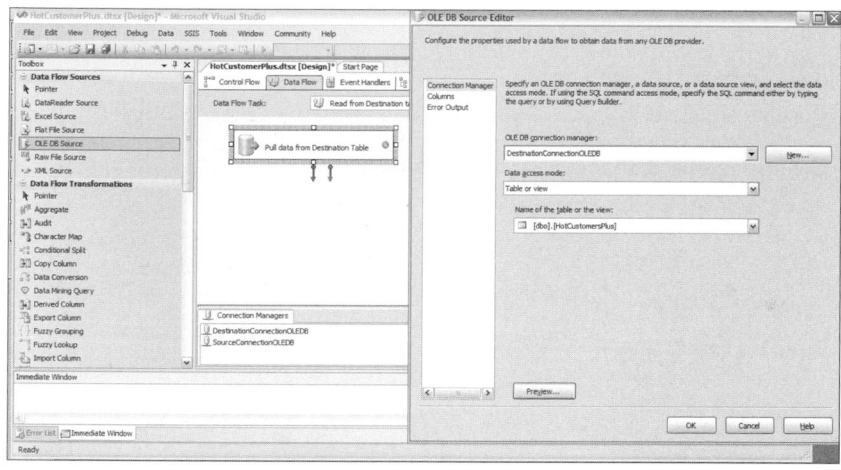

FIGURE 40.35   Specifying the Source Data Flow items for a new data flow task.

5. Back in the Data Flow designer pane, scroll down in the Toolbox to the Data Flow Destinations portion and locate the `Excel Destinations` item. Drag this over to the Data Flow designer pane and rename it something like `Write data to Excel file`.

6. Before you go any further, you need to connect the source data flow task (and its data output) to this new Excel destination. You can easily do this by just clicking the source data flow task's outbound arrow (that is just below the box) and dragging it to the new Excel destination box. A full arrow is redrawn that connects these two data flow tasks (as you can see in Figure 40.36).

7. Right-click this new data flow task item (Excel Destination) and choose Edit. This again puts you in an editor where you can specify the Excel destination file properties you want. This starts with identifying the connection manager and the Excel file to be used. Click New here, and you are asked to specify a location and filename for the destination Excel file (`HotCustomersPlus.xls`). Again, you want the whole table, so specify Table or View as the data access mode and use the default sheet name that appears in this portion when you click the drop-down; the default sheet name is `Excel_Destination`. Figure 40.37 shows this complete Excel destination specification. Click the Preview button to make sure this data will be retrieved properly.

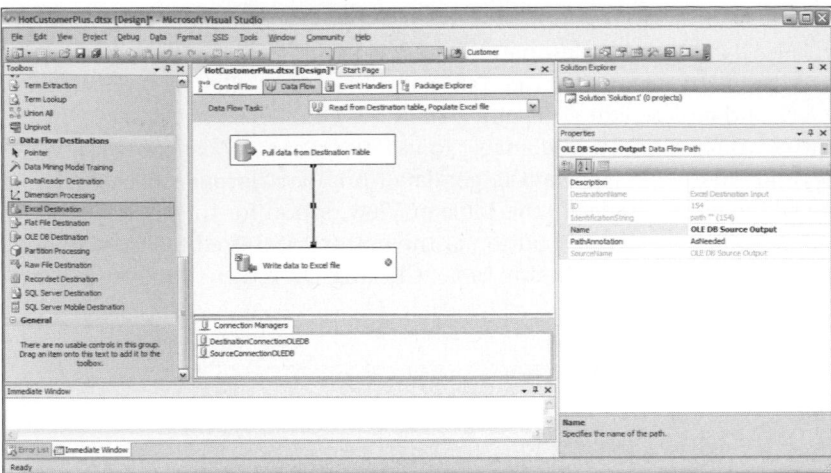

FIGURE 40.36   Connecting the data source to the data destination for the new data flow task.

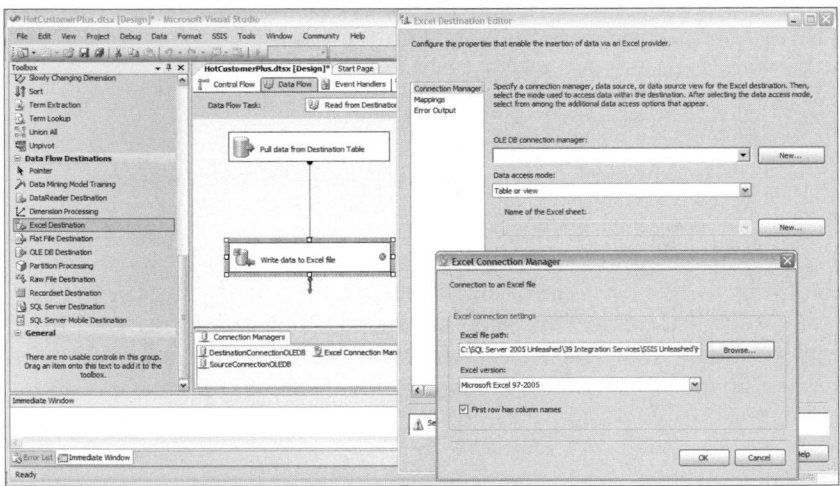

FIGURE 40.37   Specifying the Excel destination data flow items for a new data flow task.

You can also click the Mappings option in the Excel Destination Editor dialog. As you can see in Figure 40.38, each of the columns in the source table (the HotCustomersPlus table) will be mapped, one-to-one, to the Excel file columns with the same names.

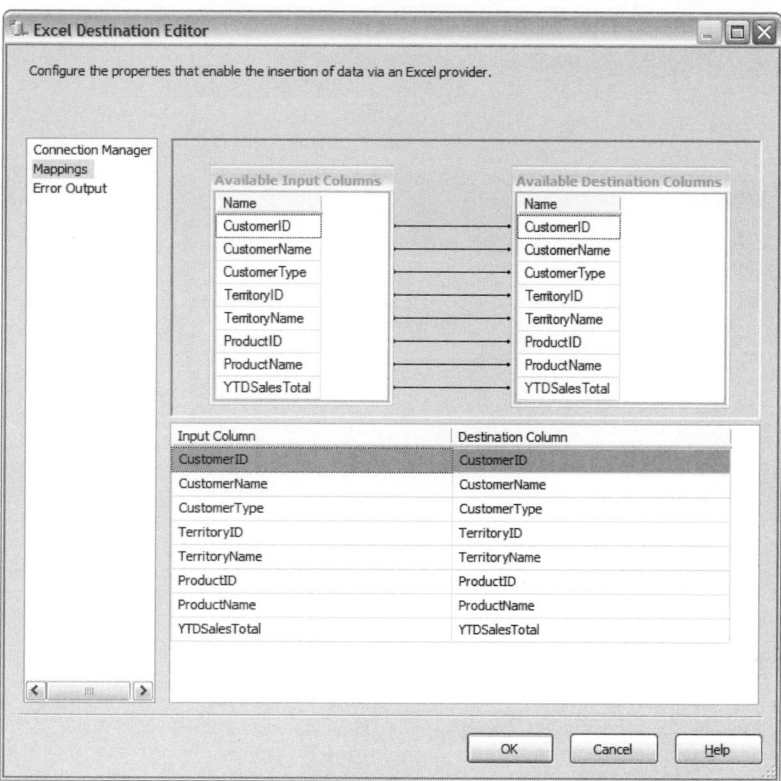

FIGURE 40.38   Source and destination column mappings.

8. Return to the Control Flow pane of the SSIS package and connect the new data flow task to the prior one. You do this by clicking the original data flow task and grabbing its control of flow arrow beneath the box and dragging it to the new data flow task you just created. Accept the default to execute the task on success of the prior task, as shown in Figure 40.39. Note that the Excel Destination connection manager now appears under the connection manager pane. At this point, save the package by clicking the disk icon or selecting File, Save.

9. To execute the package, double-click the .dtsx file, which automatically invokes the package execution utility. Choose Execute, and the package executes and shows all results in the execution console, as shown in Figure 40.40. That's it: You have populated the data mart and created data in an Excel file for distribution to the sales team.

40

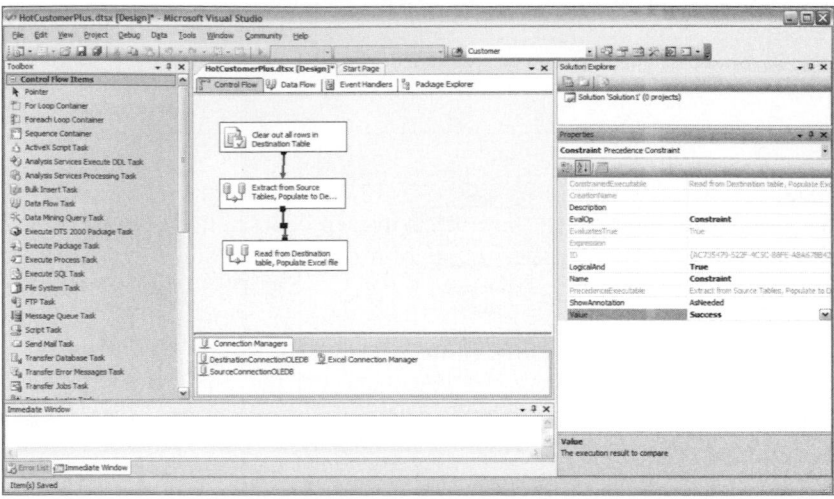

FIGURE 40.39   Control of flow between the old data flow and the new data flow tasks.

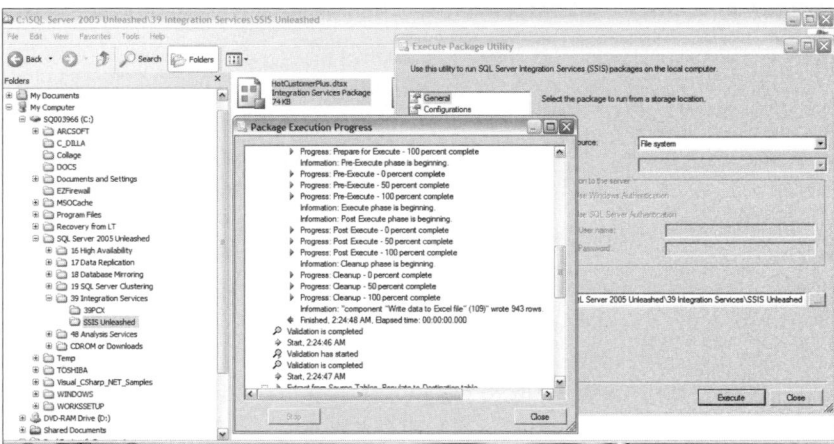

FIGURE 40.40   Executing the SSIS package.

> **NOTE**
>
> You could also execute this new package by using the `dtexec` utility at a command prompt:
>
> ```
> C:> dtexec /FILE "C:\HotCustomerPlus.dtsx"
> ```

The Package Execution Utility

The `dtsrun` utility in SQL Server 2000 is no longer used within SQL Server 2005. It has been taken over by the `dtexec` utility, which is bigger and better and has more options and values to serve your every SSIS package execution need. Before you begin to use the `dtexec` utility, you should execute it at a command prompt with the help option set only and pipe the results into a text file:

```
c:> dtexec /? > dtexec.txt
```

You will quickly see all the main options and how similar this is to `dtsrun` (in SQL Server 2000). Some `dtsrun` command-line options have direct `dtexec` equivalents, such as the options for providing a server name or package name or for setting the value of a variable. Other `dtsrun` command-line options don't have direct `dtexec` equivalents. In addition, there are some new `dtexec` command-line options that support new features in SSIS, such as the options to pass in connection strings and to manage checkpoints.

You can create new command-line `dtexec` executions visually with the assistance of the Package Execution utility, which you open through `dtexecui`. This GUI displays all the available options and ensures the use of the correct syntax (see Figure 40.41). You start it up from the command prompt:

```
c:> dtexecui
```

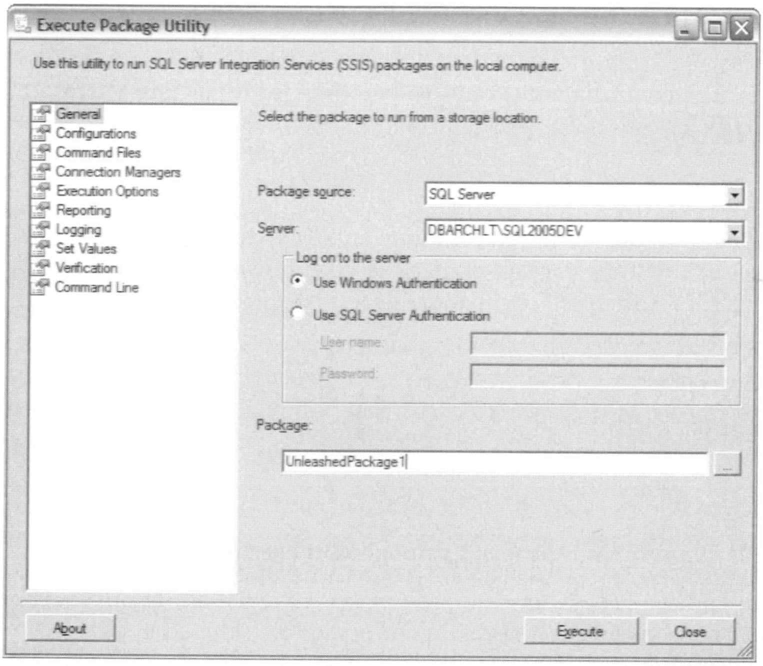

FIGURE 40.41   The user interface for executing and configuring SSIS packages.

Using this Package Execution utility is really the best way to create new command-line executions for SSIS packages and to run them easily. Figure 40.42 shows the Package Execution Progress console during a package execution. You can choose to stop the execution from here.

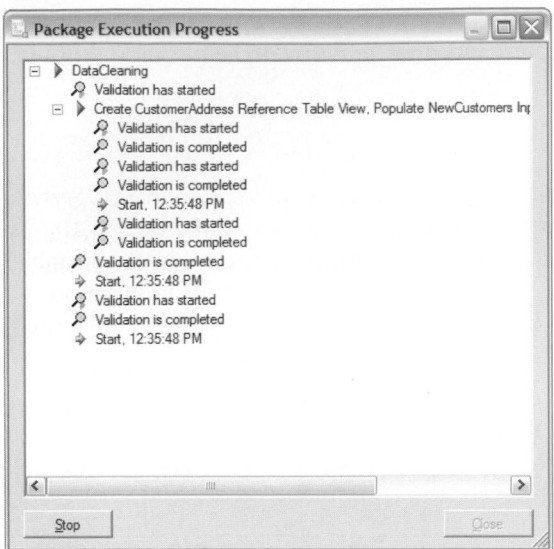

FIGURE 40.42   The Package Execution Progress console in the Execute Package utility.

When you double-click any filesystem stored SSIS package (that is, `.dtsx` file), you are always placed in this `dtexecui` environment (just as you automatically start up Microsoft Word when you double-click a Word document).

The `dtexec` Utility

You use the `dtexec` command prompt utility to configure and execute SSIS packages. The `dtexec` utility provides access to all the package configuration and execution features, such as connections, properties, variables, logging, and progress indicators. The `dtexec` utility lets you load packages from three sources:

▶ A Microsoft SQL Server database

▶ The SSIS service (package store)

▶ The filesystem itself

The `dtexec` utility has four phases that it proceeds through as it executes:

1. **Command sourcing phase**—The command prompt reads the list of options and arguments that have been specified. All subsequent phases are skipped if a `/?` or `/H[ELP]` option is encountered.

2. **Package loading phase**—The package specified by the `/SQL`, `/FILE`, or `/DTS` option is loaded.

3. **Configuration phase**—These options are processed in the following order: Process options that set package flags, variables, and properties; process options that verify

the package version and build; and process options that configure the runtime behavior of the utility, such as reporting.

4. **Validation and execution phase**—The package is run or validated without running if the /VALIDATE option was specified.

When a package runs, dtexec can return an exit code. The exit code is used to populate the ERRORLEVEL variable—the value of which can then be tested in conditional statements or branching logic within an operating system batch file. The dtexec utility can set the following exit code values:

Exit Code Value	Description
0	Successful package execution.
1	Package execution failure.
3	User-cancelled package execution.
4	Package could not be found.
5	Package could not be loaded.
6	Utility encountered an internal error.

Running Packages

The dtexec options are additive. Depending on what you are trying to do, you will string one or more options and their values together in the form indicated in the following:

```
dtexec /option [value] [/option [value]] ...
```

Showing available options for dtexec is done using '/?' or '/H' or '/Help'. Or you can see the details for a particular option by using the available options indicator followed by the option name ('/? [option name]). This will invoke SQL Server Books online for that particular option.

Note that - may be substituted for /.

The dtexec package execution options include the following:

▶ **/~CheckF[ile] filespec**—This option sets the CheckpointFileName property on the package to the path and file specified in filespec. This file is used when the package restarts.

▶ **/~CheckP[ointing]{on\off}**—The value on specifies that a failed package is to be rerun. When the failed package is rerun, the runtime engine uses the checkpoint file to restart the package from the point of failure. The default value is on if the option is declared without a value. Package execution fails if the value is set to on and the checkpoint file cannot be found. If this option is not specified, the value set in the package is retained.

40

> **NOTE**
>
> Using the /CheckPointing on option of dtexec is equivalent to setting the SaveCheckpoints property of the package to True and the CheckpointUsage property to Always.

▶ **/~Com[mandFile] filespec**—This option specifies that during the command sourcing phase of the utility, the file specified in filespec is opened, and options from the file are read until the EOF is found in the file. filespec is a text file that contains additional dtexec command options. The filespec argument specifies the filename and path of the command file to associate with the execution of the package.

▶ **/~Conf[igFile] filespec**—This option specifies a configuration file to extract values from. Using this option, you can set a runtime configuration that differs from the configuration specified for the package at design time.

▶ **/~Conn[ection] id_or_name;connection_string [[;id_or_name;connection_string]...]**—This option specifies the specific connection manager name or GUID and the specific connection string to use. This option requires that both parameters be specified.

▶ **/~Cons[oleLog] [[*displayoptions*];[*list_options*;*src_name_or_guid*]...]**—This option displays specified log entries to the console during package execution.

The *displayoptions* values are N (name), C (computer), O (operator), S (source name), G (source GUID), X (execution GUID), M (message), and T (time start and end).

One *list_options* value is I, which specifies the inclusion list. With this value set, only the source names or GUIDs that are specified are logged. The value E specifies the exclusion list. The source names or GUIDs that are specified are not logged. The *src_name_or_guid* parameter specified for inclusion or exclusion is an event name, a source name, or a source GUID.

▶ **/~D[ts] package_path**—This option is used to load a package from the SSIS package store. The package_path argument specifies the relative path of the SSIS package, starting at the root of the SSIS package store, and includes the name of the SSIS package. The /DTS option cannot be used together with the /File or /SQL option.

▶ **/~De[crypt] password**—This option provides the decryption password that is used when you load a package with password encryption.

▶ **/~F[ile] *filespec***—This option is used to load a package that is saved at the filesystem level. The *filespec* argument specifies the path and filename of the package.

▶ **/~L[ogger]** *classid_orprogid*;*configstring*—This option associates one or more log providers with the execution of an SSIS package. The *classid_orprogid* parameter specifies the log provider and can be specified as a class GUID. *configstring* is the string that is used to configure the log provider.

The following are the available log providers:

```
Text file:
 ProgID: DTS.LogProviderTextFile.1
 ClassID: {59B2C6A5-663F-4C20-8863-C83F9B72E2EB}
SQL Server Profiler:
 ProgID: DTS.LogProviderSQLProfiler.1
 ClassID: {5C0B8D21-E9AA-462E-BA34-30FF5F7A42A1}
SQL Server:
 ProgID: DTS.LogProviderSQLServer.1
 ClassID: {6AA833A1-E4B2-4431-831B-DE695049DC61}
Windows Event Log:
 ProgID: DTS.LogProviderEventLog.1
 ClassID: {97634F75-1DC7-4F1F-8A4C-DAF0E13AAA22}
XML File:
 ProgID: DTS.LogProviderXMLFile.1
 ClassID: {AFED6884-619C-484F-9A09-F42D56E1A7EA}
```

▶ **/~M[axConcurrent]** **concurrent_executables**—This option is used to identify the number of executable files the package can run concurrently. The value specified must be either a non-negative integer or –1. With a value of –1, SSIS allows a maximum number of concurrently running executables that is equal to the total number of processors on the computer executing the package, plus two.

▶ **/~P[assword]** **password**—This option is used together with the /User option to retrieve the package from SQL Server. If the /Password option is omitted and the /User option is used, a blank password is used.

▶ **/~Rem** **comment**—This option creates a comment on the command prompt or in command files. The comment is a string that must be enclosed in quotation marks, and it must contain no whitespace.

▶ **/~Rep[orting]** **level** **[;event_guid_or_name[;event_guid_or_name[...]]**—This option identifies what types of messages to report. Available reporting option levels are N (no reporting), E (errors are reported), W (warnings are reported), I (informational messages are reported), C (custom events are reported), D (data flow task events are reported), P (progress is reported), and V (verbose reporting; all details of each type). If the /Reporting option is not specified, the default level is E, W, and P.

▶ **/~Res[tart]** **{deny ¦ force ¦ ifPossible}**— This is how you set a new value for the CheckpointUsage property on the package. The possible values are Deny (sets the CheckpointUsage property to DTSCU_NEVER), Force (sets the CheckpointUsage property to DTSCU_ALWAYS), and ifPossible (sets the CheckpointUsage property to DTSCU_IFEXISTS).

40

▶ **/~Set propertyPath;value**—This option overrides the configuration of a variable, property, container, log provider, Foreach enumerator, or connection within a package. When this option is used, /SET changes the propertyPath argument to the value specified. You can specify more than one /SET option at a time.

▶ **/~Ser[ver] server**—This option identifies the name of the server from which to retrieve the package. If you do not specify the /Server option, the package execution is attempted against the local server.

▶ **/~SQ[L] package_path**—This option is used to load a package that is stored in SQL Server (in the msdb database).

▶ **/~Su[m]**—This option displays the incremental counter that contains the number of rows that will be received by the next package component.

▶ **/~U[ser] user_name**—This option identifies the SQL Server user ID needed to retrieve the package.

▶ **/~Va[lidate]**—This option is used to complete the validation phase of package execution only. The package will not be executed.

▶ **/~VerifyB[uild] major[;minor[;build]]**—This option is a verification of the build number of a package against the build numbers specified during the verification phase in the major, minor, and build arguments. If a mismatch occurs, the package will not execute. These values are long integers.

▶ **/~VerifyP[ackageID] packageID**—This option verifies the GUID of the package to be executed by comparing it to the value specified in the package_id argument.

▶ **/~VerifyS[igned]**—If specified, this option causes the package to fail if the package is not signed.

▶ **/~VerifyV[ersionID] versioned**—This option verifies the version GUID of a package to be executed by comparing it to the value specified in the version_id argument during package validation phase.

▶ **/~W[arnAsError]**—This option cause the package to consider a warning as an error. In other words, the package will fail if a warning occurs during validation. If no warnings occur during validation and the /Validate option is not specified, the package is executed.

Running Package Examples

To execute an SSIS package saved to SQL Server using Windows authentication, you use the following code:

```
dtexec /SQL UnleashedPackage1SQL /SER DBARCHLT\SQL2005DEV
```

To execute an SSIS package saved to the package store (on the filesystem), you use the following code:

```
dtexec /DTS "\File System\UnleashedPackage99PS"
```

To execute an SSIS package that is saved in the filesystem, you use the following code:

```
dtexec /FILE "C:\Program Files\Microsoft SQL Server\90\Samples\Integration

    Services\Package Samples\DataCleaning Sample\DataCleaning\DataCleaning.dtsx"

    /MAXCONCURRENT " -1 " /CHECKPOINTING OFF   /REPORTING EWCDI
```

Figure 40.43 shows the command prompt and subsequent execution of the HotCustomersPlus.dtsx SSIS package. Now, the package can be set up for regular batch execution using SQL Agent or any scheduling software.

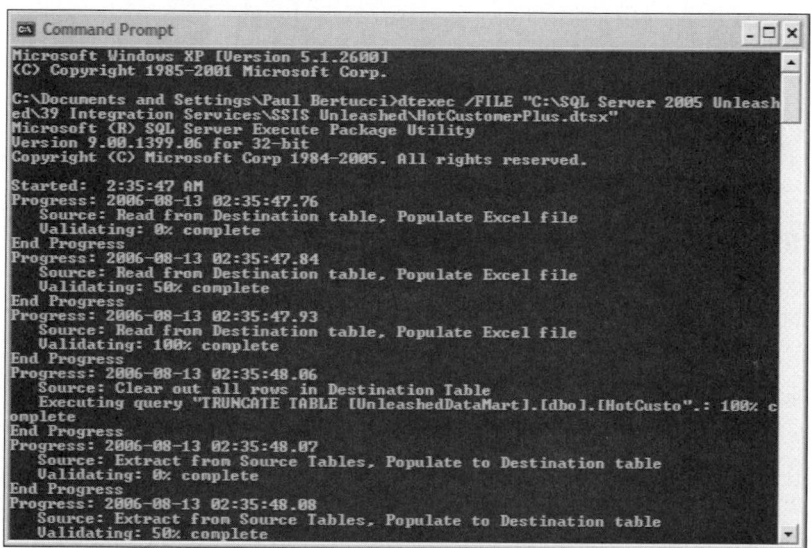

FIGURE 40.43   Command-line execution of an SSIS package.

To execute an SSIS package that is saved in the filesystem and specify logging options, you use the following code:

```
dtexec /FILE "C:\Program Files\Microsoft SQL Server\90\Samples\Integration
    Services\Package Samples\DataCleaning Sample\DataCleaning\DataCleaning.dtsx"
    /l "DTS.LogProviderTextFile;c:\log.txt"
```

To execute a package that uses Windows authentication and is saved to the default local instance of SQL Server, and to verify the version before it is executed, you use the following code:

```
dtexec /sq UnleashedPackage1 /verifyv {b399e360-38c5-11c5-99x1-ae62-08002b2b79ef}
```

To execute a package from SQL Server via the command shell, you use the following code:

```
DECLARE @returncode int
EXEC @returncode = xp_cmdshell 'dtexec /FILE "C:\Program Files\Microsoft SQL
    Server\90\Samples\Integration Services\Package Samples\DataCleaning
    Sample\DataCleaning\DataCleaning.dtsx" '
```

The following are some additional notes on using `dtexec`:

▶ ~ is optional; if it is present, the parameter is hex text of the encrypted value (for example, 0x313233...).

▶ Whitespace between the command switch and value is optional.

▶ Embedded whitespace in values must be surrounded by double-quotes.

▶ If an option is specified multiple times, the last one wins (except multiple /A options).

The `dtutil` Utility

You use the `dtutil` command prompt utility to copy, move, delete, or verify the existence of a package. These actions can be performed on any SSIS package, regardless of whether it is stored in a Microsoft SQL Server database, the SSIS package store, or at the filesystem.

The `dtutil` options are additive. Depending on what you are trying to do, you will string one or more options and their values together in the form indicated in the following:

```
dtutil /option [value] [/option [value]] ...
```

Showing available options for `dtutil` is done using '/?' or '/H' or '/Help'. Or, you can see the details for a particular option by using the available options indicator followed by the option name ('/?' [option name]). This will invoke SQL Server Books online for that particular option

```
c:> dtutil /?
```

Note that a dash (-) may be substituted for / in this command.

The `dtutil` options include the following:

▶ **/~C[opy][StorageLocation];[PackageName]**—This option identifies where the package is to be stored (`StorageLocation` value of `DTS`, `FILE`, or `SQL`) and the full destination path and filename of the package (`PackageName`). When the `Copy` action encounters an existing package at the destination, `dtutil` prompts the user to confirm package deletion. Y overwrites the package, and N aborts the overwrite of the destination package. If you include the /Q (quiet) option, no prompt appears, and the existing destination package is overwritten.

▶ **/~Dec[rypt] Password**—This option sets the decryption password used when loading a package with password encryption.

▶ **/~Del[ete]**—This option deletes the package specified by the SQL, DTS, or FILE option.

▶ **/~DestP[assword] Password**—This option specifies the password used with the SQL option to connect to a destination SQL Server instance using SQL Server authentication.

▶ **/~DestS[erver] Server**—This option specifies the server name used with any action that causes a destination to be saved to SQL Server or a non-local or non-default server when saving an SSIS package.

▶ **/~DestU[ser] User name**—This option specifies the SQL Server username at the destination SQL Server instance.

▶ **/~DT[S] PackagePath**—This option specifies that the SSIS package referenced is located in the SSIS package store, and the PackagePath argument is a relative path that commences at the root of the SSIS package store.

▶ **/~En[crypt] [StorageLocation];[;Path;ProtectionLevel[;Password]**—This option encrypts the loaded package with the specified protection level and password and saves it to the location specified in Path. StorageLocation types are DTS, FILE, and SQL. ProtectionLevel determines whether a password is required.

The possible ProtectionLevels values are 0 (strips sensitive information), 1 (sensitive information is encrypted using local user credentials), 2 (sensitive information is encrypted using the required password), 3 (package is encrypted using the required password), 4 (package is encrypted using local user credentials), and 5 (package uses SQL Server storage encryption).

▶ **/~Ex[ists]**—This option is used to determine whether a package exists.

▶ **/~FC[reate] [StorageLocation];FolderPath;NewFolderName**—This option creates a new folder that has the name specified by NewFolderName. StorageLocation is SQL or DTS only. The location of the new folder is indicated by FolderPath.

▶ **/~FDe[lete] [StorageLocation] ExistingFolderPath;ExistingFolderName**—This option deletes the folder specified by the name in ExistingFolderName from SQL Server (SQL) or SSIS (DTS). StorageLocation is SQL or DTS only. The location of the folder to delete is indicated by ExistingFolderPath.

▶ **/~FDi[rectory] [StorageLocation] FolderPath[;S]]**—This option lists the contents, both folders and packages, in a folder on SSIS (DTS) or SQL Server (SQL). The optional ExistingFolderPath parameter specifies the folder whose contents you want to view. StorageLocation is SQL or DTS only. The optional S parameter specifies that you want to view a listing of the contents of the subfolders for the folder specified in ExistingFolderPath.

40

▶ **/~FE[xists] [StorageLocation] ExistingFolderPath**—This option verifies whether the specified folder exists on SSIS (DTS) or SQL Server (SQL). The ExistingFolderPath parameter is the path and name of the folder to verify the existence of. StorageLocation is SQL or DTS only.

▶ **/~FR[ename] [StorageLocation]; ExistingFolderPath; ExistingFolderName; NewFolderName**—This option renames a folder on the SSIS (DTS) or SQL Server (SQL). StorageLocation is SQL or DTS only. The ExistingFolderPath is the location (path) of the folder to rename. The ExistingFolderName is the name of the folder to be renamed, and NewFolderName is the new name to give the folder.

▶ **/~Fi≤ PathName**—This option specifies that the SSIS package to be operated on is located in the filesystem, and the PathName value contains either a universal naming convention (UNC) path or local path.

▶ **/~I[DRegenerate]**—This option creates a new GUID for the package and updates the package ID property.

▶ **/~M[ove] [StorageLocation]; PathandName**—This option specifies a move action for an SSIS package. StorageLocation may be DTS, FILE, or SQL. PathandName indicates the package path (location) and/or package name: SQL uses the package path and package name, FILE uses a UNC or local path, and DTS uses a location that is relative to the root of the SSIS package store. If there is an existing package at the destination with the same name, dtutil prompts you to answer Y to overwrite this existing package or N to not do the move. If you specify the /Q (quiet) option, no prompt appears when an existing package may exist at the move destination, and it will just be overwritten.

▶ **/~Q[uiet]**—This option disables the Y/N prompts when a package with the same name as the specified package already exists at the destination location or if the specified package is already signed.

▶ **/~R[emark] [Text]**—This option is a comment to the command line. There can be multiple remarks in a command line.

▶ **/~Si[gn] [StorageLocation]; ExistingPath; Hash**—This option signs an SSIS package. StorageLocation may be DTS, FILE, or SQL. ExistingPath specifies the path (location) of the package that is to be signed. Hash specifies a certificate identifier expressed as a hexadecimal string of varying length.

▶ **/~SourceP[assword] Password**—This option provides the password used with the SQL and SOURCEUSER options to connect to a SQL Server instance that uses SQL Server authentication.

▶ **/~SourceS[erver] Server**—This option provides the name of the server where the package is to be stored.

▶ **/~SourceU[ser] User Name**—This option provides the SQL Server username to use to access the SSIS package.

▶ **/~SQ[L] PathName**—This option specifies the path (location) of the SSIS package stored in the msdb database.

Next, let's look at various examples of running dtutil.

dtutil **examples**

The following example copies an existing package in SQL to the SSIS package store:

```
C:> Dtutil /SQL ExistingPackage /COPY DTS;destPackage
```

The following example copies an existing package from one location on the filesystem to another location on the filesystem:

```
C:> dtutil /FILE c:\Unleashed\HotCustomersPlus.dtsx /COPY
    FILE;c:\UnleashedProduction\HotCustomersPlus.dtsx
```

The following example creates a new GUID (usually after you copy a package):

```
C:> dtutil /I /FILE HotCustomersPlus.dtsx
```

The following example deletes a package that is stored in the local server (msdb database):

```
C:> dtutil /SQL HotCustomersPlus /SOURCEUSER PBertucci
    /SOURCEPASSWORD xyz   /DELETE
```

The following example deletes a package that is stored in the filesystem:

```
c:> dtutil /FILE c:\UnleashedProduction\HotCustomersPlus.dtsx /DELETE
```

The following example verifies whether a package exists in a local server (msdb database):

```
C:> dtutil SQL HotCustomersPlus /SOURCEUSER Pbertucci /SOURCEPASSWORD xyz /EXISTS
```

The following example verifies whether a package exists on the local filesystem:

```
C:> dtutil /FILE c:\UnleashedProduction\HotCustomersPlus.dtsx /EXISTS
```

The following example moves a package from one server (msdb database) to another server (msdb database):

```
C:> dtutil /SQL HotCustomersPlus /SOURCEUSER Pbertucci
    /SOURCEPASSWORD xyz /MOVE SQL;HotCustomersPlus
    /DESTUSER sa /DESTPASSWORD zwx
```

The following example moves a package from one filesystem location to another:

```
c:> dtutil /FILE c:\Unleashed\HotCustomersPlus.dtsx /MOVE
    FILE;c:\UnleashedProduction\HotCustomersPlus.dtsx
```

40

The following example signs a package on the filesystem:

```
dtutil /FILE c:\Unleashed\HotCustomersPlus.dtsx /SIGN FILE;
    c:\Unleashed\HotCustomersPlus.dtsx;987377773999af33df399999333
```

Using bcp

As you have seen in this chapter, it is fairly easy to create and implement SSIS packages to do data transformations from one or more data sources to one or more data destinations. However, there are still many organizations that really just need a vanilla and very fast mechanism to export data out of SQL Server or import data into SQL Server. bcp fills this need well (and has done so from the beginning of SQL Server bcp).

The following sections outline the primary initiation methods of bcp, bcp's many switches, the format file, and ways to improve performance when using bcp. By the end of these sections, you will be able to optimally execute bcp successfully for several common production scenarios. Microsoft has added a new execution switch that generates an XML format file. Most other features of bcp have remained the same, though.

First, you need to see if you have the right version of bcp. A quick check of your version of bcp guarantees that you won't run into any limitations from older versions of bcp that might be left on your servers. You can do this by executing bcp at the command prompt with the -v option and no other parameters. (Note that all bcp switch options are case-sensitive; for example, -v and -V are two very different switches.) Here's an example:

```
C:> bcp -v
BCP - Bulk Copy Program for Microsoft SQL Server.
Copyright (c) 1991-1998, Microsoft Corp. All Rights Reserved.
Version: 9.00.1399.06
```

Yes, this is version 9.0 that is distributed with MS SQL Server 2005 (SQL Server 9.0). If a version other than 9.x is present here, you must re-install bcp immediately.

At any time, you can see the proper usage and bcp switch options that are available by executing bcp at the command prompt with a question mark (?):

```
C:> bcp ?
usage: bcp {dbtable ¦ query} {in ¦ out ¦ queryout ¦ format} datafile
[-m maxerrors]              [-f formatfile]          [-e errfile]
. . .
```

You use the following syntax for bcp, along with one or more switches:

```
bcp {dbtable ¦ query} {in ¦ out ¦ queryout ¦ format} datafile
```

In this syntax, *dbtable* is the *database_name*, *schema*, and *table_name* ¦ *view_name* (for example, AdventureWorks.Production.Product or "AdventureWorks.Production. Product"):

▶ *database_name*—This is the name of the database in which the specified table or view resides. If not specified, this is the default database for the user.

▶ *owner*—This is the name of the schema of the table or view.

▶ *table_name* | *view_name*—This is the name of the destination table or view when copying data into SQL Server (in), and it is the name of the source table when copying data from SQL Server (out).

query is a T-SQL query that returns a result set. queryout must also be specified when bulk-copying data from a query.

in ¦ out ¦ queryout ¦ format Specifies the direction of the bulk copy (in copies from a file in to the database table or view, out copies from the database table or view to a file). queryout must be specified when bulk-copying data from a query. format creates a format file based on the switch specified (-n, -c, -w, -V, or -N) and the table or view delimiters. If format is used, the -f option must be specified as well.

data_file is the data file used when bulk-copying a table or view into or out of SQL Server.

All the available bcp switches are listed in Table 40.1.

TABLE 40.1   bcp Switches

Switch	Description	Example
-m	Specifies the maximum number of errors to allow before stopping the transfer. The default is 10.	[-m *max_errors*]
-f	Specifies the format file used to customize the load or unload data in a specific style.	[-f *format_file*]
-e	Specifies the file to write error messages to.	[-e *err_file*]
-F	Specifies the first row in the data file to start copying from when importing. The default is 1.	[-F *first_row*]
-L	Specifies the last row in the data file to end copying with when importing. The default is 0, which indicates the last row in the file.	[-L *last_row*]
-b	Specifies the number of rows to include in each committed batch. By default, all data rows in a file are copied in one batch.	[-b *batch_size*]
-n	Specifies that native (database) data type formats are to be used for the data.	[-n]
-c	Specifies that character data type format is to be used for the data. In addition, \t (tab character) is used as the field separator, and \n (newline character) is used as the row terminator.	[-c]
-w	Specifies that the Unicode data type format is to be used for the data. In addition, \t (tab character) is used as the field separator, and \n (newline character) is used as the row terminator.	[-w]

40

TABLE 40.1   Continued

Switch	Description	Example
-N	Specifies to use Unicode for character data and native format for all others. This can be used as an alternative to the -w switch.	[-N]
-V	Specifies to use data type formats from earlier versions of SQL Server.	[-V (60 ¦ 65 ¦ 70 ¦ 80)]
-q	Tells bcp to use quoted identifiers when dealing with table and column names.	[-q]
-C	If you are loading extended characters, allows you to specify the code page of the data in the data file.	[-C code_page]
-t	Specifies the terminating character(s) for fields. The default is \t (tab character).	[-t field_term]
-r	Specifies the terminating character(s) for rows. The default is \n (newline character).	[-r row_term]
-i	Specifies a file for redirecting input into bcp (the response file containing the responses to the command prompts).	[-i input_file]
-o	Specifies the file for receiving redirected output from bcp.	[-o output_file]
-a	Specifies the network packet size (in bytes) used to send to or receive from SQL Server. Can be between 4,096 and 65,535 bytes. The default size is 4,096.	[-a packet_size]
-S	Specifies the SQL Server name to connect to. Local is the default.	[-S server_name ¦ server_name\ instance_name]
-U	Specifies the user account to log in as; this account must have sufficient privileges to carry out either a read or a write of the table.	[-U login_id]
-P	Specifies the password associated with the user account.	[-P password]
-T	Makes a trusted connection to the server, using the network user/security credentials instead of the login_id/password.	[-T]
-v	Displays the bcp version information.	[-v]
-R	Uses the regional format for currency, date, and time data, as defined by the locale settings of the client computer.	[-R]
-k	Overrides a column's default and enforces NULL values being loaded into the columns as part of the bcp operation.	[-k]
-E	Uses the identity values in the import file rather than generating new ones.	[-E]
-h	Specifies special hints to be used during the bcp operation. These include the following: the sort order of the data file, the number of rows of data per batch, the number of kilobytes of data per batch, whether to acquire a table-level lock, whether to check constraints, and whether to fire insert triggers.	[-h hint_type,..]
-x	Generates an XML format file.	[-x]

Fundamentals of Exporting and Importing Data

One of the great things about bcp is its ease of use. This section runs through a couple simple examples and provides full explanations. All tables used here can be found in the AdventureWorks sample database supplied by Microsoft in SQL Server 2005.

Let's start by exporting product data from AdventureWorks that may be needed by a sales team for reference in Excel format (a .csv file). To do this, you simply export the Product table data into a comma-delimited file. You need to specify the following with bcp in this case:

- ▶ The full table name (in this case, AdventureWorks.Production.Product)

- ▶ The direction of bcp (OUT in this case because it is exporting data out)

- ▶ Data filename to hold the exported data (in this case, products.dat)

- ▶ The server name DBARCHLT\SQL2005DEV for this example (in this case, -S DBARCHLT\SQL2005DEV)

- ▶ The username SA (in this case, -U sa)

- ▶ The password (in this case, -P xyz)

- ▶ A comma as the column delimiter (in this case, -t ",")

- ▶ That this should be exported in character data format (in this case, -c)

At the command prompt, you execute the following:

```
C:> BCP AdventureWorks.Production.Product OUT products.dat
    -S DBARCHLT\SQL2005DEV -U sa
-P xyz -t "," -c
Starting copy...

504 rows copied.
Network packet size (bytes): 4096
Clock Time (ms.):  total: 10   Average: (50400.00 rows per sec.)
```

Here's a sample of the data in the Products.dat file that was just exported:

```
1,Adjustable Race,AR-5381,0,0,,
2,Bearing Ball,BA-8327,0,0,,
3,BB Ball Bearing,BE-2349,1,0,,
4,Headset Ball Bearings,BE-2908,0,0,,
. . .
```

Now let's look at importing data into SQL Server 2005.

Say that each salesperson is providing a flat file that contains his or her new sales orders. These files are emailed to a person in the ordering department and need to be imported into SQL Server every week. The file that you will import will be a comma-delimited file

40

(.csv) that the salesperson created using Excel. The new sales order (sales order header) rows will have a sales order ID automatically assigned when the data is inserted into that table. A sample input data file (named BCPSalesOrders.csv) is included on the Sams website for this book title (www.samspublishing.com).

You need to specify the following with bcp in this case:

▶ The full table name (in this case, AdventureWorks.Sales.SalesOrderHeader).

▶ The direction of bcp (IN in this case because it is importing data).

▶ The names of the data files that contain the import data (in this case, BCPSalesOrders.csv).The following is a sample of the input data file (BCPSalesOrders.csv):

```
,1,2006-07-01,2006-07-13,,5,0,,PO522145787,10-4020-000676,
,1,2006-07-31,2006-08-12,,5,0,,PO522145787,10-4030-018759,
,1,2006-07-31,2006-08-12,,5,0,,PO522145787,10-4030-018759,
,1,2006-07-31,2006-08-12,,5,0,,PO522145787,10-4030-018759,
. . .
```

▶ The server name (in this case, -S DBARCHLT\SQL2005DEV)

▶ The username SA (in this case, -U sa).

▶ The password (in this case, -P xyz).

▶ A comma as the column delimiter (in this case, -t ",").

▶ That this should be exported in character data format (in this case, -c).

▶ The -q option (in this case, -q), to be sure quoted identifiers are handled properly.

At the command prompt, you execute the following:

```
C:> BCP AdventureWorks.Sales.SalesOrderHeader IN BCPSalesOrders.csv
    -S DBARCHLT\SQL20005DEV -U sa -P xyz -t "," -c -q
Starting copy...

24 rows copied.
Network packet size (bytes): 4096
Clock Time (ms.): total : 241  Average : (99.59 rows per sec.)
```

A quick SELECT * from the orders table shows the success of this operation:

```
1000025 1   2006-07-31 00:00:00.000   2006-08-12 00:00:00.000   NULL   5
1000026 1   2006-07-31 00:00:00.000   2006-08-12 00:00:00.000   NULL   5
1000027 1   2006-07-31 00:00:00.000   2006-08-12 00:00:00.000   NULL   5
. . .
```

The sales team can now send in their sales orders as they make sales. This brief example illustrates the beauty and power of using bcp.

The next sections look at how bcp can work with basic data representations (character, native, or Unicode), the use of a format file, and a few other extended bcp capabilities.

File Data Types

bcp can handle data in one of three forms: character (ASCII), native, or Unicode. You have the choice of which character format is used, depending on the source or destination of the data file:

▶ The character format (–c) is the most commonly used of the three data types because it reads or writes using ASCII characters and carries out the appropriate data type conversion for the SQL Server representations. The CHAR data type is the default storage type; it uses tabs as field separators and the newline character as the row terminator.

▶ The native format (–n) is used for copying data between servers. This format allows bcp to read and write using the same data types used by server, which results in a performance gain. This format does, however, render the data file unreadable by any other means.

▶ The Unicode option (–w) uses Unicode characters rather than ASCII characters. The NCHAR data type is the default storage type; it uses tabs as field separators and the newline character as the row terminator.

Format Files

By using a format file, you can customize the data file created by bcp or specify complex field layouts for data loads. There are two ways to create a format file: by using interactive bcp and by using the format switch.

Customizing a Format File by Using Interactive bcp

If you do not specify one of the –n, –c, or –w data type format switches, bcp (in or out) prompts you for the following information for each column in the data set:

▶ File storage type

▶ Prefix length

▶ Field length

▶ Field terminator

40

bcp offers a default for each of these prompts that you can either accept or reject. If you accept all the defaults, you wind up with the same format file you would have by specifying the native format (with the -n switch). The prompts look like this:

```
Enter the file storage type of field au_id [char]:
Enter prefix length of field au_id [0]:
Enter length of field au_id [11]:
Enter field terminator [none]:
```

or like this:

```
Enter the file storage type of field ProductID [int]:
Enter prefix length of field ProductID [0]:
Enter field terminator [none]:
```

By pressing the Enter key at the prompt, you accept the default. Alternatively, you can type your own value at the prompt if you know the new value and it is different from the default.

Creating a Format File by Using the format Switch

By using the format option, you can create a format file without actually transferring any data. Here is an example of creating a format file for the SalesOrderHeader table in the AdventureWorks database:

```
C:> BCP AdventureWorks.Sales.SalesOrderHeader format orders.dat
    -S DBARCHLT\SQL20005DEV
        -U sa -P xyz -f orders.fmt -c
```

The format file created looks like this:

```
9.0
27
1  SQLCHAR    0   12   ""\t""   1    SalesOrderID          ""
2  SQLCHAR    0   5    ""\t""   2    RevisionNumber        ""
3  SQLCHAR    0   24   ""\t""   3    OrderDate             ""
4  SQLCHAR    0   24   ""\t""   4    DueDate               ""
5  SQLCHAR    0   24   ""\t""   5    ShipDate              ""
6  SQLCHAR    0   5    ""\t""   6    Status                ""
7  SQLCHAR    0   3    ""\t""   7    OnlineOrderFlag       ""
8  SQLCHAR    0   50   ""\t""   8    SalesOrderNumber      SQL_...
9  SQLCHAR    0   50   ""\t""   9    PurchaseOrderNumber   SQL_...
10 SQLCHAR    0   30   ""\t""   10   AccountNumber         SQL_...
11 SQLCHAR    0   12   ""\t""   11   CustomerID            ""
12 SQLCHAR    0   12   ""\t""   12   ContactID             ""
13 SQLCHAR    0   12   ""\t""   13   SalesPersonID         ""
14 SQLCHAR    0   12   ""\t""   14   TerritoryID           ""
15 SQLCHAR    0   12   ""\t""   15   BillToAddressID       ""
```

16 SQLCHAR	0	12	""\t""	16	ShipToAddressID	""
17 SQLCHAR	0	12	""\t""	17	ShipMethodID	""
18 SQLCHAR	0	12	""\t""	18	CreditCardID	""
19 SQLCHAR	0	15	""\t""	19	CreditCardApprovalCode	SQL_...
20 SQLCHAR	0	12	""\t""	20	CurrencyRateID	""
21 SQLCHAR	0	30	""\t""	21	SubTotal	""
22 SQLCHAR	0	30	""\t""	22	TaxAmt	""
23 SQLCHAR	0	30	""\t""	23	Freight	""
24 SQLCHAR	0	30	""\t""	24	TotalDue	""
25 SQLCHAR	0	256	""\t""	25	Comment	SQL_...
26 SQLCHAR	0	37	""\t""	26	rowguid	""
27 SQLCHAR	0	24	""\r\n""	27	ModifiedDate	""

The following is a description of the lines and columns in the preceding format file example:

▶ The first line shows the version of bcp.

▶ The second line shows the number of columns.

▶ The third line, first column shows the data field position.

▶ The third line, second column shows the data type.

▶ The third line, third column shows the prefix.

▶ The third line, fourth column shows the data file field length.

▶ The third line, fifth column shows the field or row terminator.

▶ The third line, sixth column shows the column position.

▶ The third line, seventh column shows the column name.

▶ The third line, eighth column shows the column collation.

You get different format files depending on your table and whether you chose character, native, or Unicode as the data type. As you can see in the preceding example, only the last two columns in the format file relate to the actual table; the remaining columns specify properties of the data file.

File Storage Types

The storage type is a description of how the data is stored in the data file. Table 40.2 lists the definitions used during interactive bcp and what appears in the format file. The storage type allows data to be copied as its base type (native format), as implicitly converted between types (tinyint to smallint), or as a string (in character or Unicode format).

40

TABLE 40.2   Storage Data Types

File Storage Type	Interactive Prompt	Host File Data Type
char	c[har]	SQLCHAR
varchar	c[har]	SQLCHAR
nchar	w	SQLNCHAR
nvarchar	w	SQLNCHAR
text	T[ext]	SQLCHAR
ntext	W	SQLNCHAR
binary	x	SQLBINARY
varbinary	x	SQLBINARY
image	I[mage]	SQLBINARY
datetime	d[ate]	SQLDATETIME
smalldatetime	D	SQLDATETIM4
decimal	n	SQLDECIMAL
numeric	n	SQLNUMERIC
float	f[loat]	SQLFLT8
real	r	SQLFLT4
int	i[nt]	SQLINT
smallint	s[mallint]	SQLSMALLINT
tinyint	t[inyint]	SQLTINYINT
money	m[oney]	SQLMONEY
smallmoney	M	SQLMONEY4
bit	b[it]	SQLBIT
uniqueidentifier	u	SQLUNIQUEID
timestamp	x	SQLBINARY

NOTE

If the table makes use of user-defined data types, these customized data types appear in the format file as their base data type.

If you are having problems loading certain fields into your table, you can try the following tricks:

▶ Copy the data in as char data types and force SQL Server to do the conversion for you.

▶ Duplicate the table and replace all the SQL Server data types with char or varchar of a length sufficient to hold the value. This trick allows you to further manipulate the data with T-SQL after it is loaded.

Prefix Lengths

To maintain compactness in native data files, bcp precedes each field with a prefix length that indicates the length of the data stored. The space for storing this information is specified in characters and is called the *prefix length*.

Table 40.3 indicates the value to specify for prefix length for each of the data types.

TABLE 40.3   Prefix Length Values

Prefix Length	Data Types to Use
0	Non-null data of type bit or numerics (int, real, and so on). Use this value when no prefix characters are wanted. This value causes the field to be padded with spaces to the size indicated for the field length.
1	Non-null data of type binary or varbinary or null data, with the exception of text, ntext, and image. Use this value for any data (except bit, binary, varbinary, text, ntext, and image) that you want stored using a character-based data type.
2	When storing the data types binary or varbinary as character-based data types, 2 bytes of char file storage and 4 bytes of nchar file storage are required for each byte of binary table data.
4	For the data types text, ntext, and image.

Prefix lengths are likely to exist only within data files created using bcp. It is unlikely that you will encounter a reason to change the defaults bcp has chosen for you.

Field Lengths

When using either the native or the character data format, you must specify the maximum length of each field. When converting data types to strings, bcp suggests lengths large enough to store the entire range of values for each particular data type. Table 40.4 lists the default values for each of the data formats.

TABLE 40.4   Default Field Lengths for Data Formats

Data Type	Length (/c)	Length (/n)
bit	1	1
binary	Column length×2	Column length
datetime	24	8
smalldatetime	24	4
float	30	8
real	30	4
int	12	4
smallint	7	2
tinyint	5	1
money	30	8
smallmoney	30	4
decimal	41	up to 17

40

TABLE 39.4   Continued

Data Type	Length (/c)	Length (/n)
numeric	41	up to 17
uniqueidentifier	37	16

NOTE

You must specify a field length that is long enough for the data being stored. bcp error messages regarding overflows indicate that the data value has been truncated in at least one of the fields. If the operation is a load, an overflow error usually results in bcp terminating. However, if you are dumping the data to a file, the data is truncated without error messages.

The field length value is used *only* when the prefix length is 0 and you have specified no terminators. In essence, you are doing a fixed-length data copy. bcp uses exactly amount of space stated by the field length for each field; unused space within the field is padded out.

NOTE

Preexisting spaces in the data are not distinguished from added padding.

Field Terminators

If you are not making use of fixed-width fields or length prefixes, you must use a field terminator to indicate the character(s) that separates fields; for the last field in the data row, you must also indicate which character(s) ends the line.

bcp recognizes the indicators for special characters shown in Table 40.5.

TABLE 40.5   bcp Indicators for Special Characters

Terminator	Escape Code
Tab	\t
Backslash	\\
Null terminator	\0
Newline	\n
Carriage return	\r

You cannot use spaces as terminators, but you can use any other printable characters. You should choose field and row terminators that make sense for your data. Obviously, you should not use any character you are trying to load. You must combine the \r and \n characters to get your data into an ASCII data file with each row on its own line.

> **TIP**
>
> By specifying the −t and −r switches, you can override the defaults that appear for the prompts during interactive bcp.

> **NOTE**
>
> You can specify terminators for data copied in native format. You should be careful if you decide to go this route; the accepted approach is to use lengthy prefixes.

The prefix length, field length, and terminator values interact with one another. In the following examples, T indicates the terminator character(s), P indicates the prefix length, and S indicates space padding.

For data of type char, the data file has the following repeating pattern:

	Prefix Length=0	**Prefix Length=**1, 2, 4
No Terminator	*string*S*string*S	P*string*SP*string*S
Terminator	*string*ST*string*ST	P*string*STP*string*ST

For data of other types converted to char, the data file has the following repeating pattern:

	Prefix Length=0	**Prefix Length=**1, 2, 4
No terminator	*string*S*string*S	P*string*P*string*
Terminator	*string*T*string*T	P*string*TP*string*T

The next few sections examine how to load data into tables when there are differences in column number and layout.

Different Numbers of Columns in a File and a Table

If you want to load data into tables when you have fewer fields in the data file than in the table, you have to "dummy up" an extra line in your format file.

Suppose you want to load a data file that is missing most of the address information for each customer (into a customer table of some kind that has full address columns in it). To do this, you create a format file for this table by using the format option with bcp. With this format file, you can still load this abbreviated data easily. Suppose that the data file looks like this:

```
WELLI   Wellington Importadora   Jane Graham     Sales (14)555-8122
        (14)555-8111
WHITC   White Clover Markets     Donald Bertucci  Owner (206)555-4112
        (206)555-4113
```

To introduce a dummy value for the missing ones, in the format file, you need to make the prefix and data lengths 0 and set the field terminator to nothing (""). The modified format file should look like this:

```
9.0
11
1       SQLCHAR 0   10    "\t"   1   CustomerID      SQL_Latin1_General_
        CP1_CI_AS
2       SQLCHAR 0   80    "\t"   2   CompanyName     SQL_Latin1_General_
        CP1_CI_AS
3       SQLCHAR 0   60    "\t"   3   ContactName     SQL_Latin1_General_
        CP1_CI_AS
4       SQLCHAR 0   60    "\t"   4   ContactTitle    SQL_Latin1_General_
        CP1_CI_AS
5       SQLCHAR 0   0     " "    5   Address         SQL_Latin1_General_
        CP1_CI_AS
6       SQLCHAR 0   0     " "    6   City            SQL_Latin1_General_
        CP1_CI_AS
7       SQLCHAR 0   0     " "    7   Region          SQL_Latin1_General_
        CP1_CI_AS
8       SQLCHAR 0   0     " "    8   PostalCode      SQL_Latin1_General_
        CP1_CI_AS
9       SQLCHAR 0   0     " "    9   Country         SQL_Latin1_General_
        CP1_CI_AS
10      SQLCHAR 0   48    "\t"   10  Phone           SQL_Latin1_General_
        CP1_CI_AS
11      SQLCHAR 0   48    "\r\n" 11  Fax             SQL_Latin1_General_
        CP1_CI_AS
```

Now bcp can load the data file by using this new format file, with the Address, City, Region, PostalCode, and Country columns containing NULL values for the new rows.

For data files that have more fields than the table has columns, you change the format file to add additional lines of information. Suppose that your customer data file contains an additional CreditStatus value at the end:

```
WELLI   Wellington Importadora   Martin Sommer  Sales Manager Rua do Mercado,
        12    Resende   SP    08737-363   Uraguay    (14) 555-8122   NULL 1
WELP    Well Drilling P   Thierry Gerardin   Sales Manager   Rue de Vaugirard,
        997    Paris    FR    08737-363   France    (11) 555-8122   NULL 1
WF      WF Enterprises   Yves Moison   Sales Manager   Rue de Sevres,
        4123   Paris    FR    08737-363   France    (14) 555-8122   NULL 1
WGZR    Wellsley Granite   Jack McElreath   Sales Manager   Hillsboro,
        131    Hillsboro   MA   08737-363   USA    (781) 555-8122   NULL 1
WHITC   White Clover Markets   Scott Smith   Owner   305 - 14th Ave. S.
        Suite 3B   Boston   MA   98128   USA (508) 555-4112  (508) 555-4115 2
```

You need to modify a format file in two important areas: You change the second line to reflect the actual number of values, and you add new lines for the extra column in the file that is not in the table (from 11 to 12 entries). Notice that the column position has a value of 0 to indicate the absence of a column in the table. The result is that your source data file will import all data into the table, except the extra field (that is, the CreditStatus field).

Thus the modified format file will look like this (where the **_bold italic_** indicates the changes made):

```
9.0
12
1      SQLCHAR 0    10    "\t"  1    CustomerID      SQL_Latin1_General_
       CP1_CI_AS
2      SQLCHAR 0    80    "\t"  2    CompanyName     SQL_Latin1_General_
       CP1_CI_AS
3      SQLCHAR 0    60    "\t"  3    ContactName     SQL_Latin1_General_
       CP1_CI_AS
4      SQLCHAR 0    60    "\t"  4    ContactTitle    SQL_Latin1_General_
       CP1_CI_AS
5      SQLCHAR 0    120   "\t"  5    Address         SQL_Latin1_General_
       CP1_CI_AS
6      SQLCHAR 0    30    "\t"  6    City            SQL_Latin1_General_
       CP1_CI_AS
7      SQLCHAR 0    30    "\t"  7    Region          SQL_Latin1_General_
       CP1_CI_AS
8      SQLCHAR 0    20    "\t"  8    PostalCode      SQL_Latin1_General_
       CP1_CI_AS
9      SQLCHAR 0    30    "\t"  9    Country         SQL_Latin1_General_
       CP1_CI_AS
10     SQLCHAR 0    48    "\t"  10   Phone           SQL_Latin1_General_
       CP1_CI_AS
11     SQLCHAR 0    48    "\t"  11   Fax             SQL_Latin1_General_
       CP1_CI_AS
12     SQLCHAR 0    1   "\r\n"  0    CreditStatus    SQL_Latin1_General_
       CP1_CI_AS
```

These two examples show you the possibilities that the format file offers for customizing the loading and unloading of data.

Renumbering Columns

Using the techniques described in the section, "Different Numbers of Columns in a File and a Table," you can also handle data file fields that are in different orders than the target tables. All you need to do is change the column order number to reflect the desired sequence of the columns in the table. The fields are then automatically mapped to the corresponding columns in the table.

For example, suppose that a customer data file you got from another source system came with the fields in this order:

1. Address

2. City

3. Country

4. PostalCode

5. Region

6. CompanyName

7. ContactName

8. ContactTitle

9. Fax

10. Phone

11. CustomerID

The SQL Server table has columns in a different order. To load your data file into this table, you modify the format file to look like this (where the **_bold italic_** indicates the changes made):

```
9.0
11
1       SQLCHAR 0       10      "\t"    11      CustomerID      SQL_Latin1_General_
        CP1_CI_AS
2       SQLCHAR 0       80      "\t"    6       CompanyName     SQL_Latin1_General_
        CP1_CI_AS
3       SQLCHAR 0       60      "\t"    7       ContactName     SQL_Latin1_General_
        CP1_CI_AS
4       SQLCHAR 0       60      "\t"    8       ContactTitle    SQL_Latin1_General_
        CP1_CI_AS
5       SQLCHAR 0       120     "\t"    1       Address         SQL_Latin1_General_
        CP1_CI_AS
6       SQLCHAR 0       30      "\t"    2       City            SQL_Latin1_General_
        CP1_CI_AS
7       SQLCHAR 0       30      "\t"    5       Region          SQL_Latin1_General_
        CP1_CI_AS
8       SQLCHAR 0       20      "\t"    4       PostalCode      SQL_Latin1_General_
        CP1_CI_AS
9       SQLCHAR 0       30      "\t"    3       Country         SQL_Latin1_General_
        CP1_CI_AS
```

10	SQLCHAR 0	48	"\t"	*10*	Phone	SQL_Latin1_General_
	CP1_CI_AS					
11	SQLCHAR 0	48	"\r\n"	*9*	Fax	SQL_Latin1_General_
	CP1_CI_AS					

The principal thing to remember with the format file is that all but the last three columns deal with the data file. The last three columns deal with the database table.

Using Views

bcp can use views to export data from a database. This means an export of data can be a result set of data from multiple tables (and with distributed queries, even multiple servers).

You can also use a view with bcp to load data back into tables. However, as is the case with normal T-SQL inserts, you can load into only one of the underlying tables at a time.

Logged and Non-Logged Operations

Bulk-copy operations can occur in two modes: logged and non-logged (also known as slow and fast bcp, respectively). The ideal situation is to operate in non-logged mode because this arrangement dramatically decreases the load time and the consumption of other system resources, such as memory, processor use, and disk access. However, the default runs the load in logged mode, which causes the log to grow rapidly for large volumes of data.

To achieve a non-logged operation, the target table must not be replicated (the replication log reader needs the log records to relay the changes made). The database holding the target table must also have its SELECT INTO/BULK COPY option set, and finally, the TABLOCK hint must be specified.

> **NOTE**
>
> Remember that setting the SELECT INTO/BULK COPY option disables the capability to back up the transaction log until a full database backup has been performed. Transaction log dumps are disabled because if the database had to be restored, the transaction log would not contain a record of the new data.

Although you can still perform fast loads against tables that have indexes, it is advisable to drop and re-create the indexes after the data transfer operation is complete. In other words, the total load time includes the loading of the data and the index creation time. If there is existing data in the table, the operation will be logged; you achieve a non-logged operation only if the table is initially empty.

Generally, you get at least a 50% drop in transfer speed if the table has an index. The more indexes, the greater the performance degradation. This is due to the logging factor: More log records are being generated, and index pages are being loaded into the cache and modified. This can also cause the log to grow, possibly filling it (depending on the log file settings).

> **NOTE**
>
> Despite the name, even a non-logged operation logs some things. In the case of indexes, index page changes and allocations are logged, but the main area of logging is of extent allocations every time the table is extended for additional storage space for the new rows.

Batches

By default, bcp puts all the rows that are inserted into the target table into a single transaction. bcp calls this a *batch*. This arrangement reduces the amount of work the log must deal with; however, it locks down the transaction log by keeping a large part of it active, which can make truncating or backing up the transaction log impossible or unproductive. By using the bcp batch (-b) switch, you can control the number of rows in each batch (or, effectively, each transaction). This switch controls the frequency of commits; although it can increase the activity in the log, it enables you to trim the size of the transaction log. You should tune the batch size in relation to the size of the data rows, transaction log size, and total number of rows to be loaded. The value you use for one load might not necessarily be the right value for all other loads.

Note that if a subsequent batch fails, the prior batches *are* committed, and those rows become part of the table. However, any rows copied up to the point of failure in the failing batch are rolled back.

Parallel Loading

A great enhancement of bcp is that you can now use it to do parallel loads of tables. To take advantage of this feature, the following must be true:

- ▶ The bulk-copy operation must be non-logged; all requirements specified in the previous discussion on non-logged operations must be met.

- ▶ There must be no indexes on the target table.

Only applications using the ODBC or SQL OLE DB–based APIs can perform parallel data loads into a single table.

The procedure is straightforward. After you have ascertained that the target table has no indexes (which could involve dropping primary or unique constraints) and is not being replicated, you must set the database option SELECT INTO/BULK COPY to true. The requirement to drop all indexes has to do with the locking that must occur to load the data. Although the table itself can have a shared lock, the index pages are an area of contention that prevents parallel access.

Now all that is required is to set up the parallel `bcp` loads to load the data into the table. You can use the -F and -L switches to specify the range of the data you want each parallel `bcp` to load into the table if you are using the same data file. Using these switches removes the need to manually break up the file. Here is an example of the command switches involved for a parallel load with `bcp` for the customers table:

```
bcp AdventureWorks.Sales.SalesOrderHeader IN SalesOrders10000.dat -T
  -S servername -c -F 1
-L 10000 -h "TABLOCK"
```

```
bcp AdventureWorks.Sales.SalesOrderHeader IN SalesOrders20000.dat -T
  -S servername -c -F 10001
-L 20000 -h "TABLOCK"
```

The TABLOCK hint (-h switch) provides improved performance by removing contention from other users while the load takes place. If you do not use the hint, the load takes place using row-level locks, and this is considerably slower.

SQL Server 2005 allows parallel loads without affecting performance by making each `bcp` connection create extents in non-overlapping ranges. The ranges are then linked into the table's page chain.

After the table is loaded, it is also possible to create multiple nonclustered indexes in parallel. If there is a clustered index, you work with that one first, followed by the parallel nonclustered index.

Supplying Hints to `bcp`

The SQL Server 2005 version of `bcp` enables you to further control the speed of data loading, to invoke constraints, and to have insert triggers fired during loads. To take advantage of these capabilities, you use hint switches to specify one or more hints at a time. The following is the syntax:

```
-h "hint [, hint]"
```

This option cannot be used when bulk-copying data into versions of SQL Server before version 7.0 because, starting with SQL Server 7.0, `bcp` works in conjunction with the query processor. The query processor optimizes data loads and unloads for OLE database rowsets that the latest versions of `bcp` and BULK INSERT can generate.

The following sections describe the various hints you can specify with the -h switch.

40

The ROWS_PER_BATCH Hint

The ROWS_PER_BATCH hint is used to tell SQL Server the total number of rows in the data file. This hint helps SQL Server optimize the entire load operation. This hint and the -b switch heavily influence the logging operations that occur with data inserts. If you specify both this hint and the -b switch, they must have the same values, or you get an error message.

When you use the ROWS_PER_BATCH hint, you copy the entire result set as a single transaction. SQL Server automatically optimizes the load operation, using the batch size you specify. The value you specify does *not* have to be accurate, but you should be aware of the practical limit, based on the database's transaction log.

TIP

Do not be confused by the name of the ROWS_PER_BATCH hint. You are specifying the *total file size* and *not* the batch size (as is the case with the –b switch).

The CHECK_CONSTRAINTS **Hint**

The CHECK_CONSTRAINTS hint controls whether check constraints are executed as part of the bcp operation. With bcp, the default is that check constraints are not executed. This hint option allows you to turn the feature on (to have check constraints executed for each insert). If you do not use this option, you should either be very sure of your data or rerun the same logic as in the check constraints you deferred after the data has been loaded.

The FIRE_TRIGGER **Hint**

The FIRE_TRIGGER hint controls whether the insert trigger on the target table is executed as part of the bcp operation. With bcp, the default is that no triggers are executed. This hint option allows you to turn the feature on (to have insert triggers executed for each insert). As you can imagine, when this option is used, it slows down the bcp load operation. However, the business reasons to have the insert trigger fired might outweigh the slower loading.

The ORDER **Hint**

If the data you want to load is already in the same sequence as the clustered index on the receiving table, you can use the ORDER hint. The syntax for this hint is as follows:

```
ORDER( {column [ASC | DESC] [,...n]})
```

There *must* be a clustered index on the same columns, in the same key sequence as specified in the ORDER hint. Using a sorted data file (in the same order as the clustering index) helps SQL Server place the data into the table with minimal overhead.

The KILOBYTES_PER_BATCH **Hint**

The KILOBYTES_PER_BATCH hint gives the size, in kilobytes, of the data in each batch. This is an estimate that SQL Server uses internally to optimize the data load and logging areas of the bcp operation.

The TABLOCK **Hint**

The TABLOCK hint is used to place a table-level lock for the bcp load duration. This hint gives you increased performance at a loss of concurrency, as described in the section "Parallel Loading," earlier in this chapter.

Summary

It is fairly easy to create and implement a typical data export, data import, or complex data transformation by using SSIS. You can either use the wizard for basic data transformation needs or the SSIS Designer for massively complex transformations (which may have multiple data sources and/or multiple data destinations). This is a very robust environment that has adopted a very formal, managed code rigor. With the SSIS capabilities, you get a self-contained place to build these data transformation solutions, and you can do so very rapidly. SSIS is completely integrated into the Visual Studio/BI Development Studio environment as well, making it that much easier to start producing rock-solid implementations.

This chapter also shows how to bulk-load data into and out of SQL Server by using the bcp utility. The multitude of switches bcp offers are very comprehensive and address most, if not all, importing and exporting situations. More importantly, with the advent of some additional switches, such as ORDER (within hints), TABLOCK (within hints), batches (-b), network packet sizes (-a), and others, it is significantly easier to increase the performance of bcp in a big way. bcp has been around for a long time, and it will continue to be the workhorse of bulk data loading and unloading.

Chapter 47, "SQL Server Notification Services" (on the CD-ROM), discusses this significant SQL Server capability and how to maximize its use for a production environment.

40

CHAPTER 41

SQL Server 2005 Reporting Services

IN THIS CHAPTER

▶ What's New in Reporting Services 2005

▶ Installing and Configuring Reporting Services

▶ Designing Reports

▶ Management and Security

▶ Performance and Monitoring Tools

▶ Building Applications for SQL Server Reporting Services 2005 Using the Report Viewer Controls

This chapter provides an introduction to SQL Server Reporting Services. It gives an overview of the product's features and architecture; it touches on some the most important areas of Reporting Services and gives you some examples of how you can start using it. This chapter is by no means a comprehensive description of the product, but it should get you excited about the capabilities of this great new technology.

So what is Reporting Services, you ask? The short answer: Reporting Services takes data that looks like in figure 41.1 and allows you to show it to your users looking as shown in figure 41.2.

Reporting Services, the newest addition to the SQL Server family, is a new managed reporting platform. It's a great way to expose data stored in SQL Server and other data sources in a central, secure environment, accessible through a large variety of formats and delivery options. Reporting Services completes the SQL Server business intelligence platform by adding the last missing piece to SQL Server's business intelligence platform: In addition to loading and analyzing data, you can now *visualize* it as well.

The first version of SQL Server Reporting Services shipped in January 2004, as part of SQL Server 2000. It generated much enthusiasm and enjoyed rapid adoption. The newest version of Reporting Services, included in SQL Server 2005, contains a great deal of new features geared toward ease of use, performance, and the improvement of a rich development platform.

	ProdSubCat	ProdModel	ProdCat	Description	LargePhoto	ProdName
1	Road Frames	HL Road Frame	Components	Our lightest and best quality aluminum fr...	0x474946383961F00...	HL Road Frame - Black, 58
2	Road Frames	HL Road Frame	Components	Our lightest and best quality aluminum fr...	0x474946383961F00...	HL Road Frame - Red, 58
3	Helmets	Sport-100	Accessories	Universal fit, well-vented, lightweight , sn...	0x474946383961F00...	Sport-100 Helmet, Red
4	Helmets	Sport-100	Accessories	Universal fit, well-vented, lightweight , sn...	0x474946383961F00...	Sport-100 Helmet, Black
5	Socks	Mountain Bike Socks	Clothing	Combination of natural and synthetic fibe...	0x474946383961F00...	Mountain Bike Socks, M
6	Socks	Mountain Bike Socks	Clothing	Combination of natural and synthetic fibe...	0x474946383961F00...	Mountain Bike Socks, L
7	Helmets	Sport-100	Accessories	Universal fit, well-vented, lightweight , sn...	0x474946383961F00...	Sport-100 Helmet, Blue
8	Caps	Cycling Cap	Clothing	Traditional style with a flip-up brim; one-si...	0x474946383961F00...	AWC Logo Cap
9	Jerseys	Long-Sleeve Logo Jersey	Clothing	Unisex long-sleeve AWC logo microfiber ...	0x474946383961F00...	Long-Sleeve Logo Jersey, S
10	Jerseys	Long-Sleeve Logo Jersey	Clothing	Unisex long-sleeve AWC logo microfiber ...	0x474946383961F00...	Long-Sleeve Logo Jersey, M
11	Jerseys	Long-Sleeve Logo Jersey	Clothing	Unisex long-sleeve AWC logo microfiber ...	0x474946383961F00...	Long-Sleeve Logo Jersey, L
12	Jerseys	Long-Sleeve Logo Jersey	Clothing	Unisex long-sleeve AWC logo microfiber ...	0x474946383961F00...	Long-Sleeve Logo Jersey, XL
13	Road Frames	HL Road Frame	Components	Our lightest and best quality aluminum fr...	0x474946383961F00...	HL Road Frame - Red, 62
14	Road Frames	HL Road Frame	Components	Our lightest and best quality aluminum fr...	0x474946383961F00...	HL Road Frame - Red, 44
15	Road Frames	HL Road Frame	Components	Our lightest and best quality aluminum fr...	0x474946383961F00...	HL Road Frame - Red, 48
16	Road Frames	HL Road Frame	Components	Our lightest and best quality aluminum fr...	0x474946383961F00...	HL Road Frame - Red, 52
17	Road Frames	HL Road Frame	Components	Our lightest and best quality aluminum fr...	0x474946383961F00...	HL Road Frame - Red, 56
18	Road Frames	LL Road Frame	Components	The LL Frame provides a safe comfortab...	0x474946383961F00...	LL Road Frame - Black, 58
19	Road Frames	LL Road Frame	Components	The LL Frame provides a safe comfortab...	0x474946383961F00...	LL Road Frame - Black, 60
20	Road Frames	LL Road Frame	Components	The LL Frame provides a safe comfortab...	0x474946383961F00...	LL Road Frame - Black, 62
21	Road Frames	LL Road Frame	Components	The LL Frame provides a safe comfortab...	0x474946383961F00...	LL Road Frame - Red, 44
22	Road Frames	LL Road Frame	Components	The LL Frame provides a safe comfortab...	0x474946383961F00...	LL Road Frame - Red, 48
23	Road Frames	LL Road Frame	Components	The LL Frame provides a safe comfortab...	0x474946383961F00...	LL Road Frame - Red, 52
24	Road Frames	LL Road Frame	Components	The LL Frame provides a safe comfortab...	0x474946383961F00...	LL Road Frame - Red, 58

FIGURE 41.1   Data view.

FIGURE 41.2   Report view.

Reporting Services is a new SQL Server service similar to the relational database engine or Analysis Services. It allows you to design reports, deploy them on a server, and make them available to users in a secured environment, in a variety of online and offline formats.

figure 41.3 shows the overall architecture of Reporting Services.

41

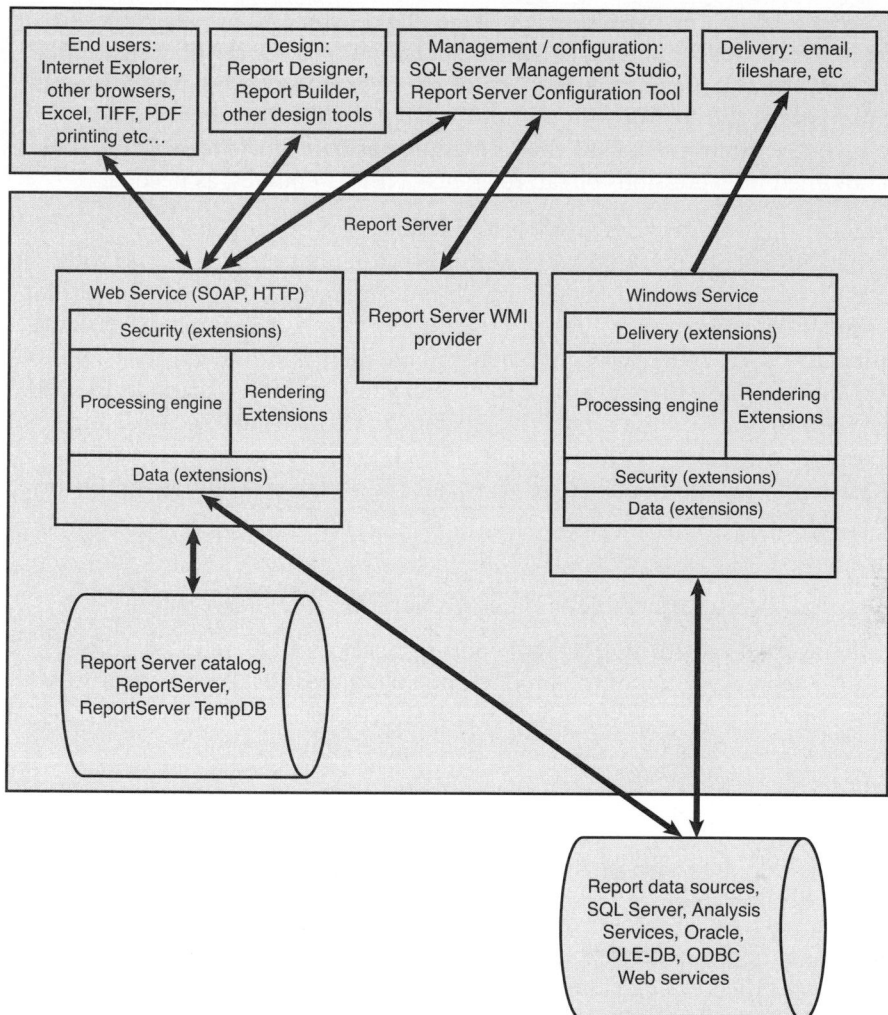

FIGURE 41.3   Reporting Services architecture.

Reporting consists of both server and client components:

There are two main server components: the web service, which is hosted in Internet Information Services (IIS), and a standalone Windows service. The web service exposes the main Simple Object Access Protocol (SOAP) interfaces and is responsible for running reports accessed on demand; the Reporting Services Windows service is responsible for offline processing and other tasks. You will read more about this later in this chapter.

The client components include the Report Designer, Report Builder, SQL Server Management Studio and the Reporting Services Configuration Tool.

Reports are described by Report Definition Language (RDL), which is an Extensible Markup Language (XML)–based language that is understood by a variety of design tools from Microsoft and third parties. The RDL contains the description of the report layout, formatting information, and instructions on how to fetch the data. It can optionally contain custom code written in VB .NET that is executed as part of the report. Custom code can be contained in expressions or can reference .NET assemblies, as needed.

In SQL Server 2005, there are two design tools for building reports: the Business Intelligence Development Studio (BIDS), a powerful development tool integrated with Visual Studio .NET 2005, and Report Builder, which is a simpler point-and-click tool that you use to design ad hoc reports. Both report design tools have a rich graphical design surface and allow a WYSIWYG experience. When you are happy with a reports' content and layout and want to make them available to others, you can deploy them on the report server. When they are on the server, the reports can be managed, secured, and delivered to a variety of formats, including HTML, Excel, PDF, TIFF, and XML. Various delivery, caching, and execution options are also available, as are scheduling and historical archiving.

What's New in Reporting Services 2005

You may already be familiar with SQL Server Reporting Services 2000, released only a couple years ago. The new version of the product includes a great deal of new features and improvements.

Report Builder

Report Builder is a major new piece of functionality that gives end users the ability to build and publish reports. Report Builder reports are constructed using a data model, which keeps users from needing to understand data source query syntax or schemas. Using a data source such as SQL Server or Analysis Services, an administrator or a developer generates a data model, either through an auto-generation process or by using the Model Designer tool. When the model is uploaded on the report server, business users can use the model to generate reports. Because models provide an abstraction layer over the underlying database schema, users operate in logical terms, navigate the relationship hierarchies, such as Customer or Department, instead of writing T-SQL or Analysis Services queries. The report server translates the model elements into native database queries. Other useful features of data models include column and row security and drill-through link generation for related entities.

The Report Viewer Controls

The report viewer controls, which are part of Visual Studio 2005, are the second major addition to the Reporting Services platform. Using these controls is the preferred way to integrate reporting in applications. They offer a rich programming interface for controlling the report execution and interactivity and are available in C#, VB .NET, and the other .NET languages.

Visual Studio 2005 includes two report viewer controls: one for use in Windows Forms applications and the other for use in ASP.NET web applications. Each control works in two modes:

▶ **Local**—In this mode, the report processing happens in your application.

▶ **Remote**—In this mode, the report processing happens in a report server instance installed remotely.

Other additions to Reporting Services in SQL Server 2005 include the following:

▶ Support for report queries against web services

▶ End-user sort capabilities

▶ Client printing through an ActiveX control

▶ Native support for multiple-value parameters

▶ Web parts for use in Windows SharePoint Services

▶ Improved ease of use for Analysis Services queries

▶ New and improved management and configuration tools

Another change worth mentioning is the inclusion of Reporting Services in all editions of SQL Server 2005—from the free SQL Express Edition up to Enterprise Edition. For a list of the available features in each edition, see "SQL Server 2005 Reporting Services Feature Matrix," at www.microsoft.com/sql/2005/productinfo/rsfeatures.mspx.

Installing and Configuring Reporting Services

This chapter will give you an overview of the possible installation and configuration options with reporting services.

The Reporting Services System Architecture

Reporting Services is a new service installed with SQL Server 2005. It can retrieve, process, and present data from a variety of stores, including SQL Server 7, 2000, and 2005; Oracle; DB/2; Teradata; as well as web services and a variety of other OLE DB and Open Database Connectivity (ODBC) providers.

Reporting Services needs an instance of the SQL Server database engine to store report definitions and other metadata used for security, subscriptions, and so on. This component is called the *report server catalog*; the SQL Server machine that hosts the catalog can be local or remote to the report server.

Reporting Services exposes its functionality as a SOAP web service hosted in IIS and ASP.NET.

figure 41.4 describes the system architecture for a simple installation in which all server components are installed on the same machine.

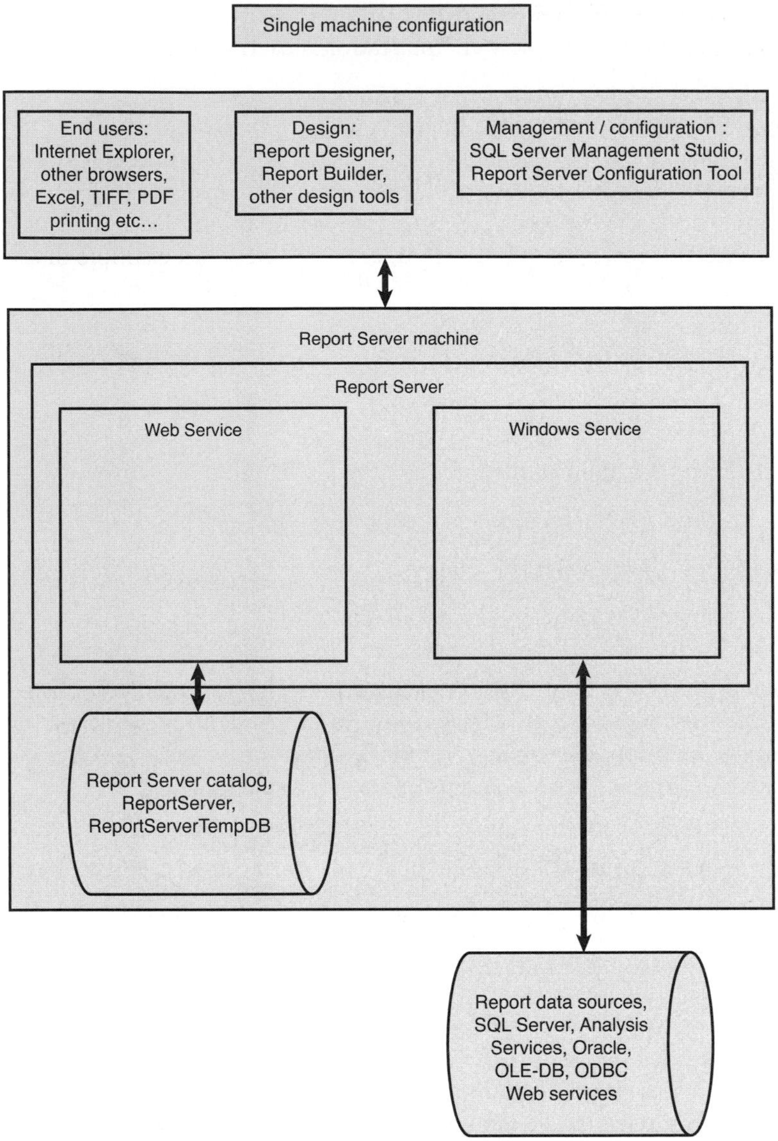

FIGURE 41.4   A single-machine Reporting Services configuration.

TIP

You can use either SQL Server 2000 or SQL Server 2005 to catalog for a report server. In other words, you don't necessarily need a SQL Server 2005 relational database in order to use Reporting Services 2005.

You can install several instances or Reporting Services on the same machine. They can share the hardware resources of the same computer, but their content (for example, reports, data sources, security) are separate for each one.

The Enterprise Edition of Reporting Services has built-in support for a scale-out architecture in which several instances of Reporting Services can be added to the installation, as needed, to support an increased user population or report complexity. In this case, all Reporting Services instances added to the scale-out configuration share the same catalog database (with the same content, security, and so on). figure 41.5 shows an example of a scale-out configuration.

> **NOTE**
>
> It is also possible to achieve a scale-out configuration on a single machine by simply joining several instances installed on the same box in a scale-out configuration.

Installing Reporting Services

When you install SQL Server 2005, you get Reporting Services by choosing the Reporting Services option in the setup feature selection screen. SQL Server 2005 Setup installs the following components of Reporting Services:

- ▶ **Server components**—The server components include the report server Windows service, the report server web service, Report Manager (a web-based management user interface), and the new Reporting Services Configuration tool and report server Windows Management Instrumentation (WMI) provider.

- ▶ **Client components**—The Setup program installs the following client components:

  - ▶ **Report design tools**—Report Designer and Model Designer are hosted within BIDS.

  - ▶ **Management tools**—SQL Server Management Studio (SSMS) supports connecting and managing a report server instance. In addition, a number of command-line tools are available for management.

There are two options to get Reporting Services up and running:

- ▶ **Default installation**—This option installs and configures the report server with the default settings and

- ▶ **Custom (or files-only) installation**—This option installs, but doesn't configure, the report server components. In this case, the configuration of Reporting Services is done using the Reporting Services Configuration tool.

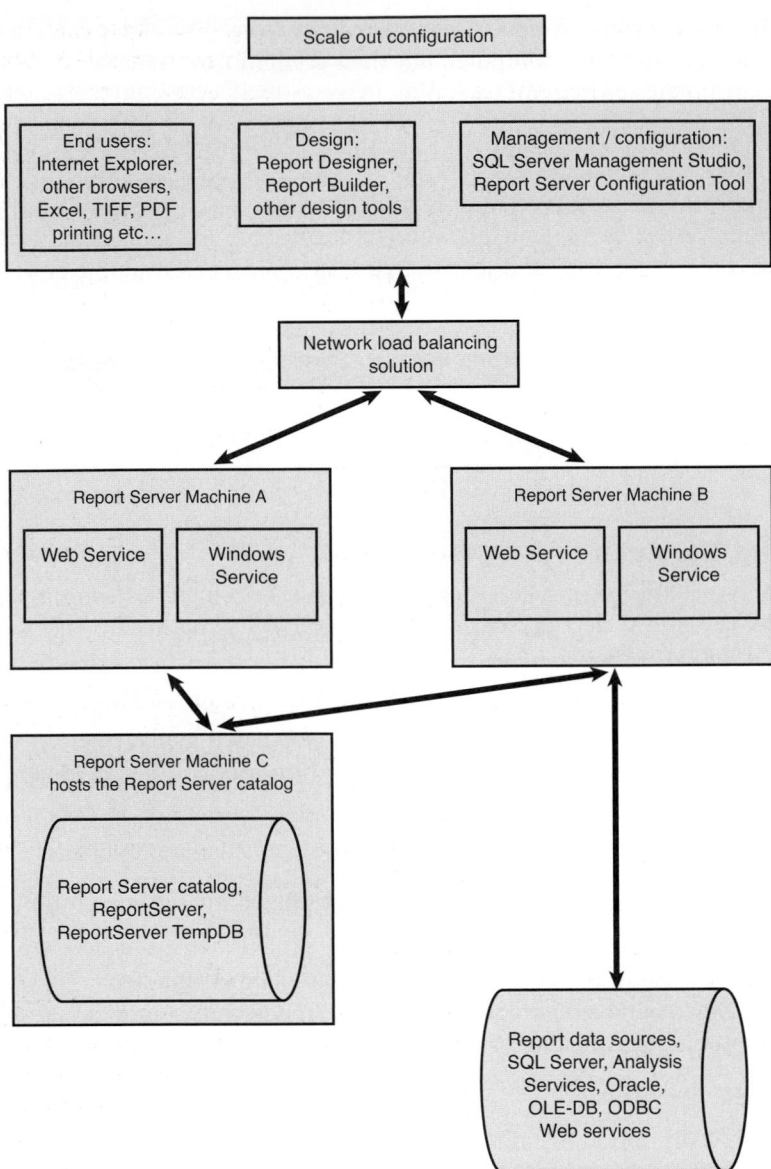

FIGURE 41.5   A Reporting Services scale-out configuration.

The Default Installation

SQL Server 2005 Setup checks the prerequisites on your system to determine whether a default configuration can be performed. If the system meets all the prerequisites requirements, you can choose Install and Configure. Otherwise, you are guided toward custom (or files-only) installation.

41

If you choose default installation, when the Setup program finishes, you have a working instance of Reporting Services; Setup creates and sets up the database catalog, configures the IIS web service, and sets the necessary permissions for it to work. The only configuration option you have with default installation is to choose the service accounts for each service (including Reporting Services).

Custom (Files-Only) Installation

In custom mode, Setup copies the necessary files, creates the registry settings, and sets up the Reporting Services Windows service, but otherwise it leaves the report server unconfigured.

When the Setup program finishes, you need to use the Reporting Services Configuration tool to customize and finish the configuration. The Reporting Services Configuration tool is a friendly management tool that assists you in configuring Reporting Services, including configuring the report server catalog, changing the service accounts, configuring the web service in IIS, setting up a scale-out configuration, backing up and restoring the encryption keys, managing your subscription settings, and many other tasks.

You can use the Reporting Services Configuration tool at the end of a custom installation or any time you want to change the settings used by the report server.

Reporting Services Configuration Options and Tools

This section describes some of the common configuration tasks for Reporting Services, the various options available to system administrators together with pros and cons for using them.

The Reporting Services Configuration Tool

The Reporting Services Configuration tool is the main interface for configuring the report server. figure 41.6 shows how the Reporting Services Configuration tool looks on a files-only installation that has not yet been configured.

The tool provides a list of configuration parameters you can change as well as a status for each item. When you use this tool after a custom (files-only) installation, the idea is to navigate from top to bottom through the tasks, configuring them until they all have green check marks next to them. Until they are configured, they are displayed with red or yellow signs. A blue icon means that particular configuration setting is optional.

You can also use the Reporting Services Configuration tool in maintenance mode, when the initial configuration settings need to be updated.

NOTE

Much of the "brains" behind the Reporting Services Configuration tool is contained in the report server WMI provider, which exposes a set of WMI interfaces that can be used to configure the report server. This enables third parties to configure the report server programmatically or build other configuration utilities.

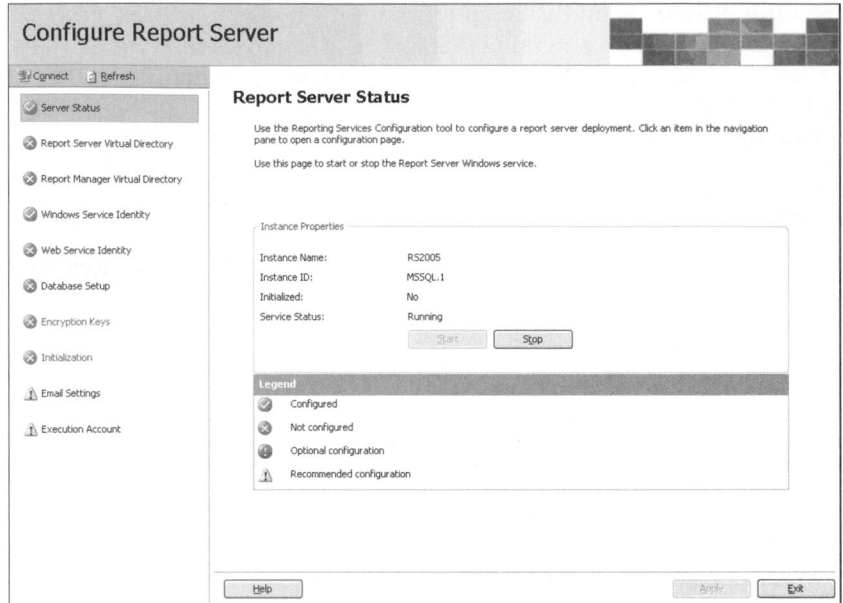

FIGURE 41.6   The Reporting Services Configuration tool.

Report Server Encryption

The report server has the capability to securely store sensitive information (for example, connection strings to data sources for reports, subscription information). In order to so, it uses the Windows Crypto APIs, which are based on the account that the service runs as. When the service is first started and it connects to an empty report server database, it creates a symmetric key that is used for encryption. It then encrypts this symmetric key with the public key of the account used to run report server Windows services. Then it stores the encrypted keys in the report server catalog database and uses the keys to encrypt and decrypt data.

As the report server administrator, you can extract (back up) the key used for encryption; if you do this, you need to make sure to store it securely. You can also change the key used for encryption, as well as restore a previously saved key All these options are available on the Encryption Keys tab in the Report Server Configuration Tool.

Configuring the Report Server Windows Service

The report server Windows service is an essential report server component. It needs to be running in order for reports to be executed either on demand or offline. You can start and stop the service from the Windows service tab, and you can also change the service account or the password for the service.

You should change the service account under which the Reporting Services Windows service runs through the Reporting Services Configuration tool because the system needs to back up and restore the keys used for encryption as well as make sure the new account has access to the report server database. This also explains why you are prompted to save the encryption key when you perform this operation.

Configuring the Report Server Web Service

The report server web service is a component, hosted in IIS, that exposes the SOAP and HTTP interfaces clients use to interact with the report server.

The report server configures two virtual directories:

▶ **/ReportServer**—(the default name); this directory exposes the SOAP interfaces and HTTP access. Development tools that work against the SOAP endpoint use http://*servername*/ReportServer/ to connect to the report server. For instance, when you deploy reports from the Report Designer development tool, the deployment path should be http://*servername*/ReportServer/.

▶ **/Reports**—(the default name); this directory exposes a richer report server management and end-user interface, built using ASP.NET. End users and administrators normally use the path http://*servername*/Reports/ to view and manage reports.

The Reporting Services Configuration tool also allows users to host the report server web services in custom websites or application pools.

Creating and Configuring the Report Server Database Catalog

As mentioned earlier in this chapter, the report server services store information about the report definitions, security, subscriptions, and so on in a SQL Server store. This is just a store for the report's metadata; the data for the reports can come from a variety of data sources.

The Reporting Services Configuration tool helps you create a new (empty) report server catalog database. You can either pick a SQL Server machine to install it in or record the creation scripts into a file for later use.

You may have noticed that Reporting Services configures and uses two databases: the main store for metadata, called ReportServer by default, and a temporary store for user sessions, called ReportServerTempDB. ReportServerTempDB is created in simple recovery mode and doesn't need to be backed up periodically because it contains only transient data—data about the in-flight sessions, actively served by the report server.

After the databases have been created, there are three options that the report server services can use to connect to it, as shown in figure 41.7.

You can configure Reporting Services to connect to its SQL catalog by using integrated security for the service accounts. That means the two service accounts (Windows service and web service) are granted enough permissions to the report server catalog to operate the ReportServer. These permissions are contained in the RsExecRole database role, which needs to be granted to ReportServer and ReportServerTempDBreport as well as msdb and master.

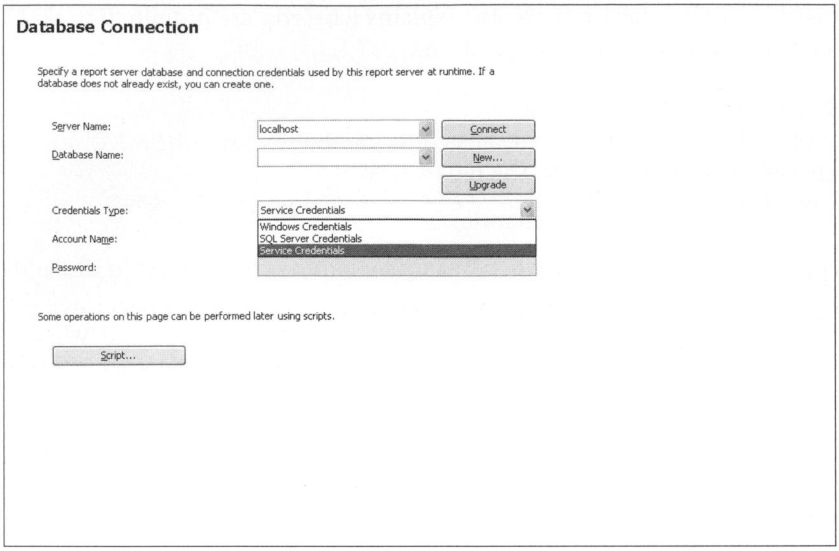

FIGURE 41.7   Configuring the database connection.

Alternatively, you can configure the report server to connect to its catalog by using a set of Windows or SQL Server credentials. The encrypted credentials are stored in Program Files\Microsoft SQL Server\[*SQLInstance*]\Reporting Services\ReportServer\ RsReportServer.config. If you use a SQL or Windows user to access the catalog database, it is recommended that you create a new user for this purpose. The user doesn't have to have any SQL permissions; in fact, the Reporting Services Configuration tool grants the user the minimum permissions necessary to operate.

The Surface Area Configuration Tool

Like the other services in SQL Server 2005, you can turn Reporting Services on and off through the Surface Area Configuration tool, which you access by selecting Programs, Microsoft SQL Server 2005, Configuration Tools, SQL Server Surface Area Configuration.

You can control the following Reporting Services features through the Surface Area Configuration tool:

▶ Turning on and off the Reporting Services Windows service and SOAP web service

▶ Turning on and off processing and delivery of subscriptions to reports

▶ Turning on and off execution of reports using Windows Integrated Security

Designing Reports

This section will walk you through the process of designing reports. It will start by showing how to build simple reports using BIDS, then add some of the more advanced features, and finally it will describe the report design process using Report Builder, the new ad hoc report design tool.

Designing Reports by Using the BIDS Report Designer

BIDS is the central, integrated development for Reporting Services, Analysis Services, and Integration Services projects.

To start building a report using BIDS, you choose a new report project. You select Solution, Add a New Report to start the Report Wizard. The wizard guides you through the choices for data retrieval and layout, and it builds a report that you can then customize.

If you want to skip the wizard and get directly into the design surface, you choose Solution, Add New Item and then select Report instead of selecting Add New Report.

The Report Designer offers four basic report templates: based on lists, tables, matrixes, and charts. We are going to explore further the "list" and "table" templates in this section.

Designing Queries

The first part of designing a report in BIDS is to define the report query. To switch to the Query Designer, you select the Data tab.

The Report Designer tool offers a familiar graphical Query Designer as well as a text-only Query Designer that is well suited for advanced SQL programmers. In the graphical Query Designer, you can pick tables, build relationships, select columns, and apply filters; the generic Query Designer, on the other hand, only lets you type or paste a query. Both tools run your queries and display the results.

The connection information for a query is called a *data source*. A query result is called a *data set*. A report can have zero, one, or several data sources, and a data source can have one or several data sets.

A welcome addition in Reporting Services for SQL Server 2005 is the graphical Query Designer for Analysis Services, which provides a great user experience for designing MDX and DMX (data-mining) queries.

The Report Designer supports out-of-the-box queries against SQL Server databases, Analysis Services cubes, Oracle databases, and any generic OLE DB and ODBC drivers.

If your queries contain parameters, the Query Designer prompts you for values when running these queries. The Refresh Fields option auto-generates report parameters for each data source parameter in the query.

Making Layout Choices

To build and customize your report layout, you need to switch to the layout view in the main designer window. The Toolbox window contains the list of report items available for report design.

The report has three parts: the body, header, and footer. The body can be a just collection of static controls, such as text boxes and lines, but most useful reports contain at least one data-bound control. Every data-bound control is tied to a data set defined in the Query Designer. The following are the data-bound controls:

▶ **List**—A list is the simplest data-bound control. It is a free-form area in which you add other controls, such as text boxes, images, and so on. Each element is repeated for each data row in the data set.

▶ **Table**—A table provides a tabular display structure with multiple columns, and it allows you to add groupings.

▶ **Matrix**—A matrix adds the ability to display data and groups on rows in addition to columns.

▶ **Chart**—A chart gives you a number of graphic representations of your data.

It may be useful to think of a table as a simplified matrix and of a chart as a different way to present the data and its dimensions in a matrix, a "graphical matrix" of sorts.

Building Reports

To get some hands-on experience with reports, in this section you'll try to build a simple report. The first step is to open SQL Server BIDS. Then you should choose a new report project and observe the two groups in the Solution Explorer: one for data sources and the other for reports. The Report Designer allows you to build reports with data source information contained in the report, or allows you to use a shared data source. The advantage of using shared data sources is that you have only one place to manage the information, as well as one central place to secure your data access layer, once it is deployed on the report server.

You need to create a new shared data source, call it `AdventureWorks`, and create a connection string, as follows:

```
"Data Source=localhost;Initial Catalog=AdventureWorks"
```

You can use Windows integrated security or store credentials in the data source. When deployed on the report server, the connection string and credentials information are encrypted using the report server–generated keys, as described in the section "Report Server Encryption."

> **TIP**
>
> If you use Windows integrated security, you should note that when your reports are deployed, they work only if the report server service and the data source server are on the same machine or you enable Kerberos delegation for both service accounts. For an overview of how to set up Kerberos delegation, see the technical article, "Troubleshooting Kerberos Delegation" at http://www.microsoft.com/technet/prodtechnol/windowsserver2003/technologies/security/tkerbdel.mspx.

Creating a Simple List

Let's create a report now. If you click New Report, the Report Wizard appears. To create a report without using the wizard, you choose New Item, Report. Either way, you should call the new report `EmployeeList.rdl`.

In the data pane, you create a new dataset called `Employees`. If you just want to display the list of employees, you can start with this query:

```
SELECT HumanResources.Employee.Title,
HumanResources.Employee.EmployeeID,
HumanResources.Employee.ManagerID,
Person.Contact.FirstName,
Person.Contact.LastName
FROM Person.Contact INNER JOIN HumanResources.Employee
ON Person.Contact.ContactID=HumanResources.Employee.ContactID
```

Note that the list columns that this query returns are added to the list of fields available in the report. You can see all the fields in the Datasets window (see figure 41.8).

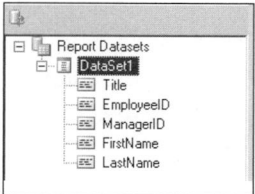

FIGURE 41.8   The Datasets window.

You can now switch to the design surface and add a list to it by using the Toolbox icon in the toolbar. Then you drag to the list the fields you want in the report, separating them with vertical lines, as shown in figure 41.9. To finish the report, you add a new text box to the top area and type the report title. You use the Font and Format tabs in the Properties dialog box to control the visual settings and styles for the report items.

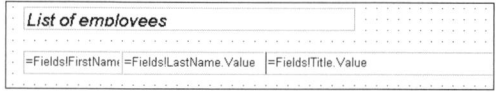

FIGURE 41.9   A list on the design surface.

You can now preview the report, which should look like that shown in figure 41.10.

Grouping and Sorting in a Report

Suppose you want to group the employees in your report based on their departments. To do this, you should create a new report, called `EmployeesByDepartment.rdl`.

FIGURE 41.10   Preview for the employee list report.

You create a new report by selecting the New Item menu. You start with the same query as in the previous report, and you add a join to the Department table in order to get the department information you want to display in the report. The query now looks like this:

```
SELECT HumanResources.Employee.Title,
HumanResources.Employee.EmployeeID,
HumanResources.Employee.ManagerID,
Person.Contact.FirstName,
Person.Contact.LastName,
HumanResources.Department.Name AS DepartmentName
FROM HumanResources.EmployeeDepartmentHistory
INNER JOIN HumanResources.Department ON
HumanResources.EmployeeDepartmentHistory.DepartmentID =
HumanResources.Department.DepartmentID
INNER JOIN Person.Contact
INNER JOIN HumanResources.Employee
ON Person.Contact.ContactID = HumanResources.Employee.ContactID
ON HumanResources.EmployeeDepartmentHistory.EmployeeID =
HumanResources.Employee.EmployeeID
```

In the Datasets pane, notice that you now have the DepartmentName field in addition to the fields from the previous report.

It's now time to switch to the visual layout of the report. From the Toolbox window, you choose a table and drop it to the design surface. From the Datasets pane, you drag the First Name and the Last Name fields to the detail row of the table. When you preview the report, you see a simple list of names that looks similar to the previous report.

Say you want to group this table, using the department name of the employees. To do this, you select the table in the design surface, right-click, and select Insert Group from the table context menu. The Grouping and Sorting Properties dialog for the table appears.

In the General tab, you select =Fields!DepartmentName.Value as the expression to group on. Then you switch to the Sorting tab and use the same expression for sorting.

When you go back to the design surface, you should notice that the table has two more rows: the group header and the group footer. They represent placeholders for showing report data before and after each group of elements in the table. In this example, you can display the department name in the group header. Because you don't need to display the group footer, you can delete it from the design surface or uncheck the Include Group Footer check box on the General tab of the Grouping and Sorting Properties dialog.

If you preview the report now, you should see that it lists all employees, grouped by their department name, and sorted in ascending order, using the department name.

Using Tables and Hierarchies

Now let's say you want to represent the organizational hierarchy in the sample employees report. This is a situation in which the grouping has to be done recursively because there are several levels of management in an organization. You need to create a new report by selecting New Item and call it EmployeeHierarchy.rdl. You use the same query as in the EmployeeList.rdl example, but instead of choosing a list, you use a table as the main data region:

```
SELECT HumanResources.Employee.Title,
HumanResources.Employee.EmployeeID,
HumanResources.Employee.ManagerID,
Person.Contact.FirstName,
Person.Contact.LastName
FROM Person.Contact INNER JOIN HumanResources.Employee
ON Person.Contact.ContactID=HumanResources.Employee.ContactID
```

In the design surface, you then need to select the table, right-click, and choose Insert Group. The Grouping and Sorting Properties dialog appears, as shown in figure 41.11. In this case, you should choose to group on the EmployeeID field, and you can choose the ManagerID field as the parent group. You don't need the details row, nor the group footer, so you can delete them.

When you preview the report now, it should look like the one shown in figure 41.12.

To make the tree structure clearer, you use the Level keyword in specifying the format of the FirstName text box. Level represents the current depth level of a recursive hierarchy. You make the Left space element an expression that equals the following:

```
=(((Level("table1_Manager"))*12)+2)&"pt"
```

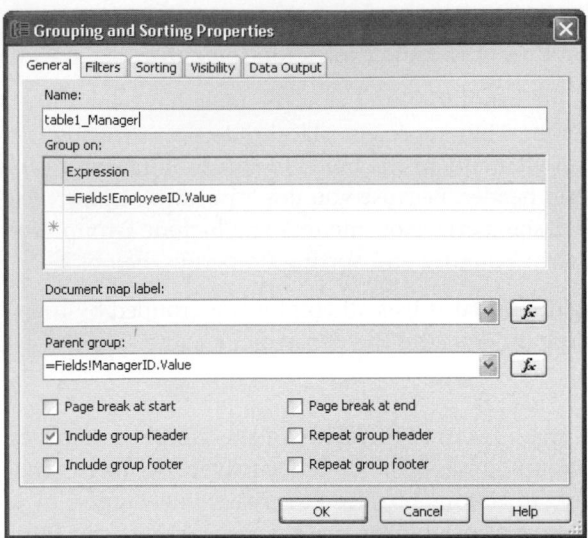

FIGURE 41.11   The Grouping and Sorting Properties dialog.

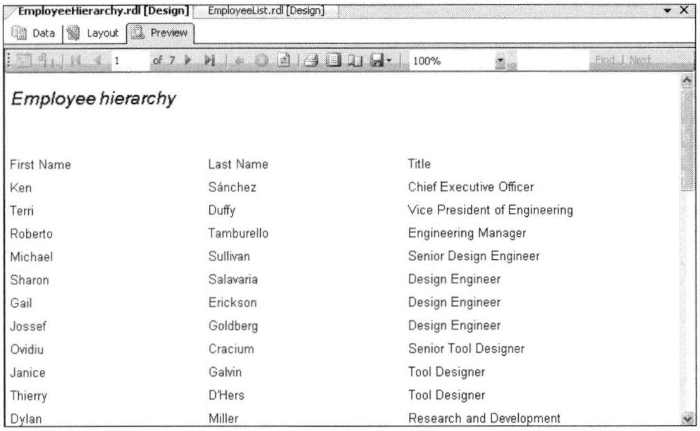

FIGURE 41.12   Previewing your report with grouping.

This indents the first level at 2 points, and for each level under it, it pushes the row to the right 12 more points per level, as shown in figure 41.13.

The report should now look like the one shown in figure 41.14.

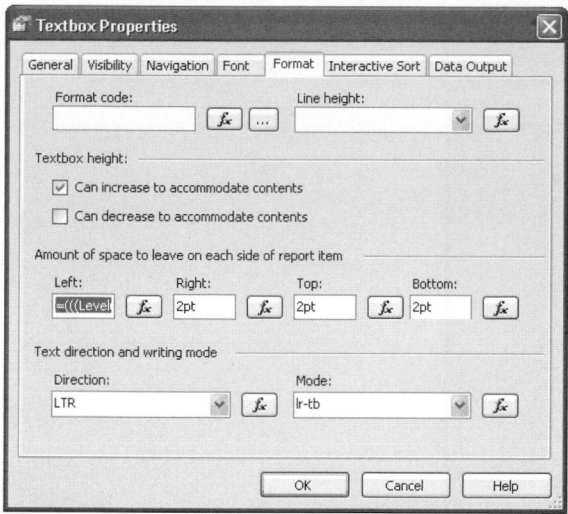

FIGURE 41.13   Specifying indentation.

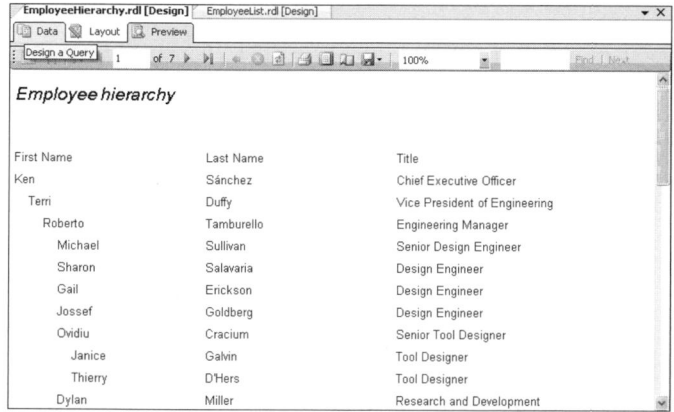

FIGURE 41.14   Previewing your indented report.

Adding Interactivity

The last thing you'll do to the report is to add drill-down interactivity to it. To do this, you right-click the group header and choose Edit Group. When the Grouping and Sorting Properties dialog appears, you navigate to the Visibility tab and choose Hidden. Then you check Visibility Can Be Toggled by Another Item and choose the first text box in the table (see figure 41.15).

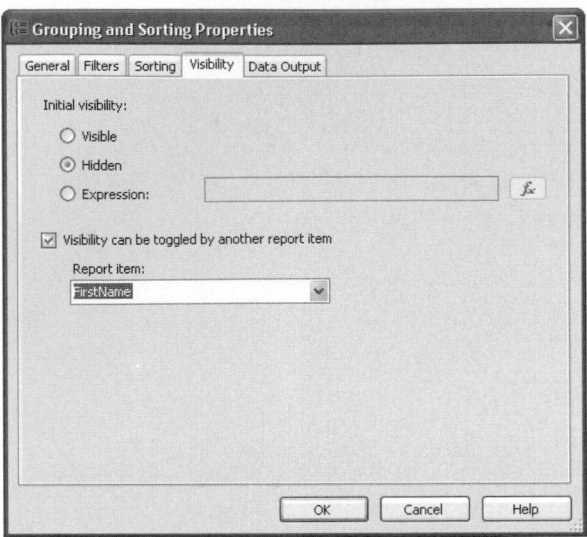

FIGURE 41.15   Toggling visibility.

Now you need to save and preview the report. It should now look like the one shown in figure 41.16.

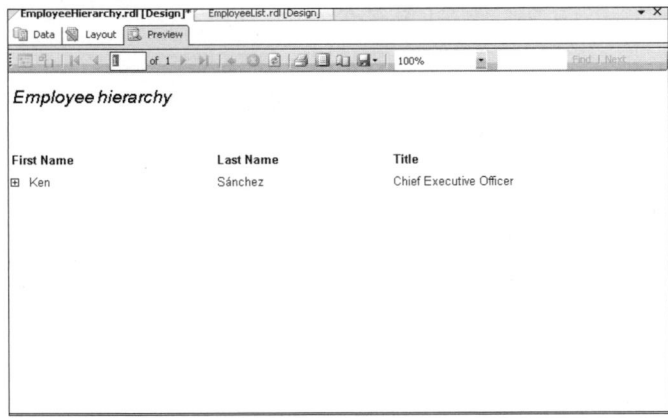

FIGURE 41.16   Report with toggle preview.

By clicking the + and - signs next to first names, your users can now recursively expand and collapse the hierarchy.

Deploying the Sample Report

You are now ready to deploy your report, to make it available to others. To deploy or publish a report, you have to specify a report server in the Project Properties window (for example, `http://salesreports/ReportServer`). Note that this URL needs to point to the web service virtual directory, not the main `http://salesreports/Reports` directory, which is the management and portal interface. When the report is successfully published, authorized users can see it by using either one of these two URLs. The report should now look as shown in figure 41.17.

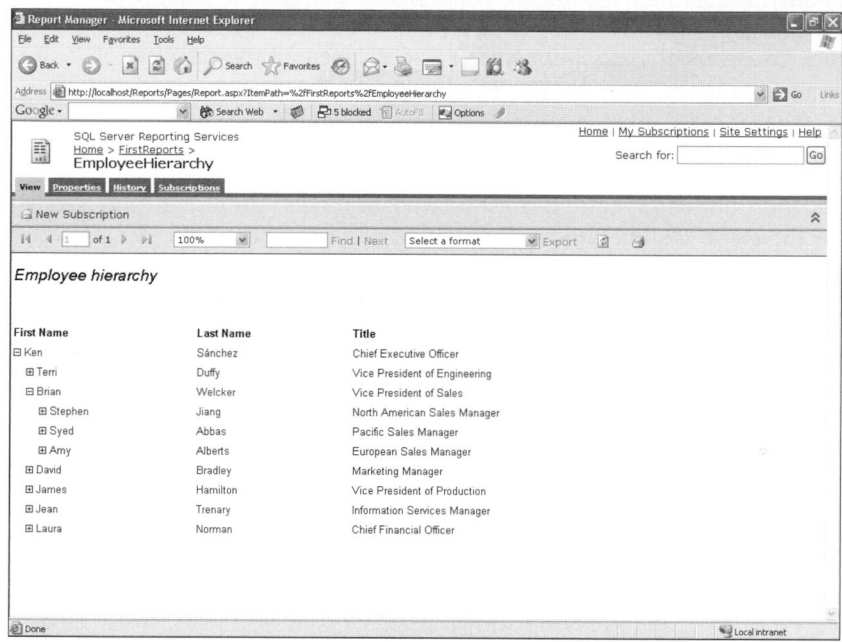

FIGURE 41.17   Deploying your report.

Designing Reports Using Report Builder

Report Builder, an end-user design tool, is new in SQL Server 2005. Report Builder simplifies both the data-retrieval and the layout-design phases.

Report Builder is much simpler to use than BIDS because it doesn't require its users to know about T-SQL SELECT statements, foreign keys, or really anything about the underlying structure of their data. Instead, it uses *data models*—also called *semantic models*—which are representations of objects and relationships between them, shown in simple business terms. Report Builder allows business users and analysts to build and design their own ad hoc reports, run reports to preview the data, and share reports with others by saving them on a report server.

The data models need to be built by someone who has good knowledge of the database schema and the needs of the ad hoc reporting customers.

For layout, Report Builder uses a set of predefined templates tables, matrixes, and charts.

TIP

It is important to note that Report Builder always requires a report server to be accessible, starting from its launch. Indeed, Report Builder is an application built using the Click-Once technology, which means it is downloadable on client machines on first access from a report server machine.

You can launch Report Builder from the Report Manager web interface: You just navigate to the Report Manager location (which is, by default, `http://localhost/reports`) and click the Report Builder button on the Folder ribbon. (If you can't see a Report Builder button in your Report Manager, see the section "Enabling Ad Hoc Reporting," later in this chapter.)

When you launch Report Builder, it gathers a list of all data models published on a server and shows them in the Getting Started pane. Once you choose a model, you can start designing your reports. (If you don't have a model yet, you can create one by using the information in the "Models and the Model Designer" section, later in this chapter.)

In the left-hand pane is the Model Explorer, a tree-like structure that contains all the objects you can use to build reports as well as a representation of the relationships between them. When you click an object, you see in the lower part of the pane a list of objects related to it—the roles, or relationships, from the selected object (entity) to other objects (entities).

You build reports by simply dragging objects from the Model Explorer to the Designer pane or by double-clicking them. Depending on the type of the object, the appropriate field is added to the report definition. The fields in the list are shown with different icons, depending on their type. Character fields are shown with a lowercase *s* icon, scalar fields are shown with the # icon, Boolean fields are shown with the check mark icon, and aggregate fields are shown with the aggregate icon (the three vertical dots next to the curly bracket).

In the example shown in figure 41.18, `Title` and `First Name` are character fields, `Name Style` is a Boolean field, `#ContactID` is a numeral field, `Modified Date` is a date/time field, and `#Contacts` is an aggregate, in this case a count field.

FIGURE 41.18   Types of fields.

Also note that fields already used in the report are highlighted in boldface. In figure 41.18, for example, `First Name` is used in the report design surface.

After you add some fields to the report, the Model Explorer is "rooted" at the entity you chose. You can see all entities related to that field in the Entities list. To get the entire model back in the Model Explorer, you have to delete all the fields from the design surface.

The icons in the Model Explorer list represent the cardinality of the relationship. The example shown in figure 41.19 shows a list of relationships from the Sales Person entity. Territory, Sales Person, and Manager represent a one-to-one relationship with Sales Person, while Employees, Sales Territory Histories, and Sales Person Quota History represent one-to-many relationships.

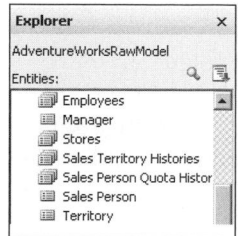

FIGURE 41.19   The Model Explorer.

For reports that return large amounts of data, it is recommended that you add filters to them. You can add a filter by clicking the filter icon in Report Builder. The type of the filter is also represented using natural language-friendly constructs, such as "Name starts with Smith" and "promotion equals true."

When you are done with a report's design, you can preview the report by clicking the Preview icon on the toolbar. At that point, the report definition is sent to the server, where it is parsed and compiled, the permissions of the user running it are checked, the semantic query is translated to the underlying T-SQL or Analysis Services MDX query, the report is executed, data is retrieved, and security filters are applied.

Unlike with the Report Designer, with Report Builder, all the report processing is performed on the server, and the client is used only for display. Hence, users of Report Builder are likely to exercise some amount of load on the servers: both the Reporting Services and SQL Server or Analysis Services data source servers. You will learn how to monitor and control this later in this chapter, in the section "Performance and Monitoring Tools."

Models and the Model Designer

In the previous section, you saw that Report Builder uses semantic data models. But how do you get one of them? It's actually pretty easy; you can auto-generate one or design one. One way to generate a data model is to find or create a data source in a report server. For example, to create a data source that points to the sample AdventureWorks database, you can click the New Data Source icon in Report Manager or connect to a report server in SSMS, right-click in the Object Explorer, and select New Data Source. Then you enter the name of the server and the database, as well as credentials to use to connect to the server, as in the following example:

```
"server=localhost;database=AdventureWorks"
```

Then you click the Generate Model button on the data source in Report Manager or SSMS. The newly generated model is saved at the location you specify on the server. Depending on the size of the database, the model generation operation may take a few minutes. The model generation process includes inspecting the structure of the tables, foreign keys, and indexes, as well as running statistics on various tables and views. However, most of the auto-generated models for real-world databases, including the one for AdventureWorks, need to be customized before they can be very useful.

If you want to customize models or design them from scratch, Model Designer is your friend. You start using it by creating a new report model project in BIDS. You create a new data source and point it to the AdventureWorks sample database. Then you create a data source view (DSV). You can either make the DSV reflect the entire database or restrict it to a certain schema. The DSV contains the information about the database objects as well as relationships between them; the graphical representation is very useful. Finally, you create a model based on the DSV. figure 41.20 shows the model generation options.

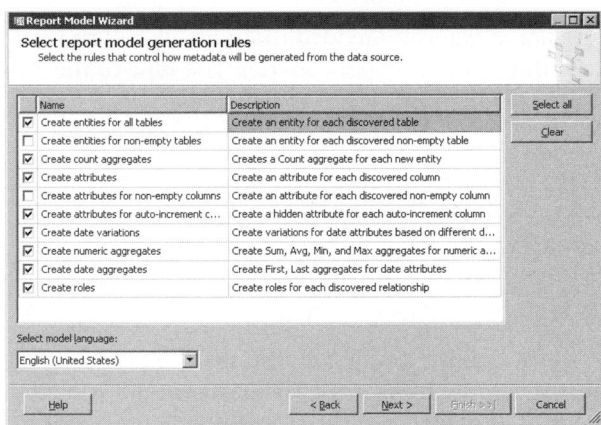

FIGURE 41.20   Model generation options.

A model has a tree structure and is made of entities and folder entities (which are simply grouping containers for other entities). Relationships between entities are called *roles*. Typically, tables and views are represented as entities, table columns are represented as attributes, and foreign key relationships are represented as roles. Some attributes, such as aggregates (for example, count, and sum), are calculated.

Most of the action in Model Designer happens in the Properties windows. You can view and set various properties for entities, attributes, roles, and folders. The values for the properties set in the Model Designer affect how they appear and are used in Report Builder.

41

> **NOTE**
>
> An important note on building models is that the underlying tables in the DSV have to have a primary key defined to be brought into a model. Report Builder models need to understand what represents one logical unit in the table, and Report Builder uses primary keys for that purpose.

A Model Design Example

To try your hand at designing a model and using it in reports, you need to start by generating a model in Report Manager, then load the "raw" model in a Model Designer project. You have obtained the model by auto-generating one from Report Manager, as described in the preceding section. You can get the model definition out of the server by clicking the Edit link on the Model Properties dialog in Report Manager. You should save the model on the local hard drive as `AdventureWorksRaw.smdl`.

Next, you should open BIDS and start a new report model project. In the Solution Explorer window, you right-click Report Models and choose Add Existing. Then you find the `.smdl` file you saved earlier and import it to the project.

Let's take a quick look at the model. As shown in figure 41.21, the main window displays the Model Designer view, which shows the model entities tree structure on the left and the attributes that belong to the selected entity on the right side. You can rename entities, roles, and attributes, but the Properties pane is where most of the features are exposed. You can read and set various properties for the selected model item, thus affecting how it will be used in Report Builder.

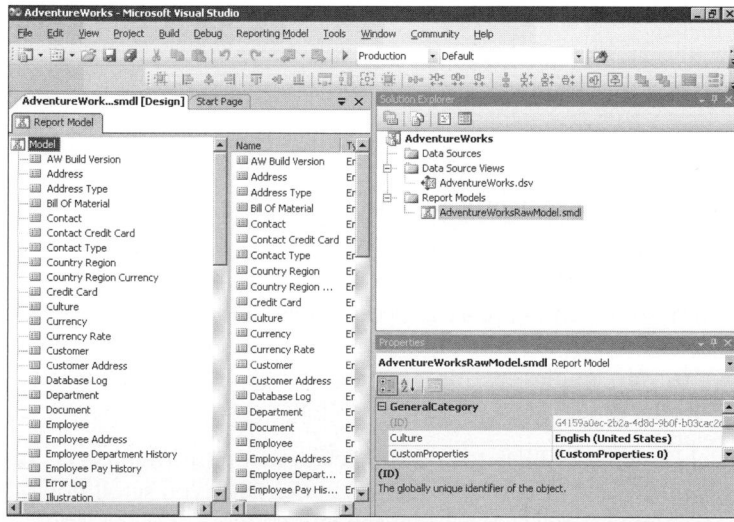

FIGURE 41.21   Model view in the Model Designer.

You can try to use this raw model in Report Builder. You need to click the Report Builder link in Report Manager, choose the AdventureWorksRaw model, and take a look at the Object Explorer. You should now see all the tables in the higher area of the tree and all columns and calculated fields in the lower part of the tree.

figure 41.22 shows the scalar columns defined in the SalesPerson table, such as Sales Quota, Bonus, and Commission Pct. Notice that for each scalar column, there are predefined aggregates, such as Sum, Avg, Min, and Max. A notable exception from the model is the missing relationship between salespersons and employees. From the database structure, you can tell that there is an inheritance relationship between salespersons and employees, yet the auto-generated model doesn't reflect that.

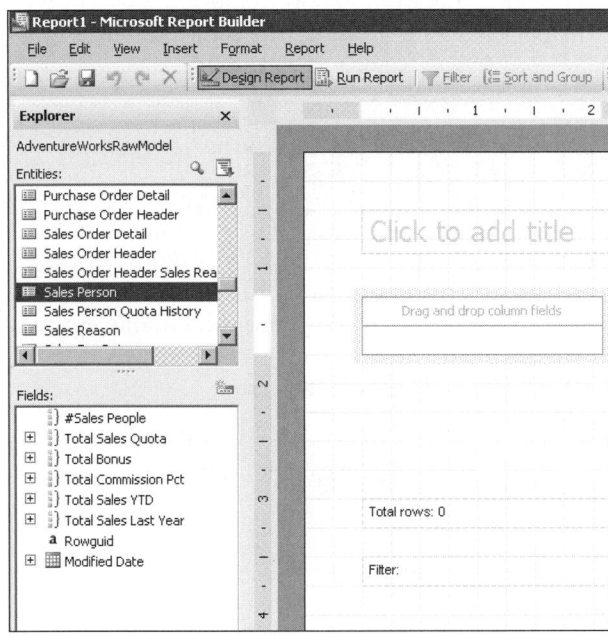

FIGURE 41.22   A Report Builder view of the model.

Defining Inheritance

By looking at the table structure shown in figure 41.23, you notice that there is a foreign key linking Sales.SalesPerson.SalesPersonID to HumanResource.Employee.EmployeeID. Because a salesperson is obviously an employee, this is a classic example of inheritance. Let's reflect this relationship in the model.

You can go back to the Model Designer in BIDS to add this relationship (see figure 41.23). First, select the Sales Person entity and open the Properties pane. Then you scroll down until you see the Inheritance property. Select InheritsFrom and choose Employee, and then choose the corresponding foreign key as the Binding property. By setting this inheritance relationship, you have made all the attributes of Employee also appear as attributes of Sales Person.

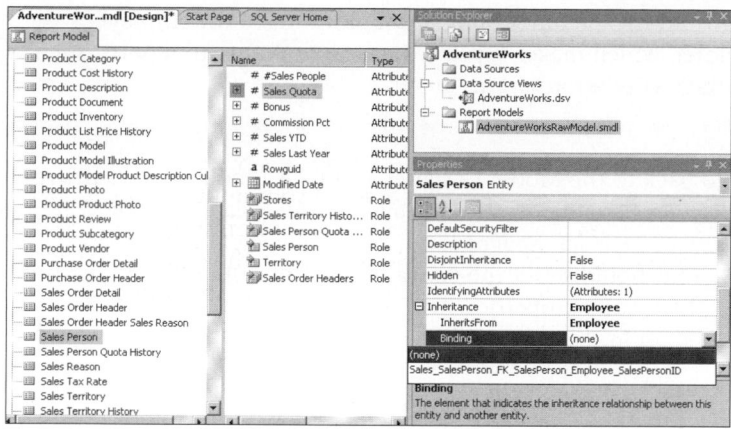

FIGURE 41.23   Defining inheritance in the Model Designer.

To see how this changes the model, you need to save your changes to the model and deploy it on your report server. In the Solution Explorer, right-click the solution itself and choose Properties. The Properties window appears, and in it you can type the link to the report server web service; the default is /ReportServer on the local machine. You can also choose where in the report server your models and data sources will be deployed. The default is two folders called /Models and /Data Sources, respectively. You should right-click on the solution again and choose Deploy.

Back on the server, you should reopen Report Builder. You need to choose the AdventureWorksRaw model again and find the Sales Person entity in the Explorer. As you can see in figure 41.24, now Sales Person has all the attributes of Employee, such as "hire date," "vacation," and "sick hours."

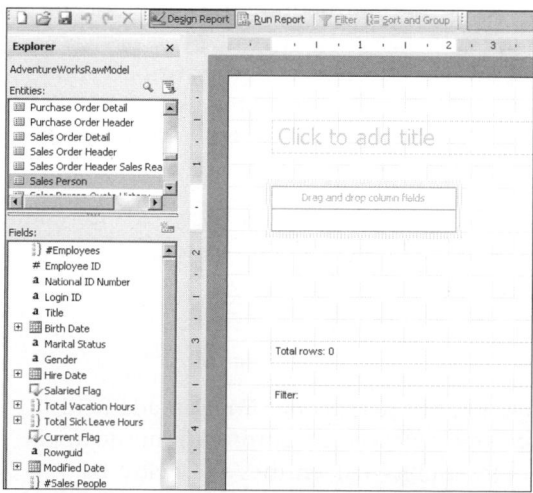

FIGURE 41.24   Inherited fields in Report Builder.

41

There is something missing from this picture, though: You don't have the employee names available in the Explorer, which makes it pretty hard to build useful reports, such as a list of salespeople and their sales information.

Promoting Properties

At this point, you need to go back to the Model Designer and take a look at the `Employee` entity properties. One of the roles hanging off the `Employee` entity is called `Contact`; it represents the foreign key between `HumanResources.Employees.ContactID` and `Person.Contact.ContactID`. You should select the `Contact` role from the right side of the Model Designer window and look at its properties. Then, choose `ExpandInline` and change its value to `True`, as shown in figure 41.25.

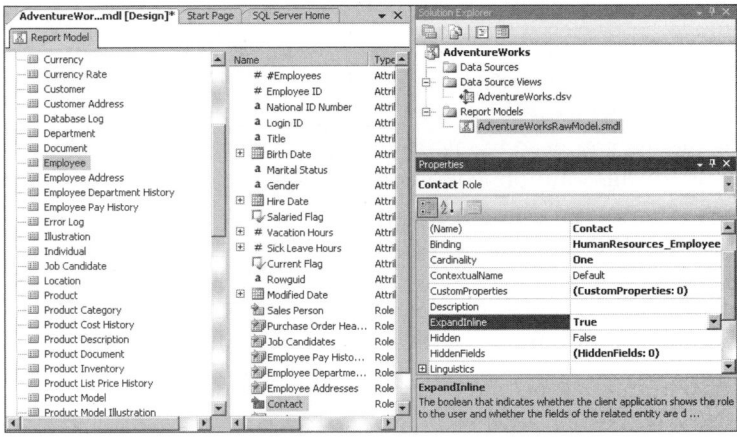

FIGURE 41.25   Promoted properties in Model Designer.

Setting the `Contact` role to expand inline has the effect of promoting the attributes and roles of the target entity inline with the source entity. For instance, when you navigate the relationship between `Employee` and `Contact` in Report Builder, all the attributes and relationships of `Contact` are shown as belonging to the `Employee` entity, instead of showing the relationship to `Contact`. This effectively removes the `Contact` role from `Employee` and replaces it with its fields and relationships.

To test your changes in Report Builder, you need to deploy the model as before and restart Report Builder, choosing the `AdventureWorksRaw` model. Then, when you select `Sales Person` in the Report Builder Explorer, you can see in the lower pane fields such as `First Name`, `Last Name`, and others that come from the `Contact` entity.

The Report Builder Design Surface

You are now ready to build a report that shows a list of salespeople. You can add fields to the report design surface in several ways: You can drag and drop entities (from the upper pane) or fields (from the lower pane), or you can double-click entities and fields. In general, dragging an item to the right of an existing item adds it to the existing group, if possible, whereas dragging it to the right of the item attempts to create a new group, if it is possible.

You should select `Sales Person` in the Report Builder Object Explorer. From the field pane, you drag and drop `First Name` and `Last Name` to the design surface. Then you add a couple `Sales Person`–specific fields, such as `#Bonus` and `#Sales Quota`. The report design surface should now look as shown in figure 41.26.

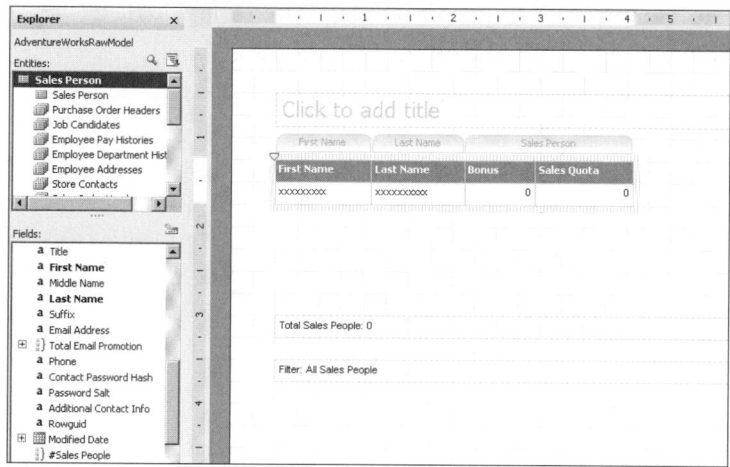

FIGURE 41.26   The design surface in the Report Builder.

Note the little rounded tabs just above the report columns in the design surface. They represent groups that will be generated in the report. Right now, it looks like the report will be grouped on `First Name`, `Last Name`, and `Sales Person`. Because it doesn't make sense to group on `First Name` and `Last Name`, you should remove those groups. The only way to do that in Report Builder (for this model) is to remove them from the design surface and again add them by dragging them to the right of the `Bonus` column. This makes them part of the `Sales Person` group. The report now has only one group, and it looks as shown in figure 41.27.

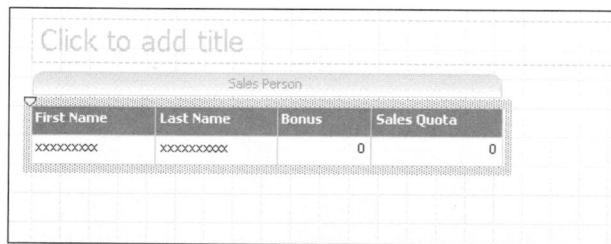

FIGURE 41.27   Grouping in the Report Builder.

Discourage Grouping

You might rightly think that it doesn't make much sense to group on First Name and Last Name in any report that users would build based on this model. It turns out that there is a way to make Report Builder not create a group when you add a field to a report. To set it, you go to the Model Designer, select Contact in the left pane, and select First Name in the right pane. In the Properties window, you set DiscourageGrouping to True. You do the same for Last Name.

Next, you redeploy your project and retest it in Report Builder. When you double-click the First Name and Last Name fields, they are added to the default group, Sales Person, instead of having separate groups created for them.

Roles and Drill-Through Reports

Now you should take your sample report—showing First Name, Last Name, Bonus, and Sales Quota for the Sales Person entity—and focus your attention on the upper pane of the Report Builder Explorer. You should see that the Explorer pane is now rooted at the Sales Person entity. Below it, you can see all the roles (or relationships) from this object to all the other objects in the model. A single-sheet icon represents a "to-one" relationship and a multiple-sheet icon represents a "to-many" relationship.

Suppose you want to add to your report the number of sales orders each sales person generated. As a model designer, you know this information is present in the Sales.SalesOrdersHeaders table, which is represented by the Sales Order Headers entity in the model.

Debugging Models and Model Queries

Strangely, when you browse through the roles of Sales Person, you see that Sales Orders Headers is present twice in the list. To see why, you can click the first Sales Orders Headers element in the list and double-click #Sales Order Headers to add it to the report. Then you can select the second Sales Order Headers in the Explorer tree and add its own #Sales Order Headers to the report. The report design surface should now look as shown in figure 41.28.

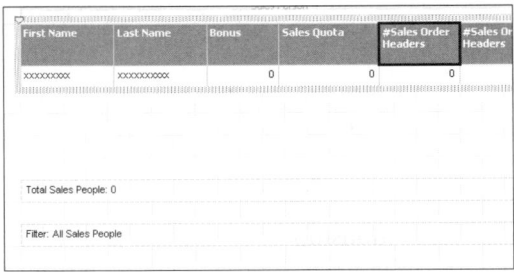

FIGURE 41.28   Adding relationships in the Report Builder.

When you run the report, you get the result shown in figure 41.29.

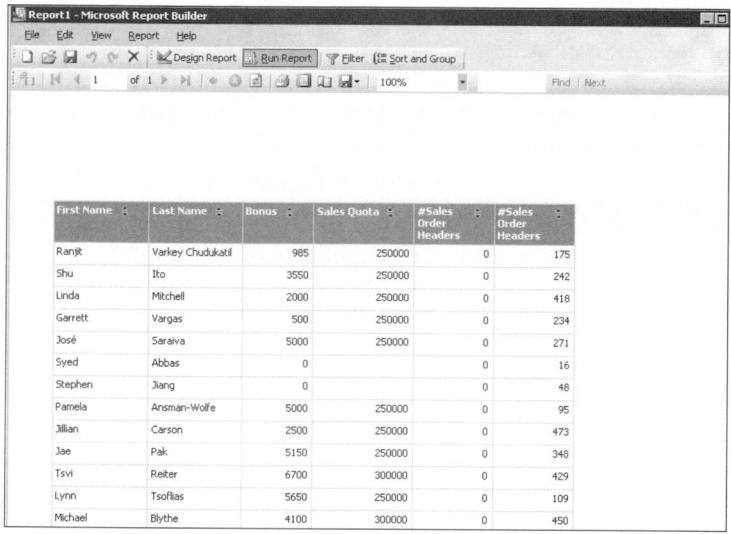

FIGURE 41.29   Previewing the report with duplicate relationships in Report Builder.

It's obvious that the first relationship is not yielding the desired results. Let's go back to the Model Designer and examine why. If you navigate to the Sales Person entity in the Model Designer, you see that it has a SalesOrderHeaders relationship that corresponds to the foreign key between Sales.SalesPerson.SalesPersonID and Sales.SalesOrderHeader. SalesPersonID. That is one of the two relationships, but where is the second? Remember that you made Sales Person inherit from Employee and set the relationship from Employee to Contact to Expand Inline. What this means for the model is that all the Contact relationships and fields are included in the Employee relationships and fields and thus in the Sales Person relationships and fields.

If you select Contact in the Model Explorer, you can see one of its relationships is SalesOrderHeaders; it corresponds to the foreign key between Person.Contact.ContactID and Sales.SalesOrderHeader.ContactID. This explains why you see the two relationships with the same name for Sales Person. It also explains why the second relationship gave you incorrect results: the join to the SalesOrderHeader table is made using the ContactID column instead of the SalesPersonID column. Therefore, this extra relationship represents the contact person for the sales order, not the sales person who generated the sales order.

Now that you have found the first model error, there are several ways to fix it:

▶ You could decide the Contact-to-Sales Person relationship is not useful for any reports built on this model, so you can mark it as hidden. Then, it will not appear in the Report Builder Explorer at all.

▶ If you see some value in using this relationship, you can disambiguate the name, by calling it Contact Sales Order Headers, for example.

You can make either of these fixes by editing the Sales Order Headers relationship properties in the Model Designer. For continuing this example you should choose the second approach and rename Contact-to-Sales Order Headers relationship. In the Model Designer, you select the Contact entity, select the Sales Orders Headers relationship in the center pane, and right-click Rename or press F2.

TIP

For debugging purposes, you might want to examine the queries that Report Builder generates. To do this, you can either start a SQL Server trace on the database server used as an underlying data source for the model or locate the file Program Files\Microsoft SQL Server\[*SQL instance*]\Reporting Services\ ReportServer\web.config. Then you need to find the RSTrace element in the file and change this line:

```
<add name="Components"
Value="all,RunningJobs:3,SemanticQueryEngine:2,SemanticModelGenerator:2" />
```

to this:

```
<add name="Components"
value="all,RunningJobs:3,SemanticQueryEngine:4,SemanticModelGenerator:2" />
```

Next, you run your report in Report Builder. Then you find the most recent report server log file: Program Files\Microsoft SQL Server\[*SQL instance*]\Reporting Services\LogFiles\ReportServer_[*timestamp*].log. Toward the end of the log file should be the SQL statement that resulted from the Report Builder query.

Make sure you revert this change after you are done developing or debugging your queries, as it will result in extraneous logging on the report server.

Now that you have fixed the relationships, you can restart Report Builder, load the new model, and rebuild the report:

1. Select Sales Person in the Explorer.

2. Drag First Name, Last Name, #Bonus, and #Sales Quota to the design surface.

3. In the Explorer pane, take a look at the relationships. You should now see both Sales Orders Headers and the newly renamed relationship Contact Sales Order Headers.

4. Select the Sales Order Headers relationship and add #Sales Order Headers to the report. Because this is an aggregate, Report Builder adds a total field. Because this is a simple detail list, you don't need the total, so you can right-click on the #Sales Order Headers column in the design surface and uncheck the Show Subtotal check box.

5. Run the report. It should look similar to the one shown in figure 41.30.

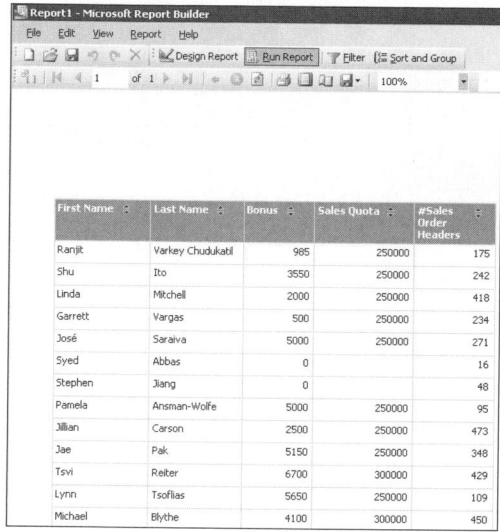

FIGURE 41.30   Previewing the fixed report in Report Builder.

Sorting in Report Builder

The sample report is not sorted in any particularly useful order. Suppose you want to see the salesperson who has generated most orders first. To do this, open the Sort and Group dialog and select #Sales Order Headers and Descending.

Note that it is possible to interactively sort the data in your reports by clicking the arrows next to the column headers. To enable or disable this feature for your reports, you can choose Report, Report Properties and then check or uncheck Allow Users to Sort the Report Data When Viewing It.

Generating Drill-Through Reports

When you run the report you have just built, you might notice that you can actually click #Sales Order Headers and get the details about the sales orders of a specific salesperson. For instance, clicking the first row yields the report shown in figure 41.31, which displays all sales orders generated by Jillian Carson.

Observe that the Sales Order Headers report itself contains links to other reports; both the #Sales Order Header Sales Reasons and #Sales Order Details fields contain links to their respective reports.

The ability to generate drill-through links on-the-fly is a powerful Report Builder feature, and it is included in the Enterprise and Developer Editions of SQL Server 2005. The Sales Order Headers report is auto-generated by Report Builder based on the information about the original salespersons list report and the filter used—in this case, the salesperson who generated the orders. Report Builder automatically generates drill-through links every time you add fields from entities related to the main entity of the report.

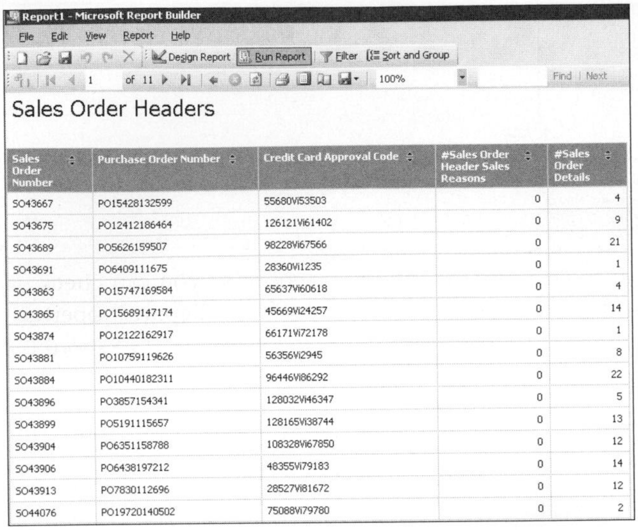

Sales Order Number	Purchase Order Number	Credit Card Approval Code	#Sales Order Header Sales Reasons	#Sales Order Details
SO43667	PO15428132599	55680Vi53503	0	4
SO43675	PO12412186464	126121Vi61402	0	9
SO43689	PO5626159507	98228Vi67566	0	21
SO43691	PO6409111675	28360Vi1235	0	1
SO43863	PO15747169584	65637Vi60618	0	4
SO43865	PO15689147174	45669Vi24257	0	14
SO43874	PO12122162917	66171Vi72178	0	1
SO43881	PO10759119626	56356Vi2945	0	8
SO43884	PO10440182311	96446Vi86292	0	22
SO43896	PO3857154341	128032Vi46347	0	5
SO43899	PO5191115657	128165Vi38744	0	13
SO43904	PO6351158788	108328Vi67850	0	12
SO43906	PO6438197212	48355Vi79183	0	14
SO43913	PO7830112696	28527Vi81672	0	12
SO44076	PO19720140502	75088Vi79780	0	2

FIGURE 41.31 A drill-through report in Report Builder.

Saving and Opening Reports

By default, Report Builder saves and loads reports in or to the report server it is connected to. Optionally, you can save or open Report Builder reports to the local file system by using File, Save to File and File, Open. You should save the report you have been designing so far to the report server root folder; you can call it `SalesPeople`.

Customizing Drill-Through Reports

If you don't like the look of the "stock" drill-through reports, the good news is that you can customize your drill-through reports, and you can also replace the ones that Report Builder generates automatically with your own. Suppose you would like a slightly different view of `Sales Orders Headers` whenever you navigate to it. To customize this, you open Report Builder and select the `Sales Order Headers` entity in the Explorer. Then add `Sales Order ID` to the report, along with `Order Date`, `Due Date`, and `Ship Date`. From the related entities, you select `Sales Person`, and then add `First Name` and `Last Name` to the report. For clarity, you should rename the column headers `Sales Person First Name` and `Sales Person Last Name`.

Now when you try to save the report, you get an error saying the report needs a filter (see figure 41.32). This warning is issued because the `InstanceSelection` property in the model is set to `Mandatory Filter` for the `Sales Order Header` entity. This is normally done when the underlying table is too large to be useful as an unfiltered list in the report. The model auto-generation process has sampled the data and has automatically set this value for the `Sales Order Header` entity.

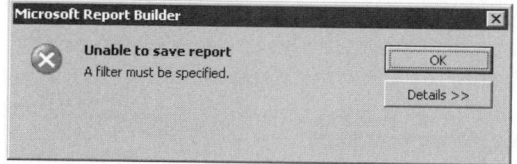

FIGURE 41.32   A required filter error.

In this case, you only want to use this report as a drill-through report, so you can check the Allow Users to Drill to This Report from Other Reports setting in the Report Properties page. Setting this property allows you to save the report on the report server. You should call the new report SalesOrderHeaders and save it on the report server.

Now you need to use SSMS to associate the report with an entity in the report model. In SSMS, you navigate in the Report Server tree to the AdventureWorksRaw model, right-click, and choose Properties. Then you select Drill-through Reports and select the Sales Order Header entity. Next, type /SalesOrdersHeaders or choose the SalesOrderHeaders report for both single-instance and multiple-instance drill-through reports. Then you click OK.

figure 41.33 shows the drill-through selection pages in SSMS.

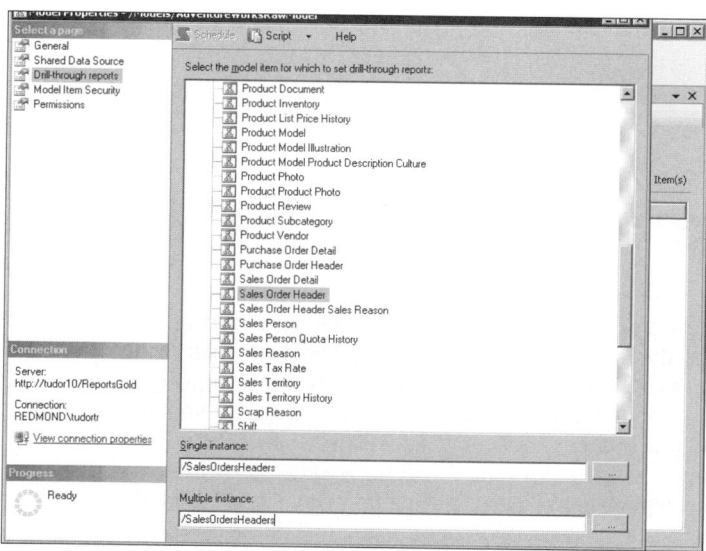

FIGURE 41.33   Selecting drill-through reports in SSMS.

Now you can restart Report Builder. Instead of choosing a model to start designing a new report, you should now open the previously saved SalesPeople report from the report server. You don't even have to make any changes to the report, so you can simply choose

Run Report. You see the same list of salespeople as before, but when you click the #Sales Order Headers rows, you get your customized report instead of the auto-generated one. The drill-through report should look similar to the one shown in figure 41.34.

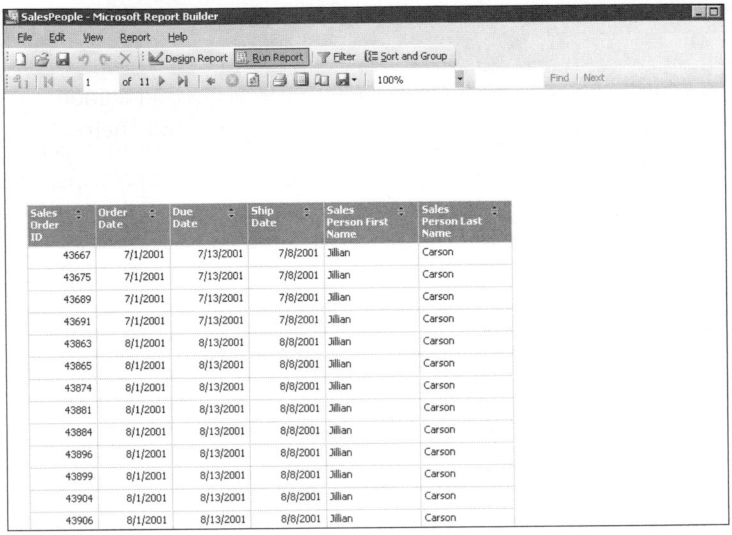

FIGURE 41.34   Previewing a drill-through report in Report Builder.

It is interesting to note that all drill-through reports to the Sales Order Header entity—no matter where they come from, will—use this report in the future, instead of the auto-generated one.

Architecture Notes

You can save Report Builder reports on the report server. When you do so, the queries saved in the reports are still semantic queries—that is, expressed in the XML-based semantic query language understood by the report server. When the report is executed, the semantic query module of the report server translates the semantic query into the underlying T-SQL or MDX statements supported by the underlying data source server. This means you don't have direct control over the SQL statements that are generated. (However, you can influence them by changing the semantic queries in the report or model characteristics.) The advantages of this approach are that you get features such as row- and column-based security, picking up changes to the model without changing the reports previously saved, and automatic drill-through generation.

Other Model and Model Designer Features

This chapter has only scratched the surface when it comes to the usage and features of report models and Report Builder. It is worth mentioning that the Reporting Services samples contain a sample AdventureWorks model that has been customized to a great extent to make reporting on it easier.

41

A useful way to learn more about model features is to open both the raw model and the customized AdventureWorks model in Report Builder and Model Designer and look at the differences between them. If you like how a certain entity, relationship, or field looks and works in Report Builder, you can compare its settings in the two models. The description and help links for models are very useful in getting a better idea of how to use them.

Remember that if you are a model designer, you need to have a good understanding of the database schema and relationships in it. The good news is that if you build a good model, your users won't have to worry about the database, and they can build their reports to suit their needs without much help from you.

Model Security

Like individual reports and data sources, objects within models can be individually secured. For instance, if you want to allow only a certain group of users access to the Human Resources part of the model, you can set up security on those entities. Other users that are not members of that group won't even see the entities in the Report Builder. Even more, if they run existing model-based reports that reference the Employee entity, the columns they don't have access to are automatically filtered out by the query generation layer in the report server.

For example, in the list of salespersons report you built earlier in this chapter, suppose you decide you want to restrict access to the Bonus and Sales Quota fields of the Sales Person entity to the Human Resources Windows security group. To do so, you open SSMS, navigate to the model in the Report Server tree, right-click, and choose Properties. In the Properties dialog that appears, you select Model Item Security and check Secure Individual Model Items Independently for This Model.

Next, select the model node, in this case AdventureWorksRawModel, and add Authenticated Users in the Model Item Browser security role. This way, all users have access to the model. Then you should navigate through the model hierarchy to the Sales Person entity, expand it, and select the Bonus node. Next, you should remove security inheritance by switching from Inherit roles from the parent folder to Use these roles for each group or user account. Then, remove the Authenticated Users group and add the Human Resources group (or some other appropriate Windows group) to the Model Item browser role. Now a user who is not part of the Human Resources group will not see the Bonus field in Report Builder.

Security is not limited to running reports in Report Builder. When reports are saved on a report server, users can access them through Report Manager. A user who has permissions to view the SalesPeople report but doesn't have permissions to the Bonus field will simply not see the Bonus column when running the report. This powerful feature is called *column sub-setting* and is specific to reports using models. figure 41.35 shows an example. This report contains the Bonus column, but when it is accessed by a user who does not have permissions, the Bonus column is automatically omitted from the report.

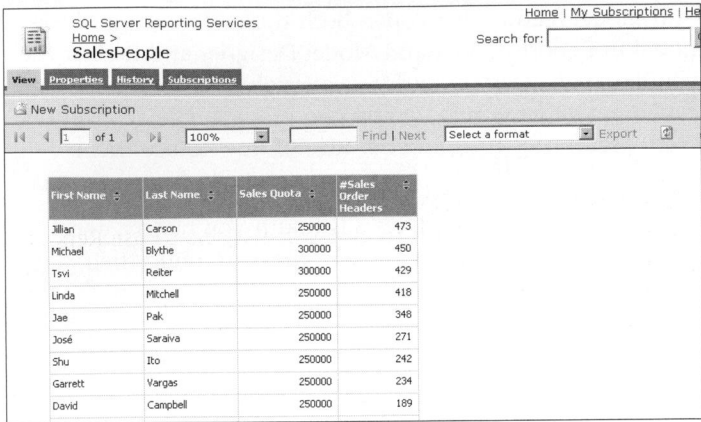

FIGURE 41.35   Filtering columns based on security.

Security Notes

Several resources are independently secured when you run reports in the report server:

▶ You can secure the report itself, by setting permissions on the report or inheriting permissions from the parent folder or the parent's parent, and so on, all the way up to the report server root folder.

▶ You can secure the model in the report server; this is similar to the way reports are secured. If a certain user is not granted permissions to a model, he or she can't see the model when Report Builder starts up, and can't build or run reports based on it.

▶ You can secure the items in the model—for example, entities, fields, and relationships—in addition to securing the model itself.

You need to keep in mind a couple security override rules for models:

▶ If a certain user has permissions to manage the model, this overrides the permissions set for any model items in the report. For instance, if Bob is given content manager permissions on the model, Bob sees all entities and fields in that model, regardless of the security set for model items. In the example we've been discussing, Bob can see the Bonus field if he has "content manager" permissions on the model, even though he doesn't have explicit permissions on the field.

▶ Local administrators on the report server machine have special permissions in the report server: They can view and change security for any resource stored in the report server. In the example we've been discussing, if Bob is member of the Administrator group on the report server machine, Bob can see the Model and Bonus fields, even if he doesn't have explicit permissions on them.

Enabling Ad Hoc Reporting

Report Builder relies on having a report server available. It uses the report server to load data models, run the reports, and save and load them from the server. On the other hand, like all the other SQL Server 2005 services, Reporting Services is locked down by default.

The following sections describe the changes you need to make in order to enable Report Builder functionality. These sections assume a Windows security group called `AdventureWorks Report Builders`, to which you want to give permissions to use Report Builder on the `AdventureWorks` model.

Granting Execute Report Definitions—A Global Permission

To start, you should open Report Manager, go to Site Settings, and click Configure Site-wide Security. The list of permissions that appears contains pairs of Windows users or groups and report server security roles. (A security role is a collection of permissions.)

You should click New Role Assignment and add `AdventureWorks Report Builders` to the `System User` role. If you click the `System User` role, you see the permissions it contains; the one you are interested in is `Execute Report Definitions`. To run reports in Report Builder, this permission is required.

Setting Permissions on the Model

To run reports against a model, users need `Browser` permissions to that model. To set permissions, in Report Manager, you navigate to the `AdventureWorks` model, click the Security link in the Properties pane, click Edit Item Security, click OK on the confirmation dialog, and add the `AdventureWorks Report Builder` group to the `Browser` role. Then, if you click the `Browser` role, you see the permissions it contains. In this case, you want the `View Models` permission.

In addition, if you want users to see the Report Manager home folder, you need to add the group to the `Browser` role in the home folder. Because permissions are inherited, unless inheritance is specifically broken, the members of that group then have permission to the entire content of the report server.

To remove permissions on a specific folder, you navigate to the folder, select Properties, Security, Edit Item Security; then you remove the respective role assignments.

After you have done all that, you can log on as `Bob`—a member of the `AdventureWorks Report Builders` Windows security group—and navigate to the Report Manager home page. When you click the Report Builder button, you see the `AdventureWorks` model in the list, and you should be able to design and run ad hoc reports.

Management and Security

This section will discuss several important aspects of managing and securing your Reporting Services deployment.

Deploying Reports

Deploying the reports to a report server is the first step in making them available to users. You can deploy reports from the report design tools, such as BIDS or Report Builder. You can upload report definitions to a server by using Report Manager or SSMS; you simply use the Upload Report link or the Import File menu item in SSMS.

When a report is published on the server, its content is validated, and it is compiled to an internal format. (If the report contains code, it is compiled into .NET assemblies.) The result is stored in the report server database.

Scripting Support in Reporting Services

All the Reporting Services tools described earlier in this section use the SOAP APIs exposed by the Report Server Web Service to perform the report upload operation. If you want to programmatically upload reports from a script or a batch file, you are in luck because Reporting Services has a script host that can execute its SOAP APIs. To see it in action, you open SSMS, log on to a report server, right-click the Home node in the Object Explorer tree, and select Import File. Then you choose a report (.rdl) file from your hard drive; for instance, one of the sample reports that come with the product.

Next, you select Overwrite Item if It Exists. Then, instead of clicking the OK button, you click the Script button at the top of the Import File dialog. A new file with the extension .rss (which stands for Reporting Services script) is created; it contains VB .NET code, ready to be executed by the report server script host.

To execute the newly created script against a report server, you need to find your copy of rs.exe, the script host executable. It is installed with the report server, and the default installation path is C:\Program Files\Microsoft SQL Server\90\Tools\Binn. To run the script file, you use the following command line:

```
rs.exe -i c:\RSSQuery1.rss -s http://localhost/Reportserver
```

The script containing the CreateReport SOAP API runs, thus deploying the report on the server.

If the report references a shared data source, you need to take another step before the report is operational: You should create the shared data source (if it doesn't exist) and bind the report to it. The Report Designer and Report Builder do this step automatically for you. If you use Report Manager, SSMS, or a batch script, you need to perform these operations yourself.

You bind a report to a data source through Report Manager by selecting Properties, Data Sources. Then you click A Shared Data Source and use the tree control to select the correct shared data source. Then you click OK, followed by Apply.

If you choose to use a batch script, you need to call the APIs CreateDataSource and SetItemDataSources.

Securing Reports

The report server has a built-in role-based security system. All operations done on the server are subject to permissions. Access to the report server is controlled through security roles and role assignments.

A *security role* is a collection of permissions (for example, the permission to create reports in a folder, the permission to view a certain report or a folder).

A *role assignment* is a set of permissions represented by the role that are given to a user or group on a certain report or folder in the report server. For example, the permissions on the folder called Data Sources contain the local administrators group with all permissions contained in the Content Manager role.

Permissions on folders are inherited to all items present in that folder, unless security inheritance is intentionally broken and the item is given its own permissions.

Built-in Roles and Permissions

Reporting Services comes with a set of built-in roles. Each role is a collection of permissions, normally used together to enable a functional scenario. The following are some of the built-in roles:

- ▶ **Browser**—This role is a collection of read-only permissions that is useful for navigating the Reporting Services namespace and viewing reports and resources.

- ▶ **Content Manager**—This role is similar to an administrator on the part of the report server where it is granted. A person who has the Content Manager role can view and change any reports, folders, data sources, and resources and can read and set security settings in the folders where he or she has that permission.

- ▶ **Publisher**—This role is useful for report authors who need to create and change reports, folders, and data sources in a specified folder.

- ▶ **Report Builder**—This role can be used for granting permissions needed for editing Report Builder reports.

- ▶ **My Reports**—This security role is normally given to each user in his or her own My Reports folder. The My Reports feature is disabled by default, but it can be enabled from the Site Settings page in Report Manager. It gives each user of the report server his or her own place to publish documents on the server.

The security roles system is fully customizable. You can change or even delete existing roles, and you can also create new ones.

To see the roles, you navigate to the Site Settings link in Report Manager and click the item-level role definitions and system-level role definitions.

In SSMS, you can see the roles under the Security node in the Report Server tree.

Reporting Services comes with a set of built-in permissions. Like all the other SQL Server 2005 servers, Reporting Services is secured by default. Local administrators on the report server machine are granted Content Manager permissions on the root of the namespace, and no one else has any permissions. To make the report server accessible to users, you need to explicitly grant permissions on the folders you want to make available to them.

System Roles and System Permissions

So far we have only talked about permissions on items in the report server namespace: reports, folders, and data sources. The report server also contains a set of serverwide roles and permissions. These are called *system roles*, and you can access them by selecting Report Manager's Site Settings link and then selecting Configure System-Level Role Definitions and Configure Site-wide Security.

As mentioned earlier in this chapter, system roles are collections of permissions, such as View Shared Schedules or Execute Report Definitions. These permissions are not specific to a certain folder or part of the namespace but are global to the entire report server installation. A site permission is a collection of these roles assigned to users or groups. Out of the box, Local administrators on the report server box are by default given the permissions contained in the System Administrator role.

To open up your system to users, you add Windows users and groups to the site security. As with normal roles, you can change or delete the built-in system roles, or you can create other system roles.

Authentication of Report Server Users: Windows and Forms

By default, the report server uses Windows security to authenticate its users. In other words, a user has to have a valid Windows account, be it local or part of a domain.

Authentication and security are two extensible areas of the Reporting Services platform. Microsoft has published an example of how to build and integrate a Forms-based security model in the report server. For more details, refer to the Technical Article at http://msdn.microsoft.com/library/default.asp?url=/library/en-us/dnsql2k/html/ufairs.asp.

Subscriptions

An important advantage to having reports available on a report server is that you can use its push, or subscription, features to make your reports available to users.

You can create subscriptions both in Report Manager and in SSMS. You can start with a report published to the server. You need to connect SSMS to the report server and then, in the Object Explorer, right-click the Subscriptions node and choose New Subscription. The first step in the Subscription dialog is to choose a delivery mode. There are three built-in delivery methods: email, file-share, and null. The null delivery, as its name suggests, doesn't deliver anywhere; however, you can use it as a way to periodically load reports in the report server cache. For details on this, see the section "Report execution options," later in this chapter.

> **NOTE**
>
> A prerequisite to using the email delivery extension is to configure it. Using the Reporting Services Configuration tool, you navigate to the E-mail Settings pane and set the sender address and the SMTP server name to a valid SMTP server.
>
> Another prerequisite for subscriptions is the SQL Server Agent service. Subscriptions use it, so it has to be enabled and running.

In this case, you should choose e-mail as the delivery method and fill in the To, Cc, and other email settings on the General pane. You also need to choose a format on which the report should be delivered. The default is web archive, also known as MHTML, but you can change it Excel, PDF, or one of the other supported formats.

The next step is to pick a schedule. You can choose a schedule just for this report subscription, or you can use a shared schedule for several subscriptions. Five recurrence patterns are available for subscriptions: Hourly, Daily, Weekly, Monthly, and Once.

If your report has parameters, you also need to decide what parameter values to use when the report is executed as part of the subscription.

One restriction in creating subscriptions is that the report data sources have to have stored credentials, whether they are Windows or database credentials. Integrated security and prompted credentials are not compatible with subscriptions because the actual user isn't around at the time the subscription will run.

Data-Driven Subscriptions

One way to deliver reports is through data-driven subscriptions. A dynamic or data-driven subscription is very useful for delivering parameterized reports to a number of recipients whose email addresses are stored in a database, for instance. Unlike with a regular subscription, the recipient's settings—such as the To or Cc address, the title of the email, and the parameters of the report being run—can all be based on a SQL Server query. For example, using the AdventureWorks sample database, let's say you want to send quarterly human resources information reports to all managers at the company.

Suppose you have created a Human Resources report that takes a parameter, the login ID of an employee. If that employee is a manager, the report displays a list of all employees reporting to him/her, together with the person's title, the base pay rate, vacation hours, and sick leave hours.

You start the data-driven subscription wizard by right-clicking New Data-driven Subscription on the Subscription tab for the Human Resources report. Then you need to choose a name and a delivery extension for the subscription, so type Send quarterly HR reports to managers and choose Report Server Email.

On the data source page, you use the shared `AdventureWorks` data source that you created earlier. You then enter the following query, which selects the email addresses and login IDs of all managers:

```
SELECT DISTINCT ManagerContact.EmailAddress, Manager.LoginID
FROM HumanResources.Employee Employee
INNER JOIN HumanResources.Employee Manager
ON Manager.EmployeeID = Employee.ManagerID
INNER JOIN Person.Contact ManagerContact
ON ManagerContact.ContactID = Manager.EmployeeID
ORDER BY ManagerContact.EmailAddress
```

You can then bind `Manager.EmailAddress` to the To field in the email and `Manager.LoginID` to the `LoginID` parameter of the `Human Resources` report. The last step is to choose a schedule for this subscription.

Subscription and Delivery Architecture

Let's take a look at what happens under the covers when a subscription is created. The metadata for the subscription is validated and stored in the report server catalog database. A SQL Agent job is created, and the schedule specified in the subscription is saved in the SQL Agent job.

When the time comes, the SQL Agent job fires, inserting a so-called "event" row in the report server catalog. The report server matches the event with the information about the subscribers and sends notifications to the subscribers. The notifications are processed in the report server Windows service; the report is run and delivered to its target.

This architecture (which is shared with SQL Server Notification Services) allows Reporting Services to scale very well with the number of subscribers and events. Because the events are recorded in the catalog database, it also allows for a scale-out configuration, so you can have a number of services process notifications in parallel, thus achieving greater scalability.

Report Execution Options

Another very useful feature of Reporting Services is the ability to cache report data, to display the data as of a certain date, and to display historical snapshots of a report's data. The following sections describe these capabilities.

Live Reports and Sessions

By default, when a report is deployed on the server, it is configured to be run live, or on-demand. Every time a user clicks the report link in Report Manager, the report queries are executed; the report is then processed, filters are applied, sorting is performed, and expressions are evaluated. Finally, the report is rendered to the desired format and returned to the user. The result of this report execution is stored in a format-independent fashion in the report server temporary database. This result is called a *session snapshot*. When the user navigates other pages of the report or exports the report to a different format, the session snapshot is used to perform these operations; this way, the report queries do not have to be rerun.

A session snapshot is tied to a specific user, is typically associated with a browser session, and is generally short lived (on the order of minutes).

Cached Reports

Now let's assume that report queries take a relatively long time to run and the data to be displayed doesn't change very often. In that case, you can set the execution options to cache for this report. To do so, in SSMS, you right-click the report and select Properties to show the Properties pane. Then you select the Execution tab and choose Cache the Report. Now, when the first user accesses this report, the report is executed (as described earlier), but the resulting snapshot will, from that point on, be shared across users. When a second user clicks the report link, instead of the report running again, the user gets the snapshot that was generated when the first user ran it.

There are two ways to remove a snapshot from the cache:

▶ **After a certain number of minutes of inactivity**—This is a "sliding" expiration, meaning that as long as users navigate to the report, it is kept in the cache. If no one has requested the report for more than the specified number of minutes, the cache is expired, and the next report request causes a live execution, which starts another cache session, and so on.

▶ **On a schedule**—This is useful if the data is not valid after a certain date (for example, if sales information changes every two weeks), and you don't want any cached report to show the data older than this date.

Execution Snapshots

If you never want your users to run reports against live data (for example, the queries are prohibitively expansive or they only make sense for end-of-month sales and the report should be run only on the first day of each month for the data to be relevant), you can set the report settings to Execution Snapshot. The report server then runs the report on this schedule. Your users always get the data from this execution snapshot.

These are the differences between execution snapshots and cached reports:

▶ Cached reports can run live if the cache is expired; execution snapshots are guaranteed to run only on the specified schedule.

▶ Reports with parameters can be cached for each individual parameter value; in contrast, only one execution snapshot per report is allowed in this version of Reporting Services.

History Snapshots

History snapshots are useful if you want to keep historical data for your reports. Say that you want to keep track of all your monthly sales reports from month to month. You can configure this on the History tab in the Report Properties dialog. You simply set Use a Monthly Schedule to Take Historical Snapshots for Your Reports.

To see historical snapshots, you go to Report Manager, click the report, and choose the History tab. You see a list of all historical snapshots taken from this report. When you click a report on the list, you see the actual report data.

Limitations for Cached Reports and Execution Snapshots and History Snapshots

Cached reports, execution snapshots, and history snapshots have something in common: They all allow sharing of report data among users. Therefore, a report server does not let you use these features with reports that contain user-specific data. Per-user references in the report include the usage of User!UserID in the report definition, the use of integrated security in the report data sources, and the Impersonate After Connection Is Made option for SQL Server data sources.

In addition, execution snapshots and history snapshots are allowed only for reports with no parameters or parameters with default values. For parameterized reports, a snapshot uses the default parameter value.

Performance and Monitoring Tools

Reporting Services includes a number of performance and monitoring tools: the trace log, the execution log, event log entries for system errors, and a set of performance counters. Also, to improve the product's quality, Reporting Services can send error reports to Microsoft if you opt in during Setup or by selecting Start, SQL Server Error and Usage Reporting Tool.

The Server Trace Log

Similarly to SQL Server, Reporting Services writes trace and error information to its log files. The Reporting Services log files are located in `Program Files\Microsoft SQL Server\[SQLInstance]\Reporting Services\LogFiles`. The main reasons to look in the trace log files are to get more information about errors and to perform troubleshooting operations.

The log files contain three types of events: errors, warnings, and informational messages. Each trace log starts with a prefix that includes the current timestamp, the process and thread used to log the error, the type of the error, and the message itself.

Each Reporting Services service component writes to its own trace file. Trace files with names that start with `ReportServer` are written by the web service component, and the ones that start with `ReportServerService` belong to the Windows service, and those that start with `ReportServerWebApp` belong to the Report Manager component. Reporting Services automatically deletes trace files older than a certain number of days.

The Execution Log

All report executions are stored in a table called ExecutionLog in the ReportServer database. Reporting Service also ships an Integration Services package that can be used to extract data from the ExecutionLog table into a database that can be used for reporting. It also includes a set of sample reports that run against this database.

If you are interested in what reports your users most commonly run, which ones take the most time or are the biggest, or how many of them have succeeded of failed, you can turn to the execution log for the answers. For more details on how to get the data out of the execution log and on how to use the execution log sample reports, see the Books Online topic "Querying and Reporting on Report Execution Log Data."

As with old trace log files, Reporting Services deletes execution log entries older than two months.

Event Log Entries

Reporting Services writes configuration or internal server errors to the application event log. It also writes a number of informational messages (for example, when there are changes to the configuration files). The event log entries are marked with Report Server* as the source.

Performance Counters

Reporting Services defines a number of performance counters that you can use to measure the performance of your system. There are two performance counter categories: MSRS 2005 Web Service and MSRS 2005 Windows Service. You will see a number of counters for each service and an instance for each instance of Reporting Services running on that machine. For more details, see the "Monitoring Report Server performance" topic in Books Online.

Building Applications for SQL Server Reporting Services 2005 Using the Report Viewer Controls

Reporting Services was designed from the ground up as an extensible enterprise reporting platform. Compared to the previous version, In SQL Server 2005, Reporting Services is much easier to integrate into applications. The preferred way to integrate Reporting Services reports in applications it to use the Visual Studio 2005 report controls. The two report controls—one for Windows Forms and one for Web Forms projects—allow developers a rich interaction between reports and existing applications.

The report controls can function in two modes:

> ► **Local mode**—In local mode, the report-processing engine is hosted in the application itself. There is no need to install or use SQL Server Reporting Services. Because there is no report server around, there are a number of limitations when using the controls in local mode.

▶ **Server mode**—In server mode, the controls are a full-fledged interface for Reporting Services, combined with a rich programming model suited for embedding reports in an application while taking advantage of the advanced features of Reporting Services: Report Builder and models, subscriptions, security, caching, history, and so on.

The rest of this chapter talks about using the report controls in server mode.

Using the ASP.NET Report Controls in a Website

In this section, you will create a simple ASP.NET website that includes a report control. To follow the example, you need SQL Server 2005, including Reporting Services, and Visual Studio 2005 installed on a development machine.

As a preparation step, you need to find the AdventureWorks sample reports that are installed as part of the documentation and samples with SQL Server 2005. You should open the solution in BIDS and deploy the reports on the report server. The default location puts them in a report server folder named AdventureWorks Sample Reports. You should verify that the reports are running by navigating to them using your browser.

To start the new project, you open Visual Studio 2005 and select New Web Site. An ASPX page named default.aspx appears. You should switch to the design view, go to the Toolbox pane, and look under the Data tab. This is the home of the new ReportViewer control (see figure 41.36).

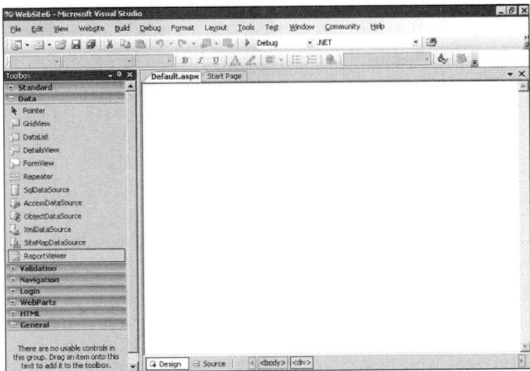

FIGURE 41.36   The Visual Studio 2005 Toolbox window.

When you drag the ReportViewer control on the page, you get a task pane in which you can configure it. As shown in figure 41.37, you should select Server Report and then enter the URL to the report server as well as the path within the report server for the report you want to use. If you used the default settings to deploy the AdventureWorks sample, you enter the following path to the Employee Sales Summary report: /AdventureWorks Sample Reports/Employee Sales Summary.

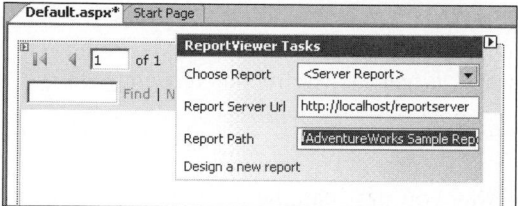

FIGURE 41.37   Report Viewer tasks.

Now you simply build and run the website, using F5. You should get a test website page that looks like the one shown in figure 41.38.

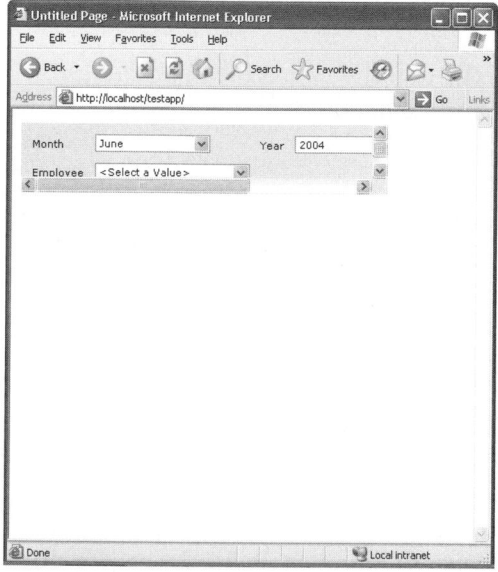

FIGURE 41.38   Initial preview of the page containing the report control.

The report is there, but it doesn't seem to be sized correctly. To fix that, you select the ReportViewer control in the design surface, select Properties, and then set the width and height to something more than the default of 400 pixels to make it look better.

This is all it takes to put reports in a website. Notice that in the process you have written zero lines of code; everything is done through the Visual Studio designer graphical user interface.

> **TIP**
>
> Another way to set the size of a report is to turn off the AsyncRendering property and set the SizeToReportContent property to true. AsyncRendering makes the control return the page to the user before the report is done rendering; it shows a frame with

the green spinning circle until the report is ready. You set `AsyncRendering` to `true` if you have slow-running reports or reports that make use of the document map feature.

Due to HTML limitations, `SizeToContent` is available only in synchronous rendering for the web form `ReportViewer` control.

Now suppose you would like to customize the way you pass parameters to the report from your application. The first step is to turn off the report parameters area of the `ReportViewer` control. To do so, you select `false` as the value for `ShowParameterPrompts` in the Properties window.

Next, you need to provide values for the three parameters the report needs from other controls in the application. The `Employee ID` parameter will be fed to the report from a data-bound list view, and the `Year` and `Month` parameters will be taken from a calendar control.

You should now drop a new `ListBox` control on the webpage. You then bind it to the AdventureWorks database and make it use the following query:

```
SELECT     E.EmployeeID, C.FirstName + N' ' + C.LastName AS Employee
FROM       HumanResources.Employee E INNER JOIN
           Sales.SalesPerson SP ON E.EmployeeID = SP.SalesPersonID INNER JOIN
           Person.Contact C ON E.ContactID = C.ContactID
ORDER BY   C.LastName, C.FirstName
```

In the `ListBox` Properties pane, you set the `DataTextField` property to `Employee` and set `DataValueField` to `EmployeeID`. This instructs the list box to display names, and the code behind the page uses `EmployeeID` to pass it to the `Report` control.

You also need to add a calendar control to the page. You should set the selection mode to `DayWeekMonth`. For both the list box and the calendar control, you should enable auto postback through the Properties pane. This means that clicking an item in the list or a date in the calendar causes a server request to be made, and the ASP.NET server code can react to these events by updating the report content on the page.

Next, right-click `default.aspx` and choose View Code. The code-behind page, called `default.aspx.cs`, appears. Now, you need to write a function to set the parameters of the `ReportViewer` control (see Listing 41.1). The idea behind this function is that it gets the parameter definition from the `ReportViewer` control and uses the other controls on the page to build a `ReportParameter` collection that it then passes to the `ReportViewer` control through the `SetParameters` function.

LISTING 41.1   Setting report parameters

```
private void SetParameters()
{
    if (this.Calendar1.SelectedDate == DateTime.MinValue
        || this.ListBox1.SelectedIndex == -1)
        return;
```

LISTING 41.1   Continued

```
    ReportParameterInfoCollection parameters =
    this.ReportViewer1.ServerReport.GetParameters();
    List<ReportParameter> changedParameters = new List<ReportParameter>();
    foreach (ReportParameterInfo parameterInfo in parameters)
    {
        ReportParameter parameter = new ReportParameter(parameterInfo.Name);
        if (parameterInfo.Name == "EmpID")
        {
            parameter.Values.Add(this.ListBox1.SelectedValue);
        }
        else if (parameter.Name == "ReportMonth")
        {
            parameter.Values.Add(this.Calendar1.SelectedDate.Month.ToString());
        }
        else if (parameter.Name == "ReportYear")
        {
            parameter.Values.Add(this.Calendar1.SelectedDate.Year.ToString());
        }
        changedParameters.Add(parameter);
    }
    this.ReportViewer1.ServerReport.SetParameters(changedParameters);
}
```

The next step is to hook up this function with the right events on the page. You need to go back to design view for default.aspx and select the ListBox control on the page. You then click the Events icon to see the events that can be defined on this control. Next, you double-click DataBound and on SelectIndexChanged. This takes you to code view again and generates empty bodies for the two event handler functions: ListBox1_DataBound and ListBox1_SelectedIndexChanged. In ListBox1_SelectedIndexChanged, all you have to do is to call the SetParameters function, as follows:

```
protected void ListBox1_SelectedIndexChanged(object sender, EventArgs e)
{
    SetParameters();
}
```

This has the effect of setting the control parameters every time some other item is selected in the list view.

Similarly, you create an event handler for the calendar control's SelectionChanged, which also calls SetParameters:

```
protected void Calendar1_SelectionChanged(object sender, EventArgs e)
{
    SetParameters();
}
```

You use the DataBound event of the list box to select default values for the controls. You want to initialize the list box with the first item and the calendar control with today's date. Given that you want to do that only when the page is first rendered, and not as a result of a user action causing a postback, you add a check for the IsPostBack property of the webpage. The code to do so looks like this:

```
protected void ListBox1_DataBound(object sender, EventArgs e)
{
    if (!Page.IsPostBack)
    {
        this.ListBox1.SelectedIndex = 0;
        this.Calendar1.SelectedDate = DateTime.Today;
        SetParameters();
    }
}
```

Finally, in order to better align the control on the webpage, you drop an HTML table on the page. The table has one column and three rows. The list box is in the first row, the calendar control is in the second row, and the ReportViewer Control is in the last row. You can also make other visual settings, including setting custom width and height for the list box and the calendar control. The end result should look as shown in figure 41.39.

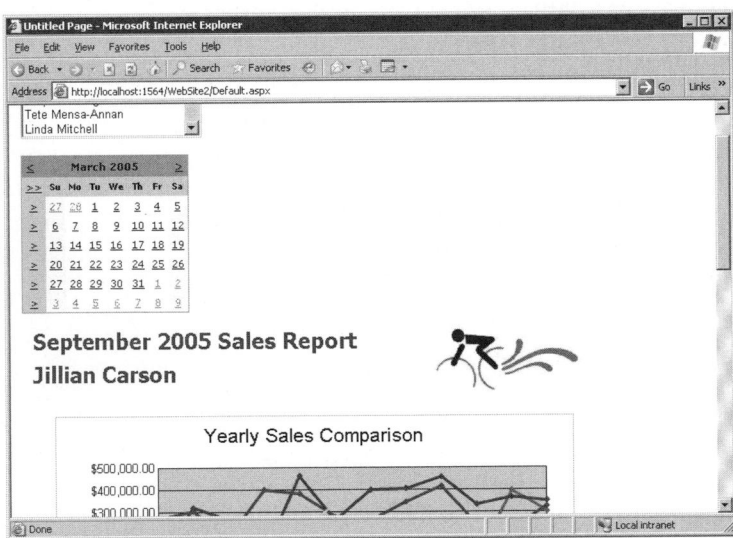

FIGURE 41.39   Web page containing a report—end result.

Notice that clicking an item in the list box or on a date in the calendar causes the page to be updated with the corresponding value of the sales summary for the person and date chosen.

This simple example only begins to explore the potential of the report controls in web or Windows applications. You have learned how to make reports react to application events, but the opposite it also possible: You can make application events react to reports. For example, you can have the `ReportViewer` control fire events when a report action is triggered by the end user, as shown in figure 41.40.

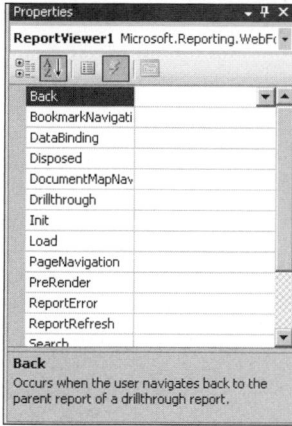

FIGURE 41.40   `ReportViewer` events.

By subscribing to the various events, such as drill-through, bookmarks, and so on, you can achieve a rich and deep interaction of reports with the other parts of an application.

Summary

This chapter describes the components of Reporting Services as well as the product's overall architecture. You have learned about report design, ad hoc reporting, Report Builder, and data models. You have also learned about the administration, security, delivery, and management capabilities of Reporting Services. Finally, you have learned about the `ReportViewer` control and started on the path of integrating reporting in other applications.

If you use Reporting Services, you will no doubt come to appreciate what it has to offer: its power and simplicity, its open and extensible architecture, and its rich feature set. Today it is easier than ever to unlock the data from database systems and make it available to users.

PART VIII

Bonus Chapters on the CD

IN THIS PART

CHAPTER 42 Managing Linked and Remote
            Servers   1663

CHAPTER 43 Configuring, Tuning, and
            Optimizing SQL Server Options   1693

CHAPTER 44 Administering Very Large
            SQL Server Databases   1743

CHAPTER 45 SQL Server Disaster Recovery
            Planning   1771

CHAPTER 46 Transact-SQL Programming
            Guidelines, Tips, and Tricks   1793

CHAPTER 47 SQL Server Notification Services   1841

CHAPTER 48 SQL Server Service Broker   1875

CHAPTER 49 SQL Server Full Text Search   1913

> **NOTE**
>
> Chapters 42–49 (pages 1663-1940) are being included
> on the CD instead of printed in the book. Therefore, the
> printed index begins on p. 1941.

Symbols

1204 trace flags, 1197-1199
1222 trace flags, 1199

A

access to data, Database Engine, 13
access path costs, estimating, 1040
    clustered indexes, 1041
    nonclustered indexes, 1042-1046
    table scan costs, 1046-1048
accounts
    for Database Mail, creating, 342-344
    proxy accounts, SQL Server Agent, 367-368
    startup accounts, configuring SQL Server Agent,
        363-365
ACID properties, transactions, 874
@action parameter, CD:1927
actions, CD:1845
active multisite DR pattern, CD:1776-1777
active/active configuration, SQL Server
    Clustering, 517
active/active DR sites pattern, CD:1775
active/passive configuration, SQL Server
    Clustering, 516
active/passive DR sites pattern, CD:1774
ActiveX Data Object Multidimensional (ADO
    MD), 1476
Activity Monitor, SSMS, 68-70
ad hoc distributed queries, CD:1704
ad hoc reporting, 1645
ADD, ALTER FULLTEXT INDEX, CD:1925-1926
Add References dialog, 1332
adding
    CLR functions to databases, 828-829
    CLR stored procedures to databases, 792-793
    columns, T-SQL, 600-601
    data sources to OLAP databases, 1488-1490
    extended stored procedures to SQL Server,
        794-795
    linked servers, CD:1673-1680
ADFs, SSNS, CD:1850
    Database, CD:1851
    Distributors, CD:1862-1863
    EventClasses, CD:1851-1852
    Generator, CD:1862
    NotificationClasses, CD:1854-1859
    ParameterDefaults, CD:1851
    Providers, CD:1859-1862
    sample applications, CD:1850-1851
    SubscriptionClasses, CD:1852-1854
administration tools, SSMS, 64-71
ADO MD (ActiveX Data Object
    Multidimensional), 1476
    in OLAP database creation, 1521
ADO.NET, 1319-1323
    connection pooling, 1328
    MARS, 1324-1326
    new features, 1324
    Query Notifications, 1328-1330
    System.Data.SqlTypes namespace, 1326-1328

Advanced page, 362
Advanced Windowing Extensions (AWE),
    CD:1707-1709
adXactReadcommitted function, 1155
affinity I/O mask, CD:1704-1706
affinity mask, CD:1706-1707
AFTER triggers, 854-856
agent history clean up: distribution, 442
agents
    replication agents. See replication agents
    snapshot agent, 437
        processing, 438-439
        synchronization, 437-438
Aggregate() method, 1363
Aggregates, UDAs, 1363-1366
aggregating data within cubes in OLAP database
    creation, 1510-1514
Aggregation Design Wizard, 1513
aging, query plans, 1075
alert mail notifications, SQL Server Agent Mail,
    356-357
alert responses, 384-386
Alert System page, 363
alerts, 361, 1237
    creating with SQL Server Agent Mail, 356-357
    scripting, 387
    SQL Server Agent, 381-386
alias data types, 588
AllocUnit locking level (SQL Server), 1177
ALLOW_PAGE_LOCKS, 1184
ALTER, 267
ALTER ASSEMBLY command, 1333
ALTER DATABASE, 548, 560, 563, 573-574
ALTER FULLTEXT INDEX, CD:1924-1926
ALTER INDEX, 46, 624, 633, 1184
ALTER INDEX ... REORGANIZE, CD:1754
ALTER INDEX REBUILD, 635, CD:1753
ALTER INDEX REORGANIZE, 953
ALTER PARTITION SCHEME, 615
ALTER PROCEDURE, 722
ALTER ROLE, 277
ALTER TABLE, creating constraints, 597
    T-SQL, 653
ALTER VIEW, 681
altering
    indexes, 624
    views with T-SQL, 681-682
American National Standards Institute (ANSI), 257
analysis phase, transaction recovery process, 890
Analysis Services, 184
    enhancements, 52-53
    upgrading, 217
Analysis Services (SSAS), migrating, 209-210
Analysis Services features, sac, 102
Analysis Services Migration Wizard, 209
Analysis Wizard, 199-202

analyzing
    slowed stored procedures or queries with SQL
        Server Profiler, 145
    STATISTICS IO, 1141-1142
    stored procedures with Query Analyzer,
        1129-1130
    traces (SQL Server Profiler) with Database Engine
        Tuning Advisor, 128-129
anonymous subscriptions, 434
ANSI (American National Standards Institute), 257
ANY, 1067
application data values, CD:1780
Application locking level (SQL Server), 1178
application locks, granularity, 1181-1184
application progress, monitoring (SQL Server Profiler),
    150-152
application roles, 264-265
ApplicationName data column (SQL Profiler), 1169
Applications, creating via SSMS for SSNS,
    CD:1866-1868
Applications ICF elements, CD:1863-1865
APPLY, 1309-1311
architecture
    delivery architecture, subscriptions, 1650
    SQL Server instance architecture, CD:1694
    of SQL Server Profiler, 112-113
    SSIS (SQL Server Integration Services),
        1545-1549
archiving data, VLDB data maintenace, CD:1755-1761
arguments for CREATE INDEX, 628
articles, 420
    data replication, 421
        filtering, 421-425
AS DEFAULT, CREATE FULLTEXT CATALOG, CD:1918
AS HTTP, 1445-1448
ASP.NET report controls, using in websites, 1654-1659
assemblies, creating managed stored procedures,
    1342-1343
Assert iconm Query Analyzer, 1123
association rules, data mining algorithms, 1527
asynchronous operations, database mirroring
    operating modes, 486
asynchronous statistics updating, indexes, 992-993
Attach Databases dialog, 575
ATTACH REBUILD LOG, 548
attaching
    databases, 574-576
    full-text catalogs, CD:1938
attachments
    sending CSV data as, 353
    sending XML as, 351
attributes, managed stored procedures,
    1335-1336, 1339
authentication, 249
    authentication modes, setting, 250-251
    mixed authentication mode, 250
    securing reports, 1648
    Windows Authentication mode, 250
AUTHORIZATION, 1445
    CREATE FULLTEXT CATALOG, CD:1918
AUTHORIZATION clause, CD:1882

AUTHORIZATION keyword, CD:1903
Auto Close, 561
Auto Create Statistics, 562, CD:1752
AUTO mode, XML, 1385-1389
Auto Shrink, 562
Auto Update Statistics, 562-563, CD:1752
auto-parameterization, 1109
auto-update statistics, monitoring, 150
AutoCommit, processing transactions, 876
automatic checkpoints, logs, 888-889
automatic query plan recompilation, stored
   procedures, 765-766
automatically updating index statistics, 990-992
AUTOSHRINK, 568
availability, enterprise computing, 515
Average Wait Time counter (SQLServer:Locks
   object), 1171
avoiding unnecessary function executions, T-SQL,
   CD:1809
AWE (Advanced Windowing Extensions) enabled,
   CD:1707-1709

B

B-tree indexes, 971
backing up
   databases, Maintenance Plan Wizard, 948-951
   system tables, 325-326
   tail of transaction logs, 330
   VLDB, CD:1745-1747
      snapshot backups, CD:1748
BACKUP, 305
BACKUP CERTIFICATE, 235, CD:1902
BACKUP DATABASE, 305-306
backup devices, 300-302
BACKUP LOG, 305, 309
backupfile, 325
backupfilegroup, 325
backupmediafamily, 325
backupmediaset, 325
backups, 291
   considerations for very large databases, 337-338
   copy-only backups, 48, 292, 296
   creating
      with SSMS, 302-305
      with T-SQL, 305-307
   developing a plan, 292-293
   differential database backups, 295
   differential partial backups, 295
   enhancements to, 48-49
   file and filegroup backups, 295-296
   frequency of, 335-336
   full database backups, 294
   full-text catalogs, CD:1938
   HA, 397
   maintenance plans, 338
   mirrored backups, 48, 292
   new features, 291-292
   partial backups, 49, 292, 295
   recovery models, 296

replication monitoring, 478-479
scenarios
   copy backups, 316-317
   differential backups, 312-313
   file/filegroup backups, 315-316
   full database backups, 311
   full database backups with transaction log
      backups, 311-312
   mirrored backups, 316
   partial backups, 313-315
   system database backups, 317
snapshot backups, 337
standby servers, 336-337
transaction log backups, 296
transaction logs, 307
   creating with SSMS, 308
   creating with T-SQL, 309-310
backupset, 325
BASIC authentication, 1445
.BAT, 90
batches
   bulk-copy operations, SSIS, 1602
   transactions, 897-899
bcp (Bulk Copy Program), 104-105, 1539
   hints, supplying to, 1603-1604
bcp utility, SSIS, 1586-1588
   exporting/importing data, 1589-1591
   file data types, 1591
   format files, 1591-1601
   views, 1601
BEGIN CONVERSATION DIALOG, CD:1890-1892
BEGIN DISTRIBUTED TRANSACTION, 755
BEGIN TRAN statements, 884
   transactions, 909
BEGIN TRANSACTION, 755
BI (business intelligence), 1473
bidirectional traffic, 245
BIDS (Business Intelligence Development
   Studio), 1610
BIDS Report Designer, designing reports, 1619
   adding interactivity, 1625-1626
   building reports, 1620
   creating simple lists, 1620-1621
   deploying sample reports, 1626
   grouping and sorting, 1621-1623
   layout choices, 1619-1620
   queries, 1619
   tables and hierarchies, 1623-1624
binary columns, RAW XML mode, 1383
binding multiple applications, 917
bipubs2005 database, installing, 6
blobs, CREATE FULLTEXT INDEX, CD:1920
bottlenecks, identifying with SQL Server Profiler,
   148-149
bound connections, 915-917
bound defaults, 662-663
breaking down database snapshots, 938
Browser role, 1647
browsing data within cubes in OLAP database
   creation, 1514-1518

built-in methods, new xml data type built-in methods, 1411-1430
built-in roles, securing reports, 1647-1648
BUILTIN\Administrators, 253
Bulk Copy Program (bcp), 1539
bulk update locks, 1176
bulk-copy operations, SSIS, 1601-1604
bulk-logged recovery model, 298-299
Bulk-Logged recovery setting, 559
bulkadmin, 259
Business Intelligence Development Studio (BIDS), 44, 219, 1610
business intelligence (BI), 1473

C

C# client applications, examples
    calling web methods-bound stored procedures that return XML, 1462-1465
    running a web method bound to a stored procedure from C#, 1453-1458
    running ad hoc T-SQL batches from SQL Server web services, 1458-1463
cached reports, 1651-1652
caches, procedure caches, 763-764
caching, query plan caching, 763, 1072-1073
calculated members (calculations), OLAP database creation, 1521-1522
calculating dates, CD:1817-1820
calling stored procedures from transactions, 783-786
CAS (Code Access Security) permission sets, .NET Framework, 1332
CASCADE, 648
cascading deletes, 1214
    DML triggers, 847-849
cascading FOREIGN KEY constraints, 850
cascading referential integrity, FOREIGN KEY constraint, 648-650
cascading updates, DML triggers, 849-850
CASE, 1301
catalog views, 156, 164-166
    system stored procedures and, 1466-1467
    viewing DDL triggers, 866
CATCH, 786
CATCH block, 787
central publisher replication model, data replication, 426-427
central publisher with remote distributor replication model, data replication, 427
central subscriber replication model, data replication, 428-430
certificates
    conversation encryption, SQL Server Service Broker, CD:1901-1908
    root-level certificates, 235
CHARACTER SET keyword, 1452
CHECK constraint, 596, 650-651
checkpoint duration option, transaction management, 873

checkpoints, 555
    logs, 886-889
CHECK_CONSTRAINTS hint, supplying to bulk-copy operations, 1604
choosing disaster recovery patterns, CD:1777-1778
CLEAR PORT, 1446
client access provisioning, 225-227
client applications, redistributing SNAC, 231
client components, 184
    installing, 1613
client data access technologies, 237
    drivers, 238
    JDBC, 244
    MDAC, 242-243
    .NET Framework, 240-241
    .NET Framework (SQLCLR), 241-242
    providers, 237
    SNAC, 238-240
client tools, client installation, 229
clients
    configuring, 231
        connection encryption, 235-236
        SSCM, 232-234
    installing, 228-230
    setup and configuration for database mirroring, 509-511
CLR (common language runtime), 37-38, 589-590, 799, 1331
CLR enabled, 1709
CLR functions, 827-828
    adding to databases, 828-829
    versus T-SQL functions, 830-831
CLR stored procedures, 791-793
CLR triggers, 834, 866-869
CLR user-defined data types, 589-590
Cluster Administrator, viewing properties, 537
Clustered Index Delete icon, Query Analyzer, 1124
Clustered Index Scan icon, Query Analyzer, 1124
clustered indexes, 624-625, 971-973
    costs, 1041
    designing, 1014-1016
    indexed views, 1021-1022
clustering, 518
    building solutions with HA options, 402-404
clusters, 518
    server clusters, 518
    upgrading, 219
Code Access Security (CAS) permission sets, .NET Framework, 1332
Codezone Community, 62
coding recommendations for T-SQL. See T-SQL, coding recommendations
coding transactions, 912-913
Collapse icon, Query Analyzer, 1124
collation, 188, 558
column lists, T-SQL, CD:1794-1796
COLUMN NAME, CREATE FULLTEXT INDEX, CD:1919
column operator values, sp trace setfilter, 139
column sub-setting, 1643
ColumnCount parameter (SqlTriggerContext), 1367
COLUMNPROPERTY, full-text indexes, 1929

columns, 579, 584
  adding in T-SQL, 600-601
  checking for updates, 843-845
  computed columns
    denormalization, 1220-1221
    indexes, 1022-1024
  data types. *See* data types
  indexes
    included columns, 1020
    joins, 1014
  naming, 585
  new xml data type, 1404-1406
  properties, 590
    changing with T-SQL, 599
    computed columns, 593-594
    IDENTITY, 591-592
    NULL and NOT NULL keywords, 590
    ROWGUIDCOL, 592-593
  renumbering, 1599-1601
  selecting from sys.databases catalog view, 566
  statistics, generating, 990-996, 998
  stored computed columns, 580
  traces (SQL Server Profiler), 137-138
  xml columns
    full-text indexing, 1436
    indexing, 1430-1436
command lines, DTA, CD:1737-1742
command sourcing phase (dtexec), 1576
command-line utilities
  bcp, 104-105
  dta, 90, 95-98
  dtswizard, 91
  installation locations, 90
  new features, 90-91
  profiler, 90-91
  sac, 91, 101-104
    parameters, 102
  sqlcmd, 90-92
    executing, 92-94
    scripting variables with, 94-95
  sqldiag, 105-107
  sqlservr, 107-108
  sqlwb, 91
  tablediff, 90, 98-101
  utilities that have been removed or deprecated in
    SQL Server 2005, 108
command-prompt utilities, SSIS, 1552
commenting, T-SQL code, 1806-1807
common language runtime, 37-38, 589-590,
  799, 1331
common table expressions. *See* CTE
Community Technology Preview (CTP), 178-179
compatibility, locks, 1187-1188
compatibility levels, 209
compatibility views, 155, 161-162
compiling
  DML statements, query compilation, 1031
  query plans, 1076-1077
Components to Install dialog, 529
composite indexes, designing, 1013
COMPRESSION, 1448

CompSales International (OLAP requirements
  example), 1485-1486
  cube creation, 1486-1487
  cube perspectives, 1524-1525
  data mining, 1526-1534
  generating relational databases, 1523-1524
  KPIs, 1525
  OLAP database creation. *See* databases, OLAP
    database creation
  security and roles, 1536-1537
  SQL Server BIDS, 1487-1488
Compute Scalar icon, Query Analyzer, 1125
computed columns, 593-594
  denormalization, 1220-1221
  indexes, 1022-1024
  SARG, 1038-1040
Concatenation icon, Query Analyzer, 1125
condition action, 1845
condition expression, 660
configuration, SSIS, 1548
configuration data, CD:1780
configuration options
  fixing incorrect option settings, CD:1702
  for instances, CD:1695-1702
  obsolete configuration options, CD:1703
  performance. *See* performance, configuration
    options
  setting with SSMS, CD:1702-1703
configuration phase (dtexec), 1576
Configure Database Mirroring Security Wizard,
  495-501
configuring
  clients, 231
    connection encryption, 235-236
    SSCM, 232-234
  database mirroring, 486-490
    client setup, 509-511
    Configure Database Mirroring Security Wizard,
      495-501
    creating database on the mirror server,
      493-495
    creating endpoints, 490-492
    granting permissions, 492
    identifying endpoints, 492-493
  linked servers, CD:1682-1683
  Reporting Services, 1615
    report server database catalog, 1617-1618
    report server encryption, 1616
    Reporting Services Configuration tool, 1615
    Surface Area Configuration tool, 1618
    Web service, 1617
    Windows service, 1616
  SQL Server Agent, 362
    email notification, 365-366
    properties, 362-363
    proxy accounts, 367-368
    startup account, 363-365
  SQL Server database disks, 525-526
connection encryption, configuring clients, 235-236
Connection page, 363
connection pooling, ADO.NET, 1328

Connection Test Program for SQL Server Cluster, 539-542
connections, bound connections, 915-917
connectivity, 245-246
consistency
    immediate transactional consistency, 443
    latent transactional consistency, 443
    VLDB, CD:1749-1751
Constant Scan icon, Query Analyzer, 1125
constraints
    CHECK, 650-651
    creating
        with ALTER TABLE, 597
        with CREATE TABLE, 596
    data integrity. See data integrity, constraints
    defining table constraints, 596-597
    FOREIGN KEY, 646-648
        cascading referential integrity, 648-650
    PRIMARY KEY, 643-644
    UNIQUE, 645-646
construction phase, OLAP design
  methodologies, 1484
constructs, SQL Server Service Broker, CD:1881
    creating queues for message storage,
        CD:1887-1889
    defining messages and choosing message types,
        CD:1882-1886
    defining services to send and receive messages,
        CD:1889-1890
    planning conversations between services,
        CD:1890-1892
    setting up contracts for communication,
        CD:1886-1887
containers, SSIS, 1546
CONTAINS, FTS, CD:1933-1936
CONTAINSTABLE, FTS, CD:1933-1937
Content Manager role, 1647
contention, locking, 1188-1189
    identifying, 1189-1191
    minimizing, 1192-1193
context connection, managed stored procedures, 1340
CONTEXT INFO, T-SQL, CD:1824-1825
context switching, 286-288
contracts, setting up for communication (SQL Server
    Service Broker), CD:1886-1887
CONTROL, 267
control flow, SSIS, 1546
CONTROL keyword, 1469
control of flow, 376
controlling
    access permissions, 1468-1469
    access to data, with views, 671-674
conversation encryption, certificates (SQL Server
    Service Broker), CD:1901-1908
conversation initiators, creating, CD:1892-1896
conversation targets, creating, CD:1896-1901
conversations, CD:1890
    building routes to map conversations between
        SQL Server instances, CD:1908
    creating conversation initiator, CD:1892-1896
    creating conversation targets, CD:1896-1901

creating remote service bindings, CD:1908
    planning between services, SQL Server Service
        Broker, CD:1890-1892
conversion deadlocks, 1194
converting dates for comparison, T-SQL,
    CD:1820-1822
Copy Database Wizard, 206-208
copy-on-write technology, 394, 924-927
    database mirroring, 484
copy-only backups, 48, 292, 296
    scenarios, 316-317
copying packages, dtutil utility, 1582-1585
correlated subqueries, 1068-1070
cost, parallelism, CD:1709-1710
covering indexes, 1018-1019
CREATE ASSEMBLY, 792, 828
CREATE ASSEMBLY command, 1333
CREATE CERTIFICATE, 235, CD:1901
CREATE DATABASE, 16, 551
    T-SQL, 559-560
CREATE ENDPOINT, T-SQL statement, 1442
CREATE ENDPOINT keywords, 1444
CREATE FULL TEXT, 1916
CREATE FULLTEXT CATALOG, CD:1916-1918
CREATE FULLTEXT INDEX, CD:1919-1924
CREATE FUNCTION
    custom function templates, 817
    inline table-valued functions, 808
    multistatement table-valued functions, 808
    scalar functions, 807
CREATE INDEX, 628-629
CREATE INDEX WITH DROP EXISTING, 635
CREATE LOGIN, CD:1670
CREATE PARTITION FUNCTION, 608-609, 615
CREATE PARTITION SCHEME, 615
CREATE PROCEDURE, 707, 792
CREATE STATISTICS command, 996-998
CREATE TABLE
    creating constraints, 596
    T-SQL, 582-584, 652
credentials, 367
CROSS APPLY, 1309-1311
crosstabs, 1306
CSV, sending data as an attachment with Database
    Mail, 353
CTE (common table expressions), 1284-1286
    recursive queries, 1286-1288
        expanding hierarchies, 1288-1294
            MAXRECURSION, 1294-1295
CTP (Community Technology Preview), 178-179
cube perspectives, 1524-1525
Cube Wizard, 1505
cubes
    aggregating with data in OLAP database
        creation, 1510-1514
    browsing data in OLAP database creation,
        1514-1518
    building and deploying in OLAP database creation,
        1506-1508
    creating in OLAP database creation, 1503-1507
    OLAP cube creation, 1486-1487

populating with data in OLAP database creation, 1509-1510

SSAS, 1477-1480

CURSOR, stored procedures, 738-743

CURSOR STATUS, 740

cursor threshold, CD:1710-1711

cursors

    stored procedures, 733-738

        CURSOR variables, 738-743

    T-SQL, performance, CD:1810-1813

custom (files-only) installation, Reporting Services, 1613-1615

custom function templates, creating, 815-818

custom managed database objects

    managed triggers, 1366-1372

    permissions, 1332-1334

    related system catalogs, 1374-1375

    stored procedures, 1335-1336, 1339-1344

        assembly creation, 1342-1343

        attributes, 1335-1336, 1339

        context connection, 1340

        debugging, 1343-1344

        implementation contract, 1335-1336, 1339

        Microsoft.SqlServer.Server objects, 1340-1341

    transactions, 1372-1374

    UDAs, 1363-1366

    UDFs

        scalar UDFs, 1344-1347

        TVFs, 1348-1349, 1352-1353

    UDTs, 1354-1355, 1359-1363

    Visual Studio 2005, 1334-1335

customizing

    drill-through reports, 1640-1642

    format files, bcp utility, 1591-1592

cycle deadlocks, 1193-1194

D

DAC (Dedicated Administrator Connection), 39

data

    application data values, CD:1780

    configuration data, CD:1780

    controlling access to, with views, 671-674

    delivering to users, in OLAP database creation, 1518-1519

    metadata, CD:1780

    purging/archiving, VLDB data maintenance, CD:1755-1761

data abstraction, views, 670-671

data access, Database Engine, 13

data access technologies, clients, 237

    drivers, 238

    JDBC, 244

    MDAC, 242-243

    MDAC (ODBC), 243

    MDAC (OLE DB), 243

    .NET Framework data provider for SQL Server, 240-241

    .NET Framework data provider for SQL Server (SQLCLR), 241-242

    providers, 237

    SNAC, 238

    SNAC (ADO), 240

    SNAC (ODBC), 239-240

    SNAC (OLE DB), 239

data archival design changes, VLDB data maintenance, CD:1760

data characteristics, data replication, 448-450

data columns, SQL Profiler, 1168

    traces, 118-120

Data Definition Language (DDL), 1273, 1404

data distribution, data replication, 444

data files, 548

data flow, SSIS, 1547

data flow task, SSIS, 1547

data integrity, 641

    constraints, 643, 656

        CHECK, 650-651

        creating, 651

        creating with SSMS, 653-656

        creating with T-SQL, 651-653

        disabling, 659

        dropping, 658-659

        FOREIGN KEY, 646-650

        gathering constraint information, 657-658

        PRIMARY KEY, 643-644

        UNIQUE, 645-646

    Database Engine, 14

    declarative data integrity, 643

    domain integrity, 642

    enforcing, 642-643

    entity integrity, 642

    new features, 641-642

    procedural data integrity, 643

    referential integrity, 642

    rules, 659-660

Data Junction, 1539

data maintenance, VLDB, CD:1751

    purging/archiving data, CD:1755-1761

    rebuilding indexes, CD:1752-1755

    updating statistics, CD:1751-1752

data manipulation, simplifying with views, 669-670

Data Manipulation Language. See DML

data mining, 1526-1534

    OLAP performance, 1535-1536

    SSIS, 1534-1535

Data Mining Wizard, 1528-1530

data modifications, views and, 683-684

data partitioning

    HA, 410

    horizontal data partitioning, denormalization, 1221-1223

    vertical data partitioning, denormalization, 1223-1224

data replication, 417-418, CD:1780-1781

    articles, 421

        filtering, 421-422, 424-425

    building solutions with HA options, 404-406

    central publisher replication model, 426-427

    central publisher with remote distributor replication model, 427

central subscriber replication model, 428-430
database mirroring and, HA, 480
distribution server, 419
log shipping, 480
merge replication, 446-447
methods of data distribution, 444
monitoring, 471
    backup and recovery, 478-479
    in heterogeneous environments, 477-478
    Performance Monitor, 477
    within SQL Server Management Studio,
        474-476
    SQL statements, 472-475
    troubleshooting replication failures, 476-477
multiple publishers or multiple subscribers
    replication model, 429-431
new features, 416-417
peer-to-peer replication model, 431-433
performance, 479-480
planning for, 443
publication server, 418-420
publications, 421
publisher subscriber replication model, 427-428
replication agents, 436-439
scripting replication, 470-471
setting up, 450-451
    creating distributors and enabling publishing,
        451-455
    creating publications, 456-462
    creating subscriptions, 465-469
    horizontal and vertical filtering, 463-465
snapshot replication, 444-445
subscription server, 420
subscriptions. See subscriptions
transactional replication, 445-446
updating subscribers replication model, 430-432
user requirements, 447-448
    data characteristics, 448-450
Data Source View Wizard, 1492
data source views, creating, 1490-1493
data sources, adding to OLAP databases, 1488-1490
data storage, 548-549
data transformation requirement, SSIS, 1555-1556
Data Transformation Services. See DTS
data types, 44, 585-587
    CLR user-defined data types, 589-590
    file data types, bcp utility, 1591
    large row support, 588
    large-value data types, 580, 587-588
    new xml data type, 1402-1403
        built-in methods, 1411-1430
        columns, 1404-1406
        schema collections, 1407-1412
    Object Explorer (SSMS), 587
    search argument problems, 1093
    user-defined data types, 588-589
    varbinary(max), 45
    varchar(max), 45
    xml, 45, 588

data-centric approach to disaster recovery,
    CD:1779-1780
data-driven subscriptions, 1649-1650
DataAccess parameter (scalar UDFs), 1345
DataAccess parameter (SqlMethod), 1359
Database ADF element, 1851
database backups. See backups
database compatibility levels, 209
Database Console Commands. See DBCC
database design
    denormalization, 1218-1219
        computed columns, 1220-1221
        horizontal data partitioning, 1221-1223
        redundant data, 1219-1220
        summary data, 1221
        vertical data partitioning, 1223-1224
        zero-to-one relationships, 1224-1225
    designing for performance, 1214
    logical database design issues, 1215-1217
    new features, 1213-1214
database design changes, VLDB data maintenance,
    CD:1760
Database Diagram Editor
    creating constraints, 655
    creating tables, 580-581
database diagrams, modifying tables, 604-605
Database Engine, 11
    access to data, 13
    data integrity, 14
    storage, 12
database engine enhancements, 46
Database engine features, sac, 102
Database Engine Tuning Advisor, 978
    analyzing trace output, 128-129
Database Engine Tuning Advisor. See DTA
database file movement, 46, 548
database files, 549-550
    filegroups, 551-553
    master database files, 557
    partitions, 554
    primary data files, 550
    secondary data files, 550
    transaction log files, 554-555
Database ICF elements, CD:1865
database integrity, Maintenance Plan Wizard, 951
database level, SSMS, managing permissions,
    281-283
Database locking level (SQL Server), 1177
Database Mail, 40, 339, 365
    deleting mail objects, with T-SQL, 345
    mail configuration objects, viewing, 357-358
    mail message data, viewing, 359-360
    mail profiles and accounts, creating, 342-344
    receiving email, 354
    security profiles, 344
    sending email, 347-348, 351-353
    sending XML as attachments, 351
    Service Broker (SSB), 347
    setting up, 339-342
    sp send dbmail, parameters for, 348
    systemwide mail settings, 345-346

testing setup, 346
updating, with T-SQL, 345
Database Mail Configuration Wizard, 339
    SMTP accounts, creating, 343
database maintenance, 945-946
    Maintenance Plan Wizard, 946-947
        backing up databases, 948-951
        checking database integrity, 951
        maintaining indexes and statistics, 953-956
        scheduling maintenance plans, 956-959
        shrinking databases, 952-953
    without a plan, 965
database maintenance plans, 946
database management system (DBMS), 1152
database mirroring, 19, 41, 481-482, CD:1783
    building solutions with HA options, 407
    client setup and configuration, 509-511
    copy-on-write technology, 484
    data replication and, HA, 480
    failovers, 486
    mirror database server, 483
    monitoring, 501-505
    operating modes, 485-486
    principal database server, 482
    removing, 505-507
    replication and, 511-512
    role switching, 486
    roles, 485
    setting up and configuring, 486-490
        Configure Database Mirroring Security Wizard,
            495-501
        creating endpoints, 490-492
        creating the database on the mirror server,
            493-495
        granting permissions, 492
        identifying endpoints, 492-493
    testing failover, 507-508
    when to use, 484-485
    witness database server, 483
Database Mirroring Monitor, 501-505
database mirrors
    providing reporting databases, database
        snapshots, 930-931
    setting up database snapshots against, 940-941
database options
    retrieving option information, 564-566
    setting, 560-563
    in SSMS, 561
database partitioning for VLDB, CD:1762
    federated servers, CD:1767-1768
    horizontal data partitioning, CD:1765-1767
    table and index partitioning, CD:1768-1770
    vertical data partitioning, CD:1763-1765
Database Properties dialog, 561
Database Read-Only, 562
database roles, managing, 276-277
Database services, 184
database snapshot sparse files, 924
database snapshots, 41, 292, 919-924
    breaking down, 938
    copy-on-write technology, 926-927

    creating, 932-937
    HA, 408-410
    limitations and restrictions, 925-926
    from mirrors, using for reporting, 512-513
    new features, 920
    number of database snapshots per source
        database, 943
    reciprocal principal/mirror reporting confirmation,
        941-942
    reverting to, 924
    reverting to for recovery, 938
    security, 942
    setting up against database mirrors, 940-941
    sparse file size management, 943
    testing with QA, 939-940
    when to use, 927-931
DATABASEPROPERTYEX, 564-566
databases
    adding CLR functions to, 828-829
    adding CLR stored procedures to, 792-793
    ALTER DATABASE, 573-574
    attaching, 574-576
    creating, 555-556
        with SSMS, 556-559
        with T-SQL, 559-560
    data structure, 548-549
    defined, 547
    detaching, 574-576, CD:1791
    expanding, 567-568
    managing file growth, 566-567
    migrating, side-by-side migration. See side-by-side
        migration
    moving, 572
    new features, 548
    OLAP database creation, 1488
        adding data sources, 1488-1490
        ADO MD, 1521
        aggregating data within the cube, 1510-1514
        browsing data in the cube, 1514-1518
        building and deploying the cube, 1506-1508
        calculated members (calculations),
            1521-1522
        creating data source views, 1490-1493
        creating the cube, 1503-1504, 1506-1507
        defining dimensions and hierarchies,
            1493-1502
        delivering data to users, 1518-1519
        multidimensional expressions, 1519-1521
        populating cubes with data, 1509-1510
        query analysis and optimization, 1523
    relational databases, 1523-1524
    replicated databases, upgrading, 217
    shrinking, 568
        DBCC SHRINKDATABASE, 568-569
        DBCC SHRINKFILE, 569-571
        log files, 571
        in Maintenance Plan Wizard, 952-953
        with SSMS, 571-573
    system databases, 157-159, 547
    transaction management, checkpoint duration
        option, 873

upgrading, 216-217
user databases, 547
Datasets window, 1621
date calculations, T-SQL, CD:1817-1822
DATEADD, CD:1817
DATEDIFF, CD:1817
datediff(), 1145
db backupoperator, 260
db datareader, 260-263
db datawriter, 260-262
db ddladmin, 260
db denydatareader, 260
db denydatawriter, 260
db owner, 260
db securityadmin, 260
DBCC (Database Console Commands), CD:1749-1751
    examining performance, 1261
        DBCC SQLPERF, 1262-1263
        INPUTBUFFER, 1265
        OUTPUTBUFFER, 1265
        PERFMON, 1263
        PROCCACHE, 1264-1265
        SHOWCONTIG, 1263-1264
DBCC DROPCLEANBUFFERS, 1144
DBCC FREEPROCCACHE, 1082
DBCC MEMORYSTATUS, 1252
DBCC OPENTRAN command, 913
DBCC PERFMON, 1241
DBCC PROCCACHE, 764
DBCC SHOWCONTIG command, 1001
DBCC SHOW_STATISTICS command, 982-984
DBCC SHRINKDATABASE, 568-569
DBCC SHRINKFILE, 569-571
DBCC SQLPERF, 1262-1263
dbcreator, 259
DBMS (database management system), 1152
dbo users, 255
DB_accessadmin, 260
DDL (Data Definition Language), 1273, 1404
DDL statements, 860
DDL triggers, 834, 859-861
    creating, 861-864
    managing, 864-866
de-duping data with ranking functions, T-SQL,
    CD:1837-1840
Deadlock Graph event (SQL Profiler), 1168
deadlocks, 1193-1195
    1204 trace flags, setting, 1197-1199
    1222 trace flags, setting, 1199
    avoiding, 1195-1196
    conversion deadlocks, 1194
    cycle deadlocks, 1193-1194
    examining, 1196-1197
    handling, 1196-1197
    monitoring, Server Profiler, 1200-1203
    SQL Server Profiler, 145-147
debugging
    managed code, 1343-1344
    models and model queries, 1636-1638
    stored procedures, with Visual Studio .NET,
        756-760

Decision Support Systems (DSS), 526
decision trees, data mining algorithms, 1527
declarative data integrity, implementing, 643
declarative defaults, 661-662
declarative referential integrity (DRI), 835
Dedicated Administrator Connection (DAC), 39
dedicated administrator connections, HA, 410
DEFAULT, 661, 663-664
DEFAULT constraint, 596
default full-text language, CD:1711-1712
default installation, Reporting Services, 1613-1614
default language, CD:1712-1713
defaults, 661
    application of, 663-664
    bound defaults, 662-663
    declarative defaults, 661-662
    restrictions on, 664-665
deferred name resolution, stored procedures, 715-717
    identifying objects referenced in stored
        procedures, 717-719
Deleted Scan icon, Query Analyzer, 1126
deleted tables, DML triggers, 841-843
deleting
    logins, SSMS, 271
    mail objects from Database Mail, with T-SQL, 345
    packages, dtutil utility, 1582-1585
delivery architecture, subscriptions, 1650
DeliveryChannels ICF elements, CD:1865
denormalization, 1218-1219
    computed columns, 1220-1221
    horizontal data partitioning, 1221-1223
    redundant data, 1219-1220
    summary data, 1221
    vertical data partitioning, 1223-1224
    zero-to-one relationships, 1224-1225
DENSE RANK, 1298-1299
densities, indexes, 987-988
DENY, 266, 285
deploying
    cubes in OLAP database creation, 1506-1508
    reports, 1646
        with BIDS Report Designer, 1626
design
    databases. See database design
    indexes, 1013-1014, 1213
        clustered indexes, 1014-1016
        composite indexes, 1013
        covering, 1018-1019
        included columns, 1020
        multiple indexes, 1020-1021
        nonclustered indexes, 1016-1017
        wide indexes, 1020-1021
    for VLDB, CD:1761-1762
        database partitioning. See database
            partitioning for VLDB
design methodologies for OLAP, 1482-1485
design phase, OLAP design methodologies, 1484
design surface, Report Builder, 1634-1635
Designer IDE (SSIS), 1551-1552, 1566-1574

designing
    example systems, SQL Server Service Broker,
        CD:1880-1881
    reports with BIDS Report Designer, 1619
        adding interactivity, 1625-1626
        building reports, 1620
        creating simple lists, 1620-1621
        deploying sample reports, 1626
        grouping and sorting, 1621-1623
        layout choices, 1619-1620
        queries, 1619
        tables and hierarchies, 1623-1624
    reports with models, 1629-1630
    reports with Report Builder, 1627-1629
detaching databases, 574-576, CD:1791
detachment of full-text catalogs, CD:1938
developing
    custom managed database objects
        managed triggers, 1366-1368, 1370-1372
        permissions, 1332-1334
        related system catalogs, 1374-1375
        stored procedures, 1335-1336, 1339-1344
        transactions, 1372-1374
        UDAs (user-defined aggregates), 1363-1366
        UDFs (user-defined functions), 1344-1349,
            1352-1353
        UDTs (user-defined types), 1354-1355,
            1359-1363
        Visual Studio 2005, 1334-1335
development tools, SSMS, 71
    integrating with source control, 81-83
    managing projects, 79-81
    Query Editor, 71-72. See also Query Editor, SSMS
    templates, 83-86
device CALs, 30
diagnostics, full-text indexes, CD:1927-1930
dialog handles, CD:1890
DialogTimer, CD:1886
differential backups, scenarios, 312-313
differential database backups, 295
differential partial backups, 295
DIGEST authentication, 1445
DIGEST authentication, 1446
Dimension Wizard, 1495, 1499
dimensions, defining in OLAP database creation,
    1493-1502
direct recursion, 871
dirty pages, 555
dirty reads, transaction isolation levels, 1153
Dirty Writer process, logs, 886-889
DISABLE, ALTER FULLTEXT INDEX, 1924
DISABLE BROKER, 1877
disabling
    constraints, 659
    indexes, 1011-1012
disaster recovery
    approaching, CD:1772-1773
    data-centric approach, CD:1779-1780
    Level 0, CD:1773
    Level 1, CD:1773

Level 2, CD:1773
Level 3, CD:1773
Level 4, CD:1773
Microsoft Virtual Server 2005, HA, 412
options for, CD:1780-1783
patterns, CD:1773-1778
planning and executing, CD:1790
recovery objectives, CD:1778-1779
reverting to database snapshots, 927-928, 938
    source databases, 938-939
third-party alternatives, CD:1791
disaster recovery planning, new features, CD:1772
disaster recovery process, CD:1784
    focus of, CD:1784-1788
    SQLDIAG.EXE, CD:1788-1790
disconnected editing, Query Editor (SSMS), 74
discouraging grouping in models, 1636
discovery, 1440
disk activity, monitoring, 1259
disk devices, 300
Disk Queue Length counter, 551
disk systems, monitoring, 1254-1257
diskadmin, 259
DISTINCT, CD:1808
    query processing, 1084
distribute streams, 1089
Distribute Streams, Query Analyzer, 1129
distributed messaging, CD:1875
distributed partitioned views (DVPs), 688-690, 858
    horizontal data partitioning, CD:1767
distributed queries, linked servers, CD:1672
Distributed Transaction Coordinator (DTC), 443, 516
distributed transactions, 444
    linked servers, CD:1672-1673
    managing, 918
distribution agent, 441
distribution clean up, distribution, 442
distribution database, 159, 435-436
distribution server, data replication, 419
distributors, creating for data replication, 451-455
Distributors ADF element, CD:1862-1863
dm exe sql text, 764
dm exec cached plans, 764
dm exec plan attributes, 764
DML (Data Manipulation Language), 1273
    max, 1274-1276
    new features, 1273
    OUTPUT, 1280-1284
    TOP, 1276-1280
    xml data type, 1274
DML statements, compiling (query compilation), 1031
DML triggers, 834-835
    AFTER triggers, 837-839
        executing, 839
        special considerations, 840-841
        trigger firing order, 840
    cascading deletes, 847-849
    cascading updates, 849-850
    creating, 835-837

inserted and deleted tables, 841-843
    checking for column updates, 843-845
    referential integrity, 845-847
DMVs (Dynamic Management Views), 38, 156,
    168-170, CD:1909
    access to perfmon counters, 1261
    monitoring disk system items, 1256-1257
    monitoring memory items, 1252-1254
    monitoring network items, 1243
    monitoring processor items, 1248
    sys.dm exec query plan, 1137-1139
dm_db_index_physical_stats, 1001
    result columns, 1002-1003
Document Type Definition (DTD), 1378
documents, XML documents, 1378
domain integrity, 642
DRI (declarative referential integrity), 835
drill-through reports
    customizing, 1640-1642
    generating, 1639
    models, 1636
drivers, client data access technologies, 238
DROP, ALTER FULLTEXT INDEX, CD:1926
DROP DATABASE, 938
DROP ROLE, 277
DROP TABLE, 606
dropping
    constraints, 658
    indexes, 637
    tables, 605-606
    views, with T-SQL, 682
DSS (Decision Support Systems), 526
dta, 90, 95-98, CD:1731
DTA (Database Engine Tuning Advisor), 90, CD:1694
    command line, CD:1737-1742
    GUI, CD:1731-1736
DTC (Distributed Transaction Coordinator), 443, 516
DTD (Document Type Definition), 1378
dtexec utility, 1574-1577
    packages, running, 1577-1582
    phases, 1576
DTS (Data Transformation Services), 198, 211, 1539
    upgrading, 218
DTS packages, migrating, 211-212
DTS Parameters, 201
dtsrun utility, 1574
dtswizard, 91
dtutil utility, 1582-1586
DVPs (distributed partitioned views), 688
Dynamic Management Views. See DMVs
dynamic SQL, stored procedures, 772-774
    sp executesql, 774-776
    sp executesql, output parameters, 776-777

E

Eager Spool, Query Analyzer, 1127
editing SQLCMD scripts, Query Editor, 74-75
editions of SSNS, 1842-1843
element-centric XML shape, 1379

email
    receiving, 354
    sending, 347-348, 351-353
    SQL Server Agent Mail. See SQL Server Agent
        Mail, 354
email notification, configuring SQL Server Agent,
    365-366
ENABLE, ALTER FULLTEXT INDEX, CD:1924
ENABLE BROKER, CD:1877
enabling SQL Server Agent Mail, 354
encryption, 40
    connection encryption, configuring clients,
        235-236
    report server encryption, 1616
ENCRYPTION, creating views with T-SQL, 677-678
END CONVERSATION, CD:1896
EndDialog, CD:1886
endpoints, 224, 1442
    catalog views and system stored procedures,
        1466-1467
    controlling access permissions, 1468-1469
    database mirroring, 490-492
    FOR SOAP, 1467
    identifying for database mirroring, 492-493
    server endpoint layers, 224-225
    TDS endpoints, 224
enforcing
    data integrity, 642-643
    referential integrity, using DML triggers, 845-847
enhancements
    Analysis Services enhancements, 52-53
    backup and restore enhancements, 48-49
    database engine enhancements, 46
    failover clustering enhancements, 51
    Full-Text Search enhancements, 52
    index enhancements, 46
    notification enhancements, 51-52
    recovery enhancements, 49
    replication enhancements, 50
    Reporting Services enhancements, 53
    security enhancements, 47-48
    SQL Server Agent enhancements, 49
    T-SQL enhancements, 47
    web services enhancements, 52
enterprise computing, 515
Enterprise Edition of Reporting Services, 1613
entity integrity, 642
EOIO (exactly-once-in-order) messaging, CD:1890
@@ERROR, 786
    T-SQL, CD:1836-1837
Error, CD:1885
ERROR BROKER CONVERSATIONS, CD:1877
error handling, TRY...CATCH, 1312-1314
ERROR LINE, 787
error logs, SQL Server Agent (viewing), 368-369
ERROR MESSAGE, 787
ERROR NUMBER, 787
ERROR PROCEDURE, 787
ERROR SEVERITY, 787
ERROR STATE, 787
errors, stored procedures from, 786-789

escalation, locks, 1186
Estimated CPU Cost, 1119
Estimated I/O Cost, 1119
Estimated Number of Rows, 1119
Estimated Operator Cost, 1119
Estimated Row Size, 1119
Estimated Subtree Cost, 1119, 1121
Estimating access path costs, 1040
    clustered indexes, 1041
    nonclustered indexes, 1042-1046
    table scan costs, 1046-1048
ETL (extraction, transformation, and loading), 1539
evaluating indexes, 979-982
event chronicles, CD:1845
event forwarding, 390
event handlers, SSIS, 1547
event log entries, Reporting Services, 1653
Event parameter (SqlTrigger), 1366
event providers, SSNS, CD:1844
event rules, SSNS, CD:1845
EventClass data column (SQL Profiler), 1169
EventClasses ADF element, CD:1851-1852
EVENTDATA function, 863
EventData parameter (SqlTriggerContext), 1367
events
    providing to applications, SSNS, CD:1871-1874
    SSNS, CD:1844
    traces (SQL Server Profiler), 116-118
        categories, 132-136
exactly-once-in-order (EOIO) messaging, CD:1890
EXCEPT IP, 1447
exclusive locks, 1174
EXEC keyword, 710-711
exec sp helplogins, CD:1785
exec sp helpdb dbnamexyz, CD:1786
exec sp helplinkedsrvlogin, CD:1785
exec sp helpserver, CD:1785
exec sp linkedservers, CD:1785
exec sp server info, CD:1786
EXEC statement, scalar functions, 804
EXECUTE AS, executing stored procedures, 713-715
EXECUTE AS clause, 288, 811
EXECUTE AS statement, 287
Execute Report Definitions, 1645
executing
    AFTER triggers, 839
    disaster recovery, CD:1790
    INSTEAD OF triggers, 852-853
    maintenance plans, 964-965
    sqlcmd, 92-94
    stored procedures, 710-711
        execution context and EXECUTE AS, 713-715
        via linked servers, CD:1689
        in SSMS, 711-713
    traces (SQL Server Profiler), 123
execution context, 286-288, 765
execution log, Reporting Services, 1653
execution options, reports, 1650-1651
execution plan selection, Query Optimizer, 1070-1072
execution plans, graphical execution plans, 1130-1131

execution snapshots, 1651-1652
EXISTS, 1067
exists() new xml data type method, 1412, 1420-1421
EXPAND VIEWS hints, 1100
expanding
    databases, 567-568
    hierarchies with recursive CTE, 1288-1294
expansion, CD:1934
    indexed views, 696-697
expired subscription clean up, 442
explicit context switching, 287
EXPLICIT mode, XML, 1389-1393
explicit transactions, 875
    implicit transactions, compared, 884
explicit user-defined transactions, processing, 876-878
    nested transactions, 879-882
    savepoints, 878-879
exporting traces (SQL Server Profiler), 123
exporting data, bcp utility, 1589-1591
Expression Builder, SSIS, 1553-1554
expressions, multidimensional expressions, 1519-1521
Extended MAPI (Extended Messaging Application Programming Interface), 339
extended stored procedures, 793-794
    adding to SQL Server, 794-795
    obtaining information on, 795
    provided with SQL Server, 795-796
    xp cmdshell, 796-798
extensions, 550
extent, 548
Extent locking level (SQL Server), 1177
EXTERNAL ACCESS, 792, 828
external activation, CD:1880
external fragmentation, indexes, 999
ExternalMailQueue, 347
extraction, transformation, and loading (ETL), 1539

F

failover
    combining with scale-out options, building solutions with HA options, 408
    database mirroring, testing, 507-508
failover clustering, enhancements, 51
failover clusters, requirements for installing SQL Server 2005, 178
failovers, database mirroring, 486
FAST n hints, 1099
Feature Selection screen, 185
federated servers, CD:1767-1768
fields, format files
    lengths, 1595-1596
    terminators, 1596-1599
file backups, 295-296
    scenarios, 315-316
file data types, bcp utility, 1591
file growth, managing databases, 566-567
File locking level (SQL Server), 1177
filegroup backups, 295-296
    scenarios, 315-316

filegroups, 551-553
    performance and, 1225-1226
FILEGROWTH, 560
files
    data files, 548
    database files, 550
    format files, bcp utility, 1591-1601
    installation log files, viewing, 190
    saving trace output to, 124
    transaction log files, 548, 554-555
fill factor, 1714-1715
    indexes, setting, 1008-1011
filter errors, 1640
Filter icon, Query Analyzer, 1126
filtering
    articles, data replication, 421-425
    horizontal filtering, data replication, 463-465
    MDS-based filtering, 1537
    vertical filtering, data replication, 463-465
filters, traces (SQL Server Profiler), 121-122
finding foreign key references, 606
FIRE TRIGGERS, 840
firewalls, connectivity, 245
FIRE_TRIGGER hint, supplying bulk-copy
    operations, 1604
fixed-database roles, 259-261
fixed-server roles, 258-259
flow control, 377
fn get sql(sqlhandle), 825
fn helpcollations(), 825
fn listextendedproperty, 826
fn servershareddrives, 826
fn trace geteveninfo(traceID), 826
fn trace geteventinfo, 141
fn trace getfilterinfo, 141
fn trace getfilterinfo(traceID), 826
fn trace getinfo, 141
fn trace getinfo(traceID), 826
fn trade gettable(filename, numfiles), 826
fn virtualfilestats(dbid, fileid), 826
fn virtualservernodes(), 826
focus of disaster recovery, CD:1784-1788
focusing on specific data with views, 670
for clause, query() new xml data type method,
    1415-1416
FOR SOAP, 1449-1453
    viewing endpoints, 1467
FOR XML, 1274
FOR XML modes, 1378
    AUTO mode, 1385-1389
    EXPLICIT mode, 1389-1391, 1393
    new xml data type, 1396-1399
    PATH mode, 1393-1396
    RAW mode, 1379-1383
FORCE ORDER hints, 1099
forced parameterization, managing Query Optimizer,
    1109-1111
forcing
    query plan recompiles, 1076-1077
    recompilation of query plans, 768-771

FOREIGN KEY constraint, 596, 646-648
    cascading referential integrity, 648-650
FOREIGN KEY constraints, 847
    cascading, 850
foreign key references, finding, 606
format files
    bcp utility, 1591-1601
    fields
        lengths, 1595-1596
        terminators, 1596-1599
    prefixes, lengths, 1595
    storage types, 1593-1594
FORMAT keyword, 1450
Format parameter (SqlUserDefinedAggregate), 1364
Format parameter (SqlUserDefinedType), 1354
formatting notifications, CD:1857-1859
fragmentation, indexes, 999
fragments, XML, 1378
FREETEXT, FTS, CD:1933, CD:1937
FREETEXTTABLE, FTS, CD:1933, CD:1937
frequency of backups, 335-336
FTS (Full-Text Search), CD:1913
    CONTAINS, CD:1933-1936
    CONTAINSTABLE, CD:1933-1937
    FREETEXT, CD:1933, CD:1937
    FREETEXTTABLE, CD:1933, CD:1937
    Gatherer, CD:1915
    how it works, CD:1914-1916
    Indexer, CD:1915
    maintenance, CD:1938
    new features, CD:1914
    noise words, CD:1937
    performance, CD:1938-1939
full database backups, 294
    scenarios, 311-312
full outer joins, T-SQL, CD:1833-1835
full recovery model, 297-298
full-text catalogs, CD:1938
full-text indexes, T-SQL command, CD:1916
    ALTER FULLTEXT INDEX, CD:1924-1926
    CREATE FULLTEXT CATALOG, CD:1916-1918
    CREATE FULLTEXT INDEX, CD:1919-1924
    diagnostics, CD:1927-1930
    managing MSFTESQL, CD:1927
full-text indexing
    Full-Text Indexing Wizard, CD:1930-1932
    xml columns, 1436
Full-Text Indexing Wizard, CD:1930-1932
Full-Text Search, 20-21
    enhancements, 52
Full-Text Search. See FTS
FULLTEXTCATALOGPROPERTY, full-text indexes,
    CD:1929
Function Properties dialog (SSMS), 824
functions
    adXactReadcommitted, 1155
    avoiding unnecessary executions, T-SQL, CD:1809
    CLR functions, 827-828
    deciding between T-SQL and CLR functions,
        830-831
    EVENTDATA, 863

getdate(), 800
getonlydate(), 801
ITransactionLocal::StartTransaction, 1155
object definition, 721
OBJECTPROPERTY, 820
partition functions, creating, 608-610
rewriting stored procedures as, 826-827
SQLSetConnectAttr, 1155
systemwide table-valued functions, 825-826
tsequal(), 1152
UPDATE, 843-845
user-defined functions. *See* user-defined functions

G

GAM (global allocation map), 549
gather streams, 1089
    Query Analyzer, 1129
Gatherer, FTS, CD:1915
generating
    column statistics, 990-998
    drill-through reports, 1639
    index statistics, 990-998
    page numbers, with NTILE, 1304
    relational databases, 1523-1524
    T-SQL statements, with T-SQL, CD:1835-1836
generation
    CONTAINS, FTS, CD:1934-1935
    CONTAINSTABLE, FTS, CD:1934-1935
generator, CD:1845
Generator ADF element, CD:1862
GET CONVERSATION DIALOG, CD:1896, CD:1900
getdate(), 800
getonlydate(), 801
global allocation map (GAM), 549
grace hash joins, 1065
GRANT, 266, 285
granularity, locks, 1176-1187
granularity hints, locks, 1206
graphic charts, 1236
graphical execution plans, saving and viewing,
    1130-1131
GROUP BY, query processing, 1083-1084
GROUP BY hints, 1098
grouping
    discouraging in models, 1636
    in reports, with BIDS Report Designer, 1621-1623
GROUPING, sorting results (T-SQL), CD:1822-1824
guest users, 255-256
GUI for DTA, CD:1731-1736

H

HA (high-availability), 393, 397
    backups, 397
    building solutions, 400-401
        combining failover with scale-out options, 408
        data replication, 404-406
        database mirroring, 407
        log shipping, 406-407
        MSCS, 401
        SQL Clustering, 402-404

data partitioning, 410
data replication and database mirroring, 480
database snapshots, 408-410
dedicated administrator connections, 410
defined, 395-396
fast recovery, 408
hardware, 397
new features, 394-395
online indexing, 408
online restore, 408
operating systems, 397
quality assurance, 398
server instance isolation, 398-399
snapshot isolation levels, 410
standards/procedures, 398
training, 398
vendor agreements, 398
Windows Servers, 410
    Virtual Server 2005, 411-412
hardware, HA, 397
hardware requirements for installing SQL Server
    2005, 174-175
hash joins, 1063-1065
Hash Match icon, Query Analyzer, 1126
Heap or B-Tree (HOBT) locking level (SQL
    Server), 1177
heartbeat, 519
help, integrated help (SSMS), 62-64
Help resources, SSMS, 62
heterogeneous environments, replication monitoring,
    477-478
hierarchies
    defining in OLAP database creation, 1493-1502
    in reports, with BIDS Report Designer, 1623-1624
high-availability. *See* HA
hints
    bulk-copy operations, SSIS, 1603-1604
    granularity hints, locks, 1206
    Query Optimizer, 1096
        EXPAND VIEWS, 1100
        FAST n, 1099
        FORCE ORDER, 1099
        GROUP BY, 1098
        join, 1099
        join hints, 1098
        KEEP PLAN, 1100
        KEEPFIXED PLAN, 1100
        MAXDOP number, 1100
        MAXRECURSION number, 1100
        OPTIMIZER FOR, 1100
        processing hints, 1098, 1101
        RECOMPILE, 1100
        ROBUST PLAN, 1099
        table hints, 1096-1097
        UNION, 1098-1099
        USE PLAN, 1101-1103
        USE PLAN N, 1101
    transaction isolation, 1204-1205
    type hints, locks, 1206
histogram charts, 1236
histograms, index statistics, 984-987

History page, 363
history snapshots, 1651-1652
HOLAP (hybrid OLAP), 1482
HOLDLOCK, 911
HOLDLOCK transaction isolation level, 1204
HOME\Administrator, 253
horizontal data partitioning, CD:1765-1766
    denormalization, 1221-1223
    distributed partitioned views, CD:1767
horizontal filtering, data replication, 463-465
hybrid joins, 1065
hybrid OLAP (HOLAP), 1482

I

IAM (index allocation map), 549
ICFs, SSNS, CD:1863-1865
icons, logical and physical operators icons (Query
    Analyzer), 1121
    Assert, 1123
    Clustered Index Delete, 1124
    Clustered Index Scan, 1124
    Collapse, 1124
    Compute Scalar, 1125
    Concatenation, 1125
    Constant Scan, 1125
    Deleted Scan, 1126
    Distribute Streams, 1129
    Eager Spool, 1127
    Filter, 1126
    Gather Streams, 1129
    Hash Match, 1126
    Insert Scan, 1126
    Lazy Spool, 1127
    Log Row Scan, 1127
    Merge Join, 1127
    Nested Loops, 1127
    Nonclustered Index Delete, 1124
    Nonclustered Index Scan, 1124
    Nonclustered Index Spool, 1126
    Parallelism, 1129
    Parameter Table Scan, 1127
    Remote Delete, 1128
    Remote Insert, 1128
    Remote Query, 1128
    Remote Scan, 1128
    Remote Update, 1128
    Repartition Streams, 1129
    RID Lookup, 1128
    Row Count Spool, 1126
    Sequence, 1128
    Sort, 1128
    Stream Aggregate, 1128
    Table Delete, 1128
    Table Insert, 1128
    Table Scan, 1128
    Table Spool, 1126
    Table Update, 1128
    Table-valued Function, 1128
    Top, 1129

identifying
    ad hoc queries, SQL Server Profiler, 147-148
    endpoints, database mirroring, 492-493
    JOIN clauses, query analysis, 1034
    objects referenced in stored procedures, 717-719
    OR clauses, query analysis, 1033-1034
    parallel queries, 1089-1090
    performance bottlenecks, SQL Server Profiler,
        148-149
    search arguments, query analysis, 1032-1033
identity columns, 591-592
IDEs (integrated development environments), 1439
IF EXISTS, CD:1807
IFilter, CD:1915
IIS (Internet Information Services), 213, 1609
immediate transactional consistency, 443
immediate updating, replication, 19
IMPERSONATE, 267, 287
implementation contract, managed stored procedures,
    1335-1339
implementation phase, OLAP design
    methodologies, 1484
implementing data integrity, 643
implicit context switching, 288
implicit transactions, 875
    explicit transactions, compared, 884
    processing, 882-884
Import and Export Wizard (SSIS), 1551
importing traces (SQL Server Profiler), 125-126
    into trace tables, 126-128
importing data, bcp utility, 1589-1591
IN, 1067
IN PATH, CREATE FULLTEXT CATALOG, CD:1917
in-place upgrading. See upgrading in-place
included columns, indexes, 1020
index allocation map (IAM), 549
index create memory, CD:1715
INDEX CREATE statement, 864
index intersection, 1048-1051
index joins, 1055-1056
index locks, granularity, 1184-1185
index partitioning, 42-43
    for VLDB, CD:1768-1770
index selection, Query Optimizer, 1034-1035
    estimating access path costs, 1040-1048
    evaluating SARG and join selectivity, 1035-1040
    multiple indexes, 1048-1056
index union strategy, 1052-1055
indexed views, 690, 1021-1022
    creating, 690-693
    expansion, 696-697
    optimizing, 1056-1059
    performance and, 693-696
indexes, 969
    altering, 624
    B-tree indexes, 971
    choosing, 1024-1026
    clustered indexes, 624-625, 971-973
        costs, 1041
        designing, 1014-1016
        indexed views, 1021-1022

columns
    computed columns, 1022-1024
    included columns, 1020
    joins, 1014
composite indexes, design, 1013
covering, 1018-1019
creating
    with SSMS, 631-632
    with T-SQL, 627-631
densities, 987-988
design, 1013-1014, 1213
disabling, 1011-1012
dropping, 637
enhancements to, 46
evaluating, 979-982
fill factor
    reapplying, 1010-1011
    setting, 1008-1010
fragmentation, 999
FTS, CD:1915
full-text indexes. *See* full-text indexes
included columns, 624
intermediate nodes, 624
maintenance, 998-1008
    disabling indexes, 1011-1012
    fill factor, 1008-1011
    Maintenance Plan Wizard, 953-956
    SSMS, 1012-1013
managing, 633-636
multiple indexes, 1020-1021
nonclustered indexes, 626-627, 973-975
    costs, 1042-1046
    designing, 1016-1017
    fill factor, 1010
    rebuilding, 1008
    SQL Server performance, 1269
on views, 639-640
online index operations, 623
online indexing operations, 637-638
parallel index operations, 624
poor selectivity, 988, 1014
problems with query optimization, 1092
query indexes, 1024-1026
Query Optimizer, multiple indexes. *See* multiple
    indexes
querying, 975-978
rebuilding, VLDB data maintenance,
    CD:1752-1755
selecting, 978
SQL Server 2005, new features, 970
statistics, 982-984
    generating, 990-998
    histograms, 984-987
    rows, estimating, 988-989
    string summary statistics, 998
structures, 970-975
tables
    over-definition, 977
    Query Optimizer, 969
update performance indexes, 1024-1026

wide indexes, 1020-1021
XML indexes, 624
IndexID data column (SQL Profiler), 1169
indexing
    online indexing, HA, 408
    xml columns, 1430-1436
        full-text indexing, 1436
indirect recursion, 871
inequality operators, SARG and, 1037
Informatica, 1539
INFORMATION SCHEMA, 819-820
INFORMATION SCHEMA users, 256
information schema views, 166-167
Infoset, XML, 1432-1433
inheritance, defining in models, 1632-1634
.ini, 191
Init() method, 1363
INITIATOR, CD:1886
inline table-valued functions, 805
    CREATE FUNCTION, 808
input parameters, stored procedures, 724-725
    passing object names as, 728-729
    setting default values for, 725-728
    wildcards, 729-730
INPUTBUFFER, 1265
INSERT, 266
Insert Scan icon, Query Analyzer, 1126
inserted tables, DML triggers, 841-843
**inserting trace data into a trace table from a trace
    file, 127-128**
installation log files, viewing, 190
installation paths, 190-191
Installation Wizard, 181
installing
    bigpubs2005 database, 6
    clients, 228-230
    Reporting Services, 1613-1615
    SP1, 193-194
        unattended installation, 195
    SQL Server for SQL Server Clustering, 528-537
    SQL Server 2005, 203
        installation log files, 190
        installation paths, 190-191
        remote installation, 193
        requirements for, 173-179
        screens, 180-190
        side-by-side migration. *See* side-by-side
            migration
        unattended installation, 191-193
        upgrading in-place. *See* upgrading in-place
    SQL Server Clustering, 524-525
        configuring SQL Server database disks,
            525 526
        Connection Test Program, 539-542
        failure of nodes, 537-539
        installing MSCS, 527
        installing network interfaces, 527
Instance Name screen, 185
INSTANCENAME, 219
InstanceName ICF elements, CD:1863-1865

instances
    configuration options for, CD:1695-1702
    creating via SSMS for SSNS, CD:1866-1868
    SQL Browser, 228
    SSNS, CD:1846-1847
    XML, 1378
instant file initialization, 46
    databases, 548
INSTEAD OF trigger, 851-853
    versus AFTER triggers, 854-856
    restrictions, 859
    views, 856-859
INTEGRATED, 1445
integrated development environments (IDEs), 1439
integrated environments, SSMS, 58
    integrated help, 62-64
    window management, 59-62
integrated help, SSMS, 62-64
Integration Services, 184, 443
    SSIS, 1552
integrity
    data integrity, Database Engine, 14
    database integrity. See database integrity
intent locks, 1174-1175
interactivity in reports, with BIDS Report Designer,
    1625-1626
intergrating SSMS with source control, 81-83
intermediate nodes, indexes, 624
internal activation, CD:1880
internal fragmentation, indexes, 999
InternalMailQueue, 347
Internet Information Services (IIS), 213, 1609
interoperability, enterprise computing, 515
InvokeIfReceiverIsNull parameter (SqlMethod), 1359
IS (Integration Services), 443
IsByteOrdered parameter (SqlUserDefinedType), 1355
IsDeterministic, 820
IsDeterministic parameter (scalar UDFs), 1345
IsDeterministic parameter (SqlMethod), 1359
IsFixedLength parameter (SqlUserDefinedType), 1355
IsInlineFunction, 820
IsInvariantToDuplicates parameter
    (SqlUserDefinedAggregate), 1364
IsInvariantToNulls parameter
    (SqlUserDefinedAggregate), 1364
IsInvariantToOrder parameter
    (SqlUserDefinedAggregate), 1364
IsMutator parameter (SqlMethod), 1359
IsNullIfEmpty parameter
    (SqlUserDefinedAggregate), 1364
isolation levels, transaction isolation levels,
    1153-1159
IsPrecise parameter (scalar UDFs), 1345
IsScalarFunction, 820
IsSchemaBound, 820
IsTableFunction, 820
IsUpdatedColumn parameter
    (SqlTriggerContext), 1367
ITransactionLocal::StartTransaction function, 1155

J
JDBC (Java Database Connectivity)
    client data access technologies, 244
    drivers, 238
Job Activity Monitor, 49, 362
job history, viewing, 380-381
job mail notifications, SQL Server Agent Mail, 354-355
job notifications, 379
job schedules, 49, 377-378
job steps, 374-376
    multiple job steps, 376-377
Job System page, 363
jobs, 361
    creating with SQL Server Agent Mail, 355
    managing in SQL Server Agent, 373
        job history, 380-381
        job notifications, 379
        job properties, 373
        job schedules, 377-378
        job steps, 374-376
    multiserver job management, 388-390
    scripting, 387
JOIN, identifying for query analysis, 1034
join hints, 1099
    Query Optimizer, 1098
join processing strategies, 1060
    hash joins, 1063-1065
    merge joins, 1061-1063
    nested loops joins, 1060-1061
join selection, Query Optimizer, 1059-1060
    determining optimal join order, 1065-1066
    join processing strategies, 1060-1065
    subquery processing, 1067-1070
join selectivity, evaluating, 1035-1040
joins
    columns, indexes, 1014
    hash joins, 1063-1065
    hybrid joins, 1065
    merge joins, 1061-1063
    nested loops joins, 1060-1061
    optimal join order, 1065-1066
    subquery processing, 1067-1070

K
KEEP PLAN hints, 1100
KEEP REPLICATION, 323
KEEPFIXED PLAN hints, 1100
KERBEROS, 1445
KEY INDEX, CREATE FULLTEXT INDEX, CD:1922
Key locking level (SQL Server), 1177
key-range locking, 1178-1180
keygen, CD:1813
keyword groups
    AS HTTP, 1445-1448
    FOR SOAP, 1449-1453
keywords
    AUTHORIZATION, 1445, CD:1903
    CHARACTER SET, 1452
    COMPRESSION, 1448

CONTROL, 1469
CREATE ENDPOINT, 1444
DEFAULT, 661, 663-664
EXEC, 710-711
FORMAT, 1450
INITIATOR, CD:1886
NAMESPACE, 1448
NOT NULL, 590
NULL, 590
RELATED CONVERSATION, 1892
SCHEMA, 1450
SITE, 1448
TARGET, CD:1886
UNIQUE, 596
XMLDATA, 1383
KILOBYTES_PER_BATCH hint, supplying to bulk-copy
operations, 1604
KPIs, 1525

L

LANGUAGE
    CONTAINS, FTS, CD:1936
    CONTAINSTABLE, FTS, CD:1936
    CREATE FULLTEXT INDEX, CD:1920-1922
large object (LOB), 551
large row support, data types, 588
large-value data types, 587-588
latent transactional consistency, 443
layout, designing with BIDS Report Designer,
    1619-1620
Lazy Spool, Query Analyzer, 1127
Legato software, CD:1791
lengths
    format file prefixes, 1595
    format file fields, 1595-1596
Level 0, CD:1773
Level 1, CD:1773
Level 2, CD:1773
Level 3, CD:1773
Level 4, CD:1773
level hints, transaction isolation, 1204-1205
libraries, net-libraries, 237
licensing models, 29-33
lightweight pooling, CD:1715-1716
LIKE, SARG and, 1038
limitations
    for cached reports, execution snapshots, and
        history snapshots, 1652
    of database snapshots, 925-926
    of relational databases, 1524
    of SQL Server web services, 1469
linear regression, data mining algorithms, 1527
linked servers, CD:1671-1672
    adding, CD:1673-1680
    configuring, with sp serveroption, CD:1682-1683
    distributed queries, CD:1672
    distributed transactions, CD:1672-1673
    executing stored procedures, CD:1689
    mapping local logins to logins, CD:1683-1687

obtaining general information about,
        CD:1687-1689
    removing, CD:1681-1682
    setting up through SQL Server Management
        Studio, CD:1689-1692
    viewing, CD:1680-1681
LISTENER IP, 1445
LISTENER PORT, 1445
lists, creating with BIDS Report Designer, 1620-1621
live reports, report execution options, 1650
load os resources, CD:1927
LOB (large object), 551
LOB reads, STATISTICS IO, 1141
local mode, report controls, 1653
lock activity, monitoring, 1160-1161
    Performance Monitor, 1169-1171
    SQL Server Profiler, 1167-1170
    SSMS (SQL Server Management Studio),
        1164-1167
    sys.dm_tran_locks view, 1161-1164
lock events, SQL Profiler, 1167
Lock Manager, 1160
    locks, 1171-1176
        granularity, 1176-1187
Lock Requests/sec counter (SQLServer:Locks
    object), 1171
Lock Timeouts/sec counter (SQLServer:Locks
    object), 1171
Lock Wait Time counter (SQLServer:Locks
    object), 1171
Lock Waits/sec counter (SQLServer:Locks
    object), 1171
Lock:Acquired event (SQL Profiler), 1167
Lock:Cancel event (SQL Profiler), 1167
Lock:Deadlock Chain event (SQL Profiler), 1168
Lock:Deadlock event (SQL Profiler), 1168
Lock:Escalation event (SQL Profiler), 1168
Lock:Released event (SQL Profiler), 1168
Lock:Timeout event (SQL Profiler), 1168
locking
    contention, 1188-1189
        identifying, 1189-1191
        minimizing, 1192-1193
    importance of, 1152-1153
    lock activity, monitoring, 1160-1171
    Lock Manager, 1160
    new features, 1151
    optimistic locking, 1207
        snapshot isolation, 1209-1211
        timestamp data type, 1207-1209
    page-level locking, 1185-1186
    row-level locking, 1185-1186
    SQL Server levels, 1177
    table hints, 1203-1206
    transaction isolation levels, 1153-1159
    transactions, 911-912
    VLDB data maintenance, 1757
locks, 1171, CD:1716
    bulk update locks, 1176
    compatibility, 1187-1188

deadlocks, 1193-1195
1204 trace flags, 1197-1199
1222 trace flags, 1199
avoiding, 1195-1196
conversion deadlocks, 1194
cycle deadlocks, 1193-1194
examining, 1196-1197
handling, 1196-1197
monitoring, 1200-1203
escalation, 1186
exclusive locks, 1174
granularity, 1176-1187
granularity hints, 1206
intent locks, 1174-1175
schema locks, 1175
shared locks, 1172
SQL Server performance counters, 1259
timeout intervals, setting, 1191-1192
type hints, 1206
update locks, 1173-1174
locks option, configuration setting, 1187
Log File Viewer, 380
SSMS, 70-71
log files
installation log files, viewing, 190
shrinking, 571, 895-897
log reader agent, 439-440
Log Row Scan, Query Analyzer, 1127
log sequence numbers (LSNs), 874
log shipping, 946, CD:1782
building solutions with HA options, 406-407
data replication, 480
logged bulk-copy operations, SSIS, 1601-1602
batches, 1602
hints, 1603-1604
parallel loading, 1602-1603
logging
SSIS, 1549
transaction logging, 885-897
VLDB data maintenance, CD:1757-1758
logical and physical operator icons, Query Analyzer.
See icons
Logical Operation, 1118
logical reads, STATISTICS IO, 1141
LoginName data column (SQL Profiler), 1169
logins
managing, 268-273
principals, 251-253
users, 254
logistic regression, data mining algorithms, 1528
logmarkhistory, 325
logs
checkpoints, 886-889
transaction log files, 548, 554-555
write-ahead logs, 555
long-running transactions, managing, 913-915
loosely coupled, CD:1876
lost updates, transaction isolation levels, 1153
LSNs (log sequence numbers), 874

M

mail configuration objects, viewing, 357-358
mail message data, viewing, 359-360
mail profiles, 342
creating in Database Mail, 342-344
maintaining
indexes, Maintenance Plan Wizard, 953-956
system databases, 159
maintenance
FTS, 1938
indexes, 998-1008
disabling, 1011-1012
fill factor, 1008-1011
SSMS, 1012-1013
maintenance issues, VLDB, CD:1745
backing up and restoring, CD:1745-1748
consistency, CD:1749-1751
maintenance phase, OLAP design
methodologies, 1485
Maintenance Plan Wizard, 946-947
backing up databases, 948-951
checking database integrity, 951
maintaining indexes and statistics, 953-956
scheduling maintenance plans, 956-959
shrinking databases, 952-953
maintenance plans, 946
executing, 964-965
managing without a wizard, 959-964
scheduling with Maintenance Plan Wizard,
956-959
majority node sets, 520
Manage Indexes tool, 631
managed database objects
managed triggers, 1366-1372
permissions, 1332
related system catalogs, 1374-1375
stored procedures, 1335-1336, 1339-1344
assembly creation, 1342-1343
attributes, 1335-1336, 1339
context connection, 1340
debugging, 1343-1344
implementation contract, 1335-1336, 1339
Microsoft.SqlServer.Server objects,
1340-1341
transactions, 1372-1374
UDAs, 1363-1366
UDFs
scalar UDFs, 1344-1347
TVFs, 1348-1349, 1352-1353
UDTs, 1354-1355, 1359-1363
Visual Studio 2005, 1334-1335
managed stored procedures, developing managed
database objects, 1335-1336, 1339-1344
managed triggers, developing managed database
objects, 1366-1372
Management Studio, XML (SSNS), CD:1848-1849
management tools, 1613

managing
  alerts (SQL Server Agent), 381
    properties, 382-384
    responses, 384-386
  constraints, 656
    disabling, 659
    dropping, 658-659
    gathering constraint information, 657-658
  database, file growth, 566-567
  database roles, 276-277
  databases
    ALTER DATABASE, 573-574
    expanding, 567-568
    shrinking, 568-571
    shrinking log files, 571
    shrinking with SSMS, 571-573
  DDL triggers, 864-866
  indexes, 633-636
  jobs (SQL Server Agent), 373
    job history, 380-381
    job notifications, 379
    job properties, 373
    job schedules, 377-378
    job steps, 374-376
  logins, 268-273
  maintenance plans, without a wizard, 959-964
  MSFTESQL, CD:1927
  operators, SQL Server Agent, 370-372
  permissions, 277
    with SSMS, 277-278
    with SSMS (database level), 281-283
    with SSMS (object level), 283-284
    with SSMS (server level), 278-280
    with T-SQL, 285-286
    user-defined functions, 824-825
  plan guides, 1106
  projects, SSMS, 79-81
  Query Optimizer, 1094-1096
    forced parameterization, 1109-1111
    join hints, 1098
    plan guides, 1103-1109
    processing hints, 1098, 1101
    query governor, 1111-1113
    table hints, 1096-1097
    USE PLAN, 1101-1103
  remote servers, CD:1664-1666
    setup, 1666-1671
  users
    with SSMS, 273-275
    with T-SQL, 275
  views, 681
    with SSMS, 683
manual checkpoints, logs, 889
manual synchronization, 438
manually updating index statistics, 993-994
mapping local logins to logins on linked servers,
  CD:1683
    sp addlinkedsrvlogin, CD:1684-1685
    sp droplinkedsrvlogin, CD:1685-1686
    sp helplinkedsrvlogin, CD:1686-1687

markups, documents (XML), 1378
MARS (multiple active result sets), 44, 221
  ADO.NET, 1324-1326
masks
  affinity I/O masks, CD:1704-1706
  affinity masks, CD:1706-1707
master databases, 158, 333
master database files, 557
Master Server Wizard, 389
master servers, creating, 388-389
materialized subqueries, 1067-1068
max, DML, 1274-1276
max degree of parallelism, CD:1716-1717
max server memory, CD:1717-1718
max text repl size, CD:1719
max worker threads, CD:1719-1720
MaxByteSize parameter
  (SqlUserDefinedAggregate), 1364
MaxByteSize parameter (SqlUserDefinedType), 1355
MAXDOP number hints, 1100
MAXRECURSION, CTE, 1294-1295
MAXRECURSION number hints, 1100
MDAC (Microsoft Data Access Components),
  221, 1440
  client data access technologies, 242-243
.mdf extension, 550
MDX (multidimensional expressions), 73
MDX-based filtering, 1537
measuring runtime, datediff(), 1145
media families, 301
media sets, 301
memory, monitoring, 1250-1254
merge agent, 442
Merge Join, Query Analyzer, 1127
merge joins, 1061-1063
merge replication, 19, 444, 446-447
Merge() method, 1363
message storage, queues (SQL Server Service Broker),
  CD:1887-1889
message types, choosing for SQL Server Service
  Broker, CD:1882-1886
messages, defining in SQL Server Service Broker,
  CD:1882-1886
Meta Data Services Repository, 218
metadata, CD:1780
Metadata locking level (SQL Server), 1177
methods
  Aggregate(), 1363
  Init(), 1363
  Merge(), 1363
  new xml data type built-in methods, 1411-1430
    exists() method, 1412, 1420-1421
    modify() method, 1412, 1425-1430
    nodes() method, 1412, 1423, 1425
    query() method, 1412-1420
    value() method, 1412, 1421-1422
  Parse(), 1355
  SqlConnection.BeginTransaction, 1155
  Terminate(), 1363
  ToString(), 1355
  value(), 1435

Microsoft Cluster Service. *See* MSCS
Microsoft Data Access Components. *See* MDAC
Microsoft English Query, 216
Microsoft Full-Text Engine for SQL Server (MSFTESQL), 20
Microsoft Message Queuing (MSMQ), CD:1875
Microsoft ODBC driver for SQL Server, 238
Microsoft OLE DB provider for ODBC, 237
Microsoft OLE DB provider for SQL Server, 237
Microsoft Tape Format (MTF), 300
Microsoft Virtual Server 2005, HA, 411-412
Microsoft Visual Studio .NET, debugging stored procedures, 756-760
Microsoft.SqlServer.Server objects, managed stored procedures, 1340-1341
migrating
    Analysis Services, 209-210
    databases, side-by-side migration. *See* side-by-side migration
    DTS packages, 211-212
    Notification Services (SSNS), 213
    Reporting Services, 212-213
migration, side-by-side migration. *See* side-by-side migration
min memory per query, CD:1720
min server memory, CD:1717-1718
mirror database servers, database mirroring, 483
mirror role, database mirroring, 485
mirror server, creating datasbase on, 493-495
mirrored backups, 48, 292
    scenarios, 316
mixed authentication mode, 250
mixed extent, 548
Mode data column (SQL Profiler), 1169
model database, 158
Model Designer
    designing reports, 1629-1630
    promoted properties, 1634
Model Explorer, Report Builder, 1628-1629
model queries, debugging, 1636-1638
models
    debugging, 1636-1638
    design examples, 1631-1632
    design surface, Report Builder, 1634-1635
    designing reports, 1629-1630
    grouping, discouraging, 1636
    inheritance, defining, 1632-1634
    permissions, setting, 1645
    properties, promoting, 1634
    roles and drill-through reports, 1636
    security, 1643-1644
    sorting, in Report Builder, 1639
modes, FOR XML modes, 1378
    AUTO mode, 1385-1389
    EXPLICIT mode, 1389-1391, 1393
    new xml data type, 1396-1397, 1399
    PATH mode, 1393-1396
    RAW mode, 1379-1383
modify() new xml data type method, 1412, 1425-1430

modifying
    data, through partitioned views, 688
    logins, SSMS, 271
    stored procedures, 722-724
    tables, 598
        with database diagrams, 604-605
        with Object Explorer and Table Designer, 601-604
        with T-SQL, 598-601
    user-defined functions, 821-822
MOLAP (Multidimensional OLAP), 1481
monitoring
    application progress, with SQL Server Profiler, 150-152
    auto-update statistics, with SQL Server Profiler, 150
    data replication, 471
        backup and recovery, 478-479
        in heterogeneous environments, 477-478
        Performance Monitor, 477
        SQL statements, 472-475
        troubleshooting replication failures, 476-477
        within SQL Server Management Studio, 474-476
    database mirroring, 501-502, 504-505
    deadlocks, Server Profiler, 1200-1203
    disk systems, 1254-1257
    lock activity, 1160-1161
        Performance Monitor, 1169-1171
        SQL Server Profiler, 1167-1170
        SSMS, 1164-1167
        sys.dm_tran_locks view, 1161-1164
    memory, 1250-1254
    network interfaces, 1239-1243
    plan cache, 1077
        sys.dm exec cached plans, 1077-1079
        sys.dm exec plan attributes, 1081-1082
        sys.dm exec query stats, 1079-1081
        sys.dm exec sql text, 1079
    processors, 1244-1249
    running traces, 141-142
    SQL Server disk activity, 1259
    SQL Server performance, 1233-1235
    store procedure recompilation, 766-768
        forcing recompilation of query plans, 768-771
    values, Performance Monitor, 1237-1238
moving
    databases, 572
    packages, dtutil utility, 1582-1585
MSCS (Microsoft Cluster Service), 51, 481
    building solutions with HA options, 401
    extending with NLB, 522
    installing, 527
    SQL Server Clustering, 517-524
MSDASQL, 237
msdb database, 158
MSDN Online, 62
MSFTESQL (Microsoft Full-Text Engine for SQL Server), 20
    managing, CD:1927

MSMQ (Microsoft Message Queuing), CD:1875
MSSQL$:Plan Cache Object, 1258
MSXML 6.0, 216
MTF (Microsoft Tape Format), 300
multidimensional expressions (MDX), 73
    in OLAP database creation, 1519-1521
Multidimensional OLAP (MOLAP), 1481
Multiple Active Result Sets. See MARS
multiple applications, binding, 917
multiple indexes
    Query Optimizer, 1048
        index intersection, 1048-1051
        index joins, 1055-1056
        index union strategy, 1052-1055
    wide indexes, compared, 1020-1021
multiple publishers or multiple subscribers replication
    model, data replication, 429-431
multiserver job management, 388
    master servers, creating, 388-389
    multiserver jobs, creating, 390
    target servers, enlisting, 389-390
multiserver jobs, creating, 390
multistatement table-valued functions, 806-807
    CREATE FUNCTION, 808
multistatement transactions, triggers, 907-909
My Reports role, 1647

N

Naïve Bayes, data mining algorithms, 1528
NAME, 1449
Name parameter (scalar UDFs), 1345
Name parameter (SqlMethod), 1359
Name parameter (SqlTrigger), 1366
Name parameter (SqlUserDefinedAggregate), 1364
Name parameter (SqlUserDefinedType), 1355
NAMESPACE, 1448
namespaces, .NET Framework, 1319
naming columns, 585
.ndf extension, 550
Nested Loops, Query Analyzer, 1127
nested loops joins, 1060-1061
nested outer joins, T-SQL, 1832-1833
nested stored procedures, 743-745
    recursion, 745-748
nested transactions
    explicit user-defined transactions, processing,
        879-882
    triggers, 905-907
nested triggers, 869, 1721
.NET Framework, 37-38
    ADO.NET, 1319-1324
        connection pooling, 1328
        MARS (Multiple Active Result Sets),
            1324-1326
        Query Notifications, 1328-1330
        System.Data.SqlTypes namespace,
            1326-1328
    Code Access Security (CAS) permission
        sets, 1332

custom managed database objects
    managed triggers, 1366-1368, 1370-1372
    permissions, 1332-1334
    related system catalogs, 1374-1375
    stored procedures, 1335-1336, 1339-1344
    transactions, 1372-1374
    UDAs, 1363-1366
    UDFs, 1344-1349, 1352-1353
    UDTs, 1354-1355, 1359-1363
    Visual Studio 2005, 1334-1335
    namespaces, 1319
    new features, 1319
.NET Framework 2.0, 216
.NET Framework data provider for SQL Server, 237
.NET Framework Data Provider for SQL Server, client
    data access technologies, 240-242
NET SEND, 371
net-libraries, 237
network interfaces
    installing, 527
    monitoring, 1239-1243
network packet size, 1721-1722
network protocol support, requirements for installing
    SQL Server 2005, 177-178
network protocols, server network protocols, 222-223
network shares, 301
neural networks, data mining algorithms, 1528
New Alert dialog, 382
NEW BROKER, CD:1877
new features
    backups and restoration, 291-292
    command-line utilities, 90-91
    data integrity, 641-642
    data replication, 416-417
    of database design, 1213
    database file movement, 548
    database snapshots, 920
    for databases, 548
    disaster recovery planning, 1772
    DML, 1273
    FTS, CD:1914
    HA, 394-395
    instant file initialization, databases, 548
    Job Activity Monitor, 362
    large rows, 579
    large-value data types, 580
    monitoring SQL Server performance, 1234-1235
    online index operations, 623
    partial availability, databases, 548
    partitioned tables, 579
    query analysis, 1116
    query optimization, 1028-1030
    for remote servers, 1664
    in SSAS, 1473-1474
    shared job schedules, 362
    SNAC, 221
    of SQL Server 2005, 35-36
        Business Intelligence Development Studio, 44
        CLR, 37-38
        DAC, 39
        data types, 44-45

Database Mail, 40
database mirroring, 41
database snapshots, 41
DMVs, 38
encryption, 40
MARS, 44
.NET Framework, 37-38
online index and restore operations, 40
query notification, 44
Service Broker, 41-42
SMO, 39
snapshot isolation, 43
SQL Server Configuration Manager, 37
SQLCMD, 39-40
SSIS, 42
SSMS, 36-37
system catalog views, 38-39
table and index partitioning, 42-43
SQL Server Service Broker. *See* SQL Server
    Service Broker
for SQL Server Clustering, 516
of SQL Server Profiler, 111-112
SQL Server web services, 1439
SSMS, 57-58
SSNS, CD:1841-1842
stored computed columns, 580
stored procedures, 699-700
triggers, 834
user-defined functions, 799-800
views, 667
VLDB, CD:1743-1744
New Job Step dialog, 374
New Project dialog (Visual Studio 2005), 1334
new xml data type, 1402-1403
    built-in methods, 1411-1430
        exists() method, 1412, 1420-1421
        modify() method, 1412, 1425-1430
        nodes() method, 1412, 1423, 1425
        query() method, 1412-1420
        value() method, 1412, 1421-1422
    columns, 1404-1406
    FOR XML modes, 1396-1397, 1399
    schema collections, 1407-1412
NEXT USED, 615
NLB, MSCS, 522
NMO, choosing programming methods (SSNS),
    CD:1847-1848
NO ACTION, 648
NO LOG:transaction logs, 310
NO TRUNCATE, transaction logs, 309
Node ID, 1119
nodes, 1117
    failure of, SQL Server Clustering, 537, 539
    XML documents, 1378
nodes() new xml data type method, 1412, 1423-1425
noise words, FTS, CD:1937
NOLOCK transaction isolation level, 1205
non-logged bulk-copy operations, SSIS, 1601-1602
        batches, 1602
        hints, 1603-1604
        parallel loading, 1602-1603

non-T-SQL (non-Transact-SQL), 367
non-Transact-SQL (non-T-SQL), 367
Nonclustered Index Delete icon, Query Analyzer, 1124
Nonclustered Index Scan icon, Query Analyzer, 1124
Nonclustered Index Spool, Query Analyzer, 1126
nonclustered indexes, 626-627, 973-975
    costs, 1042-1046
    designing, 1016-1017
    fill factor, setting, 1010
    rebuilding, 1008
    SQL Server performance, 1269
nonexistent rows, searching, 1180
nonrepeatable reads, transaction isolation
    levels, 1153
NORECOVERY, 321
    transaction logs, 309
normalization, logical database design, 1215
    benefits of, 1217
    disadvantages of, 1217
normalization forms, logical database design,
    1215-1217
NOT NULL, column properties, 590
notification, 44
    enhancements, 51-52
    managing operators, 370-372
notification cycles, SSNS, CD:1845-1846
Notification Services. *See* SSNS (SQL Server
    Notification Services)
NotificationClasses ADF element, CD:1854-1859
notifications, formatting, 1857-1859
nscontrol, CD:1866
NSDiagnosticDeliveryChannel, CD:1874
NSDiagnosticEventClass, CD:1873
NSDiagnosticEventProvider, CD:1873
NSDiagnosticNotificationClass, CD:1874
NSDiagnosticSubscriptionClass, CD:1874
NT AUTHORITY\SYSTEM, 253
NTILE, 1299-1301
    generating page numbers, 1304
NULL, column properties, 590
num proc buffs, 764, 1264
num proc buffs active, 764, 1264
num proc buffs used, 764, 1264
Number of Deadlocks/sec counter (SQLServer:Locks
    object), 1171

O

Object, 1119
object definition function, 721
Object Explorer (SSMS), 66-67
    databases, creating, 556-559
    creating tables, 580
    tables
        creating, 580
        dropping, 605-606
        modifying, 601-604
Object Explorer tree, 61
object level (SSMS), managing permissions, 283-284
object names, T-SQL, CD:1796-1799
ObjectID data column (SQL Profiler), 1169

objectives of disaster recovery, CD:1778-1779
ObjectName data column (SQL Profiler), 1169
OBJECTPROPERTY, CD:1928
OBJECTPROPERTY function, 820
objects, identifying objects referenced in stored
  procedures, 717-719
obtaining information on extended stored
  procedures, 795
ODBC (Open Database Connectivity), 238, 1440
  MDAC, client data access technologies, 243
OLAP (online analytical processing), 198, 1473
  design methodologies, 1482-1485
  HOLAP, 1482
  MOLAP, 1481
  versus OLTP, 1480-1481
  performance, data mining, 1535-1536
  preparing for database creation, 1482
  requirements example, CompSales International,
    1485-1486
    cube creation, 1486-1487
    cube perspectives, 1524-1525
    data mining, 1526-1534
    generating relational databases, 1523-1524
    KPIs, 1525
    OLAP database creation, 1488. See also
      databases, OLAP database creation
    security and roles, 1536-1537
    SQL Server BIDS, 1487-1488
  ROLAP, 1481
  SSAS and, 1474-1476
OLE DB
  linked servers, 1671
  MDAC, client data access technologies, 243
OLTP (online transaction processing), 526, 1475
  versus OLAP, 1480-1481
ON DELETE CASCADE, 847, 1214
on failure workflows, SSIS, 1547
ON FILEGROUP, CREATE FULLTEXT CATALOG, CD:1917
ON FULLTEXT CATALOG, CREATE FULLTEXT INDEX,
  CD:1922
on success workflows, SSIS, 1547
ON UPDATE CASCADE, 847
online analytical processing. See OLAP
online index, 40
online index operations, 623
online indexing, HA, 408
online indexing operations, 637-638
online restorations, 291, 332
online restore, 49
  HA, 408
online transaction processing. See OLTP
OnNullCall parameter (SqlMethod), 1359
Open Database Connectivity (ODBC), 238, 1440
opening reports, Report Builder, 1640
OPENXML, relational data, 1399-1402
operating modes, database mirroring, 485-486
operating systems, HA, 397
operations, SSIS, 1601-1604

operators, 361
  creating with SQL Server Agent Mail, 354
  managing in SQL Server Agent, 370-372
optimistic locking, 1207
  snapshot isolation, 1209-1211
  timestamp data type, 1207-1209
optimization, OLAP database creation, 1523
OPTIMIZER FOR hints, 1100
optimizing indexed views, Query Optimizer, 1056-1059
OR, identifying for query analysis, 1033-1034
ORDER BY, CD:1808
order by clause, query() new xml data type method,
  1417-1418
ORDER hint, supplying to bulk-copy operations, 1604
Ordered, 1119
OUTER APPLY, 1311
outer joins, T-SQL, CD:1826-1827
  full outer joins, CD:1833-1835
  nested outer joins, CD:1832-1833
  versus WHERE clause, CD:1827-1832
OUTPUT, DML, 1280-1284
Output List, 1119
output parameters
  sp executesql, 776-777
  stored procedures, 731-732
OUTPUTBUFFER, 1265

P

Package Execution Utility (SSIS), 1574-1576
  dtexec utility, 1574, 1576-1577
  dtsrun utility, 1574
  dtutil utility, 1582-1586
  packages, running, 1577-1582
package loading phase (dtexec), 1576
Package Migration Wizard, 212
packages
  running, dtexec utility, 1577-1582
  SSIS, 1546, 1549
PAD_INDEX option, 1010
page free space (PFS), 549
Page locking level (SQL Server), 1177
Page Verify, 562
page-level locking, compared to row-level locking,
  1185-1186
pages, 548
  dirty pages, 555
paging results, ROW NUMBER, 1301-1305
PAGELOCK optimizer hint, 1206
parallel index operations, 624
parallel loading, bulk-copy operations (SSIS),
  1602-1603
parallel query processing, 1086-1087
  configuration options, 1088-1089
  identifying, 1089-1090
parallel snapshot preparation, 416
parallelism
  cost of, CD:1709-1710
  max degree of, CD:1716-1717
  Query Analyzer, 1129

Parameter Table Scan, Query Analyzer, 1127
ParameterDefaults ADF element, CD:1851
ParameterDefaults ICF elements, CD:1863-1865
parameters
    dm_db_index_physical_stats, 1001
    for sac, 102
    input parameters, 724-730
    output parameters
        sp executesql, 776-777
        stored procedures, 731-732
    scalar UDFs, 1345
    SqlMethod, 1359
    SqlTrigger attribute, 1366
    SqlTriggerContext attribute, 1367
    SqlUserDefinedAggregate attribute, 1364
    SqlUserDefinedType, 1354-1355
Parse() method, 1355
partial availability, 46
    databases, 548
partial backups, 49, 292, 295
    scenarios, 313-315
partition functions, creating, 608-610
partition schemes, creating, 610-612
partitioned tables, 579, 607-608
    adding partitions, 614-616
    creating, 612-613
        partition functions, 608-610
        partition schemes, 610-612
    dropping partitions, 616-618
    switching partitions, 618-621
    viewing information, 613
partitioned views, 684-687
    distributed partitioned views, 688-690
    modifying data through, 688
partitioning
    databases across servers, CD:1767-1768
    table and index partitioning, 42-43
partitions, 554, 607
    adding table partitions, 614-616
    dropping table partitions, 616-618
passing object names as parameters, stored
  procedures, 728-729
passive server/failover licensing, 32
passwords, SQL login password policies, 247
PATH, 1446
PATH mode, XML, 1393-1396
PATH secondary index (XML), 1434
patterns, SQL Server web services, 1440-1441
patterns of disaster recovery, CD:1773-1777
pause indexing, CD:1927
peer-to-peer replication model, data replication,
  431-433
PERFMON, 1263
perfmon counters, access to, 1261
performance. See also SQL Server performance
    configuration options, CD:1703
        ad hoc distributed queries, CD:1704
        affinity I/O mask, CD:1704-1706
        affinity mask, CD:1706-1707
        AWE enabled, CD:1707-1709
        CLR enabled, CD:1709

        cursor threshold, CD:1710-1711
        default full-text language, CD:1711-1712
        default language, CD:1712-1713
        fill factor, CD:1714-1715
        index create memory, CD:1715
        lightweight pooling, CD:1715-1716
        locks, CD:1716
        max degree of parallelism, CD:1716-1717
        max server memory, CD:1717-1718
        max text repl size, CD:1719
        max worker threads, CD:1719-1720
        min memory per query, CD:1720
        min server memory, CD:1717-1718
        miscellaneous options, CD:1730-1731
        nested triggers, CD:1721
        network packet size, CD:1721-1722
        parallelism, CD:1709-1710
        priority boost, CD:1722
        query governor cost limit, CD:1722-1723
        query wait, CD:1723
        recovery interval, CD:1724
        remote admin connections, CD:1724
        remote login timeout, CD:1725
        remote proc trans, CD:1725
        remote query timeout, CD:1726
        scan for startup procs, CD:1726
        show advanced options, CD:1727
        user connections, CD:1727
        user options, CD:1728-1729
        XP-related configuration options, CD:1729
    data replication, 479-480
    designing for database performance, 1214
    filegroups and, 1225-1226
    FTS, CD:1938-1939
    indexed views and, 693-696
    monitoring SQL Server performance, 1233-1235
    new features, 1151
    stored procedures, 762-766
    T-SQL. See T-SQL, performance
    VLDB data maintenance, CD:1757
performance counters, Reporting Services, 1653
performance logs, 1237
Performance Monitor, 1236
    lock activity, monitoring, 1169-1171
    monitoring values, 1237-1238
    replication monitoring, 477
    views, 1236-1237
performance output, Query Editor (SSMS), 76-78
permission granularity, 248
permissions, 248, 266-267
    access permissions, controlling, 1468-1469
    database mirroring, 492
    Execute Report Definitions, 1645
    managed database objects, 1332
        three-permission sets, 1332-1334
    managing, 277
        with SSMS, 277-278
        with SSMS (at database level), 281-283
        with SSMS (at object level), 283-284
        with SSMS (at server level), 278-280
        with T-SQL, 285-286

roles, 258
securing reports, 1647-1648
setting on models, 1645
system permissions, securing reports, 1648
user-defined functions, 824-825
perspectives, cubes, 1524-1525
PFS (page free space), 549
phantom reads, transaction isolation levels, 1153
Physical Operation, 1118
physical reads, STATISTICS IO, 1141
PhysicalDisk object, 551
pipes, SQL Browser, 228
PIVOT, 1305-1309
plan cache, 1072
    monitoring, 1077
        sys.dm exec cached plans, 1077-1079
        sys.dm exec plan attributes, 1081-1082
        sys.dm exec query stats, 1079-1081
        sys.dm exec sql text, 1079
plan guides, managing Query Optimizer, 1103-1109
planning
    for data replication, 443
    disaster recovery, 1790
plans
    developing for backups and restoration, 292-293
    maintenance plans, 338
point in time, restoring to, 331-332
point of failure, restoring to, 328-330
point-in-time reporting databases, providing with
    database snapshots, 930
populating cubes, with data in OLAP database
    creation, 1509-1510
population, CD:1922
POPULATION TYPE, CREATE FULLTEXT INDEX,
    CD:1922-1924
PORTS, 1446
ports, SQL Browser, 228
Predicate, 1119-1121
predicate transitivity, query processing, 1083
prefixes, format files (lengths), 1595
primary data files, 550
PRIMARY KEY constraint, 596, 643-644
principal database servers, database mirroring, 482
principal role, database mirroring, 485
principals, 248, 251
    logins, 251-253
    roles, 258
        application roles, 264-265
        fixed-database roles, 259-261
        fixed-server roles, 258-259
        public roles, 261-262
        user-defined roles, 262-264
    user/schema separation, 257-258
    users, 254-256
PRINT, CD:1900
priority boost, 1722
problems with query optimization, 1090
    index design, 1092
    large complex queries, 1094
    search arguments, 1092-1093

statistics, 1090-1091
    triggers, 1094
proc cache active, 764, 1264
proc cache size, 764, 1264
proc cache used, 764, 1264
PROCCACHE, 1264-1265
procedural data integrity, implementing, 643
procedure caches
    SQL Server performance counters, 1260
    stored procedures, 763-764
procedure status, returning in stored procedures,
    732-733
procedures
    HA, 398
    startup procedures, 778-781
    stored procedures, transactions, 899-904
Proceedings of the 31st International Conference on
    Very Large Data Bases (i), 1432
processadmin, 259
processes
    deadlocks. See deadlocks
    locking contention, 1188-1189
        identifying, 1189-1191
        minimizing, 1192-1193
processing
    snapshot agents, 438-439
    transactions, 875
processing hints, Query Optimizer, 1098, 1101
processing instructions, XML, 1378
processor affinity, 1704
processors, monitoring, 1244-1249
profiler, 90-91
Profiler GUI, 123
    saving trace output to, 125
programming methods, SSNS, 1847-1848
projects, managing in SSMS, 79-81
promoting properties in models, 1634
properties
    alert properties, 382-384
    columns, 590
        changing with T-SQL, 599
        computed columns, 593-594
        IDENTITY, 591-592
        NULL and NOT NULL, 590
        ROWGUIDCOL, 592-593
    configuring, SQL Server Agent, 362-363
    DATABASEPROPERTYEX, 564
    job properties, 373
    promoting in models, 1634
PROPERTY secondary index (XML), 1435
providers, client data access technologies, 237
Providers ADF element, CD:1859-1862
providing events to applications, SSNS, CD:1871-1874
provisioning, 225
    client access provisioning, 225-227
proximity
    CONTAINS, FTS, CD:1935
    CONTAINSTABLE, FTS, CD:1935
proxy, 1441
proxy accounts, configuring (SQL Server Agent),
    367-368

public roles, 261-262
publication server, data replication, 418-420
publications, 420
    creating for data replication, 456-459, 461-462
    data replication, 421
Publisher role, 1647
publisher subscriber replication model, data
    replication, 427-428
publishing, enabling for data replication, 451-455
pull subscriptions, 434
purging data, VLDB data maintenance, CD:1755-1761

Q

QA (quality assurance), testing database snapshots,
    939-940
    HA, 398
queries
    100 worst-performing queries, 1265-1269
    ad hoc distributed queries, CD:1704
    analyzing with SQL Server Profiler, 145
    designing with BIDS Report Designer, 1619
    distributed queries, linked servers, CD:1672
    identifying ad hoc queries, SQL Server Profiler,
        147-148
    model queries, debugging, 1636-1638
    partitioned tables, 607
    problems with query optimization, 1094
    recursive queries, CTE, 1286-1295
    semantic queries, 1642
    subquery processing, 1067-1070
query analysis
    new features, 1116
    OLAP database creation, 1523
    Query Optimizer, 1032-1034
    SQL Server Profiler, 1147-1148
Query Analyzer, 1117-1118
    execution plan ToolTips, 1118-1121
    graphical execution plans, saving and viewing,
        1130-1131
    logical and physical operator icons. See icons,
        logical and physical operator icons (Query
        Analyzer)
    stored procedures, analyzing, 1129-1130
Query Analyzer (QA), 205
Query Builder, SSIS, 1552-1554
query compilation, 1030
    DML statements, compiling, 1031
    optimization steps, 1032
        execution plan selection, 1070-1072
        join selection, 1059-1070
        query analysis, 1032-1034
        row estimation and index selection,
            1034-1059
Query Designer, Query Editor (SSMS), 78-79
Query Editor, SSMS, 71-73
    disconnected editing, 74
    editing SQLCMD scripts, 74-75
    performance output, 76-78

Query Designer, 78-79
Query Editor types, 73
regular expressions and wildcards, 75-76
query execution plan, 1030
query governor, managing Query Optimizer,
    1111-1113
query governor cost limit, CD:1722-1723
query indexes, compared to update performance
    indexes, 1024-1026
query notification, 44
    ADO.NET, 1328-1330
query optimization
    defined, 1027
    new features, 1028-1030
    problems with, 1090-1094
Query Optimizer, 1027, 1030, 1115
    indexes, evaluating, 979-982
    managing, 1094-1096
        forced parameterization, 1109-1111
        join hints, 1098
        plan guides, 1103-1109
        processing hints, 1098, 1101
        query governor, 1111-1113
        table hints, 1096-1097
        USE PLAN, 1101-1103
    optimization steps, 1032
        execution plan selection, 1070-1072
        join selection, 1059-1070
        query analysis, 1032-1034
        row estimation and index selection,
            1034-1059
    table scans, 970
query parameterization, query plan reuse, 1074-1075
query plan aging, 1075
query plan caching, 1072-1073
    stored procedures, performance, 763
query plan execution, limiting with query governor,
    1111-1113
query plan reuse, 1073-1074
    query parameterization, 1074-1075
query plans
    automatic query plan recompilation, 765-766
    forcing recompilation, 768-771
    query plan caching, 763
    recompiling, 1076-1077
    shared query plans, 764
query processing
    DISTINCT, 1084
    GROUP BY, 1083-1084
    parallel query processing, 1086-1090
    predicate transitivity, 1083
    UNION, 1084-1086
    UNION ALL, 1086
query statistics, 1139
    datediff(), 1145
    STATISTICS IO, 1139-1140
        analyzing, 1141-1142
        LOB reads, 1141
        logical reads, 1141

physical reads, 1141
read-ahead reads, 1141
scan count, 1140
STATISTICS PROFILE, 1146
STATISTICS TIME, 1142-1145
STATISTICS XML, 1146-1147
query trees, 1031
query wait, CD:1723
query() new xml data type method, 1412-1420
for clause, 1415-1416
order by clause, 1417-1418
return clause, 1418-1420
where clause, 1417
querying
indexes, 975-978
sys.dm_tran_locks view, 1161-1164
questions, SSMS, 62
queue monitor, CD:1911
queues
creating for message storage, SQL Server Service
Broker, CD:1887-1889
transmission queues, CD:1890
quorum drives, 519
quorums, 520

R

RAID (redundant array of inexpensive disks), 1227
RAID Level 0, 1227-1228
RAID Level 1, 1228-1229
RAID Level 5, 1230-1231
RAID Level 10, 1229
RANGE LEFT partitions, 610
RANGE RIGHT partitions, 610
range searching, key-range locking, 1178-1180
RANK, 1298-1299
ranking functions, 1295
DENSE RANK, 1298-1299
NTILE, 1299-1301
generating page numbers, 1304
RANK, 1298-1299
ROW NUMBER, 1295-1297
for paging results, 1301-1305
partitioning by ROW NUMBER, 1297-1298
RAW mode, XML, 1379-1383
RDL (Report Definition Language), 213, 1610
read committed isolation, 1155
READ COMMITTED option (SET TRANSACTION
ISOLATION LEVEL statement), 911
Read Committed Snapshot, 1151
read committed snapshot isolation, 1155-1156
read uncommitted isolation, 1154
READ UNCOMMITTED option (SET TRANSACTION
ISOLATION LEVEL statement), 911
read-ahead reads, STATISTICS IO, 1141
READCOMMITTED transaction isolation level, 1205
READCOMMITTEDLOCK transaction isolation
level, 1205
READPAST transaction isolation level, 1206
READUNCOMMITTED transaction isolation level, 1205
reapplying fill factor, indexes, 1010-1011

REBUILD, indexes, 634
Rebuild Index task, 954
rebuilding
indexes, VLDB data maintenance, CD:1752-1755
nonclustered indexes, 1008
RECEIVE, CD:1896, CD:1900
receiving email, Database Mail, 354
reciprocal principal/mirror reporting configuration,
941-942
RECOMPILE hints, 1100
recompiling query plans, 1076-1077
recovering, full database recovery, 330
recovery
enhancements, 49
HA, 408
replication monitoring, 478-479
recovery interval, CD:1724
Recovery Model setting, 558
recovery models, 296-300
recovery point objective (RPO), CD:1778
recovery processes, transactions, 885-886, 889-891
analysis phase, 890
checkpoint process, 886-889
redo (roll-forward) phase, 890
undo (rollback) phase, 891
recovery time objective (RTO), CD:1778
recursion, 871
nested stored procedures, 745-748
recursive queries, CTE, 1286-1288
expanding hierarchies, 1288-1294
MAXRECURSION, 1294-1295
recursive triggers, 870-871
redistributing SNAC, with custom client
applications, 231
redo (roll-forward) phase, transaction recovery
process, 890
redundant array of inexpensive disks (RAID), 1227
redundant data, denormalization, 1219-1220
referential integrity, 642
cascading FOREIGN KEY constraint, 648-650
DML triggers, 845-847
VLDB data maintenance, CD:1759
registered servers, SSMS, 65-66
regular expressions, Query Editor (SSMS), 75-76
reinitialize subscriptions having data validation
failures, 442
RELATED CONVERSATION keyword, CD:1892
related system catalogs, developing managed
database objects, 1374-1375
relational data, XML
FOR XML modes, 1378-1383, 1385-1391,
1393-1399
OPENXML, 1399-1402
relational databases, generating, 1523-1524
relational index options, for CREATE INDEX, 629
Relational OLAP (ROLAP), 1481
relationships, zero-to-one relationships
(denormalization), 1224-1225
reliability, enterprise computing, 515
remote admin connections, CD:1724

remote connections, enable launch of (Surface Area Configuration) tool, 223
Remote Delete, Query Analyzer, 1128
Remote Insert, Query Analyzer, 1128
remote installation, installing SQL Server 2005, 193
remote login timeout, CD:1725
remote proc trans, CD:1725
remote procedure calls (RPC), CD:1663
Remote Query, Query Analyzer, 1128
remote query timeout, CD:1726
Remote Scan, Query Analyzer, 1128
remote servers, CD:1663
    managing, CD:1664-1666
        setup, CD:1666-1671
    new features for, CD:1664
remote service bindings, creating for conversations, CD:1908
remote stored procedures, 755-756
Remote Update, Query Analyzer, 1128
removing
    database mirroring, 505-507
    linked servers, CD:1681-1682
    mappings for linked servers, sp droplinkedsrvlogin, CD:1685-1686
    snapshots, from cache reports, 1651
renumbering columns, 1599-1601
REORGANIZE, indexes, 634
Reorganize Index task, 954
repartition streams, 1089
    Query Analyzer, 1129
repeatable read isolation, 1156-1157
REPEATABLE READ option (SET TRANSACTION ISOLATION LEVEL statement), 911
REPEATABLEREAD transaction isolation level, 1205
replaying trace data, 129-131
replicated databases, upgrading, 217
replication. See also data replication
    database mirroring and, 511-512
    enhancements, 50
    immediate updating, 19
    merge replication, 19
    snapshot replication, 18
    transactional replication, 18-19
replication agents, 436-437
    agent history cleanup: distribution, 442
    distribution agent, 441
    distribution cleanup: distribution, 442
    expired subscription cleanup, 442
    log reader agent, 439-440
    merge agent, 442
    reinitialize subscriptions having data validation failures, 442
    replication agents checkup, 442
    snapshot agent, 437-439
replication agents checkup, 442
Report Builder, 1610
    ad hoc reporting, 1645
    design surface, 1634-1635
    designing reports, 1627-1629
    models, 1632
    opening reports, 1640

    saving reports, 1640
    sorting, 1639
Report Builder role, 1647
Report Definition Language (RDL), 213, 1610
report design tools, 1613
report displays, 1236
report server database catalog, configuring, 1617-1618
Report Viewer, 202-203
report viewer controls, 1610-1611
    building applications for SQL Server Reporting Services 2005, 1653
        ASP.NET report controls, 1654-1659
Reporting Services, 23, 184, 1607-1608. See also reports
    configuration options and tools, 1615-1618
    enhancements, 53
    Enterprise Edition, 1613
    installing, 1613-1615
    migrating, 212-213
    performance and monitoring tools, 1652-1653
    Report Builder, 1610
    report viewer controls, 1610-1611, 1653
        ASP.NET report controls, 1654-1659
    scripting support, 1646
    system architecture, 1611-1613
    upgrading, 218-219
    web service, 1609
    Windows service, 1609
Reporting Services Configuration tool, 1615
Reporting Services features, sac, 102
/Reports, 1617
reports, 1610
    ad hoc reporting, 1645
    building with BIDS Report Designer, 1620
    cached reports, 1651-1652
    deploying, 1646
    designing with BIDS Report Designer, 1619
        adding interactivity, 1625-1626
        building reports, 1620
        creating simple lists, 1620-1621
        deploying sample reports, 1626
        grouping and sorting, 1621-1623
        layout choices, 1619-1620
        queries, 1619
        tables and hierarchies, 1623-1624
    designing with models and Model Designer, 1629-1630
    designing with Report Builder, 1627-1629
    drill-through reports
        customizing, 1640-1642
        generating, 1639
        models, 1636
    Execute Report Definitions, 1645
    execution options, 1650-1651
    models. See models
    opening, in Report Builder, 1640
    saving, in Report Builder, 1640
    securing, 1647-1648
    security, 1644
    subscriptions, 1648-1650

/ReportServer, 1617
requirements
    for installing SQL Server 2005, 173
        hardware requirements, 174-175
        software requirements, 175-179
    for SSNS, 1842-1843
    user requirements. *See* user requirements
requirements phase, OLAP design
  methodologies, 1483
resource database, 158
resource usage, CD:1927
responsibilities of system administrators, 156-157
restorating, 317
restoration
    developing a plan, 292-293
    new features, 291-292
    online restoration, 291
    restore information, 324-325
    scenarios, 326
        online restorations, 332
        restoring system databases, 333-335
        restoring to a different database, 327
        restoring to point in time, 331-332
        restoring to point of failure, 328-330
        restoring transaction logs, 328
    with SSMS, 322-323
    with T-SQL, 318-321
        transaction logs, 321-322
RESTORE, 318
restore, enhancements, 48-49
RESTORE DATABASE, 318-319
Restore dialog, SSMS, 60
RESTORE FILELISTONLY, 324
RESTORE HEADERONLY, 325
restore operations, 40
RESTORE TRANSACTION, 318
RESTORE VERIFYONLY, 325
restorefile, 325
restorefilegroup, 326
restorehistory, 326
restores, online restores, 49
restoring
    database backups to new locations, 573
    to different databases, 327
    full-text catalogs, 1938
    to point in time, 331-332
    to point of failure, 328-330
    system databases, 333-335
    system tables, 325-326
    transaction log backups, 330-331
    transaction logs, 328
    VLDB, CD:1745-1747
Restrict Access, 562
RESTRICT IP, 1447
restrictions
    of database snapshots, 925-926
    on defaults, 664-665
    INSTEAD OF triggers, 859
result columns, dm_db_index_physical_stats,
  1002-1003

retrieval of archived data, VLDB data maintenance,
  CD:1759-1760
retrieving database option information, 564-566
Retry Attempts, 376
Retry Interval, 376
Retry options, 376
return clause, query() new xml data type method,
  1418-1420
returning procedure status, stored procedures,
  732-733
reusing query plans, 1073-1075
reverting to database snapshots, 924
    to database snapshots for recovery, 927-928,
      938-939
REVOKE, 266, 285
rewriting stored procedures as functions, 826-827
RID Lookup, Query Analyzer, 1128
ROBUST PLAN hints, 1099
ROLAP (Relational OLAP), 1481
role assignments, 1647
role switching, database mirroring, 486
roles, 258
    application roles, 264-265
    of database mirroring, 485
    fixed-database roles, 259-261
    fixed-server roles, 258-259
    models, 1636
    OLAP, 1536-1537
    public roles, 261-262
    user-defined roles, 262-264
ROLLBACK, CD:1901
rollback transaction statement, 783
root-level certificate, 235
routing, building routes to map conversations between
  SQL Server instances, CD:1908
Row Count Spool, Query Analyzer, 1126
row estimation, Query Optimizer, 1034-1035
    estimating access path costs, 1040-1048
    evaluating SARG and join selectivity, 1035-1040
    multiple indexes, 1048-1056
    optimizing indexed views, 1056-1059
Row ID (RID) locking level (SQL Server), 1177
ROW NUMBER, 1295-1297
    paging results, 1301-1305
    partitioning, 1297-1298
    partitioning by ROW NUMBER, 1297-1298
ROW OVERFLOW DATA, 588
row-level locking, compared to page-level locking,
  1185-1186
@@ROWCOUNT, T-SQL, 1836-1837
ROWGUIDCOL, columns, 592-593
ROWLOCK optimizer hint, 1206
rows, 579
    indexes, estimating, 988-989
    new features, 579
ROWS_PER_BATCH hint, supplying bulk-copy
  operations to, 1603-1604
RPC (remote procedure calls), CD:1663
RPO (recovery point objective), CD:1778
RTO (recovery time objective), CD:1778
rules, data integrity, 659-660

running
packages, dtexec utility, 1577-1582
SSIS Wizard, 1556-1566
runtime, measuring with datediff(), 1145

S

sac, 91, 104
parameters, 102
SAC (Surface Area Configuration) tool, 223
safeguarding databases prior to making mass changes, database snapshots, 928-929
SAN (storage area network), 520, 549
SARG
computed columns, 1038-1040
evaluating, 1035-1036
inequality operators, 1037
LIKE, 1038
search argument problems, 1092
savepoints
explicit user-defined transactions, processing, 878-879
triggers, transactions, 909-910
SAVESYSDB, 219
saving
graphical execution plans, 1130-1131
reports, Report Builder, 1640
traces (SQL Server Profiler), 123-125
scalability, enterprise computing, 515
scalar functions, 803-804
CREATE FUNCTION, 807
scalar UDFs (user-defined functions), 1344-1347
Scalar Vector Graphics (SVG), 351
scaling out, 522
scan count, STATISTICS IO, 1140
scan for startup procs, 1726
SCC (System Configuration Checker), 174
scheduled rules, 1845
scheduling maintenance plans, Maintenance Plan Wizard, 956-959
SCHEMA, 1450
schema collections, new xml data type, 1407-1412
schema locks, 1175
SCHEMABINDING
creating views with T-SQL, 678
indexes, 639
user-defined functions, 809
schemes, creating partition schemes, 610-612
screens
Feature Selection screen, 185
installing SQL Server 2005, 180-190
Instance Name screen, 185
Service Account screen, 187
scripting
alerts, 387
jobs, 387
support, in Reporting Services, 1646
variables, with sqlcmd, 94-95
scripting replication, 470-471

search arguments
identifying for query analysis, 1032-1033
problems with query optimization, 1092-1093
search phrase, CD:1934
secondary data files, 550
secondary GAM (SGAM), 550
securables, 248, 265
Secure Sockets Layer (SSL), 388, 1445
securing reports, 1647-1648
security, 249
authentication, 249-251
database snapshots, 942
enhancements to, 47-48
execution context, 286-288
models, 1643-1644
module execution context, 248
OLAP, 1536-1537
permission granularity, 248
permissions, 266-267. *See also* permissions
principals, 251
logins, 251-253
users, 254-255. *See also* users
securables, 265
SQL login password policies, 247
SQL Server 2005 security components, 248
SQL Server Agent, 370
SQL Server Service Broker, conversation encryption with certificates, CD:1901-1908
user/schema separation, 247
security components, 248
security roles, 1647
securityadmin, 259
Seek Predicates, 1119
select @@SERVERNAME, CD:1785
select @@SERVICENAME, CD:1785
select @@VERSION, CD:1785
SELECT COUNT(*), CD:1807
SELECT statement, 711
users, 257
selecting
columns, from sys.databases catalog view, 566
indexes, 978
self-configuring options, CD:1695
self-signed certificates, 235, CD:1901
semantic queries, 1642
SEND, CD:1895
SEND ON CONVERSATION, CD:1896
sending email (Database Mail), 347-348, 351-353
sequence, Query Analyzer, 1128
sequence clustering, data mining algorithms, 1527
sequence trees, 1031
SERIALIZABLE option (SET TRANSACTION ISOLATION LEVEL statement), 912
serializable read isolation, 1157-1158
SERIALIZABLE transaction isolation level, 1205
serialization locking, granularity, 1178-1180
server aliases, 234
server clusters, 518

server components, installing, 1613
server endpoint layer, 224-225
    client access provisioning, 225-227
server instance isolation, HA, 398-399
server level (SSMS), managing permissions, 278-280
server mode, report controls, 1654
server network protocols, ensuring appropriate
    network protocols are configured on server, 222-223
SERVER ROLE, 252
server trace log, Reporting Services, 1652
server-side traces
    creating and starting, script for, 139-140
    defining, 131-136, 138-140
    monitoring running traces, 141-142
    stopping, 143-144
serveradmin, 259
servers
    federated servers, CD:1767-1768
    linked servers. See linked servers
    master servers, 388-389
    multiserver jobs, creating, 390
    remote servers. See remote servers
    target servers, 388
        enlisting, 389-390
Service Account screen, 186-187
Service Broker, 24, 41-42
service program, CD:1880
services, defining to send and receive messages (SQL
    Server Service Broker), CD:1889-1890
session snapshots, 1650-1651
    removing from cache reports, 1651
sessions, report execution options, 1650
SET CHANGE TRACKING, ALTER FULLTEXT INDEX,
    CD:1925
SET DEFAULT, 649
SET LOCK_TIMEOUT command, 1191
set nocount on, 763
SET NULL, 648
SET REMOTE PROC TRANSACTIONS, 755
SET ROWCOUNT, 1278
SET SHOWPLAN XML ON, 78
SET TRANSACTION ISOLATION LEVEL command, 1203
SET TRANSACTION ISOLATION LEVEL READ
    COMMITTED statement, 1155
SET TRANSACTION ISOLATION LEVEL statement,
    options, 911-912
SET TRANSACTION ISOLATION SERIALIZABLE
    command, 1178
setupadmin, 259
SGAM (secondary GAM), 550
SGML (Standard Generalized Markup
    Language), 1377
shared disk arrays, 519
shared job schedules, 362
shared locks, 1172
shared nothing disk arrays, 519
shared query plans, stored procedures, 764-765
Short Messaging Service (SMS), 1841
show advanced options, 1727
SHOWCONTIG, 1263-1264
SHOWPLAN ALL, 1136

SHOWPLAN SET options, 1133
    SHOWPLAN ALL, 1136
    SHOWPLAN TEXT, 1134-1135
    SHOWPLAN XML, 1137
SHOWPLAN TEXT, 1134-1135
SHOWPLAN XML, 1137
Shrink Database dialog, 571
shrinking
    databases, 568
        DBCC SHRINKDATABASE, 568-569
        DBCC SHRINKFILE, 569-571
        Maintenance Plan Wizard, 952-953
        shrinking log files, 571
        with SSMS, 571-573
    log files, 571
side-by-side migration (installing SQL Server
    2005), 204
        avoiding an unintentional in-place upgrade during
            setup, 204
        migrating Analysis Services, 209-210
        migrating databases, 206-209
        migrating DTS packages, 211-212
        migrating Notification Services (SSNS), 213
        migrating Reporting Services, 212-213
        SQL Server client tools, 205
Simple Mail Transfer Protocol (SMTP), 339, CD:1841
Simple Object Access Protocol (SOAP), 1440, 1609,
    CD:1841
simple recovery model, 299-300
simplifying data manipulation with views, 669-670
SITE, 1448
site autonomy, 443
SMO (SQL Server Management Objects), 39, 206
SMS (Short Messaging Service), CD:1841
SMTP (Simple Mail Transfer Protocol), 339, CD:1841
    creating accounts in Database Mail, 342
SMTP failover priority, 344
SNAC (SQL Native Client), 221
    client data access technologies, 238-240
    installing for clients, 230
    redistributing with custom client applications, 231
snapshot agent, 437-439
snapshot backups, 337
    VLDB, 1748
snapshot databases, 924
snapshot isolation, 43, 1151, 1158-1159
    optimistic data type, 1209-1211
snapshot isolation levels, HA, 410
SNAPSHOT option (SET TRANSACTION ISOLATION
    LEVEL statement), 912
snapshot replication, 18, 444-445
snapshots. See database snapshots
SOAP (Simple Object Access Protocol), 1440, 1609,
    CD:1841
SOAP nodes, 1442
SOAP receivers, 1442
SOAP senders, 1442
software requirements for installing SQL Server 2005,
    175-179
software scaling, 522
Solution Explorer, 81-82

Sort, Query Analyzer, 1128
sorting
    in Report Builder, 1639
    in reports, with BIDS Report Designer, 1621-1623
source code control, stored procedures, 789-790
source control, integrating SSMS, 81-83
source databases, 923
    number of database snapshots per, 943
    reverting from database snapshots, 938-939
sp helplinkedsrvlogin, 1688
sp addextendedproc, 794
sp addlinkedserver, CD:1673-1680
sp addlinkedsrvlogin, CD:1684-1686
sp catalogs, CD:1688
sp columns ex, CD:1688
sp configure, 171, 1246, CD:1697-1698
SP Counts, 114
sp createstats, 171
sp dboption, 563-564
sp delete jobsteplog, 376
sp dropserver, CD:1681-1682
sp executesql, 774-776
    output parameters, 776-777
sp executsql, CD:1805
sp foreignkeys, CD:1688
sp help, 171
sp help constraint, 657
sp helparticle, 472
sp helpconstraint, 606
sp helpdb, 171, 566
SP HELPDINDEX, 636
sp helpdistributor, 472
sp helpextendedproc, 795
sp helpfile, 171
sp helplinkedsrvlogin, CD:1686-1687
sp helppublication, 472
sp helpsubscriberinfo, 472
sp helpsubscription, 472
sp helptext, 720
sp indexes, CD:1688
sp linkedservers, CD:1680-1681, CD:1687
sp lock, 171
sp monitor, 1242
sp primarykeys, CD:1688
sp procoption, 141
sp recompile, 771
sp send dbmail, 348
sp serveroption, CD:1682-1683
sp setapprole, 265
sp settriggerorder, 840
sp spaceused, 171, 594
sp tables ex, 1688
sp trace create, 131
sp trace setevent, 131
sp trace setfilter, 131
    column operator values, 139
sp trace setstatus, 131, 143
sp who, 171
SP1, installing, 193-195
sparse file size management, database
    snapshots, 943

spid data column (SQL Profiler), 1169
SPLIT RANGE, 614
split-brain scenarios, 520
SQL Browser, 227-228
SQL Clustering, building solutions with HA options,
    402-404
SQL injection attacks, avoiding with T-SQL,
    CD:1799-1806
SQL Mail, 365
SQL Native Client ODBC driver, 238
SQL Native Client OLE DB provider, 237
SQL Native Client. See SNAC
SQL Profiler
    data columns, 1168
    lock events, 1167
SQL Profiler Templates, 114
SQL Server
    installing for SQL Server Clustering, 528-537
    transaction management. See transaction
        management
    upgrading, 197
SQL Server 2005, indexes, 970
SQL Server 2005 Analysis Services. See SSAS
SQL Server 2005 Developer Edition, 28
    licensing, 31
SQL Server 2005 Enterprise Edition, 26
SQL Server 2005 Express Edition, 28-29
    licensing, 31
SQL Server 2005 Full-Text Search. See FTS
SQL Server 2005 Mobile Edition, 29
    licensing, 31
SQL Server 2005 Notification Services. See SSNS
    (SQL Server Notification Services)
SQL Server 2005 Reporting Services. See Reporting
    Services
SQL Server 2005 security model, 248-249
SQL Server 2005 Standard Edition, 25-26
SQL Server 2005 Workgroup Edition, 27-28
SQL Server Agent, 16-17
    alerts, 381
        properties, 382-384
        responses, 384-386
    configuring, 362
        email notification, 365-366
        properties, 362-363
        proxy accounts, 367-368
        startup account, 363-365
    enhancements, 49
    error logs, viewing, 368-369
    Job Activity Monitor, 362
    jobs. See jobs
    operators, managing, 370-372
    security, 370
    shared job schedules, 362
SQL Server Agent Mail, 354
    alert mail notifications, 356-357
    job mail notifications, 354-355
SQL Server Agent proxy accounts, 367-368
SQL Server Analysis Services. See SSAS
SQL Server BIDS, OLAP, 1487-1488

SQL Server client tools, side-by-side migration, 205
SQL Server Clustering, 516
  active/active configuration, 517
  active/passive configuration, 516
  installing, 524-525
    configuring SQL Server database disks, 525-526
    Connection Test Program, 539-542
    failure of nodes, 537-539
    MSCS, 527
    network interfaces, 527
    SQL Server, 528-537
  MSCS, 517-524
  new features, 516
  problems with, 543
SQL Server Configuration Manager, 16, 37, 364
SQL Server database disks, configuring, 525-526
SQL Server instance architecture, CD:1694
SQL Server Integration Services. *See* **SSIS (SQL Server Integration Services)**
SQL Server Lock Manager, 1160
SQL Server Management Objects (SMO), 39, 206
SQL Server Management Studio
  linked servers, setting up, CD:1689-1692
  replication monitoring, 474-476
SQL Server Management Studio (SSMS). *See* **SSMS (SQL Server Management Studio)**
SQL Server Management Studio wizards, data replication. *See* **data replication, setting up**
SQL Server Notification Services. *See* **SSNS**
SQL Server performance
  100 worst-performing queries, 1265-1269
  DBCC, 1261
    DBCC SQLPERF, 1262-1263
    INPUTBUFFER, 1265
    OUTPUTBUFFER, 1265
    PERFMON, 1263
    PROCCACHE, 1264-1265
    SHOWCONTIG, 1263-1264
  nonclustered indexes, 1269
  Performance Monitor, 1236-1238
  performance monitoring approach, 1235-1236
  SQL Server performance counters, 1257-1258
    locks, 1259
    monitoring disk activity, 1259
    MSSQL$:Plan Cache Object, 1258
    procedure cache, 1260
    user-defined counters, 1260-1261
    users, 1259
  tempdb, 1269
  Windows performance counters, 1239
    monitoring disk systems, 1254-1257
    monitoring memory, 1250-1254
    monitoring network interfaces, 1239-1243
    monitoring processors, 1244-1249
SQL Server performance counters, 1257-1258
  locks, 1259
  monitoring disk activity, 1259
  MSSQL$:Plan Cache Object, 1258
  procedure cache, 1260

  user-defined counters, 1260-1261
  users, 1259
SQL Server procedure cache, stored procedures, 763-764
SQL Server Profiler, 17, 1147-1148
  analyzing, slowed stored procedures or queries, 145
  application progress, monitoring, 150-152
  architecture, 112-113
  auto-update statistics, monitoring, 150
  deadlocks, 145-147
    monitoring, 1200-1203
  indexes, selecting, 978
  lock activity, monitoring, 1167-1170
  monitoring running traces, 141-142
  new features, 111-112
  performance bottlenecks, identifying, 148-149
  queries, identifying ad hoc queries, 147-148
  replaying trace data, 129-131
  server-side traces
    defining, 131-140
    stopping, 143-144
  traces
    analyzing trace output with Database Engine Tuning Advisor, 128-129
    creating, 113-116
    data columns, 118-120
    events, 116-118
    executing, 123
    exporting, 123
    filters, 121-122
    importing, 125-126
    importing into tables, 126-128
    saving, 123
    saving Profiler GUI output, 125
    saving to files, 124
    saving to tables, 124
  user configurable events, 151
SQL Server Service Broker, CD:1875
  basics of, CD:1876-1879
  constructs, CD:1881
    creating queues for message storage, CD:1887-1889
    defining messages and choosing message types, CD:1882-1886
    defining services to send and receive messages, CD:1889-1890
    planning conversations between services, CD:1890-1892
    setting up contracts for communication, CD:1886-1887
  designing example systems, CD:1880-1881
  distributed messaging, CD:1875
  routing and security, conversation encryption with certificates, CD:1901-1908
  system catalogs, CD:1909-1911
SQL Server Service Broker, 24, 41-42
SQL Server Surface Area Configuration tool, 16
SQL Server Upgrade Advisor (UA), 197

SQL Server Web services
  creating, 1442-1445
    AS HTTP, 1445-1448
    FOR SOAP, 1449-1453
  history and overview, 1439-1440
  limitations, 1469
  new features, 1439
  patterns, 1440-1441
SQL statements
  replication monitoring, 472-475
  transactions, 874
SQLAgentOperatorRole, 370
SQLAgentReaderRole, 370
SQLAgentUserRole, 370
SqlCacheDependency object, 1329
**SQLCLR, .NET Framework data provider for SQL
Server, 241-242**
SQLCMD, 39-40, 90-92
sqlcmd
  executing, 92-94
  scripting variables with, 94-95
SQLCMD scripts, editing in SSMS, 74-75
SqlConnection.BeginTransaction method, 1155
SqlDependency object, 1328-1330
sqldiag, 105-107
SQLDIAG.EXE, disaster recovery, CD:1788-1790
SQLiMail. See Database Mail
SQLMAINT, 946
SqlMethod, parameters, 1359
SqlNotificationRequest object, 1329
SQLOLEDB, 237
SQLRowCount, 763
SqlServerSystem ICF elements, CD:1863-1865
sqlservr, 107-108
SQLSetConnectAttr() function, 1155
SqlTrigger attribute, parameters, 1366
SqlTriggerContext attribute, parameters, 1367
SqlUserDefinedAggregate attribute, parameters, 1364
SqlUserDefinedType, parameters, 1354-1355
sqlwb, 91
SQL_LOGIN, 252
**SSAS (SQL Server 2005 Analysis Services), 22-23, 73,
209, 1473**
  cube perspectives, 1524-1525
  cubes, 1477-1480
  OLAP, 1481-1482. See also OLAP
  OLAP and, 1474-1476
  wizards, 1476-1477
  new features, 1473-1474
SSCM
  configuring clients, 232-234
  testing connectivity, 246
SSIS (SQL Server Integration Services), 42, 946, 1539
  architecture, 1545-1549
  bcp utility, 1586-1588
    exporting/importing data, 1589-1591
    file data types, 1591
    format files, 1591-1601
    views, 1601

  bulk-copy operations, 1601-1604
  configurations, 1548
  containers, 1546
  control flow, 1546
  data flow, 1547
  data flow task, 1547
  data mining, 1534-1535
  data transformation requirement, 1555-1556
  event handlers, 1547
  logging, 1549
  new features, 1540
  Package Execution utility, 1574-1576
    dtexec utility, 1574, 1576-1577
    dtsrun utility, 1574
    dtutil utility, 1582-1586
    running packages, 1577-1582
  packages, 1546, 1549
  SSIS Wizard, running, 1556-1566
  tasks, 1546
  tools, 1549-1551
    command-prompt utilities, 1552
    Expression Builder, 1553-1554
    Import and Export Wizard, 1551
    integration services, 1552
    Query Builder, 1552-1554
    SSIS Designer, 1551-1552, 1566-1574
  transformations, 1547
  variables, 1549
  workflows, 1546
  XML configuration file, 1548
SSIS Designer, 1551-1552, 1566-1574
SSIS Wizard, running, 1556-1566
SSL (Secure Sockets Layer), 388, 1445
SSL PORT, 1446
**SSMS (SQL Server Management Studio), 14-16, 36-
37, 57, 205, 340, 631, 1151**
  administration tools, 64
    Activity Monitor, 68-70
    Log File Viewer, 70-71
    Object Explorer, 66-67
    registered servers, 65-66
  backups, creating, 302-305
  configuration options, setting, CD:1702-1703
  constraints, creating, 653-656
  creating instance and application, for SSNS,
    CD:1866-1868
  creating user-defined functions, 812-814
  Database Diagram Editor, creating tables,
    580-581
  database options, 561
  databases, creating, 556-559
  development tools, 71
    integrating with source control, 81-83
    managing projects, 79-81
    Query Editor. See Query Editor
    templates, 83-86
  indexes
    creating, 631-632
    managing, 636
    managing with, 1012-1013

integrated environments, 58
  integrated help, 62-64
  window management, 59-62
lock activity, monitoring, 1164-1167
logins, 271
managing database roles, 276
managing logins, 268-271
managing permissions, 277-278
  at database level, 281-283
  at object level, 283-284
  at server level, 278-280
managing users, 273-275
new features, 57-58
Object Explorer
  creating tables, 580
  data types, 587
  dropping tables, 605-606
  modifying tables with Table Designer, 601-604
Query Analyzer, 1117-1118
  execution plan ToolTips, 1118-1121
restoration, 322-323
shrinking databases, 571-573
startup accounts, SQL Server Agent, 365
stored procedures
  creating, 702-705
  creating (custom stored procedure templates), 705-709
  executing, 711-713
  modifying, 723-724
Summary page, 61
Template Explorer, 704
transaction logs, creating, 308
user-defined functions, 822
views, managing, 683
SSMS client statistics, 1132-1133
SSMS Shrink File dialog, 896
SSNS (SQL Server Notification Services), 23-24, 184, 213, CD:1841
  ADFs, CD:1850
    Database ADF, CD:1851
    Distributors ADF, CD:1862-1863
    EventClasses ADF, CD:1851-1852
    Generator ADF, CD:1862
    NotificationClasses ADF, CD:1854-1859
    ParameterDefaults ADF, CD:1851
    Providers ADF, CD:1859-1862
    sample applications, CD:1850-1851
    SubscriptionClasses ADF, CD:1852-1854
  choosing programming methods, CD:1847-1848
  creating instance and application via SSMS, CD:1866-1868
  editions of, CD:1842-1843
  event providers, CD:1844
  event rules, CD:1845
  events, CD:1844
  ICFs, CD:1863-1865
  instances, CD:1846-1847
  migrating, 213
  new features, CD:1841-1842
  notification cycles, CD:1845-1846
  providing events to applications, CD:1871-1874

  reasons for using, CD:1843
  requirements for, CD:1842-1843
  subscribers, CD:1844-1845
  subscriptions, CD:1844-1845
    creating, CD:1869-1871
  upgrading, 219
  XML and Management Studio, CD:1848-1849
Standard, 114
Standard Generalized Markup Language (SGML), 1377
standards, HA, 398
STANDBY, 321
  transaction logs, 310
standby servers, backups, 336-337
START, ALTER FULLTEXT INDEX, CD:1926
startup accounts, configuring (SQL Server Agent), 363-365
startup procedures, 778-781
statements
  BEGIN CONVERSATION DIALOG, CD:1890
  BEGIN TRAN statement, transactions, 909
  BEGIN TRAN statements, 884
  CREATE CERTIFICATE, CD:1901
  CREATE ENDPOINT, T-SQL, 1442
  END CONVERSATION, CD:1896
  HOLDLOCK, 911
  PRINT, CD:1900
  RECEIVE, CD:1900
  ROLLBACK, CD:1901
  SEND, CD:1895
  SET TRANSACTION ISOLATION LEVEL READ COMMITTED, 1155
  SET TRANSACTION ISOLATION LEVEL statement, options, 911-912
  SQL statements, transactions, 874
  WAITFOR, CD:1900
statistics
  columns, generating, 990-996, 998
  indexes, 982-984
    generating, 990-998
    histograms, 984-987
  maintaining, with Maintenance Plan Wizard, 953-956
  problems with query optimization, 1090-1091
  query statistics, 1139
    datediff(), 1145
    STATISTIC IO, 1141-1142
    STATISTICS IO, 1139-1141
    STATISTICS PROFILE, 1146
    STATISTICS TIME, 1142-1145
    STATISTICS XML, 1146-1147
  updating, VLDB data maintenance, CD:1751-1752
STATISTICS IO, 1139-1142
STATISTICS PROFILE, 1112, 1146
STATISTICS TIME, 1112, 1142-1145
STATISTICS XML, 1146-1147
statistics, indexes, 988-989
SteelEye Technologies, CD:1791
steps (values), histograms, 984
STOP, ALTER FULLTEXT INDEX, CD:1926
stopping server-side traces, 143-144

storage, Database Engine, 12
storage area network (SAN), 520, 549
storage data types, format files, 1593-1594
storage of archived data, VLDB data maintenance,
    CD:1759-1760
stored procedures
    advantages of, 700-701
    analyzing with Query Analyzer, 1129-1130
    calling from transactions, 783-786
    CLR stored procedures, 791-793
    creating, 701-702
        in SSMS, 702-705
        in SSMS (custom stored procedure
            templates), 705-709
    cursors, 733-738
        CURSOR variables, 738-743
    Debugging, with Visual Studio .NET, 756-760
    deferred name resolution, 715-717
        identifying objects referenced in stored
            procedures, 717-719
    defined, 699
    dynamic SQL, 772-774
        sp executesql, 774-776
        sp executesql, output parameters, 776-777
    errors, 786-789
    executing, 710-711
        execution context and EXECUTE AS, 713-715
        in SSMS, 711-713
        via linked servers, CD:1689
    extended stored procedures, 793-794
        adding to SQL Server, 794-795
        obtaining information on, 795
        provided with SQL Server, 795-796
        xp cmdshell, 796-798
    input parameters, 724-725
        passing object names as, 728-729
        setting default values for, 725-728
        wildcards, 729-730
    managed database objects, developing,
        1335-1336, 1339-1344
    for managing logins, 272
    modifying, 722
        with SSMS, 723-724
    monitoring recompilation, 766-768
        forcing recompilation of query plans, 768-771
    nested stored procedures, 743-745
        recursion, 745-748
    new features, 699-700
    output parameters, 731-732
    performance, 762-763
        query plan caching, 763
        qutomatic query plan recompilation, 765-766
        shared query plans, 764-765
        SQL Server procedure cache, 763-764
    remote stored procedures, 755-756
    returning procedure status, 732-733
    rewriting as functions, 826-827
    system stored procedures, 170-171, 760-762
    T-SQL
        calling from transactions, 783-786
        coding guidelines, 781-783
        errors, 786-789
        source code control, 789-790
    temporary stored procedures, 709-710
    temporary tables, 749-750
        performance tips, 751-752
        table data type, 752-755
    transactions, 899-904
    using BEGIN CONVERSATION DIALOG, CD:1892
    viewing, 719-722
Stream Aggregate, Query Analyzer, 1128
streams, 1089
string summary statistics, indexes, 998
structures, indexes, 970-975
stub, 1441
subquery processing, joins, 1067
    correlated subqueries, 1068-1070
    materialized subqueries, 1067-1068
subscribers, SSNS, 1844-1845
subscription server, data replication, 420
SubscriptionClasses ADF element, CD:1852-1854
subscriptions, 24, 433-434
    anonymous subscriptions, 434
    creating
        for data replication, 465-469
        for SSNS, CD:1869-1871
    distribution database, 435-436
    reports, 1648-1649
        data-driven subscriptions, 1649-1650
        delivery architecture, 1650
    SSNS, CD:1844-1845
summary data, denormalization, 1221
Summary page, reports, 61
Surface Area Configuration (SAC) tool, 223, 340, 1618
suspect pages, 326
SVG (Scalar Vector Graphics), 351
svmail configure sp, 346
SWITCH, 621
switching table partitions, 618-621
Symantec, CD:1791
synchronization, 437-438
synchronous operations, database mirroring operating
    modes, 485
sys users, 256
sys.conversation groups, CD:1910
sys.databases catalog view, selecting columns, 566
sys.dm broker activated tasks, CD:1911
sys.dm broker connections, CD:1911
sys.dm broker forwarded messages, CD:1911
sys.dm broker queue monitors, CD:1911
sys.dm broker transmission status, CD:1911
sys.dm exec cached plans, 1077-1079
sys.dm exec plan attributes, 1077, 1081-1082
sys.dm exec query plan, 1137-1139
sys.dm exec query stats, 1077-1081
sys.dm exec sql text, 1077-1079
sys.dm_db_index_physical_stats, 1003
sys.dm_tran_locks view, querting, 1161-1164
sys.endpoint webmethods, 1467
sys.endpoints, 1466
sys.indexes, 1097
sys.master files, 550

sys.plan guides, 1106-1107
sys.service contract message usages, CD:1910
sys.service contracts, CD:1910
sys.service message types, CD:1910
sys.service queues, CD:1909
sys.services, CD:1910
sysadmin, 259
sysjobstepslogs, 376
sysmail account, 358
sysmail configuration, 358
sysmail delete account sp, 345
sysmail delete log sp, 360
sysmail delete principalprofile sp, 345
sysmail delete profile sp, 345
sysmail delete profileaccount sp, 345
sysmail faileditems, 359
sysmail help queue sp, 360
sysmail help status sp, 360
sysmail principalprofile, 357
sysmail profile, 357
sysmail profileaccount, 358
sysmail server, 358
sysmail servertype, 358
sysmail start sp, 348
sysmail unsentitems, 360
sysmail update account sp, 345
sysmail update principalprofile sp, 345
sysmail update profile sp, 345
sysmail update profileaccount sp, 345
sysmessages, 382-383
sysopentapes, 326
system administrators, responsibilities of, 156-157
system architecture, Reporting Services, 1611-1613
system catalog views, 38-39
system catalogs, SQL Server Service Broker, CD:1909-1911
System Configuration Checker (SCC), 174
system database backups, scenarios, 317
system databases, 157-159, 547
    restoring, 333-335
system permissions, securing reports, 1648
system roles, securing reports, 1648
system stored procedures, 170-171, 760-762
    catalog views and, 1466-1467
system tables, 160-161
    backing up and restoring, 325-326
system views, 161
    access to perfmon counters, 1261
    catalog views, 164-166
    compatibility views, 161-162
    DMVs, 168-170
    information schema views, 166-167
    monitoring disk system items, 1256-1257
    monitoring memory items, 1252-1254
    monitoring network items, 1243
    monitoring processor items, 1248
System.Data namespace (.NET Framework), 1319
System.Data.SqlClient namespace (.NET Framework), 1319

System.Data.SqlTypes namespace, ADO.NET, 1326-1328
System.Xml namespace (.NET Framework), 1320
SystemDataAccess parameter (scalar UDFs), 1345
SystemDataAccess parameter (SqlMethod), 1359
systemwide mail settings, Database Mail, 345-346
systemwide table-valued functions, 825-826

T

T-SQL, CD:1793
    @@ERROR, CD:1836-1837
    @@ROWCOUNT, CD:1836-1837
    altering views, 681-682
    backups, creating, 305-307
    coding recommendations, CD:1794
        avoiding SQL injection attacks when using dynamic SQL, CD:1799-1806
        commenting, CD:1806-1807
        explicit column lists, CD:1794-1796
        qualifying object names with schema names, CD:1796-1799
    constraints, creating, 651-653
    CONTEXT INFO, CD:1824-1825
    CREATE ENDPOINT, 1442
    CREATE TABLE, 582-584
    creating tables, 582-584
    creating user-defined functions, 807-811
    creating views, 675-678
    database options, setting, 563
    databases, creating, 559-560
    date calculations, CD:1817-1820
    de-duping data with ranking functions, CD:1837-1840
    deleting mail objects, 345
    DML. See DML
    dropping views, 682
    enhancements to, 47
    execution engine, 209
    full-text indexes, CD:1916
        ALTER FULLTEXT INDEX, CD:1924-1926
        CREATE FULLTEXT CATALOG, CD:1916-1918
        CREATE FULLTEXT INDEX, CD:1919-1924
        diagnostics, CD:1927-1930
        managing MSFTESQL, CD:1927
    functions, versus CLR functions, 830-831
    generating statements, CD:1835-1836
    GROUPING function, CD:1822-1824
    indexes
        creating, 627-631
        managing, 633-636
    INITIATOR, CD:1886
    managing
        database roles, 277
        logins, 272-273
        permissions, 285-286
        users, 275
    modifying tables, 598
        adding and dropping columns, 600-601
        changing column properties, 599

outer joins, CD:1826-1827
    full outer joins, CD:1833-1835
    nested outer joins, CD:1832-1833
    versus WHERE clause, CD:1827-1832
performance
    avoiding unnecessary function executions,
        CD:1809
    cursors, CD:1810-1813
    DISTINCT, CD:1808
    IF EXISTS, CD:1807
    ORDER BY, CD:1808
    temp tables versus table variables versus
        common table expressions, CD:1808-1809
    UNION versus UNION ALL, CD:1807
    UPDATE, CD:1813-1816
PIVOT, 1305-1309
restoration, 318-321
    transaction logs, 321-322
running ad hoc T-SQL batches from SQL Server
  web services, 1458-1463
stored procedures
    calling from transaction, 783-786
    coding guidelines, 781-783
    errors, 786-789
    source code control, 789-790
TARGET, 1886
transaction logs, creating, 309-310
UNPIVOT, 1305-1309
updating Database Mail, 345
user-defined functions
    modifying, 821-822
    viewing, 818-821
T-SQL stored procedures, versus CLR stored
  procedures, 793
table constraints, defining, 596-597
table data types, temporary tables (stored procedure),
  752-755
Table Delete, Query Analyzer, 1128
Table Designer, modifying tables, 601-604
table expressions, T-SQL, CD:1808-1809
table hints
    locking, 1203-1206
    Query Optimizer, 1096-1097
Table Insert, Query Analyzer, 1128
table location, 594-596
Table locking level (SQL Server), 1177
table partitioning, 42-43
    for VLDB, CD:1768-1770
table partitions
    adding, 614-616
    dropping, 616-618
    switching, 618-621
Table Scan, Query Analyzer, 1128
table scans
    costs, 1046-1048
    Query Optimizer, 970
Table Spool, Query Analyzer, 1126
Table Update, Query Analyzer, 1128
table variables, T-SQL, CD:1808-1809
Table-valued Function, Query Analyzer, 1128

table-valued functions, 805-807
tablediff, 90, 98-101
tables, 579
    columns. See columns
    creating, 580
        with Database Diagram Editor (SSMS),
          580-581
        with Object Explorer (SSMS), 580
        with T-SQL, 582-584
    dropping, 605-606
    fragmentation, 999
    importing trace files into, 126-128
    in reports, with BIDS Report Designer, 1623-1624
    indexes. See indexes
    inserting trace data into trace tables, 127-128
    modifying, 598
        with database diagrams, 604-605
        with Object Explorer and Table Designer,
          601-604
        with T-SQL, 598-601
    partitioned tables. See partitioned tables
    saving trace output to, 124
    system tables, 160-161
        backing up and restoring, 325-326
    table location defining, 594-596
    temporary tables
        creating, 622
        stored procedures, 749-750
    temporary tables. See temporary tables
TABLESAMPLE, 1314-1318
TABLOCK hint, supplying bulk-copy
  operations to, 1604
TABLOCK optimizer hint, 1206
TABLOCKX optimizer hint, 1206
Tabular Data Stream (TDS), 1440
Tabular Data Stream endpoints, 224
tape devices, 300
TARGET, CD:1886
Target parameter (SqlTrigger), 1366
Target Server Wizard, 389
target servers, 388-390
TARGET SIZE, 570
tasks, SSIS, 1546
TDS (Tabular Data Stream), 1440
TDS (Tabular Data Stream) endpoints, 224
temp tables, T-SQL, CD:1808-1809
tempdb
    SQL Server performance, 1269
    temporary table and stored procedures,
        performance tips, 751-752
tempdb database, 159
Template Explorer, 84, 836
    SSMS, 704
templates
    custom function templates, creating for user-
        defined functions, 815-818
    custom stored procedure templates, creating in
        SSMS, 705-709
    intergrating SSMS, 83-86
temporary stored procedures, 709-710

temporary tables
    creating, 622
    stored procedures, 749-750
        performance tips, 751-752
        table data types, 752-755
Terminate() method, 1363
terminators, fields (format files), 1596-1599
testing
    alerts, SQL Server Agent Mail, 357
    connectivity, 246
    Database Mail setup, 346
    failover, of database mirroring, 507-508
    job-completion notification, SQL Server Agent
        Mail, 355
TextData data column (SQL Profiler), 1169
third-party disaster recovery alternatives, 1791
three-permission sets, managed database objects,
    1332-1334
time series, data mining algorithms, 1528
time slices, 519
timeout intervals setting locks, 1191-1192
timestamp data type, optimistic data type, 1207-1209
tokens, 475
tools
    administration tools, 64-71
    client tools, installing, 229
    development tools. *See* development tools
    Manage Indexes tool, 631
    performance and monitoring tools, 1652-1653
    Reporting Services Configuration tool, 1615
    SAC tool, 223
    SQL Server Agent, 16-17
    SQL Server client tools, side-by-side
        migration, 205
    SQL Server Configuration Manager, 16
    SQL Server Profiler, 17
    SQL Server Surface Area Configuration tool, 16
    SSIS. *See* SSIS, tools
    Surface Area Configuration tool, 340, 1618
ToolTips, execution plan ToolTips (Query Analyzer),
    1118-1121
TOP, DML, 1276-1280
Top, Query Analyzer, 1129
ToString() method, 1355
trace flags, 1197-1199
Trace Name, 115
tracer tokens, 416
traces, analyzing output with Database Engine Tuning
    Advisor, 128-129
traces (SQL Server Profiler)
    creating, 113-116
    data columns, 118-120
    events, 116-118
        categories and, 132-136
        columns, 137-138
    executing, 123
    exporting, 123
    filters, 121-122
    importing, 125-126
    inserting trace data into trace tables, 127-128
    monitoring running traces, 141-142

    replaying trace data, 129-131
    saving, 123-125
    server-side traces
        defining, 131-140
        stopping, 143-144
training, HA, 398
@@trancount, 783
Transact-SQL. *See* T-SQL
transaction isolation, level hints, 1204-1205
transaction isolation levels, 1153-1154
    dirty reads, 1153
    lost updates, 1153
    nonrepeatable reads, 1153
    phantom reads, 1153
    read committed isolation, 1155
    read committed snapshot isolation, 1155-1156
    read uncommitted isolation, 1154
    repeatable read isolation, 1156-1157
    serializable read isolation, 1157-1158
    snapshot isolation, 1158-1159
transaction log backups, 296
transaction log files, 548, 554-555
transaction logs, 307
    backing up tail of, 330
    creating, 308-310
    full database backups, 311-312
    restoration, T-SQL, 321-322
    restoring, 328
    restoring backups, 330-331
transaction management, 873-875
    AutoCommit, 876
    batches, 897-899
    bound connections, 915-917
    checkpoint duration option, 873
    coding, 912-913
    distributed transactions, 918
    explicit user-defined transactions, 876-878
        nested transactions, 879-882
        savepoints, 878-879
    implicit transactions, 882-884
    locks, 911-912
    long-running transactions, 913-915
    recovery process, 885-886, 889-891
    stored procedures, 899-904
    transaction logging, 885-897
    transactions, processing, 875
    triggers, 904-905
        multistatement transactions, 907-909
        savepoints, 909-910
        transaction nesting, 905-907
transaction processing phase, 1072
transactional integrity, VLDB data maintenance,
    CD:1759
transactional replication, 18-19, 444-446
transactions, 874
    ACID properties, 874
    batches, 897-899
    BEGIN TRAN statement, 909
    bound connections, 915-917
    calling stored procedures from, 783-786
    coding, 912-913

distributed transactions
    linked servers, 1672-1673
    managing, 918
explicit transactions, 875, 884
implicit transactions, 875, 884
locks, 911-912
long-running transactions, managing, 913-915
managed database objects, developing,
    1372-1374
processing, 875
    AutoCommit, 876
    explicit user-defined transactions, 876-882
    implicit transactions, 882-884
stored procedures, 899-904
transaction logging, 885-897
triggers, 904-905
    multistatement transactions, 907-909
    savepoints, 909-910
    transaction nesting, 905-907
transformations, SSIS, 1547
transmission queues, 1890
trigger firing order, AFTER triggers, 840
TriggerAction parameter (SqlTriggerContext), 1367
triggers, 833
    AFTER triggers, 837-839
        executing, 839
        special considerations, 840-841
        trigger firing order, 840
    CLR triggers, 834, 866-869
        creating, 866-868
    DDL triggers. See DDL triggers
    DML triggers. See DML triggers
    INSTEAD OF triggers, 851-853
        restrictions, 859
        views, 856-859
    managed triggers, 1366-1368, 1370-1372
    nested triggers, 869, CD:1721
    new features, 834
    problems with query optimization, 1094
    recursive triggers, 870-871
    transactions, 904-905
        multistatement transactions, 907-909
        savepoints, 909-910
        transaction nesting, 905-907
trivial plan optimization, 1071
troubleshooting
    connectivity issues, 244-245
    replication failures, replication monitoring,
        476-477
TRUNCATE, 288
TRUNCATE ONLY, transaction logs, 310
TRUNCATE TABLE, 840
TRY...CATCH, 786-788, 1312-1314
tsequal() function, 1152
TSQL, 114
TSQL Default TCP, 226
TSQL Duration, 115
TSQL Grouped, 115
TSQL Replay, 115
TSQL SPs, 115
Tuning, 115

TVFs (table-valued UDFs), 1348-1349, 1352-1353
TYPE COLUMN, CREATE FULLTEXT INDEX,
    CD:1919-1920
type hints, locks, 1206
types, UDTs, 1354-1355, 1359-1363

U

UA (SQL Server Upgrade Advisor), 197-198
    Analysis Wizard, 199-202
    Report Viewer, 202-203
UDAs (user-defined aggregates), developing managed
    database objects, 1363-1366
UDFs. See user-defined functions
UDTs (user-defined types), 221, 589-590
    managed database objects, developing,
        1354-1355, 1359-1363
unattended installation
    installing SQL Server 2005, 191-193
    of SP1, 195
unattended upgrades, 219-220
UNC (Universal Naming Convention), 301
unconditional workflows, SSIS, 1547
undo (rollback) phase, transaction recovery
    process, 891
uniform extent, 549
UNION
    query processing, 1084, 1086
    versus UNION ALL, 1807
UNION ALL
    query processing, 1086
    versus UNION, 1807
UNION hints, 1098-1099
UNIQUE constraint, 596, 645-646
UNIQUE keyword, 596
Universal Naming Convention (UNC), 301
UNPIVOT, 1305-1309
UNSAFE, 792, 829
UPDATE, T-SQL (performance), CD:1813-1816
update languages, CD:1927
update locks, 1173-1174
update performance indexes, compared to query
    indexes, 1024-1026
UPDATE STATISTICS command, 990-994
UPDATE(), 843-845
updates, checking for column updates, 843-845
updating
    column statistics, 990-996, 998
    Database Mail, with T-SQL, 345
    index statistics, 990-996, 998
    statistics, VLDB data maintenance,
        CD:1751-1752
    subscribers replication model, data replication,
        430-432
UPDLOCK optimizer hint, 1206
UPGRADE, 219
upgrading
    Analysis Services, 217
    clusters, 219
    databases, 216-217
    DTS, 218

Notification Services (SSNS), 219
replicated databases, 217
Reporting Services, 218-219
SQL Server, 197
unattended upgrades, 219-220
upgrading in-place (installing SQL Server 2005), 214
.NET Framework 2.0, 216
MSXML 6.0, 216
SQL Server 2005 upgrade matrix, 214-215
upgrading
Analysis Services, 217
databases, 216-217
DTS, 218
Notification Services (SSNS), 219
Reporting Services, 218-219
Usage-Based Optimization Wizard, 1523
USE PLAN, Query Optimizer, 1101-1103
USE PLAN N hints, 1101
user CALs, 30
user configurable events, SQL Server Profiler, 151
user connections, 1727
user databases, 547
user options, CD:1728-1729
user requirements, data replication, 447-448
data characteristics, 448-450
**user-defined counters, SQL Server performance
counters, 1260-1261**
user-defined data types, 588-589
user-defined functions, 799, 802
creating, 807
custom function templates, 815-818
with SSMS, 812-814
T-SQL functions, 807-811
managed database objects, developing, 1344-
1349, 1352-1353
managing permissions, 824-825
modifying, 821-822
new features, 799-800
reasons for using, 800-802
scalar functions, 803-804
scalar UDFs, 1344-1347
table-valued functions, 805-807
TVFs, 1348-1349, 1352-1353
viewing
with SSMS, 822
with T-SQL, 818-821
user-defined roles, 262-264
user-defined types. See UDTs
user/schema separation, 247
principals, 257-258
users
delivering data to, in OLAP database creation,
1518-1519
logins, 254
managing, 273-275
principals, 254-256
SELECT statement, 257
SQL Server performance counters, 1259
USESYSDB, 219

utilities, SSIS, 1549-1551
bcp utility, 1586-1601
command-prompt utilities, 1552
Expression Builder, 1553-1554
Import and Export Wizard, 1551
integration services, 1552
Package Execution utility, 1574-1586
Query Builder, 1552-1554
SSIS Designer, 1551-1552, 1566-1574

V

valid documents (XML), 1378
validation and execution phase (dtexec), 1577
**ValidationMethodName parameter
(SqlUserDefinedType), 1355**
VALUE secondary index (XML), 1434
value() method, 1435
value() new xml data type method, 1412, 1421-1422
**values, monitoring with Performance Monitor,
1237-1238**
varbinary(max), 45
varchar(max), 45
variables
CURSOR, stored procedures, 738-743
scripting, with sqlcmd, 94-95
SSIS, 1549
VDI (Virtual Device Interface), 1748
vendor agreements, HA, 398
verification, packages (dtutil utility), 1582-1585
verify signature, 1927
VeriSign, 235
vertical data partitioning, 1763-1765
denormalization, 1223-1224
vertical filtering, data replication, 463-465
very large database. See VLDB
VHD (Virtual Hard Disk), 412
VIEW DEFINITION, 267
View Designer, creating views, 679-681
VIEW METADATA:creating views with T-SQL, 678
viewing
DDL triggers, with catalog views, 866
error logs, SQL Server Agent, 368-369
graphical execution plans, 1130-1131
installation log files, 190
job history, 380-381
last generated report, Report Viewer, 202
linked servers, CD:1680-1681
lock activity
Performance Monitor, 1169-1171
SQL Server Profiler, 1167-1170
SSMS, 1164-1167
mail configuration objects, Database Mail,
357-358
mail message data, Database Mail, 359-360
partitioned table information, 613
stored procedures, 719-722
user-defined functions, 818-822

views
altering, with T-SQL, 681-682
bcp utility, 1601
catalog views, 156
compatibility views, 155, 161-162
controlling access to data, 671-674
creating, 674-675
creating
with T-SQL, 675-678
with View Designer, 679-681
data abstraction, 670-671
data modifications and, 683-684
defined, 667-668
distributed partitioned view, 858
DMVs, 156
dropping, with T-SQL, 682
focusing on specific data, 670
indexed views, 690, 1021-1022
creating, 690-693
expansion, 696-697
performance and, 693-696
indexes on, 639-640
INSTEAD OF triggers, 856-859
managing, 681
with SSMS, 683
new features, 667
partitioned views, 684-687
distributed partitioned views, 688-690
modifying data through, 688
Performance Monitor, 1236-1237
simplifying data manipulation, 669-670
system views. See system views
Virtual Device Interface (VDI), 1748
Virtual Hard Disk (VHD), 412
Virtual Machine Monitor (VMM), 412
virtual server licensing, 33
Virtual Server name dialog, 529
Visual Studio 2005
managed database objects, developing,
1334-1335
report viewer controls, 1611
VLDB (very large database), CD:1743
consistency, checking, CD:1749-1751
data maintenance, CD:1751
purging/archiving data, CD:1755-1761
rebuilding indexes, CD:1752-1755
updating statistics, CD:1751-1752
design considerations, CD:1761-1762
database partitioning. See database
partitioning for VLDB
determining if you have one, CD:1744-1745
maintenance issues, CD:1745
backing up and restoring, CD:1745-1748
consistency, CD:1749-1751
new features, CD:1743-1744
VMM (Virtual Machine Monitor), 412
Volume Shadow Copy Service (VSS), CD:1748
VSS (Volume Shadow Copy Service), CD:1748

W

W3C (World Wide Web), 1440
WAITFOR, CD:1900
web methods, examples
calling web methods-bound stored procedure that
returns XML, 1462-1465
running ad hoc T-SQL batches from SQL Server
web services, 1458-1463
running web methods bound to stored procedures
from C#, 1453-1456, 1458
web services
enhancements, 52
Reporting Services, 1609
configuring, 1617
Web Services Description Language, 1440, 1451
web services. See SQL Server Web services
Web Sites Properties dialog, 1448
WEBMETHOD, 1449
weighted, FTS, CD:1936
well formed documents (XML), 1378
WHERE
search argument problems, 1093
versus OUTER JOIN, CD:1827-1832
**where clause, query() new xml data type
method, 1417**
**wide indexes, compared to multiple indexes,
1020-1021**
wildcards
parameters, stored procedures, 729-730
Query Editor, SSMS, 75-76
window management, SSMS, 59-62
windows, Datasets window, 1621
Windows Authentication mode, 250, 268
Windows Firewall, 245
WINDOWS GROUP, 252
Windows Installer 3.1, 228
WINDOWS LOGIN, 252
Windows performance counters, 1239
monitoring
disk systems, 1254-1257
memory, 1250-1254
network interfaces, 1239-1243
processors, 1244-1249
**Windows Performance Monitor, replication
monitoring, 477**
Windows servers, HA, 410-412
Windows Service
Reporting Services, 1609
configuring, 1616
requirements for installing SQL Server 2005, 177
Windows Service Control Manager, 364
**Windows Vista support, requirements for installing
SQL Server 2005, 178**
**WITH ACCENT SENSITIVITY, CREATE FULLTEXT
CATALOG, CD:1917**
**WITH CHECK OPTION, creating views with T-SQL,
678-679**
**WITH clause, options for planning conversations
between services, CD:1892**
WITH CLEANUP clause, CD:1896

WITH RECOMPILE, 769
witness database servers, database mirroring, 483
witness role, database mirroring, 485
wizards
    Aggregation Design Wizard, 1513
    Analysis Services Migration Wizard, 209
    Analysis Wizard, 199-202
    Configure Database Mirroring Security Wizard,
        495-501
    Copy Database Wizard, 206-208
    Cube Wizard, 1505
    Data Mining Wizard, 1528, 1530
    Data Source View Wizard, 1492
    Database Mail Configuration Wizard, 339
        creating SMTP accounts, 343
    Dimension Wizard, 1495, 1499
    Full-Text Indexing Wizard, CD:1930-1932
    Installation Wizard, 181
    Maintenance Plan Wizard, 946-947
        backing up databases, 948-951
        checking database integrity, 951
        maintaining indexes and statistics, 953-956
        scheduling maintenance plans, 956-959
        shrinking databases, 952-953
    Master Server Wizard, 389
    Package Migration Wizard, 212
    SSAS, 1476-1477
    SSIS Wizard, 1551
        running, 1556-1566
    Target Server Wizard, 389
    Usage-Based Optimization Wizard, 1523
workflows, SSIS, 1546
World Wide Web Consortium (W3C), 1440
write-ahead logs, 555
WRITETEXT, 840
WSDL (Web Services Description Language),
    1440, 1451

X-Y-Z

XLOCK optimizer hint, 1206
XML, 1377
    attribute-centric XML shape, 1379
    calling web methods-bound stored procedure that
        returns XML, 1462-1465
    choosing programming methods, SSNS, CD:1847
    CREATE FULLTEXT INDEX, CD:1920
    data types, 588
    documents, 1378
    element-centric XML shape, 1379
    FOR XML modes, 1378
        AUTO mode, 1385-1389
        EXPLICIT mode, 1389-1391, 1393
        newxml data type, 1396-1399
        PATH mode, 1393-1396
        RAW mode, 1379-1383
    Infoset, 1432-1433
    Management Studio, SSNS, CD:1848-1849
    new features, 1377

    new xml data type, 1402-1403
        built-in methods, 1411-1430
        columns, 1404-1406
        schema collections, 1407-1412
    nodes, 1378
    OPENXML, 1399-1402
    sending as attachments, 351
    xml columns
        full-text indexing, 1436
        indexing, 1430-1436
XML configuration file, SSIS, 1548
XML Data Modification Language (XMLDML), 1425
xml data type, DML, 1274
xml data types, 45
XML for analysis (XMLA), 73
XML indexes, 624
XML Schema Definition (XSD), 1378
XMLA (XML for analysis), 73
XMLDATA keyword, 1383
XMLDML (XML Data Modification Language), 1425
xp cmdshell, 796-798
XP-related configuration options, 1729
XSD (XML Schema Definition), 1378

zero-to-one relationships, denormalization, 1224-1225

Safari
BOOKS ONLINE
ENABLED

THIS BOOK IS SAFARI ENABLED

INCLUDES FREE 45-DAY ACCESS TO THE ONLINE EDITION

The Safari® Enabled icon on the cover of your favorite technology book means the book is available through Safari Bookshelf. When you buy this book, you get free access to the online edition for 45 days.

Safari Bookshelf is an electronic reference library that lets you easily search thousands of technical books, find code samples, download chapters, and access technical information whenever and wherever you need it.

TO GAIN 45-DAY SAFARI ENABLED ACCESS TO THIS BOOK:

- Go to **http://www.samspublishing.com/safarienabled**
- Complete the brief registration form
- Enter the coupon code found in the front of this book on the "Copyright" page

If you have difficulty registering on Safari Bookshelf or accessing the online edition, please e-mail customer-service@safaribooksonline.com.

Your Guide
to Computer
Technology

www.informit.com

Sams has partnered with **InformIT.com** to bring technical information to your desktop. Drawing on Sams authors and reviewers to provide additional information on topics you're interested in, **InformIT.com** has free, in-depth information you won't find anywhere else.

ARTICLES

Keep your edge with thousands of free articles, in-depth features, interviews, and information technology reference recommendations—all written by experts you know and trust.

POWERED BY
Safari

ONLINE BOOKS

Answers in an instant from **InformIT Online Books'** 600+ fully searchable online books. Sign up now and get your first 14 days **free**.

CATALOG

Review online sample chapters and author biographies to choose exactly the right book from a selection of more than 5,000 titles.

 www.samspublishing.com